Painted Shadow

Also by Carole Seymour-Jones

Beatrice Webb: A Life

*Journey of Faith: The History of
the World YWCA, 1945–1994*

The life of

Vivienne Eliot, first wife of

T. S. Eliot, and the

long-suppressed truth about

her influence on his genius

Nan A. Talese

Doubleday

New York   London   Toronto   Sydney   Auckland

PAINTED
SHADOW

Carole Seymour-Jones

PUBLISHED BY NAN A. TALESE

an imprint of Doubleday
a division of Random House, Inc.
1540 Broadway, New York, New York 10036

DOUBLEDAY is a trademark of Doubleday
a division of Random House, Inc.

First published in the United Kingdom by
Constable Robinson Publishers

Book design by Ellen Cipriano

Title page photo of Vivienne Eliot (detail)
courtesy of Houghton Library, Harvard University
(*AC9. E1464.Zzx II, env.13)

Library of Congress Cataloging-in-Publication Data
Seymour-Jones, Carole.
Painted shadow / Carole Seymour-Jones.—1st ed. in the
United States of America
p. cm.
1. Eliot, Vivienne, 1888–1947. 2. Eliot, T. S. (Thomas Stearns),
1888–1965—Marriage. 3. Authors' spouses—Great Britain—
Biography. 4. Poets, American—20th century—Biography.
5. Hysteria—Patients—Biography. I. Title.

PS3509.L43 Z93 2002
821'.912—dc21
[B]   2001055694

ISBN 0-385-49992-2

May 2002

First Edition in the United States of America

1   3   5   7   9   10   8   6   4   2

In memory of my brother,
Nick Seymour-Jones, 1947-2000

Contents

Illustrations

Ezra Pound (© *Hulton Archive*)
Vivien playing croquet (*Adrian & Philip Goodman*)
Ottoline Morrell and T. S. Eliot (*Adrian & Philip Goodman*)

Between pages 448 and 449

Vivien with Mark Gertler and Julian Morrell (*Adrian & Philip
    Goodman*)
Vivien in her London flat (*Houghton Library*)
Mary Hutchinson (*Tate Gallery*)
Tom and Vivien in Sussex, 1919 (*Jane & Anne Haigh-Wood*)
Vivien with Sydney Schiff (*King's College, Cambridge*)
T. S. Eliot with his mother and sister Marian (*Houghton Library*)
T. S. Eliot at the clinic in Lausanne (*Jane & Anne Haigh-Wood*)
Dinner in Rome, 1930 (*Jane & Anne Haigh-Wood*)
T. S. Eliot outside Faber & Gwyer, 1926 (*Houghton Library*)
Vivienne in the garden at Chester Terrace, 1928 (*Harry Ransom Center,
    Texas*)
T. S. Eliot with Virginia Woolf and Vivienne, 1932 (*Houghton Library*)
W. L. Janes, 1929 (*Jane & Anne Haigh-Wood*)
T. S. Eliot with Maurice Haigh-Wood (*Jane & Anne Haigh-Wood*)
Léonide Massine (*Musée de l'Opéra, Bibliothèque Nationale*)
Portrait of T. S. Eliot by Patrick Heron (*A. C. Cooper*)
T. S. Eliot and Sir Alec Guinness (*Houghton Library*)
Mary Trevelyan (*Kate Trevelyan*)
Vivienne in 1934 (*Jane & Anne Haigh-Wood*)

Painted Shadow

A restless shivering painted shadow
In life, she is less than a shadow in death.

—T. S. ELIOT, *THE FAMILY REUNION*, 1938

"Dearest Ottoline . . . The truth will all come out,
if not in *our* life—*then after it*."

—VIVIENNE HAIGH ELIOT TO
LADY OTTOLINE MORRELL, 31 DECEMBER 1933

Preface

Posterity will probably judge Vivienne harshly,"[1] wrote Herbert Read in 1967, and so it has proved. Committed to an asylum in 1938, Vivienne has been all but obliterated from literary history; stigmatised as insane, it is she who has been the scapegoat for the failure of her marriage to T. S. Eliot. No verdict upon Vivienne is more memorable than that of her contemporary, Virginia Woolf: "She was as wild as Ophelia—alas no Hamlet would love her, with her powdered spots."[2] Woolf's often-quoted description, "this bag of ferrets is what Tom wears round his neck,"[3] has damned Vivienne in literary history as the madwoman in the attic, T. S. Eliot's own Mrs. Rochester, as surely as the poet's own portrait of a wife in *The Family Reunion* who is "a restless shivering painted shadow."

Later memoirs and biographies have continued to be largely hostile towards Vivienne. "Poor Tom Eliot married the landlady's daughter,"[4] a remark quoted by Ronald Kirk, typifies the widespread sympathy for "poor Tom," as his friends invariably described him, and the contempt for his allegedly vulgar and intellectually inferior wife. "Eliot met," wrote T. S. Matthews, author of *Great Tom* (1974), "the girl who was to plow up, harrow and strip his life to the bone,"[5] losing no time in comparing Vivienne to Zelda Fitzgerald, another literary lion's wife who ended her days in an asylum. Aldous Huxley considered Vivienne a *femme fatale,* who trapped the shy New Englander by means of her sexuality. Even modern biographers have tended to paint Eliot as the victim in the marriage, a man who bore the burden of an intolerable wife with patience and devotion: "I believe he went towards her with a kind of child-like trust,"[6] writes Peter Ackroyd. The myth of Eliot the martyr, a latter-day St. Thomas, had been born.

Such a version of history seemed to justify Vivienne's committal in 1938. And on Eliot's death in 1965, his status as the greatest poet of the twentieth century was confirmed by a plethora of tributes. Condolences came from the White House. A memorial service was held at Westminster Abbey. Over the years his reputation remained impregnable, his privacy impenetrable. Criticism of Eliot's work was policed by the New Critics who directed readers to the poetry not the poet, and acted as guardians of the poet's mysterious personal life. As scholars followed his impersonal theory of poetry into a literary cul-de-sac, Vivienne sank into deeper obscurity.

A few dissenting voices were raised. In 1963 Randall Jarrell had written prophetically in *Fifty Years of American Poetry:*

> Won't the future say to us in helpless astonishment: "But did you actually believe that all those things about objective correlations, Classicism, the tradition, applied to *his* poetry? Surely you must have seen that he was one of the most subjective and daemonic poets who ever lived, the victim and helpless beneficiary of his own inexorable compulsions, obsessions? From a psychoanalytical point of view he was by far and away the most interesting poet of your century."

Yet Eliot still remained elusive and any putative connection between the poet's art and biography was off limits.

On her death in January 1947 Vivienne Haigh Eliot had bequeathed her papers, which included diaries, fictional sketches, poetry, correspondence and account books, to the Bodleian Library, Oxford, under the terms of her 1936 will. At first the Bodleian believed it held copyrights in the manuscripts,[7] and in the 1970s it was possible for Dr. Lyndall Gordon, who undertook valuable work on Vivienne's papers, to quote from them in her biography of T. S. Eliot, with the permission of Vivienne's brother, Maurice Haigh-Wood, to whom she was referred by the library. However, following the 1984 performance of Michael Hastings's play, *Tom and Viv,* and the subsequent film, the copyright in Vivienne's papers was claimed by Mrs. Valerie Eliot, widow and literary executor of T. S. Eliot. From that date the second wife was, in effect, able to silence the first. Legal opinion remains divided on the matter of ownership of the copyright.

When I began working on Vivienne's papers I was astonished to encounter an artistic, energetic, gifted woman, very different from the stereotype who lingered in literary history. I was touched by Vivienne's poignant love for Tom Eliot, her anguish when he left her, which leapt out from the pages of her diaries. In page after page of her notebooks lay irrefutable evidence of the close literary partnership she and Eliot shared, including drafts of her poems, prose sketches and short stories, which he published in the columns of *Criterion*. Although in the 1930s her voice became agitated and fearful, it seemed to me incredible that she should have been certified as insane.

Nor could I ignore the confession made by Vivienne's brother, Maurice, shortly before his death in 1980, to Michael Hastings:

> It was only when I saw Vivie in the asylum for the last time I realized I had done something very wrong . . . She was as sane as I was . . . What Tom and I did was wrong. And Mother. I did everything Tom told me to. Not ashamed to say so . . .

It was a statement which hinted at darker motives for Vivienne's committal, and suggested that it was she, no less than Tom, who was victim in the marriage.

The mystery intrigued me. But reading Vivienne's passionate diaries had stirred another emotion apart from curiosity or sympathy: anger. I became determined to discover the truth that lay behind her incarceration, to rescue her from ignominy and disgrace, and to restore her to her rightful place in the historical record. For the next five years I would be hostage to Vivienne and her story.

It immediately became apparent that substantial obstacles lay ahead. A number of people told me that the task would prove impossible. It was a David against Goliath battle which five biographers had allegedly already attempted without success. No co-operation would be forthcoming from T. S. Eliot's second wife, Mrs. Valerie Eliot, who was following the instructions given by her late husband in a letter to his previous literary executor, John Hayward: "Your job," wrote Eliot, "will be to suppress everything suppressible."[8] The pessimists seemed justified when my then agent declined to have anything to do with the project. But it was too late to give up.

Unearthing the sources for a life of Vivienne did indeed prove problematical. Material was buried in archives on both sides of the Atlantic, in university and private collections, but with the invaluable encouragement of librarians and literary executors, they yielded a far greater fund of new information than I had ever imagined. All the same, days sometimes passed as I waited to see letters of Vivienne's which seemed mysteriously to have vanished from the face of the earth. More than one assistant expressed surprise that a first Mrs. Eliot existed, assuming that it was to Valerie that Tom was married when he wrote *The Waste Land*. I realised that, unbelievable as it may seem, some readers might have understood the dedication "To My Wife" in *Ash Wednesday* (1930) to refer to the second Mrs. Eliot. In later editions of the poems the dedication to Vivienne was dropped, as Eliot eradicated his first wife from his history. It was time to redress the balance.

As I followed the twisted trail of Vivienne's life, I felt strangely close to both Eliots. But the longer I worked, the more sure I became that it was justified to view T. S. Eliot's poetry and drama, bedrock of the modernist canon, through the lens of his life with Vivienne; that the autobiographical and confessional element in Eliot's texts had been greatly underestimated, due at least in part to a paucity of information.

Vivienne Eliot was a major influence upon her husband. The Eliots' tragic and tempestuous marriage was both source and subject of his poetry and drama; together they shared one of the most neurotic partnerships ever recorded, the deepest and strongest of the "tentacular roots" of his work. Vivienne had a predisposition to instability but Eliot, also neurotic, brilliant, repressed, unable to accept himself, contributed to that instability by withholding love, and it was this unhappy combination of "Tom and Vivienne," this crucible of dysfunction which, rather than hindering the poet's creativity, provoked it. For Vivienne was Tom's Muse: she was "the true inspiration of Tom," said Virginia Woolf. Theresa Garrett Eliot, Tom's sister-in-law, wrote: "Vivienne ruined him as a man, but she made him as a poet." Without Vivienne, in all probability, Eliot would not have given the world *The Waste Land.*

The poet had thrown down the gauntlet to researchers when he admitted that *The Waste Land,* far from being an expression of horror at the fate of Western civilisation, "was only the relief of a personal and wholly insignificant grouse against life."[9] Was he challenging readers to search for a new, personal understanding of his poetry, I wondered. How much did he want me to know? He had left clues everywhere, in the early manuscripts in the Berg Collection, New York Public Library, in the vast Eliot collection at the Houghton Library, Harvard University, in the largely untouched Mary Hutchinson and Ottoline Morrell Papers at the Harry Ransom Center at the University of Texas at Austin, in the John Hayward Bequest at King's College, Cambridge, and, most revealingly, in the excised pages of the "lost" Notebook of his early poetry ("Inventions of the March Hare") preserved in the Ezra Pound Papers at the Beinecke Library, Yale.

It may seem that T. S. Eliot was determined to preserve his reputation at all costs. However, it is significant that he failed to destroy revealing evidence. Although he arranged for Emily Hale's letters to him to be burnt, he sold the early "Notebook," so indicative of his sexual orientation, to his agent, John Quinn. Perhaps Eliot was less concerned in 1922 about the verdict of history than he became in the homophobic 1950s. To eradicate all traces of his secret life was possibly too great a task. But as Joseph L. Sax writes in *Playing Darts with a Rembrandt* (1999): "The failure of the principal to destroy material during his or her lifetime at least suggests a willingness to abide posterity's judgement." The descendants of Oscar Wilde co-operated generously with biographers; the daughter of Charles Dickens allowed herself to be persuaded by George Bernard Shaw not to burn her mother Nelly's letters to the great author. They were acknowledging that time may change puritanical attitudes and justify a new openness about family secrets once thought shameful. But if an archive is destroyed by the caprice of heirs—as Stephen Joyce burnt his schizophrenic aunt Lucia's letters to her father, James Joyce—the chance is lost forever for the wider community to come to a new understanding of a great artist. In time, claims of public interest deserve to be set against the private claims of family.

If her husband's wishes were perhaps ambiguous, Vivienne's desire to have her story told is indisputable and provided my motivation:[10] "You who in later years *will read these very words of mine* will be able to trace a true history of this epoch, by my diaries and papers," she wrote on 1 August 1934. More than once Vivienne congratulated herself on having left her papers to the Bodleian, writing triumphantly to Lady Ottoline Morrell: "The truth will all come out, if not in *our* life—*then after it.*"[11] Certainly Vivienne never wavered in her determination to preserve those sources which would enable later readers to understand, in some degree, the causes of her deepening hysteria.

Vivienne longed for the sympathy which was denied her in her lifetime. Instead, silenced behind the bars of the asylum, she has waited over fifty years for her story to be told. Only part of her diaries were eventually delivered by Maurice to the Bodleian, where at first they mouldered in the basement; the rest had gone up in flames in a garage fire at the house of Mildred Haigh-Wood, widow of her nephew Raggie. Vivienne's Bodleian papers have been controlled by the Eliot estate since 1985; I record now my debt of gratitude to Faber & Faber, representing the Estate, for their generous permission to quote without restriction from the writings and papers of Vivienne Eliot, although I have been required to paraphrase all direct quotations from the writings of T. S. Eliot, except for passages considered fair dealing by Faber & Faber.

C.S.J.
July 2001

I

A Bohemian from Bury

Oxford was losing its young men. It was the winter of 1914, and the streets were unnaturally quiet, the quadrangles deserted by those undergraduates who had joined the British army. But the university was not entirely empty. A number of Americans had arrived to fill the gaps, to the extent that at Merton College the Junior Common Room proposed the motion, "that this society abhors the Americanisation of Oxford." The resolution failed by two votes, after a recently arrived graduate student in philosophy named Thomas Stearns Eliot pointed out to his fellows how much they owed to "Amurrican culcher...in the movies, in music, in the cocktail, and in the dance."[1]

As spring arrived, the presence of the Americans attracted eager young women, short of partners in the first year of the Great War. One such visitor to Oxford was Vivienne Haigh-Wood, a vivacious artist's daughter from Hampstead who, one sunny afternoon, hired a punt on the River Cherwell. She was a slight girl with huge grey eyes, a governess with pretensions to culture. As the boat glided under the willows, Vivienne bent over her phonograph and placed the needle upon the record. The sound of ragtime drifted over the water.

The familiar tune attracted the attention of Eliot, the tall, nervous young American from Merton who had also taken a punt on the river. It reminded him of home in St. Louis, Missouri, where as a child he used to listen to the music from the honky-tonks, and promised an antidote to the gloom of wartime Oxford where he had been "plugging away at Hüsserl" and finding it terribly hard.[2] To his old Harvard friend, Conrad Aiken, Eliot had written on New Year's Eve 1914, "I hate university towns and university people, who are the same everywhere, with pregnant wives, sprawling children, many books and hideous pictures on the walls . . . Oxford is very pretty, but I don't like to be dead."[3]

Now, catching sight of Vivienne, one of the "river girls," as the press of that time described such light-hearted young women, Tom Eliot saw a way out of his gloom.[4] For in the punt with her was another American he thought he recognised: Lucy Thayer, a cousin of Scofield Thayer, Tom's fellow alumnus from Milton Academy in Massachusetts, a young man who came from the same distinguished New England milieu as Eliot, and who was also studying at Oxford, at Magdalen College, conveniently close to Merton. And Scofield was about to give a luncheon party to which Eliot was invited. Watching Vivienne and Lucy, laughing in their white dresses, his spirits began to lift. It only needed a word in Scofield's ear . . .

This tale was related by Eliot's friend Sacheverell Sitwell, and may well be apocryphal, although Vivienne *was* introduced to Tom Eliot at a lunch party in Scofield's rooms at Magdalen.[5] And she *did* love the river. One of her only surviving sketches is of a punt moored under the willows. For Vivienne, it seems, one glance was enough. She fell in love. It was a violent love—fierce, uncompromising and loyal. "Father and Tom, Tom and father, those two of my heart," she whispered in 1934 as she walked by her father's grave.[6]

The attraction between Vivienne and Tom was instant—and mutual. She admired his accent, which she described in her diary as "the *real* middle westerner's deep and thrilling voice," although in fact Eliot had been at some pains to lose his childhood accent in favour of the clipped tones of Boston. To Vivienne, the handsome American symbolised the heroic spirit of the Wild West, "the call to the wild that is in men"; but she had mistaken her man. It was to be but one of several fundamental misunderstandings. Eliot, too, had misjudged Vivienne. Unschooled in the complexities of the English class system, however well schooled he was in philosophy, Eliot was as impressed by Vivienne's leisured and apparently wealthy background as he was by her lively personality: her father, Charles Haigh-Wood, a retired member of the Royal Academy, lived on his unearned income and was the possessor of several houses, in Hampstead, Buckinghamshire and Anglesey; his son Maurice, educated at public school, was at Sandhurst training to be an army officer. But Vivienne's roots were, in fact, very different from what Eliot imagined.

Born in Bury, amidst the factory chimneys of the booming Lancashire cotton town, Vivienne Haigh-Wood made an unexpected arrival into this world on 28 May 1888. Her parents, local-boy-made-good Charles Haigh-Wood and his wife, Rose Esther, had taken lodgings near the railway station at Knowsley Street, having travelled north from London to mount an exhibition of the artist's pictures at a gentleman's club in his home town.[7] It was a long journey for the pregnant Rose, and perhaps one which brought on the birth inconveniently early. Had time allowed, Rose might have preferred her confinement to take place in the comfortable villa owned by her in-laws, Charles and Mary Wood, in Walmersley Road, nearby. As it was, the small, dark-haired baby arrived to the sound of trains, loaded with bales of raw cotton for the mills, steaming into Bury from Liverpool.[8]

The artist was busy with his one-man show in Manchester Road, and not until 4 July did he find time to register the birth of his first child, "Vivienne Haigh in the sub-district of Bury South in the county of Lancaster." Charles gave his occupation as "Artist (Painter)." The entry suggests a certain desire on the part of Haigh-Wood, as the artist styled himself, to avoid any confusion with his artisan father, plain Charles Wood, a gilder and picture framer born in nearby Bolton. It also suggests Haigh-Wood's pride in his success, for by 1888 the boy from Bury had become a Royal Academician whose fame had spread far beyond the cotton town in which he grew up.

In later life, Vivienne was ashamed of her northern roots. Writing to her new brother-in-law, Henry Ware Eliot, in October 1916 as she sat on the train to Manchester on her way to stay with a childhood friend, she declared: "I know I shall hate it. I know my Father was (is) a Lancashire (and Yorkshire) man, and I was born in Lancs, altho' I only lived there three weeks! But we have a number of *old* friends who live in Lancashire and North Wales. They are the most dreadful people really—very *very* rich manufacturing people—so provincial . . ."[9] Yet Vivienne had spent many childhood holidays at the *"beautiful"* country houses of the Lancashire manufacturers she affected to despise, and her upbringing had greater significance for her than she acknowledged. Her childhood was split between north and south, as was Eliot's, and there is a genuine sense of "not belonging" in her confession to Henry that she is a different person from the

girl who sat on the same train just two years ago, on her way to be bridesmaid to her hostess: "I have got out of the way of these people now—(not
that *I ever* was *in* the way—having lived in London and in such a different
set all my life) but I was more used to them." Vivienne's upbringing left her
self-conscious and snobbish, with an underlying sense of social inferiority
when she mixed with "old money," such as that exemplified by Lady
Ottoline Morrell, half-sister of the Duke of Portland. Yet Vivienne also inherited northern grit and determination, of which she was to have need in
the coming years, as she attempted to follow the path of Victorian upward
mobility set by her grandfather Wood.

Vivienne's father, Charles, was born over the shop owned by his father
in 22 Fleet Street, opposite the parish church in the centre of Bury. As a boy
he heard the heavy tramp of the women's clogs on the cobbles below as
they hurried to the mill. His father, also Charles, a master craftsman, had
moved his workshop from Bolton to Bury, where business flourished as the
looms whirred in the cotton factories and the mill owners embellished
their homes with pictures framed by Wood.[10] A shrewd marriage consolidated Wood's position. His bride was Mary Haigh, an Anglo-Irish
Protestant girl from Dublin with financial expectations, about seven years
his junior,[11] who had sailed from Kingstown to Liverpool, sometime after
the 1845 potato famine. It was a period of busy traffic between Liverpool,
Holyhead and Dublin, where the British government maintained a military garrison; the Haighs were a family of means, and Mary Haigh's marriage may have seemed like a misalliance to her family. Nevertheless, by
1851, she and Charles Wood had set up home in the four rooms over the
shop in Bury, where five children were born in quick succession. Young
Charles arrived in 1856, three years after the birth of the couple's first child,
Laura Amy. Another son followed, James, who died young, and two more
daughters, Emily and Sarah. There was Kate, too, an Irish servant girl
Mary had brought over from Kilkenny, and soon the cramped rooms over
the shop were uncomfortably crowded.[12] But by the 1870s Charles Senior's
business had prospered under the patronage of the mill owners, and he di-
versified into picture-dealing; soon he was able to move into a substantial
new house at 14 Albion Place, Walmersley Road.[13] He had laid the foundations for his rise from artisan to gentleman.

Young Charles Wood was not only as ambitious as his father, but precociously talented artistically. As a boy he was sent to nearby Bethel Sunday School in Henry Street, an independent Congregationalist chapel, and attended the local grammar school, but his sights were set on the world outside Bury. At some point in his upbringing he decided to combine his parents' surnames as Haigh Wood (later hyphenated), perhaps when his mother Mary inherited property in Kingstown (now Dun Laoghaire). The rents from the seven semi-detached houses made a difference to the family fortunes, and may have made it possible for Charles Wood to sign the 999-year lease on the house at 14 Albion Place for £780, a not inconsiderable sum in the late nineteenth century.[14] Wood sent his promising son to Manchester Art College, where he won several prizes. In 1873 Charles shook the dust of Bury from his feet, arriving in London at just seventeen to attend the Royal Academy School.

His rise in the art world was rapid. Charles later recalled how, when he was training at the Academy, he was noticed by the editor of the *Art Journal,* S. C. Hall, a "discriminating art critic," who praised his work; by the age of twenty-one he was exhibiting at the Academy and elected a member. Three years of travelling and studying the Renaissance masters in Italy followed, before he returned to settle in a little house at Taplow, on the upper reaches of the Thames. Nevertheless Haigh-Wood kept his links with the north. His ability to catch a likeness and his technical virtuosity brought him an increasing number of commissions from the local worthies of Bury and its neighbouring towns, Bolton and Rochdale, and he kept a studio at Castle Chambers in Market Street, Bury. His sister Sarah married into the Heap family, drapers in the same street as Charles Wood, and Mayor Heap was the subject of one of Charles's portraits in 1880. In 1899 he was still painting the aldermen and mayors of the neighbourhood, working on a portrait of Alderman Baron, who was about to be presented with the freedom of Rochdale. Three years earlier Charles had painted the portrait of Alderman Turner, Mayor of Rochdale.[15]

These portraits demonstrate Charles Haigh-Wood's ability to penetrate to the personality behind the mayoral robes, but he probably regarded them as bread-and-butter work. The pictures of which he was most proud were the drawing-room "conversation pieces" which made him a fashionable genre painter in the late nineteenth century—scenes of polite society in which gentlemen wooed elegant young ladies, and coy studies of children. His paintings carried titles like *Chatterboxes* and *The Old Love and the New.* So popular did this cloyingly sentimental style make him that all his pictures were sold before the doors of the Academy opened in 1899, two to the greeting-card manufacturers Raphael Tuck and Son for reproduction. Galleries from as far away as Australia were bidding for his pictures, the artist proudly recalled.

Despite his comfortable circumstances, Haigh-Wood complained to a reporter from the *Bury Times* in 1899 that although in France the government fostered art, "here in England the artist struggles on, sometimes receiving from purchasers the patronage necessary to keep him in comfort, but more often sighing for such assistance. An English artist, unless he is possessed of private means, can seldom afford to wait for the appreciation accorded to the highest form of art. He would be painting above the understanding of his public."[16]

These protests were hardly justified, for in fact Haigh-Wood had no need to live by his brush alone. On his father's death in 1881 the house in Albion Place passed to his mother, Mary, and on her death in 1890,[17] two years after Vivienne's birth, to his sister Sarah. But Charles, the only son, inherited the bulk of his mother's fortune. She left him her properties in Kingstown, then a fashionable watering place. Charles rented these properties out to the town corporation. "Dad collected and lived on the rent," remembered his son Maurice.[18] In addition, Haigh-Wood inherited Eglinton House, a substantial property in the same neighbourhood. He became, through this lucky legacy, not a struggling artist but an English Protestant landlord, living off the rents of his Irish tenants. As a fashionable painter with a private income, it was time to think about a change of lifestyle.

His first move was to leave Buckinghamshire for Hampstead, since "The Porch," his house at Taplow, though pretty, "did not in other respects answer my expectations."[19] Perhaps Rose, at home with the new baby, missed the proximity of her family. The couple moved to Hampstead in about 1891, taking a sixty-year lease on a house at 3 Compayne Gardens, the house which Vivienne was always to think of as home. Rose, *née* Robinson, had originally come from North London, and her sister Lillia Symes lived nearby, at Broadhurst Gardens. Soon the Haigh-Wood family settled into comfortable bourgeois life.

Charles no longer had the need to prostitute his art to the public.

Paintings such as *A Fisherman's Cottage, Runswick 1886*[20] show the social realism of which he was capable when he painted the Yorkshire fishing folk. This charming study of a young woman and her daughter, carrying apples down a path from their cottage, anticipates the Newlyn School. Yet Haigh-Wood never fulfilled his promise: he continued to churn out the mannered conversation pieces which reproduced so well as greeting cards, and when in 1910 his home town decided to honour him with a retrospective exhibition, it met with hostile reviews. The *Bury Times* said: "Mr. Haigh-Wood's art suffers much from the tyranny of fashion," while the *Manchester Guardian* was even more critical: " 'Is it Yea or Nay?' or 'Will He Come?' are the sort of questions the pictures ask; the trouble is that if the stories do not interest the spectator profoundly he is likely to find little else to satisfy him in the pictures."[21]

For Vivienne, however, her father remained a hero, the parent of whom she was so proud.[22] During her childhood his painting was at its most popular, reflecting the values of Victorian civilisation: she was born a year after Queen Victoria's Golden Jubilee when the imperialistic fervour which greeted General Gordon's death at Khartoum was still fresh in people's minds. Kaiser Wilhelm came to the throne a month after Vivienne's birth, and Arthur Conan Doyle had recently published his first Sherlock Holmes story. There were few doubts in British minds about the morality of empire, and such assumptions were reflected in Haigh-Wood's quintessentially Victorian style. When her father's reputation plummeted after the Tories fell from power and Liberal reforms began to chip away at the old capitalist class structure, it made no difference to Vivienne's cloistered world. Her father continued to paint in his studio at the top of the house, to make marmalade in the kitchen—cooking was one of his favourite ways of relaxing—and to conduct his peripatetic life between Hampstead, Bury and Buckinghamshire (where he had taken on another house to serve as a studio and picture store), and to spend summers with his family at Plas Llanfair, Llanfairpwll, a manor house on Anglesey. There was never enough money, yet in Hampstead Rose kept servants, ran an ordered household, took the children to the tennis club, and wintered abroad with Charles in the Alps and the south of France.

Vivienne was also her father's favourite model. One of his most dramatic portraits was of his daughter in a cape, exhibited at Bury Art Gallery in 1910[23] and at the Paris Salon. It was a painting he refused to sell. Rose also modelled for him, as did their son Maurice, who was seven years younger than Vivienne. She and Maurice are the subjects of a painting entitled *The Peace Offering,* or *I'll Be Sorry If You'll Be Sorry,*[24] painted in 1900 when Vivienne was twelve and her brother five. The room in which they stand, with its green patterned wallpaper and ornate fireplace, lined with blue and white Delft tiles, was probably the family drawing-room. The small boy, in frilled white shirt and breeches, holds out an apple to his elder sister, chubby and pretty in her smocked pink pinafore, with bows at the shoulders and long curling brown hair; the pair have clearly been squabbling, and a torn picture book lies open on the carpet. But the girl refuses the peace offering her brother shyly holds out to her.

This picture was originally entitled *Small Girl Sulking,* and is an early indication of the moods from which Vivienne suffered increasingly from the age of twelve. Identifying with her half-Irish father, she later described herself as "a tormented Celt" to Ezra Pound—but it was her other parent, Rose, who was called upon to provide the stable mothering Vivienne required as the father she adored was often absent. When Rose tried to deal with her high-spirited and sensitive daughter, mother and daughter often clashed.

In her early childhood Vivienne was infected in her left arm with tuberculosis osteomyelitis or tuberculosis of the bone, a common nineteenth-century disease. Treatment for TB of the bone was in its infancy in the 1890s, and there was little that the medical profession could do before the discovery of antibiotics. Patients were prescribed rest, fresh air and sunlight, and the infected parts were immobilised so that children whose spine and lower limbs were affected often spent years in plaster casts. Surgery was very limited, but Vivienne's parents insisted on the best for their daughter, calling in Sir Frederick Treves, Surgeon-Extraordinary to Queen Victoria, who became famous for treating the "Elephant Man." Although there is no record of his treatment of Vivienne, she may have been subjected to painful aspiration of any cold abscesses on her arm and possibly curetting of decayed bone. She later told Osbert Sitwell that she had had so many operations as a young girl that she had no memory of her life before the age of seven.[25]

Remarkably, Vivienne recovered from her illness well enough to excel physically in adolescence. It is possible that she made a spontaneous recovery; diagnosis was not always very precise. Her brother Maurice remembered that Vivienne was a good swimmer and reached a high standard at ballet. Brigit Patmore, a friend whom she met through Ezra Pound, wrote that "Vivienne had studied ballet technique—was expert at its many complications and yet it did not prevent her enjoyment of ballroom dancing."[26] Dance was always a powerful form of release for Vivienne. "Shut up, don't talk. Surely you know I can't dance and talk," she says in "The Night Club," one of her autobiographical short stories in which she calls herself "Sibylla."[27] Her admirer, probably one of the "pick-ups" whom she easily attracted, tells her that she dances better than anyone in the room. "You dance gloriously, you extraordinary little thing."

This portrait of a flapper, dancing deliriously to the new jazz tunes of the 1920s—and this story was written in 1924—encapsulates many elements of Vivienne's personality. The desire to shock, to be outrageous, the sharp wit combined with impatience with intellectual debate, the intense interest in clothes and making a dramatic appearance, were fundamental characteristics. Indeed, in Vivienne's story, "Sibylla" meets her brother "Horace," a barely disguised caricature of Maurice. "I like your surplice," he comments sarcastically, glancing down at her dress, which was presumably unwaisted. In fiction, as in life, Maurice was conventional like his mother, whose favourite he was, and frequently shocked by his impulsive, unpredictable sister.

On the surface Vivienne's adolescence seemed happy. The family often escaped London for Plas Llanfair, which Vivienne's father had taken on a ninety-year lease. The house was cold and hideous, thought Maurice, but for Vivienne, who liked nothing better than to walk the family dogs on a blustery day, the island of Anglesey was a haven from city life. The summer, she wrote, was the season for the country—the air, the wind tearing the hair and reddening the face as one tramped across the marshes. "Your scarf blows out like a flying jib behind you. Boots wet in the salt water puddles, one slips and slides across the rank grass—the seaweed slime. The sky is clear and scrubbed, reflected in blue pools." When a shower "stumps her," Vivienne shudders, eager to get home. But then the sun comes to laugh at her, warms her. "You smile and swing your stick, call the dog and push on towards the sea."[28] It may have been on Anglesey, or on holiday in Cornwall, that Vivienne first learnt to sail a boat and developed her love of the sea. And when the weather was so bad as to daunt even her, she put on plays for the family and entertained her bored brother.

Yet beneath the surface, Vivienne hid a shameful secret. For this energetic, sporty girl, the arrival of menstruation was truly a curse. She bled irregularly, probably as a result of a hormonal imbalance which today could be cured by the contraceptive pill. It is also possible that she might have had a polyp in her uterus, or cervicitis. Whatever the cause, the mood swings and abdominal pains and cramps which accompanied her all too frequent and unpredictable periods began to dominate her life.[29]

There was no treatment for the condition at this time. Vivienne became obsessional about washing her bedlinen herself, sometimes twice a day.[30] Nor could she turn to her father for help—women's problems were left to Rose and the doctors to deal with. Rose seemed to have little understanding of Vivienne's temperament, and wished only for her to conform to the mores of suburban Hampstead. She had no patience with Vivienne's rebellious urges to dance, to escape, to satisfy her frustrated creativity. In 1924 Vivienne wrote a sketch about her childhood in which she describes a family by the name of "Buckle": the Buckles were a local Hampstead family well-known to Vivienne, and in 1914 she became engaged to the son Charles. But her sketch, although possibly inspired by the Buckles, appears primarily to be a self-portrait as well as a vehicle for criticism of her mother. In the sketch she calls herself "Rosa," her mother's name. The family she describes hide their conflict behind laughter: "As a family the Buckles laughed too much. They were proud of their daughter. They thought themselves an exceptionally merry family . . . Unless they were laughing they were in the dumps . . ." The family were "all rather hysterical. Rosa was the only one with any character."

All Mrs. Buckle's children, declared Vivienne, suffered from having a mother with too strong a personality. "Her personality was so big that there was no room for any other personality at all in the crowded Kensington house." In the evenings she and "Rosa" sat together sewing, mending and darning for "the boys," making their own and other clothes. Mrs. Buckle liked her daughters to sing as they worked and she led the songs lustily: "She would be happy if her son brought home his friends, and there would be singing and playing the piano and laughter all evening." But if Maurice was allowed a certain freedom, Vivienne was not.

But even then [Mrs. Buckle] expected her daughters to go on with their sewing. She never liked it if one left the room. "Where are you off to?" she would say sharply. "Only to get a handkerchief, mother." "Then don't fiddle about up there, and don't leave the light on." The sisters would nudge each other, but they were too timid to disobey. None of them had ever been alone for a moment from their birth. They were anaemic and frequently painted. They were all pretty and healthy looking girls, and their brother was handsome.

It was an accurate self-description, and Vivienne knew also that she had a streak of wilfulness which "Mrs. Buckle" would be hard put to control. In "Rosa's" eyes, there is

A queer look, a fleeting expression of utter recklessness. It was a startling and disturbing look—unconscious and almost inhuman. It was not the recklessness of high courage and adventurousness but rather a wild expressive look of a secret urge towards self-destruction . . .[31]

In her struggle to control her determined and difficult daughter, Rose turned to the family doctor, Dr. Smith, who practised at Queen Anne Street, W1. Maurice subsequently recalled that Vivienne was about sixteen when her doctors began to prescribe drugs for her symptoms. Dr. Smith recommended bromide, the drug commonly used to treat hysterical or over-anxious patients. He probably diagnosed Vivienne as suffering from hysteria, a female malady in which the uterus was believed to work in opposition to the brain and cause irrational behaviour. It was a label often pinned upon young women who were unhappy and frustrated with their circumscribed lives in the late nineteenth and early twentieth centuries. Potassium bromide acts on the central nervous system. "By lowering the activity of both motor and sensory cells, the bromides are of great service . . . in the treatment of cerebral excitement," according to the British Pharmaceutical Codex of 1911. They "render the brain less sensitive to disturbing influences," reduce all reflexes and promote sleep. Bromide, often administered as a preparation dissolved in alcohol, was the drug of choice

and habit for most general practitioners of the period, and was especially
recommended for dysmenorrhoea, or irregular menstruation, as well as
hysteria. And so the process of tranquillising Vivienne began. Her regular
"doses," as she called them, were facilitated by Rose, who had an account
as a private patient of Dr. Smith's at Allen and Hanbury, a pharmacy in the
nearby Finchley Road. As well as bromide, the doctors prescribed
Vivienne "Hoffman's Anodyne" and other powders. The anodyne was dissolved in spirit of ether, a powerful anaesthetic with a distinctive smell.
Maurice believed Vivienne's medicines contained formaldehyde, and that
she also took snuff. She was, he recalled, "stuffed with filthy drugs" by the
time she reached adulthood.

As the medical bills for Vivienne's treatment mounted, so did
Maurice's resentment of his sister. He became convinced that the heavy
burden of her medical expenses on the family budget prevented him going
to a first-rate public school. After Ovingdean Prep School, Maurice was accepted at Malvern College, which he complained was a "second-class
school." It seems not to have occurred to Maurice, who spent thirteen years
trying to find employment as a stockbroker after leaving the army, that he
lacked the intellectual credentials for Winchester, or the social background
for Eton. The difference in fees between one public school and another
would not have been great, and it is more likely that this family with its
roots in trade did not have the right connections for entry into the most
privileged schools. But Maurice continued to bear a grudge against his sister, just as she continued to embarrass him, turning up at Malvern to take
him out to tea, wearing a white shirt and tie above her long skirt—an outfit the seventeen-year-old boy considered unbecomingly masculine—and
turning cartwheels on the headmaster's lawn.

A "double-binding" situation thus arose in which Rose and Maurice
combined to designate Vivienne the "victim" in the family; she was the one
they were permitted to harm, the scapegoat for Maurice's failings.[32]
Vivienne's father Charles, her anchor, failed her; anxious for a quiet life,
and dominated by Rose, he distanced himself from the situation both emotionally as well as physically, abandoning his vulnerable daughter to the
mercy of his wife. For Vivienne, her family became the source of overwhelming stress, as her mother criticised her, controlled her, and bombarded her with conflicting commands. "Vivie," as Maurice called his

and sister both liked to dance, and Vivienne shone at the army balls. As she entered her twenties, marriage became her goal: it would give her status and identity and a way out of the family ghetto.

Once again the obstacle was her mother. Rose made up her mind that Vivienne was not fit to marry or have children, and stood in the way of her efforts to form a relationship which might lead to marriage. Rose believed that Vivienne suffered from "moral insanity," another diagnosis much in favour with doctors of the period, such as Sir George Henry Savage, who treated Virginia Woolf. Savage defined "moral insanity" as a condition in which "the moral nature or moral side of the character is affected greatly in excess of the intellectual side." Savage believed that a child might be born "prone to wickedness," and that "many so-called spoiled children are nothing more nor less than children who are morally of unsound mind . . . In many cases, doubtless, the parent who begets a nervous child is very likely to further spoil such a child by a bad or unsuitable education." It was a diagnosis which could be applied to Vivienne who, during long periods of illness, had been indulged. Such children, argued Savage, were "naturally unstable and unfitted to control their lower natures."[36]

"Moral insanity," a term more usually applied to women than men, was shorthand for a precocious sexual awareness leading to promiscuity.[37] There is little doubt that Rose feared her strong-willed daughter would lose her virginity and disgrace the family. In her diary Vivienne remembered her "young days, at Esher, when a whole gang of us . . . painted Esher red." The gang consisted of herself, Maurice, Lucy Thayer and "dozens of others."[38] Such wild partying aroused her mother's deepest apprehensions. Significantly the bromide prescribed for Vivienne was recommended to damp down sexual desire, and was labelled an anaphrodisiac by the Pharmaceutical Codex. In reality Vivienne may have had a predisposition to manic depressive illness, which would account for her uninhibited "manic" episodes which so alarmed Rose, alternating with periods when she preferred to withdraw from society. It was the secret fear of inherited insanity which lay behind Rose's determination that Vivienne should not marry. During her teenage years Vivienne was rebellious, but the question of marriage did not arise. In 1914, however, when she was twenty-five, she fell in love. It was time to challenge her mother.

2

The River Girl

rivileged, protected and popular, Vivien, as she now chose to
call herself, lived the life of a social butterfly as the merry-go-
round of balls and parties whirled ever faster in the shadow of war. Later
she remembered how she

> started life as a beautiful Princess admired and worshipped by all
> men and living in a house of rosy glass through which one
> watched the envious world go by & how the glass house is bro-
> ken and one wants to get back inside, safe & beautiful & se-
> cure.[1]

Vivien was "fresh, innocent, a chatterbox, pretty," said a friend of Stephen
Spender's who used to dance with her at the Hammersmith Palais de
Danse before the war. She was nicknamed "The River Girl," wrote
Spender, by "Eliot's social friends (Lady Ottoline Morrell, St. John
Hutchinson and his wife, Virginia and Leonard Woolf, the Sitwells, the
Aldous Huxleys),"[2] although Eliot himself called Vivien and her friends
"Char-flappers"; and, according to Osbert Sitwell, "River-Girl" was a term
used by the contemporary press to describe "that kind of young person—
the rather pretty young girl who could be seen, accompanied by an undergraduate, floating down the river in a punt on a summer afternoon."[3] It
was a light, insouciant name, reflecting Vivien's supposed character, and
suggesting the sparkle and mutability of water, that quality which led
Brigit Patmore to describe her as "shimmering" with intelligence. But it is
also derogatory, conjuring up the image of the only half-human naiad or
water sprite who lives at the bottom of the river and lures men to fall in

love with her. "There seems a trace of mockery in this name," said Spender, remarking damningly, "She had a history of illness and 'nerves.' "

But Vivien was neither as conventional nor as empty-headed as her nickname suggests. In the undated (early 1920s), prose sketch of George Bernard Shaw, in which she described feeling like a princess in the pre-war era, she also tells how she longs to hold Shaw's hand and "tell him all about the Firebird and cages . . ." The Firebird, flying free, symbol of escape from the confines of bourgeois life, inspired Vivien, and in 1914 it was escape from her golden cage on which she was determined. Under her fashionable flapper dresses beat a passionate heart, and inside her neatly bobbed head was a sharp brain eager to be of use. She had trained as a secretary and was proficient in shorthand and typing, and in the winter of 1914–15 she worked as a governess in a family in Cambridge as well as successfully tutoring backward children individually.

In early 1914 Vivien was twenty-five, and would be twenty-six in May. It was a critical age for any young woman, and matrimony was necessarily in the forefront of her mind. The alternative of spinsterhood was, in that period, too horrible to contemplate. The panic which such a prospect aroused in Vivien is shown in her portrait of the Buckle family in which she writes about herself and the young man with whom she fell in love in 1914, Charles Buckle. In her sketch, Vivien calls herself Rosa Buckle, is an indication that she liked to imagine herself as Charles's wife, even though her fictional little sisters tease her about her fiancé's lack of good looks: "Certainly Charles Spencer was neither fair nor tall nor handsome (but) Rosa was twenty-six and in 1886 that was very nearly an old maid."[4]

In January 1914, Vivien had bought herself a Boots' Lady's Diary and Notebook, and began recording the progress of her romance with "C.B.," as she usually referred to the young schoolmaster and occasional journalist. It seems that at first Charles and Rose Haigh-Wood had no objection to their daughter's suitor.[5] He came from a local family whom they knew, and seemed a suitable match.

Vivien's brief, excited entries for the month of February paint a picture of frequent, intense meetings with Charles Buckle. Proximity in North London made meeting easy, and the weeks flew by with almost daily outings together to tea-shops in Baker Street, dances at the Elysée dance hall, where she had a "perfect time," visits to Whiteleys, where

Vivien had her hair washed and waved, and lunches with her American friend Lucy Ely Thayer. At the Dutch Oven on 12 February Vivien and Lucy discussed the progress of the romance; afterwards Vivien rang up Buckle and was pleased to hear he had missed her and "hadn't liked it."[6]

Vivien and Lucy Thayer had met in Vevey in 1908 when the two families were holidaying in the Alps; the Haigh-Woods regularly visited Switzerland in the winter, perhaps on the recommendation of Vivien's doctors when she was recovering from TB of the bone. It was a time when Charles Haigh-Wood was forbidden by Rose to bring his paints, and the family could relax together in the mountains. Vivien was a bold and graceful skater; she and Lucy became firm friends, bound together by their love of sports and shared experience of "nerves."[7] Soon Lucy became a regular guest at Compayne Gardens, and her parents frequently took a house in London.

In the autumn of 1913 Lucy's cousin, Scofield Thayer, later to be editor of *The Dial,* also arrived in England, to study at Oxford. Scofield was the only child of Florence and Edward Thayer, and his father was the millionaire owner of several woollen mills in Worcester, Massachusetts. Thayer Senior had high expectations of his only son and intended that he should crown his successful academic career at Milton Academy and Harvard with an Oxford degree. Scofield, however, having no need to work for a living, had other ideas.

That Michaelmas term, Scofield took rooms in the cloisters at Magdalen, looking out on the lawn in the middle of the quad. Prince George of Teck had rooms nearby, and HRH the Prince of Wales on the opposite side. Thayer himself, wrote his friend Henry McBride, seemed "more than a gentleman, a prince."[8] He regarded himself as an aesthete, and at once joined the Nineties Club, a society dedicated to living by the principles of Oscar Wilde. "The society conceives of the world as having come again to the same condition as it found itself in the 1890s," said its manifesto. "Following the lead of the obscure young men who followed Oscar Wilde, they are busy marking time and making every effort to live only a sensuous life with no purpose in the future . . ." The "amusing" side of the club members was said to be their "odd costumes of long white cloaks, great rings on their fingers, rare flowers in their rooms etc."[9]

Scofield apparently began reading for a degree in English, before switching to philosophy in 1914, and registering for a BPhil, but there is no

record of his ever taking a degree. Instead he began collecting pictures, laying the foundations for his great collection of modern art; shopping, visits
to his tailor, and to his aunt Josephine, drew Scofield to London, where it
was inevitable that he would one day meet Vivien.

Buckle, meanwhile, had been drawn into the friendship between
Vivien and Lucy Thayer, taking both girls to the "kinema" on 18 February.
On the 21st Vivien was invited to a dinner party Lucy's parents were giving in London. It was a high-point of the romance. Vivien wore her
favourite yellow silk dress, which set off her shining brown hair; Buckle
had sent her "dark flowers," and after the dinner party he took her dancing, before returning her to the Thayers, where she was staying the night.
He did not leave till 2 a.m.; "Told me he loved me," wrote Vivien with satisfaction in her diary.

Vivien lay in late the next morning, and Lucy came to sit on the edge
of her bed. No doubt they discussed C.B. and Vivien's hopes of a proposal.
Vivien dressed and went out to lunch, followed by another intimate tea
with her boyfriend, but hardly had love been declared than a quarrel followed in Holland Park. She gave him up. "Fearful nerves and depression,"
she confided miserably to her diary.[10] It is probable that she was suffering
from pre-menstrual tension, for one of the stars which appear to mark the
beginning of her period decorates the next day's entry.

Two days later the lovers made up. "Got engaged to C.B." wrote
Vivien triumphantly, heavily underlining the entry in her diary for 26
February, the day of Buckle's proposal. In her excitement she fainted the
next morning, but her recovery was swift; by that evening she was well
enough to go dancing again with her new fiancé at the Savoy. The next day
Buckle came to dine with the Haigh-Woods and asked Vivien's father for
her hand in marriage. Vivien was apprehensive and nervous, fearful that
Charles might not agree. But Haigh-Wood consented, offering to settle
£500 on his only daughter, and to give her £50 outright. Overcome with
joy, Vivien went to Silverman, her dressmaker, and ordered a new coat
and skirt to celebrate her engagement.[11]

Her happiness was short-lived, however. Over tea on Sunday at
Compayne Gardens, where Vivien and Buckle had an *"awfully* nice time,"
she persuaded him to tell his mother of their engagement that evening.
Later he rang to say that Mama very much disapproved. Vivien was "very

upset" and spent a sleepless night, and the next day, Monday, was "the most awful day." Rose Haigh-Wood decided to intervene. She summoned Charles Buckle and overrode her husband's decision, ordering the young man to break off the engagement. Vivien, she declared ominously, was unsuited for marriage and maternity. "Mother sent me away and talked to him and thoroughly upset him," recorded Vivien. "Mummy warned CB off," recalled Maurice,[12] relating how the engagement was broken off. According to Vivien's diary, Buckle stayed on and on and the row "got worse and worse." "When Rosa Buckle became engaged to Charles Spencer . . . Rosa was very angry and her cheeks were red," wrote Vivien in her fictionalised account of the event. "She tried to be dignified and scornful but her eyes filled with mortified tears . . . Mother herself felt a little blank on Rose's engagement . . . She still loved to see 'a fine tall handsome man,' if possible with brown eyes and a heavy moustache."[13] The ill-favoured Buckle was driven out, complaining that he felt ill as he left the house of arguments and tears. The family friction which had rumbled through Vivien's adolescence, as the Haigh-Woods found themselves divided, father and daughter ranged against mother and son, had culminated in the sabotaging of Vivien's hopes of independence by her mother.

Rose Haigh-Wood may have felt she had her daughter's interests at heart, but it is more likely that she was influenced by early twentieth-century hysteria over eugenics, and fears of the physical deterioration of the British race aroused by the fiasco of the Boer War. Fabians such as Sidney and Beatrice Webb and Bernard Shaw argued that "degeneracy" was inherited and the "feeble-minded" should be compulsorily sterilised. Doctors declared that "moral insanity" disqualified women from motherhood, and women who had illegitimate babies were confined to mental asylums as "morally insane"; the fear that Vivien might become pregnant was never far from her mother's mind. According to Maurice: "Mummy wasn't very clever," there was "something in her that made her fancify; Mummy got so worried she believed her own fears" of Vivien's "moral insanity," which she placed in a different category from "lunacy." His sister was never a "lunatic," emphasised Maurice.[14]

Another factor in the family opposition to the engagement, from Buckle's mother as well as from the Haigh-Woods, was the approach of war. Although there is no hint in Vivien's artless account of tea parties, balls, dinner parties, art and dance classes, of the escalating quarrel with Germany, the bubble was soon to burst. Charles Buckle had volunteered for the army and was waiting to hear if he had secured a commission. His thoughts were of politics, even of glory, as much as of marriage, and Rose's prohibition as well as his own mother's may have made him hesitate.

The morning after Rose's bombshell, Tuesday, 3 March, Buckle telephoned Vivien to say he was too ill to go in to school to teach. "It's *all wrong,"* wrote Vivien miserably. Lucy had spent the night with her to comfort her and now Vivien went round to the Thayers' house for lunch, where she rang Buckle again, who would not come out to see her. *"Terrible.* Everything slipping away," wrote Vivien. As usual she cheered herself up by having a fitting for a new dress.[15]

Within a day the lovers were together again, although not harmoniously so. They met for tea and went to see *The Darling of the Gods.* The next night Vivien decided to escape her mother and went to stay with Lucy at 38 Inverness Terrace, Bayswater, a flat rented by the Thayers. Buckle took Vivien out for the evening, and there was a *"fearful* scene" in the bedroom. "I gave way altogether," recorded Vivien. "No good."[16] Did Buckle voice the fears put in his head by Mrs. Haigh-Wood? In any event, Vivien was too depressed to see "B" for several days. By Sunday, however, they were meeting again for tea at the Old Oak, and Buckle was in a "perfect mood." Vivien, in response, was "standoffish," which had the desired effect. The young schoolmaster asked her out to dinner, and she accepted. Over the meal at the Boulogne, he told her of his plans to give up his job and go to France. It was a *"perfect* evening," wrote Vivien happily. Everything seemed right again, and he was "splendid."[17]

Now their daily meetings restarted. Soon Buckle was again in a "vile mood." Mrs. Thayer came into the room in the middle of the argument, and was "very unpleasant. So was B!" Buckle went to meet his mother for dinner, and Vivien was trembling all evening. The next night she had to leave the cinema because of the "noises,"[18] an indication of the hypersensitivity to noise of which Vivien was to complain later to her friend Sydney Schiff. The couple returned to the Thayers' house at 10:45, and by the next day Vivien had decided the Thayers, who also disapproved of the engagement, were all "beastly" ("I hate it!"), and she would be thankful to leave, although that evening she went to the ballet with Lucy to see Nijinsky.[19]

Restless, volatile and upset over the deterioration of her relationship with Buckle, the next day Vivien decided on impulse to visit her friend Constance Darley at Bookham in Surrey. The Darleys were "perfectly sweet," and Vivien felt calmer in their company, sewing quietly all morning and motoring to Guildford in the afternoon. But she could not stay away from Charles Buckle. She decided to slip up to town the next day and sleep at Inverness Terrace: "A great risk—but still—."[20] After church the next day she took the train to Waterloo, and met her lover. As usual they dined in Soho and went to the cinema, returning to the Thayer residence at 11:30 p.m. where another "very great scene" took place in the bedroom. It is probable that by this time Vivien and "Charles" were having an illicit sexual affair, and Maurice later stated that "Vivie and Charles had a *real* affair";[21] if that were the case it would account for Mrs. Haigh-Wood's anxiety. Certainly Vivien's attachment to Charles Buckle was deep enough for her to risk disgrace, for as well as sneaking away from the Darleys, she seems to have met "B" at the home of his aunt, Lady Allen, who was away, as well as at the Thayers' residence, which she used with the increasing disapproval of Mrs. Thayer.

Early the next morning a guilty Vivien hurried back to Bookham, "glad to be back and to find that nothing had happened to discover me. I was so nervous."[22] That night she had a long talk with Mrs. Darley, who encouraged her to abandon the idea of marriage to Buckle. Vivien sent an express letter to Buckle, asking him to come and see her at home that evening; she was "dead tired," but knew "definitely what I wished to do. It is [for] the best."[23] Lady Allen was returning to her flat—"and of course that means the very end."[24] On 20 March, a cold snowy day, Vivien stayed indoors with a "fearful liver and very depressed." She had requested her father to write to Buckle, saying that "he prefers that all consideration of marriage shall for a time be set aside, and that we shall have no further opportunity of knowing each other better."[25]

Although Vivien had now broken off the engagement, she remained in love with Buckle. Gloomily she began to make herself a blue dress, but could not resist ringing Buckle to say she was "not very well." All the next morning she sewed and brooded about the affair, only emerging for a trip to Harrow with Lucy. That night she wrote Buckle a long letter.[26] On Tuesday he came in for tea, and her father joined them. The next day

Vivien could not resist ringing Charles up late that evening, who was *"very horrid."*[27] The young man must have been confused by Vivien's contradictory behaviour; for hardly had she rejected him than she was pestering him to meet her again. Her capricious behaviour continued; Vivien sent Buckle a wire demanding he come to tea again. He did so, and a "dreadful, awful time" ensued. She continued to nurse hopes of a reconciliation while Buckle went to the Boat Race, only to find them finally dashed when they met on Passion Sunday for tea at their favourite tea-shop, the Dutch Oven. "Really the *best, the very end,*" wrote Vivien in her diary. "Had a better talk, but it is all quite hopeless."[28]

After that meeting, there continued to be "no word or sign" from Buckle, and Vivien consoled herself with the return of her brother Maurice, now an officer cadet at Sandhurst. She took Maurice and her mother to watch her ballet class with her friend Iris. But on 2 April "bad neuralgia" did not prevent her from going dancing with Buckle, who had once again responded to her letters and telephone calls. It was, remembered Vivien, "an extraordinary evening," which renewed the affair. The couple came back through Holland Walk, the scene of a previous quarrel, "and here things happened." They kissed and petted; perhaps Buckle confessed his love again, but it was only, supposed Vivien cynically, because she was going away again to stay with the Darleys.[29]

"The happiest Easter Sunday I have had for years" followed, as Charles took Vivien for dinner in Soho, and after to the "kinema" and out to coffee. It was *"a perfect* evening" she wrote dreamily.[30] "Heavenly" days followed, as Charles continued to ring three times a day, to take Vivien to lunch, tea and the "kinema"; they visited St. Paul's, saw the play *The Melting Pot* ("rotten play but *lovely* evening"),[31] had innumerable cups of coffee in the Monaco, and while Charles was teaching, Vivien gardened or went to her dance class. Sometimes she lunched with him at Hammersmith, near his school, "hung about" while he taught, and met him at the end of school for tea at 4:30 p.m.[32] They had become inseparable.

This idyll was shattered when once again Vivien exploded on the day she began menstruating: "I made an awful row, and cried and screamed, and made myself ill." She lay down all afternoon and cried, but was well enough the next day to "bring Buckle round" over lunch, and to leave for

Surrey again where she spent the next five days on a walking holiday in the hills with Lucy. The two young women followed Vivien's favourite route from Chilworth to Shere, stopping for the night at the White Horse Inn, and tramping to Coldharbour, ten miles away, where they spent another night before walking back to Shere. Although "dreadfully tired" on Friday, Vivien sketched the stream and the church, before returning on Saturday to Hampstead.[33]

A day or two later, Buckle went down to Torquay with his aunt. It was in his absence that Vivien met Lucy's cousin, the princely Scofield Thayer, over tea on 30 April 1914. "Liked him very much," she recorded.[34] The next day, 1 May, Vivien and Lucy set off for a day in the Buckinghamshire countryside. Once again a ten-mile walk followed, and at Chalfont St. Giles, Vivien and her friend found "the most perfect cottage in the world," which, on impulse, they rented.

A week later, when the Haigh-Woods were out to dinner, Buckle came back to 3 Compayne Gardens at nine o'clock, and he and Vivien went into the tennis court for what seems to have been another romantic interlude. Vivien made no entries in her diary for the rest of May or June, but she was drawing closer to Buckle and his family. On 29 July she wore her new dress for the service of St. Paul's Apposition, and "sat with his people." Mrs. Buckle asked her to go back for dinner, and she ended up having "a *lovely* time" and liking his sister very much. Charles brought her home very late, and two days later took her dancing again at the Savoy with his sister.

On 3 August, the day before Britain declared war on Germany, Vivien made her first entry concerning the coming conflict: "Great suspense about the war." Charles came to tea, for the last time, although Vivien did not then know it. Her brother Maurice had arrived back from camp, "because of the war," but Vivien had to leave for a prearranged visit to Henley-on-Thames. She missed Buckle badly, and when on 6 August she received a letter from him, saying he had written to the War Office to offer himself as a "Galloper" or interpreter, she at once decided to come home, where she found "everything was wrong, as I expected."[35] For the next two days, Friday and Saturday, Vivien went to the town hall to do some work for Colonel Carpenter, perhaps typing or rolling bandages. On Monday she

quarrelled with Charles, probably over his decision to enlist. A brief interlude followed with Maurice at Esher, where she and her brother had "an
excellent time of tennis and golf—but for the trouble with CB,"[36] before returning to London to meet him at Victoria Station where they had an amicable tea. Vivien was by then resigned to his decision to serve in the army.

On 24 August, Charles rang to say he had been called to the War
Office, examined, and put on the shortlist. "He is certain to go in a few
days," wrote Vivien. "He is delighted."[37] The lovers spent the next two
days in each other's company, Charles accompanying Vivien to the town
hall to help with her war work. At lunchtime on Wednesday, 26 August,
Buckle's mother rang to say that the War Office had wired for him. "He
dashed out, had had no lunch, ate half a pork pie in an Express, and started
in a taxi." Charles would not let Vivien go all the way to the War Office
with him, and she was "fearfully upset and behaved stupidly." Her tears
had no effect. Caught up in the patriotic fervour of the time—the mood of
"dulce et decorum est pro patria mori"[38]—and the cheerful belief that the
adventure of war would be over before Christmas, Charles was "icy" in the
face of Vivien's pleas.

On 28 August she set out at quarter to nine to "see the last of CB."
Dolefully she watched him and his mother going into the War Office, and
then waited outside, joining Mrs. Buckle who was walking up and down.
An hour later Buckle came out, and said goodbye. He was "very cheerful,"
said Vivien. "I saw the last of him," she records proudly, for she went back
when his mother had gone and just caught a final glimpse of him jumping
into a taxi with another soldier. When they said goodbye, Buckle's words
were: "Goodbye child, for the present." "I hope it may be. But I am sure it
is for ever," wrote Vivien with a heavy heart.[39]

At this point, her diary entries ended. The fact that she kept an almost
daily record of her rollercoaster relationship with Charles Buckle is an indication of the importance of this love affair to her; after he left for France,
Vivien's mood must be gleaned from her letters to Scofield, to whom she
grew closer in Buckle's absence. A characteristic letter she scribbled at one
o'clock in the morning in February 1915 expresses the bubbling exuber-
ance, the teasing wit, the sharp mood changes which both bewildered and
fascinated the opposite sex. On 22 February, in a letter to Scofield only
dated "Sunday," she writes:

Dear Scofield

Is'nt [sic] it nice of me to write you this—out of a clear blue sky? Is'nt it *kind?* Please say—yes it is—Vivien. Tell me, did you think the half letter I gave you was beastly? Please say. I didn't mean it to be. Although this is Sunday, it is very early on Sunday, in fact, Scofield my child, it is 1 o'clock in the morning. I have just got back from the dance . . . and I am making a night of it as I usually do. If I don't go to bed at 10, I don't want to go to bed at all . . .

Vivien's late hours are, she remarks, a frequent and bitter cause of contention between Scofield's cousin Lucy and herself.

The dance was VERY nice, says Vivien in her letter. But, being a philosopher, she supposes he doesn't care very much. Vivien is obviously impressed that Scofield is a philosopher, although she doesn't even know the meaning of the word. "Do tell me what it is, will you?" she asks pertly. A friend of Scofield's called Parr has told Vivien that *everybody* has a philosophy, and it's no particular distinction. The subject both worried and intrigued her because Buckle, she says, had always told her that her problem was that she had no philosophy. He used to implore her with tears to try and get a little—"but where, and how do you get it?" Her own flippant creed, outlined to Scofield, is that whatever happens, you say to yourself—I don't care. I've got myself, what more do I want? Yet she feels this is not an attractive attitude. "Please tell, what's the truth of this philosophy business?"[40]

Vivien's naïve questions in this letter betray her lack of confidence about her education. She is curious, anxious to be better informed, and yet defensive in the face of the careless superiority of Harvard philosophy graduates who seem to have the key to the knowledge she covets. Even Buckle, who claimed to love her, criticised her for her thoughtless, irresponsible attitude to life before he left for the front, something she could not forget. She will write for support to Ellen Thayer (another cousin of Scofield's, who in March 1925 came to work on *The Dial* as Assistant Editor), says Vivien; Ellen thinks Vivien is *"very clever,"* she tells Scofield defiantly. "If you don't believe me, ask her."

Ellen Thayer had said, before their acquaintance, that she wished

Scofield and Vivien knew each other. However, after his last visit to town Vivien is inclined to doubt whether this is a point in her favour. Scofield was scolded for trying to "work her in" as well as a visit to his tailor and aunt, and still catch the 5:30 train back to Oxford. "You must remember I am English and not accustomed to being pushed about in a hurry," she informs him. Sitting at tea with a distraught American holding his watch in his hand and giving her so many minutes in which to eat her tea and so many in which to say what she has to say, unnerves her, and causes her to relapse into one of those "awful silences" which are the terror of her American acquaintances.

Yet despite her complaints about American habits, Vivien's closest friends after Buckle's departure were American: Lucy, Scofield, and his circle. "You do seem to have a lot of friends, which is one good point about you," she informs Scofield, only half-jokingly. She liked their self-assured manners and expensive clothes, remarking à propos of Scofield's friend Parr, whom she disliked because he was too "posy (and prosy)," that she did *hate* people who had no pose, though too much of it made them unreal and nauseating. Scofield responded to Vivien's flirtatious overtures, and by 3 March 1915 he was complimenting her on "the radiancy of her countenance," and comparing her flatteringly to the *Mona Lisa*.[41] "No, Scofield, you have never seen me 'divine' or 'exquisite' yet. But I hope you may some day," replied Vivien, who was in bed with "prosaic, recurring influenza" and not looking robust, merely "interesting . . . It is nice of you to compare me to the Mona Lisa. I wish she and I had anyhow one point in common, and that is that someone would cut me out of my frame too."[42]

Vivien's weakness for good dressing continued to make her susceptible to the charms of men in uniform. That spring (1915) she was badgering her brother to introduce her to an officer called Butler-Thuring: Maurice was going to "overcome his prejudice against opening his lips, and speak to Mr. B-T," she confided excitedly to Scofield. In March she was invited to dance at the Savoy with a Captain Holmes. But by this time Scofield had also introduced her to another friend from Milton Academy and Harvard days: Thomas Stearns Eliot, whose tall, dark good looks and languid poise were guaranteed to appeal to the eager, restless Vivien, disappointed in love and looking for a new boyfriend.

3

An Alien in America

Four months after Vivienne was born in humble circumstances in Bury, another baby was born to an older, wealthier mother in the booming city of St. Louis, Missouri, on the other side of the Atlantic. Thomas Stearns Eliot was the seventh child of his forty-five-year-old mother, Charlotte, who had assumed her child-bearing days were at an end. Nevertheless, a new son was welcome, for Charlotte's family was predominantly female: her daughters Ada, Margaret, Charlotte and Marian preceded Thomas, as well as her first son, Henry, eight years older than his little brother. "Lallie and little Thomas are well," read the telegram from the proud father, brick manufacturer Henry Ware Eliot Sr., to his brother, Pastor Thomas Lamb Eliot of Portland, Oregon, announcing the birth of the new baby on 26 September 1888. In a letter written the same day, Eliot *père* added: "Young Thomas Stearns (for his grandfather) came forth at 742 hrs am."[1] The birth must have seemed like a miracle to Charlotte Champe Eliot, a deeply religious woman who had lost another daughter, Theodora, in 1886, and Tom soon became her favourite.

At first the baby seemed healthy enough, but Charlotte's protective instincts were quickly aroused when it was found that he had a congenital double hernia, which she was afraid might rupture at any moment. As a result Tom had to wear a truss from boyhood. As late as 1905, when he was sixteen, she was writing to his prospective headmaster at Milton Academy, Massachusetts, a preparatory school for Harvard University: "Tom has never fully realised until now, when he is almost the only fellow debarred from football, his physical limitations. We hope in a few years he will be entirely normal . . ."[2] Her nervousness at allowing Tom independence was intensified by being an older parent, and he was rarely allowed out of the sight of the women who cared for him. Ada, the eldest sister, nineteen years older than he, became a second mother to the little boy who was so much younger than his brother and sisters that he had to play alone. Even when he was given sailing lessons at the family's summer house at East Gloucester, Massachusetts, mother came too.

Nevertheless Charlotte was not involved in the day-to-day upbringing of her children, preferring to immerse herself in social reform and campaigning for social justice for young offenders. "Well, she wasn't particularly interested in babies, that's the fact of it, and I don't think she petted her daughters at all," remembered Tom's cousin, Eleanor Hinkley. "But I think they were well taken care of—there was a nurse." Tom was a bright and bookish boy, who seemed not to resent his lack of playmates: "He could sit all day long in his little rocking chair, and he'd read anything; she never supervised his reading."[3]

Tom's nursemaid was an Irish Catholic girl, Annie Dunne, whom he accompanied to the Catholic Church on the corner of 2635 Locust Street where the family lived. Later Tom remembered Annie taking him behind a screen and talking about the existence of God. It was his first introduction to the comforting rituals and doctrines of Catholicism, and was to leave a lasting impression upon him, associated as the Holy Roman Church was with Annie, who was, in some senses, his "real" mother; Annie provided the warmth lacking from his preoccupied, rigidly Puritan mother and his deaf father, who found communication difficult and spent his leisure playing chess alone or drawing cats. Later Eliot recalled that both his parents, being so much older, were like "ancestors to him."[4] And so the Catholic Church became "Mother Church," while the cool creed of Unitarianism, to which his parents adhered, offered only a set of moral injunctions.

Unitarianism, exemplified in the life and example of Tom's paternal grandfather, the Rev. William Greenleaf Eliot, known as "the Saint of the West," dominated the Eliot household, and was responsible for the transplantation of this cultured New England family to a corner of the raw Midwest. William Greenleaf Eliot, a Unitarian minister who had left Harvard Divinity School in 1831 to found the Unitarian Church in St. Louis, had died in 1887—the year before Tom was born—but his presence was as vivid to the small boy as if he still lived. "I was brought up as a child to be very much aware of him," said Tom. "So much so, that as a child I thought of him as still the head of the family." The standard of conduct the sister, knew she resembled her bohemian father not her bourgeois mother, but her aspirations to become a dancer or an artist never translated themselves into a career. There seemed no alternative but to try to adjust herself to the standards of the mother she continually seemed to displease, but even at this she failed. Moreover, Rose told Vivienne, as she gave her her "doses," that she was sick. The label seemed to fit, and increasingly Vivie acted out this role by indulging in temperamental outbursts and crying fits.

Such symptoms are often protests against strict management, which may become pathological if they grow rigid, habitual and part of an illness pattern.[33] But Vivienne's "nerves," as she learnt to call them, by no means disabled her to this extent or became pathological. She was not only attractive but intelligent, describing herself later as "a *frightfully* mentally *over*developed child . . . and Oh what a child I was. Poor, wretched, *clever* child."[34] She longed to learn, although academies for young ladies offered "accomplishments"—piano, sketching and languages—rather than the classics or sciences which were only available to their brothers. At King Alfred School in Hampstead and later in Margate, where she boarded at Dulwich House School, Vivienne read Hardy and Swinburne and grew to love poetry; she also excelled at languages. Holidays in Paris and Switzerland with her parents gave her the opportunity to become a fluent French speaker and she regarded Paris as a second home. She wrote as quickly as she thought, and learnt to type to dictation. In London she regularly attended her beloved art school, and also sketched with her father at the seashore at Eastbourne, Hastings, and the Hampshire coast, as well as on Anglesey where Haigh-Wood obsessively painted cows. The few of Vivienne's watercolours which have survived are of boats and waterside scenes.

Brigit Patmore described Vivienne in 1914: "She was slim and rather small, but by no means insignificant. Light brown hair and shining grey eyes. The shape of her face was narrowed to a pointed oval chin and her mouth was good—it did not split up her face when she smiled, but was small and sweet enough to kiss. Added to this, she did not quiver, as so sensitive a person might, but shimmered with intelligence."[35] Such an attractive woman found many suitors among her brother Maurice's army officer friends, who were often her dancing partners. After Sandhurst Maurice had joined the Manchester Regiment; despite their differences, brother

children adhered to was that which their grandfather had set; and moral
judgements, decisions between duty and self-indulgence, were taken "as if,
like Moses, he had brought down the tables of the Law, any deviation from
which would be sinful." Plain living was the order of the day: "I grew up,"
said Eliot, "in a family in which to buy candy for oneself was considered
selfish indulgence."[5]

Henry Ware Eliot Sr. had not felt the call to follow his father into the
church, complaining that "too much pudding choked the dog," and went
into business instead, working his way up from clerk to become President
of the Hydraulic-Press Brick Company. It was Charlotte whose personality responded to that of her father-in-law, and she began writing his biography. Her own Stearns ancestors had been preachers and theologians who
lived by the "Good Book," and her mother, Charlotte Blood, was descended from General Thomas Blood.[6] On his father's side, young Thomas
inherited the judgemental certainties of the Salem witch-finders. His
ancestor, Andrew Eliot, had emigrated to New England in about 1668,
and served on the same witch-trial as Nathaniel Hawthorne's great-
grandfather; as Eliot later told Ezra Pound: "I just naturally smell out
witches."[7]

His paternal grandfather's educational legacy also shaped Eliot's early
life. Not only had William Greenleaf Eliot founded Washington
University at St. Louis, but a preparatory school, Smith Academy, to which
Tom was sent. And it was loyalty to Grandmother Eliot after her husband's death which kept the family in the "old Eliot place" on Locust
Street, a substantial house around the corner from old Mrs. Eliot at 2660
Washington Avenue, as it gradually became a slum area from which other
families of their social class fled to the west of the city. Henry Ware Eliot
refused to sell up, and it was in the nearby commercial centre that Thomas
first saw the name "Prufrock," over a furniture wholesalers;[8] but, as the
neighbourhood went downhill, Tom's mother discouraged him from playing with local children. Instead, she talked to him "as I would with a
man."[9]

A less introverted child might have made friends with the local boys,
but Tom's own nature, and a mother who ensured that he was invariably
dressed formally in a sailor suit, and was reprimanded for using the expression "OK," made him conscious of the gulf between himself and boys

of a lower social standing, even at his private dancing school, "Mr. Mahler's Select Academy for the jeunesse dorée of St. Louis," as he later described it to his friend John Hayward: "How I dreaded those afternoons, and my shyness, and being chivvied about by my most loathed enemy, Atreus Hagadine von Schrader Jr." Nor did Tom much like the girls, "Effie Bagnall whose family were considered distinctly nouveaux riches," or the reigning beauty of the dancing school, Edwine Thornburgh herself, who subsequently became Lady Peek of Peek Frean & Co. Ltd. It was odd, re-marked Eliot, that Edwine's most assiduous admirer was Lewis Dozier Jr., "the small but pert and self-assured son of a biscuit manufacturer—I think his father made his fortune out of Uneeda Biscuit, which, as you must know, is a kind of cracker. Well, it seems Edwine got on by sticking to bis-cuits." Another youth Eliot disliked was Gerard Lambert, whose family made a fortune through the manufacture of Listerine; unlike Eliot, Lambert was good at mathematics and athletics.

Outside the dancing academy, Tom's childhood acquaintances at Smith Academy were, he later told John Hayward, more "mixed in origin than any of your playmates, I'm sure." There was Butch Wagner, Pat Sullivan, Snowball Wolfpert, Elephant-mouth Hellman, Gander Giesecke . . . "What has become of them?" But Tom congratulated himself that these early school days had not "corrupted my good manners," and once he arrived at Milton Academy, the society was "more select," being supposedly limited to scions of the best Unitarian families of Massachusetts, whose names, Dago Parker (who became Churchwarden of King's Chapel, Boston), Chicken Gilbert, and Doodle Page (son of an ambassador), he never forgot. Despite spending the first sixteen years of his life in St. Louis, Eliot became conscious at an early age that he sprang from that distinguished clan of Eliots who numbered themselves among the "best" Brahmin Boston families of New England.

In other ways, growing up in the American "South West, which was, in my own time, rapidly becoming the Middle West," as Eliot wrote in 1928, left its mark on him.[10] One of his strongest associations, he wrote, was that of the smell of grapes which greeted him on returning in the autumn to their house in St. Louis, after the summer at The Downs, the house his father had built at Eastern Point, Gloucester.[11] Another lasting memory was of the great Mississippi River in flood, a sight he was taken to by his

nurse Annie as a treat. Like Krishna, the river was "a strong brown
god"—both destroyer and preserver, thought Eliot, as he stared at the
sullen, untamed Mississippi "with its cargo of dead Negroes, cows and
chicken coops."[12] At night the sound of the St. Louis blues, carried on the
warm night air through open windows, wove its way into his dreams.
"Lincoln Snow, Negro Jazz Drummer" in *Sweeney Agonistes* comes from
his childhood; there are curled snapshots of "Stephen" and other black servants, one of whom used to hold his foot in front of the fire until the small
boy hopped up and down with alarm.

From his earliest years Eliot lived in an interior world. A friend of his
brother Henry remembered Eliot "folded in a chair in the family library
reading 'heavy stuff.' " He was a "tattle-tale, stingy (who wouldn't lend
money); when a phone call came for Henry he would leave the receiver off
the hook and go back to his reading without bothering to find Henry. But
Henry, who was a regular guy . . . was very fond and protective of his kid
brother."[13] Tom's reading paid off and at Smith Academy he won the Latin
prize in his last year. His mother was delighted to see him excel at school,
as she herself had done, but it was not easy to escape her control or her
anger, for Charlotte was a frustrated woman who had not been allowed to
go on to university despite her intellectual gifts. "I should so have loved a
college course," she confessed to her son, "but was obliged to teach before
I was nineteen. I graduated with high rank, 'a young lady of unusual bril-
liancy as a scholar' my old yellow testimonial says, but when I was set to
teaching young children . . . I made a dead failure."[14]

Nor had marriage to Henry Ware Eliot brought Charlotte the intellectual companionship she craved. In his autobiography Eliot Sr. called
himself a "Simpleton," and, handicapped by deafness as a result of scarlet
fever, an affliction shared by his son Henry, he became a remote husband
and father who left the upbringing of his youngest son to his wife.[15] Tom
was forced to fill the emotional vacuum in the life of his mother, a woman
whose personal characteristics were described as "sincere conscientiousness
and great reserve."[16] The burden of Charlotte's thwarted aspirations lay
heavily upon him, for although she taught unhappily at the Normal School
in St. Louis, and sometimes substituted at the Mary Institute, a girls' school
also founded by William Greenleaf Eliot, next door to the Eliot house, it
was into religious poetry that she poured her heart.

But her verses, although employing many of the powerful themes of sacrifice and martyrdom which strongly influenced her son, met with little success. The journals to which she submitted her work invariably rejected them, and she was published only in religious journals of a Unitarian or religious complexion to whose editors her married name opened the door: *The Unitarian, The Christian Register, Our Best Words.*[17] Charlotte became increasingly embittered. She began to channel all her hopes and dreams through her talented son Thomas, writing: "I hope your literary work will receive early the recognition I strove for and failed." As her sense of failure grew, so did the fervour of her poetry in its exhortations to reject this sinful world and turn to God: "Loose the spirit from its mesh/From the poor vesture of the flesh," she commands the reader. Poem after poem hammered home the message of the saints, the examples of St. John the Baptist, St. Francis, or Savonarola, that it is better by far to endure the privations of the desert, or burn at the stake, than to enjoy secular pleasures.[18]

The prohibition upon pleasure was a lesson Eliot learnt young, and he said that it left him "permanently scarred."[19] Sex was equated with sin, his father in this instance joining with his mother to reinforce the lesson of the "nastiness" of sexual intercourse. Syphilis, said Tom's father, was God's punishment for sin, and he hoped that no cure would be found for it; otherwise he believed it might be necessary "to emasculate our children to keep them clean." Sex instruction for children meant "giving them a letter of introduction to the Devil."[20] Such opinions left a deep and lasting impression upon his son, who never forgot the lesson that the sexual act was unclean, often linking in his poetry "The coupling of man and woman/And that of beasts." Such couplings, wrote Eliot in "East Coker," come in the end to "dung and death."[21]

One childhood incident at the age of five or six affected him deeply. Tom was in the habit of playing in the schoolyard of the Mary Institute next door. There was a high brick wall which concealed the Eliots' back garden from the schoolyard. "There was a door in this wall and there was a key to this door," said Eliot sixty years later, recalling how the habits of voyeurism were learnt young. Over the wall he could hear the girls playing and laughing together; it was a forbidden world which the solitary boy longed to join, but from which he was shut out. Not until the girls had

gone home did he dare unlock the door and enter the empty yard, sometimes even exploring the deserted corridors of the school. A photograph
shows young Tom in his sailor suit, standing alone in the schoolyard. One
day, however, he miscalculated and unlocked the door too early. The girls
saw him, but they did not invite him to join them; instead, they laughed
mockingly and Tom "took flight at once."[22]

The theme of children's mocking laughter was to occur over and over
again in Eliot's poetry: "The hidden laughter/Of children in the foliage,"
in "Burnt Norton" is but one example. The girls attracted Tom, but jeered
at him, found him ridiculous and rejected him. It was a paradigm for
many future encounters with women from which he was to flee. Another
early memory of great significance for Eliot was his "first love affair at (as
nearly as I can compute from confirmatory evidence) the age of five, with
a young lady of three, at a seaside hotel. Her name was Dorothy; that is all
I know . . ." Eliot "pined a bit" after he and Dorothy separated in the autumn.[23] That memory, he told John Hayward, was his preparation for
reading the *Vita Nuova,* and it was one which led him to compare himself
to Dante in his first sighting of Beatrice. In his essay on Dante, Eliot remarked that: "The type of sexual experience which Dante describes as oc-
curring to him at the age of nine years is by no means impossible or unique.
My only doubt (in which I found myself confirmed by a distinguished psychologist) is whether it could have taken place so *late* in life as the age of
nine years." The psychologist agreed with Eliot that it was more likely to
have occurred at about five or six years of age. Emphasising that the *Vita
Nuova* could only have been written based on a personal experience as, by
inference, his own poetry also was, Eliot wrote, "I cannot find it incredible
that what has happened to others should have happened to Dante with
much greater intensity."[24]

"I was seven, she was littler," Eliot writes in French in the published
version of "Dans le Restaurant," in which he describes an encounter with
a small girl. "She got soaked, I picked primroses for her . . . I tickled her to
make her laugh/I felt such power for a moment, such rapture."[25] An earlier English version which Eliot sent to Ezra Pound is more explicit than
the sanitized French: "Down in a ditch under the willow tree,/There you
go to get out of the rain/I tried in vain,/I mean I was interrupted/She was
all wet with the deluge and her calico skirt/Stuck to her buttocks and bel-

ley [sic],/I put my hand up and giggled . . . That one can do at the age of eight,/I was younger." It was a "big poodle" which interrupted Eliot; the dog came "sniffing about" and scared him "pealess."[26] In the *dédoublement* of experience which Eliot learnt from the Symbolists, he is both protagonist and the observing waiter in this poem ("You crapulous vapulous relic . . . to have had an experience/So nearly parallel, with . . . /Go away,/I was about to say mine"). In this screen memory, rapture is mingled with frustration and rejection. Eliot remembered that he expressed his feeling of love for Dorothy by "bullying, teasing, and making her fetch and carry."[27] Underneath the surface of the "priggish little boy" Tom knew he had become, lay strong emotions.

Lyndall Gordon, Eliot's biographer, claims that he "accepted his mother's domination in good humour," but there is evidence that this was not so.[28] In "Animula" he is a perplexed and protesting child, who offends each day, and finds himself surrounded by fierce imperatives, the "may's and may not's" of control. The unhappy boy flees the mother he cannot appease: "The pain of living and the drug of dreams/Curl up the small soul in the window seat/Behind the *Encyclopaedia Britannica.*"[29] Resentful of a mother who lived only through her son, Eliot immortalised Charlotte as "Amy" in his most autobiographical play, *The Family Reunion*. Wishwood, the family house, is a "cold place," where nothing is allowed to change. "Were you ever happy here, as a child, at Wishwood?" Harry, Eliot's persona, is asked. "Not really," replies Harry, remembering that his unhappiness was viewed as naughtiness. His one memory of freedom is the hollow tree in the wilderness beside the river, and even this Charlotte/Amy destroys: "The wilderness was gone,/The tree had been felled." In its place a neat summer-house had been erected "to please the children."

The core revelation of the play is that Harry's father once wanted to kill his mother, the central character in *The Family Reunion*. Amy is seen as the root of Harry's neurosis. It is very possible that this was the interpretation Eliot later put on his own childhood, and that he believed that it was his dominating mother who crippled him in his later relationships with women.[30] Certainly Eliot's feeling for his mother was deeply ambivalent, love mixed with a fear which was replicated in the alarm, physical revulsion and violent misogyny which women were to engender in him.[31] His brother Henry, by contrast, an unexceptional boy of quite different temperament and ability, shielded from Charlotte's possessiveness by sisters close in age, experienced no such difficulties.

Tom possibly exhibited some of the tendencies of obsessive-compulsive disorder from which, argued American writer Randall Jarrell, he suffered as a result of his upbringing, when he entered Harvard University from Milton Academy in 1906: fastidious cleanliness, secrecy, the desire for order, control and repetition as a defence against anxiety.[32] He was deeply inhibited and, on his own admission, extremely shy with girls.[33] His fellow student and friend at Harvard, Conrad Aiken, noticed him as "a singularly attractive, tall and rather dapper young man, with a somewhat Lamian smile."[34] Others called him a Buddha, for although his distant cousin Charles William Eliot was at that time President of Harvard, and he was a member of a distinguished New England family, Boston society presented an ordeal to a nervous Prufrock:

> In the room the women come and go
> Talking of Michelangelo.

Eliot's only thought was "Do I dare?" as he hesitated at the threshold. "Time to turn back and descend the stair."[35] Nevertheless, he dutifully joined university societies, took dancing, skating and boxing lessons, and worked on his accent.

As Eliot later explained to his confessor, the Rev. William Force Stead, "I was a nomad, even in America." His "real ancestral home" was Massachusetts, but his branch of the family had been settled in St. Louis for two generations, and although he was proud to be "a descendant of pioneers," the family jealously guarded its connections with New England.[36] The result was, "I was enough of a Southerner to be something of an alien in Massachusetts."[37] He was embarrassed by the divided existence he had led between Massachusetts and St. Louis, and one of his first tasks when he "came East" at seventeen to Milton Academy was to eradicate the southern drawl which he felt marred his speech, and to develop a "correct" accent acceptable to the young blades from the best Boston families with whom he was mixing. Nevertheless, he was conscious that on going to school in New England, "I lost my southern accent without ever acquiring the accent of the native Bostonians." Later he expressed to the poet Herbert Read his confused and bitter memory of how it felt to be "an American who wasn't an American, because he was born in the South and went to school in New England as a small boy with a nigger drawl, but who wasn't a southerner in the South because his people were northerners in a border state and looked down on all southerners and Virginians, and who so was never anything anywhere and who therefore felt himself to be more a Frenchman than an American and more an Englishman than a Frenchman and yet felt that the USA up to a hundred years ago was a family extension."[38]

Although there had been dislocation in Tom's youth, it did not trouble his brother and sisters to such an extent; the ready acceptance of his cousins, such as Eleanor Hinkley, with whom he played on the beach at East Gloucester during the family's three-month summer holidays, the sailing lessons arranged by his mother with an elderly mariner, the excursions in his brother's catboat *Elsa* in the waters off Cape Ann, should have smoothed the path to Harvard. Yet Eliot remained aloof and silent. In New England he missed the long, dark river, the ailanthus trees, and the flaming cardinal birds; in Missouri he missed the fir trees, the bay and goldenrod, the song sparrows, the red granite and blue sea of Massachusetts, comparing his own childhood, with a grandmother who shot her own wild turkeys for dinner, to that of a schoolfriend whose family had lived in the same house in the same New England seaport for two hundred and fifty years.

At Harvard Eliot chose to take courses considered conservative and relatively unpopular, Greek and Latin texts at first, inspired by his tutor, the fiery Irving Babbitt, whose defence of "Classicism" struck a chord with his student; he steeped himself in Dante, puzzling out *The Divine Comedy* with the help of a prose translation before he had any grasp of Italian. And then by chance he picked from the library shelves Arthur Symons's *The Symbolist Movement in Literature,* a book which introduced Eliot to the poetry of Jules Laforgue. Eliot felt an immediate sense of identification with the French poet, whose "bittersweet dandyism" spoke to him. Eliot was just twenty, and he said later that reading Laforgue "affected the course of my life." In the Symbolist poet he found not only an ironic, self-deprecating voice which reflected his inner feelings, but the use of idiomatic, everyday speech in poetry rather than the high rhetoric of the late

Romantics. Instantly Eliot abandoned the mannered, *fin-de-siècle* verses based on Tennyson and Swinburne which he had been publishing in the *Harvard Advocate,* and began to try something new.

Laforgue's most enduring image is that of Pierrot, the comic figure who hides his sadness behind a mask, and Eliot's first attempt at a pastiche of Laforgue, "Conversation Galante" (1909), was based on Laforgue's "Autres Complaintes de Lord Pierrot."[39] Masks offered Eliot the protection his sensitive spirit needed, and Pierrot promised the mask of the dandy by which the poet might distance himself from his fellow human beings. Laforgue had made a habit of dressing formally, in top hat, dark tie, English jacket, clerical overcoat, and carried his rolled umbrella over his arm. By January 1910 Eliot had completed his own transformation, expressed in his poem "Spleen," in which, "Life, a little bald and grey,/Languid, fastidious and bland,/Waits, hat and gloves in hand . . . On the doorstep of the Absolute."[40] It had not been a difficult task, as Conrad Aiken recalled that from his first days at Harvard, Eliot carried himself "with enviable grace."

The Laforguean disguise fitted so well because Eliot did more than study the dead poet as a model: he felt an immediate sense of psychic recognition. In *The Egoist* he wrote later about "a feeling of profound kinship, or rather of peculiar personal intimacy, with another, probably dead author . . . Like personal intimacies in life, it may and probably will pass, but it will be ineffaceable."[41] The young poet studied Symons for descriptions of Laforgue's personality as well as his dress. Laforgue practised, wrote Symons,

> An inflexible politeness towards man, woman and destiny. He composes love-poems hat in hand, and smiles with exasperating tolerance before all the transformations of the eternal feminine. He is very conscious of death, but his *blague* of death is, above all things, gentlemanly. He will not permit, at any moment, the luxury of dropping the mask: not at any moment.[42]

There were elements in Laforgue's life which caused Eliot to feel that the French poet's soul had passed into his own. Laforgue had died four days before his twenty-seventh birthday in 1887, the year Eliot was conceived.

This sense of synchronicity affected Eliot deeply; years later he would choose to be married for the second time in the same London church in which Laforgue had married.[43]

The balanced, chill, colloquial style of Laforgue with its "icy ecstasy" enabled Eliot to discard the pretentiousness of late Georgian poetry, and to reinvent himself. Laforgue led to Verlaine, whose translucency also attracted Eliot. Already well-read in Shakespeare, he discovered the late-six-teenth-century dramatists Marlowe, Kyd, Webster and Tourneur, writing: "The form in which I began to write, in 1908 or 1909, was directly drawn from the study of Laforgue together with the later Elizabethan drama; and I do not know anyone else who started from exactly that point." It was this cross-fertilisation of ideas from other languages and periods which was to revolutionise his poetry.

A second but equally significant effect of Eliot's sense that he was the reincarnated soul of Laforgue was to impel him to follow the course of the poet's life. Laforgue, born, like Eliot, outside France, in his case in Uruguay, had gone as a young man to Paris, and Eliot was determined to follow in his footsteps. The French capital was a mecca for artists and writers, and Eliot was attracted by the idea of "scraping along" there, and writing in French. His mother, however, was opposed to the idea: "I can not bear to think of your being alone in Paris, the very words give me a chill. English speaking countries seem so different from foreign. I do not admire the French nation, and have less confidence in individuals of that race than in English."[44]

This time, Tom was not prepared to accept his mother's decision without a fight. His rebellion had been germinating under the influence of Laforgue, and his scorn for Unitarianism found expression in a new poem, "Mr. Eliot's Sunday Morning Service," which satirised his uncle, Christopher Rhodes Eliot, a Unitarian minister, and his congregation fil-ing into their pews like "religious caterpillars" along "the avenue of peni-tence," where "The young are red and pustular/Clutching piaculative pence."[45] Now the genteel aunts and cousins who had welcomed Tom into their houses at Cambridge were also made the subject of savage satire in "Cousin Nancy" and "Miss Helen Slingsby." Boston society was described as "a society quite uncivilised, but refined beyond the point of civilisation." Beneath his own refinement—for Eliot was always influenced by the standards of the society for which he professed disdain—lay barely contained hostility towards the hostesses who entertained him to tea.

In the *Harvard Advocate* Eliot spelt out these feelings in a series of poems between May 1907 and January 1909. Women humiliate, emasculate and disappoint men. "Circe's Palace" comes straight from Eliot's unconscious and is the product of the split vision which led him to see women as either saint or sinner, Madonna or whore.[46] Although such stereotypes are common in Western literature, Eliot's images have an intensity and violence which point to their childhood origins: although calm and compliant on the surface, beneath his painfully constructed "false self," he knew rage.[47] The dream sequence of "Circe's Palace," written when Eliot was twenty, represents in Freudian imagery his fears of women as he experienced them at Harvard: creatures who threatened him with impotence, engulfment and annihilation. Around Circe's fountain, which flows with "the voice of men in pain," are "flowers that no man knows." Their petals are "fanged and red/With hideous streak and stain." In the "forest" below, "along the garden stairs/The sluggish python lies."[48] The poem, writes critic George Whiteside, describes "a frightening hilltop fountain with a sinister garden around it, and a thick forest below—which in archetypal Freudian dream symbolism is obviously a mons veneris. Indeed one climbs to this mons on stairs 'along' which a phallic snake lies! The scene . . . clearly shows Eliot's fear of female sexuality."[49]

Eliot used myth to disguise fears he dared not face, but his flower metaphor works on different levels: "The flower's petals recall the women's lips, inviting but masking fangs . . . ; finally the petals suggest the lips of the vagina, whose stain reveals a revulsion not only from women, but from intercourse," writes American critic John T. Mayer. "We shall not come here again," is the poet's damning verdict.[50] In the next stanza the phallic python lies "sluggish"; the hidden message of the poem is that "sexual woman threatens man with a fundamental loss of maleness, of potency transformed and rendered impotent."[51] At first a panther, strong and "rising," man is transformed into a coiled and lazy python, and finally a showy and effeminate peacock, whose "eyes," an obsessional image for Eliot, appear here on the peacock's tails, watching the poet, as the little girls' eyes watched and judged him in the schoolyard. Eliot's grandfather had magnificent eyes that read one's innermost thoughts, according to his son. "One feels rebuked in his presence . . . How can one be familiar with the Day of Judgement? asked one of William Greenleaf Eliot's classmates."[52] Charlotte's eyes were equally penetrating.

Tom's urge to escape became all-consuming. Frustrated by the neat, white picket fences, the well-swept streets, the ordered rituals of Cambridge, with its tea parties and amateur dramatics, he persisted in his demands to go to Europe. Even sailing in the grey waters off Cape Ann only tempted him with the promise of freedom over the horizon. As his mother prevaricated, he collapsed with an undiagnosed illness. Charlotte hurried from St. Louis to nurse him, and finally gave in. Tom would have his way. Captain "Colombo," as Tom thought of himself in the ribald rhymes he was writing, might cross the Atlantic and begin his conquest of the Old World.[53]

Free at last from the shackles of family, Tom Eliot arrived in Paris in the autumn of 1910 to attend the Sorbonne, and found a room on the *rive gauche*. Settling into the pension at 9, rue de l'Université, his expectations were high; André Gide had founded the *Nouvelle Revue Française* only the year before, and as Eliot hurried out to buy the new review in its grey paper cover, he met Jacques Rivière, who was later to become its editor. He took lessons in French conversation from Rivière's brother-in-law, novelist Alain-Fournier, who introduced him to the works of Dostoevsky. He listened to the anti-democratic speeches of Charles Maurras, and met up occasionally for a *sirop de fraises* with Conrad Aiken, his old Harvard friend who was also in Paris. But none of these acquaintances, either old or new, wholly absorbed his thoughts.

Instead it was the vibrant life of the Parisian streets which cast its spell over him. Urban squalor was already familiar to Eliot, for his earliest memories were of the seedy poverty of St. Louis, and in New England he had penetrated beyond the privileged precincts of Harvard Yard to walk the slums of Roxbury in North Cambridge; two of his early poems had experimented with images of street pianos, dirty windows, broken glass, wailing children and tattered sparrows pecking in the gutter.[54] But now a new layer of experience was superimposed upon American decay: the squalor of Montparnasse, which became for Eliot a symbol of Paris.[55]

Ten years earlier, Charles-Louis Philippe's little-known novel *Bubu de Montparnasse*[56] had been published. The *quartier* had changed little in the intervening decade, nor had the trade for which it was infamous. *Bubu,* the story of a pimp and the prostitutes he controlled, opened Eliot's eyes to the life of the underworld. Repelled yet fascinated, he took to walking the streets at night, shadowing the women as they bargained with clients, darting into back alleyways when he was in danger of being seen. In his imagination he entered into the life of the young prostitute, the "pauvre petite putain," who flashed him a smile as she went about her work, and the business of the streets "où l'on vend son âme pendant que l'on vend sa chair."* [57]

In "Rhapsody on a Windy Night"[58] Eliot tells how every street light seems to beat like a drum in his head as he paces the streets: a fatalistic drum controlling him. Drums become a recurrent image in his poetry: elsewhere he writes of the "drums of life" which "were beating on their skulls/the floods of life . . . swaying in their brains."[59] The drumbeat of the streets impels him towards connection with people rather than the mandarin-like detachment he has so assiduously cultivated.[60] At half past one in the morning he imagines the street light is speaking to him: "Regard that woman/Who hesitates toward you in the light of the door/Which opens on her like a grin." For a moment he is tempted. But as he looks again he sees the corner of her dress is torn and stained, the corner of her eye is twisted like a crooked pin. Instead he passes on, past the scavenging cats, the nocturnal smells of chestnuts in the streets, and female smells in shuttered rooms. Sometimes he peers through lighted shutters at the people within, experiencing vicariously the warmth and companionship from which he is shut out. Finally, it is four in the morning, and he finds his front door, fumbles for the key, and mounts the stairs to his unmade bed and toothbrush hanging on the wall.

Eliot was lonely; it is the sense of his loneliness, as much as the scent of the working women, that rises from the pages of his poetry written in the first months in Paris. Uprooted from the familiar sights and sounds of New

*where one sells one's soul as one sells one's flesh.

England, the certainties of family and university life, the young American felt as much of a misfit, as much of an outcast, as he had done during his adolescence lived on the cusp of Missouri and Massachusetts. The intense sensitivity which caused him to feel deep embarrassment at an accent which seemed to fit him perfectly for nowhere—although to other relatives, speaking like a Bostonian in Missouri or a Midwesterner in Boston was simply an occasion for laughter—was intensified in Paris.[61] Added to it were the sexual urges which he found harder and harder to ignore.

The women of the streets seemed to promise an antidote to depression and loneliness. In "Prufrock's Pervigilium,"[62] an unpublished section cut from the "The Love Song of J. Alfred Prufrock," where "lonely men in shirtsleeves" smoke their pipes and lean out of windows, it is the women, spilling out of their corsets as they stand at the entrances to their flats, who symbolise a motherly rather than a seductive bosom, the female company to which Eliot had been so accustomed in childhood; the oil-cloth curls up the stairs and the gas-jet flickers, inviting him in. Did Eliot finally mount the stairs and take his chance with one of the prostitutes, or did he remain the irresolute voyeur as portrayed in "Prufrock"?

Perhaps the answer is to be found in the pages of the new notebook the young poet bought in 1909, a year before leaving for Paris. This notebook, with its stiff marbled brown cover, came from a bookstore in East Gloucester and cost only 25 cents, but it signalled a radical shift in Eliot's poetry. In a fine spidery hand, Eliot printed in black the title "Inventions of the March Hare."[63]

It was a title full of significance, for the "madness" of the March Hare in *Alice in Wonderland* expressed something of Eliot's feelings at the time, on his own admission. Images of *Alice* occur in his poetry, for example, the white rabbit hopping "around the corner,"[64] and the perennial tea parties. In *Alice,* it is the White Knight who claims, "It's my own invention," but Eliot's choice of title suggests that his inventions are peculiar to the March Hare, who in March is "raving mad." During the breeding season, hares are "unusually wild," says the *OED,* and the obvious sexual excitement of the twenty-two-year-old poet found expression in a series of obscene verses, relating the exploits of King Bolo and Colombo, a sea-captain in charge of a band of merry men, who has crossed the Atlantic to discover a new world as Eliot (and Christopher Columbus) did.[65]

Christopher Ricks, editor of *T. S. Eliot: Inventions of the March Hare—Poems 1909–1917,* suggests that Eliot may have been thinking of Rémy de Gourmont when he chose his title, with its implications of the madness of sexual desire. Of hares in heat, Rémy de Gourmont wrote: "Ce sont des animaux fort bien outillés pour l'amour, pénis très développé . . . les mâles font de véritables voyages, courent des nuits entières, à la recherche des hases. . . ."*[66] It was at about this time that Eliot composed "The Jolly Tinker," relating the adventures of the tinker who had "come across the sea/With his four and twenty inches hanging to his knee." In the second stanza the tinker is "in heat/With his eight and forty inches hanging to his feet." Finally, with "his whanger in his hand" the tinker walks through the hall. " 'By God,' said the Cook, 'He's a gone and fucked us all.' "[67]

In Eliot's verse, Colombo cries, on board ship: "I feel like frigging," before chasing the chaplain around the deck and "up among the rigging." Since the chaplain, "that good old man," had no one to protect him, Colombo grasped him "by the balls and buggered him up the rectum." In another unpublished "ithyphallique" verse Eliot sent to his confidant, Ezra Pound, Colombo comes aboard with a bunch of big bananas, takes the chaplain by the drawers and shoves "one up his anus."[68] Nor is King Bolo's big black queen safe from Colombo's attentions: when the queen calls Colombo a "dirty Spanish loafer," he terminates the affair "by fucking her on the sofa." Even animals are in danger from the captain; when the wind drops and there's no sailing to be done, the Captain suggests fucking a tortoise. "The beast was caught, the beast was fucked" and the merry men set up a cheer for their captain, "bold Colombo."

Phallic and scatological details sprinkle the verse. Feeling "rooty" after three weeks at sea, Colombo "took his cock in both his hands/And swore it was a beauty." Of Colombo's favourite, the cabin boy Orlando, or Orlandino, "whose language was obscene-o," we learn "his prick was 13 inches long/And wound around with marlin," while his role was of "backhouse darling." "Fry my balls!" exclaims Colombo, when he is feeling strong, ordering one of the crew to quickly go and fetch "my cabin boy Orlando." When full of rum, however, Colombo's role is a passive one:

*They are animals very well equipped for love, with a very large penis . . . the males travel great distances, running all night in search of females.

after Sunday morning prayers, surrounded by the masturbating crew, he falls down in a stupor and turns "his asshole SSW."[69]

Eliot's poem "The Triumph of Bullshit," probably written in November 1910, gave rise to the earliest recorded instance of the word in the *OED*.[70] Written in pencil, like many of the verses on the eight or nine pages and half pages preserved from the Notebook, in the spiky hand Eliot developed during his year abroad which differed markedly from his earlier (and later) handwriting, it is an indication of the sudden release of feelings long repressed. Like his constipated hero (Colombo was constipated for forty days and forty nights at sea, praying to the Virgin for "a hundred shits a-piece from 100,000 assholes"),[71] the poet takes his revenge on the "ladies" who laugh at him, who consider his merits are "unmale . . . etiolated . . . crotchety, constipated, impotent galamatias," who find his attentions are ridiculous, his manner gauche, and that he is altogether as dull as an unbaked *brioche*. "For Christ's sake stick it up your ass," he commands.[72] At the queen's banquet Colombo "hoisted up his ass/And shat upon the table." The repetitive references to defecation reveal the fantasies of the anal character who, beneath the polished and exquisite exterior, longs to display the contents of the "shithouse" and to revenge himself upon the women who humiliate him, such as the "great big whore with bloodshot eyes" who "bitched him with a pisspot."[73] In his tinker rhyme, Eliot imagines the tinker's "john" mutilating the woman who falls in love with him and, in a reversal of the usual arrangement, offers half a dollar for sex: "he ripped up my belly from my cunt to my navel."[74]

Pound was full of enthusiasm for his friend's verses (he ticked the description of the crew—"the rest were jews and niggers") and responded in similar vein:

> Sweet Christ in hell, spew out some Rabelais
> To belch and fahrt and to define the day
> In fitting manner and her monument
> Heap up for her in fadeless excrement.[75]

The bawdy, lecherous sea-captain of these long-hidden verses of Eliot's presents a vivid contrast to the Prufrock who asks "Do I dare?" and "Do I dare/Disturb the universe?" (a question lifted directly from

Laforgue). This persona represents the dark, secret side of Eliot; he him-self referred to the Jekyll and Hyde sides of his personality,[76] with the alter ego of "Captain Eliot" representing the secret life of Mr. Hyde, who dared to live differently from the repressed Dr. Jekyll, who was Eliot's public face. "Captain Eliot" was to be a persona to which Eliot clung tenaciously and acted out in fact as well as fantasy.[77]

Hugh Kenner has called Prufrock the "generic" Eliotic voice, the forerunner of Gerontion and the bisexual Tiresias in *The Waste Land:* the timid lover who hesitates and turns back, whose action dissipates in thought, when he comes face to face with a woman. Eliot began writing "The Love Song of J. Alfred Prufrock" in Paris in 1910, although it was finished in the summer of 1911 in Munich. An early draft of "Prufrock's Pervigilium" contained a passage, cut at the suggestion of Conrad Aiken, in which the protagonist visits a prostitute; Eliot's biographer Lyndall Gordon believes this to be only "the fantasy of a nervous Bostonian," ar-guing that it is unlikely that the deeply inhibited Eliot ever entered one of the whorehouses whose comings and goings he watched so closely. However, in one of the ribald Colombo verses he imagines himself going to the "whore-house ball" with a prostitute, "La Grosse Lulu." The text of the Pervigilium suggests that Eliot did enter one of the "evil houses lean-ing all together" but that the encounter was not a success. At dawn he feels a sense of nausea and fumbles to the window to experience the world and "to hear my Madness singing, sitting on the kerbstone." A blind, drunken old man sings below, and as he sings Prufrock's world began to fall apart. His only desire is to separate himself from the woman he has visited. His alienation from the female sex is expressed in the image of the crab, the nervous sea creature whose soft body is protected by its shell from attack as surely as Eliot's mask—the "envelope of frozen formality" noted by Virginia Woolf—protected him from the world of other people.

> I should have been a pair of ragged claws
> Scuttling across the floors of silent seas . . .

Eliot cannot even visualise himself as a whole crustacean; he is simply a pair of claws fleeing across the sea bed, isolated from marine life as surely as he is from human life.

Nor are the women who terrify the protagonist in the published verses of "Prufrock" only the brazenly sexual prostitutes of Montparnasse; the well-bred women of Boston society whose arms are "braceleted and white and bare," or decorously wrapped in shawls, also throw his "nerves in patterns on a screen," and cause him to turn back upon the stair. The contrast between the virile Colombo and the impotent Prufrock could not be greater.

In another poem, "Prelude in Roxbury," Eliot is again the observer who seems to be sitting in the bedroom of the "petite putain," watching her toss a blanket from the bed, fling out an arm, while in the dawn the light creeps through the shutters and the sparrows start to chirp. The girl sits up and takes the curl papers from her hair, clasps the yellow soles of her feet between the palms of her soiled hands. Most revealingly, it is her soul rather than her body which is the theme of the poem, which bears the epigraph "son âme de petite putain" from Philippe's *Bubu de Montparnasse*. For Eliot, her soul is constituted of "a thousand sordid images," and it seems likely that his relationship to the women of the street was as ambivalent as was the mother-dominated Baudelaire's, whose poetry also much influenced Eliot.

It was Baudelaire the Symbolist whose example suggested to Eliot that the world of prostitution was a fit subject for poetry. Later Eliot acknowledged that Baudelaire had taught him the poetical possibilities of the more sordid aspects of the modern metropolis, "the possibility of fusion between the sordidly realistic and the phantasmagoric." He said that Baudelaire's significance could be summed up for him in the lines:

Fourmillante Cité, cité pleine de rêves
Où le spectre en plein jour raccroche le passant . . .*[78]

If Baudelaire set a precedent for writing about the underworld, he also demonstrated to Eliot in his autobiographical *Fleurs du Mal* the predicament of the poet who is the prisoner of his doubleness, a *homo duplex,* to use Baudelaire's words: "always double," caught in the gap between "action and intention, dream and reality; one always harming the other, the

---

*Teeming city, city full of dreams,
  Where in broad daylight ghosts accost the passer-by . . .

one usurping the part of the other." As Baudelaire's biographer says, "the *Fleurs du Mal* is not merely the autobiography of a soul; it is the autobiography of the divided modern man, peering at his own reflection . . ."[79] Baudelaire dealt in polarities, in the oscillation between two simultaneous positions, one leaning towards God, the other towards Satan. In *Spleen et Idéal* the poet reaches towards God or the "Ideal" through art and through love, but is finally conquered by his own animal nature, falling back into *ennui* or *spleen.* This sense of paralysed inaction may have its roots in the love/hate relationship Baudelaire had with his mother. Although close to her after the death of his father when he was six, he bitterly resented her domination over him and expressed great hostility to women in his diaries; he compared the act of love to the "torture of a surgical operation" and although he had relationships with prostitutes they seem unlikely to have been consummated.[80]

Eliot, too, felt deeply equivocal towards women and was hampered by the same sense of guilt and revulsion from the female body as his mentor Baudelaire. Both men had mothers whom they considered as persecutory, and yet on whom they were dependent. For Eliot, the relationship with the mother is always the dominant one: "with a mother who becomes both the object of desire and the Divine Mother . . . the usual relationship with a woman is always the deeply wrong form of love and . . . the father-figures are disposed of . . ."[81] argues critic David Moody. Eliot escaped the "deeply wrong" heterosexual form of love through the creation of woman as an ideal-object, as in "La Figlia Che Piange," which describes an ethereal young woman.[82] And deeply embedded in his conscience also were the injunctions of parents and grandfather on the subject of sex. The equation between sex and sin is perhaps most clearly expressed in a poem of 1910, "The Little Passion: From 'An Agony in the Garret,' "[83] in which the poet imagines himself once again walking the streets on a stifling August night, following the lines of lights and knowing where they will lead: "To one inevitable cross/Whereon our souls are pinned and bleed."

So Eliot sat in the vacant square, watching other men come and go into the leering houses which "exude the odour of their turpitude." There was an obvious solution to his frustration: masturbation. In *Inventions of the March Hare,* Colombo's crew masturbate—on deck, and in their bunks. "Imaginations/Masturbations/The withered leaves/Of our imaginations," wrote Eliot in "First Debate Between Body and Soul," in which the conflict between the flesh and the spirit which had so preoccupied his mother is expressed. But such short-term satisfaction did not assuage his loneliness.

His overpowering need was to find connection with another human spirit who would provide the intimacy and emotional understanding he craved, without the female sexuality which repelled him. And then, most opportunely, his need was met by an encounter with a young medical student, born in Pau in the French Pyrenees in 1889. Jean Verdenal was also a resident at Mme. Casaubon's pension at 151 bis rue St. Jacques, a narrow street in the *quartier* of St. Germain des Prés on the Left Bank, where Eliot had moved. Tall, dark and cultured, Verdenal was exceptionally well read for a science student, and shared Eliot's interest in the philosopher Henri Bergson. The twenty-two-year-old poet and the twenty-one-year-old medical student struck up an instant friendship.

Meeting in the autumn of 1910, they shared a magical spring together in 1911, which Jean later recalled in the words of André Gide: "Ou d'aller encore une fois, O forêt pleine de mystère jusqu'à ce lieu que je connais où, dans une eau morte et brunie, trempent et s'amollissent encore les feuilles des ans passés, les feuilles des printemps adorables."*[84] Memories of their shared excursions were recalled by Jean in the spring of 1912, when he retraced their footsteps in the parks and woods they visited together. "Une vivace ardeur de soleil de printemps m'a poussé aujourd'hui à sortir dans les bois."† Full of nostalgia, he took the little boat to Saint-Cloud, drifting between the rows of translucent green shoots illuminated by the April light. In this fairy tale scene it was Tom's figure which appeared to him: "*Vous* me fûtes particulièrement évoqué par le contact de ce paysage senti ensemble,"‡ he wrote on 22 April.[85]

Jean expressed these memories in a series of letters written after Tom had left Paris for Munich and northern Italy in July 1911. There is no doubt that Tom replied to Jean's letters, for the medical student makes fre-

---

*"Or to go once more, O forest filled with mystery, to that place I know, where, in darkened, stagnant water, the leaves of former years are still steeping and softening—the leaves of adorable springtimes."
†"A bright blaze of spring sunshine impelled me to go out in the woods today."
‡"*You* were especially called to mind by this scenery we enjoyed together."

quent references to his friend's replies, which do not appear to have survived.[86] Immediately after Eliot's departure Jean wrote to him at the Pension Burger on Luisenstrasse, saying he is waiting impatiently for Tom to find some writing-paper in Bavaria "et d'en recevoir un échantillon couvert de votre *belle écriture* avant que la bière allemande n'ait engourdi votre esprit."*[87]

Later in July he writes again to say Tom's letter has arrived just as he is leaving Paris for the Pyrenees, and that he would be happy to see him in September.

It is possible that they met in Munich—where Jean urged Tom to hear some Wagner—he himself had just seen *Götterdämmerung*—or in Paris, before Eliot returned to America. Eliot's copy of a novel by Charles-Louis Philippe, *Mère et Enfant,* which Jean recommended to him, is marked "T. S. Eliot/Paris/September 1911."[88] It would have been their final meeting. "Ne croyez pas que je vous oublie" ("Don't think I'm forgetting you"), wrote Jean in October, explaining that he was cramming for his medical exams, studying twelve hours a day and had only time to write a quick letter; but he was pleased to receive Tom's, signing off: "Cordialement je vous envoie mille choses affectueuses." After Christmas Jean's mood seemed to change; exhausted by the drudgery of study—although he had passed his examination—he had returned to his family for a few weeks' holiday and was back in Paris in the New Year of 1912 before taking up a post as a surgical registrar. The shadow of war hung over the capital. Alain-Fournier wrote to Eliot that although four or five years ago he was an internationalist, now he would willingly march against the Germans, and he thought most French people felt the same way.[89]

In the pension at 151 bis rue St. Jacques, watching Mme. Casaubon mix the salad with her wrinkled hands for, he said, "the 2474th time," Jean was trying to pick up the threads of his life, not knowing to whom to attach himself, for his best friend was away ("mon meilleur ami est en voyage"). He missed Tom, and waves of nostalgia swept over him as he remembered the past. Apathetic and depressed, Jean decided to move into Eliot's old bedroom, although it was smaller than his own; he liked the

---

*"and to receive an example of it covered in your beautiful handwriting before German beer has dulled your wits."

way the bed was set into a small recess, he told his friend, "mais les dessins du papier (vous en souvient-il?) m'ont bien souvent exaspéré,"* an indication of shared times spent together in Tom's bedroom. "Zut," exclaims Jean, "je viens d'avoir l'idée de vous envoyer un tout petit bout de ce papier en question—au même instant je m'aperçois que l'idée n'est pas de moi et me vient d'une lettre de J. Laforgue, et je n'en ferai rien."†

Verdenal's deepest fear was that the bond between them was loosening: "Mon cher ami, nous ne sommes pas très loin, vous et moi, de la limite au delà de laquelle les êtres perdent, l'un l'autre, je ne sais quelle influence, quelle puissance d'émotion naissant à nouveau quand ils sont rapprochés."‡

Not only time but also space separated them. "Send me news of yourself," he begs, "avec détails suggestifs, comme vous savez; secouez votre gracieuse nonchalance et donnez-moi un peu de temps volé à vos études— si indigne j'en sois" ("with suggestive details, you know the sort of thing; shake off your elegant nonchalance and spare me a little time stolen from your studies—however unworthy of it I am"). Wistfully he wonders what kind of figure Tom cuts at home in America, where he had returned in the autumn of 1911, after a brief visit to England, to enter graduate school at Harvard; there must be a few Americans left in the States, jokes Jean, in spite of the number here in Paris.[90]

Jean Verdenal found consolation for his melancholy mood in music, particularly Wagner. In February 1912, he told Tom that he had been listening to *Tristan und Isolde* and was left "prostrate with ecstasy"; he hoped his friend would be able to hear a Wagner opera in America. It is likely to have been Jean Verdenal who put into Eliot's mind the quotations from *Tristan und Isolde* he later used in *The Waste Land:* in "The Burial of the Dead" the sailor ("Captain Eliot") longs for his loved one.[91]

As he lay on Eliot's bed, Jean brooded over the purpose of life. He had listened to Charles Maurras with Eliot in early 1911 and attended the

---

*"but the pattern of the wallpaper (do you remember it?) often gets on my nerves."
†"I just had the idea of sending you a little piece of this wallpaper—then I instantly realised that this wasn't my idea but came from a letter by J. Laforgue, so I won't do it."
‡"My dear friend, we are not very far, you and I, from the point beyond which people lose that indefinable influence and emotional power over each other, which is reborn when they come together again."

meetings of the Action Française; certainly, like Eliot, he was convinced
that the latter half of the nineteenth century had seen a decline in materialism and a return to Catholic or evangelical Christianity. The criterion by
which he judged a modern writer such as Verlaine or Huysmans was by
how far he could influence the inner life towards the knowledge of the
supreme good. Pious, sensitive and idealistic, Jean Verdenal may have been
as important an influence on Eliot as his nursemaid Annie Dunne in leading him along the path which was to end ultimately in his conversion to
the Anglo-Catholic Church.[92] Together Jean and Tom had queued for seats
at the Collège de France, and listened to Bergson's message to cast aside intellectual analysis and to open oneself to the flow of immediate experience—to act rather than to observe.[93] Jean had responded to the call to
action, berating himself for his lethargy: he was, he wrote, not made to be
melancholy: "Je ne suis pas fait pour être mélancolique (et puis c'est trop
romantique), je ne sais guère agir; et si j'agis (ô l'action, ô Bergson) je suis
assez malin pour qu'un sincère regard vienne bientôt analyser la joie
d'agir et la détruire."*[94] Caught up in the wave of patriotism which glorified the "joy of action" and cast aside doubt, Jean continued to philosophise
along Bergsonian lines. In April 1912, eleven months before he renounced
his deferment from military service and joined the 18th Infantry
Regiment, he wrote to Eliot that he believed the "Ideal" to be an inner impulse, not an attraction from outside. So long as men live they will be inspired by the Ideal, since it is inherent in "l'élan de la vie" (the life force).
This leads us to think of the finality of life and makes that end unknow-
able—"Et nous avançons, nous avançons toujours."[95] Carefully addressing
the envelope to "Thomas Eliot Esq." (he had progressed from writing
"Monsieur Thomas Eliot") at 16 Ash Street, Cambridge, Mass., Jean hoped
that his friend was doing great things in America and "que germent des
fleurs radieuses" ("that radiant blooms were germinating").

For Tom, too, Bergsonian exhortations to taste life to the full enabled
him to cast off Bostonian inhibition and, free from the watchful eye of his
mother and his classmates, to allow himself to create an emotional bond
with Jean Verdenal. For a man who had no intimate friends previously, the

---

*"which is too romantic anyway, and I hardly know how to act; and if I do act I'm sharp
enough to take a good look at action and destroy it by analysis."

relationship with Jean was a revelation. Full of conflict, ascetic, yet deeply sensual as his poetry reveals, Eliot discovered that his new-found intimacy with Verdenal crystallised the struggle between his instinctive sexual orientation, which seemed predominantly homosexual at that time, and the dictates of tradition and conscience, which demanded a conventional life. Although the relationship with Verdenal was unlikely to have been a physical one, given Eliot's inhibitions—notwithstanding the consistent homosexual theme of the Colombo verses—it was the knowledge that in this gay relationship alone he felt, for the first time, accepted and understood by another human being, which was to lead to a mental crisis after his return to America.[96]

That August, revising once more in Eliot's old room in Paris, Jean listened to the nearby bells chiming, just as he and Eliot used to listen together; first the distant bells, then the deeper note of one close by: "Do you remember it," he asks on 26 August 1912. Suddenly he thinks of Tom as ten o'clock strikes. "Et votre image est là devant moi"—"your image is before me."[97] Write to me when you can, he begs. As Christmas approaches, his defences fall away: on Boxing Day he expresses his innermost wishes for what might have been, and asks God's help in resisting them. Praising Tom's "delicate taste and clairvoyance" which will be put to good use in his study of philosophy, he wishes his friend for the new year "une ardeur souvent renouvelée—ardeur, flamme—mais c'est au coeur qu'en est la source et voici où nos voeux doivent être prudents. 'Amène sur moi les biens, ô Dieu, que je te les demande ou non, et écarte les maux quand même je te les demanderai.' "*[98] It is possible that it was Jean who took the initiative in the relationship, who wished for "evil" and begged for divine help to resist his desires.

The emotional intensity of these long, sometimes seven-page letters, for whose style, crabbed handwriting and crossings-out Jean apologises, explaining that he was in the habit of coming down to Tom's old room in an old jacket, collarless and in slippers to write to his friend, indicate that Jean had given his heart to Eliot; it seems that Eliot felt the same way, for he continued to exchange letters during 1912 with Verdenal who was tak-

---

*"an oft-renewed ardour—ardour, flame—but its source is in the heart, and it is here that our wishes must be prudent. 'Bring good upon me, O Lord, whether I ask for it or not, and remove evil from me even though I ask for it.' "

ing his final medical exams before joining the French army on 18 March 1913. Their correspondence may have continued until Verdenal's death on 2 May 1915. One of Tom's most abiding memories was of Jean, with branches of lilac in his arms, bathed in the rays of the setting sun as he ran across the grass in the Luxembourg Gardens towards him; the gardens were near the pension in which the two young men stayed in Paris, as was the medical school Jean attended. Many years later Eliot recalled that day with deep emotion, and the friend who was "to be mixed with the mud of Gallipoli."[99] This undoubtedly was Jean Verdenal, *"mort aux Dardanelles,"* to whose memory Eliot dedicated *Prufrock and Other Observations* in 1917, later adding the epigraph culled from his pocket Dante which he had written out in the "March Hare" Notebook:

> . . . Tu se' ombra ed ombra vedi.
> . . . Puoi, la quantitate
> Comprender del amor ch'a te mi scalda,
> Quando dismento nostra vanitate
> Trattando l'ombre come cosa salda.*
>
> *(Purg., XXI)*[100]

As time passed, the memories of lost love became ever more vivid for Eliot, rather than fading. In 1925 he altered the epigraph slightly, and changed the dedication to "For Jean Verdenal, 1889–1915 Mort aux Dardanelles," rather than "To Jean Verdenal" as it stood in the 1917 *Prufrock and Other Observations.* Verdenal had feared that Eliot was forgetting him; in this epigraph the poet gave him his answer.

Back at Harvard in the autumn of 1911, Eliot decided to read for a doctorate in philosophy, studying Indic philosophy, Buddhism, and the philosophy of F. H. Bradley rather than literature as he had previously planned, a decision which his mother attributed to the influence of Bergson,[101] but which was undoubtedly connected with Eliot's sense of personal crisis. He appeared to Conrad Aiken to have gained a new veneer of European sophistication, hanging a print of Gauguin's *Crucifixion* in his

---

*. . . For thou art a shade and a shade thou seest . . . Canst thou comprehend the measure of the love which warms me toward thee, when I forget our nothingness, and treat shades as a solid thing.

room, adopting a malacca cane in imitation of Jules Laforgue, and snapping at Aiken with a waspishness that led him to nickname his friend "the Tsetse."[102] Eliot also made a conscious effort to "discipline" himself to fit into Harvard society, becoming an editor of the *Harvard Advocate,* joining the Signet literary society, attending dances and taking boxing lessons with a pugilist named Steve O'Donnell who may have been the prototype of Sweeney.[103]

Yet underneath his apparent insouciance lay a soul in turmoil. Eliot experienced a mysterious "personal upheaval" which, he later told Virginia Woolf, turned him aside from his inclination to develop "in the manner of Henry James" to devote himself instead to philosophy.[104] For almost two years Eliot wrote no poetry except for "La Figlia che Piange" ("Young Girl Weeping"), which may have been inspired by a young woman from the same exclusive Boston society as himself, Emily Hale, whom he met at the house of his cousin Eleanor Hinkley, probably in 1912. With Emily he participated in amateur dramatics, playing Mr. Woodhouse to Emily's Mrs. Elton in a scene from Jane Austen's *Emma.* "Weave, weave the sunlight in your hair," Eliot exhorts the young woman in his poem, but she remains removed from him, "on the highest pavement of the stair," and already wears an expression of "fugitive resentment." Eliot later came to believe that at this point he fell in love with Emily, although "I cannot make that assertion with any confidence," he wrote in the 1960s, unsure whether such feeling was merely his reaction to later misery.[105] Certainly there is no hint of fervour in his poem; instead, as if prophesying what was to follow, Eliot imagines his protagonist "faithless," leaving "La Figlia" to stand and grieve.

By contrast, in the poem "Do I know how I feel? Do I know what I think?" Eliot expresses suicidal despair. In his desperation he asks the hall porter to tell him what to think and feel. But he knows that to the porter he is only the gentleman who lives on the second floor; and he dreads what "a flash of madness" might reveal. Would the porter tell him how much beauty is wasted in marriage? "If we are restless on winter nights, who can blame us?" exclaims Eliot. Alone in his room he tries to masturbate, but "something which should be firm . . . slips, just at my finger tips." He imagines his own suicide, his brain "twisted in a tangled skein," he takes a drug ("the sinking blackness of ether"), and finds release ("I do not know what, after, and I do not care either"); finally the doctor with his black bag and a knife comes to investigate the cause of death.[106]

Eliot was struggling to repress sexual inclinations to which he could only give expression in his poetry. "The Descent from the Cross," in which the poet tells Conrad Aiken that he will go to the masquerade as St. John among the Rocks, dressed in his underwear,[107] reveals his innermost fantasies; while to outsiders he appeared the diligent doctoral student as he worked on his dissertation on "Knowledge and Experience in the Philosophy of F. H. Bradley." Lyndall Gordon asserts that at this point in his life Eliot was "circling . . . on the edge of conversion," citing the evidence of the "visionary poems" he was writing,[108] and asks why did he not make a "serious religious commitment in 1914?" Certainly Eliot was much preoccupied with mysticism and the lives of the saints—St. Theresa, Dame Julian of Norwich, St. Ignatius and St. John of the Cross—but Eastern texts interested him as much as Christian ones. He studied Sanskrit and Pali and read the *Bhagavad-Gita*. It is easy to argue with hindsight that the poet's psychological distress of the time,[109] the fears and night panics expressed in his poetry, were the product of a spiritual struggle, steps along the pathway of an aspirant saint to his God. But it is more likely this was a very different psychic crisis for Eliot, precipitated by the intimate relationship with Jean Verdenal, in which the poet was forced to confront his sexuality with all its implications for his future life.

The psychotic "Saint" poems Eliot wrote in 1914 must be seen within the context of the development of his intense anxiety, as he struggled with the knowledge of his aberrant sexuality (as he, his family and the society of which he was part would have perceived it) while turning a polished face to the world. Preoccupied with the journey towards self-understanding, immersed in both Western and Eastern asceticism, he at times apparently experienced his own hallucinations and visions and lived with "shadows for my company."[110] Far from being simple signposts along the path to sainthood, the "Saint" poems reveal Eliot journeying to the psychic edge as he experiments with heightened states of awareness.

Eliot was inspired to write "The Love Song of St. Sebastian" after seeing *"three* great *St. Sebastians"* as he travelled through Europe in the summer of 1914: Mantegna's in Venice, Antonello of Messina's at Bergamo, and Memling's in Brussels.[111] Eliot tells Aiken that he has studied St.

Sebastians, and asks why any artist should paint a beautiful youth and stick him full of pins (or arrows) unless he felt the same way as the hero of his verse—"only there's nothing homosexual about this." Since no one ever painted a female St. Sebastian, he had given the poem this title *faute de mieux.*[112]

It might seem that Eliot protested too much. St. Sebastian was already established as a gay icon in European art by the early twentieth century, and Eliot was unlikely to have been unaware of this, or to have missed seeing San Sodoma's famous *St. Sebastian* in the Uffizi in Florence. Following the example of Baudelaire, who developed the ability to observe himself objectively with the detachment of a scientist, and to heighten his own hypersensitivity through the technique of *dédoublement,* Eliot too developed "the sensual excitement of a voyeur." "I have cultivated my hysteria with delight and terror," wrote Baudelaire, insisting on "the supernatural sensual delight man can experience at the sight of his own blood."[113] Eliot's reading of Eastern texts opened his eyes to the development of trancelike mystical states, and at the same time the Decadent movement, which had grown out of the Symbolist movement, intrigued him with its interest in androgyny, perversion and pain. Like the aesthete Walter Pater he began to see ecstasy as a bridge between the physical and the spiritual,[114] and to aim for Eastern detachment through the surrender of self. In "The Love Song of St. Sebastian" the protagonist mortifies the flesh, coming in a hair shirt to flog himself until he bleeds. Hour on hour of "torture and delight" follow, until his blood "should ring the lamp/And glisten in the light." At first the poet is victim, dead between the breasts of a woman; then he murders her: "and you would love me because I should have strangled you . . . And I should love you the more because I had mangled you." Perhaps Eliot was influenced by Huysmans, who wrote of artist Gustave Moreau that he painted virgins who, under the pretence of prayer, appealed for "sacrilege, shameful orgies, torture and murder."[115] The theme of murder—an enduring one for Eliot—was already preoccupying him in 1914.

The mental crisis Eliot was experiencing, which he viewed as a conflict between body and soul, life and art,[116] expressed itself in "The Death of Saint Narcissus," a poem which Eliot cancelled just before it was to be published in *Poetry* in 1915, but later incorporated into *The Waste Land.*[117] The self-absorption of the poem reflects the poet's own narcissism. The same auto-eroticism surfaces: "With slippery white belly held tight in *his* own fingers/Writhing in his own clutch, his ancient beauty/Caught first in the pink tips of his new beauty."[118] The androgynous hero/heroine knows too that he has been a young girl, caught in the woods by a drunken old man—but he also knows that "his flesh is in love with the pentrant arrows," in a phrase which recalls the image of St. Sebastian. His punishment therefore is to be exiled to the desert, where he dances on the hot sand until the arrows come, and surrenders himself to them "until his white and redness" satisfy him.[119] Self-punishment has here become not only a habit, but a source of pleasure.

There is no doubt that this poem betrays the influence of Eliot's mother Charlotte, whose own poems related the ordeals of the desert fathers of the early Christian church. But a more significant reference may be to Dante. In Canto XV of the *Inferno,* it is the Sodomites, "the Violent against God," who are condemned to cross and recross the fiery sands beneath the rain of fire until they perish.[120] Eliot the puritan knew that if he followed the path of the Sodomites he would be condemned to the Inferno. In the poem, Narcissus, like the black moth in "The Burnt Dancer," is consumed by fire and becomes a "dancer to God." The image of the moth circling the flame, in the ecstasy which is a bridge to the spiritual life, is borrowed from the *Bhagavad-Gita;*[121] it represents Eliot's solution to the conflict between God and Satan, the Ideal and Spleen of Symbolist poetry. To take the path towards the phallic arrow was to risk divine retribution; to renounce it was an act of painful self-sacrifice. Such inner conflict was the root of neurosis and it was in this frame of mind that Eliot travelled towards England as the continent of Europe slipped into war.

4

A Clandestine Marriage

Tom Eliot cut an impressive figure when he arrived in England. To Vivien Haigh-Wood, meeting him for the first time in March 1915, he seemed an American "prince" in the same mould as Scofield, but his "deep and thrilling voice" with its slow drawl added a dash of glamour.[1] Vivien was a young woman who, as she wrote years later when attending historian Arthur Bryant's lectures on "The American Ideal" at London University, found "the shout of the baseball team . . . deep, stirring, madly exciting." She read Henry James, and her favourite entertainment, apart from dancing, was the "kinema" where Hollywood's silent stars aroused in her dreams of romance. In short, she was susceptible to all things American, and Eliot, unlike Charles Buckle, was "a fine tall handsome man" of the kind that "Rosa" preferred.

When she met him Eliot was twenty-six, as was Vivien. His appearance was strikingly feline: he had "peculiarly luminous, light yellow more than tawny, eyes: the eyes, they might have been, of one of the greater cats, but tiger, puma, leopard, lynx, rather than those of a lion, which for some reason, display usually a more domesticated and placid expression." His face, too, wrote Osbert Sitwell, "possessed the width of bony structure of a tigrine face, albeit the nose was prominent, similar, I used to think, to that of a figure on an Aztec carving or bas-relief." The impassivity of his face, the resemblance to a carved Aztec mask, was also noted by the artist Wyndham Lewis. This mask-like face enabled the poet to armour himself "behind the fine manners, and fastidiously courteous manner that are so particularly his own." In 1917, when Sitwell met him, "His air . . . was always lively, gay, even jaunty. His clothes too,—in London he usually wore check or 'sponge-bag' trousers, and a short black coat—were elegant, and he walked with a cheerful, easy movement." Speculating that a poet's technique was represented in his etheric body, Sitwell found that "Eliot's muscular conformation and his carriage and the way he moved seem to explain the giant muscular control of rhythm he has acquired." But although Eliot seemed patient and controlled, at his heart Sitwell detected "a tiger's fiery core of impatience."[2]

Astute, arrogant and determined, Eliot had made few moves that were not to his benefit following his arrival in England after an uncomfortable journey from Marburg in August 1914. It had "never entered his head" that England would declare war on Germany, and not until 2 August, two days before that declaration, did he take the decision to flee Marburg for London, piqued, as he told his mother, that the summer school for which he had gone to Germany *"expressly"* had been cancelled.[3] He was surprised to find the London in which he arrived "literally boiling with war," as his old Harvard friend, Conrad Aiken, who was also in the capital, described it. On 3 August Aiken was amazed to see the crowds coalescing like some animal force in desperate need of direction and unity, as they poured up the Mall to Buckingham Palace, where their prolonged cheers brought out the "little figures on the high stone balcony." Rumours of late wires and ultimatums flew around London. Sir Edward Grey, the Foreign Secretary, was speaking to the House, and "It looked like the real thing, yes, it looked like it." All day there was the tramp of feet towards the railway stations, the sound of bands playing (one of them playing a Harvard tune, thought Aiken) as men hurried to enlist.[4] The excitement made it impossible for Aiken to stay in his Bedford Place boarding house, where he was soon joined by Eliot, at number twenty-eight. But Eliot's reaction to British patriotism was rather different. He had found the evacuation from Germany "an intolerable bore," and felt the Germans were "perfectly justified" in violating Belgium. The war interested him little; it was of greater concern to discover whether, despite all the noise and rumour, he would be able to work. The commotion in Bloomsbury was like "hell turned upside down," as to the general hubbub of crying babies, pianos and street accordions was added the shouts of newspaper vendors proclaiming "GREAT GERMAN DISASTER" and an hour later selling the next extra, the list of English dead and wounded. However Eliot found the noise "depersonalised" and was able to detach himself from it.[5]

Nevertheless, as the days passed he became a little depressed. He continued to feel a barrier between himself and the English, and to be home-sick for Paris. He and Aiken had made a previous, brief visit to London from Paris in 1911, but Eliot considered that it was much easier to under-stand a Frenchman or an American than an Englishman; the English, he decided, lacked the intellectual honesty of the French. There was a "brick wall" through which he could not pass: something to do with convention-ality, he thought, not snobbishness, for "I am a thorough snob myself," he confessed to his cousin Eleanor Hinkley.[6] He was gloomily aware of "the damp souls of housemaids" brooding in the basements, of the brown fog tossing up twisted faces from the bottom of the street towards the window of his boarding house.[7]

Nor did things improve when he arrived in Oxford in October to take up his Sheldon Travelling Fellowship in philosophy at Merton College. The city was three parts deserted, as the majority of undergraduates had enlisted in the army; Eliot later recalled that, "I left with my only trophy a pewter mug obtained for stroking a college junior four at a time when all the real oarsmen were fighting for England and France." He was not able to meet the reclusive F. H. Bradley, a fellow of the college and the subject of his doctoral thesis, although he did like and respect his tutor Professor Harold Joachim, who taught him the importance of punctuation as Eliot worked on the text of Aristotle. "In criticising the papers I brought him, Joachim taught me what little I know of the art of writing English prose. It was a painful and humiliating experience," he recalled, declaring that no prose he had written justified the agony he had endured, although he did admit that practice in writing prose was necessary to those who wanted to write verse.[8] The food and climate were "execrable," he complained later to Aiken. "I suffer indigestion, constipation and colds constantly."[9] But when a telegram arrived from Harvard, notifying him that he had been nominated for his fellowship, it threw his mind into turmoil. Unsure whether he really wanted the academic career for which he was preparing himself, it became all the more important to find a toehold in English so-ciety and penetrate the closed world of Anglo-Saxon letters.

His first stroke of luck, or so it seemed, was to bump into Bertrand Russell in New Oxford Street. The philosopher recognised Eliot from an earlier encounter that spring at Harvard, where Russell had taught a post-graduate class of twelve, including the young poet, at that time president of the university philosophical club and an assistant in philosophy. Eliot, normally "extraordinarily silent," remarked when Russell praised the Greek philosopher Heraclitus, "Yes, he always reminds me of Villon." "I thought this remark so good that I always wished he would make another," said Russell,[10] impressed not only by the American's intelligence but by his appearance, which was "very well-dressed and polished with manners of the finest Etonian type,"[11] although Russell confided to his mistress Lady Ottoline Morrell that he feared that despite being "ultra-civilised" his pupil had "no vigour or life—or enthusiasm" and was unlikely to be very creative.

The English professor had made an impression on the young American too; Russell looked like the Mad Hatter from *Alice in Wonderland,* "his large head poised on a little neck with a high collar,"[12] but his clear mind and irrepressible laugh appealed at once to a young man who likened himself to the March Hare. In his poem "Mr. Apollinax," a satirical portrait of Russell, first published in 1916, the poet recalls that "When Mr. Apollinax visited the United States/His laughter tinkled among the teacups," on an afternoon visit to Harvard academic "Professor Channing-Cheetah" and his mother "Mrs. Phlaccus." Later Russell's laughter was to enrage Eliot, who compared it in his poem to that of an "irresponsible foetus," and hinted at the philosopher's satanical nature.[13] In October 1914, however, Eliot found "Bertie," as he was asked to call his new friend, very hospitable.[14] Russell was living near Eliot in Bloomsbury, and invited him back to his flat for tea. Eliot thought the flat was furnished in very good taste and its owner, although a pacifist, amusing as he compared the thoroughness of German war-making to their scholarship. Not for another year was Eliot to discover that Russell's friendship was a poisoned chalice.

A second contact of immense importance to Eliot was with another American expatriate, the poet Ezra Pound, to whom he was introduced by Conrad Aiken. Rabbi Ben Ezra, as Aiken mockingly called him in his autobiographical novel *Ushant,* was in some ways markedly similar to Eliot.[15] Pound, too, had felt an "alien" growing up in the suburb of Wyncote, near Philadelphia, dislocated from his roots in the pioneer town of Hailey, Idaho, where he was born on 30 October 1885;[16] he, too, seemed isolated and detached from his fellow students at the University of Pennsylvania.

Like Eliot he admired European literature, and in particular Dante, although Pound preferred the songs of the troubadors to French Symbolism as a source of inspiration. Like Eliot he left a woman behind in America who felt herself romantically attached to him: in Pound's case the daughter of the Professor of Astronomy at the University of Pennsylvania, Hilda Doolittle, who followed him to London, whereas Eliot's Emily Hale continued to languish in New England. Both men took enormous trouble with their appearance and although the images they so carefully crafted were very different, they served the same function: that of mask, behind which to hide from the human race to whom each found it hard to relate. As Pound expressed it in 1914: "I began this search for the real in a book called *Personae,* casting off, as it were, complete masks of the self in each poem. I continued in a long series of translations, which were but more elaborate masks."[17] The adopted persona was often a virile one but, despite finding comfort in the company of women, and flirting ostentatiously with a number of them, both Pound's and Eliot's sexuality was ambiguous, and both claimed to be virgins before marriage.[18]

Pound had arrived in London in 1908 with only £3 in his pocket. Unlike Eliot, he had left America under a cloud, having been dismissed from his university post at the Presbyterian College of Wabach, in Crawfordsville, Indiana, after a scandal in which he shared a meal with an actress in his rooms (although he slept elsewhere). "They say that I am bisexual and given to unnatural lusts," he confided to Hilda.[19] Never an academic star like Eliot, Ezra Pound struck people as being something of a charlatan, the small-town huckster brashly peddling his wares to a doubting crowd. He dressed to fit the popular idea of the bohemian poet, in a wide-collared shirt with loosely knotted tie, spats over his shoes, and a velvet coat, carefully combing his crinkled hay-coloured hair up from his forehead in a bird-like tuft. The buttons on his overcoat were replaced with new ones of lapis lazuli; he grew "a forked red beard" and a thin moustache, wore a pince-nez and carried a malacca cane. Egotistical, self-obsessed and impatient, he was known to eat tulips at a dinner party where he felt ignored, and to wear a single turquoise earring in one ear.

Pound's talent for self-publicity served him well in his pursuit of reputation.

'Tis the white stag, Fame, we're a-hunting,
Bid the world's hounds come to horn![20]

Although at first he was ignored, this "small but persistent volcano in the
dim levels of London literary society," in Richard Aldington's words,
began to be noticed.[21] Elkin Matthews, the literary publisher, stocked his
first collection of poems, *A Lume Spento (With Tapers Quenched),* which
Pound had self-published in Venice, and at Matthews's bookshop he met
the charming novelist Olivia Shakespear, a solicitor's wife who had had a
secret affair with W. B. Yeats in 1895. When Maud Gonne reappeared in
Yeats's life, Olivia remained his friend and, as to meet "Bill Yeats" was one
of Pound's chief reasons for coming to England, she introduced the
twenty-three-year-old American to his hero. An instant rapport grew up
between master and disciple; soon Pound had taken over Yeats's Monday
evening salons at his house in Woburn Place, and during the winter of
1913 was employed as Yeats's "secretary" at Stone Cottage, Coleman's
Hatch, his rural retreat in Sussex.

Another breakthrough for Pound was being published by Ford
Madox Hueffer (who had changed his name during the war to Ford
Madox Ford), influential editor of the *English Review.* Ford and his mistress Violet Hunt—often known as "Immodest Violet"—were the centre
of a literary circle at South Lodge in Campden Hill, of which Pound soon
made himself an indispensable part. Ford has described how Pound would
walk up to South Lodge from his lodgings in Church Walk, Kensington:
"He wore a purple hat, a green shirt, a black velvet jacket, vermilion socks,
openwork brilliant tanned sandals, trousers of green billiard cloth, in addition to an immense flowing tie that had been hand-painted by a Japanese
Futurist poet."[22] Despite Pound's bizarre appearance, Ford detected his talent and energy. His horror at Pound's "jejune and provincial" collection
Canzoni, which left the editor rolling on the floor in protest at the archaic
and over-blown language, stung Pound into new attempts at finding a
modern poetic voice.

Establishment poetry was at that time represented by the Poets' Club,
founded in 1908: "An arthritic milieu," said Pound, representing the
"doughy mass of third-hand Keats" into which English poetry had degen-

erated, and against which T. E. Hulme and F. S. Flint were in revolt.[23] Hulme's group met in Soho on Thursday nights, and soon Pound was introduced to A. R. Orage, editor of the radical journal *The New Age*, who gave him a weekly column in which to express his evolving views about modern poetry. By the end of 1911, in a sequence of articles entitled "I Gather the Limbs of Osiris," Pound was working out his new principles: "As to twentieth-century poetry, and the poetry I expect to see written during the next decade or so, it will, I think, move against poppycock; it will be harder and saner . . . At least for myself, I want it so, direct, free from emotional slither."

An experiment became a movement with the unexpected arrival in England of Pound's former fiancée, Hilda Doolittle. Embarrassed by her presence, since he was by now involved with Olivia Shakespear's daughter Dorothy (whose devotion was more fervent than his own lukewarm courtship), Pound introduced Hilda to another young poet experimenting with *vers libre,* blond, nineteen-year-old Richard Aldington, the self-taught son of a Portsmouth solicitor with whom she duly fell in love.

Pound was as impressed by Aldington as Aldington was by Pound. The younger poet remembered that, "I showed him my *vers libre* poems over a beefsteak in Kensington and he said: 'Well, I don't think you need any help from me!' "[24] But Hilda—whom Pound had long ago nicknamed "the Dryad"—was more reticent. It was only over tea and buns in the British Museum tearoom that she shyly showed Pound a page of manuscript which seemed to meet his urgent need to find poetry for a new American journal. *Poetry* had been launched recently in Chicago by a middle-aged spinster named Harriet Monroe, who had accepted Pound's offer to become her overseas editor. "But Dryad . . . This is poetry." He slashed with a pencil. "Cut this out, shorten this line, 'Hermes of the Ways' is a good title. I'll send this to Harriet Monroe of *Poetry . . .* " Finally he scrawled "H. D. Imagiste" at the bottom of the page.[25] Not only had Pound launched a new movement, he had found a new *métier*—that of editor and impresario.

It was a role which Pound found much to his liking, and for which he had as great a talent as he did for creative verse. In *Des Imagistes,* the anthology of Imagist poems edited by Pound and published in 1914, "H. D." had seven poems. The edition sold out, even though neither the "Dryad" nor Aldington (whom Pound nicknamed "the Faun") much liked the label. "I didn't like his insistence that the poems should be signed: 'H. D. Imagiste' " protested Aldington, "because it sounded a little ridiculous. And I think (she) disliked it too. But . . . it was only through him that we could get our poems into . . . *Poetry*."[26] The *succès de scandale* of *Des Imagistes* attracted another female American poet, Amy Lowell, the wealthy and rotund lesbian author of a collection of poetry entitled *A Dome of Many-Coloured Glass* (1912), whose energy rivalled Pound's. Although Aldington condemned her book as "the fluid, fruity, facile stuff we most wanted to avoid,"[27] Amy Lowell was not easily deterred; having read about Imagism in *Poetry,* she crossed the Atlantic in July 1913 with an introduction to Pound from Harriet Monroe and soon found herself accepted by the Imagist group. Although amazed by Pound's appearance ("never, since the days of Wilde, have such garments been seen in the streets of London," she wrote to a friend) she allowed herself to be converted to free verse by the Imagist leader.[28] Returning in the following year with her actress lover "Peter," Lowell challenged Pound's hegemony with the publication of her own Imagist anthology, *Some Imagist Poets.* Although another counterblast against the increasingly popular Georgian poets, it led not only to a rift between her and Pound but between Pound, "H. D." and Aldington, the junior two members of the triad resenting Pound's "czarist" behaviour in trying to prevent them from contributing to Amy's anthology.[29]

Pound was not overmuch concerned, for a new star had burst onto London's artistic and literary scene: Percy Wyndham Lewis, son of an absentee American father and English mother, and friend of Augustus John, with whom he had enjoyed the *vie de bohème* in Paris between 1905 and 1909. Lewis was an artist, writer and, in his own words, an "art politician," who had begun to be published by Ford Madox Ford in the *English Review.* He had not much liked Pound when he first met him at South Lodge, but he changed his mind when he encountered him at the Vienna café in New Oxford Street. Pound, with his "fierce blue eyes and reddishly hirsute jaw" was viewed by the other habitués of the café as a "bogus personage" and they were determined not to be taken in by this "tiresome and flourishing, pretentious, foreign aspirant to poetic eminence," but Lewis detected "a heart of gold" beneath Pound's eccentricity.[30] After being shown Lewis's paintings, Pound christened his new friend "Vorticist." Lewis, who had quarrelled with the artist Roger Fry over an invitation to exhibit with the Omega Workshops, and regarded the Bloomsbury group with violent dislike as the province of perverse spinsters, was delighted with Pound's intervention. "We were a youth racket," remembered Lewis. "It was Ezra who in the first place organised us willy-nilly into that."[31] Lewis was at a point in his career when he was ready to launch a new movement. Like Fry, he considered himself in opposition to the Royal Academy, but the split with the older artist was the catalyst for Lewis to set up his own Rebel Art Centre in Great Ormond Street and to publish a sensational new review, *Blast*. This publication, which had bright puce pages, trumpeted the manifesto of the Great London Vortex, and was signed by Richard Aldington, Ezra Pound, Wyndham Lewis, and Pound's sculptor-protégé Henri Gaudier-Brzeska, among others. *Blast* made a splash when it was published in July 1914, and Pound's confidence grew in his ability to "puff" his friends.

Having cut his teeth on "H. D.," Aldington and Wyndham Lewis, not to mention his old friend from the University of Pennsylvania, William Carlos Williams, and another American poet, Robert Frost, whose work he sent to Harriet Monroe, Ezra Pound did not hesitate to "edit" Yeats's poetry, to the poet's initial fury, although even Yeats soon came to believe that Ezra had the magic touch. In 1913 Pound began to throw his formidable energies into promoting yet another new discovery, James Joyce, who regarded him as a "miracle worker" after Ezra accepted his poem "I Hear an Army" for *Des Imagistes* and followed it up with the decision to serialise *A Portrait of the Artist as a Young Man* in *The Egoist* (formerly *The New Freewoman*), a literary journal founded by two English feminists, Dora Marsden and Harriet Shaw Weaver. *The Egoist* served as a London platform for Pound—who became its literary editor in 1913—just as *Poetry* did in America.

No one, therefore, was in a better position to advance the career of Tom Eliot in 1914 than Ezra Pound, with his mission to modernise twentieth-century poetry and his sympathy for the "rebel." Pound had absolute confidence in his own literary judgement, dismissing those he considered unsuitable with the crushing remark: "Il n'est pas dong le mouvemong." But when Conrad Aiken showed Pound "The Love Song of J. Alfred Prufrock" his reaction was excited and determined. "I was jolly well right about Eliot," he wrote to Harriet Monroe in September 1914. "He has sent in the best poem I have yet had or seen from an American. PRAY GOD IT BE NOT A SINGLE AND UNIQUE SUCCESS."[32] What impressed Ezra most was that Eliot had "actually trained *and* modernised himself *on his own"*—something Pound was aware he had not been able to do himself. He brusquely overrode Miss Monroe's objections to the Laforgue-inspired poem which she was not sure she understood. "No, emphatically I will not ask Eliot to write down to any audience whatever . . . Neither will I send you Eliot's address in order that he may be insulted."[33] Harriet Monroe continued to protest at the ending: " 'Mr. Prufrock' does not 'go off' at the end" retorted Pound in January 1915. "I dislike the paragraph about Hamlet, but it is an early and cherished bit and T. S. E. won't give it up, and as it is the only portion of the poem that most readers will like at first reading, I don't see that it will do much harm."[34] His editor remained reluctant: *"Do* get on with that Eliot," wrote Pound in April.[35] Only in response to his threat to "quit the magazine" unless Monroe published Eliot did Prufrock finally appear in June 1915. And Pound was unrelenting; in August he sent Monroe "three jems of Eliot" for September, and this time Monroe acted quickly: three of Eliot's new poems appeared in the September issue of *Poetry,* "The Boston Evening Transcript," "Aunt Helen," and "Cousin Nancy."[36] Pound had launched his new protégé.

Eliot held less complimentary views about the merits of Pound's verse, which he confided to Aiken he found "well-meaning but touchingly incompetent,"[37] but he was grateful for his help, particularly as Harold Monro, owner of the Poetry Bookshop, which opened on 8 January 1913, and editor of *Poetry and Drama,* had previously been offered "Prufrock" and rejected it as "absolutely insane"—a decision neither Monro nor Eliot ever forgot.[38] Pound's support was deeply significant; his encouragement and example led Eliot to rethink his decision to continue with philosophy *faute de mieux.* Instead he began to contemplate an alternative course of action: to stay in England and make a reputation as a poet and editor, as Ezra had done.

Wyndham Lewis described his first meeting with Eliot in Pound's narrow triangular flat at 5 Holland Park Chambers, just up the road from

Church Walk. "A sleek, tall, attractive transatlantic apparition—with a sort of Gioconda smile" sat not two feet away from Lewis, and struck the artist as "Prufrock himself," only a Prufrock who had quite enough confidence to "dare" to eat a peach: "For this was a very attractive young Prufrock indeed, with an alert and dancing eye—*moqueur* to the marrow—bashfully ironic, blushfully *tacquineur.* But still a Prufrock!" At first Lewis eyed the stranger with contempt, for he was used to finding Pound's flat used as a *rendez-vous* for transatlantic birds of passage, and barely listened to "the prepossessing, ponderous, exactly-articulated, drawl [which] made a sleepy droning in my ear, as if some heavy hymenopter, emitting a honeyed buzz, had passed in at the Kensington window."[39] Pound showed him Eliot's poems in typescript, which Lewis barely glanced at; being one of Ezra's protégés himself, he had a healthy suspicion of rivals, and considered that his mentor "warmed, with alarming readiness, to almost anything that was immature, in the development and evolution of which he might masterfully intervene."

At the flat Eliot met Pound's new wife, Dorothy. Ezra had married Dorothy on 20 April 1914, and she was paying the rent of the new flat, which was in the same block as the Aldingtons', for Richard had married Hilda Doolittle the previous autumn, a match much encouraged by Pound.[40] Holland Park Chambers was therefore something of a nest of poets, although the Aldingtons soon fled from over-proximity to Pound. Both marriages united an Englishman or woman (Aldington, Dorothy) with an American. Dorothy, silent and submissive, must have appeared an excellent example of a wife to Eliot; not only did she design the covers for her husband's collections of poetry such as *Ripostes,* her private income also spared Pound the necessity of having to earn a living from his poetry.

Eliot's own thoughts now began to turn to women. Alone in Oxford on New Year's Eve 1914, he confessed to Conrad Aiken that he was experiencing "one of those nervous sexual attacks which I suffer from when alone in a city. This is the worst since Paris." He was, he explained, "very dependent upon women (I mean female society)" and felt the deprivation in Oxford. "One walks about the street with one's desires, and one's refinement rises up like a wall whenever opportunity approaches."[41] He felt the burden of his virginity, telling Conrad that he sometimes thought he would be better off if he had disposed of his virginity and shyness several years ago: "and indeed I still think sometimes that it would be well to do so before marriage."

Only the month before, Eliot had asked Conrad to order some red or pink roses for Emily Hale, who was appearing in a Cambridge Dramatic Play, probably at the house of Eleanor Hinkley at Berkeley Place, Cambridge, Massachusetts. Conrad was to send them to her for the Saturday night performance with a card he had enclosed.[42] But Emily was far away; it was time to meet some English girls. As ever, Eliot sought safety in numbers with women, in order to keep them at a distance. "I should find it very stimulating to have several women fall in love with me—several, because that makes the practical side less evident. And I would be very sorry for them too," he confessed to his friend, wondering what would happen if he gave a few lectures from the *Inventions of the March Hare* with wax candles. A new Colombo poem, transcribed to Conrad in the same letter—which had been turned down, so he said, by several publishers on the grounds that it paid too great a tribute to the charms of German youth—revealed desires closer to Eliot's heart. In this verse the captain is pacing the quarterdeck, parading in his corset, until the ship is sunk by a German warship; the cabin boy, saved alive, is "bugger'd in the sphincter."[43] Eliot also showed his Bolo and Colombo rhymes to Pound, who passed some on to Wyndham Lewis for inclusion in *Blast*. Lewis also refused them, writing to Pound: "Eliot has sent me Bullshit and the Ballad for Big Louise. They are excellent bits of scholarly ribaldry. I am trying to print them in *Blast;* but stick to my naif determination to have no 'words ending in -Uck, -Unt, and -Ugger.' "[44]

Despite Eliot's nervousness with the opposite sex and fear of the "practical side" of a relationship, there is plenty of evidence that women found the shy but handsome poet sexually attractive. Lewis's impression was of a Prufrock "to whom the mermaids would decidedly have sung, one would have said, at the tops of their voices—a Prufrock who had no need to 'wear the bottom of his trousers rolled' just yet."[45] In his Bloomsbury boarding house during the Christmas vacation Eliot was the object of attention from a "delightful" young woman from New Zealand, and attended "cubist teas" with Futurist novelists, Vorticist poets, and Cubist painters he had met through Pound. In Oxford and London his social life was expanding; by March 1915 he was planning to take a Miss Petersen punting in the summer, and telling his cousin Eleanor that he would like English girls better if they were not so completely managed by their mothers. Perhaps the ones he had been meeting were too young, he mused.[46]

A month later Eliot was putting on his dancing shoes and practising the ballroom dancing skills he had learnt at Harvard. He decided he much preferred metropolitan to provincial life ("the latter is so much like New England, and the former quite unique") now that he had met "several English girls" and been admitted to two dancing parties at the large hotels where one could dine and dance. These new lady friends were about his own age, and there were two especially who were very good dancers, although he found the English style of dancing very stiff and old-fashioned, confessing to Eleanor Hinkley on 24 April that he had terrified one poor Spanish girl by starting to dip in his one-step. "The two I mentioned are more adaptable and caught the American style very quickly." Fascinated by the difference between these "emancipated Londoners" and anything he had known at home or in England before, he speculated that his previous generalisations about English girls didn't apply to London girls over twenty-five. "They are charmingly sophisticated (even 'disillusioned') without being hardened; and I confess to taking great pleasure in seeing women smoke, even though for that matter I do not know any English girls who do not." The English girls had such amusing names, confided Tom to his cousin. One was named "Vivien."[47]

Vivien found her new dancing partner equally amusing. The first indication that she reciprocated Eliot's interest comes in a reproachful letter she wrote in March 1915 to Scofield Thayer, who had cancelled an invitation he and Eliot had extended to Vivien and Lucy (who were staying at Thyme Cottage, Upper Bourne End, Buckinghamshire), to visit them the following weekend at Oxford. Vivien had hinted on 22 February that she would like an introduction to Eliot—reported to be visiting Epsom races with another friend of Thayer's—as he sounded "a very nice person."[48] She wrote again on 3 March, but not until her third letter, which is only dated "Thursday," is it clear that Scofield had made the fateful introduction at a lunch party in his rooms at Magdalen.[49]

It is hard to know whether Vivien's irritation with Scofield, with whom she was involved in the kind of flirtatious relationship which both found amusing, was simply because he had stood her up, or because she was annoyed at missing the chance of getting to know his friend Tom better. Vivien writes haughtily that Lucy and she were given to understand by Eliot and Scofield, "severally and definitely," that they were expected to keep both Saturday and Sunday free, and if Saturday was wet they would come on Sunday. The young ladies had therefore refused an invitation to Cambridge for Sunday, and, even worse, said no to a particularly charming dance on Saturday. Vivien is at pains to emphasise her popularity to Scofield, and her irritation that he has cancelled as late as *Thursday,* accepting another invitation for himself on Sunday. Such casualness, she tells him, in the tones of Lady Bracknell, is "really not done." It is quite unforgivable to leave Vivien in the lurch for the whole weekend "to the horrors of unmitigated London."

Switching from petulance to threats, Vivien reminds Scofield of her specialist's words: "Do not be the instrument of pushing me more quickly than is necessary into an untimely melancholia, or else, as he also prophesied, an early grave." Then, with a swift change of mood, she begs "dear, kind hearted little Scofield," as the weather is obviously turning out cold, to come to her in London on Saturday instead of meeting in Oxford—"Please do." There is no better way to spend a wet Saturday, according to Vivien, than by coming to town and having a cheerful afternoon looking at pictures, watching an Irish theatre group, having tea at the Piccadilly Hotel, and going out to dinner with "little Vivien to jog along beside you and gaze lovingly upon you with her golden eyes. And you are *an awful* fool—my dear," she warns him, since in two weeks he is to return to America:

> When, like a rat, you desert a sinking ship—from that day I do *solemnly promise* you I will never have speech or correspondence with you, nor will I *ever* look upon your promising-much and fulfilling-little countenance. Never. I have made up my mind, really. And you will never meet another such as I—and one day, I assure you, you will grind your teeth at the raw, childish *folly* which prevented you distinguishing between a yellow diamond—a white flame—and an ordinary toy of coloured glass.

Why cast pearls before swine, demands Vivien: "Yellow diamonds and white flames before hide-bound, unawakened, limited savages?" You ought to snatch *every hour* in these last days, she exhorts her bemused suitor: *"Try,* try to burn just one of your fingers in the white flame—just for the experience, you know." Each hour is a pearl, each pearl a prayer, in Vivien's philosophy.

Mercurial, intense, albeit immature, Vivien was full of confidence in her powers of attraction: she was the "yellow diamond, the white flame," the pearl beyond price to which ordinary women could not be compared. Part coquette, part drama-queen, she alternates promises with threats. You *must* come to London, she commands him again. She will not forgive him if he does not. "I could have danced like a faun at the Savoy," she says in a reference to Nijinsky's performance in *L'Après-midi d'un Faune,* which she and Lucy had seen at the Palace theatre. "I have a new dress—and *what a dress!"* "You shall *not* spoil everything," she tells Scofield sulkily. Her final weapon is to cast the responsibility for her mental health upon her correspondent, complaining that she "Can't stand these things now, I can only keep going by the skin of my teeth—"

Despite this emotional blackmail, Vivien was far more in control than she suggests, and it must be emphasised that she believed herself in 1915 to be a far stronger and more stable personality than Lucy Thayer, who was also considered neurasthenic. "Nerves" were, it seems, a common bond between Vivien and Lucy, but in Vivien's opinion the two families took a very different attitude to their temperamental daughters. Lucy was not really weak, Vivien told Scofield in February, apologising if she had given the wrong impression about his cousin. "I never know myself how far nerves can be helped," she remarks thoughtfully. Although Vivie had been trained "to consider them a crime, to be concealed," Lucy had always been allowed to consider them "an interesting misfortune."[50] Enclosing a letter of Lucy's to help Scofield understand, Vivien gives him the benefit of her own experience:

> She will have to find out one day that no human being can ever really help another, & if you can't help yourself you are done for—won't she? But it's a nasty jar when you arrive at that conclusion! You will help me to drag her out and make her enjoy life a little when you are here—won't you?

This letter reveals Vivien's independence and determination not to allow a troubled adolescence to prevent her living the life she wants, as well as her protective attitude towards Lucy. There is no indication that at this point in her life she was dependent on drugs, although they had been prescribed in the past; certainly she was well enough to be working in January 1915 as a governess with a Cambridge family, with whom she lived at 26 Malcolm Street.[51] One beautiful Sunday afternoon in February Vivien was planting seeds at home in the Haigh-Woods' "half inch of garden": "Did ever you see such a day as this?" she asks.

But at the end of February, a bittersweet *rendez-vous* with Charles Buckle had left Vivien depressed, as she complained to Scofield on 3 March. Only ten minutes after Scofield had left her house the previous Thursday, while she was feeling ill with influenza, the telephone rang and it was *"Mr. Buckle!!!"*—home on four days' leave, who whisked Vivien away to the Savoy to dance. Despite her high temperature—"I guessed it would kill me"—she could not resist the invitation, although the next day she felt so ill that she could hardly stand. Vivien was disappointed that she was not able to see her former fiancé before he returned to the front on Sunday, or even wave him goodbye. For a short while Buckle's visit revived Vivien's old feelings for him; "Wasn't it queer," she asks Scofield, that Buckle rang just after she had been showing Scofield his photographs, and she confesses that "there is so much more to tell," which she will disclose when she sees him.[52]

But her hopes seem to have melted away again with Buckle's departing regiment, the Royal Garrison Artillery, in which he had been commissioned 2nd Lieutenant on 19 September 1914. As a "galloper" he would have ridden one of the horses pulling the 80-pound guns.[53] The rows of the past year which ended in their broken engagement probably convinced her that the relationship had no future. Despite the lengthening lists of soldiers killed in action, which might have alerted Vivien to the danger of marrying an officer—although it seems that Charles Buckle survived the Great War—she continued to divert herself with friends of Maurice's, particularly cavalrymen such as Butler-Thuring of the 5th Lancers, for whom she had a particular weakness, and Captain Holmes, who also took her dancing. But if Vivien seemed fickle, she was also determined; her thoughts were turning increasingly to the more exciting, and safer, option of an American. Disappointed that Scofield was about to return to America, she now had his friend Tom Eliot in view.

The development of Vivien's relationship with Eliot was stimulated by the long-standing rivalry between himself and Scofield. They had competed academically at both school and university in poetry and Latin, and Eliot had emerged triumphant, being chosen to declaim his "Ode to Fair Harvard" on Harvard Class Day at graduation in June 1910.[54] Now to academic competitiveness romantic rivalry was added. Vivien gave the impression of being Scofield's girlfriend in the months before she met Eliot, as her flirtatious letters demonstrate: Scofield is a "noble Roman" she tells him in February. "You had me in your . . . sight," she remarks teasingly in March 1915, and urges him to take "a batchelor's [sic] flat" at Queen Anne's Mansions: "You *must* go there, I want you to." Mischievously she attempted to arouse Scofield's jealousy, telling him that her brother Maurice had been beagling with Mr. Butler-Thuring, whom she would like *very* much.[55] At the Savoy again on 2 August, she is reminded of Scofield and "that very nice dinner which cost you such an *awful lot* that we had there."[56] Maurice remembered that "Scofield Thayer was going out with Vivie," and Ezra Pound also thought so.[57] The intimacy between Vivien and Scofield was evident to Eliot and spurred him to steal yet another prize from his friend. Vivien, of course, was never serious about Scofield, however much she valued him as a generous escort, friend and consolation for her hurt pride over the broken engagement.

Not only did Vivien's popularity in the set to which he himself now belonged increase her desirability for Eliot, she also appealed to his snobbishness. The dances at the Savoy, the dinners in Soho, seemed to promise a more upper-class lifestyle than the "Cubist teas" he attended with Pound or Wyndham Lewis. Vivien must have talked of her army officer brother, her father the Royal Academician, with a private income and several houses, who could be expected to settle a generous sum on his only daughter. On first acquaintance it seemed to Eliot that Vivien came from a social background equivalent to his own in New England, although to an English aristocrat such as Bertrand Russell, Vivien, only two generations away from her roots in trade, seemed "a little vulgar."[58] She made a similar impression on Aldous Huxley, who saw it as a point in her favour: "I rather like her; she is such a genuine person, vulgar, but with no attempt to conceal her vulgarity, with no snobbery of the kind that makes people say they like things such as Bach or Cézanne, when they don't." Another aristocrat, the generous-hearted Ottoline Morrell, could not help noticing in 1921 that Vivien was "really rather common."[59]

Vivien's eager response to Tom's poetry fostered their relationship. Her enthusiasm for her new suitor's poetic mission encouraged the astonishing but intoxicating thought that Tom might stay in England at the end of his year at Oxford instead of returning to a dull and predictable future in academic philosophy at Harvard. Together he and Vivien made secret plans. Perhaps Eliot detected in Vivien's bright, articulate manner a good, if untrained mind; certainly her secretarial skills would aid him in his career. Although no intellectual, in the months before their marriage Vivien was educating herself in the poetry of the Imagists. In February 1915 she visited the Poetry Bookshop, complaining to Scofield that bookseller Harold Monro was "rather haughty" about exchanging her book, demanding to "inspect it first"; Monro, a good judge of his customers, suspected that Vivien was trying to conceal the fact she had cut some of the pages. In March, Vivien confided to Scofield that she had read T. E. Hulme's poem "Conversion" while waiting in someone's drawing-room, which made her search for the book in which it was included, Pound's *Ripostes*. Her favourite poems were "Luies—Echoes II, and the *last* part of 'A Girl' *(I love that)."* Pound's poem "A Girl" is a verse of pagan sensuality, in which a girl is a spirit of the earth:

Tree you are,
Moss you are,
You are violets with wind above them.
A child—*so* high—you are,
And all this is folly to the world.[60]

The appeal of the poem for Vivien reveals her innocence as well as her animism, the "child's eye" through which she viewed nature. She also liked Pound's "An Immorality," "A Virginal" and "Camaraderie" in *Personae*. The wistful sonnet "A Virginal" expresses the thoughts of a lover for the woman he has left behind, and reminded Vivien no doubt of Buckle, who had so lately left her to go to war. She hoped her soldier lover missed her as much as the narrator of Pound's poem:

> No, no! Go from me. I have left her lately.
> I will not spoil my sheathe with lesser brightness,
> For my surrounding air hath a new lightness;
> Slight are her arms, yet they have bound me straitly
> And left me cloaked with a gauze of aether;
> As with sweet leaves; as with subtle clearness.
> Oh, I have picked up magic in her nearness.

Another of Vivien's favourites, "An Immorality," from *Personae,* 1909, was also liked by Pound's mother, and was set to music by Aaron Copland:[61]

> Sing we for love and idleness
> Naught else is worth the having.
> Though I have been in many a land,
> There is naught else in living.
> And I would rather have my sweet,
> Though rose-leaves die of grieving,
> Than do high deeds in Hungary
> To pass all men's believing.

The troubadour's idealisation of love as the purpose of living, as interpreted by Pound, influenced Vivien and may have clouded her judgement of Eliot. He, finding Vivien as much an admirer of Hulme's "Conversion" as himself, and influenced by Bergsonian exhortations to cast oneself into the flow of immediate experience, began to feel "the magic of her nearness" in a way which gratified Vivien. But although Eliot was impressed by her interest in Imagist poetry, and saw it as an indication of shared interests, boarding-school education had left many gaps in Vivien's knowledge—"I have found out how to spell 'queu' [sic]. Isn't that it?" she writes hopefully to Scofield, explaining that she wasn't really referring to billiards and remaining just as confused between "cue" and "queue" as before.[62] This ignorance may have had its charm for Eliot. No doubt her naïve questions about philosophy fed his ego and gave him the confidence to overcome his usual Prufrockian paralysis in the presence of women. It must have seemed to Tom Eliot that Vivien, child-like, artistic and vulnerable, was the very opposite of his formidable, managing mother, and in this very weakness lay her attraction for him.

As he held Vivien's slim androgynous figure in his arms, an avenue of escape opened before him: escape from his mother's domination, provincial New England life and an academic career. With Vivien, emancipated yet seductive, he felt an unaccustomed sexual spark as they sparred in conversation, or quickstepped across the ballroom, a stylish couple who turned heads. Aldous Huxley believed there was a "sexual nexus" between them: "One sees it in the way he looks at her . . . she's an incarnate provocation."[63] Certainly Vivien, for her part, had fallen in love with the "thrilling" American from the Midwest. Tom seemed to have stepped straight out of the movies, putting in the shade the callow army officers who had formerly been her suitors. In her diary, she described Tom's clean-cut mouth, fine head and deep, hawklike eyes.[64]

Both Vivien and Tom carried an air of mystery; undeniably they mirrored each other, both *poseurs* who attached great importance to fashion and outward appearance. Each felt a Narcissus-like spark of recognition in the other's presence. Added to this subliminal attraction, which was the basis for physical desire, Vivien found in Tom Eliot someone who seemed to promise everything she had hoped for from Buckle and had lost: love, marriage and, most important, freedom from her mother. For Vivien, marriage was a revenge upon Rose Haigh-Wood as much as it was—for Tom—upon Charlotte Eliot.

Vivien's very vivacity seemed to breathe into him the life force her name promised: "adventurous, full of life," in Russell's words, she roused Eliot from the *aboulie* and nervous depression which had troubled him in the past, and offered an apparent solution to his sexual problems, an opportunity to normalise his life. She promised, too, an end to the loneliness he had experienced since coming to England, in a re-creation of the close family life he had known in St. Louis with his sisters. Perhaps most of all, his vision—and hers too—was of a literary and artistic partnership like the Pounds' and Aldingtons', at the heart of the vortex. The energy of this vortex, which Gaudier-Brzeska wrote from the trenches was "the vortex of will, of decision, that begins," caught Tom and Vivien in its tumbling centre and swept them towards action.[65] Rationality was lost as they spun in the whirlpool. Looking back, Eliot came to see Pound's role as fateful, both for his career and his marriage. Pound, he said, was the man who had "changed his life" by giving him the praise and encouragement he had long since ceased to hope for. "Pound urged me to stay . . . and encouraged me to write verse again." Astute enough to realise that Eliot's future as a writer lay in England, Pound encouraged him to follow his example of settling in London and marrying an Englishwoman.[66]

It was an attack on two fronts, for in the same month, at Pound's insistence, "The Love Song of J. Alfred Prufrock" appeared in *Poetry*. Much later, Eliot came to believe that he had been in love with Emily Hale in 1915 and had only wanted a flirtation with Vivien: "I came to persuade myself that I was in love with her simply because I wanted to burn my boats and commit myself to staying in England. And she persuaded herself (also under the influence of Pound) that she would save the poet by keeping him in England."[67] Nevertheless, Pound the matchmaker cannot be blamed for the marriage: Eliot never loved Emily Hale enough to want to propose to her; when he had the opportunity later he failed to do so. It was Vivien's personality and position which seemed at that moment to meet his needs.

Vivien's restless energy may have been psychologically necessary to Eliot in May and June 1915, for he nursed a secret grief he could not share with her. His dear friend, the Frenchman Jean Verdenal, who had become a medical officer in November 1914, had been killed on 2 May in the Dardanelles. His service record contains a citation dated 30 April 1915: "Scarcely recovered from pleurisy, he did not hesitate to spend much of the night in the water up to his waist helping to evacuate the wounded by sea, thus giving a notable example of self-sacrifice." A later entry dated 23 June 1915 says: "Verdenal, assistant medical officer, performed his duties with courage and devotion. He was killed on 2 May 1915 while dressing a wounded man on the field of battle."[68] In his small library his brother Pierre later found volumes of Laforgue and Mallarmé.

Eliot never eradicated the memory of Jean, which became an obsession as time passed. In 1934, reminiscing in the editor's column of the *Criterion* about his year in Paris in 1910–11, he wrote: "I am willing to admit that my own retrospect is touched by a sentimental sunset, the mem-ory of a friend coming across the Luxembourg Gardens in the late after-noon, waving a branch of lilac, a friend who was later (so far as I could find out) to be mixed with the mud of Gallipoli." Lilacs became Eliot's symbol of loss: "April is the cruellest month, breeding/Lilacs out of the dead land, mixing/Memory and desire." Eliot would have heard of Verdenal's death in May or June, and the shock and sorrow of this news may well have pre-cipitated his proposal to Vivien. The poet's anguish was immense. It seems that Verdenal was later transfigured in his imagination into Phlebas, the drowned Phoenician in "Death by Water" in *The Waste Land*. "Gentile or Jew," he addresses his readers, "O you who turn the wheel and look to windward,/Consider Phlebas, who was once handsome and tall as you." It is a cry of grief which has given rise to the suggestion that *The Waste Land* is in essence an elegy for Jean. The medical officer, like Phlebas, was "a fortnight dead," when Eliot, on the rebound, proposed to the young Englishwoman he scarcely knew.

The war was also dividing Eliot from another close companion, a suc-cessor to Jean, at the end of the Oxford term. Just before his marriage Eliot was forced to part company with Karl Henry Culpin, an Anglo-German undergraduate, who was in his final year as an Exhibitioner at Merton College when Eliot met him; according to Eliot's confidant, New Zealand critic Robert Gordon George, who wrote as "Robert Sencourt," Eliot "shared one of the deepest friendships of his life"[69] with Culpin, who was nearly five years his junior. Karl Culpin had been educated at Doncaster Grammar School and was described by Eliot as "the most intelligent of the Englishmen at Merton"—he graduated with First Class Honours in Modern History in the summer of 1915; his warm appreciation of "Prufrock" made him an "ideal companion" for the poet, whom Culpin in-troduced to his sister, Mary. During the Christmas vacation Eliot and Karl and an American friend, Brand Blashford, had spent a fortnight's holiday together by the seaside at Swanage in Dorset. After graduation Karl en-tered the army and despite poor eyesight was commissioned as 2nd Lieutenant in the Gloucestershires.[70] Soon Eliot would lose this friend also.

Vivien seemed to promise life, whereas the love of men promised only death. Sencourt alludes to Vivien's "melancholy, disillusionment, fragility and sensitiveness": Eliot found her sensitive to his moods and his pain. It may have seemed to Eliot that the death of Verdenal represented punishment for a love that was sinful. Was he tormented by guilt, were his Unitarian grandfather's prohibitions ringing in his ears, when he took the fatal decision to propose to Vivien? Did she trap him into marriage? Sencourt suggests that Vivien seduced Eliot: "it is normal for a woman to enjoy her power to play upon the strings and nerves of manhood till they hasten the throbbing pulse with sensations of peculiar pleasure."[71] A myth was put about by Cyril Connolly that Vivien compromised Tom Eliot; that "the awful daring of a moment's surrender" took place in a punt, with Eliot playing "the young man carbuncular" and Vivien "the indifferent typist." Eliot then felt honour bound, as a New England gentleman, to propose: "In Richmond I raised my knees," run lines in *The Waste Land:* "Supine on the floor of the narrow canoe." Eliot's American biographer, T. S. Matthews, dismisses this theory, and the evidence suggests that Eliot was no victim.[72] He had told Aiken that he wanted to marry and lose his virginity; and in a letter to Scofield, congratulating him on his own marriage a year later, Eliot remembered how the two Americans took the initiative in "charming the eyes (and ears) of Char-flappers"; he recommends to Scofield the advice of Oscar Wilde that "only the soul can cure the senses, and only the senses can cure the soul."[73] If this is not sardonic—for Eliot was not to know that Scofield the aesthete's marriage to Elaine Eliot Orr was rapidly to collapse, although he might have guessed it—it suggests that in his girlfriend Vivien, Tom Eliot believed for a moment he had found a cure for his sickness of soul.

Eliot's willingness to marry without a formal engagement or introductions to either sets of parents was of vital importance, for Vivien knew she must keep her plans secret or else Rose Haigh-Wood would forbid marriage to Eliot just as she had forbidden marriage to Charles Buckle. And Vivien was resolved to be a bride; she was twenty-seven in May (although she gave her age as twenty-six on her marriage certificate), and did not want to spend the rest of her life as a spinster governess. Tom, too, knew his own mother would be opposed to marriage to an unknown English girl, but it was not only fear of his mother that drove him to hurry into this marriage. He could not afford to stop and think, for the only way to overcome the conflict between head and heart which up till now had left him paralysed and inhibited towards women, was to jump in with his eyes shut. Like Stephen Spender, who also married his first wife Inez on impulse, after knowing her for only a few weeks, Eliot felt that, despite the ambivalence in his attitudes towards men and women, he needed the "eternally feminine," the otherness of women which contrasted with the self-identification of male-male relationships. "I could not develop beyond a certain point unless I were able to enter a stream of nature through human contacts, that is to say, through experience of women," says Spender.[74] Like Spender, Eliot knew that if he did not act on impulse he could not act at all; and having reached a point in his life where work no longer filled the emptiness of living alone, where "friends had failed," marriage seemed the only solution.

On 26 June 1915, after knowing each other for three months, Vivien Haigh-Wood and Thomas Stearns Eliot were married at Hampstead Register Office, shortly after the end of the term at Oxford. Lucy Thayer was present, but the only member of either family to witness the marriage was Vivien's aunt, Lillia Symes. So ill-prepared were the couple for life together that neither had given the slightest thought to money or where they would live.

5

The Poet's Bride

"Bless war babies, Selfridges, The scaffolding around the Albert Memorial, All ABC Tea-Shops" and "BLESS the Poet's Bride (June 28th)"—the date was incorrect by two days—*Blast* exhorted its readers in July 1915. "BLAST Bevan, and his dry rot, and Birth Control . . ." An article by editor Wyndham Lewis congratulated his friend Eliot on his decision to marry: "There is nothing so impressive as the number Two," wrote Lewis. "For the Individual, the single subject, and the isolated, is, you will admit, an absurdity . . . Hurry up and get into this harmonious and sane duality. The thought of . . . Male and Female, Eternal Duet of Existence, can perhaps still be of help to you."[1] *Blast* published several of Eliot's poems in the July edition of the magazine: four "Preludes" and "Rhapsody on a Windy Night." But although recognition by an underground magazine might bring the white stag of fame a little closer, it did not pay the bills.

Eliot had taken lodgings at 35 Greek Street, Soho, for the week between the end of the Oxford term on 19 June and his wedding, but these were unsuitable for a new bride. The problem of where to live immediately presented itself. Vivien sent a telegram breaking the news of the marriage to her parents, Charles and Rose, who were staying in Lincolnshire, where Maurice's regiment was quartered. They returned directly and, to Vivien's immense relief, Rose's reaction to her daughter's shocking announcement—marriage without a previous engagement was scandalous behaviour for a girl of her social class—was more favourable than she expected. Instead of venting their anger on Vivien for presenting them with a *fait accompli,* Rose and Charles "very quickly recognized Tom's sincerity and high character and took him to their hearts as a son-in-law."[2] Vivien's new husband was, after all, no stranger to the Haigh-Woods, for he had been to stay at Compayne Gardens with Lucy Thayer, although he kept a poste restante address in London at which to receive his American post. Now Tom joined Vivien in the spare room at number 3, and Rose's warnings to Buckle that her daughter was not fit to marry or become a mother were quietly buried.

The truth was that Charles and Rose Haigh-Wood were relieved to have their problematical daughter taken off their hands in 1915, a year in which their financial situation was changing for the worse. With the onset of the First World War the "peripatetic ease" of their life, lived between London, Taplow, Anglesey, the Alps and the South of France, came to an end. According to Maurice, monies sent between Dublin and London were frozen and Charles and Rose Haigh-Wood "found themselves a little low on cash."[3] The careless extravagance of the *belle époque* was no longer possible, and Haigh-Wood began cutting the annuities he paid to a number of sisters and cousins. Apparently Aunt Lillia and cousin Cornelius refused to leave the outer hall of Compayne Gardens until they received the funds they believed were owed them. Although circumstances may not have been as straitened as Charles claimed (the manor house in Anglesey was retained and none of the Irish property was sold) he now made his "beloved" Rose "for whom I have thanked God every day during our married life" his priority.[4] After settling £1,000 on Vivien, which gave her an income of £50 a year, he made it clear to his son-in-law that henceforth his new wife was to be his own responsibility.

Maurice has said that his father "was not involved with Tom and Vivie: he only wanted what was best for her, and never enquired further. He never wanted to know much about her 'womanly problems.'"[5] Rose's attitude was equally detached, behind coaxing words, as a letter she wrote to Vivien from Plas Llanfair in Anglesey on her wedding anniversary shows:

[Friday, June 1916]

Dearest Little Vivie,

Of course I was delighted to have your nice little letter this morning . . . Now I want to hear you are *building* up. You know what I mean, dear. And you must do it with your own bricks and mortar. And your own trowel. Firmly lay your bricks with good

strong cement. Each day adding one more. Till you build yourself
a strong wall of defence. So I shall want your assurance that each
day the brick has been truly laid.

Write me a *really* newsy letter. There's a dear little Vivie. So
now darling with all my most loving wishes for many happy returns of the anniversary of your marriage and wishing you all
good luck, your own loving mother, love to Lucy and Tom.[6]

It was a strange letter to write to a woman of twenty-eight, and gives
an indication of why Vivien found independence so hard. But for both her
children to be independent was Rose's desire. Maurice had been commissioned 2nd Lieutenant in the Manchester Regiment on 12 May 1915[7] and,
aged only nineteen, left for France on the day Tom and Vivien were married. He and Tom formed a close friendship from the beginning, in which
Maurice looked up to his older brother-in-law and accepted his judgement, even at the expense of his sister: "He is a very handsome boy, with a
great deal of breeding," wrote Eliot to his mother. "Very aristocratic, and
very simple too."[8] When Maurice returned from northern France on his
first leave in November, Rose tried to give the early Christmas celebrations
an American flavour: "There was cranberry sauce in my honour—they did
not know that it ought to be served with the turkey! And had it as a
dessert!" Eliot pretended this was right, as his mother-in-law had taken
such pains with it, and the pudding came in "blazing properly," with an
American flag on it. Rose did everything possible to show that she was
fond of Tom, although he had expected to take a back seat when Maurice
was at home, "but they all treated me with more cordiality than ever, and
I felt very fond of them." Nevertheless, he began quite soon to realise that,
for all their friendliness, the Haigh-Woods were self-preoccupied and
would do little to help him. He was not told of his new wife's history of illness and dependence on doctors. "You must be kind to Vivie," was the
coded message Maurice gave his brother-in-law.[9]

The only solution to Tom and Vivien's pressing financial crisis seemed
to be to apply to Henry and Charlotte Eliot, who had supported their
gifted son in the past through his years at Harvard, Paris and London, in
the expectation that he would finally win a prestigious post at Harvard and
bring academic glory to the family. More conventional than the Haigh-

Woods, the news of Tom's hurried marriage to an unknown English-woman hit them like a bombshell. Equally shocking was his proposal to abandon philosophy and stay in England to make his fortune as a poet. Such deviation from the path his parents had laid out for him demanded an explanation, and Tom knew that he must go to them in person if he was not to be cut off without a penny.

His first action was to turn to his old friend, Ezra Pound, who, only two days after the marriage, wrote to Henry Ware Eliot, defending Eliot's decision to devote himself to a literary life. He cited his own case as proof that it was possible to exist by letters: "I believe I am as well off as various of my friends who plugged away at law, medicine, and preaching. At any rate I have had an infinitely more interesting life." Unfortunately Pound's view of subsistence living was different from Tom and Vivien's: the $500 allowance for the first year "to begin on" and $250 for the second, for which Ezra pleaded, was far below the standard of living to which both the Eliots were accustomed.[10] Nor were the rest of Pound's arguments likely to carry much weight with the brick manufacturer to whom he was writing. Pound had paved the way for Eliot, he explained: "I have brought something new into English poetry; I have engineered a new school of verse now known in England, France and America," adding that he had cast his poetry in medieval Provence but Tom was doing the far more difficult job of setting his "personae" in modern life. "T.S.E. is . . . that rare thing among modern poets, a scholar," and thus a man with the mental stamina to finish "a distance race." Eliot needed to be in London, declared Pound with brutal honesty, because, "No one in London cares a hang what is written in America . . . London likes discovering her own gods."[11]

It was not a letter calculated to please a father who wanted his son to take a steady job, or a mother who wanted him to live out her own dreams of academic brilliance. Nor did Bertrand Russell's subsequent letter to Charlotte Champe Eliot, arguing that the "financial outlook"[12] for Eliot would be just as good in England as in America bring her round. Charlotte replied crisply that she did not see "any reason why if my son makes Philosophy his life work he should not write all the poetry he pleases, if not too much of the ephemeral *'vers libre.' "*[13] Charlotte was not impressed by Russell's praise of Vivien. "I have taken some pains to get to know [Tom's] wife, who seems to me thoroughly nice, really anxious for his welfare, and very desirous of not hampering his liberty or interfering with whatever he feels to be best," wrote Russell. "The chief sign of her influence that I have seen is that he is no longer attracted by the people who call themselves 'vorticists.'" The mention of the Vorticists was like a red rag to a bull to Charlotte. "As for the 'The *Blast*,' Mr. Eliot remarked when he saw a copy he did not know there were enough lunatics in the world to support such a magazine."

The announcement of the marriage in the *St. Louis Globe Democrat* of 16 July 1915 was heavy with disapproval. "Thomas Eliot of St. Louis Weds Abroad," proclaimed the headline: "Bride of Oxford Student was Miss Vivien Haigh-Wood, Daughter of Member of Royal Academy of Arts. The announcement of the marriage of Thomas Stearns Eliot, son of Mr. and Mrs. Henry Ware Eliot of 4446 Westminster Place, St. Louis, and Miss Vivien Haigh-Wood in London, England, on June 26, was made by the Eliots, who are at their summer house in Gloucester, Mass." Henry Ware Eliot Jr., notified by his mother, "said he knew little of Miss Haigh-Wood."[14] Between the lines of the local newspaper item we can read the horror of the Eliot parents that, as Henry's wife Theresa expressed it, "T.S.E. and Vivienne married in 1915 without prior announcement to their parents."[15]

A week after his marriage, Eliot sent a letter of explanation to his brother Henry. It reads as if he is still trying dazedly to convince himself that he has made the right decision. Henry knows what his younger brother has always wanted, writes Eliot, and so his sudden marriage will seem natural enough: "The only really surprising thing is that I should have had the force to attempt it, and when you know Vivien, I am sure you will not be surprised at that either." The responsibility of marriage, he declares, is just what he needs. "Now my only concern is how I can make her perfectly happy, and I think I can do that by being myself infinitely more fully than I ever have been. I am much less suppressed, and more confident, than I ever have been." After asking Henry to approach the editor of the *Atlantic Monthly* on his behalf if he happened to be in Boston, and telling him that "Portrait of a Lady" was coming out in a new publication called *Others* in New York, Tom repeats his conviction that he feels more alive than he ever has before.[16] Will Henry use his influence to persuade their mother and father to come over to see them, he begs. Vivien adds a postscript: "I am sure we can depend on you to help us. I read the letter you wrote to Tom and liked it so much, and I almost feel I know you. I should like it if you will write to me." She signs herself, "Vivien S. Eliot," proudly adopting Stearns as her middle name.

Eliot struck the same note of guarded enthusiasm in a letter sent in early July to Mrs. Jack Gardner, a Boston hostess and art patron whom he used to visit in 1912. He had not been secretive, or rash, he assured her, in marrying Vivien: "You said once that marriage is the greatest test in the world. I know now that you were right, but now I welcome the test instead of dreading it." Marriage, he had already discovered, is much more than a "test of sweetness and temper," as people think; rather it tests the whole character and affects every action. Simply saying this, rather than telling his correspondent about Vivien, or his happiness, will show her that he has done "the best thing."[17] Reading between the lines, Isabella Gardner might have detected signs that her correspondent was already finding the "test" of marriage a trying one.

On 9 July Tom invited Bertrand Russell to dinner to meet Vivien, and perhaps to ask the older man for advice as to how to solve some of the problems crowding in upon him. Russell instantly judged the marriage to be a failure. His interest was aroused by Eliot's pretty but discontented bride, however, and he encouraged Vivien to confide her secrets to him. "Friday evening I dined with my Harvard pupil, Eliot, and his bride. I expected her to be terrible, from his mysteriousness; but she was not so bad," he wrote to Ottoline Morrell. "She is light, . . . adventurous, full of life— an artist, I think he said, but I should have thought her an actress. He is exquisite and listless; she says she married him in order to stimulate him, but finds she can't do it. Obviously he married in order to be stimulated. I think she will soon be tired of him."[18] Eliot may have hoped marriage would restore the sense of Bergsonian *élan vital* which he had experienced in Paris in the company of Jean Verdenal, but for all his claims to Henry to be more "alive," he struck Russell as "listless." From her complaint that she was unable to "stimulate" Tom, Russell quickly scented that the couple's problems were sexual.

"He is ashamed of his wife," noted Russell, "and very grateful if one is kind to her." Within just two weeks of marriage, Vivien's mock-Cockney chatter and theatrical manner had begun to jar on her husband:

"Thanks very much for your cable—*and* for yr gratters and invitation," wrote Vivien to Scofield, who had telegraphed not only his congratulations but an invitation to stay with him at Edgartown, Massachusetts, if she came to America. "Charmed as I should be to avail myself of the latter, I fear it is impossible at present."[19] It was the kind of language which Eliot was to incorporate into *The Waste Land,* a task in which Vivien aided him, but although the rhythms of Cockney speech fascinated Eliot, his wife's affectations began to irritate him as his suspicion grew that nothing of substance lay beneath her lively chatter.

As Vivien poured out her feelings to Russell, who was sixteen years older than both the Eliots and presented himself as a father-figure and mentor, Eliot felt a surge of relief that someone seemed to understand his wife, and to sympathise with them both. Naïvely he believed Russell could solve the problem of what to do with Vivien while he was away, for he was due to sail for the U.S. on 24 July, for a six-week family reunion at the Eliot summer house at East Gloucester. Vivien refused to accompany him. "She refuses to go to see his people, for fear of submarines," wrote Russell to Ottoline.[20] Vivien expressed the same fear to Scofield, saying she was "much too frightened" of the voyage and the submarines, and did not want to go at all. Such fear was justified, for the *Lusitania* had been sunk in May 1915, only a month before the Eliots' marriage; it was an indication of Eliot's own sense of crisis that he braved the journey in obedience to his parents' summons. But Vivien's fear of submarines was not the only reason for her reluctance to accompany her husband. She wrote to Scofield on 2 August, the day that Eliot arrived in America, that "all the Eliots appear to have an overwhelming desire to see me, and have written me such charming letters of welcome into their select family, that I am sure I *shall* have to go over soon, probably in the spring."[21] It was an alarming prospect. Would they find her acceptable, she wondered apprehensively. "I hope you will repeat your invitation," she told Scofield, putting off the evil day, for her feelings about America were ambivalent. Although Vivien admired the novels of Henry James, likening herself to Daisy Miller,[22] the Rousseauesque "child of nature" in James's eponymous tale, and Eliot to Daisy's repressed suitor, Winterbourne, the United States seemed a "savage land" to her and she remained resolutely in London.[23]

The night before he sailed, Tom wrote a letter to his father, asking him to look after Vivien if anything happened to him on the voyage. Specifically he hoped Henry Ware Eliot would see she got the $5,000 insurance he had taken out for his son. Vivien would need it, he wrote. She would be in a most difficult position. Her own family were in straitened circumstances owing to the war, and he knew her pride would make her want to earn her own living. This would be very hard for her at first, with the weight of Tom's loss. He had taken on a great responsibility, he admitted, perhaps the first hint of Vivien's frail constitution, but he was also aware of all that he owed her:

> She has been ready to sacrifice everything for me . . . Now that we have been married a month, I am *convinced* that she has been the one person for me. She has everything to give that I want, and she gives it. I owe her everything.

Only too conscious that he was penniless, he burst out: "I have married her on nothing, and she knew it, and was willing, for my sake. She had nothing to gain by marrying me. I have imposed upon you very much, but upon her more . . . Your loving son, Tom." Vivien, he wrote, had not seen his letter.[24]

It was a generous letter, expressing Eliot's deep sense of obligation to Vivien for marrying him "on nothing," and for freely offering him her love and support at a critical time in his life. Had she not done so in June 1915, it is highly questionable whether Eliot would have stayed in London and made the career he did. Instead he would have obeyed his mother's summons to return to New England and philosophy. In 1915 his literary life hung in the balance, and Vivien tipped the scales. It was she who anchored him in England. Had Vivien sailed to America with Eliot, the increasing danger of submarines would have probably kept them both on the other side of the Atlantic for the duration of the war at least. Like Scofield, Eliot might never have returned to England. Vivien's refusal to accompany him to the family reunion in Gloucester gave Eliot both the courage and the excuse to do as he wished, to defy his parents and return to England and poetry.

Eliot's letter to his father to some extent contradicts Russell's damning and not wholly disinterested verdict on the marriage written in the same month. But although Eliot voiced his gratitude for Vivien's "sacrifice," he did not say he loved her. And it was certainly a very disgruntled bride he left behind. Vivien was annoyed that her new husband had left her to make the risky journey home, and did not understand the necessity for it. It seemed to her that no sooner had she captured a husband than he abandoned her. "Tom has gone to America without me," she complained to Scofield on 2 August. "Rather unwise to leave so attractive a wife alone to her own devices! However—I did not at all want to go," she wrote, explaining that as well as being afraid of the voyage, she "much preferred to play my own little games alone." It was an ominous portent for the events that unfolded during Tom's six-week absence.

Artlessly Vivien described her life since her marriage to Eliot to Scofield, painting an initial picture of charming bohemian poverty: "Do you remember my mentioning a studio flat which I rather hankered to take, while you were here? Well, Tom and I took it—furnished—& lived there for about 3 weeks before he went . . . It was a delightful place." Vivien kept the studio for another week after Tom's departure, and spent three days at home at Compayne Gardens before joining her friend Lucy at Thyme Cottage. Tom was supposed to be coming back on 1 September. "After we have had a second honeymoon!—we shall have to set up a house or a flat of our own—in London, of course. It is very nice being Mrs. Stearns-Eliot" (a name Vivien adopted in the first euphoria of marriage, later dropping the hyphen and the Stearns and reverting to her paternal grandmother's name, Haigh). She was seeing a good deal of the Pounds, of course, "and between ourselves, find them rather boring." However, they were very nice to her, and sought her out such a lot that she supposed she should feel honoured.

Teasingly Vivien tells Scofield something of the "little games" she is playing with the officers she knew before her marriage.

I was at the Savoy the other night with 2 male friends who are consoling the grass widow, so I thought of you Scofield . . . You really ought to be over here now, just think of the dinners in Soho we could do—and grass widows do seem, I find, to be so very *very* attractive, *much more* than spinsters! Now WHY is that? Butler-

Thuring is in the *5th Lancers!*—so is of course bucked to death.
But he has done well—It is a very crack regiment.[25]

There is no doubt that Vivien was extremely pleased to be married at last,
a change of status which encouraged her to play the coquette. "Have you
seen the new *Blast!*" she demands, gratified that she was featured in it as
"the Poet's Bride," although she found Lewis "an impossible man." Was
Scofield married yet, she inquires archly. If not, why not? "If you can manage to refrain from marriage (it is *so* catching I know!) do come over here
before long and let us resume our childish aquaintance [sic] and youthful
prattle." She wasn't really keen on meeting him in the United States, she
repeated. "London is far better—is it not?" Almost as an afterthought, she
remembered her husband, and asked Scofield to remember her kindly to
Tom if he should see him in Massachusetts.

There is an air of unreality about Vivien's "prattle," as she herself
called it. "What I want is MONEY! $! £! We are hard up!"[26] Tom was
writing to his old friend Conrad Aiken from The Downs, the large house
overlooking the sea which his father had built in 1896 at Eastern Point,
Gloucester; Vivien, meanwhile, was still dancing at the Savoy in the "snobbish, social sunset," in the words of Wyndham Lewis, of the pre-war
golden years.[27] Setting up a house in London, as she wished, would be impossible on a schoolmaster's salary, for by now Tom was planning to look
for a teaching job in a boys' school, a prospect which filled his mother with
horror: "It is like putting Pegasus in harness," she confided to Bertrand
Russell.[28]

Despite Vivien's bravado, she was lonely without Tom, and therefore
vulnerable. Her brother Maurice was away in France, and the officers she
saw briefly had to return to their regiments, but there was another man
who was interested, available, and as lonely as she was: Bertrand Russell.
He did not take long to strike. The first hint of Russell's pursuit of Vivien
comes in her boast to Scofield in her letter of 2 August that she is "very
popular with Tom's friends—and who do you think in *particular*? No less
a person than Bertrand Russell!! He is all over me, is Bertie, and I simply
love him. I am dining with him next week."

Flattered and excited by the philosopher's reputation and back-

ground, Vivien was easy prey for the fickle and predatory Russell, a man
with a long history of broken relationships, who was as unwise a choice of
guardian to a new bride as it was possible to make. It is difficult to believe
that Eliot was unaware of Russell's reputation, through Pound and the
Vorticists, when he left his lively wife in the mathematician's care: did
naïveté have its secret intentions?

By 2 August, Russell's euphoric mood of early summer had evaporated. Born in 1872, Bertrand Russell was the second son of Viscount
Amberley, heir to the Russell earldom, and grandson of Lord John Russell,
twice Prime Minister and the architect of the Great Reform Bill of 1832.
His childhood had been a tragic one, since he lost his mother, sister and father before the age of four. At the point in his life when he met Vivien, he
was disillusioned with two important relationships in his life: his "blood-
brotherhood" with D. H. Lawrence, with whom he had struck up an instant friendship when they first met in 1915; and his love affair with Lady
Ottoline Morrell, wife of Philip Morrell, MP for Burnley.

Russell was an essentially solitary man, one of whose life tasks was to
"escape from the inner life, which is too painful to be endured continuously." His first wife, Alys Pearsall Smith, from a distinguished Quaker
family, never offered him the intimacy or sexual fulfilment he craved:
"Alys, even when I was most in love with her, remained outside my inner
life," he told Ottoline. "What I get from you is an intensification of it, with
a transmutation of the pain into beauty and wonder."[29] From the moment
Russell stayed at Ottoline and Philip Morrell's house at 44 Bedford Square
in Bloomsbury on 19 March 1911, his marriage was dead; he and Ottoline
resolved to become lovers, and his first hope was that she would leave her
husband for him. Ottoline was not a classically beautiful woman but she
had enormous appeal for Russell, as for many other men: "Ottoline was
very tall," wrote Russell in his *Autobiography,* "with a long thin face something like a horse, and very beautiful hair of an unusual colour, more or
less like that of marmalade, but rather darker . . . She had a very beautiful
gentle, vibrant voice, indomitable courage, and a will of iron . . . We were
both earnest and unconventional, both aristocratic by tradition, but deliberately not so in our present environment, both hating the cruelty, the caste
insolence, and the narrow-mindedness of aristocrats, and yet both a little
alien in the world in which we chose to live, which regarded us with sus-

picion and lack of understanding because we were alien."[30] Their shared
background drew Ottoline and Russell together and ensured that even
when they ceased to be lovers in 1916, they remained close friends. Both
were sometimes regarded as figures of fun by those of a different social
background, to whom both Ottoline and Russell displayed a curious blindness, never comprehending that a working-class protégé like Lawrence
might feel patronised by the sudden interest of two aristocrats who took
him up with great alacrity and then appeared to reject him.

Immediately after the *coup de foudre* from Ottoline, Russell told Alys
their marriage was over. "She stormed for some hours," he reported
matter-of-factly, but his wife's feelings aroused no pity in Russell, who had
lost interest in her as long ago as 1902 when he had fallen in love with
Evelyn Whitehead, the wife of the co-author of *Principia Mathematica*.
Russell's remarks about his first wife demonstrate the coldness and detachment he displayed to most of his lovers, with the exception of Ottoline.
His solipsism was all-encompassing. Relating how Alys used to come to
him in her dressing-gown and beseech him to spend the night with her,
Russell wrote that, "About twice a year I would attempt sex relations with
her in the hope of alleviating her misery, but she no longer attracted me
and the attempt was futile."[31] Unfortunately for Russell, Alys refused him
a divorce and her brother Logan Pearsall Smith demanded conditions for
not naming Ottoline, when Russell decided to end his nine years of "tense
self-denial" with his wife: the most painful of these was that Russell and
Ottoline were never to spend a night together.[32] After their first rapturous
love-making at Studland Bay, Ottoline agreed to this embargo. Russell's
pyorrhoea, about which Ottoline was too embarrassed to speak to him,
may have had something to do with her decision. In a cruelly honest entry
in her journal, Ottoline once wrote that she could hardly bear Russell's lack
of physical attraction:

> Not that he was at all ugly—he is rather short and thin, rigid and
> ungraceful, and would be unremarkable in a crowd. Then the ex-
> ceeding beauty of his head would arrest me, for it gave the im-
> pression of perfect modelling: the skull thin and delicate, and the
> shape, especially when looked at from behind, always gave me the
> thrill of a very beautiful object. His eyes are large, and hold a con-

centrated beauty of intelligence and passion, and at times great
tenderness. The chin is small and rather weak, and the upper lip
very long and straight.[33]

However, she induced Bertie to shave off his large moustache, which she
thought had the effect of changing his appearance from that of a
Cambridge don to a cross between an actor and Voltaire.

Hurt that Ottoline would not leave Philip, Russell had no compunction about having sexual relations with other women, although he never
wished these transgressions to endanger his relationship with Ottoline. In
March 1914 he travelled to America to lecture in logic at Harvard, and in
Chicago met Helen Dudley, the daughter of a distinguished gynaecologist.
"I spent two nights under her parents' roof, and the second I spent with
her,"[34] remarks Russell casually, justifying his decision as a form of philanthropy, for Miss Dudley was apparently "withering like a flower in
drought" for lack of love, and "the impulse that came over me was like the
impulse to rescue a drowning person, and I am *sure* I was right to follow
it,"[35] as he informed Ottoline. Russell invited Helen Dudley to come to
England as soon as possible, so that they could live together openly and
perhaps marry later if a divorce could be obtained from Alys.

Russell was hardly back in England before his ardour towards Helen
began to cool. Ottoline had written to him that henceforth she wanted
their relationship to be platonic, but on hearing the news both that he had
a new mistress and that his pyorrhoea had been cured in America, changed
her mind, exhibiting a new sexual passion which revived all Russell's love
for her. "My Heart, I cannot lose you . . ." he wrote to Ottoline. By the time
the unfortunate Helen Dudley and her father sailed for England on 3
August 1914, Russell had resolved to have nothing to do with her, making
the excuse of loneliness to Ottoline for his misdemeanour: "The actual bottom fact is that the lonely nights grow unendurable and that I haven't
enough self-discipline to overcome the desire to share the nights with a
woman . . ."[36] In his *Autobiography* Russell argued that it was "the shock of
war" that ended his love for Helen Dudley, but this was as much a lie as
his vows of love to Helen. When she came hammering on the door of his
flat he refused to let her in: "I shall break her heart," wrote Russell dispassionately.[37] Finally Helen returned unhappily to America.

A second abortive affair with his research assistant, Irene Cooper-Willis, to whom Russell was introduced by Ottoline through her friendship with the writer Vernon Lee, had an even more extreme effect on his old lover. Ottoline was witness to Russell's and Vernon Lee's struggle for ascendancy over Irene Cooper-Willis, who finally agreed in January 1915 to help Russell research his proposed book on British foreign policy from 1906. Every afternoon, after a day in the British Museum, Irene called in at Russell's flat nearby for tea and conversation. Ottoline, feeling guilty that she and Russell had only snatched afternoons together, encouraged Russell's growing intimacy with Irene, and he kept up the fiction that his assistant was susceptible to his advances, even when she made it clear that she had no interest in him. On 15 January Ottoline wrote to ask Russell to spend a night with her. Jealousy made her more passionate than usual. "Last night I could only go on my knees in deep awe and thankfulness that such wonders had been given to one," she wrote to Russell. "It was simply unearthly, wasn't it? Every moment of it up to the last . . . It is worth all the sufferings of hell to love like this."[38] Russell's response was even more ecstatic: "My Heart, my Life, how can I ever tell you the amazing unspeakable glory of you tonight? You were utterly, absolutely of the stars—& yet of the Eternal Earth too—so that you took me from the Earth & in a moment carried me to the highest heights." The next night he continued:

> I want the mountains & the storm & the danger, & the wild sudden beauty, & the free winds of heaven. I have all that with you . . . you have *all* that my soul craves—I can't tell you the depths & wildness & vastness of my love to you. We have had many many great & wonderful times, but yesterday was more than all of them—more full of flame & fire—with the wildness of our having meant to part—with all the pain of the war—with everything, everything, caught up & transfigured in a great world of love, love, love.[39]

Despite this outpouring of passion, by the late summer Russell felt that Ottoline was "completely indifferent" to him. The companionship for which he yearned was unavailable to him at Garsington Manor, even though Ottoline had prepared a flat at the Bailiff's House for him in which to write his lectures on Social Reconstruction. But his hostess was wholly absorbed in her new property. On her forty-second birthday and house-warming party on 16 June 1915, Bertie joined D. H. Lawrence, the painter Mark Gertler, and Gilbert Cannan, a friend of artist Henry Lamb, in painting the oak panelled drawing-rooms, one Venetian red and the other sea-green, but this camaraderie proved illusory. All summer Garsington thronged with guests, and Bertie suddenly jarred on Ottoline when compared with the Bloomsbury wit and gossip offered by Clive and Vanessa Bell, Duncan Grant, Lytton Strachey, and the Slade School artists Dora Carrington and Dorothy Brett, as well as Lawrence's friends John Middleton Murry and Katherine Mansfield. Those who had passed through Ottoline's green double doors to her Thursday evening parties at Bedford Square now followed her to Oxfordshire. They represented the world of art, beauty and feeling to which she felt she belonged, while Bertie was of that other culture—science. Bertie "gets dreadfully on my nerves," wrote Ottoline on 19 July. "He is so stiff, so self-absorbed, so harsh and unbending in mind or body, that I can hardly look at him, but have to control myself and look away. And of course he feels this, and it makes him harsher and more snappy and crushing to me. What can I do? . . . Bertie . . . would remake me . . . It is far better to be alone than to be false."[40]

But Ottoline was never alone. And Russell's depression deepened when he became the subject of an unexpected, "ferocious" attack by D. H. Lawrence, to whom he and Ottoline had become very close after they had both read Lawrence's *The Prussian Officer*. The triangular mutual admiration society which had developed between Russell, Ottoline and Lawrence had done much to heal the wounds suffered by Russell at the hands of Wittgenstein, whose criticism had dented his confidence in 1913. "Lawrence is wonderfully lovable," Russell wrote to Ottoline. "The mainspring of his life is love—the universal mystical love—which inspires even his most vehement and passionate hate."[41] Weekends at Garsington consolidated his admiration for Lawrence, and Lawrence's for Ottoline, whom he called his "high priestess," imagining she could form the nucleus of a "little colony" of people who would sail away from the world of war and establish their own Utopia called Rananim.[42] Lawrence's ideal was "*a religious belief which leads to action"* and for a time Russell too was caught up in Lawrence's energetic fantasies. In spite of difficulties created by Lawrence's wife, Frieda, who resented Ottoline's adulation of her "Lorenzo," Russell began to believe that in Lawrence he had found a man who could finally assuage his loneliness. And when Lawrence accepted Russell's invitation to Cambridge, where the miner's son railed against the homosexual culture of Maynard Keynes and Duncan Grant, comparing them to "black beetles . . . which are cased each in a hard little shell of his own," and telling his new friend, "You must leave these friends, these beetles,"[43] the philosopher was delighted. Lawrence "has the same feeling against sodomy as I have," he informed Ottoline: "You had nearly made me believe there is no great harm in it, but I have reverted; & all the examples I know inform me in thinking it sterilising." Lawrence encouraged Russell to dream of leaving Trinity College, Cambridge, and becoming an independent teacher like Abelard. Together they began to plan a course of lectures in London in the autumn of 1915—Lawrence discoursing on ethics and Russell on immortality.

Russell's biographer Ray Monk draws attention to the mood of euphoria in Russell's letters of the time. It was unlikely that the working man from Nottingham and the academic philosopher could collaborate, and when Russell finally apprehended Lawrence's philosophy he thought it "bosh." When Russell sent Lawrence the synopsis he had drawn up of their proposed joint lectures, his collaborator attacked him with brutal ferocity. Russell received the rejected synopsis from Lawrence on 8 July, the day before he met Vivien. His reaction was extreme. "I feel a worm, a useless creature," he told Ottoline.[44] On 10 July he met Lawrence in London and had a "horrid" day. "I got filled with despair, and just counting the moments till it was ended."[45] Bertie decided to go it alone with his lectures, and made alternative arrangements through C. K. Ogden, editor of *The Cambridge Magazine,* to hire a hall in London, while Lawrence too began to make his own plans to publish his views in a new journal called *Signature,* which he was starting with John Middleton Murry.

The final blow came on 14 September, when Lawrence responded with a vehement attack on an essay Russell sent to him, outlining the danger to civilisation of the war; the essay was a lie, countered Lawrence, and

Russell was a hypocrite posing as the "angel of peace," although Lawrence would prefer Tirpitz a thousand times in that role. "You are really the super war-spirit," wrote Lawrence. "You are simply *full* of repressed desires, which have become savage and anti-social. And they come out in this sheep's clothing of peace propaganda." Russell's face looked evil, said Lawrence, and he was "too full of devilish repression to be anything but lustful and cruel," a man inspired by "a perverted, mental blood-lust. Why don't you own it? Let us become strangers again. It is better."[46]

For twenty-four hours Bertie was stunned by this attack, and even contemplated suicide, although later he came to think that Lawrence was simply Frieda's mouthpiece. "He was like a mollusc whose shell is broken," wrote Lawrence in a 1920s story called "The Blind Man,"[47] which was a fictional account of their relationship. He had read Russell's weaknesses, the chief of which was his inability, in Lawrence's eyes, "ever to enter into close contact of any sort." Interestingly, Russell made a similar accusation about Lawrence's living in a "solitary world."[48] Part of Lawrence's bitterness came from the feeling that he had been the plaything of Russell and Ottoline, whom he now saw as "traitors" who used him for their own gratification as if he were a cake or a wine or a pudding. In the split which followed Russell broke with Lawrence and cooled temporarily towards Ottoline, who remained aloof at Garsington but continued to entertain Lawrence.

In this fraught emotional climate, Russell felt uncomfortable working at Garsington. An alternative occurred to him when he discovered that Vivien could type to dictation: he would return to his flat at 34 Russell Chambers, Bury Street, near the British Museum, and persuade Vivien to take up the role of research assistant recently vacated by Irene Cooper-Willis. She seemed to have everything that he needed and she was far prettier than Helen Dudley, who had struck Ottoline as "an odd creature of about twenty-seven, rather creeping and sinuous in her movements, with a large head, a fringe cut across her forehead, and thick lips . . . She did not at all belong to the self-assertive, strident type of American woman: on the contrary, she was languid and adhesive, sympathetic but insensitive and phlegmatic . . ."[49] Vivien was also twenty-seven, but small and slim, a better match for Bertie physically than Ottoline, who towered over her lover.

Vivien's youth was an added inducement to the forty-three-year-old Russell, whose overriding desire was to find a woman who would bear him a child. His marriage to Alys had been childless, and he felt an "intolerable ache" when he saw a child playing in the street. He had had hopes that Ottoline, who had a daughter, Julian, might be impregnated by him, but when he sent her to a gynaecologist for an examination on 12 February 1914 the report came back that "there was absolutely *no* possibility, or practically none" of Ottoline having a child. The fact that Vivien was just married was no more of a deterrent to Russell than it had been in the case of Ottoline; he saw the Eliots' difficulties as an opportunity to ingratiate himself with Vivien, suspecting that her "exquisite and listless" husband was unlikely to father a child by his wife.

On 12 August, only ten days after Eliot's departure, Russell wrote to tell Ottoline that he would not arrive at Garsington the following weekend until late on Sunday afternoon, as he was taking Vivien out to lunch. Although he gave the impression that this was the first time they had met alone, Vivien's letter to Scofield indicates that she and Bertie had already dined together the week before. In Eliot's absence their meetings grew more frequent as, despite his physical shortcomings, Bertie Russell had a charismatic personality which women found irresistible. As Vivien sat opposite him in Soho restaurants, the "intense, piercing, convincing quality" of his conversation had the same mesmeric effect on her as it had originally had on Ottoline. Bertie's technique was to concentrate the full force of his personality upon the woman he wanted: "He assumed at once that I was his possession, and started to investigate, to explore, to probe," until she felt she was in the hands of a "psychological surgeon investigating the tangle of thoughts, feelings and emotions which I had never yet allowed anyone to see," wrote Ottoline of an early meeting with Bertie. Now Vivien was the woman whose psyche was being probed, and she felt Russell's interest upon her like a searchlight illuminating her unhappiness. There could be no greater contrast to her silent, introverted husband. Like Ottoline, Vivien found herself carried into worlds of thought of which she had never dreamt, and was flattered that so remarkable a man should find her worth talking to. "Bertie had a wonderful clear mind," recalled Frances Partridge. "That was what fascinated me."[50] Vivien too was fascinated.

Soon she became a convert to his pacifist ideas; by 24 October Vivien was enthusiastically informing Scofield that she was going to bring "Bertie Russell's seditious writings" with her when she and Tom came to the United States in the spring, and try to place them in New York. "Will you help me, Scofield *deeear?*"[51]

The physical spark which was dying between Ottoline and Russell ignited rapidly between Vivien and her new admirer. Vivien's pride had been hurt by Charles Buckle's rejection of her, and the mortifying knowledge that she did not sexually arouse Tom. As Russell put it in a mollifying note to Ottoline, referring to Buckle and Eliot, "She has suffered humiliation in two successive love-affairs, & that has made her vanity morbid."[52] Russell, whom Irene Cooper-Willis named "Tom Wolfe" in a fictionalised account of her employer's pursuit of her, was known for the passion as well as the amorality with which he pursued women.[53] In 1916, in "Mr. Apollinax," Eliot likened Russell to a satyr in the shrubbery, or a centaur whose "dry passionate talk" devours the afternoon. The images of a lustful predator reflect the poet's reaction to Bertie's intimacy with his wife in the months following July 1915, as well as his memories of Russell at Harvard, for the poem was first published in *Poetry* in September 1916.[54]

Russell's pursuit of Vivien was tinged with a certain desperation after his rejection at the hands of both Ottoline and Lawrence. Fortunately for Russell, Vivien's excited response to his compliments rebuilt his shattered self-confidence and soothed his wounded pride, just as his interest in her restored Vivien's own self-esteem. Abandoning the lectures he was writing after completing only three of the series, Russell began spending the weekdays in London rather than Garsington. Within weeks of Eliot's departure, Vivien was helping Russell work on a reply to a pamphlet written by Gilbert Murray defending government foreign policy, "The Foreign Policy of Sir Edward Grey 1906–1915," which had been published that summer. Irene Cooper-Willis had already collected substantial material towards an analysis of British foreign policy for the book which Russell had been planning, and he now used this as a foundation. Vivien also began typing the collection of articles on the war Russell was writing, entitled *Justice in War Time.*

Despite Russell's attentions, Vivien was unhappy at Tom's absence and wanted him back. Although her letter of 2 August to Scofield bubbles with high spirits, her guilt, illness, or a determination to demonstrate her power over her husband against that of her mother-in-law ensured that by 16 August Eliot had received an urgent summons to return immediately to England. He wrote to his supervisor at Cambridge, Professor Woods, that he had just heard that his wife was "very ill in London," and he must sail at once for England.[55] After barely three weeks in America he left Massachusetts. Not until 1932 was he to return to the country of his birth.

The family reunion had been painful, and it left Tom with bitter memories. First, he had quarrelled with his old friend Scofield, who objected to Eliot's snatching Vivien from under his nose. Eliot wrote a smooth and insincere letter of apology, affecting to be surprised at how "nettled" Scofield was. "You had never given me the impression that your interest in the lady was exclusive—or indeed, in the slightest degree a pursuit: and as you did not give *her* this impression, I presume that I had wounded your vanity rather than thwarted your passion."[56] It was a shrewd thrust, but Vivien had probably been less than honest with Tom about how close she was to Scofield, whom she had begged not to return to the U.S. and its "savages of Wall Street calibre." She had castigated herself for wasting time on Scofield. "A fool there was, & *she* made her prayer—to a rag & a bone & a hank of hair . . . Oh God WHY?"[57] Eliot signed off, "Sincerely yours, Thomas Stearns Eliot," but on his return to England repented of his coolness and sent apologies for his "shabby letter."[58]

Secondly, arguments raged within his family. These were not so easily mended. The family reunion Eliot endured with his parents formed the basis of his later play of that name, a play to which in earlier drafts he gave alternative and revealing titles: *Follow the Furies,* or *Fear in the Way.*[59] The horror and fear the character Harry feels when he returns to Wishwood to confront his mother, Amy, mirrors the emotions experienced by Eliot when he returned to East Gloucester to confront Charlotte Eliot. All the buried resentment of the child who was denied his freedom spill out in this drama. It is "the stupidity of older people" which destroys happiness and brings "The sudden extinction of every alternative,/The unexpected crash of the iron cataract." "You do not know what hope is, until you have lost it," declares Eliot. "You only know what it is not to hope." Returning to the family home ("Wishwood") confirmed Eliot in his belief that to stay in America would mean the "crash of the iron cataract." Vivien represented a bridge to freedom, to enable him to roam in the wilderness of his imagination far away from his mother's "stupidity." Escape was the only possible choice he could make.

Charlotte also expressed her own expectations of her favourite son in her dramatic poem "Savonarola." In this drama the mother, Elena, Charlotte's autobiographical persona, is "of illustrious birth and a woman of great intelligence and force of character. Between her and the most famous of her sons there existed strong sympathy and affection." When Elena's son Savonarola leaves her, she asks in desolation:

. . . Must we part
And loneliness and longing in my heart
Usurp love's deep content?

Savonarola answers that he must take the vow that separates him from his mother. The vow that Charlotte wished her son to take was to allow "the current of his being to be directed by the Lord."[60] In 1915 this was not the vow that Eliot made, although to do so became an increasingly insistent inner demand. His vow was to another mistress—Art—and for this his mother never forgave him.

Eliot left New England weighed down with sorrow and anger. Henry Ware Eliot had taken a hard line with his younger son, refusing to continue his allowance. Knowing that his father owned substantial property in St. Louis, as well as the single biggest block of shares in the Hydraulic Press-Brick Company (whose slogan was "Largest Manufacturers of Face Brick in the World"), Tom had not expected to be cut off. But his father had five other children to consider, and his brick firm had not paid a dividend since 1913, the year in which Henry Eliot Sr. had retired as President at the age of seventy. Eliot Sr.'s only concession was a grudging agreement to pay Tom's rent. In return his son was to finish his thesis on Bradley and present it to Harvard in May. They parted in bitterness, and Eliot never saw his father again. "Tom has always had every reasonable desire gratified, without any thought of ways and means, up to the present time,"[61] a resentful Charlotte complained to the duplicitous Russell. She was not to know that the decision she and Henry made was to have an altogether different result from that which they intended. It did not persuade their impecunious son to return to academic philosophy, as they wished, but instead increased his dependence on his benefactor, Russell.

6

Triple Ménage:
Bertie, Vivien and Tom

Bertrand Russell wrote Vivien out of his life in his *Autobiography.* Complaining of his fading intimacy with Ottoline in 1915, he confessed: "I sought about for some other woman to relieve my unhappiness, but without success until I met Colette [O'Niel],"[1] the aristocratic actress Lady Constance Malleson, with whom Russell fell in love in 1916. Economical with the *actualité,* Russell makes no mention here of his relationship with Vivien, the first "other woman" to console him for the fading of Ottoline's love, yet their intimacy lasted from 1915 until 1918, continuing after Russell began his affair with Colette, and was the product of an instant mutual attraction from which both found it hard to break free. Indeed, it left Vivien with lasting wounds.

Russell destroyed most of Vivien's letters to him,[2] although by nature he was an inveterate hoarder who preserved his correspondence with both Ottoline and Colette. What did he have to hide?[3] In Eliot's opinion, Russell undermined his wife's mental health: "He has done evil," he wrote to Ottoline. It became common literary gossip, as Evelyn Waugh recorded in his diary on 21 July 1955, "that Mrs. T. S. Eliot's insanity sprang from her seduction and desertion by Bertrand Russell."[4] For Eliot, to blame his former friend rather than himself for Vivien's psychological distress was a tempting salve to his conscience, but there is evidence that even Russell, for whom morality had little place in affairs of the heart, was left with deep feelings of guilt for his treatment of Vivien. Tampering with the truth in his *Autobiography* could not obliterate his memory of her. After Vivien's death in 1947 he fictionalised their relationship in an autobiographical short story, "Satan in the Suburbs," written in 1953 when he was eighty-one. His emotional account of the harm done to Mrs. Ellerker,[5] a woman married to a "pompous" and dull husband, Henry Ellerker, by his rival Mr. Quantox, who seduces her, indicates Russell's uncomfortable sense of responsibility for Vivien's ultimate fate, and links her story to his own fear of madness. His biographer Ray Monk associated this fear with Russell's recurring nightmare that he might suffer the same fate as his Uncle Willy who, as Russell discovered as a child, strangled a man in 1874 and spent the rest of his life in an asylum.[6]

In his *Autobiography,* Russell tellingly compares himself to Faust, betraying his awareness of his own sin, as well as of a sense of omnipotence: he often returned to the idea that there was something devilish within him (an accusation made by both D. H. Lawrence and Eliot). It has been assumed that it was Ottoline who awoke in the desiccated philosopher repressed desire, as Gretchen did in Faust, but in Ottoline's case her favours were rationed as she never found Russell physically attractive. It was in fact Vivien who not only aroused but responded to Russell's passion, and in return was betrayed.

In "Satan" Russell introduces a Mephistophelian figure, Dr. Mallako, who tempts the Faustian Mr. Quantox to talk Mrs. Ellerker into committing a murderous crime. When "Mrs. E." goes to the authorities to accuse Mr. Quantox, no one believes her for she is a "nobody"; but Mr. Quantox is "too valuable a public servant to be at the mercy of a hysterical woman, and Mrs. Ellerker, after being quickly certified, was removed to an asylum." The story can be read as Russell's confession as, like the "sneering ghost" Dr. Mallako, who will not leave Quantox alone until he succumbs to temptation, Vivien's ghost dwelt reproachfully in Russell's unconscious in his old age.

Russell draws a flattering self-portrait: Mr. Quantox is "sparkling and witty, a man of wide education and wide culture, a man who could amuse any company by observations which combined wit with penetrating analysis . . ." Perhaps this was Russell's answer to Eliot's unflattering description of his former tutor in "Mr. Apollinax," since he chose so similar a name. Confessing that "Mr. Quantox had a roving eye, and would have incurred moral reprobation but for the national value of his work . . . ," he describes Mrs. Ellerker (referred to as "Mrs. E." in Russell's letters to Ottoline), emphasising the sense of identification he felt with Vivien and the closeness which developed between them.

Mrs. Ellerker, in many of these respects, bore more resemblance to Mr. Quantox than to her husband . . . Her neighbours in Mortlake were divided into those who enjoyed her sparkling talk, and those who feared that such lightness in word could not be wedded to perfect correctness in behaviour. The more earnest and elderly among her acquaintance darkly suspected her of moral lapses skilfully concealed, and were inclined to pity Mr. Ellerker for having such a flighty wife. The other faction pitied Mrs. Ellerker, as they imagined his comments on *The Times* leaders at breakfast.[7]

Once she has met Mr. Quantox, Mrs. E. "imagined what she would feel if Mr. Quantox's eyes looked at her with passion, if Mr. Quantox's arms were about her, if Mr. Quantox's lips were in contact with her own. Such thoughts made her tremble, but she could not banish them."[8] She dreams of Mr. Quantox: "How we should stimulate each other, how shine, how make the company marvel at our brilliance! And how he would love, with passion and fire, and yet with a kind of lightness, not with the heaviness of uncooked dough." Soon, "overcome by reckless desire," Mrs. Ellerker allows Mr. Quantox to kiss her in the library. She agrees to the crime he requires of her which results in loss of life and her husband's suicide; once it is committed, Mr. Quantox abandons her. He is rewarded in the Birthday Honours, "but to Mrs. Ellerker his door remained closed, and if they met in the train or in the street he gave her only a distant bow. She had served her purpose. Under the lash of his disdain, her passion died, and was succeeded by remorse, bitter, unavailing, and unendurable."[9]

In this story Russell spelt out his shame for having used Vivien; she too had "served her purpose" for him, restoring his confidence until he met someone he loved better—Colette—and finally someone who would give him the children he longed for—Dora Black, who became his second wife. In "Satan" Quantox allows Mrs. Ellerker to languish in the psychiatric hospital, even though he visits her and realises that she is perfectly normal and not suffering from "insane delusions." But Russell sets up his own imagined punishment: after murdering the evil Dr. Mallako, Mr. Quantox ends up in the asylum too; there he and Mrs. Ellerker dance together as they used to: "Once a year I shall meet my dear Mrs. Ellerker, whom I ought never to have tried to forget, and when we meet, we will wonder whether there will ever be in the world more than two sane people."

Vivien became Russell's guilty secret, just as his murderous Uncle William was his grandmother's, and the insistent image of himself as an insane murderer haunted his imagination. Rogojin, the murderer in Dostoevsky's *The Idiot,* was the character in fiction with which he felt most "intimate," Russell told Ottoline, as he brooded over the question of what constituted insanity. It is difficult to avoid the conclusion that Russell, who often felt suicidal, believed that he, like Vivien, sometimes teetered on a "knife edge" between reason and unreason, and was equally misunderstood by a society which judged them both unfairly. This was the bond that at times linked them together, and at times repelled Russell because of his fears for his own state of mind. For Vivien, the affair which developed became her guilty secret also, but she was left not only with the feelings of remorse with which Russell credited her, but also with profound regrets for lost love.

In September 1915, however, Russell appeared unselfishness itself as he wrote to Tom Eliot, who had returned from America on the 4th, and offered to share his Bury Street flat with the Eliots until Christmas. To Tom, beside himself with worry over his parents, his finances, his wife's poor health and his thesis, this plan, which Bertie and Vivien had hatched together while he was away, seemed manna from heaven. He had hurriedly accepted a teaching position at Wycombe Grammar School, which was still open at £140 a year with free dinners, to give lessons in French, mathematics, history, drawing and swimming, but until his salary was paid he and Vivien were hard up. "You will see that until January we shall be in urgent need of funds, and that we shall need some money very soon," he wrote in another begging letter to his father on 10 September, apologising for his "blunders" and explaining why he had decided to stick to his original plan of studying for his exams in England. "We have planned a very economical mode of life, and Vivien's resourcefulness and forethought are inexhaustible. We are not planning to make living easier: the question is how to live at all."[10]

Now Bertie's offer answered the question of "how to live," and obviated any need for thrift and "resourcefulness" from Vivien. The proposal had obvious advantages for Russell. He saw it as a way of continuing his delightful intimacy with Vivien at a time when he was bearing the full brunt of Lawrence's savage attack as a "super war-spirit," and feeling ever more divided from Ottoline, who was exhilarated by bringing in the harvest with the Garsington villagers (an occupation which bored Bertie immensely), and newly involved with her "adorable companion" Lytton Strachey, then writing *Eminent Victorians* in the bedroom set aside semipermanently for him by his hostess. The luxury-loving Vivien also preferred to continue her agreeable arrangement with Bertie, rather than follow her husband to live in his rented lodgings in Conegra Road, High Wycombe, at the start of the autumn term. Nevertheless to leave Vivien in the flat made "nice and pretty" by Ottoline in the early days of her affair with Russell, rather than to set up home with his new wife, seems a strange choice for Eliot to make.

"Dear Mr. Russell," Eliot wrote from Eastbourne where he and Vivien had gone for a belated honeymoon in mid-September, although she was apparently still so "unwell" that he had sent for the doctor in order to put their minds at rest, "Your letter coming on top of all your other kindnesses, has quite overwhelmed me." Such generosity and encouragement, he wrote, meant a great deal to him, "above all coming from you." He was feeling quite exhausted each day at having to write so many letters to friends and family in America, but was "overpowered" by Russell's generous offer. Moving on to the practical details, he assured Russell that there would be no problem if their landlord wished to spend nights in London alone with Vivien: "As to your coming to stay the night at the flat when I am not there, it would never have occurred to me to accept it under any other conditions," he wrote. Such a concession to convention had never entered his head and seemed to him not only totally unnecessary, but also would have destroyed all the pleasure he and Vivien took in the "informality of the arrangement."[11] This letter demonstrates a curious blindness to the likely outcome of leaving Bertie alone with Vivien.

Why did Eliot acquiesce in the *ménage à trois* which ensued? It is probable that he grasped at the apparent solution to his difficulties without suspecting the older man's motives. At this stage Eliot knew little of Russell's private life. It is of course possible that the relationship which developed between Vivien and Bertie was as innocent as Eliot apparently assumed—or that Eliot was a cuckold. On the other hand, the triple *ménage* could in fact have been a far more complicated bargain, by which Eliot, for his own reasons, permitted Bertie to enjoy Vivien's sexual favours.

Russell himself later categorically denied to Eliot's friend Robert Gordon George ("Robert Sencourt") that he had slept with Vivien, writing: "I never had intimate sexual relations with Vivienne." Biographers have tended to believe him. Caroline Moorehead writes: "No one has ever been sure whether Russell, by this time something of a philanderer, actually slept with Vivienne."[12] "There can be no doubt . . . that he and Mrs. Eliot did not, in the expected progress of night following day, become lovers," states Ronald W. Clark, arguing that Russell told Ottoline, "to whom he never lied," "I never contemplated risking my reputation with her, & I never risked it so far as I can judge."[13] Peter Ackroyd describes Russell's relationship with Vivien as "intense but 'platonic.' "[14]

But Russell's letters to Colette and Ottoline are inconsistent, for he changed his story to suit his correspondent. On occasions he did lie to Ottoline, but there is little reason to doubt his confession to Colette in October 1916, a few months after meeting her, that he was already "intimate" with Vivien, a tell-tale word which for Russell implied full sexual relations.[15] He had already confessed to being "intimate" with Ottoline. Later, in October 1917, Russell gave Colette a blow-by-blow account of making love to Vivien, an account intended to bring his latest, but already wayward, mistress back to his side.[16] That particular night with Vivien had "a quality of loathsomeness about it which I can't describe," wrote Russell to Colette, but the "loathsomeness" should not be attributed to Vivien's menstruating, as Peter Ackroyd surmises, for Russell went on to say that the one and only thing that made the night loathsome was that it was not with Colette. He was in the habit of telling one of his girlfriends that she was better in bed than the other, remembered Dora Russell, his second wife.[17] Playing one off against the other usually resulted in a revival of passion from the mistress Russell felt was neglecting him, and presumably this was his intention in this letter to Colette, who described Russell as a "lover" of Vivien's in 1917. In 1972, Colette wrote to Kenneth Blackwell, Director of the Russell Archives, on the question of sexual relations between Vivien and Russell: "I always took it for granted that they had, & when I wrote so to BR, he never contradicted me."[18]

Another explanation for Eliot's enthusiastic acceptance of Russell's

offer of accommodation may lie in the disastrous honeymoon he and
Vivien spent at Eastbourne, a spot she probably chose for its happy memories of holidays there with her family and father, to whom she naturally
compared her new husband. Vivien had looked forward to her "second
honeymoon!" with Tom, as she told Scofield in an excited letter which suggests that her initial experience of marital relations in the three weeks she
and Tom had spent together in the studio flat before he left for America
were not an unmitigated failure. She hoped for a rapturous reunion with
the bridegroom from whom she had parted so soon after their marriage,
imagining that, having solved their money troubles and made his peace
with his parents, he would turn to her with new ardour. She still had no idea
of the value of money; still prattled of dances and balls; while Tom knew
that his schoolmaster's salary of £140 a year could not possibly support the
upper-middle-class lifestyle his new wife expected. Even £200 a year
would not support such a lifestyle, although in socially divided England in
1910, 94 per cent of incomes were less than £160 a year. Nor did Eliot seem
to observers to possess the energy and determination necessary to make a
success of this new undertaking; in March 1914 Russell had judged him to
be "very capable of an exquisiteness of appreciation, but lacking in the
crude insistent passion that one must have in order to achieve anything."[19]

Bertrand Russell's report of the honeymoon suggests that it was
not turning out as Vivien hoped. "I am worried about those Eliots," he
wrote, with a hint of *schadenfreude,* to Ottoline, whom he had just left at
Garsington:

It seems their sort of pseudo-honeymoon at Eastbourne is being a
ghastly failure. She is quite tired of him, & when I got here I found
a desperate letter from her, in the lowest depths of despair & not
far removed from suicide. I have written her various letters full of
good advice, & she seems to have come to rely on me more or less.
I have so much taken them both in hand that I dare not let them
be. I think she will fall more or less in love with me, but that can't
be helped. I am interested in the attempt to pull her straight. She
is half-Irish, & wholly Irish in character—with a great deal of
mental passion & *no* physical passion, and universal vanity, that

makes her desire every man's devotion, & a fastidiousness that makes any expression of their devotion disgusting to her . . . She has boundless ambition (far beyond her powers), but it is diffuse and useless. What she needs is some kind of religion, or at least some discipline, of which she seems never to have had any. At present she is punishing my poor friend for having tricked her imagination—like the heroine of the "Playboy."

Presenting Vivien as the disappointed heroine of J. M. Synge's *The Playboy of the Western World* gave Russell the opportunity to make altruism his excuse:

I want to give her some other outlet than destroying him. I shan't fall in love with her, nor give her any more show of affection than seems necessary to rehabilitate her. But she really has *some* value in herself, all twisted and battered by life, lack of discipline, lack of purpose, & lack of religion.[20]

It was a letter which rang alarm bells with Ottoline, who was instantly fearful that if Vivien and Russell had an affair it would create a scandal. This might then reflect badly on the pacifist cause with which she and Philip were increasingly involved as disaster unfolded at Gallipoli, where her brothers Henry and Charles Bentinck were fighting. Russell's intention, as usual, was to provoke jealousy in Ottoline by hinting at Vivien's attachment to him, a technique which had worked well in the past. Although Ottoline had been disengaging herself from Bertie as she compared him unfavourably to the "lovable" Lawrence, who continued his visits through the autumn of 1915, and to the stream of new friends such as Aldous Huxley, Katherine Mansfield and John Middleton Murry, who filled the manor house to overflowing, it was obvious to her from Bertie's breathless and detailed analysis of Vivien's personality, that he, too, was becoming infatuated. His criticisms of Vivien, such as her lack of religion, were calculated to appeal to Ottoline, who had a strong religious faith, but his correspondent was not taken in. On 9 September 1915 she wrote an anxious reply:

My darling,

I was awfully glad to hear from you this morning, but I am rather worried about the Eliots. I am so afraid of what might happen if she became in love with you, which is evidently quite likely . . . I feel you are running a very great risk and I beg and entreat you to be awfully careful—for if you want to do any lecturing or public work any scandal of this kind would entirely damage it and I don't suppose she is worth it.

Anyhow I don't think it would *help her* and help towards making the joint Eliot life happier to let her fall in love with you. I expect in a way it may have made her already more critical of Eliot. Don't think I want to interfere or stop you but I feel *very* strongly that in getting her confidence you are rather separating her from Eliot—and besides that running an awful risk to your reputation . . . Please don't think I am cross, for I am not one bit, only I know you are led on by yr. sympathy and by yr. longing to set people straight and the big things you *can* do are more important.

My Love darling.

Yr. O.

Ottoline's warning that to encourage Vivien to fall in love with Bertie would separate her from Eliot was altogether reasonable; and she may also have seen the ominous similarity between her lover's argument here and his excuse that sleeping with Helen Dudley was like saving a drowning woman. The pattern which Bertie's seductions followed was already apparent to Ottoline, who was unlikely to be convinced by his assurance that Vivien had "no physical passion." Ottoline had been deeply hurt to discover, when Helen Dudley showed her the love letters Russell had sent her, that he had used almost identical language to the young American as he had to her. She should, however, have guessed that the threat of scandal would do little to sway Russell; when in love, he was recklessness itself. His affair with Ottoline had already cost him his teaching post at Newnham College, Cambridge, where the college had decided to dispense with the services of an adulterer.

Russell hastened to reassure Ottoline. "There is no occasion for your fears," he wrote on 10 September. Eliot was not "that sort of man & I will be much more careful than you seem to expect. And I feel sure that I can make things come right. We can talk about it when I come. I would not for the world have any scandal, & as for the Eliots, it is the purest philanthropy—I am sorry you feel worried—there is *really* no need—I am fond of him, & really anxious to be of use to him. The trouble between them was already at its very worst before I came into the matter at all—it is already better, & when I saw him he was very full of gratitude. I must have given you quite a wrong impression when I wrote."[21] Nevertheless Ottoline remained unconvinced and declined to invite Vivien to Garsington. Russell meanwhile kept his two women separate and continued to lead a double life between Garsington and Bury Street.

Although Russell often dramatised the emotional situations in which he found himself, this time his description of Vivien's mood of suicidal despair seems to have been accurate. Maurice said later that the Eliots' honeymoon was "rotten," a euphemism for the sexual failure that had undoubtedly occurred. It cannot have been helped by Tom's emotional state on his return from what had been a painful confrontation with his parents; he was, said Maurice, "terrified" of his mother, this "tough old woman who wrote poetry." The fierce ticking-off he received for marrying Vivien may have made him reconsider the sudden decision he had made, and its economic consequences, as he brooded over his situation on the boat carrying him back to England. Certainly it was a shaken bridegroom who travelled down to Eastbourne with his sickly wife. In his absence Vivien had fallen under Russell's spell and must have looked with new, critical eyes at her nervous husband, embarrassed by his truss, who attempted to make love to her. "He was a virgin when he married," remembered Maurice (as Eliot himself confessed). "He had a hernia: this awful truss must have depressed him. Tom was convinced that his hernia was a form of tumor, cancer—and wouldn't let anyone look at it." In the hotel bedroom, Vivien, newly reunited with the husband she barely knew, was horrified by the arrival of her menstrual period, which embarrassed her as much as Tom. Maurice remembered that "both Tom and Vivie were so clean, both so worried about cleanliness." As he bluntly expressed it: "Viv's sanitary towels always put a man off."[22] It was not a stage set for passion.

In a confessional poem entitled "Ode on Independence Day, July 4 1918,"[23] published in *Ara Vos Prec* ("I pray you"), a collection of Eliot's poems published in February 1920, of which only two hundred and sixty-four copies were printed, and which he later suppressed, Tom recalled his honeymoon three years after the event and the long-deferred rite of passage he had endured at Vivien's hands. The title of the volume is taken from a speech from Canto XXVI of Dante's *Purgatorio* in which the poet meets the souls of the Sodomites and the souls of the Lustful, one of whom, Arnaut Daniel, a twelfth-century troubadour, speaks to Dante and Virgil in Provençal, regretting his sins. Eliot takes Arnaut Daniel's words, "Ara vos prec . . . ,"[24] asking his audience to be "mindful in your time of my pain," before diving back into the refining fire of purgatory; it was a canto to which he would frequently return. *Ara Vos Prec* also carried the Dante epigraph which Eliot later made an explicit dedication to Jean Verdenal in *Prufrock*: "Now you are able to comprehend the quantity of love that warms me towards you/When I forget our emptiness/Treating shades as if they were solid." The title of the poem, too, celebrating Independence Day, is surely ironic: in the trap of marriage the poet feels he has lost his freedom.

In "Ode" the poet mourns the "silence from the sacred wood," the source of his creativity, since he retired from "the profession of calamus." This is a reference to Walt Whitman's *Calamus* poems which celebrate the intimacy of man-to-man relationships. Whitman chose the Calamus, "a large and aromatic grass, or rush," for its value as a symbol of life associated with the phallus.[25] The friendship with Verdenal, transfigured in Eliot's memory, grew to have a significance greater than the reality of their association; the winter of their friendship, 1910–11, was a time of great creativity for Eliot, which he compared unfavourably to the negativity of life with Vivien.

The poet feels "tired," "misunderstood." The morning after his wedding night he is "Tortured/When the bridegroom smoothed his hair/There was blood upon the bed./Morning was already late." He feels revulsion at consummating the relationship with his bride, irritation at messing his hair and rising late because of her sexual demands. In his imagination the children sing a wedding chant: "(Io Hymen, Hymenaee)/Succuba eviscerate." Eliot may have had in mind the ironic reproach of Whitman's expression of sexual ecstasy in the *Children of Adam* poems which precede the *Calamus* poems. He may also have been thinking of Catullus's wedding chant, "Hymen to Hymenaee," in a poem in which the husband is reminded that he must give up his previous "Calamus-like" relationship with "a boyfriend favourite." The "succuba eviscerate" to whom the bridegroom refers is a female demon who has sexual intercourse with men in their sleep, disembowelling or castrating the bridegroom (who later becomes the sterile Fisher-King of *The Waste Land*).

Decoding this poem, with its vivid imagery of a castrating female, leads to the suggestion that Eliot was impotent, or partially impotent, with Vivien. Psychiatrist Dr. Harry Trosman has claimed that Eliot's deprived childhood left him "isolated and uncomfortable in his ill-fitting masculinity . . . It is likely that . . . unacceptable homosexual longings were activated. Such longings, to which he responded with panic, were transformed into aesthetic sublimations or dandyism."[26] Strongly fixated on his powerful mother, Eliot had followed the classic pattern of same-sex orientation in identifying with her in adolescence, and looking for love-objects in whom to rediscover himself.[27] His resulting profound fear of sexual relationships with women was not only expressed in early poems such as "Circe's Palace,"[28] but also in the *Prufrock* poems which he placed immediately after "Ode" in *Ara Vos Prec*.

The last stanza of "Ode" returns compulsively, through twisted paths, to the image of the dead Verdenal: "Tortuous/By arrangement with Perseus/The fooled resentment of the dragon," perhaps an allusion to the trickery by which Perseus slew the Gorgon, and Eliot's own resentment at being tricked into a marriage he regrets. "Sailing before the wind at dawn./Golden apocalypse. Indignant/At the cheap extinction of his taking-off./Now lies he there/Tip to tip washed beneath Charles' Wagon."[29]

Lyndall Gordon has interpreted these last lines as a reference to the bridegroom's disappointment as he, "sailing expectantly towards 'a golden apocalypse,' is frustrated by what appears to be a premature ejaculation. He is left a good way below the stars, 'Indignant/At the cheap extinction of his taking-off.' "[30] But the stanza must be read in conjunction with Eliot's sources: resonating with grief and anger, his lines also echo the lament for Duncan's death in *Macbeth* (Act 1, Scene 7) and Shakespeare's praise for his virtues which:[31]

Will plead like angels, trumpet-tongued against
The deep damnation of his taking-off . . .

Surely the "cheap extinction" is a reference to the needless loss of
Verdenal's life in the Dardanelles. Now his body lies beneath the waves, in
lines which serve as a prologue to *The Waste Land:* "Now he lies there/Tip
to tip washed beneath Charles' Wagon." Charles' Wagon is another name
for the constellation of Ursa Major, the Great Bear, visible over the
Dardanelles. "Washed" and purified by water, the body rests in its grave:
it is an image to which Eliot returned again and again in anguish, as he
turned away from the living body of his wife.

Eliot's response to the threat of Vivien's messy and demanding proximity was to escape, to withdraw into "icy urbanity." Maurice recalled that
Tom spent a night in a deckchair on the beach at Eastbourne, while a distraught Vivien locked herself in her bedroom and apparently damaged the
room. The couple returned early from Eastbourne, Vivien insisting on
bringing the soiled sheets home with her in a laundry basket to be washed
at home; the manageress of the hotel wrote to Charles Haigh-Wood to
complain that the sheets had been "stolen," but this was a habit Vivien had
developed while still at school at Margate, where she first acquired the
laundry basket. Since puberty she had become accustomed to taking the
basket with her wherever she stayed, filling it with the dirty laundry, and
having it sent home by rail. One of her maid's jobs was to collect the laundry basket from the station and have the contents washed. It was a habit
which irritated Eliot immensely, remembered Maurice: "Vivie stole sheets
from the hotels, had them washed and sent them back. Sometimes she
went along to the Post Office and posted the clean sheets back to the hotels. Tom went *mad.*"[32]

In the midst of this marital crisis, Tom turned in panic-stricken gratitude to Russell. The flat into which the newly married couple moved was
small, and the sleeping accommodation inconvenient; there was "just a *tiny*
cupboard room behind the kitchen, so small you couldn't swing a cat," remembered Maurice. "Tom slept in the hallway in a deckchair. Vivie used
a cot-bed she got from Compayne Gardens." The room in which Vivien
slept was in fact the former pantry. In such circumstances conjugal relations were well-nigh impossible, but this was no doubt a relief to Tom. The

rest of the flat was attractive, for Ottoline had spent three weeks in 1911 fitting it out for Bertie in the first flush of their relationship; she had bought a rug and filled the rooms with carnations and lilies of the valley, while Bertie moved in his grandfather's desk and a small table made from Domesday Book oak that had belonged to his mother and on which he had written most of *Principia Mathematica.* "It will be very nice—we shall have a great sense of liberty & I can have books there & means of making tea, & even some peppermints in some secret recess!" (Ottoline's favourite sweets were peppermints).[33]

Ottoline had found Bertie a demanding and dependent lover; he was so isolated from people in general that he once confessed he felt he had to speak to them in "baby talk" if they were to understand him. "How much emotion those little rooms in Bury Place held—intense and burning and very tragic!" she wrote. "Bertie demanded so much, and all I could give him was so inadequate to his desires. He would stand at his window look- ing for my coming, growing tenser and tenser, counting the minutes if I was late. As I hurried along the street I dreaded looking up, and seeing his face pressed against the panes looking for me. And then it was dreadful leaving him in those rooms, unsatisfied and tragically lonely. How could I satisfy him? The very intensity of his demands seemed to crush me." Sometimes when she was with him Ottoline had felt as if she were in prison, for his passion was so possessive and oppressive. On returning home she would "skip for joy, and often dance round my bedroom and fling out my arms and sing 'Free, free.' "[34]

Vivien, by contrast, had never been happier than she was with Bertie. And, instead of snatched hours in station waiting rooms, afternoons in Tottenham Court Road hotels at 2/6d a time, or brief trysts in Russell Buildings, which was all Ottoline would allow her lover, Russell had the relationship he had always wanted with a woman, in which domestic inti- macy and writing were shared in a companionable twosome. "Physical in- stinct, at least in me, is not satisfied by the physical act alone, but cries out for constant companionship, especially in the night,"[35] he had written to Ottoline during his affair with Helen Dudley, a bitter allusion to the prom- ise they had made to Logan Pearsall Smith never to spend a night together. Now he could climb into Vivien's little bed, or persuade her to move into his own much more comfortable bedroom, which Maurice remembered as well-furnished, while Tom was safely away in the country. He was no longer dependent on Ottoline for love; Vivien was dependent on him. She had moved into his home, and although he sometimes returned to Garsington, Bertie and Vivien lived contentedly in the flat while they worked. "The foreign policy of Sir Edward Grey 1906–1915" was published that summer[36] and *Justice in War Time,* the collection of his articles on the war, in November.

Tom left for High Wycombe almost immediately after his ill-fated Eastbourne honeymoon, taking lodgings during the week with a Mrs. Toone. Lack of money continued to worry him. On 27 September he wrote another anxious letter to his father, telling him that he was settling into school work and had two free afternoons a week in which to work for his degree, but his deposit was reduced to almost nothing and that was all he had to live on: "If no money comes from you at the end of the fortnight I shall be forced to cable, as I shall be reduced to the last pound by the time you get this. I hate to *cable* for money . . ."[37] He could be earning extra money by writing, he reminded Henry Ware Eliot Sr., if only his parents had not insisted that he finish his degree.

Eliot therefore eagerly accepted Russell's temporary gift of £3,000 of engineering debentures, used to fund the making of munitions; as a pacifist Russell felt he could not keep an unethical investment, but Eliot retained the debentures, which produced an annual income of £180 at 6 per cent, for nearly twelve years after the war.[38] Nor were these the only gifts the Eliots accepted, for Russell, increasingly attached to Vivien, kept her like a highly prized mistress. "I am getting very fond of Mrs. Eliot," he confessed to Ottoline on 13 October 1915. "Not in an 'improper' manner— she does not attract me much physically—but I find her a real friend, with a deeply humane feeling about the war, & no longer at all unkind to her husband. I feel her a permanent acquisition, not merely an object of kindness, as I thought at first."[39] As the months passed, he admitted "a very great affection" for Vivien. His feeling was, he told Ottoline, "utterly different from the feeling I have for you. What makes me care for her is that she affords me an opportunity for *giving* a kind of affection that hitherto I have only been able to give in a slight, fragmentary way to pupils—I don't mean that is the whole of it, but it is what is important." Vivien, needy, dependent, as lonely as he, was grateful for Russell's care, in contrast to the rich, socially successful hostess and politician's wife he had chosen before. He had loved Ottoline, but she never desired him as he desired her; now, with Vivien, he had found a woman to whom he could not only feel effortlessly superior but who also accepted the totality of his love without finding it oppressive. Insecure, and as alone as Vivien for all his intelligence, Bertie began to spend more and more time with her, returning to 34 Russell Chambers, Bury Street, after an abortive attempt to write his lectures on social reconstruction at Garsington, although to Ottoline he rationalised his feelings as paternal: "I shall be seeing a great deal of her—the affection I have for her is what one might have for a daughter, but it is very strong, & my judgement goes with it."[40] Since henceforth his relationships would invariably be with younger women, such professions of fatherly love on Bertie's side were never to be trusted.

Russell showered Vivien with presents, much to Ottoline's annoyance. By July 1916 she was writing in her journal: "I had a long talk with Bertie about Mrs. Eliot. I don't really understand her influence over him. It seems odd that such a frivolous, silly little woman should affect him so much, and she looks up to him as a rich god, for he lavishes presents on her of silk underclothes and all sorts of silly things and pays for her dancing lessons. It takes all his money . . ."[41] Vivien accepted his gifts without compunction. Like Tom, she had been used to a privileged lifestyle, and saw no reason to allow her standards to drop. A letter to Scofield Thayer in October shows an indulgent Russell funding her dream of becoming a professional ballet dancer like Karsavina in the Russian Ballet, or the English Jenny Pearl, despite his remarks to Ottoline that Vivien had "boundless ambition (far beyond her powers) but it is diffuse and useless." Vivien had a studio portrait photograph of herself taken, and sent a copy to Scofield:

> I must *insist* that if you do not like it you will return it. I will *not* allow my photograph to be retained out of politeness (Scofield was always so courteous!) . . . I am not at all sure that I like it myself—and now that I am the wife of a poet whose fame is rapidly increasing throughout the length and breadth of more than one land, *and* in order not to become merely "T.S. Eliot's wife"—am

embarking on the proffession [sic] of ballet dancing myself (shade of Jenny Pearl!)—I shall frequently present my features to the camera.

After telling Scofield that an anthology of poetry, including poems by Yeats, Pound, Eliot and others was coming out the following week— "Elkin Matthews, 3/6d!"—she confides to her old admirer that "We have been more or less of a triple menage. Bertie Russell has taken us to his bosom. I cheer him up, he says—and the flat rings with his raucous mirth. Bertie has rather an elementary sense of humour!" In the spring she and Tom are going to the U.S., she tells Scofield, where she will take Bertie's "seditious writings" and try to place them for him in New York. If they stay long she will want to take some ballet-dancing lessons there. "I am going in for it very seriously. Is there a school of ballet in New York," she asks. "I am a true JP [Jenny Pearl] now. Three times a week I descend into a subterranean hall in Carnaby Street, Soho, and there, in a little black skirt above my knees, and toe-blocked shoes, I leap & skip under the guidance of a massively-calved lady who calls me 'darling.' When Bertie and Tom come to watch me, as they often do, she calls them 'darling' too."[42]

High-spirited and happy in this strange, triangular relationship, Vivien contrasts the "slow, deep tones" of Tom, who remarks ponderously, "It *would* be nice to see Scofield again," with Bertie's reaction to Scofield's letter: "He enjoyed it, he laughed with joy . . ." What pleasure Scofield has given to more than one of them in this dark land, she tells him. "Send us another ray of light!" Bertie's neighing laugh was famous among Ottoline's cronies: D. H. Lawrence, caricaturing him as Sir Joshua Malleson in *Women in Love,* writes of "a learned dry Baronet of fifty who was always making witticisms and laughing at them heartily in a harsh horse-laugh."[43] Vivien, receptive and quick-witted, provoked such laughter; in return she received not only money but the concentrated force of Russell's charismatic and intense personality focused upon her. It is no wonder that Vivien did indeed fall in love with Bertie, whose high sex drive and determined charm was effortlessly to win him a succession of much younger wives, Dora, Patricia (Peter) and Edith, in the future. Vivien was attracted to highly intellectual men, and Russell and Eliot had much in common: both were brilliant, introverted and highly emotional. The difference lay in their attitude to women.

Vivien was not the first woman on whom Russell had secretly lavished presents, as a way of achieving intimacy, and perhaps also as a form of control. He had acted in a similar fashion with Evelyn Whitehead, wife of Alfred North Whitehead, paying her bills without her husband's knowledge.[44] But to Vivien he gave much more than silk stockings and dancing lessons: Maurice recorded that Russell gave his sister dresses and also "Russell family heirlooms." It was a mark of Russell's deep infatuation that he was prepared to give his mistress part of his inheritance. In the end, said Maurice, "Bertrand Russell got scared. His family asked Vivien for a ring back." Later, he reported, "Mummy made her give it back."[45]

Tom and Vivien continued to live in a state of dependency upon Bertrand Russell, and it is almost impossible to believe that Tom was unaware that Russell and Vivien were having a sexual relationship; he may have suppressed the knowledge, and no doubt it was never openly discussed, but from his unconscious came the poem which characterised Russell as a satyr, "Mr. Apollinax." Nevertheless, Eliot remained complaisant and grateful for several good reasons. First, although Russell could ill afford it, he was subsidising both Eliots because he had taken pity on his former pupil for being "desperately poor." "Eliot was not truly poor" writes Paul Delany, "but he certainly exuded an air of desperation,"[46] which caused Russell to write to Eliot's Harvard supervisor, J. H. Woods, that "It has driven me almost to despair to see his fine talents wasting."[47] It was to become a characteristic of the Eliots that they expected other people to subsidise their lifestyle.

Secondly, Eliot was relieved to turn over to Russell the conjugal duties he often found distasteful. "The difficult relationship with Vivienne served as a constant reminder of sexual failure," writes Dr. Harry Trosman. "Eliot's tolerance for and complicity in Vivienne's affair with Russell suggested an unresolved oedipal tie and a need to placate a sexually aggressive father surrogate."[48] While Russell took care of Vivien's demands for affection and sexual fulfilment, all three could be happy. A third reason was that Russell was an important literary contact for Eliot; he put his protégé in touch with the editor of the *International Journal of Ethics,* Sydney Waterlow, who commissioned two reviews from him in October, work which Eliot found more congenial as well as more lucrative than toiling over academic philosophy for his thesis. "The reviewing has cheered me up very much," he wrote gratefully to Russell from High Wycombe.[49] Russell was also attempting to mollify Charlotte Eliot, assuring her that the shortage of educated men who had now enlisted in the army would enable Tom to obtain "suitable work" once he had taken his Ph.D.[50]

However, it would be wrong to assume that Vivien and Eliot *never* had physical relations, as Ackroyd and Monk appear to do. Monk states that Eliot was "incapable of sexual relations with her," and this was the explanation for his acceptance of the triangular relationship.[51] Ackroyd also attributes this to the "physical failure" of the marriage. But Eliot's honeymoon nerves seem to have evaporated to some extent as the months passed, and it is perfectly possible that Vivien was intimate with both men in the autumn of 1915. By 8 May 1916 Vivien was writing a letter of congratulation to Scofield in which she implied limited love-making with her husband had taken place, although it appears she had to work hard to stimulate him. "How nice that you are going to be married!" she writes. "Nothing could be better! Try black silk sheets and pillow covers—they are extraordinarily effective—so long as you are willing to sacrifice *yourself.*"[52] Colette also remembered that Bertie "once appeared in my bedroom wearing black pajamas, saying that V.S.E. (Vivienne Stearns Eliot) likes them."[53] Black sheets and pajamas would not, of course, show blood stains, and were possibly Vivien's own solution to her problem.

As the term drew to a close, the *ménage à trois* began to unravel. Perhaps Vivien grew too demanding, and Russell's brother Frank began to protest at the disappearance of the family jewels. Perhaps Russell himself grew "scared," as Maurice believed. Eliot's conscience may at last have driven him to hunt for a flat for himself and his wife. What is not in doubt is the nervous collapse which the ending of this crucial love triangle precipitated in Vivien. "The situation is anxious and painful, although it is too interesting to be left alone, apart from kindness," wrote Russell to Ottoline on 10 November, apologising for being unable to come to Garsington. He had come to love Eliot "as if he were my son":

He is becoming much more of a man. He has a profound & quite unselfish devotion to his wife, & she is really very fond of him, but has impulses of cruelty to him from time to time. It is a Dostoevsky type of cruelty, not a straightforward every-day kind. I am every day getting things more right between them, but I can't let them alone at present, & of course I myself get very much interested. She is a person who lives on a knife edge, & will end as a criminal or a saint—I don't know which yet. She has a perfect capacity for both.[54]

This passage, in which Russell implies Vivien is mentally unstable, has been much quoted. It should be remembered that it was written to Ottoline, who was prejudiced against Vivien; it should also be compared to the letter Russell wrote on 3 December to Tom's mother, Charlotte Eliot, in which he praises Vivien's charm and ability:

I have continued to see a good deal of your son and his wife. It has been a great pleasure having them staying in my flat, and I am sorry to lose them . . . She has done a great deal of work for me, chiefly typing, and consequently I have come to know her well. I have a great respect and liking for her: she has a good mind, and is able to be a real help to a literary career, besides having a rare strength and charm of character.[55]

As the time of leaving approached, Vivien's illness necessitated her mother's presence to nurse her in 34 Russell Chambers, and Russell had to take refuge in the Waverly Hotel just around the corner. "I have been having a horrid higgedly-piggedly pillar-post kind of time," he complained to Ottoline on 8 December,[56] as he worried about completing the lectures on social reconstruction he was due to deliver in the new year. Finally he decamped to the house of his old friend Robert Trevelyan, at Holmbury St. Mary, near Dorking, and thence to his brother's in Sussex, where he found the necessary quiet in which to write. It was time for the Eliots to move on. By early December the Eliots had found a flat of their own in St. John's Wood, and by the 20th they had left. Such was Vivien's panic at the prospect of living alone with her husband that Russell was forced to promise to take her on holiday to the seaside after Christmas.

7

A Child in Pain

Early in the new year Bertie and Vivien travelled together to the Torbay Hotel, Torquay, where they stayed for five days, from 7 to 12 January 1916. It was a provocative move by Bertie, who had complained sulkily to Ottoline that he did not want to visit Garsington because it was full of "morbid corners," but instead mentioned in a letter of 3 December that he was planning to invite Vivien for a holiday before Christmas.[1] All he wanted, he told his old lover, was six months' sleep. The letter, meanwhile, had the desired effect, bringing fresh pleas from Ottoline to visit her.

"I *long* to be with you," replied Bertie, not altogether truthfully, on 1 January, "but I am afraid I can't . . . I made a beginning of an attempt to get out of it [the holiday with Vivien], but found I should hurt her feelings so I dropped it. Now she is well enough, and wants to go on Monday."[2] He assured Ottoline he was in no mood for a holiday and would have preferred to stay in London where the Military Service Bill, which introduced conscription for all single men aged between eighteen and forty-one, was making its stormy way through Parliament. As a leading activist in the No-Conscription Fellowship, and as an acquaintance of H. H. Asquith, the Prime Minister, an old admirer of Ottoline's whom he had met at Garsington on the occasion when he emerged naked from a pond to find Asquith on the bank ("the quality of dignity which should have characterised a meeting between the Prime Minister and a pacifist was somewhat lacking on this occasion," wrote Russell[3]), he might have been expected to stay in London to fight this extension of the powers of the state.[4] Yet Russell left the capital just as the bill was receiving its first reading on 6 January in the Commons, in order to take Vivien to the seaside.

Before his departure, Bertie teased Ottoline with excuses for his West

Country holiday. Vivien, he was sure, would "much prefer" to be with her husband, but Eliot needed to work on his thesis and was looking forward to the time alone: "She needs a change in order to get well, & Eliot has been so busy nursing her he wants solitude. So it seems inevitable." The conventions would be observed, Russell assured his former lover: "We shall be quite 'proper'—There is no tendency to develop beyond friendship, quite the opposite. I have really now done all I meant to do for them, they are perfectly happy in each other, & I shall begin to fade away out of their lives as soon as this week is over."

On 3 January Russell made another attempt to justify his holiday alone with Vivien, explaining that he had made "a valiant attempt" to get out of going away with "Mrs. E.," without success.

> The whole thing rather amused me, because it was so unlike the way things are conventionally supposed to happen. First I talked to him, & said I felt the responsibility of her health, & wished he were going as he knew better what to do. He was willing to take my place, but reluctant on account of his work . . . However, he would have gone; but when I said the same things to her, she wouldn't hear of it, again on account of his work. So I had to let the matter be . . .[5]

Clearly Vivien preferred to go on holiday with Russell rather than her husband, but as a sop to Ottoline, who was unhappy that she and Bertie had lost "the fine intense moments" of the past, and their affair was "fading out,"[6] Russell promised to make the break with the Eliots soon: "What I meant to do for these two is done, except to some slight extent as regards money (I must go on giving her my typing)," and assured her that the Eliot marriage was happier than it had been. But for all his promises, Vivien's vulnerability had touched Bertie's heart, for it stood in such contrast to the strong-willed Ottoline, whom he was determined to punish for rejecting his "oppressive" physical advances: "I don't quite know why, she appeals to me as a child in pain would," he wrote on 7 January 1916. "I hate to see her suffer. She has the one great thing, real love—She will endure anything rather than hurt people." Russell disliked Vivien's mother, Rose, who in his opinion was "odious, but Mrs. E. is always thinking how to keep her happy—For some reason she had no kindness to her husband at first, but now she is quite changed towards him."[7]

It is possible that for once Russell was telling the truth when he emphasised the innocence of his relations with Vivien at Torquay to Ottoline, and that Vivien had taught him why women found him oppressive. "I have been quite fantastically unselfish towards her, & have never dreamt of making any kind of demands." Russell claimed to have discovered that a "clash" existed between artistic people, those like Ottoline and Vivien who took pleasure in "things of sight," and the inartistic, like himself, those who lived *"exclusively* in thoughts & purposes." It was hardly a profound insight, but Russell attributed the lifting of his mood to this lesson learnt from Vivien's conversation and company. Now he understood this, wrote an exuberant Russell, and realised that such personality clashes could not be cured, he was no longer in a state of depression at all, but was simply trying to see things clearly. "I simply *must* understand, & avoid getting into such a state again."[8]

Whether Ottoline believed him is unlikely; certainly she had heard from Aldous Huxley that Vivien was a flirtatious and seductive woman, and she had no reason to trust Bertie's fidelity in affairs of the heart; past experience had taught her that he could lie when he felt it necessary. She responded, however, with dignity:

> I feel you think I am hurt that you are with Mrs. Elliot [sic]. You must not *please* think so, for I am not a bit. I am only sorry that it is such a mere health sojourn & that it is very little rest or relaxation for you, but I hope in spite of everything that it may rest you . . .

But despite her brave protests, Ottoline *was* hurt. She knew that Russell, who lived "entirely mentally," was critical of her longing to live what she described as "the simple instinctive life" at Garsington, although few of her guests would have recognised in those terms the lifestyle she had created at the Oxfordshire manor house. Ottoline could not help confessing to her "darling Bertie" her disappointment that she had failed "so lamentably lately to make you *at all happy* & that you dread to come here—to a place I Love. Please dont think I am *hurt*—about it—only it *is* a disappointment

& I feel—really—discouraged—about the future." In future, said Ottoline, they could only meet in London.[9]

Ottoline knew that Russell had been in a state of nervous tension before leaving for Torquay. The decision he made in 1915 to devote himself to anti-war propaganda had made him an increasingly hated figure in the country. Under suspicion by the government, he was about to give the first of his lectures on social reconstruction on 18 January, the preparation of which, he complained to Ottoline, "nearly drove me into insanity." In fact Russell had felt so distressed before leaving London that he had discussed with Ottoline the possibility of consulting her "nerve doctor," the Swiss psychiatrist Dr. Vittoz, asking if he could cure "despair." Vivien's health was allegedly equally precarious: "Coming here is merely a question of health—Mrs. E. fancied it would do her good," wrote Russell. "She is too ill for any thought of real enjoyment in the place." On the day they arrived, 7 January 1916, he told Ottoline, "I detest it but she seems to like it. However, she is not any better so far."

Alone in each other's company, in a climate so warm that they could sit out without a coat, "warmer than Rome" in fact, Bertie and Vivien found "very lovely places" near the coast to explore. Soon Bertie was feeling quite fit, "and Mrs. E. is better, I no longer feel anxious and weighed down with responsibility." What exactly was wrong with Vivien? Ottoline had enquired; Russell had told her in December when Vivien was laid up in his flat that "Mrs. Eliot's illness is not serious in itself, but she has been threatened since childhood with tuberculosis in the bones, and it means everything has to be treated very carefully. All through her childhood she has been kept alive by Sir F. Treves, gratis, because the case interested him. I had always thought he was a brute, but her experience of him is quite the opposite . . ."[10] As Russell's correspondence makes clear, Vivien was "delicate," an easy prey to influenza and chest infections, but her ill-health was largely "nervous," as was his.

Ottoline urged Russell to see Dr. Vittoz at the Villa Cimerise in Lausanne, explaining that he need only be away just over a fortnight, and the doctor was not very expensive. But by 12 January Russell, like Vivien, was feeling so much better that he saw no need to visit Dr. Vittoz—not that the Foreign Office would have allowed him to leave the country. Ottoline was magnanimous: "I am *so* glad Mrs. E. is better," she replied the next day. "It is really a great comfort to feel you have been such a help to them, & it was well worthwhile."[11]

The same afternoon, 12 January, Eliot arrived at Torquay, "as happy as a boy escaped from school," said Russell, who paid both the Eliots' expenses. Russell's revealing phrase, "Eliot replaced me,"[12] suggests that he had, in some sense, fulfilled the role of husband until Tom, who had journeyed down through Somerset, passing East Coker, from where his ancestor Andrew Eliot had emigrated to Salem, was reunited with his much recovered wife. Russell reluctantly returned to London, still struggling to analyse the mystery of Vivien's attraction for him: "I can't quite make out why I like her, & feel you wouldn't, & I couldn't defend her," he told Ottoline. "I believe I like her really because I can be useful to her, so I get over the sense of being a failure & making people unhappy when I want to make them happy." It was, he wrote, a sort of comfort to him to think that the Eliots were happier than they would have been if he had not known them.[13] "Mrs. E does for me what the Germans did last Xmas," implying that Vivien roused him from torpor and depression to a sense of purposeful activity.

In Vivien and Russell's absence Eliot had been staying alone at 34 Russell Chambers, looked after by Russell's charwoman, Mrs. Saich. As ever, he had no qualms about accepting Russell's offer of free accommodation at Torquay, and the alacrity with which he agreed to take his benefactor's place suggests that Eliot's need to work on his thesis, most of which had been completed at Oxford before he sent it to his supervisor Professor James H. Woods at Harvard in February, was not as pressing as Ottoline had been given to understand. "This is wonderfully kind of you—really the last straw (so to speak) of generosity," wrote Eliot. He was very sorry Russell had to return to London—"and Vivien says you have been an angel to her"—but of course he jumped at the opportunity of a holiday. "I am sure you have done *everything* possible and handled her in the very best way—better than I. I often wonder how things would have turned out but for you—I believe we shall owe her life to you, even."[14]

It was a letter of heartfelt gratitude, but one which carries an air of desperation. Eliot may have believed that once again Russell had saved Vivien from suicidal despair,[15] but the miracle Russell had worked required no great skill: essentially it was to make Vivien, a feminine and dependent woman, feel loved and desired. Eliot's true agony sprang from the knowledge that when his wife was with Bertie her health improved, and when she was alone with him it deteriorated.

Eliot hinted at his marital disharmony in a letter to his old college contemporary Conrad Aiken, with whom he often employed a vivid homosexual imagery he did not share with his new English acquaintances. On 10 January, while Vivien was away, Eliot listed his tribulations, cursing the Boston publishers who had refused to publish his poems "on account of his being an Englishman: If you are in with them you might tell them to butter their asses and bugger themselves . . . ," complaining that the *Catholic Anthology,* the collection of modern poetry edited by Ezra Pound, which included some new poems of Eliot's, "Miss Helen Slingsby" and "Hysteria" as well as "Prufrock" and "Portrait of a Lady," was not selling well (it was condemned by critic Arthur Waugh in the *Quarterly Review* as "the unmetrical incoherent banalities of these literary 'Cubists' "),[16] and that his only paying publications were *Poetry* and the *International Journal of Ethics.* But it was not only uncooperative publishers and unkind critics who frustrated Eliot. "I have *lived* through material for a score of long poems, in the last six months," he exploded to Aiken.[17] It was a prophetic remark if, as early as 1916, Eliot was aware that his calamitous marriage could be the raw material for a masterpiece. Certainly the comparison between himself and Russell the womaniser was a cruel one. Now Bertie had gone and Tom and Vivien were left alone in the quiet desperation of an unhappy marriage.

Eliot struggled to put the best face possible on their holiday: "Vivien is massaging my head, so my writing will be rather scrawly," he wrote to his father two days after his arrival in Torquay.[18] The West Country was lovely, rich and green, with bright red soil, and had one of the "loveliest bits of shore" he had ever seen. "I was in raptures over it," he wrote to Russell. "It is wonderful to have come out of town and been bathed in this purity." In front of the hotel was a little harbour. Reminded of his sailing days with Henry in the *Elsa,* off the coast near East Gloucester, Tom was tempted to seize a boat and put to sea—"except that Vivien couldn't come with me."[19] The little boats symbolised the freedom he had so impetuously sacrificed, as the poet stared out to sea and dreamed of escape.

Alone with Tom, Vivien's maladies multiplied. Although when

Russell left she was about to start typing a manuscript he had left her, within two days of his departure she was having bad nights, bad stomachs, headaches, and feeling tired and faint. Even so Torquay was idyllic. "You could not have chosen a better place for Vivien: it's a sign how badly she needed it, when even under the absolutely *perfect* conditions you have provided for her, she is still so weak and fatigued," reasoned Tom, unwilling to admit that Vivien's collapse was due to her change of companion rather than any disease. "I am convinced that no one could have been so wise and understanding with her as you. She was very happy." The past tense is significant.

The Eliots had intended to return in time for Russell's first lecture at Caxton Hall, but Vivien was, according to Tom, too "tired and low" to travel. They stayed an extra night, at Tom's expense *("Of course . . . I insist on that"*), although Vivien was anxious to attend her admirer's debut. Tom had begun to take control of the situation, laying down for his wife "a very strict regimen, with very clear limits of exertion [which] will be imperative for the rest of the winter."[20]

Conscription was the issue of the moment when Tom and Vivien finally returned to London, and Russell was fast becoming the man of the moment, as his revulsion at the slaughter of young men at the Battles of the Marne, Ypres and Gallipoli in 1915 inspired his lectures with new passion: "When the War came I felt as if I heard the voice of God . . . As a lover of civilisation, the return to barbarism appalled me. As a man of thwarted parental feeling, the massacre of the young wrung my heart." Appalled at the apparent eagerness with which parents such as the Whiteheads offered their sons to be sacrificed, Russell took to watching the troop trains steam out of Waterloo and began to experience strange visions of London. In his imagination he saw the bridges collapse and sink, and the city vanish like a morning mist. Its inhabitants began to seem like hallucinations to him, a product of his nightmares. These illusions he described to Eliot, who later used them in *The Waste Land,* or so Russell believed.[21] The need to stiffen pacifist resistance roused Russell to action, as it did most of Bloomsbury. The Derby Scheme, whereby unmarried men of military age "attested" their willingness to serve, had failed in the autumn of 1915 as the roll call of the dead lengthened and the enthusiasm of young men to enlist palled. Men who did not wear the prescribed armband were open to the gift of the white feather, but still the war machine remained short of numbers. Public feeling grew against men of military age who were still in "civvies," and in November 1915 Duncan Grant was arrested at Folkestone for not being in uniform.[22]

When the First Military Service Bill became law in March 1916 the government joined battle with the pacifists. Lytton and James Strachey, Duncan Grant, Vanessa Bell, her brother Adrian Stephen, David "Bunny" Garnett and Bob Trevelyan all volunteered for work at the Fleet Street headquarters of the National Council for Civil Liberties, and many joined the NCF, the other centre of opposition to compulsory military service. Old friends were divided by the war; Lytton sent his former lover, Maynard Keynes—a fellow member of the Apostles, the élite Cambridge *conversazione* society—the "conscientious objector's equivalent of a white feather," when he posted to him a newspaper cutting of a militaristic speech by Edwin Montagu, Foreign Secretary to the Treasury, with a note saying: "Dear Maynard, Why are you still at the Treasury? Yours, Lytton."[23]

To Russell fell the task of defining the arguments against militarism in his lectures, which proved a huge popular draw.[24] Lytton, also a member of the NCF, attended every lecture, finding that, as he wrote on 16 February 1916:

> Bertie's lectures help one. They are a wonderful solace and re-freshment. One hangs upon his words, and looks forward to them from week to week, and I can't bear the idea of missing one—I dragged myself to that ghastly Caxton Hall yesterday, though I was rather nearer the grave than usual, and it was well worth it . . . He . . . plants it down solid and shining before one's mind. I don't believe there's anyone quite so formidable to be found just now upon this earth.[25]

Lytton Strachey needed the support of Bertie's philosophy as well as the presence of his friends for his tribunal hearing which took place in March. With Philip Morrell in attendance as chief character witness, carrying the air cushion upon which Lytton sat, for his piles, Lytton gave his celebrated answer to the tribunal's question: "What would you do if you saw a

German soldier attempting to rape your sister?" "I should try and come between them." Rejected as medically unfit, Lytton retired to Garsington to recover.

In the weeks after her return to London Vivien remained on intimate terms with Bertie, despite the "strict regimen" prescribed by her husband, and Bertie continued to bait Ottoline with news of his encounters with Vivien; on 30 January he informed her that Mrs. Eliot had dined with him, "which I enjoyed. She is living a more or less invalid life, going out very little, & going to bed at ten—but she is getting much less ill, especially nervously. Her husband is out all day at his school, & works all evening, so her existence is very dull, but I am sure it is good for her."[26] As Russell continued to lunch and dine with Vivien twice a week, his relationship with her became an increasing bone of contention with Ottoline, who complained in February that Bertie now only wrote her "very meager letters . . . I suppose you are tired and busy."[27] Moreover she firmly declined to meet her rival, writing at the beginning of the year: "I had felt it rather better not to meet her as it might complicate matters, especially if I didn't like her much—but—if it was any use or help to her of course I should be delighted to ask them both here, a little later on, when the spring comes—just Now I am feeling tired and want to be quiet."[28] Instead she suggested that Bertie should introduce Dorothy Brett to the Eliots, or Carrington or Gilbert Cannan—"I'm sure he would be delighted to know Mrs. Elliot [sic]."

But Russell continued to put pressure on Ottoline to receive his new mistress at Garsington until she finally capitulated: "My darling, I am delighted to have Mrs. E. here. I wrote to her yesterday. I hope she will come for I should like *very* much to know her." Would Bertie come for the weekend, she asked, suggesting Maynard and Lytton as fellow guests.[29] However, a reply from Vivien, which has not survived but which Ottoline found over-emotional, prompted the chatelaine of Garsington to withdraw her invitation. Bertie accused her of being unkind to his "child in pain." "My darling, I am very sorry you thought me unkind. I *really* didn't mean to be—nor did I realise that I had been," replied Ottoline on 3 March. "I *really* don't mind yr. friendship with The Eliots, quite the contrary, for I am sure it is an *enormous* help to them both & incidentily [sic] to you too. I hope you don't think me unkind about *her.* The effect of her rather exaggerated letter made me draw in . . ."[30]

Ironically, Vivien's epistolary style could resemble Ottoline's with its dashes, capitals, underlinings and misspellings sprinkled haphazardly through the text. Under particular stress, her letters become confused and incoherent, yet in conversation Vivien did not suffer from the inarticulacy for which Ottoline was often mocked by the literati she patronised. Lawrence, for example, satirises Ottoline as Hermione Roddice in *Women in Love* whose tendency to "rumble" and inability to complete a sentence is a source of amusement to her guests. It is possible that Ottoline recognised a certain similarity in style, indicative of a shared emotionality and nervous temperament, between herself and Vivien, which at first influenced her against receiving her rival at Garsington. Under Bertie's relentless pressure, however, Ottoline finally agreed to meet Vivien on neutral ground, in London. Bertie owed her a favour in return, implied Ottoline, asking him to keep Wednesday afternoon free for her alone. In exchange she would ask a few people in on Thursday evening: "You could ask the Eliots to come too—and they could meet a few others Thurs."

Three days later Ottoline and Philip came up to London for Russell's final lecture. Ottoline was delighted to be back at her "dear old house" in Bedford Square, the top floors of which were let out during the war, although she and Philip retained the drawing-room and dining-room floors for themselves. Many of Bertie's old friends came to the lecture, including Desmond MacCarthy, Clive Bell and his mistress Mary Hutchinson, wife of barrister St. John Hutchinson, and artist Merk Gertler. The next evening the long-awaited meeting took place: Ottoline and Philip dined with Bertie, Tom and Vivien at a restaurant in Soho. Ottoline had already read some of Tom's poems in "a little American magazine" *(Poetry),* and they had struck her as "very remarkable," but she remained reluctant to condone Bertie's meddling in the Eliots' marriage. He "was convinced that the Eliots were not really happy together, but by a little manipulation on his part everything would come right between them," she wrote in her journal. "By what he had told me I was not convinced of this and felt doubtful as to whether he would not make things much worse."[31]

The dinner was not a success. "T. S. Eliot was very formal and polite, and his wife seemed to me of the 'spoilt-kitten' type, very second-rate and ultra-feminine, playful and naïve, anxious to show she 'possessed' Bertie, when we walked away from the restaurant she headed him off and kept him to herself, walking with him arm-in-arm," wrote a resentful Ottoline. "I felt rather *froissée* at her bad manners." Nevertheless, the next day she gave a tea-party at Bedford Square, to which she invited the Eliots and Russell. Ottoline had turned one of the drawing-rooms into her bedroom, in which stood a large four-poster bed, hung with cardinal-coloured silk curtains trimmed with silver. It was, she remembered, very lovely looking into that room from the great drawing-room. Molly MacCarthy, wife of journalist Desmond MacCarthy, and Dora Sanger, wife of Thoby Stephen's old friend Charles Sanger, and artists Dorothy Brett, Carrington and Mark Gertler came too, and the afternoon was a happier gathering than the evening before. To Tom Eliot, anxious to meet people of influence in English society, it must have seemed like entering Circe's cave. At last he had the introduction to Bloomsbury's powerful high priestess,[32] who could open the door to acceptance by the most exclusive and influential literary clique in England.

The next prize to be won was a visit to Garsington, for if Bedford Square remained magnificent despite being half-shut down in wartime, it could not match the Tudor manor house about whose exotic house parties Eliot had heard so much from Russell. Vivien, however, was too agitated by late March to care whether or not she received an invitation. A new crisis had arisen. Despite the German wartime blockade of allied Atlantic shipping, Tom was due to sail for America on 1 April to present his "decidedly anti-Russellian" thesis at Harvard, and take the oral exam for his doctorate. Vivien was afraid he would be putting his life at risk.

Throughout March Vivien's panic increased. Despite having told Scofield that she was planning to visit America that spring, when the moment came her fear of submarines led her to change her mind. Once again she refused to accompany Tom. Her apprehension was not without foundation, for on 24 March 1916 the cross-Channel steamer *Sussex* was torpedoed off Dieppe with the loss of fifty lives, including those of three Americans. "Mr. Eliot did not believe it possible that even the Germans (a synonym for all that is most frightful) would attack an American liner," wrote Charlotte Eliot in indignation: "I am glad all our ancestors are

English with a French ancestry far back on one line . . ."[33] On 23 March, the day before the *Sussex* was sunk, Russell received a worried postcard from Eliot; once more he stepped into the breach, cabling to Tom's father: "STRONGLY ADVISE CABLING TOM AGAINST SAILING UNDER PRESENT PECULIARLY DANGEROUS CONDITIONS UNLESS IMMEDIATE DEGREE IS WORTH RISKING LIFE."[34] "He will probably not go to America—she is probably not really ill—she wasn't before—but her nerves are all to pieces," Russell explained to Ottoline. "It is the way of his going that upset her. She is afraid he would be sunk by a submarine."[35] Henry Ware Eliot Sr. was "not greatly pleased" with the language of Russell's cable, but he was helpless in the face of circumstances when Tom's boat was cancelled. A relieved Eliot posted his thesis,[36] which was received as the "work of an expert," and promised to come *at the first opportunity*" when the war was over. "Naturally I do not like to leave my wife here, or venture the waves myself, while it is still on," he told Professor Woods. Having failed to present himself for the viva voce, Eliot never did receive his doctorate.[37]

The prospect that she would be left alone to manage their forthcoming move from their old flat at 3 Culworth House, Henry Street, St. John's Wood, to a new one in Marylebone, added to Vivien's worries. She poured out her troubles in excited letters to Ottoline, who took fright at Vivien's near-hysteria. "I hope Mrs. Eliot will be able to array her affairs—Does she often write like that—I couldn't make out how substantial it was or if it was exaggerated—I felt it was so . . ." wrote Ottoline to Bertie on 28 March. Her natural sympathy for a fellow sufferer, and the shared experience of having been Bertie's lover, which was to form the basis of the future bond between Ottoline and Vivien, was tempered by the lack of understanding of a wealthy aristocrat for the difficulties of an impoverished young couple:

> I don't know what to say about Mrs. E. She is evidently over-wrought by the pain—& rather hysterical. Isn't her letter rather exaggerated? Perhaps she will feel better in a day or two. Has she got another flat that she can send her furniture into? If she has, I should advise her just to Tilt into the new place & Lock the door & either go home to her people to rest for a week—or if she would

like to come down here I should be delighted to have her Next week—on Monday, for a bit.

Ottoline's letter suggests that Vivien's doctor was prescribing medication for the pain from which she was suffering, probably bromide to calm her and counteract her migraines and abdominal discomfort. Ottoline understood the side effects of the tranquillisers of that time, and was sympathetic to Vivien's case: "The *Numbness* comes frm thgs she has taken fr the Pain, I expect—I always feel that—Perhaps a rest in this warm house would do her good. Couldn't her mother help her to arrange for her furniture to be moved?"[38]

By the next morning, however, Ottoline had thought better of her rash invitation:

> It is snowing *& so so cold here*—that I feel rather nervous of asking Mrs. E to come here until the weather is better—I think she would hate it—& be miserable so perhaps better *not* suggest her coming just yet—she was coming on Thursday—Of course tho if it is any good I would have her just to rest—Do you think she would like to go to a Nursing Home for a *rest*—I know of quite a nice one—but after she would hate it. Are her own people horrid?[39]

On 7 April Ottoline wrote to enquire of Bertie whether Vivien was better, but the highly coloured letters she had received from Vivien had confirmed Ottoline in her decision to entertain Tom only. Four days later she wrote that she would be pleased to have Mr. Eliot, who she thought would get on with Lytton, but she had cancelled Vivien, who was to have come the following week. "I suppose it would rest him more to come alone."[40] And although she remarked to Bertie on 19 May that she had had a "nice letter from Mrs. Eliot," she remained determined after her initial poor impression in London not to receive her at Garsington in the coming months, despite Bertie's pleas: "Yes, I am *sure* Mrs. Eliot is nice," she responded tartly. "I hope she will come some day & that I shall know her a little—I rather wish I hadn't seen that letter—It was so like my sisters-in-laws' letters . . . I am sure you can help her. Please don't think I grudge that at all."[41]

The day of Eliot's spring visit to Garsington arrived finally in April. To her journal Ottoline confided her excitement that Russell was bringing Eliot, but, unlike his hosts the Morrells, Russell, and the majority of the guests, Eliot was not in sympathy with the pacifist movement. When asked by Russell in October 1914 what he thought of the war, he had replied: "I don't know. I only know that I am not a pacifist." "That is to say, he considered any excuse good enough for homicide," commented Russell.[42] Their lack of agreement did not, however, divide them as it did Lytton and Maynard Keynes.[43] As an American there was as yet no question of Eliot confronting his conscience, although the question of whether the U.S. would be drawn into the war, and whether or not he should volunteer at some time in the future was beginning to weigh on his mind, stimulated by the conversation at Garsington, which had become a rallying point for "conchies," whose work as farm labourers exempted them from military service.

This time the meeting between Tom and Ottoline was less successful than in London. Russell was irritating Ottoline more than usual, despite their common opposition to conscription and the fact that her husband, Philip "Pipsey" Morrell, was risking his seat at Burnley by speaking against the war in Parliament. "I never feel my best with Bertie. I cannot tell why. He always quenches my lightheartedness and gaiety and puts a blight on me," wrote Ottoline. As for his new friend Eliot, she found the poet "dull, dull, dull":

> He never moves his lips but speaks in an even and monotonous voice, and I felt him monotonous without and within. Where does his queer neurasthenic poetry come from, I wonder. From his New England, Puritan inheritance and upbringing? I think he has lost all spontaneity and can only break through his conventionality by stimulants or violent emotions.[44]

Anxious to impress his aristocratic hostess, Eliot was at pains to suppress any traces of his hybrid American accent, but, despite his erudition, his carefully enunciated English sounded false to Ottoline. "Eliot spoke English very beautifully and deliberately," recalled Helen Gardner, but he "lost his American accent without ever developing English speed and

English slurring or English speech rhythms."⁴⁵ Struck by the poet's formality and ignorance of England, Ottoline tried talking French to Eliot in the hope of breaking down the barriers between them. He seemed to imagine that it was essential to be polite and decorous, and she hoped that he might feel freer in another language. Again she failed, although he was "better" in French than English. "He speaks French very perfectly, slowly and correctly . . . It shows how very foreign Eliot seemed to me then; but I generally found that Americans are as foreign to us as Germans are."⁴⁶ Ottoline found no reason to change the nickname she had given Eliot: "The Undertaker."

While Russell's affairs galloped towards a crisis with the circulation of his "seditious" leaflet protesting against the sufferings of Ernest Everett, a conscientious objector condemned to two years' hard labour, and his provocative letter to *The Times* in May 1916, inviting prosecution, Vivien was feeling calmer now that the move had taken place on 12 March into the new flat at 18 Crawford Mansions, Crawford Street, Marylebone. Her pride in their first real home together was immense, as she experimented with interior decoration: "It is the tiniest place imaginable," she wrote to Tom's brother Henry Ware Eliot Jr. in June. They had just a dining-room, a drawing-room, a large bedroom, a kitchen and a nice bathroom. "We have constant hot water, which is a *luxury* in England." The building was quite new with "every modern convenience," and Vivien chose all the wallpapers herself. Among the "rather original effects" was an *"orange paper"* in the dining-room ("which is also Tom's dressing room and study!") and black and white stripes in the hall.⁴⁷ The orange paper, Vivien's pride and joy, featured in another letter to Scofield Thayer, in which she sent "congratulations of the most fervent" on the occasion of his marriage to Elaine Eliot Orr in New York. "I was never more delighted than when I heard you have an orange wallpaper," she wrote, telling Scofield that they had one in the dining-room. He was to come and see them when he brought his bride to see Europe. "You can do us and the Tower of London on the same day."⁴⁸

The news that his old friend was also marrying aroused surprise and nostalgia in Tom, who could scarcely believe that it was only a year since he and Scofield were charming the eyes and ears of "Char-flappers" from their virginal punt at Oxford. Had Scofield, the Magdalen aesthete, "the connoisseur of puberty and lilies... about to wed the Madonna of the mantelpiece," discovered the Fountain of Eternal Youth not in Florida, but in Troy (New York), he asked ironically. Quoting Oscar Wilde to his old friend, Eliot prayed that domestic felicity might not "extinguish the amateur" in Scofield, nor the possession of beauty quench the passionate detachment which his friends admired and admirers envied. He hoped that "within an interior of dim light drifting through heavy curtains, by a Buhl table holding a Greek figurine, and a volume of Faust bound in green and powdered with gold, with a bust of Dante, and perhaps a screen by Korin, a drawing by Watteau—a room heavy with the scent of lilies," Scofield would enshrine such a treasure as that with which he rightly credited Eliot—"a wife who is not wifely."[49] It was perhaps as hard for Eliot to imagine Scofield, described as "strikingly pale, with coal-black hair, black eyes veiled and flashing, and lips that curved like Lord Byron [who] seemed to many the embodiment of the aesthete with overrefined tastes and sensibilities,"[50] settling down to marriage, as it had been for Scofield to imagine Eliot as a bridegroom, and it was therefore with a degree of fellow feeling that Eliot enquired into Scofield's domestic arrangements. Although Eliot declared that when Mr. and Mrs. Scofield Thayer came to visit London, "Mr. and Mrs. Stearns Eliot will be outraged if they are not the first to entertain them," his doubts proved well founded: Scofield returned to his bachelor flat in Washington Square within months of his marriage, and his wife had a baby daughter, Nancy, by the poet e. e. cummings, whom she later married.[51]

Vivien, lover of "pose" and fashion, shared Scofield and Tom's aesthetic values and aspired to create a similar beauty in her flat. The following year she describes herself to Scofield in her drawing-room: upon an inlaid Renaissance chest two mysterious faces confront her, two inscrutable smiles. One is that of a Burmese buddha, curiously carved in green jade, the other that of a young man still in his prime, whose eyelids are heavy with the languor of those upon whom the gods have lavished knowledge too early. He is "one of those mad amateurs of beauty," a strange figure of the late Empire who in the midst of corruption preserves a childlike grace. "Quis desidirio aut pudor aut modus/Tam cari capitis?" ("Unshamed, unchecked, for one so dear/We sorrow") murmurs Vivien, between "half-open lips," misquoting Horace's "Ode to Vergil on the Death of

Quintilius,"[52] as she lies on her divan, burning incense of cloudy Gold Flake.[53] The head of the youth standing on her cabinet reminds her of Scofield: "Behold thou are overfair, thou are overwise," she quotes, recalling "vanished days and evenings to one who is grateful for these memories." It was a letter designed to impress Scofield, who had always made Vivien feel horribly uneducated, but it also conjured up a heartfelt nostalgia for pre-war gaiety.

Despite their aspirations to luxury, both Tom and Vivien were obliged to face the painful business of trying to balance income and expenditure during the course of 1916. Henry Ware Eliot had agreed to pay the rent of their flat, but told Tom that he should "get some work to support his wife."[54] After only one term in Buckinghamshire Tom had found a new post in London at Highgate Junior School, teaching the boys French, Latin, mathematics, drawing and baseball, at a slightly increased salary of £160 a year; he also earned a little money from literary journalism, but *The Monist* and the *International Journal of Ethics* paid poorly for book-reviewing. Tom was once again grateful to Russell for an introduction to Philip Jourdain, editor of both periodicals, who commissioned two articles on Leibnitz.

Vivien believed fervently in her husband's poetic genius, and thought him *"too* good and *not* fitted" for school teaching: "Tom is *wonderful"* she enthused to Henry in June. Never had she met a man who impressed people so much with the feeling that he was *worth* helping. But if Tom went on teaching he would throw away innumerable chances and openings for writing, and would only be able to do "the little scraps" that he had time and energy for after school. "And school tires him very much—and chances don't come twice." The question was, did they dare gamble on giving it up? "He would win in time, but in the first year or two—how should we live?"[55] Henry responded to this begging letter as Vivien hoped, by sending money, one of the "constant five poundses" that he sent during the year. By October, Vivien confessed to Henry, they had only twenty-two pounds in the bank, and Tom wouldn't get any more till Christmas, so they were in a "fairly tight place." This, unfortunately, meant "writing to your father for help again."[56] Eliot Senior responded with cheques, despite the fact that he was "very despondent" about the brick business which he feared would go downhill if Woodrow Wilson lost the coming presidential election. Tom was duly grateful, remarking to his brother that he certainly had every reason to be proud of his family: the way they had accepted the responsibility for helping him—"without a single murmur"—was wonderful.

Vivien's letters to her mother-in-law paint a picture of a self-sacrificing, frugal and devoted housewife: "Darning alone takes me hours a week." Tom needed a new suit, "and I think *must* have one. His pyjamas are all very old and need constant mending." Tailoring her prose to Mrs. Eliot's own puritan standards, Vivien assured her that she was a careful manager, often sending the receipts for the clothes she had bought for Tom: "I *would* get Tom some new vests myself but I really *do* think the old ones are quite good for the rest of this winter." He was wearing his flannel shirts all the time, she promised Charlotte, albeit "under protest!"[57] Vivien of course omitted to mention that she and Tom had been subsidised by Russell while staying in his flat, and were still receiving help, as he admitted to Ottoline on 26 January 1916. Russell was thankful that his successful lectures had made him "rich," having earned £65 from his writing in the last few weeks: "I needed it, as I spent a lot on the Eliots. I don't need to spend much more, as they are now safely established."[58]

Both Tom and Vivien's letters to the Eliot family are notable for what they leave out rather than what they put in and, taken alone, provide a distorted version of their early married life. There is only thrift, never overspending, although we have Maurice's evidence that Vivien was still extravagant; she "lived" in the shops in the Finchley Road, where her mother had several accounts. In October 1916 Vivien returned to Lancashire for a week to ten days to stay with a girlfriend to whom she had once been bridesmaid; it was a trip which entailed "getting more clothes than I should have needed otherwise."[59]

Nor do these letters give an accurate picture of the Eliots' health problems. The emphasis was always on Vivien's illnesses, which appear mysterious. In 1970, Theresa, Henry Eliot's widow, recalled: "Henry, my husband, sent money to Tom for some years, but Tom never said anything to his family about Vivienne's ill-health and the doctor's bills."[60] But, although Vivien had been prescribed tranquillisers such as bromide from adolescence, her letters show that she could be happy and high-spirited with Russell; nor does the evidence of her 1914 and 1919 diaries and the letters of her early marriage suggest that her use of drugs was continuous. It is more probable that under the stress of living with Eliot, depressed by their sexual problems and incompatible temperaments, Vivien developed a range of psychosomatic symptoms for which her doctors on occasions prescribed drugs. She was far from being always incapacitated, as her lively letters to Scofield show.

Nevertheless, the angle presented by Tom, from his earliest letters home after his marriage, is that Vivien is invariably the "invalid" ("my invalid dependent wife") and he the devoted caregiver. This was the version of events Eliot was to promulgate until it became widely accepted as the truth. He plays down Vivien's own important role in nursing him through his own frequent bouts of influenza, bronchitis and episodes of paralysing depression, which culminated in his nervous breakdown in November 1921. Apologising to Conrad Aiken in August 1916 for not having written for so long, Eliot writes: "My wife has been very ill all the winter . . . This was not a case of maternity in any degree. Most people imagine so unless I explain. It has been nerves, complicated by physical ailments, and induced largely by the most acute neuralgia."[61] In reality, however, Vivien was sometimes the stronger of the two in this co-dependent relationship in which she also nursed Tom, as she did in early 1917 when he was ill for weeks with influenza, and in 1921.

In many of his letters home Eliot exaggerates Vivien's condition. With Russell he was more honest. In March 1916 Tom sent Russell a long and agitated account of Vivien's visit to the dentist which is notable for what it reveals about Eliot's state of mind rather than Vivien's teeth. According to Tom, Vivien was upset by this visit and as a result was in great pain, "both neuralgia and stomach." The dentist himself made light of Vivien's toothache, saying the problem "meant no great pain or risk"; significantly, he thought Tom was the person to be calmed down, and that he had communicated his own fears to Vivien. Sensing Tom's terror, for Eliot suffered as much as Vivien with his teeth until he had them all removed in later life, the dentist decided not to alarm him by mentioning that Vivien might develop an abscess (although he trusted Vivien with the truth). When Tom discovered this, he panicked: Vivien, who had been typing up some work for Russell all afternoon, was allegedly "very ill tonight, and I am very, very sorry that she went through this. It has been too great a strain upon her will . . . The mistake was in letting her go at all—the effort and the anticipation during the last weeks . . . have taken every ounce of strength out of her. Don't expect her to lunch to-morrow. I am sure it will be some days before she can go out to lunch or dinner."[62] Did Eliot exaggerate Vivien's symptoms in order to prevent her seeing Russell? It would appear that he was taking back control of the situation now that he and Vivien were in their own flat and it could be that his wife's "invalidism" suited Tom, for it was the best possible excuse to keep her at home.

A typical letter of October 1916 from Vivien to Henry, in whom she frequently confided, listed her symptoms: migraines, neuralgia and sinus problems, but there is no clue as to *why* she is suffering so acutely. Vivien explains she is trying not to spend too much money on doctors: "I shan't have my sinus trouble touched until I simply have to." Three weeks before "they" had sent her to the doctor for her headaches, which were quite separate from her sinus pain and "much *more* horrible." The doctor concluded that in the first place, she was undernourished—one of the first mentions of the anorexia nervosa from which Vivien probably suffered. "The headaches are called hemicranial migraine, and they are really 'nerve storms' affecting one whole side of me—they make me sick and feverish and they always last fifteen to twenty-four hours." When they pass, she rises up "weak and white" as if she has been through some long and dreadful illness. Her headaches are "rather rare . . . *no drug touches them*"—fifteen to twenty grains of phenacetin bring not the slightest relief, she tells Henry.[63]

In Tom and Vivien's misleading letters to his family from 1915, Bertrand Russell is to be the missing link. Henry and Charlotte Eliot were not to guess that Vivien was deeply in love with the man who featured only in their letters as a respected friend, rather than as Vivien's lover, benefactor and counsellor to the couple ("You are a great psychologist," wrote Eliot in 1925). Russell continued to be a key figure in the Eliots' lives, existing with them in a state of intimate interdependence throughout 1916. In May, for example, Russell was writing to Ottoline from Leith Hill in Surrey: "I have unexpectedly come down here for Sunday with Mrs. Eliot (she is in the hotel and I am in the cottage) . . . I am enjoying this little plunge in the country."[64] The triangle, wrote Robert Sencourt, "was to alter drastically both Vivien's hopes for the future with Tom, and her already fragile grasp on sanity [and was] the background of everything that Eliot wrote in verse or prose from 1915 onwards."[65] The pattern of Vivien's illnesses in 1915–18 is explicable within the context of her relationship with Russell: when he withdrew, she sickened; when he returned, she revived.

Russell himself was in collusion with Tom in writing himself out of the Eliots' personal history, and creating the myth of Tom, the capable caregiver of a sick wife, although he was aware of the fragility of Eliot's own conflicted personality. Russell writes to J. H. Woods that Eliot "has spent his spare hours in looking after his wife, with the most amazing devotion and unselfishness . . . Except in the one matter of health, his marriage is a very happy one and altogether desirable."[66] This was far from true, but both Eliot and Russell—although a personal and intellectual rift widened between them in later life—remained united in the belief that concealment was necessary in their private lives, although they approached this objective in different ways: Russell laid a false trail in his autobiography while Eliot, like his creation Eeldrop, sought to protect himself by an embargo on biography. "Such is precisely the case," returned Eeldrop (to Appleplex, the Russell persona), "but I had not thought it necessary to mention this biographical detail."[67]

During the spring of 1916 Russell's provocative anti-war propaganda continued to bait the government. Eventually it had no option but to bring him to trial on 5 June over his No-Conscription Fellowship leaflet attacking the sentence handed out to conscientious objector Ernest Everett. The trial took place at the Mansion House, attracting widespread publicity. Russell was fined £100 by the Lord Mayor, but pleaded that he could not pay; Ottoline began raising a fund to meet the fine: "His goods and furniture at Cambridge are to be sold to pay for it, but his friends have offered to buy them and restore them to him: I am busy collecting money for this purpose," she wrote, irritated that this job should fall upon her because Bertie had spent all his money on Mrs. Eliot.[68] At the subsequent auction of his belongings Philip and Ottoline bought most of his possessions, thus saving him from going to prison. Even in the midst of this crisis, on 6 June, Russell was writing tactlessly to Ottoline that "Mrs. Eliot makes it much easier for me not to mind not seeing more of you . . . I am really very devoted to her."[69]

Worse was to follow. On 11 July 1916, Russell was removed from his lectureship at Trinity College, Cambridge. His notoriety was such that the Foreign Office denied him a passport, thus making it impossible for him to recoup his financial position by teaching at Harvard, where he had been invited to return. Financially Russell's fortunes took a sharp downturn, although he professed to feel exhilarated at the prospect of devoting himself entirely to the peace movement. He was forced to let his London flat and move into his brother's flat at 57 Gordon Square, before setting off on a lecture tour of South Wales for the NCF.

In these difficult economic circumstances, Bertie could no longer afford to help Vivien financially. It was a mark of his deep infatuation with her that he nevertheless continued to pay for her dancing lessons and provide the other frivolous gifts jealously chronicled by Ottoline in July. In the face of Ottoline's remonstrances that he was ruining himself, he took Vivien out to dinner again "& discussed money."

> The passion of her life is dancing & ever since I have known her I have paid for her dancing lessons whenever she has been well enough. I don't suppose she will ever be any good, because of her health, but it is such a passion that I can't bear to baulk it if I can possibly help it . . . Of course, it would save my pocket if her husband got better-paid work . . .

Praising Eliot's reviewing ("it has quality & distinction, although it is done in the evenings after a full day's work at school"), Russell asked Ottoline if she would persuade Desmond MacCarthy to get his protégé published in the *New Statesman* or the *Guardian*. Making the extraordinary confession that he had not only paid for dancing lessons and other luxuries but was subsidising the Eliots' ordinary living expenses, Russell wrote, "So if you can see any way of helping me it will relieve me of a great anxiety."[70]

Dancing continued to be the great joy of Vivien's life, not only ballet but ballroom, an interest she shared with Tom. In November 1915 Eliot had excused himself from a meeting with Wyndham Lewis as "we have got to go and dance on Saturday."[71] Brigit Patmore, a member of the South Lodge Circle and later the lover of Richard Aldington, remembered frequent outings to a dance hall at Vivien's suggestion, soon after the Eliots had moved into their own flat. "You see, I'm very anxious to get Tom to take some exercise and there's a hall in Queensway where a small band plays on Sunday afternoons for people to dance to; very respectable, all that it should be. If you'd come and perhaps a few other friends sometimes— the quieter we begin the better, I believe Tom might come and not be bored." They danced with "unostentatious pleasure" on those Sunday afternoons. "Tom was an adequate performer, held one lightly and gracefully," Brigit recalled. "There was no agitated under-the-breath counting of *one*-two-three, *one*-two-three, but it might not have been a long time back and perhaps kept him silent . . ." She found Tom charming but unnerving. "His slow way of speaking in a slightly booming monotone, without emphasis, was quite beguiling." Yet she also sensed he was "pleased with nobody" and was always judging people.

> His mouth had turned-up corners, not with merriment, but with some kind of restriction—perhaps the bit between his teeth—for he was careful never to say anything indiscreet. Yet how winning and cordial he could be when the wide mouth smiled and the lines from both sides of the strong, well-shaped nose looked humorous and really genial. But the eyes, not yet inquisitorial as they became later, but cold dark grey, wide open and suiting finely the forehead so wide and high, but not too high . . . He was distinguished in appearance, perhaps handsome, but one longed for a grace, a carelessness which would have let him approach beauty.[72]

Those afternoons at the dance hall brought out the best in Tom and Vivien. One day, remembers Brigit, they went into a chemist's shop after the dancing. "Vivienne was talking about a ballet and said, 'I think I can do what Karsavina does at that moment.' And she held on to the counter with one hand, rose on her toes and held out the other hand which Tom took in his right hand, watching Vivienne's feet with ardent interest whilst he supported her with real tenderness. From him it was unexpected. Most husbands would have said, 'Not here, for Heaven's sake!' But he looked as if he did indeed want to help Vivienne in her chosen work."[73]

Another pleasure Tom and Vivien allowed themselves, despite their straitened finances, were seaside holidays, which they had both enjoyed as children. In August 1916 they left London for Bosham, in Chichester Harbor, taking a cottage in an area already favoured by Bloomsbury: Mary and St. John Hutchinson rented a farmhouse named Eleanor House at West Wittering, and invited Clive and Vanessa Bell and Duncan Grant. The indispensable Russell had already supplied Eliot with an introduction to Clive Bell in June, through whom it was inevitable he would meet Mary Hutchinson, as well as Roger Fry and Goldsworthy Lowes Dickinson, a Cambridge don. "Bloomsbury on sea" provided Tom and Vivien with rare hours of happiness. "We are vegetating and gaining health against the coming term on a backwater near Portsmouth harbour, where the tide is either very much in or very much out; the place alternates between mud and water, and is very charming," wrote Eliot to Conrad Aiken,[74] describing a routine of mornings spent working, afternoons bathing, boating and bicycling, with occasional trips up to the British Museum to prepare the lectures he was to give at Southall in the autumn term. As so often, Russell came too, preferring to spend time at Bosham with Vivien and Tom than at Garsington, where he would have to face the exhortations of Ottoline to give up Mrs. E. In the weeks after returning from his lecture tour in Wales he holidayed with the Eliots, apart from two or three days a week in London or staying with his brother at his country house near Chichester. "Mrs. E's brother is here—invalided home," he wrote to Ottoline on 20 August. "I like him—he is very like her in temperament, but a gentleman" (the implication was that Vivien was not a lady). Making the first of many promises on the subject of Vivien's allowance, he said: "I told her a definite date (not far off) after which I can't undertake to find any more money, explained how hard up I am, which I had not done before. She accepted it without demur."[75]

Vivien was more tenacious than Bertie would admit. Throughout August Ottoline increased her pressure on Bertie to end his affair with this "frivolous, silly little woman," but he refused to do so. Two years later Ottoline may have been thinking of Vivien when she mourned the decline of love in her life: "Isn't it sad that no one *really* falls in love nowadays?" she said to Virginia Woolf. "Its the rarest, rarest thing ... Bertie does of course—but then his choice is so often unfortunate."[76] For there is no doubt that in 1916 Vivien's star was in the ascendant, as Ottoline's was waning, and it was to Vivien's pleas that Russell listened. He protested to

Ottoline that he had promised "Mrs. E." he would meet her that week, and he was afraid of a "violent quarrel" if he acted on Ottoline's suggestions, although he assured her they had influenced him. "But it is difficult to act on them without cruelty. The only part in the matter that I feel on my own account to be wrong is the spending of money. Quite at first, that was justifiable, but it has ceased to be. At the same time, having created the expectation, I can hardly stop suddenly . . . You were *quite right* to speak," he told Ottoline. "I am *sure* it will work out as you think right but I ought not to do anything violent or sudden."[77]

It was Russell's payment of the Eliots' everyday bills, as well as the "extras" they both considered essential, which subsidised a lifestyle well beyond their means and enabled them to mix with the Bloomsbury group, many of whose members practised a similar "open marriage" to that of Tom and Vivien. There was Philip Morrell turning a blind eye to Ottoline's lovers, although she was ignorant of his; Vanessa Bell living with the homosexual Duncan Grant while Clive was the lover of Mary Hutchinson; and the Strachey-Carrington-Partridge triangle, all of which made the Eliots' arrangement seem perfectly natural. It was a bohemian ethos in which the Eliots felt comfortable, one in which bourgeois conventions had long ago been abandoned; honesty in personal relations, based upon the ideas of G. E. Moore, was the ideal; and homosexuality or bisexuality was as acceptable as it had been to the Apostles at Cambridge under the leadership of Lytton Strachey and Maynard Keynes. The Eliots, therefore, could not give up Russell's allowance without a fight—too much depended on it. Given Russell's poverty, his generosity seems inexplicable but, cast adrift from his academic milieu and his old friends, uncomfortable with new suburban allies like Clifford Allen, chairman of the No-Conscription Fellowship, he needed Vivien, and was therefore unable to refuse her demands.

In his letters to Ottoline, he agonised over the strange hold Vivien had over him, and he over her. "She is trustful & thinks of me as wise & good—at least as regards her—& as regards her I have been," he wrote on 20 August 1916. "Partly this satisfies my love of despotism, partly it makes me feel not such a wretch as I have always felt for a long time in relation to you." That Vivien might be flattering her older lover, and even manipulating him, Russell seems not to have realised. All Vivien's faults were "gradually improving," he wrote, congratulating himself on his successful therapy, and the fact that

> I have made her . . . look up to me & care for me to a considerable extent. In spite of her faults I have an affection for her, because I feel they spring from a root of despair & that she might become different. And apart from affection, I have incurred responsibility.

Pleading with Ottoline that he could not abrogate this responsibility, he continued to play for time: "I don't want to quarrel—I think with time I can avoid giving her the feeling that I have played her false, without getting into a permanent entanglement. But it will want time."[78]

Russell's promises that he would see Vivien just once more, and then the long-awaited "readjustment" would come when he would finally break with her, must have brought a weary smile to Ottoline's lips, as she read page after page of excuses from her former lover. "I am going . . . to Bosham for a few days," he wrote on 22 August. "After that I don't expect to see Mrs. E. again at any rate till the spring; but I can't be sure. There has been no quarrel of any sort . . ." The next day he was still "unhappy" about dashing Mrs. E's hopes.

> One thing that attracted me to her was that it seemed clear one could make her happy by the very simple method of spending a certain amount of money. If I had succeeded I should have got rid of a morbid oppression. As it is, it has come back. It would have been worth a good deal of money to get rid of it . . . I can afford the money, but it seemed clear that it was wrong to spend so much on a matter of no real importance, & also that I ought not to have to think too much about making money. I said all this to her. She took it very well, but on my side it makes trouble—the pleasure I had was in giving things.
>
> (undated, ?23 August)

By 26 August a quarrel had taken place. Vivien was upset that Bertie was stopping her money and pleaded with him to reconsider. "Mrs. E. and I are drifting apart," wrote Russell. "We have practically agreed not to meet during the winter. My feelings on the matter are very complex."[79] Two days later his financial situation had improved, as Helen Dudley and her sister agreed to rent his flat in Bury Street at £3 a week, and Russell began to relent. It is remarkable, however, that Russell was prepared to sacrifice having a home of his own and to make himself dependent on the generosity of his brother Frank, in order to subsidise his mistress.

Nevertheless it was the price Russell had to pay if he wanted Vivien, as Tom now made clear to him. There had been a hint of blackmail in Tom's earlier demand that Bertie "fix" some lecturing work for him. In June Russell had rushed to Ottoline a letter from Eliot "à propos of University Extension lecturing which he wants to get." Did *she* know anyone with influence, as he did not. "He wants everything done before Saturday. If you *do* know anyone & can write, I should be *infinitely* grateful."[80] Eliot's lecturing posts were arranged for him, but it was not enough; Vivien's "allowance" must continue if Bertie wished to enjoy her favours, and he was forced to concede:

> Yesterday I came up by way of Chichester, & had a talk with Eliot there (I didn't see Mrs. E. who was ill). It was rather gloomy, but I got quite clear as to what must be done . . . It is fixed that I go to Bosham Monday to Friday; . . . I shall go on doing what I have done in the way of money during the winter, but beyond that I have said I can't foresee what will be possible.

Promising to come to Garsington after his week with the Eliots, Russell told Ottoline: "Matters with Mrs. E will be decided then. I never contemplated risking my reputation with her, & I never risked it as far as I can judge."[81]

For the moment Vivien had won the battle. Astonishingly Russell had agreed to continue to pay up. Such a change of heart must have aroused suspicion in Ottoline's mind as to the nature of his relationship with Vivien. Vivien's collapse with "neuralgia" had been the weapon she used in the battle over money, one which led Bertie to change his mind after a discussion with Tom, who probably accused him of ruining Vivien's health.

The decks cleared, Bertie was intending to make a final visit to

Bosham the following Monday, he told Ottoline on 28 August.[82] Tom had apparently returned to London, so he and Vivien would be alone together, just as they had been in Torquay in January. Perhaps both hoped for an amorous reconciliation after the dispute which had soured the relationship. But at this point the government intervened. According to a second letter Russell wrote to Ottoline on 1 September, headed "Gordon Square," two men in plain clothes appeared on behalf of the War Office at twelve o'clock and served a notice on him, ordering him not to go into any prohibited areas, which in effect meant the sea coast, from where it was suspected Russell could signal to submarines. He told Ottoline that he had to give up going to Sussex on Monday ("It makes my blood boil") but in his *Autobiography* he gives a contradictory account: "At the moment when the order was issued I had gone up to London for the day from Bosham in Sussex, where I was staying with the Eliots. I had to get them to bring up my brush and comb and tooth-brush, because the Government objected to my fetching them myself." As so often, Russell was lying to Ottoline in order to play down the relationship with Vivien.

Nevertheless, the ban ended his chances of any more holidays with "Mrs. E." Forced to stay in London, Russell threw himself once more into NCF work. Within three weeks an event occurred which was ultimately to spell the end to all Vivien's hopes. In August, at Lavender Hill police station, Battersea, when Clifford Allen was arrested, Russell had seen a striking young woman. She, too, had noticed him: "A small man, with a fine brow, aristocratic features, silver-grey hair, and a passionate expression." He was conventionally dressed, "but all the furies of hell raged in his eyes."[83] She was Lady Constance Malleson, an actress generally known by her stage name, Colette O'Niel, and married to the actor Miles Malleson. Both the Mallesons supported the NCF, where Colette was working in the office. She caught Russell's eye for the second time at Gustave's restaurant in Soho, at one of the Wednesday night meetings of Left-wingers, which included Philip Snowden, Ramsay MacDonald, George Lansbury and Gilbert Cannan. Perhaps not wholly by accident, Colette found herself placed next to Russell at dinner; afterwards he escorted her through the quiet Bloomsbury squares to her attic flat in Bernard Street, saying goodnight on the doorstep and walking off, a "curiously lonely figure," in the direction of Gordon Square.[84] Intrigued, she came ten days later to hear

Russell speak at the NCF Convention in the Portman Rooms, Baker Street, on 23 September. Afterwards he took her out to supper in the restaurant opposite and she invited him up to her flat. They talked half the night. "In the middle of talk [we] became lovers," wrote Russell, in words almost identical to those relating how he fell in love with Ottoline. "I clung to Colette. In a world of hate, she preserved love."[85] Within the next few months Russell was to have eyes only for Colette.

8

Wartime Waifs

Vivien returned from Bosham to war-ravaged London on 18 September 1916, and lunched with Russell that day. On his return from Bosham Russell had gone to stay at the Eliots' flat, as his own was still let to the Dudley sisters, and Gordon Square was occupied by his brother Frank and his wife, Elizabeth, Countess of Arnim (author of *Elizabeth and Her German Garden*).[1] "It is all right *really* about the Eliots," Russell reassured Ottoline, who remained concerned about the state of his finances as well as his relationships, perhaps not realising that Bertie enjoyed being a cuckoo in other people's nests. "I shan't get more involved—there is no expectation of my going on indefinitely. After this winter it will be all right—you were *quite* right to speak." He and Vivien were simply "very good friends." As if to underline this statement, five days later he consummated his love for Colette. Vivien was, it seemed, to be pushed into the margins of his life.

In Crawford Mansions the Eliots' memories of Bosham faded to "a beautiful dream."[2] The air raids over London intensified, and the night sky was red with the flames of burning Zeppelins. Vivien felt that Tom's family in America did not understand the ordeal they were enduring. Public feeling was running high against America for remaining out of the war. "It is horrid, I hate it," wrote Vivien to Henry, enclosing one of her brother Maurice's letters to help her brother-in-law appreciate that "England is *all* army now"; Maurice was not one of Kitchener's Army, who were put in khaki directly they joined, she explained, but a member of the regular army ("Of course there is some feeling of class distinction").[3] Only twenty, Maurice was commissioned as a 2nd Lieutenant in the Manchester Regiment on 12 May 1915,[4] had already served in France and, said Eliot, was used to the sight of corpses and sitting up at nights shooting rats with a revolver.

All the "Bloomsberries" who could manage it deserted the capital in favour of the country: Ottoline dug in at Garsington, while that other unconventional *ménage à trois* of Vanessa Bell, Duncan Grant and Bunny Garnett, were moving from Wissett Lodge to Charleston Farmhouse, near Firle in Sussex, close to Virginia and Leonard Woolf at Asheham.[5] But the Eliots were trapped in London. In their cramped, noisy flat near Paddington Station, with slums and "low streets and poor shops" close by—although within a stone's throw of great squares and big houses—Vivien felt as if she were in a wilderness. To her mother-in-law she complained: "We are just two waifs who live perched up in our little flat—no-one around us knows us, or sees us, or bothers to care how we live or what we do, or whether we live or not."[6] She missed the green Hampstead suburb in which she had been brought up, where there were familiar faces, even a need to keep up appearances, and began to feel miserably isolated. Incarcerated with her husband, bereft of Russell's presence to defuse the tension, Vivien was forced to face the inescapable fact that her marriage to Tom was deeply troubled.

"Hysteria," the prose poem Eliot wrote in the summer of 1915, reveals that despite his earnest desire to make a success of the marriage, he could not suppress his negative emotions towards Vivien.[7] The poem may be interpreted autobiographically in the light of Eliot's remark to Henry in January 1916 that he had *"lived* through material for a score of poems in the last six months." Eliot's statement that there should be a separation in the artist between "the man who suffers and the mind which creates"[8] formed the cornerstone of his impersonal theory of poetry: the poet, he wrote, surrenders himself in the act of creation: "The progress of the artist is a continual self-sacrifice, a continual extinction of personality." He emphasised this "process of depersonalization" by which "art may be said to approach the condition of science,"[9] and warned off critics who were tempted to make connections between art and life. For at least a generation, readers obeyed his stern injunction to concern themselves with the poetry not the poet.

Yet Eliot's critical writing expresses a contradiction, for he also be-

lieved that "what every poet starts from is his own emotions,"[10] and for him
the struggle, one which he believed he shared with his idols Dante and
Shakespeare, was "to transmute his personal and private agonies into
something rich and strange, something universal and impersonal." His poetry begins, like Yeats, "In the foul rag-and-bone shop of the human
heart," writes A. David Moody. "His method is to observe himself and the
whole world of his experience with passionate detachment and to fashion
out of his observations 'an individual and *new* organisation.' "[11] In *The
Sacred Wood* Eliot quotes Rémy de Gourmont's view that the artist "se
transvasait goutte à goutte" ("decanted himself drop by drop"). Even in his
favourite analogy of the chemistry experiment, in "Tradition and the
Individual Talent," in which Eliot describes himself as scientist *qua* artist,
it is the poet's feelings which form the basis of a new compound.[12] It was a
largely unconscious, subterranean and unpredictable process, which Eliot
compared to the gradual accumulation of a tantalus jar.[13] The incubation
period could not be hurried, but the poetry ultimately created, issued from
"the deeper, unnamed feelings which form the substratum of our being, to
which we rarely penetrate."[14]

In the poem "Hysteria," as so often with Eliot, it was an encounter
with a woman which spurred him to transmute life into art.[15] This word-
painting of a nervous young couple seated tête-à-tête at a rusty green table,
the elderly waiter with trembling hands serving them tea in the hotel garden, provides several clues as to why Eliot perceived Vivien as a threat. She
is laughing. He is silent, his silence "an in-gathering against that threat."
He watches her open mouth, her "shaking . . . breasts," and imagines himself being "drawn in by short gasps, inhaled at each momentary recovery,
lost finally in the dark caverns of her throat . . ."[16] Such a fear of being swal-
lowed up has been described in *The Divided Self* by R. D. Laing as the
schizoid fear of engulfment, or loss of autonomy. For someone as ontologically insecure as Eliot, who daily wrestled with the task of preserving his
sense of identity and selfhood, Vivien's nervousness and the sense that the
afternoon was splintering into "fragments" would have created immense
anxiety. But Eliot's fear was not only the dread of intimacy which such a
person is liable to feel in almost any relationship, however "harmless,"[17] but
a sexual one also: "One cannot avoid the conclusion that he is frightened of

her sexuality," writes critic George Whiteside, who argues that the mouth, with its "squad drill" of teeth, implies an overwhelming sexual as well as a schizoid threat: "There may be a terror, hardly recognized by him, of an imagined *vagina dentata,* into which one's penis can be 'drawn . . . lost finally . . . bruised by the ripple of unseen muscles.'"[18] The "hysteria" of the poem's title is primarily the poet's, as he strives to "collect" the afternoon in the face of the woman's nervous laughter; but it is also hers, as her laughter becomes hysterical in the face of his icy silence. The latent hostility expressed in the final lines of the poem becomes a threat, as the poet concludes that the only solution open to him is to silence the woman: "I decided that if the shaking of her breasts could be stopped, some fragments of the afternoon might be collected, and I concentrated my attention with careful subtlety to this end." It was an ominous omen for the future.

If Vivien had tried to "stimulate" Tom physically with her seductive sexuality, and to coax or even goad him into opening up emotionally, the experiment had failed: his defence was to close up even more tightly, like the crustaceous Prufrock. A symptom of Eliot's acute distress was that he stopped writing poetry. This creative paralysis worried Vivien intensely; one of her prime reasons for marrying Tom had been her belief in his genius and, if Russell is to be believed, from the unspoken recognition of their unhappiness had come a new resolution on her part to stop "punishing" Tom verbally. United in their belief in Tom's destiny as a poet, both Vivien and Tom suffered when he felt that his creative spring dried up, as it did at least three times in his life. These were periods when he became convinced that he would never again be able to write anything worth reading. Consumed by self-doubt, he attempted unsuccessfully to keep his fears secret from Vivien: "I often feel that 'J.A.P.' is a swan-song, but I never mention the fact because Vivien is so exceedingly anxious that I shall equal it, and would be bitterly disappointed if I did not," he confided to Henry in September 1916. "The present year has been the most awful nightmare of anxiety that the mind of man could conceive, but at least it is not dull and has its compensations."[19]

Meanwhile, Vivien opened Henry's reply while Tom was out ("We always do this with *family* letters") and read the postscript which was intended to be private; it did not matter that she had seen it, she said, for Tom knew perfectly well that she shared his feelings over his poetry:

I look upon Tom's poetry as real genius—I *do* think he is meant
to be a great writer—a poet. His prose is very good—but I think
it will never be *so* good as his poetry. Anyhow, it is a *constant*
canker with me that it is at a standstill—and every time the
thought is in Tom's mind I see it. I know how he feels—he has
told me more than once—he feels *dried up*.[20]

What Vivien did not realise was that in one hidden corner of Tom's mind
he blamed her for his barrenness; in "Ode" he had linked his being "now
retired" from the "Profession of the calamus," to the loss of the male comradeship which he associated with poetic inspiration. But Vivien's identification with Tom's despair led her to push him into any action she felt
would cause the spring to flow again. With considerable foresight, Vivien
diagnosed that journalism was bad for Tom. Although he loved it, she
wrote to Henry, "I am sure and certain that it will be the *ruin* of his poetry—if it goes on. For him—he ought never *to have to write.*" One of her
more impractical ideas was that Henry, who also nursed literary ambitions, should come and live in London and take over Tom's journalistic
work, while Tom concentrated on lecturing. Tom had taken on a much
larger risk a year ago, she told Henry, for he had her to keep as well—
"And I can swear he has never regretted it." It was a defiant remark and,
one suspects, one she did not wholly believe; what is more pertinent is
Vivien's proud boast, "Of course, he has had *me* to shove him—I supply the
motive power, and I *do* shove." As she later told Jack Hutchinson: "As to
Tom's *mind,* I am his mind."

Vivien's "shove" may have encouraged Tom's apparently rash decision
to give up his teaching post at Highgate Junior School. There, despite the
attentions of a young pupil named John Betjeman, who presented "the tall,
quiet usher" called "the American Master" with a manuscript entitled
"The Best Poems of Betjeman," he found the work intolerably draining.
His mother Charlotte, who had taught unsuccessfully in a girls' school, felt
only contempt for Eliot's teaching post, believing that "the male teachers in
secondary schools are as a rule inferior to the women teachers, and they
have little social position or distinction." She wrote to Russell: "I hope Tom
will not undertake this work another year."[21] But it was not only to appease
the two women in his life that Tom gave up teaching: he found the effort

to control the boys "altogether too exhausting."[22] As he later told his Harvard classmates, "I stayed at that for four terms, then chucked it because I did not like teaching."[23]

Eliot's prospects were now uncertain. Optimistically he believed that he could make a living through journalism and lecturing. Before abandoning the task of teaching small boys, he had, with Ottoline's help, applied to the Oxford University Extension Delegacy, and to the University of London Joint Committee for the Promotion of the Higher Education of Working People, for a post in adult education. The rewards were meagre; he was paid only £60 a year with £3 expenses for his Monday night lectures on modern English literature to working people at Southall, a course which was to last for three years, and see a £10 rise to a salary of £70. He also found employment in Ilkley, Yorkshire, as an Extension Lecturer on modern French literature from 3 October to 12 December 1916; it was his first introduction to the north of England, and to Yorkshire's manufacturing class, whom Vivien despised. Its members were, she told Henry as she travelled north for the first time in two years in October 1916, "So *provincial* that my American friends tell me that they are very much like Americans!! Tom has met just a few at Ilkley (in Yorkshire) when he went for his first lecture—and *he* says the same—he was struck with how much more like Americans they are than the South of England people."[24]

Lecturing may have released Eliot from the classroom, but it brought him little more free time. His syllabuses reveal the extent of the reading required to prepare for his lectures; although his Yorkshire lectures—on Romanticism and the reaction against it, sketching the life of Rousseau, the rise of Charles Maurras and royalism and the return of French intellectuals to the Catholic Church—covered ground already familiar to him, his Southall classes, which Vivien attended, required a plunge into less familiar Victorian literature.[25] But whatever lecturing lacked in remuneration, it made up for in interest, and he became a keen advocate of the working classes for their enthusiastic response to his "personal magnetism," as he described the experience to his cousin Eleanor: "My greatest pleasure is my workingmen's class in English literature on Monday evenings. I have steered them through Browning . . . Carlyle, Meredith and Arnold, and am now conducting them through Ruskin."[26] The class was in fact largely composed of women, elementary school teachers bent on self-improvement, but their "unabated eagerness to get culture in the evening" built up Eliot's confidence after his failure as a school teacher, as well as setting him on a path of self-education which stimulated him to write poetry again, albeit at first in French. His poem "Mélange Adultère de Tout" reflects his pleasure in these different roles: "En Amérique, professeur;/En Angleterre, journaliste" and "En Yorkshire, conférencier."[27]

Literary journalism paid equally poorly. The *Westminster Gazette* gave him no more than half a crown per review, but, he told Charlotte Eliot, the editor had said she could read and review six novels in an evening and he could do the same ("and Vivien can do some of them for me"). In addition he could sell the novels (published at six shillings) for two shillings each. "At that rate one would take in one pound and seven shillings for an evening's work!" He was learning, said Tom to his mother, the "ins and outs of journalism," proudly enclosing a complimentary review in the *Nation* of his poems in the *Catholic Anthology,* although he suspected it was a word in the ear of the editor Henry Massingham from his friend Ottoline which had made the difference. "This is Fleet Street!"[28]

Despite his creative crisis, Eliot knew he had to take a gamble. "I think everybody gets the kind of life he wants, and that if he doesn't know, or doesn't want strongly enough, he will never get anything satisfactorily," he had written to Henry on 5 November 1916, at the end of his last term at Highgate. Teaching, as well as being uncongenial, had prevented him pursuing his literary connections, and was "telling on the quality of my production," so it had to be abandoned: "The only recklessness, I think, consists in taking a risk when your will is not strong enough in that direction to carry you through." The financial risk was, however, rather less than Tom explained to his family, since he had succeeded in persuading Russell to continue supporting them, although he forbore to mention this fact.

Eliot's originality and relentless ambition had already brought remarkable results for an American who had arrived unknown in England in 1914. Nineteen fifteen had been "the year of his flowering," as Cyril Connolly[29] described it in 1963, when "The Love Song of J. Alfred Prufrock" had finally appeared in *Poetry* in June, to be followed by the two "Preludes" and "Rhapsody on a Windy Night" in the second or war number of *Blast* in July, and "Portrait of a Lady" in *Others* in September. Three more short poems appeared in *Poetry* in October, and Pound's determination "to get Eliot between hard covers" had borne fruit in the *Catholic Anthology* in November. Nevertheless Eliot was still comparatively unknown, as a letter from Ottoline demonstrates: "Huxley said there was some *very* good poetry by Elliot [sic] in an American Chicago paper called *Poetry,*" she wrote in surprise to Russell in February 1916. "It is your Elliot."[30]

As the citizen of a neutral country, Eliot was able to benefit from the war. He was adept at networking: Pound attributed Tom's ability to befriend those who would enhance his own status and position to his aptitude for "playing possum." By showing as few signs of life as possible he did not alarm people, and therefore could get away with revolution. Eliot adopted this stance intentionally, staking out his strategy in "Prufrock": "No! I am not Prince Hamlet, nor was meant to be;/Am an attendant lord . . ." His behaviour was "deferential, glad to be of use,/Politic, cautious, and meticulous."[31]

Certainly there was little danger of Eliot alienating people with rash outbursts of temper like Ezra Pound.[32] Instead, Eliot's watchful charm and sharp insight into the location of the citadels of power enabled him to profit from the increasing shortage of journalists, many of whom were now in the forces. Unemotionally Eliot listed the Vorticists leaving to fight: Wyndham Lewis, Wadsworth, Ford Madox Hueffer, T. E. Hulme, Aldington, for there were no conscientious objectors among that group. Already Hulme and Gaudier-Brzeska had been killed. The Imagist and Vorticist movements, which had been gathering momentum in 1914, spent its energies on the battlefields of France, or was scattered abroad; James Joyce remained in Trieste and Zurich, although *A Portrait of the Artist as a Young Man* continued to be serialized by *The Egoist*. This left the papers "rather hard up for reviewers," Eliot explained with satisfaction to his mother, and as a result he was also hired by the *New Statesman,* whose literary editor was J. C. Squire.[33]

In this critical period Tom still depended on Pound's support, even though he was skilfully laying the foundations for a Jamesian "conquest of London" and had already outstripped the reputation of Pound who, ignored by the reviewers and "killed by silence,"[34] continued to work indefatigably and unselfishly to "puff" his protégé, Eliot. In January 1917

Pound wrote to Margaret Anderson, editor and founder of the Chicago-based periodical *The Little Review:* "I want an 'official organ' (vile phrase). I mean I want a place where I and T. S. Eliot can appear once a month (or once an 'issue') and where Joyce can appear when he likes, and where Wyndham Lewis can appear if he comes back from the war . . ."[35] By May Pound had become foreign editor for Anderson, and was placing the remaining modernist poets, "H. D.," Amy Lowell, even Yeats, as well as Aldington, Lewis and Ford Madox Ford, whose poetry appeared in its columns with Eliot's. Margaret Anderson was braver than Harriet Monroe—editor of another Chicago-based journal, *Poetry*—who had "loathed and detested Eliot" when first she read "Prufrock," as Pound reminded her in April. She had published James Joyce's *Ulysses* in March 1918, an action in keeping with her masthead slogan: "A Magazine of the Arts Making No Compromise with the Public Taste." Boldly she declared that "the ultimate reason for life is Art. I don't know what they mean when they talk about art for life's sake. You don't make art so you may live; you do just the reverse of that. . . . Art uses up all the life it can get—and remains forever."[36]

It was a philosophy with which Tom and Vivien agreed in principle, but living for art became increasingly hard to practise by January 1917. Tom's income was substantially reduced. The Yorkshire lectures had ended, and he had not yet begun another course on Victorian literature he was to give on Friday evenings at the County Secondary School, Sydenham, from 28 September. Even then, the fee was a mere one pound a lecture, with no travelling expenses.[37]

Not only did the Eliots keep a servant, Rose, but food prices were rising week by week; every day "the strain and difficulty is a *little* increased, and the screw turned a little tighter," said Vivien. She adopted her own *"rigid,* locking-up-everything principles," as she explained to her mother-in-law:

> In the flat, if we have a woman, I lock up every mortal thing, and not a grain of rice or a crust of bread is eaten without my knowledge. Naturally one does not enjoy practising such parsimonious ways, but when it is a choice between that and practically starvating [sic] as it has been with us—there is of course no question.[38]

Tom hastened to assure his mother that he did not think anyone could manage more economically than Vivien did, and that she had Rose "very well in hand." Vivien was a good cook, he told Charlotte, and wanted to give up her charwoman and do the housework herself: "Of course when I think of all the clothes she needs—she has not had any for a long time, and I have my new suit [which his mother had paid for] I see advantages in giving up the woman, but I do not like it."[39]

Behind the harmonious façade they presented to Tom's family, in reality the Eliots were facing a personal and financial crisis in early 1917. Tom found the life of a freelance journalist more taxing than he had imagined. Enforced domesticity brought on black moods ("It is terrible to be alone with another person"). So inhibited that he would never dream of shaving in front of his wife, as he later confessed to Leonard Woolf, Tom found Vivien's very femininity abhorrent. Her physical presence, her smell, her clothes, her bodily functions, all repelled him, as a savage line in "Lune de Miel" (July 1917) reveals. Speaking of a young couple on honeymoon, as he and Vivien had been eighteen months ago, he comments on "une forte odeur de chienne" ("the strong stink of bitch") rising from the open thighs of the woman lying on her back.[40] It was an expression of a primitive instinctual revulsion. Filling the empty hours became a torment. "But what is there for you and me/For me and you/What is there for us to do?" he asks, "Where the leaves meet in leafy Marylebone?"[41] (from "Death of the Duchess").

Tom missed his mother Charlotte, the ageing matriarch on whose love and guidance he depended: "I long to see you, every day," he wrote in June 1917. Separated by the war, now entering its third year, Charlotte had begun to fear she would never see her favorite son again. "Don't talk about not seeing me again; it is too painful, and besides you *shall* see me again," he reassured her, nostalgically recalling his childhood when she used to sing him nursery rhymes like the "little Tailor."[42] "He was most gloomy and depressed and very irritable and I know he felt that life was simply not worth going on with," wrote Vivien to Charlotte on 8 March 1917. Eliot's depression at this point was such that he even lost confidence in his ability to write philosophy, feeling that an article he sent on 13 March to Russell to criticise was "too scattered and incoherent" and he had better keep it in his drawer for a year or two.[43] When Russell replied reassuringly, Eliot re-

peated that "what I have said is too negative and perhaps looks obscuran-
tist." He wanted to discuss authority or reverence, "But this is a task which
needs impulse and hope, and without more peace of mind and contented-
ness, better nerves and more conviction in regard to my future, I do not
feel capable of satisfying myself."[44]

Following the bouts of influenza through which Tom and Vivien had
nursed each other that winter (1916–17), Vivien was left anxious and in-
somniac: "I worry a great deal, and my brain is restless and active," she
confessed to Charlotte. "Often when I lie down to sleep I feel that a wheel
is going round in my head, and although my body is dead tired my brain
gets more and more excited . . . my migraines are coming back and I don't
feel nearly so well."[45] Tom wrote to his father: "When she worries she
bleeds internally, in a metaphorical sense, as well as other internal pains,
like migraine and stomach trouble, in a literal sense."[46]

Vivien's own mother, Rose, seems to have done little to help her distressed daughter and son-in-law, a neglect which perhaps bears out
Russell's comment that Rose was "odious." "Couldn't her mother help
her?" Ottoline had enquired of Bertie in March the previous year when the
Eliots were struggling to move flats.[47] "Are her own people horrid?" In fact
Rose Haigh-Wood often invited Vivien and Tom to Sunday lunch and tea,
but otherwise left her daughter and son-in-law to their own devices, perhaps feeling that, at nearly thirty, they should be able to manage on their
own. In this terrifying vacuum Tom began to feel he was staring failure in
the face. If the "silence from the sacred wood" of which he wrote in "Ode,"
and which he associated with his marriage, and Russell's intrusion in it,
continued for many more months, the gigantic gamble he had taken to
abandon family and country for an English wife and the hope of fame
would be in vain. He began to think of himself as another Coriolanus, an
identification which found expression in 1921 in *The Waste Land* as "a broken Coriolanus." In Shakespeare's *Coriolanus* the mother "breaks the
hero's iron spirit," and in Eliot's "Coriolan" poem, written after his
mother's death in 1929, the same utter dependence upon her is voiced:
"What shall I cry?/Mother mother . . ." The poet, "I a tired head among
these heads," utters his lamentation: "Mother/May we not be some time, almost now, together" repeating: "O mother/What shall I cry?"[48]

The Eliots' mutual misery, in which neurosis fed off sexual incompatibility, can in part be attributed to the withdrawal from their lives of Bertrand Russell in September 1916. Both Tom and Vivien experienced this trauma in their different ways. Eliot had lost his mentor, but for Vivien the agony of Bertie's abandonment was magnified by the knowledge that he was rhapsodizing over his new love affair with Colette, a woman who had many advantages over Vivien. First she came from a similarly aristocratic background to Russell's as the younger daughter of the fifth Earl of Annesley by his second marriage to Priscilla Cecilia Moore. Born in 1895, Constance had been brought up at Castlewellan, a grey granite castle looking out over the mountains of Morne in Northern Ireland, and despatched to boarding school at Downe House in Kent, which she nicknamed "Damned Hell." After her father's death she begged her mother to allow her to join her sister at school in Dresden and, at only fourteen, she began training for the theatre in Germany and later Paris; only reluctantly did she return for the London season, striking a bargain with her mother that she would become a débutante on condition she was allowed to train at the Royal Academy of Dramatic Arts. Constance had beginner's luck, and soon after taking the stage name Colette O'Niel found herself understudying Yvonne Arnaud for £2 a week.[49] She had a firm idea of her vocation and a professional training in contrast to Vivien's everchanging aspirations to paint, dance or act. Again in comparison to the sickly Vivien, Colette enjoyed vigorous good health as well as unbounded confidence, which led her to being described as "imperious" as well as striking. Like Russell's other lovers, Ottoline and Vivien, Colette was married, having eloped in her teens with the dramatist and actor Miles Malleson, to whom she was married in 1915. Both had joined the Independent Labor Party and the No-Conscription Fellowship after Malleson was invalided out of the army, and Colette was working in the NCF office on the index of conscientious objectors by day and acting at the Haymarket by night when she met the "brilliantly witty" Bertie.

Russell could scarcely believe that the twenty-year-old Colette returned his love, but his fiery eloquence had made an indelible impression on the young actress. After he walked away from her attic flat at 43 Bernard Street (only round the corner from Frank Russell's at 57 Gordon Square, so the lovers never needed to use the post) she dissolved into tears:

"I was crying. The moon shone down through my window. I cried and cried, but I knew I had found myself."[50] The next day Russell wrote her the first of many passionate and lyrical love letters, in language similar to that he had used in the early days of his affair with Ottoline: "Colette, my soul & my life. I love you every day with a deeper love. I feel you the embodied hope of the world—the youth & life with new promise, like the first flowers of spring . . ." He had grown weary in the struggle, he said, but with her he felt full of vigour and strength. Colette replied that she felt unworthy of Russell, of whose reputation she was in awe: "Strength you seem to have and courage. Then I can only add joy. But perhaps, from all the inward striving, something will grow. I stand with empty hands. Colette."[51] Touched by this answer, Russell ran out into the street early the next morning and bought red roses from a man who used to "haunt" the Bloomsbury streets calling out, "Sweet roses, sweet lovely roses," and had them delivered to her door.

Only by degrees did Russell reveal to Colette the web of relationships in which he was caught. By 2 October Colette was thanking Russell "very specially" for telling her about his relations with Ottoline, whom Colette had met once at Garsington, remembering her "splendid bearing and real kindness." Of Vivien Russell at first said nothing, for she belonged in a very different compartment of his life.[52] Comradely fervour and pacifist convictions united Russell and Colette, something with which Vivien, who identified with her young brother in the army, had no sympathy. Sending her new lover a Hoppé photograph portrait of herself, Colette asked for one of him when his "heathery head hasn't been all shorn off by the damn'd barber—I'd like it looking robustious [sic] and revolutionary."[53] As the NCF split into two factions, the Absolutists or extremists, which included Clifford Allen, Russell, the Mallesons and the NCF founder Fenner Brockway, and the Alternatives or moderate wing, Colette turned to Russell to save the situation. He wrote an article in the NCF magazine which she found "marvellously good": "I want your humanity, your radiant tenderness, your golden wisdom, the lightening [sic] flash of your mind," she told him, humbled to be the object of love of the NCF's most famous activist. But she was conscious of their age difference: "I'm just twenty. You beloved, are . . . forty-five? To me it seems that your life must

have been a wonderful tapestry, rich in experience, a glorious feast of adventurous thought; and now I come along like a sip of wretched after-
dinner coffee."[54]

There was more in the tapestry of Russell's life than Colette suspected
and, after they had spent her birthday on 24 October together in
Richmond Park, where they were caught in a storm and forced to shelter
under a giant oak, he decided to tell her something of Vivien. His opportunity came on the long train journey to Manchester, where he was due to
speak for the NCF. Painfully he struggled with the words, writing page
after page as the train puffed northwards: he had meant to tell her many
things about his life, and every time the moment had conquered him. He
was old and she was young, and

> because with me passion can seldom break through to freedom,
> out of the net of circumstances in which I am enmeshed; because
> my nature is hopelessly complicated, a mass of contradictory
> impulses; & out of this, to my intense sorrow, pain to you must
> grow.

It was an honest attempt at self-analysis, as he tried to explain the "terrible
pain" at the centre of his being as he searched for "something transfigured
and infinite, the beatific vision—God," which he was unable to find. "It is
like the passionate love for a ghost."

At last he comes to the point of the letter: his relationship with Vivien,
of whom Russell sounds as ashamed as Eliot seemed to be when first he introduced his wife to his former tutor:

> I began telling you about my friends the Eliots. I have a very great
> affection for them both—my relation with her especially is very
> intimate. If you met her you would be utterly unable to under-
> stand what I see in her. You would think her a common little
> thing, quite insignificant. But when I first knew her, which was
> 14 months ago, after her marriage, I found her so bruised and
> hurt by various people that I couldn't bear it, & I felt only a great
> deal of affection would cure her—The result is responsibility. I
> thought lately that I had come to an end, as there had been a long

disagreement. But I find her mood quite changed, and all that I had tried to do for her has at last succeeded . . .

The root of Vivien's troubles, wrote Russell, was that she had become filled with fear through having been hurt, and out of defiance had become harsh to everyone, including her husband, "Who is my friend, whom I love, & who is dependent on her for his happiness. If I fail her, she will punish him, & be morally ruined." Russell thought this had happened during their last disagreement, and although it had turned out otherwise, he still felt he was essential to the Eliots' happiness. "I am really vitally needed there, & one can't ignore that . . ."[55]

Colette responded generously to this confession, even though Bertie was saying that he was now reconciled with Vivien and would continue to see her, for reasons which he asked Colette to believe were therapeutic. "I cannot give you a *simple* happiness," he wrote. "I can give you moments of heaven with long intervals of pain between—if you think them worthwhile." It was a prophetic remark which was as true of Russell's relationship with Vivien as of that with Colette. But, in the first flush of love, Colette had no inkling of the complicated nature of her new lover's relationships with women: "Of course, Beloved, you mustn't neglect other people, neither women nor old friends, on account of our two selves. It would be entirely against my creed and against your own . . . Freedom must be the basis of everything. And that *is* so. For my part I'd rather cut off my right hand than not live by my creed."[56]

A few days later Colette told her husband Miles about Russell. Miles took the news that his young wife was passionately in love with another man well enough for, like Colette and Russell, he believed in an open marriage, the "new morality," which was intended, as Russell's daughter Kate later wrote, "to be joyful and positive, but no less demanding than the old . . . They believed it would be easy to live without jealousy, but it turned out the new morality was no easier and no more natural than the ideal of rigorous life-long monogamy it was intended to replace."[57]

For the moment the creed of free love seemed an intoxicating one which would allow Colette a tolerant husband and a devoted lover, and Bertie the thrill of a new mistress while retaining the old, as well as continuing his long-standing relationship with Ottoline. Vivien's despair in

October 1916, when she suffered from "nerve-storms" and acute migraine, is easily understood in the context of Russell's withdrawal from her as his passion for Colette reached a new pitch of intensity: "We seem to enter some world beyond passion—more passionate than any passion," he wrote at midnight on 29 October. "My Beloved I feel we are one eternally—I want to travel with you through all the lands of the spirit—heights & depths & wildernesses—to pierce with you to the mystic heart of the world—I long to be with you in wild & lonely places—to gather up in one eternal moment all the ages of man & all the abysses of space."[58]

In the face of Vivien's desolation, Russell could not avoid meeting her. "I am dining with Mrs. Eliot to-night," he told Colette on 2 November 1916. "I rather dread it. I don't *wish* to take less interest in the Eliots than I have done, but unavoidably it works out so. You fill my heart & mind so full that it is very difficult to find room for anything else." No doubt there was a tearful scene, and Vivien protested that Bertie was deserting her, for he wrote guiltily to Colette: "I had a painful time with Mrs. Eliot & am very worried. I *can't* make myself feel the Eliots' affairs at all vividly any more—it seems so cruel."[59] By now Colette's sympathy for Russell began to run thin:

> Beloved I'm terribly sorry that your evening with Mrs. Eliot turned out painful. What can I say? You write that you're very worried. But you've known her for more than a year, and I've never met her; and I've never really been in the sort of situation in which you find yourself; and I don't suppose there's anything useful I can say.

Stung by Russell's accusation that she did not understand complex situations, she added: "I also suspect you'd find any remedies of mine far too simple . . . When you first wrote me about her, you said I'd see nothing in her and would think her an ordinary little thing. You may be right, but I mostly *like* people . . ."[60]

Vivien's misery would have deepened had she known that Russell and Colette were about to leave for a three-day "honeymoon" in mid-November 1916, at the Cat and Fiddle, a rough stone pub in the Derbyshire Peak district. "The 'Cat and Fiddle' sounds *too* delicious. I want to be the dish,"[61] was Russell's response to Colette's suggestion. It was a bit like *Wuthering Heights,* said Colette, imagining herself and Bertie as Cathy and Heathcliff. The bleak moors suited their mood, remembered Bertie, even though it was bitterly cold and the water in his jug was frozen in the morning. "We spent our days in long walks and our nights in an emotion that held all the pain of the world in solution, but distilled from it an ecstasy that seemed almost more than human."[62]

For Colette, too, the days with Bertie had been wonderful "beyond mortal words . . . the evenings sitting by the fire, the wonder and joy of the nights, the untellable joy of sleeping in your arms." He was her "dear dear Love, heart's comrade as never before," she wrote from Manchester. The brief interlude on the moors was to remain the high point of their relationship, which soon began to run into difficulties. One reason was yet another new female interest in Russell's life that autumn (1916): Katherine Mansfield, a cousin of his sister-in-law Elisabeth. He had met the young and gifted writer from New Zealand at Garsington, and she had asked him for a reference for a flat, having been refused by St. John Hutchinson on the grounds that she was living in sin with John Middleton Murry, whom she was to marry on 3 May 1918. Happy to oblige, Russell was soon entertaining Katherine to dinner; by October Katherine was living with Murry, Dora Carrington and Dorothy Brett in a house they nicknamed "The Ark" in Gower Street, just round the corner from Russell at Gordon Square, and her influence over him began to grow.

Colette was very hurt when Russell announced that his work and other engagements would prevent him from seeing her for "some very considerable time." Although she did not yet know it, this was a phrase he used when considering breaking off relations with a woman. "I shan't lose foothold in the storm," she wrote bravely.[63] For Russell, Katherine's allure lay primarily in her mind: "Her talk was marvellous, much better than her writing," he recalled in his *Autobiography.*[64] "I want to get to know (her) really well," he wrote to Ottoline. "She interests me mentally very much indeed—I think she has a very good mind, & I like her boundless curiosity."[65] "My head aches with a kind of sweet excitement," responded Katherine to one of Russell's letters in December 1916,[66] suggesting the interest was mutual.

At Garsington, where they met at Christmas 1916, Russell listened to

Katherine's envious, dark, penetrating talk about her hostess, Ottoline, whom Katherine detested because she believed, without foundation, that Ottoline had made overtures to her lover, Middleton Murry. Although Russell professed to believe very little of what Katherine said, her malicious conversation encouraged him in the disengagement from Ottoline which he believed was necessary to his happiness, since she no longer returned his feelings. In his *Autobiography* Russell writes that after Christmas he saw no more of Katherine, but was able to allow his feelings for Colette full scope. In fact he continued to meet Katherine throughout 1917, just as he continued to dine with Vivien. Colette disliked Katherine intensely, and was shocked by her disloyalty towards Ottoline, who had entertained her generously. "Beloved, if you feel you want to see a good deal of her, of course you must do so; but I wouldn't be honest if I didn't say that, if anybody spoke of you in the way she speaks of Ottoline to you, I'd think they'd gone clean off their head—or, the quicker they got out of my Attic the better," wrote Colette in September 1917. "But as *I* don't have to know K.M., my feeling is beside the point."[67]

Katherine Mansfield's "dark hatreds" bore fruit: Russell ceased to think of Ottoline as a lover, but only as a friend—and even his friendship wavered over the months. He had finally confessed to her, in the same sentence in which he admitted that he liked Katherine, that "In a gay boyish mood I got intimate with Constance Malleson, but she doesn't suit serious moods."[68] In June 1917 he blamed Ottoline for the fact that he and Colette nearly broke up in the winter of 1916–17: it was Ottoline's criticism which influenced him too much, whether of people or his work:

> I wanted to tell you more about Constance Malleson—I began to know her well in the autumn, & meant to tell you, but your attack both made me afraid of you & set me to thinking I wanted to break with her. I set to work to withdraw, & almost completed the process. It was at that time that I hated everybody—& I found it set me against you too. At last I came to the conclusion that I didn't really want to withdraw . . .

Russell's need to find an outlet for his libido and Ottoline's failure to return his passion was a recurring theme with him, highlighted by her recent infatuation with a young army officer and poet, Siegfried Sassoon: "Nearly a year & a half ago now I realised once for all that I *must* detach my *instinct* from you, because otherwise life was too painful to be borne. That left me with a feeling of grudge, unless I could let my instinct go to someone else."[69] Both Vivien and Colette were outlets for Russell's frustrated "instinct," implied in his admissions of "intimacy," as he turned against Ottoline, complaining that she had found fault with him for becoming absorbed in writing, and as a result his "impulse" to write his lectures on Social Reconstruction had "stopped dead . . . It was only after I got interested in the Eliots, & by means of that interest, that I was able to get back to the lectures. I do not think you know at all how vehemently you find fault, or how it kills one's impulse when you do it . . ." It is a letter which reveals Russell's egotistical attitude to the women in his life: Vivien, like Ottoline, was there to serve *his* needs, to overcome *his* sense of failure: "Mrs. E. happened to turn up . . . and I used her for my purpose," he confessed with no hint of shame.[70] Later, Colette was to write in her novel *The Coming Back* a thinly disguised account of her relationship with Russell, whom she describes as

> a man exhausting other men by his intellect; exhausting women by his intensity; wearing out his friends, sucking them dry, passing from person to person, never giving any real happiness—or finding any.[71]

Ottoline, already reeling from the blow of finding herself cruelly satirised by D. H. Lawrence in *Women in Love*, needed Bertie's understanding rather than his criticism. "Lawrence has sent me his *awful* book," she complained on 2 January 1917. "It is so loathsome that one cannot get clean after it—& a most insulting Chapter with *minute* photographs of Garsington & a horrible disgusting portrait of me making me out as if filled with cruel develish [sic] *Lust* . . . It is of course Frieda's revenge."[72] She was quick to forgive Bertie: "Perhaps after all Lawrence's view of me in his book is partly True," she wondered sadly.[73] But as her depression deepened ("All Life came shattering down about me—and all that I had been trying to build up—came grinning in mockery at me—")[74] she began to withdraw from Bertie and his volley of grievances, and warn him that her patience had limits: "You have battered me hard—for many months indeed years now—and even the poor rag doll will turn someday."[75]

Insensitive to the needs of individuals, Russell remained deeply touched by the plight of millions.[76] His role in the NCF was becoming ever more vital as the original leaders of the movement disappeared behind prison bars, including Fenner Brockway, the original founder of the Fellowship in 1914, and he began to withdraw from both Colette, whom he now only saw once a week, and Vivien. "The ghosts from the Somme & the Dardanelles & the blood-drenched plains of Poland come & call me not to forget them," he told Colette. "I think of Allen and Fenner & all the rest of them—& I feel ashamed."[77] On 3 January 1917 Russell dined with Vivien, afterwards assuring Colette that he had told Vivien he wouldn't see her again "for an indefinite time."[78]

He did not keep his promise. Although in January 1917 Russell became acting chairman of the NCF, and was actively involved in furthering the cause of peace by lobbying President Woodrow Wilson of the United States,[79] who had been elected as the "peace candidate" in November, he continued to meet Vivien frequently. In March he told Colette:

> Practically the only people I see nowadays except on business are the Eliots—She is rather dependent on me in a variety of ways— I took on the responsibility of her when she was in a bad way, and the responsibility remains. I have an affection for her, but almost entirely because of her dependence. My affection for both of them grows less as time goes on.[80]

Colette's acceptance that Vivien was a fixture in Russell's life is clear in a letter in which she asks him to accompany her and Miles to the great celebration to mark the Russian Tsar's abdication and the Kerensky Revolution in March 1917. "On Saturday there's the Albert Hall, 7 oc. Aren't you coming? I know you were by way of dining with Mrs. Eliot, but if Sunday happened to suit her just as well, you could come?"

"I find I must dine with Mrs. Eliot on the Saturday or the Sunday, to make up for last Saturday," replied Russell, after the "electric" meeting at the Albert Hall on 31 March, at which his euphoria rose to such dizzy heights that he longed to call on the audience to follow him and pull down

Wormwood Scrubs. "If I made it Saturday, I could (if you are free) go away Sunday morning & stay away the night. If you are free Sunday evening, I will see Mrs. E. later, and keep Saturday dinner for you as planned."[81]

This careful dovetailing of Vivien and Colette in Russell's diary demonstrates the falseness of the impression he gives in his *Autobiography* that his love affairs were sequential. Vivien was the ever-present backdrop to his affair with Colette, remaining in the shadows only because so little of her correspondence with Russell appears to have been preserved. In her letters Colette makes many references to her lover's "complicated tangles."[82] Years later, writing of Vivien's importance in Russell's life, Colette commented, "I was . . . very surprised when, in his autobiography, he made it appear that none of his women overlapped with each other; which, so far as I knew, they all did."[83] Nor do the facts bear out Russell's dismissive comment that he merely used Vivien for the "purpose" of freeing himself from Ottoline, for he continued to see her long after he had broken with Ottoline as a lover; once released from the influence of her hostile judgment on Vivien and Colette, Russell followed his own inclinations.

In March 1917 the Eliots' fortunes at last took a turn for the better. Charles Haigh-Wood took pity on his daughter and son-in-law and introduced Tom to L. E. Thomas, chief general manager of the National Provincial Bank. He in turn put Tom in touch with the Colonial and Foreign Department of Lloyds Bank at 20 King William Street, in the heart of the City; Eliot was taken on as a bank clerk at a starting salary of £2.10s. a week, on the false assumption that he was a linguist, his task being to tabulate the balance sheets of foreign banks and make digests of the foreign language press. Soon he was using his French and self-taught Italian, and picking up Spanish and Danish in his lunch hour. To Vivien's surprise, her husband's depression at once began to lift: "His health is *much* improved," she wrote to her mother-in-law on Easter Sunday. "There is a marked change in him. Everyone notices it. His nerves are so much better—he does not have those black silent moods, and the irritability. Those months when he was entirely at home were very very trying . . ."[84]

The assurance of a regular salary ("However *little*"), and the prospect of a pension which would provide for Vivien in the event of his death, removed a burden from Tom's shoulders. Like his father, who had started life as an agricultural clerk, he enjoyed the routine of work and the department in which he was "petted" by the female staff, as well as finding the "science of money" to be extraordinarily interesting.[85] Vivien could hardly contain her delight that Tom had taken so extraordinarily to the City: "He is considering, to my *great* astonishment, taking up Banking as his *money-making* career!" she confided to Charlotte. "We are all very much surprised at this development, but not one of his friends has failed to see, and to remark upon, the great change in Tom's health, appearance, spirits, and literary productiveness since he went in for Banking." Amazed that Tom was so interested in finance and found it a congenial career, which left his mind fresh enough to write, she was relieved that he would no longer have to depend on journalism for a livelihood.

> This is what he has *always* been hoping for—he has never altered . . . So far the Bank *seems* to be the thing. No one could be more surprised than I am. I shed *tears* over the thought of Tom going into a Bank! I thought it the most horrible catastrophe. Most of Tom's friends agreed with me. We all wrung our hands and lamented . . . Only when he began to be more bright and happy and boyish than I've known him to be for nearly two years, did *I* feel convinced.[86]

Not only did life as a bank clerk free Eliot from the stress of freelancing, it relieved him of the daily company of his wife; soon his writer's block had vanished and he had written five "excellent poems," finding that writing in French helped his "spring" to run again. He was now "A Londres, un peu banquier," as he described his new situation with relief in "Mélange Adultère de Tout."[87] And in June Ezra Pound was able to do Tom another favour which turned his financial fortunes around, as well as giving him an important leg-up on the literary ladder. Richard Aldington, assistant editor of the fortnightly *Egoist,* joined the army and Pound persuaded the editor, Harriet Shaw Weaver, who had founded the review in 1913, to take on Eliot in Aldington's place. The salary was £36 a year, of which Pound secretly contributed half. It was Harriet Shaw Weaver's readiness to publish *Prufrock and Other Observations* under the banner of the Egoist Press in June 1917, when no other publisher was forthcoming, for which Eliot was always to remain grateful, which made possible his initial breakthrough in poetry.

Provided Russell's help continued, and the cheques for the rent and extras such as clothes (a black quilted satin chest protector for Tom to wear when he went out in evening dress) continued to arrive regularly from the Eliot family, Tom and Vivien were now much better off than previously. However, in May a financial tug-of-war took place between Vivien and Colette. Brought up to a life of privilege, Colette was extravagant by nature and, despite having an unearned income of £500 a year, £100 more than was now available to Russell, she was always short of money. "We lived mostly on tuppenny fish cakes from a shop up the back street, and scrambled eggs concocted by me out of a horrid looking orange powder called somebody's 'best dried eggs,' " wrote Colette of early 1917.[88] It was hardly true. In reality the aristocratic actress was more likely to abandon her gas ring in the attic for Gustave's or Canuto's restaurants where she and Bertie and the NCF activists liked to plot and dine. Miles did not earn more than £1 a week acting, and so both of them were dependent on Colette's unearned income. As a result Colette poured out her financial troubles to Russell, who in April offered to sell his debentures (already passed to the Eliots) to help her. "Now listen, Beloved," replied Colette on 2 May. "You are on no account to sell your debentures for me. It was an adorable thought, for which I love you, but I would *hate* you to do it."[89]

On 1 April, shortly after Eliot had joined Lloyds Bank, Bertie had entertained Vivien to dinner. She was unable to hide her affection for him, and her consequent unhappiness. "Mrs. Eliot yesterday assured me that she is perfectly happy, & finds her life quite satisfactory," he told Colette. "She lied quite bravely and convincingly." Russell was touched by Vivien's plight and, if he had been planning to remove the debentures which had been put into Tom Eliot's name and realise the capital in favour of Colette, he changed his mind, perhaps at Colette's insistence, perhaps because Vivien pleaded with him that she still needed the money. "The matter of the debentures is fixed in my will and cannot be altered," was Russell's excuse to Colette on 4 May. He continued to help both Vivien and Colette, to whom he often advanced small sums which she repaid punctiliously.

Russell's relationship with Ottoline had deteriorated further since a comment he had made on leaving Garsington after one of his visits: "What a pity your hair is going grey." "My rapier is out," recorded his hostess. In July he would write her a letter which marked the end of their affair: "It is true that I am not in love with you now." His roller-coaster relationship with Colette did not seem to promise lasting happiness, as he begged her to leave the stage to join him in political work, and she refused. After a holiday together near Ludlow, Shropshire, he had hoped she would leave Miles for him, but instead Colette hesitated. Frustrated, and growing bored with revolutionary politics, Russell's thoughts were turning inwards once again to philosophy. On Good Friday, 6 April, the United States declared war on Germany, and the possibility that Eliot would enlist drew nearer. Meanwhile, as other doors closed to him, Bertie began to feel it was time to woo Vivien again.

9

Priapus in the Shrubbery

The prospect that Tom might have to fight filled Vivien with dread. On the "eventful day," 4 April 1917 (in fact 6 April)[1] which she believed to be that of the United States' declaration of war, Vivien wrote to her sister-in-law, Charlotte Eliot Smith, the third of Tom's sisters: "Today's news is very exciting—rather unpleasant—but exciting to one personally."[2] Vivien was sure that Charlotte, like herself, would hate the thought of her husband going to fight. She hoped and prayed that the married men would not be conscripted for a long time, and that the war would be over before their turn came. Returning to her recurrent theme, that many Americans simply "don't know what war means—I mean what *this* war means. I dont suppose you ever will, as we have known it," she apologised for her depressing letter. "I have got a bad sore throat, & it does not help towards looking on the bright side of things—if there is such a side!"[3]

By 1917 the euphoria of the early days of the war had evaporated. Vivien had seen too many cases of the "bad and dreadful" effect of the war on young men to have any illusions left: "If they are nervous and highly-strung (as Tom is, and also my brother) they become quite changed. A sort of desperation, and demoralisation of their minds, brains, and character. I have seen it so, so often."[4] Tom shared her scepticism. He was distressed to learn in May that his closest friend from Merton, Karl Culpin, was critically wounded and not expected to live.[5] It was one more blow, coming after the death of Jean Verdenal, which made him see the war as simply "sordid," even if the cause were righteous. As well as Culpin, who died a few days later, the fiancé of one of Vivien's friends had just been killed. "You cannot realise what it is to live in the midst of alarms of war!" Tom told his mother, confessing that he didn't envy his Harvard contemporaries who were patrolling the seas, and hoped that he would not be called up for a couple of years and by then the war would be over. "I certainly do not feel in a position to go until 'called out,' though Vivien has been rather troubled. I should go then, but not till then."[6] Tom wondered hopefully whether his hernia might affect his medical.

Ezra Pound, meanwhile, sent his name to the American Embassy in May, only to be cautioned by John Quinn, the wealthy American lawyer and patron of the arts, against foolhardy patriotism: "I would let it go at that, let it be pigeon-holed . . . Don't be in a hurry about getting to France. This is not lack of patriotism, it is just horse sense."[7] Safe in his subterranean cubby-hole beneath the London pavements, sitting at his mahogany desk surrounded by tall filing cabinets, in the office he shared, with another clerk, Mr. McKnight, who lived in a suburb and cultivated his kitchen garden, Tom expressed his reluctance to exchange his balance sheets for the trenches to his cousin Eleanor. "I have been living in one of Dostoevsky's novels, you see, not in one of Jane Austen's," he wrote. "If I have not seen the battle field, I have seen other strange things, and I have signed a cheque for two hundred thousand pounds while bombs have dropped around me."[8]

Now that Tom was settled at Lloyds Bank, Vivien also tried to look for work. "She is possessed with the idea that she ought to earn money, and if she had average health and could find congenial work, I should not object," Tom told his mother.[9] He was against the plan, feeling that it would be impossible for Vivien to work in a noisy office after the sleepless nights and headaches from which she suffered. But in the autumn of 1917 Vivien did apply for a position in a government office where she could use her secretarial skills, and was called for an interview in November, only to be rejected outright as the wife of an American. To be refused on the grounds of her "nationality" was a great disappointment to her. Vivien longed to exchange the isolation of her flat for a busy office, and to feel she was participating in the war effort. It would have given her life some purpose and probably improved her health, as it had done for Tom. Her failure to find war work was a key factor in the increasing separation of her life from Tom's.

Thrown back on her own resources, Vivien took pride in homemaking at Crawford Mansions: "I should like you to see our flat," she wrote to Charlotte Eliot Smith. "It is the one thing I do really take a pride in—I mean seem to have succeeded in. It means an extraordinary lot to me—I am a person who simply does not exist without a home, & am always fussy with it." Nevertheless, life in wartime London was hard, not only for Vivien: "Hell is let loose on earth this Christmas—all around me the devil-world is whirling, swaying, reeling. Somewhere, through the madness, you are . . ."[10] Colette had written to Bertie at the turn of 1916 and, as Russell's despair deepened at the failure of revolutionary politics to bring about peace, he spoke of looking "only into horror and black darkness and the red pit of hell."[11] Even in the quiet of the Oxfordshire countryside, Ottoline too, sheltering the "nervy" Sassoon at Garsington, felt the horrors of war had worn away all feeling. "Ones nerves are rampant and one is all raw," she comforted Bertie, feeling that *extreme* nerve fatigue" was affecting them all.[12]

Temporary respite of a sort came when Vivien's parents offered Tom and herself the use of their house in Compayne Gardens for a fortnight in June. They were able to exchange their "scrambling, overworked, hand-to-mouth sort of existence" for the large, airy rooms and quiet greenness of the Hampstead square, where Rose Haigh-Wood's two servants kept everything running smoothly, and Vivien was able to sink back into the easy comfort of her life before marriage. It seemed very strange to her to return to her childhood home with Tom, after two years of noisy struggle in a working-class area of central London. "I had almost forgotten that life could be so pleasant, so smooth," she wrote wistfully to her mother-in-law. "It is the old tale, I suppose, of no-one's ever appreciating anything till they have lost it."[13] Tom, Vivien's brother Maurice (who was at Chelsea Barracks), Ezra Pound and a civil servant friend named Arthur Dakyns played tennis together, and soon both Tom and Vivien were "doing better" than in their flat, Tom told his mother. But despite the fact that the Haigh-Woods paid £1 a week for their servants' food while the Eliots were staying at their house, Vivien found it cost considerably more to live in Hampstead than in Marylebone. It was becoming more and more difficult and harrassing to procure proper nourishment on Tom's salary of £2.10s. a week, which Vivien thought an absurdly low salary for the work he was doing, she confided to her mother-in-law: "I dont know what will happen if he does not get a rise soon."

Vivien worried as much about Tom's health as he did about hers. "It seems he has not average strength," she wrote, "and added to that he lives as no average man does. The incessant, never ending grind, day and evening—and always *too* much to do, so that he is always behind hand, never up to date—therefore always tormented—and if *forced* to rest or stop a minute it only torments him the more to feel that inexorable pile of work piling up against him."[14] Vivien continued to type Tom's articles on her Corona typewriter, often to dictation which saved time when he had many reviews to do; she bought his clothes with the money his mother sent—two pairs of pyjamas, one shirt, and six pairs of socks in June, all "absolute necessities"; she ran the household as economically as possible, for example, bringing back quantities of blackberries from Bosham to make into "delicious" jam, and faithfully attended Tom's Friday night lectures on Victorian literature. But as his reputation grew, so did the demand for his services as a journalist and literary critic.

In June 1917, *Prufrock and Other Observations* was published, subsidised by the kindly Pound, which was unknown to Eliot.[15] Tom himself felt it was only a *réchauffée,* and that his friends were growing tired of waiting for something better from him,[16] but *Prufrock* sold well and brought his name before a wider public. "I have read Eliot's little book of poems with immense enjoyment," wrote publisher Alfred A. Knopf to John Quinn. "I do not know whether it is great poetry or not. I do know that it is great fun and I like it."[17] It was a typical reaction. Quinn, who had already offered to repay Pound the cost of the *Egoist*'s printing bill for *Prufrock* ("No-one would know about it, neither Eliot nor anyone") became an important patron of Tom's work, which he "boomed" at every opportunity.[18] Meanwhile Clive Bell recalled—probably incorrectly—that he had that Easter taken a dozen copies of *Prufrock* to Garsington which he distributed "hot from the press" like so many Good Friday buns to the assembled guests of Lady Ottoline Morrell, who included Mrs. St. John Hutchinson, Katherine Mansfield, Aldous Huxley, John Middleton Murry, Lytton Strachey and Mark Gertler. Katherine read aloud "The Love Song of J. Alfred Prufrock" from the badly printed book, bound in its "trashy yellow jacket": it caused a stir, remembered Clive.[19] There was much discussion and some perplexity; but the Bloomsbury audience knew instinctively that the verse they were hearing was as revolutionary as the music of Stravinsky or the paintings of Picasso.

Vivien's stay at Hampstead was followed by another summer holiday at Bosham, where she and Tom sailed together every day despite having a rainy week. Returning with reluctance from Sussex, she succumbed to influenza; ill and feverish, Vivien was forced to stumble downstairs from their top-floor flat to take shelter in the cellar for two nights running because of the air raids—even though the doctor had forbidden her to get out of bed. It was the last straw. She resolved to find a country cottage to live in for the remainder of the war, where the laryngitis, catarrh, neuralgia and migraines which made her life miserable in London might improve. In October 1917 Vivien told Charlotte Eliot that she had spent nearly eight weeks in the country during the summer, and "I'm so *much* better for it. I have not felt so well since we were married."[20] Tom, too, longed for the peace of nights undisturbed by air raids. "We are going to try and find rooms outside of London, not too far for me to come up every day," he wrote. "It is absolutely imperative; we cannot stand the strain of moonlight nights in London."[21]

Vivien struggled to justify the expense of renting a "cheap" cottage to Charlotte, while at the same time keeping on the flat at Crawford Mansions, despite the fact that she and Tom were, almost by the same post, asking for money from his parents for the rent and clothes. A cottage was essential, and would become more so, she said, wishing she could describe conditions at home without fear of the censor: "I am sure if you were here you would urge us to find something in the country." As to the flat, they were bound to keep it on to store Tom's books—"to say nothing of papers—typewriters, and all the other business!" He needed somewhere to stay for two nights a week after his lectures, from which he did not return till eleven at night. In any event, argued Vivien, the flat was unlettable, being on the top floor.[22] Tom added his voice to hers: "She is ever so much healthier in the country, and I should be delighted if we could find a small cottage, such as she and Miss Thayer had before quite near town at 8/- a week. And of course she is very nervous in town," he told his father.[23]

The truth was somewhat more complicated. Vivien's conviction that her health was better out of London was undoubtedly sincere, but what she left unsaid to her mother-in-law was, once again, the significant part played by Bertrand Russell in the Eliots' lives. For Vivien's desire to escape London coincided with a crisis in the relationship between Russell and Colette, which led Russell to feel the time had come to breathe new fire into the embers of his affair with Vivien. His sudden desire to resurrect the old arrangement of a "triple ménage" with Vivien and Tom came at a particularly vulnerable time for the Eliots, when they were making an attempt to work out their own *modus vivendi.* Their mutual concern and loyalty is evident in their letters, but it was to be freshly destabilised by Russell's selfish attempt to assuage his misery over Colette in the arms of Vivien.

Russell's desire for a child had also grown stronger with the passing of time. After an ecstatic interlude with Colette in August 1917 at the Feathers Inn, Ludlow, when they made up their quarrel over her refusal to give up her stage career, his love for her seemed to reach new heights. Colette was equally fervent: her love, she said, was, "minted like a gold coin which may become rubbed, worn thin, deformed with incrustations, but will last till the end of our lives. Let tempests rage, let cities crumble, my small gold coin will outlast them all."[24] But the demands of her increasingly unhappy husband Miles, who also wanted to have a child with her, cast a shadow over their relationship, just as Philip's terms to Ottoline had put constraints on *her* affair with Bertie. Russell must have wondered whether Colette, like Ottoline, would ultimately choose the status quo rather than passion out of wedlock when she wrote: "The long and short of it is that [Miles] is now *minding* that he is no longer the *central* person in my life." As to children, in response to the urging by both the men in her life to be allowed to impregnate her, Colette wrote crisply: "Well—I've sometimes thought that my parents had no business to have children. And if that should be so, it's a thing I wouldn't want to repeat in my own life."[25]

Bertie found it hard to reconcile his emotions with his belief, reiterated to Colette in August, that "one must follow love freely wherever it leads one,"[26] when she accepted an offer to star in a film called *Hindle Wakes,* based on a Lancashire play about a mill girl who is seduced by her employer's son. When Colette left for Blackpool and began filming in the cotton mills with director Maurice Elvey, Russell's jealousy was inflamed.

"B.R. thought acting was a worthless sort of occupation," remembered Colette. "He thought it brought out the worst in one's character: personal ambition, love of admiration."[27] Vituperative letters followed Colette: "The whole region of my mind where you lived, seems burnt out," wrote Bertie on 23 September. "There is nothing for us both but to try and forget each other. Goodbye."[28] On 25 September he sent her a letter containing a harsh character analysis, accusing her of being a personality whose happiness depended on "an unusual amount of sexual adventure . . . for the satisfaction of sexual vanity." Colette's energy, he said, made her enjoy an element of roughness and fierceness in love and her vanity led her to seek notoriety and luxury, and the path of commercialism, "With all its attendant evils of competition, envy, shoddy work, and possibly prostitution . . . She is almost entirely destitute of self-control . . ."[29]

Insecure in his relationship with Colette also because of the age difference, Russell was convinced that she was about to have an affair with Elvey; and Colette's husband Miles Malleson, who was looking after the philosopher in London, believed he was on the verge of a nervous breakdown. "I don't need to tell you that Maurice is not my lover in the sense that you are the lover of Ottoline and Mrs. Eliot," retorted Colette on 28 September 1917, another indication that Russell's tie with Vivien was a sexual one.[30] Colette was irate at Russell's double standards, since on 21 August and 6 September he had dined with Katherine Mansfield, unwisely confessing to Colette on the latter date, in words almost identical to those he had used to Ottoline previously: "She doesn't want a love-affair . . . I don't *at all,* but her mind is very interesting & I should like to see a fair amount of her, so long as there is not too close an intimacy . . ."[31] As well as suspecting Bertie of sleeping with Katherine, Colette was annoyed that he had spent time with Vivien in the country during the summer—Vivien had stayed at the White Horse in Shere, near Guildford, for part of the time.[32] Russell was feeling "completely set up," he had told Colette, after two days' walking with Vivien, and lunch with Bob Trevelyan in late June. It is very probable that Russell helped Vivien in her search for a cottage in the vicinity. On 3 September he told Colette that he was planning to find a country cottage in the spring, not too far from London, as he was thinking of returning to philosophy after finishing *Mysticism and Logic.*

Colette was therefore not in the mood to abstain from a "minor adventure" of the sort designed to arouse wild jealousy in her lover, and by 11 October 1917 was on the verge of breaking with Bertie. "I'm sorry I've understood so little," she wrote. "First, that you care nothing for me; second, that you don't believe in my love; third, that you hate my work. I've not known these things before. I know them very well now . . . I hope to God that we shall never meet again. I shall of course break with Maurice . . ."[33] Bertie rushed over to see her that night in her new attic in Mecklenburgh Square, where she and Miles had moved that summer, and attempted to make up. Five days later he analysed the problem of his jealousy: "Possessiveness in sex-relations is clearly an evil; it makes them something of a prison," he wrote to Colette on 16 October. "I must get rid of *all* possessiveness to you." Because jealousy robbed him of any sense of rest or peace, he could not be with her constantly—"only as much as will not leave me tired out."

Now that Russell felt "cold" towards Colette, he found his own solution to his need for peace: to be with Vivien, who did not exhaust him like Colette. Although he made his work needs his excuse, Russell was using Vivien to punish Colette for her intimacy with Elvey.

> I found accidentally that the Eliots don't want to go on being always together, & that she was looking out for a place where she could live alone in the country & he would come for week-ends. So I suggested that, as I too wanted to live in the country, we might be less dreary if we lived in the same house.
>
> She was pleased with the idea, & no doubt it will happen. I want, for every day, reliable companionship without any deep stirring of emotion; if I don't get it, I shan't do any more good work. I feel this plan may hurt you, & if it does I am sorry; but if I let myself grow dependent on you, we shall have all the recent trouble over again next time, & I can't face that, & I don't suppose you can. So I must have a life which is not fundamentally shaken by your moods . . .[34]

Although Russell presented his plan to set up house with Vivien as a new idea to Colette, it had probably been germinating in his mind as long as it had been in Vivien's. In July he had been shaken by the experience of mob violence in London, when "drunken viragos" with boards full of rusty nails attacked him in the Brotherhood Church, Southgate Road, Islington, at a meeting of sympathisers with the Kerensky Revolution. Shocked and frightened, he resigned from the NCF in the autumn, and began cutting his ties with pacifist politics. This left the question of where to live, and with whom, as Russell had to have the companionship of a woman in order to keep his demons at bay, and he never lived alone by choice. Garsington was no longer congenial; his sister-in-law Elizabeth had returned to Gordon Square from America, and this did not provide the quiet refuge he required for a return to his work on logic. Once more Russell started gravitating towards Vivien and Tom.

October found Vivien settled in the Surrey hills, in a farm four miles from the village of Abinger Common. Tanhurst Farm was in a little hollow in the hills, surrounded by a ring of pine woods, and broken only by a narrow winding road wandering down into the valley. It was "completely in a forest," wrote Tom, but after walking two miles you emerged suddenly on the top of Leith Hill, with a view over the Surrey and Sussex downs.[35] The owners, a farmer and his wife, did not normally take lodgers, but they had been gardeners to Lord Russell and the Trevelyans; Bob Trevelyan lived only a few hundred yards down Tanhurst Lane, at Shiffolds, and a word from him or Russell persuaded the farmer to take in the Eliots as lodgers. Tom and Vivien spent the weekend of 20 October together there: "It is the sort of country where old farmers touch their hats and call you 'gentry,' " noticed Eliot approvingly, as he prepared his lecture on William Morris.

On 22 October Vivien wrote to her mother-in-law, Charlotte, from Tanhurst Farm, explaining that she and Tom had decided to search ("probably in vain") for a "tiny cottage" within easy reach of town:

> The only way to do that was to take some neighbourhood as a centre and to stay there for a time, hunting all around. I spent much time and money in correspondence, trying to get rooms near enough for Tom to go up and down each day while I hunted but of sixteen addresses I had not one could take us, except this one—which we discovered, *when* we arrived, to be six miles from

the nearest station!!! It was a great disappointment, for of course
it means that Tom can only be here at weekends.

It was a disingenuous letter, for Vivien knew the Surrey countryside well
from her childhood, including the triangle between Coldharbour, Abinger
Common and Holmbury St. Mary. Both she and Bertie were aware how
far Tanhurst Lane was from Gomshall and Dorking stations, and that
commuting would be impossible for Tom. Vivien may have longed to introduce Tom to the area in which she had walked and sketched before her
marriage, one which was, "In my opinion, and in Tom's too, now—the
most beautiful country in England. It is all hills and miles and miles of pine
forests—with stretches of heath—heather and bracken and bushes—in
between. It is very wild although so near to London, and very *very*
healthy,"[36] but she had other motives for finding a sequestered spot in
Surrey.

Vivien stayed on at the farm, ostensibly to house-hunt while Tom was
in London. She had engaged a new servant to look after him during the
week, a hard-working woman and an excellent cook ("a most finished servant altogether"), and professed to feel perfectly confident that Tom was as
well looked after and fed as if she had been at home. The farm was like the
setting for a fairy tale, with its pine trees surrounding the large old house
which could only be reached by a cart track. Pigs rooted among the trees,
and the farmer's wife fed Vivien on fresh milk and homemade butter.
Vivien waited there, like Rapunzel in the tower, until Bertie, who was feeling deeply misanthropic and claimed he longed to mix with "very simple
country folk who live with the seasons," came to visit her on the Tuesday
or Wednesday after Tom's departure.

Bertie's arrival filled Vivien with joy, and her calmness seemed to
soothe him. Colette was still touring in the north and had written to him
that she wished them still to be together, *"but not as lovers."* Convinced his
relationship with Colette was over, Russell made overtures to Vivien, who
was, he claimed, very "happy" at the resumption of relations. Nevertheless
the unexpected result for Bertie was a sudden shame at the revenge he had
wrought on Colette, with whom he was still in love. "I intended to be (except perhaps on very rare occasions) on merely friendly terms with Mrs.
Eliot," wrote Bertie in an emotional confession to Colette on 25 October:

But she was very glad that I had come back, & very kind, & wanting much more than friendship. I thought I could manage it—I led her to expect more if we got a cottage—at last I spent a night with her. *It was utter hell.* There was a quality of loathsomeness about it which I can't describe. I concealed from her all I was feeling—had a very happy letter from her afterwards. I tried to conceal it from myself—but it has come out since in horrible nightmares which wake me up in the middle of the night & leave me stripped bare of self-deception. So far I have said not a word to her—when I do, she will be very unhappy. I should like the cottage if we were merely friends, but not on any closer footing—indeed I cannot bring myself now to face anything closer.

It was not the experience of love-making with Vivien in itself which filled Russell with self-loathing, only his betrayal of Colette: "I want you to understand that the one & only thing that made the night loathsome was that it was not with you. There was absolutely nothing else to make me hate it."[37] For once Russell's guilt seemed genuine: "I wish there were monasteries for atheists," he wrote.[38] "Such people as I am ought not to be left to live. I have spread pain everywhere—because of a devouring hunger which is ruthless and insatiable."

But if, as he said, Russell felt guilty over his unfaithfulness towards Colette, he displayed remarkably little guilt at leading Vivien on and using her as the tool for his revenge on the actress. Instead, he speculated on the impact his decision to abandon "Mrs. E." for the second time will have on her:

The plan of the cottage with the Eliots was an attempt to make myself a life more or less independent of you, but it has failed. If the plan goes through, I shall be more dependent upon you than ever. Apart from you, life has no colour & no joy. A sort of odour of corruption pervades everything, till I am maddened by nausea. I have to break Mrs. Eliot's heart & I don't know how to face it. It mustn't be done all of a sudden.[39]

His letter crossed with one of Colette's written on the train heading south from Manchester: "To-morrow I will be in your arms. Our big moon will look down through the window, and I think he will be glad to see me in your arms—I love you, love you, love you."[40] The intensity of Bertie and Colette's relationship, with its peaks of passion and troughs of misery, explains Russell's reference to "an odour of corruption" pervading everything, a euphemism for his revulsion at his own moral degradation: he had played one woman off against the other. Moreover, his letters had intended to deceive: "Pride has led me a strange dance since you went to Blackpool," he confessed, "but what I am writing now is the real truth," an avowal which Colette may have found hard to believe.

Vivien stayed three weeks at Tanhurst Farm, and Bertie may well have spent more time with her than the single night to which he confessed to Colette; certainly he had promised Vivien more: "I led her to expect more if we got the cottage," implies that Vivien was anticipating a full-scale resumption of the affair. But now that Bertie had decided it was Colette's love he wanted after all, despite her "insolent triumph" at capturing Elvey, he barely gave a thought to the necessary consequence: breaking Vivien's heart.

In the rapturous reunion which followed, Vivien was forgotten. She was still in the country ("so I shan't have to see her to-night") and Russell could meet Colette instead: "I am coming back to you to-night with all my heart and with all my soul," he wrote. "I want your hand in my hair—my arms about you—the love in your eyes . . . I have been numb & now I am not. O Love, my love, my love—B."[41] Since his flat was unavailable, still being let to Helen Dudley, and there was no privacy at his brother Frank's, the lovers decided to find a place of their own. "To-morrow morning at eleven sharp I'll be waiting on the doorstep for you," wrote Colette, "and we'll walk out together to find a home."[42] They took a studio in Fitzroy Street which she began to redecorate and furnish for herself and her lover.

Meanwhile Russell had an appointment with Vivien. His task was to shatter her delight in their revived romance. It was not an encounter to which he looked forward, but Vivien behaved with a dignity and understanding for which he was grateful: "I had a *very* satisfactory time with Mrs. Eliot last night—got out of the troublesome part of the entanglement by her initiative," he told Colette on 7 November, apparently thankful to be released from any sexual obligation to Vivien. "She behaved very generously—it is a great relief."[43] Colette may have wondered, like Ottoline in the past, why so many meetings with Vivien were necessary to release Bertie of his "entanglement," but then he had told her that breaking Vivien's heart could only be done slowly. On the 13th he was writing that he dreaded seeing Vivien that evening: "Nevertheless, the relief of having done something irrevocable persists, though I feel this is shameful."[44] Yet again Vivien acted with a generosity and diplomacy which kept Bertie within her orbit: "Mrs. E behaved like a saint from heaven," he wrote on 14 November after his second tête-à-tête. "She put away her own pain & set to work to make me less unhappy—she succeeded."[45] There were no re-criminations; Vivien kept Bertie on a long leash while she continued to hunt for a permanent place in the country. Although she seemed content to leave her lover to Colette, her rival may have wondered whether, for all his protestations of love, Bertie was not still keeping his options open.[46]

Yet again Colette began to withdraw from Bertie. Puzzled by her sudden and mysterious coldness, he confessed that he was now dreading spending a night with her (rather than Vivien). He suspected her of still being attracted to Elvey: "I keep wondering—I imagine Maurice cares less for you than you for him?"[47] Russell's suspicions were well founded. In November Colette discovered she was pregnant. The father was Maurice Elvey, who had shared a house with her, his leading lady, in Blackpool. Colette was resolved to have an abortion but there remained the difficult task of telling Bertie.

On 29 November Bertie and Colette spent their first night together in the studio in Fitzroy Street. Colette had bought a new bedspread and "the very softest Johnny pillow for your heathery head. Everything is longing for you to see it. And so is your Colette."[48] But the evening proved a fiasco: the lovers quarreled violently over Maurice, and no doubt over Colette's condition. Distraught, Russell asked her to meet him there four days later, on 4 December: "I may be all raw nerves . . . I desperately want just *time* with you. I would rather you did not try to talk about Maurice . . ."[49] Deeply hurt by Colette, Bertie turned again to Vivien. Once again he put the suggestion to her: could she find a cottage for the three of them to share?

In the tug-of-war for Russell's heart, Vivien knew that Colette's pregnancy by Elvey had given her the advantage. For a moment caution made her hesitate, but Russell's attraction for her was too strong. In an excited letter to her new friend, Mary Hutchinson, she wrote:

> Bertie says he wants to go shares in a country cottage. That will probably mean being out of the frying pan but *in* the fire! However, as I have NO money, and insufficient energy, the plan has its merits. We are going forth to hunt in a few days.

Vivien could not disguise her triumph at her victory over Colette, quoting to Mary a comment by Mark Gertler which Aldous Huxley had just repeated to her: "viz, that the Mallesons might be said to keep 'open bed.' It's true, from all I hear!"[50]

In the first week in December Vivien was able to give Russell the good news: she had at last found a pretty terraced Victorian house to rent in Marlow, not far from the river.[51] Russell was delighted; he planned to live harmoniously with Vivien during the week in Buckinghamshire, a county which she knew well, enjoying rural peace while he worked on his new book, *Roads to Freedom.*[52] The couple planned to leave Eliot alone to occupy Crawford Mansions from Monday to Friday. Eliot, hard-pressed by his assistant editorship of *The Egoist,* twice weekly lecturing, nightly book reviews, on top of daily labour at the bank, was relieved to fall in with a plan which in effect restored the *ménage à trois* they had enjoyed in Russell Buildings. Vivien and Bertie wasted no time in taking out a joint five-year lease on the Marlow house.

In a letter of 22 November 1917 Vivien had told her mother-in-law of Russell's offer to share a country cottage, "as he needs some quiet place of refuge himself." They did not intend it *instead* of living in town, she wrote cautiously: Tom found it essential to have his headquarters in London, but they all three longed for a bolthole, "somewhere we *could* go to at any time when things are bad in town. For weekends too."

Having decided to move in with the Eliots, Russell faced several tricky obstacles. First there was the task of moving his furniture out of the studio to Marlow, without letting Vivien know that he had ever shared a love-nest with Colette. Secondly there was the problem of stripping the studio of the furniture he had bought for Colette without causing a scene.

"Nothing but financial necessity would have made me suggest moving the studio furniture to Marlow—I don't want to tell Mrs. E of the Studio if I can help it—still less to take her there—but the saving of money is important—," a heartless Bertie wrote to Colette on 13 December. "I think perhaps I can manage it without telling her."[53] "Beloved, you must do just whatever you think best about the Studio furniture and Mrs. Eliot," replied a weary Colette. She had troubles of her own. The termination of her pregnancy had just taken place and had been "very painful"; Bertie came to visit her in the nursing home. "I remember being surprised that he didn't seem upset by my . . . abortion," recalled Colette. According to Russell's biographer Ray Monk, the philosopher paid for the operation, but Colette denied this, writing in 1975: "I had a number of abortions in my youth; but I'm almost certain that B.R. did *not* pay for any of them."[54] In keeping with her code of freedom, she believed that abortions were a woman's choice, and "need not be secret"; she chose never to have children and continued to make her career her priority.

"I got out of telling Mrs. E more than that there was furniture available," wrote a jubilant Russell, congratulating himself on having covered his tracks. "I found I would have died sooner than take her to the Studio. I can't think how I fancied I could do such a thing. I promised to see to getting it sent."[55] By 1 January 1918 he had moved to Marlow with Tom and Vivien, but was reluctant to "drift apart" from Colette, who "froze up" over dinner when he let slip that he was spending New Year's Eve with the Eliots at Marlow. "You had given *all* your *real* free time to Maurice (Sundays), & had only allowed me to see you at times when you were too tired for it to count . . . I can't bear the suspicion that when you are with me you are wishing you were with him . . ." Bertie reproached her, justifying his cohabitation with Vivien on the grounds that Colette was too "upsetting" for a long-term relationship.

> I come now to another matter: Mrs. Eliot. I am not in love with her, & I do not care whether I have a physical relation with her or not. But I am happy in talking with her & going about with her. She has a very unselfish affection for me, & but for her I don't know how I should have lived through the unhappiness of these last few months. I am intensely grateful to her, & I expect

that she will be an essential part of my life for some time to come . . ."[56]

Colette replied with a spirited defence of her own actions, coupled with an attack upon Vivien—and indirectly upon Bertie:

> You say she (Vivien) has a very unselfish affection for you. I'm quite prepared to take your word for it. I don't know her and I can't therefore judge in any way. But what I do know is that you've been, times without number, involved in the most complicated tangles with her (dreading meeting her and so on), which would seem, perhaps, quite as upsetting to your work as the things you hold against me. I also know that you quite frequently find your relations with her oppressive . . .

Colette argued that personal rage of the sort Russell was feeling could not be squared with her creed of freedom for others. *"Freedom for oneself only is no creed* . . . I don't feel personal rage against Ottoline or Mrs. Eliot." Mrs. Eliot might be an essential part of Russell's life for some time to come, but Colette had no such expectations of Maurice.[57]

But Bertie's sense of humiliation that Colette had become pregnant by Maurice in preference to himself runs through his letters. On Sunday, 6 January, he set out his vision of the future: "My work-a-day life will be at Marlow, with Mrs. E. I shall come up to London one or two nights a week, according to how busy I am. If you are prepared to give me those nights & a day, we shall keep in touch . . ."[58] There was a gulf between himself and Colette which Russell found impossible to bridge, and he clung to Vivien as a haven in the storm. "When I took up with the Marlow plan, one of my chief reasons was so as to make myself an existence in which I should not demand of you more than you could give," he wrote. "We shall be much happier with each other if I want rather *less* of your time than you could give me if I am always wanting more."[59]

Bertie's resentment towards Colette, and his continued co-existence with Vivien, only broken by visits to Garsington, where he had been working on his lectures on logical atomism, led Colette to bid him another bitter farewell. Predictably her letter provoked an emotional declaration of

love, written in the large scrawling hand which Bertie used when exceptionally distraught: "Colette, we *must must* not break with each other," he
pleaded. "I must *must* have you or life is hell."[60] She relented, and they continued to meet on Sundays for walks in the country, of which her favourite
was that between Dorking and Merrow Down. But his "work-a-day" life
continued to be with Vivien at Marlow, where a comfortable routine had
evolved. Russell had finished his book, and Eliot, too, was working well in
the peaceful atmosphere; he wrote a perceptive review of Russell's
Mysticism and Logic, which was published in January 1918. Russell was anticipating a productive summer working on philosophy in the company of
his prize pupil when a new bombshell fell. Ironically, at the point when he
was severing all connection with the NCF, and had decided to abandon political propaganda, he wrote a final editorial, "The German Peace Offer,"
in *The Tribunal,* in which he remarked that the American army might
shoot down strikers in Britain; on 17 January this article landed on the
desk of the Home Secretary.[61]

This final, foolish—as Russell admitted to Ottoline—act of defiance
would abruptly curtail Russell's Marlow idyll with the Eliots; but the damaging impact on the Eliots' marriage of his affair with Vivien was not so
easily overcome.[62] From Tom's point of view, she had cuckolded Tom with
"Mr. Apollinax," as Eliot named Russell after his visit to the United States,
a man old enough to be her father: "I thought of Fragilion, that shy figure
among the birch-trees," wrote the poet. "And of Priapus in the shrub-
bery/Gaping at the lady in the swing." Russell as Priapus among the
Surrey birch-trees, or in the shrubbery, gaping at Vivien, mocked Eliot
with his rude heterosexuality, his virility as insistent a reproach to the limp
poet as his neighing laugh. Outraged, Eliot visualised Russell dead and dismembered, "the head of Mr. Apollinax rolling under a chair . . ."[63] There
is, the poet implies, something mad about "Mr. Apollinax," who, like the
devil, has "pointed ears . . . he must be unbalanced," and does evil, a charge
whose accuracy Bertie himself sometimes acknowledged in those rare moments of insight when he believed that, like Satan, he should not be allowed to live because he too "spread pain everywhere."[64]

But Eliot's reaction was a complex one. Although his Puritan code led
him to condemn the very behaviour in which he had colluded, and to feel
disgust at Vivien's adultery, he had cooperated for the second time in a con-

venient *ménage à trois* which continued to bring him not only financial benefit, including the debentures which he was to retain in his name for many more years, but also introductions to key figures in Bloomsbury such as Ottoline and Clive Bell, as well as to editors and journalists essential for his conquest of literary London. Opportunistically, while he needed Russell's support, Tom had offered Vivien as bait. Eliot, as much as Russell, had used Vivien for his own ends. Now both men would together grow tired of Vivien, as together they had once wanted her. For Vivien it was to be a painful and double rejection.

There is a sense too, in which the most significant relationship in this bizarre triangle was not between Russell and Vivien, or between Vivien and Tom, but between Tom and Bertie. Sometimes it operated as a substitute father/son relationship, on another level there was an element of homosexuality by proxy in the way in which Eliot offered Vivien to Russell.[65] It is possible that Eliot made no objection to Russell's physical relationship with Vivien for fear of abandonment by Russell. Certainly Eliot's passivity in the face of Russell's sexual aggression is remarkable.[66]

That Eliot and Russell discussed Vivien in a derogatory fashion is evident in a rare prose sketch Eliot wrote for the *Little Review,* "Eeldrop and Appleplex" (September 1917). It is an autobiographical piece: Eliot refers to himself as "Eeldrop" in a letter to Ezra Pound dated 23 September 1917,[67] in which he said he had "Appleplex on the brain."[68] "I am, I confess to you in private, a bank clerk," says Eeldrop to his friend Appleplex, another version of "Apollinax," or Russell. The two men are close friends and live together, although their philosophical positions are dissimilar: Eeldrop is "a sceptic with a taste for mysticism," an accurate representation of Eliot's religious attitude in 1917; Appleplex, by contrast, is "a materialist with a leaning toward scepticism." "Eeldrop was learned in theology, and . . . Appleplex studied the physical and biological sciences," writes Eliot.

Eeldrop and Appleplex discuss marriage together, and Eeldrop the clerk relates the story of his friend, Bistwick, who has married a housemaid, "and now is aware of the fact"; his relatives are moved by "their collective feeling of family disgrace . . . Bistwick is classified among the unhappily married." But what does Bistwick feel when he wakes up in the morning? He feels "the ruin of a life." At this point in his sketch Eliot juxtaposes a newspaper report of a man who has murdered his mistress. It is another early indication of an interest in the theme of murder, particularly of women and wives, which was to dominate much of his future drama. The murderer, remarks Eliot, has crossed a frontier: "The act is eternal, and that for the brief space he has to live he is already dead." He acknowledges the truth of the medieval belief that punishment lasts for eternity—but he understands the murderer's motives.

In Part II of "Eeldrop and Appleplex" the two men are again in their South London suburb, discussing a woman called Edith, alias Scheherazade. For both Tom and Vivien the name "Scheherazade" would have conjured up images of Nijinsky dancing the Golden Slave in the Ballets Russes production of Rimsky-Korsakov's ballet in London in 1912.[69] *Scheherazade* was inspired by the sexuality and exoticism of *fin de siècle* decadence, and by assigning the name "Scheherazade" as well as "Edith" to a character which had elements of Vivien, Eliot was telling his readers that his wife was sexuality incarnate, a woman whose powers of seduction as well as her wit enabled her to escape death at the sultan's hands.

"Edith," murmured Eeldrop, . . . "I wonder what became of her. 'Not pleasure, but fullness of life . . . to burn ever with a hard gemlike flame,' those were her words. What curiosity and passion for experience! Perhaps that flame has burnt itself out by now." His words bear a striking resemblance to those of Vivien to Scofield, whom she had taunted for leaving her, the "yellow diamond" who burns with a "white flame." Eeldrop speaks of "Edith" with withering scorn: "the passion for experience" is "a creed only of the histrionic." Appleplex defends her, saying he finds she has "a quantity of shrewd observation," and an "excellent fund of criticism," although he cannot connect them to any peculiar vision. "Her sarcasm at the expense of her friends is delightful, but I doubt whether it is more than an attempt to mould herself from outside, by the impact of hostilities, to emphasise her isolation." Eeldrop replies that he tests people by the way in which he imagines them waking up in the morning; he imagines "Edith" waking "to a room strewn with clothes, papers, cosmetics, letters and a few books, the smell of Violettes de Parme and stale tobacco. The sunlight beating in through broken blinds, and broken blinds keeping out the sun until Edith can compel herself to attend to another day."

It is a contemptuous portrait which anticipates that of Fresca in the original unedited version of *The Waste Land,* and may have been partly based on Katherine Mansfield,[70] whose short story "Prelude" (1916) was the second publication of the Woolfs' Hogarth Press, and of whose sudden success Eliot was jealous.[71] Scornfully Eeldrop remarks that he thinks of "Edith" as an artist without the slightest artistic power, and when Appleplex protests, Eeldrop interrupts him to declare that there is no such thing as artistic temperament. What holds the artist together is the work which he does; by this criterion Edith fails to be an artist.

Eliot's misogyny, which found expression in his struggle while editing the *Egoist* to "keep the writing as much as possible in Male hands, as I distrust the Feminine in literature,"[72] would have fuelled his criticism of "Edith," but the virulence of this portrait suggests that his emotions were engaged. Vivien's pretensions to be an artist—a dancer, artist, or actress, in all of which spheres she had talent—had impressed Tom when he first met her, but after two years of marriage he considered her to be the possessor of nothing more than a histrionic temperament. Certainly, Vivien's ambitions were always more grandiose than her achievement, and by 1917 her adultery with Russell was the subject of gossip in literary London, and probably at Garsington too. For so private a man as Eliot this was deeply painful; he must have suspected that people were laughing at him. In addition, Vivien's erratic moods and non-specific, but expensive, ailments, took their emotional and financial toll. How often Eliot must have wished his conscience would allow him to leave the wife for whom he had lost respect. As Eliot witnessed the unprincipled behaviour of Russell, he must have envied the older man's insouciance, while condemning his amorality. For every day the knowledge must have tormented Eliot, like Eeldrop, that he had made a marriage of which his family was ashamed; every day he must have berated himself for his impetuous and unwise choice. If only he had chosen a different path, to be able to say when he married, like another character in the sketch: "Now I am consummating the union of two of the best families in Philadelphia." Perhaps Eliot's thoughts turned nostalgically to Emily Hale, the well-connected, well-behaved young woman who had participated in amateur dramatics at Harvard with him. Instead he was locked into marriage with an Englishwoman whom most observers considered vulgar. Was Eliot's fate, too, to be "the ruin of a life"?

Bloomsbury Beginnings

For many months in 1918, and indeed for the rest of their marriage, Vivien and Tom harvested the bitter fruits of Vivien's affair with Russell and Tom's complicity in it. For his part, Russell was forced to withdraw from the Marlow triple ménage so harmoniously reconstituted with the Eliots, when on 1 February the police demanded to know if he was the author of the offending article in *The Tribunal* which suggested that an occupying "American garrison" might intimidate British strikers. Forced to acknowledge that he was, Russell found himself summoned to appear in court, charged with making statements prejudicial to His Majesty's relations with the United States of America; on 9 February he was found guilty under the Defence of the Realm Act and sentenced to six months' imprisonment in Brixton Prison.[1] Russell at once appealed; urgent negotiations began for his sentence to be commuted from the second to the first division. He was obliged to spend less time at Marlow and, while waiting for his appeal to be heard on 12 April, again became reconciled with Colette, spending a nostalgic week with her at the Cat and Fiddle in the Peak District, before entering prison the following month.

It was a double blow to Vivien. Not only was it blindingly clear that she would always be second string to Colette, but Bertie's imprisonment ended Vivien's dream of riverside domesticity with him in the terraced house with the pretty black-and-white canopy over the step, at 31 West Street (the same Marlow street in which Shelley had lived), only ten minutes' walk from the banks of the Thames and Marlow Lock. There would be no summer days spent gardening—a favourite hobby—while Bertie wrote. Instead she was left alone with a resentful husband who expressed his stark feelings of disgust for his wife's body in the repressive "Ode," written in May 1918, the month in which Bertie entered Brixton. The

poem's title, "Ode on Independence Day, July 4th 1918," was a sarcastic allusion to his bondage to Vivien, while the accompanying epigraph from
Shakespeare's Coriolanus:

> To you particularly and to all the Volscians
> Great hurt and mischief

has been rightly described as a curse as much as an avowal of guilt.[2]

In the spring of 1918, however, Vivien proved more resilient than
might have been expected in the face of Bertie's disappearance from her
life—a disappearance which allowed a new chapter in her life to begin.
Vivien had recently acquired a new and stimulating friend who was already replacing Lucy Thayer in her affections: Mary Hutchinson. Mary
was the stylish, self-assured, unconventional but well-connected wife of
Jack (St. John) Hutchinson, a wealthy and eminent liberal barrister. "She
was," remembered Frances Partridge, "clever and plain. She always managed to say, 'I'm a jolie laide.' It was all too true—apart from the jolie part.
She was very neatly dressed—great care was taken. She was sharp and
witty, but not creative."[3]

The Hutchinsons lived on the banks of the Thames at River House,
Upper Mall, Hammersmith; there Mary gave parties which were the talk
of London society. She was linked to, although at first only tolerated on the
margins of, the Bloomsbury Group, by virtue of her liaison with art critic
Clive Bell, who had attended Trinity College, Cambridge, with Thoby
Stephen—brother of Vanessa and Virginia Stephen—Lytton Strachey and
Leonard Woolf, in 1899. Clive, with his pink complexion and sporting
friends, was never elected a member of the Apostles, who formed the nucleus of the group of friends known as "Bloomsbury." "They didn't care
about what people thought," remembered Frances Partridge. "They only
thought about each other. They were not deliberately shocking." Frances
compared Bloomsbury to a "fringed jellyfish," the fringes representing
those who belonged to "outer Bloomsbury." "Old" Bloomsbury was an élitist group; in 1921 Frances was struck by the Strachey accent, a particular,
languid, overemphasised way of speaking peculiar to Lytton Strachey's
family, which was adopted by other members of the group. The members
could be intimidating; Frances recalled as a young woman receiving an en-

velope covered with "beautiful handwriting," and realising that it was a letter from Virginia Woolf: "I was terrified."[4] Bloomsbury could sting those who came too close; it could even kill.

Clive's apparent lack of a first-class intellect disbarred him from the Apostles, but he was a founder of the Midnight Society, a reading group so called because its members met on Saturday nights at twelve o'clock. His acceptance by the small membership which included Lytton Strachey, Leonard Woolf, and Saxon Sydney-Turner is perhaps evident in an anecdote concerning one evening meeting, at which, after whisky and beefsteak pie, Lytton recorded of Bell: "He was *divine*—in a soft shirt, & hair and complexion that lifted me and my penis to the heights of heaven. Oh! Oh! Oh!"[5] But, according to Frances Partridge, many members of Bloomsbury found Bell and Mary, nicknamed the "parakeets" by Virginia, an irritating couple: "We'd arrive at the Ivy, where we often lunched," recalled Frances, "and I'd say, 'Oh bother! There they are again.' "

Mary Strachey Barnes was born in India on 28 March 1889, daughter of Sir Hugh Barnes and Winifred, daughter of Sir John Strachey, and was thus a half-cousin of Lytton Strachey; she was largely brought up in Florence by her maternal grandparents. By 1908 she had settled in London with her brother James, and had developed an appetite for culture and ideas and joined the Fabian Society. In 1910 she helped St. John Hutchinson fight the General Election as the candidate for Rye, Sussex. On the eve of the poll he proposed, and although the electors of Rye rejected him, Mary did not.[6] Her brother Jim thought they made a strange pair: "The one, smallish, palish, Parisian, pliable like a reed that never breaks, possessed of a roguish and naif humour . . . he, immense and Pasha-like . . . at once both judge and advocate, all rolled into one, sarcastic, mordant, witty . . ."[7]

The Hutchinsons moved in artistic circles. Henry Tonks showed a pastel of Mary in a red jacket at the 1913 summer exhibition of the New English Art Club and, after Tonks rented a farmhouse named Eleanor House that year at West Wittering on Chichester harbour, Mary and Jack took it the next spring. Clive Bell's affair with Mary began in 1914, following his prolonged flirtation with Virginia Stephen and an affair with Molly MacCarthy. Bell had married Virginia's sister Vanessa in 1906, but by 1911 Vanessa had begun an affair with Roger Fry in Turkey after he nursed her through a serious miscarriage. Two years later Vanessa fell deeply in love with homosexual artist Duncan Grant, a love which was to be lifelong, although she had to share her lover with David "Bunny" Garnett. It was in 1914 also that Clive made his reputation with the publication of *Art,* his first book, and he and Mary soon became inseparable. In July 1918 Clive took his lover to Richmond to meet Virginia, who spoke "perfect literary sentences." It was strangely like being in a novel, thought Mary, unaware that before many years had passed Virginia would have used her as the basis for the character of the socialite, Jinny, in *The Waves.*[8] Vanessa meanwhile took her revenge on her errant husband by painting an unflattering portrait of his new mistress, in which Mary's full mouth is exaggerated into a sulky pout.[9] Nevertheless, by May 1915 Vanessa was lodging in a cottage near Eleanor House with Duncan and his boyfriend Bunny, while Clive squeezed into a caravan in the garden in order to be near Mary. Bohemian tolerance had won the day. When Jack and Mary moved into River House in 1916, it was Vanessa and Duncan whom Mary commissioned to decorate it. Their work was featured in *Vogue,* for which Mary wrote on fashion and interior design under the byline "Polly Flinders."

Bloomsbury's disdain for middle-class morality had its antecedents in the Apostles society. By 1904 homosexuality was in fashion among the Apostles, personified by Lytton Strachey and Maynard Keynes, who had superseded G. E. Moore as leaders of the society. Of this change in ethos former member Bertrand Russell wrote:

> The tone of the generation some ten years younger than mine was set mainly by Lytton Strachey and Keynes . . . We were still Victorian, they were Edwardian . . . There was a long-drawn out battle between George Trevelyan and Lytton Strachey in which Lytton Strachey was on the whole victorious. Since his time, homosexual relations among the members were for a time common, but in my day they were unknown.[10]

Maynard Keynes was elected an Apostle in February 1903, and became Lytton's able lieutenant. The frankness of their correspondence, with its "frequent references to buggery and rape, its oscillation between higher and lower sodomy, was part of the new Apostolic code," wrote Strachey's biographer Michael Holroyd.[11] This frankness was carried into the Stephen sisters' drawing-room at 46 Gordon Square, Bloomsbury, where they moved after the death of their father, Sir Leslie, and where they began the Thursday evening *soirées* at which they entertained their brother Thoby's former Cambridge friends, including Strachey and Woolf. "Isn't that semen on your dress?" enquired Lytton of Vanessa, and with that infamous remark another barrier fell. "One can talk of fucking and Sodomy and sucking and bushes and all without turning a hair," remarked Vanessa to Maynard.[12]

Mary's "role in Bloomsbury has dwindled to little more than a walk-on part as 'Clive Bell's mistress' " writes David Bradshaw, editor of Bell's letters to Mary.[13] Richard Shone simply describes her as "a cousin of Duncan Grant . . . the lover of Clive Bell for many years . . . and a valuable patron of the Omega Workshops,"[14] but Mary's significance was greater than this. She was a key figure in the lives of Tom and Vivien Eliot over a period from 1916 to, in Vivien's case, 1936[15]—the trusted confidante to whom both wrote hundreds of spontaneous and amusing letters.

Although never a creative artist to bear comparison with the "great figures" of Bloomsbury—Roger Fry, Virginia Woolf, Vanessa Bell, Lytton Strachey and Duncan Grant (followed by a "sub-rout of high-mathematicians and low psychologists, a tangle of lesser painters and writers")[16]—Mary, as a successful hostess, straddled the worlds of Georgian society and Bloomsbury, and few in either world refused her invitations. Her guests marvelled at her dress sense and her parties. Mary in turn expected much of them:[17] "No-one should go to a party as he is every day," she wrote in *Vogue*. "He must be changed—touched by a little frenzy. Remembering that night permits of extravagance and excess . . . the witty must be wittier, the gentle more insinuating, the fat much fatter, the pale paler, a flirt more flirtatious . . . Like tropical plants all should extravagantly flower."[18] Katherine Mansfield was no more impressed than she had been with Ottoline at Garsington: "Oh God! Those parties. They are all very well in retrospect but while they are going on they are too infernally boring."[19]

It was not an opinion shared by the Eliots. For Vivien, Mary was an enviable woman of fashion, socialite and cultural touchstone. She cultivated Mary's friendship eagerly, and Mary in turn saw that Vivien could be useful to her. She showed her new friend Mrs. Eliot a short story she had written, inspired by the war. "Dear Mrs. Hutchinson," Vivien wrote in September 1917, "I am not sending back your story to-day, because I want to show it to my husband." The story ["War"] was "so vivid and amusing . . . You *must* let me show it to him."[20] A day or two later, Vivien returned Mary's story, telling her that her husband was "ever so pleased with it. He is going to write and tell you so. I admire you very much."[21] Shortly afterwards Eliot agreed to publish "War" in the *Egoist*. A shared interest in literature drew the two women together, and Vivien's own wit and vivacity appealed to Mary, who wasted no time in adding the Eliots to her guest list. At River House, Vivien's world began to open up in a fairytale fashion, as she and Tom mixed with the *beau monde*. Vivien felt like Cinderella, as she was transported from her tiny flat near Paddington Station to the glamour and glitter of Mary's drawing-room. The evening, she wrote, was "unreal, dreamlike," although at the same time Vivien was forced to apologise for "one of my indiscretions," towards Lytton Strachey. Vivien had probably repeated gossip concerning Lytton, to his annoyance, but it was only the first of many such indiscretions which were to create difficulties for Vivien with the Bloomsbury group. To become the object of Lytton's scorn was a foolish move, as Ottoline had discovered. "I feel it's my fault," Vivien wrote apologetically to Mary, "But I knew Tom rather wants him. He's lonely. How could he be otherwise? And Lytton is such a dear, *surely* they could be friends?"[22]

Vivien shared Mary's enthusiasm for parties because of her love of dance. In the physicality of dance she forgot the "troubles" which dogged her days and, although Tom could be leaden-footed, she knew that together they looked superb. The autumn of 1917, when the Eliots' fortunes took a turn for the better as Tom thrived unexpectedly at the bank, found Vivien often encouraging her friends to give dances. Their friend Arthur Dakyns was dragging his heels over arranging a dance, so, she urged Mary, "If he won't, I wish you would have one! I can imagine it being a wonderful occasion—You *must* like dancing." She and Tom were going to a dance that night in a studio in Kensington, wrote Vivien, and to another dance on Wednesday night.[23]

Mary's *soirées* also provided a valuable *entrée* to the world of wealthy literati. There Vivien met the Sitwell trio, Osbert, Edith and Sacheverell, to whom Eliot was first introduced in the autumn of 1917, when he was invited to read his new poems for charity at the house of another fashionable hostess, Sybil Colefax. "Osbert and Edith Shitwell [sic] will be there," he told Pound, wondering if he might not shock the bigwigs with "our old friend COLOMBO? Or Bolo, since famous."[24] It was just as well that Eliot did not recite his ribald rhymes about Colombo who couldn't "stop a-pissin" in front of the distinguished audience, including chairman Sir Edmund Gosse who publicly rebuked Eliot for arriving a few minutes late after a day's work at the bank. But Eliot showed no sign of annoyance at this reproof. His good manners impressed Osbert, and his reading of his satirical poem "Hippopotamus" delighted Arnold Bennett.[25] Vivien, meanwhile, was making friends with Edith. "I liked Miss Sitwell much better yesterday," she wrote to Mary, taking back her earlier poor opinion of Edith: "We both positively loved your party. I have seldom seen Tom so stimulated by anything as he was last night."[26] Soon she was inviting Mary and Edith to tea at 18 Crawford Mansions to meet the Pounds.

The gaiety which at first made Vivien a popular new arrival in Bohemia is evident in an undated letter to Mary which bubbles with high spirits as Vivien anticipates the summer in the Marlow house in 1918. She compares the "remote tower" of their Crawford Street flat, "secret and shut off" from the street noises which surround it ("You know I have *loved* this flat") to the house they have taken in Marlow, which she will like so much more if Mary will come to visit her and Tom. "You must come alone sometimes, when it is very *hot,* and we can be just three by ourselves," pleads Vivien. She is planning

> a very ripping weekend party, if only people don't mind the scarcity of furniture *and* the food. We could go on the river in punts in the day, and perhaps we should dance in the evening . . .
> One day you must try Tom's negro rag-time. I know you'd love it.

The Sitwells are coming today, writes an excited Vivien. *"He* says you are to give a dance!"

Tom Eliot had met Mary Hutchinson as early as 1916, the result of

Russell's initial introduction to Clive Bell that summer.[27] Mary was instantly impressed by the handsome and erudite American poet. If
Clive was sometimes dismissed as third-rate, too "wordy and gossipy" in
Ottoline's words,[28] to be taken seriously, no one could make the same criticism of the silent, brooding Eliot. Clive, whose thinning ginger hair and
pot belly reminded Ottoline of a balloon rather than Prince Charming, had
first been spotted by Lytton Strachey walking through the Great Court at
Trinity, Cambridge, in full hunting-rig, including a hunting horn and the
whip carried by a whipper-in.[29] He could not compare in elegance with the
dandyish Eliot, whose letters to his mother reveal his preoccupation with
fashion. Dutifully Eliot acknowledged the hand-knitted sweater and
woollen muffler Charlotte sent as presents, but he preferred his own recent, well-cut purchases: a light overcoat, bought "at Vivien's earnest solic-
itation . . . as an investment," a new pair of shoes ("fearfully expensive"),
and a new suit—"very nice, very dark gray, almost black . . ."[30] Like
Vivien, Eliot was prepared to spend extravagantly in the pursuit of fashion, justifying his new clothes by the argument that the price of wool was
going up due to the war. It was another example of Tom and Vivien's
shared tastes, as each dressed to impress their new Bloomsbury friends.

But it was not only Eliot's immaculate *extérieur pimpant,* as Aldington
described it, which so powerfully attracted Mary, but his personality. The
luminous light yellow eyes were as mesmeric as those of his grandfather or
his formidable mother; the beautiful but impenetrable features and the
controlled, muscular body suggested a powerful will hidden beneath fastidious courtesy. Eliot was, wrote Sitwell, "a most striking being."
Instantly captivated, Mary had invited him to Eleanor House in September
1916, an invitation he smoothly declined, yielding precedence to Roger
Fry's boating party.[31]

On 16 January 1917, when Mary was in London rehearsing in one of
the private, often transvestite plays which Lytton wrote for performance
by members of the Bloomsbury group, and Clive was at Garsington, he
wrote:

> I daresay you will be gay at your rehearsal, but I shall take care
> not to think about that . . . To-night when I return from my party
> I can either read Thucydides by candlelight like a Renaissance

grammarian or write to you like a Petrarchian lover: but you will be flirting with Eliot! . . . I'll write a better letter to-morrow night if I'm not feeling too jealous.[32]

Mary, meanwhile, was joking to Lytton about writing and relationships, and how the latter got in the way of the former. During the rehearsals of the play, in which both Eliot and Lytton's brother James had parts, she claimed to have lost hope of writing an "immortal work." How could she invent a character with her head so full of "charming and subtle flirtations," of the sort which she had practised with an elderly gentleman in the shape of Lytton? Shouldn't she always be wondering whether she was ready to give Mr. Eliot "a prolonged kiss," or whether James would expect her for certain to embrace him in return? "No! No!" cried Mary. Such rehearsals were far too distracting.[33]

The following year found her demanding a new play from Lytton, one with a part for her husband Jack. This play was not to be one of Lytton's usual transvestite farces like *The Unfortunate Lovers or Truth Will Out,* which dramatized Bloomsbury's liaisons of the moment and had been performed at a private party in 1914 at which Duncan Grant came dressed as a pregnant whore and Majorie Strachey wore nothing but a miniature of the Prince Regent round her neck.[34] It was to be for public performance, said Mary, and must be "fairly convenable—*no mixing of skirts and trousers.*"[35]

Clive Bell's insecurity grew as the months passed. "Darling, how delicious it will be—like a summer's day—when one has almost forgotten what summer is—to see you again, and catch hold of you and kiss you and walk along with you, chattering and commenting, and kiss you again," he wrote from Garsington on Easter Day 1917. "But I had forgotten, you have probably been kissing Elliot [sic], or at least squeezing his hand, and my ecstasies are a little mistimed." Frustrated at his confinement as a "conchie" in the Oxfordshire countryside, which kept him apart from Mary, Clive was, he confessed, only in a moderate humour.

What about you? O Mr. Elliot is come to call after his dinner party, and you are getting on very well talking about his verses. Pray make him tell you exactly what it means, word for word, as

they used to construe Greek in the Lower School; and a little later
get him to show you how the footman sat on the dining-room
table with the second housemaid on his knees . . ."[36]

Clive seethed with jealousy as he pictured Mary on Eliot's knee. Why did
Mary send her story to "Mrs. E," he demanded from Garsington on 20
September 1917. "Doesn't mean I hope that you're not going to send it to
Virginia . . . I wonder, what this great secret attraction in Mr. T.S.E., beyond his beaux yeux and his plus beaux vers may be, and in Mrs. Eliot too,
beyond her confidences: the plot thickens."[37] Three days later he was asserting his prior claim to his "dearest Polly," his nickname for Mary, for the
weekend: "I shall fix nothing with Vanessa till I know . . . I am very much
in the mood for a romance in spite of all your wicked sidelong glances at
Mr. T.S.E. and his obliging criticism; but if you can't choose but go to River
House I will acquiesce with the best grace possible."[38] Magnanimously he
conceded that Mary would do better to publish in the *Egoist* through Tom
than in the Hogarth Press, which was taken up with Virginia's novel
(Night and Day). Others, however, beside Clive had noticed Mary flirting
with Eliot. Katherine Mansfield recorded that Mary, at one of her parties
in June 1917, had "an *eye* on Greaves [Robert Graves] and an *eyebrow* on
Eliot."[39]

Eliot, too, found in Mary a cultured and sympathetic personality,
a woman with a gift for friendship, well-bred, well-read and robustly
healthy, whose capable and resilient character presented a refreshing contrast to Vivien. She was already the mother of two children, Barbara and
Jeremy, but remained *soignée* as well as sexually adventurous. Maurice
Haigh-Wood believed that Mary, like other women in Eliot's life, took the
initiative in her flirtatious relationship with the poet: "Tom was always in
demand," he said. "Mary and Nancy [Cunard] both made a pass at him."[40]
Behind flirtation, however, lay more serious business, on both sides. Mary,
for her part, was in earnest about her writing despite the "correspondence,
door-bells, telephone, sentimental journeys, and other extravagances"
which came between her and the immortal work she dreamed of composing. It was she who had first approached Eliot in 1917 to congratulate him
on *Prufrock* after Clive brought copies to Garsington, and in September
when Eliot read "War," he was genuinely impressed by her ability to get

inside the feelings of her characters, even if she had not quite got *out* again. "I like to feel that a writer is perfectly cool and detached, regarding other people's feelings or his own, like a God who has got beyond them," he told her, promising to publish her story in his journal.[41] The intellectual bond which developed between them was a genuine one.

But the maternal role Mary filled for both Vivien and Tom was paramount. Mary, like Ottoline, helped at first to launch the Eliots in society, manage their lives and straighten out their "muddles." It also amused her to be the confidante of both Eliots in their quarrels as each turned to her for sympathy. "Tom is impossible at present—very American and obstinate!" Vivien confided to Mary in March 1918.[42] In the beginning Mary was kind to Vivien. She genuinely liked her, writing to Lytton that she had gone out sailing with "my friend Mrs. Eliot."[43] To be "kind"—in other words tolerant—of Vivien's moods and muddles, was essential to the friendship. Vivien was afraid of those who were not "kind" to her, and it was a major cause of her later withdrawal from society. Accepting an invitation of Mary's to a party much later, in 1921, she invited Mary to lunch: "Do Mary, there's a child," she wrote. "Be kind to me as ever: Very much love—V."[44] And, years later in 1929, as the Eliot marriage disintegrated, Vivien wrote that she rather dreaded Barbara, Mary's daughter, coming to visit with her mother: "You must tell her not to be unkind to me, and that you and I must go on being friends."[45] In the event, Barbara turned out to be "charming."[46]

Meanwhile, Mary's encouragement, and the competence of Vivien's new servant, Ellen Kelland, prevailed on Vivien to invite the Hutchinsons to a lunch party in the flat in March 1918. It was the most ambitious attempt she and Tom had ever made, and the small dining-library was packed. "But it went off very well," Eliot told his mother proudly. "We are excellent hosts, I think, and our servant did admirably." It was easier to have people to lunch rather than dinner, he explained, because of the wartime restrictions on meat, but at lunch fish and spaghetti sufficed.[47]

There was another reason for Vivien's new confidence that spring. Her long-standing ambition to act or dance at last bore fruit. Vivien was given a part in a play in Hampstead, and was able to tell Mary that she had been quite busy and happy recently with her "suburban performances."[48] Soon she was so occupied with acting that she was forced to decline one of

Mary's invitations. On 31 March 1918 Vivien wrote that she had never disliked having to refuse an invitation so much as she did that one: "It was so tempting to me. Dances are so few, and as you know, they mean a lot to me," but she was still trying to earn an honest penny acting and had achieved some unexpected success. She explained that she had had to refuse the Sitwells the night before for the same reason. (Osbert was at this time living in Swan Walk, Chelsea, and entertaining frequently.) "I do not like it," wrote Vivien. "But we must do something, and I have been spending recklessly lately." She apologised for being "a wretched crock" who could only do one thing at a time.[49] However, it was unlikely that Vivien could earn enough by acting to pay for her impulsive purchases in the north London shops; certainly Colette never made a living from the stage. But Vivien's intentions were laudable, if unrealistic.

Vivien's admiration for Mary grew as their intimacy deepened: "I love you more than ever," she wrote. "I turn to you with thoughts of joy and relief . . . I am very fond of you and I think you are wonderful. And *wonderful* you are." It was a similar emotional attachment to that which Vivien had had with Lucy Thayer, who remained in America during the war, nursing her sick mother. Vivien was to give the name "Félise" or "Felice," probably inspired by Swinburne's eponymous poem, to the character of a close friend and companion in many of her fictional sketches; it is a name which bears witness to the importance of such relationships to her, although later Vivien would be horrified by Lucy's apparently lesbian advances to her. In Swinburne's Félise, a lover laments a lost "lifelong" love:

> Kiss me once hard as though a flame
>   Lay on my lips and made them fire;
> The same lips now, and not the same;
>   What breath shall fill and re-inspire
> A dead desire?[50]

But Vivien's affection for Mary was also founded on trust. Her references to Mary's visits to Marlow so that the three of them might be alone together demonstrate the happy intimacy which at first existed between Vivien, Tom and Mary, before jealousy came between them.

When Russell's prison sentence at Brixton began in May 1918, Mary's support was vital to Vivien. Although T. S. Eliot's name was upon the list of visitors whom Russell might see in prison, Vivien's was missing. Bertie's brother, Frank, Earl Russell, who had already served a sentence for bigamy in Brixton, persuaded the authorities to allow three visitors a week, who were to arrive together. Russell drew up the list of "compatible" visitors, such as Elizabeth Russell and Clifford Allen, ensuring that the visits of Colette and Ottoline were on alternating weeks. Apart from T. S. Eliot, other old friends on the visiting list included Gilbert Murray, Charles Sanger and Desmond MacCarthy,[51] but it was for Colette's visits that Russell longed most eagerly. Although forbidden to write to him, she sent him messages through the agony column of *The Times,* and soon Russell perfected a method of smuggling love letters out to her written in French, which the warders assumed to be part of his research. "Dans l'amour, la terreur cesse parce que la solitude n'existe plus. Il est difficile de trouver un amour réciproque si intime qu'il fasse cesser la solitude, mais il est possible. Tu l'as fait pour moi. Je ne sais pas si je l'ai fait pour toi . . ." ("In love, terror ceases because loneliness no longer exists. It is difficult to find a mutual love so intimate that it can banish solitude, but it is possible. You have done it for me. I don't know if I have done it for you.")[52]

Busily he began to straighten out his tortuous property arrangements, which reflected the emotional "tangles" in which he had found himself, and plan for his release in September. "I will not go to T.H. (Telegraph House) when I come out," he wrote. "I want to be with you. I cannot wait. I will make it all right with my brother. Here is everything cut & dried:

> You take my flat Sp 1, & let the Attic.
> My nominal residence is still Gordon Sq.
> ?We go 1st for 1 week to Ashford if they can have us & you have
>   no work?
> LET US NOW TREAT PLANS AS SETTLED.

His sister-in-law, Elizabeth, in flight, as so often, from her disastrous marriage to Frank Russell, decided to rent Colette's attic, and Colette prepared to move into Bury Street to make it ready for Russell. He had given notice to his tenant and former mistress Helen Dudley, to whom he allowed a solo prison visit to bid him goodbye. She sailed for the United

States on 15 August, leaving Russell temporarily remorseful over his treatment of her.[53] "I was upset about Helen Dudley," he told Colette. "I have
broken her life and I suffer when I think of it."[54] Helen's subsequent mental deterioration and breakdown present interesting parallels to that of
Vivien.[55]

There remained a final adjustment for Russell to make. So confident
of his love for Colette and hers for him as to write that he could "live
through fifty Maurices now,"[56] Russell decided to eradicate Vivien from his
life, finally and irrevocably. In July Tom sent a message to Russell that he
was having difficulty finding someone with whom to share the cost of
the Marlow house. Russell responded by asking his brother to tell Tom that
he would probably have to give up his share in it. It was a coded farewell.

Russell's sudden withdrawal increased the financial burden on the
Eliots, and necessitated their letting their London flat. Instead of staying in
Crawford Mansions during the week, Eliot was forced to commute over
the summer of 1918. At first he did not mind. The relief of being out of
London and getting away from it all at the end of the day was very great,
and he found the train journey restful too. During May and June he wrote
several poems, sitting in the back garden among the roses.[57] One was
"Ode," in which he alludes, in one version of the poem, to the "sullen succuba suspired," suggesting Vivien sighing gloomily after the departed
Russell.[58] The use of the word "succuba"—in the final version "succuba
eviscerate"—alludes to the witch-craze which lasted for three centuries in
Europe; sexual assaults by succubi and demons, who associated with the
devil at nocturnal witches' sabbaths, is a constant theme of the 1486 *Malleus
Maleficarum* or *Hammer of the Witches,* the handbook of persecution. In
this period women were generally seen as more sexually voracious than
men: "Of women's unnatural, insatiable lust," wrote an Englishman,
Robert Burton, in 1621, "what country, what village doth not complain?"[59]
In seventeenth-century England the word "succuba" also meant "strum-
pet" or "whore," a fact which would have been known to Eliot, whose
knowledge of Jacobean drama was extensive. If Vivien existed in a hidden
corner of Tom's imagination as a succuba, a female witch who threatened
his potency, might he not also have believed that her diabolical compact
was with Russell, who described himself as Satan in his own short story?

But any such feelings Eliot may have had towards his wife remained hidden to visitors. When in May Aldous Huxley paid a call on the Eliots, he found the poet "in excellent form, and his wife too."[60] However, as the summer progressed Tom discovered that the cost of the season ticket to Marlow was an added burden on his expenses, and he began to resent the hours spent in slow suburban trains.

During a summer heatwave, Vivien invited Brigit Patmore to stay.

The cab drew up beside an old-fashioned house—one of half a dozen or so with front doors opening straight onto the pavement, so no matter how quiet life in this little town was, you were right in the midst of it.

"Did you mind the journey?" asked Vivienne. "Such a funny little end-of-the-rail station! . . . Come upstairs. You're at the back. I do hope you don't mind. I'll be downstairs."[61]

After unpacking, Brigit went downstairs, carrying notepaper and envelopes. "Vivienne was in the sitting room which had a window opening onto the street. She looked well and young and said at once, 'I'm so glad you're here. Let's have tea at once. Don't you hate keeping to formal mealtimes?'"

Fortunately neither Brigit nor Vivien wanted to walk a great deal, punt on the river, or bother with people. "We lived seemingly by exchanging quiet moods, a little dreamily, a little melancholy. My writing case was old and ragged and apparently got on Vivienne's nerves, for she constantly referred to it as 'that horrible old thing,' 'your disgusting writing—flummery.' I said I liked old things and took it up to my room." It was an example of the obsessional tidiness and cleanliness which Maurice considered characterised both the Eliots.

"There sometimes seemed to be nothing that she and Tom did not take with terrible seriousness," recalled Brigit, who found it slightly exhausting. "It explained why Vivienne said, with a sigh, 'The frightful time I have with Tom.'" Yet, Brigit observed, Vivienne "could make him gay at times—even with a schoolboy sense of humour." Tom confessed to Brigit that one of their amusements on summer evenings in their flat in London had been to watch the two prostitutes in a flat across the road get dressed to go out or come in to undress.[62] Such voyeurism may have inspired one of the quatrain poems Eliot wrote that summer at Marlow, "Whispers of Immortality," although Ezra Pound took the credit for introducing Tom to the uncorseted woman of easy virtue whom he claimed was the model for the cat-like Grishkin, whose "friendly bust" promises "pneumatic bliss" in the poem, but whose female body odour also offends the poet. Even the "sleek Brazilian jaguar" says Eliot, does not "distil so rank a fe-line smell/As Grishkin in a drawing-room."[63]

In his garden Eliot brooded on death, and read Webster, the Jacobean playwright whose *Duchess of Malfi* was to be a potent source of inspiration for *The Waste Land*. "Webster was much possessed by death/And saw the skull beneath the skin," noted Eliot: "Daffodils bulbs instead of balls/Stared from the sockets of the eyes!" Identifying with John Donne, who knew that "No contact possible to flesh" allays the "ague of the skele-ton" or "fever of the bone," and dehumanising the beings about whom he writes, Eliot's sexual imagery encompasses skull, eye socket, bust, part-objects of whose Freudian significance he was aware, having praised in a book review the Freudians' study of "the influence of the sexual instinct."[64] In the final verse Eliot makes his own confession: "instead of circumam-bulating 'her charm' like a tom-cat before it mates, 'our lot' (i.e. 'our kind' of men) do not circumambulate such women; instead we 'crawl between dry ribs' (... read books)," argues George Whiteside. "One cannot, I be-lieve, escape the implications of the circumambulation image and the 'But our lot' phrase immediately consequent. They inescapably imply that Eliot is saying: our kind of men stay away from desire-filled women."[65] In his twenties, it seemed, Eliot struggled with contradictory urges, to confess and yet to repress his homosexual feelings: it was a kind of torture, but one which explains to some extent the obscurity of poetry in which so many se-crets demanded concealment.

Among those secrets was his grief for Jean Verdenal, to which he had referred earlier in "Portrait of a Lady" (1915). In that poem it is once again April, the month Tom associated with his friend's death. Watching the "Lady" of the poem twisting a lilac stalk from the bowl of lilacs before her, Tom remembers Jean, and addresses a silent remark to the woman before him: "Ah, my friend, you do not know, you do not know/What Life is, you who hold it in your hands." He smiles and sips his tea: "Yet with these April sunsets, that somehow recall/My buried life, and Paris in the

Spring . . ."[66] He tells himself that now he is at peace; but, three years later in 1918, in the Marlow garden, Eliot returned to the theme of Jean's death, writing "Dans le Restaurant," which, like "Whispers of Immortality," was published in the *Little Review* that September.[67] Eliot's water poetry is some of his most beautiful verse; in his treatment of death by water he returns repeatedly to images of drowned men, sea voyages and shipwreck, the source of which lay partly in his childhood sailing experiences, but which also held for him the deepest personal meaning. Distancing himself from his emotions by writing in French, he transposes the image of Jean— "Phlébas, le Phénicien . . . quinze jours noyé?" (fifteen days drowned)— from the Dardanelles to an English sea: "oubliant les cris des mouettes et l'écume de Cornouaille"* where Jean will be carried far away by the current. The poet's own cry is one of pain: "Cependant, ce fut jadis un bel homme, de haute taille."†

As the weeks passed and Russell's release from Brixton approached, he demanded that Vivien and Tom return his belongings from Marlow: "Has Eliot brought the things I sent for?" he asked Colette in July. "If not, please make Miss Rider (of the NCF) write to him & remind him. I shall give you the Persian bowl, if it survives unbroken . . ."[68] Having settled, as he thought, the problem of his discarded mistress, he was content to dream in his prison cell of the work he would do under the inspiration of Colette's love:

> I want to stand with you at the rim of the world, and peer into the darkness beyond, and see a little more than others have seen of the strange shapes of mystery that inhabit that unknown night— terrible shapes, which the touch of your hand makes bearable. I want to bring into the world of men some little bit of new wisdom. There is little wisdom in the world . . . I want to add to it, even if only ever so little.[69]

---

*forgetting the cries of the seagulls and the sea-foam of Cornwall
†However, he was once a handsome man, and tall.

He would kiss her lips until their souls touched, he told her, as he waited impatiently for his sentence to end.

But for Colette the temptations of London nightlife had proved irresistible since she had left the NCF. "Dashing around between the Carlton, the Berkeley and Ciro's was a sort of reaction from the very rarified, elevated atmosphere of the N.C.F.," she wrote. "I was always a person given to bouts—of one sort or another."[70] As Russell's initial mood of euphoria switched sharply to a depression which led him to threaten a hunger strike in July, Colette sought for light-hearted diversion from her lover's profoundly gloomy letters. Not only did she see Maurice Elvey again, but she began to dine with an American colonel by the name of Mitchell, whose appearance intrigued her, his "sad, honest brown eyes" reminding her of a St. Bernard mastiff. It was a sympathetic portrait calculated to arouse the usual suspicions in Russell's mind.

In July 1918, meanwhile, an event occurred which was to affect Vivien and Tom profoundly: the call-up of all Americans in Britain was announced. Vivien's reaction was one of panic and she wrote at once to Mary, begging for help. Within eight weeks all Americans must either have gone to America to enlist, or be enlisted in England, "presumably as privates," she wrote inaccurately on 30 August. Tom was "rushing about the embassy."

> You know we have *no* influence here, American or highish political. Do you think yr husband could give him any useful introduction, or any help? *Or can you?* I mean to get him into a job *here*—propaganda or something.

Vivien's fear of losing Tom communicates itself in her rising hysteria:

> If he goes to America he will not be able to come back while the war lasts. That means years. If he stays here he will be killed, or as good as. If we don't save him, he'll never write again. You know how bitter he is *now*.

Desperately Vivien asked Mary to "be a friend" and communicate at once with anyone who could help. "Get Tom at the *Bank*—it's quicker (17

Cornhill—Avenue 6430)." Finally she passed on Tom's plea not to let word of their difficulties be passed on to Ottoline—"This is important. Will explain later. Do do *something,* please. Yrs, V.E."[71]

"Saving Tom" in August 1918 became the first of several such projects undertaken by the Eliots' friends over the next few years. Vivien and Tom were both alarmed at the prospect of his being passed fit for active service, and Vivien pressed her husband to find a commission rather than enter the forces as a private. To his correspondents, Eliot stressed his need for a rank high enough to support him and Vivien financially. "With an invalid dependent wife it is obvious that I should suffer very badly on a private's pay," he complained to his brother.[72] To John Quinn, too, he explained that "my wife (who is an invalid) is entirely dependent upon me, which I believe makes a difference . . ."[73] At thirty Tom was of draft age, and as the date of his medical examination approached his apprehension increased. Vivien related the outcome to Mary:

> I am too restless and unhappy to write much. It was a shock to both of us that Tom was graded so high in the medical exam. I did not realize until then how much I had *counted* on his being passed quite *UNFIT.* I can't understand it. He took a very strong certificate from our doctor, and he had been *fearfully* ill over the weekend so that he was *obviously* in a wretched state . . .

Vivien was also ill, she told Mary. She had been to a specialist just before the call-up, as she was getting "iller and iller all this summer. He gave me a lot of fearful directions . . ."[74]

Vivien had done everything possible to prepare her nervous husband for the medical examination on 12 August, coaching him carefully for the ordeal ahead: "I write out what he is to say under every conceivable situation, but it always happens that some unexpected twist occurs which throws him off his balance in the entire interview," she lamented to Mary. "Tom is *fearfully* vague, one can never trust him to be worldly wise and to say the inspired thing or to suppress the unfortunate truth, you see."[75]

But Vivien's coaching was not completely wasted. Fortunately, as the Eliots perceived it, Tom was eventually graded unfit for active service on account of his hernia, which his mother had explained to him was congenital (he had thought it was due to an accident), and tachycardia. His call-up was deferred, affording him the time to go about procuring a non-combatant commission through his connections. Eliot set to work soliciting testimonials to send in to the Quartermasters' Corps or Interpreters' Corps; he had by now learnt enough Spanish to read a newspaper, had been having lessons in Danish for his bank work, and was already fluent in French and German, and had some Italian. An even more attractive prospect was a commission in the U.S. Navy Office in London, perhaps in the Intelligence Department. Eliot turned to his old friends Wyndham Lewis, and Osbert Sitwell, at that time an officer in the Grenadier Guards, to intervene on his behalf. Osbert spoke to Lady Cunard and introduced Eliot to Arnold Bennett via the journalist Robert Ross. But in the third week in August a cable arrived from Washington forbidding any more naval commissions for Americans in England. Disappointed, Eliot renewed his efforts to become a non-combatant army officer.

Friends and strangers alike rallied round in his support. Quinn informed Major Turner of the U.S. Information Department that Eliot was "a man of ability, a good patriotic loyal American, a man of keen intelligence and of the right age . . . a desirable acquisition for the information department."[76] The artist Edmund Dulac, who had corrected Eliot's French poems, vouched for the poet's knowledge of French, as did Arnold Bennett. Hugh Walpole, Ezra Pound, St. John Hutchinson, Osbert Sitwell, Sir Alfred Zimmern, Graham Wallas, the Fabian leader, and Harold Joachim, Eliot's tutor at Merton, were among those who wrote between 22 and 27 August recommending him for non-combatant military service, while from America his relative Charles William Eliot, President of Harvard, chimed in with one of the three American testimonials Eliot also needed.

The more he thought about it, the more attractive the prospect of such a commission began to seem to Eliot. There were many points in its favour. Not only would such a role demonstrate to his family and Harvard contemporaries that he was finally prepared to serve his country, but it occurred to him that it might be a more restful form of occupation than the continual grind of bank work, editing and reviewing. As an officer, he could find more time for poetry than as a bank clerk. Despite the warm summer, and a garden bright with foxgloves, lupins and larkspur, his and

Vivien's mutual ill-health had persisted at Marlow. The dissatisfaction with each other's company which inevitably led both Tom and Vivien to dislike their residence of the moment, however apparently suitable it was for their needs, stirred Tom to hint to his mother on 7 July that "we long for Bosham and the sea." Three weeks later, on 28 July, he stressed Vivien's toothache, and begged for funds to allow them to go to the seaside, where Mary and Jack were holidaying at Eleanor House: "I think a week at Bosham would do her much good, and if father sends the money I think we can do it."[77] It would put Vivien in shape for the winter, he pleaded, but advised his mother to write to him at the bank as he did not know how much longer they would be able to stay at Marlow. Economical with the truth, as usual, Eliot did not admit the fact that Vivien had signed a five-year lease on the Marlow house, lest his mother think a seaside holiday as well as a riverside one an extravagance in a country at war.

The army also seemed to promise an enticing avenue of escape from Vivien. Tom wrote to "Dear Mary" on 25 August (the first occasion he used her Christian name), saying that although he hated a situation which made him force his personal affairs upon his friends to the exclusion of everything else, and he felt quite as she did "about khaki; at the same time I think that this is the moment for getting into it to the best advantage . . ."[78] Mary helped him with the "strings" he had out, and as the flattering testimonials continued to arrive, joining up became an increasingly agreeable prospect. Patriotism did not motivate him, for his disillusionment with the war was total, but, so long as there was no need for heroics in the trenches, the vision of "more leisure for serious work and (more) freedom from anxiety in the Army than out of it" opened up a new prospect of freedom. Soon Vivien was agreeing that "nearly *anything settled* would be less unpleasant than the present incessant strain."[79]

In August Eliot also had a meeting with Russell in which he told him that he refused to be a conscientious objector, and asked Russell to add his name to those working on his behalf. "At present what I want are names which would carry instant conviction to *anybody*—celebrities, and people with official or social titles," he told Mary.[80] Russell passed on the request to Colette: "Tell me, did you accomplish anything for Eliot?" he asked three days later. "Don't bother yourself about it too much. I expect he will manage all right. She [Vivien] always gets in a fuss."[81] Colette offered to ask her new American admirer, Colonel Mitchell, who was General Biddle's Chief of Staff, to pull strings: "Abt. Eliot. I daresay it might be quite easy for Col. M. to help him with a job more suitable to the special Eliot talents."[82]

On 11 September Colette invited Eliot, whom she had never met, to tea. He arrived at Russell's Bury Street flat, into which Colette had moved. "I gave him tea on yr. kitchen table," reported Colette. "He sat with his back to the bathrm, looking as if just put through a mangle & come out all smooth . . ."[83] She noticed the same feline quality as Osbert Sitwell had, finding the poet

> reserved and rather shut up in himself—remote. Extraordinarily erudite, of course. His eyes were most remarkable. One felt they might spring out on one at any moment—like a cat. His manner was detached and there was a certain frigidity about him. But underneath that frigidity, one felt there lurked a curiously deep despair.[84]

By September Eliot had eighteen letters of recommendation. He was waiting for a post in Army Intelligence when the U.S. Navy Intelligence suddenly offered to make him a Chief Yeoman with the promise of a commission in a few months. At once Eliot left the bank and waited for two weeks without pay, only to find that "Everything turned to red tape in my hands," as he complained to John Quinn.[85] The promised post never materialised. At last Eliot was ignominiously forced to ask the bank to take him back again. It was an anti-climax which he found exceptionally irritating. The number of detailed letters he wrote explaining that it was not *his* fault that he was not able to make himself useful to his country indicate his sensitivity on the point: "Possibly in the course of time the army will discover that they need me to peel potatoes," he wrote sarcastically to an American friend.[86] The armistice of 11 November ended Eliot's abortive attempts to join the forces and left him feeling decidedly anti-American. Having seen more of his countrymen in the last three months than he had done for four years, he wrote disgruntledly that he got on much better with the English. "Americans now impress me, almost invariably, as very immature."[87]

In Trafalgar Square the crowds danced under the lights, turned on for the first time in four years. On the evening of 4 August 1914 the crowd had "cheered for its own death," remembered Osbert Sitwell. By 1918 most of the men who had made up that crowd were dead. Now "their heirs were dancing because life had been given back to them."[88] Ironically, Eliot's call-up papers from St. Louis, requesting him to report for immediate military service, were issued on 25 November 1918, fourteen days after the armistice, but by then he had already returned to his office beneath the London pavements. Unlike Osbert Sitwell, who felt the "startling joy" of peace, with its promise of deliverance from the mud, poison-gas and sodden trenches of France, Eliot's chief emotion was one of gratitude to the bank, who had signed his appeal for exemption and raised his salary to £360 a year. But it was hard to let go of a lingering sense of bitterness that the avenue of escape from office drudgery—and from Vivien—had been suddenly blocked.

Vivien felt equally numb. "I really have not been able to rejoice much over Peace!" she wrote to Henry Eliot on 21 November. "In the abstract I do, and I try to make myself *realise* it." She was afraid that conditions would be harder than ever for a long time. "Poor Tom's disaster over his Navy job very nearly did for both of us. It was indeed the last straw."[89] By December Tom was in a state of collapse after his "exhausting year" of alarms, illness, moving house, and military difficulties.[90] His doctor advised him to rest. Pound, newly alarmed, wrote that Eliot's health was "in a very shaky state. Doctor orders him not to write any prose for six months." Eliot temporarily gave up writing for the *Egoist,* and found a colleague to undertake his reviewing for several months.

At this point Vivien took control of the situation. Of the two of them, she was sure she was the stronger. "Tom takes cold *very* much more easily easily than I do," she explained to Henry. "Most of *my* colds are caught from him." Troubled by "splitting headaches" and feeling "very very weak" so that he had to postpone his lecture, Tom continued to worry about his mind not working properly, and to feel that his writing was deteriorating. Vivien was convinced that he needed "a complete *mental* rest." After a good deal of argument, she persuaded Tom to sign a contract with her, saying he would do no writing of any kind, except what was necessary for the one lecture a week he had to give, and no reading, except poetry and novels for three months from December. She also made him promise her he would take a walk every day. "I am sure you will be glad to hear this," she wrote in a firm letter to her mother-in-law on 15 December. "When one's brain is very fatigued, the only thing to do, I think, is to *give up* the attempt to use it."[91] Vivien was certain that if Tom continued to tax his brain and felt it did not respond, he would collapse in despair. Her priority was to avert a breakdown. Three days before Christmas Tom had a sharp attack of sciatica, and Vivien administered cod liver oil.

Her firmness had the desired effect. By Christmas Day Tom was feeling better. He put up a small Christmas tree, and he and Vivien gave each other stockings full of nuts, oranges and candies. He gave her a coal-scuttle for the drawing-room, and she gave him some books. Aunt Lillia presented Vivien with a turkey, which she cooked for Charles and Rose Haigh-Wood, and although the little party missed Maurice, who had returned from leave to Italy, where he was directing railway operations, Vivien organised a cheerful Christmas dinner in the "dining-library" at Crawford Mansions. Tom had responded well to Vivien's care, and on Boxing Day he was well enough to rise early with her to watch American President Woodrow Wilson drive through the streets of London to Buckingham Palace. It was fine and sunny, "Wilson weather," said Vivien, and she and Tom stood for over two hours waiting for the president to pass. Vivien was too small to see over people's heads, as the spectators were thirty rows deep, but, as the carriage came in sight, Tom lifted his wife up high. "It was a most moving and wonderful sight to see him sitting next to the King," wrote Vivien to Charlotte Eliot.[92]

Tom had attributed his acute anxiety at the time of the armistice to the strain of military uncertainty, but this was not the only reason for his nervous terror. Vivien admitted: "As soon as I can, I *really must,* I *ought to,* go to America. I say I, but I mean we." Overnight the armistice had removed their most powerful excuse for not visiting Tom's family, and now nothing stood in the way of the long-overdue introduction of Vivien to her in-laws. Despite Tom and Vivien's constant protestations to the contrary, there was nothing they feared more than a family reunion. "You are certainly the most wonderful woman of seventy-four I have ever heard of," Tom had written to his mother in November 1917; but fear was mingled with the admiration he felt for the formidable Charlotte, now President of the St.

Louis branch of the Colonial Dames of America, who never failed to reprimand her son if he failed to write his weekly letter.

Vivien was equally apprehensive. She could not fail to realise that her mother-in-law regarded her as a rival, if not an enemy, for having married Tom in 1915. She guessed that Charlotte held her responsible for her son's failure to return to America and philosophy. She confessed her part in this to Richard Aldington in 1922: "Once I fought like mad to keep Tom here and stopped his going back to America. I thought I could not marry him unless I was able to keep him here, in England."[93] In addition there were particular reasons for Vivien's nervousness over meeting Charlotte. First she was afraid of Tom's parents discovering her "invalidism," although she felt close enough to Henry to be painfully honest: "I am always now in such wretched health, and I am simply ashamed of it," she wrote in October 1918. *"I don't want them to know* . . . I wish something would bring you over here. I do wish it."[94]

There was another reason for Vivien's terror at the prospect of visiting America: she was afraid that Tom's family would consider her socially inferior. From 1936 Vivien signed her letters "Daisy Miller," taking the name of Henry James's heroine; she could not have failed to have read James's novella by 1917, when Eliot was working on the *Egoist*'s Henry James issue which came out in January 1918 and was written almost exclusively by Eliot himself. "Read *The Europeans* and *The Americans,* . . . and *Daisy Miller,"* Tom told his cousin, explaining that he had a great admiration for James.[95] When Vivien read James's tale of a fresh, innocent "child of nature," who attracts a stiff young New Englander called Winterbourne, she immediately identified with the character. "I'm a fearful, frightful flirt," says Daisy. "Did you hear of a nice girl that was not? But I suppose you will tell me that I am not a nice girl." Winterbourne, whom Daisy notices is as stiff as an umbrella when she first meets him, is too well-connected to contemplate marrying someone who is not a "nice girl"—and his suspicions of Daisy are confirmed when Mrs. Costello, who comes from a distinguished New York family, declares of Daisy and her mother: "They are very common . . . They are the sort of Americans one does one's duty by not—not accepting."[96] This helps Winterbourne make up his mind about Daisy: "Evidently she was rather wild . . ." and, as Daisy compromises her reputation by going out unchaperoned with young men of dubious reputation, he concludes that she is not someone he wishes to know. James articulated Vivien's own deepest fear: that she was too "common" to be acceptable to Tom's family. "Daisy" is the name of a common flower; the surname "Miller" betrays roots in trade like those of Vivien's picture-framing grandfather. And Daisy's impropriety was another characteristic with which Vivien identified, and for which her husband condemned her. Although amusing in other members of the Bloomsbury group, immorality in his own wife had shocked Tom; after the end of her affair with Russell he no longer trusted Vivien although he remained protective of her, weighed down by a growing sense of responsibility for her ill-health, and the conviction, as he confessed to Russell, that living with him damaged her.

The events which followed Russell's release from prison compounded Vivien's unhappiness. His rapturous reunion with Colette, his "lamp in this dark world," had failed to take place as anticipated. Although the actress had written on 7 September 1918 that she longed for the moment when Bertie would stand at the door of his flat: "I'll put my arms round your dear straight shoulders & stroke yr heathery hair, & kiss you like a starving man & love every bit of you,"[97] in the event she was caught unawares by his early release. Russell left Brixton three weeks earlier than expected, on 14 September, due to remission for good behaviour. That evening found Colette dining with her new boyfriend, Colonel Mitchell, at Bury Street. Bertie was mortified. A jealous scene took place, the holiday at Ashford was cancelled, and he flounced out of his flat to sleep at his brother Frank's.

Disappointments crowded in on Russell thick and fast. He was no longer welcome at Frank's as a permanent house guest. Ottoline declined to come on holiday with him to Lulworth. Plaintively Bertie asked if he could stay at Garsington for four days a week. He even regretted leaving his wife Alys in 1911, who had been a faithful companion, complaining that, "Of course what I *really* want is a wife . . . I need looking after . . . Since I quarrelled with Alys I have never found anyone who would or could take me away on holidays."[98]

As other doors closed to him, Russell, at Colette's instigation, turned to the "suburban" Clifford Allen, who was struck by his guest's self-centredness: "He is very child-like in his engrossment with his own emotions, virtues, vices, and the effect he has upon other people," he noted in his diary. "The oddest mixture of candour and mystery, cruelty and affection . . ."[99]

It was inevitable that as soon as Russell had quarrelled with Colette, he would turn again to the Eliots. Colette was annoyed: "Eliot's prospects are clearly of far greater importance to B than the damage done between us,"[100] she wrote to her mother, Lady Annesley. But although Tom was prepared to accept Russell's help in September, when military service still seemed a likely prospect, Vivien was no longer inclined to co-operate. Bertie had hurt her deeply by the cavalier and insensitive fashion in which he had pulled out of the Marlow house, leaving Tom to find a tenant at short notice. She felt Russell had ignored her at a time when she and Tom were caught up in the "storm" of problems over his call-up. And now, having decided to share a flat with Clifford Allen at 70 Overstrand Mansions, Prince of Wales Road, Battersea, he was making peremptory demands for his furniture to be returned from Marlow.

Ten days after disturbing Colette's dinner with Mitchell, Bertie repented: "My dearest, I cannot clip your wings and put you in a cage. Go back to Mitchell if that is what you feel right."[101] Colette, on the other hand, seemed willing to give up her American colonel. The usual reconciliation took place at Lulworth, and during a holiday at Abinger with Allen, Bertie took Colette walking in the same Surrey hills in which he had taken Vivien, retracing the steps they had taken together over Leith Hill. "Gomshall is the station," wrote Russell. "I would meet you there, and would lunch with C.A. . . . You can do your walking here, where it is beautiful."[102] He bought Colette a stout pair of leather boots for £3 in preparation for his Christmas holiday with her and Allen at Lynton, North Devon, and sent her 10s. "allowance" as well.[103]

On 26 November Bertie took Vivien out to dinner. Writing from the studio, he related confidently to Colette: "My dinner with Mrs. Eliot passed off without disaster—she has been going through a rest-cure—I told her I should probably not be able to see her again for a considerable time."[104] It was his usual brush-off until such time as he needed Vivien's company again, but it met with a different rejoinder than he had anticipated. This time Vivien was no longer prepared to be kept dangling at

Russell's pleasure. Disillusioned by past disappointments, she took the initiative at last. In January 1919 she wrote to Russell saying that she disliked fading intimacies, and must therefore break off all friendship with him.[105]

"I do hope you aren't very distressed about Mrs. Eliot," wrote Colette. "I really don't know what to say about her letter—except that I'm distressed if *you* are."[106] It was not perhaps a wholly sincere remark. Colette must have been relieved to have, as she thought, at last disposed of her rival. On 22 January Bertie replied that he was not in the least distressed at the break with Mrs. Eliot. He too was being evasive. In February Colette was horrified to discover the extent of her lover's domestic and financial involvement with the Eliots, as Bertie was forced to tell her the truth about Marlow. "Mrs. Eliot's country house . . . had been let at a reduced rate to tenants who maintained that it was only half furnished," recorded Colette.[107] The tenants were moving out, and therefore Eliot wrote that he wished to see Russell, as the house would be left on his hands. Russell then suggested to Colette that he might take over the house himself.

It was not a proposition which pleased Colette. It was difficult to give an opinion about Mrs. Eliot's house, she wrote sarcastically,

> mainly because I know so little about it. I quite see all the points you make, but I also see things against them. As her house is in a town, it wouldn't be a decent substitute for real country holidays; and I think your summer would be more fruitful for work if you were in peaceful country or in a farm by the sea. I'm not much in favour of business and property involvements; and I think you've enough of them already.

Russell was, as Colette emphasised, already over-extended. He was "not *completely* free of the Studio" (which was let to author Frank Swinnerton from 2 December 1918). "Were I run over tomorrow, you'd have this flat (Bury Street) on your hands; half of Allen's flat is still on your hands. I grant you that Battersea was my idea; but I didn't know then that you were still involved with Mrs. Eliot's house . . . I think you are really trying for two birds with one stone."[108]

Colette's judgement was more accurate than she realised, for Russell had continued to write to Vivien despite having assured Colette he was no longer seeing Mrs. E. Colette wrote loyally to Russell that "I think Eliot has no right to worry you. He's known, ever since Brixton in July, that he'd have the house on his hands. And if, as you say, houses are hard to get, then they're not hard to get rid of."[109] Eliot was furious that Russell had refused to abide by Vivien's decision that there should be an end to the relationship. He had begun to blame his wife's ill-health on Bertie: "It is not the case that Vivien 'won't reply'—I have taken the whole business of Marlow into my hands, as she cannot have anything to do with this or with anything else that would interfere with the success of her doctor's treatment," he wrote sharply. He had heard from the tenants who had at first offered to keep on the house at a lower rent because of the lack of furniture, but had decided on Saturday to leave on 29 March—"So after that date I shall be able to get at your things."[110]

"Sorry about Marlow but it can't be helped," wrote Russell airily on 27 February, explaining that he could not meet Eliot as requested because Allen had influenza and so he had been "forced back" to Garsington while he recovered. With breathtaking insensitivity, Russell continued to harass Eliot for his possessions, requesting that he return his copy of Synge to Gordon Square. "It is a book I value, & I had often wondered what became of it."[111] Colette, meanwhile, had organised the moving of Russell's other books, and his favourite "green Brixton vase" from Bury Street to Battersea in December.[112]

In February the meeting between Eliot and Russell finally took place, but not until the Eliots' servant Ellen, who was ill with pneumonia, had gone to hospital, did Tom have an opportunity to discuss with Vivien the future of the Marlow house. She was distraught at the prospect of losing it: "Dear Bertie," wrote Tom on 14 February 1919, "I am afraid that night I was only thinking of my own point of view towards Marlow. The idea of parting with the house altogether had not before occurred to me; with so many worries on my mind I lost sight of how attached Vivien is to the house and garden . . . I found she was extraordinarily upset at the thought of parting with it. She worked very hard at it during the spring and summer and put so much thought and so many hopes into it. The garden in particular is such a great joy and source of activity to her that now there are so few things she may do, as you know, I am sure it would be a mistake to deprive her of this interest."

Vivien was always thinking about the garden, said Tom, and even while the tenants had been in residence she had visited several times to look after it.[113]

Russell brushed aside Tom's concerns for Vivien and her garden. His mind remained focused on his own needs. On 19 March he sent Tom a list of his possessions he wished returned at once, asking him on no account to send anything to Gordon Square. Tom was to inform him when he was sending the things, and how, as "I don't want to have to go to Marlow myself if necessary . . . I should like the tea-table & coffee-grinder as soon as possible. Love to Vivien. How are your troubles?"[114]

The Eliots' "troubles" had taken a new turn on 7 January 1919 with the sudden death of Tom's father, aged seventy-six. "A fearful day and evening," wrote Vivien in her diary. She wisely withheld the cable until Tom returned from the bank. His first thoughts were of his mother, and he wrote at once to tell her how much he loved her. The death of Henry Ware Eliot Sr. heightened Tom's desperate need to prove himself to his family. Only the day before the news of the death of his father had reached him, Tom had written to John Quinn asking him to chase up the manuscript of prose and poetry he had sent to Knopf two months earlier. "You see I settled over here in the face of strong family opposition, on the claim that I found the environment more favourable to the production of literature," he wrote. "The book is all I have to show for my claim." It would, he argued, go some way towards satisfying his parents that he had not made a mess of his life.[115] His father's death made his task more urgent, as he explained a few days later—"This does not weaken the need for a book at all—it really reinforces it—my mother is still alive."[116]

Tom's sense that his father had died disappointed in his son weighed heavily upon him. In February he again had "a sort of collapse," nursed once more by Vivien as Ellen was still recovering from pneumonia. Eliot's doctor ordered him to spend a week in bed, where he slept almost continuously. "I am so tired now that it has ceased to be becoming," Vivien told Mary, explaining that she had not been able to get outside the door to telephone as she was nursing Tom continuously. "You see Tom depends on me for every meal, and I am cooking, cleaning and nursing all day long."[117] As he slowly recovered, Tom agonised over the failure of his relationship with his parents, two lonely people who had little connection with each other.

Fretting also over his inability to publish more poetry ("I have written so little, I have so little time to write"), he confessed to his brother Henry, "I feel very played out."[118]

The bickering over the furniture continued, and the Eliots' dilatoriness—as Russell perceived it—in this respect became the rock on which their mutual friendship finally foundered. Tom decided to keep on the Marlow house, in view of Vivien's dismay at the prospect of its loss, and told Russell he hoped that there would be fewer misfortunes in the future. He promised that, if the weather was moderate, Vivien would go down next week to fetch Russell's furniture,[119] but when she made the journey in April Vivien could find no one to help her carry the tea-table to the station. She wrote to him apologetically that she was going again the next day— "unless my cold turns to influenza"—to try to bring up the table and whatever else she could carry. Then there was the problem of getting "this first collection" conveyed to Bertie's address in Battersea. "I am sorry it has been so long, & I am afraid it will take a good many journeys before you have everything. So please have patience!"[120]

"I will call for the small tea-table at Crawford Mansions on Monday afternoon with a taxi—it can be taken loose," replied Russell in a frigid note to Tom, for he no longer communicated with Vivien. "Please mention that I shall be coming for it between 3 & 4." The triple *ménage,* which had once been so close, had finally unravelled. Once Tom would have turned to Russell, his surrogate father, on the death of his own father, but it was a role that Russell was no longer prepared to fill. Instead of benefactor he had become importunate and impecunious, an ageing Romeo whose prolonged and painful affair with Vivien had done irreparable harm to the Eliot marriage, and whom Tom wished only to forget. And, since Bertie had already served his purpose in Eliot's ascent of the literary ladder, his former student had few regrets over the withering of the friendship. Moreover, John Middleton Murry, the new editor of the *Athenaeum,* had just made Tom "the very flattering offer" of the assistant editorship of the literary weekly at £500 a year. It offered him social prestige, more leisure and more money.[121]

Vivien, on the other hand, was left with a lacerating sense of failure. "Like the sunshine," wrote Russell's daughter Kate of her father, "he could be loved while his warmth was upon you, but he could not be grasped to hold. Those who tried found themselves with a shadow upon their hands; the sunshine had escaped and was shining on someone else."[122] Like Colette and Helen Dudley, Vivien found it hard to dwell in the light without him. To be loved by Bertie was an intense experience none of these women found it possible to replicate and, despite his solipsism, they often remained devoted. Although Russell cannot be blamed for Vivien's subsequent mental deterioration, his acrimonious desertion of her destabilised her and contributed to her later depression and neurotic fear of abandonment. Had he remained her friend, as he did with Ottoline, she would have been better placed to overcome the trials ahead.

Now, though, a new triangle was forming. On 4 March 1919 Tom wrote to Mary, who he had heard was lunching with Vivien the next Thursday. Would she come on later and dance with him at a place near Baker Street, he asked. They could learn the new steps together, and dine afterwards. "I think it would be rather fun ... Do come."[123] In this new threesome Vivien was to be the dupe.

II

Possum's Revenge

In the immediate post-war years Vivien entered a new phase of gratifying social success. Those qualities which had attracted the attention of two of the most brilliant men in England,[1] her husband and Bertrand Russell, contributed to her popularity and Tom's. The Eliots' penetration of Bloomsbury as well as the acquisition of new friends such as the Sitwells and Sydney and Violet Schiff, is reflected in Vivien's "busy" 1919 diary: teas with Ottoline, outings to the Russian ballet with Sachie Sitwell for the first night of *The Three-Cornered Hat,* a literary party at Edith's, dinner parties for Aldous Huxley and picnics in Itchenor woods with Mary and Jack Hutchinson filled her often "perfect" days.[2] It seemed that Vivien had found the acceptance she had sought and, in her affectionate friendship with Mary, consolation for her break with Russell.

The three Sitwells, Osbert, Edith and Sacheverell, began to meet the Eliots regularly in the afternoons in "dank London tea-shops, seemingly papered or panelled in their own damp tea-leaves" near Marble Arch or Oxford Street. Vivien would be the first to arrive, and then Tom would come from his bank by Underground, and join them in consuming hot tea and muffins. "Tea-drinking is not a habit of Americans," remarked Osbert, who concluded that for Tom it possessed an exotic charm that it lacked for the English. But it was very noticeable how, though obviously very tired, Tom at once made an effort to stimulate the party. Osbert was struck by the contrast between his diction, the slow, careful, attractive voice, "which always held in it, far down and subjugated, an American lilt and an American sound of r's," the sharp observation evident in everything he said, and his old-fashioned courtesy.

In the early days of Osbert's friendship with the Eliots Vivien was kind and attentive to him. "I could not but like her," he recalled later. "She was slightly built, and had brown hair, and eyes which ranged from blue to green and were her chief attraction, being very expressive of her moods . . . Certainly her gaiety made her good company."[3] It was a description similar to that given by Richard Aldington in *Stepping Heavenward,* a satirical short story in which Vivien is lightly disguised as "Adèle Paleologue," a governess, and Eliot as Jeremy Cibber, a young American from Colonsville (St. Louis) in the Midwest who has come to Europe. It is Adèle's "deep grey eyes [which] were so effective under her neat black hair"; the "emotional spotlights" of her large eyes arouse Cibber's sympathy although the match is an unhappy one.

Aldington, who became bitterly jealous of Eliot's fame in the late 1920s, defends Adèle who he considers has, like the wives of many great men, been severely blamed.

> Enthusiastic admirers . . . forget that in these days the hero's inevitable valet is nearly always his wife. And they forget that Adèle was one of the earliest to proclaim Cibber's genius and to push him on in the world. Is she really to be blamed because she, an ordinary woman, could not dwell happily on the austere mountain heights of spiritual elevation? Could she help it if his presence— owing to the will of God, no doubt—drove her into neurasthenia? After all, it must be rather a shock to think you are marrying a nice young American and then to discover that you have bedded with an angel unawares.[4]

Aldington implies that Eliot was impotent, and the pair "though wedded in the sight of God and man, grew more hysterical daily simply through having to inhabit the same tank-like flat."

The Sitwell trio also often lunched with the Eliots in the "tank-like flat" in Crawford Mansions. Osbert experienced the same sense of confinement as Aldington in the grey distempered drawing-room, sparsely furnished and cramped. On the walls there hung a cluster of small outline drawings of elephants, executed in green ink, drawn by Eliot's grandmother. Osbert was struck by the "shrine" to Tom's family which grew in size over the years: old photographs, silhouettes and miniatures of the Eliot and Stearns families hung over the chimneypiece, until it seemed that something begun in mockery had established a genuine hold on Tom. "Vivienne's taste was not shown in the decoration of the flat," observed Sitwell: her early efforts to impress her personality on the flat gradually became subsumed under his, and it was Eliot's character which pervaded his surroundings.[5]

Noise they still found difficult to tolerate, although the flat was on the top floor, since both suffered from insomnia. There were the nightly shouts of "Hurry up please, it's time," from the pub opposite, lines which found their way into *The Waste Land,* and in the flat below the Eliots lived two sisters, "actresses," who occasionally appeared in suburban pantomime but spent most of their time playing the piano, singing, or playing loud records on the gramophone. About midnight the women would throw open their windows and call down to their "gentlemen friends" standing on the pavement several storeys below. This disturbance often continued into the small hours, interrupting Eliot's efforts to write or sleep, until at last, after several bouts of illness, he wrote to the landlord to complain. This gentleman came to see him in person, and reproved the poet: "Well, you see, Sir, it's the Artistic Temperament: We ordinary folk must learn to make allowances for artists. They're not the same as us!" Although the sisters prevented Eliot working, Osbert conjectured that they supplied much of the material for *Sweeney Agonistes.* Similarly, in this dark, cramped flat Osbert listened to two voices, one "querulous and insistent," the other, he considered, "patient and wise," which he later recognised in *The Waste Land.*[6]

In 1918 Osbert Sitwell had become an editor of the quarterly *Art and Letters,* which was financed by Sydney Schiff, his Holy Ghost, as he dubbed the wealthy patron of the arts who wrote novels under the pseudonym Stephen Hudson, and to whom he had introduced Tom and Vivien. Osbert invited Eliot to contribute to the new periodical, a compliment which Eliot returned by publishing the Sitwells in *Egoist.* The second number of *Art and Letters* in spring 1919 carried prose by Eliot and Wyndham Lewis, as well as poetry by Siegfried Sassoon, Herbert Read and Osbert; and in the summer "Burbank with a Baedeker: Bleistein with a Cigar," and "Sweeney Erect" were published. Neither Schiff himself, Osbert, nor the other editors, Frank Rutter and Herbert Read, troubled to censor Eliot's contemptuous anti-Semitism, expressed in lines such as: "The rats are underneath the piles./The Jew is underneath the lot./Money in furs."[7]

Anthony Julius, a lawyer and critic, has written that "Burbank resonates with anti-Semitic scorn."[8] Bleistein walks "with the palms turned out./Chicago Semite Viennese." He is, suggests Eliot, as parasitic and diseased as a rat:

A lustreless protrusive eye
Stares from the protozoic slime

These verses were written during the period 1917–22, in which the bulk of Eliot's anti-Semitic poetry was composed, years in which his long-established misogyny also took on a new virulence. Misogyny and anti-Semitism were historical partners in nineteenth-century Europe, expressed in the Symbolist and Decadent movements; and this historical linkage formed part of the context for Eliot's writing. However, Julius argues that Eliot had another purpose in combining the Jewish and the female, as he did in a string of names which resonate with disgust: Rachel *née* Rabinovitch, Lady Kleinwurm, and Lady Katzegg, "whose names are ugly and betray their owners." Unlike the women in *Prufrock,* however, "these Jews do not intimidate. By making women Jewish, Eliot overcame them; by subordinating them to Jews, he diminished them."[9]

Vivien seems to have shared Eliot's prejudices, which were deeply ingrained in British society at the time: Virginia Stephen was conscious of her own anti-Semitism when she married Leonard Woolf. Vivien later reviewed in the *Criterion* a book by G. B. Stern, *The Tents of Israel,* under one of her many pen-names, Irene Fassett, and stated that "no Jew can ever be a great artist:" the best a Jew can do by dint of cleverness and hard work is "a marvellous imitation of art."[10] She would have read "Burbank," for Tom respected her literary judgement but in any case, as a future member of the British League of Fascists, Vivien was unlikely to have made any objection.[11] Neither she nor Tom saw any contradiction in accepting the hospitality of Jews such as Schiff, who with his invalid wife Violet became close friends of the Eliots, or Leonard Woolf in 1919, and writing (in "Gerontion"):

. . . the jew squats on the window-sill, the owner,
Spawned in some estaminet of Antwerp,
Blistered in Brussels . . .[12]

As Eliot's fame spread, even more illustrious literary allies than the
Sitwells decided they wished to know the poet. Virginia and Leonard
Woolf had made their first approach in the autumn of 1918 after reading
Prufrock and Other Observations: they invited Eliot to Hogarth House,
Richmond, and offered to publish his new poetry under the imprint of
their fledgling Hogarth Press. It was to be a prestige project for the Woolfs,
who considered it their best work yet, owing to the quality of the ink as
well as of the poetry.[13] When Eliot visited the Woolfs on 15 November, he
impressed Virginia as

> a polished, cultivated, elaborate young American, talking so slow,
> that each word seems to have special finish allotted it. But beneath
> the surface, it is fairly evident that he is very intellectual, intoler-
> ant, with strong views of his own, & a poetic creed.

Virginia disagreed with Eliot's view that Ezra Pound and Wyndham
Lewis[14] were "very interesting" writers, and was horrified that he admired
James Joyce, whose novel *Ulysses* she considered "filth" and had already refused to publish.[15] But these differences did not prevent the Woolfs' printing nearly 250 copies of Eliot's poems on 12 May 1919 at 2/6d each.[16]

The publication of *Poems* was an important landmark in Eliot's ascent
of the literary foothills, although he was still far from being the social lion
that Lytton Strachey had become with the publication of *Eminent
Victorians* in 1919. Such recognition perhaps gave Eliot the confidence to
turn down Middleton Murry's offer of the assistant editorship of the
Athenaeum at £500 per annum, but it was far from being the only reason
for his decision. Eliot's inherent caution led him to distrust the prospects of
a new literary weekly, for the paper had lost its character as a monthly
under the old ownership and there was no guarantee, even with Murry at
the helm, that it would succeed. In that case he calculated that he would be
left in difficulties after his two-year contract expired. But Eliot's chief reason for turning down the offer, despite the higher salary, was the "drudg-

ery" of journalism. "The constant turning out of 'copy' for a weekly paper would exhaust me for genuine creative work," he wrote to his mother on 29 March 1919.[17] Finance he could attend to "mechanically" but review-writing he could not, and so he chose to remain in the bank, where a new department was being opened which offered him the chance of more interesting economic work connected with the German war debt, and where he was certain of regular increases in salary. He was earning £360 a year, and was now, he told his mother, almost self-supporting.

Eliot's rejection of Murry's offer appeared a strange decision to the couple's friends, and it is one for which Vivien has been blamed. One of the charges laid against Vivien was that she pressed Tom to stay at Lloyds with its promise of a pension and medical benefits.[18] In fact, if Vivien had had her way Eliot would have left the bank in 1919. Nevertheless, Osbert Sitwell represented the commonly held point of view when he wrote:

> Never was there such a waste of a poet's days. In order to find money for the household, he was obliged to follow the, to him, exhausting and uncongenial profession of a clerk in Lloyd's Bank in the City.

Aldington was scornful rather than sympathetic. "With superb energy, Cibber made a decision—and what a mad world it was!—accepted work as the guiding spirit of a haberdashery department, where his courteous manners and distinguished appearance found full scope."[19] Yet in 1919 Vivien was in favour of Tom accepting the post Murry had offered him on the *Athenaeum,* as Eliot confirmed to Aldington in 1922.[20] It was Tom's choice to stay at Lloyds.

During 1919 Vivien's health was generally good. She was fit and extrovert enough to socialise four nights a week; in one week in November she had the Pounds to dinner on Monday, Ottoline on Tuesday, dined at Pagani's and went to a concert given by the Syncopated Orchestra on Wednesday, had tea-parties on Thursday and Friday, entertained the Pounds to dinner again on Friday, and had Schiff in for coffee afterwards, attended her dress-making class and went for the weekend to the musician Arnold Dolmetsch and his family at Haslemere.[21] Within the household

Fleet Street, the birthplace of Charles Haigh-Wood in Bury, Lancashire.
Vivienne was born in nearby Knowsley Street.

Rose Esther Haigh-Wood with Vivienne in
1898. Maurice, age three, stands behind.

Family group: Charles Haigh-Wood
with Rose, Vivie and Maurice.

(*right*) *The Peace Offering*, 1900:
a portrait of Vivienne and Maurice by
their father, Charles Haigh-Wood, at
their house in Hampstead. Maurice has
torn up Vivie's reading book and offers
her an apple as a peace offering. Vivie
often modelled for her father, whose
paintings were reproduced as greeting
cards.

(*below*) Vivienne in 1900. As a child she
was ill with TB of the bone.

(*below right*) Vivie visiting Maurice, age
seventeen, at Malvern College.

Henry Ware Eliot Sr.,
brick manufacturer.
He was profoundly deaf.

Charlotte Champe Eliot;
Thomas Stearns was her
seventh child.

Tom Eliot at four years old.

Tom Eliot with his mother, his sister Margaret and cousin Henrietta
outside 2635 Locust Street, St. Louis, 1896.

(*left*) T. S. Eliot as a young man.

(*below left*) Jean Verdenal, Eliot's close companion in Paris.

(*below right*) The announcement of the marriage of Thomas Eliot and Vivien Haigh-Wood in the *St. Louis Globe Democrat*, 16 July 1915.

THOMAS ELIOT OF ST. LOUIS WEDS ABROAD

Bride of Oxford Student Was Miss Vivien Haigh-Wood, Daughter of a Member of Royal Academy of Arts.

Announcement of the marriage of Thomas Stearns Eliot, son of Mr. and Mrs. Henry W. Eliot of 4446 Westminster place, to Miss Vivien Haigh-Wood in London, England, June 26, was made yesterday by the Eliots, who are at their summer home in Gloucester, Mass.

Henry W. Eliot, Jr., said last night that he had been notified of his brother's marriage, through his mother. He said that Thomas Eliot had been in London taking a year's course in philosophy at the Oxford University. He said he knew little of Miss Haigh-Wood, but understood that she was a daughter of a member of the Royal Academy of Arts.

Eliot, who is 26 years old, was graduated from Smith Academy in 1905 and Harvard in 1910. He went to London more than a year ago and entered Oxford. Eliot's father is chairman of the Board of Directors of the Hydraulic Press Brick Company.

A stylish couple. Tom and Vivien in the early years of their marriage, *c.* 1920.

Tom has gone to America without me, & arrived yesterday. Rather unwise perhaps to leave so attractive a wife alone & other new devices!. However — I did not at all want to go — I am much too frightened of the voyage & the submarines — & preferred to remain & play my own little games alone.

Tom is supposed to be coming back by September 1st, & after we have had a second honeymoon! we shall have either to a house or a flat of our own — in London of course. It is very nice being Mrs Stearns-Eliot (notice the hyphen) I am very popular with Tom's friends — & who do you think in particular? No less a person than Bertrand Russell!! He is all over me, is Bertie, & I simply love him. I am dining with him next week. I see a good deal of the Pounds, of course, & between ourselves, find them rather boring.

Two extracts from a letter from Vivien to Scofield Thayer, 2 August 1915, announcing Bertrand Russell's interest in her.

"Mr. Apollinax": Bertrand Russell, Lytton Strachey and Lady Ottoline Morrell, at the time of Russell's affair with Vivien, 1916.

Bertrand Russell in 1916. Vivien worked as his secretary during his campaign against conscription in the First World War.

Lady Constance Malleson, the actress "Colette O'Niel," who was Russell's mistress.

Maurice Haigh-Wood, age twenty-four.

American poet and critic Ezra Pound
sitting on his bed in his Paris studio.

Mark Gertler (*behind*), Philip Morrell, Lady
Ottoline and Vivien at Garsington, August 1921.

Vivien, in dance costume, playing croquet.

Ottoline and T. S. Eliot at Garsington.

her role was often that of caregiver rather than patient. For several weeks in February and March Vivien had nursed Ellen, her servant, through the first stages of pneumonia ("very fatiguing and unpleasant" in Tom's eyes) as well as caring for Tom himself, who had collapsed at the news of his father's death. She also nursed her mother, who had no servants and was ill in bed. In addition, she was responsible for all the housework and laundry. "Vivien is very tired and looks very ill," Tom told Henry on 27 February:[22] "I have been and am still very afraid of Vivien's breaking down," he confessed in a letter to his mother on the same day—as so often, projecting his own fears of nervous collapse onto Vivien.[23]

Vivien nevertheless found both time and energy for pleasure. It was the birth of the jazz age and, only a few days after Tom's letters to his family, on 2 March, her diary records an outing to the Elysée Galleries to dance with a friend named Hawkinson and "the boy," with whom she had "a splendid time."[24] The next day she was very tired, but still went over to Compayne Gardens to lunch with her parents and help them, before hurrying back to "get T's meal" and doing housework all evening. At the beginning of November she was nursing their friend and neighbour, Arthur Dakyns, at Marlow with Tom, returning to London when her aunt Emily, Charles Haigh-Wood's sister, fell seriously ill, taking her mother to Victoria Station, travelling to Eastbourne for Emily's funeral, and still finding time for another outing to the dance halls the next day. "Went to dance at Caxton Hall with Freddy," recorded Vivien. "Much against the grain, but enjoyed it."[25]

Vivien's courage and physical stamina in a crisis is underlined by an admiring letter of Tom's which relates the events surrounding a sailing expedition which took place in Chichester harbour in June 1919. Eliot and Dakyns had driven down for the weekend in Dakyns' motor car to Bosham, where Vivien was spending the summer. On the Sunday the party hired a boat and sailed with Sacheverell Sitwell and Mary Hutchinson down Chichester harbour to Wittering, where the Hutchinsons lived. There they had a picnic lunch, and Vivien took some photographs. The sailing, confessed Tom, was "rather disastrous." There was no proper place to land and the crew was forced to put the boat up on a beach. Tom was at the helm and, attempting to sail into the wind, got stuck on a sandbank on a falling tide. Soon they were left "high, but not very dry." "Captain" Eliot broke the boat hook trying to push off, eventually throwing out an anchor and wading ashore with his crew on planks because of the soft sinking mud. "Vivien is splendid in a boat, she took off her stockings and jumped off and tried to push," Tom told his mother.[26] It seems he played the incident down, for Sacheverell later often related the tale of how he and Eliot nearly drowned in Chichester harbour.

On occasions Vivien ventured alone in a sailing dinghy to visit Mary at Eleanor, with apparently more attention to the tide and fewer accidents than her husband. On one "wonderful day" in July she started in the boat early, rowed from Bosham all the way to Eleanor to pick up Mary, and sailed to Hayling Island, where they bathed and picnicked together and, as they lay on the sand, Mary told Vivien the story of her life; afterwards Vivien landed Mary back at Itchenor before sailing the boat back to Bosham at 6 p.m. Although she was exhausted by the outing, Mary had been "delightful."[27] The normality, even heartiness revealed in Vivien's diary, in which she records swimming even when it is very cold, sailing and walking, getting "soaked" in damp woods, but having successful picnics[28] contradicts the myth of her constant illness.

Anne Olivier Bell, editor of Virginia Woolf's diaries, comments with reference to a remark of Virginia's that Vivien looked "washed-out" in April: "She suffered increasingly from psychotic illness and this began to show in her appearance."[29] Judging retrospectively, many commentators forgot that Vivien did enjoy periods of good health during the earlier years of her marriage. Nor should the evidence of a novelist such as Woolf, who had her own reasons for distancing herself from Vivien, be accepted at face value. In 1919 Vivien speaks for herself. It is the only year of her marriage for which her diary survives, and it serves as a warning against accepting the judgement of biased observers.

Meanwhile Tom, free of the daily intrigues and demands of journalism, was able to write what he wanted. "There is a small and select public which regards me as the best living critic, as well as the best living poet in England," he proudly informed his mother. As contributor to the *Athenaeum,* where Murry, the editor-in-chief, was one of his most cordial admirers, as assistant editor of the *Egoist*[30] and with the new outlet of *Art and Letters,* which was glad to take anything he gave it, Eliot's position was a privileged one. He had more than enough prestige to satisfy him, he told Charlotte: "I really think that I have far more *influence* on English letters than any other American has ever had, unless it be Henry James. I know a great many people, but there are many more who would like to know me, and I can remain isolated and detached. All this sounds very conceited but it is true . . ."[31]

To his brother Henry, Eliot repeated Vivien's argument that he must conserve his creative energy for his own writing: "My reputation is built on writing very little, but very good." He calculated that he probably had more influence, power and distinction *"outside* the journalistic struggle" than within it.[32] To J. H. Woods he made the point that a poet's best work, the only work that counts in the end, is written for oneself. If one had to earn a living, therefore, the safest occupation was that most remote from the arts. Eliot's carefully thought-out strategy, designed to keep up his reputation as the "best living" critic and poet, was to keep his public hungry: his plan was to release only two or three new poems a year. The only thing that mattered was that these should be perfect in their kind, so that each should be an event.[33]

Money was also a factor in Eliot's decision. He was "deeply affected," believed Stephen Spender, "by the fact that his father left his family money in trust so that if he, Tom Eliot, died, it could not be inherited by his wife."[34] Henry Ware Eliot Sr. did not leave Tom a direct legacy, but this did not mean his son derived no benefit from the will. Eliot's habit of financial dependency on others continued after 1918, just as it had when, writes Paul Delany, he "came close to being paid for being a complaisant husband" by Russell. Delany estimates that Eliot and Vivien received about £100 a year from Charlotte and Henry from 1916 to 1919; in this period they "received twice the amount of Tom's earnings as gifts from his parents, Vivien's parents, and Russell." On Henry Ware Eliot's death on 7 January 1919, he left his silver cane to Tom, and about $3,000 worth of shares in the Hydraulic Press-Brick Company to each of three daughters and the residue to his widow to provide for his two sons. Delany writes that the probate value of the estate was $258,159 net, divided between $117,807 in shares (mostly in Hydraulic Press-Brick preferred) and

$128,000 in real estate. "As befitted a brick-maker, Henry Ware Eliot had been an inveterate buyer of building-lots in St. Louis,"[35] which featured in his son's early poems.

Soon after Henry Ware Eliot's death, his elder son, Henry Ware Eliot Jr., began selling off the family shares in the Hydraulic Press-Brick Company and moving into a portfolio of stocks and tax-exempt bonds in order to provide income for his mother and his siblings. Charlotte Eliot gave each of her six children 225 preferred shares of Hydraulic Press-Brick early in 1920, when they had already risen from the $30 probate valuation to $55 because of the postwar housing boom. Tom sold his shares in November at that price, and turned over $12,000 to Henry to invest for him. Henry invested the money at seven per cent. Charlotte gave Tom another 120 shares in the summer of 1923, which he sold at $64. "He now had an inherited capital of about $19,000, on which he earned $1400 a year." When his mother died Tom had expectations of receiving about another $35,000.

Charlotte's disapproval of Vivien was thus "the only blemish on Tom's rosy prospects." After the estate was settled Charlotte decided to give Tom further shares in trust rather than outright, against her son Henry's urging. In October 1920 Tom wrote a strong letter to his mother, telling her that if he died he wanted Vivien to receive his inheritance, but Charlotte pursed her lips and reserved judgment; she would wait until she met her English daughter-in-law. Meanwhile, Tom's sense of injustice grew: out of the other siblings only his sister Margaret, who was mentally handicapped, was to have her shares in trust; Henry and his other sisters were given their shares without restriction. This discrimination rankled with Tom, who deeply resented being treated in the same way as Margaret, on account of his marriage to Vivien.[36] Not until his mother had visited England would he know whether he could persuade her to change her mind.

Nevertheless, Eliot's sister-in-law, Theresa (wife of Henry Eliot), confirmed in 1970 that Tom had received a private income from the family trust. She did not know exactly what Tom's was, "but Marian (Tom's sister) yielded Eighteen hundred a year, and the estate was about 350,000 my husband told me. So Tom had additional financial help in 1919."[37] The pity that Tom's friends felt for his apparent financial plight was ill-founded. Pound, who later crusaded to raise funds in order that Tom might leave

the bank, "did not know that Eliot was already endowed with a private income larger than his own," writes Delany.[38] Poverty and the "burden" of
Vivien were, therefore, never the deciding factors in Eliot's decision to stay
in Lloyds.

It was not long after meeting Leonard and Virginia Woolf that Tom and
Vivien became drawn into the quarrels and intrigues of the Bloomsbury
group. Vivien, emotional and sharp-tongued, was ill-fitted for the jealous
squabbles of a self-regarding clique who thrived on gossip and mystery.
Tom's cat-like stealth, his aptitude for "playin' possum," for smiling as he
stalked his prey, was more suited to these ephemeral but fierce battles of will.

The honeymoon period between the Woolfs and the Eliots lasted into
the spring of 1919, as Virginia and Leonard laboured to print and cover
Eliot's *Poems* and Virginia's *Kew Gardens* on the hand-press at Paradise
Road, Richmond. Both were to be published on the same day, 12 May.[39] On
6 April 1919 Tom and Vivien dined with the Woolfs and chose the cover
for *Poems*. Subsequently, on 12 April, Eliot sent Virginia a list of people to
whom he wanted a circular advertising the book to be sent prior to publication. But no circulars arrived. Vivien and Tom grew agitated. From 39
Inverness Terrace, W2, where she was lodging while their flat was being
redecorated, Vivien wrote to Mary, asking what they should do:

> Tom has for a long time been very much worried, puzzled, and
> *annoyed* at the Woolfs' behaviour about his poems which they
> were, as you know, printing...*No one* has received a circular
> about the book. This is very awkward ... He gave them several
> poems to print which are *not* published elsewhere, and has been
> counting on this book of the Woolfs' for showing them. *I mean*
> certain people are *asking* to see these poems in order to publish
> them, and Tom has been waiting and waiting for this Woolf
> book, to show them.

Vivien suspected the worst: "Now Mary, do you think that out of revenge,
the W's are actually going to shelve the whole of those books of Tom's

which they have printed? If they do, what a humiliation for Tom!" She was angry and unhappy on Tom's behalf: "If a man is sensitive and an artist, he can't stand these people."

If Leonard and Virginia were going to throw up the book, threatened Vivien, she would go round and have it out with them.

> Yet, *if* I *did*, I believe that Tom would never speak to me again. He would *hate* me. He hates and loathes all sordid quarrelling and gossiping and intrigue and jealousy *so much*, that I have seen him go white and *be ill* at any manifestation of it.

Ezra Pound had been ruined by literary feuds and see what he has become, said Vivien—a laughingstock. Only "a person of coarse fibre," like Wyndham Lewis, could stick it and remain undamaged. As for Mary, who had gossiped indiscreetly to Clive Bell over Tom's problems with the Woolfs, she must say nothing more to her lover, declared Vivien. "If you do the whole matter will end in complete estrangement between us. *I know it.* Leave Clive *out of it* . . . If you do not do what I say *about this*—I will never be a friend of yours again. I will not . . . Goodbye dear Mary I am not angry with *you*, but I am very much worried."[40]

Tom appears to have been speaking equally wildly against the Woolfs to Mary, and she had repeated his remarks to Clive who, jealous of Tom, had not hesitated to pass them on. Soon Tom's criticisms of the Woolfs reached Virginia's ears: "By the way, Mary rang me up yesterday in great agitation about Eliot, imploring me to say nothing, denying the whole story, and insisting that he only abused Bloomsbury in general, and not me, and that Clive had completely misunderstood!" Virginia told Vanessa.[41] The situation was complicated by the fact that, as Eliot explained to his cousin, Eleanor Hinkley, "A" (Mary) hated "B" (Virginia), of whom she was jealous; "A" therefore repeated Tom's remarks to "D" (Clive), who disliked him because "A" (Mary) liked him. "The sequel is that 'G' (Ottoline) is jealous of 'A.'[42] She hears that I spent a weekend at 'A's house. She promptly invites me for a weekend . . ." In associating themselves so closely with Mary Hutchinson the Eliots ran the risk of incurring the same hostility she encountered from other members of Bloomsbury, who were irritated by Clive's constant praise of his mistress. In October 1918, it had been reported, Mary had been "conveyed about London in a fainting condition in taxicabs,"[43] and Duncan Grant explained why in a letter to Lytton Strachey:

> That idiot Virginia went and told Gertler that we all despised and disliked Mary and only put up with her as a concubine of Clive's, which is perfectly untrue but which of course Gertler immediately tells Mary and she of course bursts into tears in the Cafe Royal and had to be taken home in a cab and you are thought to be the only person to cheer her up. Really Virginia and Ottoline are almost as bad as one another.[44]

That crisis blew over. By February 1919, Clive, Mary and Virginia were all three "chattering like a perch of parrakeets," although Virginia took a malicious delight in April in telling Duncan how Vanessa snubbed Mary at a party given by Roger: Vanessa approached the sofa where Mary was sitting, "decked like a butterfly in May—and said 'Its time you got off that sofa, Mary.' " This snub became part of the Bloomsbury repertory: "Katherine (Mansfield) acted it too yesterday," wrote a gleeful Virginia: "Its time you got off the sofa, Mary."[45]

Eliot enjoyed these spats, which he found an intellectual challenge, despite Vivien's claim that he hated gossip and intrigue. It was, he said, the sort of thing that was going on continually in a society where everyone was very sensitive, very perceptive, and very quick, and a dinner party demanded more skill and exercised one's psychological gifts more than the best fencing match or duel. "It does use one's brains!"[46] Vivien, as a very new acquaintance of Bloomsbury's founders, but one who wore her heart on her sleeve, was rash to criticise the Woolfs so openly. In May Vivien told Mary that Leonard had written very curtly to Tom to say he had lost the list. "I saw the letter, It could not have been curter . . . I really always rather hate a man who takes up his wife's feuds, don't you?"[47] Virginia, needless to say, could take offence as quickly as Vivien. After entertaining the Eliots in early April, she wrote: "I amused myself by seeing how sharp, narrow, & much of a stick Eliot has come to be since he took to disliking me." She laughed at Vivien's snobbery, judging her guest to be a "worn looking little woman, who was relieved to find Walter Lamb with his stories about the King provided for her."[48] This Bloomsbury imbroglio took an unexpected twist on 17 April when Virginia told Duncan that "the mystery of Eliot was further thickened by hearing how he'd praised me to the skies" to the Murrys. Now she had a letter from Eliot asking her and Leonard to dinner, and was determined "to draw the rat from his hole."[49]

Vivien could never outsmart Virginia, but her blood was up. She accepted an invitation from Ottoline to Garsington, intending to gather ammunition against her new enemy. On 10 May, on the train to Oxford, she scribbled a note to Mary: "Everyone seems to be hanging on my experiences at G! . . . I am going to throw out a few feelers at G. [and] try to trap O. into saying something to V's disadvantage. I like to go about collecting evidence, which I may not use for years perhaps never."[50] Vivien had an appointment with her then ally, Edith Sitwell, at four o'clock on Monday to give her her report. Although at this time Vivien felt herself to be a match for Bloomsbury, she failed to recognise the fundamental fact that it was Tom whose genius it recognised, and with whom its loyalties would ultimately lie. Bloomsbury, said Vivien's brother Maurice, destroyed her. Yet in 1919 it seemed to offer Vivien the hand of friendship, and so she felt herself to be among friends. Hot-headed and unfounded accusations were not the best way of keeping them.

Vivien's meddling extended to the romantic arena also. Mary's liaison with Clive left St. John Hutchinson out in the cold, so Vivien decided to pair him up with Brigit Patmore. On her way to Garsington that May Vivien planned a dinner party the following Tuesday to bring Jack and Brigit together. "Last time it did not come off," she told Mary, but she had not given up hope of a diversionary affair which would help her new friend. Perhaps Vivien was unaware that Tom was himself writing to Brigit, arranging discreet dinners with her while Vivien was at Marlow.

In May, Brigit accompanied Tom and the Hutchinsons to watch Diaghilev's Ballets Russes perform *Carnaval, The Firebird,* and *The Good-Humoured Ladies,* and he pressed her to dine again before she went to stay with Vivien. In the early summer of 1919 London was in a fever of excitement as it greeted the arrival of "Diaghileff's troupe" for the first time since the war. Diaghilev had brought two new dancers who rapidly created a sensation—Léonide Massine and Lydia Lopokova—who danced the new repertoire which included *La Boutique Fantasque,* which Vivien much preferred to *Le Tricorne (The Three-Cornered Hat)*. "Suddenly the arts became the preoccupation of Society . . . French became the language of the Savoy where Diaghileff, Massine, Stravinsky, Picasso, and Picasso's very beautiful and aristocratic wife were staying for the season," remembered Clive Bell. Picasso "dwelt" in the Savoy. "Madame Picasso had no notion of joining in the rough and tumble of upper Bohemia," and would only allow her husband to attend fashionable parties, dressed "en smoking." It was to Clive, then living at 46 Gordon Square with Maynard Keynes, that Picasso turned when he needed fitting out in white tie and tails; Clive was happy to oblige the painter.[51]

While it amused Tom to flirt with Brigit, Mary was the bigger prize. His invitation to Mary in March that year to dance at a club near Baker Street where they could learn the new steps together and dine afterwards was not an isolated occurrence. In part it was revenge on Vivien for her liaison with Russell. Tom and Vivien now danced less together than in the early days of the marriage when Aldous Huxley described Tom rolling up the carpet in the flat, and seriously fox-trotting with his wife to the strains of the gramophone.[52] Tom no longer met Vivien's demanding standards. In "Thé Dansant," one of Vivien's sketches published in the *Criterion* in 1924, she describes a wife trying to energise her husband on the dance floor: "Now *dance* for a change," she commands. "You never do dance, you know, you simply march about. *You've got no energy.*"[53] Vivien did not hesitate to find herself more skilful partners than her husband, who still needed to count under his breath as he danced. On 2 March, the same month in which Eliot was meeting Mary to learn the new steps, Vivien, in no need of such lessons, recorded that she went to the Elysée Galleries to dance with two of her usual companions and was "Picked up by three Canadian flying-men, all exquisite dancers—Danced as I never have since before the war."[54] Maurice considered that Vivien was a more gifted dancer than his wife, Ahmé Hoagland, who danced professionally in cabaret. It is then hardly surprising that rather than face Vivien's scorn, Tom preferred to dance with Mary and Brigit; but part of the excitement of these illicit encounters lay also in deceiving his wife.

Mary was a willing partner in the game of love. Soon she began inviting Eliot to parties alone. "Vivien would have made the party brighter/It's a Pity you didn't invite her," responded Tom, remarking that Vivien wouldn't have come anyway. He added a rhyming envelope, inviting the postman to "take your little skiff/And ply upstream to HAMMERSNIFF, there to rest an oar ('nay but you shall') at River House, Upper Mall."⁵⁵

Vivien had no suspicions at first. She was unaware of the number of secret meetings which took place between her husband and Mary. Often Mary wrote directly to Tom, enclosing a letter for Vivien; sometimes he, knowing the extent of Vivien's dependence upon her, reproached his correspondent for not writing often enough to Vivien. His deception was made easier by the fact that in June Lloyds Bank sent him into the provinces on a business tour which lasted several weeks, and Vivien had little idea of his whereabouts.

On 16 May 1919 Tom had accepted an invitation from Mary to come alone to Wittering for Whitsun, assuring her that Vivien had made alternative arrangements.⁵⁶ "Please dont have anyone else—flattery quite apart!" he wrote to Mary. "I should like best to be the only guest . . . So you see I can be seduced. I am looking forward to it very keenly."⁵⁷ "So Tom is coming to you at Whitsun!" Vivien remarked with surprise, as she remained in Crawford Mansions, signing herself "Your devoted friend, Vivien."⁵⁸ Mary awaited her guest with anticipation. She had decided to ask Roger Fry for Sunday, but would give Tom an afternoon and evening alone with her first. Anxious as ever to be correctly dressed, Eliot decided to bring his flannels, as well as an account of the "provincial amours," which he provocatively claimed he had enjoyed while travelling for Lloyds, for his hostess.

The spell Eliot cast over women is apparent in Mary's memoir of her first meeting with the poet:

> The first time I saw my friend T. S. Eliot he was sitting alone on a sea-wall in the estuary of Chichester Harbour. It was in August 1916 . . . Eliot was dressed in white flannels and was looking out to sea. He says that I had in my hand an unusual flower picked in the woods through which my husband and I had been walking . . .

In his pockets Eliot carried a "very small Virgil and a very small Dante and read them by the water's edge." He told Mary that "Baudelaire and Dante are the two poets of whom I cannot have enough copies about." "Soon after our first meeting Eliot took a house near the Estuary, from different sides of which we could see white sails and sometimes a red one, 'sea-ward flying.' The oak woods which line the shores—as George Moore described them—became the meeting-place for picnics, and the ferry boat at Itchenor a bridge between his side of the water and ours."[59]

Mary's favourite poems became those in which Eliot captured "water in poetry." "The river sweats/Oil and tar" lines from *The Waste Land,* which describe barges drifting with the turning tide on the Thames, suggested to her Chichester Harbour, and the "Red sails/Wide/To leeward" reminded her of the dinghies she and the poet watched together from the windows of Eleanor.[60]

Strangely there is no mention in Mary's memoir of Vivien, her "devoted friend." It is Eliot only who lives on "his side of the water," Eliot to whom she sends tamarisk and sea lavender to be woven into laurels and roses of Pireira "with which his head will be crowned." Certainly Vivien was not much in either Mary's or Tom's mind when he arrived at Eleanor at Whitsun 1919. Mary, later immortalised as Erato, the Muse of Erotic Poetry, in Boris von Anrep's mosaic floor at the entrance to the National Gallery, was skilled in the arts of love, but it is significant that it is she, not Eliot, who he assumes will take the initiative in any love-making which may ensue. Whether the anticipated seduction took place is not known, but if so, Eliot's heart was not stirred. The world-weariness of the poem he was composing at the time, "Gerontion," dubbed the "new Byronism" by Middleton Murry in his review, speaks of Eliot's very different mood that summer. The poet is "an old man in a dry month,/Being read to by a boy, waiting for rain." Military and amatory progress are compared in the poem, argues Eliot's biographer Tony Sharpe;[61] it is replete with sexual innuendo: "I was neither at the hot gates/Nor fought in the warm rain." The last lines of "Gerontion" enact a sexual crescendo and diminuendo, but its protagonists end as fractured atoms whirling in a dissolving cosmos. The poet returns to the thoughts of "a dry brain in a dry season."[62] There may have been, from Eliot's point of view, a cold coupling at Eleanor, but the aridity of his mood at the time, which found expression in "Gerontion," revised in France that August, suggests anti-climax and disillusion rather than rapture by the water.

Nor is Tom's bread-and-butter letter to Mary after their Whitsun rendez-vous the message of a lover. Eliot speaks instead of being at cross-purposes, and hints at a disagreement. It is Mary's independence and self-sufficiency, and the mysteriousness which made her appear "incomprehensible and unaccountable," which he stresses. His inquiry: "Do you insist on being a very superior woman?" reflects distance rather than intimacy; his stay had not ignited the fires of passion, but instead served to highlight the gulf which existed between the lifestyle of the wealthy lawyer and his confident wife, and the Eliots' own misery.[63]

Nevertheless, rumours about Tom and Mary were now flying around Bloomsbury. On 19 May, a week after the Hogarth Press had published Eliot's *Poems,* Virginia and Ottoline met to "talk personalities," and discuss "the case of Mary Hutch and Eliot."[64] There was more trouble, too, with Virginia, who had heard the latest gossip that Tom thought her new novel, *Night and Day,* was "rubbish." Ottoline was in her turn jealous of Tom's new-found intimacy with Mary, and Clive was more green-eyed than ever when he heard that Tom had spent the weekend with his girlfriend Mary, and Roger Fry. Ottoline at this point invited Tom and Virginia for the weekend at Garsington, without Mary or Vivien. "Tom is going to Garsington; think of Virginia, Tom and Ottoline!" wrote Vivien to Mary. "O think of it."[65] But Vivien's efforts to trap Ottoline into speaking ill of Virginia had backfired and, although she had written "most sensibly and friendly with all due regard to her hothouse feelings," Ottoline was furious with her. "I am cast into outer darkness, so I can join you there," joked Vivien to Mary.[66] Tom, meanwhile, basked in being the centre of attention; "So I must go smiling on Saturday" to Garsington, he wrote to his cousin Eleanor Hinkley, who must have found Bloomsbury feuds as childish as they were confusing.

Unfortunately at this juncture Harold Peters, an old sailing friend of Eliot's, arrived from America, and the poet was forced to give up his weekend at Garsington in order to entertain him. On Saturday, 14 June, Tom brought Vivien to Bosham to spend the weekend at South View, the cottage they had rented for the summer. "Beautiful day," recorded Vivien in her diary. "It is almost too much for one." But by Sunday, despite the hot weather which allowed them to lie out in the grass near Itchenor ferry, her terse entry read: "Didn't get on."[67] Tom returned to London to continue his tour of the provinces and Vivien remained alone in Bosham. Although at this point Vivien still trusted Mary, she was becoming increasingly anxious as she lost track of her husband's whereabouts. The London flat was shut up, Ellen having gone to Margate for her own holiday. Vivien wrote several wistful and placatory letters to Ottoline. "I am awfully happy here, and never want to go back. It is so nice to have Mary so near too. We have glorious picnics together," she wrote, begging Ottoline, however, not to invite Tom to stay again too soon. "*Please,* my dear, don't ask him until *after* the weekend July 5th–7th, as a favour to me, because I do want him to come down here and stay with me. I never see him now."[68]

That June Vivien suffered another disappointment. Russell had arrived early one morning at the flat in Crawford Mansions to collect another instalment of his possessions which she had brought up from Marlow. Vivien had not been dressed when Bertie arrived, and had been forced to shout to him from the bathroom, as cheerfully as she could. She had met with a brusque response, and was left full of regrets, having hoped that she and Bertie might have talked over tea and come to an amicable truce. "But it is no good. I will make no more attempts at all. But it is strange how one does miss him! Isn't it hard to put him *quite* out of one's mind?"[69] Perhaps Ottoline, who had just had Bertie for the weekend at Garsington, was mollified by Vivien's evident unhappiness that Russell was no longer part of her life, as he was part of Ottoline's, and began to repent of her anger.

As the days passed Vivien waited anxiously for her elusive husband to return to her at Bosham. He was due to arrive on 28 June. "Tom is coming here and WE MUST HAVE A GOOD TIME," wrote Vivien to Mary. "It will be the only weekend he'll come, I think."[70] Vivien hunted unsuccessfully in Chichester for partridges and grouse, not realising that they were out of season. She settled for crabs, 6/6d for two, and lobsters, 4/9d for two, to bring to Mary. "If the crabs are *doubtful,* the *middle* parts might be taken out of the shell and kept on a plate. Then they will keep. I hope Jack will not be cross . . ." Envying Mary her children, whom she met on her visits to Eleanor, Vivien wrote a letter apologising for not saying goodbye to Jeremy and Barbara, and sending them some chocolate.

Vivien professed to be delighted with the "glorious" sailing expedition which ensued, after Tom's arrival, with Mary and Sachie Sitwell, although as this was the occasion when Tom ran the boat aground, she was unsure whether anyone else felt the same way: "It's possible that some people thought the boat adventure was boring & silly, I suppose! To me it was pure joy. Tom too, liked it." But her exasperation was growing with Tom, whom she blamed for the growing frostiness with the Woolfs, Clive Bell, and others. He had only asked Mary to arrange the outing as a mark of comradeship, Vivien said: "He thinks it is friendly to ask people to clear up his muddles for him."[71]

Alone again at Bosham, Vivien continued to ask Mary to join her for picnics in the woods, or, if wet, at the inn at Itchenor. However Mary, as hostess to Roger Fry and other guests, was not always available. "I love to get you *away* from everything," wrote Vivien. "I will be on this side of the ferry, waving, at 12.30." By this time Vivien seems to have heard the rumours linking Mary and Tom, signing one letter, "Your loving Vivien, The Woman's Friend, Damn you."[72] But she felt no real cause for concern, believing that Tom was unlikely to relish a physical union with Mary.

By mid-July Tom and Vivien were quarrelling vociferously. Vivien had come up to town to see de Falla's *The Three-Cornered Hat,* but Tom refused to take her to the ballet a second time as she wished: "Tom is *Im*possible—full of nerves . . . very morbid and grumpy. I wish you had him!" Vivien complained to Mary. Money troubles kept cropping up, and Tom reproached Vivien for spending too much, while his own "muddles" over conflicting invitations continued. "He gets angry and stubborn," Vivien confided to Mary. In contrast to her husband, Mary seemed perfect to Vivien after another wonderful day out together. "You are all that I admire," wrote Vivien on 19 July; "you are such a *'civilised'* rebel."[73]

That month an unexpected event occurred which was to change Vivien's view of events. Sydney and Violet Schiff invited the Eliots to spend a weekend at Eastbourne, and, although Vivien recorded in her diary that she found the Schiffs "fatiguing and irritating," she told a different story to Mary, and one with a purpose. As for Tom, she wrote, a lot seemed to happen in the time between her leaving Bosham and his going to France, where he was about to take a walking holiday with Ezra Pound in the Dordogne.

I had rather an affair with him for one thing. It began when we were staying with the Schiffs for the Peace Weekend. Don't you yourself find that staying in people's houses together is very conducive to reviving passions?

The novelty of sexual relations with her husband surprised Vivien. Was Tom's "affair" with her stimulated, perhaps, by his rumoured affair with Mary? Or did Tom find Vivien's own intimacy with Mary an aphrodisiac? The spark of passion, so briefly inflamed, was extinguished, however, when the Eliots left Eastbourne. Vivien remained frustrated by the quarrels she considered to be Tom's fault, telling Mary, "In future I am going to simply wash my hands of Tom, and refuse politely to explain him or influence or direct him. Tom must manage his own muddles." Mischievously Mary enquired whether Tom had many "enemies." "Has Tom enemies? You ask me, but I think you know better than I," replied Vivien. "Anyhow, it doesn't matter now, for I think enemies stimulate him. The important point is—friends . . . You do stand alone . . . Goodbye, darling Mary."[74]

In this Bloomsbury triangle, Mary may have wanted Tom, but he never felt as at ease with her as his polished exterior suggested. To his brother Henry, Eliot complained that summer of still feeling a foreigner among the English. "Don't think that I find it easy to live over here," he wrote. "It is damned hard work to live with a foreign nation and cope with them." He confessed that the English had a knack for making him feel humiliated and lonely, always on "dress parade," and unable to relax. People sought you out because they wanted something from you, and if they didn't get it, they dropped you and quickly became enemies. "London is something one has to fight very hard in, in order to survive."[75] His preservation would be due to luck, said Tom—"or Vivien's assistance, in large part." Even to Mary, Eliot made the same point: that he was a "métic" or foreigner.

Although it might appear that Mary and Vivien were in jealous competition for Eliot, in fact it was Mary whose attention both Tom and Vivien individually craved. Unhappy together, both wanted to be alone with Mary and experience what Vivien described as the "exciting joy" of her conversation, as well as her sympathy in the Bloomsbury squabbles which each

tended to blame on the other. As Eliot put it to Mary, "We are both grateful to anyone who is intelligent enough to take us as individuals."[76] This
Mary well understood.

The intense friendship which developed between Vivien and Mary in
the summer of 1919 presaged that which developed in the 1920s between
Maria Huxley and Mary. Indeed, Mary subsequently had relationships
with both Aldous Huxley and his wife Maria, as well as with Vita
Sackville-West.[77] As early as 1918 Clive was writing to his bisexual lover:
"I often envy you your catholicity,"[78] and in 1922 he referred to an affair
Mary might be having with a woman.[79] But it would be a mistake to assume that Vivien stepped into a lesbian nest when she spent the night with
Mary, as she did on 18 September 1919, and possibly on other occasions. In
her diary Vivien recorded that she and Mary stayed up till one o'clock talking, and she was afterwards "frightfully tired." It was probably on 9 July,
when Mary had told Vivien the story of her life as the two women lay together in the sunshine on the beach at Hayling Island, that the relationship
moved into a different phase. It was very bold of her to ask Mary to invite
her to stay when she was alone, wrote Vivien on 1 September, "But you
must not let me get too excited! Do you know I always get too excited
when I see you & am very ill afterwards. This is true. That heavenly picnic
we had nearly killed me."[80] Mary, sensual and self-indulgent, was tolerant
of Vivien's quirkiness and mood swings. She wrote in 1927 to Lytton
Strachey that she found exhilarating satisfaction in personal relationships,
especially in those which one might describe as

> truthful, unbinding, courageous—"a l'état pur" of impurity . . . I
> think it is fatal to wish for any particular state or particular de-
> velopment—when one is provoked, one should adjust oneself
> very ingeniously—(the more complicated the character probably
> the more exciting) and develop by peculiar jumps![81]

During another later summer at Wittering, on 1 August 1925, Mary
wrote to Maria Huxley of her memories of her lying in her "chaste, narrow bed" at Eleanor; she recalled the "gay and intense days and exquisite
nights" she spent with Maria,[82] whose sweetly scented, oiled body Mary
loved more than that of Aldous.[83] Bloomsbury's encouragement of bisexu-

ality was fast breaking down old taboos against such relationships. In the 1920s lesbianism was the new chic, and the dual-sexed figure of the androgyne a central figure of revolt against bourgeois morality.[84] But there is no evidence that Vivien was lesbian, and her documented affairs were only with men, although she may have been tempted to experiment.

At one point during the summer of 1919 it is clear that Mary was setting up a meeting between Vivien and her brother Jim, whom she hoped might console Vivien for Tom's neglect and Russell's disappearance. Vivien was apparently not averse to the scheme. "Don't tell Jack about Jim, it wouldn't do, I assure you," she implored Mary. She was planning to buy a new wardrobe for the coming season, but didn't know what would please Jim most. "Do begin laying foundation stones for me with Jim," she begged.[85]

In August Tom left for his French holiday with Pound. This came as a welcome relief to Vivien and, combined with Mary's friendship, resulted in a dramatic improvement in her health. The migraines which often prostrated her, as on 1 January, when she had lain in bed all day without moving, with "very bad head pains," and was disturbed by Pound visiting after dinner ("their voices drove me mad as I lay in the dark"), vanished. There was no longer the strain of managing Tom's health and his moods, so carefully charted in her diary: for Saturday 21 June, "T. looking very ill"; Saturday 5 July, "Tom had a cold and was cross"; Monday 21 July, "T. went to Dr." Her own maladies seemed to disappear during these separate holidays. Having seen Tom off at Waterloo in "boiling and roasting heat," Vivien dined with her friend Freddie at Lyons Corner House, before leaving the next day for Eastbourne to spend a fortnight with another old friend, May Pacy. She was pleased to have the same bedroom as the year before at the Lansdowne Hotel, and to find a Colonel and Mrs. Ashe they had met last summer were again at the next table. The next day her brother Maurice arrived and they all went dancing and had "a roaring time." But as the time of Tom's return drew near Vivien again collapsed with premenstrual tension; she was in bed on the day he arrived home from France with several days' growth of beard. It was a starred day in her diary: "Tom came home . . . Very nice at first. Depressed in evening,"[86] she recorded.

Briefly the Eliots drew closer over the illness of their beloved Yorkshire terrier, Dinah, one of many they were to keep during their marriage. Tom had queued for many hours earlier that year to buy a muzzle for Dinah when there was a rabies scare. For three days at the beginning of September they nursed the dog, until on the Friday Vivien and Tom together took Dinah to the vet in a taxi. Nothing could be done and she was put to sleep at once. "Frightful day of misery," recorded a heartbroken Vivien.

Another picnic at Itchenor with Jack and Mary raised their spirits a little, and Vivien and Tom dined together that night at the Anchor at Chichester, before Tom took the train back to London. The following week Vivien's father Charles came to stay with Vivien in Bosham. Father and daughter sketched together and Vivien swam daily, as well as spending many hours blackberrying. It was an idyllic time. But Vivien's conscience pricked her when Tom's birthday arrived on 26 September and found her still in Bosham; once again her period arrived accompanied by a migraine, and a railway strike frustrated her efforts to return to London. When finally she managed to find a seat in a motor car for 30/– to take her as far as Putney Bridge, a typical Eliot muddle occurred: she had wired for Tom to meet her at Putney, but he went instead to London Bridge. She had to wait two hours, and finally abandoned her hamper of blackberries. "We both wept," she recorded.[87]

After Tom's return from France relations between Vivien and Mary were at first peaceful. "Although I've been trying hard to quarrel with everyone else, succeeding too, I *never* want to quarrel with you . . . Yr. devoted V," Vivien had assured Mary in May, but she found it hard to restrain her pen: "I will write a letter from Eastbourne, if I CAN write the sort of letter one woman likes to get from another."[88] Mary remained tactful, assuring Vivien of the "amiability of her savagery."[89] But, as the weeks passed, heightened emotions threatened to burst out into open warfare. On 26 September Vivien exploded with anger after missing Mary in Chichester. Annoyed at waiting three hours in vain, she wrote an "unfortunate" letter to Mary telling her she had "a good store" of things ready to be said to her, and accusing Mary of selfishness.

About giving oneself up to people. I had never seen before we spoke how much I have done that with Tom. And how little *you* were prepared to do it with anyone. Also how much one gains by doing it, how much one loses; and how much one *loses by not ever doing it.*[90]

Mary sent a cool reply, and on 29 October Vivien, who had returned to London, thanked her sarcastically for her "nasty letter," calling her "little cat." But it was Vivien who had her claws out, for Tom as much as for Mary. Hoping to see Mary at the lecture on "Modern Tendencies in Poetry," which Tom had given on 28 October as part of his Monday evening classes on Elizabethan literature in Southall,[91] Vivien had been disappointed when she failed to turn up; she had hoped to sit by Mary and poke her in the ribs. Instead, Vivien was left playing the Dormouse to "Pasha Schiff's Mad Hatter in the front row"; however, she wrote crossly, "As Tom is not a French artist, or a Flirt, or Amusing or even Rather Fun, your absence from his lecture was no surprise to him." Her barbed remark revealed the extent of the Eliots' disharmony, and it was in search of diversion that Vivien accepted another invitation from Mary to a party at River House, reminding her that she would see her at Edith Sitwell's party, and this time there would be no excuse to miss her: "You will know me by my paisley shawl." When might she stay the night with Mary, begged Vivien. "I embrace you."[92]

But Mary's own marriage was under stress. In late 1919 she temporarily left her husband Jack, who had become growingly resentful of his wife's affair with Clive Bell. Mary found refuge with Roger Fry at Durbins, his new house near Guildford. For once Clive was not his usual gossipy self, writing to Vanessa:

> You will see that if they are ever to live together again it is really important that you should be absolutely secret. Above all, I beg you, if anything does come out to make it quite clear that it didn't come from me. Knowing what Jack's feelings in the matter are, I do think it would have been disgraceful in me to have talked. I don't know what will happen, but I think it likely that there will be a partial separation, and that in a short time Mary will ostensibly go back to their house.[93]

So indeed it proved, and later in life Jack would jokingly refer to Mary's lovers.[94] In the interim, however, Mary turned her attentions to another admirer, Tommy Earp, before travelling to Paris in pursuit of Clive. Vivien was grimly amused to hear that her friend had a plot to reawaken Clive's affections. "I also have a gunpowder plot in preparation, but mine is not timed to go off until the New Year," she threatened Mary. "So perhaps it will be a case of he who laughs last laughs loudest."[95]

12

Breakdown

From the time of Henry Ware Eliot Senior's death, Vivien and Tom's lives were dominated by Tom's overriding desire to see his mother. He and Vivien fretted over plans: should Tom go to America for a short visit, which would use up all his leave from the bank, or could he persuade his mother, Marian and Henry to come for two or three months to England? "I want to see you *soon*," he begged his "dearest Mother," in February 1920. "Unless I can see you *once* again . . . I shall *never* be really happy unto the end of my life. Is anything so important as that? Does anything else really matter?"[1] Tom's longing for his mother became the perpetual theme of his letters home, intensifying as Charlotte Eliot appeared impervious to his pleas, protesting that she must first settle her business affairs, sell up in St. Louis and find a new house in Cambridge, Massachusetts.[2] Vivien began to feel she took second place to her mother-in-law during these long months of waiting for the American relatives to arrive. And although Eliot remained "devotedly your son, Tom," finding consolation in the pyjamas Charlotte sewed him for Christmas, the clothes, books, silver cane, his father's chessmen and even the mounted Eliot arms she sent were no substitute for her physical presence: her touch, the sound of her voice, her approbation. His wish that he and Charlotte might "live together a little bit" in England began to take on a neurotic and obsessional quality.

Nevertheless there were fears inherent in the prospective visit. Eliot worried whether his family would detect the falsehoods upon which his marriage was based, the contradictions which lay behind the "envelope of frozen formality" which seemed to Virginia Woolf to encase Eliot's personality, and the wildly glittering eyes she also noticed in 1920.[3] Tom thought of cutting out the page with "Ode" on it in *Ara Vos Prec* ("Now I

Pray You")—which was published in February by the Ovid Press at 15s. a copy—and sending the book thus mutilated to his mother, rather than allow her to see a poem so revealing of his and Vivien's disastrous honeymoon. "The 'Ode' is *not* in the edition that Knopf is publishing," he explained to Henry on 15 February, relieved that his family in America would not see the revealing poem. But although he had suppressed "Ode," he still worried about the other poems in his new collection: "I suppose she will have to see that book. Do you think that 'Sweeney Erect' will shock her?"[4] Tom asked, imagining his mother's reaction to a profoundly misogynistic poem in which a naked, broadbottomed and erect Sweeney shaves while on the bed a prostitute has an epileptic fit. Contemptuously Sweeney ignores her "Gesture of orang-outang" as she flails the steaming sheets, her shrieking mouth (an "oval O cropped out with teeth"), her jackknifing hips (a parody of intercourse) as she claws at the pillow slip, while he tests the razor on his leg. Hysteria might easily be misunderstood, observes Eliot: "It does the house no sort of good."[5] It was an observation which could as easily be taken as an allusion to Vivien as to the inmates of a brothel.

Eliot had made a proud, if premature, boast to his mother that he was England's greatest living poet and critic. Now, with her impending arrival, he had to prove it, and during 1920 he plunged into a frenzy of activity designed to ensure he had enough published work to impress her. Vivien helped with the typing, as Eliot struggled to finish *The Sacred Wood,* his collection of *Egoist* critical essays first suggested by Harriet Shaw Weaver; he hoped to have it ready in April for Methuen but it took until August to complete. Meanwhile he continued writing articles feverishly. He had fallen out with Middleton Murry at the *Athenaeum,* but Richard Aldington came to his aid. Aldington enabled Tom to step onto "the top rung of literary journalism" through his introduction in 1919 to Bruce Richmond, the powerful editor of the *Times Literary Supplement,* at that time the Delphic shrine of literary criticism.[6] Although, relates Aldington (who was the paper's French literature correspondent), Eliot nearly sabotaged his opportunity by arriving fresh from his holiday "wearing, if you please, a derby hat and an Uncle Sam beard he had cultivated in Switzerland," his erudite conversation saved the situation and on 13 November 1919 his first leading article on Ben Jonson appeared.[7] He was also contributing to

Harold Monro's *Chapbook*. Yet Eliot's sense of victimisation remained great. "Getting recognised in English letters is like breaking open a safe—for an American, and . . . only about three have ever done it," he confessed in a sudden burst of honesty to his mother,[8] admitting the magnitude of the task he had set himself as leader of the Modernist revolution.

In a December 1920 a new blow came for both the Eliots when Ezra
Eliot found the success of lesser poets exasperating, especially his American contemporaries. Conrad Aiken was in London, "stupider than I remember him; in fact, stupid," he brusquely told Ezra Pound, although he lunched with Aiken two or three times a week in the City. Aiken had won a reputation as a poet in America, but he, Osbert and Sacheverell Sitwell, Aldous Huxley and Herbert Read all seemed children to the hard-pressed bank clerk, who suspected both Aiken[9] and Osbert Sitwell of copying his style and even the content of his poetry.[10] Eliot was angry that Sitwell seemed to be attempting "clever imitations" of his own poems, and was horrified at the prospect that Knopf might publish him and Sitwell simultaneously. *Would I think of contributing to Wheels?"*—a poetry anthology edited and published by Edith Sitwell and Nancy Cunard between 1916 and 1922—"And so give the S(itwells) a lift and the right to sneer at me?" he demanded scornfully of Wyndham Lewis,[11] urging the painter to keep away from these second-rate, "Chelsea people." Eliot despised the wealthy Sitwells as amateurs, "weekend poets" who did not work for their living; Aldous Huxley also sneered at the family he called "Shufflebottom, one sister and two brothers . . . each of them larger and whiter than the other,"[12] who considered themselves revolutionaries but whose verse differed little from the neo-Georgians against whom they affected to rebel. Although Eliot did not object to accepting the Sitwells' hospitality, he felt embattled, envious of the wealth and leisure of literary dilettantes, bitter at the traditionalists who stood in his way.

In December 1920 a new blow came for both the Eliots when Ezra Pound finally abandoned London for Paris, "killed," in Eliot's view, by the British literary establishment. Pound had been a good friend to Vivien, but it was Eliot who most missed his compatriot and mentor, who now believed Paris to be the "centre of the world" and found in Dadaism a substitute for Vorticism.[13] Although only three years older than Tom, "Ez" had behaved like a father-figure or elder brother to his inhibited protégé, whom he cosseted and protected; when Tom visited him in France Pound fussed over his health, took him for long walks, and "put him through a course of sun and sulphur baths."[14] Pound's absence highlighted the loneliness of Eliot's struggle, and the triumphs of those whom he felt were inferior to himself and Ezra. The financial precariousness of the literary and artistic journals which sprang up and as quickly died, such as *Art and Letters* and Wyndham Lewis's ill-fated *Tyro,* confirmed the wisdom of Eliot's decision to turn down the *Athenaeum* job, as Vivien now acknowledged; nevertheless his work at the bank had become far more onerous since being put in charge of the settlement of pre-war debts between the Germans and Lloyds, despite a new salary increase to £500. When the Cambridge don I. A. Richards met Eliot at the bank he described him as

> a figure stooping, very like a dark bird in a feeder, over a big table covered with all sorts and sizes of foreign correspondence. The big table almost entirely filled a little room under the street. Within a foot of our heads when we stood were the thick, green glass squares of the pavement on which hammered all but incessantly the heels of the passers-by. There was just room for two perches beside the table.[15]

Lloyds, however, were pleased with Eliot's efforts: "If you see our young friend, you might tell him that we think he's doing quite well at the Bank," a senior official told Richards. "In fact, if he goes on as he has been doing, I don't see why—in time, of course, in time—he mightn't even become a Branch Manager." Horrified, like so many other of Eliot's friends and disciples, Richards tried to persuade the poet to find some alternative occupation—this time to accept an academic post at Cambridge—but, "like a wary animal sniffing a trap," he declined.[16]

Although a perverse caution kept Eliot at Lloyds, the price he paid was high. Proud of his new appointment, for he now had several assistants, he nevertheless felt chained to a treadmill with only the distant promise of retirement; Vivien, who had pleaded with him to leave in 1919, worried constantly about his health. Observer of Tom's bitterness and resentment, her own anger grew at the mother-in-law she blamed for their poverty and her husband's unhappiness. She was convinced that with one stroke of her pen Charlotte could change their lives, if she would only give them enough of the shares Tom felt were his by right, and which would release him from the bank. Vivien knew that Tom hungered for editorship of his own journal, envying the ease with which their rich friend Scofield Thayer was able to buy *The Dial,* which Eliot condemned as merely a "very dull" imitation of the *Atlantic Monthly,* although Thayer's generous rates forced him to agree to contribute a "London Letter" to his old Harvard rival's periodical.[17] Pound was even ruder about Scofield's new venture, finding it no better than the *London Mercury* "or one of those other mortuaries for the entombment of dead fecal mentality."[18] As the months passed, Eliot's paranoia increased alongside his unwavering determination to win the battle for literary supremacy in London.

Eliot felt the battle he was fighting was for high standards in the midst of the contemporary "putrescence" of English literature and journalism; he wanted to wipe the smile of imbecility from the face of London. Was he not a Puritan soldier fighting post-war degeneracy, of which modern journalism was simply one symptom, just as his Blood ancestors had struck down deluded witches? His sense of persecution, however denied, was intensified by his continuing sense of alienation: "I have got used to being a foreigner everywhere," he told Maxwell Bodenheim, an American poet then in London, in similar words to those he had used to Mary, "and it would fatigue me to be expected to be anything else."[19] The effort of disguise, of fitting himself to a post-war culture so different from the familiar certainties of Unitarianism, was commented on by Henry Eliot to their mother: "The strain of going out among people who after all are foreigners to him, and, I believe, always must be to an American—even Henry James never became a complete Englishman—has, I think, been pretty heavy." Tom had confessed, his brother said, to "always having to be alert to appearances, always wearing a mask among people. To me he seemed like a man playing a part."[20]

Acting the part of an Englishman might have been less of a burden, had not Eliot carried the heavier weight of feeling misunderstood by his family in America. In July 1919 a distant relative, Charles William Eliot, President of Harvard 1869–1909, wrote a severely critical letter to Tom, who had earlier solicited his help when attempting to enter the American armed forces in 1918. It was unintelligible to him how any young American scholar could forego the privilege of living in the genuine

American atmosphere, wrote the President sternly. Tom's duty was to be of use primarily to Americans of the present and future generations, as Emerson had been. The poet would find, like Henry James, that English residence contributed "neither to the happy development of his art nor to his personal happiness." If he wished to speak through his work to people of the "finest New England spirit," declared this elder of the Eliot clan, he had better not live much longer in England. "The New England spirit has been nurtured in the American atmosphere."[21]

Such reproaches weighed heavily on Eliot. His inherited sense of duty, the family "Fear and Conscience," which he believed was still keeping his mother in America since she refused to travel until her late husband's estate had been settled, conflicted with his burning desire for literary success, the quickest route towards which—he was certain—lay in London, in his eyes the literary capital of the world, even if Ezra had awarded that crown to Paris. There was no alternative. Eliot would play his part and bide his time. Ezra had failed and was out of the race, but Tom would pick up the baton his intemperate friend had dropped in anger, and do what no other American had done—impose "his personality, taste and even many of his opinions on literary England." His weapons were, as Aldington noted, "merit, tact, prudence and pertinacity."[22]

The "character armour" Eliot wore did not go unnoticed. Aldous Huxley observed to Ottoline that Eliot had created a character for himself, a wooden armour inside which he hid.[23] Virginia Woolf found him "sinister, insidious, eel-like, also monolithic, masked, intensely reserved."[24] Ottoline herself often found it impossible to penetrate the smooth, impervious surface of Eliot's personality. Vivien's emotions, by contrast, were transparently open, and this was the secret of her initial popularity, although she could not help responding to the hypocrisy and inauthenticity of her life with Tom, on both a social and sexual level, by sometimes losing control. The infiltration of Bloomsbury, so necessary for the fulfilment of Tom's ambition, the cultivation of men she knew he despised, the pretence of marriage, became impossible for her to sustain because of the falsity of her position.

Eliot's mind was like a Chinese puzzle, as Ottoline noted. He revelled in Machiavellian diplomacy and manipulation, and lived by the family motto, *"Tacuit et fecit"* ("Be silent and act"). Vivien, despite good intentions, could not keep a secret, and was too impulsive to play the games at which Mary excelled (to Tom's admiration). Mary was "as mute as a trout" when prudence demanded, a woman who "though silent . . . has the swift composure of a fish," the observant Virginia Woolf recorded;[25] Mary successfully handled the triangular relationships at which Vivien had failed, winning her errant lover Clive back from a new affair in 1920–21 with a Spanish beauty, Juana de Guandarillas.[26]

Nevertheless, there is no doubt that in 1920 Vivien was still a considerable asset to Tom in his pursuit of power and position. Despite, or perhaps because of her *naïveté*, she sparkled at literary gatherings, her spontaneity a refreshing contrast to the thrusts and parries of most of the guests. Herbert Read, then a civil servant, remembered Eliot bringing "his pretty . . . wife" to the Saturday afternoon tea parties given by Edith Sitwell and her companion Helen Rootham in their Bayswater flat. "Posterity will probably judge Vivienne harshly," he wrote, "but I remember her in moments when she was sweet and vivacious."[27]

Vivien's path through the salons of London was smoothed by the warm friendship she now shared with Ottoline Morrell, with whom she had become reconciled after their quarrel the previous year. Dependent, as always, on other people to make her marriage to Tom bearable, Vivien had written in December 1919 that she wished *ever so much* that she could see Ottoline at Garsington for the Christmas festivities: "Xmas is awful, *awful.*" She was longing for Ottoline to come to London. "I keep saying to Tom, 'when Ottoline is here we will do so and so . . .' You do not know how I admire you, my dearest Ottoline. I hope we shall always be friends." Innocently Vivien urged Ottoline to become closer friends with Mary, whom she believed Ottoline would like very much if she liked Vivien. Although Ottoline would not think it, wrote Vivien, she and Mary were very much alike—"Leaving out the sex business which of course makes a vast difference"[28]—an allusion to Mary's promiscuity. Vivien was probably unaware that Ottoline and Virginia had been gossiping over Mary's relationship with Tom[29] and that Virginia had taken perverse pleasure in seeing the "poor parakeet fallen off her perch, or left to preen & prink in solitude," when Clive strayed in the direction of the beautiful Spaniard.[30]

Ottoline responded to Vivien's pleas by taking Ethel Sands's house at 15 Vale Avenue in Chelsea for six weeks from the end of January 1920, and was touched to find that Vivien was the first person to welcome her back to London. Vivien's obvious affection appealed to a woman who felt neglected by her unfaithful husband Philip, now father of two illegitimate sons, and who shared a bond with Vivien as a former lover of Bertrand Russell. A common love of the ballet also drew Ottoline and Vivien together, for Vivien was as impressed with the Russian stars as the rest of High Bohemia, noting in her diary in July 1919: "Massine really wonderful."[31] In addition, shared maladies, migraine, insomnia, gastric attacks and "nerves" led to mutual understanding of the difficulties of being "delicate"; with Vivien too, whose education had been as sporadic as her own, Ottoline felt none of the intellectual inferiority induced by the acid tongue of Katherine Mansfield or Virginia. Ottoline was still the target of criticism by ungrateful Garsington guests such as Clive Bell, who was liable to lose his temper with his hostess on account of "her confounded stupidity," writing, "I wouldn't mind her utter inability to see the point when it becomes the least bit difficult—Philip is almost as bad—but she's so damned pleased with herself and feels so noble and idealistic when she reaches the heights of imbecility—that it is hard not to let her see the least little bit what one thinks."[32] With relief Ottoline turned to the unpretentious Vivien, who seemed to have more sensibility than brains, a fact Ottoline put down to her being partly Irish, like herself.[33] The impression Vivien gave was also noted by Ottoline's daughter Julian, who described her as "coy, actressy, flirtatious, amusing."[34]

Vivien and Ottoline soon became inseparable. On Wednesday, 18 February 1920 the Eliots dined together with Ottoline. Tom then left Vivien to spend the night with their hostess; the next day Vivien gave a dinner party for Osbert and Sacheverell Sitwell and Aldous Huxley, and afterwards the party went on to Ottoline's Thursday night reception, where a Japanese performer did a hara-kiri dance, pretending to disembowel himself with a fan, and uttering horrid cries until the duchess who had brought him calmed him down with a cup of tea.[35]

Relations between the Eliots and the Woolfs had also improved: Eliot's *Poems* had met with poor reviews, a particularly severe one entitled "Not Here O Apollo" appearing in the *Times Literary Supplement* in June 1919.[36] Critics and readers alike agreed with Aldington, who had written crushingly to the poet that July, "I dislike your poetry very much; it is over intellectual and afraid of those essential emotions which make poetry."[37] Leonard attempted to rescue the situation by writing a favourable review which was published in Murry's *Athenaeum* (although it was awkward for Leonard to review their own publication, confessed Virginia), and Tom was grateful for his words of praise. Clive Bell also gave Tom and Virginia a "puff" in *The New Republic* (New York) in the same month in an article condemning English critics for ignoring the young Bloomsbury writers, Tom, Virginia and Murry.[38] United in their loathing of the middle-class literary establishment, which was headed by J. C. Squire, editor of the newly founded *London Mercury,* and which seemed blind to the merits of the modernists, Bloomsbury began to close ranks. Virginia confessed to her diary that she was a snob: "The middle classes are cut so thick, & ring so coarse, when they laugh or express themselves. The lower classes don't do this at all," she wrote at the end of January 1920,[39] sentiments with which Tom and Vivien entirely agreed. Tom's idealistic view of the English working class, which he considered less "aggressive and insolent" than the same class in America, had grown since he lectured to working people in Ilkley and Southall: "This class of person," he had written to his cousin, "is really the most attractive in England . . . it is not so petrified in snobbism and prejudice as the middle classes."[40] The "hopelessly stupid" middle class, whose family life was, said Tom, "hideous" and whose only motive in sending their sons to public school he believed to be snobbism, attracted nothing from him but contempt.[41] Ignored by readers, under attack by the "squirearchy," it was with new-found relief that Tom, and Vivien too, dined with the Woolfs on 20 February 1920, in the company of Sydney Waterlow, Lord Robert Cecil's right-hand man at the Foreign Office, to whom Tom had escaped for Boxing Day after the "awful" Christmas Day alone with his wife.

A few months later Vivien, repenting of her former feud, invited Leonard and Virginia, who was working on *Jacob's Room* (1922), to dinner. They declined, but Virginia sent a kindly note to Vivien, saying she hoped Tom's new book *(The Sacred Wood)* would have poems in it. "I have been wanting to say how much I enjoy his poems—but I never know whether it is better to say so or not."[42] In July Virginia issued a tentative invitation to both Eliots to stay for the weekend at Monk's House, Rodmell, the cramped, damp house beside the water meadows of the Ouse which the

Woolfs had bought in 1919, partly because it was near enough for Virginia to stride over the Downs to her sister at Charleston. "We would like to ask you and Mrs. Eliot here for the weekend," Virginia wrote to Tom. "The only thing is that the discomfort is so great and arrangements so primitive that I dont think she would find it possible."[43] Tom assured Virginia that Vivien would find conditions perfectly comfortable, and despite Virginia's sense of inadequacy over her "tiny" house compared to Charleston,[44] an invitation for September was despatched. "Please bring no clothes," commanded Virginia, alarmed that Eliot might appear in a "four-piece suit." "We live in a state of the greatest simplicity."[45]

In September 1920 Eliot came alone to stay with the Woolfs. When the three of them were walking across the fields, Woolf fell behind to relieve himself. On catching up with Tom and Virginia, he noticed that the poet seemed uncomfortable and even shocked. A frank conversation about conventions and formality followed, in which Eliot admitted that not only would he not have urinated himself in similar circumstances, but that he would never dream of shaving in the presence of anyone else, even his wife.[46] The anecdote illustrated the extent of Eliot's inhibitions and the difficulties faced by Vivien, frozen out when she attempted to overcome them. Eliot was defensive about criticisms of his coldness: "The critics say I am learned and cold," he told Woolf; "the truth is I am neither," but although Virginia felt sympathy for the poet, she still found him as chill as marble.[47]

Social success only made the contrast between the privileged lifestyle of so many of their friends and the sordid flat the Eliots inhabited more insupportable. They decided they could no longer tolerate living in a neighborhood full of prostitutes, which they "loathed." Tom began flat-hunting, encouraged by the prospect of dividends from the first tranche of 225 Hydraulic Press-Brick Company shares which his mother gave him in early 1920. But a bigger flat meant sacrificing the house in Marlow, much against Vivien's will. She had refused to let it to a prospective tenant the previous year: "I will not let them have it," she confided to Ottoline. "I should be *wretched* without it,"[48] but in 1920 the Eliots surrendered the lease. Rents outside Paddington were much higher than they had expected, and by May 1920 Vivien and Tom were both in a state of prostration. A brief visit to Paris for Easter, a treat promised to Vivien who had not left

England for six years, proved a disappointment as Tom collapsed again with flu: "It was very worrying and exhausting to Vivien having me on her hands in Paris, and having to fetch a doctor, get medicines etc., and the journey back was trying for her," Eliot explained later to Ottoline.[49] Even as close a friend as Herbert Read could not but admit that Eliot "had a streak of hypochondria and was addicted to pills and potions."[50] That summer Vivien worried about Tom's health, as he continued tired and low-spirited.

Working against the clock to finish *The Sacred Wood,* Tom began to make excuses to see less of Mary, who attempted to provoke him with an account of her stay with Lytton. "Glad . . . to hear Lytton's life is so perfect," responded Eliot. They dined out together and Eliot wrote that although he was ashamed of the quality of the meal, he was very happy to see her and hoped it would happen again.[51] But his heart was not in the relationship. He began to backpedal, encouraging Mary, who continued to press invitations upon him, to see Vivien as well as himself. "Can you come to lunch with Vivien on *Saturday,"* he asked. "I will hope to see you afterwards when I get in?"[52] Mary, who was still having difficulties with Clive, seems to have suspected Eliot of having a new lover, and he accused her of having "a very suspicious nature."[53] When Mary asked him to dinner, he replied that they would *both* enjoy seeing her again: "Vivien is not here just now, and she will grumble if I go without her . . . so will you please not be nasty and invite us for next week," he begged.[54] He was relieved when she agreed to postpone dinner. Would she wear her cotton earrings, he asked, and look nice and be nice and they would talk a great deal.[55]

Vivien had communicated her growing fears for Eliot's health to Ezra Pound while they were in Paris. As a result, in June, Pound wrote to John Quinn in New York, who had begun to act as Eliot's agent, to propose the scheme which became known as "Bel Esprit," by which subscribers would contribute to a fund to allow Eliot to give up the bank. It was "a crime against literature," declared Pound, for Eliot to stay at Lloyds.[56] But his friend's terms were steeper than Pound anticipated: Eliot wanted £800 a year, a flat in London and six months abroad, and was not prepared to go back to lecturing which he found "much *more* fatiguing" than banking.[57] Meanwhile, unknown to Pound, Eliot received the first dividend cheque for $225 from the $900 promised by his mother from the Hydraulic Press-

Brick Company, and decided to take a walking holiday in France to restore his health after the "depressing adventure" which Paris had turned
out to be.[58]

Before leaving he and Vivien spent the weekend of 6 August 1920 at
Eastbourne with the Schiffs ("very nice Jews"); the weather was beautiful
and the party, which included Wyndham Lewis, went motoring along the
cliffs, and in the evening performed amateur dramatics in which both
Vivien and Tom excelled. Momentarily they drew closer. Vivien's vivacious performance as an actress was remarked on by Sydney Schiff, who
paid her gratifying attention. A few days later Tom sent his mother some
photographs of Vivien taken by Ottoline at Garsington, telling her Vivien
looked "very attractive."[59] It was not a comment calculated to please
Charlotte, however hard Tom tried to bring his mother round to the idea
of accepting her daughter-in-law.

On the 15 August Eliot and Wyndham Lewis—who had decided at
the last minute to accompany the poet—arrived in Paris, leaving Vivien in
the care of Violet and Sydney Schiff. The two men visited James Joyce in
Paris, Eliot carrying a heavy parcel which he had been entrusted by Pound
to hand to Joyce, who on first acquaintance struck Lewis as an oddity in
patent-leather shoes, large powerful spectacles and a small ginger beard.
Joyce accepted Eliot's invitation to meet at their small hotel on the Left
Bank of the Seine. The parcel was placed in the middle of a large Second
Empire marble table, standing upon gilt eagles' claws in the centre of the
apartment. Joyce cut the string with Eliot's nail scissors and unrolled the
damp brown paper. "Thereupon a fairly presentable pair of *old brown shoes*
stood revealed." "Oh!" exclaimed James Joyce faintly. " 'Oh!' I echoed and
laughed, and Joyce left the shoes where they were . . . ," wrote Lewis. Eliot,
in his "still-trailing Bostonian voice . . . asked our visitor if he would have
dinner with us."[60]

After this interlude, Eliot and Lewis continued on to the Loire and
Brittany together. Lewis noted with surprise that his companion entered
most scrupulously in a small notebook the day's expenses. "This he would
do in the evening at a café table when we had our night-cap. There was not
much more he could spend before he got into bed."[61] Eliot, however, found
Lewis an intellectually stimulating companion, enjoying their stay in
Saumur, where the artist sketched the old houses and they both drank co-

piously, until Lewis fell off his bicycle on the road to Chinon and bruised his hand so he could no longer hold a pencil; Eliot then left him in Dieppe to return to Vivien.

Eliot's holiday resolved him to try again for a new flat: Henry had sent £90 which encouraged his brother to look for something more expensive, and by September he thought he had found a property but, as he lamented to Henry, John Quinn and his mother, what he really longed for was a period of tranquillity to "do a poem that I have in mind."[62] Negotiating with the vendor, an "insane she-hyena," left him feeling maddened. Like every house-move the Eliots made, it was a fraught business, made worse by Eliot's impracticality and indecision, the *aboulie* or paralysis of will of which he complained throughout his life. As in the previous crisis over his son-in-law's unemployment, it was Charles Haigh-Wood who saved the situation. Haigh-Wood stepped in and took charge of the negotiations, which Eliot thankfully placed in his hands while he hurried to correct the proofs of his book.

It was not an opportune moment for Mary Hutchinson to renew her reproaches to Tom for ignoring her, and he responded touchily when she enquired in September whether he had forgotten her. No doubt Tom had heard the gossip about Clive's affair with Juana, although, according to Vanessa Bell, it was "on its last legs and . . . Mary will probably triumph after all,"[63] and about Mary's own latest love affair with Thomas Earp, the *Daily Telegraph* art critic. Oddly, in view of his own behaviour, Clive could not get over Mary's affair, writing sarcastically to enquire whether "to round the matter off," Mary was going to bed with Mrs. Earp as well.[64] "It is the only thing that really prevents Clive from returning to her," reported Vanessa.[65] But Tom was too preoccupied to be any sort of substitute for Clive. It would be more reasonable to ask if Mary had forgotten him, he retorted huffily. What had suddenly recalled him to her memory? As to her questions, he was not well and was about to have an operation; he had been engaged in activity towards a new flat, varied by agreeable weekend visits; his "pamphlet" (*The Sacred Wood*) would "emerge into obscurity in October *höffentlich*." As for writing, said the frustrated poet, I am only signing my name to leases.[66]

Eliot's irritation mounted at Mary's complaint that he and Vivien had not visited West Wittering that summer. Vivien had suggested September, said Tom, and neither of them had heard anything from her. Mary was still able to live her life on pre-war terms, and did not understand the difficult choices he and Vivien had to make between town and country, because he could not afford both. Mary, with her fine houses in London and Wittering, was insulated against the "horrible waste of time, energy, life, of the struggle with post-war machinery of life."[67] Mary's uncomprehending letters brought Tom face to face with the contrast between their lifestyles, hers that of a leisured wife, his that of hard-pressed City office worker.

Mary subsequently changed her line of attack, inviting Vivien to bring Tom to Wittering to convalesce from the operation on his nose, which was to be cauterised. In a dignified letter, Vivien declined the invitation, explaining that she could not possibly come with Tom to Eleanor, which she now believed had been the scene of Mary's seduction of Tom the previous summer, as well as of her own quarrel with Mary in autumn 1919. "It is a pity, but there are some things I can't do, and that is one of them." Magnanimously Vivien agreed that it might do Tom good to stay at Eleanor, if someone in the village could come in and cook his meals, but she herself could not be Mary's guest. "I do not bear you a grudge," wrote Vivien, but she had not forgotten her threat that he who laughs last laughs loudest. Like Eliot she would bide her time, and work on her "gunpowder plot," although not until 1925 was she to explode her "bomb" and betray her true feelings towards Mary, the wealthy and duplicitous hostess she believed had betrayed her friendship, in a malicious portrait intended to make Mary the same object of ridicule as she had made of Vivien as a deceived wife.[68] Sometimes Tom felt equally hostile towards Mary, writing to "Dearest Mary" as "Mrs. H (tho' rich)/A dreary kind of bitch."[69] What an extremely fine actor Tom is, noted Ottoline astutely, for he hates Mary and yet he is attentive to her.[70]

At the end of September 1920 Vivien asked Mary to meet her in London. "It would have been nice if you had come to Eastbourne to find me," she reproached her. "I wish you had."[71] Not for the first time, Vivien felt Mary neglected her when Tom was away. That summer Abigail Adams Eliot, Tom's first cousin, who was spending a year in Oxford, had asked Vivien to travel to Holland with her, but Vivien was obliged to stay at home; she had to prepare for the move into the new flat, and save money while Tom was abroad with Wyndham Lewis. Abigail was disappointed. In 1965 she wrote

> I have thought many times about Vivienne. You know I knew her quite well in the 1920s and I saw her once even after Tom had separated himself from her . . . I knew her as a charming, sensitive, affectionate person. I never doubted Tom's love for her and hers for him. I have been distressed by statements about . . . Vivienne as a person which have appeared in the press.[72]

In mid-October the long-awaited move took place to 9 Clarence Gate Gardens, a more spacious London flat, and the Eliots finally gave up Marlow. They were "moving in 2 peices" [sic] explained Vivien to Mary on 25 October. "Moving, especially double moving, is a great event,"[73] which was to take several weeks, as they lingered on in Crawford Mansions awaiting the arrival of Wyndham Lewis, who was taking it over. Vivien lost Mary's letter inviting them to dinner, because the confusion was immense in both flats; there was no place to be civilised in, she complained. "And Lewis sits here, in the wreckage. With a black patch on his eye."[74]

Just as the Eliots were completing the move, a new crisis occurred: Vivien's father Charles fell dangerously ill with what appeared at first to be food poisoning from some tinned sardines. An emergency operation was performed in the house in Compayne Gardens. Vivien was told by the surgeon that her adored father would have died within ten minutes, as there was an abscess in his abdomen which was on the point of breaking. Haigh-Wood was not expected to survive the night. Vivien, Tom and Rose sat up with him till daybreak, and for many days afterwards shared his care with two hired nurses. Although the abscess had been removed, the surgeons said they would have to operate again as soon as Charles was stronger. Vivien lent her mother her servant Ellen, as Rose's servant was ill, and then collapsed with a migraine. Forced to return to the new flat in the evenings, because there was no room for her to sleep at her parents' house, she remained anxious because she and Tom had no telephone. "Vivien is particularly fond of her father," explained Tom to his mother on 31 October, describing Charles Haigh-Wood as a "sweet, simple man" who was perfectly happy in the country, drawing and painting. "She takes more after him and his side of the family, and understands him better than the others do."[75]

Somehow Haigh-Wood survived a second operation, even though the surgeon was apparently so horrified by what he found that at first he simply wanted to sew the patient up and let him die. Weeks of worry followed for Vivien, as her father slowly convalesced. She wrote:

> We have been fighting every minute a long losing battle against *horrible* illnesses, unimaginable pain, doctors' mistakes—obstinacy—stupidity—delays—family's blindness. The only thing on my side has been my father's courage and determination. But I am afraid we're going to lose after all, & after so much fighting it will be very hard to bear.

Anxious to stay in touch, Vivien had a telephone installed. On Boxing Day Haigh-Wood's life was again despaired of. Vivien told Mary:

> I can't make an engagement more than an hour ahead. There are changes every few hours, and every single complication and misadventure happens. I never go to bed without fear, & to ring up first thing every morning takes all one's courage . . .

Vivien asked Mary to ring her at two o'clock, and if she felt "secure enough to leave Father," she would come over. She had been out of the "great world" for so long, she wrote, that before long she would fade away altogether.[76]

By February 1921 Haigh-Wood was convalescing in Tunbridge Wells. Vivien was deeply grateful to Tom for his support in this crisis, telling Mary that her husband had been simply wonderful, doing everything and making everyone adore him. "We should never have come through without him," she wrote. Her father was still alive, but in great danger and great pain. "I am so fond of him," she told Mary; it was the utmost torture to see people one loved in pain, or to think of doing without them.[77] Eventually Haigh-Wood made a miraculous recovery.

As Vivien continued to nurse her father, Tom felt his own brain had become numb. The upset of the move to Clarence Gate Gardens and the strain of his father-in-law's illness had prevented him from writing for two months, despite trying to seal himself hermetically against the "domestic weepies." Now, the move completed, Eliot decided to take his remaining holiday from the bank in Paris. It was a nostalgic trip. He returned alone to the Pension Casaubon in rue St. Jacques, where he had stayed with Jean Verdenal in 1910–11. The old proprietors were dead, but their grandson had kept on the pension. Perhaps Eliot stayed in his old bedroom, which had been taken over by Jean when he left, and wandered again in the nearby Luxembourg Gardens where Jean had picked lilac. Certainly his thoughts were of the medical student as he at last set to work on the "long poem," provisionally entitled "He Do the Police in Different Voices," a quotation from Charles Dickens's *Our Mutual Friend* which expresses Eliot's intention to weave together a pattern of voices both personal and impersonal.[78] This poem, which would become *The Waste Land,* had been in his mind since November 1919,[79] when he had been attending séances conducted by a mystic, P. D. Ouspensky, in London, in a possible attempt to communicate with his lost friend.[80] The city "would be desolate for me with pre-war memories of Jean Verdenal," Eliot confessed to his mother, but for the company of Vivien's brother Maurice, who joined him in Paris, and the new acquaintances he made—writers and painters who had heard of him even if they did not read English. For Vivien, left at home, he bought "very cheap" a drawing by Raoul Dufy.[81]

Many months of caring for her father without respite took its toll on Vivien, and when he was finally out of danger in February, she collapsed with influenza. Tom professed to feel sorry for her, but he remained detached. "Do come on Monday if you don't mind Vivien's being shut in her room," he wrote to Mary.[82] Vivien developed neuritis, in her arms, legs, feet and back. "Have you ever been in such incessant and extreme pain that you felt your sanity going, and that you no longer knew reality from delusion? That's the way she is," Tom informed Brigit Patmore on 17 March 1921. "She is in screaming agony."[83] The doctors were unable to help Vivien's pain, which may have been in part a psychosomatic expression of her longing for some sympathy from Tom. Instead he sent Vivien to a nursing home for several weeks until the mounting expense made it necessary to bring her home again. A specialist treated her for nervous exhaustion, and her "stomach trouble" had become so alarming, despite massage, that she was allowed to see no one but Tom. As soon as she was up, he resolved to send her to the country for a month, gloomily confiding to Sydney Schiff, whose wife Violet had just had an operation, that he did not expect his wife to be really well for another year or two.

Banishing Vivien to the country, whether to an institution or a cottage, was Tom's frequent response to her illnesses, and one liable to increase her sense of rejection and abandonment. Aldington speculated in his novella that Eliot's attempts to free himself temporarily of Vivien came about at the suggestion of Ezra Pound, who had watched his protégé's dissension with his wife with growing dismay:

> "You can't go on like this. You're driving each other crazy."
>
> "Ye-es," said Cibber.
>
> "Well, can't you do *something?*"
>
> "What is there to be said, what is there to be done?" Cibber retorted languidly . . .
>
> "Look here, what I mean is, why don't you send her to the country for a month?"
>
> "What! In cold weather like this?"
>
> "Why not?"
>
> "She wouldn't like it."
>
> "Well, she'll have to lump it."
>
> "But she wouldn't go."
>
> "Damn it!" exclaimed the irascible Cholmp, "make her go."
>
> "But I don't know where to send her."
>
> "Hell! You've got the whole miserable little island!"
>
> "Ye-es, ye-es."
>
> ". . . Try Cheltenham."
>
> "Yes," Cibber agreed, "one might do worse than Cheltenham."[84]

By 1921 the cracks in the Eliot marriage were becoming chasms. Eliot began to think of himself and Vivien as Paolo and Francesca, Dante's doomed lovers, buffeted for eternity by the "warring winds" of hell as punishment for their carnal sins.[85] In Tom's eyes, he and Vivien seemed to be suffering a similar fate: to inhabit their own hell, to wage their own war of words. In their unhappiness both Eliots had looked outside the marriage for comfort, each becoming acutely dependent on an aged parent for the love and affection missing in their own relationship; it was the frailty of Vivien's father, and the prospect of his loss, which had triggered her breakdown, for only her father offered her the love and devotion her husband denied her. Tom's own despair was expressed in his choice of pseudonym, "Gus Krutsch," under which he contributed a poem, "Song to the Opherian," published in Wyndham Lewis's *Tyro* in May 1920. It is an ugly name, not only suggesting deformity,[86] but, in its resemblance to "crotch," also an apt one for the protagonist of a sexual story. "Krutsch" also resembles Conrad's "Mr. Kurtz" in *Heart of Darkness,* a novel which influenced Eliot so profoundly that he chose a quotation from it as the original epigraph for *The Waste Land* until dissuaded by Pound. For Kurtz, "nerves went wrong"; he is possessed by the "powers of darkness." Among the "subtle horrors" of the jungle, he discovers he is "hollow at the core." Did Eliot, like Kurtz, feel "I am lying here in the dark waiting for death?"[87]

Certainly the effort of creativity implied self-sacrifice: "It is a sacrifice of the man to the work, it is a kind of death," Eliot wrote in a letter to the *Athenaeum* published on 25 June 1920, in which he voiced the same conviction expressed in his most famous essay in *The Sacred Wood,* "Tradition and the Individual Talent," that what the poet experiences "is the continual surrender of himself as he is at the moment to something more valuable. The progress of an artist is a continual extinction of personality."[88] Each poem was a little death, the depersonalized mind of the artist operating as the catalyst through which emotions were transmuted into new combinations; sometimes Eliot felt himself to be like a scientist with his test-tube, creating new acid from old gases. But as he gestated his greatest poem, he was preoccupied not only with transforming his own creative death into life, but with the theme of the death of a woman: Eliot had recently seen Webster's *The Duchess of Malfi* at the Lyric, in which the lustful duchess is strangled by her brother's agents as punishment for her immoral marriage.[89] For the Duchess, like Francesca, death was, it seemed, the karma she deserved.

By midsummer 1921 all Tom's hopes were centred on the arrival of his mother, Charlotte, who he believed would magically heal his unhappiness. His spirits rose as the date of her arrival drew close, while Vivien's sank at the prospect of finally coming face to face with her rival. Charlotte, who had now moved to 27 Concord Avenue, Cambridge, sailed with her un-married daughter Marian Cushing Eliot, and Henry, on the *S.S. Adriatic* at the beginning of June; Tom had insisted that Charlotte should not book rooms in an hotel or take lodgings, but accept his offer of their own com-fortable flat and servant during their stay. Vivien and Tom in turn would move in with Lucy Thayer, Vivien's American friend, who had returned to England after the death of her mother, and was renting a much smaller flat at 12 Wigmore Street. Vivien had no desire to leave her new home in Clarence Gate Gardens so soon after moving in, but the arrangement met Tom's own need to re-create his childhood proximity to his mother: "I should keep my books here and should often work here in the evenings, and I should be dropping in of course all the time . . ." he wrote happily.[90] Conscious of his mother's age, he implored her not to start the holiday fa-tigued. Ellen, their servant, would bring her breakfast in bed every morn-ing, and she was to rest in the afternoon.

Vivien was determined to be on her best behaviour for her mother-in-law, despite her ambivalent feelings towards the woman she felt was de-priving Tom of his rightful inheritance. She returned from the sanatorium full of good intentions. Much depended on the visit, for if Charlotte could be persuaded to like her English daughter-in-law, she might agree to hand over to Tom outright, as she had to Henry, the rest of the Hydraulic Press-Brick Company shares, which were holding up well despite the industrial depression. Henry had been trying to convince their mother to take this step, but she refused to make a decision until she had met Vivien. Tom, who was conscious that Vivien had made a financial sacrifice in marrying him, was also anxious to know whether Charlotte would agree to his ear-lier strongly worded request for his wife to receive his inheritance on his death. Eliot had also asked Charlotte to keep up his life insurance, arguing that Vivien would only receive £60 a year from Lloyds in the event of his death.

Vivien's inheritance from her father would not support her, argued Tom, because of heavy death duties and the division of the estate between her and Maurice, who was unemployed after his discharge from the army. In any case, Vivien and Maurice would receive nothing until both parents were dead. Vivien could not support herself, Tom explained, because her eyes were so weak that her oculist only permitted her to do close work for two hours a day—not a convincing excuse in view of the secretarial work she was accustomed to doing.[91] Peter Ackroyd has speculated that Eliot's preoccupation with the possibility of his own death, despite having no serious disease, indicates his suicidal feelings at this time. But it is more likely that Eliot's depression sprang from his fierce sense of injustice at being treated the same way as his mentally handicapped sister, Margaret, was— her shares were also put in trust—as well as his frustration at the lack of time to work on the important poem which it had been his New Year's resolution as long ago as 31 December 1919 to complete.

When she finally disembarked at Southampton on 10 June 1921, the seventy-seven-year-old Charlotte proved not to be the frail old lady her son anticipated, but a "terrifyingly energetic" personage who demanded every moment of Tom's time; of whom, in fact, Tom was "terrified," said Maurice, when he saw his brother-in-law with this "tough old woman who wrote poetry."[92] Coming face to face after six years with this formidable matriarch, the model for Amy in *The Family Reunion,* was a considerable shock to Tom, banishing the false and sentimental memories of childhood recalled from the safety of England, and reviving the fear and sulky obedience of the years in St. Louis. He had to take "Mother dearest" sightseeing, to Stratford and Kenilworth; he was forced to devote weekends to introducing his family to Ottoline at Garsington in August, instead of going to the seaside at Bosham. Despite the poet's handsome presence, which caused Ottoline to remark admiringly to Vivien, "Isn't Tom beautiful, Vivienne, such a *fine mind,* such a grand impression. Such a good walk,"[93] as he escorted Charlotte through the Italian garden created by Ottoline, Virginia sensed the suppressed rage which lay behind Tom's "grim marble face: a mouth twisted & shut; not a single line free & easy; all caught, pressed, inhibited; but great driving power somewhere."[94] To Tom, his mother, sister and brother appeared not as the intimate family members he had anticipated, but as strangers who interrupted the creative solitude for which he longed.

On 7 August, Vivien, Tom and Charlotte Eliot were entertained by Ottoline, and six days later, on the 13th, Vivien and Henry Ware Eliot Jr. visited Ottoline again at Garsington. Tom was present the day after, on the 14th.[95] It was on one such evening, when Tom was talking to Siegfried Sassoon, that Vivien began gossiping to the artist Mark Gertler, whose patron Ottoline had become since meeting him in 1914. Gertler, a frequent Garsington guest, was known for his malicious tongue and self-interest; he and Vivien dashed off arm in arm into the garden and Ottoline suspected that they were laughing about herself and Philip. It was a subject on which she was particularly sensitive after D. H. Lawrence's cruel portrait of her as Hermione Roddice, and Ottoline began to sense that Vivien could be indiscreet. Their friendship, which had been so close, was no longer unsullied.[96]

Nor was there a happy resolution to the financial problem. During July, Vivien and Tom sweltered in the tiny flat in Wigmore Street, "an attic with a glass roof." Vivien asked Charlotte to tea and, anxious to make a good impression, invited the Sitwell brothers to help her manage her guests. "Mrs. Eliot senior, and her daughter were polite, formal, even stiff, black-clothed New Englanders by style and antecedents," remembered Osbert. Vivien had given Osbert the impression that she "bitterly resented" her mother-in-law, explaining that since the death of his father, Tom's mother was well enough off to help her son, and could "spare him the necessity of being a bank-clerk," but that she would not come to his aid owing to her scruples of conscience, "knowing that, because Tom was a poet and not a business man (though he had been forced to become one), his father would have strongly disapproved of any effort that she might make to ease the burden." Osbert was impressed that Vivien seemed "immensely, genuinely, and without selfishness, to resent this treatment of her husband." But he remarked that "when you met old Mrs. Eliot it was difficult to think any ill of her. She appeared to be a strait-laced, straightforward, conventional, but kindly lady."[97]

Mrs. Eliot Senior was not as kindly as Osbert supposed. She blamed and disliked Vivien as much as Vivien blamed and disliked her. She was not convinced that Vivien was really ill. "I am afraid [Tom] finds it impossible to do creative work (other than critical) at home," commented Henry. "Vivien demands a good deal of attention, and I imagine is easily offended if she does not get it well buttered with graciousness and sympathy."[98] In addition she was deeply suspicious of Vivien's brother Maurice, now a louche "young man about town," who would soon leave for Kenya's Happy Valley to make his fortune.[99] The following year, on 8 April 1922 Mrs. Eliot wrote to Henry that she feared that Maurice "would sponge off his sister and brother-in-law."[100] She made up her mind not to transfer the shares, writing her decision into her will in 1923. Charlotte's malevolent jealousy of Vivien can be understood in the words of condemnation Amy, mistress of Wishwood in *The Family Reunion,* delivers on the dead wife of her son Harry: "She never would have been one of the family,/She never wished to be one of the family,/She only wanted to keep him to herself/To satisfy her vanity." Vivien never accepted, says Amy/Charlotte "Harry's relations or Harry's old friends;/She never wanted to fit herself to Harry,/But only to bring Harry down to her own level."[101] The character Mary, for whom Eliot's Cambridge friend Emily Hale was probably the inspiration, talks revealingly of the effect Amy's hatred has on Harry's wife: "And even when *she* died: I believed that Cousin Amy—/I almost believed it—had killed her by willing." Mary asks, "Doesn't that sound awful?" but the strength of Mrs. Eliot's disapproval of Vivien was such that Tom felt able to imagine such a result.[102]

Charlotte Eliot defended her decision not to transfer the Hydraulic Press-Brick Company shares to her second son in a Memorandum summarising Tom's life, which she wrote in 1921 on her return from the fateful visit to England. Her disappointment is evident that her son "unfortunately" postponed his examination at Harvard for his doctorate in philosophy, not literature as he originally planned, until after his return from Göttingen and Oxford; that the war then intervened, and that in the summer of 1914 "he met and married an English lady." Vivien is not even named in this account of Tom's life. Were she able to afford it, wrote Charlotte, she would settle on Tom enough to enable him to devote his entire time to literature, but "this is impossible."[103]

At this juncture, in July 1921, Vivien retreated again to the country, ostensibly for the sake of her health, but Tom urgently summoned her back to help him. It seemed that at last his luck had changed: an opportunity had arisen to crack the safe of English letters. The proposal, brokered by Scofield Thayer and Sydney Schiff, was to establish a new literary quarterly to take the place of the now defunct *Art and Letters;* Eliot was to edit it, and Lady Rothermere,[104] wife of Harold Sydney Harmsworth, first Viscount Rothermere, the owner of the *Daily Mirror,* was to finance it. It was the chance for which he had been waiting, but the negotiations required "exceptional tact," Eliot told Ottoline, and Vivien was *"invalu-*

able."[105] However, as Lady Rothermere continued to stall, Vivien became pessimistic, writing to Scofield Thayer on 20 July that Lady Rothermere "does *not* wish . . . to spill her cash for the cause of Literature . . . I am sorry and Tom is sorry." They were in the midst of a heatwave in London, and Tom had had his family on his hands since early June. Tom was so "tired and hot" that she was taking over his business correspondence, despite joking to her old admirer that her mind had left her and she was gradually becoming insane:

> So you see other people have troubles as well as yourself, and I believe you invited me to come and drown myself with you, once. I am ready at any moment. T. says delighted to review Joyce . . . Well, go and frizzle—we shall be in Paris in *October,* many D's V.[106]

Just before the Eliot party left, Vivien's control snapped. Intuitive enough to sense Charlotte Eliot's implacable hostility towards her, and irritated by her mother-in-law's puritanical manner and financial control over their lives, Vivien at last gave way to her emotions. To Henry, whom she regarded as a friend, although she was disappointed not to see more of him during his visit (perhaps he chose to avoid her), she wrote on 23 August 1921:

> Dear Henry.
> Now I want you to tell me something truly. You are not to lie. Did your mother and sister show, think say or intimate that I behaved like "no lady," and just like a wild animal when [we] saw you off? I was perfectly stunned on that occasion. I had no idea what I was doing. I have been more or less stunned for many months now and when I come to, I suppose it seems dreadful, to an American. I have worried all the time since. Tom said it was perfectly allright etc. but I am sure he has lived here so long he hardly realises how *very* much less English people mind showing their emotions than Americans—or perhaps he does realise it so perfectly. But I was extremely anxious to show no emotion before your family at any time, and then I ended in a fit!

I found the emotionless condition a great strain, all the time. I used to think I should burst out and scream and dance. That's why I used to think you were so terribly failing me. But I won't talk about that now, except to ask you if ever two people made *such* a fearful mess of their obvious possibilities... Goodbye Henry. And *be personal,* you must be personal, or else it is no good.

Nothing's any good.

Vivien.[107]

Although Henry's loyalties lay with his family, he was discerning enough to detect some of the psychological motivation behind Vivien's "invalidism." "I have a feeling that subconsciously (or unconsciously) she likes the role of invalid, and that, liking it as she does to be petted, 'made a fuss over,' condoled and consoled, she ... encourages her breakdowns, instead of throwing them off by a sort of nervous resistance," he wrote to Charlotte on 30 October after his return to Chicago. Henry thought that it was hard to tell how much of Vivien's illness was physical and how much mental and controllable by will power, but if she had more of "the Will to Be Well" she would have less suffering. She needed something to take her mind off herself, something to absorb her entire attention.[108] Henry thought he had discovered the key to Vivien's breakdown after her father's near-fatal illness: that it was the only way she knew of penetrating her husband's remoteness and formality, of reaching a man who otherwise ignored her. He did not see that Eliot, in starving Vivien of affection, was unwittingly contributing to her hysteria.

After Charlotte, Henry and Marian left, Tom and Vivien both became deeply depressed. They lingered on in Wigmore Street, lacking the energy to move back to Clarence Gate Gardens, their only consolation Henry's typewriter, which he had left for his brother to use. "You are ... an angel. A bloody angel ..." wrote Vivien in thanks. Henry's roses were dying miserably in their vase, as she confessed, "We miss you dreadfully." She and Tom did not even have the spirit to buy wine, yet when the evening came they cursed and abused each other for not having gone out to get it.

Quarrels and migraines punctuated their lives. "I feel you are right about Tom. He must somehow be *tamed,*" Vivien wrote to Mary

Hutchinson, warning her not to say anything to Jack. "You don't know it, but he is often very unkind to me in a way, and often makes me wretched."[109] Tom's expectations of his family's visit had been unrealistic; when they left he blamed Vivien for the fact that nothing had changed. They were still trapped in this misery. Overpowered by a sense of anticlimax, he complained to his friends that he was exhausted, "paralysed" by his reaction to his family's departure, although by the end of August he had signed a contract with Lady Rothermere and was plunged into business calculations. Surprisingly, in view of her lack of experience, he turned to Mary Hutchinson for advice, asking whether she thought a new literary periodical the size of *Art and Letters* was possible or worthwhile. Were there enough good contributors, or enough possible subscribers, and what would it all cost? The biggest question of all was, "Whether I am competent and have time enough . . . *Please keep it to yourself till I let you know it may be revealed* . . . Write and comfort me," he begged.[110] Mary offered to meet him—they had not met since April—and they made an assignation at the Piccadilly Hotel for 5:15 p.m. "I will look out for you inside the Regent Street entrance," wrote Tom.[111]

But neither old friends nor society could mend his "emotional derangement." On the verge of collapse, Eliot turned to Richard Aldington, whose own experience of war-shattered nerves and marital problems inclined him to sympathy. Aldington was at the time consoling the Imagist poet and translator Frank Stuart Flint, who was depressed, Harold Monro, who had problems with alcohol, and Frederic Manning (a contributor to Monro's *Chapbook*), complaining to Amy Lowell that his own work was delayed "because of having to rush off from time to time to save people from nervous breakdowns,"[112] but he invited Eliot to Malthouse Cottage, near Reading, where he was living. Even a weekend in September at Aldington's "cottage for neurasthenics"[113] did nothing to restore Tom's spirits, although his friend had written a generous review of *The Sacred Wood,*[114] perhaps in an effort to cheer Tom, who was depressed by the book's generally disappointing reception since its publication in November 1920.

Eliot continued to go downhill rapidly: "I have been feeling very nervous and shaky lately, and have very little self-control . . . Your not being here but in Chicago seems as unreal as death . . ."[115] he told Henry. Vivien was seriously worried, writing to Mary: "Tom is ill. He is overworked and tired of living . . . I wish he could break his leg, it is the only way out of this that I can think of."[116] Fearful that her husband was indeed suicidal after his separation from his family, Vivien decided to take matters into her own hands. At the beginning of October she made an appointment for him to see a celebrated nerve specialist, who, shocked at his patient's mental state, immediately prescribed three months' complete change and rest. The bank agreed to give Tom three months' leave. By now Eliot was barely able to function, sleeping all day and struggling to write the few essential letters before his departure. Asking St. John Hutchinson to write his "London Letter" for *The Dial,* he left on 14 October for Margate with Vivien. "I am supposed to be alone, but I could [not] bear the idea of starting this treatment quite alone in a strange place, and I have asked my wife to come with me and stay with me as long as she is willing,"[117] he explained to Richard Aldington, asking him to house their small cat (a good mouser) while they were in Margate.

The day before Vivien had written to explain the situation to Scofield Thayer:

> Tom has had a rather serious breakdown, and has had to stop all work and go away for three months. He has to follow a strict regimen, and may only read (for pleasure, not profit) two hours a day.

Could Scofield wait for Tom's review of Marianne Moore's poems until February, she asked. She had written to Seldes, Thayer's partner, to tell him that Tom had "fortunately" secured St. John to do the "London Letter." Would Scofield (who was in Vienna) write to Seldes for her about the review, she pleaded. "You have nothing to do, I presume, and look at *my* position. I have not nearly finished my own nervous breakdown yet."[118] It was an ironic letter which demonstrates that Vivien managed to retain a sense of humour in the midst of her trials. She was suffering "hateful stupid temperatures" for no real reason at all, as she confided to Violet Schiff, who had the same troublesome symptom, and had so many business letters to write for Tom.[119]

At Margate, on the Kent coast, Vivien and Tom stayed at the

Albemarle Hotel, Cliftonville, "a nice, comfortable and *inexpensive* little hotel," and Vivien bought her agitated husband a mandolin. Sitting in the shelter on the promenade, he began to pick out the notes. The days passed in walking by the sea and enjoying the air. "You will be pleased to hear that Tom is getting on *amazingly*," wrote Vivien to Violet. "It is not quite a fortnight yet, but he looks already younger and fatter and nicer. He is quite good, and not unhappy, keeping regular hours and being out in this wonderful air nearly all day."[120]

Nevertheless Tom's psychological distress was extreme, and required more than physical exercise and a healthy diet. He and Vivien discussed the idea of consulting Dr. Roger Vittoz, the Swiss psychiatrist who was a favourite of Ottoline Morrell's, whom she had recommended for Bertrand Russell and was now strongly advising Tom to visit. "I want a specialist in psychological troubles," Eliot wrote to Julian Huxley, whom Ottoline had also sent as a patient to Vittoz in 1918, after Huxley had collapsed with a nervous breakdown following his honeymoon.[121] Meanwhile Vivien reported to Mary: "I have started Tom well and he shows great improvement already." After two weeks she returned to London.

Tom continued to sit in the shelter on the promenade, to sketch the passers-by and practise scales on his mandolin. At last there was time to turn again to the manuscript of *The Waste Land* on which he had been working sporadically between crises for the last two years. He told Schiff on 4 November that he had done "a rough draft of part of Part III," calling it "The Fire Sermon." "I do not know whether it will do & must wait for Vivien's opinion."[122]

While Tom remained in Margate, Vivien wrote to Russell to congratulate him on the arrival of his first son, John Conrad, following his marriage to Dora Black. "As you know, Tom is having a bad nervous—or so called—breakdown . . . He is at present at Margate, of all cheerful spots! But he seems to like it," she wrote. In an allusion to Tom's poem "Mr. Apollinax," in which Russell's satanic aspect is stressed, she wrote: "Tom says he is quite sure the baby *will* have pointed ears, so you need not be anxious. Even if not pointed at birth, they will sharpen in time."[123] It was a painful letter for Vivien to write. Bravely she hid her true feelings, for she often missed Bertie's companionship in the days of misery since the end of their affair. In a revealing undated letter to Ottoline she had written:

About Bertie, you know he was *extraordinarily generous* to me. I
mean in *giving* things. So much so that it will always make me feel
mean for talking against him. I know you understand perfectly.
But I think he was more generous to me than he has ever been to
anyone. He really made a sacrifice. I shall never forget that, and
it makes a lot of difference to *everything*. I have really suffered
awfully in the complete collapse of our relationship, for I *was*
fond of Bertie (I think I still am). But it is of course hopeless. I
shall never try to see him again.[124]

On 18 November 1921 Vivien escorted her husband across the
Channel to Paris, where she and Tom stayed with Ezra and Dorothy
Pound at 70 bis rue Notre Dame des Champs. A few days later Tom trav-
elled on alone to Lausanne to meet the psychiatrist Roger Vittoz.

13

The Waste Land

Vivien found it difficult at first to get "a clutch on Paris." After being immured in England for seven years, it was painful to be torn up by the roots, and "thrown, hurled, alone & stunned, into such a strange way of living." The first few days alone with Tom were perfect, she told Mary, but then the moment came when she was forced to take her husband to the station and watch him climb onto the "dreadful Swiss train." Vivien was left alone on the platform at 9:20 in the evening, feeling as if someone had taken a broomstick to her and knocked her on the head.

The empty weeks stretched ahead. She had no idea when Tom would return to Paris. "I was so *absolutely* alone," she wrote to Mary on 16 November 1921: "All the French I knew deserted me." But gradually, like someone slowly coming back to life after a long hibernation, Vivien forgot London and became absorbed in Parisian life. It was a relief to leave behind the Bloomsbury backbiting and literary feuds which she had come to detest, to forget the " 'intellectual' party" given by Lady Rothermere ("What a woman"), and the last evening at the Huxleys which epitomised everything she disliked about "the whole stupid round": the monotony, the *"drivel,"*[1] which had given her "an awful down on London." Mary would disagree with her, acknowledged Vivien, but she was glad to turn her back on it all. Yet even from the safe distance of the Hotel du Pas-de-Calais, 59 rue des Saints-Pères, a narrow turning off the Boulevard Saint-Germain, she could not help worrying if the Eliots' "enemies" were talking behind their backs. "Stick up for me if you hear nasty things (they will be lies) and also for Tom," she begged her friend.[2]

Although Vivien professed to miss Mary, the Pounds' kindness compensated for her absence. Ezra and Dorothy had made their home on the Left Bank, renting an "exquisite" studio, with two rooms on rue Notre

Dame des Champs, the street where Whistler had lived as a young man. The studio was not far from Vivien's hotel and the fashionable bohemian bar Les Deux Magots, and only cost £75 a year. Vivien herself was marooned in a "high up little room" and having meals *en pension,* which she loathed. She envied the Pounds their snug nest, for she had already decided that she would prefer to live in Paris rather than London. "For Tom, I am *convinced,* Paris!" Although the city was incredibly dear—"it costs *fortunes*," she complained, it had a vibrant artistic life, to which Vivien had the entrée through Pound, who performed the same role of impresario to impoverished and undiscovered artists and writers in Paris as he had done in London, bringing James and Nora Joyce to a supper party where the Irishman met Sylvia Beach, publisher and owner of the famous bookshop Shakespeare and Company. Pound, as flamboyant as ever in his velvet jacket and "open road shirt," his jutting red beard reminding one writer of a fox's muzzle, had persuaded Ernest Hemingway, W. B. Yeats, and André Gide to subscribe to Beach's costs in publishing *Ulysses.*[3] In between writing his Cantos and encouraging the sculptor Constantin Brancusi, Pound made his own furniture and cooked over an oil lamp, producing, declared Wyndham Lewis, better suppers than in London.

Pound took Vivien three times to meet the thirty-eight-year-old Joyce, but although she admired him as a writer, she did not find the "cantankerous Irishman," in his long overcoat and tennis shoes, an agreeable acquaintance. The attraction of Paris for her lay not in the presence of Hemingway, Ford Madox Ford, Lewis, Aldington, or even Gertrude Stein, but in the prospect of a *rendez-vous* somewhere on the continent with her close friend and former suitor, Scofield Thayer, who had arrived in Paris in July 1921 with e.e. cummings. While Pound had stayed at the cheap hotel on the rue des Saints-Pères that he recommended to Vivien, Thayer had been able to afford the luxurious Hotel Continental on the rue Castiglione. But by the time of the Eliots' arrival in November the bird had flown. Scofield had left for Cologne, having told Vivien on 27 July that he preferred the "coolth" of Germany. His plan was to move on to Vienna sometime in October: "If en route to Paris you should get the wrong train and get out at Vienna, be sure to look me up,"[4] he wrote.

Scofield's sympathy meant a great deal to Vivien; there was no one else apart from Ezra Pound whose friendship predated her marriage, and who she felt understood her troubles. "Yes, drowning just now should certainly be the thing," he had responded ironically to her last letter offering to drown herself with him. Scofield was sorry that Vivien and Tom were so troubled, remarking that to have one's family on one's hands in midsummer struck him as no less appropriate than to wear mittens. "Goethe once observed, speaking of his love affairs, that it was pleasant to see the moon rise before the sun set," he wrote on 20 October in another attempt to comfort Vivien. "But such is not I presume the case with nervous breakdowns, especially when they are both in the same family."[5] Vivien applied for a German visa, as Thayer was still in Cologne, but then as the value of the Deutschmark fell, she decided to wait for Scofield's return. Meanwhile she exhibited few signs of mental strain: to the concert pianist Olga Rudge, Vivien, to whom she was introduced by her friend Pound, seemed "very charming, perfectly normal."[6]

While she waited at the Hotel du Pas-de-Calais for the return of "the man from Cologne," as she discreetly described him to Mary, anxious no doubt that Clive's wagging tongue would not broadcast tales of her meeting with Thayer to Bloomsbury ears, Vivien began to record her impressions of Paris in a notebook. It was not the first time she had considered writing creatively, for she was a "reckless" letter-writer already, as Virginia and Brigit Patmore both noticed, as well as a diarist, but while she still hoped to dance or act professionally it did not occur to her to think of writing for publication. Nor were the war years in London conducive to writing: in 1918 Vivien had written that "life is so feverish and yet so dreary at the same time, and one is always waiting, waiting for something. Generally waiting for some particular strain to be over. One thinks, when this is over I will write. And then there is something else. For *months* now I have waited for T. to be settled [over joining the army]. I am also waiting to be well."[7] Later, Virginia Woolf was to claim that she was the person who had first suggested to Vivien that she might write, but it is possible that Vivien had begun recording her thoughts in her writing book in adolescence, during the long days of being confined to bed for treatment of TB of the bone. She has been "writing for a long time," Tom admitted to Ottoline, who challenged him over Vivien's authorship of a poem in the *Criterion* in May 1925, "and I have always suspected that you knew it!"[8]

Ottoline herself was an example to Vivien. Ottoline confided to

Dorothy Brett as early as 1916 that she was writing her memoirs, and showed her extracts from her journal;[9] Vivien may also have seen Ottoline's work in about 1919 when they became intimate, and felt encouraged that her friend, despite being "very diffident" at any thought of competing with her celebrated guests, nevertheless dared to record her own opinions of the authors who rarely hesitated to caricature her. But it was Mary Hutchinson, a published writer, who was Vivien's prime inspiration; fashionable, flirty Mary, rather than the cool Virginia or "acid" Katherine Mansfield, served as her role model. However, there is also little doubt that in 1921 Vivien, just as much as Tom, felt a compelling need to express her despair with her tormented marriage. To do so was a form of therapy. In addition, both the Eliots were suddenly free from the domestic responsibility for which they were singularly ill-fitted, and had the time and solitude necessary for creativity.

The prospect of the launch of Lady Rothermere's new review may have been an added inducement to Vivien. The *Criterion,* a name which Vivien suggested,[10] inspired by a hotel at which she and Charles Buckle used to dine, could provide her with an outlet for the prose sketches with which she was experimenting. Her husband, as editor, might be persuaded to give her the same chance as he had given Mary at the *Egoist.*

Whatever her reasons, Vivien's prose sketches were autobiographical, a fact which was to be her undoing. In "A Diary of the Rive Gauche," she writes in the first person, painting a vivid picture of herself, aimlessly walking the streets of the Latin Quarter. For three days it had been raining, "the cold hard venomous rain of Paris. Very different from the soft enveloping moisture of London where often one can hardly tell if it is raining or not. Wet English weather, and a wet wind, say I. Steam heating and harsh winds soon take the bloom off poor thin-skinned English faces." At last the rain stopped, to be replaced by a fierce, drying wind which cut through the narrow streets and blew full blast over the bridges. Vivien took refuge in the pension's salon, bringing her writing materials downstairs because the chambermaid Victorine and her husband were cleaning her room. The salon was so small that only four people could sit in it, and anyone could read what Vivien was writing unless she hedged the paper with her left arm like an awkward schoolgirl over a letter. No light penetrated into the room except that from the open door into the hall, and the radiator heated it to suffocation; but she found the warmth comforting and began to write. The theme she took was one much on her mind: the relationship between an American man and an Englishwoman.

> There is a strange man in the salon, who is obviously waiting for someone. He holds his hat in his hand. He is American, I think. He looks at me from time to time and I feel sure that he contemplates asking me a question. But why me? Although of course the others are obviously French: the pale, austere old lady, and the uncomfortable-looking middle-aged woman who glares at me so indignantly. So many people look at one indignantly here. One gets used to it. Hardened.[11]

Vivien sympathises with the other guests' disapproval. She is, after all, in loose shabby clothes with no hat and slippers on her feet, daring to sprawl at the writing-table and write on and on without stopping or looking up or making any of the impatient clicks or ejaculations that they do. The middle-aged woman is wearing "black bombazine or some such harsh material, made very tight and fitting to her figure—a *real* figure, not a few bones with rags hung on, like mine. No wonder she is indignant." At this point the stranger addresses Vivien:

> "Pardon me!—but do you happen to be acquainted with Miss Newton who is staying in this hotel?"
> "No," I say flatly.
> "You will excuse me addressing you, I hope; but I took you for English—" he looks at me hard.
> "Yes—?"
> "I'm an American," he tells me, most unnecessarily; "and I made the acquaintance of Miss Newton at the Soirée last Friday at the Consulate. I asked her if she would like to go to one of these Latin Quarter balls."

His next question provokes Vivien's irritation: might he take Miss Newton to the ball without a chaperone?

Now is this fair? First of all, I have seen his "American girl"—an arch miss of about forty, fresh from Main Street, and I am only—well, never mind, but that's that. Why should *I* know? Why ask *me*? *I* am indignant now. There are three indignant people in this salon now . . .

At this point the middle-aged person in black begins to tremble with disapproval. The old lady comes out of her swoon, and with one look of horror swoons again. Vivien gathers up her writing materials. "I am sorry," she says, "but I have never been to a ball in Paris." The American actually dares to appear incredulous. "I know nothing whatever about balls in Paris," she continues coldly, leaving the salon with all the dignity she can muster.

On the way up the five flights of stairs Vivien reminds herself that she has always found Americans to be a mystery:

I simply do not understand Americans. When I see an American coming I ought to say immediately, "Please do not speak to me, because if you do I shall not understand you. I shall never understand you, so will you please pass on." For instance, why do Americans insist that all European women are *au courant* with every form of vice (to them all pleasure and amusement really means vice, so far as I can see) whereas they insinuate that the female of their own species is supremely innocent and unsullied. They actually appear to be trying to protect their own women from *us!* Why? Because they cannot cope with European women. Ha! They can't cope with us!

The note of personal resentment in this description in "Diary of the Rive Gauche" of the American male suggests Vivien was brooding over Tom and the nostalgic feelings she believed he still harboured towards Emily Hale, the refined New England drama teacher he knew at Cambridge; Emily was a woman of whom Vivien would have heard much from her indiscreet friend Lucy Thayer, although Tom's sister Marian may have proved more reticent when she came to stay. But Vivien was already sensitive to any hint that she did not measure up to the standards of purity and education of a young woman such as Emily, who remained on the other side of the Atlantic, unmarried, forlorn, waiting. Vivien's barbed remark that to an American all pleasure means vice, was no doubt aimed at Tom, who she felt had misled her. When they met had he not delighted in dancing, smoking, talking with her? And yet by 1921 he condemned such pleasures as "vice," although he was prepared to practise them with alternative companions. Vivien may have felt that it was her affair with Russell—although he did not object to it at the time—which had altered her husband's perception of her morals and had a disastrous effect on their relationship.[12]

While Vivien remained in Paris, struggling to exist on £5 a week, for she was paying her living expenses out of her own small income from her father, Tom had put himself into the hands of Dr. Vittoz at his sanatorium in Lausanne. In Margate Tom had reassured himself that he was not psychotic, telling Richard Aldington that his "nerves" were "a very mild affair, due not to overwork but to an *aboulie* and emotional derangement which has been a lifelong affliction. Nothing wrong with my mind."[13] Certainly Eliot's hesitancy and slowness, which he described as *aboulie* or want of will, was noticeable to observers who invariably commented on it. Russell, for example, wrote to Ottoline that Eliot's "slowness is a sort of nervous affliction due to lack of vitality. It *is* annoying—it used to drive his wife almost to physical violence—but one gets used to it."[14] It was this paralysing indecisiveness which led Vivien to write to Jack Hutchinson: "As to Tom's *mind,* I *am* his mind,"[15] and to claim that she gave him the "shove" responsible for his success.

Yet had Eliot's psychiatric illness been as mild as he implied to Aldington, he would have accepted Lady Rothermere's offer of the free use of her villa above Monte Carlo, as he first intended, rather than travelling to the sanatorium which he knew to be expensive.[16] It was his knowledge that he was in urgent need of help which drove him to seek Vittoz, a "specialist in psychological troubles." The insistent "voices," both male and female, which Eliot heard talking to him when he tried to sleep, and which concerned him enough to complain of them much later on, in the 1950s, to Mary Trevelyan, a close friend at the time, may have troubled him earlier in life, and triggered fears for his own sanity.[17]

The therapy offered by the Swiss psychiatrist was simple, and in all probability his apparent success in Eliot's case was due to the transference which occurred between therapist and patient. The poet's symptoms and their causes were manifold, suggests the psychiatrist Dr. Harry Trosman:

> Depression with exhaustion, indecisiveness, hypochondriasis, and fear of psychosis. His personality had been aloof and distant and he guarded himself against the intrusions of others with icy urbanity. Compulsive defences enabled him to isolate his emotions. Sexuality was a potent danger not only because of intense conflict but because instinctual forces threatened him with loss of ego control and dominance.[18]

Trosman argues that Eliot's equilibrium was easily vulnerable to injury as a result of his deprived childhood, in which he felt "isolated and uncomfortable in his ill-fitting masculinity . . . His illness can be characterised as a transitory narcissistic regression with partial fragmentation and loss of ego dominance." This diagnosis accords with Eliot's own sense of a disintegrating self, and Trosman's theory that *The Waste Land* served as a form of "self-analytic work" is supported by Eliot's own confession, when he writes towards the end of the poem: "These fragments I have shored against my ruins." He was, according to Trosman, describing "a process of partial integration."

Eliot acknowledged the creative and therapeutic aspect of his psychological illness, writing that some form of ill-health, such as debility or anaemia, might produce "an efflux of poetry." What one wrote in this way gave the impression of having undergone a long incubation—"though we do not know until the shell breaks what kind of egg we have been sitting on." Such moments "are characterised by the sudden lifting of the burden of anxiety and fear which presses upon our daily life so steadily," and the accompanying feeling was one of "a sudden relief from an intolerable burden."[19]

The programme of "cerebral re-education" to which Eliot now submitted himself was a treatment plan devised by the Swiss psychiatrist, who laid his hands upon the patient's forehead in order to feel the disordered vibrations of the "cerebral hemispheres" before setting simple mental exercises intended to relax him. Vittoz would ask Eliot to look at a rose in a vase or a hat on a rack, and to concentrate on the sensations aroused; with eyes shut the patient would retain the image, and then eliminate it. "Be like a photographic plate," commanded Vittoz. "Eliminate thought." One also had to practise eliminating letters from words, or one number from a set of numbers, recalled Ottoline. "Julian would laugh at me when, perhaps in the train, she would see me gazing into space—'There is Mummy eliminating.' "[20] The emphasis was on calmness and rest, as the patient gradually learnt to exercise and master the will. Vittoz compared his treatment to the tuning of a piano, bringing harmony and control to an overanxious mind and, as Eliot settled into Ottoline's old room at the Hotel Ste. Luce, and enjoyed the "excellent" food, he was reassured by the psychiatrist's diagnosis, writing to Ottoline: "I never did believe in 'nerves,' at least for myself!"[21]

Vittoz's success owed more to his personality than to any magical ability to detect brain vibrations. "I like him very much personally," wrote Eliot, "and he inspires me with confidence."[22] The psychiatrist urged his patients to follow the model of Christ, to take the path of sainthood and self-control, moral exhortations which to Eliot's ears echoed those of his grandfather, William Greenleaf Eliot, and his mother, and would also have appealed to Ottoline, who was deeply religious. "I am trying to learn how to use all my energy without waste, to be *calm* when there is nothing to be gained by worry, and to concentrate without effort," Eliot wrote to his brother on 13 December. "I hope I shall place less strain on Vivien, who has had to do so much *thinking* for me."[23]

It is likely that Vittoz functioned as a paternal figure whom Eliot felt able to idealise and obey, for he told Ottoline that although he could not tell *much* about the method yet, he felt much calmer than he had for many years since childhood. "That may be illusory—we shall see." Certainly the sanatorium provided the ambience, free of the multiple pressures of banking, literary journalism, Bloomsbury parties and domestic demands, in which Eliot was able to complete *The Waste Land*. "This is Tom's autobiography," exclaimed Mary Hutchinson, when she first read *The Waste Land*.

The poem's intense emotion, so tightly controlled, its springs disguised by a trail of footnotes which lead away from the source, led the critic Edmund Wilson to hail Eliot's greatness despite the poem's obscurity. "The acuteness of his suffering gives poignancy to his art," he wrote in *The Dial*.[24] "These drops, though they may be wrung from flint, are nonetheless authentic crystals. They are broken and sometimes infinitely tiny, but they are worth more than all the rhinestones on the market." Wilson's thesis in "Philoctetes: The Wound and the Bow" (1929) that it is the suffering of the artist which inspires creativity, was true of Eliot, who, like Sophocles' Philoctetes, had a wound which would not heal; like Philoctetes the wounded archer of Wilson's essay, Eliot's genius became "purer and deeper in ratio to his isolation and outlawry."[25] The poet's anguish was as complex as the man: its roots lay in his grief for Jean Verdenal and a love cut short by death, the cruel comparison to an unloved wife who reproached him with sexual failure, and his disillusion with the post-war world.

From Joyce, Eliot borrowed the idea of myth as the starting point for his work. Just as Joyce had based *Ulysses* upon the *Odyssey,* so Eliot took the Arthurian legend of the Holy Grail and the impotent Fisher King who rules a waste land, a desolate and sterile country in which not only have the crops ceased to grow, the animals to reproduce, but even human beings no longer bear children. The wound of the Fisher King can only be healed by the success of the Knight who has come to find the Holy Grail, which will allow the land to be renewed.[26] For Wilson, like other contemporary readers of Eliot's poem, the meaning behind the myth was not altogether clear. Virginia Woolf spoke for many when she commented after a visit from Tom during which he read his new poem aloud to her: "I have only the sound of it in my ears, when he read it aloud; and have not yet tackled the sense. But I liked the sound."[27] But Wilson, in his review in *The Dial,* was the first to interpret the poem as social criticism. He saw the waste land as a concrete image of spiritual drought, the action of the poem taking place half in the real world of London, half in the wilderness of medieval legend: "The Waste Land is only the hero's arid soul and the intolerable world around him, our post-War world of shattered institutions, strained nerves and bankrupt ideals." The poet's sense of futility is expressed in the words of the Cumaean Sibyl, who was condemned to live for as long as the number of grains of sand in her hand; when asked by little boys what she wanted, she replied only, "I want to die."[28] It was one of the layered meanings behind the declaration, "I will show you fear in a handful of dust."

The obscurity of the poem, whose four hundred lines contained quotations from, allusions to, and parodies of a daunting list of earlier writers from Buddha to Wagner, led critics away from any attempt to relate the poem to the facts of Eliot's life.[29] It continued to be viewed as the expression of the disillusionment of a generation; Hugh Kenner, for example, wrote that Eliot went to Margate "preoccupied with the ruin of post-war Europe."[30] But the footnotes were a carefully laid wild-goose chase, the scholarship much more than the "peevish assumption of superiority" of a "timid and prosaic" poet noted by Wilson.[31] Together they functioned as a smokescreen behind which Eliot hid his need to confess, while over future decades his impersonal theory of poetry put an embargo on decoding a poet's work as a personal statement. Yet Eliot tapped into the mood of despair and disillusion of 1921 precisely because he was writing about his own inner despair and disillusion. He used the material of his own life and made it universal, as has been recognised by some later critics, transmuting his "personal and private agonies into something rich and strange."[32] "It is an anguished personal revelation and an austere cultural monument," argues John T. Mayer.[33]

Later, Eliot repented of having sent his readers in the wrong direction, and wished to correct the poem's reputation, writing: "Various critics have considered it, indeed, as an important bit of social criticism. To me it was only the relief of a personal and wholly insignificant grouse against life; it is just a piece of rhythmical grumbling."[34] This disclaimer was almost as far from the truth as some early critics' comments. Valerie Eliot's publication of the original drafts, showing the radical revision made by Ezra Pound, which removed much of the personal element from her husband's writing and made it more opaque, gives a tantalising glimpse of what he longed to reveal.

In Lausanne, "this decayed hole among the mountains," Eliot ruminated over his past life, "in every detail of desire, temptation and surrender during that supreme moment of complete knowledge," as he put it in the words of Conrad he originally chose as an epigraph. In a flash of insight he saw "The horror! The horror!"—and felt a sense of identification with the dying Kurtz.[35] It was an extreme state of mind, one he would later describe as the poet "haunted by a demon, a demon against which he feels powerless, because in its first manifestation it has no face, no name, nothing; and the words, the poem he makes, are a kind of form of exorcism of this demon."[36]

Conversation with the other patients, the "people of many nationalities, which I always like," penetrated his gloom, and perhaps stimulated him to write—just as writing in French had done previously—and a *mélange* of foreign phrases found its way into his poem.[37] Memories of his visits to Germany flooded back to him, of the Hofgarten in Marburg, of the Starnbergersee near Munich and of a Lithuanian girl he had met there, originally from Russia, who claimed, to Eliot's amused surprise, that she was a "real German"—"Bin gar keine Russin, stamm' aus Litauen, echt deutsch."[38] A remembered conversation with Countess Marie Larisch, niece of the Austrian Empress Elizabeth, whom Eliot apparently met in 1911, also worked its way into the poem; as a child she had stayed with her cousin, the archduke: "he took me out on a sled,/And I was frightened. He said, Marie,/Marie, hold on tight."[39]

But most of all Eliot's thoughts returned to his last summer trip to Munich, on which Verdenal may have accompanied him, and to that Paris winter of 1910–11 ("Winter kept us warm") in the pension with Jean. Trosman speculates that during periods of "regressive isolation," such as in the confinement of the clinic, Eliot was flooded with "unacceptable homosexual longings . . . To such longings Eliot responded with panic." In 1952 a Canadian critic, John Peter, suggested in *Essays in Criticism* that *The Waste Land* was indeed written as an elegy for Jean Verdenal. Peter's reading of the poem was breathtakingly simple:

At some previous time the speaker has fallen completely—perhaps the right word is "irretrievably" in love. The object of this love was a young man who soon afterwards met his death, it would seem by drowning. Enough time has elapsed now since his death for the speaker to have realised that the focus for affection that he once provided is irreplaceable. The monologue which, in effect, the poem presents is a meditation upon this deprivation, upon the speaker's stunned and horrified reaction to it, and on the picture which, as seen through its all but insupportable blackness, the world presents.[40]

A later critic, James E. Miller, has compared *The Waste Land* to Tennyson's mourning for the dead Arthur Hallam in *In Memoriam;* in a revealing comment, Eliot praised Tennyson's poem as "a long poem, made by putting together lyrics, which have only the unity and continuity of a diary, the concentrated diary of a man confessing himself."[41]

John Peter's homosexual interpretation of the poem brought an angry response from Eliot, who threatened to sue the editor of the journal; as a result the remaining copies of the offending issue were pulped. Not until after Eliot's death in 1965 was the critic able to restate his case. In 1969 his article was republished with an interesting "Postscript" in which he identified Phlebas the Phoenician as Jean Verdenal, and described how he was obliged to tender an apology to Eliot through his solicitors. The poet accepted his apology, indicating that "he considered it neither necessary nor desirable for a public retraction to appear" but that he would take "the very gravest view of any further dissemination of this article or the views expressed in it." Eliot's solicitors informed Peter that their client had read his essay and found it "absurd" and "completely erroneous."[42]

Nevertheless Peter's case is a convincing one. The recurrent image in *The Waste Land,* to which Eliot returns obsessively, is of Verdenal walking towards him in the Luxembourg Gardens, his arms full of lilacs. Eliot's memory forces him to a bitter contradiction of Chaucer, who had welcomed April with its "shoures sweete":

> April is the cruellest month, breeding
> Lilacs out of the dead land, mixing
> Memory and desire, stirring
> Dull roots with spring rain.

Eliot never knew exactly how Verdenal died on 2 May 1915, remaining uncertain whether he was "mixed with the mud of Gallipoli."[43] Was Jean drowned ("those are pearls that were his eyes") or did he die on land? Influenced by the army citation dated 30 April 1915, which describes the young medical officer up to his waist in water, helping to evacuate the wounded by sea, Tom came to believe that the sea had claimed Jean, even if the officer's bones were left in the mud of Gallipoli. In the poem there are images of death on land: "White bodies naked on the low damp ground ... Rattled by the rat's foot only, year to year." None, however, are so powerful as the lines in "Death by Water" commemorating "Phlebas the Phoenician, a fortnight dead .../A current under sea/Picked his bones in whispers." The repetition of earlier lines from "Dans le Restaurant," which mourned "Phlebas" in almost identical phrases in French—the heartfelt plea to the reader to remember Phlebas, "once handsome and tall as you"—supports the contention that Verdenal is central to *The Waste Land*.[44]

The "dull roots" stirred by the spring rain suggest a reawakening of Eliot's repressed sexuality, the mixing of memory and desire as he relives the sweet spring shared with Jean. Since April, in its cruelty, has deprived him of his companion, he is cast out in the stony desert ("Come in under the shadow of this red rock") in a fragment of verse taken from his own earlier poem, "Saint Narcissus," in which the saint is transformed from a beautiful youth, entranced with his own physicality, into a young girl who is raped in the woods. In that poem, because "he could not live men's ways," the poet-protagonist becomes "a dancer before God," dancing on the hot sand, in a poem which anticipates both the homoerotic imagery of *The Waste Land* and the androgyny of Tiresias.[45]

The anguish of the poet's situation in the shadow of the rock melts into fresh memories of the past, evoked by a verse from Wagner's *Tristan und Isolde*: "*Frisch weht der Wind/Der Heimat zu./Mein irisch Kind,/Wo weilest du?*" (The wind blows fresh homeward, my Irish child, where do you tarry?). The sailor is singing with an ardour once shared by the speaker.[46] The poet then returns to the ecstatic moment, "... when we came back, late, from the hyacinth garden,/Your arms full, and your hair wet, I could not/Speak, and my eyes failed, ... and I knew nothing,/ Looking into the heart of light, the silence."

These lines evoked a mood of bliss and transcendence, shattered by the second fragment of the opera, which Jean and Tom saw together in Paris; its message is brutal: "*Oed' und leer das Meer.*" The sea is empty and desolate, the sailor drowned, a message reinforced by the fortune-teller Madame Sosostris, who deals the tarot cards (a practice to which Eliot had been introduced in Primrose Hill in north London). Here, she says, is your card, the drowned Phoenician Sailor. The accompanying quotation from *The Tempest,* "Those are pearls that were his eyes," is repeated, the reprise in Eliot's tale of lamentation. But the next card dealt by Madame Sosostris (another incarnation for the satanic Russell, derived from Aldous Huxley's *Chrome Yellow*)[47] is Belladonna, the amorous "lady of situations."[48] She is juxtaposed, in the original draft, with the Fisher King, symbol of impotence and sterility, and only in the cut version is the less revealing card, the "man with three staves," substituted. "Fear death by water," is the fortune-teller's prophecy to the protagonist, underlining the bereavement to come.[49]

Was "the moment's surrender," to which Eliot refers with such emotion in a later passage, to the "seductive" Vivien—as Sencourt argues—or to Jean Verdenal? Or was it indeed to the Virgin, in spiritual surrender, as Helen Gardner believed?[50] Eliot wrote in his original version of this irrevocable moment of fulfillment: "We brother, what have we given?/My friend, my friend, beating in my heart,/The awful daring of a moment's surrender/Which an age of prudence can never retract—"[51] Clearly his partner here is masculine. The facsimile edition of the poem, which includes the cuts made by Ezra Pound, confirms the homosexual theme eliminated from the 1922 version.[52] This is underlined by Eliot's final benediction: "Those are pearls that were his eyes. See/Still and quiet brother are you still and quiet."[53]

The image of eyes associated with a lover lost to the "kingdom of the dead" is one to which Eliot returns in three poems he entitled "Doris's Dream Songs," which were published by Harold Monro in his *Chapbook* in 1924 and later incorporated into "The Hollow Men." He speaks of "Eyes that last I saw in tears/Through division." In his "dream kingdom/The golden vision reappears."[54] The eyes are "eyes of decision," perhaps after Verdenal decided to enlist. The poet mourns the fact that they are "Eyes that I shall not see unless/At the door of death's other kingdom." As in *The Waste Land,* the protagonist now exists in "the dead land . . . the cactus land" (perhaps derived from memories of the desiccated landscape of Arizona or Texas), his mind circling around the "golden vision" of Verdenal, lit up by the "sentimental sunset" of their tryst in the

Luxembourg Gardens. "This is my affliction," confesses the poet, a reminder that inversion, although acceptable to Bloomsbury, was considered by society at large to be a deviant sexuality, and in his own mind perhaps remained so. He asks poignantly whether it is like this in death's other kingdom, walking alone "At the hour when we are/Trembling with tenderness/Lips that would kiss/Form prayers to broken stone."[55] The same lyrical and sensual mood celebrating an "angelic" lover is expressed in Eliot's earlier "dream poem," "Song to the Opherian,"[56] in which the "golden foot" he may not kiss or clutch glows in the shadow of the bed "Waiting that touch—that breath."[57]

The memory of Verdenal may have been transfigured in Eliot's imagination into something of far greater significance than the bare facts of the relationship warrant. The dedication of his first volume of poems to his friend in 1917, rather than to his parents, to Vivien, or indeed to Pound; the repetition of that dedication in *Ara Vos Prec* in 1920, linked to the passionate Dante epigraph ("Now you are able to comprehend the quantity of love that warms me toward you . . .")[58] was not only an affirmation of love, but a tribute to the powerful spell the dead can cast over those who survive.[59] W. H. Auden speculated that even as late as 1942, Eliot was thinking of Verdenal when he wrote the Dante section of "Little Gidding": "Of course Dante was meant, but he probably had something more personal in mind."[60]

It is difficult to imagine a more powerful contrast to the tremulous tenderness of love directed towards a "brother" than the deep hostility of the verses whose subject is a woman. Eliot's fantasy of wife murder is expressed in "The Death of a Duchess," a section of the original *Waste Land* text, which he modelled on John Webster's *The Duchess of Malfi,* precisely because both the "breathless tension" and the plot of the Jacobean dramatist mirrored Vivien's and his own situation. Just as Webster's Duchess has married her steward, Antonio, a misalliance which leads to her misery and death, so this modern Duchess and her husband are "bound forever on the wheel" in Hampstead, where even the aspidistra grieves at the entrapment of marriage. "It is terrible to be alone with another person."[61] This flat statement of despair resonates with the "cold fury" of "André," the scowling husband in one of Vivien's most powerful short stories.[62] The poet's feelings are angry, confused and primitive: they have tails and hang like monkeys from the chandelier. The woman brushes her hair in fierce strokes so that under the brush her hair is spread out in "little fiery points of will" and glows into words almost identical to those of Webster, who wrote originally:

> You have cause to love me, I entered you in my heart
> Before you would vouchsafe to call for the keys.[63]

It is a reproach which underlines Eliot's indebtedness to Vivien who gave him her love when he was penniless and unknown: "She has everything to give that I want and she gives it. I owe her everything," he had written to his father in 1915.[64]

As in Webster's original scene, the woman in "Death of a Duchess" turns her back, giving her husband the opportunity to leave. "Time to regain the door," writes Eliot, echoing Antonio's desertion of his wife. Should he feign love, he wonders, say "I love you." What would be the point? "If it is terrible alone, it is sordid with one more." Whether he pretends love or not, the meaningless routine of their lives will continue, the daily drives, the games of chess which fill up the hours. It was Vivien who asked Eliot to delete the line "The ivory men make company between us" (from "A Game of Chess"), so revealing their incompatibility, although her first instinct had been to scribble an enthusiastic "Yes" against the chess verses. Eliot did as she asked in the first printed version, but in 1960 restored the line from memory.[65]

In "Death of a Duchess," an importunate, vulnerable woman meets a similar fate to Webster's Duchess, who is stabbed by her brother Ferdinand. Eliot's Duchess pleads despairingly with her husband: "But I know you love me, it must be that you love me." Grimly the poet disposes of his victim: "Then I suppose they found her/As she turned/To interrogate the silence behind her." The cancelled lines which follow—"I am steward of her revenue/But I know, and I know she knew . . ."[66]—imply the wife may guess the fate she is about to meet, and emphasise the connection between the monologue and its original source in Webster's drama. Eliot's continual rehearsal of a wife's desertion and death prepared his mind for the desertion of Vivien, which he was probably already considering; his belief that he would in some way cause her death may also be foreshadowed in *The Waste Land.*

"Death of the Duchess" was in the end sacrificed by Pound, with only a few lines being incorporated into Part II of *The Waste Land,* originally entitled "In the Cage" (perhaps inspired by the Henry James novella "In the Cage") and later changed to the less revealing "A Game of Chess."[67] Vivien also used the metaphor of a cage to describe the entrapment of marriage. "Now one begins to beat against the bars of the cage. One's soul stirs stiffly out of the dead endurance of the winter—but toward what spring?" she would write in "Letters of the Moment—1," in the *Criterion.*[68] The image of the captured bird, trying to fly, was one with which she identified in Stravinsky's *Firebird:* "It tries to fly, over and over again, wings beating."[69] The sibyl of Eliot's epigraph, from the *Satyricon* of Petronius, is also in a cage, waiting to die, and it can be no coincidence that Vivien chose the name "Sibylla" for the unhappy wife in several of her short stories, for there were occasions during her own marriage when she felt suicidal.[70]

Eliot's lines in "A Game of Chess" describe a woman imprisoned, and the cage metaphor is appropriate to the animalistic passions of the scenes which follow, in which woman is no longer Madonna or muse, but *femme fatale,* enslaving men through her seductive arts in whatever class of society she finds herself. The opulent description of Belladonna—a beautiful but poisonous woman—sitting on her throne is sardonic in its intention; marble, gold, glitter, and overpowering perfume surround her, tempting and even inviting the rape which is the fate of Philomel, at the hands of her brother-in-law Tereus. Mutilated, her tongue ripped out, Philomel is transformed into a nightingale whose cry, "Jug Jug," is as ugly as the tales of lust from the "bloody ends of time."[71]

In *The Waste Land* facsimile edition, Belladonna is powerful, phallic, castrating, her hair as fiery and venomous as Medusa's snakes. The atmosphere is oppressively sexual: the woman's desire is clear as she demands of the protagonist "the bestial act rudely forced on him by his marriage, and his unwillingness or inability to comply turns their relationship into a parody of marriage." The language hints at his impotence or "withered stumps" in the face of what all "the world pursues/Jug Jug"—a sex act which repels him. The gorgon's scornful gaze "deadens him for he has lost his bones, his erections."[72] The connection between the panic aroused by his wife's sexual demands, and the "accents of neurasthenia" which follow, are no coincidence. Freud claimed that frustrated sexuality bred anxiety neurosis, like wine turned to vinegar:

> My nerves are bad tonight. Yes, bad. Stay with me.
> Speak to me. Why do you never speak? Speak.

"What are you thinking of?" demands the wife. "What thinking? What?" "I think we met first in rats' alley," replies the poet, "Where the dead men lost their bones." "What is that noise?" Her voice is querulous. "The wind under the door." "What is that noise now? What is the wind doing?" His unspoken reply is: "Carrying/Away the little light dead people," a reference once more to Paolo and Francesca, Dante's doomed lovers.[73]

"WONDERFUL" wrote Vivien, who was closely involved in the editing of *The Waste Land,* and suggested three lines of her own. In front of her was a virtual transcript of her own nervous assaults upon her husband, echoing one particular letter to Mary Hutchinson in 1928: "Of course, he is *so* reserved and peculiar, that he never says anything and one cannot get him to speak. That makes one much more lonely."[74] The insistent questions of the wife in the poem, "What shall I do now? What shall I do?" and the answer, "I shall rush out now as I am, and walk the street," mirrors an invariable response of Vivien to the stress of her marriage. Her own frustration and rage led her once to throw her nightdress out of the window onto the pavement below. In 1942 Eliot pointed out to Mary Trevelyan the building near Trafalgar Square in which this happened.[75] Pound, too, recognised the verses' origins, commenting: "PHOTOGRAPHY."

Belladonna steps down from her throne. "Do you know nothing? Do you see nothing? Do you remember nothing?" she demands. The poet blots out his wife's voice, remembering only the moment of rapture in the "hyacinth garden." In the first section of *The Waste Land,* "The Burial of the Dead," Eliot again makes it clear that his remembrance is not of a "hyacinth girl" with whom he is in love, but of a male partner, who may indeed be symbolised by the god Hyacinth, killed by Apollo when the two are playing at discus. The allusion is to ecstatic male love which ends in tragedy.[76] The girl in the garden may be the poet himself, in another sexual transfiguration, as in "Saint Narcissus" when he changes sex; Eliot's remark that Tiresias, in whom the two sexes meet,[77] is the "most important personage in the poem, uniting all the rest," stresses the androgynous impulse which is central to the poem. The image of transfiguration is one Vivien herself used in 1936, writing *"Tiresias"* above her announcement that she had "become" Daisy Miller.

Androgyny continued to be fashionable in Bloomsbury in the 1920s, part of the revolt against middle-class morality by the self-consciously decadent; Viola Tree sneered at George Moore, so old-fashioned that at a Phoenix Society performance he was surprised that "the Silent Woman was a boy; his conception of woman is so womanish, and of man so masterful, no wonder he fails to believe that there could in this strange age be any mistake!" In their boyish flapper dresses, in which barely a hint of breast or hip dared break the line, and in make-up which could be "dead white or putty colour," with touches of orange or mauve, women, in their common desire to defy English dowdiness, could easily be mistaken for men.[78] Aldous Huxley wrote poetry celebrating the role of the androgyne. "One arrow and two pierced hearts," was the emblem of his 1927 Valentine tribute to his two Marias, his wife and Mary Hutchinson: "Soft androgyne on androgyne/Using hermaphrodite arts."[79] Virginia Woolf also acknowledged the creativity of the androgyne, writing: "It is fatal for anyone who writes to think of their sex. It is fatal to be a woman pure and simple; one must be woman-manly or man-womanly," perhaps proving her own point when she found *Orlando* to be a book she was able to write at great speed. And there is evidence that Eliot enjoyed challenging accepted gender roles too, performing in Lytton Strachey's transvestite plays.[80] Not only Vivien (in "Fête Galante"), but several of his contemporaries bore witness to his use of cosmetics in the 1920s.[81]

The poet's disgust for heterosexual love is expressed in a different milieu, that of the working-class, in lines in *The Waste Land* describing the marriage of a Cockney couple, Lil and Albert. The dialogue was based on many conversations with Ellen Kelland, the Eliots' maid for many years, to whom Vivien was devoted. The grim future Vivien predicted for Ellen, who was later to marry one of her "followers," is captured in lines given to "Lil" and her friend, and edited by Vivien, whose ear for dialogue was acute: "Now Albert's coming back, make yourself a bit smart," says the speaker. Albert's out of the army and wants a good time; Lil has spent the money he gave her for a new set of teeth, and is looking "so antique." If she doesn't please him, there's plenty of others who will. "Hurry up please, it's time," the landlord's cry from the pub opposite the Eliots' first flat in Crawford Street, is followed by a Cockney line of Vivien's own invention: "If you don't like it you can get on with it." Lil looks old, despite being only thirty-one, because she has had five children and an abortion: "It's that medicine I took, to bring it off." Thoughtfully Vivien changed "medicine" to "pills," and the final line reads: "It's them pills I took, to bring it off, she said." "You *are* a proper fool," replies the speaker. "Well, if Albert won't leave you alone, there it is." Again Vivien added to Eliot's typescript her own revealing line which he retained: "What you get married for if you don't want to have children?" Lil's tale of mechanistic copulation and squalid abortion ends with the landlord's "Good night, ladies," a phrase which echoes Ophelia's unhinged "good night, sweet ladies, good night, good night" in *Hamlet*. "Splendid last lines," wrote an impressed Vivien.[82] But Eliot's cry to his wife, like that of Hamlet to Ophelia, was one presaging flight: "Go to, I'll no more on't; it hath made me mad."

Vivien's own longing for a baby may have contributed to the Eliots' marital problems; Maurice remembered that his mother had said that Vivien had been pregnant at one time and had had an abortion, but he did not believe the story. There is no way of confirming whether or not Vivien had an abortion (took pills), and if so whether Eliot was the father. The line which asks, why marry if you don't want to have children, suggests a reproach to a husband who cannot satisfy his wife: the Fisher King of Jessie Weston's myth. And in an undated letter to Mary, Vivien makes the suggestion, tragic in its impracticality, that the enemies of the Left and Right in literary London should unite and live in a utopian community in which she might have an adopted child.[83] For Vivien, as for Virginia Woolf, motherhood denied may have had a more harmful effect upon her mental state than a pregnancy which Virginia's, and possibly Vivien's doctors, advised against.

In his original manuscript, the poet-protagonist began Part III of *The Waste Land*, "The Fire Sermon," with his starkest statement so far of revulsion against women's physicality. James E. Miller writes that "there is passion throughout 'The Fire Sermon' but it is the passion of a misogynist, burning with a hatred that seems almost inexplicable, except in the context we have already encountered, the protagonist held in the grip of a paralysing memory of a dead and deeply beloved friend."[84] Interestingly, however, the couplets describing a privileged woman, Fresca, being brought tea or hot chocolate in bed by her maid may have originated in a poem reclaimed by Vivien as her own and published under the initials "F.M." (one of her pseudonyms) in "Letters of the Moment—II" in the *Criterion* in April, 1924.

> When sniffing Chloe, with the toast and tea
> Drags back the curtain to disclose the day,
> The amorous Fresca stretches, yawns and gapes,
> Aroused from dreams of love in curious shapes.
> The quill lies ready at her finger tips;
> She drinks, and pens a letter while she sips;
> "I'm very well, my dear, and how are you?
> I have another book by Girandoux.
> My dear, I missed you last night at the Play:
> Were you there? Or did you slip away? . . ."
> Her hands caress the egg's well-rounded dome;
> As her mind labours till the phrases come.[85]

These lines were possibly written by Vivien originally, and edited by Tom in Lausanne, only to be cut by Pound; neither of the Eliots liked to waste material, which may account for the publication of Vivien's "few poor verses" in 1924. However, the transformation of the "Fresca" verses in Tom's hands gave them a misogynistic twist. Now she awakes, dreaming of "pleasant rapes." "Leaving the bubbling beverage to cool,/Fresca slips softly to the needful stool." His contempt for woman is, once again, all the greater when she is Jewish: Fresca writes her letter, as in Vivien's verse, but relates how "out of dull despair" she went to "Lady Kleinwurm's party." "Who was there?/Oh, Lady Kleinwurm's monde—no one that mattered—/Somebody sang, and Lady Kleinwurm chattered."[86]

Eliot was possibly satirising Violet Schiff, a musician who studied singing under Tosti, and gave many parties at her house in Cambridge Square, even on occasion including Rose and Maurice Haigh-Wood.

"Fresca," also in Eliot's version reading a book by Girandoux, asks her correspondent to tell her all about herself, Paris, and her new lovers. Nancy Cunard or Mary Hutchinson may also have been Eliot's sources, but the contemptuous lines which follow were based on his revulsion at enforced cohabitation with Vivien. "Odours disguised by the cunning French/ Disguise the hearty female stench."

The diatribe which follows encompasses all women: Fresca, says the poet, in another time or place, had been a "weeping Magdalene" or prostitute: "The same eternal and consuming itch/Can make a martyr, or plain simple bitch;/Or prudent sly domestic puss puss cat./Or strolling slattern in a tawdry gown." One definition fits all women, he declares: "Unreal emotions and real appetite./For women grown intellectual grow dull,/And loose the mother wit of natural trull."[87] Women, believes the poet, have a "consuming itch," the insatiable appetite for sex which revolts him. And should they attempt to educate themselves, reading, like "Fresca," the Scandinavians who "bemused her wits," or the Russian novelists who "thrilled her to hysteric fits," they lose the "mother wit of natural trull"— the quick repartee of the barmaid or prostitute. Vivien might have recognised this savage portrait of herself, for she too read Dostoevsky and, like "Fresca," scribbled verse.

The Fresca couplets express, in an extreme form, Eliot's belief that "the love of man and woman (or for that matter of man and man) is only explained and made reasonable by the higher love, or else it is simply the coupling of animals."[88] The revelation he had experienced in the Hyacinth Garden had sanctified a relationship which, without such "higher love," was otherwise bestial. Nevertheless, the homosexual encounter between the poet-protagonist and the unshaven "Smyrna merchant," which follows, is treated with amused tolerance rather than the scorn reserved for male/female relationships. In the "Unreal City" of London, where people are "bound upon the wheel" and "phantasmal gnomes" burrow in brick and stone and steel, the speaker is approached by a Mr. Eugenides, who asks him "in abominable French/To luncheon at the Cannon Street hotel/And perhaps a week at the Metropole."[89] According to an informant of Edmund Wilson's, John Peale Bishop, this brief encounter under the "brown fog" of a winter afternoon, was based on real life. "Mr. Eugenides actually turned up at Lloyd's with his pocket full of currants and asked

Eliot to spend a weekend with him for no nice reasons," writes Bishop. "His place in the poem is I believe as a projection of Eliot however . . . the one-eyed merchant is homosexual. Thomas's sexual troubles are undoubtedly extreme." This supposition is chiefly of interest as an example of the gossip which was circulating about "Tears Eliot" (as a Parisian wit christened him) by November, 1922.[90]

At this point the poet adopts a new and prophetic voice: that of Tiresias, the mythical blind figure who can see, who has exchanged "eyesight for insight." Tiresias, the androgyne, "Old man with wrinkled female breasts, can see" the truth. Eliot emphasises the centrality of Tiresias. "What Tiresias *sees,* in fact, is the substance of the poem." Tiresias's insights relate to sex, which in Ovid's *Metamorphoses* he experiences first as a man, and for the next seven years as a woman, before changing sex once more. "Wise Tiresias' knows what love is like, from either point of view, declares Ovid, and the seer repeats the message that human sex is no better than that of coupling snakes: mechanistic, casual, unfulfilling, as Eliot's parade of typists, clerks, and young men carbuncular illustrates. Even the ironic pageant of historical romance which follows, Elizabeth and Leicester in their "gilded shell" on the Thames, underlines the sterility of heterosexual relationships. The question Jove asked Tiresias to settle was whether females gained more pleasure from loving than males do; Tiresias, having tasted the pleasures of both sexes, agreed with the male god against his wife Juno, that women had the better side of the bargain, an opinion shared by the poet.

Eliot can no longer maintain the pose of detachment. In a new metamorphosis as St. Augustine, he is "burning" with pain and passion: "To Carthage then I came/Burning burning burning burning/O Lord Thou pluckest me out."[91] Eliot explains, in a note which he attaches to this quotation from St. Augustine's *Confessions,* that the saint came to Carthage where "a cauldron of unholy loves" sang in his ears. But, argues John Peter, Eliot's note does not make clear that St. Augustine travelled twice to Carthage, the second time to escape from the misery into which he had been plunged at the death of a friend, one with whom he had enjoyed a friendship he described as "delightful to me above all the delights of this my life." It is in this context that the visit to Carthage can be understood as a prayer for release from attachment and the agony of human love. "Like

Augustine at this stage of his life the speaker is not yet able to accept Christianity, despite the craving for consolation and forgiveness that he endures," writes Peter. "At least his repetition of the word 'burning' seems to imply that he is still caught in the trammels of the senses." Eliot seeks for release from suffering through the Fire Sermon of Buddha, who taught his disciples to divest themselves of passion in order to become free.[92]

Like Baudelaire, Eliot struggled to escape from *ennui* and anguish towards a spiritual life. In 1930 he wrote of Baudelaire: "He could not escape suffering and could not transcend it, so he *attracted* (it) to himself. But what he could do, with that immense passive strength . . . was to study his suffering" (Eliot's italics).[93] In *The Waste Land* Eliot, too, studied his suffering and made art of it; but the struggle he chronicled by speaking in different voices, which enabled him to express and observe his own pain as his own analyst, was by no means over. He remained "bleeding between two lives," in the words of "Song for the Opherian," still casting backwards looks towards Hades like Orpheus in search of his Eurydice. "Who is the third who walks always beside you? . . . I do not know whether a man or a woman/—But who is that on the other side of you?" is the insistent question of "What the Thunder Said," the final section of *The Waste Land*.[94] Whether it was the shrouded shade of Verdenal, the hooded figure of Christ on the road to Emmaus, or simply an illusion, its ghostly presence in the marriage ensured Eliot's rejection of his wife; for Vivien, there was always a third person in her marriage.

Eliot longed for "Shantih," the peace of Eastern asceticism, but he burnt still with longing for his sailor "brother": "The sea was calm, your heart would have responded/Gaily, when invited, beating obedient/To controlling hands." Datta, Dayadhvam, Damyata: Give, sympathise, control, is the prayer he takes from the Thunder fable of the *Upanishads* and adapts to his own personal drama. "DATTA my brother, what have we given?/My friend, my friend, beating in my heart,/The awful daring of a moment's surrender." The memory of exaltation is ineradicable. "DA/Dayadhavam, friend, my friend I have heard the key/Turn in the door, once and once only."[95] But the finality of death is the lesson given in the Chapel Perilous, one which the poet must learn to accept if he is to exorcise his demon and find release and renewal, both physical and spiritual.[96]

Death into faith is a step he is not yet ready to take. His prayer collapses in a kaleidoscope of quotations. "London Bridge is falling down falling down falling down./*Poi s'ascose nel foco che gli affina.*" He speaks with the voice of Arnaut Daniel, the Provençal poet, who is weighed down with guilt, a guilt explained by the provenance of the quotation from Canto XXVI, "The Reign of Lust" of Dante's *Purgatorio,* which relates the sins of a band of sodomites. *"Nostro peccato fu ermafrodito"* (Our sin was hermaphrodite), cries Daniel, as he plunges into the purifying fire.[97] It was the critic I. A. Richards who observed that this canto of the lustful sodomites illuminated Eliot's "persistent concern with sex, the problem of our generation, as religion was the problem of the last." Eliot observed that it was "very shrewd" of Richards to notice this, but that "in his contrast of sex and religion he makes a distinction which is too subtle for me to grasp."[98] It was a disingenuous rejoinder, but Richards's barb had indeed been a shrewd one. Sex lies at the heart of much of Eliot's poetry, becoming his personal synonym for sin. Sex attracts and repels, its urgency creating in the poet the same engulfing horror that he feels he, like Kurtz, deserves for breaking moral rules. For sinning brings in its wake a Calvinistic fear of punishment. "Elegy," part of *The Waste Land* original 1,000-line typescript cut by Pound, which closely resembles Charlotte Eliot's religious poetry, portrays a judgemental God who "in a rolling ball of fire" pursues the poet's errant feet in "flames of anger."[99] However, the conflict between sex and spirituality, body and spirit, was by no means over. Eliot could only cry in agony: "Hieronymo's mad againe."[100]

14

A Wild Heart in a Cage

Complimenti, you bitch," wrote Ezra Pound after reading Tom's typescript. "I am wracked by the seven jealousies." Recognising that the sprawling, chaotic poem was enough "to make the rest of us shut up shop," Pound set to work with his blue pencil to cut the poem by nearly half, while Tom waited with Vivien in Paris for a fortnight. "The thing now runs from April . . . to 'shantih' without a break," Ezra wrote on 24 December, 1921. "That is 19 pages, and let us say the longest poem in the English langwidge. Don't try to bust all records by prolonging it three pages further."[1] Feebly Eliot protested at some of Ezra's cuts. Could he not work "sweats with tears etc" into the nerves monologue, the only place where it could go?[2] Pound was firm: "I dare say sweats with tears will wait." Discouraged, Eliot wondered if he should leave out Phlebas altogether. No, replied Pound, Phlebas was an integral part of the poem. "The card pack introduces him, the drowned phoen sailor. And he is needed ABSOlootly where he is. Must stay in."[3] In essence, Eliot abandoned the poem to Pound, whose aim was to make it the justification for the Modernist movement.[4] Addressing his compatriot as "Cher Maître," Tom allowed the personal element in the poem to be sacrificed, while Pound for his part claimed that "on each Occasion/Ezra performed the Caesarian Operation" which allowed the poem to be born.[5] Gratefully Eliot wrote: "Complimenti appreciated, as have been excessively depressed."

On 12 January 1922, the day on which Tom returned to England, Vivien wrote to Mary that she thought he was much better, although "you must judge for yourself."[6] Unwilling to return to London after two months in France, she lingered for a few days in Lyons. Perhaps Vivien still hoped to meet Scofield, who continued to edit *The Dial* from Vienna, but he was

busy establishing the *Dial* Award, as well as collecting pictures and entering analysis with Freud, and seems to have eluded Vivien. Finally, reluctantly, she crossed the Channel to join Tom. The weather was vile and he
had collapsed with influenza. Both Eliots subsequently became severely
depressed. They felt persecuted by their enemies as they struggled to
launch the *Criterion* from their flat, find a publisher for *The Waste Land,*
decide whether Tom should leave the bank, and rent a country cottage. "If
Vivien had realised how bloody England is she would not have returned,"
wrote Tom to Ezra.[7] None of these problems would have been insupera-
ble, had it not been for Eliot's acute sexual conflict which by 1922 urgently
demanded resolution. In the anonymity of Paris he had socialised with
artists and intellectuals: "May your erection never grow less," wrote
Pound. "I had intended to speak to you seriously on the subject, but you
seemed so mountany gay while here in the midst of Paris that the matter
slipped my foreskin." Eliot was tempted to send his bawdy Bolo verses to
James Joyce, but Pound cautioned him against doing so: "You can forward
the Bolo to Joyce if you think it wont unhinge his somewhat sabbatarian
mind. On the hole he might be saved the shock, shaved the sock."[8]

The 1920s were tempting yet dangerous times for homosexuals and
members of the *avant garde.* "Kicking the corpse of Oscar," as Robbie Ross,
Wilde's friend, described the homophobia of the time, reached fever pitch
with the belief that the Germans held a "Black Book" listing the names of
the "First 47,000" homosexuals in British society. Homosexuals were
viewed as potential traitors, because they were open to blackmail in a
Britain which outlawed the "invert," the "urning" or third sex, as sexolo-
gist Richard von Krafft-Ebing described gay men in his *Psychopathia
Sexualis* (1886). Such "experts" viewed same-sex desires as an aberration
from the procreative norm required by society. One such was Christopher
Millard, Wilde's biographer and Ross's secretary, who in 1918 was prose-
cuted for a second time for indecent assault.[9] The need for discretion had
never been greater, yet eighteen years after his death the cult of Oscar
Wilde refused to go away.

The First World War had been a powerful catalyst in creating a homosexual sub-culture in Europe's cities, particularly Berlin and London, as re-
cruitment into the armed forces had for the first time mixed together large
numbers of men from different social classes in a heady cocktail of danger

and proximity. Fears of German decadence infecting British soldiers led to calls for punitive measures against homosexuals, and Lord Alfred Douglas, Wilde's former lover and now a married man, exhorted the nation to unite against "The foe without, the foe within," declaring in verse:

Two filthy fogs blot out the light:
The German and the sodomite.

Within the armed forces a conviction for sodomy was punished by a minimum sentence of ten years, and a maximum of life. Nevertheless, this was no deterrent to the élite Guards regiments within which the attraction and availability of other ranks—"a bit of scarlet"—for officers and other members of the upper classes was well known. Mary Hutchinson, confidante of many homosexuals, related with glee to Lytton Strachey a visit from civil servant Monty Shearman, who told her that since time immemorial there had been a connection between the Foreign Office and the Horse Guards: "He described the tradition—when you have noticed your Horse Guard you walk past him and drop half a crown into his boot with a note fixing a *rendez-vous*—you then hope he will turn up—but imagine the state of the boots of a very handsome guard . . . When and how does he drill? . . . Imagine his state of mind—does he look to see who has made the chink or does he stare straight ahead of him?"[10]

A new sense of identity was also germinating among homosexuals. Michel Foucault argues that the category of homosexual has been culturally constructed. In the Renaissance sodomy had been condemned by the Church and prohibited by law as a shameful sexual practice which its practitioners were urged to confess to their priest, but not until the late nineteenth century did homosexuality finally metamorphose from the practice of sodomy into something new: "a kind of interior androgyny, a hermaphrodism of the soul. The sodomite had been a temporary aberration; the homosexual was now a species."[11] As the negative aspects of homosexuality were emphasised, the "invert" was increasingly seen as a suitable case for treatment, one who should undergo the "talking cure" of psychoanalysis and confess his aberrant sexuality to the new authority figure—doctor rather than priest. Thus Ottoline Morrell was instrumental in taking some of the young homosexuals who gathered at Garsington to see her favourite physician, the German Dr. Marten, to be cured of their "disease" at his clinic in Freiburg. Lytton was sceptical about these expeditions, especially after meeting Marten at Garsington in 1923: "Psychoanalysis is a ludicrous fraud," he told Dora Carrington, "the Sackville-West youth was there [at Freiburg] to be cured of homosexuality. After 4 months and an expenditure of £200, he found he could just bear the thought of going to bed with a woman."[12]

By the 1920s the homosexual was increasingly subject to social control. Tabloid newspapers had informed a fascinated public of accusations made during the notorious 1918 Pemberton Billing trial that dancer Maud Allen, who lost her libel action against Billing for describing her performance of Wilde's *Salome* as lesbian, was also enjoying a lesbian relationship with Margot Asquith, wife of the former Prime Minister, H. H. Asquith.[13] In 1885 the law against buggery had been strengthened by Henry Labouchère's amendment to the Criminal Law Amendment Bill, which criminalised all sexual acts between men including fellatio and mutual masturbation, and led to Wilde's conviction.[14] In 1921 the government attempted to extend the law to include lesbianism. The Lords threw out the Bill, protesting that it would bring such an offence to the notice of women who had never heard of it.[15] Indeed, Lord Albemarle was alleged to have walked into the Turf Club and asked who was "this Greek chap clitoris" everyone was talking about.[16]

Foucault argues that power produces but cannot contain resistance. Increasingly defined and categorised as perverse, homosexuals began to fight back:

> The appearance in nineteenth century psychiatry, jurisprudence and literature of a whole series of discourses on the species and subspecies of homosexuality, inversion, pederasty, and "psychic hermaphrodism" made possible a strong advance of social controls into this area of "perversity"; but it also made possible the formation of a "reverse" discourse: homosexuality began to speak on its own behalf, to demand that its legitimacy or "naturality" be acknowledged . . .[17]

Many homosexuals went abroad to indulge their tastes: Montague Shearman boasted to Mary Hutchinson that on the ship to Naples in 1927 he had a boy in every port, and the swimming instructor at Toulon, as well as "complicated affairs" in hotels. In England, W. H. Auden recalled, the 1920s were a period of decadence when he first became aware of the "undercurrents of homosexuality" at Christ Church, Oxford.[18] Nor were the universities the only area of escape from heterosexuality; in London, where society and Bohemia made common cause in the pursuit of pleasure, the worlds of the arts and theatre offered the "invert" an acceptance missing in mainstream culture. Nevertheless, homosexuals still walked in fear: of the hundreds of prosecutions each year for "unnatural offences" between gay men, nearly half resulted in custodial sentences.

Back at home, and still buried in the bowels of Lloyds Bank, in 1922 Tom Eliot's mood was bitter. He was aware that he had written his masterpiece: "A long poem of about 450 words [lines] which, with the notes that I am adding, will make a book of 30 or 40 pages. I think it is the best I have ever done, and Pound thinks so too," he confided to John Quinn on 15 June, explaining that Pound had introduced him to the publisher Liveright in Paris, who offered him a 15 per cent royalty and $150 in advance. Eliot had given first refusal on the poem to Knopf, who had published the American edition of his *Poems,* but Knopf told him his offer came too late for inclusion in the autumn list. Liveright then agreed to take the poem for his own autumn list, but the "extremely vague" contract he sent displeased Eliot, and he asked Quinn to renegotiate it. On 19 July Eliot sent Quinn a typescript of *The Waste Land* to hand on to Liveright, apologising that he was too busy to "type it out fair . . . I shall rush forward the notes to go at the end. I only hope the printers are not allowed to bitch the punctuation and the spacing, as that is very important for the sense."[19] In the same letter Eliot offered to present Quinn with the original MSS of *The Waste Land:* "When I say MSS, I mean that it is partly MSS, and partly typescript, with Ezra's and my alterations scrawled all over it." Whilst waiting for this famous gift, Quinn sat up on the night of 27 July reading the typescript. "*Waste Land* is one of the best things you have done," he reassured the anxious poet, "though I imagine Liveright may be a little disappointed at it, but I think he will go through with it . . ." Quinn thought the text was too short to make a book, and too difficult. It was a poem for "superior guys" only, he wrote, anticipating a "small number of readers."[20]

Eliot encountered the same muted enthusiasm for his masterpiece from Scofield Thayer, to whom he had written on 20 January 1922 asking whether *The Dial* wished to print his new poem (*"not* to appear in any periodical on this side"), and what he might pay. He offered to postpone all arrangements for publication until he heard from Scofield, and explained that as *The Waste Land* was in four parts, it could easily divide to go into four issues. The poem "will have been three times through the sieve by Pound as well as myself so should be in final form."[21]

Scofield's response to this generous offer was grudging. His own mental state was precarious: "As I am half dead already I beseech you not to counsel my coming to London" he had gasped to Tom the previous July, despite his anxiety to discover what plans his old rival was making to start a periodical with Lady Rothermere.[22] By December a row had blown up over the "horrid and vulgar and tedious and totally impossible London Letter" which Thayer's business manager Gilbert Seldes claimed to have received from St. John Hutchinson, who had written Eliot's Letter for him during his breakdown. Seldes and Watson sent Hutchinson $25, two thirds of the amount due, as the article was unusable. "Prevent the man from sending any more," wrote Scofield sharply from Vienna, informing Eliot that he had hired Raymond Mortimer instead until Tom could send a new Letter. "At least it will indicate that you are again well."[23] It was an embarrassing situation for Eliot and he stiffly informed Scofield in January that he wished Seldes to deduct $25 from his own next payment, to be given to Hutchinson—unless Thayer preferred to keep on Mortimer in his stead.

Scofield replied with heavy sarcasm on 22 January: "It is good to know that you have again taken up the old-fashioned custom of answering letters. I hope I shall not have to await another case of influenza before receiving another letter . . . You seem to take ill my frankness in re the lad Hutchinson." He offered Eliot an extra $25 for the next London Letter: "Then you and Mr. Hutchinson and *The Dial* and Mr. Seldes and the mad hatter will no doubt be tutti contenti . . ." Seemingly unaware of the herculean task which *The Waste Land* represented for the poet, he wrote coolly: "I thought you were aware that we pay fixed rates always and that therefore it is not for us to bargain. . . . We pay for verse that has been un-published elsewhere 10 dollars the page which is something more than double our rates for prose. 450 lines will take something more than 11 pages. *The Dial* when dealing with famous writers may offer round sums rather than split figures. Can we have the poem? *The Dial* would pay $150." Pound's "sieving" would, he suggested, have eliminated any impropriety which might have got by Eliot's own censor.[24]

It was an offer which Eliot found insulting and when, a few days later, he heard "on good authority" that the editor of *The Dial* had paid £100 to George Moore for a short story, he exploded with rage. "Cannot accept under 856 pounds," he wired Thayer. "I presume there is some error upon the part of the telegraph service," replied his urbane correspondent, pleading that he and Watson ran *The Dial* on a very large annual deficit and had to make personal sacrifices to keep it going.[25] Knowing that Thayer was a millionaire, Tom refused to be mollified, and on 16 March repeated that he must decline "$150 for a poem which has taken me a year to write and which is my biggest work . . . Certainly if I am to be offered only 30 to 35 pounds for such a publication it is out of the question."[26] A stalemate resulted which would last for months.

Tom's fury and bitterness spilled over into the London Letter he sent to *The Dial* that spring, in which he described the "particular torpor or deadness which strikes a denizen of London on his return" after three months' absence. Tom, and Vivien too, knew he had broken the mould of twentieth-century poetry with *The Waste Land,* yet his work seemed to meet only with obtuse incomprehension. His sense of being misunderstood and unappreciated was never greater. "I am about ready to chuck up literature altogether and retire," he burst out to Sydney Schiff. "I don't see why I should go on forever fighting a rearguard action against time, fatigue and illness, and complete lack of recognition of these facts."[27] Jealously he hit out in his "London Letter" in the May issue of *The Dial* at the "moral cowardice" of English poets, with their instinct for safety, who were indistinguishable, in his view, from "the decent middle-class mob." Even the war poems did not represent a revolt, he wrote, but paid tribute to "all the nicest feelings of the upper middle-class British public schoolboy."[28]

Tom was living on the edge, and Vivien became fearful once more for her husband's mental health. She explained to Mary, whom she met at the Gimpel Galleries followed by a two-and-a-half-hour chat in a tea-room, that he was too sensitive: "Tom is *all* Achilles heel. That is the point, the trouble, the complex, the unhappiness." Other people had at least one *"hard spot"*—indeed, most of them were all "hard spot," but Tom had not one.[29] Tom, however, continued to believe that it was Vivien who was thin-skinned and needed protecting. "*Please* don't mention it to Vivien," he wrote to Ottoline in October 1923, the following year, in the middle of another Bloomsbury tiff over an article by Clive Bell which Eliot found "vulgar and tasteless," and which left him feeling as if he were covered with lice. He would not show Vivien the article, because "I don't feel these things but she does."[30] They were united in dislike of the London literary mafia, of whom Eliot wrote to Richard Aldington: "You know that I have no persecution mania, but . . . I am quite aware how obnoxious I am to perhaps the larger part of the literary world of London, and that there will be a great many jackals swarming about waiting for my bones."[31] Tom and Vivien longed to get away and have solitude and peace: "People won't let us alone and won't understand and take offence," Tom complained to Ottoline in the summer of 1922. He and Vivien felt "exposed . . . If only we could go abroad for a long time and hide and forget everything."[32]

Fortunately Eliot was not without friends who believed in his genius, although some of them blamed Vivien for being a burden on her delicate husband. "Eliot ought to be private secretary to some rich imbecile," Pound had written to Quinn in February 1922. "Failing that you might send someone over to elope, kidnap, or otherwise eliminate Mrs. E." Like Eliot himself, Pound partly blamed Eliot's American nationality for the fact that he was trapped in the bank: "Eliot has beautiful manners, wd. adorn any yacht club, etc . . . If he wuz English he wd. be stuck into some govt. sinecure . . ."[33] Learning that Eliot was in a bad way mentally from Richard Aldington, and perhaps also from Gilbert Seldes, to whom Eliot confessed that his mind was "in a very deteriorated state, due to illness and worry,"[34] Pound decided to relaunch his Bel Esprit scheme from Paris. His generosity was remarkable, for he himself was so hard-up that he had had to accept a loan of $250 from Quinn that October.

The aim of Ezra's scheme was "the release of captives," beginning with Eliot: "Only thing we can give the artist is leisure to work in. Only way we can get work from him is to assure him of this leisure . . ." "Eliot is at his last gasp," he wrote to William Carlos Williams on 18 March 1922. "Has had one breakdown. We have got to do something at once."[35] The circular Pound sent secretly to his and Eliot's friends stated the case even more baldly: "Eliot in bank, makes £500. Too tired to write, broke down . . . Returned to bank, and is again gone to pieces physically." Pound hoped to find thirty guarantors who would pledge £10 a year, as he and Aldington had already done: "NOT charity, NOT 'pity the poor artist.' Eliot wd. rather work in bank than do poor work. Has tried to live by pen and can't. (Poor health, invalid wife.)"[36] Quinn at once offered to take six or seven shares, and to find other American donors. On 30 March Pound went public with the scheme, to Eliot's acute embarrassment, appealing openly for funds for the poet in the *New Age*. The public appeal "took my breath away," wrote Quinn, more sensitive than Ezra to Eliot's feelings that he was being shown up as a charity case, and fearing that the bank might come to hear that the young man marked down as a future manager was in reality yearning for his freedom.

The mystery of Vivien's poor health had for a long time puzzled Pound, who had suspected she was suffering from syphilis. He continued to discuss the problem with Quinn by letter: "Eliot has always been very reserved about his domestic situation, so much so that I thought Mrs. E. had syph; and marveled that they didn't get a dose of 606" [an arsenical compound].[37] In the end Ezra got down to "brass tacks" with Tom, who told him that "the girl really has a long complication of things, tuberculosis in infancy *supposed* to have been cured. Symptoms, so far as I now see, point to pituitary trouble . . ." Rather than blaming Vivien, Pound now grew more understanding, as Eliot told him that she had "all along behaved very finely," even offering to live separately.

> so that she shouldn't get on T's nerves, *and* prevent his working, is ready to live by herself if it will help T. to write etc. And in general ready to do anything she can to help his work, he can't simply chuck her in the Thames, even if he were so disposed, which he aint.

Pound, aware of how reliant he was on his own wife, Dorothy, whom he had married thinking she had £50 a year, but who in fact received an allowance of more than £150 from her family (bringing his total income up to barely £300 a year), sympathised with Vivien's own lack of support from her family. "Eliot's wife quite honestly expected to get something when she married, but they didn't get it fixed up, went off and married in haste, and then her old Member of the Brit. Academy father pled poverty, and hard times due to war. Has never done a damn thing so far as I know."[38]

By April 1922 Tom was going rapidly downhill, to Vivien's growing alarm. Vivien and he had suffered incessant illness since a week before Easter, Tom told Ottoline, who asked them to Garsington. Could Ottoline recommend a hotel in Brighton, so that they might get "braced up"?[39] A week or two later found them sheltering at the Castle Hotel in Tunbridge Wells, having given up the idea of Brighton because it was too far for Tom to commute from. Vivien was "very seedy" with an attack of neuralgia, having cut short a trip to Paris because of a temperature, and returned to England. Tom, Aldington told Amy Lowell on 5 May, "is very ill, will die if he doesn't get proper & complete rest . . ."[40]

That spring Vivien wrote Aldington—who was to become assistant editor of the *Criterion*—an agitated letter which suggested that Tom was on the verge of collapse. Vivien had read a letter from Aldington to Tom, criticising an article of his in *The Dial*.[41] Tom was, she said, "so *ill*" that it was she who had had to write the article: "He *asked me what he should say* and I told him what to say, and he just wrote it down, *anything,* not caring, for he felt too ill and in despair. So the article is more mine than his. I wd. be glad if everyone knew that." Tom always left his letters behind for her to read, said Vivien, which precipitated her protest:

> It is not easy for me to write to you in this way but I feel for once I must come out of my obscurity and say something. I think your letter is unkind . . . It is exactly the letter to upset Tom, and to harden his pride, and to help precipitate the disasters we all foresee and which you cheerfully say he is asking for. At this moment I know he *cannot stand* a letter like this from anyone he actually *did* look upon as his friend . . . Quarrel with me if you like, and

send me any kind of letter, or no letter at all—show your scorn for my interference.

Aldington had criticised the Eliots' choice of name for the quarterly review, which he thought pretentious, and Vivien robustly defended their decision:

> And as for the title—the *Criterion,* I am responsible for that too. It would be nice if you had offered some good suggestions for the title yourself in time. Perhaps you did not know how many were tried and discarded, and how much worry and bother even the stupid naming of the Review caused us. Anyhow, I thought of the *Criterion* out of my own head . . . and Tom, too tired—*too tired* to bother very greatly once an apparently harmless title had been found, which pleased Lady Rothermere, agreed, and was glad to get the matter settled.

The emotional tone of this letter reveals the paranoid state of mind of both the Eliots at the time, as well as the extent of Vivien's involvement in the creation of the *Criterion.* She fretted that now the title must be changed once more, even though the notices were being printed, and the headed writing paper. "I don't see what to do—Tom won't care, he will say let the wolves get him. You little understand his state of mind," she wrote despairingly.

> I am English, and once I liked England—once I fought like mad to keep Tom here and stopped his going back to America. I thought I could not marry him unless I was able to keep him here, in England. Now I hate it. I hate the word. I hate the people whom you explain so well and so truly. I think Ezra is lucky and wise to have got out. And it is an everlasting stain on the English that he did get out. I hope Tom will soon get out.[42]

Reminding Aldington that she was ill and an "endless drag" on Tom, Vivien begged him to remain the real friend he had always been. Tom would stand or fall by the new review. Could he not understand that?

"Each person who gives him a push now gives him a push out of England. And that will be damned England's loss." Defiantly she signed herself: Vivien Eliot.

Vivien could fight like a vixen on her husband's behalf, and her fierce, almost maternal devotion explains in part the strange and powerful bonds which tied her and Tom to each other. They existed in a state of co-dependence in which psychological need and distress played a large part in illnesses which often had no organic basis. Many letters bear witness to the dance of disease the Eliots shared, taking it in turns to be ill, as one led and the other followed in a flight into hysterical illness which served a particular purpose for each partner in the marriage. For Tom, illness was an escape from the demands of marriage, for his breakdowns in 1921 and 1922 were not simply due to the pressures of work. Vivien's own illnesses were in part an unconscious attempt to hold on to the husband she idolised, even if she could not live with him in harmony, in the face of her escalating fear that he would abandon her.

Some psychiatrists today argue that so-called "mental illness," and in particular hysteria, is a form of language ("protolanguage," which is more primitive than speech) by which the sufferer attempts to communicate with the caregiver or love-object through iconic body signs. "In general, whenever people are unable to prevail by ordinary speech over the significant person in their environment, they are likely to shift their pleas to the idiom of protolanguage," for example, weeping, tantrums or seizures, writes the psychiatrist Thomas S. Szasz. A hysterical symptom, such as a seizure, paralysis or pain, has meaning and transmits a message. The hysteric's goal is to arouse emotion in the listener and induce action. The message is, "You should be ashamed of yourself for making me suffer so," or "Take care of me!"[43] By communicating through such "symptoms" as migraine or backache a woman who is dissatisfied with her life may be able to make her husband more attentive towards her, or, if not her husband, her doctor. Thus Szasz points out that we find "human beings in complicated patterns of paired activities characterised by the helplessness of one member and the helpfulness of another." His game-playing model of human behaviour provides useful insights into the kind of situation which Eliot and Vivien created. One of Bertrand Russell's most perspicacious remarks was that after endeavouring to help the Eliots in their troubles, he

found that "their troubles were what they enjoyed."[44] Tom and Vivien perfected the "routines of torment" which bound them together and in which
there may have been more collusion than is immediately apparent.[45] It is
significant that after leaving Vivien, Eliot moved in with another invalid,
John Hayward, and his leaving Hayward was marked by as much stealth
and emotional difficulty as was his abandonment of Vivien. It is probable
that Eliot chose Hayward, as he did Vivien, because he detected a frailty,
both physical and psychological, which met his own need for control, as
well as a readiness to give total devotion to the service of genius.

Vivien's love, so freely given when Tom was most in need of it, laid a
crushing burden upon him which he grew increasingly to resent during
the 1920s. Since she had no sexual hold over him, so was unable to with-
hold sexual favours as a weapon in their marriage, she had to use hysteria
to gain his attention. She probably did not do this consciously—though
Szasz argues that lying can be part of the hysteric's armoury—but through
"conversion hysteria," as Freud dubbed it, somatising her own pain.

Breuer and Freud, in their *Studies on Hysteria,* cite the case of a
woman who, after a quarrel with her husband which felt like a "slap on
the face," developed facial neuralgia, demonstrating how through symbol-
isation an insult can be converted into a symptom.[46] It is a case which bears
a resemblance to that of Vivien, who often developed neuralgia, one may
surmise, after angry exchanges with Eliot, and earlier with her mother.

But Eliot could play the hysteric too when circumstances demanded,
and in this case his illness had the desired effect. Far from never doing "a
damn thing," as Pound believed, Eliot's father-in-law, Charles Haigh-
Wood, probably at Vivien's instigation, invited him to take a fortnight's
holiday at his expense in Lugano, Italy. "I think this visit to Italy will just
save me from another breakdown," wrote the relieved poet to Ottoline.
Vivien could not decide whether to cross the Channel again and wait in
Paris for her husband while he holidayed from 20 May to 4 June, or go
"miserably to the seaside" in search of better health.[47] In the event she
stayed behind, struggling alone to move their belongings back to 9
Clarence Gate Gardens from the flat at 10 Wigmore Street where she and
Tom had been living temporarily. There was the usual Eliot confusion and
muddle: they had quarrelled with the landlord at Wigmore Street and were

trying to extract damages from the tenant in their own flat. Tom, meanwhile, recuperated in the heat and sunshine of Italy, confessing to Ottoline
that he had *never* felt *quite* so lazy and languid as in his lakeside hotel
"smothered in roses," and wished he could stay in Italy for six months.[48]

On Tom's return, Vivien's health became much worse, "accelerated in
its decline," noted her detached husband, by the horrors of moving and the
fatigue and strain of interviewing two Harley Street specialists. At this
point Ezra Pound, following a heart-to-heart with Tom in Verona, decided to add a new role to his repertoire: that of medical expert. He would
now take Vivien in hand. The work of Dr. Louis Berman, a New York en-
docrinologist, who claimed that most illnesses could be attributed to mal-
functioning glands, had attracted his attention. In March 1922 he wrote
about Berman's book in *New Age,* and when he met Berman in Paris, consulted him about Vivien's case. "I am sending him to Eliot, and hope he
will get best gland specialists onto the job," he told Quinn on 5 July. "Of
course if the poor woman has a cramped cella turcica [the bone over the pituitary gland], the job is nearly hopeless. Only one wd. at least KNOW
what one was fighting."[49]

Grateful for Pound's interest, Vivien wrote to him on 27 June 1922
listing her symptoms: colitis, raised temperature ("I very often have a temperature of 99.4 for two or three days at a time for no obvious reason"), insomnia, which had lasted eight years, migraines, physical exhaustion, and
increasing mental incapacity ("I have a horror of using my mind and spend
most of my time trying to avoid contact with people or anything that will
force me to use my mind.")[50] The "hateful, stupid temperatures" of which
Vivien had complained in 1921 to Violet Schiff, who was similarly afflicted, refused to go away.[51] They may not, however, have always had a
physical cause: sometimes Vivien's emotional storms could lead to a raised
temperature. She used to become so upset that after two hours her raised
temperature would necessitate calling in her doctor, she later recalled in
her diary. Tom added a postscript to Vivien's letter: "Vivien has shown me
this letter and I think it is *quite inadequate* as a description of her case, but
she is *very* ill and exhausted, and I do not think she can do any better now."
Pound had surmised that Vivien might have syphilis, because the symptoms of the secondary stage include malaise, headaches, sore throat and

low irregular fever, as well as a rash, but if he was as indiscreet about his suspicions of the cause of her illness as he was about his fund-raising activities on the Eliots' behalf, it is no wonder Vivien felt like hiding away.

In fact the skin rashes which were also troubling Vivien had already sent her to a new specialist, at the urging of Ottoline. Thanking her, Eliot gloomily confided that this specialist, a biologist named Lancelot Hogben, had immediately diagnosed Vivien's "whole trouble as *glands. Most of her glands are not working at all.*" In addition Vivien's system was poisoned by colitis and, according to the specialist, these two problems accounted for all her problems. She was to start a new and violent cure at once.[52] Vivien did not think the treatment would be any use, although she agreed to try it; she was to take "some glands called…Ovarian Opocaps" in sachets for a month. The doctor told Vivien that his treatment was a shot in the dark. "I think that English doctors are more fond of 'shots in the dark' than any treatment based on scientific knowledge," wrote Vivien to Ezra. "It appeals to the 'sporting' side of the English character."[53]

After a fortnight she noticed no improvement. Taking the glands of animals was of course purely experimental, explained Eliot to Ottoline, who was also putting herself in the hands of a new specialist: "It may take a long time before they find the right glands." In addition, Hogben prescribed "a very strong internal disinfection" for Vivien, who was to go without food completely for two days a week. Vivien hoped that this cure would prove scientific enough, wrote Eliot, seemingly unaware of his wife's scepticism as she obediently began fasting.[54]

In the summer of 1922 the Eliots again returned to Bosham. The peace of mind for which they yearned was symbolised for them by the idea of a country cottage by the sea, the possession of which became the focus of a vain but obsessive two-year quest assisted by Mary Hutchinson, as well as by Virginia Woolf and Richard Aldington. "Although we cannot in the least afford it, we are frightfully keen to get a tiny country cottage," Eliot had written to Aldington the previous April. "It would be very good for both of us…a country cottage might just be the saving of my wife's health."[55] Southview, the cottage the Eliots had formerly rented, was no longer available, so instead, in July 1922, they took a two-month let on 2 Creed Cottages, on the outskirts of the village. The 300-year-old labourer's cottage, with its low ceiling, beams, inglenook and bread oven, was full of charm, but it had an outside privy and was not ideal for a "scientific" cure. Bravely Vivien followed her doctor's orders. She had benefited in some ways, wrote Tom doubtfully to Ottoline, but at the same time the cure was so drastic that it made her feel extremely ill and indeed caused her a great deal of pain.[56] In two or three weeks they hoped to know definitely how sound the treatment was.

Vivien put a brave face on conditions at 2 Creed Cottages to Mary Hutchinson: the first weekend was "ghastly" without any servants, but soon she had engaged two, one for the mornings and one for the evenings. Vivien took pride in her treatment of servants: although she did not like to pay a woman more than £1 a week, she gave them plenty to eat and sent their print dresses and aprons to the laundry,[57] and in her close relationship with faithful retainers such as Ellen, who became devoted to her mistress, she found a substitute of sorts for the affection missing in her life. But the furnished cottage was "inconceivably tiny," she complained to Mary, although the south-facing upstairs bedrooms looked out towards the sea, and offered a peaceful spot in which to rest and write. Vivien longed to find somewhere where she could put her own furniture and make a real home; then "how happy I should be!" Bosham seemed so lovely, she told Mary, and even if Tom did leave the bank at Christmas, as seemed likely, and they went to live in Paris, there was no countryside she liked better than English countryside—although she would cheerfully exchange London for Paris.[58]

As time passed—with Tom remaining in London during the week allegedly "head over heels in work"—Vivien's weakness increased under Hogben's fasting regime. She was at a very low point where "all weak spots break out—neuralgia, neuritis, eye trouble, etc," Eliot told Pound on 19 July, and had now started on a new diet for colitis which involved great care in the preparation of food: all meat had to be minced three times, only the "best sealed medical milk" allowed, together with "vitamins and proteids [sic] daily." He did not want Vivien to break the diet, which seemed to be "the best so far and really doing her good," although he agreed to see Berman if he came to London. "I should like to put her in your hands," Tom assured Pound, but for the time being she was not well enough to bring to Paris. In a postscript, Tom added the most significant diagnosis yet made by Hogben: that Vivien's colitis was not a disease but a symptom of a more deep-seated malady. The sharp-eyed doctor had observed the tensions between the couple, the source of which he could only guess at, and was aware of the link between anxiety or depression and disorders of the digestive system such as colitis or irritable bowel syndrome.[59] There seems little doubt that Vivien was depressed: in a letter to Ottoline written in pencil because of the pain of neuritis in her right arm, she complained of "extreme dejection . . . I long to see you. Yet I often get into a condition of such apathy that I can scarcely lift my head. I get long periods of this inertia and I simply dread it."[60] Tom, however, clung to the idea that Vivien's colitis was a symptom of "glandular trouble" and she continued to take Hogben's animal gland capsules thrice daily.[61]

Vivien's condition was far more severe than her husband admitted. The starving regime had been disastrous, inevitably increasing the effect of any drugs she was taking for insomnia and the pain of neuralgia in her right arm. The poor skin of which she complained to the Harley Street specialists was very probably a symptom of bromism caused by overdosing on the bromide and chloral sleeping draughts which she had been taking for many years. Taken in excess they caused crimson blotches on the face and hands, as Evelyn Waugh noticed to his horror when he began mixing his undiluted sleeping draught with crème de menthe and taking it in larger and larger quantities as an antidote to insomnia and depression. His face, like Vivien's, developed a "congested, mottled hue," and he began hearing voices. Paranoia was another side effect vividly described by Waugh in his novel, based on his experiences, *The Ordeal of Gilbert Penfold;* he began to feel he was being spied on. "The doctor has you under observation," whispered the voices. "He'll keep you in a home because you're mad, Gilbert." Not until his doctor informed him that his was a "simple case of poisoning" did Waugh/Penfold find relief from the fear that he was going insane.[62]

But drugs could be "comforters" to someone as unhappy as Vivien, as Muriel Spark related in her first novel, *The Comforters,* which in 1957 took a similar theme to that of Waugh's, in this case revealing how dexedrine caused her to have hallucinations.

Vivien's own "Nightmare figure" visited her at night with "strange looks and horrid glares," she confessed in 1924 to Sydney Schiff, who suffered a similar affliction.

I am no more responsible for him than you are, I take it, for your particular Nightmare. I mean your pet bogey, your tame Superman. But if we are to accept them, and you say in your letter we must, we shall I suppose have to accept all their accoutrements—their moods and fancies, their flights, their disguises, their *armaments,* their chains and padlocks & their groans, shrieks and imprecations. And why not?[63]

Vivien's vivid imagination may have been the source of these nightmare figures, but it is more likely that drugs caused her to hallucinate. In a painting by Henry Fuseli, *The Nightmare,* demons and goblins appear to a young woman who seems drugged. The culprit in Vivien's case was probably chloral, a commonplace drug of the time: Virginia Woolf found "Prince Chloral" a seductive comforter in her battle for sanity, claiming in her essay "On Being Ill" that we need a new "hierarchy of the passions":

Love must be deposed in favour of a temperature of 104; jealousy give place to the pangs of sciatica; sleeplessness play the part of villain, and the hero become a white liquid with a sweet taste—that mighty Prince with the moth's eyes and the feathered feet, one of whose names is Chloral.[64]

Illness, such a constant presence in Vivien's life, inspired some of her most vivid and forceful writing. In a striking, semi-autobiographical sketch, "The Paralysed Woman," written in 1922, she describes "Sibylla," an unhappy wife living at the seaside, awaiting the return of her husband, André. In the house opposite is a paralysed woman. Sibylla observes her closely. The paralysed woman dines with an attentive man in grey. Sibylla feels she is more disabled, more unfortunate than the woman in the bath chair.

On Saturday came André, wearing a bowler hat, with an anxious expression, and carrying as usual two large suitcases—one filled with books and periodicals and the other with medicine bottles . . . Felice, the help, is wearing her overall; she puts a kettle on the gas fire with a fat, helpless hand, spilling a little water as she does. Her short-sighted eyes hold the expression of a worried monkey . . .[65] André scowled at her: "Are you quite certain that the milk is 'certified' "? he asked with cold fury, removing the cardboard disk from a milk bottle and peering down at the contents . . . André slept till three: he rose liverish and bad-tempered and ate a combined meal of stale lunch and early tea . . . He poked about the medicine chest, collected empty bottles, made copious notes, and packed and unpacked suitcases.[66]

André/Tom brings supplies of drugs for his wife from the London specialist, and the tranquillising compounds Sibylla swallows must have seemed a necessity, for her behavior is irrational and bizarre. Half-jokingly she threatens "Mike," another resident who claims to feel a Proustian indifference for life; carelessly picking up a knife, she asks if he cares whether he is dead or alive.

> She stood the knife upright on its handle, and tapped it on the table. She glanced at the knife, and then again at Mike, who did not answer . . .
> "Answer me," said Sibylla in a loud and martial tone. Mike hung his head.
> "No," he said.
> "Ah," said Sibylla, "so you are not indifferent to everything." She played with the knife. "You would not be indifferent for instance, if I were just to wipe this knife round your throat."

Vivien presents "Mike" as an obtuse character forever being set "traps" by Sibylla, Felice and André. Mike tries to laugh: "You know you look so awfully fierce, dear, sitting there." Sibylla ignores him; and only a few pages later she explodes with rage when André, Mike and Felice bring her the laundry to sort as she lies in bed; Felice has been using Sibylla's Sunlight soap without permission. Sibylla screams at Felice. She asks everyone to leave her room. With bowed heads they creep out. Left alone, Sibylla falls back exhausted on her bed, surrounded and covered with piles of linen, half-open parcels and paper and string.

"I can't bear it. I can't go on." She relaxed her body and appeared dead: but her mind went on as fast as ever.

Covering her face with her hands, she repeats to herself like a lesson—"I must be independent. I must. Somehow I must be independent."

Framed in the window opposite she sees the paralysed woman, wearing white, taking tea with the man in grey and a little boy. She has a son; she is surrounded by love. Sibylla locks her suitcase and lies flat on the bed. Her aching back eases a little as she puts her legs up over the end of the bed . . . "She'll probably get better anyhow," thinks Sibylla impatiently. She lies inert, waiting for André to come with the car and take her away.[67]

It would be possible to interpret this sketch as an indication of Vivien's inherent instability, manifesting itself in psychotic behavior, but there is no need for such a reductive reading of the piece. Vivien, like Tom, was neurotic but not psychotic. There are many references in Vivien's diaries to her feelings of depression, insomnia and lethargy, as well as to her hyperactivity or mania, when she could not stop writing, shopping or socialising, and experienced feelings of omnipotence. But in different marital circumstances her highly strung temperament might have found the calm and stability she required.

The hysteria from which Vivien suffered was the most common form of neurosis exhibited by women at that time. Hysteria, like "witchcraft," is a pejorative term, taking its name from *hystera,* the Greek word for uterus; its wide variety of symptoms was blamed by classical healers on the supposed ability of the uterus to travel through the body. Viewed throughout history as a women's disease, subject to punitive treatments, it can also be read as the "body language of powerlessness," the only outlet for frustrated libido and talent in a prefeminist era. Vivien, trapped in her marital cage, is like Hedda Gabler, of whom Ibsen wrote: "It is Hedda's repression, her hysteria that motivates everything she does."[68] Vivien is as much a paradigm of hysteria as Hedda when she writes to Mary from her cottage: "I felt like a wild heart in a cage."[69]

Hysteria as a response to the immobilising and silencing of women is a thesis which illuminates Vivien's case. Like Freud's patient, "Anna O," she cannot communicate with a man she perceives as hostile; yet "Sibylla" writes feverishly. Although unable to walk in "The Paralysed Woman," her typewriter sits in her bedroom. She plucks the last page of her story from it. "It was finished. She was sorry in a way." There is nothing more she can do to it, and it must stand or fall on its own. "Her back ached now, and suddenly she was aware of that, and of her fixed tense face and of the old dull pain." Writing is her rebellion as she fumbles to find a voice which will not only express her pain and anger but transcend it, for in her imagination she is not a sick woman but an exhibition dancer who is dancing in her yellow knitted dress to the applause of the audience. "It's the only thing to be," she cries to André.

> Don't you see? You simply dance and then you are finished. You don't have to think. You don't have to act. All you have to do is dance . . . and everybody claps.[70]

Significantly, both in folklore and in medicine, dance was seen as an imitation or representation of female hysteria, occupying the shadowy place between theatrical and histrionic frenzy.[71]

In reality, in August 1922, when she was writing "The Paralysed Woman," Vivien was struggling to regain enough strength to visit her friend Mary, who was recovering from a mild case of mumps. If she could walk as far as Eleanor, wrote Vivien, she would come and speak to Mary through the door, or climb up to the window. "I should love to do that. But I cannot walk so far, walk such a long way. It is so long now since I walked at all." She passed the time rereading Mary's letters, which she had meant to destroy, because she had "a mania for destruction." But they were so nice, so charming, that she kept them, so that they might go into "someone's biography." It is significant that as early as 1922 Vivien was concerned with preserving evidence for the future; as the years passed she took increasing care in dating her letters, although the recipients often failed to take equal care in preserving them. "I am not liking it here *very* much," she confessed sadly to Mary. "I try to like it. But something is wrong. I cant *relax*. What is it?"[72]

Bloomsbury, meanwhile, was taking Eliot to its very heart. At Hogarth House Virginia Woolf set up the type for *The Waste Land* with her own hands, as she had done with his *Poems*.[73] She now felt that the poet amused her more than old friends such as Clive Bell: earlier that year, in March, Virginia found Tom had grown "supple as an eel," positively familiar and jocular. She enjoyed the clash of steel with him as they crossed swords over *Ulysses,* a work about which they still held very different views.[74] And when, in July 1922, Virginia discovered the talk at Garsington was of the subscription Ottoline was getting up "to give Tom £300, & so free him from journalism," she decided to help rally supporters for The Eliot Fellowship Fund, as the English arm of Bel Esprit was known. Richard Aldington, with whom the scheme had originated in England, was a mere "greasy-eyed" tradesman, in Virginia's eyes. It was she and Ottoline, both of whom felt increasing sympathy for "great Tom," as Virginia dubbed him, who hastened to rescue their protége.[75]

Nevertheless Bel Esprit was beginning to look an increasingly precarious and undignified scheme: Eliot snapped at Pound that he strongly objected to any mention of Lloyds Bank in the circular: "*Please see my position*—I *cannot* jeopardise my position at the Bank before I know what is best."[76] His mood with Aldington was irascible, as he laid his plans for the *Criterion;* secrecy was imperative. His editorship was to be hidden from readers: "I shall initial my editorial," he informed Aldington, promising to arrange the division of labour between the two of them in "an orderly way."[77] The first issue was to kick off with some contemporary criticism from Aldington, and the first two sections of *The Waste Land;* he did not intend to launch the review with an attack on his enemy, Middleton Murry, he explained: "I wish to be very careful at first not to appear to use the paper as a weapon."[78] But behind the "softly, softly" approach, Eliot was in deadly earnest. The jackals were snapping at his heels, and he knew that his reputation would stand or fall by the success or failure of the new periodical which he intended to rival or surpass Scofield's *Dial.* Angry words were exchanged when Aldington's article did not come up to scratch, and when Herbert Read seemed to have let the cat out of the bag about his editorship, Eliot's fury was so great that he threatened legal action against his old friend: "I don't want *anyone* to write of me as the editor, and I am very angry that he [Read] has done so," he spluttered to Aldington. "I am seeing my solicitor . . ."[79]

Eliot's quarrels with Vivien and his short temper with male colleagues betrayed the stress of maintaining a mask which had never fitted and had now become an intolerable burden. Although to friends he appeared preoccupied with the *Criterion* launch and Vivien, the astute Virginia noticed that all was not as it seemed. When Tom visited her at Gordon Square in early August she no longer found him approachable but rather "sardonic, guarded, precise, & slightly malevolent . . ."[80] Clive Bell had confirmed her suspicions in March 1922 that Tom was wearing face-powder, explaining, via Mary, that Tom "uses violet powder to make him look cadaverous."[81] "I am not sure that he does not paint his lips," she recorded in September.[82] A few months later she noted with growing disillusion: "He dreads life as a cat dreads water. But if I hint so much he is all claws"; Tom was "broken down," unable to speak for tears when he telephoned her, distraught, peevish, egotistical.[83]

The pull of that other twilight world had become too great to be resisted. The conflict which brought Eliot for a second time to the verge of breakdown, before he fled to Lugano, had found its own resolution with the discreet help of Mary, always sympathetic to the needs of her friends. That year the Russian ballet had returned to the Coliseum for another triumphant season, its stars Lydia Lopokova and Léonide Massine delighting Ottoline Morrell, the Sitwell brothers, Roger Fry, Duncan Grant and other members of Bloomsbury, who were devoted adherents of the Ballets Russes. Ottoline entertained Diaghilev and Massine to tea at Garland's Hotel in Suffolk Street, where the dancers could be found after the first house eating strawberry or raspberry jam in silver spoons, dipped in black tea; she entertained them at Garsington too, impressing the snobbish Diaghilev, threatened with boredom among the shaggy writers in the garden, by announcing of Dorothy Brett: "That woman is sister to a Queen." "It is true that the Queen in question was Queen of Sarawak, but the words nevertheless produced a tonic effect," recalled Osbert Sitwell.[84]

Massine and Ottoline exchanged photos, and he signed himself "votre très dévoué Léonide."[85] Although London was at the feet of the "fluttering, pink-petticoated, mischievous Lopokova, and her . . . sinister-looking partner," as Massine described himself and Lydia, they looked for social life to Bloomsbury, and Lydia eventually married Maynard Keynes.[86] Massine, maître de ballet and principal choreographer of the Russian Ballet, had made his début in *La Légende de Joseph* in 1914, returning after the war in the role of Amoun in *Cléopâtre,* in which he was naked except for a loincloth. His dancing had "a dark, grotesque quality," to which his partner Lydia, "fair, with the plump greenish pallor of arctic flowers," was the perfect foil.[87] Eliot had watched many performances of the Russian Ballet, both in Paris and London, but it was not until April 1922 that he asked Mary to find out whether Massine, who was starring in *La Boutique Fantastique, Le Tricorne (The Three-Cornered Hat)* and *Parade,* would be prepared to meet him. Her reply was encouraging, and he responded with excitement. "I hope your news of Massine at the Coliseum is true, as I have been to see him and thought him more brilliant and beautiful than ever—if what you said was sincere it is I consider a great compliment as I (never having been so close before) quite fell in love with him," he wrote to Mary on 28 April 1922. "I want to meet him more than ever—& he is a genius." Thanking her for one of their "Piccadilly teas," he repeated that he hoped to see Massine with her.[88]

Three weeks after returning from his Italian holiday, Eliot's wish was granted. He met the dancer—who at that time was still married to Vera Savina (formerly Clark—it was the custom of the Russian Ballet to give English dancers Russian names)—at a restaurant. "I liked Massine very much indeed—with no disappointment—and hope that I shall see him again," he wrote to Mary, thanking her for being "very sweet" in arranging a perfect evening. He was feeling rather tired, explained Eliot, for while Vivien starved, he had been out to a dinner and dance the night before, "and enjoyed myself and got off with the Aga Khan, and finished the evening at Wigmore Street where I ended the vermouth and packed my clothes, rather fun . . ."[89] Tom had made a decision: he would not yet abandon Vivien, but the time had come to lay the foundations for his secret life.

15

"Fanny Marlow"

By September the roses were fading around the door of the Bosham cottage. After a farewell picnic with Mary, Vivien reluctantly left the windswept shores of Chichester Harbour for London. But her heart remained in Sussex: she pined for her seaside cottage, whose lease was up, she told Ottoline, and wished she could make her home in the country. "London is so horrible . . . I certainly do wish that there was not so much hatred, and when one gets right away from everybody one cannot see what it is all about." Nevertheless, Vivien's mood was collected, her letter neatly typed and accurately spelt. Determined to act unselfishly towards Tom, she told Ottoline on 15 September 1922, in what may be a coded message of understanding, that she longed for him "to have a freer life and a less ugly one."[1]

From Clarence Gate Gardens Vivien continued her restless search for a replacement cottage. "Please please find me a cottage, house, bungalow, anything, *unfurnished*," she begged Mary on 23 September.[2] Messages flew to Mary at both Eleanor and River House on French postcards Vivien had bought in Paris in January. Still "starving and helpless,"[3] Vivien was frustrated by the difficulties of house-hunting from a distance. It was "terrible" when one could not *go and look*. Did Mary think a cottage on the main road to Selsey would be any good? Or a bungalow at Clymping, near Littlehampton—or even a fine Georgian residence in Chichester itself? There seemed to be so many properties, but they were *never* quite right. In response Mary showered Vivien with flowers—pink carnations for her bedroom and chrysanthemums for Tom's study—but kept her distance. Vivien remained the supplicant, asking herself to tea, complaining that they were "indeed behindhand" in seeing each other: "I want to see you, if you want to see me," she told Mary, enquiring whether next Saturday afternoon would be any good, for Vivien never went out in the evening.[4]

No such difficulties presented themselves to Mary when it came to meeting Tom. While Vivien remained in bed with a "strained heart," under doctor's orders, trying to reduce her blood pressure after a bout of bronchitis which had nearly turned to pneumonia, Tom asked Mary and Jack to dinner at the Café Royal as his guests. "I want very much indeed to see you, both—don't disappoint me," he wrote to Mary on 7 October.[5] His busy social life, which had crossed the increasingly blurred line between Bloomsbury and the drawing-rooms of high society, left little time for rest. Tom apologised to Mary for not being "at home" when she had called early one evening: he was in a very deep sleep, he explained, snatching a few hours before his new secretary, a young woman named Irene Pearl Fassett, came to the flat at eight. As his nights were seldom more than five hours, he usually took a nap before dinner.[6] Sometimes Mary complained that she could not reach him on the telephone: "O la, my dear Mary, and so I am not the only person who cannot be got on the telephone." He had tried her twice that evening and got "no reply." Well, he was glad she also understood that one *need not* respond to the busy bell. He hoped she was not also in bed with an aching head and back and an exasperated liver, after a night on the town, and that the next time he rang she would be "sweetly present."[7]

There is no doubt that Mary remained more than a little in love with Tom, as were Edith Sitwell and Nancy Cunard. Nancy never forgot the evening she met Tom in 1922 at a ball at her mother's house: he in a dinner jacket, she in a panniered Poiret dress, "gold with cascading white tulle on the hips." Although she had danced that night with the Prince of Wales, Nancy was bored until the moment when she met Eliot; they had had supper alone together, she recalled, and talked about poetry. She had suggested a *rendez-vous* the following evening. The poet agreed. They met, drank together and talked into the night. Nancy remembered that they were both engaged to dine at the Hutchinsons', but "I begged you not to get us there, and in the end I won."[8]

Eliot enjoyed flirting with amusing and decorative married women (Nancy was at this time married to Sydney Fairbairn). It is possible that he may have fallen prey to the seductive and promiscuous Nancy, who prided herself on demonstrating the pleasures of heterosexual relationships to otherwise confirmed homosexuals.⁹ Certainly Maurice Haigh-Wood remembered that Nancy, like Mary, "made a pass" at Tom. But it is more likely that Tom continued to meet Nancy at Lady Cunard's box at the ballet because of his intense interest in the Ballets Russes, and in particular in his new friend, Léonide Massine, whom he had reviewed with unusual effusiveness in *The Dial* in August 1921. Eliot greeted the second, post-war "golden age" of the Ballets Russes, a period in which Massine's ascendancy was complete, with acclaim. In his view it surpassed the pre-war era of Nijinsky and Pavlova, both in simplicity and in sophistication.¹⁰ In April 1923 Eliot would go on to claim that Massine was "The greatest actor . . . in London . . . the most completely unhuman, impersonal, abstract," observing in the dancer the same "mask-like beauty" he had noticed in another actor, Ion Swinley, of the Phoenix Society company, whose productions Tom, Vivien, and other members of Bloomsbury attended. Massine's training in movement and gesture, declared Tom in "Dramatis Personae" in the *Criterion,* allowed the Russian to transmute personality into art as only the greatest artist could do: "The difference between the conventional gesture of the ordinary stage, which is supposed to *express* emotion, and the abstract gesture of Massine, which *symbolises* emotion, is enormous." For the poet it was the ritualistic quality of Massine's performance which moved him: "For the stage . . . always . . . is a ritual, and the failure of the contemporary stage to satisfy the craving for ritual is one of the reasons why it is not a living art."¹¹

Eliot was influenced by Clive Bell in his praise of the modernist "impersonality" of Massine's performing style, which echoed the qualities he and other "Bloomsberries" valued in poetry and literature. Yet, as Lynn Garafola, historian of the Russian ballet, points out, Eliot's enthusiasm for Massine's performance was "most astounding," when one considers the production in which he was dancing. This was George Robey's *You'd Be Surprised,* a "tinned" New York revue, as Eliot himself described it, which led Massine to cross the line dividing ballet and variety, and work with Noël Coward and C. B. Cochran.¹² Nevertheless, after sitting through an hour of this "cold-stored humour," Eliot discovered "life" as well as machinery: "We move toward satisfaction in the direction which moves Leonid [sic] Massine."[13]

The Russian ballet had become a cult with High Bohemia. Edward J. Dent, music critic of the *Athenaeum,* had written in June 1920 that the Diaghilev audience was dominated by the "intellectual-smart":

> musicians who know all about painting, painters who know all about music, poets who like to be men about town, men about town who like to be poets . . . M. Diaghilev understands them as if he were himself the *maestro* whose immortal hand had framed their sawdust and tinsel anatomies.[14]

If, as is likely, Eliot and Osbert Sitwell recognised themselves in this hostile portrait of "poets who like to be men about town, men about town who like to be poets," neither was unduly concerned. Both were committed to living beyond their means in the pursuit of pleasure. Hedonism and aestheticism were their natural values and, under the guise of robust heterosexuality, married women their confidantes. The difference between them lay not only in talent but in fortune; in his pursuit of a single social life apart from Vivien, Tom was forced to amuse himself largely at other people's expense, in contrast to Osbert, who could borrow on the security of Reninshaw, his future inheritance. But Tom, the handsome poet-about-town, was a welcome guest in many salons, and in the Rothermeres he had the good fortune to find a couple whose patronage linked the worlds of literature and dance: the press baron Rothermere was as devoted to dancers (Alice Nikitina, a Ballets Russes dancer, was his mistress) as his wife was initially to her lion cub Tom at the *Criterion,* and in the late 1920s would become financial backer of Diaghilev's company.[15]

In the final run-up to the *Criterion* launch on 15 October 1922, however, pleasure had to take second place to the pains of editorship. Fortunately Tom's problems over the publication of *The Waste Land* had melted away. The diplomatic John Quinn had resolved Tom's quarrel with Scofield over payment by hosting a lunch for Gilbert Seldes and Liveright at which a face-saving formula was found: Eliot was to be awarded the *Dial* prize of $2,000 for services to letters in America. This allowed *The Waste Land* to appear, without Notes, in *The Dial* in November 1922, a month after its first publication in the inaugural issue of the *Criterion*. The Boni & Liveright edition, with the "solemn mockery" (in T. S. Matthews' words)[16] of the added Notes suggested by Roger Fry, was published in mid-December, to be followed by the Hogarth Press edition in September 1923. When Quinn received the bundle of manuscripts from Eliot (which included the "unpublishable" 1909 notebook of Bolo poems) on about 15 January 1923, he commented that he himself would not have agreed to the cuts to *The Waste Land* made by Ezra Pound.[17] Nevertheless Eliot inscribed the copy of the Boni & Liveright edition he sent to Ezra in Paris with a graceful dedication: "for E.P./*miglior fabbro*/from T.S.E./Jan. 1923." The quotation was again from Canto xxvi of the *Purgatorio* in which Dante says of Arnaut Daniel: *"Fu miglior fabbro del parlar materno"* (he was the better craftsman in his mother-tongue). Eliot repeated the compliment to Pound when *The Waste Land* was reprinted in his *Poems 1909–25* with the dedication: "For Ezra Pound/*il miglior fabbro.*"[18] Eliot's gratitude for his friend's critical ability was genuine, but the dedication perhaps assuaged his guilt at receiving the *Dial* prize, which he felt should have gone to Pound, languishing in obscurity in Paris.

It is worth considering why Eliot took the decision at this point in his life to commit to Quinn's safe-keeping the notebook containing his early poems, and in particular the revealing Bolo and Colombo verses with their homosexual and scatological themes. By contrast it seems that Eliot arranged for Emily Hale's letters to him to be burnt by Peter du Sautoy, a director of Faber & Faber and one of his executors, as in March 1963 he gave du Sautoy a tin-box containing papers which he had, he said, "for a long time been meaning to destroy." Du Sautoy duly burned the papers in the coal-burning furnace in the block of flats where he was living.[19] The question remains, why Eliot did not also consign his "Bolo" notebook to the flames, since its repetitive tales of Captain Colombo, "the great big bitch," reveal inclinations which he had kept secret during his lifetime.[20] Surely the answer has to be that Eliot, like other great artists, intended such "sensitive" material to be read after his death. Arguably he wanted future generations to know the private man who sheltered behind the grave public persona, and we can only be grateful for his foresight in appreciating that a later generation might be less judgemental than his own.

Nervously Vivien awaited the publication of the first part of *The Waste Land* in their new quarterly. To Sydney Schiff, who expressed his appreciation of the poem in an "unexpectedly moving" letter, she wrote on 16 October, the day after the publication of the *Criterion* No. 1:

> Perhaps not even you can imagine with what emotions I saw *The Waste Land* go out into the world. It means to me a great deal of what you have exactly described, and it has become a part of me (or I of it) this last year. It was a terrible thing, somehow, when the time came at last for it to be published. I have been distracted these last 2 days . . .[21]

She need not have worried. The poem was an immediate financial and critical success, even if her prosaic brother-in-law Henry found that it seemed to be written in a "cipher" he could not understand. "Probably no poem of comparable length was ever more promptly, more variously, or more copiously rewarded," writes Professor Reid.[22] The evidence of genius needed to attract subscribers to Bel Esprit was there for all to see, argued Pound, who was now comparing Eliot to Keats, Shelley or Browning.[23] As Cyril Connolly realised, Eliot and Joyce had broken with nineteenth-century Romantic models and surpassed them in originality: 1922 was "the *annus mirabilis* of the modern movement, with *Ulysses* and *The Waste Land* just around the corner, and the piping days of Huxley . . . and the Sitwells, of the Diaghilev ballet . . ."[24] And Eliot, with the birth of his new quarterly, had taken yet another step up the pyramid of fame.

But barely was the *Criterion* born, than it seemed in danger of choking. Lady Rothermere complained that she was displeased with the first number, writing Tom three "offensive letters" from La Prieuré, a former Carmelite monastery at Fontainebleau which had become the Institute for the Harmonious Development of Man. Run by a Russian mystic, the

Institute was, wrote Vivien to Ezra Pound, an "asylum for the insane," where Lady Rothermere was doing "religious dances naked with Katherine Mansfield," who was also an inmate. Vivien worried that Mansfield was influencing their patron against Tom: " 'K.M.,' " Lady R. was writing in every letter—"is *the most intelligent* woman I have ever met," she told Pound. " 'K.M.' is pouring poison in her ear (of course) for 'K.M.' hates T. more than anyone."[25] Tom and Vivien began to panic that "Lady R." would "shipwreck" the quarterly, despite its instant "SUCCESS," as Tom explained to Ezra in a letter written a day after Vivien's on 3 November. He had had nothing but good notices, and nearly all the six hundred copies printed were sold, but now he was afraid he would be forced to abandon the paper.[26] What were they to do?

Vivien's plan was a bold one: she proposed somehow to raise the money to buy out Lady Rothermere, whom she believed would take £500 for the journal now, although she would not sell it later if it began to pay. "Do you think this is a *possible* idea? If so, how shall we do it—and *can you get that money?*" she demanded of Ezra. Her belief in Tom was absolute. "I know he could make the *Criterion* a success," she wrote, offering herself to provide £500. It would halve her income from the capital her father had given her, but she would do it "gladly."[27]

Tom agreed with Vivien's idea. It would be "the thing of our lives," Tom told Ezra, if he and Ezra could get the *Criterion* into their own hands and run it for a couple of years. Come over to London for a weekend and see me, he pleaded. Ezra's reaction was unenthusiastic: "I think both you and V. are in delirium," he wrote, "thinking of paying £500 for the privilege of having worked six months. Bring out another number . . . Dear ole SON. You jess set and hev a quiet draw at youh cawn-kob." The *Criterion*'s only asset was Tom himself, he told the anxious poet. "If you quit, *it* quits." And why would one story from Katherine M. really "queer the review? . . . I dare say K.M. IS the most intelligent female she [Lady R.] has ever met."[28]

This defence of Katherine Mansfield aroused a furious reaction from Tom two days later. K.M. was not by any means the most intelligent woman Lady Rothermere had ever met: "She is simply one of the most persistent and thickskinned toadies and one of the vulgarest women Lady R. has ever met and is also a sentimental crank."[29] (It was an opinion at odds with his expression in April 1923 of the *Criterion*'s "profound regret" at Katherine Mansfield's death, and the subsequent "loss to English letters.")[30] Vivien's own hostility towards Katherine may have had its roots in her resentment of Katherine's brief liaison with Russell, as well as in Vivien's protective feelings towards Tom. Yet at the same time Vivien's own work showed signs of Katherine's influence: Vivien's story "Mrs. Pilkington," which she wrote for the *Criterion* in October 1924 under the pen name Felix Morrison, as well as her "Diaries of the Rive Gauche," resemble in both style and content Mansfield's "Je Ne Parle Pas Français."[31]

Pound's advice to Eliot regarding Lady Rothermere's vociferous complaints that the paper was "Dull" and looked like a corpse, was astute. "She's right, mon POSSUM," he wrote in a letter which reached the Eliots on 5 November 1922, the anniversary of Guy Fawkes's Gunpowder Plot. How could Lady R. be expected to see what was scarce discernible to the naked eye, that "the Crit . . . is *supposed* to be PLAYIN' POSSUM."[32] Pound had detected Tom and Vivien's intention: to blow up the literary establishment and make of Tom a new, puritan leader in the mould of Oliver Cromwell. It was a "plot" of long standing, first mentioned by Vivien to Mary as long ago as November 1919, after Mary had asked, in apparent innocence, whether Tom had many literary "enemies." "You ask me, but I think you know better than I," Vivien had retorted, worried that the Woolfs were being influenced against Tom.[33] "I also have a gunpowder plot in preparation," she had written to Mary, who was busy with her own scheming, "but mine is timed to go off in the New Year."[34]

Tom also confided the Eliot "Gunpowder Plot" to his friend, the poet Herbert Read, a contributor to the *Criterion*.[35] They would aim for a "softly, softly" approach, as he explained to Ezra in July 1922, at first keeping the "jailbirds" behind the scenes, and only cautiously allowing Pound and Wyndham Lewis into print.[36] Tom would, as Pound put it, play Possum. And indeed the 1920s were the period in which Eliot amused himself in the Possum role, signing his letters to Pound with his own logo: a cross whose four corners were inscribed "POS SUM HIS MARK." The Latin meaning of "possum"—"I can, I am able"—indicated perhaps that Eliot knew that he had within his grasp the power he had always craved.[37] Nearer a cat than a possum, as Osbert Sitwell had instantly discerned, Eliot stalked his prey with stealth and patience, beginning with Middleton Murry, his chief rival and intellectual antagonist in a war of words waged on the battlefield of the *Criterion*. But such was Eliot's cunning in disguising the *Criterion,* so that it looked "so heavily camouflaged as Westminster Abbey,"[38] that few realised that they were living through a revolution.

If Eliot was the general, Vivien was his aide-de-camp in this struggle for ascendancy. She hatched a scheme, in collusion with Tom, whereby she could earn extra money to supplement his salary from Lloyds. She would write for the paper under a variety of pseudonyms, the most popular of which was "Fanny Marlow," sometimes reduced to the initials, "F.M." Vivien also gave herself two male pen names, Felix Morrison and Feiron Morris, as well as writing under the name of her close friend, Irene Fassett, who was Eliot's secretary. "Fanny Marlow" has interesting psychological associations, for it was during her stay at Marlow that Vivien's "fanny" was the object of Bertrand Russell's attentions. "I *MUST* explain that I have been riting (writing!) for a long time under various names and nomenclatures," she confided to Ezra in 1924.

> Have written a lot of stories . . . I wrote nearly the whole of the last "Criterion"—except anything that was good in it, if there was such—under different names, all beginning with F.M. I thought out this scheme of getting money out of the Criterion a year ago. Because was always annoyed by spouse getting no salary. So thought what a good idea will receive money for contributions. Have received money. No one knows.[39]

Vivien knew her education at private ladies' academies had left her lacking in the skills of her university-educated male colleagues on the *Criterion.* Watercolour sketching, sewing and dancing were not the best preparation for journalism, but she was encouraged by Tom's vigorous support. "My wife . . . [has] been working very hard for some months, doing a lot of the Criterion work and also writing," he wrote to Richard Aldington in April 1924. "She is very diffident and is very aware that her mind is quite untrained, and therefore writes only under assumed names, but she has an original mind, and I consider not at all a feminine one; and in my opinion a great deal of what she writes is quite good enough for the Criterion." Tom intended to see that Vivien got "training and systematic education," because there were so few women who did have what he considered to be an "un-feminine mind" that he thought they ought to be made the most of. Richard was the only person, confessed Tom, apart from two of Vivien's friends, who knew of her writing.[40]

One good reason for Vivien's money-making plan was the shortcomings of the Bel Esprit scheme: first, the five-year time-limit put on the scheme, after which Eliot "OUGHT to be self-supporting . . . BUT in all probability he *won't* be," as Pound was forced to admit to Quinn, recalling that Yeats at the age of forty-seven had been forced to draw out his last £5 from the bank;[41] secondly, the size of the proposed income: £300 might be acceptable to Ezra, but for Eliot, a tolerable life demanded £600 a year at least, preferably £800, a comfortable flat in London, and six months abroad. Too reticent to speak plainly, he allowed confusion to grow among his English supporters.

In September 1922 Ottoline had written to Vivien to ask her to suggest more subscribers to the Eliot Fellowship Fund; Vivien replied enigmatically that she had a lot to say on that subject, more than she could write in a letter. "As for giving you a list of names of people who would be interested, I do not know of one person outside of those who have already been approached . . . who would be likely to take the slightest interest in the subject."[42] Vivien had her reasons for this brush-off, for she knew better than Ottoline her husband's true financial position, although Ottoline was soon to be privy to secrets of Tom's which he did not choose to share with his wife.

Richard Aldington had seen the rapids ahead in the summer of 1922, when Amy Lowell refused to contribute to Bel Esprit. Pound's article in the *New Age,* publicising the scheme, had proved disastrous. "The publicity he has created (revolting to the last degree) makes [it] impossible," Aldington explained to Amy on 7 July. American supporters began writing in, demanding that Pound contact the press with photographs of Eliot. Horrified, Aldington proposed to withdraw from fund-raising, although he had already gathered promises of £100 a year for his own "private scheme" with Ottoline and Virginia. He made a statement in the *Literary Review,* attempting to correct Ezra's mis-statements, and to clear Eliot and himself from "the inevitable ridicule and odium. I don't mind very much myself," he confided to Amy, "but I do mind for Eliot's sake."[43]

The damage, however, had been done. Whispers were growing about the poet: it was said that his family were wealthy, that he earned £600 a year at Lloyds—and was not prepared to give up his job. There were jibes that he was a hypocrite, a miser even. It was probably known—for Pound was notoriously indiscreet—that Eliot had agreed to accept £20 from his impoverished compatriot; Eliot was to solemnly receipt the gift in clerkly hand: "Received from Bel Esprit per Ezra Pound Esq £20 (twenty pounds)," signing himself "T. S. Eliot" across two one-penny stamps.[44] People marvelled that Aldington, scraping a living doing translations at Malthouse Cottage, near Reading, was collecting for the author of *The Waste Land,* who had just won the *Dial* prize of $2,000. Tom's anguish grew, as the gossip spread.

On 16 November 1922 the story broke. The *Liverpool Post* printed a garbled but damaging piece about the collections being made for him:

> As the amusing tale went at the time the sum of £800 was col-
> lected and presented to Mr. Eliot there and then. The joke was
> that he accepted the gift calmly, and replied: "Thank you very
> much; I shall make good use of the money, but I like the bank."
> That was two years ago, and he held out until last spring, when
> he suffered a severe nervous breakdown which necessitated three
> months leave of absence. Thereupon the society of "Bel Esprit"
> was hatched in secret and carried through, the poet's own wishes
> not being consulted.

The long poem by Eliot in the first number of the *Criterion* was, said the newspaper, the "initial result" of "a considerable and generous scheme with excellent possibilities."[45]

Tom's fury at these "calamitous falsehoods," as he described them to Richard Aldington, knew no bounds. Certainly the paper's claim that Eliot had received £800 was erroneous, but his anger was due chiefly to the knowledge that the *Post* had made him a laughingstock. Tom was tempted to blame Aldington for leaking the story—although there is no reason to suppose the latter was to blame—and wrote to him on 18 November, determined to discover the source which had made possible the appearance of "such a libel . . . As I want to *track it down* and not merely secure an apology from the L. Post, please DO NOT MENTION THIS TO A *SIN-*

GLE PERSON until I have seen my solicitor. I pledge you to secrecy." But no sooner had Eliot called in a King's Counsel to help draft a letter to the *Liverpool Post,* than he received an anonymous letter from "Your Wellwisher," stating that the writer had heard that a collection was being taken for the poet and that although the writer's means were small no claim on his charity was ever in vain and he therefore enclosed four postage stamps in the hope that this would help to strengthen Tom's poetry until he became Poet Laureate. It was the last straw. Tom felt "utter exhaustion," as he complained to Aldington.[46]

Such mockery of their protégé evoked sympathy from both Ottoline and Virginia Woolf, who remained committed to the Eliot Fund. Virginia, in particular, was determined to come to Tom's rescue. Although their relationship was a complex and ambivalent one, and at times she did not wholly trust Tom, she nevertheless had felt peculiarly close to the poet ever since their encounter in a taxi in March 1921 on the way to the Lyric, Hammersmith, to see Congreve's *Love for Love;* there, in the dark interior of the cab, they had confessed to their mutual "vices" and acknowledged that they were both trying to write something harder than the classics, something "streaked with badness." "But I plunge more than he does," decided Virginia. "Perhaps I could learn him [sic] to be a frog."[47] Convinced now that if he would only allow her to organise affairs, she might instead make a prince of him, Virginia laboured assiduously to raise money. Her novel *Jacob's Room* was going into a second edition, and her reputation was well established. People did not like to refuse her, but nevertheless it was an uphill struggle. By December 1922 she, Leonard, Ottoline, Aldington and the Cambridge mathematician Harry Norton, who together formed the committee, had, despite paper promises, raised only £77. Of this they gave Eliot £50. Was he to receive an annual sum in future, enquired Tom delicately, or was the committee to continue just giving him "presents"?[48]

A month later Virginia was still waiting for Tom to leave the bank. He had told her "in confidence" of his decision to do so in December. Still he hesitated, "full of scruples." "He is about ready to leap," Ezra had written optimistically in July 1922. Instead Eliot did just as the *Liverpool Post* predicted, and in January 1923 put the £50 into the bank "to invest it," together with the *Dial* prize of £400 ($2,000). Harry Norton, irritated by the poet's procrastination, urged Virginia and Ottoline to get Ezra Pound to take over the fund.[49] Tom could not be blamed for his caution, for the Eliot Fund had given him no guarantees of an income which would match the bank's. A few days later Virginia attempted to clarify the situation with Richard Aldington. Would Mr. Eliot object to her mentioning the possibility that he might leave the bank, she enquired. "I find that when I ask people to subscribe, many of them object that he is staying in the Bank and drawing what many of them consider a good income."[50] She drew Mary Hutchinson into the scheme, too, asking her to persuade Sydney Schiff, who had already subscribed, to circulate the appeal. Mary in turn tried to persuade Vivien of the merits of the fund, but she remained reluctant; *if* the fund offered Tom a guaranteed sum, and *if* the *Criterion* succeeded, Vivien agreed Tom would automatically leave the bank, but in the meanwhile she was sure that any "forcing or pressure to *make* him leave the Bank at *this* point would be very tactless, and bad policy. *So much depends on the* Criterion."[51]

Vivien knew her husband better than Virginia, but she did not interfere. In early February 1923 Tom again visited Virginia at Hogarth House, Richmond; she was ill with a cold which was "a match for any in Bloomsbury." "We had a sitting: costive, agonised . . ." she told Clive Bell.[52] She and Leonard were too ill to penetrate Tom's sphinx-like reticence, but by 12 February Virginia had had an inspiration: since it was obviously impossible to collect enough money to provide Tom and Vivien with a sufficient income, she would pull strings to find him a more congenial job than the bank. She wrote to Maynard Keynes, who had taken over the *Nation* from its former editor, H. W. Massingham, asking whether he would employ Tom as literary editor:

> He would prefer not to teach, but would do secretarial or librarian's work. He is clearly getting into a bad state of health, and the efforts of the Eliot Fund are so slow that it is useless to wait . . . If he could rely on a small certain income from regular work he would risk giving up the Bank. If it were not for his wife's constant illness he would have left the Bank before now.[53]

Keynes's fellow directors were disinclined to give the post to Eliot, since "none of them ever heard of him," and Virginia was forced to plead with Lytton Strachey to promise to write for the *Nation* if Tom were appointed literary editor. "The poor man is becoming (in his highly American way, which is tedious and longwinded to a degree) desperate," she explained.[54] To her diary she confessed to growing boredom with Tom's troubles: "I could wish that poor dear Tom had more spunk in him, less need to let drop by drop of his agonised perplexities fall ever so finely through pure cambric. One waits, one sympathises, but it is dreary work . . ."[55]

By 17 March 1923 Tom could not speak for tears, as he agonised over whether to accept Keynes's offer to become literary editor. "He is broken down, & yet must buckle to & decide: shall he take the Nation?" wrote a weary Virginia in her diary,[56] meanwhile ordering "cheap" paper from which to make covers to bind *The Waste Land,* and arranging the marbling with Vanessa.[57] She consulted Bruce Richmond, editor of the *Times Literary Supplement,* who said emphatically, "He's not the man for the job." Virginia could not help agreeing, as Tom prevaricated over the question of guarantees (the *Nation* could not guarantee more than six months' employment). He was on the verge of collapse, she told Maynard, begging him for at least a two-year contract for Tom;[58] Maynard rang back to say that Tom seemed "distraught." "Whether distraught people can edit the Nation lit. sup. I doubt," mused Virginia.[59]

On 23 March Tom finally turned down the *Nation* job, which Maynard then unexpectedly offered to Leonard Woolf. "Here have I been toiling these 3 weeks to make Eliot take it; finally he shied; & this is the result," exclaimed Virginia, happy that her husband, who had formerly been a contributor to the *Nation* under Massingham, would be earning a regular salary. To the Woolfs it meant "safety . . . indeed luxury."[60] The Eliot Fund was subsequently wound up, as Tom decided he could not accept any more money while he remained at the bank. There was now, as Virginia told Ottoline, no prospect of his being able to leave it.

It is all too easy to follow in the footsteps of Tom's friends and blame Vivien for Tom's decision not to accept Maynard Keynes's offer, and for his consequent unhappiness. The problem was, according to Lyndall Gordon, "Eliot's obligation to secure the future for a wife who would never manage to shift for herself, or endure any privation . . . a vengeful muse who dragged him down to her dark seabed."[61] Tom himself complained to Ezra

Pound that, at the age of thirty-four, the prospect of staying in the bank was "abominable" to him, miserably comparing his own situation with Vivien to that of Ezra with Dorothy: "Dorothy has comparatively good health, a family who can help her, and prospects of enough money to live on afterwards," he had written on 15 November 1922. "Vivien has none of these things. Her father's property . . . is all tied up in Irish real estate, which he has been trying to sell all his life, has never paid much, now pays less . . ." It was, argued Tom, nothing but an encumbrance on Vivien and Maurice, although in the end Vivien's inheritance would prove sufficient to pay the fees of her mental asylum. Vivien was, in fact, as Henry Eliot realised, not penniless "as we once supposed."[62]

Vivien "will *never* be strong enough to earn her own living," insisted Tom, ignoring the fact that he, as editor of the *Criterion,* was about to start paying his wife for her journalism. The only reason he had asked for guarantees, he claimed to Ezra, was because of Vivien, for whom he felt a particular responsibility: "I have made a great many mistakes, which are largely the cause of her present catastrophic state of health, and also it must be remembered that she kept me from returning to America where I should have become a professor and probably never written another line of poetry, so in that respect she should be endowed." At the bank he was assured of a widow's pension for Vivien; outside it there was no security.[63]

It was a touching letter which nevertheless omitted several important facts. First, there was the question of Eliot's portfolio; only a few weeks earlier he had thanked his brother Henry for the "exceedingly welcome dividend," and instructed him to hold on to the Hydraulic stock while the market rose, looking for an opportunity to sell when sterling was low.[64] Eliot's interest in the stock market was a growing one: he was later in discussions with a very successful bond broker in New York, writing to Aldington in April 1924 that he could put him in touch with "a good broker" if he wished, although Tom himself had an aversion to "foreign securities."[65] Vivien's autobiographical sketch "On the Eve," which appeared in the *Criterion* under T. S. Eliot's name in January 1925, but bears all the marks of his wife's writing and his editing, indicates her knowledge that Eliot, by the mid-1920s, was not as poor as he claimed. The sketch pokes fun at a group of wealthy friends concerned about the possibility of being "completely and utterly ruined" if an extreme socialist government comes to power. "My few bits of stuff which pay me about twopence a year are all *absolutely* unsaleable," complains Agatha (perhaps based on Mary Hutchinson, whose husband "Alexander" resembles Jack). If only they could *sell* their horrible stocks and get the *cash* to invest in America: "We shall be destitute," she complains. Vivien's brother Maurice makes an appearance as "Horace," exclaiming that there are a few "stoutish fellows" left to save England, before departing for his club after a spirited rendition of:

> It's the sime the whole world over—
>> It's the pore that gets the blime,
> It's the rich that gets the pleashur:
>> Isn't it a ber-loody shime![66]

"Ow-ee, it's ni-eece to be rich, isn't it," remarks Lizzie the lift-girl to Rose, Agatha and Alexander's maid.

Eliot was more honest to Ezra than he ever was to Virginia about his real reasons for choosing to stay at the bank: "I don't want to write, no sensible man does who wants to write verse . . . It is preferable to run a review and be paid for letting other people write than to write oneself."[67] The editorship of the *Criterion* was demanding enough without the added burden of being literary editor at the *Nation;* he preferred the mechanical routine of Lloyds.

There was another factor in the equation which Eliot took care to keep hidden from Ezra. Only Ottoline was at first privy to this latest secret expense, which made it even more difficult to leave the bank. In January 1923 Vivien, whose vision had been so badly affected by the "starving" regimen that she could barely read, was sent "into exile" at Eastbourne, where her doctor had found her a flat without telling her the address.[68] Vivien had been sleeping worse than Tom had ever known her to do, he confided gloomily to Ottoline.[69] The intense strain of the "two very nasty personal affairs"—the insulting anonymous letter enclosing 6d in stamps, and the attack by the *Liverpool Post*—which she was to keep "absolutely to yourself" had worn them both out: no damages he might get could possibly compensate him for the strain and worry of bringing the case, he complained. He had retreated for a fortnight in November to Worthing himself, prostrated and unable even to write a letter.[70] As to Vivien, Tom expressed to his brother Henry on 31 December his anger at the damage done by her four months of dogged efforts in following the most severe and Spartan regime that he had ever known, one far more difficult than any cure in a nursing home or sanatorium: "Living in the midst of ordinary life imposes much more responsibility on her and requires infinite tenacity of purpose," he wrote. Vivien had not been able to deviate in the slightest from the most limited diet, she had followed special exercises prescribed for her and she had hardly seen anybody. "I have never known anybody stick to a thing with such persistence and courage, often with relapses which made her feel that the whole thing was useless."[71] On Christmas Day 1922 Vivien sat up to dinner for the first time for many months; by the first week in January 1923 she was in Eastbourne, beginning yet another "experiment."

Tom, meanwhile, took tea with Ottoline. A plan had been forming in his head which was facilitated by Vivien's absence. On 5 January he wrote Ottoline a confidential letter: by "an extraordinary stroke of good luck" he had come across a "tiny suite" of two rooms, amazingly cheap, which he intended to take. The idea, he said, was to use them as an office for the *Criterion* work, and when the lease of 9 Clarence Gate Gardens was up, to give that flat up. He and Vivien wanted to decrease their living expenses and settle themselves in a way that would be "adaptable to any kind of life," a hint that he and Vivien may have already discussed living separately. Tom had taken the liberty of giving Ottoline's name as a reference, knowing he could depend upon her not to mention this to *anyone at all*— and there were few of his friends of whom he could be sure in that way. The arrangement he was entering into was "so personal" that he did not want anyone to know of it. He asked Ottoline to reply at once to his agent, and be *very* quick about it.[72]

The flat Tom rented in early 1923 was to be the hub of his secret life, a place where he could throw off conventionality. Burleigh Mansions, a block of portered flats on Charing Cross Road, looked out on St. Martin's Lane, and was favoured by actors. Ellen Terry and Donald Wolfit both at times lived there. Eliot rented number 38, thus securing for himself a *pied à terre* in the heart of theatreland. At Burleigh Mansions he underwent a metamorphosis: here he was no longer "Mr. Eliot," banker and dutiful husband, but "Captain Eliot," hero of the Colombo verses, captain of his crew. Among that crew was in all probability Léonide Massine, who danced the French sailor in *Les Matelots,* a "light-hearted romp" which he choreographed for Diaghilev after divorcing his wife Vera in 1924 and returning to the bosom of the Ballets Russes and a bed-sitting room in Bloomsbury.

Osbert Sitwell noticed, when he visited Eliot in the "bizarre" atmosphere of the Charing Cross Road flat, that "Visitors on arrival had to enquire at the porter's lodge for 'The Captain,' which somehow invested the whole establishment with a nautical—for I cannot say why, I took the title to be naval rather than military—a gay, a gallant feeling." The room in which Osbert and Sacheverell dined was high up at the back of the block, looking down on the revolving glass-ball lantern of the Coliseum music hall, where the Russian ballet performed. Osbert sat next to Tom on one side, Sachie on the other:

> Noticing how tired my host looked, I regarded him more closely, and was amazed to notice on his cheeks a dusting of green powder—pale but distinctly green, the colour of a forced lily-of-the-valley. I was all the more amazed at this discovery, because any deliberate dramatisation of his appearance was so plainly out of keeping with his character, and with his desire never to call attention to himself, that I was hardly willing, any more than if I had seen a ghost, to credit the evidence of my senses.

Osbert was almost ready to disbelieve what he had seen, but he went to tea with Virginia Woolf a few days later. "She asked me, rather pointedly, if I had seen Tom lately, and when I said 'Yes' asked me—because she too was anxious for someone to confirm or rebut what she thought she had seen—whether I had observed the green powder on his face—so there was corroboration!" Osbert and Virginia were apparently equally astounded, and although they discussed Tom's use of cosmetics at considerable length, could find no way of explaining his "extraordinary and fantastical pretence," except on the basis that the great poet was expressing a craving for sympathy in his unhappiness.[73]

It was a cold summer evening, but the light lingered. After dinner

Osbert and Sachie sat in low armchairs; conversation did not flow. After a long silence Sachie remarked, as the golden globe of the Coliseum shone its beam on them, "What is so nice for you here, Tom, is that you're right in the centre of everything." Tom agreed, "in a tone of enthusiasm which lacked his usual wariness": "Yes. Near all the theatre." This amused Osbert, who did not find it easy to imagine Eliot hurrying out to see any of the popular successes of the moment, one of Noël Coward's plays or a current musical comedy, the electric signs for which could be distinguished if they walked to the window.[74] He remained mystified: "Osbert never did discover why T. S. Eliot called himself 'The Captain' and wore make-up," writes John Pearson, biographer of the Sitwells. Osbert, who himself found happiness in his relationship with David Horner after Sacheverell's marriage in 1925, seems to have had no inkling of Eliot's own inclinations, for the poet never took the Sitwells into his confidence as he did Ezra Pound. Osbert was only aware that there was some mystery about the Eliots, around whom there was "an ambience permeated with tragedy, tinged with comedy, and exhaling at times an air of mystification."[75]

Few people knew of Tom's new hidey-hole, certainly not those like Aldington and Norton who had so generously collected for him. Mary Hutchinson was, however, a guest, receiving in 1923 a postcard printed "from T. S. Eliot, 9 Clarence Gate Gardens, London NW1," with the handwritten message that the poet expected her at nine o'clock, Monday, at 38 Burleigh Mansions, almost over the publisher Chatto & Windus. She was to ask the concierge to take her to "Captain Eliot's" as the rooms were difficult to find. "Knock at the door three times." The card was unsigned.[76]

Barely had Eliot taken on the rooms in Burleigh Mansions than another financial burden fell upon him: in March 1923 Vivien discovered a tiny but south-facing labourer's cottage at 2 Milestone Cottages, Old Fishbourne, a mile or two from Bosham. She was eager to rent it, and Tom agreed, despite the cost. Vivien probably learnt in early 1923 that her husband had taken the flat on the fringes of Soho; later she visited it occasionally and wrote there but, despite its ostensible purpose as an office, the rental of the rooms in Burleigh Mansions marked a critical point in the Eliots' relationship—forcing Vivien to face the fact that Tom was creating an alternative life in which she had no place. Her response was panic, as her fear of abandonment mounted, a panic which is profoundly implicated in her acute illnesses of 1923. And, although renting both the extra flat and the country cottage created a practical *modus vivendi* which preserved the outward appearance of the Eliots' marriage, it was not a cheap arrangement. Vivien had acted generously in her tolerance of Tom's separate life, and yet she remained the object of his resentment and frustration at the "burden" she represented. The gay Captain longed to be rid of his sick, unhappy wife, and the situation was complicated by the fact that no one but Tom, and possibly Vivien, knew the truth about their financial affairs. It partly explains a confused "letter of denunciation" Vivien wrote to Osbert Sitwell and, so he claimed, similar letters she wrote to Ottoline and Virginia regarding their efforts to help Tom. Vivien also had her own resentments: she felt unfairly blamed for costing Tom the few shillings rent (Aldington was paying 3/6d a week for a similar cottage)[77] on a two-up two-down semi-detached cottage with an outside privy, which was less than the rent of a flat in central London, and for incurring doctors' fees to treat illnesses certainly exacerbated by her marital misery. She was caught in a web of Tom's weaving for, knowing that her husband was both richer and more extravagant than he admitted, she was forced to keep his secrets, live with his rejection, and accept that it was he, not she, who was generally the object of pity.

To Virginia Woolf Tom posed as a dutiful husband, expressing his regret at not being able to visit the Woolfs at Rodmell because he could not leave Vivien to "stick it out" in the country at the weekends.[78] To Mary he expressed a different mood: it was sweet of her to ask them to the Boat Race the next day, he wrote grumpily on 23 March, but they would be busy moving into their "tiny" country cottage. He was spending all his time packing furniture, and the next day he and Vivien were going down early before the van and furniture arrived. "It will be such a day's work."[79] Vivien was still very weak, exhausted by the fashionable but "most disagreeable" "Plombières treatment" (possibly enemas for constipation) which she had begun in early March in order to be ready to go to the country. It was, Tom feared, "too desperate a treatment for her," and he never knew, as he told Ottoline, whether the benefits of this sort of thing compensated for the strain, especially as Vivien was being given "electric treatment" in addition.[80]

On 5 March Vivien had written sadly to Mary that she was too ill to see her, but if anyone asked what was the matter with her, Mary was to reply that Vivien had—"in crude words—'catarrh of the intestines, with occasional enteritis'; that is, if your delicacy will allow you to frame such an intolerable statement of fact." If Mary could not bring herself to utter such indelicate phrases, she was to refer enquiries to Vivien, to whose cynical and unromantic mind such a statement of fact presented no difficulties.[81] Still, as the days passed amidst the horrors of "Plombières," and Vivien grew weaker, she began to feel anxious at the thought of being deprived of the care of her London doctors:

> It is my opinion that Tom is right in refraining at this point from taking steps which would make our common dwelling place a 4 roomed country cottage or an attic in London, and which would deprive me of medical assistance . . . Indeed, if he did take such steps I should bear him a considerable grudge. I know, too well, that in your eyes the poet's wife dying in a humble cot would be a pretty sight—almost a nosegay. Alas! That you should never have to experience such a pathetical [sic] situation . . .[82]

Vivien's terror mounted as Tom pressed her to leave London for the new cottage. Finally it precipitated "a terrible crisis": Tom had engaged a car to take Vivien down to Chichester on Tuesday, but postponed it to Thursday because she was too ill. As he explained to Ottoline:

> On Wednesday she had the worst crisis, after tea, that I have *ever* seen, the worst she has ever had. *I am sure she was on the point of death.* She went completely numb, terrible palpitations, and gasping for every breath.

Tom telephoned four doctors, who were all out. Finally one came. "But before he came she suddenly had a terrific colitis explosion—poison that must have been accumulating for two or three weeks, owing to the terrible strain of the *Nation*." According to the locum doctor, and also the Eliots' own doctor, Dr. Higgins, who came later, *"This saved her life.* Otherwise she would have died of acute toxaemia, or of the strain on the heart from the effort to resist it."

Both doctors advised Eliot that the danger was over for the moment, and Vivien had better get away at once. He therefore took her down to Milestone Cottages on the Thursday as arranged, but instead of the crisis being over, "Vivien had two more, all Friday night and on Saturday." Tom at once sent for Rose Haigh-Wood. That night, exhausted by the sequence of crises which meant, as he told Ottoline, that he had had hardly a moment to *read* a letter, much less write one, he was at last able to give her the latest news of Vivien in a long, undated letter written from the cottage: "Tonight for the first time she begins to show a little sign of being alive. She has not had any meal at all since last Thursday and for the last three days has been fed on little drops of milk and teaspoons of brandy to keep her alive. I *think* we are through now, but she has wasted in this week to an absolute skeleton so it will take weeks to build her up."[83]

There is little doubt that Vivien's "crises" were severe panic attacks and that her "colitis" or irritable bowel syndrome was also triggered by the acute fear that Tom was on the point of leaving her. Vivien's unconscious attempt to keep her husband with her was successful in the short term. Thanking Ottoline for sending him some of her favourite "hectine," a new "remedy" which she had recommended should be taken by injection as a cure for nervous trouble, he set off to Chichester to buy a syringe, promising Ottoline a cheque soon. He had not dared, he explained, to "try Vivien with any new thing during this crisis," but she would begin taking it directly she was able.[84]

Vivien was never well enough to try Ottoline's home cure. In the "humble cot" in Fishbourne she caught "malignant influenza" which turned to a "devastating" pneumonia. She hovered between life and death, once more "a wild heart in a cage," the trapped bird in whose body life only flickered faintly. Outside, the wind cut like a knife across the muddy fields. Tom's irritation grew. "We [heavily crossed out] *I* have only pitched the furniture into the cottage so must start without V.," he complained to Mary, absconding after Easter to holiday alone with the Schiffs at Hindhead.[85] By 26 April 1923 it was still "extraordinarily uncomfortable and inconvenient for a case of serious illness" in the cottage, and they had not even been able to arrange the furniture. Vivien was being kept going on "serum and Bulgarian bacillus"; the doctor from London had stayed for two weekends and was still visiting twice weekly, with the local man coming in daily and possibly a nurse in attendance too. His "successful holiday," wrote Tom sarcastically, would soon be at an end.[86] Barely had he returned to London than he too fell ill, taking another fortnight's leave "by the kindness of the bank."[87]

As her physical and mental state deteriorated, so Vivien's dependence grew upon the doctors who, whatever their faults, at least offered her attention and a measure of comfort. Her neediness made her vulnerable to exploitation. Such exploitation was difficult for Eliot to resist, as his own personality, combined with 1920s medical ignorance, predisposed him, even more than Vivien, to assign magical powers to the medical profession.[88] As Vivien spent more time alone with her caregivers in the isolated cottage, in conditions in which her liberty was almost as limited as if she had been in a sanatorium, she began to form a new dependent relationship to rival that which she had with Tom: she and her physician became a "doctor-patient couple," as Foucault terms it in *Madness and Civilization:* "In the patient's eyes . . . the authority [the doctor] has borrowed from order, morality and the family, now seems to derive from himself; it is because he is a doctor that he is believed to possess these powers . . ." According to this theory, the physician seems to possess an almost demonic knowledge. "Increasingly the patient will accept this self-surrender to a doctor both divine and satanic; beyond human measure in any case . . . submitting from the very first to a will he experienced as magic."[89]

The doctor in Vivien's case—as her Harley Street doctors in London no longer visited—was "a *very good* Scotch doctor in Chichester." Recovering from the pneumonia Vivien was left with a "depression of mind"[90] so severe that she was threatening suicide, as Eliot confided to Pound: she was too weak even to sit up. To her dearest Ottoline, Vivien confessed on 28 May that she still felt so ill,

> so intolerably unsteady, weak, dizzy, *reeling,* that life is a fearful
> burden. I hardly know where I am, now. After so great a shock—
> so many shocks—it is coming back from death and I am still

gasping for breath—just *hanging on*. It is not life, I don't know what it is. Time passes, it seems the summer is going—and I cant grasp it . . . I don't feel I could ever pick up the old life again. I feel so many hundred miles now from everyone and everything. You understand this, don't you?

Vivien reminisced that one of the very few *"really happy, stable* memories" she had to hang on to was Garsington. "You and Garsington, there is something definite there. *You* have *made* something real, comforting . . . Excuse incoherence."[91]

In mid-April Vivien received a charming letter from Virginia, who sensed something of Vivien's ordeal.[92] On 18 May, after entertaining Eliot to dinner, Virginia wrote: "I feel that he has taken the veil, or whatever monks do. Mrs. Eliot has almost died at times in the last month. Tom, though infinitely considerate, is also perfectly detached. His cell is, I'm sure, a very lofty one, but a little chilly."[93] But if Tom felt cool towards Virginia, as his obituary of her later demonstrated he did, and he practised a chilly detachment from Vivien, he retained warmer feelings for Mary Hutchinson, who continued to send Vivien presents—perhaps as a salve to her conscience. Touched by gifts of a lilac sun-bonnet and several copies of the *Nation,* Vivien roused herself to pencil a note to her "darling friend" Mary. "One feels & is—so unkempt, untended, ugly and in despair that one needs the stimulus of pretty things to remind one that life is not so barren," she wrote. "As Virginia so cleverly says—there is some romance in being very ill, but getting well is sordid misery. *It is.*"[94] Vivien's depression was possibly not unconnected with the uncomfortable knowledge that Tom preferred Mary's company to her own. While putting Mary off on 9 August with the news that Vivien was too "dizzy and weak" for a visit from her friend,[95] Tom did not hesitate to send his confidante an urgent telegram from London the following day, inviting her "if alone" to meet him on Sunday at three-thirty at the Black Boy pub, Fishbourne, for a picnic.[96]

A week or two earlier, however, Vivien *had* felt well enough to make her first drive into the country. She and Tom took tea with the Woolfs at Rodmell on 17 July. Virginia, who noticed Vivien was "very nervous, very spotty, much powdered . . . overdressed, perhaps," watched with interest as Tom pressed alcohol on his reluctant wife, and recorded the conversation in her diary:

> Tom: Put brandy in your tea, Vivien.
>
> No, no, Tom.
>
> Yes, you must. Put a teaspoonful of brandy in your tea.
>
> Vivien: Oh all right—I don't want it.
>
> Virginia: One doesn't like taking medicine before one's friends . . . (pause) I've been setting up your poem. It's a good poem.
>
> Vivien: A damned good poem, did you say?
>
> Virginia: Well, you've improved what I said. But it is a d—d good poem.

Virginia's impression was that the Eliots were nervous, but compared themselves with herself and Leonard, and liked them and their surroundings. "And on the drive home, I daresay Vivien said 'Why can't we get on as the Woolves do?' I think they meant us to feel them in sympathy together. Certainly they were lighter, more affectionate."[97] As she slowly convalesced, Vivien, despite her poor eyesight, began trying to learn Italian, in order to converse with the "foreign young gentleman" whom, she told Mary, was staying at the cottage with them.[98]

Eliot himself had felt exhilarated earlier in the summer to be invited by Ottoline to lecture to a group of Oxford undergraduates. "One has hopes of undergraduates," he wrote, "almost the only kind of audience that is interesting to talk to." He spent the night at Balliol, before coming on to Ottoline's, where he sang comic songs on the lawn with six of the students; the freshness of youth, noted his hostess, was like wine to him. Afterwards Tom hastened to tell her how "very keenly I enjoyed meeting the young men—all of them—I enjoyed every minute. I wish I might see them all again!" Finding "fresh and untried minds and unspoiled lives" appealed to him so much that he longed to give a whole course of lectures at Oxford.[99] Among the young, often homosexual, men Ottoline gathered about her at Garsington, such as "pretty" Lord David Gascoyne-Cecil, Puffin Asquith and Eddy Sackville-West, heir to Knole, Eliot often found a receptive audience, as Virginia confided to the poet on 2 June: "I sat next to a young Lord (Sackville-West) at Oxford, who said Mr. Eliot was his favourite poet, and the favourite of all his friends."[100] So effeminate was that "tiny lap dog called Sackville-West" that when he came to visit Virginia, her cook asked: "Who was the lady in the drawing-room?" "He has a voice like a girls, and a face like a persian cats, all white and serious with large violet eyes and fluffy cheeks," reported Virginia to the French painter Jacques Raverat, wondering whether her correspondent had any views on "loving ones own sex. All the young men are so inclined, and I cant help finding it mildly foolish . . . For one thing, all the young men tend to the pretty and ladylike, for some reason, at the moment. They paint and powder, which wasn't the style in our day . . ."[101] On this occasion Virginia had travelled to Garsington with Lytton Strachey, but was dismayed to find Ottoline had invited a "bunch of young men no bigger than asparagus," and that she had to walk around the vegetable garden with Lord David while Lytton flirted with another undergraduate, James Byam Shaw, on a green seat in a corner.[102]

It was on this particular visit to Garsington on 17 June 1923 that a fateful conversation took place between Eliot and Ottoline. The high priestess of Bloomsbury had herself come close to breakdown after her husband Philip's "brat" by her parlourmaid had been born.[103] Tom had been all sympathy: "It's like a horrible treadmill, isn't it?" he wrote. "Going on struggling and fighting for health only to be knocked over and to begin at the beginning. And how few people understand what delicate people have to put up with, & how much courage and *character* they have to exercise at every minute."[104] Expressing her own sympathy for the Eliots' predicament, Ottoline suggested her pet doctor, the German Dr. Marten, as the ideal specialist for Vivien. Tom was reluctant, for Vivien's colitis had almost gone under the care of the "Scotch doctor." Weakly Vivien protested that she knew she just needed a quiet, sensible life, and no "*mental* conflicts or worry," but Ottoline continued to urge her that it was "a chance not to be missed."[105] Finally Tom took Vivien to London: it was to be the beginning of yet more "magical" pseudo-science.

By mid-July the Eliots had had two long interviews and "three analyses" with Dr. Marten, who was, reported Tom, very much interested in

Vivien and talked to her for a long time. "He has discovered, by having bacteriological analyses made, an extraordinary excess of streptococcus fecalis, and other mischievous cocci. He has promised to send over cultures from Germany. But he says that it cannot be *properly* done in this country . . ." The only hope of a cure was for Vivien, despite the "ruinous expense," to go to Freiburg in the autumn.[106]

16

Deceits and Desires

Dr. Marten wasted no time in taking control of Vivien's case. Discerning in his new patient and her husband a gullible couple whose marital situation and neuroses predisposed them, as did Ottoline's, to offer themselves as his willing victims, he imposed a bizarre experimental regime upon Vivien. "My new cure," she informed Mary, in a faint pencilled note, "is to spend half my life upside down. *Do* come to tea, if you don't mind my having tea standing on my head."[1] The forced jollity was short-lived. Soon Vivien was again so weak that she could only "totter" through the days.[2]

In spite of Vivien's relapse, Tom's enthusiasm for Dr. Marten grew apace. When in October 1923 Dorothy Pound asked him for the name of Vivien's gland specialist, Dr. Hogben, Eliot joked that he wouldn't give it unless Dorothy wanted to do somebody in. *That* specialist had nearly put Vivien in her grave, and she had only just escaped at the moment of ex-piring—hence their year of disasters. But now she had an *excellent* man in Marten, whom he would recommend to anyone who was willing to go to Freiburg, and was, very slowly, fighting her way up.[3]

Before long Eliot was recommending the German doctor to his Bloomsbury friends as keenly as Ottoline. The following year he pressed Virginia Woolf to consult the "very remarkable Dr. Martin [sic]" who was staying in London in Eaton Square, and whom Eliot considered a "first rate physician." He also had the additional merit of being very accommo-dating about his fees. Tom liked him more than any physician he had ever had dealings with, he confided to Virginia, and claimed the doctor had brought about a turning point in Vivien's illness.[4] As a result, Tom was now consulting Dr. Marten himself. Ominously, the German was in real-ity not a medical specialist but simply "a Doctor of . . . wide special knowledge." Soon Virginia, in her turn, was urging Roger Fry to consult the fashionable Dr. Marten.

Fortunately for her health, perhaps, Vivien never reached Freiburg. During the summer of 1923 Ottoline made energetic but ultimately futile attempts to find Tom a lecturing post at Oxford University as an alternative to Lloyds. If Ottoline could fix it for the winter term, Eliot told his patron, he would take Vivien to the German clinic in September, "If she would go with me. But I feel so little hope of eligibility that I do not think of it." Plaintively he explained to Ottoline that the expenses of Vivien's illness were already so high that he saw little hope of affording the trip.[5]

Illness was not, however, the only cause of Eliot's spiralling costs during that summer. He had begun a relationship with a young man which was also to prove expensive, both to his purse and his temper. In May 1923 he invited the "foreign young gentleman," to whom Vivien referred in an undated letter to Mary, to stay at 2 Milestone Cottages, Old Fishbourne ("During May/J. came to stay.")[6] Ostensibly the young man had come to lend a hand during Vivien's illness, but there is little doubt that he was, in fact, romantically and sexually involved with Tom. The youth's name was Jack and he was German, recalled Vivien, who recorded the eventful summer in the "stunning sort of instant doggerel" with which, remembered Maurice, she had been accustomed to amuse her family at Anglesey.[7] At first the handsome young German, whom Eliot may have met at Garsington, made an excellent impression, as Vivien recalled in rhyming couplets written in pencil because she was too weak to hold a pen:

> His manners were good
> He *never* was rude
> His *expression* was sweet
> His ways were quite neat . . .

"That boy has a beeootiful nature," remarked Vivien's mother Rose, who was also a guest at the cottage. "He looked very *young*/And his praises were sung" enthused Vivien; she and Jack read Shakespeare aloud together, and practised Italian, and Vivien at first found the pliable young man an agreeable companion.

In July, though, the mood in the cottage turned ugly. A quite different Jack returned for a second stay. This time he looked "old, ugly and
bad" in Vivien's eyes. There was "Not a trace of the lad/Who had helped
us in May." Jack had "nothing to say/He was glum, never gay." The party
in the cottage had also changed. In place of Rose Haigh-Wood was Eliot's
new secretary, Irene Pearl Fassett, a fiery woman who idolised her employer, and who had joined the Eliots to help with the *Criterion* workload
the previous year when Vivien was ill. Pearl Fassett had quickly become
an intimate friend of Vivien's, and the two women soon began to collaborate on those reviews published under the name "Irene Fassett" in the
"Books of the Quarter" in the *Criterion*. Pearl and Vivien, equally protective of Eliot, watched in horror as the friendship between Tom and Jack
deteriorated. Jack's

> . . . incessant insistence
> Upon *passive resistance*
> Made an unhappy house
> With nothing but rows.

As the weeks passed, the young German grew "more *secretive* and bitter
and rude/More lazy and obstinate, *ugly* and crude." His insulting manner
towards Eliot infuriated Pearl, and filled Vivien with fear as tension
mounted in the cramped two-bedroom cottage, in which the sleeping
arrangements allowed for little privacy. (Eliot never shared Vivien's bedroom during their marriage, choosing to sleep in a deckchair in the hallway in Russell's flat rather than with his wife, and having a separate room
in their subsequent flats and houses, as photographs taken by Eliot's niece,
Theodora Eliot Smith, demonstrate.) It is probable that at number 2,
Milestone Cottages, Vivien shared a room with Pearl, and Tom with Jack.
Vivien could not have failed to be aware of the erotic nature of Jack's attraction for Tom, but she turned a blind eye to this unwelcome fact. She
had no alternative but to remain a tolerant, if increasingly nervous, observer of the fury smouldering dangerously between the two men.

Finally, as autumn turned to winter, Jack's sneers and tantrums escalated to a pitch which the two women found unbearable. Vivien and Pearl

watched in horror as Tom, a man of nearly thirty-five, silently put up with Jack's open rudeness. "[Jack] behaved in a way that Pearl *never* expected," wrote Vivien.

> To see Tom endure it detracts from the awe,
> Indeed, veneration, she gave him before . . .
> And worse & worse this matter grows
> Tom makes no move
> Pearl's fury glows
> While V. quite ill becomes like ice . . .
> Oh what a hell it all is *now*
> Xmas comes near, and then the row.
> Tom blacks Jack's eyes
> But does no good—

Tom's outburst of violence ended his countryside idyll with Jack. "In sullen mood," Tom threw Jack out of the house. In this breakdown of what was clearly an intense emotional relationship between the two men, Tom, believed Vivien, was incited to extreme behaviour by Pearl ("Who is, at least, a 'vengeance girl' "). The next day Jack returned, bruised and angry at the physical abuse he had suffered. He was determined to justify his behaviour towards Tom, and Vivien listened as the youth poured out his story: Jack declaimed his "views and griefs and aims," explaining that he had been happy enough in May to come to the Eliots' aid, but by July had grown tired of being at Tom's beck and call; he felt "a fool," as "Eliot's tool," a sexually ambiguous remark by Vivien which hints at reasons for Jack's indignation other than a reluctance to help around the house: it seems that Jack had grown to resent the older man's attentions.

Vivien, nevertheless, loyally judged that it was Jack who had abused his position. Convinced that Jack himself was too weak and unformed a character to have resented his situation, she was sure that his mother, who ruled "this stupid, stubborn, *witless mule,*" had told him to make a stand. Vivien—"Our wily Vivien," as she described herself—infuriated by Jack's growing meanness during his visit of many months, then decided to search his room. Rifling through the possessions the young man had left behind when he was abruptly turned out, she discovered letters which proved that he had been sending money home to his German aunts and friends.[8] Jack, it seemed, had been helping himself to the housekeeping money, feeling perhaps that he was owed payment for services rendered.

"We are now out of love with young people," confided Vivien to Virginia, in a masterly understatement. Young people with literary aspirations were especially out of favour, she said. Such guests used to go about harmlessly with a box of watercolours and a sketching block: now they immersed themselves in ink and shouted their ideas at meal times, giving their wan hosts no chance to digest their food.[9] Tom had hurriedly and thankfully returned to London; Vivien could not wait to follow him.

This emotional and pecuniary disaster with Jack affected Eliot deeply and he began to drink heavily. Virginia was surprised to see "poor Tom" getting drunk at Burleigh Mansions when "the Captain" invited her to a small Christmas party, probably the same occasion attended by Lytton Strachey on 17 December 1923.[10] The party had taken weeks of preparation, with all the food set out on little tables, Leonard Woolf remembered later; the Hutchinsons and Roger Fry were also invited.[11] Two days later Virginia recorded:

> We went to a flat in an arcade, & asked for Captain Eliot. I noticed that his eyes were blurred. He cut the cake meticulously. He helped us to coffee—or was it tea? Then to liqueurs . . . There was a long pale squint-eyed Oxford youth on the floor. We discussed the personal element in literature. Tom then quietly left the room. L. heard sounds of sickness. After a long time, he came back, sank into the corner, & I saw him, ghastly pale, with his eyes shut, apparently in a stupor. When we left he was only just able to stand on his legs.

The next day Virginia spent ten minutes on the telephone receiving Eliot's apologies—"How distressing, what could we all think? Could we forgive him—the first time—would we ever come again? No dinner, no lunch—then sudden collapse—how dreadful—what a miserable end to the evening—apologise please to Leonard, to your sister . . ." It was, thought Virginia, one of those comedies which life sometimes does to perfection.[12]

It would appear that Jack had successors. The Hon. Philip Ritchie, eldest son of Lord Ritchie of Dundee, a beautiful and gay young man to whom Lytton Strachey was attracted, stayed on occasions at Burleigh Mansions with Eliot, so Frank Morley, a Faber director, admitted to playwright Michael Hastings;[13] in 1923 Ritchie was an Oxford undergraduate, but he was not the "squint-eyed Oxford youth" noticed by Virginia on 17 December, for Ritchie was a friend of the Woolfs and Roger Fry and would have been recognised. The homosexual novelist C. H. B. Kitchin was also reputed to be a guest of "Captain Eliot's," as was Roger Senhouse, the art critic.[14]

Eliot's physical abuse of Jack may have been an isolated incident, but it explains Vivien's later fears, which she expressed to Ottoline, that she too would be battered by her husband, although there is no record of such marital violence taking place. There are, however, many references to Eliot's rages by those who knew him well. Throughout his adult life Eliot found it difficult to control his explosive temper. Vivien's personal account book for 1930 records "A FRESH START" on 24 October, and on Monday, 23 February 1931, a "Prize to Tom for keeping his temper."[15] In January 1935, recalling visits with Tom to the Haigh-Wood family solicitors, James and James, Vivien related that Tom was "livid with savage fury" on many occasions, particularly when the issue under discussion was the "mistake they [Tom, Maurice and the solicitors] all made" in keeping her in ignorance of the size of her private income. James, apparently arguing Vivien's case, was "very insulting" to Tom. Eliot responded with "a very real grudge and hatred" towards the solicitor.[16]

There are similar incidences in Mary Trevelyan's revealing memoir of her twenty-year friendship with T. S. Eliot, "The Pope of Russell Square 1938–1958," in which she documents the numerous occasions when she experienced Tom's "FURY," and had to plead with him not to upset her and John Hayward, whom he often snapped at in public.[17] On 16 August 1954, for example, the poet was in "one of his most towering rages, white with anger, and practically non-speaking," banging the door of Mary's car shut and creating "a high state of tension" for his sister Marian and niece Theodora, whom Mary was driving to the Prospect of Whitby. The ostensible reason for this angry outburst was that Eliot blamed Mary for arranging the party on a Monday, without consulting him, although the outing had in fact been Theodora's idea.[18] Many times Mary was left wondering, "Why the rocket?" only to learn that she had once again transgressed the obsessional "Rules" to which Eliot insisted she conform.[19] Mary, the inspiration for "Julia" in *The Cocktail Party,* was left with a lasting impression of a man who sometimes acted in a way which was "cruel and incompatible with his professed 'way of life.'" She concluded that Tom was quite blind to people—"perhaps because he doesn't love them."[20] Her accusation echoes that made by Lavinia, the wife in *The Cocktail Party,* against her husband: "You *are* cold-hearted, Edward." To the psychiatrist, Harcourt-Reilly, Lavinia confides, "My husband has never been in love with anybody."[21]

As the months passed it became clear that, despite Eliot's faith in him, Dr. Marten's spurious science was not, after all, improving Vivien's health. In May 1923, when Jack had been staying with the Eliots at Fishbourne, Tom complained to Ezra Pound that he was having "a hell of a time" with Vivien; she was contemplating suicide and "was going to leave you a letter."[22] Ottoline herself noted in her journal in June 1923 her opinion that Eliot was afraid Vivien would commit suicide, and this was why he was protective of her.[23] Did Vivien threaten suicide to keep Eliot at her side, as she competed against the lure of the beautiful young men to whom Ottoline introduced him at Garsington? Much later Eliot shared his memories of Vivien with Mary Trevelyan: "The dreadful nights when she would say 'I ought never to have married you' or, 'I am useless and better dead'—and then my disclaimers and her floods of tears—but the next morning that would be quite forgotten."[24] The horror of those nights of reproach and torment worked their way into Eliot's drama in 1923, as he began writing *Sweeney Agonistes;* his night sweats and nightmares resembled Sweeney's:

> You've had the cream of a nightmare dream and you've got the hoo-ha's coming to you.

During those stormy nights when a weeping Vivien played on his conscience, Tom in turn blamed himself for his wife's misery and psychological distress. "I thought it was my fault for a period," he told Mary in 1950. "I got away by going to America and not coming back."

In Eliot's imagination Vivien had become strongly identified with "wrong'd Aspatia," the heroine of Beaumont and Fletcher's play *The Maid's Tragedy,* a play Eliot knew well, having set it for his night class of Extension students in 1918. In the drama, Aspatia, deserted by her lover, engineers her death at his hands; there is one scene which particularly struck Eliot, in which the betrayed Aspatia hysterically laments her abandonment by her lover and compares herself to Ariadne, similarly abandoned by Theseus on the "cavernous waste shore" of Naxos. Eliot had already borrowed lines from this scene as the epigraph for "Sweeney Erect" (1919).[25] Aspatia commands her needlewomen to rework their tapestry of Theseus and Ariadne, in order to make it truly reflect Ariadne's sorrow.[26] "Make all a desolation," Aspatia commands. "Paint me the bold anfractuous rocks/Faced by the snarled and yelping seas," are the words Eliot himself gives Aspatia in "Sweeney Erect."[27] Eliot knew that he, like Theseus, had been false to the woman who loved him.

By 1921 Eliot's perception of Vivien had undergone a second metamorphosis: in the original manuscript of *The Waste Land* he portrayed her as a reproachful gorgon, whose hysterical complaints follow him night and day. She shadows his dreams, the "injur'd bride," issuing from sepulchral gates as in a tale by Edgar Allan Poe, as Eliot wrote in "Elegy," lines cut by the cautious Pound. In Eliot's nightmare Vivien is no longer muse but Medusa: "Around that head the scorpions hissed!/Remorse unbounded, grief intense/Had striven to expatiate the fault—" He implores the vision to keep its distance: "Poison not my nightly bliss," he begs, "Keep within thy charnel vault."[28]

Eliot's conscience tormented him. He could not repress the knowledge that he had rejected Vivien within weeks of his marriage to her, and that Vivien's affair with Russell, rather than being, in Ronald Schuchard's words, a vicious sexual betrayal of Eliot,[29] had in fact been one in which he had knowingly colluded in order to further his career, relieve himself of conjugal responsibilities, and to gain financial advantage. Nor could Eliot deny the strength of his own homosexual desires, which were leading him into a web of deceit. Those desires are powerfully documented not only in the Colombo verses torn from "The Inventions of the March Hare" notebook which Eliot sent to John Quinn, but in later pornographic verses Eliot attached to a letter he sent to Ezra Pound on 3 January 1934—verses which leave no doubts as to "Captain Eliot's" sexual orientation. Writing in the first person, Eliot boldly exhorts his reader to buggery, "again and again and again." Proclaim to the morning, he cries, that "a r s e spells arse."[30]

Eliot's obscene verse testifies to the violence of his feelings, and it is hard to believe that they were never acted upon. But, even if the strength of the poet's will, inhibition, or fear of exposure ensured that his desires remained in the realm of sexual fantasy, they affected both his and Vivien's lives powerfully. Eliot's secrets shaped his biography and his poetry. And the balance of probability seems to lie with the argument that Eliot, like Lytton Strachey and other members of the Bloomsbury Group, had a physical relationship with the young men like Jack or Ritchie with whom he consorted. Why should he have felt such a degree of shame and self-loathing had he not sinned—in his own eyes at least? Eliot's grinding sense of his own sexual sinfulness overwhelmed him, a legacy of his puritanical upbringing and the prejudices of the period in which he lived. It was Vivien's misfortune that not only did her very femininity repel him, simply looking at her reminded Eliot of the Russell affair, and of her immorality which he later roundly condemned. In his eyes Vivien was the harlot who bewitches, emblematic of Eliot's own immorality and sexual betrayal. Vivien now represented for her husband his shadow side, the dark anima behind Eliot's urbane exterior of which he speaks in "The Hollow Men" (1925): "Between the desire/And the spasm . . . Between the essence/And the descent /Falls the Shadow."[31]

For the hollow men, their heads stuffed with straw, the satisfaction of desire is annihilated by the falling Shadow. The epigraph Eliot chose for "The Hollow Men," taken from Conrad—this time he would not allow Pound to change his first choice—was "Mistah Kurtz—he dead." It speaks of Kurtz's end, in the heart of darkness, all civilised values abandoned. Kurtz is dead to God, and in the early 1920s Eliot began to feel he was too, as he abandoned his lawful wife to live an alternative life in Burleigh Mansions whenever the opportunity presented itself. At times the pricking of his conscience urged him to connect with the spiritual and let "the darkness come upon you/Which shall be the darkness of God."[32] Other voices spoke louder, as Vivien struggled with all the weapons at her disposal in the tug-of-war for her husband's love. Hysteria and illness were in the forefront of her armoury, and Eliot could not gainsay his Ariadne. He was unable to refuse Vivien her doctors, whatever they cost, and guilt and a desire to pass on responsibility to the "experts" drove him to acquiesce in whatever cure they suggested.

In 1924, Eliot decided to call in yet another fashionable London physician, Dr. James Cyriax. Cyriax was an orthopaedic surgeon who had trained at Cambridge and practised spinal manipulation; he was on the staff of St. Thomas's Hospital and had a reputation for being able to treat seemingly intractable back pain. He began to work on Vivien's "permanent spinal injury," as she later described it; but he was not, perhaps, as accommodating about his fees as Marten had been.

By 27 August 1924 Tom was bitterly bemoaning his financial position to Mary Hutchinson, whom he and Vivien had asked to help find them a house in London. Their latest whim was to exchange their flat in Clarence Gate Gardens for a house with a garden. Eliot explained that a garage selling "B. P. Motor Spirit" at all hours had opened beside their cottage at Old Fishbourne, and there was a lemonade stall opposite, so he and Vivien had decided that it was uninhabitable, and given up the lease.[33] In June they considered moving close to the Woolfs, and Tom enlisted Virginia's help to find a cottage on the Downs. As usual, plans failed to materialise. Tom fell ill again, and he and Vivien moved to Eastbourne, which became their base during another six-week visit from Tom's mother. "I have been boiled in a hellbroth," Tom complained to Virginia on his return from putting Charlotte on the transatlantic steamer on 27 August. He then bolted back to Burleigh Mansions, claiming his tax return was overdue, leaving Vivien alone in Eastbourne.[34]

On the same day that Eliot thankfully bade goodbye to his mother, he asked Mary to view a house on Chiswick Mall for himself and Vivien, assuring his correspondent that when they found a property they would depend upon her to get them into it: "You are an angel and give me confidence that we *shall* get a house." However, Eliot was in an agitated mood. He could not possibly afford a house unless he could sell the lease on their flat, he told Mary, and he lacked the time to attend to the business of buying and selling: "You see, Mary, I *must* settle down and write a *lot* of articles at once, because I *must* find the money, and I cant do anything else . . . I have been living beyond my income for 5 months, and eating up my savings. Vivien's illness and the cost of running *two establishments at once*, doctors, food, medicines, constant railway fares etc. have run me into colossal expense." He had to try to make £50 a month by writing, said Tom, something which it had been impossible to do for the last few months—"and I must do it *now*."

Vivien, meanwhile, was working her way through a reading list which, in the interests of self-education, she had asked Mary to compile for her. "Don't feed her too fast," instructed Tom, saying that Vivien's vitality was so low that she could only read a very little at a time, as reading was too tiring and exciting. He preferred her to do manual work, when she could not be out of doors: she had been painting furniture very beautifully and this, while physically tiring, was mentally restful. Her mind was still "utterly worn out and *ruined*" by his indecision over the *Nation* job, he confided to Mary. "No-one will know what she went through."[35]

Eliot's anxiety as usual attracted sympathy from his correspondent, but the picture he painted was, as so often, not wholly truthful. "Tom is a 'great runner-away,' " wrote Mary Trevelyan in 1958 in a perceptive analysis of Eliot's character. "He is extremely deceitful when it suits him and he would willingly sacrifice anybody and anything to get himself out of something which he doesn't want to face up to."[36] Although in August 1924 Eliot wrote as if he were financially *in extremis* to Mary Hutchinson—who probably believed him—a far simpler solution to his over-expenditure presented itself than she realised. In the spring of that year Eliot had wired to his brother Henry to send him $2,000 as he was desperately short of money. This Henry did, as he informed Charlotte Eliot in a letter dated 15 March 1925.[37] The sum sent enabled Eliot to settle his doctors' bills and pay the rent on not two but three dwellings: Clarence Gate Gardens, Milestone Cottages, and Burleigh Mansions. As Henry later related, when he arrived in England in 1926 he found that the Eliots had committed themselves to several different leases, and it was his task to negotiate with landlords and extricate his brother from his legal tangles.

The real reason for Eliot's irritation over money in the spring and summer of 1924 was the mistake he (and his mother) felt Henry had made in deciding to sell 120 of Eliot's Hydraulic shares too early—at $63 in 1923—although by January 1924 they had soared to $80,[38] reaching $94 in February 1925. "Do not worry about Tom's stock. It is all right," Henry wrote defensively to Charlotte Eliot, saying that he had reinvested the proceeds in "good bonds." Although "stocks are irritating things," he wrote, Tom was still getting dividends from his investments. This was small consolation to Henry's younger brother, left out in the cold as he watched the rest of his family make money at the rate of $3,000 to $4,000 a month, just by holding their rocketing shares, as Henry was forced to admit on 17 February 1925.[39] Tom's jealousy over the disparity between his own and his brother's situation would have intensified had he learnt that Henry was also earning $8,000 a year as a partner in the advertising agency David C. Thomas of Chicago,[40] even though at this period the U.S. dollar was standing at about $4.90 to the pound so that a dollar was worth only one-third as much in sterling as it is now. Henry, then a bachelor, was able to save most of his salary; Tom was unable to live within his. By 16 March 1924 Henry was confessing to Charlotte that he regretted selling Tom's stock so soon, assuring her that there was however "no breach" between himself and Tom,[41] who was getting a return of 7.37 per cent on his capital of $19,000, giving him an income of about $1,400. Tom's total income, Henry estimated, was about $5,000 (£1,000) a year, made up of the $1,400 on his capital, $3,000 (£600) from the bank, and $600 in literary earnings. £1,000 a year was a comfortable income: a maid in London in 1925 might be paid £35 a year, and the Eliots had two maids.[42] But to normal upper-middle-class expenses Eliot had to add Vivien's medical bills and the costs of his other, secret life.

To add insult to injury, Henry continued to push Tom towards agreeing to the trust which Charlotte had set up in his name, and from which Tom would derive income only from a mixed portfolio of shares and bonds; not only was she refusing to hand his shares over to him directly, she was also cutting him off from the potential capital gains to be made on the substantial real estate she owned in St. Louis and Kansas City.[43] Undoubtedly Tom felt aggrieved; Henry and his sisters had the best side of the bargain. In addition, Henry continued to press his younger brother to make a will, arranging to have the proceeds of the trust distributed to "our family" in the event of Tom's and Vivien's deaths.[44] Tom, scratching a living editing an experimental quarterly in the spare time he could snatch from the bank, felt jealous of his shrewd brother, who in his turn envied his handsome and increasingly famous sibling. It was this sibling rivalry which lay behind Eliot's outburst to Mary as much as any costs of Vivien's.

Nor did Eliot give Mary a wholly accurate picture of Vivien's health as, far from her mind being so "ruined" that she could only paint furniture, his wife was quietly laying the foundations of a new career as a writer. As Tom had let slip in another letter on 2 January 1924, she was making "an exhaustive study of Clive's work, in her thorough way";[45] Vivien added that she was also reading law books, which she found more interesting than novels, apart from her beloved Hardy. And there were moments when Vivien and Tom were both fit enough to pursue their favorite hobby of viewing houses, which provided an escape from London, although they continued to expect Mary to do the real work of finding a suitable property. In a cheerful letter to Sydney Schiff on Boxing Day 1923, Vivien had said that she and Tom had spent "a queer sort of Christmas" wandering around the country in a borrowed car, in search of a more convenient country cottage.[46] Their quest took them to Surrey. From Dorking Vivien sent Mary a postcard of an open tourer in the front of the White Horse, inscribed "En auto—Vivien!"[47] Although she told Virginia that she and Tom had given up their dream of a Citroën car now that they were convinced that they must have a house in London with a garden[48]—a decision which did not stop the unending search for the mythical, ideal country cottage— her improved health is confirmed by Eliot's remark to Schiff that Vivien had stood the winter in London better than the year before, and had "kept up remarkably well," enabling her to go out and see her friends.[49]

As Vivien, encouraged by Tom, made tentative attempts to begin writing, she turned to her closest friend, Mary, as her model for a writer's life. Vivien had always occupied a position of deference towards Mary, but although she hoped to garner a few tips, she was anxious not to give away her own aspirations. On 29 December 1923 Vivien had written a disingenuous letter to Mary, enquiring what sort of life she was intending to lead until, say, April (1924): "What routine—what foundations—what reading—and what (of course) pleasures? And may I add, altogether towards

what end?" inscribing herself "Your curious friend, Vivien."[50] Fear of failure and of ridicule led Vivien to disguise her identity behind pseudonyms
when first she began to be published in the columns of the *Criterion.* She
was concerned that Mary should not discover her secret, for not only was
Mary likely to gossip to the indiscreet Clive, and expose Vivien to the scorn
of Bloomsbury, but Mary had already preceded Vivien along the path of
women's journalism, being published by the *Nation* and *Athenaeum* in July
1923. What could be more embarrassing for Vivien than to be found to be
challenging her accomplished, well-connected *confidante,* and to provoke
her mockery—or even her jealousy?

But Vivien was in need of advice in her new endeavour. Tom was the
first to encourage her, as she had encouraged him. Tom's belief in Vivien's
creative ability was the significant factor in developing her gift, and she
knew she could trust him to keep her secret, as she kept his. There was also
one other person she could trust: Sydney Schiff, whose novels Vivien
admired profoundly. Schiff, too, took Vivien seriously from the first.
Together they discussed style and the creation of character in the novel. He
advised her on no account to reveal her authorship. On 31 March 1924
Vivien replied that she was sure he would not give her away: "You do not
need to persuade me that anonymity is vital; the more so as I have a very
strong feeling that this is a sort of flash in the pan—that it won't go on—
that, in fact, it is being done *faute de mieux.*" What is *mieux,* she asks. "Why,
Life of course, dear Sydney. No-one will persuade me that writing is a substitute for living," and yet, she confided, her "temporary aberration" was
making her very happy.[51]

Vivien was aware that what she and Mary were attempting was a
daunting enterprise: to write for publication in a male-dominated literary
world, to sup with giants at whose feet even the confident Mary trembled.
Self-consciousness and a despair of ever being able to express herself inhibited Mary in April 1924 from sending, even to Lytton, her cousin and
close friend, a report she had written of Virginia Woolf's speech to the undergraduates at Cambridge.[52] Mary believed that her inhibition was largely
due to Proust, "who," she wrote, "after so much pleasure, nevertheless
leaves one a nervous wreck—with this lack of simplicity—this sense of
being a hundred eyes instead of two." It was "this modern wretchedness of
feeling one is a slightly transparent ghost" which made Mary tear her re-

port up.[53] Vivien's own rebellion was to remain private. She would tear up her own first drafts in secret.

Virginia Woolf was not so easily deceived however. She was in close touch with Tom, who was continually badgering her for a contribution to the *Criterion,* and he at the time was grateful to the Woolfs for publishing *Homage to John Dryden: Three Essays on Poetry in the Seventeenth Century* in November. In 1924 Virginia was still Tom's "admiring and attached old friend, Virginia W"[54] and, although Tom joked that Virginia could only stand nineteen and a half hours with "the Prince of Bores" when he visited Rodmell, he valued her "timeless and generous friendship and understanding" as well as respecting her genius.[55] It was not, however, a genius he found easy to penetrate. *Jacob's Room* required "superhuman cleverness" on his part to review for *La Nouvelle Revue Française,* he wrote on 1 May 1924.[56] Neither Virginia nor Tom wholly understood what the other was seeking to achieve. Virginia confessed to the poet that she could not summon enough faith in her own judgement to criticise his poems to him: "Such radiance rises from the words that I can't get near them." Critics would call it enchantment, incantation, but she could only testify that she was held off understanding by magic.[57] But if neither comprehended the other's creativity, they each feared the other's judgment. Tom found Virginia's contempt an uncomfortable experience, he confessed to Ottoline.[58] Running the gauntlet of Virginia's biting wit was not a risk Vivien was prepared to take, even though it was the novelist who first recommended that Vivien should take up writing, probably as a form of therapy. When Virginia suspected her of contributing to the *Criterion* in June 1924, Vivien's reply was oblique: "Writing—!? Editing, perhaps."[59]

Disease and disharmony made demanding friends of the Eliots, as Tom spent his evenings struggling to bring out the new periodical on the dining-room table at Clarence Gate Gardens, on top of a full day's work at the bank, and Vivien typed to his dictation and suggested pieces of her own to fill gaps in the paper. Apart from a weekend in Paris in November 1924, there was no escape from the grindstone. Early in the new year of 1925 Tom again fell ill with influenza. That January he felt like a shell with no machinery in it; Vivien, as usual, nursed him through the "anxiety and strain" of the first ten days of his illness before collapsing herself with flu. Eliot was forced to take a month off work, and their mutual desperation was expressed once more in their longing for a country cottage, one near the Woolfs, whom the Eliots were still pestering as often as they did Mary "Hutch" to find them a place in the country. A cottage, a barn, a stable, a shed, even a bit of land on which to put up a bungalow, no matter so long as it was in the *country* and *cheap,* begged Tom. Ever since leaving Fishbourne they had pined more and more for the country, and if only Lady Rothermere would pay "a possible salary" they would move out at once. Of his unearned income Tom, of course, made no mention to Virginia: it was no good offering to lend Rodmell, he warned her. "We want a *hovel* of *our own,* not the house of friends."[60] Vivien chimed in with identical demands to Virginia to find them a cottage near the Downs— "and quickly."[61]

By February 1925 Vivien was again critically ill, laid up with "violent neuralgia and neuritis," Tom told Virginia. "Only her brain was alive."[62] At this moment of crisis Eliot finally exploded. Angry that his wife was once again stricken with a "near-fatal" illness, despite the haemorrhaging of his income into the pockets of fashionable doctors—the very predicament portrayed by Vivien in her satirical sketch "Médecine à la Mode"— he turned on the practitioners he felt had duped him, and on Ottoline. His fury precipitated a rift with the chatelaine of Garsington. Vivien's illness was Ottoline's fault, insinuated Eliot, since she had recommended Marten, whose bogus doctoring was responsible for Vivien being brought to the brink of death. Tom's rage also encompassed Dr. Cyriax, who had been no more successful than Marten in restoring Vivien to health. In an accusatory letter written in April 1925, in which Tom said Vivien was still paying for the effects of the Cyriax osteopathic treatment, he made his own diagnosis of Vivien's condition: "These people have done her damage that will take a *very long* time to repair, irritating and weakening the stomach, over-stimulating & exhausting the nerves. Her stomach is now *persistently* relaxed and *out of place,* pressing on the heart and the nerves, and I think thereby causing the neuritis." Furthermore, Vivien was, he related, "in *agony* with neuralgia of the sinus and antrim," which was making her "almost *blind."*[63]

On 1 May Tom complained again to Ottoline that Vivien was in continuous torture with a peculiar neuralgia which came from the base of the neck and affected all one side of her face, and had not left her for three weeks. It was impossible for her to stir out of bed. The simple truth was that "the Cyriax treatment" had exhausted every nerve in her body to breaking point, and had she gone on much longer she would have never recovered. "What doctors *can* do, in the way of criminal maltreatment is incredible—and one can never prove it in a court of law!" Ominously he wrote that he would explain more fully about both the Cyriax treatment and Dr. Marten when they met.[64]

What ill luck Tom and Vivien seemed to have with doctors, remarked Henry Eliot with a degree of *schadenfreude* to his mother in May 1925:

> They thought this Dr. Cyriax was such a wonder at the time. Tom has indeed a dreadful time. I suppose it is cruel and unsympathetic to think of Tom's troubles more than Vivien's, but it is of course natural.[65]

But Eliot refused to confide in his brother or mother, to Henry's annoyance. Instead he increasingly turned to Leonard Woolf for advice, rather than the disgraced Ottoline, or his family. There were obvious parallels in Tom and Vivien's situation and that of Leonard and Virginia. Eliot began lunching regularly with Leonard, and in April 1925 wrote to ask him for advice on how to deal with Vivien. Should she be allowed to write, did Leonard think? Leonard replied tactfully that it depended on the actual cause of the nervous disturbance, but if it was nervous exhaustion, then "anything which excites or tires the brain is bad and that therefore writing is bad." Tom was to begin with food and rest alone which would produce stability: "When the stability begins, then a little work like writing is good, but at first only in minute quantities." When Virginia was recovering from acute nerve exhaustion, wrote Leonard, she began by limiting her writing strictly to half an hour a day and only increased it months later when she was sure she could stand the strain. If, on the other hand, the cause of Vivien's nervous trouble was not exhaustion but something entirely different, wrote Leonard, he imagined that writing might "do good."[66] Woolf recommended that Eliot consult Sir Henry Head, a strange choice considering that Virginia was Head's patient when she attempted suicide in 1913, and one that Eliot rejected; Woolf agreed that Head was "too brusk in manner."[67]

Ottoline was deeply hurt by Eliot's accusations. Her journal demonstrates how her sympathies shifted over the years between Tom and Vivien, to both of whom she at times exhibited generous friendship, before withdrawing in exasperation from their unceasing and often unrealistic demands. Eliot hurried to placate his old friend, explaining in a quickly pencilled note that he assigned the blame for Vivien's illness equally between "Dr. Marten, the Cyriax, and myself" and *by no means* threw the whole blame on Dr. Marten: "He was a factor in a terrible nexus of misfortune," he wrote, "which has dogged Vivien for years. I blame him as much for urging her to go on with the Cyriax treatment, when she was already showing its ill-effects and on the verge of a nervous breakdown, as I do for anything else, because I think this shows *really bad doctoring.*" Tom only went to Leonard Woolf for advice, he protested, because he was "a very nice and clever man."[68]

It is doubtful whether Woolf's advice would, in any event, have been helpful to Vivien's condition. Vivien's predisposition to mental illness, complicated by her dependence on prescription drugs—a dependence which increased in the 1920s—the bizarre experimental treatments imposed upon her, and a toxic marriage which in itself produced neurotic symptoms, proved a deadly combination. And Eliot, like Woolf, had no option but to put himself and Vivien in the hands of doctors, who were themselves handicapped by the limits of medical knowledge of the time. It is probable that the tranquillising drugs prescribed for Vivien were similar to those prescribed for Virginia Woolf. For women who suffered mood-swings typical of manic-depression, chloral hydrate was a "chemical restraint" given to the neurotic patient which, wrote Sir George Savage, Physician Superintendent at Bethlem Royal Hospital, and physician to Virginia Woolf, could itself "produce physical ill-health, hypochondriasis, and insanity." Another, even more dangerous drug was hyoscyamine, which, as the drug trials which Savage carried out on patients at Bethlem in 1879 demonstrated, had serious side effects. Even a tiny dose could induce collapse. Serious loss of appetite followed, together with an inability to read, loss of power in the limbs, great mental depression, "dread" of death, confusion, hallucinations of sight and touch, and "a dry, unpleasant feeling in the throat which drinking did not relieve."[69] Patients detested being given hyoscyamine, and one accused Savage of being a poisoner. Yet

Stephen Trombley suggests, in his study of Virginia Woolf's doctors, that hyoscyamine was prescribed for the novelist, who complained of a bitter taste in the mouth during a fainting fit in 1930.[70] Given the widespread influence of Savage, an "expert" on psychoneurosis and author of a standard textbook on the subject, it is possible that hyoscyamine was also a drug of choice for Vivien, and was implicated in her loss of appetite and subsequent emaciation, weakness, weak eyes and difficulty with reading, and episodes of depression in the 1920s. For Vivien, Virginia and Ottoline, the "cure" was often more disastrous than the illness.

During the 1920s, Henry Eliot came to believe that both Tom and Vivien were hypocrites as well as hypochondriacs, who exaggerated both their illnesses and their poverty. "Vivien always recites some account of her migraines and malaises in her letters," he had remarked to his mother in 1921. "But I suppose it is natural; it is a relief to talk about one's pains." Henry considered that Vivien encouraged her breakdowns, which he thought were both mental and physical in character, and which she could control if only she had the motivation to do so: "I think some strong impulse from outside, some change in her circumstances, might call forth the necessary power to be well. She needs something to take her mind off herself; something to absorb her entire attention."[71]

His diagnosis was more accurate than that of many of the expensive professionals the Eliots consulted. When Vivien began to write and be published, she did at last find something which absorbed her entire attention and, as Henry predicted, her health improved. Yet writing and illness were parallel dramas, inextricably linked, and the attempt to make sense of her own situation gave Vivien one of her most recurrent themes, just as it became an excuse to avoid the people and parties she disliked. Illness therefore served as a spur rather than a restraint upon her creativity in the early 1920s. Her awareness of her own situation, and ability to find comedy in the midst of tragedy, is remarkable. Vivien's sketch "Médecine à la Mode" is full of insights as, with wry humour, she depicts both her dependence upon fashionable doctors—for example, the black-eyed Dr. Papadopoulos, vast and loose-jointed, who smiles kindly at Vivien when they meet in the corridor (a portrait perhaps based upon Dr. Cyriax)—and her bitter experience of financial exploitation at their hands.

In this unsparing portrait of herself, written in pencil in 1923–24 in the second of the exercise books with stiff black covers which Vivien bequeathed to the Bodleian Library at Oxford, "Sibylla," Vivien's autobiographical protagonist, has just come from the treatment room at the clinic after a sadistic session at the hands of the lady doctor with cold blue eyes. Sibylla stands outside the open door:

> Her short dark hair untidily disposed on her head . . . & her thin hands clasping and rubbing her emaciated body in the places where the treatment had been most severe. She looked a strange little bony object in her shrunken grey flannel dressing gown with all her life in her small, keen face, & her startled grey eyes.

Emerging into the corridor, "big Dr. Papadopoulos" regards Sibylla with a slight smile under his untidy mustache; his large comfortable body is reassuring, he jokes with the patients and makes them laugh: "I may be a good doctor—yes, but I am absolutely hopeless, my dear lady. Mad, that's what I am. Mad as a hatter . . ." he seems to be saying. He and Sibylla have a special understanding. "His black gypsy eyes" take in Sibylla, who receives their "full message." He makes a semi-humorous bow to her, remarking that they always seem to meet in the corridor. Sibylla, who is being addressed by the lady doctor, cannot escape. In some "deep down and suppressed agony" she allows the large untidy figure to pass behind her and on down the corridor without another sign. But the suppressed urge becomes too strong. Casting prudence to the wind, she turns her head and deliberately looks after the doctor:

> She met his eyes as he entered his own room. He also looked round—& then—Sibylla turned in haste and fled towards the dressing-room . . . *completely* de-fabricated.[72]

Side by side with Vivien's romantic fantasy of being part of a "doctor-patient couple," expressive of her wish for a relationship which would supply the love lacking in her marriage, went her self-mocking admission that she was victim to those very "specialists" whose charm was merely professional, whose jokes were all part of the service. In this story, Vivien/Sibylla

cannot afford her expensive treatments. This truth is brought home to her
when she enters the dressing-room and is met by the strong whiff of scent
and "opulence," signs which make her immediately suspect that "Lady
Rotherbrooke" (Lady Rothermere) is a fellow patient. "You could not have
convinced Sibylla," writes Vivien, "if you had proved it by algebra, that
this opulence was *not* Lady Rotherbrooke." Sibylla enters the cubicle vacated by the absent lady, and begins to examine her discarded garments, although she does not touch them ("Sibylla had her 'lines' beyond which she
did not go"). From her inventory of the fashionable clothes before her it is
apparent that they do not resemble the "rosy gold and blue scintillations"
of "Lady Beavermere" (another alias for the newspaper magnate's wife),
who, remembers Sibylla, was "fantastically chic," sparkling like a
Christmas tree angel, when last she saw her at luncheon.

Mortified, Sibylla leaves the cubicle and inspects herself in the long
glass. "O monstrous." Her clothes are *démodés*. Nothing looks quite right.
And because Sibylla is always six months behind with her outfits, in spite
of much laborious planning and outlay, she is doomed to be in hiding from
all but her boon companions for quite nine months of the year. The rest of
her "sartorial time" is spent "in agony of mind and in infinity of buying
and selling."

Emerging into the street (perhaps Welbeck Street, where Cyriax practised), her attention is caught by "an immense closed car standing waiting
at the kerb." The chauffeur peers at Sibylla. "I expect he thinks I am an
odd-looking party leaving this house." Nevertheless, she lingers for an instant, "the more fully to drink in every detail of this super car." Walking a
few steps out of her way, she examines the bonnet: "Rolls Royce—ah." She
glances up and down the street, reflecting upon the doctors who inhabit it:
"Poor old Sir Roysten Robery on the right there—poor old Sir Evans
Mason down on the left . . ." (perhaps an allusion to neurologist Sir Henry
Head, whom Eliot had discussed with Leonard). But this ostentatious
medical wealth reassures rather than alienates her, for Vivien considers
herself someone who knows a good thing when she sees it and, as far as
fashionable medicine is concerned, she is an epicure who can recognise
"good doctoring" when she meets it as surely as she can recognise a good
Paris hat. Are not high bills a guarantee of medical skill as they are of high

fashion? She walks home "on little wings . . . She had found, at last, the treatment, the cure, the one perfect, certain ultimate treatment, and opening her hand, she grasped it as her own."[73]

Eliot never published "Médecine à la Mode" in the *Criterion,* probably because it was too revealing, but nevertheless it demonstrates Vivien's lively talent. In writing she found not only a therapeutic outlet, but a *métier* in which she could succeed, unlike dancing or acting, and which provided an outlet for her creativity and intelligence. Vivien's manuscripts also clarify the intricate links between her writing and Tom's, and make clear the literary partnership which existed between the Eliots in the early days of the *Criterion.* The first draft, in Vivien's hand, establishes her authorship, but the fair copy, which also begins in Vivien's handwriting, continues after several pages in Tom's. Eliot's firm, neat hand contrasts with her fluent, careless one, but his punctilious editing of her script is everywhere in evidence. In "Médecine à la Mode" "thin" is crossed out and "small" substituted, describing Sibylla's face. Tom changes Dr. Papadopoulos's "mouth smiling slightly" to "his slight smile." It was a husband-and-wife collaboration which extended to nearly all Vivien's writing, and much of Tom's in the early years of the marriage.[74] Abigail Eliot, Eliot's first cousin, remembered of Tom and Vivien: "In the beginning he lived through her. Her hand was all over his work," a judgement confirmed by Vivien's notebooks, as by the facsimile edition of *The Waste Land,* with its fifty lines of "Fresca" verse, some in Vivien's style; cut by Pound from "The Fire Sermon," some of these lines surfaced under Vivien's pen name ("F.M." for "Fanny Marlow") in the *Criterion* in April 1924, an indication of her authorship.[75] Nor can Vivien's artless remarks to Aldington that she told Tom what to write when he was "too tired" to think for himself, or Tom's praise of Vivien's ability to his assistant editor, fail to convince of the authenticity and extent of their literary union.

Tom's support was critical in the making of Vivien as a writer. "It is wonderful how keen her mind keeps with such pain," he had remarked admiringly to Ottoline at the end of 1922.[76] After the crisis with "German Jack" in May 1923, Eliot's approbation fostered Vivien's growing confidence and determination, as she worked quietly in the upstairs bedroom overlooking the sea at 2 Milestone Cottages. From this south-facing, peaceful room the couple put together the new journal. Perhaps a bargain was

struck during this time of truce: Eliot would give Vivien her chance in return for her silence over his homosexual alliances, which were hidden
from all but his closest confidants, Ezra, Mary, Ottoline and Vivien herself.
At any event, in February 1924, the moment came when Eliot took the
bold decision to publish his wife in his prestigious periodical.

It is possible that Eliot first encouraged Vivien's writing to assuage his
own guilt. If he could not give her love, he could give her the benefit of his
literary ability and editorial experience. Together they could make a quarterly, even if they could not make a child. And for Vivien her writing could
become a substitute for the flesh and blood infant for which she longed.
What began in part as therapy became a new career; Eliot learnt a genuine
respect for Vivien's ability as she progressed from the role of shorthand-
typist to that of indispensable contributor to the new review. When the editor was short of copy, who was on hand to fill the vacant columns?
Vivien—quick and adept at writing sketches, poems, book reviews, whatever Tom needed to make up the paper when other writers handed in their
pieces late or failed to meet his standards. And, as "Fanny Marlow's" success grew, so her health improved now that she had a job to do and was
part of a team. Valued, busy, empowered, this new Vivien was sometimes
simply too busy to be ill.

"We have both been working at top pitch for the last five weeks to get
out the *Criterion,*" Eliot told Sydney Schiff on 24 February 1924, explaining that the review was "all ready" and would be sent out on the 29th. The
husband-and-wife team would at once set to work on the April number.[77]
On the last day of March Vivien wrote importantly that although she
longed to meet the Schiffs, "the next *Criterion* is blocking every moment
until Saturday, when it MUST go to print. Until then—chaos!"[78]

17

Criterion Battles

From her first article, "Letters of the Moment," Vivien began to define herself as a writer who did not hesitate to shock as well as amuse. Her pieces were witty, provocative and often dangerously candid, despite their anonymity. Writing as "F.M." in "Letters of the Moment—I," published in February 1924, she attacked one of Bloomsbury's sacred cows, the theatrical Phoenix Society, founded in 1919, whose productions were a favourite of Tom and Virginia. Vivien scoffed at the "Mermaid Society's" "tawdry bawdry Caroline renovations" of Congreve's *The Way of the World,* and other plays which, she wrote scornfully, were performed on Sunday nights to "Whiggish patrons of the arts," and on Monday afternoons to an audience of resting actors, "unkempt sub-editors (of monthlies) goggling over the gallery rail, and ladies from Hampstead who have met there for a good talk and a cup of tea."[1]

Vivien's "fierce Welsh shriek," as she called her speaking voice, set a tone for the pieces to follow. In "Letters of the Moment—II" (April 1924), she continued her attack on "voguish" seventeenth-century revivals and the avant-garde fashion for watching

> what the cultivated call The Play . . . When the poor dear Mermaid Society meritoriously started to dig out these dusty old plays and a sparse and earnest audience beaten up by the indignant Aquin half filled an unfrequented theatre, how little it suspected that it would turn a hitherto inconspicuous though tedious pose into a Movement.

She did not spare her husband, "Aquin" (a derivative of Thomas Aquinas), in her onslaught.[2]

Bloomsbury parties were another target of Vivien's criticism, but here her tone grew confessional. A quotation from Ronsard, neatly written out in French by Tom in her writing book, expressed her mood—and probably Tom's—of disillusionment that spring of 1924: "Le temps s'en va, le temps s'en va, madame: / Las! Le temps, non, mais nous nous en allons . . ." Time is fleeing, is Ronsard's message; Vivien's response is that she no longer wishes to join the party.[3] She had reached a turning-point. The severe mental and physical breakdown she had endured in 1923, as she was finally forced to acknowledge Tom's sexual preferences, had alienated her even further from pretentious, bickering, bisexual Bloomsbury, as she now viewed the writers and artists she had once felt privileged to know.

In 1924–25 Vivien used the *Criterion* as a vehicle for her anger and pain: "What happy meetings, what luminous conversations in twilight rooms filled with the scent of hyacinths, await me now?" she asks nostalgically in "Letters of the Moment—I": "The uncompromising voice of truth inside me answers, None at all. For I am not the same person who once played—as it seems to one—a leading part in those Spring fantasies."

> But, you say, what about the wonderful parties of your intellectual friends which you used to describe to me so gaily?
> I have not been to any.
> And why not? you say.
> Well, the enjoyment of parties belongs to the Spring that one has lost.

Only egoists enjoy "intellectual" parties, declared Vivien in another dig at the Bloomsbury Group: "All the odd minutes and odd hours and odd half-days which an egoist fills up so satisfyingly by toying with some aspect of himself are arid to a person without egoism." In fact, she argues, thinking about oneself corrodes the mind and, for the non-egoist, destroys his life purpose. Is an artist ever therefore an egoist, she asks. Never, comes the answer. And only an egoist can avoid boredom at a "party of the future," as Vivien designates an afternoon at the "Mermaid Society," where, she confided to Sydney Schiff, *King Lear* had nearly done her in.[4]

Looking back to her youth in "Letters of the Moment—II," Vivien recalled performing an act of "self-immolation," long ago, at a birthday dance at Hampstead. Then, "abashed and solitary," she had threaded her way up a staircase packed with "lusty maidenhead and manhood," only to find herself passed by her eager hostess into the expectant hands of a young gentleman with eyeglasses, in the belief that he and she would find many "high-souled things" in common, including a shared love of light opera. Behind the handsome Jacobean sideboard stood the butler, dispensing champagne cup and claret. The young gentleman turned his glasses on Vivien, and "without *gêne* or hesitation inquired whether I had yet secured my seats for the first night of *The Pirates of Penzance*. This was his test—having been misled into expecting to find me a superior person: it was in fact his Secret." Painfully aware that her answer would offend, Vivien replied bluntly that she found Gilbert and Sullivan a bore. The same expression convulsed her questioner's features as, at a certain moment in 1919, would have distorted those of an *aficionado* of the Ballets Russes, if one had said, "settling a pillow or throwing off a shawl: No, I do not care for the *Boutique* at all, not at all."[5]

Vivien was half-aware that she was performing a similar act of self-immolation now. It was a reckless move to exhibit such scorn of Bloomsbury tastes in the *Criterion,* despite the cloak of anonymity, but a continuing theme of Vivien's writing is her urge towards self-destruction. The impulsion towards social suicide at that Hampstead party, where she did not hesitate to shock a pretentious guest, and the "solitary" nature of her personality were characteristics set early in her life. And Vivien was defiant. She refused to compromise. Her writing became all-important to her and, unlike Mary Hutchinson, she was no longer prepared to fit it around the demands of society. Boldly she adopted the voice of Stravinsky, a "great classic master," whose Firebird she took as her own symbol of a woman aspiring to freedom:

A work does not have to be good or bad; it must be organic and identified with the artist. You must never present anything that isn't perfect. I have never given the public my experiments, my sketches. Each of my works represents something I tried to do the best I could, with all my strength. A piece is finished for me when I can go no further. I stop at the edge of the abyss.[6]

As Vivien developed her ideas in print, a particular target of her pen became the tendency she found in England "to turn everything involving personal tastes into a Secret." Once again her barbed attack was aimed at those who would understand it. Satire had long been the weapon of Bloomsbury and its hangers-on; it was an in-game whose satisfaction lay in writing for an élitist audience who would understand its thrusts, and the amusement of knowing that the majority of readers remained in ignorance of the victims' identity. Ottoline had been the victim singled out for caricature and ridicule by D. H. Lawrence, Aldous Huxley and Virginia Woolf. "Is the sunlight ever normal at Garsington?" demanded Virginia in 1924. "No, I think even the sky is done up in pale yellow silk, and certainly the cabbages are scented."[7] Now those who felt ill-treated were taking their revenge: Ottoline was recording her own impressions of her ungrateful guests in her journals, and in February Wyndham Lewis boldly satirised Lytton Strachey and the Sitwells in an article entitled "The Apes of God" in the *Criterion*.

Lewis's article caused a furore. "Everyone—that is Lytton, Osbert Sitwell, Mary Hutchinson, is claiming to be an Ape of God, and identifying the rest of the pack," Virginia informed Tom on 11 May 1924.[8] Eliot, however, defended his publication of Lewis's article, claiming unconvincingly that it had slipped through because of his careless editing. He had not had time to "read and expurgate" the article—there being only twenty-four hours in the day—he protested to Virginia; and if, as Sydney Schiff was threatening, a mass meeting of protesters met and dismembered him like a hero of Grecian tragedy (or even a "bungalow bride"—a murder victim, as featured recently in the tabloid newspapers) it was Virginia whom Tom would reproach and execrate with his last breath. "For you are my oracle and counsel in matters journalistic, and did you not advise me (with the supporting opinions too of Leonard and Clive as junior counsel) that it was 'in the best tradition of British journalism' to let one contributor say what he likes about another?"[9]

Privately Tom and Vivien joked about the article and composed their own verses on its scurrilous contents:

... And what an awful thing to do
To let upstarts who are Taboo

Write nasty article on Apes
Or speak of love in curious shapes.[10]

This verse, in Vivien's hand, is a reference to Lewis's Rabelaisian descriptions of Bloomsbury perversions (expanded in 1931 into a book, *The Apes of God),* in which he ridiculed "lesbian-apes" who lived in a "nest" of studios, "ape-flagellant" artists who kept a collection of whips in a cupboard, and other members of the "Apery," the "select and snobbish club" which Lewis alleged to be Bloomsbury, and in which he claimed the substitution of money for talent was a qualification for membership.[11]

Tom joined in the fun, copying out Vivien's verse into her writing book and adding his own blasphemous ending concerning "love in curious shapes": "The pal of God whose name is John/Is one safe bet to gamble on/Is glory hallelujah John."[12] This reference was to St. John, whom playwright Christopher Marlowe, according to his rival Thomas Kyd (author of *The Spanish Tragedie),* alleged was the homosexual lover of Jesus—an Elizabethan controversy of 1593 well known to Eliot, who was steeped in the "tragedy of blood," and had written an essay on Marlowe in 1919.[13] Vivien meanwhile pasted into her writing book a newspaper cutting which quoted Oscar Wilde's letter to Whistler describing his new bride: "Her name is Constance—and she is quite young, very grave and mystical with wonderful eyes—and dark brown coils of hair: quite perfect . . ." It was to Constance Wilde that Vivien now compared herself.[14]

Secrets related to parties, to money, to passions and to hatreds. Tom and Vivien shared such secrets with each other, and their liberated "friends." "This passion for Secrets appears in different classes and sections of society in very different manifestations," wrote Vivien. "But in every part of this viscous morass, this gently undulating bog of Anglo-Saxon democracy, Secrets of one kind or another are to be discovered . . ."[15] Sexual secrets amused Virginia, herself a lesbian whose interest was growing in Vita Sackville-West, "like a ripe grape in features, moustached, pouting . . . [who] strides on fine legs, in a well-cut skirt, & . . . has a manly good sense & simplicity about her . . ."[16]

As Vivien distanced herself from such an atmosphere, Virginia recorded Tom's presence at a "queer little party" earlier in May, after he had taken her to the Phoenix Society production of *King Lear,* at which they had both jeered, only for Virginia to find Tom praising the performance as "flawless" in the *Criterion,* and coming out with a "solemn & stately rebuke of those who jeer and despise." Such hypocrisy irritated Virginia, and the private thoughts she confided to her diary were less complimentary than the letters she wrote to the poet: "The sinister & pedagogic Tom cut a queer figure. I cannot wholly free myself from suspicions about him—at the worst they only amount to calling him an American schoolmaster: a very vain man . . . There's something hole & cornerish, biting in the back, suspicious, elaborate, uneasy, about him . . ." The party included Philip Ritchie, as well as Lytton Strachey, Duncan Grant and Vanessa Bell.[17] To Virginia the transvestite ballet *Don't Be Frightened,* designed by Duncan and performed at a party given by Maynard Keynes that July, was "enchanting, lyrical," only spoilt by finding Duncan's lover Bunny Garnett behaving like a "surly devil."[18] She did not record whether or not Vivien was present on that occasion, but a few weeks earlier, on 21 June 1924, Virginia made a hostile diary entry concerning her. She had seen, she wrote, "Mrs. Eliot—the last making me almost vomit, so scented, so powdered, so egotistic, so morbid, so weakly."[19]

Virginia's malicious portrait of Vivien can be attributed to the Woolfs' irritation with the Eliots that summer. Virginia and Leonard had been annoyed at the complaints which they believed Tom and Vivien were making about the Hogarth Press's failure to market *The Waste Land* efficiently. Gossip was going the rounds of Bloomsbury that Leonard and Virginia had only sold forty copies, and that Tom was furious about the poor sales. On 27 June 1924 Vivien wrote a dignified letter of apology to Leonard, protesting that the gossip was "complete fantasy": neither she nor Tom thought or imagined that Leonard or Virginia had ever written anything "insulting or unkind" about *The Waste Land.* She and Tom, she wrote, had merely indulged in a little "crude and meaningless badinage" which should not have given offence. Unconvincingly, Vivien professed to know nothing of the facts of private publishing: she would have no more idea of the success of the publication if she heard that forty copies had been sold by the Hogarth Press or four thousand, she declared, adding that the subject of the sales of the Hogarth Press had never once been discussed between Tom and herself:

We have never conceived it possible that Tom or any good poet could be popular in this country or any other country. We have never imagined that any money could be made out of good poetry. Therefore we have never considered poetry as a financial aset, and that is why Tom earns his living in other ways. We still cherish hopes of leisure and independence, bringing such command of conversation as will make it impossible for misunderstandings of this kind to occur.[20]

Once again Vivien's taste for gossip had got her into trouble, just as it had the previous year when she was blamed for starting a rumour that Maynard Keynes was going bankrupt. Vivien had been so upset on that occasion that on 11 June 1923 she had told Virginia that, as the "instigator of such a rumour," she felt too timid to return to London and "try my luck." Nor had she dared accompany Tom when he went to Oxford to lecture to the undergraduates, and then on to Garsington, although she would have loved to have gone with him.[21] As Ottoline knew to her cost, Bloomsbury could never be trusted. Professions of friendship could change overnight to cruel caricature and mocking laughter. Virginia might tell Tom that she was "subterraneously trying to get you and Vivien to come to London," and might write warmly "Give my love to Vivien and come and see us soon," but her diary knew a different reality.[22] And although Virginia is not a wholly reliable witness, her description indicates Vivien's struggle to disguise her misery and to mix in society she found essentially uncongenial; it also suggests her growing pride in her published writing which left her open to the very charge she repudiated: that of being an egoist.

Another "secret" was Vivien's part in the running battle in which Tom was engaged with John Middleton Murry, by now editor of the *Adelphi* and defender of Romanticism in opposition to Eliot's Classicism. Eliot's position was not a new one; although in 1928 he famously stated in the preface to *For Lancelot Andrewes* that he was "a classicist in literature, royalist in politics, and anglo-catholic in religion," this was no sudden turning from a previously revolutionary stance, as is sometimes supposed. Eliot has been viewed as a revolutionary who disappoints, failing to follow through the promise of modernism as he retreats from experimental verse into Anglo-Catholic orthodoxy, religious pageantry and derivative drama. But Eliot's profoundly pessimistic view of man was formed long before his formal conversion in 1927. He defined the Classicist point of view as essentially a belief in original sin, and his belief in this doctrine and man's need for "austere discipline" intensified, as he turned increasingly towards Catholicism. "There are only two things—Puritanism and Catholicism," he noted in Vivien's writing book. "You are one or the other. You either believe in the reality of *Sin* or you don't. *That* is the important moral distinction—not whether you are good or bad." Puritanism does not believe in "Sin," he continued, it merely believed that certain things must not be done.[23]

Vivien, although by instinct a Romantic rather than a Classicist—who identified with James's Rousseauesque heroine Daisy Miller—closely followed Tom's literary and political opinions in the 1920s. Now she was ready to lead a Celtic charge against Murry after he declared that the English writer (or the English divine) must listen to "the inner voice" rather than depend on outside authority. Eliot was the first to attack his rival: "The possessors of the inner voice ride ten in a compartment to a football match at Swansea, listening to the inner voice, which breathes the eternal message of vanity, fear and lust," he protested in the *Criterion* in October 1923, making a plea for order and discipline.[24] Vivien's idea was to write a spoof letter, something Eliot had used before to fill up blank pages of the *Egoist,* pretending to be a vicar, "the Rev. Mr. Grimble," or a schoolmaster, "J. A. D. Spence, Thridlington Grammar School," or even a Tory, "Charles Augustus Coneybeare, The Carlton Club, Liverpool"; it was a prank which belonged to the Eliot tradition of practical jokes, misleading footnotes, and the other tricks which E. M. Forster detected the poet was playing on his audience. Forster pointed out that in Eliot's book *Homage to John Dryden* he expressed the hope that his essays might "preserve in cryptogram certain notions which, if expressed directly, would be destined to immediate obloquy, followed by perpetual oblivion." What is he trying to put across here? demanded Forster. "Why, if he believes in it, can he not say it out straight and face the consequences?"[25] Again and again, complained Forster, the reader had the sense of being outwitted by Eliot. Whose fault was it, he asked. "The verse always sounds beautiful but often conveys nothing."

It amused Vivien to outwit an audience as much as it did Tom. Posing as two "young women earning our own living," aged twenty-six and thirty, one married with a baby to support (possibly herself and Pearl Fassett), Vivien puts a provocative question to Murry, who, said Virginia Woolf, had been beating his breast over his past sins like a "revivalist preacher," following the tragic early death of his wife, Katherine Mansfield, in January 1923: "What, Mr. John Middleton Murry, are your actual qualifications for the post of Junior Prophet, a general exponent of LIFE?" From a study of his editorials Vivien was forced to the conclusion that "your raison d'être is that your wife has died. To put the matter crudely, other men's wives have died. But few, we venture to suggest, have been able to extract such a plethora of copy—and other profit—from the supposedly lamentable event."[26] It was not an attack in the best of taste, and there is no record of the letter being published by Murry, who on 14 April 1924 married one of his contributors, Violet le Maistre. Perhaps Vivien never sent the letter, but her dislike of Murry was echoed by Eliot's own jeering remarks, hidden in Vivien's writing book and directed at Bloomsbury and Murry, whom he saw as an example of the harm that "autocratic" Bloomsbury could do in cramping a person for life "by having him put in a pot in youth" so that he begins to grow too late and becomes "pot bound." As time passes, says the poet, such "fonctionaires" shrivel, and "one sees them as a silly little collection of failures and little Japanese trees."[27]

Identical images often surface in Tom's and Vivien's writing, and illustrate their shared opinions. Although Vivien might write to Sydney Schiff that "the weekend was a strain (our weekends always are),"[28] in the work situation Vivien remained an indispensable partner. Eliot's notes on being "pot bound" are remarkably similar to the opening of Vivien's "Letters of the Moment—I," in which she writes: "My hyacinths are busting clumsily out of their pots, as they always do, coming into misshapen bloom before their time. And this is the essential spring—spring in winter, spring in London, grey and misty spring, grey twilights, piano organs, women at street crossings . . ." before launching into her own attack on Bloomsbury.[29] To both the Eliots, Bloomsbury was autocratic, egotistical and self-regarding; it did not, Tom wrote accusingly, allow "growth," which fatigued and terrified it. Although Eliot appeared close to the Woolfs at a time when they were useful to him, Virginia was right in sensing that he was "uneasy" in her presence. It is doubtful whether Eliot ever felt genuine affection for Virginia.

The Eliots' hostility towards Murry, expressed in the columns of the *Criterion,* was, however, ungenerous, for the editor of the *Adelphi* was about to do Eliot a good turn. Despite their intellectual antagonism, Murry, Clark Lecturer at Cambridge for 1924–25, decided to nominate Eliot, the apologist for Classicism, to succeed him the following academic year. Excitedly Eliot would write on 20 February 1925, thanking Murry for the appointment and the £200 fee, which came like a ray of hope to him "just at the *blackest moment of my life,"* when Vivien was ill.[30]

Vivien may yet have sensed that her husband's star was in the ascendant, as she poked fun at the editor of the rival review. "Murry's star sank as Eliot's rose," writes Murry's biographer.[31] In any event, Vivien did not hesitate to satirise Murry; in "Letters of the Moment" (April 1924) Vivien describes the periodicals which lie on her drawing-room table: there are the monthlies, the weeklies, the quarterly reviews, "set out in rows like a parterre," the pink *Dial,* the golden *Mercury,* the austere *Nouvelle Revue Française,* the buff *Blackwood* and the lemon yellow *Adelphi.* Beneath all, "shamefully in sight the gaudy cover and uncouth dimensions of *Vogue.* One turns to *The Dial,* flip-flop go the pages. Very dull, very dull" until, reading the shocking Paris Letter, Vivien thinks of Mr. J. Middleton Murry. "Golly!" he says, revealing his "sensitiveness to the living soul of the language" and disclosing to his readers how much better a Professor of Poetry he would make than the insensitive present incumbent. "Crikey!" comments Vivien, "As one might say, what a go!"[32]

Emboldened by success, in the July 1924 *Criterion,* Vivien wrote a scathing review of Murry's novel *The Voyage* under the pseudonym "F.M." In the same issue she described David Garnett's *A Man in the Zoo* as "an enchanting book," but Murry's heroine is trite, and "humor is not Mr. Murry's strong suit." What is the novel all about, she demands. Who can tell? Has it style, form or rhythm? "In the words of Mr. Doherty, 'No-o, my child, no-o.' "[33] As she established herself as a reviewer in the "Books of the Quarter" section of the *Criterion,* Vivien began to deliver increasingly patronising judgements on some of Bloomsbury's greatest stars. Commenting in October on E. M. Forster's *A Passage to India* under the disguise of "I. P. Fassett," but in a style that is all her own, Vivien asks: "Why do we have to remind ourselves so incessantly that Mr. Forster's work is admirable?" before concluding that Forster's great novel lacks the missing ingredient which might lift it above the level of "Sound Contemporary Fiction where it must inevitably lie."[34] It was an equally rash and tactless move to criticise the Eliots' assistant editor, Richard Aldington, who was likely to discover that Vivien was contributing to the quarterly, but she had not forgiven Aldington for upsetting Tom earlier, and for criticising her choice of name for the review. Although Aldington's *Literary Studies and Reviews* had met with praise for their learning and erudition, Vivien wrote tartly, "a discriminating critic would have put [these] as the last of the book's qualities."[35] As for John Galsworthy's *The White Monkey,* "I am afraid he misses badly," was I. P. Fassett's damning comment.[36]

Soon Vivien was enjoying the gratifying experience of receiving payment for her work. On 18 September 1924 she banked her first pay cheque of £1.10.0d., made out to "Miss Fanny Marlow" by the printer J. Cobden Sanderson.[37] The Eliots' "Gunpowder Plot" to dominate literary London was coming to fruition, and Vivien was playing her part, contributing towards the family finances just as she and Tom had planned. Her income was yet another secret to hug to herself, to keep hidden from Mary and Ottoline and, as the months passed, she basked in her journalistic success. As "Fanny Marlow" Vivien had crossed the divide from private to public writing, and her new aliases began to fill more and more columns of the *Criterion,* completing her metamorphosis into an androgynous persona who took refuge behind a male *nom de plume* for her more daring pieces. In October 1924 it was difficult to miss Vivien's journalism: writing as "Feiron Morris" she published "Thé Dansant,"[38] as "Felix Morrison" she wrote "Mrs. Pilkington,"[39] and as "F.M." and "Irene Fassett" she reviewed several "Books of the Quarter." But it was "Fanny" who made the most money, spinning webs in which to catch the Eliots' supposed enemies: "There is no *end* to Fanny!" Vivien confided proudly to Sydney Schiff. "But Feiron will never make money. And he does not spin. He is a nasty fellow."[40]

By January 1925 Tom and Vivien were working so closely together that it was sometimes hard to tell who was the author of a piece: the

January issue of the *Criterion* carried "On the Eve: A Dialogue" by T. S. Eliot,[41] whose style is characteristically Vivien's, but as it was extensively edited by her husband was published under his name. It is probable that when Vivien was too ill to finish a prose sketch, Eliot polished it for publication; if Vivien sometimes had the keener ear for dialogue, Tom had the more precise and ironic eye. Certainly in January Vivien was busy on the first "Diary of the Rive Gauche," originally titled "Paris on £5 a Week," her reminiscences of Paris in the winter of 1921, written under her favourite pen name, "Fanny Marlow."[42]

The January *Criterion* also included a knowing review by Vivien writing as "Feiron Morris" of Virginia Woolf's essay on the novel "Mr. Bennett and Mrs. Brown," an expanded version of a lecture Woolf had given to the Society of Heretics at Cambridge in May 1924. It was extraordinary for Vivien to criticise Virginia, since Tom had previously begged Virginia to let him have the article for the July 1924 issue, offering her a special rate of £20 instead of £10 per 5,000 words, a rate he explained that he could only offer to Europe's four best contemporary writers.[43] "Five thousand words are no drawback, when the words are yours," he wrote flatteringly; "I wish for nothing better than to attract the sparkish wits of undergraduates . . . May I have [the article] at once, and set it up? I shall print it in the July number."[44] On 22 May 1924, after Virginia agreed, Tom wrote a gushing letter of thanks: "My dear Virginia, I must tell you how I appreciate your generosity in letting me have this article . . . If the Criterion should be extinguished, I want it to go out in full flame and with your paper and unpublished manuscripts of Marcel Proust and W. B. Yeats, the July number will be the most brilliant in its history . . . It will help me to feel that the Criterion has not been altogether without value or distinction."[45]

In Virginia's essay, which Tom published as "Character in Fiction," she praised her friend Tom's work, one of the habitual "puffs" which members of Bloomsbury gave each other; Clive Bell, for example, had previously drawn attention to the neglect of Virginia, Tom and Murry by critics. Tom modestly alluded to Virginia's praise, writing that her comments on him "do somewhat embarrass me as being excessive for what I know my own work to be . . . I feel myself that everything I have done consists simply of tentative sketches and rough experiments. Will the next generation profit by our labours?"[46]

It was as Tom's ally that Virginia had given him her article, which the Hogarth Press subsequently published at 2/6d. To have such contributors as Virginia Woolf added to the prestige of the *Criterion,* as Eliot acknowledged in his letter. Nevertheless, as editor, he allowed Vivien, posing as a male journalist, "Feiron Morris," to voice her naïve criticisms of Virginia in his quarterly in January 1925. At first Vivien praised Virginia for her "brilliant essay," but then proceeded to criticise her for citing Joyce and Eliot as examples of the creation of character from external observation.[47] "Did Mr. Eliot . . . deduce Sweeney from observations in a New York barroom?" asks Vivien, chastising Virginia for selecting the three "nightmare figures"—James Joyce, T. S. Eliot and Wyndham Lewis—as the only representatives of modern literature. "Such an idea is ludicrous," declares Vivien. "What about Proust, for example?" Condescendingly she concludes, using the editorial "we": "Mrs. Woolf has written a very able argument upon a thesis which we believe to be wrong. The argument is so clever that it is difficult to disprove the thesis: we can only wait in the hope that Mrs. Woolf will disprove it herself."[48]

It is possible that Eliot was too busy to "read and expurgate" Vivien's review; this was the excuse he had made previously to Virginia over the publication of Wyndham Lewis's notorious article on the Bloomsbury "Apes of God." But the evidence of Vivien's writing book shows unequivocally that Eliot shared her hostility to Bloomsbury. It is probable that Tom was as duplicitous and hypocritical as Vivien; both Eliots welcomed the Woolfs' friendship when it profited them, and disparaged them when Tom felt his rival Virginia's "superhuman cleverness" (in writing *Jacob's Room)* surpassed his own achievements.[49] Jokes and games held a constant appeal to both Eliots, and for Vivien to sneer at Virginia in the columns of the very paper in which Virginia had been published to widespread acclaim was the kind of private secret which held particular appeal for both Tom and Vivien.

By April 1925 Vivien had removed herself, "sore throat and all," to 38 Burleigh Mansions in search of "a room of her own" in which to work during the day. Although she and Tom still retained their flat at 9 Clarence

Gate Gardens, they had given up Milestone Cottages at Old Fishbourne. Despite the fact that she was "withering to death in this frightful winter in this intolerable country," Vivien's mood was buoyant. She was, she told Sydney, by now quite accustomed to reading a typed MS and having to form her opinions on it before she saw it in print; over the last year Cobden-Sanderson had been submitting proofs for her to pass for press "at her earliest convenience." Her pride grew at seeing her pseudonyms sandwiched between those stars of Bloomsbury—Huxley, Fry and Woolf—to whom she had for so long deferred, sharing space with Pound, Aldington and even distinguished continental writers such as André Gide, Dostoevsky and Proust. Proof-reader, editor, contributor, she felt herself to be any writer's equal. It was as such that she confided to Sydney in a letter dated only "Sunday" in the spring of 1925, that she believed she was trying the same experiment with form as he was in his new book: "But with this difference; I have not attempted to make each sketch from the *point of view* of a different person involved but rather the attempt is to make them all from the point of view of a very interested and *intimate* outsider . . ." This was of course a very important difference, wrote Vivien, and no doubt the only similarity was that both were a series of sketches which could appear separately, but which did, "when all is finished (not yet, alas with me!) make up a whole." Everything she told him, she wrote, was *"of course . . .* absolutely and irrevocably in confidence."[50]

Perhaps it was hubris which drove Vivien to risk disclosure. She now felt herself to be invincible, and could not resist the urge to express her secret feelings. In addition her illnesses provided an alibi. While Tom was complaining to Virginia on 4 February 1925, "the moment I try to use my mind at all, it's no use, and then up goes the temperature . . . Vivien is worse than I am by far,"[51] or writing on 19 April 1925, "Vivien can't move, with violent neuralgia and neuritis. It will be months before she can get right again," his correspondents had the impression from his exaggerated accounts that Vivien was far too incapacitated to even think of taking up a new career as a writer.[52]

In the *Criterion* of April 1925, therefore, Tom published Vivien's poem, "Necesse est Perstare" (originally entitled "Ennui"),[53] in which she vented her scorn for "intellectual" parties in economical and astringent *vers libre* which caused an instant stir:

A flurry of snow in the sky,
Cold blue English sky,
And then the lunch party broke up
And people said they must go
And there was an end (for a session)
    of the eternal Aldous Huxley—
Elizabeth Bibesco—Clive Bell—
    Unceasing clamour of inanities.
I looked at you and you had stretched
    Your arms up above your head
With such an air of weariness,
Like some very old monkey.
I looked at you and you looked at me.
I longed to speak to you,
    But I didn't. I longed
To come and stand beside you at the window and
    Look out at the fleering
    Cold English sunshine and say,
Is it necessary—
Is this necessary—
Tell me, is it necessary that we go through this?[54]

Princess Elizabeth Bibesco, daughter of H. H. Asquith, had had an affair with Middleton Murry in November 1920, and moved in the same circles as the Eliots. Vivien's ridicule of the socialite, as well as of Bell and Huxley, her description of Tom as "some very old monkey," became public when Ottoline at last guessed the identity of the author. "Yes, it is true that Vivien wrote that poem," replied Eliot on 1 May 1925. "In fact she has been writing for a long time—and I have always suspected that you knew it! And *I* think that she is a *very* clever and original writer, with a mathematical and abstract mind which ought to be trained—and I intend that it shall."[55] Soon plaudits were ringing in Vivien's ears. "I cannot believe that all the congratulations that Vivien receives on her writing is quite sincere," wrote Henry Eliot sourly to his mother on 10 May.[56]

It had always been part of the Eliot game-playing for Tom to allow the publication of Vivien's descriptions of him, revelations which he might

have been expected to censor. Her pride in her own prolific output led her
to contrast it with Eliot's own periodic writer's block in some cruel lines
suggesting that he aspired to the conquest of too many literary peaks:

> "Isn't he wonderful?" whispered Felice. "He is the most marvel-
> lous poet in the *whole world.*"
>
> "He might be if he wrote anything," said Sibylla drily.
>
> "Yes, why *doesn't* he write more?"
>
> "Because he wants to be everything at once, I expect. Perhaps
> the devil took him up into a high mountain and showed him all
> the kingdoms of the world—unfortunately for him!"
>
> "And so, I suppose," asked Felice naggingly, "that he doesn't
> know which kingdom to choose?"
>
> "He's still up the mountain as far as I know . . ."[57]

Eliot nevertheless drew the line at publishing Vivien's most confessional
writing, which drew a vivid picture of their personal incompatibility.
"Ellison and Antony" is an account of a couple who live in "Mansions," a
large, gloomy and somewhat sordid building with jangling lifts, staring
lift-girls, wide dark staircases with stained carpets, and beetles and crick-
ets in the kitchen of every flat. When "Antony" came home, wrote Vivien,

> Very quietly and carefully he hung up his hat and coat, put his
> stick in the corner, laid down the morning paper and the evening
> paper, both unfolded, and the book he had wanted to look at dur-
> ing the day. He hung for a moment in the hall, silent and unde-
> cided. There were many things he dreaded. That Ellison might
> have a headache, that she might be irritable and hate him, that she
> might be in despair or have with her her greatest friend who
> might have been quarrelling with her. If the flat was silent and
> dark with only the light from the glass over Jane's kitchen door,
> he was uneasy. Where was Ellison? . . . At last he would move, al-
> most stealthily, towards his study, open the door, put just his head
> in, and there was Ellison, alone lying on the sofa. That was all-
> right. And yet it was not allright. If only he could find his study
> empty, and Ellison in another room, occupied peacefully . . .

> Antony stooped, kissed Ellison rather gingerly. Ellison's smile was strained . . . She said harshly and wearily, "Has anything happened?" . . . "No," said Antony. He smiled apologetically.[58]

Such a portrait was too private to be disclosed. Nevertheless, Vivien was skating on the thinnest of ice in criticising writers far greater than herself, as well as those who counted her among their friends. In "Fête Galante" by "Fanny Marlow," published in the *Criterion* in July 1925, Vivien delivered her final salvo against "intellectual" parties in a thinly disguised account of "Sibylla's" experiences at a glittering event hosted by Mary Hutchinson at River House. It followed hard on a sketch entitled "Night Club" written by "Feiron Morris,"[59] the second "Diary of the Rive Gauche" by "Fanny Marlow,"[60] and a stinging review of Rose Macaulay for whom "a delicate facetiousness stands for wit" by "I. P. Fassett" in the April issue;[61] even Stephen Hudson (Sydney Schiff) did not escape F.M.'s sharp criticism.[62] But none of these was as personally wounding, as malicious, and as clearly written by someone with a guest's inside knowledge, as "Fête Galante," with its savage portrait of Mary and St. John as the rich, superficial, social-climbing Becky and Rawdon Crawley from Thackeray's *Vanity Fair,* entertaining in their garden hung with Chinese lanterns like a scene from Whistler.

All High Bohemia are present: "Ethelberta Chaplin" (Edith Sitwell), stretching out a long white hand "on every finger of which was some blazing specimen of Florentine jewellery"; her brother, "Cedric Chaplin" (Osbert), "in his most aristocratic and blue-blooded mood," is also disapprovingly present:

> He stood very straight and tall, keeping his fair head rigid while his strained, prominent light blue eyes shifted incessantly from one person to another. Glancing obliquely down at the guests, he makes sarcastic comments in a low voice, although he remains protective of Sibylla ("Poor Sibylla," he thought, "But she is rather nice really.")

Sibylla, Cedric and Ethelberta attempt to escape "that awful woman . . . the Macaw" (Lady Diana Cooper) who, attended by her train, "had discovered champagne, iced punch, and a huge pile of bonbons," but, darting into the garden, Sibylla is accosted by "the great art critic, white locks gleaming in the moonlight, a loaded plate in each hand" (Roger Fry); he is too self-absorbed to listen to her. Disheartened, she leaves him eating "large mouthfuls of strawberries and cream" and wanders down the path, passing "Becky" (Mary) and "Steyne" (Clive Bell).

> Becky reached out a hand to her.
> "Do come and sit on the arm of my chair," she said seductively.
> "And be an audience for you and Steyne—no, thank you," Sibylla thought.

On the balcony "Sibylla" finds Rawdon, dispensing whisky and brandy-and-soda to a large group of men discussing Art. Among them is Eliot, "the American financier," leaning with exaggerated grace against the eighteenth-century marble fireplace. She is struck afresh by his strange appearance:

> the heavy, slumbering white face, thickly powdered; the long hooded eyes, unseeing, leaden-heavy; the huge, protuberant nose, and the somehow inadequate sullen mouth, the lips a little reddened. His head was exceptionally large, and not well shaped; the hair thin and plastered tightly down.

He is wearing a paper cap with streamers with which the Macaw has crowned him, and is haranguing his audience in a muffled, pedantic, and slightly drunken voice.

There is a sudden tumult among the crowds awaiting the arrival of the Ballets Russes. "The Ballet at last!" says someone. The Macaw leads her troupe into the room. "Rawdy, more drink, more drink!" she screeches. Sibylla runs across the deserted drawing-room to the balcony, and leans over the railing. Her eyes sweep the wide flat horizon.

> Beneath her, the sluggish river, flat-banked. Beyond it the vast unknown country of that London which lies on the other side. Over all lay a low, flat, smoky mist clinging to the ground and to

the river. Masts, spires, and tall buildings rose above the lake of mist. Down on the horizon lay the gibbous moon. The sky overhead was pearl-grey. The atmosphere had already the unearthly greenish-grey light of an English summer dawn.

"O Moon, I love you like that," said Sibylla. "I hate Shelley's old moon, like a wretched, dreary invalid escaped from an asylum. This is the moon for me, so fat, so comforting and solid. So *near.*"

As she gazes at the hump-backed moon, Sibylla's friend Felice approaches, asking why the Ballet have not come. "Why should they come?" answers Sibylla lightly; "I shouldn't come if I was the Ballet." The two friends fetch their cloaks, make their farewells, and walk in a dream down the path to the gate. Becky shouts after them: "Have you liked my party?" "Loved it!" calls Sibylla.

Vivien's sketch was an act of *auto-da-fé*. St. John Hutchinson, stated Osbert Sitwell, was outraged by Vivien's "unflattering portrait" of his close friend Lady Diana Cooper, "comparing her, if I remember rightly, to a parrot." As Lady Diana's host, and as an old friend of Tom's, he decided to make a strong protest to Eliot. The real reason for Jack Hutchinson's protest was, of course, his outrage at the insulting portrait of himself and his wife, as well as of their friends.[63] But why, one may ask, did Eliot publish "Fête Galante" when, with a few strokes of his editorial pencil, he could have cut the insulting description and dialogue which he must have known would cause offence? Did he intend to sacrifice Vivien, who must have been encouraged by his defence of Wyndham Lewis to think that he would stand by her in the event of criticism? It is possible that Eliot had grown jealous of Vivien's rising success, for it is hard to believe that he thought he and Vivien could continue to mock Bloomsbury with impunity; it was only a matter of time before her cover was blown.

On the other hand, Tom may have allowed Vivien to express the anger and emotion both Eliots felt as they struggled to make a success of the *Criterion* in a viciously competitive literary environment. In April 1924 Eliot told Virginia how tired he was of "being supposed to edit the *Criterion* and being told by Oxford dons what a lucky young man he was at his age to have a review 'to do as I like with!' " "Do as I like!" he ex-

ploded. As if there were any satisfaction in editing a review "in the fragmentary evening hours given at the cost of sleep, society, recreation," in
trying to bring out a paper of the same appearance as reviews with salaried
editors and sub-editors and proper offices, in working "in one's sitting-
room in the evenings, subject to a thousand interruptions; without staff, assistants or business manager; only since Christmas with a desk (the one
Vivien shewed you: nine pounds ten saved up for) . . ."[64] His bitterness had
deepened as he worried the paper might fold; in May he had written to
Virginia that the *Criterion* "might be extinguished," but only one issue,
Autumn 1925, failed to appear.[65] Jealousy of the wealthy and privileged
members of High Bohemia rankled with both Eliots, but while Tom
"Possum" hid his resentment, Vivien—passionate, impetuous and foolhardy—expressed the contempt they both shared for society's drones. She
alone would pay the price.

18

On with the Dance

Tom yielded to Jack Hutchinson's complaints, making Vivien the scapegoat for his own ambivalent feelings towards Bloomsbury. At first he denied her authorship of "Fête Galante" in the July 1925 *Criterion,* but Virginia Woolf had recorded as early as 29 April her knowledge that Vivien has "done nothing but write since last June, because I told her to!"—a confession made by Tom on a visit to Rodmell. Two days later Tom had been forced to own up to the identity of "Fanny Marlow" when challenged by Ottoline. There was, therefore, no likelihood that the Hutchinsons would accept his denials.[1] In July, in Virginia's opinion, Tom treated Jack as "scurvily" as she felt he later treated her and Leonard by taking away *The Waste Land* and his other poems from the Hogarth Press and placing them behind her back with his new firm, Faber & Gwyer: "He treated Jack in the same way over Vivien's story in the *Criterion,*" wrote Virginia angrily. "The Underworld—the dodges & desires of the Underworld, its shifts and cabals are at the bottom of it. He intends to get on by the methods of that world; & my world is really not the underworld."[2]

Jack Hutchinson was not a man to take an insult lying down. A distinguished barrister, a King's Counsel and later a trustee of the Tate Gallery,[3] although mocked on occasions for being opinionated and sententious, he was nevertheless well liked in Bloomsbury[4]—and he was more than a match for Tom Eliot. Nor was Hutchinson alone in recognising his transparent portrait in "Fête Galante": Roger Fry had also held a garden party in June in which Chinese lanterns, referred to in the sketch, were much in evidence; Clive Bell, Lady Diana Cooper and the Sitwells, offended by Vivien's caricatures, also supported Jack and Mary. In the face of the Hutchinsons' outrage Tom agreed to their terms: he would never publish "Fanny Marlow" again. Vivien's star fell to the ground as fast as it had risen. The scandal precipitated a crisis: the autumn number of the *Criterion* failed to appear, and in the remodelled *New Criterion* of January 1926, only a short review under I. P. Fassett's name appeared in which Vivien probably had no hand.[5]

It is legitimate to ask whether Tom set Vivien up for her disgrace. Why did he allow her to drop the poison in the chalice? It seems inconceivable that Eliot as editor would allow a piece of hers to go through of whose contents he was ignorant. To the innocent eye the assumption must be that Eliot encouraged Vivien to risk her reputation by satirising their closest friends. Even if he were as supportive of her writing as he claimed and, despite his own insecurity, welcomed her unexpected fame, he may have had a darker motive: to eradicate her from the scene because he was negotiating a new contract with Lady Rothermere and Geoffrey Faber for a quarterly in which there would be no place for Vivien. In engineering Vivien's fall Tom cleared the decks for the future.

During 1925 Vivien tried to find another outlet for her writing, one which would relieve her dependence upon Tom and bring her work to a wider audience. Naturally, in view of her close friendship with Scofield Thayer, she turned to *The Dial,* submitting "The Paralysed Woman," the sketch so expressive of her own medical situation. But Thayer was in the process of bowing out of *The Dial* in 1925, handing over the editorship to the poet Marianne Moore, to whom he had awarded the *Dial Award* for 1924, hailing her as America's most distinguished poetess since Emily Dickinson. That spring Moore arrived at *The Dial* offices to take over from the previous managing editor, Alyse Gregory. Ellen Thayer, Scofield's cousin, agreed in March to work as her partner, and by July Scofield had finally relinquished *The Dial.*[6] The forty-one-year-old Ellen Thayer was the sister of Lucy Thayer, Vivien's oldest friend. By the time Vivien submitted her story in the late summer of 1925, it was too late for Scofield to do her any favours. Nevertheless Vivien still had hopes of publication: as she explained in a letter to Ezra Pound, in which Vivien adopted (as did Tom) Ezra's own idiosyncratic spelling.

After revealing to Pound that she had written nearly the whole of the last *Criterion* under different names all beginning with F.M., Vivien related how she was unfortunately misled into telling Scofield's cousin Lucy about her writing. Lucy Thayer had at first professed great admiration for Vivien's stories:

> She wrote to her sister Ellen . . . who Sco has left the Dial to, and her sister Ellen expressed much joy and sed my stories made her laugh & laugh & split her sides etc. etc. so I got ambitious and sent a long story to the Dial (O hell—blood why did I), thinking that Ellen Thayer was a just woman and knew her sister to be mad and bad and insane and shocking and murderous.
>
> Ellen Thayer *immediately* returned my story which is damn good *by means of a ghastly female* called Marriannnne Mooooore (or sum such name) a POETESS (Christ!) . . . Spouse had written letter concerning story to Ellen Thayer & at the same time enclosed my doctor's diagnosis of present disease, to explain why her sister is dangerous to me, but as the reply (curt and rude) came via Marianne Mooore, he rote and cursed her out. He cursed Ellen and Marrrriannnne and Lucy, and so ends the Dial for us.

Sending Vivien's doctor's diagnosis of her condition was not a move guaranteed to encourage publication, but this was not the reason for her rejection by *The Dial*'s new co-editor. Vivien and Lucy had quarrelled over an incident in which, according to Vivien, Lucy made unwelcome lesbian advances to her:

> Damn Sco's cousin. She has done me in . . . She came to my doctor's and told me her Pa was dead at larst and as she had already told me she ment to kill him it upsett me. Then she nelt down beside me and asked me if I loved her, & made love. I could not get anyone to help me & so nearly went mad. Helpless. Not dressed. Alone.[7]

Lucy, who shared with Vivien a history of "nerves," was unbalanced and, like Scofield, now under analysis with Sigmund Freud in Vienna, and indeed, like Vivien, would end her days as a psychiatric patient. The intensity of her relationship with Vivien is hinted at in the character of the

confidante "Felise" in Vivien's fictional sketches, several of which seem to
have been based on actual incidents in the lives of the two women. Lucy
had returned to England after her mother's death from cancer, and she
would have been in an emotional state when she arrived unexpectedly at
Vivien's doctor's surgery to announce that her father also had died; Vivien,
having listened to Lucy's past threats to kill her father, burst into tears
which prompted Lucy's overtures.

Vivien may have misinterpreted Lucy's kisses, but Tom acted
promptly to protect her. He "removed" Lucy, wrote Vivien: "He sent her
a chit to say she should never see me again. She then left England, to poison France"—not, however, before taking her revenge: Ellen would never
in future publish Vivien.

Vivien's rejection by *The Dial* was a devastating blow. All doors
seemed closed to her. Her letter to Pound, written in late 1925, in which
she said she was starving herself because she was "anxious to die," was a
cry for help from a woman *in extremis.* "Am ill *(still* ill) not ill again (always
ill)," she wrote. In September Vivien went down with shingles, her pain so
acute—"all stuck up with bandages, ointments and loathsomeness"—that
her parents looked after her.[8] To Pound she recalled her weakness earlier
that year when she had nearly died just after Christmas and had taken to
"swoons and trances." ("Am very *hypnotic, always was.* Could be first class
MEDIUM.") Vivien told Pound that she enjoyed her trances and "went
off" for two or three weeks at a time, and had some strange experiences on
another dimension.[9] The drugs Vivien took are probably implicated in
these trances, and in such altered states of mind, she said, she stopped eating. Fasting may also have presented its own attractions, making Vivien
light-headed and distancing her from an unhappy reality: choosing not to
eat offered her a measure of control over at least one aspect of a life which
was, in so many ways, controlled by Tom. It is possible, too that fasting
may have enhanced her creativity: Vivien found it impossible to moderate
her writing, having never been trained in regular habits of work, Eliot told
Leonard Woolf;[10] when she had an idea she wanted to work on it constantly.

The female doctor treating Vivien that February was baffled, confessing to Eliot that she had never seen such a case as Vivien's. Although her
unlikely diagnosis was "rheumatism and neuralgia," Tom told Mary that

on the 20th Vivien was again "practically at death's door" from continuous pain, which stopped her sleeping, and there were moments when he thought she would die simply from exhaustion.[11] His growing sense of entrapment was heightened by the effects of Dr. Marten's treatment which, recorded Virginia in April, "set V. off thinking of her childhood terror of loneliness, & now she cant let him, Tom, out of her sight. There he has sat mewed in her room these 3 months, poor pale creature, or if he has to go out, comes in to find her in a half fainting state." This exaggerated account was at odds with Virginia's other report that Vivien was writing constantly,[12] but it does suggest Vivien's terror of abandonment by Tom. He could only leave her for a few hours in the afternoon, he told Mary in April: Vivien was "in torture" again, so he was sorry to miss Mary at Viola Tree's.[13] Although, in an hysterical mimicry of organic illness, Vivien was able to use her sick body to get what she wanted—Tom's attention and presence—she could not stop his growing determination to break out from the circle of co-dependence, and to escape the "chaos and torment," as he expressed it to Ottoline, of his marriage.[14]

Some part of Tom's anger continued to be expended on Dr. Marten, whom he was threatening to sue in July, only being dissuaded from so doing by the necessity of travelling to Germany. It was in fact not until January 1926 that Marten was finally exposed as a charlatan, after Siegfried Sassoon arranged for an analysis of the liquid with which Ottoline, on Marten's instructions, was injecting herself. The liquid turned out to be nothing but milk.[15] Ottoline, whose organs were being X-rayed at Chirk Castle, North Wales, where she was undergoing a cure, "proved to be full of nothing but stale milk," marvelled Virginia to Lytton Strachey in January. "All her injections for the past five yrs at the hands of Dr. Martin of Freiburg were of nothing but that."[16]

In May 1925 an exasperated Eliot called in an Irish-American, Dr. West, who he remembered had helped Dorothy Pound, and who he hoped would undo the damage done by Marten, although by now both he and Vivien were convinced that "all ordinary medical men are *fools.*" Eliot questioned West about Vivien's trances, and the doctor replied that starvation induced trances in "mediumistics." West seems to have suspected that Vivien was anorexic. Although her skeletal appearance may have been partly due to Marten's fortnightly fruit and water diets, it is significant that

anorexia nervosa was once called "anorexia hysterica" and that eating disorders are a widely observed feature of hysteria, as are the "death-states"
or trances, which Vivien so readily entered, and the piercing pains with
which she, like Freud's Dora, suffered.[17] Perhaps for the first time, apart
from the "Scotch doctor" at Chichester, Vivien had found a doctor who
understood the hysterical roots of her symptoms.

After a thorough examination West told his patient that she was
"starved to death," related Vivien to Pound, and although she had "a
very very strong hart" and "no spine fuss" she had the most terrible and
shocking

"LIVER
I have ever
Seen or herd
Tell of in life or on any
Living or ded female. MUST
Go VICHY in the end."[18]

On 1 June Tom once again consulted the Woolfs on Vivien's health; he
was inclined to particularise the state of Vivien's bowels too closely for her
taste, recorded Virginia: "We both almost laughed; she has a queer rib, a
large liver, & so on."[19] That autumn Vivien dragged herself to West's
consulting rooms three times a week: the doctor was "always yelling"
about one thing or another, and Vivien became sickened by his robust
treatment.

It was during this time that Vivien told Ezra Pound that she was convinced she had experienced a nervous breakdown "owing to various
causes."[20] One of these was undoubtedly the collapse of her career as a
writer: she felt a pariah and, after her exposé, did not dare venture into the
society she had satirised. What had begun in part as a joke—an imitation
of other satirists—had led to her silencing. And yet writing was a necessity
for Vivien. It sprang, she wrote with painful prescience, from some "very
overgrown and hidden inner spirit":

When this begins to spurt, it is intolerable to choke it up, & will
lead to my going mad. It is agony either way, of course, but I

think at first, until one has got the spout of this long disused fountain clear, it is better to let the water burst out when it will & so
force away the accumulation of decayed vegetation, moss, slime &
dead fish which are thick upon & around it.[21]

Vivien disliked Dr. West, although at times she thought he was improving her health. She hated the noisy clinic and his *"very LOW Irish,"*
Californian ways; she was afraid of being bullied into going to the Vichy
clinic, suspecting that West earned a commission on patients who attended
it. But West continued to press her to go. "I say *no,*" wrote Vivien. "Spouse
all of a dither." She became increasingly suspicious and recalcitrant.
"Please relieve a tormented Celt (am ½ Welsh ½ Irish)," she begged
Ezra.

Years later, in November 1934, Vivien recalled how her disgrace at the
hands of Jack Hutchinson over "Fête Galante" had precipitated her fall
into a "fearful abyss." In this crisis Eliot turned to Jack for help:

> Tom and Jack had complete control of everything, with Ellen
> Kelland, when I lay for more than a year, a helpless unspeakable
> wreck of drugs, fear, and semi-paralysis. When no-one even came
> to the flat and the whole strange and very horrible affair was kept
> in the hands of Tom and Jack.[22]

Tom's response to the crisis of 1925 was also an intense one. It marked a
turning-point in his life with Vivien, in which a cold antipathy increasingly overlaid his feelings of guilt and responsibility for her, and he began
to consider seriously the possibility of separation. His frustration was such
that, despite the coolness between them, he turned once again to his former
mentor and Vivien's old lover, Bertrand Russell, for advice. Russell, who
had in the meantime left Colette and married Dora Black, invited him to
stay at his home at Carn Voel, Porthcurno, Penzance, over Whitsun so that
Tom could explain more fully what was wrong. "Vivien has avoided me
for the last 7 or 8 years, and I suppose still wants to do so," Russell wrote;
"I shouldn't like her to imagine that there is any lack of friendliness on my
side." Russell assured Tom that he could count on him to help in any pos-

sible way.[23] But a visit to Penzance was out of the question. Tom replied despairingly that Vivien's health was a thousand times worse than before:

> Her only alternative would be to live quite alone—if she could. And the fact that living with me has done her so much damage does not help me to come to any decision. I need the help of someone who understands her—I find her still perpetually baffling and deceptive. She seems to me like a child of 6 with an immensely clever and precocious mind. She writes *extremely* well (stories etc.) and has great originality. And I can never escape from the spell of her persuasive (even coercive) gift of argument.
> Well, thank you very much, Bertie—I feel quite desperate.[24]

Tom's agonising over life with Vivien provoked the scorn of Virginia Woolf, who was herself ill after collapsing in a fainting fit at a Charleston party in August: "Poor Tom" was behaving "more like an infuriated hen, or an old maid who has been kissed by the butler, than ever," she confided to Roger Fry.[25] But Tom was less indecisive than he seemed. After another breakdown of his own that year, he had determined to make fundamental changes in his life. First he was no longer prepared to carry on bringing out the *Criterion* from the flat at Clarence Gate Gardens. Although publicly Tom defended Vivien, praising her to Ottoline for fighting "bravely and tenaciously" to recover her health, in reality the struggle had become unendurable to him, an expression of the "horror in the real world," captured by the dramatists Eliot had studied intensely, and with whose tormented and often vengeful protagonists he identified: Sophocles' Oedipus, Aeschylus' Orestes, Dante's Arnaut Daniel, Marlowe's Faustus and Shakespeare's Hamlet.[26]

In a letter of apology to Ottoline in February 1925 for the "silent estrangement" which had divided them after the fiasco with Dr. Marten, he described the horror of his life with Vivien, which was the trigger for the "sort of avocation," the "much more revolutionary style [crossed out] thing" he was experimenting with, and which would become *Sweeney Agonistes,*[27] Eliot's own hysterical narrative, in which he explored the theme of wife murder:[28] "We have been very ill," he wrote (bulletins of the Eliots' health were often collective). He was still confined to the house after six weeks of influenza; it would be several weeks more before he could take up any work; he was unable to read for more than a few minutes and could only write "necessary notes." Some part of his strength had left him "forever." The fact was that he had been very much more ill than he knew: "It was a real breakdown." Vivien, too, had collapsed a fortnight before that: she had simply got out of bed and fallen down with utter exhaustion of body and spirit. Even a few minutes conversation with him, said Tom in a revealing confession, sent her temperature up.[29] When he was not physically ill, imagined ailments such as the "suppressed influenza" Tom claimed to have had from July to November 1924, eroded his vitality.[30] It had got to the point when neither of them could stand it any more, he told Ottoline: "I *had* to make a change."

Eliot was resolved that he must either give up the *Criterion* or get a minimum salary from Lady Rothermere ("£300 a year is little enough, God knows") so that he and Vivien might "save what remains of our health." Playing on Ottoline's sympathy, he pleaded with her as early as February 1925 to help find him a group of backers who would take over the *Criterion* if Lady Rothermere backed out. Would Ottoline's half-brother, the Duke of Portland, allow his name to be put forward? "It is names (preferably titled) which will impress Lady R. not figures." If Lady Rothermere refused Tom a contract and a salary he planned to get a larger group of twenty or twenty-five people to subsidise the paper. Such a scheme would be more sympathetic than Bel Esprit, he argued, because he would be giving his services to a review instead of receiving charity.[31]

Ottoline, having had her fingers burnt over Bel Esprit, may have been less than enthusiastic. In the event her help was not needed. Lady Rothermere "didn't cut up anything but 'smooth,' " as a relieved Tom told Virginia. Suddenly he found himself facing the prospect of running two papers, the "Light" and the "Heavy," or "Criterion Junior" and "Senior," as Virginia described them. One was to be the continuing quarterly for Lady Rothermere and the other a new paper proposed by the publishing firm of Faber & Gwyer, for whom he finally, with enormous relief, left the bank in May 1925. It was the change in Eliot's fortunes for which he had longed. A Tory journalist, Charles Whibley, had introduced him to the publisher Geoffrey Faber, who had gone into partnership with a firm of scientific publishers, Gwyer, in 1923, and two years later launched a new general publishing house. Faber was impressed by Eliot who, remembered F. R. Leavis, had become "the important contemporary critic" with the publication of *Homage to John Dryden,*[32] as well as having proven experience as an editor and a reputation as a poet which would enable him to attract writers of renown;[33] he invited Eliot to join the Board of Directors. Suddenly, with one stroke of Faber's wand, the poet's economic troubles seemed at an end.

Virginia Woolf was critical of this development, which she suspected would adversely affect the Woolfs' Hogarth Press, and irritated at Tom's duplicity. Had he not begged and entreated her to let him have something of hers for his new review, while surreptitiously moving the publication of his poems to his new firm—a development that Virginia only discovered in the pages of the *Times Literary Supplement.* It was "a fact which he dared not confess, but sought to palliate by flattering me," she exploded to her diary on 14 September.[34] It certainly sounded irrational to run two reviews, agreed Tom smoothly, detecting "a note of disapproval" in Virginia's voice, but it was, he argued, less of a task to run two things as twins, with one proper office and full secretarial assistance, and his new firm to deal with the whole business part, than to run Lloyds Bank's "Extracts from the Foreign Press" in the City in the day and the *Criterion* from Clarence Gate Gardens at night.[35] His satisfaction at leaving banking for a more congenial form of business was immense: Lady Rothermere had offered to guarantee four-fifths of his present Lloyds salary if he ran the *Criterion* for another year, and it was soon decided that she and Faber & Gwyer would share the financial responsibility for a single revamped review, to be named the *New Criterion.* Hiding her displeasure, Virginia sent Tom her essay, "On Being Ill," for the *New Criterion.*[36] Even so, all through September she grumbled to her diary about Tom's behaviour, in particular his poaching of authors from the Hogarth Press (he was luring Herbert Read from the Woolfs, who had published his first book). "To-day we are on Tom's track, riddling & reviling him ... There is the fascination of a breach; I mean, after feeling all this time conscious of something queer about him, it is more satisfactory to have it on the surface. Not that I want a breach: what I want is a revelation. But L. thinks the queer shifty creature will slip away now."[37]

It was hard to maintain the Eliot-Woolf friendship at the old level now that they had become publishing rivals, although Virginia continued to feel sorry for Vivien ("that little nervous self-conscious bundle"),[38] and sent her some earstoppers[39] and an inscribed copy of *The Common Reader,* which "she *will* read," Tom assured its author.[40] Tom was moving on to a new life, but Virginia and Richard Aldington were left to pick up the pieces of Bel Esprit: Tom had asked them to return the rest of the money to the subscribers, which involved Virginia in long letters of explanation to each donor and a rebuke from Leonard for her "vanity" in trying to help the afflicted.[41]

Vivien refused to go to Vichy in August. Instead, at the end of October, Tom sent her "to the country," a euphemism for a sanatorium near Watford, having called in "other (medical) opinions," according to which the country was absolutely necessary. On 5 November he told Ottoline he was leaving England for a short sea voyage the next day. A few days later he arrived jubilantly in the Alpes Maritimes, and stayed at the Savoy Hotel, La Turbie, near Lady Rothermere's villa and Monte Carlo, winter home of Diaghilev's Ballets Russes. The Côte d'Azur was "damned cold" but it could not dampen his delight at his new career. The pay was less than Bruce Richmond, editor of the *Times Literary Supplement,* had said an editor might get, he wrote to Richard Aldington, but there were additional perks from Faber & Gwyer, and now that they were combining with Lady Rothermere to own and manage the review, he had a cast-iron five-year contract. "So I am a Director of Faber & Gwyer and a humble publisher at your service!" Aldington, struggling in his Malthouse cottage, felt more than a flicker of jealousy, especially as the new editor asked him to write a book on Rémy de Gourmont for Faber for an advance of only £25.[42] "When one is a professional whore of letters it is not much fun to whore far under the skeduled [sic] price and be treated as if it were a favour," he complained to Pound.[43]

Although Eliot had seemed to Virginia in the spring of 1925 to be momentarily a little humbler and "more humane" to Vivien,[44] he nevertheless placed Vivien in the sanatorium against her will. On 14 December 1925

Vivien sent a desperate letter from the Stanboroughs, which advertised itself as "A Modern Hydrotherapeutic Health Institution," to Ezra in Rapallo, asking him to intercede on her behalf with her husband, now in Italy:

> Tell T. not to be a fool. He pretends to think I hate him, but its just a lie. . . . Speak to Tom. Ask him, dear Ezra, *make* him rescue me before Xmas. I am well now. At least I *shd* be well with/given one half grain of happiness, peace of mind, assurance, and time and opportunity to read and think. But O the starvation with all these things missing . . . I want a few books, my liberty, & peace. Is that too much? T. *is* unbalanced, and in the toils of . . . one Higgins. Pull him up O Ezra. S.O.S. V. H. Eliot.[45]

In this letter Vivien stressed that she was more sane than Tom, whose actions she blamed on one of their doctors, Higgins. But Ezra's first loyalty lay with Tom, and he did nothing to help Vivien. Instead he kept Tom's secrets, while receiving Vivien's confidences. At some point he replied reassuringly to Vivien, for she sent him a gift, perhaps of money, with a note saying it was for "medical attendance," a "special long distance consultation," which came with her love and thanks.[46] Tom, meanwhile, was writing to Ezra, his "caro lapino," dear rabbit, from La Turbie, suggesting a meeting: but "don't give my address to *anyone,*" he instructed his compatriot.[47]

Tom's ostensible reason for visiting the South of France was to find peace and quiet in which to begin writing the eight Clark lectures he was to deliver at Trinity College, Cambridge, the following Lent term. Middleton Murry's nomination had resulted in Eliot's being awarded the lectureship after the college's first choice, A. E. Housman, had turned it down in February 1925. Eliot had been delighted at the opportunity to take the seventeenth-century metaphysical poets and contrast them with Dante and his school, even though his stipend for eight lectures would be only £200, a sum unchanged for forty-two years. After a painful operation on his jaw, and the nail-biting *Criterion* negotiations, he needed isolation in which to write the first four lectures before returning to England.[48]

But Tom made better progress than expected. By 8 December he was promising Ezra that "me and my lil old saxaphone" would be with him in Italy the following week. It was so cold in France that they had to break the ice in the horsetrough "to wash mah pants," and as soon as he had his new passport he wanted to come south.[49] After his passport had expired the previous week, Eliot had been forced to make a detour to Nice to get a new one, nearly missing his bus; "had to run my balls off across the Place Massena" to get a seat, he wrote, and sit with a bottle of wine in his lap and a parcel of medicines which he had bought for his chilblains, and for constipation, and some Eno's Fruit Salts, which he always took "on principle."[50]

Finally, Ezra's "Tarbaby," as Eliot signed himself, arrived at the older poet's home at 12, Via Marsala, Rapallo. There was no longer any need to wear the mask of conformity, to preserve the careful dress of the banking hall. "C'est à grands pas et en sueur/Que vous suivrez à peine ma piste,"* he had written in an earlier poem ("Mélange Adultère de Tout"), expressing his sense of multiple identities—as lecturer, teacher, journalist and bank clerk.[51] Now the twisted trail had led to the top of the mountain. Henceforth he would dominate English letters. Relaxing in the winter sunshine, Eliot could dress as he was accustomed to in Italy, in a "theatrical get-up with a little (not very clean) lace falling over his knuckles, in the role of *il decaduto,* the decadent, or dandy-aesthete.[52] Yet there was steel under the actor's costume, as Aldington noted: "Cibber . . . combined extreme caution and superiority with *un extérieur trés pimpant* and perfectly lovely manners . . . Oxbridge held the world's record for the lifted eyebrow, but Cibber raised his at least a semi-tone higher. His cool American wit . . . enabled him to score off even his most hirsute and erudite opponents, and soon made him a dreaded power."[53]

Vivien's demand for her liberty prompted Tom to return reluctantly to England after Christmas. He at once dismissed her complaints as "moonshine." She was physically fitter than he had ever seen her, he told Ezra on 27 December, but otherwise left "much to be desired," and he was not optimistic. He decided to send her to Brighton to a furnished flat with a nurse.[54]

In Tom's absence Vivien had consoled herself in the sanatorium with

---

* With large steps and much sweat/You will scarcely follow my tracks

Ezra Pound's poems, spending so much time reading them that the staff finally took them away from her.[55] She wrote to ask him to include her favourites—"In Tempore Senectutis," "Camaraderie" and "Vilanelle" [sic]—in any new collection, signing herself "Little Nell," Dickens's innocent but doomed child-heroine.[56] Brooding on her incarceration Vivien read and reread the poems which seemed relevant to her present state, such as "A Villonaud, Ballad of the Gibbet," with its image of the "lusty robbers twain," their tarred corpses swinging in the wind: "Black is the pitch of their wedding dress." Like the robbers, Vivien felt "the strain/Of love that loveth in hell's disdeign," sensing "the teeth thru the lips that press/Gainst our lips for the soul's distress."[57] Black sheets, black wedding dresses, were symbols of death on which she pondered in her writing book, as she contrasted Pound's paean to the contentment of old age ("In Tempore Senectutis") with her own uncertain future with Tom:

> For we are old
> And passion hath died for us a thousand times
>   But we grow never weary.

In Pound's verse the old couple or "twain" are never weary of each other's companionship, despite the flight of passion;[58] but Vivien knew her own case to be very different. She guessed why she was in the Stanboroughs. That autumn she had longed to go to Rapallo, telling Ada Leverson that she was lucky to be going there, for everyone they knew was at Rapallo at the moment.[59] Monte Carlo and Italy were magnets for artists and intellectuals, and Vivien suspected that Tom would be meeting his friends from the Ballets Russes and preferred not to have her company.

Diaghilev was touring Italy on "honeymoon" with his new favourite, Serge Lifar, before bringing his company to London for the new season at the Coliseum from 26 October, and then returning to Monte Carlo in December. Léonide Massine, divorced from Vera Savina in 1924, had returned to his old company as guest choreographer, having made up his quarrel with Diaghilev, who had been keeping a close eye on his former favourite's work for his rival impresario, the homosexual Comte Etienne de Beaumont, in ballets such as *Salade*. At a meeting engineered by the ballet maestro Cecchetti, at his studio in Shaftesbury Avenue in the summer of 1924, Diaghilev asked Massine to choreograph two new ballets for him. Massine accepted, arranging a *rendez-vous* in Monte Carlo at the end of that year, where he met the new stars of the ballet: Nikitina, Markova, Anton Dolin and Lifar, and at once began working on a new ballet, *Zéphire et Flore*.[60]

Tom, therefore, did not tell Vivien the truth about either his travels or his health, fobbing her off with promises of sun and sea-bathing the next year. It was difficult to keep up the fiction that his trip abroad had been entirely convalescent. There was an embarrassing moment when he found himself having to explain to his wife how he had heard "a bit of Antheil"—George Antheil, the "bad boy" American composer who was the toast of Paris and a protégé of Pound's.[61] Eliot pretended to Vivien that he and Antheil had not met, but that Pound had simply played his compositions on the bar-room piano. "Yew dropped a brick," Tom reproached Ezra on 27 December, for telling Vivien that he looked in excellent health: "It'll come out in the wash, but dr. [Dr. Higgins] was trying to impress her that I have been on the verge and was just pulling round with care and treatment." People in Vivien's state were always "inclined to vampire," warned Tom, implying that his wife was a blood-sucker upon his money and energy. "I shall thank God when the next six months is over, if still alive." He fretted that in his absence Vivien had been writing letters, spreading undesirable rumours about him. "If you shd at any time hear such, you'll be ready for them, & will have to say she has had a nervous breakdown." And you might let me know, said Tom: "I'm ready to wipe up after these rumours when necessary."[62]

It was a letter which suggested that Tom and Dr. Higgins were allies: Higgins would arrange for Vivien to enter a sanatorium to suit Tom's convenience, or exaggerate Tom's own mental distress to justify his absence abroad, so long as the doctor's bills were paid; likewise, Tom or Ezra would exaggerate Vivien's instability in order to discredit any stories she was spreading about Tom. Despite the fact that Tom claimed to Ezra, in a postscript, that he had found Vivien "very affectionate on the whole," he made plans to return to the Continent as soon as possible, asking his "dear Rabbit" if Possum could rent his flat.[63] Vivien, meanwhile, put a good face on the situation to "Dearest Ottoline," writing on 23 December that she was now nearly well.[64] In reply Ottoline, who had said she was doing no Christmas shopping that year, sent Vivien some "glorious scent." Vivien's response was light-hearted:

> Oh what a truly *Otto* trick
> Upon a friend to play
> To make her feel as green as grass
> Upon a Christmas Day![65]

Vivien begged Ottoline to come and visit her at Brighton, where she was going after a week at Clarence Gate Gardens, "to get really strong. Get your husband or a nice rich friend or relation to take you to Brighton for a long visit," she pleaded. *"Please do."*[66]

In the intervening months Mary Hutchinson had given up both River House in Hammersmith and Eleanor House in West Wittering, and had moved to 3 Albert Road, Regent's Park, where she commissioned Vanessa Bell and Duncan Grant to decorate her dining-room and study. Mary's status as an arbiter of taste and fashion had risen. *Vogue,* to which she contributed as "Polly Flinders," noted approvingly in 1926 that in the drawing-room at 3 Albert Road, "The book-filled alcoves on either side of the fireplace are surmounted by a lively design of fighting cocks and the purplish grey stippled overmantel is an ideal background for a fine Matisse *[Interior at Nice]."*[67] The panels by Bell and Grant, with a "delicate over-door decoration show a classical feeling befitting the period of the house."[68] Undeniably Mary had triumphed: she remained a leader of society. Invitations to her parties were eagerly sought, while Vivien, frozen out by Bloomsbury, could only write contritely to her old friend on 23 December that she would love to meet again after so long. "To do so," she wrote, "would seem like starting a new life."[69]

Vivien did not forgive Tom for incarcerating her in the Stanboroughs instead of taking her abroad with him. She and Tom had also moved house, leaving north London for Belgravia, where they had at last found the house with the garden they had been seeking, near Sloane Square, at 57 Chester Terrace (now Row), for a rent of only £58 a year. They had initially taken it in May 1925, when Virginia had piously hoped that the Eliots might be able to "start fresh."[70] But Vivien had found the move a shock: Mary's move from Hammersmith to Regent's Park had been a move "towards civilisation," wrote Vivien on 25 March 1926, but hers to Belgravia felt like a plunge into the outer suburbs. Indeed, after their initial move to Chester Terrace in 1925, intending to sub-let Clarence Gate Gardens furnished, Vivien had bolted back to "cower" in the flat when she had shingles, as she had difficulty in finding servants.[71]

They did not return to Chester Terrace until 1926. When Ottoline dined there with the Eliots on 3 March, she noticed that Tom was watching Vivien all the time. The couple seemed more cheerful than normal, and Vivien in particular appeared oddly elated, smoking and eating chocolates. Afterwards Ottoline heard from Bertie Russell that Vivien was threatening to sue her husband for putting her away, although Ottoline remembered indignantly that Vivien had herself told Ottoline earlier how happy she had been in the "home."[72]

There was a reason for Vivien's elation—and for Tom's careful watchfulness. Vivien had fallen in love. The resurgence in her vitality after she returned from Brighton—which at once struck Ottoline—was not only due to Dr. West's "regimen," but to the attention of the fast and thoughtless young men, the opposite of the intellectuals whom she professed to dislike, with whom she began to flirt at night clubs. According to Osbert Sitwell, in 1926 Vivien carried on "ostentatious flirtations," some with "squalid sub-fusc writers"; her aim was to make Tom jealous, to hold his attention now that she was excluded from writing for the *Criterion*.[73] Indeed, from the moment when the *New Criterion* began to be edited from the offices of Faber & Gwyer in Russell Square, Vivien's life lost much of its meaning. In her new house she was far from familiar north London, and the house was "terrible," full of workmen, Vivien told Mary, and Ellen, her maid, was leaving. None of this would have mattered to Vivien if she had still been at the heart of the *Criterion* coterie, but from 1926 she was redundant, in every sense of the word. Her stories were unacceptable, her secretarial skills displaced. The home which had once been their joint workplace, the heart of their literary partnership, had become a desert. With Ellen gone, Vivien was left with only "a mad ex-policeman aged seventy to help," the first reference to William Alfred Janes, the former detective, now handyman, who was to become an omnipresent and sinister figure in her life. The Eliots' old flat, which Vivien had left "as neat as a pin," was occupied by Tom's brother Henry and his new wife, Theresa Garrett Eliot, an artist, on an extended European honeymoon. Every time Vivien visited these cuckoos in her nest, she felt in a rage.[74] Confronted with such emptiness, she emulated her husband and turned outside the marriage for consolation.

Ottoline condemned Vivien's pursuit of frivolity, having previously considered her both intellectual and spiritual.[75] But in her search for sensation Vivien was in tune with the spirit of the age. *On with the Dance,* Charles B. Cochrane's new show with Noël Coward, expressed frenzied city life in "Crescendo," one of the "scenes" choreographed by Massine, who danced Bobo, the Spirit of the Age, to a swift and satirical score based on popular jazz melodies. *On with the Dance* had opened in April 1925, and the programme proclaimed that

> In an age when the romance of machinery is superseding the lilies and languor of Victorianism, Art must of necessity reflect the angular tendencies of the times . . . Man becomes a puppet and Beauty a slave to the new forms of the relentless progress of civilisation . . . Massine as the Spirit of the Age dominates the scene, and his puppets jig to the tune of cocktails and jazz, until, willy nilly, they are swept up to a frenzied climax of impressionistic movement.

The abstract backcloth featured the word "Café," the women wore flapper dresses, and sang the show's popular tune, "Pack Up Your Sins." The ballet was, remembered Massine, "a real period piece which, in its way, epitomised the whole of the early 1920s."[76] Ballet held up a mirror to contemporary life, borrowing from music-hall, jazz and vaudeville in productions such as *Parade*. It was "piquant, amusing, replete with accoutrements of modern living," writes Lynn Garafola, historian of the Ballets Russes. "Lifestyle modernism identified the new consumerist chic of the upper classes."[77] It was a brand of modernism which spoke to Vivien, flapper-slim, stylish, who painted her mouth with red lip-lotion in a perfect cupid's bow, wore a "surplice" as Maurice described her short, bustless, waistless dress, and was determined to dance her way out of unhappiness.

The flat at Burleigh Mansions now served a new purpose, not only as writing-room but a setting for nocturnal adventure for Vivien as well as for Tom. From the Eliots' eyrie behind the Coliseum, which they often used separately, Vivien addressed a poem to the illuminated Coliseum dome whose flickering light she loved to watch at night.

> Oh why, spangled globe must you darken so soon
> And leave me alone with the swift-marching moon?

But there was no need to be alone. Vivien was in the mood for sexual rebellion after the failure of her bid for literary recognition; indeed, extramarital affairs were but another aspect of Bloomsbury's resolve to *épater les bourgeois,* one already practised by Mary Hutchinson, Ottoline, and by Virginia and Vita Sackville-West. The search for novelty was the essence of modernism, and if one rebellion had been crushed Vivien would essay another kind of freedom, looking beyond Tom for personal satisfaction, as Mary had done in taking Clive as her lover.

> But my sparkling glittering swift-turning dome
> You're the first thing I look for when late I come home,
> And if you're still whirling and shining and gay
> Then something's come right at the end of the day.[78]

When the dome darkened, the moon shone over the lovers, high in the sky for it was late indeed when Vivien returned from the nightclub: "O moon dear/We spoon dear," she wrote, "When you guard the night."[79]

Ottoline judged both the Eliots to be self-absorbed. One day in 1926 Tom suddenly kissed her violently on the lips: he, too, was in love with somebody, she deduced. He had seemed detached the previous summer, hiding behind a smokescreen she could not penetrate, secretly meeting Mary Hutchinson to exchange confidences during her last summer at Eleanor.[80] Sometimes he apologised to Ottoline for being too busy to speak to her at the ballet but he had "Diaghilev etc. on my hands."[81] It was an admission of the importance that the Ballets Russes had come to have for him since their return to London. Was Eliot still in love with Massine, who was living close to Burleigh Mansions? No longer constrained by the short lunch hour of which he used to complain at Lloyds, Eliot could now keep the hours of a gentleman publisher; there was time to lunch with Léonide Massine, Serge Diaghilev, Kochno and the others at Gennaro's, and to join them backstage after performances at the Coliseum, before going on to the Savoy Grill.[82] In her unpublished memoir on T. S. Eliot, Mary Hutchinson wrote of Tom's "immense admiration of Massine," and her memories of Eliot at Diaghilev's ballets, often in a box, or walking the corridors of Covent Garden.[83] Significantly, one of Vivien's few surviving poems, "Perque Domos Ditis Vacuas," which translates as "Through the Empty Halls of Dis" (Dis was another name for Pluto, God of the Underworld), implied that in entering the gay world of Diaghilev, Eliot was entering the Underworld, a world of which she no longer wanted any part. Vivien took the title of her poem from a line in Virgil's *Aeneid,* Book VI, which relates Aeneas's voyage to the Underworld, and served as a model for Dante. On his way, Aeneas met the Sibyl of Cumae, with whom Vivien identified; the Sibyl's message to the hero was a stark one: "Facilis discencus Averni:/Noctes atque dies patet atri ianua Ditis . . ." ("Easy is the path that leads down to hell; grim Pluto's gate stands open night and day.") To retrace one's steps and escape to the upper air is a hard task, says the Sibyl; nevertheless, she agrees to accompany Aeneas to the realms of Pluto. Vivien, who saw herself also as a prophetess, was delivering her own commentary on her husband's lifestyle. Despite Sibyl's—or Sibylla's—warnings, Eliot has entered the jaws of hell.

Vivien's poem expressed her own urgent need to escape from those "halls of Pluto," or corridors of death:

> It was after the acrobats
> And I left my box
> And ran along the corridor
> Fast
> Because I wanted to get into the air
> And in the suffused light of the empty corridor

In the stale air and soft suffused light of the corridor . . .
In the stifling scent of death and suffocation of the corridor
I met my own eyes
In another face.[84]

Perhaps it was after Anton Dolin's acrobatic feats in *Le Train Bleu,*
Cocteau's last ballet for Diaghilev, that Vivien ran from the "suffocating"
corridor. In the final years of the Ballets Russes, 1925–29, the atmosphere
at performances became more overtly "decadent" or homosexual, and Old
Bloomsbury began to withdraw from it. Young dandies such as Harold
Acton, Brian Howard and Cecil Beaton made Diaghilev their hero; the
promenoir at the back of the circle became a pick-up area for homosexuals,
and a newspaper suggested that the "young men in roll-top jumpers who
stroll about at the back of the circle and talk and talk and talk should be
thrown out."[85]

In the summer of 1926, Diaghilev and Lifar moved from the Savoy to
a flat in a house run as "bachelor chambers," at Albemarle Court, 27
Albemarle Street, off Piccadilly. It had, said Osbert Sitwell to his brother,
a "queer" reputation, and it may therefore have been he who recommended the chambers to Diaghilev. Nevertheless, Sacheverell emerged
from his visits there "unscathed."[86] He was collaborating on a new ballet,
The Triumph of Neptune, performed at the end of 1926; a few months later,
Serge Lifar appeared in his Neptune costume at the "Sailor party," organised by Howard and Edward Gathorne-Hardy in 1927 at the swimming-
baths in Buckingham Palace Road, attended by many Bright Young
Things, to celebrate the revival of *Les Matelots,* in which Massine danced
the French sailor for the first time.[87]

There was certainly talk in London that Eliot enjoyed the company of
sailors. On 22 January 1926 Vivien wrote to Mary, denying the rumour that
Tom had a studio in Marseilles. It was "false," she said, although it was
true that he was lecturing in Cambridge, and that he was giving a tea-party
on 31 January in honour of a gentleman from France, one connected with
the *Nouvelle Revue Française*—"and *very* handsome, so Tom says." She
wondered if Mary and Jack could come to tea.[88] In March Vivien wrote
an apologetic letter to Ottoline for not being able to come to stay at
Garsington, because Tom had "another marvellous Frenchman" coming

over that weekend.[89] This was the writer Henri Massis, editor of the *Revue,* who was lecturing in London, explained Tom to Ottoline.[90]

It was not love she was looking for, only oblivion, Vivien had written in "Night Club" *(Criterion,* April 1925), basing her story on the experiences outside marriage which "Sibylla" had sought as early as 1919, when she went off dancing with three airmen. To dance was to forget, to annihilate memory. In her reflection in the eyes of her young escorts Vivien had seen admiration instead of dislike, desire instead of rejection.

> "Love," said Sibylla at the night club—"You don't know what you are talking about. And I'm sure I don't know anyhow," she added carelessly, leaning her elbows on the table, and her chin on her hands. She stared about her.
>
> "But look here," her companion began to reply, in a tone full of emotion. His young face was beaded with perspiration . . .
>
> "Love," she said, "why there isn't such a thing nowadays that I know of. It's out of date. Nobody wants *love."* She flicked a crumb off the table. "Nobody gets it either for that matter. Don't you worry about love, my poor fellow, as you'll soon be in the soup or the cart or whatever it is you people like to be in at the moment."

Vivien's naïve and obtuse admirer is mystified, and protests.

> "Honestly," she continued. "You take it from me, no-one wants your love. I don't know what they do want, I'm sure and I don't care either—your money probably, or your brains, not that you've got any. But love, O hell . . ."
>
> She turned slightly round, and leaning now her head on one hand looked full into her admirer's face with brilliantly clear grey eyes holding an expression of the most virginal primeval innocence . . . that he or anyone in that large, hot and crowded room had ever seen. Her cynical, careless and unending chatter com-

which Henry, in his letters home to his mother, compared Tom to Job;[97] Vivien's "vampiring" drained "poor Tom" of his vitality, they all agreed, although Henry was pleased to see that his brother was taking a firmer line with Vivien. When she had objected to Tom playing their phonograph, he had insisted on carrying on.[98] Even so, Eliot still did not confide in his brother on the subject of Vivien, complained Henry to Charlotte on 15 March, although Henry suspected that it would be a "great mental relief" to him to do so.[99]

As Henry and Theresa left for Cambridge to listen to Tom lecture at Trinity, where he had given his first Clark lecture on 26 January, stories of Vivien's flirtations were circulating among the gossips of bohemian London. According to Osbert Sitwell, it was said that Vivien had now taken a lover. In her notebook she recorded a conversation in which "Sibylla" rings to tell the man in question that their secret is out:

"Hullo," said Sibylla. "Can you speak now or cant you?"

"Ye-es," said Mike . . . "Have you been to see Mrs.———?"

"Yes I have, and she was *all over me* . . . My dear—she *knew*—"

"She—she *knew?*"

"Yes. *She knew.*"

"But how could she possibly—have heard, have found out?"

"Ho, because she's a woman. She hadn't *heard,* you idiot. She just *knew.* Intuition."

"And what do you think she wants *now?*"

"If you please, she asked when André was going to Cambridge—you know André is going to Cambridge to lecture?"[100]

However, Vivien was not as light-hearted about her behaviour as she pretended. Nor, despite not having seen him for seven years, had she forgotten Bertrand Russell. In her notebook she carried on a dialogue with her conscience, personified by Bertie, the only man she felt had loved and understood her; although she claimed to bear no malice, and to reject any idea of revenge, it was in part Russell she blamed for her present predicament. In Vivien's sketch she pictures him paying an unexpected call just after she has given a party. "B.R. enters."

"I am afraid it is rather late to be paying a call," he said mincingly and dryly, "but I saw your light on as I was passing."

"Bertie, come in," said Sibylla, who hated to hear explanations as much as she hated to give them. "Fancy *him* turning up," she thought to herself. There had been a time when she had seen much of this aristocratic heretic, but he had revolutionized his way of life and for the past few years she had seen him scarcely at all. Missing him, she yet wasted no time on regrets—"It's no use having regrets; there simply *isn't time,*" she often said to Felise. It was the same with bearing malice, there *isn't time* for bearing malice in this world.[101]

Felise then arrives with Vivien's "young man of the moment," whom she has discovered on the doorstep.

"Well, how did you get on with your body-snatchers?" the young man asked. "You've had a sort of funeral party or something, haven't you?"

"It didn't seem funereal to me," said Sibylla coldly . . .

"Sibylla has always had a profound respect for body-snatchers," said the philosopher dryly.

"Perhaps that's why they come to her parties," said Felise.

"They are like white maggots," said the mathematician. "They feed like coffin-worms—they feed in the brains of artists."

"But I am not an artist," cried Sibylla.

This, despite her protestations, was not what Vivien believed; above all she longed to be an artist, to be the equal of Tom, of Ezra, of Virginia, at the very least of Mary. Into the mouth of another guest Vivien puts the words she believed described herself: "You have personality—you have vision—you have above all a distinctive point of view." You Sibylla, are "essentially an artist." "Besides, you're *Sybil,*" cried Felise ardently. "Isn't that enough. The old Sybil!" "You've said it, by God," exclaimed the young man, claiming that Sibylla could be in Parliament. While Felise and the other guests laugh, Vivien turns to Bertie. They share a different understanding:

"They're like barnacles on an old hulk."

"Or clinging to a piece of wreckage."

"Yes, they don't even know there's been a wreck," said Sibylla. And she added to herself, with her eyes fixed directly on the philosophical mathematician. "You are one of the people who have caused the wreck."

Vivien blamed Bertie in part for the post-war "waste land" of modern life ("It takes an aristocrat to overthrow tradition") but she was also referring to the detritus of their affair: "To be a nowadays person means you must not have any nasty little tentacles reaching back to behind the war," she wrote sadly. "You may have had such tentacles, but the war must have chopped them off." Try as she might to be a "nowadays person," Vivien was not a compulsive hedonist like Nancy Cunard; she remained under Bertie's influence and judged herself by his intellectual standards. She knew he would have condemned the "mountebanks" or coffin-worms of her sketch, who fed on the brains of artists; the coffin was a persistent image for her now, death the "wages of sin." In her sketch "Lonely Soldier," Vivien returned to the black-draped coffin, the "long box roughly wrapped with black cloth and corded," which she had watched being carried into the Paddington Street mortuary that morning.

The Eliots' life together continued to influence Tom's art, as did the interrelationship between his work and hers: "Sibylla" and "Felise" in Vivien's "Lonely Soldier" are as superstitious as Doris and Dusty in Eliot's *Sweeney Agonistes*. They cut the cards and tell each other's fortunes.

"Draw a card," said Felise, spreading out the other pack on her lap.

Sibylla drew one.

"Nine of diamonds," said Felise, "you're in luck."

"Let me see what does that mean?"

"Good luck, prosperity or business success," Felise replied promptly.

"Fancy, and I saw the new moon too."[102]

This card-playing dialogue of Vivien's is echoed in Tom's "Fragment of an Agon" (later incorporated into *Sweeney Agonistes),* first published in the

New Criterion in January 1927: "You've got to *think* when you read the cards,/It's not a thing anyone can do," Doris tells Dusty, in Eliot's words, which could also be Vivien's to Pearl Fassett or Lucy Thayer. Doris spreads out the cards, like Felise. "Here's the two of spades," Doris says. "The *two of spades!*" exclaims Dusty. "THAT'S THE COFFIN!! Oh good heavens what'll I do?" A page or two further on Doris begs Sweeney not to talk of murder, because she cut the cards before he came: "I drew the COFFIN very last card./I don't care for such conversation/A woman runs a terrible risk." Sweeney replies that he knew a man once who did a girl in. "Any man might do a girl in/Any man has to, needs to, wants to/Once in a life-time, do a girl in."[103]

There is a poignancy in Vivien's self-reproach, for she knew that she too was running "a terrible risk" in the lifestyle she was adopting. But she was in flight from *ennui,* from that "panic fear of boredom" which often assailed her:

> To be bored was perhaps the only fear that Sibylla ever really knew. In general she feared and detested a tête-à-tête. She would do anything to avoid it. She was more at ease with several people, feeling that the burden of their minds pressed on her less.

Vivien confesses that she has become adept at inventing little tricks and games by which to turn the conversation away from herself and back upon others. She is a performer, "constantly engaged in acting violent parts, or simulating various definite characteristics," inwardly rebelling against picking up cues offered by other performers, and prepared to "take the most fantastic courses to preserve herself from being thrust into such a position."[104] It is a revealing comment on Vivien's propensity to threaten people with knives, threats which her victims were never sure were entirely in jest. But role-playing was not enough to fill up the emptiness inside her; nor was alcohol. It is Felise who is pictured with a bottle of whisky and a siphon of soda beside her; "her friends had warned her so often against drinking in private (!) that she took every opportunity to drink in public," writes Vivien. Felise shares her whisky with "Horace" (Maurice), the "lonely soldier" of the title of her sketch, as they play "pseudo-bridge" together in Felise's "pseudo-studio," before putting on the gramophone and having "a little rously-tously," in Horace's words.[105] In these sketches Vivien never drinks, although she dances, goes to parties in Felise's studio, and plays bridge with the brother she despises. By her own account, cocktails did not "buck her up," although her escort in "Night Club" presses her to have one. "No thanks, I don't need bucking, and I can't drink," she replies. "I wish to God I could . . . I can't even smoke. Can't drink and can't smoke. What a horrible woman. Oh I am an awful woman—"[106] Vivien's prescription drugs were often alcohol-based, and therefore she could not drink socially, as Maurice recalled.

According to a signed statement made on 28 March 1970 by Theresa Eliot—to whom Vivien took an instant liking—during the Henry Eliots' stay to England in 1926, Vivien asked them to visit her doctor in order to discuss her health; he would tell them something that she could not tell them herself. The doctor informed Henry and Theresa that Vivien took drugs, and had started at the age of sixteen under doctor's orders. Charlotte Eliot Smith, Tom's sister, had already realised the "true" situation on an earlier visit to London with their mother in 1924; at that time Vivien, wary of her perceptive sister-in-law, had kept her distance, although she described one awkward afternoon visit to her in-laws: there was a bright fire burning in the sitting-room and "Charlotte and the old lady" were reading, making conversation, and obviously waiting for something to happen. At the same time there was an atmosphere of strain: "the repressed emotions of impending departure [were] in the air":

> "Why, isn't this just lovely to see you again," exclaimed Charlotte, rising deliberately and extending her arms to Sibylla, who murmured vaguely, allowing herself to be kissed on both cheeks.
>
> "Why Sibylla," the old lady said, "I did hope I'd see you again but I thought it would not be good for you to come to London to see me." She also embraced Sibylla, who submitted to her with a better grace than to Charlotte, and even lingered a little to allow the old lady to pat her shoulders and stroke her cheek, rather like some cool graceful cat which allows one to caress it for a moment before it bounds away.[107]

But Charlotte Smith was not deceived; she had communicated her suspicions to Henry, so Vivien's habit did not come altogether as a surprise to him in 1926.[108]

Apart from bromides and "Prince Chloral," did Vivien also experiment with cocaine? There is no doubt that narcotics were easily available in the set in which she mixed. Dope was a theme of Noël Coward's 1925 play *The Vortex*. In an article headed "The Cocaine Curse—Evil Habit Spread by Night Clubs" the *Evening News* reported that the drug habit was prevalent among "young women especially of the leisured class that regards itself as Bohemian." "Forty years later, when she was dining with pop stars in Cheyne Walk, Lady Diana Cooper announced, with a perceptible degree of ennui, that in her day, post-prandial cocaine was served in salt cellars," writes Philip Hoare.[109] Tom Eliot was certainly aware of the drug and its effects, as is evident from a note in his handwriting in Vivien's writing book. He poses a provocative question: "Ah yes, Fresca, but would you have the courage to stick a hypodermic cocaine needle into yourself— would you take the risk *once*—as [illegible] did every day?" If, as suggested, Fresca in the original version of *The Waste Land* was inspired by Nancy Cunard, a member of the "Corrupt Coterie" who knew both Tom and Vivien, this may have been a rhetorical reference to her lifestyle. But it begs other questions, for there are elements of Vivien, too, in Eliot's hostile portrait of "Fresca." Did he encourage Vivien in her addiction, and did he experiment with cocaine himself? It is unlikely that Vivien used narcotics, but it is not impossible: her hyperactivity and insomnia were longstanding, but the sexually stimulating and disinhibitory qualities of cocaine may have been a factor in the events which were to follow. What *is* certain, however, is Vivien's disgust at her drug dependence, and her self-knowledge: the theme of self-destruction is a continuing one in her writing: "The things Sibylla had *got* to do!" she writes in an undated scrap of dialogue. "They often included self-destruction." No one could stop her. "I *must,*" she would say, "I am sorry, awfully sorry, but I've *got* to do it."[110]

For the first few weeks of his 1926 visit to England, Henry Eliot seems not to have sensed the bombshell which was about to fall, although he soon began to edit the version of events he sent to his mother Charlotte, whose long religious poem, "Savonarola," Eliot was dutifully publishing. Vivien came up to Cambridge on 9 March to hear the last of Tom's lectures, at which Theresa sketched Tom speaking on the nineteenth-century poets and comparing Donne to Laforgue and Corbière. Vivien looked, reported Henry, "well and cheerful," as did Tom.[111]

On another occasion, over tea at Garsington, where Henry was amazed by the insouciance of Oxonians such as Robert Gathorne-Hardy, who had a "fine shock of brown Byronic hair," Shelley-like features, and a monocle, he listened while Ottoline praised Eliot as the greatest poet of the period, but berated Vivien for being "hysterical over her health" and making Tom cancel engagements at the last minute. Ottoline's opinion was that Vivien was jealous of Tom's many friendships and recognition and was "altogether too touchy," recorded Henry. Tom nevertheless assured his brother that Vivien was now perfectly well, apart from occasional querulous moods, and said that her friendship with Theresa had had a "tonic effect" on her.[112] On their last day together in London, Henry and Theresa and Tom and Vivien went out to dinner at a hotel in Kensington and apparently had a very jolly time. The two couples danced together, and an exhilarated Vivien was in "fine humour and very nice."[113] Henry and Theresa then invited Tom and Vivien to join them in Paris and Rome on the next leg of their five-month honeymoon.

By 13 March Ottoline had learnt the identity of Vivien's supposed lover. She noted in her journal that Vivien was in love with a Mr. Haden Guest, or was using his "ardent attentions" to provoke Tom. Haden Guest was probably one of the young officers Ottoline had entertained at Garsington after the war, as the name of 2nd Lieutenant H. Guest MC, of the Queen's Own Royal West Kents, appears in her visiting book for July 1918.[114] The relationship between Vivien and Haden Guest no doubt ripened during the period of Tom's absence in Cambridge from 26 January 1926, for there is no reason to suppose that Vivien stayed long in Brighton, if indeed she ever consented to convalesce there. On the night of 13 April, however, Vivien and Tom joined Henry and Theresa on the 10:30 p.m. night express from Paris to Rome, Henry assuring his mother that the two weeks he was about to spend with his brother and Vivien in Rome would make it a regular picnic, since he would have extra time with Tom, and Vivien adored Theresa.[115] They expected to meet up with Maurice, who was also in Rome, a city well known to Charles and Rose Haigh-Wood, who often wintered there, but which Tom and Vivien had never visited.

Tom may have felt it was necessary to remove Vivien from London, hoping that a trip abroad would distract her from her admirer. At first his tactics seemed to work. In Rome, the fivesome stayed at the Pensione Fray, near the Borghese Gardens, after an expensive night at the Albergo Boston, chosen by Maurice for them because it was near the Victoria, where the Haigh-Wood parents had stayed. The *pensione* was good value at only eighty lire a day for a couple, including three meals, and the party apparently met up for merry lunches and dinners, attending a *thé dansant* in between sightseeing. They visited the English tennis club, where Suzanne Lenglen was playing, and bumped into Mary Hutchinson's brother, Jim Barnes.[116] It was during this visit to Rome that Theresa was astonished to see her brother-in-law fall on his knees before Michelangelo's *Pietà,* the first sign of his imminent conversion.[117] On 4 May Henry heard the news of the General Strike in England, and wrote that he was glad to be in Rome, although he was forced to tell Charlotte Eliot, who was missing her elder son and had been telegraphing impatiently to demand his return, that he had had to modify his plans. The holiday with Tom and Vivien had left them "behind schedule," he wrote discreetly; he and Theresa were unavoidably detained and would be two weeks late arriving in Cambridge, Mass.[118]

However, under the amicable surface, the joint holiday was not all it seemed. At some point in April, probably before Henry and Theresa moved north to Florence, Vivien decided to leave Tom—either for Haden Guest or a new lover. Richard Aldington fictionalised the episode in *Stepping Heavenward:* after the months in which

> many a time poor Adèle gazed into the mirror, clutching her hair distractedly, and whispering: "I'm going mad, I'm going mad, I'm going mad" . . . La Princesse Adèle ran away with a young man and plunged into a life of hectic dissipation in Berlin. As the sole reward for years of misery she begged Cibber to divorce her.[119]

Almost at once Vivien regretted her decision. From Rome she sent Ottoline an express letter on 16 April 1926, saying that she was "in great trouble," and did not know what to do. How she wished she could see Ottoline.[121] Vivien was then thirty-eight, and perhaps her young lover proved to be fickle. In "Mrs. Pilkington" Vivien had imagined a scene in which an older woman, a writer, is deserted by a younger man:

> A young man entered.
>
> "Hugh," cried Marion, "oh Hugh, I am so glad to see you. What are your plans for to-day? Can you take me to see the sights? It's poor fun going about without a man."
>
> "I'm very busy to-day," said Hugh dully, after a moment's hesitation . . . [He] looked at the writing-pad: "Are you writing now?" he asked, determined to stand his ground.
>
> "Writing? On a day like this? Good heavens, no; it would be a sin to stay in and write. Look at the sunshine."
>
> "I am going away," said Hugh, after a terrible silence.
>
> "Away?" she said, standing quite still, her voice dropping to its normal pitch.
>
> "Yes."
>
> "For a long time?"
>
> "Probably."
>
> "When did you decide?"
>
> He did not answer. He picked up his hat from the table where it had lain by the Russian novel and *The Mast*.
>
> "Goodbye," he said.[121]

In her distress Vivien also turned to the Sitwells. On the first or second day of the General Strike, wrote Osbert, he and Edith, in her flat in Moscow Road, Bayswater, both received

> long and incoherent letters from Vivienne, couched in almost identical terms. She wrote from Rome, where she had gone to stay, and declared that we should have inevitably have heard of the scandal to which she was referring, and in which she was involved. We should be aware, therefore, that if she returned to

Tom, it would inevitably bring disgrace upon him, of which he would never be able to rid himself. She appealed to us, in consequence, as old friends of his, to tell her what to do. Unless, she proceeded, she heard from us by cable or letter, advising her to go back to him, she would continue to remain abroad. We were on no account to let him find out that she had written to us.[122]

The Sitwells did nothing. Assuming that Tom—"the chief person to be considered"—might very probably not want her to go back to him, they decided not to answer Vivien's letters, especially as they had heard no rumours. In any event, wrote Osbert, owing to the General Strike, no letter or telegram from them could reach her. And, as far as he knew, as soon as it was possible to travel Vivien returned on her own initiative.[123] In fact Tom decided to hush the scandal up: he consigned Vivien to a sanatorium at Malmaison, outside Paris, and returned to England alone, writing to Ottoline on 24 June 1926 that he had seen the Woolfs that day and told them only that Vivien was in a sanatorium—that was therefore all Ottoline needed to know "officially." Tom would lunch the next day with Leonard, and would tell him more, as in the past he had found Leonard's experience and advice helpful; but, for various reasons (probably Virginia's tendency to gossip), it was not advisable that Virginia should know more than he had told her. He therefore asked Ottoline to keep his confidences secret. A few days later Tom returned to Paris, eventually bringing home a shamefaced and penitent Vivien.[124]

19

Mourning and "Madness"

Vivien's impetuous desertion gave Tom the opportunity for which it might seem he had been looking: a way out of torment. Certainly many men in his position might have left an adulterous wife at this juncture. Yet despite having a certain moral justification for separating from Vivien in the summer of 1926, Eliot chose to stay in the marriage. Guilt still kept him captive, and perhaps in addition marriage offered him a cloak of respectability he did not wish to lose. His protective instincts towards Vivien apparently came into play, as he turned on the Sitwells for failing to help his wife when she was in need: "Vivienne," wrote Osbert, "told Tom that when, finding herself in an agonising personal quandary she had appealed to us for counsel, neither of us had troubled to reply. As a result he was for some months angry with us, and the coolness made itself evident."[1]

Rather than leave Vivien, Eliot joined her in August 1926 at the Sanatorium de la Malmaison in Rueil, near Paris, for a joint cure: he apparently needed help for his own dependency problems. Aldous Huxley, who lunched with Eliot just before he entered the sanatorium, reported to Mary Hutchinson on 6 August: "Tom . . . looked terribly grey-green, drank no less than five gins with his meal, told me he was going to join Vivien in her Paris nursing home to break himself of his addictions to tobacco and alcohol . . ." Eliot was "eloquent about Parisian lunches with resoundingly titled duchesses," lunches which may have contributed to his need to dry out.[2] But neither Tom nor Vivien enjoyed successful rehabilitation at the hands of the French doctors, and they continued to travel Europe as medical tourists in the fashion of the time. The following summer found them in Switzerland together, subjecting themselves to a new form of treatment: *douche écossaise* (strong gushes of hot, alternating with

icy cold water, played on the naked body), which apparently benefited
Tom more than Vivien. They stayed at yet another centre offering treatment for nervous disorders, the Grand Hotel, Divonne-les-Bains, twelve
miles from Geneva in the Jura mountains.

It was there in June 1927 that Robert Sencourt, who was a fellow patient, glimpsed Vivien's forlorn figure wandering ghost-like along a
wooded trail; she was deeply depressed and suffering from extreme
insomnia, wrote Sencourt. "Her black hair was dank, her white face
blotched—owing, no doubt, to the excess of bromide she had been taking.
Her dark dress hung loosely over her frail form; her expression was both
vague and acutely sad." Sencourt, who shared Eliot's love of Dante and
Donne, became an intimate friend and an influence in Eliot's imminent
conversion to the Anglican faith, although not as significant a one as he
claimed. Sencourt's own nerves were, he confessed, "like Vivienne's . . .
often on a knife-edge," and he claimed to understand "her predicament
and Tom's . . . The strain from which my new friends were suffering was
that they no longer lived together in deepest unity."[3] Although Sencourt
professed sympathy for Vivien, it was Tom whom he found the more congenial, taking the poet away on holiday to France for a fortnight. Alone
with Sencourt, so the critic later told Frances Lindley, his editor at Harper
& Row, Tom spoke openly of his sexuality and consequent incompatibility
with Vivien: "the tragedy apparently resulting from Eliot's homosexuality
and his entering into the marriage in the hope that he would become 'normal.' "[4] Immediately after returning from France, Eliot took a final and
apparently paradoxical step, which made divorce from Vivien impossible:
he formally converted to the Anglican Church on Wednesday, 29 June
1927. In November that year he also became a naturalised English citizen.

A more potent force in Eliot's conversion than Sencourt was fellow
American, William Force Stead, Chaplain to Worcester College, Oxford,
to whom Eliot was introduced by the printer of the *Criterion,* Richard
Cobden-Sanderson, in 1923. Stead became Eliot's confidant and confessor,
familiarising him with the sermons of Lancelot Andrewes, the
seventeenth-century Bishop of Winchester, whose orderly, precise and yet
deeply felt preaching appealed to the poet more than the sermons of
Donne, with their dangerous indulgence in "sensibility" and romantic appeal to "personality." For Eliot, Andrewes represented the *via media* of the

English Church under Elizabeth I; he was "the first great preacher of the English Catholic Church."⁵ Conversion to Anglicanism was nevertheless a greater step for Eliot than might appear, for, despite having been raised as a Unitarian, he told Stead that he felt that he had been brought up as an atheist; when Stead wrote of Eliot's "return" to the Church, the poet protested in the margin of his confessor's reminiscences: "Return? I was never there before."⁶ Indeed, Eliot doubted whether his own baptism, not being in the name of the Trinity, qualified him for entry into the Anglican Church, although the position of his people in Boston Unitarianism was, he said, like that of the Borgias to the papacy. "I never communicated," he told Stead resentfully, although his parents did regularly. "They did not bother about me."⁷ Kneeling was not a part of the Unitarian tradition, but it was part of an earlier rite. In the deepest recesses of Eliot's mind lay buried memories of attending Roman Catholic mass in St. Louis with his nurse Annie, whose photograph he kept on his office mantlepiece, and it was towards this dimly remembered ritual that he reached, within the framework of an Anglo-Catholic theology.

Andrewes drew Eliot's attention to the Incarnation, the subject of every Christmas Day sermon the bishop preached before King James I between 1605 and 1624. "It is only when we have saturated ourselves in his prose, following the movement of his thought, that we find the examination of his words terminating in the ecstasy of assent," wrote Eliot. It was an intellectual rather than emotional assent and, although it would be unfair to follow Richard Aldington in asserting that Eliot discovered God as a theorem not a faith, it was Andrewes's emphasis upon sin which spoke to the Puritan in Eliot: "Besides our skin and flesh a soul we have, and it is our better part by far, that also hath need of a Saviour . . . Indeed our chief thought and care would be . . . how to escape the wrath, how to be saved from the destruction to come, whither our sins will certainly bring us. Sin it is will destroy us all."⁸ Andrewes's influence upon Eliot is underlined by the "flashing phrases" with which he supplied his disciple: the "cold coming" of "Journey of the Magi," "Christ the tiger" of "Gerontion," and the pious hope that he would not "turn again" of *Ash Wednesday.*⁹

Middleton Murry foretold Eliot's conversion the year before it took place, to the poet's annoyance. "It might conceivably be done, by an act of violence, by joining the Catholic Church," wrote Murry: "To be proved," was Eliot's terse comment on Murry's draft text.[10] But Eliot's conversion had a long history: he had experienced visionary moments earlier in his life, in particular at Marlow, while composing "Whispers of Immortality" and again at Périgueux on holiday in August 1919 with Ezra Pound. "This sense of dispossession by the dead I have known twice, at Marlow and at Périgueux," he told Stead. Although he did not consider himself a true Christian, a reading of Charlotte Eliot's "Savonarola," for which Eliot was writing the introduction in 1926, demonstrates an emphasis on bloody martyrdom which left its mark on her son. "Priests and prophets, saints and sages/Martyred in successive ages," the subjects of Charlotte's didactic and rejected poetry, began to assume a similar dominance in Eliot's poetry and drama.[11]

Stead remembered the day in 1927 when he and Eliot had been taking tea in London: "When I was leaving he said, after a moment's hesitation: 'By the way, there is something you might do for me.' He paused with a suggestion of shyness. After a few days he wrote to me saying he would like to know how he could be 'confirmed into the Church of England.' "[12] That February Eliot had begged Stead to keep his intentions secret, anticipating the outrage of Bloomsbury. He had written on 7 February that he did not want any publicity or notoriety: "I *hate* spectacular conversions."[13] Stead made secrecy a point of honour. For several months Eliot attended communion, sometimes at Hickleton Church, where he worshipped with Lord Halifax, to whom Sencourt had introduced him, "in a form which only an expert could have detected was other than the Roman Catholic mass, and where the building was exactly arranged with lights, lamps, pictures, images and the redolence of incense so as to have what one could only call a Catholic atmosphere."[14] At last the moment came when Stead summoned from Oxford Canon B. Streeter, Fellow of Queen's College, and Vere Somerset, history tutor and Fellow of Worcester, to act as Eliot's godfathers at Finstock Church, in the Cotswolds. "It seemed odd to have such a large though infant Christian at the baptismal font," recalled Stead. "So, to avoid embarrassment, we locked the front door of the little parish church."[15] Stead himself baptised Eliot, and the next morning the poet was confirmed privately at the Palace of Cuddesdon by the Bishop of Oxford.

Vivien had little sympathy for Tom's position; she resented the influence of Anglo-Catholic priests over her husband, rightly construing the veiled misogyny of their counsel as inimical to her interests. Bloomsbury was as shocked as Tom had anticipated: "If only he had become a Dancing Dervish, an alchemist or an adept in Black Magic, he would have had his followers, and the cult looked upon as interesting—or amusing," wrote Stead. "But for the leaders of the 'Moderns' to become a Christian—that was beyond the pale. It was not amusing." Stead was accused of having "corrupted" Eliot.[16] Virginia Woolf's horrified reaction was typical: she had a "most shameful and distressing" interview with "poor dear Tom Eliot, who may be called dead to us all from this day forward," she confided to Vanessa Bell. "He has become an Anglo-Catholic, believes in God and immortality, and goes to church . . . A corpse would seem to me more credible than he is. I mean, there's something obscene in a living person sitting by the fire and believing in God."[17]

Eliot's conversion has been portrayed as the culmination of a long spiritual journey, whose ending might have come sooner had he not "turned aside" from his mission to marry Vivien. She, like Ezra Pound, is thus viewed as an aberration and interruption, an obstacle to his mystical quest: "Each distracted Eliot from his saint's dream," writes Lyndall Gordon,[18] who believes that Eliot's first "memory of bliss" can be traced to his unpublished poem "Silence," written in 1910.[19] At Harvard Eliot had made extensive notes on the saints and mystics, St. Thomas Aquinas, Dame Julian of Norwich, St. Bernard, and the sixteenth-century Spanish mystics, St. Ignatius, St. Theresa and St. John of the Cross; the latter was the subject of the long poem, tentatively entitled "Descent from the Cross," that Eliot began drafting in Marburg in 1914, in which he envisaged attending a masquerade in his underwear. It was to St. John that Murry now compared Eliot, a parallel the poet angrily rejected: "What St. John means by the 'dark night' and what Mr. Murry means by my 'dark night' are entirely different things."[20] Murry's implication was that Eliot shared the alleged homosexuality of St. John.[21] And, despite Eliot's denials, St. John *did* have a special meaning for him: as the blasphemous verse written in Eliot's handwriting in Vivien's notebook suggests with its reference to Bloomsbury perversions.[22]

In Gordon's hagiographic reading of *The Waste Land,* Pound is the culprit responsible for editing "the saint's dream" out of the poem, and Vivien the prima donna who distracted the "would-be saint" from his

Julian Morrell, Vivien and Mark Gertler at Garsington. On this occasion Vivien
and Gertler annoyed Ottoline, who suspected them of gossiping about their hostess.

Vivien in the Eliots' Paddington flat. In the foreground is the Corona typewriter on which she took dictation from Tom and Bertie.

Mary Hutchinson, confidante of both Tom and Vivien, in a portrait by Vanessa Bell, 1915.

Tom and Vivien in Sussex in 1919. They rented cottages in Bosham and Old Fishbourne.

Vivien with Sydney Schiff, the novelist Stephen Hudson, at Eastbourne, 1919.

T. S. Eliot, his mother and favourite sister, Marian, on their visit to England in 1921, which precipitated his breakdown.

Eliot in Lausanne, 1922, where he received treatment from the psychiatrist Dr. Roger Vittoz.

Vivien, Tom, her sister-in-law Ahmé Hoagland Haigh-Wood and Maurice, Italy, 1930.

(*right*) No longer bank clerk but
gentleman publisher at Faber & Gwyer;
Tom's relief is evident in this photograph
taken by his brother, Henry, in 1926.

(*below*) Her writing career in ruins,
Vivienne's distress showed itself in
anorexia and drug dependence. In the
garden at 57 Chester Terrace, SW1,
June 1928.

(*right*) September 1932. Vivienne, a wraith-like figure in white, on her last visit with Tom to Virginia Woolf at Monk's House, just before he left for America.

(*below left*) William Leonard Janes (1855–1939), ex-policeman and servant of the Eliots, at Chester Terrace, 1929.

(*below right*) Maurice Haigh-Wood and T. S. Eliot at the races. Both men were trustees of the Haigh-Wood estate.

Léonide Massine, principal dancer of the Ballets Russes and intimate of Eliot.

Jekyll and Hyde: double-faced portrait of T. S. Eliot by Patrick Heron, 1947, the year of Vivienne's death.

T. S. Eliot and Sir Alec Guinness, who played the psychiatrist, Sir Henry Harcourt-Reilly, in *The Cocktail Party*.

Mary Trevelyan, Eliot's "guardian" for twenty years until his second marriage in 1957.

The last photograph: Vivienne Eliot wearing a suit by Philips et Gaston for her presentation to the Prince of Wales at Londonderry House in October 1934.

search for faith in the years immediately afterwards.[23] Gordon argues that Eliot was circling "on the edge of conversion" in 1914, was already "bold convert, martyr or saint" and, but for his unwise marriage to Vivien, might have made a religious commitment at that point. But such an interpretation ignores Eliot's own powerful ambitions and inclinations: he was still under the influence of Henri Bergson, whose message was to abandon rational thought and plunge into the "flow of immediate experience" in order to arrive at the Absolute.[24] It was an injunction on which the shy intellectual had acted, first in the ecstatic union of souls he experienced with Jean Verdenal, and secondly in his ill-fated attempt to break out of the prison of self through marriage. It was a necessary road for Eliot to take in pursuit of both artistic and personal development, as he unconsciously realised when he chose to marry Vivien, a woman who worshipped him both as a man and as a poet, and was prepared to commit herself totally to furthering his career.

But by 1927 the thirty-nine-year-old poet no longer needed Vivien as a helpmate, as from September 1926 he was comfortably established at Faber & Gwyer. The fervent anguish of *The Waste Land* had given way to the paralysis of "The Hollow Men," as Eliot worked out, through many versions, how to transform the pain of separation and loss of a beloved object, who had crossed into "death's other Kingdom," into something meangingful and holy.[25] "Lost/Violent souls," like the poet himself, have become "the hollow men/The stuffed men," men of straw like a scarecrow or guy, husks empty of feeling, who exist in a dead "cactus land." "Eyes that last I saw in tears" have faded into memory ("There are no eyes here/In this valley of dying stars"), and he can only end with a prayer, "For Thine is the Kingdom."[26] Yet it was a difficult, and by no means inevitable path from the "broken jaw of our lost kingdoms" to belief; this was a point that Eliot made forcibly. His intention was, like his master Dante, to begin a new life. "INCIPIT VITA NUOVA," capitalised by Eliot in his 1929 essay in book form, signifies the importance of that acceptance which, he argued, precedes faith: "This *acceptance* is more important than anything that can be called belief. There is almost a definite moment of acceptance at which the New Life begins."[27]

Nor did Eliot's progress towards conversion appear to the poet himself to have been destined from adolescence. He acknowledged that the personal circumstances of his life were the trigger for that conversion. The primary catalyst was Vivien's affair with Russell, from which, argues Schuchard, Eliot created his own myth not only of double sexual betrayal, but also of psychological retribution and moral regeneration. Undoubtedly Eliot knew of Vivien's adultery, and was deeply hurt by it; it was the background to the tone of bitter disillusionment which runs through "Whispers of Immortality" (1918), in which Eliot wrote in a cancelled passage of the seduction of "wives of men." What angel hath cuckwoled thee?" enquired a curious Pound, after seeing the manuscript, adding his own jottings about "copulationion [sic] in carnal form/—et les anges."[28]

Russell became the greatest of Eliot's "lost illusions," as he acknowledged in a letter to Ottoline in 1933, remembering that he had at first admired Russell so much, until his tutor seduced Vivien: "He has done Evil, without being big enough or conscious enough to Be Evil," wrote Eliot, owning that the "spectacle of Bertie" had made a major contribution to his conversion. Grimly he listed the ways in which Russell had been a bad influence upon Vivien: he had excited her mentally, made her read pacifist books and become "a kind of pacifist"; he had flattered her in order to gain influence over her, although, claimed Eliot, "unfortunately" she found him unattractive.[29] Seven years after his conversion, in 1933, the name of Russell still aroused fury in Eliot, whom he blamed, perhaps more than Russell deserved, for the failure of the marriage; in his first Clark lecture on the poet John Donne, Eliot had praised the "fusion and identification of *souls* in sexual love," as expressed by Donne,[30] and the delights of the flesh captured by Sappho and Catullus, contrasting them bleakly with the horrors of a "happy marriage." Marriage is "one sort of bankruptcy," he told his audience, and if you seek the Absolute in marriage, adultery or debauchery, you are seeking it in the wrong place.[31] In an allusion to Vivien's relationship with Haden Guest, he remarked on Donne's preoccupation with "coffins, the day of judgement, sin, and even, perhaps, with jealous husbands!"[32]

The timing of Eliot's conversion also underlines the importance of Russell's influence. By 1927 Russell had become bitterly anti-Christian, a propagandist for atheism whose prominence infuriated Eliot. He seemed to flaunt his disregard for morals in Eliot's face, marrying his second wife

Dora when she was eight months pregnant. The reissue of *Principia Mathematica* in 1925 had consolidated the future earl's status as a mathematician and philosopher, and when his lecture "Why I Am Not a Christian," addressed to the National Secular Society at Battersea Town Hall, provoked outrage, Eliot was one of the first to attack its author and defend the Christian position: his review of August 1927 condemned Russell's text as a "pathetic document."[33] It was simply a "piece of childish folly," he wrote to Russell: "Why don't you stick to mathematics?" All the arguments Russell advanced had been familiar to him by the age of six, said Eliot, for he had been brought up an atheist, while Russell had evidently been brought up, and remained, an evangelical.[34] Unsurprisingly, when Eliot came to write *Murder in the Cathedral,* Russell was his chosen, diabolic model for First Tempter, the representative of atheism who attempts to turn St. Thomas from his martyrdom.[35]

Even though Eliot had been wounded by Vivien's infidelity, he was himself no solitary saint. The telling juxtaposition of epigraphs to his Clark lectures reveals his own struggle between spirituality and violent sensuality: on the one hand, the dedication to the Virgin, the Madonna who was "the end and aim of my love" ("Madonna, lo fine del mio amore fu già il saluto di questa donna, forse de cui voi intendete"), on the other a line from a music-hall song, "I want someone to treat me rough,/Give me a cabman."[36] Lines from Part II of "Ash Wednesday," his "conversion" poem, lines first published in 1927 as "Salutation," voice a prayer to the "Lady of silences" for release from his private hell: "Terminate torment/Of love unsatisfied/The greater torment/Of love satisfied."[37] He dedicated "Ash Wednesday" "To My Wife," for Vivien alone shared Tom's secrets. The poem is one of regret, even apology, for their joint past, of his need to escape a woman who had become "the devil of the stairs who wears/The deceitful face of hope and despair."

Nor did Eliot construct a simple myth of sexual betrayal by Vivien and Russell, as Schuchard argues; in his heart the poet knew, with a degree of self-loathing, why Vivien had run into Russell's arms. His own failure to consummate the marriage satisfactorily had created a situation in which he had colluded, in which Vivien had become the victim of her lover and her husband in an arrangement which profited both men at the expense of the woman. Sencourt has remarked on Eliot's fascination with *Bubu de Montparnasse,* the story of the pimp and the girl harlot. Why had Eliot continued for thirty-five years to be obsessed with "the miasma of sexual sin," he demanded of John Hayward after the poet's death.[38] The answer lay in Tom and Vivien's own story, for as the years passed Eliot became convinced that his wife was no better than a harlot, a polluting presence from whom he must turn away to be cleansed through faith.[39] At the heart of his hatred lay his own guilt and denial of the role he had consented to play (one as morally "unpleasant" as the adulterous Vivien's) in the three-handed drama of himself, Bertie and Vivien. For if Vivien had been "whore," who had been the pimp?

Eliot's powerful feeling that Vivien, female succuba or demon, deserved violent punishment, found an outlet in *Sweeney Agonistes,* first published in the 1926 *Criterion.* One of the epigraphs the playwright chose, St. John of the Cross's prayer for the soul to be divested "of the love of created beings" in order to achieve divine union, sits uneasily with Eliot's obsession with murder and retribution;[40] but he had long been interested in the "thriller" element in Elizabethan and Jacobean drama. His study of Kyd's *Spanish Tragedy* (forerunner of Shakespeare's *Hamlet)* had influenced the composition of *The Waste Land,* among whose last lines Eliot placed the sub-title of Kyd's play, "Hieronimo is mad againe." Kyd's hero, Hieronimo, has undergone a psychological change: he is mad with grief for his murdered son, and his passion for vengeance, which the audience may have felt was justified, shapes the play.[41] Eliot, too, felt he had undergone a psychological change through his marriage to Vivien. "Murder, help Hieronimo," cries a woman in a 1615 woodcut advertising the *Spanish Tragedy.* "Stop her mouth," is the stark response from the figure of Murder on the handbill, something Eliot longed to do to the wife who berated him for never speaking to her.

Just as Hieronimo's revenge quest was Kyd's central theme, so was it Eliot's in *Sweeney Agonistes.* Sweeney, like Hieronimo, can be viewed as a savage priest *(hieros* means holy or divine) presiding over an ancient fertility ritual, symbolising death and resurrection, a ritual similar to the virgin sacrifice in *The Rite of Spring,* another fertile source of inspiration to Eliot. In *Sweeney Agonistes* the hero also presides over a violent if farcical ritual,

in which he cooks eggs in a chafing dish and serves them to the two prostitutes, Doris and Dusty, who were based on Vivien and Lucy Thayer.
Doris's fate is to be killed and cooked by Sweeney in a "nice little, white little, missionary stew"; Mrs. Porter, the house's Madam, is shot and resurrected.[42]

Murder was an act which seems to have haunted Eliot's nightmares,
born of the fear that one day he might lose control and physically harm, or
even kill, Vivien. An early handwritten draft of *Sweeney Agonistes* shows
the play's gestation in the poet's "Terrors of the Night."[43] As an epigraph in
an early typescript he misquoted lines of Brutus the murderer from *Julius
Caesar:*

Between the acting of a dreadful thing
And the first motion, all the interim is
Like a miasma, or hideous dream.[44]

It was "the *feeling* of a haunted conscience" which dominated the "strange
little piece" for Desmond MacCarthy, when he reviewed a production of
Sweeney by ex-Diaghilev dancer Rupert Doone's Group Theatre at 9
Newport Street in 1934. Eliot seemed to have assented to this interpretation by quoting, in the double epigraph, a passage by Orestes in which he
speaks of the Furies which are pursuing him: "You don't see them, you
don't—but *I* see them: they are hunting me down . . ." "In this case the
Furies of retribution are the police, as well as the lashes of remorse . . ."
wrote MacCarthy.[45] "And you wait for a knock and the turning of a
lock/For you know the hangman's waiting for you," wrote Eliot: "And
perhaps you're alive/And perhaps you're dead/Hoo ha ha/Hoo ha ha/Hoo
KNOCK KNOCK KNOCK."[46]

Later Eliot confessed his night terrors to Mary Trevelyan, when he
would wake, sweating, imagining that he had completed the wished-for
ritual of Vivien's extinction, and was about to meet his punishment. He
dreamt "that he was about to be hung and was standing in a grey holland
overall, with a rope round his neck." Auditory hallucinations also troubled
Eliot, who imagined that he heard voices, male and female, speaking to
him at night: "I sometimes wonder if I am schizophrenic," he told Mary in

1950.[47] Two years later, the "voices" were still keeping him awake, and he was trying to record a phrase or two to show her.

Sweeney Agonistes has a visceral intensity which puts it beyond any dream sequence and demonstrates that, as Eliot wrote of the Elizabethan dramatists, "actual life is always the material."[48] It was the horror of Eliot's life with Vivien which motivated him to write *Sweeney* and, as Vivien and Lucy, alias "Sibylla" and "Felise" or, in Tom's incarnation, Doris and Dusty, entertain their clients, including Canadian officers—Vivien had a weakness for officers—and cut the cards, they turn up the King of Spades; and the King of Spades is the murderer, is Sweeney, say the girls. In an early version of the play Sweeney, the only actor unmasked, sits drinking and arguing with Mrs. Porter. In the Group Theatre production he was dressed as a young clerk. Sullen and silent, Sweeney's mood becomes uglier as he drinks: the two girls become hysterical; he pulls out a gun, it gives a "dull roar"; the girls shriek. Mrs. Porter falls to the floor. She is dead. Or is she? "Life is death, death is life." In the second scene Sweeney addresses Doris, who has drawn the two of spades, the coffin. His speech is half sinister soliloquy, half confession, perhaps a threat to her:[49] "Any man might do a girl in/Any man has to, needs to, wants to/Once in a lifetime, do a girl in./Well he kept her there in a bath . . ." The verse is "popular," with its syncopated beat, its music-hall jollity, but the message is chilling. The black jazz drummers, "SWARTS AS TAMBO, SNOW AS BONES" join in: these fellows all get pinched in the end, avers Swarts. Snow disagrees. "What about them bones on Epsom Heath?" "A woman runs a terrible risk," murmurs Doris.[50]

The woman's refrain is brushed aside. "Let Mr. Sweeney continue his story," says Bones Snow. "This one didn't get pinched in the end," says Sweeney knowingly. He knew a murderer who'd done a girl in and got away with it. "This went on for a couple of months/Nobody came/And nobody went/But he took in the milk and paid the rent." "I'd give him a drink and cheer him up." "Cheer him up?" asks Doris. "Cheer him up?" repeats Dusty incredulously; the atmosphere of menace is compounded by the techniques of Greek and Roman drama: masks, a chorus and, from the music hall, the jazz drumming which heightens the incantatory rhythm of the dialogue as Doris's fear mounts. "He didn't know if he was alive/And the girl was dead/He didn't know if the girl was alive/And he was dead."

Behind Sweeney's threats lies the desperation of non-communication: "I gotta use words when I talk to you/But if you understand or if you don't/That's nothing to me and nothing to you." Eliot's most original piece of theatre is, for this reason, violently authentic in its *exposé* of marital disconnectedness. "Birth, and copulation, and death," says Sweeney. "I'd be bored," replies Doris. "You'd be bored," repeats Sweeney.[51]

Originally, Eliot intended a three-minute ballet to be performed between the two scenes. The drumbeat he planned to accompany it, like the dance itself, was modelled on Diaghilev's ballet and was typical of the 1920s: Lifar danced Icarus to an unaccompanied drum.[52] Massine was also much in Eliot's mind as he began working on *Sweeney,* soon after meeting the dancer on 22 June 1922. Memories of *Le Tricorne,* choreographed by Massine to Manuel de Falla's syncopated music, a ballet in which Massine danced the Miller "like one possessed" in his own version of the Spanish folk dance the *farucca,* was one of the strands which led the poet to try to create something as innovative in drama as that which Diaghilev had created in ballet by marrying music hall to classical dance. "What is needed in art is a simplification of current life into something rich and strange, wrote Eliot."[53] From 1923 onwards, as he struggled to match in his text Massine's ritualistic and impersonal control of popular contemporary forms, he compared with longing the grace and beauty of the Ballets Russes to the sordid daily world he inhabited with Vivien.

Yet another strand from daily life fed into *Sweeney.* Eliot, like a large section of the British public, had followed with fascination the fortunes of Dr. H. H. Crippen (who fell in love with his secretary, Ethel le Neve, poisoned his wife and dissected her body) and he made notes on the case when Crippen was hanged at Pentonville in 1910. Virginia Woolf sat next to Eliot at the Group Theatre's masked performance of *Sweeney Agonistes* in November 1934, and recorded in her diary: "Certainly he conveys an emotion, an atmosphere . . . something peculiar to himself; sordid, emotional intense—a kind of Crippen in a mask."[54] Perhaps the delight in police court horrors was something the Eliots shared, for Maurice recalled that at a fancy-dress party at the Schiffs, Eliot dressed as Crippen, Vivien as Ethel le Neve, disguised as a cabin boy as she was when the pair fled England on a transatlantic liner.[55] It was a disguise Eliot enjoyed: he was still wearing it in 1939, six months after Vivien was committed to Northumberland

House, when he attended Andrian Stephen's fancy-dress party in the costume of Crippen the poisoner.[56]

Vivien's failed romance in Rome in 1926 precipitated a serious depression and she had thoughts of suicide. A snatch of dialogue in her notebook, in which "Sibylla" pleads in vain with her lover not to give her up, hints at her misery:

> Sibylla went into Mike's little narrow bedroom, & shut the door after her.
>
> "Look here, Mike," she said, and made a dash at his dressing gown pocket to extract a handkerchief, but finding none, she looked round and saw it lying on the dressing table. Turning, she seized the handkerchief and blew her nose. "Look here," she said . . . hurriedly and furtively, "Will you ring me up at 3—at 3 o'clock. See? Will you? Because, I must tell you, I do still come over awfully—well awfully depressed—So—all the time."
>
> "Yes I know," said Mike.
>
> "It's my temperature; it's high—."
>
> "Yes," said Mike gloatingly, "I *knew* it was high to-night."
>
> "Damn you," thought Sibylla and she said, "Yes, yes, it's high all the time and it's a great strain to me to have people to dinner. I don't know—I might . . ."[57]

Sexual rebellion had brought Vivien no happiness, for none of her "admirers" could take Tom's place. Like Ibsen's Nora she had attempted to break out of her doll's house and forge a new role for herself; like Nora, she had impetuously left her husband, only to bitterly regret her decision and return, humiliated. To carve out an existence as a "modern" woman was no easy task. A woman might write, like the poet Hilda Doolittle, "I believe in women doing what they like. I believe in the modern woman." Living out the dream of freedom was a different reality; even H. D. was forced to acknowledge that "the modern woman" had no place on the map, and her quest for experience was "a very thin line to toe, a very, very frail wire to do a tight rope act on." In H. D.'s case only therapy with Freud restored her confidence in herself as a gifted woman, and taught her to exist in that borderline country in which old values have been discarded and new ones have yet to be learnt.[58] But for Vivien there was no Freud to heal her, only an estranged husband who imagined he had some skill as an analyst. And in March 1927 a further blow struck Vivien: she lost her most enduring male support—her father.

Charles Haigh-Wood was terminally ill with lung cancer in early 1927 and died on 25 March, aged seventy-two, at the Warrior House Hotel, St. Leonard's, Sussex, surrounded by his family: his wife Rose, sister-in-law Lillia Symes, Vivien, Tom, Maurice and Lucy Thayer, with whom Vivien was now reconciled, were all present. Vivien grieved deeply for her father, and her memories often drew her back to St. Leonard's.[59] Possibly her mourning became pathological in its intensity. Later, in 1932, she and Tom stayed at the Warrior House Hotel, and Vivien returned there once more in the autumn of 1934, the year after Eliot left her. On 15 September 1934 she drove out into the countryside in her Morris Minor with Polly, her Yorkshire terrier, on a blackberrying expedition. Afterwards she recalled how

> enjoying some of the richest of the English landscape . . . I longed that Father could have seen it with me, and I thought a great deal about him, and how he died here, in Sussex, and his dying eyes lingered on the sea & the sunset, sitting up in bed in room no. 9, poor, poor darling Father. I remember how he always begged me to stroke his head, and how I *wish* I had done that for him much more often and more patiently, and how I wish there was still *someone* who needs the touch of my hands, which are the best part of me. But there is only Polly.[60]

The following spring, on 24 March 1935, Vivien returned to her father's grave to plant two shamrock roots.[61] *"Full* of memories, Father & Tom, Tom & Father—those two of my heart," she wrote. *"The sea is so much in it all."*[62]

Bereft of her father, who had understood her as her mother never did, the final severance of the tie with Bertrand Russell hit Vivien hard. At the height of their affair, Russell had given Vivien some of the family jewels, as well as other small articles. "Russell gave Vivie dresses, then Russell family heirlooms," remembered Maurice: "Russell's family asked Vivie for a ring back," and so "Mummy made her give back the jewels."[63] Vivien herself remembered resentfully in her diary for April 1936 that her mother had never offered her "a stick of furniture," but Bertie Russell had given her one or two fenders,

> and of course all his jewellery which I returned but he made me keep one valuable pendant which has been stolen. I wish I could get back the pendant which BR made me keep. It was one large pearl in a dark blue enamel setting and a thick solid gold chain.[64]

In fact the truth was rather different, as Vivien had reluctantly confessed in a letter to Russell in 1926. Perhaps therapeutic sessions with her doctors abroad enabled her to confront her past and triggered the remorse which caused her to reopen correspondence with Russell on 6 December:

> I shall have to ask you to believe me that I became conscious, during the time I was in France, that I had stolen a part of this jewellery from you. Since getting back to England I have not had the courage to come to your house & give it to you, which is what I ought to do. So now I am asking Tom to hand you the packet, & as it is nothing to do with him, I hope you will not speak of it together, it wd be very painful to him. I am not showing this letter to him, or anyone. I shall not ask you to forgive me because you cannot.

Vivien had given one ring with turquoises in it to her maid, Ellen Kelland, she explained. The rest she returned, apart from the pearl pendant, which she may have kept back purposely or which Russell may have allowed her to keep.[65]

Vivien also raised the matter of the shares which Russell had transferred to Eliot during the war, and from which he was still drawing an income which he allowed Vivien to spend. Vivien was urging Tom, now well remunerated at Faber & Gwyer, to return them to Bertie, who had a wife and two young children to support: John Conrad, born in November 1921, and, two years later, Katharine Jane.[66] Russell had been forced to turn to popular journalism in order to fund the purchase of a house in Sydney Street, Chelsea, and was certainly in greater need of the income from the debentures than the Eliots, but, said Vivien, due to them "being in Tom's name, and our not yet having been able to agree about it, I must leave it till he sees it as I do. I shd have to get him to do the transferring." She added a final, sad sentence: "You see I have not had the courage to live alone."[67]

Eventually Eliot gave in to the promptings of Vivien's "entirely morbid conscience," as he described it.[68] On 16 May 1927, he wrote to tell Russell that he would shortly be transferring to him the debentures—£3,500 of Penty & Son Ltd. of Newbury. "There is no reason for you to demur." However, Eliot requested from Russell a letter exempting him from tax on the "gift" in the event of his death within three years, as he did not want his affairs "buggered up" if he should die suddenly.[69] A few weeks later Eliot wrote again to Russell, explaining that Vivien's father had died and she would shortly come into property which yielded income almost equal to that she was surrendering. He himself, he added, was influenced in his decision to return the debentures by the fact that Russell had heirs, and "I have, and shall have, none."[70]

This surprisingly personal remark, reminiscent of Eliot's almost filial relationship to Russell in the past, touched on a source of great pain to both Eliots—their childlessness. Much later, on 29 November 1939, Eliot confessed to his companion John Hayward that he had never loved a woman or enjoyed sexual intercourse with her: "I never lay with a woman I liked, loved, or even felt any strong physical attraction to." He no longer even regretted this lack of experience, he wrote, although for years he continued to "feel acutely the desire for progeny, which was very acute once."[71] Certainly the desire for children was a constant in Vivien and Tom's relationship at the time when Eliot was writing *The Waste Land*: "What you get married for if you don't want to have children?," a line added by Vivien to the manuscript was, according to Maurice, his own response to Rose Haigh-Wood's argument that Vivien should never have children, in case her "moral insanity" was hereditary.[72] The reproach implicit in "not marrying if you do not want to have children" is also that Eliot did not wish to make love to her, and may account for the continuing motif of lost or even murdered children in Eliot's work.[73] Sometimes children laughing in an apple tree, sometimes the "children at the gate/Who will not go away and cannot pray" of "Ash Wednesday," the anguished cry "O my daughter" of "Marina," or the theme of the madness of Hieronimo at the murder of his children, all point to the "acute desire" Eliot and Vivien had for a baby.[74] The emphasis on death and birth on the "cannibal isle" in *Sweeney Agonistes,* or in "Journey of the Magi," which took as its theme the birth of the Christ child, has been interpreted as an allusion to Eliot's spiritual rebirth. But it had its roots, too, in the longing of a childless couple for a baby of their own, which must have grown more powerful over the years and which was highlighted for Vivien by the presence of Russell, nearby in Chelsea, whose own wish for children was at last gratified. "Was Bertie there? Do you see Bertie much now?" she wrote wistfully to Ottoline in January 1928 from the Malmaison sanatorium.[75]

In the years when the Eliots lived at 57 Chester Terrace, Belgravia, Vivien turned for consolation to her pets, her garden and her servants. Her Yorkshire terriers, Peter and Polly Louise, became substitute children. The faded brown photograph album, inscribed "T. S. and V. H. Eliot 1924–1929," into which Vivien pasted her carefully captioned snaps, shows "Aunt Vivienne with Peter," the dog held tight in her arms, or "Uncle Tom" training Polly, although Eliot generally reserved his affections for Georgie the cat, shown on his lap in his study. The album demonstrates the new care with which Vivien began dating and signing the record of her life with Eliot, returning at this time to the original spelling of her name, "Vivienne." Her home became important to her as she withdrew into it, defeated: "Vivienne with household gods," she has titled a photograph of herself beside her well-polished sideboard on which stands gleaming silver, on the wall beside an oil painting of an ancestor.[76] In the morning room a meal is laid on a white linen tablecloth, a bottle of beer prominent on the table: Vivienne's meticulous account books from December 1927 to April 1932, which record how she ran the house on the £6 a week housekeeping money Tom gave her, often struggling to repay him the small sums he grudgingly loaned her when she overspent ("Lent by T.S.E. 1/9d"), contain several entries for beer, for instance: "V.H.E. for 2 b. beer." "Returned to T.S.E. 3s." writes a contrite Vivienne, for her husband did not approve of her regular spending on taxis, cigarettes, bridge debts, "chemises de Vaneck" (her favourite dress designer), grey silk stockings, impulsive purchases of flowers, lilies or violets for Edith Sitwell, or roses for her mother. Nor did the Vogue patterns she bought for dressmaking, plants for the window-boxes, doctors' and chemists' bills, and the continual expenditure on sanitary towels please him.[77] Vivienne tried to make amends, buying Tom orange writing paper and envelopes, sealing wax and blotting paper for his birthday in 1928; but Maurice, with whom Vivienne occasionally lunched, noted that: "Tom never spent money; Vivie lived in the shops, especially Vanecks."[78]

Behind the façade of domesticity, Vivienne and Tom now led separate lives. In July 1928, Theodora Eliot Smith, "Our neice" [sic], who stayed with the Eliots in Chester Terrace,[79] photographed the large bedroom with a writing table used by Tom, and the small bedroom with a narrow bed on which sat Vivienne, alone.[80] Omnipresent in the household was the handyman and ex-policeman W. L. Janes, a mysterious figure who was very close to Tom. Rose Haigh-Wood never liked Janes, remembered Maurice: he reminded her of a lavatory attendant. Later Tom told Mary Trevelyan that Janes had been a "great friend," who used to tell him stories of Disraeli; when Janes was ill in hospital Tom used to visit him and take him champagne. "If I ever write my reminiscences, which I shan't," he said, "Janes would have a great part in them."[81] Tom meanwhile continued to rent the flat at Burleigh Mansions, despite having an office at Faber, and Vivienne continued to arrange for it to be cleaned. The house in Chester Terrace was one of whispers and secrets, for all Vivienne's attempts to keep up appearances. Old friends began to avoid the Eliots. Surreal dinner parties, such as that given by the Eliots in the summer of 1927 to celebrate Vivienne's recovery after her course of treatment at the sanatorium, gave rise to rumour and gossip, as Osbert Sitwell recalled.

Shown into the drawing-room, Osbert found that he was not the first arrival: Geoffrey Faber, James Joyce and his wife Nora were already talking to their host:

> A few minutes later, Vivienne entered in a flustered manner, on her lips a rather twisted smile, which was opposed by the consternation and suspicion in her greenish eyes. Not quite certain what tone was suitable to adopt, I opened by remarking to her with heartiness, "It *is* splendid to see you again, Vivienne."

Looking me straight in the eye, she replied slowly, "I don't know about *splendid:* but it is strange, very *strange."*

Thereupon we went in to dinner. The table seemed set for a gala: for by each plate was set a bouquet or a large buttonhole, of sweet-peas, struggling through a white misty rash of gypsophila. The food was good, and accompanied by excellent hock . . .

As for our hostess, she was in high spirits, but not in a good mood. She showed an inclination to "pick on" Tom across the table, challenging his every statement, and at the same time insinuating that the argumentativeness was his; that he was trying to create a scene. All this he parried with his calm and caution, remaining patient and precise, with on his face an expression of wary good nature . . .

Her name was usually pronounced *Vivien:* but if he were irritated by her, we would notice that he would call her *Vivienne* . . . As dinner went on, things became a little better: and she began to leave him alone, and instead to talk to me about him. He was being very *difficult,* she averred; only one human being seemed now to interest him, an ex-policeman of about seventy years of age, who acted as odd-job man, and was a habitual drunkard . . .

After dinner, Tom was talking to Nora Joyce and Enid Faber in the drawing-room, but looking "as if he were keeping an eye open for a squall." Vivienne, who had been complaining that Tom would never give his guests enough to drink, found another bottle of hock for Osbert and her other guests, and left them at the table. "A door in the further wall of the passage suddenly swung back," wrote Osbert, "and out stepped the figure of an elderly man in a dark suit with white hair and moustache, blinking as if he had suddenly emerged from darkness into a strong light, and—rather singularly inside a house—crowned with a bowler hat."

My attention had been focused on him from the moment he appeared, as it were, out of his trap-door, since I had at once identified this rather tortoise-like individual as the ex-policeman of whom Vivienne had spoken. Silence now fell on the company.

The newcomer stopped in the doorway opposite us for a moment, and made to each of the three of us—Joyce, Faber and me— a sweeping bow with his hat, saying as he did so, "Goo' night, Mr. Eliot!" "Goo' night, Mr. Eliot!" "Goo' night, Mr. Eliot!," and then, while the last syllable was still on his lips, and without giving himself time to discover the failure of his ingenious method of insurance by address in triplicate against the possible charge of inebriation, he turned and went on his way humming to himself. The incident possessed atmosphere, and I was delighted by it, as was Vivienne when we returned to the drawing-room and told her about it. For once Tom refused to see the joke, looking rather as I imagine Dante would have looked had someone ventured to make a stupid pun in his presence.

Soon the moment came for the party to break up. Mrs. Faber rose . . . and observed, "It's been lovely, Vivienne."

Vivienne looked at her mournfully, and replied, "Well, it may have been lovely for you, but it's been dreadful for me."

Mrs. Faber, rather at a loss, rapped out at her, "Nonsense, Vivienne, you know it's been a triumph."

Vivienne repeated in desolate tones, "A triumph . . . Look at Tom's face!"[82]

Even Ottoline, most faithful of hostesses, who had asked Tom and Vivienne to Garsington after they returned from France in 1926, withdrew her invitation after a difficult visit to Vivienne at Chester Terrace. Nevertheless, both Vivienne and Tom depended on Ottoline, competing for her attention as they rehashed the problems of the marriage, both demanding her support for their version of events. Ottoline called regularly on Vivienne: on one occasion, in November 1926, Vivienne felt that "some sort of subconscious hope" that she had not known she still had, went out of her as Ottoline talked. She apologised for being "dull and unpleasant," for she did not want to hear what Ottoline had come to say: that the marriage was dead in all but name.[83] When Ottoline asked the Eliots to Garsington once more, Vivienne's confidence was too low to face the stares of other guests at the manor. Could Ottoline find them two rooms in the village, she asked: "I could then see you as much as you cared to see *me,* and shd not be in the way . . ." Vivienne said she was too "unendingly dull" and although Ottoline might bear with her out of "yr goodness of heart," she could not hope that other people would.[84] Perhaps Vivienne guessed that Tom was complaining, on his separate visits to see Ottoline, that Vivienne was always suspicious of his movements; and the growing feeling in Bloomsbury was that Tom was a martyr to his wife.

One May morning in 1927, when Vivienne, in a state of collapse after her father's death, was abroad, waiting for her husband to join her in the Swiss sanatorium, Eliot told Stead that he had had a letter from a girl in Boston whom he had not seen or heard from for years and years. This was Emily Hale, whom he had first met in 1912 when she was seventeen, and with whom he had acted in amateur theatricals at his cousin Eleanor Hinckley's.[85] Emily was then thirty-six: a disappointed, if well-bred woman, who had been brought up by her aunt and uncle, Unitarian minister, the Rev. and Mrs. John Carroll Perkins; they had prevented her from training as a professional actress as she had wished. Instead she had become a drama teacher in girls' colleges. It was on the pretext of needing help for a lecture on modern poetry that she wrote to Eliot, who responded by sending her his essay on "Shakespeare and the Stoicism of Seneca."[86]

Eliot's response revived Emily's dreams of romance with him. According to his account in the 1960s, Eliot had told her he was in love with her before he left for Europe in 1914, although he did not believe that she returned his feelings.[87] In the intervening years she had not married; perhaps no opportunities presented themselves as she ran the girls' dormitories at Milwaukee Downer College, Wisconsin, and played Juliet in a production of *Romeo and Juliet* which she put on as Assistant Professor of Vocal Expression.[88] She made several visits to England, studying at the Speech Institute in London, possibly in 1923. Certainly in September that year Eliot sent her a copy of *Ara Vos Prec,* his 1920 collection of poems and, according to her own résumé, she made five visits to England before 1930, taking a half year's leave of absence in 1927, when she stayed on in London until October.[89]

But Emily had mistaken her man. Even as she began to plan her resignation from the college and a long break from teaching, in order to spend time in 1930 with Eliot at Burford, near Oxford, Eliot was being drawn closer into the Anglo-Catholic community. In March 1928 he made his first confession, telling Stead that he felt that he had crossed "a very wide and deep river" from which there was no going back.[90] In the same month he took a vow of chastity. But his struggle between flesh and spirit did not abate, and in April he told Stead that he could not expect to make great progress. All he could do was "to keep my soul alive." Eliot's spiritual counselor was then Francis Underhill, warden of Liddon House, in London, an Anglican centre for the pastoral care of university students.[91] Eliot wrote to Stead "in confidence" that he felt he needed, "the most severe, as Underhill would say, the most Latin kind of discipline, Ignatian or other. It is a question of compensation. I feel that nothing could be too ascetic, too violent, for my own needs."[92]

The only role Eliot envisaged for Emily was that of spiritualised muse and soon she began to inspire his poetry, replacing Vivienne. Vivienne had become a virago but, in Eliot's imagination, Emily, despite being a drama teacher, was transmuted into the passive, mute "Lady of Silences" of "Ash Wednesday." Correspondence and meetings with her triggered thoughts of New England. Emily's influence stirred Eliot to write "Marina" (1930), a poem resonant with images of Maine,[93] of water lapping the bows of ships, of grey rocks and islands: memories of his youth flooded back to him, when he had gone out with the fishermen in their ships, "Bowsprit cracked with ice and paint cracked with heat . . . /The rigging weak and the canvas rotten."[94] In "Animula" (1929) he returned to his childhood in St. Louis, for Emily had roused the poet from another "dry spell" after his failure to finish *Sweeney Agonistes*. Eliot had been blocked, unable to recapture the revolutionary impulse with which he began his drama, and it was Geoffrey Faber who, concerned at the silence from the "sacred wood," had suggested to Tom that he write a poem for Faber's Ariel series. This led to "Journey of the Magi" in 1927. Emily provided another new stimulus in returning Eliot to his roots as a source of inspiration. Significantly, however, it is the poet's daughter whom he addresses in "Marina." The goodness and loveliness of his virginal Lady brings life to his dry bones in "Ash Wednesday"; and the image of lustrous brown hair ("Blown hair is sweet, brown hair over the mouth/Blown") suggests romantic attachment, but it was the devotion of a daughter Eliot sought, not a sexual tie. Emily, if she read "Marina" with care, would have heeded Eliot's message of damnation for copulating humans: "Those who suffer the ecstasy of animals, meaning/Death."

Before Emily returned to England in 1930, a flesh-and-blood figure hoping for a future with her former suitor who, said Boston gossip, had failed to marry her earlier because of fears that her mother's mental illness might be hereditary,[95] Eliot had decided that Emily was his Beatrice, the inspiration for his spiritual "New Life." When he and Stead discussed the way in which Dante's love for Beatrice led him to the "divine goal" of love of God, in the *Vita Nuova,* Eliot confided: "I have had that experience."[96]

Nevertheless Eliot encouraged Emily's hopes. Flirtatious and intimate letters, of the sort he wrote to married women such as Mary Hutchinson and Dorothy Pound, were easily misinterpreted by a single, inexperienced woman. Eliot blamed Vivienne for the fact that he, like Harry in *The Family Reunion,* felt "desexed" towards women. In 1938 he told E. Martin Browne, director of many of his plays, that for Harry, "the effect of his married life upon him was one of such horror as to leave him for the time at least in a state that may be called one of being psychologically partially desexed: or rather, it has given him a horror of women as of unclean creatures."[97] In Eliot's most autobiographical play, Harry meets Mary, a woman from his past, now aged thirty; he feels "repulsion for Mary as a woman," but attraction to her as a personality. In the end he leaves her for his "bright angels."

From the late 1920s, however, Eliot believed his new muse to be pure, undefiled—in contrast to Vivienne, fallen *femme fatale.* Unwilling to confront his own nature, he may have imagined that this "lady" from a Bostonian Brahmin background, the sort of wife his mother would always have wished for him, might stimulate him to some sort of heterosexual passion; certainly he allowed her to believe that he would marry her when freed to do so by Vivienne's death. Eliot's letters to Emily, still sequestered at Princeton University Library until 2019, number over a thousand, and testify to the depth of their friendship; and the fact that Eliot asked Peter du Sautoy, director at Faber, to burn her letters to him demonstrates his desire to destroy the evidence. Eliot's destruction of Emily's letters apparently followed her own decision to consign his letters to her to the safety of an archive in 1956.[98] Her intention must have been to put down a marker for the future and, like Vivienne, to claim her place in Eliot's life, allowing readers to judge whether he exploited her love and loyalty. Critics however have already traced a pattern of cruelty in Eliot's relations with women: Vivienne, Emily Hale, Mary Trevelyan, all in turn loved Eliot too much and suffered for it.[99]

Emily may have captured Eliot's imagination, and the Anglo-Catholic Church his heart, but it was the convivial *coterie* grouped around Geoffrey Faber, Frank Morley, and a new and devoted acolyte, John Davy Hayward, whom Vivienne perceived as her closest rivals in her struggle to retain her influence over Tom. Eliot had met John Hayward as early as October 1925, when Hayward, then an Exhibitioner at King's College, Cambridge, invited the poet to read a paper to the Heretics Society; Eliot declined because he was too busy with the Clark lectures, but the two kept in touch.[100] Hayward, the son of a Wimbledon surgeon, was already disabled by muscular dystrophy, but when he came down in 1927 Eliot asked him to tea at his office in Russell Square, and accepted Hayward's offer to review for the *Criterion*.[101] The two began lunching regularly; the malicious wit which earned Hayward the nickname "The Tarantula" appealed to Eliot as much as the younger critic's learning and sense of the macabre, which united both men in a shared fascination with seventeenth-century drama (Hayward had played the Fourth Madman in *The Duchess of Malfi*).[102] Once Hayward had settled at 22 Bina Gardens, in Earl's Court, his flat became the meeting place—or drinking-den—where Eliot (the Elephant), Geoffrey Faber (the Coot) and Frank Morley (the Whale) gathered to dance, drink gin, and declaim obscene verse together, which Hayward eventually had privately printed. A typical poem ("Vers pour la Foulque," "Verses for the Coot") ends: "Nous allons nous donner la peine/De chier sur le seuil. Sonnez! Laissons nos culs se ventiler . . ." ("We are going to crap on the doorstep. Ring the bell! Let our arses break wind . . .")[103] Through Hayward Eliot was drawn into the intellectual, and largely homosexual circle around John Sparrow, Warden of All Souls, Oxford, which included "our old friend Al," the historian A. L. Rowse. This led to a visit by Eliot in September 1929 to the Dragon School to watch the young boys perform *The Mikado,* followed by dinner at All

Souls, during which, as Eliot told Hayward, he urinated in the college grounds and so missed Faber's offer to share a few more drinks.[104]

The cumulative losses which Vivienne sustained from 1926 onwards triggered a mental deterioration which grew more marked in the early 1930s. Perhaps the turning-point was the realisation that Tom hated her: the savagery of his feelings led on occasions to bizarre behaviour. Conrad Aiken recalled how, in 1925, he wrote to compliment Eliot on a new volume of poetry. In reply the poet sent him a page torn out of the *Midwives' Gazette*, on which he had underlined various forms of vaginal discharge. The words *blood, mucus* and *shreds of mucus* were also underlined, as well as the phrase *purulent offensive discharge*. "I still shudder when I think of it," wrote Aiken.[105]

Like Doris before the unpredictable and drunken Sweeney, Vivienne was afraid of Tom. It was a fear she voiced to Ottoline on several occasions in early 1928, although she too was capable of violence. From the Malmaison sanatorium she wrote on 31 January, saying she was very miserable and "it is all quite useless." Ottoline would have gathered from Tom what a *"horrible* mess" all this was. "He simply hates the sight of me. And I *don't know what to do."*[106] Shortly afterwards Eliot reluctantly agreed to bring Vivienne home. In her diary Vivienne later recalled the day seven years before when she had returned to England from France: "My dear Tom brought me back with him, but he did not want to. He would have much preferred for me to remain in France." Vivienne had become overwrought as she struggled beforehand to arrange her return, taking the tram daily into Paris, getting her passport and papers in order and signed by the chaplain at the British Embassy. No one at the sanatorium would help as they were "furious" at her leaving. She, too, was frightened to leave, "so I was out of my mind, and so behaved badly to Tom and got very excited." When they arrived at Victoria, Vivienne and Tom were met by her mother and Maurice; their behaviour seemed to her "sinister and unkind." Rose and Maurice had hired a nurse to take care of Vivienne, which she resented, seeing it as a "futile effort" to justify their previous behaviour of putting her into the clinic.[107]

It was not the first time Vivienne had turned on Tom. In another 1920s story, "André and Sibylla" meet at Dickens and Jones to buy presents for his mother and sister who are staying. Sibylla, caught up by a fit of rage or passion, throws her parcels down the stairs, which are fortunately quite deserted:

> She hits André on the face with her umbrella. Having done it once she does it again. The whole world totters—it spins about her. She longs to destroy herself and looks wildly about but there is no window low enough from which to cast herself, no knife or weapon presents itself for her purpose.

"Sibylla" collapses on the stairs in a silent convulsion while André/Tom collects the parcels. "He then takes her arms tightly and gets her into the street, where she walks mechanically beside him sunk into utter blackness. Now and then a gust of violent rage returns like a glaring flash of lightning . . ."[108]

Eliot found the presence of so unpredictable a wife in the house unendurable, and Vivienne's fears that he would harm her increased. "I am very unhappy, and as you agreed with me—*quite* defenceless," wrote Vivienne to Ottoline on 28 February 1928. "If you hear of me being murdered, don't be surprised."[109] Ottoline was in a difficult position as a friend to both parties in the Eliots' marital disputes; she objected when Vivienne criticised Tom to her, and Vivienne hurried to apologise for talking at such length about Tom. He was, of course, a very old friend of Ottoline's, and a "great friend and no-one likes hearing their friends spoken against." Bravely Ottoline offered on 1 June 1928 to act a mediator, seeing both Eliots separately. This was "wonderful news," wrote Vivienne, full of gratitude.[110]

The long, tiring summer, with repairs to the house and a succession of American visitors—Irving Babbitt, Paul Elmer More and Tom's nieces—proved very fatiguing, and Ottoline's counselling had to wait, for she herself was seriously ill with necrosis of the jaw and had to submit to an operation to remove the diseased bone, which left her disfigured. Eventually, in early autumn, she was well enough to begin her Thursday tea-parties in her new house at 10 Gower Street, having given up

Garsington. But Tom's visits to Ottoline had aroused Vivienne's suspicions, although Ottoline had taken pains to visit Vivienne regularly for afternoon tea. On 7 June Virginia Woolf recorded that Tom and Vivienne "give parties, where she suddenly accuses him of being in love with Ottoline (and me, but this Ott. threw in as a sop) and Tom drinks, and Vivien suddenly says when talk dies down 'You're the bloodiest snob I ever knew'—so I have refused to dine there." Vivienne was, said Virginia, "as mad as a hare, but not confined."[111]

It was obviously ludicrous to suggest that Tom was in love with Ottoline, by then fifty-five and "an old volcanoe, all grey cinders," whose deafness caused her to depend on a black tin ear-trumpet to hear her guests' conversation. Only long-standing affection for Tom caused Ottoline to gather him up in a "long and cadaverous embrace," such as that which Virginia reported almost drew her under the following November.[112] Nervously Tom avoided Ottoline. He would like to see her soon, he wrote on 2 October 1928, but he would not like Vivienne to think that Ottoline wished to see him and not her. "V. is very much better everyone thinks." It would be unwise, he thought, to have any concealment from Vivienne or discrimination, so he would rather delay a bit.[113] In November he wrote again that he thought it would be better if Ottoline saw Vivienne first. "I hope you understand."[114] Ottoline was hurt, however, and accused Tom of "Neglect."

When Ottoline eventually called on Vivienne on 11 February 1929, the atmosphere was strained. Although at first Vivienne seemed more normal and "sane" to Ottoline, she became fractious and upset when Ottoline did not remember Pearl Fassett, Tom's secretary, who had died recently. Barely had Ottoline calmed her hostess down when Tom entered with Prince Mirsky, a White Russian writer whom Ottoline disliked intensely; her sympathies began to shift towards Vivienne and against Tom, whose contempt for other "uneducated" writers, such as Lawrence and Blake, annoyed her, as did Eliot's secret holding of Ottoline's hand, which she found patronising.[115] Tom considered himself as infallible as the Pope, decided Ottoline—a title also awarded him by Mary Trevelyan, who called her memoir of T. S. Eliot "The Pope of Russell Square." Vivienne, conscious of the awkward atmosphere, wrote the next day to apologise in a letter carefully composed on their new orange writing-paper. She was sorry that

Mirsky had been there; she had been afraid Ottoline would be bored if there was no one else. As for Tom, wrote Vivienne huffily, she was only too glad for him to have Ottoline's "intimate friendship." She understood now that Ottoline had not known that Miss Fassett was dead.[116] Two days later, on 13 February, Tom himself hurried to assure Ottoline that he had not "dropped" her, as she thought: "Neither of us wants to lose you, you may be sure." Apologising for Mirsky's presence, he invited Ottoline to dine with them both alone so that there would be no more misunderstandings.[117]

The truce did not last long. Vivienne, feverish with influenza, at home with a "very queer" Tom, who had toothache, brooded jealously over her husband's relationship with Ottoline. On 29 February she wrote a bread-and-butter note for Ottoline's tea-party, but defended herself vigorously against the accusation of speaking against her friend and advanced her own claims to Ottoline's friendship. "I never said anything against you," she wrote, "except on that one occasion under what I consider the *most extreme* provocation, and if T was ever worth knowing, I am worth knowing now."[118] And although she thanked Ottoline for her honesty in advising her last year to separate from Tom, she did not see what she could have done, for Vivienne was not prepared to agree to Ottoline's suggestion that she should live apart from Tom, perhaps in adjoining flats. Tom meanwhile continued to visit Ottoline in her garden at Gower Street, as her grandson Philip Goodman remembers, and wring his hands. What should he do about Vivienne, he asked. Should he leave her? Should he stay? Ottoline could only listen.[119]

But if one source of friendship was temporarily strained, another presented itself again. Vivienne turned back to Mary Hutchinson, who had once more swum into her orbit now that her long affair with Clive had ended in 1927, and she had detached herself from Aldous and Maria Huxley. Joyfully Vivienne welcomed Mary to Chester Terrace in June 1928; her guest had brought heliotropes for Vivienne to plant in her garden. Soon the old routine of tea and dinner-parties was re-established. Vivienne's gratitude to Mary for finding and keeping a little pearl necklace she had broken at Mary's dinner-party on 26 June, and which had been a Christmas present from Pearl Fassett, provoked a confession of unhappiness from Vivienne: "[Pearl's] death is the most *terrible loss,* and gap, in my life that you could possibly imagine . . . It leaves me *frightfully* lonely." Pearl had been constantly with her, wrote Vivienne, and no one could take her place; she had also been Tom's right hand at the *Criterion*. Vivienne had no idea how he got on without Pearl: "Of course, he is *so* reserved and peculiar, and one cannot get him to speak. That makes one much more lonely." Was Mary lonely too over there at Regent's Park, asked Vivienne. "I thought you seemed so." She herself could never get resigned to the loss of Clarence Gate and their life there. And she missed her servant Ellen, who could never be replaced, and was depressed by the glum, silent girl she had now. Complaints about the servants were followed by complaints about Tom's new friends, who took no interest in his "poetry side." He needed his old friends, wrote Vivienne. *"More* people of the *right* sort, (and less of the *wrong*.)"[120]

Vivienne's mental and physical deterioration became more pronounced over the next few months. In May 1929 she was bedridden, perhaps as a result of a fall when under the influence of drugs. Tom rang up Virginia, who found his story both tragic and sordid. "Vivien's legs." *"Legs,* did you say?" "Yes, both legs, but especially the left." . . . "My God, Tom, have you seen a doctor?" "We have already had ten doctors," and so on for an "hour or two." The long and the short of it all, gossiped Virginia to Clive, was that Vivienne was "recumbent for ever."[121] A month or two earlier Tom had asked Mary to call on Vivienne when she could, as "the commissariat is rather demoralised at present." It was difficult for Vivienne to get about to see people, explained Tom, as she was a bit unsteady since her accident, which Mary need not mention to her.[122]

Vivienne's "queer turns" and fainting fits continued, while Tom, by contrast, took up dancing to the gramophone again and began new driving lessons. Soon he was "a perfect master" of their Morris Minor. His relentless social life continued: autumn 1928 found him entertaining Ethel Sands in a box at the ballet, and at Edith Sitwell's party without Vivienne, who complained in November that she had no dress to wear and felt "ugly with rough hands."[123] Vivienne continued to stay at home while Eliot escorted the Princesse di Bassiano to tea at Virginia's or went to Mary's birthday party. Alone and "very miserable," so "terrible to look at" that she dared not go, for that was the sort of mortification one could not endure, Vivienne asked Mary to think of her while she was feasting. Send me something off the table, she begged, a cap, a mask, or a cracker. She would sit up late to hear Tom's account of the evening.[124]

Vivienne began to believe that if only she could return to north London, where she would be near Mary in Albert Road, she would be happy again. Too ill and lame to househunt herself, she left it to Tom to choose a flat. "Very stupid and unfair of me," she wrote regretfully to Mary from their new address at 98 Clarence Gate Gardens, to which they moved in June 1929. "Well, my dear, it is the most terrible flat." The flat was barrack-like, very expensive, and they were surrounded by builders. "Hammer, hammer, hammer. Cranes, drills, etc."[125] Wistfully she asked Mary, who had taken Salt Mill House at Fishbourne for the summer, if there was a small, vacant, workman's cottage nearby: *"Is there?* This is serious." Eliot added his own chorus of complaints to Vivienne's. She was at the end of her strength, he said. The flat had turned out much more frightful than anticipated. Finally, in a postscript, Vivienne claimed to be "homesick" for their old home.[126] But there was no escape from London for the Eliots. They renewed their old cycle of restless flat-moving, one which reflected their own desperation, moving again in October to 177 Clarence Gate Gardens. Virginia recorded in May 1930 that Tom had written to say he was just moving to a house from a flat—"the 5th move in 6 months; which means I suppose that the worm in Vivien turns and turns, and not a nice worm at that."[127]

On 10 September 1929, Eliot received a cable to say that his mother had died. "I fear for Tom, at this time," wrote Vivienne to Mary.[128] In her later diary she remembered it as an agonising time for Tom, who had not had a chance to see Charlotte again since abandoning both his Unitarian faith and his American nationality. Tom was guiltily aware of the pain he had caused her, despite the propitiatory gesture of publishing her "Savonarola"; nevertheless, he had made the decision to sever the bonds with Charlotte long ago. Vivienne was, perhaps, the more shocked when she received the news of her brother Maurice's sudden marriage in Italy in March 1930 to a twenty-five-year-old American, Ahmé Hoagland, one of the dancing Hoagland sisters, who had performed in Monte Carlo—"All done without our knowledge." Vivienne and her mother were both annoyed that Maurice, having brought his new wife to London to introduce her to his sister and mother, returned almost instantly to Italy.

Over the next few months Vivienne continued to try to find another "little house as nice as 57 Chester Terrace."[129] At last they moved again "without much hope" to 43 Chester Terrace. It proved a brief flirtation. January 1931 found them back in Clarence Gate Gardens, at number 68. Vivienne had had, she told Mary, "a sort of breakdown."[130]

From 1930, stories of Vivienne's bizarre behaviour were legion in literary London, many centering around her abuse of ether, then used as an anaesthetic, which could be inhaled or rubbed on the body. To apply ether as a local anaesthetic would have numbed the pain of neuralgia; in fact, according to his relatives, Dr. Miller, Vivienne's doctor who practised at 110 Harley Street, prescribed paraldehyde for her as a massaging gel, which smelt strongly of ether.[131] Eventually paraldehyde "was given up because of its smell, and because patients became dependent on it, as it was a potent sedative moving towards a tranquilliser."[132] Miller was acting responsibly within the limits of the medical knowledge of the time. Nevertheless, Vivienne's use of the paraldehyde he prescribed for her led some observers to believe that she was an ether-drinker who entered that state, described by Eliot in "East Coker," "when under ether, the mind is conscious, but conscious/of nothing."[133]

Aldous Huxley noted that Vivienne's face was "mottled, like ecchymmotic spots, and the house smelled like a hospital."[134] Ottoline was another such witness. Visiting Vivienne on 15 November 1930, she walked into marital war. Vivienne was restless, constantly leaving the room and returning smelling more and more strongly of ether. She spoke to Tom as if he were a dog; he "grim . . . fat . . . horrid" remained formally polite to her until Vivienne went to sit sulking in a corner of the sofa where she was ignored by Ottoline and Desmond MacCarthy. After ten minutes' absence she made a dramatic re-entrance, demanding that someone come to talk to her. Ottoline spent a moment or two alone with Vivienne in her room, and then fled, vowing never to return. Vivienne's breath had, she recorded in her journal, filled the air with ether and she was "half-crazed." Ottoline felt an almost equal measure of repulsion for Tom, who tried as usual to hold her hand. She sensed in him an hypocrisy and humbug, which demonstrated itself in his poetry, and which Ottoline now found a meaningless form without faith, and also in his attitude towards Vivienne, towards whom he still claimed to feel affection.[135] Ottoline did not believe him.

Yet Ottoline was too generous-spirited to abide by her decision not to see either Eliot again. July 1931 found Vivienne sitting next to Ottoline at a Gower Street tea-party with Virginia Woolf, David Cecil, Elizabeth Bowen, Alida Monroe, Leslie Hartley, Juliette Huxley and Dorothy and Simon Bussy among others. Diplomatically, Ottoline decided to look after Vivienne, whom she feared might make a scene, and left Virginia and Elizabeth Bowen to talk to each other, while L. P. Hartley discussed with Vivienne a detective story she was planning to write. It was, decided an exhausted Ottoline afterwards, rather like conducting an orchestra, trying to induce harmony among her disparate guests.[136] But Vivienne did not forget Ottoline's kindness: in her 1934 diary she recalled how, "ill, late, flustered," she used to motor to fetch Tom to take him to 10 Gower Street. "Inconspicuous (and) as inoffensive as possible," she would sit in the shadows in the garden: "Ottoline used to keep me by her which was kind of her," while the literary ladies and gentlemen talked.[137]

Behind the scenes Tom's priests pressed him to end his marriage. He was now worshipping daily at St. Cyprian's, near the flat at 68 Clarence Gate Gardens. The service was Anglo-Catholic, the vicar Father Mayhew, who added his voice to that of others, urging Eliot to separate from Vivienne. Robert Sencourt, who stayed with the Eliots in 1930, noted disapprovingly that Vivienne refused to join in Eliot's religious life, which she mockingly called "monastic," a reference perhaps to Kelham Theological College in Nottinghamshire, to which he was introduced by his spiritual adviser, Father Underhill, and where he began to join the brethren in retreats. Vivienne followed Bloomsbury in its mockery of Eliot's conversion, needling him as Stephen Spender watched the Woolfs do: " 'Tom, do you really go to church?' 'Yes.' 'Do you hand round the collection?' 'Yes.' 'Oh, really! What are your feelings when you pray?' They waited rather tensely for his answer to this question. Eliot leaned forward, bowing his head in that attitude which was itself one of prayer, and described the attempt to concentrate, to forget self, to attain union with God."[138] Vivienne refused to accompany him on weekend visits to Bishop Bell of Chichester, with whom Eliot stayed in December 1930. At that point, recalled Sencourt unctuously, "his spiritual counsellors became decisive: he had a duty to his career and his spiritual life. He must not wreck the work he was doing for the Church."[139] That month Eliot wrote to Stead: "I want to talk to you about your suggestion, my dear." The suggestion that he should leave Vivienne, said Eliot, had already been put *strongly* to him by Vivienne's Roman Catholic doctor, by Underhill, and by others less qualified, but it was to Stead he wished to speak because he alone knew how difficult it would be. "I will say that I have now a certain happiness which makes celibacy easy for me for the first time. I think you will know what I am speaking of."[140]

The battle of wills continued. As Tom wavered, an answer came to his prayers for deliverance. An invitation arrived from Harvard University to deliver the Charles Eliot Norton poetry lectures in the academic year 1932–33. It would mean leaving England in the autumn of 1932. Eliot barely hesitated before accepting.

20

Ghosts and Shadows

By 1932 Vivienne resembled the "restless shivering painted shadow" of Eliot's most painfully confessional play, *The Family Reunion*. When Conrad Aiken came to dinner with the Eliots in the autumn of 1930 he had painted an almost identical portrait of his "shivering, shuddering" hostess.[1] Vivienne herself wrote to the poet Ralph Hodgson in May 1932 that she lived in "a world of ghosts and shadows and unrealities."[2] She was to be pushed "beyond the confines of sanity," believed Sencourt, by Eliot's decision to go to America without her.[3]

The question of his guilt for Vivienne's condition was to torment Eliot for years to come. In *The Family Reunion* the protagonist, Harry, Lord Monchensey, recalls the death of his wife, who had apparently been swept off the deck of a liner in the middle of a storm. But Harry remembers, "That cloudless night in the mid-Atlantic/When I pushed her over." "Pushed her?" asks Violet, his aunt. "You would never believe that anyone could sink so quickly," replies Harry. He had supposed that whatever he did, his wife was "unkillable." He expected to find her when he went down to the cabin. Later, he became excited. The purser was sympathetic, the doctor very attentive. That night he slept heavily, alone.[4]

Did Tom push Vivienne over the edge—into insanity, and even death?[5] It was a question which would become his purgatory. You mustn't indulge such dangerous fancies, Harry is told in *The Family Reunion,* and Eliot leaves it unclear whether Harry's wife fell, jumped "in a fit of temper," or was pushed over; yet Harry's cool reaction to the disclosure that his father, too, once wanted to murder his mother ("In what way did he wish to murder her?") suggests similar premeditation.[6] *You* have no reason to reproach yourself, your conscience is clear, says Charles, uncle to Harry/Eliot. It goes a good deal deeper than what people call their conscience, protests Harry. You must believe that I suffer from delusions. I am afraid of sleep—and also waking. *She* is nearer than ever: "The contamination has reached the marrow/And they are always near."[7] The delusions to which Eliot refers may have had some basis in the voices which, as he would confess to Mary Trevelyan, he heard at night: "quite indeterminate voices, neither male nor female—I hear what they say—but it's never anything notable . . ."[8] "They are very distinct—the individual voices I mean," he repeated to Mary on 21 October 1952. "They are never the *same* voices I have heard on other nights . . ." These voices, perhaps, spoke the words of reproach which tortured Eliot, and lent authenticity to his portrait of the Eumenides.

Eliot's torment is well-documented: "We were married for seventeen years—I mean, we lived in the same houses," he told Mary Trevelyan. "Happy? NO, I was never happy—but I don't think I have ever been happy."[9] Yet Vivienne's torment was greater. Her end was not, in the final years of the marriage, as the murder victim she sometimes feared she would become, but in psychic death, a lapse into non-being for which Eliot was to feel as responsible—as if, for one second, his icy control had snapped and he had hit or shot or drowned the shadow of a woman who had haunted him. It was an end he had foreseen, quoting in 1929 Dante's description of the lost lovers, Paolo and Francesca, whose fate was metamorphosis into shades: "So I saw the wailing shadows come, wailing, carried on the striving wind."[10]

Vivienne slipped into non-being the longer she lived with Eliot. In the last photograph of her with Tom and Virginia Woolf she stands apart from the other two, a wraith-like woman in white, preparing to vanish. It was the final act of the drama. Trapped in the strange, claustrophobic world they had created, Vivienne was weaker than Tom in the battle of wills which ensued. The kitten had met a cat, Great Tom, Old Possum, whose claws were sharper than hers.

Jean-Paul Sartre writes, "I exist my body: this is its first dimension of being. More importantly, I exist as a body known by the Other." In any human relationship, the Other's look defines us for ourselves, and we see ourselves through the Other's eyes.[11] Vivienne, through Tom's eyes, saw herself as worthless. Her psychic pain translated into physical pain or disease, as the "lived pain" became "the suffered illness," a process illuminated by Sartre's ideas on hate, domination and submission. He argues that every relationship is a circle, in which each tries to assimilate and make an object of the Other. Conflict ensues, as each struggles to regain his or her freedom. "While I seek to enslave the Other, the Other seeks to enslave me . . . the Other holds a secret—the secret of what I am. He makes me be and thereby he possesses me . . . He has stolen my being from me."[12] Even love, says Sartre, is destructive: Vivienne's love for Eliot, which existed at the beginning of the relationship, ultimately proved destructive for them both as he came to resent the alienation of his freedom, the drying up of his creative spring in the trap of marriage—after "Ash Wednesday" he found himself unable to complete the two poems later published as "Coriolan"[13]—and the reproach of ill-matched sexuality. "The more I am loved the more I lose my being," writes Sartre. "The more I lose my being, the more I am thrown back on my own responsibilities." In the end such conflict provokes total despair.[14]

For Vivienne and Tom, love turned to indifference, then to hatred and sadism. Both felt the burden of having failed themselves and the Other. Vivienne punished herself through starvation and drugs because she accepted Tom's definition of her as a burden, as an inadequate, useless wife, while he grew to hate her as she cuckolded him and attempted to usurp his role as writer, encroaching on his own territory and taking on aspects of his dominating mother.[15] But at the core of the revulsion Eliot felt for Vivienne was her very femininity, which reminded him of the shameful, feared feminine part of himself. It became impossible for her to preserve self-esteem in the face of this instinctual, primitive hatred. Forced once more to submit to his control, as he asserted male literary hegemony and ended her writing career, she was left the object of Bloomsbury's scorn and ridicule, as well as Tom's. In the end Vivienne saw no justification for existing, and simply ceased to be.

In so doing she was fulfilling Tom's wishes. "When I hate," says Sartre, "I hate the whole psychic totality of the Other. I wish to rediscover a freedom without limits . . ." This is equivalent to projecting the realisation of a world in which the Other does not exist. In his poetic drama Eliot did indeed continually rehearse Vivienne's removal from his life. Yet hate is in turn a kind of failure because even if one being brings about the abolition of the Other, "it could not bring it about that the Other had not been," writes Sartre. "What I was for the Other is fixed by the Other's death."[16] Hate at the moment of realisation by the Other's death is transformed into failure. Hate does not free us from the circle. Leaving Vivienne did not bring Eliot release from the furies of conscience which were to pursue him; thus, even after separation, the imago of Vivienne acted as Eliot's prime creative stimulus. As Virginia Woolf admitted in 1936 to Clive Bell, Vivienne was "the true inspiration of Tom . . . He was one of those poets who live by scratching, and his wife was his itch."[17]

Vivienne's devastation was evident to Robert Sencourt, an insidious presence in the Eliots' flat. When he stayed with them in 1930, Vivienne seemed on the edge of "the abyss of despair," quoting to her guest Hardy's poem "In Tenebris":

> Black is night's cope
> But death will not appal
> One who, past doubtings all,
> Waits in unhope.

Sencourt watched as Vivienne made valiant efforts to hold together a fast fragmenting social life. One evening she asked some literary friends to meet the poet Ralph Hodgson, an old friend of Tom's. Hodgson was born in County Durham, the son of a coal merchant, and perhaps his "homely accent," as Sencourt described it, reminded Vivienne of her own northern background; certainly she felt at ease with Hodgson, who had the same passion for his bull terrier Pickwick as she had for her Yorkie Polly. She also liked his companion, Aurelia Bollinger, a former student at Missionary College, whom Hodgson had seduced, and grew close to them both in the last two years of her life with Eliot.[18] On the evening in question a group of younger writers read their work aloud, but the centre of attention was Ottoline to whom, wrote Sencourt, "Vivienne deferred as if to royalty"; Tom read "Difficulties of a Statesman" ending with the shout: RESIGN, RESIGN.[19] It was an awkward gathering: Ottoline balefully observed Vivienne flirting excitedly with Hodgson who was, apparently, a patient listener; but his hostess, grotesque in flowered chiffon, her little face with its grey-green make-up reminding Ottoline of an overdressed monkey, presented a bizarre yet pitiful spectacle. Nor was the Eliots' tea-party for James and Nora Joyce in July 1931 any more successful. Tom and Vivienne greeted Joyce like a king as well, and this time it was Ottoline who felt left out as the two writers fell into deep conversation and she was ignored. The company listened to a gramophone recording of Joyce reading "Anna Livia Plurabella," followed by Tom reading "Ash Wednesday"; it was, thought Ottoline, greatly inferior to Joyce's work.[20]

There were mysterious comings and goings at the Clarence Gate Gardens flat. Sencourt remembered Maurice, as well as Montgomery Belgion, one of Eliot's many right-wing, French contacts, and the "Bolshevised" Mirsky, who was a frequent visitor; unknown to his hosts, the wrinkled, watchful aristocrat, with his crooked, yellow teeth, while flirting with Vivienne was also gathering material for a Marxist analysis of Bloomsbury, which would ridicule its members after his return to Russia.[21] Vivienne did not, however, know all her husband's male guests as well as she did Mirsky. Sometimes there were secret visitors. On 27 January 1931, she asked Mary if she knew of the man Tom had staying, whom she only saw for a few minutes late at night after all the servants and nurses had departed. "He sometimes stays with us. Tom can bear him. Perhaps you could find out why."[22]

Old friends became captive but embarrassed witnesses to the Eliots' escalating marital warfare. On 1 June 1931 Mary and Jack yielded to Vivienne's repeated invitations to visit her new "strange" flat at number 68, and came to dinner with Mary's brother Jim Barnes. An explosive scene ensued, in which Tom lost his temper. "Something seemed to upset Tom very much indeed yesterday," wrote Vivienne. She was dreadfully sorry and shocked at what happened the previous night. "We are now quite 'calm' and so *please* can you telephone tomorrow morning and suggest any meal for you and Jim . . ."[23] Predictably, Jim Barnes proved unavailable when Vivienne rang him three times to make another date.

The evening from which the Hutchinsons fled in horror was probably similar to that endured by Conrad Aiken a few months earlier. A battle had broken out almost as soon as he had arrived. Vivienne looked like a scarecrow, and both Eliots directed streams of hatred at each other throughout the meal. There was no such thing as pure intellect, declared Eliot. Vivienne interrupted angrily: "Why, what do you mean? You know perfectly well that *every* night you tell me that there *is* such a thing: and what's more that *you* have it, and that nobody *else* has it." "You don't know what you're saying," retorted Eliot, but it seemed to Aiken that the arrow had struck home. Vitriolic, sarcastic, maybe, but Vivienne did not appear mad to Aiken.[24]

Christmas Day 1931 found the Eliots alone together. Vivienne was glad that Ottoline's Christmas had been "nice and calm." "Ours," she wrote, "was rather terrible."[25] It followed hard on another "fearful" evening when Vivienne had four people to dinner, who did not seem to have "at all a good effect, anyhow not in *combination*" on Tom, who had erupted in a drunken rage. Vivienne was horrified, she confided to Ottoline, for it was so long since anything like that had happened. Don't speak of it to anyone, she instructed her friend. *"I know you won't."* She was thankful for the presence of Sencourt, who had been staying again in December and managed to calm Tom down. However, Sencourt's sooth-ing words could not mask the fundamental problem of Tom's alcoholism, which often made Ottoline, who was a teetotaler, feel apprehensive before dining with the Eliots.[26] Would Tom be sober or drunk, that was the ques-tion; or if sober, hungover and surly, his eyes bloodshot.[27] Tom sometimes took the opportunity to defend his consumption of gin and wine; alcohol kept one young, he told Ottoline, citing de Quincey and Coleridge as ex-amples of this generalisation, a remark which Vivienne found in bad taste, and it required all Ottoline's tact to avoid yet another argument.[28] But however well-preserved his looks, Eliot's drinking was widely known from the late 1920s. Anthony Powell recorded in his memoirs: "Someone remarked, 'They say Eliot is always drunk these days . . .' "[29]

Nor was Tom's temper helped by Vivienne's jealousy of his fame, which provoked further outbursts. One young man called at the flat and Vivienne opened the door; on hearing that he wanted to see Eliot, she com-plained bitterly: "Why, oh why, do they all want to see my husband?"[30] The poet was angry, too, at the knowledge that he was the subject of mocking laughter among the *literati* since the publication of Richard Aldington's satirical story *Stepping Heavenward* in 1931, with its caricature of Eliot as the sanctimonious but ruthless "Blessed Jeremy Cibber," a genius with whom it is "quite awful" to live. Aldington also sneered at Eliot's "death-worshipping" in "The Hollow Men." Those who had fought in the war like himself, he said, were "healthy-minded" individuals, struggling to escape the "perpetual suicidal mania," in which only those who had not fought, like Eliot—cowards by implication—yearned to wallow.[31] It was a criticism which struck a raw nerve with Eliot, who was concerned about perceptions of his own effeminacy. He preserved among his papers a cutting by the American critic Louis Untermeyer:

> The charge that the poet is, by nature, effeminate is still prevalent. And it is patently absurd . . . The essential manliness of the arts—and particularly the art of finding words for our deepest emotions—may be proved by examining the biographies of the great poets of all nations.

Under this cutting Eliot scrawled in enormous, angry letters his own initials: "TSE."

Eliot's sensitivity over being the subject of rumour, whether financial, such as the Bel Esprit leaks, or concerning his private life, had already led him to threaten legal action, as in the case against the *Liverpool Post*. It was further exacerbated by Vivienne's predilection for outspoken public attacks on him. Stephen Spender, who first met Eliot in 1928, was struck by Vivienne's ability to expose him to humiliation before strangers.[32] Eliot grew nervous of blackmail; such was his reputation that the writer E. W. F. Tomlin felt it necessary to state that his friendship with the poet was "devoid of sexual feeling . . ." despite the "persistent insinuations that Eliot, owing to his friendship with Jean Verdenal and perhaps with others, was either homosexual or, as one fellow-poet remarked, suppressed homosexuality."[33]

In this climate of fear, Aldington's malicious satire, the product of jealousy of his old friend's dominance of English letters, seemed the last straw. It had been tactless, perhaps, of Eliot to have recommended "a good broker" to the struggling writer, or to have invited the country mouse to a "London soirée" in November 1927.[34] "Certainly the party was a silly one," Eliot had replied breezily, justifying his own attendance on the grounds of a liking for "drinking beer in company." He had never intimated that London parties were superior to provincial ones, he protested.[35] But after visiting Eliot's spacious office at Faber, furnished in red Chinese Chippendale, with its fine view over the church spire and square,[36]

Aldington had determined on revenge. Eliot's reaction to *Stepping Heavenward* was swift. Geoffrey Faber wrote at once to the novelist's publisher, Chatto's, requesting that the book be withdrawn because it would offend Eliot and Vivienne; his letter also contained "what looked like the threat of a libel action." Aldington told Sydney Schiff that if Eliot were to send him a straightforward request, that is, one that was not too "Christian-slimy," he might feel obliged to cancel publication but, since none was forthcoming, and the story had already been previously published twice, he went ahead.[37]

Many accounts exist of Tom and Vivienne's marriage in the years 1930–32, but it is the hostile pen of Virginia Woolf which has been responsible for the most "violently" vivid descriptions of Vivienne's "insanity." Woolf's accounts of her last sightings of Tom and Vivienne together have, as her biographer Hermione Lee writes, "powerfully affected all the versions of the Eliot story."[38] Woolf's disdain for Eliot's religiosity certainly influenced her against him; she observed him in November 1930, "all suspicion, hesitation & reserve. His face has grown heavier fatter & whiter. There is a leaden sinister look about him." But it was Vivienne from whom she was determined to distance herself, from a "madness" which seemed contagious and threatening to someone who was herself, in all probability, manic-depressive.

> But oh—Vivienne! Was there ever such torture since life began!—to bear her on ones shoulders, biting, wriggling, raving, scratching, unwholesome, powdered, insane, yet sane to the point of insanity, reading his letters, thrusting herself on us, coming in wavering trembling—"Does your dog do that to frighten me? Have you visitors? Yes we have moved again. Tell me, Mrs. Woolf, why do we move so often? Is it accident?" That's what I want to know (all this suspiciously, cryptically, taking hidden meanings.) Have some honey, made by our bees, I say. Have you any bees? (& as I say it I know I am awakening suspicion.)[39]

"Have you any bees?" It was a question which must have seemed ridiculous to a woman living in a north London flat, and Vivienne answered with ironic mockery: "Not bees. Hornets. But where? Under the bed." After half an hour in which Vivienne pitted her own sharp and mordant wit against Virginia's, her hostess was relieved to bid farewell to her unwelcome guest, damning Vivienne for posterity with her final verdict which has been so often quoted: "This bag of ferrets is what Tom wears round his neck."[40]

As Hermione Lee points out, Virginia understood "suspicion" very well. She too suffered from paranoia. The passage describing Vivienne echoes a remark Virginia made about herself in 1921: "A wife like I am should have a label to her cage: She bites!" Vivienne's alarming presence, like a *doppelgänger* of Woolf, must have provoked the novelist's anxiety and paranoia and threatened her own fragile equilibrium.

Virginia's ambivalence towards Vivienne was profound. On another occasion she could be impulsively kind, hunting up and down Oxford Street on Boxing Day 1928 for a 3/6d present for Vivienne. She was looking for a "green smooth knife" like the one Ottoline had given her for Christmas.[41] Perhaps it was this exchange of knives which gave rise to Virginia's stories that Vivienne was trying to stab her and Ottoline in the street, as she believed them to be Tom's mistresses, and skin them with a carving knife. Tom and Vivienne both, according to Maurice, bought joke knives from the same shop where Tom bought the whoopee cushions for his office at Faber, and the "giant" fire crackers he exploded in the coal scuttle on Independence Day.[42] As Eliot related to John Hayward, there were often "high jinks" at the Faber book committee meetings, with stinkbombs, gin and vermouth, and a sharing of his collected "Psuedoxia Contemporanea": previous items in the collection included the fact that "a fart, strained through bath water, loses both odour and inflammability," the information that to rub the fingers between the toes and sniff them was "sovereign against costiveness," and the discovery that cigarette ash, stirred into black coffee, was "most urgently aphrodisiac."[43] It was, therefore, not unusual for Vivienne, at Christmas 1931, to give Ottoline "a funny little Christmas token," which Ottoline felt was a wand, but, wrote Vivienne enigmatically, she did not take or give it as such: "To me it is a Sword, and one has to be careful to whom one gives swords." The sword, she wrote, was mightier than the pen. This "sword," like Ottoline's gifts to Vivienne, had some strange connection in Vivienne's mind, as her propensity to read significance into "signs" grew. Such paranoia was certainly a feature of bromism, and led Vivienne, who was frustrated in her desire to communicate privately with Ottoline by her friend's deafness, to feel she had to choose between writing, which was always a "risk," or communicating "by signs" which she thought *"low and brutal and degrading."*[44]

Such a letter suggests that Vivienne was becoming temporarily deranged yet her correspondence with Ralph Hodgson and Aurelia Bollinger gives a very different impression of her state of mind. Her writing changes to a more upright, determined hand, although it is sometimes shaky as a result of drugs, and the content is rational, the letters carefully dated and signed. On 12 May 1932 Vivienne wrote a sensitive letter of condolence to Hodgson, who had just lost his brother, offering the sympathy of "a real friend if you will allow me to think of myself as being your friend." Hodgson had brought so much into her life, she wrote, and done so much for her, clearing up things which she never understood. "You have seemed to me like some very solid tower of strength and reality in a world of ghosts and shadows and unrealities." She would never cease to be grateful to him, although "nothing is finished yet, or quite clear." She was with him in his grief, in which she had seen his courage, wonderful patience, kindness and tact. Please let us see you over Whitsun, she begged, although Tom had announced that he was taking to his bed for the next three days.[45]

Battling with ghosts took every ounce of Vivienne's strength in the months which followed. Like Mrs. Aveling, through whom, in *Ghosts,* Ibsen develops the character of Nora, Vivienne began to think "we are all ghosts . . . every one of us," weighed down by the burden of the past, of parents, old beliefs and old lovers. "I've only to pick up a newspaper and I seem to see ghosts gliding between the lines," says Mrs. Aveling. "Over the whole country there must be ghosts, as numerous as the sands of the sea. And here we are, all of us, abysmally afraid of the light."[46] Much of the time Vivienne too stayed in the shadows, within the walls of her flat, only venturing out with the support of trusted friends. If only she could be induced to go out of doors with you, complained Tom to Mary, it might build up her self-confidence. "She can't *drive* without me or a driver—" and she needed persuading that people she liked wanted to see *her*.[47] But despite Vivienne's eccentricity and the paranoia which caused her to open Tom's letters behind his back, some friends stayed remarkably loyal without his prompting. They not only responded dutifully to Vivienne's often articulated need, but also to the warmth which she had not entirely lost. Aurelia Bollinger became "one of the family," spending evenings with the Eliots while Vivienne wrote nineteen letters and Tom read and grumbled. There were outings to Hindhead with Ralph and Aurelia to see Rose Haigh-Wood and her sister, Lillia,[48] trips to the theatre and, despite Vivienne's confusing letters cancelling appointments, days in the country. On 27 May 1932 Vivienne thanked Aurelia effusively for their *"perfect"* day out, when they had visited Arundel, and arranged for Aurelia to come to stay for a week with Ralph's bull terrier Picky while Hodgson was visiting Siegfried Sassoon.[49]

Vivienne knew Aurelia well enough to complain to her about Tom. "Mr. Eliot is playing the Wireless and driving me *MAD*," she had confided to her friend on 19 May, while arranging a day at the Derby in the Eliots' car.[50] Tom, meanwhile, as spring turned to summer, laid silent plans for his escape to America. Lunching with Eliot and Jim Barnes that March to plan a "fascist" book on modern politics, Harold Nicolson found the poet "very yellow and glum . . . dyspeptic, ascetic . . . Inhibitions."[51] The lines Eliot wrote about himself and sent to Ralph Hodgson reveal a sardonic awareness of the impression he made on others: "How unpleasant to meet Mr. Eliot!/With his Coat of Clerical Cut," wrote the poet; "And his Face so Grim/And his Mouth so Prim . . ."[52] The pen and ink sketch of himself with which Eliot decorated the poem bears a striking resemblance to the self-righteous Unitarian ministers he had satirised in his youth: his exuberant sketch of Hodgson and his dog, by contrast, suggests a certain envy of the portly, good-natured friend of whom he wrote, "How Delightful to Know Mr. Hodgson!/(Everyone Wants to Know *Him*)."[53]

In the last months of the Eliots' marriage, Vivienne's character assassination at the hands of Bloomsbury proceeded apace. Edith Sitwell described the "very exciting" afternoon in 1932 when Vivienne came to visit her, to Osbert's lover, David Horner:

A certain lady (Osbert will tell you who I mean) came to tea without her husband. As she entered, a strange smell as though four bottles of methylated spirits had been upset, entered also . . . Nellie, (the maid) who was once what is known as an Attendant, enquired if she might speak to me on the telephone, and, as soon as she got me outside, said (looking very frightened): "If she starts anything, Miss, get her by the wrists, sit on her face, and don't let her bite you. Don't let her get near a looking-glass or a window." I said, "What *do* you *mean?*" and she replied that what I thought was an accident with the M.S. was really the strongest drug given by attendants when nothing ordinary has any effect!! She concluded gloomily: "Often it takes six of us to hold one down."— You can imagine my feelings, and when I got back into the room, I found that Mrs. Doble [mother of Georgia Sitwell, Sachie's wife] had offered the lady a cigarette, and had been told the lady *never* accepted anything from strangers. It was too dangerous.

Poor Mrs. D was terrified as she thought the Patient was going to spring at her throat . . .[54]

In fact Mrs. Doble was in no danger. Vivienne was never violent but, if Edith is to be believed, she had begun to experience delusions as a result of her addiction. In the summer of 1932 Edith met Vivienne walking down Oxford Street.

"Hullo, Vivienne!" she called to her.

Vivienne looked at her suspiciously and sadly, and replied, "Who do you think you're addressing? I don't know you."

"Don't be so silly, Vivienne: you know quite well who I am."

Vivienne regarded her with profound melancholy for a moment, and then said, "No, no: you don't know me. You have mistaken me *again* for that *terrible* woman who is so like me . . . She is always getting me into trouble."[55]

As the date of Eliot's departure grew closer, Vivienne manifested some of the symptoms of *grande hystérie*. She found it difficult to function normally, to eat, sleep or even walk. At the Derby, on 1 June, she was carried fainting from the Epsom race course, and she never forgot that day when she had tried to cross the course with Tom and Ralph Hodgson and Aurelia Bollinger and had collapsed—the intense heat, the fearful crowds, Tom and a policeman carrying her out of the crowd. The police were always kind to Tom and to her, she remembered.[56]

It is probable that Vivienne's collapse was caused by her panic at the thought of losing Tom. It is also possible, although very unlikely, that she was suffering from "etheromania" or ether drunkenness, a form of intoxication produced by drinking ether,[57] similar to that produced by alcohol, but which came on more rapidly and was more transitory. Ether was commonly used as a narcotic and antispasmodic in the treatment of hysteria or asthma.[58] It is more probable that anxiety, and increased dependence on the drugs already prescribed by Dr. Miller, accounted for Vivienne's bizarre behaviour in the final months of her marriage. Chloral and bromide—prescribed for Vivienne's hypertension—and purgatives such as croton-oil acted as a chemical cosh on the patient.[59] Virginia, who was taking a variety of medication, found that taking "somnifène" left her "quite drugged" in January 1929.[60] She could hardly walk, reported Leonard, and was in "a drugged state. She says she has only taken twenty drops. She has been in bed ever since."[61] As Virginia's mental and physical collapse continued, her doctors gave her "stiff doses of bromide," she told Vita Sackville-West. "Its rather nice. Ones head feels grown to the pillow. One floats like a log."[62] Virginia enjoyed her days under the influence of bromide, when she felt like a fish at the bottom of the sea. It was from her underwater vantage point perhaps that she dispassionately recorded Vivienne's "madness" when Tom and Vivienne made a final visit to Rodmell on 2 September 1932:

> She as wild as Ophelia—alas no Hamlet would love her, with her powdered spots—in white satin, L said; Tom, poor man, all battened down as usual, prim, grey . . . Then her chops & changes. Where is my bag? Where—where—then a sudden amorous embrace for me—& so on: trailing about the garden—never settling—seizing the wheel of their car—suddenly telling Tom to drive—all of which he bears with great patience: feeling perhaps that his 7 months of freedom draw near . . .[63]

Vivienne also recalled the same occasion with Virginia when "We had tea, & as I was *very nearly insane* already with the Cruel Pain of losing Tom . . . I paid very little attention to the conversation . . . We got back to the Lansdowne [Hotel, Eastbourne], I felt *very ill & was in a fever.* Tom also *seemed very strange.*"[64]

Hope Mirrlees's recollection in 1971 of Vivienne echoes Virginia's:

> Fear, that's it. Because she gave the impression, you see, of absolute terror. Of a person who'd seen a hideous ghost; a goblin ghost, and was always seeing a goblin in front of her. Her face was all drawn and white; and wild, frightened, angry eyes, and an over-intensity over nothing, you see; over some little thing you'd say. Suppose you were to say to her: "Will you have some more cake?"; and she'd say (in a wild voice): "What's that, what's that, what d'you mean, what did you say that for?" She was terrifying. At the end of an hour, when she used to come and see me, I was absolutely exhausted, sucked dry; and I felt to myself, poor Tom this is enough. But—she was his Muse all the same.[65]

In August, Frank Morley invited the Eliots to Pikes Farm, near Crowhurst, Surrey, for the christening of his daughter Susannah, to whom Eliot was to be godfather. Since the reorganisation of Faber & Gwyer as Faber & Faber under the chairmanship of Geoffrey Faber in April 1929, the Fabers, Eliots and Morley had become close friends. Vivienne remembered later that "my poor Tom had great difficulty in getting me up and dressed and ready to start," on the drive to Oxted, where they were to meet Morley in his car. Eliot only succeeded by reminding Vivienne that she was keeping two old people waiting: Morley's parents, who came from Baltimore.[66] At last they made their *rendez-vous:* Tom driving Vivienne in their tiny Morris Minor, following Morley's car, a second-hand American Ford V-8, which blazed the trail, at 20 mph, for the Morris Minor to follow through the twisting lanes. Morley came to a hill, which the Ford breasted with ease. Tom "missed his gear-change, pressed everything pulled everything, stalled, began to roll back—I draw a veil," remembered Morley. "Another thing I had forgotten was that in the back of the Morris there would be the heaviest of suitcases—Tom never journeyed without the *heaviest* of suitcases. Another thing I remembered was that Tom would intensely dislike any notice taken, any assistance. I went on waiting . . . At a third attempt and with unexampled gallantry Tom with the heart of a lion did charge to the top of the mountain. Vivien's nerves withstood the strain better than mine."[67]

Nevertheless, it turned out a "happy, memorable day," and Morley made no comment on Vivienne's eccentricities; indeed, he remembered that

> When I knew her it was quite obvious that she had been a person of immense charm and vivacity, and quickness of uptake. And I'm quite sure of one thing: that she, rather like Ezra, was an immense help to Eliot—to Eliot as a poet—and her contribution, and indeed, her courage, in encouraging the publication of *The Waste Land,* which many wives would have blanched from, is something that is worthy of a tribute, and memory. I doubt if he'd have ever written *The Waste Land* if it hadn't been for Vivien.[68]

Ottoline, too, bravely continued to entertain Vivienne, who clung to her friend for support, feeling that the part of her life which was around Ottoline was "the only part I can endure to contemplate." She regularly attended Ottoline's "glorious" summer tea-parties, writing to her on 4 July 1932: "You *know* that it is entirely due to you that I have been able to keep up."[69] Ottoline could not have entertained Vivienne weekly if she had been as insane as Virginia Woolf suggested, and there were times when the mistress of Gower Street recorded that Vivienne was cordial, lively and quite normal, in contrast to Eliot, whose cruelty hurt Ottoline deeply when he contemptuously dismissed her religious faith.[70] Tom appeared duly grateful to Ottoline for her care of Vivienne, who was, he wrote, so much "a creature of environment" that it was a vital matter what company she frequented; not only had Ottoline exerted her own influence but she had helped Vivienne to add a number of "desirable people" to her acquaintance. "I am especially glad of this because I shall be so long absent."[71]

But it was Mary, not Ottoline, who came to Vivienne's rescue as Tom's absence drew nearer. The courage with which Vivienne had at first greeted the news that Tom would be away from September till May, writing to Mary, "It is all of our duties to keep things going for him *here,"* was fast evaporating.[72] She needed Mary's help so much, begged Vivienne on 8 June 1932, adding that she hardly dared telephone her friend for fear of disappointment. "You don't suppose *I* don't need a change *too*—do you?" How could she be expected to stay alone at Clarence Gate Gardens for eight months? She would hate it.[73] Within four days Mary had come up with an ingenious solution. She suggested that Vivienne and Tom should take rooms in the Strachey family home at 51 Gordon Square, as the top-floor flat was vacant following the death of Lytton in January 1932. Vivienne would be next door to Adrian and Karin Stephen at number 50, near the Keyneses at number 46, and not far from the Woolfs at 52 Tavistock Square. At first Vivienne responded enthusiastically to Mary's proposal, and on 12 June she and Tom were shown around Lytton's two rooms by his sister, Pippa Strachey, who was, said Vivienne, "sweet . . . and so *kind* to us both." The rooms were more beautiful and desirable than she ever dreamed, wrote Vivienne: "Tom very *much* likes the rooms and knows that he would be happy there." She began to fantasise about the coming winter; how she would decorate and furnish the flat "beautifully," live there quietly and "cultivate my mind." Could she not found a Society or Fund to keep Lytton's rooms "always perfect" in his memory? Tom could use them for writing, reading and thinking, and Mary could be the "Curator."[74]

Nothing came of these plans. Perhaps Vivienne began to think twice about doing without the *"economy* and convenience of constant hot water," which was not available in Lytton's flat as it was in Clarence Gate Gardens. Although on 18 July she was writing to Mary, saying she wished to move to 51 Gordon Square because she could not endure her present servants a moment longer, Vivienne's mind was now pursuing another suggestion of Mary's: that she should take a job. You are more practical than most of my friends, Vivienne told Mary gratefully, after another "lovely tea," where they talked over Vivienne's problems alone together: "It is *kind* of you to *interest* yourself in what I shall do this next year. I do appreciate that!!!"[75] She hurried to ask her doctor's advice about doing some work. He replied that it would be "very very *nice* and a *very good thing,"* Vivienne confided excitedly to Mary.[76]

Three weeks before he left, Tom took Vivienne away for a short holiday. She had no inkling that it was to be their last. He gave no hint of his intentions, as she talked nervously of their imminent separation. Huge moons and "boiling days" marked that August. In September the weather became chilly and disagreeable. Vivienne decided to give Tom a farewell party which took place on Thursday, 15 September, two days before he sailed from Southampton. "He is really going—next Saturday," she wrote wonderingly to Ottoline,[77] who tried to decline the invitation, having experienced Vivienne's last fiasco of a party that January, at which Alida Monro, widow of Harold, read Tom's poems aloud to a hand-picked audience.[78] "Yes I do know you hate parties," countered Vivienne sternly, but this one was to be "a kind of *gathering* together of people which Tom would *like to remember,*" people who genuinely desired his "ultimate good" in every possible way, above all spiritually. They would be *very* sorry indeed if she was not with them, even if only for a very short time. Ottoline finally yielded, also acceding to Vivienne's wish that she would have a final farewell meeting alone with Tom on Friday 16th, after which he was only to see Vivienne's mother Rose.[79] But Ottoline made the decision that, after Tom's departure, she would never again meet Vivienne.

In order to allay Vivienne's fears that he would stay in America and never return to her, Tom had written "my dear Vivienne" a letter dated 4 March 1932, stating the terms on which he had been appointed Charles Eliot Norton Professor of Poetry at Harvard University. The post was only for the academic year 1932–33, for a fee of $10,000. Eliot undertook to return to England the following May. He wished to make it clear, he wrote, that the appointment was not renewable, signing off, "affectionately yours, your husband."[80] With this paper reassurance Vivienne had to be content, and yet she did not trust him. Even as the Eliots left their flat in a cab, weighed down with his ample luggage, and followed by Maurice and his wife Ahmé in another cab, Tom discovered that Vivienne had locked some of his important papers in the bathroom. He asked a friend to go back and a pageboy from a nearby hotel had to be pushed through the bathroom window. The papers were retrieved and handed to Tom at the station a few minutes before the boat-train left for Southampton.[81]

On board, Tom and Vivienne walked the deck together, while Maurice and Ahmé waited on the quayside. At last it was time for Vivienne to leave. With a sense of deep foreboding she joined her brother and sister-in-law as they waved goodbye to Tom, and the liner steamed out to sea, bearing his receding figure across the Atlantic to Montreal and thence to the homeland he had not seen since 1915. Vivienne could barely guess at the scale of the welcome which awaited Eliot in the United States, the country he had left as an unknown graduate student and to which he now returned, seventeen years later, as a conquering hero, creator of a modernist canon which had changed the face of literary history.

From the moment Tom left, Vivienne's social life imploded. Her network of friendships vaporised. It took many months for her to understand the cruel fact that she had only been tolerated as the poet's wife; and, as that title was taken from her, doors closed in her face. Many Bloomsbury "friends" did not return her calls; even her dearest friend, Ottoline, was suddenly not "at home" to her. It was a savage blow which Vivienne found bewildering, for she alone had no share in the secret to which Ottoline and Virginia were privy, and which was soon the subject of gleeful gossip at Bloomsbury parties: that Tom Eliot had no intention of ever seeing his wife again. "I have felt frightful being quite cut off from you all these terrible months," wrote Vivienne plaintively to Ottoline the following year. "I do not see why it is necessary." She begged for an opportunity to speak to Ottoline, or "a message even," signing her letter, "Vivienne Haigh-*Eliot*," the Eliot underlined three times.[82] But Ottoline remained obdurate.

From Cambridge, Massachusetts, Eliot wrote early in February 1933 to Ottoline, saying he understood her decision not to see Vivienne but wished to have trustworthy reports of his wife's mental and physical condition. If Ottoline were to see Vivienne, he would be glad of "a line of description."[83] It was a detached letter. Eliot reserved his warmth for references to his family, his three sisters and brother, who surrounded him with affection, and the mass of "secondary" relatives, who gave him the sense of belonging to a clan, and an important clan to boot. Outside of Boston, he wrote, he was simply T. S. Eliot, "but *here I am an Eliot.*"[84] After his prolonged tour of New York, California ("a nightmare"), Missouri, Minnesota, Chicago, Buffalo and Baltimore, he was relieved to be back in Harvard Yard, which felt like home, at B-11 Eliot House, lecturing to undergraduates on English literature.[85] This break in his life, he told Ottoline cautiously, would be "very significant" and would alter his life.[86]

Eliot forbore to mention either to Ottoline or Virginia one interlude in California which may have helped him come to his final decision over Vivienne: his visit to Scripps College, Claremont, to see Emily Hale, who now held the post of Assistant Professor of Oral English at this recently founded college for women. Emily's career had flourished in California: she played an imposing Lady Bracknell in a production of *The Importance of Being Earnest*,[87] bringing the same authority to her performance as that which caused Ottoline to dismiss her as a "sergeant-major" with a handbag when she and Eliot came to tea in October 1935.[88] But despite Emily's apparent bossiness, Eliot responded happily to the fuss she made of him when he visited Scripps College. Their contact continued during the Easter holidays, which Emily spent in Boston, where her uncle had become minister of King's Chapel, the historic heart of Unitarianism. After an Eliot family holiday, in which Emily was included, at Mountain View House, Randolph, New Hampshire,[89] Eliot wrote a nostalgically autobiographical poem, "New Hampshire." "Twenty years and the spring is over." The motif of children—regrets for those unborn—returned; their voices echo in the orchard, and they "swing up into the appletree."[90] It is a poem of hope, reflecting the illusion to which Eliot clung, that the happiness he felt in Emily's company could "normalise" him, as once he had hoped Vivienne's might. When Eliot even included her in a visit to his old school, Milton Academy, where he gave the Prize Day Oration—proudly telling Virginia Woolf by letter that he had "done the Old Boy properly"[91]— Emily could be forgiven for thinking that Eliot was serious about her and, if he were free, would wish to marry.

But part of the exhilaration Eliot felt was simply due to being back in America. A letter he wrote to Virginia in March 1933 bubbles with excitement at the mixture of familiarity and novelty which he encountered as he crossed the continent. After a time in America, nothing could surprise you, he told her. He had learnt how to pronounce Los Angeles and Albuquerque, but Terre Haute was beyond him. In Los Angeles, "They have a sky-scraper and it is bright green"; and in a restaurant called the Brown Derby, built of concrete to look like a brown bowler hat, he ate "Buckwheat Cakes and Maple Syrup and Coffee at Midnight, and it seems just as normal as an ABC..." In Providence, Rhode Island, a plump, somewhat tipsy lady from the "best society of the place" made eyes at him for three hours, responding to his every remark with "My! What a line you've got." Cocktails and champagne smoothed his way; a "nincompoop" of a congressman named Henry Cabot Lodge pressed three kinds of liqueurs on him, and beer and whisky. At Yale he lectured on English writers and met Thornton Wilder, at Baltimore he just missed Einstein, and at Vassar the young ladies performed *Sweeney Agonistes*. Eliot was learning what it meant to be a celebrity; it was a gratifying experience, despite his protests to Virginia that he would be happier to be back in England, consuming a dozen Whitstable oysters and a pint of Guinness.[92]

His mood was not always so buoyant. In Virginia, where in April to May 1933 he gave the three Page-Barbour lectures at the university, which were published as *After Strange Gods: A Primer of Modern Heresy* in 1934, he knew "iron thoughts," attacking D. H. Lawrence for being "spiritually sick" and, in some of his stories, even an instrument of "the daemonic powers."[93] The anti-Semitism which Eliot expressed, arguing that in "the society that we desire... reasons of race and religion combine to make any number of free-thinking Jews undesirable," has been excused on the grounds that "he merely reflected the pejorative feeling of his class and religion about Jews; that they are partly comic, partly sinister ..."[94] However, the intimate letters between Pound and Eliot of the early 1930s reveal a shared anti-Semitism directed at the critic F. R. Leavis ("Leavis louse"), who, wrote Pound, dumped his "anglo-yittisch and other diseased putrid secretions/notably a mess... spewing his Whitechapel spittle upon Sitwell," his "Leavis jew ooze," etc.[95] Eliot also continued his habit of using the lower case "j," attacking a "jew politician" called Julius Bender,[96] and had returned to his Jewish protagonist Bleistein in a Dirge which Pound had had the good sense to cut from *The Waste Land:* "Full fathom five your Bleistein lies/Under the flatfish and the squids," wrote Eliot. "Graves" Disease in a dead jew's eyes!/Where the crabs have eat the lids."[97] Now Bleistein lay "lower than the wharf rats"; slowly Eliot's verse dissected his body: the "lace that was his nose," the lips unfolding from the teeth, "gold in gold," while the lobsters kept watch. "Hark! Now I hear them scratch scratch scratch."

Over twenty years later, in 1955, Eliot stayed in Cape Town with Mr.

Justice Millin and his wife, Sarah Gertrude Millin, a novelist published by Faber & Faber. "That night before going to bed," wrote Tom Matthews, "Mrs. Millin was brushing up her acquaintance with Eliot's verse . . . when her eye fell on 'Burbank with a Baedeker: Bleistein with a Cigar,' and particularly these lines:

> The rats are underneath the piles.
> The jew is underneath the lot.

Mrs. Millin was a Jew. She went and rapped on Eliot's door, asked whether he acknowledged these lines (he did) and then asked him to leave her house next morning."[98] Eliot never recanted or changed these lines, although, according to William Empson, he later justified his lectures on the grounds that he was "very sick in soul" when he wrote them.[99]

As the months of Tom's absence passed, Vivienne waited expectantly for his return. She was not to know that Ottoline had advised him in March 1933 that she thought Vivienne would "flourish better" alone. It was exactly what Eliot wanted to hear, reinforcing a decision he had already made. In February 1933 he wrote to his solicitor, instructing him to draw up a Deed of Separation and enclosing a letter which the solicitor was to take personally to Vivienne, breaking the news. Eliot related that as he dropped the letter into the postbox he quoted the lines of Brutus from *Julius Caesar,* that he had once chosen as the epigraph to *Sweeney Agonistes:*

> Between the acting of a dreadful thing
> And the first motion, all the interim is
> Like a phantasma, or a hideous dream.[100]

Father Underhill and Ottoline had both argued it would be in both Tom's and Vivienne's interests to separate. Their promptings offered a salve to Eliot's conscience, and his attitude towards Vivienne had hardened. To Ottoline he wrote that he would prefer never to see Vivienne again, arguing that it could do no good to a woman to live with a man to whom she was "morally unpleasant," as well as physically repugnant. The heavily scored underlinings and crossings-out in this letter from Eliot, normally the neatest of correspondents, bears witness to the strength of his feelings. In his Calvinist eyes Vivienne's flesh was corrupt as the result of her carnal sins, and he judged her harshly. Judge/witch, doctor/patient, husband/wife, were patriarchal oppositions in which male/female power was ill-matched, whether the woman's "sin" was her supposed league with the devil, her wilful womb, or her adultery. As Eliot split off his idealisation of the Virgin, or an asexual "woman in white"—a role into which Emily Hale was forced to fit—from Vivienne—viewed as whore, temptress and Eve—her fate was sealed. Like the women of Canterbury in *Murder in the Cathedral* (1935) who invite rape, Vivienne had in his eyes consented to "the horror of the ape," and was "violated." Like these women, all women, the "living worms" of original sin lay coiled in her guts.[101]

While Eliot in New England brooded on the state of Vivienne's soul, his thoughts turned again to the witches of nearby Salem, who were said to have had carnal knowledge of the devil at their sabbaths. His ancestors had judged the witches; on his mother's side he was descended from Isaac Stearns, who had migrated from England to Salem in 1630. He felt himself to be a witchfinder still: "As for me, I can't help it," he had told Pound. "My great-grandfather was on the same witch jury as Nat Hawthorne's great-grandfather; and I just naturally smell out witches etc."[102] Was this not God's mission for him? In his bible he marked God's call to Isaiah:[103] "Thou *art* mine . . . The voice said, Cry. And he said, What shall I cry? All flesh is grass . . ."[104] But he kept his thoughts to himself: "Tell no-one what I have said," he instructed Ottoline: not Vivienne, nor anyone else.[105]

Vivienne, meanwhile, waited at home, ignorant of her husband's decision. To her great regret Ralph Hodgson and Aurelia Bollinger had returned to Japan, where Ralph had been invited to lecture. They left a final present of a "beautiful Kimono and scarf . . . which," wrote Vivienne, "I shall always treasure." It was almost too much pleasure for her to have them, she said sadly, feeling unworthy of such gifts.[106] She tried to fill the vacuum by turning to Alida Monro, who she felt understood Tom because he was so like Alida's late husband, Harold.[107] Alida, described by Virginia Woolf as "a handsome swarthy Russian looking woman in a black astrachan cap,"[108] was, declared Ottoline, extremely kind to Vivienne while Tom was away.[109] But Bloomsbury whispers led to stories that Alida was saying "disagreeable things" about Vivienne. Tom confided to Ottoline that Alida shared the same instinctive "antipathy" towards Vivienne as he did, one which she (and by implication he) had tried in vain to overcome.[110] Shocked by his misplaced criticism of Alida, Ottoline sent robust messages through Sencourt, Eliot's go-between, and forced him to apologise.[111]

At first Vivienne was not alone in her flat after Tom's departure. Robert Sencourt had introduced her to Tim and Mabel Nelson, two friends of his from New Zealand, and Mabel moved in with Vivienne. She was then replaced by Vivienne's old friend Lucy Thayer, who stayed with her at the request of the Haigh-Woods. On 29 November 1932 Vivienne sent a cheerful, meticulously typed letter to Mary Hutchinson, who had offered her the post of secretary.[112] "This is a sample of my typewriting," she wrote, wanting to tell Mary how happy the news made her. "I may really consider myself your Secretary from now on, may I not?" She asked Mary if she would dictate the articles she wrote for *Vogue* on fashion and home decoration, so that Mary would have no need to write them in longhand. "I can take them straight down for you on the typewriter, as I have done for Tom." They could work either at Mary's house or at Vivienne's flat, wrote Vivienne, saying that she was so happy about the whole thing that she was writing immediately to Tom. "Do hurry up with your notes, I am impatient to begin."[113]

The winter passed uneventfully. Vivienne had several tea-parties and gave a dinner-party on 14 December for the poet Walter de la Mare and his wife, to which she also asked Mary and Jack. She repeatedly asked if Mary was getting on with her article, as she was so impatient to start work.[114] Then in December a crisis occurred: Lucy Thayer, perhaps unable to stand the strain of Vivienne's demanding and volatile friendship, fled secretly to America. She was "vanished, flown." Vivienne had rung up her hotel to find that she had sailed on the *Europa,* and was distraught, not only because she had been planning to spend Christmas with Lucy, but because she was afraid that her friend would meet Tom in her flat in New York and betray Vivienne's confidences about him. Aware that she had spoken indiscreetly to Lucy, Vivienne complained guiltily to Mary that it was "vile" of her friend to do this.[115] Her first reaction was to follow Lucy, and she wrote to Tom, offering to come to America. When he read her letter, Eliot told Sencourt, he felt as if he had received an electric shock.[116]

Mary showered Vivienne with Christmas presents, calling on Christmas Eve when Vivienne was entertaining her family to dinner. She promised to call again to admire Vivienne's Christmas tree. This concern was not as spontaneous as it seemed. Mary, like Ottoline and Virginia, corresponded frequently with Eliot in America and, to some extent, acted as his agents in carrying out his instructions. Indeed, the Bloomsbury triumvirate of Virginia, Ottoline and Mary were in competition as to which one was most intimate with Eliot; he, in turn, played one off against the other, sharing confidences parsimoniously amongst his eager acolytes. Immediately after arriving in Boston in September 1932, Eliot had asked Mary to visit Vivienne from time to time: "It would be a kindness to me too."[117] Mary, unlike Ottoline, obeyed; perhaps she was fonder than Ottoline was of Vivienne, and had forgiven Vivienne for having compared her to Becky Crawley. Mary's own sexual adventurousness had foundered with age, but she would never judge Vivienne's amours as harshly as Eliot did; and, after the comparative failure of Mary's book *Fugitive Pieces,* which the Hogarth Press had published in 1927, she may have felt a certain sympathy for Vivienne's own abortive attempts to carve out a literary career. The depression Mary also suffered in 1928, as she came to realise that the pose of decadent coolness and detachment she had adopted under the influence of Aldous Huxley—he sent her his translation of Baudelaire's *Femmes Damnées*—left her simply confused and weary, lent her a measure of understanding of Vivienne's mental problems.

In March 1933 Vivienne appealed again to Ottoline to see her. Ottoline's only response was to suggest that Vivienne enter the sanatorium at Malmaison. Vivienne was horrified. How miserable to go to a nursing home without Tom to visit her. "No, I still have Liberty." She would stay at the flat, she protested, although she was "aneaimic" [sic] and looked awful. "I have had only 2 or 3 baths since Tom went away." The self-neglect Vivienne describes, only washing her hair twice, hair grey, hands red and rough, teeth "all broken . . . Children in the street do not look as dreadful," cannot be taken too literally: it was no doubt an exaggeration designed to provoke a meeting with Ottoline, and as such, it failed.[118] Maurice, by contrast, reported that Vivienne had redecorated the flat, and had given a small party at which Tom's health was drunk. Vivienne herself recalled the sunny day in early June 1933 when she asked her friend Isobel Lockyear to lunch at 68 Clarence Gate Gardens, where they discussed which bed Eliot would prefer to sleep in, and Isobel admired the new decorations and Harold Monro's old wardrobe which Vivienne had bought from Alida for Tom.[119]

On 26 June Eliot reluctantly caught the *Tuscania* to Greenock, Scotland. Vivienne, who had been waiting expectantly for his return since May, received a cable to say he had sailed for England, but by early July she had no news of her husband. She feared he had drowned. To Ottoline, Vivienne wrote on 7 July of her great anxiety about Tom, and belief that he was "in *danger.*" She had been "nearly insane" with anxiety for two weeks: "I do not know *where he is* and *no-one* knows where he is."[120] All day long she was receiving enquiries for Tom and was in "absolute terror." By Monday, 10 July, Bloomsbury was ringing with the news that "Tom has finally deserted Vivienne." Jack Hutchinson told Virginia that Vivienne "has by today worked herself into a frenzy—in bed, with a nurse." Jack then telephoned to Faber, at Leonard Woolf's suggestion:

> They say mysteriously that they cannot discuss the matter on the telephone, but if V will pull herself together she will realise that there is no reason for anxiety. This we interpret to mean that Tom is back; he has told Faber that he is parting from her; but it is kept secret, until he gives leave—which he may do today.

Jack told Virginia that he had read one of Tom's last letters, which he described as "a very cold and brutal document." Eliot had provided for Vivienne, said Virginia, and made Leonard her executor, but Vivienne had shut the letters in her cupboard with sealed string.[121]

Vivienne's concern was wholly understandable if she had not received the explanatory letter from Eliot's solicitors. It is possible that, as Virginia suggested, she did not read the post and shut the letters unopened in a cupboard. But she remained unaware that she was the victim of a conspiracy: that, while she waited in despair at Clarence Gate Gardens, Eliot was secretly travelling down to Surrey, to be hidden by Frank Morley. "I can neither conceal nor evade the fact that when Tom returned from Harvard . . .

he did not return to Vivien but came to Pikes Farm," wrote Morley. Eliot had given him "carte blanche to commit me to anything" on 3 May, and confirmed the arrangement to stay with him on 2 June. It seemed better to Tom to accept that Vivienne's relations and Enid Faber would do what they could for Vivienne in London, while he sheltered with the Morleys at the farm, wrote Frank in extenuation of his friend's plans. As instructed by Eliot's telegram from the *Tuscania,* Morley met him from the boat-train and took his heavy luggage to the country; after a night at his London club Eliot took the branch line to Surrey. Morley met him at the local station with the dog-cart, a touch which reminded Eliot of Sherlock Holmes and pleased him very much.[122] The poet was taken to the battered seventeenth-century brick farmhouse; there were no cows, of which he was "scary."[123] Soon Eliot had settled into "Uncle Tom's Cabin," where he had a bed and working-room, and was taking his meals at the house of Mrs. Eames, wife of the foreman of the adjacent brickworks.

Mary Hutchinson, left to face a hysterical Vivienne in London, complained indignantly to Tom that it was unfair of him to leave her and Jack to deal with the situation. "I am very sorry that you and Jack have had such a bad time—I did not anticipate this, and I do not know how else I could have managed," wrote an unrepentant Tom. His overriding desire from now on would be to avoid Vivienne at all costs, to conduct all negotiations through solicitors, and to sever completely all connection with his former life. The letter he sent, he wrote, must have made clear his reasons for concealing his movements, although he feared it might take some time to make Vivienne realise that his decision was irrevocable—"She is tenacious." He would, therefore, have to remain "in obscurity" for some little time.[124]

By 20 July Virginia had satisfied herself that her statement of events was quite correct. Gleefully she reported that Tom had left Vivienne "irrevocably": "& she sits meanwhile in a flat decorated with pictures of him, & altars, & flowers." She and Leonard were to dine with the Hutchinsons that night, "& shall I expect found some sort of Vivienne fund" (a reference to the ill-starred fund for Eliot).[125] Virginia's attitude towards Vivienne continued to oscillate. Her cold novelist's eye prompted the remark: "It was a most interesting process, to one who loves the smell of the rubbish heap as I do, to watch."[126] And yet, when she heard the next day that Vivienne had finally met Tom she wrote with some sympathy: "Vivi E said of the scene with Tom at the solicitors: he sat near me & I held his hand, but he never looked at me."[127]

Vivienne refused to accept Tom's desertion. Her only thought was to win her husband back. She would pay a large sum, and put everything into Tom's hands, if he would honestly come back to her, she told her solicitor. "But I will NOT sign any blackmailing paper relinquishing all rights to him for anybody."[128] The more she thought about the situation, the more Vivienne became convinced that Tom had not left her of his own free will, but at the instigation of their "enemies." "Because I *showed* I *enjoyed* our brief period of *Prosperity,* and because I *made* the *most* of it, *Jealousy* and *Envy* and *Hate* surrounded us both, and finally *tricked* Tom into going to *America,* and worse, to deserting *me,*" she wrote in her diary on 28 January 1934.[129]

Denial is a typical immediate reaction to loss, but it was one which left Tom intensely frustrated. "It would seem that Vivienne adopts the attitude that I have simply and unaccountably chosen to absent myself, leaving her in suspense and very much in the dark," he wrote in annoyance to Mary in September. On the contrary, it was *Vivienne* who was holding matters up. *He* had made it clear that he insisted upon a permanent separation, although he had thought it "fruitless and unnecessary" to give Vivienne any reasons for his decision, beyond saying that he was convinced that it would be the best thing for them both in the long run.[130]

It was natural for Vivienne to feel that she must see Tom, and hear from his own lips his reasons for leaving her. Without such a meeting, how could she accept that their marriage was over? "To induce her to regard the separation as final is quite impossible," wrote Vivienne's solicitors. "She asks that her husband shall return to her and manage her affairs and is ready to accept any conditions he may impose. If only Mrs. Eliot could be given some hope, however faint, of occasional visits by her husband and of eventual re-union it would help enormously."[131]

By September 1933 Eliot had become tired of Pikes Farm and the Surrey countryside, being anxious, said Morley "to get into theatre." He was again experiencing a poetic block after completing the "Five-Finger Exercise," which included the two poems on Ralph Hodgson and himself, and had given up the attempt to complete *Sweeney Agonistes.* "I seemed to myself to have exhausted my meagre poetic gifts, and to have nothing more to say," he wrote.[132] From this dry spell he was rescued by E. Martin Browne, a former actor who had been appointed by Bishop Bell to the post of Director of Religious Drama for Chichester. Browne asked Eliot to write the verse chorus for a pageant to raise money for forty-five churches in London, an offer which he welcomed after the drudgery of writing his American lectures. The pageant, to be named *The Rock,* was to be performed at Sadler's Wells Theatre, which its manager, Lilian Bayliss, had offered to the poet. Eliot now needed urgently to return to the capital. But, on the other hand, as he wrote petulantly to Mary, he could not think of returning to his marriage, a situation "to which I have already given the best years of my life." He railed at Vivienne's "obstruction and cajolery" at refusing to accept the separation. What steps could he take to make her see sense? He could not afford to blow his cover. Eliot became obsessional about preserving his secrecy, concealing his address, and the date of his visit, when he saw Virginia on 9 September at Rodmell. "The mystery I imagine flatters him," wrote Virginia sarcastically.[133]

When he arrived, Eliot seemed changed. "He is 10 years younger: hard, spry, a glorified boy scout in shorts and yellow shirt. He is enjoying himself very much. He is tight & shiny as a wood louse." At forty-six, he wanted "to live, to love." Over breakfast Tom and Virginia discussed Vivienne, with Tom showing "some asperity." He refused to admit the "excuse of insanity for her." Vivienne was not insane, said Tom, but "put it on." He was resentful of the past waste of his life. Virginia, sympathetic to suffering genius—as she believed Tom to be—promised to find him lodgings in Sussex.[134]

Ezra Pound proposed a meeting to "The Rt. Rev. Wunkus T. Possum." "You must come incognito, as I shall be the same," replied Eliot, offering to meet "Rabbit" in some "predetermined sequestered spot," such as Cliftonville or Reigate.[135] Pound suggested he should come to Rapallo, but Eliot demurred: "I must live cheap until I get things settled." His hair had started falling out on one side during 1932, he said, and he didn't know if there was a good wigmaker in Rapallo. Write to me at 24 Russell Square, he asked Pound, and mark the envelope "PERSONAL"; in a postscript he added a discovery made by most newly separated men: "Solicitors *are* expensive."[136]

Tom's refusal to divulge his address irritated Ottoline, as did his intimacy with Robert Sencourt. Robert had no greater facility to communicate with him than anyone else, protested Eliot: all his letters were forwarded from Faber at Russell Square because he did not wish to inconvenience any friends by entrusting them with an address which they would be expected to conceal.[137] A fortnight later, Ottoline complained she was still receiving messages through Sencourt rather than directly from Tom. "Robert is very sweet and good," replied Tom; his only fault was that he was something of a chatterbox, and liked to give people news of each other. Eliot promised Ottoline to come out of hiding soon.[138] However, the truth was that he enjoyed the mystery: the actor in him revelled in the role of Sherlock Holmes. He referred to Morley as "Inspector Morley," an assistant who, like the patient Watson, did his bidding in plodding but loyal fashion.[139] Of his oldest sister Ada, the only other intellectual in his immediate family, Tom often said that she was the Mycroft to his Sherlock Holmes.[140] Morley himself entered into the spirit of the saga, writing of his subsequent career, which took him away from Eliot: "I have often missed my Sherlock Holmes."[141]

Eliot's ducking and diving continued. He enlisted the help of Vivienne's doctor, Dr. Reginald Miller, who agreed to write her "an explicit letter," explaining that Tom's decision was irrevocable.[142] In November 1933 he was still waiting to hear whether Vivienne was prepared to sign the agreement,[143] but by the new year he was no further forward. Vivienne's only response was to write Tom letters, begging him to return to her to "be protected."[144] In his mind she became the pursuer; but in hers he was simply an errant husband, who must be coaxed back to the marital home. "The only thing I *yearn* for and *bleed* for is the day when Tom *calmly turns the keys* in the front door, walks *leisurely* in . . . and then has a good look round, *smiles* with quiet satisfaction, draws a *long breath,* and goes *quietly* to his *dear* books and to his bed," she wrote. "And if he *can then* say, God bless my little Welsh wife Vivienne. Surely he *wld* say that . . ."[145]

Eliot continued to house-hunt, and to obfuscate. On 31 October he had told Virginia that he intended to look for a room in Kensington, a district which he disliked, on his next visit to town, and take it temporarily while he looked about elsewhere. The room he was considering was three guineas a week for one room with breakfast and dinner, but he thought he could find two rooms for that price in a cheaper part of London, such as Clerkenwell, Blackheath or Greenwich.[146] Four days later, on 3 November, he was apologising to Mary for not receiving her invitation to dinner, because "my Miss Gilbert" at the office had made a muddle and failed to forward the card. "I wish I had given you my address," he wrote, not altogether convincingly; "it is only that I have not been able to give it to anyone lest it might be an inconvenience to them to know it . . ." He was, he wrote, hoping to find "a temporary abode" in London within the next fortnight, from which to conduct a search. He was going to Inverness, and then Paris for a day or two, and then wanted to settle in London while he waited to hear whether Vivienne would accept his terms.[147] Nevertheless, by December he was still lying low, declining Mary's invitation to her daughter Barbara's wedding: "In the present circumstances I don't go to parties." He was, however, prepared to go to *Measure for Measure* with the Hutchinsons and Woolfs at Sadler's Wells.[148] Eliot could get a house with grounds on the banks of Loch Lomond for £10 per annum, he joked to Pound in December. "But I don't like the climate." Even Wiltshire was "really too exposed."[149] In the end it was Sencourt who rescued Eliot from his country exile. He found him a room in a gaunt Victorian lodging-house in which he had himself formerly stayed, at 33 Courtfield Road, South Kensington.[150]

The lodging-house at Courtfield Road was devoid of women, apart from the housekeeper, Freda Bevan, who cooked for the residents. It was run by an "Old Catholic" eccentric, a once dubiously ordained bishop, William Edward Scott-Hall, and was something of an Anglo-Catholic enclave. Next door lived a prominent Anglo-Catholic, Miss Muriel Forwood, and nearby was the leading Anglo-Catholic layman Athelstan Riley, as well as Axel Munthe, author of *The Story of San Michele*.[151] Eliot played with Miss Bevan's cat, Bubbles, a tabby who became an inspiration for his cat verses, as did a majestic Persian named Xerxes; but a more important consideration than cats was Anglo-Catholicism, and fortunately Courtfield Road was only a few minutes' walk from St. Stephen's Church, Gloucester Road, where the priest, Father Eric Cheetham, held services which Eliot attended regularly.

It is unclear whether Eliot stayed for more than a few weeks at Courtfield Road. He continued "tramping Clerkenwell" in the search of better value accommodation, asking Virginia on 7 December to look out for anything "well recommended (furnished bed and sitting room)" with a bathroom geyser that worked, in "East Bloomsbury," between Southampton Row and Grays Inn Road.[152] Eventually it was Virginia who indirectly solved Eliot's accommodation problem—by reintroducing him to a fellow Hogarth Press author, the homosexual novelist C. H. B. Kitchen, who took pity on the poet and offered him "sanctuary" in his flat in Great Ormond Street. At the end of the year Eliot moved in with Clifford, and his two gay flatmates.[153]

21

Separation

Eliot experienced his time in Great Ormond Street as liberation. It was an all-male establishment: the poet's flatmates were his old friend, novelist Clifford Kitchin, Richard Jennings, a gay book collector, and Ken Ritchie, later Chairman of the Stock Exchange, who had a policeman lover. It was, recalls the novelist Francis King, "a gay household," in which Eliot felt free to venture out in the evenings, wearing "a bit of slap." "Clifford told me how Eliot went out rouged and lipsticked, with eye shadow," says King. "Clifford was absolutely convinced he was carrying on a gay life then." All three men liked to bring back "trade" to the flat; and why, asked Clifford, would Eliot choose to lodge in such a house were he not gay?[1] However, it was still a period in which discretion was all-important for a man like Eliot, who depended on his income from his work, and could not afford the aristocratic disdain shown by Osbert Sitwell, who was living openly with David Horner. Eliot kept his own counsel, and did not discuss his nightly jaunts with Kitchin.[2] But Stephen Spender, who had met Eliot in 1928 and had been published by Faber, was aware that Eliot wore cosmetics; in May 1996 Spender's widow Natasha confirmed the truth of the Sitwells' stories of Eliot's use of "pale green powder" to Alec Guinness, who played the psychiatrist Sir Henry Harcourt-Reilly in *The Cocktail Party*.[3]

Eliot was experimenting with a new lifestyle free of Vivienne and free, too, from the constraints of family life with Frank Morley. Sometimes he went out with Kitchin, whose new novel, *Crime at Christmas,* was published in October 1934 by the Hogarth Press. On 19 November he and Clifford dined with the Woolfs in Tavistock Square, Virginia finding Kitchin something of a misfit, "a little fat & white and cunning & not up to the mark. A rather conceited touchy man, I guess . . ."[4] And Eliot had the courage to support Djuna Barnes in her struggle to have her novel *Nightwood* (1936) published, after it had been turned down by her previous publisher, Boni & Liveright, as being "nothing more than a welter of homosexuality."[5] In Eliot's preface for the novel, which was published by Faber, he praised Barnes's characterisation of the cross-dressing doctor, Dr. Matthew O'Connor, whose original was her friend Dan Mahoney; once Barnes found Mahoney in bed dressed for a scene from *Nightwood,* "all bathed and perfumed and made up like a hussy, the clock was ticking, the radio going, the kitchen kettle steaming, and he was eating peppermints!"[6]

Yet Eliot was still living a falsehood. The closet remained a prison within which his isolation grew. In 1932 he had confessed in the foreword to Harold Monro's posthumous *Collected Poems* that "the compensations for being a poet are grossly exaggerated; and they dwindle as one becomes older, and the shadows lengthen and the solitude becomes harder to endure."[7] In *Sweeney Agonistes* Eliot had written of the loneliness within an unhappy marriage with startling innovation, anticipating the plays of Pinter; now he experienced a different solitariness, one relieved only by casual encounters, guarded friendships and office routine: Eliot's Hell was not "other people," as Sartre famously stated, but the condition he now experienced. "Hell is oneself,/Hell is alone, the other figures in it/Merely projections," says Edward in *The Cocktail Party.*[8] As Eliot told Princeton theologian Paul Elmer More in 1928, he looked into the void, that "void that I find in the middle of all human happiness and all human relations . . . I am one whom this sense of void tends to drive towards asceticism or sensuality, and only Christianity helps to reconcile me to life, which is otherwise disgusting."[9] He walked in a "daily terror of eternity," for religion had brought him, not happiness, but something "more terrifying than ordinary pain and misery."[10] Eliot was "really shocked" that More did not believe God had made hell; his own fear of damnation lived with him daily, as he relived the horrors of his marriage, which he described as a Dostoevsky novel written by Middleton Murry,[11] and brooded over the nature of good and evil and his private sins. Introspection brought little comfort, for by the standards of his own harsh Puritan morality, same-sex orientation and love was an abomination before the Lord. And yet it was the only form of relationship to which Eliot was attracted at that time.

Ottoline concluded that Eliot was either very sick or "rather crazy" when he viciously denounced D. H. Lawrence to her as "Evil" in April 1934, and recoiled in horror when she showed him some books of fourth-century Greek statues, saying they repelled him and were not far removed from serpent worship. What a strange relic of his Calvinist ancestry the poet was, thought Ottoline, as he talked obsessively of evil spirits, demonology and original sin, arguing that those who did not partake of Christian sacraments were possessed by devils. His censure of Lawrence and Vivienne, as of himself, revealed a dark and punitive seam within American Puritanism. Intuitively Ottoline understood that Tom saw evil spirits where no one else saw them because he felt them in himself, and that was why he had fled into the arms of the church, where priests could ward them off.[12] Only ritual and routine sustained him as he fought with the demons of his conscience. "What people call their conscience," wrote Eliot, is "just the cancer/That eats away the self."[13]

Eliot drew closer to Father Eric Cheetham, who in 1934 appointed him Vicar's Warden at St. Stephen's. At some point in late 1934 Eliot moved in with his vicar, whose rectory at 9 Grenville Place, Cromwell Road, shared with a number of curates, offered him a more congenial and discreet sanctuary than Clifford's flat. He had considered sharing a flat with A. L. Rowse, whose *Politics and the Younger Generation* he had nursed into print in 1931. In a letter dated 12 October 1934, Eliot set out his marital and legal difficulties, and the idea fell through.[14] This was probably due to Eliot's unwillingness to commit himself to any arrangement from which he could not immediately "decamp," as he put it later to Dorothy Pound. It is uncertain whether Eliot was still in Great Ormond Street or living with Eric Cheetham when in November Virginia Woolf asked where she might find him. Tom was so fearful that she might spy out his hiding-place that he replied, "You shall have my address only if and when you will come to see me, because it is Secret."[15]

Vivienne, meanwhile, was still in shock from Eliot's desertion. On Tuesday, 30 January 1934 she had had a meeting with her solicitor, Moxon Broad, and discussed the burning question of Tom's whereabouts. She instructed Broad "to *find out* his *domicile secretly* and *at once*. With *no view* to my attempting to *upset* him,"[16] for all she wanted, as she had told Ottoline on 31 December 1933, "is my *own* husband, and to be able to look after him and take *care* of him again," saying that she could not be persuaded into "what I think is wrong, or converted to cruelty"—a reference to the deed of separation.[17] Five months later, she and Broad had made no progress in tracing Tom: "I have no idea where my husband Tom is, and whether he is alive or dead," she wrote on 4 June 1934, one year after she had expected Eliot to walk through the doorway of their flat at 68 Clarence Gate Gardens.[18] Blotting out her brief meeting with him at his solicitor's office, she told Mr. Hope, her bank manager, the following summer, she had no proof that her husband had ever returned from America, although, as time passed, "it is easy . . . to say that he is living in England and to scare me, by every kind of bogey, from seeing him."[19] From Vivienne's point of view, the mystery deepened. Eliot had vanished as surely as Macavity, the mystery cat. No answer came to her requests, via her solicitor, for a meeting in which Eliot would give her the explanation he owed her. Vivienne therefore remained in denial, unable to accept the reality of his desertion. Maurice Haigh-Wood, who may have known Eliot's address, asked his brother-in-law if there were any other, less cruel way, than of writing through solicitors, but Eliot replied: "What other way *can* I find?"[20]

Eliot's pusillanimity was linked to his paranoid fear of Vivienne, a fear which had at its core the belief that further contact with her could drive him insane. As he had confessed to John Hayward in February 1931, he had had "considerable mental agony" at one time or another, and "once or twice felt on the verge of insanity or imbecility," feeling, until his conversion, that everything was "just waste and muddle,"[21] a phrase which echoes the last lines of the first of the *Four Quartets,* "Burnt Norton": "Ridiculous the waste sad time/Stretching before and after." Although, Eliot told Hayward, after his conversion "a pattern emerged," he never found the courage to face Vivienne honestly. As a result she remained baffled and frustrated, imagining that he was held prisoner and prevented from returning to her. She continued to refuse to sign the Deed of Separation.

On Boxing Day 1933 Vivienne had made a final appeal to Ottoline for a meeting: "I had such a terrible shock in the summer, and since then an increasing nightmare." Her strength, she wrote, could not last much longer. What appalled and amazed and completely bewildered her was that she was expected to *"agree and acquiesce* in a *wicked plot. And still am—! Bombarded. Threatened."* Her days had been spent mostly in bed over the last three months, she wrote, and she could only dress for a few hours. "I had no little presents from anyone this year." It was a self-pitying letter and Ottoline ignored it.[22]

To Ottoline, as to so many other judges of Vivienne, such talk of a "plot" seemed either evidence of paranoia and "madness" or wilful exaggeration, but in fact Vivienne's "paranoia" was justified. She *was* the victim of Eliot's determination, aided by her unscrupulous brother Maurice, to eradicate her from his life. His decision, the legacy of so many tempestuous years of marriage, was to lead—by a path of humiliation and subterfuge—to the first attempt to commit Vivienne to an asylum, while she, for her part, remained equally resolute in her own aim, to win Tom back by whatever weapons at her disposal. It was to be a bitter, but unequal war, one with a financial twist, in which Vivienne had at first no inkling that Tom was supported by her own mother and brother. The odds were stacked against her in a way she only slowly came to realise. It was a war she could not win.

The opening shots had already been fired by 1934, a year in which Vivienne felt embattled. "This is the sternest fight one delicate nerve-wrecked Englishwoman of 46 ever had to fight," she wrote on 14 June. "It is just relentless *warfare,* me and Polly, and a few crippled mercenaries, v the world."[23] She was at first an innocent in the struggle, a woman who had no experience of solicitors and had relied on her husband and brother to see to financial affairs. It was only her friends and neighbours, Charles and Ella de Saxe, who warned her *"not* to put my signature to any paper or document connected with Tom," by which she might have signed away her rights to her property and papers.[24] The de Saxes supported Vivienne, seeing her almost every day for six "terrible" months and keeping her head "clear," until they left for South Africa at the end of 1934. With their support Vivienne remained firm and refused to sign any "dirty paper" presented to her by James & James, the Haigh-Wood family solicitors. But after the de Saxes went abroad, Vivienne was vulnerable to pressure from James & James, who took advice from Maurice, and to demands from her husband's solicitors, Bird & Bird. Maurice, now a stockbroker at

Northcotes in the City, managed the Haigh-Wood estate which he, Vivienne, and their mother Rose, had inherited from Charles Haigh-Wood on his death. At first Vivienne trusted her brother to look after her interests, until Charles de Saxe suggested that Maurice had "bungled" the purchase of some de Havilland shares. Feeling that the truth of her financial situation was being kept from her, Vivienne became concerned to discover the full extent of her legacy from her father, and instructed her own solicitor, Moxon Broad. In the four-year struggle over the family money, which ensued until Vivienne's final committal, Broad was her ally.

Vivienne's domestic situation was also one to justify fears of persecution, for she was kept under surveillance by the Eliots' servant, William Leonard Janes, who was in Tom's pay, but whom Vivienne mistakenly regarded as a friend ("not a servant"), and whom she innocently but unwisely took into her confidence. Janes regularly monitored her behaviour and reported to Eliot, who may at first have been motivated by concern for her condition without him. "I have not seen or herd [sic] from Mrs. Eliot since she came last Saturday week when she came to take away the Tin Base . . ." wrote Janes.[25] "Janes stayed on at 68 Clarence Gate Gardens just to watch over Vivie," said Maurice.[26] The ex-detective's reports furnished evidence for the first, unsuccessful attempt to commit Vivienne to a private mental home.[27] Yet on 1 August 1934 Vivienne recorded gratefully in her diary that W. L. Janes and Jan Culpin (possibly the mother of Eliot's Oxford friend Karl Culpin),[28] were the only two people who cared for her: "These two are both *old* people, who can *expect nothing from me, gain nothing by my death*—and there is *no* way in which I can reward them, *nor do they look for reward,*" she wrote, comparing "these 2 *old* people with *my* mother, *my brother, my aunts, and My Husband* . . . These questions did not come to my mind during my Father's lifetime."[29]

It is ironic that Vivienne, who fervently desired to preserve her papers in order that posterity might judge her fairly, trusted Janes, who passed information to his master, which made possible the removal by force of some of those records from 68 Clarence Gate Gardens. Although Vivienne prized her liberty so highly that she refused Ottoline's suggestion that she enter the Malmaison sanatorium in 1932, she allowed Janes to know the details of her health, including her almost daily visits to collect her drugs from her chemist Allen & Hanbury at 7 Vere Street, as well as her unwavering determination to pursue Tom. Had she not confided so freely in Janes, she might have preserved both her liberty and her possessions with more success.

Yet at times Vivienne was frightened of Janes. In January, he "banged and bawled" at her cook, Mrs. Forminger, and made such a *"hideous* row" in the kitchen that she was driven to speak to him: "he then became most abusive, railed against Mrs. Forminger whom he really seems to hate, and finally banged out, leaving me quite sick and faint; saying he would never come back any more . . ."[30] When she kept him waiting he reminded her of his high blood pressure and said "he wished me to understand that he is close to 80 years old and *my* troubles are no affair of his."[31] Nevertheless, Vivienne often called on Janes and his wife at 101 Lumley Buildings, their flat in Pimlico, joining them for Mrs. Janes's birthday tea on 7 October 1934; when Mrs. Janes was ill on October 29, Vivienne hurried out to buy her a bottle of whisky, and when Vivienne herself collapsed on 11 November, Janes handed her "a *very* hot water bottle" and told her: "If you can stay in bed all day, it is the best place for you and I advise you to do so." Such daily intimacy lulled Vivienne into a false sense of security.

As Vivienne painfully came to realise that her life with Eliot was over, it became her priority to find a place of safety for the records which charted that life. On 31 December 1933 she had told Ottoline: "The truth will all come out, if not in *our* life—*then after it.*"[32] In her diary of 1 August 1934 she addressed future researchers: "You who in later years *will read these very words of mine* and will be able to trace a true history of this epoch, by my Diaries and Papers."[33] Anticipating the blame which would be heaped upon her for the failure of the marriage, and already suspicious of Maurice and her mother, she considered to which institution she should leave her archive of diaries, drafts of fiction and poetry, photograph albums, account books and letters. Oxford had happy associations with Tom's courtship, of punting on the river with Scofield and Lucy Thayer, and she therefore chose the Bodleian Library. Within a year of Tom's desertion Vivienne decided to write her decision into her will, having her first meeting with her solicitor, Moxon Broad, on 30 January 1934, and writing in her diary: "N.B. Change Wills . . . Instruct to keep J & J [James & James] off me entirely, & to procure a moderate *rent* for a new home." Soon Moxon Broad had nineteen letters between Vivienne and James & James in his file, as

Vivienne began the long process of attempting to gain control over her share of her father's legacy. Interestingly, one of Vivienne's early impulses was to make a will "leaving to Theodora," Eliot's niece, some of her estate.[34]

On 24 June 1934, the anniversary of the day, one year ago, on which "T. S. Eliot, my *husband,* was to have *sailed from Boston . . .*" Vivienne reflected on a year in which "there has been more serious damage and *evil* and abomination in my life than I should have believed *possible* in *England* in 1934 to go *unpunished.* This is a black document." Two days later, 26 June, was an even more unhappy day for Vivienne, marking as it did the nineteenth anniversary of "the Wedding Day of Thomas Stearns and Vivienne Haigh Eliot." Nevertheless, conscious that the seventeen years she had shared with Eliot would prove of enormous interest to future readers, she wrote with pride in her diary that day: "What an example to hand down from generation to generation, and what an *invaluable* gift I have made to the *Bodleian* Library, Oxford." Her hope was that her papers, manuscripts and diaries would be published "without *alterations.*"[35] On 22 July 1934, Vivienne signed a new will at 1 Great Winchester Street, EC1, the office of Moxon Broad, in which she bequeathed her papers to the Bodleian in order to avoid their falling into the hands of either T. S. Eliot or Maurice Haigh-Wood.[36] Vivienne Haigh Eliot signed her final will, witnessed by Moxon Broad and his stenographer, on 1 March 1936, in which she gave to the Bodleian Library "absolutely and free of duty all my papers manuscripts diaries journals photographs albums and sketches"; advised by Broad, she supposed that in making this bequest she was also leaving copyright in her unpublished manuscripts to the library, as the Copyright Act 1911 had apparently created a rule of presumption that the legatee was the owner of the copyright. To Eliot she left first choice of her family portraits, and her "personal chattels," as well as her Yorkshire terrier Polly and cat Whiskers.[37]

Vivienne was afraid that Tom, who was in possession of the keys to 68 Clarence Gate Gardens, which he had taken with him when he left for America on 17 September 1932, might return without her knowledge to the flat when she was absent and remove documents such as her diaries. On Monday 23 July, she decided to ask the Hutchinsons if they knew where these keys were now, because Mary had taken such a "keen inter-

est" in her keys during the time Tom was in America.[38] She gave instructions to her maid, Ivy, that the door was not to be opened to anyone. "I am
not at home," said Vivienne, forbidding Ivy to open the door even to her
mother when she rang the bell.[39] But Vivienne now found another ruse by
which she hoped to outwit Tom: she had, according to Maurice, asked the
management of the blocks for another little flat "for a servant," and they
had offered her number 177, on the second floor, a tiny flat but one which
served her purpose of storage. "One flat—number 68—was in Tom's name
still," said Maurice. "And Vivien was paying *somehow* for 177. She moved
all she could upstairs."[40]

Vivienne's longing to see Tom grew during the anguished hours she
spent puzzling over his disappearance. Between 1934 and 1938 she and
Eliot played out a game of cat and mouse, in which she was at first the pursuer, he the quarry. Her first impulse was to "collar" him at the theatre. In
April 1934 Vivienne attended a party on the stage at Sadler's Wells, a few
weeks before the opening of *The Rock,* the pageant play Eliot had written
at the invitation of Martin Browne. The invitation from Lilian Bayliss, the
manager of the theatre, was perhaps addressed to both Eliots, as a large
volume of post, as well as many telephone calls for Eliot, continued to be
directed to the flat. Vivienne was nervous about attending, but a new
friend, artist Margaret Smith, "incited" her to go. Ella de Saxe, too, continued to encourage Vivienne in her struggle to survive her mysterious
abandonment by Eliot, *"urging* me to *courage* and *endurance* by *reminding*
me I *must* fight on and not funk anything . . ."[41] It was in this spirit that
Vivienne slowly dressed in her blue velvet dress on 16 April and took a taxi
at 10:30 p.m. to Sadler's Wells. It was terrible at first, she recorded, but
Miss Bayliss was very kind and came up and greeted her. Vivienne sat close
to the door, keeping her eyes "fixed for Tom." At first she saw no one she
knew, but at last in came Mary and Virginia, together. Both greeted her,
and were "very nice." Jack Hutchinson and Leonard then entered, and
Mary reintroduced her to her son, Jeremy.[42] Food and drink were handed
round; Vivienne waited in hope, but of Eliot there was no sign. Holmes
had given her the slip.

On 28 May, Vivienne's birthday, *The Rock* opened at Sadler's Wells.
"He did it for my birthday, I know," she comforted herself. That evening,

sitting in cheap seats with Margaret Smith and munching her sandwiches, Vivienne looked down on the stalls where St. John Hutchinson sat smoking a big cigar. The Fabers, in evening dress, were chatting to the great and the good. Nothing could have underlined more clearly the change in her lifestyle. She and Margaret waited until the very end, and saw everyone leave: "We walked all round and hung about but no sign of TS Eliot at all," wrote a frustrated Vivienne.[43] Four days later she renewed her quest, returning to Sadler's Wells for another performance of the pageant. The theatre was full but, once again, there was no sign of Tom: bewildered, she left in the interval.[44] Was Tom alive or was he dead, she demanded of her diary.[45] On 7 June she took two buses to the theatre, and stood in the gods, jostled by the crowds, craning her neck for a glimpse of the playwright. After the curtain came down, "I hung about a long time," she wrote sadly: "No sign of Tom."

On 9 June Vivienne attended *The Rock*'s final performance, a small figure among the audience of 1,500. That night the pageant made a powerful impression upon her: she found it both moving and terrible as the masked chorus declaimed Eliot's words, castigating society for its materialism and holding up to ridicule the lives of commuters, those "decent godless people" whose only monument was "a thousand lost golf balls."[46] The evening was an emotional experience "in the heat and the *horror.*" She found it hard to believe that Tom had written it and she felt the author was "certainly a very wicked man to so play (and prey) on the *emotions.*" As she, like Tom, turned over the past in her mind, she came to the conclusion that Eliot was immoral; although the pageant was *"very* beautiful," with its exhortations to the audience not to neglect God, "It is the man who wrote it, *if that is TSE,* whose soul must be saved . . ."[47]

That summer was a time of despair for Vivienne. A day or two after seeing *The Rock,* an experience which brought her old life with Tom vividly back to her, she recorded that "a very queer *stunned, lost, dazed* feeling is creeping over me. It is the strangest episode—like a vast preparation for a *death.* Crépescule [sic] des Dieux." A foray into Camden Town to see her cleaner, Margaret Clee, whom she had sacked, left Vivienne frightened and nervous, and she began at last to take note of Jan Culpin's warning not to trust the servants: "Now I do see what Jan means and that no doubt it is a plant and a crib, and all my servants are tampered with and paid agents . . ." Hurriedly she threw 30 shillings on to the camp-bed, once Tom's bed, which Clee had stolen, and fled in a taxi.[48]

Day after day Vivienne walked with her dog Polly to Allen & Hanbury at 7 Vere Street to collect her medicine, which included the sleeping-pill Soneril, and saw her pharmacist friend Louie (Louise) Purdon, with whom she sometimes lunched at the ABC café. Vivienne rose late and ate out, often visiting Selfridges for waffles and coffee or shopping in Marshall & Snelgrove; sometimes she visited her favourite doctor, physiotherapist Dr. Anna Cyriax, who practised with her husband, Dr. James Cyriax, and father-in-law, Dr. Edgar Cyriax, at 41 Welbeck Street, for a "treatment," but although she and Polly roamed the streets of London, between Marylebone, Kensington and Pimlico, remarkably Vivienne never caught a glimpse of Eliot. It was a "blisteringly hot" summer that year. 12 June 1934 was one of the most perfect June days Vivienne had ever seen:

> A pure blue sky, a still, hot, yet fresh air. No dust or mist, but almost like Italy. The high white buildings here look most beautiful against the sky and now that Clarence Gate Gardens is painted outside it holds its own with the newer buildings. It must be *exquisite* in the *country* to-day, or on the river. The *height* of the *Season,* and here I am, *lost* in London. Was there ever a more *strange* life than mine?[49]

By the end of July Vivienne felt that her nerve had completely gone. "I look like the *ghost* of a street child," she wrote. "My face is yellow like parchment, no colour, dead eyes, am as thin as a rat." She was too restless to rest, too tired to think constructively.[50] The black and white head and shoulders portrait of her, drawn by Margaret Smith that summer, showed "the bland expression of one who has learnt to keep out of the way. Out of anyone's way. A hard school," and was it a wise one, asked Vivienne, who was beginning to question her own docility. "Isn't it better to throw one's weight about?"[51] But she remained nervous. Frightened of sleeping alone in the flat, from which she had had the telephone removed, she preferred to spend the night at a hotel at 20 Roland Gardens, Kensington, staying in room number seven, Jan Culpin's room, during her absence in Germany.

During the day Vivienne returned to 68 Clarence Gate Gardens. She maintained the flat meticulously, often cleaning it herself with Mrs. Forminger. Although Vivienne had packed up the silver in March, depositing it in the District Bank, and had arranged the auction of the surplus furniture, she had no intention of leaving the flat, renewing the lease in June for a further five years. Instead, Vivienne kept their former home as a "Shrine to Tom," similar to the shrine to Oswald Mosley, leader of the British Union of Fascists, which she much admired at the BUF Christmas Bazaar held in Chelsea on 8 December. Vivienne was impressed by Lady Cynthia Mosley, whom she saw at the bazaar, and congratulated herself on having joined the movement at the Women's Fascist Headquarters at 12 Lower Grosvenor Place three days earlier. Vivienne felt "glad and relieved" to join the Fascists, believing the movement would bring a return to the "happy, organised public service" she remembered from the war.[52] She had shared Eliot's right-wing beliefs: the year 1934 was the one in which his lectures at the University of Virginia were published as *After Strange Gods: A Primer of Modern Heresy,* lectures for which Isaiah Berlin was to take him to task in 1951, pointedly referring to the fact that, in the year after Hitler came to power, "You thought it a pity that large groups of 'free-thinking Jews' should complicate the lives of otherwise fairly homogeneous Anglo-Saxon Christian communities? And that it were better otherwise? . . . And that it would be better for such communities if their Jewish neighbours . . . were put 'beyond the borders of the city'?" Berlin quoted Eliot's words back to him: "reasons of race and religion make any large number of free-thinking Jews undesirable." How could he insist that "race" had nothing to do with the "Jewish problem"? Although Eliot apologised to Berlin for the offensive sentence, writing, "the sentence of which you complain would of course never have appeared at all at that time, if I had been aware of what was going to happen, indeed had already begun in Germany . . . ," he did not, even then, abandon the idea of "race" altogether, writes Michael Ignatieff.[53] Nevertheless Eliot was no supporter of Mosley,[54] but Vivienne felt her husband would be pleased as she hung a large portrait of him by Sir William Rothenstein in the drawing-room, highlighted just as the portrait of Lady Cynthia's husband had been high-lighted at the bazaar. Her "altar" to Tom was flanked on each side by two Venetian mirrors given to her by Charles and Ella de Saxe. On another wall she hung a sketch of Eliot by Wyndham Lewis. She also displayed three oil paintings by her father, and two of his watercolours.

Over the summer months of 1934 Vivienne fought a running battle with cockroaches in the kitchen, but finally the local vermin officer brought the problem under control. By October the flat was *"Quite* perfect," and it accorded the perfect setting, too, for Vivienne to indulge an-other passion: her fervent royalism. With pride she displayed on the drawing-room mantelpiece her invitation to a reception given by the English Speaking Union at Londonderry House to meet HRH The Prince of Wales, and arranged white roses in the room in honour of "Elizabeth, Princess [sic] of York."[55] She had seals made with the crests of the Earls of Carnarvon and St. Germans, to whom Eliot claimed connection, and used them to seal her private papers. And on 30 October 1934 she and W. L. Janes walked to Londonderry House, Vivienne in her blue dress and cloak from Barkers, her hair newly waved, for her presentation to the Prince of Wales. She felt so faint as she waited in the immense crowd that two American ladies brought her some sherry; until at last her turn came to walk up the wide staircase and stand beside the two ushers. Vivienne was momentarily annoyed that they did not call out her name: but then, "in front of me stood his royal highness, the Prince of Wales, first gentleman of Europe. He looked so young, and is about my height and build. His head is on the small side, his shoulders very square and a very fine car-riage . . ." When the prince held her hand in his own "very strong grip" she almost fainted with joy; and she remained, fixed to the ground, until at last the usher said, walk straight on.

Despite these high points in an otherwise humdrum life, Vivienne sometimes felt that she was on the verge of "nervous collapse," but her new help, Mrs. Read, had "a true mother's heart," and shopped and cooked for Vivienne daily. Meanwhile her fascination with the royal family contin-ued: in November she sent a copy of Eliot's poem "Marina" to Prince George, Duke of Kent, and Princess Marina as a wedding present, signing it "from VHE and TSE, with sincere wishes for their happiness,"[56] just as she sent out Christmas cards from "Mr. and Mrs. T. S. Eliot" in 1935.[57] For the Silver Jubilee of George V in 1935, Vivienne decorated her balcony with large Irish and French flags, the Union Jack, Stars and Stripes, and "two small royal standards," plus an electric light from Woolworth's with red, white and blue lamps: "I meant to make my balcony a success no matter what it cost for their royal highnesses Queen Mary and King George," she wrote in her diary. She volunteered to sell flowers on 3 June, collecting her tray of red, white and blue flowers, and walking the streets all afternoon, gratified to find that she sold far more than she expected.[58]

The English Speaking Union continued to be the centre of Vivienne's social life, giving her an excuse to indulge her interest in fashion, as well as an outlet for the snobbery of which she had often accused Eliot. Early December 1934 found Vivienne once again at Barkers, having her hair dressed in Empire style, with five hanging curls, and her nails manicured in preparation for a reception for Mr. and Mrs. Bingham, the American ambassador and his wife. Lovingly Vivienne selected the cream chiffon and black lace Agnes Decolt model dress she had bought for Tom's return; and, although her maid Gretel dressed her in a red and black velvet dress which she had altered, her mistress immediately changed her mind. In the cream chiffon with a blue sash, gold shoes and stockings, long cream suede gloves and pearls, Vivienne and her friend, Mrs. Winden, took a taxi to Berkeley Square. This time her name was loudly and clearly announced, but otherwise the evening did not live up to expectations. Vivienne had hoped to make some new, American friends, writing in her diary: "I only came for Americans, Royalty, French cultured people." Perhaps she dreamt of finding a successor to Eliot; if so, she was disappointed.[59]

As time passed, Vivienne grew increasingly apprehensive at the prospect of suddenly coming face to face with Tom in public. She fretted over whether or not to attend a meeting of the Sadler's Wells Theatre at Lord Howard de Walden's in Belgrave Square on 28 June. The only reason she had for hesitating, she wrote, was the reason she had for hesitating to attend *any* function: "The determination I have formed *NOT* to meet my husband *anywhere* but *in his* (and my) own home. Alternatively at the Sanatorium de la Malmaison in the presence of *witnesses* of my own *choosing* . . . Never having seen him in his own home *since September 17th 1932* I have formed this *determination* for my own *protection* and it is very necessary."[60] But in reality Vivienne was no closer to finding Tom's "domicile"

than she had been since he returned to England in July 1933. Dinner with
Geoffrey and Enid Faber in March 1934 had yielded no clues, even though
Faber and Eliot worked together daily. Vivienne was happy that evening:
Enid looked "charming," and the Fabers' new house at Oak Hill Park was
"nice and homelike." But "Tom's name was not mentioned, *that* we had
agreed beforehand."[61] Although Vivienne dared asked no questions of
Faber, without doubt he reported to Eliot on Vivienne's condition, as did
the "eccentric impulsive odd ecstatic" writer Hope Mirrlees, who brought
her black dachshund to have tea with Vivienne and "Polly Eliot" the same
month.[62] Vivienne wrote to Violet Schiff and Virginia Woolf, as well as
Ottoline, but the wall of silence which protected Eliot was impenetrable.
Nevertheless, by March, Vivienne was, she recorded, "feeling saner," an
impression also gained by Virginia, who had told Ottoline two months earlier that she had received a "remarkable letter" from Vivienne Haigh-
Eliot.

> Happily she doesn't ask me to do anything. She merely says that
> Tom refuses to come back to her, and that it is a great tragedy—
> so I suppose I can agree and say no more. She has made Leonard
> her executor, but writes sensibly—rather severely, and with some
> dignity poor woman, believing, she says, that I respect marriage.[63]

Once Vivienne's initial panic subsided, she began to consider more
logically the best means by which to locate Tom. It is strange that it did not
at first occur to her that her mother and brother were in touch with Eliot.
Maurice had become closer still to Tom after returning from Lagos, where,
as Colonel Haigh-Wood, he had been Chief of Police; not only had he and
Ahmé shared continental holidays with Tom and Vivienne as recently as
1930, Maurice and Tom went to the races together, and no doubt Maurice,
as a stockbroker and joint trustee of the Haigh-Wood estate, also discussed
market movements and the rise and fall of the Haigh-Wood and Eliot
portfolios with his brother-in-law. For by the terms of Charles Haigh-
Wood's will of 3 January 1920, Rose, Maurice and Tom had all been appointed trustees of the Haigh-Wood estate, but Vivienne was excluded and
was simply paid an allowance through the District Bank. Vivienne resented this dependence, especially when Alfred E. James, solicitor for the

Haigh-Wood estate, wrote her a "Fatherly but threatening" letter in March when he "spied out" that she had not collected her income from the bank and sent her the Selfridges account to settle. She was annoyed: "It is the old game," she wrote, "and it is vile, *caddish,* and it *won't do.*"[64] She was being treated like a child, and she knew it. Now that she no longer lived with Eliot, in whose management of the family money she had implicitly trusted, she became concerned to discover the value of her third of the estate, for by the terms of Charles Haigh-Wood's will and codicil of 18 May 1927, she was entitled to equal shares in the trust funds with her brother Maurice, subject to her mother Rose's life interest.[65]

Vivienne then began an arduous campaign. Her first step was to try to obtain a copy of her father's will in the early months of 1934, as well as his death certificate. Maurice tried to distract her, aware that if Vivienne remained in ignorance of the true extent of her wealth, he and Tom, also a trustee, could get away with paying her an allowance below her real entitlement. In February Maurice brought Vivienne a bunch of violets and snowdrops and took her for a walk in Regent's Park. On 10 April he took his sister out to lunch at Trinity House in the Strand: "He gave me a *very good* meal," reported Vivienne with delight. "We had an amusing conversation which I shall record and try to get published in a short collection called 'Conversations Embittered.' "[66] Even in July, when she dropped in on her mother at 3 Compayne Gardens, and found "Maurice lunching with Mother and both of them *very* well and complacent," Vivienne still felt her brother's motives were altruistic. She had walked past Maurice's house in London every day, she told him pathetically, for she longed to see him. Maurice, who had resolved never to receive his sister, coolly informed her that he and Ahmé had been living in the country since June.

As the months passed, Vivienne struggled to penetrate the mystery of the Haigh-Wood finances. April found her at the Inland Revenue Office, enquiring about a tax rebate on the Irish rents she received, and at Somerset House, where on the 18th she finally obtained her father's will. However, it was explained to her that she needed permission from one of the trustees to obtain an affidavit to enquire into the disposition of the Estate. At last Vivienne discovered her father had left nearly £40,000 in one trust, but she could find no record of the 1927 codicil regarding the Irish estate and the properties in Kingstown. Grudgingly Maurice gave her a letter entitling her to obtain a Power to Search, although, as a trustee, he already knew the contents of the codicil and could have saved her this trouble. For Vivienne, it was like wading through treacle. In July she visited the Warrior House Hotel at St. Leonards in the hope that an inspection of the ledgers for March 1927 would reveal the signatories to the Irish codicil which her father had made on his death-bed, but her visit was to no avail: the manageress refused to let her see the register.[67] Maurice continued to obstruct her efforts to find out what the Irish estate was worth and therefore whether she was receiving a fair share of income from the trust funds set up by their father.[68] Shortly before his death in 1980—at the age of eighty—Maurice finally confessed his greed in a remorseful interview with Michael Hastings: "We did not want Vivie to have her share [although] she always said a third was hers."[69]

Thus, Vivienne had little hope of discovering the truth. By 1 January 1935 she suspected she was being deceived:[70] "A whole mistake they all made was to try to keep me in ignorance of how much money I really had and would have," she wrote, having come upon some figures jotted down by Tom. "It appears that it is a much larger income than I had ever been told."[71] But Maurice told her that her income was only £400 a year, Eliot carried her cheque book in his briefcase, and Vivienne's spending was controlled by the men of the family who were determined to override Charles Haigh-Wood's intentions to make just and generous provision for his beloved daughter.

Once Vivienne gained sight of her father's codicil, she demonstrated her loyalty towards her estranged husband by an initial, generous impulse to leave him half of the share of the Irish estate which she would inherit on her mother's death. On 7 April 1935 she drafted a new will: "To Tom, all the rest of my estate, unconditionally and absolutely, our house in Ireland—Eglington House—or rent of the same."[72] As trustees she appointed Tom, Maurice, St. John Hutchinson, Geoffrey Faber, and Philip Morrell—a naïve choice, perhaps, but who else did Vivienne have to trust? At this point, in early 1935, Vivienne felt sure that Tom had made a will, leaving "everything without exception" to her—apart from his ring and his stick to Henry—and that she and Geoffrey Faber were joint trustees of his literary estate and would inherit Eliot's copyrights.[73] In this she was deeply mistaken: by 18 February 1938 Eliot was pressing John Hayward to act as his literary executor, pleading that he knew no one except John whom he could altogether trust in that capacity, and stressing his "mania for posthumous privacy." Your job, Eliot wrote to Hayward, would be "to suppress everything suppressable, however F & F might be tempted."[74]

However, Vivienne soon changed her mind about Maurice. By June 1935 she was complaining that her acquisitive brother was a "DIRTY DEVIL," who had "wiped up" all their mother's dining-room furniture. "Poor old lady, how dare he?" she demanded of her diary. Maurice and Ahmé were "proper gangsters," she wrote, who had stolen from Rose.[75] In November she wrote to Maurice at his office at Gresham House, Old Broad Street, protesting at his threatening letters warning her to keep away from mother, which Vivienne began burning, unread. "Kindly cease interfering with me," she ordered her brother.[76] It is puzzling, therefore, ten months later, to find Vivienne signing a new will, making over her entire share in the Irish estate to Maurice. Why did she change her mind? It is possible that at this time Eliot offered to give up any share in the Irish rents willed to him by Vivienne, after his financial position had improved with his director's salary and the royalties due from his *Collected Poems* in 1935, in return for Maurice's promise to silence Vivienne. Alternatively, Eliot may not have wished, on moral grounds, to benefit from the estate of the wife from whom he was separated. Without doubt, though, as joint trustees Tom and Maurice would have discussed the wills which Vivienne was making in 1934–36, and which Maurice, from the evidence of Vivienne's diary, was "helping" her draft.

Unaware of her mother's true feelings towards her, Vivienne frequently visited Rose, and her aunts Lillia and Jackie, dining and sometimes staying at Compayne Gardens; in March 1934 Rose celebrated her seventy-fourth birthday and Vivienne sewed "a tea-cosy for mother."[77] "If only my husband had had the gentleness not to give her this last blow," she lamented. "So late in her poor life. It is cruel and shameful—and a black scar. She *did* admire him and has been so hurt."[78] But Rose and Vivienne had a volatile relationship, as proved by Rose's will of 1936, in which she cut Vivienne out altogether, leaving all her personal chattels to Maurice, and the capital and income of the trust fund to her grandson Charles, as well as legacies to her sisters Lillia Symes and Ada Woolff, and niece Edna Zeistell. Even the maid received a legacy, but of Rose's only daughter

Vivienne there is no mention, indicating that the family had come to the joint conclusion that she was unfit to inherit.[79]

Rose and Maurice remained in touch with Eliot and his family, but kept Vivienne in the dark. For instance, Rose knew in July 1934 that Eliot's niece Theodora Eliot Smith, of whom Vivienne was very fond, was staying in London at the Constance Hotel. She refrained from telling Vivienne, who, left in ignorance, went on holiday to the Warrior House Hotel in Eastbourne. But in September another of Tom's relatives, Elizabeth Wentworth, arrived in London, writing in advance to tell Vivienne of her visit. Delighted to receive an Eliot at 68 Clarence Gate Gardens, where she had had a new carpet laid in the drawing-room, Vivienne entertained Miss Wentworth to tea, and showed her around the flat with its portraits and photographs of Tom and other Eliot relatives. The next day Vivienne and Elizabeth Wentworth lunched together at the English Speaking Union, and Vivienne arranged to have two handkerchiefs embroidered with the name "Marian Eliot," for Elizabeth to take home to Tom's sister Marian, who lived in the same block of flats in Cambridge, Massachusetts.[80] "Point counter point," she wrote triumphantly in her diary.

In September 1934 Vivienne stepped up her efforts to contact her husband. On the 13th she tried to place an advertisement in the personal column of *The Times:* "Will T. S. Eliot please return to his home 68 Clarence Gate Gardens, which he abandoned September 17, 1932." The newspaper did not publish her message, but a few days later, on 22 September, W. L. Janes told Vivienne that he had seen Eliot in the street, and had handed him a letter in a sealed envelope which Vivienne had given to Janes to keep until her death. The news made Vivienne's head reel. She drafted a hasty statement: "There is no reason why Mr. T. S. Eliot should not come to *68 Clarence Gate Gardens NW1* at *any time* and *no* reason why he should *not live* at Clarence Gate Gardens NW1 and there is *nothing* to prevent his doing so, as 68 Clarence Gate Gardens NW1 is his *home.* Anyone making any *statement to the contrary is lying.* Signed V. H. Eliot." This note she handed to Janes.[81] Then she had another flash of inspiration: "I *saw* at *last* just what I needed to do." Tom's birthday was in a few days' time, on 26 September, when he would be forty-six. Vivienne took two spare keys to the flat and labelled them, "26th September 1934. Keys of 68 Clarence Gate Gardens for T. S. Eliot wishing him *many* happy returns." She ordered Janes to take the labelled keys at once to the Faber office at 24 Russell Square, to demand to see Tom, and to hand him the keys.[82] Surely now Tom would return.

Cat and Mouse

Eliot was unlikely to have responded to any of Vivienne's distraught messages. In September 1934 he was in the Cotswolds, holidaying with Emily Hale. Emily had sailed from Boston in July and was staying with her aunt and uncle, Dr. and Mrs. Carroll Perkins, who had rented Stamford House at Chipping Campden; they gave their niece the adjoining Stanley Cottage, where Eliot was a frequent visitor.[1] Edith Perkins, Eliot and Emily toured nearby gardens, including Hidcote Manor, and Eliot took Emily on long walks around the Gloucestershire countryside. It seems that Eliot felt almost as nervous of Emily as he did of the cows they tried to evade on these walks, writing in an unpublished poem, "The Country Walk," addressed to "Miss E—— H——," and later dedicated "For J. H." (John Hayward), of the alarm he felt "when walking/With country dames in brogues and tweeds/Who will persist in hearty talking."[2] Emily, however, remained unaware of the malicious joke about her that Eliot shared with his confidant, John.

Eliot's decision to leave his sick wife had encouraged Emily to hope for a shared future with him; perhaps she anticipated that he would ask her to stay on in England when she wrote euphemistically to her employer Dr. Jaqua, President of Scripps College, Claremont, California, that she was "optimistic" about "the final decision" from the "doctor" under whose care she was.[3] In late August or early September Eliot and Emily paid a visit to the rose garden at Burnt Norton, seat of the Earls of Harrowby, outside Chipping Campden. In 1934 the house was unoccupied, the garden all but deserted, as the couple wandered past the box hedges and empty pools in the sunshine. It was the romantic moment for which Emily had been waiting, an opportunity for a declaration of love. Eliot would have held her hand as they walked, as he used to hold Ottoline's and later Mary

Trevelyan's. And it seems from a fragment of verse (the "Bellegarde" fragment), which he sent his brother in 1935, that Eliot did experience momentary physical arousal: he wrote of the "leaping pleasure" he felt, which reached a "matchless moment," before desire died in detumescence, "impaired by impotence." In naming these few lines "Bellegarde," Eliot had in mind an early Henry James work, *The American,* in which an American in Europe, Christopher Newman, falls in love with a mature woman of good family, a family who abort the romance just as it appears likely to succeed. "In James," writes Lyndall Gordon, "the pure woman retreats into a convent . . . in Eliot's 'Bellegarde' . . . it is the writer—stricter than the Bellegardes themselves—who shuts off the woman."[4] "Footfalls echo in the memory," wrote Eliot in "Burnt Norton," "Down the passage which we did not take/Towards the door we never opened/Into the rose-garden."[5]

Their love, if love it was, would remain unconsummated; Eliot would not try again. In the years leading up to the Second World War he would continue to see Emily, to bring her, usually unsuccessfully, to meet his literary friends. She was dismissed as that "dull, impeccable Bostonian lady" by Virginia Woolf when they met in November 1935. Nevertheless Eliot enjoyed Emily's respectful worship of his genius, and her "hearty" company. Domineering she may have been, as Ottoline noted when Emily insisted that she and Eliot go in a bus together into Oxford instead of by car,[6] but Eliot was used to dominating women and liked to have his life organised by them. Emily represented a mother figure to him. Even more importantly, she served as a useful smokescreen, a counter to the whispers of homosexuality which gathered about him, and a deterrent to other females, who imagined the poet was already spoken for. But there was never a chance, as Peter Ackroyd asserts, that Eliot would have married Emily if Vivienne had not been alive.[7]

Eliot kept Emily dangling for many years, and behaved towards her with an indecision, indeed deviousness, which does him no credit, but which followed a pattern he had already established with Vivienne. Emily lingered long in England, hoping for Eliot to make a move, perhaps towards a formal engagement which, however long it lasted, would have offered her the promise of an eventual union after Vivienne's death, and would also have provided her with a certain status. As the Deanery of

Chichester Visitors' Book records, Miss Emily Hale, T. S. Eliot and the Perkinses visited on 30 November 1934.[8] As a result of her delayed return Emily was unable to give Dr. Jaqua an answer in the autumn of 1934, and so lost her job. And she was still in England in the summer of 1935, returning in 1937 and 1938; in 1936 Eliot visited her in America. The outward signs of affection Eliot gave her as he was to give Mary Trevelyan from 1938—the regular letters, the shared meals and excursions, the confidences and comic verses—kept hope warm in the breasts of these two middle-aged spinsters; but it was a hope based on the shakiest of foundations.

The intimate relationships Eliot knew in the years immediately after leaving Vivienne were in fact within the Anglo-Catholic community. By March 1935 he had settled in with Eric Cheetham at the Kensington Rectory in Grenville Place. When Virginia Woolf finally visited him for tea there one Sunday at the end of the month, she was depressed by the "decorous ugliness" of Tom's surroundings as he pressed her to eat bread rolls, nestling in frills of paper, while they sat together in a small angular room. Conversation was heavy going. Virginia poured tea from Tom's "respectable" teapot, while the great poet perched on a hard chair before a spluttering gas fire and made literary small talk to her and his other visitor, Alida Monro. Virginia was relieved when Alida left. Tom showed her his bedroom, which was directly over the District line which ran towards Gloucester Road tube station. "I forgot to ask you to drink sherry," he said to Virginia, pointing to the bottle and glasses on the bedroom window sill, and joking that he had to share a bathroom with the curates. "The hot water runs very slowly," he twinkled at her; sometimes he took the bath prepared for the curates. "I discover a certain asperity in him towards the woman—a priestly attitude," recorded Virginia.[9] Earlier she had noted that Tom was "petrifying into a priest"; he reminded her of a "great toad with jewelled eyes." When she had pressed him in April 1934 to define his belief in God, he refused.[10]

The repressed violence and the contradictions within the poet struck Virginia again when she entertained Eliot and his friend Clifford Kitchin to dinner that November in 1934, ten days after seeing *Sweeney Agonistes* and noticing Tom's resemblance to a masked Crippen; "Such a conflict; so many forces have smashed against him: the wild eye still; but all rocky, yellow, riven, & constricted . . . self-confident, didactic."[11] To the poet John Lehmann, Virginia's assistant at the Hogarth Press, she also stressed the violence in Tom which she felt accounted for his success as a poet compared with younger, coming men such as Wystan Auden (who had joined the Faber list in 1930), Stephen Spender, and C. Day Lewis: "Tom is much more violent; and I think by being violent, limits himself so much that he only attacks a minute province of the imagination."[12] Virginia had detected, as few others did, that it was Tom's secrets which shaped his poetry.

Tom and Eric Cheetham lived together for six years. In 1937 they left the clergy-house and set up home together in a nearby flat at 11 Emperor's Gate, South Kensington. The vicar, who was not apparently "altogether masculine," was an eloquent preacher who spent his spare time dressmaking. His impetuous appointment of Eliot as Vicar's Warden proved to be "highly irregular," as the poet was not formally elected, a fact Eliot discovered on Father Cheetham's death; Eliot at once appealed to the archdeacon for an act of indemnity, and was forgiven, staying on as churchwarden until 1959. Cheetham, recalled Eliot, "was very lovable and was also, at times, extremely irritating, and one loved him the more for the irritation he caused." It was only the Blitz in 1940 which caused Eliot, reluctantly, to leave Cheetham and retire to lodge with the Mirrlees family in Shamley Green, near Guildford; the vicar moved into the basement of the Albert Hall.[13]

Soon after joining Cheetham, Eliot had gone into retreat at St. Simon's, Kentish Town, where he met two priests who became his spiritual counsellors: Father Frank Hillier, who was the same age as Tom, and Father Bacon, who became Eliot's "ghostly father." Every two months Eliot escaped to Kentish Town to make his confession to the priests,[14] as well as going into frequent retreat at the Anglican religious community at Kelham, Nottinghamshire, where, from 1931, he enjoyed the company of theological students at the headquarters of the Society of the Sacred Mission. He formed a lasting relationship with Brother George Every, himself an aspiring poet and playwright, who became a close personal friend and remained in touch with Eliot during the war and after. An episode at Kelham wove itself into "Burnt Norton": George Every related to Dame Helen Gardner how on a hot day in the summer of 1935, when Eliot was staying there, he saw a kingfisher on a stream running into the river Trent by Averham church, a short walk over the fields from Kelham. Eliot was apparently much excited by the sight of the bird. In the church-yard stood a yew, and clematis bloomed abundantly in the rectory garden next door.[15] "Will the clematis/Stray down, bend to us?" asks Eliot in "Burnt Norton." "Fingers of yew be curled/Down on us? After the king-fisher's wing/Has answered light to light . . . At the still point of the turn-ing world."[16] When, in the autumn of 1935, Eliot began writing "Burnt Norton," it was his memory of that Kelham kingfisher, associated with Every, which was as fresh in his mind as the rose garden traditionally as-sociated with Emily. At Burnt Norton itself there would have been no kingfisher on the dried pool.

In the spring of 1936 George Every sought Eliot's advice concerning a verse play he had written, "Stalemate—The King at Little Gidding." Every's unpublished play took as its subject King Charles I's flight to Little Gidding after his defeat at the battle of Naseby in June 1645.[17] Little Gidding, near Huntingdon, Cambridgeshire, was already a place of pil-grimage for Anglicans after the seventeenth-century mystic, the Rev. Nicholas Ferrar, set up a religious community there in 1625, and Eliot, too, made his own pilgrimage on "a really lovely day," as he told Mrs. Perkins, in May 1936 to the chapel which had inspired Every. The young priest gave Eliot both the subject of his fourth *Quartet* and the impetus to com-plete the series which the poet eventually decided, after finishing "East Coker," should be based upon the four seasons and the four elements.[18]

The sea poetry of the third *Quartet,* "The Dry Salvages," which cele-brates the courage of the Gloucester fishermen to whose tales of cod-fishing on the Grand Banks Eliot had listened in his boyhood, had come easily to the poet. It sprang from his own experience of sailing out of Gloucester harbour in his nineteen-foot catboat; on one occasion, Eliot and his friend Harold Peters sailed up to Maine, taking shelter in a gale in Somesville, a "hurricane hole" in Penobscot Bay. Eliot knew how to lay a course avoiding the Salvages, bare granite rocks off Cape Ann which, just protruding from the water, could wreck the unwary sailor. In 1631, relates an early New England chronicle, a "Mr. William Eliot" was among the party of one Thatcher and his friends who were wrecked off Cape Ann.[19] Eliot understood "the menace and caress of wave that breaks on water," the dangers of navigation through the swift-descending fog of a coast where "the salt is on the briar rose,/The fog is in the fir trees." As a youth he would have visited the Gloucester church of Our Lady of Good Voyage, which stands high on a hill, its twin towers a beacon to returning fishermen; in her arms the Virgin holds, not the infant Jesus, but a model of a schooner. For the fishermen and their wives Eliot felt deep sympathy, urging his reader to repeat a prayer to the Queen of Heaven on behalf of "Women who have seen their sons or husbands/Setting forth and not returning."[20] At sea, during the dawn watch, he felt a sense of time eternal as his boat was carried forward by the sea's rhythm: "And the ground swell, that is and was from the beginning,/Clangs/The bell." The bell buoys rang, it seemed to him, a perpetual Angelus for the drowned mariners who had ended their lives "in the sea's lips/Or in the dark throat which will not reject them."[21]

"The Dry Salvages" was a reworking of earlier lines from *The Waste Land,* describing a schooner's voyage from the Cape to the eastern banks ("We laid our course/From the Dry Salvages"). Never had the codfish run so well; the men laughed, and thought of "home, and dollars . . . and the girls and gin;" but the narrator "laughed not."[22] He had had a premonition of disaster. A gale sprang up, two dories were lost and then the trysail. One night on watch the poet saw in the cross-trees three women, their white hair streaming behind, who sang songs of enchantment to him; they were water witches, who "release omens/By sortilege" as in the "Dry Salvages." This earlier "Death by Water" passage ends when the ship collides with an iceberg, in contrast to the quieter ending of the third *Quartet,* in which Eliot ponders the way in which meaning must be wrung from experience, and thinks of Krishna: "Time the destroyer is time the preserver." Debating the nature of grief, he is sure of one thing only, that time is no healer.[23]

To complete his series, Eliot needed a fourth poem, whose theme would be fire, as "the spirit unappeased and peregrine" traced its final journey. Every provided the source he required. Eliot had already read J. H. Shorthouse's popular novel *John Inglesant* (1880), which described the way of life at Little Gidding, but it was his close study between February and October 1936 of several drafts of Every's play, in which John Ferrar, the head of the community, debates what should be done after the defeat of the King's cause at Naseby, which gave the poet a text from which to work. In Every's manuscript, Ferrar responds to another member of the community, who declares they must leave behind "the conflagration of forest fire" which rages in England, to demand "Would you walk away or walk through the fire?" Suffering must be endured "to find the meaning which God intends in it . . . for God has meaning in defeat," writes Every, an argument dear to Eliot's heart. In Every's manuscript, King Charles arrives that night with his chaplain, to ask for refuge before travelling north to give himself up to the Scots.[24] Interestingly, there are references to Richard III's death at the battle of Bosworth, and Eliot also alluded to "the crown hanging in a thornbush," in almost identical words to those of Every in his own early drafts.[25] Working with Every on his manuscript and criticising the young priest's "uneven" verse—by October there was "a great improvement"—gave Eliot not only the fire metaphor, developed as either purgatorial or pentecostal fire, but the symbol of the rose, which can be understood both as the Yorkist rose (according to Hope Mirrlees, Eliot always wore a white rose on the anniversary of Bosworth, in memory of "the last English king") and the "sensuous" ghost of a rose in which the poet commemorated Nijinsky's famous leap in *Le Spectre de la Rose*.[26]

Every acted as a male muse for Eliot, a more powerful one than Emily Hale, whose influence waned after "Burnt Norton"—the young man's urgent enthusiasms proving a spur to the disillusioned middle-aged poet. As well as bringing the suffering of the "broken king" to Eliot's mind, and the stoic devotion of Ferrar, Every may have led Eliot to Ferrar's more famous follower, the poet George Herbert, of whom Eliot became an ardent admirer. Eliot wove into "Little Gidding" the ideals of Ferrar and Herbert which he associated with St. John of the Cross's detachment from earthly desire, arguing for "love beyond desire," and borrowing, too, the words of Julian of Norwich, one of the fourteenth-century mystics who followed the *via negativa*: "Sin is Behovely, but/All shall be well, and/All manner of things shall be well."[27]

But was the pull of sensuality banished as completely as Eliot was pretending? It seems not. The period immediately after his separation from Vivienne was a time in which homosexuality seems to have been at the forefront of his mind. Eliot's correspondence with Ezra Pound in 1934 is full of obscene jokes about bestiality, elephants in chastity belts, and Pound's plan to send him an elephant's vagina under the "snotty nose" of the postal authorities;[28] it was a time in which Tom was open about his sexual prowess to Ezra. "About COARSENESS I don't want to boast," he wrote on 3 January 1934, so he wouldn't tell Ezra what one sea-captain had said about Eliot to another: that apart from old Ike Carver of Mosquito Cove—and "He was the man who fucked the whole of Marshall's Island in one night, at the age of 70," so it was only fair to except a man like that—Tom was unbeatable in bed. The obscene verse he included in this letter dwells, with violent and tedious repetition, upon the pleasures of buggery: "Grasp hard the bastards by the short hair./Not once, or twice, shalt thou bugger 'em, in our/rough island story,/But again and again and again and again, leaving/their arseholes all glory." Compulsively he continues: "And when I say, again and again, I mean repeatedly, I/mean continually, I mean in fact many times." The orgiastic hero of Eliot's verse, "Lord of a hundred battles," is proud of his "1000 hard won scars."[29]

Even Pound was shocked by his correspondent's language: "Dearest Possum you pertinacious old whoreHound," he wrote. "I ain't nebber heeerd sech langwitch not even from de deacons in the methikerkiskpiple church . . . Jess try to normalfy your vices."[30] But Eliot felt he could afford to let the mask slip in letters to his old friend, to whom he opened his heart just as he did to John Hayward, whose proud boast to American writer John Brinnin (Director of the New York Poetry Center) in 1950 was that, in Eliot's bedroom "confessional" at 19 Carlyle Mansions, Cheyne Walk, Chelsea, where the two men lived together after the war, "He tells me *ev*erything."[31] Pound, too, probably knew "everything." "Dearest Possum," wrote Ezra on 3 February 1935, when an over-worked Eliot was busy helping to edit the *New English Weekly,* whose editor A. R. Orage had died in late 1934, "Where is your blushing Ganymede? Why don't he co/lab?? [orate]." In all probability this was an allusion to George Every. How was Eliot's "pimp and pansy series" (his poetry list at Faber, which included Auden, Isherwood and Spender), asked Pound: "I commend you for putting all the flowers in one box."[32]

In Eliot's letter of 25 June 1934 to John Hayward, he made very plain the nature of the attraction priests had for him. His suggestive pen and ink sketches of a row of headless male torsos in various stages of undress, the first wearing plus fours, the second shorts, the third underpants, and the fourth nude but for a single fig leaf, are labelled figures one, two, three and four, and described accordingly: "cold, cool, hot, torrid"; the nude torso is decorated with exuberant radial lines which, according to Eliot's "key," indicate the "peculiar emanation or rather effulgence which usually accompanied with the odour of violets is accustomed to envelop the limbs and torso of very Holy persons."[33] The erotic charge which priests held for the poet is indisputable.

Love "without desire" therefore remained an ideal only, for in reality Eliot was living, as he admitted in Fable XIV "The Whale, the Elephant, the Coot and the Spider," in *Noctes Binanianae,* a Jekyll and Hyde life. Churchwarden and publisher by day, at night Eliot became Tom "tusker," who enjoyed the "red light time" with his bisexual friend Geoffrey Faber.[34] In his vestry, jokes Tom, "pious Jekyll purloins letter-paper," that "Hyde may cut a rogue elephant's caper," trusting to "an ecclesiastical alibi." And although, like the Chairman at Faber & Faber, the Elephant is "always in temptation," and "must do what nature bids him do," being sometimes "by nature speedy/In Après-midi," it is at night that their most spectacular transformations take place. The nightly revels ("Late at Night-time/Is the Red-light time") are accompanied by a chorus of "Nigger Minstrels" singing "Who dat Man? See Them Roll . . . See Them Ro-hole," as Possum transforms his elegant shape into that of Tom Elephant, "a tusker at that, the biggest extant." Together, the Elephant and Coot visit a palace, not the palace of peace at the Hague, or the "Palace of Sorts" at Geneva, or even Alexandra Palace, but a House in the Euston Road, "where Friend meets Friend," though what a friend would say if a friend were a whale (Morley) remains an "unimaginable tale." In another "Ode to a Roman Coot," Eliot recalled shared memories of the "festal drunks" at All Souls' Hall, of the Coot at dawn on Hampstead Heath, "forever panting and in cotton pants," of charming the "loud roisterers" in the Common Room, and amazing "th' attendants in the Turkish Bath." In the final chorus, the Elephant, Coot and black minstrels cry "Berry Berry: Let the grave close over the nights that were."[35]

Safe at least, within the bosom of the church, at the office Tom remained vulnerable to Vivienne. On 26 March 1934, six days after dining with Geoffrey and Enid Faber, Vivienne telephoned Faber & Faber, and was amazed to discover that "Tom *had* been there and does go every day, a great relief to me. Poor, silly boy. His poor, hot, stuborn [sic] head."[36] Two days later she rang again at 3:30 p.m., to be told he was in a committee meeting. At five she rang again: he had just left. At six she spoke to Miss Swan, the receptionist. They were all very nice to her, recorded Vivienne in her diary: "So I shall go on!"[37] She continued to call, "a slight, pathetic, worried figure, badly dressed and very unhappy," who screwed up her handkerchief as she wept, recalled Bridget O'Donovan, Eliot's secretary from 1934 until 1936. O'Donovan, who was in love with Eliot herself, knew her duties. She went downstairs to the foyer, where Vivienne sat weeping in the corner, and explained that it was not possible for her to see her husband, but that he was quite well. Eliot, meanwhile, was slipping down the backstairs out of the building; sometimes he hid in the lavatory. The rest of the day he would be on edge, speaking slowly and hesitantly.[38]

At first Vivienne believed Swan and O'Donovan. In early 1935 she was still wondering if Tom was a "prisoner," or if he was "FREE" and receiving the letters she continued to send him: "My heart urges me to make every endeavour to get Tom to accept the absolute possession of 2 rooms in this flat," she wrote on 1 January. She clung to the fantasy that he would use the Yale keys she had sent him, and treat the flat as "his most private offices," coming and going, unmolested by herself; on 7 February she sent him a chit informing him that she left the front door open every night from 10:30 until 11 p.m. "for TS Eliot. Here is your home and here is your protection. Which you need."[39] On 27 February she delivered another letter, telling Tom that she worked night and day on his behalf: "Every thought I have is for you and all my strength . . . I take note of all things so that it will be known, in time."[40] In March, an alarming letter from Maurice about Tom made her tremble with fear for her husband's health: "I felt all of a sudden that I must go at once to Tom." She would have gone then, in the night, she wrote, had she known where to go. The next day, 8 March, Vivienne's courage came to her. She walked "fast and straight" to Russell Square: "To think I have allowed myself to be frightened and intimidated into a state of mind in which I have never dared to go openly and honestly to Faber & Faber and demand to see Tom. What a history for the English nation to read and marvel at in years to come when these records of mine have been released . . ." At Faber, Vivienne was met by "dear Miss Swan" and Bridget O'Donovan ("a very nice timid girl"), who once again put her off with excuses. "We did not see Tom," reported

Vivienne. "They said he was not there and that he is very erratic." Her suspicions were at last aroused. "Tom was never erratic. He was the most regular of men," she noted. ". . . A most sweet and homely man. It is not right
of Tom to refuse to come home." Bridget succeeded in calming Vivienne a
little, and Miss Swan promised to come and have tea with her.[41]

Protecting the boss continued to be part of Miss O'Donovan's duties.
On 13 March 1935 Vivienne marched again to Faber, determined to talk to
Eliot face to face. At first Miss Swan said he was in; her heart leaped. She
sat in reception, promising herself that she would be "very quiet and gentle" with Tom. Then Miss Swan "bethought her," wrote Vivienne sarcastically, that she had not after all seen Tom come back after lunch. "Swannie"
called O'Donovan, who came down, looking "rather sick." Was not Mr.
Eliot always in for the board meetings, demanded Vivienne. There was no
answer. "Of course you know I shall have to keep on coming here," said
Vivienne. "Of course it is for you to decide," replied O'Donovan. "It is too
absurd, I have been frightened away too long," declared Vivienne. "I am
his wife."[42] But her protests changed nothing. Although the secretaries felt
sympathy for her plight (ground to powder by the "Mills of God"), they
could only listen as Vivienne protested her loyalty to Tom, poor Tom
("poor headstrong and noble Tom"), her belief in his innocence ("The sin
is not my husband's") and her longing for "the great happiness of taking
care of him again." That night Vivienne returned to her flat, and dreamed
that Tom was in danger. "I wish I could see Bertie again," she wrote wistfully, recalling that she had not seen Russell for ten or eleven years.[43] Two
days later Vivienne returned to Faber & Faber and pushed a piece of
chocolate through the letter box for Tom.[44]

From Janes, meanwhile, Vivienne had learnt tantalising news of Eliot:
"He reported to me that he had *seen* him, for a very hurried few moments,"
she recorded incredulously.[45] How could Eliot, so available to Janes, elude
her still? Why did he act "in this queer way," she wondered. Still unaware
of Janes's duplicity, Vivienne clung to the belief that Tom, "the poor fellow," had been under a delusion for two years, which made him fail to understand that "we here are his friends and true champions and loyal to the
death and that we still wait for him with open arms."[46] Two days before
Christmas 1935 Vivienne made her final visit to Faber & Faber that year;

she spoke to O'Donovan and bought five books. "I told her everything."
The following year, O'Donovan, a female Oxford graduate who realised
there was no chance of promotion at Faber & Faber, left the firm. Perhaps
she was tired of the subterfuge; "Swannie," her successor, continued to
shield Eliot from Vivienne.

It became even more difficult for Vivienne to cling to notions of Eliot's
innocence, or the illusion that he might ever return, when the bailiffs came
knocking on her door. Vivienne was still asleep at 68 Clarence Gate
Gardens when the first raid took place early on 11 December 1934. She
was awoken by loud banging, and still in her nightdress and dressing-
gown, she went to the door. "A man put his foot in and pushed me violently, forced the door open, and five or six men pushed their way in."
Vivienne screamed for Louie Purdon, who was staying the night, "and she
came very quickly," she recorded. The flat was wrecked; the shelves were
wrenched from the walls and not only were all Eliot's books taken, but
many of Vivienne's, including all her copies of the *Criterion*. Janes came
quickly to the flat by taxi; he seemed dazed, but Vivienne suspected he
knew in advance about the raid,[47] which was the result of a court order obtained by Eliot's lawyers, Bird & Bird, after Vivienne had failed to respond
to his demands for the return of his possessions.[48] Maurice recalled that
"Tom got Fabers to enter 68, but Vivie held on to all the things in 177."[49]
Vivienne no longer knew whom to trust, and was conscious only that she
was the victim of "incessant persecuting, . . . devilish cruelty, open treach-
ery and conspiracy." On Christmas Day 1934, she prayed: "God grant that
I am dead."

Vivienne cared "excessively" about the theft of her copies of the
Criterion because they contained all her writing under her various pen-
names.[50] When they were not returned, she wrote a polite letter to Geoffrey
Faber in March 1935, pleading with him to intervene on her behalf:

> Dear Geoffrey, I should be so grateful if you would have my
> books and my *Criterions* returned to me . . . It is not a question of
> their monetary value but a question of the names and signatures
> which are inscribed on the front pages and the personal notes and
> markings which they all contain . . .[51]

Evidently the message reached Eliot and Vivienne's *Criterion*s were returned. Geoffrey Faber was in an awkward position as go-between, having to reassure Vivienne that he did, in fact, pass on her letters to Eliot as requested, and the fault was not his if they were returned to her unopened, as happened when Vivienne sent Eliot a cheque for £1 for his birthday, 26 September 1935: "Dear boy," she wrote. "I wish you everything in this life and for all eternity. Can't you let me have another address, except 24 Russell Square. With love, your wife, VH Eliot. Buy yourself some socks at Marshall & Snelgrove."[52] On this occasion she was upset enough to take her "private letter," marked "Private and Confidential," which was returned, to Marylebone police station. Telling her that there was no evidence that 24 Russell Square was not Eliot's correct address, the police turned her away.[53]

After the first "smash and grab raid," Tom became even more determined to repossess his family silver and photographs. The bailiffs had been foiled in their search for the silver during the first raid, because Vivienne had already crated it up and deposited it in the District Bank vaults. A long list of cutlery, itemising every fish knife and teaspoon, was sent to Moxon Broad by Bird & Bird. Broad attempted to mediate in the dispute. On 22 December 1934 he wrote to tell Vivienne that he had persuaded Bird & Bird that it would be more desirable in the interests of everybody that they should not exercise their rights until they had given her the opportunity to set aside the silver and plate. He knew that she would be "quite willing to hand over to Mr. Eliot what properly belongs to him," and offered to accompany her to the bank. But Vivienne was implacable. Her mind remained firmly fixed on her goal—Tom's return. She had asked Broad to raise this matter with Tom's solicitor, and this he assured her he had done. Although he hoped that her wishes would be passed on to Mr. Eliot, wrote Broad, he could hold out no hopes whatsoever that anything would result from it: "I am very sorry indeed, but I think it would only be giving yourself greater pain to entertain hopes which I feel certain would be disappointed."[54]

The fighting over the family silver escalated. Vivienne demanded to be hidden somewhere, perhaps in a wardrobe, in the flat at Clarence Gate Gardens, so that she could spy on Tom and ensure that it was indeed he who was calling to claim his property.[55] Bird & Bird refused her request.

Vivienne in turn refused to return the crested Eliot cutlery. Eliot's relentless, but unseen, pressure on her continued: on 7 June 1935 Vivienne was informed by the bank clerks at the District Bank that Tom was thinking of stopping her allowance of £5 a week for fifteen weeks "as a punishment for something."[56] In response she promptly opened a new account at Eliot's branch of Lloyds, getting a cheque book "just like Tom's" from the friendly bank manager (though her account was later declined). But Vivienne was also alarmed by her husband's threats, as her diary references to being kidnapped, arrested, "done in or murdered" demonstrate. Now the roles were reversed: it was she who needed "protection." But who would protect her? Vivienne had no faith in her family or her servants. She felt as nervous as she had in 1918, when Osbert Sitwell used to say, "The spies are out, Vivienne," as they went into the Café Royal to meet their friends.

One day in June 1935, as Vivienne hid in her "shrine to Tom," a taxi came to the door. Out stepped Dr. Cyriax and Dr. Reginald Miller; the latter had trained at the Royal Psychological Association and practised as a specialist in nervous troubles, later becoming senior physician at Great Ormond Street Hospital. It was, recalled Maurice, "William Leonard Janes who got the doctors round in a taxi," because "Janes did everything Tom said," and Tom and Maurice had decided that Vivienne should be certified. But Vivienne appeared too rational on this occasion to meet the criteria of the Involuntary Reception Order; she answered the doctors' questions calmly and sensibly. That day Miller and Cyriax declined to sign the order. Vivienne remained, for the moment, free.[57]

Terrified that next time she would not be so lucky, Vivienne decided to flee to France. "She went to Paris to get away," remembered Maurice.[58] On 18 June Vivienne visited the British Fascist HQ to buy a uniform, which she saw as some kind of protection, only to be disappointed to learn that Fascists were not permitted to wear uniforms abroad. The next day she spent alone in the flat, in dread of being "arrested." But nobody came to take her away, and the day passed uneventfully. On 21 June, which was to be her last day in England, Vivienne went to Vere Street for "two light doses" and to say goodbye to Louie Purdon. Before leaving, she took every possible precaution to safeguard her papers, packing them with her jewellery and depositing them in a safe at Selfridges' safe deposit department. In the flat she left only "certain trinkets" in her blue and silver jewel box, which she locked in her tin deed box, in which she usually kept her papers, sealing it in the green room cupboard. She wore the key of her deed box around her neck. Finally, armed with the address of the Paris Fascist HQ, on 22 June Vivienne set off, having booked a room by telegram at the Hotel Cécile, rue St. Didier, under the name of Thayer.

Even the use of a false name barely seemed sufficient protection, and Vivienne walked the streets in fear of unknown assailants. "If the assassination of Edith Cavell is a crime which shook the world, I say the assassination of Vivienne Haigh Eliot is a crime which will shake the world with far more consequence," she wrote defiantly on 23 June 1935. "I sit, alone, in France."[59] She could not rest. She hardly knew where she found the strength to do all she achieved, she wrote. "But of course it all came from God." The previous year, on 22 August, Vivienne had written to Dr. Prevost at the Sanatorium at Malmaison, saying she was coming to see him, an arrangement she cancelled in September as she felt too weak to make the journey. This time, as she recalled better days when the Princess de Bassiano had visited Tom and herself at the Hotel Cécile and entertained them at her house at Versailles, Vivienne wrote again to Dr. Prevost, saying she had been a week in Paris, was sorry to miss him, but she would meet him, not at Malmaison, but at her hotel.[60] On 7 July, Prevost replied, expressing his regret at missing her. Vivienne's refusal to see the doctor at his sanatorium was a direct result of her fear of being detained against her will. When at last, anxious about the security of her flat, Vivienne returned to London, she wrote of her French visit: "Chaque jour et chaque soir j'ai marché dans les rues, exactement comme nous marchons ici à Londres, pour montrer comme nous sommes, maintenant, en Angleterre, si bien et si libres."*[61] Vivienne had become not cat, but mouse in the game of hide and seek she and Tom were playing out.

By 12 July Vivienne thought she had turned the tables on Tom. She wrote triumphantly: "It looks as though I have cornered him." Vivienne had sent Eliot a registered letter with a cheque for 11s. for three of his books, which she had bought from Faber, reasoning that since he would have to endorse her cheque and pass it through her bank, he could not fail

---

*Each day and each evening I walked the streets, exactly as we do here in London, to show how here in England now we are so well and so free.

to open her letter, in which, "for the thousandth time," she begged him to face up to his "enemies and blackmailers" by coming to Clarence Gate Gardens, where there was nothing but security and safety for him. Chiding him for his cowardice in the face of the blackmail to which Vivienne apparently believed he was subject, on grounds of homosexuality, she wrote:

> It almost makes one doubt your sanity, the way you are hiding yourself up as if you are committing a crime. The shame and slight on your family, the name of Eliot, is more than one could believe an Eliot could do. Have you lost all shame? And have you forgotten Christianity and become a heathen or are you STILL terrorised and blackmailed . . . ?

No one need put up with blackmail, she told him, if they had the courage of a dog. She would make it hot for anyone who wasn't kind to Tom, threatened Vivienne. "You know that I have always said that if a hair of your head is harmed, I will make the whole world pay."[62] Vivienne's continuing misplaced loyalty led her to plan to follow Eliot to Paris, where she thought he was about to travel. "It is worth anything to me to get him back," she confessed to her diary. She *would* go to Paris. "My belief is that *he* wants to get back to me, and is in *chains.*"[63] Once again, her letter was returned unopened.

Tom's response was not what Vivienne had hoped for. On 15 July there was "the usual foot in the door," and once again two large men forced themselves into her flat. Vivienne was better prepared for this second raid; she at once rang Dr. Miller, who came within twenty minutes and spoke to the intruders. After the doctor had left, Vivienne slipped out of the door and locked all the men in with her patent key. When she returned triumphant at 7:30 p.m. they had escaped out of the kitchen window with a ladder, leaving behind most of the "booty," which Vivienne and Ivy, her maid, packed up and hid, probably in number 177.[64] The following month Janes brought back the mandolin which had been snatched from the flat, and which Vivienne had given to Eliot when they had gone to Margate together in October 1921.

For Vivienne, the raids were a violation. Her flat was no longer a home but a place where she felt like "hell," and from which she now fled. From 23 July 1935 she made the Constance Hotel in Lancaster Gate her refuge, where she had "a dear little room" and friends among the residents. The hotel was already familiar to her because Lucy Thayer had stayed there, as had another friend, Violet Jones, and "poor darling Theodora" and Marian Eliot: "So they have the names Thayer, Jones and Eliot on their ledgers."[65] Regular meals and the "warm welcome" she received lifted Vivienne's spirits, and when Eliot's dentist, Dr. Henry Moore, informed her that her husband lived "somewhere in Kensington," and that he had seen him on 5 July when he pulled one of Eliot's teeth at his rooms in Portland Place, she was able to record simply: "I am so relieved."[66] Vivienne made nostalgic trips to Oxford, touring Trinity College, and Merton, "the best, the oldest college." On 28 July she looked up at the "very window of the room poor little loyal Tom had, and where I saw him sitting, quietly reading his books in 1915." She also visited the Bodleian Library, purchasing a catalogue and recording her expenses in her account book, although she did not contact the Keeper of Western Manuscripts at the library to discuss the bequest of her papers.

Staying at the Constance Hotel for five weeks had one important consequence for Vivienne. No longer terrified of sudden intrusion, she began to sleep much better and was thus able to cut down her drug use. On 22 August, Allen & Hanbury confirmed that they would in future deliver two Adalin tablets and two Phenacetin tablets (an analgesic) to her every morning, together with "one draught." This, noted Vivienne, represented a great reduction in her sleeping draughts since staying at the Constance. Another influence, which brought comfort and increased stability into her life, was religion. In 1935 she began attending services at St. Cyprian's Church, Marylebone, where the priest, Father Mayhew, encouraged her to come to Mass. She began the practise of visiting St. Cyprian's whenever she felt in distress, going to pray in the church, for example, during the second raid on her flat. On 29 September, when Father Mayhew left St. Cyprian's, Vivienne was heartbroken. She attended two services on that Sunday, listening attentively to Father Mayhew's sermons and, after she shook hands to say goodbye, lit four candles in his memory.[67]

Perhaps it was the choral evensongs which Vivienne attended, as well as the reduction in her medication, that enabled her to discover her greatest consolation during the years of separation from Eliot—music. In September 1935 Vivienne began singing lessons at the Marylebone Studios, and was excited to be told by her teacher, Miss Gale, that she had a natural soprano voice. "She let me sing up to F but she will be able to take my voice up higher later on," she wrote. Her middle register was weak, and Miss Gale warned her against harming her voice by singing to herself, or humming and crooning in the flat. She felt so strong after her lesson, Vivienne wrote, that it was like a new life beginning. "To think that after all these years of longing to sing, and being laughed at and ignored, I have got a real voice. A gift," she recorded incredulously.[68] Vivienne also began practising her piano-playing and singing for an hour and a half a day at her flat, and on 26 September sat the entrance examination in pianoforte at the Royal Academy of Music, York Gate, Marylebone. She passed, and was accepted to study piano as her first subject and piano accompaniment as her second, with classes also in aural training and elements of music. Full of joy, she wrote, "I can attend all the concerts. A most wonderful thing in my life. And I thank God."[69]

Music gave Vivienne a new identity and a new purpose. When Harriet Weaver asked her to tea in 1936, she declined on the grounds of being a full-time music student, adding that as she was no longer a member of "Lady Ottoline Morrell's little court" she could not undertake to interest Ottoline in Miss Weaver's forthcoming edition of Chaucer's "Hymn to the Virgin," illustrated by the daughter of James Joyce.[70] Vivienne exulted in her "huge" voice. Her piano-playing improved at the hands of her "nice and gentle" teacher, Mr. Webbe: "I want to please him," she wrote: "Went home, lit my fire with logs and played the Peer Gynt suite."[71] With great pride she recorded her attendance at the Queen's Hall, on 6 December 1935, as "the very greatest event in my life after my marriage to Thomas Stearns Eliot on June 26 1916. This was to sit on the platform among the students as a student of the Royal Academy. Dressed all in white with the great scarlet ribbon across my chest . . ." Vivienne, stylish in her new white corduroy suit from Vanecks, faced Sir Henry Wood, who was conducting the concert, her heart swelling with pride.[72] Earlier she had written: "I shall make a great singer. I shall win a fortune for my producers."[73] At last her artistic and narcissistic personality had found an outlet, and music had begun to fill the gap left in her life by Tom's desertion.

It was unfortunate, therefore, that just at the point when her pursuit of Eliot was no longer all-consuming, Vivienne at last succeeded in tracking down her quarry. As she wrote earlier, Eliot wanted her to disappear. As an abandoned wife who knew his secrets she was both a reproach and an embarrassment, and her appearance in public at his plays resurrected the horrific moments of their marriage, which he longed to forget, and which filled him with guilty terror at the prospect of meeting her. But Vivienne refused to vanish: her musical success bolstered her confidence. On 2 October 1935, in what may be seen as a dress rehearsal for her actual meeting with Tom, she attended a performance of *Sweeney Agonistes* at the Westminster Theatre, with her friend Louie. Membership of the Fascists, who had asked her to write for their magazine, *Blackshirt,* had also stirred up Vivienne's fighting spirit, as had her admiration for Lenin, whose thrilling and poignant revolutionary songs reduced her to tears at the film society to which she belonged. She had therefore chosen to wear her Fascist uniform as she and Louie entered the theatre. The audience hissed "Mrs. Eliot," recalled Louie, as the two women marched down the aisle to their seats in the front stalls. She and Vivienne found this funny. As for the play itself, Louie, "a somewhat earnest spinster," who was dedicated to her work for the National Society for Lunacy Law Reform in North Harrow, understood little. "It was all about birth, copulation and death," she told her cousin. "My only consolation is that at the time I did not know what copulation was."[74]

However, Vivienne recognised the play's roots in her life with Tom. "How I contrived not to faint I do not know," she wrote, startled at "the absolute horror of the thing." Fascinated, she returned to the Westminster Theatre at least twice more to watch *Sweeney Agonistes.* Her lasting emotion was pride in Tom and gratitude for the years they had shared: "He made me a woman among thousands, a sort of superbeing," she wrote, "He is a prophet."[75] "Dear Tom, how proud of him I am," she recorded on Boxing Day 1935, remembering how Ottoline used to admire Tom. Now she felt no more malice towards Ottoline ("however much she regrets me now") than she did towards Tom.[76]

Yet Vivienne's instinct for the limelight made it impossible to ignore her. She dressed carefully for her entrances. When she visited the

American Women's Club in Grosvenor Gardens in September 1935 it was the result of five days of intense preparation, which included two expensive visits to Francis, her hairdresser. She had ordered a car. At last she started out, "dressed in my thin, fine black suit and black felt hat with red feather, black shoes and gloves, sunburn stockings and cerise macintosh cape," only to be disappointed by being told that she was not eligible to join as Eliot was a naturalised British citizen. To join the club was "the ambition of a lifetime," declared Vivienne. The three American ladies were sorry. As Vivienne was British born, there was nothing American about her or Tom at all. If only Vivienne had come before Tom got naturalised. "I said yes, but I never wanted him to get naturalised. . . . They were very nice and said you cannot make husbands do what you think they ought to."[77]

Meanwhile Vivienne continued to act as a private eye, stalking Eliot outside the office. On 4 November 1935 she waited in her car outside 2 Whitehall Court from 8:30 until 9:15 p.m., because a friend had tipped her off that he would attend a meeting at that address. "Did not see Tom—a great many large men in grey suits who *might* have been him," she reported. Her neatly typed list of over thirty car numbers which she noted in the vicinity of Whitehall Court indicates how obsessive she had become in her pursuit of her husband.[78]

The next time Vivienne was not to be thwarted. The public confrontation which Eliot had sought for so long to avoid at last occurred on 18 November, at the *Sunday Times* Book Fair at Dorland House, Lower Regent Street. Apart from their brief meeting at the solicitors' office, it was the first time since September 1932 that they had come face to face. Once again Vivienne had dressed for the starring role. She chose to wear her Fascist uniform, a black beret, with the penguin pin which Tom had given her when she was at the Malmaison sanatorium, and a large black macintosh cape, the outfit she had worn in the streets when distributing Fascist leaflets during the 1935 General Election.[79] A small, fierce, dramatic figure, she strode in, clutching three of Eliot's latest books and holding her dog Polly in her arms; she fought her way to the front of the lecture room, passing Bridget O'Donovan. Directly she was in the midst of the crush, she heard steps behind and, turning around, found Tom just behind her.

I turned a face to him of such joy that no-one in that great crowd could have had one moment's doubt. I just said, Oh *Tom,* & he seized my hand, & said how do you *do,* in quite a loud voice. He walked straight to the platform then & gave a most remarkably *clever,* well-thought out lecture . . . I stood the whole time, holding Polly *up* high in my arms. Polly was very excited & wild. I kept my eyes on Tom's face the whole time, & I kept nodding my head at him, & making encouraging signs. He looked a *little* older, more mature & smart, much *thinner & not* well or robust or rumbustious at *all.* No sign of a woman's *care* about him. No cosy evenings with dogs and gramophones I should say.

As Eliot finished his talk to great applause, Vivienne pushed her way up to the platform, and let the dog off the lead. The terrier ran to Eliot, scampering around his feet and jumping up at him. Vivienne, too, mounted the platform, and stood beside Eliot, her hands on the table on which were piled the poet's books. "I said quietly, Will you come back with me?" "I cannot talk to you now," replied Eliot, hurriedly signing the books Vivienne had brought. He then left with a young writer, Richard Church, who had been chairing the evening.[80]

Vivienne wasted no time in writing to James & James on 25 November to inform them that she had met her husband and that, "Everything was perfectly all right between us . . . In short he turned up and I turned up and I took my dog, and my dog pursued him." There were, she said, many witnesses to their meeting.[81] But Vivienne also drew the solicitors' attention to the "slight young man" called Richard Church, who introduced Tom to the audience, and whom she had never seen before. It struck her as "extremely odd," she wrote, that her husband should have with him in what *"seemed* rather a familiar relation, a young man, no relation, no particular bond in common . . ." This young man, said Vivienne, walked after Tom and was behind him when she spoke to her husband. Vivienne requested Messrs. James & James to lay her chronicle of the event before Dr. Prevost and the other distinguished mental specialists who would be competent to judge it, declaring that in the streets of London there was now "a disgusting and filthy parade of *Sex,*" and England was just a dung heap, crawling with "maddened worms and filthy maggots."[82] The importance Vivienne attached to her "chronicle" is shown by the fact that she took down shorthand notes, which she preserved. Her letter indicates also the type of sexual stories she was likely to spread, to Eliot's alarm. He remembered in 1954: "I was afraid of the dreadfully untrue things she said of me and afraid that my friends believed her. I couldn't say anything—a kind of loyalty perhaps and partly a terror that they would show me that they believed her and not me . . ."[83] If Vivienne was suggesting to James & James her husband was homosexual, she was no doubt also writing in similar vein to others, and Eliot must have shuddered at the thought of her accusations dropping onto his friends' doormats.

A few days later, on 30 November, Vivienne visited the Mercury Theatre to watch *Murder in the Cathedral,* which had transferred from Canterbury to Ashley Dukes' studio theatre. Once again she was a conspicuous figure, sitting in the stalls beside Aldous and Maria Huxley and Sybille Bedford. It was an encounter which Sybille Bedford remembers as "terrifying." Gaunt and swaying, still smelling of ether, her make-up misapplied, half recognising people and half not, Vivienne made such an intense impression on Sybille that she was forced to leave the room and have a brandy.[84] Like "wrong'd Aspatia," Vivienne refused to stay locked in her charnel vault, but issued from the shadows to haunt Tom. She watched the play at least nine times. "Tom," she forecast, "will be a big noise as a playwright. He has got everything. Historic sense, music in his very blood, rhythm and sound and time sense to an extent which is almost incredible."[85] By 26 December *Murder in the Cathedral,* with Robert Speaight in the role of Becket, was a sell-out. And, as Tom's fame grew, so did Vivienne's longing to share his celebrity status. She *would* be noticed. She was his wife, as she repeated over and over again. She was shunned because she was "mad"—Tom's Ophelia, as Virginia wrote—and so she would be mad, acting out her label in ever more bizarre and embarrassing public appearances which, four years after leaving her, still forced Eliot to hide from public life.

It was Tom's "callous cruelty" which made her "act in a queer and abnormal way," wrote Vivienne in justification of her behaviour.[86] She was taking her revenge. Had Eliot confronted her just once, and spoken to her honestly, he might have given her the sense of closure she needed. Instead, his cowardice prolonged her agony—and his.

Vivienne knew she was courting danger. It was time to become "Daisy Miller."

23

Into the Dark

In June 1936 Vivienne began her double life. It was the final act in the melodrama she and Tom played out for five years between 1933 and 1938. Her frustration at her situation had grown. Nothing had changed since she had cornered Eliot at the *Sunday Times* Book Fair, as she was forced to confess to Louie Purdon over lunch in December 1935. "Do you know where he lives?" asked Louie, when Vivienne told her that she had at last seen Tom. "I said no, and I am not going to torture myself unnecessarily—I said, I *trust* the man. He has some very strong reasons . . ."[1] For Eliot himself, Vivienne's love remained undiminished; it was his "enemies" she blamed for her predicament. No closer to penetrating the impregnable fortress that was Faber & Faber, she began to suspect Geoffrey Faber. "I am innocent," protested the publisher when, on 13 March 1936, Vivienne again accused him of not forwarding her invitation to "T. S. E. . . . I handed it to him myself. What happened to it after that is not my responsibility."[2] "Either you see that Tom receives it, or else you will give me an explanation," retorted Vivienne.[3] Although at first Vivienne believed that "my husband has now found me . . . When I say found, I mean he claimed me in public," in reality the meeting had proved an anti-climax. She was still "a woman alone," as she expressed it to Moxon Broad—a single middle-aged woman alone in north London, nursing her dream of reconciliation.[4]

The trail had gone cold, and yet Vivienne's terror intensified. She felt increasingly hounded by unseen pursuers. Following Tom and Maurice's first bid in June 1935 to certify her, she did not dare enter the Malmaison sanatorium as a voluntary patient, as she wished. Aware that she was in need of the help which her old friend Dr. Prevost was offering, Vivienne had again booked a room, for December 1935: "Vous savez que vous serez toujours ici la bienvenue, et que nous vous reçevrons comme une amie,"* the kindly doctor had written on 15 November; but Vivienne was still too afraid to take up her place at the clinic and receive the psychiatric support from which she could have benefited. Had she done so, her life might have ended differently.[5] Instead, in London, faceless "Kidnappers" seemed to wait on every street corner for her; and yet only out of doors, among the familiar London landmarks she had known since childhood, was her anxiety bearable. In her own flat, a "black prison" since the bailiff's raids, where she kept a single bed in the corridor, she was unable to sleep or rest. How she wished that after her piano lesson she could come home to a meal and settle down to practise, she wrote. Instead, "I am always driven out, to tramp the streets—this way and that until I get such a horror of the streets that the streets only understand."[6]

There were, felt Vivienne, demons at her heels, and at Tom's: "The only way to get rid of Tom and Vivienne is to wear them out—hurry the pace . . . Make them work till they drop—crack the whip. Then hustle them into an untimely grave," she wrote on 11 November 1935. As she remembered her last conversation with Eliot, she imagined that he was warning her of kidnap or murder: "This may be done in various manners—unlimited are the ways." She shivered as she remembered Tom's words: "The poor gentleman said to me, 'Do not go to sleep anywhere where nobody knows where you are, will you?' I said, 'Why shouldn't I? You do.' He said, 'It is very easy to remove one.' "[7] So great were Vivienne's fears that in her will of 1 March 1936 she requested that her coffin should not be closed until the expiration of at least four days after her death, and not until death had been certified by Dr. Miller and another doctor.[8]

Wandering the streets by night as well as by day that November, Vivienne recorded walking from Westminster, through Horseguards, and up the side steps leading to Waterloo Place. "I love it so. It's often fine and cold, and then it's beautiful. I shall walk back from there to-morrow night." It was a reassuring route, for Vivienne was retracing the steps she had taken when her father first fell seriously ill, and she, Ottoline and Tom had paced the streets around Crawford Mansions. It was to this area, which she associated with the early years of her marriage, that she re-

* You know you will always be welcome here, and we will receive you as a friend.

turned with nostalgia, to her "young days . . . when Tom and I were first married [and] we used to walk about London at night. I loved it so. We even had the honour of spitting into Monty Sherman's letter-box in the Adelphi! So many mad mad nights."[9] On Vivienne's "Route marches," as she called them, she often dressed in her Fascist uniform as she inspected the streets, deciding that it was the Fascists who had tidied up Sloane Square and, "IF they can make a world where every man, woman and child, can go about their business in peace, unmolested and unhindered, . . . then the fascists will deserve this new world."[10] On one occasion she rescued a tramp, bringing him back to her flat for bread-and-butter and giving him 7/6d to find a bed; on another, she found a starving black dog which she took to Battersea Dogs Home, but such incidents were mere crumbs in her search for solace.

The influence of the *fascismo* upon someone as impressionable, lonely and vulnerable as Vivienne was a harmful one. On 22 March 1936 she fulfilled a long-felt ambition to see Sir Oswald Mosley in the flesh, when she attended a Mass Rally at the Royal Albert Hall. The police were out in *"immense* force" for an area of at least two miles around the Albert Hall, mounted and unmounted, as hundreds and thousands of people gathered to hear their leader, whom Vivienne excitedly compared to Prince André in *War and Peace,* another "man of action." As she stood amidst the hysterical crowd, applauding Mosley as he ranted that England's civilisation was rotten, its morals decayed, Vivienne drank in his propaganda, which she reproduced in agitated diary entries. London's children were "degenerate imbeciles in clattering perambulators," she wrote, and in the streets she was followed by "low class men," who "propagated their own loathesomeness."

On Easter Sunday 1936, alone in her flat and lame with a poisoned foot, Vivienne brooded over several mysteries: Richard Church, the "very handsome, elegant and properly behaved young man," who at the Dorland Hall the previous November had introduced the speaker by saying, "Mr. T. S. Eliot is a man who cannot endure the slightest pain." What was Church's connection with Tom? Tom himself looked no older, and *"just as handsome."* And the bewildering "disgusting persecution" to which she was subjected in her flat, which was no home but a place where she had been *"incessantly molested* and my nervous system shaken and ruined":[11] who was behind it? Her thoughts, she wrote, were not clear, for Vivienne could not bear to listen to the warnings of Moxon Broad, her solicitor and ally, against Eliot. "There is more in this than you know of," Broad had maintained after the second raid, but Vivienne had shut her mind to suspicion of her husband. "He is a queer man and his idea of Tom is so mad and so away from the truth that I often wonder if he was Tom's solicitor all those years," she wrote after a long interview with Broad at his City office the previous October, at which he had tried to tell her that Eliot was the culprit.[12] Humankind, as Eliot knew, cannot bear very much reality.[13]

Inevitably, considering the amount of time Vivienne spent walking around central London, the day at last came, in the summer of 1936, when she bumped into Tom. It was an event which triggered an extreme reaction in him: "I am rather shaky at the moment, because I ran into my late wife in Wigmore Street an hour ago, and had to take to my heels," he wrote to Dorothy Pound on 28 July. "Only people who have been 'wanted' know the sort of life I lead." If he could afford to live anywhere but London, he would, Eliot told Dorothy, only he had to have an address from which he could "decamp" quickly.[14]

Vivienne's distress, which had greater foundation than Eliot's, now led her to adopt a different identity—to see whether she could disappear as completely as he had done, and outwit her unknown pursuers. She also hoped to discover a new peace of mind in which to prepare for her music exams in July. As so often, Vivienne's actions imitated Tom's: she would continue to be his shadow, as he was hers; she, too, would lead a double life, her disguise enabling her not only to preserve her freedom, but to track him down, as she confided to her bank manager, Thomas Hope. "You may not know it, but I make it the first interest in my life to follow his movements, and it is the perpetual anxiety of my life."[15] In June 1936 Vivienne informed Moxon Broad:

> I have chosen the incognita of Miller to allow it to be supposed by as many as possible that I have gone to America . . . —for two reasons, one to give me more time for work at the Royal Academy of Music . . . but also to try if possible this experiment to reduce the strain on my brain, and at the same time to see if I could succeed in disappearing as completely and baffling all attempts to trace me as my husband has. And at the same time I have in mind

such undying resentment against all those who had any part in this business that I want them to know what it is like to suffer in this same way.

Tiresias.

At this point I have become Daisy Miller.[16]

On 20 July Vivienne, writing as "Daisy Miller," informed her daily woman, Mrs. Flint, that Mrs. Eliot had left the day before for America, and had let the flat to her as she was a fellow student at the Royal Academy of Music. Mrs. Eliot's address in America, wrote "Daisy," would be 83 Brattle Street, Cambridge, the apartment block in which both Marian Eliot lived and another Eliot relative, Elizabeth Wentworth, with whom Vivienne remained on friendly terms.[17]

Like Tiresias, Vivienne had experienced a mythical transformation. Like Tiresias, she would see all things, spying them out as Eliot's spies had done. The incognita she chose, Daisy Miller, symbolised in Vivienne's eyes her innocence of any crime, and would have been immediately understood by those who read her words. Vivienne knew that, just as Daisy had compromised her reputation by her outing with Winterbourne in a boat on Lake Leman at eleven o'clock at night without a chaperone, so had Vivienne, in Eliot's eyes, compromised her own by her outing with him in a punt on the River Cherwell. It was said of Vivienne, as of Daisy: "She is very crazy."[18] Daisy's ruin was assured when she went out at night with Giovanelli, an Italian fortune-hunter, and caught malaria; she had paid the price for breaking the rules of polite society: ostracism, isolation and early death. In choosing the name "Daisy Miller" Vivienne made it clear that she believed that she would also have to die; and that the verdict of history upon her should be the same as that of James upon Daisy, underlined by Giovanelli's final words to Winterbourne:

"She was the most beautiful young lady I ever saw, and the most amiable." And then he added in a moment, "And she was the most innocent."

Winterbourne looked at him, and presently repeated his words, "And the most innocent?"

"And the most innocent!"[19]

Vivienne's message was that Eliot, like Winterbourne in his relationship with Daisy, contributes to her death through rigidity, snobbery and lack of compassion. Choosing to be "Daisy" was a powerful and defiant indictment of her husband; but it also suggests that Vivienne was sinking into depression as she turned her anger inwards. Like the Cumaean Sibyl, she wanted to die. "*Very* depressed," she recorded in her diary in 1934. "There will be plenty of time for fighting after I am dead," she remarked prophetically to Moxon Broad on 10 August 1936. "And I have had quite enough of it."[20] Over time, her sense that she had lost the battle against Eliot grew, as her defiant protests at the way in which "everything is liable to be twisted and perverted and coercion and the foulest methods are used to direct or misdirect opinion and action" against her were replaced by a mood of hopelessness and, at times, suicidal thoughts.

Her bizarre behaviour continued to attract comment. Stephen Spender related that a friend of his who shared a hairdresser with Vivienne used to find herself sitting side by side with her under the dryers. On one occasion, Vivienne complained bitterly that when she was in the street people in the road persistently stared at her. "My friend found this as unaccountable as Mrs. Eliot did, until leaving the hairdressers, Mrs. Eliot put on her hat," wrote Spender. "This had stitched on it the rather garish purple and green wrapper of Eliot's play, with the letter print MURDER IN THE CATHEDRAL very prominent around the rim."[21]

Vivienne's frequent presence at the tiny Mercury theatre in Notting Hill Gate continued to be a potential source of embarrassment to Eliot, to his friend, producer Rupert Doone, and Doone's lover, designer Robert Medley; she had joined the Group Theatre Society and Film Club, and managed to discover Doone's address. As Vivienne was liable to wait outside the houses of those she suspected of sheltering Eliot, recording car numbers and spying on any man in a grey suit who she thought might be Tom, this was, yet again, a limitation upon his freedom of movement. And Vivienne was closer upon his heels than he realised: in January 1935 Eliot had commissioned W. H. Auden to write "Dogskin" (*The Dog Beneath the Skin*) with Christopher Isherwood, which was subsequently staged by Doone, and watched by Vivienne, who kept her programme. Between 24 January and 28 February 1936 alone, Vivienne attended performances of *Murder in the Cathedral* at least nine times, carefully hoarding the tickets among her papers. She even followed the play on tour, being given complimentary tickets in the front stalls at the Cambridge Arts Theatre and Oxford Playhouse. It is no wonder that to Eliot she appeared a malevolent presence, haunting his life, a phantom who "fed upon me while I fled."[22]

Vivienne, meanwhile, continued to act as if she and Eliot were a couple—as indeed they were in law. On Armistice Day 1935 she had bought two yellow roses which she left at the Cenotaph with cards signed from Tom and herself. All she wished for, she wrote, was to have her old life back. On 13 April 1936 she longed to catch, "If only a glimpse of my husband, the only man now living for whom I have the slightest respect. Many men have passed my line of vision since the autumn of 1932, but never one for whom I would trouble to turn my head . . ."[23] Vivienne's photograph, taken on the day on which she was presented to the Prince of Wales in 1934, shows a slim, dark-haired woman with bobbed hair, her complexion unblemished, her eyes large and arresting; she looks young for her age, forty-seven, and might have made new male friends, had she not remained mired in grief over Eliot's desertion. For Vivienne never adjusted to the loss of her husband. One of her last acts was to buy some sheet music at Selfridges: "Can't Help Loving that Man of Mine," from *Showboat*.[24]

Although Vivienne repeatedly visited the theatres where Eliot's plays were performed, she was determined to hide her private address from him, as he had hidden his from her. From June 1936, when Vivienne became "Daisy Miller," she seemed to have given W. L. Janes—who she believed was implicated in the raids on the flat—the slip. She began using the Three Arts Club, 19a Marylebone Road, opposite Madame Tussaud's, as her poste restante address, writing to the English Speaking Union, her bank, and even Moxon Broad, as "Daisy Miller." That summer she advertised on the Three Arts Club notice-board for "an educated shorthand typist *(expert,* and accustomed to a Remington portable machine)" to manage "Daisy Miller's" correspondence.[25] And she continued to search for a house rather than a flat in which to live, nearly renting 53 Chester Terrace, and then 8 Edge Street, Church Street, Kensington, in March 1936; she was tempted by a "charming" summer cottage at Meads End, Eastbourne, which she and Tom had rented before from Sir William Collins. He showed her around again, but when she decided to take the cottage for the summer of 1936, the estate agent told her that the owner was withdrawing the property from the market. A furious Vivienne threatened to sue for wasted expenses, suspecting that the real reason was that she had unwisely given as her reference the British Union of Fascists.[26]

Loneliness ("ghastly morbid solitary confinement") and rows with other tenants contributed to Vivienne's desire to leave 68 Clarence Gate Gardens for good.[27] At her mother's "definite request," in early summer 1936 Vivienne finally left the flat she had shared with Eliot: "It is impossible to live at 68 Clarence Gate Gardens, for a woman alone, as I told you," she explained to Broad.[28] Unable to find a house to rent, she lived "a nomad life," as she described it, moving from hotel to hotel. On occasions she enjoyed the company of other guests, as at the Constance Hotel the previous Christmas, when Vivienne took Polly for

> a most lovely walk in Regent's Park, where the ice was thick on the lake and pond, and where the fine mist, the red sun and the delicate bare trees against the pale misty sky and the flocks of birds standing about in the ice and flying slowly, made one of the most beautiful pictures I have *ever* seen. Everything is so much finer, cleaner and quieter in a *freezing* cold winter, than in the summer. I love it. At dinner I found all my old friends and had a nice evening . . .[29]

But her restless movement from one hotel to another made friendship an increasingly rare commodity. Her favourite venue was the Three Arts Club. But even the Club, "a very very nice club," was reluctant to allow Vivienne to be a long-term resident, probably because of her unconventional behaviour. "Unhappily it has been for a long time too full up with country members to take me in," she wrote to Harriet Weaver, former editor of *The Egoist,* on 12 June 1936, "so that I live about from one Hotel to another."[30] From the Three Arts Club Vivienne moved to Durrants' Hotel, Manchester Square, to the Cliftonville Hotel in Dorset Square, and thence to the Welbeck. Polly was boarded out in Hampstead. Increasingly, public occasions became a substitute for intimacy: "Mrs. Eliot . . . has had very great friends, and she prefers to mourn their losses rather than to fill the gaps they leave," she informed her lawyer.[31]

Church offered a certain solace. The new priest at St. Cyprian's in-

vited Vivienne to attend his services again, and she began going to High
Mass. Otherwise, in whichever direction she turned, Vivienne found herself courteously, but very firmly, rebuffed. She had approached Jack
Hutchinson. Why did she want to meet, he asked. "For no reason at all except that it is more normal to see one's friends than not to," replied
Vivienne with dignity.[32] In September 1936 she wrote to Faber, suggesting
that if they were considering a new edition of Eliot's poem "Marina,"
which was out of print, she would like to offer an illustration she had made
for the front page.[33] Faber & Faber replied that it was "most unlikely" that
a new edition of the poem would be printed, as it had already been included in Eliot's *Collected Poems 1925–1935,* published last spring.
Otherwise they would, of course, have been very glad to consider Mrs.
Eliot's "kind suggestion."[34] In February, Vivienne offered to help the
English Speaking Union entertain American visitors: the Reception
Secretary wrote encouragingly to enquire how Mrs. Eliot could help: "As
you know, our members from America and the Dominions appreciate
nothing so much as friendly and informal contact with British members
and the opportunity of visiting British homes, or of sightseeing under the
guidance of local people . . ."[35] But nothing came of Vivienne's suggestion.
Her application in February to St. James's Palace for a seat at the coronation of Edward VIII met with the inevitable refusal from the Earl
Marshall, who explained that invitations to the Ceremony of the
Coronation in Westminster Abbey would be issued only to those included
in Government lists approved by His Majesty.[36] Once again Vivienne had
set herself up for rejection. The pathos of these letters, in which she makes
vain attempts to cling to the fringes of that society at whose centre she had
once glittered, is powerful. A pitiful, doomed figure, she stood at the
Dorland Hall listening to Bertrand Russell lecture, but did not speak to
him. She attended Arthur Bryant's "thrilling lecture" at London
University on Two American Poets, and dreamed of her husband.[37] Her
need for human contact made it impossible for her to maintain the charade
that "Mrs. Eliot" was in America, and Eliot and Geoffrey Faber were
aware that Vivienne alias "Daisy" remained somewhere in London. They
did not, however, know her address, for by July 1936 Vivienne had signed
a six-year lease on 8 Edge Street, at a rent of £160 per annum, in addition
to the £215 p.a. she was still paying for Clarence Gate Gardens.[38]

Vivienne's battle now was to maintain her mental equilibrium. "You know how terribly nervous and timid she is, and how she is apt to lose her wits and go all to pieces," wrote "Daisy Miller" of her friend Mrs. Eliot to Moxon Broad on 5 August 1936, after Vivienne had created one of her most confused "muddles" over the new Ibach grand piano she was buying on hire purchase from Selfridges, who were storing the old upright for which she had exchanged it. Vivienne, with her usual delusions of grandeur, believed that "the progress I am making in my piano studies does justify my having a really first class instrument to work on,"[39] and when she found she could buy a Bechstein grand from the Wigmore Hall, through the Royal Academy of Music, where she was still a student, nothing would stand in her way. "I wish you could get Selfridges to fetch this piano away," complained Daisy Miller of the Ibach grand, as it was "not a very satisfactory instrument." Mr. Broad replied that he would endeavour to straighten the matter out. "Yes, I have been very much upset and shaken by what I told you about Mr. T.S. Eliot," explained Daisy, who was "lingering in London trying to get things cleared up for my friend." "It would un-nerve Mrs. Eliot so much if she knew I am only thankful she is out of the country."[40] The problem was, explained the patient Broad, that Mrs. Eliot had signed HP (Hire Purchase) agreements for two grands.[41]

Yet it was music which continued to give Vivienne's life focus: "One whole hour of Bach. I loved it," she confided to her diary after one of her piano and singing lessons. Although she longed for the sunshine, Vivienne had turned down Ella de Saxe's invitation to stay with her in Monte Carlo in January, because she wanted to "stick to the music" and make up, during the vacation, what she had not understood during the term.[42] In the spring term Vivienne, despite a minor operation on her infected foot, had struggled on, failing only her Elements of Music examination, and by the summer was well enough to write to her piano teacher that, "If it would not be considered unreasonable, I would also like to learn the violin, as an extra study."[43] July 2 found her "working up to the last" for her exams the next day.

Vivienne's new identity as a full-time music student led to a truce with her mother. Rose Haigh-Wood was both surprised and proud to be invited by Vivienne to the Music Students' Concert at the Queen's Hall in April, at which Vivienne, once again dressed all in white, sat with the students. Rose wrote to congratulate "My dearest little Vivy" on the "splendid concert,"[44] and she served as a more stabilising influence in her daughter's life at this time than hitherto, as the following letter shows:

> My dearest Vivy—for you are my dear little Vivy—and I think you are very brave and persevering in taking up serious study now—so I am very proud of you dear—So go on with your work dear . . . It is a *real* pleasure to study. So I do hope you will continue—You are welcome to tea or supper at *any* time—Of course I only have simple meals—but you *are* welcome as you know. The little walk backwards and forwards is pleasant for you. So—let us all be happy together—Granny used to sing it to us.
>
> Fondest love from yr *devoted* Mother.[45]

Rose's loving encouragement in 1936 presented a contrast to Maurice's continued avoidance of his sister. In May Vivienne decided to be assertive: "As I have not seen you for so long, or your wife and child, and have never even seen the inside of your home, I propose calling on you Sunday afternoon, if you will be at home."[46] Maurice replied that no one would be in: "No-one ever is in chez moi. I invariably spend the whole weekend playing golf, or at any rate out of London . . . Vive le sport!" Grudgingly he agreed to meet her at the Three Arts Club "at cocktail time," but he and Ahmé kept Vivienne at arm's length. Eliot was godfather to Maurice and Ahmé's son Raggie, of whom Vivienne was very fond; she now took over this duty, sending Raggie gifts of lead soldiers and having him to tea with his nanny, but seeing little of Ahmé. Later, Maurice recalled the relationship between his sister and his thirty-one-year-old wife from South Carolina:[47]

> Ahmé tried to like Vivien, but Vivien fought her off. [As for] Ahmé and Tom . . . Ahmé playfully pulled his leg about his Englishness. Tom never thought that funny. Tom wanted her to take his side against Vivien. Ahmé never would.

Of his own disloyalty, Maurice recalled in 1980, shortly before he died: "Tom appealed to me—and I always took his side. Never Vivy's. I was a fool for doing so. Later I realised. Not then."[48] In old age Maurice blamed Tom for his behaviour to his sister; Tom, at least, blamed only himself.

The year 1936 witnessed a late, brief artistic flowering for Vivienne. Her self-confidence had increased as she developed a new life at the Royal Academy of Music. She began to draw and paint again at the Three Arts Club, which held a spring exhibition. Vivienne offered the club "an extraordinary clever and witty Cartoon" by Eliot for the exhibition; this the committee turned down on the grounds that it was not the work of a club member. They did, however, select two of Vivienne's own sketches for exhibition, to her great joy. She at once sent invitations to Tom, Maurice, Geoffrey and Enid Faber to come to the private view, which was to be opened by Mark Gertler. Enid promised to come although Geoffrey pleaded a business engagement after his ticking-off by Vivienne for not delivering Tom's invitation. Typically, Vivienne priced her sketches too highly for them to be put into the Club lottery, but her success prompted her to have one drawing photographed and printed as her Christmas card for 1936. It also prompted her to challenge Faber & Faber in a provocative fashion: if the publishers refused to use her sketch to illustrate "Marina" themselves, wrote Vivienne on 5 September, she proposed to have Eliot's poem privately printed with her own illustration "in a similar way to Miss Lucia Joyce's *Hymn to the Virgin* by Geoffrey Chaucer."[49] The prospect of Vivienne setting herself up as a rival publisher of T. S. Eliot's poems, with illustrations by his deserted wife, must have been an alarming one to the directors of Faber & Faber.

And in 1936, attracted by the name, Vivienne joined Eliot's Club in the Charing Cross Road, a club which advertised itself as being near twenty-five West End theatres, with supper and dancing every night till 2 a.m.: "Indian Curry every Thursday, cabaret with unique turns, evening dress always optional." Vivienne's bohemian nature was reasserting itself, and she planned to attend the dancing on Sunday night "to dispel the gloom of Sunday night in London."[50]

But on 9 November a tragedy befell the Haigh-Wood family: Rose had a stroke. Her illness precipitated a violent row between Maurice and Vivienne, who was horrified to find that 3 Compayne Gardens which, two years ago, was "fully furnished with good old furniture collected by my Father, her proper right," had become an "empty barn, practically everything having been snatched away before her eyes" by her brother, including her parents' double bed. Impetuously Vivienne ordered a new double bed for Rose. It was useless to expostulate with Maurice, Vivienne told Moxon Broad:

> But when it comes to her lying in her last illness on a little old brass single bed, not good enough for a modern servant girl, and two so-called nurses sleeping on the same bed, I am not going to stand by and look on. Such things are not tolerated nowadays, and unless altered she would be better in The London Clinic . . .[51]

Maurice was furious with Vivienne when one of the nurses told him that his sister expected him to pay for the bed and other items she had ordered for their mother. "I may as well make it clear that I am naturally *not* going to pay for such things either out of Mother's money or my own,"[52] he wrote to Vivienne on 20 November. Mother might have a long illness, and her money was "extremely limited. God knows what the doctors' and nurses' bills will be." As Vivienne knew, he repeated angrily, the whole of the Haigh-Wood capital was in trust and could not be realised. "Most of the things you have sent here have been really useless." A new bed made no difference to Mother, declared Maurice: "her mind is dreadfully confused, poor darling."

On the contrary, declared Vivienne two days later, Mother was perfectly rational. "When I saw [her] on Thursday morning she was very sweet and perfectly herself." The crisis aroused in Vivienne's mind memories of her own recent crisis with Tom: "You never offered me a word of sympathy or understanding in my most desperate need, my most incredible shock," she accused Maurice.[53] Concerned that her mother was emaciated, Vivienne asked Dr. Reginald Miller to call. But Miller and Vivienne had crossed swords before. In October 1935 Vivienne had refused to pay Miller his fee of nine guineas as a protest against his action in refusing to allow her to see Eliot, who was also his patient.[54] Now Miller demanded payment in advance, before contacting Rose's own doctor. "There is urgent need for action," replied Vivienne impatiently. "You can say that I am your patient and it is necessary for my mental health that you see my Mother."[55] But not until Miller had received his two guineas in advance, on 13 November, did he consent to call on Rose.[56] Using her "mental health" as a weapon was a dangerous tactic with doctors, and one which could backfire on Vivienne. Dr. Miller, like Maurice, was no friend to Vivienne, and both took their orders from Eliot.

Rose remained seriously ill, and Vivienne was very much "lowered" by her mother's illness. She suffered with a recurrence of severe back pain from her permanent spinal injury, and had to have physiotherapy with Dr. Cyriax four mornings a week, and was no longer able to attend her music lectures before midday.[57] In this crisis Vivienne turned in despair to Mary Hutchinson. On 11 November 1936 she sent Mary a typed letter from Durrant's Hotel, explaining that her mother was very seriously ill. "If you could see me I should be so glad . . . If you send me a postcard, I will meet you anywhere you say. *Please.*" Vivienne enclosed a stamped addressed postcard for Mary's reply. Mary ignored her appeal.[58]

Vivienne's records are missing from 1937, but according to Maurice, the sixty-year lease on 3 Compayne Gardens expired in 1939. The Haigh-Wood estate then bought Rose a house in Pinner, Middlesex, at 97 Marsh Road, where she was nursed until her death in April 1941.[59] Although Vivienne still used her old home in Compayne Gardens as a refuge until 1938, she no longer had her mother to accompany her to concerts, but only Aunts Jackie and Lillia, whom Vivienne by now disliked and whom she felt disliked her. Rose's affection had been a significant factor in mitigating Vivienne's loneliness and sense of insecurity, and without it she was "distraught."

On 10 December another event occurred which Vivienne, as an ardent royalist, found profoundly shocking: the abdication of Edward VIII. Vivienne had worshipped the Prince of Wales, "the young and handsome king emperor, who with his blue eyes, his elegant if diminutive form, and his golden locks [is] the idol, the joy, the one and only ray of light and colour on which all eyes in this land should focus."[60] "I quite agree about the King. The whole thing is appalling," wrote Maurice on 17 December, in a letter thanking Vivienne for her Christmas present for Raggie. "However, it's no earthly use allowing it to upset us. Life is difficult enough already."[61]

But life was certainly less difficult for Maurice than it was for Vivienne. Determined that "I must get all clear before I die," in 1936 she asked Moxon Broad to add a codicil to her will, appointing her brother-in-law Henry Eliot as another trustee in addition to Tom, Maurice, and the others, writing that this had been her original intention, "but, as you know, I was obstructed in carrying the matter out in the way I believed to be right then, and still do."[62] She requested that if Tom Eliot predeceased his brother, Henry Eliot would become beneficiary and trustee on the same terms as her husband. Vivienne's letter is neatly and accurately typed, and makes perfect sense, as does all her business correspondence (of which she kept carbon copies) to Broad, and to her bank manager, Thomas Hope. By 1 March 1936 Vivienne had signed her new will, of which Maurice was the main beneficiary and, on his death, his son Charles ("Raggie") Warren Haigh-Wood. Tom was now left only the "residue" of her property, but to her brother Vivienne bequeathed her title and interest in the Haigh estate in the Irish Free State, comprising 1, 3, 4 and 5 Haigh Terrace, 1–10 Eglington Park, and Eglington House leased from the ground landlords, the Lords Vescy and Longford.[63] Signing this will was her downfall. Now only Vivienne's freedom stood in Maurice's way.

Maurice and Ahmé lived extravagantly; nor did he meet with great success as a stockbroker, later losing £200,000 in Slater Walker.[64] Vivienne was also by nature extravagant. She found it impossible to live on her allowance from the Haigh-Wood estate, and had no hesitation about eating into capital. "Simply choose a security to sell and send it to me for my signature," she blithely instructed Hope when he complained that her overdraft was too high.[65] Maurice watched with growing alarm as Vivienne bought Bechsteins and beds and a new Ford four-seater car (she sold her Morris Minor for £45), rented flats at whim, as well as ordering white and scarlet dresses, claret-coloured silk model suits, a fashionably short shingle wig, and having her leopard skin coat remodelled for receptions at the French Embassy, the English Speaking Union to meet Dame Margaret Lloyd George, and a luncheon with the Archbishop of York. By 1936 the Haigh-Wood estate was funding Vivienne's leases on 68 Clarence Gate Gardens, 8 Edge Street, her numerous hotel bills, music lessons and doctors' bills. Although Vivienne kept careful notes on her Irish property, calculating that she was entitled to £569.3.4d in rent between 1927 and 1933, her insouciant attitude towards money was an increasing drain upon the estate.[66] For Maurice and Tom, the only trustees of the estate now that Rose was too ill to have any say, the idea of putting Vivienne away was increasingly tempting. Not only would it remove her embarrassing presence from their lives, it would enable them to stop her reckless spending, and allow Tom at last to retrieve the Eliot family treasures still hoarded by Vivienne.

However, Eliot had different, though equally pressing, motives for locking his wife up: gagging Vivienne would put a stop to her innuendos about his private life and prevent her attendance at his plays. By the summer of 1938 Eliot had finished the second draft of *The Family Reunion,* whose theme was the death of an unwanted wife, possibly at the hands of her husband Harry, Lord Monchensey, possibly by accident. Its autobiographical nature was at once evident to Virginia Woolf, who considered the characters to be "as stiff as pokers. And the chief poker is Tom . . . A cold upright poker."[67] Even Emily Hale had a role as a faded spinster to whom Harry was close in his youth, while Charlotte Eliot is immortalised as Amy, the matriarch who detests her daughter-in-law. What could be worse than the resurrection of Lady Monchensey in the stalls, a shrieking reproach to the author? It was inevitable that Vivienne, who had attended productions of *Sweeney Agonistes* and *Murder in the Cathedral* repeatedly, would appear, probably in Fascist uniform, probably very often, at the Westminster Theatre, where *The Family Reunion* was due to open in March 1939. Martin Browne, the producer, and Eliot had originally planned a production for autumn 1938. The playwright, wrote Browne, was "already troubled by the looming clouds of war and anxious to get the play finished and on the stage before they broke."[68]

Undoubtedly Maurice and Tom discussed what was to be done about Vivienne in the years before her committal. Cassius knew Brutus's wishes, even if Brutus himself did not wish to be the instrument of his victim's removal. But as Vivienne, fearful of a second attempt to certify her, fled from hotel to hotel and studied regularly at the Royal Academy of Music, no opportunity or pretext for certification presented itself. Nevertheless, it was easy enough to trace her. Vivienne's attempts at secrecy after becoming "Daisy Miller" were half-hearted: on 6 July she sent her sister-in-law Theresa a poignant but prickly letter in which she reproached Theresa for not keeping in touch with her ("Good manners requires me to write to you from time to time, and requires you to write to me"), and confessed that she had not, as she allowed it to be supposed, gone to America but was at the Three Arts Club where any of the Eliot family could find her. "I should enjoy a good talk with you and Henry," she wrote wistfully.[69] At the same time Vivienne was aware she was no longer acceptable to her in-laws: it was Eliot whom Theresa would entertain at her apartment in Cambridge, Massachusetts, and would continue to do so after Henry's death in April 1947.[70] Theresa knew, as she had known her so long, wrote Vivienne, that she never sought friends. "And if people seek me, I have come to the point of wondering what they 'want.' "

Vivienne's neat entries in her 1936 account book detail her movements. In September she spent 2s on a visit to Dr. Moore, the dentist; on the 13th she sent a registered letter to "T. S. Eliot" and, a few days later, spent 1/6d on tips to the porter and chambermaid at the Constance Hotel, where she spent the night. On the 16th Vivienne bought an 8s ticket to Oxford, where she purchased postcards of the Bodleian Library and a catalogue, and had tea with a former servant, Annie. And in December she paid the bill for the coming term at the Royal Academy of Music, which she now intended to attend full time as her health had improved. There were periods of virtual normality in Vivien's eccentric life, but it was only a matter of time before a crisis broke. She was "not waving, but drowning." And Maurice was waiting.

In June 1937 Vivienne bought tickets for the fifteenth exhibition of the Art Union of the Three Arts Club. After that date, she vanishes. Did she tumble, once again, into the "abyss" of drugs she had experienced in 1925, drugs which caused delusion? Her tone on 10 December, the day of Edward VIII's abdication, is agitated and confused. She wrote to Geoffrey Faber:

> Dear Geoffrey
>
> I am obliged to complain of a fact of which I am quite sure you are unaware, that on the very rare occasions when I go to 24 Russell Square, where I find an extremely agreeable and courteous atmosphere—I am *OSTENTATIOUSLY FOLLOWED* by persons who have no claim on me, & whose acquaintance I deny. I write, merely to make you acquainted with a state of affairs which I am sure you will agree with me is in detestably bad taste, hoping that I may rely on your wisdom in not extending a welcome to such persons who follow in my train to your affairs, and

who are the enemies of my husband and myself, and the parasites and no friends to your household. I write on this day of disaster and defeat for England. The last weeks, which have included the serious illness of my mother, preceded by a stroke, have been the severest strain which my existence has ever had to support.[71]

Faber replied that he had no idea who the persons of whom Vivienne complained might be. "But I need hardly assure you that if I *did,* I should share your objections of the kind you describe."

The belief that one is being followed is a symptom of anxiety and paranoia, although in Vivienne's case her paranoia was entirely justified, as events were to prove. Overwhelmed by panic and loss, she became irrational and mentally disturbed. But there is no evidence that Vivienne was schizophrenic. She never manifested the social withdrawal of the schizophrenic, nor does her dedication to music, reaching the high standards of the Royal Academy of Music, or her correspondence or diaries, indicate a psychosis; rather, her behaviour continued to suggest a tendency to manic-depression shared by numerous artists and writers. In Vivienne's case, her symptoms became more florid under stress, for example her extravagance, a symptom of mania. She knew her pursuit of the truth was a provocative, dangerous policy, but principle mattered too much for her to abandon her efforts to collect and preserve her records: "As you know I am always morbidly anxious to have the truth . . . which makes me such an unpleasant person to have about," she wrote to Moxon Broad in August 1936, pressing him to obtain copies of all the cables sent to 68 Clarence Gate Gardens from the Western Union Cable Company in July 1933. Vivienne had stuck the original cables onto cartridge paper and put them into a sealed cupboard, only to find the contents now missing. She was certain they had been "thieved" from the cupboard by one of those who had reasons for wishing to make things appear otherwise than they actually were.[72] "The average mind concerns itself so much more with articles of jewellery or silver that mere Scraps of Paper are of no account whatever," she wrote. "That is not my view."[73]

It seems that Vivienne had a premonition that she would be "removed" before long. In the autumn of 1936 she had watched Rupert

Doone's production at the Group Theatre of the *Agamemnon* of Aeschylus, in which Robert Speaight, whom she had admired as Becket, took the part of Agamemnon. She would have read the note by its translator Louis MacNeice that in the world of Aeschylus there is such a thing as sin, and that not only are their fathers' sins visited upon the children, the children themselves have to sin in their turn and to some extent are responsible agents: "The worst sins are those against one's family, which are punished by the . . . Furies that belong to that family," wrote MacNeice.[74] Perhaps Vivienne saw herself as Cassandra in her own Greek tragedy—the part was taken by a Vivienne Bennett—as she kept her programme, along with a postcard of the Ritz Hotel in Paris from Mary Hutchinson, in her album, inscribing her own delphic captions:

"COMING EVENTS CAST THEIR SHADOWS BEFORE. HEAVIER THE INTERVAL THAN THE CONSUMMA-TION" (T. S. Eliot).[75]

Beside Mary's postcard, Vivienne also wrote: "ALIBI?" Did she believe that Tom was hiding in Paris, while she waited, full of dread, for the second arrival of the doctors?

Vivienne's "consummation" or committal took place in July 1938. Maurice's letter of 14 July 1938 to Tom, who was on holiday with Emily Hale in Gloucestershire, appears to exonerate him and Eliot from any responsibility.

Dear Tom

I am very sorry to write to you on your holiday but I'm afraid I must.

V. was found wandering in the streets at 5 o'clock this morning and was taken into Marylebone police station . . . The inspector of the police station told me she had talked in a very confused and unintelligible manner and appeared to have various illusions, and if it had not been possible to get hold of me or someone to take charge of her, he would have felt obliged to place her under mental observation.

As soon as I got to the city I rang up Dr. Miller . . . He got a reply from Allen & Hanbury's this morning in which they said that V. called every day for her medicine, that she appeared to be in a deplorable condition and that they had no idea of her address. Dr. Miller was therefore on the point of writing to me because he feels that something must be done without much more delay . . . (He) feels that V. must go either to Malmaison or to some home, and I am also inclined to think that, because there is no telling what will happen next.

V. had apparently been wandering about for two nights, afraid to go anywhere. She is full of the most fantastic suspicions and ideas. She asked me if it was true that you had been beheaded. She says she has been in hiding from various mysterious people, and so on.

I have made a provisional appointment with Dr. Miller for 3.15 tomorrow (this was before I discovered you were away).

I really don't know whether to suggest your running up to town tomorrow and returning to Gloucestershire in the evening, or not. You will be able to decide that for yourself, but I would be grateful if you would send me a telegram in the morning to say what you decide.[76]

Yours ever

Maurice.

Mrs. Valerie Eliot, the poet's second wife, in interview with the writer Blake Morrison, produced from her handbag a photostat of the above letter, and a second letter from Maurice to Tom, dated 14 August 1938, one month later. This describes Vivienne's certification by two doctors, Dr. Hart and Dr. Mapother, and subsequent committal to Northumberland House, a private mental asylum in Green Lanes, Finsbury Park.

Both doctors felt strongly that she should be put into a home. They handed me their certificates. I then had to go before a magistrate to obtain his order. I got hold of one in Hampstead.

I then went to Northumberland House, saw the doctor there, and arranged for a car to go with nurses to Compayne Gardens that evening. The car went at about 10 pm. Vivienne went very quietly with them after a good deal of discussion.

I spoke to the doctor yesterday evening, and was told that Vivienne had been fairly cheerful, had slept well and eaten well, and sat out in the garden and read a certain amount . . .

I gather . . . that Vivienne was in the habit often of saving up her drugs and then taking an enormous dose all at once, which I suppose accounts for the periodical crises.

As soon as you get back I should very much like to see you . . .

Yrs. Ever

Maurice.

"Tom would *not* sign the committal order," remembered a resentful Maurice. Eliot was not prepared to take responsibility for Vivienne's final committal. According to Maurice, it was Jack Hutchinson, who had met Vivienne in 1936, who signed the order.[77] Enid Faber confirmed to Michael Hastings, in a letter of 26 August 1983, that she did not sign an involuntary reception order on behalf of Vivienne Eliot—"And I do not think my husband Geoffrey did." Enid remembered that "some member of the family did."[78] Maurice later said: "I don't think I did. If I did I can't remember," but guilt clouded his memory. It was he who orchestrated Vivienne's committal. Of his sister he said shortly before his death: "She was never a lunatic. I'm as sure as the day I was born."[79]

The doors of the "home" closed behind Vivienne:

O dark dark dark. They all go into the dark . . .[80]

"Our only health is the disease," wrote Eliot in "East Coker." We must obey the nurse, "whose constant care is not to please," but to remind us of Adam's curse, "And that, to be restored, our sickness must grow worse."[81] Vivienne did not take kindly to institutionalisation, and her sickness did "grow worse." She refused to obey the nurses, or the rules of the home, which was not, alleged Valerie Eliot, a mental hospital but "a glorified nursing home in which degrees of restraint were necessary . . ." (although Eliot referred to it as an "asylum" to Mary Trevelyan). At first

Vivienne was in the nicest part, the Villas, where the patients who needed least watching lived. They only moved her when she began stealing from and worrying other patients. She stirred up a lot of havoc in the place, apparently.[82]

Vivienne was unhappy enough to try to escape. She appealed to Louie Purdon, then increasingly active in the Harrow Lunacy Law Reform Society, which was composed of volunteers aiming to befriend and help those who had been certified and confined. Basil Saunders, son of Louie's cousin and close friend, Marjorie Saunders, recalled that its members believed that "many people had relatives certified because they were tiresome and, quite often, to get hold of their money, when they may have been no more than eccentric."[83] England had a long tradition of husbands imprisoning unwanted wives in private madhouses. Such asylums, writes the historian Lawrence Stone, were "squalid private prisons which, as long as the fees were paid, would accept anyone and keep them behind bars, regardless of their mental condition or the motives of the person who ordered their confinement." In 1774 Parliament had passed a law to put a stop to these abuses but, although madhouse-keepers had thenceforth to be licensed and to keep records, and were forbidden to accept patients without a doctor's order, such regulations could be evaded.[84] In the 1930s, writes Saunders,

> The law provided that if anyone certified could "escape" and evade "capture" for six weeks . . . they automatically became decertified and had a chance to resist re-certification. This was the main style of help of the lunacy law reformers: sheltering individuals during these six weeks . . .

Marjorie Saunders, a Christian Scientist, provided a refuge for escaped psychiatric patients at her pebble-dashed semi-detached house in Parkside Way, Harrow; it was to this liberal household she intended to bring Vivienne.[85] Basil Saunders takes up the story.

> One evening my mother went up to a café near Allen & Hanbury's off Oxford Street. There she was to receive Vivien and

take her home to stay. Instead she was told "Mrs. Eliot" would not be coming and that the arrangement was off. I believe Vivien had been apprehended before she got to Louie.

Thereafter Louie was not able to communicate with Vivien. The "home" she was in would not pass on telephone messages. Louie's letters were returned.[86]

Eliot never visited Vivienne in Northumberland House. Why not? Blake Morrison asked Valerie Eliot.

> Because the doctors had told him he mustn't . . . But he did get regular reports, through his solicitors, on how she was doing. And because she'd been made a Ward in Chancery, there was this outside person looking after her interests. I'm quite sure that if a doctor had said, "She can come out," Tom or Maurice would have done something about it . . . I talked to Maurice for many hours . . . I'd pour whisky down him and he'd talk and talk—but he never expressed regret to me. He must have realised it was for her own good.[87]

By contrast, Eliot visited W. L. Janes regularly on Thursday afternoons in St. Stephen's Hospital, Fulham, smuggling champagne in for his servant during the winters of 1937 and 1938, and telling John Hayward how he "dashed down to Fulham" the day after buying Sir John Gielgud and Browne oysters, Guinness and tournedos for dinner at the Reform Club, during which Gielgud failed to persuade his host to allow him to direct and act the leading part in *The Family Reunion*.[88] Dinner, recalled Eliot, made "quite a hole" in a pound note.[89] It may have been Gielgud's extravagant habits, rather than the fact, as Sybil Thorndike told him, that he had no faith, that prevented Eliot from letting Gielgud have the play. Gielgud's indiscreet homosexuality, which was well known in the theatrical world before his conviction in 1953 for importuning, may also have alarmed Eliot as the post-war moral climate became increasingly homophobic.

During Janes's final illness Eliot visited twice a week.[90] Oddly personal details on which Eliot remarked to Hayward, such as the "fact" that, although all policemen have big feet, Janes turned out to have smaller feet than Eliot, indicate the closeness of their relationship.[91] Even Ottoline noticed Eliot's desire to befriend "sixth-rate writers and detectives," whom he could dominate.[92]

Vivienne's committal opened the way for Maurice to take sole control of the Haigh-Wood estate. When Rose died in 1941, Eliot relinquished his trusteeship. Maurice was Vivienne's heir by her will of 1936. But although her death would benefit him, it also brought him anguish, as he confessed to Michael Hastings:

> It was only when I saw Vivie in the asylum for the last time I realized I had done something very wrong. She was as sane as I was. She said, "God knows that may not amount to much, Maurice, but I'm as sane as you are," and I did what I hadn't done for years. I sat in front of Vivie and actually burst into tears . . . What Tom and I did was wrong. And Mother. I did everything Tom told me to. Not ashamed to say so. But when it came to our family, I think he bit off more than he could chew. He didn't understand the rules, actually. You see—you have to be kind to Vivie.[93]

Yet Vivienne never lost her faith in Tom. "The sin is not my husband's" remained her mantra.[94] She spent the Second World War in the asylum,

> Locked away in Northumberland House, listening to German bombs dropping on London, waiting in vain for her husband to take her home.
>
> Hearing his poems in her head. Alone, forced to reconsider everything.

> *What is that sound high in the air.*
> *London Bridge is falling down falling down falling down.*[95]

In London Eliot watched for fires from the roof of Faber & Faber. As he waited for the drone of the bombers and the gentle rain of grey ash upon his clothes, he felt reproached by the circumstances of Vivienne's committal. He knew that Miller could have referred Vivienne, as the doctor suggested, to Malmaison as a voluntary patient, to stay until she was stabilised and well enough to be discharged. Her income was more than adequate to pay for her to live at 8 Edge Street with a nurse and a maid. Permanent confinement had not been necessary. It had only been arranged in response to his wishes and Maurice's. The second letter Maurice wrote, in which he described how Vivienne "went quietly," after a good deal of discussion, to Northumberland House, and was certified, not by Miller or Cyriax, but by doctors unfamiliar to her and possibly connected with the asylum, could have been composed after he and Eliot had conferred on the telephone, in order, as Vivienne put it, "to make things appear otherwise to what they actually were." Certainly it reads like a deliberately worded statement of justification.

Eliot repressed these inconvenient thoughts. "Where does one go from a world of insanity?" he asks in *The Family Reunion*. "Somewhere on the other side of despair." As soon as Vivienne was safely behind bars, the play was performed in 1939. In it Eliot takes his revenge upon Vivienne, and upon his mother.[96] His play was as much a sponge in prussic acid as the revenge drama Djuna Barnes wrote after seeing *The Family Reunion—The Antiphon*.[97] Eliot's unforgettable portrait of an unbalanced wife who, "a restless shivering painted shadow/In life," is "less than a shadow in death," fixed Vivienne's character in history like a fly in aspic. Instantly recognised as the author's wife, the play seemed to justify the murder of such a crazed, demonic creature. And although the author, "Harry," a modern Orestes, is supposedly cursed because he has sinned against the family just as surely as Orestes did in killing his mother Clytemnestra, the audience's sympathies are supplicated for the suffering protagonist, in his quest for "bright angels," rather than his unnamed, disappeared wife, the portrait of whom is irredeemably hostile.

In reality, Vivienne, although technically still living, had vanished as suddenly as Lady Monchensey, and also without leaving a body. In *The Family Reunion* Eliot imagined her life: "Up and down, through the stone passages/Of an immense and empty hospital/Pervaded by a smell of disinfectant." She would look straight ahead as she walked, "passing barred windows./Up and down. Until the chain breaks."[98]

From the evidence of the Hayward letters, it seems Eliot's life was less penitential in the years after Vivienne's committal than has been claimed. During raids he sheltered in the "fashionable" Russell Square coal cellar, number four, which he shared with Geoffrey Faber and the senior secretaries. As in the First World War, he ordered a new winter coat before the price of wool went up; this time he also bought a portable wireless and a pair of pince nez.[99] In his office he made fashion sketches for John Hayward of gentlemen in gas masks, with wing collars and spotted ties, decorated with "Old Possum's" dictum: "Gas Masks to be worn under, not over the Necktie," and joked that at 6:30 he had had "an unmistakable attack of emerods," and fifteen minutes later an air-raid warning came, which "goes to show that emerods cause air raid warnings and not vice versa." At the weekends he continued to enjoy excellent meals with the Tandys in Dorset, the Kauffers in the Chilterns, and at Rodmell with the "Woolves . . . where food is easy to get." One November Sunday in 1939 Eliot lunched with Clive, Vanessa, Duncan and Angelica on a "most noble" sirloin of beef, washed down by brown ale, and enjoyed some hilarious small talk. Heavy drinking with Geoffrey Faber continued over dinner at All Souls; that was the evening when the poet was forced to urinate in the college garden, and A. L. Rowse, with whom Eliot nearly shared a flat in 1934, proved "endearing";[100] Eliot rejoiced in the fact that he was still in demand for weekend house-parties: even the Bishop of Bath and Wells had to go on his waiting list. Otherwise his time was spent with Robert Sencourt, and "poor Stephen" (Spender), whom he was consoling because his wife Inez had left him.[101] Against the view that Eliot's post-1938 life was one of grim despair must be set his remark to John Hayward on 29 November 1939 that "the last six years have been the only happy years of my life."[102] Once he had used his marriage as the source and subject of his work in *The Family Reunion,* as he had done in *The Waste Land* and *Sweeney Agonistes,* Eliot banished thoughts of Vivienne, and allowed himself to enjoy certain "menus plaisirs de la vie—quant au grands, said Gourmont, ils n'existent guère"*—such as French tobacco, shirts, socks, and a good snooze in a club armchair, preferably at the Garrick.[103]

After the Second World War Eliot moved in with Hayward, the "sapient Tarantula." It was an interesting choice. John Hayward, confined

---

*Small pleasures in life—as for the large ones, said Gourmont, they scarcely exist.

to a wheelchair, was as needy as Vivienne had been in 1915. For the second time Eliot entered into a co-dependent relationship with someone weaker than himself. It was an arrangement which Hayward had proposed as early as 1935, but Eliot's fear of an address that could be discovered by Vivienne prevented him from accepting. All through the 1930s, Hayward had remained at the heart of the Faber coterie around Eliot, publishing in 1937 *Noctes Binanianae*, the "Satyrical Compliments and Verses" exchanged between the Coot (Faber), the Elephant (Eliot), the Whale (Morley) and Hayward, the Vesperal Spider, verses which bear witness to the nature of the parties at his flat in Bina Gardens, as well as Eliot's and Geoffrey Faber's nights out on the town.[104] In March 1946, after leaving the Mirrlees family in Shamley Green and returning to London, the Elephant joined the Spider, "who spinneth his web above all," in his new flat in 19 Carlyle Mansions, Cheyne Walk, once the home of Henry James. There Hayward, progressively more disabled, lived in some disorder in the large room overlooking the river, and Eliot existed in a small bedroom as monastic as that which he had had in Father Cheetham's Rectory.

The poet John Malcolm Brinnin, director of the New York Poetry Center, was given an introduction to Hayward, through whom he hoped to persuade Eliot to speak at the Center. One winter Sunday he called on Hayward.

> "How d'je do," said a Quasimodo figure in a wheelchair. Grotesquely bent, he had a big head, thick lips the colour of raw liver.
>
> "You'll have to get used to me," he said, "just like everybody else."
>
> The hand he offered hung like a broken wing.
>
> "Make yourself a drink." He pointed to a table on wheels. "And one for me, some whisky and a little water. You can have ice, if you insist."

The flat "echoed with the absence of its other tenant." A salver full of sixpences for the buses to Russell Square indicated Eliot's occupancy. "Let me show you round," said Hayward. He made a ninety-degree turn and pointed his wheelchair in the direction of a closed door.

"His," said Hayward, indicating the room we had entered. Its walls looked as if they'd been uniformly stained with nicotine. There was one bare bulb on a chain, an ebony crucifix over the single bed. The wardrobe closet was open: crow-black silk ties on a rail, a scarlet water-silk sash, three glen plaid suits, others in shades of gray and black . . . "The confessional," said Hayward. "Here we have our bedtime chats."[105]

Hayward's protection of Eliot's privacy—he took all the phone calls at the flat—his skills as literary critic, offering advice which Eliot prized highly on the *Four Quartets,* and his malicious and ribald wit, ensured that their companionship lasted for eleven years. Nevertheless, they retained different sets of friends, and contemporaries speculated as to why Eliot, and his cat Pettipaws, whose expensive tastes were the despair of their French housekeeper, Madame Amory, chose to share his life with Hayward. There was gossip about the two which, wrote his friend, the writer E. W. F. Tomlin, "disgusted me."[106] Some speculated, erroneously, that it was a gay partnership, others that living with someone so physically incapacitated gave Eliot the control he desired. It was Eliot on whom Hayward depended for weekend walks to watch the football in Royal Hospital Gardens, although one or two devoted women took the bibliophile to parties. And Hayward's role as confidant, the recipient of Eliot's secrets, meant that he understood when Eliot explained, in December 1939, that he felt obliged to present the prizes to the "infant damned" of Raynes Park, where among 320 undersized, weedy, gangly pale boys at the grammar school, the future broadcaster Robert Robinson was a pupil.[107]

Robinson realised that his headmaster, John Garrett, was "as queer as a coot," but had distinguished friends. W. H. Auden had written the school song. Other poets helped out. "You simply couldn't say no," remembered Stephen Spender. Nor could Eliot. Robinson was amazed when the illustrious poet descended upon the suburban "waste land" from which he longed to escape. "Why do I do this?" Eliot asked Hayward, answering his own question. Because the headmaster was John Garrett, one of the dimmer *Criterion* contributors, one of the "young men," a friend of Auden, Rupert Doone, et al., who therefore seemed to have a claim upon him.[108] So

Eliot made his first, and probably last, visit to Raynes Park, SW20, as a token of his solidarity with "Les Boys," as he described MacNeice, Auden, Spender and David Gascoyne ("one of the nicest of les jeunes, but not so far a good poet").[109] It was an example of his membership of what Wystan Auden dubbed "the homintern," the international fraternity of gay men in literature and the arts between the wars, who befriended each other, collaborated and commissioned work from each other.[110]

In July 1938, the month in which Vivienne was committed, Eliot gave a poetry reading at the Student Christian Movement Conference at Swanwick, Derbyshire. There he met a gifted and energetic forty-one-year-old woman, Mary Trevelyan, Warden of Student Movement House in Gower Street, London. Mary was the daughter of the Rev. Philip Trevelyan, and a descendant of the Victorian historian Thomas Babington Macaulay; her brother Humphrey was already carving out a distinguished career in the diplomatic service. A talented musician, Mary, unlike Vivienne, came from a clerical family that could claim equal distinction with Eliot's, and he felt he had found a sympathetic ear as he confided to Mary that in American society there were "Eliots, non-Eliots, and foreigners." Mary later recalled that when she first met him, "T.S.E. was all the rage in the student world. Young men in corduroy trousers, floppy ties and long hair, carried his poetry about and looked intense." She was flattered when the poet agreed to read his work to her students. When she was appointed the only woman member of the Anvil, a BBC religious brains trust programme, it was to Eliot she turned for advice on the weekly questions sent round to the team.

Religion drew the two together. Mary and Eliot both worshipped at St. Stephen's, Kensington, where they sometimes met to pray in the darkened church for the service of Tenebrae. Mary had a gift for breaking through Eliot's reserve. They shared Sunday suppers of bacon and eggs, and drives into the country, with Mary doing the driving. She was introduced to his favourite sister Marian. And Mary, like Emily, fell in love with Eliot. During the war she served as YMCA Programme Director with the British Liberation Army in Belgium and France, and became Head of the Field Survey Bureau in Paris, organising post-war reconstruction work, service which prompted Eliot to write from the Mirrlees' house that "the Shambly family is consumed with admiration for you . . . as a Man of Action."[111] After the war Mary returned to London and she and Eliot renewed their friendship.[112]

In 1942, Mary apparently learnt from Eliot's friend George Every that the poet was married, but that his wife had "gone out of her mind." Eliot still had no contact with Vivienne, although Enid Faber visited her all through the war, and Mary Hutchinson also did so, according to Maurice. Otherwise both her visitors and her mail were censored. Her pleading letters to Faber & Faber continued to be returned unopened. She was silenced and immobilised, a prisoner in all but name. Over dinners with Mary Trevelyan at the Etoile in Charlotte Street, Eliot spoke distractedly of his marriage, explaining that it was at his instigation that his wife had been made a Ward of Chancery. In June 1944, aware how frightened Vivienne would be of the doodle bug bombs, one of which had exploded in Russell Square, blasting the Faber office and flat while Eliot was in the country, he wrote to his solicitors suggesting she be moved. The Official Solicitor's reply was that Maurice must give permission. Maurice was out of touch in Sicily and Italy, and therefore Vivienne remained in Northumberland House. Her own wishes were never considered.[113]

On 22 January 1947 Vivienne died. She was only fifty-eight. The cause of her death was given as a heart attack (syncope and cardiovascular degeneration) on the death certificate. But there is no reason to suppose that this was any more accurate than it had been in the case of Ottoline, who had died in April 1938 after being given a dose of a powerful antibiotic called Prontosil. The cause of her death was also given as heart failure. The doctor who prescribed the drug was threatened with medical investigation following the deaths of other patients, and committed suicide.[114] Medical negligence might have caused Vivienne's death, but it is more probable that Vivienne saved up her drugs, as Maurice said was her habit, and overdosed. Her depression can only be guessed at, as her efforts to escape were foiled, her contact with the outside world cut off, and her misery grew too great to bear. Suicide may have seemed her only option. Like Dora Carrington, who found life without Lytton Strachey intolerable, Vivienne saw no meaning in a life without Tom.

"Life is like a hurried walk in the dark: a blind stumble," Vivienne once wrote. "Death must be like the opening of a door into a lighted house, and saying breathlessly, 'Well, I've got here, but I don't know how I did it.' "[115] In dying by her own hand, if indeed she did so, she took her last gamble: to move from the darkness into the light.

The announcement of her death in *The Times* was curt, the shortest in the Deaths column: "On Jan. 22 1947, Vivienne Haigh Eliot, in London. Funeral Private." Tom was annoyed that Maurice had not included his name in the notice. Vivienne's death, he confided to Mary Trevelyan, was "quite sudden and unexpected. She was supposed to be in quite good physical health . . . It was therefore a particular shock and left me more disintegrated than I could have imagined. Curiously enough, I believe it is much more unsettling to me now, after all these years, than it would have been fifteen years ago."[116]

Snow was falling as Eliot, Maurice and the Fabers travelled to Pinner on a bleak winter's day for Vivienne's funeral. She was buried in Pinner Cemetery, her grave close to her mother's, although her wish had been to be buried beside her father in Eastbourne.[117] The headstone, ordered by Maurice, reads: "In Loving Memory of Vivien Haigh Eliot, Died 29th January 1947." The stone-mason carved the wrong date. No one troubled to correct it.[118]

Epilogue

When Maurice telephoned to say that Vivien had died suddenly, John Hayward took the call, and broke the news to his flat-mate.

"Oh God! Oh God," Eliot said, and buried his face in his hands.[1] His shock at Vivienne's early death was greater than anyone expected. Mary Trevelyan noted that "he talked much of his wife and did, indeed, seem to be very much upset at her death."[2] The thought had at once leapt into Eliot's mind that Vivienne might have committed suicide. It was a threat she had made many times before, he never knew how seriously. "Downing, do you think it might have been suicide,/And that his Lordship knew it?" Harry's Uncle Charles in *The Family Reunion* asks of Harry's servant and chauffeur (a character who was in all probability based on W. L. Janes, who had similarly been with his master for "over ten years . . .") as they discuss Lady Monchensey's death. "I don't think she had the courage," replies Downing. Charles asks whether Harry's wife ever talked of suicide. Oh yes, replies Downing, but she only did it to frighten people. Was she in good spirits? She was always up and down, says Downing. "Down in the morning, and up in the evening,/And *then* she used to get rather excited." She was irresponsible, and wouldn't let the master out of her sight. Up and down, down and up. It was an accurate description of the manic-depressive personality. When Eliot learnt of Vivienne's sudden and unexpected death, he must have suspected that she had, at last, found the courage. The chain had broken.

An inherited predisposition to manic-depression or bipolar affective disorder may, indeed, have existed in the Haigh-Wood family: Vivienne's nephew, Raggie, committed suicide in 1976, six years after his mother Ahmé's death from cancer.[3]

Vivienne's death gave Eliot his freedom, while reviving and intensifying his remorse. The way now lay open for him to remarry. There were two contenders for the title of the second Mrs. Eliot: Emily Hale and Mary Trevelyan. Emily had the prior claim, having been waiting in the wings for as long as Eliot could remember, but her expectations had become a burden to him. Theresa Eliot confirmed to E. W. F. Tomlin, who spent many hours in her company in Cambridge in 1959, that at one point Eliot did give Emily to understand that, if Vivienne were to die, he would marry her. "Consequently, she began to go about as if she were his fiancée presumptive, and she would dutifully kiss the members of the Eliot family—at a time when the bestowal of kisses was by no means so free as it is now—almost as if she were already an in-law." Emily was so insistent that she was to all intents and purposes the next Mrs. T. S. Eliot, that Henry wrote to Tom to enquire whether there was any basis for her behaviour. To his surprise he received a letter confirming that there was. Henry tore up the letter in a rage, exclaiming: "Tom has made one mistake, and if he marries Emily he will make another."[4]

On 15 April 1947 Eliot told Mary that he was dreading his forthcoming visit to America, and it would be a relief to get started, as then he would have his return to look forward to. He did not tell Mary that Emily was waiting, this time for official confirmation of their unofficial understanding. However, soon after Eliot's arrival in Boston on 5 May, Henry Eliot died of leukaemia. Eliot, shaken by this second death, knelt by his brother's body, saying prayers, and kissing him goodbye.[5] He returned to his sister Margaret's house at 41 Kirland Street, Cambridge. Not long afterwards, Henry's well-meaning widow, Theresa, invited Eliot to her apartment to meet Emily, who was producing *Richard II* in nearby Concord. Theresa intended to facilitate Tom's wedding plans: instead he turned on her with a white fury which she never forgot to the end of her life.[6] Refusing to accompany her to the cemetery to scatter Henry's ashes, Eliot stumped out, announcing, "I've got to get something over with." When he returned, he told Theresa that he had completed his mission to tell Emily that all thought of marriage between them must be forgotten.[7]

For Emily, Tom's subsequent visit to Concord Academy (where she was now teaching) was a "nightmare." They had another private conversation: "He loves me—I believe that wholly," she wrote to her friend

Lorraine Havens, "but apparently not in the way usual to men less gifted ie with complete love thro' a married relationship."[8] She hoped that Eliot would recover his feelings for her after the shock of two deaths, his wife's and his brother's, had faded, but by 1948 he had made it clear to her that his decision was final.[9] Later, Eliot explained to Mary Trevelyan that for many years he had believed himself to be in love with "someone": "Then, when finally I was free, I realised quite suddenly that I was deluding myself with emotions I had felt in the past, that I had changed more, and in ways unsuspected, than I had thought. I found that I actually could not bear the thought of it . . ." The relationship, when it reached the possibility of completion, was found no longer to exist, he said. And now, "I prefer not to see her, feel embarrassed and unhappy when I do, seem to have very little in common now. There is also of course the feeling, which only a man can understand, that a man, in all these situations, is somehow in the wrong . . ."[10]

Had Eliot learnt the lesson, as he claimed, that reticence, and the desire not to inflict pain, "can often approach very near to cowardice"? It seemed not, for he allowed a near identical situation to develop with Mary. By 1949 Mary was established in a flat in Brunswick Square and working for the University of London, her flat and office both only a few minutes walk from Eliot's office at Russell Square. Eliot was taking her out so often that she began to feel he owed it to her to clarify their relationship. He gave many indications that he reciprocated her feelings, sending her a stream of presents, and holding her hand for "an embarrassingly long time" so that, as she wrote in her memoir, "I really didn't know where I was at all." In addition Mary, who was conductor of the Chelsea Madrigal Society and the Kensington Choral Society, put her musical skills at Eliot's disposal for *The Cocktail Party,* scoring the tune of "One Eyed Riley" as Eliot sang it to her in his thin tenor.[11]

On 18 April 1949 Mary proposed to Eliot. "Oh dear, oh dear," he responded. "As for yourself and me, I didn't think it was anything like that." He was, he said, "burnt out": his years of agony with Vivienne had crippled and exhausted him. Even to think of sharing his life with someone had become a "nightmare." Mary accepted that the "psychological change of life," which Eliot told her he had undergone, made it impossible for him to love again. But as she listened to his repetitive complaints—"I feel so lonely going to Receptions alone" and "What shall I do if I get ill?" and "I can't plan a holiday" because he had no one to holiday with, Hayward being too handicapped to travel—an obvious solution presented itself again to Mary. "Why should we both be lonely?" she asked on 29 May 1950. Again she met with a rebuff. This time Eliot explained that it was because of the catastrophe over Emily Hale that he could not contemplate except "with horror, the thought of marrying anyone else, or of any relationship except that of friendship."[12] "His conscience about Emily, and the way he 'jilted' her must be very bad," commented Mary drily, when Eliot went to meet a train on which she was arriving in August 1953. "He hardly ever meets trains!"

Mary accepted with fortitude Eliot's rejection of her third proposal. She told him that he could enjoy, without embarrassment, the knowledge that there was one person who loved him and that he had better accept her as one of the family. "Tom, with a beaming smile, said, 'Yes, indeed—and I'll give you a toast—TO THE GUARDIANS.' " Unlike Emily, Mary saw Eliot almost weekly and gained a realistic insight into the limitations of his character. She played her allotted role with dignity, remaining a loyal and devoted "guardian" for twenty years from 1938 until 1957. Henceforth, she and John Hayward functioned as a surrogate family to Eliot, sometimes conferring when they felt the poet was in danger of becoming too self-important. By the 1950s Eliot had become "the Pope of Russell Square," possessor of an authority which was semi-divine within the Vatican-like confines of Faber & Faber, and even beyond; it was after he made Mary a present of a good "practical" rosary, one of two which he had been given by the Pope in Rome, that Mary gave Eliot this mocking, but wholly fitting title. In 1948 he received the Order of Merit and the Nobel Prize, and honorary doctorates by the handful—from Yale, Princeton and even, finally, from Harvard. The shell which guarded his personality grew more rigid; he imposed strict "Trade Union" rules upon Mary in order to ration their meetings.[13] "He is a man in prison, a prison largely of his own making," she surmised in 1950. "I had to spend all these years loving him and being hurt often—and now, perhaps, the prison door has opened just a chink." But Eliot's door barely opened before it slammed shut again. "I have noticed of late his *immense* indignation with anyone who disagrees with *him*—and that is a bad state to get into," wrote Mary to John

Hayward on 21 April 1955. "So I consider it's practically your mission to tell him what you really think . . . It is indeed a terrible strain on any human being to feel he is a Classic in his lifetime, & Tom needs, more than he will ever know, honesty from his closest friends."[14]

In the 1950s Eliot took to "snapping" at John and Mary, who often found themselves the victims of his moods. In August 1954 he was "in one of his most towering rages—white with anger, and practically non-speaking" during a visit from Marian and Theodora.[15] The year before, Eliot had met Mary at the Armistice Day Requiem on 8 November; he was tired after dining with the King of Sweden, who was on a state visit, and "very wheezy" during the long service. Mary drove him home to Cheyne Walk and said that she was looking forward to dining with him on Thursday as arranged. "He replied petulantly that he'd no idea what he was doing this week and the thought of dining with *anyone* filled him with horror . . . and departed. Oh La! La!" recorded an exasperated Mary. Generally, however, she waited patiently for Eliot to thaw; a few days after an argument might find the poet with a gin in Mary's kitchen, mixing the salad, cooking the bacon, getting in the way and enjoying himself very much.[16] "You spoil him," said Marian, who wanted Mary for a sister-in-law. "She thinks that I ought, for my own sake, to leave him," wrote Mary. "I didn't say so to her, but I fear it is too late."

Eliot's letters to Hayward reveal why he rationed his intimacy with Mary. Damningly he confided to his friend in November 1939, after giving his first poetry reading at Student Mission House, that "Miss Mary Trevelyan, the hearty Warden" of the settlement, whisked him upstairs for a couple of glasses of bad sherry afterwards. "Hearty," the same epithet he had used for Emily on their country walks, spelt death to any woman's hopes of marriage to the poet. Nevertheless both Mary and Emily were immortalised in Eliot's drama: in *The Cocktail Party,* originally entitled "One-Eyed Reilly," Emily features as the martyred Celia, and Mary as Julia, who hopes to fill the gap in Riley's life left by his vanished wife Lavinia.

Despite the popular and financial success of his first drawing-room comedy, Eliot's unhappiness seemed to deepen after Vivienne's death. It seemed that he faced his own Eumenides, and only by the practise of Christian ritual could guilt be expiated, or redemption glimpsed. It has been suggested that Eliot deliberately undertook a ten-year penance from

1947, one in which he condemned himself to walk across "a whole Thibet of broken stones" in atonement. This is judgement by hindsight, and it should not be supposed that Eliot deliberately set a term on his remorse, after which he felt he warranted absolution. But undeniably he experienced the "terrifying guilt," as Josef Chiari has described it, of knowing he had "loathed one woman to the point of wishing, or perhaps even causing her death."[17] His ill-controlled anger was a sign of the strain under which he laboured, and others besides Mary and John were subjected to his wrath.[18]

Eliot's producer, E. Martin Browne, concluded at the end of his long collaboration with the playwright that Eliot's plays after *The Family Reunion* represented a failure of nerve. Neither *The Confidential Clerk* (1953) nor *The Elder Statesman* (1958) was as successful, dramatically or financially, as *The Cocktail Party,* which, *Time* magazine estimated, grossed a million dollars during its run of 325 performances in New York, of which Eliot's own share was £29,000. "I feel that, by adopting this pattern of ironic social comedy, Eliot placed upon his genius a regrettable limitation," writes Browne. "He tied himself to social, and still more theatrical, conventions which were already outworn when the plays were written . . ."[19] Without his Muse—Vivienne—Eliot the revolutionary had become a reactionary. As early as 1939 Eliot wrote to Hayward that he had no family, no career, and nothing particular to look forward to in this world. "I doubt the permanent value of everything I have written." These doubts grew as, during the 1950s, his energies diminished, and he traded innovation for West End success. Fame and financial security, craved for so long, did not assuage loneliness. Eliot remained in the bleak bedroom in Carlyle Mansions, Cheyne Walk. Increasingly he clung to worldly honours, signifiers of worth, slipping out of the flat to peek at the photograph of himself on the front of *Time* in 1950, and even accepting the Hanseatic Goethe Award in Hamburg despite his dislike of Goethe. Ronald Duncan asked Eliot: "Isn't it a bit of a grind for you to write about Goethe?" To which Eliot replied: "It is. I can't stand his stuff."[20] And the friendship of younger poets and writers such as E. W. F. Tomlin, Josef Chiari, Djuna Barnes and the American priest William Turner Levy, whom he often published at financial and editorial cost to himself, provided confirmation of his position.[21] Such people deferred to Eliot's almost legendary status as a literary icon, and never challenged him as Hayward and Mary were liable, brusquely, to do. The memory of his marriage to Vivienne might have faded had not the threat of future biographies begun to haunt him.

Worries about his health and his reputation began to weigh on Eliot. By 1956, despite the solicitude of friends such as Tomlin and Levy, his tachycardia (abnormally rapid heartbeat) and bronchitis were giving serious cause for concern. Often he asked Mary Trevelyan to feel his pulse. He was, by this period, seriously addicted to the tranquilliser Nembutal, prescribed for anxiety and phobias connected with lifts and large animals.[22] On 12 June 1956 he returned from a trip to America on the *Queen Mary:* "Exhausted T. S. Eliot rushed to hospital. Taken Off Liner, American Trip Wearies Poet" screamed the headline. The United Press added, "The 67-year old Nobel Prize Winner was stricken two days outside New York on the voyage back from his trip to America . . . When the ship reached Southampton, he was taken ashore, pale but smiling, by wheelchair and put into an ambulance."[23] His doctors, Eliot told Tomlin, said that although he had obeyed their orders to give up smoking, his chances of surviving were only fifty-fifty.[24]

Rumours continued to grow that Eliot was homosexual. On 11 November 1952 he met Mary in her flat, bringing "a nasty little article from an American magazine, practically accusing him of homosexuality and mentioning John." He also told her of Canadian academic John Peter's "more serious" article in *Essays in Criticism,* "hinting the same so transparently that he is consulting his solicitor about a possible libel action."[25] On Sunday 30 November Eliot mentioned to Mary that Helen Gardner was very angry about the latter article, and had written a strong protest about it. Tom was not "one of the fraternity," he assured Mary, although the following January, when she remarked that the Chelsea "pansies" were said to have a club in the block of flats to which she had moved, he burst out that homosexuals lived "a life of fear and ostracism—like souls in hell. I believe in hell, yes I do," with a vehemence that astonished her. "I live in constant fear of it myself."[26]

Eliot expressed his outrage at Peter's article to Tomlin and took legal advice. When he wrote to the "young man" with the veiled threat of legal action, John Peter replied, wrote Tomlin, "with a touchingly contrite letter."[27] All copies of *Essays in Criticism* containing the article were pulped, in response to a formal letter from Eliot's solicitor. This did not prevent Peter republishing his allegations in 1969, after Eliot's death. Tomlin has recalled how Eliot's threats of legal action were interpreted as a desire to suppress the truth: "Eliot has been credited with more than one *sub rosa* liaison, and with the extremes of hypocrisy in trying to pretend to be what he was not." At Cambridge, too, F. W. Bateson cited the "King Bolo" poems in a lecture as evidence that Eliot had written a quantity of obscene poetry. In a decade in which homosexual writers and artists were acutely aware of a legal situation which could destroy careers—as it nearly did for John Gielgud, who was unable to work in the United States for four years in the mid-1950s after his conviction for cottaging—the fear of scandal was very real. Gielgud's sentence triggered a debate on homosexuality which led to the Wolfenden Report in 1957, but not until 1967, two years after Eliot's death, was homosexuality decriminalised.

In February 1938 Eliot had pressed John Hayward to become his literary executor. There was, he wrote, no one else whom he could altogether trust in that capacity. Hayward's function would be chiefly negative: to say no to republication of the "junk" he had written for periodicals in the past, and which ought never to be reprinted. "And I don't want any biography written," he stipulated, or any intimate letters published. "So again your job would be to discourage any attempts to make books of me or about me, and to suppress everything suppressible." He would, he wrote, leave instructions in his will to this effect.[28]

By 1956, however, Eliot had begun to wonder whether Hayward's health would enable him to carry out the task of literary executor for long. There was no guarantee that the younger man would outlive him for many years; and yet Eliot was seriously concerned about his own failing health. His thoughts turned to his own death. In 1948 he requested that Father Cheetham should preside over a Requiem Mass, followed by burial in Brookwood Cemetery, Woking. Later, in June 1956, he decided that he would prefer to be buried in the old graveyard, near the church of East Coker, Somerset, from which his ancestor Andrew Eliot had journeyed to the New World. His second choice, were he to die in the United States, was the Bellefontaine Cemetery, St. Louis, near his parents and grandparents. He had, he wrote, very strong objections to being buried in any cathedral or abbey church, such as Westminster Abbey or St. Paul's.[29]

Hayward had hinted in May 1956 to the poet John Brinnin that the situation was becoming critical:

"Tom's now developed something called emphysema. It's rapidly becoming apparent that he needs a nurse more than I do. And I have an informed suspicion that the ever-adoring Miss Fletcher is ready to assume the role. You know her?"

"The young woman in his office?"

"There's somewhat more to that flower of the Yorkshire marshes than meets the eye," he said. "The perfect secretary has begun to see herself as the lady with the lamp."[30]

Valerie Fletcher had become T. S. Eliot's secretary in 1949. Growing up in Leeds, where playwright Alan Bennett, son of the local butcher, used to deliver her mother's orders of meat on his bicycle, she heard John Gielgud's recording of "The Journey of the Magi" at the age of fourteen.[31] It was her first introduction to Eliot's poetry, and she was captivated. "My obsession became a family joke," she recalled. She took a secretarial course and travelled to London, where she worked for the writer Charles Morgan before Eliot engaged her as his secretary.[32]

By 1956 Valerie Fletcher had become indispensable to Eliot, as indispensable a secretary as Vivienne had once been. Margaret Behrens, the "Field Marshall," as Eliot nicknamed her when he knew her at Shamley Green, owned a house in the south of France to which she invited Miss Fletcher. Prompted by Mrs. Behrens, Eliot came to stay at a nearby hotel. The barriers of formality began to break down, but not until Eliot had slipped his written proposal into the letters his secretary was typing for him, and she had accepted, did he suddenly say, "Do you know my Christian name?" Even so, the couple kept their engagement secret at the office, where Valerie wore a finger stall over her engagement ring.

T. S. Eliot and Valerie Fletcher were married on 10 January 1957, ten years after Vivienne's death, at St. Barnabas's Church, Kensington, the church in which Jules Laforgue had married. The "curiously furtive" ceremony took place at 6 a.m. with only Valerie's parents and a friend present. She was thirty, he sixty-eight. Eliot had married a woman young enough to be his daughter; he had at last found the laughing, loving child which featured so often in his poetry. It was a father/daughter relationship which inspired the newfound tenderness between Lord Claverton and Monica in *The Elder Statesman* (which Eliot began shortly before his second marriage), a play based on Sophocles' *Oedipus at Colonus.* The drama, as Kenneth Tynan acutely observed, tells "the old story of the great man whose past catches up with him, the hero who has Lived a Lie."[33]

Eliot abandoned Hayward with the same abruptness and moral cowardice with which he left Vivienne; Hayward had no foreknowledge of the wedding. According to one version, he was simply left a letter of explanation by Eliot on the morning when he slipped out to be married, as secretly as he had gone to his baptism thirty years earlier. Geoffrey Faber and Mary Trevelyan, to whom Eliot gave a false address in France, received similar letters on the same day.[34] However, Hayward told another version: that Eliot came into his room very early on 10 January and handed him the letter, asking him to read it at once. Hayward did so. He assured Eliot he was not angry. "Then Eliot leaned forward, put his arm around him, and kissed him, saying, 'Oh, I knew I could always rely on you.' Hayward said later, with a resigned grin, 'Since I am the most un-homosexual man in London, I found this a most offensive gesture.' "[35] Thenceforth Hayward referred to himself as "the widow," a different species of spider.

Mary thought Tom had gone out of his mind, having being thrown off the scent by his remarks to her that Miss Fletcher was "such a tiresome girl, she will keep on working late. I do wish she wasn't so devoted." Attributing Tom's second marriage to his hypochondria and panic over death, and to his increasing inability to accept criticism or contradiction, Mary felt that he needed someone who "would always tell him he was right and everyone else was wrong." The two letters of good wishes she sent Tom prompted "a very angry reply" from the poet, accusing her of "gross impertinence." She had no further contact with him. Soon she found herself struck off the Eliots' Christmas card list, and sorrowfully concluded that Tom was no longer the person she had known: "But have I known the real person? Have John and I known and loved the real man?" Now there was "no to-morrow—but I have had my years and I wouldn't have missed them." Tom had left, wrote Mary, "so great a sadness in the hearts of his old friends"; nevertheless, she continued to say a nightly prayer for him, in words of his own, in which he asked God for protection from "the Voices [and] the Visions."[36] Emily Hale, on hearing Eliot's news, had a breakdown and was admitted to Massachusetts General Hospital in Boston. She never recovered completely.

Eliot's second marriage brought him the happiness that the first had denied him. No longer was he jostled by ghosts. But in old age, during the seven years of his second marriage, he wrote neither poetry nor plays of distinction, in contrast to the outpouring from the "sacred wood" which had marked his seventeen years with Vivienne. He died at the age of seventy-six, on 4 January 1965, comforted by the impregnability of his reputation; Vivienne, meanwhile, lay forgotten in the Pinner cemetery.

Acknowledgments

The suggestion to write about Vivienne Eliot came from novelist Pauline Neville, to whom I am grateful for the germ of an idea, which grew, with the encouragement of Peter Day, then Editorial Director of Allison & Busby, into a book proposal. When, sadly, Peter's ill-health prevented him taking the book on, I was extraordinarily fortunate to find in Carol O'Brien, Editorial Director of Constable & Robinson, someone who believed in this book almost as passionately as I did. For sharing my vision, and contributing her own determination, unwavering encouragement, negotiating and editorial skills over the last four years, particularly in our struggle to quote from Vivienne Eliot's Bodleian Papers, I owe her a particular debt of gratitude. I am also indebted to Nick Robinson, Managing Director of Constable & Robinson, for his conviction that the book merited a legal defence by Queen's Counsel. Nick's support has played an essential part in making this book a reality. I am very grateful to Kim Witherspoon, my agent in New York, and Nan Talese, Editorial Director of Doubleday, for their guidance, and for Nan's perceptive editorial advice.

I wish to thank John Stallworthy for his critical reading of several chapters, in particular those concerning *The Waste Land,* and for his support; Andrew Motion for his generous assistance, and Matthew Evans and John Bodley of Faber & Faber for a close reading of the typescript, and their subsequent decision, on behalf of Mrs. Valerie Eliot, to give permission for quotations from Vivienne Eliot's Papers.

Valuable encouragement in the early stages of my research came from Michael Hastings. I am immensely grateful to him for making available to me his notes of a series of interviews with Maurice Haigh-Wood, other research notes, correspondence, Haigh-Wood family photographs, and for introductions to Vivienne's descendants.

I am greatly indebted to Humphrey Carpenter and Kate Trevelyan, literary executors for Mary Trevelyan, for permission to read and quote from Mary's important unpublished memoir of T. S. Eliot, which spans twenty years; to Adrian and Philip Goodman for making available extracts from the unpublished journals of Lady Ottoline Morrell; to Pamela Matthews, widow of T. S. Matthews, for giving me unrestricted access to her late husband's archive; and to Paul Delany for permission to quote from his unpublished research on the Eliots' finances.

I am most grateful to the Harry Ransom Humanities Research Center at the University of Texas at Austin for their award of the Paul Mellon Visiting Fellowship 1999–2000. This enabled me to return for a second visit to the Center in autumn 1999 to work on important sources for Vivienne's life: the Richard Aldington Papers, Mary Hutchinson Papers, Ottoline Morrell Papers, Léonide Massine Papers, Sitwell Papers and others. Although there is no collection bearing Vivienne Eliot's name at Texas, her intimate correspondence with more famous figures provided a rich source of information. The knowledge and efficiency of so many members of staff speeded my task, and I wish to thank all those who helped me, especially Thomas F. Staley,

Director, and Cathy Henderson for her advice on copyright issues. The enthusiasm of academics, archivists and librarians for my quest and their belief in freedom of information heartened me on many occasions. I also wish to thank Pat Fox for shared outings; Brian Bremen, for making available correspondence from the Edmund Wilson Papers; Margaret Ratliff, for permission to quote from her thesis on the Correspondence of Mary Hutchinson; Brian Parker, for discussions on T. S. Eliot and Members of the British Studies Group, including Charlotte Rhodes, whose hospitality I appreciated over Thanksgiving.

At the Bertrand Russell Archive, Mills Memorial Library, McMaster University, Hamilton, Ontario, I was greatly helped by Carl Spadoni, Director, whose extensive knowledge of the Russell Papers aided my research immeasurably. I am most grateful to Carl, to Kenneth Blackwell, Editor of the journal *Russell,* and to Nicholas Griffin, Editor of Russell's letters, for their interest and encouragement, and to all the staff; I am indebted to the university for its generous decision to waive permissions fees. I also wish to thank Phyllis Urch, literary executor of Lady Constance Malleson (Colette O'Niel), for permission to quote from the unpublished letters between Malleson and Russell, and from Mrs. Urch's unpublished typescript.

I would like to thank the following librarians, archivists and institutions for their help: Mary Clapinson at the Bodleian Library (Vivienne Eliot Papers); Richard Burns, Curator, at Bury Art Gallery; Alan Bell at the London Library; Elizabeth Inglis, former Head of Special Collections at Sussex University Library (Monk's House and Charleston Collections); Ros Moad at King's College Library, Cambridge (John Davy Hayward Bequest); the Librarians at the British Library Manuscript Dept. (Schiff Papers), and at the New British Library; the Librarian at the Wellcome Library; the Librarian at the New York Public Library (The Henry W. and Albert A. Berg Collection); William Stoneman and Elizabeth Falsey at the Houghton Library, Harvard University; the Librarian at the Beinecke Rare Book and Manuscript Library, Yale University (Scofield Thayer/*Dial* Papers, Ezra Pound Papers, W. F. Stead Papers, Osborn Collection, and John Quinn Papers); the Librarian at the Lilly Library, Indiana University (Eliot letters to Ezra and Dorothy Pound); and the Librarian at Princeton University Library (the Paul Elmer Moore Papers).

I am indebted to many wise and generous people over the last four years for interviews, answers to my queries, advice, inspiration and hospitality: Sybille Bedford, Moris Farhi, Lyndall Gordon, Rosalind Ingrams at Garsington, Francis King and Frances Partridge; Peter Ackroyd, Rachel Billington, Ray Bown, David Bradshaw, Anthony and Sarah Cassidy, Cherry and Robert Clarke, Ania Corless, Ken Craven, David Davidson, Dawn and Philip Firth, Jonathan Fryer, John Gielgud, Victoria Glendinning, Pat Grayburn, Lord Hutchinson, Christopher Hutchings, Dr. Frank Keane, Hermione Lee, Mark Le Fanu, Jane Mays, Blake Morrison, Jenny MacKilligan, Lucy Popescu, Diana Pullein-Thompson and Dennis Farr, Elizabeth Parker, Peter Parker, Jocelyn and Christopher Rowe, Bill Saunders, Ann and Richard Salter, Reresby Sitwell, Miranda Seymour, Michael Silverleaf, QC, Christopher Sinclair-Stevenson, Sue and Christopher Singer, Ann R. Jones and Peter Stallybrass, Bill Stallybrass, Gunnvor Stallybrass, Kate Tait (daughter of Bertrand Russell), Dr. Tom Stuttaford, Dr. Graham Tyrell, and Moira Williams.

I would like to thank Jane Robertson for her patience and industry in copy-editing the typescript; Lorna Owen for extra editorial work; Gary Chapman, Andrew Hayward and all the Constable team for their commitment to this book; my father, Tony Seymour-Jones, FRCS, for assistance with medical research; my children, Emma and son-in-law Andrew, Edward and Lucy, for their ever-present support; and especially my partner, Geoffrey Parkinson, for reading and discussing the manuscript over many hours, for his illuminating suggestions, for his understanding during my absences abroad, and for his sense of humour.

I am grateful to the following for permission to quote material in copyright: the executors of the Virginia Woolf Estate and The Random House Group *(The Diaries and Letters of Virginia Woolf* published by The Hogarth Press); Faber & Faber on behalf of Mrs. Valerie Eliot (for unpublished and published letters and texts by T. S. Eliot, Vivienne Eliot and Ezra Pound); Adrian and Philip Goodman (Lady Ottoline Morrell); Bruce Hunter (Osbert Sitwell). For illustrative material I wish to thank: the Bury Art Gallery; Jane and Anne Haigh-Wood; the Houghton Library, Harvard University; the Beinecke Library, Yale; McMaster University, Hamilton, Ontario; Mrs. Phyllis Urch; the Tate Gallery; King's College, Cambridge; A. C. Cooper; the Harry Ransom Humanities Research Center; University of Texas at Austin; Musée de l'Opéra; Bibliothèque Nationale and Kate Trevelyan.

Notes

Abbreviations Used in the Notes

Beinecke	Beinecke Rare Book and Manuscript Library, Yale: Ezra Pound Papers, Scofield Thayer/*Dial* Collection, W. F. Stead Papers
Berg	Berg Collection, Manuscript Division of New York Public Library
Bodleian	Bodleian Library, Oxford
BR	Bertrand Russell
C. C. Eliot	Charlotte Champe Eliot (TSE's mother)
CM	Colette O'Niel, stage name of Lady Constance Malleson
CP	T. S. Eliot, *Collected Poems 1909–1962* (London: Faber & Faber, 1974)
EP	Ezra Pound
Houghton	Houghton Library, Harvard: Eliot Collection
IMH	Christopher Ricks (ed.), *Inventions of the March Hare, T. S. Eliot: Poems 1909–1917* (New York: Harcourt Brace Jovanovich, 1996)
JH	John Hayward
JHB	John Hayward Bequest, King's College, Cambridge
JQ	John Quinn
Letters I	Valerie Eliot (ed.), *The Letters of T. S. Eliot, Volume 1, 1898–1922* (New York: Harcourt Brace Jovanovich, 1988)
Lilly	Lilly Library, Indiana: Ezra Pound Papers, including correspondence of T. S. Eliot to Dorothy Pound
McMaster	Bertrand Russell Archives, McMaster University, Hamilton, Ontario
MH	Mary Hutchinson, wife of St. John (Jack) Hutchinson
OM	Lady Ottoline Morrell
RA	Richard Aldington
Schiff	British Library: Schiff Papers
Sussex	The Manuscript Section of the University of Sussex Library: Leonard and Virginia Woolf Collection
ST	Scofield Thayer
Texas	Harry Ransom Humanities Research Center, University of Texas at Austin, Texas: Mary Hutchinson Collection and Ottoline Morrell Collection
TSE	Thomas Stearns Eliot
VE	Vivien(ne) Eliot. Maiden name on birth certificate, Vivienne Haigh-Wood. By 1915 Vivienne spelt her name "Vivien," and continued to do so for the greater part of her marriage. In Chapter 1 she is "Vivienne," and returns to this spelling in Chapter 19, in 1928.

VW   Virginia Woolf
WL Facs   Valerie Eliot (ed.), T. S. Eliot, *The Waste Land: A Facsimile and Transcript of the Original Drafts including the Annotations of Ezra Pound* (New York: Harcourt Brace Jovanovich, 1971)

Preface

1. Herbert Read, "T.S.E.—A Memoir," in Allen Tate (ed.), *T. S. Eliot, the Man and His Work* (London: Chatto & Windus, 1967).
2. Anne Oliver Bell (ed.), *The Diary of Virginia Woolf,* vol. 4, 1931–35 (London: Penguin, 1983), p. 123, 2 September 1932.
3. Bell (ed.), *Diary of Virginia Woolf,* op. cit., vol. 3, p. 331, 3 November 1930.
4. Donald E. Stanford, "The First Mrs. Eliot," *Library Chronicle of the University of Texas at Austin,* new series, p. 40.
5. T. S. Matthews, *Great Tom: Notes Towards the Definition of T. S. Eliot* (London: Weidenfeld & Nicolson, 1974), p. 40.
6. Peter Ackroyd, *T. S. Eliot* (London: Penguin, 1993), p. 63.
7. Mary Clapinson, Keeper of Special Collections and Western Manuscripts, Bodleian Library, to the author, 24 March 2000.
8. TSE to John Hayward, February 1938, John Hayward Bequest, King's College, Cambridge.
9. Valerie Eliot (ed.), *The Waste Land: A Facsimile and Transcript of the Original Drafts including the Annotations of Ezra Pound* (New York: Harcourt Brace Jovanovich, 1971).
10. Will of Vivienne Haigh Eliot, 1 March 1936.
11. VE to Ottoline Morrell, 31 December 1933, Texas.

1. A Bohemian from Bury

1. T. S. Eliot to Eleanor Hinkley, 27 November 1914, Valerie Eliot (ed.), *The Letters of T. S. Eliot, Vol. 1, 1898–1922* (New York: Harcourt Brace Jovanovich, 1988), p. 70.
2. T. S. Eliot to J. H. Woods, 5 October 1914, *Letters I,* p. 60.
3. T. S. Eliot to Conrad Aiken, 31 December 1914, *Letters I,* 74.
4. Osbert Sitwell, unpublished memoir on T. S. Eliot and his marriage, 19 February 1950, Texas.
5. T. S. Matthews, *Great Tom: Notes Towards the Definition of T. S. Eliot,* (London: Weidenfeld & Nicolson, 1974) p. 41.
6. Vivienne Eliot Diary, 1 September 1934, Bodleian.
7. Richard Lewis, "Tom & Viv: The Bury Connection," *Bury Times,* 15 April 1994.
8. Vivienne Haigh-Wood's birth certificate gives the residence of the father, C. Haigh-Wood, as Knowsley Street.
9. Vivien Eliot to Henry Eliot, 11 October 1916, MS Houghton, *Letters I,* p. 154.
10. The 1841 Census records Charles Wood, carver and gilder, living in Union Square. By 1851 he had moved to 22 Fleet St. (now the Rock) and had five children aged between nine and one living with him, including Charles.

11. There is a discrepancy in the difference between the ages of Charles and Mary on the different censuses, but it appears to have been between seven (1881) and ten years (1871).

12. Census, April 1861, shows eight people living at 22 Fleet Street: Charles and Mary Wood and their five children, and Kate Lee servant.

13. The Census of April 1871 shows Charles Wood, aged sixty, Master Carver and Gilder, still living at 22 Fleet Street, Bury.

14. Michael Karwowski, "The Bride from Bury," *Lancashire Life,* March 1984.

15. Charles Haigh-Wood Collection, Bury Art Gallery and Museum, Lancashire. I am indebted to the present Curator, Richard Burns, for showing me the collection now in store.

16. Ibid.

17. Information from Electoral Rolls and Directories gathered by Penney Farrell, Assistant Reference and Information Services Librarian, Bury Central Library.

18. Maurice Haigh-Wood, interview with Michael Hastings, 12 March 1980.

19. "Mr. C. H. Wood and His Work," *Bury Times,* July 1899.

20. Charles Haigh-Wood Collection, Bury Art Gallery and Museum.

21. Quoted by C. Billingham, Senior Curator, Bury Art Gallery and Museum, in his letter to Norman Wood, 4 May 1990.

22. VE Diary, 23 July 1935, Bodleian.

23. Catalogue no. 37, Charles Haigh-Wood, 1910 Bury Art Gallery exhibition details, from a transcription by the artist's great-granddaughter, Anne Haigh-Wood, with additional notes by Ken Craven.

24. Charles Haigh-Wood Collection, Bury Art Gallery and Museum. This painting is still reproduced as a greetings card with the caption, "I'll Be Sorry . . . If You'll Be Sorry," and is entitled *Boy with Apple and Girl.*

25. Osbert Sitwell, unpublished memoir on T. S. Eliot and his marriage, op. cit.

26. Brigit Patmore, *My Friends when Young* (London: Heinemann, 1968), p. 85.

27. "The Night Club," a short story, May 1924, Vivien Eliot Papers, Bodleian.

28. Notes for a short story, May 1924, Vivien Eliot Papers, Bodleian.

29. Conversations with Dr. Thomas Stuttaford, October 1998, and Dr. Graham Tyrell, November 1998.

30. Maurice Haigh-Wood, interview with Michael Hastings, 21 January 1980.

31. "Rosa Buckle" sketch, ?1924, MSS Eng. Misc. c. 624, loose-leaf paste-up book, Vivien Eliot Papers, Bodleian.

32. Anthony Clare, *Psychiatry in Dissent: Controversial Issues in Thought and Practice* (London: Routledge, 1989), pp. 186, 187.

33. Adam Phillips, *Winnicott* (London: Fontana, 1988), p. 48.

34. VE Diary, 24 August 1935, Bodleian.

35. Patmore, op. cit., pp. 84, 85.

36. Stephen Trombley, *All That Summer She Was Mad* (London: Junction Books, 1981), p. 115.

37. Henry Maudsley, "Moral Insanity versus Will," in Vieda Skultans, *Madness and Morals: Ideas on Insanity in the Nineteenth Century* (London: Routledge and Kegan Paul, 1975), p. 194.

38. VE Diary, 18 March 1935, Bodleian.

2. The River Girl

1. Loose-leaf book, MSS Eng. Misc. c. 624, Vivien Eliot Papers, Bodleian.
2. Stephen Spender, *T. S. Eliot* (London: Fontana, 1975), p. 49.
3. Osbert Sitwell, "T. S. Eliot," an unpublished memoir, Sitwell Papers, Harry Ransom Humanities Research Center, University of Texas at Austin.
4. Loose-leaf book, Vivien Eliot Papers, Bodleian.
5. Statement by Theresa Eliot, Houghton Library.
6. VE Diary, 12 February 1914, Bodleian.
7. Maurice Haigh-Wood, interview with Michael Hastings, 21 January 1980.
8. Nicholas Joost, *Scofield Thayer and* The Dial, *An Illustrated History* (Southern Illinois University Press, 1964), p. 8. In 1918 Thayer bought *The Dial,* a Chicago review founded by Francis F. Browne in 1880.
9. President's Secretary, Magdalen College, Oxford, to T. S. Matthews, 26 September 1972, citing entry on Scofield Thayer from J. Brett Langstaff, *Oxford 1914* (New York: Vantage Press, 1965).
10. VE Diary, 23 February 1914, Bodleian.
11. VE Diary, 26 February 1914, Bodleian.
12. Maurice Haigh-Wood, interview with Michael Hastings, 28 January 1980.
13. "Rosa Buckle" sketch, loose-leaf book, Vivien Eliot Papers, Bodleian.
14. Maurice Haigh-Wood, interview with Michael Hastings, 4 March 1980.
15. VE Diary, 3 March 1914, Bodleian.
16. VE Diary, 5 March 1914, Bodleian.
17. VE Diary, 8 March 1914, Bodleian.
18. VE Diary, 11 March 1914, Bodleian.
19. VE Diary, 12 March 1914, Bodleian.
20. VE Diary, 14 March 1914, Bodleian.
21. Maurice Haigh-Wood, interview with Michael Hastings, 28 January 1980.
22. VE Diary, 16 March 1914, Bodleian.
23. VE Diary, 17 March 1914, Bodleian.
24. VE Diary, 19 March 1914, Bodleian.
25. VE Diary, 20 March 1914, Bodleian.
26. VE Diary, 22 March 1914, Bodleian.
27. VE Diary, 25 March 1914, Bodleian.
28. VE Diary, 29 March 1914, Bodleian.
29. VE Diary, 2 April 1914, Bodleian.
30. VE Diary, 12 April 1914, Bodleian.
31. VE Diary, 16 April 1914, Bodleian.
32. VE Diary, 17 April 1914, Bodleian.
33. VE Diary, 21–25 April 1914, Bodleian.
34. VE Diary, 30 April 1914, Bodleian.
35. VE Diary, 6 August 1914, Bodleian.
36. VE Diary, 22 August 1914, Bodleian.
37. VE Diary, 24 August 1914, Bodleian.
38. Horace, *Odes,* III.ii.13.

39. VE Diary, 28 August 1914, Bodleian.
40. VE to Scofield Thayer, 22 February 1915, Beinecke.
41. VE to Scofield Thayer, 3 March 1915, Beinecke.
42. Ibid.

3. An Alien in America

1. Henry Ware Eliot Sr. to Thomas Lamb Eliot, 26 September 1888, Houghton.
2. Charlotte Champe Eliot to Richard Cobb, end September 1905, *Letters, I*, p. 11.
3. Eleanor Hinkley, quoted in "The Mysterious Mr. Eliot," BBC1 TV Programme, 3 January 1971.
4. Mary Trevelyan, "The Pope of Russell Square," unpublished memoir of T. S. Eliot, 1957.
5. T. S. Eliot, *To Criticize the Critic and Other Writings* (London: Faber & Faber, 1963), pp. 43–60.
6. Family genealogies, Houghton. Charlotte Blood (1818–93) was descended from General Thomas Blood. She married Thomas Stearns (1811–96). Her daughter Charlotte was born in Baltimore, Maryland, on 22 October 1843.
7. TSE to Ezra Pound, 10 December 1933, Beinecke.
8. Prufrock-Littau, furniture wholesalers, advertised in St. Louis in the early twentieth century. Hugh Kenner, *The Invisible Poet: T. S. Eliot* (London: Methuen, 1960), p. 3.
9. Charlotte C. Eliot to R. Cobb, 4 April 1905, *Letters, I,* p. 7.
10. T. S. Eliot, Preface to Edgar Ansel Mower, *This American World* (London: Faber & Gwyer, 1928), quoted in Helen Gardner, *The Composition of the Four Quartets* (London: Faber & Faber, 1978), p. 48.
11. TSE to John Hayward, 27 December 1939, John Hayward Bequest, King's College, Cambridge.
12. T. S. Eliot, "The Dry Salvages," from *Four Quartets, Collected Poems 1900–1962* (London: Faber & Faber, 1963), p. 209.
13. Smith Academy Record, February 1905.
14. Quoted in Lyndall Gordon, *Eliot's Early Years* (Oxford: Oxford University Press, 1977), p. 4.
15. Henry Ware Eliot Sr., "Reflections of a Simpleton," unpublished memoir, 1911, Houghton.
16. Clara H. Scudder, The Wednesday Club, "Charlotte C. Eliot, In Memoriam," 1929. Charlotte died on 10 September 1929, and these notes were collected by Henry Ware Eliot Jr.
17. Herbert Howarth, *Notes on Some Figures Behind T. S. Eliot* (London: Chatto & Windus, 1965), p. 28.
18. Poems of Charlotte C. Eliot, and typescript of *Savonarola,* with corrections by T. S. Eliot, Houghton.
19. William Turner Levy and Victor Scherle, *Affectionately, T. S. Eliot: The Story of a Friendship* (London: J. M. Dent & Sons, 1968), pp. 53–54.
20. Henry Ware Eliot to Thomas Lamb Eliot, 7 March 1914, quoted in John Seldo, "The Tempering of T. S. Eliot, 1888–1915," unpublished Harvard dissertation, 1972.
21. T. S. Eliot, "East Coker," *Four Quartets, CP,* p. 197.
22. TSE Address to the Mary Institute, 1 November 1959, published as *From Mary to You* (St. Louis, 1959), p. 135.
23. TSE to John Hayward, 27 December 1939, John Hayward Bequest, King's College, Cambridge.

24. T. S. Eliot, *Selected Essays, 1917–1932* (London: Faber & Faber, 1932), p. 273.

25. Translation by A. David Moody, *Thomas Stearns Eliot, Poet* (Cambridge: Cambridge University Press, 1979), pp. 77–78.
    The original (*CP,* p. 101.) reads:
    J'avais sept ans, elle était plus petite,
    Elle était tout mouillée, je lui ai donné des primevères . . .
    "Je la chatouillais, pour la faire rire.
    J'éprouvais un instant de puissance et de délire."

26. Undated typescript, "Dans le Restaurant," Pound's corrections, Ezra Pound Papers, Beinecke, Yale.

27. TSE to John Hayward, 27 December 1939, John Hayward Bequest, King's College, Cambridge.

28. Lyndall Gordon, *Eliot's Early Years* (Oxford: Oxford University Press, 1977), p. 4.

29. T. S. Eliot, "Animula," 1929, *CP,* p. 113.

30. Alessandra Lemma-Wright, *Invitation to Psychodynamic Psychology* (London: Whurr Publishers Ltd., 1995), pp. 32, 149. See the case study of "Mark," and his "very strong, yet highly ambivalent attachment to his mother . . . Mark's difficulty in settling down with another woman, and his recurring problem with impotence, were understood as being in some way connected to his very close relationship with his mother and the rivalry she felt towards any woman Mark introduced her to. In order to appease his mother Mark reached the only compromise which he felt was open to him: he would see other women but he was frequently unable to fully consummate the relationship sexually . . . thereby never establishing any relationship that would seriously threaten his mother. In many respects he remained his mother's 'little boy.'"

31. Sigmund Freud, *Inhibitions, Symptoms and Anxiety* (London: Penguin Freud Library, vol. 10, 1979), pp. 230–38.

32. Randall Jarrell, unpublished notes for an article on T. S. Eliot, n.d., Berg Collection.

33. Address to the Mary Institute, Locust Street, St. Louis, Missouri, op. cit.

34. Quoted in Bernard Bergonzi, *T. S. Eliot* (London: Macmillan, 1972), p. 6.

35. T. S. Eliot, "The Love Song of J. Alfred Prufrock," *CP,* p. 14.

36. Helen Gardner, *The Composition of the Four Quartets* (London: Penguin, 1993).

37. TSE to William Force Stead, 30 June 1930, W. F. Stead Papers, Beinecke.

38. Herbert Read, "T.S.E.—A Memoir," in Allen Tate (ed.), *T. S. Eliot: The Man and His Work* (London: Chatto & Windus, 1967), p. 15.

39. Hugh Kenner, *The Invisible Poet: T. S. Eliot* (London: Methuen, 1960), p. 17.

40. T. S. Eliot, *Poems Written in Early Youth* (London: Faber & Faber, 1967), p. 26.

41. Quoted in Bernard Bergonzi, *T. S. Eliot* (London: Macmillan, 1972), p. 9.

42. Arthur Symons, *The Symbolist Movement in Literature* (London: William Heinemann, 1899), p. 113.

43. Robert Sencourt, *T. S. Eliot: A Memoir,* edited by Donald Adamson and L. P. Addison (London: Garnstone Press, 1971), pp. 33–34.

44. Charlotte C. Eliot to TSE, 3 April 1910, *Letters, I,* p. 13.

45. *CP,* p. 57.

46. T. S. Eliot, "Circe's Palace," *Poems Written in Early Youth,* p. 26. The poem was first published in the *Harvard Advocate,* lxxxvi, 5, 25 November 1908.

47. According to Melanie Klein, splitting is the first mechanism of defence of the infant ego. Identifying with the ideal object or Madonna figure keeps at bay the persecutors, whores

and prostitutes who represent the bad object. For a child such as Eliot, omnipotent denial would have been used against the fear of persecution, as he would have needed to maintain excessive idealisation of his mother in order to defend against paranoid feelings about her. His early paranoid fears of annihilation of the ego by his mother, identified not only as the good but also as the bad object—the withholding breast which failed to give him love—threatened to burst out. He was left with a "schizoid fear of loving," as Hanna Segal terms it, which led him to cut himself off from close relationships. See Hanna Segal, *Klein* (London: Harvester, Karnac, 1989), pp. 80, 114. English paediatrician Donald Winnicott developed Klein's view of the manic defence further to argue that the infant develops a "false self" in order to comply with the demands of the mother who is not "good enough." It is "the good, compliant child in the family who can become the bad child in adolescence—ending up as the mad child . . . However Laing shows how the phase of being good is often experienced as one of existential death or nothingness by the patient." See Emmy van Deurzen-Smith, *Everyday Mysteries: Existential Dimensions of Psychotherapy* (London: Routledge, 1997), pp. 165–66. The mask behind which Eliot appeared to many observers to hide may be interpreted as the "false self."

48. *CP*, p. 26.
49. George Whiteside, "T. S. Eliot: The Psychobiographical Approach," *Southern Review* (Adelaide) 6, no. 1 (March 1973), p. 23.
50. T. S. Eliot, "Circe's Palace," op. cit.
51. John T. Mayer, *T. S. Eliot's Silent Voices* (Oxford: OUP, 1989), p. 33.
52. Gordon, op. cit., p. 8.
53. Unpublished Bolo and Colombo verses, Ezra Pound Papers, Beinecke, and published, *Noctes Binanianae,* Houghton.
54. T. S. Eliot, "First Caprice in North Cambridge," "Second Caprice in North Cambridge" in Christopher Ricks (ed.), *Inventions of the March Hare, T. S. Eliot Poems 1909–1917* (New York: Harcourt Brace Jovanovich, 1996), pp. 13, 15.
55. T. S. Eliot, Preface to Charles-Louis Philippe, *Bubu de Montparnasse* (Paris, 1890).
56. Charles-Louis Philippe, *Bubu de Montparnasse* (Paris, 1890).
57. Ibid., Chapter vii.
58. T. S. Eliot, "Rhapsody on a Windy Night," Berg Collection, New York Public Library; published in *IMH,* p. 338.
59. T. S. Eliot, "Bacchus and Ariadne," "2nd Debate Between Body and Soul," Ricks (ed.), *IMH,* p. 68.
60. See the *Mandarin* series of poems, August 1910, written the summer before TSE left for Paris, Ricks (ed.), *IMH,* pp. 19–22.
61. Interview, 15 October 1998, Cambridge, Mass., with Mary Eliot, granddaughter of Edward Cranch Eliot, son of William Greenleaf Eliot and therefore cousin to T. S. Eliot, whom she met frequently at the home of Theresa Garrett Eliot (Mrs. Henry Ware Eliot Jr.) in Cambridge, and on occasions with Mrs. Valerie Eliot in London. Miss Eliot spoke of being teased for speaking like a Bostonian on return to St. Louis as an occasion for mirth rather than embarrassment. Eliot's concern over this was due, she believed, to his "extreme sensitivity."
62. T. S. Eliot, "Prufrock's Pervigilium," cancelled lines originally part of "The Love Song of J. Alfred Prufrock," Ricks (ed.), *IMH,* p. 43.
63. Donald Gallup, "The Lost Manuscripts of T. S. Eliot," reprinted from *Times Literary Supplement,* 7 Nov. 1968, Yale University Library.

64. T. S. Eliot, "While You Were Absent in the Lavatory," Ricks (ed.), *IMH,* p. 60 and pp. 6, 7. The text in manuscript at the Beinecke Library, Yale, has "around the corner" instead of "hopped beneath the table." The former is closer to the original White Rabbit "as it turned a corner."

65. Leaves excised from "The Inventions of the March Hare Notebook," Ezra Pound Papers, Beinecke. These poems are written in a much smaller, spikier hand than Eliot's letters; they are frequently corrected and many are in pencil. There is more than one version of many of the poems, but certain characters and themes constantly recur: Colombo and his black bodyguard of "Jersey Lilies," "Orlando" the cabin boy, Bolo and his big black Kween, and the Ship's Chaplain.

66. Rémy de Gourmont, *Physique de l'amour: essai sur l'instinct sexuel* (1904), ch. xv, quoted by Ricks (ed.), *IMH,* op. cit., p. 7.

67. Leaves excised from the Notebook, Ezra Pound Papers, Beinecke, and *IMH,* Appendix A, p. 314.

68. Leaves excised from the Notebook, Ezra Pound Papers, Beinecke. A number of Colombo poems featuring the Chaplain remain unpublished.

69. Leaves excised from the Notebook, Ezra Pound Papers, Beinecke. See also Ricks (ed.), *IMH,* pp. 315–19.

70. The earliest recorded instance of the use of the word "bullshit" is in a letter from Wyndham Lewis, before July 1915 ("Eliot has sent me Bullshit"), Ricks (ed.), *IMH,* p. 308.

71. Fragments, leaves excised from the Notebook, Pound Papers, Beinecke.

72. "The Triumph of Bullshit," Pound Papers, Beinecke, Ricks (ed.), *IMH,* p. 307.

73. Leaves excised from the Notebook, Pound Papers, Beinecke, and Ricks (ed.), *IMH,* p. 315.

74. Ricks (ed.), *IMH,* p. 314.

75. Ezra Pound to TSE, n.d., Pound Papers, Beinecke.

76. T. S. Eliot, "The Whale, the Elephant, the Coot and the Spider," *Noctes Binanianae,* Houghton Library, Harvard. Privately "printed without castration" in 1939. The Whale represented Frank Morley, The Elephant, T. S. Eliot, the Coot, Geoffrey Faber (directors of Faber & Faber) and the Spider, John Hayward. In this poem Eliot refers to himself as "pious Jekyll" (he was then a Churchwarden) who "purloins letter paper/That Hyde may cut a Rogue Elephant's caper."

77. Osbert Sitwell gives an account of a visit to "Captain Eliot" in "T. S. Eliot," an unpublished memoir on the marriage of Tom and Vivienne Eliot, in the Sitwell Papers, Harry Ransom Humanities Center, Austin, Texas. See also a postcard from TSE inviting Mary Hutchinson to visit him and ask for "Captain Eliot," Hutchinson Papers, Texas.

78. Quoted by Eliot in "What Dante Means to Me" in *To Criticize the Critic* (London: Faber & Faber, 1965).

79. Martin Turnell, *Baudelaire: A Study of His Poetry* (New York: New Directions, 1972), p. 101.

80. Ibid., pp. 41–58.

81. Moody, op. cit., p. 289.

82. *CP,* p. 36.

83. *IMH,* p. 57.

84. André Gide, *Préludes* (Paris, 1895) quoted by Jean Verdenal, Letter to TSE, 5 February 1912, Houghton, *Letters I,* p. 30.

85. Jean Verdenal to TSE, 22 April 1912, Houghton, *Letters I,* p. 32.

86. "As I remember, there are no copies of my husband's letters to him." Letter from Mrs.

Valerie Eliot to Prof. James E. Miller, of the University of Chicago, refusing him permission to see the letters of Jean Verdenal, 23 July 1974, Houghton.

87. Jean Verdenal to TSE, "Dimanche" (?mid-July 1911), Houghton, and *Letters I*, p. 20.

88. Houghton, and *Letters I*, p. 21n.

89. Alain-Fournier to TSE, 25 July 1911, Houghton, and *Letters I*, p. 25.

90. Jean Verdenal to TSE, 5 February 1912, Houghton, and *Letters I*, p. 28.

91. *CP*, p. 64.

92. Jean Verdenal was reading *Le Mystère de la Charité de Jeanne d'Arc* by Charles Péguy (Paris 1909), particularly liking the account of the Passion of Christ. Jean Verdenal to TSE, mid-July 1911, Houghton, and *Letters I*, p. 23.

93. Eliot's notes on the Bergson lectures, which he attended in January and February 1911, are in the Houghton Library.

94. Jean Verdenal to TSE, 5 February 1912, Houghton.

95. Jean Verdenal to TSE, 22 April 1912, Houghton.

96. Memorandum by Charlotte Champe Eliot in respect of a request by her son, Henry Ware Eliot Jr., who was preparing in 1921 a family record of the descendants of William Greenleaf and Abigail A. Eliot, Houghton.

97. Jean Verdenal to TSE, 26 August 1912, Houghton.

98. Jean Verdenal to TSE, 26 December 1912, Houghton.

99. *Criterion*, April 1934, quoted by John T. Mayer, *T. S. Eliot's Silent Voices* (Oxford: OUP, 1989), p. 200.

100. This Temple Classics translation (reprinted 1909) is the one which Eliot knew; his copy is in the Houghton Library. It is probable that TSE wrote out this epigraph in the Notebook when he sold it to John Quinn in 1922. The epigraph first appeared in *Ara Vos Prec* (1920) but with no dedication; the dedication and epigraph, with slightly different wording from that in the Notebook, first appeared together in *Poems 1909–1925* (1925). See *IMH*, pp. 3, 4.

101. Memorandum by Charlotte Champe Eliot prepared for her son, Henry Ware Eliot Jr., Houghton.

102. Conrad Aiken, *Ushant* (London: W. H. Allen, 1963), p. 168 and *passim*.

103. Conrad Aiken, "King Bolo and Others" in Richard March and Tambimuttu, *T. S. Eliot: A Symposium* (London: P.L. Editions, 1948), p. 21.

104. Anne Olivier Bell (ed.), *The Diary of Virginia Woolf*, vol. 2, 1920–1924 (New York: Harcourt Brace Jovanovich, 1981), p. 68.

105. Valerie Eliot, Introduction to *Letters I*, p. xvii.

106. "Do I know what I feel?" *IMH*, p. 80. This undated and untitled poem from the Notebook was probably written after Eliot's return to Harvard but before he went to England in 1914.

107. TSE to Conrad Aiken, 25 July 1914, Huntingdon Library, *Letters I*, p. 44.

108. "After the turning," "I am the Resurrection," "So through the evening," the two "Saint" poems, and "the Burnt Dancer," all written in 1914, see Gordon, *Eliot's Early Years* (Oxford: OUP, 1977), p. 58. For a chronology of the poems 1905–1920 see *IMH*, pp. xxxvii–xlii.

109. Diary of Virginia Woolf, September 1920, Berg Collection.

110. T. S. Eliot broadcast talk to Germany, "The Unity of European Culture," 1948, quoted in Gardner, op. cit., p. 55; T. S. Eliot dissertation, *Knowledge and Experience in the Philosophy of F. H. Bradley*, p. 55, quoted by Gordon, *Eliot's Early Years*, op. cit., p. 53.

111. TSE to Conrad Aiken, 19 July 1914, Huntingdon Library, *Letters I*, p. 41.

112. TSE to Conrad Aiken, 25 July 1914, Huntingdon Library, *Letters I*, p. 44.

113. Henri Dorra, *Symbolist Art Theories: A Critical Anthology I* (California, Berkeley: University of California Press, 1994), p. 7.

114. Ibid., p. 27.

115. Ibid., p. 46. See also Joris-Karl Huysmans, *Certains* (Paris, 1889), on Gustave Moreau.

116. Mayer, op. cit., p. 132.

117. Donald Gallup, "The Lost Manuscripts of T. S. Eliot," *Times Literary Supplement*, 7 November 1968.

118. Valerie Eliot (ed.), second draft, "The Death of St. Narcissus," *The Waste Land: A Facsimile and Transcript of the Original Drafts including the Anotations of Ezra Pound* (New York: Harcourt Brace & Co., 1971), p. 97.

119. First draft, "The Death of St. Narcissus," ibid., p. 93.

120. Dante Alighieri, *The Divine Comedy, Inferno,* translated by Allen Mandelbaum (New York: Bantam, 1982), p. 133.

121. *Bhagavad-Gita,* chapter 11.

4. A Clandestine Marriage

1. VE Diary, 13 December 1934, Bodleian.

2. Osbert Sitwell, *Laughter in the Next Room, vol. 4, Left Hand, Right Hand!* (London: Macmillan, 1949), p. 43.

3. TSE to Charlotte Champe Eliot, 23 August 1914, *Letters I*, p. 52.

4. Conrad Aiken, *Ushant* (London: W. H. Allen, 1963), pp. 200–201.

5. TSE to Henry Eliot, 8 September 1914, *Letters I*, p. 56.

6. TSE to Eleanor Hinkley, 8 September 1914, *Letters I*, p. 57. Eleanor Hinkley was the second daughter of Susan Heywood Stearns, his mother's sister, who married Holmes Hinkley.

7. "Morning at the Window" (1914), *CP*, p. 29.

8. T. S. Eliot's speech replying to the toast of "The Guests," Christ Church, Oxford, 23 June 1948.

9. T. S. Eliot to Conrad Aiken, 25 February 1915, *Letters I*, p. 88. Eliot's thesis was published under the title *Knowledge and Experience in the Philosophy of F. H. Bradley* (1963).

10. Bertrand Russell, *Autobiography, Vol. 1, 1872–1914* (London: George Allen & Unwin, 1967), p. 212.

11. Robert Gathorne-Hardy (ed.), *Ottoline: The Early Memoirs of Lady Ottoline Morrell* (London: Faber & Faber, 1964), p. 257.

12. Frances Partridge interview with author, 27 November 2000. Frances Marshall became part of the Bloomsbury group in 1921 after leaving Cambridge, and later married Ralph Partridge.

13. "Mr. Apollinax," published in *Poetry* (Sept. 1916), and in *Prufrock and Other Observations* (1917). Christopher Ricks (ed.), discusses changes in the text in *Inventions of the March Hare, Poems 1909–1917* (New York, Harcourt Brace Jovanovich, 1996), p. 345; *CP*, p. 33.

14. TSE to Eleanor Hinkley, 10 October 1914, *Letters I*, p. 64.

15. Aiken, op. cit., p. 205. A joke based on Browning's monologue of the same title, which had

occurred to Pound years earlier, see Humphrey Carpenter, *A Serious Character: The Life of Ezra Pound* (London: Faber & Faber, 1988), p. 257.

16. Carpenter, op. cit., p. 23.

17. Peter Ackroyd, *Ezra Pound and His World* (London: Thames & Hudson, 1981), p. 25.

18. Despite a verse repeated in literary circles: "Ezra Pound/And Augustus John/Bless the bed/That I lie on," Richard Aldington believed Pound to be sexually naïve, although he posed as a roué. Carpenter, op. cit., pp. 136, 241, also cites Pound's poem, "Mr. Styrax": "Mr. Hetacomb Styrax . . . has married at the age of 28,/He being at that age a virgin" from *Moeurs Contemporaines*.

19. Ackroyd, op. cit., p. 14.

20. Quoted in Carpenter, op. cit., p. 100.

21. Richard Aldington, *Life for Life's Sake* (London: Viking, 1941), p. 105.

22. Ford Madox Ford, *Return to Yesterday* (London: Victor Gollancz, 1931).

23. Carpenter, op. cit., p. 113.

24. Richard Aldington to Amy Lowell, 20 November 1917, in Norman T. Gates (ed.), *Richard Aldington: An Autobiography in Letters* (Philadelphia: University of Pennsylvania Press, 1992), p. 28. Hugh Kenner, *The Pound Era* (London: Faber & Faber, 1976), p. 277, reads Pound's comment as ironic. Charles Doyle, *Richard Aldington: A Biography* (London: Macmillan, 1989), points out that Aldington's *vers libre* was inspired by the chorus of Euripides' *Hippolytus*.

25. Hilda Doolittle, *End to Torment* (New York: New Directions Publishing, 1979), p. 18.

26. Aldington, op. cit., p. 135.

27. Aldington, op. cit., p. 127.

28. Carpenter, op. cit., p. 209.

29. Ezra Pound to Amy Lowell, 19 October 1914, in D. D. Paige (ed.), *The Letters of Ezra Pound 1907–1941* (London: Faber & Faber, 1951), pp. 84–85.

30. P. Wyndham Lewis, *Blasting and Bombardiering* (London: Calder & Boyars, 1967), p. 280.

31. Ibid., pp. 254, 255.

32. EP to Harriet Monroe, 30 September 1914, *Letters of Ezra Pound*, op. cit., p. 80.

33. EP to Harriet Monroe, 9 November 1914, *Letters of Ezra Pound*, op. cit., p. 85. He also sent "Portrait of a Lady" to *Smart Set*, another American periodical.

34. EP to Harriet Monroe, 31 January 1915, *Letters of Ezra Pound*, op. cit., p. 92.

35. EP to Harriet Monroe, 10 April 1915, ibid., p. 101.

36. EP to Harriet Monroe, (August) 1915, ibid., p. 107.

37. TSE to Conrad Aiken, 30 September 1914, ibid., p. 59.

38. Doyle, op. cit., p. 18.

39. Wyndham Lewis, *Blasting*, op. cit., pp. 283–85.

40. Richard Aldington married Hilda Doolittle (known as "H.D.") in October 1913, with Pound and the Doolittle parents as witnesses. The same month Dora Marsden offered Aldington the job of sub-editor of *The New Freewoman*, following the resignation of Rebecca West. Doyle (in op. cit., p. 24) rejects the idea that the Aldington/Doolittle marriage was simply one of convenience after Pound rejected Hilda Doolittle. Doolittle's novel, *Bid Me Live*, suggests she reciprocated Aldington's love while retaining a strong emotional bond with Pound.

41. TSE to Conrad Aiken, 31 December 1914, *Letters I*, p. 73.

42. TSE to Conrad Aiken, 21 November 1914, *Letters I*, p. 69.

43. TSE to Conrad Aiken, 30 September 1914, *Letters I*, p. 59.

44. Wyndham Lewis to EP, ?January 1915, *The Letters of Wyndham Lewis*, op. cit., p. 67. None of the Bolo/Colombo verses were published in *Blast*.

45. Wyndham Lewis, *Blasting*, op. cit., p. 284.

46. TSE to E. Hinkley, 21 March 1915, *Letters I*, pp. 91, 92.

47. TSE to E. Hinkley, 24 April 1915, *Letters I*, p. 97.

48. Vivien(ne) Haigh-Wood to Scofield Thayer, 22 February 1915, Scofield Thayer/*Dial* Papers, Beinecke.

49. V. Haigh-Wood to Scofield Thayer, "Thursday," ?March 1915, from Thyme Cottage, Upper Bourne End, Bucks. This letter follows a previous letter dated 3 March 1915, Beinecke.

50. V. Haigh-Wood to Scofield Thayer, 22 Feb. 1915, Beinecke.

51. Signed statement by Theresa Eliot, Vivien's sister-in-law, 28 March 1970.

52. V. Haigh-Wood to Scofield Thayer, 3 March 1915, Beinecke.

53. The Army Lists show that a Charles Buckle was commissioned 2nd Lieutenant on 19 Sept. 1914 in the Royal Garrison Artillery, Territorial Force, based in Kent. A "galloper" would have ridden one of the horses pulling the guns. Maurice Haigh-Wood thought that Buckle was killed during the war, but the lieutenant listed above did survive. According to the Commonwealth War Graves Commission records, none of the three officers killed in the First World War named C. Buckle had a London connection, and none of the soldiers killed seemed a likely candidate.

54. T. S. Eliot, *Poems Written in Early Youth* (London: Faber & Faber, 1950), p. 33. *Harvard Advocate,* lxxxix, 8, 24 June 1910.

55. V. Haigh-Wood to Scofield Thayer, 3 March 1915, Beinecke.

56. V. Haigh-Wood to Scofield Thayer, 2 August 1915, Beinecke.

57. M. Haigh-Wood, interview with Michael Hastings, 21 January 1980. Pound also surmised that Vivien was going out with Scofield: see letter to John Quinn, 24 March 1920, in Lyndall Gordon, *Eliot's Early Years* (Oxford: OUP, 1972), p. 72n.

58. Bertrand Russell, *Autobiography, vol. 2* (London: George Allen & Unwin, 1968), p. 54.

59. Journal of Lady Ottoline Morrell, August 1921, Goodman Papers.

60. Michael King (ed.), *Ezra Pound, Collected Poems* (London: Faber & Faber, 1977), p. 186.

61. Charles Norman, *Ezra Pound, I* (London: MacDonald, 1969), p. 81.

62. V. Haigh-Wood to Scofield Thayer, 3 March 1915, Beinecke.

63. Aldous Huxley to Ottoline Morrell, 21 June 1917, Robert Gathorne-Hardy (ed.), *Ottoline at Garsington: Memoirs of Lady Ottoline Morrell 1915–1918* (London: Faber & Faber, 1974).

64. VE Diary, 26 December 1935, Bodleian.

65. Gaudier-Brzeska's last testament from the trenches. He was killed on 5 June 1915.

66. Valerie Eliot (ed.), Introduction, *The Waste Land: A Facsimile and Transcript of the Original Drafts including the annotations of Ezra Pound* (New York: Harcourt Brace Jovanovich, 1971), p. ix.

67. Valerie Eliot (ed.), Introduction, *Letters I*, p. xviii.

68. Ibid., p. 20, note 1.

69. Robert Sencourt, *T. S. Eliot: A Memoir,* edited by Donald Adamson and L. P. Addison (Garnstone Press, 1971), pp. 47, 48.

70. Karl Culpin was born on 10 September 1893. He died of wounds received in action near Fresnais, 15 May 1917.

71. Sencourt, op. cit., p. 53.

72. T. S. Matthews, *Great Tom: Notes Towards the Definitions of T. S. Eliot* (London: Weidenfeld & Nicolson, 1974), pp. 43–44.

73. TSE to Scofield Thayer, 7 May 1916, *Letters I*, p. 137.

74. Stephen Spender, *World Within World: The Autobiography of Stephen Spender* (New York: St. Martin's Press, 1951), p. 185.

5. The Poet's Bride

1. *Blast*, no. 2, July 1915.

2. Robert Sencourt, *T. S. Eliot: A Memoir*, edited by Donald Adamson and L. P. Addison (London: Garnstone Press, 1971), p. 50.

3. Michael Hastings, "The Haigh-Woods: The Story of a Family," introduction to the programme of *Tom and Viv*, first performance 3 February 1984 at the Royal Court Theatre, London. The introduction is based on Hastings's series of interviews with Maurice over five months in 1980, which came to an end with Maurice's death that year.

4. Codicil to the will of Charles Haigh-Wood, 18 May 1927.

5. Maurice Haigh-Wood, interview with Michael Hastings, 21 January 1980.

6. Rose Haigh-Wood to VE, "Friday," n.d. ?June 1916. Quoted in "The Haigh-Woods: The Story of a Family," programme of *Tom and Viv* by Michael Hastings.

7. Army List 1915–21, information supplied by the National Army Museum, 18 January 1999.

8. TSE to Charlotte C. Eliot, 18 May 1915, *Letters I*, p. 120.

9. Interview with Michael Hastings, 19 March 1980.

10. Pound was proposing that a writer could live in London on $1,000 a year (£200), of which Eliot's father was being asked to provide half. This seemed a reasonable request, since Henry Ware was apparently wealthy. Probate of his will suggests that he owned about 4,000 preferred shares, of 52,000 outstanding, in the Hydraulic Press-Brick Co. of St. Louis. The dividend, stopped in 1913, was resumed in 1918. Paul Delany, "T. S. Eliot's Personal Finances, 1915–1929," chapter in *Literature, Money and the Market from Trollope to Amis* (Basingstoke: Palgrave, 2001). Eliot's first job as a schoolmaster at High Wycombe paid less than £3 a week. At the other extreme, Lytton Strachey was able to earn between £2,000 and £3,000 per annum after the publication of *Eminent Victorians* in 1918, see Michael Holroyd, *Lytton Strachey* (London: Vintage, 1995), p. 430.

11. Ezra Pound to Henry Ware Eliot, postmark 28 June 1915, *Letters I*, p. 99.

12. Bertrand Russell to Charlotte C. Eliot, 3 October 1915, *Letters I*, p. 118.

13. Charlotte C. Eliot to Bertrand Russell, 18 January 1916, *Letters I*, p. 130.

14. *St. Louis Globe Democrat*, 16 July 1915, Houghton.

15. Statement signed by Theresa Garrett Eliot, 28 March 1970, Houghton.

16. TSE to Henry Eliot, 2 July 1915, *Letters I*, p. 104.

17. TSE to Mrs. Jack Gardner (Isabella), ?10 July 1915, *Letters I*, p. 107.

18. Bertrand Russell, *Autobiography, vol. 2, 1914–1944* (London: George Allen & Unwin, 1968), p. 54.

19. VE to Scofield Thayer, 2 August 1915, Beinecke.

20. Bertrand Russell to Ottoline Morrell, July 1915, *Autobiography, vol. 2*, op. cit., p. 54.

21. VE to Scofield Thayer, 2 August 1915, Beinecke.

22. VE Diary, 1936, Bodleian.

23. VE to Scofield Thayer, 3 March 1915, Beinecke.

24. TSE to Henry Ware Eliot, 23 July 1915, *Letters I,* p. 110. This unposted letter was found among Vivien's papers.

25. VE to Scofield Thayer, 2 August 1915, Beinecke.

26. TSE to Conrad Aiken, 5 August 1915, *Letters I,* p. 111.

27. P. Wyndham Lewis, *Blasting and Bombardiering,* 2nd ed. (London: Calder & Boyars, 1967).

28. C. C. Eliot to Bertrand Russell, 18 January 1916, *Letters I,* p. 131.

29. Quoted in Ray Monk, *Bertrand Russell: The Spirit of Solitude* (London: Vintage, 1997), p. 359.

30. Russell, *Autobiography, vol. 1, 1872–1914* (London: George Allen & Unwin, 1967), p. 204.

31. Ibid., p. 151.

32. Robert Gathorne-Hardy (ed.), *Ottoline at Garsington: Memoirs of Lady Ottoline Morrell 1915–1918* (London: Faber & Faber, 1974), p. 276.

33. Ibid., p. 272.

34. Russell, *Autobiography, vol. 1,* op. cit., p. 213.

35. Bertrand Russell to Ottoline Morrell, 1 June 1914, McMaster.

36. Bertrand Russell to Ottoline Morrell, 23 June 1914, McMaster.

37. Bertrand Russell to Ottoline Morrell, 2 August 1914, McMaster.

38. Quoted in Miranda Seymour, *Ottoline Morrell: Life on the Grand Scale* (London: Hodder and Stoughton, 1992), p. 201.

39. Bertrand Russell to Ottoline Morrell, 19 January 1915, McMaster.

40. Gathorne-Hardy (ed.), *Ottoline at Garsington,* op. cit., p. 43.

41. Ibid., p. 56.

42. Seymour, op. cit., p. 290.

43. Quoted in Monk, op. cit., p. 408.

44. Bertrand Russell to Ottoline Morrell, 8 July 1915, McMaster.

45. Gathorne-Hardy, op. cit., p. 57.

46. Russell, *Autobiography, vol. 2,* op. cit., pp. 22–23.

47. Monk, op. cit., p. 430.

48. Russell, *Autobiography, vol. 2,* op. cit., p. 23.

49. Gathorne-Hardy, op. cit., p. 286.

50. Frances Partridge, interview with author, 27 November 2000.

51. VE to Scofield Thayer, 24 October 1915, Beinecke.

52. Monk, op. cit., p. 440.

53. Irene Cooper-Willis wrote a novel, *The Green-Eyed Monster,* published under the pen-name "Althea Brook," in which Russell appears as "Tom Wolfe." See Monk, op. cit., p. 394.

54. T. S. Eliot, *Collected Poems,* p. 33. "Mr. Apollinax" was published in *Poetry* in September 1916. During Russell's visit to Harvard he was invited to stay a weekend with Benjamin Apthorp Fuller, a historian of philosophy and friend of George Santayana. Fuller and his mother were the inspiration for "Professor Channing-Cheetah" and the "dowager Mrs. Phlaccus."

55. TSE to Prof. J. Woods, 16 August 1915, *Letters I,* p. 113.

56. TSE to Scofield Thayer, 9 August 1915, Beinecke, and *Letters I,* p. 112.

57. VE to Scofield Thayer, "Thursday"? March 1915, Beinecke.

58. TSE to Scofield Thayer, 4 September 1915, Beinecke, and *Letters I,* p. 113.

59. Typescript of *The Family Reunion,* edited by Emily Hale, Houghton.

60. Charlotte Champe Eliot, typescript of "Savonarola" (London: Cobden-Sanderson, 1926), Foreword by T. S. Eliot, Houghton.

61. C. C. Eliot to Bertrand Russell, 18 January 1916, *Letters I*, p. 131.

6. Triple Ménage: Bertie, Vivien and Tom

1. Bertrand Russell, *Autobiography, vol. 2, 1914–1944* (London: George Allen & Unwin, 1968), p. 25.

2. Only three letters remain from Vivien to Russell at the Bertrand Russell Archive, McMaster.

3. Nicholas Griffin, editor of Russell's *Selected Letters, vols. 1 and 2,* is of the opinion that Russell and Eliot made a pact not to reveal their secrets, and Russell destroyed the majority of Vivien's letters to him. None of his to her have been preserved either. Conversation with Nick Griffin, June 1999.

4. Michael Davie (ed.), *The Diaries of Evelyn Waugh* (London: Weidenfeld and Nicolson, 1976), p. 73.

5. The suggestion that Vivien was the inspiration for Mrs. Ellerker was originally made in "Bertrand Russell and T. S. Eliot: Their Dialogue," by Gladys Garner Leithauser and Nadine Cowan Dyer, *Russell 2 (1),* summer 1982, pp. 7–28. Leithauser and Dyer also consider the relationship between Appleplex (Russell) and Eeldrop (Eliot) described in T. S. Eliot's "Eeldrop and Appleplex," published in *The Little Review,* May and September 1917, see Ray Monk, *Bertrand Russell: The Spirit of Solitude* (London: Vintage, 1997), p. 650.

6. Monk, op. cit., p. 12.

7. Bertrand Russell, *Satan in the Suburbs and Other Stories* (London: Bodley Head, 1953), p. 29.

8. Ibid., pp. 44–45.

9. Ibid., p. 48.

10. TSE to Henry Ware Eliot, 10 September 1915, *Letters I*, p. 115.

11. TSE to Bertrand Russell, 11 September 1915, *Letters I*, p. 115.

12. Caroline Moorehead, *Bertrand Russell* (London: Sinclair-Stevenson, 1993), p. 219.

13. Ronald W. Clark, *The Life of Bertrand Russell* (London: Jonathan Cape and Weidenfeld and Nicolson, 1975), p. 311.

14. Peter Ackroyd, *T. S. Eliot* (London: Hamish Hamilton, 1984), p. 84.

15. Bertrand Russell to Constance Malleson, 21 October 1916, McMaster.

16. See Chapter 9, "Priapus in the Shrubbery," for an account of the circumstances leading up to this night.

17. Michael Hastings to the author, 22 April 1999.

18. Constance Malleson to Bertrand Russell, 30 October 1917, quoted in Monk, op. cit., pp. 510–11, including footnote p. 511, quoting Colette's letter to Kenneth Blackwell, dated 12 February 1972. Peter Ackroyd in *T. S. Eliot* writes (p. 84) that Russell "made love to Vivien," but the experience was "hellish and loathsome." "He did not explain why it was quite so 'loathsome,' although no doubt Vivien's own physical problems had something to do with it. It was the pointless and messy end of what had been an intense but 'platonic' relationship." Ackroyd cites not Colette's letter but a paraphrase of it given in "Bertrand Russell and the Eliots" by Robert H. Bell, *The American Scholar,* summer 1983, pp. 309–25, in which the phrase "hellish and loathsome" is used, and this paraphrased description is

also used by Caroline Moorehead in *Bertrand Russell,* op. cit. Russell's letter to Colette in fact explains that love-making with Vivien was only "loathsome" because it was not with Colette. Vivien's letters to Scofield in the autumn of 1915 are those of a contented mistress, and there is no evidence that her relationship with Russell was "platonic" as Ackroyd says, apart from Russell's remarks to Ottoline, which cannot be taken at face value.

19. BR to Lucy Donnelly, 26 March 1914 quoted *Letters I,* p. 115n.

20. Quoted in Clark, op. cit., p. 311. Draft letter of Russell's to Ottoline, dated "1916," but apparently September 1915, private source. There is a copy of this letter at McMaster, dated 9 September.

21. Clark, ibid., p. 312. BR to Ottoline Morrell, 10 September 1915, McMaster.

22. Maurice Haigh-Wood, interview with Michael Hastings, 21 January 1980.

23. T. S. Eliot, "Ode," in Christopher Ricks (ed.), *Inventions of the March Hare, T. S. Eliot: Poems 1909–1917* (New York: Harcourt Brace, 1996), p. 383.

24. "Ara vos prec, per aquella valor,
    que vos guida al som de l'escalina,
    sovegna vos a temps de ma dolor"
    Poi s'ascose nel foco che gli affina. (XXVI, 145–48).
    ("I pray you, by that virtue
    that guides you to the summit of the stair,
    be mindful in your time of my pain."
    Then he dived back into the fire that refines them.)

       Quoted in James E. Miller Jr., *T. S. Eliot's Personal Waste Land: Exorcism of the Demons* (Philadelphia: University of Pennsylvania Press, 1977), p. 47. For a discussion of the significance of "Ode" see Chapter 5, "A Suppressed Ode," pp. 47–58.

25. "And this, O this shall henceforth be the token of comrades, this calamus-root shall,/ Interchange it youths with each other! Let none render it back." Walt Whitman, from *Leaves of Grass.*

26. Dr. Harry Trosman, "T. S. Eliot and *The Waste Land:* Psychopathological Antecedents and Transformations," *Psychoanalytic Studies of Biography,* George Moraitis and George H. Pollock (eds.), (International Universities Press Inc., 1987), p. 202.

27. Sigmund Freud, "Some Neurotic Mechanisms in Jealousy, Paranoia and Homosexuality" (1922), *On Psychopathology: Inhibitions, Symptoms and Anxiety* (London: The Penguin Freud Library, vol. 10, 1979), pp. 205–206.

28. T. S. Eliot, *Poems Written in Early Youth* (London: Faber & Faber, 1967), p. 26.

29. The reference to Perseus, son of Zeus and Danaë, who killed the Gorgon Medusa and used her head to turn to stone those who gazed upon it, is more difficult to decode. The story is told in Ovid's *Metamorphoses,* a favourite source of lines and allusion for Eliot. For a discussion, see Miller, op. cit., pp. 55–56. He argues that there may be an allusion to the trickery by which Perseus won Andromeda, or to the death of Athis and Lycabus which followed:

       Perseus turned, and swung
       The scimitar that once had slain the Gorgon
       And now slew Lycabus, who, in the darkness
       That swam before his eyes, looked once around
       For Athis, and once more lay down beside him
       And took this comfort to the world of shadows
       That in their death the two were not divided.

30. Lyndall Gordon, *Eliot's Early Years* (Oxford: OUP, 1977), p. 75.

31. Miller, op. cit., pp. 55–58.

32. Maurice Haigh-Wood, interview with Michael Hastings, 4 March 1980.

33. BR to Ottoline Morrell, n.d., McMaster.

34. Robert Gathorne-Hardy (ed.), *Ottoline at Garsington: Memoirs of Lady Ottoline Morrell 1915–1918* (London: Faber & Faber, 1974) p. 279.

35. BR to Ottoline Morrell, 23 June 1914, McMaster.

36. Gilbert Murray was Professor of Greek at Oxford, a classical scholar and historian. Bertrand Russell's reply, "The Policy of the Entente, 1904–1914: A Reply to Professor Gilbert Murray," was published in December 1915. See Monk, op. cit., pp. 438–39.

37. TSE to Henry Ware Eliot Sr., 27 September 1915, *Letters I*, p. 117.

38. Paul Delany, "T. S. Eliot's Personal Finances, 1915–1929," chapter in *Literature, Money and the Market from Trollope to Amis* (Basingstoke: Palgrave, 2001).

39. BR to Ottoline Morrell, n.d., Texas, quoted in Clark, op. cit., p. 312.

40. BR to Ottoline Morrell, 24 November 1915, McMaster.

41. Gathorne-Hardy, op. cit., p. 120.

42. VE to Scofield Thayer, Sunday, 24 October 1915, Beinecke.

43. Ronald Clark, *Bertrand Russell and His World* (London: Thames and Hudson, 1981), p. 80.

44. Monk, op. cit., pp. 140–41.

45. Maurice Haigh-Wood, interview with Michael Hastings, 21 January 1980.

46. Delany, op. cit.

47. *Letters I*, p. 132.

48. Trosman, op. cit., p. 712.

49. TSE to BR, 11 October 1915, McMaster, *Letters I*, p. 119.

50. BR to Charlotte C. Eliot, 3 October 1915, McMaster, *Letters I*, p. 118.

51. Monk, op. cit., p. 442.

52. VE to Scofield Thayer, 8 May 1916, Beinecke.

53. Constance Malleson to Kenneth Blackwell, 12 February 1972, McMaster.

54. Russell, *Autobiography,* pp. 55–56.

55. BR to Charlotte C. Eliot, 3 December 1915, McMaster, *Letters I*, p. 123.

56. BR to Ottoline Morrell, 8 December 1915, McMaster.

7. A Child in Pain

1. Bertrand Russell to Ottoline Morrell, 3 December 1915, McMaster.

2. BR to OM, 1 January 1916, McMaster.

3. Bertrand Russell, *Autobiography, vol. 2, 1914–1944* (London: George Allen & Unwin, 1968), p. 24.

4. Richard Shone, *Bloomsbury Portraits* (London: Phaidon, 1976), p. 153.

5. BR to OM, 3 January 1916, McMaster.

6. OM to BR, ?21 January 1916, McMaster.

7. BR to OM, 7 January 1916, McMaster.

8. Ibid.

9. OM to BR, "Monday," January 1916, McMaster.

10. BR to OM, 15 December 1915, McMaster.

11. OM to BR, 13 January 1916, McMaster.

12. Russell, op. cit., p. 58.

13. BR to OM, 12 January 1916, McMaster.

14. TSE to BR, 11 January 1916, McMaster, *Letters I,* p. 127.

15. BR to OM, "Wednesday mg.," n.d., 1916, McMaster.

16. Caroline Behr, *T. S. Eliot: A Chronology of his Life and Works* (London: Macmillan, 1983), p. 10. The *Catholic Anthology* was published in November 1915.

17. TSE to Conrad Aiken, 10 January 1916, *Letters I,* p. 126.

18. TSE to Henry Ware Eliot Sr., 14 January 1916, *Letters I,* p. 127.

19. TSE to BR, 14 January 1916, McMaster, *Letters I,* p. 127.

20. TSE to BR, 17 January 1916, McMaster, *Letters I,* p. 130.

21. Russell, op. cit., p. 18.

22. Shone, op. cit., pp. 143–44.

23. Maynard was granted a certificate of exemption by the Permanent Secretary to the Treasury on the grounds that he was doing work in the national interest. According to Clive Bell he objected to "being made to fight." Maynard sent £50 to the National Council for Civil Liberties. See Shone, op. cit., p. 148.

24. The lectures were published as *Principles of Social Reconstruction,* and in America as *Why Men Fight.*

25. Quoted in Michael Holroyd, *Lytton Strachey* (London: Vintage, 1995), p. 344.

26. BR to OM, 30 January 1916, McMaster.

27. OM to BR, 16 February 1916, McMaster.

28. OM to BR, 1 January 1916, McMaster.

29. OM to BR, n.d. March 1916, McMaster.

30. OM to BR, 3 March 1916, McMaster.

31. Robert Gathorne-Hardy (ed.), *Ottoline at Garsington: Memoirs of Lady Ottoline Morrell 1915–1918* (London: Faber & Faber, 1974), p. 96.

32. D. H. Lawrence, *Women in Love* (first published 1921; London: Heinemann, 1960), with an introduction by Richard Aldington, p. 83. "Hermione strange like a long Cassandra . . . Like a priestess she looked unconscious, sunk in a heavy half-trance." In the novel, Birkin represents Lawrence, Ursula, Frieda Lawrence, Gudrun, Katherine Mansfield and Gerald, Middleton Murry.

33. Charlotte C. Eliot to BR, 23 May 1916, *Letters I,* p. 138.

34. BR to Henry Ware Eliot, 7 April 1916, *Letters I,* p. 136.

35. BR to OM, 29 March 1916, McMaster.

36. Published in 1964 as *Knowledge and Experience in the Philosophy of F.H. Bradley* (Oxford: OUP, 1969).

37. TSE to J. H. Woods, 3 May 1916, *Letters I,* p. 136.

38. OM to BR, 28 March 1916, McMaster.

39. OM to BR, 29 March 1916, McMaster.

40. OM to BR, 11 April 1916, McMaster.

41. OM to BR, 19 May 1916, McMaster.

42. Russell, op. cit., p. 19.

43. Holroyd, op. cit., p. 343.

44. Gathorne-Hardy (ed.), *Ottoline at Garsington,* op. cit., pp. 101–2.

45. Helen Gardner, *The Composition of the Four Quartets* (London: Faber & Faber, 1978), p. 48n.

46. Gathorne-Hardy (ed.), op. cit., pp. 101–2.

47. VE to Henry Eliot, 1 June 1916, *Letters I,* p. 139.

48. VE to Scofield Thayer, 8 May 1916, Beinecke.

49. TSE to Scofield Thayer, 7 May 1916, *Letters I,* p. 138.

50. This description of Thayer by Alyse Gregory, managing editor of *The Dial,* is quoted in Nicholas Joost, *Scofield Thayer and* The Dial: *An Illustrated History* (Carbondale and Edwardsville: Southern Illinois University Press, 1964), p. 78.

51. The Thayers divorced in 1921. Notes to *The Dial* Collection, Beinecke.

52. The correct version is: "Quis desiderio sit pudor aut modus/Tam cari capitis?" *The Oxford Book of Latin Verse,* chosen by H. W. Garrod (Oxford: OUP, 1912), p. 141. Translation by C. S. Calverley, p. 485.

53. Translation by C. S. Calverley, ibid., p. 485.

54. Statement by Theresa Eliot, wife of Henry Ware Eliot Jr., 28 March 1970, Houghton.

55. VE to Henry Ware Eliot Jr., 1 June 1916, *Letters I,* p. 139.

56. VE to Henry Ware Eliot Jr., 11 October 1916, *Letters I,* p. 154.

57. VE to Charlotte C. Eliot, 8 March 1917, Houghton, *Letters I,* p. 161.

58. BR to OM, 26 January 1916, McMaster.

59. VE to Henry Ware Eliot Jr., 11 October 1916, *Letters I,* p. 155.

60. Statement of Theresa G. Eliot, 28 March 1970, Houghton.

61. TSE to Conrad Aiken, 21 August 1916, *Letters I,* p. 143.

62. TSE to Bertrand Russell, Monday (6 March? 1916), McMaster.

63. VE to Henry Ware Eliot Jr., 11 October 1916, *Letters I,* p. 154.

64. BR to OM, 21 May 1916, McMaster.

65. Quoted by Robert H. Bell, "Bertrand Russell and the Eliots," *The American Scholar,* Summer 1983, pp. 309–75.

66. BR to J. H. Woods, 4 March 1916, *Letters I,* p. 132.

67. TSE, "Eeldrop and Appleplex," *The Little Review,* Part I in May 1917; Part II is September 1917.

68. Gathorne-Hardy (ed.), *Ottoline at Garsington,* op. cit., pp. 120–21.

69. BR to OM, 6 June 1916, McMaster.

70. BR to OM, in Ray Monk, *Bertrand Russell: The Spirit of Solitude* (London: Vintage, 1997), p. 469.

71. TSE to Wyndham Lewis (November? 1915), *Letters I,* p. 122.

72. Brigit Patmore, *My Friends When Young* (London: Heinemann, 1968), pp. 84–86.

73. Ibid.

74. TSE to Conrad Aiken, 21 August 1916, *Letters I,* p. 143.

75. BR to OM, 20 August 1916, McMaster.

76. Anne Olivier Bell (ed.), *The Diary of Virginia Woolf,* Vol. 1 (London: Penguin, 1977), 29 July 1918, p. 175.

77. BR to OM, undated, ? August 1916, McMaster.

78. BR to OM, 20 August 1916, McMaster.

79. BR to OM, 16 August 1916, McMaster.

80. BR to OM, 20 June 1916, McMaster.

81. BR to OM, 1 September 1916, McMaster.

82. BR to OM, 28 August 1916, McMaster.

83. Constance Malleson ("Colette O'Niel"), *After Ten Years* (London: Jonathan Cape, 1929), p. 104.

84. Ibid., p. 107.

85. Russell, *Autobiography,* Vol. 2, op. cit., p. 26.

8. Wartime Waifs

1. Earl Russell married Elizabeth, Countess of Arnim, in February 1916.
2. TSE to Eleanor Hinkley, 5 September 1916, *Letters I,* p. 146.
3. VE to Henry Ware Eliot Jr., 1 June 1916, *Letters I,* p. 140.
4. Michael Ball, National Army Museum to the author, 18 January 1999.
5. Virginia Woolf had noticed the farmhouse just below Firle Beacon on the South Downs on one of her walks near Firle village, and thought it might be rented by her sister. It was arranged that Duncan and Bunny would work for a nearby farmer, and Charleston Farmhouse was rented from Lord Gage. Richard Shone, *Bloomsbury Portraits* (London: Phaidon, 1976), p. 155.
6. VE to Charlotte Champe Eliot, 28 June 1917, *Letters I,* p. 186.
7. "Hysteria," *Collected Poems 1909–62* (London: Faber & Faber, 1974), p. 34.
8. "Tradition and the Individual Talent," *Selected Essays* (op. cit., 1932), p. 18. The full quotation is "The mind of the poet . . . may partly or exclusively operate upon the experience of the man himself; but, the more perfect the artist, the more completely separate in him will be the man who suffers and the mind which creates; the more perfectly will the mind digest and transmute the passions which are its material."
9. Ibid., p. 17.
10. "Shakespeare and the Stoicism of Seneca," *Selected Essays* (Faber & Faber, 1932), p. 137.
11. A. David Moody, *Thomas Stearns Eliot, Poet* (Cambridge: CUP, 1979), pp. xvii–xviii.
12. "Tradition and the Individual Talent," *Selected Essays,* op. cit., p. 21.
13. Moody, op. cit., p. 11.
14. "Shakespeare and the Stoicism of Seneca," *Selected Essays,* op. cit., p. 137.
15. H. W. H. Powel Jr., in an unpublished MA thesis, "Notes on the Life of T.S. Eliot" (Brown University, 1954). Powell demonstrates that Adeleine Moffat, who entertained Eliot to tea in Boston when he was a student at Harvard, was the inspiration for "Portrait of a Lady."
16. "Hysteria," published in *The Catholic Anthology,* November 1915, *Collected Poems 1909–1962* (London: Faber & Faber, 1974), p. 34.
17. R. D. Laing, *The Divided Self* (London: Pelican, 1965), pp. 39–45. Laing makes a distinction between the ontologically secure individual who "may experience his own being as real, alive, whole; as differentiated from the rest of the world in ordinary circumstances so clearly that his identity and autonomy are never in question"; and the ontologically insecure, who "may feel more unreal than real; in a literal sense more dead than alive; precariously differentiated from the rest of the world, so that his identity and autonomy are always in question . . . He may feel more insubstantial than substantial, and unable to assume that the stuff he is made of is genuine, good, valuable. And he may feel his self is partially divorced from his body" (pp. 41–42). Laing distinguishes between the "sane schizoid way of being-in-the-world" and the psychotic.
18. George Whiteside, "Eliot: The Psychobiographical Approach," *Southern Review* (Adelaide), vol. V, 1972, p. 12.
19. TSE to Henry Eliot, 6 September 1916, *Letters I,* p. 151.
20. VE to Henry Eliot, 11 October 1916, *Letters I,* p. 155.
21. C. C. Eliot to Bertrand Russell, 18 January 1916, McMaster.
22. TSE to J. H. Woods, 23 March 1917, *Letters I,* p. 171.

23. *Harvard College Class of 1910, Seventh Report* (June 1935), p. 219.

24. VE to Henry Eliot, 11 October 1916, *Letters I*, p. 154.

25. Ronald Schuchard, *Eliot's Dark Angel: Intersections of Life and Art* (Oxford: OUP, 1999), gives Eliot's syllabuses in full, pp. 25–51.

26. TSE to Eleanor Hinkley, 23 March 1917, *Letters I*, p. 168.

27. *CP*, op. cit., p. 49.

28. TSE to C. C. Eliot, 6 September 1916, *Letters I*, p. 149.

29. Cyril Connolly, *Previous Convictions* (London: Hamish Hamilton, 1963), p. 241.

30. OM to BR, February 1916, McMaster.

31. *CP*, p. 17.

32. A. David Moody, "Tracing T. S. Eliot's Spirit," in *"The Waste Land" in Different Voices* (London: Edward Arnold, 1974), p. 42.

33. His article "Reflections on Vers Libre" appeared in the *New Statesman* in March 1917: "The division between Conservative Verse and *vers libre* does not exist, for there is only good verse, bad verse and chaos."

34. TSE to John Quinn, 25 January 1920, *Letters I*, p. 357.

35. Ezra Pound to Margaret C. Anderson, ?January 1917, D. D. Paige (ed.), *The Letters of Ezra Pound 1907–1941* (New York: Harcourt Brace, 1950), p. 161.

36. Margaret Anderson, editorial in the *Little Review,* March 1918.

37. Schuchard, op. cit., p. 39.

38. VE to C. C. Eliot, 28 June 1917, *Letters I*, p. 186.

39. TSE to C. C. Eliot, 1 July 1917, *Letters I*, p. 187.

40. "La sueur aestivale, et une forte odeur de chienne . . ." From "Lune de Miel," *CP*, op. cit., p. 50.

41. T. S. Eliot, "The Death of the Duchess," Valerie Eliot (ed.), *The Waste Land: A Facsimile* (New York: Harcourt Brace, 1971), p. 105.

42. TSE to C. C. Eliot, 3 October 1917, *Letters I*, p. 198.

43. TSE to BR, 13 March 1917, McMaster.

44. TSE to BR, "Thursday," 1917, McMaster.

45. VE to C. C. Eliot, 8 March 1917, Houghton, *Letters I*, p. 161.

46. TSE to Henry Ware Eliot, 1 March 1917, *Letters I*, p. 160.

47. OM to BR, 2 March 1916, McMaster.

48. *CP*, op. cit., p. 142–43.

49. Constance Malleson, *After Ten Years* (London: Jonathan Cape, 1931), p. 35.

50. Ibid., p. 109.

51. Constance Malleson to BR, September 1916, "Letters to Bertrand Russell from Constance Malleson, 1916–1969, Edited with a Preface by P.M. Urch," unpublished typescript, 1973, p. 5, McMaster.

52. BR to OM, 31 August 1916, Texas.

53. CM to BR, 2 October 1916, McMaster.

54. CM to BR, "afternoon," October 1916, Mrs. Urch (ed.), unpublished typescript, 1973, p. 14, McMaster.

55. BR to CM, 20 October 1915, in the train to Manchester, McMaster.

56. CM to BR, 25 October 1916, Urch, op. cit., pp. 30–31, McMaster.

57. Katharine Tait, *My Father Bertrand Russell* (New York: Harcourt Brace Jovanovich, 1975), p. 101. This description by Russell's daughter, Katharine, is of the "new morality" practised by Russell and her mother, his second wife, Dora Black.

58. BR to CM, 29 October 1916, midnight, McMaster.

59. BR to CM, 4 November 1916, McMaster.

60. CM to BR, 5 November 1916, Urch, op. cit., p. 38, McMaster.

61. BR to CM, 26 October 1916, McMaster.

62. Bertrand Russell, *Autobiography, vol. 2, 1914–1944* (London: George Allen & Unwin, 1968), p. 27.

63. CM to BR, December 1916, Urch, op. cit., p. 50, McMaster.

64. Russell, op. cit., p. 27.

65. BR to OM, n.d., Texas (archived letter no. 1439).

66. Katherine Mansfield to BR, December 1916, in Ronald Clark, *The Life of Bertrand Russell* (London: Jonathan Cape and Weidenfeld & Nicolson, 1975), p. 309.

67. CM to BR, 7 September 1916, McMaster.

68. BR to OM, n.d., Sunday, Texas (archived letter no. 1436).

69. BR to OM, "June 1917," McMaster.

70. BR to OM, n.d., 1917.

71. Constance Malleson, *The Coming Back* (London: Jonathan Cape, 1933), p. 307, quoted by John G. Slater, "Lady Constance Malleson, 'Colette O'Niel,' " *Russell,* Journal of the Bertrand Russell Archive, p. 11.

72. OM to BR, 2 January 1917 postmark, Texas.

73. OM to BR, 6 January 1917 postmark, Texas.

74. OM to BR, 19 March 1917, Texas.

75. OM to BR, 31 August 1917 postmark, Texas.

76. BR to CM, 28 November 1916, McMaster.

77. BR to CM, 3 December 1916, McMaster.

78. BR to CM, 5 January 1917, McMaster.

79. The letter was presented to the American Neutral Conference Committee on 22 January.

80. BR to CM, March 1917, McMaster.

81. BR to CM, 27 March 1917, McMaster.

82. CM to BR, 6 January 1917, McMaster.

83. CM to K. Blackwell, 12 February 1972, McMaster.

84. VE to C. C. Eliot, 8 April 1917, *Letters I,* p. 173.

85. TSE to C. C. Eliot, 11 April 1917, *Letters I,* p. 174.

86. VE to C. C. Eliot, 30 April 1917, *Letters I,* p. 178.

87. T. S. Eliot, "Mélange Adultère de Tout," in *Collected Poems,* p. 49.

88. Malleson, *After Ten Years,* op. cit., p. 111.

89. CM to BR, 2 May 1917, Urch, op. cit., p. 94, McMaster.

90. BR to CM, 2 April 1917, McMaster.

9. Priapus in the Shrubbery

1. The official date of the U.S. declaration of war was 6 April 1917.

2. Charlotte (1874–1926) married George Lawrence Smith in September 1903, and was an artist. Her daughter Theodora, born 25 July 1904, became a favourite niece of Vivien's.

3. VE to Charlotte Eliot Smith (Mrs. George Lawrence Smith), 4 April 1917, Houghton.

4. VE to Charlotte C. Eliot, 8 April 1917, Houghton, and *Letters I,* p. 173.

5. Karl Henry Culpin (1893–1917), Anglo-German, Exhibitioner at Merton College, First in

Modern History 1915; his call-up was delayed owing to poor eyesight, but he became a 2nd Lieutenant in the Gloucestershire Regiment.

6. TSE to C. C. Eliot, 11 April 1917, *Letters I,* p. 174.

7. John Quinn to Ezra Pound, 2 June 1917, Ezra Pound Papers, Beinecke.

8. TSE to Eleanor Hinkley, 23 July 1917, *Letters I,* p. 189.

9. TSE to C. C. Eliot, 15 November 1917, *Letters I,* p. 207.

10. Constance Malleson to Bertrand Russell, 25 December 1916, McMaster.

11. BR to CM, 21 September 1917, McMaster.

12. OM to BR, 30 July 1917 (wrongly dated 17 July by BR), Texas.

13. VE to C. C. Eliot, 28 June 1917, *Letters I,* p. 185.

14. Ibid.

15. Pound put £5 towards the cost of printing by the Egoist Press. The little book cost one shilling, and the print run was 500 copies. *Letters I,* p. 179.

16. TSE to Mary Hutchinson, 2 July 1917, *Letters I,* p. 188.

17. Alfred A. Knopf to John Quinn, 17 August 1917, Beinecke.

18. John Quinn to Ezra Pound, 29 April 1917, Beinecke.

19. Clive Bell, "How Pleasant to know Mr. Eliot," R. Marsh and Tambimuttu, *T. S. Eliot: A Symposium* (London: P.L. Editions, p. 17. Clive's memory must have been at fault, as *Prufrock and other Observations* was not published until June 1917, see *Letters I,* p. 179, note 4).

20. VE to C. C. Eliot, 22 October 1917, *Letters I,* p. 200.

21. TSE to C. C. Eliot, 3 October 1917, *Letters I,* p. 198.

22. VE to C. C. Eliot, 22 October 1917, *Letters I,* p. 200.

23. TSE to Henry Ware Eliot, 22 November 1917, *Letters I,* p. 208.

24. CM to BR, 19 August 1917, McMaster, Urch typescript, p. 126.

25. CM to BR, 23 August 1917, McMaster, Urch typescript, pp. 131–32.

26. BR to CM, 17 August 1917, McMaster.

27. Constance Malleson, *After Ten Years* (London: Jonathan Cape, 1931), p. 123.

28. BR to CM, 23 September 1917, Bertrand Russell, *Autobiography,* vol. 2, 1914–1944 (London: George Allen & Unwin, 1968), p. 179.

29. BR to CM, "What She Is and What She Might Become," 25 September 1917, McMaster.

30. CM to BR, 28 September 1917, McMaster, Urch typescript, vol. 2, p. 161.

31. BR to CM, 6 September 1917, McMaster. Russell visited Garsington in between his two meetings with Katherine Mansfield. Phyllis Urch writes: "To judge from the only unpublished evidence available—a letter from Katherine Mansfield to Russell, postmarked January 25, 1917—one would not care to pronounce on the exact nature of her relations with Russell. His statements, in letters to Colette, can hardly be taken as evidence; for, although they no doubt contain a part of the truth, it might be rash to assume they contain the whole of it." See Mrs. P. Urch, unpublished thesis, 1973, p. 112.

32. BR to CM, 26 June 1917, Urch, op. cit., vol. 2, p. 112.

33. CM to BR, 11 October 1917, Urch, op. cit., vol. 2, pp. 167–68.

34. BR to CM, 16 October 1917, McMaster.

35. TSE to C. C. Eliot, 24 October 1917, *Letters I,* p. 203.

36. VE to C. C. Eliot, 22 October 1917, Houghton, *Letters I,* p. 200. From the original letter it seems that the farm mentioned is possibly Tanhurst Farm, which is within two miles of Leith Hill, as described in Eliot's letter of 24 October to his mother, rather than "Senhurst," as given in the published version of Vivien's letter. There is no farm of the

name of Senhurst in the area around Leith Hill, according to Matthew Alexander, curator of Guildford Museum. A study of the 1916 6" ordnance survey map gives two possible
farms in the area described, Tanhurst or Hartshurst. Conversation with Matthew
Alexander, 21 July 1999.

37. As Peter Ackroyd surmises in his biography, *T. S. Eliot* (London: Penguin, 1993) p. 84, because she was menstruating, which there is no reason to think was the case. Since she was
at the farm for three weeks, Vivien was unlikely to have invited Russell at such a time.
Ackroyd's interpretation is based on a paraphrase of Russell's letter of 30 October 1917 in
"Bertrand Russell and the Eliots" by Robert H. Bell (*The American Scholar,* summer 1983,
pp. 309–25).

38. BR to CM, 25 October 1917, McMaster.

39. BR to CM, 30 October 1917, McMaster.

40. CM to BR, 31 October 1917, McMaster.

41. BR to CM, n.d., Gordon Square, November 1917, McMaster.

42. Ronald Clark, *The Life of Bertrand Russell* (London: Jonathan Cape and Weidenfeld and
Nicolson, 1975), pp. 334–35.

43. BR to CM, 7 November 1917, McMaster.

44. BR to CM, 13 November 1917, McMaster.

45. BR to CM, 14 November 1917, McMaster.

46. BR to CM, ibid.

47. BR to CM, "Thursday," 22 November 1917, McMaster.

48. CM to BR, 29 November 1917, Urch, op. cit., vol. 2, p. 186.

49. BR to CM, 6 December 1917, McMaster.

50. VE to Mary Hutchinson, n.d., ?November 1917, Texas.

51. VE to C. C. Eliot, 22 November 1917, *Letters I,* p. 210.

52. *Roads to Freedom: Socialism, Anarchism and Syndicalism,* "undertaken for an American
publisher, 'solely for the sake of filthy lucre,' " Clark, op. cit., p. 333.

53. BR to CM, 13 December 1917, McMaster.

54. Lady Constance Malleson to Kenneth Blackwell, 1 February 1975, in reply to his query
whether Russell paid for her abortion. I differ from Ray Monk in dating Colette's pregnancy by Elvey and subsequent abortion as December 1917 (as Colette does), following her
stay with him in Blackpool during filming, rather than December 1918, when Russell suspected her of having an affair with the American Colonel Mitchell while he was in
Brixton. Colette denies that Russell paid for the abortion, as stated by Monk, op. cit.,
p. 542. It is of course possible that Colette's stay in the nursing home in 1918 was for another abortion, as she said she had had "a number of abortions" in her youth.

55. BR to CM, 14 December 1917, McMaster.

56. BR to CM, 1 January 1918, McMaster.

57. CM to BR, Urch, op. cit., vol. 2, pp. 198–204.

58. BR to CM, 6 January 1918, McMaster.

59. BR to CM, 9 January 1918, McMaster.

60. BR to CM, 10 January 1918, McMaster.

61. Monk, op. cit., p. 524.

62. BR to OM, 4 February 1918, McMaster.

63. "Mr. Apollinax" in Christopher Ricks (ed.), *Inventions of the March Hare, T. S. Eliot: Poems
1909–1917* (New York: Harcourt Brace, 1971), p. 344. First published in *Poetry,* September
1916.

64. Russell appropriated this personalisation of himself as "Satan" in his short story, "Satan in the Suburbs."

65. Andrew Laing, *R.D. Laing: A Biography* (New York: Thunder's Mouth Press, 1994), p. 232.

66. Alessandra Lemma-Wright, Chapter 14, "I'm Homosexual," *Invitation to Psychodynamic Psychology* (Whurr Publishers, 1995), pp. 148–56.

67. TSE to Ezra Pound, 23 September 1917, *Letters I,* p. 198.

68. Part I of "Eeldrop and Appleplex" was published in May and Part II in September 1917 in the *Little Review.*

69. Joan Acocella, "Dancing with Demons," *Independent on Sunday,* 8 August 1999, writes that Nijinsky "ushered ballet into modernism" with his productions of *L'Après-midi d'un Faune, Jeux,* and *The Rite of Spring.* See also Lynn Garafola, *Diaghilev's Ballets Russes* (New York: Da Capo Press, 1998), p. 50.

70. Lyndall Gordon, *T. S. Eliot: An Imperfect Life* (London: Vintage, 1998), p. 106, makes this suggestion.

71. Virginia Woolf confessed, "I was jealous of her writing—the only writing I have ever been jealous of," quoted on the cover of Katherine Mansfield, *Bliss and Other Stories* (London: Penguin, 1962).

72. TSE to Henry Ware Eliot Sr., 31 October 1917, *Letters I,* p. 204.

10. Bloomsbury Beginnings

1. Ray Monk, *Bertrand Russell: The Spirit of Solitude* (London: Vintage, 1997), pp. 520, 521.

2. T. S. Matthews, *Great Tom: Notes Towards the Definition of T. S. Eliot* (London: Weidenfeld & Nicolson, 1974), p. 45. Matthews argues that Eliot has taken an acknowledgement of guilt and made it read as a curse. See also C. Ricks (ed.), *Inventions of the March Hare, T. S. Eliot: Poems 1909–1917* (New York: Harcourt Brace Jovanovich, 1996), p. 183. The quotation from *Coriolanus,* IV.v, reads:

> My name is Caius Marcius, who hath done
> To thee particularly, and to all the Volsces,
> Great hurt and mischief.

Undoubtedly Eliot identified with the banished Coriolanus, and compared his mother Charlotte to the courageous Volumnia, mother of Coriolanus, who boasted that she had the courage to perform the labours of Hercules. "Ode" was included in *Ara Vos Prec,* published by John Rodker (1919). Part of this edition bore the title *Ara Vus Prec,* which Eliot later blamed on his ignorance of Provençal.

3. Frances Partridge, interview with author, 27 November 2000.

4. Ibid.

5. Michael Holroyd, *Lytton Strachey* (London: Vintage, 1995), p. 59.

6. David Bradshaw, "These Extraordinary Parakeets," Part I in *Charleston Magazine,* 16, Autumn/Winter 1997; Part II in *Charleston Magazine* 17, Spring/Summer 1998.

7. James Strachey Barnes, *Half a Life* (London: Eyre & Spottiswoode, 1933), pp. 87–93.

8. The character of Jinny, a socialite, is based on Mary, that of Louis very probably on Eliot, although Angelica Garnett suggests Leonard Woolf in her introduction to *The Waves,* in which Jinny and Louis play hiding and kissing games together. Virginia Woolf, *The Waves* (London: Vintage, 1992), p. 5. See Hermione Lee, *Virginia Woolf* (London: Vintage, 1997), p. 383.

9. Jane Dunn, *A Very Close Conspiracy* (London: Jonathan Cape, 1990), p. 243.

10. Ibid., p. 103.

11. Ibid., p. 105.

12. Vanessa Bell to Maynard Keynes, Regina Marler (ed.), *The Selected Letters of Vanessa Bell* (New York: Pantheon, 1993), p. 163.

13. Bradshaw, op. cit., p. 1.

14. Richard Shone, *Bloomsbury Portraits* (London: Phaidon, 1976), p. 169.

15. VE to Mary Hutchinson, 11 November 1936, Texas.

16. Osbert Sitwell, *Laughter in the Next Room* (London: Macmillan, 1949), p. 17.

17. River House was previously the home of bookbinder and printer T. J. Cobden-Sanderson, and was next door to Kelmscott House, which formerly belonged to William Morris. See Bradshaw, op. cit., p. 22.

18. "Polly Flinders," "Fireworks," *Vogue,* 67 (early January, 1926), p. 49. Reprinted in Mary Hutchinson, *Fugitive Pieces* (London: Hogarth Press, 1927). Quoted by Bradshaw, op. cit., p. 23.

19. Vincent O'Sullivan and Margaret Scott (eds.), *Collected Letters of Katherine Mansfield,* vol. 1 (Oxford: Clarendon Press, 1984), p. 312. Quoted by Bradshaw, op. cit., p. 24.

20. VE to Mary Hutchinson, "Southview," n.d., 1917, Texas.

21. VE to MH, "18 Crawford Mans.," n.d., 1917, Texas.

22. VE to MH, n.d., ?1917, Texas.

23. VE to MH, n.d., ?1917, Texas.

24. TSE to Ezra Pound, 31 October 1917, Beinecke, and *Letters I,* p. 206.

25. Sitwell, op. cit., pp. 32–33.

26. VE to MH, n.d., ?1918, Texas.

27. Clive Bell, "How Pleasant to know Mr. Eliot," Richard March and Tambimuttu, *T. S. Eliot: A Symposium* (London: P. L. Editions Poetry, 1948), p. 15.

28. Robert Gathorne-Hardy (ed.), *Ottoline at Garsington: Memoirs of Lady Ottoline Morrell 1915–1918* (London: Faber & Faber, 1974), p. 52.

29. Michael Holyroyd, *Lytton Strachey* (London: Vintage, 1995), p. 59.

30. TSE to C. C. Eliot, 17 January, 6 February 1918, *Letters I,* pp. 218–19.

31. TSE to MH, 6 September 1916, *Letters I,* p. 151.

32. Clive Bell to MH, 16 January 1917, Hutchinson Papers, Texas.

33. MH to Lytton Strachey, 17 January 1917, Texas.

34. Shone, op. cit., pp. 119–20.

35. MH to Lytton Strachey, 14 June 1918, Texas.

36. Clive Bell to MH, 8 April 1917, Hutchinson Papers, Texas.

37. Clive Bell to MH, 20 September 1917, Texas.

38. Clive Bell to MH, 23 September 1917, Texas.

39. O'Sullivan and Scott (eds.), *Collected Letters of Katherine Mansfield,* vol. 1, op. cit., p. 312.

40. Maurice Haigh-Wood, interview with Michael Hastings, 21 January 1980.

41. TSE to MH, 19 September 1917, *Letters I,* p. 197.

42. VE to MH, 13 March 1918, Texas, *Letters I,* p. 224.

43. MH to Lytton Strachey, 19 May 1919, Texas.

44. VE to MH, n.d., 1921, Texas.

45. VE to MH, 6 September 1929, Texas.

46. VE to MH, 10 July 1931, Texas.

47. TSE to C. C. Eliot, 24 March 1918, *Letters I,* p. 225.

48. VE to MH, 31 March 1918, Texas, *Letters I,* p. 224.

49. Ibid.

50. L. M. Findlay (ed.), *Algernon Charles Swinburne, Selected Poems* (Manchester: Fyfield Books, 1982), p. 84.

51. Ronald Clark, *The Life of Bertrand Russell* (London: Jonathan Cape and Weidenfeld & Nicolson, 1975), p. 345.

52. Bertrand Russell to Constance Malleson, n.d. (?May), archive letter no. 200305, McMaster.

53. The day after Helen sailed Russell confessed his affair with her to Colette. Clark, op. cit., p. 352.

54. BR to CM, n.d., McMaster.

55. I am indebted to Dr. Carl Spadoni, Director, Bertrand Russell Archive, for this suggestion.

56. BR to CM, April 1918, McMaster.

57. "Sweeney among the Nightingales," "Whispers of Immortality," "Dans le Restaurant," "Mr. Eliot's Sunday Morning Service." Published as "Four Poems" in the *Little Review,* v, 5 (September 1918), pp. 10–14. Valerie Eliot (ed.), Introduction to *The Waste Land: A Facsimile,* xiv, note.

58. Ricks (ed.), *IMH,* p. 384. In *Ara Vos Prec,* "Ode on Independence Day, July 4 1918" followed "Mélange Adultère de Tout" and preceded "The Love Song of J. Alfred Prufrock." It is the only poem published by TSE not in a subsequent collection.

59. Quoted in Keith Thomas, *Religion and the Decline of Magic* (London: Penguin, 1973), p. 679.

60. Quoted in Ackroyd, *T. S. Eliot* (London: Penguin, 1993), p. 86.

61. Brigit Patmore, *My Friends When Young* (London: Heinemann, 1968).

62. Brigit Patmore, op. cit., pp. 88–89.

63. T. S. Eliot, "Whispers of Immortality," *CP,* p. 55; Ricks (ed.), *IMH,* p. 365.

64. *International Journal of Ethics,* January 1917, quoted in George Whiteside, "T. S. Eliot: The Psychobiographic Approach," *Southern Review* (Adelaide) 6, no. 1 (March 1973), p. 22.

65. Whiteside, ibid., p. 23. "Whispers of Immortality" can be compared to "Circe's Palace" (1908), whose Freudian imagery is similar, and betrays the twenty-year-old Eliot's dawning self-knowledge of his homosexuality.

66. T. S. Eliot, "Portrait of a Lady," in Ricks (ed.), *IMH,* p. 327. The original epigraph for this poem was from Webster's *The White Devil.*

67. Ricks (ed.), *IMH,* p. 363; *CP,* op. cit., p. 53.

68. BR to CM, n.d. (?July), archive letter no. 200325, McMaster.

69. BR to CM, Urch, op. cit., p. 73.

70. Constance Malleson, *After Ten Years* (London: Jonathan Cape, 1931), pp. 123–24.

71. VE to Mary Hutchinson, 30 August 1918, Texas.

72. TSE to Henry Ware Eliot Jr., 25 August 1918, Houghton, *Letters I,* p. 241.

73. TSE to John Quinn, *Letters I,* p. 244.

74. VE to MH, n.d., ?August 1918, Texas.

75. Ibid.

76. John Quinn to Major Turner, August 1918, Houghton.

77. TSE to Charlotte C. Eliot, 28 July 1918, Houghton, *Letters I,* p. 239.

78. TSE to Mary Hutchinson, 25 August 1918, Texas.

79. Ibid.

80. Ibid.

81. BR to CM, 24 August 1918, McMaster.

82. Urch, op. cit., p. 266.

83. Ibid., p. 285.

84. Malleson, op. cit., p. 127.

85. TSE to John Quinn, 13 November 1918, *Letters I,* p. 254.

86. TSE to Mrs. Jack Gardner, 7 November 1918, *Letters I,* p. 251.

87. TSE to Henry Eliot Jr., ibid., p. 250.

88. Sitwell, op. cit., p. 5.

89. VE to Henry Eliot Jr., 21 November 1918, *Letters I,* p. 258.

90. TSE to C. C. Eliot, 8 December 1918, *Letters I,* p. 259.

91. VE to C. C. Eliot, 15 December 1918, *Letters I,* p. 261.

92. VE to C. C. Eliot, 30 December 1918, *Letters I,* p. 264.

93. VE to Richard Aldington, in pencil, n.d., ?spring 1922, Texas.

94. VE to Henry Eliot Jr., 27 October 1918, *Letters I,* p. 245.

95. TSE to Eleanor Hinkley, 31 December 1917, *Letters I,* p. 216.

96. Henry James, *Daisy Miller,* with an Introduction by Geoffrey Moore (London: Penguin Classics, 1986), p. 62.

97. CM to BR, 7 September 1918, McMaster.

98. BR to OM, 20 November 1918, Texas.

99. Clark, op. cit., p. 353.

100. Urch, op. cit., p. 292.

101. BR to CM, 26 September 1918, McMaster.

102. BR to CM, 23 October 1918, McMaster.

103. BR to CM, 26 November 1918, McMaster.

104. BR to CM, 27 November 1918, McMaster.

105. Urch, op. cit., p. 309.

106. Ibid.

107. Ibid., p. 317.

108. CM to BR, 7 February 1919, Urch, op. cit., p. 318.

109. Ibid., p. 319.

110. TSE to BR, 3 February 1919, McMaster and *Letters I,* p. 270.

111. BR to TSE, 27 February 1919, McMaster.

112. Urch, op. cit., p. 309.

113. TSE to BR, 14 February 1919, McMaster, *Letters I,* p. 271.

114. BR to TSE, 19 March 1919, McMaster.

115. TSE to John Quinn, 6 January 1919, *Letters I,* p. 166.

116. TSE to John Quinn, 16 January 1919, *Letters I,* p. 169.

117. VE to Mary Hutchinson (postmark) 28 February 1919, Texas.

118. TSE to Henry Ware Eliot Jr., 27 February 1919, *Letters I,* p. 272.

119. TSE to BR, 26 March 1919, McMaster.

120. VE to BR, 13 April 1919, McMaster.

121. TSE to C. C. Eliot, 12 March 1919, *Letters I,* p. 276.

122. Katherine Tait, *My Father Bertrand Russell* (New York: Harcourt Brace Jovanovich, 1975), p. 101.

123. TSE to Mary Hutchinson, 4 March 1919, *Letters I,* p. 275.

11. Possum's Revenge

1. Donald Stanford, quoted in Margaret Clare Ratliff, "The Correspondence of Mary Hutchinson: A New Look at Bloomsbury, Eliot and Huxley," thesis, University of Texas at Austin, 1991, ch. 4, "Mary Hutchinson and the Eliots," p. 143.
2. VE Diary, 1919, Bodleian.
3. Osbert Sitwell, "T. S. Eliot:" unpublished memoir on T. S. Eliot and his marriage, 19 February 1950, Texas.
4. Richard Aldington, *Stepping Heavenward: A Record* (London: 1931), pp. 28–53.
5. Sitwell, memoir, op. cit., pp. 3–5.
6. Ibid., p. 12.
7. "Burbank with a Baedeker: Bleistein with a Cigar," *Collected Poems,* pp. 42–43.
8. Anthony Julius, *T. S. Eliot, Anti-Semitism, and Literary Form* (Cambridge: Cambridge University Press, 1995), p. 2.
9. Ibid., pp. 19–20. These poems dominate *Ara Vos Prec* (London: The Ovid Press, 1920).
10. *Criterion,* April 1925, iii, p. 330.
11. Basil Saunders to Lyndall Gordon, 18 August 1993.
12. T. S. Eliot, *Ara Vos Prec,* op. cit.
13. Anne Olivier Bell (ed.), *The Diary of Virginia Woolf, vol. 1, 1915–1919* (London: Penguin, 1979), p. 257.
14. Lewis had his first novel *Tarr* published by The Egoist Ltd. in July 1918.
15. *Diary of Virginia Woolf,* vol. 1, op. cit., p. 140, entry for 18 April 1918. Eliot suggested to Harriet Weaver that the Woolfs might print *Ulysses* on their private press, which Weaver's printers were refusing to do because of printers' liability for prosecution under the laws of obscene libel. The Woolfs declined to do so.
16. Leonard Woolf, *Beginning Again: An Autobiography of the Years 1911 to 1918* (London: Hogarth Press, 1964).
17. TSE to C. C. Eliot, 29 March 1919, *Letters I,* p. 279.
18. Sitwell, op. cit., p. 6.
19. Aldington, op. cit., p. 46.
20. TSE to Richard Aldington, 30 June 1922, Texas, *Letters I,* p. 535.
21. VE Diary, 17–22 November 1919, Bodleian.
22. TSE to Henry Eliot, 27 February 1919, *Letters I,* p. 272.
23. TSE to C. C. Eliot, 27 February 1919, *Letters I,* p. 274.
24. VE Diary, 2 March 1919, Bodleian.
25. VE Diary, 1–10 November 1919, Bodleian.
26. TSE to C. C. Eliot, 26 June 1919, *Letters I,* p. 309.
27. VE Diary, 9 July 1919, Bodleian.
28. VE Diary, 6 July 1919, Bodleian.
29. *Diary of Virginia Woolf,* op. cit., note 262.
30. Wyndham Lewis, in R. March and Tambimuttu, *T. S. Eliot: A Symposium* (London: P. L. Editions Poetry, 1948), p. 31.
31. TSE to C. C. Eliot, 29 March 1919, *Letters I,* p. 280.
32. TSE to Henry Eliot, 6 April 1919, *Letters I,* p. 283.
33. TSE to J. H. Woods, 21 April 1919, *Letters I,* p. 285.

34. Stephen Spender, *Eliot* (London: Fontana, 1975), p. 93.

35. Paul Delany, "T. S. Eliot's Personal Finances, 1915–1929," in *Literature, Money and the Market from Trollope to Amis* (Basingstoke: Palgrave, 2001).

36. Delany, op. cit., p. 261.

37. Signed statement by Theresa Eliot, 28 March 1970, Cambridge, Mass., Houghton.

38. Delany, op. cit., p. 261.

39. The Woolfs did not acquire their first treadle machine until after moving the Hogarth Press to 52 Tavistock Square, Bloomsbury, in 1924. Even then conditions were primitive, as their assistant, John Lehmann, recalled.

40. VE to MH, 1 May? 1919, Texas, and *Letters I*, p. 288.

41. V. Woolf to Vanessa Bell, 4 April 1919, in Nigel Nicolson and Joanne Trautmann (eds.), *The Letters of Virginia Woolf*, vol. II. (London: Hogarth Press, 1976), p. 344.

42. TSE to Eleanor Hinkley, 17 June 1919, *Letters I*, p. 304.

43. *Diary of Virginia Woolf*, op. cit., p. 209.

44. British Library, 13 October 1918, quoted in Ratliff, op. cit., p. 116.

45. V. Woolf to Duncan Grant, 17 April 1919, Nicolson and Trautmann (eds.), *Letters*, vol. II, op. cit., p. 350.

46. TSE to Eleanor Hinkley, 17 June 1919, *Letters I*, p. 304.

47. VE to MH, 10 May 1919, *Letters I*, p. 292.

48. *Diary of Virginia Woolf*, 10 April 1919, op. cit., p. 262.

49. V. Woolf to Duncan Grant, 17 April 1919, Nicolson and Trautmann (eds.), *Letters, vol. II*, op. cit., p. 350.

50. VE to MH, 10 May 1919, *Letters I*, p. 292.

51. Clive Bell, *Old Friends, Personal Recollections* (London: Chatto and Windus, 1956), p. 170.

52. Stephen Spender, "Remembering Eliot," in Allen Tate (ed.), *T. S. Eliot: The Man and His Work* (London: Chatto & Windus, 1967), p. 58.

53. Vivien Eliot, "Thé Dansant," *Criterion,* 3 October 1924.

54. VE Diary, 2 March 1919, Bodleian.

55. TSE to MH, 4 June 1917, Texas.

56. Vivien did not visit Bosham in 1919 until 14 June when she was "delighted to see it again," VE Diary, Bodleian.

57. TSE to MH, 16 May 1919, Texas.

58. VE to MH, n.d. ?May 1919, Texas.

59. Mary Hutchinson, "T. S. Eliot," unpublished biographical sketch, n.d., Texas.

60. "The Fire Sermon," *The Waste Land, CP,* p. 73.

61. T. Sharpe, *T. S. Eliot* (London: Macmillan, 1991), p. 63.

62. *CP,* p. 39.

63. TSE to MH, "Sunday," ?15 June 1919, Texas, *Letters I,* p. 302.

64. *Diary of Virginia Woolf,* op. cit., 16 May 1919, p. 272.

65. VE to MH, n.d., ?June 1919, Texas.

66. VE to MH, n.d., ?June 1919, Texas.

67. VE Diary, 14 June 1919, Bodleian.

68. VE to OM, ?25 June 1919, Texas, *Letters I,* p. 307.

69. VE to OM, ?4 June 1919, Texas, *Letters I,* p. 301.

70. VE to MH, "Thursday," ?26 June 1919, Texas.

71. VE to MH, "Wed.," ?early July 1919, Texas.

72. Ibid.

73. VE to MH, 16 July 1919, Texas, *Letters I*, p. 320.

74. VE to MH, ?late July 1919, Texas.

75. TSE to Henry Ware Eliot Jr., 2 July 1919, *Letters I*, p. 310.

76. TSE to MH, ?11 July 1919, Texas, *Letters I*, p. 317.

77. In 1927 Mary spent at least one night with Vita Sackville-West, see V. Glendinning, *Vita: The Life of Vita Sackville-West* (London: Penguin, 1984), p. 178. Dr. David Bradshaw states that it is clear from their letters to her in the Mary Hutchinson Collection, Texas, that "overlapping with her affair with Clive, Mary had also had relationships with both Aldous Huxley and his wife Maria," "Those Extraordinary Parakeets," *Charleston Magazine*, Part I, Autumn/Winter 1997, issue 16; Part II, Spring/Summer 1998, Issue 17.

78. Clive Bell to MH, 19 April 1918, quoted in Margaret Ratliff, "A Bloomsbury Friendship: The Correspondence of Mary Hutchinson and Lytton Strachey," *The Library Chronicle of the University of Texas at Austin,* no. 48 (1989), p. 199.

79. Hermione Lee cites a letter from Clive Bell to MH, 20 October 1922, Texas; Hermione Lee, *Virginia Woolf* (London: Vintage, 1997), note 383.

80. VE to MH, 1 September 1919, Texas.

81. MH to Lytton Strachey, 31 July 1927, Texas.

82. MH to Maria Huxley, 1 August 1925, Hutchinson Papers, Texas.

83. Mary Hutchinson, unpublished memoir of Aldous Huxley, Texas.

84. Ratliff, op. cit., ch. 5, p. 224.

85. VE to MH, n.d., ?September 1919, Texas.

86. VE Diary, 31 August 1919, Bodleian.

87. VE to MH, 3 October 1919, Texas, *Letters I*, p. 338.

88. VE to MH, 8 May 1919, Texas.

89. VE to MH, 20 March 1919, Texas.

90. VE to MH, 26 September 1919, Texas, *Letters I*, p. 334.

91. Ronald Schuchard, *Eliot's Dark Angel: Intersection of Life and Art* (Oxford: OUP, 1999), p. 50.

92. VE to MH, 29 October 1919, Texas, *Letters I*, p. 342.

93. Tate Gallery Archives, quoted in Bradshaw, op. cit., p. 29.

94. Bell, *The Diary of Virginia Woolf,* op. cit., vol. 4, p. 230.

95. VE to MH, n.d., ?November 1919, Texas.

12. Breakdown

1. TSE to C. C. Eliot, 15 February 1920, *Letters I*, p. 365.

2. Charlotte C. Eliot settled at 27 Concord Avenue, Cambridge, Massachusetts.

3. Anne Olivier Bell (ed.), *The Diary of Virginia Woolf, vol. 2, 1920–1924* (London: Penguin, 1981), p. 67, 19 September 1920; see also Hermione Lee, *Virginia Woolf* (London: Vintage, 1997), pp. 439–40.

4. TSE to Henry Eliot, 15 February 1920, *Letters I*, p. 363.

5. *CP*, p. 44.

6. T. S. Matthews, *Great Tom: Notes Towards the Definition of T. S. Eliot* (London: Weidenfeld & Nicolson, 1974), p. 62.

7. Charles Doyle, *Richard Aldington: A Biography* (London: Macmillan, 1989), p. 71.

8. TSE to C. C. Eliot, 27 July 1920, *Letters I*, p. 393.

9. When Scofield Thayer sent Aiken's *House of Dust* to Eliot from *The Dial* for review he

wrote that "the workmen called in to build the house were Swinburne and myself, the Dust being provided by Conrad." He pointed to a quotation on p. 83 which appeared to be derived from *Prufrock,* and declined to review the book as it would "strain his friendship" with Aiken. TSE to Scofield Thayer, 17 October 1920, *Letters I,* p. 413.

10. Eliot wrote to John Quinn on 22 January 1920 that he did not want Knopf to publish Osbert Sitwell's poems at the same time as his, as "some of them are rather clever imitations of myself and other people." *Letters I,* p. 358.

11. TSE to Wyndham Lewis, ?16 April 1921, *Letters I,* p. 446.

12. Philip Ziegler, *Osbert Sitwell* (London: Chatto & Windus, 1998), pp. 68–69.

13. Peter Ackroyd, *Ezra Pound and His World* (London: Thames and Hudson, 1980), p. 57.

14. Donald Gallup, "The Lost Manuscripts of T. S. Eliot," *Times Literary Supplement,* 7 November 1968; quoted in Trosman, "T. S. Eliot and the Waste Land: Psychopathological Antecedents and Transformations," *Emotions and Behavior Monographs, 4* (University of Chicago, 1987), p. 208.

15. Caroline Behr, *T. S. Eliot: A Chronology of His Life and Works* (London: Macmillan, 1983), p. 21.

16. Matthews, op. cit., p. 65.

17. TSE to C. C. Eliot, 26 January 1920, *Letters I,* p. 359.

18. Ezra Pound to Hugh Walpole, 30 June 1920, in D. D. Paige (ed.), *The Letters of Ezra Pound 1907–1941* (London: Faber & Faber, 1951), p. 218.

19. TSE to Maxwell Bodenheim, 2 January 1921, *Letters I,* p. 431.

20. Henry Eliot to C. C. Eliot, 30 October 1921, Houghton, quoted in Lyndall Gordon, *T. S. Eliot: An Imperfect Life* (London: Vintage, 1998), p. 171.

21. Charles W. Eliot to TSE, 25 July 1919, Houghton, *Letters I,* p. 322.

22. Richard Aldington, *Life for Life's Sake* (New York: Viking Press, 1941), quoted in Behr, op. cit., p. 20.

23. Journal of Lady Ottoline Morrell, 7 December 1919, Goodman Papers.

24. Lee, op. cit., p. 439.

25. *Diary of Virginia Woolf,* op. cit., vol. 1, 18 September 1928, p. 197.

26. David Bradshaw, "Those Extraordinary Parakeets," *Charleston Magazine,* Part I, Autumn/Winter 1997, issue 16; Part II, Spring/Summer 1998, issue 17.

27. Herbert Read, "T.S.E.—A Memoir," in Allen Tate, *T. S. Eliot: The Man and His Work* (London: Chatto & Windus, 1967), p. 23.

28. VE to OM, n.d. (?December 1919), Texas.

29. Bell, *The Diary of Virginia Woolf,* op. cit., vol. 1, 16 May 1919, p. 272.

30. Bell, *The Diary of Virginia Woolf,* op. cit., vol. 2, 1920–24, p. 87.

31. VE Diary, 22 July 1919, Bodleian.

32. Clive Bell to M. Hutchinson, 23 September 1917, Texas.

33. Journal of Lady Ottoline Morrell, 16 March 1920, Goodman Papers.

34. Matthews, op. cit., p. 55.

35. TSE to C. C. Eliot, 22 February 1920, *Letters I,* p. 368.

36. Bell, *The Diary of Virginia Woolf,* op. cit., vol. 2, p. 281.

37. Richard Aldington to TSE, 18 July 1919, Houghton, *Letters I,* p. 321.

38. Middleton Murry's book, *The Critic in Judgment,* had attracted even more severe reviews than Eliot's *Poems.* Virginia Woolf's story, *Kew Gardens,* published like the other two by The Hogarth Press on 12 May 1919, had been received more favourably.

39. Bell, *The Diary of Virginia Woolf,* op. cit., vol. 2, p. 15.

40. *Letters I,* pp. 168–69.

41. TSE to Professor Woods, *Letters I,* p. 171.

42. Virginia Woolf to VE, 20 July 1920, Nigel Nicolson and Joanne Trautmann (eds.), *The Letters of Virginia Woolf, vol. II* (London: Hogarth Press, 1976), p. 436.

43. Virginia Woolf to TSE, 28 July 1920, in ibid., p. 437.

44. Virginia Woolf to Vanessa Bell, 15? September, in ibid., p. 444.

45. Virginia Woolf to TSE, 15 September 1920, in ibid., p. 443.

46. Bernard Bergonzi, *T. S. Eliot* (London: Macmillan, 1972), p. 70.

47. Ibid., p. 71.

48. VE to OM, n.d. (?December 1919), Texas.

49. TSE to OM, 10 April 1920, *Letters I,* p. 379.

50. Read, op. cit., p. 32.

51. TSE to MH, "Wed." 1920, Texas.

52. TSE to MH, "Wed." 1920, Texas.

53. TSE to MH, "Sunday" 1920, Texas.

54. TSE to MH, "Monday" 1920, Texas.

55. TSE to MH, "Thursday" 1920, Texas.

56. Behr, op. cit., p. 19.

57. TSE to Ezra Pound, ?June 1920, *Letters I,* p. 385.

58. TSE to C. C. Eliot, 27 July 1920, Houghton, *Letters I,* p. 393.

59. TSE to C. C. Eliot, 9 August 1920, *Letters I,* p. 399.

60. P. Wyndham Lewis, *Blasting and Bombardiering* (London: Calder & Boyars, 1967), pp. 270–75.

61. Wyndham Lewis, "Early London Environment," R. March and Tambimuttu, *T. S. Eliot: A Symposium* (London: P. L. Editions, 1948), p. 30.

62. TSE to C. C. Eliot, 20 September 1920, *Letters I,* p. 408.

63. There was an awkward encounter in May 1921 at the Private View of the Picasso Exhibition in Paris, witnessed by Vanessa Bell, when Juana and her aunt arrived, only to come face to face with Jack, Mary and Clive.

64. Clive Bell to Mary Hutchinson, quoted in Margaret Ratliff, "The Correspondence of Mary Hutchinson: A New Look at Bloomsbury, Eliot and Huxley," thesis (University of Texas at Austin, 1991), p. 204.

65. Vanessa Bell to Roger Fry, 25 May 1921, Regina Marler (ed.), *Selected Letters of Vanessa Bell* (New York: Pantheon Books, 1993), pp. 249, 250.

66. TSE to MH, 22 September 1920, Texas, *Letters I,* p. 409.

67. TSE to MH, 28 September 1920, Texas, *Letters I,* p. 410.

68. "Fanny Marlow," "Fête Galante," *Criterion iii* (July 1925), pp. 557–63.

69. TSE to MH, "June," n.d., Texas.

70. Journal of Lady Ottoline Morrell, 16 March 1920, Goodman Papers.

71. VE to MH, 28? September 1920, Texas, *Letters I,* p. 411.

72. Letter from Abigail Eliot, 12 June 1965, quoted in programme of *Tom and Viv.*

73. VE to MH, 25 October 1920, Texas.

74. VE to MH, "11 o'clock," Texas.

75. TSE to C. C. Eliot, 31 October 1920, *Letters I,* p. 418.

76. VE to MH, n.d., ?December 1920, Texas.

77. VE to MH, 22 November 1920, Texas.

78. Charles Dickens, *Our Mutual Friend,* chapter xvi: "Sloppy is a beautiful reader of a news-

paper. He do the Police in different voices." Valerie Eliot (ed.), *The Waste Land: A Facsimile and Transcript of the Original Drafts including the Annotations of Ezra Pound* (New York: Harcourt Brace Jovanovich, 1971), note 125.

79. TSE to John Quinn, 5 November 1919, *Letters I,* p. 343.

80. Behr, op. cit., p. 20.

81. TSE to C. C. Eliot, 22 January 1921, *Letters I,* p. 432.

82. TSE to MH, 3 February 1921, *Letters I,* p. 435.

83. TSE to Brigit Patmore, 17 March 1921, *Letters I,* p. 441.

84. Richard Aldington, *Stepping Heavenward. A Record* (Florence: 1931), pp. 47, 48.

85. Conrad Aiken, who was lunching regularly in the City with Eliot in 1920, noted that he always carried his pocket Dante with him. Conrad Aiken, "An Anatomy of Melancholy," in Allen Tate op. cit., p. 194.

86. T. S. Eliot as Gus Krutsch, "Song to the Opherian," *Tyro,* May 1920. Eliot's choice of pseudonym seems significant. In the *Swanee Review* (vol. Lxxiv, No. 1, Special issue, Winter 1966), Francis Noel traces the influence of Petronius's *Satyricon* on *The Waste Land,* noting that "Gus Krutzsch" is "remarkably reminiscent of the English of 'Encolpius,' namely the Crutch or Crotch." "Encolpius" in the *Satyricon* may be translated as "Mr. Encrotch, an appropriate choice for the protagonist of a predominantly sexual story." See Valerie Eliot (ed.), *WL Facs,* op. cit., p. 125, note 8. Seven of the thirteen lines of "Song for the Opherian" appeared later, slightly revised, in Eliot's poem "The wind sprang up at four o'clock."

87. Joseph Conrad, *Heart of Darkness* (London: Wordsworth, 1995), pp. 84–87, 97.

88. T. S. Eliot, *The Sacred Wood,* (New York: Dover Publications Inc., 1998), pp. 30–32.

89. Eliot wrote on *The Duchess of Malfi* for *Art and Letters,* Winter 1919/20.

90. TSE to C. C. Eliot, 6 March 1921, *Letters I,* p. 438.

91. TSE to C. C. Eliot, 31 October 1920, *Letters I,* p. 417.

92. Maurice Haigh-Wood, interview with Michael Hastings, 25 January 1980.

93. VE Diary, 13 December 1935, Bodleian.

94. Bell, *The Diary of Virginia Woolf,* op. cit., vol. 2, p. 77.

95. Visitors' Books of Lady Ottoline Morrell, Garsington Manor, 1921.

96. Journal of Lady Ottoline Morrell, August 1921, Goodman Papers.

97. Osbert Sitwell, unpublished memoir, 19 February 1950, Texas.

98. Quoted in Lyndall Gordon, *T. S. Eliot,* op. cit., p. 171.

99. Michael Hastings, "The Haigh-Woods: The Story of a Family," Introduction in programme for *Tom and Viv,* 3 February 1984.

100. C. C. Eliot to H. Eliot, 8 April 1922, Houghton, quoted by Paul Delany, "T. S. Eliot's Personal Finances, 1915–1929," in *Literature, Money and the Market from Trollope to Amis* (Basingstoke: Palgrave, 2001), p. 260.

101. T. S. Eliot, *The Family Reunion* (London: Faber & Faber, 1939), pp. 20, 21.

102. Giles Evans draws attention to these lines in *Wishwood Revisited: A New Interpretation of T. S. Eliot's "The Family Reunion"* (Lewes: The Book Guild, 1991), p. 32.

103. C. C. Eliot, Memorandum on T. S. Eliot, 1921, prepared for family record of the descendants of William G. and Abigail A. Eliot, Houghton.

104. Mary Lilian Share married Harold Sidney Harmsworth, first Viscount Rothermere (1868–1940) in 1893. He was the younger brother of Alfred Harmsworth, Viscount Northcliffe, who founded the *Daily Mail* (1896) and the *Daily Mirror* (1903). Rothermere took over the *Mirror* in 1914 and was made a viscount in 1919.

105. TSE to OM, 14 July 1921, Texas, *Letters I,* p. 461.

106. VE to Scofield Thayer, 20 July 1921, Beinecke, *Letters I*, p. 462.

107. VE to H. Eliot, 23 August 1921, Texas, *Letters I*, pp. 465–66.

108. H. Eliot to C. C. Eliot, 30 October 1921, Houghton, quoted in Gordon, *T. S. Eliot*, op. cit., p. 171.

109. VE to MH, n.d., Texas.

110. TSE to MH, 1 September 1921, Texas, *Letters I*, p. 467.

111. TSE to MH, postcard, n.d., ?Mid-September 1921, Texas.

112. Quoted in Doyle, op. cit., p. 76. Aldington had left his wife "H.D.," after she had a daughter by another man, for "Arabella" (Dorothy Yorke).

113. TSE to Richard Aldington, 16 September 1921, Texas, *Letters I*, p. 469.

114. In the September 1921 issue of *To-day* Aldington reviewed *The Sacred Wood,* which was published by Methuen with a dedication to H.W.E. (Henry Ware Eliot, TSE's father). Aldington described it as "the most original contribution to our critical literature during the last decade." Other reviews were more disappointing.

115. TSE to Henry Eliot, 3 October 1921, Houghton, *Letters I*, p. 471.

116. VE to MH, n.d., ?December 1921, Texas.

117. TSE to Richard Aldington, 13 October 1921, Texas, *Letters I*, p. 476.

118. VE to Scofield Thayer, 13 October 1921, Beinecke, *Letters I*, p. 478.

119. VE to Violet Schiff, 26 October 1921, British Library, *Letters I*, p. 479.

120. Ibid.

121. Miranda Seymour, *Ottoline Morrell: Life on the Grand Scale* (London: Hodder & Stoughton, 1992), p. 415.

122. TSE to Sydney Schiff, Friday night (?4 November 1921), *Letters I*, p. 484.

123. VE to Bertrand Russell, 1 November 1921, *Letters I*, pp. 482–83.

124. VE to OM, "Monday," n.d., from 39 Inverness Terrace, W2, Texas.

13. The Waste Land

1. VE to MH, "Tuesday," ?November 1921, Texas.

2. VE to MH, 16 November 1921, Texas.

3. Charles Norman, *Ezra Pound* (London: MacDonald, 1969), pp. 243–49.

4. Scofield Thayer to VE, 27 July 1921, Beinecke.

5. ST to VE, 20 October 1921, Beinecke.

6. Humphrey Carpenter, *A Serious Character: The Life of Ezra Pound* (London: Faber & Faber, 1988), p. 415.

7. VE to Henry Eliot, 22 October 1918, *Letters I*, p. 245.

8. TSE to OM, 1 May ?1925. Vivien's poem "Necesse est Perstare" was published in the *Criterion,* April 1925.

9. OM to Dorothy Brett, n.d., 1916, Texas.

10. TSE to Richard Aldington, 4 July 1922, Texas.

11. Vivien Eliot, "A Diary of the Rive Gauche," *Criterion,* vol. III, no. 10 (December), January 1925, pp. 290–94.

12. TSE to OM, 14 March 1933, Texas.

13. TSE to Richard Aldington, 6 November 1921, Texas, *Letters I*, p. 486.

14. Bertrand Russell to OM, n.d., quoted in Donald E. Stanford, "The First Mrs. Eliot," *The Library Chronicle of the University of Texas at Austin,* New Series 40, 1987, p. 89.

15. VE to St. John Hutchinson, 8 December 1935, Texas.

16. TSE to Julian Huxley, 26 October 1921, in Valerie Eliot (ed.), Introduction to *WL Facs* (Harcourt Brace, 1971), p. xxii.

17. Mary Trevelyan, "The Pope of Russell Square 1938–1958," unpublished memoir, 1954. See Chapter 22 for a discussion of Eliot's "voices."

18. Harry Trosman, MD, "T. S. Eliot and the Waste Land: Psychopathological Antecedents and Transformations," *Emotions and Behavior Monographs,* 1987, no. 4 pp. 191–218.

19. T. S. Eliot, 1933, quoted in Trosman, ibid., p. 214.

20. Robert Gathorne-Hardy (ed.), *Ottoline: The Early Memoirs of Lady Ottoline Morrell* (London: Faber & Faber, 1964), p. 237.

21. Huxley remained sceptical about the claim that Vittoz could feel his brain vibrations, although he did feel that he "got a little more control over my depression." Trosman, op. cit., p. 205.

22. TSE to OM, 30 November 1921, Texas.

23. TSE to Henry Eliot, 13 December 1921, Lausanne, *Letters I,* p. 493.

24. Edmund Wilson, "The Poetry of Drouth," *The Dial,* vol. 73, December 1922, pp. 611–14.

25. Edmund Wilson, "Philoctetes: The Wound and the Bow," in *The Wound and the Bow, Seven Studies in Literature* (Athens: Ohio University Press, 1997 [first pub. 1929]), with an introduction by Janet Groth, p. 223. See also Grover Smith Jr., *T. S. Eliot's Poetry and Plays* (University of Chicago Press, 1956).

26. Eliot had read Jessie L. Weston's *From Ritual to Romance.* She linked the Fisher King to an ancient fertility god, identified with Nature itself, arguing that the lance and the grail were sexual symbols, and the adventure in Chapel Perilous an initiation rite. According to Jessie Weston, the worship of the Fisher King was part of the popular Persian cult of Mithraism brought north to Gaul and Britain by Roman legionnaires; when Christianity prevailed, the cult went underground.

27. Virginia Woolf to David Garnett, 20 October 1922, Nigel Nicholson and Joanne Trautmann (eds.), *The Letters of Virginia Woolf, vol. 2, 1912–1922* (New York: Harcourt Brace Jovanovich, 1976), p. 572.

28. From the *Satyricon* of Petronius. The new epigraph replaced Eliot's original choice from Joseph Conrad's *Heart of Darkness.* Valerie Eliot (ed.), *WL Facs,* op. cit., p. 126.

29. Wilson cites the Vedic hymns, Buddha, the Psalms, Ezekiel, Ecclesiastes, Luke, Sappho, Virgil, Ovid, Petronius, the Pervigilium Veneris, St. Augustine, Dante, the Grail Legends, early English poetry, Kyd, Spenser, Shakespeare, John Day, Webster, Middleton, Milton, Goldsmith, Gérard de Nerval, Froude, Baudelaire, Verlaine, Swinburne, Wagner, *The Golden Bough,* Miss Weston's book, various popular ballads, and TSE's earlier poems.

30. Hugh Kenner, *The Invisible Poet: T. S. Eliot* (London: W. H. Allen, 1960), p. 125.

31. "I regret having sent so many readers off on a wild goose chase after Tarot cards and the Holy Grail." T. S. Eliot, *The Frontiers of Criticism* (Minneapolis: University of Minnesota Press, 1956), quoted in James E. Miller, *T. S. Eliot's Personal Waste Land: Exorcism of the Demons* (Philadelphia: University of Pennsylvania Press, 1977), p. 93.

32. A. David Moody, *Thomas Stearns Eliot, Poet* (Cambridge: 1979), p. 79.

33. John T. Mayer, *T. S. Eliot's Silent Voices* (Oxford: OUP, 1989), p. 241.

34. Valerie Eliot (ed.), *WL Facs,* op. cit., p. 1.

35. "Did he live his life again in every detail of desire, temptation, and surrender during that supreme moment of complete knowledge? He cried in a whisper at some image, at some vision—he cried out twice, a cry that was no more than a breath—'The horror! the hor-

ror!.' " Joseph Conrad, *Heart of Darkness,* quoted by Valerie Eliot (ed.), *WL Facs,* op. cit., p. 3.

36. T. S. Eliot, *On Poetry and Poets,* (London: Faber & Faber, 1957), pp. 107–8, quoted in Miller, op. cit., p. 43.

37. Norman, op. cit., p. 351, argues that the foreign phrases were not the portents of the collapse of Western civilisation as some critics afterwards said, but the talk of patients.

38. Robert Sencourt, *T. S. Eliot: A Memoir,* edited by Donald Adamson and L. P. Addison (London: Garnstone Press, 1971), pp. 40, 41.

39. Valerie Eliot (ed.), *WL Facs,* op. cit., note, p. 126.

40. John Peter, "A New Interpretation of *The Waste Land,*" *Essays in Criticism,* 2 (July 1952), p. 245.

41. Miller, op. cit., p. 2.

42. John Peter, "Postscript," *Essays in Criticism,* 19, (April 1969), pp. 165–66.

43. T. S. Eliot editorial, "A Commentary," *The Criterion,* April 1934.

44. Similar lines occur in French in an earlier poem, "Dans le Restaurant": "Phlebas the Phoenician, suspended 15 days drowned,/Forgot the cries of sea gulls and the surge of Cornwall . . . Nevertheless, he was once a handsome man, and tall," quoted in Miller, op. cit., p. 111. See Grover Smith, "Observations on Eliot's 'Death by Water,' *Accent 6* (Summer 1946), pp. 257–63, for speculations on the sexual connotations of the section, including the origin of the name Phlebas, which Smith believed to be derived from the Greek "phlép: phlebós," a vein. "But even more remarkable," writes Smith, "is the fact that the Greek word has another meaning, which is the same as that of 'phallos' . . . it confirms my theory that the Phoenician Sailor represents the commerce of lust."

45. Miller, op. cit., pp. 68, 69, Valerie Eliot (ed.), *WL Facs,* p. 93.

46. Richard Wagner, *Tristan und Isolde,* Scene 2, lines 1–4.

47. The character of Mr. Scogan, who impersonates Sesostris the Sorceress in *Chrome Yellow,* is based on Bertrand Russell. Informed readers of *The Waste Land* would have recognised Russell as Madame Sosostris, who in the first draft was a "clairvoyant," later changed to "clairvoyante."

48. John Peter, "A New Interpretation . . .," op. cit., pp. 247–48.

49. Valerie Eliot (ed.), *WL Facs,* op. cit., "He Do The Police in Different Voices," Part 1, "The Burial of the Dead," pp. 6–9. Eliot said he associated "the man with three staves" from the Tarot pack, "quite arbitrarily, with the Fisher King himself." Notes to *The Waste Land,* p. 147.

50. Helen Gardner, *The Art of T. S. Eliot* (London: Faber & Faber, 1949), p. 172. "As in the *Waste Land,* it is by 'the awful daring of a moment's surrender' that we exist, by praying . . . The meaningless monotony and pointless waste of living finds its purpose in the Virgin's words: 'Be it unto me according to thy word.' "

51. Valerie Eliot (ed.), *WL Facs,* p. 77.

52. There are several versions of the line: "My friend, my blood, shaking within my heart," is another. Ibid.

53. Ibid., "Dirge," p. 123.

54. The first of "Doris's Dream Songs" was republished as "Eyes that last I saw in tears," *CP,* p. 147; and the other two became incorporated in "The Hollow Men," p. 87.

55. T. S. Eliot, "Doris's Dream Songs," I, II, III, *The Chapbook, A Miscellany* (No. 39), November 1924.

56. Valerie Eliot points out that there is no such word as "Opherian," and it is possible that

Eliot meant "Orpharion," a musical instrument known as the "poor man's lute" (*WL Facs,* p. 130). In an interesting discussion, Mayer (op. cit.) speculates that "the Opherion is a split-self symbol . . . of Eliot himself, who, as Gus Krutzsch, bleeds between two worlds, that of the *August* Spirit and the real *crotch,* combining lover and uncertain artist, person and . . . ineffective instrument . . ." The mythical Orpheus entered the world of shades to rescue his wife Eurydice, which he was allowed to do on condition that he did not look back; to do so condemned her to remain in hell—as Vivien is condemned because Eliot looks back to Verdenal. The poem focuses on the love that is looked back upon. Similarly the allusion to Arion emphasises the backward glance to a beloved friend from the past; Arion was a musician and favourite of Periander, King of Corinth, whom he left to travel overseas, despite Periander's pleas. Arion is abandoned at sea to die, but his song casts a spell on a dolphin, which saves him and reunites him with Periander. It is another myth which for Eliot would have had parallels with his relationship with Verdenal, both men being separated unwillingly by journeys over water. See Mayer, op. cit., pp. 257–58.

57. Valerie Eliot (ed.), *WL Facs,* p. 99, published in *The Tyro* (April 1921) by "Gus Krutsch." This poem contains Eliot's line, comparing the river to "a face that sweats with tears," which Pound cut from *The Waste Land.*

58. Miller, op. cit., pp. 17, 18.

59. Mayer, op. cit., p. 206.

60. Alan Ansen, *The Table Talk of W. H. Auden* (London: Faber & Faber, 1991), p. 54.

61. "The Death of the Duchess," Valerie Eliot (ed.), *WL Facs,* pp. 105–7.

62. Vivien Eliot, "The Paralysed Woman," unpublished short story, 1922, Bodleian.

63. Elizabeth M. Brennan (ed.), John Webster, *The Duchess of Malfi* (London and Tonbridge: Ernest Ben), p. 45, III, ii, lines 69–70.
    You have cause to love me, I entered you into my heart
    Before you would vouchsafe to call for the keys.

64. TSE to Henny Ware Eliot Senior, 23 July 1915, *Letters I,* p. 110.

65. E. W. F. Tomlin, *T. S. Eliot: A Friendship* (London: Routledge, 1988), p. 230. Valerie Eliot confirms that Eliot restored the line from memory in 1960, *WL Facs,* p. 126.

66. Valerie Eliot (ed.), *WL Facs,* op. cit., p. 107.

67. Eliot suggested his inspiration came from the game of chess in Thomas Middleton's *Women, Beware Women* (c. 1623).

68. VE as "F. M.," "Letters of the Moment—1," *Criterion,* vol. 2, no. vi (February 1924), pp. 220–22.

69. VE n.d., writing book, Bodleian.

70. Vivien portrays herself as "Sybilla" or "Sibylla" in unpublished stories, "The Paralysed Woman" (1922) and "Médecine à la Mode," n.d., and in "Thé Dansant" (1924), and "Fête Galante," (1925) in *Criterion.*

71. Valerie Eliot (ed.), *WL Facs,* op. cit., p. 11.

72. Valerie Eliot (ed.), *WL Facs,* op. cit., p. 11; see also Mayer, op. cit., p. 264.

73. *WL Facs,* op. cit., p. 13: This is another reference to the doomed Paolo and Francesca, to whom Eliot compared himself and Vivien. They are in the second circle of Hell, among the souls of the lustful: ". . . the two that go together and seem so light upon the wind." Dante, *Inferno,* v, lines 73–75. See Valerie Eliot's note, *WL Facs,* p. 126.

74. VE to MH, 27 September 1928, Texas.

75. Mary Trevelyan, "The Pope of Russell Square 1938–1954," November 1942.

76. Mayer points out that in *Metamorphoses* Ovid relates that Apollo vows to keep Hyacinth

with him in memory and in his poetry: " 'You will be/With me forever, and my songs and music/Will tell of you, and you will be reborn/As a new flower.' Eliot mentions both the flower (lowercase hyacinth) and the myth (uppercase Hyacinth)." Mayer op. cit., p. 255.

77. Valerie Eliot (ed.), *WL Facs,* p. 148.

78. Viola Tree, "Mayfair and Bohemia," *Criterion,* vol. 3, no. 10, January 1925.

79. Aldous Huxley, untitled poem, 14 February 1927, quoted in Margaret Ratliff, "The Correspondence of Mary Hutchinson: A New Look at Bloomsbury, Eliot and Huxley," thesis (University of Texas at Austin, 1991), ch. 5, "Mary Hutchinson and the Huxleys," p. 221.

80. Mary Hutchinson to Lytton Strachey, 3 August 1917, Texas.

81. Osbert Sitwell, unpublished memoir on TSE and his marriage, 19 February 1950, Texas.

82. Valerie Eliot (ed.), *WL Facs,* op. cit., p. 15.

83. VE to MH, n.d., ?1922, Texas.

84. Miller, op. cit., p. 87.

85. Valerie Eliot (ed.), *WL Facs,* op. cit., p. 23.

86. Ibid.

87. Valerie Eliot (ed.), *WL Facs,* op. cit., pp. 23, 27.

88. T. S. Eliot, *Selected Essays* (London: Faber & Faber, 1932), pp. 234–35. Quoted by John Peter, "Postscript" to his "A New Interpretation of *The Waste Land,*" *Essays in Criticism,* 19 (April 1969).

89. Miller argues that the "effect of the original passage is to lend emphasis to the Eugenides encounter, with the frantic singing of the nightingale in a fragmentary context, coming immediately after it, highly suggestive as to some obscure and sordid consummation, some kind of hasty and covert fulfillment of the poet's momentary need." Miller, op. cit., p. 97. See Valerie Eliot (ed.), *WL Facs,* op. cit., p. 31: "London, the swarming life you kill and breed,/Huddled between the concrete and the sky;/Responsive to the momentary need . . ." follows the sudden interjection, "Twit twit twit/Jug jug jug jug jug jug/Tereu" of the "rudely forc'd" Philomel.

90. John Peale Bishop to Edmund Wilson, November 1922, 28 rue de la Rochefoucauld, Paris, Edmund Wilson Papers, Yale. I am indebted to Brian Breman at University of Texas for drawing my attention to this letter.

91. "The Fire Sermon" in Valerie Eliot (ed.), *WL Facs,* op. cit., p. 53. T. S. Eliot's note is on p. 148.

92. Peter, "A New Interpretation . . . ," op. cit., pp. 259–60.

93. Eliot, *Selected Essays,* op. cit., pp. 374–75.

94. Valerie Eliot (ed.), *WL Facs,* op. cit., p. 85. Eliot recalled, in his notes to *The Waste Land,* that during one of Shackleton's Antarctic expeditions the explorers, at the extremity of their strength, had the constant delusion that there was one more member than could be actually counted. See *WL Facs,* p. 148.

95. Ibid., p. 79.

96. Jessie Weston writes of the initiation ritual in the Chapel: "the Mystery ritual comprised a double initiation, the Lower, into the mysteries of generation, i.e. of physical Life; the higher, into the Spiritual Divine Life, where man is made one with God." See Mayer, op. cit., p. 284.

97. See Peter, "A New Interpretation . . . ," op. cit., p. 265. See also Miller, op. cit., pp. 39, 131.

98. T. S. Eliot, *The Use of Poetry and the Use of Criticism* (Harvard: Harvard University Press, 1986), p. 119.

99. Valerie Eliot (ed.), *WL Facs,* op. cit., p. 117.

100. Thomas Kyd, *The Spanish Tragedy* (London: Penguin, 1998). Hieronymo, an antecedent of Shakespeare's "Hamlet," is driven nearly mad with grief after his son is murdered. His life became an "endless Tragedie," as Eliot felt his own to be.

14. A Wild Heart in a Cage

1. Ezra Pound to TSE, 24 Saturnus An 1 (24 December 1921), *Letters I,* p. 497.

2. TSE to EP, ?24 January 1922, *Letters I,* p. 504.

3. EP to TSE, ?27 January 1922, *Letters I,* p. 505. Pound addressed Eliot as "Filio dilecto mihi, my beloved son."

4. "Eliot's *Waste Land* is I think the justification of the 'movement' of our modern experiment since 1900." EP to Felix Scheling, *Letters I,* pp. 180–81. Pound cut three poems: "Exequy," with its confessional lines "SOVEGNA VOS AL TEMPS DE MON DOLOR/Consiros vei la pasada folor (Be mindful in due time of my pain/In thought I see my past madness," from Eliot's favourite Canto XXVI of Dante's *Purgatorio,* the canto of "the lustful," (facs 130); "Elegy"; and "Dirge."

5. Ezra Pound, "Sage Homme": a humorous poem sent by Pound to Eliot on 24 December 1922, in which he described himself as the midwife of *The Waste Land.*

6. VE to Mary Hutchinson, 12 January 1922, Hotel du Bon Lafontaine, Paris, Texas.

7. TSE to EP, ?24 January 1922, *Letters I,* p. 504.

8. EP to TSE, ?27 January 1922, *Letters I,* p. 505.

9. Philip Hoare, *Oscar Wilde's Last Stand* (New York: Arcade Publishing Inc., 1977), p. 109.

10. MH to Lytton Strachey, 9 September 1927, Texas.

11. Michel Foucault, *The History of Sexuality: An Introduction* (Harmondsworth: Penguin, 1984), p. 43.

12. Lytton Strachey to Dora Carrington, 3 June 1923, Michael Holroyd, *Lytton Strachey* (London: Vintage, 1995), p. 856.

13. Hoare, op. cit., p. 90.

14. Joan Smith, *Moralities: Sex, Money and Power in the Twenty-first Century* (London: Penguin Press, 2001), p. 110.

15. Hoare, op. cit., p. 126.

16. Hoare, op. cit., p. 188.

17. Foucault, op. cit., p. 101.

18. Louis Stanley, *Public Masks & Private Faces* (London: Quartet Books, 1986), p. 59.

19. TSE to John Quinn, 15 June 1922 and 19 July 1922, in B. L. Reid, *The Man from New York: John Quinn and His Friends* (New York: Oxford University Press, 1968), pp. 534–35.

20. John Quinn to TSE, 28 July 1922, in Reid, op. cit.

21. TSE to Scofield Thayer, 20 January 1922, Pound Papers, Beinecke.

22. ST to TSE, 14 July 1921, Beinecke.

23. ST to TSE, 18 December 1921, Beinecke.

24. ST to TSE, 29 January 1922, Beinecke.

25. ST to TSE, 12 March 1922, Beinecke.

26. TSE to ST, 16 March 1922, Beinecke.

27. TSE to Sydney Schiff, 20 April 1922, British Library, *Letters I,* p. 522.

28. T. S. Eliot, "London Letter," May 1922, *The Dial,* vol. LXXII, Jan.–June 1922.

29. VE to MH, n.d., Texas.
30. TSE to OM, n.d., Texas.
31. TSE to Richard Aldington, 13 July 1922, *Letters I*, p. 541.
32. TSE to OM, n.d., ?early summer 1922, Texas.
33. EP to John Quinn, postmark 21 February 1922, Timothy Materer (ed.), *The Selected Letters of Ezra Pound to John Quinn 1915–1924* (Durham and London: Duke University Press, 1991), p. 206.
34. *Letters I*, p. xxvi.
35. EP to William Carlos Williams, 18 March 1922, D. D. Paige (ed.), *The Letters of Ezra Pound 1907–1941* (London: Faber & Faber, 1951), p. 238.
36. Bel Esprit circular, ibid., pp. 238–39.
37. Arsenic and bismuth compounds were the standard treatment for syphilis before the discovery of penicillin.
38. EP to JQ, 4–5 July 1922, Materer (ed.), *Selected Letters of Pound to Quinn*, op. cit., pp. 209–11.
39. TSE to OM, 26 April 1922, Texas.
40. Richard Aldington to Amy Lowell, 5 May 1922, Norman T. Gates (ed.), *Richard Aldington: An Autobiography in Letters* (Philadelphia: University of Pennsylvania Press, 1992), p. 67.
41. This letter has not been traced.
42. VE to Richard Aldington, n.d., ?Spring 1922, Texas, *Letters I*, pp. 543–44.
43. Thomas S. Szasz, MD, *The Myth of Mental Illness: Foundations of a Theory of Personal Conduct* (New York: Harper and Row, 1974) revised edition, pp. 111–21.
44. Bertrand Russell, *Autobiography, vol. 1* (London: George Allen & Unwin, 1968), p. 10.
45. John T. Mayer, *T. S. Eliot's Silent Voices* (Oxford: 1989), p. 185.
46. Szasz, op. cit., pp. 121–24. See also S. Freud, *On Psychopathology: Inhibitions, Symptoms and Anxiety and Other Works* (London: Penguin Freud Library, vol. 10, 1979), p. 99.
47. TSE to OM, "Castle Hotel, Tunbridge," n.d., ?April 1922, Texas.
48. TSE to OM, postcard of Lugano, 27 May 1922, Texas.
49. EP to JQ, 4 and 5 July 1922, Materer (ed.), *Selected Letters of Pound to Quinn*, op. cit., p. 210.
50. VE to EP, 27 June 1922, *Letters I*, pp. 532–33.
51. VE to Violet Schiff, 26 October 1921, British Library.
52. TSE to OM, 15 June 1922, Texas.
53. VE to EP, 27 June 1922, *Letters I*, p. 532.
54. TSE to OM, 15 June 1922, Texas.
55. TSE to Richard Aldington, 7 April 1921, Texas.
56. TSE to OM, 18 July 1922, Texas.
57. VE to MH, 16 November 1921, Texas.
58. VE to MH, 19 July 1922, Texas.
59. "Disorders of the digestive system due to psychological factors are common and they may mimic organic disease. Stress may be associated with a symptom such as dyspepsia ('indigestion'), abdominal discomfort or diarrhoea . . . Gastrointestinal functions . . . can alter with change in emotion. Patients with anxiety states may develop a wide range of alimentary symptoms such as dryness of the mouth, a feeling of a lump in the throat . . . anorexia, nausea, vomiting . . . abdominal pain, diarrhoea or constipation. Patients with a depressive illness may have similar complaints . . ." John Macleod (ed.), *Davidson's Principles and Practices of Medicine* (London: Churchill Livingstone, 1977), p. 418.

60. VE to OM, "2 Creed Cottages," n.d., ?summer 1922, Texas.

61. TSE to EP, 19 July 1922, *Letters I,* p. 549.

62. Evelyn Waugh, *The Ordeal of Gilbert Penfold* (first published London: Chapman & Hall, 1957; Penguin, 1962), pp. 23, 63, 138, 156. Waugh encouraged Muriel Spark, whose first novel *The Comforters* (1957) treated a similar theme of a Catholic novelist hearing voices and confessed to her that, as most of his friends knew, his novel was based on his own experience of auditory hallucinations. See Muriel Spark, *Curriculum Vitae* (London: Penguin, 1993), pp. 207–8.

63. VE to Sydney Schiff, "Sunday," ?April 1924, from 38 Burleigh Mansions, St. Martin's Lane, London WC2.

64. Virginia Woolf, "On Being Ill," *The Moment and Other Essays* (New York: Harcourt Brace & Co., 1947), pp. 11, 12.

65. Lyndall Gordon suggests (*T.S. Eliot: An Imperfect Life,* p. 216) that "Felice" may be based on Mary Hutchinson, but I feel Mary was too sophisticated to have been the model for "Felice," who does the chores in her overall. Vivien seems to have had a help/companion named Felise (*sic*) to whom she refers in a letter to Ottoline Morrell, n.d., saying she has "settled" with Felise, whom she can afford to keep if she gives up Ellen.

66. Vivien Eliot, "The Paralysed Woman," 1922, Bodleian.

67. Ibid.

68. Elaine Showalter, *Hystories: Hysterical Epidemics and Modern Culture* (London: Picador, 1997), p. 103. In a 1991 production of *Hedda Gabler,* influenced by feminist interpretations of hysteria, Deborah Warner and Fiona Shaw presented Hedda as a woman having a nervous breakdown.

69. VE to MH, 19 April 1923, Texas.

70. Vivien Eliot, "The Paralysed Woman," 1922, Bodleian.

71. Showalter, op. cit., p. 101.

72. VE to MH, "Thursday," August 1922, Texas.

73. The Hogarth Press published *The Waste Land* in September 1923. See introduction to Jan.–March 1923, Nigel Nicolson and Joanne Trautmann (eds.), *The Letters of Virginia Woolf, vol. III, 1923–28* (London: Hogarth Press, 1977), p. 1, and Anne Olivier Bell (ed.), *The Diary of Virginia Woolf,* vol. 2 (London: Hogarth Press, 1978), 23 June 1922, p. 178.

74. Virginia found *Ulysses* "an illiterate, underbred book," which seemed to her "the book of a self-taught working man, & we all know how distressing they are, how egotistic, raw, striking, & ultimately nauseating." Bell (ed.), *Diary of Virginia Woolf,* vol. 2, op. cit., p. 189.

75. "Great Tom," Bell (ed.), *The Diary of Virginia Woolf,* vol. 2, op. cit., p. 189. "If it were not for his wife's . . ." VW to Maynard Keynes, 12 Feb. 1923, Nicolson and Trautmann (eds.), *Letters of Virginia Woolf,* vol. 3, op. cit., pp. 11–12.

76. TSE to EP, 28 July 1922, *Letters I,* p. 553.

77. TSE to Richard Aldington, "Friday," ?1922, Texas.

78. TSE to RA, 30 June 1922, *Letters I,* p. 537.

79. TSE to RA, "Friday," ?end 1922, Texas.

80. Bell (ed.), *The Diary of Virginia Woolf,* vol. 2, op. cit., 3 August 1922, p. 187.

81. Ibid., 12 March 1922, p. 170.

82. Ibid., 27 September 1922, p. 204.

83. Ibid., 6 and 17 March 1923, pp. 238–39.

84. Osbert Sitwell, *Laughter in the Next Room* (London: Macmillan, 1949), pp. 15, 16.

85. Léonide Massine to OM, n.d., 38 Bloomsbury Street. Massine Papers, Texas.

86. Léonide Massine, *My Life in Ballet* (London: Macmillan, 1968), p. 137.

87. Sitwell, op. cit., p. 14.

88. TSE to MH, 28 April 1922, Texas, *Letters I,* p. 523.

89. TSE to MH, "Friday," postmark 24 June 1922, Texas, *Letters I,* p. 529.

15. *"Fanny Marlow"*

1. VE to OM, 15 September 1922, Texas, *Letters I,* p. 570.

2. VE to MH, postcard of Eglise St. Germain, 23 September 1922, Texas.

3. VE to MH, postcard of Lyon, 20 October 1922, Texas.

4. VE to MH, 21 October 1922, Texas.

5. TSE to MH, 7 October 1922, Texas.

6. TSE to MH, 18 June 1921, Texas.

7. TSE to MH, "Tuesday," n.d., ?late 1922, Texas.

8. Anne Chisholm, *Nancy Cunard* (London: Sidgwick & Jackson, 1979), p. 331.

9. Ibid., p. 163.

10. T. S. Eliot, "London Letter," *The Dial,* August 1921, p. 214, quoted in Lynn Garafola, *Diaghilev's Ballets Russes* (New York: Da Capo Press, 1998), pp. 338–39. Garafola remarks that allusions to the Russian ballet appear in many of TSE's writings.

11. T. S. Eliot, "Dramatis Personae," *Criterion,* April 1923, pp. 305–6.

12. Garafola, op. cit., p. 339.

13. Eliot, "Dramatis Personae," op. cit., p. 306.

14. Edward J. Dent, "Covent Garden: 'Pulcinella,' " *Athenaeum,* 18 June 1920, quoted in Garafola, op. cit., p. 341.

15. Garafola, op. cit., p. 242.

16. T. S. Matthews, *Great Tom: Notes Towards the Definition of T. S. Eliot* (London: Weidenfeld and Nicolson, 1974), p. 78.

17. "Personally I should not have cut out some of the parts that Pound advised you to cut out." Quinn to TSE, 26 February 1923, in B. L. Reid, *The Man from New York: John Quinn and His Friends* (New York: Oxford University Press, 1968), p. 580. Quinn immediately re-alised that the real value of the *Waste Land* manuscript lay in the fact that it was the only evidence of the difference which Pound's criticism made to the poem (p. 540). Eliot also gave Quinn the leather-bound notebook containing the Bolo and Colombo verses dating back to 1909, which, he told Quinn, "have never been printed and which I am sure you will agree ought never to be printed, and, in putting them in your hands, I beg you fervently to keep them to yourself and see that they are never printed" (21 September 1922).

18. Humphrey Carpenter, *A Serious Character: The Life of Ezra Pound* (London: Faber & Faber, 1988), p. 415. Pound was finally awarded the *Dial* prize in 1927.

19. Peter du Sautoy, "T. S. Eliot: Personal Reminiscences," in James Olney (ed.), *T. S. Eliot: Essays from The Southern Review* (Oxford: Clarendon Press, 1988), from *The Southern Review,* vol. 21, no. 4 (Autumn 1985), pp. 947–56.

20. Manuscript leaves from the 1909 notebook, Colombo and Bolo poems in ink and pencil, Pound Collection, Beinecke.

21. VE to Sydney Schiff, 16 October 1922, *Letters I,* p. 584.

22. Reid, op. cit., p. 538.

23. EP to John Quinn, 4–5 July 1922, Timothy Materer (ed.), *The Selected Letters of Ezra Pound to John Quinn 1915–1929* (Durham and London: Duke University Press, 1991), p. 209.

24. Quoted in John Pearson, *Façades: Edith, Osbert and Sacheverell Sitwell* (London: 1978), p. 176.

25. VE to EP, 2 November 1922, Lilly, *Letters I*, p. 588.

26. TSE to EP, 3 November 1922, Lilly, *Letters I*, p. 589.

27. VE to EP, 2 November 1922, *Letters I*, p. 588.

28. EP to TSE, 4 November 1922, *Letters I*, p. 589.

29. TSE to EP, 7 November 1922, *Letters I*, p. 592.

30. *Criterion,* April 1923, p. 307.

31. "Felix Morrison," "Mrs. Pilkington," in *Criterion,* October 1924, pp. 103–6; "Fanny Marlow," "Diary of the Rive Gauche," in *Criterion,* January 1925, pp. 291–97; "Fanny Marlow," "Diary of the Rive Gauche II," in *Criterion,* April 1925, pp. 425–29. Compare Katherine Mansfield, "Je Ne Parle Pas Français," *Bliss and Other Stories* (first pub. London: Constable, 1920; Penguin, 1962), p. 62. See also Lyndall Gordon, *T. S. Eliot: An Imperfect Life* (London: Vintage, 1998), p. 217.

32. EP to TSE, 4 November 1922, *Letters I*, p. 589.

33. VE to MH, n.d., 1919, Texas.

34. VE to MH, "November," ?1919, Texas.

35. Gordon, *T. S. Eliot,* op. cit., p. 193.

36. TSE to EP, 28 July 1922, *Letters I*, p. 553.

37. TSE to EP, n.d., 1927, Beinecke.

38. Carpenter, op. cit., p. 413.

39. VE to EP, n.d., ?1924, Beinecke.

40. TSE to Richard Aldington, 8 April 1924, Texas.

41. EP to John Quinn, 5 July 1922, Materer (ed.), *Selected Letters of Ezra Pound to John Quinn,* p. 209.

42. VE to OM, 15 September 1922, Texas, *Letters I*, p. 570.

43. Richard Aldington to Amy Lowell, 7 July 1922, Norman Gates (ed.), *Richard Aldington: An Autobiography in Letters* (Philadelphia: University of Pennsylvania Press, 1992), p. 69.

44. This receipt, June 1923, signed by TSE over two George V penny stamps, is in the Pound Collection, Beinecke.

45. *Liverpool Post,* 16 November 1922, cutting enclosed by TSE in a letter to RA, 18 November 1922, Texas.

46. TSE to RA, 18 November 1922, Texas.

47. Quoted in Hermione Lee, *Virginia Woolf* (London: Vintage, 1997), p. 442, from Anne Olivier Bell (ed.), *The Diary of Virginia Woolf,* vol. 2 (London: Hogarth Press, 1978), 22 March 1921, pp. 103–4.

48. Virginia Woolf to RA, 21 January 1923, Nigel Nicolson and Joanne Trautmann (eds.), *The Letters of Virginia Woolf,* vol. 3 (London: Hogarth Press, 1977), p. 7.

49. VW to OM, 21? January 1923, Nicolson and Trautmann (eds.), *The Letters of Virginia Woolf,* vol. 3, op. cit., p. 8.

50. VW to RA, 26 January 1923, in ibid., p. 9.

51. VE to MH, ?late 1922, Texas, *Letters I*, p. 587.

52. VW to Clive Bell, early February 1923, in Nicolson and Trautmann (eds.), *The Letters of Virginia Woolf,* vol. 3, op. cit., p. 11.

53. VW to Maynard Keynes, 12 February 1923, in ibid., p. 12.

54. VW to Lytton Strachey, 23 February 1923, in ibid., p. 14.
55. Anne Olivier Bell (ed.), *The Diary of Virginia Woolf,* vol. 2, op. cit., 19 February 1923, p. 236.
56. Ibid., 17 March 1923, p. 239.
57. VW to Vanessa Bell, ?12 March 1923, Nicolson and Trautmann (eds.), *Letters,* vol. 3, op. cit., p. 21.
58. VW to Maynard Keynes, 13 March 1923, in ibid., p. 20.
59. Bell (ed.), *The Diary of Virginia Woolf,* vol. 2, op. cit., 17 March 1923, p. 239.
60. Ibid., 23 March 1923, p. 240.
61. Gordon, *T. S. Eliot,* op. cit., pp. 197, 199.
62. Ibid., p. 198.
63. TSE to EP, 15 November 1922, *Letters I,* pp. 597–98.
64. TSE to Henry Eliot, 11 October 1922, *Letters I,* p. 579.
65. TSE to Richard Aldington, ?April, 1924, Texas.
66. T. S. Eliot, "On the Eve," in *Criterion,* January 1925. The style of this piece is typical of Vivien, and from the manuscript it seems unlikely that TSE did more than tinker with it.
67. TSE to EP, 7 November 1922, *Letters I,* p. 593.
68. VE to MH, 5 December 1922, Texas.
69. TSE to OM, 12 December 1922, Texas, *Letters I,* p. 611.
70. TSE to RA, 8 November 1922, *Letters I,* p. 594.
71. TSE to Henry Ware Eliot Jr., 31 December 1922, *Letters I,* p. 627.
72. TSE to OM, 5 January 1923, Texas.
73. John Pearson quotes Osbert Sitwell's unpublished memoir of Eliot, Texas, in *Façades,* op. cit., p. 239.
74. Sitwell memoir, op. cit., p. 14.
75. Pearson, op. cit., p. 239.
76. TSE to MH, postmark 1923, Texas.
77. RA to Harold Monro, 24 October 1920, Norman Gates (ed.), *Richard Aldington,* op. cit., p. 63.
78. TSE to VW, 2 April 1923, Berg.
79. TSE to MH, 23 March 1923, Texas.
80. TSE to OM, 2 March 1923, Texas.
81. VE to MH, 5 March 1923, Texas.
82. VE to MH, 5 March 1923, Texas.
83. TSE to OM, n.d., ?early April 1923, address "2 Milestone Cottages, Nr. Chi, Sussex," Texas.
84. Ibid.
85. TSE to MH, 3 April 1923, Texas.
86. TSE to MH, 26 and 30 April 1923, Texas.
87. TSE to OM, n.d., ?May 1923, Texas.
88. See Keith Thomas, *Religion and the Decline of Magic* (London: Penguin, 1973), pp. 209–51, for an explanation of the magical tradition.
89. Michel Foucault, *Madness and Civilization: A History of Insanity in the Age of Reason,* trans. Richard Howard (New York: Random House, 1965), pp. 274–75.
90. TSE to OM, n.d., "2 Milestone Cottages, Old Fishbourne," ?April 1923, Texas.
91. VE to OM, 28 May 1923, Texas.
92. VE to MH, 19 April 1923, Texas. In her entry for 13 June 1923, Virginia says she should

be writing to Vivien, and will do so "directly, on the instant." TSE mentions in a letter to Ottoline (n.d.) ?May 1923 that Vivien has received a "curious" letter from Virginia. He chides Ottoline for not writing to Vivien, who "hopes for a line."

93. VW to Roger Fry, 18 May 1923, Nicolson and Trautmann (eds.), *The Letters of Virginia Woolf,* vol. 3, op. cit., p. 38.

94. VE to MH, n.d., "2 Milestone Cottages, Old Fishbourne," ?May 1923, Texas.

95. TSE to MH, 9 August 1923, Texas.

96. TSE to MH, telegram, 10 August 1923, Texas.

97. Bell (ed.), *The Diary of Virginia Woolf,* vol. 2, op. cit., 17 July 1923, pp. 256–57.

98. VE to MH, pencil note, n.d., ?May 1923, Texas.

99. TSE to OM, p.m. 18 June 1923, Texas.

100. VW to TSE, 4 June 1923, Nicolson and Trautmann (eds.), *The Letters of Virginia Woolf,* vol. 3, p. 45. This was Virginia's first meeting with Edward Sackville-West, who was already a friend of TSE's.

101. VW to Jacques Raverat, 24 January 1925, in ibid., p. 155.

102. Bell (ed.), *The Diary of Virginia Woolf,* vol. 2, op. cit., 4 June 1923, pp. 243–44. Virginia visited Garsington on 2 June, Eliot a fortnight later.

103. Ibid., 19 February 1923. Philip Morrell had a son by his secretary, Alice Jones, in 1917, and another child by one of the Garsington maids in 1923.

104. TSE to OM, n.d., "The Criterion," paper, 9 Clarence Gate Gardens, ?May 1923, Texas.

105. VE to OM, pencil, n.d., ?June 1923, Texas.

106. TSE to OM, 10 July 1923, Texas.

16. Deceits and Desires

1. VE to MH, n.d., ?1923, Texas.

2. VE to OM, n.d., ?1923, Texas.

3. TSE to Dorothy Pound, 27 Oct.? 1923, Lilly.

4. TSE to VW, 22 May 1924, Monk's House Papers, Sussex.

5. TSE to OM, September 1923, Texas.

6. Untitled verse about Jack's "row" with Tom at 2 Milestone Cottages, Old Fishbourne, n.d.,?December 1923, loose-leaf book (MSS. Eng. Misc. c. 624), VE Papers, Bodleian.

7. Maurice Haigh-Wood, quoted in Michael Hastings, *Tom and Viv* (London: Penguin, 1985), p. 51.

8. Untitled verses about Jack, ?December 1923, MSS Eng. Misc. c. 624, loose-leaf book, VE Papers, Bodleian.

9. VE to VW, "Sunday 5th" 1923, Monk's House Papers, Sussex.

10. Michael Holroyd, *Lytton Strachey* (London: Vintage, 1995), p. 777 fn.

11. Journal of Lady Ottoline Morrell, 26 March 1934, Goodman Papers.

12. Anne Olivier Bell (ed.), *The Diary of Virginia Woolf,* vol. 2, 1920–1924 (London: Penguin, 1978), p. 278. Bell notes that the Woolfs had been dining with Clive and Vanessa Bell and Mary Hutchinson at the Commercio before going on to Eliot's party.

13. Michael Hastings, interview with the author, April 2000.

14. Hastings, Introduction to *Tom and Viv,* op. cit., p. 18.

15. VE Personal Account Book, Dec. 1927–April 1932, MSS Eng. Misc. c. 621, VE Papers, Bodleian.

16. VE Diary, 1 January 1935, Bodleian.

17. Mary Trevelyan, unpublished memoir, "The Pope of Russell Square, 1938–1958 (Twenty Years 'and no to-morrow')," 28 February 1952, p. 91.

18. Ibid., 16 August 1954, p. 119.

19. Ibid., p. 121. There are many references to Eliot's "Trade Union rules" with regard to not seeing people, which Mary found "frightening" (p. 94 and passim). The "Rules" governed his life minutely, for example, he did not allow himself to play Patience before breakfast during Lent. One Rule to which Mary objected was that he would not see the same person two days running.

20. Ibid., Preface, and p. 68.

21. T. S. Eliot, *The Cocktail Party* (London: Faber & Faber, 1958), p. 123; Sir Henry Harcourt-Reilly, the psychiatrist, tells Edward: ". . . You realised, what your wife has justly remarked,/That you had never been in love with anybody;/Which made you suspect that you were incapable/Of loving. To men of a certain type/The suspicion that they are incapable of loving/Is as disturbing to their self-esteem/As, in cruder men, the fear of impotence." (Act II, sc. 1.)

22. Quoted in Humphrey Carpenter, *A Serious Character: The Life of Ezra Pound* (London: Faber & Faber, 1988), p. 415.

23. Journal of Lady Ottoline Morrell, 19 June 1923, Goodman Papers.

24. Mary Trevelyan, "Pope of Russell Square," op. cit., 20 August 1950, p. 75, and 28 August 1954, p. 122.

25. T. S. Eliot, "Sweeney Erect," published in *Art and Letters* (Summer 1919) and *Poems* (1920) and in Christopher Ricks (ed.), *Inventions of the March Hare. T. S. Eliot: Poems 1909–1917* (New York: Harcourt Brace, 1996).

26. Ronald Schuchard, *Eliot's Dark Angel: Intersections of Life and Art* (Oxford: Oxford University Press, 1999), p. 92.

27. "Sweeney Erect," *CP,* p. 92.

28. T. S. Eliot, "Elegy," in Valerie Eliot (ed.), *WL Facs,* p. 117.

29. Schuchard, op. cit., p. 124.

30. TSE to EP, 3 January 1934, Beinecke.

31. "The Hollow Men," *CP,* op. cit., p. 87.

32. "East Coker" from *Four Quartets* (1940), *CP,* op. cit., p. 200.

33. TSE to VW, 12 June ?1924, Monk's House Papers, Sussex.

34. TSE to VW, 27 August 1924, Monk's House Papers, Sussex.

35. TSE to MH, 27 August 1924, Texas.

36. Trevelyan, "Pope of Russell Square," op. cit., August 1958.

37. Henry Eliot Jr. to C. C. Eliot, 15 March 1925, Houghton.

38. Henry Eliot Jr. to C. C. Eliot, 9 January 1924, Houghton.

39. Henry Eliot Jr. to C. C. Eliot, 17 February 1925, Houghton.

40. Henry Eliot Jr. to C. C. Eliot, 21 November 1923, Houghton.

41. Henry Eliot Jr. to C. C. Eliot, 16 March 1924, Houghton.

42. Paul Delany, "Appendix: T. S. Eliot's Personal Finances, 1915–1929," in *Literature, Money and the Market from Trollope to Amis* (Basingstoke: Palgrave, 2001), pp. 264, 265.

43. A complicated formula was discussed by which Tom would be compensated for any loss of profit.

44. Henry Eliot Jr. to C. C. Eliot, 3 March 1924, Houghton.

45. TSE to MH, 2 January 1924, Texas.

46. VE to Sydney Schiff, 26 December 1923, British Library.
47. VE to MH, December 1923, Texas.
48. VE to VW, "Sunday 5th" 1923, Monk's House Papers, Sussex.
49. TSE to Sydney Schiff, 24 February 1924, British Library.
50. VE to MH, 29 December 1923, Texas.
51. VE to Sydney Schiff, 31 March 1924, British Library.
52. This speech, delivered to the Heretics at Cambridge on 18 May 1924, developed from a *Nation* article (December 1923), became "Mr. Bennett and Mrs. Brown." Virginia offered it to Eliot for the *Criterion* on 5 May 1924. Virginia described it as "elementary and loquacious," being designed for undergraduates, but Eliot accepted the 5,000-word article with alacrity and offered Virginia a special rate of £20 per 5,000 words, reserved only for her and James Joyce. TSE to VW, 7 ?May 1924. Monk's House Papers, Sussex.
53. MH to Lytton Strachey, 23 April 1924, Texas.
54. VW to TSE, "Sunday," 1924, Monk's House Papers.
55. TSE to VW, 3 March 1923, Monk's House Papers.
56. TSE to VW, 1 May 1924, Monk's House Papers.
57. VW to TSE, n.d., ?1924, Monk's House Papers.
58. Journals of Lady Ottoline Morrell, 19 June 1923, Goodman Papers.
59. VE to VW, 13 June 1924, Monk's House Papers.
60. TSE to VW, 4 February 1925, Monk's House Papers.
61. VE to VW, "Sunday 5th" 1923, Monk's House Papers.
62. TSE to VW, 19 April 1925, Monk's House Papers.
63. TSE to OM, 19 April ?1925, Texas.
64. TSE to OM, 1 May ?1925, Texas.
65. Henry Eliot Jr. to C. C. Eliot, 10 May 1925, Houghton.
66. Leonard Woolf to TSE, 30 April 1925, Frederic Spotts (ed.), *Letters of Leonard Woolf* (New York: Harcourt Brace Jovanovich, 1989), pp. 227–28.
67. Sir Henry Head, neurologist, was recommended by Roger Fry to the Woolfs; Head's rejection of "label" and understanding of hysteria in which "the symptoms of the disorder may be seen as the direct result of living in an untenable situation" (Stephen Trombley, *"All That Summer She Was Mad," Virginia Woolf and Her Doctors* [London: Junction Press, 1981], p. 176) might have made him a better choice of doctor than Marten or Cyriax for Vivien. He believed that a sexless marriage could contribute to neurosis: "Marriage without physical affection is an impossible human relation; one of the simplest methods of escaping from such difficulties is the development of physical illness" (Henry Head, "The Diagnosis of Hysteria," *British Medical Journal,* 1, 1922, pp. 827–29).
68. TSE to OM, Pencil note, "Sunday? 1925, Texas."
69. Trombley, op. cit., pp. 140–43. Savage was the author of the popular textbook, *Insanity and Allied Neuroses* (1884).
70. Trombley, op. cit., p. 142, quotes Anne Olivier Bell (ed.), *The Diary of Virginia Woolf,* vol. 3 (London: Penguin, 1982), p. 315. Leonard Woolf also noted that Virginia had a very bitter taste in the roof of the mouth, p. 143. Trombley suggests that it was Craig who prescribed a sleeping draught, probably containing hyoscyamine.
71. Henry Eliot Jr. to C. C. Eliot, 30 October 1921, Houghton.
72. Notebook 2, VE Papers, MSS Eng. Misc. c. 936, pp. 1–4, 1–36. Notebook 1, representing Vivien's earliest writing, is missing from the collection, having disappeared from the Duke

Humphrey room in June 1990, but Notebook 2 can be dated 1923–24 from an untitled sketch on p. 8, dated May 1924.

73. Ibid.

74. Very occasionally there is a third hand, probably that of Irene Pearl Fassett, but invariably Vivien writes a piece which Eliot edits, often interspersing a few lines of his own with her text.

75. VE as "F.M.," "Letters of the Moment—II," *Criterion,* April 1924.

76. TSE to OM, 29 December 1922, Texas.

77. TSE to Sydney Schiff, 24 February 1924, British Library.

78. VE to Sydney Schiff, 31 March 1924, British Library.

17. Criterion *Battles*

1. "Letters of the Moment—I," *Criterion,* February 1924.

2. "Letters of the Moment—II," *Criterion,* April 1924. Vivien's lists of dramatis personae for her sketches confirm that Tom is "Aquin," VE Collection, Bodleian.

3. Ronsard, "On sent le printemps," in TSE's hand in Vivien's loose-leaf book, MSS. Eng. Misc. c. 624.

4. "Letters of the Moment—I," op. cit.

5. "Letters of the Moment—II," *Criterion,* April 1924, pp. 360–64.

6. "Letters of the Moment—II," op. cit.

7. VW to Barbara Bagenal, 24 June 1924, quoted in Clive Bell, *Old Friends* (London: Chatto & Windus, 1956), p. 103.

8. VW to TSE, 11 May 1924, Nigel Nicolson and Joanne Trautmann (eds.), *The Letters of Virginia Woolf,* vol. 3, 1923–28 (London: Hogarth Press, 1977), p. 108. Lewis published *The Apes of God* in book form in 1930.

9. TSE to VW, 7 April 1924, Berg.

10. Untitled verse, n.d., VE loose-leaf book, Bodleian.

11. Wyndham Lewis, *The Apes of God* (London: Nash & Grayson, 1930), p. 123. Richard Aldington, who had his own grievances against Bloomsbury, described *The Apes of God* (which was an expanded version of the original article) as "one of the cruelest, [and] one of the most tremendous farces ever conceived in the mind of man," which could be compared to Rabelais.

12. VE loose-leaf book, Bodleian.

13. John Pitcher (ed.), *Thomas Kyd, The Spanish Tragedie* (London: Penguin, 1998), p. iii. When in prison in 1593 and accused of atheism, Kyd "squealed" on Marlowe, arguing that the atheistical materials found belonged to his former companion. Eliot's essay on Marlowe was published in 1919. "Four Elizabethan Dramatists" followed in 1924, in *Selected Essays 1917–1932* (London: Faber & Faber, 1932), pp. 109, 118.

14. VE loose-leaf book, Bodleian.

15. "Letters of the Moment—II," op. cit.

16. Anne Olivier Bell (ed.), *The Diary of Virginia Woolf,* vol. 2 (London: Penguin, 1981), 15 September 1924, p. 313.

17. Ibid., 5 May 1924, p. 302; see Bell's footnote.

18. VW to Marjorie Joad, 20? July 1924, Nicolson and Trautmann (eds.), *The Letters of Virginia Woolf,* vol. 3, op. cit., p. 120.

19. Bell (ed.), *The Diary of Virginia Woolf,* vol. 2, op. cit., 14 June 1924, p. 404.
20. VE to Leonard Woolf, 27 June 1924, Monk's House Papers.
21. VE to VW, 11 June 1923, Monk's House Papers.
22. VW to TSE, 5 May 1924, Nicolson and Trautmann (eds.), *The Letters of Virginia Woolf,* vol. 3, op. cit., p. 107.
23. Vivien's loose-leaf book, Bodleian.
24. "The Function of Criticism," *Criterion,* October 1923.
25. E. M. Forster, "T.S. Eliot," *Abinger Harvest* (London: Penguin, 1936), p. 105.
26. VE loose-leaf book, Bodleian, p. 101.
27. TSE's notes on being "Pot Bound," n.d., VE loose-leaf book, p. 105, Bodleian.
28. VE to Sydney Schiff, 31 March 1924, British Library.
29. "Letters of the Moment—I," op. cit.
30. Ronald Schuchard (ed.), Introduction, T. S. Eliot, *The Varieties of Metaphysical Poetry: the Clark Lectures at Trinity College Cambridge 1926 and The Turnbull Lectures at Johns Hopkins University 1933* (New York: Harcourt Brace Jovanovich, 1993), p. 6.
31. F. A. Lea, *The Life of John Middleton Murry* (London: Methuen, 1959), p. 130.
32. "Letters of the Moment—II," *Criterion,* April 1924, p. 362.
33. "F.M.," "Books of the Quarter," *Criterion,* July 1924, pp. 483–86.
34. "I. P. Fassett," "Books of the Quarter," *Criterion,* October 1924, pp. 136–39.
35. Ibid., p. 139.
36. "I. P. Fassett," review of *The White Monkey* by John Galsworthy, *Criterion,* January 1925.
37. VE loose-leaf book, Bodleian.
38. "Feiron Morris," "Thé Dansant," *Criterion,* October 1924, pp. 73–78.
39. "Felix Morrison," "Mrs. Pilkington," *Criterion,* October 1924, pp. 103–6.
40. VE to Sydney Schiff, n.d., British Library.
41. T. S. Eliot, "On the Eve: A Dialogue," *Criterion,* January 1925, pp. 278–81.
42. "Fanny Marlow," "Diary of the Rive Gauche," *Criterion,* January 1925, pp. 291–97.
43. TSE to VW, 1 May 1924, Monk's House Papers.
44. TSE to VW, 7 May 1924, Monk's House Papers.
45. TSE to VW, 22 May 1924, Monk's House Papers.
46. Ibid.
47. Virginia Woolf's "Mr. Bennett and Mrs. Brown" was published in the *Criterion* (July 1924); see Nicolson and Trautmann (eds.), *The Letters of Virginia Woolf,* vol. 3, op. cit., p. 106n.
48. "Feiron Morris," review of "Mr. Bennett and Mrs. Brown" by Virginia Woolf (The Hogarth Press, 2/6d.) in "Books of the Quarter," *Criterion,* January 1925.
49. TSE to VW, 1 May 1924, Monk's House Papers.
50. VE to Sydney Schiff, "Sunday," ?end March/early April 1925, British Library.
51. TSE to VW, 4 February 1925, Monk's House Papers.
52. TSE to VW, 19 April 1925, Monk's House Papers.
53. Early drafts of the poem give the alternative titles of "Ennui," "Exhaustion" and "Fatigue."
54. VE ("F.M."), "Necesse est Perstare," *Criterion,* April 1925.
55. TSE to OM, 1 May ?1925, Texas.
56. Henry Eliot Jr. to C. C. Eliot, 10 May 1925, Houghton.
57. "Fête Galante," *Criterion,* July 1925, pp. 557–63.
58. "Ellison and Antony," MSS Eng. Misc. c. 624, VE Papers, Bodleian.
59. "Feiron Morris," "Night Club," *Criterion,* April 1924, pp. 401–4.

60. "Fanny Marlow," "Diary of the Rive Gauche—II," *Criterion*, April 1925, pp. 425–29.

61. "I. P. Fassett," review of *Orphan Island*, by Rose Macaulay, *Criterion*, April 1925.

62. "F.M.," review of *Myrtle* by Stephen Hudson, *Criterion*, April 1925.

63. Osbert Sitwell, "unpublished memoir of T. S. Eliot," 19 February 1950, p. 22, Texas.

64. TSE to VW, 7 April 1924, Berg.

65. Nicolson and Trautmann (eds.), *The Letters of Virginia Woolf*, vol. 3, op. cit., p. 110n. "Is there any danger that the Criterion is dying?" asked Virginia. "I hope not." VW to TSE, 23 May 1924.

18. On with the Dance

1. Anne Olivier Bell (ed.), *The Diary of Virginia Woolf*, vol. 3 (London: Penguin, 1982), 29 April 1925, p. 14.

2. Ibid., 14 September 1925, p. 41. Virginia objected to a letter from Tom which "fawns & flatters," but hid the fact that his new firm, Faber & Gwyer, would be publishing his poetry—"a fact which he dared not confess, but sought to palliate by flattering me." "Tom has treated us scurvily, much in the manner that he has treated the Hutchinsons," wrote Virginia. Editor Anne Olivier Bell writes (note 5): "The parallel with Jack Hutchinson and Mrs. Eliot has defied explanation." The furore over "Fête Galante" explains Virginia's comparison.

3. Alan and Veronica Palmer, *Who's Who in Bloomsbury* (Brighton: The Harvester Press, 1987), p. 80.

4. Bell (ed.), *The Diary of Virginia Woolf*, vol. 3, op. cit., 27 June 1925, p. 33.

5. "I. P. Fassett," review of *Daimon* by E. L. Grant Watson (London: Jonathan Cape, 1926), "Books of the Quarter," *Criterion*, January 1926.

6. Nicholas Joost, *Scofield Thayer and* The Dial: *An Illustrated History* (Southern Illinois University Press, 1964) pp. 84–87.

7. VE to EP, n.d., Beinecke.

8. VE to OM, pencil, n.d., "temporarily" 9 Clarence Gate Gardens, Texas.

9. VE to EP, n.d., Beinecke.

10. TSE to Leonard Woolf, n.d., Berg.

11. TSE to MH, 20 February 1925, Texas.

12. Bell (ed.), *The Diary of Virginia Woolf*, vol. 3, op. cit., 29 April 1925, pp. 14, 15.

13. TSE to MH, 3 April 1925, Texas.

14. TSE to OM, 30 November 1924, Texas.

15. Miranda Seymour, *Ottoline Morrell: Life on the Grand Scale* (London: Hodder & Stoughton, 1992), pp. 448–49. Ottoline faithfully followed Dr. Marten's starvation diets of fruit and water until she was "so weak she could scarcely sit up." She did not leave Marten until 1932.

16. VW to Lytton Strachey, 26 January 1926, Nigel Nicolson and Joanne Trautmann (eds.), *The Letters of Virginia Woolf*, vol. 3 (London: Hogarth Press, 1977), p. 234.

17. Juliet Mitchell, *Mad Men and Medusas* (London: Penguin Press, 2000), p. 25.

18. VE to EP, n.d., Beinecke.

19. Bell (ed.), *The Diary of Virginia Woolf*, vol. 3, op. cit., 1 June 1925, p. 26.

20. VE to EP, n.d., Beinecke.

21. Draft of a letter pasted into Vivien's writing book in the Bodleian, quoted by Lyndall Gordon, *T. S. Eliot: An Imperfect Life* (London: Vintage, 1998), p. 200.

22. VE Diary, 14 November 1934, Bodleian.

23. Bertrand Russell to TSE, 23 April 1925, McMaster.

24. Bertrand Russell, *Autobiography,* vol. 2 (London: Allen & Unwin, 1968), p. 174.

25. VW to Roger Fry, 16 September 1925, Nicolson and Trautmann (eds.), *The Letters of Virginia Woolf,* vol. 3, op. cit., p. 209.

26. *After Strange Gods* (London: Faber & Faber, 1934), quoted in Ronald Schuchard, *Eliot's Dark Angel* (Oxford: OUP, 1999), p. 128.

27. TSE to OM, 30 November 1924, Texas. Eliot describes his experiments with *Sweeney Agonistes.*

28. Mitchell, op. cit., pp. 41, 42.

29. TSE to OM, 20 February 1925, Texas.

30. TSE to OM, 30 November 1924, Texas.

31. TSE to OM, 4 March ?1925, Texas.

32. *"The Sacred Wood* . . . had very little influence or attention before the Hogarth Press brought out *Homage to John Dryden* . . . It was with the publication in this form of those essays that Eliot became the important contemporary critic. It was the impact of this slender new collection that sent one back to *The Sacred Wood* and confirmed with decisive practical effect one's sense of the stimulus to be got from that rare thing, a fine intelligence in literary criticism." F. R. Leavis, *Anna Karenina and Other Essays* (London: Chatto & Windus, 1967), pp. 177–78, quoted in Ronald Schuchard (ed.), *T. S. Eliot: The Varieties of Metaphysical Poetry, The Clark Lectures at Trinity College, Cambridge, 1926 and The Turnbull Lectures at the Johns Hopkins University, 1933* (New York and London: Harcourt Brace Jovanovich, 1993), p. 5.

33. Peter Ackroyd, *T. S. Eliot* (London: Penguin, 1993), p. 151.

34. Bell (ed.), *The Diary of Virginia Woolf,* vol. 3, op. cit., 14 September 1925, p. 41.

35. TSE to VW, 5 September 1925, Monk's House Papers.

36. It was published in the *New Criterion* in January 1926.

37. Bell (ed.), *The Diary of Virginia Woolf,* vol. 3, op. cit., 30 September 1925, p. 45.

38. Ibid., 29 April 1925, p. 15.

39. TSE to VW, n.d., ?1925, Monk's House Papers. Tom said the earstoppers were "a blessing." He could testify that Vivien was sleeping better since she had them than for about four years.

40. TSE to VW, "Sunday," ? May 1925, Monk's House Papers.

41. VW to Richard Aldington, early November, mid-November, 1924, Nicolson and Trautmann (eds.), *The Letters of Virginia Woolf,* vol. 3, pp. 139, 142.

42. TSE to RA, 26 November ?1925, Texas.

43. RA to EP, 5 October 1925, in Charles Doyle, *Richard Aldington: A Biography* (London: Macmillan, 1989), p. 89. Aldington was annoyed that Eliot, as he thought, was paying him low rates for reviewing in the *Criterion,* and that his poem "A Fool i' the Forest" was seen as a second-rate *Waste Land.* He began to suspect Eliot of condescension towards him (pp. 101–3). The rift with Eliot grew wider after Routledge asked Aldington to collaborate in a series of critical biographies to be edited by William Rose and with Aldington as possible co-editor; it was to be called "The Republic of Letters." Aldington invited Herbert Read and Eliot to contribute, and was upset when both refused. Eliot, as director of Faber & Gwyer, then initiated a similar scheme, "The Poets on the Poets," under the joint imprint of the two publishing houses and the joint editorship of himself and Rose.

Aldington was distraught over losing the editorship, calling it his biggest "setback . . . since the war [which] loses me the fruit of years of work." He felt betrayed by Eliot in his efforts to lift himself "out of the mire of journalism and poverty." See Norman Gates, *Richard Aldington: An Autobiography in Letters* (Philadelphia: Penn State University Press, 1992), p. 76. His jealousy of Eliot increased subsequently.

44. Bell (ed.), *The Diary of Virginia Woolf,* vol. 3, op. cit., 29 April 1925, p. 14.
45. VE to EP, 14 December ?1925, Beinecke.
46. VE to EP, n.d., Beinecke.
47. TSE to EP, postcard, 24 November 1925, Beinecke.
48. Introduction by Schuchard (ed.), *T. S. Eliot: The Varieties of Metaphysical Poetry,* op. cit., pp. 8–11.
49. TSE to EP, second postcard, 8 December 1925, Beinecke.
50. TSE to EP, 11 December 1925, Beinecke.
51. "En Amérique, professeur;/En Angleterre, journaliste;/C'est à grands pas et en sueur/Que vous suivrez à peine ma piste./En Yorkshire, conférencier;/A Londres, un peu banquier," from "Mélange Adultère de Tout," *Collected Poems,* p. 49. Eliot gave Extension Lectures at Ilkley, Yorkshire, in the autumn of 1916.
52. Gordon, op. cit., p. 210.
53. Richard Aldington, *Stepping Heavenward* (London, 1931), p. 55.
54. TSE to EP, 27 December 1925, Beinecke.
55. Ibid.
56. Charles Dickens, *The Old Curiosity Shop.*
57. "A Villonaud, Ballad of the Gibbet," Michael John King (ed.), *Collected Early Poems of Ezra Pound* (London: Faber & Faber, 1977); p. 16; "Camaraderie," p. 30.
58. Ibid., p. 27.
59. VE to Ada Leverson, n.d., Berg. From the content it is clear that this letter was written shortly after the marriage of Sacheverell Sitwell to Georgia Doble, which took place on 12 October 1925 in Paris.
60. Léonide Massine, *My Life in Ballet* (London: Macmillan, 1968), pp. 162, 163.
61. Lynn Garafola, *Diaghilev's Ballets Russes* (New York: Da Capo Press, 1998), p. 353.
62. TSE to EP, 27 December 1925, Beinecke.
63. TSE to EP, 12 February 1926, Beinecke.
64. VE to OM, 23 December 1925, Texas.
65. VE, "Poem to Ottoline," 26 December 1925, Texas.
66. VE to OM, 30 December 1925, Texas.
67. Now in the St. Louis Art Museum. David Bradshaw, "Those Extraordinary Parakeets," *Charleston Magazine,* 16, Autumn/Winter 1997; 17, Spring/Summer 1998.
68. "The Work of Some Modern Decorative Artists," *Vogue,* 68 (late August 1926), pp. 27–33, quoted by Bradshaw, op. cit.
69. VE to MH, 23 December 1925, Texas.
70. Bell (ed.), *The Diary of Virginia Woolf,* vol. 3, op. cit., 29 April 1925, p. 14.
71. VE to OM, pencil, n.d. (temporarily 9 Clarence Gate Gardens), ?late 1925, Texas.
72. Journal of Lady Ottoline Morrell, 3 March 1926, Goodman Papers.
73. Osbert Sitwell, unpublished memoir of T. S. Eliot, Goodman Papers. 19 February 1950, Texas.
74. VE to MH, 25 March 1926, Texas.

75. Ottoline varied in her opinions of Vivien, finding her sometimes dedicated to frivolity and passing pleasure, at other times intellectual and spiritual. Journal of Lady Ottoline Morrell, 1921–26.

76. Massine, op. cit., pp. 164, 165.

77. Garafola, op. cit., pp. 114–15.

78. VE, "The Coliseum Dome," 17 October 1925, MSS Eng. Misc. c. 624, loose leaves pasted into a book, Bodleian.

79. VE, "Verse," ibid.

80. MH to Lytton Strachey, 6 August 1925, Mary Hutchinson Collection, Texas. Mary wrote that she was amused and enchanted by "Mr. E" at Eleanor.

81. TSE to OM, 30 November 1924, Texas.

82. Massine, op. cit., pp. 166, 167. Massine's letters to Ottoline (Texas) show that he rented different rooms in Bloomsbury St.

83. "T. S. Eliot, A Biographical Sketch," n.d. Significantly Mary makes no mention of Vivien in this sketch of Tom's character. She demonstrated her own admiration of the poet by sending him tamarisk and sea lavender to be woven into laurels and roses with which his head would be crowned. Texas.

84. "F.M." "Perque Domos Ditis Vacuas" ("Through the empty halls of Dis"), n.d., Bodleian; the title is taken from Virgil, *The Aeneid,* Book VI, line 269. I am indebted to Patricia Grayburn, Governor, and the Head of Classics, Sherborne School for Girls, for identifying and translating this quotation. Translation of other lines is by James Brodie Ltd. Ezra Pound's choice of Latin titles for many of his poems may have influenced Vivien to do the same, although it was probably Eliot, with his love of Dante and classical scholarship, who introduced her to Virgil.

85. Richard Buckle, *Diaghilev* (London: Weidenfeld & Nicolson, 1993), p. 453, from an unidentified press cutting Dolin's album. The paragraph is headed "Ballet of Degenerates."

86. Ibid., p. 470.

87. Garafola, op. cit., p. 365.

88. VE to MH, 22 January 1926, Texas.

89. VE to OM, "Cambridge," 10 March ?1926, Texas.

90. TSE to OM, Trinity College, Cambridge, 10 March 1926.

91. VE draft of "Night Club," Notebook 3, 10, Bodleian.

92. "Feiron Morris," "Night Club," *Criterion,* April 1925, pp. 401–4.

93. "Feiron Morris," "Song in the Night," Vivien's loose-leaf book, Bodleian.

94. VE to Pearl Fassett, n.d., letter in loose-leaf book, Bodleian.

95. VE draft of "Letter of the Moment," ibid.

96. Journal of Lady Ottoline Morrell, 13 March 1926, Goodman Papers.

97. Henry Eliot to C. C. Eliot, 25 February 1925, Houghton.

98. Henry Eliot to C. C. Eliot, 2 March 1926, Houghton.

99. Henry Eliot to C. C. Eliot, 15 March 1925, Houghton.

100. VE, "Telephone Conversation," Notebook 2, Bodleian.

101. VE, draft of Bertrand Russell story, loose-leaf book, Bodleian.

102. VE notes for "Lonely Soldier," loose-leaf book, Bodleian.

103. "Fragment of a Prologue," *CP,* pp. 125, 126. "Fragment of an Agon," *Sweeney Agonistes, CP,* p. 134. Eliot first published "Fragment of an Agon" in the *New Criterion* (January 1927).

104. Ibid.

105. VE drafts for "The Lonely Soldier" and "Pseudo-Bridge," partly in TSE's handwriting. Vivien lists the characters as: "Sibylla, Horace, Felice, a dago, a German, an American (André) Mary, Dorothea, St. John, a Cambridge undergraduate" (p. 91). An earlier list identifies Maurice as Horace, the Hutchinsons as the Rawdon Crawleys, "T" as Aquinas, "W.L." (Wyndham Lewis) as Lieut. Bonaparte, Osbert as "Mr. Botch," and The Phoenix as the Mermaid; loose-leaf book, Bodleian.

106. "Night Club," *Criterion,* April 1925, p. 402.

107. VE, Notebook 3, 1924, Bodleian.

108. Theresa Eliot, signed statement, 28 March 1970, 84 Prescott St., Cambridge, Massachusetts. Houghton.

109. Philip Hoare, *Oscar Wilde's Last Stand* (New York: Arcade Publishing, Inc., 1998), pp. 36–38.

110. VE loose-leaf book, Bodleian.

111. Henry Eliot to C. C. Eliot, 9 March 1926, Houghton. In a letter of 21 March, Henry wrote that twelve copies of "Savonarola" were shipped to Charlotte Eliot last week, and Tom said that they had already sold fifty copies.

112. Henry Eliot to C. C. Eliot, postmark 31 March 1926, Houghton.

113. Henry Eliot to C. C. Eliot, 6 April 1926, Houghton.

114. I am indebted to Mr. Adrian M. Goodman for this information.

115. Henry Eliot to C. C. Eliot, postcard, 13 April, letter 16 April 1926, Houghton.

116. VE to Mary Hutchinson, postcard, 12 May ?1926, Texas.

117. Theresa Garrett Eliot, interview in BBC production, *The Mysterious Mr. Eliot,* televised 3 January 1971.

118. Henry Eliot to C. C. Eliot, 4 May 1926, Houghton.

119. Aldington, *Stepping Heavenward,* op. cit., pp. 57, 60.

120. VE to OM, express letter, 16 April 1926, Texas.

121. "Felix Morrison," "Mrs. Pilkington," *Criterion,* October 1924, pp. 103–6.

122. Sitwell, unpublished memoir, op. cit., Texas.

123. Ibid.

124. TSE to OM, 24 June 1926, Texas.

19. Mourning and "Madness"

1. Osbert Sitwell, unpublished Memoir on T. S. Eliot," 19 February 1950, p. 16, Texas.

2. Aldous Huxley to Mary Hutchinson, 6 August 1926, Texas.

3. Robert Sencourt, *T. S. Eliot: A Memoir,* edited by Donald Adamson and L. P. Addison (London: Garnstone Press, 1971), pp. 102, 103.

4. Frances Lindley, editor, Harper and Row Publishers, New York, to T. S. Matthews, 3 September 1971. Lindley was T. S. Matthews's editor, who was in touch with Dodd, Mead, the publishers of Sencourt's memoir, over their authors' joint difficulties with the Eliot estate. Sencourt hoped that his memoir would assist Tom Matthews in writing *Great Tom.*

5. T. S. Eliot, "Lancelot Andrewes" (1926), *Selected Essays 1917–1932* (London: Faber & Faber, 1932), p. 344.

6. W. Force Stead, "Some Personal Reminiscences of T. S. Eliot," Alumni Journal of Trinity College, Washington, vol. XXXVIII, Winter 1965, no. 2.

7. TSE to W. F. Stead, 7 February 1927, Osborn Papers, Beinecke.

8. Ibid., p. 349.

9. Hugh Kenner, *The Invisible Poet: T. S. Eliot* (London: W. H. Allen, 1960), p. 209; "Lancelot Andrewes," in *Selected Essays,* op. cit., p. 350.

10. Lyndall Gordon, *T. S. Eliot: An Imperfect Life* (London: Vintage, 1998), p. 222, quotes David W. S. Goldie's Oxford thesis, "John Middleton Murry and T. S. Eliot: Tradition versus the Individual in English Literary Criticism, 1919–1928" (1991). Murry's attack, "The Classical Revival," *Adelphi* (Feb.–March, 1926). Goldie discovered a draft of the attack annotated by Eliot.

11. Charlotte Eliot's handwritten draft of "Savonarola" is at the Houghton Library.

12. Stead, op. cit.

13. TSE to W. F. Stead, 7 February 1927, Beinecke.

14. Sencourt, op. cit., p. 104.

15. Stead, op. cit.

16. Ibid.

17. VW to Vanessa Bell, 11 February 1928, Nigel Nicolson and Joanne Trautmann (eds.), *The Letters of Virginia Woolf,* vol. 3, 1923–28 (London: Hogarth Press, 1977), pp. 457–58.

18. Lyndall Gordon, *Eliot's Early Years* (Oxford: OUP, 1977), p. 66.

19. Ibid., p. 15.

20. T. S. Eliot draft of Clark Lecture III, Houghton. Schuchard writes: "In the 'Classical Revival' Murry had compared the nihilistic voice of *The Waste Land* to the voice of St. John of the Cross: 'Once its armour of incomprehensibility is penetrated the poem is found to be a cry of grinding and empty desolation . . . This is a voice from the Dark Night of the Soul of a St. John of the Cross—the barren and dry land where no water is.'" Ronald Schuchard (ed.), *The Varieties of Metaphysical Poetry, the Clark Lectures at Trinity College, Cambridge, 1926 and the Turnbull Lectures at Johns Hopkins University, 1933* (New York: Harcourt Brace, 1993), p. 52, note 104.

21. John Pitcher (ed.), *Thomas Kyd, The Spanish Tragedie* (London: Penguin, 1998), p. xiii.

22. VE loose-leaf book, Bodleian.

23. Gordon, *T. S. Eliot: An Imperfect Life,* op. cit., pp. 192, 199, 189.

24. T. S. Eliot draft of Clark Lecture III, Houghton. Schuchard, op. cit., p. 99.

25. A. David Moody, *Thomas Stearns Eliot, Poet* (Cambridge: CUP, 1994), pp. 117–21. The evolution of "The Hollow Men" can be traced from "Song to the Opherian" (1921) through "Doris's Dream Songs" (1924), "Three Poems" by Thomas Eliot (*Criterion,* January 1925) to "The Hollow Men" (*Dial,* March 1925) and the final "The Hollow Men" in *Poems 1909–1925.*

26. Ibid., p. 122.

27. Quoted by Moody, op. cit., p. 125.

28. Christopher Ricks (ed.), *IMH,* p. 369 and see Ronald Schuchard, *Eliot's Dark Angel: Intersections of Life and Art* (Oxford: 1999), p. 91.

29. TSE to OM, n.d., 1933, from "B-11 Eliot House, Cambridge," Mass. Texas.

30. T. S. Eliot, draft of Lecture 1, Houghton. Schuchard, *Varieties of Metaphysical Poetry,* op. cit., p. 54.

31. Ibid., Sappho's "Ode to Anactoria" is an example of the description of a "love trance" praised by Eliot.

32. Ibid., p. 149.

33. *Monthly Criterion,* vol. 6 (August 1927) quoted by Ronald Clark, *The Life of Bertrand Russell* (London: Jonathan Cape and Weidenfeld & Nicolson, 1975), p. 413.

34. TSE to BR, 22 June 1927, McMaster.

35. Lyndall Gordon, *Eliot's New Life* (Oxford: OUP, 1988), p. 30.

36. Misquoted from section XVIII of Dante's *La Vita Nuova*, "Madonne, lo fine del mio amore fu gia il saluto di questa donna, di cui voi forse intendete . . .": "Ladies, the end and aim of my Love was but the salutation of that lady of whom I conceive that ye are speaking." Translation, Dante Gabriel Rossetti, *Early Italian Poets* (London: George Newnes, 1904).

37. *Ash Wednesday* (London: Faber & Faber, 1930), dedicated "To My Wife," p. 12. Grover Smith, *T. S. Eliot's Poetry and Plays: A Study in Sources and Meaning* (The University of Chicago Press, 1956), p. 135. The dedication to Vivien was removed from later editions of the poem.

38. Robert Sencourt to John Hayward, 15 July 1965, John Hayward Bequest, King's College, Cambridge.

39. TSE to OM, 14 March 1933.

40. "Hence the soul cannot be possessed of the divine union, until it has divested itself of the love of created beings." The epigraph is from St. John of the Cross, *Ascent of Mount Carmel,* (book 1, ch. 4).

41. Introduction by Emma Smith (ed.), *Thomas Kyd: The Spanish Tragedie* (London: Penguin, 1998), pp. xiv–xxii.

42. *Sweeney Agonistes, CP,* p. 123.

43. Draft of *Sweeney Agonistes,* John Hayward Bequest, King's College, Cambridge.

44. The title of this typescript is "The Superior Landlord," and the cancelled title: "Pereira" or "The Marriage of Life and Death—A Dream." King's College, Cambridge.

45. Desmond MacCarthy, *"Sweeney Agonistes," Listener,* 9 January 1935.

46. Draft of *Sweeney Agonistes,* John Hayward Bequest, King's College, Cambridge. In this early draft Eliot wrote that there should be eighteen knocks, like the Angelus.

47. Mary Trevelyan, "The Pope of Russell Square" memoir, 25 July 1950, 10 February 1952.

48. T. S. Eliot, "Four Elizabethan Dramatists," *Selected Essays,* op. cit., p. 111.

49. MacCarthy, op. cit.

50. Draft of *Sweeney Agonistes,* op. cit.

51. Robin Grove, "Eliot's theater," A. David Moody (ed.), *The Cambridge Companion to T.S. Eliot* (Cambridge: CUP, 1994), p. 173.

52. Ibid.

53. *Dial,* 71 (August 1921), p. 214. See Schuchard, op. cit., pp. 110–13.

54. Anne Olivier Bell (ed.), *The Diary of Virginia Woolf,* vol. 4, 12 November 1934.

55. Maurice Haigh-Wood, interview with Michael Hastings, 1980.

56. VW to Elisabeth Bowen, 29 January 1939, Nicolson and Trautmann (eds.), *The Letters of Virginia Woolf,* op. cit., vol. 6, p. 313.

57. VE Notebook 2, p. 68, Bodleian.

58. Louis Martz, Introduction to *H.D. Collected Poems, 1912–1944* (New York: New Direction Books, 1925).

59. VE Diary, 18 April 1936, Bodleian.

60. VE Diary, 15 September 1934, Bodleian. Charles Haigh-Wood's death certificate cites "cancer of the mediastinum" as the cause of death. Lillia Symes, sister-in-law, of 37 Stratford Road, London W8, informed the registrar of the death, at which she was present.

61. VE Diary, 24 March 1935, Bodleian.

62. VE Diary, 1 September 1934, Bodleian.

63. Maurice Haigh-Wood, interview with Michael Hastings, 28 January 1980.

64. VE Diary, 20 April 193, Bodleian.

65. VE to BR, 6 December 1926, McMaster.

66. According to Russell's daughter, Mrs. Katharine Tait, the family jewellery did not pass down to his children, but "was probably all given to his various wives at different times." Katharine Tait to the author, 21 September 2000.

67. VE to BR, 6 December ?1926, McMaster.

68. TSE to BR, 22 June 1927, McMaster.

69. TSE to BR, 16 May 1927, McMaster.

70. TSE to BR, 22 June 1927, McMaster.

71. TSE to John Hayward, 29 November 1939, "St. Andrews Eve," John Hayward Bequest, King's College, Cambridge.

72. According to Maurice, at some point Vivien had an abortion, but this fact is uncorroborated.

73. Eliot used as an epigraph for "Marina" (1930) lines from Seneca's *Hercules Furens,* Hercules' words when he wakes to discover he has murdered his own children. Grover Smith, op. cit., p. 131.

74. Bernard Sharratt traces the motif of lost or murdered children in Eliot's work in "Eliot: Modernism, Postmodernism, and after," in Moody (ed.), *The Cambridge Companion to T. S. Eliot,* op. cit., pp. 225, 226. Eliot singled out "Yeats's lines about having reached forty-nine with only a book, not a child, to show for it."

75. VE to OM, 31 January 1928, Texas.

76. Vivien's photograph album 1924–29 is at King's College, Cambridge.

77. VE's Account Books, December 1927–April 1932, Bodleian.

78. Maurice Haigh-Wood, interview with Michael Hastings, 28 January 1980.

79. Daughter of Eliot's sister Charlotte, who had married Lawrence Smith.

80. Theodora's photographs and sketch plan of 57 Chester Terrace are at the Houghton Library, Harvard. She stayed at least twice with Tom and Vivien in 1928 and 1929.

81. Mary Trevelyan, "The Pope of Russell Square" memoir, 2 April 1951.

82. Osbert Sitwell, unpublished memoir on T. S. Eliot, Texas; also quoted in John Pearson, *Façades: Edith, Osbert and Sacheverell Sitwell* (London, 1978), pp. 240–42.

83. VE to OM, postmark 25 November 1926, Texas.

84. VE to OM, 27 March ?1927, Texas.

85. Lyndall Gordon, *Eliot's New Life* (Oxford: OUP, 1988), p. 8.

86. T. S. Eliot, "Shakespeare and the Stoicism of Seneca" (1927), *Selected Essays,* op. cit., p. 126.

87. Valerie Eliot, Introduction, *Letters I,* p. xvii.

88. Gordon, *T. S. Eliot,* op. cit., pp. 234–45.

89. Ibid., p. 205.

90. TSE to W. F. Stead, 15 March 1928, Beinecke.

91. Sencourt introduced Eliot to Underhill, who became Dean of Rochester in 1932. Sencourt, op. cit., pp. 112, 114.

92. TSE to W. F. Stead, 10 April 1928, Beinecke.

93. The poem describes Casco Bay, Maine.

94. "Marina" (1930), *Collected Poems,* p. 115.

95. Gordon, *Eliot's New Life,* op. cit., p. 10.

96. Ibid., p. 12.

97. TSE to E. Martin Browne, 19 March 1938, *The Making of T. S. Eliot's Plays* (Cambridge: CUP, 1969), p. 107.

98. Valerie Eliot, Introduction, *Letters I,* p. xvi.

99. A. David Moody, "Being in Fear of Women," in *"The Waste Land" in Different Voices* (London: Edward Arnold, 1974), pp. 184–91, writes: "It becomes difficult not to identify Eliot also with Harry in *The Family Reunion,*" p. 190.

100. TSE to JH, October 1925, John Hayward Bequest, King's College, Cambridge.

101. TSE to JH, 27 September 1927, loc. cit.

102. Gordon, *T. S. Eliot,* op. cit., p. 257.

103. JH to Frank Morley, 15 November 1937, list of poems for *Noctes Binanianae,* John Hayward Bequest.

104. TSE to JH, 14 November 1939, Kings College, Cambridge.

105. Quoted in Peter Ackroyd, *T. S. Eliot* (London: Penguin, 1993), pp. 150–51.

106. VE to OM, 31 January 1928, Texas.

107. VE Diary, 16 February 1935, Bodleian.

108. "Story 3," VE Notebook 3, Bodleian.

109. VE to OM, 28 February ?1928, Texas.

110. VE to OM, 1 June 1928, Texas.

111. VW to Vanessa Bell, 7 June 1928, Nicolson and Trautmann (eds.), *The Letters of Virginia Woolf,* vol. 3, p. 508.

112. VW to Vita Sackville-West, 13 November 1929, in ibid., vol. 4, p. 108.

113. TSE to OM, 2 October 1928, Texas.

114. TSE to OM, 1 November 1928, Texas.

115. Journal of Lady Ottoline Morrell, 14 February 1929, Goodman Papers.

116. VE to OM, Monday, 11 February 1929, Texas.

117. TSE to OM, 13 February 1929, Texas.

118. VE to OM, 29 February 1929, Texas.

119. Conversation with Philip Goodman, 1999.

120. VE to MH, 29 September 1928, Texas.

121. VW to Clive Bell, 2 May 1929, Nicolson and Trautmann (eds.), *The Letters of Virginia Woolf,* vol. 4, pp. 49, 50.

122. TSE to MH, 20 November 1928, Texas.

123. VE to MH, 9 November 1928, Texas.

124. VE to MH, n.d., Texas.

125. VE to MH, 6 September 1929, Texas.

126. TSE to MH, 23 June 1929, Texas.

127. VW to Clive Bell, 6 February 1930, Nicolson and Trautmann (eds.), *The Letters of Virginia Woolf,* vol. 4, p. 133.

128. VE to MH, 10 September 1929, Texas.

129. VE to MH, 25 March 1930, Texas.

130. VE to MH, 3 January 1931, Texas.

131. Michael Hastings, in conversation with relatives of Dr. Miller, 1981.

132. Professor Derek Russell Davis to Michael Hastings, October 1981, Hastings Papers.

133. "East Coker," *CP,* p. 200.

134. Ackroyd, op. cit., p. 158.

135. Journal of Lady Ottoline Morrell, 15 November 1930, Goodman Papers.

136. Ibid., 16 July 1931.
137. VE Diary, 12 November 1934, Bodleian.
138. Stephen Spender, *Eliot* (London: Fontana, 1975). p. 130. Pound was equally scornful, writing the following couplet:

"In any case let us lament the psychosis

Of all those who abandon the Muses for Moses."

Ackroyd, op. cit., p. 172.
139. Sencourt, op. cit., p. 121.
140. TSE to W. F. Stead, 2 December 1930, Beinecke.

20. Ghosts and Shadows

1. Conrad Aiken to Theodore Spencer, 31 October 1930, Joseph Killorin (ed.), *Selected Letters of Conrad Aiken* (New Haven, Conn., 1978).
2. VE to Ralph Hodgson, 12 May 1932, Beinecke.
3. Robert Sencourt, *T.S. Eliot: A Memoir* edited by Donald Adamson and L. P. Addison (London: Garnstone Press, 1971), p. 121.
4. T.S. Eliot, *The Family Reunion* (London: Faber & Faber, 1939), p. 30.
5. A. David Moody, *"The Waste Land" in Different Voices* (London: Edward Arnold, 1974), p. 190.
6. John Peter, "An Artistic Failure" (1949) in Arnold P. Hinchliffe (ed.), *T. S. Eliot Plays, A Casebook* (London: Macmillan, 1985), p. 127.
7. *The Family Reunion,* op. cit.
8. Mary Trevelyan, "The Pope of Russell Square . . . ," unpublished memoir, 10 February 1952.
9. Ibid., 28 October 1954.
10. T. S. Eliot. "Dante," *Selected Essays 1917–1932* (London: Faber & Faber, 1932), p. 245.
11. Jean-Paul Sartre, *Being and Nothingness* (1943), (London: Routledge edition 1989), pp. 354–57.
12. Ibid., "First Attitude Toward Others: Love, Language, Masochism," p. 365.
13. *CP,* p. 139. "Triumphal March" and "Difficulties of a Statesman" on which Eliot worked in the final years of his marriage, were never completed, and were finally published as "Coriolan" in his *Collected Poems*. Nor was he able to finish *Sweeney Agonistes*. Eliot published his translation of St. John Perse's *Anabase* in 1930. His frustration over this inability to complete work, which was only partly due to Vivien, is revealed in his sub-title to "Four Elizabethan Dramatists," *Selected Essays:* "Preface to an unwritten book." Only four essays of the proposed work were completed.
14. See Emmy van Deurzen-Smith, "Jean-Paul Sartre" in *Existential Dimensions of Psychotherapy* (London: Routledge, 1997), pp. 45–57.
15. Diane Long Hoeveler, *Romantic Androgyny: The Women Within* (Philadelphia: University of Pennsylvania Press, 1990), p. 7. Hoeveler traces the process by which the "Eternal Feminine" became for the Romantic poets "the encroaching feminine, an usurping and castrating power that needed to be suppressed rather than simply exalted."
16. Sartre, op. cit., "Second Attitude Toward Others: Indifference, Desire, Hate, Sadism," p. 412.

17. Clive Bell to Mary Hutchinson, September 1936, Texas. Quoted in Hermione Lee, *Virginia Woolf* (London: Vintage, 1997), p. 828 n.

18. Journal of Lady Ottoline Morrell, 12 April 1932, Goodman Papers.

19. Sencourt, op. cit., pp. 118–20.

20. Journal of Lady Ottoline Morrell, 23 July 1931, 17 November 1931, Goodman Papers.

21. Mirsky wrote a Marxist critique of Bloomsbury in his book *The Intelligentsia of Great Britain,* which was published in an English translation in 1935; it upset Bloomsberries much as Lewis's *Apes of God* had done. Mirsky was, said Lydia Lopokova, "a dirty little cad." Anne Olivier Bell (ed.), *The Diary of Virginia Woolf,* vol. 4 (London: Penguin, 1983), pp. 112, 288, 292.

22. VE to MH, 27 January 1931, Texas.

23. VE to MH, 2 June 1931, Texas.

24. Conrad Aiken to Theodore Spencer, October 1930, Killorin (ed.), *Selected Letters of Aiken,* op. cit.

25. VE to OM, 28 December 1931, Texas.

26. VE to OM, 11 December 1931, Texas.

27. Journal of Lady Ottoline Morrell, 17 November 1931, Goodman Papers.

28. Ibid., ?November 1931.

29. Quoted in Peter Ackroyd, *T. S. Eliot* (London: Penguin, 1993), p. 168.

30. Ibid., p. 184.

31. Charles Doyle, *Richard Aldington: A Biography* (London: Macmillan, 1989), p. 149.

32. Stephen Spender, *T. S. Eliot* (London: Fontana, 1975), p. 130.

33. E. W. F. Tomlin, *T. S. Eliot: A Friendship* (London: Routledge, 1988), p. 48.

34. TSE to RA, ?April 1924, Texas.

35. TSE to RA, 1 November 1927, Texas.

36. Henry Eliot to C. C. Eliot, 21 March 1926, Houghton.

37. Doyle, op. cit., p. 148.

38. Lee, op. cit., p. 449.

39. Bell (ed.), *The Diary of Virginia Woolf,* op. cit., vol. 3, 8 November 1930, p. 331.

40. Ibid.

41. VW to OM, 26 December 1928, Nigel Nicolson and Joanne Trautmann (eds.), *The Letters of Virginia Woolf,* vol. 3, p. 565.

42. Morley notes some of Eliot's practical jokes at the office: "OK Sauce (for Faber) which was very far from OK, the coffee which foamed over, the cigarettes which produced snow-storms . . . Something noisy" was always rigged up on the Wednesday nearest to the Fourth of July. Frank Morley in Richard March and Tambimuttu (eds.), *T.S. Eliot: A Symposium* (London: P.L. Editions, 1948), p. 69.

43. TSE to John Hayward, Notes on Practical Jokes, n.d. 1938, John Hayward Bequest, King's College, Cambridge.

44. VE to OM, 28 December 1931, Texas.

45. VE to Ralph Hodgson, 12 May 1932, Beinecke.

46. Henrik Ibsen, *Ghosts,* Act II.

47. TSE to MH, 28 October 1931, Texas.

48. VE to Aurelia Bollinger, 12 May 1932, Beinecke.

49. VE to Aurelia Bollinger, 27 May 1932, Beinecke.

50. VE to Aurelia Bollinger, 19 May 1932, Beinecke.

51. Harold Nicolson, 2 March 1932, Nigel Nicolson (ed.), *Diaries and Letters 1930–39* (New York and London: Harcourt Brace, 1977), p. 111.

52. TSE to Ralph Hodgson, Two typescripts with sketches, 16 August 1932, Beinecke. Published as "Lines for Cuscuscaraway and Mirza Murad Ali Beg," *CP,* p. 151.

53. "Lines to Ralph Hodgson Esqre," *CP,* p. 150.

54. The visit took place in March 1932. Edith Sitwell quoted in John Pearson, *Façades: Edith, Osbert and Sacheverell* (London: 1978), p. 277.

55. Ibid., p. 278.

56. VE Diary, 14 September 1934, Bodleian.

57. Henry W. Cattell, MD, *Lippincott's New Medical Dictionary* (London: Lippincott Co., 1910) p. 325. Wellcome.

58. Robert Hooper, MD, *Lexicon Medicum* (London: Longman, 1839), p. 46. Wellcome.

59. "The belief that madness was caused by the build-up of bodily toxins led to the often puni-tive use of laxatives such as croton-oil, which could result in griping, sickness, colitis, faint-ing and even total collapse in a weak patient. Dr. Montagu Lomax, "The Experiences of an Asylum Doctor with Suggestions for Asylum and Lunacy Law Reform" (1921) in Roy Porter (ed.), *The Faber Book of Madness* (London: Faber & Faber, 1991), pp. 314–16.

60. VW to Vita Sackville-West, 27 January 1929, Nicolson and Trautmann (eds.), *Letters of Virginia Woolf,* vol. 4, op. cit., p. 8.

61. Leonard Woolf to Vanessa Bell, in ibid., p. 9.

62. VW to V. Sackville-West, 1 February 1929, Nicolson & Trautmann (eds.), *Letters of Virginia Woolf,* vol. 4, op. cit., p. 12.

63. Bell (ed.), *The Diary of Virginia Woolf,* vol. 4, op. cit., p. 123.

64. VE Diary, 1 April 1935, Bodleian.

65. Hope Mirrlees, "The Mysterious Mr. Eliot," BBC television programme, 3 January 1971.

66. VE Diary, 5 September 1934, Bodleian.

67. Morley, in March and Tambimuttu (eds.), *T. S. Eliot: A Symposium,* op. cit., p. 104.

68. Morley in Mirrlees, "The Mysterious Mr. Eliot," op. cit.

69. VE to OM, 4 July 1932, Texas.

70. Journal of Lady Ottoline Morrell, 12 April 1932, Goodman Papers.

71. TSE to OM, 11 July 1932, Texas.

72. VE to MH, 21 April 1932, Texas.

73. VE to MH, 8 June 1932, Texas.

74. VE to MH, 12 June 1932, Texas.

75. VE to MH, 18 July 1932, Texas.

76. VE to MH, 28 July 1932, Texas.

77. VE to OM, 11 September 1932, Texas.

78. Journal of Lady Ottoline Morrell, 12 January 1932, Goodman Papers.

79. VE to OM, 13 September 1932, Texas.

80. TSE to VE, 4 March 1932, Bodleian.

81. Sencourt, op. cit., p. 121.

82. VE to OM, 26 December 1933, Texas.

83. TSE to OM, 9 February 1933, Texas.

84. TSE to OM, 14 March 1933, Texas.

85. Eliot's Charles Eliot Norton Professor of Poetry lectures were published in 1933 as *The Use of Poetry and the Use of Criticism* (Harvard: Harvard University Press, 1933).

86. TSE to OM, 9 February 1933, Texas.

87. Lyndall Gordon, *Eliot's New Life* (Oxford: OUP, 1988), p. 18.

88. Journal of Lady Ottoline Morrell, 22 October 1935, Goodman Papers.

89. Gordon, op. cit., pp. 20, 21.

90. *CP,* p. 152.

91. TSE to VW, 25 April 1933, Berg.

92. TSE to VW, 5 March 1933, Berg.

93. "Virginia," *CP,* p. 153.

94. T. S. Matthews, *Great Tom: Notes Towards the Definition of T. S. Eliot* (London: Weidenfeld & Nicolson, 1974), p. 113.

95. EP to TSE, ? January 1934, Beinecke.

96. TSE to EP, n.d., 1927, Beinecke. "Julius or Joe" Bender had written a book on Propertius.

97. "Dirge," Valerie Eliot (ed.), *WL Facs* p. 119 and Stephen Spender, *T. S. Eliot* (London: Fontana, 1975), p. 54.

98. Matthews, op. cit., p. 163.

99. Spender, *Eliot,* op. cit., p. 131.

100. Sencourt, op. cit., p. 122. In the earlier misquotation Eliot wrote "miasma" for "phantasma," thinking of the "miasma of sexual sin" of which he often spoke to Sencourt.

101. T. S. Eliot, *Murder in the Cathedral,* part II (London: Faber & Faber, 1935). See also Robin Grove, "Pereira and After: The Cures of Eliot's Theater," A. David Moody (ed.), *The Cambridge Companion to T. S. Eliot* (Cambridge: CUP, 1994), p. 169.

102. TSE to EP, 8/10 December 1933, Beinecke.

103. Eliot lifted the words of Isaiah 40:6–8: "The voice said, Cry, And he said, What shall I cry? All flesh is grass, and all the goodliness thereof is as the flower of the field" to use as the first lines of "Difficulties of a Statesman": "Cry what shall I cry?/All flesh is grass . . ." It was yet one more example of his remark, "Immature poets imitate, mature poets steal" (*Selected Essays,* op. cit., p. 182). One acerbic reviewer wrote of *The Waste Land:* "The borrowed jewels he has set in its head does not make Mr. Eliot's toad the more prepossessing." For a discussion of Eliot's practice of "stealing," see James Longenbach, " 'Mature poets steal' ": "Eliot's allusive practice," in Moody, *Cambridge Companion to T. S. Eliot,* op. cit., p. 176.

104. Isaiah 40:6–8. On 1 December 1932, Eliot quoted from Psalm 130 in King's Chapel, Boston: "I wait for the Lord, my soul doth wait . . ." Gordon, *Eliot's New Life,* op. cit., p. 39.

105. TSE to OM, 14 March 1933, Texas.

106. VE to Aurelia Bollinger, 28 July 1932, Beinecke.

107. Journal of Lady Ottoline Morrell, 12 April 1932, Goodman Papers.

108. Bell (ed.), *The Diary of Virginia Woolf,* vol. 4, op. cit., 31 March 1935.

109. Journal of Lady Ottoline Morrell, 20 August 1933, Goodman Papers.

110. TSE to OM, 9 August 1933, Texas.

111. Journal of Lady Ottoline Morrell, 20 August 1933, Goodman Papers.

112. Mary Hutchinson wrote for a variety of journals, including *The London Mercury, Vogue,* and *The London Magazine.*

113. VE to MH, 29 November 1932, Texas.

114. VE to MH, 30 November 1932, Texas.

115. VE to MH, 18 December 1932, Texas.

116. Sencourt, op. cit.

117. TSE to MH, 29 September 1932, Texas.

118. VE to OM, 31 March 1933, Texas.

119. VE Diary, 4 June 1934, Bodleian.

120. VE to OM, 7 July 1933, Texas.

121. Bell (ed.), *The Diary of Virginia Woolf,* vol. 4, op. cit., p. 167.

122. Frank Morley, in Allen Tate (ed.), *T. S. Eliot: The Man and His Work* (London: Chatto & Windus, 1967), pp. 104–5.

123. Eliot's poem, "The Country Walk," with the dedication "For J.H." (John Hayward), expresses not only his fear of cows but also of women: "when walking/With country dames in brogues and tweeds/Who will persist in hearty talking . . . ," John Hayward Bequest, King's College, Cambridge. There is another copy of this unpublished poem which Eliot gave to Emily Hale, at Princeton.

124. TSE to MH, 13 July 1933, Texas.

125. Bell (ed.), *The Diary of Virginia Woolf,* vol. 4, op. cit., 20 July 1933, p. 168.

126. VW to Francis Birrell, 3 September 1933, in Nicolson and Trautmann (eds.), *The Letters of Virginia Woolf,* vol. 5, p. 222.

127. Bell (ed.), *The Diary of Virginia Woolf,* vol. 4, op. cit., 21 July 1933, p. 169.

128. VE Diary, 20 January 1934, Bodleian.

129. VE Diary, 28 January 1934, Bodleian.

130. TSE to MH, 20 September 1933, Texas.

131. Ibid.

132. "The Three Voices of Poetry," reprinted in *On Poetry and Poets* (London: Faber & Faber 1957), quoted in Peter Ackroyd, *T. S. Eliot* (London: Penguin, 1993).

133. Bell (ed.), *The Diary of V. Woolf,* vol. 4, 2 September 1933, p. 177.

134. Ibid., 10 September 1933, p. 178.

135. TSE to EP, "Vigil of Ascension Day 1933," Beinecke.

136. TSE to EP, 21 September 1933, Beinecke.

137. TSE to OM, 9 August 1933, Texas.

138. TSE to OM, 21 August 1933, Texas.

139. EP to TSE, ?1934, Beinecke.

140. Frank Morley, in Tate (ed.), *T. S. Eliot,* op. cit., p. 109.

141. Frank Morley, "T. S. Eliot as a Publisher," March and Tambimuttu (eds.), *T. S. Eliot: A Symposium,* op. cit., p. 70.

142. TSE to MH, 26 September 1933, Texas.

143. TSE to MH, 3 November 1933, Texas.

144. TSE to MH, 1 January 1934, Texas.

145. VE Diary, 1 November 1934, Bodleian.

146. TSE to VW, 31 October 1933, Berg.

147. TSE to MH, 3 November 1933, Texas.

148. TSE to MH, 5 December 1933, Texas.

149. TSE to EP, 8/10 December 1933, Beinecke.

150. Sencourt, op. cit., p. 129.

151. Ibid.

152. TSE to VW, 7 December 1933, Berg.

153. Francis King, *Yesterday Came Suddenly* (London: Constable, 1993), p. 197.

21. Separation

1. Francis King, *Yesterday Came Suddenly* (London: Constable, 1993), p. 197.
2. Francis King in conversation with the author, 4 April 2000.
3. Alec Guinness, *My Name Escapes Me* (London: Hamish Hamilton, 1996), p. 185.
4. Anne Olivier Bell (ed.), *The Diary of Virginia Woolf,* vol. 4, 21 November 1934 (London: Penguin, 1983), pp. 262–63.
5. Phillip Herring, *Djuna: The Life and Work of Djuna Barnes* (London: Penguin, 1995), p. 222.
6. Ibid., p. 231.
7. Quoted in Tony Sharpe, *T. S. Eliot: A Literary Life* (London: Macmillan, 1991), p. 128.
8. T. S. Eliot, *The Cocktail Party* (London: Faber & Faber, 1958), p. 99.
9. TSE to Paul Elmer More, "Shrove Tuesday" (20 February) 1928, in Ronald Schuchard, *Eliot's Dark Angel: Intersections of Life and Art* (Oxford: OUP, 1999), p. 152.
10. TSE to Paul Elmer More, 29 June 1930, Schuchard, op. cit., p. 129.
11. Valerie Eliot in interview with Timothy Wilson, "T. S. Eliot and I," *Observer,* 20 February 1972.
12. Journal of Lady Ottoline Morrell, 7 April 1934, Goodman Papers.
13. T. S. Eliot, *The Family Reunion* (London: Faber & Faber, 1939).
14. Phillip Herring, *A Man of Contradictions: A Life of A. L. Rowse* (London: Penguin, 1999).
15. TSE to VW, 3 November 1934, Berg.
16. VE Diary, 30 January 1934, Bodleian.
17. VE to OM, 31 December 1933, Texas.
18. VE Diary, 4 June 1934, Bodleian.
19. VE to Hope Esq., 8 January 1935, Bodleian.
20. Peter Ackroyd, *T. S. Eliot* (London: Penguin, 1993), p. 206.
21. TSE to JH, 1 February 1931, John Hayward Bequest, King's College, Cambridge.
22. VE to OM, 26 December 1933, Texas.
23. VE Diary, 14 June 1934, Bodleian.
24. VE Diary, 2 August 1935, Bodleian.
25. T. S. Matthews, *Great Tom: Notes Towards the Definition of T. S. Eliot* (London: Weidenfeld & Nicolson, 1974), p. 118.
26. Maurice Haigh-Wood, interview with Michael Hastings, 4 March 1980.
27. Maurice Haigh-Wood, interview with Michael Hastings, 19 March 1980.
28. Tom and Vivienne had remained in touch with Karl Culpin's sister, Mary, who had helped them move into 18 Crawford Mansions. Donald Adamson and L. P. Addison (eds.), Robert Sencourt, *T. S. Eliot: A Memoir* (London: Garnstone Press, 1971), p. 52.
29. VE Diary, 1 August 1934, Bodleian.
30. Ibid., 29 January 1934.
31. Ibid., 6 July 1934.
32. VE to OM, 31 December 1933, Texas.
33. VE Diary, 1 August 1934, Bodleian.
34. Ibid., 30 January 1934, Bodleian.
35. Ibid., 26 June 1934.
36. Ibid., 22 July 1934.

37. Will of Vivienne Haigh Eliot, 1 March 1936. Section 17 (2) of the Copyright Act 1911 created a rule of procedural law that there shall be a rebuttable presumption that a legatee of an unpublished manuscript is the owner of the copyright. This presumption can be rebutted by evidence to the contrary.

38. VE Diary, 23 July 1934, Bodleian.

39. Ibid., 8 July 1934.

40. Maurice Haigh-Wood, interview with Michael Hastings, 4 March 1980.

41. VE Diary, 21 March 1934, Bodleian.

42. Ibid., 16 April 1934.

43. Ibid., 28 May 1934.

44. Ibid., 1 June 1934.

45. Ibid., 4 June 1934.

46. E. Martin Browne, *The Making of T. S. Eliot's Plays* (Cambridge: CUP, 1969), p. 30.

47. VE Diary, 11 June 1934, Bodleian.

48. Ibid., 3 June 1934.

49. Ibid., 12 June 1934.

50. Ibid., 25 July 1934.

51. Ibid., 10 May 1934.

52. Ibid., 5 September.

53. Michael Ignatieff, *Isaiah Berlin, A Life* (London: Chatto & Windus, 1998), pp. 186–87.

54. Eliot warned Pound, who had become pro-Fascist, against Mosley on 12 March 1934. Lyndall Gordon, *Eliot's New Life* (Oxford: OUP, 1988), p. 22.

55. VE Diary, 24 October 1934, Bodleian.

56. Ibid., 28 November 1934.

57. The final item in Ottoline Morrell's file of correspondence with Vivienne is the Christmas card Vivienne sent her from herself and Tom for Christmas 1935, Texas.

58. VE Diary, 3 June 1935, Bodleian.

59. Ibid., 4 December 1934.

60. Ibid., 28 June 1934.

61. Ibid., 20 March 1934.

62. Anne Olivier Bell (ed.), *The Diary of Virginia Woolf,* vol. 4 (London: Penguin, 1983), 12 November 1934. Despite Hope's critical description of Vivienne, she met her regularly and Vivienne praised Hope's "wonderful personality." According to Virginia, Hope's dachshund had a "snappy screech" (p. 162) and was a distracting dog. Hope met Eliot at Virginia's after dinner on 12 November 1934.

63. VW to OM, 31 December 1933, Nigel Nicolson and Joanne Trautmann (eds.), *The Letters of Virginia Woolf,* vol. 5 (New York: 1980), p. 207.

64. VE Diary, 13 March 1934, Bodleian.

65. Last Will and Testament of Charles Haigh-Wood, 3 January 1920, and codicil of 18 May 1927.

66. VE Diary, 10 April 1934, Bodleian.

67. Ibid., 26 July 1934.

68. In her will of 1936, Vivienne stated that, subject to her mother's life interest, "I and my said Brother Maurice are . . . respectively entitled to equal shares" in Charles Haigh-Wood's estate.

69. Maurice Haigh-Wood, interview with Michael Hastings, 12 March 1980.

70. Will of Charles Haigh-Wood, 18 May 1927.

71. VE Diary, 1 January 1935, Bodleian.

72. Ibid., 7 April 1935.

73. Ibid., 1 January 1935.

74. TSE to JH, 18 February 1938, John Hayward Bequest, King's College, Cambridge. Eliot wrote that he always counted on making a new will every five years, so Hayward's commitment need only be for that period.

75. VE Diary, 10 June 1935, Bodleian.

76. Ibid., 13 November 1935.

77. VE Diary, 14 March 1934, Bodleian.

78. Ibid., 26 April 1934.

79. Will of Rose Esther Haigh-Wood, 20 February 1936.

80. VE Diary, 18, 20, 21 September 1934, Bodleian.

81. Ibid., 23 September 1934.

82. Ibid., 26 September 1934.

22. Cat and Mouse

1. Lyndall Gordon, *Eliot's New Life* (Oxford: OUP, 1988), p. 43.

2. John Hayward Bequest, King's College, Cambridge.

3. Gordon, *Eliot's New Life*, op. cit., p. 44.

4. Ibid., p. 47. The "Bellegarde" fragment is in the Houghton Library, with the Notes for *Murder in the Cathedral* made by Eliot between December 1934 and May 1935, and collected by Henry Ware Eliot Jr. The rose garden sequence in "Burnt Norton" was also the genesis for the similar scene in *The Family Reunion* between Mary and Harry. Early drafts of *The Family Reunion* date from 1934–35. See Gordon, *Eliot's New Life*, Appendix 1, pp. 274–76. I do not, however, agree with Lyndall Gordon that Emily was the inspiration for Eliot's "memory and desire" when he looked into "the heart of light, the silence" in *The Waste Land* (p. 48), which, I submit, was inspired by Jean Verdenal.

5. T. S. Eliot, "Burnt Norton," *Four Quartets, CP*, p. 189.

6. Journal of Lady Ottoline Morrell, 22 October 1935, Goodman Papers.

7. Peter Ackroyd, *T. S. Eliot* (London: Penguin, 1993), p. 230.

8. Helen Gardner, *The Composition of the Four Quartets* (London: Faber & Faber, 1978), p. 35.

9. Anne Olivier Bell (ed.), *The Diary of Virginia Woolf*, vol. 4 (London: Penguin, 1983), 31 March 1935, p. 294.

10. Ibid., 19 April 1934, p. 208.

11. Ibid., 21 November 1934, pp. 262–63.

12. VW to John Lehmann, 1932, John Lehmann, *Thrown to the Woolfs* (New York: Holt, Rinehart and Winston, 1979), p. 31. V. Woolf's *A Letter to a Young Poet* was published in 1932.

13. T. S. Matthews, *Great Tom: Notes Towards the Definition of T. S. Eliot* (London: Weidenfeld & Nicolson, 1974), p. 117.

14. Donald Adamson and L. P. Addison (eds.), Robert Sencourt, *T. S. Eliot: A Memoir* (London: Garnstone Press, 1971), p. 133.

15. Gardner, op. cit., p. 38.

16. Eliot, "Burnt Norton," op. cit., p. 194.

17. Ronald Schuchard, *Eliot's Dark Angel: Intersections of Life and Art* (Oxford: OUP, 1999), p. 181.

18. Eliot gave Hayward five typed drafts of "Little Gidding," beginning with "First Complete Draft 7 July 1941": on a page torn from his scribbling pad are notes showing that he had come to see the four seasons and four elements as the organising principle behind the sequence of poems. Gardner, op. cit., p. 157.

19. Herbert Howarth, *Notes on Some Figures Behind T. S. Eliot* (London: Chatto & Windus, 1965), p. 118.

20. "The Dry Salvages" (1941) *Four Quartets, CP,* pp. 205–13.

21. Ibid.

22. "Death by Water," Section IV, Valerie Eliot (ed.), *WL Facs,* p. 59.

23. "The Dry Salvages," *Four Quartets, CP,* pp. 209–10. Gardner thought the poem had a "lame close," which did not lead forward to the theme of the next poem. Gardner, op. cit., p. 149.

24. A window in Little Gidding church commemorates the visit of the king and displays his arms with the inscription: "Insignia Caroli Regis qui latitabat apud Ferrarios 2do Maii A.S. 1646." Helen Gardner writes of Eliot: "Having read the first draft of [Every's play], it seems to me that when, four or five years later, he planned to write a fourth poem on 'Fire,' it was Mr. Every's play that linked fire with Little Gidding in his mind and that his memory of it coloured the discussion of victory and defeat in Part III." Gardner, op. cit., pp. 62–63.

25. Every wrote: "King dead, the crown/One day was plucked by a crafty hand from a thornbush." Gardner, op. cit., p. 209.

26. Gardner, op. cit., p. 202.

27. "Little Gidding" (1942) in *CP,* p. 214. Whereas "The Dry Salvages" demonstrates Eliot's debt to Indic philosophy, in "Little Gidding" he returned to Dante, Yeats, and Julian of Norwich's *Revelations of Divine Love* (Cressy, 1670), as well as Evelyn Underhill's edition of *The Cloud of Unbeknowing,* from which he also quoted ("With the drawing of this love and the voice of this calling"). Evelyn Underhill reviewed for the *Criterion,* and her death in June 1941, when Eliot was writing "Little Gidding," may have prompted his return to the English mystics, whom she had popularised. Eliot read Underhill's *Mysticism* (1911) when he was at Harvard. Gardner, op. cit., pp. 69–71.

28. EP to TSE, ?1934, Beinecke. In July, Eliot replied that he was "right proud" to have that elephant and thanked Pound from the bottom of his heart.

29. TSE to EP, 3 January 1934, Beinecke.

30. EP to TSE, n.d., ?January 1934, Beinecke.

31. John Malcolm Brinnin, *Sextet: T. S. Eliot & Truman Capote & Others* (London: André Deutsch Ltd., 1982), p. 253.

32. EP to TSE, 3 February ?1935, Beinecke.

33. TSE to JH, 25 June 1934, John Hayward Bequest, King's College, Cambridge.

34. Francis King in conversation with the author, 4 April 2000.

35. Fable XIV, "The Whale, the Elephant, the Coot and the Spider," "Ode to a Roman Coot," "Nobody Knows How I Feel About You" (from Geoffrey Faber to Eliot), *Noctes Binanianae* (1939), no. 10 of 25 copies printed, Houghton.

36. VE Diary, 26 March 1934, Bodleian.

37. Ibid., 28 March 1934.

38. Bridget O'Donovan, "The Love Song of Eliot's Secretary," *Confrontation,* 11, Martin Tucker (ed.), Fall/Winter 1975.

39. VE Diary, 7 February 1935, Bodleian.

40. Ibid., 27 February 1935.

41. Ibid., 8 March 1935.

42. Ibid., 13 March 1935.

43. Ibid., 14 March 1935.

44. Ibid., 16 March 1935.

45. VE Diary, 10 October 1934.

46. Ibid., 11 October 1934.

47. Ibid., 11 December 1934.

48. Bird & Bird obtained a Court Order to enter 68 Clarence Gate Gardens, with which Vivienne refused to comply (Bird & Bird to VE, 30 October 1934). James & James refused to put forward Vivienne's claim for compensation because "had our advice been taken the necessity for breaking into your flat would not have arisen" (James & James to VE, 19 August 1935). Vivienne replied that if she had succumbed to James & James's pressure she would have signed "an offensive and damaging paper" in 1933 (signing away her rights to her property and papers to Eliot), and only Ella de Saxe's advice prevented her (VE to James & James, 20 August 1935, Bodleian).

49. Maurice Haigh-Wood, interview with Michael Hastings, 4 March 1980.

50. James & James to VE, 25 July 1935, Bodleian.

51. VE to Geoffrey Faber, copy, 29 March 1935, Bodleian.

52. VE to TSE, 25 September 1935, Bodleian.

53. VE Diary, 28 September 1935, Bodleian.

54. Moxon Broad to VE, 22 December 1934, Bodleian.

55. VE to T. Hope, District Bank, 8 January 1935, Bodleian.

56. VE Diary, 7 June 1935, Bodleian.

57. Maurice Haigh-Wood, interview with Michael Hastings, 19 March 1980.

58. Ibid.

59. VE Diary, 23 June 1935, Bodleian.

60. VE to Dr. Prevost, 28 June 1935, Bodleian.

61. VE Diary, 27 June 1935, Bodleian.

62. VE to TSE, 12 July 1935, Bodleian.

63. VE Diary, 12 July 1935, Bodleian.

64. Ibid., 15 July 1935.

65. Ibid., 23 July 1935.

66. Ibid., 12 August 1935.

67. Ibid., 29 September 1935.

68. Ibid., 10 September 1935.

69. Ibid., 26 September 1935.

70. VE to Harriet Weaver, 12 June 1936, Bodleian. Vivien wrote that her only free day was Saturday.

71. VE Diary, 15 October 1935, Bodleian.

72. Ibid., 6 December 1935.

73. Ibid., 25 October 1935.

74. Basil Saunders to Lyndall Gordon, 18 August 1993. I am indebted to Lyndall Gordon for making this correspondence available to me, and to Basil Saunders, for further information about Louie and Vivien's friendship.

75. VE Diary, 2 October 1935, Bodleian.

76. Ibid., 26 December 1935.

77. Ibid., 20 September 1935.

78. Ibid., 4 November 1935.

79. Ibid., 13 April 1936.

80. Ibid., 18 November 1935.

81. VE to James & James, 28 November 1935, Bodleian.

82. VE to James & James, 25 November 1935.

83. Gordon, *Eliot's New Life,* op. cit., p. 65.

84. Sybille Bedford, interview with author, 1 August 2000.

85. VE Diary, 30 November 1935, Bodleian.

86. Ibid., 11 October 1934.

23. Into the Dark

1. VE Diary, 11 December 1935, Bodleian.

2. Geoffrey Faber to VE, 13 March 1936, VE Paste-up book, MSS. Eng. Lett c. 383, Bodleian.

3. VE to Geoffrey Faber, 17 March 1936, Bodleian.

4. VE to Moxon Broad, 22 November 1935, Bodleian.

5. Dr. Prevost to VE, 15 November 1935, Bodleian.

6. VE Diary, 1 November 1935, Bodleian.

7. Ibid., 11 November 1935.

8. Will of Vivienne Haigh Eliot, 1 March 1936, Probate Registry, York. If she died in France Dr. Prevost and Prof. Claude were to certify death.

9. VE Diary, 18 March 1935, Bodleian.

10. Ibid., 1 November 1935, Bodleian.

11. Ibid., Easter Sunday 1936, Bodleian.

12. Ibid., 15 October 1935, Bodleian. Vivien had an interview with Broad in his City office in which he voiced his opinion of Eliot.

13. "Burnt Norton," *Four Quartets, CP,* p. 190.

14. TSE to Dorothy Pound, 28 July 1936, Lilly.

15. VE to T. Hope, District Bank Manager, 7 November 1935, Bodleian.

16. VE Notes to Moxon Broad, n.d., Bodleian.

17. VE to Mrs. Flint, 20 July 1936, Bodleian.

18. Henry James, *Daisy Miller* (1878; Penguin, 1986).

19. Ibid., p. 115. Mrs. Costello, Winterbourne's aunt, a member of New York society, declares of Daisy and her mother: "They are very common. They are the sort of Americans that one does one's duty by not—not accepting." Mrs. Costello, in whom Vivien would have seen a parallel to Charlotte Eliot, puts pressure on Winterbourne to drop the "vulgar" Daisy. James refers (p. 79) to Cherbuliez's novel *Paule Méré* (1865), in which the innocent but unconventional heroine has her reputation blackened by malicious gossip, which destroys her relationship with the hero. A character remarks: "What is this weakness which makes us listen to a society which we despise?" (p. 123, note 42). Reference to this novel by James emphasises his message of Daisy's innocence to the reader.

20. VE to Moxon Broad, 10 August 1936, Bodleian.

21. Stephen Spender, *T. S. Eliot* (London: Fontana, 1975), p. 130.

22. *The Family Reunion* (London: Faber & Faber, 1939), p. 113.

23. VE Loose-leaf book 1936, entry 13 April 1936, Bodleian.

24. VE Diary, 12 July 1936, Bodleian.

25. Advertisement for secretary, VE Loose-leaf book 1936, Bodleian.

26. VE to Edgar Horn, Estate Agent, 14 June 1936, Bodleian.

27. VE Diary, 24 December 1935, Bodleian.

28. VE to J. Moxon Broad, 22 November 1935, Bodleian.

29. VE Diary, 22 December 1935, Bodleian.

30. VE to Harriet Weaver, 12 June 1936, Bodleian. T. S. Eliot dedicated his *Selected Essays* in 1932 "To Harriet Shaw Weaver in gratitude, and in recognition of her services to English Letters."

31. VE, "Notes for Moxon Broad," n.d., Loose-leaf book, 1936, Bodleian.

32. VE to St. J. Hutchinson, 8 November 1935, Bodleian.

33. VE to Literary Manager, Faber & Faber, 2 September 1936, Bodleian.

34. Bridget O'Donovan to VE, 4 September 1936, Bodleian.

35. Joan Skelton, Reception Secretary, English-Speaking Union, to VE, 21 February 1936, Bodleian.

36. Earl Marshall to VE, 24 February 1936, Loose-leaf book, Bodleian.

37. VE Diary, 13 December 1935, Bodleian.

38. On 17 July, J. Moxon Broad wrote to Vivien, c/o Miss Daisy Miller, to say that he had insured 8 Edge Street for £1,500 during the repairs she was having done. The rent was £160 p.a., Bodleian.

39. VE to T. Hope, District Bank, 19 July 1936, Bodleian.

40. "Daisy Miller," The Three Arts Club, to Moxon Broad, 5 August 1936, Bodleian.

41. Moxon Broad to "Daisy Miller," 6 August 1936, Bodleian.

42. VE to Ella de Saxe, 30 December 1935, Bodleian.

43. VE to Miss Hutchins, Piano Teacher, Royal Academy of Music, 24 July 1936, Bodleian.

44. Rose Haigh-Wood to VE, 5 April 1936, Bodleian.

45. Rose Haigh-Wood to VE, n.d., Bodleian.

46. VE to Maurice Haigh-Wood, 13 May 1936, Bodleian.

47. Ahmé was born in Charleston, South Carolina, in 1905.

48. Maurice Haigh-Wood, interview with Michael Hastings, 23 March 1980.

49. VE to Literary Manager, Faber & Faber, 5 September 1936, Bodleian.

50. Eliot's Club Brochure, March 1936.

51. VE to Moxon Broad, 15 November 1936, Bodleian.

52. Maurice Haigh-Wood to VE, 20 November 1936, Bodleian.

53. VE to Maurice Haigh-Wood, 22 November 1936, Bodleian.

54. VE to T. Hope, District Bank, 27 October 1935, Bodleian.

55. VE to Dr. Reginald Miller, 11 November 1936, Bodleian.

56. Dr. Miller to VE, 13 November. Miller thanked Vivien for payment of his fee and agreed to call that day, Bodleian.

57. VE to Royal Academy of Music, 27 November 1936, Bodleian.

58. VE to Mary Hutchinson, 11 November 1936, Texas.

59. Maurice Haigh-Wood, interview with Michael Hastings, 12 March 1980.

60. VE Diary, 13 April 1936, Bodleian.

61. Maurice Haigh-Wood to VE, 17 December 1936, Bodleian.

62. VE to Moxon Broad, 11 February 1936, Probate Registry, York.

63. Last Will and Testament of Vivienne Haigh Eliot, 1 March 1936.

64. Maurice Haigh-Wood, interview with Michael Hastings, 23 March 1980. Maurice said that in 1965 he lost £200,000 in Slater Walker, and by 1980 was "down to £250,000."

65. VE to T. Hope, 27 October 1935, Bodleian.

66. Vivienne noted that the total rents for the Irish property at Haigh Terrace, 16 Tivoli Road, and 1–10 Eglinton Park, and Eglinton House for six years, 1927–33, was £1144.15.0d, of which she was entitled to one third. 1 February 1935, VE Diary.

67. Anne Olivier Bell (ed.), *The Diary of Virginia Woolf,* vol. 5, 1936–41 (London: Penguin, 1985), 22 March 1939, p. 210.

68. E. Martin Browne, *The Making of T. S. Eliot's Plays* (Cambridge: CUP, 1969), p. 144.

69. VE to Theresa Eliot, 6 July 1936, Bodleian. Henry and Theresa Eliot were then living at 315 East 68th Street, New York City.

70. Lyndall Gordon, *Eliot's New Life* (Oxford: OUP, 1988), p. 169.

71. VE to G. Faber, 10 December 1936, Bodleian.

72. VE to Moxon Broad, 23 August 1936, Bodleian. The Cable Company replied that all copies of the cables were destroyed a year after sending.

73. Vivienne emphasised to her bank, too, that she was "morbidly careful" about papers, and never burnt or destroyed one without consideration. Her account books and lists of rents on her Irish property demonstrate this.

74. Louis MacNeice, translator's note, programme for *Agamemnon,* music by Benjamin Britten, masks by Robert Medley, choreography and production by Rupert Doone, 1 November 1936, Bodleian.

75. MH to VE, postcard, n.d., 1936, Texas.

76. Blake Morrison, "The Two Mrs. Eliots," *Too True* (London: Granta Books, 1998), pp. 139–40, first published in *Independent on Sunday,* 24 April 1994.

77. VE to St. J. Hutchinson, 29 November 1935, Bodleian. Vivienne wrote to tell Jack that she had seen Tom, and was now living at the Constance Hotel.

78. Enid Faber to Michael Hastings, 26 August 1983, MH Papers.

79. Maurice Haigh-Wood, interview with Michael Hastings, 19 March 1980.

80. "East Coker," *CP,* p. 199.

81. Ibid., pp. 201–2.

82. Blake Morrison, op. cit., p. 141.

83. Basil Saunders to Dr. Lyndall Gordon, 18 August 1993.

84. Lawrence Stone, *Road to Divorce, England 1530–1987* (Oxford: OUP, 1992), pp. 167, 168.

85. Bill Saunders, grandson of Marjorie Saunders (*née* Purdon), e-mail to author, 14 September 1999.

86. Basil Saunders to Lyndall Gordon, 18 August 1993.

87. Blake Morrison, op. cit.

88. John Gielgud, *An Actor's Life* (London: Penguin, 1981), p. 133. Gielgud also recalled the oysters, as well as the formality of the occasion. He thought he had created quite a good impression on Eliot, until a few days later Sibyl Thorndike told him that Eliot was not going to let him have the play, fearing he was going to turn it into "a fashionable Shaftesbury Avenue comedy." Years later, meeting in Marrakesh, Gielgud told Eliot that he had played Harry in *The Family Reunion* on the radio, and made a recording of his "Journey of the Magi." The poet asked Gielgud to send him a copy. Although Gielgud never met Vivienne, he well remembered Derek Patmore and Edith and Osbert Sitwell, and made an unsuccessful attempt to make a film in which he would play Sir George Sitwell. Sir John Gielgud to the author, 22 May 1998.

89. TSE to John Hayward, 19 November 1937, 20 October 1938, John Hayward Bequest, King's College, Cambridge.

90. TSE to Mrs. Webster, 28 October 1938, King's College, Cambridge.

91. TSE to JH, 4 May 1938, King's College, Cambridge.

92. Journal of Lady Ottoline Morrell, 26 March 1934, Goodman Papers.

93. Michael Hastings, Introduction, *Tom and Viv* (London: Penguin, 1984).

94. VE Diary, 24 August 1934, Bodleian.

95. Martha Cooley, *The Archivist* (London: Little, Brown & Company, 1998), p. 3.

96. Having seen *The Family Reunion,* Djuna Barnes wrote *The Antiphon* (1939), her own revenge drama. Phillip Herring, *Djuna: The Life and Work of Djuna Barnes* (London: Viking, 1995), p. 262.

97. In his review (1958) of *The Antiphon,* Eugenio Montale described Barnes as a sponge of prussic acid. Herring, op. cit., p. 259.

98. *The Family Reunion,* op. cit., p. 113.

99. TSE to JH, 6 September 1939, King's College, Cambridge.

100. Richard Ollard, *A Man of Contradictions: A Life of A. L. Rowse* (London: Penguin, 1999) serialised in the *Daily Telegraph,* 22 September 1999, cites a letter dated 12 October 1934 from TSE to Rowse, in which he sets out the marital and financial difficulties he faced, and the idea lapsed.

101. TSE to JH, 8 November 1939, King's College, Cambridge.

102. TSE to JH, 29 November 1939, King's College, Cambridge.

103. Ibid.

104. TSE to JH, 19 November 1937, King's College, Cambridge. Eliot's letter comments on the design of the title page of *Noctes Binanianae.*

105. John Malcolm Brinnin, *Sextet: T. S. Eliot & Truman Capote & Others* (London: André Deutsch, 1982), pp. 252–53.

106. E. W. F. Tomlin, *T. S. Eliot: A Friendship* (London: Routledge, 1988), p. 149.

107. TSE to JH, 13 December 1939, King's College, Cambridge.

108. Robert Robinson, *Skip All That: Memoirs* (London: Century, 1996), p. 22.

109. TSE to JH, 2 June 1940, King's College, Cambridge.

110. Jonathan Fryer, *Eye of the Camera: A Life of Christopher Isherwood* (London: Allison & Busby, 1993), p. 106. In 1935 Auden and Isherwood were writing *The Dog Beneath the Skin,* which was commissioned by Eliot at Faber & Faber, staged by Rupert Doone et al., and watched by Vivienne, who preserved her programme.

111. It was while Eliot was staying at the "Cat Farm," as he called the Mirrlees house, that Robert Sencourt took him over to meet the Duchess of Northumberland, whose guest he was at Albury Park. While Sencourt was pointing out the Turners to Eliot, the Duchess came in, and Sencourt explained to her that he had brought his friend over to give her the opportunity of meeting him. "I detected, however, that she knew nothing of Tom's work and it was therefore with diffidence that I introduced them. Tom noticed this at once and said with his usual good humour, 'Are you getting to be ashamed of me, Robert?' " Robert Sencourt, *T. S. Eliot: A Memoir,* edited by Donald Adamson and L. P. Addison (London: Garnstone Press, 1971), p. 141. Mary also visited Eliot in Shamley Green, bravely walking the five miles from Peaslake as instructed by Eliot.

112. Mary Trevelyan, "The Pope of Russell Square 1938–1958: Twenty Years 'and no-tomorrow,' " unpublished memoir.

113. Ibid., p. 19.

114. Sandra Jobson Darroch, *Ottoline: The Life of Lady Ottoline Morrell* (London, 1976), p. 288.

115. VE Quotation on death, ?mid-1920s. Loose-leaf book, MSS Eng. Misc. c. 624, Bodleian.

116. Trevelyan, op. cit., p. 35.

117. Will of Vivienne Haigh Eliot, 1 March 1936.

118. Vivienne is buried in plot G6–78 and Rose nearby in G6–92 in Pinner Cemetery, Middlesex. Maurice was responsible for the upkeep of the grave according to the Cemetery Superintendent. Ray Bown to the author, 26 April 2000.

Epilogue

1. Lyndall Gordon, *Eliot's New Life* (Oxford: OUP, 1988), p. 147.

2. Mary Trevelyan, "The Pope of Russell Square 1938–1958," unpublished memoir, p. 35.

3. Maurice Haigh-Wood, interview with Michael Hastings, 12 March 1980.

4. E. W. F. Tomlin, *T. S. Eliot: A Friendship* (London: Routledge, 1988), p. 218.

5. Trevelyan, op. cit., p. 37.

6. Gordon, *Eliot's New Life,* op. cit., p. 169.

7. Tomlin, op. cit., p. 219.

8. Ibid., p. 171.

9. Emily gave Eliot's letters to her to Princeton after hearing the devastating news of his second marriage to his secretary in 1957. She retired from her post, and after treatment for a nervous breakdown in Massachusetts General Hospital in Boston, returned to Chipping Campden, where she appeared disturbed. She died in 1968. For a fuller account of the relationship between Eliot and Emily Hale, see Gordon, *Eliot's New Life.*

10. Trevelyan, op. cit., 2 June 1950, p. 72.

11. In Mary Trevelyan's copy of *The Cocktail Party,* Eliot inscribed with characteristic formality: "To Miss Mary Trevelyan, with the author's compliments" and, in addition, "See Appendix and with thanks for her contribution to the character of Julia, eg p. 151." The Appendix consists of "The tune of One Eyed Riley, as scored from the author's dictation by Miss Mary Trevelyan." Page 151 includes lines in which Julia interrupts Riley. Tom, Mary recalled, used to derive great pleasure from interrupting her longer "and more fascinating" stories so that she lost the thread entirely.

12. Trevelyan, op. cit., 2 June 1950, p. 72.

13. One of Eliot's rules was never to see *anyone* two days in succession. She was hurt when he made John and Madame Amory, the French housekeeper, his excuse for vetoing his Sunday night suppers with Mary; the routine was changed from Wednesdays and Sundays to Tuesdays and Thursdays in 1952.

14. Mary Trevelyan to John Hayward, 21 April 1955. King's College, Cambridge.

15. Trevelyan, op. cit., p. 119.

16. Ibid., 26 August 1954, p. 120.

17. Josef Chiari, *T. S. Eliot: a Memoir* (London: Vision Press, 1972), p. 129.

18. T. S. Eliot exploded to Hayward over an article by his former protégé novelist Richard Church, who had published an article in *Books* which Eliot interpreted as an attack upon himself. Eliot threatened to resign as Vice-President of the National Book League, and it took all Geoffrey Faber's diplomatic skill to persuade him to stay on. TSE to JH, 9 May 1950, King's College, Cambridge.

19. E. Martin Browne, *The Making of T. S. Eliot's Plays* (Cambridge: CUP, 1969), p. 342.

20. Ronald Duncan, *How to Make Enemies* (London: Rupert Hart-Davis, 1968), p. 384.

21. Eliot underwrote a loss of £1,500 on Duncan's play *Stratton,* see Peter Ackroyd, *T. S. Eliot*

(London: Penguin, 1993), p. 301. He took enormous trouble with Djuna Barnes' *Nightwood,* cutting it extensively and writing a 1,500 word preface. Faber published it in 1937. Phillip Herring, *Djuna: The Life and Work of Djuna Barnes* (London: Viking, 1995), p. 230.

22. Ackroyd, *Eliot,* op. cit., pp. 304, 305.

23. William Turner Levy and Victor Scherle, *Affectionately, T. S. Eliot: The Story of a Friendship: 1947–1965* (London: Dent & Sons, 1969), p. 88.

24. Tomlin, op. cit., p. 195.

25. Trevelyan, op. cit., p. 95.

26. Ibid., pp. 96, 98.

27. Tomlin, op. cit., p. 184.

28. TSE to JH, 18 February 1938, King's College, Cambridge.

29. Eliot's instructions to his executors, 29 June 1956. Originally Eliot had purchased plot no. 2150 at Brookwood Cemetery, Woking, for his burial.

30. John Malcolm Brinnin, *Sextet: T. S. Eliot & Truman Capote & Others* (London: André Deutsch, 1982), p. 274.

31. Alan Bennett, *Writing Home* (London: Faber & Faber, 1994), p. ix.

32. Timothy Wilson, "T. S. Eliot and I," interview with Valerie Eliot, 20 February 1972, *Observer.*

33. Browne, op. cit., pp. 340–41.

34. Trevelyan, op. cit., p. 167. Although Mary was struck off his Christmas card list, her mother received a Faber card. As for John, apart from two visits to collect his possessions from the flat, Eliot had no contact with him for six months, until John was invited to lunch with Robert Frost and Rosamund Lehmann.

35. T. S. Matthews, *Great Tom: Notes Towards the Definition of T. S. Eliot* (London: Weidenfeld & Nicolson, 1974), p. 160.

36. Postscript to Trevelyan, op. cit., Chelsea, August 1958. The prayer Mary said every night for Tom ran as follows:

> Protector of travellers
> Bless the road.
> Watch over him in the desert.
> Watch over him in the mountain.
> Watch over him in the labyrinth.
> Watch over him by the quicksand.
> Protect him from the Voices
> Protect him from the Visions
> Protect him from the tumult
> Protect him in the silence.

Bibliography

A Note on Sources

The conspiracy of silence which has grown up around the life of Vivienne and T. S. Eliot over the years created difficulties when I began my search and it is clear that some sources for Vivienne's life still remain closed to me. Many letters, perhaps, remain in the possession of Mrs. Valerie Eliot, as we await the publication of further volumes of T. S. Eliot's own correspondence, and significant collections remain under the control of the Eliot estate. John Hayward's letters to Eliot at King's College, Cambridge, may only be read by permission of Mrs. Valerie Eliot. At the Houghton Library, Harvard, Eliot's letters to Emily Hale remain restricted, as does a larger collection at Princeton. As well as collections which are closed to researchers, others may be read but quotation is prohibited, as was the case with Vivienne's own papers in the Bodleian Library, Oxford, when I began my research.

In addition, correspondents tended to throw away their letters from Vivienne—as the mere wife of a great man—while retaining those from her husband. As her reputation became blackened by scandal and the label of insanity, others, such as Bertrand Russell, destroyed them deliberately in an attempt to distance himself from her. Maurice Haigh-Wood delivered Vivienne's papers to the Bodleian Library in 1947, but when he did so much was missing. Vivienne's diaries are incomplete, covering only the years 1914, 1919, and the period of her separation from T. S. Eliot, ending in 1936. Unfortunately, one of the black notebooks in which she wrote drafts of her stories, often edited in T. S. Eliot's hand, went missing from the library in 1990, but three remain, as well as her day-books, which include drafts of fiction and poetry, some published in the *Criterion;* there is also Vivienne's correspondence relating to the period before her committal, as well as postcards, theatre tickets to see Eliot's plays, press cuttings, photographs and her account books. Together they provide a window into the Eliots' life together. The many other sources for Vivienne's life remain buried within the collections of more famous figures.

In the United States, at the Beinecke Rare Book and Manuscript Library at Yale, are Vivienne's letters to Scofield Thayer, an early confidant. The Ezra Pound Papers, also at the Beinecke Library, include Vivienne's surviving letters to Pound, whom she, like Tom, regarded as a mentor and friend. Vivienne's pitiful letters here can be laid side by side with Eliot's to Pound of the same period, revealing how Tom and Ezra delighted in deceiving her. Eliot's letters to Pound's wife, Dorothy, demonstrate that she, too, was a supporter of the poet against Vivienne, and refer to the fact that some of the Pound/Eliot correspondence was censored by Eliot at some point. The library also holds Eliot's letters to W. F. Stead, his confessor.

Within the Pound Papers are the manuscript "Colombo" and "Bolo" poems on pages which Eliot had excised from the notebook of early poems begun in 1910, which he sold to John Quinn in 1922 for £29 24s. 10d. ($140). Before sending Quinn the notebook, Eliot cut out those leaves containing parts of the Bolo series. He seems to have given them, along with scraps of other versions, to Pound, who put the obscene verses in an envelope labelled: "T.S.E. Chançons ithyphallique."

The Harry Ransom Humanities Research Center at the University of Texas at Austin holds a number of significant collections: the Ottoline Morrell Papers and Mary Hutchinson Papers, which contain the intimate letters to her two closest female friends, recording the long process of deterioration of her marriage and health, as well as Eliot's duplicity; the Aldington Papers, which reveal the extent of the Eliots' literary partnership during the *Criterion* period; and the Sitwell Papers which furnished further depth and detail for Vivienne's story.

The monumental Eliot collection at the Houghton Library at Harvard holds the letters from Vivienne to her formidable mother-in-law, Charlotte Champe Eliot, although, to my regret, these were not catalogued and proved difficult to access. There were also the original letters from Jean Verdenal, the French medical student who shared an intimate friendship with Eliot. The Houghton Library has a rich cache of photographs, as well as the writings and poems of Charlotte Eliot, the correspondence between Eliot's elder brother Henry and his mother, which betrays the Eliots' hostility to Vivienne, and drafts of Eliot's drama, including *The Family Reunion,* with Emily Hale's annotations, and *Sweeney Agonistes.* There is also a copy of *Noctes Binanianae,* the bawdy poems by Eliot and Geoffrey Faber, which were privately printed by John Hayward, and of Eliot's drafts of the Clark Lectures.

The Berg Collection in the New York Public Library houses some of Eliot's correspondence to Virginia and Leonard Woolf relating to Vivienne's health. There are also early manuscripts of T. S. Eliot's poems, among them the manuscript of *The Waste Land* which Eliot gave to John Quinn in 1922.

The many letters between Tom and Vivienne Eliot and Lady Ottoline Morrell at the Harry Ransom Center revealed the length and significance of Vivienne's affair with Bertrand Russell, and led me to the Bertrand Russell archive at McMaster University, Hamilton, Ontario. It holds Vivienne's few remaining letters to Bertie, together with the extensive correspondence between Bertie and Ottoline, his "senior" mistress, and Bertie and Colette, the mistress who supplanted Vivienne, as well as the typescript by Phyllis Urch, literary executor of Colette (Lady Constance Malleson), which includes many of Colette's letters to Russell.

In England, meanwhile, access to a number of private collections made it possible to add pieces to the jigsaw: Mary Trevelyan's detailed and objective memoir of her twenty-year friendship with Eliot; Lady Ottoline Morrell's unexpurgated journals, which filled in many gaps in her published two-volume memoirs; the notes which Michael Hastings made of his interviews with Col. Maurice Haigh-Wood just before Maurice's death in 1980.

In public collections in the UK, besides the Bodleian Library, there are the John Hayward Bequest at King's College, Cambridge, which includes correspondence between Hayward and Eliot, and the Schiff Papers in the British Library.

Vivienne Eliot's Writings

Unpublished drafts of the following sketches are in the Bodleian Library, MSS. Eng. misc. d. 936/1–4.

Notebook 1	noted to be missing on 15 June 1990
Notebook 2	"Médecine à la Mode," edited by T. S. Eliot

	"The Lonely Soldier"
	"Parties"
	"Sibylla and Mike"
	"Dream Song"
Notebook 3	"Letter of the Moment"
	"The Ginger Kitten"
	"The Night Club"
	Bertrand Russell sketch for "Parties"
	Sketch: "André and Sibylla Go Shopping"
Notebook 4	4 November 1924. "A Paris Diary" or "A Diary of the Rive Gauche," or "Paris on £5 a Week," edited by T. S. Eliot

MSS Eng. Misc. c. 624. Loose-leaf book, includes drafts of sketches, poems, letters to Vivienne (some in T. S. Eliot's hand also)

"Ellison and Antony"

Poems: "Necesse est Perstare" (alternative titles "Ennui," "Exhaustion," "Fatigue"); "Perque Domos Ditis Vacuas"; Poem about Jack at Fishbourne; "The Coliseum Dome," 17 October 1925

Drafts of "Letters of the Moment, I and II"

"Song in the Night" by "Feiron Morris"

Verses in both Eliot's and Vivienne's handwriting on "Love in Curious Shapes"

"Rosa Buckle" sketch

"The Paralysed Woman" by "Feiron Morris"

"Dancing" in Eliot's hand

"Pseudo-Bridge"

Notes on "Self-Destruction." The book ends with the death certificate of Charles Haigh-Wood, d. 25 March 1927

Vivienne's account books are dated December 1927–April 1932.

Vivienne's work was published in the *Criterion* under different pen names:

"F.M.," "Letters of the Moment I," *Criterion,* vol. 2, no. 6, February 1924

"F.M.," "Letters of the Moment II," *Criterion,* vol. 2, no. 7, April 1924

"F.M.," "Books of the Quarter" reviews, *Criterion,* July 1924

"Felix Morrison," "Mrs. Pilkington," *Criterion,* vol. 3, October 1924

"Feiron Morris," "Thé Dansant," *Criterion,* vol. 3, October 1924

T. S. Eliot, "On the Eve: A Dialogue," *Criterion,* January 1925

(This dialogue is written in Vivienne's style, although Eliot probably edited it.)

"Fanny Marlow," "Diary of the Rive Gauche," *Criterion,* January 1925

"F.M.," "Books of the Quarter," reviews of Virginia Woolf, G. Stern

"F.M.," Poem: "Necesse est Perstare," *Criterion,* April 1925

"Feiron Morris," "Night Club," *Criterion,* April 1925

"Fanny Marlow," "Diary of the Rive Gauche II," *Criterion,* April 1925

"I. P. Fassett" and "F.M.," "Books of the Quarter," reviews of Rose Macaulay and others, *Criterion,* April 1925

"Fanny Marlow," "Fête Galante," *Criterion,* July 1925

"I. P. Fassett," "Books of the Quarter," *The New Criterion,* vol. 4, January 1926

A Note on The Waste Land

Quotations from *The Waste Land* are taken from the original 1,000-line manuscript which, on his return from Dr. Vittoz's Lausanne clinic, T. S. Eliot gave to Ezra Pound in Paris in early January 1922. Pound, as editor, reduced the size of the text and sacrificed much of the personal element of the poem. Sections and additional poems such as "The Death of the Duchess," "Death by Water," "The Fire Sermon," "The Death of St. Narcissus," "Exequy," "Elegy," and "Dirge" were either dramatically cut or omitted altogether. The title of the poem was changed from "He Do the Police in Different Voices" (a quotation from Dickens's *Our Mutual Friend*) to *The Waste Land*. On 23 October, Eliot sent the manuscripts of *The Waste Land*, consisting of fifty-four leaves, to John Quinn, the New York attorney who acted as his agent. On 28 July 1924 Quinn died, and the manuscripts were subsequently lost; in the 1950s they were rediscovered by his niece, Mrs. Thomas F. Conroy, who, on 4 April 1958, sold them privately to the Berg Collection of the New York Public Library for $18,000. Neither Eliot nor Pound knew of this transaction; in the summer of 1968, three years after Eliot's death, his widow Mrs. Valerie Eliot was informed of the acquisition by Mr. James W. Henderson, Chief of the Research Libraries of the New York Public Library. She subsequently edited and wrote an Introduction for *The Waste Land: A Facsimile and Transcript of the Original Drafts including the Annotations of Ezra Pound* (Harcourt Brace and Co., 1971); the facsimile edition of *The Waste Land* also included the editorial comments and additions made by Vivien Eliot who wrote two, possibly three lines of *The Waste Land*, writing on page fifteen, for example: "Make any of these alterations—or *none* if you prefer. Send me back this copy & let me have it." I am indebted to Valerie Eliot for her scholarship.

Published Sources of T. S. Eliot's Works and Letters

Donald Gallup's bibliography, *T. S. Eliot: A Bibliography* (1969), lists T. S. Eliot's major works. I cite only those which have been most relevant to the writing of this book.

Prufrock and Other Observations (London: Egoist Ltd., 1917)
Poems (London: Hogarth Press, 1919)
Ara Vos Prec (London: The Ovid Press, 1920)
The Sacred Wood (London: Methuen & Co., 1920)
The Waste Land (London: Hogarth Press, 1923)
Homage to John Dryden (London: Hogarth Press, 1924)
Poems, 1909–1925 (London: Faber & Gwyer, 1925)
Journey of the Magi (London: Faber & Gwyer, 1927)
For Lancelot Andrewes (London: Faber & Gwyer, 1928)
Ash Wednesday, with the dedication "To My Wife" (London: Faber & Faber, 1930)
The Use of Poetry and the Use of Criticism: The Charles Eliot Norton Lectures for 1932–33
    (Cambridge, Mass.: Harvard University Press, 1961)
Selected Essays 1917–1932 (London: Faber & Faber, 1932)
The Varieties of Metaphysical Poetry: The Clark Lectures at Trinity College, Cambridge, 1926 and

The Turnbull Lectures at The Johns Hopkins University 1933, edited by Ronald Schuchard
        (New York: Harcourt Brace Jovanovich, 1993)
Sweeney Agonistes (London: Faber & Faber, 1932)
After Strange Gods (London: Faber & Faber, 1934)
The Rock (London: Faber & Faber, 1934)
Murder in the Cathedral (London: Faber & Faber, 1935)
Old Possum's Book of Practical Cats (London: Faber & Faber, 1939)
The Family Reunion (London: Faber & Faber, 1939)
Four Quartets (London: Faber & Faber, 1944)
The Cocktail Party (London: Faber & Faber, 1949)
Poems Written in Early Youth (London: Faber & Faber, 1950)
The Confidential Clerk (London: Faber & Faber, 1954)
On Poetry and Poets (London: Faber & Faber, 1957)
The Elder Statesman (London: Faber & Faber, 1959)
To Criticize the Critic (London: Faber & Faber, 1965)
Valerie Eliot (ed.), T. S. Eliot, *The Waste Land: A Facsimile and Transcript of the Original Drafts
        including the Annotations of Ezra Pound* (New York: Harcourt Brace Javanovich, 1971)
Collected Poems 1909–1962 (London: Faber & Faber, 1974)
Valerie Eliot (ed.), *The Letters of T. S. Eliot, Volume I, 1898–1922* (New York: Harcourt Brace
        Jovanovich, 1988)
Christopher Ricks (ed.), *Inventions of the March Hare, T. S. Eliot: Poems 1909–1917* (New
        York: Harcourt Brace Jovanovich, 1996)

Select Bibliography

This does not pretend to be an exhaustive bibliography, but merely lists some of the books, collections, essays and articles I found most helpful.

Ackroyd, Peter, *Ezra Pound* (London: Thames and Hudson, 1980)
Ackroyd, Peter, *T. S. Eliot* (London: Penguin, 1993)
Aiken, Conrad, *Selected Letters of Conrad Aiken,* Joseph Killorin (ed.) (New Haven, Conn., 1978)
Aiken, Conrad, *Ushant* (London: W. H. Allen, 1963)
Aldington, Richard, *Stepping Heavenward, A Record* (London, 1931)
Aldington, Richard, *Richard Aldington: An Autobiography in Letters,* Norman Gates (ed.)
        (Philadelphia, Penn.: University of Pennsylvania Press, 1992)
Aldington, Richard, *Life for Life's Sake* (New York: Viking Press, 1941)
Behr, Caroline, *T. S. Eliot: A Chronology of His Life and Works* (London: Macmillan, 1983)
Bell, Clive, *Old Friends: Personal Recollections* (London: Chatto & Windus, 1956)
Bell, Quentin, *Bloomsbury* (London: Weidenfeld & Nicolson, 1968)
Bell, Vanessa, *Selected Letters,* Regina Marler (ed.) (New York: Pantheon Books, 1993)
Bergonzi, Bernard, *T. S. Eliot* (London: Macmillan, 1972)
Bradshaw, David, "Those Extraordinary Parakeets," *The Charleston Magazine,* Part I,
        Autumn/Winter 1997, 16; Part II, Spring/Summer 1998, 17
Brinnin, John Malcolm, *Sextet: T. S. Eliot & Truman Capote & Others* (London: André
        Deutsch, 1987)

Browne, E. Martin, *The Making of T. S. Eliot's Plays* (Cambridge: Cambridge University Press, 1969)

Buckle, Richard, *Diaghilev* (London: Weidenfeld & Nicolson, 1993)

Carpenter, Humphrey, *A Serious Character: The Life of Ezra Pound* (London: Faber & Faber, 1988)

Chiari, Joseph, *T. S. Eliot: A Memoir* (London, 1982)

Clare, Anthony, *Psychiatry in Dissent: Controversial Issues in Thought and Practice* (London: Routledge, 1980)

Clark, Ronald W., *The Life of Bertrand Russell* (London: Jonathan Cape and Weidenfeld & Nicolson, 1975)

Cooley, Martha, *The Archivist* (London: Little, Brown, 1998)

Darroch, Sandra, *Ottoline: The Life of Lady Ottoline Morrell* (London, 1976)

Delany, Paul, "T. S. Eliot's Personal Finances 1915–29," chapter in *Literature, Money and the Market from Trollope to Amis* (Basingstoke: Palgrave, 2001)

Doyle, Charles, *Richard Aldington, A Biography* (London: Macmillan, 1989)

Duncan, Ronald, *How to Make Enemies* (London: Rupert Hart-Davis, 1968)

Gallup, Donald, "The Lost Manuscripts of T. S. Eliot," *Times Literary Supplement,* 7 November 1968

Garafola, Lynn, *Diaghilev's Ballets Russes* (New York: Da Capo Press, 1998)

Gardner, Helen, *The Art of T. S. Eliot* (London, 1949)

Gardner, Helen, *The Composition of the Four Quartets* (London: Faber & Faber, 1978)

Garnett, Angelica, *Deceived with Kindness: A Bloomsbury Childhood* (Oxford: Oxford University Press, 1984)

Glendinning, Victoria, *Edith Sitwell: A Unicorn Among Lions* (London: Phoenix, 1993)

Gordon, Lyndall, *Eliot's Early Years* (Oxford: Oxford University Press, 1977)

Gordon, Lyndall, *Eliot's New Life* (Oxford: Oxford University Press, 1988)

Gordon, Lyndall, *Virginia Woolf: A Writer's Life* (Oxford: Oxford University Press, 1991)

Gordon, Lyndall, *T. S. Eliot: An Imperfect Life* (London: Vintage, 1998)

Grover, Smith, Jr., *T. S. Eliot's Poetry and Plays* (Chicago: University of Chicago Press, 1956)

Hastings, Michael, *Tom and Viv,* with introduction by Michael Hastings (London: Penguin, 1984)

Hoare, Philip, *Oscar Wilde's Last Stand, Decadence, Conspiracy, and the Most Outrageous Trial of the Century* (New York: Arcade Publishing Inc., 1998)

Hoeveler, Diana Long, *Romantic Androgyny: The Women Within* (Philadelphia, Penn.: University of Pennsylvania Press, 1990)

Holroyd, Michael, *Lytton Strachey: A Critical Biography* (London: Vintage, 1995)

Howarth, Herbert, *Notes on Some Figures Behind T. S. Eliot* (London: Chatto & Windus, 1965)

James, Henry, *Daisy Miller* (London: Penguin, 1984)

Joost, Nicholas, *Scofield Thayer and* The Dial: *An Illustrated History* (Southern Illinois University Press, 1964)

Julius, Anthony, *T. S. Eliot, Anti-Semitism, and Literary Form* (Cambridge: Cambridge University Press, 1995)

Kenner, Hugh, *The Invisible Poet: T. S. Eliot* (London: W. H. Allen, 1960)

Lee, Hermione, *Virginia Woolf* (London: Vintage, 1997)

Lehmann, John, *Thrown to the Woolfs, Leonard and Virginia Woolf and the Hogarth Press* (New York: Holt, Rinehart & Winston, 1979)

Levy, William Turner and V. A. Scherle, *Affectionately, T. S. Eliot* (London, 1969)

Lewis, Wyndham, *Blasting and Bombardiering* (London: Calder & Boyars, 1967)

Lewis, Wyndham, *The Apes of God* (London, 1931)

Lewis, Wyndham, *The Letters of Wyndham Lewis,* W. K. Rose (ed.) (London, 1963)

Litz, A. Walton (ed.), *Eliot in His Time: Essays on the Occasion of the Fiftieth Anniversary of The Waste Land* (Princeton: Princeton University Press, 1973)

Malleson, Constance, *After Ten Years* (London: Jonathan Cape, 1929)

Mansfield, Katherine, *Bliss and Other Stories* (London: Constable, 1920)

March, Richard and Tambimuttu (eds.), *T. S. Eliot: A Symposium* (London: P.L. Editions, 1948)

Massine, Léonide, *My Life in Ballet* (London: Macmillan, 1968)

Matthews, T. S., *Great Tom: Notes Towards the Definition of T. S. Eliot* (London: Weidenfeld & Nicolson, 1974)

Mayer, John T., *T. S. Eliot's Silent Voices* (Oxford: Oxford University Press, 1989)

Miller, James E. Jr., *T. S. Eliot's Personal Waste Land* (Philadelphia, Penn.: University of Pennsylvania Press, 1977)

Mirrlees, Hope, BBC 1 television programme, "The Mysterious Mr. Eliot," 3 January 1971

Mitchell, Juliet, *Mad Men and Medusas: Reclaiming Hysteria and the Effects of Sibling Relations on the Human Condition* (London: Allen Lane, The Penguin Press, 2000)

Monk, Ray, *Bertrand Russell: The Spirit of Solitude* (London: Vintage, 1997)

Moody, A. David, *Thomas Stearns Eliot, Poet* (Cambridge: Cambridge University Press, 1979)

Moody, A. David (ed.), *The Cambridge Companion to T. S. Eliot* (Cambridge: Cambridge University Press, 1994)

Moody, A. David (ed.), *"The Waste Land" in Different Voices* (London: Edward Arnold, 1974)

Morrell, Ottoline, *Ottoline at Garsington: Memoirs of Lady Ottoline Morrell 1915–1918,* Robert Gathorne-Hardy (ed.) (London: Faber & Faber, 1974)

Morrison, Blake, "The Two Mrs. Eliots," *Independent on Sunday,* 24 April 1994

Nicolson, Harold, *Diaries and Letters 1930–39,* Nigel Nicolson (ed.) (New York and London: Harcourt Brace Jovanovich, 1977)

Norman, Charles, *Ezra Pound* (London: Macmillan, 1960)

Olney, James (ed.), *T. S. Eliot: Essays from the* Southern Review (Oxford: Clarendon Press, 1988)

Patmore, Brigit, *My Friends When Young: the Memoirs of Brigit Patmore,* Derek Patmore (ed.) (London: William Heinemann, 1968)

Pearson, John, *Façades: Edith, Osbert and Sacheverell Sitwell* (London, 1978)

Peter, John, "A New Interpretation of *The Waste Land*" (1952) with postscript (1969), *Essays in Criticism,* vol. 19, 1969

Pound, Ezra, *Collected Early Poems,* Michael John King (ed.) (London: Faber & Faber, 1977)

Pound, Ezra, *The Letters of Ezra Pound 1907–1941,* D. D. Paige (ed.) (New York: Harcourt Brace Jovanovich, 1950)

Ratliff, Margaret, "A Bloomsbury Friendship: The Correspondence of Mary Hutchinson and Lytton Strachey," Ph.D. thesis, Harry Ransom Humanities Research Center, University of Texas at Austin, Texas, 1989

Russell, Bertrand, *Satan in the Suburbs and Other Stories* (London: The Bodley Head, 1953)

Sartre, Jean-Paul, *Being and Nothingness* (1943, Routledge translation, 1969)

Sartre, Jean-Paul, *Nausea* (1938, Penguin translation, 1965)

Sax, Joseph L., *Playing Darts with a Rembrandt: Public and Private Rights in Cultural Treasures* (Ann Arbor: University of Michigan Press, 1999)

Schuchard, Ronald, *Eliot's Dark Angel: Intersections of Life and Art* (Oxford: Oxford University Press, 1999)

Segal, Hanna, *Klein* (Karnac Books, 1989)

Sencourt, Robert, *T. S. Eliot: A Memoir,* Donald Adamson and L. P. Addison (eds.) (London: Garnstone Press, 1971)

Seymour, Miranda, *Ottoline Morrell: Life on the Grand Scale* (London: Hodder & Stoughton, 1992)

Shone, Richard, *Bloomsbury Portraits* (Oxford: Phaidon Press, 1976)

Sitwell, Osbert, *Left Hand, Right Hand: An Autobiography,* vol. 4, *Laughter in the Next Room* (London, 1949)

Spalding, Frances, *Vanessa Bell* (London: Weidenfeld & Nicolson, 1983)

Spender, Stephen, *World Within World* (London: Hamish Hamilton, 1951)

Spender, Stephen, *T. S. Eliot* (London: Fontana, 1975)

Symons, Arthur, *The Symbolist Movement in Literature* (London: Heinemann, 1899)

Szasz, Thomas S., *The Myth of Mental Illness: Foundations of a Theory of Personal Conduct* (New York: Harper and Row, 1974)

Tate, Allen (ed.), *T. S. Eliot: The Man and His Work* (London: Chatto & Windus, 1967)

Tomlin, E. W. F., *T. S. Eliot: A Friendship* (London, 1987)

Trombley, Stephen, *"All That Summer She Was Mad," Virginia Woolf and Her Doctors* (London: Junction Press, 1981)

Turnell, Martin, *Baudelaire: A Study of His Poetry* (New York, 1972)

Watson, George, "Quest for a Frenchman," *The Swanee Review,* vol. 84, 1976

Wilson, Edmund, *The Wound and the Bow: Seven Studies in Literature,* with an introduction by Janet Groth (Ohio University Press, 1997)

Wilson, Timothy, "T. S. Eliot and I," *Observer,* 20 February 1972

Woolf, Leonard, *Letters of Leonard Woolf,* Frederic Spotts (ed.) (New York: Harcourt Brace Jovanovich, 1989)

Woolf, Leonard, *Beginning Again: An Autobiography of the Years 1911–1918* (London: Hogarth Press, 1964)

Woolf, Leonard, *Downhill All the Way: An Autobiography of the Years 1919–1939* (London: Hogarth Press, 1967)

Woolf, Virginia, *The Diary of Virginia Woolf,* Anne Olivier Bell (ed.), vols. 1–5 (London: Penguin, 1979, 1981, 1982, 1983, 1985)

Woolf, Virginia, *The Letters of Virginia Woolf,* Nigel Nicolson and Joanne Trautmann (eds.), vols. 2, 3, 5 (New York: Harcourt Brace Jovanovich, 1976, 1977, 1980); vol. 4 (London: Hogarth Press, 1994)

Ziegler, Philip, *Osbert Sitwell* (London: Chatto & Windus, 1998)

Index

T. S. Eliot and Vivienne Eliot referred to as TSE and VHE throughout index.

Note About the Author

CAROLE SEYMOUR-JONES was educated at Oxford University, and is the author of the biography *Beatrice Webb*. The author is the recipient of a Visiting Fellowship from the Paul Mellon Foundation for her work on the archives held at the Harry Ransom Research Center, University of Texas, Austin. She divides her time between Surrey and London.

L'INFIRMIÈRE ET L'ENFANT

2e édition

L'INFIRMIÈRE

ADAPTATION DE

Textbook of
PEDIATRIC NURSING

4th édition

ET

L'ENFANT

VERSION ORIGINALE

Dorothy R. Marlow, R.N., Ed.D.

*Doyen et professeur titulaire de Nursing Pediatric,
Faculté de Nursing, université de Villanova,
(Auparavant professeur agrégé de Nursing Pediatric,
Faculté de Nursing, université de Pennsylvanie.)*

VERSION FRANÇAISE

Nicole David, M.S.

*Infirmière clinicienne, spécialisée
dans le soin de l'enfant.*

Claire-Andrée Leclerc

*Baccalauréat en Nursing
Professeur au CEGEP Saint-Jean-sur-Richelieu*

LES ÉDITIONS HRW Ltée

Montréal, Toronto

en collaboration avec

W. B. SAUNDERS COMPANY

Philadelphie, Toronto, Londres.

L'INFIRMIÈRE ET L'ENFANT 2e édition

Traduction et adaptation de

textbook of PEDIATRIC NURSING, 4th edition
Dorothy R. MARLOW

Copyright © 1961, 1965, 1969 and 1973
by W.B. SAUNDERS

Maquette de la couverture:
Andrée PAYETTE

LES ÉDITIONS HRW LTÉE
8035 est, rue Jarry,
Anjou, Montréal H1J 1H6, P.Q., Canada

Distributeur exclusif pour l'Europe

Librairie Maloine S.A.
27 rue de l'École-de-Médecine
75006 Paris.

Dépôt légal 3e trimestre 1976
Bibliothèque nationale du Québec

ISBN   0-03-928116-7

Imprimé au Canada

3 4 5 6 7 LLC 88 87 86 85 84

PRÉFACE

Un enfant, être bio-psycho-social en période de croissance et de développement, possède ses propres réactions face à la maladie. Ceci exige de la part du personnel infirmier une préparation spécifique et les personnes spécialisées dans le soin de l'enfant doivent comprendre « ce petit monde en évolution » afin d'appliquer efficacement leurs connaissances scientifiques et professionnelles.

L'enfant n'est pas un adulte en miniature: les recherches en sociologie, en anthropologie et en psychologie le démontrent constamment. Le soin de l'enfant a subi une évolution importante à la suite des découvertes des sciences humaines et biologiques. L'isolement de l'enfant et les soins purement techniques prodigués dans des unités de soins stéréotypés ont été remplacés par une approche globale de l'enfant, laquelle suppose la collaboration d'une équipe multi-disciplinaire, la participation de la famille et la création d'un milieu adapté aux besoins de l'enfant, que ce soit en milieu hospitalier, en clinique, à domicile ou dans un centre de soins à long terme. L'infirmière et l'infirmier en pédiatrie ne satisfont donc plus isolément les besoins de l'enfant puisqu'ils doivent travailler activement au sein d'une équipe de santé.

Le personnel infirmier en pédiatrie ne remplace plus les membres de la famille, ne sert plus de substitut. Au contraire, quel que soit le milieu où les services sont donnés, ce personnel doit transformer l'expérience santé en une expérience positive dans la vie de l'enfant. Puisque la durée du séjour hospitalier diminue de plus en plus, le rôle de l'infirmière ou de l'infirmier est primordial pour que l'expérience hospitalière ne soit pas traumatisante et pour que le programme de soins infirmiers soit orienté vers la communauté, compte tenu de la société actuelle. En pédiatrie, l'infirmière et l'infirmier doivent donc mettre en application tous les concepts relatifs au dépistage, à la prévention, à l'éducation sanitaire, à la réadaptation, à la participation de la famille et des personnes significatives ainsi qu'à la coordination et à la continuité des soins et des services.

Un programme de soins infirmiers en pédiatrie doit impliquer l'enfant et sa famille. Par l'enseignement, incluant l'expérience dirigée, l'infirmière ou l'infirmier doit rendre l'enfant capable de participer aux soins préventifs, curatifs ou de réadaptation que ce soit à l'occasion d'un test de dépistage, d'un traitement ou d'une séance d'éducation sanitaire.

En centrant les soins infirmiers sur la santé, la croissance et le développement de l'enfant, les auteurs de cet ouvrage donnent à la santé la place qui lui revient. Par la description des perturbations physiologiques et par l'identification de leurs conséquences sur la croissance normale, les auteurs forcent le lecteur à reconnaître l'être complexe qu'est l'enfant vivant en société. Les concepts de soins infirmiers pédiatriques énoncés dans ce volume peuvent servir de guide pour l'évaluation et le contrôle de l'exercice de la profession d'infirmière ou d'infirmier en pédiatrie. De plus, ces concepts sont à la base de la dispensation de soins infirmiers de qualité au sein de l'équipe de soins de santé.

L'ouvrage permet de suivre l'évolution des soins infirmiers et explore la façon d'utiliser les ressources communautaires disponibles. Partant du développement de l'enfant, les auteurs identifient les problèmes spécifiques pouvant survenir à divers âges tout en respectant une suite logique. Marlow, l'auteur de la version originale et les auteurs de l'édition française, qui sont hautement qualifiés en nursing pédiatrique, ont su adapter le soin de l'enfant aux situations actuelles de la société. Les modifications apportées dans l'édition française, parce qu'adaptées spécifiquement aux politiques et au régime de santé du Québec, seront très utiles au professeur, à l'étudiant, au chef d'équipe, à l'infirmier(e) — chef, à l'infirmier(e) clinicien(ne) et même à l'architecte qui devra dessiner les plans d'une salle d'attente, d'une clinique pour nourrissons, d'une unité de soins, d'un centre de soins à long terme. Ce livre nouvellement révisé met l'accent sur toutes les dimensions inhérentes à la famille, à la collectivité et à la communauté.

Cet ouvrage, écrit spécialement pour les infirmières et les infirmiers, sera d'une grande utilité pour tous les membres de l'équipe de santé. L'éducateur, le spécialiste en récréologie et toute personne ayant à travailler auprès des enfants trouveront également des renseignements précieux concernant l'approche de l'enfant, le maintien et la promotion de sa santé ainsi que la compréhension de son comportement.

Il n'existe à peu près pas de volume en langue française présentant les concepts modernes et nord-américains en soins infirmiers pédiatriques. Les auteurs de l'édition française rendent donc un grand service à la profession du nursing en offrant un outil de travail adapté aux besoins des infirmières et des infirmiers. Hommage et reconnaissance à celles qui ont consacré de longues heures de travail à la révision de ce volume.

NICOLE DU MOUCHEL, inf., M.N.
Directrice générale et secrétaire de l'Ordre des infirmières et infirmiers du Québec.

Janvier 1976.

TABLE DES MATIÈRES

CHAPITRE 7   SOIN DU NOUVEAU-NÉ

CHAPITRE 8   LE PRÉMATURÉ ET LE NOURRISSON POST-MATURE

CHAPITRE 12   PATHOLOGIES DES NOURRISSONS NÉCESSITANT DES SOINS IMMÉDIATS OU DE COURTE DURÉE

CHAPITRE 13   PATHOLOGIES DES NOURRISSONS NÉCESSITANT DES SOINS DE LONGUE DURÉE

QUATRIÈME PARTIE: LE TROTTINEUR

CHAPITRE 14   LE TROTTINEUR NORMAL: CROISSANCE, DÉVELOPPEMENT, SOINS

SEPTIÈME PARTIE: L'ADOLESCENT

CHAPITRE 23   L'ADOLESCENT: CROISSANCE, DÉVELOPPE-MENT, SOINS

CHAPITRE 24   PROBLÈMES DE LA PUBERTÉ ET DE L'ADO-LESCENCE RELIÉS À LA CROISSANCE ET AU DÉVELOPPEMENT

Acné – Perçage des oreilles – Défaut de posture – Fatigue – Anémie – Obésité – Les marottes alimentaires – Gynécomastie – Menstruations irrégulières – Dysménorrhée – Douleur à l'ovulation – Ménorragie – Syndrome prémenstruel – Masturbation – Hyperthyroïdisme – Névroses mineures.

CHAPITRE 25   PATHOLOGIES DE L'ADOLESCENT NÉCESSI-TANT DES SOINS DE LONGUE DURÉE

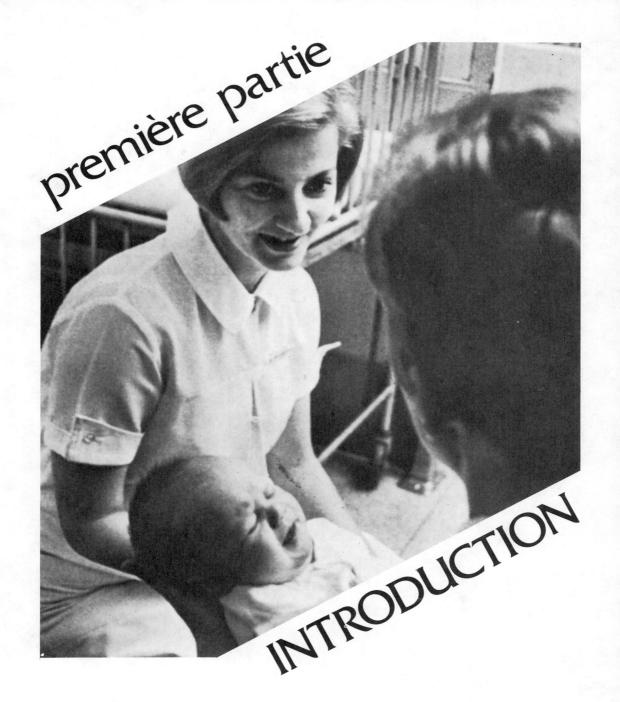

première partie

INTRODUCTION

1
soin de l'enfant à travers les âges

HISTORIQUE ET TENDANCES ACTUELLES

L'importance attribuée à l'enfant par la société a, de tout temps, déterminé les soins accordés à l'enfant bien portant et les traitements offerts à l'enfant malade. L'enfant était soigné ou négligé selon sa capacité de perpétuer la race, les croyances religieuses, les superstitions, les migrations du groupe ainsi que la connaissance que l'on avait des maladies et des traitements.

Pour bien saisir ce qui a conduit à la conception actuelle de la puériculture et de la pédiatrie, l'infirmière doit comprendre l'évolution qu'ont subi les soins de l'enfant à travers les âges.

L'enfant dans la société primitive

On connaît peu de choses sur la vie préhistorique, mais on suppose que les soins de l'enfant étaient à peu près semblables à ceux que l'on trouve aujourd'hui dans les groupes humains peu touchés par la civilisation. L'enfant n'avait pas de valeur en tant que tel mais en tant que futur adulte, et c'est la raison pour laquelle son développement devait s'effectuer conformément aux coutumes du groupe.

À ces époques lointaines les groupes primitifs étaient des nomades voyageant constam-

ment à la recherche de vivres et s'efforçant de se protéger des animaux sauvages et des intempéries. Ils ne pouvaient donc pas se permettre d'être retardés par des enfants faibles ou malades. Ces collectivités acceptaient les enfants sains et éliminaient aisément les autres.

Quand on jugeait qu'un enfant malformé ou malade diminuait les ressources du groupe, il était tué ou abandonné. Certains bébés du sexe féminin étaient éliminés tout simplement parce qu'ils ne pourraient pas fournir ultérieurement un travail aussi productif que leurs frères. C'était la pratique de l'infanticide. Cependant, certains enfants ont pu échapper à la mort, leur mère les ayant protégés du groupe. Les sociétés d'autrefois, comme celles d'aujourd'hui, n'étaient pas nécessairement composées d'individus qui acceptaient aveuglément les lois communes.

Certaines peuplades primitives croyaient en des êtres supérieurs qui dirigeaient les hommes, la nature et l'univers. La tempête ou la sécheresse pouvaient naître de la colère de l'Être supérieur. Ainsi, la naissance d'un enfant malformé pouvait être considérée comme la punition d'une faute antérieure des parents; d'ailleurs, cette façon de penser n'est pas entièrement disparue aujourd'hui.

Il n'en reste pas moins que l'enfant, même chez les peuplades primitives, devait recevoir un minimum de soins pour survivre. L'amour et l'affection qu'il recevait en surplus dépendaient du groupe social où il vivait et des sentiments de sa mère à son égard.

L'enfant dans la société ancienne

L'importance de l'enfant dans la société s'est manifestée petit à petit, à mesure que chaque groupe se fixait sur une terre fertile et cessait d'être nomade. L'enfant n'étant plus une charge pour la société, il en devint lentement une ressource.

Égypte. Les premières peuplades qui s'installèrent dans la vallée du Nil prenaient bien soin de leurs enfants, les habillaient de vêtements confortables et préconisaient l'allaitement maternel. En outre, elles veillaient à leur instruction et les encourageaient aux sports extérieurs. Dès l'an 1500 av. J.-C., tel qu'attesté par le papyrus d'Ebers, les traitements prescrits pour les maladies infantiles étaient différents des traitements pour adultes.

Grèce et Rome. La beauté physique était très importante chez les Grecs; aussi l'éducation des enfants tendait-elle à promouvoir un développement physique harmonieux.

À Rome, la famille était importante parce qu'elle devait produire des garçons forts qui deviendraient de bons guerriers au service de l'État. Hippocrate (460-370 av. J.-C.) fait souvent allusion dans ses écrits aux particularités des maladies infantiles. Celse, qui vécut au premier siècle chrétien, opposa aux traitements pour adultes des traitements spécifiques pour les maladies infantiles.

Israël. Chez les anciens Juifs, les mesures hygiéniques prescrites par la loi de Moïse eurent une grande influence sur les soins de la mère et de l'enfant. Le peuple hébreu reconnaissait l'importance de la propreté et de la nutrition. De plus, ils avaient quelques connaissances des maladies contagieuses et s'efforçaient de les combattre. Enfin, la cérémonie de la circoncision était en même temps une pratique hygiénique.

La paternité était à l'honneur chez les Hébreux, et une famille nombreuse était considérée comme une bénédiction de Yahvé sur les parents. Le plus grand malheur d'une femme était d'être stérile.

Influence du christianisme sur les soins de l'enfant

Le christianisme contribua à développer une nouvelle philosophie de la vie; il a donné une plus grande importance à l'enfant en tant qu'individu, et non plus seulement comme un fils ou une fille qui aime tendrement ses vieux parents et leur donne des petits-enfants pour continuer la lignée familiale.

Comme le christianisme enseignait la protection du plus faible par le plus fort, les soins du malade par le bien portant, l'enfant et l'infirme devinrent l'objet d'une attention particulière. Des orphelinats et des hôpitaux furent fondés très tôt dans l'histoire de l'Église chrétienne.

L'enfant en Europe

Avant le 19e siècle, l'espérance de vie était courte en Europe. Beaucoup de parents ne vivaient pas assez longtemps pour élever leurs enfants et de grandes épidémies ravageaient régulièrement le continent; les jeunes gens mouraient nombreux, à la guerre ou à la suite d'accidents de travail. Quant aux femmes, elles se mariaient tôt et avaient plusieurs enfants; le taux de mortalité maternelle était élevé. Généralement, le taux de mortalité était plus élevé dans les villes et chez les pauvres.

Ainsi, on comptait un grand nombre d'enfants orphelins chez les pauvres des cités en voie de croissance. Plusieurs d'entre eux étaient placés dans des foyers nourriciers ou dans des fermes. La plupart étant de naissance illégitime, le paiement initial de leur pension n'était souvent suivi d'aucune autre rémunération; les fermiers qui acceptaient de tels enfants avaient intérêt à les voir mourir prématurément, et même à hâter la mort de leurs protégés.

Les orphelinats, apparus dès l'an 787 après J.-C., se sont multipliés à mesure que les besoins se faisaient sentir. Malgré leur nombre grandissant, ces institutions connaissaient un problème de « surpopulation » chronique. Plusieurs enfants mouraient, certains à cause de l'état déplorable de leur santé lors de l'admission, la plupart par manque d'hygiène ou à cause des mauvaises conditions de nutrition ou de logement, par manque de techniques aseptiques et à cause de la qualité extrêmement pauvre des soins qui leur étaient prodigués. On estime que dans de telles conditions, la moitié des enfants pauvres des villes mouraient avant l'âge de cinq ans.

C'est en Grande-Bretagne et en Europe occidentale que le soin des enfants a été le plus déplorable, au début de la révolution industrielle du 19e siècle. Dans les usines de coton, des enfants entre six et douze ans travaillaient jusqu'à dix heures par jour et parfois plus. Ils s'endormaient souvent au travail et les accidents étaient fréquents. Mais comme ils étaient aussi habiles que les adultes pour attacher les fils brisés, et que le coût de leur entretien ainsi que leur salaire étaient très bas, s'ils étaient des orphelins-apprentis, les propriétaires de filatures les employaient énormément. Ce n'est que plus tard, au 19e siècle, que des lois furent promulguées pour interdire l'exploitation de la main d'œuvre infantile.

L'enfant en Amérique

Jusqu'au début du 20e siècle, la plupart des enfants américains vivaient dans les fermes ou dans de petits villages. C'était, en général, un mode de vie très sain, même si ces enfants ne pouvaient profiter des soins médicaux et des services hospitaliers des grandes villes. L'exploitation de la main-d'œuvre infantile fut moins aiguë en Amérique qu'en Europe; cependant, les enfants pauvres devaient travailler dans des usines ou des magasins où les conditions de travail étaient insalubres et les heures très longues.

Vers la moitié du 19e siècle, il y avait, à New York et dans la plupart des grandes villes américaines de l'Est, des quartiers sordides où les habitants étaient généralement d'origine étrangère, la plupart issus de milieux ruraux et ne connaissant pas la vie urbaine. Les logis d'ouvriers y étaient surpeuplés, insalubres et en décrépitude. Les taux de morbidité et de mortalité chez les enfants étaient excessivement élevés, et il y avait de nombreux accidents dans les maisons et dans les rues où ils jouaient. Le lait contaminé causait de sérieux troubles intestinaux, car les laiteries et les magasins n'étaient pas inspectés, et le lait n'était pas pasteurisé. Le lait des vaches tuberculeuses était à l'origine de la tuberculose infantile.

Le sort des enfants abandonnés et malades ameuta l'opinion publique et professionnelle. Peu à peu, grâce à des initiatives privées et publiques, les conditions de vie de ces enfants s'améliorèrent considérablement.

L'enfant dans les pays
en voie de développement

La rapidité des transports modernes et l'explosion démographique à laquelle nous assistons rapprochent les peuples les uns des autres; ainsi, les problèmes de santé qui ne concernaient autrefois qu'un petit secteur de la planète deviennent maintenant une menace universelle. C'est pourquoi, aujourd'hui, on ne peut se permettre de penser uniquement au bien-être des enfants de sa propre ville, état, province ou pays.

Grâce à des organisations internationales comme l'OMS et l'UNICEF, les pays en voie de développement reçoivent une assistance leur permettant d'améliorer les soins donnés aux enfants.

OMS: L'Organisation Mondiale de la Santé, instituée agence spécialisée des Nations Unies en 1948, fut la première organisation sanitaire internationale dans l'histoire de l'humanité. Les quartiers généraux de cette organisation sont à Genève, en Suisse.

Le but de l'OMS est d'aider tous les peuples à atteindre le plus haut niveau de santé possible. A cette fin, l'Organisation dirige et coordonne des projets internationaux, établit et maintient une collaboration efficace entre les gouvernements et autres groupes concernés. De plus, l'OMS fournit aux pays des informations sur la santé ainsi que des services techniques, et évalue les problèmes de santé d'un pays si la demande en est faite. Ses activités ont également pour but d'encourager les efforts vers l'éradication de certaines maladies et la prévention des accidents, d'améliorer les conditions d'alimentation et de logement, l'équipement sanitaire et tout autre aspect de l'hygiène.

Les objectifs actuels de l'OMS sont plus précisément de maîtriser les maladies infectieuses comme la malaria, la tuberculose, la lèpre et les maladies vénériennes à travers le monde. Elle met en place des organisations publiques dans les pays où le programme de santé est déficient, contribue à l'éducation et à l'entraînement du personnel médical et paramédical.

Toutes ces activités démontrent que les nations peuvent travailler de concert dans un but commun: l'amélioration de la santé humaine.

UNICEF (United Nations International Children's Emergency Fund): Cette organisation fut créée en 1946 par les Nations Unies. Son but est d'apporter des secours d'urgence aux enfants victimes de la guerre ou de cataclysmes qui se produisent dans le monde. Cet organisme participe aux programmes de santé et de bien-être pour les enfants dans plus de 50 pays. Une aide est apportée uniquement à la demande du pays et selon ses besoins, quelles que soient la race, les croyances ou les allégeances politiques.

L'enfant nord-américain d'aujourd'hui

Nous vivons dans une société complexe et changeante. Les enfants, qui deviendront rapidement des adultes, doivent apprendre à vivre heureux dans le monde d'aujourd'hui, et surtout à s'adapter aux nombreux changements imprévisibles du futur.

TYPE DE MALADIE	HOSPITALISATIONS DE LA NAISSANCE À L'ENTRÉE À L'ÉCOLE	
	FAVORISÉS	DÉFAVORISÉS
Mastoïdectomie	–	5
Otites à répétition	1	7
Rougeole	6	16
Accidents divers	13	19
Coqueluche	1	23
Pneumonie	9	31
Gastro-entérite	19	46
Amygdalectomie	23	93
TOTAL	72/577 enfants soit 12,4%	240/256 enfants soit 93,7%

Tableau 1-1. État de santé comparatif de groupes d'enfants des secteurs favorisés et défavorisés, Montréal, 1966-1967. (Rapport Castonguay-Nepveu, Tome 1, Vol. IV, p. 122.)

Les principes sociaux, qui inspirent le mode de vie actuel et qui influeront sur l'avenir, sont nombreux. Une des principales caractéristiques de la société nord-américaine est l'importance de la vitesse: dans la production des biens, les moyens de transport et la course vers l'espace. La population universelle, ainsi que celle de l'Amérique, s'accroît considérablement; la population infantile grandit de façon surprenante. Ce problème suppose une planification de l'éducation, des services de santé et de bien-être dont auront besoin les enfants de toutes les races.

La mobilité et le déracinement des groupes familiaux est un autre trait caractéristique de notre société: la migration de familles entières de l'étranger vers l'Amérique, la migration des travailleurs ruraux vers les grandes villes, celle des classes moyennes vers la banlieue.

À cause de ces migrations, le groupe familial du siècle dernier, formé de plusieurs générations et de la parenté demeurant dans l'environnement immédiat, s'est fragmenté en petits noyaux familiaux comprenant les parents et leurs enfants, quelquefois un grand-parent. Alors que le groupe familial traditionnel apportait la sécurité à des membres dépendant les uns des autres, le petit groupe familial d'aujourd'hui est pratiquement isolé parmi des étrangers. La société, et plus particulièrement les agences sociales spécialisées, se doivent d'empêcher la désintégration totale des cellules familiales.

Au cours des dernières années, les effets désastreux de la pauvreté dans la société nord-américaine ont été particulièrement étudiés (tableau 1-1): les gouvernements tentent, par des mesures de progrès social, de briser le cercle vicieux de la pauvreté. Ceci est primor-

dial pour que tous les enfants puissent se développer selon leurs véritables capacités.

L'accroissement rapide des connaissances scientifiques, dans le domaine de la croissance et du développement de l'enfant et sur les causes et les traitements des maladies infantiles, confère au personnel de la santé la responsabilité d'entreprendre une action efficace. Mais la pénurie de médecins, d'infirmières et de spécialistes de la santé rend plus difficile l'amélioration rapide du bien-être de l'enfant.

Face aux problèmes sociaux, les infirmières partagent, avec les autres travailleurs de la santé, la responsabilité de créer un monde dans lequel tous les enfants, malades ou bien portants, recevront le maximum de soins dans un environnement adéquat.

L'enfant dans la collectivité

L'infirmière, en tant que professionnelle, mais aussi comme membre d'une société, se doit de connaître les énormes progrès réalisés dans le domaine du soin de l'enfant.

L'aide que les nouveaux parents recevaient autrefois de leur milieu familial vient maintenant d'agences spécialisées, privées ou gouvernementales. En effet, la plupart des enfants naissent dans des hôpitaux, ils sont revus par la suite dans des cliniques pour nourrissons et des efforts sont tentés, tant au Canada que dans d'autres pays, pour créer des structures qui permettraient d'effectuer une surveillance sanitaire adéquate des trottineurs et des enfants d'âge préscolaire.

Les programmes de santé dans les écoles varient selon les localités et selon l'importance de l'école. L'infirmière scolaire peut travailler seule ou au sein d'une équipe formée d'un médecin, d'un psychologue, d'un orienteur et d'un travailleur social.

Les fonctions de l'infirmière scolaire sont diverses : elle peut d'abord s'occuper des premiers soins à donner durant les heures de classe, assister le médecin pour les examens physiques, et diriger les examens de la vue et de l'audition. Son travail peut aussi consister à dépister la tuberculose ou autres affections, vérifier la validité des immunisations contre les maladies contagieuses, s'occuper plus particulièrement des enfants atteints de diabète, d'épilepsie et de troubles divers du comportement; elle peut également promouvoir l'élaboration d'un programme d'éducation sexuelle pour les enfants et aussi, quelquefois, pour leurs parents, et dispenser un enseignement sur les moyens de promouvoir et de conserver sa santé tant physique que mentale. L'infirmière scolaire peut être une infirmière hygiéniste, s'occupant d'une ou de plusieurs écoles, à temps complet ou à temps partiel.

Jusqu'à ces dernières années, on ne trouvait des camps d'été que pour enfants normaux et en bonne santé. Depuis, on a fondé de nombreux camps pour enfants diabétiques, atteints de fibrose kystique du pancréas, affectés de malformations orthopédiques ou autres handicaps. Ces camps sont sous surveillance médicale et une infirmière autorisée est toujours sur les lieux, en cas d'accident ou de maladie. Dans les camps pour enfants infirmes, les enfants sont sous une surveillance médicale encore plus étroite, et un personnel médical complet est constamment sur les lieux pour la sécurité des enfants.

Les agences de santé communautaire emploient la majeure partie des infirmières œuvrant au sein de la collectivité. Les soins de longue durée des malades chroniques sont de plus en plus donnés au sein même de la famille de l'enfant, et les infirmières en santé publique jouent un rôle important pour la santé des petits malades. Le rôle de ces infirmières ne consiste plus seulement à prodiguer des soins, mais surtout à les enseigner aux parents.

Des programmes d'aide préventive et de stimulation intellectuelle pour les enfants d'âge préscolaire sont maintenant offerts dans plusieurs pays et sont ordinairement sous la responsabilité gouvernementale.

L'infirmière en santé communautaire, comme les autres membres de l'équipe de santé, enseigne les mesures préventives d'hygiène pédiatrique et participe à leur promotion. Cette responsabilité comprend la participation aux consultations destinées à favoriser la santé des enfants, à l'immunisation contre les maladies contagieuses, à l'éducation dans le domaine de la prévention des accidents, au dépistage des enfants présentant des troubles émotifs ou

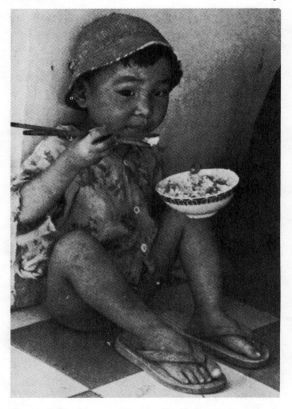

Figure 1-2. Des millions d'enfants à travers le monde sont sous-alimentés. (Courtoisie de H.E. Devitt et Nursing Outlook. Décembre 1966.)

des signes de maladie physique, pour les diriger vers les centres de santé appropriés.

Dans certains milieux, des centres spécialisés ont été mis sur pied: centres de contrôle des intoxications, centres pour enfants prématurés, centres de cardiologie, et centres pour le diagnostic et le traitement des déficiences mentales de l'enfant.

Une planification des services sanitaires et des agences communautaires complètement organisées sont indispensables pour répondre à tous les besoins. Il est évident que seul un effort sérieux et honnête, de la part de travailleurs représentant plusieurs disciplines, pourra donner à tous les enfants le plus haut niveau de santé physique et psychique.

La section que nous venons de terminer montre à l'étudiante-infirmière l'importance du rôle de l'infirmière dans l'organisation communautaire de la santé. Elle peut œuvrer comme éducatrice de la santé, professeur, conseillère, dans la recherche ou le dépistage, ou enfin comme infirmière compétente et aimante au chevet de l'enfant malade.

PROJET DE DÉCLARATION DES DROITS DE L'ENFANT

Texte adopté par la Commission des Droits de L'Homme

Préambule

Considérant que, par la Charte, les Nations unies ont proclamé à nouveau leur foi dans les droits fondamentaux de l'homme et dans la dignité et la valeur de la personne humaine, et qu'elles se sont déclarées résolues à favoriser le progrès social et à instaurer de meilleures conditions de vie dans une liberté plus grande.

Considérant que, dans la Déclaration universelle des droits de l'homme, les Nations unies ont proclamé que chacun peut se prévaloir de tous les droits et de toutes les libertés qui y sont énoncés, sans distinction aucune, notamment de race, de couleur, de sexe, de langue, de religion, d'opinion politique ou de toute autre opinion, d'origine nationale ou sociale, de fortune, de naissance ou de toute autre situation.

Considérant que l'enfant a besoin d'une protection spéciale, notamment d'une protection juridique spéciale, en raison de son manque de maturité physique et intellectuelle.

Considérant que la nécessité de cette protection spéciale a été énoncée dans la Déclaration de Genève sur les droits de l'enfant, de 1924, et a été de nouveau reconnue au paragraphe 2 de l'article 25 de la Déclaration universelle des droits de l'homme ainsi que dans les statuts des institutions spécialisées et des organisations internationales qui se consacrent au bien-être de l'enfance.

Considérant que l'humanité se doit de donner à l'enfant le meilleur d'elle-même.

En conséquence,

L'Assemblée générale reconnaît et proclame les droits essentiels de l'enfant afin qu'il ait une enfance heureuse et qu'il puisse se développer pour pouvoir bénéficier, dans son intérêt comme dans l'intérêt de la société, des droits et des libertés fondamentaux et notamment de ceux qu'a énoncés la Déclaration universelle des droits de l'homme. Elle invite les hommes et les femmes, à titre individuel, ainsi que les autorités locales et les gouvernements nationaux, à reconnaître ces droits et à s'efforcer d'en assurer le respect par l'application des principes suivants.

Principes

1) L'enfant doit jouir de tous les droits énoncés dans la présente Déclaration, sans distinction ni discrimination fondées sur la race, la couleur, le sexe, la langue, la religion, les opinions politiques ou autres, l'origine nationale ou sociale, la fortune, la naissance ou tout autre statut, qu'il s'agisse du statut de l'enfant lui-même ou de celui de son père ou de sa mère. Tous les enfants, qu'ils soient nés du mariage ou hors mariage, doivent jouir de ces droits.

2) L'enfant doit être mis en mesure de se développer d'une façon saine et normale, sur le plan physique, intellectuel, moral, spirituel et social, dans des conditions de liberté et de dignité.

3) L'enfant doit bénéficier d'une protection spéciale par l'effet de la loi et par d'autres moyens. Si besoin est, des possibilités et des facilités doivent lui être accordées par la loi pour lui permettre de se développer conformément aux principes de la présente Déclaration. L'intérêt supérieur de l'enfant doit être la considération déterminante dans l'adoption de cette législation.

4) L'enfant doit avoir, dès sa naissance, droit à un nom et à une nationalité.

5) L'enfant doit bénéficier de la sécurité sociale. Il doit pouvoir grandir et se développer d'une façon saine; à cette fin, une aide et une protection spéciales doivent lui être assurées ainsi qu'à sa mère, notamment des soins prénataux et postnataux adéquats. L'enfant a droit à une alimentation, à un logement, à des loisirs et à des soins médicaux adéquats.

6) Pour l'épanouissement harmonieux de sa personnalité, l'enfant a besoin d'amour et de compréhension. Il doit, à moins que son intérêt supérieur ne l'exige autrement, grandir sous la sauvegarde de ses parents, et l'enfant en bas âge ne doit pas, sauf circonstances exceptionnelles, être séparé de sa mère. En tout état de cause, l'enfant doit avoir la possibilité de grandir dans une atmosphère d'affection et de sécurité morale et matérielle. La société et les pouvoirs publics ont le devoir de prendre un soin particulier des enfants sans famille ou de ceux qui n'ont pas de moyens d'existence suffisants.

7) L'enfant a le droit de recevoir, au moins aux niveaux élémentaires une éducation gratuite et obligatoire. L'éducation de l'enfant doit viser à l'épanouissement de sa personnalité et au renforcement du respect des droits de l'homme et des libertés fondamentales; elle doit lui permettre, avec les mêmes chances que ses semblables, de développer ses facultés et son jugement personnel et de devenir un membre utile de la société. Elle doit favoriser la compréhension, la tolérance et l'amitié entre tous les peuples et tous les groupes raciaux ou religieux et aider l'enfant à comprendre la culture de son peuple et celle des autres peuples, ainsi que les buts et principes des Nations unies. L'intérêt supérieur de l'enfant doit être le guide de ceux qui ont la responsabilité de son éducation et de son orientation; cette responsabilité incombe en priorité à ses parents.

8) L'enfant doit être le premier à recevoir en toutes circonstances protection et secours.

9) L'enfant qui souffre d'une déficience physique, mentale ou sociale, doit recevoir le traitement, l'éducation et les soins spéciaux que nécessite sa situation particulière.

10) L'enfant doit être protégé contre toutes les formes de négligence, de cruauté et d'exploitation. Il ne doit pas être admis à l'emploi avant d'avoir atteint un âge approprié; il ne doit en aucun cas être soumis ou autorisé à se soumettre à une occupation ou à un emploi qui nuise à sa santé ou à son éducation ou qui entrave son développement physique, mental ou moral.

11) L'enfant doit être élevé dans une atmosphère qui favorise la compréhension, la tolérance et l'amitié entre les peuples et tous les groupes nationaux, raciaux et religieux, et l'aversion pour toutes les formes de discrimination d'ordre national, racial ou religieux. Il doit être protégé contre les pratiques fondées sur toute discrimination de cette nature. Il doit être élevé dans un esprit de paix, d'amitié et de fraternité entre les nations, dans le sentiment qu'il atteindra son plein épanouissement et s'assurera le maximum de satisfaction en consacrant son énergie et ses qualités au service de ses semblables, dans un esprit de fraternité et de paix universelles.

Relations parents – enfant – infirmière

On dit parfois que le 20e siècle est le siècle de l'enfant. La société se rend compte que l'enfant n'est pas un adulte en miniature: son corps est différent de celui de l'adulte, qualitativement aussi bien que quantitativement, et ses besoins, ses processus mentaux et intellectuels sont particuliers. De ce fait, l'étude de l'enfance est une discipline à part, où les connaissances multi-disciplinaires sont appliquées aux soins.

L'importance de l'enfant, dans la société actuelle, ne lui est pas accordée uniquement en tant qu'adulte en puissance, futur parent ou travailleur. L'enfant a une valeur intrinsèque, en tant qu'enfant, avec tout ce que cela comporte d'aspects aimables ou quelquefois irritants, d'expériences enrichissantes pour les parents ou pour les adultes qui prennent soin de lui. Depuis 1959, à la suite d'une assemblée générale des Nations Unies, il existe même une charte officielle des droits de l'enfant (voir page 8), qui sanctionne les droits spécifiques et les privilèges de l'enfance. Dans notre culture, les relations de l'enfant avec ses parents sont pour lui la base de son développement émotif. Grâce à cette relation privilégiée, l'enfant apprend à se découvrir et à s'épanouir et les parents vivent une expérience de croissance à la fois très riche et très exigeante.

Les relations parents-enfant peuvent toutefois s'attiédir, sinon se détériorer, du fait que le soin de l'enfant est une tâche ininterrompue, de jour et de nuit, et que cette attention absorbante est très lourde à supporter pour les parents. Quand l'enfant est bien portant, une gardienne peut grandement soulager la mère; il peut aussi être inscrit à une garderie, pour des périodes plus ou moins longues, ou aller à l'école maternelle ou dans un camp de vacances lorsqu'il a atteint l'âge requis. Lorsque l'enfant est malade, une infirmière peut venir à la maison pour aider à donner les soins, ou l'enfant peut être hospitalisé pour un traitement plus approfondi.

De bonnes relations parents-enfant dépendent non seulement de la somme de temps qu'ils passent ensemble, mais aussi de la qualité de leur relation.

Peu d'adultes parviennent à travailler de façon satisfaisante avec les enfants, s'ils ne sont pas eux-mêmes heureux dans ce travail. Il ne s'agit pas ici d'adopter le rôle de substitut parental et de s'y complaire. Il faut donner à l'enfant un sentiment de sécurité, sentiment qui lui vient d'un ami adulte qui, comme les parents, fait pour lui avec amour ce qu'il ne peut faire lui-même.

Le jeune adulte qui a connu une enfance heureuse et qui manifeste un épanouissement personnel, ainsi qu'un succès professionnel certain, a beaucoup de chances de réussir dans le soin des enfants.

Une meilleure compréhension de la vie émotive de l'enfant facilite les relations parents-enfant-infirmière. Ceci, en ce qui concerne l'infirmière, sera démontré dans ce livre.

RÉFÉRENCES

Livres et documents officiels

Annuaires du Québec, Gouvernement du Québec, 1972-73-74.
Annuaires du Canada, Gouvernement du Canada, 1972-73-74.
Assemblée générale de l'Organisation des Nations Unies: *Projet de déclaration des droits de l'enfant,* document officiel de l'O.N.U., 1959.
Comité spécial du Sénat sur la pauvreté: *La pauvreté au Canada.* Ottawa, 1971.
Conseil national du Bien-être social: *Un enfant, une chance.* Ottawa, 1973.
Conseil national du Bien-être social: *Les enfants pauvres.* Ottawa, 1975.
De Castro, F. J., et Rolfe, U. T.: *The Pediatric Nurse Practitioner.* St.Louis, C. V. Mosby Company, 1972.
Frost, J. L. et Hawkes, G. R. (édit.): *The Disadvantaged Child.* Boston, Houghton Mifflin Company, 1970.
Garrison, F. H., et Abt, A. F.: *Abt-Garrison History of Pediatrics.* Philadelphie, W. B. Saunders Company, 1965.
Ishwaran, K.: *The Canadian Family.* Toronto, Holt, Rinehart et Winston, 1971.
Kriesberg, L.: *Mothers in Poverty: A Study of Fatherless Families.* Chicago, Aldine Publishing Company, 1970.
Land, H.: *Large Families in London.* Toronto, Clarke, Irwin and Company, 1969.

Leininger, M.: *Nursing and Anthropology: Two worlds to Blend*. New York, John Wiley and Sons, 1970.

Ministère des Affaires sociales: *Orientations générales en santé communautaire*, Québec, 1973.

Ministère des Affaires sociales: *Les services à l'enfance*. Monographies des Affaires sociales, Québec, 1973.

Muller, P.: *Les tâches de l'enfance*. Paris, Hachette, 1969.

Ordre des infirmières et infirmiers du Québec: *Le nursing en santé communautaire*. Montréal, O. I. I. Q., 1973.

Rapport de la commission d'enquête sur la santé et le bien-être social. Vol. IV, Tomes I et IV, Gouvernement du Québec, 1970.

Articles

American Nurses' Association Division on Maternal and Child Health Nursing Practice and the American Academy of Pediatrics: A Joint Statement-Guidelines on Short-Term Continuing Education Programs for Pediatric Nurse Associates. *Am. J. Nursing*, 71:509, 1971.

Blanchet, M. et Bilodeau, L.: Besoins de santé des enfants au Québec. *Médecin du Québec*, 10:19, 20, 1972.

Conant, L., Robertson, L. S., Kosa, J., et Alpert, J. J.: Anticipated Patient Acceptance of New Nursing Roles and Physicians' Assistants. *Am. J. Dis. Child.*, 122:202, septembre 1971.

Day, L. R., Egli, R., et Silver, H. K.: Acceptance of Pediatric Nurse Practitioners. *Amer. J. Dis. Child.*, 119:204, mars 1970.

Eliot, M. M.: Six Decades of Action for Children. *Children Today*, 1:2. Mars-avril 1972.

Erickson, F.: Nurse Specialist for Children. *Nursing Outlook*, 16:34, novembre 1968.

Paquin, A. et autres: La santé de l'enfant dans le Montréal métropolitain français et son acheminement vers la maturité. *Union méd. du Can.*, 95:445, 1966.

Patterson, P. K., et Skinner, A. L.: Physician Response to Delegation of Well Child Care. *Northwest Med.*, 70:92, février 1971.

Reid, J. H.. et Phillips, M.: Child Welfare Since 1912. *Children Today*, 1:13. mars – avril 1972.

Scelsi, M. N.: UNICEF at Work around the World. *Children Today*, 1:19, mars – avril 1972.

Silver, H. K., et Hecker. J. A.: The Pediatric Nurse Practioner and the Child Health Associate: New Types of Health Professionals. *J. Med. Educ.*, 45:171, mars 1970.

Vaillancourt-Wagner, M.: L'enfant porte-bonheur ou l'enfant fardeau. *Inf. Can.*, 17:25, août 1975.

Walker, D. J.: Our Changing World – Its Implications for Nursing. *Nursing Forum*, 9:328, 1970.

Word, S. A.: Components of a Child Advocacy Program. *Children Today*, 1:38, mars – avril 1972.

Wiss, M. O.: Kibbutz Nurse. *Am. J. Nursing*, 71:1762, 1971.

2

croissance et développement de l'enfant

L'ENFANT GRANDIT AU SEIN D'UNE FAMILLE

La croissance et le développement de l'enfant apparaissent comme le résultat de ses caractéristiques génétiques, et des soins et de l'amour que les adultes, habituellement sa famille, lui prodiguent. Bien qu'il ait été brièvement fait mention, dans le premier chapitre, de la famille incluant toute la parenté et de sa division en unités appelées « familles nucléaires », ce concept mérite de plus amples explications. Il y a plus de deux cents ans, en Amérique du Nord, les enfants étaient élevés au sein d'une famille qui gagnait son pain quotidien en cultivant la terre et en pratiquant la chasse et la pêche. Dans un tel type de famille, plusieurs générations étaient interdépendantes; chaque membre de la famille, indépendamment de son âge, était considéré comme un individu qui contribuait au bien-être de tous. Il existait une continuité dans cette vie collective. On éduquait le jeune enfant selon les règles de sa famille et de son milieu social, et selon les normes, les valeurs, les traditions transmises de génération en génération. Graduellement, certaines familles ou quelques-uns de leurs membres émigrèrent vers les villes et devinrent de véritables citadins. Les villes se développèrent et prirent une telle expansion que de nombreuses familles délaissent actuellement les centres urbains surpeuplés pour habiter la banlieue. Cette mobilité contribue à désintégrer les familles nombreuses et à soumettre les plus petites unités familiales et les individus séparés de leur famille à une sorte d'angoisse, inconnue au sein de la grande famille traditionnelle qui se suffisait à elle-même. Cette angoisse n'est pas uniquement due à la mobilité, mais aussi aux changements économiques et sociaux d'une société en constante transformation.

Les vagues d'immigration qui se sont succédé en Amérique du Nord depuis plusieurs décades ont enrichi les pays d'individus ou de familles dont les valeurs, les mœurs, les coutumes, les traditions et quelquefois la langue diffèrent de l'ensemble de la population. Leur intégration à ce nouveau milieu culturel ne s'accomplit pas toujours sans heurts et rend encore plus aigu le problème de l'incompréhension entre les générations.

Le foyer

Influences culturelles. Même si la majorité des pays démocratiques préfère ne pas prononcer les termes de « classe sociale », il est indéniable qu'il existe des groupes d'individus plus favorisés que d'autres, dans toutes les sociétés.

Les personnes ayant une instruction collégiale ou universitaire présentent des caractéristiques absentes chez celles qui n'ont pas eu la chance de s'instruire, et les personnes qui doivent vivre continuellement avec un revenu insuffisant adoptent aussi des comportements particuliers et distinctifs. Il est fort probable que l'enfant né dans une famille appartenant à un niveau social élevé ou moyen va recevoir, grâce au statut socio-économique de sa famille, de meilleurs soins physiques qu'un enfant né au sein d'un foyer vivant dans la misère. Par suite de leur manque probable d'instruction, les parents des milieux défavorisés peuvent difficilement connaître les principes à la base d'une alimentation adéquate. Les conséquences de cette situation furent dramatiquement démontrées lors d'une enquête effectuée à Montréal (Canada) en 1966-1967 (tableau 1-1).

Dans le rapport du Conseil national de bien-être social sur les enfants pauvres au Canada paru en 1975, il y est inscrit que le taux de mortalité prénatale est plus élevé en classe défavorisée et que le taux de morbidité chez les enfants pauvres surpasse dramatiquement celui de la population infantile en général.

Les parents qui n'ont pas la possibilité de procurer à leurs enfants des avantages matériels ne peuvent, la plupart du temps, ni offrir à leurs enfants, ni recevoir eux-mêmes des soins médicaux adéquats. Ils ignorent aussi parfois qu'ils ont à leur disposition des soins médicaux gratuits ou dont le coût est minime. D'autres ne demandent jamais d'aide, même s'ils savent où obtenir gratuitement ces secours. Par conséquent, les parents et les enfants peuvent souffrir de maladies qui auraient pu être aisément traitées si elles avaient été diagnostiquées assez tôt. Ceci ne signifie pas que les enfants qui ne reçoivent pas de soins physiques adéquats soient privés d'amour. Très souvent, tant qu'ils sont très jeunes, ces enfants sont confiants et heureux.

Malheureusement, l'effet de la pauvreté sur la vie d'un enfant devient plus intense lorsqu'il est plus âgé et qu'il doit vivre à l'extérieur de son milieu familial. C'est durant ses années scolaires qu'il peut se sentir désavantagé par rapport aux autres enfants plus fortunés que lui.

Le comportement des parents est en général modelé sur celui de leur groupe, et plus spécifiquement sur celui de leurs propres parents. Ainsi, la punition corporelle est, de façon caractéristique, infligée par beaucoup d'Européens de l'Est, mais rarement utilisée par les Chinois ou les Japonais. De même, les rôles du père et de la mère varient selon les coutumes du groupe.

La culture du groupe ethnique, l'aire géographique, la localisation urbaine ou rurale et la classe sociale influencent les parents, mais sont redéfinies par la famille elle-même, qui forme une petite unité sociale étroitement liée dans laquelle l'enfant naît et est élevé. L'influence de la culture familiale est déterminante dans la croissance et le développement de l'enfant. À mesure qu'il grandit et délaisse le foyer, pour jouer en groupe à l'école et faire partie d'une bande, d'une équipe ou d'un club, sa culture familiale est de plus en plus modifiée par celle de la communauté.

Nouveaux types de familles. Dans les familles où le père est loin du foyer durant de longues périodes, comme c'est le cas pour les militaires, les marins, les représentants de commerce, et ceux qui travaillent dans des régions éloignées où il leur est impossible de faire venir leur famille, la mère devient le chef de la maisonnée. On trouve aussi des mères qui détiennent l'autorité nécessaire pour prendre des décisions dans les familles où les enfants voient rarement leur père, sauf pendant les fins de semaine, parce qu'il quitte le foyer tôt le matin et rentre tard le soir.

La famille démocratique, dans laquelle le couple et les enfants, quand ils sont assez âgés, participent aux décisions, représente une tendance moderne. Dans ce type de famille, les parents, « père et mère », peuvent travailler afin de permettre à leur famille un niveau de vie plus élevé que celui qui aurait été possible avec l'unique salaire du père. Chez un nombre croissant de jeunes couples, la femme travaille pour subvenir en tout ou en partie aux besoins de la famille, lorsque le mari termine ses études professionnelles. Chez les générations antérieures, lorsque, dans un couple, la femme seule travaillait, l'homme était blâmé pour son comportement et la femme attirait la pitié de ses amies. Aujourd'hui, l'on comprend que l'instruction du mari est nécessaire et remplace le travail qui permettra plus tard à la famille d'obtenir un niveau de vie qu'elle n'aurait pu atteindre sans cette longue préparation.

Dans certaines familles, les deux conjoints poursuivent leurs études ou désirent tous deux demeurer sur le marché du travail. Ils peuvent désirer des enfants et dans ce cas, le père et la mère partagent les travaux ménagers et le soin des enfants. La garde des enfants constitue en général un problème pour un type de parents nord-américains étant donné l'éloignement de la parenté et le petit nombre de garderies de qualité.

Enfin, dans certaines familles, tous ceux qui sont assez âgés pour travailler sont employés au même endroit. De telles familles dépendent de quelque industrie et sont groupées dans une petite ville ou dans certains quartiers de villes populeuses. Les membres appartenant à de tels groupes ont souvent de multiples caractéristiques sociales similaires.

Une nouvelle formule de vie a pris de plus en plus d'importance au cours des dernières années. Il s'agit de jeunes adultes qui vivent en « communes » pendant des périodes plus ou moins longues selon les circonstances. Les enfants qui vivent au sein de ces groupes sont habituellement pris en charge par l'ensemble de la communauté.

De nombreux enfants ne vivent pas au sein d'une famille unie. Certaines familles ne comprennent qu'un seul parent, par suite du divorce, de la mort d'un conjoint ou de la naissance de l'enfant en dehors du mariage. Parfois, les parents étant absents du foyer, les jeunes enfants sont élevés, soit par leurs aînés, soit par leurs grands-parents ou par d'autres membres de la famille. Certains enfants sont placés chez des parents nourriciers ou passent la majeure partie de leur enfance dans des institutions. Ces enfants sont privés, non seulement de contacts avec des adultes stables et aimants, mais aussi de l'apprentissage des valeurs familiales et des normes et rôles essentiels à la vie en famille. Il est primordial pour l'infirmière qui cherche à comprendre la croissance et le développement d'un membre d'une famille, qu'il soit adulte ou enfant, de connaître l'identité et le rôle de chaque membre du groupe et les relations entre ces membres.

La collectivité

Les tendances générales de la société au sujet de l'éducation des enfants influencent sans aucun doute l'enfant plus âgé. Celui-ci est susceptible d'évaluer son foyer et la manière dont ses parents, ou les autres adultes qui s'occupent de lui, le traitent, et de se rendre compte s'il y a une grande différence entre son foyer et le modèle général. Si tous les parents infligent des punitions physiques, l'enfant est prêt à les accepter comme faisant partie intégrante des relations parents-enfant. Mais s'il est battu alors que ce n'est pas le cas pour ses amis, il est vraisemblable qu'il blâmera ses parents et pensera qu'ils ne l'aiment pas.

C'est tout d'abord dans une chaleureuse vie familiale que l'enfant apprend le sens de l'amour et peut renoncer à satisfaire un plaisir pour obtenir l'approbation de parents aimants. Il apprend à obéir à ceux qui savent mieux que lui ce qui doit être fait dans une situation donnée. Il adapte cette attitude envers l'autorité à ses relations avec sa gardienne, les voisins, les employés de sa garderie, les infirmières et les enseignants. Il établit des relations avec les adultes à l'intérieur d'un champ social qui s'agrandit constamment.

COMPRÉHENSION DE L'INFIRMIÈRE DES PRINCIPES DE LA CROISSANCE ET DU DÉVELOPPEMENT

La période de croissance s'étend de la conception à la fin de l'adolescence et le développement humain dure toute la vie. Durant la période la plus active de la croissance et du développement, deux cellules, n'en formant plus qu'une, se multiplient et deviennent normalement une personne douée de pensée et de sentiments qui, finalement, prend ses responsabilités au sein de la société. L'infirmière doit comprendre ces processus de croissance et de développement pour diverses raisons.

L'infirmière doit savoir ce qu'il faut attendre d'un enfant à un âge donné et à quel moment peuvent apparaître certains types de comportement. Elle utilise ses connaissances pour évaluer chaque enfant selon des normes établies pour chaque étape du développement. Un enfant peut être aidé à adopter un comportement plus approprié si l'infirmière connaît les phases normales du développement.

De plus, l'infirmière se sert de ses connaissances sur la croissance et le développement de l'enfant pour participer, avec les autres membres de l'équipe de santé, à l'élaboration d'un plan de soins adapté à chaque enfant.

Ces connaissances importantes doivent aussi aider l'infirmière à mieux comprendre pourquoi des conditions particulières, et des maladies, surviennent plus spécifiquement à certains âges.

Quand l'infirmière a acquis assez d'expérience pour mettre en pratique ses connaissances sur la croissance et le développement dans sa tâche de donner les soins aux enfants, elle peut enseigner aux mères la manière d'utiliser un tel savoir, de façon qu'elles puissent aider leurs propres enfants à profiter de leur potentiel physique, émotif et intellectuel.

Dans le chapitre, comme dans les chapitres suivants consacrés à la croissance et au développement, seront commentés des concepts, des principes et des faits que l'infirmière devrait connaître afin d'adapter les soins qu'elle donne aux besoins des enfants de différents âges. La plupart des normes de croissance et de développement ont été établies à partir de groupes d'enfants américains appartenant vraisemblablement à la classe moyenne. Quand une tâche est présentée comme devant être accomplie à tel âge, l'infirmière doit comprendre que chaque enfant peut présenter des variations acceptables dans certaines limites. Par exemple, si l'infirmière se réfère au chapitre 14, elle y notera qu'on déclare qu'un enfant fait ses premiers pas seul à l'âge de quatorze mois. En général, l'enfant peut normalement marcher seul à n'importe quel moment durant la période située entre neuf et dix-huit mois. L'infirmière trouvera probablement plus facile de se souvenir des âges spécifiques pour les différentes étapes, que d'essayer d'apprendre des limites à l'intérieur desquelles une étape donnée se situe.

HÉRÉDITÉ, EUGÉNISME ET EUTHÉNISME

L'aspect physique de la croissance et du développement est influencé par l'hérédité, l'environnement et l'état de santé de l'enfant.

L'hérédité d'un homme et d'une femme détermine celle de leurs enfants. Pour cette raison, l'histoire de santé de plusieurs générations des familles de chacun des parents devrait être étudiée, pour découvrir les caractéristiques héréditaires que l'enfant est susceptible de posséder.

L'eugénisme est la science qui étudie les facteurs pouvant améliorer les qualités congénitales ou héréditaires de la race. Si l'eugénisme était appliqué, ceci influencerait les hommes et les femmes dans leur sélection d'un partenaire en vue du mariage, en les aidant à éviter des unions qui, probablement, produiraient des enfants faibles ou tarés, et en encourageant celles qui seraient susceptibles de produire des enfants au-dessus du niveau minimal de santé. Quelques maladies sont héréditaires et une prédisposition à certaines affections est génétiquement déterminée.

Comme il a déjà été souligné, l'histoire de la famille, plus que la condition actuelle des parents de l'enfant, doit être étudiée pour déterminer la probabilité d'une tendance vers une maladie spécifique. Une telle étude est difficile parmi les groupes défavorisés dont les histoires en ce qui concerne la santé sont transmises oralement, et aussi parmi quelques groupes dont l'attitude envers la santé et la maladie peut être influencée culturellement. Avec l'expansion des services de santé scolaires, les programmes sanitaires dans les cliniques et les dispensaires, l'histoire de santé des familles peut être obtenue plus facilement et de façon plus complète.

L'amniocentèse et certaines analyses sanguines permettent parfois de découvrir si les parents sont porteurs de traits génétiques indésirables et si le fœtus est atteint de certaines maladies connues.

L'euthénisme, par opposition à l'eugénisme, traite des moyens de promouvoir la santé. Cette science étudie les conditions intra-utérines pour un développement optimal du fœtus et les caractéristiques d'un environnement salubre, non seulement pour les enfants, mais aussi pour tous les groupes d'âge.

Dans les hôpitaux et les cliniques, les mères ainsi que les infirmières apprennent les principes généraux de la croissance et du développement de l'enfant. Elles apprennent que chaque enfant a un potentiel génétique différent pour sa croissance, et que ce potentiel ne peut être dépassé, mais plutôt entravé à chaque étape. Un enfant qui s'éloigne trop d'un critère normal de taille, de poids, de développement physique ou de comportement doit être examiné par un professionnel de la santé. Le problème le plus communément rencontré chez l'enfant est un soudain ralentissement, non caractéristique de son âge. Une aide préventive devrait être apportée aux mères, en leur enseignant les changements dans le rythme de croissance et de développement qui peuvent survenir à certains âges.

CARACTÉRISTIQUES DE LA CROISSANCE ET DU DÉVELOPPEMENT

La croissance et le développement sont des termes qui furent souvent utilisés d'une manière interchangeable. L'une dépend de l'autre et, chez un enfant normal, ces deux processus ont une évolution parallèle tout en demeurant deux phénomènes distincts. Le terme croissance se rapporte à une augmentation quantitative de tout le corps en général et de chacun de ses organes en particulier, pouvant être mesurée en centimètres et en kilogrammes. Le terme développement définit le perfectionnement progressif des habiletés et les possibilités croissantes d'utiliser ses capacités. Le terme maturation est souvent employé comme synonyme de développement. Toutefois, le concept de maturation a une application plus limitée, puisqu'il désigne uniquement le développement de certaines caractéristiques déterminées génétiquement. Le développement ne survient pas de façon erratique, mais plutôt selon un ordre défini. Il y a une relation directe entre chacune des étapes et l'une dépend toujours de la précédente.

Chaque enfant est unique; il ne devrait jamais être catalogué comme membre d'un groupe ou confondu avec l'ensemble. Chaque enfant a son propre rythme de croissance, mais l'ordre dans lequel les étapes surviennent est assez constant. Par exemple, un enfant doit pouvoir s'asseoir avant de se tenir seul debout. L'âge auquel tel enfant en particulier acquerra telle habileté spécifique peut, comme nous l'avons déjà mentionné, varier tout en demeurant à l'intérieur de certaines limites acceptables.

Bien que la croissance et le développement – aux points de vue physique, mental, social, émotif et intellectuel – ne suivent pas exactement le même rythme, ils n'en demeurent pas moins étroitement liés chez la majorité des enfants. Cette interaction est perturbée quand la croissance, en totalité ou en partie, est anormalement lente ou rapide; l'enfant apparaît alors comme anormal. Par exemple, un garçon qui, à quatorze ans, mesure 1,80m, peut ressembler physiquement à un homme, mais aux niveaux émotif, social et culturel, être encore à l'âge pubère. Quelle qu'en soit la cause, si un enfant est différent de ceux de son âge, il aura probablement besoin d'aide pour se développer harmonieusement au sein de sa famille et à l'extérieur de son foyer. L'enfant victime d'une longue maladie, d'un handicap physique ou mental, diffère lui aussi des autres enfants et, par conséquent, aura besoin d'aide pour vivre normalement.

Le concept d'interaction entre la croissance et le développement est aussi important pour l'enfant hospitalisé ou sous contrôle médical à la maison. Il est un des principes de base du travail d'équipe dans les soins à l'enfant malade. Toute l'équipe de santé participe au développement total de l'enfant hospitalisé ou malade à la maison. Ainsi, l'instituteur à l'hôpital participe au développement intellectuel de l'enfant, et l'animatrice de la salle de jeu crée des situations par lesquelles l'enfant continue son apprentissage des relations sociales. Le psychologue et le psychiatre aident les infirmières à faire face aux problèmes émotifs des enfants malades. La diététicienne, la physiothérapeute, l'infirmière et tous les autres membres de l'équipe de santé, chacun dans son domaine particulier, visent à favoriser le développement total de l'enfant. Beaucoup de membres de l'équipe de santé atteignent l'enfant malade à la maison par l'intermédiaire de l'infirmière en santé publique. L'équipe travaille aussi à faciliter à l'enfant les transitions entre le foyer et l'hôpital et, ensuite, entre l'hôpital et la maison.

Étude de la croissance et du développement

Tous les enfants suivent un ordre normal de croissance, mais selon un rythme individuel. En général, il y a une corrélation positive entre la croissance physique et le développement mental et émotif. Ceci peut toutefois être faux, pour un enfant déterminé, et nous avons déjà parlé du danger qui consiste à comparer sans discernement un enfant à un modèle standard de croissance. Il y a beaucoup trop de variations quant aux caractéristiques génétiques et, aussi, quant à l'environnement, pour rendre ceci possible. Par exemple, une tension excessive peut provoquer des changements de personnalité chez l'enfant et même altérer sa santé physique. Les adultes doivent bien comprendre les étapes de la croissance et du développement, de manière à pouvoir appliquer leurs connaissances quand ils prennent soin des enfants. Les stades, énumérés ci-après, sont étudiés en détail dans les chapitres concernant le soin des enfants de différents âges.

1) L'embryon puis le fœtus – de la conception à la naissance;
2) le nouveau-né – de la naissance à deux ou quatre semaines;
3) le nourrisson – de deux à quatre semaines jusqu'à un an;
4) le trottineur – de un à trois ans;
5) l'enfant préscolaire – de trois à cinq ou six ans;
6) l'enfant d'âge scolaire – de 5 ou 6 ans à 12 ans ou jusqu'à la puberté;
7) l'adolescent – de la puberté au début de la vie adulte.

Normes de croissance

Afin d'établir des normes de croissance, nous pouvons étudier des groupes d'âges séparément et faire une comparaison de leurs moyennes aux points de vue pondéral, statural et autres aspects de la croissance.

Comparons, par exemple, la taille moyenne des enfants de 5 ans avec ceux de 6 ans; la différence entre ces moyennes est considérée comme la croissance moyenne d'un enfant durant sa sixième année. Dans une étude longitudinale de la croissance, la taille et le poids des enfants sont surveillés de la naissance jusqu'à la fin de l'enfance. De telles études montrent des périodes de croissance accélérées qui sont en corrélation avec les diverses étapes de la maturation de l'enfant. Par exemple, la dernière poussée de croissance est rattachée à la puberté et peut commencer chez certaines filles dès dix ans, et chez d'autres, seulement à quatorze ans; les âges correspondants pour les garçons sont douze et seize ans. Une accélération précoce indique une puberté prochaine et un délai dans la poussée de croissance acompagne aussi ordinairement un retard pubertaire. Garçons ou filles, qui expérimentent une lenteur à croître et à se développer, risquent de se sentir honteux et malheureux.

Les aspects mentaux, émotifs et sociaux du développement montrent aussi des variations et

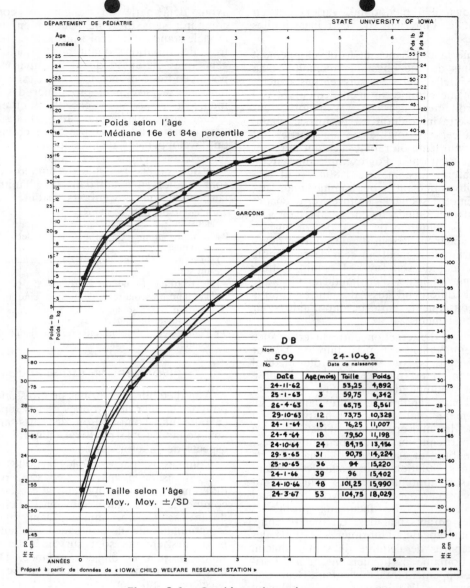

Figure 2-1. Graphique de croissance

sont beaucoup plus influencés par les facteurs d'environnement que ne l'est la croissance physique. Dans des conditions de grande privation, cependant, comme en temps de guerre, lors de maladie prolongée ou d'hospitalisation, la croissance physique peut être plus influencée par les facteurs d'environnement que le développement mental ou émotif.

On doit utiliser avec prudence les normes ou les moyennes de croissance, car quelques enfants parviennent plus vite à maturité que d'autres et complètent plus rapidement leur croissance. De nombreux facteurs héréditaires

sont en cause et expliquent partiellement pourquoi certains enfants sont petits et gras, d'autres bien musclés et de taille moyenne et quelques-uns, enfin, grands et minces. Des normes caractéristiques pour chacun des types morphologiques décrits ont plus de valeur qu'une seule échelle pour tous les enfants en général.

Étude des modèles de croissance

Les premières statistiques relatives à la croissance normale des enfants de différents âges

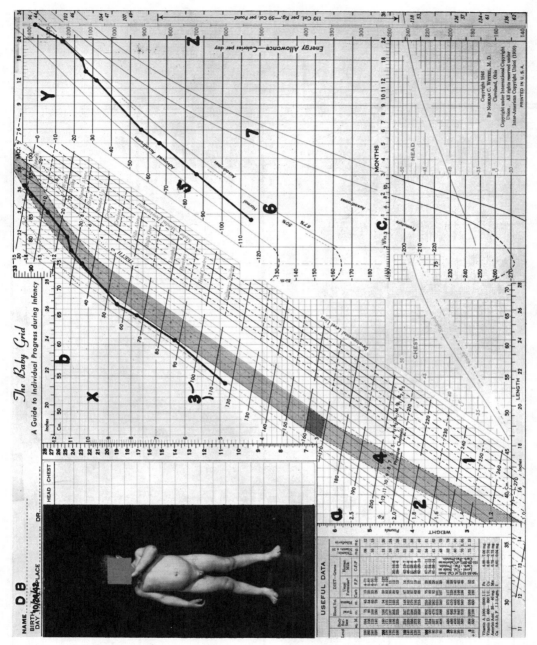

Figure 2-2. Schéma de l'évolution de l'enfant.

se basaient uniquement sur les moyennes de poids et de taille, sans tenir compte des différents schémas corporels, de l'environnement et des différences normales dans le rythme de croissance de chaque enfant.

Lorsqu'on considère la croissance d'un enfant en particulier, on doit accorder une plus grande importance à une prise optimale de poids qu'à une simple prise passagère.

Comme exemple de graphiques de croissance, nous avons celui de l'Iowa: le personnel de l'Université d'Iowa a construit une série de six graphiques à partir d'observations faites sur des milliers d'enfants. Ces graphiques indiquent le poids et la taille, selon l'âge, et ceci, pour les deux sexes. Les groupes d'âges furent ainsi délimités: de 0 à12 mois, de 0 à six ans et de cinq à dix-huit ans. On présente à la figure 2-1 un exemple d'un graphique de croissance

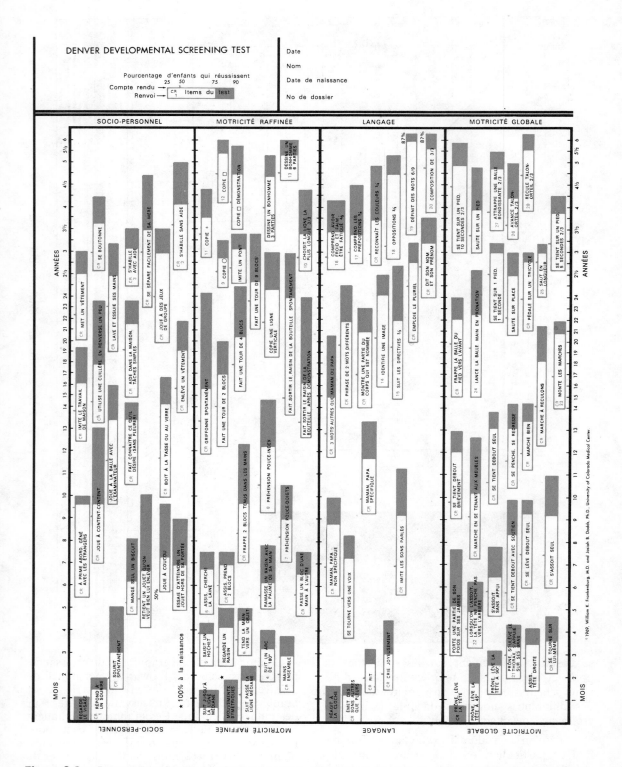

Figure 2-3. Denver Developmental Screening Test. (Courtoisie de W. K. Frankenburg, M.D., et J. B. Dodds, Ph.D., Université de Colorado Medical Center, 1968.)

de l'Iowa. On inscrit le nom et la date de naissance de l'enfant lors de la première rencontre. À chaque examen, on inscrit sa taille et son poids sur le graphique, où l'on peut les comparer à la courbe moyenne. L'utilisation de cette forme de graphique s'avère d'une grande simplicité, mais demeure insuffisante à certains égards.

Pour permettre une meilleure évaluation de la croissance, le docteur Norman Wetzel a imaginé un système de grilles (Grid Graphs) où de multiples informations peuvent être enregistrées. Deux cartes différentes permettent d'étudier le développement de 0 à 3 ans (Baby Grid) ou de 2 à 15 ans (Wetzel Grid). Sur le schéma du bébé (Baby Grid) une grille permet de suivre les variations du poids et de la taille sur un graphique où les moyennes de contrôle sont différentes pour les bébés de type longiligne et de type bréviligne. On indique également les étapes du développement normal en passant par le sourire, le contrôle de la tête, la marche et la parole. Sur le même graphique, une grille indique le développement de l'enfant prématuré et du nourrisson normal ou précoce, ce qui permet d'évaluer l'enfant selon ses propres caractéristiques de croissance et de le comparer à lui-même. Lente ou rapide, la croissance normale est avant tout régulière et prévisible (fig. 2-2).

Il existe une nouvelle façon d'interpréter le modèle de croissance physique grâce à la stéréophotogrammétrie, qui consiste à dessiner une carte représentant le relief de tout le corps. On obtient ainsi une évaluation physique exacte.

Une autre méthode, qui diffère peu de la précédente, consiste à étudier les formes du visage de l'enfant. On obtient cette image en projetant un graphique sur le visage de l'enfant. Les contours, les surfaces planes, les lignes et les courbes de la structure squelettique du visage modèlent le patron de la figure en lignes courbes. Il en résulte une carte du visage différente d'un individu à l'autre. Les empreintes physiques enregistrent les modifications de la croissance et pourront guider, par exemple, la correction de la dentition. Elles pourront éventuellement servir à l'interprétation des traits héréditaires dans l'arbre généalogique.

Les graphiques les plus récents de croissance et de développement recèlent des informations très variées allant des étapes-clés du développement psychomoteur au rythme du développement osseux et à l'apparition des dents. On admet de plus en plus que seules des évaluations multi-factorielles peuvent effectivement mesurer la croissance et le développement d'un enfant.

Les déviations ou les retards pathologiques du développement peuvent être dépistés précocement par l'infirmière qui utilise le test appelé D.D.S.T. (Denver Developmental Screening Test). Ce test d'usage simple a été conçu par W. K. Frankenburg et J. B. Dodds. (Fig. 2-3.)

Un manuel d'instruction a été conçu pour assurer l'uniformité et la fiabilité du test administré. Il est indispensable de bien connaître toutes les règles du test et d'en effectuer plusieurs sous surveillance avant de se servir de cet instrument d'évaluation. Il faut se rappeler que ce test a été normalisé à partir d'une population d'enfants américains anglophones. Il est possible que les enfants d'une autre culture soient évalués un peu injustement par un tel instrument.

FACTEURS DE CROISSANCE ET DE DÉVELOPPEMENT

La croissance et le développement dépendent d'une combinaison de facteurs tous interdépendants.

Hérédité et facteurs de développement

Les membres d'une même famille ont généralement une certaine ressemblance physique et physiologique, et le rythme de croissance n'échappe pas à cette règle. Il arrive souvent que la maigreur d'un enfant ne dépende pas d'un mauvais fonctionnement endocrinien ou d'une nutrition inadéquate, mais tout simplement de sa constitution génétique. Avant de juger la taille d'un enfant, on doit observer celle des parents.

Race

Chaque race possède des traits caractéristiques distincts qui se sont maintenus au cours des âges. Les sous-groupes raciaux présentent cependant entre eux des différences aussi nombreuses que variées. Ainsi, l'Européen de race blanche sera probablement de taille élevée s'il vient du Nord, et court et trapu s'il est natif de la Sicile.

Sexe

Au moment de la naissance, le nourrisson de sexe masculin est généralement plus long et plus lourd que le bébé de sexe féminin. Les garçons conservent ordinairement cette tendance jusqu'à l'âge de onze ans, âge auquel la petite fille atteint une période de croissance accélérée et se développe plus rapidement que son frère pendant quelque temps. Dès qu'il a lui-même atteint la phase pré-pubertaire, le garçon reprend l'avantage staturo-pondéral, qu'il gardera par la suite.

Le développement osseux est plus précoce chez les filles comme on le voit sur les radiographies des poignets du nourrisson et de l'enfant. L'éruption précoce des dents définitives chez les filles démontre aussi cette avance dans le développement osseux.

Environnement

On peut trouver un exemple de l'influence de l'environnement sur la taille chez la première et la seconde génération de Japonais en Amérique du Nord. Les enfants, généralement plus grands que leurs parents, ont eu l'avantage d'avoir une nourriture plus saine et des conditions de vie meilleures que ces derniers. Les enfants qui vivaient dans des camps de concentration et dans certaines régions où régnait la misère, durant la Seconde Guerre mondiale, souffraient pour la plupart d'un arrêt quasi-total de la croissance et du développement. Ils montrèrent une amélioration remarquable quand on les replaça dans de meilleures conditions de vie.

L'environnement prénatal

Il semble que le milieu intra-utérin joue un rôle important sur le développement futur de l'enfant, car il protège le fœtus contre les attaques du monde extérieur. Ce milieu peut cependant s'avérer déficient, et il devient quelquefois nécessaire d'y soustraire le fœtus dès que celui-ci a atteint le stade de viabilité.

Les progrès de l'hygiène prénatale, l'amélioration des soins prodigués à la mère, surtout en milieu défavorisé, ont grandement amélioré les conditions de vie intra-utérine et augmenté les chances de survie du fœtus. Il faut souligner, toutefois, que la mortalité infantile demeure plus fréquente en milieu défavorisé.

Facteurs prénatals nuisibles

De nombreux facteurs peuvent s'avérer nuisibles pour le fœtus. Il peut souffrir de déficiences nutritives, quand l'alimentation maternelle est qualitativement ou quantitativement déficiente. Certains problèmes mécaniques résultent d'une mauvaise position in-utero. Les troubles endocriniens de la mère, par exemple le diabète, peuvent aussi affecter le fœtus. Si la mère doit subir une radiothérapie anti-cancéreuse, les radiations peuvent détruire l'embryon ou tuer le bébé dans l'utérus. Les maladies infectieuses constituent un des principaux facteurs néfastes. La rubéole qui atteint la mère au cours des trois premiers mois de gestation est responsable d'un grand nombre de malformations congé-

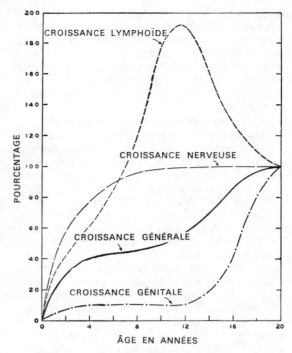

Figure 2-4 Principaux types de croissance des différentes parties et divers organes du corps (Scammon: *The measurement of the Body in Childhood. The Measurement of Man.* University of Minnesota Press.)

nitales. Le nouveau-né peut naître porteur d'une toxoplasmose ou de la syphilis, maladies dont sa mère a souffert pendant le deuxième et le troisième trimestre de sa grossesse. L'érythroblastose fœtale, due à une incompatibilité sanguine mère-fœtus, peut perturber l'évolution normale de la maturation fœtale. La malnutrition, ou l'anoxie fœtale, peuvent résulter d'une mauvaise implantation ou d'une dysfonction placentaire. L'usage excessif du tabac a été incriminé comme facteur de prématurité, ou de petitesse du bébé né à terme.

L'environnement post-natal

Un environnement qui fournit des expériences satisfaisantes contribue à la croissance. Les relations étroites entre la croissance et le développement font que chacun influence l'autre dans tous les domaines. Les éléments les plus importants de l'environnement post-natal sont les suivants:

Environnement externe. STATUT SOCIO-ÉCONOMIQUE DE LA FAMILLE. L'environnement est moins adéquat chez les groupes défavorisés que chez les classes moyennes et supérieures de la société. Les parents, placés dans des conditions financières difficiles, ont moins de possibilité d'initiation aux principes modernes et scientifiques des soins aux enfants. Ils manquent d'argent pour acheter ce qui est essentiel à la santé et à la nutrition. Souvent, ils ne peuvent, ne veulent ou ne savent pas comment obtenir les soins médicaux et hospitaliers nécessaires. Les programmes de santé publique et d'éducation scolaire aident graduellement de tels parents à fournir de meilleurs soins à leurs enfants.

NUTRITION. La nutrition est reliée à l'approvisionnement qualitatif et quantitatif en protéines, lipides, glucides, minéraux et vitamines. Une mauvaise absorption ou une assimilation défectueuse de substances nutritives peuvent cependant ruiner tous les effets d'une alimentation adéquate.

CLIMAT ET SAISONS. Les variations climatiques influencent la santé de l'enfant. Ceci est un facteur moins important pour les pays qui se trouvent dans la zone tempérée, mais chaque saison apporte des problèmes spécifiques, surtout en milieu défavorisé. La chaleur accablante de l'été s'accompagne souvent d'épidémies de gastro-entérite, quand il est difficile de conserver les aliments au frais et d'exterminer les mouches. En hiver, le chauffage inadéquat, (maison trop froide ou trop sèche), cause de nombreuses affections respiratoires, allant de la sinusite à la pneumonie parfois mortelle.

Les saisons influencent le taux de croissance et le poids, surtout chez les enfants plus âgés. Les gains de poids sont moins importants au printemps et au début de l'été, et plus élevés à la fin de l'été et en automne.

MALADIE ET BLESSURES. La maladie et les blessures, avec la débilité et le déséquilibre nutritif qu'elles entraînent, ont une grande influence sur le poids et quelquefois sur la taille de l'enfant.

EXERCICES. L'exercice active les processus physiologiques et la myélinisation et stimule le développement musculaire.

SITUATION DE L'ENFANT AU SEIN DE LA FAMILLE. La situation de l'enfant au sein de la famille est un facteur de développement pour plusieurs raisons, dont voici les principales. 1) L'enfant reçoit un enseignement de ses aînés, avantage que ne peuvent avoir ni l'enfant unique, ni l'aîné d'une famille. 2) Le plus jeune enfant peut évoluer plus ou moins lentement, parce qu'il manque d'encouragements pour s'exprimer et qu'il est « couvé » par toute la famille. 3) L'enfant unique, stimulé par la présence constante de l'adulte, a tendance à se développer intellectuellement plus rapidement qu'un autre. Son développement moteur, comme celui du cadet d'une famille normale, peut cependant être plus lent. Il est fréquent que l'on fasse tout pour lui, sans lui laisser la chance d'exercer ses propres capacités physiques.

L'environnement interne. L'INTELLIGENCE. Surtout durant le jeune âge, l'intelligence est reliée jusqu'à un certain degré au développement physique, et l'enfant très intelligent est souvent plus développé que l'enfant moins doué. L'intelligence influence aussi le développement social et mental.

L'ÉQUILIBRE HORMONAL. L'équilibre hormonal chez le jeune enfant est important. Les sécrétions des glandes endocrines sont essentielles à une croissance normale.

L'ÉMOTIVITÉ. Des troubles émotifs influencent la croissance. L'enfant qui a des problèmes ne dort ni ne mange jamais aussi bien qu'un enfant heureux et satisfait.

TYPES DE CROISSANCE ET DE DÉVELOPPEMENT

Croissance physique

Variations dans la croissance générale du corps. Les variations sont dues à des taux de croissance différents pour certaines parties du corps pendant les étapes successives du développement. Par exemple, la hauteur de la tête du nouveau-né équivaut à un quart de la longueur du corps, alors que la tête de l'adulte correspond à un huitième de sa longueur totale. La croissance durant l'enfance est surtout verticale; l'adolescent a une croissance à la fois verticale et horizontale, jusqu'à ce qu'il atteigne les proportions de l'adulte.

On présente à la figure 2-4 la courbe de croissance physique générale, de même que les principaux types de croissance tissulaire. D'après cette illustration, il y a une accélération de la croissance générale au début de l'enfance, à la préadolescence et à l'adolescence. On constate que la maturation nerveuse s'effectue surtout avant l'âge scolaire pour ensuite se stabiliser graduellement. Le tissu lymphoïde progresse rapidement jusqu'à l'âge de douze ans, pour décliner progressivement par la suite. La croissance génitale s'effectue lentement jusqu'à la puberté, pour s'accélérer à partir de l'adolescence.

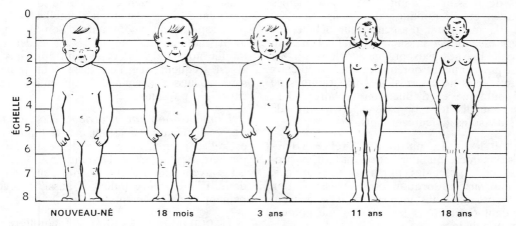

ÉCHELLE

NOUVEAU-NÉ   18 mois   3 ans   11 ans   18 ans

Figure 2-5. Échelle indiquant les changements des proportions du corps de la naissance à la maturité physique.

La circonférence de la tête. Comme elle est reliée au volume intra-crânien, on accorde beaucoup d'importance à la circonférence de la tête. Une augmentation de cette circonférence permet d'estimer le taux de croissance du cerveau. Pour un groupe d'âge particulier, les mesures ne varient pas tellement.

Le diamètre thoracique. Les dimensions de la poitrine changent quand l'enfant grandit et que l'allure générale de son thorax se modifie. À la naissance, les diamètres antéro-postérieur et latéro-latéral sont presque identiques. Avec la croissance, le diamètre latéro-latéral augmente beaucoup plus rapidement que l'autre.

Les mesures abdominale et pelvienne. La circonférence de l'abdomen varie selon l'état nutritif de l'enfant, le tonus musculaire, la dilatation gastrique, la dilatation gazeuse abdominale et les phases de la respiration. Le diamètre pelvien (distance maximale entre les épines iliaques antéro-supérieures) ne dépend pas des différentes positions que l'enfant peut adopter, ou de sa musculature. Le diamètre pelvien permet d'évaluer la délicatesse ou la robustesse de l'enfant.

Le poids. Le poids, influencé par la taille de l'enfant, constitue le meilleur critère d'une nutrition adéquate et d'une croissance normale. Il y a une grande variation au sein des normes énoncées pour chaque âge. Un poids excessif, par rapport à la hauteur et au diamètre pelvien, est aussi anormal qu'un poids insuffisant. Ce peut être le résultat d'une déficience hormonale, mais il s'agit plus vraisemblablement d'une suralimentation ou d'un régime trop riche

en glucides et en lipides, et insuffisant en protéines.

La taille. Les gains annuels en hauteur diminuent de la naissance à la maturité. La poussée de croissance à la puberté constitue l'unique exception à cette décélération. On constate une grande variation dans les gains annuels parmi les enfants du même âge. Certains enfants atteignent la taille adulte très tôt après la puberté, d'autres tardent jusqu'à la fin de l'adolescence. Les périodes de croissance les plus rapides se situent au cours de la première année de vie et à la puberté.

Développement du contrôle musculaire

Le contrôle musculaire se développe selon le mode céphalo-caudal (de la tête aux extrémités) et procède du centre vers la périphérie. Cette évolution explique, d'une part, que l'enfant peut soulever sa tête avant de parvenir à s'asseoir, et d'autre part, qu'il contrôle ses bras avant ses mains. Au cours du développement, on assiste à la spécialisation du mouvement global. L'enfant saisit les objets à pleine main avant de maîtriser le mouvement de préhension, à l'aide du pouce et de l'index, qui suppose un contrôle volontaire beaucoup plus poussé des petits muscles de la main.

L'acquisition de la dextérité manuelle et le développement locomoteur s'effectuent par étapes bien définies, comme c'est le cas pour le développement mental, émotif et social. On doit donner à l'enfant la possibilité d'apprendre, soit par l'expérience, soit par l'enseignement, quand il est prêt à franchir une nouvelle étape

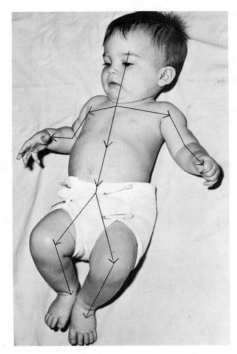

Figure 2-6. Le développement du contrôle musculaire s'achemine de la tête aux extrémités (céphalo-caudal) et du centre du corps à la périphérie.

prendre était survenue au moment favorable. L'acquisition harmonieuse du contrôle moteur, selon la séquence normale et au même rythme que les autres enfants de son âge, est probablement plus importante pour le développement de la personnalité de l'enfant que sa compétence finale dans une habileté particulière. Ainsi, l'enfant physiquement incapable de marcher jusqu'à l'âge de six ans est un enfant anormal par rapport aux autres enfants de son âge. Il peut en être marqué pour la vie, même s'il parvient ensuite à marcher normalement.

D'autre part, un handicap durant les années préscolaires peut ne pas avoir d'effet négatif permanent sur l'enfant, qui offre quand même une résistance remarquable aux éléments qui pourraient théoriquement entraver le développement normal de sa personnalité. Ceci a été souvent observé chez des enfants souffrant d'un retard causé par la maladie ou par un mode de vie aberrant. L'attitude des parents et de l'entourage de l'enfant joue un rôle important dans sa perception de lui-même et de son incapacité, et peut lui permettre de triompher de cette situation. Toutefois, certains effets négatifs peuvent ne pas être apparents, ou se révéler tardivement.

Développement mental

Il existe des tests standardisés pour évaluer l'intelligence et le développement mental des enfants d'âges différents. Il n'y a pas de moyen parfait pour mesurer les caractéristiques génétiques de l'intelligence, mais, parmi les enfants ayant un environnement comparable, ce qui est le cas dans la classe moyenne, les tests

de son évolution. Si on confronte prématurément l'enfant avec une nouvelle habileté à maîtriser et qu'on le force à l'acquérir, il ne parviendra que très lentement à atteindre l'objectif fixé. D'un autre côté, si on retarde l'apprentissage, il pourra apprendre rapidement mais n'atteindra pas l'habileté ou la compétence qu'il aurait pu avoir si l'occasion d'ap-

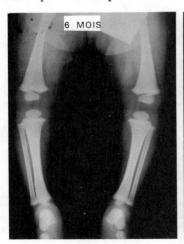
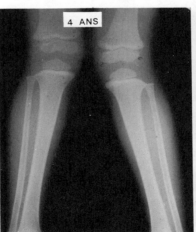
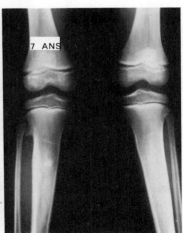

Figure 2-7. Les radiographies montrent les variations normales qui se produisent dans la position des genoux au cours de l'enfance. (Courtoisie de Charles E. Shopfner, M.D.: dans Man Is **Not** a Straight-Legged Animal: Avoid Unnecessary Therapy *J.A.M.*, *207*:29, 6 janvier 1969.)

standardisés d'intelligence permettent de prédire la capacité de développement intellectuel. On emploie de tels tests dans le système scolaire et ils aident à vérifier si les acquisitions correspondent à la capacité innée. Il est toutefois injuste d'appliquer ces tests à des groupes d'enfants différents de ceux qui ont servi à la normalisation des tests.

Le développement mental dépend de plusieurs facteurs. L'enfant doit apprendre à résoudre des problèmes et savoir comment réagir dans une situation donnée. On doit le laisser résoudre certains problèmes par lui-même quand il en est capable et l'aider à trouver une solution que seul son manque d'expérience l'empêche de découvrir. On résout pour lui les problèmes trop difficiles, afin de ménager sa patience, et celle de l'adulte, en face d'essais infructueux.

Les problèmes initiaux auxquels le bébé est confronté sont d'ordre physique et ses réflexes innés l'aident à les résoudre. Le premier problème est l'ingestion du lait. Prendre le sein maternel et avaler le lait supposent peu ou

Tableau 2-1. *Stades du développement de la personnalité*

Description jusqu'au stade précédant la vie adulte

STADE	ÂGE APPROXIMATIF	PROBLÈME PSYCHO-SOCIAL	PERSONNES IMPORTANTES	TÂCHES
Nourrisson	0- 1 an	Confiance surpassant méfiance	Mère ou substitut maternel	Prendre Tolérer de petites frustrations Reconnaître le visage maternel
Trottineur	1- 3 ans	Autonomie surpassant honte et doute	Parents	Expérimenter sa puissance verbale Tempérer l'action basée sur le plaisir par celle basée sur la réalité
Préscolaire	3- 6 ans	Initiative surpassant culpabilité	Famille	Questionner Explorer son corps et son entourage S'identifier sexuellement
Scolaire	6-12 ans	Travail surpassant infériorité	Voisinage École	Apprendre à avoir de la valeur par son travail Explorer, collectionner Etablir des relations avec des compagnons du même sexe.
Adolescent	12-? ans	Identité surpassant diffusion de rôle	Groupe d'amis Héros Modèles de chefs	Évoluer vers l'hétérosexualité Choisir une profession Se séparer de ses parents Unifier sa personnalité
Jeune adulte	—	Intimité surpassant isolement	Amis Partenaires sexuels Equipe de travail	Établir une relation durable avec un partenaire du sexe opposé Apprendre à créer, à produire

Adapté de E. Erikson – Enfance et Société, 1966.

aucune pratique. Le nouveau-né qui prend le sein pour la première fois peut avoir de la difficulté à se maintenir en contact avec le mamelon et il peut crachoter ou suffoquer quand le lait commence à couler. Mais il apprend vite, ayant souvent la possibilité de pratiquer la succion.

Un nourrisson se rend compte qu'il aime voir sourire sa mère car elle exécute pour lui des choses agréables. Donc, un des premiers problèmes pour l'enfant est de faire apparaître le sourire maternel. Il apprend à éviter les gestes qu'elle réprouve et qu'elle défend par un « non-non » accompagné d'un froncement de sourcil.

Un petit bébé est plus capable de résoudre ses problèmes que nous sommes portés à le croire; le comportement qui lui fait obtenir ce qu'il désire devient vite coutumier et ces habitudes sont ensuite très difficiles à modifier tant pour l'enfant que pour les adultes qui l'éduquent. On doit l'aider à résoudre ses problèmes, afin de lui permettre d'être fier de lui et d'obtenir la récompense sociale qui consiste à recevoir l'approbation d'autrui. Certains adultes croient qu'une attention continue peut nuire à l'enfant alors qu'elle satisfait plutôt un besoin naturel. L'enfant privé d'affection peut avoir tendance à pleurer sans raison physique, car il prend vite conscience que c'est le seul moyen d'attirer l'attention des adultes. On doit plaindre l'enfant qui pleurniche souvent, car on lui dénie le droit naturel d'être aimé par un cercle d'adultes qui s'agrandit sans cesse et par les enfants qui l'entourent.

Donc, bien que le potentiel mental soit génétiquement déterminé, l'environnement de l'enfant joue un rôle primordial sur l'actualisation de ce potentiel tel que mesuré par les tests standardisés.

Évaluation du niveau de développement mental

On définit l'intelligence comme l'aptitude à s'adapter à de nouvelles situations, à penser de manière abstraite ou à profiter de l'expérience acquise. Il existe de très nombreux types de tests d'intelligence. On soumet le nourrisson et le trottineur à des tests de type fonctionnel. On leur demande de manipuler un matériel choisi ou de prouver leurs capacités motrices.

De tels tests montrent le niveau général du développement de l'enfant, mais ne peuvent prédire le niveau intellectuel futur.

Dès que l'enfant en est capable, on lui fait passer des tests verbaux d'intelligence; quand il peut écrire, c'est-à-dire à l'âge scolaire et à l'adolescence, on l'évalue par des tests écrits, individuels ou de groupe. Après l'âge de cinq ans, les résultats des tests d'intelligence sont beaucoup plus valables que ceux obtenus durant la période préscolaire.

Signification du quotient intellectuel

Le quotient intellectuel est le rapport entre l'âge chronologique de l'enfant et son âge mental tel qu'évalué par un test d'intelligence. Voici la formule qui sert à calculer le quotient intellectuel:

$$\frac{\text{Âge mental}}{\text{Âge chronologique}} \times 100 = \text{Q.I.}$$

Comme la maturation mentale est ordinairement achevée vers l'âge de seize à vingt ans, l'âge mental de l'adulte ne peut être calculé de la même manière. On a donc choisi arbitrairement seize ans comme le début de l'âge adulte. On considère qu'un adulte a un quotient intellectuel de 75 s'il réussit toutes les questions du test destiné aux enfants de douze ans. Dans le cas d'un résultat parfait dans le test destiné aux adolescents de seize ans, son Q.I. serait de 100 et considéré comme normal ou moyen. Le Q.I. de l'enfant peut se situer au-dessus ou au-dessous de ce point. Les enfants avec un Q.I. équivalent ou supérieur à 140 sont considérés comme surdoués et ceux dont le Q.I. est inférieur à la moyenne souffrent d'un retard plus ou moins important.

Développement émotif

La *personnalité* ne représente pas un attribut spécifique, mais la qualité du comportement global d'un individu. L'aptitude à l'amour et au travail sont deux des critères d'une personnalité saine parvenue à la maturité.

Étapes du développement de la personnalité

Le développement émotif ou développement de la personnalité est un processus continu. Au cours de chaque étape du développement émotif de l'enfant, il y a un problème central qui doit être résolu, mais la solution n'est jamais complète ni définitive. Une solution satisfaisante à une étape donnée assure les bases de l'étape suivante. Une aide appropriée, et une solution heureuse des problèmes successifs de chacune des étapes du développement, s'avèrent essentiels pour atteindre à l'harmonie fonctionnelle caractéristique de la maturité.

La réussite complète et l'échec total sont quasi impossibles quand il s'agit d'atteindre un but précis dans le développement de la personnalité. En voici un exemple: l'enfant n'apprend jamais à avoir totalement confiance ou à toujours se méfier, car le nourrisson acquiert à la fois des habitudes de confiance et de méfiance. L'enfant qui jouit d'un sentiment de confiance peut se montrer méfiant quand des circonstances malheureuses se présentent plus tard dans sa vie. La personnalité saine est déterminée par la proportion d'attitudes favorables et par les sortes de compensation qu'un enfant développe pour remédier à ses incapacités.

Nous donnons une vue d'ensemble des étapes du développement émotif ou de la personnalité, d'après Erik H. Erikson, psychanalyste bien connu.

De la naissance à un an: (le nourrisson). Sentiment de confiance. Le nourrisson apprend à se fier aux adultes qui prennent soin de lui, tout d'abord à sa mère, car c'est elle qui répond à ses besoins le plus souvent.

D'un an à trois ans: (le trottineur). Sens de l'autonomie. De petit être dépendant qu'il était, le nourrisson va se transformer en une personne douée d'un esprit et d'une volonté qui lui sont propres. L'enfant qui réussit cette étape jouira d'une maîtrise de lui-même basée non pas sur la crainte, mais sur le sentiment de sa propre estime. S'il échoue, il doutera de sa valeur et de celle des autres et souffrira d'un sentiment de timidité et de honte.

De trois à six ans: (l'enfant d'âge préscolaire). Sens de l'initiative. À cet âge, l'enfant veut apprendre ce qu'il peut faire par lui-même. Son imagination est très vive. Il imite le comportement de l'adulte en prenant part à ses activités.

Il aime tenter l'expérience de pousser sa volonté à l'extrême limite. L'adulte aide à prévenir le sentiment de culpabilité qui pourrait en résulter en imposant des limites nécessaires à un comportement indésirable et en créant un climat favorable à l'exploration de nouvelles expériences désirables. L'aboutissement positif de cette étape est le sens de l'initiative, tempéré par la conscience, ou le surmoi, développé à partir des attitudes parentales et de leurs exemples. Une personnalité dominée par des sentiments de culpabilité signifie l'échec de cette étape du développement.

De six à douze ans: (l'âge scolaire). Sens du travail. Un sens très fort du devoir caractérise les enfants de cet âge. Ils veulent s'engager dans des tâches qu'ils peuvent accomplir avec succès, et ils désirent que leur effort soit reconnu par les adultes et par les enfants de leur âge. C'est une période calme où mûrit le futur citoyen. La société atteint l'enfant à travers l'école où il acquiert des connaissances tout en faisant l'apprentissage de sa vie future. L'enfant apprend à travailler et il peut coopérer et jouer loyalement à l'intérieur de règles définies. Le danger durant cette période est que l'enfant risque de développer un sentiment d'infériorité, si les parents ou l'école lui fixent des objectifs inaccessibles.

Douze ans: (début de l'adolescence). Sentiment d'identité. Un sentiment d'identité se développe pendant l'adolescence. L'adolescent veut comprendre qui il est, veut se connaître et il s'interroge sur son rôle futur dans la société. Sa principale question face à la vie est la suivante: « Qu'est-ce que cela signifiera pour moi? ».

Le succès de cette période apporte l'estime de soi, une façon de se percevoir essentielle à la rupture normale avec la tutelle parentale, rupture qui s'avère nécessaire pour envisager l'avenir. Il existe cependant un danger de diffusion de rôle, car l'adolescent affronte, dans la réalité et dans ses rêves d'avenir, une vie pleine de désirs et de conflits, de possibilités et de chances. Il perd le sentiment d'appartenance propre à l'enfant et doit envisager les responsabilités de la vie adulte pour ses propres actions et celles de ceux qui dépendront de lui. Il peut aussi, dans des circonstances défavorables, développer un sentiment de « nonappartenance » qui peut perturber le développement normal de sa personnalité.

Jeune adulte. Le sentiment d'intimité. Après la puberté, les jeunes dépassent le stade où ils trouvaient essentiel d'appartenir à un groupe composé de membres de leur âge et de leur sexe. Les garçons perdent ordinairement de l'intérêt pour le scoutisme et les filles pour les associations strictement féminines. À la fin de l'adolescence, le jeune développe un sentiment d'intimité qui lui permet d'accéder à des relations personnelles et profondes avec d'autres êtres humains. La réussite de cette période signifie une union profonde avec les autres, et une communion avec leurs désirs et possibilités. Un échec dans l'établissement d'une telle intimité a comme conséquence un isolement psychologique dans lequel les relations avec les autres demeurent sur une base formelle qui manque de chaleur. Il pourrait en résulter un échec à tous les niveaux de cette intimité qui doit conduire au choix d'un partenaire stable et à la réussite de la vie à deux.

Évaluation du développement émotif

Les tests du développement émotif et social sont moins concrets que ceux qui évaluent le développement physique et mental. Ils sont surtout utilisés en thérapie, bien qu'ils servent aussi à planifier l'environnement physique ainsi que les activités et les qualifications du personnel s'occupant des enfants. Les professionnels de la santé doivent être aussi familiers avec ces tests qu'avec ceux évaluant la croissance et le développement, car l'environnement doit être planifié en fonction des besoins physiques, mentaux, émotifs et sociaux des enfants.

Il existe plusieurs moyens pour mesurer le développement émotif ou celui de la personnalité. Les tests ont pour but de comparer une étape du développement d'un enfant avec celle d'autres enfants du même âge, et de découvrir s'il souffre d'un trouble de la personnalité. Les résultats de tels tests ne sont pas très rigoureux, car la personnalité est une entité très complexe qui ne peut être évaluée aussi aisément. Les échelles d'estimation (rating scales), les questionnaires d'auto-évaluation, les techniques projectives comme la peinture digitale ou au chevalet, les jeux, le test de Rorschach, servent tous à connaître la personnalité de l'enfant. Le test de perception thématique (T.A.T.) demeure le plus global et le plus fréquemment utilisé dans l'évaluation d'une anxiété généralisée ou de problèmes de comportement chez l'enfant.

Développement social

La socialisation, ou le développement social, signifie l'intégration progressive d'un enfant à la culture du groupe. On peut diviser en deux classes les caractéristiques de la personnalité: l'une sociale, l'autre culturelle. Les caractéristiques sociales se retrouvent chez les membres adaptés au sein d'un groupe. Elles s'avèrent nécessaires à la survivance du groupe, comme, d'une part, la volonté de sacrifier son confort actuel à un bonheur futur et, d'autre part, ce qui est plus important, la coopération individuelle aux efforts d'un groupe pour le bénéfice de tous. Cette caractéristique sociale s'appelle l'altruisme. L'amour et la constance sont nécessaires à la socialisation d'un enfant. Il existe évidemment divers degrés de socialisation.

Les caractéristiques culturelles dépendent de la culture des différents groupes. L'attention portée aux enfants d'un groupe est un trait culturel, mais la manière particulière dont on soigne un enfant constitue une caractéristique sociale différente dans chacune des cultures.

Facteur de développement social

Le groupe de jeux. Il est tout à fait différent d'apprendre à vivre heureux en compagnie d'adultes et de se lier d'amitié avec des enfants de son âge. En général, les relations adulte-enfant apprennent à l'enfant à vivre à l'intérieur de certaines restrictions imposées par des adultes qui l'aiment, même si ces restrictions ne sont pas toujours rigoureusement maintenues. La vie de famille serait peu réaliste si les parents comme les enfants étaient parfaits.

Les adultes n'entrent pas en concurrence directe avec un enfant pour les choses qu'il désire. Quand il y a désaccord entre adultes et enfants, c'est généralement parce que l'adulte demande à l'enfant de faire ou d'éviter telle chose que ce dernier ne voulait pas ou voulait faire.

Un enfant qui s'adapte bien aux adultes peut s'avérer incapable de s'entendre avec d'autres enfants. Un enfant unique qui n'a pas de camarades de jeu trouvera particulièrement difficile d'apprendre l'échange de bons procédés à l'intérieur des jeux d'enfants. Les responsables de garderies devront l'aider à acquérir cette capacité. Ce peut être un processus très lent. L'adulte se trompe s'il pense qu'il est facile de faire la transition entre être un enfant unique au foyer et être un enfant parmi quinze ou vingt autres à la garderie. Beaucoup d'éducatrices pensent que la mère devrait rester avec lui pendant les premiers jours, jusqu'à ce qu'il se soit fait des amis parmi les autres enfants et qu'il conçoive l'école comme un endroit assez agréable pour y rester. Finalement, il apprend à être un élément du groupe, chef ou participant, selon l'apport qu'il peut fournir au succès du groupe dans l'activité du moment. Dans le groupe de jeu, dans l'équipe ou même dans la bande, le chef ou le meneur sera choisi moins pour sa supériorité physique à la lutte, à la course ou au ballon, que pour sa capacité à créer des activités intéressantes quand le groupe est en panne de jeu. L'enfant qui peut imaginer des activités agréables pour le groupe, qui donne ses idées à ses compagnons et qui les conduit à la réussite du projet imaginé, sera vraisemblablement choisi comme chef du groupe.

L'enfant accaparé par des activités intéressantes au sein du groupe aime tout autant ses parents, mais dépend moins d'eux pour ses besoins physiques, le support émotif et le système de valeurs qu'ils peuvent lui procurer. Il a beaucoup plus confiance en lui et apprend à utiliser les ressources de son groupe, et celles de la communauté organisées par les adultes pour les enfants et pour tous les groupes d'âge. Cette première socialisation hors du foyer, effectuée par les jeux de groupe, est ensuite continuée et développée par le système scolaire.

Résumé

L'hérédité impose des limites au développement, mais un environnement adéquat permet à l'enfant d'atteindre le maximum de ses capacités. Des expériences heureuses stimulent son habileté croissante pour s'approprier les choses qu'il désire et achever ce qu'il s'efforce de réaliser. La satisfaction de posséder et d'agir peut à elle seule signifier le bonheur, mais cet état heureux peut être intensifié par l'approbation d'autrui, perçue dans un visage souriant, une intonation agréable dans la voix, ou des caresses physiques.

L'enfant apprend la frayeur à la suite d'expériences terrifiantes directes, ou au contact d'individus effrayés. Certains adultes créent consciemment des craintes. On mentionne souvent les policiers ou les gendarmes, le médecin ou l'hôpital, dans le but d'effrayer l'enfant et le faire obéir. Il est mauvais d'obtenir ainsi son obéissance, sans l'aider à acquérir la prudence et à exercer son jugement dans de nouvelles situations.

Il faut protéger les jeunes enfants des scènes de violence ou de colère injustifiée, mais ils peuvent être exposés sans danger à une colère justifiée et bien contrôlée. Lorsque l'enfant irrite ses parents, il faut lui faire comprendre qu'il est encore aimé même s'il est l'objet de réprimandes. Il apprendrait ainsi que l'on peut l'aimer et en même temps être en courroux contre lui à cause de ce qu'il a fait. Ce type de raisonnement est inaccessible au jeune enfant qui dissocie mal actes et intentions. Toutefois, il peut saisir ce qu'il doit faire pour atténuer la colère de ses parents.

Un bébé comprend très tôt les conséquences de son comportement à l'intérieur d'une structure sociale comme la famille. S'il pleure parce qu'il a faim et que sa mère comble son besoin de nourriture, ceci constitue une expérience sociale, car il a besoin de quelqu'un d'autre pour satisfaire un besoin. Ces expériences sociales sont aussi importantes que les expériences avec le monde physique qui l'entoure,

comme par exemple, quand il trouve amusant de sucer son hochet ou de faire du bruit en le secouant. Les deux types d'expériences contribuent au processus total de maturation, croissance et développement.

L'acquisition d'une perception adéquate de son image corporelle s'effectue lentement à partir des premiers mois de la vie. Cette tâche est soumise aux principaux facteurs discutés précédemment soit les caractéristiques génétiques, la configuration biologique, la maturation, les expériences, l'environnement social. L'enfant doit apprendre à connaître son corps et à le percevoir de façon positive comme une ressource. Il doit aussi développer sa capacité de se saisir comme une entité complète séparée de ceux qui l'entourent.

ATTITUDES PARENTALES ENVERS LA CROISSANCE ET LE DÉVELOPPEMENT

Autrefois, on élevait l'enfant selon un régime strict de nourriture, de sommeil et de jeu; il était surprotégé. La routine le protégeait contre les accidents et les maladies, mais l'empêchait de s'adapter progressivement à la vie. Il ne pouvait développer de résistance à l'infection, bien que cette dernière fut prédominante dans la société dans laquelle il allait prendre une part active et croissante, en passant de la petite enfance à l'âge scolaire et à l'adolescence. L'enfant surprotégé, dont la mère déclarait qu'il n'avait jamais attrapé froid ou jamais eu mal à la gorge, était susceptible de souffrir de graves infections respiratoires lorsqu'il commençait à fréquenter l'école. Il n'avait pas non plus un jugement exercé à traverser la rue ou à grimper dans un arbre pour jouer. Il était spécialement prédisposé aux accidents quand il sortait de l'abri qu'était son foyer. Il avait des goûts très stricts en matière de nourriture et refusait d'essayer de nouveaux plats. S'il n'était pas dans son propre lit, il ne pouvait dormir aisément, comme il ne pouvait s'adapter aux heures de sommeil autres que celles auxquelles il était habitué. En vérité, il était lié à un régime qui n'était possible que dans son foyer, et il n'était pas préparé à faire une entrée graduelle dans la vie communautaire.

Les parents avaient l'habitude d'attendre d'un tel enfant, à qui ils avaient accordé très peu de responsabilités dans sa conduite, qu'il pût se diriger avec succès à l'école et au jeu. On attendait tout particulièrement des garçons qu'ils livrent leurs propres combats, qu'ils deviennent des chefs parmi les garçons de leur âge et qu'ils ne reviennent jamais à la maison en pleurant.

Cette période d'autorité et de surprotection fut suivie par une tendance où tout était permis à l'enfant. On n'imposait aucun régime alimentaire au nourrisson; lorsqu'il avait faim, on lui présentait la nourriture d'une manière très variée et il consommait peu ou beaucoup selon ses désirs. Le trottineur pouvait choisir ce qui lui plaisait parmi plusieurs plats et on ne l'obligeait jamais à se presser en mangeant. Il ne se couchait jamais contre sa volonté et on ne lui enlevait ses jouets que lorsqu'il était endormi profondément. On le punissait rarement. L'adulte lui permettait de faire ce qu'il voulait dès sa plus tendre enfance et se fiait aux conséquences naturelles de son comportement pour qu'il acquière de l'expérience. Cette attitude aboutissait logiquement à en faire un enfant irréfléchi, exigeant de ses parents énormément de temps et de patience.

Le plus récent concept tendrait à préparer l'enfant à prendre sa place dans le monde, à vivre en accord harmonieux avec son environnement physique et social. Il doit être traité comme un individu, mais qui n'est pas encore assez développé pour qu'il lui soit permis de décider ce qui est préférable pour lui et pour les autres. Une discipline saine est donc jugée nécessaire au bonheur et au développement de l'enfant.

Pendant la croissance de l'enfant, les parents doivent apprendre à le considérer et à se considérer eux-mêmes sous une optique différente. Les attitudes parentales peuvent être inadéquates quand les parents ne savent pas à quoi s'attendre de la part de l'enfant et ne connaissent pas ses besoins réels durant les différentes étapes de son développement. Les parents subissent, de plus, l'influence de l'enfant qu'ils ont été, ou de leurs propres expériences d'enfance, et ils voient les choses comme si cette situation passée existait encore. Ils considèrent cependant ces mêmes situations à travers l'accumulation d'expériences d'adulte et leur perception de la mentalité infantile reste un peu floue. Pour que l'infirmière puisse aider les parents à comprendre la psychologie de l'enfant, nous discuterons les étapes de son développement au cours de différents chapitres.

ATTITUDES DE L'INFIRMIÈRE ENVERS LA CROISSANCE ET LE DÉVELOPPEMENT

L'attitude de l'infirmière envers les enfants, sa conception de la croissance et du développement dépendent, entre autres, de la manière dont elle a été élevée et des enfants qu'elle a connus à l'intérieur et à l'extérieur de sa famille. Si elle a été heureuse au foyer et si ses expériences avec les enfants ont été satisfaisantes, son attitude sera en général plus positive que dans la situation contraire.

Pour travailler de manière plus efficace avec l'enfant, l'infirmière doit être consciente de sa manière d'envisager les rôles respectifs des parents, des enfants et de la famille. Elle a souvent tendance à minimiser le rôle du père dans la famille et à travailler seulement avec la mère en ce qui concerne l'éducation de l'enfant. Elle doit aussi reconnaître ses propres attitudes culturelles. De nombreuses infirmières, capables d'aider efficacement les parents et les enfants de la classe moyenne, ont de la difficulté à assister les gens issus des groupes défavorisés. Ceci est dû au fait que les infirmières appartiennent en général à la classe moyenne et ont quelque difficulté à comprendre les membres d'autres classes sociales.

L'infirmière doit comprendre et être sensible aux problèmes spécifiques des enfants et de leur famille. Pour développer cette sensibilité, elle doit être consciente de sa propre émotivité et analyser ses sentiments envers des attitudes autoritaires ou indulgentes. Si l'étudiante ne se sent pas à l'aise en travaillant avec les enfants, elle devrait discuter de cette situation avec son professeur ou le conseiller de son école. Une étudiante maussade et qui n'est pas heureuse avec les enfants ne pourra les rendre heureux à cause de son manque de sensibilité à leurs besoins.

Enfin l'infirmière doit prendre une attitude chaleureuse et sympathique, quoique flexible, pour soigner les enfants. Face à un comportement normal ou problématique, une solution fondée sur les besoins de l'enfant, avec pleine connaissance de ses propres sentiments, aidera l'enfant dans son évolution vers la maturité, et l'infirmière elle-même dans sa manière de considérer les problèmes futurs dans ce domaine.

RÉFÉRENCES

Livres et documents officiels

Babcock, D. E.: *Introduction to Growth, Development and Family Life*. 3e éd., Philadelphie, F. A. Davis Company, 1972.
Brazelton, T. B.: *Infants and Mothers*; Differences in Development. New York, Delacorte Press, 1969.
Breckenridge, M., et Murphy, M. N.: *Growth and Development of the Young Child*. 8e éd. Philadelphie, W. B. Saunders Company, 1969.
Brunet, O. S., et Lezine, I.: *Le développement psychologique de la première enfance*. Paris, P. U. F., 1965.
Davie, R., Butler, N., et Goldstein, H.: *From Birth to Seven: The Second Report of The National Child Development Study*. London, National Children's Bureau, 1972.
Dodson, F.: *Tout se joue avant 6 ans*. Bruxelles, Marabout, 1972.
Duvall, E. M.: *Family Development*. 4e éd. Philadelphie, J. B. Lippincott Company, 1971.
Ellis, R. W., et Mitchell, R. G. (édit.): *Child Life and Health*. 5e éd., Baltimore, Williams & Wilkins Company, 1970.
Erikson, E.: *Enfance et société*. 2e éd., Paris, Neuchâtel, Delachaux & Niestlé, 1966.
Gesell, A. et Amatruda, C. S.: *Developmental Diagnosis*. 3e éd., New York, Harper and Row, 1975.
Hadfield, J. A.: *L'enfance et l'adolescence*. Paris, Payot, 1966.
Kennedy, W. A.: *Child Psychology*. Englewood Cliffs, New Jersey, Prentice Hall, 1971.
Lewis, M. (édit.): *Origins of Intelligence*. New York, Plenum Press, 1976.
Lewis, M.: *Clinical Aspects of Child Development*. Philadelphie, Lea & Febiger, 1971.
McDonald, M.: *Not by the Color of Their Skin: The Impact of Racial Differences on the Child's Development*. New York, International University Press, 1970.
Osterrieth, P.: *Introduction à la psychologie de l'enfant*. 2e éd. Paris, P. U. F., 1974.
Richmond, P. G.: *An Introduction to Piaget*. New York, Basic Books, Inc., 1971.
Saul, L. J.: *Emotional Maturity: The Development and Dynamics of Personality*. 3e éd. Philadelphie, J. B. Lippincott Company, 1971.
Senn, M. J. E., et Solnit, A. J.: *Problems in Child Behavior & Development*. Philadelphie, Lea & Febiger, 1968.
Tomkiewicz, S.: *Le développement biologique de l'enfant*. Paris, P. U. F., 1968.
Voizot, B.: *Le développement de l'intelligence chez l'enfant*. Paris, Armand Colin, 1973.

Articles

Babson, S. G., Hendersen, N. B., et Clark, W. M.: Preschool Intelligence of Oversized Newborns. *Pediatrics*, 44:536, octobre 1969.
British Survey: Lower I Q's Found in Breech Babies. *J. A. M. A.* 208:2256, 1969.
Dayton, D. H.: Early Nutrition and Human Development. *Children*, 16:210, novembre-décembre 1969.
Dits, A., et Cambrien, A.: L'absence de la mère lors du retour de l'enfant à l'école. *Enfance*, 1:99, janvier – mars 1966.
Frankenburg, W. K., et Dodds, J. B.: The Denver Developmental Screening Test. *J. Pediat.*, 71:181, août, 1967.
Frankenburg, W. K., Goldstein, A. D., et Camp, B. W.: The Revised Denver Developmental Screening Test: Its Accuracy as a Screening Instrument. *Pediatrics*, 79:988, décembre 1971.
Gentry, E., et Paris, L. M.: Tools to Evaluate Child Development. *Am. J. Nursing*, 67:2544, 1967.
Hines, J. D.: Father – The Forgotten Man. *Nursing Forum*, 10:176, 2, 1971.
Hutto, R. B.: Poverty's Children. *Am. J. Nursing*, 69:2166, octobre 1969.
Irwin, T.: First Child? Second Child? Middle Child? Last Child? Only Child? What's the Difference? *Today's Health*, 47:26, octobre 1969.
Lavallée, H.: La capacité physique des enfants canadiens. *Union Méd. du Can.*, 104:259, février 1975.
Murphy, L.: Apprentissages spontanés du bébé et du jeune enfant. *L'enfant*, 44:229, 3, 1969.
Olshin, I. J.: Problems in Growth. *Pediat. Clin. N. Amer.*, 15:433, 1968.
Page, E. W.: Human Fetal Nutrition and Growth. *Am. J. Obst. & Gynec.*, 104:378, 1er juin 1969.
Partington, M. W., et Roberts, N.: Heights and Weights of Indian and Eskimo School Children on James Bay and Hudson Bay. *Canad. Med. Assoc. J.*, 100:502, 15 mars 1969.

Plante, M. et autres: Le dessin du bonhomme. *Union Méd. du Can.*, 104:432, mars 1975.
Rubin, R.: Body Image and Self-Esteem. *Nursing Outlook*, 16:20, juin 1968.
Simard, T. G.: Fine Sensorimotor Control with Healthy Children. *Pediatrics*, 43:1035, juir 1969.
Steinmetz, N.: Soins pédiatriques chez les Esquimaux. *Inf. Can.*, 9:21, mars 1967.
Velin, J.: Les tests mentaux chez l'enfant. *Soins*, 17:31, janvier 1972.
Waechter, E. H.: Recent Research in Child Development. *Nursing Forum*, 8:374, 4, 1969.
Weiner, L. et Goldberg, R.: Psychological Testing of Children. *Ped. Clin. N. Amer.*, 21:175, 1, 1974.

3

l'enfant et la maladie

La pédiatrie est une branche spécifique de la médecine, en raison des différences qui existent entre l'adulte et l'enfant. Celui-ci, en pleine période de croissance, assure en même temps les reconstitutions nécessaires à un fonctionnement organique normal.

On ne connaît pas la période où la possibilité de reconstitution est à son maximum. On n'a pas fixé non plus le moment de l'arrêt. Il y a peut-être une certaine vérité dans la croyance populaire qui veut que l'éruption des dents de sagesse marque la fin de la croissance. Il ne faut cependant pas oublier que le processus de destruction est depuis longtemps en marche, puisque les caries dentaires peuvent apparaître très tôt dans la vie.

La différence entre les pathologies de l'adulte et celles de l'enfant réside dans l'immaturité de l'organisme infantile aux points de vue anatomique, physiologique et psychologique.

Les différences anatomiques, surtout la petitesse de l'enfant, déterminent les méthodes de traitement et le choix de l'équipement nécessaire pour prendre soin de l'enfant. La disproportion de poids et de taille entre la tête et le corps de l'enfant, et son immaturité motrice, rendent le bébé difficile à manipuler et un adulte malhabile peut facilement blesser ou heurter accidentellement la tête de l'enfant.

Pendant les premiers mois de la vie, certaines sutures du crâne restent ouvertes et le cerveau n'est pas protégé au niveau des fontanelles; les os peuvent aussi facilement se déformer. L'accumulation de liquide à l'intérieur de la boîte crânienne va donc se manifester par un élargissement des sutures et une augmentation du volume de la tête, alors que chez l'adulte, les symptômes d'hypertension intra-crânienne apparaissent très rapidement. Cette flexibilité osseuse explique les déformations crâniennes et thoraciques qui se produisent quand la mère ou l'infirmière négligent de changer l'enfant de position et le couchent toujours du même côté.

Le sphincter du cardia s'ouvre facilement chez les nourrissons, ce qui explique la fréquence des vomissements à cet âge; l'adulte, dont le cardia est très rigide, vomit difficilement même s'il présente des nausées.

Un exemple des répercussions du développement anatomique inachevé de l'enfant sur la santé est la fréquence de l'otite moyenne. Chez le tout jeune enfant, la trompe d'Eustache, droite et courte, fait communiquer directement le rhino-pharynx avec la caisse du tympan et l'infection se propage très facilement.

Les différences physiologiques, moins évidentes que les différences anatomiques, n'en sont pas moins importantes et elles influencent directement les soins à prodiguer à un âge donné. Le tableau 3-1 illustre les variations de la composition du sang aux différentes périodes de l'enfance. L'apport de calories et de liquide nécessaires au nourrisson et au tout jeune enfant est supérieur à celui de l'adulte, compte tenu de leur taille. Cet apport, en fait, est proportionnel aux besoins de l'enfant, pour assurer sa croissance, maintenir son activité et assurer les fonctions du métabolisme basal.

L'immaturité physiologique de l'enfant peut expliquer certaines perturbations hydro-électrolytiques rapides et graves, l'élévation ou la diminution soudaine de la température corporelle, ainsi que la dissémination rapide de l'infection. Ces manifestations sont typiques des maladies infantiles.

Une perte importante de liquide causée, par exemple, par la diarrhée ou l'hyperthermie, provoquera un déséquilibre électrolytique. Pour corriger ce déséquilibre, une thérapie intraveineuse sera probablement appliquée. Il faut se rappeler, alors, que l'enfant ne peut absorber une grande quantité de liquide à la fois et qu'une perfusion intraveineuse, administrée aussi rapidement que chez l'adulte, peut causer un œdème pulmonaire.

Le degré de résistance aux infections constitue une autre différence importante entre enfants et adultes. Au tout début de sa vie, le nourrisson possède une très courte immunité passive, transmise par sa mère durant la grossesse. Il faut cependant commencer l'immunisation active chez le bébé le plus tôt possible, certaines maladies infectieuses pouvant être fatales ou comporter un risque de séquelles très graves.

Contre la maladie, les réactions de l'organisme de l'enfant et de l'adulte sont différentes.

L'infirmière doit bien les connaître si elle veut appliquer les soins préventifs et curatifs spécifiques et être prête à toute éventualité. Le nourrisson et le trottineur peuvent présenter des convulsions au moment de la montée thermique qui accompagne le début d'une maladie infectieuse, alors que l'enfant et l'adulte présenteraient plutôt un frisson important, suivi d'hyperthermie.

Tous les enfants ne réagissent pas de la même façon contre la maladie. Chaque âge a ses réactions particulières. Le nourrisson et le tout jeune enfant ne savent pas exprimer ce qu'ils ressentent. L'infirmière expérimentée doit savoir observer et interpréter les symptômes subjectifs qu'ils manifestent. L'enfant qui pleure en tirant sur son oreille, qui crie quand on le déplace ou quand on touche à un de ses membres, manifeste sa douleur, mais ne peut l'exprimer.

L'enfant plus âgé peut faire connaître sa souffrance pour attirer l'attention de son entourage; l'enfant de moins d'un an en est incapable, et tous les signes de douleur qu'il exprime doivent être sérieusement observés.

Les changements soudains qui peuvent se produire dans l'état d'un enfant, et le fait qu'il est inapte à les communiquer à l'infirmière, obligent celle-ci à être constamment en éveil pour suivre l'évolution de la maladie, observer les symptômes qui peuvent aider le médecin à poser ou à modifier un diagnostic.

C'est grâce aux progrès de la psychologie infantile et de la pédo-psychiatrie que l'on reconnaît depuis peu l'aspect psychosomatique des maladies de l'enfance.

L'état psychologique de l'enfant agit plus profondément sur son état physique qu'on ne pourrait le croire au premier abord. Il est

Tableau 3-1. *Moyenne normale du décompte des cellules sanguines*

	À LA NAISSANCE	À 2 JOURS	À 14 JOURS	À 3 MOIS	À 6 MOIS	À 1 AN	À 4 ANS	À 8-12 ANS
Globules rouges/mm³ (en millions)	5,1	5,3	5	4,3	4,6	4,7	4,8	5,1
Globules blancs/mm³ (en milliers)	15	21	11	9,5	9,2	9	8	8
Plaquettes/mm³ (en milliers)	350	400	300	260	250	250	250	250
Différents frottis:	*Pourcentages*							
Polynucléaires Neutrophiles	45	55	36	35	40	40	50-60	60
Éosinophiles et Basophiles	3	5	3	3	3	2	2	2
Lymphocytes	30	20	53	55	51	53	40	30
Monocytes	12	15	8	7	6	5	8	8
Leucoblastes	10	5	–	–	–	–	–	–

Adapté de W. E. Nelson: Textbook of Pediatrics, 1964.

important de noter les symptômes physiques sur le dossier du malade, mais si on néglige de consigner les changements de comportement, le médecin ne peut juger adéquatement leur valeur psychosomatique.

Il est très important d'écouter les observations des parents et de les noter adéquatement. Il ne faut pas oublier que ce sont eux qui connaissent l'enfant. Par la suite, l'infirmière peut les aider à orienter plus efficacement leur observation si cela s'avère nécessaire.

Si l'adulte peut exprimer ses craintes, l'enfant en est souvent incapable, et il peut essayer de se faire comprendre par un comportement inhabituel. Il est facile de se rendre compte qu'un enfant s'agite pour manifester son anxiété, mais on oublie souvent de signaler le comportement régressif ou replié sur lui-même de l'enfant plus introverti.

L'enfant peut quelquefois faire face à certaines situations dramatiques, alors qu'il est seul et sans protection. Il peut tomber et se blesser, ou ses vêtements peuvent prendre feu à la suite d'une désobéissance solitaire. Dans ces situations d'urgence, la plupart des enfants appellent leur mère et sont convaincus que son arrivée mettra un terme à toutes leurs souffrances. Ces crises passagères cèdent ensuite la place à des situations moins effrayantes. Certains enfants souffrent d'anxiété grave et chronique. Pour eux, le passé désagréable est toujours présent et les quelques événements heureux qu'ils vivent ne leur semblent que le prélude à de nouveaux traumatismes. Ces enfants peuvent bénéficier d'une aide psychiatrique.

La capacité d'attention de l'enfant est courte mais intense. Il faut savoir utiliser cette caractéristique pour le distraire d'une douleur physique. Il est évident que l'infirmière devra trouver continuellement de nouveaux stimulants à mesure que l'intérêt s'émoussera.

L'enfant ne doit jamais se sentir seul lorsqu'il souffre. Il doit pouvoir compter sur une présence réconfortante et sympathique. Ceci ne signifie pas qu'il faille toujours laisser quelqu'un près de lui, mais il doit savoir que l'on viendra à son chevet s'il pleure ou s'il appelle à l'aide.

L'enfant hospitalisé en institution spécialisée, dans un hôpital de malades chroniques, ou qui doit fréquenter une école pour enfants handicapés, peut trouver un grand réconfort à côtoyer des enfants qui lui ressemblent. D'autres enfants, au contraire, deviennent encore plus anxieux, car ils craignent que leur état ne s'aggrave et ne devienne semblable à celui de leurs camarades plus handicapés.

Certains enfants se servent d'excuses physiques pour éviter d'accomplir certaines tâches désagréables. On ne doit pas punir l'enfant qui s'est plaint « d'avoir mal au ventre » et qui oublie sa douleur dès que l'heure de partir pour l'école est passée. Il est plus important de chercher les motifs qui l'ont poussé à simuler, et il faut découvrir et corriger les problèmes scolaires sous-jacents. L'enfant d'âge préscolaire est rarement un simulateur; il est même difficile de lui faire dire ce qu'il ressent et de l'inciter à le signaler lorsqu'il a mal.

Certains facteurs aident l'enfant à bien réagir contre la maladie.

1) Orienté vers le présent, il oublie rapidement le passé et ne craint pas l'avenir.
2) Sa capacité d'attention est courte.
3) Il s'intéresse facilement à ce qui est nouveau, à ce qui peut le distraire d'une situation désagréable: images, sons, sucreries, la sensation d'être bercé ou la succion de son pouce.

Cette dernière caractéristique laisse croire à l'infirmière inexpérimentée que l'enfant va beaucoup mieux. Il faut chercher à distraire l'enfant, mais l'atteinte de cet objectif n'implique pas nécessairement que la cause de la douleur ou du malaise soit vraiment disparue.

DIFFÉRENTES PATHOLOGIES INFANTILES

Il y a des pathologies, comme l'appendicite ou la pneumonie, qui atteignent aussi bien l'adulte que l'enfant, mais certaines maladies sont spécifiques à ce dernier.

Les anomalies congénitales, comme l'atrésie de l'œsophage, l'anus imperforé ou l'omphalocèle, qui sont probablement le résultat de facteurs complexes d'hérédité et d'environnement intra-utérin, causeront la mort précoce de l'enfant si elles ne sont pas traitées dès la naissance. Par contre, une pathologie comme le rein polykystique peut fort bien passer inaperçue et être découverte à l'âge adulte.

Les pathologies du nouveau-né, telle l'érythroblastose fœtale, ne se rencontrent pas chez l'adulte parce que la survie de l'enfant dépend de l'efficacité du traitement, commencé dès que la maladie est découverte.

Les problèmes nutritifs se rencontrent souvent au cours des premières années de la vie, à cause des besoins alimentaires accrus par la croissance et le développement de l'enfant. Des maladies de carence, comme le rachitisme et le scorbut, sont les plus fréquentes.

Les accidents, comme les chutes, les brûlures et les intoxications médicamenteuses et domestiques, atteignent surtout les jeunes enfants victimes de leur insatiable curiosité, de leur activité débordante et de leur manque de maturité. Malgré les lois interdisant l'emploi du plomb dans la peinture, l'intoxication au plomb se produit lorsque l'enfant suce des surfaces recouvertes de vieille peinture ou des jouets anciens. Les parents doivent aussi être renseignés sur les dangers d'utiliser certaines poteries pour conserver des liquides.

Les problèmes psychologiques ou psychiatriques comme les traits névrotiques, la délinquance, les maladies psychosomatiques et les psychoses semblent malheureusement plus fréquents qu'auparavant en pathologie infantile.

Les cancers se rencontrent chez les enfants, sous forme de leucémies, tumeurs cérébrales, osseuses ou rénales (Tumeur de Wilms). Certaines maladies comme l'acné ou le retard staturo-pondéral se rencontrent au cours du processus de croissance et de développement.

Les infections, très fréquentes chez l'enfant, s'expliquent par l'insuffisance des défenses naturelles. Spécialement sujet aux infections respiratoires, l'enfant se trouve également en contact avec les virus et bactéries des maladies contagieuses et peut développer une immunité dès la fréquentation de l'école maternelle et de l'école primaire.

Au cours des prochains chapitres, nous étudierons les principales maladies qui se rencontrent aux différentes périodes de la croissance. Il faut se rappeler que certaines maladies sont indéniablement plus fréquentes à un âge déterminé, alors que d'autres débutent à un certain moment pour se prolonger ensuite au cours de la croissance. Dans ce livre, les pathologies ont été groupées selon l'âge où elles avaient la plus grande incidence, ou selon le moment où elles avaient le plus d'impact sur l'enfant et sa famille.

Les soins spécifiques à chacune des maladies sont basés:

1) Sur le développement anatomique, physiologique et psychologique, et sur la croissance normale.

2) Sur le traitement préventif et curatif de chaque maladie.

Un manuel d'étude doit se contenter de présenter l'aspect général de chaque maladie. L'adaptation aux besoins individuels des malades s'acquiert directement au chevet du patient et nécessite la présence du professeur qui dirige l'expérience.

MORTALITÉ ET MORBIDITÉ

Mortalité

À mesure que l'enfant vieillit, ses chances de survie augmentent. Le risque de mourir est plusieurs milliers de fois plus important au cours de la première journée de vie qu'à l'époque scolaire, et aucune année de la vie n'est plus dangereuse que la première.

Le taux de *mortalité infantile* indique le nombre de décès d'enfants au-dessous d'un an, pour un total de mille naissances vivantes. Le taux de mortalité néo-natale représente les décès au cours du premier mois de la vie.

Dans la plupart des pays occidentaux, en Scandinavie en particulier, les taux de mortalité infantile se sont considérablement abaissés.

Toutefois, les naissances prématurées et l'insuffisance des soins prénatals expliquent les taux de mortalité infantile encore relativement élevés dans certains pays, tels les Etats-Unis et le Canada. (Voir l'appendice pour les taux de mortalité infantile au Québec et au Canada). La prématurité est souvent directement liée au manque de surveillance médicale pendant la grossesse. Il est impérieux d'améliorer les soins prénataux et de les rendre facilement accessibles aux patientes des milieux défavorisés.

Il y a quelques années, les diarrhées infectieuses ou d'origine alimentaire, constituaient la principale cause de mortalité chez le nourrisson. Pendant les journées chaudes de l'été, les services pédiatriques accueillaient de nombreux bébés venant de taudis insalubres, qui étaient amenés à l'hôpital à l'état de moribond. Cette situation ne prévaut plus aujourd'hui; la diarrhée alimentaire est moins fréquente, grâce au contrôle très strict de la production et de la distribution du lait dans les fermes, les laiteries et les magasins d'alimentation, grâce à l'inspection des viandes et des entrepôts, et grâce à l'avènement des possibilités de réfrigération qui empêchent la contamination des aliments.

Les infections respiratoires demeurent une des grandes causes de mortalité infantile. L'immunisation massive des nourrissons et de la population scolaire et l'emploi des antibiotiques ont diminué les infections respiratoires secondaires aux maladies contagieuses.

Toutefois, les infections respiratoires primaires étant souvent virales, on attend avec impatience la découverte et la mise en marché d'une substance, chimique ou autre, qui serait capable de stimuler la fabrication de l'interféron, une protéine normalement produite par l'organisme pour lutter contre les virus.

Actuellement, les causes de mortalité néonatale et infantile demeurent la naissance prématurée, l'asphyxie, l'atélectasie, les malformations congénitales, les traumatismes obstétricaux, la grippe et la pneumonie. A mesure que l'enfant grandit, ses chances de survie augmentent. Ainsi, la mortalité est plus fréquente durant la période de un à quatre ans que durant l'intervalle entre 5 et 14 ans.

Les principales causes de décès entre un an et quinze ans comprennent les accidents, les tumeurs malignes, la grippe, la pneumonie et les malformations congénitales.

Morbidité

Contrairement au taux de mortalité juvénile, le taux de morbidité est élevé chez les enfants.

Les infections respiratoires constituent la principale cause de maladie en pédiatrie; un enfant sur cinq souffre d'au moins une pathologie chronique, comme l'allergie, les troubles respiratoires ou autres. L'incidence des maladies chroniques augmente avec l'âge.

On note que le nombre d'hospitalisations courtes augmente avec la hausse du niveau de vie des parents; la longueur du séjour est directement proportionnelle à la pauvreté des familles. Les enfants qui habitent dans des régions rurales demeurent à l'hôpital plus longtemps que leurs camarades de la ville.

Les caries dentaires demeurent un problème majeur pour les enfants d'âge scolaire, et la moitié des enfants de moins de quinze ans ne se sont jamais présentés chez le dentiste. Les enfants des milieux urbains, de niveau socio-économique plus élevé, reçoivent plus de soins dentaires que les autres.

La chute des taux de mortalité et de morbidité dues aux maladies contagieuses prouve la valeur de la recherche médicale. On vaccine maintenant contre la plupart des maladies contagieuses infantiles.

L'infection au staphylocoque doré ne régresse pas et on ne semble pas prêt de la juguler. On cherche encore un vaccin qui permettrait de combattre efficacement ce microbe.

Les membres de l'équipe médicale doivent veiller à l'éducation des parents, d'abord pour leur enseigner à prendre soin efficacement de la santé de leurs enfants, et aussi pour leur montrer où ils peuvent obtenir une aide médicale si la maladie apparaît.

RÉFÉRENCES

Livres et documents officiels

Gaidner, D. et Hull, D. (édit.): *Recent Advances in Pediatrics*, 4e éd. Baltimore, Williams & Wilkins Company, 1971.

Gellis, S. S. et Kagan, B. M.: *Current Pediatric Therapy 5*. Philadelphie, W. B. Saunders Company, 1971.

Gustafson, S. R. et Coursen, D. B. (édit.): *The Pediatric Patient*. Philadelphie, J. B. Lippincott Company, 1972-73-74.

Hughes, J. G. (édit.): *Synopsis of Pediatrics*. 3e éd. St. Louis, C. V. Mosby Company, 1971.

Illingworth, R. S.: *Common Symptoms of Disease in Children*. 3e éd. Philadelphie, F. A. Davis Company, 1971.

Journées parisiennes de pédiatrie. 1972-73-74, Paris, Flammarion.

Karelitz, S.: *When Your Child Is Ill*. New York, Random House, 1969.

Kelley, V. C. (édit.): *Brennemann's Practice of Pediatrics*. New York, Harper and Row, 1971.

Lightwood, R., Brimblecombe, F. et Barltrop, D. (édit.): *Paterson's Sick Children*. 9e éd. Philadelphie, J. B. Lippincott Company, 1971.

Ministère de la Santé nationale et du Bien-être social: *L'enfant malade à la maison*. Division de l'hygiène mentale, Ottawa.

Ministère de la Santé nationale et du Bien-être social: *La maladie: comment aider mon enfant malade*. Série: Formation de l'enfant, Ottawa.

Ministère des Affaires sociales: *Dossier régional. Données statistiques par région socio-sanitaire*. Annexe du rapport annuel 1973-74, Québec, 1974.

Nelson, W. E., Vaughan, V. C. et McKay, R. J. (édit.): *Textbook of Pediatrics*. 9e éd. Philadelphie, W. B. Saunders Company, 1969.

Shirkey, H. C. (édit.): *Pediatric Therapy*. 4e éd. St. Louis, C. V. Mosby Company, 1971.

Silver, H. K., Kempe, C. H. et Bruyn, H. B.: *Handbook of Pediatrics.* 9e éd. Los Altos, Californie, Lange Medical Publications, 1971.
Talbot, N. B., Kagan, J. et Eisenberg, L.: *Behavioral Science in Pediatric Medicine.* Philadelphie, W. B. Saunders Company, 1971.

Articles

Battaglia, F. C. et Lubchenco, L. O.: A Practical Classification of Newborn Infants by Weight and Gestational Age. *J. Pediat.*, 71:159, 1967.
Démographie. *Statistiques des Affaires sociales.* 2, 6, 1975.
Falkner, F.: Infant Mortality: An Urgent National Problem. *Children*, 17:83, mai – juin 1970.
Hunt, E.: Infant Mortality Trends and Maternal and Infant Care. *Children*, 17:88, mai – juin 1970.
Pearman, J. R.: Survey of Unmet Medical Needs of Children in Six Counties in Florida. *Pub. Health Rep.*, 85:189, mars 1970.
Rouquette, C.: Mortalité-Morbidité. *La revue de pédiatrie*, VI:495, 8, 1970.
Stine, O. C. et Chuaqui, C.: Mothers' Intended Actions for Childhood Symptoms. *Am. J. Pub. Health*, 59:2035, novembre 1969.
Wallace, H. M.: Some Thoughts on Planning Health Care for Children and Youth. *Children*, 18:95, mai – juin 1971.

4

l'importance de l'hérédité et du milieu dans les maladies infantiles

La santé ou la présence de maladie ou d'anomalie chez le nouveau-né dépend de plusieurs facteurs, dont les principaux sont l'hérédité et le milieu. Ceci a déjà été discuté au cours d'un chapitre précédent, mais il est cependant bon que l'infirmière ait une connaissance plus spécifique de ces influences, si elle veut comprendre la physio-pathologie de plusieurs maladies infantiles.

HÉRÉDITÉ

L'hérédité est la transmission de caractères génétiques des parents aux enfants. La vie commence par un ovule fertilisé ou zygote, composé de cytoplasme et d'un noyau qui contient entre autres, des chromosomes et des gènes. Plusieurs malformations congénitales proviennent d'anomalies chromosomiques et génétiques. Toutefois, même si les composantes du zygote sont normales, l'enfant peut quand même souffrir de malformations dues à un milieu utérin inadéquat.

Les chromosomes sont des structures filiformes qui contiennent les gènes. Chez l'être humain, chaque spermatozoïde et chaque ovule sont porteurs de 23 chromosomes, dont 22, les chromosomes autosomes, ont été numérotés de 1 à 22, alors que le 23e s'appelle chromosome sexuel. Après la fertilisation de l'ovule par le spermatozoïde, le zygote contient donc 44 chromosomes autosomes et 2 chromosomes sexuels.

Dans l'ovule et le spermatozoïde, les chromosomes autosomes correspondent entre eux un à un. Les chromosomes sexuels sont différents: la femme est porteuse de 2 chromosomes X (XX), alors que l'on trouve chez l'homme un grand chromosome X et un petit chromosome y (Xy). De plus, les cellules femelles diffèrent habituellement des cellules mâles par une masse de chromatine que l'on trouve dans le noyau de certains leucocytes, des cellules nerveuses et des cellules épithéliales. Cette masse de chromatine est appelée chromatine sexuelle ou corps de Barr. La façon la plus simple d'obtenir des cellules épithéliales pour y déterminer la présence du corps de Barr est d'effectuer un frottis buccal. Cette analyse apporte un élément supplémentaire pour le diagnostic des pathologies impliquant la différentiation sexuelle.

Le caryotype représente la constitution chromosomique de la cellule somatique humaine. C'est aussi la représentation photographique de l'étalement des chromosomes réunis en 23 paires et 7 groupes par ordre de grandeur et selon la position du centromère. Il est maintenant possible, grâce au microscope électronique, d'observer les chromosomes lors de la division cellulaire et de les identifier, grâce à leur forme respective.

Habituellement un individu possède un seul caryotype. Certaines personnes, toutefois, possèdent une série de cellules avec un certain caryotype et une autre lignée de cellules dont le caryotype diffère soit par le nombre ou par la forme des chromosomes. Ce phénomène s'appelle « mosaïsme » chromosomique. Un exemple de mosaïsme est donné lors de la présentation du mongolisme au chapitre 10.

L'expression visible des caractéristiques génétiques d'une personne s'appelle « phénotype ». Ainsi deux personnes peuvent présenter un phénotype semblable pour un certain trait génétique (les yeux bruns par exemple), mais l'une peut posséder un génotype où les allèles sont identiques et l'autre peut avoir des allèles dissemblables, d'où un génotype différent.

Les chromosomes sont constitués d'acides nucléiques et de protéines. Au point de vue chimique, les gènes contenus dans les chromosomes sont formés d'acide désoxyribonucléique ou ADN. Les gènes, supporteurs du code génétique, seraient des molécules d'ADN. La structure de l'ADN est hélicoïdale: on la compare à une échelle de corde enroulée sur elle-même ou à une double hélice.

Un polymère d'ADN contient des acides phosphoriques, des sucres (désoxy-ribose) et des bases azotées (adénine, guanine, cytosine et thymine). L'ADN donne naissance à l'acide ribonucléique (ARN) qui diffère du précédent par son oxydation, son sucre qui est le ribose et l'échange de la thymine par l'uracile. L'ARN-messager transporte le code génétique nécessaire à la synthèse des protéines. L'ARN de transfert est dissous dans les sucs nucléaires et cytoplasmiques et sert à la constitution des acides aminés. L'ARN-messager reçoit les acides aminés selon le code génétique qu'il véhicule afin de former une protéine et il pénètre à l'intérieur des ribosomes où il vient se mouler sur un des moules spécifiques ribosomiques et une protéine est finalement synthétisée.

L'ADN joue un rôle important dans la transmission des caractères héréditaires. Chaque gène est « programmé » pour un trait particulier ou une caractéristique organique. C'est à ce niveau qu'est contenu le code spécifique nécessaire à la synthèse des protéines, cette matière première des corps vivants. Tout comme les chromosomes, les gènes sont jumelés. Les gènes qui sont situés au même endroit sur une paire de chromosomes homologues sont appelés des allèles. Si les allèles sont

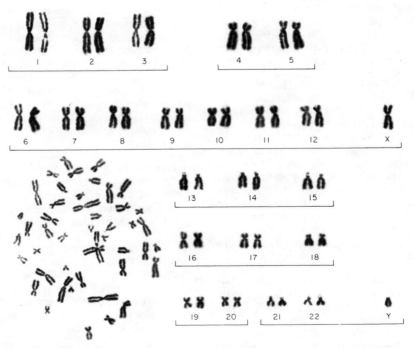

Figure 4-1. Caryotype normal mâle ($\times$ 2200). Les chromosomes sont groupés par taille. La longueur approximative d'un chromosome n° 1 est de 7 microns. (De A. G. Bearn; in P. B. Beeson et W. McDermott (Eds.): Cecil-Loeb Textbook of Medicine. 12e ed.)

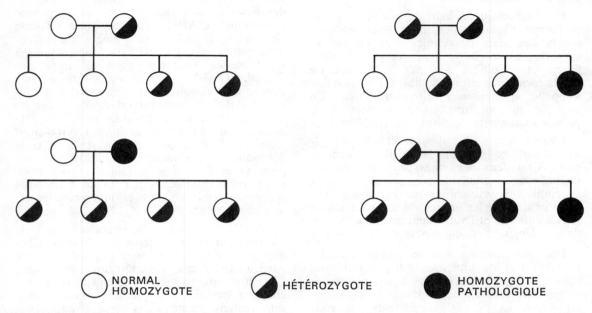

Figure 4-2. Transmission génétique non liée au sexe. Chez les populations qui vivent dans un territoire donné sans mouvement migratoire marqué, les mariages consanguins sont fréquents et la multiplication des porteurs est importante. Le risque de voir apparaître les pathologies récessives devient très grand. Les Québécois francophones et les colonies juives sont des exemples de tels types de société.

identiques, l'individu est dit *homozygote*, s'ils sont différents, la personne est *hétérozygote*. Si dans une paire d'allèles les gènes sont dissemblables, celui qui prévaut est *dominant,* alors que l'autre est considéré comme *récessif.*

Les traits anormaux dominants sont relativement rares. La personne atteinte étant ordinairement hétérozygote (ce qui signifie qu'un seul gène est pathologique), elle aura une chance sur deux d'avoir un enfant normal en épousant une personne porteuse de 2 traits normaux. Si l'héritier est sain et qu'il épouse une personne normale, leur progéniture ne sera pas atteinte. Les pathologies suivantes sont dues à un caractère dominant: l'ostéogénèse imparfaite, l'anémie à hématies falciformes et la thalassémie mineure. Il peut arriver qu'un trait dominant ne se manifeste pas cliniquement chez le porteur.

L'individu, porteur d'un gène récessif pathologique (hétérozygote), qui épouse une personne normale et homozygote, n'aura pas d'enfant atteint cliniquement, mais *quelques-uns* pourront *être porteurs.* D'autre part, si ce même individu épouse une personne hétérozygote, les probabilités seront les suivantes pour chacun de leurs enfants: un risque sur

quatre d'être homozygote pour le gène anormal, une chance sur quatre d'être homozygote et normal, deux chances sur quatre d'être hétérozygote comme ses parents. Il est évident que seuls des enfants anormaux naîtront de l'union de deux personnes homozygotes pour un gène anormal récessif. Voici quelques pathologies dues à des gènes récessifs: l'idiotie amaurotique ou maladie de Tay-Sachs, la mucoviscidose, la galactosémie et la phénylcétonurie. (Fig. 4-2.)

Les gènes anormaux peuvent provenir de mutations. La *mutation* est le changement fondamental du matériel génétique et la transmission d'un nouveau caractère au lieu du code génétique héréditaire. La cause de la mutation est inconnue, mais on étudie actuellement l'effet des rayons cosmiques, du radium, des rayons X et des isotopes sur les cellules reproductrices. On ne connaît pas encore la dose maximum de radiations à laquelle un être humain peut être exposé sans danger. La chaleur et certaines substances chimiques peuvent aussi causer des mutations.

Les changements apportés au matériel génétique d'un individu peuvent se traduire par des modifications physiologiques. Ainsi, les anoma-

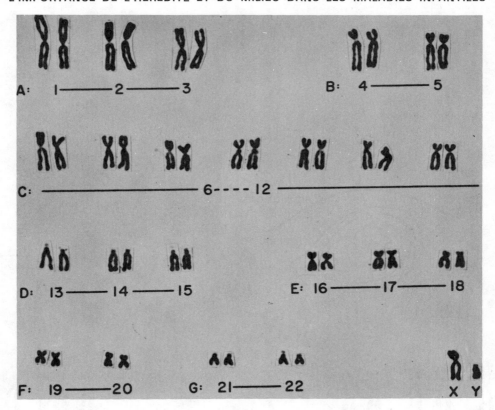

Figure 4-3. Ordinairement, on étudie les chromosomes à l'aide des petits lymphocytes du sang péri-phérique. Après 72 à 96 heures de culture on interrompt la croissance au stade de la métaphase. On plonge les chromosomes dans une solution hypotonique de façon à les hypertrophier et à les séparer. On les colore, les photographie, les découpe et les réunit en 7 groupes suivant leur longueur et la position de leur centromère. Cet arrangement des chromosomes par groupes distincts s'appelle caryo-type. On voit ci-haut un caryotype mâle normal.

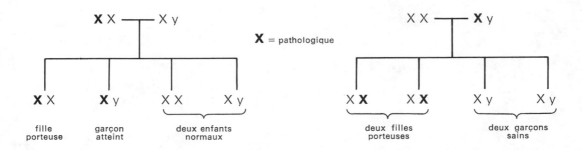

Figure 4-4. Transmission génétique liée au sexe

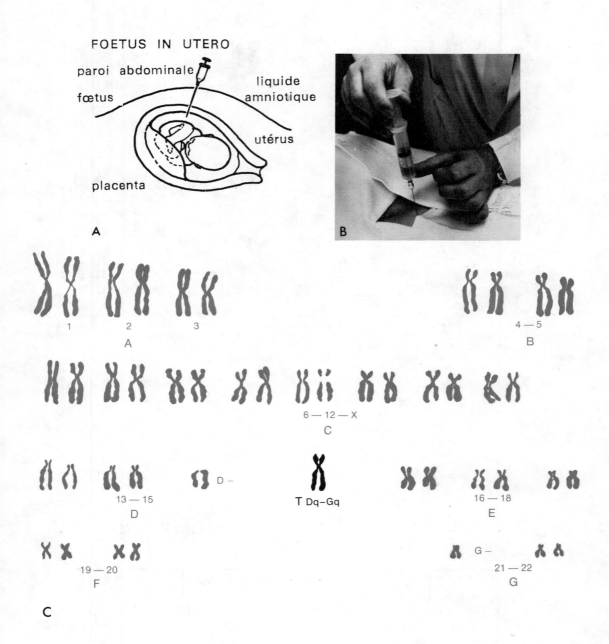

Figure 4-5. Recherche d'une anomalie génnétique chez le fœtus. *A)* et *B)* Retrait du liquide amniotique à l'aiguille. *C)* Le caryotype de la *mère* indique une anomalie du chromosome « 15 » auquel est rattaché le numéro « 21 » (en noir) d'où une probabilité de mongolisme pour l'enfant.

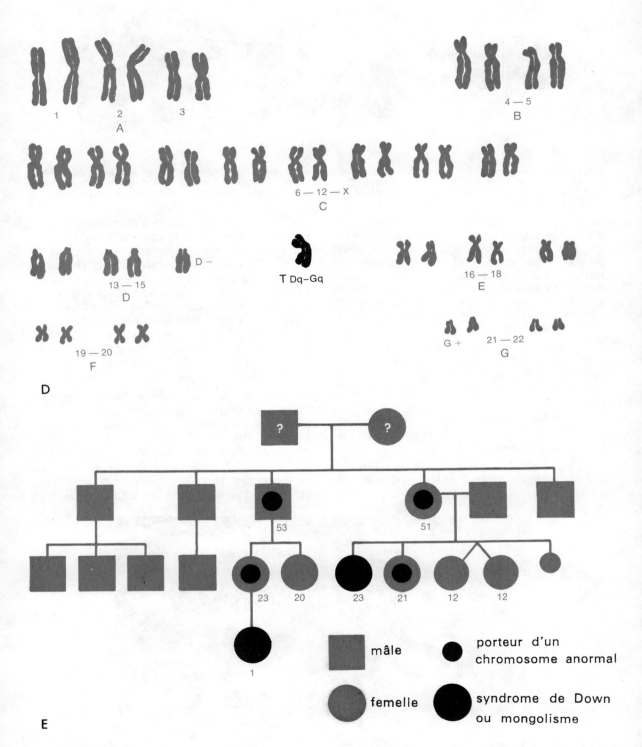

Figure 4-5. *D)* Le caryotype du *fœtus* indique que celui-ci est réellement mongolien. *E)* Le tableau indique comment l'anomalie chromosomique s'est transmise jusqu'à la mère. (*B*, courtoisie de National Institutes of Health, *C, D, E*, courtoisie de Laird Jackson, M.D.)

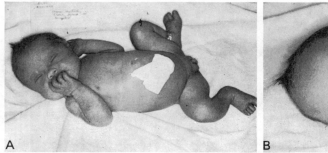
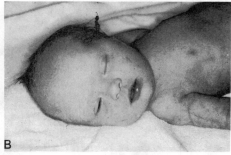

A   B

Figure 4-6. *A)* Photographie d'un enfant mongolien âgé de deux jours. L'hypotonie générale est suggérée par une position détendue mais disgracieuse. *B)* La tête et le visage de l'enfant sont de forme arrondie, le crâne est court, l'épicanthus bien développé, les orbites peu profondes. (Schaffer: Diseases of the Newborn.)

lies métaboliques congénitales se manifestent par des perturbations touchant un ou plusieurs corps chimiques. Souvent une seule enzyme est déficiente et la chaîne métabolique est rompue. En d'autres cas, on constate seulement, sans savoir la cause exacte, qu'un produit anormal s'accumule dans le sang ou qu'un produit normal s'y trouve en quantité insuffisante ou excessive.

Les anomalies métaboliques congénitales ne sont pas symptômatiques à la naissance et souvent, seules les analyses de laboratoires permettent de les déceler. Nous pouvons donner comme exemples:

1) l'agammaglobulinémie, manifestation d'un défaut du métabolisme des immuno-protéines du plasma

2) la phénylcétonurie où le métabolisme et le transport de l'acide aminé phénylalanine sont perturbés.

Certaines caractéristiques individuelles, comme le daltonisme et certaines pathologies comme l'hémophilie « type A », sont dites liées au sexe. La longueur respective des chromosomes sexuels est différente, le X étant plus long que le y. Le X est donc porteur d'un plus grand nombre de gènes que le y. Chez l'homme (Xy), si l'un des gènes contenus dans le X est pathologique, il apparaîtra, même s'il s'agit d'un gène récessif, car il n'est pas caché par le caractère normal de l'allèle comme cela se produit chez la femme. (Voir fig. 4-4.)

Ainsi, le X pathologique d'une femme, phénotypiquement normale, est transmis à la génération suivante; la moitié des garçons pourront être atteints et la moitié des filles porteuses. Pour qu'une fille soit hémophile « type A », elle doit être homozygote pour le gène anormal et cette combinaison génétique est ordinairement léthale pour le fœtus. D'autres

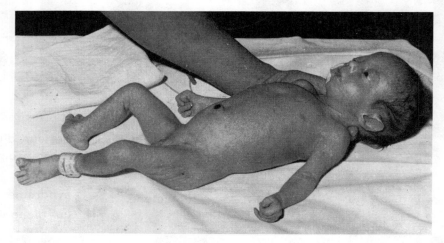

Figure 4-7. Enfant atteint d'une trisomie chromosomique du groupe E, probablement à la paire 18. Remarquez le chevauchement des doigts, le pied plat convexe, l'anomalie de l'oreille, et la dorsiflexion du gros orteil. (Courtoisie de D. H. Carr, dans Thompson and Thompson: Genetics in Medicine.)

malformations congénitales incompatibles avec la vie peuvent également causer la mort in-utero.

Certaines anomalies sont causées par des perturbations du nombre, de la grandeur ou de la forme des chromosomes. Il arrive qu'au moment de la division cellulaire, par le phéno-mène de la non-disjonction, les chromatides n'arrivent pas à se détacher; on retrouve alors deux cellules-filles différentes: l'une comptant un chromosome de trop alors que l'autre est incomplète. Aucune cause précise n'a été in-criminée, mais le fait se présente plus souvent chez les mères d'un âge plus avancé.

Si la cellule anormale de 22 chromosomes est fécondée, le zygote contiendra 45 chromo-somes. Si le chromosome qui manque est le chromosome sexuel X, il se produit un syn-drome de Turner.

Si la cellule anormale, porteuse de 24 chro-mosomes, est fécondée, le chromosome sup-plémentaire va provoquer l'apparition de traits pathologiques et de malformations qui risquent de compromettre la vie ou le développement du fœtus. L'exemple classique d'un enfant porteur de 47 chromosomes est celui du bébé mongolien, dont la 21e paire contient 3 chro-mosomes. On parle alors de trisomie 21. Dans le mongolisme, on rencontre également la translocation du bras (chromatide) du 21e chro-mosome sur un des chromosomes du groupe D (13-15) ou du groupe G (21-22).

En plus du syndrome de Down, on connaît actuellement d'autres pathologies très rares attribuables à des trisomies.

La trisomie 18 (groupe E) est un syndrome incluant de multiples malformations congéni-tales, au niveau des oreilles, des mains, des pieds et du cœur. La trisomie D (chromosomes 13-14-15) est plus rare encore et produit un tableau clinique extrêmement grave. Enfin une trisomie partielle est possible i.e. qu'une por-tion seulement de chromosome est surnumé-raire. Lorsque ceci survient au niveau du chromosome 5, un syndrome du « cri-du-chat » apparaît. Ce terme provient du fait que le pleur de ces bébés ressemble étrangement à un miaulement. Ces nouveau-nés présentent aussi une microcéphalie, des oreilles basses, des yeux espacés et un retard mental. Il semble bien qu'une recherche constante sur les causes non élucidées de plusieurs entités cliniques conduira à la découverte d'autres anomalies chromosomiques.

MILIEU

L'ovule fécondé ou zygote possède un bagage génétique important qui en fera un individu particulier, ayant certaines caractéristiques in-altérables. Il est toutefois difficile de déceler, chez l'enfant naissant, les caractéristiques qu'il tient de son hérédité et celles qui ont été modifiées par le milieu dans lequel il a vécu jusque-là. L'utérus est un milieu privilégié où l'enfant est relativement à l'abri du monde extérieur, mais diverses influences néfastes peu-vent tout de même l'atteindre. Nous étudierons successivement le rôle de l'infection, des trou-bles endocriniens, mécaniques et nutritifs, des irradiations et des agents chimiques dans le développement de l'embryon et du fœtus.

La période critique se situe au cours des *trois premiers mois de la grossesse* au moment de l'organogénèse de l'embryon. Au cours des six derniers mois, le fœtus peut toujours être atteint, mais il n'en résultera pas de véritables difformités.

La rubéole et la toxoplasmose sont les principales infections qui peuvent atteindre l'embryon. La rubéole n'est qu'une maladie bénigne, mais chez la femme enceinte depuis moins de trois mois, le virus, en traversant la barrière placentaire, peut atteindre l'embryon en formation.

Le vaccin anti-rubéoleux, actuellement sur le marché, permettra peut-être de changer complètement les données du problème. Cer-tains gouvernements préconisent la vaccination en bas âge, afin d'enrayer complètement la maladie, alors que d'autres autorités sanitaires pratiquent la vaccination massive des enfants d'âge scolaire.

De toutes façons, on recommande à toutes les femmes susceptibles de devenir enceintes de faire doser leurs anticorps rubéoleux. Si leur taux est insuffisant, le vaccin est indiqué. Etant donné que l'on ne connaît pas les effets du vaccin sur l'embryon et le fœtus, on suggère aux femmes de le recevoir immédiatement après leurs menstruations. Il est important de rappeler au personnel féminin des poupon-nières que les nouveau-nés rubéoleux sont contagieux. Les statistiques prouvent l'action tératogène du virus rubéoleux, et les enfants dont la mère a été en contact avec lui durant la grossesse peuvent souffrir de lésions cardia-ques, microcéphalie, dommage cérébral, cécité ou surdité.

Les infections des *six derniers mois de la grossesse* se manifestent chez le nouveau-né par les caractéristiques de la maladie en cause. Ainsi, le spirochète contaminera l'enfant qui naîtra syphilitique, à moins que sa mère n'ait été traitée adéquatement à l'aide de la péni-cilline.

Les problèmes endocriniens tels le diabète ou l'hypothyroïdie peuvent affecter grandement le développement du fœtus. Les traumatismes physiques survenant chez la mère peuvent également avoir une influence néfaste. On croit qu'un vice de position in-utero pourrait aussi provoquer des malformations chez le nouveau-né.

L'état nutritionnel de la mère influence le développement fœtal. Pendant la Deuxième Guerre mondiale, on a pu observer une incidence plus élevée de mort in-utero et de malformations fœtales chez les mères souffrant de sous-alimentation chronique.

Les recherches récentes ont démontré que les femmes sous-alimentées donnaient naissance à des enfants de faible poids dont la croissance cérébrale était parfois perturbée.

Il semble que l'irradiation précoce de l'abdomen maternel puisse provoquer des malformations chez l'embryon, d'où l'importance d'éviter les radiographies pendant la deuxième partie du cycle menstruel. On s'interroge actuellement sur l'influence de l'irradiation des spermatozoïdes vers l'époque de la conception.

On connaît le drame de la thalidomide, qui a rendu le monde médical plus conscient de ses responsabilités quant à la prévention des accidents pharmacologiques de la grossesse. L'usage du L.S.D. semble également avoir un effet tératogène. Etant donné qu'à peu près tous les médicaments que la femme enceinte absorbe peuvent passer la barrière placentaire, il y a risque d'effets tératogènes ou dépresseurs sur le fœtus. L'infirmière doit donc insister auprès des patientes enceintes, afin qu'elles ne prennent aucun médicament sans avoir au préalable consulté leur médecin.

On peut conclure que les anomalies congénitales sont en général le fruit d'une interaction entre des facteurs génétiques et des influences du milieu. De plus, il est fréquent qu'un enfant soit affligé de plusieurs anomalies.

Fœtologie

Une des raisons pour lesquelles le taux de mortalité infantile est très élevé durant la première année de vie est que plusieurs anomalies sont compatibles avec la vie intra-utérine mais incompatibles avec la vie extra-utérine. Les anomalies congénitales se classent toujours au premier ou au second rang des causes de décès des nourrissons.

Avec l'avènement de la fœtologie, spécialité médicale nouvelle, on espère diagnostiquer in-utero les pathologies du fœtus, les traiter parfois ou, si cela s'avère impossible, indiquer les cas où une interruption de la grossesse peut être envisagée.

Les principales techniques utilisées en fœtologie sont:

1) *l'amniocentèse*: procédure qui consiste à retirer du liquide amniotique à l'aide d'un trocart inséré dans l'utérus par la paroi abdominale après avoir bien identifié la position du fœtus. On peut ainsi doser les anticorps, les antigènes Rh, l'érythropoïétine, la bilirubine, déterminer le sexe de l'enfant lorsqu'une pathologie héréditaire liée au sexe est soupçonnée et diagnostiquer une trentaine de maladies dont le mongolisme et la maladie de Tay-Sachs.

2) *l'amniographie*: procédure qui consiste à injecter une substance radio-opaque dans le liquide amniotique de façon à délimiter les contours et la vitalité du fœtus et à déterminer certaines anomalies digestives étant donné que le fœtus avale du liquide amniotique.

3) *la radiographie du fœtus*: examen qui peut être effectué à la fin de la grossesse pour découvrir des anomalies squelettiques.

4) *l'amnioscopie*: procédure qui consiste à introduire une sonde par voie vaginale dans l'utérus de façon à visualiser l'intérieur de l'utérus, à prélever des échantillons de liquide amniotique et parfois de sang fœtal. Selon les résultats des analyses, une interruption précoce de la grossesse peut être indiquée.

5) *l'électrocardiographie fœtale*: enregistrement des battements cardiaques fœtaux sur moniteur. L'ECG fœtal peut être utilisé durant tout le travail et l'accouchement si l'on soupçonne des risques de souffrance fœtale.

6) *l'ultrasonographie*: procédure qui consiste à expédier des ondes ultrasoniques dans l'abdomen maternel et à recueillir sur oscilloscope l'écho qui provient des zones denses. Un diagnostic précoce de grossesse peut être fait; la croissance, la localisation et la taille du placenta et du fœtus peuvent aussi être déterminées. Des anomalies peuvent ainsi être décelées.

Il peut arriver qu'un traitement intra-utérin soit possible comme dans le cas de l'érythroblastose fœtale où le fœtus peut recevoir des transfusions intra-utérines. Beaucoup de recherches sont encore nécessaires pour créer des traitements applicables au fœtus et même effectuer certaines chirurgies intra-utérines.

Réactions des parents et de l'infirmière devant l'enfant handicapé

Un couple qui désire avoir des enfants doit faire face à la possibilité de procréer un enfant anormal. Avant toute conception le couple peut discuter des sentiments qu'éveille en eux la perspective de prendre soin d'un enfant handicapé. De plus, les couples doivent savoir que la prévention de la naissance d'un enfant handicapé commence avant la conception du bébé. Une vie saine et des consultations génétiques peuvent éviter la venue d'un être malformé. Lorsque de futurs parents interrogent l'infirmière et le médecin sur les possibilités de mettre au monde un enfant handicapé, ils devraient recevoir des réponses honnêtes et adaptées. Une fois l'ovule fécondé, le médecin ne peut qu'aider la mère à mener à terme un enfant dont les caractéristiques sont en grande partie déjà fixées ou lui permettre d'obtenir un avortement si elle le désire et si la loi l'y autorise.

Les parents modernes réagissent souvent devant un enfant malformé par un sentiment de culpabilité que ressentaient déjà les membres des tribus primitives dans des circonstances analogues: « Qu'ai-je fait de mal pendant ma grossesse? » « Quelle faute mon mari peut-il avoir commise pour que nous méritions une telle punition? » « Quel mal avons-nous fait aux autres? » « Quel péché avons-nous commis pour provoquer une telle souffrance chez notre enfant? »

Quand une anomalie est découverte à la naissance, le médecin a la responsabilité d'en faire part aux parents; il est normal qu'ils aient alors une réaction de déception, de douleur et de désespoir: ils attendaient un enfant normal et ils reçoivent un bébé handicapé.

Les parents ont alors besoin d'aide et de temps pour faire le deuil de l'enfant normal qu'ils n'ont pas eu et accepter la réalité du bébé handicapé. Ce n'est qu'ensuite qu'ils peuvent établir une relation chaleureuse avec leur nouveau-né. Ils ont aussi besoin de support pour prendre les décisions qui s'imposent, telles la signature pour une chirurgie indispensable sinon pour la vie, du moins pour le confort de l'enfant (ex. hydrocéphalie). Les parents ont besoin d'une présence pour avoir la force de regarder leur enfant, si les anomalies sont apparentes, de le toucher et éventuellement d'en prendre soin. Empêcher les parents de voir leur bébé encourage la production de phantasmes plus horribles que la réalité et qui rendent très difficile l'adaptation parents-enfant si ce dernier survit.

La plupart des parents se sentent coupables de l'état de leur enfant; lorsqu'on réussit à convaincre la mère qu'elle ne pouvait l'éviter, pas plus d'ailleurs que son mari ou son médecin, il lui est beaucoup plus facile d'accepter cette malformation et de penser aux besoins de l'enfant. Le fait d'intéresser tôt la mère aux soins qu'elle aura à donner à l'enfant diminuera souvent son désespoir et son sentiment de culpabilité.

Si les parents ne bénéficient pas de l'appui moral de l'équipe médicale, et s'ils n'obtiennent pas d'explications réalistes sur l'état de l'enfant, ils risquent de partir à la recherche d'une cure miracle et de dilapider l'énergie qu'ils devraient employer à planifier l'avenir de cet enfant. Il faut étudier avec eux les possibilités de traitement, insister sur les capacités de l'enfant et les familiariser avec la croissance et le développement qui lui sont propres. L'infirmière doit être capable d'aider les parents, en acceptant de discuter avec la mère des sentiments de culpabilité, de colère ou de crainte qui peuvent l'envahir, mais elle ne doit jamais chercher à provoquer les confidences. Si la mère désire parler, l'attitude verbale et non verbale de l'infirmière sera empreinte de chaleur et de compréhension et elle l'encouragera à s'exprimer.

Si l'enfant est encore à la pouponnière après le départ de la mère, l'infirmière hygiéniste peut encourager cette dernière à rendre visite au nouveau-né; il peut être profitable que la mère puisse exprimer ce qu'elle ressent, puisqu'en discutant de ses problèmes, elle deviendra plus apte à prendre soin de son enfant, en dépit des perspectives pénibles pour l'avenir.

L'infirmière peut contribuer à susciter chez les parents une attitude positive mais réaliste. Leur sentiment de culpabilité ne doit pas les porter à traiter l'enfant de façon trop indulgente, ce qui ne l'aiderait pas à se développer adéquatement. L'arrivée de l'enfant malformé ne doit pas faire négliger les autres enfants de la famille, et le père ne doit pas se sentir délaissé. De même, les besoins de la mère ne doivent pas être oubliés au profit de ceux de l'enfant.

L'attitude des parents envers l'enfant malformé déterminera, de façon générale, la manière dont ses frères et sœurs, les membres plus éloignés de la famille et l'entourage immédiat se comporteront envers lui. Une fois qu'ils ont accepté cette malformation, les parents peuvent apprendre à l'enfant à profiter de la vie au maximum, et à devenir un membre utile à la société.

Puisque l'enfant malformé demande des soins prolongés et une rééducation intensive, l'infirmière doit connaître les organismes qui peuvent offrir des services et une aide financière; elle doit fournir ces renseignements à la famille éprouvée et, si cela s'avère nécessaire, agir comme agent de liaison entre la famille et les ressources communautaires.

L'infirmière qui s'occupe d'un enfant malformé est soumise à une rude épreuve, si les difformités sont réellement apparentes. De plus, les soins peuvent être complexes, selon la malformation; mais le vrai problème est souvent la réaction psychologique qu'elle doit maîtriser avant de venir en aide aux parents et de prendre soin de l'enfant efficacement. Son attitude peut être dictée par les sentiments qui l'agitent lorsqu'elle s'imagine que cet enfant pourrait être le sien.

Si l'étudiante se sent incapable de maîtriser ses sentiments en face d'une telle situation, elle devrait demander l'aide de son professeur clinique, qui pourra l'aider à adopter l'attitude positive dont les parents ont besoin, et aussi à diminuer la tension qu'elle ressent quand elle prend soin du bébé.

Consultation génétique

Plusieurs couples s'interrogent sur l'opportunité d'une grossesse s'ils ont déjà eu un enfant malformé, ou s'il existe une histoire de maladie dans la famille de l'un ou l'autre des conjoints. Une histoire complète de la famille et une étude génétique approfondie permettent quelquefois de prévoir de façon assez juste les possibilités d'enfanter un autre être difforme, ou les risques pour l'enfant malformé de transmettre cette maladie à ses propres enfants.

Les parents désirent souvent approfondir leurs connaissances sur la maladie, être informés des possibilités de récupération de l'enfant, de la façon dont il peut être soigné, et surtout savoir s'ils peuvent de nouveau transmettre cette maladie à d'autres enfants.

L'infirmière, en général, n'a pas les connaissances nécessaires pour vraiment conseiller les couples sur cette question, mais elle peut communiquer certaines informations et orienter la famille vers une personne compétente qui pourra leur répondre. Même un généticien ne pourra jamais être catégorique, mais il lui sera plus aisé d'extrapoler les risques de malformations dans les conceptions futures. Il peut signaler aux parents les probabilités de procréer un autre enfant difforme.

Les parents qui ont beaucoup apprécié l'aide d'une infirmière lors de la mort d'un ou de plusieurs de leurs enfants, par exemple à la suite de mucoviscidose, peuvent lui demander son avis lorsqu'ils veulent prendre la décision d'avoir un autre enfant. Comme nous l'avons mentionné, l'infirmière n'est pas qualifiée pour répondre adéquatement, mais elle peut fournir son appui moral quand la décision a été prise, après discussion avec le médecin ou le généticien.

Le conseiller génétique est appelé à jouer un rôle très important dans la médecine préventive des années futures.

RÉFÉRENCES

Livres et documents officiels

Allan, F. D.: *Essentials of Human Embryology*. 2e éd. New York, Oxford University Press, 1969.
Balinsky, B. I.: *An Introduction to Embryology*. 3e éd. Philadelphie, W. B. Saunders Company, 1970.
Carter, C. O.: *An ABC of Medical Genetics*. Boston, Little, Brown and Company, 1969.
Crelin, E. S.: *Anatomy of the Newborn: An Atlas*. Philadelphie, Lea & Febiger, 1969.
Crispens, C. G.: *Essentials of Medical Genetics*. New York, Harper & Row, Publishers, Incorporated, 1971.
Emery, A. E. H. (édit.): *Modern Trends in Human Genetics*. New York, Appleton-Century-Crofts, 1970.
Ferreira, A. J.: *Prenatal Environment*. Springfield, Ill., Charles C. Thomas, 1969.
Gardner, L. I. (édit.): *Endocrine and Genetic Diseases of Childhood*. Philadelphie, W. B. Saunders Company, 1969.
Goodman, R. M. (édit.): *Genetic Disorders of Man*. Boston, Little, Brown and Company, 1970.
Langman, J.: *Medical Embryology*. Baltimore, Williams & Wilkins Company, 1963.
Levine, H.: *Clinical Cytogenetics*. Boston, Little, Brown and Company, 1971.
Levitan, M. et Montagu, M. F. A.: *Fundamentals of Human Genetics*. New York, Oxford University Press, 1970.
Lynch, H. T.: *Dynamic Genetic Counseling for Clinicians*. Springfield, Ill., Charles C. Thomas, 1969.

Monif, G. R. G.: *Viral Infections of The Human Fetus.* New York, Macmillan Company, 1969.

Moore, M. L.: *The Newborn and the Nurse.* Philadelphie, W. B. Saunders Company, 1972.

Reisman, L. E. et Matheny, A. P.: *Genetics and Counseling in Medical Practice.* St.Louis, C. V. Mosby Company, 1969.

Smith, D. W.: *Recognizable Patterns of Human Malformation.* Philadelphie, W. B. Saunders Company, 1970.

Stevenson, A. C. et autres: *Genetic Counselling.* Philadelphie, J. B. Lippincott Company, 1970.

Switzer, D. K.: *The Dynamics of Grief.* New York, Abingdon Press, 1970.

Thompson, J. S. et Thompson, M. W.: *Genetics in Medicine.* Philadelphie, W. B. Saunders Company, 1966.

Valentine, G. H.: *The Chromosome Disorders.* 2e éd. Philadelphie, J. B. Lippincott Company, 1969.

Waisman, H. et Kerr, G. (édit.): *Fetal Growth and Development.* New York, McGraw-Hill Book Company, Inc., 1970.

Articles

Boué, A. et Boué, J. G.: Effects of Rubella Infection on Division of Human Cells. *Am. J. Dis. Child.* 118:45, juillet 1969.

Briard, M. L.: Conseil génétique et aberrations chromosomiques. *La revue de pédiatrie,* 9:179, 4, 1973.

D'Arcy, E.: Congenital Defects: Mothers' Reactions to First Information. *Brit. Med. J.,* 3:796, 28 septembre 1968.

Farrow, M. G. et Juberg, R. C.: Genetics and Laws Phohibiting Marriage in the United States. *J. A. M. A.,* 209:534, 28 juillet 1969.

Hardy, J. B.: Rubella and Its Aftermath. *Children,* 16:90, mai – juin 1969.

Hughes, W. T.: Infections and Intrauterine Growth Retardation. *Pediat. Clin. N. Amer.,* 17:119, février 1970.

Kennedy, J. F.: Maternal Reactions to the Birth of a Defective Baby. *Soc. Casework,* 51:410, juillet 1970.

Laberge, C et autres: Le réseau de médecine génétique au Québec. *Union méd. du Can.,* 104:428, mars 1975.

Marmol, J. G., Scriggins, A. L. et Vollman, R. F.: Mothers of Mongoloid Infants in Collaborative Project. *Am. J. Obst. & Gynec.,* 104:533, 15 juin 1969.

Melançon, S. et autres: Approche biochimique au diagnostic prénatal. *Union méd. du Can.,* 104:1787, décembre 1975.

Nielsen, J. et Tsuboi, T.: Intelligence, EEG, Personality Deviation, and Criminality in Patients with the XYY Syndrome. *Brit. J. Psychiat.,* 115:965, août 1969.

Palmisano, P. A., Sneed, R. C. and Cassady, G.: Untaxed Whiskey and Fetal Lead Exposure. *J. Pediat.,* 75:869, novembre 1969.

Pellie, C. et Briand, M.: Conseil génétique et hérédité monofactorielle. *La revue de pédiatrie,* 9:171, 4, 1973.

Reisman, L. E.: Chromosome Abnormalities and Intrauterine Growth Retardation. *Pediat. Clin. N. Amer.,* 17:101, février 1970.

Sever, J. L. et autres: Rubella in the Collaborative Perinatal Research Study: Part II. *Am. J. Dis. Child,* 118:123, juillet 1969.

Steinschneider, R.: Éléments de génétique: langage génétique. *Soins,* 17:44, septembre, 1972.

Steinschneider, R.: Éléments de génétique: hérédité dominante. *Soins,* 18:23, janvier 1973 (série de 6 articles).

Stutz, S. D.: The Nursing Challenge of OB: When the Baby Isn't Normal. *RN,* 34:40, novembre 1971.

Tjio, J.-H., Pahnke, W. N. et Kurland, A. A.: LSD and Chromosomes, *J. A. M. A.,* 210:849, 3 novembre 1969.

Uchida, I. A., Holunga, R. et Lawler, C.: Maternal Radiation and Chromosomal Aberrations. *Lancet,* 2:1045, 16 novembre 1968.

Von Schilling, K. C.: The Birth of a Defective Child. *Nursing Forum,* 7:425, 4, 1968.

Waechter, E. H.: The Birth of an Exceptional Child. *Nursing Forum,* 9:202, 2, 1970.

5

l'infirmière et l'enfant malade

Le rôle de l'infirmière en pédiatrie s'est transformé au cours des dernières années. Les recherches dans les domaines médical et para-médical ont conduit à l'amélioration des soins pour les enfants malades. Également, les recherches dans le domaine des sciences sociales ont donné naissance à de nouvelles conceptions du développement psychologique et des besoins de ces enfants. Dans ce chapitre, le nouveau rôle de l'infirmière en pédiatrie sera mis en lumière à mesure que nous étudierons la croissance et le développement des enfants, et, évidemment, la façon de les soigner lorsqu'ils sont malades.

MOYENS
MIS À NOTRE DISPOSITION
POUR LE SOIN DES ENFANTS

Les enfants malades peuvent être soignés dans différents endroits: unité pédiatrique d'un hôpital général, hôpital exclusivement pour enfants, unité de soins intensifs, centre de recherches en pédiatrie, institutions appropriées pour les soins de l'enfant atteint d'une maladie chronique, cliniques pour les patients ambulatoires, domicile de l'enfant à l'intérieur d'un programme de soins pour enfant malade à la maison.

L'unité pédiatrique

L'unité pédiatrique doit être construite en fonction des besoins des enfants et des parents. Les enfants ont besoin de recevoir des soins adéquats, d'être protégés contre les infections, les accidents et les traumatismes psychologiques causés par un environnement défavorable.

L'unité pédiatrique, de couleurs vives et attrayantes, devrait posséder un ameublement à la mesure de l'enfant. Des couvre-lits de couleur recréent une atmosphère familière. Lorsque l'enfant peut porter ses propres vêtements, il se sent encore plus près de sa vie habituelle. Les infirmières, qui revêtent des uniformes de couleur, introduisent plus de variété dans l'environnement de l'enfant et souvent établissent de meilleures relations avec les parents et les enfants. Conserver des plantes et des fleurs dans l'unité pédiatrique est une excellente initiative qui embellit le décor hospitalier et fournit une distraction à l'enfant qui peut s'en occuper.

Afin d'assurer plus d'attention aux enfants, l'unité pédiatrique devrait compter moins de lits que celle des adultes. De plus, l'organisation physique de l'unité doit être assez souple pour permettre l'utilisation maximale de l'espace disponible. On devrait aussi séparer les

Figure 5-1. L'enfant hospitalisé retrouve l'atmosphère familiale si on lui permet de prendre soin de lui-même. (Courtoisie de l'Hôpital Sainte-Justine, Montréal.)

petits malades en fonction des soins qu'ils requièrent et aussi selon leur âge (comme ils le font eux-mêmes en jouant).

Chaque section pourrait comporter une dizaine de lits disposés de telle sorte que les enfants puissent jouir à la fois du décor intérieur et extérieur. Dans chaque chambre on devrait retrouver un lit ajustable ou un berceau (selon l'âge de l'enfant), une table de lit pour les plateaux ou les jouets, une penderie pour suspendre les vêtements de l'enfant, un bureau et une salle de toilette avec eau courante située juste à l'entrée de la pièce.

Une chambre simple ou privée, contenant un seul lit, devrait être assez grande pour

accommoder deux enfants en cas d'urgence, ou donner à l'un des parents la possibilité de passer la nuit auprès de son enfant. Une telle chambre pourrait aussi servir à soigner un enfant souffrant d'une maladie grave ou porteur d'une infection. Il faudrait penser à munir ces chambres d'un fauteuil confortable, d'un panier à déchets et d'un équipement complet pour l'administration de l'oxygène et l'aspiration des sécrétions. Toute chambre, si possible, devrait être équipée de cette façon.

De simples cloisons peuvent diviser les grandes salles à plusieurs lits afin de diminuer la dissémination possible d'une infection. De plus, des cloisons vitrées incassables permettent aux infirmières de voir tous les patients, à tout moment, et ceci sans danger d'accidents.

Le poste des infirmières devrait se situer au centre de l'unité pédiatrique, non loin des chambres destinées aux plus jeunes enfants ou à ceux qui sont les plus malades. Un système de communication électronique ne doit pas remplacer les interactions humaines, mais peut s'avérer nécessaire. Il doit alors être accessible même aux très jeunes enfants. Toutefois, un système de moniteur télévisé, plus coûteux, est préférable.

On devrait aussi aménager une salle d'attente, pour parents et amis, près des ascenseurs et des escaliers et visible du poste des infirmières. On pourrait décorer cette salle insonorisée, d'une façon attrayante, la meubler de fauteuils confortables et y déposer des revues intéressantes ou des articles éducatifs.

On devrait situer la salle de traitement et la salle d'examen dans un endroit paisible, de préférence près de l'entrée de l'unité. On peut aménager deux salles, ou une seule grande pièce tranquille et bien éclairée, avec tout le matériel nécessaire à l'examen et aux traitements des enfants. Cette salle est indispensable, afin d'éviter aux enfants d'être témoins de traitements potentiellement traumatisants. Il serait sage aussi d'insonoriser la pièce afin que les cris, pouvant être provoqués par des traitements douloureux, ne parviennent pas aux oreilles des autres petits malades.

Il est essentiel de prévoir une salle de jeu et une classe pour les malades ambulants et les convalescents. On peut y transporter aussi les enfants qui le désirent, soit sur une civière, soit en chaise roulante. Nous traiterons de l'utilité de ces pièces un peu plus loin dans ce chapitre.

Les enfants pourraient prendre leurs repas groupés autour de petites tables dans la salle de jeu ou au centre de l'unité pédiatrique. Pour les malades alités, on devrait utiliser les tables de lit.

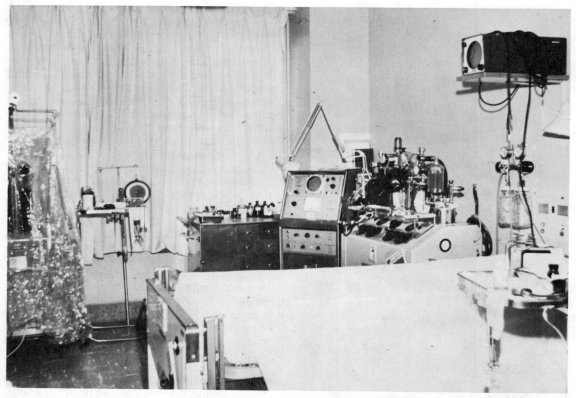

Figure 5-2.   Unité des soins intensifs pédiatriques. Tente à oxygène. Balance. Charriot d'urgence. Moniteur. Respirateur. Appareil fixe à aspiration. Appareil à tension. (Courtoisie de l'Hôpital Sainte-Justine, Montréal.)

Enfin, l'unité pédiatrique doit comprendre aussi une salle de consultation assez grande pour permettre de causer avec les parents de l'enfant en toute quiétude et de les renseigner au sujet des soins qu'ils devront donner à leur enfant après sa sortie de l'hôpital, des salles de bains, une lingerie, des salles de cours pour les étudiants, des salles d'utilité et une pièce inaccessible aux enfants et servant de pharmacie.

L'unité des soins intensifs

On trouve actuellement des unités de soins intensifs dans plusieurs hôpitaux pour enfants et dans certaines grandes unités de pédiatrie des hôpitaux généraux. L'équipement électronique doit être adapté plus particulièrement aux problèmes de soins intensifs pour enfants et nouveau-nés. Dans cette unité, on doit pouvoir disposer d'une information continue et contrôlée de l'état physiologique et biochimique des enfants qui s'y trouvent.

Parmi les enfants et les nouveau-nés qui nécessitent des soins intensifs, on trouve des patients porteurs d'anomalies congénitales, en état comateux, atteints d'asthme, de bronchiolite grave, de pneumonie aiguë, de malformation cardiaque congénitale ou d'insuffisance cardiaque. À ceux-là s'ajoutent évidemment les enfants accidentés ou encore ceux qui subissent des opérations cardio-vasculaire ou neurochirurgicale.

Autrefois, la mort se définissait comme étant le moment où l'enfant cessait de respirer. Ce n'est plus vrai, puisqu'on peut maintenant garder un enfant en vie après un arrêt respiratoire, un collapsus cardio-pulmonaire et cérébral. En effet, il est désormais possible de ranimer les enfants après une défaillance temporaire d'un de ces systèmes, pourvu que le temps écoulé entre l'arrêt fonctionnel et l'institution du traitement soit réduit au minimum.

En utilisant efficacement le moniteur électronique, les membres de l'équipe de santé peuvent surveiller constamment les signes vitaux, recourir rapidement à un traitement d'urgence ou cesser une thérapie qui n'est plus nécessaire ou efficace.

Étant donné la rapidité des changements de l'état de santé des enfants, on peut, grâce à une surveillance électronique des signes vitaux, faire facilement la différence entre la survie ou la mort, ou entre une récupération complète ou accompagnée de séquelles.

La réanimation des enfants peut être faite par le personnel régulier des unités de soins intensifs ou par une équipe spéciale de réanimation qui répond aux appels de tout l'hôpital. Quelle que soit la modalité, ces mesures d'extrême urgence ne doivent jamais faire perdre de vue le soin des autres enfants témoins du drame ainsi que la famille du malade en détresse.

On commence toutefois à identifier les effets néfastes des unités de soins intensifs sur les enfants. Ceux-ci peuvent être terrifiés par le bruit et les appareils, être témoins de procédures douloureuses et de décès, et être trop stimulés par une lumière intense constante tout en étant privés de stimulations tactiles appropriées. Le rôle des infirmières affectées à ces unités doit évoluer pour assurer un soin de meilleure qualité aux enfants.

Le centre de recherches en pédiatrie

Il existe dans certains hôpitaux pour enfants, des centres de recherches en pédiatrie, où se poursuit l'étude de maladies actuellement peu connues. Ces centres permettent aux infirmières d'établir des contacts très étroits avec leurs petits patients, parce que les malades sont peu nombreux et ordinairement soumis à un horaire semblable à celui de leur foyer. Le personnel doit élaborer un plan de soins qui permet à l'enfant d'être relativement heureux en dépit des examens douloureux qu'il doit subir. Une équipe d'infirmières dévouées et compétentes peut réduire les effets dommageables de l'hospitalisation.

Unité de soins de courte durée

Dans une unité de ce genre, les enfants sont admis habituellement pour une journée ou deux. Des soins adéquats sont prodigués à l'enfant et il n'est privé de son foyer qu'un court laps de temps. On y accepte les enfants hospitalisés pour amygdalectomie, adénoïdectomie, herniorraphie, correction de strabisme, etc..

Service de soins de longue durée

Les enfants souffrant d'un handicap quelconque peuvent être soignés dans des hôpitaux, ou dans des centres plus propices aux soins prolongés que ne l'est la maison familiale. Ces endroits favorisent une paisible et longue convalescence chez les enfants qui ne pourraient se reposer chez eux. Ils permettent aussi, parfois, aux enfants handicapés d'atteindre un niveau de développement plus élevé qu'il ne serait possible de tenter dans des conditions familiales habituelles, soit parce que l'enfant présente des problèmes d'adaptation familiale, soit parce qu'il requiert un appareillage compliqué et un environnement modifié. Ces services comprennent les hôpitaux publics ou privés, les foyers pour convalescents ou malades chroniques, les écoles pour handicapés, et enfin les camps d'été, où l'on regroupe les enfants souffrant d'une même maladie, par exemple, le diabète ou la fibrose kystique du pancréas. Toutefois, l'enfant ne doit être retiré de son milieu familial que lorsqu'il y a vraiment nécessité.

Service de soins pour patients ambulants

La clinique externe de pédiatrie peut vraiment compléter les services hospitaliers grâce à ses nouvelles méthodes de travail, tant médicales que sociales. Cette unité tend à s'intégrer de plus en plus au milieu et à devenir un centre communautaire de santé. Elle accueille maintenant toute personne qui nécessite des soins, quel que soit son revenu.

Un nombre croissant de médecins préfèrent traiter les enfants dans ce genre d'unité. Afin d'éviter le traumatisme de l'hospitalisation, il est aussi préférable d'y soigner les enfants souffrant d'une pneumonie, d'un abcès, d'une infection urinaire ou autre, à condition qu'ils soient sous la surveillance d'une personne responsable à la maison. Une des plus récentes fonctions du personnel de ces cliniques consiste à dépister les maladies héréditaires et à donner des conseils génétiques.

L'enseignement demeure la fonction essentielle de l'infirmière travaillant à la clinique externe. Elle doit toujours s'assurer que les parents et/ou l'enfant comprennent les soins à effectuer, connaissent les médicaments à utiliser, leurs effets, le mode et le temps d'administration, et sachent exactement la date et l'heure du prochain rendez-vous. L'infirmière doit tenter de créer un climat qui incite le client à respecter ses rendez-vous.

Toute clinique externe de pédiatrie devrait fournir un local ou un espace de jeu où l'enfant pourra se distraire et se sentir moins anxieux. Les rendez-vous accordés aux patients ambulatoires devraient être donnés de telle sorte qu'il n'y ait pas d'attente inutile. Par ces cliniques, des soins de qualité devraient être prodigués à tous.

Soins à domicile

Le programme de soins à domicile pour enfants est une innovation toute récente, quoique de tels programmes existaient déjà pour les soins des patients âgés ou indigents. Ce programme a pour but de prévenir ou réduire le traumatisme de l'hospitalisation, de permettre de soigner à la maison les enfants qui peuvent l'être sans danger et, enfin, d'inviter les parents à utiliser les ressources communautaires lorsque l'état de leur enfant ne nécessite plus de soins hospitaliers. Pour que le programme de soins à domicile fonctionne bien, l'équipe de santé a besoin de la collaboration de tous ceux qui entourent le petit malade et doit pouvoir compter sur une personne relativement compétente à la maison.

NOUVELLES FAÇONS D'ENTREVOIR LE SOIN DES ENFANTS HOSPITALISÉS

On trouverait difficilement aujourd'hui un jeune adulte qui n'a pas passé quelque temps à l'hôpital au cours de son enfance. Plusieurs d'entre eux se souviendront longtemps de cette malheureuse expérience passée dans la solitude et la douleur, alors qu'ils étaient trop jeunes pour y faire face seuls. Les méthodes de soins ont changé depuis vingt ans, et certains hôpitaux sont à l'avant-garde. Ce sont les découvertes en sciences sociales et en psychologie de l'enfant, ainsi que la pression du milieu social, qui ont permis tous ces changements.

Les heures de visites

Il y a plusieurs années, les enfants hospitalisés recevaient la visite de leurs parents une fois par mois, ou lors de l'admission et la journée du départ. Maintenant, dans plusieurs hôpitaux, les visites sont permises entre dix heures et vingt heures; dans quelques-uns elles le sont du lever au coucher de l'enfant et même, dans quelques autres hôpitaux, à toute heure du jour et de la nuit. La durée et la fréquence des visites devraient être établies en fonction des besoins des parents et surtout des enfants. Certaines infirmières ont tendance à croire que ces visites bouleversent l'enfant parce qu'il pleure au moment du départ de ses parents. Mais qu'y a-t-il là d'anormal? Le contraire serait plus alarmant! Nous retrouverons une discussion plus détaillée à ce sujet aux chapitres qui traitent des maladies particulières aux différents groupes d'âge.

La cohabitation

On ne devrait jamais exiger des parents qu'ils restent au chevet de leur enfant, ni les en empêcher s'ils le désirent. De même, les parents devraient pouvoir participer aux soins de leur enfant s'ils le désirent mais ne jamais y être contraints.

Pour les parents qui passent la journée dans l'unité pédiatrique, certains hôpitaux disposent d'une salle spéciale où ils peuvent se détendre. Dans certaines institutions, on sert les repas des parents dans la chambre de leur enfant; ils peuvent également manger à la cafétéria de l'hôpital.

On encourage tout particulièrement les mères des enfants très jeunes et des enfants gravement malades à cohabiter avec eux et à profiter des avantages qu'on met à leur disposition. Les pères peuvent aussi se prévaloir de ce droit. En général, les parents dorment sur un lit pliant, un fauteuil-lit ou dans une chambre dortoir aménagée pour eux. Certains hôpitaux ont des unités de participation familiale où la mère vit avec son enfant. Cette méthode de nursing prend racine en Orient, où la famille entière se sent concernée si un de ses membres est malade. Le petit malade est alors soigné par des personnes qu'il connaît, mais sous la surveillance d'une infirmière. Celle-ci peut en toute simplicité, transmettre ses connaissances aux mères qui ne sauraient pas comment procéder pour donner certains soins.

Dans un tel service, les responsabilités de l'infirmière consistent à aider la mère à satisfaire les nouveaux besoins de son enfant, à expliquer les techniques médicales et les tests de diagnostic. Elle observe également le savoir-faire et les attitudes des parents, de même que la relation parents-enfant. Elle doit, de plus, déceler les besoins physiques et émotifs de chaque mère, afin que cette expérience ne la fatigue pas trop. Certaines mères, anxieuses ou affligées d'un sentiment de culpabilité, refuseront l'expérience proposée; d'autres, au contraire, la souhaiteront pour la sécurité qu'elle apportera au petit.

Enfin, ce sujet sera traité à nouveau un peu plus loin dans ce livre.

La santé et l'équipe de nursing

L'infirmière en pédiatrie envisage son rôle sur le plan des relations avec la mère, l'enfant, et toute la famille. Elle n'est pas un substitut maternel, mais plutôt une amie de la mère. Elle peut soigner elle-même chaque enfant ou agir à l'intérieur d'une équipe de nursing.

Dans ce dernier cas, l'infirmière travaille en étroite collaboration avec des étudiantes, d'au-

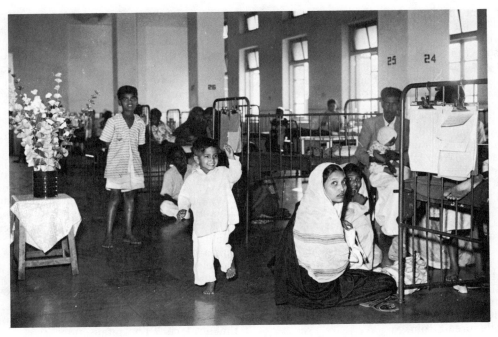

Figure 5-3. Unité pédiatrique de l'hôpital Sassoon à Bombay, Inde. Les parents participent activement aux soins de l'enfant hospitalisé. (UNICEF. Photo Jack Ling.)

tres infirmières, des auxiliaires et des puéricultrices. Elle doit saisir l'ensemble des soins dont l'équipe est responsable et pouvoir agir en tant que chef ou simple membre de l'équipe.

De plus, elle doit collaborer aussi avec une équipe plus vaste, l'équipe de santé, qui comprend: un médecin, un travailleur social, une diététicienne, une institutrice, une éducatrice spécialisée, une infirmière en santé publique, un aumônier, etc... L'infirmière contribue à l'efficacité de cette équipe en y apportant ses connaissances et son savoir-faire.

L'étudiante-infirmière comprendra facilement le rôle des différents membres de cette équipe de santé, mais il lui sera peut-être plus difficile de saisir celui des personnes spécialisées dans la fonction récréative et éducative de l'enfant hospitalisé. Pourtant, leur rôle est très important. L'éducatrice ou la jardinière d'enfants peut organiser un programme d'activités pour chacun des enfants en fonction de ses besoins; elle peut planifier des activités de groupe pour permettre aux enfants d'exprimer leur hostilité ou leur anxiété. Aux enfants opérés elle donnera un jouet familier afin de diminuer leurs craintes. Cette personne transmettra ses observations aux autres membres de l'équipe de santé et de l'équipe de nursing.

Les fonctions de l'instituteur ressemblent à celles observées dans les salles de cours habituelles. D'autres informations concernant ces deux spécialistes seront données plus loin au cours de ce chapitre, ainsi que dans plusieurs autres sections du livre.

Le jeu et l'école à l'hôpital

L'idée d'organiser des activités récréatives et instructives dans les institutions n'est certainement pas récente, mais les méthodes pour organiser ces programmes sont nouvelles dans plusieurs hôpitaux.

Pour l'enfant, le jeu représente sa façon de vivre: c'est son mode de vie. Le jeu peut satisfaire l'enfant à tous les niveaux de son développement physique, mental, social et émotif. C'est aussi un moyen très sûr pour l'enfant de surmonter ses peurs et ses angoisses. Le jeu est aussi essentiel à l'enfant malade qu'à l'enfant en bonne santé. Il lui permet de combler son ennui et d'exprimer ses sentiments, réduisant ainsi le traumatisme causé par l'hospitalisation.

La mise sur pied de nombreux programmes de jeu et d'instruction dans les départements pédiatriques est due en grande partie à l'amélioration du nursing et des soins médicaux que les enfants reçoivent actuellement. Elle a été également influencée par les recherches en psychologie de l'enfant. Aujourd'hui les enfants se rétablissent plus vite, tout en n'étant pas confinés au lit pendant une longue période.

On se rend compte, actuellement, que le jeu aide l'enfant à comprendre les expériences qu'il vit et lui permet d'exprimer ses phantasmes, ses craintes et ses appréhensions.

Les enfants peuvent jouer dans des salles de jeu ou au centre de l'unité. Évidemment ils ne doivent pas jouer à proximité des enfants gravement malades ni près du poste des médecins et des infirmières. On construit maintenant des salles de jeu spécialement conçues pour les enfants, afin de ne pas les limiter dans leurs activités récréatives. Si toutefois une telle pièce n'est pas disponible, on peut fabriquer un chariot à jouets qu'on déplace d'un lit à l'autre.

Si l'on a prévu une grande salle de jeu et un parc extérieur pour les activités récréatives, on pourra transporter les malades alités sur les civières ou en chaises roulantes, afin qu'ils puissent eux aussi participer aux jeux. Dans le cas d'enfants immobilisés, il faudra prévoir des activités propres à leurs besoins.

L'infirmière qui s'intéresse réellement au bien-être des enfants, saura introduire le jeu dans les activités quotidiennes des malades dont elle prend soin.

En préparant son programme d'activités, l'infirmière devra tenir compte de l'âge, des intérêts, des restrictions et de la maladie de l'enfant. Un petit malade incapable de jouer activement, aimera sûrement se faire raconter une histoire où il s'identifiera émotivement aux personnages. Le narrateur de l'histoire peut poser des questions, insérer des commentaires particuliers pour chaque enfant et lui donner l'impression qu'il participe à l'histoire. On peut aussi proposer à ce genre de petits malades des activités, telles que regarder pousser une plante, observer le travail des fourmis, s'occuper de poissons rouges dans un aquarium, d'un oiseau en cage, ou enfin, regarder des émissions de télévision. Les enfants qui peuvent se lever devraient pouvoir développer leur intelligence et leurs différentes habiletés grâce aux arts plastiques, tels que la peinture ou le modelage. Même à l'hôpital les enfants aiment s'amuser avec des jouets provenant de la maison, mais on peut aussi leur proposer des poupées et de l'équipement hospitalier, afin qu'ils aient la possibilité d'exprimer leurs sentiments face à l'hospitalisation.

Figure 5-4. Le moment des repas devient agréable si les enfants capables de marcher peuvent s'asseoir à une table commune. (Courtoisie de l'Hôpital Sainte-Justine, Montréal.)

Figure 5-5. Jouer détend l'enfant hospitalisé. La peinture digitale l'aide à exprimer ses émotions. (École d'infirmières de l'Hôpital Johns Hopkins, Baltimore, Maryland.)

Les enfants choisissent souvent des jouets ayant rapport à leur hospitalisation: des poupées représentent un médecin ou une infirmière, des seringues, un stéthoscope. Les petites filles aiment fabriquer des coiffes de papier comme celles des infirmières. Elles utilisent aussi un vieux drap pour immobiliser leur poupée ou lui improviser un bandage. Tout dernièrement, on a eu recours à des spectacles de marionnettes pour expliquer les différentes techniques utilisées à l'hôpital. On donne aussi aux enfants la possibilité de jouer eux-mêmes avec les marionnettes. De telles activités sont thérapeutiques, car elles permettent à l'enfant de s'extérioriser et réduisent ainsi son anxiété.

Chaque salle de jeu devrait aussi contenir des jeux semblables à ceux que les enfants ont à la maison: blocs, livres d'histoire, disques, maisons de poupées, téléphones en matière plastique, peinture, glaise, marionnettes. Les tricycles et les petits chariots sont aussi très populaires et aident l'enfant à développer ses muscles.

Pour l'enfant qui reçoit peu ou pas de visite de ses parents, on suggère à son infirmière de lui faire parvenir des petits colis ou des lettres par la poste, afin qu'il sache que d'autres adultes pensent à lui. Si c'est possible, on demande aux parents de lui expédier des cartes postales régulièrement.

Bien sûr, les salles de jeu ne peuvent pas toujours être bien rangées de sorte que l'infirmière, trop soucieuse de bon ordre, risque de nuire à l'initiative des enfants et d'entraver le cours du jeu. Il n'en demeure pas moins que l'on doit encourager les enfants à prendre soin des jouets que leurs parents ont apportés de la maison. Ils peuvent les prêter aux autres enfants, car leur développement social doit se continuer à l'hôpital, mais un endroit devrait être désigné pour ranger ces jouets à la fin du jeu. Comme l'enfant apprend à respecter ses propres jouets, il sait qu'il doit également agir de la même façon pour ceux des autres.

Regarder jouer un enfant est très révélateur: il est intéressant d'observer son comportement à l'égard de ses petits compagnons, de ses parents et de son entourage général. On peut noter aussi son degré d'activité, sa capacité d'attention, son habileté verbale et sa facilité à tolérer une frustration. De plus, l'infirmière peut écouter les commentaires de l'enfant sur sa vie à la maison et son expérience à l'hôpital; elle peut ainsi connaître ses impressions sur son environnement et les moyens qu'il emploie pour faire face à des situations difficiles.

Les infirmières devraient avoir l'occasion de participer au programme récréatif préparé pour les enfants. Cela leur permettrait de voir les petits en pleine activité, elles pourraient apprécier le travail que fournit l'éducatrice, son apport au bien-être des petits malades et faire d'heureuses suggestions.

L'institutrice est un membre important de l'équipe de santé au sein de l'unité pédiatrique. Engagée par les commissions scolaires ou au-

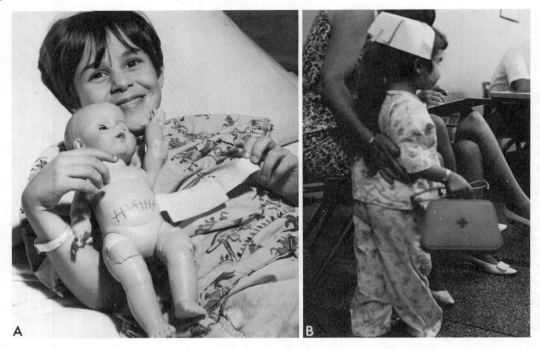

Figure 5-6. Le jeu à l'hôpital: *A)* En période postopératoire, cette fillette soigne la plaie abdominale de sa poupée; *B)* De retour à la maison, le jeu continue. (Courtoisie de Shirley Bonnen, Children's Hospital of Philadelphia.)

tres organismes de l'éducation, elle est dégagée de ses fonctions habituelles pour enseigner aux enfants malades. On l'affecte surtout auprès des enfants hospitalisés pour des périodes relativement longues. Toutefois, elle enseigne à tout enfant d'âge scolaire à moins que le médecin n'interdise ce genre d'activité. Même si l'on sait qu'un enfant est très malade et ne pourra plus jamais retourner en classe, il est important qu'il continue ses activités scolaires et sente qu'il appartient toujours au groupe de son âge. Dans certains hôpitaux, l'institutrice se rend au chevet du malade, alors qu'à d'autres endroits, elle rassemble les petits malades dans une pièce destinée à l'enseignement. L'enfant qui reçoit des cours se sent plus utile, plus important, et par conséquent est plus heureux que celui qu'on laisse dans l'oisiveté. S'il retourne à l'école après son hospitalisation, il ne sera pas trop dépaysé ou retardé.

LE RÔLE DE L'INFIRMIÈRE DANS LE SOIN DE L'ENFANT

Plusieurs infirmières croient qu'elles remplissent leur rôle en procurant à l'enfant malade ce qui est communément appelé de « l'amour maternel ». En retour de l'affection qu'elles lui portent, elles espèrent recevoir de l'enfant les mêmes manifestations affectives qu'il prodigue à sa mère. En fait, elles essaient de remplacer les parents auprès de l'enfant.

L'amour des parents pour l'enfant ne consiste pas seulement à le caresser, à le nourrir et à jouer avec lui. Il comprend aussi ces interactions parents-enfant qui stimulent la croissance, la perception, la curiosité, le goût de découvrir son environnement, l'indépendance et le désir de faire tout ce qu'il peut pour son âge. Des parents aimants accepteront que leur nouveau-né complètement dépendant devienne graduellement un être autonome et ils s'en réjouiront. À mesure que l'enfant grandit, les parents doivent continuer à aimer leur enfant, même si ses intérêts sont différents des leurs. En un mot, tout ce qu'ils doivent vouloir, c'est le plein épanouissement de cet enfant quelle que soit leur propre façon d'envisager la vie. Le véritable amour parental, dégagé d'égoïsme et d'intérêt personnel, est difficile à développer. Une telle capacité d'aimer dépend habituellement d'expériences semblables au cours de l'enfance ou de la jeunesse. Ainsi, lorsque l'adulte équilibré sait accepter des sentiments exprimant la colère, l'amour, le chagrin, le désir sexuel, l'enfant pourra connaître ces émotions par le processus d'identification.

Dans notre culture, il est rare de rencontrer de tels parents et de tels enfants. Privés sérieusement sur le plan émotif, certains parents essaient de compenser cette lacune en obtenant tout ce qui leur assure le confort. Les enfants nés d'une union où les parents n'ont pas connu beaucoup d'amour, ne seront pas gâtés, eux non plus, car les parents peuvent difficilement donner ce qu'ils n'ont pas reçu.

Bien sûr, l'infirmière ne peut pas combler complètement ce manque d'amour chez l'enfant. En nursing, l'amour s'exprime par les efforts réciproques de l'infirmière et de l'enfant en vue d'amener la guérison ou le confort du patient. La confiance de l'enfant envers l'infirmière se gagne lentement et elle doit prouver au petit son attachement réel. Même lorsque la relation enfant-infirmière est bien établie, celle-ci doit se rappeler qu'elle ne remplace pas la mère, mais qu'elle en est plutôt un complément.

Communication avec les parents

Pour vraiment aider l'enfant, il faut d'abord entrer en contact avec les parents et surtout avec la mère. *Cette communication a pour but d'obtenir des informations des parents, de leur en donner, de discuter de leurs sentiments et de leurs tensions, de les encourager à résoudre eux-mêmes leurs problèmes.* Pour que la communication soit efficace, l'infirmière doit respecter parents et enfants, tenir compte de leur culture, de leurs besoins, de leurs craintes et de leur éducation.

La capacité de compréhension des parents dépend de la situation où ils se trouvent. S'ils vivent une période de crise ou de tension, ils peuvent demander de l'aide et être très réceptifs aux conseils. Toutefois, ils ne sont pas toujours en mesure d'apprécier la valeur des suggestions parce que leurs émotions dominent leur raison. Il est alors important qu'ils rencontrent des professionnels compétents durant ces temps de crise.

De tels moments surviennent lorsqu'un enfant est malade ou hospitalisé et à certaines étapes difficiles du développement de l'enfant, comme au moment de l'apprentissage de la propreté, à l'adolescence, etc.

Chaque échange doit avoir un but bien précis, mais les rapports entre parents et infirmières doivent demeurer souples et flexibles. Par exemple, tout renseignement donné au sujet de l'alimentation, des inoculations, de la santé, peut être important, mais les parents doivent d'abord être en mesure d'apprendre ce que l'infirmière juge utile de leur enseigner

et une bonne relation doit exister entre les parents et l'infirmière.

L'établissement d'une bonne relation entre les parents et l'infirmière dépend en grande partie de la chaleur, de la sensibilité et de la compréhension de cette dernière, toutefois les paroles seules ne suffisent pas à gagner la confiance des parents. La tenue extérieure, la propreté, les communications non-verbales, telles que gestes, ton de la voix, etc. servent à exprimer la bonne volonté de l'infirmière. Les attitudes et le comportement sont largement conditionnés par les expériences antérieures. La communication avec les parents dépendra aussi d'eux, de leur apparence, de leur attitude, de leur âge ou de leur sexe; l'infirmière peut aimer ou ne pas aimer une certaine personne car elle ressemble à quelqu'un qu'elle admire ou qu'elle rejette. Les conflits et les problèmes personnels de l'infirmière se répercutent sur ses relations professionnelles. Si des parents lui sont antipathiques, il est bon qu'elle le reconnaisse simplement, même si elle ne connaît pas la cause spécifique de ses sentiments.

Les parents tout comme les enfants considèrent l'infirmière comme une figure d'autorité. Celle-ci peut accepter l'hostilité, la culpabilité et la dépendance d'un enfant, mais elle les tolérera beaucoup moins de la part des parents dont l'âge est souvent près du sien. Elle devra néanmoins leur faire sentir qu'elle respecte leurs sentiments et leur procurer l'opportunité de discuter de leurs perceptions et de leurs émotions avec une personne chaleureuse et qui ne porte pas de jugements moraux.

Certains principes régissent ces relations parents-infirmières, enfants-infirmières:

1) *L'infirmière commence à établir une relation d'aide avec les parents et l'enfant dès qu'elle les rencontre pour la première fois, que ce soit au foyer, à l'hôpital ou dans un service communautaire.*

2) *Elle sait que toute conduite a un sens, une signification, même si ceci n'est pas apparent.*

3) *Elle accepte parents et enfants comme ils sont,* sans chercher à les juger en terme de bien et de mal. Son rôle consiste à comprendre et non à appliquer des règles morales.

4) Elle doit éprouver pour eux de l'empathie, c'est-à-dire tenter de saisir ce que représentent pour eux les problèmes et sentiments qu'ils expriment. Elle leur communique aussi sa compréhension sincère et essaie de les aider à trouver une solution.

5) *Elle doit reconnaître que les parents ont le droit de prendre des décisions concernant l'enfant et elle doit les respecter, même si parfois elles lui semblent inadéquates.*

6) *Elle doit permettre à l'enfant et aux parents d'exprimer leurs sentiments négatifs* et réagir de façon adulte et objective dans de telles circonstances.

7) *Elle doit poser des questions simples et brèves et s'exprimer dans un langage compréhensible.*

8) *Elle doit faire comprendre aux parents qu'il y a cohésion et unité à l'intérieur de l'équipe de santé, de façon à ce qu'ils se sentent en sécurité.*

Plusieurs situations dans le nursing pédiatrique exigent que l'infirmière connaisse les techniques d'entrevue. *Ainsi, une expression sincère de sympathie calme l'anxiété de l'enfant et des parents.* Il est préférable de laisser les parents parler d'abord et narrer eux-mêmes les faits avant de poser des questions. La méthode non-directive d'entrevue est indiquée dans certaines situations de nursing; la technique la plus utilisée est de répéter ce que les parents ou l'enfant ont dit, soit en posant des questions, en répétant d'une voix interrogative les derniers mots entendus, soit en disant en d'autres mots ce qui vient d'être exprimé. Cette méthode limite la participation verbale de l'infirmière mais fait appel aux communications non verbales, telles que mimique, attitude, posture.

Cette méthode peut se révéler efficace lors d'une discussion sur un sujet anxiogène, tel que la peur de la mort ou de la chirurgie. Dans ces cas, un encouragement superficiel ne soulage que temporairement et a peu de valeur. L'infirmière apaisera plus facilement les parents en leur facilitant l'expression de leurs craintes, en les aidant à comprendre les raisons de leurs angoisses, en les écoutant avec sympathie. Toutefois, cette technique exige beaucoup de prudence de la part de l'infirmière. Elle ne doit pas questionner indûment les parents et les amener à dire plus qu'ils ne voulaient. Une telle discussion pourrait s'avérer explosive et occasionner aux parents plus d'anxiété qu'ils n'en avaient au départ. Au cours des entrevues, des moments de silence se présenteront et l'infirmière doit apprendre à les respecter sans difficulté. Ces pauses précèdent souvent un changement significatif dans la conversation. Il se peut qu'un des parents ou l'enfant veuille dire quelque chose d'important, mais hésite à faire confiance à leur interlocutrice. Il est possible qu'il cherche les mots qui exprimeraient bien son problème ou encore qu'il désire cesser la discussion sur un sujet en particulier. L'infirmière doit accepter ces temps d'arrêt.

L'infirmière doit savoir qu'elle ne peut pas aider parents et enfants à résoudre immédiatement tous leurs problèmes, mais elle peut tendre à clarifier les situations. *Si les problèmes présentés à l'infirmière ne sont pas de son ressort, elle doit faire appel aux autres membres de l'équipe de santé.*

ADMISSION DE L'ENFANT À L'HÔPITAL

On peut considérer cette admission de deux façons: d'abord les activités qu'elle implique, puis les réactions émotives de l'enfant et de sa famille. Nous verrons en premier lieu le plan émotif, où l'infirmière joue un rôle primordial.

L'hospitalisation des enfants est devenue tellement courante aujourd'hui, que l'on tend à oublier son importance et ses effets sur l'unité de la cellule familiale. Afin de minimiser les conséquences de cette rupture plus ou moins complète des liens familiaux, l'équipe de santé doit tenir compte de chacun des membres de la famille dans ses conseils et dans son approche. Toute l'équipe doit aussi travailler de concert afin de créer un climat favorable lors de l'admission de l'enfant.

L'admission d'un enfant à l'hôpital et ses répercussions psychologiques

Réaction des parents

Les parents dont l'enfant est hospitalisé souffrent non seulement de cette séparation, mais aussi de leur incompétence vis-à-vis du personnel infirmier qui va prendre soin de leur enfant.

Il est parfois nécessaire d'opérer d'urgence afin de sauver la vie d'un bébé né avec une malformation ou affligé d'une affection quelconque; mais en d'autres cas, il peut quitter la pouponnière avec sa mère et revenir seulement lorsqu'il a atteint l'âge ou le poids requis pour subir l'intervention correctrice. Bien sûr, cette anomalie représente une déception pour les parents qui attendaient la venue d'un enfant sain. Il est donc normal qu'au moment de sa réadmission à l'hôpital, les parents soient anxieux, découragés et animés d'un certain sentiment de culpabilité.

D'ailleurs l'anxiété rend les parents moins aptes à réconforter leur enfant et, de plus,

Figure 5-7. L'admission à l'hôpital. (Courtoisie de l'Hôpital Sainte-Justine, Montréal.)

ils peuvent la transmettre à l'enfant malade. Les parents anxieux se reconnaissent à leur voix tremblante, mal assurée, à leur agitation, à leur agressivité et à leurs mouvements intempestifs.

Dès que l'infirmière décèle cette anxiété, elle doit immédiatement tenter d'en connaître les causes, afin de soulager le plus rapidement possible la personne aux prises avec une telle angoisse. Elle pourra même faire appel aux autres membres de l'équipe, si c'est nécessaire.

Il arrive souvent que le père ou la mère sans expérience impute la maladie de l'enfant à leur propre maladresse. Par contre, si l'enfant n'a pas été désiré, ils peuvent concevoir la maladie comme une punition pour leur manque d'amour durant la grossesse et parfois après la naissance de l'enfant.

Si les parents se sentent responsables de la maladie de l'enfant, l'infirmière doit leur expliquer les causes réelles de la maladie et leur faire comprendre qu'ils ne sont pas jugés fautifs. Si toutefois, ils ont vraiment commis une erreur qui a entraîné la maladie de l'enfant, l'infirmière peut essayer de les convaincre que l'erreur est humaine.

Si la mère est anxieuse par manque de confiance en elle, l'infirmière peut l'aider en la félicitant pour certaines bonnes méthodes qu'elle utilise avec son enfant. Employer certaines habitudes de la mère, non seulement la valorise, mais aussi la rassure et permet une meilleure adaptation de l'enfant au milieu hospitalier.

Causes de l'anxiété parentale. En plus de la maladie de leur enfant, les parents doivent faire face à la séparation, à l'hospitalisation. Parmi les raisons qui augmentent leur anxiété, on trouve:

1) La crainte du milieu hospitalier. L'infirmière peut diminuer cette crainte en expliquant aux parents le fonctionnement des différents appareils et surtout en répondant à toutes leurs questions.

2) La peur de voir leur enfant loin d'eux, aux mains d'une étrangère et peut-être aussi la peur inconsciente de passer au second plan dans l'affection de leur enfant. Si tel est le cas, l'infirmière peut suggérer aux parents certains soins qu'ils pourraient prodiguer eux-mêmes à leur petit.

3) La peur de l'inconnu et du sort réservé à leur enfant. La vie future d'un enfant handicapé apparaît très pénible aux

parents parce qu'ils n'ont aucune idée réelle de ce qu'elle sera.

4) La peur que la maladie soit contagieuse et contamine tout le reste de la famille.

5) La peur de voir l'enfant souffrir.

6) La crainte d'être obligés de s'endetter à cause des frais occasionnés par la maladie; (le travailleur social peut apporter une aide précieuse aux parents dans ce cas).

7) La peur que les gens pensent qu'ils sont des parents irresponsables ou tarés.

Les parents anxieux exagèrent l'importance des problèmes et s'égarent dans de longues discussions qui ne concernent pas du tout la maladie de l'enfant. Mais l'infirmière doit comprendre ce comportement et ne pas croire pour autant qu'ils se désintéressent de leur enfant. La plupart des mères cherchent un support moral auprès de l'infirmière; même si certaines mères ne semblent rien faire dans ce sens, ce sont souvent ces dernières qui ont le plus besoin d'aide. L'infirmière, et d'autres membres de l'équipe sauront aider ces personnes à exprimer leurs émotions.

Réactions de l'enfant

Toute maladie ou handicap physique menace à la fois le développement physique et psychologique de l'enfant et risque d'altérer sa confiance dans les adultes et dans la vie. La maladie amène la douleur, l'immobilité, de longues périodes d'insomnie, la frustration du besoin de succion chez le nourrisson qui ne peut être alimenté par voie orale.

Au moment où il en a le plus besoin, sa mère lui manque beaucoup à moins que l'hôpital ne permette à la mère de demeurer avec son enfant de façon presque permanente. L'hospitalisation est une toute nouvelle expérience pour le bébé ou le jeune enfant. Celui-ci au cours de ses visites chez le médecin considérait le personnel comme des amis, mais il ne fait pas toujours le lien entre ce personnel et celui de l'hôpital. De plus, l'anxiété de ses parents risque de l'influencer défavorablement.

Toutefois, la façon de voir l'hôpital dépend du degré de maturité de l'enfant, de ses expériences antérieures et de la façon dont il a été préparé à l'hospitalisation. Si l'enfant s'imagine qu'il est puni, justement ou injustement, il aura plus de difficulté à faire face à l'hospitalisation que s'il en connaît les causes exactes.

Les relations entre l'infirmière et l'enfant

L'infirmière doit se rappeler que les besoins de l'enfant malade sont semblables à ceux d'un enfant sain et qu'il doit être en mesure de faire confiance à ceux qui prennent soin de lui. Incapable de juger de la compétence du personnel infirmier, il se fie uniquement au genre de relation que les personnes établissent avec lui. L'enfant doit donc sentir que les adultes qui l'entourent l'aiment et s'en occupent d'une façon particulière. Mais il a également besoin de contacts fréquents et étroits avec ses parents. La croissance et le développement de l'enfant doivent se poursuivre au cours de son séjour à l'hôpital. C'est la raison pour laquelle l'infirmière doit savoir quelles sont ses habitudes et son genre de vie, afin de les respecter le plus possible. Elle doit s'enquérir si les parents donnent un surnom à l'enfant et l'utiliser afin de faciliter son adaptation à l'hôpital. Enfin, il est essentiel pour l'enfant de jouer et d'entrer en contact avec d'autres petits malades.

Le point de vue de l'enfant. L'enfant perçoit cette relation avec l'infirmière de différentes manières:

1) Elle lui donne les mêmes soins que sa mère.

2) Elle lui administre des soins qui peuvent être douloureux et angoissants.

3) Elle lui apporte la sécurité et l'affection d'un adulte.

4) Elle lui sert de lien entre l'hôpital et sa mère et son foyer.

Un enfant plus âgé se rend compte qu'en plus de tout cela, l'infirmière lui enseigne des principes d'hygiène et des notions anatomiques et physiologiques: pour les petites filles, elle devient le modèle de ce qu'elles pourraient être plus tard. L'enfant peut sentir qu'elle cherche à lui faciliter son adaptation au milieu, à sa maladie ou à son handicap. Il apprend rapidement les liens qui existent entre l'infirmière et ses parents, et entre l'infirmière et ses médecins, et il utilise souvent cette dernière pour entrer en contact avec l'une ou l'autre de ces autorités.

Quelles que soient les ressources du milieu, l'infirmière doit chercher à recréer une atmosphère familiale dans l'unité pédiatrique. Par atmosphère familiale, on entend celle créée par la présence de lumière, couleurs, images, musique, télévision, jouets, voiturettes, tricycles, ameublement à la mesure de l'enfant. Ainsi des baignoires individuelles de couleur, des jouets flottants et des serviettes de couleurs confèrent au bain une allure familiale. Et pourquoi la nourriture ne serait-elle pas servie à partir d'un chariot chauffant converti en wagon? L'utilisation d'un landau au lieu d'une chaise roulante ou d'une civière permet de transporter le jeune enfant d'un endroit à l'autre dans l'hôpital pour lui donner les soins nécessaires, sans pour autant l'effrayer outre mesure. Si on permettait au petit malade d'apporter au laboratoire ou à la salle d'opération le jouet qu'il préfère, il conserverait une certaine sérénité devant l'inconnu.

Il faut souligner que la relation humaine entre l'enfant et l'infirmière est de première importance et prévaut sur toutes les nouvelles méthodes et sur l'équipement adapté à l'enfant L'idéal serait que ce soit toujours la même infirmière, jour après jour, qui dispense les soins à l'enfant, mais cela est pratiquement impossible. Cependant il serait souhaitable qu'un nombre restreint d'infirmières soigne l'enfant et ce, afin d'établir une meilleure connaissance réciproque. Si celui-ci connaît bien quelques infirmières, il acceptera plus facilement le personnel de rotation. Leur uniforme et une façon semblable de procéder incitent l'enfant à identifier les nouvelles infirmières à celles qu'il connaît déjà.

Le point de vue de l'infirmière. 1) *Le rôle de l'infirmière, tel que perçu par l'enfant,* devrait correspondre sensiblement à celui qu'elle est censée remplir puisqu'elle se doit de répondre aux besoins de l'enfant. Mais cette image de l'infirmière peut être gravement altérée si l'enfant en rencontre qui ne sont pas à la hauteur de la situation. Alors, plutôt que de la considérer comme une personne bonne et douce, il verra en elle une personne autoritaire et méchante, même si elle utilise avec lui de bonnes techniques de soins physiques.

2) *L'infirmière doit aider l'enfant à acquérir de bonnes habitudes au point de vue hygiénique pendant son séjour à l'hôpital.* Elle doit introduire progressivement de nouveaux aliments, etc. Les nouvelles méthodes de traitement et les instruments inconnus doivent lui être expliqués afin de ne pas le prendre par surprise. L'enseignement de bons principes hygiéniques et la correction des mauvaises habitudes font partie intégrante du nursing en pédiatrie.

Malheureusement, un enfant peut perdre les bonnes habitudes qu'il avait, et régresser au cours de son séjour à l'hôpital, ou encore il peut acquérir de très mauvaises habitudes. Un cas fréquent de régression est la perte du contrôle des sphincters qui peut être causée par la condition physique de l'enfant, par sa nervosité créée par le changement de milieu. Mais parfois la cause se trouve ailleurs. L'enfant demande le « pot » ou à aller aux cabinets, mais personne ne l'entend ou le personnel tarde à venir; après avoir pleuré et s'être retenu longtemps l'enfant en arrive à souiller son lit. Trop souvent l'infirmière et les parents ne prennent pas conscience que son état émotif et sa faiblesse le rendent plus vulnérable. L'infirmière occupée à une autre tâche peut penser que cet appel n'est pas urgent ou même préférer changer la literie plutôt que d'accourir à l'instant. Certaines infirmières vont même jusqu'à remettre des couches aux enfants. Toutes ces attitudes du personnel infirmier portent l'enfant à régresser et à abandonner des habitudes acquises.

3) *L'infirmière doit être disponible.* La maladie et l'hospitalisation causent des problèmes d'adaptation à l'enfant et à sa famille. L'infirmière est pour eux une source de réconfort, de courage; elle doit d'abord s'efforcer de gagner leur confiance. C'est à cette condition qu'elle pourra établir une relation émotive positive entre l'enfant, les parents et elle-même. *Elle doit aussi identifier leurs sentiments et réactions de façon à apporter une aide adaptée à leurs besoins spécifiques.* Dans le cas d'un enfant gravement malade, l'infirmière doit savoir reconnaître l'anxiété, aider à la soulager en se montrant intéressée, en écoutant patiemment ses plaintes et en lui donnant des soins d'une façon attentive. Les mots seuls ne persuadent pas les parents que tout est fait en vue du rétablissement de l'enfant. L'attitude du personnel est aussi très importante. À mesure que l'anxiété des parents diminue grâce à la sollicitude de l'infirmière, celle de l'enfant disparaît aussi peu à peu.

L'étudiante-infirmière au début de son apprentissage peut souffrir de son incapacité à réconforter parents et enfants. C'est normal, car sa propre anxiété à soigner un enfant déformé, malade ou mourant, lui fait oublier celle de l'enfant et de ses parents.

Le nursing en pédiatrie exige beaucoup de patience et de tendresse, mais surtout un solide équilibre émotif dans les périodes de tension. Pour se protéger et dissimuler ses sentiments, l'infirmière peut chercher à construire un mur impénétrable entre elle, l'enfant et ses parents. Elle peut même tenter de se dérober aux situations difficiles auxquelles elle ne veut pas faire face émotivement. Elle laisse alors les parents seuls, au moment où ils pourraient avoir un pressant besoin de réconfort. Mais

Histoire de nursing en pédiatrie

Identification

Prénom _____ Nom _____ Surnom _____

Date de naissance _____ Âge _____

Admission

Date _____ Circonstances d'admission _____

Accompagné (e) par _____

Comportement général de l'enfant _____

Famille

Frères et Soeurs	Prénoms	Âge	Prénoms	Âge	Prénoms	Âge

Gardienne habituelle _____

Langue parlée à la maison _____

Événements importants (mort, maladie, naissance, déménagement) _____

Habitudes de l'enfant

Alimentation

Purée _____ Aliments hachés _____ ordinaire _____ Sorte de lait _____

Biberon _____ Tasse _____ Verre _____

Cuillère _____ Fourchette _____ Couteau _____

Heure des repas _____ des collations _____

Aliments préférés _____ Aliments détestés _____

Allergies alimentaires _____

S'alimente facilement _____ Besoin de stimulation _____

Mange seul _____ avec aide: _____ dans les bras: _____

chaise haute: _____ chaise et table: _____

Appétit habituel _____

Élimination

Apprentissage commencé _____ complété _____ depuis quand _____

Demande pour éliminer _____

Contrôle vésical seulement _____ anal seulement _____

Incontinence nocturne _____

Habitudes spéciales _____ Horaire _____

Moyens utilisés   Jour   Nuit

      — couche   _____

      — culottes   _____

      — petit pot   _____

      — siège adaptable _____

      — toilette   _____

Termes utilisés pour désigner: selles _____ urines _____

Figure 5-8. Fiche d'admission.

Sommeil

Genre de lit à la maison _____

Heure du coucher _____ du lever _____ des siestes _____

Habitudes au coucher _____

Agitation, cauchemars _____

Peurs particulières _____

Autres activités

S'habille: seul _____ avec aide _____

Se brosse les dents: seul _____ avec aide _____

Se peigne: seul _____ avec aide _____

Se lave: seul _____ avec aide _____ heure _____

lavabo _____ baignoire de bébé _____ baignoire adulte _____

avec plaisir _____ avec crainte _____

Jeux

Habituels _____ Favoris _____

Partenaires habituels _____

Animal à la maison _____

École ou maternelle

Inscrit à une garderie ou à l'école maternelle _____ depuis quand _____

Va à l'école _____ En quelle année _____

Amis favoris _____

Hospitalisations antérieures

Nombre _____ À quel âge _____

Raisons _____ Événements marquants _____

Hospitalisation actuelle

Connaît la raison de l'hospitalisation _____

Type de préparation _____

Opération prévue _____

Ce qu'il sait de son opération _____ Visiteurs prévus _____

Parents (si présents)

Perceptions de la situation _____

Connaissance de la maladie _____

Attitudes face au personnel _____ à l'enfant _____

Prochaine visite _____

Commentaires et suggestions _____

il faut aussi souligner que la présence physique d'infirmières qui imposent leurs idées, rassurent faiblement, apportent de fausses conclusions ou évitent les sujets critiques, n'est guère mieux que leur absence. C'est pourquoi nous répétons que l'infirmière doit connaître ses sentiments, les contrôler, et surtout, savoir qu'ils existent chez tous les êtres humains.

Elle doit aussi apprendre à se faire aider et elle pourra jouer le rôle que l'on attend d'elle.

Les relations parents-infirmières

L'enfant constitue le noyau de la relation entre les parents et l'infirmière. Cependant c'est parfois la mère ou le père plus que l'enfant, s'il est gravement atteint, qui a besoin de conseils, de sympathie et d'aide de la part de l'infirmière. L'influence de la mère sur l'enfant étant considérable, il est de première nécessité de lui venir en aide de façon à ce qu'elle rassure son enfant. L'infirmière doit écouter les parents, accepter d'apprendre leurs méthodes de soins. Elle doit essayer de connaître, non seulement leurs faiblesses, mais aussi leurs points forts et pourra s'en servir pour soigner l'enfant.

Avant ses débuts en nursing, l'infirmière a probablement eu l'expérience d'enfants séparés de leurs mères, mais la plupart du temps la séparation se faisait dans une atmosphère détendue et n'était dramatique, ni pour l'enfant, ni pour la mère, dont l'absence était le plus souvent très courte. Si l'infirmière a déjà été gardienne d'enfants ou monitrice dans des camps, elle peut entrer plus facilement en contact avec la mère puisqu'elle connaît les enfants, point de rencontre entre les deux. À cela s'ajoutent évidemment ses connaissances médicales qu'elle pourra transmettre à la mère.

La mère connaît son enfant beaucoup mieux que l'infirmière. Son attention peut toutefois devenir tellement centrée ou orientée sur lui qu'elle le voit comme le prototype de tous les enfants et non pas objectivement par rapport aux autres; elle ne voit pas en quoi il ressemble ou diffère des autres enfants, elle évalue difficilement ses capacités et ses limites. Malgré cette optique quelque peu étroite, elle peut grandement aider l'infirmière à comprendre le comportement de l'enfant. Surtout dans le cas d'un malade chronique ou handicapé, ceci peut faciliter l'adaptation de l'enfant à l'hôpital. Prodiguer des soins à son enfant malade représente pour la maman un réconfort et aide l'enfant à se familiariser avec le milieu

étranger qui l'entoure; de plus, la mère apprend ainsi, sous surveillance, les soins qu'elle aura à donner à l'enfant après son départ de l'hôpital.

L'infirmière connaît, mieux que la mère, la pathologie et les soins médicaux pour malades chroniques ou handicapés, mais le peu que celle-ci connaît, elle l'a acquis par expérience, en soignant son enfant. Il est donc préférable de la laisser donner les soins quotidiens à l'enfant jusqu'à ce que l'infirmière ait appris à bien connaître le malade. S'il y a lieu, elle peut ensuite enseigner à la mère de meilleurs moyens pour le soigner. En pédiatrie, la mère et l'infirmière doivent travailler en étroite collaboration.

Mais il faut toujours penser au retour éventuel de l'enfant dans son foyer. Changer des habitudes en risquant de créer des tensions entre l'enfant et son milieu ne lui profite guère. Par exemple, il faut réfléchir avant d'empêcher un enfant de dire des mots vulgaires, alors qu'ils sont monnaie courante chez lui ou de lui défendre de se battre, alors que son propre père l'y encourage.

On ne peut cependant permettre à l'enfant hospitalisé de blesser les autres petits malades. *Dans ce cas l'infirmière doit condamner l'acte et non l'enfant ou ses parents.* De plus, elle doit fournir à cet enfant des activités qui lui permettent d'utiliser son énergie et son agressivité. Enseigner à des enfants de milieux défavorisés des valeurs de classe moyenne, en condamnant implicitement leurs parents, entraîne souvent des troubles psychologiques et de comportement chez ces enfants.

L'éducation des parents. Traiter des relations parents-infirmières nous conduit à discuter de l'éducation des parents. Celle-ci débute dès l'enfance des futurs parents. En effet, si un enfant vit dans un milieu stable, il saura plus tard recréer la même atmosphère de sécurité. C'est un aspect dont il faut tenir compte quand on blâme certains parents. Mais cela ne veut pas dire qu'il n'y a plus rien à faire devant un parent incompétent. Le comportement d'un individu peut toujours se modifier ou être influencé. L'infirmière doit accepter les parents tels qu'ils sont, mais en les guidant vers une meilleure compréhension de leur enfant.

L'infirmière doit respecter certains principes de base dans l'éducation des parents. Elle doit d'abord connaître le degré de compréhension, l'expérience des parents et surtout les moyens dont ils disposent à la maison. Ont-ils l'équipement nécessaire pour tel soin, sinon peuvent-ils se le procurer? L'infirmière qui se rend compte des problèmes d'une mère doit procéder avec prudence et lui donner le temps d'assimiler son enseignement. Pour s'assurer que la mère a bien compris, l'infirmière pourrait écrire ses recommandations ou les faire réviser par la mère avant le départ de l'enfant.

Le rôle de l'infirmière en pédiatrie comprend également une partie pratique qui consiste en une démonstration des soins à donner à l'enfant. Cependant l'influence de l'infirmière ne concerne pas seulement l'aspect physique des soins et ses composantes psychologiques. Elle doit aussi apprendre à la mère quels stimulants provoquent des réponses positives et lesquels produisent des effets néfastes chez son enfant. Même si l'infirmière a une bonne connaissance générale et de l'expérience, elle ne doit pas négliger son rôle d'intermédiaire entre les parents et le personnel spécialisé. En effet, c'est au médecin que revient la charge de diriger l'aspect médical de l'éducation des parents. L'infirmière est malgré tout la personne la plus efficace pour travailler à cette éducation: elle peut montrer aux parents comment soigner l'enfant, afin de satisfaire les besoins physiques et émotifs du petit malade.

Il arrive souvent que les parents se sentent coupables de l'état de leur enfant; l'infirmière doit pouvoir leur proposer une nouvelle façon de comprendre la maladie de l'enfant. Ils doivent accepter le fait que personne n'est parfait et que leurs gestes proviennent d'une décision subjective basée sur le désir d'accomplir ce qu'ils croient être préférable pour leur enfant. Il est fréquent d'entendre des parents dire: « Nous n'aurions pas dû le faire opérer ». On devrait alors leur faire comprendre qu'ils ont choisi ce qu'ils croyaient être la meilleure solution, même si le résultat n'a pas été satisfaisant, et qu'ils n'auraient pu faire mieux.

Le rôle de l'infirmière au moment de l'admission de l'enfant

L'infirmière, au moment de l'admission de l'enfant à l'hôpital, joue un rôle tout aussi important face à la mère que face à l'enfant. Elle comprendra que le comportement de la mère correspond directement à la perception qu'elle a de la maladie et de l'hospitalisation de son enfant. Alors, il est inadmissible de lui demander de ne pas pleurer ou de s'estimer heureuse que la situation ne soit pas plus grave, car la mère se sentirait honteuse et réprimerait ses sentiments, ce qui aurait pour effet d'augmenter son anxiété et ses sentiments de culpabilité.

L'infirmière devrait s'abstenir de toute critique à l'égard de la conduite antérieure de la mère et de son attitude présente, afin de ne pas augmenter la tension et également l'hostilité de la mère. Elle devra plutôt essayer de comprendre ce que la mère ressent au sujet du pronostic et du traitement de la maladie.

Il existe différents moyens de sécuriser la mère et l'enfant:

1) L'infirmière devrait accueillir la mère aimablement, lui offrir un siège. La mère aura une plus grande confiance dans le personnel hospitalier, si la personne qui l'accueille est calme et sereine.

2) L'infirmière devrait se présenter à la mère, lui faire connaître l'infirmière-chef et celles qui dispenseront les soins à l'enfant. Elle devrait s'assurer que la mère a bien compris le nom de chacune. Si l'enfant est assez âgé, il pourrait être présenté à ses petits compagnons ainsi qu'au personnel qui en a la charge.

3) Conduire la mère et l'enfant à la chambre de celui-ci afin qu'ils connaissent le milieu où il va vivre. Lorsque l'anxiété de la mère diminue, celle de l'enfant s'atténue aussi.

4) On devrait expliquer clairement le processus de l'admission et répondre explicitement à toute question.

5) Lorsque c'est possible, l'enfant devrait avoir le temps de jouer avant de procéder à l'admission proprement dite.

Voici le déroulement d'une admission:

1) Histoire médicale. Présentée au médecin, la mère raconte la maladie de son enfant. On aura pris garde d'éloigner celui-ci un moment, afin qu'il ne sente pas l'anxiété possible de sa mère ou n'entende pas de commentaires pouvant l'effrayer.

2) Histoire de soin. L'infirmière demande aux parents de remplir le questionnaire d'admission ou histoire de soin ou elle le complète elle-même en posant les questions aux parents. L'histoire de soin permet de recueillir les informations sur l'environnement familial de l'enfant, ses habitudes à la maison, les particularités de ses soins ainsi que les connaissances et les attitudes de ses parents. Pour être utile, l'histoire doit être adaptée à l'âge de l'enfant. L'infirmière doit toujours revoir l'histoire de soin avec les parents, clarifier les données imprécises et répondre aux questions.

3) Signes vitaux. L'infirmière prend les signes vitaux de l'enfant: température, pulsation, respiration et si cela est nécessaire la tension

---

artérielle; si on doit prendre la température par voie rectale, il faut réserver cette procédure pour la fin et y préparer l'enfant, car il risque de pleurer et de fausser la lecture des autres signes vitaux.

(a) *Température.* La prise de la température par voie rectale qui représente trop souvent une agression pour l'enfant ne devrait être utilisée que lorsque c'est nécessaire, c'est-à-dire quand les voies buccale et axillaire ne sont pas recommandées. Pour obtenir des données exactes, le thermomètre doit être laissé en place 7 minutes, par voie buccale, 3 minutes, par voie rectale et 10 minutes par voie axillaire.

(b) *Respiration.* Chez l'enfant le rythme respiratoire s'observe mieux au niveau de l'abdomen que du thorax. En effet, durant le jeune âge, les muscles intercostaux peu développés participent moins à la respiration qu'ultérieurement. Les moyennes du rythme respiratoire, selon les âges, sont les suivantes:

Âge	Rythme respiratoire
Nouveau-nés	30-50
2 ans	24-30
6 ans	22-28
10 ans	20-26
12 ans	18-24
Adultes	16-22

(c) Pulsation. Chez le nourrisson, le rythme cardiaque se vérifie à l'apex ou à l'artère temporale. Chez le jeune enfant, la pulsation peut être prise aux niveaux de l'artère temporale ou de l'artère radiale. Les moyennes de pulsation, selon les âges sont les suivantes:

Âge	Pulsation
Nouveau-nés à un an	120
2 ans	110
6 ans	100
10 ans	90
12 ans	85
Adultes	72

(d) *Tension artérielle.* La brise de la tension artérielle, sur ordonnance du médecin, nécessite un matériel approprié pour les bébés et les jeunes enfants; beaucoup d'erreurs sont dues à l'usage d'un brassard trop large pour le bras du petit patient. Le brassard devrait couvrir les deux tiers du bras. Les mesures sont les suivantes:

Nouveau-nés:	2,5 cm
2 mois à 1 an:	4 cm
1 an à 8 ans:	5 à 7,5 cm
8 à 12 ans:	10 cm
Adultes:	13 cm

Ces mesures générales doivent être adaptées au poids et à la taille de chaque enfant. La tension artérielle doit se prendre dans une atmosphère de calme, lorsque l'enfant est au repos, sinon le résultat pourrait être faussé.

Les moyennes normales de tension artérielle, selon les âges, sont les suivantes:

Âge	Tension systolique	Tension diastolique
À la naissance	40	–
1 mois	75	50
4 ans	85	60
8 ans	95	62
12 ans (garçon)	108	67
16 ans "	118	75
20 ans "	120	75

Comme on peut le constater sur ce tableau, la tension systolique augmente graduellement avec l'âge. La tension diastolique augmente aussi, mais très lentement entre 6 et 18 ans. Jusqu'à l'âge de 14 ans, il n'existe pas de différence notable entre les deux sexes. Ensuite la tension artérielle chez la fille demeure stable, alors que celle du garçon s'élève encore. De plus, la tension peut varier d'un individu à l'autre selon son degré personnel de maturation.

4) Le poids et la taille. L'infirmière pèse et mesure l'enfant au moment de son admission.

5) Examen physique de l'enfant. La mère devrait elle-même dévêtir l'enfant et si possible assister à l'examen. Une atmosphère de calme doit être maintenue et, dans la mesure du possible, les techniques d'immobilisation devraient être évitées. Si l'enfant est agité au moment de son admission, il serait préférable de retarder certaines parties de l'examen physique. Si des moyens restrictifs doivent être absolument utilisés, il est impérieux de parler et de caresser l'enfant et de veiller à ne pas entraver sa circulation sanguine.

6) Préparation aux traitements. Il est important d'expliquer à l'enfant les raisons et le déroulement des traitements, ceci dans un vocabulaire adapté à son âge. On peut aider le nourrisson en intégrant la technique de soin à une suite agréable d'activités: lui parler, le caresser avant le traitement et ensuite le prendre, le bercer. Le traitement lui paraîtra ainsi plus acceptable. Le meilleur moyen de sécuriser l'enfant est d'accepter sa mère auprès de lui pendant les soins, ou une infirmière en qui il a confiance. Lorsque l'enfant est plus vieux, on peut lui expliquer les traitements d'une façon plus claire et l'apprivoiser en le laissant exécuter la procédure d'abord, comme écouter son cœur au moyen du stéthoscope, ou bien en lui montrant des images explicatives ou, encore mieux, en démontrant le traitement sur des poupées. La présence de l'infirmière auprès de l'enfant est fortement recommandée pour calmer ses craintes.

7) Préparation à la chirurgie. Si l'enfant doit être opéré, il peut entrer à l'hôpital habité de craintes multiples. Il est important que l'infirmière découvre ce qu'il sait et ce qui l'inquiète afin de le préparer adéquatement. Avant le matin de l'intervention, l'enfant doit connaître la séquence des événements préopératoires, savoir qui sera avec lui, ce que signifie l'anesthésie et comment il se sentira en période postopératoire. Une préparation psychologique bien effectuée exige que l'infirmière sache évaluer le niveau de développement de l'enfant, utiliser des moyens de communication efficaces et avoir recours à du matériel didactique approprié.

Rencontre des parents avec l'infirmière soignante ou le chef d'équipe

Cette rencontre a pour but de discuter de l'enfant et le fait d'en parler en utilisant son prénom aide les parents à comprendre que leur enfant recevra des soins individualisés. Une telle approche aide l'infirmière à poser plus de questions pertinentes aux parents. De façon à obtenir les informations nécessaires et à les rendre accessibles à toute l'équipe de soins, il est préférable d'utiliser un questionnaire ou une histoire de nursing préparée à l'avance. L'infirmière doit à son tour donner des informations aux parents, telles les heures de visite et les inviter à venir le plus souvent possible. Elle peut s'informer des raisons qui les en empêchent, mais sans leur donner un sentiment de culpabilité. En cas de besoin, elle peut les référer à un médecin ou à un travailleur social. Il est également important d'expliquer à la maman quels soins elle peut elle-même donner à son enfant. S'il est très malade au début de son hospitalisation, sa participation sera plus minime, mais à mesure que l'état de l'enfant s'améliorera, elle pourra prendre soin de lui de plus en plus. C'est le meilleur moyen d'atténuer des sentiments de culpabilité et de frustration, puis de l'initier aux soins qu'elle devra accorder à son petit à son retour au foyer.

Si l'hôpital établit certains règlements concernant les heures de visites, la nourriture, les jouets, le port des masques et des uniformes, on devrait en fournir une copie aux parents. Leur présence est surtout indispensable au début de l'hospitalisation lorsque l'enfant n'est pas encore adapté à ce nouveau milieu et on doit leur rendre ce séjour confortable. On doit aussi indiquer aux parents où sont les endroits utiles comme le restaurant, le téléphone, les toilettes ou le fumoir et leur signaler que quitter l'enfant durant de brèves périodes peut lui être fort salutaire.

Si la mère ou le père désire assister aux traitements, on leur en expliquera d'abord les buts et le déroulement. Même si les parents peuvent donner certains soins à l'enfant, l'infirmière demeure la première responsable du nursing. Toutefois, en travaillant en collaboration, elle peut leur enseigner une foule de principes et procédés utiles qui rendront service à toute la famille.

Techniques de soin après l'admission

Remplir certaines formalités, recueillir des spécimens d'urine et de sang, par une méthode aseptique, donner des médicaments, instituer un plan de soins et rédiger des observations: telles sont les occupations d'une infirmière après l'admission de l'enfant.

Technique aseptique. Son but est de prévenir la transmission d'une infection d'un enfant à un autre ou aux membres du personnel hospitalier. Elle s'applique dès qu'on suppose que l'enfant a une infection. En entrant dans l'unité sous technique aseptique, le personnel non contaminé le devient au simple contact de l'enfant infecté ou d'objets utilisés pour ses soins.

L'unité de contagion regroupe tous les patients qui souffrent d'une maladie infectieuse. On devrait y trouver des meubles simples, peu nombreux et faciles à nettoyer; seul l'équipement strictement nécessaire, dépendant du nombre d'enfants et des soins à accorder, devrait y être conservé. Tout le mobilier est considéré contaminé (lavabos, murs, planchers et équipement): on utilisera un chiffon ou une vadrouille humide pour nettoyer afin de prévenir la dispersion des microbes dans l'air. Le matériel que l'on emploie quotidiennement pour le patient doit être stérilisé régulièrement.

On doit suivre certaines étapes lorsqu'on reçoit un patient dans cette unité: redonner les vêtements de l'enfant aux parents afin qu'ils soient désinfectés soit par aération, lavage ou ébullition; donner à chaque patient son propre matériel pour la toilette et un thermomètre individuel; attacher les jouets lavables au lit du patient de façon à ce qu'ils ne tombent pas sur le plancher, en prenant soin que l'enfant ne puisse s'enrouler autour du cou le lien qui retient ses jouets à son lit.

Les visites dans cette unité sont quand même permises à cause de l'importance du maintien des liens parents-enfants, mais on doit mettre les parents au courant des règlements établis en vue de prévenir toute dissémination de l'infection.

Ils doivent revêtir la jaquette ou blouse de contagion en prenant soin de ne pas en contaminer l'intérieur, ce qui par le fait même mettrait leurs vêtements en contact avec les microbes. Il doivent se laver les mains et les avant-bras avant de revêtir la blouse et également après l'avoir enlevée.

L'importance du masque dans la limitation de la propagation des infections respiratoires est actuellement mise en doute. Toutefois, si le port du masque est exigé dans certains endroits, il devrait couvrir à la fois le nez et la bouche pour prévenir la contamination par le porteur et l'inhalation de microbes provenant d'un malade qui souffre d'une infection respiratoire. Le masque ne devrait servir qu'une fois et pour une période ne dépassant pas une heure parce qu'il capte au passage un grand nombre de bactéries, et s'humidifie à l'usage. Il ne faut jamais porter un masque autour du cou pour le revêtir ensuite si besoin, ni circuler avec le masque en dehors de l'unité contaminée.

Le brossage des mains varie d'un hôpital à l'autre tant pour le savon employé que pour la technique utilisée. Le matériel de base est toujours l'eau courante, un antiseptique, une brosse et des serviettes de papier. On garde la brosse dans un désinfectant près du lavabo, ou on utilise des brosses que l'on jette après usage. Des serviettes de papier devraient toujours être disponibles.

Tous les articles qu'utilise un patient en isolement doivent être désinfectés avant un nouvel usage; on stérilise la literie et les vêtements à l'autoclave ou par ébullition. On brosse les articles de métal ou de verre et on les place dans l'alcool ou une autre solution antiseptique, telle l'ammonium quaternaire, le chlorure de zéphiran. Pour tuer les microorganismes, on expose certains objets, en particulier les appareils mécaniques, au soleil, à l'air, aux rayons ultra-violets ou à la vaporisation de substances germicides. La désinfection des excréta, des vomissures et du pus dépend du type de micro-organisme qui cause l'infection. Lorsque l'enfant n'est plus infecté et quitte l'unité contaminée, il doit subir une désinfection complète.

Les spécimens d'urines. On les demande habituellement à l'admission. Chez les enfants assez vieux pour coopérer, il y a peu de problèmes, mais chez les petits, ce n'est pas si simple. On utilise, pour l'enfant qui n'est pas continent, un collecteur d'urine fait de plastique, non rigide, avec une surface adhésive à une extrémité. Après avoir lavé et

asséché la peau, on applique une solution protectrice, telle la teinture de benjoin puis on presse fermement la surface adhésive du collecteur sur la région génitale, en prenant soin de ne pas couvrir le rectum et de ne pas blesser la peau. Après la miction de l'enfant, le collecteur peut être enlevé très facilement et l'urine expédiée au laboratoire. (Voir fig. 5-9.)

Il existe une autre méthode pour recueillir l'urine chez les nourrissons. Il s'agit d'utiliser un filet qui peut être stérile ou simplement propre, de le tendre au-dessus du matelas du lit et de l'attacher par une série de huit cordonnets aux ridelles du berceau. L'enfant est confortablement couché sur le filet, vêtu d'une simple chemisette. Un récipient est placé sous le siège de l'enfant, sur le matelas, et l'urine est recueillie à mesure qu'elle est excrétée. Aucun moyen de contrainte n'est nécessaire et l'enfant est facilement accessible pour les soins: il suffit de détacher deux cordons et de baisser une ridelle. (Voir fig. 5-10.)

En pédiatrie, les médecins demandent habituellement un spécimen prélevé de façon aseptique, mais le cathétérisme est très rarement utilisé chez les jeunes enfants. On procède plutôt de la façon suivante: on lave soigneusement les parties génitales de l'enfant au savon et à l'eau. On désinfecte ensuite à l'aide d'une solution non irritante, tel le chlorure de zéphiran 1/1000 et on se sert d'eau stérile pour le rinçage. Il est important de changer de tampon stérile à chaque mouvement, procédant de haut en bas et du centre vers l'extérieur. Après avoir essuyé la peau de façon aseptique, il suffit de mettre le collecteur d'urine en place.

Un enfant d'âge préscolaire ou plus vieux, peut uriner directement dans un bassin de lit ou dans un urinoir stérile, après la toilette décrite ci-dessus. Les spécimens d'urine prélevés au milieu de la miction sont plus stériles, mais plus difficiles à obtenir chez le jeune enfant. Toutefois, dès que l'enfant est capable de coopérer, cette procédure est à recommander. La technique pour prélever l'urine de 24 heures sera décrite un peu plus loin.

Les prélèvements sanguins. Leur but est de déterminer le stade de la maladie et de permettre un diagnostic ou de vérifier l'effet de la thérapie. Chez les enfants qui ont les veines assez développées on procède comme chez les adultes; chez l'enfant plus jeune, seules certaines veines assez développées, telles les veines fémorales ou jugulaires externes, sont utilisées. On se voit souvent obligé d'immobiliser le nourrisson pour permettre ces ponc-

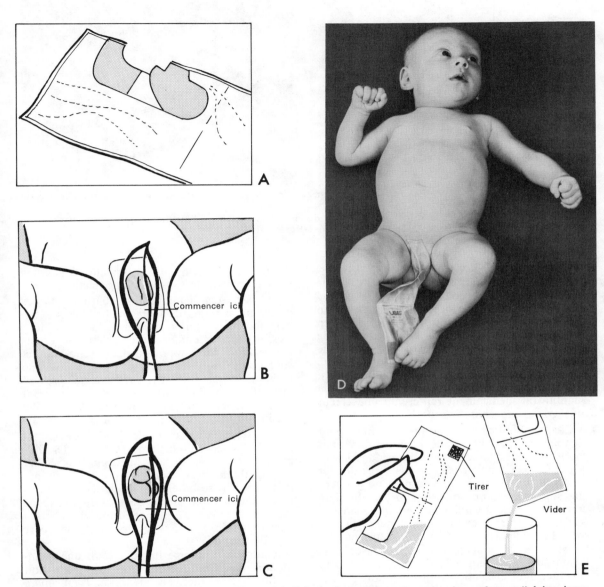

Figure 5-9. Installation du sac collecteur: *A)* Enlever le papier qui couvre la surface adhésive hypo-allergique. *B)* Filles: tendre la peau du périnée, coller le bas de l'orifice du sac entre le vagin et le rectum, sans faire de pli et coller dans un mouvement ascendant. *C)* Garçons: presser la surface adhésive sur la peau après avoir introduit le pénis dans l'orifice du sac. *D)* Sac collecteur en place. *E)* Tenir le sac dans une main, tirer la languette et verser. (Courtoisie de Hollister, Chicago, Illinois.)

tions veineuses. Pour une ponction jugulaire, on maintient fermement la tête en provoquant une hyper-extension du cou alors que pour une ponction fémorale on place les cuisses en abduction. Après le prélèvement de sang, on recommande d'exercer une pression à l'endroit affecté, environ 3 à 5 minutes, afin d'éviter la formation d'un hématome. Durant l'exécu-tion de la prise de sang, l'infirmière parlera à ce petit patient afin de le distraire et elle l'encouragera à extérioriser ses sentiments de crainte ou de colère après la prise de sang. Il faut toutefois souligner que la plupart des prélèvements sanguins peuvent maintenant se faire par micro-méthode en utilisant le bout d'un doigt, d'un orteil ou le talon.

Figure 5-10. Photo 1. Le filet forme un hamac et l'enfant est libre de ses mouvements. (Courtoisie de l'Hôpital Maisonneuve-Rosemont.)

Photo 2. Les soins peuvent être donnés sans enlever le filet. Remarquer le coussinet sous la tête du bébé. (Courtoisie de l'Hôpital Maisonneuve-Rosemont.)

Médicaments. Administrer des médicaments à un enfant représente une grande responsabilité. On doit faire preuve d'une précision extrême en mesurant la dose et en l'administrant. En effet, la dose varie en fonction de l'âge, du poids et de la taille de l'enfant; l'infirmière ne peut se fier à une posologie de base comme dans le cas d'un adulte. Et comme la dose est relativement faible, une erreur insignifiante concernant la quantité du médicament représente une erreur plus grave que chez l'adulte.

Chaque hôpital a sa propre méthode pour identifier les patients: cette identification obligatoire s'avère plus difficile à faire dans le cas des enfants. Le nourrisson ne peut pas donner son nom; quant au jeune enfant il ne donnera que son surnom ou son prénom. L'infirmière doit donc bien identifier un enfant avant de lui administrer quelque médicament que ce soit. La plupart des hôpitaux utilisent des bracelets où le nom de l'enfant est inscrit; on le marque également à la tête du lit. On peut effectuer une vérification supplémentaire si l'enfant n'est pas dans son lit en lui demandant de dire son nom; toutefois il est préférable de demander « Comment t'appelles-tu? » plutôt que « C'est toi, Alice Leblanc? ». Ensuite on vérifie le nom de l'enfant avec le nom sur la carte de médicament comme on le fait chez l'adulte.

L'infirmière doit donner les médicaments de manière à favoriser ses relations avec le petit. Il est inutile de dire à un enfant qu'un remède a bon goût si ce n'est pas le cas, c'est le plus sûr moyen de perdre sa confiance.

L'infirmière doit être très vigilante lorsqu'elle administre un médicament à un enfant, de façon à reconnaître assez tôt les effets secondaires ou les signes d'intoxication.

Dosage. Les compagnies pharmaceutiques préparent certains de leurs médicaments selon des formules qui conviennent aux adultes. Les doses pour enfants se calculent en termes de fraction par rapport à la dose adulte et sont basées, soit sur l'âge, soit sur le poids de l'enfant. Même si c'est le médecin qui prescrit la médication, l'infirmière doit être au courant de la relation qui existe entre la dose adulte habituelle et la dose pour enfants.

Les doses basées sur le poids de l'enfant (règle de Clark) donnent les résultats les plus précis. Toutefois, certains médecins emploient une méthode plus moderne pour déterminer le dosage: ils se basent sur la surface du corps parce qu'on croit que cette mesure est reliée plus étroitement au métabolisme de l'enfant que son poids. Même si ce n'est pas l'infirmière qui décide des doses à prescrire, elle doit connaître la posologie habituelle. Si une quantité ordonnée lui semble trop forte, elle doit le faire remarquer au médecin. L'infirmière doit connaître les effets secondaires des médicaments et surveiller leur apparition possible chez l'enfant. Souvent l'enfant ne se plaint pas et il risque de s'intoxiquer.

Administration orale. Les bébés acceptent généralement les médicaments administrés par voie orale, du moment qu'ils peuvent l'avaler tout de suite. Le nourrisson portera un bavoir à cet effet et on lui donnera lentement le médicament, à l'aide d'un compte-gouttes ou d'un petit verre; on assoira le bébé ou on lui soutiendra la tête et les épaules, si la position assise est contre-indiquée, et ceci afin qu'il ne s'étouffe pas. Il est recommandé

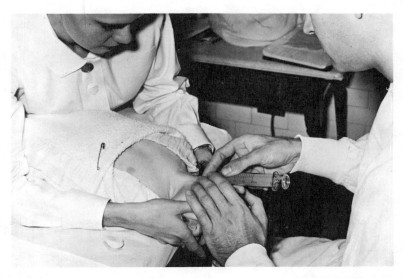

Figure 5-11. Méthode pour le prélèvement sanguin à la jugulaire. L'enfant est momifié.

de donner au nourrisson une tétine ou un biberon après la prise des médicaments afin de s'assurer qu'il avalera toute la dose. L'enfant plus âgé peut refuser de prendre son médicament parce qu'il n'en aime pas le goût ou parce qu'il est malheureux à l'hôpital.

Plusieurs solutions s'offrent à l'infirmière qui veut obtenir la coopération de l'enfant et elle doit essayer de trouver le meilleur moyen pour qu'il accepte son médicament. Si l'infirmière se montre douce, bienveillante mais ferme, et si elle encourage l'enfant à collaborer, le petit malade sera conditionné à le faire, spécialement s'il reçoit toujours des félicitations immédiatement après son acceptation. Par son attitude, l'infirmière doit faire comprendre à l'enfant, sans le supplier ni l'enjôler, qu'il doit prendre son médicament. D'ailleurs l'exemple donné par les autres enfants incite souvent l'enfant récalcitrant à prendre ses médicaments.

Pour aider l'enfant plus vieux à accepter ses médicaments, on peut lui faire choisir, lorsque c'est possible, de les prendre en suspension ou en comprimés et le laisser décider du breuvage qu'il boira immédiatement après l'ingestion de ses médicament. Pour masquer le goût d'un médicament, on peut le diluer dans du sirop de cerises ou du miel. On peut également broyer les comprimés et les mêler au sirop avant de les donner aux enfants qui pourraient éprouver quelques difficultés à avaler des médicaments un peu trop volumineux. Mais, en général, on doit s'abstenir de mêler les médicaments à du lait ou à des aliments, à moins d'une ordonnance à cet effet.

Un médicament à prendre par voie buccale peut s'administrer à l'aide d'une cuiller à thé, d'un compte-gouttes, ou d'un petit verre à médicament en plastique: l'enfant peut aussi le boire à l'aide de pailles multicolores. L'atti-

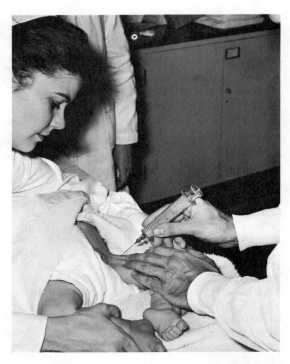

Figure 5-12. Prélèvement sanguin à la veine fémorale. L'infirmière maintient les cuisses de l'enfant en abduction.

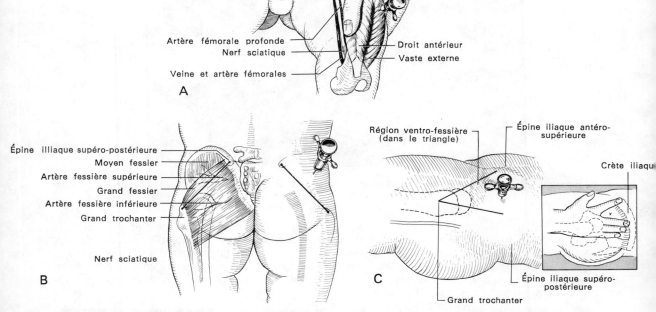

Figure 5-13. Les injections intramusculaires peuvent être données à différents endroits selon l'âge et la grosseur de l'enfant, selon l'état de la masse musculaire et la sorte de médicament utilisée. *A)* Le vaste externe: bien développé à la naissance, il ne contient pas de nerf ou de vaisseau important; utilisé chez le très jeune enfant. *B)* Chez l'enfant qui marche depuis un an, le muscle fessier est suffisamment développé pour qu'on l'utilise comme point d'injection. *C)* La région ventro-fessière facilement accessible et ne contenant pas de nerfs ou de vaisseaux importants est de plus en plus recommandée pour les injections chez l'enfant. (Extrait de P.A. Brandt, M.E. Smith, S.S. Ashburn et J. Graves, IM Injections in children, *Am. J. Nursing,* 72:1402, août 1972.)

tude de l'infirmière face au médicament se doit d'être positive, sinon l'enfant adoptera facilement la même attitude négative, telle que dégoût, réticence...

Si, malgré toutes les mesures de soin, l'enfant continue à refuser ses médicaments, il faut en discuter avec les membres de l'équipe de santé. Il peut être plus bénéfique pour l'enfant de ne pas recevoir cette médication et d'être moins tendu. L'infirmière ne doit jamais forcer un enfant à prendre un médicament, en lui ouvrant la bouche ou en lui pinçant le nez, parce que l'enfant peut aspirer le liquide. De plus, l'enfant la percevrait comme hostile et punitive et pourrait difficilement maintenir une relation de confiance avec elle.

Dans le cas d'un médicament vomi aussitôt après l'absorption, le médecin doit être averti.

Celui-ci peut répéter par la suite la dose prescrite. Pour éviter les vomissements de médicaments, il est préférable de les administrer en dehors des heures de repas, lorsque c'est possible. D'un autre côté, certains médicaments, tels les enzymes digestives, doivent être administrés au moment du repas. Lorsque l'enfant peut avaler une pilule, il est préférable de placer cette dernière à l'arrière de la langue et de fournir au petit de l'eau ou un jus pour faciliter la déglutition. L'infirmière ne doit pas oublier de féliciter l'enfant qui offre sa collaboration.

Injections intramusculaires. La première injection intramusculaire est importante parce qu'elle détermine l'attitude de l'enfant envers les injections à venir. La technique d'administration est la même que pour les adultes. Si l'enfant est assez vieux pour comprendre, on doit lui expliquer le procédé. On doit aussi permettre aux enfants de tout âge d'exprimer leurs craintes et leur agressivité face aux injections.

Avant de donner une injection, l'infirmière doit établir une relation de confiance avec l'enfant, lui expliquer ce qu'elle va faire et comment il peut collaborer, puis ensuite procéder rapidement, mais avec douceur. La présence d'une autre infirmière peut se révéler utile ou plus sûre dans la majorité des cas. Une façon d'aider l'enfant est de distraire son attention pendant l'injection, par exemple, en lui faisant tenir la main d'une infirmière et en la serrant très fort quand l'aiguille pénètre, ou en lui faisant pointer les orteils vers l'intérieur: les muscles fessiers se relâchant, l'injection est moins douloureuse.

L'endroit idéal pour les injections intramusculaires est encore un sujet controversé dans plusieurs hôpitaux. Le quadrant supéro-externe de la fesse, longtemps préféré à tout autre, est abandonné progressivement à cause des accidents très graves qui peuvent se produire. Le muscle fessier est peu développé chez le petit enfant et le quadriceps fémoral offre une surface beaucoup plus sûre. On recommande d'employer la partie latérale ou antérieure de la cuisse, au tiers moyen entre les articulations du genou et de la hanche. Lorsque c'est possible, on essaie d'alterner les lieux d'injection.

L'infirmière, peu sûre d'elle-même quand elle arrive en pédiatrie, ne doit jamais se risquer à donner une injection intra-musculaire en l'absence de son professeur ou d'une infirmière autorisée. Après le traitement, il est essentiel de prendre l'enfant, de l'amuser pour éviter l'association unique: traitement-douleur. Si l'enfant n'a pas coopéré, l'infirmière ne doit pas montrer sa désapprobation, mais le prendre afin de le réconforter ou lui donner un jouet. À un enfant plus âgé, on peut permettre de choisir l'endroit de l'injection parmi ceux proposés par l'infirmière et de nettoyer lui-même la région avec un tampon alcoolisé. Permettre à tout enfant de jouer avec des seringues et des poupées aide à diminuer la peur de l'inconnu.

Injections intraveineuses. Dans notre contexte actuel, plusieurs institutions suivent la politique suivante quant aux injections intraveineuses. L'infirmière pédiatrique peut prélever du sang par ponction veineuse, installer des solutés intraveineux et ajouter des médicaments aux solutés déjà en place. Cette très lourde responsabilité ne doit jamais être prise à la légère. L'infirmière protège l'enfant et se protège elle-même en s'enquérant d'abord de la politique de l'hôpital à ce sujet, en exigeant du médecin des prescriptions claires et précises et en s'assurant qu'elle peut obtenir de l'aide médicale si le besoin s'en fait sentir.

Administration rectale. On administre les médicaments par le rectum de la même manière qu'un lavement; ceux-ci sont mélangés à un peu d'eau ou un peu d'amidon et injectés très lentement pour que le tout soit bien retenu. Certains médicaments pour administration rectale nous parviennent sous forme de suppositoires. L'enfant acceptera ce procédé plus facilement si l'infirmière le compare à la prise de température rectale à laquelle il peut être habitué. Il est important de tenir fermement les fesses de l'enfant pendant quelques minutes après l'insertion du suppositoire afin d'éviter son éjection.

Soin du client pédiatrique

Établir un plan de soins pour l'enfant, en tenant compte de ses composantes familiales et culturelles, constitue la responsabilité de l'équipe de soins. Pour implanter le plan de soins et le modifier selon l'évolution de l'enfant, les infirmières doivent connaître le nursing pédiatrique, les principes de la croissance et du développement, la maladie de l'enfant et le plan de traitement médical, *la méthode de solution de problèmes* ainsi que la *démarche nursing,* enfin, les techniques d'observation de l'enfant et les aspects pertinents à observer. Dans ce chapitre, nous ne discuterons que de l'observation de l'enfant et des mesures de sécurité à l'hôpital.

Observation de l'enfant. Il est indispensable que, dans son travail, l'infirmière pédiatrique applique les procédés d'une observation adéquate et systématique. Avec un entraînement approprié, un bon observateur peut découvrir le langage non-verbal (mimiques, gestes, actions) des enfants, leur rythme d'activités et les particularités de leur expression verbale.

Chaque observateur développe son style de notation et de description, toutefois la connaissance de la technique d'observation demeure utile.

L'observation la plus pertinente est obtenue lorsque l'enfant est inconscient d'être observé pendant qu'il est en train de jouer. L'observateur doit se garder d'intervenir et tenter de se faire oublier le plus possible. Il doit tenter de saisir l'enfant dans sa globalité, noter à la fois tous ses gestes, ses expressions et ses réactions. L'infirmière observatrice doit s'astreindre à rédiger ses séquences d'observation dans un style non critique et sans porter de jugement. Elle ne posera un jugement sur le comportement de l'enfant qu'après plusieurs séances d'observation. De bonnes observations systématiques permettent de saisir des éléments qui passeraient totalement inaperçus autrement.

Il existe trois niveaux d'observation:

1) Au premier niveau, l'infirmière note ce que l'enfant fait, principalement ses activités motrices et de manipulation.

2) L'infirmière note ensuite l'intérêt que l'enfant porte à ce qu'il fait ou a fait. Elle doit observer l'ensemble de la situation et noter l'expression faciale de l'enfant, son ton de voix, son comportement avec les autres.

3) L'infirmière doit en troisième étape, tenter d'interpréter ce qu'elle a observé. L'observateur doit être très habile et compétent en ce qui concerne la croissance et le développement afin de pouvoir fournir des interprétations justes et utiles. Il faut se rappeler le danger d'interpréter le comportement de l'enfant à partir d'une seule séance d'observation.

L'infirmière qui développe sa capacité d'observation découvre des points-clés chez l'enfant, des éléments qui expliquent certains comportements difficiles et une connaissance plus profonde de l'enfant.

Mesures de sécurité

Les accidents sont la première cause de décès chez les enfants de tout âge, à partir de l'âge d'un an. Il est donc essentiel que l'hôpital insiste sur les mesures de sécurité, pour protéger l'enfant et pour éduquer les parents. La discussion qui suit porte surtout sur les accidents à l'hôpital, quoique certains d'entre eux puissent se produire à la maison.

Plusieurs mesures de sécurité concernent la construction et l'aménagement de l'édifice; elles sont ordinairement hors du contrôle des infirmières. Voici donc quelques-unes des mesures de sécurité qu'on devrait respecter:

1) Escaliers larges à l'épreuve du feu.

2) Fenêtres protégées par des grilles fermées à clé et placées de telle sorte que l'aération puisse se faire tout en n'exposant pas les enfants aux courants d'air.

3) Des barrières à l'entrée des salles de jeu, placées de telle sorte que les tout-petits ne puissent les ouvrir ou se blesser les doigts entre la porte et le cadrage.

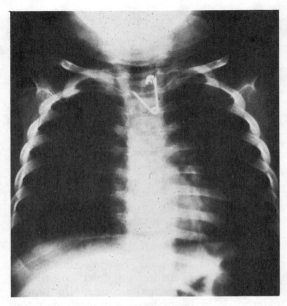

Toujours fermer les épingles à couches et ne jamais les laisser à la portée des enfants.

Figure 5-14. Mesures de sécurité. (Courtoisie de l'Hôpital Sainte-Justine, Montréal.)

Les mesures suivantes de sécurité sont directement sous le contrôle de l'infirmière:

1) Veiller à ce que les ridelles de la couchette soient toujours en bon état et levées lorsque l'enfant est au lit. Garder une main sur l'enfant quand on lui donne des soins et que les ridelles sont baissées, ceci afin de prévenir toute chute.

2) Lorsqu'on utilise des contraintes, veiller à ce qu'elles n'occasionnent ni constriction ni arrêt circulatoire. Un danger qui guette l'enfant vêtu d'un gilet de protection est l'étranglement dû au glissement de la contrainte, du tronc autour du cou de l'enfant.

3) Mettre sous clé tous les médicaments et ne jamais en laisser traîner sur les tables de nuit.

4) Garder les solutés et l'équipement médical hors de la portée des enfants.

5) Comme les bébés portent tous les petits objets à leur bouche, fermer les épingles de sûreté dès qu'elles ont été détachées des vêtements et les placer hors de la portée des jeunes enfants.

6) Veiller à ce que les jouets aient des coins arrondis et non pointus, à ce qu'ils ne soient pas peints avec une peinture à base de plomb, qu'ils ne contiennent pas de petites parties détachables que les enfants pourraient avaler ou aspirer. Ne jamais laisser traîner sur

le plancher des jouets qui pourraient entraîner la chute d'un enfant ou d'une infirmière portant un petit dans ses bras.

7) Empêcher les bébés et les jeunes enfants de jouer avec les abaisse-langue et les tiges montées, sauf sous surveillance attentive.

8) Couvrir les éventails et les prises de courant qui ne sont pas utilisés et empêcher les enfants d'approcher de ceux qui sont en service.

9) Appliquer les techniques d'isolement à tous les malades atteints de maladies transmissibles et installer l'équipement nécessaire au brossage et au lavage des mains. Certaines unités de pédiatrie utilisent les rayons ultraviolets pour réduire le nombre de micro-organismes dans l'air. L'infirmière doit pouvoir détecter les maladies infectieuses le plus rapidement possible chez les enfants ou chez elle.

10) Ne jamais laisser un jeune bébé seul dans son lit avec son biberon dans la bouche, car il y a danger d'aspiration pouvant causer une maladie pulmonaire et même une mort subite. Ne jamais forcer le bébé à boire contre son gré.

11) Lors de l'administration de médicaments, se faire aider d'une autre infirmière pour retenir doucement l'enfant dans le cas où celui-ci ne coopérerait pas. Les médicaments huileux ne devraient jamais se donner oralement à cause du danger d'aspiration.

12) L'eau chaude des bouillottes ne doit pas dépasser 46°C et ces sacs doivent toujours être étanches et couverts d'un tissu avant d'être déposés près de l'enfant.

13) Vérifier si l'extrémité du thermomètre n'est pas fendillée. Tenir fermement le thermomètre rectal lors de la prise de température de façon à ce qu'il ne bouge pas et que l'enfant ne soit pas blessé s'il remue.

À la sortie de l'hôpital

Le médecin, l'infirmière ou le psychiatre attachés à l'équipe de santé, doivent prévenir les parents que l'enfant pourra présenter certains troubles de comportement à son retour à la maison. Il peut exiger plus d'attention et d'affection qu'auparavant, mais par contre, il est aussi possible qu'il rejette les adultes, même sa mère et se montre indépendant. Le jeune enfant peut montrer son besoin de confort en suçant son pouce ou en régressant vers un stade qu'il avait dépassé. La mère doit comprendre ce comportement et prouver constamment à l'enfant qu'elle l'aime toujours. Elle rétablira ainsi les relations normales entre elle et son enfant.

Le passage de l'unité de pédiatrie à la maison requiert des parents une connaissance des soins à donner au petit convalescent, surtout si la mère n'était pas présente au moment de l'hospitalisation. La mère est souvent anxieuse et nerveuse le jour où son enfant quitte l'hôpital et il est préférable de ne pas attendre cette journée pour la mettre au courant des soins que nécessitera l'enfant. Si l'enseignement n'a pu être donné tout au long de l'hospitalisation, il est recommandable alors de remettre à la mère des instructions écrites. Parmi les explications importantes à donner se trouvent celles de l'utilisation des appareils spécifiques pour le soin de l'enfant à la maison et celles concernant les médicaments à administrer. De plus, il est nécessaire de réviser les ordonnances du médecin, fixer l'heure et le jour du prochain rendez-vous avec un membre de l'équipe de santé, d'informer la mère des nouvelles habitudes de l'enfant (par exemple, boire dans une tasse ou manger avec une cuiller) et des nouveaux développements de son activité musculaire. Ainsi, il est important que la mère sache que son bébé peut maintenant se retourner seul, afin d'éviter une chute. Ces derniers renseignements amèneront la mère à modifier sa façon de voir son enfant et aussi la manière de s'en occuper.

Le rôle de l'infirmière dans le cas d'un enfant souffrant d'une maladie chronique ou terminale

Nous avons étudié précédemment quel rôle devait jouer l'infirmière durant l'hospitalisation de l'enfant. L'anxiété des parents est déjà grande lorsque leur enfant souffre d'une maladie à court terme, mais elle est habituellement non comparable à celle des parents dont l'enfant souffre d'une maladie chronique ou terminale.

Soin de l'enfant atteint d'une maladie chronique

La paralysie cérébrale, la poliomyélite, le diabète, la mucuviscidose sont quelques-unes des maladies chroniques dont un enfant peut souffrir. Ces longues maladies qui affligent l'enfant tout au cours de son enfance affectent nécessairement son développement physique et émotif. Ayant continuellement besoin de soins et d'attention, l'enfant a d'énormes difficultés à atteindre sa maturité et son indépendance émotive. Si les parents ne saisissent pas ce problème, il est fort probable que l'enfant développera une personnalité infantile.

Il ne parviendra pas à avoir confiance dans ses capacités et se liera difficilement avec des compagnons de son âge.

Les infirmières doivent faire comprendre aux parents qu'il est essentiel que leur petit malade, malgré son handicap, vive des expériences normales pour un enfant et qu'il acquière ainsi une attitude positive et saine envers la vie afin de devenir un adulte responsable. Pour accomplir ceci, les parents doivent connaître la nature, les traitements et les limites de la maladie; ils sauront alors ce qu'ils peuvent exiger de l'enfant et ce qui outrepasse ses possibilités.

C'est seulement en exerçant ses capacités que l'enfant deviendra sûr de lui et obtiendra un sentiment de satisfaction personnelle. On doit également expliquer aux parents que leurs propres réactions, telle une inquiétude excessive vis-à-vis de la santé de l'enfant, peuvent nuire à l'adaptation de celui-ci. Au contraire, leur attitude positive aidera l'enfant à accepter ses limites et à développer ses capacités.

L'infirmière et l'enfant en phase terminale

Le phénomène de la mort représente un événement très difficile à affronter pour la plupart des gens et même pour le personnel médical et infirmier. Il n'en est que plus illusoire d'attendre de la jeune infirmière qu'elle vienne en aide au petit mourant et à ses parents. Ce ne sont pas des cours théoriques et neutres sur ce qu'elle devrait faire dans une telle circonstance qui auront un impact sur son comportement, alors qu'elle sera émotivement concernée par la situation. C'est pourquoi notre discussion portera d'abord sur la conception de la mort elle-même. Puis, nous nous demanderons quelle est la perception de l'infirmière; ce que peut faire le médecin dans une telle situation; comment les parents envisagent cette mort; et, enfin, quel est le rôle de l'infirmière à ce moment-là.

La perception de la mort. La mort est une expérience inévitable et universelle. Dans la culture occidentale on met l'accent sur la vie, la jeunesse, et on refuse souvent de penser à la mort.

En théorie, la mort est considérée comme un événement naturel et qui peut être positif dans le cas où il soulage un patient de souffrances intolérables. Pour ceux qui ont certaines convictions religieuses, la mort s'interprète comme un signe de la volonté de Dieu et le commencement d'une vie nouvelle.

Même si l'infirmière rencontre fréquemment la mort, son anxiété demeure présente malgré sa connaissance des causes fréquentes de celle-ci et son orientation religieuse ou profane. La peur de la mort est un des sentiments les plus ancrés et les plus profonds chez l'être humain. Dans plusieurs hôpitaux, on a tendance à isoler les mourants, qu'ils soient conscients ou non, alors qu'ils auraient tant besoin de réconfort et d'une présence. On justifie cette pratique en invoquant le repos du malade et de sa famille, mais n'est-ce pas tout simplement un mécanisme de défense de la part du personnel qui n'accepte pas de faire face à la mort? Pour améliorer les soins, il est essentiel de comprendre ce que signifie la mort pour l'être humain, que ce soit l'infirmière, le médecin, les parents, ou l'enfant.

Comment l'infirmière perçoit la mort. Cette perception dépend évidemment de plusieurs facteurs: sa culture, son âge, ses idées religieuses, son éducation, son équilibre personnel, sa conception de la vie. Elle peut ne pas encore avoir connu l'expérience de la mort, d'où une réaction violente lorsqu'un petit enfant est impliqué dans cette tragédie inéluctable. La situation est encore plus pénible pour elle, si l'âge de l'enfant mourant n'est pas très éloigné du sien ou de celui de ses frères et sœurs. Voici quelques-unes des réactions qu'une jeune infirmière peut présenter:

« Je fus saisie de panique. Je me sentais impuissante devant cette situation ».

« Je priais pour que Marie ne meure pas pendant que j'étais seule avec elle dans la chambre. J'aurais voulu me sauver ».

« Sylvain était un si beau petit garçon. Je pleurais chaque soir après ma journée de travail auprès de lui ».

« Après la mort de Louise, je me demandais si je n'aurais pas pu faire plus pour elle; je me demandais si je pourrais surmonter un tel drame dans le cas où mon enfant y était impliqué; je me demandais même si je voulais avoir des enfants puisque de telles choses pouvaient se produire ».

Chaque individu est influencé par des personnes ou des événements marquants de son passé. L'étudiante-infirmière et même l'infirmière graduée n'échappent pas à cette règle. Leur première rencontre avec la mort peut être faite de peur, mêlée à un fort sentiment d'impuissance. *Il est important que l'infirmière soit consciente de ses propres sentiments et réactions en face de la mort; elle doit arriver à les contrôler de façon à pouvoir accorder les soins appropriés au petit mourant et le réconfort nécessaire à ses parents.* Parce que l'objectif usuel de sa carrière est de préserver la vie, une infirmière expérimentée peut éprouver beaucoup de difficultés en soignant un enfant dont la mort est imminente. Ce fait, dû à des sentiments possibles de négation de la mort, peut amener l'infirmière, tout comme les autres membres de l'équipe de santé, à se retirer dans une tour d'ivoire et à refuser de s'arrêter au phénomène de la mort. À ce moment-là, ceux qui souffrent de cette froideur sont le patient et ses parents.

La première démarche de l'infirmière doit consister en une prise de conscience de ses croyances à l'égard de la mort, de ses sentiments envers les patients qui vont mourir. Une collègue, un conseiller religieux, un psychiatre ou un autre membre de l'équipe de santé peuvent aider l'infirmière dans sa recherche; cette démarche est pénible, mais est essentielle à son développement professionnel et personnel. L'infirmière doit savoir qu'elle peut recevoir de l'aide et qu'elle doit apprendre à contrôler ses sentiments pour dispenser des soins adéquats aux malades mourants. C'est après cet effort seulement qu'elle saura procurer à l'enfant et à ses parents le soutien moral dont ils ont besoin.

L'infirmière doit savoir qu'en soignant intensivement un enfant mourant, elle pénètre peu à peu dans l'intimité des parents qui partagent avec elle leurs problèmes et leur peine. Si l'infirmière ne possède pas un bon équilibre émotif, elle peut devenir déprimée ou revivre ses propres chagrins; elle ne peut plus alors être d'aucun support, ni pour l'enfant, ni pour les parents.

Communiquer avec l'enfant mourant et ses parents peut être difficile, sinon pénible. L'enfant peut être émacié ou défiguré, ses parents peuvent être exigeants ou hostiles. Certains enfants ou parents sont tellement pitoyables que l'infirmière est plus encline à les plaindre qu'à les aider.

La pierre angulaire du soin à l'enfant mourant est la stabilité émotive de l'infirmière liée à une grande capacité d'empathie.

Ce que le médecin peut faire

La mort chez une personne âgée peut être bienvenue pour le patient et sa famille parce qu'elle met fin à la douleur et à l'incapacité. La famille se console, sachant que le malade a eu une longue vie, utile à la société; mais la mort d'un enfant semble inacceptable pour les médecins et tout le personnel médical. La mort d'un enfant, causée par un accident d'automobile ou par une anomalie congénitale, peut être instantanée; par contre, la mort causée par une leucémie ou par une tumeur cérébrale maligne est lente à venir et impose une tension inévitable, non seulement à la famille, mais aussi à toute l'équipe de santé.

Maintenir la vie tant qu'il le peut: tel est le rôle du médecin. On écrit beaucoup actuellement sur le problème d'affirmer avec certitude qu'un patient est décédé. Il n'est pas question de discuter, dans ce livre, de cet aspect précis; toutefois, les infirmières doivent être au courant des recherches et de l'exploration philosophique qui se font actuellement dans ce domaine.

En plus de déterminer le traitement médical, le médecin doit décider, avec les autres membres de l'équipe de santé, s'il doit avertir les parents et l'enfant de la gravité de la situation. Certains médecins sont en faveur de ce geste considérant le droit des parents de connaître l'état exact de leur petit. Il peut expliquer la maladie, l'impossibilité actuelle de la guérir, tout en insistant sur le fait que la douleur et la souffrance seront épargnées à l'enfant autant qu'il sera possible de le faire. Même quand on dit la vérité à la famille, il faut lui laisser un petit rayon d'espoir. Il y a eu assez de rémissions inexpliquées dans le passé pour justifier cette attitude. Habituellement les parents demandent: « Combien de temps vivra-t-il? » ou « Pourra-t-il retourner à l'école? » Même si les réponses sont difficiles à donner, le médecin doit répondre honnêtement à toutes ces questions.

L'aide d'un conseiller religieux peut être précieuse dans ces moments-là: avec le consentement des parents, il peut assister aux discussions concernant la maladie de l'enfant. Le médecin et le personnel infirmier savent combien ce conseiller peut être utile s'il a la confiance des parents.

Si un enfant plus âgé demande: « Est-ce que je vais mourir? » que faut-il répondre? Si l'enfant est très stable et mature, certains médecins répondront: « Oui, mais nous ne sommes pas certains du moment où cela va arriver. » Souvent l'enfant acceptera mieux cette assertion qu'une réponse évasive. Toutefois, l'enfant est ordinairement plus enclin à demander si ses symptômes disparaîtront et s'il guérira. Là encore, l'honnêteté est de rigueur.

Par contre, certains médecins croient que la certitude de la mort accroît l'anxiété des parents et de l'enfant, leur enlevant tout espoir. En réalité, il est impossible de donner une solution générale pour toutes les familles et, dans certaines circonstances, il est même difficile de déceler les besoins exacts d'une famille en particulier.

Réactions des parents dont l'enfant est en phase terminale

Peu d'expériences humaines apportent avec elles plus de souffrances pour les parents que la mort de leur enfant. Si on leur dit que leur petit est condamné, ils ont tendance à se sentir impuissants, pris dans un piège. Ils peuvent réagir de différentes façons, soit d'une manière stoïque, soit avec peur ou colère. Ils peuvent tout simplement nier la situation pénible ou régresser de façon dramatique.

Les infirmières considèrent que les parents sont « bons » si, connaissant le pronostic, ils acceptent le fait de la mort, ne causent pas d'ennui au personnel et soutiennent leur enfant du mieux qu'ils peuvent. Si ces parents croient en Dieu, ils pensent que le destin de leur enfant est entre ses mains. Ils se trouvent ainsi soulagés de leur propre culpabilité et de leurs responsabilités personnelles.

Dans le cas où les parents sont pris de panique, pleurent ou sont exigeants, le travail des infirmières auprès de l'enfant est compliqué et difficile à accomplir. De tels parents risquent d'être détestés et évités à un moment où ils sont seuls et effrayés. D'autres parents semblent dépourvus de toute émotion après avoir appris la terrible nouvelle. Ils parlent de la mort d'une façon détendue. Il semble qu'il y ait alors dissociation entre l'émotion, l'esprit et le corps.

Il y a des parents qui, pour apaiser leurs sentiments de culpabilité, accordent à l'enfant tout ce qu'il désire. Ils croient qu'en étant tolérants, ils éviteront toute frustration à l'enfant et lui procureront un milieu agréable pour ces derniers jours. Une telle attitude stimule l'enfant à régresser et à exiger toujours plus. Même les parents les plus aimants réagissent avec hostilité face à ce changement chez l'enfant. Et c'est un cercle vicieux qui s'installe: hostilité des parents, culpabilité consécutive, gâteries suivies de demandes plus exigeantes de l'enfant, fatigue et découragement des parents, etc. L'enfant peut finalement souffrir de l'hostilité qu'il engendre chez ses parents, plutôt que de profiter de leur tolérance. Son bonheur aurait été mieux préservé par une saine discipline.

Il se peut que les familles, connaissant la situation, demandent de célébrer Noël ou un anniversaire de naissance à l'avance pour l'enfant mourant. Il serait important de faire comprendre à ces parents les besoins réels de l'enfant et les raisons de leur désir. De plus, ils doivent saisir que l'enfant peut se demander la raison pour laquelle on fait toutes ces célébrations si tôt et en être effrayé. D'ailleurs, il peut être encore en vie à la date réelle de ces événements.

Si on a tout tenté du côté médical, le médecin peut demander aux parents s'ils préfèrent ramener l'enfant chez lui pour le peu de temps qui lui reste. Cette situation dépend, entre autre, de la présence d'autres enfants à la maison, de la capacité que la mère a d'en prendre soin, des ressources financières de la famille et du logis qu'elle habite. Si le petit quitte l'hôpital, l'aide des membres de l'équipe de santé communautaire, telle l'infirmière en santé communautaire, peut se révéler très utile et réconfortante.

La signification de la mort pour l'enfant

En vieillissant, l'enfant change sa façon de se percevoir et d'envisager le monde dans lequel il vit. Il modifie aussi ses conceptions sur la vie et la mort. Il est inutile d'espérer que l'enfant ne vienne jamais en contact avec le phénomène de la mort. La meilleure attitude pour les parents est d'agir naturellement, de répondre aux questions de l'enfant et de le familiariser petit à petit avec cet aspect de la vie.

Pour un enfant à la période préscolaire, l'idée de la mort, comme fait physique, est au-dessus de son niveau de compréhension. Une personne morte, pour un petit enfant, est partie en voyage et reviendra éventuellement. Même si elle ne bouge pas, elle vit encore. En général, la mort ne fait pas peur à un très jeune enfant et, s'il est malade, ce sont des symptômes, tels que saignements, qui l'effraient. Ce qui lui fait peur, lorsque quelqu'un qu'il aime meurt, c'est l'angoisse de se retrouver seul, privé de sa source de sécurité et d'affection. Souvent, un jeune enfant a sa première expérience de la mort lorsque son animal favori meurt et ne revient pas. Mais ordinairement, un autre animal est donné à l'enfant, et la vie continue comme avant. Toutefois, une partie de cet apprentissage douloureux demeure, même si le comportement du petit n'est pas changé. À l'âge de cinq ou six ans, l'enfant commence à accepter le fait de la mort, mais il croit qu'elle est un processus graduel et que la personne revient, puis décède de nouveau. L'enfant pourra atteindre plus ou moins rapidement ce stade de compréhension qui constitue un palier vers une compréhension plus raisonnable du phénomène de la mort.

Les enfants d'âge scolaire personnalisent la mort: ils la voient comme une personne qui emmène les vivants avec elle, surtout quand il fait noir et qu'ils ont été «méchants». Certains d'entre eux croient que la mort est comme la personne morte qui repose dans un cercueil. Entre six et neuf ans, ils croient en général que la mort est invisible si ce n'est pour les êtres qu'elle emporte.

Vers neuf ou dix ans, les enfants prennent conscience que la mort est le point final de la vie du corps, qu'elle est inévitable et qu'éventuellement chaque être vivant doit mourir. La conception de la mort chez les adolescents est plus variée que chez les enfants, car elle dépend de certains facteurs, tels que les expériences passées, le degré de croyance à une religion, les différences culturelles et la perception de l'avenir.

La façon dont un enfant entrevoit la mort dépend donc de son degré de développement, mais également des expériences de la mort qu'il a connues dans le passé et surtout dans sa propre famille. Si la mort frappe une sœur ou un frère, il lui reste toujours la protection de ses parents, quoique ceux-ci modifieront leur comportement à son égard après le décès de l'autre enfant et lui donneront plus ou moins d'affection. L'enfant plus vieux, dans cette situation, peut se dire « ceci peut m'arriver bientôt, peut-être demain ou la semaine prochaine ». Cette pensée traumatise les enfants de tout âge et, si celui qui est mort était près d'eux, ils peuvent se sentir coupables de ne pas l'avoir rendu assez heureux avant son départ.

Mais dans le cas où l'un des parents meurt, l'enfant traverse une véritable crise. Si la mère meurt lorsque l'enfant est très jeune, il aura peur parce qu'il est séparé d'elle. S'il est plus vieux, il comprend que désormais la vie ne sera plus jamais la même. Si son père meurt et que sa mère doive travailler à l'extérieur, il souffre non seulement de la perte de son père mais aussi de l'éloignement de sa mère. Il peut ressentir un sentiment de culpabilité à l'égard de la personne maintenant disparue en raison de l'hostilité ou de la jalousie qu'il a pu éprouver à son égard avant sa mort. Il peut même s'en vouloir d'avoir désiré jusqu'à un certain point sa disparition et qu'elle se soit justement réalisée.

Lors du décès d'un membre de la famille, on peut éviter des angoisses à l'enfant en lui expliquant honnêtement ce qui se passe. La décision au sujet de sa présence au service funèbre dépend de son âge, des convictions religieuses de la famille et du degré d'anxiété que l'enfant démontre. Les adultes doivent, en général, se montrer discrets quant à l'expression de leur chagrin, afin de ne pas épouvanter l'enfant, mais ils ne doivent pas tenter de dissimuler toute peine. On peut demander à l'enfant de petits services pour qu'il ait l'impression d'aider sa famille dans ces circonstances difficiles. Les enfants expriment leur peine d'une manière différente de celle des adultes. Ils peuvent jouer sans arrêt, ce qui est mal jugé par les adultes, ou se refermer sur eux-mêmes. Il est cruel de réprimander un enfant pour son comportement à ce moment-là: cela a seulement pour effet d'augmenter son sentiment de culpabilité et son insécurité.

En résumé, disons que l'enfant assez vieux pour savoir ce que signifie sa maladie, percevra la mort en fonction de son degré de maturité et de ses expériences passées. Quant à savoir si on doit avertir un enfant de son état, les opinions varient. En fait, ce sont les parents, aidés du médecin et de l'infirmière, qui décident à quel point renseigner leur enfant sur sa condition. Ce sont eux aussi qui décideront si l'enfant doit l'apprendre par un conseiller religieux, par le médecin ou par un ami. L'important pour l'infirmière est de connaître la ligne de conduite des parents et du médecin et d'offrir son aide et son support. Lorsqu'une décision est prise, tous les membres de l'équipe de santé doivent s'y conformer, de façon à offrir à l'enfant sécurité et constance.

Rôle de l'infirmière auprès du petit mourant et de ses parents

La société attribue une certaine valeur à une personne, en fonction de son âge, de sa classe sociale, de son apparence physique et de sa personnalité. Toutefois, un enfant au seuil de la vie renferme un énorme potentiel et peut être plus valorisé que la personne âgée qui « a vécu sa vie ». Il ne faut donc pas s'étonner qu'on mette sur pied toutes sortes de techniques de réanimation pour sauver la vie d'un enfant. Il ne faudrait pas être surpris non plus d'apprendre que certaines infirmières ne peuvent travailler en pédiatrie, car elles ne peuvent supporter la vue d'un enfant mourant. Celles-ci n'ont pas réussi à contrôler leurs émotions et ne sont alors d'aucune utilité auprès de l'enfant et de ses parents.

La mort d'un nourrisson et la mort d'un enfant atteint de leucémie sont différentes pour l'infirmière. En effet, le premier n'est pas conscient de ce qui lui arrive, alors que le second peut fort bien s'en rendre compte. Cette différence influence l'attitude des infirmières auprès de leur patient. C'est un art et un défi que de soigner un enfant dont la mort est inévitable et de représenter pour les parents une espèce de bouée de sauvetage. L'infirmière doit se rappeler que l'enfant mourant est encore vivant. Elle doit savoir agrémenter les derniers jours ou mois du petit, maintenir ses intérêts et l'aider à vivre aussi normalement que possible. Elle doit aussi se rappeler que les enfants se sentent en sécurité à l'intérieur d'une saine discipline. Au moment où l'enfant sent que son corps change et qu'il ne peut plus en dépendre, il faut qu'il puisse s'appuyer sur un entourage sûr et conséquent.

Autrefois, les infirmières ne se préoccupaient que des traitements physiques à accorder aux enfants mourants. Aujourd'hui, l'on reconnaît que les soins psychologiques sont tout aussi importants. Par exemple, l'infirmière fait face à un problème épineux avec les parents renfermés; les voyant assis et silencieux, elle peut les aborder ainsi: « Cette nouvelle doit vous troubler beaucoup ». À la suite d'une réponse affirmative, elle peut ajouter: « Pouvez-vous me dire ce que vous ressentez ». Si les parents peuvent discuter de leurs sentiments, ils seront plus en mesure de les assumer. À noter que si les parents refusent de parler, l'infirmière aura la délicatesse de les laisser à leur chagrin. La responsabilité de l'infirmière consiste à offrir son aide aux parents afin qu'ils sachent qu'ils ne sont pas seuls. La force de l'infirmière viendra du fait qu'elle partage le chagrin de la famille sans perdre tous ses moyens. Quand les parents répriment leurs sentiments, l'infirmière peut délicatement souligner que c'est très bien de pleurer. De tels parents ont besoin du soutien moral de l'infirmière qui peut leur expliquer que leur apparente absence de réaction est un mécanisme naturel de défense qui leur permet de continuer à fonctionner malgré les circonstances. Il ne faut cependant pas presser les parents de pleurer au risque de détruire le mécanisme de défense qu'ils utilisent pour ne pas flancher.

Une autre réaction qui ne doit pas surprendre l'infirmière est celle où les parents semblent ignorer l'enfant et parlent d'un deuil passé. Leur expérience présente ravive le souvenir de la précédente, et ceci est surtout vrai si le deuil n'a pas été accepté dans le passé. L'infirmière doit donc travailler sur les plans: passé et présent. Ce parent pourra porter le deuil de son enfant sans être obligé de se protéger contre d'anciens souvenirs.

Le chagrin des parents au chevet de leur enfant mourant est un spectacle pénible. L'infirmière doit comprendre la volonté des parents qui ne veulent pas quitter la chambre de leur enfant comme celle des parents qui ne se sentent pas capables d'y entrer. Elle doit leur permettre de donner certains soins de nursing au petit, s'ils le veulent, mais elle doit aussi les remplacer lorsqu'ils sont fatigués et surmenés. Pour dominer la situation, certains parents procurent au malade des soins attentifs ou s'agitent ici et là dans la chambre. Ils peuvent blâmer médecins et infirmières ou au contraire les vanter avec excès. L'infirmière ne doit pas se formaliser si la mère n'a pas les réactions qu'elle devrait normalement avoir. Le comportement de chaque parent reflète ses tentatives de prendre en mains ses propres sentiments et il faut les accepter ainsi.

Toujours dans le but d'aider les parents, l'infirmière doit leur fournir l'occasion d'exprimer leur colère et leurs craintes à quelqu'un qui saura y faire face sereinement. À mesure que les parents connaîtront l'infirmière, ils lui feront davantage confiance et lui livreront plus facilement leurs inquiétudes.

Les parents ont besoin de parler de leur enfant mourant, que ce soit à leur famille, à des amis, aux médecins ou aux infirmières. On doit leur permettre d'être bouleversé par ce problème afin qu'ils soient en mesure d'envisager le drame avec plus de réalisme. L'infirmière doit savoir qu'une aide préventive ou qu'une conversation au sujet du deuil futur peut aider les parents à s'adapter et à surmonter leur peine.

Les patients qui sont à l'article de la mort, adultes ou enfants, ont besoin de la présence des autres. Ils ont besoin d'avoir des gens sympathiques autour d'eux. C'est surtout le cas pour un enfant mourant dont la sécurité repose sur la proximité de ses parents et de son infirmière.

Connaissant l'état du malade, l'infirmière doit encourager les parents et amis à venir au chevet du petit. Mais un problème peut alors survenir: certains adultes sont si bouleversés par la vue de l'enfant, qu'ils se sentent incapables de revenir. L'enfant peut douter de leur franchise s'ils ont promis de revenir et qu'ils ne le font pas.

En réalité, si les visiteurs ne peuvent pas contrôler leur émotion devant l'enfant, il vaut mieux qu'ils quittent la chambre sinon ils risquent de l'effrayer. Les enfants mourants comme les enfants souffrant de maladie en phase aiguë sont vulnérables aux mêmes peurs. Par exemple, à cinq ans, l'enfant a peur d'être séparé de sa mère; jusqu'à neuf ans, il craint les mutilations de son corps. Plus l'enfant est vieux, plus il pose de questions au sujet de son état de santé. L'infirmière doit lui répondre et chercher à connaître la cause exacte de sa peine. Est-ce qu'il souffre ou a vu pleurer sa mère? À ce moment-là, elle pourrait lui apprendre que les parents sont malheureux quand leur enfant est malade et qu'il ne peut pas jouer.

On doit traiter l'enfant plus vieux comme un adulte qui a droit à ses opinions et qui peut exprimer ses volontés: que sa maîtresse d'école vienne le voir ou non, ou que son frère plus jeune puisse ou non prendre sa bicyclette durant son absence. Inutile de lui dire aussi qu'il paraît aller mieux quand il se sait très malade. L'honnêteté est aussi importante avec un enfant qu'avec un adulte.

L'enfant qui sent ou sait qu'il va mourir appréhende la venue de la nuit. C'est un défi pour l'infirmière que de lui faire trouver le sommeil nécessaire. Les veilleuses et le passage fréquent de l'infirmière aident l'enfant à se sentir en sécurité.

On doit essayer d'assurer la permanence du personnel auprès des enfants mourants, afin de compenser le sentiment de perte et d'abandon que ressentent leurs parents. Ils apprécient la présence de l'infirmière qu'ils connaissent et qui répond franchement à leurs questions et surtout avec qui ils peuvent communiquer pour recevoir des nouvelles du petit. Il est important que l'infirmière fasse preuve d'une attitude accueillante et chaleureuse à l'égard de la famille et des visiteurs. Il n'est pas question de fermer les rideaux ou de chuchoter dans la chambre de l'enfant, pas plus qu'on ne le ferait dans la chambre d'un adulte mourant.

On pourrait aussi prévoir un endroit retiré et confortable pour les parents désireux de se retrouver seuls à certains moments. L'infirmière qui pense à trouver une pièce de ce genre, prouve ainsi sa sympathie aux parents éprouvés. Sa présence auprès d'eux doit être discrète mais réconfortante dans des circonstances où les mots sont incapables de recouvrir l'ampleur du drame.

Si les parents et l'enfant ignorent le diagnostic, la situation de l'infirmière est plus délicate et plus exigeante puisque c'est elle qui porte tout le fardeau du problème, le médecin n'ayant pas un contact aussi fréquent avec la famille. Évidemment, dans le cas où l'enfant ne reste pas longtemps à l'hôpital et retourne chez lui pour mourir, le problème des questions est moins susceptible de se présenter. Sinon, l'infirmière est soumise aux interrogatoires des parents et de l'enfant et ne peut que se sentir frustrée, triste et dépourvue de moyens efficaces pour faire face à cette situation.

Après la mort de l'enfant, l'infirmière est en butte au premier choc d'incrédulité des parents, puis elle les voit prendre lentement conscience de la mort de leur enfant. Malheureusement, elle ne peut observer tout le processus de deuil qui s'étend sur plusieurs mois et elle n'est plus là lorsque les plaies se cicatrisent.

Lorsque la mort survient, l'infirmière doit s'attendre à toute réaction: choc, refus, larmes ou colère. Le danger ne réside pas dans la manière dont les parents se comportent, mais dans l'incapacité où ils se trouvent de tolérer leurs sentiments, dans leur désir de les réprimer et d'agir différemment.

Refouler ses sentiments dans de telles circonstances n'est qu'une solution temporaire et l'équilibre des parents sera soumis à de rudes épreuves lors de la résurgence de toutes ces émotions.

L'infirmière réagit de diverses manières à la mort d'un de ses jeunes patients. Il est arrivé souvent que des infirmières, attachées au petit qui vient de mourir, soient allées cacher leurs larmes loin des parents. Pourquoi une telle attitude? Les parents qui, au contraire, voient le chagrin de celle qui s'est tant occupée de leur petit, peuvent en être réconfortés et s'apercevoir qu'ils ne sont pas seuls dans leur épreuve.

L'infirmière devrait accepter les demandes des parents qui veulent rester encore quelques instants auprès du petit, ou désirent le voir, s'ils étaient absents au moment du décès. Elle doit également veiller à ce que tout soit propre et rangé, mais le plus important, c'est qu'elle soit une présence paisible et réconfortante pour la famille. Louer les soins attentifs des parents pour leur enfant peut les consoler et les encourager, sinon une simple présence peut suffire à les apaiser. Les parents se demandent souvent ce qu'ils doivent dire à leurs autres enfants. On doit leur conseiller l'honnêteté: dire que l'enfant était très malade et que le médecin n'a pu le guérir est une explication valable. Si la famille est croyante, les parents peuvent dire que le petit est parti au ciel.

En ce qui concerne les soins post-mortem, on recommande d'envoyer une étudiante-infirmière en compagnie d'une personne plus expérimentée afin que l'apprentissage soit moins pénible.

Que dire aux autres enfants de l'unité? On leur répond souvent que l'enfant a été changé d'unité parce qu'il était gravement malade, ou bien qu'il a été transporté à la salle d'opération, ou enfin qu'il est retourné chez lui. Devant ces réponses, certains enfants plus âgés insistent pour savoir où se trouve exactement l'enfant disparu. Toute l'équipe de santé doit s'entendre sur la façon d'aborder le problème en se basant sur le nombre d'enfants concernés, leur âge, leur maladie, leur fidélité à l'enfant décédé; toutefois, l'honnêteté est de rigueur et habituellement c'est l'infirmière qui doit éventuellement répondre aux questions à la satisfaction des enfants. Si les enfants reçoivent des réponses évasives ou embarassées, ils apprennent que la mort n'est pas un sujet dont on puisse facilement discuter.

La mort n'est pas seulement un phénomène biologique, c'est également une expérience sociale. Si les parents ne connaissent pas l'issue fatale qui attend l'enfant, ils ne peuvent en parler avec d'autres personnes, ni faire leurs adieux à l'enfant et encore moins se préparer à faire face à la situation après sa mort.

L'approche de la mort d'un enfant et le comportement de ses parents posent de véritables problèmes à l'infirmière, mais si elle a réussi à résoudre ses propres difficultés vis-à-vis de la mort, elle sera en mesure de servir d'appui à la famille. Chaque situation semblable sera pour elle un défi à relever et une occasion de pratiquer l'art et la science de sa profession.

Résumé

Tout au long de ce livre nous insistons sur l'importance du problème de l'hospitalisation pour l'enfant, et par conséquent sur les moyens à prendre pour faciliter son adaptation. Pour éviter de causer des traumatismes psychologiques à l'enfant en le séparant de sa famille, on essaie de soigner les bébés et les jeunes enfants en clinique externe, si possible. Lorsque l'hospitalisation est inévitable, les parents peuvent être invités à demeurer avec leur petit.

En vue d'accorder tous les soins nécessaires à l'enfant autant aux points de vue émotif que physique, l'infirmière doit évaluer ses propres sentiments à l'égard de la famille de chaque enfant. Dans certaines situations, elle peut recourir aux conseils des autres membres de l'équipe pour apprendre à contrôler ses émotions et savoir ensuite exercer une influence bienfaisante sur les attitudes des parents et de l'enfant. Dans le cas où l'infirmière rejetterait un patient ou sa famille, elle serait extrêmement nuisible. Si au contraire elle accepte le malade, elle apprendra à le connaître au fur et à mesure qu'elle le soigne, et elle pourra ainsi continuer ou améliorer l'éducation des parents et favoriser la guérison de l'enfant.

La mère d'un enfant malade d'une façon chronique et soigné chez lui, peut renseigner l'infirmière en lui indiquant quels soins elle a prodigués à l'enfant jusqu'alors. La mère doit donc être considérée comme un autre membre de l'équipe de santé qui travaille en étroite collaboration avec l'infirmière.

Le nursing pédiatrique doit être adapté en fonction du développement de l'être humain depuis la naissance jusqu'à l'adolescence. L'infirmière doit donc connaître les aspects normaux de la croissance et du développement des enfants aux points de vue physique, émotif, social, mental et spirituel; elle doit aussi connaître la relation parent-enfant qui sert de base aux divers soins qu'elle accordera aux enfants de tout âge.

Chaque chapitre de ce livre traite d'enfants appartenant à un groupe d'âge précis. L'ordre chronologique est respecté. Nous considérerons les caractéristiques de chacun des groupes pour déterminer les principes généraux du nursing pédiatrique. Après, nous décrirons les pathologies qui se présentent le plus fréquemment dans les différents groupes et nous discuterons des soins appropriés.

RÉFÉRENCES

Livres et documents officiels

American Academy of Pediatrics: *Care of Children in Hospitals*. Evanston, Ill, American Academy of Pediatrics, 1971.

Bergmann, T. et Freud, A.: *Children in the Hospital*. New York, International Universities Press, 1966.

Bowlby, J.: Separation: Attachment and Loss. New York, Basic Books, 1973.

De Castro, F. J. et Rolfe, U. T.: *The Pediatric Nurse Practitioner*. St. Louis, C. V. Mosby Company, 1972.

Easson, W. M.: *The Dying Child: The Management of the Child or Adolescent Who Is Dying*. Springfield, Ill., Charles C Thomas, 1970.

Fredlund, D. J.: Nurse Looks at Children's Questions about Death; dans *American Nurses' Association Clinical Sessions*, 1970. New York, Appleton-Century-Crofts, 1971, p. 105.

Geist, H.: *A Child Goes to the Hospital: The Psychological Aspects of a Child Going to the Hospital*. Springfield, Ill., Charles C Thomas, 1965.

Groolman, C.: *Explaining Death to Children*. Boston, Beacon Press, 1967.

Grollman, E. A.: *Talking about Death; A Dialogue Between Parent and Child*. Boston, Beacon Press, 1970.

Haller, J. A., Talbert, J. L. et Dombro, R. H. (édit.): *The Hospitalized Child and His Family*. Baltimore, John Hopkins Press, 1967.

Hamovitch, M. B.: *The Parent and the Fatally Ill Child: A Demonstration of Parent Participation in a Hospital Pediatrics Department*. Duarte, Californie, City of Hope Medical Center, 1964.

Hardgrove, C. B. et Dawson, R. B.: *Parents and Children in the Hospital*. Boston, Little, Brown and Company, 1972.

Kübler-Ross, E.: *On Death and Dying*. New York, Macmillan Company, 1969.

Leifer, G.: *Principles and Techniques in Pediatric Nursing*. Philadelphie, W. B. Saunders Company, 1972.

Ministère de la Santé nationale et du Bien-être social: *Préparation à l'hôpital*. Division de l'hygiène mentale, série Formation de l'enfant, Ottawa.

Petrillo, M. et Sanger, S.: *Emotional Gare of Hospitalized Children*. Philadelphie, J. B. Lippincott, 1972.

Plank, E.: *Working with Children in Hospital*. Cleveland, W. R. U. P., 2e éd. 1971.

Quint, J. C.: *The Nurse and the Dying Patient*. New York, Macmillan Company, 1967.

Robertson.: *Jeunes enfants à l'hôpital*. Paris, éd. du Centurion, 1973.

Schoenberg, B.: *Anticipatory Grief*. New York, Columbia Press, 1974.

Schoenberg, B. et autres (édit.): *Loss and Grief: Psychological Management in Medical Practice*. New York, Columbia University Press. 1970.

Vernon, D. et autres: *The Psychological Responses of Children to Hospitalization and Illness*. Springfield, Ill., Charles C. Thomas, 1965.

Articles

Azarnoff, P.: A Play Program in a Pediatric Clinic. *Children*, 17:218, novembre-décembre 1970.

Barnes, C.: Level of Consciousness Indicated by Responses of Children to Phenomena in the Intensive Care Unit. *Maternal Child Nurs. Journ.* 4:1, 4, 1975.

Bohu, D.: Les besoins psychologiques de l'enfant hospitalisé. *Revue de l'inf. et ass. soc.*, 16:951, 10, 1966.

Brain, D. J. et Maclay, I.: Controlled Study of Mothers and Children in Hospital. *Brit. M. J.*, 1:278, 3 février 1968.

Brandt, P. A. et autres: IM Injections in Children. *Am. J. Nursing*, 72:1402, août 1972.

Branstetter, E.: Young Child's Response to Hospitalization: Separation Anxiety or Lack of Mothering Care? *Am. J. Pub. Health*, 59:92, janvier 1969.

Bright, F. et France, Sister M. L.: The Nurse and the Terminally Ill Child. *Nursing Outlook*, 15:39, septembre 1967.

Carter, M. D.: Identification of Behaviors Displayed by Children Experiencing Prolonged Hospitalization. *Intern. J. Nurs. Studies*, 10:125, 5, 1973.

Charlin, A. et autres: Les pseudo-arriérations mentales profondes d'origine affective. *La revue de neuropsychiatrie infantile*, 16:647, 9-10, 1969.

Clifton, J.: Collecting 24-Hour Urine Specimens from Infants. *Am. J. Nursing*, 69:1660, août 1969.

Crook, W. G.: Changing Patterns in Child Health Care. *Pediat. Clin. N. Amer.*, 15:novembre 1969.

David, N: Modes de Communication de l'enfant et de l'adolescent. *Inf. Can.*, 14:13, décembre 1972.

Forest-Cyr, M.: Dehors les Parents. *Inf. Can.*, 13:23, janvier 1971.

Freiberg, K. H.: How Parents React When Their Child Is Hospitalized. *Am. J. Nursing,* 72:1270, juillet 1972.

Gochman, D. S.: Children's Perceptions of Vulnerability to Illness and Accidents. *Pub. Health Rep.*, 85:69, janvier 1970.

Hardgrove, C. et Ruthledge, A.: Parenting During Hospitalization. *Am. J. Nursing*, 75:836, mai 1975.

Harper, J. R. et Varakis, G.: Children in Adult Intensive Therapy Units. *Brit. M. J.*, 1:810, 28 mars 1970.

Jackson, P.: The Child's Developing Concept of Death. *Nursing Forum*, 14:205, 2, 1975.

Knudsen, K.: Play Therapy: Preparing the Young Child for Surgery. *Nurs. Clin. N. Amer*, 10:679, 4, 1975.

Koop, C. E.: The Seriously Ill or Dying Child: Supporting the Patient and the Family. *Nursing Clin. N. Amer*, 16:555, août 1969.

Lerner, M. J. et autres: Hospital Care-by-Parent: an Evaluative Look. *Med. Care*, 10:430, 5, 1972.

Luciano, K.: Preparing Children for Surgery. *Nursing*, 4:64, novembre 1974.

McCaffery, M.: Children's Response to Rectal Temperatures: An Exploratory Study. *Nursing Research*, 20:32, janvier – février 1971.

McClure, M. J. et Ryburn, A. C.: Care-by-Parent Unit. *Am. J. Nursing*, 69:2148, octobre 1969.

McDonald, M.: La participation des parents aux soins de l'enfant hospitalisé. *Inf. Can.*, 12:31, mars 1970.

Mead, J.: The Lemonade Party. *Nursing Outlook*, 21:104, février 1973.

Melekian, B.: Hospitalisations abusives en pédiatrie. *La revue de l'inf.* 23:123, février 1973.

Nelson, A. C.: How Can You Stand the Crying? *Am. J. Nursing*, 70:66, janvier 1970.

Northrup, F.: The Dying Child. *Am. J. Nursing*, 74:1066, juin 1974.

Roy, Sister, M. C.: Role Cues and Mothers of Hospitalized Children. *Nursing Research*, 16:178, 1967.

Scahill, M.: Preparing Children for Procedures and Operations. *Nursing Outlook*, 17:36, juin 1969.

Schezem, J.: Locating the Best Thigh Injection Site. *Nursing*, 3:20 décembre 1973.

Schulman, J. L., Kaspar, J. C. et Child, D.: Videotape Sampling of the Child's Day in the Hospital. *J. Pediat.*, 76:728, mai 1970.

Schultz, N. V.: How Children Perceive Pain. *Nursing Outlook*, 19:670, octobre 1971.

Soparkar, B.: Trickery, White Lies and Deception in Pediatrics. *Nursing*, 4:11, mars 1974.

Stainton, C.: Venez avec moi soigner Panda. *Inf. Can.*, 16:23, décembre 1974.

Steinhauer, P. et autres: Psychological Aspects of Chronic Illness. *Ped. Clin. N. Amer.*, 21:825, 4, 1974.

Waechter, E.: Developmental Consequences of Congenital Abnormalities. *Nursing Forum*, 14:109, 2, 1975.

Waechter, E. H.: Children's Awareness of Fatal Illness. *Am. J. Nursing*, 71:1168, juin 1971.

Wolfer, J. et Visintainer, M.: Pediatric Surgical Patients's and Parents' Stress Responses and Adjustment. *Nursing Research*, 24:244, 4, 1975.

deuxième partie

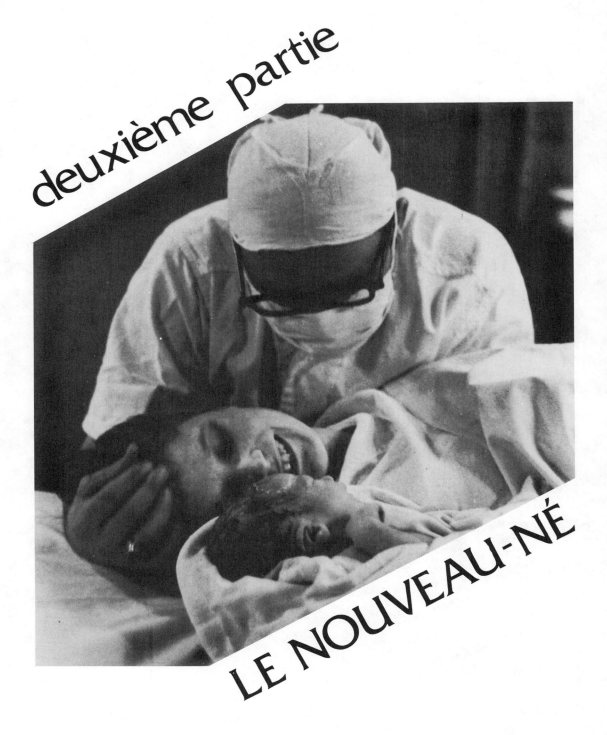

LE NOUVEAU-NÉ

(Courtoisie de M. Ciavolino, Jr. Extrait de *Baby Talk*: juin 1971.)

6

examen et caractéristiques du nouveau-né

L'examen physique du nouveau-né, que l'infirmière fait quotidiennement, suppose que celle-ci connaît les caractéristiques physiques et les déviations fonctionnelles du bébé. Anatomiquement, physiologiquement et psychologiquement, le nouveau-né diffère de l'adulte et de l'enfant. Chaque bébé est un être unique qui possède ses propres caractéristiques; il y a cependant des normes qui servent de guide et doivent être respectées afin que le bébé reçoive des soins adéquats s'il s'éloigne trop de la normale.

RÉSISTANCE PHYSIOLOGIQUE

La nature a pourvu le fœtus et le nouveau-né d'une certaine résistance physiologique. Le nouveau-né normal semble peu affecté par un écart de température se situant entre 36°C et 38°C; chez les prématurés, la température corporelle peut descendre jusqu'à 34,5°C. Le bébé possède un système thermo-régulateur instable et la température de son corps peut s'abaisser facilement.

Les taux sanguins sont très variables chez le nouveau-né et les concentrations normales

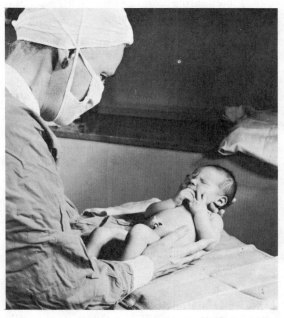

Figure 6-1. On observe le nouveau-né pour déceler les malformations évidentes avant de procéder à l'examen détaillé. (Courtoisie des Laboratoires Pfizer, Brooklyn, New York.)

chez l'enfant n'apparaissent pas toujours immédiatement après la naissance, surtout si celle-ci s'est produite prématurément.

Quoique le taux de glucose dans le sang puisse être inférieur à la normale, la réaction hypoglycémique qui se produit habituellement chez l'adulte n'apparaît pas chez le nouveau-né. Les ions d'hydrogène (H+) et le gaz carbonique se trouvent en quantité moindre. Le nourrisson supporte mieux l'anoxie que l'adulte, mais il existe une limite à sa capacité de tolérer une carence en oxygène.

Cette résistance physiologique présente des avantages évidents; grâce à elle, de nombreux nouveau-nés ont triomphé d'une mort certaine. Elle complique cependant le diagnostic en cachant ou en diminuant certains signes révélateurs. Par exemple, l'infection ne s'accompagne pas toujours de fièvre comme cela se produit chez l'enfant plus âgé ou chez l'adulte. Le nouveau-né, relativement déshydraté, paraîtra respirer presque normalement; lorsque son pH sanguin est au-dessous de 7,2, il ne présentera pas nécessairement une respiration du type Kussmaul, qui indique un état d'acidose.

Somme toute, cette résistance passive constitue un atout pour le nouveau-né; mais elle possède des limites, surtout chez le prématuré moins bien armé contre les conditions défavorables du milieu.

Pendant les premiers jours de l'existence, l'enfant se trouve dans un état d'équilibre négatif. Il subit une chute de poids, une perte de liquides organiques, une baisse d'hémoglobine, d'azote, de chlorure de sodium et d'anticorps hérités de sa mère. Il est dangereux de vouloir trop le nourrir pour compenser ces nombreuses pertes qui, d'ailleurs, sont rarement responsables des décès qui surviennent pendant les premiers jours de vie extra-utérine.

TAILLE ET POIDS

La taille moyenne d'un nouveau-né mâle est de 50 cm; une fille mesure ordinairement 49 cm. L'écart normal pour les deux sexes se situe entre 47,5 et 53,75 cm.

Le poids de naissance a également tendance à varier. Environ les deux tiers des bébés à terme pèsent entre 2700 et 3850 g. Une fille pèse approximativement 3150 g et le garçon 3375 g. Durant les premiers jours, l'enfant perd environ 180 à 300 g ou 5 à 10% de son poids initial. Les facteurs qui concourent à cette diminution de poids sont la perte des urines et des selles, le retrait des hormones d'origine maternelle et la faible ingestion calorique.

SIGNES VITAUX

La température, le pouls et la respiration du nouveau-né varient de façon imprévisible. Nous avons parlé de la résistance physiologique, mais quand les limites de cette résistance sont dépassées, le nouveau-né peut paraître subitement malade, ses forces en réserve étant moindres que celles de l'adulte. L'infirmière doit apprendre à connaître les réactions du bébé aux sensations extérieures, réactions que le bébé ne peut transmettre par les mots mais par des gestes, comme, par exemple, repousser les couvertures quand il a trop chaud. Un sens aigu de l'observation est donc essentiel pour l'infirmière qui travaille dans une pouponnière.

Température

La température du bébé à la naissance, légèrement plus élevée que celle de sa mère, s'explique par la situation de l'utérus dans le corps maternel. Par contre, elle descend immédiatement après la naissance et s'ajuste à la température de la salle d'accouchement, pour remonter à la normale dans les huit heures qui suivent. Les pieds et les mains du bébé restent plus froids que le reste du corps, car son système circulatoire ne fonctionne pas parfaitement. Ce manque de stabilité, dû à un sous-développement du centre thermo-régulateur, demande un surplus de chaleur extérieure. Toutefois, l'infirmière qui déposera l'enfant dans son lit doit se rappeler qu'une chaleur trop élevée pendant une période trop longue fera monter indûment la température corporelle.

Le pouls

On emploie l'électrocardiographie fœtale pour enregistrer les impulsions électriques du cœur fœtal. Ceci permet le diagnostic et l'évaluation d'états pathologiques intra-utérins qui peuvent être traités immédiatement après la naissance. Le pouls du nouveau-né bat souvent de façon irrégulière, car le centre cardio-régulateur, situé dans le bulbe rachidien, n'a pas atteint son parfait développement. Le rythme rapide, d'environ 120 à 150 pulsations à la minute, devient plus irrégulier encore à la suite d'un stimulus physique ou émotif. Quand l'enfant pleure, son rythme cardiaque s'accélère et son pouls devient irrégulier.

La peau rougit sur toute la surface du corps quand le bébé pleure intensément. Les veines du cuir chevelu se gorgent de sang et battent. Ordinairement le nouveau-né n'a pas de larmes.

La peau est mince et sèche, on peut voir les veines sous l'épiderme. La couleur est rose-rouge. Le lanugo n'est pas exceptionnel. On retrouve encore du vernix caseosa.

La tête semble plus grosse que le corps. Sa forme peut être temporairement anormale à cause du modelage dû à l'accouchement.

Les pieds semblent plus complets qu'une radiographie ne le démontrerait. Seul l'os du talon est présent, les autres os sont encore cartilagineux. La peau est lâche et plissée.

Le tronc présente les détails suivants: cou court, épaules petites et tombantes, gonflement des seins, abdomen rond et proéminent, cordon ombilical, bassin étroit.

Les yeux sont bleu foncé. Le regard est vide. Les yeux ont un mouvement convergeant ou divergeant. Les paupières sont gonflées.

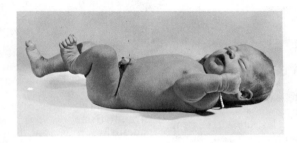

Les jambes sont souvent repliées contre la paroi abdominale, en position fœtale. Étendues, les jambes semblent proportionnellement plus courtes que les bras. Les genoux sont légèrement fléchis et les jambes plus ou moins arquées.

Les organes génitaux semblent disproportionnés, surtout le scrotum.

La figure présente les caractéristiques suivantes: joues bouffies, nez large et plat, menton fuyant et mâchoire sous-développée.

Le poids de l'enfant varie de 2700 à 3600 g, mais l'enfant semble proportionnellement très petit. Sa longueur est de 47,5 à 52,5 cm.

Les mains, si on les examine à plat, présentent: face palmaire plissée, ongles ayant l'aspect du papier, peau lâche et sèche et plis cutanés aux poignets.

Le crâne présente les fontanelles. La plus importante est au-dessus du front, l'autre à l'arrière de la tête.

Figure 6-2. Représentation d'un bébé en bonne santé. Cette photographie, non retouchée, a été prise 6 heures après la naissance. Hôpital Lawrence Memorial. (Tiré de *Baby Talk*, janvier 1964.)

La respiration

Le rythme respiratoire peut varier de 35 à 50 respirations par minute. Tout comme le pouls, des stimuli extérieurs ou intérieurs le modifient aisément. On observe plus facilement la respiration en suivant le mouvement abdominal, car les muscles du diaphragme et de l'abdomen sont les plus importants dans la respiration du nouveau-né. La dyspnée ou la cyanose peuvent apparaître soudainement chez un jeune enfant qui respire normalement; elles peuvent indiquer la présence d'une anomalie congénitale ou d'un autre état qui peut causer la mort du bébé s'il ne reçoit pas des soins adéquats. L'infirmière doit avertir le médecin si l'enfant respire moins de 35 fois par minute ou plus de 50 fois par minute quand il est au repos, et s'il souffre de dyspnée ou de cyanose.

Le nouveau-né normal pleure souvent, avec énergie et apparemment sans motif précis. S'il ne pleure pas, on doit le stimuler périodiquement afin de permettre une bonne expansion pulmonaire, nécessaire à son intégrité respiratoire.

La tension artérielle

La tension artérielle est remarquablement basse. Il est difficile de la déterminer avec précision et elle peut varier selon la largeur du brassard utilisé.

LA PEAU

La couleur de la peau du nouveau-né varie selon son origine raciale ou ethnique. La peau est douce, recouverte de lanugo et d'enduit sébacé appelé vernix caseosa. On remarque une légère desquamation; l'élasticité de la peau (turgor) signifie que l'enfant est en bonne santé.

On appelle *lanugo,* le fin duvet qui recouvre le bébé, surtout aux épaules, au dos, aux extrémités, au front et aux tempes. Puisque le lanugo commence à apparaître à la 16e semaine de gestation pour s'estomper vers la 32e semaine, sa présence à la naissance est souvent un signe de prématurité. Le lanugo est en tout cas beaucoup plus abondant chez le prématuré que chez l'enfant à terme, et disparaît ordinairement pendant les premières semaines de vie extra-utérine.

Le vernix caseosa qui recouvre la peau du nouveau-né est une substance graisseuse, d'un blanc jaunâtre, qui a l'apparence du fromage en crème. Cet enduit est composé de la sécrétion des glandes sébacées et de cellules épithéliales. Il est inégalement réparti, plus abondant dans les replis cutanés et à la vulve. Il sèche ou disparaît spontanément en adhérant aux vêtements du bébé.

La turgescence des tissus provient de l'eau contenue dans les tissus sous-cutanés. On évalue l'élasticité de la peau par l'expérience suivante: il faut saisir un repli de la peau entre le pouce et l'index et, en le relâchant, la peau devrait reprendre sa position initiale. Une observation plus approfondie révélera un autre phénomène tout à fait normal, celui de la *desquamation* qui se produit pendant les deux

premières semaines de la vie pour se terminer vers la quatrième. Les surfaces les plus rapidement dénudées sont celles qui subissent un contact continuel avec les couvertures et les draps, c'est-à-dire le nez, les genoux et les épaules. La peau du siège requiert des soins particuliers afin de prévenir l'irritation; il faut changer immédiatement une couche souillée ou mouillée.

Le nouveau-né présente quelquefois une *irruption* cutanée temporaire. *Les points miliaires,* petites papilles blanches sur le nez et le menton, sont dus à l'obstruction des glandes sébacées et disparaissent au cours des deux premières semaines. L'ictère physiologique devient nettement apparent entre le troisième et le septième jour. Il apparaît graduellement le second ou le troisième jour et se rencontre chez la majorité des nouveau-nés.

Sur le corps de l'enfant on peut voir des *marques.* Certaines demeurent en permanence, ce sont les taches de naissance. D'autres sont temporaires, causées tout simplement par le traumatisme de la naissance ou dues à l'immaturité, même si l'enfant est né à terme. Parmi les marques temporaires, on rencontre encore les *hémangiomes* ou petites taches rosées, situées entre les sourcils, au-dessus des paupières, sur le nez, sur la lèvre supérieure et enfin derrière le cou. Dans la plupart des cas, elles disparaissent spontanément avant la fin de la première année et ce fait devrait rassurer les parents. L'utilisation des forceps pendant l'accouchement peut provoquer des marques temporaires sur la tête ou la partie du corps qui a été pressée par l'instrument. Il peut se produire une hémorragie à l'intérieur des tissus fessiers ou des organes génitaux, s'il s'est agi d'une présentation du siège; l'œdème est également une conséquence de ce genre d'accouchement. En réalité, tous les tissus peuvent être meurtris au cours de l'expulsion.

Il existe également un autre type de marque qu'on appelle taches mongoliques. Ces marques, d'un gris d'ardoise, sont localisées habituellement sur les fesses ou sur la partie inférieure du dos. Elles apparaissent surtout chez les enfants noirs, les esquimaux, les orientaux ou ceux qui sont originaires de la région méditerranéenne. Elles disparaîtront sans traitement pendant la période préscolaire.

Vers l'âge de deux semaines, la peau du bébé devrait être douce, rosée et fraîche comme on la décrit habituellement. Les glandes sudoripares deviennent actives vers la fin de la deuxième semaine.

PLANCHE 1

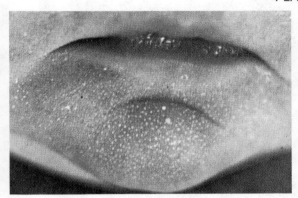

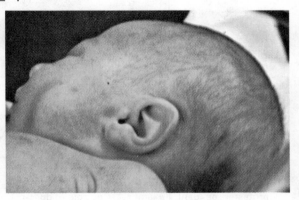

1. Les points miliaires ou milium sont de petites papilles blanches, situées spécialement sur le nez et le menton.*

2. Les forceps, utilisés pendant l'accouchement, peuvent laisser des marques temporaires sur la figure.*

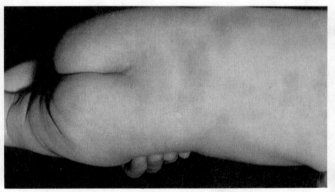

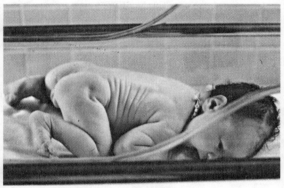

3. Taches mongoliques. Coloration diffuse et gris bleu de la région du sacrum.**

4. La cyanose des mains, des pieds et quelquefois des lèvres est fréquente au cours des premières heures de vie et est généralement associée à un sous-développement de la circulation périphérique capillaire de la peau.*

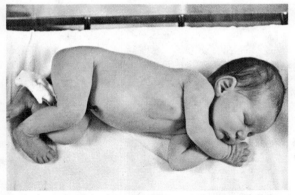

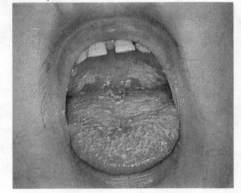

5. Ictère physiologique: Environ un tiers des bébés en souffrent au cours de la première semaine de vie. L'ictère apparaît habituellement entre 48 et 72 heures et disparaît au cours de la deuxième semaine.*

6. Muguet, (moniliase buccale). Erythème, œdème et enduit blanchâtre recouvrant les muqueuses de la bouche.**

* Courtoisie des Laboratoires Mead-Johnson
**(De Frieboes & Schonfeld's Color Atlas of Dermatology, par J. Kimming & M. Janner. Édition américaine traduite et revisée par H. Goldschmidt. Georg. Thieme Verlag, Stuttgart, 1966.)

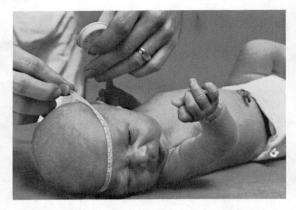
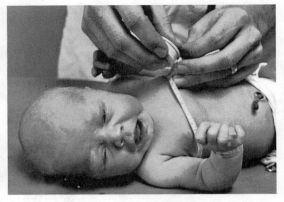

Figure 6-3. On mesure la circonférence de la tête et de la poitrine. Les nouveau-nés ne cessent de protester pendant l'examen. (Courtoisie du Dr Charles H. Perte, Jr., et de la revue *Baby Talk.*)

LA TÊTE

La tête, proportionnellement beaucoup plus grosse que le reste du corps, mesure en moyenne 34 à 35 cm de circonférence. Les mensurations normales de la tête varient de 33 à 37 cm. La tête du bébé représente le ¼ de sa longueur totale alors que la tête de l'adulte équivaut à ⅛ de sa hauteur totale (voir figure 2-5). Le crâne de l'enfant semble volumineux et sa figure, relativement petite, surtout lorsqu'on les compare au crâne et à la figure de l'adulte. Les mâchoires sont assez petites et le menton fuyant. La circonférence de la tête est égale ou dépasse celle de la poitrine et de l'abdomen.

Les os du crâne n'étant point tous soudés, il existe des ouvertures ou plages membraneuses qu'on appelle *fontanelles*. On devrait les palper pour évaluer leur présence ou leur fermeture. La fontanelle antérieure a la forme d'un diamant ou d'un losange et se situe à la jonction des deux os pariétaux et de la suture des frontaux. Elle mesure entre 2 et 3 cm de large et entre 3 et 4 cm de long (figure 6-4). La fontanelle postérieure, triangulaire, est localisée entre l'occipital et les pariétaux. Beaucoup plus petite que la fontanelle antérieure, il

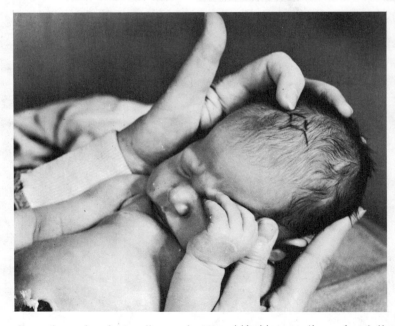

Figure 6-4. Les dimensions des fontanelles varient considérablement d'un enfant à l'autre. On les palpe pour vérifier leur tension. (Courtoisie des Laboratoires Pfizer, Brooklyn, New York.)

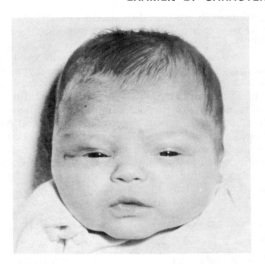

Figure 6-5. Le caput succedanum: œdème sous-cutané du cuir chevelu.

se peut qu'elle soit presque fermée à la naissance. Les fontanelles bombent si l'enfant pleure ou force ou si la pression intra-crânienne augmente. De nombreuses causes, entre autres l'hydrocéphalie, peuvent provoquer une augmentation de la pression intracrânienne (voir p. 221. La fontanelle antérieure se soude normalement entre 12 et 18 mois, la fontanelle postérieure à la fin du deuxième mois.

Des membranes relient les os du crâne au niveau des sutures non complétées. Durant l'accouchement, la pression exercée sur la tête peut la modeler de façon asymétrique. En général, la tête reprend sa forme normale une semaine après la naissance.

Le caput succedanum, ou bosse séro-sanguine, est un renflement ou œdème d'une portion du cuir chevelu. Il peut être localisé ou passablement étendu. Habituellement, au bout de la troisième journée, il n'en reste plus trace (voir fig. 6-5).

Le céphalhématome est une accumulation de sang sous le périoste d'un os plat du crâne. L'épanchement ne traverse pas la ligne de suture et la masse apparaît molle au toucher, fluctuante et irréductible. Les pleurs de l'enfant n'accroissent pas son volume. L'étendue du *caput succedanum* empêche de déceler la présence du céphalhématome pendant les premiers jours de la vie. Il faut éviter d'aspirer l'hématome à cause du danger évident d'infection et aussi parce que la masse disparaît habituellement après quelques semaines (voir fig. 6-6).

La figure et le cou

La figure du nouveau-né est inexpressive. Jusqu'à ce que le cartilage se calcifie, les oreilles demeurent flasques. Le cou est plissé et court. Ces plis profonds, encore plus nombreux chez un enfant gras, doivent être net-

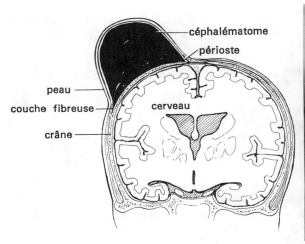

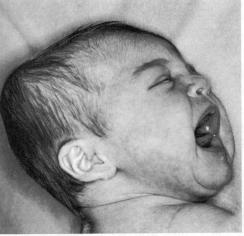

céphalématome
périoste
peau
couche fibreuse
cerveau
crâne

Figure 6-6. Céphalhématome. *A)* Collection sanguine sous le périoste d'un os plat du crâne. *B)* Céphalhématome du pariétal droit.

toyés avec soin si l'on veut éviter l'irritation toujours possible.

La tête d'un nouveau-né normal peut tourner librement d'un côté à l'autre. Une limitation de mouvement peut faire supposer que les muscles sternocléidomastoïdiens ont été endommagés pendant l'accouchement ou que le bébé a un torticolis congénital. Si on maintient droite la tête de l'enfant lorsqu'il pleure, couché sur le dos, les deux côtés de sa figure se meuvent également. L'absence de symétrie dans le mouvement ou le contour du visage indique la présence d'une anomalie.

LA POITRINE

La poitrine, en forme de cloche, possède approximativement la même circonférence que l'abdomen; par contre, la circonférence de la tête habituellement est supérieure. Lorsque l'enfant atteint l'âge de deux ans, les dimensions thoraciques excèdent celles de la tête et ses porportions corporelles ressemblent davantage à celles de l'adulte.

Dans l'utérus, la pression exercée par les bras du bébé contre sa poitrine entraîne une symétrie entre les diamètres antéro-postérieur et transverse; le thorax du nouveau-né est presque circulaire. Quand il respire, le bébé n'utilise pas sa cage thoracique comme le fait un enfant plus vieux ou un adulte; il se sert du diaphragme et des muscles abdominaux pour inspirer et expirer. La présence d'hormones d'origine maternelle cause quelquefois un gonflement des seins d'où l'on peut extraire un liquide pâle et laiteux, appelé *lait de sorcière*. Ce phénomène disparaît en deux à quatre semaines, sans traitement; mais aussi longtemps que cet état persiste, les seins, très sensibles, ne doivent être touchés qu'en cas de nécessité absolue et avec beaucoup de délicatesse.

Habituellement, le thymus est volumineux. Il triple son poids avant que l'enfant ait atteint l'âge de cinq ans; il gardera la même dimension jusqu'à l'âge de dix ans, pour décroître par la suite. On a réfuté la théorie voulant qu'un gros thymus cause des difficultés respiratoires et qu'il puisse provoquer la mort par asphyxie. Habituellement, un autre facteur est responsable de la cyanose ou de l'apnée.

LE SYSTÈME RESPIRATOIRE

Même si le mécanisme de la respiration est établi avant la naissance, il subira de profonds changements quand l'enfant viendra au monde. Les mouvements pré-respiratoires commencent dès le quatrième mois de la gestation. Ces mouvements périodiques provoquent la péné-tration et le retrait du liquide amniotique au niveau des bronches. Évidemment, c'est la circulation placentaire qui fournit l'oxygène. L'hypoxie, résultant de la section du cordon, stimule le centre respiratoire par l'accumulation du gaz carbonique dans le sang. Le processus de la naissance, de même que les modifications de l'environnement, stimulent également le centre respiratoire. La première respiration, habituellement exécutée dans les trente secondes qui suivent la naissance, permet la dilatation des poumons affaissés, quoique leur expansion complète ne se produise qu'au bout de quelques jours.

LE SYSTÈME CIRCULATOIRE

Le système circulatoire subit de profonds changements à la naissance. La circulation du fœtus est reliée au placenta; après la naissance, l'apport d'oxygène dépend essentiellement des poumons. Le trou de Botal et le canal artériel doivent être oblitérés. La circulation pulmonaire s'établit progressivement et peu de temps après la naissance le sang oxygéné circule dans le corps de l'enfant de la même manière que dans celui de l'adulte. Le trou de Botal (voir figure 10-3), se ferme aux environs du troisième mois. Le canal artériel s'oblitère avant l'âge de quatre mois. On peut entendre chez quelque 2% des nouveau-nés des murmures cardiaques transitoires et insignifiants. Ces bruits, provoqués par le sang qui s'échappe des ouvertures non refermées, disparaîtront au bout de quelques semaines.

Comparativement, le cœur et le système vasculaire du nouveau-né paraissent beaucoup plus volumineux que chez l'adulte. Le volume sanguin du nouveau-né correspond à 10 ou 12% de son poids corporel, car il comprend la quantité de sang reçue du placenta avant la section du cordon.

Sang

À la naissance, le sang contient un taux relativement élevé d'hémoglobine et de globules rouges (voir tableau 3-1). Cette hausse relative est essentielle à l'oxygénation in-utero et demeure nécessaire jusqu'à la dilatation pulmonaire complète, soit quelques jours après la naissance. Durant les deux premières semaines de la vie, l'oxygénation s'améliore à un point tel que les taux élevés d'hémoglobine et de globules rouges deviennent inutiles. Une hémolyse importante survient alors, suivie d'une chute progressive de ces éléments durant les trois mois suivants, provoquant ainsi une anémie physiologique.

Ictère physiologique ou ictère du nouveau-né

À la naissance, le sang contient un taux relativement élevé de bilirubine qui augmente encore durant la première semaine de la vie à cause d'une destruction additionnelle de globules rouges. Les globules rouges hémolysés libèrent l'hémoglobine. L'anneau protoporphyrinique de l'hémoglobine s'ouvre et devient biliverdine qui se transforme en bilirubine après réduction. La bilirubine se lie à une protéine plasmatique et se rend au foie sous le nom de bilirubine indirecte ou insoluble. Le foie immature du nouveau-né ne parvient pas à sécréter la glucoronyltransférase, enzyme nécessaire à la conjugaison de la bilirubine indirecte et à sa transformation en bilirubine directe ou soluble. Cette déficience physiologique provoque l'accumulation de bilirubine indirecte. La peau ne révèle aucune trace de jaunisse tant que la bilirubine demeure dans le système intravasculaire. La coloration cutanée et cornéenne apparaît quand le taux de bilirubine indirecte s'élève au-dessus de 7 mg/100 ml de sang, chez l'enfant à terme, et quitte le milieu sanguin. Chez le bébé dont le poids à la naissance est inférieur à la normale, la coloration rougeâtre de la peau causée par le manque de tissu sous-cutané masque l'ictère qui apparaît cependant quand on exerce une pression sur la peau.

55 à 70% des nouveau-nés présentent cet ictère physiologique à partir du deuxième ou troisième jour après la naissance. Cet état s'amplifie pendant quelques jours pour disparaître à la fin de la première semaine. Les urines peuvent devenir foncées et l'enfant sembler apathique, voire anorexique. Chez le nouveau-né, le taux normal de bilirubine indirecte correspond à 1 mg/100 ml de sang, une hyperbilirubinémie inquiétante existe quand les proportions de bilirubine dans le sang atteignent 18 à 20 mg/100 ml durant la première semaine de vie. Un ictère prolongé indique un état pathologique tel l'atrésie biliaire, la syphilis et surtout l'érythroblastose fœtale.

Chez certains enfants nourris au sein une hyperbilirubinémie se manifeste vers la 2e semaine de vie. Ce phénomène est associé à la présence dans le lait maternel de prégnan-3 (alpha), 20(bêta)-diol. Ce métabolite de la progestérone inhibe l'action de la glucoronyltransférase. On doit vérifier fréquemment le taux de bilirubine indirecte chez ces enfants et l'allaitement doit quelquefois être suspendu jusqu'à ce que le taux de bilirubine soit revenu à la normale. Ordinairement l'état du nouveau-né redevient normal en 4 à 6 jours.

Le traitement de l'ictère physiologique est rarement indiqué. La photothérapie peut être employée pour traiter ces bébés normaux mais la journée de l'apparition de l'ictère le taux de bilirubine indirecte et le poids de l'enfant sont pris en considération avant d'appliquer le traitement tel qu'il est expliqué au chapitre 8.

L'hypoprothrombinémie physiologique

Le taux de prothrombine décroît chez tous les enfants pendant les premiers jours de la vie, ce qui entraîne une prolongation du temps de coagulation. Cet état s'accentue entre le second et le cinquième jour après la naissance. Comme mesure préventive, on peut administrer de la vitamine K, soit à la mère pendant l'accouchement, soit à l'enfant après la naissance. Cette situation se corrige d'elle-même entre le 7e et le 10e jour de vie.

LE SYSTÈME GASTRO-INTESTINAL

Les coussinets buccaux, la bouche et la mâchoire

Les coussinets buccaux sont des dépôts de tissu graisseux que l'on trouve au niveau des joues. Ils y demeurent même si l'enfant souffre de malnutrition extrême et disparaissent dès que la succion n'est plus le principal mode de nutrition.

Le menton est fuyant, tremblant à la moindre stimulation, surtout si le bébé pleure ou s'il est effrayé. Relativement grosse, sa langue sort de la bouche lorsque celle-ci est ouverte. Le nouveau-né ne peut acheminer sa nourriture des lèvres au pharynx. Plus tard, lorsqu'on le nourrit d'aliments solides, on doit placer la nourriture sur la base de la langue afin qu'il puisse avaler sans difficulté. La salivation se manifeste vers l'âge de deux ou trois mois. Tant que l'enfant n'aura pas appris à avaler ce qui est à l'avant de sa bouche, il sera enclin à baver.

L'œsophage, l'estomac et les intestins

À la naissance, le cardia n'a pas atteint le même niveau de développement que le pylore d'où la propension du jeune bébé aux régurgitations et aux vomissements. On doit placer le bébé dans la position verticale plusieurs fois durant son repas afin de lui permettre d'éructer l'air avalé en buvant. L'éructation, quelquefois accompagnée d'une légère régurgitation, empêche les gaz de demeurer dans l'estomac et de provoquer des vomissements, ou de déclencher des coliques s'ils pénètrent dans l'intestin.

Il arrive que le fonctionnement du sphincter pylorique s'avère déficient. Les régurgitations constantes (le rejet des aliments, sans effort, immédiatement après leur ingurgitation) entraînent alors une perte de poids. Au chapitre 12, on abordera cet état pathologique.

Le contenu de l'estomac s'acheminant presqu'immédiatement dans le duodénum, il est difficile d'évaluer la capacité gastrique. Lorsqu'un enfant boit, on constate que le liquide qu'il ingurgite ne demeure pas dans l'estomac et qu'il le quitte avant même la fin du biberon. On admet qu'à la naissance, l'estomac peut contenir 30 à 60 g; à l'âge de 3 semaines, 90 g; à 5 mois, 210 g et à 10 mois, 300 g. Il ne reste plus trace de la formule, 2 heures et demie ou 3 heures après le repas. Les aliments riches en protéines ou en graisses ralentissent la digestion.

Le tractus intestinal commence à éliminer du liquide amniotique au début du cinquième mois de la vie intra-utérine. Les intestins assument aisément leurs fonctions après la naissance. Le méconium, premier produit fécal, est une substance collante, sans odeur, de couleur noir-verdâtre ou vert-brunâtre, pouvant être excrétée entre 8 et 24 heures après la naissance.

Pendant la première semaine, la composition des selles change quotidiennement. On les a donc qualifiées de selles transitoires. Du troisième au cinquième jour, elles sont molles, contiennent du mucus et se caractérisent par leur couleur jaune-verdâtre. Après le cinquième jour, la nature des selles dépend de la nourriture. Les selles d'un enfant nourri au sein se distinguent par leur consistance semi-pâteuse et leur couleur jaune-paille; leur fréquence varie de 2 à 4 par jour. Les selles d'un enfant nourri au lait de vache sont jaunes, plus dures et surviennent une ou deux fois par jour. Certaines formules commerciales améliorées se distinguent tellement peu du lait maternel qu'il s'avère pratiquement impossible de déceler la moindre différence entre les selles d'un enfant nourri avec ce lait et celles de l'enfant nourri au sein. Plus tard, lorsque l'enfant recevra une alimentation à base de purée, ses selles deviendront brunes ou prendront la coloration des aliments qu'on lui donnera.

Abdomen

Le cordon ombilical sèche et se décolore peu de temps après la naissance: il noircit peu à peu et se détache habituellement entre le sixième et le dixième jour. Il laisse, en guise de cicatrice, une surface granulée qui disparaît au cours de la semaine suivante. On doit examiner attentivement le cordon ombilical pendant les 24 heures qui suivent la naissance et quotidiennement par la suite, afin de déceler un écoulement sanguin. Si ceci se produit, on doit immédiatement prévenir le médecin qui pincera le cordon ou l'attachera de nouveau. Après la première journée, les dangers d'hémorragie diminuent; si des signes d'infection se manifestent, ils doivent être signalés immédiatement. Le cordon requiert des soins méticuleux jusqu'à guérison complète de la cicatrice, car les vaisseaux sanguins et leur prolongement dans l'abdomen sont une porte ouverte à l'entrée des microbes. On emploie souvent une teinture bactéricide afin d'éviter cette complication.

Dépistage d'anomalies

En plus de l'examen externe, viennent s'ajouter trois tests qui complètent l'évaluation du système gastro-intestinal du nouveau-né. On recherche les anomalies qui pourraient entraver le fonctionnement normal des processus physiologiques. Non évidentes à première vue, ces malformations ont une importance telle que leur découverte précoce et leur correction sont susceptibles de sauver la vie de l'enfant. Parmi les anomalies qu'on rencontre le plus fréquemment, il faut citer l'anus imperforé, l'omphalocèle et l'atrésie de l'œsophage.

L'anus imperforé. En l'absence de selles méconiales, le médecin ou l'infirmière peuvent déceler cette anomalie en tentant d'introduire dans le rectum du nouveau-né un thermomètre rectal, un doigt ganté, (il est préférable d'utiliser l'auriculaire ou l'index à cause de l'étroitesse du rectum) ou un cathéter de caoutchouc souple.

Omphalocèle. On doit examiner le lieu de jonction du cordon ombilical à l'abdomen afin de s'assurer qu'une portion de l'intestin n'apparaît pas à la base du cordon.

L'atrésie de l'œsophage. Si le nouveau-né bave ou s'il laisse couler une quantité excessive de salive, il peut souffrir d'une atrésie de l'œsophage. Le dépistage de ce défaut physique s'effectue en tentant d'introduire un cathéter de caoutchouc souple jusqu'à l'estomac. Si on découvre une obstruction on le mentionne immédiatement, car l'enfant ne pourra prendre aucun liquide avant que les mesures nécessaires aient été prises. Il faut rectifier cet état avant que l'enfant ne s'affaiblisse par le manque de nourriture ou qu'une pneumonie ne se déve-

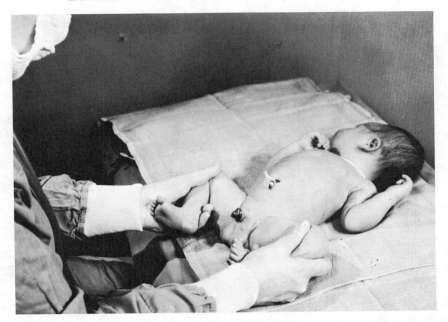

Figure 6-7. On peut déceler la luxation congénitale de la hanche en faisant exécuter aux cuisses des mouvements d'abduction; du côté atteint, l'abduction sera limitée à environ 45° alors qu'elle est de 90° du côté sain. (Courtoisie des Laboratoires Pfizer, Brooklyn, New York.)

loppe, imputable à l'aspiration des sécrétions ou du liquide de son premier biberon.

Ces simples examens ne sont pas dangereux pour le nouveau-né. Ils peuvent être effectués sans risque par l'étudiante-infirmière sous la surveillance du médecin ou de l'institutrice, si la politique de l'hôpital lui permet de le faire. Bien entendu, l'infirmière n'établit pas de diagnostic, mais par une observation intelligente et la description de ses découvertes, elle peut informer le médecin des conditions qui requièrent ses soins.

RÉGION ANO-GÉNITALE

Les fesses des nouveau-nés se caractérisent par leur couleur rosée, leur fermeté et leur rondeur. La région anale ne doit pas présenter de rougeurs ou de fissures.

Les organes génitaux masculins. Les dimensions du pénis et du scrotum varient. Le prépuce adhère quelquefois au gland. Vers le huitième mois de la vie intra-utérine, les testicules sont ordinairement descendus dans le scrotum; il arrive cependant qu'ils demeurent dans l'abdomen ou dans le canal inguinal. On qualifie cet état de cryptorchidie (voir p. 326).

Les organes génitaux féminins. L'activité des hormones d'origine maternelle entraîne quel-quefois un léger gonflement des organes génitaux externes. On constate que les grandes lèvres sont sous-développées et que les petites lèvres paraissent volumineuses. Le vagin laisse passer des sécrétions muqueuses qui peuvent occasionnellement se teinter de sang pendant la première semaine. Les hormones transmises de la mère à l'enfant peuvent provoquer cette réaction, qui devrait disparaître vers la seconde ou troisième semaine de vie.

Urines

À la naissance, la vessie de l'enfant contient de l'urine, qui pourra être excrétée immédiatement ou dans les heures qui suivent. Certains nouveau-nés n'auront pas de miction avant le deuxième jour. L'immaturité rénale entraîne une dilution partielle de l'urine. La perte d'une grande quantité d'eau peut provoquer une hémoconcentration transitoire. La couche peut être colorée d'une tache rosée provenant d'un dépôt de cristaux d'acide urique.

L'infirmière doit noter l'heure de la première miction du nouveau-né, et observer aussi la force du jet et les particularités qui peuvent se présenter. Ces observations peuvent permettre de soupçonner une pathologie urinaire telle l'atrésie du méat urinaire ou une obstruction quelconque au niveau des voies urinaires. La cause la plus fréquente d'anurie chez le nouveau-né est la déshydratation.

STRUCTURE SQUELETTIQUE

La souplesse des os s'explique par leur forte composition en cartilage et leur faible teneur en calcium. Afin de permettre l'expulsion du fœtus sans risque au moment de l'accouchement, la structure du squelette est flexible et les articulations élastiques.

Le dos de l'enfant est normalement droit et plat. Les courbes sacrées et lombaires se dessineront plus tard, lorsque l'enfant apprendra à s'asseoir ou à se tenir debout.

Les jambes sont petites, courtes et arquées. Lorsque l'enfant repose et que ses jambes occupent la position d'abduction et de flexion, les plantes de ses pieds se touchent. Il est important de vérifier le mouvement d'abduction des cuisses pour déceler une luxation congénitale des hanches. Le coussin graisseux de l'axe longitudinal des pieds donne l'impression que les pieds sont plats. On doit examiner les jambes afin de déceler toute limitation de mouvement. Comme les jambes, les bras sont courts et souvent en position qualifiée de « réflexe tonique du cou » (voir p. 101).

Les mains sont potelées, les doigts relativement courts, les ongles sont lisses et tendres et dépassent le bout des doigts. Le nouveau-né conserve ses poings fermés. On doit examiner les doigts séparément. Le réflexe de préhension est tellement développé qu'un adulte peut soulever le nouveau-né de son berceau en introduisant un doigt à l'intérieur des poings de l'enfant.

On rencontre aux extrémités plusieurs anomalies fréquentes, tels les pieds bots ou la syndactylie. Même si ces infirmités ne gênent pas les fonctions vitales comme pourraient le faire, par exemple, certaines malformations cardiaques, rénales ou autres, elles provoquent beaucoup d'anxiété chez les parents.

LES MUSCLES

Le contour musculaire de l'enfant en bonne santé paraît lisse. Les muscles, en dépit de leur faiblesse et de leur manque de précision, semblent fermes et passablement résistants à la pression. L'infirmière doit prendre note de la capacité de l'enfant à résister au mouvement passif de ses extrémités. S'il s'en montre incapable, il peut souffrir d'une lésion cérébrale, de narcose ou même de choc. Si l'enfant semble amorphe, il faut éviter de considérer cet état comme une simple caractéristique de son immaturité.

Le nouveau-né exécute ses mouvements au hasard et de façon non coordonnée; il s'agite et s'étire. Lorsque l'infirmière le soulève, elle doit supporter sa tête et son dos car le nouveau-né manque de force musculaire pour maintenir sa tête droite. Si on ne lui fournit pas d'appui en position assise, il tombera vers l'avant.

LE SYSTÈME NERVEUX

Le système nerveux du nouveau-né se caractérise par une immaturité saisissante. Les fonctions vitales et les réactions aux stimuli extérieurs ne dépendent pas du cortex mais des centres inférieurs et de la moelle épinière. Le contrôle des centres nerveux supérieurs entre en action à mesure que s'effectue la myélinisation des fibres nerveuses et que les synapses s'établissent. Il en résulte peu à peu un comportement plus complexe et organisé. On peut observer aisément, de semaine en semaine, le développement neurologique qui progresse selon un axe céphalo-caudal.

Réflexes

Certains réflexes s'avèrent essentiels pour la vie de l'enfant, d'autres jouent tout simplement un rôle protecteur. Parmi ces derniers, on note le *réflexe de clignotement* qui se produit lorsqu'on expose l'enfant à une lumière trop vive; le *réflexe de l'éternuement* a pour fonction de libérer les voies respiratoires supérieures. Le *bâillement* protège l'enfant en augmentant son approvisionnement en oxygène.

Plusieurs réflexes sont reliés à l'alimentation. Le *réflexe de la recherche du mamelon* porte l'enfant affamé à tourner la tête vers tout ce qui peut frôler sa joue, facilitant ainsi l'atteinte de la source de nourriture. Quand le sein frôle sa joue, ce réflexe invite l'enfant à saisir le mamelon. Présent à la naissance, le *réflexe de succion* est également accompagné du *réflexe de déglutition*. Tout ce qui touche les lèvres de l'enfant déclenche le réflexe de succion. Le *réflexe de rejet* se produit quand l'enfant absorbe plus de nourriture qu'il ne peut en avaler. Si le liquide qu'il absorbe suit une mauvaise trajectoire en se dirigeant vers la trachée, il réagira en utilisant le *réflexe de la toux*.

L'enfant ne maîtrise pas tous ces réflexes et requiert pour leur exécution l'aide de sa mère ou de l'infirmière. Il est possible que le nouveau-né éprouve quelques difficultés à atteindre le mamelon et même s'il y réussit, il se peut qu'il l'introduise sous la langue plutôt que sur la langue. Ces réflexes peuvent être absents ou perturbés chez le prématuré. Chez l'enfant à terme, leur absence indique un état possible de narcose, un traumatisme cérébral ou un retard mental. Si le réflexe de succion cesse d'être stimulé, il disparaît.

Les mains et les pieds sont dotés du *réflexe de préhension*. Il se manifeste ainsi: l'enfant saisit tout objet placé dans sa main, le tient quelques instants et le laisse involontairement tomber ensuite. À la naissance, ce réflexe est tellement bien développé qu'en introduisant un doigt à l'intérieur des poings du nouveau-né, on peut le soulever facilement de son berceau (*réflexe de Darwin*). Ce réflexe disparaît progressivement, lorsque l'enfant prend conscience de sa possibilité de préhension et en tire quelque plaisir, par exemple en agitant son hochet. Même si l'enfant ne peut saisir les objets avec ses pieds, il réagit aux stimuli en essayant d'attraper avec ses orteils tout ce qui effleure la plante de ses pieds (fig. 6-8).

Lorsqu'on maintient l'enfant debout en le supportant par le thorax et que ses pieds entrent en contact avec une surface quelconque, il réagit à cette sensation en agitant les jambes. Appelée *réflexe de la danse,* cette réaction disparaît pendant quelque temps pour refaire son apparition plus tard, mais non sous forme de réflexe, lorsque le bébé tentera de marcher ou de se tenir debout.

Le *réflexe de Moro (sursaut)* incite l'enfant à réagir vigoureusement aux stimuli importants. Un bruit puissant ou un manque de support soudain éveilleront ce réflexe dès la naissance, ou peu de temps après. La réaction se traduit par une activité musculaire importante. Le réflexe de sursaut démontre le besoin d'équilibre du nouveau-né. On peut observer davantage ce réflexe lorsque l'enfant repose tranquillement, libre de vêtements gênants. Un stimulus soudain, tel que le déplacement de son berceau, provoquera un redressement de ses jambes, les plantes des pieds tournées l'une vers l'autre et les orteils se touchant presque. Les bras imitent la position d'enlacement. Suivis d'une positioin fixe et rigide, ces mouvements s'exécutent habituellement de façon symétrique. Réaction normale, le réflexe de Moro se manifeste durant les huit premières semaines de

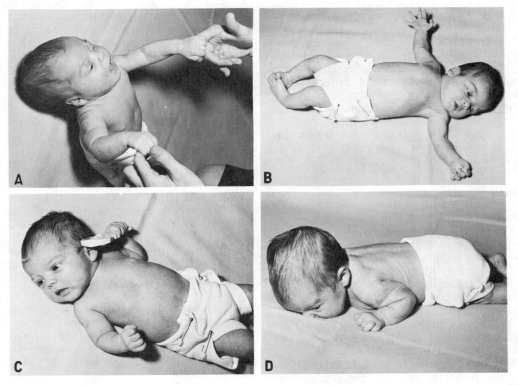

Figure 6-8. Les réflexes et le développement moteur du nouveau-né. *A)* Réflexe de préhension. *B)* Réflexe de Moro. *C)* Réflexe tonique du cou. *D)* Léger soulèvement de la tête.

vie. Il peut persister jusqu'au 5e mois, mais devient de plus en plus difficile à reconnaître. En son absence, il faudrait envisager un trouble cérébral.

Le *réflexe tonique du cou* incite le nourrisson couché à tourner la tête d'un côté et à étendre le bras et la jambe du même côté. L'autre bras et l'autre jambe adoptent tout simplement la position de flexion. Le bébé peut également serrer les poings. On a qualifié cette réaction de position de défense de l'enfant. Elle apparaît chez le fœtus entre la 20e et la 28e semaine et se poursuit chez l'enfant jusqu'à 18 ou 20 semaines.

La présence des réflexes donne la preuve d'un fonctionnement normal du système nerveux. Un réflexe perturbé ou absent signifie que le système nerveux central a pu subir quelque détérioration. Même s'il peut s'avérer impossible de réparer ces anomalies, on doit quand même apporter à l'enfant des soins en rapport avec sa condition. S'il ne peut sucer, par exemple, on doit le nourrir par gavage. Certains réflexes, présents à la naissance, disparaissent lorsque l'enfant vieillit et que le cerveau exerce un contrôle plus important sur le système nerveux. Quand le comportement change, les soins de la mère ou de l'infirmière doivent s'y adapter.

Le réflexe conditionné. C'est la seule voie par laquelle le jeune nourrisson peut apprendre. Cette forme de réflexe lui fait associer, par exemple, le plaisir répété provenant du soulagement de sa faim aux personnes qui lui procurent cette satisfaction. Même si le visage de l'infirmière, ou celui de sa mère, peut lui paraître brouillé, il apprend à les aimer, car ces figures symbolisent pour lui l'arrêt de sa faim et le bien-être qui s'ensuit.

Activité motrice

Les mouvements du nouveau-né sont rapides, variés et désordonnés. Ils consistent uniquement en actes réflexes ou en mouvements qui y sont associés; ainsi, la succion provoquera la déglutition. Même si, dès sa naissance, le nouveau-né commence ses apprentissages par des réflexes conditionnés, presque tout son comportement dépend malgré tout des réponses-réflexes entraînées par les stimuli. Son activité implique la participation de tout son corps et ses réactions sont déclenchées par un état généralisé, comme la faim, la douleur, ou le malaise provoqué par une position prolongée. Il ne localise pas l'endroit d'où viennent la faim et la douleur.

Lorsque l'enfant éprouve un malaise, il réagit avec tout son corps et essaie de se soulager par des actes-réflexes qu'il associe à l'apaisement de la douleur. Même si le sein ou le biberon ne représentent pas encore pour lui la satisfaction de la faim, il exécutera des mouvements de succion et sucera tout ce qui sera introduit dans sa bouche. Des réactions spécifiques à des stimuli particuliers n'apparaissent qu'avec le perfectionnement de ce comportement généralisé; les mouvements superflus disparaissent tandis que seuls les mouvements qui apportent la satisfaction demeurent et s'améliorent par l'exercice. Ce progrès est surtout redevable à la maturation du système nerveux, des muscles, des os, donc du corps entier. Tous les systèmes ne se perfectionnent pas au même rythme, mais un aperçu général permet d'établir le comportement typique des enfants à un âge donné. Naturellement, les enfants doivent avoir l'occasion d'expérimenter de nouvelles réactions pour conserver un comportement typique.

RÉACTIONS ÉMOTIVES

Il s'avère extrêmement difficile d'interpréter les signes d'émotion chez le nouveau-né. Tout ce que nous pouvons affirmer, c'est qu'il existe deux états bien différents: celui qui donne l'impression qu'il repose paisiblement et celui qui traduit son insatisfaction par des cris et des traits crispés. On peut également ajouter à ces réactions émotives, sa façon de sursauter lors de stimuli inattendus.

Traduisant les émotions, on considère également que la vocalisation fait partie des réactions émotives.

La vocalisation

La seule forme de vocalisation du nouveau-né se traduit par des pleurs qui résultent de la douleur ou d'un état d'inconfort. Le nouveau-né est un petit être égocentrique, entièrement dépendant de l'adulte et incapable de manifester sa volonté par d'autres moyens. Le cri qu'il émet à la naissance remplit deux fonctions: oxygéner le sang et dilater les poumons.

À partir d'un cri faible et non soutenu (plaintif), on peut soupçonner un état anormal. À la naissance, le nouveau-né devrait produire un cri perçant. On n'a pas encore réussi à découvrir si le cri de l'enfant qui naît provient du traumatisme de la naissance ou d'un réflexe physiologique qui lui permet de dilater ses poumons.

Très tôt, le bébé apprend à pleurer pour souligner son inconfort. Si les pleurs entraînent un soulagement de la douleur et un état de bien-être, il saura les utiliser pour attirer l'attention de sa mère. Même au cours des premières 24 heures, les cris varient déjà en tonalité, en intensité et en durée; une personne expérimentée saura apporter une réponse adéquate à ces pleurs.

Le milieu environnant ou ses propres sensations provoquent les pleurs de l'enfant. Il peut éprouver une sensation de faim, de douleur ou tout simplement avoir besoin d'exercice ou d'un changement de position. Les enfants pleurent souvent sans raison apparente, et la cause de leur malaise demeure difficile à préciser. Si un enfant repu et bien propre cesse de pleurer quand on le prend, c'est qu'il avait tout simplement besoin d'un contact physique, et une fois rassuré, on peut le remettre dans son lit. Mais l'enfant qui persiste à pleurer souffre d'un malaise quelconque causé par la soif, la chaleur, l'humidité ou toute autre raison. La faim semble être la cause la plus commune des pleurs, et on utilise ces derniers pour établir l'horaire des biberons (voir p. 118).

Les cris se composent presque exclusivement de voyelles produites par la partie antérieure de la bouche. Bientôt, le bébé produira d'autres sons, qui se révéleront aussi importants que les pleurs comme précurseurs du langage. Il utilise des consonnes explosives, gazouille, roucoule, grogne et gargouille. Ces sons signifient que l'enfant est satisfait ou non et servent de base à l'interaction entre l'adulte et le nourrisson. Les bruits produits par le bébé peuvent varier selon le type de sensation ressentie. Ils constituent un prélangage nécessaire à l'acquisition des étapes subséquentes. Le prochain stade, consistant en une répétition de syllabes, comme « ma-ma-ma », est élaboré à partir de la pratique phonétique.

LES SENS

Par ses réactions, l'enfant nous avertit de son manque de confort, et cela prouve qu'il ne demeure pas insensible à la pression, au changement de température et à la douleur.

Le toucher

De tous les sens, celui du toucher s'avère le plus sensible et le plus développé. Il est particulièrement développé aux lèvres, à la langue, aux oreilles et au front. L'incapacité de saisir le mamelon pourrait indiquer un trouble cérébral. Dès la naissance, le nouveau-né réagit au contact des mains qui lui prodiguent des soins.

La vue

Gris ou bleus à la naissance, les yeux adoptent leur véritable couleur entre trois et six mois. Leur mouvement manque de coordination et ils peuvent se croiser ou se diriger vers l'extérieur sans que cela ait la moindre signification pathologique.

Il est assez difficile de déterminer ce que le nouveau-né peut voir. Ses yeux sont entrouverts et les paupières paraissent légèrement gonflées. L'utilisation de nitrate d'argent peut entraîner un écoulement de liquide trouble. Les pupilles réagissent à la lumière et une lumière trop violente incommode l'enfant. Des recherches systématiques et contrôlées ont toutefois démontré que le nouveau-né voit dès le premier jour et distingue rapidement des formes si le tableau visuel est à moins de 30 cm de ses yeux.

De récentes recherches ont aussi démontré que les nouveau-nés à terme peuvent verser des larmes, même si celles-ci ne deviennent apparentes qu'à l'âge de trois ou quatre semaines.

L'ouïe

On a pu démontrer que le développement auditif du fœtus lui permet de réagir à des stimuli auditifs de grande intensité. Les structures fonctionnelles de l'audition semblent établies chez le fœtus à la fin de la grossesse. Toutefois, la présence d'un liquide gélatineux dans l'oreille moyenne rendrait le nouveau-né sourd aux sons d'intensité normale. Les mouvements respiratoires, les pleurs et peut-être les bâillements, provoquent le drainage de l'oreille moyenne et l'ouverture de la trompe d'Eustache et ensuite l'établissement de l'audition s'effectue progressivement. Le nouveau-né réagit à des bruits en clignant des paupières, en bougeant les yeux, en remuant ses membres ou en cessant toute activité.

Les tests d'audition utilisés à la pouponnière sont constitués de stimuli auditifs de 90 décibels. Le moment optimal pour tester le nouveau-né se situe entre les repas durant une période de sommeil léger. Ces tests ne peuvent pas encore dépister de façon certaine les troubles de l'ouïe. Ils indiquent seulement que certains nouveau-nés entendent mais un échec à ces tests ne signifie pas nécessairement un problème auditif réel ou durable.

Le nouveau-né n'entend rien jusqu'à l'émission de son premier cri. Nous pouvons évaluer l'ouïe du nouveau-né en faisant tinter doucement une cloche près de son oreille. S'il entend, il réagira de tout son corps. Chez l'enfant normal, le bruit provoquera quelques réactions, du 3e au 7e jour, ce qui prouve qu'ordinairement, il entend avant le 10e jour. Vers la 4e semaine, la voix de sa mère ou de l'infirmière provoquera beaucoup plus de réactions de sa part qu'un bruit assourdissant.

Le goût

Chez le nouveau-né, le goût se révèle beaucoup plus perfectionné que l'ouïe. Il accepte volontiers des liquides sucrés mais refuse systématiquement les aliments acides, surs ou amers.

L'odorat

La seule preuve qui nous permette d'affirmer que ce sens existe chez le bébé, c'est qu'il recherche le mamelon et semble attiré par l'odeur du lait maternel. Le développement de l'odorat varie énormément d'un enfant à l'autre.

Les sensations organiques

L'enfant réagit fortement aux stimulations organiques, telles que la faim ou la soif, sensations qui provoquent les pleurs. Le nouveau-né semble indifférent aux gaz intestinaux; par contre, l'enfant âgé de quelques semaines souffre intensément, s'il a des coliques.

LE SOMMEIL

Le sommeil du nouveau-né se distingue difficilement des états de veille. Il dort environ 15 à 20 heures par jour. Il se réveille toutes les deux heures, pendant une courte période. Ces périodes de réveil s'espacent et raccourcissent pendant la nuit, faute de stimulations extérieures. Un malaise, comme la faim ou la douleur, le réveille habituellement. Au fur et à mesure qu'il vieillit, le sommeil occupe une place moins importante dans son horaire quotidien.

L'IMMUNITÉ

Les anticorps qui combattent certaines maladies infectieuses passent de la mère à l'enfant à travers le placenta. Parmi ces anticorps, on note ceux contre la variole, les oreillons, la diphtérie et la rubéole, si la mère a été immunisée contre ces maladies. Cette immunité passive peut durer quelques semaines ou quelques mois. Il existe une immunité insignifiante contre la varicelle ou la coqueluche, et elle n'empêche pas les enfants d'en être atteints. Il n'est pas recommandé d'immuniser de très jeunes enfants tant qu'ils n'ont pas acquis la maturité suffisante pour développer avec succès leurs propres anticorps.

Contractée par un nouveau-né, une maladie contagieuse s'avère beaucoup plus sérieuse et entraîne beaucoup plus de complications que chez l'enfant plus âgé.

RÉFÉRENCES

Livres et documents officiels

Abramson, H.: *Symposium on the Functional Physiopathology of the Fetus and Neonate: Clinical Correlations.* St. Louis, C. V. Mosby Company, 1971.

Arey, L. B.: *Developmental Anatomy.* 7e éd. Philadelphie, W. B. Saunders Company, 1965.

Assali, N. S. (édit.): *The Fetus and Neonate.* New York and London, Academic Press, 1968.

Balinsky, B. I.: *An Introduction to Embryology.* 3e éd. Philadelphie, W. B. Saunders Company, 1970.

Crelin, E. S.: *Anatomy of the Newborn: An Atlas.* Philadelphie, Lea & Febiger, 1969.

Fitzpatrick, E., Eastman, N. J. et Reeder, S. R.: *Soins infirmiers en maternité.* Le renouveau pédagogique, Montréal, 1973.

Garigue, P.: *Analyse du comportement familial.* Montréal, Presses de l'Université de Montréal, 1967.

Garigue, P.: *La vie familiale des Canadiens français.* Montréal, Presses de l'Université de Montréal, 1970.

Iorio, J.: *Principles of Obstetrics and Gynecology for Nurses.* Saint Louis, C. V. Mosby Company, 1971.

Laboratoires Ross: *Le cycle normal des selles chez le nouveau-né.* (feuillet no 3) *Particularités fréquentes chez le nouveau-né.* (feuillet no 9) Section de l'éducation en nursing. Columbus, Ohio.

McKilligin, H. R.: *The First Day of Life.* New York, Springer Publishing Company, 1970.

Ministère de la Santé nationale et du Bien-être social: *Normes et recommandations pour les soins à la mère et au nouveau-né.* Ottawa, 1968.

Moore, M. L.: *The Newborn and the Nurse.* Philadelphie, W. B. Saunders Company, 1972.

Sinclair, D. C.: *Human Growth after Birth*. Don Mills, Ontario, Oxford University Press, 1969.

Waisman, H. et Kerr, G. (édit.): *Fetal Growth and Development*. New York, McGraw-Hill Book Company, Inc., 1970.

Articles

British Survey: Lower IQ's Found in Breech Babies. *J. A. M. A.*, 208:2256, 1969.

Carroll, M. H.: Preventing Newborn Deaths from Drug Withdrawal. *RN*, 34:34, décembre 1971.

Clark, A. L.: The Beginning Family. *Am. J. Nursing*, 66:802, 1966.

Cohen, S. N. et Olson, W. A.: Drugs that Depress the Newborn Infant. *Pediat. Clin. N. Amer.*, 17:835, novembre 1970.

Craig. M. E.: Normal Neonatal Behavior Patterns: The First Week of Extrauterine Life. *Bull. Am. Coll. Nurse Midwife*, 15:93, novembre 1970.

Hervada, A. R.: Nursery Evaluation of the Newborn. *Am. J. Nursing*, 67:1669, 1967.

Ingall, D. et Zuckerstatter, M.: The Passively Addicted Newborn. *Hosp. Practice*, 5:101, août, 1970.

Marcil, V.: L'examen physique du nouveau-né. *Inf. Can.*, 18:11, 3, 1976.

Shimek. M. L.: Screening Newborns for Hearing Loss. *Nursing Outlook*, 19:115, février 1971.

Winick, M.: Fetal Malnutrition and Growth Processes. *Hosp. Practice*, 5:33, mai 1970.

Yao, A. C. et Lind, J.: Effect of Gravity on Placental Transfusion. *Lancet*, 2:505, 6 septembre 1969.

Yerushalmy, J.: The Classification of Newborn Infants by Birth Weight and Gestational Age. *J. Pediat.*, 71:164, août 1967.

7
soins du nouveau-né

Les soins que prodigue l'infirmière devraient être fondés sur sa compréhension de l'état physique du nouveau-né, et sur les réactions émotives du bébé et de ses parents consécutives au processus de l'enfantement. Le chapitre précédent traitait des caractéristiques physiques et physiologiques du nouveau-né normal. Le présent chapitre traite des soins à donner au nouveau-né immédiatement après l'accouchement, à la pouponnière et après le départ de l'hôpital.

SOINS À LA SALLE D'ACCOUCHEMENT

Les soins immédiats au nouveau-né, qui doivent toujours être prodigués avec la plus grande douceur, comprennent la prévention des infections, l'établissement et le maintien de la respiration, le soin du cordon ombilical et des yeux, la stabilisation de la température, l'identification du bébé et la tenue du dossier.

À la salle d'accouchement, on examine l'enfant afin de déceler la présence d'anomalies évidentes, comme une méningocèle, la fissure labiale, la fissure palatine, l'anus imperforé, l'hydrocéphalie, les taches de naissance, ou l'évidence de choc ou de traumatisme obstétrical. Plusieurs anomalies ne sont pas immédiatement évidentes à l'examen et leur découverte est du ressort du médecin et de l'infirmière à la pouponnière.

Dans les 60 secondes qui suivent l'expulsion du bébé, on devrait évaluer cinq signes objectifs. Ces signes, présentés sur le tableau évaluateur mis au point par le Dr Virginia Apgar, comprennent le rythme cardiaque, l'effort respiratoire, le tonus musculaire, la réaction réflexe à la stimulation et la coloration de la peau. Chacun de ces signes est un indice de la faiblesse ou de la force du bébé naissant, et on les évalue par la note 0, 1 ou 2. L'enfant jouit d'une excellente condition physique si la somme des points est égale à 10. Si le résultat se situe entre 5 et 10, il ne nécessite ordinairement pas de traitement. Si le résultat est de 4 ou moins, on doit tout de suite poser un diagnostic et instituer le traitement approprié. Environ 70% à 90% des nouveau-nés reçoivent un résultat de 7 ou plus, une minute après la naissance. Le test d'Apgar doit être répété cinq minutes après l'expulsion.

Le médecin et l'infirmière ont plusieurs responsabilités dans le soin du bébé immédiatement après sa naissance.

Établissement et maintien de la respiration

On doit susciter et maintenir les respirations du bébé. Pour cela, il est nécessaire qu'il pleure avec force périodiquement. La pleine expansion des poumons procure l'oxygène qui, avant la naissance, était fourni par la circulation pla-

Tableau 7-1. Tableau d'appréciation d'Apgar

SIGNE	0	1	2
rythme cardiaque	absent	lent (moins de 100/min)	plus de 100/min
effort respiratoire	absent	faible pleur, hypoventilation	pleur puissant
tonus musculaire	flasque	une certaine flexion des extrémités	activité motrice
réaction réflexe à la stimulation de la plante des pieds	pas de réaction	une grimace	un cri
coloration	bleue ou pâle	corps rose, extrémités bleues	complètement rose

V. Apgar et autres: Evaluation of the Newborn Infant — Second Report. *J.A.M.A.,* 168:1988, 1958.

centaire. Le retrait de cette source d'oxygène stimule les mouvements respiratoires qui avaient d'ailleurs débuté sous forme superficielle pendant la vie intra-utérine.

Tout enfant qui ne respire pas dans les 30 secondes après sa naissance est menacé d'asphyxie. Il est évident qu'il faut observer de près le nouveau-né et avoir sous la main ce qui est nécessaire pour la réanimation.

Certains bébés requièrent une stimulation plus poussée que celle produite par le processus normal de l'accouchement. L'absence de pleurs peut être due à diverses causes, dont la plus fréquente consiste en l'obstruction des voies respiratoires par du mucus. Afin de les libérer, on peut tenir le bébé par les pieds, la tête en bas et le cou vers l'arrière.

Dans cette position, le mucus sort par gravité. L'expulsion du mucus peut également être facilitée en massant le cou en direction de la bouche. On peut stimuler davantage les respirations en frottant délicatement le dos du bébé ou en frappant son siège ou la plante de ses pieds. Le doigt ganté de l'infirmière peut extraire le mucus de la bouche du bébé.

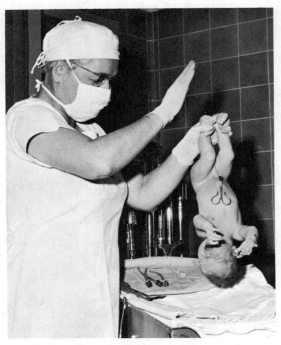

Figure 7-1. Le Dr Virginia Apgar, créatrice du tableau évaluateur Apgar, tape fermement la plante des pieds d'un bébé pour déterminer la valeur de ses réflexes. Ce bébé normal pleure fortement. (Courtoisie de la National Foundation — March of Dimes.)

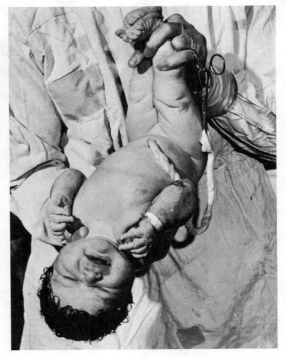

Figure 7-2. Position dans laquelle il faut tenir l'enfant après l'accouchement. Si sa première respiration se produit lorsqu'il a la tête en haut, il s'en suit une obstruction respiratoire. Remarquez le bracelet d'identification au poignet. (Tiré de *Resuscitation of the Newborn Infant.* American Academy of Pediatrics.)

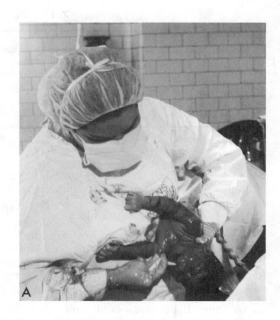

Figure 7-3. *A)* Aspiration du nouveau-né immédiatement après la naissance avec une poire en caoutchouc. *B)* Aspirateur de Lee. L'infirmière indique silencieusement le rythme cardiaque par le mouvement de son doigt. *C)* Aspiration du pharynx du nouveau-né. (*A*, extrait de *R.N.* janvier 1970, page couverture. *B* et *C*, extrait de *Resuscitation of the Newborn Infant*, American Academy of Pediatrics.)

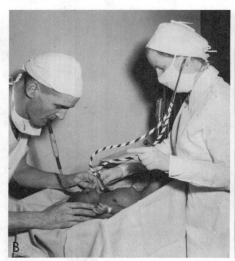

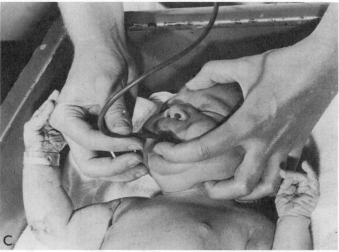

Si ces mesures échouent, il est nécessaire alors d'enlever le mucus par aspiration. On utilise un cathéter souple que l'on branche à un aspirateur. Quand le cathéter a pénétré dans le pharynx, on procède à une légère aspiration.

Celle-ci ne doit pas être trop vigoureuse pour éviter de détériorer les muqueuses. Il est important de retirer le mucus avant la première respiration du bébé, afin d'empêcher qu'il ne l'aspire. Quand on a retiré le plus de mucus possible, on place le bébé la tête en bas pour permettre un drainage plus complet, à moins que cela ne soit contre-indiqué.

Si le bébé ne pleure pas après ces mesures de réanimation, le médecin procède à la section du cordon ombilical et des moyens plus énergiques seront utilisés pour stimuler les réflexes respiratoires du bébé.

Lorsque les voies respiratoires supérieures sont libérées, on procède à une ventilation par administration d'oxygène. Si la langue du bébé est appuyée contre la paroi postérieure du pharynx, obstruant ainsi la trachée, l'application d'un tube bucco-pharyngé empêchera l'obstruction. Si le bébé ne respire pas encore convenablement, on peut remplir les poumons d'oxygène à l'aide d'une pression positive intermittente contrôlée, en utilisant un masque bien ajusté. Ordinairement, pour plus de sécurité, on opère à des pressions ne dépassant pas 15 à 20 cm d'eau. Quand on donne de l'oxygène, le médecin devrait ausculter la poitrine pour déterminer si l'oxygène pénètre bien dans les poumons.

Si les poumons du bébé ne sont pas encore assez dilatés, on devrait procéder à une laryngoscopie directe afin que soit enlevé tout corps étranger obstruant le passage de l'air. Dans certains cas, on peut appliquer une pression directe en utilisant un tube endo-trachéal. Il faut se rappeler que l'air poussé sous une trop grande pression dans les poumons du bébé peut provoquer la rupture des alvéoles. En cas d'urgence, s'il n'y a pas d'instrument mécanique disponible, on peut procéder à une réanimation bouche à bouche. On ne peut employer de stimulants respiratoires, mais un stimulant circulatoire peut être indiqué.

Soin du cordon ombilical

Pour attacher le cordon ombilical, on emploie ordinairement une pince qui comprime les vaisseaux et qui est laissée en place jusqu'à ce que le cordon soit asséché. Dans certains hôpitaux, on place deux pinces hémostatiques sur le cordon et on ligote celui-ci à environ 2,5 cm de l'abdomen à l'aide d'un cordonnet stérile attaché entre les deux pinces. Certains obstétriciens préfèrent attendre que le cordon ne soit plus pulsatile avant de le sectionner, ceci afin d'assurer une transfusion placentaire d'environ 100 ml au nouveau-né prématuré ou susceptible d'être anémique. Toutefois, plusieurs accusent ce procédé d'augmenter l'ictère physiologique du nouveau-né, à cause du danger d'hémolyse accrue due à la surcharge de globules rouges.

Il y a divergence d'opinions quant à savoir s'il faut appliquer sur le cordon une solution antiseptique et un pansement ou le laisser sécher à l'air. Si on suppose qu'une exsanguinotransfusion pourrait être nécessaire à la suite d'une incompatibilité fœto-maternelle connue, on conserve au cordon une longueur supérieure à la normale et on le couvre d'un pansement stérile pour les premières 24 heures de vie. Tout comme pour les autres bébés, il faut vérifier l'état du cordon pour déceler toute menace d'hémorragie durant les premiers jours et l'apparition d'une infection jusqu'à ce qu'il se détache et tombe. Il faut éviter à tout prix la contamination du cordon, car il est rattaché au système veineux et toute infection pourrait se propager rapidement.

Soin des yeux

Si la mère est atteinte de gonorrhée, les yeux du bébé peuvent être contaminés durant l'accouchement. Si on ne soigne pas les yeux adéquatement, il y a danger d'ophtalmie purulente du nouveau-né (Cf. chap. 9). On procède dans tous les hôpitaux à un traitement prophylactique de cette maladie. Immédiatement après la naissance, on applique un germicide dans les yeux du nouveau-né. Pendant plusieurs années, on a employé le nitrate d'argent. Plus récemment, on a utilisé la pénicilline, qui est un agent anti-gonococcique.

Si on emploie le nitrate d'argent, il peut être appliqué entre les paupières, à n'importe quel moment entre la sortie de la tête et la fin de la troisième phase de l'accouchement. On nettoie d'abord soigneusement les paupières, en allant de la racine du nez vers l'extérieur, avec un tampon de coton stérile imbibé d'eau stérile. On abaisse la paupière inférieure et on applique deux gouttes d'une solution à 1% de nitrate d'argent dans la cavité conjonctivale. Après une minute ou deux, on devrait irriguer les yeux avec une solution saline physiologique tiède, ce qui enlève le surplus de nitrate d'argent et forme un précipité avec ce qui reste. Dans environ 50% des cas, il peut se produire une irritation chimique due au nitrate d'argent. Bien qu'un écoulement oculaire puisse apparaître après quelques heures, il n'en résulte pas d'effet nocif permanent.

On peut administrer de la pénicilline sous forme d'onguent ophtalmique ou par voie intramusculaire.

Stabilisation de la température

Ordinairement, la température du nouveau-né baisse immédiatement après la naissance et redevient normale après environ 8 heures. La température de la salle d'accouchement, plus basse que celle de la cavité utérine, explique partiellement cette baisse de température. Pour ramener la température à la normale, on devrait envelopper le bébé, immédiatement après sa naissance, dans une couverture chaude et stérile. Le froid peut faire apparaître l'acidose et l'hypoglycémie, mettant ainsi en péril la vie du nouveau-né.

Identification du bébé

Tous les bébés doivent être rigoureusement identifiés avant de quitter la salle d'accouchement. Il y a plusieurs méthodes, qui ont en commun de fournir toutes les informations sur son identité: une étiquette collée au dos du bébé, un bracelet ou un collier avec le nom, des rubans gommés au poignet comportant un numéro d'identification dont l'un est pour la mère et l'autre pour l'enfant (voir figure 7-2), et les empreintes du pied et de la main prises lorsque l'enfant est encore dans la salle d'accouchement. Cette dernière méthode est la plus sûre, mais doit être effectuée avec soin afin d'obtenir des empreintes précises. Elle ne procure cependant pas une forme d'identification rapide, comme le bracelet.

Le baptême

En cas de danger de mort du nouveau-né, la majorité des parents chrétiens désirent que leur enfant soit baptisé immédiatement. Cela peut évidemment avoir lieu à la salle d'accouchement, mais relève plus souvent de la responsabilité de l'infirmière à la pouponnière. Si les parents sont catholiques, on doit appeler un prêtre, s'il semble que le bébé vivra jusqu'à son arrivée. Si les parents sont protestants, on appelle un ministre de leur culte. Si la mort est imminente et qu'il n'y a pas de prêtre présent, l'infirmière ou le médecin peuvent baptiser en versant de l'eau sur le front du bébé et en disant: « Je te baptise, au nom du Père, du Fils, et du Saint-Esprit ». L'Église catholique enseigne qu'on devrait baptiser chaque fœtus et chaque embryon, si c'est possible. Le baptême sous condition peut être administré, lorsqu'on n'est pas certain que le sujet puisse le recevoir.

Particularités du soin au nouveau-né

L'infirmière doit se rappeler que la naissance représente un effort épuisant pour le nouveau-né. Il doit subir une série de pressions, sentir le froid, faire face à la lumière et commencer à accomplir des fonctions physiologiques que sa mère assumait pour lui auparavant. Tout mouvement brusque, tout tissu sur sa peau constitue un stress additionnel pour lui. Ceci explique pourquoi l'on préconise actuellement moins d'ampoules brillantes dans les salles d'accouchement, moins de bruit et plus de chaleur.

Le nouveau-né devient une proie facile pour l'infection après sa naissance et il possède peu de défense. La literie et l'équipement utilisés pour le nouveau-né doivent être stériles et l'infirmière doit employer une technique aseptique préventive.

SOINS À LA POUPONNIÈRE

Le nouveau-né, enveloppé dans une couverture chaude, est amené à la pouponnière dans un berceau réchauffé ou dans les bras de l'infirmière. Il est alors vêtu d'une couche, d'une chemisette, enveloppé d'une couverture et placé dans un berceau chaud. Si le père ne l'a pas encore vu, le bébé doit lui être montré s'il le demande.

Une procédure, souhaitable à la pouponnière, consiste à placer les bébés qui sont nés le même jour dans une pièce vitrée particulière, constituant un îlot dans la pouponnière. Ainsi, chaque jour, on emploie une pièce différente pour les nouveaux bébés. Chaque fois qu'un groupe de nouveau-nés quitte l'hôpital, la pièce est nettoyée à fond. Si une infection apparaît, il est ainsi plus facile de la circonscrire.

Soins généraux

Tant que le bébé demeure à l'hôpital, on lui prodigue des soins quotidiens assidus. Comme le taux de mortalité infantile est plus élevé pendant les premiers jours de la vie, les soins physiques et les observations de l'infirmière sont aussi importants qu'immédiatement après la naissance.

C'est seulement quand l'infirmière a pris connaissance des caractéristiques physiques, des variations physiologiques et des désordres fonctionnels fréquents chez le nouveau-né qu'elle peut évaluer adéquatement la santé des bébés confiés à sa garde à la pouponnière (voir le chapitre 6 pour les caractéristiques et l'examen du nouveau-né normal).

Examen physique préliminaire

L'infirmière doit examiner l'enfant avec soin, au moment de l'admission à la pouponnière ou peu de temps après. Cette évaluation n'est valable que si l'infirmière connaît ce qui est normal et anormal chez le nouveau-né, car il y a toute une gamme de différences individuelles chez les bébés normaux. Cette connaissance ne peut pas être acquise uniquement dans les livres; elle s'acquiert surtout par la pratique dans le soin du nouveau-né. Pour cette raison, l'étudiante infirmière devrait s'informer immédiatement auprès de son professeur lorsqu'elle a des doutes sur la signification des variations de l'état ou du comportement d'un bébé.

Pour pouvoir appliquer ses connaissances, l'infirmière devrait connaître l'histoire du bébé, c'est-à-dire l'âge de la mère, l'histoire des grossesses antérieures et de la grossesse actuelle, le facteur Rh des parents, la durée du travail, la couleur du liquide amniotique et le résultat de l'Apgar au moment de la naissance.

Elle doit se rappeler que les signes les plus communs de détresse infantile sont: *1) un rythme respiratoire accéléré ou des difficultés respiratoires, 2) le tirage sternal ou intercostal, 3) le mucus en quantité excessive, ex.: lorsque le bébé bave ou fait des bulles, 4) un faciès anxieux, 5) la cyanose, 6) une distension abdominale ou la présence d'une masse, 7) l'absence de méconium dans les 24 heures qui suivent la naissance, 8) l'absence d'urine, même après plusieurs heures, 9) les vomissements bilieux, 10) l'ictère prononcé et 11) les convulsions.* L'infirmière doit aussi vérifier les mouvements du bébé afin de déceler précocement des anomalies congénitales. Dans notre contexte actuel, l'infirmière est rarement seule responsable de l'évaluation du bébé, mais ses observations peuvent attirer l'attention du médecin et faciliter son diagnostic. Pour que ses remarques soient pertinentes, elle doit comprendre la maturation normale qui a lieu pendant les premiers jours de la vie. Elle ne peut employer les mêmes normes pour un bébé de 3 jours et pour un nouveau-né d'une heure.

En plus de l'évaluation de la santé du bébé pendant son séjour à la pouponnière, l'infirmière peut aussi discuter avec la mère des variations physiologiques du nouveau-né, afin que celle-ci ne s'alarme pas de caractéristiques effectivement normales, telles que la forme de la tête ou le strabisme. Une telle information peut prévenir ou dissiper l'anxiété que pourrait ressentir la mère, même si le pédiatre l'a assurée de la bonne condition physique de son enfant.

Observation continuelle

On doit observer le bébé régulièrement, de jour et de nuit, afin de déceler immédiatement les perturbations des fonctions vitales.

Difficultés respiratoires. Les difficultés respiratoires se manifestent par des modifications de la nature ou du rythme des respirations du bébé, par ses pleurs, sa coloration et son comportement en général. Si l'enfant étouffe, il se peut qu'il y ait du mucus dans son nez ou sa bouche. On pourra libérer immédiatement les voies respiratoires en plaçant la tête du bébé plus bas que le reste du corps, massant délicatement le cou avec un mouvement ascendant. Si cette méthode ne réussit pas à soulager le bébé, l'infirmière doit faire une aspiration des sécrétions et donner de l'oxygène. Avant d'utiliser des méthodes

plus spécifiques de réanimation, on doit appeler le médecin. Pour faire face à une urgence de ce genre, il faut toujours garder à la pouponnière l'équipement servant à l'aspiration des sécrétions et à l'administration de l'oxygène.

Position du bébé. Il est possible que des difficultés respiratoires surviennent durant les premières 24 heures de la vie. S'il n'y a pas de contre-indication, il est conseillé d'incliner le sommier du berceau de 15 ou 20 degrés, de placer le bébé sur le côté en position déclive.

Il faut changer le bébé de position toutes les deux ou trois heures, pour faciliter l'expansion pulmonaire. De plus, comme les os du bébé sont mous et sensibles à la pression, son crâne et son thorax risquent de s'aplatir si l'on ne change pas sa position fréquemment. Puisque le bébé aime la lumière et qu'il est essentiel qu'il ne soit pas toujours couché sur le même côté, on placera sa tête alternativement au pied ou à la tête du berceau.

Le nouveau-né doit s'habituer à dormir sur l'abdomen, mais l'infirmière doit veiller à éliminer les causes de suffocation, telles oreiller, plis ou surplus de literie ou de vêtements.

La position dans laquelle on tient le bébé dépend de son niveau de maturation, particulièrement de la maturation de son système neuromusculaire. Même un bébé normal ne peut tenir sa tête droite sans support avant l'âge de six semaines. Lorsque l'infirmière prend le bébé dans ses bras, elle soutient sa tête et ses épaules avec une main et son siège avec l'autre. Elle doit le tenir fermement et de façon constante, afin qu'il ne puisse craindre de perdre cet appui. Certains psychologues pour enfants soutiennent qu'une telle peur fait partie des quelques craintes fondamentales de l'enfance. Un enfant éprouve du plaisir à être pris, et cela donne à l'infirmière la possibilité de l'aider à développer sa confiance dans ceux qui en prennent soin.

Température. Il faut contrôler la température et l'humidité dans la pouponnière, ou dans la chambre de la mère si le bébé y réside. La température et l'humidité de la pièce influent beaucoup sur la respiration, particulièrement chez le nouveau-né. Pendant la journée, la température doit être maintenue entre 20°C et 24°C, l'humidité, entre 45% et 55%. Le bébé, dont les centres régulateurs de chaleur s'avèrent peu développés, réagit rapidement à toute variation de température de son environnement. L'air de la chambre doit être renouvelé, mais il ne doit pas y avoir de courants d'air. L'air frais contient ordinai-

rement assez d'humidité pour prévenir l'assèchement des muqueuses du nez et de la gorge.

La température du nouveau-né lors de son
admission à la pouponnière peut être au dessous de la normale. Il faut alors lui mettre
des vêtements secs et le réchauffer si nécessaire, jusqu'à ce que sa température remonte
au degré désiré.

Si l'enfant est né à la maison, on pourra
utiliser des bouillottes placées dans le berceau, pour procurer une source additionnelle
de chaleur. Comme la perception de la chaleur
est peu développée chez le nouveau-né, il faut
observer trois précautions quand on se sert
de bouillottes: 1) la température de l'eau ne
doit pas dépasser 46°C. 2) Le contenant doit
être recouvert de flanelle ou d'une serviette
et il faut s'assurer qu'il n'y a pas de fuite avant
de l'utiliser. 3) Il ne faut pas placer le contenant sur la poitrine ou l'abdomen du bébé,
son poids pouvant nuire aux mouvements respiratoires. Ordinairement, on emploie trois
bouillottes, une sous les jambes et une de
chaque côté du corps, ce qui procure de la
chaleur aux extrémités, où la circulation est
pauvre, sans surchauffer la poitrine. Les bouillottes refroidissent rapidement et doivent être
remplies fréquemment; si l'on en emploie
trois, on pourra en changer l'eau par rotation.
Il ne faut pas employer de couverture électrique, car il y a toujours danger de surchauffage ou de choc dû à de mauvais raccords
électriques.

L'incubateur demeure le moyen de réchauffement le plus satisfaisant car il conserve une
température uniforme et contrôlée. On maintient le régulateur de chaleur entre 27°C et
28°C et on vérifie souvent la température du
bébé afin d'ajuster l'appareil conformément
à ses besoins. Le bébé réagit rapidement à
la chaleur ambiante et on devrait prendre sa
température toutes les heures, jusqu'à ce que
la chaleur de son corps soit revenue à la normale. Ordinairement, le nouveau-né peut alors
être retiré de l'incubateur pour être déposé
dans son berceau, mais ceux qui pèsent moins
que la moyenne ou qui sont affaiblis par un
accouchement difficile peuvent y demeurer
plus longtemps.

La quantité de vêtements et de couvertures
requise pour le bébé dépend de la température de la pièce. En général, on conserve une
température plus élevée dans la pouponnière
que dans l'unité post-partum, si bien que le
bébé aura besoin de plus de couvertures s'il
séjourne dans la chambre de sa mère. Les
mères tendent à habiller leur bébé trop chau-

dement, parce qu'elles se basent sur la température de ses mains et de ses pieds. L'infirmière
apprendra aux mamans qu'il y a une méthode
plus exacte pour déterminer si l'enfant a chaud
ou froid; celle-ci consiste à observer la coloration du visage. S'il est rouge, l'enfant a
trop chaud; s'il est pâle ou bleuâtre, il a froid.
La mère devrait palper les bras et les jambes
du bébé, plutôt que les mains et les pieds,
pour corroborer son observation du visage.
Elle aura alors des critères adéquats pour déterminer la quantité de vêtements et de couvertures dont a besoin le nouveau-né.

Le bébé ne peut se maintenir à une température optimale lorsqu'on le transporte de la
pouponnière à la chambre de sa mère et on
doit le couvrir d'une chaude couverture pour
éviter le refroidissement.

Après la stabilisation de la température du
nouveau-né, on la vérifie toutes les 4 heures
pendant les deux premiers jours, et ensuite,
deux fois par jour. On peut prendre la température sous les aisselles ou par voie rectale.
Il devrait y avoir un thermomètre pour chaque bébé afin de réduire la possibilité d'infection. Si on utilise ordinairement la voie
rectale, il faut prendre garde de ne pas endommager la muqueuse. On examine soigneusement le bout du thermomètre pour détecter
toute imperfection. L'infirmière saisit fermement les jambes du bébé, l'index entre les
malléoles, et le maintient immobile pendant
l'opération. Il faut bien lubrifier le thermomètre et le laisser dans le rectum pendant 3
minutes. Certains médecins préfèrent la prise
de température axillaire. Dans ce cas, il faut
tenir le thermomètre fermement sous l'aisselle, le bras du bébé serré contre son côté,
pendant 5 minutes ou jusqu'à ce que le mercure cesse de monter.

La température du nouveau-né peut être
contrôlée de façon continue soit avec un thermomètre électronique soit par l'application
d'un petit élément de matière plastique sur la
peau abdominale du bébé au niveau de la
région hépatique. La couleur du film varie
selon la température de la peau et il peut être
laissé en place 24 heures.

Poids. On pèse l'enfant à la naissance et
tous les jours qui suivent, vers la même heure,
ordinairement quand on lui donne les soins
du matin. On pèse ordinairement les nouveau-
nés complètement nus dans une pouponnière
adéquatement chauffée. On pèse une feuille
de papier ou une couche stérile avant de
placer le bébé sur la pesée. Lorsque le bébé
est prématuré ou malade, ou si la pouponnière

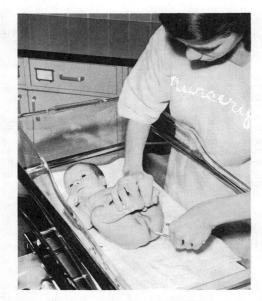

Figure 7-4. La température de l'enfant est prise rectalement deux fois par jour. Si l'enfant a de la fièvre, la température doit être contrôlée toutes les 2 heures. Pour prendre la température, l'infirmière place son index entre les chevilles de l'enfant et tient le thermomètre en place pour plus de sécurité. (Davis et Rubin: Delee's Obstetrics for Nurses. 17e éd.)

n'est pas suffisamment chauffée, on peut peser le nouveau-né habillé et enveloppé dans sa couverture. Lorsqu'on le déshabillera pour les soins du matin, on pèsera ces articles, soustrayant ensuite leur poids de celui obtenu précédemment.

Certains incubateurs contiennent tout l'équipement nécessaire aux soins de l'enfant, y compris une balance. On peut alors laver et peser le bébé sans avoir à l'exposer à la température extérieure.

On compare chaque jour le poids du bébé avec celui noté la veille. Si la perte de poids excède la perte physiologique durant les premiers jours ou si, après une semaine, il manifeste peu ou pas de gain de poids, l'équipe de santé devrait agir sans tarder.

Soins infirmiers spécifiques

Soin de la peau

Il ne faut pas nettoyer à fond la peau du bébé immédiatement après l'accouchement, car on croit que l'enduit sébacé joue un rôle protecteur pour l'épiderme. Le vernix caseosa disparaît d'ailleurs en quelques jours.

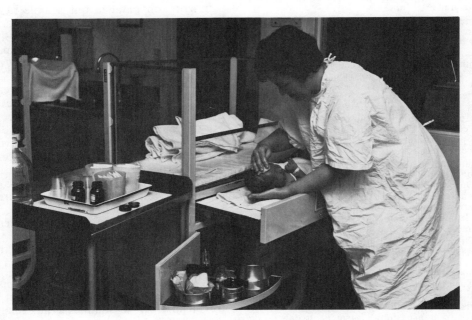

Figure 7-5. L'heure du bain est le moment idéal pour observer le comportement du bébé et ses réactions aux stimuli. Le lit du bébé devient une unité indépendante où tout est à portée de l'infirmière qui donne les soins. (Courtoisie de l'Hôpital Sainte-Justine, Montréal.)

La méthode suivante concorde avec les concepts modernes sur les soins immédiats des nouveau-nés.

1) Peu après la naissance du bébé, on essuie le sang sur son visage et sa tête avec un tissu très doux ou des tampons de coton imbibés d'eau stérile.

2) On ne cherche pas à enlever l'enduit sébacé qui adhère à la peau et qui a peut-être une valeur protectrice. Cet enduit a aussi été comparé à une crème adoucissante.

3) Le bébé peut prendre froid si l'infirmière néglige de le couvrir pendant qu'elle enlève le liquide amniotique et le sang. Elle ne doit exposer que la partie du corps qu'elle est en train de laver. De cette manière, le corps du bébé n'est jamais complètement découvert. On le vêt ensuite d'une couche et d'une chemise de nuit et on l'enveloppe, sans le serrer, dans une couverture propre.

4) Pendant la première journée, l'enduit sébacé pénètre dans la peau ou adhère aux vêtements du bébé. Au deuxième jour, on peut enlever ce qui reste du vernix au niveau des plis de la peau à l'aide de tampons de coton ou d'un tissu doux.

Les soins du matin. La technique suivante pour baigner le bébé dans la pouponnière est basée sur des principes généralement acceptés et est employée dans plusieurs hôpitaux.

1) On profite de la nudité progressive du bébé au moment du bain pour observer son état. On accorde une attention spéciale à l'état de la peau, des yeux, du nez, des oreilles, de la bouche, de l'ombilic et des organes génitaux. Au moment du bain, le bébé est libre de toute entrave provenant de ses vêtements ou couverture et ses mouvements spontanés peuvent être mieux observés. Tout signe inhabituel ou mouvement anormal devrait être noté.

2) On peut laver le bébé avec un tissu doux et de l'eau claire stérile. On ne doit pas employer d'huile. Un savon doux à base de camomille peut être utilisé sans danger. Des recherches récentes laissent penser que le bain répété du bébé avec une solution contenant 3% ou plus d'hexachlorophène peut s'avérer dangereux. Cette substance était employée pour prévenir l'infection staphylococcique au cours du premier mois de la vie. On a prouvé chez l'animal que l'hexachlorophène peut être absorbé au niveau de la peau et causer des dommages cérébraux. On n'emploie plus maintenant l'hexachlorophène que sur ordonnance médicale.

3) L'épiderme se desquame normalement en petites particules granuleuses ou en écailles passablement grandes. On peut baigner les régions desquamées avec de l'eau claire, les assécher et appliquer de l'huile. Les gerçures autour des poignets et des chevilles reçoivent le même traitement. Il est souvent difficile pour une mère de croire que ces lésions sont normales et sans importance. Elles s'améliorent heureusement très vite avec un traitement approprié.

4) Le soin du siège et des organes génitaux est extrêmement important. On doit laver ces régions avec de l'eau tiède. Chez le garçon, on accordera une attention spéciale aux régions autour du scrotum et du pénis. Dans certaines institutions, on emploie un savon doux, non parfumé, lorsqu'il est difficile de décoller les selles avec de l'eau claire. Il y a divergence d'opinions à savoir s'il faut employer de l'huile sur le siège. Certains médecins croient que son usage

accroît le danger d'infection, alors que d'autres en prescrivent régulièrement l'application. Toutefois, il a été démontré qu'aucune pratique n'est meilleure qu'un lavage fréquent à l'eau claire suivi d'un assèchement complet à l'aide d'un tissu doux.

5) La poudre de talc est ordinairement contre-indiquée. Le dommage qu'elle peut causer à la peau est léger, mais il y a un certain danger qu'en manipulant trop vigoureusement le récipient, des particules puissent se répandre dans l'air et être aspirées par le bébé. Les poudres ont un effet hautement irritant sur les voies respiratoires. De plus, les particules accumulées dans les plis de la peau peuvent devenir saturées par les sécrétions du corps. Si on emploie de l'huile avec la poudre, il en résulte une pâte qui retiendra vraisemblablement l'urine, les selles ou les sécrétions corporelles et s'avérera irritante. Il ne faut jamais employer de la poudre contenant de l'acide borique à cause de son effet toxique sur l'être humain ou du stéarate de zinc à cause de son effet irritant sur les muqueuses des voies respiratoires.

Parmi les techniques incluses dans les soins du matin, nous trouvons les suivantes: la prise de température, la pesée, le changement du pansement sur le cordon ombilical, s'il y en a un, ou le nettoyage du cordon ombilical (voir p. 117), et le changement de la literie. Il faut également couper les ongles des doigts et des orteils lorsqu'ils sont trop longs. On coupe les ongles droit carré, les coins légèrement arrondis, pour que le bébé ne puisse pas s'égratigner avec ses ongles.

Irritation de la peau. En dépit des soins appropriés, des irritations cutanées sont susceptibles de se développer chez certains bébés.

L'irritation cutanée qui semble la plus répandue chez le bébé est la *miliaire,* appelée communément « boutons de chaleur ». Elle est causée par une action bactérienne superficielle, faisant suite à une transpiration excessive durant une période de chaleur ou lors d'un accès de fièvre. L'éruption consiste en petites papules et vésicules érythémateuses provoquant la démangeaison. Une grande propreté est de rigueur; le traitement consiste à laver avec de l'eau plutôt chaude et un savon doux, à rincer avec de l'eau claire et à essuyer à fond. On peut employer des lotions calmantes, telle la lotion calamine, qui assèche la peau comme le fait la poudre et demeure sur la surface irritée sans former de croûte. Le bébé qui souffre de « miliaire » a probablement été vêtu trop chaudement, car, même lorsqu'il fait chaud, les lésions se manifestent rarement sur les surfaces exposées souvent à l'air.

L'intertrigo, ou échauffement, apparaît le plus souvent chez les bébés qui ont la peau très tendre. Il se manifeste aux endroits où deux surfaces cutanées viennent en contact, en arrière des oreilles, dans les plis du cou, aux aisselles et à l'aine et, chez le garçon, sous le scrotum. Il apparaît plus particulièrement aux endroits où il y a de l'humidité provenant de la sueur, des selles ou du lait qui s'est infiltré dans les replis cutanés. Il est aussi causé par la friction, quoique ce soit rarement le cas chez le nouveau-né dont les vêtements sont doux et dont l'activité physique est limitée.

L'intertrigo se manifeste aux plis de la peau par des surfaces cutanées à vif, rouges et humides. Les lésions ne causent pas de prurit, et elles guérissent sans former de croûte ou de gale. La surface s'assèche et reprend graduellement sa texture et son apparence normales. La prévention repose sur la propreté et surtout sur un asséchage rigoureux, particulièrement au niveau des plis cutanés; on garde la peau sèche et débarrassée de tout contact avec les bactéries qui pourraient l'infecter.

L'infirmière ne rencontrera probablement pas d'intertrigo chez le bébé né dans un hôpital, mais plutôt chez celui qui est né à la maison et que l'on amène à l'hôpital après quelques jours, à cause d'une complication nécessitant des soins hospitaliers.

Le bébé peut aussi présenter des *écorchures* aux talons, aux genoux, aux orteils et aux coudes, provenant du frottement sur la literie. Cela se produit rarement chez le nouveau-né en santé et entouré de soins, mais fréquemment chez le bébé négligé, sous-alimenté, qui gît en pleurs et qui s'agite sans but. Les surfaces irritées peuvent être légèrement pansées ou vaselinées et elles doivent être gardées parfaitement nettes.

L'érythème fessier est causé par l'irritation provenant de l'urine et des selles. On le voit rarement chez le bébé nourri au sein, mais il apparaît fréquemment chez le bébé nourri artificiellement. Si les selles ou les urines sont irritantes, si on tarde à changer la couche ou si on néglige de laver l'enfant après chaque selle ou miction, le siège peut devenir rouge, et ensuite brillant et à vif. Les lésions brûlent quand le bébé urine et elles s'avèrent une cause fréquente de pleurs chez les bébés qui ne reçoivent pas suffisamment de soins. Le traitement consiste à exposer la peau à l'air en plaçant une couche sous l'enfant et en le déposant sur l'abdomen, la chemisette relevée plus haut que le siège. On change évidemment cette couche chaque fois qu'elle est souillée et on garde le bébé dans une pièce où la température est adéquate. Des bains de siège prolongés à l'eau tiède suivis d'un asséchage complet hâtent la guérison.

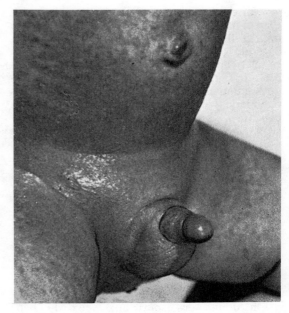

Figure 7-6. Dermatite ammoniacale ou érythème fessier. (Courtoisie du Dr Ralph V. Platou et de l'Académie américaine de Pédiatrie.)

Si possible, on expose la surface irritée à la lumière du soleil, mais si c'est impossible, le siège peut être placé sous la chaleur d'une ampoule électrique (25 à 40 watts) placée dans une lampe au cou long et flexible. On place la lampe près du berceau, on replie le cou de telle façon que l'ampoule soit à environ 30 à 40 cm du corps du bébé. On ne met pas d'onguent sur la peau pendant que la lampe est utilisée. Si la surface est à vif, la lampe devrait être plus éloignée du siège, car la chaleur excessive sera douloureuse et pourra blesser. On prendra grand soin que la lampe soit dans une position de sécurité et que les draps et couvertures ne viennent jamais en contact avec l'ampoule.

Quand on ne peut exposer la surface à la lumière du soleil ni utiliser une lampe, ou que cela s'avère une thérapie insuffisante, un onguent apaisant tel l'oxyde de zinc, un onguent vitaminé ou le chlorure de méthylbenzéthonium (Diaparène) hâtera la guérison. Le diaparène contient un germicide combattant les bactéries qui acidifient l'urine et provoquent l'irritation.

Les couches qui ont été mal lavées et rincées peuvent causer une éruption. Si on lave les couches à la maison, on doit les faire tremper dans l'eau froide, ensuite les laver avec un savon doux, les rincer à fond et, si possible, les faire sécher au soleil. Une tablette de diaparène dissoute dans 2 l d'eau constitue un excellent antiseptique pour le dernier rinçage de 6 couches. Il faut le verser sur les couches après qu'elles aient été lavées et rincées. Il faut les laisser tremper pendant quelques minutes et ensuite les faire sécher. Les buanderies commerciales ou « services de couches » font de l'excellent travail, et plusieurs hôpitaux aussi bien que des familles utilisent leurs services. Les couches à usage unique peuvent être utilisées avec avantage.

La propreté demeure le facteur primordial dans la prévention de l'érythème fessier. Les culottes en plastique, lorsqu'on les emploie, peuvent prédisposer à l'érythème fessier parce qu'elles retiennent l'humidité et que souvent on change moins fréquemment les couches.

Soin des yeux, du nez, des oreilles et de la bouche

On donne des soins aux yeux du bébé seulement si cela s'avère nécessaire. On enlève les sécrétions accumulées dans les coins des yeux avec un linge doux et de l'eau claire en partant des commissures vers l'extérieur. On ne doit pas irriguer les yeux à moins que le médecin ne l'ordonne. On emploie alors une solution physiologique saline. Il ne faut pas employer d'acide borique, qui est dommageable lorsqu'il est absorbé par voie interne. Comme les solutions à l'acide borique sont inodores et incolores, on peut les confondre avec l'eau.

On nettoie le nez et les oreilles du bébé à l'eau stérile, en utilisant un tampon de coton ou un petit linge doux et humide. Il ne faut jamais employer d'huile à cause du danger d'aspiration qui pourrait endommager les voies respiratoires. On n'utilise pas de cure-dents, ni de bâtonnets en bois couverts de coton, car si le bébé bouge, on peut le blesser par une pénétration trop profonde ou trop brusque. Il y a aussi le risque que le coton se détache et demeure dans le nez ou l'oreille; il sera alors nécessaire que le médecin le retire avec les instruments appropriés.

Il ne faut pas nettoyer la bouche, sauf en offrant au bébé de l'eau stérile entre les repas, parce qu'il y a danger de blesser les tissus, ce qui prédispose à l'infection.

Soin des organes génitaux

La vulve. On nettoie délicatement la vulve avec un savon doux et de l'eau plutôt chaude. Une partie de l'enduit sébacé peut être enlevée chaque jour au moment du bain et lorsqu'on nettoie le siège après le passage des selles. On devrait enseigner aux mères à nettoyer la vulve à partir du méat urinaire vers l'anus, en employant une partie différente de la serviette pour chaque manœuvre. De cette façon, il y a moins de possibilité que l'urètre soit contaminée par les bactéries fécales, minimisant ainsi la possibilité d'inflammation vésicale due à l'infection ascendante.

Le pénis. Chaque jour, en nettoyant le pénis, on dilate le prépuce s'il n'est pas trop serré et si le bébé n'a pas été circoncis. Autrement, le sébum et les bactéries qui siègent sous le prépuce peuvent irriter le gland et l'enfant peut souffrir de balano-posthite (inflammation simultanée du gland et du prépuce). On nettoie très délicatement, et le prépuce ne doit être dilaté qu'aussi loin qu'on peut le faire sans pression. On le ramène à sa position normale immédiatement après afin de prévenir le douloureux paraphimosis dû au resserrement et à l'œdème du gland.

Si le prépuce adhère au gland durant la période néonatale, le médecin peut le décoller immédiatement ou remettre la dilatation à une date ultérieure. Néanmoins, la mère devrait connaître le procédé pour nettoyer le pénis.

Le phimosis. Ce terme signifie que le prépuce, trop serré à l'extrémité du gland, empêche la décharge normale de l'urine et prédispose à l'irritation. Le traitement consiste dans la circoncision, c'est-à-dire l'excision chirurgicale du prépuce. On procède à cette opération afin d'éviter l'infection, de faciliter l'écoulement de l'urine et de rendre cette région plus facile à nettoyer. Il faut obtenir des parents, par écrit, le consentement opératoire. Le phimosis demeure la seule indication médicale actuelle pour pratiquer une circoncision, chez le nouveau-né, mais des parents peuvent requérir l'intervention pour des raisons religieuses ou culturelles. L'opération a ordinairement lieu le premier jour de la vie, avant que ne se produise une diminution de prothrombine dans le sang, ou entre le sixième et le huitième jour, lorsque le bébé ne souffre plus de cette déficience et que les temps de saignement et de coagulation demeurent en deçà des limites normales.

Bien que la circoncision soit une opération mineure, le bébé a besoin de soins postopératoires. L'infirmière veille à ce que la plaie ne saigne pas. Un onguent adoucissant peut être appliqué sur les surfaces à vif lorsque la couche a été changée (certains médecins préfèrent qu'on n'emploie pas de couche). Ces soins doivent continuer jusqu'à guérison complète.

Soin du cordon ombilical

Durant les premières 24 heures après l'admission du bébé à la pouponnière, on surveille attentivement le cordon afin d'éviter l'hémorragie. Quelquefois, le cordon contient une quantité excessive de gelée de Wharton. Quand elle se contracte, ce qui est normal, une ligature ou une pince pourtant bien appliquée peut se relâcher et il y a danger d'hémorragie. Normalement, un caillot se forme à l'extrémité du cordon et prévient l'hémorragie. Toutefois, si le caillot est délogé par manipulation, le cordon peut saigner. Pour prévenir une plus grande perte de sang, l'infirmière devrait placer une pince stérile hémostatique aussi loin que possible de la paroi abdominale. Le médecin ou l'infirmière peut alors appliquer une autre pince ou ligature au cordon, plus près de la paroi abdominale.

Le cordon peut se cicatriser de deux façons: par gangrène sèche ou humide. La cicatrisation sèche est préférable parce que les bactéries se développent moins facilement sur une surface sèche. Normalement, la blessure ombilicale est complètement guérie en une semaine.

On peut nettoyer chaque jour la région ombilicale avec de l'alcool à 70%, qui a un effet asséchant et favorise l'antisepsie, ou avec d'autres solutions, selon la technique adoptée par le personnel médical. Toutefois, certains préconisent de laisser le cordon sécher à l'air sans utiliser d'antiseptique asséchant. Si l'on applique un pansement sur le cordon, il faut le changer promptement dès qu'il est souillé. Si l'infection se développe autour de l'ombilic, comme en feraient preuve de la rougeur, de l'œdème, des mauvaises odeurs, de l'humidité ou des exsudats provenant du cordon, on doit avertir le médecin aussitôt. Le traitement d'une telle infection consiste ordinairement en applications fréquentes de pansements imbibés d'antiseptique et en administration d'antibiotiques locaux ou systémiques.

Inanition ou fièvre déshydratante

Entre le second et le quatrième jour de la vie, le bébé peut présenter de la fièvre résultant d'une faible quantité d'ingesta et de la perte normale de liquide. La température peut monter de 38,9°C à 40°C. La peau s'assèche, l'urine devient rare; la figure et le corps démontrent une perte soudaine de poids. Le traitement consiste dans l'augmentation du liquide ingurgité, en donnant de l'eau entre les biberons de lait, ou dans l'administration parentérale de liquides.

Prévention de l'infection

Le nouveau-né offre peu de résistance à l'infection. C'est pour cette raison que toutes les infirmières chargées des nouveau-nés doivent comprendre l'importance de la technique aseptique. La règle fondamentale que doivent suivre les parents et le personnel hospitalier consiste dans la nécessité de se laver les mains à fond avant de toucher le bébé. Les détergents antiseptiques sont préférables au savon de toilette, et l'on doit se laver les mains à l'eau courante. Les bagues et les montres-bracelets doivent être exclues puisque les deux peuvent porter des bactéries. Même le vernis à ongle est interdit, car lui aussi peut être une source d'infection. Il est possible qu'un bébé s'infecte oralement par les bactéries de ses propres selles; pour cette raison, l'infirmière devrait se laver les mains à fond après avoir changé la couche de l'enfant et avant de lui donner à manger.

Dans certaines pouponnières, tout le personnel porte régulièrement un masque même si l'inutilité du port du masque a déjà été démontrée. De plus, si on néglige de le changer fréquemment, il devient une source de contamination plutôt qu'une protection pour le bébé.

Le personnel qui présente des symptômes d'infection respiratoire, intestinale ou cutanée, ne devrait pas entrer dans la pouponnière ou dans les pièces où co-habitent les mères et leur bébé; les personnes infectées ne devraient avoir absolument aucun contact, direct ou indirect, avec les bébés. Si la mère contracte une infection, tous les contacts avec le bébé doivent être supprimés; s'il couche dans la même pièce qu'elle, on devrait l'isoler, non seulement de celle-ci mais aussi des autres enfants de la pouponnière afin qu'il ne soit pas une source de transmission, s'il a déjà été contaminé.

L'infection est plus souvent véhiculée par contact direct avec une personne contaminée que par contact indirect avec l'équipement qui reste cependant une source certaine d'infection. Tous les bébés devraient avoir leurs propres articles pour le bain et autres soins. On peut garder ceux-ci sur son bureau ou dans un tiroir sous la bassinette et les transporter avec lui à la chambre de sa mère, s'il séjourne dans la même chambre qu'elle.

Lorsqu'un bébé, dans la pouponnière, manifeste des signes d'infection, il est prudent de l'isoler aussitôt. On doit surveiller de près les autres bébés dans le cas où ils manifesteraient les mêmes symptômes. Il est à noter que la température du nouveau-né s'élèvera rarement lors d'une infection. Les symptômes les plus communs sont le refus de s'alimenter, la diarrhée fréquente, des écoulements provenant de l'ombilic, des exsudats provenant des yeux et du nez et quelquefois des convulsions. Les infections respiratoires se manifestent d'abord par un écoulement nasal et par une élévation de la température. On remarque facilement les lésions cutanées lorsqu'on déshabille le bébé pour les soins matinaux ou lorsqu'on change sa couche.

Tenue du dossier

L'infirmière qui prend soin d'un bébé à la pouponnière est responsable de toutes les notations sur son dossier permanent. Quand le bébé couche dans la chambre de sa mère, celle-ci rapporte à l'infirmière, qui doit en prendre note, les soins qu'elle lui prodigue ainsi que ses observations sur l'état et le comportement du nouveau-né.

En plus des dossiers permanents, certaines pouponnières tiennent des *dossiers quotidiens*, qui diffèrent des premiers. On enregistre sur ces feuilles les soins donnés aux bébés et les observations concernant l'alimentation, l'évacuation des selles et les émissions d'urine. L'infirmière, à partir de ces fiches détachées rédige les notes se rapportant à chaque bébé sur un dossier permanent. Dans certains cas, elle résume l'information, par exemple, le nombre de selles durant la journée et la quantité totale de nourriture ingérée. Parmi les renseignements importants contenus dans les notes de l'infirmière sur les dossiers individuels permanents, on trouve:

— des notes sur le degré d'activité et les particularités individuelles, telles les pleurs, le rythme respiratoire, la température, l'état du cordon, la coloration, l'état de la bouche, des yeux, de la peau, la fréquence et la nature des urines et des selles.

— les moments où on nourrit le bébé et la quantité de nourriture ingérée et tolérée; la fréquence, le volume des régurgitations et la qualité de la succion.

— le poids quotidien du nouveau-né.

— les médicaments et les traitements administrés.

Pour chaque bébé une déclaration de naissance doit être complétée par les parents et remise à un prêtre, pour les parents catholiques, ou encore à un officier civil. Cette démarche est nécessaire pour que le bébé acquière son statut de citoyen.

ALIMENTATION DU NOUVEAU-NÉ

Le bébé peut avoir faim immédiatement après sa naissance ou ne montrer aucun signe de faim pendant le premier ou même le second jour. L'enfant affamé devient agité, il pleure, il bouge sa tête à la recherche de nourriture et accomplit des mouvements de succion qui, n'apportant aucun soulagement, finiront vraisemblablement par des pleurs aigus.

Ordinairement, il dort pendant plusieurs heures après avoir été nourri, se réveillant quand il a encore besoin de nourriture ou qu'il se sent mal à l'aise. Les causes les plus fréquentes de pleurs chez un bébé en santé sont la faim et l'inconfort provenant d'une couche souillée.

Même si durant la période prénatale, la mère s'est informée sur les méthodes d'allaitement, c'est au moment de la naissance qu'elle doit prendre la décision d'allaiter son bébé ou de lui donner une alimentation au biberon.

L'infirmière travaillant à la pouponnière doit discuter avec la mère des avantages respectifs de l'alimentation au sein ou au biberon, mais elle doit éviter à tout prix les pressions intempestives qui peuvent susciter un sentiment de culpabilité chez la mère qui ne peut ou ne veut pas suivre les conseils qui lui sont donnés. L'infirmière doit comprendre que le contact physique entre la mère et l'enfant pendant l'alimentation importe beaucoup plus que la méthode employée pour le nourrir.

Alimentation sur demande

Le bébé qui fixe lui-même son horaire, tète quand il a faim. Il dort jusqu'à ce que les contractions de son estomac vide le réveillent. Il pleure, et lorsqu'il est nourri, les contractions cessent et il éprouve une sensation plaisante de plénitude. S'il est nourri chaque fois qu'il a faim, il développera un bon appétit et un sentiment progressif de confiance. Qu'il soit nourri au sein ou au biberon, il établira son propre rythme d'alimentation.

Si le bébé règle lui-même le moment de ses repas il est absolument nécessaire que l'infirmière et la mère reconnaissent les signes de la faim et n'emploient pas le biberon pour apaiser le bébé chaque fois qu'il pleure, au risque de le suralimenter.

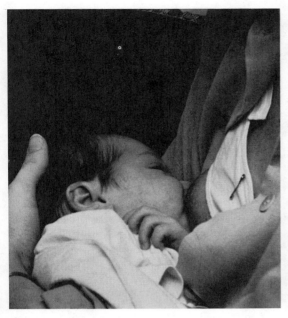

A

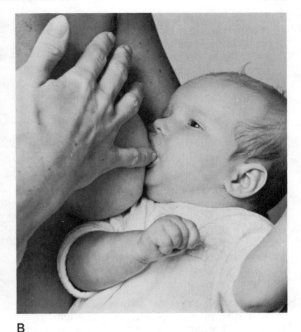

B

C

Figure 7-7. *A)* L'enfant acquiert ses premières impressions de sécurité par le toucher, la chaleur et la satisfaction de l'appétit. (Courtoisie de Erika Stone et Baby Talk.) *B)* Pour éviter d'irriter le mamelon la mère place un doigt entre les lèvres du bébé quand elle désire qu'il cesse de téter. (Applebaum, R.M. Ped. Clin. N. Am. 17:203, 1970.) *C)* Dessin de Picasso. (Courtoisie de Fogg Art Museum, Université de Harvard.)

Allaitement au sein

Les facteurs psychologiques et émotifs sont probablement plus importants que les facteurs physiques pour aider la mère à décider d'allaiter elle-même son bébé, puisqu'il existe sur le marché des laits conformes aux normes alimentaires pour les bébés.

Certains médecins croient qu'il faut mettre le bébé au sein aussitôt que l'état de la mère et de l'enfant le permettent étant donné que l'allaitement aide à l'involution utérine, stimule la lactation et procure aussi une satisfaction émotive tant à la mère qu'à l'enfant. On commence dans certains hôpitaux à mettre le bébé au sein alors que la mère est encore dans la salle d'accouchement car il semble que le réflexe de succion du bébé soit à son maximum au cours des deux premières heures après la naissance. Il diminuerait ensuite pour revenir progressivement au cours des deux jours suivants. D'autres médecins croient que l'allaitement devrait être commencé entre 4 et 24 heures après la naissance. Ce délai donne assez de temps pour que la gorge du bébé se libère du mucus, et il permet à l'enfant de se remettre de l'effort de la naissance et des soins qu'il a reçus immédiatement après l'accouchement. Cet intervalle permet également à la mère de se reposer avant de donner le sein à son enfant. La première tétée est souvent difficile, car le bébé doit apprendre à saisir le mamelon et à sucer.

Après avoir d'abord perdu du poids, le nouveau-né nourri au sein gagnera de 170 à 225 g par semaine.

S'il est sous-alimenté, il sera vraisemblablement constipé. Il peut avoir des coliques, vomir, être irritable, et alternativement pleurer et sucer ses doigts. Les vomissements et les coliques sont aussi des caractéristiques de l'enfant suralimenté. En général, cependant, le bébé nourri au sein manifeste un gain régulier de poids et est moins sujet aux problèmes intestinaux que le bébé nourri artificiellement.

Avantages pour la mère. La mère aussi bien que le bébé profite de l'allaitement au sein. La stimulation du sein aide à l'involution utérine et provoque souvent des sensations de type orgasmique. Plusieurs mères trouvent une grande satisfaction émotive à nourrir leur bébé au sein, car c'est le parachèvement de l'union symbiotique qui existait durant la vie intra-utérine du bébé. Le fait que l'allaitement au sein soit moins coûteux attire également certaines femmes.

Critique et contre-indications de l'allaitement au sein. Pour certaines femmes, les avantages de l'allaitement maternel peuvent être neutralisés par d'autres facteurs. La mère peut avoir certaines réticences conscientes ou inconscientes envers l'allaitement au sein et celles-ci interfèrent avec sa sécrétion lactée. De plus, sa profession, son emploi hors de la maison et l'accélération du rythme de vie de la société contemporaine peuvent l'empêcher de se reposer et la rendre impatiente. Si la mère travaille à l'extérieur ou a plusieurs engagements sociaux, il se peut qu'elle ne puisse être à la maison à heure fixe pour la tétée. Elle peut, dans ce cas, tirer de ses seins du lait qu'elle gardera au froid et qui sera donné au bébé pendant son absence. Elle peut aussi n'enlever que le surplus de lait de ses seins. Le lait humain se garde pendant une journée au réfrigérateur, deux semaines au compartiment de congélation du réfrigérateur et plus d'une année au congélateur. Pour libérer la mère temporairement et donner au père la possibilité de nourrir le bébé, un biberon peut être substitué périodiquement à une tétée. Cette pratique habitue le nourrisson à une autre méthode d'alimentation ce qui lui évitera éventuellement un trop grand traumatisme si sa mère doit être hospitalisée d'urgence alors qu'il n'est pas encore sevré.

Une autre objection alléguée par certaines mères contre l'allaitement au sein réside dans le fait qu'elles croient que cela détruit le contour ferme de la poitrine et les fait ainsi paraître plus vieilles qu'elles ne le sont en réalité. Il faut se rappeler que les modifications au niveau des seins se produisent surtout au début de la grossesse. Le risque de déformation n'est pas très grand si la mère porte en permanence (jour et nuit) un soutien-gorge bien taillé, au cours des dernières semaines de sa grossesse et au cours de son premier mois d'allaitement alors que le volume des seins est à son maximum.

La contre-indication majeure à l'allaitement au sein est *une maladie grave de la mère*. Atteinte de tuberculose, son état peut être aggravé par la lactation, et son bébé risquerait de contracter la maladie. Il peut arriver qu'une mère n'ait pas la vitalité nécessaire pour nourrir au sein à cause de complications sérieuses apparues lors de sa grossesse. Par exemple, elle peut être anémique à la suite d'une perte sanguine abondante. Elle peut souffrir d'une maladie chronique, telle que le cancer, une cardiopathie ou une insuffisance rénale, ce qui n'est pas contagieux, mais ne lui permet pas de faire l'effort de la lactation. Le travail et l'accouchement peuvent avoir été compliqués par une maladie intercurrente ou par une opération urgente requérant une convalescence prolongée.

Le lait d'une *mère qui se drogue* (morphine, héroïne ou codéine) contiendra de petites quantités de drogue. La quantité que recevra l'enfant pourra ne pas être suffisante pour lui causer du tort, mais elle peut s'avérer créatrice d'accoutumance. La pénicilline peut passer dans le lait maternel et produire une sensibilisation allergique. Plusieurs autres substances absorbées par la mère peuvent se rendre dans le lait maternel et il faut lui recommander de s'informer auprès de son médecin avant de prendre quelque médicament que ce soit. Les dangers de l'automédication sont énormes et le bébé peut également souffrir d'un abus d'absorption de thé, de café et de nicotine.

Les *menstruations* ne gênent pas l'allaitement maternel alors que la *grossesse* amène souvent un arrêt de la sécrétion lactée.

Il n'y a pas de contre-indication à l'allaitement maternel pour une mère souffrant de *troubles psychiatriques,* bien qu'il y ait un danger à lui confier un nourrisson. Puisque, dans ces conditions, le lait est normal, quant à sa quantité et sa composition, on peut l'extraire par compression du sein et le donner au bébé, si cette méthode ne perturbe pas la mère, et s'il existe une probabilité d'amélioration permettant d'espérer qu'elle puisse éventuellement allaiter directement son bébé.

Des *lésions locales,* telles que les fissures du mamelon, les tumeurs ou les abcès au sein peuvent constituer une contre-indication à l'allaitement maternel. On peut extraire manuellement le lait pour soulager la mère de la douleur causée par le gonflement du sein et pour maintenir la sécrétion lactée afin qu'elle puisse éventuellement recommencer à allaiter.

Certaines mères souffrent de *rétraction du mamelon* de telle sorte que le bébé ne peut le saisir avec sa bouche. Une téterelle appliquée sur le sein, telle que la « Cléopâtre » que l'on utilise dans certains hôpitaux aidera le bébé à sucer et à se procurer le lait, ou alors on peut extraire le lait avec un tire-lait et le donner au biberon. Si on se sert d'une téterelle, une légère quantité de colostrum ou de lait peut être extraite et placée dans le protecteur avant qu'il ne soit appliqué ou on peut le remplir partiellement d'eau stérilisée. (Voir fig. 7-8.)

L'état du bébé peut empêcher l'allaitement maternel. Le nourrisson peut être trop faible pour sucer ou cela peut l'exténuer. Le prématuré peut être, en plus, dépourvu des réflexes nécessaires de succion et de déglutition. Le bébé affecté d'une fissure palatine ou labiale est souvent incapable de sucer, tout comme le bébé souffrant de paralysie faciale. Pour de tels bébés, le lait du sein peut être extrait manuellement et donné au moyen d'un compte-gouttes.

L'érythroblastose fœtale ne constitue pas une contre-indication puisque les anticorps Rh présents dans le lait de la mère sont détruits par la digestion du bébé.

Avantages pour l'enfant. Les arguments les plus importants en faveur de l'allaitement maternel, au point de vue de la santé du bébé, sont les suivants:

Le lait maternel se digère plus facilement que le lait de vache et il est disponible en tout temps, ce qui est important si l'enfant doit régler lui-même le rythme de son alimentation.

Les bébés nourris au sein auraient une plus grande immunité à certaines maladies de l'enfance. Le degré de cette protection n'a pas encore été établi. Les enfants sont également

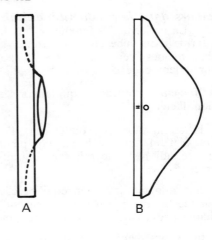

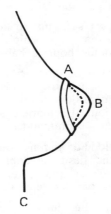

Figure 7-8. « Cléopâtre ». *A)* Partie inférieure arrondie, percée au centre, appliquée sur le mamelon. *B)* Partie supérieure, vissée à la partie inférieure. *C)* Cléopâtre appliquée sur le sein.

moins portés à l'anémie ou à une déficience en vitamines.

Ces bébés présentent moins de désordres gastro-intestinaux et d'allergies alimentaires. Ils ont moins de rhumes, d'infections respiratoires graves et, en général, moins de maladies infectieuses de toutes sortes, même si l'hygiène de l'environnement fait défaut, car le lait maternel est stérile et les mamelons de la mère se nettoient facilement.

Les bébés nourris au sein jouissent de la vigilance de leur mère et du contact intime avec son corps; ils peuvent ingurgiter autant ou aussi peu de lait qu'ils le désirent. Ils peuvent régler le débit de ce qu'ils boivent, on ne peut les forcer à en absorber plus qu'ils ne veulent.

Facteurs dans la production du lait maternel. La majorité des femmes ayant accouché à terme d'un bébé en bonne santé, et qui sont elles-mêmes bien portantes sont capables de nourrir leur bébé.

Les *facteurs physiques* qui favorisent la sécrétion lactée incluent:

a) la stimulation provoquée par l'enfant qui tète. Si l'enfant ne vide pas complètement le sein, ce qui reste devrait être extrait manuellement.

b) une alimentation bien équilibrée, riche en protéine et un approvisionnement suffisant de calcium provenant du lait et autres sources.

c) un supplément adéquat en vitamines, spécialement en vitamine D, car la mère doit en absorber également pour le bébé à qui elle le transmettra par son lait.

d) un apport suffisant de liquide pour satisfaire ses besoins et fournir aussi de 480 à 960 ml de liquide pour le bébé.

e) des exercices appropriés. Le travail de maison, s'il n'est pas trop épuisant, est excellent, mais la mère devrait aussi sortir à l'extérieur chaque jour. La marche à pied est tout particulièrement recommandée.

f) une période de sommeil de 8 à 10 heures par nuit et une sieste pendant la journée. Il ne faut pas oublier que le repos de la mère est interrompu par les tétées de nuit.

g) une quantité suffisante de cellules sécrétrices de lait dans le sein conditionne l'approvisionnement. De gros seins peuvent contenir une bonne quantité de graisse ou de tissu conjonctif et une quantité inadéquate de glande mammaire.

h) une bonne sécrétion hormonale ne peut être contrôlée complètement mais elle est stimulée par la tétée du bébé et l'écoulement du lait hors du sein. L'oxytocine, une hormone, n'intervient pas dans la sécrétion lactée, mais elle facilite l'écoulement du lait hors des canaux galactophores. Le libre écoulement du lait active la sécrétion des glandes mammaires. Cette hormone est disponible dans le commerce et est utilisée en vaporisation nasale.

Les *facteurs psychologiques* dans la production du lait maternel sont extrêmement importants. La mère a besoin de sentir qu'elle est capable de satisfaire les besoins alimentaires du bébé. Elle doit être en sécurité, heureuse et détendue dans sa vie familiale. Naturellement, s'il lui arrive d'être perturbée, la quantité de lait décroîtra, mais la qualité demeurera inchangée; quand elle aura recouvré un bon moral, sa montée de lait sera, à nouveau, normale. On devrait lui mentionner que l'émotion produite par le retour à la maison et le fait d'entreprendre les soins du bébé, peuvent créer un état de tension susceptible de diminuer temporairement la montée de lait.

Sécrétion et composition du lait maternel. Les sécrétions des glandes mammaires dépendent de l'hormone lactogène, appelée prolactine, provenant de la glande pituitaire.

L'écoulement du lait dépend du réflexe d'éjection du lait. La présence du bébé, ses mouvements de succion ou ses pleurs provoquent la décharge d'oxytocine provenant de la partie postérieure de la glande pituitaire. L'oxytocine agit sur le tissu contractile autour des alvéoles et amène la pressuration du lait vers les canaux plus grands, puis dans les mamelons. Si la mère est tendue, ce réflexe sera inhibé et le lait présent dans le sein n'arrivera pas au mamelon.

Le colostrum est sécrété pendant les deux ou trois premiers jours après l'accouchement. Il est jaune, peu épais et peu consistant. Il contient plus de protides et de minéraux et moins de gras et de glucides que le lait maternel. Il est facilement digestible et a une action laxative légère.

La montée laiteuse proprement dite est plus tardive; elle survient deux à quatre jours après l'accouchement. Après le premier mois, le lait maternel est constant dans sa composition et demeure tel. La quantité augmente à mesure que le besoin en nourriture du bébé augmente.

Plus le bébé boit efficacement, plus la sécrétion lactée s'établit rapidement. À son maximum la femme produit environ 900 à 960 ml de lait par jour.

Le lait maternel est légèrement bleuté et a un contenu en glucides assez élevé; dans l'estomac du bébé, il forme un caillot mou floconneux et digestible. Si la mère a une alimentation adéquate, le contenu vitaminique de son lait est ordinairement suffisant pour le bébé. Les mères devraient savoir qu'une partie des médicaments qu'elles prennent tels les opiacés, l'alcool, la belladonne, la pénicilline peut passer dans le lait en quantité suffisante pour agir sur l'organisme du bébé.

Le tableau 7-2 montre la composition respective du lait maternel et du lait de vache. Le lait maternel contient plus de glucides et moins de protides que le lait de vache, approximativement la même quantité de gras et leur valeur calorique est égale.

Il est à noter que les laits commerciaux « maternisés » se rapprochent plus du lait maternel que du lait de vache. Leur taux de glucide est assez élevé pour se comparer au lait maternel et leur taux de protéine s'abaisse, parfois à un taux aussi bas que celui du lait maternel. Ils contiennent tous un supplément de vitamine D.

Technique d'allaitement maternel. Il faut expliquer à la mère que la montée laiteuse apparaît chez les primipares vers les cinquième et sixième jours, chez les multipares, vers les deuxième et troisième jours et dans certains cas exceptionnels, seulement le quatorzième jour. Durant la période latente, avant qu'une quantité suffisante de lait soit disponible, le bébé perd du poids. Cela constitue un phénomène normal et ne devrait pas causer d'angoisse à la mère. On peut donner de l'eau glucosée pour remplacer la quantité requise de liquide. Certains préconisent d'offrir l'eau au compte-gouttes ou à la cuillère et non au biberon, au tout début de la période d'allaitement.

Il est important que les mamelons demeurent souples et sans lésion, afin que l'allaitement constitue une expérience agréable pour la mère. Les mamelons normaux favorisent la succion. Quand les mamelons sont plats, on peut appliquer un onguent avec un mouvement délicat et circulaire en partant du bord extérieur du mamelon vers le bout. Si les mamelons deviennent craquelés et douloureux, on peut les lubrifier avec de la vaseline ou on peut employer une téterelle pour minimiser la souffrance au cours de l'allaitement.

Il faut laver soigneusement les seins à l'eau stérile, avant et après chaque tétée, en prenant soin de bien les assécher à l'aide d'un tissu doux.

Les vêtements de la mère devraient être suffisamment amples pour éviter de comprimer les seins. Si un peu de lait s'écoule des mamelons entre les tétées, elle devra protéger ses vêtements en utilisant les coussinets d'allaitement qui se portent à l'intérieur du soutien-gorge. On les trouve sous forme à usage unique ou en tissu lavable ce qui s'avère beaucoup plus économique.

La mère doit se laver les mains à fond, avec du savon et de l'eau, avant d'allaiter. Elle devrait s'installer dans une position confortable, assise ou couchée sur le côté, la tête légèrement relevée. En présentant le mamelon au bébé et pendant qu'il tète, elle devrait exercer une légère pression sur son sein de façon à permettre à son bébé de respirer librement.

Tableau 7-2. *Comparaison entre le lait maternel et le lait de vache entier*

	LAIT MATERNEL (%)	LAIT DE VACHE ENTIER (%)
Eau	87 − 88	83 − 88
Protéines	1 − 1,5	3,2 − 4,1
Lactalbumine	0,7 − 0,8	0,5
Caséine	0,4 − 0,5	3
Glucides (lactose)	6,5 − 7,5	4,5 − 5
Lipides	3,5 − 4 (plus d'oléine et moins d'acides gras volatils)	3,5 − 5,2
Minéraux	0,15 − 0,25	0,7 − 0,75
Calcium	0,034 − 0,045	0,122 − 0,179
Fer	0,0001	0,00004
Vitamines (par 100 cm^3)		
A	60 − 500 U.I.	80 − 220 U.I. *
D	0,4 − 10 U.I.	0.3 − 4.3 U.I.*
C	1,2 − 10,8 mg	0.9 − 1,4 mg *
Réaction	Alcaline ou amphotérique	Acide ou amphotérique
Bactéries	Non	Oui
Digestion		Moins rapidement
Décharge de l'estomac		Moins rapidement
Caillot	Mou, floconneux	Dur, volumineux
Calories par 30 ml	20	20

Adapté de W. E. Nelson: *Textbook of Pediatrics,* 8e édition.

* Valeurs pour le lait pasteurisé.

La chambre doit être silencieuse pendant que le bébé tète et on doit éviter de déranger la mère sans raison. Un nouveau-né normal possède un réflexe « directionnel », si bien que tout ce qui touche sa joue quand il a faim lui fait tourner la tête dans cette direction. L'infirmière doit éviter de poser sa main sur la joue opposée du bébé pour essayer de tourner sa tête vers le sein. Si la mère laisse le mamelon toucher la joue du bébé, il se tournera dans cette direction pour sucer.

Bien que le bébé obtienne 85% à 90% de sa ration dans les 5 à 8 premières minutes de succion vigoureuse, on devrait lui permettre de boire pendant 10 à 20 minutes. Il aime cela, et le surplus de lait ainsi obtenu lui profitera. Puisque la succion stimule la production lactée, les deux seins doivent être présentés à chaque tétée en prenant soin de bien vider le premier sein avant de présenter le second. La mère doit commencer chaque séance d'allaitement par le sein qui a été tété en second lors de l'allaitement précédent. Il faut que le bébé saisisse le mamelon entier dans sa bouche; autrement, il ne peut sucer correctement et peut avaler de l'air.

On peut peser le bébé avant et après les tétées surtout si on a des doutes sur la quantité de lait ingurgitée. Cela, cependant, peut rendre la mère anxieuse ce qui perturbe le processus physiologique de la lactation et tend à réduire la sécrétion lactée. Plusieurs spécialistes de l'allaitement ne favorisent pas l'allaitement complémentaire parce qu'ils craignent que le bébé ne soit pas suffisamment affamé pour vider le sein lors de la prochaine tétée.

Il s'avère aussi nécessaire de faire éructer le bébé nourri au sein que celui qui boit à la bouteille. On le tient en position verticale ou assis droit dans les bras de sa mère, le frottant délicatement dans le dos. (Voir fig. 7-10) L'air qu'il a avalé remonte vers le haut de l'estomac et est éructé.

Tous les bébés ont besoin d'éructer à la fin des repas; certains en ressentent le besoin plusieurs fois pendant qu'ils boivent. Le bébé régurgite souvent le surplus de lait ingurgité, au moment de l'éructation ou même après qu'il ait été replacé dans son berceau.

Il peut souffrir du hoquet; dans ce cas, il faudrait lui donner un peu d'eau et le réconforter jusqu'à ce que le hoquet cesse.

On peut lui offrir de l'eau stérilisée entre les tétées, mais ce n'est pas absolument nécessaire. Il ne faut pas le forcer car l'eau peut diminuer son appétit lors de sa prochaine tétée. Donner de l'eau constitue une excellente façon d'habituer le bébé à boire au biberon dans le cas où l'allaitement maternel devrait soudainement être interrompu. De plus, cela le préparera à prendre du jus dilué avec de l'eau lorsque le médecin le recommandera.

Les bébés aiment à s'accrocher au sein lorsqu'ils ont fini de sucer. Pour enlever le bébé s'il ne laisse pas spontanément le mamelon, on peut opérer une légère pression sur les joues ou insérer un doigt dans la bouche du bébé. Cette méthode permet à l'air d'entrer dans la bouche; la succion se trouve diminuée et il ne peut pas maintenir sa prise sur le mamelon. Cette méthode n'est pas douloureuse pour la mère et elle n'irrite pas non plus la peau tendre du mamelon.

Des horaires rigides ne sont pas à recommander pour le bébé. Si on lui permet d'établir son propre rythme, il arrivera éventuellement à un horaire passablement régulier et le tout s'accomplira sans trop de frustration pour lui ou pour sa mère.

Extraction manuelle du lait. Voici la technique pour vider les seins manuellement.

Saisir le sein avec le pouce au-dessus du bord externe de l'aréole et l'index en-dessous. Presser le pouce vers les doigts à la base du mamelon, par une pression ferme et profonde. Supporter le sein avec les autres doigts. Employer un mouvement vers l'avant. Répéter cette manœuvre environ 30 fois par minute jusqu'à ce que les seins soient vides, ce qui prend de 10 à 15 minutes. Si l'on destine le lait au bébé, on pourra le conserver dans un récipient stérile, sous réfrigération.

On peut utiliser un tire-lait au lieu des mains. Plusieurs mères trouvent la pompe électrique supérieure aux autres méthodes; cependant, elle coûte assez cher et peut endommager facilement les tissus du sein. On l'emploie rarement à la maison.

Difficultés fréquentes lors de l'allaitement maternel.

Mamelons douloureux. Il s'agit d'enseigner à la mère de ne pas utiliser de savon pour laver ses seins et de lui expliquer la technique pour retirer l'enfant du sein sans que ses mamelons en soient meurtris. L'infirmière doit aussi vérifier si le bébé est bien placé pour sa tétée et s'il capte l'aréole et non seulement l'extrémité du mamelon.

Seins trop durs. Le bébé peut être incapable de sucer si le sein est trop gonflé. L'infirmière doit veiller à ce que la mère allaite le bébé sur demande, aussi souvent qu'aux trois heures, pour éviter le gonflement. Lorsque l'engorgement s'est produit, l'extraction manuelle d'une petite quantité de lait permet aux seins de ramollir et la tétée devient possible.

Lait qui ne coule pas. Il arrive que le sein soit rempli et que le bébé affamé n'obtienne pas de lait. Un massage de chaque quadrant du sein permet de stimuler la progression du lait à travers les canaux galactophores vers le mamelon.

Bébé dort au sein. Le bébé qu'on oblige à boire aux quatre heures pleure pendant de longues périodes épuisantes et s'endort au moment de la tétée. Parfois le bébé a trop chaud et a besoin d'être dégagé un peu de ses vêtements. Une stimulation sous la mâchoire aide le bébé à reprendre sa succion.

Alimentation artificielle

L'alimentation artificielle est fondée sur des principes scientifiques de nutrition et de stérilisation. Quand l'alimentation maternelle s'avère impossible et qu'on ne peut employer une alimentation artificielle adéquate, les taux de morbidité et de mortalité, chez les bébés, tendent à monter.

Les conditions suivantes peuvent avoir un effet néfaste sur le succès de l'alimentation artificielle: contamination du lait de vache; formule qui ne convient pas aux besoins du bébé, dans sa composition ou dans sa quantité; manque de propreté dans la préparation de la formule et réfrigération inadéquate de l'approvisionnement de 24 heures; horaire irrégulier; responsabilité des repas confiée à des étrangers, ce qui implique facilement un manque d'intérêt et d'affection.

Exigences de l'alimentation artificielle

Voici les principaux critères qui influent sur l'alimentation artificielle.

Basse teneur en bactéries. Trois étapes successives permettent d'obtenir un approvisionnement de lait dont la stérilité s'avère suffisante pour servir à l'alimentation des jeunes enfants.

La surveillance des troupeaux laitiers par des vétérinaires a permis d'éliminer la tuberculose bovine et la brucellose, autrefois très meurtrières chez les jeunes enfants. On soumet périodiquement les vaches au test à la tuberculine et au test spécifique permettant de reconnaître la brucellose. Une troisième exigence réside dans la propreté, dans le soin et dans la traite des vaches.

La surveillance du produit laitier débute à la ferme où la traite et l'entreposage sont régis par des règles hygiéniques sévères. La plupart des producteurs n'ont jamais de contact avec le lait, car les trayeuses automatiques sont reliées par des canalisations au réservoir réfrigéré, ce qui constitue la meilleure protection contre la contamination. Le fermier nettoie toute l'installation après le ramassage du lait par des camions citernes réfrigérés.

La plupart des villes exigent une inspection stricte de la manipulation du lait commercial à partir de la laiterie jusqu'à l'épicerie. Les employés de ces établissements possèdent une carte de santé et sont soumis à des examens de contrôle. La teneur du lait en bactéries et en graisse doit être conforme à certaines normes. Le lait, vierge de tout agent de conservation ou de toute substance qui peut l'affecter, doit être, en plus, pasteurisé. Pour servir à l'allaitement du nourrisson, on doit le faire bouillir et ce, jusqu'à ce que le bébé soit suffisamment résistant pour tolérer le lait pasteurisé que boit le reste de la famille.

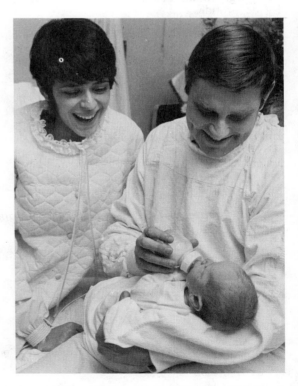

Figure 7-9. Alimentation au biberon. (Extrait de Medical World New, 10 avril 1970.)

Économie et disponibilité du lait.

Dans les foyers à revenu modique, il est nécessaire que l'alimentation artificielle ne soit pas onéreuse. C'est là une raison qui explique la popularité du lait stérilisé et évaporé. On peut l'acheter en petites quantités, et si on ne peut le réfrigérer, on peut ouvrir une petite boîte de conserve pour chaque biberon. Ce que le bébé ne boit pas sera absorbé par les enfants plus âgés ou par les adultes de la famille.

Facilité de digestion du lait.

Le bébé âgé de plus de 3 mois peut normalement tolérer du lait de vache non-dilué. Pour les bébés plus jeunes, on dilue le lait avec de l'eau bouillie. Dans l'estomac du bébé, le lait de vache forme une masse ferme qu'on peut rendre plus digestible par la pasteurisation, l'ébullition, l'homogénéisation, l'évaporation ou l'addition d'un acide ou d'une base.

Besoins nutritifs du nourrisson.

L'alimentation devrait fournir 130 à 190 ml *de liquide* par kilogramme par jour. On calcule en général 1 litre par jour à 12 mois et 100 ml de plus par année additionnelle.

L'exigence en protides pour la croissance et pour la reconstitution des tissus est de 3 à 4,5 g/kg. 30 ml de lait de vache procurent 1 g de protides.

Une addition modérée de sucre à la formule de lait, soit approximativement une à deux cuillerées à thé par biberon, fournit au nourrisson une ration glucidique appropriée.

Les besoins fondamentaux du métabolisme sont faibles durant la période néonatale. La production basale de chaleur monte toutefois rapidement durant la première année de la vie et les besoins en calories sont proportionnellement plus hauts dans la première enfance qu'à n'importe quelle autre période de la vie.

Durant la période néonatale, il faut environ 80 calories par kilogramme de poids corporel, pour satisfaire les exigences nutritives du bébé. Cette quantité doit être augmentée rapidement, parce que même si les besoins du métabolisme basal ne changent pas, les besoins caloriques nécessaires à la croissance et à l'énergie sont beaucoup plus élevés par la suite. Bientôt une exigence calorique de 100 à 130 calories par kilogramme de poids corporel, par jour, s'avère nécessaire; ces normes demeurent constantes jusqu'à l'âge de 4 mois, alors que le bébé requiert environ 100 calories par kilogramme. Les besoins en calories varient selon l'activité du bébé, son état général et son gain de poids, mais demeurent très élevés par rapport à l'adulte qui requiert en moyenne 44 calories par kilogramme.

Figure 7-10. Le bébé peut éructer si on le tient fermement contre l'épaule, en supportant son dos et sa tête. On peut frotter délicatement son dos afin de l'aider à se détendre.

Tableau 7-3. Un bébé d'un mois a besoin des quantités suivantes:

		S'IL PÈSE 4 kg.
Liquide		130 à 190 ml / kg
	Total:	520 à 760 ml / jour
Lait de vache entier		100 à 130 ml / kg
	Total:	400 à 520 ml
Eau		Environ 240 ml
		Pour obtenir 760 ml au total
Calories		110 cal. / kg
Exigences caloriques totales		440 cal. / jour
Sucre		6,5 g / kg / jour
Volume de chaque biberon selon la tolérance du bébé		
1 mois		6 × 120 ml
3 mois		5 × 150 ml
6 mois		4 × 180 ml
		3 × 240 ml

Les vitamines sont ordinairement déficientes ou absentes dans l'alimentation artificielle. La vitamine A, nécessaire à la croissance et la vitamine D, qui prévient le rachitisme proviennent de l'huile de foie de morue ou sont présentées sous une forme concentrée. Le bébé a besoin d'environ 400 Unités Internationales de Vitamine D par jour. Les vitamines du complexe B sont également nécessaires pour la maturation nerveuse. La vitamine C prévient le scorbut; le bébé en requiert entre 25 et 50 mg par jour. Parce que la vitamine C est facilement détruite par le processus de pasteurisation du lait, on doit l'obtenir d'une autre source. Les bébés nourris au sein en reçoivent ordinairement suffisamment par le lait maternel, bien que ceci dépende de l'alimentation de la mère. On peut fournir la vitamine C au bébé en lui donnant de l'acide ascorbique à raison de 25 à 50 mg par jour ou 60 g de jus d'orange par jour. Quelques bébés présentent cependant de l'allergie à cet aliment s'il est présenté non dilué et trop tôt après la naissance.

Le nouveau-né possède ordinairement une réserve de fer suffisante pour les trois premiers mois de la vie sauf si sa mère a souffert de malnutrition. Si le bébé est menacé d'anémie, il doit recevoir du fer en supplément. La plupart des céréales pour bébés contiennent du fer et dès que l'enfant vieillit, on ajoute à son alimentation de la viande et du jaune d'œuf.

En somme, jusqu'à l'âge de 6 mois, le bébé a approximativement besoin de 130 à 190 ml de liquide par kilogramme de poids corporel. La somme des besoins caloriques, protidiques et liquides pour 24 heures détermine la composition de la formule. Le nombre de biberons diminue à mesure que le bébé grandit. À un mois, il prendra probablement 5 ou 6 biberons. La quantité présentée à chaque biberon augmente à mesure que l'intervalle entre les repas augmente et que le bébé réclame une ration plus abondante.

On donne rarement à un bébé, indépendamment de son âge, plus de 1200 ml de lait entier durant une période de 24 heures.

Calcul de la formule. L'exemple donné clarifiera peut-être les énoncés généraux sur les besoins nutritifs quotidiens du bébé et la quantité de liquide total qu'il doit absorber. (Voir tableau p. 126)

Types de lait et ingrédients pour l'alimentation artificielle

La valeur calorique du lait de vache entier est de 20 calories par 30 millilitres.

Lait certifié. C'est la forme la plus pure de lait à l'état naturel. Il contient moins de 10 000 bactéries par centimètre cube, et aucun agent pathogène même avant la pasteurisation. Il est produit en respectant des conditions spéciales d'hygiène. Tous les récipients doivent être stérilisés avant usage. Les employés chargés de la manutention du lait doivent être examinés afin de déceler la présence de maladie qui pourrait être transmise par le lait. On procède à des cultures lorsqu'ils ont des maux de gorge et également à d'autres tests afin de prévenir toute contamination. La plus grande partie du lait certifié est également pasteurisée.

Lait pasteurisé. Dans la pasteurisation, le lait naturel est chauffé jusqu'à 28°C pendant 30 minutes. Puis on le refroidit rapidement. Dans la plupart des villes, la pasteurisation du lait commercial est requise par la loi. La pasteurisation tue les organismes pathogènes, mais ne stérilise pas le lait; elle rend inoffensifs le *Salmonella typhosa,* les bacilles de la tuberculose, de la diphtérie, ceux du groupe parathyphique et les streptocoques hémolytiques. La pasteurisation détruit la vitamine C, qui est une vitamine facilement détruite par la chaleur et rend plus petit et plus mou, le caillot formé par le lait dans l'estomac du bébé. Le lait pasteurisé devrait être bouilli pour les biberons du bébé.

Lait additionné de vitamine D. Il s'agit du lait entier auquel on a ajouté de la vitamine D, qui prévient le rachitisme. Le lait des vaches au pâturage contient davantage de vitamine D que celui des vaches qui ne paissent pas dans l'herbe fraîche. On peut augmenter le contenu de vitamine D du lait en donnant cette vitamine à la vache. En pratique, il est plus efficace d'ajouter la vitamine directement au lait. Ceci est fait dans la plupart des grandes laiteries commerciales et dans la production du lait évaporé. Cette méthode assure le contenu désiré de vitamine D dans tout le lait offert sur le marché.

Lait homogénéisé. Dans le lait homogénéisé, les globules de gras sont scindés et distribués en suspension colloïdale à travers tout le lait. Le caillot devient plus mou et de ce fait plus digestible, et la saveur du lait en est améliorée. La digestion est alors plus facile, parce qu'une plus grande surface lipidique est offerte à l'action des enzymes intestinaux.

Lait évaporé. Le lait évaporé est du lait entier auquel on a retiré 60% de son volume d'eau. La valeur calorique est de 44 calories (ordinairement considérée comme 40 calories) par 30 ml. Il contient 2 g de protides par

30 ml. Il est stérilisé, relativement peu coûteux, disponible dans toutes les épiceries et peut être conservé à la maison sans réfrigération si la boîte n'est pas ouverte. Le lait évaporé est ordinairement à la fois irradié et homogénéisé. Il se transformera en un caillot fin parce que homogénéisé, et aussi parce que la caséine a été partiellement rendue inactive par l'évaporation. Afin de l'employer comme du lait entier, il suffit de le diluer avec une égale quantité d'eau.

Lait condensé. Le lait condensé est du lait évaporé entier auquel on a ajouté 45% de sucre. La valeur calorique est environ de 100 calories par 30 millilitres. On ne devrait pas l'utiliser pour l'alimentation des bébés parce que sa teneur en glucides est beaucoup trop élevée. Un bébé nourri au lait condensé sera pâle et gras, aura des muscles distendus et sera sujet à la diarrhée causée par la fermentation des glucides.

Lait en poudre. Dans le lait en poudre l'eau du lait écrémé est complètement évaporée. Le lait en poudre contient des quantités variées de gras. Il est valable pour l'alimentation de bébés qui ne tolèrent pas la quantité de gras présente dans le lait entier. Le lait en poudre produit un caillot fin. Il est empaqueté dans des récipients hermétiques et se conserve pendant plusieurs mois sans se détériorer; pour cette raison, il est pratique de l'employer lorsqu'on voyage avec un bébé et quand il est impossible de se procurer du lait frais ou évaporé. Dans le processus de fabrication du lait en poudre, la vitamine C est détruite. 3,5 cuillerées à table de lait en poudre mélangées avec 210 ml d'eau donnent un mélange qui a la composition du lait liquide. Pour nourrir le bébé, on mélange le lait en poudre avec assez d'eau froide pour faire une pâte; puis, on ajoute graduellement la quantité désirée d'eau, pendant que l'on remue le mélange pour prévenir la formation de grumeaux.

Glucides. On ajoute des glucides à la formule pour augmenter sa valeur calorique, pour en améliorer la saveur, et pour son effet laxatif. Ils contiennent, en moyenne, 120 calories par 30 cm³. Pour dissoudre le sucre, on le mélange avec un liquide chaud.

Dans l'intestin, toutes les sortes de glucides doivent être fractionnés jusqu'au niveau des monosaccharides avant de pouvoir être utilisés par l'organisme. Les glucides les plus communément employés dans la nourriture des bébés incluent les suivants:

(*a*) Dextrose ou glucose. Ils sont aisément digestibles.

(*b*) Sucrose ou sucre de canne. La forme la moins onéreuse et la plus courante pour la formule du bébé mais elle a le désavantage d'être trop sucrée.

(*c*) Lactose ou sucre de lait. Le sucre de lait n'est pas sucré au goût, est semblable au glucide dans le lait maternel et a une valeur laxative.

(*d*) Dextri-maltose. Une forme relativement onéreuse, mais aisément digestible. Ce produit consiste en un mélange de maltose et de dextrine. Ceux-ci sont simplifiés par un processus digestif avant l'absorption.

(*e*) Sirop de maïs. Un glucide peu dispendieux et aisément digestible. On devrait le conserver dans le réfrigérateur et le couvrir avec soin, puisque c'est un bon milieu liquide de culture pour les bactéries.

(*f*) Amidon. Un polysaccharide. Il est difficile à digérer pour le bébé à moins qu'il ne soit bouilli à fond (ce qui fractionne les molécules d'amidon).

Produits laitiers enregistrés pour bébés. Ils sont fabriqués par des entreprises commerciales et ont comme base le lait évaporé ou en poudre. Dans certains, on a enlevé le gras ou on l'a remplacé, et dans d'autres, on a fait diverses modifications du lait original. Certains laits enregistrés ressemblent de près au lait maternel dans leur composition. Ces préparations sont relativement coûteuses, mais ont les avantages de la commodité, de la stérilisation et de la compacité. La loi requiert que les ingrédients soient inscrits sur le récipient. Ordinairement, on ajoute de l'eau bouillie à la préparation en poudre pour préparer la formule. Certaines formules enregistrées sont préparées sous forme liquide dans des bouteilles qui sont prêtes pour l'usage immédiat et que l'on jette après usage.

Préparation de la formule

Les principes fondamentaux de la préparation de la formule du bébé incluent la propreté et la précision. Le biberon doit être propre et de préférence stérilisé, puisqu'il peut être une source d'infection pour le bébé. À l'hôpital, dans la biberonnerie, le personnel devrait porter des blouses et des couvre-chefs; plusieurs hôpitaux exigent également le port des masques. La pièce où l'on prépare les biberons doit être éloignée des endroits où le personnel hospitalier et les visiteurs circulent, et des salles où se trouvent les patients. Il est à noter que, dans la plupart des hôpitaux, on utilise des laits préparés commercialement. À la maison, le biberon est ordinairement préparé à la cuisine. La mère devrait porter une robe propre ou un tablier qui l'enveloppe entièrement.

Équipement. L'équipement et les ingrédients devraient être prêts avant de commencer la préparation du biberon. Les ingrédients sont le lait, l'eau stérilisée et une forme de glucides. L'équipement consiste en bouteilles, tétines et couvercles de bouteille.

Bouteilles. Il faudrait se procurer suffisamment de biberons de 240 ml pour toutes les rations données durant 24 heures et, au moins, une bouteille supplémentaire pour remplacer celle qui se briserait. On emploie communément des bouteilles à large goulot, parce qu'elles peuvent être nettoyées facilement et complètement avec une brosse et aussi parce que la tétine qui s'y adapte ressemble passablement au mamelon de la mère. À l'hôpital, on étiquette clairement et précisément chaque bouteille soit selon le nom du bébé, soit selon le type de formule que la bouteille contient. Chaque bouteille devrait être gardée au réfrigérateur jusqu'à l'heure du repas du bébé.

Tétines. Le nouveau-né a besoin d'une tétine ferme. Une tétine devenue molle à force d'être employée et d'être stérilisée rend la succion difficile. L'ouverture de la tétine devrait être cruciforme, composée de deux incisions de 4 mm en forme de croix. Certaines tétines sur le marché ont cette croix, mais d'autres portent les 3 trous traditionnels disposés en forme de triangle. Les orifices peuvent être agrandis pour satisfaire les besoins du bébé. Les critères pour trouver la meilleure dimension des trous consistent dans l'habileté à sucer (le bébé immature et faible peut s'épuiser s'il doit sucer vigoureusement pour obtenir le lait à travers de petits trous), et dans la consistance du liquide.

Quand on renverse la bouteille, le goulot vers le bas, le lait devrait s'écouler lentement de la tétine, à raison d'une goutte à la seconde.

Couvercles de bouteille. Comme la tétine doit être stérile quand elle entre dans la bouche du bébé, on emploie des couvercles stérilisés et imperméables à l'air. Ils peuvent être de verre ou de plastique et ils sont en forme de cône, couvrant la tétine. Si on doit mettre la tétine stérilisée sur la bouteille juste avant de la donner au bébé, on peut employer un couvercle en caoutchouc ou en plastique, pour couvrir le goulot de la bouteille.

Préparation de la formule. Il y a deux grandes méthodes pour préparer les biberons.

La méthode aseptique et la méthode de chaleur terminale.

Méthode aseptique. L'équipement nécessaire pour préparer un biberon inclut ce qui suit:
Bouilloire ou casserole,
Bouteilles, tétines, couvercles de bouteilles,
Cruche,
Cuillère à table et tasse à mesurer,
Grande casserole pour faire bouillir (avec couvercle),
Cuillère à long manche,
Couteau de table,
Ouvre-boîte,
Entonnoir,
Petite casserole pour faire bouillir les tétines et les couvercles de bouteilles,
Pincettes,
Brosse à bouteilles,
Petit pot avec couvercle ajusté pour conserver les tétines.

Il est à noter qu'il existe sur le marché des ensembles contenant tout cet équipement et qui sont accompagnés d'un mode d'emploi.

Voici la marche à suivre pour préparer un biberon:

1) Laver tout l'équipement dans de l'eau chaude et savonneuse et rincer dans de l'eau chaude et claire. Laver les bouteilles, l'entonnoir, les tétines et les couvercles de bouteille avec la brosse à bouteille. Passer de l'eau à travers les trous des tétines pour s'assurer qu'ils sont ouverts.

2) Placer tout l'équipement, excepté les articles en caoutchouc, dans un récipient couvert et faire bouillir pendant 10 minutes.

3) Placer les tétines et les couvercles en caoutchouc, si on les utilise, dans une casserole couverte et faire bouillir pendant 3 minutes.

4) Placer les tétines dans le petit pot stérilisé et fermé.

5) Faire bouillir l'eau dans la bouilloire ou la casserole pendant 5 minutes. Mesurer la quantité requise dans la tasse à mesurer stérilisée et verser dans la cruche stérilisée.

6) Mesurer la quantité requise de sucre ou de sirop dans la cuillère à mesurer. Niveler le contenu avec un couteau de table. Ajouter les glucides à l'eau dans la cruche et remuer jusqu'à dissolution.

7) Si on emploie du lait en boîte, frotter le dessus de la boîte avec du savon et rincer avec de l'eau chaude.

8) Mesurer la quantité requise de lait dans une tasse à mesurer et verser dans le mélange eau-sucre. Brasser à fond avec la cuillère à long manche.

9) Verser la préparation dans les bouteilles stérilisées au moyen de l'entonnoir. Couvrir les bouteilles avec les couvercles.

10) Placer les bouteilles dans une casserole d'eau froide afin de les refroidir rapidement. L'eau devrait être au même niveau que le lait dans les bouteilles. Placer les bouteilles dans le réfrigérateur.

11) Quand il est temps de nourrir le bébé, retirer une bouteille du réfrigérateur. Enlever le couvercle. Retirer une tétine du pot et la placer sur la bouteille. Replacer le couvercle sur le pot.

12) Placer la bouteille dans une casserole d'eau chaude afin de réchauffer un peu le biberon et le donner au bébé.

Méthode de chaleur terminale. Cette méthode est maintenant employée dans plusieurs hôpitaux et foyers pour toutes les formules qui peuvent tolérer le degré de chaleur nécessaire pour cette forme de stérilisation.

Le lait est préparé proprement mais sans stérilisation et versé dans des bouteilles nettoyées à fond. Les tétines sont placées sur les bouteilles et les couvercles sont placés, sans les serrer, sur les tétines.

À l'hôpital, on range les bouteilles dans des supports que l'on met dans un autoclave pendant 10 minutes à une température de 119°C et une pression de 103 k Pa.

Au foyer, on peut acheter un stérilisateur et adapter la technique hospitalière. La formule devrait être stérilisée pendant 25 minutes à 100°C. Le couvercle du stérilisateur ne devrait pas être enlevé avant qu'on puisse le manipuler les mains nues. Cela est un indice approximatif du temps requis pour que les tétines refroidissent lentement. Soumis à un refroidissement rapide, les trous des tétines ont tendance à se couvrir d'une mince pellicule. Les bouteilles doivent être enlevées, les couvercles ajustés, et le tout est rangé dans le réfrigérateur à une température de 4,4 à 7,2°C jusqu'à ce qu'on l'utilise.

Dans plusieurs hôpitaux, on emploie actuellement un service commercial de laits préparés au lieu de préparer les biberons dans un laboratoire. Les mères peuvent aussi acheter des laits préparés commercialement pour usage au foyer. On peut, soit les utiliser tels quels, soit les diluer avec de l'eau stérilisée et on se sert de bouteilles et de tétines stérilisées. On peut aussi se procurer des biberons à jeter après usage, avec des tétines fixées au récipient. Au foyer, ces procédés épargnent aux mères du temps et des efforts, mais il s'avèrent assez onéreux.

Technique de l'alimentation à la bouteille

Le lavage des mains à l'eau et au savon est toujours de rigueur avant de donner le biberon à un enfant. Si le lait sort du réfrigérateur, on peut le réchauffer en plaçant la bouteille pendant 10 minutes dans une casserole contenant de l'eau à une température de 49°C ou dans un réchaud électrique, contrôlé au thermostat. Pour vérifier la température et le débit du lait l'infirmière laisse tomber quel-ques gouttes de lait sur la partie interne de son poignet. Il n'est pas nécessaire de réchauffer le biberon jusqu'à la température du corps, car le nouveau-né tolère très bien les liquides qui sont à la température de la pièce. Quand un nourrisson est hospitalisé, il faut demander à la mère à quelle température elle donne le biberon car certains bébés habitués au lait réchauffé refusent de s'alimenter si l'on ne se conforme pas à leurs habitudes.

L'infirmière vérifie le nom du bébé et celui inscrit sur la bouteille avant de le faire boire. Elle change sa couche, s'il est souillé, pour qu'il soit à l'aise au moment du repas.

Après s'être de nouveau lavé les mains, elle prend le bébé, enveloppé dans une couverture, si cela est nécessaire, et reposant sur un piqué et elle s'assoit sur une chaise berceuse, tenant le bébé dans ses bras, la tête appuyée sur son bras. Si, pour quelque raison, le bébé ne peut être sorti de son lit, l'infirmière devrait s'asseoir à côté du berceau, lever la tête du bébé ou l'asseoir dans une petite chaise de lit et tenir la bouteille. La mère peut tenir le bébé dans ses bras pour le faire boire pendant qu'elle repose au lit durant la période post-partum.

On ne devrait jamais placer la bouteille sur un coussinet et laisser l'enfant boire seul. Ceci peut s'avérer la pire forme de négligence. Le bébé peut lâcher la tétine et ne plus pouvoir la remettre dans sa bouche; il y a surtout danger que le débit du lait soit trop rapide et que le bébé s'étouffe.

On s'assure que le bébé capte toute la tétine et on penche la bouteille de telle façon que la tétine soit toujours remplie de liquide; sans quoi, le bébé avalera de l'air ce qui provoquera une dilatation gastrique ou des coliques. On doit le faire éructer fréquemment, au cours du repas, et toujours à la fin du biberon, ordinairement après 10 à 20 minutes. On devrait ensuite le coucher, sur le côté droit ou sur l'abdomen, dans son berceau. Dans chacune de ces positions, le lait passera très facilement par le pylore jusque dans le duodénum, et, si le bébé régurgite, le liquide s'écoulera vers l'extérieur, éliminant le danger d'aspiration bronchique.

On jette le lait qui reste et on rince la bouteille et la tétine à l'eau froide avant de les retourner au laboratoire où l'on prépare les biberons. L'infirmière devrait aller voir de nouveau le bébé après quelques minutes pour voir s'il a régurgité ou vomi pendant son absence.

Après le biberon, on note l'heure, la durée, la quantité de liquide ingurgitée et, si c'est le cas, la quantité régurgitée ou vomie.

DÉPART
DE LA POUPONNIÈRE

Avant le départ du bébé, on procède aux prélèvements sanguins qui permettent de vérifier s'il souffre de phénylcétonurie, de galactosémie, de fructosémie ou de maladie du « sirop d'érable » (aménopathie). L'enfant doit avoir reçu du lait pendant au moins 24 heures pour que le test de Guthrie, destiné à dépister la phénylcétonurie, puisse être significatif.

Au Québec, on demande un échantillon sanguin de tous les bébés quittant la pouponnière et ce, depuis mai 1969. De plus, on remet à la mère les éléments nécessaires pour qu'elle puisse tester l'urine de son bébé après son retour à domicile et expédier le résultat au centre de génétique. On effectue des tests de contrôle après quelques semaines, si les résultats indiquent un taux de phénylalanine supérieur à la normale. Le seuil rénal de la phénylalanine n'est dépassé que quelques jours après l'arrivée à la maison et les tests urinaires ne sont pas valables s'ils sont pratiqués à la pouponnière. Pour ce qui est des désordres impliquant le galactose et le fructose, on devrait donner au bébé des biberons contenant ces substances avant de procéder aux tests d'urine. Les bébés nés de famille dans lesquelles ces maladies métaboliques ou autres maladies métaboliques héréditaires ont été retracées, doivent être examinés avec soin.

SOINS À LA MAISON

Nous discuterons ici de l'environnement et des soins physiques que la mère devra prodiguer à son bébé après le retour à la maison. N'oublions pas que plusieurs jeunes mères n'ont jamais eu de contact avec un nourrisson et que, malgré toutes les lectures qu'elles ont pu faire, elles s'interrogent sur leur habileté à vraiment prendre soin d'un nouveau-né.

Aspect émotif
du retour à la maison

On trouve deux types différents de mère qui retourne au foyer avec un nouveau-né. Nous parlerons peu de la femme qui, ayant déjà eu un ou plusieurs enfants, possède l'expérience des soins de l'enfant. Toutefois, elle ne doit pas, dès son arrivée, se surcharger de travaux domestiques et elle a vraiment besoin d'une aide quelconque. Ceci lui permettra de s'adapter aux exigences de ce nouvel enfant et de combler par sa présence les aînés qui ont sûrement souffert de la séparation et peuvent réagir fâcheusement en face de l'intrus qu'est le nouveau bébé.

Pour celle qui est mère pour la première fois, le problème est différent. Elle a surtout besoin d'un support psychologique qui lui vient souvent de sa propre mère, si celle-ci peut disposer de quelques jours pour lui venir en aide et si mère et fille ont une relation saine. Elle souffre rarement de véritable surmenage physique puisque son bébé dort presque toute la journée. Elle craint toutefois d'être inefficace dans les soins précis comme le bain, l'allaitement ou la simple évaluation de l'état du bébé. Son mari s'avère rarement d'un grand secours car son inexpérience est encore plus flagrante. Le premier mois de la vie du bébé constitue une période de crise pour les parents.

Environnement
Chambre de l'enfant

Le bébé devrait avoir sa propre chambre. Le plancher et les murs devraient être faciles à nettoyer; les couleurs claires sont préférables. Le chauffage et la ventilation devraient être adéquats. Pour le jeune bébé, on maintient la température entre 21°C et 24°C durant le jour et entre 15,5°C et 18°C pendant la nuit; pour l'enfant plus âgé, la température idéale pendant le jour est de 20°C à 21°C et 10°C pendant la nuit. On évite les courants d'air, tout en s'assurant que la chambre est bien aérée. On devrait maintenir le degré d'humidité à 55%. En hiver, tout système permettant l'évaporation de l'eau augmentera l'humidité, tels qu'un humidificateur, un réceptacle plein d'eau placé sur un calorifère, ou un appareil fixé au radiateur. La buée qui se forme à l'intérieur des vitres pendant les jours froids indique que le taux d'humidité, dans la chambre du bébé, est approprié.

Ameublement de la chambre

L'ameublement doit être simple, durable et facilement nettoyable. La peinture au plomb dans les vieilles maisons ou sur de vieux berceaux peut être une source d'empoisonnement si le bébé mord la surface peinte ou met dans sa bouche des morceaux de plâtre peint provenant du mur.

Le bébé devrait avoir son propre lit. Il est sage et plus économique d'acheter un berceau convenant pour un enfant de 2 ou 3 ans. Cela donnera de l'espace au bébé pour se rouler et ramper lorsqu'il sera capable de bouger et il sera heureux à son réveil, même si sa mère n'arrive pas aussitôt. Les barreaux du berceau devraient être rapprochés et les ridelles assez hautes pour l'empêcher de passer. Le loquet devrait être hors de sa portée.

Le matelas, recouvert d'un tissu imperméable, devrait être d'une qualité suffisante pour lui permettre de garder sa forme à l'usage.

Les draps-housses constituent la solution idéale pour la literie. Toujours bien tendus, ils se changent en un tour de main et empêchent le bébé de déchirer l'enveloppe de matelas. Pour éviter la transpiration due à la surface imperméable du matelas, on conseille d'ajouter un tissu épais, lavable qui couvre entièrement le lit, sous le drap-housse. Il faut proscrire l'oreiller dont l'enfant n'a aucun besoin et qui risque de l'étouffer, s'il se tourne sur l'abdomen et y enfouit la figure. L'enfant a besoin de peu de couvertures dans une chambre bien chauffée. Les pyjamas-combinaisons constituent la solution idéale pour l'enfant qui rejette constamment ses couvertures pendant son sommeil.

Le bébé devrait avoir sa propre baignoire. Celles en plastique sont légères, durables et douces pour la peau du bébé. Il aura besoin d'un seau à couches, de préférence contrôlé par une pédale, avec un couvercle bien ajusté, et plus tard il lui faudra un siège de toilette. Il devrait y avoir une barrière à la porte de sa chambre et en haut de l'escalier, si la famille demeure dans une maison à étages.

Bain

On baigne le bébé quotidiennement et on peut l'éponger plusieurs fois par jour quand il fait chaud. La température de la chambre devrait alors se situer entre 24°C et 26°C. On emploie souvent une baignoire portative pour le nourrisson. Après 4 mois, on utilise la baignoire familiale, mais la mère peut trouver que le fait de se pencher la fatigue. Une serviette de bain ou un tapis de caoutchouc placé au fond du bain empêche le bébé de glisser et ajoute au plaisir du bain. La température de l'eau devrait être entre 38°C et 40,5°C pour le nouveau-né ou le petit bébé; pour le bébé normal et en santé, on pourra bientôt la réduire à 35°C. La mère vérifie la température de l'eau avec son coude ou un thermomètre à bain. Il faut des serviettes douces et une débarbouillette.

Elle devrait avoir un plateau à bain contenant les articles suivants:

Pot de tampons de ouate hydrophile

Porte-savon (le savon devrait être blanc et non-parfumé)

Bouteille d'huile ou de lotion pour bébés

Pelotte à épingles

Brosse à cheveux et peigne

Sac en papier pour déchets

Poudre (si la mère veut l'employer car la fécule de maïs coûte moins cher que presque toutes les autres poudres et convient à la peau du bébé; cependant, aucune poudre ne devrait être employée de façon routinière.)

Onguent doux (lorsqu'il faut traiter les surfaces excoriées.)

Il n'y a pas de technique spéciale à suivre pour le bain du bébé mais il faut se rappeler certains principes.

Le lavage de la tête doit être effectué chaque fois que l'on donne le bain au bébé. La mère ne doit pas craindre de laver le crâne du bébé au niveau des fontanelles. Il se produit parfois de la dermite séborrhéique sur le cuir chevelu et on la prévient par un lavage régulier des cheveux suivi d'un bon rinçage. Le traitement de la dermite séborrhéique du cuir chevelu consiste en l'application d'une huile ou d'un onguent non médicamenteux qu'il faut laisser en place pour la nuit et que l'on fait suivre d'un shampoing doux au matin. On répète ce traitement jusqu'à la disparition des lésions. Il existe des préparations commerciales qui donnent aussi d'excellents résultats.

On accorde une attention spéciale aux yeux, au nez et aux oreilles. On lave les plis cutanés en prenant soin de bien les assécher. On nettoie les organes génitaux et le siège chaque fois qu'on change la couche du bébé.

Il faut donner à la mère des directives complètes sur les soins à donner à l'ombilic. Ordinairement, l'exposition à l'air du cordon ombilical amène une guérison rapide. Le bain d'éponge s'avère suffisant jusqu'à la tombée du cordon.

Vêtements

On évite de trop vêtir l'enfant. Les bébés aujourd'hui portent très peu de vêtements. La plupart des maisons sont très bien chauffées en hiver et moins le bébé portera de vêtements l'été, plus il sera à l'aise. L'enfant grandit vite et on doit renouveler fréquemment sa garde-robe, de telle sorte qu'il est préférable d'acheter peu de vêtements, quitte à laver plus souvent. Tous les vêtements pour bébé devraient être doux et non-irritants, confortables, amples et lavables, convenant à la température

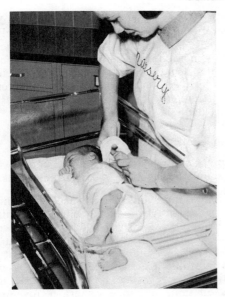

Figure 7-11. La façon la plus simple d'habiller le bébé est de mettre la main entière à travers la manche, de saisir la main du bébé et de la tirer gentiment. (Davis et Rubin, *DeLee's Obstetrics for Nurses.* 17ᵉ éd.)

extérieure, faciles à mettre, absorbants et sûrs. On évite les attaches autour du cou qui risquent d'étouffer le bébé, et qui, de toute façon, l'incommodent.

Plusieurs mères optent pour la simplicité dans l'habillement de leur bébé. Une chemisette de coton, une couche, un pyjama léger et enveloppant suffisent pour l'hiver. L'été, le bébé est très à l'aise dans son parc s'il est vêtu d'une couche, d'une chemisette et d'un petit chandail de coton. On évite d'emblée de le placer au soleil, mais un bonnet recouvrant les oreilles peut s'avérer utile pour pallier aux changements de température. On protège les pieds contre le froid, la saleté et les blessures. On n'emploie chaussons et chaussettes, que si les pieds du bébé sont froids.

On a décrit plus tôt dans ce chapitre la technique du lavage des couches. On emploie cependant, de plus en plus, les couches jetables dont certaines ne requièrent pas l'emploi d'épingles de sureté. Plusieurs familles font aussi appel aux services de distribution et de lavage des couches qui existent dans le commerce.

Élimination

Le bébé nourri au sein a plusieurs selles par jour; elles sont molles et plutôt spongieuses et peuvent contenir un peu de mucus. Elles ne provoqueront probablement pas d'irritation. Leur odeur est plutôt aromatique. Les selles du bébé nourri au lait de vache ou au sucre de canne sont jaunes et plus consistantes que celles du bébé nourri au sein. Une ou deux selles par jour constituent un rythme normal.

Sommeil

Le nouveau-né dort ou semble dormir pratiquement tout le temps où il ne se nourrit pas et ne pleure pas. Son sommeil est léger, et il a de fréquents mouvements spontanés de la figure et du corps. Il étire et plisse sa figure. Quand il n'a que quelques semaines, ses périodes de sommeil sont plus longues et plus calmes, mais par contre, il est éveillé et alerte pour de plus longues périodes. Cette tendance continue à mesure qu'il progresse dans sa première année de vie.

Poids

Les mères devraient apprendre à l'hôpital comment peser leur bébé, si elles ont ou comptent avoir un pèse-bébé à la maison. Il faut attirer l'attention sur le sentiment de sécurité que cela leur donne. La mère devrait garder une main au-dessus du bébé en tout temps pendant qu'elle le pèse afin qu'il ne puisse glisser.

À la maison, des pesées hebdomadaires sont suffisantes. Si la mère pèse le bébé chaque jour, elle peut s'inquiéter en constatant les fluctuations mineures. Les balances ne sont pas absolument nécessaires, car le bébé peut être pesé lors de son examen au bureau du médecin ou à la clinique pour bébés. Le bébé moyen gagnera entre 210 et 240 g chaque semaine. Quelques bébés, cependant, gagnent entre 150 et 360 g par semaine. Si l'augmentation de poids est supérieure ou inférieure à cette moyenne, la mère devrait en avertir le médecin.

Température

Bien que l'on doive apprendre aux mères à prendre la température du bébé, il ne faut pas considérer cela comme faisant partie des soins quotidiens. Il faudrait prendre la température seulement lorsque le bébé présente des signes d'hyperthermie.

Alimentation

L'alimentation du bébé devrait être considérée comme faisant partie des activités routinières de la journée, auxquelles participent tous les membres de la famille. Si tout le monde dans la maison doit être subordonné au bébé, il deviendra probablement un facteur de trouble. Consciemment ou inconsciemment, on aura le sentiment qu'il est privilégié et cela influencera les relations émotives des parents et des jeunes à son égard et, indirectement, les uns envers les autres. On doit établir un plan pour ses soins dès le premier jour à la maison, veillant à ce qui est le mieux pour lui et pour la famille.

Les heures des biberons devraient convenir tant au bébé qu'à la famille. Le bébé apprend à aimer la personne qui lui donne à manger et le caresse. Le bébé moyen, à six semaines, sourira à sa mère quand elle le prend et lui sourit. Il est conditionné graduellement à sourire parce que cela lui amène toujours plus de caresses et d'expressions d'amour de la part de sa mère. C'est sa façon de chercher à lui plaire, et c'est le fondement de sa bonne volonté à faire ce qu'elle veut; cette disposition est essentielle à l'acceptation volontaire de la discipline, laquelle en retour mène à l'autodiscipline.

Pendant que la mère est à l'hôpital, l'infirmière devrait lui donner, A) une recette pour la formule alimentaire et un ensemble d'instructions, B) une démonstration de l'alimentation au biberon, C) une démonstraion du bain, de la pesée, de la prise de température et de la préparation de la formule. On peut enseigner à la mère ou bien la méthode aseptique ou bien la méthode de chaleur terminale, ou les deux. On peut procéder à cet enseignement par l'usage de livrets fournis par les laiteries; ils illustrent les étapes de préparation des biberons par l'une et l'autre méthodes.

Soins continus

Après le congé de l'hôpital, le bébé devrait être soumis à des soins médicaux continus.

La mère qui a un médecin privé lui confiera la santé de son bébé lorsqu'elle et lui auront quitté l'hôpital. Mais les autres mères recourront aux services de santé municipaux ou aux unités sanitaires qui tous les deux offrent des soins gratuits. Ces agences de santé seront averties des congés de l'hôpital, et une infirmière en santé publique visitera le foyer pour expliquer à la mère comment adapter tout ce qu'elle a appris à la situation familiale. Elle vérifiera l'équipement destiné aux soins du bébé et donnera une démonstration de la façon de le baigner et de préparer son biberon. S'il faut des conseils ou de l'aide ultérieurs, qu'elle ne peut pas donner, elle pourra référer cette famille à une agence sociale plus spécialisée.

RÉFÉRENCES

Livres et documents officiels

Abramson, H. (édit.): *Resuscitation of the Newborn Infant.* 3e éd. St. Louis, C. V. Mosby Company, 1973.

American Academy of Pediatrics: *Standards and Recommendations for Hospital Care of Newborn Infants.* 5e éd. Evanston, Ill., American Academy of Pediatrics, 1971.

Craig, W. S.: *Care of the Newly Born Infant.* 4e éd. Baltimore, Williams & Wilkins Company, 1969.

Curley, A. et autres: *Hexachlorophene: A Possible Toxin for Infants Via Absorption Through the Skin.* The American Pediatric Society, Inc., and the Society for Pediatric Research Combined Program and Abstracts. Atlantic City, New Jersey, 28 avril–1er mai 1971, p. 262.

Fomon, S. J.: *Infant Nutrition.* Philadelphie, W. B. Saunders Company, 1967.

Laboratoires Ross: *Les glandes mammaires et l'allaitement maternel.* Section de l'éducation en nursing, feuillet no 10, Columbus, Ohio.

MacKeith, R. et autres: *Infant Feeding and Feeding Difficulties.* 4e éd. Baltimore, Williams & Wilkins Company, 1971.

McKilligin, H.R.: *The First Day of Life.* New York, Springer Publishing Company, 1970.

Ministère de la Santé nationale et du Bien-être social: *Normes et recommandations pour les soins à la mère et au nouveau-né.* Division de l'hygiène mentale et infantile, Ottawa, 1968.

Ministère de la Santé nationale et du Bien-être social: *La mère canadienne et son enfant.* Division de l'hygiène maternelle et infantile, Ottawa, 1967.

Moore, M. L.: *The Newborn and the Nurse.* Philadelphie, W. B. Saunders Company, 1972.

Pearlman, R.: *Feeding Your Baby; The Safe and Healthy Way.* New York, Random House, 1971.

Robinson, C. H. et Lawler, M. R.: Normal and Therapeutic Nutrition. 14e éd. New York, Macmillan Company, 1972.

Sekely, T.: *La maman et son nouveau-né*. Montréal, Éditions de l'homme, 1967.
Shepard, K. S.: *Care of the Well Baby*. 2e éd. Philadelphie, J. B. Lippincott Company, 1968.

Articles

Alvord, E. C.: Neurotoxicity of Hexachlorophene in the Human. *Pediatrics*, 54:589, juin 1974.
Applebaum, R. M.: The Modern Management of Successful Breast Feeding. *Pediat. Clin. N. Amer.*, 7:203, février 1970.
Bird, I.S.: Breastfeeding Classes on the Postpartum Unit. *Am. J. Nursing*, 75:456, mars 1975.
Brioude, R.: Mode d'administration des médicaments au nouveau-né. *Soins*, 20:43, novembre 1975.
Brown, M. S.: Controversial Questions About Breastfeeding. *Journ. Obst & Gynec. Nursing*, 4:15,avril 1975.
Catz, C. et Giacoia, G.: Drugs and Breast Milk. *Ped Clin. N. Amer.*, 15:151, 1, 1972.
Clark, L.: Introducing Mother and Baby. *Am. J. Nursing*, 74:1483, août 1974.
Countryman, B. A.: Hospital Care of the Breast-Fed Newborn. *Am. J. Nursing*, 71:2365, décembre 1971.
Davidson, M.: Formula Feeding of Normal Term and Low Birth Weight Infants. *Pediat. Clin. N. Amer.*, 17:913, novembre 1970.
Eckes, S.: The significance of Increased Early Contact Between Mother and Newborn Infant. *Journ. Obst. & Gynec. Nursing*, 3:42, avril 1974.
Evans, R. T., Thigpen, L. W. et Hamrick, M.: Exploration of Factors Involved in Maternal Physiological Adaptation to Breastfeeding. *Nursing Research*, 18:28, Janvier-février 1969.
Herrmann, J. et Light, I. J.: Infection Control in the Newborn Nursery. *Nursing Clin. N. Amer.*, 6:55, mars 1971.
Keaveny, M. E.: Breastfeeding. *Nursing '72*, 2:31, novembre 1972.
Keitel, H. G.: Preventing Neonatal Diaper Rash. *Am. J. Nursing*, 65:124, mai 1965.
Kendall, N., Vaughan, V. C. et Kusakcioglu, A.: A Study of Preparation of Infant Formulas. A medical and Sociocultural Appraisal. *Am. J. Dis. Child.*, 122:215, Septembre 1971.
Klauss, M. H. et autres: Maternal Attachment: Importance of the First Post-Partum Days. *New England J. Med.*. 286:480, 2 mars 1972.
Klaus, M. H. et Kennell, J. H.: Mothers Separated from Their Newborn Infants. *Pediat. Clin. N. Amer.*, 17:1015, Novembre 1970.
Lutz, L. et Perlstein, P. H.: Temperature Control in Newborn Babies. *Nursing Clin. N. Amer.*, 6:15, mars 1971.
Mizer, H.: The Staphylococcus Problem versus the Hexachlorophene Dilemma in Hospital Nurseries. *Journ. Obst. & Gynec. Nursing*, 2:31, février 1973.
Murdaugh, Sister A. et Miller, L. E.: Helping the Breast-Feeding Mother. *Am J. Nursing.* 72:1420, août 1972.
Otte, M. J.: Correcting Inverted Nipples. *Am. J. Nursing*, 75:454, mars 1975
Phillips, C.: Neonatal Heat Loss in Heated Crib vs Mothers' Arms. *Journ. Obst. & Gynec. Nursing*, 3:11, juin 1974.
Reed, B., Sutorius, J. et Coen R.: Management of the Infant During Labor, Delivery, and in the Immediate Neonatal Period. *Nursing Clin. N. Amer.*, 6:3, mars 1971.
Richard, M.: Contribution du test d'Apgar au pronostic physique et intellectuel du nourrisson. *Laval médical*, 37:34, janvier 1966.
Robson, K. S. et Moss, H. A.: Patterns and Determinants of Maternal Attachment *J. Pediat.*. 77:976, décembre 1970.
Rousselet, D.: La congélation du lait maternel. *Inf. Can.*, 17:13. juillet 1975
Scanlon. J.: The Apgar Score Revisited. *Clin. Pediat.*, 12:61, février 1973.
Taggart, M. E.: L'allaitement peut être un succès. *Inf. Can.*, 18:16, 3, 1976.
Tempesta, L.: The Importance of Touch in the Care of Newborns. *Journ. Obst. & Gynec. Nursing*, 1:27 mars 1972.
Théberge-Rousselet, D.: La mastite. *Inf. Can.*, 18:25, 3, 1976.
Théberge-Rousselet, D.: Les médicaments et l'allaitement. *Inf. Can.*, 18:26, 3, 1976.
Van Leewen, G.: The Nurse in Prevention and Intervention in the Neonatal Period. *Nurs. Clin. N. Amer.*, 8:509, 3, 1973.
Whitner, W. et Thompson, M. C.: The Influence of Bathing on the Newborn Infant's Body Temperature. *Nursing Research*, 19:30, janvier-février, 1970.
Yasunaga, S. et Rivera, R.: Cephalhematoma in the Newborn. *Clin. Ped.* 13:256, mars 1974.
Zorn, J. R. Réanimation du nouveau-né à la naissance. *Soins*, XV:319, 7, 1970.

8
le prématuré et le nourrisson post-mature

ENFANT PRÉMATURÉ

La prématurité est la première cause de mortalité néonatale et infantile. Malgré les efforts déployés au cours des vingt-cinq dernières années, environ 10% des bébés naissent encore avant terme. Les critères de prématurité sont la durée de vie fœtale, le poids, la longueur et l'immaturité physiologique du nouveau-né. On se sert de l'un ou l'autre indice pour affirmer la prématurité. On considérait autrefois comme prématuré, tout enfant qui naissait entre la 28e et la 37e semaine de vie fœtale. On réserve aujourd'hui ce terme au bébé pesant 2500 g ou moins à sa naissance, quel que soit l'âge de la grossesse. Le prématuré mesure rarement plus de 47 cm; la pauvreté de ses réflexes et une insuffisance flagrante de vitalité démontrent l'immaturité de son organisme.

Incidence et causes de prématurité

La cause exacte de l'accouchement prématuré demeure souvent inconnue. Beaucoup de gestantes de faible niveau socio-économique ne reçoivent pas de soins prénatals et ne se présentent à l'hôpital qu'au moment de l'accouchement. Ces patientes n'ayant pas été suivies médicalement pendant la grossesse, peuvent avoir développé ou aggravé des pathologies risquant d'affecter leur enfant.

Les principales causes de la prématurité sont: la gémellité, les toxémies de la grossesse, surtout chez les patientes n'ayant pas bénéficié de soins prénatals, les hémorragies de la grossesse, surtout le placenta praevia et le placenta abruptio, la rupture prématurée des membranes qui amène invariablement une naissance avant terme.

Parmi les maladies maternelles qui expliquent l'accouchement prématuré, on trouve les infections aiguës et chroniques et des causes non infectieuses comme les cardiopathies et le diabète. L'incompatibilité sanguine, mère-fœtus, peut aussi provoquer un accouchement prématuré. La fatigue excessive et une alimentation inadéquate, surtout chez les femmes de faible niveau socio-économique, grèvent la santé, prédisposent l'organisme à l'accouchement avant terme ou à la formation d'un fœtus de faible poids. Les anomalies fœtales ou un traumatisme qui atteint la mère ou le fœtus peuvent également jouer un rôle néfaste. Il semble aussi que l'incidence de naissances

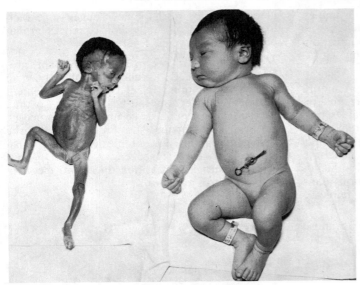

Figure 8-1. À droite, un nouveau-né pesant 3500 g. À gauche, un prématuré né à la 26e semaine de gestation et qui pesait 1100 g. La photographie prise à l'âge de 8 semaines montre le bébé qui pèse maintenant 2000 g. (Davis et Rubin, *DeLee's Obstetrics for Nurses.* 17e éd.)

prématurées soit plus forte chez les mères qui fument.

Prévention de l'accouchement prématuré

La prévention de la prématurité réside principalement dans les soins prénatals et une alimentation adéquate pour les femmes enceintes. L'accessibilité de ces soins à toutes les femmes enceintes demeure une préoccupation actuelle des divers gouvernements. Les soins dispensés à la future mère protègent aussi le fœtus dont les chances de santé et de survie sont liées à la durée de la gestation.

Caractéristiques du bébé prématuré

Aspect physique

L'aspect du prématuré correspond à son âge fœtal. Le fœtus est considéré comme viable, à l'extérieur de l'utérus, vers la 28e semaine de grossesse. L'immaturité du prématuré frappe immédiatement l'observateur averti. Minuscule et hypotonique, il a la peau rouge, mince et fripée; un duvet le recouvre et le vernix caseosa est à peu près absent. Sa tête semble proportionnellement trop grosse, les yeux proéminents, les oreilles molles et le menton fuyant. Le thorax est flexible, l'abdomen protubérant et les organes génitaux externes peu développés. Les extrémités paraissent longues et effilées, les muscles petits, les ongles minces et courts. La pauvreté du tissu sous-cutané lui donne un aspect de transparence. Malgré une maigreur extrême, quel-

ques prématurés présentent un œdème dû à la baisse des protéines sériques. Cet œdème disparaît en quelques jours. On ne rencontre pas l'engorgement des seins, dû, chez le nouveau-né normal, à la transmission au fœtus des hormones maternelles, à la fin de la grossesse. Chez des bébés extrêmement petits, les réflexes de succion, de déglutition et de toux font défaut.

Handicaps physiologiques

L'immaturité physiologique du prématuré explique la différence qui doit exister entre les soins qui lui sont administrés et ceux que l'on donne au nouveau-né normal. L'immaturité se manifeste par un contrôle déficient de la température corporelle, une respiration difficile, une diminution de la résistance aux infections, une tendance à l'hémorragie et à l'anémie, une prédisposition au rachitisme, des problèmes alimentaires et, enfin, un fonctionnement déficient du système rénal.

Instabilité thermique. L'influence du milieu sur la thermo-régulation du prématuré s'explique par les facteurs suivants: le manque de maturité du centre nerveux thermo-régulateur, les pertes caloriques causées par l'absence du pannicule adipeux qui se forme normalement au cours du dernier mois de gestation, la perte de chaleur par irradiation due à une grande surface corporelle par rapport au poids, la faible production de chaleur, l'enfant étant hypotonique à la suite de son faible développement musculaire, un métabolisme basal très bas. L'absence de sudation explique les hausses soudaines de température en milieu trop chaud. Les causes habituelles d'hyperthermie, comme la déshydradation et l'infection, peuvent facilement se manifester sans élévation de température.

Problème respiratoire.   Le prématuré respire difficilement et de façon irrégulière. Le développement incomplet des alvéoles pulmonaires, la faiblesse de la cage thoracique et des muscles inspiratoires, expliquent les problèmes respiratoires et le retard des échanges gazeux. De plus, l'enfant se défend difficilement contre l'accumulation des sécrétions dans les voies respiratoires à cause de la faiblesse de son réflexe de la toux.

La cyanose. La tendance à la cyanose prouve l'oxygénation inadéquate du sang artériel. Parmi les principales causes, on trouve: l'hypertension intracrânienne à la suite d'un traumatisme à la naissance, une obstruction des voies respiratoires, une insuffisance de développement des muscles inspirateurs et un obstacle à l'expansion normale du poumon comme la distension abdominale qui empêche ou pertube l'action du diaphragme.

L'apnée. Un excès d'analgésiques ou d'anesthésiques administrés à la mère pendant le travail provoque souvent de l'apnée. L'apnée et la cyanose dues à des traumatismes obstétricaux diminuent avec des soins médicaux adéquats. L'immaturité du système nerveux et des voies respiratoires, inhérente à la condition de prématuré, constitue un risque supplémentaire que l'on ne peut éviter. Les méthodes modernes de réanimation permettent de sauver beaucoup de prématurés qui, autrefois, seraient morts dès la naissance.

Pauvre résistance aux infections.   La grande sensibilité aux infections s'explique par le manque de facteurs immunitaires transmis normalement par la mère au cours du dernier mois de gestation et par une déficience dans la synthèse des globulines, dans la formation des anticorps et des défenses cellulaires. L'infection se manifeste rarement par de la fièvre ou une hausse de la formule blanche.

Tendance à l'hémorragie et à l'anémie. La fragilité vasculaire, l'hypoprothrombinémie et l'avitaminose K prédisposent le prématuré aux hémorragies qui conduisent à l'anémie. L'hématopoïèse déficiente s'explique par le défaut de réserves de fer et d'autres substances hématogènes qu'il aurait dû recevoir au cours du dernier mois de grossesse. La croissance, proportionnellement plus rapide, demande un apport sanguin important. Le prématuré possède encore une quantité importante d'hémo-globine fœtale; ses globules rouges sont facilement détruits, d'où les conséquences graves d'une perte sanguine légère.

Tendance au rachitisme.   L'enfant prématuré manque de calcium, de phosphore et parfois de vitamine D, éléments normalement présents chez le nouveau-né à terme. Le taux de croissance rapide exige une quantité accrue de tous ces facteurs. Le prématuré absorbe mal les vitamines liposolubles, et risque, ainsi d'accroître sa déficience en vitamine D. Tout ceci concourt à l'apparition du rachitisme chez le prématuré.

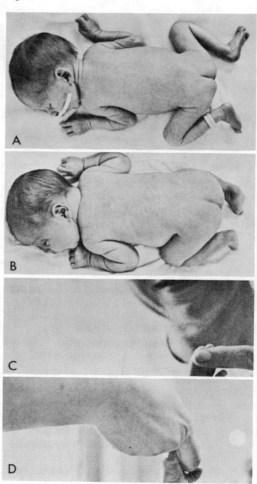

Figure 8-2.   Différence de développement neuro-musculaire et de tonus musculaire entre le prématuré et le nouveau-né normal. *A)* En position de pronation, le prématuré étendu à plate ventre, gît en position de grenouille, le bassin appuyé sur le matelas. *B)* Le nouveau-né a les genoux fléchis, ramenés sous lui et son siège est élevé. *C)* Le prématuré saisit la main faiblement, mais le tonus musculaire est pauvre. *D)* Le nouveau-né s'agrippe au doigt qui tente de le soulever. (Courtoisie de Mead-Johnson and Company.)

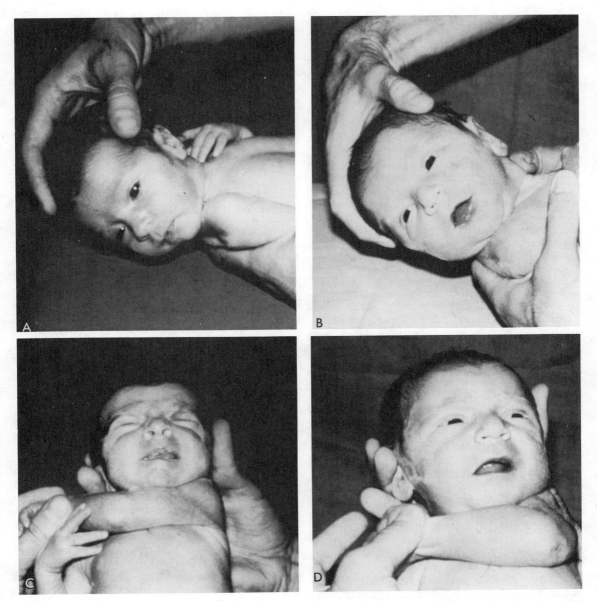

Figure 8-3.   Évaluation du tonus musculaire du nouveau-né. *A)* Signe du « hibou » chez le prématuré. On peut tourner la tête du bébé de telle sorte qu'il semble regarder en arrière. *B)* Chez l'enfant à terme, la rotation de la tête ne dépasse pas la ligne de l'épaule. *C)* Signe du « foulard » du prématuré. On peut étendre le bras de telle sorte que le coude dépasse le menton. *D)* Chez l'enfant à terme, le coude n'atteint pas la ligne du mnton. (Hodgman, Hosp. Pract., mai 1969.)

Problème de nutrition.   Ce problème sera traité ultérieurement.

Immaturité de la fonction rénale.   Le rein qui manque de maturité concentre difficilement l'urine; la perte de liquide très importante qui s'ensuit, explique la labilité de l'équilibre hydro-électrolytique.

Soins qui suivent immédiatement la naissance

Chaleur.   On place le nouveau-né dans un incubateur chauffé, pourvu d'une source d'oxygène et d'humidité. Les recherches ont prouvé que l'enfant prématuré survit plus facilement si on évite qu'il perde de la chaleur.

Stimulation respiratoire. On libère les voies respiratoires du mucus qui s'y trouve à l'aide d'un cathéter à succion en utilisant une pression faible et en effectuant des manœuvres délicates. On place l'enfant en position horizontale ou déclive, ce qui augmente le drainage naturel des sécrétions.

Si l'enfant fait de l'hypoxie, on peut stimuler artificiellement sa respiration à l'aide d'un appareil qui fournit une pression positive strictement contrôlée. En l'absence d'appareil, on fait la respiration bouche à bouche, très doucement, par petites insufflations à travers plusieurs épaisseurs de gaze. Si l'opérateur tient dans sa bouche un tube fournissant de l'oxygène, l'enfant reçoit un air plus oxygéné. Certaines méthodes plus radicales peuvent provoquer quelques inspirations forcées, mais s'avèrent insuffisantes pour rétablir une respiration régulière.

L'administration d'oxygène. Une source d'oxygène doit être facilement accessible si l'enfant ne respire pas dans les quelques secondes qui suivent la naissance ou si la cyanose apparaît un peu plus tard. Immédiatement après la naissance, on place le nouveau-né prématuré dans un incubateur dont l'atmosphère contient 30 à 40% d'oxygène.

Médication. L'infirmière doit connaître les médicaments utilisés couramment pour le prématuré et ces médicaments doivent être facilement accessibles en cas de besoin. L'épinéphrine en injection intramusculaire agit comme stimulant cardiaque alors que la caféine et le benzoate de sodium servent de stimulants respiratoires. Pour prévenir les hémorragies, on peut donner de la vitamine K en injection intramusculaire, à raison de 1 mg; un surdosage de cette vitamine peut causer l'hyperbilirubinémie. La nalline agit comme antidote pharmacologique de la morphine, la codéine ou autres opiacés que la mère pourrait avoir reçus pendant le travail, ceux-ci ayant traversé la barrière placentaire. On évite ordinairement l'administration d'analgésiques à la mère, quand on prévoit la naissance d'un prématuré.

Soins à la pouponnière

On prend soin du prématuré dans une pouponnière spéciale ou dans une section de l'unité des soins intensifs des nouveau-nés à terme. Il faut que chaque bébé puisse bénéficier à tout moment des appareils nécessaires au diagnostic et au traitement de son état, tels une source d'oxygène et d'air comprimé, un appareil aspirateur, des prises de courant pour l'appareil moniteur, pour le respirateur et pour les pompes électriques nécessaires à l'alimentation parentérale. Tout l'équipement nécessaire à la réanimation devrait être disponible ainsi que les appareils permettant de déceler rapidement les apnées du prématuré et de prévenir les dommages cérébraux. Le personnel infirmier qui travaille dans ces unités doit savoir manipuler les appareils conçus pour permettre au prématuré de survivre à son immaturité physiologique. Dans les hôpitaux plus petits, un effort devrait être fait pour fournir rapidement des soins d'urgence et assurer le transport rapide de l'enfant dans un hôpital pédiatrique ou une unité spécialisée de néo-natalité.

L'environnement. Seul le personnel spécialement désigné pénètre dans la pouponnière des prématurés. Il devrait exister un service séparé pour les prématurés nés dans un autre hôpital ou à domicile.

On effectue le transport du nouveau-né, de la salle d'accouchement à l'unité des prématurés, dans un incubateur chauffé et contenant une prise d'oxygène. La personne qui assure le transport doit apporter une bombonne portative d'oxygène. L'isolement le plus strict entoure la pouponnière des prématurés et assure la protection contre les sources possibles d'infection. L'air climatisé serait l'idéal. L'humidité de la pièce devrait varier entre 55 et 65% et la température devrait être maintenue entre 26°C et 32°C.

Le prématuré devrait être entouré d'un personnel infirmier compétent possédant un sens aigu de l'observation. En effet, à nul autre endroit, une surveillance constante et une observation aiguisée sont d'une telle importance. L'infirmière doit bien connaître les réactions physiologiques et pathologiques du prématuré pour interpréter très rapidement les symptômes qu'il présente. On a pu démontrer qu'un personnel compétent constitue un atout beaucoup plus précieux qu'un équipement électronique complexe. L'infirmière doit être capable d'apprécier à leur juste valeur les appareils multiples qui entourent le bébé; elle ne doit pas les craindre ni s'en servir pour interposer une barrière entre elle et son petit client.

Minimum de manipulations. Il faut sortir le prématuré le moins possible de son incubateur. L'habileté manuelle, la douceur et la précision dans les gestes aident à conserver les forces du bébé. En lui procurant les soins nécessaires au moment des repas, il peut ensuite se reposer durant de plus longues périodes ce qui permet de maintenir une concentration adéquate d'oxygène dans l'incubateur. Les recherches récentes tendent à démontrer toutefois que l'on a peut-être exagéré en évitant le plus possible les manipulations. On constate maintenant que le prématuré caressé et bercé, engraisse plus rapidement que celui qui vit solitaire dans son incubateur. De plus, il semble que pour le développement ultérieur du prématuré, celui-ci ait besoin d'être soigné par un personnel stable, de recevoir la visite régulière de sa mère et de profiter de stimulations sensorielles adaptées.

Maintien de la température corporelle

À cause de l'immaturité de l'appareil thermo-régulateur du prématuré, une déviation minime de la température extérieure se manifeste par une variation de sa température corporelle; le refroidissement peut lui être fatal. On essaie de maintenir sa température entre 35,5°C et 36,5°C, mais on cherche surtout la stabilité. Il faut aussi éviter de trop réchauffer l'enfant. La température et l'humidité appropriées dans la pouponnière préviennent la perte d'eau par la peau et les voies respiratoires.

On place d'emblée dans l'incubateur le bébé qui pèse 1400 g ou moins. Dans une pouponnière ordinaire, on ne sort pas immédiatement le prématuré de l'incubateur, même s'il a franchi le cap des 1360 g, surtout si sa température varie beaucoup, s'il respire mal ou cyanose facilement. L'incubateur a l'avantage de pouvoir être réglé à la température optimale pour le nouveau-né. En général, on n'élève pas la température de l'incubateur au-dessus de 32,2°C, mais on peut varier selon les besoins du bébé.

La prise de température permet de vérifier si la température extérieure est idéale. On prend d'abord la température rectale afin d'évaluer la perméabilité de l'anus. Par la suite, la température axillaire suffit mais il faut quelquefois la prendre toutes les heures jusqu'à ce qu'elle soit stable. Un thermomètre électronique relié au système de chauffage de l'incubateur permet un réglage continu de la température du nouveau-né et de son environnement immédiat.

Emploi et préparation de l'incubateur.

Plusieurs compagnies fabriquent des incubateurs et des berceaux chauffants. Il faut bien connaître les caractéristiques de chacun afin d'en tirer le maximum de rendement.

Les points à évaluer pour choisir l'incubateur sont le maintien facile de la température et de l'humidité, l'administration d'oxygène, le vitrage transparent permettant d'observer l'enfant et les signaux d'alarme en cas de surchauffage et de mauvaise circulation d'air.

Avant l'arrivée de l'enfant, on prépare l'incubateur dont on règle d'ordinaire la température à 32°C. On l'ajuste ensuite aux besoins de l'enfant pour le maintenir entre 35,5°C et 36,5°C. Dans certains incubateurs, un petit appareil électronique, attaché au bébé, permet des ajustements automatiques. On colle une sorte de thermostat très sensible sur l'abdomen du bébé et, au moindre changement, le moteur qui réchauffe l'incubateur part ou s'arrête et la température se stabilise au point désiré.

Le réservoir, rempli d'eau distillée stérile, permet une bonne humidité dans l'incubateur. On place le matelas, de telle sorte que le bébé demeure en position horizontale ou déclive. On vérifie fréquemment le débit d'oxygène jusqu'à l'atteinte du niveau prescrit. Chaque lecture est ensuite enregistrée toutes les deux heures. On doit toujours s'assurer que l'oxygène pénètre dans l'appareil. La concentration idéale d'oxygène pour un prématuré serait de 30 à 40% jusqu'à la disparition des symptômes de détresse respiratoire ou de cyanose. Elle devrait être ajustée selon la concentration sanguine en oxygène et en gaz carbonique. A l'aide d'une balance ajustable, le prématuré peut être pesé quotidiennement, tout en demeurant dans l'incubateur.

En l'absence d'incubateur, on emploie d'autres méthodes de réchauffement. Le plus fréquemment, on emploie la bouillotte dont on a déjà discuté au chapitre précédent.

Maintien de la respiration

Le prématuré respire rapidement, de façon superficielle et irrégulière. Sa respiration est abdominale; il a souvent des périodes d'apnée. L'aspiration des sécrétions libère les voies respiratoires mais l'on doit procéder à un lavage d'"estomac si les sécrétions sont trop abondantes.

On se sert d'un vaporisateur pour fournir l'humidité nécessaire au bébé prématuré ou né par césarienne. On ajuste l'appareil pour atteindre un taux de 55% d'humidité à l'intérieur de l'incubateur. On peut cesser le traitement 24 à 36 heures après que la respiration soit revenue à la normale. L'excès d'humidité peut prédisposer le bébé aux infections cutanées. À domicile, un humidificateur, une bouilloire, un inhalateur ou des

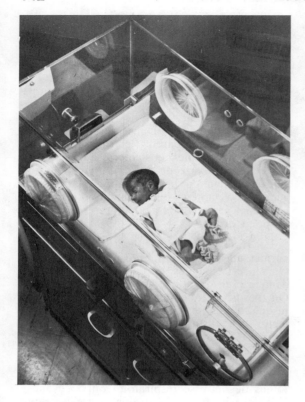

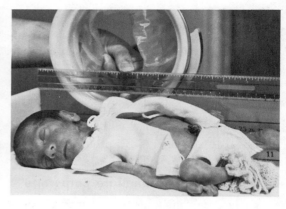

Figure 8-4. L'incubateur facilite les soins du prématuré et constitue pour celui-ci un milieu privilégié où la température et l'humidité peuvent être bien contrôlées. Les manchons qui s'ouvrent permettent d'atteindre l'enfant sans avoir à le déplacer. (Courtoisie de l'Hôpital Sainte-Justine, Montréal.)

serviettes mouillées posées sur un radiateur aident à humidifier l'atmosphère. Les serviettes demeurent humides quand une extrémité baigne dans un plat d'eau.

On place le bébé sur le côté afin de permettre une meilleure ventilation pulmonaire. S'il bouge peu, il faut le changer de position toutes les heures. Étant donné l'hypotonicité du prématuré, il faut maintenir sa position latérale avec un coussinet ou un sac de sable.

Si le bébé présente une période d'apnée, il importe de le stimuler en tapotant la plante de ses pieds ou en aspirant doucement ses sécrétions. De l'oxygène est administré si sa coloration s'altère. Si ces mesures échouent, on utilise rapidement la pression positive pour ventiler le bébé. Une infirmière expérimentée sait ajuster adéquatement le masque sur la figure du nouveau-né de façon à ce qu'il n'y ait pas de fuite d'air. La manipulation du sac à pression positive (Ambu) exige beaucoup de dextérité pour ne pas endommager les tissus pulmonaires. La majorité des prématurés ne nécessitent pas d'autres traitements. Toutefois, l'insertion d'un tube endotrachéal s'avère quelquefois vitale. Si le rythme cardiaque ne se rétablit pas. on aura recours au massage cardiaque externe.

Pour le massage cardiaque externe, 2 doigts sont placés sur le bord inférieur gauche du sternum et il faut obtenir une dépression de 1,5 à 2 cm. Trois mouvements de massage cardiaque devraient être suivis d'une ventilation.

Il est à noter que tout effort de réanimation doit s'effectuer en conservant la chaleur corporelle du nouveau-né puisqu'une baisse de température accentue la détresse respiratoire. Le prématuré qui présente des problèmes respiratoires peut finalement avoir besoin d'un respirateur pendant une certaine période.

Le danger de fibroplasie rétrolenticulaire est plus à redouter quand la concentration d'oxygène excède 40%. Plusieurs méthodes permettent de contrôler efficacement le débit d'oxygène. On peut analyser fréquemment l'atmosphère de l'incubateur et ajuster le débit pour maintenir la concentration au taux désiré. On peut administrer un mélange de 40% d'oxygène et 60% d'azote de sorte que le taux de chacun des gaz demeure à la même concentration. Un appareil permettant le mélange de l'air atmosphérique et de l'oxygène peut être fixé à un certain taux et s'y maintenir. L'oxygène ne doit être administré qu'en cas de nécessité et des prises sanguines régulières doivent permettre d'évaluer sa concentration dans l'organisme.

Enregistrement de l'administration de l'oxygène

Chaque dossier de prématuré contient une feuille permettant l'enregistrement des différentes données de l'oxygénothérapie. Elle comprend la prescription médicale concernant le débit et le mode d'administration de l'oxygène; la durée de l'administration à chaque séance; la concentration de l'oxygène pour chacune des périodes; la réaction du bébé à la concentration et à la durée du traitement. On note soigneusement toute interruption, si brève soit-elle. On contrôle fréquemment le bon fonctionnement de l'oxymètre en mesurant la concentration de l'oxygène dans l'air atmosphérique (20,9% au niveau de la mer) et en analysant de l'oxygène pur. L'exactitude de l'appareil pour ces deux extrêmes laisse supposer que les mesures intermédiaires sont également justes.

On note également les changements dans la coloration, la respiration, le pouls et le degré d'activité qui indiquent l'effet de l'oxygéno-thérapie sur l'enfant. Les prises sanguines régulières demeurent l'élément capital dans le dosage de l'oxygène. Les mesures de la pression partielle de l'oxygène, de la pression partielle du gaz carbonique et du pH sanguin sont essentielles pour déterminer l'efficacité de l'administration de l'oxygène et détecter un surdosage nuisible pour certains tissus de l'organisme. Un oxymètre cutané est en expérimentation.

Nutrition

La faiblesse, l'absence ou le manque de synchronisation des réflexes de succion et de déglutition compliquent l'alimentation du prématuré. Il peut ne pas réagir à la stimulation de la lèvre par une tétine ou un compte-gouttes et une quantité, même minime, d'aliments peut glisser hors de sa bouche ou dans ses voies respiratoires. S'il boit ou s'il reçoit des gavages, il peut souffrir de distension gastrique; des vomissements peuvent causer une broncho-aspiration. L'acidité gastrique et la capacité d'absorption des graisses demeurent plus faibles que chez le nouveau-né normal. Le système enzymatique peu développé rend même le lait maternel difficile à digérer.

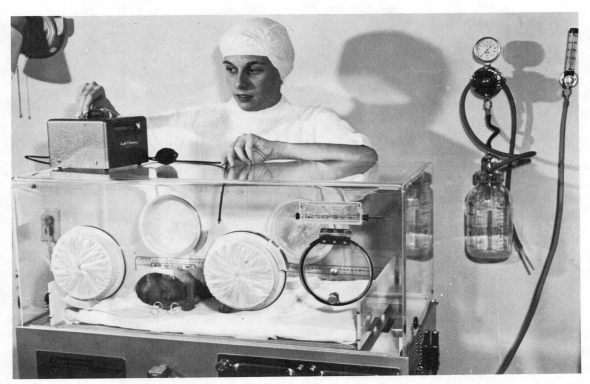

Figure 8-5. L'oxymètre permet de vérifier la concentration d'oxygène.
(Courtoisie de l'Hôpital Sainte-Justine, Montréal.)

Le prématuré a besoin d'un apport calorique supérieur à celui de l'enfant normal dont le poids est suffisant pour compenser la perte physiologique consécutive à la naissance. Ses besoins en calories sont évalués à 130-175 calories par kilogramme de poids dont 3 à 4 grammes de protéines, un apport suffisant de glucides et de liquide. L'absorption difficile des graisses rend le lait écrémé plus facile à digérer que le lait entier.

Dans leur alimentation, les prématurés ont besoin d'un supplément de vitamine C pour métaboliser la phénylalanine et la tyrosine; de vitamine D parce qu'ils perdent les vitamines liposolubles et du calcium dans leurs selles; de fer parce qu'ils n'ont pas eu le temps de constituer leur réserve étant donné leur prématurité.

Les données sur l'alimentation du nouveau-né se sont modifiées au cours des dernières années. On a longtemps cru qu'au cours des premières 24 heures le prématuré n'avait pas besoin de recevoir de nourriture puisqu'il était inactif, qu'il n'avait pas besoin de produire

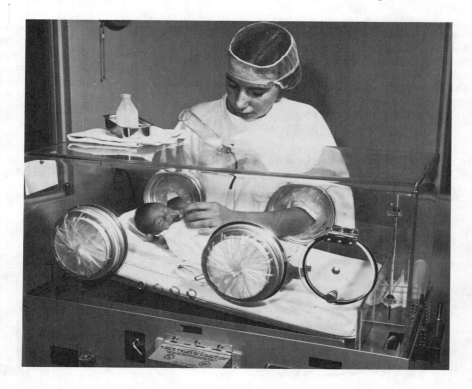

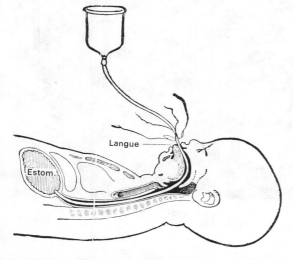

Figure 8-6. Technique du gavage chez le prématuré. Pendant le gavage par la bouche, l'infirmière maintient le tube près des lèvres de l'enfant. La tête du lit est légèrement surélevée. (Courtoisie de l'Hôpital Sainte-Justine, Montréal.)

de chaleur si sa température corporelle était maintenue à un niveau approprié et que l'œdème qu'il présentait à la naissance compensait ses besoins en électrolytes, en calories et en eau. On s'est rendu compte depuis, que l'administration précoce de solution glucosée ou isotonique salée diminuait la fréquence de l'hyperbilirubinémie et de l'hypoglycémie. Si le prématuré ne peut être alimenté par la bouche, on lui fournit le liquide, les électrolytes et les calories nécessaires par voie intraveineuse.

Il n'existe pas de règle définie pour l'alimentation du prématuré. Il tolère mal, en général, le lait de vache non modifié. Le lait maternel est idéal, mais on doit quelquefois le diluer avec de l'eau bouillie. La mère peut extraire son lait manuellement ou à l'aide d'un appareil. Elle conserve ainsi sa sécrétion lactée et l'enfant pourra être mis au sein quand ses réflexes de succion et de déglutition seront bien affermis. Il existe à certains endroits des « lactariums » où on centralise les réserves de lait maternel mais ce système s'avère très onéreux sans aide économique. Dans certains hôpitaux, on demande aux patientes qui ont accouché quelques jours plus tôt, de donner le surplus de leur lait pour les prématurés. Il existe, de toutes façons, des laits commerciaux spécialement conçus pour répondre à leurs besoins. Riches en protéines, pauvres en lipides et contenant une quantité normale de glucides, leur stérilité et leur facilité de manutention réduisent le danger de contamination.

Le bébé qui pèse peu à sa naissance est plus susceptible de présenter de l'hypoglycémie qu'un bébé de poids normal. La baisse du taux de sucre sanguin peut endommager les cellules cérébrales du bébé. Il est à noter que le froid aggrave l'hypoglycémie. Il est donc important de maintenir la chaleur corporelle du prématuré et de commencer à l'alimenter quelques heures seulement après sa naissance. On devra peut-être aussi lui faire boire de l'eau glucosée à 10 ou 20% si sa glycémie demeure trop en-deçà des limites acceptables.

Méthodes d'alimentation. Une technique d'alimentation appropriée permet d'éviter la broncho-aspiration et aide le bébé à tolérer la nourriture qui lui est essentielle. L'enfant prend ordinairement peu de lait à la fois et le choix de la tétine doit être fait en fonction de la grosseur et de la force du prématuré. On le fait éructer fréquemment. On ne doit jamais forcer l'alimentation, car une quantité insuffisante de nourriture est moins dommageable pour le prématuré qu'une quantité trop abondante. Si on doit laisser l'enfant dans l'incubateur, on le place en position semi-assise pendant qu'il boit et on le couche ensuite sur le côté droit. Le repas ne devrait jamais excéder 20 minutes pour éviter de fatiguer le bébé. Le tout petit prématuré bénéficie d'un horaire régulier, même si on omet une ration de temps à autres pour le laisser reposer. Pour un prématuré plus vieux et plus vigoureux, on préfère un horaire flexible, selon ses besoins.

Gavages. On nourrit par gavage l'enfant qui ne peut sucer ou déglutir facilement, celui qui se fatigue vite ou qui cyanose après avoir bu à la bouteille ou au compte-gouttes.

Des recherches récentes ont permis de prouver que les gavages provoquaient des changements dans la physiologie cardio-respiratoire du nouveau-né. Il est encore nécessaire de poursuivre des recherches pour découvrir le moyen de diminuer ou de prévenir ces modifications.

Pour un gavage on emploie le matériel suivant: un cathéter stérile de plastique ou de caoutchouc pourvu d'une extrémité mousse; un baril de seringue stérile; une mesure graduée; de l'eau stérile dans deux récipients et la formule préalablement réchauffée ou portée à la température de la pièce.

Pour donner un gavage à l'aide d'un tube naso-gastrique, on applique la technique suivante:

1) Mesurer la distance du nez à la pointe du sternum, en passant par le lobe de l'oreille, et marquer le cathéter.

2) Lubrifier le tube à l'eau stérile, car l'huile peut causer une broncho-pneumonie lipoïdique.

3) Introduire le cathéter par la narine jusqu'à l'endroit marqué sur le cathéter.

4) Vérifier l'insertion du tube dans l'estomac en plongeant l'extrémité dans l'eau stérile. Si des bulles apparaissent en même temps pour ensuite disparaître complètement, ceci indique que l'estomac s'est vidé de l'air qu'il contenait. Si, par contre, les bulles apparaissent à intervalles réguliers et rapprochés, le cathéter se trouve dans la trachée et l'enfant peut étouffer. On enlève le tube immédiatement pour tenter à nouveau de l'introduire dans l'estomac. Une autre méthode consiste à aspirer le liquide gastrique quand le tube semble en place, mais ceci peut s'avérer dangereux chez le petit prématuré qui ne prend que quelques centimètres cubes de liquide chaque fois qu'il boit On pratique une aspiration à basse pression étant donné le danger de blesser la délicate muqueuse de l'estomac.

Une méthode qu'on ne peut employer chez le prématuré à cause du danger de dilatation gastrique consiste à insuffler de l'air dans le cathéter et à localiser le bruit au stéthoscope. Il est en fait très difficile d'introduire le cathéter dans la trachée d'un prématuré mais toutes ces précautions restent quand même essentielles puisqu'une erreur pourrait être fatale.

5) Après vérification, fixer le tube au nez ou à la joue gauche du bébé.

6) Brancher le baril de la seringue au cathéter à l'aide d'un adaptateur.

7) Tenir la seringue 12,5 ou 20 cm au-dessus de l'enfant et laisser couler lentement le liquide. Ne jamais utiliser le piston de la seringue et cesser immédiatement le gavage si le liquide ne s'écoule pas par gravité.

8) Après le gavage, on injecte quelques ml d'eau pour laver l'intérieur du tube et éviter l'obstruction par le lait caillé.

9) Entre les gavages, le tube est ordinairement laissé en place. L'extrémité peut être fermée ou ouverte et, dans ce dernier cas, l'extrémité du tube est maintenue à quelques centimètres au-dessus du corps du bébé pour que le liquide demeure dans l'estomac. Le cathéter peut ainsi servir de valve de sûreté, si jamais l'enfant vomissait.

10) Placer l'enfant sur le côté droit, une couverture pliée supportant son dos.

11) Changer le cathéter au moins tous les quatre jours.

On emploie une technique différente quand il faut enlever le tube à chaque gavage. On introduit par la bouche un cathéter de grosseur moyenne. On vérifie la localisation gastrique et on administre le liquide en tenant le tube près de la bouche du bébé. On le retire ensuite après l'avoir rincé avec de l'eau stérile pour que l'enfant reçoive toute la quantité prescrite. On prend la précaution de pincer le tube en le retirant de l'estomac afin d'éviter que le lait qui se trouve à son extrémité inférieure ne coule, au passage, dans le pharynx et ne soit ensuite aspiré dans les voies respiratoires. Cette technique est utilisée pour les petits prématurés et pour ceux qui présentent beaucoup de sécrétions.

Alimentation au compte-gouttes. On emploie cette méthode pour les prématurés qui ont une déglutition normale, mais qui n'ont pas la force de téter, pour ceux qui ont un réflexe de succion inadéquat ou une synchronisation succion-déglutition insuffisante. Un petit tube de caoutchouc protège l'extrémité du compte-gouttes s'il est en verre, mais il est préférable d'utiliser un compte-gouttes en plastique flexi-

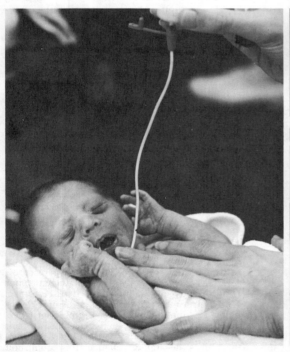

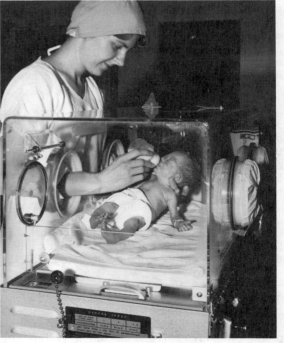

A　　　　　　　　　　　　　　　　B

Figure 8-7. Comportement alimentaire. *A)* Les mouvements de la main à la bouche et le mâchonnement indiquent que le prématuré pourra bientôt tolérer l'alimentation au biberon. *B)* Alimentation au biberon. (O'Grady, R.S., *Am. J. Nurs.* 71(4), 1971. Photographies: *A*, de Dominick et *B*, de Armstrong-Roberts.)

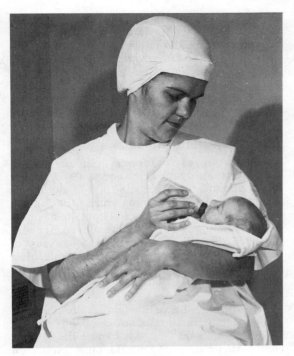

Figure 8-8. Quand il peut le supporter, on sort le bébé de l'incubateur pour lui donner son biberon. Il faut bien le couvrir pour éviter un changement brusque de température. (Courtoisie de l'Hôpital Sainte-Justine, Montréal.)

ble. On donne la solution à raison de quelques gouttes à la fois, ce qui permet au bébé d'avaler entre chaque gorgée. Si cette méthode fatigue le bébé, le gavage devient alors indiqué.

Alimentation à la bouteille. On l'emploie chez les gros prématurés et ceux qui ont des réflexes de succion et de déglutition bien synchronisés. Une tétine spéciale permet au bébé de boire sans trop d'efforts, mais on peut se servir d'une tétine ordinaire, souple, pas trop molle. L'orifice trop petit fatigue l'enfant qui doit tirer le lait avec difficulté; l'orifice trop large lui fait courir le risque de prendre une trop grande quantité à la fois et d'aspirer le liquide au lieu de le déglutir. De plus, le lait qui s'écoule trop facilement prive l'enfant du plaisir de téter. On doit tenir la bouteille pendant que l'enfant boit et, si possible, le prendre et le cajoler. Toute méthode préconisant l'utilisation d'un appareil qui force le lait dans la bouche du bébé doit être condamnée à cause du danger de broncho-aspiration.

Médication

Nous verrons uniquement les médicaments nécessaires à la croissance et au développement du prématuré. Celui-ci doit recevoir un supplément vitaminique important, car ses réserves néo-natales s'avèrent insuffisantes et son rythme de croissance demeure plus rapide que celui de l'enfant à terme. Le lait bouilli qu'on lui sert en très petites quantités a, de plus, perdu une partie de sa teneur en vitamine C. L'absorption déficiente des graisses explique le peu d'absorption des vitamines liposolubles. Le prématuré requiert en général 50 mg de vitamine C par jour, introduite dans le régime dès les premiers biberons et 1000 unités de vitamine D dont on retarde l'introduction jusqu'à la deuxième semaine de vie. Le fer n'est généralement pas absorbé avant le deuxième ou troisième mois, mais on peut l'administrer plus tôt, si l'enfant a saigné ou si son taux d'hémoglobine descend au-dessous de 8 grammes.

Prévention de l'infection

Les infections gastro-intestinales du prématuré sont souvent dues à la contamination des tétines, des bouteilles ou autre matériel utilisé pour son alimentation.

Les infections cutanées commencent souvent par une lésion minime et apparemment sans importance. Le matériel utilisé en commun pour les soins, l'infirmière qui néglige de se laver les mains avant et après avoir soigné un bébé, la lingerie non stérilisée servent également de véhicules aux microbes.

Pour laver le prématuré, l'infirmière mouille ses mains, prend une cuillerée à thé de savon et en fait une mousse abondante dont elle couvre entièrement le bébé, en finissant par la région fessière. Elle évite soigneusement d'irriter les yeux, elle enlève la mousse à l'aide d'ouate ou de compresses stériles et d'eau. Pour terminer, elle sèche le bébé en l'épongeant avec une serviette douce.

Les infections respiratoires proviennent souvent des microbes que transporte le personnel de la pouponnière. On ne doit jamais tolérer dans une pouponnière une personne qui souffre d'une infection des voies respiratoires sous prétexte qu'elle porte un masque.

À cause du danger de transmission aérienne de l'infection, on suit pour chaque bébé une technique d'isolement et on éloigne des salles communes celui qui souffre d'une infection. Dans la plupart des hôpitaux, une antichambre à la pouponnière empêche l'entrée des micro-organismes quand s'ouvre la porte de l'unité.

Suggestions générales pour la prévention de l'infection. Aucune infirmière ne devrait approcher un bébé sans s'être scrupuleusement nettoyé les ongles, lavé les mains et les avant-bras au savon et à l'eau courante. On ne tolère pas les bagues et les montres-bracelets à la pouponnière. On garde près de chaque bébé l'équipement nécessaire à ses soins et on s'assure de la propreté méticuleuse des rares objets communs à tous les enfants. On emploie de la lingerie stérile dont on enlève l'enveloppe contaminée avant d'entrer dans la pouponnière. Les infirmières qui prennent soin des bébés infectés ne devraient jamais s'approcher des bébés sains. On évite le ménage à sec à cause du déplacement de la poussière, grande source de contamination. On époussette quotidiennement avec un linge humide qui contient un désinfectant de façon à empêcher la dissémination des microbes d'un endroit à l'autre. On nettoie le plancher en utilisant la technique qui consiste à étendre de l'eau et du détergent sur le plancher et à aspirer le tout à l'aide d'un appareil pourvu d'un bidon pour la récupération des eaux sales.

Traitement de l'infection. On ne peut prévoir la réaction du prématuré aux antibiotiques. Des doses bien tolérées par l'enfant à terme peuvent être très toxiques et provoquer des réactions malencontreuses chez le prématuré du fait de sa petite taille et de sa difficulté à les excréter en quantité suffisante. Chez le prématuré, on connaît mal le seuil de toxicité de beaucoup de médicaments.

MALADIES DU PRÉMATURÉ

L'observation du prématuré doit porter sur les éléments suivants: la nature du cri, la respiration, la coloration, l'activité, l'aspect de la peau et de l'ombilic, les fonctions rénales et intestinales; la stabilité de la température corporelle à la suite de légères variations de la température extérieure; les réactions à l'alimentation selon la méthode employée, les réflexes de succion et de déglutition, la quantité prise et gardée et l'activité de l'enfant lorsqu'il boit; les symptômes qui doivent être signalés immédiatement au médecin de façon à permettre de déceler une maladie grave.

Fibroplasie rétrolenticulaire

Historique et incidence. La pathologie, découverte au cours des années 1940, atteint les prématurés qui pèsent 1500 g ou moins ou dont l'âge fœtal se situe entre 6 et 7 mois. La fibroplasie a remplacé l'ophtalmie purulente comme principale cause de cécité néonatale. L'affection implique les deux yeux et se complique souvent de cécité totale. Les symptômes apparaissent quand l'enfant atteint l'âge de quelques semaines ou de quelques mois.

Étiologie. La pathologie résulte d'un empoisonnement à l'oxygène qui agit sur la vascularisation de l'œil. La hausse de la pression partielle de l'oxygène du sang artériel du prématuré, et non la concentration d'oxygène dans l'incubateur, demeure la cause capitale d'une fibroplasie rétrolenticulaire. La pression partielle normale de l'oxygène du sang artériel se situe entre 60 et 100 mm Hg mais elle peut s'élever à 140 et 150 mm Hg si le bébé respire un mélange d'air contenant une concentration d'oxygène excédant 40%. Il importe d'analyser fréquemment le sang artériel du bébé et de maintenir la pression de l'oxygène à moins de 100 mm Hg. On doit se rappeler que plus le bébé est immature plus il est susceptible de développer une fibroplasie rétrolenticulaire.

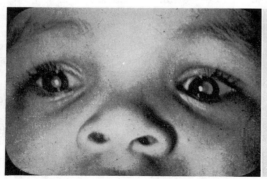
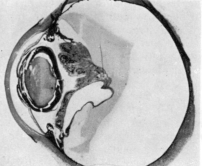

A   B

Figure 8-9. Fibroplasie rétrolenticulaire. *A)* L'opacification des tissus derrière la pupille est le stade final de la pathologie. *B)* Coupe sagittale de l'œil atteint. La rétine, complètement décollée, flotte dans le corps vitré. Une bande de tissu fibreux cicatriciel entoure la paroi postérieure du cristallin. (Tiré de la collection du Dr Arnall Patz, Baltimore.) (Schaffer: *Diseases of the Newborn.*)

Physio-pathologie. Il se produit d'abord une vasoconstriction au niveau de la rétine. Si la pression partielle de l'oxygène demeure élevée dans le sang artériel, la phase active de la maladie apparaît, caractérisée par une prolifération capillaire, suivie d'œdème et d'hémorragie. La rétine subit une tension importante et peut finalement se détacher et flotter dans le corps vitré. L'enfant peut percevoir la lumière mais ne possède aucune vision fonctionnelle. Le glaucôme et l'opacification de la cornée apparaissent quelquefois au cours de l'évolution.

Diagnostic. L'examen ophtalmologique de routine devrait permettre un diagnostic précoce, de préférence dès la sortie de la pouponnière.

Prévention. On administre l'oxygène seulement si l'enfant en a un besoin immédiat. La concentration ne devrait jamais excéder 40% sauf en cas d'urgence vitale. L'ordonnance faite en termes de concentration est plus sûre que celle basée sur le débit. On règle le débit-mètre à un taux suffisant pour maintenir une concentration constante. L'oxymètre demeure essentiel à la pouponnière, même s'il existe un contrôle automatique du débit et du mélange de l'oxygène dans l'incubateur. Si l'état de l'enfant exige une concentration plus forte, celle-ci doit être prescrite par le médecin et non laissée au jugement de l'infirmière, sauf dans les cas d'urgence. Le personnel infirmier de l'unité pédiatrique peut être appelé à soigner de tels cas à l'aide de prescriptions courantes. Il y a moins de risque à donner de l'oxygène à un enfant qui pèse 2 300 g et plus mais, il en a rarement besoin puisqu'il a atteint un développement plus complet de son système cardio-respiratoire.

Maladie des membranes hyalines

Incidence. On retrouve cette pathologie chez environ 50% des prématurés qui meurent au cours des premiers jours qui suivent la naissance. Très rare chez l'enfant à terme, elle se présente quelquefois chez l'enfant de mère diabétique ou chez celui né par césarienne.

Physio-pathologie. Chez le fœtus normal, la plus grande partie du sang veineux retourne dans la circulation artérielle par le canal artériel et le trou de Botal, sans passer par la circulation pulmonaire. Au cours des premières respirations, la résistance diminue au niveau des poumons et la circulation pulmonaire augmente progressivement.

Au cours de la maladie de la membrane hyaline, la *résistance pulmonaire demeure très haute*. Le sang veineux continue à passer de la circulation veineuse à la circulation artérielle sans emprunter les artères pulmonaires. Il en résulte une détresse respiratoire et de la cyanose. La pression de gaz carbonique augmente et le pH sanguin diminue.

Au cours des manœuvres de réanimation le bébé souffre souvent d'un refroidissement important occasionné par son manque de tissu adipeux, l'absence de réserves d'énergie et une thermo-labilité extrême. Si, à ce phénomène, viennent s'ajouter une augmentation de la tension du CO_2, et une baisse du pH, il se produit une vasoconstriction des artérioles pulmonaires, une hypoperfusion pulmonaire et le sang veineux passe directement au système artériel évitant ainsi le poumon. L'atélectasie néo-natale vient souvent compliquer la situation.

Il est également possible d'expliquer la maladie de la membrane hyaline par une hyperactivité du système sympathique en réponse au stress de l'hypoxie et de l'hypercapnie.

Une autre hypothèse étiologique existe. En effet, on trouve normalement sur la paroi des alvéoles pulmonaires une substance appelée *surfactant* qui est une lipoprotéine chargée de réduire la tension de surface de la membrane des alvéoles pulmonaires.

Si la production de surfactant est inhibée par une substance provenant du liquide amniotique ou du tissu pulmonaire traumatisé, le poumon ne peut fonctionner adéquatement et les symptômes de la maladie des membranes hyalines apparaissent.

Anatomo-pathologie. La consistance du tissu pulmonaire ressemble alors à celle du foie et sa couleur est d'un rouge pourpre très prononcée. L'atélectasie est présente; les bronchioles et les alvéoles sont tapissées de membranes. On peut trouver des déchets amniotiques, des signes de pneumonie et d'hémorragie ainsi que de l'emphysème interstitiel.

Manifestations cliniques. Elles justifient habituellement une réanimation dès la naissance ou dans les quelques heures qui suivent. Ces manifestations incluent une accélération du rythme respiratoire atteignant 60 mouvements et plus par minute, un tirage intercostal, un grognement respiratoire et de la cyanose; la fatigue et la détresse respiratoire deviennent bientôt évidentes.

Évolution et pronostic. La mort peut se produire en quelques heures. Dans les formes légères, les symptômes augmentent pendant trois jours environ et diminuent par la suite. Le pronostic éloigné reste bon quand les symptômes s'amendent durant la première semaine de vie. Le taux de mortalité augmente avec la prématurité.

Prévention. Les principaux éléments sont la prévention de la prématurité, la surveillance étroite de la mère diabétique et la nécessité d'éviter les naissances par césarienne quand c'est possible.

Les autres mesures de protection incluent la prévention de l'hypoxie, de l'hypotension systématique et de l'acidémie chez la mère; la réduction de la vasoconstriction pulmonaire chez le nouveau-né; le raccourcissement du temps, durant lequel le flot sanguin ombilical est diminué ainsi que la prévention du refroidissement et de l'hypoxie du nouveau-né.

Traitement, complications et soins. Puisque les problèmes d'hématose conduisent à l'acidose métabolique, le traitement consiste à prévenir le refroidissement du bébé et à lui administrer de l'oxygène et une substance-tampon qui contrebalancera l'acidose. L'administration intraveineuse de liquide, de calories et d'une solution tampon évite la fatigue occasionnée par l'alimentation orale. La ventilation mécanique peut s'avérer nécessaire et l'unité néo-natale de soins intensifs demeure l'endroit indiqué pour conduire le traitement de façon appropriée.

La température cutanée doit demeurer entre 36°C et 37°C. On peut employer le système thermo-régulateur adapté à un thermostat collé sur l'abdomen du bébé. En l'absence d'un tel appareil, on doit placer le bébé dans un incubateur dont la température varie entre 32°C et 34°C et dont le taux d'humidité se situe entre 80 et 90%. On essaie d'obtenir un taux d'humidité adéquat sans recourir au nébulisateur puisque le nuage de vapeur d'eau peut s'avérer dangereux pour le bébé.

Une surveillance étroite de la pression partielle de l'oxygène (Po_2), de la pression partielle du gaz carbonique (Pco_2) et du pH du sang artériel et du sang capillaire s'impose. On peut obtenir ces mesures en retirant de petites quantités de sang de l'artère temporale ou du cathéter central introduit par une des artères ombilicales jusqu'à la bifurcation de l'aorte. L'anémie peut s'installer à la suite de prélèvements sanguins trop abondants et trop fréquents. L'administration de transfusions peut être nécessaire. Le cathéter ombilical sert aussi à l'administration de liquides et de médicaments.

Quand l'enfant reçoit de l'oxygène, il faut vérifier fréquemment le taux d'oxygène dans l'incubateur pour éviter la fibroplasie rétro-lenticulaire dont nous avons parlé au début

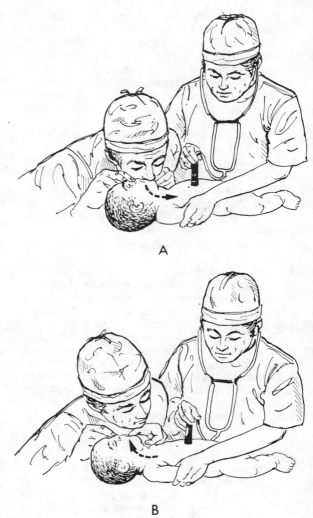

Figure 8-10. Ventilation bouche à bouche. *A)* Insufflation de l'air dans les poumons. *B)* Expiration. Le stéthoscope permet de vérifier si l'air n'entre pas dans l'estomac.

de ce chapitre. La Po_2 artérielle doit demeurer en-deçà de 100 mm Hg quand l'enfant respire un mélange concentré d'O_2 avec ou sans l'aide d'un respirateur.

On aide le nouveau-né à respirer en employant de façon intermittente un masque à circuit semi-fermé. Un appareil à pression positive est réglé en fonction du bébé et relié à un tube endo-trachéal; un masque d'anesthésie peut également servir, mais son emploi prolongé peut causer un traumatisme ou une intoxication à l'oxygène au niveau des poumons. Le respirateur et l'incubateur à pression négative sont, incontestablement, des appareils très prometteurs pour le traitement des détresses respiratoires.

La surveillance continue de la tension artérielle et de la pression veineuse centrale permet de reconnaître le choc qui peut se produire tôt après la naissance du prématuré.

Certains médecins prescrivent des antibiotiques pour prévenir l'apparition d'infections graves, en particulier la pneumonie.

Un arrêt cardiaque peut se produire au moment de l'intubation ou de l'aspiration des sécrétions. Les complications locales peuvent être évitées par l'emploi de tubes endotrachéaux en vinyle (qui ne contiennent pas d'étain toxique pour les cellules), par le choix de tubes de faible diamètre, par la réduction des manœuvres pour aspirer les sécrétions ou pour changer le tube; par la prévention de l'infection, qui dépend en grande partie des précautions que prennent les membres du personnel qui s'occupent du bébé. Si on utilise un masque d'anesthésie, il faut éviter que la pression exercée sur la figure n'endommage les yeux ou la peau du visage. Un pneumothorax est toujours à redouter si l'enfant reçoit une assistance respiratoire.

D'autres complications peuvent se produire au niveau de l'artère ombilicale cathétérisée. Ces complications incluent un spasme artériel réflexe, un blocage d'une artère de moindre calibre pouvant conduire à la gangrène du territoire qu'elle dessert, à une hémorragie ou à une thrombose. Il faut retirer le cathéter le plus tôt possible si l'une ou l'autre des complications apparaît.

Grâce à l'installation des unités néo-natales de soins intensifs on a pu réduire considérablement la mortalité parmi les bébés présentant un risque élevé de mortalité dont ceux souffrant de maladie des membranes hyalines. Le succès du traitement dépend de la collaboration étroite qui doit régner entre tous les membres de l'équipe soignante.

Vomissements

Habituellement, l'enfant vomit parce qu'on le nourrit trop vite ou en quantité excessive. Il faut donc réduire la quantité et ralentir la vitesse d'alimentation. Si on peut prendre l'enfant, on doit le faire éructer lorsqu'il boit et avant de le remettre dans l'incubateur.

La distension abdominale cause non seulement les vomissements mais nuit à la respiration en élevant le diaphragme. L'atrésie congénitale de l'œsophage empêche la descente du lait qui est rejeté par la bouche après quelques gorgées. La pression intra-crânienne cause les vomissements en jets, non précédés de nausées. L'infirmière doit noter la quantité, la couleur et la nature des vomissements ainsi que les circonstances qui l'entourent.

Diarrhée

Un bébé prématuré a normalement 4 à 5 selles par jour. Une plus grande fréquence ou des selles liquides peuvent devenir très graves à cause des besoins énergétiques très élevés du prématuré et de la perte hydrique que la diarrhée occasionne. Le prématuré tolère mal les graisses et la fraction lipidique de son alimentation peut produire la diarrhée. On incrimine aussi l'excès d'alimentation.

La diarrhée infantile peut accompagner une infection intestinale ou systémique. On avertit le médecin immédiatement et on place l'enfant en isolement strict pour éviter la dissémination de l'infection. Les vomissements accompagnent souvent la diarrhée et doivent être soigneusement notés et enregistrés. L'enfant meurt très rapidement de diarrhée et sa survie dépend d'un traitement immédiat.

Déshydratation

Déjà plus grave pour le nourrisson que pour l'enfant plus vieux, la déshydratation devient facilement mortelle chez le prématuré. Elle accompagne toujours un mauvais apport hydrique et provient souvent de la diarrhée et des vomissements.

Ictère

L'ictère physiologique provient de la hausse sanguine de la bilirubine au cours de la période post-natale immédiate. Habituellement peu important, il faut s'en inquiéter s'il persiste ou devient trop marqué. Il peut alors indiquer une condition sérieuse comme l'érythroblastose.

La photothérapie est utilisée actuellement comme traitement de l'hyperbilirubinémie. Ce traitement consiste à placer l'enfant sous les rayons d'une lampe suspendue au-dessus de la bassinette ou de l'incubateur. On ignore le mécanisme d'action de la photothérapie sur le métabolisme de la bilirubine et quels peuvent être ses effets néfastes ultérieurs. On applique ce traitement en tenant compte à la fois du taux de bilirubine et du poids de l'enfant. Il n'est jamais utilisé de façon prophylactique. L'exsanguino-transfusion demeure le traitement de choix si le taux de bilirubine continue à s'élever.

Après avoir enlevé tous les vêtements du bébé, on couvre ses yeux de coquilles qui protégeront la cornée et la rétine au cours du traitement. On peut enlever les coquilles

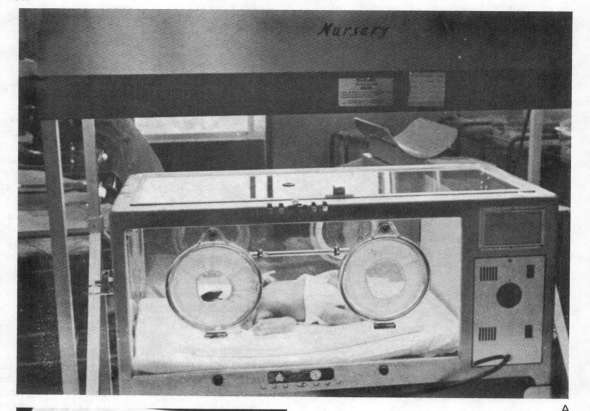

A

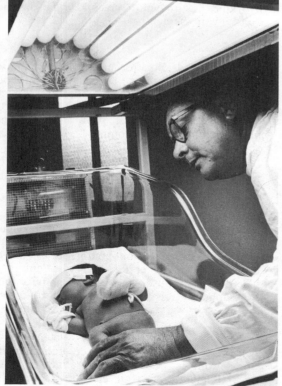

B

Figure 8-11. Photothérapie. La lumière fluorescente diminue le taux de bilirubine sérique et par conséquent l'ictère. *A)* Pour permettre une exposition maximale à la lumière, on ne met pas de couche au bébé sauf dans certains cas exceptionnels comme le priapisme. *B)* Les yeux sont couverts d'un pansement protecteur. (*A*, extrait de Williams, S.L., *Am J. Nurs.*, 71:1398, juillet 1971. *B*, extrait de Sam Nocella, Medical World News, juin 1969.)

lorsqu'on cesse le traitement pour alimenter le bébé de façon à ce qu'il puisse prendre contact avec son environnement. L'entourage immédiat du bébé étant réchauffé par la lumière, il est essentiel de surveiller l'apparition d'une hyperthermie en prenant sa température toutes les quatre heures. Le bébé peut avoir des selles vertes très molles, il peut présenter un érythème cutané et le bébé masculin peut souffrir de priapisme, érection douloureuse du pénis.

Le taux de bilirubine peut remonter après la cessation du traitement et l'exsanguino-transfusion peut s'imposer.

L'ictère physiologique est un phénomène banal en soi; un ictère qui persiste ou qui devient excessif indique que le bébé souffre d'une pathologie, telle que l'érythroblastose fœtale, une anomalie congénitale, une obstruction des voies biliaires, une toxoplasmose congénitale, une « maladie d'inclusion cytomégalique », une syphilis ou une septicémie. Les soins que le bébé recevra seront alors en fonction de la maladie sous-jacente.

Pâleur

Elle accompagne le choc, hémorragique ou autre. On la constate souvent chez les enfants qui ont souffert de troubles respiratoires ou d'un traumatisme intracrânien à la naissance.

Convulsions

Les convulsions constituent un danger majeur pour le prématuré. L'anoxie et la tension qui les accompagnent grèvent la santé du prématuré et une surveillance continuelle s'impose. L'infirmière applique les mesures d'urgence tout en observant l'évolution de la crise. Une bonne description des convulsions aide le médecin à poser son diagnostic et à traiter la cause si possible. Les convulsions peuvent indiquer une hémorragie intracrânienne, une anomalie cérébrale congénitale, une anoxie prolongée, une hypoglycémie, une hypocalcémie ou une bactériémie.

Pronostic de la prématurité

Statistiques. Les chances de survie du prématuré sont moins élevées que celles de l'enfant à terme. 12 à 20% des prématurés meurent. La prématurité est responsable de la moitié de tous les décès au cours du premier mois de vie. Les chances de survie augmentent avec l'âge fœtal. Les trois quarts des décès chez les prématurés, surviennent au cours de la première journée de vie. Les techniques modernes de réanimation sauvent la vie de plus de prématurés qu'autrefois.

Causes de décès. L'immaturité des différents systèmes explique le taux élevé de mortalité chez les prématurés. Un faible pourcentage des bébés pesant moins de 1 000 g parvient à survivre. L'insuffisance respiratoire cause beaucoup de décès. Les traumatismes obstétricaux comme l'hémorragie intracrânienne avec dommage cérébral peuvent conduire à une mort immédiate. Certaines malformations congénitales s'avèrent incompatibles avec les fonctions vitales. L'infection tue beaucoup plus fréquemment le prématuré que le nouveau-né à terme; le prématuré ne peut la combattre,

ni supporter ses effets systémiques. La cause de la prématurité peut également en modifier le pronostic.

Facteurs de survie. Le prématuré de plus de 1500 g qui possède un bon tonus musculaire et dont la respiration demeure normale survivra probablement. La présence des réflexes de déglutition et de toux lui permettra de se nourrir sans danger d'aspiration. On a démontré précédemment l'importance de stabiliser la température corporelle du prématuré.

Problèmes parentaux causés par la prématurité

La naissance d'un prématuré inquiète la famille et constitue une surprise, à moins que la mère sache qu'une grossesse multiple, par exemple, risque de se terminer prématurément. Après un voyage rapide à l'hôpital, à la suite du début du travail, elle subit une préparation hâtive et donne naissance à son enfant, ordinairement sans anesthésie. Si la mère a subi une césarienne, elle ne sait pas qu'elle a mis au monde un bébé de faible poids jusqu'à ce que le médecin lui en apporte la nouvelle. Si elle voit son bébé avant qu'on le place dans l'incubateur, elle peut sursauter devant son aspect décharné. Le père et la mère devraient être préparés à voir leur bébé, afin d'éviter qu'ils soient traumatisés par sa maigreur et son apparence de vieillard.

Malgré les questions pressantes des parents, le personnel médical évite souvent de répondre directement, de peur de provoquer de faux espoirs. Les parents se rendent cependant compte de l'incertitude que provoque la condition de l'enfant et réagissent avec anxiété. De plus, à son départ de l'hôpital, la mère doit laisser son petit à la pouponnière jusqu'à ce qu'il pèse 2300 ou 2500 g. Cela peut signifier une séparation de plusieurs semaines à quelques mois.

Il faut aider les parents à affronter la réalité. Les médecins qui discutent franchement avec eux de la condition de l'enfant, les amènent à parler de leurs craintes. La compréhension de l'infirmière encourage les parents à surmonter leur anxiété. L'infirmière en post-partum devrait connaître les soins que nécessite le prématuré pour mieux être en mesure de rassurer la mère. Les amis, plutôt que d'envoyer des cartes de souhaits, peuvent les aider par des paroles réconfortantes. Ils expriment ainsi combien la survie de l'enfant leur tient à cœur.

La mère à qui l'on explique les chances réelles de survie de l'enfant ne sera pas nécessairement moins anxieuse, mais elle envisagera l'avenir avec plus de réalisme, que celle qui craint de demander si son bébé survivra.

Il est toujours important de discuter avec les parents de leur désir de voir leur enfant et de leur faciliter le plus possible l'accès à leur bébé prématuré. Aussitôt que possible, il faut permettre aux parents qui le souhaitent de toucher leur enfant et d'apprendre graduellement à lui donner des soins. Même si la cause de la naissance prématurée demeure inconnue, la mère rend souvent responsable de cet événement malheureux soit une personne, soit un événement quelconque: un enfant plus âgé qu'elle a dû porter dans ses bras, son mari qui n'a pas voulu porter les paquets ou faire la lessive ou elle incrimine les soins du médecin ou de l'infirmière. Cette façon de nier la réalité ne l'aide pas à surmonter la crise qu'elle traverse.

Si l'enfant meurt, il vaut mieux exprimer de la sympathie aux parents plutôt que de leur dire d'oublier ce bébé et d'en avoir un autre. Malheureusement, de tels conseils sont trop souvent prodigués. L'infirmière doit se rappeler que les parents pleurent autant le prématuré qui vient de mourir que l'enfant sain dont ils avaient rêvé durant la grossesse.

Si l'enfant survit, on doit permettre aux parents de se familiariser avec les soins qu'il requiert et ce, avant sa sortie de l'hôpital. Même s'il demeure frêle et petit, il ressemble maintenant à un nouveau-né normal que ses parents peuvent manipuler. Dans beaucoup

d'hôpitaux, il existe des locaux où l'on enseigne la façon de laver et d'habiller le bébé, comment préparer sa formule de lait et le nourrir. Les parents prennent progressivement confiance en leur habileté et leur anxiété diminue.

L'infirmière en santé communautaire devrait visiter la maison avant l'arrivée de l'enfant afin d'évaluer les dispositions prises pour l'accueillir. Elle peut faire des suggestions quant au milieu physique et essayer d'analyser les sentiments de la mère à l'égard de l'enfant. Elle profite aussi de sa visite à la famille pour donner les conseils et l'assistance nécessaires. De nombreuses mères ont lu un grand nombre de livres sur les soins à donner au prématuré. Elles comprennent les principes de base de ces soins, mais ont besoin d'aide pour les appliquer.

La mère s'inquiète du développement normal de son enfant et se demande s'il sera mentalement retardé, restera frêle et petit. Elle doit savoir qu'en général, le prématuré se développe relativement plus vite que l'enfant à terme. Les différences tendent à disparaître progressivement et, après quelques années, plus rien n'y paraît. Tôt dans l'enfance, il semble retardé au point de vue moteur et il diffère un peu de l'enfant à terme sur le plan sensoriel. La naissance prématurée n'influe pas sur l'intelligence, si les conditions néonatales ont été excellentes mais le comportement émotif et social des « anciens prématurés »

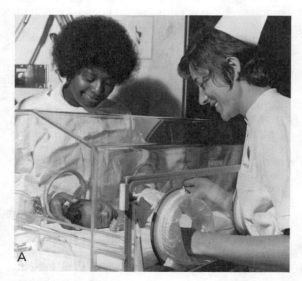
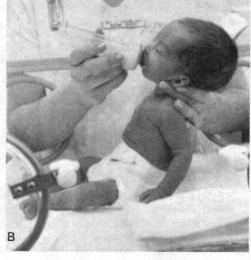

Figure 8-12. Avant le départ pour la maison. *A)* La mère apprend à connaître son bébé et *B)* à lui donner des soins. (*A*, extrait de Warrick, L.H., *Am. J. Nurs.* 71:11, 1971. *B*, courtoisie des Laboratoires Ross.)

manque quelquefois de maturité. Quelques-uns présentent un comportement anormal; leur dépendance excessive et leur négativisme sont, en large part, causés par la surprotection dont les parents les ont entourés, tout en les talonnant pour qu'ils atteignent le développement des enfants nés à terme. L'ambivalence des parents crée des conflits qui perturbent le développement. De plus, la rareté des contacts affectifs, durant leurs premières semaines de vie, influe sans doute sur leur développement ultérieur.

Il est souhaitable d'aider la mère à acquérir la certitude qu'elle est capable de donner les soins au prématuré. Cette confiance en elle est essentielle à l'évolution harmonieuse des relations mère-enfant. Elle ne craindra pas de corriger l'enfant et acceptera de lui laisser faire ses propres expériences.

POST-MATURITÉ

Une grossesse qui se prolonge jusqu'à 43 semaines ou 300 jours se termine par la naissance d'un bébé que l'on dénomme post-mature. Ceci se produit rarement, car si apparemment plusieurs grossesses semblent se prolonger, seul le calcul de la date d'accouchement était peu valide.

Caractéristiques de l'enfant post-mature. Il a le comportement et l'apparence d'un enfant dont l'âge correspond au retard de l'accouchement. Il est parfois alerte, parfois léthargique; il est plus maigre que le nouveau-né normal, ses ongles et ses cheveux sont plus longs et il n'a pas de lanugo ou de vernix caseosa. Souvent la peau a pelé et ressemble à du parchemin. Ces enfants sont grands, mais mesurent rarement plus de 57,5 cm de longueur.

Traitement. Provoquer l'accouchement représente un danger plus grand que la post-maturité elle-même. Une césarienne libère l'enfant qui présente des signes de souffrance fœtale.

Pronostic. Le taux de mortalité est deux ou trois fois plus élevé que chez l'enfant né à terme.

RÉFÉRENCES

Livres et documents officiels

Abramson, H.: *Symposium on the Functional Physiopathology of the Fetus and Neonate, Clinical Correlations.* Saint-Louis, C. V. Mosby Company, 1971.

Avery, M. E.: *The Lung and Its Disorders in the Newborn Infant.* 2e éd. Philadelphie, W. B. Saunders Company, 1968.

Babson, S. G. et Benson, R. C.: *Management of High-Risk Pregnancy and Intensive Care of the Neonate.* 2e éd. Saint-Louis, C. V. Mosby Company, 1971.

Fontana, V. J. et Keitel, H. G.: *Management of the Low-Birth-Weight and Premature Infant.* New York, Harper & Row, Publishers, Incorporated, 1971.

Klaus, M. et Fanaroff, A.: *Care of the High-Risk Neonate.* Philadelphie, W. B. Saunders Company, 1973.

Korones, S. B.: *High-Risk Newborn Infants – The Basis for Intensive Care.* Saint-Louis, C. V. Mosby Company, 1972.

Laboratoires Ross: *Le nouveau-né prématuré.* Section de l'éducation en nursing, (feuillet nº 1) Columbus, Ohio.

Laboratoires Ross: *Problems of Neonatal Intensive Care Units.* Ross Conference on Pediatric Research, Columbus, Ohio, 1969.

Organisation mondiale de la santé: *Prévention de la mortalité et de la morbidité périnatales.* Série de rapports techniques, nº 457, Genève, 1970.

Pierog. S. H. et Ferrara, A.: *Approach to the Medical Care of the Sick Newborn.* Saint-Louis, C. V. Mosby Company, 1971.

Waisman, H. et Kerr, G. (édit.): *Fetal Growth and Development.* New York, McGraw-Hill Book Company, Inc., 1970.

Articles

Babson, S. G. et Kangas, J.: Preschool Intelligence of Undersized Term Infants. *Am. J. Dis. Child,* 117:553, mai 1969.

Beargie, R. A., James, V. L. et Greene, J. W.: Growth and Development of Small-for-Date Newborns. *Pediat. Clin. N. Amer.,* 17:159, février 1970.

Berges, J. et Lézine, I.: L'avenir du prématuré. *La médecine infantile,* 75:27, 1, 1968.

Besch, N. J. et autres: The Transparent Baby Bag. *New England J. Med.,* 284:121, 21 janvier -971.

Blennow, G. et autres: Noise Levels in Infant Incubators. *Pediatrics*, 53:29, 1, 1974.

Calvez, M.-T.: L'éducation sanitaire des parents en service de prématurés. *Revue de l'infirmière*, 1re partie: 21:255, mars 1971. 2e partie: 21:357, avril 1971.

Chinn, P. L.: Infant Gavage Feeding. *Am. J. Nursing*, 71:1964, octobre 1971.

Choi, M.: A Comparison of Maternal Pyschological Reactions to Premature and Full-Size Newborns. *Maternal-Child Nursing Journal*, 2:1, 1, 1973.

Davis, L.: Neonatal Respiratory Emergencies. *Nurs. Clin. N. Amer.*, 8:441, 3, 1973.

DeLeon, A. S., Elliott, J. H. et Jones, D B.: The Resurgence of Retrolental Fibroplasia *Pediat. Clin. N. Amer.*, 17:309, mai 1970.

Doray, B.: Troubles respiratoires du prématuré. *Union méd. du Can.*, 98:1870, novembre 1969.

Dubois, D.: Indications of an Unhealthy Relationship Between Parents and Premature Infant. *Journ. Obst. & Gynec. Nursing*, 4:21, mars 1975.

Duhamel, T. et autres: Early Parental Perceptions and the High-Risk Neonate. *Clin. Ped.*, 13:1052, décembre 1974.

Evans, H. E., Akpata, S. O. et Baki, A.: Bacteriologic and Clinical Evaluation of Gowning in a Premature Nursery. *J. Pediat.*, 78:883, mai 1971.

Fanaroff, A. A., Kennell, J. H. et Klaus, M. H.: Follow-up of Low Birth Weight Infants – The Predictive Value of Maternal Visiting Patterns. *Pediatrics*, 49:387, février 1972.

Fogarty, S.: The Nurse and the High-Risk Infant. *Nurs. Clin. N. Amer.*, 8:533, 3, 1973.

Garney, J.: Infant Respiratory Distress Syndrome. *Am. J. Nursing*, 75:614, avril 1975.

Hasselmeyer, E. G. et Hon, E. H.: Effects of Gavage Feeding of Premature Infants upon Cardiorespiratory Patterns. *Milit. Med.*, 136:252, mars 1971.

Huault, G.: Intubation du nouveau-né. *Soins*, 20:37, novembre 1975.

Katz, V.: Auditory Stimulation and Developmental Behavior of the Premature Infant. *Nursing Research*, 20:196, mai-juin 1971.

Kennedy, J.: The High-Risk Maternal-Infant Acquaintance Process. *Nurs. Clin. N. Amer.*, 8:549, mars 1973.

Le Loch, H. et Retbi, J. M.: Principes actuels du traitement de la maladie des membranes hyalines. *La revue de pédiatrie*, 10:31, 1, 1974.

Maillard, E. et autres: Le traitement des hyperbilirubinémies néonatales par le phénobarbital. *La revue de pédiatrie*, 7:741, 10, 1971.

McLean, F.: La durée de la gestation oriente les soins du nouveau-né. *Inf. Can.*, 14:32, octobre 1972.

Minkowski, A. et autres: Les prématurés. *Revue de neuropsychiatrie infantile*, 17:711, novembre 1969.

Nalepka, C.: Oxygen Hood for Newborns in Respiratory Distress. *Am. J. Nursing*, 75:2185, décembre 1975.

Neal, M. V. et Nauen, C. M.: Ability of Premature Infant to Maintain His Own Body Temperature. *Nursing Research*, 17:396, septembre-octobre 1968.

Nicopoulos, D. et autres: Croissance, morbidité et mortalité de 300 prématurés. *Pédiatrie*, XXIV:435, 4, 1969.

O'Grady, R. S.: Feeding Behavior in Infants. *Am. J. Nursing*, 71:736, avril 1971.

Perlstein, P. H, Edwards, N. K. et Sutherland, J. M.: Apnea in Premature Infants and Incubator-Air-Temperature Changes. *New England J. Med.*, 282:461, 26 février 1970.

Relier, J. P.: La maladie des membranes hyalines. *La médecine infantile*, 77:449, 7, 1970.

Riker, W.: Cardiac Arrest in Infants and Children. *Pediat. Clin. N. Amer.*, 16:661, août 1969.

Scarr-Salajatek, S. et Williams, M. L.: The Effects of Early Stimulation on Low-Birth Weigth Infants. *Child Dev.*, 44:94, mars 1973.

Segal, S.: Oxygen: Too Much, Too Little. *Nurs. Clin. N. Amer.*, 6:39, mars 1971.

Solas, M.: Une technique courante en pédiatrie: le gavage. *Soins*, 19:35, juin 1974.

Stern, L.: Therapy of the Respiratory Distress Syndrome. *Pediat. Clin. N. Amer.*, 19:221, février 1972.

Toubas, P.: Soins à donner aux prématurés. *Soins*, 20:15, novembre 1975.

Warrick, L. H.: Family-Centered Care in the Premature Nursery. *Am. J. Nursing*, 71:2134, novembre 1971.

Whitley, N. N.: Breast-Feeding the Premature. *Am. J. Nursing*, 70:1909, septembre 1970.

9

pathologies du nouveau-né nécessitant des soins immédiats ou de courte durée

Dans ce chapitre, seront étudiés les maladies et anomalies congénitales, les traumatismes obstétricaux, les problèmes respiratoires du nouveau-né et les infections néonatales.

Anémie hémolytique du nouveau-né (érythroblastose fœtale)

La maladie hémolytique du nouveau-né survient lorsque le fœtus possède les antigènes sanguins absents chez sa mère. Les antigènes fœtaux provoquent chez la mère la fabrication d'anticorps appelés agglutinines. Lorsque les agglutinines maternelles traversent la barrière placentaire, elles produisent une agglutination des globules rouges de l'enfant.

Les deux maladies hémolytiques les plus importantes sont dues à l'iso-immunisation au facteur Rh et aux antigènes sanguins A et B.

Maladie hémolytique due à une incompatibilité Rh

Dans les trois cas suivants, la sensibilisation mère-enfant ne peut se produire et les combinaisons sanguines sont toujours compatibles:

1) les deux parents sont Rh positif. 2) les deux parents sont Rh négatif. 3) la mère est Rh positif et le père Rh négatif. L'érythroblastose fœtale se produit si la mère est Rh négatif et si le père et le fœtus sont Rh positif. Environ 15% de la population blanche est Rh négatif. On trouve très peu de femmes noires ou asiatiques Rh négatif.

Étiologie. L'incompatibilité sanguine mère-enfant ne cause pas toujours l'érythroblastose fœtale. Ceci s'explique par la variabilité du potentiel de sensibilisation maternelle, par le fait que le père puisse être hétérozygote et par le nombre restreint d'enfants dans les familles actuelles. S'il n'y a pas eu d'avortement antérieur, le premier enfant n'est pas atteint, car dans tout phénomène immunitaire, la sensibilité ne se développe que progressivement au contact de la substance antigénique. Le taux d'anticorps maternels augmentera avec chaque grossesse et le danger d'érythroblastose en sera d'autant plus prononcé pour le fœtus.

L'immunisation anti-Rh résulte de l'hémorragie transplacentaire qui se produit normalement à l'accouchement. L'immunisation peut aussi se produire si la mère Rh négatif re-

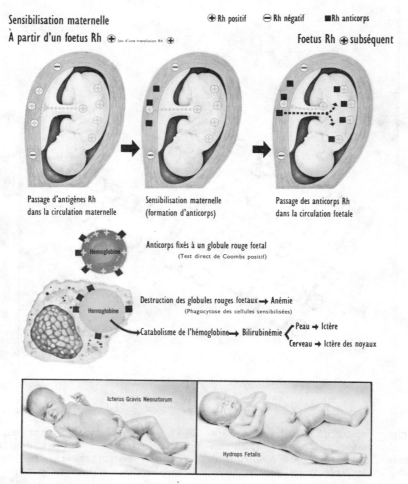

Figure 9-1. Étiologie de l'érythroblastose fœtale (maladie hémolytique congénitale). (Dessin des Laboratoires Ross, U.S.A.)

çoit une transfusion de sang Rh positif. Il existe une hypothèse selon laquelle des hématies fœtales pourraient traverser la barrière placentaire, après le 2e mois de grossesse, et déclencher le phénomène de sensibilisation durant la première grossesse d'une femme Rh négatif.

Manifestations cliniques. Le vernix caseosa est jaunâtre et l'on trouve souvent un œdème important *(hydrops fetalis)* avec hépato-splénomégalie. L'ictère apparaît dès le premier jour et il se produit une anémie progressive due à l'hémolyse massive. Dans les cas très graves, le kernictère apparaît (atteinte des noyaux gris centraux) avec des symptômes de perturbation du système nerveux central: opisthotonos, spasticité, réflexe de Moro anormal, passivité et anorexie. Ces symptômes

augmentent du troisième au cinquième jour après la naissance.

Laboratoire. La mère est Rh négatif et le bébé, Rh positif. Chez le nouveau-né, le test de Coombs est positif, l'hémogramme prouve l'anémie et l'augmentation des érythroblastes, le taux sérique de bilirubine indirecte est augmenté. Le taux d'anticorps anti-Rh est élevé dans le sang maternel.

Évolution. Dans les cas graves de maladie hémolytique, l'enfant est mort-né ou meurt dans les premiers jours après la naissance. Avec un traitement prompt et adéquat, la guérison complète est généralement la règle.

Les séquelles du *kernictère* peuvent se manifester durant la première semaine de la vie ou quelques mois après la naissance. Une telle complication peut être évitée, dans la plupart des cas, en pratiquant la transfusion d'échange dès que le niveau de bilirubine sérique atteint un niveau critique, qui diffère selon l'âge, en heures, du nouveau-né. Dans plusieurs hôpitaux, les médecins utilisent encore la règle de 20 mg signifiant qu'une transfusion d'échange est pratiquée lorsque le seuil de 20 mg de bilirubine indirecte plasmatique est atteint ou dépassé. Si l'enfant survit au kernictère, il souffrira vraisemblablement de dommages cérébraux irréversibles.

Traitement. La photothérapie s'avère suffisante dans certains cas mais il est alors nécessaire de surveiller étroitement toute modification des analyses sanguines, surtout s'il s'agit d'une hausse de la bilirubine indirecte.

La transfusion d'échange peut être indiquée et ce traitement nécessite environ 170 ml/kg de sang frais, Rh négatif. La transfusion devrait être pratiquée aussitôt que le besoin est confirmé, et répétée au besoin.

Un cathéter de polyéthylène est introduit dans la veine ombilicale ou une autre grosse veine, si celle-ci est inutilisable. On retire de petites quantités du sang du nouveau-né (environ 10 à 20 ml à la fois) et une quantité égale de sang Rh négatif est injectée. Le traitement se poursuit jusqu'à ce que la quasi-totalité du sang de l'enfant ait été remplacée. On administre des antibiotiques à dose prophylactique et ensuite de petites transfusions, si cela est nécessaire.

Il faut garder le bébé au chaud pendant le traitement et le sang utilisé pour la transfusion doit atteindre 37°C. Une infirmière doit surveiller le pouls, la respiration et la tension artérielle; elle doit aussi observer l'état de l'enfant, noter sa coloration, l'aspirer si nécessaire et enregistrer minutieusement les quantités de sang prélevées et injectées. Après le traitement, il importe de surveiller l'apparition d'une hémorragie ainsi que l'état général du bébé.

Pour connaître l'état de l'enfant in-utero, le médecin peut pratiquer une amniocentèse qui consiste à introduire une aiguille dans l'utérus gravide pour en retirer du liquide amniotique. Le taux de bilirubine de ce liquide permet de confirmer le diagnostic et d'évaluer la gravité de l'atteinte fœtale. Le traitement consiste alors à provoquer l'accouchement, si la grossesse dure depuis au moins 32 semaines et à pratiquer une ou plusieurs exsanguino-transfusions si cela s'avère nécessaire.

Si la grossesse n'est pas suffisamment avancée pour provoquer l'accouchement, le médecin peut pratiquer la transfusion intra-utérine. Il vérifie radiologiquement la position de l'aiguille dans la cavité péritonéale fœtale, qui a été localisée par ultrasonographie. Là encore, des transfusions supplémentaires peuvent s'avérer nécessaires, si le taux de bilirubine demeure élevé dans le liquide amniotique.

La transfusion intra-utérine étant une technique nouvelle pour la majorité des femmes, la mère peut devenir très anxieuse au cours du traitement. L'infirmière doit l'inciter à ne pas se décourager et à garder toute confiance dans son médecin. La mère craignant que le bébé ne meure, le niveau d'anxiété monte dès que celui-ci cesse de bouger pendant quelque temps. De nombreuses femmes se plaignent de douleurs lombaires causées par la station prolongée sur la table de radiologie. Des soins appropriés, tels que la friction du dos, peuvent aider à minimiser ce malaise. L'infirmière a un grand rôle de soutien à jouer jusqu'à l'accouchement, où le résultat du traitement sera enfin connu.

Prévention. La prévention commence à la période prénatale. Toutes les femmes enceintes devraient connaître leur groupe et leur facteur sanguins. Le taux d'anticorps devrait être vérifié chaque mois chez toutes les multi-gestes Rh négatif. En cas de hausse rapide, des mesures urgentes s'imposent sans attendre la naissance de l'enfant. Après la naissance, si le nouveau-né est Rh positif, si le test de Coombs est positif et si la bilirubine indirecte s'élève rapidement, l'exsanguino-transfusion doit être pratiquée immédiatement.

Des expériences sont actuellement en cours pour éliminer l'érythroblastose fœtale. La mère Rh négatif, qui vient de donner naissance à un enfant Rh positif, reçoit dans les trois jours qui suivent l'accouchement, une injection intra musculaire d'immunoglobuline spécifique anti-Rh. Ce « vaccin » appelé Rhogam est une solution très concentrée d'anticorps anti-Rh provenant d'une personne Rh négatif déjà sensibilisée. Après l'administration du sérum, on constate sur des prises sanguines ultérieures, que la mère n'a pas développé d'anticorps anti-Rh et n'est donc pas sensibilisée. La mère acquiert ainsi une immunité passive qui la protègera contre une incompatibilité sanguine future durant une autre grossesse. Malheureusement, ce sérum n'est pas efficace chez la mère Rh négatif ayant déjà développé ses propres anticorps à la suite de la naissance d'un enfant Rh positif.

Maladie hémolytique due à une incompatibilité ABO

Les manifestations cliniques de la maladie hémolytique traduisent plus souvent une incompatibilité ABO qu'une incompatibilité Rh; le processus étiologique est le même dans les deux cas. Il est difficile de prévoir l'incompatibilité des groupes sanguins A et B, à moins qu'il n'existe une histoire semblable lors des grossesses précédentes.

La maladie, ordinairement bénigne, peut même passer inaperçue; le traitement est indiqué si l'on constate une aggravation des symptômes. Un ictère léger apparaît au cours des premières trente-six heures de vie. A l'examen physique, le médecin peut trouver une hépato-splénomégalie, il y a peu ou pas d'œdème et les complications nerveuses sont rares. La majorité des enfants atteints ne requièrent aucun traitement. Pour éviter le kernictère, une transfusion d'échange peut être indiquée si le taux sérique de la bilirubine s'élève entre 16 et 20 mg/100 ml de sang dans les trois jours qui suivent la naissance.

Soins infirmiers: maladie hémolytique du nouveau-né.

L'infirmière compétente se prépare à toute éventualité. L'incubateur est indiqué si l'enfant a des problèmes de régulation thermique; s'il devient cyanosé, l'oxygène peut être administré sur-le-champ. On commence les préparatifs pour une transfusion d'échange, dès que l'on prévoit la naissance d'un enfant susceptible de présenter une érythroblastose fœtale ou dès que le besoin s'en fait sentir chez un nouveau-né.

On observe attentivement l'enfant pendant et après le traitement et on note le pouls, la respiration, la température et l'état neurologique. L'infirmière doit signaler immédiatement les symptômes suivants: ictère évolutif, pigmentation des urines, œdème, cyanose, convulsions, ainsi que tout changement dans les signes vitaux. L'enfant léthargique est changé fréquemment de position pour éviter l'atélectasie et l'infection. Toutefois, en présence de kernictère, il faut éviter de bouger l'enfant indûment, car les manipulations peuvent précipiter les spasmes. Comme ce bébé est faible et tète difficilement, on emploie une tétine molle et largement percée ou on le nourrit au compte-gouttes, si cela est nécessaire. L'allaitement maternel est possible, puisque les agglutinines présentes dans le lait maternel seront désintégrées lors de la digestion.

Maladie hémorragique du nouveau-né

Étiologie.

La maladie est causée par une déficience en prothrombine qui résulte d'un manque de vitamine K, essentielle à sa formation, ou d'une immaturité hépatique. La vitamine K, normalement produite par une action bactérienne au niveau de l'intestin, ne peut être synthétisée dans le tractus digestif stérile du nouveau-né.

Manifestations cliniques.

L'hémorragie est possible aux niveaux suivants: la peau, la rétine la conjonctive, les muqueuses, l'ombilic ou les viscères. L'enfant peut présenter du méléna (sang passant dans les selles) ou de l'hématémèse (vomissements de sang noirâtre). Les saignements se produisent avec ou sans traumatisme et apparaissent ordinairement entre les 2e et 5e jour de la vie quand le taux de prothrombine a atteint son niveau le plus bas. Au laboratoire, on constate que le temps de coagulation est allongé, alors que le temps de saignement peut être normal ou allongé.

Traitement.

Le traitement consiste en une ou plusieurs injections intramusculaires de vitamine K. La vitamine injectée par voie intraveineuse agit toutefois beaucoup plus rapidement et une transfusion de sang frais peut être indiquée. Si le lieu de l'hémorragie est facilement accessible, des anticoagulants topiques, appliqués sous un pansement compressif, donnent de bons résultats.

Le traitement préventif consiste en l'injection à la mère de vitamine synthétique hydrosoluble, par voie intraveineuse ou intramusculaire, 4 à 6 heures avant la délivrance ou en l'administration de comprimés quelques jours avant la date prévue pour l'accouche-

Figure 9-2. Le transport du nouveau-né, vers un centre spécialisé, s'effectue en ambulance. On place le bébé dans un incubateur portatif muni d'une source d'oxygène. (Courtoisie de l'Hôpital Sainte-Justine, Montréal.)

ment. Ce traitement vise à corriger l'hypoprothrombinémie maternelle consécutive à une alimentation inadéquate. À la naissance, le bébé présente alors un taux plus élevé de prothrombine, quoique l'administration de la vitamine directement au nouveau-né donne de meilleurs résultats que le traitement préventif chez la mère. On administre la vitamine par voie intramusculaire au moment de la naissance. De fortes doses de cette vitamine semblent provoquer l'hyperbilirubinémie sans que l'effet thérapeutique en soit augmenté.

Soins. L'enfant reçoit les soins normaux du nouveau-né ou du prématuré, une attention spéciale étant portée à la prévention des traumatismes. On recherche de façon plus spécifique les saignements du tractus gastro-intestinal traduits par l'hématémèse et le méléna, l'hémorragie de l'ombilic, ainsi que l'hémorragie cérébrale qui se manifeste par des symptômes neurologiques.

ANOMALIES CONGÉNITALES

Chirurgie du nouveau-né

Beaucoup de malformations congénitales peuvent être corrigées immédiatement ou tôt après la naissance, car le risque opératoire est faible au cours des deux premiers jours de la vie. Le taux de mortalité monte ensuite très rapidement et plusieurs facteurs en sont responsables: la perturbation de l'équilibre hydro-électrolytique, l'hémolyse néonatale des globules rouges, la diminution des réserves physiologiques et la baisse du taux de prothrombine.

Les bébés handicapés nés à domicile ou dans un hôpital non spécialisé, doivent être dirigés immédiatement vers un centre pourvu d'un personnel qualifié en pédiatrie et en chirurgie pédiatrique.

L'ambulance doit être équipée d'un incubateur pourvu d'une source d'oxygène et d'un appareil à aspiration. L'enfant est trop souvent enveloppé dans une couverture et amené à l'hôpital dans un véhicule ordinaire.

La personne responsable du transport a pour fonction d'observer les changements anormaux survenant chez le nouveau-né et d'appliquer les mesures d'urgences qui s'imposent. L'infirmière ou l'ambulancier doivent être capables d'empêcher la torsion d'une omphalocèle, de prévenir l'aspiration bronchique de liquide gastrique ou œsophagien, si l'on soupçonne une atrésie de l'œsophage ou une obstruction intestinale. D'autres aspects du traitement d'urgence du nouveau-né seront discutés au cours de ce chapitre.

Préparation avant une intervention chirurgicale

À son arrivée au centre médical, le nouveau-né est immédiatement conduit à l'unité de soins intensifs néo-natals où un personnel qualifié le prend en charge. Dans ces unités, l'infirmière dispose des appareils nécessaires aux prélèvements de sang pour l'analyse des gaz artériels, à l'intubation endotrachéale, à l'assistance respiratoire et à tout autre traitement d'urgence. Un cathéter placé dans l'artère radiale du bébé permet de prélever fréquemment des échantillons sanguins pour l'analyse des gaz artériels. Cette surveillance continue permet de déceler précocement si le bébé a besoin d'une aide respiratoire. Les précautions prises pour le transport en ambulance sont aussi requises lorsqu'on amène l'enfant en radiologie ou à la salle d'opération.

La phase préopératoire indûment prolongée peut être néfaste et l'opération devrait avoir lieu aussitôt que possible. Vu le danger de broncho-pneumonie d'aspiration, il faut éviter l'emploi de substances radio-opaques comme le baryum pour diagnostiquer une atrésie de l'œsophage ou une obstruction des voies digestives supérieures. On évite les pertes sanguines en faisant les prélèvements absolument nécessaires, par micro-méthode. L'hydratation peut être médicalement indiquée; la manipulation de l'enfant doit être réduite au minimum.

Des doses extrêmement faibles de médicaments pré-opératoires préviennent l'accumulation des sécrétions bronchiques; le lavage gastrique élimine le danger de vomissements et d'aspiration de liquide gastrique dans les voies respiratoires. Une atmosphère hautement oxygénée évite à l'enfant la fatigue extrême causée par la polypnée.

Le succès de la chirurgie du nouveau-né est assuré par un diagnostic précoce, une préparation minimale et surtout la présence d'une équipe composée d'un chirurgien, d'un anesthésiste, d'un pédiatre et d'infirmières expérimentées en chirurgie infantile.

Problèmes physiologiques soulevés par la chirurgie néonatale

La chirurgie du nouveau-né soulève de nombreux problèmes qui en font une spécialité pour le chirurgien et les infirmières.

Chez le nouveau-né, l'élasticité vasculaire est telle, qu'à la suite de pertes sanguines, l'enfant présente peu de symptômes avant de tomber brutalement en choc hypovolémique: le pouls disparaît, la tension artérielle chute brutalement et la peau devient marbrée. Il faut donc prévoir l'hémorragie et donner du sang électivement si les circonstances l'exigent; il est difficile de corriger l'hypovolémie quand le bébé est déjà en état de choc, car un excès de liquide peut provoquer un œdème aigu du poumon.

D'autres problèmes risquent de compromettre le pronostic vital du nouveau-né: l'instabilité pondérale, les variations de la fonction rénale, le contrôle labile de la température corporelle; la tachypnée consécutive à l'anoxie cause une fatigue extrême dont l'enfant peut mourir.

Soins postopératoires du nouveau-né

Le nouveau-né a une résistance remarquable et il se rétablit d'habitude très rapidement et sans complication. Toutefois, certaines réserves physiologiques lui font défaut et l'état d'urgence peut apparaître sans avertissement. L'infirmière doit donc vérifier attentivement l'état de son patient s'attachant surtout à observer les variations de la température, la qualité de la respiration, sa coloration, ainsi qu'à déceler les signes d'hémorragie. Elle doit être en mesure d'appliquer les soins d'urgence, si le médecin n'est pas sur les lieux.

La période cruciale est la première heure postopératoire. Placé dans un incubateur qui maintient sa température corporelle entre 36°C et 37,2°C, l'enfant se remet lentement de l'anesthésie. Une bonne position de la tête et l'aspiration des sécrétions nasopharyngées préviennent les complications respiratoires et l'asphyxie. La concentration d'oxygène dans l'incubateur est adaptée aux besoins du nouveau-né; l'humidité permet de fluidifier les sécrétions et compense la perte d'eau causée par l'hyperpnée.

L'enfant s'épuise rapidement s'il n'est pas protégé contre les stimuli extérieurs inutiles. Une planification adéquate permet de grouper les soins, tels que changer la couche, administrer les médicaments, vérifier le pansement, prendre les signes vitaux.

Les positions qui diminuent l'amplitude respiratoire et les pansements qui compriment le thorax doivent être évités et il faut changer fréquemment la position du bébé tout en évitant de l'éveiller.

Le débit des solutés et des médicaments intraveineux est ordinairement prescrit en fonction du nombre désiré de gouttes par minute (gttes/min) ou de centimètres cubes à l'heure (cm³/h). Le contrôle du débit a pour but d'éviter la surcharge circulatoire pouvant occasionner un œdème aigu du poumon; il faut surveiller l'infiltration du liquide dans le tissu sous-cutané. On pèse régulièrement l'enfant pour vérifier l'équilibre hydrique et voir si la perfusion est bien adaptée à ses besoins. S'il est préférable que l'enfant n'absorbe aucune nourriture par voie orale, il faut alors avoir recours à l'hyperalimentation par voie intraveineuse.

L'infirmière est responsable du bon fonctionnement des différents tubes (gastrostomie-thoracique), cathéters ou tubulures intraveineuses. Si l'enfant est alimenté par un tube de gastrostomie, celui-ci doit être élevé d'environ 15 cm au-dessus de l'estomac et demeurer ouvert entre les repas afin d'éviter la dilatation gastrique ou encore une régurgitation suivie d'une broncho-aspiration. Il est recommandé de faire précéder et suivre le repas d'une petite irrigation du tube au soluté salin. Le retour à l'alimentation par voie orale doit s'effectuer de façon progressive et sous un contrôle continu.

La faiblesse du réflexe de toux augmente le danger de broncho-aspiration, si l'enfant vomit. Ceci peut être prévenu en installant un drainage gastrique continu ou en plaçant l'enfant sur le côté, tête basse, pour permettre l'écoulement des sécrétions à l'extérieur du nasopharynx. Si elle devient nécessaire, l'aspiration endo-bronchique doit être effectuée sans délai et par une personne qualifiée.

À mesure que l'état de l'enfant s'améliore, on le sèvre graduellement de son incubateur, en modifiant progressivement l'atmosphère de l'appareil et en sortant l'enfant durant des périodes de plus en plus prolongées, jusqu'à ce qu'il puisse être placé dans un berceau ordinaire.

Les soins postopératoires du nouveau-né sont un aspect très important du nursing pédiatrique. Les soins spécifiques seront étudiés en regard de chaque pathologie. Les besoins des parents de ces bébés ne doivent pas être oubliés par l'infirmière affectée à l'unité néonatale de soins intensifs.

Pathologies congénitales pouvant nécessiter un traitement chirurgical

Stridor laryngé congénital

Définition. Le stridor laryngé congénital est une affection du nouveau-né, caractérisée par un bruit striduleux ou sifflement laryngotrachéal, qui se répète à chaque mouvement respiratoire et qui augmente quand l'enfant pleure ou s'agite. La guérison est souvent spontanée; en d'autres cas, seules des mesures d'urgence peuvent sauver la vie de l'enfant.

Étiologie. La cause du stridor laryngé qui persiste plusieurs jours après la naissance peut être interne ou externe, et la laryngoscopie permet de poser le diagnostic. La cause la plus fréquente est la faiblesse de l'épiglotte et des parois de la glotte. On peut découvrir aussi la redondance de l'épiglotte, une faiblesse de la paroi laryngée, l'absence d'anneaux trachéaux, une anomalie des cordes vocales ou une membrane obstruant partiellement le larynx. Une infection laryngée, la tétanie ou la présence d'un corps étranger dans le larynx peuvent expliquer le stridor chez l'enfant plus âgé.

Manifestations cliniques. Le principal symptôme est la respiration bruyante, accompagnée d'une sorte de croassement ou sifflement à l'inspiration. Ce symptôme devient plus évident quand l'enfant pleure. Le stridor est quelquefois accompagné d'une dépression intercostale et supra-claviculaire plus ou moins importante et l'enfant peut devenir dyspnéique et cyanosé.

Évolution et traitement. Le traitement est basé sur la correction du facteur causal. Le stridor léger ne justifie aucune intervention, mais la chirurgie peut devenir nécessaire si l'affection est grave. La trachéotomie peut agir comme mesure palliative contre la mauvaise oxygénation; la laryngoplastie peut être nécessaire devant une difformité du larynx (anomalie laryngée).

La forme légère du stridor laryngé congénital disparaît souvent spontanément entre 6 et 18 mois. L'enfant ne cyanose pas et le seul symptôme qu'il présente est la respiration bruyante caractéristique. Le pronostic est intimement lié à la pathologie sous-jacente.

Les os de l'enfant étant facilement malléables, le tirage intercostal peut, à longue échéance, déformer le thorax. Le bébé présente quelquefois des difficultés d'alimentation qui sont causes de malnutrition. Il est évident que les infections respiratoires intercurrentes vont assombrir le tableau et l'état de l'enfant peut s'aggraver rapidement.

Soins. Les problèmes respiratoires rendent l'alimentation difficile et on doit faire boire l'enfant lentement. Le besoin de respirer est impératif et des interruptions fréquentes faciliteront la respiration. Si l'enfant cesse spontanément de téter, son appétit n'est pas nécessairement satisfait. L'alimentation peut être suspendue quelques instants et le biberon

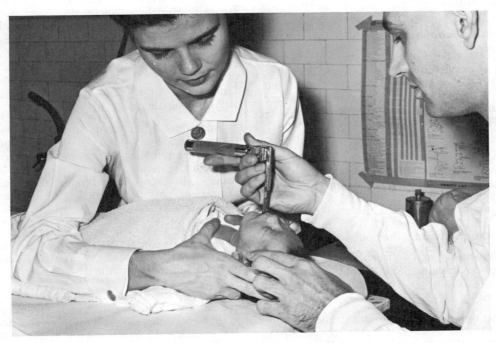

Figure 9-3. Examen laryngoscopique. On pratique une contrainte de momie et on place une petite serviette roulée sous les épaules.

offert de nouveau. Si l'enfant semble présenter la moindre difficulté à la déglutition, on suspend immédiatement l'allaitement. Une petite tétine est, en général, plus efficace et son orifice doit permettre un écoulement adéquat. L'infirmière tient l'enfant dans ses bras pour l'alimenter et il serait très dangereux de laisser l'enfant dans son lit pour le faire boire. Ce principe est valable pour tous les bébés, mais dans ce cas particulier, son importance ne peut être exagérée.

On devrait fournir à la mère, pendant son séjour à l'hôpital, toutes les chances de s'habituer à la respiration bruyante de son enfant. Autrement, à la maison, elle risque de ne pas savoir discerner une aggravation de l'état du bébé. La difficulté respiratoire est augmentée par une infection respiratoire, une broncho-aspiration ou tout autre problème laryngé. L'infirmière devrait guider la mère lors de ses premiers essais pour faire boire le bébé. Elle peut ainsi lui faire remarquer les réactions de l'enfant, si l'alimentation est trop rapide, si les interruptions ne sont pas assez fréquentes ou s'il ne semble pas avaler normalement. La mère qui allaite aura le temps d'approfondir ses connaissances durant son séjour à l'hôpital.

L'enfant est spécialement sensible aux infections respiratoires et tout contact avec des sources infectieuses doit être évité. Une atmosphère humidifiée lui est salutaire.

Atrésie des choanes

L'atrésie des choanes est une obstruction de la partie postérieure des narines, à l'entrée du nasopharynx. Ordinairement causée par une membrane ou une excroissance osseuse anormale, l'anomalie peut être uni ou bilatérale.

L'obstruction bilatérale oblige l'enfant à respirer par la bouche; puisqu'il ne peut téter et respirer simultanément, les problèmes d'alimentation font rapidement leur apparition. La dyspnée traduit l'apport insuffisant d'oxygène à chaque inspiration. Si l'affection est unilatérale, l'inspiration sera normale, sauf en cas d'infection persistante du côté sain.

Le diagnostic est confirmé, si une sonde ou un cathéter de caoutchouc flexible vient buter sur un obstacle après avoir été introduit dans la narine.

L'atrésie bilatérale doit être traitée immédiatement afin d'éviter l'anoxie. Si l'obstruction est membraneuse, le médecin perce l'obstacle à l'aide d'un nasoscope. Une intervention chirurgicale correctrice s'impose dans le cas d'une obstruction osseuse, mais on ne corrigera pas l'atrésie unilatérale tant que le bébé n'aura pas atteint une condition physique lui permettant de supporter facilement une intervention chirurgicale.

Le rôle de l'infirmière vise à soulager l'enfant. Maintenir les narines libres et propres est essentiel. L'enfant présente des problèmes d'alimentation, puisqu'il est incapable de téter et de respirer simultanément et il existe un danger de broncho-aspiration. Les soins sont similaires à ceux du stridor laryngé.

Pathologies incompatibles avec la vie sans traitement chirurgical

Il existe plusieurs malformations, surtout au niveau du tractus gastro-intestinal, qui sont incompatibles avec la vie, sans traitement chirurgical correcteur. Ces anomalies sont l'imperforation anale, l'atrésie de l'œsophage, l'omphalocèle, la hernie diaphragmatique et l'occlusion intestinale. Elles sont souvent associées à d'autres malformations congénitales et on les voit aussi chez le prématuré. Un diagnostic précoce et un traitement immédiat sont essentiels à la survie de l'enfant.

Chaque heure de délai dans la chirurgie gastro-intestinale augmente le risque opératoire à cause de la distension abdominale qui s'installe; le rythme respiratoire s'accélère, fatigue l'enfant à l'extrême, le rendant éventuellement incapable de subir l'opération. Le développement des techniques d'hyperalimentation parentérale rend toutefois moins aigu le problème de l'alimentation.

Au cours d'un chapitre précédent, nous avons indiqué les points à observer pour déceler une anomalie interne chez le nouveau-né. Au moindre doute, l'infirmière avertit le médecin qui prend ensuite les décisions qui s'imposent pour le diagnostic et le traitement de l'anomalie.

Les signes qui peuvent indiquer la présence de lésions incompatibles avec la vie sont la cyanose, les vomissements, l'absence de selles et la distension abdominale.

La cyanose est un symptôme commun à plusieurs pathologies dont la hernie diaphragmatique et l'atrésie de l'œsophage. Elle peut être également l'indice majeur d'une anomalie cardiaque congénitale que nous étudierons plus loin dans ce livre.

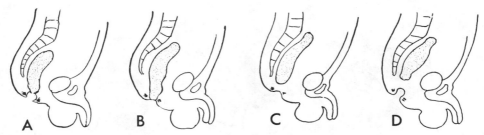

Figure 9-4. Illustration de 4 sortes de malformations ano-rectales. (P. Hanley et M. O. Hines, dans *Christopher's Minor Surgery.* 8e éd., Ochsner et DeBakey.)

Les vomissements bilieux sont un signe d'occlusion intestinale. La régurgitation immédiate peut indiquer une atrésie de l'œsophage alors qu'un vomissement tardif, après l'alimentation, signale plutôt une sténose du pylore. Une hernie diaphragmatique cause souvent des vomissements à répétition.

L'absence de selles et la distension abdominale se rencontrent dans tous les cas d'occlusion intestinale. Il est évident que l'on peut remarquer ces différents cas chez un nouveauné normal, mais puisqu'ils peuvent indiquer une pathologie curable, bien qu'incompatible avec la vie, le médecin doit être averti immédiatement afin que le traitement soit institué dans les plus brefs délais.

Anus imperforé

Étiologie. Cette anomalie congénitale mortelle est la plus fréquente. Au cours de la 8e semaine de vie embryonnaire, la membrane qui sépare le rectum de l'anus devrait normalement se résorber pour permettre la formation du canal ano-rectal; en l'absence de ce phénomène, le nouveau-né aura un anus imperforé. L'anomalie est souvent accompagnée chez la fille d'une fistule qui relie le rectum au vagin, au périnée ou à la fourchette; chez le garçon, elle fait communiquer le rectum avec les voies urinaires, le scrotum ou le périnée.

Diagnostic. Les éléments suivants permettent de poser le diagnostic:

1) L'absence d'ouverture anale constatée à l'examen de routine au moment de la naissance.

2) L'impossibilité d'insérer l'extrémité de l'auriculaire ou d'un petit thermomètre dans le rectum du bébé.

3) L'absence de méconium.

4) L'installation progressive d'une distension abdominale.

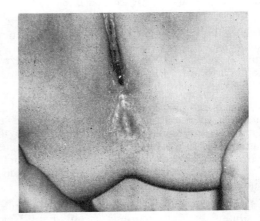

Figure 9-5. Anus imperforé. (P. Hanley et M. O. Hines, dans *Christopher's Minor Surgery,* 8e éd., Ochsner et DeBakey.)

L'examen radiologique permet de confirmer le diagnostic et d'évaluer la distance qui sépare la fossette anale de l'extrémité distale du rectum. L'air que l'enfant avale en pleurant s'accumule dans l'intestin et cet air peut être observé radiographiquement en tenant l'enfant, tête en bas ou en position fœtale. Pour évaluer correctement la distance entre l'air intestinal et l'extérieur, un objet opaque est placé au niveau de la fossette anale et sert de point de repère.

Chez le garçon, il est urgent de corriger l'anomalie, car les selles vont s'accumuler dans l'intestin; chez la fille, il est probable que les selles passeront par la fistule et aboutiront au vagin, au périnée ou à la fourchette. L'orifice de la fistule est souvent visible d'emblée; cependant, l'émission d'urines teintées de méconium permet de soupçonner la présence d'une fistule recto-vésicale non décelable à l'œil nu.

Traitement. Le type d'intervention chirurgicale est fonction de la nature de l'anomalie. Dans certains cas, la présence d'une mem-

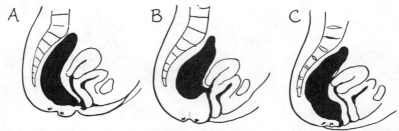

Figure 9-6. Représentation d'une imperforation anale associée à une fistule, chez une fille. *A)* Recto-vaginale basse. *B)* Recto-vaginale haute. *C)* Recto-périnéale. (P. Hanley et M. O. Hines, dans *Christopher's Minor Surgery*, 8e éd., Ochsner et DeBakey.)

brane mince, à travers laquelle le méconium est visible, constitue le seul obstacle et celui-ci peut être éliminé par l'insertion d'un instrument perforant.

Si la distance entre la fossette anale et l'extrémité borgne du rectum ne dépasse pas 1,5 cm, une périnéorraphie est suffisante. Une distance supérieure à 1,5 cm complique le traitement: une colostomie temporaire peut permettre d'attendre un moment plus favorable, tandis qu'une chirurgie correctrice abdomino-périnéale est quelquefois possible.

L'anus est quelquefois normal, l'anomalie se situant quelques centimètres plus haut. Cette pathologie, qualifiée *d'atrésie rectale,* sera corrigée comme une occlusion du côlon.

Soins. Une des principales caractéristiques de l'infirmière compétente est sa capacité de déceler les symptômes importants. L'infirmière qui rencontre un enfant qui lui semble porteur d'une imperforation anale, doit aussitôt avertir le médecin, permettant ainsi un traitement précoce et efficace.

Le diagnostic posé, le médecin demande d'installer une aspiration gastrique continue et un soluté intraveineux ou de préparer immédiatement l'enfant pour une intervention chirurgicale.

Période postopératoire. Si l'opération a été effectuée à la région anale, cette région doit être gardée propre et sèche sans toutefois mettre de couche à l'enfant. La région doit être nettoyée aussitôt après chaque défécation et l'utilisation du thermomètre rectal est prohibée. Puisque le bébé placé sur l'abdomen a tendance à replier ses jambes sous lui, on le couchera sur le côté en le changeant souvent de position pour éviter toute tension sur les sutures périnéales. Si le chirurgien a pratiqué une colostomie, les soins de la peau au niveau de la plaie périnéale et autour de l'anus artificiel sont de prime importance puisque l'irritation locale se produit encore plus facilement chez le bébé que chez l'enfant ou l'adulte. Un sac de colostomie collé sur un anneau de karaya bien adapté autour de la stomie assure une excellente protection. L'infirmière doit connaître les différentes sortes et grandeurs de sac et elle doit apprendre à mesurer correctement le diamètre de la stomie. Si une irritation se produit, de la poudre ou de l'onguent de karaya peuvent être utilisés. Le nouveau-né n'a pas besoin de ceinture pour tenir le sac en place.

Avant de donner congé au bébé, il faut expliquer aux parents la nature de l'intervention et leur enseigner les soins de la peau de même que l'entretien du sac: vidange, nettoya-

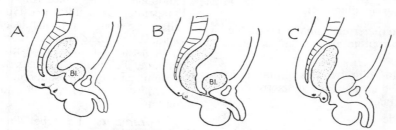

Figure 9-7. Anus imperforé avec fistule, chez un garçon. *A)* Recto-vésicale. *B)* Recto-urétrale. *C)* Recto-périnéale. (P. Hanley et M. O. Hines, dans *Christophers's Minor Surgery*, 8e éd., Ochsner et DeBakey.)

ge et changement de sac. Il est important de souligner aux parents que leur enfant requiert aussi les soins attentifs et habituels dont tout enfant a besoin.

Après la fermeture de la colostomie et aussi s'il n'y a pas eu de création d'anus artificiel, la mère peut être obligée de dilater régulièrement l'anus du bébé. L'incontinence fécale est la rançon de l'échec du traitement chirurgical et peut causer des problèmes graves au moment de l'intégration de l'enfant à la vie scolaire, les enfants de son âge risquant de le rejeter.

Atrésie de l'œsophage

Incidence.   L'atrésie de l'œsophage se classe au deuxième rang dans l'ordre de fréquence des malformations obstructives du tractus gastro-intestinal. Elles est caractérisée par l'absence de développement d'un segment de l'œsophage. Environ 80% des bébés atteints de cette malformation présentent une atrésie proximale et une fistule œsophago-trachéale distale.

Diagnostic.   L'hydramnios maternel semble un indice d'atrésie de l'œsophage. En effet,

le fœtus qui souffre de cette pathologie est incapable d'avaler du liquide amniotique comme il le ferait normalement.

À la naissance, les sécrétions du naso-pharynx sont excessivement abondantes et l'enfant présente une cyanose qui disparaît lors de l'aspiration du mucus et l'administration d'oxygène. Toutefois, comme le mucus s'accumule très vite dans les voies respiratoires supérieures, la cyanose réapparaît très vite. L'infirmière de la salle d'accouchement ou de la pouponnière doit pouvoir reconnaître ces symptômes et en avertir *immédiatement* le médecin. Au moindre doute, on retarde l'alimentation jusqu'à ce que le bébé ait été sérieusement examiné et qu'un jugement médical ait été posé sur sa condition.

Un cathéter gastrique, non rigide, de calibre 8, va buter sur un obstacle, lors de l'insertion dans l'œsophage. Aux rayons-X, l'extrémité radio-opaque du cathéter apparaît enroulée sur elle-même. *Aucune substance à base de baryum ne devrait être instillée à cause du danger d'aspiration* pouvant provoquer des complications pulmonaires. S'il existe, en plus, une fistule trachéo-œsophagienne distale, la plaque

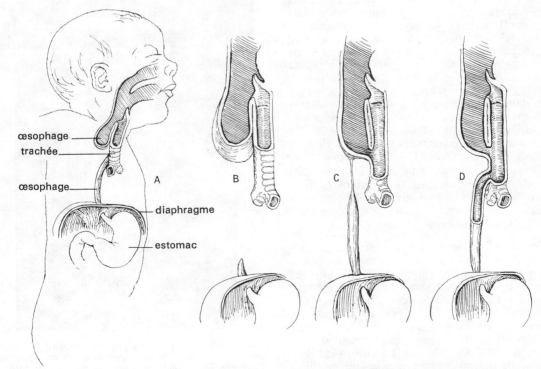

Figure 9-8.   Atrésie de l'œsophage. *A)* Forme la plus fréquente. La portion supérieure est borgne. La portion inférieure communique avec la trachée. *B)* Les deux segments sont borgnes. *C)* le segment supérieur communique avec la trachée. Le lien fibreux avec la partie inférieure n'existe pas toujours. *D)* Les deux portions de l'œsophage communiquent avec la trachée.

simple de l'abdomen va révéler la présence d'air dans le tube digestif.

Si le diagnostic n'est pas fait et que l'on essaie d'hydrater l'enfant, il avalera la première gorgée, mais comme le liquide s'accumule dans le tronçon borgne de l'œsophage, les gorgées suivantes seront rejetées d'emblée par le nez et la bouche. L'enfant étouffe, éternue, tousse et devient extrêmement agité. Une pneumonie de déglutition peut s'ensuivre, le liquide risquant d'être aspiré dans les bronches lorsque l'enfant boit, ou de s'écouler dans la trachée par la fistule œsophago-trachéale.

Variétés et traitements. Plusieurs solutions sont possibles et dépendent du type d'atrésie.

a) L'anastomose termino-terminale des segments proximal et distal de l'œsophage.

b) En l'absence du segment distal de l'œsophage ou si une distance trop grande sépare les deux tronçons, l'anastomose est impossible et le chirurgien pratique une œsophagostomie cervicale ou une gastrostomie en attendant la transplantation d'un segment du côlon quand l'enfant aura atteint l'âge d'un an.

Chez certains prématurés ou certains enfants souffrant déjà d'une pneumonie, un drainage continu de l'œsophage par un cathéter à double tubulure permet de recueillir le liquide qui s'accumule dans le tronçon proximal. L'enfant est nourri par une gastrostomie et la chirurgie correctrice a lieu, quand l'enfant a gagné du poids ou après la guérison de la pneumonie. Si l'anastomose termino-terminale est impossible, l'autre possibilité est une transplantation du côlon, dont une section de la portion ascendante ou transverse est suturée à la place de l'œsophage. Une constriction, toujours possible, sera facilement corrigée par une dilatation ultérieure. Le pronostic vital dépend de l'âge, du poids, de la condition générale de l'enfant, ainsi que de la présence d'autres malformations.

Soins infirmiers. Il est préférable de placer l'enfant dans un incubateur où il sera à la chaleur, protégé contre les infections et entouré d'une atmosphère humide permettant la liquéfaction des sécrétions abondantes qui s'accumulent dans les voies aériennes. Le rythme et l'amplitude respiratoires du nouvel opéré permettent de juger cliniquement du besoin d'aspirer les sécrétions. Le chirurgien doit indiquer le niveau anatomique de l'intervention et le cathéter est soigneusement marqué de façon à ce que l'infirmière libère le bébé de ses sécrétions, mais ne touche pas à la plaie

opératoire. Si le bébé demeure agité ou embarrassé, le chirurgien pratique l'aspiration trachéobronchique. Une trachéotomie temporaire peut aider la ventilation.

Il est très important que l'enfant ait continuellement une infirmière à son chevet au cours de la période postopératoire immédiate. Il doit être aspiré fréquemment; l'infirmière doit le stimuler pour qu'il pleure de temps à

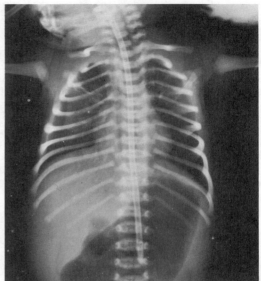

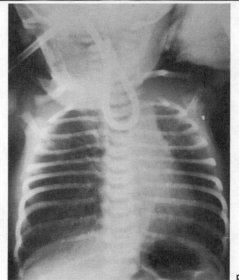

Figure 9-9. Atrésie de l'œsophage. *A)* Un tube de Levine passé dans l'œsophage d'un nouveau-né normal. *B)* Chez le bébé porteur d'une atrésie de l'œsophage, le tube fait demi-tour au niveau de l'obstruction et remonte vers la gorge. (Courtoisie du « Children's Hospital », Philadelphia, U.S.A.)

autre et elle doit le changer souvent de position ce qui facilite l'expansion pulmonaire. S'il revient de la salle d'opération avec un drain thoracique, l'infirmière doit bouger le tube ou le sac de drainage quand elle change la position du bébé afin d'éviter toute tension au niveau de l'insertion du tube. Le sac ou la bouteille de drainage ne doivent jamais être levés plus haut que le thorax; le tube ne doit jamais être débranché, pincé ou plié. S'il se forme des caillots dans le système de drainage, il faut « traire » le tube en direction de la bouteille. Au chevet de l'enfant, on doit garder en permanence deux pinces hémostatiques, ce qui permettrait de bloquer le système de drainage pour éviter un pneumothorax si un des tubes se débranchait par inadvertance. Il faut marquer la bouteille ou le sac de drainage afin de pouvoir mesurer la quantité de liquide qui s'écoule et aussi surveiller l'aspect de l'écoulement.

Si une gastrostomie a été pratiquée, on reprend l'alimentation quelques heures après l'opération. Le gavage peut être donné par gravité, goutte à goutte, à l'aide d'une bouteille et d'une tubulure à perfusion intraveineuse ou à l'aide d'un tube de gastrostomie.

Alimentation par tube de gastrostomie. Le nécessaire comprend un plateau contenant la solution de gavage à la température de la pièce, un entonnoir stérile ou une seringue Asepto (large seringue sans piston), une tétine d'amusement stérile.

Pincer le tube de gastrostomie. Adapter la seringue ou l'entonnoir à l'extrémité du tube de gastrostomie et verser la formule de lait avant d'enlever la pince, afin d'éviter la pénétration d'air qui dilaterait l'estomac. Élever la seringue ou l'entonnoir de quelques centimètres et laisser couler le liquide, lentement, par gravité, sans exercer de pression.

Pour éviter la remontée du liquide dans l'œsophage en cas de vomissements, certains chirurgiens préfèrent laisser le tube ouvert entre les gavages, tout en laissant l'extrémité plus élevée que le niveau de l'orifice.

Pour satisfaire le besoin de succion de l'enfant, on lui donne une tétine d'amusement, ce qui le détend et facilite l'écoulement du lait dans l'estomac. À la fin du repas, l'infirmière prend l'enfant dans ses bras pendant quelques minutes pour satisfaire son besoin de tendresse et l'aider à associer plaisir et nourriture.

Les soins de la peau entourant la bouche de gastrostomie s'avèrent d'une extrême importance. La région doit être lavée et asséchée fréquemment et protégée du suc gastrique par de l'onguent de zinc ou d'aluminium.

Le tube est solidement fixé à l'aide d'un pansement, mais de grandes précautions sont quand même nécessaires pour éviter de l'ôter en changeant le pansement abdominal. Il est bon de marquer le tube de gastrostomie à l'aide d'un diachylon, au niveau de la peau; l'infirmière peut ainsi voir immédiatement s'il a été bougé. Les attaches de Montgomery sont idéales dans ce cas particulier. *Attaches*

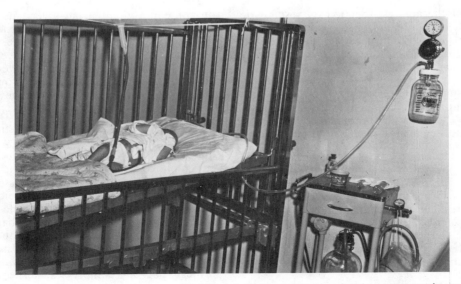

Figure 9-10. Nouveau-né après une cure d'atrésie de l'œsophage. Le tube de gastrostomie permet le gavage. Notez les cordelettes qui servent de support à la seringue de gavage. (Courtoisie de l'Hôpital Sainte-Justine, Montréal.)

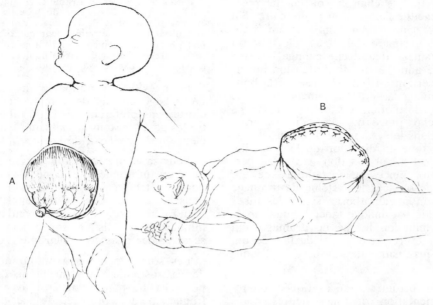

Figure 9-11. Omphalocèle. *A)* Hernie du contenu abdominal au niveau de l'ombilic. *B)* La peau est ramenée sur la surface de l'omphalocèle et suturée.

de Montgomery: deux diachylons de longueur inégale sont collés l'un sur l'autre et l'extrémité adhésive est fixée à la peau. Une autre bande semblable est placée de l'autre côté de l'abdomen. Une boutonnière, pratiquée à l'extrémité non adhésive de chaque bande, permet le passage d'un cordon qu'on lace ensuite sur le pansement.

L'antibiothérapie est fonction du résultat de la culture du tronçon œsophagien réséqué. Comme dans toute chirurgie gastro-intestinale, on donne du sang ou du plasma, au besoin, et les liquides sont administrés par voie parentérale. L'hydratation per os est commencée aussitôt que possible, souvent dès le 3e jour postopératoire, car le passage du liquide dans l'œsophage permet de diminuer le risque de sténose du segment nouvellement reconstruit.

Si l'enfant a subi une œsophagostomie cervicale, certains chirurgiens prescrivent des repas « fictifs » qui, même si les aliments sont expulsés par l'orifice cutané et ne peuvent donc pas être digérés, permettent d'habituer le bébé de plus de 2 mois à une alimentation normale, ce qui facilitera sa convalescence. L'orifice doit être gardé scrupuleusement propre, afin d'éviter l'infection.

Il faut essayer de combler au maximum les besoins de succion, de chaleur et de confort de ces nouveau-nés. Ces enfants, dont la durée d'hospitalisation peut être assez longue, risquent de souffrir de carences affectives, malgré des soins physiques de haute qualité. Les parents doivent être renseignés régulièrement et encouragés à participer aux soins.

L'omphalocèle

Définition. L'omphalocèle est une hernie du contenu abdominal au niveau de l'ombilic. L'anomalie se produit entre la sixième et la dixième semaine de vie intra-utérine. Le contenu herniaire est entouré d'une mince membrane transparente et avasculaire. Souvent facile à déceler, l'omphalocèle est quelquefois si petite qu'elle semble faire partie du cordon ombilical.

Manifestations cliniques et traitement. À première vue, le contenu intestinal d'une forte omphalocèle semble plus volumineux que la cavité abdominale dans laquelle il doit être replacé. Le traitement chirurgical, consistant en l'enfouissement de la masse dans sa cavité naturelle, est possible à condition d'agir immédiatement avant l'apparition de la distension intestinale causée par l'aérophagie, avant l'assèchement du sac ou sa contamination par les bactéries de l'air environnant. La contamination est possible, même si le sac doit être protégé par des compresses stériles humides. La cure chirurgicale peut être effectuée en un ou deux temps opératoires. Une technique chirurgicale récente consiste à suturer un sac de

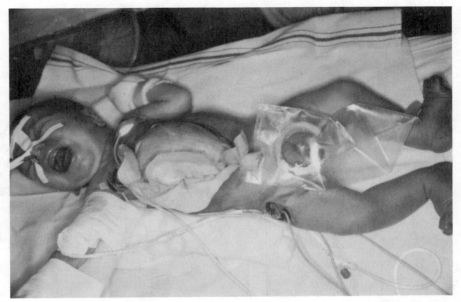

Figure 9-12. L'utilisation d'un sac de silastic couvrant l'omphalocèle constitue la base du traitement. Ce bébé gravement malade reçoit des perfusions intraveineuses, a un tube naso-gastrique et un sac collecteur d'urine. (Courtoisie du Dr C. Everett Koop, Children's Hospital of Philadelphia.)

silastic à la paroi abdominale, au-dessus de l'omphalocèle et à suspendre le fond du sac au plafond de l'incubateur. Chaque jour, une pression plus forte oblige le sac herniaire à regagner l'espace intra-abdominal tout en rapprochant les muscles de l'abdomen. Quand l'omphalocèle est complètement réduite, la paroi est suturée.

Le taux de mortalité de ces enfants a beaucoup diminué mais il demeure élevé surtout quand d'autres malformations viennent s'ajouter au tableau clinique.

Hernie diaphragmatique

Définition et incidence. La fréquence accrue de hernies diaphragmatiques n'est pas nécessairement due à une augmentation réelle du nombre de ces anomalies, mais plutôt à un diagnostic plus précoce et plus précis. L'importance de la lésion est très variable, mais celle-ci, plus fréquente du côté gauche, se présente toujours comme une protrusion du contenu abdominal dans la cavité thoracique à travers un orifice diaphragmatique anormal.

Manifestations cliniques. Les symptômes forment une entité clinique caractéristique et, si la lésion est très importante, le diagnostic peut même être fait dès la naissance de l'enfant. Dans le cas contraire, les symptômes peuvent apparaître assez tardivement. L'affection est caractérisée par une détresse respiratoire extrême, souvent accompagnée de cyanose. Le thorax semble augmenter de volume, le côté affecté n'est pas fonctionnel et l'abdomen est relativement petit. La dilatation aérienne de l'intestin provoque une aggravation marquée des symptômes, les mouvements respiratoires sont complètement absents du côté atteint, le poumon étant comprimé par les anses intestinales.

Diagnostic. Le diagnostic, possible grâce à l'examen physique et à l'auscultation, est confirmé par une radiographie pulmonaire qui montre l'air contenu dans les anses intestinales logées dans la cavité thoracique.

Traitement. La chirurgie, très urgente dans les cas graves, est ordinairement précédée de l'insertion d'une sonde naso-gastrique qui va retirer les sécrétions et l'air accumulés dans le tractus gastro-intestinal. Le bébé doit être gardé en position semi-assise pour diminuer la pression des organes abdominaux sur le diaphragme. La réinsertion des viscères dans la cavité abdominale et une plastie du diaphragme permettent la réexpansion pulmonaire du côté atteint et une respiration normale. Le pronostic s'assombrit avec le délai de l'intervention et l'enfant non opéré meurt ordinairement au cours du premier mois de vie.

Soins. Les soins postopératoires sont extrêmement importants. L'aspiration gastrique prévient la distension abdominale. Les liquides sont administrés par voie intraveineuse jusqu'à tolérance de l'hydratation orale et les

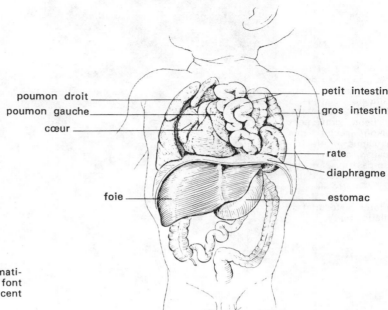

poumon droit

poumon gauche

cœur

foie

petit intestin

gros intestin

rate

diaphragme

estomac

Figure 9-13. Hernie diaphragmatique. Les viscères abdominaux font hernie dans le thorax et déplacent les organes thoraciques.

transfusions de sang ou de plasma sont quelquefois nécessaires. Les gavages, commencés au cours de la deuxième ou troisième journée postopératoire, évitent la dilatation gastrique causée par l'aérophagie qui accompagne la tétée.

Occlusion intestinale

Étiologie. Plusieurs pathologies peuvent causer une occlusion intestinale chez le nourrisson: l'atrésie ou la sténose congénitale de l'intestin, les vices de rotation du côlon avec volvulus, les hernies internes, les brides péritonéales, l'iléus méconial et la maladie de Hirschsprung.

Atrésie congénitale et sténose de l'intestin. L'atrésie ou absence de lumière d'une portion de l'intestin est causée dans l'utérus par un trouble de l'irrigation sanguine à la suite d'un accident vasculaire, d'une intussusception ou d'un volvulus. Dans la sténose, on trouve une occlusion partielle du tractus gastro-intestinal.

On connaît trois sortes d'atrésie: 1) une membrane peut fermer complètement l'orifice, 2) le segment proximal peut se terminer abruptement sans présence de segment distal ou 3) une série de segments peuvent être reliés entre eux par des cordons fibreux.

Vice de rotation et volvulus. Au cours de la dixième semaine de vie embryonnaire, il se produit normalement une rotation complète du cæcum et fixation par attaches mésentériques dans le quadrant inférieur droit. En l'absence de ce processus, le côlon peut demeurer au niveau du quadrant supérieur droit et une membrane anormale peut obstruer le duodénum. Le volvulus est la grande complication de ce vice de rotation. Les anses intestinales, libres d'attaches, s'enchevêtrent, causant une obstruction qui peut aller jusqu'à la nécrose par manque d'apport sanguin suffisant.

Hernies internes et brides péritonéales. La hernie interne se produit quand une anse intestinale glisse de sa position normale et s'insère dans une portion défectueuse du mésentère ou est comprimée par des brides péritonéales. Dans chacun de ces cas, l'occlusion intestinale est la règle.

Iléus méconial. Il se rencontre chez 5 à 10% des enfants porteurs d'une mucoviscidose. Les enzymes, normalement produites par le pancréas, sont déficientes et, dès avant la naissance, le méconium est durci, épaissi, adhérant à la paroi intestinale. D'autres symptômes de mucoviscidose peuvent aussi être présents.

Manifestations cliniques. Les trois grands symptômes d'occlusion intestinale sont l'absence de selles, les vomissements bilieux et la distension abdominale. Si quelques heures après la naissance, l'enfant n'a pas encore eu de selles, le toucher rectal permet de s'assurer s'il y a bien présence de méconium dans l'ampoule rectale. En l'absence de méconium, le médecin peut prescrire un lavement d'environ 10 cm³ de soluté physiologique. Ce lavement doit être administré en utilisant une technique rigoureuse et délicate parce que les risques de perforation sont élevés. Les vomissements bilieux se présentent dans l'occlusion intestinale mais l'absence de bile dans les vomissements n'élimine pas la possibilité d'obstruction intestinale. La présence de bile dépend de la localisation de l'obstruction et suppose que celle-ci se trouve au-dessous de l'ampoule de Vater. La distension abdominale peut être normalement présente avant l'élimination du méconium. Il faut surtout retenir que ces manifestations peuvent être normales chez tous les nouveau-nés, mais que l'association de deux symptômes chez le même enfant ou la persistance de ces manifestations, requièrent un examen médical approfondi.

Diagnostic. Les examens radiologiques permettent de vérifier la présence ou l'absence d'un obstacle intestinal.

Traitement. Le traitement est essentiellement chirurgical. La chirurgie digestive est d'ailleurs la plus fréquente chez le nourrisson. Le taux de mortalité est relativement élevé, mais la survie dépend surtout du niveau anatomique de l'anomalie et de la rapidité du diagnostic et du traitement.

Soins. C'est à l'infirmière qu'incombe la responsabilité de surveiller le nouveau-né et elle sera d'autant plus en mesure de saisir l'importance de certains symptômes qu'elle aura une connaissance suffisante des pathologies susceptibles de se présenter.

TRAUMATISMES OBSTÉTRICAUX

Cette entité comprend les traumatismes qui se produisent au moment de l'accouchement, ainsi que le dommage permanent qui se manifeste tôt après la naissance.

Hémorragie intracrânienne

Étiologie. Les traumatismes crâniens se produisent souvent à la suite d'une dystocie fœto-maternelle, d'un travail prolongé, d'une présentation du siège, d'un accouchement précipité, ainsi que chez l'enfant porteur d'une maladie hémorragique. Le plus souvent *sous-durales* ou *sous-arachnoïdiennes* les hémorragies se produisent aussi au niveau du cerveau et des ventricules.

L'hémorragie intracrânienne constitue le type le plus fréquent et le plus grave d'accident obstétrical et se rencontre surtout chez le prématuré.

Diagnostic. Le diagnostic est basé sur une histoire obstétricale de travail et d'accouchement difficiles, et sur la hausse de la pression du L.C.R. du nourrisson. La présence d'éléments sanguins dans le liquide céphalorachidien n'est toutefois pas significative, car une hémorragie méningée minime se produit souvent lors de l'accouchement.

Manifestations cliniques. L'hémorragie intracrânienne est évidente dès la naissance ou se manifeste plus tard chez un nourrisson apparemment normal à la naissance. L'infirmière peut noter de la somnolence, de la léthargie, de l'irritabilité ou de l'agitation. On rencontre aussi de l'opisthotonos, une absence du réflexe de Moro, des spasmes musculaires et même des convulsions; le cri est aigu et perçant. Si les fonctions cardiaques et respiratoires sont perturbées, l'enfant est pâle et cyanosé; son irrégularité thermique est encore plus manifeste que chez le nouveau-né normal. Une hausse importante de la pression intracrânienne fera bomber les fontanelles et la paralysie peut apparaître en quelques jours.

Traitement. Le traitement donne quelquefois de très bons résultats. La chaleur et le repos sont essentiels et l'enfant est placé, en position Fowler, dans un incubateur pourvu d'une source d'oxygène. La vitamine K permet de contrôler l'hémorragie; les sédatifs, comme le phénobarbital, préviennent ou font cesser les crises convulsives et le médecin prescrit souvent des antibiotiques à titre prophylactique.

Il est évident que des soins obstétricaux suivis et éclairés, constituent la meilleure *prévention*.

Pronostic. Le pronostic, favorable dans la plupart des cas, inclut la possibilité de séquelles telles que le retard mental, la paralysie cérébrale ou une certaine tendance aux convulsions.

L'enfant mortellement atteint décède ordinairement avant la troisième journée de vie.

Soins. On place l'enfant dans un incubateur. L'absence ou la faiblesse des réflexes de succion et de déglutition rendent l'alimentation difficile. Pour prévenir les vomissements, on couche le bébé en position semi-Fowler, sur l'abdomen ou sur le côté droit, tout de suite après le repas, afin de faciliter le passage du

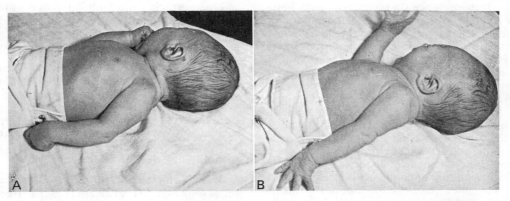

Figure 9-14. Paralysie du plexus brachial — bras gauche. *A)* Bras au repos. *B)* Réponse asymétrique au réflexe de Moro. (R. J. McKay, Junior et C. A. Smith, dans W. E. Nelson, *Textbook of Pediatrics*, 8e éd.)

liquide de l'estomac au duodénum. Il sera nécessaire d'utiliser un coussinet ou une couverture pliée, dans le dos de l'enfant, pour maintenir la position latérale.

Les convulsions sont toujours possibles. L'infirmière doit vérifier fréquemment les fontanelles et tenir prêt ce qui est nécessaire à l'injection d'un médicament anti-convulsif.

L'infirmière assiste le médecin quand il procède à une ponction lombaire ou à l'aspiration d'un hématome sous-dural.

Traumatismes nerveux périphériques

Paralysie du plexus brachial (Erb-Duchenne)

Un traumatisme au niveau de la cinquième et de la sixième paires de nerfs rachidiens, à la suite d'une manœuvre pour dégager le bras lors de l'expulsion, explique la paralysie du membre supérieur. Le bras malade est en adduction, extension et rotation interne avec pronation de l'avant-bras. La main et les

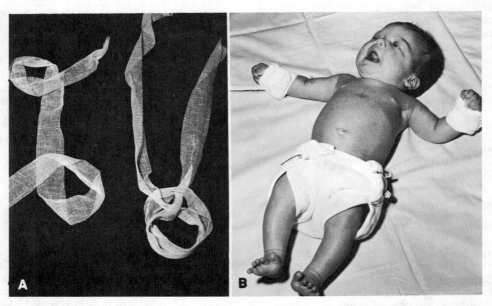

Figure 9-15. Contraintes aux poignets. *A)* On fait un 8 dans une bande de coton et on applique l'une sur l'autre les deux têtes du 8 en les inversant. *B)* Un coussinet protège le poignet. Le bandage ne doit pas être trop serré afin de ne pas entraver la circulation.

doigts ne sont pas atteints. Il n'y a pas de mouvements volontaires d'abduction ou de rotation externe du bras et de supination de l'avant-bras. Le réflexe de Moro est absent du côté malade et il peut même y avoir perte de sensibilité de la région latérale du bras.

Pour le traitement, le bras est immobilisé en position de repos, c'est-à-dire en abduction et rotation externe, le coude fléchi. Un appareil est quelquefois nécessaire; le physiothérapeute manipule et masse délicatement le membre pour éviter les contractures. Dans les cas graves, une neuroplastie peut s'avérer nécessaire.

L'infirmière applique les contraintes nécessaires pour maintenir la position de correction. La contrainte nécessite le matériel suivant: un bandage d'une largeur de 5 cm et de 1,35 m de longueur et un coussinet d'une largeur de 5 cm suffisamment long pour entourer le poignet de l'enfant. On fabrique la contrainte tel qu'indiqué à la figure 9-15. On attache l'extrémité du bandage à la tête du lit de façon à maintenir le bras dans la position désirée. Il faut observer la température et la coloration de la main et des doigts, et les signes d'irritation sous le coussinet protecteur. La contrainte doit être enlevée régulièrement de façon à mobiliser passivement le bras et à prévenir les blessures cutanées.

Il est évident que ces enfants ont besoin d'une attention toute particulière afin de pallier au manque de contact physique par un surplus d'amour et de tendresse.

Le pronostic est bon si la paralysie est due à une hémorragie ou à un œdème autour des fibres nerveuses et s'il n'y a pas de lacérations. La chirurgie ne doit être envisagée qu'après plusieurs mois d'évolution.

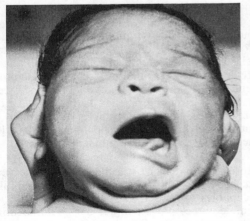

Figure 9-16. Paralysie faciale droite. (Davis et Rubin: *DeLee's Obstetrics for Nurses.* 17e éd.)

Paralysie du nerf facial

La paralysie apparaît à la suite d'une compression du nerf facial pendant le travail ou lors d'une application de forceps, étant donné que le nerf facial passe juste en avant de l'oreille. La paralysie est ordinairement unilatérale et les mouvements faciaux n'apparaissent que d'un seul côté lorsque l'enfant pleure. La bouche s'ouvre du côté opposé à la lésion et la paupière est entr'ouverte du côté atteint. La lésion guérit ordinairement en quelques semaines; une atteinte plus grave justifie la neuroplastie.

La succion difficile cause des problèmes d'alimentation et met la patience de l'infirmière à rude épreuve. On couvre souvent l'œil entrouvert d'un protecteur oculaire et l'on doit empêcher l'enfant de le déplacer. Celui-ci peut être pris et bercé comme tous les autres bébés.

Traumatismes osseux

Malgré l'étonnante flexibilité des os du nouveau-né, certaines fractures peuvent se produire à l'occasion d'un accouchement difficile. Elles surviennent surtout au crâne, à la clavicule ou aux os longs.

Il y a deux sortes de fractures du crâne: 1) linéaire, la plus fréquente, ne produit aucun symptôme et guérit sans traitement; 2) avec enfoncement, caractérisée par une dépression de la voûte osseuse; elle doit être traitée chirurgicalement, le plus tôt possible.

La fracture de la clavicule, la plus fréquente chez le nouveau-né, se produit quand la libération de l'épaule est difficile. L'examen révèle une limitation de mouvements et l'absence du réflexe de Moro du côté atteint. Le mouvement du bras est possible, si la fracture est du type « bois vert », fréquente chez les bébés et les jeunes enfants. Le pronostic est toujours excellent et le traitement se limite à l'immobilisation.

Les fractures des os longs, à moins qu'elles ne soient en « bois vert », rendent le mouvement impossible. Le traitement, pour les fractures des extrémités supérieures, consiste en l'immobilisation; les fractures des membres inférieurs sont corrigées par l'immobilité et la traction.

L'infirmière est responsable du maintien d'un bon alignement corporel, du soin des plâtres ou des tractions et de la prévention des points de pression. Si l'enfant est immo-

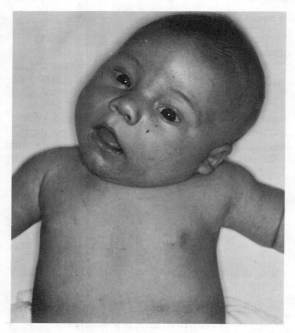

Figure 9-17. Torticolis congénital gauche. La tête penche vers le côté et le menton est tourné vers la droite. (Mihran O. Tachdjian, Ped. Cl. of North Am., mai 1967, p. 347.)

bilisé par une traction, les soins physiques et les marques de tendresse devront être adaptés à son état. L'allaitement au sein est évidemment impossible, mais si la mère le désire, l'extraction manuelle maintiendra la sécrétion lactée et l'enfant pourra profiter des avantages nutritifs du lait maternel.

Traumatisme au sterno-cléido-mastoïdien ou torticolis congénital

Environ 2 semaines après la naissance, on note la présence d'une petite masse au centre du muscle. De la grosseur d'une olive, cette masse peut être le résultat d'un hématome qui se serait produit au moment de la naissance ou d'une petite malformation du muscle lui-même. L'enfant pourra alors souffrir de *torticolis congénital,* une pathologie où la tête est inclinée en permanence. La majorité de ces « tumeurs » disparaissent avant l'âge d'un an, si un traitement adéquat est institué.

Le traitement consiste à étendre ou étirer le cou délicatement, en dirigeant la face du bébé du côté opposé au torticolis. On doit enseigner à la mère la bonne position à donner à son bébé. La manœuvre est répétée jusqu'à vingt fois de suite, deux ou trois fois par jour. La chirurgie peut être indiquée quand

l'enfant est âgé de deux ans et qu'il n'y a pas eu d'amélioration sensible.

Les soins sont adaptés à la limitation de mouvements dont souffre l'enfant; il faut lui parler beaucoup et le bercer avant et après les exercices musculaires. L'infirmière doit enseigner à la mère les exercices musculaires qui devront être faits à la maison.

PROBLÈMES RESPIRATOIRES

Les causes de détresse respiratoire sont nombreuses chez le nouveau-né, mais on les a classifiées ici en deux catégories principales qui en rendront l'étude plus facile.

1) Les détresses respiratoires d'origine centrale, causées par l'anoxie, l'hémorragie intracrânienne, les anomalies, les traumatismes ou la narcose;

2) Les difficultés respiratoires périphériques (hématose), causées par l'atélectasie, le syndrome de la membrane hyaline et la pneumonie.

Les pathologies qui viennent d'être énumérées ne seront pas toutes étudiées au cours de ce chapitre.

Anoxie du nouveau-né

Étiologie. L'anoxie est caractérisée par une insuffisance en oxygène qui touche toutes les cellules de l'organisme, principalement les cellules cérébrales. L'hypoxie précède l'anoxie: c'est la diminution du taux d'oxygène dans le sang. L'anoxie n'est pas une entité clinique, mais la manifestation d'une pathologie connue ou non identifiée.

L'anoxie est une cause importante de mort néonatale ou de dommage cérébral permanent qui se traduit par la paralysie cérébrale ou l'arriération mentale.

Variétés. L'anoxie fœtale, peut être due à toute cause qui diminue la concentration d'oxygène de la circulation sanguine maternelle ou fœtale et empêche l'oxygène d'atteindre le cerveau en quantité suffisante. L'anoxie peut être consécutive à une défaillance cardiaque ou circulatoire chez la mère; elle peut être causée par des obstacles au niveau de l'utérus ou du placenta ou par une obstruction mécanique du cordon ombilical.

L'anoxie post-natale, peut être due à toute cause qui limite l'arrivée d'oxygène au cerveau du bébé ou qui rend les cellules cérébrales incapables d'utiliser l'oxygène qu'elles reçoivent, comme, par exemple, dans l'intoxication aux barbituriques. L'état de choc et l'obstruction des voies respiratoires diminuent sérieusement l'oxygénation cérébrale. On rencontre une anoxie prolongée dans l'anémie grave, due à une hémorragie ou une maladie hémolytique et lorsque le sang est mal oxygéné, à cause d'une cardiopathie congénitale ou d'une malformation pulmonaire.

Manifestations cliniques. Il est extrêmement important que l'infirmière connaisse les signes d'anoxie du fœtus et du nouveau-né. L'anoxie fœtale se manifeste par une agitation anormale, suivie d'un calme subit. Le cœur fœtal ralentit et faiblit, ce qui commande l'institution immédiate de manœuvres destinées à provoquer l'accouchement.

Un liquide amniotique verdâtre, teinté de méconium, un vernix caseosa jaunâtre, la pâleur ou la cyanose du bébé, l'atonie musculaire ou la spasticité et un rythme cardiaque irrégulier signalent l'anoxie du nouveau-né.

Traitement. Le traitement est fonction du degré d'anoxie et de sa cause. La Nalline (Nalorphine), administrée par voie intraveineuse, combat la dépression respiratoire causée par l'administration de narcotiques à la mère pendant le travail. La respiration artificielle est inutile sans un minimum d'expansion pulmonaire.

Les moyens mécaniques comprennent la respiration bouche à bouche, l'administration d'oxygène à une pression modérée, par masque ou tube endotrachéal, le berceau automatique qui provoque un travail diaphragmatique passif. Voici la méthode de respiration bouche à bouche pour les nourrissons et les enfants, telle que recommandée par la Croix-rouge américaine:

Nettoyer la bouche de l'enfant de toute substance qui pourrait l'encombrer.

Coucher l'enfant sur le dos; tirer la machoire vers l'avant à l'aide des majeurs de chaque main; renverser la tête et la maintenir dans cette position avec une seule main. Couvrir entièrement la bouche et le nez de l'enfant avec la bouche du sauveteur et insuffler doucement jusqu'à ce que la poitrine de l'enfant se soulève. La main libre appuie délicatement entre le nombril et le sternum, empêchant l'arrivée de l'air dans l'estomac du bébé.

À la fin de chaque insufflation, le sauveteur enlève ses lèvres et laisse les poumons rejeter l'air qu'ils contiennent. Continuer la manœuvre, gardant continuellement une main sous la mâchoire et l'autre sur l'estomac. Le rythme idéal serait de vingt insufflations par minute, après lesquelles le sauveteur devrait se reposer quelques secondes, le temps nécessaire pour prendre une très bonne respiration.

On peut aussi ventiler le bébé à l'aide d'un masque à circuit semi-fermé fournissant de l'air ou de l'oxygène. L'insufflation pulmonaire doit alterner avec 3 ou 4 compressions cardiaques, au rythme normal pour un enfant de cet âge, selon la technique du massage cardiaque pour le nouveau-né. Chez le bébé plus vieux et chez le jeune enfant, la paume de la main droite appuie sur le sternum au niveau du 4e

espace intercostal. Quand l'enfant est assez vieux, la paume de la main gauche couvre celle de la main droite afin que le sauveteur se serve de la force de ses bras tendus et des muscles de ses épaules.

La colonne vertébrale doit toujours être bien appuyée et on place habituellement une planche de bois sous le dos de l'enfant. Le rythme normal de massage se situe aux environs de 100 battements à la minute pour un bébé et de 80 battements pour un enfant.

Chaque infirmière travaillant en pédiatrie devrait maîtriser la technique du massage cardiaque et de la ventilation puisqu'elles sont très souvent obligées de commencer les manœuvres de réanimation avant l'arrivée du médecin.

L'administration de gaz carbonique (CO_2) est dangereuse en l'absence d'une respiration spontanée. On injecte souvent, par voie intramusculaire, des stimulants comme la caféine ou le benzoate de sodium. Pour aider le bébé qui respire spontanément, un mélange de 95% d'oxygène et de 5% de CO_2 peut être administré toutes les heures, pendant une à deux minutes. L'enfant en détresse respiratoire est enveloppé dans une couverture chaude ou placé dans un incubateur. L'aspiration des sécrétions est indiquée mais en évitant d'irriter le pharynx et de provoquer une réaction vagale.

Pendant l'accouchement, les mesures préventives consistent à éviter l'abus d'analgésiques ou d'anesthésiques, à donner de l'oxygène à la mère pendant le deuxième stade du travail et à surveiller le rythme cardiaque fœtal. Après la naissance, il s'agit de maintenir les voies respiratoires libres de toute obstruction, d'administrer de l'oxygène si cela est nécessaire, de stimuler l'enfant et de le garder bien au chaud.

Atélectasie

Étiologie. Pendant la vie fœtale, le poumon est replié sur lui-même; l'expansion se produit au moment de la naissance avec les premières respirations du nouveau-né. Plusieurs jours sont parfois nécessaires pour obtenir l'expansion complète et tous les bébés qui meurent peu après la naissance, présentent de l'atélectasie à des degrés divers.

La pathologie est primaire, si la dilatation alvéolaire ne s'est pas produite. *L'atélectasie primaire* est très fréquente chez les prématurés et les bébés souffrant d'accidents cérébraux à la suite d'un accouchement difficile. *L'atélectasie peut être secondaire* à l'anoxie fœtale et néonatale, à la pneumonie et à la maladie des membranes hyalines.

Manifestations cliniques. Les symptômes d'atélectasie comprennent un cri faible et plaintif, une respiration rapide, irrégulière, superficielle, accompagnée de tirage intercostal et suprasternal et de battement des ailes du nez. La peau est marbrée; la cyanose, permanente ou intermittente, diminue si l'enfant pleure ou s'il reçoit de l'oxygène. L'auscultation révèle des râles fins et une diminution de la ventilation; les radiographies montrent une densité importante des plages pulmonaires.

Diagnostic. La bronchoscopie permet de poser le diagnostic et, si possible, de lever l'obstacle.

Traitement. Le débit d'oxygène doit être élevé et le taux d'humidité suffisant pour liquéfier les sécrétions et permettre au bébé de libérer ses voies respiratoires.

On stimule la respiration par l'administration d'un mélange d'oxygène (95%) et de gaz carbonique (5%) ou par l'injection intramusculaire de caféine ou de benzoate de sodium. La stimulation cutanée qui provoque les pleurs et les fréquents changements de position du bébé favorisent l'expansion pulmonaire. L'antibiothérapie préventive est de règle. Le traitement doit s'attacher à combattre la cause de l'atélectasie.

Même avec un *diagnostic* précoce et un traitement approprié, le pronostic est pauvre et la mortalité, élevée. La *prévention* inclut de bons soins prénatals aux gestantes, puisqu'on rencontre fréquemment cette pathologie chez les prématurés et chez les bébés dont la mère a subi un travail long et difficile.

Soins. L'infirmière recherche systématiquement les symptômes d'atélectasie chez les prématurés, chez les bébés dont la mère a eu une grossesse difficile, un accouchement compliqué ou une césarienne, chez les nouveaunés souffrant de traumatisme cérébral, de pneumonie ou autre affection respiratoire.

La chaleur de l'incubateur, l'oxygène et l'humidité aident l'enfant à franchir les moments difficiles. On aspire les sécrétions des voies respiratoires supérieures, si le besoin s'en fait sentir. On fait boire le bébé lentement et le gavage peut s'avérer nécessaire. Il faut éviter, à tout prix, la distension abdominale et l'infection qui pourraient être fatales. La planification des soins a pour but d'éviter toute fatigue à l'enfant.

Pneumonie

Étiologie. La pneumonie est responsable d'environ 10% des morts néonatales. À l'opposé de la pneumonie de l'adulte, elle est rarement lobaire et est causée par des virus ou des bactéries, telles l'entérocoque, le colibacille, le klebsiella, le pseudomonas, le proteus, le salmonella ou le staphylocoque.

Le contact avec l'agent infectieux se produit à l'accouchement ou après la naissance. Pen-

dant l'expulsion, l'aspiration de liquide amniotique ou de sécrétions vaginales infectées explique la contamination exogène. L'infection peut être endogène et provenir du courant sanguin. La mère ou l'infirmière, souffrant d'un simple rhume, peuvent être la cause d'une pneumopathie grave. Les infections cutanées à staphylocoque peuvent se compliquer de pneumonie chez le bébé qui résiste mal à n'importe quel type d'infection.

Manifestations cliniques. Le premier signe de pneumonie est une respiration rapide pouvant atteindre un rythme impossible à calculer avec exactitude. La détresse respiratoire se manifeste par le battement des ailes du nez. Le bébé est affaissé, pâle ou cyanosé, il présente de l'hypo ou de l'hyperthermie. Il refuse de s'alimenter et souffre de distension abdominale.

Traitement. L'oxygénothérapie soulage la détresse respiratoire et le médecin prescrit des antibiotiques à large spectre avant de connaître le résultat de l'antibiogramme. L'infection à staphylocoque réagit ordinairement bien à la bacitracine ou à une pénicilline semi-synthétique.

Broncho-pneumonie de déglutition

La broncho-pneumonie de déglutition est généralement précédée d'une crise de toux ou d'une suffocation chez un nouveau-né dont le réflexe de toux est encore faible. Les symptômes de broncho-pneumonie se précisent ensuite très rapidement. La technique d'alimentation est souvent directement responsable de l'accident et l'aspiration est très rare chez le bébé nourri au sein. Le nouveau-né ne maîtrise pas encore la coordination entre la succion et la déglutition, et il lui est plus facile de repousser le sein que la bouteille, si le lait coule trop vite dans sa bouche. L'orifice de la tétine ne doit pas être trop large et il faut laisser au bébé le temps d'avaler avant de continuer de le faire boire.

Si l'enfant suffoque et devient cyanosé, le traitement d'urgence consiste à le suspendre par les pieds ou du moins à le placer en position déclive pour permettre au liquide de refluer des bronches vers l'extérieur. Pour prévenir de tels épisodes, on couche l'enfant sur le côté droit ou sur l'abdomen après l'avoir fait boire; s'il régurgite, le liquide va glisser hors de la bouche et la suffocation sera évitée. De fréquentes éructations au cours de l'alimentation préviennent aussi la pneumonie de déglutition.

Il faut attendre au moins deux heures après l'avoir fait boire pour administrer des traitements comme la ponction de la veine jugulaire ou de la veine fémorale qui risque de perturber l'enfant et de provoquer des vomissements.

INFECTIONS NÉONATALES

L'ophtalmie purulente du nouveau-né, le muguet, la syphilis congénitale, la toxoplasmose et la maladie à inclusions cytomégaliques sont des infections qui se transmettent de la mère à l'enfant pendant ou après la grossesse.

L'ophtalmie purulente du nouveau-né (conjonctivite gonococcique)

Étiologie. On identifie *le gonocoque,* un diplocoque gram-négatif, ressemblant à deux haricots placés face à face, par un frottis ou une culture du liquide purulent qui coule des yeux du nouveau-né. Le contact avec les sécrétions vaginales infectées a lieu pendant l'expulsion. C'est une maladie à déclaration sanitaire obligatoire. On prévoit une augmentation du nombre de bébés atteint d'ophtalmie purulente, due à la hausse de l'incidence de la gonorrhée chez les adultes.

Manifestations cliniques. Les symptômes apparaissent deux à trois jours après la naissance, quelquefois même plus tôt, et consistent en une rougeur et un œdème des paupières et un écoulement purulent abondant.

La principale complication est l'ulcération de la cornée suivie d'une opacification qui cause une cécité partielle ou complète.

L'étendue des dégâts dépend de la durée et de la gravité de la maladie et du retard à entreprendre le traitement.

Traitement. La pénicilline est l'antibiotique de choix mais l'érythromycine, la chloromycine ou la tétracycline peuvent être administrées de façon systémique ou topique. L'isolement est strict et le traitement symptomatique consiste à nettoyer les yeux par des irrigations au soluté physiologique. Le traitement donne d'excellents résultats et l'ophtalmie purulente n'est plus, comme autrefois, une cause majeure de cécité pour l'enfant.

Soins. L'infirmière doit empêcher l'enfant de se frotter les yeux. Si un seul œil est atteint, on applique un protecteur sur l'autre pour éviter qu'il ne s'infecte également. On enlève régulièrement l'écoulement purulent par des irrigations; le liquide, à la température du corps, est instillé dans le récessus interne de la paupière inférieure, vers l'extérieur. L'enfant est maintenu à l'aide de contraintes ou par une infirmière qui l'empêche délicatement de bouger. Quand elle se penche sur l'enfant, l'infirmière doit faire attention de ne pas se contaminer. L'onguent ou les gouttes ophtalmiques ne sont administrés qu'après nettoyage de l'œil.

La meilleure prophylaxie est d'éviter la gonorrhée chez la mère. Ceci étant difficile à réaliser entièrement, un autre traitement préventif consiste à instiller du nitrate d'argent dans les yeux du nouveau-né, immédiatement après la naissance. Habituellement, à l'hôpital, on applique ce traitement à tous les bébés naissants, même s'il n'existe aucun danger de contamination par la mère.

Il est difficile d'instiller des gouttes dans les yeux d'un nouveau-né. L'infirmière doit être absolument certaine que le produit a été en contact avec la face interne des paupières. Le médicament cause quelquefois une légère irritation, mais la rougeur de l'œil et de la paupière disparaissent en quelques jours.

Le muguet ou moniliase orale

Étiologie. L'agent causal est le *Candida Albicans,* un champignon normalement présent dans le vagin et l'intestin, et qui existe aussi à l'état saprophyte dans la bouche des enfants et des adultes. Les champignons croissent sur la délicate muqueuse buccale de l'enfant, à la suite d'une contamination par une tétine mal stérilisée ou par le sein maternel. Chez le nourrisson plus âgé, le muguet peut apparaître à la suite d'une antibiothérapie vigoureuse.

Manifestations cliniques. La bouche de l'enfant est parsemée de taches blanchâtres, à l'aspect de lait caillé, qui adhèrent à la paroi buccale et laissent une lésion sanguinolente, si on les enlève. Ces lésions, surélevées, d'un blanc perlé, couvrent les côtés de la langue, l'intérieur des lèvres et des joues et le palais. Si l'infection est localisée à la bouche, l'anorexie constitue le seul symptôme systémique, bien que la dissémination du champignon puisse causer des infections pulmonaires ou digestives.

Le Mycostatin, l'antifungique de choix, s'applique sur les lésions buccales à l'aide de tiges montées. L'enfant peut avaler sans danger l'excès de médicament.

Une solution aqueuse de Violet de Gentiane à 1% ou de chlorure de Zéphiran, employée localement et selon les concentrations prescrites, donne des résultats moins spectaculaires. Le pronostic est généralement très bon et l'enfant guérit en trois ou quatre jours.

La prophylaxie est basée sur la propreté absolue de tout ce qui est porté à la bouche de l'enfant: sein maternel, tétine d'allaitement, applicateurs de coton, jouets et tétines d'amusement pour l'enfant plus âgé.

Ce qui a servi au repas de l'enfant atteint de muguet doit être stérilisé avant d'être retourné au laboratoire du lait. Il est recommandé dans ces cas, d'utiliser des ustensiles et des biberons à jeter après usage.

On doit quelquefois nourrir au compte-gouttes, l'enfant qui refuse de téter. On prévient la mère des difficultés qu'elle pourra rencontrer pour alimenter son bébé et de la teinte caractéristique produite par le violet de gentiane sur les muqueuses et sur la literie.

Il faut regarder chaque jour l'enfant qui reçoit une antibiothérapie massive pour déceler très tôt l'apparition des lésions. Si l'enfant souffre de malnutrition ou d'une maladie chronique, il devra recevoir un traitement approprié à son état.

La syphilis congénitale

Étiologie. L'agent causal de la syphilis est un spirochète, le *tréponème pâle* de Schaudinn. *La syphilis, congénitale et acquise, qui avait subi une baisse remarquable avec l'avènement des antibiotiques reprend progressivement du terrain depuis quelques années.* L'inoculation du fœtus se fait par voie transplacentaire, pendant la deuxième partie de la grossesse. Au moment de la naissance, la maladie a donc dépassé le stade primaire.

Manifestations cliniques. Plusieurs pathologies donnent des symptômes similaires à la syphilis, mais l'association de plusieurs symptômes d'une même catégorie, oriente vers ce diagnostic. Certains font leur apparition tôt après la naissance, d'autres se manifestent plus tardivement.

Les premiers symptômes apparaissent, en général, six semaines après la naissance, mais la précocité des symptômes est en relation directe avec la gravité de la maladie. Les symptômes suivants sont caractéristiques:

1) Une rhinite persistante, sous forme de coryza avec écoulement muco-purulent, quelquefois teinté de sang, irritant pour la lèvre supérieure.

2) Une éruption caractéristique, très prononcée sur le dos, les fesses et les cuisses, et qui atteint aussi la plante des pieds et la paume des mains.

3) Des ulcérations sanguinolentes et des lésions humides des muqueuses de la bouche, des lèvres, de l'anus et des organes génitaux.

4) L'anémie de l'enfant.

5) L'ostéochondrite et la périostite.

6) Les pseudo-paralysies et les fractures pathologiques.

7) L'hépatomégalie et la splénomégalie.

8) Il peut y avoir chorio-rétinite avec atrophie subséquente du nerf optique.

Les symptômes tardifs sont:

1) La destruction de la structure osseuse du nez qui devient caractéristique: creux ou plat au niveau de l'arête, il est relevé au bout, présentant l'aspect d'une selle.

2) La périostite des tibias déforme les os et donne des jambes en « sabre ».

3) Les dents de lait sont normales, mais les incisives permanentes présentent une encoche caractéristique et s'appellent « dents de Hutchinson ».

4) Les lésions syphilitiques précoces autour de la bouche et du nez forment des crevasses permanentes formées de tissu cicatriciel (rhagade).

5) La kératite interstitielle apparaît entre 6 et 12 ans et se manifeste par de la photophobie, du larmoiement, un malaise généralisé et des troubles visuels.

6) La neurosyphilis peut apparaître n'importe quand, entre 1 et 10 ans. Les symptômes en sont l'hémiplégie, la paralysie spasmodique et le retard mental; l'enfant parle lentement, il est irritable et affaissé.

Diagnostic. Les tests sérologiques confirment le diagnostic. Un prélèvement sanguin peut être fait n'importe quand, mais le sang du cordon, prélevé au moment de l'accouchement, peut être utilisé pour la réaction de Wasserman. Il ne faut toutefois pas oublier que les tests sérologiques de la syphilis sont peu significatifs chez le tout jeune bébé.

À l'âge de six mois, on considère comme probablement syphilitique, le bébé dont les tests de laboratoire sont positifs. En l'absence de manifestations cliniques, une seconde épreuve de laboratoire est cependant nécessaire pour confirmer le diagnostic. Un frottis des cellules des lésions humides peut révéler le *tréponème*.

Traitement. Le traitement immédiat de la syphilis congénitale apporte la guérison, suivie d'une croissance et d'un développement normaux. La syphilis congénitale tardive peut toujours être guérie, mais les séquelles en sont ineffaçables.

Il faut découvrir la syphilis chez la mère, si l'on veut éviter la syphilis congénitale. Un test sérologique, avant le mariage ou pendant la grossesse, permet le dépistage qui se fait aussi par l'examen physique obligatoire pour

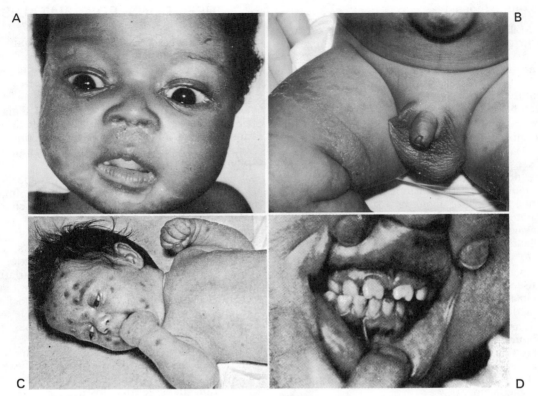

Figure 9-18. Syphilis congénitale. *A)* Coryza. (Courtoisie du Ralph V. Platou et de l'American Academy of Pediatrics.) *B)* Éruption à la face interne des cuisses. (Courtoisie de Luis Schut, M.D.) *C)* Éruption maculo-papulaire. (Katharine Dodd dans W. E. Nelson.) *D)* Dents de Hutchinson chez un enfant de 10 ans. (Katharine Dodd, dans W. E. Nelson.)

obtenir certains emplois et pour entrer dans l'armée. Les soins prénatals qui se généralisent de plus en plus, permettent aux mères syphilitiques d'être soignées avant la naissance du bébé. Le traitement précoce après la naissance empêche ou minimise les dégâts causés par la maladie.

Soins. La pénicilline par voie intramusculaire constitue le traitement de base. S'il existe une allergie à cet antibiotique, l'érythromycine ou une tétracycline peuvent servir de substituts. Après la guérison apparente de la maladie, la mère et le bébé subissent des analyses de routine pendant un certain temps.

Le nursing est basé sur la contagiosité de la maladie. Même si le tréponème exposé à l'air ne survit pas longtemps, il peut être transmis par contact direct et indirect. Présent dans l'écoulement nasal et les lésions cutanées, le tréponème envahit l'organisme par une lésion siégeant sur une muqueuse ou sur la peau. Dans plusieurs hôpitaux, les infirmières qui s'occupent des bébés syphilitiques portent des gants de caoutchouc et une blouse protectrice. Pendant la période aiguë de la maladie, on évite les épingles à ressort, cause possible de contamination directe.

Le coryza rend l'alimentation difficile. Avant de présenter le biberon, on enlève l'écoulement nasal et on nettoie les narines. La lèvre supérieure mérite une attention spéciale et une crème protectrice empêche l'excoriation. Les douleurs, causées par les lésions osseuses, peuvent rendre la manipulation du bébé difficile. L'obscurité de la chambre soulage l'enfant qui souffre de photophobie due à une kératite interstitielle; plus tard, les lunettes teintées seront utiles.

La syphilis congénitale est la preuve de la faillite du dépistage chez une patiente enceinte. C'est pourquoi, les infirmières en santé communautaire appuient sur la nécessité des examens et des soins prénatals, sur l'urgence et l'importance du traitement de la mère syphilitique et la poursuite du traitement des enfants atteints de la maladie.

Toxoplasmose

Maladie rare du système nerveux central, la toxoplasmose est causée par un protozoaire, *le toxoplasme.* L'enfant infecté *in utero* présente la forme infantile grave. La morti-natalité est fréquente, l'accouchement souvent prématuré. La forme acquise après la naissance présente moins de danger.

L'examen du fond de l'œil révèle une choriorétinite, inflammation simultanée de la rétine et de la choroïde. Il est possible de trouver des calcifications cérébrales, de l'hydrocéphalie, de la microcéphalie; le retard psychomoteur et les convulsions sont souvent présents. A la phase aiguë, la toxoplasmose évolue comme une encéphalite. On retrouve le toxoplasme dans le liquide céphalo-rachidien ou ailleurs dans l'organisme.

Le pronostic de la forme infantile est très mauvais. Si la toxoplasmose congénitale ne cause pas la mort en quelques jours ou semaines, la maladie peut régresser, mais au prix de terribles séquelles.

L'association d'un antagoniste de l'acide folique et d'un sulfamidé semble efficace, mais l'on doit procéder périodiquement à une numération des globules blancs, à cause de la leucopénie secondaire à l'administration de ces médicaments.

Le nursing a pour but de soulager les symptômes et de donner à l'enfant tout le confort souhaitable. L'infirmière qui connaît les symptômes et les complications possibles peut donner un rapport précis de ses observations.

Inclusions cytomégaliques

Cette maladie systémique causée par un virus des glandes salivaires et du tissu adénoïdien apparaît surtout chez le nouveau-né prématuré ou débile. La transmission transplacentaire explique l'atteinte au moment de la naissance. La forme légère guérit mais parfois laisse des séquelles; la forme grave conduit à la mort en quelques jours ou quelques mois.

Chez l'enfant gravement atteint on constate une hépato-splénomégalie, du porpura, un ictère important et des manifestations de l'atteinte du système nerveux central. Les convulsions, la microcéphalie, l'hydrocéphalie et la choriorétinite sont possibles. Si l'enfant survit, c'est au prix de séquelles neurologiques importantes accompagnées de retard mental et psychomoteur. Cliniquement, la maladie ressemble à la toxoplasmose. Le traitement est symptomatique et axé sur le confort de l'enfant.

INFECTIONS POST-NATALES

Les principaux micro-organismes qui peuvent atteindre le nouveau-né sont le colibacille et le staphylocoque. On rencontre fréquemment l'entérocoque, le klebsiella, le pseudomonas, le salmonella et le proteus.

Les infections les plus fréquentes dans les pouponnières sont celles de la peau et du cordon ombilical, la pneumonie et la septicémie. La diarrhée est toujours fréquente quoique plus rare qu'auparavant.

Le nouveau-né n'a pas de réaction spécifique à l'infection. C'est pourquoi, il est si important de faire part au médecin de tout changement même minime, dans l'état d'un nouveau-né.

Les signes suivants sont importants: cyanose, convulsions, affaissement, anorexie, vomissements, ictère et diarrhée. Les variations physiologiques de la thermorégulation empêchent de considérer automatiquement la fièvre comme un symptôme d'infection chez le bébé naissant. L'absence de fièvre n'est pas plus rassurante, puisqu'une infection grave ne cause pas toujours d'hyperthermie. La prématurité amplifie tous ces problèmes. Les analyses de laboratoire et la radiologie jouent un rôle prépondérant dans le diagnostic.

Les antibiotiques à large spectre permettent de commencer le traitement avant de connaître le résultat de la culture microbienne.

Infections causées par l'Escherichia Coli

L'escherichia coli, la cause la plus fréquente d'infection sérieuse chez le nouveau-né, est capable de produire une septicémie, une pneumonie, une méningite et une entérite. La Néomycine est l'antibiotique de choix contre les infections intestinales; les infections systémiques sont traitées à la Kanamycine.

Infections dues au staphylocoque doré

Le staphylocoque doré, un coccus grampositif, constitue la deuxième cause d'infection néo-natale. Son incidence augmente actuellement dans les pouponnières et plusieurs souches ont développé une résistance aux principaux antibiotiques.

L'infection initiale se produit pendant le séjour à l'hôpital, mais peut apparaître des semaines ou des mois plus tard; on voit ainsi l'importance des visites de nourrissons dans les cliniques et chez les pédiatres. Malgré les précautions prises, l'infection qui se produit chez un seul bébé peut contaminer tous les occupants de la pouponnière. La mère qui allaite peut souffrir de mastite secondaire. La contamination s'étend souvent aux autres membres de la famille, lorsque le nouveau-né contaminé revient chez lui.

La peau constitue habituellement le substrat de contamination initiale. Le naso-pharynx, le cordon ombilical, une myéloméningocèle ou la plaie de circoncision peuvent servir de point de départ à une pneumonie, une septicémie ou une gastro-entérite à staphylocoque. La septicémie se complique quelquefois d'ostéomyélite ou de méningite.

Les infirmières, les puéricultrices, le personnel d'entretien ou la mère d'un bébé peuvent être la cause d'une infection qui se propage ensuite très facilement.

Le traitement systémique consiste en l'emploi d'antibiotiques spécifiques comme la bacitracine ou les pénicillines semi-synthétiques anti-staphylococciques. L'antibiothérapie prophylactique risque de créer de nouvelles souches résistantes et devrait, de ce fait, être évitée.

Les lésions cutanées sont lavées au savon ordinaire à base d'hexachlorophène et rincées à l'eau stérile. On applique un onguent antibiotique; le drainage chirurgical des abcès peut s'avérer nécessaire.

On ne peut surestimer l'importance de la prévention. On devrait d'abord interdire l'accès de la pouponnière ou du post-partum à toute personne porteuse d'une lésion cutanée. La mère infectée et son bébé devraient être isolés. Le matériel servant aux soins de chaque bébé devrait lui être réservé et tout le personnel doit se laver les mains avant et après avoir touché le bébé ou sa literie. Tous les objets servant aux soins du bébé, tels la pesée, les berceaux, etc. doivent être désinfectés tous les jours et il est recommandé de tenir fermées les portes des pouponnières.

On admet peu de bébés dans chacune des chambres, car la surpopulation des salles est un facteur important d'infection croisée. Toutes les salles devraient être complètement vidées et décontaminées à intervalles réguliers. Un roulement d'admission et de départ des nouveau-nés devrait être planifié, afin de permettre la libération périodique de chaque salle (environ tous les 6 ou 7 jours).

Au début d'une épidémie, il est d'usage d'isoler les nouveaux patients et de renforcer les techniques d'isolement. On ouvre une autre pouponnière pour recevoir les bébés nés par la suite et n'ayant pas été contaminés. Tout l'équipement est brossé et, si possible, stérilisé. On lave les murs, le plafond, le plancher et le mobilier. On procède à une culture des sécrétions nasales et pharyngées de tout le personnel et on insiste sur l'importance d'avoir un personnel régulier au service de la pouponnière. Comme mesure supplémentaire, un antibiotique spécifique est donné à tous les bébés ayant été en contact avec l'épidémie, même s'ils ne présentent pas de symptôme et ce, pendant toute la durée de leur séjour dans cette pouponnière. A mesure que les chambres se vident, une fumigation de chaque salle et de tout son contenu permet de recevoir les futurs nouveau-nés dans un environnement sain. Une telle épidémie est un des plus graves dangers que l'on puisse rencontrer dans une pouponnière.

L'impétigo du nouveau-né

L'impétigo est une maladie de la première enfance causée parfois par l'envahissement des couches superficielles de la peau par le staphylocoque, mais surtout par le streptocoque. Fréquent chez le nouveau-né, l'impétigo peut facilement contaminer tous les enfants d'une pouponnière; il est encore plus fréquent chez les enfants un peu plus âgés.

Les papules érythémateuses font d'abord leur apparition, suivies de vésicules molles et plissées dont le liquide devient purulent. Entourées d'une zone érythémateuse, les pustules se fendillent et une croûte apparaît. Les lésions siègent aux endroits humides ou dans les plis cutanés et durent environ 2 semaines. Les symptômes généraux sont rares.

Le traitement consiste à dénuder les lésions à l'aide d'éponges alcoolisées et à les assécher par la chaleur. On lave les régions atteintes avec un savon antiseptique. L'onguent de Bacitracine ou de Néomycine en application locale et l'antibiothérapie systémique peuvent compléter le traitement.

Jadis l'impétigo était une infection dangereuse qui conduisait à la septicémie et au pemphigus, aujourd'hui grâce aux antibiotiques le pronostic est bon. Les lésions superficielles guérissent sans cicatrice. Une technique d'isolement strict devrait prévenir son apparition et sa dissémination à la pouponnière.

La furonculose

La furonculose, causée par le staphylocoque, peut se produire à n'importe quel âge de l'enfance; elle est beaucoup plus dangereuse chez le nouveau-né sous-alimenté. Les furoncles apparaissent le plus souvent au cuir chevelu; le dos et les extrémités peuvent être atteints.

Le furoncle est une inflammation circonscrite de la peau, siégeant au niveau de l'appareil

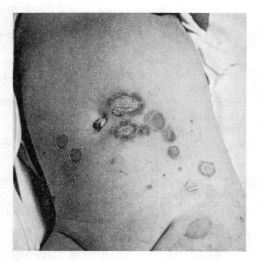

Figure 9-19. Impétigo du nouveau-né. (R. J. Mc-Kay, Junior et C. A. Smith. *Textbook of Pediatrics* — W. Nelson. 8e éd.)

pilo-sébacé. Il est caractérisé par une tuméfaction coiffée d'un bourbillon. Une série de furoncles constitue une furonculose. Très rarement, des cas graves d'anorexie et de toxémie peuvent se produire.

L'antibiothérapie spécifique dépend de la souche pathogène retrouvée par une enquête épidémiologique dans la famille. Un lavage quotidien à l'aide d'un savon antiseptique et une application locale d'un onguent de Néomycine-bacitracine dans les narines, sous les ongles et à la région périanale, préviennent la dissémination de l'infection. Des compresses chaudes hâtent la maturation du furoncle et favorisent le drainage après l'ouverture spontanée ou l'incision du bourbillon.

La diète est basse en glucides et riche en vitamines. L'hydratation doit être suffisante pour maintenir la balance hydro-électrolytique.

Les techniques aseptiques de routine assurent la protection des pouponnières. Pendant les chaudes températures de l'été, on varie souvent la position de l'enfant afin d'empêcher l'érosion de la peau par l'humidité.

Si un nouveau-né a un furoncle, il doit être isolé immédiatement. Au premier signe de lésion, la peau doit être nettoyée avec soin et les cheveux seront rasés si c'est nécessaire. Il faut quelquefois appliquer des moyens de contraintes ou mettre des mitaines à l'enfant pour l'empêcher de toucher à ses lésions. La plus petite lésion cutanée peut servir de porte d'entrée à la contamination chez ceux qui prennent soin de ce bébé.

La diarrhée épidémique

Aucune cause unique n'a encore été incriminée dans la diarrhée infectieuse du nouveau-né, mais de multiples agents causals sont connus, tels des souches virulentes d'escherichia coli ou certains virus causant habituellement des infections respiratoires chez l'adulte. La diarrhée est hautement contagieuse et l'isolement le plus strict est essentiel.

Les aliments peuvent servir de véhicule à l'infection, mais on oublie trop souvent que les mains des adultes (mère, infirmières, puéricultrices) contiennent une foule de microbes auxquels ceux-ci sont résistants et qui s'avèrent très dangereux pour le très jeune enfant n'ayant pas développé suffisamment de défenses. Même le plus rigoureux lavage ne peut stériliser les mains mais il peut éliminer presque complètement cette source de contamination.

Les selles liquides, fréquentes, expulsées avec force sont caractéristiques de la maladie. L'enfant présente de la distension abdominale, il refuse de s'alimenter et vomit le peu qu'il ingurgite. L'hyperthermie est fréquente et la perte de poids est fonction de la perte de liquide qui, si elle est excessive, provoque la déshydratation et le déséquilibre hydro-électrolytique. L'acidose fait son apparition si un traitement n'est pas institué dans les plus brefs délais.

Le traitement de la diarrhée du nouveau-né est le même que chez le nourrisson. L'unité d'obstétrique doit être fermée et les mères dirigées vers un autre hôpital, à moins qu'une autre section de l'hôpital soit ouverte aux nouveaux bébés et que les infirmières qui en prennent soin n'aient eu aucun contact avec les bébés malades. Si l'agent causal est une souche provenant de l'intestin, la Néomycine est l'antibiotique de choix.

Le remplacement hydrique et électrolytique par voie parentérale permet l'amélioration de l'état général touché par la déshydratation. La diarrhée infectieuse doit être rapportée aux autorités sanitaires. Le taux de mortalité peut varier entre 25 et 45%.

La responsabilité des infirmières de la pouponnière est essentielle pour prévenir et contrôler la diarrhée infectieuse. La technique d'isolement est théorique et seule la conscience professionnelle de toutes les personnes qui s'occupent du bébé peut éviter la contamination. La routine fait quelquefois oublier le danger et les principes de technique préventive devraient être l'objet de fréquents rappels lors des réunions d'équipe. C'est la personne directement responsable du bébé qui notera la première selle liquide, contenant peut-être du mucus; c'est elle qui remarquera l'anorexie, les vomissements et la hausse de la température. Un prélèvement de selles pour la culture et l'antibiogramme ainsi que l'isolement du bébé sont de routine dans plusieurs hôpitaux, avant même d'avertir le médecin de l'état du nouveau-né.

L'infirmière suit les ordonnances générales codifiées pour une telle situation et le médecin complète en spécifiant les solutés intraveineux qui pourraient être nécessaires.

Chaque selle doit être suivie d'un changement de couche, après lavage, rinçage et asséchage complet de la peau fragile du bébé. Si l'irritation causée par la diarrhée est importante et si la chaleur de la pièce le permet, on peut laisser le siège de l'enfant à l'air libre et le placer sur une ou plusieurs couches ou piqués. En certains cas, une ampoule électrique suspendue au-dessus du lit ou un arceau couvert permet de garder l'enfant au chaud, sans qu'il soit nécessaire de le couvrir.

On dépose les couches souillées dans un panier ou un sac spécial, portant la mention « contaminé » et que les employés de la buanderie identifieront facilement. L'idéal serait l'emploi de couches jetables pour tous les enfants présentant des selles diarrhéiques.

Infection ombilicale

L'escherichia coli ou le staphylocoque cause ordinairement l'infection ombilicale, mais d'autres organismes pathogènes ont aussi été incriminés. La rougeur et l'humidité constituent les premiers signes d'une infection qui peut être bénigne ou grave, mais dont il ne faut jamais minimiser l'importance, surtout si une odeur putride s'en dégage. L'enfant peut guérir rapidement mais on doit redouter la septicémie, toujours possible dans les infections purulentes. L'infection tétanique, plus rare, est très souvent mortelle.

Le *traitement* consiste en l'administration immédiate d'antibiotiques à large spectre, avant même l'obtention du résultat de la culture. On conseille les bains au savon antiseptique et le badigeonnage du cordon à la teinture antiseptique. La formation d'un abcès appelle l'incision et le drainage.

La septicémie néonatale

La septicémie peut avoir pour origine tout organisme pathogène qui pénètre dans le courant sanguin par la peau, les muqueuses, les voies respiratoires et gastro-intestinales, l'ombilic, la plaie de circoncision ou tout autre blessure. La contamination peut avoir lieu avant, pendant ou après la naissance.

Les symptômes de la septicémie néonatale sont très variables. Le diagnostic est posé à partir des modifications de l'état général, mais les analyses de laboratoire, surtout l'hémoculture et les cultures des sécrétions des voies respiratoires, s'avèrent essentielles.

Les symptômes sont soudains ou insidieux; l'enfant paraît d'abord affaissé ou agité et anorexique; la lenteur du gain de poids précède la déshydratation et l'émaciation. On rencontre des vomissements et de la diarrhée. La température du bébé s'élève et le nombre de globules blancs peut être élevé, abaissé ou normal. On rencontre quelquefois des convulsions, de l'ictère et de l'hépato-splénomégalie.

Traitement. Le traitement immédiat consiste à administrer des doses massives d'antibiotiques à large spectre, en attendant le résultat des cultures qui permettront de déterminer le médicament le plus efficace contre le microorganisme responsable de la maladie. L'enfant est isolé et l'incubateur permet de l'observer et de contrôler adéquatement la température, l'humidité et l'administration d'oxygène. Les solutés et l'oxygène peuvent être nécessaires, de même qu'une transfusion sanguine.

Diagnostic. Le diagnostic précoce et l'institution immédiate du traitement intensif ont contribué à abaisser le taux de mortalité. Le foyer d'infection peut être au niveau des méninges, du périnée ou ailleurs. La bactériémie ne laisse aucun organe à l'abri d'une contamination possible. La méningite suscite des convulsions; l'hydrocéphalie et des signes de retard mental apparaissent parfois par la suite.

Soins. Les techniques aseptiques de la salle d'accouchement ou de la pouponnière assurent la meilleure sauvegarde contre la septicémie néo-natale et les membres du personnel de ces services devraient se faire un devoir de signaler immédiatement aux autorités, le plus petit signe d'infection qui pourrait se présenter. Dans les hôpitaux modernes, il semble bien que la plus grande cause d'infection du nouveau-né soit les porteurs non connus de bactéries pathogènes au niveau des voies respiratoires.

Il faut observer attentivement le bébé pour déceler le moindre signe d'infection, car les symptômes de septicémie sont vagues et les chances de guérison diminuent rapidement, si la maladie reste trop longtemps inaperçue.

Le tétanos néonatal

Étiologie. Le *clostridium tétani* ou bacille de Nicolaïer, un bacille à spore, gram-positif et anaérobique, pénètre dans l'organisme par une lésion qui saigne peu. L'immunisation anti-tétanique a diminué considérablement le risque de contamination dans la population infantile.

Incidence. Le tétanos néonatal est extrêmement rare en Amérique du Nord et est peu susceptible de se produire dans les hôpitaux, car le bacille vit dans le sol qu'il contamine. Il se transmet quand les mains de la personne qui assiste la parturiente ont été mal lavées ou que le couteau servant à couper le cordon a été en contact avec la terre contaminée. Le bacille pénètre directement dans l'organisme par le cordon ombilical et se développe dans un milieu privé d'air libre.

Manifestations cliniques. La *période d'incubation* varie de 5 jours à plusieurs semaines. Plus les symptômes apparaissent rapidement, plus la maladie est grave. Le départ de l'hôpital est ordinairement fixé au cinquième jour de vie et il est évident que les premiers symptômes apparaîtront quand l'enfant sera à la maison. Les conditions de contamination étant aussi inusitées, il est fort probable que la naissance ait eu lieu à domicile.

L'endotoxine tétanique produit des effets toxiques sur le système nerveux. L'enfant est irritable et agité. Le trismus l'empêche d'ouvrir la bouche et de sucer; sa mâchoire est serrée et il ne peut avaler. Il présente un « rictus sardonique », à cause de la tension spastique exercée sur les muscles faciaux. Son expression est tirée, ses yeux apeurés; la raideur de la nuque constitue un indice précoce et révélateur. L'opisthotonos, contracture généralisée, cou replié vers l'arrière, est le résultat d'une tension excessive sur les muscles du corps. Les convulsions sont fréquentes et douloureuses, déclenchées à la moindre stimulation visuelle, auditive ou tactile. La température atteint facilement 40°C; les globules blancs varient entre 8 000 et 12 000/mm³ et on constate une hausse modérée de la tension du liquide céphalo-rachidien.

Traitement et soins. Le tétanos ne se transmet pas de personne à personne, aussi n'est-il pas nécessaire d'isoler l'enfant. On peut le faire pour lui assurer de meilleurs soins, car la présence constante de l'infirmière est essentielle pour assurer le succès de la thérapie. L'enfant reçoit d'abord de l'antitoxine au point d'inoculation et ensuite de façon systémique pour neutraliser la toxine circulante. Avant l'administration de l'antitoxine, il fallait autrefois procéder au test de sensibilité, afin d'éviter une réaction au sérum de cheval, base de l'antitoxine. Il existe actuellement des préparations beaucoup moins allergènes et dangereuses, d'origine humaine, et on les emploie de plus en plus.

L'administration continue de sédatifs permet de garder l'enfant semi-conscient et détendu; il faut éviter toute stimulation qui n'est pas absolument nécessaire. Les soins de nursing coïncident avec les traitements et on touche le moins possible à l'enfant. Il faut, malgré tout, aspirer les sécrétions, donner de l'oxygène, prendre soin de la trachéotomie, si l'enfant en a eu besoin. On peut même être obligé de le placer sous respiration assistée. Les gavages suffisent pour l'alimentation et l'hydratation se fait par voie intraveineuse. Le dosage des ingesta et excréta est de rigueur. La prévention du tétanos consiste en un plus grand effort d'éducation, afin d'éviter la contamination des bébés, lorsque la naissance se produit à domicile.

Le taux de mortalité atteint 50% et la mort survient à la suite d'une insuffisance respiratoire, une fatigue extrême ou une broncho-pneumonie d'aspiration. La guérison est toutefois complète et sans séquelle si l'enfant réussit à survivre.

INTOXICATION NÉONATALE

Incidence, étiologie et manifestations cliniques. Puisque l'incidence de l'accoutumance aux drogues, telles que la morphine, l'héroïne et la méthadone a augmenté parmi les adultes, il se trouve un plus grand nombre de bébés nés de mères intoxiquées.

Le bébé souffrant d'intoxication néonatale présente des symptômes d'irritation du système nerveux central, tels que la trémulation, une hyperréflexie, l'irritabilité et un comportement perturbé. Le cri de ces bébés est perçant, il ressemble à celui des enfants dont le système nerveux est atteint. Le bébé a beaucoup de sécrétions, de la diarrhée et des vomissements. La perte de poids à la naissance est plus importante que normalement; le nouveau-né semble affamé, mais suce avec difficulté. Puisque ces symptômes peuvent apparaître chez n'importe quel bébé, il faut observer attentivement la mère du nouveau-né et essayer de découvrir les marques de toxicomanie: traces de piqûres aux extrémités, cellulite, thrombophlébite et signes de sevrage. Les symptômes du bébé intoxiqué peuvent survenir le premier jour de vie ou 3 à 4 jours après la naissance.

Pour que le diagnostic soit précoce, il faut prélever un échantillon de sang à la naissance puisque les traces sanguines de la drogue disparaissent rapidement du courant sanguin.

Traitement et soins infirmiers. Les médicaments les plus efficaces contre ces drogues sont le phénobarbital et la chlorpromazine. Le parégorique peut diminuer la diarrhée. Il faut éviter de manipuler le bébé à cause de l'hyper-excitabilité du système nerveux. L'emploi de liquides intraveineux peut s'avérer nécessaire pour corriger la déshydratation et le déséquilibre électrolytique.

RÉFÉRENCES

Livres et documents officiels

Abramson, H. (édit.): *Resuscitation of the Newborn Infant.* 3e éd. Saint-Louis, C. V. Mosby Company, 1973.

Abramson, H. (édit.): *Symposium on the Functional Physiopathology of the Fetus and Neonate: Clinical Correlations.* Saint-Louis, C. V. Mosby Company, 1971.

Avery, M. E. *The Lung and Its Disorders in the Newborn Infant.* 2e éd. Philadelphie, W. B. Saunders Company, 1968.

Charles A. G. et Friedman, E. A. (édit.): *Rh Isoimmunization and Erythroblastosis Fetalis.* New York, Appleton-Century-Crofts, 1969.

Korones, S. B.: *High Risk Newborn Infants − The Basis for Intensive Care.* Saint-Louis, C. V. Mosby Company, 1972.

Laboratoires Ross: *Obstructions du tube digestif chez le nourrisson* (feuillet no 4). *La détresse respiratoire chez le nouveau-né* (feuillet no 6). *Érythroblastose fœtale* (feuillet no 9). Section de l'éducation en nursing, Columbus, Ohio.

Lorrain, J.: *Notions pratiques sur l'érythroblastose foetale.* Mead Johnson, Québec, 1970.

Pierog, S. H. et Ferrara, A.: *Approach to the Medical Care of the Sick Newborn.* Saint-Louis, C. V. Mosby Company, 1971.

Rickham, P. P. et Johnston, J. H.: *Neonatal Surgery.* New York, Appleton-Century-Crofts, 1969.

Smith, D. W.: *Recognizable Patterns of Human Malformation.* Philadelphie, W. B. Saunders Company, 1970.

Articles

Allen, R. G.: Silon as Sac in Treatment of Omphalocele and Gastroschisis. *J. Pediat. Surg.,* 4:3, février 1969.

Amiel-Tison, C.: Dépistage des urgences abdominales chez le nouveau-né. *La revue de l'inf.,* 24:811, septembre 1974.

Auld, P.: Resuscitation of the Newborn Infant. *Am. J. Nursing,* 74:68, mai 1974.

Bang, J., et Northeved, A.: A New Ultrasonic Method for Transabdominal Amniocentesis. *Am. J. Obst. & Gynec.,* 114:599, 1er novembre 1972.

Bensabel, H., et Gross, P.: Omphalocèle. *La médecine infantile,* 76:757, 9, 1969.

Bensabel, H.: Perspectives actuelles du diagnostic et du traitement de l'atrésie de l'oesophage. *La médecine infantile,* 76:723, 9, 1969.

Boreau, TH. et autres: Maladie hémolytique du nouveau-né. *La médecine infantile,* 77:439, 6, 1970.

Bowman, J. M., et autres: Fetal Transfusion in Severe Rh Isoimmunization. *J.A.M.A.,* 207:1101, 10 février 1969.

Chappuis, J. J., et autres: Accidents mécaniques du diverticule de Meckel. *Pédiatrie,* XXIV:169, 2, 1969.

Delaitre, R., et autres: Méningites purulentes du nouveau-né. *La médecine infantile,* 77:65, 2, 1970.

Dommergues, J. P.: Incompatibilités sanguines fœto-maternelles. *Soins,* 17:7, mars 1972.

Dommergues, J. P.: Les ictères du nouveau-né. *Soins,* 19:5, juin 1974.

Duhamel, J. F., et autres: Diagnostic radiologique des occlusions intestinales néonatales. *La revue de pédiatrie,* 10:411, juillet 1974.

Finnigan, L., et Mac New, B.: Care of the Addicted Infant. *Am. J. Nursing,* 74:685, avril 1974.

Gregory, G.: Respiratory Care of Newborn Infants. *Ped. Clin. N. Amer.,* 19:311, 2, 1972.

Haller, J. A.: The Scope and Purpose of Pediatric Surgery. *Surgical Clinics,* 50:755, 4, 1970.

Hernial Mass Reduction « In the Bag ». *J.A.M.A.,* 207:483, 20 janvier 1969.

Hey, E. N., et autres: Heat Losses from Babies During Exchange Transfusion. *Lancet,* 1:335, 15 février 1969.

Humphrey, N. M., Wright, P., et Swanson, A.: Parenteral Hyperalimentation for Children. *Am. J. Nursing,* 72:286, février 1972.

Ingelrans, P.: Atrésie de l'oesophage. *Pédiatrie,* XXIV:563, 5, 1969.

Khanna, N., Stein, L., et McLeod, P.: Nouvelles méthodes de traitement de l'hyperbilirubinémie du nouveau-né. *Union méd. du Can.*, 100:506, mars 1971.

Kitterman, J. A., Phibbs, R. H., et Tooley, W. H.: Catheterization of Umbilical Vessels in Newborn Infants. *Pediat. Clin. N. Amer.*, 17:895, novembre 1970.

Lucey, J.: Neonatal Jaundice and Phototherapy. *Ped. Clin. N. Amer.*, 19:827, 4, 1972.

Maisels, M.: Bilirubin: On Understanding and Influencing Its Metabolism in the Newborn Infant. *Ped. Clin. N. Amer.*, 19:447, 2, 1972.

Martin, Cl., et Bildstein, G.: Modifications de l'équilibre acido-basique accompagnant l'exsanguino-transfusion. *Pédiatrie*, XXIV:5, 1, 1969.

McCracken, G. H., et autres: Congenital Cytomegalic Inclusion Disease. *Am. J. Dis. Child*, 117:522, mai 1969.

Michener, W. M., et Law, D.: Parenteral Nutrition: The Age of the Catheter. *Pediat. Clin. N. Amer.*, 17:373, mai 1970.

Nathenson, G., et autres: The Effect of Maternal Heroin Addiction on Neonatal Jaundice. *J. Pediat.*, 81:899, novembre 1972.

Picard, J. L.: La détresse respiratoire et les soins néo-nataux. *Union méd. du Can.*, 98:1724, octobre 1969.

Pinon, F.: Prévention de l'incompatibilité foeto-maternelle. *La revue de l'inf.*, 2:525, juin 1972.

Ploussard, J. P. et Lestradet, H.: Bilirubine, hyperbilirubinémie, ictère nucléaire. *La revue de pédiatrie*, 6:3, 1, 1970.

Queenan, J. T., et autres: Role of Induced Abortion in Rhesus Immunization. *Lancet*, 1:815, 24 avril 1971.

Regnier, C.: Néonatalogie. *Médecine infantile*, 82, 2, 1975 (numéro spécial).

Roberts, J. E.: Suctioning the Newborn. *Am. J. Nursing*, 73:43, janvier 1973.

Rodman, M. J.: Drugs for Treating Tetanus. *RN*, 34:43, décembre 1971.

Rothstein, P., et Gould, J.: Born with a Habit. *Ped Clin. N. Amer.*, 21:467, 2, 1974.

Sinclair, J. C. et autres: Supportive Management of the Sick Neonate: Parenteral Calories, Water, and Electrolytes. *Pediat. Clin. N. Amer.*, 17:863, novembre 1970.

Stern, L.: The Use and Misuse of Oxygen in the Newborn Infant. *Ped. Clin. N. Amer.*, 20:447, 2, 1973.

Stephen, D.: Embryologic and Functional Aspects of Imperforate Anus. *Surgical Clinics*, 50:919, 4, 1970.

Tort-Grumbach, J.: Détresse respiratoire. *Soins*, 19:23, juin 1974.

Touraine, R.: Syphilis congénitale. *La revue de pédiatrie*, 6:357, 6, 1970.

Van Eys, J: Recent Progress in Genetic Hemolytic Disorders: A Practical Approach. *Pediat. Clin. N. Amer.*, 17:449, mai 1970.

Waechter, E.: Birth of an Exceptional Child. *Nursing Forum*, 9:203, 4, 1970.

Williams, S. L.: Phototherapy in Hyperbilirubinemia. *Am. J. Nursing*, 71:1397, juillet 1971.

10 pathologies du nouveau-né nécessitant des soins de longue durée

MALFORMATIONS CONGÉNITALES

De nombreuses anomalies congénitales nécessitent des soins de plusieurs semaines, mois ou années. Les affections de longue durée, telles certaines anomalies métaboliques, qui ne sont pas couramment diagnostiquées durant les tout premiers jours de la vie, seront discutées dans des chapitres ultérieurs. Pour les anomalies traitées dans ce chapitre l'intervention chirurgicale précoce sera en général recommandée. Le risque opératoire doit être soupesé en fonction des avantages qui résulteront de l'intervention. Il est difficile pour les parents d'être objectifs en prenant une décision pour ou contre l'opération. Avant que celle-ci n'ait lieu, ils devraient être persuadés que leur décision est bonne, et que les avantages ultérieurs en justifient le risque, de sorte que si l'enfant vient à mourir, au cours ou à la suite de cette intervention, ils ne se considèrent pas coupables de l'avoir autorisée.

Lésions cutanées

Les nævi chez le nouveau-né sont de deux types: a) le groupe vasculaire dû à une hyperplasie des vaisseaux sanguins (hémangiomes) ou des vaisseaux lymphatiques (lymphangio-

mes); b) les nævi non vasculaires causés par une prolifération du tissu conjonctif ou épidermique. Le facteur héréditaire semble important.

Nævus vasculaire ou angiome simple. L'angiome simple, communément appelé *tache de naissance*, est entièrement composé de vaisseaux sanguins. Ces taches, généralement plates et localisées à l'occiput, sur les paupières ou le front, ne requièrent aucun traitement; la plupart du temps, elles disparaissent spontanément.

L'angiome appelé « *tache de vin* » est plat, de forme irrégulière et apparaît souvent sur le côté du visage. Légèrement rosée chez le nouveau-né, cette tache devient éventuellement violet foncé. Due à une malformation des capillaires superficiels, elle résiste au traitement local. Elle peut être enlevée par intervention chirurgicale ou par irradiation, mais seulement par un spécialiste de ce genre de traitement. Plusieurs conseillent un traitement conservateur associé à l'utilisation de fard.

Une lésion petite ou très pâle, qui semble similaire à ces taches sur le visage, peut apparaître sur la nuque, la racine du nez ou sur les paupières. Ces lésions, contrairement à celles de la face, disparaissent sans traitement.

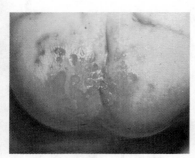

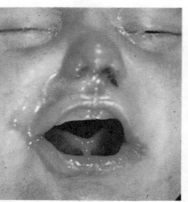

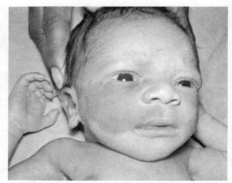

1. Syphilis. Lésions maculo-papulaires de la région périanale. (U.S. Department of Health, Education and Welfare.)

2. Rhinite et coryza de bébé syphilitique. (U.S. Department of Health, Education and Welfare.)

3. Tache de vin située sur le territoire du trijumeau. (Extrait de Hodgmann, J.E., Freedman, R.I., Levan, N.E., *Ped Clin. N. Amer.* 18 (3): planche 1, août 1971.)

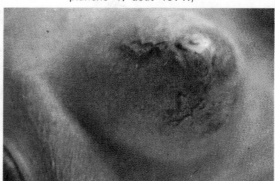

4. Tache de fraise : néo-capillaires, excessivement dilatés, des couches superficielles de la peau associés à une hypertrophie du tissu conjonctif. (Courtoisie des Laboratoires Mead Johnson.)

5. Hémangiome caverneux. (Courtoisie des Laboratoires Mead Johnson.)

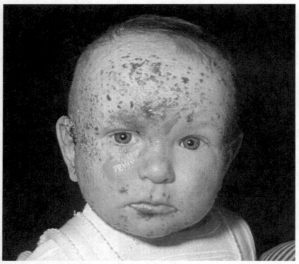

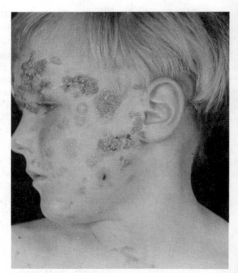

6. Dermatite séborrhéique chez un nourrisson. Lésions érythémato-squameuses du visage et du cuir chevelu. *

7. Impétigo contagieux. Les lésions fraîches sont recouvertes de croûtes épaisses, adhérentes, gris-brun et jaune miel ; causées par le streptocoque. Lésions plus anciennes en voie de cicatrisation. *

* Extrait de *Frieboes & Schonfeld's Color Atlas of Dermatology*, par J. Kimmig & M. Janner. (Édition américaine traduite et revisée par H. Goldschmidt. Georg. Thieme Verlag, Stuttgart, 1966.)

L'angiome dénommée « *tache de fraise* » est un angiome légèrement turgescent, qui va du rouge vif au violet foncé, et qui disparaît spontanément, mais plus lentement que les nævi précédents. La radiothérapie peut s'avérer efficace, mais ne doit être utilisée que par un expert en ce genre de traitement. La chirurgie est aussi possible; on préfère cependant adopter une attitude conservatrice.

Un *hémangiome caverneux* est formé de divers vaisseaux sanguins, tels capillaires, veinules, sinus. Ces lésions sont des anomalies vasculaires kystiques, profondément enracinées, qui sont bleues ou violacées. Dans les rares cas où l'hémangiome caverneux augmente rapidement de volume et déforme le visage de façon grotesque, le traitement avec de la neige carbonique peut être envisagé. La régression de l'hémangiome peut également être obtenue par l'utilisation cyclique des stéroïdes. Le traitement doit être commencé très tôt, car il y a possibilité d'hémorragie grave, si quelque traumatisme venait à faire saigner la lésion. Une anémie secondaire peut aussi être observée.

Nævus pigmentaire. Ces lésions varient en dimension et en couleur, à partir des plus innocents lentigos (taches de rousseur) jusqu'aux gros nævi noirs avec poils. Quoique de telles lésions soient rarement malignes, on devrait empêcher l'enfant de les irriter. Elles se développent lentement, mais grandissent en proportion de l'évolution de l'enfant et elles sont de plus en plus difficiles à enlever. Etendues, foncées et situées sur le visage, elles peuvent causer aux parents, aussi bien qu'à l'enfant, les frustrations qui accompagnent toute infirmité apparente.

Traitement. Le traitement le plus satisfaisant des nævi pigmentaires est l'ablation chirurgicale, incluant une portion de la peau normale avoisinante. Les nævi situés sur les parties du corps où se produit une constante irritation doivent être observés à intervalles réguliers et opérés dès qu'un changement se manifeste dans leur taille ou leur texture. Si l'aspect esthétique est le seul but du traitement, le moment de l'opération importe peu. En général, cependant, il est recommandé de l'effectuer durant la première année ou dans les toutes premières années d'âge scolaire.

Système gastro-intestinal

Fissure labiale et fissure palatine

Étiologie. D'après les histoires familiales recueillies et compilées par des généticiens, un facteur héréditaire complexe serait à la base de l'apparition de ces anomalies.

Physio-pathologie. Les fissures labiale et palatine résultent d'un défaut de soudure des structures embryonnaires de la face (bourgeons faciaux). La fusion des éléments maxillaires et prémaxillaires a normalement lieu entre la 5e et la 8e semaine de la vie intra-utérine. Le palais se forme approximativement un mois plus tard. Cette soudure partielle ou incomplète peut s'étendre au-delà de la voûte du palais et de la lèvre supérieure. Elle peut affecter le maxillaire supérieur, les tissus mous prémaxillaires, ainsi que le voile du palais, la luette et les structures nasales. Tous ces défauts simultanés, ou toute combinaison de certains d'entre eux, peuvent se présenter. Ce n'est parfois qu'une des nombreuses autres anomalies dont l'enfant est atteint. L'incidence du bec-de-lièvre et de la fissure palatine est approximativement de un pour 800 ou 1 000 naissances.

Choc psychologique. En apprenant la présence de cette anomalie chez leur nouveau-né les parents éprouvent un grand choc, même si parfois un membre de l'une ou l'autre lignée familiale a déjà subi une opération réussie d'une telle affection. Une infirmière compréhensive et adroite peut alléger leur détresse. Il est important que ces parents puissent exprimer leur peine, leur déception, parfois leur colère ou leur ressentiment. Lorsqu'ils sont prêts à envisager l'avenir, le médecin et l'infirmière peuvent leur expliquer les étapes de la chirurgie réparatrice et leur montrer des photographies d'enfants, avant et après l'intervention. Cette approche peut, en partie, les soulager de l'anxiété que leur cause l'apparence de leur enfant.

Fissure labiale

Incidence et anatomo-pathologie. Le bec-de-lièvre est une des anomalies congénitales les plus courantes. On le constate plus fréquemment chez les garçons que chez les filles.

Il consiste en une fusion incomplète entre la membrane centrale et l'une ou les deux membranes latérales qui forment la région qui s'étend de la lèvre supérieure aux narines. La fissure unilatérale est généralement localisée sous le centre de l'une des narines; bilatérale, elle siège sous les deux narines.

La fissure incomplète peut n'être qu'une échancrure du rebord charnu de la lèvre, mais peut aussi s'étendre jusqu'aux narines. La fissure complète peut atteindre les structures osseuses du maxillaire. L'aile du nez peut alors être déplacée vers le côté, et le plancher du nez et même la gencive supérieure peuvent être déformés.

Traitement et pronostic. La chirurgie correctrice devrait être préconisée autant pour le confort de l'enfant que pour son apparence esthétique. Dans le type incomplet bénin, l'infirmité n'embarrasse pas l'enfant et la correction devrait se faire au moment où il est en bonne condition pour la tolérer. On devrait réparer très tôt la fissure labiale complète, étant donné que ce handicap nuit à l'alimentation.

L'enfant s'habitue à respirer par la bouche, ce qui provoque la sécheresse et le fendillement des muqueuses et peut amener une infection secondaire. Les structures de la face de l'enfant grandissant rapidement, la fissure perturbe l'équilibre du développement. L'effet psychologique de la difformité de l'enfant sur les parents, même s'ils essaient de se montrer objectifs à l'égard de celle-ci, peut diminuer les stimulations visuelles et sociales offertes au bébé. Si celui-ci est montré à des amis, il peut ne pas recevoir les chaleureux compliments que les adultes adressent normalement aux enfants sains et bien faits; les parents peuvent en ressentir de l'amertume qui retentira éventuellement sur le nourrisson.

Quand la correction est effectuée par un chirurgien compétent, spécialiste en chirurgie esthétique, le pronostic est excellent.

L'âge auquel la correction est faite dépend de l'école de pensée du chirurgien. Certains préfèrent opérer le bébé durant son premier mois de vie, afin qu'il n'ait pas le temps de s'adapter à sa difformité et de développer des comportements indésirables. D'autres choisissent d'intervenir lorsque le nourrisson a trois mois, parce qu'il est alors plus facile d'éviter toute cicatrice en travaillant sur des structures mieux développées. Dans l'un ou l'autre cas, le bébé ne doit avoir aucune infection et présenter une courbe pondérale ascendante. Après cette première intervention, le résultat esthétique est spectaculaire, mais les parents doivent être avertis que des corrections dentaires et d'autres interventions, au niveau des gencives, du palais et du nez, s'avèreront peut-être nécessaires.

Après cette première opération, la tension sur les sutures est évitée par la mise en place de diachylon papillon ou du pont métallique de Logan. Ce pont est maintenu de chaque

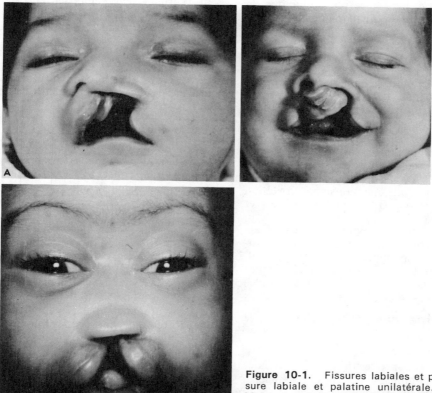

Figure 10-1. Fissures labiales et palatines. *A)* Fissure labiale et palatine unilatérale. *B)* Fissure labiale et palatine bilatérale. *C)* Fissure médiane. (Courtoisie du Dr Ralph Millard, Jr., M.D., F.A.C.S.)

côté par des diachylons placés sur les joues du bébé et l'arête métallique surplombe la plaie opératoire.

Soins infirmiers avant l'opération. Pendant le séjour du bébé à la maison, on doit encourager la mère à le traiter comme s'il était un enfant normal sans le surprotéger. Il ne devrait pas être caché aux parents et amis qui, éventuellement, l'accepteront comme tel. Les parents doivent cependant se rendre compte que la vue d'un enfant ainsi défiguré provoque la première fois une réaction de surprise; ils doivent permettre aux gens de s'habituer à son apparence, avant d'espérer d'eux une réaction habituelle.

Ce bébé ne pouvant créer de vide d'air dans sa bouche, suce difficilement. Il peut être nourri 1) à l'aide d'une tétine très souple pourvue d'un orifice relativement large, 2) avec une tétine spéciale dont l'extrémité ferme la bouche et recouvre entièrement le palais dur de l'enfant, 3) ou avec un compte-gouttes en matière flexible ou dont l'extrémité est en caoutchouc. La mère doit connaître les principes de chacune de ces méthodes. Dans le premier cas, le bébé doit être alimenté en position semi-assise afin d'éviter la suffocation par aspiration. Lorsque la seconde technique est utilisée, la mère doit éviter de traumatiser la lèvre du bébé en insérant la tétine et elle doit prendre soin de la placer de façon appropriée. Le bébé peut ensuite être nourri comme tout autre nourrisson. Si elle utilise un compte-gouttes, elle doit apprendre à placer son extrémité douce sur la langue, vers le côté,

et aussi près de la base que possible. Que l'enfant soit alimenté par l'une ou l'autre méthode, il est nécessaire de le faire éructer fréquemment, parce qu'il avale plus d'air que les autres bébés. Il est bon aussi de lui faire boire de l'eau afin que sa bouche soit rincée.

Afin de préserver la lèvre du nourrisson, la mère doit s'habituer à la maintenir propre et humide. De plus, les positions latérales et dorsales sont préférables à une position ventrale continue.

Elle doit aussi éviter que l'enfant n'irrite sa lèvre avec ses doigts. Avec un petit enfant, il suffit habituellement de descendre les manches de sa chemise sur les mains et de les attacher aux côtés de la couche.

Chez l'enfant plus vieux, il peut être nécessaire d'appliquer des contraintes aux poignets ou aux coudes pour obtenir le même résultat. Plusieurs spécialistes médicaux et paramédicaux s'opposent toutefois à ces pratiques qui privent l'enfant d'une étape sensori-motrice de son développement. Si la lèvre n'est pas irritée et qu'elle est maintenue humide, l'enfant n'y touchera pas plus qu'à une autre partie du corps.

Certains spécialistes recommandent d'offrir une tétine d'amusement au nourrisson alimenté au compte-gouttes ou avec une tétine molle largement percée, pour satisfaire son besoin de succion et pour l'habituer aussi à son futur mode d'alimentation après la correction chirurgicale.

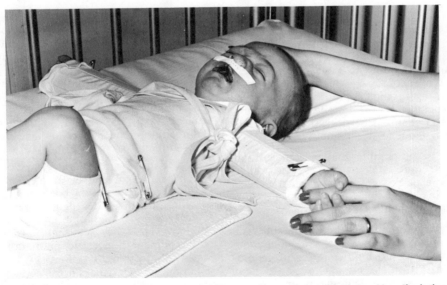

Figure 10-2. Un enfant de deux mois après l'opération d'une fissure labiale. Un diachylon est utilisé pour tenir la ligne de suture. Des entraves au coude empêchent l'enfant de se frotter la figure. La mère demeura avec l'enfant durant son hospitalisation.

La mère doit aussi surveiller les signes de détresse respiratoire ou de troubles gastro-intestinaux, et prendre toutes les précautions nécessaires pour protéger l'enfant contre l'infection. On doit enseigner à la mère tous les soins nécessaires, étant donné que l'enfant vivra à la maison jusqu'à ce qu'il soit suffisamment âgé pour supporter l'intervention.

Au départ du bébé de la pouponnière, la mère devrait avoir reçu un enseignement adéquat quant à la façon d'alimenter son enfant et aux moyens de prévenir l'irritation de ses lèvres.

Soins infirmiers postopératoires. On surveille étroitement l'enfant pour tenir ses voies respiratoires libres. Il s'est habitué à respirer par la bouche, ce qui peut être difficile après l'opération. On signale au médecin toute inflammation des tissus de la langue, de la bouche ou de ceux en bordure des narines. Un laryngoscope, une canule trachéale et l'appareil à succion doivent être toujours à portée de la main en cas de besoin.

La solution pour le nettoyage des narines et de l'incision devrait être prescrite par le médecin. On évite le peroxyde d'hydrogène qui détruit les cellules nouvelles qui se forment au niveau de la ligne de suture. On nettoie la ligne de suture fréquemment et avec beaucoup de soin. La lèvre devrait être tamponnée avec une gaze et non essuyée. Les tampons d'ouate peuvent laisser des fils qui nuisent à la cicatrisation; si la suture est tirée ou pressée, la cicatrice sera irrégulière. L'enfant doit recevoir les soins infirmiers de routine dont tout bébé a besoin.

Il doit être confortablement installé, au chaud et au sec. Les pleurs imposent à la ligne de suture une tension que le diachylon ou le pont métallique ne peut complètement absorber. On encourage la mère à rester près du bébé et à le cajoler pour éviter qu'il ne pleure. Il peut être pris dans les bras et promené dans la chambre. Il devrait recevoir l'alimentation à laquelle il est habitué.

Si on utilise un compte-gouttes pour le nourrir, on l'introduit dans le coin de la bouche de manière à ne pas entrer en contact avec la région voisine de la ligne de suture. On nourrit l'enfant lentement et en position assise.

Il faut faire éructer le bébé, autant pour le débarrasser de l'air qu'il a avalé que pour la sensation de confort qui en résulte généralement. On nettoie la bouche avec de l'eau après l'alimentation et, comme pour tout enfant, on doit lui donner de l'eau entre les repas.

Si les mains sont immobilisées, il ne peut exécuter les mouvements habituels à tout bébé. Pour faciliter la circulation et donner plus de confort à l'enfant, on doit libérer chaque bras, à tour de rôle. Comme il ne peut pas sucer, on doit le porter et le cajoler fréquemment pour lui procurer d'autres satisfactions émotives. Des mobiles colorés et des jouets musicaux doivent lui être fournis pour favoriser son développement et le distraire, afin qu'il se désintéresse de la région opérée. L'enfant ne doit jamais reposer sur son abdomen, ni même sur le côté, s'il y a danger qu'il roule vers l'avant. En position latérale, il est cependant moins susceptible d'aspirer ses sécrétions ou le lait qu'il régurgite. On le change fréquemment de position pour diminuer les dangers de pneumonie hypostatique. On garde le diachylon propre et on le remplace s'il se décolle.

Il faut également replacer le pont métallique s'il se détache et le nettoyer fréquemment. Après deux semaines environ, quand la lèvre est complètement guérie, l'alimentation au sein ou au biberon peut recommencer. Seul un enfant avec une fissure incomplète peut téter convenablement et, conséquemment, peu de ces enfants sont capables de prendre le sein d'une manière satisfaisante. Durant ce temps ou au cours de la période postopératoire, quand l'enfant est incapable de téter, la mère doit extraire son lait manuellement si elle veut conserver sa sécrétion lactée.

Fissure palatine

Incidence, étiologie, anatomo-pathologie et manifestations cliniques. À la différence du bec-de-lièvre, observé plus fréquemment chez les garçons, la fissure palatine affecte plus souvent les filles. Elle est souvent associée à une fissure labiale, mais les deux malformations ne se présentent pas toujours ensemble. La fissure palatine est plus sérieuse, car elle perturbe davantage la respiration et l'alimentation de l'enfant et elle est beaucoup plus difficile à corriger.

La fissure peut se limiter au voile du palais ou s'étendre au nez et à la voûte du palais. Elle se présente sur la ligne médiane du voile et sur un seul ou les deux côtés de la voûte. Elle crée donc une communication entre l'oropharynx et le nez, causant ainsi des difficultés d'alimentation et de phonation et des risques d'infection. L'enfant est incapable de bien sucer, et même s'il essaie, une partie des aliments peut être expulsée vers le nez. On peut adapter un appareil qui comble l'orifice du palais et permet à l'enfant de téter normalement. Cet appareil, semblable à une prothèse dentaire, doit être ajusté par un spécialiste et on le perce au moment de l'éruption des dents. L'hygiène de la prothèse revêt ici une importance capitale pour le bébé sujet aux infections respiratoires. Il est évident que cet appareil acquiert une double importance au moment de l'acquisition du langage. En son absence, le ton guttural qui résulte de la malformation peut devenir une habitude et persister même après que l'opération ait rendu possible une élocution normale.

Enseignement à donner à la mère au moment de la sortie de la pouponnière.

Les parents d'un enfant atteint d'une fissure palatine risquent, ou de le surprotéger, ou de le rejeter émotivement. Pendant le séjour à la pouponnière, on doit apprendre à la mère comment en prendre soin, et elle devrait s'habituer à lui donner elle-même le biberon. Le problème de nutrition se présente immédiatement. Il faut lui donner une quantité suffisante de liquide pour prévenir la déshydratation. On doit enseigner à la mère comment faire boire l'enfant avec une tétine molle, pourvue d'orifices suffisamment larges pour permettre au lait de couler dans la bouche de l'enfant sans qu'il ait besoin de sucer, ou encore avec une tétine spéciale porteuse d'un voile qui obstrue la fissure du palais, de telle sorte que l'enfant puisse sucer. Il peut aussi être alimenté au compte-gouttes. Le gavage ne doit être utilisé qu'en dernière instance. On doit tenir l'enfant en position assise de manière à faciliter la déglutition des aliments sans qu'il puisse les refouler vers le nez ou les aspirer. Après quelques mois, on peut l'alimenter à la cuillère et lui apprendre à boire son lait à la tasse.

La bouche de tels enfants s'infecte facilement. Certains médecins pensent que jusqu'à ce que l'enfant soit suffisamment préparé à coopérer, on devrait immobiliser ses bras pour l'empêcher de sucer ses doigts, de porter des objets à sa bouche ou d'irriter la fissure de toute autre manière. D'autres médecins, très intéressés aux problèmes du développement de la première enfance professent que, si l'enfant peut être observé fréquemment, on devrait éviter les contraintes, car elles l'empêchent d'explorer son univers et son propre corps. Si l'enfant n'a pas la latitude d'explorer et de se découvrir lui-même, une étape d'acquisition sensorielle lui fera défaut, et il lui sera difficile de la compenser plus tard. On tient la bouche propre en tout temps et pour cela, le médecin doit prescrire un antiseptique léger. On donne un peu d'eau pour rincer la bouche à la fin des repas. Durant la première année de l'enfant, les parents doivent rencontrer un orthodontiste, et un orthophoniste dès la seconde année. Il est recommandé aux parents de s'inscrire à une clinique spécialisée dans le soin de ces enfants et qui groupe de nombreux spécialistes.

Programme complet de rééducation.

Le traitement et la rééducation de l'enfant affligé d'une *fissure palatine* peuvent exiger de nombreuses années de traitements médicaux, chirurgicaux, dentaires et orthophoniques. Le travail d'équipe s'avérant plus efficace que l'effort individuel, l'équipe peut être constituée des professionnels suivants: pédiatre, chirurgien esthétique, oto-rhino-laryngologiste, dentiste, technicien dentaire, orthodontiste, ortophoniste, travailleuse sociale, psychologue, pédo-psychiatre et une infirmière en santé communautaire ou en pédiatrie. Le médecin de l'enfant peut agir en tant que coordinateur du groupe pour que la mère ne soit pas troublée par l'apparente complexité du traitement. Cette dernière peut se faire conseiller par chaque membre de l'équipe au cours de l'évolution du traitement. De telles équipes existent habituellement dans les grands centres hospitaliers.

Comprendre et partager les inquiétudes des parents constitue une des fonctions de l'équipe. Ceci s'applique spécialement aux infirmières de la pouponnière, à l'infirmière en santé communautaire travaillant à domicile ou à la clinique externe ainsi qu'aux infirmières de l'hôpital si on admet l'enfant pour une intervention chirurgicale. Il faut rassurer les parents en leur disant qu'on offrira à l'enfant tous les traitements connus nécessaires pour corriger son anomalie.

Le défaut physique peut souvent être éliminé avec plus de succès si l'enfant ne se sent pas différent des autres et rejetés pour cette raison.

Correction chirurgicale.

On doit confier l'enfant le plus tôt possible aux soins de l'équipe spécialisée afin d'observer les modifications palatines entraînées par la croissance et ainsi, établir la conduite à tenir pour les soins de longue durée.

Le chirurgien effectue ordinairement l'intervention quand l'enfant a plus d'un an et moins de cinq ans. Il se base sur l'importance et les particularités de la lésion. Il essaie de corriger la difformité en obtenant une union maximale des tissus du palais, de façon à rendre la parole intelligible, tout en évitant de traumatiser les maxillaires.

Si l'on doit retarder l'opération, il devient nécessaire d'appliquer une prothèse palatine afin que l'enfant puisse faire un apprentissage normal de la parole.

Si la difformité est trop accentuée et que la correction chirurgicale est impossible, l'emploi d'une prothèse peut considérablement faciliter l'éducation phonétique. On doit remplacer de tels appareils périodiquement suivant la croissance de l'enfant.

Soins infirmiers pré et postopératoires.
Les soins préopératoires sont simples. L'infirmière doit observer étroitement l'enfant et signaler immédiatement tout signe d'infection qui interdit habituellement toute intervention.

Les *soins postopératoires* sont excessivement importants. Lors des suites opératoires immédiates, des soins pour garder la bouche propre et sans irritation sont essentiels. On prescrit des antibiotiques uniquement s'il y a suspicion d'infection. Immédiatement après l'intervention, on place l'enfant en position abdominale ou latérale, le pied du lit légèrement surélevé, pour prévenir l'aspiration des sécrétions. On tourne sa tête sur le côté; l'infirmière surveille étroitement tout signe d'obstruction respiratoire et d'hémorragie. Il ne faut pas oublier que l'enfant respirait par des voies particulièrement larges. Il faut l'observer lors du réveil et s'assurer qu'il n'éprouve pas trop de difficultés respiratoires.

Le médecin peut prescrire des aspirations du rhinopharynx pour minimiser les risques de pneumonie ou d'atélectasie. Il faut alors procéder avec beaucoup de délicatesse. De nombreux médecins, toutefois, préfèrent qu'on ne fasse pas d'aspiration pour éviter de léser la ligne de suture. S'il existe un suintement sanguin par les narines, il faut éviter d'aspirer; on couche l'enfant sur le côté et on laisse le caillot se former.

L'infirmière doit convaincre l'enfant, en termes appropriés à son âge, de ne pas frotter sa langue sur son palais. Elle aura plus de succès si l'enfant a été prévenu en période préopératoire. On peut avoir recours à des moyens de contention pour empêcher l'enfant de porter ses doigts ou même ses jouets à la bouche. S'il n'est pas assez âgé pour coopérer, il faut maintenir fermement ses bras à l'aide de manchons placés sur la chemise autour du coude. Il faut retirer périodiquement les manchons, effectuer des mouvements passifs et même, sous surveillance étroite, laisser l'enfant faire certains jeux.

Quelques médecins préfèrent reprendre aussitôt que possible, le mode d'alimentation auquel l'enfant était habitué avant son opération. Ceci peut diminuer les frustrations et éviter les pleurs de l'enfant. D'autres chirurgiens préfèrent limiter le régime à une alimentation liquide stérilisée. Ils n'autorisent pas le lait immédiatement après l'intervention en raison du danger de dépôt de lait caillé sur la ligne de suture. Après chaque repas, il faut rincer ou nettoyer la bouche avec de l'eau stérile ou du soluté physiologique.

On poursuit l'alimentation liquide, ou semi-liquide, pendant dix à quatorze jours. Durant les deux semaines suivantes, on donne une alimentation de consistance molle puis on revient à un régime régulier.

Dans la mesure du possible, il faut prévenir toute tension sur les sutures. Les premiers repas postopératoires sont donnés à l'aide d'un compte-gouttes en caoutchouc ou en plastique flexible, d'une tasse en papier ou du côté d'une cuillère. On ne donne pas de pailles pour éviter l'augmentation de pression qu'elles entraînent dans la bouche.

Dans la mesure du possible, il faut empêcher les pleurs. Dans certains hôpitaux, on conseille fortement à la mère de séjourner à l'hôpital pendant les quelques jours postopératoires de façon à maintenir son enfant calme et rassuré.

L'enfant doit être gardé au chaud et au sec, dans la position la plus confortable. Des distractions appropriées comme, par exemple, lire ses histoires favorites tout en lui montrant les illustrations, préviendront ses pleurs. Le médecin peut prescrire l'administration de sédatifs qui le calmeront.

Enseignement à donner à la mère lorsque l'enfant quitte l'hôpital.
Il faut avertir la mère d'éviter tout traumatisme du palais. Comme la région affectée peut demeurer insensible, l'enfant ne manifestera peut-être aucun signe de douleur s'il érafle son palais avec un objet dur, comme une cuillère par exemple. Si la mère adopte une attitude normale face à l'enfant et que celui-ci peut reprendre son rythme de vie habituel, il ne portera pas plus d'objets à sa bouche que les autres trottineurs. Par contre, si l'enfant sent une constante anxiété autour de lui ou si on restreint constamment ses activités, il peut exercer un chantage en menaçant de blesser son palais ou régresser en voulant sucer ses doigts ou divers objets, ce qui est particulièrement nocif dans son cas. Il est important que la mère comprenne ces données, parce que l'utilisation courante de moyens de contrainte pour le trottineur est malsaine et peu efficace. Il peut déjouer à peu près toutes les inventions de l'adulte à ce sujet. La mère doit toutefois se rappeler que les jeux demandant à l'enfant de sucer, siffler ou souffler doivent être évités pour quelque temps.

Une infection des voies respiratoires supérieures retarde son apprentissage de la respiration normale. Il faut prévenir l'infection en isolant le trottineur de toute personne enrhumée ou atteinte de maux de gorge.

Complications. Les otites moyennes à répétition et la perte de l'acuité auditive demeurent des complications fréquentes. La mère doit indiquer au médecin tout signe d'otite. Des caries dentaires étendues ne sont pas rares et nécessitent des soins spéciaux. Il faut enseigner à la mère comment brosser correctement les dents de l'enfant, lorsque, selon l'avis du médecin, il n'y a plus de danger à employer une brosse à dents. Plus tard, elle lui apprendra comment s'en servir lui-même. Les dents nécessitent une attention spéciale si l'on doit poser une prothèse buccale. Un déplacement des arcades maxillaires et de mauvaises positions dentaires requièrent une correction orthodontique.

Pronostic. Le pronostic demeure assez bon, mais il dépend de l'étendue de la difformité à la naissance. Après l'intervention ou la pose d'une prothèse, on peut avoir recours à la rééducation orthophonique pour réduire la persistance de difficultés du langage.

SYSTÈME CIRCULATOIRE

Changements survenant dans le système circulatoire à la naissance. Dès la section du cordon ombilical, il y a une augmentation de pression du sang qui arrive au cœur gauche. Ceci favorise l'oblitération progressive du « foramen ovale » ou trou de Botal, situé entre les deux oreillettes. Durant la vie fœtale, l'artère pulmonaire communique avec l'aorte par le canal artériel. À la naissance, les muscles de la paroi du canal artériel se contractent et l'augmentation de pression du sang artériel empêche le sang veineux de l'artère pulmonaire de pénétrer dans l'aorte. L'obturation complète se produit durant les six premiers mois de la vie. Plusieurs autres changements se produisent, mais ils ne sont pas étudiés ici, parce qu'ils ne sont pas en relation directe avec des anomalies congénitales cardiaques.

Cardiopathies congénitales

Étiologie. Le cœur est complètement formé durant les huit premières semaines de la vie intra-utérine. Une ou plusieurs anomalies peuvent provenir d'un défaut de développement du cœur ou d'un des gros vaisseaux sanguins avoisinants. Il en résulte que l'enfant naît avec une cardiopathie congénitale. De telles anomalies peuvent être héréditaires, ou être causées par une infection virale, comme la rubéole survenant durant le premier trimestre de la grossesse. Une véritable maladie cardiaque peut également apparaître pendant la vie intra-utérine. Après la naissance, une malformation peut provenir de l'absence de fermeture du canal artériel ou du trou de Botal. Il existe encore une part d'inconnu dans l'étiologie des cardiopathies congénitales.

Incidence. L'incidence des malformations cardiovasculaires est de l'ordre de 6 pour mille naissances. Elles sont responsables de la moitié des mortalités infantiles.

Diagnostic. Le diagnostic est basé sur l'histoire obstétricale de la mère, sur l'histoire familiale des deux parents et sur les caractéristiques cliniques de l'enfant. Afin de participer à l'établissement précoce du diagnostic, l'infirmière doit connaître les particularités du bébé cardiaque. Les principaux signes et symptômes chez le bébé cardiaque incluent des souffles anormaux, des degrés variables de cyanose et de dyspnée, une succion et une déglutition lentes ou difficiles. Le nourrisson est faible, souvent irritable et présente rapidement un retard staturo-pondéral. Après un an ou deux, on remarque que l'enfant se fatigue plus facilement dans toutes ses activités. Il adopte souvent spontanément une position de repos en chien de fusil ou accroupie. Le retard staturo-pondéral s'aggrave et l'hippocratisme digital apparaît. La cyanose et la dyspnée demeurent variables.

L'examen radiographique montre des modifications tant dans la position normale du cœur que sur son contour. Un tel examen répété à intervalles de plusieurs mois peut refléter les changements continus de la structure du cœur au fur et à mesure que le corps de l'enfant se développe. L'ingestion de baryum par voie buccale peut montrer l'empreinte de l'aorte et d'autres vaisseaux sur l'œsophage.

L'électrocardiographie permet de vérifier les variations du potentiel électrique des différentes parties du cœur. Il permet d'évaluer l'état des structures musculaires cardiaques et le système nerveux intrinsèque du cœur.

On soumet l'enfant à l'anesthésie pour subir une *angiocardiographie*. On injecte une substance opaque aux rayons X dans une veine périphérique et on étudie son trajet au niveau du cœur, par une succession très rapide de clichés. Les communications anormales sont alors facilement repérées. L'angiocardiographie sélective s'avère un examen plus précis, puisque le cathéter radio-opaque est amené jusqu'à l'oreillette avant que le liquide ne soit injecté.

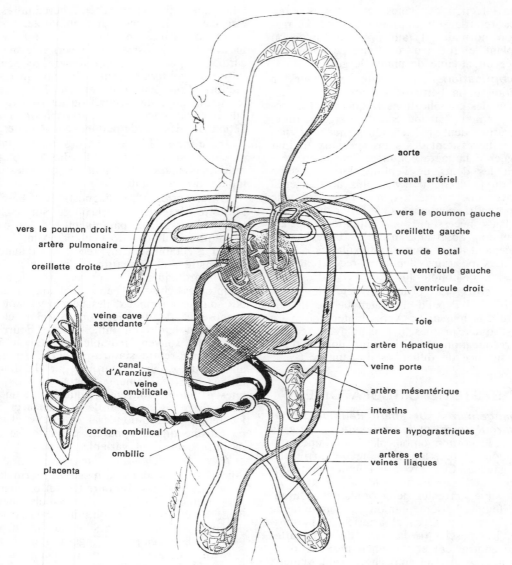

aorte

canal artériel

vers le poumon gauche

oreillette gauche

trou de Botal

ventricule gauche

ventricule droit

foie

artère hépatique

veine porte

artère mésentérique

intestins

artères hypograstriques

artères et veines iliaques

vers le poumon droit

artère pulmonaire

oreillette droite

veine cave ascendante

canal d'Aranzius

veine ombilicale

cordon ombilical

ombilic

placenta

Figure 10-3. Diagramme illustrant la circulation fœtale.

La *ciné-angiocardiographie* est l'impression sur pellicule de la succession d'images qui paraît sur l'écran fluoroscopique. Ces méthodes font maintenant partie intégrante de la technique du cathétérisme cardiaque.

Le *cathétérisme du cœur* se fait sous anesthésie générale ou locale. Si l'on utilise l'anesthésie locale, l'enfant doit recevoir de puissants sédatifs. Le médecin qui cathétérise le cœur doit être assisté par une équipe bien entraînée d'assistants habitués à travailler avec lui. Un petit cathéter opaque aux rayons X est introduit dans une grosse veine du bras ou de la cuisse, ordinairement la saphène interne, et poussé jusque dans l'oreillette droite.

Avec la pointe du cathéter, le médecin peut explorer le cœur minutieusement pour y découvrir des anomalies de structure, souvent localisées dans le ventricule droit et l'artère pulmonaire. Il est capable de déterminer la pression sanguine des différentes cavités intracardiaques, et des échantillons de sang peuvent être prélevés pour déterminer le degré exact d'oxygénation. Pour l'investigation du côté gauche du cœur, le médecin introduit le cathéter dans une artère périphérique, remonte l'aorte et pénètre jusque dans l'oreillette gauche, en passant par le ventricule. Cette cathétérisation, plus dangereuse, est rarement utilisée.

Le cathétérisme cardiaque ne se fait pas sans risques; l'infirmière doit donc être très prudente en rassurant les parents d'un enfant très malade, qui y est soumis. De plus les parents doivent savoir avant l'examen qu'il s'agit d'un procédé d'investigation et non d'un traitement correctif.

Après le cathétérisme cardiaque, l'infirmière doit surveiller l'enfant pour déceler l'apparition d'une hémorragie au niveau de l'insertion du cathéter, pour vérifier sa coloration, le rythme et la force des signes vitaux, surtout quand elle prend le pouls périphérique. Elle doit signaler immédiatement tout changement significatif.

Types de malformations. On peut classer les malformations congénitales cardiaques en deux groupes: 1) les affections non cyanogènes qui n'entraînent pas de cyanose, 2) les affections cyanogènes qui produisent des degrés divers de cyanose. Les soins précis à prodiguer à un enfant souffrant de cardiopathie congénitale seront expliqués avec la présentation de la tétralogie de Fallot. L'enfant cardiaque doit être traité dans un centre hospitalier qui possède un service de cardiologie infantile et une unité de soins intensifs pédiatriques.

Cardiopathies congénitales non cyanogènes

Dans ce groupe de cardiopathies, ou bien il n'y a pas de communication anormale entre la circulation pulmonaire et la circulation générale, ou bien cette communication existe, mais la pression pousse le sang des artères vers les veines. Le sang périphérique est conséquemment oxygéné comme chez un enfant normal, et la cyanose ne se produit pas. Si l'anomalie est telle que le sang veineux se mélange éventuellement à celui des artères, la cyanose peut en résulter.

Certains auteurs, toutefois, appellent non cyanogènes, seulement les cardiopathies qui n'impliquent aucune communication entre la petite et la grande circulation.

Coarctation de l'aorte

Types, manifestations cliniques et diagnostic. Il y a deux types de coarctation. Dans le type infantile ou préductal, il y a une constriction entre l'artère sous-clavière et le canal artériel. Le type postductal consiste en une constriction au niveau du canal artériel lui-même ou plus bas que celui-ci. Les symptômes varient avec le degré de coarctation. La tension artérielle est élevée dans la partie supérieure du corps, provoquant céphalées, vertiges, épistaxis, et, plus tard, des accidents cérébro-vasculaires.

La tension artérielle dans les jambes est relativement basse, résultant en une absence ou une diminution du pouls fémoral ou pédieux.

Le *diagnostic* basé sur l'absence de corrélation entre la tension artérielle aux bras et aux jambes, est confirmée par la radiologie. Chez les enfants plus âgés, la radiographie peut montrer une hypertrophie du cœur, qui n'est pas évidente au moment de l'examen de routine du nouveau-né, et en même temps une indentation des côtes due à des vaisseaux collatéraux distendus.

Traitement et pronostic. L'opération chirurgicale consiste à exciser la portion rétrécie de l'aorte et à anastomoser les deux segments. Dans certains cas, un greffon est inséré là où le rétrécissement est si large que l'ablation avec anastomose n'est pas réalisable.

Si l'état de l'enfant est tel que le médecin croit qu'il peut vivre jusqu'à ce qu'il ait atteint l'âge optimal pour l'opération, celle-ci est différée jusqu'à ce que l'enfant soit âgé de huit à quinze ans.

L'opération devrait être reportée à cet âge, parce que le segment utilisé comme greffe ne se développera pas comme le fera l'aorte. Plus l'opération sera tardive, moins il y aura de différence entre la croissance de l'aorte et celle de la greffe. Le pronostic dépend du succès de l'intervention. Si l'opération réussit, la durée de la vie devrait être normale.

Sténose aortique

Dans cette affection, le sang ne passe pas librement du ventricule gauche à la grande circulation, à cause du rétrécissement de l'orifice aortique. Le degré de constriction varie. Il peut être si peu prononcé que l'enfant est asymptômatique ou si grave qu'il cause des évanouissements et peut amener la mort subite. Ceci peut être normalement corrigé chirurgicalement, en utilisant la technique à cœur-ouvert et en incisant les feuillets valvulaires sténosés ou en dilatant l'anneau rétréci.

Persistance du canal artériel

Étiologie, incidence et manifestations cliniques. Le canal artériel se ferme normalement durant les premiers mois après la naissance. S'il reste perméable, la pression dans l'aorte pousse le sang artériel dans l'artère pulmonaire, étant donné que la pression du sang veineux est moins élevée. En conséquence, la pression augmente le débit de la circulation pulmonaire et le flot sanguin de l'aorte est diminué.

La persistance du canal artériel est une des anomalies cardiaques les plus fréquentes. Souvent unique, elle peut être associée à d'autres défectuosités cardiaques. Elle est deux fois plus fréquente chez les filles.

Les *symptômes* de la persistance du canal artériel chez le bébé sont généralement si légers que l'affection n'est pas découverte à l'examen initial et ne se révèle que plus tard, lors d'un examen de routine. Les symptômes caractéristiques apparaissent au fur et à mesure que l'enfant grandit et devient plus actif. Il présente souvent une dyspnée progressive à l'effort. L'examen physique peut révéler un mauvais fonctionnement du ventricule gauche ou une défaillance cardiaque. La surcharge pulmonaire rend l'enfant particulièrement sensible aux infections respiratoires. La progression des symptômes est due à l'effort du cœur pour pomper le sang une seconde fois à travers les vaisseaux pulmonaires, alors qu'en même temps, il doit assurer une circulation systémique adéquate pour un nourrisson ou un enfant actif. Il est facile d'empêcher le surmenage physique d'un bébé, mais

beaucoup plus difficile de limiter les activités d'un enfant qui grandit, sans le surprotéger et développer chez lui les attitudes qui peuvent en faire un enfant handicapé, rejeté par ses camarades de jeu. Si le canal artériel est assez large et que beaucoup de sang passe de l'aorte vers les vaisseaux pulmonaires, la croissance de l'enfant peut en être retardée. Les signes physiques incluent une augmentation de tension du pouls, quelquefois sentie quand on palpe le pouls radial.

Les pulsations sont du type du pouls bondissant de Corrigan. On trouve généralement, dans le second espace inter-costal gauche, un frémissement cardiaque qui peut s'irradier sur une grande partie du thorax. Il y a un « souffle de locomotive » classique, qui s'étend de la systole jusqu'à la diastole. L'électrocardiogramme ne révèle habituellement pas d'anomalie, mais les radiographies montrent une artère pulmonaire vigoureusement pulsatile et une vascularisation pulmonaire augmentée.

Le cœur peut être de dimensions normales, mais il est plus susceptible d'être hypertrophié.

Diagnostic, traitement et pronostic. Le diagnostic s'appuie sur les symptômes clini-

Figure 10-4. Cathétérisme cardiaque. L'enfant est sous anesthésie. La dénudation du vaisseau permet l'entrée du cathéter, que l'on peut suivre sur l'écran de télévision. (Courtoisie de l'Hôpital Sainte-Justine, Montréal.)

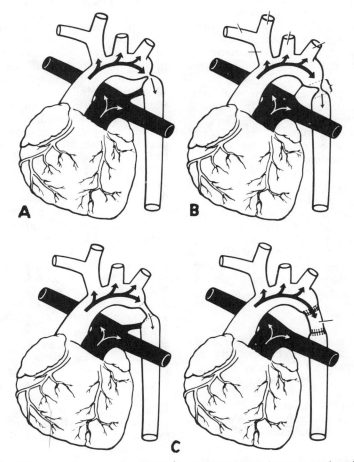

Figure 10-5. Coarctation de l'aorte. *A)* Rétrécissement préductal avec canal artériel ouvert ou fermé. *B)* Rétrécissement aortique postductal avec canal artériel fermé. *C)* Long rétrécissement dont l'ablation ne peut être suivie d'anastomose et qui requiert l'emploi d'une greffe après résection. *(Diagnosis of Congenital Cardiac Defects in General Practice.* Heart Association of South Eastern Pennsylvania and American Heart Association.)

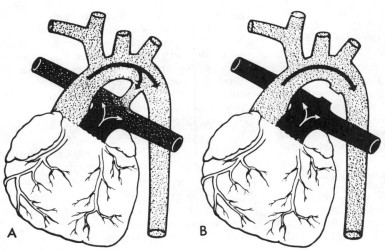

Figure 10-6. Persistance du canal artériel. *A)* Relation du canal avec les gros vaisseaux. *B)* Canal réséqué (schéma) ou ligaturé.

ques, le souffle cardiaque et une tension artérielle diastolique basse. Le cathétérisme cardiaque montre une pression normale ou augmentée, les radiographies révèlent un élargissement de l'ombre de l'artère pulmonaire et l'angiocardiographie met en évidence le canal artériel.

On procède au traitement chirurgical par ligature et/ou section du canal, de préférence vers la troisième année. Cependant, l'opération peut être entreprise plus tôt, si cela est nécessaire. Après la correction, les dimensions du cœur redeviennent normales, le souffle disparaît, et on constate une amélioration de l'état général.

Avec la chirurgie moderne, faite par un spécialiste compétent, le pronostic est excellent. Le taux de mortalité demeure extrêmement bas. Sans opération, une endocardite infectieuse subaiguë et/ou une insuffisance cardiaque peuvent se développer, lorsque l'enfant franchit l'étape moins protégée et plus fatigante de l'âge scolaire.

Dextrocardie

Dans cette affection, le cœur se trouve dans la partie droite du thorax. Ceci peut arriver avec ou sans inversion des autres organes. Quoique le cœur puisse être normal, l'existence d'autres malformations, souvent associées, complique cette affection. En l'absence d'autres anomalies, aucun traitement n'est nécessaire, et le pronostic demeure excellent.

Crosse aortique double

Les nourrissons et les enfants peuvent présenter des symptômes respiratoires ou de la dysphagie, ou les deux. Ces symptômes, commençant durant la première année, sont provoqués par la compression de la trachée ou de l'œsophage, ou des deux, par les branches de l'aorte. Ceci est dû à la persistance des précurseurs vasculaires embryologiques de l'aorte et de ses branches collatérales.

L'enfant, dans un effort pour se soulager, tiendra sa tête en position d'extension. L'examen radiologique qui démontre la constriction de l'œsophage par l'aorte signe le diagnostic. La constriction ou la déviation de la trachée peut aussi être mise en évidence. Le traitement est chirurgical et le pronostic excellent.

Communication interauriculaire (C.I.A.)

C'est une des anomalies congénitales les plus communes. Son incidence est plus élevée chez les filles. Il s'agit d'une communication entre l'oreillette gauche et l'oreillette droite, par défaut de fermeture du trou de Botal après la naissance. La pression plus élevée de l'oreillette gauche pousse le sang oxygéné dans l'oreillette droite, à travers l'orifice du septum. Une telle dérivation artério-veineuse ne produit pas de cyanose. Le cœur droit reçoit donc un surplus sanguin qui provoque une surcharge pulmonaire. Si la pression au niveau de l'oreillette droite augmente à la suite d'une sténose pulmonaire ou d'une hypertension pulmonaire, le sang veineux peut franchir le trou de Botal, se mêler au sang artériel et la cyanose apparaît. À ce stade, la correction chirurgicale devient plus aléatoire. La cyanose devient évidente si l'enfant souffre de défaillance cardiaque.

Le *diagnostic* est basé sur la radiographie et sur l'électrocardiogramme. Le cathétérisme cardiaque en fait la preuve. Le cœur peut être hypertrophié et la congestion pulmonaire est possible. À l'auscultation, on entend un gros souffle dans la région de l'artère pulmonaire. Il est à souligner que l'enfant est le plus souvent asymptômatique et que le diagnostic est souvent posé lors d'un examen de routine.

Le *traitement* consiste dans la réparation chirurgicale de l'anomalie. Les bords de l'ouverture sont rapprochés et suturés, ou bien l'orifice est obturé par une pièce synthétique fixée sur l'ouverture. Cette opération s'effectue sous circulation extra-corporelle. Sans traitement, la durée de la vie dépasse rarement trente-cinq ans. Il peut arriver que la malformation soit si minime qu'elle ne nécessite aucun traitement.

Communication interventriculaire (C.I.V.)

Cette anomalie consiste en une communication entre le ventricule droit et le ventricule gauche. L'affection peut être légère ou très grave. *Dans la forme bénigne,* la communication se situe à la partie inférieure ou musculaire du septum ventriculaire et est si petite qu'une très légère quantité de sang oxygéné passe du ventricule gauche au ventricule droit. C'est une anomalie congénitale commune. Le cœur s'hypertrophie rarement et le seul signe clinique consiste en un souffle accompagnant le battement du cœur.

L'oblitération chirurgicale constitue le traitement. Comme l'opération se fait à l'intérieur du ventricule, la circulation extra-corporelle permet au chirurgien d'atteindre la lésion. L'affection peut se compliquer d'une endocardite infectieuse subaiguë.

Dans la forme grave, il s'agit d'une large ouverture à la partie supérieure ou membraneuse du septum et le sang oxygéné passe en grande quantité du ventricule gauche au ventricule droit. Il en résulte de l'hypertension pulmonaire. Les symptômes incluent la défaillance cardiaque, une tendance à la pneumonie et un retard de croissance. On se base sur la radiographie et le cathétérisme cardiaque pour établir le diagnostic. Le traitement demeure l'obturation chirurgicale de l'anomalie. Une fois le cœur ouvert, les bords de l'orifice septal sont rapprochés, ou une pièce synthétique obture l'orifice. Ce genre d'opération nécessite l'usage d'une machine « cœur-poumons ». Sans l'opération, le pronostic est réservé.

Si l'hypertension pulmonaire devient tellement grave qu'il en résulte une inversion des pressions et que le sang passe du côté droit vers le cœur gauche, l'enfant devient cyanosé et inopérable. Ce phénomène est connu sous le nom de syndrome d'*Eisenmenger*. Une technique couramment employée pour empêcher le développement du syndrome d'Eisenmenger est le bridage de l'artère pulmonaire. On le pratique habituellement sur le nourrisson porteur d'une large communication interventriculaire, avant le développement de l'hypertension pulmonaire irréversible. On suture une pièce de ruban de Téflon autour de l'artère pulmonaire pour diminuer le flot sanguin vers les poumons.

Il existe d'ailleurs des C.I.V. associées à une sténose pulmonaire qui rend la communication sans effets; cette forme s'appelle la communication interventriculaire à poumon protégé.

Sténose pulmonaire

Quoique ces sténoses puissent exister chez les nouveau-nés, ceux-ci restent souvent asymptômatiques pendant plusieurs années. La défaillance cardiaque peut survenir et le pronostic est généralement mauvais. Le traitement consiste dans une valvulotomie ou dilatation mécanique de l'orifice valvulaire.

Cardiopathies congénitales cyanogènes

La particularité commune des cardiopathies congénitales cyanogènes est une communication entre le système circulatoire pulmonaire et la grande circulation, ce qui amène le mélange du sang veineux au sang artériel. La cyanose peut apparaître à la naissance ou ne devenir apparente que plus tard, habituellement au cours de la première année.

Elle tend à augmenter au fur et à mesure que l'enfant avance en âge.

La *polycythémie* (augmentation du nombre de globules rouges par millilitre de sang) provient du besoin des tissus en un approvisionnement adéquat d'oxygène. Les symptômes varient en degré avec l'étendue et la nature de l'anomalie. En général, il y a hippocratisme des doigts et des orteils, croissance retardée, dyspnée à l'effort. Si le sang, épaissi par une concentration anormale de globules rouges, forme des caillots dans les vaisseaux, des complications ultérieures peuvent en résulter. Une hydratation adéquate aide à prévenir la formation de caillots.

Tétralogie de Fallot

Incidence et physio-pathologie. C'est le type le plus commun de cardiopathie congénitale cyanogène durant l'enfance. Pathologiquement, on retrouve quatre anomalies associées: 1) sténose pulmonaire infundibulaire ou valvulaire; 2) communication interventriculaire haute; 3) dextroposition de l'aorte; 4) hypertrophie ventriculaire droite.

La sténose pulmonaire diminue le flot sanguin du cœur vers les poumons; le ventricule droit s'hypertrophie, les pressions sanguines s'inversent et le sang veineux est poussé vers le ventricule gauche par la communication interventriculaire. Le chevauchement de l'aorte sur les deux ventricules facilite aussi le mélange veino-artériel. Comme la cyanose dépend de la concentration absolue de l'hémoglobine réduite dans la circulation capillaire, il est évident que la circulation systémique contenant une riche addition de sang veineux au départ, le taux normal d'hémoglobine réduite est invariablement dépassé et la cyanose se manifeste cliniquement.

Manifestations cliniques et diagnostic. La saturation en oxygène du sang artériel n'est pas normale chez cet enfant et conséquemment la peau n'a pas sa couleur rosée naturelle, mais une teinte bleutée.

Les doigts et les orteils s'hypertrophient, réalisant l'hippocratisme digital et présentent une coloration violacée, à cause des capillaires distendus par du sang pauvrement oxygéné. L'affection prend de l'ampleur dès la première année de la vie. L'organisme réagit à un approvisionnement inadéquat d'oxygène par une production surabondante de globules rouges (polycythémie).

L'état général de l'enfant est médiocre. Il souffre d'un retard staturo-pondéral; les exercices lui causent une dyspnée grave. Pour se reposer, l'enfant préfère s'accroupir. Ce comportement est typique et a une valeur diagnostique.

La crise anoxique ou crise de dyspnée paroxystique apparaît le plus souvent au cours des 24 premiers mois de la vie et peut durer entre quelques minutes et quelques heures. L'enfant cyanose, devient dyspnéique et agité; il court littéralement après son souffle et il peut gémir ou pleurer. Dans les cas bénins, l'enfant finit par s'endormir; la crise grave peut conduire à l'inconscience, aux convulsions, à l'hémiparésie ou à la mort. Les crises peuvent apparaître sans avertissements; elles se produisent quelquefois à la suite d'un repas, d'une défécation ou d'une émotion forte. Ces enfants souffrent d'hypoxie et d'acidose métabolique.

Le traitement de la crise anoxique consiste à placer l'enfant sur l'abdomen, les jambes repliées, à relâcher ses vêtements, à lui administrer de l'oxygène et à lui donner de la morphine. Dans les cas graves, l'administration intraveineuse de bicarbonate de sodium permet de ramener le pH à la normale. Puisque l'acidose peut apparaître de nouveau, il faut vérifier fréquemment le pH sanguin.

En vieillissant, l'enfant tend à restreindre lui-même ses activités, à devenir anxieux et irritable, à dépendre exagérément des autres. Ses parents, préoccupés par son état physique, ont tendance à ne pas le contraindre à une discipline normale, car la frustration causée par un refus entraîne chez lui des crises de larmes qui augmentent la cyanose et effraient l'entourage. L'enfant prend conscience que s'il pleure, on le laisse faire ce qu'il veut. Il développe ainsi une personnalité

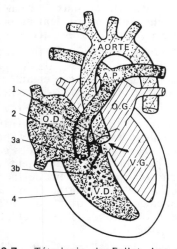

Figure 10-7. Tétralogie de Fallot. Les anomalies incluent, *1)* chevauchement de l'aorte, *2)* communication interventriculaire haute, *3a)* sténose pulmonaire valvulaire, *3b)* sténose infundibulo-pulmonaire, *4)* hypertrophie du ventricule droit. (Heart Association of South Eastern Pennsylvania and American Heart Association.)

caractérielle qui le rend inquiet, malheureux et il est facilement rejeté par les autres enfants.

Le diagnostic basé sur ces symptômes est confirmé par l'examen radiographique du cœur, le cathétérisme cardiaque et l'angiocardiographie qui révèlent une cavité droite élargie, une réduction de calibre de l'artère pulmonaire et un flot sanguin réduit à travers les poumons. La forme inhabituelle du cœur l'a fait surnommer « cœur en sabot ».

Avant tout examen, l'enfant devrait pouvoir se familiariser avec l'équipement qui sera utilisé, afin de minimiser son inquiétude lors du traitement. S'il doit prendre du baryum, l'addition de chocolat au mélange peut le faire ressembler au chocolat au lait. Les analyses biochimiques révéleront la diminution d'oxygène dans le sang artériel, et les tests de tolérance à l'effort prouveront la tendance de l'enfant à la dyspnée extrême.

Enseignement aux parents. Sur les parents repose la responsabilité de donner de bons soins à l'enfant jusqu'au moment de l'opération.

La mère peut craindre l'apparition des crises anoxiques après le retour à la maison. On peut réduire son anxiété en lui permettant de prendre soin du bébé pendant son séjour à l'hôpital; elle apprendra ainsi à le nourrir, à conserver son énergie au cours des soins normaux et à le soigner s'il présente une crise anoxique. L'infirmière l'aide à découvrir à la fois les problèmes particuliers de son bébé et les solutions possibles à ces différents problèmes. On doit attendre que les parents soient prêts à recevoir le bébé avant de lui donner son congé de l'hôpital. On peut aussi rassurer les parents en leur faisant rencontrer l'infirmière en santé communautaire qui les visitera à la maison.

Ils doivent considérer autant l'hygiène physique que mentale de leur enfant. Veiller à lui assurer une croissance et un développement normaux requiert un jugement sain et constant, afin que l'enfant ne soit ni surprotégé, ni livré à une indépendance qui surmène son cœur. On doit l'habituer très tôt à accepter un programme déterminé pour toutes ses activités journalières.

Il s'habitue alors à ses limites sans dépendre outre mesure de son entourage. Il apprend aussi à se fier aux autres pour obtenir l'aide et le secours dont il a besoin. La mère doit lui éviter le surmenage et ne jamais tolérer qu'il se fatigue au-delà de ses capacités. Il peut être difficile pour les membres de la famille et les adultes en dehors du cercle familial d'adopter cette ligne de conduite à l'égard d'un enfant dont le handicap n'est pas toujours visible, mais c'est au cours de cette période que se posent les bases d'une personnalité forte et heureuse.

Les parents doivent éviter que l'enfant n'acquière un sentiment de fausse importance qui le porte à croire que l'état de son cœur fait de lui un enfant spécial, qui doit toujours agir selon son gré. Ils doivent également penser aux autres enfants de la famille. L'enfant cardiaque a certains besoins importants, mais leur satisfaction ne doit pas engendrer une privation constante chez ses frères et sœurs. Toutefois, les parents doivent tenter de comprendre les réactions de leur enfant à son handicap et éviter qu'il ne se sente inférieur aux autres. Il devrait avoir un genre de vie compatible avec son état, mais le plus normal possible. Il doit apprendre à accepter les frustrations et les inévitables restrictions que son état impose à ses activités et à ses relations sociales. Il ne peut suivre les autres enfants dans toutes leurs activités. Les recherches démontrent que la cyanose ne semble pas avoir d'effets permanents sur le développement intellectuel de l'enfant. S'il est retardé, les parents peuvent attribuer entièrement le retard à sa condition physique, oubliant qu'une faible intelligence peut être due à beaucoup d'autres facteurs. Vivre une vie normale, dans ces circonstances, est le meilleur moyen de développer sa capacité mentale au maximum. Les expériences auxquelles il ne peut prendre part devraient être remplacées par d'autres de valeur didactique comparable. Il devrait apprendre, par exemple, qu'une balle roule, bien qu'il ne puisse être capable de courir pour l'attraper. Il ne peut grimper tout un escalier, mais il peut en monter une marche ou deux; aussi doit-il être porté beaucoup plus souvent qu'un enfant normal.

On doit lui procurer des jouets légers et faciles à manipuler. Les livres d'images sont appréciables. L'enfant peut marquer le rythme avec une musique lente. La surexcitation est aussi néfaste pour lui que le surmenage et, au fur et à mesure qu'il grandit, il doit apprendre que les jeux réclamant agilité et force lui sont pour la plupart interdits. En règle générale, les jeux compétitifs excitent trop de tels enfants et on doit leur faire comprendre que le plaisir ne dérive pas exclusivement du fait de dépasser quelqu'un d'autre. L'enfant a quand même besoin de se sentir habile dans un sport quelconque, ne serait-ce qu'à la pêche à la ligne ou au jeu de fléchettes.

Si les parents lui donnent de bons soins et savent observer les signes de détérioration de son état, il peut ne pas avoir besoin de fréquentes visites chez le médecin. Il doit quand même être vu régulièrement par le médecin de famille, le pédiatre ou le cardiologue infantile. Toute intervention chirurgicale, même mineure, doit être précédée d'un examen général approfondi. Le danger ne réside pas dans l'anesthésie — souvent des opérations mineures ont lieu sans anesthésie — mais surtout dans les possibilités d'infection. Une médication antibiotique prophylactique peut être indiquée.

Traitement et pronostic. Le traitement chirurgical peut être curatif ou simplement palliatif. La chirurgie palliative ne corrige pas la malformation elle-même mais permet une survie temporaire. Sans l'opération, la survie devient très aléatoire. En principe, on diffère la correction jusqu'à ce que l'enfant ait atteint sa troisième année ou soit plus âgé, mais si son état se détériore, l'opération peut être entreprise même s'il est tout petit.

Traitement chirurgical et soins. Pour l'enfant porteur d'une tétralogie de Fallot, il existe plusieurs types de traitement chirurgical. La chirurgie à cœur fermé (chirurgie palliative) comprend l'opération de « Blalock-Taussig », l'opération de « Potts » et celle de « Brock ».

CHIRURGIE À CŒUR FERMÉ (palliative). Dans *l'opération de Blalock-Taussig*, une branche de l'aorte est mise en communication avec l'artère pulmonaire. Chez l'enfant endessous de deux ans, on utilise l'artère inno-

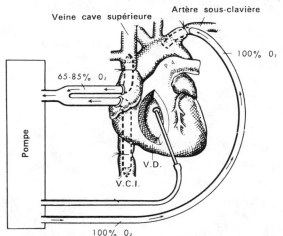

Figure 10-8. Circulation extra-corporelle. Les veines caves sont canulées; le sang veineux est retiré de la circulation et passe dans l'appareil pour y être oxygéné. Il est ensuite retourné dans l'aorte pour satisfaire la circulation corporelle. On aspire le sang qui remplit le cœur pour le rendre exsangue. (Courtoisie de l'American Heart Association. Adapté de Ventricular Septal Defects with Pulmonary Hypertension, par James Dushane et autres: *J.A.M.A.*, vol. 160.)

minée; chez l'enfant plus âgé, on utilise de préférence l'artère sous-clavière. Ceci a pour but de réaliser une communication entre une artère systémique et l'artère pulmonaire; il en résulte une augmentation du flux sanguin vers les poumons, suivie d'une meilleure tolérance à l'effort et d'une diminution de la cyanose.

Dans l'*opération de Potts*, on établit une communication directe entre l'aorte et l'artère pulmonaire. On obtient les mêmes résultats que dans l'intervention de Blalock-Taussig.

Ces techniques chirurgicales à base d'anastomoses demeurent palliatives, mais le risque opératoire est faible. Bien que l'amélioration clinique immédiate soit bonne, il peut quand même persister un certain degré d'incapacité. La *technique de Brock* s'attaque directement à la sténose de l'artère pulmonaire à travers le ventricule droit. Cette opération augmente le flux sanguin pulmonaire mais ne corrige pas la malformation interventriculaire.

CHIRURGIE À COEUR OUVERT (correctrice). Les techniques permettant la chirurgie à cœur ouvert comprennent: (1) l'hypothermie. L'hypothermie peut être induite à l'aide d'un matelas réfrigérant pourvu d'un contrôle automatique, de sacs de glace ou de lavages gastriques à l'eau glacée. Le degré de refroidissement est choisi par le chirurgien; cependant, on obtient ordinairement un effet maximum avec un minimum de danger quand on abaisse la température de l'enfant aux environs de 30° à 32°C. Certains chirurgiens préfèrent une température encore plus basse. Pour que cette technique soit efficace, on doit éviter un frisson vigoureux. L'emploi de l'hypothermie n'est pas sans danger. L'enfant doit être surveillé de près par une équipe experte pouvant faire face aux complications. Le but de l'hypothermie est d'abaisser suffisamment la température pour réduire le taux du métabolisme, diminuer le besoin en oxygène des tissus de l'organisme et, de ce fait, atténuer le danger d'anoxie au cours de l'opération. (2) Cœur-poumon artificiel. Le cœur-poumon artificiel est interposé dans la circulation afin de dériver le flux sanguin hors du cœur et des poumons. L'hématose se produit dans l'appareil. Le sang veineux passe à travers deux cathéters placés dans les veines caves, il traverse la pompe, et le sang oxygéné retourne vers une artère coronaire pour l'oxygénation du muscle cardiaque et vers les artères de gros calibre pour la distribution systémique. La pompe remplace les fonctions du cœur et des poumons et le chirurgien est à même d'ouvrir le cœur exsangue et de réparer la malformation. (3) L'oxygénation hyperbare. On place le malade dans une chambre spécialement construite ayant un contenu de 21 à 100% d'oxygène sous une pression de une à cinq atmosphère. De ce fait, la quantité d'oxygène est très augmentée dans les tissus et les liquides de l'organisme. Des recherches récentes ont été faites sur l'utilisation de cette technique pour la chirurgie des cardiopathies cyanogènes congénitales de l'enfant. Actuellement, les problèmes de l'oxygénation hyperbare sont la toxicité de l'oxygène, les dangers de la décompression, de l'explosion et du feu.

La chirurgie à cœur ouvert paraît le meilleur traitement pour l'enfant porteur d'une té-

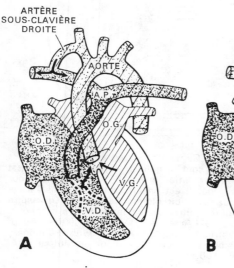
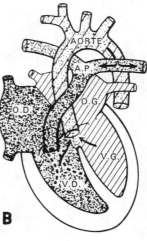

Figure 10-9. Tétralogie de Fallot. *A)* Quantité augmentée de sang vers les poumons en joignant la sous-clavière droite à l'artère pulmonaire droite. (Anastomose termino-latérale — Procédé Blalock.) *B)* Quantité augmentée de sang vers les poumons en créant la communication entre l'artère pulmonaire gauche et l'aorte. (Anastomose latéro-latérale — Procédé Potts.) (*Diagnosis of Congenital Cardiac Defects in General Practice.* Heart Association of South Earstern Pennsylvania and American Heart Association.)

tralogie de Fallot, puisqu'elle permet de corriger à la fois la sténose pulmonaire et la communication inter-ventriculaire. Le risque opératoire demeure plus élevé que celui des interventions employant l'anastomose mais, dans les cas réussis, les résultats sont spectaculaires.

Après ces interventions, on insère dans la cavité pleurale un drain thoracique relié à une bouteille placée en-dessous du niveau thoracique. Le drainage par gravité empêche toute accumulation de liquide dans la cavité pleurale. Si le liquide s'accumulait dans le thorax, ceci empêcherait la réexpansion complète du poumon; par ailleurs, ce liquide pourrait s'infecter et produire un empyème. À chaque respiration, l'oscillation du liquide contenu dans le tube signifie que ce dernier est perméable.

Si le drain s'arrachait de son insertion thoracique, un pneumothorax résulterait de l'entrée massive de l'air dans la cavité pleurale. On évite cet accident en fixant solidement le drain à la peau à l'aide de points à la soie et en posant du ruban adhésif autour de l'insertion.

Pour éviter le pneumothorax, si le tube se détachait de la bouteille, on applique des pinces hémostatiques sur le tube avant de bouger le patient. On fixe le tube au drap pour l'empêcher de pendre sur le bord du lit ce qui pourrait également causer un accident si quelqu'un s'y accrochait par inadvertance.

On garde au chevet du patient de la vaseline et des compresses stériles que l'infirmière devrait appliquer immédiatement sur l'orifice si le tube se détachait.

PRÉPARATION PSYCHOLOGIQUE À LA CHIRURGIE. Les parents devraient non seulement expliquer à l'enfant les raisons de son hospitalisation, mais ils devraient aussi lui expliquer sa maladie et son traitement en utilisant des mots qu'il peut comprendre.

Si l'enfant a des frères et sœurs, on devrait leur expliquer son état afin qu'ils saisissent la nécessité des attentions qui lui sont prodiguées.

L'enfant admis pour une chirurgie cardiaque peut être anxieux et instable. Il s'est probablement rendu compte de l'anxiété de ses parents en ce qui concerne sa santé et il devient inquiet. En raison de sa cardiopathie, cet enfant n'a propablement jamais été soumis aux mêmes frustrations que les autres enfants. Toutefois, il a dû réduire ses activités physiques, non seulement pour ne pas se surmener mais aussi à cause de sa dépendance, envers ses parents, pour des activités que l'enfant normal d'âge préscolaire effectue lui-même. Bien que certains enfants cardiaques se révoltent contre de telles restrictions, la plupart d'entre eux acceptent cette situation en échange des multiples attentions qu'ils reçoivent. Ces enfants manquent souvent d'assurance, se sentent inférieurs à leurs semblables et s'éloignent des autres enfants. Ils deviennent exigeants et agressifs avec leurs parents et les autres adultes.

Afin de planifier ses soins, l'infirmière devra au cours de conversations avec les parents, s'enquérir de la préparation que l'enfant a reçue en prévision de son opération. Elle essaiera également de connaître ses antécédents et la confiance qu'il témoigne à des adultes autres que ses parents. À partir de ces informations, l'infirmière doit être capable de trouver un moyen d'aborder l'enfant en gagnant sa confiance.

Les parents qui conduisent l'enfant à l'hôpital ont une attitude ambivalente vis-à-vis de la chirurgie. Cette ambivalence est due à la nouveauté relative de la chirurgie cardiaque, dont ils ont peur, et à l'espoir que l'opération s'avère un succès. Les parents ont besoin d'une personne à qui ils peuvent faire part de leur espoir et de leur crainte et de qui ils peuvent facilement obtenir une réponse à leurs questions.

L'enfant et les parents ont besoin d'une préparation psychologique pour les tests d'évaluation et pour l'intervention que devra subir l'enfant. L'examen, même le plus simple, devra être expliqué car l'enfant ne sait pas ce qui l'attend. On peut faire visiter aux parents la salle d'opération ainsi que la salle des soins intensifs; ainsi pourront-ils connaître le personnel du bloc opératoire et se familiariser avec l'environnement. Avec l'enfant, il est souvent préférable de se servir d'un hôpital-jouet ou de lui montrer les pièces d'équipement une par une. Il demeure important que l'enfant connaisse les infirmières de la salle d'opération et des soins intensifs. Certains détails de l'opération, le type d'anesthésie, l'endroit de l'incision et les drains qui seront laissés en place devront être discutés dans une atmosphère de confiance. Les appareils dont on se servira seront montrés graduellement. Ainsi, on pourra placer temporairement l'enfant sous une tente à oxygène afin de l'y habituer s'il n'a jamais subi ce traitement. Il doit également être mis au courant de l'emploi du respirateur à pression positive intermittente si on doit l'employer après l'opération. Cet appareil fait peur aux enfants à cause de la poussée de l'air et le masque facial les effraie car ils craignent de suffo-

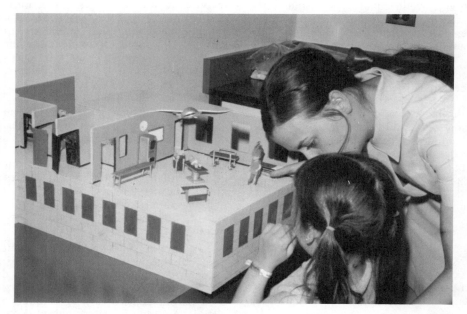

Figure 10-10. Préparation à la chirurgie. L'hôpital-jouet permet à l'enfant de se familiariser avec le milieu physique. La fillette assimile l'enseignement reçu de l'infirmière en manipulant le décor et le matériel. (Courtoisie de l'École des sciences infirmières de l'Université Laval, Québec.)

quer s'ils l'emploient. Pour gagner la coopération de l'enfant, l'infirmière lui fait une démonstration du masque facial et ceci peut devenir un jeu, par exemple en prétendant avec l'enfant que ce masque est du même type que celui que porte les astronautes. Avant l'opération, l'enfant doit également être mis

au courant des autres soins qu'il est appelé à recevoir: le contrôle des signes vitaux, les solutés intraveineux, l'importance de changer de position, de tousser et de respirer profondément. Il est important que l'enfant ait l'occasion de toucher à tout l'équipement, qu'il expérimente ce qui lui est expliqué, sur lui-même et sur des jouets. L'infirmière doit rester avec lui pendant ce type de jeu, déceler peurs et phantasmes et apporter renseignements et réconfort. Si l'enfant comprend qu'il peut faire part à l'infirmière de ce qu'il éprouve, il se sentira libre d'exprimer ouvertement ses émotions après l'opération. L'infirmière doit rassurer l'enfant, lui dire qu'il n'a pas à se souvenir de tout ce qu'elle lui enseigne et qu'il y aura toujours quelqu'un près de lui pour l'aider en période postopératoire.

Au cours de cette phase préparatoire, l'infirmière devra expliquer aux parents que leur enfant ne sera jamais seul, qu'une infirmière sera constamment à ses côtés. L'infirmière doit gagner la confiance des parents et de l'enfant et leur faire comprendre qu'ils sont acceptés. La régression due au stress devra également être reconnue, acceptée et discutée avec les parents.

L'infirmière devra aussi expliquer aux parents qu'il y aura beaucoup de soins à prodiguer à l'enfant après l'opération et qu'il ne faudra pas voir dans cette activité intense un signe d'aggravation de son état.

Préparation physique de l'enfant en vue de l'intervention. Étant donné que plusieurs enfants ne se trouvent pas dans une condition physique optimale avant l'opération, une diète adéquate, du repos et de l'exercice contrôlé seront nécessaires. Une hydratation abondante est spécialement indiquée si l'enfant est porteur d'une polycythémie compensatoire. En présence d'une insuffisance cardiaque, le repos absolu, la digitaline, les diurétiques et l'oxygène peuvent s'avérer nécessaires. Le médecin peut prescrire une antibiothérapie préventive. L'enfant sera tenu à l'écart des malades et du personnel porteurs d'une maladie infectieuse. On donne des liquides par voie parentérale si indiqué, avant et durant l'opération pour éviter la déshydratation. La veille de l'intervention, on procède à l'asepsie du champ opératoire. Un lavement peut être prescrit. Une antiseptie des voies respiratoires supérieures est obtenue à l'aide de gargarismes répétés, effectués avec des solutions antiseptiques. La libération complète des voies nasales, à l'aide de soluté physiologique, peut aussi être utile. Les exercices respiratoires et musculaires débutent ordinairement la veille de l'intervention. On administre un tranquillisant au coucher afin de procurer à l'enfant le plus de repos possible. On le pèse sur la même balance que l'on emploiera après l'opération, afin de pouvoir évaluer la quantité de liquide perdu ou reçu au cours de l'intervention. L'enfant sera autorisé à amener son jouet préféré en salle d'opération.

L'infirmière qui a eu soin de l'enfant avant l'opération devrait se charger des soins postopératoires. Si ceci s'avère impossible, l'infirmière de l'unité postopératoire devrait rencontrer l'enfant avant la chirurgie. Ainsi, tout changement de son état pourra être évalué correctement; de plus l'enfant se sentira en sécurité. Pendant l'opération, l'infirmière apportera son aide aux parents en les écoutant, en répondant à leurs questions et en les préparant à l'aspect physique de l'enfant lors de son retour de la salle d'opération. Il peut être utile de permettre aux parents de rencontrer un enfant qui a subi avec succès la même intervention que celle effectuée sur le leur.

Pendant l'opération, l'infirmière devra également vérifier l'équipement dont elle aura besoin pour les soins postopératoires. Immédiatement après l'opération, elle se renseignera sur le type d'intervention, les médicaments et les liquides reçus au cours de l'opération et sur les prescriptions postopératoires.

Soins postopératoires. À son arrivée à la salle de soins intensifs ou à celle de réveil, on donne immédiatement de l'oxygène à l'enfant. Chacun des drains thoraciques est soigneusement contrôlé et raccordé à un appareil d'aspiration. La prise des signes vitaux s'avère essentielle et on utilise le cardioscope qui permet un contrôle continu du rythme cardiaque et de l'électrocardiogramme. Il faut veiller à ce que les électrodes demeurent en place. La tension artérielle peut aussi être vérifiée de façon continue par appareil électronique. On doit surveiller et régler soigneusement l'administration de liquide et de sang par voie intraveineuse. La tension veineuse est mesurée régulièrement. L'enfant porteur d'une trachéotomie reçoit les soins appropriés.

Quand l'enfant s'éveille de l'anesthésie, on lui dit que l'opération est terminée. Il peut être confus, agité, somnolent et souffrant. Un narcotique peut alors être donné sur ordre du médecin. L'enfant peut ne sentir que sa douleur et ne pas reconnaître ses parents, ni le personnel médical, ni l'infirmière qui se trouvent à son chevet.

On contrôle les signes vitaux toutes les heures ou plus souvent si nécessaire. L'infirmière doit prendre la température rectale, car la température de la tente à oxygène (20°C - 22°C) peut influencer le contrôle par voie buccale. On peut employer un thermomètre permanent électronique. Si l'enfant est hyperthermique, il peut recevoir un suppositoire d'aspirine; un matelas réfrigérant demeure la mesure idéale. La fièvre doit baisser puisqu'elle augmente à la fois la vitesse du flux sanguin et le taux du métabolisme.

L'infirmière doit surveiller le rythme et l'amplitude des mouvements respiratoires et noter si l'expansion thoracique demeure égale et symétrique. Si la respiration de l'enfant devient bruyante et rapide, ceci indique une accumulation de sécrétions dans les voies respiratoires. L'infirmière doit alors procéder à une aspiration afin de débarrasser l'enfant de ses sécrétions. Elle doit également noter la différence entre la qualité, le rythme et le volume du pouls radial et pédieux. Elle prend fréquemment la pression artérielle. Si le pouls devient irrégulier et si la pression artérielle diminue, elle avertit le médecin immédiatement car ces signes indiquent un arrêt cardiaque imminent. L'hémorragie se traduit par une accélération du pouls et de la fréquence respiratoire, par une baisse de la tension artérielle, une altération de l'état général et une soif intense. Plusieurs appareils électroniques en usage dans certains centres sont d'une grande utilité dans l'évaluation de l'état de ces patients. On note la coloration des ongles et de la peau de l'enfant, si la peau est sèche ou humide, froide ou chaude. Si la cyanose et les difficultés respiratoires deviennent importantes, une trachéotomie peut s'avérer nécessaire, si elle n'a pas été pratiquée antérieurement.

On donne les liquides par voie intraveineuse après dissection d'une veine du bras ou de la jambe et on note leur administration afin d'éviter qu'ils ne soient donnés trop rapidement. Il faut penser qu'un changement de position et le fait de pleurer peuvent modifier la vitesse d'écoulement. L'infirmière devra surveiller le débit du soluté et s'assurer que le liquide n'infiltre pas les tissus.

On peut installer un tube de Levine pour éviter la dilatation gastrique. Les soins de la bouche et le rinçage fréquent avec de l'eau peuvent apaiser la soif de l'enfant. Vu qu'une restriction de liquide peut troubler les parents et l'enfant, l'infirmière devra leur expliquer non seulement que la soif est une réaction normale mais aussi les raisons de la restriction postopératoire.

Si l'enfant n'a pas uriné au cours des huit à douze heures après l'opération, on peut recourir au cathétérisme vésical. Toutefois, une sonde vésicale est souvent installée au moment de l'opération pour éviter à l'enfant des procédures supplémentaires en période postopératoire. On note soigneusement la densité spécifique et la couleur de l'urine et on en fait un dosage strict.

Tout de suite après l'opération, on raccorde le ou les drains thoraciques à un drainage sous l'eau. Ces drains permettent l'écoulement du liquide de la cavité pleurale. On peut ainsi évaluer la perte sanguine et la thérapie de remplacement. Si le médecin le demande, on manipule les drains dans le sens du drainage afin d'assurer leur perméabilité en empêchant la formation de caillots sanguins. L'infirmière doit veiller à ce que les drains ne soient pas coudés et que le raccordement aux embouts de verre soit étanche. Elle veille également à ce qu'ils soient suffisamment longs pour permettre à l'enfant de bouger; elle note l'oscillation du liquide avec chaque mouvement respiratoire. L'infirmière doit se rappeler que la bouteille de drainage doit se trouver au-dessous du niveau du lit. Pour s'assurer que la bouteille ne sera pas élevée, on la fixe au sol. On note soigneusement la couleur, la quantité et la consistance du liquide excrété. Le drainage est contrôlé toutes les heures, et l'heure du relevé est indiqué sur une bande verticale collée à la bouteille.

L'infirmière devrait savoir que s'il existe une fuite d'air dans la cavité pleurale, il se produira un pneumothorax qui se traduit par de l'agitation, de l'appréhension, de la cyanose, et par une vive douleur thoracique au niveau de la zone d'insertion du drain, de la tachycardie et de la dyspnée. Si ces signes apparaissent, l'infirmière pince le drain thoracique le plus près possible du thorax de l'enfant et prévient le médecin.

Après l'opération, on prend une radiographie des poumons. Comme on cesse l'administration d'oxygène au moment où l'on effectue cette radiographie pulmonaire, l'enfant peut devenir anxieux. On prend ses signes vitaux et on le rassure d'une façon appropriée.

Bien que l'enfant ait été avisé de la nécessité de tousser et de respirer profondément et qu'il ait maîtrisé ces techniques avant son opération, il peut montrer quelques difficultés à coopérer dans ce sens car, en phase postopératoire, la toux et l'inspiration profonde sont douloureuses. L'infirmière peut alors l'aider en appuyant ses mains sur le thorax, de chaque côté de l'incision chirurgicale, ou l'enfant peut se courber sur son jouet préféré, ou sur un oreiller, afin de diminuer la douleur. On doit le féliciter pour sa coopération. Étant donné que la toux permet d'éviter la rétention des sécrétions bronchiques, on devra aviser le médecin si l'enfant ne réussit pas à tousser.

On peut se servir d'un respirateur à pression positive intermittente pour aider l'enfant à tousser et pour administrer des aérosols. L'infirmière doit observer sa coloration, sa respiration, son pouls et son comportement général. Elle doit se rappeler que la toux peut être extrêmement douloureuse et fatigante en phase postopératoire. Si des narcotiques sont prescrits, on doit les administrer avant ces exercices de toux et de respirations profondes. On peut procurer de l'air humide, chaud ou froid, et des médicaments en aérosol pour éviter l'assèchement des muqueuses du tractus respiratoire et faciliter ainsi l'expectoration.

On doit changer la position de l'enfant toutes les heures pour favoriser une bonne circulation et une bonne ventilation du poumon et pour permettre les mouvements des extrémités. Une série d'oreillers adéquatement placés peut aider l'enfant à varier ses positions. Aussitôt que possible, on l'encourage à bouger par lui-même. Après avoir déplacé l'enfant, on peut noter une augmentation du drainage thoracique.

L'infirmière devra noter les observations suivantes: l'absence de pouls pédieux, la cyanose ou le refroidissement des jambes (ce qui indique une embolie artérielle probable), la distension des veines du cou, la nausée, la distension abdominale, le saignement ou l'infection au niveau d'une dissection veineuse. Elle doit signaler tout spasme des extrémités, les signes de défaillance cardiaque, les pétéchies, les symptômes de vertige, l'agitation et la céphalée. L'infirmière devra également assister le médecin au moment où les tubes thoraciques seront enlevés ainsi que le fil de l'entraîneur électro-systolique (pacemaker), si celui-ci a été posé au moment de l'opération.

Le repos demeure d'une importance capitale; l'infirmière devra donc planifier les soins de façon à ce que le malade ait le plus de repos possible. On administre les narcotiques ou les sédatifs selon les ordonnances. Toutefois, des soins attentifs peuvent soulager les craintes de l'enfant et diminuer la demande d'analgésiques. Selon l'importance de l'intervention chirurgicale, on permettra à l'enfant de se lever plus ou moins rapidement.

Comme il en a été fait mention précédemment, l'enfant qui subit une chirurgie cardiaque régresse souvent vers un état antérieur. Il peut crier, devenir plus exigeant ou demander un contact physique presque constant. L'infirmière, reconnaissant son besoin de sécurité sous-jacent, lui permettra d'utiliser la régression comme moyen de recouvrer sa confiance en autrui et en lui-même. Elle devra aider progressivement l'enfant à retrouver l'indépendance et l'initiative qu'il a temporairement perdues. Elle devra aussi lui procurer des moyens pour exprimer son agressivité. Graduellement, l'enfant reviendra à son stade de développement et recommencera à jouer avec les autres.

Avant son départ de l'hôpital, le médecin, les parents, les travailleurs sociaux, l'infirmière en santé communautaire, l'infirmière de l'hôpital, travaillent ensemble à planifier un programme de soins pour l'enfant. Celui-ci apparaît généralement plus actif, plus agressif et plus indépendant qu'il ne l'était avant l'opération. Ces changements peuvent effrayer les parents qui craignent le surmenage. De plus, la mère peut trouver difficile de renoncer au plaisir qu'elle avait à soigner un enfant dépendant. L'infirmière peut les aider en soulignant la joie évidente de l'enfant à participer à de nouvelles activités et l'absence de dyspnée et de fatigue. On peut aider la mère à réorienter ses activités afin de remplacer celle qui consistait à soigner un enfant malade.

Pronostic. Le *pronostic* est généralement bon après l'opération et dépend du type d'intervention que l'enfant a subi. Si on a pratiqué une correction complète à cœur ouvert, le pronostic est excellent.

Trilogie de Fallot

Il s'agit d'une sténose pulmonaire avec communication interauriculaire, accompagnée d'une hypertrophie ventriculaire droite.

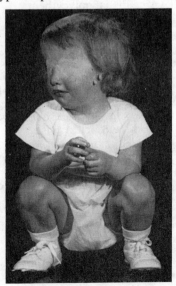

Figure 10-11. Tétralogie de Fallot. Enfant accroupi. (Nadas: *Pediatric Cardiology*, 2e édition.)

Dans cette affection, le sang veineux chassé de l'oreillette droite vers l'oreillette gauche provoque la cyanose. Cliniquement, la maladie peut simuler la tétralogie de Fallot. Le traitement consiste dans la valvulotomie pulmonaire, avec ou sans plastie de la cloison interauriculaire. Le pronostic après l'opération est bon.

Transposition des gros vaisseaux

Incidence et physio-pathologie. Cette pathologie est presqu'aussi fréquente que la tétralogie de Fallot. Dans cette affection, l'aorte naît dans le ventricule droit, et l'artère pulmonaire dans le ventricule gauche. De ce fait, l'aorte transporte du sang veineux dans la grande circulation et les artères pulmonaires retournent du sang oxygéné aux poumons. Un nourrison ne peut survivre initialement que s'il y a un défaut associé tel qu'une communication interauriculaire ou interventriculaire ou une persistance du canal artériel.

Manifestations cliniques et diagnostic. Un enfant qui a une transposition des gros vaisseaux peut sembler normal à la naissance à cause de la persistance du canal artériel mais deviendra extrêmement cyanosé très tôt après la naissance. Dyspnéique et incapable de sucer, l'enfant souffre rapidement d'un retard staturo-pondéral important, et il y a hippocratisme progressif des doigts et des orteils. Le diagnostic se fait par une cathétérisation cardiaque et une radiographie associées. Le laboratoire révèle un taux d'hématocrite élevé et de la polycythémie.

Traitement et pronostic. Grâce aux récentes recherches dans le traitement de cette affection, plus d'enfants survivent actuellement. Le traitement palliatif vise à assurer un mélange adéquat de sang oxygéné et non-oxygéné. Ceci peut être réalisé en enlevant le septum interauriculaire, ce qui permet à l'enfant de survivre jusqu'à ce que la chirurgie corrective puisse être entreprise.

Une technique palliative non chirurgicale utilisée couramment est celle de Rashkind-Miller. Elle consiste à introduire un cathéter cardiaque à double lumière par la veine fémorale jusqu'à l'oreillette droite et ensuite jusqu'à l'oreillette gauche par le trou de Botal. Un ballon gonflable se trouve situé juste avant la pointe terminale. Dans l'oreillette gauche, le ballon est gonflé par une solution radio-opaque, jusqu'à la grosseur désirée. En retirant le cathéter, le ballon déchire la paroi interauriculaire et permet le mélange du sang artériel et du sang veineux.

On répète la manœuvre jusqu'à ce que le ballonnet gonflé puisse être déplacé sans résistance de l'oreillette gauche vers l'oreillette droite. La coloration de l'enfant s'améliore et la défaillance cardiaque, si elle était présente, disparaît.

On entreprend l'étape corrective de cette thérapie, quand l'enfant est âgé de dix-huit mois à trois ou quatre ans. L'intervention complexe de Mustard s'effectue sous circulation extra-corporelle. Cette intervention consiste à coudre une double cloison auriculaire grâce à un segment de péricarde. À la suite de cette opération, le sang veineux de l'organisme est dirigé vers le ventricule gauche et le poumon alors que le sang artériel est orienté vers le ventricule droit et l'aorte. On corrige toute communication interventriculaire ou interauriculaire et le canal artériel est fermé. Si le diamètre de l'artère pulmonaire a été réduit, on enlève la bande correctrice.

Le *pronostic* pour les enfants souffrant d'une transposition des gros vaisseaux a été grandement amélioré depuis la découverte de ces nouveaux procédés. Si l'affection est diagnostiquée assez tôt, de nombreux enfants peuvent être traités et guéris.

Soins infirmiers. L'infirmière qui est chargée des nouveau-nés dans une pouponnière doit être en mesure de dépister les sujets atteints de cette maladie, en dépit du fait que la cyanose peut ne pas être très importante à cause de la persistance du canal artériel. Elle devrait pouvoir remarquer la dyspnée progressive et l'incapacité de l'enfant à bien téter. De tels enfants ont beaucoup de sécrétions, moins cependant que ceux atteints d'atrésie de l'œsophage. Plus tôt ces nouveau-nés atteints seront soumis à une chirurgie palliative, plus grande sera leur chance de survie. Il est donc extrêmement important que l'infirmière rapporte ses observations au plus tôt.

Il existe d'autres malformations cardiaques plus rares; presque toutes sont susceptibles d'être corrigées ou améliorées par la chirurgie.

Décompensation cardiaque

Le cœur qui doit fournir un effort physiologique trop grand ou qui a subi des lésions réelles peut quand même s'adapter normalement. Dans le cas contraire, on dit qu'il décompense et il tombe en défaillance.

Manifestations cliniques. L'infirmière devrait être consciente du fait que les enfants, tout comme les adultes atteints de troubles cardiaques graves, peuvent souffrir de décompensation. Elle constate d'abord que l'enfant ne se nourrit plus aussi bien; il peut se fatiguer plus vite à sucer et cesser de gagner du poids. On parvient à l'alimenter si on lui permet de se reposer après avoir bu chaque once du biberon. D'autres signes de défaillance cardiaque peuvent être un cri affaibli, un teint pâle ou cyanosé, de l'œdème, de la tachycardie, de la tachypnée accompagnée d'un râle ronflant expiratoire, du tirage sus-sternal et le battement des ailes du nez. Sur les radiographies, le cœur paraît hypertrophié.

Chez l'enfant plus âgé, les signes de défaillance cardiaque ressemblent à ce qui se produit chez l'adulte. On retrouve de l'anorexie, de la fatigue, de la dyspnée, de la toux, de la cyanose, des douleurs abdominales, une hépatomégalie ainsi qu'un œdème secondaire. La cardiomégalie est présente.

Traitement et soins infirmiers. Le traitement comporte l'administration de digitaline, de diurétiques en cas d'œdème et l'oxygénothérapie. L'antagoniste de l'aldostérone, la spironolactone (Aldactone) est quelquefois employée en plus des diurétiques.

Le traitement commence par la digitalisation. La digoxine et la digitoxine agissent lentement alors que la lanatoside C (Cedilanide) produit une digitalisation rapide. On préfère habituellement la digoxine qui existe sous forme liquide et dont l'administration s'avère plus facile à contrôler. On établit la dose selon le poids corporel et on l'ajuste selon la tolérance de l'enfant. L'usage de doses d'entretien de digitaline s'avère nécessaire, à moins que la cause de la défaillance ne soit complètement corrigée. Au cours du traitement d'entretien, la posologie administrée peut être augmentée parallèlement à l'augmentation du poids. L'intoxication digitalique peut apparaître et doit être spécialement redoutée, vu le peu de symptômes d'alarme précédant une fibrillation ventriculaire, ou l'arrêt cardiaque. Un pouls qui ralentit, de l'anorexie, de la diarrhée ou des vomissements suspects invitent à suspendre la médication jusqu'à ce que les signes de toxicité régressent. On peut la reprendre ensuite, si cela est nécessaire, avec un dosage plus faible. L'infirmière doit toujours vérifier le rythme cardiaque du nourrisson *avant* et *après* l'administration de la digitaline.

L'enfant qui souffre d'une insuffisance cardiaque, a besoin de plus de repos qu'un enfant normal. Il doit avoir de petits repas fréquents, de digestion facile, et plus riches en calories qu'à l'ordinaire. Certains médecins recommandent l'usage d'une tétine d'amusement pour le maintenir heureux et content, ce qui diminue le travail du cœur.

Un nourrisson ainsi atteint est plus à l'aise en position assise ou lorsqu'il est tenu contre l'épaule de sa mère ou de l'infirmière. Le petit siège pour bébé peut être utilisé avantageusement, surtout si l'enfant a une respiration rapide et laborieuse. On doit traiter promptement toute affection compliquant une défaillance cardiaque, telle une infection, l'anémie ou le déséquilibre électrolytique.

En présence d'un œdème pulmonaire, toute infection intercurrente doit être traitée adéquatement. On peut avoir à réduire le sel de l'alimentation en vue de prévenir une rétention excessive de liquide. Le lait sans sel Lonalac est à conseiller. Le régime hyposodé est réajusté progressivement au fur et à mesure que l'enfant récupère. On peut administrer du sulfate de morphine, pour ses effets favorables sur l'œdème pulmonaire.

La surveillance du bébé suppose aussi la pesée quotidienne et le dosage strict des liquides. Avant le départ du bébé de l'hôpital, la mère doit apprendre à administrer les médicaments du bébé, à connaître leurs effets secondaires et le type de régime qu'il devra suivre ainsi que la teneur en sel des différents aliments. Elle doit savoir reconnaître l'apparition de l'œdème et de l'infection. Si l'enfant reçoit de la digoxine, l'équipe médicale devra décider si l'on doit enseigner à la mère à prendre le pouls apical; elle peut en effet s'inquiéter à la moindre variation ce qui influera sur les soins qu'elle donnera au bébé. Le médecin et l'infirmière doivent discuter avec la mère des soins à donner au bébé avant le départ de celui-ci de l'hôpital.

Résumé des soins infirmiers dans les cardiopathies congénitales

Les soins infirmiers aux nourrissons et enfants atteints d'anomalies du système cardiovasculaire sont très importants. Ils dépendent naturellement du traitement établi par le médecin et comportent des procédures délicates et de l'habileté technique.

L'infirmière doit se familiariser avec la réaction habituelle des parents à qui l'on annonce que leur enfant est atteint d'une cardiopathie congénitale, et apprendre à les rassurer sans pour autant minimiser les dangers de la maladie. Elle doit enseigner aux parents com-

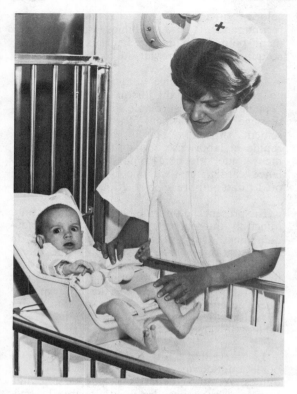

Figure 10-12. Les enfants, particulièrement les bébés, souffrant de congestion pulmonaire, semblent plus à l'aise en position assise. (Courtoisie de l'Hôpital Sainte-Justine, Montréal.)

ment prendre soin de l'enfant entre le moment où il va quitter la pouponnière et son retour à l'hôpital pour subir l'opération. Ces soins visent à, 1) maintenir une nutrition adéquate malgré la lenteur à boire et la succion déficiente. La mère peut utiliser des tétines flexibles, ramollies par l'ébullition et installer le bébé dans des positions moins traditionnelles, mais qui facilitent la respiration et la consommation d'oxygène. L'introduction de la nourriture solide plus rapidement et plus complètement aide ces bébés. 2) réduire les difficultés respiratoires précipitant la fatigue cardiaque. L'infirmière et la mère doivent apprendre à humidifier les sécrétions nasales et à les extraire manuellement plusieurs fois par jour. Une atmosphère suffisamment humide doit toujours être maintenue.

La prévention des infections et des situations fatigantes ou anxiogènes a été expliquée dans les soins à l'enfant affecté d'une tétralogie de Fallot .Ce qui a été dit précédemment à ce sujet peut être appliqué aux autres types de malformations cardiaques congénitales.

Système nerveux central

Spina-bifida

Incidence et types. Le spina-bifida consiste en un défaut de fermeture d'une ou plusieurs lames vertébrales. Cette anomalie osseuse peut atteindre une ou plusieurs vertèbres. Elle peut se situer à n'importe quel niveau de la colonne vertébrale, mais plus souvent à la région sacro-lombaire. C'est l'anomalie la plus fréquente dans le développement du système nerveux central; elle apparaît approximativement une fois sur mille naissances.

Nous étudierons trois variétés d'anomalies. 1) Le spina-bifida simple, où l'anomalie n'atteint que la structure osseuse et dans lequel la moelle et les méninges sont normales. 2) La méningocèle, dans laquelle les méninges seules forment une hernie à travers le spina-bifida. 3) La myéloméningocèle, dans laquelle la moelle épinière et les méninges font une saillie au travers de la brèche osseuse du canal vertébral. La myéloméningocèle est la plus grave de ces anomalies.

Spina-bifida occulte

Manifestations cliniques, diagnostic et traitement. La majorité des patients ne présentent pas de symptômes. Quelques-uns peuvent avoir une excroissance de la peau ou des poils au niveau de la vertèbre malformée. Si l'affection est soupçonnée, à cause de ces signes ou à la suite d'un examen physique, une radiographie infirmera ou confirmera le diagnostic. Aucun traitement n'est requis, à moins que des symptômes neurologiques n'indiquent que l'anomalie est plus grave qu'on ne l'avait d'abord soupçonné. Si on craint que la moelle épinière puisse être impliquée dans l'anomalie, un traitement chirurgical est indiqué.

Méningocèle

Manifestations cliniques, diagnostic, traitement et pronostic. Le nouveau-né présente une anomalie de la colonne vertébrale assez grande pour que les méninges surgissent à travers l'ouverture. L'anomalie se situe sur la ligne médiane et la hernie est ordinairement couverte d'une couche de peau normale. La défectuosité se trouve le plus souvent au niveau lombo-sacré ou cervical. Il n'y a généralement ni évidence de faiblesse des jambes, car l'enfant s'étire et bouge normalement, ni manque de contrôle sphinctérien, quoique ceci soit difficile à évaluer chez le nouveau-né. Le pronostic s'avère excellent

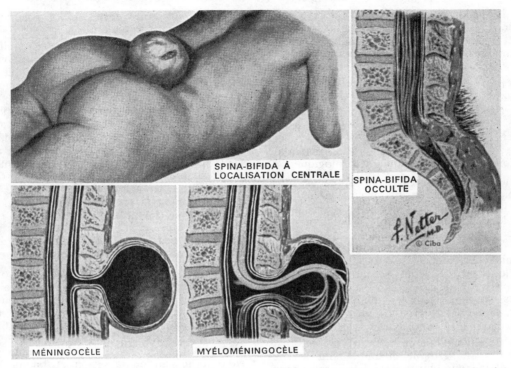

Figure 10-13. Diagrammes représentant les types de spina bifida. (Droit d'auteur — Collection Ciba d'illustrations médicales, par Frank H. Netter, m.d.)

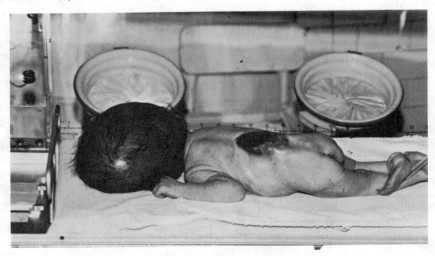

Figure 10-14. Enfant souffrant d'une myéloméningocèle avec hydrocéphalie. (Courtoisie du Dr Luis Schut.)

et l'anomalie se corrige par la chirurgie. L'hydrocéphalie peut déjà être présente ou apparaître après la correction de la méningocèle.

Myéloméningocèle

Manifestations cliniques, diagnostic, traitement et pronostic. Dans cette affection, un segment imparfaitement développé de la moelle épinière ainsi que les méninges, font saillie à travers la fissure du rachis (spina-bifida). La protubérance arrondie et fluctuante ressemble à celle de la méningocèle mais elle n'est habituellement recouverte que d'une mince pellicule de tissu friable et parfois suintant. L'anomalie est ordinairement localisée dans la région sacro-lombaire. La myéloméningocèle peut produire un affaiblissement léger et même une paralysie flasque complète des jambes et une insensibilité totale des membres inférieurs, accompagnées de pieds bots.

Le fonctionnement des intestins et de la vessie requiert une soigneuse évaluation, car des perturbations graves se présentent fréquemment. L'objectif du traitement et des soins infirmiers vise à éviter l'infection du sac herniaire et à permettre la restauration maximale des fonctions orthopédique et urologique.

L'intervention chirurgicale supprime une anomalie esthétiquement inacceptable, prévient l'infection et dans beaucoup de cas, améliore le déficit neurologique en diminuant la tension exercée sur certaines voies nerveuses. Autrefois, on retardait l'opération de la myéloméningocèle afin de pouvoir contrôler toute infection; on l'effectue aujourd'hui, aussitôt que possible, de préférence durant les premières vingt-quatre heures qui suivent la naissance, pour empêcher toute détérioration ultérieure des tissus nerveux.

La décision d'opérer ou non l'enfant, peut constituer un véritable dilemme pour les parents et le neurochirurgien. Il est très important que les parents reçoivent tous les renseignements concernant l'état actuel et le pronostic de l'affection de leur enfant. Ils ont besoin de beaucoup de sympathie durant cette période.

Le syndrome d'*Arnold-Chiari*, habituellement sans symptôme, est une malformation congénitale de la région occipito-cervicale, consistant en un glissement des amygdales cérébelleuses et des structures voisines dans une portion du canal rachidien cervical entraînant un gonflement et coincement du bulbe rachidien. La lésion se produit entre les seizième et vingtième semaines de la vie fœtale. Ce syndrome se présente chez près de 50% des enfants ayant un spina-bifida lombo-sacré avec myéloméningocèle. Le bulbe rachidien et une partie du cervelet sont attirés dans le foramen magnum parce que la mœlle épinière est attachée au siège de la lésion dans la colonne vertébrale. Le résultat peut être une obstruction dans l'écoulement du liquide céphalo-rachidien, et c'est ainsi qu'une hydrocéphalie se développe souvent chez ces enfants, même à la suite de la réparation de la myéloméningocèle.

Les symptômes résultent du blocage complet ou partiel de la circulation du liquide céphalo-rachidien. Chez les bébés, les manifestations cliniques consistent en un écoulement nasal (quelquefois confondu avec une infection des voies respiratoires supérieures) et une respiration ronflante.

L'infirmière doit observer ces manifestations qui indiquent l'urgence de faire baisser la pression du liquide. Elle doit habituellement mesurer la circonférence crânienne (au niveau du front et de la région occipitale) afin de suivre l'évolution de l'hydrocéphalie. Chez les enfants plus âgés, les manifestations comprennent la raideur de la nuque, la céphalée et les vertiges. Quand l'enfant est assez vieux pour marcher et parler, sa démarche est hésitante et son langage anormal. Comme chirurgie palliative, la correction de l'hydrocéphalie est le seul traitement connu pour le syndrome d'Arnold-Chiari.

Soins des enfants affectés d'une méningocèle et d'une myéloméningocèle

Soins préopératoires. Jusqu'au moment de l'intervention, le nouveau-né doit être tenu à plat sur l'abdomen, la lésion recouverte d'une simple couche de gaze stérilisée vaselinée ou un « coussin de Telfa » imbibé de solution de Varidase. Il s'agit de prévenir la rupture du sac; donc, il faut éviter toute pression au niveau de la lésion et bannir l'emploi d'épingles à ressort pouvant perforer le sac.

Si, pour une raison quelconque, le neurochirurgien préfère attendre pour opérer, les soins préopératoires sont ceux à accorder à un enfant normal, tout en protégeant le sac herniaire des chocs, frictions et infections qui pourraient l'atteindre. Pour diminuer le danger d'infection par les matières fécales et l'urine, on maintient les parties génitales et les fesses dans une propreté irréprochable, et on ne met pas de couche si l'anomalie siège à la partie inférieure de la colonne vertébrale. Si la paroi du sac est infectée ou mince, certains médecins prescrivent une solution de Varidase en goutte à goutte sur la région.

Il existe trois méthodes de soins pour conserver le sac herniaire propre et non contaminé par les selles et les urines. On peut utiliser l'une ou l'autre ou une combinaison des trois. Dans le premier cas, le sac lui-même est recouvert d'un pansement stérile. On applique d'abord une gaze vaselinée sur la lésion puis on installe autour du sac un anneau de tissu spongieux recouvert de gaze stérile. Cet anneau doit être suffisamment large et haut pour ne pas comprimer l'anomalie, mais la protéger complètement. Un bandage abdominal recouvert d'une mince feuille imperméable est ensuite appliqué. Lorsque l'on utilise cette méthode, le bébé peut facilement être mobilisé, pris dans les bras.

Dans le second cas, on couche l'enfant à plat ventre et on installe un tablier de méningocèle. Il s'agit de coller une pièce de plastique au-dessous de la lésion. On place le bout le plus long dans la direction de la tête de l'enfant, et on se sert d'un papier collant résistant, hydrophile et anti-allergique, pour le faire tenir en place, juste au-dessus du pli fessier. On replie ensuite la pièce de plastique sur elle-même et on la fixe à nouveau contre la peau de telle sorte qu'elle recouvre le siège et protège la lésion des matières fécales.

Un troisième choix est de placer l'enfant sur un cadre de Bradford, sorte de sommier à lanières, fabriqué de telle façon que l'urine et les selles passent entre les sections de l'appareil et tombent dans un récipient placé en-dessous. On dispose la literie de façon à couvrir le matelas, laissant l'orifice libre.

Dans tous les cas décrits, le bébé peut être pris dans les bras plusieurs fois par jour, à condition qu'une bonne technique soit utilisée par l'infirmière. Elle doit toujours tenir l'enfant en passant une main sous le siège et l'autre sous la tête. La position dans laquelle on place l'enfant dans son lit, s'avère ici d'une importance capitale. L'enfant ne doit pas être couché sur le dos, une telle position pouvant exercer une pression contre la protubérance. Si le médecin le permet, on peut placer l'enfant en décubitus latéral avec une couverture enroulée ou un oreiller derrière la tête et le siège. Les couvertures ou l'oreiller doivent être protégés des matières fécales par une enveloppe de plastique.

Il faut surtout éviter les mauvaises positions qui, à la longue, engendrent des contractures difficiles à corriger.

On doit placer les membres inférieurs selon la position anatomique en évitant la flexion prononcée aux articulations de la hanche et du genou. On peut « draper » les jambes du bébé pour obtenir ce résultat. On utilise alors une couche repliée en forme de huit qui recouvre les jambes et les cuisses. Elle maintient un bon alignement des membres inférieurs et prévient l'irritation cutanée causée par la friction sur la literie ou sur la jambe opposée. Elle doit être enlevée et réinstallée à chaque séance d'exercices. Un coussinet sous la cheville maintient le pied dans une position adéquate. Les exercices passifs des pieds, des jambes et des cuisses effectués toutes les 3 ou 4 heures par l'infirmière ou la physiothérapeute préviennent aussi les contractures et gardent aux jambes la mobilité dont elles auront besoin pour que l'enfant puisse éventuellement apprendre à marcher à l'aide d'appareils orthopédiques.

L'enfant affecté d'une myéloméningocèle importante, avec perte de contrôle des sphincters, sera sujet aux infections urinaires consécutives au résidu vésical chronique. Pour éviter cette complication, on peut pratiquer sur l'enfant la méthode de Crédé qui consiste en une compression manuelle de la vessie facilitant l'expulsion plus complète de l'urine. L'infirmière — ou la mère, quand l'enfant est à la maison — a la responsabilité de vider la vessie de l'enfant toutes les deux heures

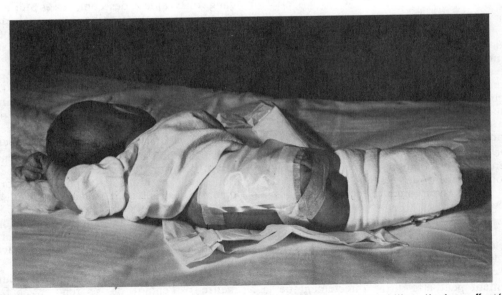

Figure 10-15. Technique employée pour protéger la protubérance et immobiliser l'enfant affecté d'une myéloméningocèle. (Courtoisie de l'American Journal of Nursing.)

durant le jour et une fois au cours de la nuit. On presse fermement mais doucement, en commençant par la région ombilicale et en progressant lentement vers la symphyse pubienne et vers l'anus.

Il faut aider la mère à apprendre cette méthode aussitôt que possible et elle devrait la pratiquer sous surveillance jusqu'à ce qu'elle la maîtrise bien. L'enfant grandissant, son urine peut être évacuée moins fréquemment. S'il est doté d'une intelligence normale, vers la troisième ou la quatrième année, il devrait être à même d'exécuter partiellement cette technique qui demeurera nécessaire même après la réparation de la myéloméningocèle.

On peut prendre le bébé pour lui donner son biberon. Quand la lésion est petite, il peut être tenu en position normale, l'infirmière prenant garde de ne pas toucher au sac herniaire. En cas de lésion plus volumineuse, on donne le biberon à l'enfant couché latéralement sur les genoux de l'infirmière ou de sa mère. Lorsque le sac est protégé par un anneau, la position habituelle pour boire est permise.

Lui faire rendre des gaz constitue un problème si la lésion siège à la région dorsale. On peut interrompre fréquemment l'alimentation, le faire boire lentement et, sans le masser, le tenir simplement en position verticale. L'éructation, plus longue à venir, se produira la plupart du temps. La myéloméningocèle lombaire n'empêche pas de tenir l'enfant en position verticale et de le masser doucement entre les omoplates comme n'importe quel bébé.

On peut éviter la contamination du sac herniaire en le couvrant avec de la gaze stérile, lorsque l'enfant est sorti du lit. Si l'enfant doit demeurer dans son lit, on le tourne légèrement sur le côté, et on lui élève la tête avec la main pendant qu'il boit. Ne pouvant lui procurer la joie qu'il éprouverait à être bercé, on lui offrira une compensation à ce plaisir, par exemple en lui caressant doucement la peau ou en fredonnant.

Une des principales responsabilités de l'infirmière est l'observation et la notation exacte du comportement de l'enfant, ainsi que des signes et des symptômes directement reliés à son état. Elle devrait enregistrer les mouvements des jambes, ainsi que les fonctions vésicale et intestinale, notant s'il y a incontinence ou rétention d'urine ou de matières fécales. Tous les signes vitaux devraient être observés et enregistrés avec un soin extrême.

L'enfant peut être dirigé directement de la salle d'accouchement ou de la pouponnière vers une unité pédiatrique. S'il est emmené à la maison avant sa réadmission à l'hôpital pour intervention chirurgicale, ses parents prendront soin de lui. Le père peut fabriquer un substitut pour le cadre de Bradford et la mère peut le couvrir comme indiqué plus haut. Les deux parents devraient apprendre comment porter l'enfant sans appuyer sur le sac herniaire et ils devraient maîtriser les principaux soins avant le départ du bébé de l'hôpital. Une infirmière visiteuse peut leur procurer un secours précieux.

Soins infirmiers postopératoires. Le but du traitement chirurgical est la fermeture de la lésion superficielle, tout en préservant le fonctionnement des tissus nerveux. L'infirmière a pour tâche d'observer tous les signes et symptômes que présente l'enfant. Elle contrôle fréquemment la température, le pouls et la respiration. Il faut prévoir le choc postopératoire et avoir un incubateur disponible, si le bébé n'y a pas d'emblée été placé. Comme celui-ci peut présenter des troubles respiratoires, le matériel nécessaire à l'administration d'oxygène et d'humidité doit être gardé à proximité. La distension abdominale causée par l'iléus paralytique ou la distension vésicale souvent présente à la suite d'opérations sur la colonne vertébrale, devraient être signalées immédiatement.

On mesure fréquemment la circonférence de la tête de l'enfant de manière à déterminer si l'hydrocéphalie se manifeste à la suite de la cure de myéloméningocèle. On protège les bandages chirurgicaux à l'aide d'un tablier à méningocèle. Si le pansement se souille de sang, on y ajoute des compresses stériles pour obtenir une surface sèche. On ne déplace pas le pansement appliqué à la salle d'opération et on avertit aussitôt si l'écoulement sanguin semble important.

Les plâtres appliqués de façon prophylactique pour protéger les jambes de l'enfant contre les contractures doivent être mis en position appropriée et manipulés avec précaution. Toutefois, l'application de plâtre n'est pas utilisée par tous les neurochirurgiens.

Après l'opération, certains chirurgiens préfèrent que l'enfant soit nourri dans une position aussi naturelle que possible, alors que d'autres désirent qu'il soit alimenté au lit jusqu'à la guérison complète des plaies. Si l'on fait boire l'enfant dans son lit, en position ventrale, sa tête doit être légèrement surélevée par la main de l'infirmière, ou en élevant la tête du lit.

On retire la tétine fréquemment pour permettre à l'enfant de se reposer et faciliter l'expulsion des gaz. Le gavage peut s'avérer nécessaire.

Réadaptation postopératoire. L'amélioration de la locomotion et des fonctions intestinale et vésicale requiert des soins longs et diligents. L'adaptation permet l'utilisation maximale des capacités normales et réduit au minimum le *handicap,* rendant l'enfant aussi autonome que possible dans les activités de la vie quotidienne. Pour élargir son horizon vital et éviter la privation sensorielle et motrice qui le guette, il faut lui fournir des occasions d'observer et de participer à des activités variées comme le font tous les enfants de son âge. Quoique l'enfant doive apprendre des mouvements qui le rendront moins dépendant des autres, il doit apprendre aussi à accepter l'aide dont les enfants normaux n'ont pas besoin. L'adulte doit l'aider à se maintenir au niveau de développement propre à son âge.

L'incontinence fécale après l'enfance crée des problèmes sociaux importants. On doit conduire l'enfant à la toilette à intervalles réguliers. On peut utiliser un suppositoire jusqu'à ce qu'il soit entraîné à avoir des évacuations régulières. Il peut avoir besoin d'une diète spéciale pour éviter la constipation qui peut conduire aux fécalomes. Il faudra peut-être avoir recours au toucher rectal quotidien. S'il peut aller à la selle avec régularité, il deviendra socialement plus acceptable.

Des mictions contrôlées sont encore plus importantes. Si l'enfant ne peut uriner spontanément, il faudra évacuer sa vessie par la méthode de Crédé (c'est-à-dire presser périodiquement pour faire évacuer l'urine) comme on le faisait avant l'opération. Un enfant de trois ans à quatre ans peut apprendre à vider sa propre vessie, en gonflant un ballon de jeu et en se couchant dessus pour faire pression au niveau de la symphyse pubienne. Sa mère peut alors procéder à l'évacuation des urines résiduelles. Il faut éviter la distension vésicale qui augmente le danger de cystite. Le reflux d'une vessie distendue peut causer l'hydrurètère et l'hydronéphrose avec lésions et infections rénales consécutives. Les cultures d'urine permettront de choisir l'antibiotique approprié si une infection urinaire apparaît en cours d'évolution.

Pour toutes ces raisons, on doit instituer un horaire de toilette et aider l'enfant à s'y adapter. L'enfant paraplégique nécessite les soins constants d'un urologue.

Les antiseptiques urinaires pris par voie buccale aident à prévenir l'infection de la vessie atone. Chez le petit garçon qui présente un écoulement goutte à goutte presque constant, un système collecteur peut être installé en attendant une intervention chirurgicale. Le sac collecteur n'entrave en rien son programme de réadaptation orthopédique. Ceci n'est pas possible avec les petites filles. On a tenté, par des moyens chirurgicaux, de créer une voie de dérivation des urines en transplantant les uretères dans l'anse sigmoïde du côlon. Malheureusement, les suites opératoires se compliquent fréquemment d'une sténose du point d'anastomose de l'uretère au sigmoïde, ce qui devient une cause d'hydronéphrose, d'infection à colibacilles, ou encore d'une perturbation hydro-électrolytique grave à la suite de la réabsorption intestinale d'une partie de l'urine.

L'alternative opératoire consiste à isoler complètement une portion de l'iléon pour en fabriquer une néo-vessie complètement détachée de l'intestin communément appelée « vessie iléale ». Les extrémités intestinales sectionnées sont anastomosées pour rétablir l'intégrité du tractus digestif. La portion de l'iléon est cousue sous forme de sac, on y transplante les extrémités des uretères et le sac est abouché à la paroi abdominale. Un sac de cystostomie adapté avec soin sur l'orifice, reçoit l'urine et l'empêche de couler sur la peau. Des mesures hygiéniques rigoureuses évitent les mauvaises odeurs. On lave régulièrement le pourtour de l'ouverture à l'eau tiède et une pâte-ciment peut être appliquée pour assurer l'étanchéité du système collecteur. Des sacs de polyéthylène jetables s'avèrent être la solution idéale quoique le sac lavable semble être plus économique à l'usage, tout en demandant une propreté scrupuleuse. Le patient emploie ordinairement deux sacs, qu'il alterne pour permettre l'aération quotidienne et le trempage dans une solution désinfectante. Les tablettes de chlorophylle chassent les mauvaises odeurs de façon satisfaisante. L'enfant doit apprendre très tôt les soins d'hygiène que requiert son état.

Quoique ses jambes puissent être totalement ou partiellement paralysées, on peut promener l'enfant dans une poussette et lui apprendre ensuite à utiliser des moyens de locomotion qu'il actionnera lui-même, en position ventrale, avec ses bras et ses mains. Ces petits véhicules fortifient ses membres supérieurs et le préparent à l'apprentissage de la marche en station debout. La plupart des physiatres bannissent l'emploi de la chaise roulante. Si le médecin choisit d'utiliser des attelles pour la marche, il utilisera probablement des supports lourds dont on réduit graduellement le poids au fur et à mesure que l'enfant grandit. Le physiothérapeute enseigne aux parents les exercices passifs et actifs nécessaires au maintien du tonus musculaire des

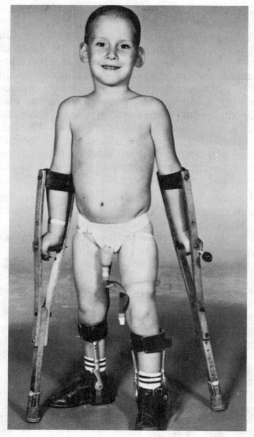

Figure 10-16. Système collecteur urinaire pour garçon. (Davol.)

appareils orthopédiques ainsi que l'entretien de ces appareils. L'enfant affecté d'une myéloméningocèle requiert des soins complexes toute sa vie et il est préférable que les parents s'inscrivent à une clinique spécialisée dans le soin de ces enfants. Il peut arriver que les parents confient leur enfant à une institution pour de courtes périodes ou définitivement tout en conservant un contact avec lui. L'infirmière doit toujours aider les parents à bien comprendre la pathologie et les soins que requiert leur enfant.

Les soins de longue durée ont pour but d'empêcher l'obésité ou la malnutrition, ainsi que les contractures secondaires ou autres difformités. Toute infection qui se déclare doit être promptement traitée avec des antibiotiques. Si l'enfant est mentalement normal, il peut devenir un membre actif dans la société. Une assistance psychologique peut être nécessaire pour lui permettre d'atteindre l'équilibre émotif dont il aura grandement besoin au cours de sa vie d'adulte.

Encéphalocèle

Une encéphalocèle consiste en la protrusion de substance cérébrale à travers un défaut de fermeture congénital au niveau de la boîte crânienne. L'anomalie se présente généralement sur la ligne médiane dans la région occipitale ou pariétale, quoiqu'elle puisse aussi se produire aux régions frontale, orbitale ou nasale.

Manifestations cliniques, diagnostic, traitement, pronostic et soins infirmiers. Les *symptômes* dépendent du degré d'implication du tissu nerveux et de la localisation de la lésion.

L'évidence *diagnostique* est un sac herniaire dans lequel les méninges, du liquide cé-

membres inférieurs et au renforcement des muscles thoraciques et des membres supérieurs.

Les parents doivent aussi connaître les soins que l'enfant requiert lorsqu'il porte des

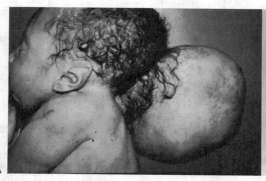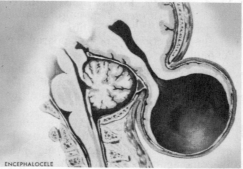

Figure 10-17. Encéphalocèle. *A)* Encéphalocèle occipitale (Courtoisie de Luis Schut, m.d.) *B)* Coupe en diagramme. (Droits réservés. Collection Ciba d'illustrations médicales, par Frank H. Netter, m.d.)

phalorachidien et du tissu cérébral se sont logés. La radiographie localise le défaut osseux. Une chirurgie réparatrice précoce s'impose, quoiqu'il ne faille pas s'attendre à une amélioration spectaculaire de l'état neurologique du bébé.

Le *pronostic* dépend de l'étendue et de la localisation de l'encéphalocèle. Il y a danger de méningite, si la lésion se rompt.

Les *soins* prodigués au bébé porteur d'une encéphalocèle ressemblent aux soins du bébé normal. On doit cependant le manipuler avec précaution pour éviter le traumatisme et la rupture de la lésion. On le change fréquemment de position pour empêcher l'infection pulmonaire par hypostase. En répondant aux questions des parents, il faut garder à l'esprit que la substance cérébrale contenue dans la hernie ne peut ordinairement pas être replacée dans la voûte crânienne et que le déficit neurologique de l'enfant a peu de chance de s'améliorer. La cure chirurgicale a surtout pour but l'aspect esthétique, la plus grande facilité de manipulation et la prévention de l'infection.

Hydrocéphalie

L'hydrocéphalie se définit comme une accumulation exagérée de liquide céphalo-rachidien dans la cavité crânienne.

Pour comprendre la *physio-pathologie*, il serait bon de revoir comment le liquide céphalo-rachidien se forme, comment il circule, et comment il est résorbé dans l'organisme. Le liquide céphalo-rachidien (L.C.R.) est formé par les plexus choroïdes des ventricules, par filtration à travers les capillaires. Il passe des ventricules latéraux (1er et 2e) dans le troisième ventricule, par les trous de Monro. Du troisième ventricule, il coule à travers l'aqueduc de Sylvius dans le quatrième ventricule, et de là dans la grande citerne, l'espace sous-arachnoïdien latéral, et le canal intramédullaire par les trous de Lushka et de Magendie. Il passe ensuite sous la base du cerveau et, par-dessus la convexité, dans la gouttière corticale jusqu'à ce qu'il soit finalement absorbé dans les sinus veineux par les villosités arachnoïdiennes. Il coule aussi le long des gaines de tous les nerfs crâniens et rachidiens avant d'être résorbé dans le système vasculaire. Normalement la quantité absorbée égale celle qui est sécrétée.

Hydrocéphalie communicante. Les *sortes* d'hydrocéphalie dépendent des causes qui l'ont provoquée. On rencontre d'abord l'hydrocéphalie par hyperproduction de liquide (papillôme du plexus choroïde) ou par ré-sorption déficiente. Ces deux variétés réalisent l'*hydrocéphalie communicante*; une communication normale existe entre les ventricules et l'espace sous-archnoïdien qui entoure le cerveau et la moelle. La déficience de résorption dépend souvent d'une cause méningée comme une hémorragie, des adhérences consécutives à une méningite, ou d'une anomalie méningée congénitale. L'excès de liquide se localise ordinairement entre la voûte crânienne qui s'amincit et l'encéphale qui s'atrophie sous la pression. Le volume de la tête augmente peu, si on le compare avec celui qui est produit par une hydrocéphalie non-communicante. L'hydrocéphalie communicante peut compliquer une myéloméningocèle.

Hydrocéphalie non communicante. Plus fréquente que l'hydrocéphalie communicante, elle provient d'un obstacle en amont de l'espace sous-arachnoïdien. Le blocage partiel ou complet se traduit par une accumulation plus ou moins rapide de liquide, qui peut débuter pendant les derniers mois de la vie intra-utérine. On peut retrouver plusieurs causes d'obstacles mécaniques: une absence de développement ou une occlusion partielle congénitale le long du trajet du L.C.R., telle une atrésie des trous de Lushka ou de l'aqueduc de Sylvius, ou un blocage provenant d'un caillot, d'une tumeur ou d'un exsudat situé sur le parcours du liquide céphalo-rachidien.

L'excès de liquide dilate les ventricules, ce qui peut provoquer une atrophie progressive de la substance cérébrale qui appuie sur la paroi osseuse. Le volume de la tête augmente de façon saisissante et, si le blocage existait in-utero, il peut même empêcher le déroulement normal de l'accouchement. En présence d'un obstacle congénital partiel ou si la lésion apparaît après la naissance, la tête est normale à la naissance et s'hypertrophie lentement; le déficit neurologique se révèle progressivement.

Manifestations cliniques. Le principal symptôme consiste en une augmentation importante du volume de la tête. Les os de l'enfant encore malléables, les sutures crâniennes non fixées et l'accumulation du L.C.R. peuvent amener une distension de la boîte crânienne. Au lieu de se fermer, les fontanelles s'élargissent et deviennent bombées. L'enfant souffre d'irritabilité, d'anorexie et de nausées. Il perd des forces et soulève de plus en plus difficilement sa tête. On constate une atrophie progressive des muscles du cou, par manque d'exercice; un nystagmus ou un strabisme convergent peuvent apparaître. La vision devient probablement brouillée, les yeux semblent poussés vers le bas et légèrement

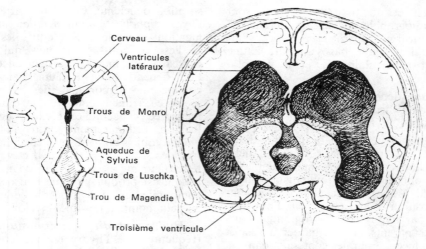

Cerveau

Ventricules
latéraux

Trous de Monro

Aqueduc de
Sylvius

Trous de Luschka

Trou de Magendie

Troisième ventricule

Figure 10-18. Hydrocéphalie. *A)* Diagramme du cerveau indiquant les points possibles d'obstruction. *B)* Diagramme du cerveau indiquant la dilatation du troisième ventricule et des ventricules latéraux.

saillants, la sclérotique est visible au-dessus de l'iris, les paupières supérieures étant rétractées sur le front proéminent (yeux en soleil couchant). Le cuir chevelu devient brillant et les trajets veineux apparaissent sur la surface du crâne (circulation compensatrice du cuir chevelu). Les manifestations affectives et les réponses sensitives normales diminuent; le bébé peut présenter des convulsions. Tous les symptômes réunis réalisent le *tableau de l'hypertension intracrânienne chronique du nourrisson.*

Le tonus musculaire des extrémités est souvent anormal. À mesure que l'état de l'enfant se détériore, il maigrit à tel point que le poids du corps devient souvent inférieur à celui de la tête. Il crie de façon aiguë et perçante. Il devient spécialement sujet aux complications infectieuses.

Diagnostic. Les tests et examens sont entrepris pour localiser le point d'obstruction. On vérifie en même temps l'évolution, en mesurant quotidiennement la circonférence de la tête, et très souvent aussi la circonférence thoracique, pour établir un point de référence. La *ponction du ventricule* détermine la présence réelle de liquide et l'épaisseur du cortex cérébral. La *pneumoencéphalographie* (ventriculographie), qui consiste en une injection d'air après ponction lombaire ou par ponction directe de la fontanelle antérieure, permet de rendre visible les contours des ventricules. L'injection de colorant dans le ventricule (*test de Blakfan*) permet de reconnaître l'hydrocéphalie communicante, si le colorant parvient au niveau de la moelle ou apparaît plus tard dans les urines. La radiographie du crâne et l'électroencéphalogramme (E.E.G.) donnent également des renseignements précieux.

L'utilisation médicale des *isotopes* va peut-être marquer une étape importante dans l'investigation. On fait actuellement le marquage du L.C.R. pour compléter les épreuves diagnostiques.

Traitement. Il n'existe actuellement aucun traitement médical de l'hydrocéphalie. La correction chirurgicale de la lésion sous-jacente demeure quasi impossible. Devant un problème d'ordre mécanique, l'alternative opératoire consiste en une dérivation du liquide

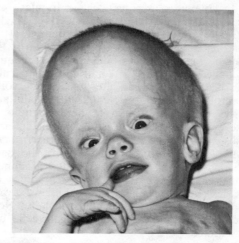

Figure 10-19. Hydrocéphalie. L'enfant est abattu et léthargique. Le strabisme est présent. Le « signe des yeux en soleil couchant » est patent. Les veines du cuir chevelu sont dilatées. On a placé un coussin de caoutchouc mousse sous la tête de l'enfant. Une couverture est enroulée sous ses épaules.

céphalo-rachidien vers un point quelconque de l'organisme. Plusieurs dérivations ou pontages ont été préconisés: la ventriculo-vénostomie (ventricule cérébral – jugulaire-oreillette droite), la ventriculo-péritonéostomie, la ventriculo-urétérostomie (ablation d'un rein et abouchement du tube à l'uretère) ou l'urétérostomie lombaire (le tube relie l'uretère à l'espace sous-arachnoïdien). Il existe aussi l'intervention de Torkildsen selon laquelle on relie un ventricule latéral à la grande citerne.

Le traitement qui semble le plus satisfaisant actuellement consiste en la dérivation du liquide d'un ventricule cérébral latéral vers l'oreillette droite, en passant par la veine jugulaire interne et la veine cave supérieure (ventriculo-vénostomie). Une valve (Holter-Pudenz) empêche le sang de refluer dans les ventricules et permet au liquide céphalo-rachidien, quand il est sous pression, d'entrer dans le système circulatoire. La valve passe sous la peau à la région mastoïdienne; compressible, elle aide au déblocage si le tube vient à se boucher et évite l'obstruction post-opératoire formée par les caillots. D'autres complications sont possibles, telles une thrombose de la jugulaire ou une infection. Le tube doit être replacé périodiquement avec des risques supplémentaires d'infection.

Pronostic. Autrefois, il était très mauvais, mais avec les techniques chirurgicales actuelles, on a obtenu d'excellents résultats. Si le cerveau n'est pas sérieusement atteint au moment de l'intervention, les fonctions mentales peuvent demeurer intactes. Les fonctions motrices sont retardées temporairement si l'enfant ne peut relever la tête et se mouvoir, comme un enfant devrait normalement pouvoir le faire. Dans beaucoup de cas, il y a des séquelles neurologiques. La mort peut résulter d'une malnutrition ou d'une infection concomitante, si l'intervention est trop tardive ou n'est pas entreprise.

Soins. Quand le diagnostic a été fait assez tôt après le début de la maladie, les soins infirmiers présentent peu de difficultés. L'infirmière a pour tâche d'observer le degré d'irritabilité et les variations dans les signes vitaux et doit les signaler promptement.

Soins préopératoires. Quand l'hydrocéphalie est importante, les soins infirmiers s'avèrent plus difficiles. L'enfant peut être incapable de soulever ou même de mouvoir la tête; des dommages cérébraux peuvent retarder le développement mental, et la malnutrition peut résulter d'une alimentation insuffisante et de vomissements fréquents.

En donnant les soins hygiéniques au bébé, on doit porter une attention spéciale aux plis du cou, où la transpiration et le lait régurgité peuvent s'accumuler.

En vue d'assurer l'alimentation, on établit un horaire de repas de manière à éviter les vomissements. On donne tous les soins appropriés avant le repas, de manière à éviter de déplacer l'enfant après qu'il ait été nourri. On doit le prendre pour le faire manger. Sa tête est lourde et l'infirmière devrait poser son bras sur un coussin placé sur l'appui de sa

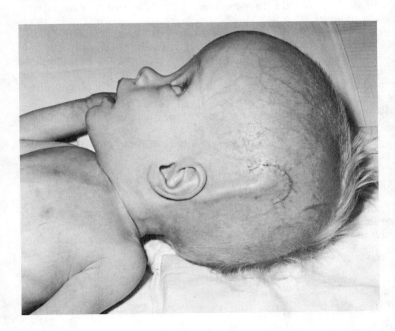

Figure 10-20. Enfant hydrocéphale porteur d'un tube de dérivation qui permet l'écoulement du liquide ventriculaire vers la circulation.

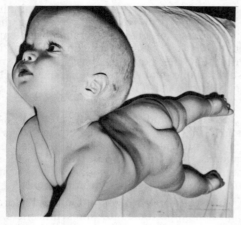

Figure 10-21. Opisthotonos résultant d'une méningite chez un nourrisson hydrocéphale.

chaise. Si la tête est très grosse, on ne peut placer l'enfant en position verticale pour lui faire rendre ses gaz. On retire le biberon plusieurs fois de la bouche du bébé pendant qu'on le nourrit, et on élève légèrement sa tête et ses épaules. Il serait utile de le masser doucement entre les omoplates. En le remettant dans son berceau il faut veiller à le coucher sur le côté, pour empêcher qu'il n'aspire le lait régurgité.

On le change fréquemment de position pour prévenir la pneumonie hypostatique et pour diminuer les risques d'apparition de plaies de décubitus. Ces lésions peuvent se manifester sur la tête et les oreilles, à moins que toutes les précautions ne soient prises pour les éviter. On place sous la tête un coussin de laine de mouton ou d'éponge en caoutchouc mousse. Un coussinet sous ses épaules est utile pour diminuer l'écart de niveau entre la tête et le reste du corps. Un matelas en caoutchouc mousse ou à pression alternative donnent d'excellents résultats. Si les plaies de lit apparaissent, on doit prendre de grandes précautions pour éviter l'infection qui, dans l'état de débilité de l'enfant, peut provoquer la septicémie.

Quand on soulève l'enfant de son berceau, on supporte soigneusement sa tête de manière à éviter tout traumatisme. En le changeant de position dans le lit, la main de l'infirmière soutient la tête, libérant ainsi l'autre main pour porter le corps. Il est essentiel que la tête et le corps soient tournés en même temps, pour ne pas provoquer de tension sur le cou, des vertiges et des nausées.

Pour lever l'enfant, l'infirmière se penche sur le berceau, lui place la main sous la tête, et l'ajuste contre sa poitrine. Ensuite, elle le lève avec l'autre bras en supportant le corps comme pour un enfant normal.

S'il y a ponction lombaire, l'infirmière aidera le médecin selon l'usage de l'hôpital. L'équipement requis est le même que pour un adulte. Avec un petit nourrisson, l'infirmière place un coude derrière le cou de l'enfant, l'autre main sur les cuisses, et elle arrondit le dos de l'enfant dans la position désirée. Pour immobiliser un enfant plus âgé, elle peut placer un bras autour du cou et tenir les jambes, puis placer son autre bras autour des cuisses et saisir les mains. En appuyant sur les épaules et les cuisses, elle peut plier le corps de l'enfant tel que requis. Chez l'enfant plus âgé, le médecin peut préférer la position assise, penchée vers l'avant.

Pour une ponction ventriculaire, l'infirmière applique une contrainte de momie, grâce à laquelle elle peut tenir la tête fermement, lorsque le médecin introduit l'aiguille à travers le tissu cérébral. Après la ponction, elle surveille les signes de choc et la fuite de liquide par les orifices de la ponction.

Les parents devraient être en contact constant avec le neurochirurgien qui leur expliquera les modes de diagnostic employés et le traitement éventuel. On les encourage à participer aux soins de l'enfant pendant son séjour à l'hôpital.

Soins postopératoires. On vérifie la température, le pouls, la respiration, ainsi que la tension artérielle, si elle est demandée, toutes les quinze minutes jusqu'à ce que l'enfant réagisse. Les **signes d'augmentation aiguë de la pression intracrânienne** sont l'irritabilité, le bombement de la fontanelle antérieure, la léthargie, les vomissements, l'augmentation de la pression différentielle, le pouls qui ralentit et devient plus percutant, le ralentissement du rythme respiratoire ou un changement dans la température corporelle.

Le médecin peut prescrire la prise et l'enregistrement des signes vitaux d'heure en heure pendant plusieurs jours. Si la température du bébé augmente, on peut lui donner un bain à l'eau tiède contenant 30 à 60 ml d'alcool dilué et ne lui laisser que sa couche. Le médecin peut prescrire de l'aspirine ou un autre antipyrétique.

Les signes neurologiques, le tonus musculaire, les mouvements des extrémités et la réaction pupillaire sont vérifiés chaque heure et enregistrés soigneusement. Une lampe de poche demeure toujours au chevet de l'enfant pour observer l'état des pupilles.

On aspire les mucosités du nez et de la gorge, afin de prévenir les difficultés respiratoires et le danger d'aspiration. Comme pour les bébés hydrocéphales il y a danger de plaies sur les parties du cuir chevelu qui supportent le poids de la tête; on insère donc du coton derrière et sur les oreilles, sous le pansement. On change l'enfant de position au moins toutes les deux heures. Le niveau d'élévation de la tête de l'enfant et sa position générale dépendent de la quantité de liquide passant à travers le tube de dérivation. On peut évaluer approximativement le fonctionnement du drainage, en vérifiant le gonflement, la tension ou la dépression de la fontanelle antérieure. Le niveau de la tête, des épaules et la position générale de l'enfant tendent à augmenter ou à diminuer le flux du drainage. Si la fontanelle se déprime trop rapidement, on devrait coucher l'enfant en position déclive pour augmenter la tension du liquide et éviter l'hématome sous-dural susceptible de se développer. Quand la tension de la fontanelle antérieure redevient normale, on peut soulever légèrement la tête.

On administre des solutés intraveineux lentement et proportionnellement au poids de l'enfant, jusqu'à ce qu'on puisse reprendre l'alimentation par la bouche. Si on les administre trop rapidement, il y a danger de surcharge circulatoire et de défaillance cardiaque.

La bouche de l'enfant se dessèche, il faut la nettoyer fréquemment avant la reprise de l'alimentation. On donne d'abord des liquides clairs, puis on commence graduellement à donner du lait. On ajoute ensuite des aliments solides qui conviennent à son âge, de manière à obtenir un régime à haute teneur en protéines.

L'infirmière doit aussi s'assurer périodiquement de la perméabilité de la valve installée, en effectuant des pressions fermes et rythmiques sur la partie compressible. Ce soin est particulièrement indiqué après chaque période de repos de l'enfant. Le médecin doit être averti immédiatement si la valve semble bloquée.

Les *manifestations* suivantes doivent être notées et rapportées consciencieusement: les signes d'infection, la tension de la fontanelle antérieure (indication d'un drainage insuffisant du L.C.R.), les vomissements (indication de hausse de la pression intracrânienne ou d'intolérance aux aliments), les signes de déshydratation, les convulsions (leur durée, le moment où elles débutent, les parties du corps impliquées, ainsi que le type de mouvements), les modifications des signes vitaux et des signes neurologiques, la froideur ou la moiteur du corps de l'enfant, la pâleur ou les marbrures de la peau, l'état de conscience, les mouvements ou les signes de paralysie, le type de liquide qui s'écoule par l'incision et le degré d'agitation et d'irritabilité de l'enfant.

Recommandations aux parents avant le départ de l'enfant. On ne peut surestimer l'importance pour la mère de comprendre les soins qu'elle doit donner à l'enfant et les symptômes qu'elle devrait reconnaître et rapporter au médecin. Elle devrait en comprendre l'importance, sans que son anxiété en soit trop augmentée. L'exemple d'autres mères qui se sont occupées d'enfants se trouvant dans la même situation que la leur aidera certaines à avoir confiance dans leur aptitude à donner à l'enfant les soins que requiert son état. La

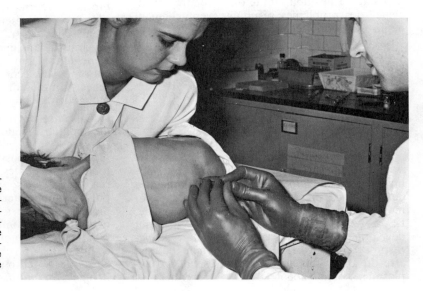

Figure 10-22. Ponction lombaire. L'infirmière place une main derrière la nuque et l'autre sous les fesses. Elle maintient le corps de l'enfant contre elle; la pression exercée sur le cou et les jambes permet d'arrondir le dos et de maintenir la position parallèle avec le bord de la table.

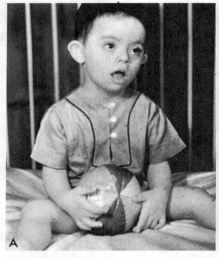
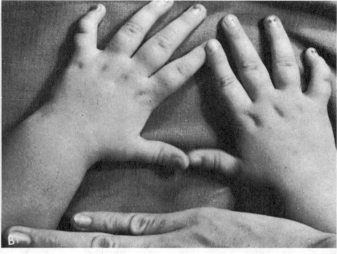

Figure 10-23. Mongolisme. *A)* Les muscles sont peu développés, les articulations lâches et l'enfant peut être à l'aise dans des positions bizarres pendant un temps prolongé. *B)* Les mains sont courtes et épaisses et le petit doigt recourbé. (Courtoisie du Dr Ralph V. Platou and the American Academy of Pediatrics.)

mère doit d'abord comprendre l'opération qui a eu lieu pour saisir l'importance des soins à prodiguer; elle devrait connaître les symptômes d'augmentation de la pression intracrânienne et de déshydratation, et la façon de contrôler la perméabilité de la valve. L'infirmière peut suggérer à la mère les exercices qui aideront à fortifier les muscles de l'enfant, de telle sorte qu'il puisse apprendre à lever la tête évitant ainsi l'atrophie musculaire et les plaies de décubitus.

Si la mère prenait soin de l'enfant avant l'opération, elle sera probablement compétente pour s'en occuper après son retour au domicile. Elle doit toutefois prendre conscience des problèmes résultant éventuellement de la dérivation et savoir reconnaître les signes d'alarme d'un drainage trop rapide ou d'une brusque hypertension intracrânienne. L'enfant devrait mener une vie aussi normale que les autres enfants de son âge et il faut lui permettre d'atteindre son niveau de développement optimal.

Microcéphalie

Étiologie, manifestations cliniques et traitement. La microcéphalie est une anomalie congénitale peu courante, accompagnée de déficience mentale; elle se reconnaît aisément à la naissance, par la petitesse du crâne. La croissance du crâne dépend largement du développement du cerveau. L'*hypodéveloppement cérébral cause la microcéphalie* et peut être dû à des facteurs héréditaires, à la toxoplasmose, à la rubéole durant le premier tri-

mestre de la grossesse, à l'irradiation de la mère pendant le deuxième ou le troisième mois de la gestation. Les symptômes sont un crâne d'un volume et d'une circonférence qui ne sont pas proportionnels au corps de l'enfant et un retard mental important. Il n'y a pas de traitement pour un tel état. On tente seulement de stimuler l'enfant jusqu'à son point de développement maximal.

Trisomie 21 ou mongolisme. (Syndrome de Down)

Incidence, étiologie, manifestations cliniques, traitement et pronostic. Cette anomalie se présente beaucoup plus fréquemment dans la race caucasienne, quoiqu'elle apparaisse quelquefois parmi la race noire. *L'incidence* demeure la même pour toutes les classes socio-économiques et pour les deux sexes. Un enfant pour 600 naissances serait mongolien.

La cause du mongolisme est toujours chromosomique. Toutefois, il existe différents génotypes correspondant au même phénotype. L'enfant peut posséder 47 chromosomes dans toutes ses cellules, avec 3 chromosomes 21, réalisant la *trisomie 21 vraie*. Il peut aussi posséder un matériel génétique pour 46 chromosomes, mais à cause d'une translocation, réaliser une *trisomie 21 apparente*. Enfin, certains enfants vont présenter des lignées de cellules de 46 chromosomes et d'autres lignées de 47 chromosomes, produisant le phénomène du *mosaïsme*.

La trisomie 21 vraie a été attribuée à une erreur de disjonction et liée à l'âge avancé de la mère. Une femme de 40 ans aurait 15 fois plus de chance qu'une jeune femme de 20 ans de produire un enfant atteint de mongolisme. La trisomie vraie ne serait pas héréditaire.

La trisomie 21 apparente, due à une translocation, a été liée au jeune âge des parents et une incidence héréditaire assez forte a été reconnue.

On constate ordinairement le mongolisme à la naissance, mais tous les signes n'ont pas besoin d'être présents pour établir le diagnostic. La physionomie de l'enfant ressemble à celle d'un oriental. La tête est relativement petite, l'occiput plat et la face ronde. Les yeux sont rapprochés et légèrement déviés vers le haut. La fente palpébrale est étroite et un épicanthus est observable. Les points de Brushfield sont visibles sur l'iris de chaque œil. Le nez est plat et la langue sort de la bouche. Ces enfants respirent par la bouche et peuvent baver continuellement. Leur cou est court et de nombreux plis cutanés sont apparents à la partie postérieure. Leur faiblesse musculaire est grande et ils sucent et mastiquent avec difficulté; ils marchent tard et sont constipés. La voix est rauque et le cheveu sec et cassant. Ils souffrent d'un retard

osseux: l'éruption tardive de dents peu résistantes en apporte la preuve. Les mains sont courtes et épaisses, le petit doigt recourbé et les lignes de la paume des mains et de la plante des pieds diffèrent de celles des enfants normaux. Il existe un espace large entre le premier et le second orteil. Une atonie musculaire relative et des articulations particulièrement flexibles permettent à l'enfant de prendre les positions les plus inhabituelles. La croissance et le développement s'effectuent lentement. On trouve souvent des anomalies secondaires associées, telles que les malformations cardiaques congénitales, les cataractes, la polydactylie ou les pieds bots. On a remarqué que la leucémie myéloïde chronique se présentait 20 fois plus souvent chez les mongoliens que dans la population normale.

Ces enfants, rarement destructeurs, sont toutefois inattentifs et insouciants. Placides et apathiques durant les deux premières années, ils deviennent ensuite gais et affectueux. Ils présentent rarement les troubles de comportement qui accompagnent fréquemment le retard mental.

De tels enfants ont besoin de soins continus et de surveillance. Ils offrent très peu de résistance aux infections et peuvent mourir tôt, d'une complication infectieuse. L'antiobio-

Figure 10-24. Des conseils d'ordre génétique sont prodigués aux parents d'un enfant affecté du syndrome de Down. (Courtoisie de The National Foundation — March of Dimes.)

thérapie a prolongé leur pronostic vital. Quoiqu'il n'existe pas de traitement de l'anomalie, on doit essayer de les éduquer au maximum, ce qui peut s'avérer facile ou difficile, selon l'enfant et les circonstances. Ils apprennent en imitant les techniques répétées devant eux et avec eux, d'une manière persistante et toujours semblable. Certaines collectivités ont organisé des centres pour éduquer ces enfants à la limite de leur capacité.

Il est difficile pour les parents d'accepter le handicap de l'enfant. Ceci s'avère particulièrement exact s'il est l'enfant unique d'un couple âgé. Si l'enfant naît d'un jeune couple, les parents peuvent craindre d'avoir d'autres enfants. De toute manière, ils ont besoin du concours de professionnels pour arriver à comprendre les limites de l'enfant et pour planifier sa vie de manière à tirer le meilleur partie de ses capacités et lui donner une enfance heureuse.

Plusieurs ressources communautaires peuvent aider les parents à faire face aux problèmes à court et à long terme que présentent les enfants mongoliens. L'infirmière devrait connaître les différentes possibilités qu'offre le milieu où elle exerce sa profession.

APPAREIL GÉNITO-URINAIRE

Certaines malformations peuvent être décelées à la naissance alors que d'autres n'apparaissent que tardivement. Il faut observer le nouveau-né qui semble normal et consulter si certaines anomalies se présentent dans la quantité ou la coloration de l'urine, l'horaire des mictions ou la force du jet urinaire. L'hyperthermie du nourrisson peut provenir d'une infection des voies urinaires causée par une malformation non décelée.

Obstruction des voies urinaires

On peut trouver des obstructions congénitales à tous les niveaux des voies urinaires. L'obstruction conduit plus ou moins rapidement à la dilatation en amont. La stase urinaire qui constitue un facteur important d'infection, conduit à la distension des voies urinaires, puis à la dilatation rénale, à la destruction du parenchyme, et enfin à l'insuffisance rénale.

Une série de tests est utilisée pour localiser l'obstruction. Celle-ci peut se situer à la partie supérieure ou inférieure des voies urinaires, en amont ou en aval de la vessie. Les symptômes ne sont pas toujours révélateurs du siège de l'obstruction. Les tests de diagnostic incluent le *cathétérisme vésical,* immédiatement après la miction, pour déterminer la quantité de l'urine résiduelle. L'*urographie endoveineuse* permet de radiographier les voies urinaires et d'évaluer la fonction excrétoire des reins. L'*examen cystoscopique* et la *pyélographie rétrograde* peuvent être pratiqués. La cystographie mictionnelle et la cystométrie sont des examens diagnostiques utiles. Le taux d'urée du sang et le taux d'excrétion de la phénolsulfonephtaléine (P.S.P.), aident à mesurer la fonction rénale.

Obstruction à la région inférieure des voies urinaires

Les causes d'*obstruction urinaire basse* incluent les valvules urétrales fibreuses, plus communément retrouvées chez les garçons; l'hyperplasie du col vésical et autres anomalies de la jonction urétro-vésicale qui constitue le lieu le plus fréquent d'obstruction; le phimosis serré, la sténose du méat urinaire et les dysfonctions neuro-musculaires, comme l'atonie vésicale, associées à la myéloméningocèle.

Toutes ces obstructions conduisent à la dilatation vésicale chronique (mégavessie). Par hausse de pression dans le haut du système, on assiste peu à peu à la dilatation des uretères (hydruretère) et des bassinets (hydronéphrose). L'hydronéphrose provoque l'atrophie et la destruction du parenchyme qui précèdent l'insuffisance rénale. L'hydronéphrose s'infecte facilement et constitue la pyo-néphrose ou la pyélo-néphrite qui précipite alors l'évolution vers une issue fatale.

Les signes et symptômes sont des troubles mictionnels comme la pollakiurie, la dysurie, l'incontinence à l'effort, la rétention urinaire ou la palpation de masses abdominales au niveau des reins hypertrophiés. On peut trouver dans l'urine du pus, des cylindres et des cellules épithéliales.

L'infection urinaire chronique se manifeste par des épisodes fébriles isolés, accompagnés ou non de convulsions. Les troubles digestifs, le retard staturo-pondéral et l'hypertension sont des signes d'insuffisance rénale.

Le traitement curatif suppose la levée de l'obstacle ou la création d'une nouvelle vessie où les uretères pourront être abouchés. (Voir page 219).

Obstruction à la région supérieure des voies urinaires

Les obstructions de la région supérieure des voies urinaires sont généralement unilatérales. La vessie n'est pas atteinte, il n'y a pas de problème de miction à moins qu'une infection ne se présente. Les anomalies impliquant l'uretère sont les plus communes. On constate l'obstruction ou la sténose, l'absence congénitale, le dédoublement, le rétrécissement dû à un vaisseau sanguin aberrant qui bloque le drainage urinaire ou, le plus fréquemment, une anomalie de la jonction urétéro-vésicale.

Les *symptômes* suivants peuvent orienter le diagnostic: un retard staturo-pondéral, des épisodes fébriles, avec ou sans convulsions, qui correspondent aux flambées infectieuses périodiques; la découverte d'une masse abdominale qui se révèle être le rein dilaté et hypertrophié; parfois de l'hypertension.

Les symptômes plus vagues qui précèdent s'expliquent par le fait que la lésion est unilatérale. Un seul rein est hypothéqué, l'autre fonctionne normalement et l'urémie n'apparaît pas.

Le *traitement* de choix est la levée de l'obstacle ou la réimplantation de l'uretère, s'il s'agit d'un reflux vésico-urétéral. Le pronostic est alors excellent. Si le diagnostic est tardif et que l'obstacle est unilatéral, l'exérèse du rein atteint va protéger l'organisme et le fonctionnement rénal sera assuré par l'autre rein, à condition qu'il soit normal.

Soins. Le dosage strict des ingesta et des excreta est de rigueur. Il faut prévenir la contamination des tubes de drainage et l'antibiothérapie intraveineuse requiert une surveillance assidue de l'infirmière. Elle doit bien identifier tous les tubes de drainage ainsi que leurs sacs correspondants et noter la couleur et les particularités de l'urine excrétée. Des instillations vésicales ou de simples lavages vésicaux peuvent être requis. Ces procédures doivent être accomplies avec aseptie et un dosage strict des liquides injectés et retirés doit être inscrit.

Rein polykystique congénital

Étiologie, physio-pathologie, manifestations cliniques et traitement. On ne connaît pas la cause de l'anomalie, probablement transmise comme un caractère récessif mendélien. Le tissu rénal apparaît truffé de kystes de dimensions différentes. Les reins plus gros ont une apparence spongieuse au moment de l'opération ou de l'autopsie. L'abondance des tissus environnants déforme les bassinets et les calices. Rarement unilatérale, l'anomalie accompagne souvent d'autres malformations, telles que l'hydrocéphalie, le polydactylisme ou des malformations cardiaques.

Les *signes cliniques* dépendent de la localisation des kystes. En palpant les deux reins (rarement un seul), on se rend compte qu'ils sont gros. On rencontre une insuffisance rénale progressive, accompagnée d'hypertension et de manifestations de défaillance cardiaque. Il peut exister un sérieux retard de croissance. Les analyses révèlent une bactériurie, une hématurie, une protéinurie et l'azotémie s'élève. L'urographie montre l'augmentation de volume des reins, ainsi que la déformation des bassinets et des calices.

Il n'existe pas de *traitement* spécifique. Des mesures conservatrices et palliatives combattent l'acidose et l'insuffisance rénale. Les très gros kystes peuvent être drainés quand ils nuisent à la fonction rénale. L'exérèse et la greffe constituent des mesures palliatives.

Le *pronostic* dépend du type et de la gravité de l'insuffisance fonctionnelle. Dans les cas graves, l'enfant meurt in-utero. Parmi ceux qui survivent, la fonction rénale décroît avec les années. Dans les cas bénins, quoique le premier symptôme puisse apparaître dès l'enfance, la condition peut ne devenir évidente qu'à l'âge adulte.

Persistance de l'ouraque

Étiologie et pathologie. Il existe chez l'embryon, une communication normale entre la vessie et l'ombilic et il arrive que ce canal appelé « ouraque » demeure chez le nouveau-né. Une émission continuelle d'urine peut alors se produire au niveau de l'ombilic. L'anomalie est souvent associée à une obstruction des voies urinaires que l'on retrouve quelquefois sous la vessie, plus rarement sous forme d'un kyste extrapéritonéal, situé juste sous l'ombilic.

Manifestations cliniques et traitement. En présence de la persistance de l'ouraque, l'urine coule continuellement de l'ombilic; le kyste de l'ouraque se manifeste par un œdème profond, situé juste sous la région ombilicale.

La correction chirurgicale s'impose et le kyste doit être enlevé avant l'apparition quasi inévitable de l'infection. Le kyste infecté doit d'abord être drainé chirurgicalement et l'enfant doit recevoir les antibiotiques appropriés.

Tumeur de Wilms

Incidence, manifestations cliniques et diagnostic. La tumeur de Wilms est un adénosarcome embryonnaire hautement malin et situé aux reins. Il se développe à partir de tissus embryonnaires anormaux, commençant à croître avant ou après la naissance. Il constitue un des types de cancer les plus fréquents chez le nourrisson et le trottineur. Il est rarement diagnostiqué à la naissance. Communément unilatéral, il peut être bilatéral.

On rencontre rarement d'autres symptômes qu'une masse dans l'abdomen, habituellement découverte par le médecin lors d'un examen de routine de l'enfant, ou perçu par la mère pendant qu'elle le change de couche ou lui donne son bain. Une fois le *diagnostic* établi, le médecin et la mère doivent soigneusement éviter de palper l'abdomen de l'enfant, les palpations pouvant favoriser l'apparition des métastases.

Les cellules tumorales passent à travers la capsule du rein ou la veine rénale et de là se disséminent dans d'autres régions du corps par le système circulatoire. Les symptômes terminaux sont l'anémie et la cachexie.

La pyélographie endo-veineuse, qui montre la distorsion et le déplacement des bassinets, confirme le diagnostic.

Pronostic, traitement et soins infirmiers. Non traitée, la maladie est toujours fatale. Il semble que les chances de survie soient meilleures chez l'enfant âgé de moins d'un an puisque la lésion est décelée très tôt. Avec un traitement adéquat, le pronostic semble moins défavorable qu'auparavant. La tumeur tend à engendrer des métastases pulmonaires en passant par la veine rénale, le cœur droit et l'artère pulmonaire.

Le traitement consiste en l'ablation chirurgicale avec irradiation avant et/ou après l'opération. L'intervention devrait avoir lieu dès que le diagnostic a été établi. L'enfant reçoit de l'Actinomycine D pendant les périodes pré-opératoire et postopératoire. Certains enfants survivent depuis plus de 12 ans à la suite de ce traitement.

On prend soin de l'enfant comme d'un enfant normal, en portant une attention spéciale à l'alimentation. Le danger spécifique dans l'administration des soins réside dans la palpation involontaire de la masse intra-abdominale, en baignant l'enfant ou en le caressant, augmentant ainsi le danger de métastase. On avertit la mère, et à l'hôpital on place un écriteau « Ne palpez pas l'abdomen » à la tête du berceau de l'enfant.

Exstrophie vésicale

Anatomo-pathologie et manifestations cliniques. L'exstrophie vésicale complète constitue une anomalie très importante. On peut la définir comme le défaut de fermeture de la vessie et des éléments de la ligne infra-ombilicale. Elle expose la partie basse des voies urinaires, de la vessie entière au méat urinaire. Chez l'enfant mâle, la malformation peut être associée à un pénis court, un épispadias, une cryptorchidie ou une hernie in-

guinale. Chez la fille, on peut constater la fissure du clitoris souvent bilatérale, la séparation des lèvres et l'absence de vagin. Dans les deux sexes, les muscles grands droits sont séparés sous l'ombilic et les branches pubiennes ne se touchent pas. Dans l'exstrophie complète, la muqueuse vésicale postérieure apparaît rouge vif à travers la fissure de la paroi abdominale. Cette affection se rencontre plus souvent chez les garçons.

On constate l'anomalie dès la naissance. L'urine coule directement de la vessie sur la paroi abdominale, provoquant une constante odeur d'urine et l'excoriation de la peau environnante. Il peut y avoir ulcération de la muqueuse de la vessie. La séparation des branches pubiennes provoque une démarche balançante (démarche de canard) quand l'enfant apprend à marcher.

Traitement. Dans certains cas, il est possible de pratiquer une fermeture complète de la vessie et une plastie des autres malformations. L'enfant peut alors uriner normale-

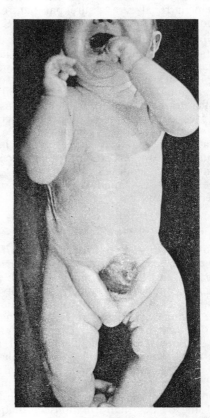

Figure 10-25. Exstrophie de la vessie. Un enfant de cinq mois affecté d'une exstrophie vésicale complète et de hernies inguinales. On trouve fréquemment ces deux pathologies associées. (Gross: *The Surgery of Infancy and Childhood.*)

ment. Malheureusement, devant l'étendue des lésions et pour éviter l'infection rénale ascendante qui ne manquera pas de se produire, le chirurgien doit souvent procéder à une des différentes formes de dérivation des urines dont nous avons parlé à la page 219.

L'implantation des uretères au niveau du côlon peut s'effectuer quand l'enfant peut contrôler l'écoulement de l'urine par le sphincter anal.

Si l'enfant a subi une transplantation des uretères dans le côlon, une pression peut apparaître au niveau des uretères à partir des zones d'anastomose; cette hausse de pression se manifeste bientôt par de l'hydro-uretère et de l'hydronéphrose. Toute infection ascendante, le plus souvent à colibacilles, risque de dégénérer en pyélonéphrite aiguë. Le risque d'infection était d'ailleurs présent avant l'intervention lorsque l'urine coulait sur la peau de l'abdomen produisant une irritation cutanée continuelle.

Le *pronostic* dépend en grande partie de l'état du rein quand la pression est finalement réduite dans les bassinets; la présence antérieure d'une infection chronique peut également modifier l'évolution. La transplantation des uretères dans le côlon provoque souvent un déséquilibre électrolytique chronique dû à l'absorption des produits de déchets de l'urine par la muqueuse du côlon.

La transplantation des uretères dans une anse isolée de l'iléon (néo-vessie) permet d'éviter les complications inhérentes à la méthode précédente.

Soins postopératoires. Les soins généraux sont les mêmes que ceux que l'on retrouve chez tous les opérés. Il faut voir à ce que le pansement reste propre et sec. Si l'enfant a subi une transplantation des uretères dans le côlon, il doit apprendre à contrôler son sphincter anal pour prévenir l'écoulement de l'urine. Ceci se fait très lentement et il faut éviter d'exercer une pression trop forte sur l'enfant qui ne pourra s'empêcher de souiller ses vêtements de temps à autre. Les menaces ou les cajoleries ne feront qu'aggraver le problème alors qu'en l'absence d'anxiété, l'enfant acquerra plus rapidement un contrôle adéquat de son sphincter.

Recommandations aux parents avant le départ de la pouponnière. Il est important que l'on enseigne aux parents les soins généraux à prodiguer à ces enfants. Une bonne hygiène permet à l'enfant de jouir de la meilleure santé possible pour résister à une infection de la peau ou des reins, et plus tard, supporter la correction chirurgicale de l'anomalie. L'infirmière devrait comprendre la détresse que l'état de l'enfant peut causer à sa mère. La mère n'aura peut-être pas tout de suite le contrôle suffisant pour nettoyer la région autour de la vessie. Elle doit d'abord s'habituer à la vue de l'anomalie. La mère doit apprendre à tenir la région de la vessie très propre et à la recouvrir de gaze vaselinée stérile de manière à éviter l'infection et des ulcérations possibles. Elle peut appliquer une pommade neutre autour de la vessie pour protéger la peau contre l'urine. Les couches devront être changées fréquemment pour le confort de l'enfant et pour éliminer l'odeur. Les selles doivent être enlevées immédiatement, de telle sorte qu'elles ne contaminent pas la muqueuse vésicale. Les vêtements de l'enfant devraient être légers, de manière à éviter toute pression sur les parties exposées de la vessie.

Si l'on a besoin d'un spécimen d'urine, il sera prélevé par l'orifice de la vessie avec un compte-gouttes stérile, ou bien on couche l'enfant sur l'abdomen dans une position permettant à l'urine de tomber dans un récipient stérile prévu à cet effet.

Figure 10-26. Anomalies des organes génitaux mâles. *A)* Hypospadias, schéma montrant une partie des localisations communes de la difformité. *B)* Hypospadias grave et pseudo-hermaphrodisme. *C)* Épispadias. (De Arey: *Developmental Anatomy.* 6ᵉ éd.)

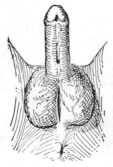
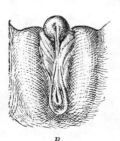
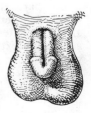

A   *B*   *C*

Hypospadias

Étiologie, traitement et pronostic. L'hypospadias est une malformation congénitale dans laquelle l'urètre s'ouvre sur la surface inférieure du pénis, juste avant le gland ou dans le corps du pénis ou sur le périnée. Si l'ouverture est située près du scrotum, le pénis est ordinairement recourbé à cause des brides entre le pénis et le scrotum. L'enfant doit s'asseoir pour uriner.

Le *traitement* est chirurgical. En présence d'une anomalie minime aucun traitement n'a lieu, car seules les formes graves sont incompatibles avec la procréation. La correction devrait s'effectuer avant l'âge scolaire à cause des difficultés psychologiques qui pourraient survenir. L'enfant devra subir une ou plusieurs hospitalisations afin de libérer le pénis de sa position incurvée, de rechercher d'autres anomalies des voies urinaires et d'effectuer une plastie de l'urètre en un ou plusieurs temps.

Au point de vue psychologique, il faut aider l'enfant à exprimer ses craintes (castration) et faire preuve de délicatesse afin de ne pas blesser sa pudeur s'il est opéré à l'âge préscolaire.

Le chirurgien crée un canal qu'il laisse guérir autour d'une sonde à demeure. Un pansement compressif empêche l'œdème et l'hématome. Il arrive que des fistules laissent passer l'urine après la plastie de l'urètre; celle-ci peut faire l'objet d'une révision chirurgicale après quelque temps.

Épispadias

Dans cette anomalie, l'urètre s'ouvre sur la surface dorsale du pénis; il peut se terminer juste derrière le gland ou, en présence d'une exstrophie de la vessie, s'étendre tout le long du pénis.

Le *traitement* est chirurgical. On remarque les mêmes problèmes émotifs et psychologiques que dans l'hypospadias.

Intersexualité

Les parents se sentent coupables à la naissance d'un enfant dont le sexe ne peut être aisément déterminé. L'intersexualité reste une anomalie extrêmement troublante, quoique son influence sur la santé physique demeure insignifiante. Si une question se pose au sujet du sexe de l'enfant, à cause d'une absence d'organes génitaux distinctifs, le nouveau-né devrait subir une investigation complète pour déterminer son sexe et l'étude de la chroma-

tine sexuelle doit être demandée. Ceci devrait être fait avant que les parents n'annoncent le sexe de l'enfant à leurs amis. Le rôle social du garçon est différent de celui de la fille et les vêtements, les activités, le comportement différencient un sexe de l'autre. Il est psychologiquement néfaste, autant pour les parents que pour l'enfant, que le sexe du bébé soit mal déterminé et qu'il change ultérieurement. Toutes les identifications psychologiques ont lieu en accord avec le sexe originellement déterminé par le médecin.

Les parents – et l'enfant, quand il est assez âgé pour cela – ont besoin de comprendre les problèmes anatomiques impliqués, de même que les éléments du traitement.

Le *traitement,* dépendant des causes du problème, peut être chirurgical ou médical. Parents et enfants ont besoin de l'appui de professionnels de la santé, qui considèrent le problème objectivement, sans la curiosité morbide et la pitié que les amis et les parents peuvent manifester. Un enfant affecté d'un tel problème a besoin d'être aidé pour s'adapter aux autres enfants de son âge à l'école. Les parents, même les plus compréhensifs, ne peuvent sonder la profondeur des problèmes émotifs d'un tel enfant.

Trois types d'intersexualité seront étudiés: le pseudo-hermaphrodisme chez la fille, le pseudo-hermaphrodisme chez le garçon, et l'hermaphrodisme vrai.

Pseudo-hermaphrodisme féminin (Hyperplasie surrénale congénitale)

Étiologie, manifestations cliniques, diagnostic et traitement. Le pseudo-hermaphrodisme féminin constitue le problème le plus commun dans l'intersexualité ou la différenciation sexuelle. Il consiste dans l'impossibilité d'élaborer l'hydrocortisone à partir de ses précurseurs. La déficience en hydrocortisone est suivie éventuellement par l'hyperplasie du segment du cortex surrénal qui sécrète les hormones androgènes. L'hypersécrétion d'hormones androgènes par le cortex surrénal du fœtus engendre une masculinisation des organes génitaux externes. Récemment, un plus grand nombre de ces cas ont été observés chez les filles nées de mères traitées aux stéroïdes durant leur grossesse.

L'hypertrophie du clitoris, la fusion des lèvres, qui ressemblent à un scrotum bifide, et l'hypospadias en constituent les manifestations cliniques. De tels enfants ont un col utérin, un utérus et le schéma chromosomique féminin.

L'exploration et la biopsie des organes génitaux durant la période néo-natale, l'évaluation du taux des stéroïdes excrétés dans les urines et le caryotype permettent de faire le diagnostic.

En dépit des anomalies des organes génitaux externes, on devrait élever ces enfants comme des filles. Si l'enfant reçoit de l'hydrocortisone, la production de corticotropine sera inhibée et celle des androgènes réduite. Les enfants qui ne sont pas atteints d'hyperplasie surrénale ne requièrent aucun traitement autre que la correction par la chirurgie plastique, qui devrait être entreprise entre l'âge de dix-huit mois et quatre ans. Si le diagnostic est posé dès la naissance ou très rapidement par la suite, si la chirurgie plastique est faite avant l'âge scolaire, le pronostic est très bon.

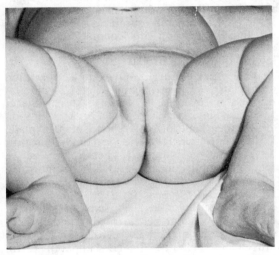

Figure 10-27. Pseudo-hermaphrodisme chez le mâle. Vue d'un nourrisson d'un mois présentant une configuration féminine normale. On remarque un renflement dans la région inguinale droite causé par un testicule logé dans le canal inguinal. L'appareil génital externe semble être composé d'organes femelles: lèvres, clitoris, vulve et vagin. Une biopsie de la peau révèle un caryotype masculin. La laparotomie n'a révélé aucun organe génital interne femelle. (Gaspar, Kimber et Berkaw, dans A.M.A., *J. Dis. Child.*, vol. 91, avec la permission des auteurs.)

Pseudo-hermaphrodisme masculin

Étiologie et traitement. Il en existe plusieurs types, mais tous ces enfants sont porteurs d'un chromosome sexuel mâle. Un type provient d'une dysgénésie gonadique. La féminisation du fœtus provient de l'insuffisance des testicules, endommagés précocement durant la période prénatale. Un autre type présente des organes génitaux externes féminins,

mais possèdent des testicules et non des ovaires. Dans ces cas, les testicules devraient être enlevés et l'enfant élevée comme une fille. À l'âge de la puberté, on devrait administrer des œstrogènes à l'enfant pour compenser l'absence de ceux normalement produits par les ovaires de la femme.

Dans un troisième type, les organes génitaux sont à prédominance masculine ou ambiguë et de tels enfants se masculinisent à la puberté. Toute structure qui n'appartient pas au sexe mâle, devrait être enlevée chirurgicalement.

Hermaphrodisme vrai

L'hermaphrodisme proprement dit est rare. Les investigations cliniques montrent l'existence des tissus ovariens et testiculaires chez le même enfant. Le sexe chromosomique peut être mâle ou femelle.

L'hermaphrodisme vrai doit être recherché chez tout enfant atteint d'intersexualité, excepté ceux atteints d'une hyperplasie surrénale congénitale. Le traitement est le même que celui du pseudo-hermaphrodisme mâle.

Anomalies orthopédiques

Jusqu'à ces vingt dernières années, on hospitalisait pendant des mois les enfants atteints d'une difformité orthopédique, même mineure. Aujourd'hui, avec la compréhension de l'importance psychologique de la séparation de l'enfant de sa mère, et avec l'amélioration des traitements, on soigne ces enfants en grande partie en clinique externe et à domicile. On les admet à l'hôpital seulement pour l'application d'un appareil plâtré ou pour une opération, et ils vivent à la maison entre les visites ou les séjours à l'hôpital.

Pied bot

Incidence, étiologie, diagnostic, physiopathologie et types. Le *pied bot* proprement dit est une des difformités orthopédiques les plus communes. La cause en demeure inconnue, quoique l'hypothèse d'une origine génétique se confirme de plus en plus, grâce aux recherches en génétique médicale. Plusieurs théories ont été avancées pour en expliquer l'étiologie. Cette infirmité peut être due à un défaut de l'œuf, une tendance familiale ou un arrêt de croissance. Il peut s'agir d'une difformité paralytique liée à la myéloméningocèle.

Le *diagnostic* du type spécifique de pied bot (plusieurs types sont connus) dépend de l'anomalie individuelle chez l'enfant. La *pathologie* varie de légers changements dans la structure du pied jusqu'aux anomalies dans les os, autant des pieds que des jambes.

Les deux types les plus communs de pied bot: le pied bot équin (équinovarus) et le pied bot valgus (calcaneovalgus), sont habituellement bilatéraux. Dans le *pied bot équin,* le pied est en flexion plantaire. Il présente un varus de l'avant-pied et un varus du talon, ainsi qu'une adduction et une supination. L'enfant marche sur ses orteils et sur le rebord extérieur du pied. Plus de 95% des cas de pied bot congénital appartiennent à cette catégorie. Dans le *pied bot valgus,* le pied subit une flexion dorsale et dévie latéralement; c'est-à-dire que les talons sont tournés vers l'extérieur et la partie antérieure du pied relevée sur son bord extérieur. L'enfant marche sur le talon dévié en dehors et sur le bord interne du pied.

Traitement et soins infirmiers. Le traitement est commencé aussitôt que possible, souvent dès la naissance. Les retards peuvent rendre la correction plus difficile, car les os et les muscles se développent anormalement et les tendons peuvent raccourcir. Chez le nourrisson, le traitement est habituellement conservateur. Il comporte une réduction progressive à l'aide de manipulations et de plâtres successifs.

Les manipulations seules s'avèrent la plupart du temps inefficaces. On applique des plâtres successifs qui suivent la croissance de l'enfant jusqu'à l'obtention d'une correction exagérée. On emploie souvent une attelle de Denis Browne pour la suite du traitement. L'appareil est composé de deux semelles attachées à une barre transversale. Quand on fixe l'attelle aux souliers, la position de l'angle du pied peut être maintenue par une vis de réglage. Quand l'enfant bouge les pieds, il les place automatiquement dans une position corrigée.

Le *traitement chirurgical* est indiqué en cas d'échec des méthodes précédentes ou en cas de diagnostic tardif. Si les mesures conservatrices échouent, la correction peut être entreprise sous anesthésie et suivie de l'application d'un plâtre. La chirurgie sur les tendons et les os peut être entreprise durant les premières années de l'enfance.

La plupart des soins infirmiers de l'enfant qui a un pied bot sont donnés par la mère à la maison.

Quand on hospitalise l'enfant pour l'application d'un plâtre, on suit les règles générales qui conviennent à cette mesure de traitement.

L'application du plâtre provoquant une correction forcée, l'infirmière doit observer les régions de pression et la texture de la peau autour des bords de l'appareil, la circulation sanguine dans les orteils, évaluée d'après leur coloration et leur température, la possibilité pour l'enfant de mouvoir ses orteils et toute manifestation d'inconfort. Si une irritation se produit ou si la circulation ralentit, on ouvre le plâtre pour soulager la pression. On colle des pétales de diachylon non-allergique sur le rebord du plâtre pour empêcher l'irritation de la peau et faciliter le lavage autour du plâtre. On n'applique ni poudre ni onguent sur la peau sous le plâtre. Ni l'une ni l'autre ne donneront plus de confort à l'enfant et les deux peuvent causer de l'irritation.

Après une manipulation pour obtenir une position correcte et l'application d'un appareil plâtré, l'enfant doit rester 24 heures au lit, le pied et la jambe surélevés par un oreiller ou une suspension quelconque. L'élévation empêche l'œdème et le ralentissement circulatoire qui l'accompagne.

Après une chirurgie suivie de l'application d'un plâtre, l'infirmière surveille si la circulation est entravée, si la blessure est sensible et si elle saigne, c'est-à-dire s'il y a coloration du plâtre à l'endroit correspondant à la plaie. Il faut entourer la tache de sang d'un trait de crayon, en indiquant l'heure afin de se rendre compte des progrès de l'hémorragie possible et avertir à temps le chirurgien. Après l'opération, il est nécessaire de changer l'appareil à intervalles de trois semaines environ, de manière à ramener le pied graduellement dans la position normale, et d'assurer un redressement définitif. Quand l'appareil plâtré n'est plus nécessaire, des exercices et des souliers orthopédiques spéciaux peuvent être requis.

Enseignement à la mère. Avant le départ du nourrisson, l'infirmière doit discuter avec la mère de la nécessité de le conduire régulièrement à la clinique ou chez son médecin. Les mères acceptent mal le désagrément des mesures correctrices. Elles peuvent avoir besoin d'encouragement pour suivre le traitement, jusqu'à ce que toutes les corrections possibles aient été accomplies. L'orthopédiste enlève les plâtres après obtention d'une correction adéquate. La mère doit savoir que l'enfant sera éventuellement chaussé de souliers spéciaux pour maintenir la correction et qu'il pourra lui être nécessaire de porter une attelle aux jambes et aux pieds (Denis Browne) durant la nuit et ceci pendant de longs mois.

Si la mère doit manipuler le pied, le médecin devrait lui enseigner la façon de procéder

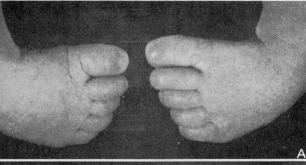

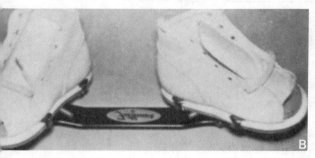

Figure 10-28. *A)* Pieds bots congénitaux (Extrait de W. R. Miller, *J. pediat.*, vol. 51). *B)* Les souliers de Denis Browne conservent la position correctrice d'éversion pendant le sommeil. (Courtoisie de F. James Funk, m. d.)

et surveiller ses essais jusqu'à ce qu'il soit évident qu'elle puisse le faire correctement. Après les manipulations ou la chirurgie et l'application d'un plâtre, la mère devra ramener l'enfant au chirurgien pour examen à plusieurs reprises pendant une période de plusieurs mois. Souvent les parents croient que l'opération corrigera l'infirmité une fois pour toutes et qu'il n'y aura plus de problèmes par la suite. Ceci est fort possible, mais l'enfant doit quand même être suivi en cas de rechute éventuelle, qui devra être traitée immédiatement, si l'on ne veut pas se retrouver au point de départ.

Pronostic. Le pronostic dépend en grande partie de l'âge de l'enfant au début du traitement. Si la correction a débuté chez le nourrisson, le résultat fonctionnel est généralement

bon. La forme du pied peut laisser à désirer si la difformité était très grave.

Luxation congénitale de la hanche

Étiologie, incidence et diagnostic. On attribue les luxations congénitales de la hanche à une défaillance du développement embryonnaire de l'articulation. La cause en demeure inconnue, mais l'hérédité semble un facteur important.

Les nouveau-nés souffrent rarement d'une luxation congénitale de la hanche. Il arrive plus souvent que la tête du fémur ne s'enchâsse pas entièrement dans la cavité cotyloïde de l'iliaque (acetabulum), réalisant ainsi la sub-luxation; quand l'enfant commence à marcher, le poids du corps peut convertir cette condition en une véritable luxation.

L'anomalie est plus fréquente parmi les filles, la proportion étant de 7 à 1. C'est une anomalie congénitale qui peut passer inaperçue chez le nouveau-né, mais qui peut se révéler durant les examens mensuels réguliers. Le premier signe et le plus certain consiste en une limitation de l'abduction de la cuisse du côté affecté. Par exemple, lorsque l'enfant est couché sur le dos, et que sa mère change sa couche, l'articulation normale de la hanche permet que le genou touche la table à un angle de 90 degrés. S'il y a luxation, l'écart du côté affecté est limité à 45 degrés au plus. Le symptôme que la mère remarque en premier lieu est cette difficulté à écarter les cuisses pour le changement de couche.

Anatomo-pathologie, manifestations cliniques et traitement. Le signe prémonitoire d'une luxation de la hanche est une cavité cotyloïde peu profonde et extrêmement oblique. La tête du fémur semble, du côté atteint, plus petite et plus haute que normalement et les centres d'ossification accusent un retard d'apparition.

Les principaux *symptômes* de la luxation congénitale sont le trochanter haut situé du côté atteint et une asymétrie des plis fessiers. Quand on couche l'enfant sur le dos, et que l'on place ses pieds à plat sur le matelas, le genou est plus bas du côté atteint; l'abduction de la cuisse est limitée et on éprouve de la difficulté à lui mettre les couches; par contre, les autres mouvements peuvent être très ou trop faciles. On trouve le signe de *Trandelenbourg* chez l'enfant plus vieux: la hanche s'abaisse quand l'enfant lève la jambe malade et se tient sur la jambe saine. Ce signe traduit la faiblesse des muscles qui stabilisent le bassin. Le périnée très large laisse soup-

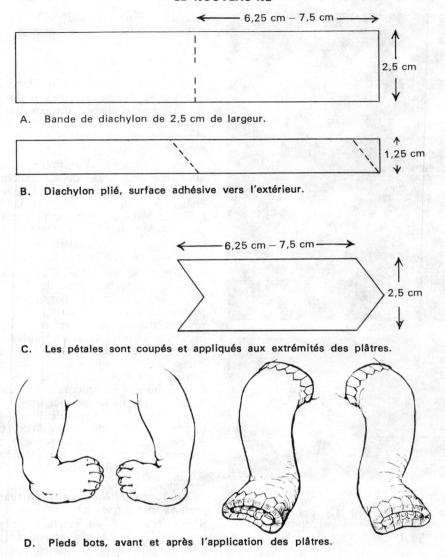

A.   Bande de diachylon de 2,5 cm de largeur.

B.   Diachylon plié, surface adhésive vers l'extérieur.

C.   Les pétales sont coupés et appliqués aux extrémités des plâtres.

D.   Pieds bots, avant et après l'application des plâtres.

Figure 10-29.   Procédés d'application de pétales adhésifs autour des extrémités du plâtre, afin de prévenir les irritations cutanées.

çonner une luxation bilatérale. Si la malformation n'est pas reconnue précocement, on constate un retard de la marche; l'enfant boite (démarche de canard) et présente une lordose compensatrice.

La sub-luxation se manifeste par des symptômes frustres qui expliquent le retard dans le diagnostic. Les parents consultent souvent le médecin quand l'enfant a commencé à marcher et que la véritable luxation est apparue.

Le *traitement* devra commencer dès que le *diagnostic* est établi. Les retards prolongent le traitement et il peut en résulter une luxation complète, plus difficile à corriger. L'ob-

jectif du traitement consiste à maintenir la tête du fémur dans la cavité acétabulaire avec une pression constante pour élargir et creuser la cavité. Ceci amène la correction complète de la dysplasie en remodelant la cavité. Pour atteindre cet objectif, on maintient les cuisses du nourrisson en abduction pendant plusieurs mois.

La mère peut utiliser trois ou quatre couches à la fois et forcer ainsi l'abduction par l'épaisseur du tissu. Elle peut aussi recouvrir un coussinet d'un sac imperméable et le maintenir dans la couche de l'enfant, entre ses cuisses.

A

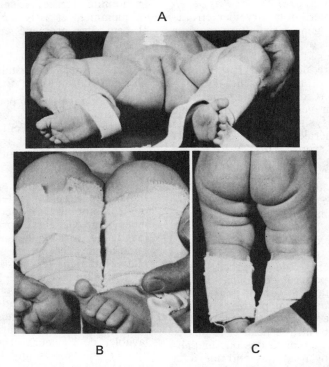

B   C

Figure 10-30.   Luxation congénitale bilatérale de la hanche. *A)* Limitation de l'abduction de la hanche. *B)* Le niveau asymétrique des genoux, quand l'enfant est sur une table plate et rigide, indique soit un déplacement, soit un raccourcissement du fémur. *C)* L'asymétrie des plis fessiers et l'abduction de la hanche atteinte sont les signes physiques qui permettent de soupçonner une dysplasie ou une luxation. (J. Cohen, dans *The Biologic Basis of Pediatric Practice*, édité par R. E. Cooke, publié par The Blakiston Division, McGraw-Hill Book, New York, 1968.)

Lorsque c'est possible, l'attelle de Fredjka peut être achetée et utilisée avec plus de sécurité et d'efficacité que les moyens précédents. Le plus important est que la mère comprenne bien le but du traitement et maintienne ses efforts aussi longtemps que nécessaire.

L'opération est pratiquée, quand la hanche est irréductible, par voie fermée ou pour corriger une obliquité persistante du toit acétabulaire. L'enfant est souvent mis en traction de 10 à 15 jours avant l'intervention. Un plâtre est mis en place après l'opération pour tenir la tête du fémur dans la position correcte, c'est-à-dire fixée dans la cavité cotyloïde de l'os iliaque. Le plâtre doit être porté plusieurs mois.

Soins infirmiers.   En général, l'enfant est hospitalisé quand il faut lui appliquer un plâtre ou procéder à une chirurgie correctrice. Le plâtre encastre la ceinture et s'étend jusqu'aux orteils; on le désigne sous le nom de Spica. L'appareil maintient les cuisses en abduction et joue le même rôle que la couche spéciale mentionnée plus haut. Le plâtre est bilatéral, que la luxation soit unilatérale ou bilatérale.

Quand l'enfant revient à sa chambre, on l'installe sur un matelas imperméable qui sera posé sur une planche pour qu'il ne se déforme pas. La tête de l'enfant devrait être légèrement plus haute que son corps pour que l'urine et les selles ne salissent pas l'appareil. On soutient la tête de l'enfant, son dos, et chaque jambe, avec un oreiller recouvert de tissu imperméable. Si les oreillers sont placés adéquatement, les talons ne reposent pas sur le matelas et le tronc est plus haut que le siège. L'infirmière doit manipuler le plâtre avec les paumes de ses mains plutôt qu'avec ses doigts car les points de pression qu'elle peut provoquer en déformant le plâtre sont une source de plaies cutanées. On utilise quelquefois un séchoir à air chaud pour accélérer le séchage mais cette technique est rarement nécessaire; elle peut provoquer un durcissement plus rapide de l'extérieur du plâtre et celui-ci devient moins résistant.

Soins directement reliés à l'appareil plâtré. 1) L'infirmière doit surveiller étroitement les signes de gêne circulatoire, comme la décoloration ou la cyanose, la perte de sensibilité ou la douleur, l'œdème ou le changement de température des pieds. En pressant l'ongle de l'orteil, celui-ci devient normalement blanc mais se recolore rapidement. Tout retard dans le retour veineux doit être signalé immédiatement. Ces signes d'une circulation déficiente sont généralement causés par la pression du plâtre trop serré. 2) Le plâtre peut être enduit de cirage à chaussures ou d'un liquide qui le durcira en séchant. 3) Afin de protéger la peau de l'enfant et d'éviter l'émiettement du plâtre, des pétales de diachylon sont appliqués à chaque extrémité. Un diachylon imperméable et anti-allergique est utilisé. 4) Afin d'éviter que l'enfant ne mette, intentionnellement ou non, de petits objets ou des aliments à l'intérieur de l'appareil plâtré, de petits coussinets peuvent être placés autour de la taille de l'enfant. L'enfant pense alors moins à faire un jeu de son plâtre et sa mobilisation est facilitée car ces coussinets évitent le contact direct entre la peau et le plâtre, que le petit soit couché sur le dos ou sur l'abdomen. 5) Si l'enfant n'est pas entraîné à la propreté, l'hygiène du périnée doit être assurée et le plâtre protégé à cet endroit. Une couche pliée en quatre peut obturer l'orifice de l'appareil plâtré, alors qu'une autre plus grande la maintiendra en place. Une couche couverte d'un morceau de plastique peut être insérée sous le plâtre et ramenée à l'extérieur, puis fixée sur l'appareil à l'aide de diachylon. Le plastique est en contact direct avec le plâtre et la couche couvrira le tout. De cette façon, le plâtre est entièrement protégé de l'humidité, des fissures et des odeurs. L'enfant doit être changé fréquemment. 6) Si l'enfant est entraîné à la propreté et qu'un bassin de lit est utilisé, on insère un tissu de plastique entre les rebords du plâtre et la peau de l'enfant au niveau de l'ouverture. On glisse le bassin sous les fesses en s'assurant que les bouts du tissu pendent dans le réceptacle. Pour l'émission d'urine, un urinoir est plus confortable et se manipule plus facilement.

Après l'application du plâtre, l'enfant qui n'est pas entraîné à la toilette peut être placé sur un cadre de Bradford. Celui-ci aide à tenir l'appareil plâtré propre et facilite les soins.

Si l'enfant a subi une opération, l'infirmière observera si les plaies ne saignent pas et s'il y a évidence d'hémorragie elle doit en avertir le médecin immédiatement.

L'infirmière doit visiter l'enfant fréquemment et tenter de trouver un dérivatif à son immobilité forcée. L'enfant peut être porté fréquemment et assis à cheval sur les genoux. Il peut être promené en landau ou sur des chariots qui n'ont pas de montants, mais un appui à l'avant et à l'arrière. L'enfant peut y être solidement installé. Des jouets assez gros peuvent lui être fournis.

Un hôpital général peut posséder un pavillon pour des enfants convalescents ou malades chroniques. Si l'enfant ne peut retourner à la maison, on peut l'y transférer. L'enfant qui vit à l'hôpital devrait mener une vie aussi normale que possible.

Ligne de conduite après le retour à la maison. L'enfant atteint d'une incapacité qui l'immobilise de façon prolongée devrait mener une vie aussi normale que possible. Il faut l'aider à se réadapter à toutes les activités quoditiennes de la vie courante. Un grand plâtre qui tient les cuisses dans une position de « grenouille » est déplaisant; on peut difficilement vêtir l'enfant et l'ameublement normal s'avère souvent inadéquat. Des pantalons larges et flottants descendant jusqu'aux chevilles peuvent cacher l'appareil. Faits de tissu lavable, de couleur attrayante, on peut leur ajouter une veste semblable et l'enfant se sentira habillé.

L'enfant doit être couché dans un grand lit afin qu'il dorme à l'aise. Quand le plâtre est bien sec et durci, il peut s'asseoir sur une chaise, les jambes pendantes de chaque côté. Différents appareils ont été conçus par des parents ingénieux pour faciliter le transport de l'enfant. Plusieurs jouets vendus dans le commerce peuvent être utilisés, tels que chevaux de bois, petits véhicules sur roulettes avec large poignée à l'avant, etc.

Tout appareil fabriqué par les parents ou toute technique utilisée dans ses soins devraient être contrôlés par le médecin pour assurer la sécurité de l'enfant et empêcher le fendillement du plâtre.

Si les parents reprennent l'enfant à la maison avant que le plâtre ne soit complètement sec, on doit leur apprendre à surveiller les fissures ou brisures, ainsi que les extrémités et la peau autour des rebords et à prévoir les signes d'infection ou d'irritation. Ils doivent savoir que l'odeur nauséabonde qui se dégage d'un plâtre peut révéler une infection sous-jacente. Tous les soins précédemment énumérés doivent leur être enseignés. Étant donné que le traitement est long avant que les résultats ne soient visibles, les parents ont besoin du soutien et de la compréhension de l'équipe de santé pour assurer les soins nécessaires à leur enfant. Ils doivent aussi com-

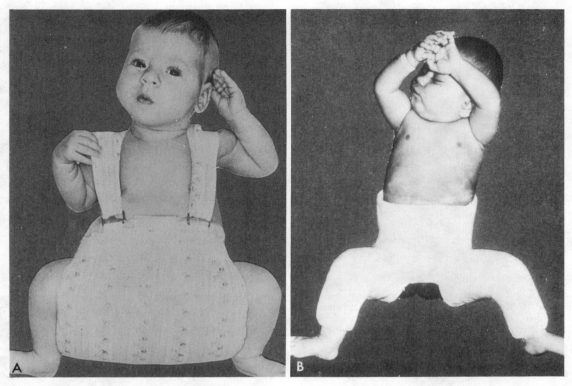

Figure 10-31.   *A)* La couche de Fredjka portée par ce bébé de 3 mois n'immobilise pas complètement mais garde aux hanches la position appropriée. Cette attelle s'utilise surtout pour le nouveau-né. *B)* Plâtre en « grenouille » après une ténotomie des adducteurs. (Dr R.B. Salter: *Modern Medicine*, 17 novembre 1969, p. 205.)

prendre que celui-ci a besoin de compensations afin d'éviter des traumatismes psychologiques et des retards de développement autres que locomoteurs.

L'ostéogénèse imparfaite

L'ostéogénèse imparfaite est une maladie rare, transmise selon le mode dominant ou le mode récessif. La forme congénitale peut être diagnostiquée *in-utero* par les multiples fractures visibles radiologiquement. Si le fœtus survit, le nouveau-né semble ne pas avoir de squelette.

La forme tardive apparaît plus ou moins rapidement selon la gravité. On note une histoire de fractures multiples à la suite de traumatismes minimes. Les luxations sont fréquentes à la suite de l'hyperlaxité ligamentaire, par déficience de la production de collagène dans les capsules articulaires. La peau est mince et fragile. Le temps de guérison des plaies est normal, mais produit une large cicatrice. L'enfant souffre de difformités, surtout par manque de traitement adéquat au moment des fractures. Les sclérotiques sont bleutées, les dents très souvent décolorées se brisent facilement.

De petits traumatismes résultant d'un changement de position peuvent donner lieu à une fracture sans douleur. Un grand nombre de ces enfants sont nains, à cause des multiples fractures des os longs et des fractures par compression des corps vertébraux.

Traitement et soins infirmiers.   Des manœuvres orthopédiques peuvent aider ces enfants, mais l'affection ne peut être guérie. Il faut maintenir ces enfants dans un bon état de nutrition et on doit les manipuler avec précaution pour éviter d'autres fractures.

Anomalie de développement des extrémités

Les anomalies congénitales des extrémités varient en gravité d'un défaut léger à une absence complète d'un membre. La polydactylie se manifeste par la présence de doigts ou

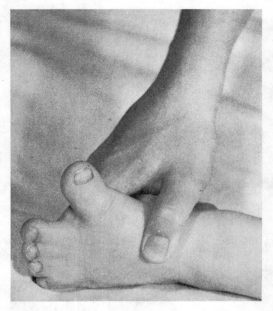

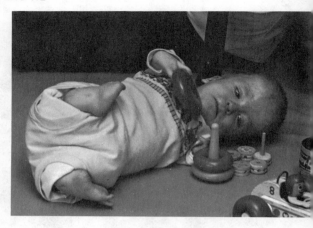

Figure 10-32. Syndactylie du pied. (Courtoisie du Dr Frank Mayfield, (de Caffey et Silverman, dans L. E. Holt, R. MacIntosh et H. L. Barnett: *Pediatrics*, 13e éd., New York, Appleton-Century-Crofts, 1962.)

A

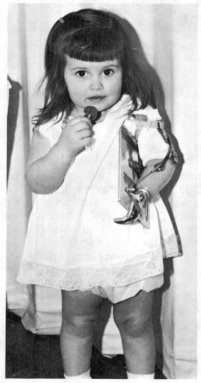

B

Figure 10-33. Cette petite fille semble s'être bien adaptée à sa prothèse. Elle parvient facilement à transporter un livre d'images sous son bras déformé. (M. I. Linberger: *Nursing Outlook*, janvier 1959.)

Figure 10-34. *A)* Né avec un membre supérieur incomplet, cet enfant s'intéresse quand même à ses jouets. *B)* Avec une seule jambe, cette fillette parvient à brosser les cheveux de sa poupée. (Courtoisie de la National Foundation-March of Dimes.)

d'orteils surnuméraires; la syndactylie, ou fusion complète ou partielle de plusieurs doigts ou orteils, peut impliquer seulement la peau, ou les os eux-mêmes qui peuvent être soudés. Ces affections sont corrigées par la chirurgie.

Chez les enfants plus gravement atteints, il peut y avoir une absence de tout ou d'une partie d'un ou des quatre membres. Au cours des récentes années, de telles anomalies soulevèrent l'intérêt du public, à cause de la découverte des effets de la thalidomide sur l'embryon. On ne peut parler de réadaptation chez ces enfants parce qu'ils n'ont jamais vécu autrement que privés d'un ou de plusieurs membres. On vise à leur faciliter la meilleure *adaptation* possible. L'adaptation de tels enfants est complexe, impliquant des facteurs squelettiques, neuro-musculaires, psychologiques, sociaux et intellectuels. La réussite du traitement suppose la présence d'une équipe de santé complète, incluant un pédiatre, un orthopédiste, un physiatre, un psychiatre, un psychologue, un physiothérapeute, des infirmières et d'autres professionnels suivant les besoins. Les parents et les enfants eux-mêmes occupent une grande place dans la thérapeutique, pour que les objectifs soient atteints.

Pour que cette thérapeutique réussisse, on encourage les enfants à utiliser les prothèses habituelles ou les nouvelles prothèses bio-mécaniques qui s'avèrent nécessaires pour qu'ils puissent devenir indépendants.

Si les parents voient d'autres enfants amputés qui se sont accommodés de leur prothèse, ils seront plus à même d'accepter un traitement similaire pour leur propre enfant.

La manière dont les parents réagissent à l'usage de la prothèse détermine souvent, dans une large mesure, son utilité éventuelle, étant donné que l'enfant modèle généralement son attitude sur celle de ses parents.

La méthode de *traitement* acceptée aujourd'hui est de munir l'enfant d'une prothèse articulée, parce que celle-ci entraîne un développement plus normal et moins d'atrophie pour les parties restantes du membre, ainsi qu'une plus grande acceptation de la prothèse par les parents et l'enfant.

Une déficience congénitale d'un membre a une profonde répercussion sur la vie de l'enfant qui en est affligé et sur ses parents. Même le personnel médical peut avoir de la difficulté à dominer ses réactions à la vue d'un enfant sérieusement difforme. On doit informer les parents de l'état de leur enfant le plus tôt possible après la naissance, même si c'est une tâche difficile à entreprendre. Du fait que le personnel médical et infirmier évite de discuter plus amplement de telles anomalies, les parents peuvent, en plus de leur sentiment de culpabilité, se sentir rejetés, désespérés et abandonnés.

Les parents de l'enfant devraient être acceptés par l'équipe de santé et encouragés à extérioriser leurs sentiments au sujet de leur déception. On doit leur parler tout de suite de l'usage des prothèses, de telle sorte qu'ils soient réalistes dans leurs espoirs pour l'enfant. Avec soutien et directives, les parents devraient être encouragés à discuter de l'infirmité avec réalisme, à accepter les besoins de l'enfant, autant son indépendance que sa dépendance, et à se libérer eux-mêmes de tout blâme, de telle sorte qu'ils puissent aider l'enfant à supporter son handicap. Lorsque l'enfant pose des questions sur son infirmité, les parents devraient lui donner une réponse simple et véridique comme par exemple: « Tu es né comme cela ». Plus tard, il aura besoin de réponses plus détaillées à ses questions. Si l'on aide les parents à résoudre leurs propres problèmes, ils seront en meilleure position pour aider l'enfant à résoudre les siens. L'attitude réaliste qu'adopteront les parents aidera l'enfant à accepter son infirmité.

Des cliniques spéciales ont été établies à travers le monde pour aider les enfants handicapés. Le but que poursuit chaque clinique pour enfants souffrant de difformités est le même: adapter et entraîner l'enfant à une vie normale, le plus tôt possible.

RÉFÉRENCES

Livres et documents officiels

Dekaban, A.: *Neurology of Early Childhood*. Baltimore, Williams & Wilkins Company, 1970.
Gross, R. E.: *An Atlas of Children's Surgery*. Philadelphie, W. B. Saunders Company, 1970.
Kramm, E.: *Families of Mongoloid Children*. Washington, Children's Bureau ,1963.
Krovetz, L. J., Gessner, I. H., et Schiebler, G. L.: *Handbook of Pediatric Cardiology*. New York, Harper & Row, Publishers, Incorporated, 1969.

Laboratoires Ross: *Les Cardiopathies congénitales* (feuillet nᵒ 7). *Bec-de-lièvre et division palatine* (feuillet nᵒ 11). *Anomalies orthopédiques congénitales* (feuillet nᵒ 15). *Les malformations du système nerveux central* (feuillet nᵒ 14). *Guide pour l'étude des cardiopathies congénitales.* Section de l'éducation en nursing, Columbus, Ohio.

Mallet, R., et Labrune, B.: *Le mongolisme.* Paris, Baillère et fils, 1967.

Matson, D. D.: *Neurosurgery of Infancy and Childhood.* 2ᵉ éd. Springfield, Ill., Charles C Thomas, 1969.

Pierog, S. H., et Ferrara, A.: *Approach to the Medical Care of the Sick Newborn.* Saint-Louis, C. V. Mosby Company, 1971.

Pillsbury, D. M.: *A Manual of Dermatology.* Philadelphie, W. B. Saunders Company, 1971.

Rickham, P. P., et Johnston, J. H.: *Neonatal Surgery.* New York, Appleton-Century-Crofts, 1969.

Ross, R. B., et Johnston, M. C.: *Cleft Lip and Palate.* Baltimore, Williams & Wilkins Company, 1971.

Rowe, R. B., et Mehrizi, A.: *The Neonate with Congenital Heart Disease.* Philadelphie, W. B. Saunders Company, 1968.

Smith, D. W.: *Recognizable Patterns of Human Malformation.* Philadelphie, W. B. Saunders Company, 1970.

Snyder, G., et autres: *Your Cleft Lip and Palate Child: A Basic Guide for Parents.* Evansville, Indiana, Mead Johnson.

Stevenson, A. C., et autres: *Genetic Counselling.* Philadelphie, J. B. Lippincott Company, 1970.

Wicka, D. K., et Falk, M. L.: *Advice to Parents of a Cleft Palate Child.* Springfield, Ill., Charles C Thomas, 1969.

Wolf, J. M., et Anderson, R. M. (édit.): *The Multiply Handicapped Child.* Springfield, Ill., Charles C Thomas, 1969.

Articles

Acknan, D: Les malformations et l'infection des voies génito-urinaires. *Inf. Can.*, 9:25, décembre 1967.

Altshuler, A.: Complete Transposition of the Great Arteries. *Am. J. Nursing*, 71:96, janvier 1971.

Atkinson, H. C.: Care of the Child with Cleft Lip and Palate. *Am. J. Nursing*, 67:1889, 1967.

Barcat, J.: Technique, indications et résultats chirurgicaux dans le traitement de l'hypospadias. *La revue de pédiatrie*, 1:197, 4, 1965; 2:39, 1, 1966.

Barnes, C. M. et autres: Measurement and Management of Anxiety in Children for Open Heart Surgery. *Pediatrics*, 49:250, février 1972.

Beck, M.: Attitudes of Parents of Pediatric Heart Patients Toward Patient Care Units. *Nursing Research*, 22:334, 4, 1973.

Bogdanovic, S.: Prenatal Detection of Down's Syndrome. *Journ. Obst. & Gynec. Nursing*, 4:35, juin 1975.

Bonine, G. N.: The Myelodysplastic Child: Hospital and Home Care. *Am. J. Nursing*, 69:541, Mars 1969.

Braine, J. P.: Tétralogie de Fallot. *Soins*, 20:9, janvier 1975.

Condon, M. R.: The Cardiac Child: What His Parents Need to Know. *Nursing '73*, 3:60, octobre 1973.

Dejean-Pusso, S.: Positioning Infants with Myelomeningocele. *Am. J. Nursing*, 74:1658, septembre 1974.

Destrooper, J. et autres: Le développement intellectuel d'enfants mongoliens hospitalisés. *Union Méd. du Can.*, 99:264, février 1970.

Etheridge, J. E.: Hypoglycemia and the Central Nervous System. *Pediat. Clin. N. Amer.*, 14:865, 1967.

Feinberg, T. et autres: Worries of Children with Exstrophy. *Pediatrics*, 53:242, 2, 1974.

Feldt, R. H., Strickler, G. B. et Weidman, W. H.: Growth of Children with Congenital Heart Disease. *Am. J. Dis. Child*, 117:573, mai 1969.

Gallet, J. P.: La rubéole congénitale. *Soins*, 15:255, juin 1970.

Héon, M.: Le traitement de l'hydrocéphalie par la valve de Holter. *Laval Médical*, 40:447, mai 1969.

Hill, M. L. et autres: The Myelodysplastic Child: Bowel and Bladder Control. *Am. J. Nursing*, 69:545, mars 1969.

Kachaner, J. et autres: Cardiologie infantile. *La médecine infantile*, 77:123, 3, 1970.

Kallaus, J. E.: The Child With Cleft Lip and Palate: The Mother in the Maternity Unit. *Am. J. Nursing*, 65:120, avril 1965.

Kapke, K. A.: Spina-bifida: Mother-Child Relationship. *Nursing Forum* 9:310, 3, 1970.

Kugel, R. B.: Combatting Retardation in Infants with Down's Syndrome. *Children*, 17:188, septembre-octobre 1970.

Lamberton, M. M.: Cardiac Catheterization: Anticipatory Nursing Care. *Am. J. Nursing*, 71:1718, septembre 1971.

Lane, P. A.: Mother's Confession – Home Care of a Toddler in a Spina Cast: What It's Really Like. *Am. J. Nursing*, 71:2141, novembre 1971.

Lewis, C.: Nursing Care of the Neonate Requiring Surgery for Congenital Defects. *Nurs. Clin. N. Amer.*, 5:387, septembre 1970.

Linde, L. M. et autres: Mental Development in Congenital Heart Disease. *J. Pediat.*, 71:197, 1967.

Lloyd, P.: Postoperative Nursing Care Following Open Heart Surgery in Children. *Nurs. Clin. N. Amer.*, 5:399, septembre 1970.

Marmol, J. G., Scriggins, A. L. et Vollman, R. F.: Mothers of Mongoloid Infants in Collaborative Project. *Am. J. Obst. & Gynec.*, 104:533, 15 juin 1969.

Menser, M. A. et autres: Congenital Rubella: Long-Term Follow-up Study. *Am. J. Dis. Child.*, 118:32, juillet 1969.

Mercer, R.: Mother's Responses to Their Infants with Defects. *Nursing Research*, 23:133, 2, 1974.

Millard, D. R., Kuszay, J. et Wireh, B.: Nursing Care of the Patient with Cleft Lip and Palate. *Nurs. Clin. N. Amer.*, 2:483, 1967.

Mollard, P. et autres: L'exstrophie vésicale. *Pédiatrie*, xx:216, 2, 1965.

Moloshok, R. et Ken, J.: The Infant with Ambiguous Genitalia. *Ped. Clin. N. Amer.*, 19:529, 3, 1972.

Morais, T. et Demers, P. P.: Le diabète néonatal. *Laval Médical*, 38:337 avril 1967.

Mori, W.: My Child Has Down's Syndrome. *Am. J. Nursing*, 73:1386, août 1973.

Murray, B. S., Elmore, J. et Sawyer, J. R.: The Patient Has an Ileal Conduit. *Am. J. Nursing*, 71:1560, août 1971.

Neimann, N. et Fonder, A.: L'hermaphrodisme. *Pédiatrie*, XXII:499, 5, 1967.

Nora, J. et autres: Risk to Offspring of Parents with Congenital Heart Defects. *J.A.M.A.*, 209:2052, 29 septembre 1969.

Pask, E. G.: La collecte des urines chez les enfants. *Inf. Can.*, 12:25, juillet 1970.

Perron, J.: Malformations de la verge. *Soins*, 14:347, 8, 1969.

Pons, J.: Le bec-de-lièvre. *Soins*, 20:23, juin 1975.

Posey, R.: Creative Nursing Care of Babies with Heart Disease. Nursing '74, 4:40 octobre 1974.

Praud, E.: Les hydrocéphalies. *Soins*, 16:458, octobre 1971.

Raimondi, A. et Soare, P.: Intellectual Development in Shunted Hydrocephalic Children. *Amer. J. Dis. Child.*, 127:664, mai 1974.

Ralph, J., O'Brien, M., Owens, M.: La réadaptation sociale des petites victimes de la thalidomide. *Inf. Can.*, 9:34, janvier 1967.

Rashkind, W. J.: Transposition of the Great Arteries. *Pediat. Clin. N. Amer.*, 18:1075, novembre 1971.

Reif, K.: A Heart Makes You Live. *Am. J. Nursing*, 72:1085, juin 1972.

Roberts, F. B.: The Child with Heart Disease. *Am. J. Nursing*, 72:1080, juin 1972.

Rowe, R. D.: Serious Congenital Heart Disease in the Newborn Infant: Diagnosis and Management. *Pediat. Clin. N. Amer.*, 17:967, novembre 1970.

Schoumacher, H.: Ostéotomie de varisation et dérotation fémorale chez l'enfant. *Soins*, 20:27, décembre 1975.

Seringe, R.: Les pieds-bots. *Soins*, 20:9, décembre 1975.

Seringe, P. et autres: Différenciation sexuelle. *La médecine infantile*, 77:327, 5, 1970.

Sinclair, J. C. et autres: Supportive Management of the Sick Neonate: Parenteral Calories, Water and Electrolytes. *Pediat. Clin. N. Amer.*, 17:863, novembre 1970.

Stanko, B.: Intervenir après la naissance d'un enfant anormal. *Inf. Can.*, 15:32, octobre 1973.

Stanley, P. et autres: La chirurgie cardiaque chez l'enfant. *Union méd. du Can.*, 99:1817, octobre 1970.

Steele, S.: Children with Amputations. *Nursing Forum*, 7:411, 4, 1968.

Stein, S.: Selection for Early Treatment in myelomeningocele. *Pediatrics*, 54:553, mai 1974.

Stone, N. W.: Family Factors in Willingness to Place the Mongoloid Child. *Am. J. Ment. Defic.*, 72:16, juillet 1967.

Talner, N. S.: Congestive Heart Failure in the Infant: A Functional Approach. *Pediat. Clin. N. Amer.*, 18:1011, novembre 1971.

Tesler, M. et Hardgrove, C.: Cardiac Catheterization: Preparing the Child. *Am. J. Nursing*, 73:80, janvier 1973.

Turpin, R. et autres: Trisomie 21. *La médecine infantile*, 73:463, 6, 1966.

Vialas, M.: Traitement intensif du spina bifida. *La revue de pédiatrie*, 7:605, août 1971.

Waechter, E. H.: Developmental Correlates of Physical Disability. *Nursing Forum*, 9:90, 1, 1970.

Whitmore, W. F.: Wilm's Tumor and Neuroblastoma. *Am. J. Nursing*, 68:527, 1968.

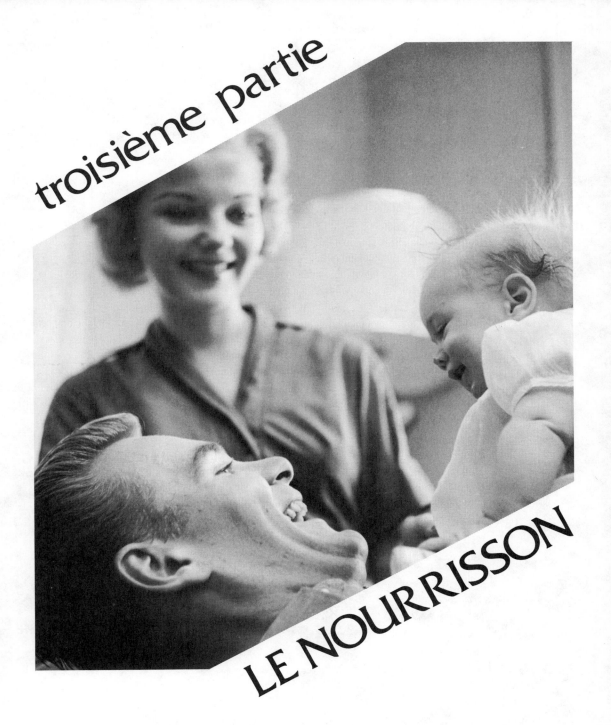

troisième partie

LE NOURRISSON

11

le nourrisson: croissance, développement, soins

Ce chapitre traitera de la croissance et du développement du nourrisson tant aux points de vue émotif et physiologique que physique et sanitaire. Les soins nécessaires au bébé y seront également expliqués.

L'évolution du bébé durant les douze premiers mois de la vie requiert des parents une adaptation constante. Ils doivent d'abord apprendre à satisfaire un petit être dépendant et passif, mais ils ont rapidement à composer avec un nourrisson qui a des exigences et des besoins propres. Durant cette période préverbale, ils doivent perfectionner leur sens de l'observation et leur capacité à déchiffrer le comportement et le babillage du nourrisson, pour parvenir à satisfaire ses besoins.

Dans ce processus d'adaptation, les parents peuvent rencontrer deux obstacles importants: d'une part, leur ignorance des étapes du développement normal d'un enfant et, d'autre part, leur immaturité émotive qui peut les empêcher de considérer leur enfant comme un être humain autonome, ayant des besoins spécifiques. Le genre d'enfance que les parents ont vécu peut également les influencer et les porter à vouloir satisfaire leurs propres exigences frustrées, plutôt que les besoins réels du bébé. Les infirmières en santé communautaire et en pédiatrie peuvent aider les parents à exprimer leurs sentiments et à adopter une attitude parentale réaliste.

Il est à souligner que le nourrisson profite plus de la joie et de la spontanéité de l'adulte qui s'occupe de lui que de soins experts prodigués sans chaleur.

APERÇU DU DÉVELOPPEMENT ÉMOTIF DU NOURRISSON

Utilisant la théorie de E. Erikson comme cadre de référence, le développement émotif du nourrisson sera présenté comme consistant essentiellement en l'acquisition d'un sentiment de confiance envers lui-même, l'adulte et l'environnement.

Le sentiment de confiance

Le sentiment de confiance se développe durant la première année d'existence. Selon les expériences vécues, il sera renforcé ou affaibli ultérieurement, mais il prend racine dès la première enfance. Si les circonstances ne permettent pas au nourrisson d'acquérir ce sentiment fondamental, il deviendra progressivement méfiant. Un tel enfant se révélera par la suite peu amical et peu liant et il suscitera des attitudes similaires chez les adultes et les enfants qui le côtoieront. Sa méfiance ira croissant s'il ne reçoit pas une aide appropriée.

Durant la première année, le jeune enfant est totalement dépendant de sa mère ou de la personne qui la remplace: le père, la grand-mère, les frères et sœurs ou la gardienne; mais sa préférence ira certainement vers sa mère. Au cours des six premiers mois de la vie, un certain équilibre doit s'établir entre les besoins du nourrisson et ceux de sa mère, particulièrement en ce qui concerne les exigences de l'alimentation du bébé. La satisfaction mutuelle des deux partenaires de la relation mère-enfant est nécessaire pour que le bébé développe un sentiment de confiance envers celle qui en prend soin. Le père et les autres membres de la famille doivent soutenir la mère pour qu'elle puisse apporter au bébé toute la tendresse nécessaire. La première façon pour le nourrisson de faire connaissance avec la vie est d'incorporer les objets et les êtres à lui-même, soit par sa bouche, soit par ses yeux. Si ce besoin de « prendre », de ramener l'environnement à lui-même est satisfait, il sera ensuite prêt pour les modalités sociales consistant à donner et à recevoir.

Une autre évolution du nourrisson consiste à délaisser progressivement les plaisirs purement physiques (être propre et sec) ou solitaires (succion des doigts, d'une tétine) pour jouir du contact avec sa mère ou son substitut et des interactions avec des personnes humaines. Il apprend aussi à se tourner vers ceux qui s'occupent de lui, quand il a peur ou est souffrant. Pour que ces transformations se produisent, le nourrisson doit avoir vécu des expériences satisfaisantes.

En effet, un jeune enfant apprend à faire confiance aux autres en fonction du degré de satisfaction de ses besoins essentiels. Si sa faim est toujours apaisée dans un délai raisonnable, il acquerra un sentiment de confiance envers ceux qui prennent soin de lui. Il apprend aussi à se fier à ceux qui lui procurent des sensations agréables. Le nourrisson ne différencie pas son corps de celui de la personne qui le tient; il croit que la main de sa mère est un prolongement de lui-même. Les caresses de sa mère, ses soins et ses sourires l'amènent à saisir les limites de son corps et à se percevoir peu à peu comme un organisme indépendant. *Progressivement, il associera soins et caresses en la personne de sa mère*, il lui sourira et gazouillera en la voyant, car intuitivement il pressent un effet agréable. Il aura appris à se fier à elle et, par la même occasion, il aura acquis les fondements de sa *confiance* en autrui.

Toutefois, si quelqu'un lui parle d'une voix rude, s'il est brusque ou vif dans ses mouvements, le nourrisson sera effrayé. Il aura ainsi reçu sa première leçon de *méfiance* à l'égard des autres; si cette situation se répète souvent, il deviendra craintif et anxieux. Cet état de chose peut exister si les relations entre les parents sont tendues et angoissées; dans ce cas, ils auraient besoin de consulter un conseiller matrimonial ou un psychiatre. Ce dernier pourrait éviter à leur enfant de sérieuses maladies mentales dues à cette absence de confiance et de sécurité. *Le sentiment de confiance est la pierre angulaire d'une saine personnalité.*

Durant les six premiers mois de sa vie, le nourrisson est gouverné par le principe du plaisir et il n'est pas capable de renoncer à un plaisir ou d'en donner un. À l'âge de six semaines, quand il sourit à sa mère, c'est tout simplement parce qu'il se sent bien et non pour la rendre heureuse. On peut remarquer d'ailleurs qu'il sourit dans son sommeil ou quand il est seul. Puis, il présente un sourire imitateur en réponse à celui de l'adulte. Plus tard, il apprendra que le sourire de sa mère répond au sien et à son gazouillis. Il sourira pour obtenir la compagnie et les caresses de sa mère.

En l'absence d'une relation mère-enfant basée sur une confiance mutuelle, le bébé risque de développer un mode de comportement perturbé caractérisé par des troubles d'alimentation et des pleurs excessifs. Une relation engendrant des frustrations mutuelles apparaît entre la mère et le bébé.

Après le 6e mois, le nourrisson découvre une autre façon de connaître les objets, celle de « mordre ». Ses premières dents percent entre le 5e et le 7e mois et il apprend rapidement à s'en servir. Mettre dans la bouche tout ce qui lui tombe sous la main devient un jeu qui lui permet d'avoir quelque chose à mordiller entre les gencives et d'expérimenter des sensations nouvelles.

Il se rend toutefois compte que sa mère lui enlève le sein s'il mordille le mamelon et qu'il ressent une douleur lorsqu'il mord sur une gencive gonflée par la dentition. L'enfant s'aperçoit qu'en étant confiant, il risque parfois de souffrir. Il doit apprendre à doser ses exigences et accepter qu'à la satisfaction habituelle de ses besoins, s'ajoute maintenant une certaine frustration.

Au fur et à mesure qu'il vieillit, le nourrisson prend conscience de son autonomie. Sa mère, le voyant maintenant plus vigoureux et moins dépendant d'elle, le laisse plus souvent livré à lui-même; elle peut envisager de l'habituer graduellement à son absence, spécialement si elle désire reprendre l'exercice de sa profession ou son travail à l'extérieur. À cette période de sa vie le nourrisson est souvent réveillé et par conséquent prend conscience qu'il est seul. Une crise peut alors survenir à l'intérieur de la relation mère-enfant.

L'adaptation mutuelle de la mère et de l'enfant aux changements qui surviennent en eux et entre eux dépendra de la qualité des soins qui ont précédé cette crise, ainsi que de la valeur des rapports établis.

Un autre facteur de réussite dans l'adaptation du nourrisson est la continuité et la qualité des soins prodigués par les autres membres de la famille qui peuvent servir de substitut maternel.

BESOINS DURANT LA PREMIÈRE ANNÉE

En plus du besoin primordial du nourrisson de tout porter à sa bouche et de tout mordre, on remarque que cinq autres exigences doivent être satisfaites pour développer et fortifier sa confiance dans les autres. Ces exigences sont les suivantes: *nourriture, succion, chaleur et confort, amour et sécurité, stimulation sensorielle.*

Besoin de nourriture

Le nourrisson a un horizon limité, il n'a aucune notion du temps il vit dans le présent. Sa vie est rythmée par ses mécanismes physiologiques. La faim lui occasionne un certain malaise et il saisit rapidement que son entourage est susceptible d'apaiser sa tension et de lui donner une sensation de bien-être. C'est aussi le moment opportun de lui exprimer amour et affection.

Le bébé peut jouir de la chaleur et du confort dont il a besoin, qu'il soit nourri au sein ou au biberon, pourvu qu'il soit pris tendrement dans les bras durant son repas.

Les infirmières sont souvent critiquées pour leur froide attitude professionnelle, quand elles alimentent les nourrissons hospitalisés. Ce comportement est regrettable parce que le nourrisson ressent le manque de chaleur et d'affection.

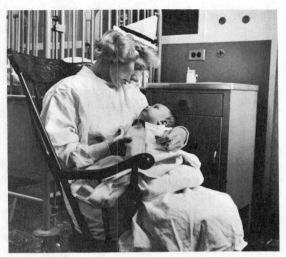

Figure 11-1. L'infirmière nourrit au biberon l'enfant hospitalisé et en même temps elle lui donne le plaisir de sucer, la chaleur, le confort et le sentiment de sécurité dont il a besoin. (Photo Hôpital St. Luke, New York City.)

L'attitude de la mère ou de son substitut se révèle à travers la voix, le toucher et le rythme des mouvements, quand elle nourrit le bébé. Ce dernier associe tendresse et chaleur à sa faim assouvie et ensuite à la nourriture. Mais il arrive que l'attitude maternelle ne soit pas tendre et affectueuse. Le bébé risque alors de développer des problèmes alimentaires, tels vomissements, méricysme.

Besoin du plaisir de la succion

L'habitude de l'enfant de mettre ses doigts et ses jouets dans sa bouche est étroitement liée au plaisir de la succion, mais n'a aucun rapport avec sa faim. Si cette habitude est contrariée, il en résultera un malaise qui disparaîtra aussitôt que le jeune enfant pourra assouvir son besoin de succion. L'intensité du désir de sucer varie d'un nourrisson à l'autre et ceci démontre le caractère individuel de chaque bébé.

Après le sixième mois de son existence il peut mordiller la tétine, mais s'il tète il peut blesser sa mère. Le sevrage sera alors vraisemblablement effectué. S'il a appris à boire dans une tasse, alors qu'il avait besoin de sucer, il aura tendance à sucer tous les objets qu'il trouve, qu'ils soient appropriés ou non. Il est bon de lui fournir un morceau de pain ou un jouet adéquat. L'intensité du désir de sucer et de mordre diminue progressivement à mesure que d'autres satisfactions lui deviennent graduellement accessibles.

Besoin de chaleur et de confort

Un nourrisson jouit de la chaleur et de la douceur du corps de sa mère quand elle le serre dans ses bras. Il jouit aussi du bercement et du changement de position. Le contact tactile est essentiel à son développement. Le jeune enfant a un besoin réel de ces agréables expériences.

Besoin d'amour et de sécurité

Le nourrisson a besoin de démonstrations d'affection multiples et variées, on peut les lui manifester lors du bain, de la promenade, du jeu, etc... Il doit également se sentir en sécurité, désiré et aimé. Les jeunes enfants ne sont pas consciemment anxieux pour leur avenir, mais une sécurité ou une appréhension qui, à l'âge adulte, deviendra anxiété ou angoisse, pourra résulter des soins quotidiens.

Besoin de stimulation sensorielle

Le bébé communique tout d'abord avec son environnement par le contact des mains de l'accoucheur et ensuite par le contact maternel. Il prendra ensuite conscience du monde qui l'entoure par une suite d'expériences tactiles et sensorielles. Le bébé découvre son propre corps en s'explorant et son image corporelle se forme peu à peu.

Au cours des dernières années, des recherches ont démontré l'importance de la stimulation sensorielle pour le développement normal du système nerveux et des différents organes sensoriels. Un adulte, s'il est isolé du monde extérieur, présentera des troubles dans le processus de la pensée, dans son aptitude à résoudre des problèmes et dans son habileté perceptuelle. Les perturbations chez le nourrisson sont encore plus graves parce qu'il est plus dépendant.

L'être humain apprend toute sa vie, mais on s'est rendu compte que certains apprentissages s'effectuent le plus efficacement à des périodes précises. Avant ou après cette période, la qualité et l'étendue des habiletés à développer seront grandement perturbées. La période critique pour tout apprentissage se situe peut-être au moment où les capacités motrices, sensorielles et psychologiques se trouvent réunies et que l'enfant sent le besoin d'apprendre et trouve en lui la motivation nécessaire.

L'enfant a besoin d'être stimulé de différentes façons: par un changement de milieu et de position, par des contacts avec diverses sortes d'étoffes et de textures, par des sons variés, par la vision d'objets colorés et mou-

Figure 11-2. Vision du monde extérieur par le nourrisson. (Photo Jack Tinney et *Baby Talk Magazine,* avril 1967.)

vants et par la chaleur humaine. S'il ne reçoit pas ces stimuli intégrés aux soins quotidiens, il ne pourra croître et se développer normalement. Une mère tendre et aimante peut répondre au besoin de stimulation sensorielle. Ainsi elle pourra le serrer dans ses bras, jouer avec lui, lui parler et, finalement, elle variera et élargira son champ d'activités et d'expériences.

Moyens de répondre à ces besoins

Répondre aux besoins du nourrisson nécessite une suite d'actions intimement liées qui débutent dès la naissance. La communication entre le bébé et le monde extérieur s'établit ordinairement par l'intermédiaire de la mère.

L'alimentation sur demande, au sein ou au biberon, comble une grande partie des besoins: le nourrisson est alors serré contre sa mère et a la possibilité de téter quand et autant qu'il le désire. Le nouveau-né nourri au biberon doit être tenu dans la même position que l'enfant nourri au sein. Si la mère accepte l'idée d'un horaire imposé par le nourrisson, rapidement ce dernier l'établira. Les orifices de la tétine doivent être de grosseur appropriée, de façon à ce que deux heures ou plus soient nécessaires au nourrisson pour boire sa ration de la journée.

Le nourrisson doit toujours être pris dans les bras pour ses repas, afin de recevoir la chaleur, la tendresse et les stimulations visuelles et tactiles dont il a besoin.

Combler ses besoins vitaux ne saurait gâter l'enfant. Sa mère doit s'occuper de lui, veiller à son confort et à son bien-être: voir s'il a froid, s'il est mouillé ou fatigué d'être couché dans la même position. D'ailleurs, le nourrisson a besoin de vivre des expériences agréables pour apprendre à faire confiance aux autres.

Quand le bébé établit la différence entre lui-même, sa mère et les autres personnes qui s'occupent de lui, il n'accepte plus de rester seul, d'être abandonné à lui-même. Il est nécessaire alors de lui parler, de lui rendre souvent visite dans sa chambre, afin qu'il comprenne qu'une absence momentanée de son entourage ne signifie pas un oubli total. S'il doit supporter de longues périodes de séparation, il peut cultiver une peur chronique d'être abandonné. Le chien de la famille n'est qu'un bien maigre substitut à la présence humaine, mais il est supérieur aux jouets inanimés.

Durant la seconde partie de la première année, le nourrisson peut devenir timide et développer un sentiment de peur et d'insécurité devant les étrangers. L'entourage adulte devra accepter cette réticence et cette frayeur et, sans bousculer le bébé, essayer de gagner sa confiance.

Durant ses premiers mois, comme le nourrisson ne peut exprimer verbalement ses désirs, sa mère doit les deviner; plus tard, il les transmettra au moyen de mouvements et de sons. Le développement du langage demeure étroitement lié à son évolution mentale et à son désir de communiquer avec autrui. Un facteur capital, souvent négligé, est la réaction de sa mère à son babillage et à son gazouillis. Le sourire et le babillage du jeune enfant récompensent la mère de ses bons soins; si celle-ci démontre sa satisfaction, soit en bavardant avec lui, soit d'une autre manière, le bébé continuera à faire des vocalises et, bientôt, il dira ses premiers mots. En bref, l'enfant saura s'adapter à la vie, si ses besoins vitaux sont comblés, comme, par exemple, s'il reçoit le sein ou le biberon dès qu'il pleure pour signifier sa faim. Mais s'il pleure de faim et que sa mère est incapable de le satisfaire, il développera un mode de comportement pour satisfaire lui-même son besoin: ou il sucera son pouce jusqu'à ce qu'il s'endorme ou alors il criera de rage. Ainsi, l'enfant apprend à s'adapter au monde extérieur et à exercer un certain contrôle sur son entourage en modifiant ses attitudes.

Le bébé a besoin d'un maximum de sensations plaisantes. Il doit, cependant, éprouver de petites doses d'anxiété pour apprendre à surmonter les frustrations et être préparé à affronter les problèmes propres à l'enfance. S'il n'est pas surprotégé, les expériences quotidiennes lui fourniront suffisamment de frustrations et lui permettront de développer son habileté à surmonter les problèmes.

Frustrations de ces besoins

Certaines réactions enfantines se retrouvent chez l'adulte, mais elles sont modifiées par la vie sociale du groupe.

La prédilection des adultes pour manger des aliments croquants ou mâcher du chewing-gum est un plaisir de nourrisson qu'ils ont probablement conservé.

Si l'on ne comble pas le besoin de nourriture de l'enfant, il deviendra anxieux et peut-être gourmand ou, au contraire, refusera de manger suffisamment.

Si son besoin d'amour et de sécurité n'est pas satisfait, il doutera de son pouvoir d'influencer l'adulte et manquera de confiance en lui; il ne pourra alors assumer l'étape suivante de son développement. S'il n'apprend pas à faire confiance aux autres, il n'adoptera pas à leur égard une attitude neutre mais, au contraire, il ne saura ni se faire, ni garder des amis. Cela sera le résultat du manque de confiance qu'il éprouvait dans sa première enfance à l'égard de ceux qui prenaient soin de lui.

Si le jeune enfant manque de stimulations sensorielles, il ne pourra développer ses facultés mentales. Très tôt, le jeune enfant doit vivre des expériences sensorielles et perceptuelles, afin de prévenir des retards de croissance, de développement ou des troubles de comportement.

Si le nourrisson est hospitalisé, ses parents doivent recevoir le support émotif nécessaire des membres de l'équipe de santé pour être capables par la suite de renforcer le sentiment de sécurité de leur enfant malade. Il faut, si possible, permettre aux parents de collaborer aux soins de l'enfant. On mettra à son chevet un nombre limité d'infirmières qu'il pourra connaître; un changement de visages trop fréquent risque de détruire son sentiment de confiance. L'enfant a besoin de stimulation sensorielle même à l'hôpital; la surstimulation qu'il subit dans l'unité de soins intensifs peut par contre s'avérer nuisible. Une tétine d'amusement ne peut remplacer le contact physique de sa mère ou de sa remplaçante, mais peut quand même satisfaire son besoin de sucer ou de mordiller.

PRINCIPES DE CROISSANCE ET DE DÉVELOPPEMENT

Dans le chapitre deux on a étudié les principes généraux de la croissance et du développement qui peuvent se résumer comme suit: le développement de l'organisme humain est un *processus continu* qui commence même avant la naissance, chaque étape dépendant de la précédente. Un exemple précis sera le développement de la dentition humaine.

L'enfant naît édenté. Il a cependant les éléments de vingt dents dans ses gencives et certaines ont commencé leur calcification in utero. L'éruption des premières dents débute aux environs du 7e mois. Certains enfants n'éprouvent aucune difficulté lors de la dentition tandis que pour d'autres, elle constitue une expérience pénible. La ration de liquide consommé alors par le bébé peut diminuer graduellement; s'il n'est pas nourri adéquatement, il peut souffrir d'insomnie et d'une légère perturbation électrolytique. Les dents permanentes commencent à se former aussitôt après la naissance, mais elles n'apparaissent que vers l'âge de 6 ou 7 ans. L'éruption des dernières dents, c'est-à-dire des troisièmes molaires, indique d'une manière approximative la fin de la croissance.

Une *séquence de développement* signifie que des changements spécifiques, graduels et ordonnés doivent survenir pour qu'une étape soit accomplie. Tous les enfants vivent les mêmes étapes durant leur croissance, mais celles-ci ne s'achèvent pas toujours à la même période;

ceci dépend du développement intellectuel de l'enfant et de sa faculté à réagir à son milieu physique et social. Il est essentiel pour une infirmière de noter *les différences individuelles* afin de répondre efficacement aux besoins de chaque enfant.

Il existe une grande corrélation entre les différents aspects de la croissance. Tous les champs d'action de la croissance physique, mentale, émotive, sociale et spirituelle évoluent parallèlement et s'influencent mutuellement pour aboutir à la maturité.

Trois principes doivent être retenus dans le développement moteur: a) Le développement musculaire est *céphalocaudal**, c'est-à-dire procède de la tête vers les pieds. Ainsi, l'enfant apprend à contrôler les muscles de son cou avant de contrôler ceux de ses jambes et de ses pieds. b) Le développement du contrôle musculaire évolue des segments *proximaux* vers les segments *distaux*, c'est-à-dire le développement débute au tronc et progresse vers les extrémités. c) Les deux principes précédents se manifestent de concert dans l'évolution des mouvements *globaux* vers des mouvements *spécifiques*.

Les muscles contrôlant les mouvements globaux sont habituellement les larges muscles proximaux. L'enfant utilise les muscles des bras et des jambes avant de contrôler ceux des mains, des pieds, des doigts et des orteils.

----

* Du grec *kephalos*: tête et du latin *cauda*: queue. Ainsi nommé à cause de la situation des cellules nerveuses du système nerveux central qui contrôle l'activité musculaire. La queue est l'équivalent de la partie inférieure de la moelle épinière.

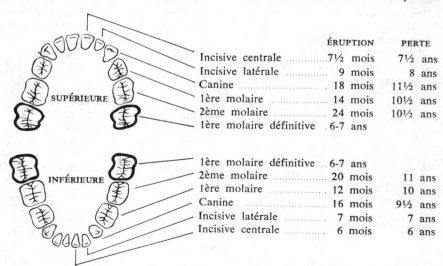

	ÉRUPTION	PERTE
SUPÉRIEURE		
Incisive centrale	7½ mois	7½ ans
Incisive latérale	9 mois	8 ans
Canine	18 mois	11½ ans
1ère molaire	14 mois	10½ ans
2ème molaire	24 mois	10½ ans
1ère molaire définitive	6-7 ans	
INFÉRIEURE		
1ère molaire définitive	6-7 ans	
2ème molaire	20 mois	11 ans
1ère molaire	12 mois	10 ans
Canine	16 mois	9½ ans
Incisive latérale	7 mois	7 ans
Incisive centrale	6 mois	6 ans

Figure 11-3. Le développement de la dentition humaine se continue à partir du cinquième mois in-utero jusqu'à la maturité. (Courtoisie de Niles Newton, Ph.D., et *Baby Talk Magazine*, novembre 1967.)

Le nourrisson bouge ses bras et donne des coups de pied bien avant de contrôler les muscles de ses doigts et de pouvoir tenir un objet dans sa main. Il serre ses jouets, roule et s'assied, avant de pouvoir ramasser des miettes comme le ferait un adulte.

Chez le nourrisson, on utilise des tests d'habileté psychomotrice pour établir un quotient de développement. Ce ne sont pas des tests d'intelligence puisqu'on ne connaît pas de façon sûre les éléments d'un comportement intelligent chez le bébé. Ces tests évaluent les capacités actuelles du nourrisson mais ils n'ont pas de valeur prédictive.

Facteurs fondamentaux du développement

Le développement est dépendant de deux facteurs fondamentaux: la maturation et l'apprentissage.

Le terme *maturation* désigne la capacité innée de développement, déterminée génétiquement. La maturation couvre tous les aspects de l'évolution.

L'*apprentissage* est le résultat d'expérience et d'entraînement. L'apprentissage est prouvé lorsque le comportement se modifie.

L'aptitude à apprendre dépend du potentiel inné de l'enfant à se développer mentalement. Si l'enfant a un faible quotient intellectuel, il apprendra difficilement.

Le nourrisson apprend d'abord par expérience personnelle: il tombe et apprend que le plancher est dur; il mange et apprend que les fruits en purée ont bon goût. Plus tard, il apprendra, en l'expérimentant, comment ouvrir et fermer une porte ou comment grimper les escaliers.

Quand il sera un peu plus âgé, un de ses moyens d'apprentissage sera l'expérience des autres, qu'il appréciera en les observant et en les écoutant parler. À cet âge, il a compris que les adultes connaissent beaucoup plus de choses que lui et que ce qu'ils disent peut le renseigner. Quand sa mère l'avertit que le four est chaud et qu'il se brûlera la main s'il le touche, il la croit et ne tentera pas l'expérience de s'en approcher. Il apprendra ce qu'est une hospitalisation par la description que lui en fera un enfant qui aura vécu cette expérience. Finalement, à l'école, il apprendra à partir de l'expérience humaine vécue.

Maturation et apprentissage sont en corrélation. Aucun apprentissage ne pourra se faire si l'enfant n'est pas suffisamment mûr pour comprendre et modifier son comportement. S'il se trouve forcé d'atteindre un niveau trop élevé pour ses capacités, il pourra développer des mécanismes qui entraîneront un certain retard dans son apprentissage futur.

L'enfant auquel on n'aura pas donné l'occasion d'apprendre, par expérience personnelle ou au contact des autres, et ce, au moment opportun, sera retardé dans son développement. Un adulte responsable d'un enfant, même pour un court laps de temps, ne doit pas négliger de noter les aptitudes de ce dernier à apprendre, ainsi que les progrès qu'il réalise. La maman qui veut obliger son nourrisson d'un mois à se maintenir assis, ne réussira pas et celui-ci probablement tombera, car ses muscles ne sont pas assez solides pour cet exercice. Il peut être effrayé par l'expérience et peu porté à la répéter par lui-même. Si, au contraire, la mère observe son nourrisson un peu plus âgé et remarque ses efforts répétés, mais vains, pour s'asseoir, elle doit reconnaître son désir d'apprendre et l'aider jusqu'à ce qu'il réussisse. Ainsi, elle aura contribué à son développement en l'aidant de façon appropriée en temps opportun.

L'efficacité de l'enseignement et de l'apprentissage dépend donc du degré de maturité de l'enfant. Mais la maturation, vérifiée par le comportement du nourrisson, est influencée à son tour par les opportunités d'apprentissage qui lui sont offertes.

Niveaux et étapes de la croissance et du développement

Il est important de revoir l'ensemble des principes du développement émotif et physique, afin de comprendre les différentes étapes de la croissance et l'enchaînement des réalisations-types des nourrissons durant leur développement, mois par mois.

Les changements de comportement durant le développement du nourrisson ont fait l'objet d'un grand nombre de recherches.

Comme il a déjà été mentionné, chaque étape déterminée du développement d'un enfant se réalise dans un certain laps de temps. L'âge moyen prévu pour ces différentes réalisations est donné dans les tableaux qui suivent.

Ces données ne seront probablement pas applicables à tous les nourrissons, car elles représentent une moyenne et finalement peu d'enfants illustrent la moyenne déterminée pour leur âge dans tous les aspects de leur évolution. Ces plans serviront de point de repère et permettront à l'infirmière de juger d'une façon approximative si le développement de l'enfant se maintient à l'intérieur des normes établies.

JEU

But. Le nourrisson apprend beaucoup en jouant. Au jeu, il exerce son adresse; il acquiert le contrôle de son corps; il améliore la coordination générale de ses mouvements et la coordination spécifique main-yeux. Il apprend aussi à établir des relations avec des personnes et des objets, à exprimer ses sentiments et à assimiler ses frustrations. *Jouer est vital pour le développement de la personnalité de l'enfant*; cette activité occupe d'ailleurs la plupart de ses moments de veille.

Le nourrisson apprend à jouer avec des objets, à s'amuser de ses propres gestes et des bruits qu'il émet, dès le premier âge. Plus tard durant l'enfance, il apprendra à jouer avec les autres enfants. Certains soutiennent que, de cette période du jeu, dépendra l'aptitude d'un adulte à travailler avec ses semblables. Bien que le but général du jeu soit le même pour tous les nourrissons, chacun d'eux découvre à sa manière comment utiliser un jouet. Ainsi, le jeu traduit l'individualité de chacun, car il répond à un besoin du moment et tous les enfants n'en tirent pas un profit identique. Il est à conseiller de laisser le nourrisson diriger son jeu; les adultes, par le vif intérêt qu'ils témoignent au développement de l'enfant, sont enclins à trop contrôler cette activité.

Choix des jouets. Les jouets jugés adéquats pour tel âge, le sont en fonction des normes de croissance et de développement. La mère qui connaît les caractéristiques de la croissance et du développement choisira les jouets qui sont appropriés à l'âge de son enfant mais en tenant compte des besoins particuliers de celui-ci.

Bien choisir les jouets est important, car ceux-ci favorisent l'apprentissage des enfants. Un facteur essentiel dans le choix d'un jouet est qu'il puisse être utilisé par l'enfant en toute sécurité. Cette condition dépend du niveau de croissance et de développement de l'enfant, de sa condition physique et de ses caractéristiques individuelles. Certains enfants sont plus prudents que d'autres; ceci peut découler d'une croissance plus ou moins rapide ou d'expériences antérieures. Il y a beaucoup de risques à donner aux nourrissons des jouets pour enfants plus âgés. Par exemple, le nourrisson pourrait porter à sa bouche et avaler facilement les petites pièces qu'un jeune enfant utilise pour construire une voiture. (Suite p. 267.)

Tableau 11-1. *Niveau moyen de développement des nourrissons de 1 à 12 mois*

1 MOIS

Physique

    Poids: 3630 grammes; il gagne 150 à 210 grammes par semaine, pendant les 6 premiers mois de son existence.
    Taille: grandit approximativement de 2,5 cm par mois pendant les 6 premiers mois.
    Pulsation: 120 – 150.
    Respiration: 30 – 60.

Contrôle moteur (Fig. 11-4, 11-5)

    La tête s'incline quand le nourrisson est soutenu. Il peut redresser la tête de temps en temps quand il est tenu serré contre l'épaule de sa mère.
    Il effectue des mouvements de reptation lorsqu'il est couché sur l'abdomen.
    Il redresse la tête d'une façon intermittente et irrégulière quand on le couche à plat ventre. La courbe cervicale commence à se développer quand le jeune enfant apprend à tenir sa tête droite.
    Il peut tourner sa tête de côté quand il est à plat ventre.
    Il peut appuyer ses pieds contre une surface afin de progresser vers l'avant.
    Il a un réflexe de « danse » quand il est tenu droit, ses pieds touchant le lit ou la table d'examen.
    Il présente le réflexe tonique du cou: tourne la tête d'un côté, le bras et la jambe du même côté sont en extension, l'autre bras et l'autre jambe sont fléchis.
    Il serre les poings. Ne saisit rien avec ses mains, il peut tenir un objet qu'on lui met dans la main, mais le laisse échapper aussitôt.

Vision

    Il fixe indéfiniment, mais aussi commence à remarquer les visages et les objets brillants qui l'entourent, mais seulement s'ils sont à l'intérieur de son champ de vision.
    Son activité diminue quand il regarde un visage humain. Il peut suivre le mouvement d'un objet qui se trouve dans son champ de vision.

Langage et sociabilité

    Il pousse de petits cris gutturaux.
    Il sourit vaguement.
    Il a un regard vague et indéfini face aux objets brillants et aux visages.
    Il pleure quand il a faim ou souffre d'un malaise.

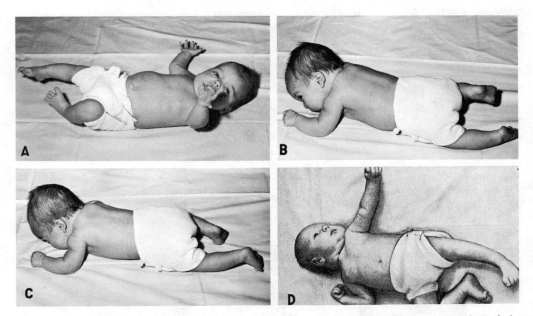

Figure 11-4. Le nourrisson âgé d'un mois: *A)* Il montre une activité généralisée et erratique à la suite d'une stimulation. *B)* Placé à plat ventre sur une surface plane, il fait des mouvements pour ramper, pousse à l'aide de ses orteils, serre ses poings. *C)* il soulève sa tête légèrement au-dessus du lit, tourne sa tête de côté, quand il est à plat ventre. *D)* Réflexe tonique du cou.

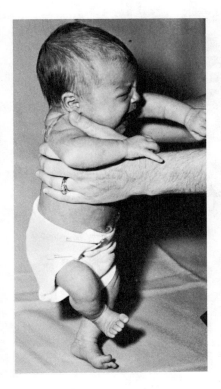

Figure 11-5. Le nourrisson âgé d'un mois a un réflexe de « danse » quand il est tenu droit, ses pieds touchant le lit ou la table d'examen.

Tableau 11-1. *Niveau moyen de développement des nourrissons de 1 à 12 mois (suite)*

2 MOIS

Physique

Fontanelle postérieure fermée.

Contrôle moteur (Fig. 11-6)

Il peut tenir sa tête droite dans une postion médiane.

Peut soulever la tête et la poitrine au-dessus du lit ou de la table quand il est couché sur l'abdomen.

Le réflexe tonique du cou et le réflexe de Moro disparaissent progressivement.

Il peut se retourner du côté sur le dos.

Il peut tenir un hochet pour un court laps de temps.

Vision

Il peut suivre des yeux une lumière ou un objet qui se déplace.

Langage et sociabilité

Il fait un « sourire » en réponse à un autre sourire. C'est le début de son comportement social, comportement qui peut ne pas apparaître avant le troisième mois.

Il saisit qu'il peut attirer l'attention des autres par ses pleurs. Ces derniers sont différents selon qu'ils sont dus à la faim, à la fatigue ou à la douleur.

Il est attentif aux voix qu'il entend.

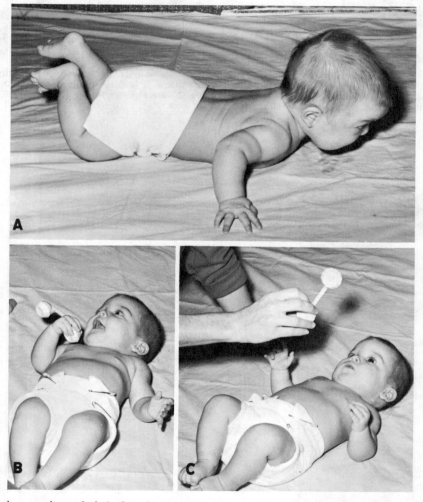

Figure 11-6. Le nourrisson âgé de 2 mois: *A)* il peut tenir sa tête droite dans une position médiane. Il peut soulever la tête et la poitrine au-dessus du lit ou de la table, quand il est couché sur son abdomen. *B)* Il peut tenir un hochet pour un court laps de temps. *C)* Il peut suivre des yeux une lumière ou un objet qui se déplace.

Tableau 11-1. *Niveau moyen de développement des nourrissons de 1 à 12 mois (suite)*

3 MOIS

Physique
   Poids: 5450 à 6000 grammes.

Contrôle moteur (Fig. 11-7)
   Il tient ses mains en face de son visage et les regarde.
   Il joue avec ses mains et ses doigts.
   Il tend la main vers les objets brillants mais ne les atteint pas.
   Il peut porter à volonté des objets ou ses mains à sa bouche.
   Il tient sa tête droite et en équilibre, soulève sa poitrine en s'appuyant sur ses avant-bras.
   Il s'assied quand il est soutenu; le dos est voûté, les genoux fléchis.
   Son réflexe de préhension s'affaiblit.
   Il a perdu le réflexe de « danse ».

Vision
   Il démontre une coordination binoculaire (vision verticale et horizontale) quand on bouge un objet de droite à gauche et de bas en haut, face à son visage.
   Il tourne les yeux vers un objet qui est à l'extérieur de son champ de vision.
   Il cligne volontairement des yeux quand il les sent menacés.

Langage et sociabilité
   Il rit fort et montre son plaisir à produire des sons.
   Il pleure moins.
   Il sourit lorsqu'il voit sa mère ou son substitut.

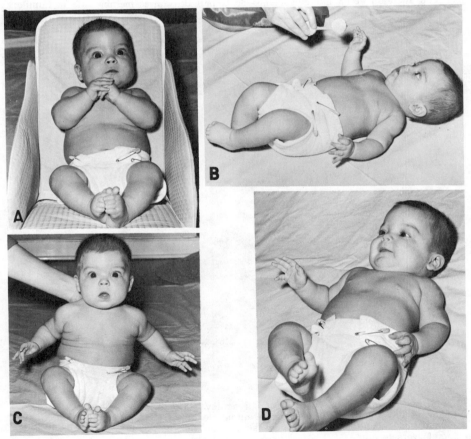

Figure 11-7. Le nourrisson de 3 mois: *A)* Il rapproche ses mains et joue avec ses doigts. *B)* Il tend la main vers les objets brillants, mais ne les atteint pas. *C)* Il s'assied quand il est soutenu, le dos est voûté, les genoux fléchis. *D)* Il sourit à sa mère et rit.

Tableau 11-1. *Niveau moyen de développement des nourrissons de 1 à 12 mois (suite)*

4 MOIS

Physique

Poids: 6000 à 6360 grammes.

Il bave vers l'âge de 3-4 mois. Ceci démontre l'apparition de la salive; il ne sait pas l'avaler et il bave.

Contrôle moteur (Fig. 11-8)

Ses mouvements et sa posture sont symétriques.

Il tient sa tête droite quand il est assis.

Il soulève la tête et les épaules à un angle de 90° et regarde autour de lui quand il est couché sur l'abdomen.

Il essaie de se retourner. Il peut se tourner de la position dorsale vers le côté.

L'opposition du pouce commence vers 3-4 mois.

Il garde ses mains ouvertes. Agite les bras à la vue de ses jouets favoris.

Il s'assied avec support et aime cette position.

Le réflexe tonique du cou a disparu.

Il porte en partie son propre poids quand on le soutient.

Vision

Il reconnaît les objets familiers.

Il fixe le hochet qu'il tient dans sa main, l'amène jusqu'à sa bouche.

Il suit parfaitement le déplacement des objets. Il peut accomplir les mouvements oculaires les plus difficiles.

Les bras s'agitent à la vue de jouets mobiles.

Langage et sociabilité

Il rit et sourit lorsque les autres lui sourient.

Il commence des jeux sociaux par ses sourires.

Il gazouille et roucoule quand on lui parle.

Il ne pleure pas quand on le gronde. Il est bavard.

Parler et pleurer sont deux actions très proches l'une de l'autre.

Il demande une attention et un intérêt soutenus de la part des autres membres de la famille.

Il est heureux d'avoir des gens autour de lui.

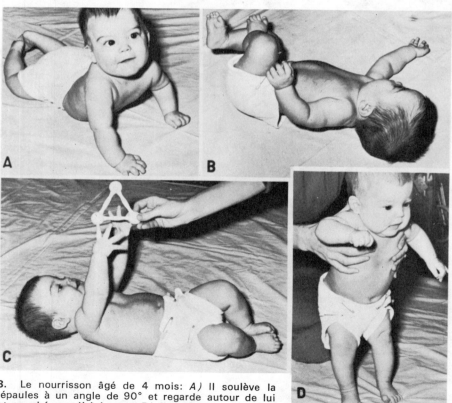

Figure 11-8. Le nourrisson âgé de 4 mois: *A)* Il soulève la tête et les épaules à un angle de 90° et regarde autour de lui quand il est couché sur l'abdomen. *B)* Il peut se tourner de la position dorsale vers le côté. *C)* Il s'agrippe à un jouet avec toute sa main. Il a une posture symétrique. Il tient sa tête droite. Il peut ouvrir et fermer les mains. Il coordonne ses yeux et ses mains afin d'atteindre et prendre ce qu'il aperçoit. *D)* Il porte son poids, en partie, quand il est soutenu.

Tableau 11-1. *Niveau moyen de développement des nourrissons de 1 à 12 mois (suite)*

5 MOIS

Physique
Poids: il pèse le double du poids à la naissance: 7000 à 7300 grammes.

Contrôle moteur (Fig. 11-9)
Il s'assied avec l'aide d'un support léger. Tient son dos droit en position assise.
Il peut opposer plus facilement son pouce aux autres doigts.
Il peut balancer sa tête.
Il cherche à atteindre les objets hors de sa portée. Il ne saisit plus les objets en fonction de la stimulation exercée sur la paume de sa main. Il saisit avec toute sa main. Il accepte les objets qu'on lui offre.
Le réflexe de Moro a complètement disparu.

Langage et sociabilité
Il crie quand on lui ôte un objet qu'il désire.

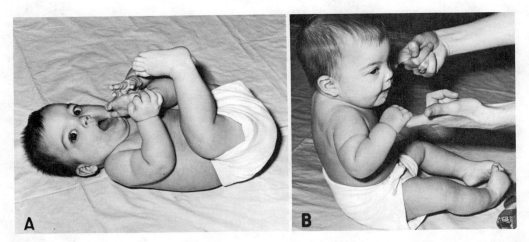

Figure 11-9. Le nourrisson de 5 mois: *A)* Il cherche à atteindre les objets, il les saisit avec toute sa main et les porte à sa bouche. *B)* Placé en position assise, il tient son dos droit. Il continue à baver.

Tableau 11-1. *Niveau moyen de développement des nourrissons de 1 à 12 mois (suite)*

6 MOIS

Physique
Durant les seconds six mois de son existence, il gagne 90 à 150 g. par semaine.
Il allonge d'environ 1,75 cm par mois.
Il fait ses dents.

Contrôle moteur (Fig. 11-10)
Il s'assied pour un court laps de temps sans aide, s'il est placé dans une position appropriée.
Il saisit avec une flexion simultanée des doigts.
Il peut tenir deux blocs, un dans chaque main.
Il essaie de s'asseoir par lui-même.
Il peut tourner complètement de la position abdominale à cette même position en se ménageant des moments de repos. Cette habileté est importante, car il faut l'empêcher de tomber de son lit.
Assis, il saute de bas en haut.
Il frappe avec les objets, hochet ou cuillère, qu'il tient dans sa main.
Assis, il recule par mouvements saccadés; pour déplacer son corps il s'aide des mains et des bras. Il manifeste cette habileté vers le 6e mois.

Langage et sociabilité
Il babille du 3e au 8e mois.
Il prononce des syllabes avec précision. Il aime gazouiller et roucouler. Le babillage n'est pas rattaché à des objets, des personnes ou des situations spécifiques.
Il pleure facilement pour un changement de position ou la perte momentanée d'un jouet. Il bat des pieds et des mains quand il a subi une frustration.
Il commence à reconnaître les étrangers (5e ou 6e mois).

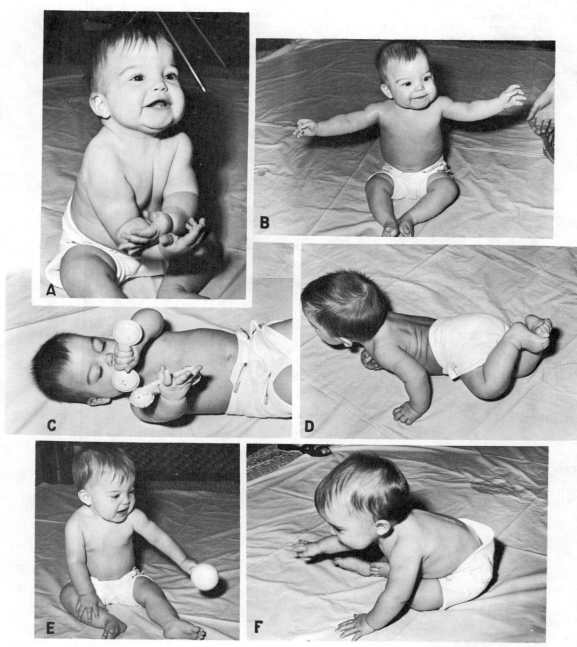

Figure 11-10. Le nourrisson âgé de 6 mois: *A)* Il a maintenant 2 incisives centrales sur la gencive inférieure. *B)* Il s'assied momentanément sans aide et maintient son équilibre avec ses bras étendus. *C)* Il peut
saisir deux objets à la fois. *D)* Il fait un tour complet sur lui-même. *E)* Il frappe avec un hochet qu'il tient
dans sa main. Il maintient son équilibre en s'appuyant légèrement sur une ou deux mains. *F)* Il remue.
Assis, il recule en s'aidant de ses mains pour se pousser.

Tableau 11-1.   *Niveau moyen de développement des nourrissons de 1 à 12 mois*
(suite)

7 MOIS

Contrôle moteur (Fig. 11-11)

Couché, il lève la tête comme s'il essayait de s'asseoir.

Il s'assied et se penche vers l'avant en s'appuyant sur ses mains. Il contrôle mieux les mouvements de son tronc.

Il joue avec ses pieds et les porte à sa bouche.

Il trépigne quand il est maintenu dans la position debout.

Il peut s'approcher d'un jouet et le saisir d'une main.

Il peut faire passer un jouet d'une main à l'autre. Le succès de cette entreprise est variable.

Il tourne plus aisément de la position dorsale à la position ventrale.

Langage et sociabilité

Ses sons expriment son ardeur.

Quand il pleure, il émet des sons « m.m.m. ».

Il émet des sons polysyllabiques à consonnance de voyelles.

Son développement émotif des 7ᵉ et 8ᵉ mois l'amène à avoir peur des inconnus.

Le passage brusque des rires aux pleurs démontre son instabilité émotive.

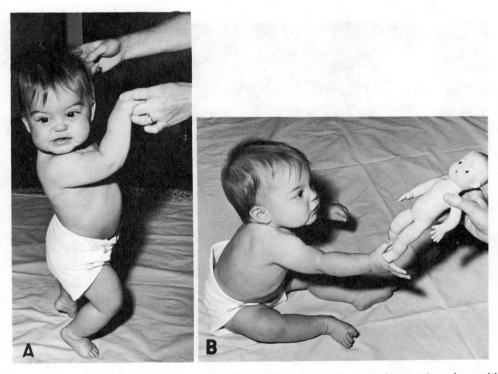

Figure 11-11.   Le nourrisson âgé de 7 mois: *A)* Il trépigne lorsqu'il est maintenu dans la position debout. Il peut porter une plus grande partie de son poids. *B)* Il peut s'approcher d'un jouet et le saisir d'une main.

Tableau 11-1. *Niveau moyen de développement des nourrissons de 1 à 12 mois (suite)*

8 MOIS

Contrôle moteur (Fig. 11-12)

Il s'assied tout seul fréquemment.

Le mouvement d'opposition du pouce est complet.

La coordination des yeux et des mains est complète. Les mouvements pour chercher ou saisir un objet sont maintenant sûrs.

Langage et sociabilité

Il accueille les inconnus farouchement ou timidement; il se détourne d'eux, il baisse la tête, pleure et peut même hurler. Il refuse de jouer avec des inconnus et même d'accepter leur jouet; il est nerveux avec eux.

Développement émotif: l'anxiété du 8e mois, différente de la dépression anaclitique, apparaît entre le 6e et le 8e mois et est la conséquence d'une capacité accrue de distinguer les amis des inconnus.

Son affection et son amour pour son entourage se développent.

L'instabilité émotive est observée par de brusques passages des pleurs aux rires.

Il veut attirer ceux qu'il aime en leur tendant les bras.

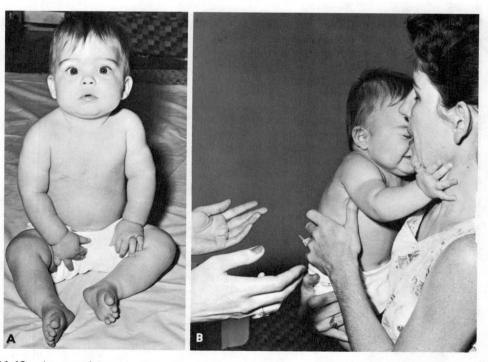

Figure 11-12. Le nourrisson de 8 mois: *A)* Il s'assied tout seul fréquemment. Son intérêt pour l'activité de son entourage s'accroît. *B)* L'anxiété du 8e mois: il accueille les inconnus en se détournant d'eux et en pleurant.

Tableau 11-1.   *Niveau moyen de développement des nourrissons de 1 à 12 mois*
(suite)

9 MOIS

Contrôle moteur (Fig. 11-13)

La coordination des mouvements est bonne et il s'assied seul.

Il tient son biberon avec une parfaite coordination des mains et de la bouche. Il peut à volonté enlever et porter la tétine à sa bouche.

Il utilise une main plus couramment que l'autre.

Il rampe au lieu de glisser assis. Certains nourrissons commencent à ramper dès le quatrième mois, mais l'âge moyen est de 9 mois; dans cette position, l'enfant est à plat ventre, son abdomen touchant le sol, sa tête et ses épaules sont soutenues par les coudes. Le corps est tiré vers l'avant par l'action des bras, tandis que les jambes sont traînées. Le mouvement des jambes ressemble à une ruade ou à celui d'un nageur.

Marcher à quatre pattes est un moyen de se mouvoir plus évolué que ramper. Bien que le corps soit parallèle au sol, il est surélevé. Le nourrisson utilise ses deux mains et ses genoux pour avancer. Tous les enfants ne suivent pas cette même évolution. Certains enfants utilisent divers moyens de locomotion et d'autres sautent une de ces étapes. Ceci est susceptible d'arriver aux enfants malades ou à ceux qui, pour d'autres raisons, ne peuvent se mouvoir.

Le nourrisson réussit à s'asseoir de lui-même; il a besoin d'aide pour se dresser sur ses jambes.

Langage et sociabilité

Il commence à imiter certaines expressions. Les sons prennent un certain sens pour lui. Il prononce des syllabes, telles que Pa-Pa.

Il réagit à la colère des adultes. Il pleure quand on le gronde.

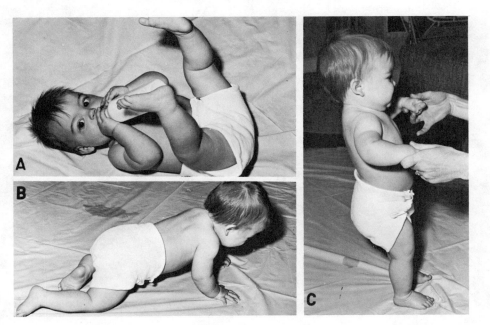

Figure 11-13.   Le nourrisson âgé de 9 mois: *A)* Il tient son biberon avec une parfaite coordination des mains et de la bouche. *B)* Marcher à quatre pattes est un moyen de locomotion plus avancé que ramper. Le corps, bien que parallèle au sol, est surélevé. Le nourrisson utilise ses mains et ses genoux pour avancer. *C)* Il peut se hisser sur ses jambes, si on l'aide.

Tableau 11-1. Niveau moyen de développement des nourrissons de 1 à 12 mois
(suite)

10 MOIS

Contrôle moteur (Fig. 11-14)

Il s'assied solidement pour un temps indéterminé. Ne veut plus rester couché, sauf s'il dort.

Quand il est soutenu, il essaie de marcher.

Il se hisse sur ses jambes en se tenant au rebord du lit ou à un support quelconque. C'est le moment propice pour l'habituer à rester dans son parc.

Il marche à quatre pattes et avance debout en s'agrippant aux choses qui l'entourent.

Il peut ramasser des objets et les frapper avec ses doigts.

Il mange tout seul un biscuit ou toute autre nourriture qu'il peut tenir dans sa main.

Il peut relâcher maladroitement un jouet.

Il peut joindre ses mains.

Langage et sociabilité

Il prononce un ou deux mots et imite les inflexions de la voix d'un adulte.

Il réagit à son nom.

Il joue à des jeux simples, tels que « coucou » et « content-content ».

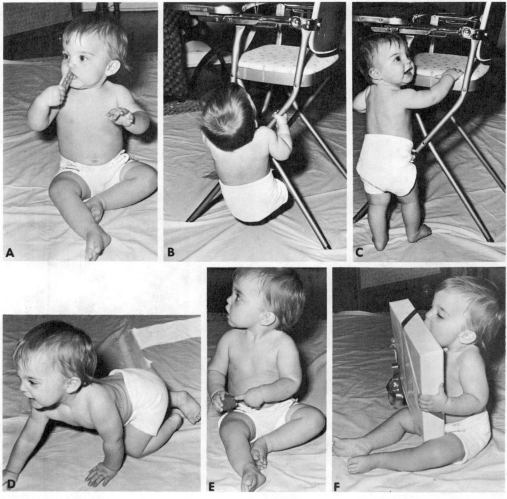

Figure 11-14. Le nourrisson âgé de 10 mois: *A)* Il s'assied solidement pour un temps indéterminé. Il mange tout seul un biscuit. *B)* Il se hisse sur ses jambes en s'aidant des meubles qui l'entourent. *C)* Il s'avance et s'aventure en s'appuyant sur les meubles. *D)* Il avance à quatre pattes. *E)* Il peut ramasser les objets et les frapper avec ses doigts. *F)* Il joue au « coucou » à l'aide d'une boîte.

Tableau 11-1. *Niveau moyen de développement des nourrissons de 1 à 12 mois (suite)*

11 MOIS

Contrôle moteur (Fig. 11-15)

Il se tient debout en tenant la main d'un adulte ou en prenant appui sur les côtés de son parc.

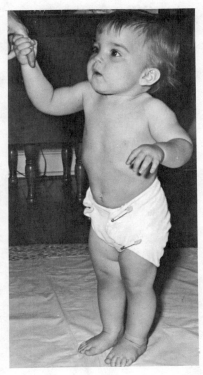

Figure 11-15.   Le nourrisson de 11 mois se tient droit avec l'aide de la main de sa mère.

Tableau 11-1. *Niveau moyen de développement des nourrissons de 1 à 12 mois (suite)*

12 MOIS

Physique

Poids: 3 fois son poids à la naissance (10 kg).
Taille: 72,5 cm.
La tête et la poitrine ont une circonférence égale.
Il a 6 dents.
Pulsation: 100-140 par minute.
Respiration: 20-40 par minute.

Contrôle moteur (Fig. 11-16)

Il se dresse sur ses jambes, seul, pour un moment plus ou moins long.
Il marche avec aide, en frôlant les murs. Il avance de chaise en chaise, en se tenant d'une main.
La courbe lombaire et la courbure dorsale compensatrice se développent quand il apprend à marcher.
Il peut passer de la position debout à la position assise sans aide.
Il peut tenir un crayon et barbouiller une feuille.
Il peut ramasser des miettes de nourriture et les porter à sa bouche. Il peut boire avec une tasse et manger avec une cuillère, mais demande une certaine aide.
Il commence à coopérer lorsqu'on l'habille: il passe son bras dans une manche et enlève lui-même ses chaussettes.

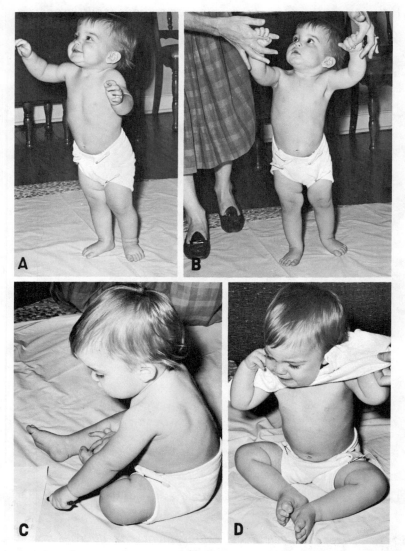

Figure 11-16. Le nourrisson âgé de 12 mois: *A)* Il se dresse seul sur ses jambes, pour un moment plus ou moins long. *B)* Il marche avec aide. *C)* Il tient un crayon adéquatement pour gribouiller sur une feuille de papier. *D)* Il coopère à son habillement: il passe ses bras dans les manches de ses vêtements.

Langage et sociablité

Il connaît 2 ou 3 mots autres que « papa » et « maman ».
Son vocabulaire s'accroît très lentement au moment où il apprend à marcher.
Il connaît son nom.
Il utilise un jargon expressif. Il dialogue avec lui-même et ceux qui l'entourent.
Il s'oppose aux ordres. Il reconnaît le sens de « Non ».
Il éprouve de la jalousie, de l'affection, de la colère et d'autres émotions. Il peut pleurer pour recevoir de l'affection. Il aime être entouré, et il répétera un exploit qui lui a gagné l'intérêt des autres. Les pleurs sont maintenant en rapport étroit avec une irritation et une frustration. Il se raidit lorsqu'il est contrarié.
Il aime la musique, le rythme.
Il est encore égocentrique, c'est-à-dire intéressé surtout par lui-même.

Les jouets devraient être de couleur gaie, lavables, durables, maniables, légers, lisses avec les coins arrondis et les pointes émoussées. Si le jouet est peint, la peinture utilisée ne doit pas contenir de plomb. La taille du jouet doit être appropriée à l'usage qu'en fera l'enfant. Les jouets doivent être bien construits: le hochet ou la crécelle ne devraient pas se briser lorsqu'ils sont frappés contre les barreaux du lit. Si le jouet se brisait, l'enfant pourrait ramasser les débris et les avaler.

Un jouet devrait avoir plusieurs usages; il est difficile de prédire l'activité de l'enfant, et son pouvoir de création doit être stimulé. Cependant, certains principes de sécurité doivent être sauvegardés. Par exemple, les cubes sont censés servir aux jeux de construction, mais l'enfant peut aussi les lancer; ils devraient donc être faits en matière caoutchoutée, de façon à ce qu'ils ne causent pas de blessures.

Il est bon de suspendre des mobiles de couleur au-dessus du berceau et de changer fréquemment de modèle pour stimuler l'intérêt du bébé. Il faudra enlever les mobiles quand l'enfant commencera à se tenir debout dans son lit; il aura ainsi plus d'espace pour se mouvoir et ne risquera pas de se blesser en s'y accrochant.

Les jouets en peluche peuvent servir à plusieurs fins. En plus d'être serrés dans les bras du nourrisson au moment où celui-ci s'endort, ils peuvent être traînés, écrasés, et lancés au loin. Nombre d'adultes ne comprennent pas que le nourrisson puisse se servir d'un jouet selon sa convenance et ses besoins. Ils font pression sur le jeune enfant afin que celui-ci utilise le jouet comme le ferait un plus âgé, ou alors ils surveillent et retirent le jouet si l'enfant risque de l'endommager. On conseille les jouets, tels que des grosses billes de bois, des bobines montées sur corde ou sur lacet, des hochets, des jouets doux de différentes formes, des balles, des grands ou des petits cubes, des anneaux qu'il peut saisir et des jouets musicaux.

Comportement ludique durant la première année.
Les jouets utilisés durant la première année doivent être très simples, car la capacité d'attention du nourrisson est limitée.

De la naissance à 5 mois. Les premiers jeux du bébé sont ses exercices physiques et l'apprentissage de sa motricité. Il essaye d'atteindre les objets et tente de se retourner sur le côté. Il gigote, remue et joue avec ses mains.

De 5 à 8 mois. À cet âge, le nourrisson s'amuse encore de ses propres mouvements. Il joue avec ses pieds, fait rebondir son corps,

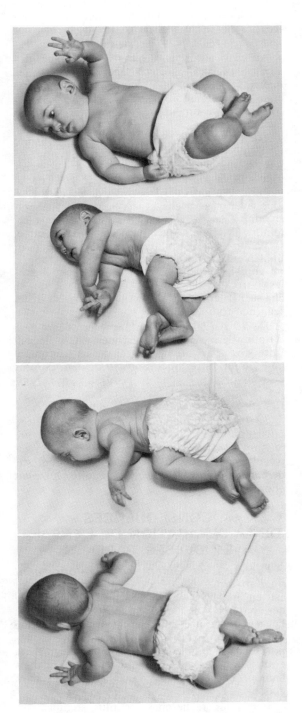

Figure 11-17. Exemple de premiers jeux de mouvement. L'enfant se tourne facilement du dos sur l'abdomen. (Courtoisie de Lew Merrim et *Baby Talk Magazine*, juin 1967.)

s'appuie contre les objets lorsqu'il apprend à s'asseoir, saisit tout ce qui se trouve à sa portée et se déplace sur le plancher, le plus souvent en position assise. Habituellement durant les six premiers mois il joue joyeusement tout seul.

Au septième mois, il aime la compagnie des adultes mais il préfère encore scruter ses mains, ses pieds et monologuer. Il apprécie son bain, étant donné qu'il est alors libéré de toute contrainte vestimentaire et peut se mouvoir facilement.

De 8 à 10 mois. L'activité motrice demeure la source principale d'amusement du nourrisson. Maintenant, il est capable de s'asseoir tout seul et aime s'appuyer sur le côté de sa voiture d'enfant ou sur le bras de sa chaise. Il joue avec ses orteils et se tourne facilement. Il rampe, se glisse, s'assied et s'étire afin d'atteindre les jouets qui sont hors de sa portée. Il passe un jouet d'une main à l'autre pour finalement le porter à sa bouche. Il a appris où vont les jouets lorsqu'il les jette par-dessus les barreaux de son lit, ou du haut de sa chaise. Il éprouve beaucoup d'intérêt à les regarder tomber.

De *10 à 11 mois.* L'enfant joue encore seul durant d'assez longues périodes, mais il peut faire savoir à sa famille qu'il désire sa compagnie ou un autre jouet. Son jeu devient de plus en plus précis. Il joue en position assise, rampe, pousse et frappe les objets avec ses doigts. Il s'étire afin de se mettre debout.

12 mois. Maintenant, l'enfant s'amuse avec plusieurs jouets, les ramasse, puis les rejette aussitôt. Il peut saisir une balle, la laisser retomber. Il prendra ou donnera le jouet sur demande; marcher, aidé d'un adulte, lui plaît énormément.

CONSÉQUENCES DE LA SÉPARATION DE L'ENFANT ET DE SES PARENTS

Facteurs qui aident au développement de l'enfant. L'adulte que deviendra l'enfant est en majeure partie fonction du caractère des parents, de leur comportement l'un à l'égard de l'autre et de l'atmosphère générale qui règne au foyer. Il ne faut pas négliger l'importance de l'attitude des parents à l'égard du nourrisson, car celle-ci l'amènera à vivre dans l'amour et la paix ou dans l'anxiété et l'angoisse.

Parmi les recherches les plus significatives faites en psychiatrie ces dernières années, nous remarquons l'étude de l'influence que peut avoir, sur le comportement futur de l'enfant, la qualité des soins prodigués par les parents pendant le premier âge et l'enfance.

Durant le premier âge et la tendre enfance, le jeune enfant doit avoir des rapports affectueux et stables avec sa mère ou le substitut permanent de celle-ci. Lorsque cette condition est remplie, il est peu probable que l'enfant développe des sentiments de culpabilité ou une grande anxiété.

À mesure que l'enfant vieillit, il devient plus capable de supporter une séparation graduelle et temporaire d'avec sa mère et il développe des mécanismes qui lui permettent de contrôler son anxiété. Certaines mères privent leur enfant de cet apprentissage en demeurant constamment avec lui, sans jamais le confier à un substitut tel une gardienne ou une amie. En évitant toute frustration à l'enfant, elles l'empêchent de franchir une étape importante et retardent son développement ultérieur.

Carence en soins maternels. Cette expression englobe toutes les situations dans lesquelles l'enfant est privé d'une relation affectueuse et stable avec sa mère ou un substitut maternel permanent. Cet état de choses existe lorsque la mère s'avère incapable de prodiguer à son bébé l'amour et la tendresse dont il a besoin pour se développer. Cette situation peut apparaître si l'enfant vit avec elle, ou s'il en est éloigné: se trouvant à l'hôpital, dans une institution, ou à la maison, alors qu'elle n'y demeure plus. Il existe différents degrés de carence. Lorsqu'elle est *partielle,* l'enfant peut développer une anxiété extrême et éprouver parallèlement un besoin excessif d'amour et d'affection. Dans le cas de *carence totale,* le nourrisson deviendra incapable de communiquer avec les autres et d'établir des relations humaines satisfaisantes.

Le bébé ne parvient à connaître sa mère, en tant qu'individu, qu'à l'âge de 5 ou 6 mois; il reconnaît les étrangers et s'effraie à leur vue vers l'âge de 7 ou 8 mois. Pour cette raison, la mère ou son substitut devrait s'occuper directement de lui et ne pas le quitter durant sa première année de vie. Bien que toute carence en soins maternels soit grave, ses conséquences varient selon qu'elle se produit durant les six premiers mois ou les six derniers mois de la première année de la vie.

Carence durant les six premiers mois. Le nourrisson de cet âge n'a pas un développement physique et psychique qui lui permette de s'adapter à des soins impersonnels, prodigués par plusieurs personnes compétentes, gentilles, mais qui n'éprouvent pas à son égard un véritable amour maternel. Les nourrissons privés de la tendresse de leur mère ou de son substitut ne reçoivent pas les stimuli nécessaires à un développement normal.

Dans les orphelinats, ils sont émotivement isolés des adultes et leur activité est ordinairement réduite. Généralement, ils manifestent un certain retard psychomoteur et ce, même s'ils reçoivent d'excellents soins physiques. Au début, le nourrisson pleure beaucoup, son gain pondéral est faible ou nul, son développement moteur ralenti, car il est rarement pris dans les bras ou stimulé. Graduellement, il refuse le contact avec les adultes. Il perd alors du poids, son sommeil est troublé, sa résistance amoindrie le rend vulnérable aux infections; au bout de quelques mois, il devient passif, paraît retardé et fait des gestes bizarres avec ses doigts. Cette séquence de comportement fut décrite par René Spitz. L'incidence du marasme et le taux des décès demeurent relativement élevés parmi ces nourrissons. Résoudre le problème de la carence d'amour maternel est presque impossible dans les orphelinats.

On devrait placer l'enfant en foyer nourricier dès les premiers mois de la vie. Il devrait demeurer dans le même foyer, avec la même personne affectueuse, c'est-à-dire avoir un substitut maternel stable. S'il est impossible de placer le bébé dans un foyer nourricier, il faudrait qu'à l'orphelinat une personne permanente tienne auprès de lui le rôle de sa mère. Cette personne pourrait être choisie parmi le personnel infirmier et ne devrait s'occuper que d'un nombre restreint de nourrissons, afin de pouvoir accorder à chacun d'entre eux une attention particulière. Elle pourrait alors donner à l'enfant le sentiment qu'il est aimé et accepté.

Si une chaude affection et une stimulation sensori-motrice appropriée ne sont pas prodiguées au bébé hospitalisé en raison d'une malformation congénitale ou d'une maladie, il peut montrer les mêmes symptômes psychopathologiques que le nourrisson placé dans un orphelinat. Une telle attention est souvent plus difficile à donner dans un hôpital que dans un orphelinat, à cause du changement continuel du personnel infirmier et aussi du plus grand besoin d'affection et de tendresse qu'ont les enfants malades. Des infirmières diplômées, stables, sont indispensables dans l'unité de pédiatrie pour assurer aux jeunes enfants une attention affectueuse et continuelle.

Avec le développement du service des soins à domicile, il est absolument nécessaire de faire une évaluation précise de chaque situation pour décider si l'enfant doit être traité à l'hôpital ou si l'équipe de santé peut fournir suffisamment de support et d'aide à la mère pour que l'enfant puisse être soigné à la maison.

Carence durant les seconds six mois. C'est la période pendant laquelle survient la dépression anaclitique. Celle-ci résulte du changement dans la vie du nourrisson: il y a rupture de la relation tendre qui unit le jeune enfant à sa mère et à sa famille et il se retrouve solitaire au milieu d'un groupe de nourrissons soumis aux soins de personnes étrangères. Le bébé devient déprimé, triste, pleure souvent, puis se replie sur lui-même. Ceci est à l'opposé de son attitude antérieure, heureuse et extrovertie. Certains nourrissons peuvent refuser de manger et perdre du poids. Ils tiennent étroitement enlacées une poupée ou une couverture apportées de la maison. La dernière étape marquant l'éloignement du milieu familial se manifeste par le retard qu'apporte l'enfant à réagir quand sa mère lui rend visite, par l'établissement de relations superficielles avec les autres adultes et par un accroissement du comportement auto-érotique tel succion du pouce, balancement. Si la séparation dure plus de 3 mois, les pleurs cessent; l'expression de tristesse est remplacée par un masque de rigidité. Le nourrisson peut souffrir d'anorexie et d'insomnie. Les infirmières peuvent éprouver de sérieuses difficultés à établir un contact affectif avec cet enfant.

Si le nourrisson est rendu à sa mère après moins de 3 mois de séparation, la guérison peut se faire rapidement. Mais si la séparation persiste, la guérison devient moins probable et a moins de chance d'être complète.

Prévention de la dépression anaclitique. Après l'âge de 6 mois, le nourrisson normal prend les devants et recherche le contact de l'adulte. Il a besoin d'espace vital pour ramper et se promener sans retenue. Sa motilité libre est essentielle à son développement moteur et à l'exploration de son milieu. Il a aussi besoin de stimulation sensori-motrice variée et adéquate. Par-dessus tout, il a besoin de l'affection soutenue d'une personne maternelle qui lui prête une attention personnelle. Ainsi, si ces deux besoins sont satisfaits, il peut demeurer normal tout en étant séparé de sa mère. La perte de potentiel affectif et les répercussions à long terme demeurent toutefois difficiles à évaluer.

Résumé et conclusion. Les réactions des nourrissons subissant une carence de soins maternels se produisent en trois étapes successives: protestation (pleurs), désespoir (attitude tranquille et soumise) et détachement (même de la mère). Après le retour de la mère, l'enfant peut continuer à être replié sur lui-même, à avoir un sommeil troublé ou manquer d'appétit, se cramponner à elle et avoir peur des étrangers.

Bien que les conséquences immédiates de la carence de soins maternels puissent être graves, il serait faux de les considérer comme irréversibles. Il ne serait pas juste non plus de prédire que chaque nourrisson privé de l'amour d'une mère deviendra un délinquant ou un adulte incapable d'aimer, souffrant obligatoirement de problèmes de personnalité.

Bien que les résultats probables d'une privation extrême soient ceux décrits plus haut, tous les nourrissons, dans un tel cas, ne réagiront pas de la même manière et ne présenteront pas les mêmes troubles. Les raisons de ceci ne sont pas très clairement connues, mais elles peuvent dépendre de l'âge de l'enfant, de la durée de la séparation, des liens antérieurs avec la mère, de la qualité du substitut offert, et du « stress » de la maladie elle-même. On ne doit pas oublier que l'entourage de chaque nourrisson est influencé par les caractéristiques propres à ce dernier. Même si cette réaction ne devrait pas se présenter, un enfant qui était affectueux avant d'être séparé de sa mère – et qui le reste – provoque plus facilement une attitude chaleureuse chez ceux qui doivent maintenant s'occuper de lui. Sa vie sera vraisemblablement différente de celle de l'enfant qui, en entrant à l'orphelinat ou à l'hôpital, ne répond pas aux tentatives de rapprochement du personnel. Le personnel d'une institution est humain et probablement très différent dans ses attitudes respectives à l'égard des enfants gais et chaleureux et de ceux qui sont maussades ou tristes.

Pour bien remplir son rôle, l'infirmière en pédiatrie devrait fournir à chaque enfant la chaleur, l'amour, l'attention dont il a besoin pour pallier à l'absence de ses parents. Des contacts physiques fréquents sont indispensables au jeune enfant. Le plus important est sans doute d'assurer la continuité des soins et de réduire au minimum le nombre de personnes qui s'occupent de lui. Les quelques infirmières qui prendront soin du petit pourront ainsi mieux le connaître, lui procurer des stimuli sensori-moteurs et devenir, si possible, les conseillères et les amies des parents.

SOIN DES NOURRISSONS

Soins quotidiens

Chaque membre de la famille a des besoins particuliers et les soins du nourrisson doivent être intégrés à l'horaire général, de façon à ne pas créer de conflits. Cette planification évitera des frustrations et permettra au nourrisson de recevoir plus de chaleur et de tendresse.

Le rythme de vie de l'enfant sera fonction de sa croissance: le moment du réveil, les périodes de sommeil et de jeu varieront. Les activités des parents et l'horaire du nourrisson sont en étroite relation et s'influencent mutuellement. Si le père et la mère planifient leur vie de façon à pouvoir consacrer dans la soirée un laps de temps à leur enfant, les périodes de veille du bébé doivent être organisées en conséquence. Si la mère ne travaille pas à l'extérieur, elle pourra facilement passer de très longs moments avec son enfant. Si elle travaille à l'extérieur, il serait préférable d'adopter pour le nourrisson un horaire basé sur les moments libres qu'elle pourra lui consacrer. S'il a des frères et sœurs, elle ne devrait en aucun cas les négliger. Les parents doivent trouver un moyen de passer quelques moments seuls avec les aînés. Ce point est important pour prévenir la jalousie et leur faire accepter leur statut d'aînés. Ils doivent prendre conscience qu'ils ont des privilèges que le nourrisson ne possède pas et que ce dernier, d'autre part, requiert des soins particuliers. Quand le bébé commence à prendre trois repas par jour et des collations entre les repas, il peut progressivement être intégré au groupe familial pour les heures de repas.

Aussi longtemps que le jeune enfant n'est pas capable de dire ce qu'il ressent, la mère doit être attentive aux symptômes de malaise et de maladie. Sa coloration est un indice, son regard en est un autre. L'enfant fatigué s'endort de lui-même.

Il n'y a pas de modèle défini des soins quotidiens donnés au nourrisson. Ses besoins varient chaque mois et chaque famille procède à sa manière.

Comment porter un nourrisson

La meilleure méthode pour porter un enfant est déterminée par sa structure anatomique et par son habileté motrice. Sa tête est volumineuse par rapport à l'ensemble de son corps et il s'avère incapable de la tenir droite sans aide avant l'âge de 3 mois. Il faut soutenir les épaules et le dos encore peu solides. L'infirmière doit se rappeler que la façon de soulever et de transporter un bébé doit impliquer confort et sécurité pour le bébé et facilité pour l'exécutant.

Il y a deux façons reconnues pour porter un jeune enfant qui sont les *positions du berceau* et *du ballon*. Chaque technique a un rôle et un but particuliers.

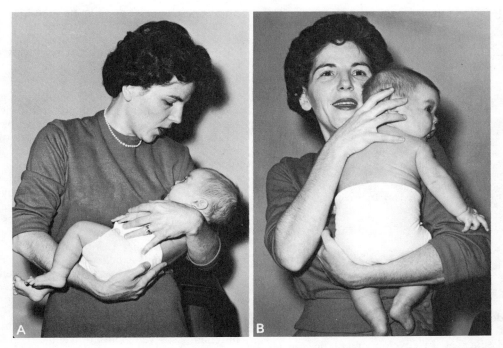

Figure 11-18. *A)* Position du berceau. La tête et le dos du jeune enfant doivent être supportés de façon adéquate. *B)* L'enfant peut être tenu droit contre la poitrine. La tête doit être soutenue jusqu'à ce que l'enfant soit capable de la maintenir par lui-même.

La position du berceau. On l'utilise pour lever, tourner et porter le nourrisson. On saisit les pieds du bébé de la main droite, et pour ne pas les frapper l'un contre l'autre, on place l'index entre les os de ses chevilles, on glisse la main et le bras gauche sous le dos de l'enfant, soutenant ainsi son siège, son dos et sa tête. Ensuite, on monte la main droite sous le siège et en même temps on avance la main et le bras gauches afin de mieux soutenir sa tête, ses épaules et son dos. On redresse alors l'enfant qui est bercé et serré dans les bras.

Si l'infirmière ou la mère tient le nourrisson contre l'épaule en position verticale, l'avant-bras gauche (si

elle est droitière) sera sous son siège, le petit corps appuyé contre sa poitrine et son épaule et la joue reposant légèrement au-dessus de l'épaule. La main droite soutiendra le dos et la tête. Si la maman, pour un motif quelconque, doit utiliser sa main droite, elle se penchera vers l'arrière afin que le corps de l'enfant se presse contre le sien, pour que le nourrisson n'éprouve pas la sensation de perdre l'équilibre.

La position du ballon permet de baigner le nourrisson – en gardant sa tête au-dessus de la baignoire – ou de faire le lit en portant l'enfant. Les hanches du nourrisson reposent dans le creux du bras de la mère ou de l'infirmière, tandis que l'avant-bras et

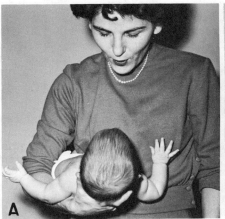

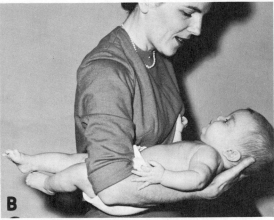

Figure 11-19.   Position du ballon. *A)* Vue de face. *B)* Vue de côté.

la main soutiennent sa tête et son dos. Cette technique est pratique car elle libère le second bras de la personne qui porte le nourrisson.

Autres techniques. Lorsque l'enfant grandit et qu'il peut tenir sa tête droite, les parents peuvent l'emmener en plein air, confortablement installé sur le dos de l'un d'eux. Ce moyen de véhiculer un enfant donne aux parents une plus grande opportunité de vivre en plein air. Après l'âge de trois mois, le bébé peut aussi être tenu sur une hanche, ses jambes encerclant le corps de la personne qui le porte. La mère ou l'infirmière soutient le siège, le dos et la tête de l'enfant à l'aide de son avant-bras et de sa main, du côté où l'enfant est assis. Cette position libère aussi un des bras de la mère ou de l'infirmière. Elle est très appropriée pour les nourrissons porteurs d'une dysplasie de la hanche, car elle force les têtes de fémur dans les cavités cotyloïdes.

Le bain

Le but du bain n'est pas seulement de nettoyer le jeune enfant, mais aussi de lui donner la joie de s'ébattre, de barboter et de s'éclabousser d'eau sans contrainte vestimentaire. L'heure du bain est un moment idéal pour bavarder et jouer avec le bébé. Il donne l'occasion à la mère de remarquer l'évolution de la croissance et du développement de son enfant et d'observer sur son corps les signes d'une irritation ou d'une éruption quelconque.

L'heure du bain sera établie selon l'emploi du temps de la mère ou de l'infirmière, mais jamais dans les soixante minutes qui suivent le repas du bébé.

On donne le bain tous les jours à la même heure, de façon à établir un rythme de vie régulier pour le bébé. Il sera annulé si la mère est surmenée ou le jeune enfant fatigué. Le père moderne baigne son bébé de temps à autre, ce qui lui permet de mieux le connaître et de lui donner le sentiment d'être aimé et soigné aussi bien par sa mère que par son père.

Durant le bain, on doit lui assurer une sécurité maximum et lui éviter d'avoir peur. On ne laisse jamais un bébé ou un jeune enfant seul dans une baignoire remplie d'eau, même s'il est assez grand pour s'asseoir et se tenir aux rebords.

Il est imprudent de lui donner en guise de jouet une boîte de poudre, même vide, car s'il l'agite, il peut aspirer les quelques grains qui restent dans le fond de la boîte. Il est capital que l'enfant apprenne à aimer son bain. Si on le plonge trop brusquement dans l'eau ou s'il ne se sent pas en sécurité, il peut se raidir, s'alarmer, s'effrayer et demeurer longtemps réfractaire à l'eau.

La mère doit le déposer délicatement dans l'eau. Elle doit tenir sa tête et ses épaules avec son avant-bras, sa main saisissant le bras

opposé du nourrisson. On ne doit pas le savonner abondamment, car il serait trop difficile de le tenir fermement et il risque de s'effrayer s'il glisse ou si son visage est recouvert d'eau.

Les vêtements

Il existe, pour les jeunes enfants, une grande variété de vêtements. Il est préférable de mettre et de retirer les vêtements par le bas, car le contact du tissu sur le visage, alors que les yeux sont obstrués, peut effrayer l'enfant inutilement.

Avec la croissance, le besoin d'activité de l'enfant augmente et il lui faudra des pyjamas ou des vêtements de nuit pourvus de jambes. Le modèle composé de deux pièces permet de ne changer que la partie inférieure quand elle est salie. Les vêtements faits d'une seule pièce sont excellents pour garder l'enfant bien au chaud. Ces vêtements doivent être suffisamment larges pour lui permettre de se mouvoir librement. Le tour de cou ne sera pas ajusté afin d'éviter la strangulation. Quand l'enfant apprend à ramper et à se mouvoir librement, ses vêtements doivent être suffisamment amples aux entre jambes et aux emmanchures. Les salopettes protègent ses jambes quand il rampe, mais doivent avoir des ouvertures aux entrejambes afin de faciliter le changement des couches. Les vêtements de plage sont appropriés à la saison d'été. Les chaussures doivent être souples jusqu'à ce qu'il apprenne à marcher, car elles ne servent qu'à protéger ses pieds quand il rampe ou avance à quatre pattes. Si le revêtement du plancher est chaud, doux et propre, le bébé peut se promener pieds nus. Ramper et marcher à quatre pattes constituent de bons exercices pour les muscles des pieds et des jambes. Les chaussettes sont portées avec les souliers et doivent être d'un demi-pouce plus longues que le pied. Les pieds des enfants grandissent rapidement et si, à l'achat, les bas ne sont pas suffisamment amples, ils seront rapidement trop petits. On ne doit pas les faire porter à l'enfant s'ils gênent ses orteils.

Plein air et soleil

Le jeune enfant devrait être le plus souvent possible au grand air. On l'habillera en fonction du temps. Si la température est printanière, un nourrisson âgé de 3 ou 4 semaines pourra prendre un court bain de soleil. De tels bains sont à conseiller pour favoriser la synthèse de la vitamine D. Les vitres, les vêtements, la poussière et la fumée de l'atmosphère détruisent les rayons ultra violets. La première exposition de l'enfant au soleil ne dépassera pas 3 à 5 minutes et on ne découvrira que les mains et le visage. Graduellement, la durée du bain de soleil et les parties exposées augmenteront jusqu'à ce que la peau du corps et des membres soit exposée et pigmentée. Les bains de soleil auront lieu avant 11 heures du matin ou après 3 heures de l'après-midi. Le jeune enfant sera placé dos au soleil, les yeux et la tête protégés de l'éclat de la lumière. Une brûlure profonde durant son bain de soleil est dangereuse. L'insolation est toujours à redouter. Même si l'enfant est souvent exposé au soleil, il doit continuer à prendre de la vitamine D par voie orale.

Exercice

Un enfant fait de l'exercice de différentes manières: pendant son bain, en changeant de position, plus tard en jouant dans son parc ou dans une salle de jeu. Ses vêtements ne doivent pas gêner ses mouvements, mais au contraire, l'inciter à bouger et à se mouvoir. Ses jouets devraient aussi stimuler sa motricité.

Sommeil

La majeure partie de la vie du nourrisson est consacrée au sommeil. Le jeune enfant a besoin de beaucoup de repos pour se développer et accumuler de l'énergie. La durée de son sommeil dépend de ses besoins et ceux-ci varient de jour en jour. Il établira souvent lui-même ses horaires de sommeil.

La position dans laquelle on le place pour dormir est importante. Dès qu'il en sera capable, il bougera la tête à droite et à gauche pour éviter de s'écraser le nez sur la surface de son lit. À ce moment, il peut être placé à plat ventre ou sur le dos. Toutefois, le laisser dormir sur le dos représente un danger: si l'enfant vomit, il risque de s'étouffer en aspirant le contenu gastrique. Il demeure finalement préférable de le coucher sur le côté, position la plus sûre et la plus confortable. Le développement progressif de l'enfant entraîne une nette réduction des périodes de sommeil. Bien que chaque enfant ait son propre rythme, la durée moyenne de sommeil varie entre 18 et 20 heures par jour pendant les deux premiers mois de l'existence. Elle diminue ensuite jusqu'à environ 16 heures au troisième mois, et le bébé dormira souvent sans interruption toute la nuit. À 6 mois, la moyenne sera de 12 heures la nuit et de 3 à 4 heures au cours de la journée – le nombre de petites siestes et leur longueur varient selon chaque nourrisson.

À 1 an l'enfant dormira environ 14 heures par jour. À cet âge, il craint de quitter sa mère ou d'être abandonné par elle. On ne doit pas le mettre au lit et le quitter aussitôt, le laissant seul dans l'obscurité. Une faible lumière donnera à sa chambre un caractère familier. Un enfant de 12 mois a besoin d'une ou deux courtes siestes durant la journée.

Techniques pour faciliter le sommeil et les soins au réveil. Il faut proscrire toute source de surexcitation au moment de mettre l'enfant au lit. Pour dormir confortablement, l'enfant doit être propre et sec. Il peut s'endormir plus facilement s'il tient dans ses bras son jouet favori. Chanter, le caresser rythmiquement ou remuer doucement son lit peuvent favoriser rapidement le sommeil.

Il est plus facile de coucher le nourrisson s'il a, si possible, sa propre chambre. Une demi-obscurité est préférable à une obscurité totale ou à une lumière intense. Une veilleuse permet au bébé de reconnaître son environnement familier. La température de la chambre doit être telle que l'enfant n'ait ni chaud ni froid. La température idéale varie de 21 à 23° C dans la journée et de 15 à 18° C durant la nuit. La chambre bien aérée doit être exempte de courant d'air. Il faut éviter de suspendre des couvertures sur les côtés du lit, car elles peuvent tomber sur le nourrisson et l'étouffer.

Le matelas doit être ferme et totalement recouvert d'une épaisse toile plastifiée. Il est dangereux de ne mettre qu'un carré de toile plastifiée sous le drap, car si l'enfant enlève le drap, il peut se couvrir le visage avec le plastique qui risquerait alors de l'étouffer.

On n'utilisera pas d'oreiller, tant que l'enfant risque d'y enfouir sa figure ou de le recevoir sur le visage, ce qui le ferait suffoquer. Il est couché sur une surface plane, ce qui facilite un développement harmonieux de son squelette.

Quand l'enfant s'éveille, les rideaux sont tirés afin que la chambre s'éclaire. On lui lave le visage pour lui donner une sensation de fraîcheur.

Mesures de sécurité

Importance de la prévention des accidents. Les accidents sont une des causes principales de mortalité chez les nourrissons.

Les infirmières et les mères doivent savoir et prendre en considération ce qui attire, intéresse et amuse l'enfant, afin de prévenir tout risque d'accident. Une protection et une éducation adaptées à chaque sexe et à chaque groupe d'âge aide à prévenir les accidents. L'éducation entreprise pendant la période prénatale et se continuant lorsque la mère séjourne dans l'unité d'obstétrique doit être constructive. Elle ne consistera pas à dresser une liste des périls qui guettent l'enfant, mais mettra l'accent sur les précautions à prendre pour les éviter. L'enseignement de la prévention contre les accidents devra par la suite être donné graduellement aux parents et aux enfants.

Il peut sembler ridicule de vouloir enseigner à un nourrisson la prudence. Il faut cependant l'habituer aux mesures de sécurité adoptées pour le protéger. Il apprendra ce qui est permis et ce qui est défendu en regardant agir sa mère et en recevant sourires ou réprimandes selon le cas.

Quand il sera d'âge préscolaire, on lui expliquera simplement comment il peut éviter de se blesser. Il apprendra à être prudent afin de ne pas se blesser. Une certaine crainte est salutaire et la meilleure garantie d'une conduite prudente.

Les maladies tendent à diminuer au fur et à mesure que l'enfant grandit, tandis que les accidents augmentent. On enseigne la prévention contre les accidents dans les écoles et sur les terrains de jeux. Nous verrons au moment opportun les accidents caractéristiques de chaque âge.

Mesures de sécurité spécifiques. Les mesures de sécurité liées au bain, aux vêtements et aux jouets ont déjà été présentées.

Les montants du lit doivent être levés et bloqués lorsque l'enfant est dans son lit. La distance entre les barreaux du lit doit être réduite au minimum afin que la tête, les bras ou les jambes de l'enfant ne puissent être coincés. Le lit de l'enfant ne sera pas placé près d'un radiateur car le bébé risque de se brûler les doigts s'il parvient à l'atteindre. Il doit être éloigné d'une fenêtre garnie de stores vénitiens, car le jeune enfant peut s'étrangler s'il s'enroule la corde pendante autour du cou. Les épingles de sûreté doivent être toujours fermées et surtout hors de portée de l'enfant. Elle ne seront pas piquées au matelas ni laissées dans un pain de savon (le savon lubrifie la pointe de l'épingle de sûreté, ce qui permet de la faire pénétrer plus facilement dans la couche).

Dès que l'enfant commence à tout porter à sa bouche, on évite de laisser à sa portée de menus objets. Ceux qui sont fréquemment avalés sont les billes, les pièces de monnaie, les cacahuètes. Il est à remarquer que, même un enfant trop jeune pour se rouler est capable d'avancer en se poussant avec ses pieds. Pour cette raison, les mesures de sécurité doivent être perpétuellement observées. La mère ou l'infirmière doit toujours surveiller le jeune enfant et ne jamais le laisser seul sur une table,

dans un lit sans montants ou dans une chaise haute même si on le pense bien attaché par sa ceinture de sécurité.

La peinture des jouets et des meubles ne doit pas contenir de plomb, car le bébé risque d'en ingérer en suçant ou en mordant ses jouets.

Quand l'enfant commence à ramper, les barrières placées en haut et au bas des escaliers préviendront les chutes; toutes les prises de courant devraient aussi être couvertes. Il faut enlever les nappes et napperons qui pendent sur le côté des tables dès que l'enfant commence à marcher ou à ramper, car il peut les tirer et recevoir ainsi sur la tête tout ce qui était posé dessus.

Un adulte portant un enfant ne doit pas marcher sur un parquet glissant ou jonché de jouets et de menus objets, car il risque de faire une chute. La mère ne devrait jamais cuisiner ou transporter des plats chauds en portant le bébé dans ses bras. Les tasses de liquide chaud constituent un grand danger pour l'enfant qui s'agrippe au bord de la table.

L'automobile familiale cache souvent un danger mortel. L'enfant non attaché est souvent projeté hors du véhicule lors d'un accident; la mère qui tient le bébé sur ses genoux peut l'écraser contre le tableau de bord quand un choc violent se produit. On trouve dans le commerce, des chaises de bébé qui s'adaptent au siège de l'auto et des courroies de sécurité pour les enfants plus âgés. Ces objets peuvent être facilement et rapidement détachés si l'évacuation du véhicule s'impose d'urgence.

Les enfants qui vivent dans une région urbaine surpeuplée sont souvent la proie des rats. Ces derniers attaquent particulièrement les bébés endormis et leur rongent le visage, les doigts ou les orteils. La prévention de base essentielle consiste à éliminer les rats.

ALIMENTATION ET NUTRITION DU BÉBÉ

L'alimentation du nouveau-né a été traitée au chapitre 7. Le nourrisson continuera à se nourrir au sein ou au biberon jusqu'au sevrage, puis il apprendra à boire à la tasse. Les mères qui allaitent leur nourrisson peuvent vouloir les habituer au biberon en leur donnant de l'eau, du lait ou du jus d'orange. De cette façon, si l'allaitement doit être brusquement arrêté, l'acceptation du biberon sera plus facile. Le tableau 11-2 donne les éléments nutritifs requis pour des nourrissons âgés de moins d'un an.

Addition d'aliments solides et d'autres substances à la diète du nourrisson

L'âge auquel on ajoute les aliments solides au régime alimentaire dépend du médecin, du nourrisson et de la mère. Les nourrissons ont un réel besoin de nourriture solide vers l'âge de trois ou quatre mois, pour rendre leur régime plus complet et pour les habituer, en bas âge, aux différents goûts et textures des aliments. Toutefois, la tendance qui a prévalu, il y a quelques années, de commencer l'alimentation solide vers 8 - 10 jours n'a aucune base physiologique ou médicale.

Des recherches récentes tendent à démontrer que l'alimentation solide trop précoce favorise la multiplication des cellules adipeuses qui se traduit par une tendance à l'obésité à l'âge scolaire. Les nourrissons de moins de cinq ou six mois acceptent facilement les nouveaux aliments mais, après cet âge, ils commencent à refuser les nouvelles saveurs et les mélanges. Les premières substances spécifiques à être ajoutées au lait sont l'eau, les vitamines C et D, le fer et, si c'est nécessaire, le fluorure de sodium.

L'eau

Les nouveau-nés apprennent à boire de l'eau bouillie à l'aide d'un biberon. On la donne entre les repas parce qu'ils ont besoin de plus de liquide qu'ils n'en reçoivent par le lait de la mère ou par leur formule. La soif du nourrisson détermine la quantité d'eau dont il a besoin. À la maison, la mère devrait préparer quotidiennement de l'eau fraîchement bouillie. L'eau ne devient stérile qu'après vingt minutes d'ébullition à gros bouillons.

On met l'eau dans un biberon stérilisé de 120 ml. Quand le bébé atteint l'âge de cinq mois, une partie de l'eau bouillie gardée dans un récipient stérile et couvert, peut être donnée à la tasse; celle-ci, cependant, n'est que complémentaire à l'usage du biberon jusqu'à ce que le nourrisson apprenne à boire à la tasse. Quelques pédiatres pensent que dès que le bébé a environ quatre mois, il peut boire de l'eau non bouillie si celle dont sa collectivité est approvisionnée est saine.

Les vitamines

Les vitamines sont essentielles au processus métabolique. Elles sont habituellement gardées en réserve par l'organisme et les effets d'une carence tardent souvent à se faire sentir. Chez l'adulte, les symptômes de carence n'apparaîtront qu'après quelques mois alors que les réserves de l'enfant s'épuisent plus rapidement.

On rencontre surtout les carences vitaminiques pendant l'enfance et elles sont exceptionnelles chez l'adulte.

Le public a été abondamment renseigné sur l'importance des vitamines et aujourd'hui, le danger réside surtout dans leur consommation abusive qui non seulement grève le budget familial, mais produit également de nombreux cas d'hyper-vitaminose.

Vitamine C. On trouve la vitamine C ou acide ascorbique dans de nombreux fruits et légumes; les fruits citrins, tels que l'orange, le citron, le pamplemousse, la limette et la tomate en sont très riches. Les jus de fruits frais sont une excellente source de vitamine C mais les jus congelés sont également très acceptables s'ils sont consommés dès le dégel. Les jus de fruit frais ou reconstitués doivent être conservés dans des récipients fermés et à l'abri de la lumière afin d'éviter les pertes de vitamine C.

Il est préférable de s'abstenir d'utiliser des jus de fruits auxquels un colorant ou une saveur artificielle a été ajouté. D'après plusieurs recherches, on tend à relier ces éléments à l'hyperkinésie chez les enfants.

Le bébé a besoin d'un minimum de 35 mg de vitamine C par jour pour prévenir le scorbut. Il est indispensable de fournir une quantité supplémentaire de vitamine C à l'enfant nourri au biberon, car cette vitamine est détruite en chauffant le lait. La vitamine C est généralement donnée aussi aux bébés qui sont nourris au sein pour assurer un approvisionnement normal parce que la quantité prise par la mère peut être insuffisante.

Quand le nourrisson atteint l'âge de deux ou trois semaines, sa mère commence à lui donner de l'acide ascorbique en solution pour satisfaire ses besoins en vitamine C. Quand on utilise le *jus d'orange*, on le donne habituellement à raison d'une cuillerée à thé composée d'une moitié de jus frais tamisé et d'une moitié d'eau bouillie. La dose est graduellement augmentée jusqu'à 60 ou 90 ml de jus, additionné d'une petite quantité d'eau, donnée chaque jour aux bébés âgés de 2 mois. Du jus d'orange congelé peut être utilisé et dilué avec de l'eau bouillie et refroidie selon les indications mentionnées sur la boîte. En raison des problèmes allergiques causés par le jus d'orange, il est rarement introduit dans la diète avant l'âge de 2 mois.

En enseignant aux mères à donner du jus d'orange à leurs nourrissons, les précautions suivantes doivent être soulignées. 1) Le jus d'orange ne doit pas être bouilli ou ajouté à de l'eau chaude, étant donné que la vitamine C est facilement détruite par la chaleur. Elle

Tableau 11-2. *Ration diététique journalière recommandée pour bébés âgés de 0 à 12 mois*

	0-2 MOIS POIDS: 5 kg TAILLE: 55 cm		2-6 MOIS P.: 7 kg T.: 63 cm		6-12 MOIS P.: 9 kg T.: 72 cm	
Calories	kg × 120		kg × 110		kg × 100	
Protéines	kg × 2,2 g		kg × 2 g		kg × 1,8 g	
Vitamines liposolubles:						
Vitamine A	1500 U.I.		1500 U.I.		1500 U.I.	
Vitamine D	400 U.I.		400 U.I.		400 U.I.	
Vitamine E	5 U.I.		5 U.I.		5 U.I.	
Vitamines hydrosolubles:						
Acide ascorbique	35	mg	35	mg	35	mg
Acide folique	0,05	mg	0,05	mg	0,1	mg
Equivalent de la niacine	5	mg	7	mg	8	mg
Riboflavine	0,4	mg	0,5	mg	0,6	mg
Thiamine	0,2	mg	0,4	mg	0,5	mg
Vitamine B_6	0,2	mg	0,3	mg	0,4	mg
Vitamne B_{12}	1	μg	1,5	μg	2	μg
Minéraux:						
Calcium	0,4	g	0,5	g	0,6	g
Phosphore	0,2	g	0,4	g	0,5	g
Iode	25	μg	40	μg	45	μg
Fer	6	mg	15	mg	15	mg
Magnésium	40	mg	60	mg	70	mg

est aussi anéantie par un long contact avec l'air ou avec un ustensile contenant du cuivre. 2) Les boissons à goût d'orange (soda à l'orange ou des produits similaires) ne contiennent généralement pas de jus d'orange frais, mais des ingrédients pouvant nuire au bébé. Il est aussi nécessaire d'insister sur la propreté dans la préparation du jus d'orange.

Si la mère préfère utiliser le *jus de tomate*, le nourrisson devrait en prendre deux fois la quantité de jus d'orange prescrite par le médecin ou requise pour son âge. Le jus de tomate devrait être donné avec une égale quantité d'eau. Puisqu'un nourrisson ne peut prendre beaucoup de liquide en plus de son biberon, le jus de tomate n'est pas donné au bébé avant l'âge de six mois. La vitamine C synthétique se vend à un prix très abordable. Cette vitamine ne produit pas d'effets toxiques, le surplus est éliminé dans l'urine. La carence en vitamine C produit le scorbut.

Vitamine D. La vitamine D est produite par l'organisme grâce à l'action des rayons ultra-violets du soleil sur le cholestérol de la peau. Puisque cette source de vitamine D est saisonnière, surtout dans les régions au climat tempéré, la diète de l'enfant doit fournir une quantité appropriée de cette vitamine. Certains aliments contiennent un peu de vitamine D; il s'agit du lait, du beurre et du

jaune d'œuf; c'est le foie cependant qui en procure le plus. On trouve dans le commerce de la vitamine D synthétique. Cette vitamine

Figure 11-20. La mère, même si elle nourrit habituellement l'enfant au sein, peut désirer donner à son nourrisson l'expérience du biberon.

est plus stable que la vitamine C et n'est pas aussi facilement détruite par la chaleur et l'oxydation.

On ajoute cette vitamine au régime alimentaire quand le nourrisson est âgé d'à peu près 2 semaines; il a besoin en général de 400 unités internationales ou 40 unités calciférol par jour. La vitamine D aide le bébé à assimiler le calcium que lui procure le lait; elle est un substitut ou un complément des rayons solaires. On trouve sur le marché du lait additionné de vitamine D. Plusieurs autres préparations contenant de la vitamine D sont aussi disponibles, comme les mélanges vitaminiques, l'huile de foie de morue et ses concentrés et d'autres concentrés d'huile de foie de poissons. Les préparations de vitamine D varient tellement en puissance, que l'on doit suivre attentivement l'ordonnance du médecin.

L'huile de foie de morue ordinaire est moins utilisée qu'auparavant. Généralement, on donne ¼ de cuillerée à thé au début et on augmente jusqu'à 1 à 2 cuillerées à thé.

Le mode d'administration est important. L'huile doit être froide. On essuie le goulot de la bouteille pour enlever le dépôt huileux. Il faut éviter de montrer du dégout pendant l'administration du médicament, étant donné que le bébé copiera l'attitude de l'adulte. Pour empêcher l'aspiration, il faut relever la tête du bébé et le tenir en position assise pendant l'absorption. Les préparations contenant de l'huile ne devraient jamais être données pendant que l'enfant pleure, afin de prévenir l'entrée de l'huile dans l'arbre respiratoire, ce qui pourrait causer une broncho-pneumonie lipoïdique.

La dose habituelle des concentrés de vitamine D est de 5 à 10 gouttes par jour. Quelques préparations de vitamine D peuvent être données dans le lait, mais le bébé pourrait ne pas prendre tout le lait et par conséquent ne pas ingérer toute la dose de vitamine. On ne doit jamais mettre de substance huileuse dans un biberon parce que: 1) l'huile adhère au verre; 2) elle surnage quand le biberon est renversé; le bébé ne suce l'huile qu'à la fin du repas, à travers la tétine.

L'excès de vitamine D produit, après un certain temps, des anomalies du métabolisme du calcium, de l'anorexie et une perte de poids. Le rachitisme apparaît à la suite d'une carence prolongée.

Autres vitamines. D'autres vitamines sont également nécessaires à la croissance de l'enfant mais un régime normal en contient habituellement en quantité suffisante. Le médecin ajoute quelquefois des suppléments vitaminiques quand il le juge nécessaire. Il faut cependant se rappeler que l'excès de vitamines produit parfois des hypervitaminoses. L'emploi abusif de la vitamine A se traduit pas de l'anorexie, un retard de croissance et un gain de poids insuffisant. L'enfant souffre d'hépatomégalie, d'un épaississement du cortex des os longs et de prurit. On trouve peu d'hypervitaminoses causées par les autres catégories de vitamines.

Fer. Bien que les nonuveau-nés normaux aient une réserve suffisante de fer à leur naissance, ils ont besoin d'une quantité de fer supplémentaire nécessaire à leur organisme durant la période de croissance, surtout après les premiers mois de la vie. Dans le régime habituel du bébé, la moitié ou plus de la quantité journalière de fer est fournie par les céréales enrichies de fer. Pour le prématuré, le régime est rarement suffisant pour fournir le fer nécessaire à sa croissance, il est donc indispensable de lui en procurer une quantité supplémentaire.

Fluorure. Le fluor ajouté à l'eau potable favorise la calcification durant la formation des tissus dentaires et rend ainsi l'émail des dents plus résistant à la carie. Dans plusieurs villes, l'addition de fluor dans l'eau d'approvisionnement est suffisante pour améliorer la santé des dents des enfants.

Pour les bébés qui ne reçoivent pas suffisamment de fluor dans l'eau potable, on recommande l'administration journalière d'une solution de fluorure. La dose habituelle recommandée par le médecin est approximativement de 0,5 mg de fluorure de sodium par jour. On doit augmenter la dose au fur et à mesure que l'enfant grandit et on peut donner la substance sous forme de tablettes. Une solution de fluorure pourrait aussi être appliquée sur les dents pour prévenir la formation de caries. Il est à noter que les fluorures, même en petites quantités, peuvent tacher l'émail dentaire. De plus, la quantité optimale pour les besoins humains est encore controversée.

Introduction des aliments solides

Aliments que les bébés aiment. Le bébé prendra les aliments solides qu'il aime plus facilement que ceux qu'il n'aime pas. En général, les bébés n'apprécient pas les aliments à saveur prononcée, et préfèrent ceux qui sont légèrement sucrés. La préférence du bébé quant à la consistance et la composition de la nourriture varie selon son âge. Naturellement, le nouveau-né n'accepte que les liquides. Le nourrisson aime la nourriture molle; lorsque ses dents commencent à percer, il préfère les aliments qu'il peut mastiquer, comme les biscuits (de dentition) ou la nourriture hachée. L'abandon des aliments en purée pour une nourriture hachée devrait être graduel. L'alimentation hachée peut être commencée à partir de 6 à 9 mois, selon l'habileté du bébé à mastiquer.

Les bébés préfèrent une nourriture à température modérée. Un bébé peut être effrayé par une nourriture trop chaude ou trop froide et peut même la refuser quand elle lui sera offerte.

Méthode d'introduction.

La réaction du bébé à son premier repas de nourriture solide est de faire des mouvements de succion avec sa langue, ce qui cause le renvoi de la nourriture hors de sa bouche. Rappelons que le bébé doit apprendre la méthode qui consiste à diriger doucement la nourriture solide du devant de la bouche au pharynx. L'infirmière devrait expliquer à la jeune mère que cet apprentissage se produira avec la répétition. L'initiation d'un bébé à la nourriture solide devrait être une expérience agréable. Il doit être tenu dans la même position que lorsqu'il boit au biberon, mais sa tête et ses épaules devraient être légèrement plus élevées que lors de l'allaitement. Une bavette est nécessaire car le bébé ne manquera pas de rejeter la nourriture et de rendre ses doigts collants en les mettant dans sa bouche. La nourriture devrait être lisse et donnée par petites quantités. Les céréales devraient être diluées avec le lait et les fruits ou légumes avec de l'eau bouillie.

Le bébé n'absorbera initialement qu'une toute petite quantité d'aliments (1 cuillère à thé). Il faudrait utiliser une petite cuillère (ne pas employer une cuillère à manche recourbé que les adultes tiennent maladroitement). On place la nourriture à l'arrière de la langue du bébé, sans toutefois exercer de pression, de peur de le faire vomir. Les nouveaux aliments doivent être introduits un à la fois de façon à pouvoir observer si l'enfant présente une réaction allergique et offerts au bébé avant son biberon ou avant la nourriture qu'il a l'habitude de prendre. Le bébé ne devrait pas être pressé ni forcé. Trente minutes sont suffisantes pour un repas. S'il n'a pas pris cette nouvelle nourriture, à la fin de cette période, le repas doit être arrêté et une autre tentative sera faite le lendemain. Les médicaments ne doivent pas être mélangés à la nourriture, à moins que le médecin ne l'ait spécifiquement demandé.

La personne qui fait prendre le repas au nourrisson devrait être calme, patiente et douce. Le bébé est alors plus porté à prendre la nourriture, que s'il est grondé ou cajolé.

Si l'on donne à l'enfant des aliments qui déplaisent à l'adulte, on ne doit pas montrer d'aversion. L'enfant est porté à imiter la réaction de l'adulte envers la nourriture. S'il veut toucher la nourriture, il devrait être laissé libre de le faire. Toucher constitue un mode d'apprentissage. Il faut, naturellement, lui laver les mains avant et après les repas.

On s'interroge de plus en plus sur l'inocuité des aliments commerciaux destinés aux bébés et on craint que l'addition de sodium ne favorise ultérieurement l'apparition d'hypertension. Le sel que l'on ajoute à ces aliments rend souvent l'aliment plus attrayant pour la mère mais on trouve peu de bébés qui refusent les aliments non salés. Les recherches continuent et il semble qu'en attendant il soit préférable de donner au bébé des aliments cuits dans la marmite à pression et passés ensuite au mélangeur électrique. La mère évite ainsi à son bébé un surplus de sel et de féculent, élément ajouté commercialement pour rendre les purées plus lisses. Il est à noter que la mère peut préparer plusieurs repas et les congeler, ce qui allège sa tâche.

Céréales.

On conseille d'inclure très tôt les céréales au régime alimentaire du bébé parce que celles-ci contiennent du fer. Un nourrisson a besoin de fer puisqu'il n'en reçoit pas suffisamment dans le lait maternel ou dans son biberon. Mais les céréales, à moins qu'elles ne soient enrichies, ne contiennent pas autant de fer que certains aliments en purée. Toutefois, toutes les céréales de bébé sont maintenant enrichies de fer. On peut donner au bébé des céréales qui sont préparées d'avance ou bien la portion du bébé peut être prise sur celle préparée pour le petit déjeuner de la famille. Les céréales sèches, pourtant, ne conviennent pas à un nourrisson. Celles spécialement préparées pour les bébés sont plus finement coupées et plus digestibles que celles des adultes. Si les céréales cuisinées pour la famille sont utilisées, la portion du bébé doit être alors cuite plus longtemps afin de transformer l'amidon, un polysaccharide, en molécules plus digestibles. Il est préférable d'utiliser un bain-marie pour les faire cuire afin qu'elles ne collent pas au fond du récipient. Celles préparées pour le bébé ne devraient pas être sucrées.

On doit en varier les sortes pour que l'enfant apprenne à accepter différentes saveurs. Toutefois, il est bon de commencer avec la céréale de riz qui est la moins allergène et d'éviter les céréales mélangées et les céréales de blé jusqu'à ce que le bébé ait atteint 4 mois de façon à prévenir les réactions allergiques qui pourraient se présenter.

On commence par une cuillère à thé matin et soir lorsque l'enfant boit 750 ml de lait par jour et demeure insatisfait. On augmente graduellement la quantité, sans diminuer l'apport lacté, jusqu'à atteindre 5 cuillères à table vers 5 ou 6 mois. Au fur et à mesure que le bébé grandit, il pourrait manger une pomme de terre cuite au four ou bouillie à la place des céréales. La pomme de terre peut être écrasée avec une fourchette et mélangée avec un peu d'eau ou de lait bouillis.

Fruits. On doit réduire les fruits frais (par ex. pommes, pêches, abricots) en compote et passer celle-ci au tamis. On peut se servir d'un mélangeur automatique pour obtenir une purée homogène et lisse. On n'ajoute pas de sucre. La banane peut être donnée crue si elle est mûre et écrasée en purée. La dose initiale de fruit doit être de 1 cuillerée à thé par jour. Plusieurs sortes de fruits doivent être données pour que le bébé apprenne à aimer la variété. Les fruits sont le plus souvent la deuxième variété d'aliments solides, ajoutée au régime du bébé. Ils suivent, ordinairement, l'addition des céréales de 2 à 3 semaines.

Légumes. On devrait commencer par faire prendre au bébé une cuillerée à thé de légumes par jour, et augmenter graduellement la quantité. Les légumes sont ajoutés lorsque le bébé s'est habitué à l'aliment solide précédemment introduit. Les légumes devraient être cuits au bain-marie ou bouillis dans aussi peu d'eau que possible, afin de conserver leurs minéraux et leurs vitamines, puis être passés au tamis. Le bébé devrait manger des légumes verts ou jaunes qui ont une saveur douce et qui contiennent les vitamines nécessaires. Les légumes qui, pour les bébés, ont une saveur moins agréable que les fruits sont souvent donnés après les céréales pour éviter leur rejet si le bébé s'est habitué aux fruits. Toutefois, leur valeur calorique est moindre que celle des fruits. Plus tard, lorsque les dents du nourrisson poussent, il pourra les manger écrasés ou coupés. Les petits pois, les carottes ou les haricots verts, bien cuits, afin d'être plus facilement écrasés avec une fourchette, peuvent être ajoutés au régime alimentaire.

Oeufs. On suggère de donner le jaune de l'œuf au nourrisson vers l'âge de 3 à 5 mois. On recommande de ne pas lui donner le blanc de l'œuf avant qu'il ne soit âgé d'un an, parce qu'il pourrait être allergique à l'albumine de l'œuf. Le jaune de l'œuf contient du fer, de la riboflavine et surtout des protéines. Il doit être cuit dur, écrasé avec une fourchette et administré en petites quantités jusqu'à ce que le bébé y soit habitué; la quantité est augmentée graduellement. Il peut être donné seul ou mélangé avec du lait ou des céréales. Quand le

blanc est ajouté au régime, l'œuf peut être plus ou moins bouilli ou même poché. De petites quantités de blanc sont données au début jusqu'à ce qu'il soit évident que l'enfant n'est pas allergique à la protéine que contient le blanc d'œuf; ensuite, il peut être donné au complet.

Viandes. On ajoute les viandes en purée au régime alimentaire du bébé, vers 4 ou 5 mois. La viande, comme les œufs et le lait, fournit des protéines. On peut acheter la viande spécialement préparée pour bébés. On peut aussi la préparer en râpant de la viande crue — du foie ou du bœuf — avec un couteau. La viande est formée en pâté et cuite au bain-marie. Quand elle est bien cuite, le pâté est brun. Au début, le nourrisson doit prendre une cuillerée à thé seulement de cette préparation, mais cette quantité doit être augmentée rapidement. Le foie est également bon parce qu'il contient beaucoup de fer, de la vitamine A, ainsi que le complexe vitaminique B. Le poulet et l'agneau sont ajoutés plus tard au régime. Le bébé ne doit pas manger de viandes grasses parce que les lipides se digèrent difficilement. Quand l'enfant est capable de mastiquer, sa viande peut être hachée plutôt que réduite en purée.

Poissons. Vers la fin de la première année, on peut substituer le poisson à la viande ou aux œufs, plusieurs fois par semaine. On le fait bouillir, cuire au four ou au bain-marie, mais on évite les fritures. Le poisson doit être bien nettoyé, de façon à être sûr qu'il ne contient aucune particule d'arête.

Pain. Du pain desséché peut être ajouté au régime alimentaire, quand le nourrisson est âgé de 6 mois et que ses dents commencent à percer les gencives. Si on lui permet de tenir le pain, il apprendra facilement à porter la nourriture à sa bouche. Ceci est le premier pas vers l'acquisition de l'habileté à se nourrir lui-même. Il exercera ainsi ses mâchoires en mastiquant le pain sec.

Le lait naturel. Si l'enfant n'est pas nourri au sein, vers le 4e mois on doit remplacer sa préparation de lait par du lait entier, homogénéisé et pasteurisé. Quelques médecins ne demandent pas à la mère de faire bouillir le lait ou l'eau qu'elle donne à son enfant, si elle habite dans une région où la qualité du lait et de l'eau est soigneusement contrôlée. Du moment que le nourrisson reçoit des glucides dans ses céréales et dans d'autres aliments, on n'a pas besoin de sucrer son lait.

Desserts. Les desserts sont donnés vers la fin de la première année. Ceux qui conviennent aux besoins du bébé sont les fruits, la gélatine, les puddings au lait, les sorbets, les flans et les yoghourts.

Le développement des habitudes alimentaires

Les parents sont généralement responsables des mauvaises habitudes alimentaires adoptées par l'enfant. Si l'heure du repas est agréable, il y aura peu de problèmes. Il vaut mieux donner un bon départ que de corriger une mauvaise habitude quand l'enfant est plus âgé.

Aux environs d'un mois, le nourrisson est en mesure de manger à la cuillère. À 5 ou 6 mois, la plupart des nourrissons commencent à se servir de leurs mains pour manger, en prenant, par exemple, une fine tranche de pain dans leur main et en essayant de la porter à leur bouche. À 8 ou 9 mois, le bébé sait tenir une cuillère et peut s'en servir comme d'un jouet. À 9 mois, le bébé peut habituellement tenir son propre biberon. L'enfant âgé d'un an boit à la tasse, bien qu'il puisse vouloir son biberon à l'heure du coucher. On peut le laisser boire au biberon le soir jusqu'à ce qu'il y renonce lui-même. Il est toutefois discutable de lui permettre de garder son biberon au lit. Pendant la première année, le bébé aura bon appétit à cause de son activité progressive et de la croissance rapide de son corps. À la fin de la première année, son appétit va décroître, parce que son rythme de croissance ralentit. Son besoin de nourriture ira décroissant. Ceci est normal et l'adulte ne devrait jamais forcer l'enfant à manger en craignant qu'il ne dépérisse. En l'encourageant à manger trop à ce moment-là, la mère prépare souvent des problèmes alimentaires pour les étapes suivantes.

Coliques

Les coliques sont courantes pendant les 3 ou 4 premiers mois de la vie. Par coliques, on entend des crampes intestinales paroxystiques, dues à une accumulation excessive de gaz. Celles-ci causent des malaises et de la douleur. L'enfant crie, lève ses mains et ses pieds, et son visage devient tout rouge. En passant la main sur l'abdomen du bébé, on remarquera que les muscles sont tendus et durs. Le bébé pourra libérer les gaz, par l'anus ou par la bouche en éructant.

Étiologie, traitement et pronostic. Les facteurs qui causent les coliques ne sont pas encore connus avec certitude, mais les causes suivantes ont été proposées: absorption excessive d'air, surexcitation, absorption excessive d'hydrates de carbone qui cause la fermentation et les gaz, excès de nourriture ou repas pris trop rapidement, ainsi que l'anxiété et l'irritation d'une mère ou d'une infirmière, qui communiquent leur tension au bébé. Il ne faut pas négliger le fait que l'enfant qui pleure fait de l'aérophagie, ce qui augmente encore la distention intestinale. Des études plus récentes permettent de penser que les bébés souffrant de coliques nécessitent plus de succion que la moyenne des bébés. Le fait de leur permettre de sucer entre les repas diminuerait leur tension, favoriserait le péristaltisme intestinal et soulagerait les coliques. Le traitement consiste à frotter gentiment et souvent le dos du bébé, tout en le tenant dans une position verticale, ce qui l'aide à se débarrasser de l'air se trouvant dans les voies digestives. Quelquefois, en lui donnant à boire de l'eau tiède, on peut l'aider à libérer des gaz. On peut aussi le tourner sur l'abdomen. Un biberon d'eau tiède additionnée de menthe poivrée peut aider par son action carminative. La technique d'alimentation peut être revue avec la mère. Le bébé a besoin d'affection et du contact physique de sa mère ou de l'infirmière. Le médecin peut recommander un changement de lait. Malgré les crises douloureuses paroxystiques, le bébé arrive souvent à gagner du poids. Toutefois, ses pleurs ininterrompus peuvent exténuer la mère et nuire à la relation parents-enfant. De là l'importance de traiter ces problèmes sérieusement.

Sevrage

Le terme sevrage désigne deux réalités différentes selon les auteurs. Il peut signifier soit le moment où l'alimentation lactée n'est plus prépondérante, soit l'arrêt de l'alimentation au sein ou au biberon.

Importance psychologique. Sevrer un bébé du sein ou du biberon en utilisant une tasse a une signification psychologique particulière. Le sevrage n'implique pas seulement l'acquisition d'une activité nouvelle — boire plutôt que sucer — mais détermine aussi la fin de la période pendant laquelle le nourrisson connaissait la plupart de ses plaisirs par l'intermédiaire de sa bouche et de la succion.

Habituellement, un bébé indique qu'il est prêt pour un nouveau comportement lorsqu'il rejette l'ancienne façon de faire et semble frustré par les limitations qu'elle impose à son désir d'expériences nouvelles et de contrôle de son entourage.

Pendant la seconde moitié de la première année, l'enfant veut et a besoin de plus de liberté de mouvement pour acquérir un contrôle croissant de son corps et la connaissance de son entourage. Il n'est plus nécessaire de le tenir dans les bras pour lui communiquer une sensation d'amour et de protection. En fait, il est probable qu'il résistera à cette contrainte. Il acquiert maintenant un sentiment de confiance envers les autres personnes à travers leur visage souriant et à travers leurs paroles dites sur un ton qu'il a toujours associé à des expériences agréables.

Il veut abandonner sa manière enfantine de se nourrir et essaie de boire avec une tasse. Dans tout apprentissage, il y a un stade optimum de développement pour qu'une nouvelle activité soit apprise promptement. À ce moment, l'opportunité d'acquérir d'autres manières de se nourrir doit être donnée à l'enfant, en lui fournissant les conditions favorables à son succès. Il ne doit pas être pressé d'abandonner sa conduite antérieure pendant qu'il expérimente la nouvelle. À 6 mois, il a appris que les bonnes choses que l'on mange viennent d'une assiette ou d'une tasse et il est prêt à boire son lait dans une tasse quand on le lui donne. Il montre son désir de boire dans une tasse en s'asseyant et en tentant d'atteindre le récipient. Il se tourne ensuite vers un adulte pour se faire aider. S'il échoue dans son apprentissage, on doit attendre quelques semaines et recommencer de nouveau. On utilise l'ancienne et la nouvelle technique conjointement pendant un certain temps. Le meilleur moment pour le sevrage est généralement la seconde moitié de la première année. Bien que certains nourrissons apprennent à boire à la tasse à l'âge de 5 mois, ils le font rarement avec plaisir et ne devraient pas être forcés de renoncer à la joie de sucer avant qu'ils ne soient prêts à le faire.

Le bébé peut être sevré du sein, avant le 6e mois, si la quantité du lait maternel diminue ou si la mère le désire. S'il y a du lait maternel disponible, il doit être donné au bébé au biberon et non pas à la tasse, parce que le jeune nourrisson a besoin du plaisir de sucer.

Méthodes de sevrage. L'enfant doit être sevré graduellement pour qu'il ne soit pas frustré par le changement de la tétine à la tasse. Aussitôt qu'il boit bien à la tasse le nombre d'allaitement ou de repas au biberon doit être diminué lentement. Quelques bébés allaités au sein apprennent à boire au biberon avant de boire à la tasse. L'utilisation du biberon comme étape intermédiaire entre l'allaitement au sein et l'usage d'une tasse est facultative. C'est une bonne méthode de laisser l'enfant apprendre à aimer le goût du lait de vache, avant que l'allaitement au sein soit complètement arrêté. Le sevrage ne doit jamais être entrepris quand l'enfant est malade, à moins d'une raison sérieuse, étant donné qu'il est déjà très tendu lors de la maladie.

Réactions au sevrage. Quand le processus complet de sevrage est trop rapide, l'enfant peut montrer des signes de malaises (anxiété, insomnie et irritabilité) et pleurer fréquemment. Il a tendance à sucer son pouce. S'il reçoit une attention spéciale, pendant et après la période de sevrage, il trouvera plusieurs autres expériences agréables pour compenser la perte du plaisir de téter son lait et fera peu ou ne fera pas de réactions au processus de sevrage.

Élimination

Étant donné que différents types de nourriture sont ajoutés au régime du nourrisson, la couleur ainsi que la consistance de ses selles changeront. Par exemple, s'il mange des betteraves, ses selles auront une teinte rougeâtre. Au fur et à mesure que l'on ajoute une variété d'aliments au régime du bébé, les selles deviendront plus pâteuses et leur couleur prédominante sera brune.

SURVEILLANCE DE LA SANTÉ DE L'ENFANT

Dans la plupart des pays, il existe des cliniques de santé ou unités sanitaires, situées dans les agglomérations urbaines ou à l'extérieur des villes. Dans la province de Québec, ces cliniques s'appelleront désormais: Centre local de Services communautaires (C.L.S.C.). Ces organisations ont pour buts généraux d'assurer une continuité dans les soins de l'enfant et d'assurer des services minima à toute la population. Les soins offerts y sont ordinairement gratuits. Ces cliniques ne sont pas situées, en général, à l'intérieur d'un hôpital et sont subventionnées par les pouvoirs publics. L'accent y est mis sur la prévention, et les programmes de soin concernent en général les femmes enceintes, les jeunes enfants et les vieillards. On tente de plus en plus d'y intégrer des programmes de soin pour les personnes handicapées ou atteintes de maladie chronique. En général, ces unités sont regroupées à l'intérieur d'un organisme qui tend à distribuer les services uniformément sur un territoire donné. Dans la province de Québec, les C.L.S.C. dépendent des 31 départements de santé communautaire et ceux-ci sont regroupés à l'intérieur de 9 conseils régionaux.

Buts spécifiques du programme de soin infantile. 1) Aider les mères à comprendre la croissance physique et le développement émotif de leurs enfants et leur permettre d'éviter de graves problèmes en leur enseignant ce qu'elles doivent attendre d'un enfant à différents âges. 2) Dépister les anomalies physiques ou les maladies par un examen complet et informer les parents sur les ressources communautaires mises à leur disposition. 3) Fournir une protection contre certaines maladies contagieuses par l'immunisation. 4) Offrir des conseils sur l'alimentation spécifique de l'enfant et aider à l'établissement du budget nécessaire à l'alimentation de la famille entière. 5) Aider à établir des relations positives entre enfant-médecin-mère et infirmière-enfant-mère. 6) Aider à résoudre les problèmes de comportement et soutenir la famille dans ses efforts à constituer une cellule harmonieuse.

Les mères apprennent l'existence de ces services soit par l'intermédiaire du personnel hospitalier, soit grâce à l'infirmière en santé communautaire qui visite les récentes accouchées. Parfois, elles sont renseignées par leurs parents ou amis. La majeure partie des mères viennent à ces cliniques pour faire immuniser leurs enfants.

Le personnel. Le personnel indispensable requis pour répondre aux besoins de la mère et de l'enfant inclut un médecin, pédiatre de préférence, ainsi qu'une infirmière. Lorsque c'est possible, un travailleur social, un psychologue, une diététicienne et un dentiste complètent l'équipe de santé.

Le médecin doit avoir une expérience valable en santé communautaire et avoir soigné avec succès des enfants. L'infirmière doit être spécialisée en santé maternelle et infantile ou en soins de l'enfant. Idéalement, la mère et l'enfant rencontrent le médecin et l'infirmière à chaque visite. Les étudiantes peuvent être présentes afin de comprendre les responsabilités du personnel de la clinique et les buts de la consultation. Une petite salle de jeu ou un coffre à jouets sont très utiles pour détendre les enfants. Une tendance récente est de confier à une infirmière spécialisée la charge de ces cliniques et de faire appel au médecin seulement lorsque des problèmes médicaux se présentent.

Équipement nécessaire

Il faut qu'il y ait des affiches éducatives sur les murs. Une petite salle est nécessaire pour peser et mesurer les enfants. Le cabinet de consultation du médecin devrait être équipé pour examiner l'enfant et on devrait y trouver une chaise confortable afin que la mère puisse s'asseoir avec aisance et tenir le bébé au moment où elle s'entretiendra avec le médecin.

On devrait aussi trouver une pièce séparée dans laquelle l'infirmière ou tout autre membre de l'équipe pourrait s'entretenir avec la mère et répondre à ses questions. Dans le cas où pareil espace ne serait pas disponible, une ou deux pièces pourraient être séparées par des paravents, afin que le travail de la clinique puisse être poursuivi. L'idéal serait un bureau pour interviewer la mère et recueillir l'histoire de santé de l'enfant, un local pour déshabiller et examiner l'enfant, une salle d'attente avec des fauteuils confortables et enfin une salle de jeux. La salle de jeux devrait avoir de petites chaises ainsi que des jouets lavables. Une personne bénévole pourrait être disponible pour s'occuper des enfants. L'endroit réservé aux immunisations devrait être éloigné de celui où les mères et les enfants attendent, afin qu'ils n'entendent pas les pleurs de ceux qui reçoivent une injection.

Les services offerts sont les suivants:

1) tenue d'un dossier complet pour chaque enfant
2) inscription du poids, de la taille et de la température de l'enfant
3) examen physique complet
4) conseils à la mère sur la nutrition et les soins généraux de l'enfant
5) immunisation de l'enfant
6) aide préventive et conseils sur les problèmes du comportement
7) évaluation de la condition physique et émotive de l'enfant
8) explication des soins conseillés par le médecin
9) référence à un médecin spécialiste, en cas de maladie, de correction d'un défaut physique ou de problèmes émotifs.

Histoire de santé. L'histoire de santé de l'enfant, complète et soignée, donne au personnel de la clinique une image globale de l'enfant et les aide à établir des relations amicales avec la mère. Cette histoire ne doit pas être faite à la hâte. La mère devrait avoir le temps de discuter de ses problèmes et de ceux de son enfant ou des autres membres de la famille qui sont continuellement en contact avec l'enfant. Si l'infirmière rédige l'histoire, elle devrait utiliser cette occasion pour dispenser un enseignement sanitaire et expliquer à la mère les buts de la clinique. Elle prépare ainsi la mère à une entrevue avec le médecin.

Taille, poids et température. L'inscription du poids, de la taille et la prise de température de l'enfant sont sous la responsabilité de l'infirmière, bien que ceci puisse être fait par un personnel auxiliaire. L'enfant déshabillé doit être examiné pour déceler une éruption ou autres signes de maladie. On peut enseigner à la mère la manière de peser l'enfant et de prendre sa température. En observant l'infirmière, elle apprend à tenir correctement son bébé.

La pesée du bébé. Le but est de déterminer le poids exact de l'enfant. Le poids fournit un indice d'évaluation du progrès du bébé et peut souligner un retard de croissance. Il faut donc être très précis. L'équipement comprend une balance pour nourrissons (placée de manière à ce que leur tête soit du côté du mur), un papier isolant qui recouvre la balance, une couverture pour enfant, un crayon et une feuille pour inscrire le poids et un carré de papier avec lequel on bouge les poids de la balance.

Il faut procéder soigneusement, de façon à préserver la sécurité de l'enfant et à empêcher la contamination. L'infirmière doit d'abord s'enquérir du poids du bébé lors de la visite précédente, le déshabiller, l'envelopper dans une couverture et préparer la balance. Pour éviter de contaminer celle-ci, elle doit placer une feuille de papier sur le plateau et bouger les poids de la balance avec un carré de papier. L'enfant est alors posé doucement, sans sa couverture au centre du plateau, sa tête étant du côté du mur, pour qu'il ne tombe pas s'il remue ou donne des coups de pieds. L'infirmière doit tenir l'enfant de la main gauche, pendant qu'elle le pèse, afin d'éviter qu'il ne tombe. La difficulté lors de la pesée d'un bébé est de le garder immobile parce que s'il bouge, le poids est inexact. La mère doit rester près de la balance, parler au nourrisson et lui montrer un jouet afin de capter son attention. Ceci le calmera et permettra une lecture exacte du poids. On enveloppe l'enfant dans sa couverture et on le remet à sa mère en attendant que le médecin puisse l'examiner. On jette la feuille de papier isolant dans un réceptacle pour papiers contaminés. On enregistre alors le poids exact au dossier du nourrisson.

On profite du moment où le bébé est sur la balance pour le mesurer.

Examen physique. L'examen physique d'un enfant doit être fait aussi souvent que nécessaire, mais le nombre et le contenu des examens donnés aux différents âges varient dans chaque clinique. En général, il est recommandé que l'enfant soit vu par le médecin tous les mois durant la première année de vie, tous les 3 mois durant la 2e et la 3e années et tous les 6 mois durant les 4e et 5e années. Ces examens, même durant l'enfance, doivent inclure une évaluation de la capacité de l'enfant à voir et à entendre.

L'enfant devrait être examiné chaque fois que le médecin le juge nécessaire. Le besoin d'un examen complet est déterminé par un examen partiel à chaque visite ou sur la demande de la mère. En général, un examen partiel est mené dans le but de trouver des conditions anormales au stade de développement atteint par le bébé, par exemple les positions des pieds, jambes ou dos alors qu'il apprend à marcher. Tout examen doit inclure l'observation du développement, de l'état nutri-

tif et le dépistage d'anomalies ou de maladies. Un test urinaire pour déceler la phénylcétonurie devrait être effectué. L'examen physique doit précéder l'immunisation qui provoque les pleurs de l'enfant.

Conseils pour l'alimentation et les soins généraux. Tous les membres de l'équipe peuvent conseiller la mère, en autant que tous s'entendent pour enseigner la même chose, de la même façon. L'infirmière doit s'assurer que la mère comprend bien ce qui doit être fait. Elle doit s'informer de la situation familiale pour être certaine que l'enseignement donné est approprié et répond aux besoins précis de la famille. Si le plan de soins n'est pas réaliste, il est peu probable qu'il soit adopté et que la mère revienne à la clinique.

Immunisation. La prévention des maladies demeure le but le plus important des soins donnés à l'enfant. Durant le bas âge et le début de l'enfance, des mesures préventives peuvent être prises contre certaines maladies infectieuses. L'immunisation est donnée à l'âge indiqué par les recherches et par l'expérience. On immunise les enfants contre la diphtérie, la coqueluche, le tétanos, la poliomyélite, la

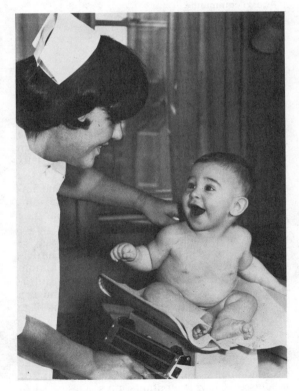

Figure 11-21. Le poids de l'enfant, enregistré à chaque visite au Centre de santé, constitue un bon critère pour évaluer ses progrès. (Courtoisie de l'Hôpital Sainte-Justine, Montréal.)

Tableau 11-3. *Programme recommandé pour immunisation active et test à la Tuberculine pour bébés et enfants normaux*
(American Academy of Pediatrics)

2 mois	DCT Sabin
4 mois	DCT Sabin
6 mois	DCT Sabin
12 mois	Test à la tuberculine, rougeole
12 mois à 12 ans	Rubéole
18 mois	DCT Sabin
4 à 6 ans	DCT Sabin
14 ans à 16 ans	DT tous les 10 ans

Tableau 11-4. *Calendrier des vaccinations*
(Service d'épidémiologie, Ministère de la Santé, Québec)

Âge recommandé	Vaccin
2 mois	DCT Sabin
4 mois	DCT Sabin
6 mois	DCT Sabin
12 mois	Rougeole
12 mois	Rubéole
12 mois	Oreillons
12 mois	Test à la tuberculine

RAPPELS ET REVACCINATIONS

Âge recommandé	Vaccin
15 à 18 mois	DCT Sabin
5 à 6 ans	DCT Sabin
12 à 14 ans	Oreillons
15 à 18 ans	DT Sabin

rougeole et la rubéole pendant la première année de vie ou peu après, avec des rappels durant les années subséquentes. Il est possible de prévenir la douleur due aux injections en utilisant un anesthésique topique une à deux heures avant l'injection.

Diphtérie, coqueluche et tétanos. Une immunisation active contre ces trois maladies peut être accomplie en même temps par une administration de 0,5 ml d'une solution comprenant un stabilisateur, les anatoxines tétanique et diphtérique et des bacilles de Bordet-Gengou tués. Ce vaccin est connu sous le nom de D C T Un minimum de 3 injections intramusculaires de ce vaccin doit être donné à intervalle de 4 semaines, commençant à l'âge de 2 ou 3 mois.

Pour réduire la possibilité de réactions locales ou générales, on donne le vaccin avec une aiguille de 2,5 cm de longueur, enfoncée profondément dans les muscles latéraux de la cuisse. Chez les enfants plus âgés, il peut être administré dans le muscle deltoïde.

On ne devrait pas inoculer plus d'une fois au même endroit. Après l'injection, on peut apercevoir certaines réactions d'irritabilité, de fièvre, d'œdème et de rougeur. L'infirmière doit renseigner la mère sur ces réactions et sur les soins à donner à l'enfant. Si les symptômes persistent, ils doivent être signalés au médecin. On devrait donner des doses de rappel du D C T entre 15 et 18 mois et entre 4 et 6 ans. Le vaccin contre la coqueluche n'est plus donné après 6 ans. Des doses de rappel d'anatoxines diphtérique et tétanique devraient être données entre 12 et 14 ans et à intervalles de 10 ans subséquemment.

Un enfant gravement malade ne doit pas recevoir d'immunisation. Le vaccin contre la coqueluche ne doit être donné à aucun bébé ou enfant qui a eu déjà des convulsions, parce que celles-ci constituent une complication rare de l'administration du vaccin contre la coqueluche.

Poliomyélite. Deux vaccins sont actuellement disponibles pour la prévention de la poliomyélite: 1) l'un administré par voie buccale, contenant des virus vivants, mais atténués (Sabin) 2) l'autre contenant des virus morts et administré par voie parentérale (Salk). Le vaccin Salk a été efficace pendant plusieurs années, alors qu'il était le seul vaccin antipoliomyélitique connu; toutefois, après son administration, le taux des anticorps tombe rapidement chez les jeunes bébés et les enfants. Actuellement, le vaccin Salk est administré seulement s'il a été donné précédemment ou à la demande des parents. Le vaccin Sabin contenant les 3 types de virus est utilisé plus largement à cause de ses multiples avantages. Il est donné par voie buccale, il stimule la résistance intestinale aux rechutes et une persistance prolongée des anticorps, et il diminuerait apparemment un besoin de répéter les vaccinations. Le vaccin Sabin, toutefois, ne doit pas être administré lorsque d'autres vaccins vivants comme ceux de la rougeole ou de la variole, l'ont été moins d'un mois auparavant.

Le vaccin trivalent buccal contre la polio est recommandé. Il doit être donné tous les 2 mois à partir du 2e mois puis entre 15 et 18 mois et entre 4 et 6 ans. Le bébé nourri au sein doit aussi être vacciné.

Rougeole. Si un bébé n'a pas eu la rougeole, le vaccin doit être donné à l'âge de 12 mois. Ceci est spécialement important pour les enfants atteints d'une maladie chronique ou vivant en institution, parce qu'ils sont plus susceptibles de souffrir des sérieuses complications de la maladie. Le vaccin composé de virus vivants atténués est recommandé pour les enfants normaux. Il provoque une immunité active en produisant une légère rougeole non contagieuse. Les contre-indications à l'usage du vaccin à virus vivants atténués sont, entre autres, la présence d'une grave maladie fébrile, la tuberculose active, la leucémie. Autrefois, le vaccin composé de virus morts était utilisé; toutefois, puisque la durée de sa protection est incertaine, il sera probablement moins employé à l'avenir.

Le vaccin contre la rougeole se donne souvent en association avec l'immunisation contre la rubéole et contre les oreillons.

On attend la fin de la première année pour procéder à l'immunisation puisque les anticorps maternels sont encore présents dans le sang du bébé jusqu'à cette période. Étant donné que le but de l'immunisation est de produire une légère rougeole non contagieuse, les anticorps présents empêcheraient la formation d'une immunité active. On observe peu de complications consécutives à la vaccination et la rougeole provoquée ne semble pas contagieuse.

Rubéole. Le vaccin est recommandé pour tous les enfants entre 1 et 14 ans. On insiste sur l'importance de l'immunisation à l'âge préscolaire et au début du cours élémentaire. Les filles doivent le recevoir avant la puberté et on le donne aux femmes séronégatives qui ne sont pas enceintes et qui peuvent être sûres de ne pas le devenir dans les deux mois qui suivent la vaccination.

Oreillons. Un vaccin efficace contre les oreillons, fait de virus vivants, mais extrêmement atténués, peut être donné par injection. Ce vaccin n'est pas recommandé pour les bébés, parce que la durée de l'immunisation semble courte. Mais il peut être donné après l'âge de 1 an et surtout aux jeunes garçons approchant l'âge de la puberté et aux adultes mâles qui n'ont pas eu les oreillons, à cause du danger de stérilité résultant de l'orchite ourlienne. L'ancien vaccin à virus tués ne produisait qu'une courte immunisation et n'est plus guère utilisé.

Variole. Les autorités sanitaires de plusieurs pays occidentaux s'opposent à la vaccination antivariolique de routine et plusieurs gouvernements dont celui de la province de Québec ont légiféré dans ce sens. Les risques de contagion variolique sont minimes et ne justifient pas le danger rare mais parfois fatal que fait courir la vaccination. Toutefois, le personnel sanitaire des hôpitaux et des cliniques de santé ainsi que le personnel travaillant auprès des immigrants et aux points d'entrée des pays devraient être vaccinés.

Test à la tuberculine. Les tests à la tuberculine devraient être faits aux enfants âgés de 12 mois. L'académie américaine de pédiatrie a conseillé que tous les enfants âgés d'un an soient soumis au test à la tuberculine, de préférence avant d'avoir été vaccinés contre la rougeole ou la variole.

Autres immunisations. Si les parents comptent voyager, de plus amples informations sur les autres immunisations nécessaires peuvent leur être données par le ministère de la santé de leur pays.

Il est essentiel que les parents conservent le relevé des différents vaccins reçus par l'enfant. Si on laisse ce tableau au centre de santé, il ne sera d'aucune utilité dans les cas d'urgence. On pense par exemple à l'immunisation antitétanique de l'enfant de 5 ans qui se blesse en vacances: la mère doit savoir si sa dernière injection consistait en un rappel de D C T ou s'il a reçu son immunisation antivariolique. Le tableau d'immunisation est également essentiel si la famille déménage dans une localité éloignée.

Aide préventive et conseils sur les problèmes du comportement. Ceci est le travail du

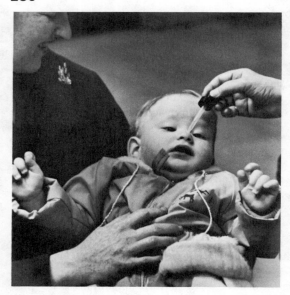

Figure 11-22. Aux enfants, le vaccin Sabin est donné goutte à goutte, directement dans la bouche. (Wyeth Laboratories, Division of American Home Products Corporation, P.O. Box 8299, Philadelphia, Pa. 19101.)

médecin et de l'infirmière. La mère peut être encouragée à poser des questions, si on lui mentionne les problèmes courants des enfants du même âge que le sien. L'infirmière doit prendre le temps d'observer le comportement de l'enfant, la relation mère-enfant. Elle doit aider la mère à exprimer ses inquiétudes et fournir des conseils judicieux. Il importe qu'elle revoit avec la mère les étapes de développement que traverse l'enfant et qu'elle lui explique les étapes suivantes. Elle doit tenter de répondre aux besoins de la mère de façon à éviter des problèmes subséquents.

Évaluation de la condition physique et émotive de l'enfant. Le médecin et l'infirmière procèdent à cette évaluation, basée sur les antécédents médicaux et obstétricaux de la mère, sur l'histoire de la santé de l'enfant, son comportement actuel et le niveau socio-économique de la famille.

L'infirmière doit connaître les normes de la croissance et du développement du nourrisson et de l'enfant, de façon à pouvoir reconnaître et évaluer les déviations de l'état normal. Ceci s'applique aussi aux étudiantes observant ou aidant à la clinique. Cette expérience ne leur est profitable que si elles possèdent des notions suffisantes sur la croissance et le développement d'un enfant.

Interprétation par l'infirmière des conseils du médecin. Il s'agit non seulement d'expliquer ce que le médecin a dit, mais aussi d'aider la mère à mettre en pratique les conseils médicaux, y compris ceux concernant la médecine préventive et l'hygiène mentale. Les infirmières ne prennent pas toujours conscience du fait qu'elles ont une contribution personnelle à offrir à la mère et à l'enfant. Leurs recommandations sont basées sur les ordonnances du médecin et sur l'ensemble de leurs connaissances.

Demande de consultation aux spécialistes appropriés. Référer un enfant à un membre spécialisé de l'équipe de santé est certainement une fonction nécessaire du personnel de la clinique. L'évaluation de chaque enfant et l'orientation vers un spécialiste sont les deux principales fonctions de la clinique.

Fonctions de l'infirmière

Les fonctions de l'infirmière consistent à créer une atmosphère chaleureuse, à assurer la bonne marche de la clinique, à recueillir les données qui sont de sa compétence et à renseigner le plus possible les mères et parfois les enfants. Le système des rendez-vous est important. Le nom de chaque patient doit être inscrit par ordre d'arrivée et tous les patients doivent être examinés par ordre de rendez-vous.

Le système de rendez-vous est un bon moyen pour vérifier si le bébé est amené régulièrement à la clinique pour être examiné et immunisé. Avant que la mère ne quitte la clinique, il faudrait lui fixer l'heure et la date du prochain rendez-vous et les indiquer dans le carnet destiné à cet usage.

Éducation des parents. L'éducation des parents obtient peu de résultats, à moins que ceux-ci ne soient prêts à recevoir les recommandations du personnel de l'équipe de santé. Leur intérêt augmente si les conseils donnés sont spécifiques et concernent vraiment leur enfant.

L'enseignement doit être simple et s'attacher à l'essentiel. Trop de détails tendent à embrouiller les parents. L'enseignement atteint son but lorsque les parents prennent eux-mêmes conscience de leurs difficultés et suggèrent des solutions appropriées.

Les méthodes audio-visuelles sont utiles pour concrétiser la théorie; une image demeure plus longtemps dans l'esprit qu'un mot. On doit vérifier le degré de compréhension des parents en leur posant des questions pertinentes. L'enseignement aux parents doit tenir compte de leur niveau social, de leur capacité économique et de leur niveau intellectuel. On devrait leur fournir des brochures; celles-ci sont très efficaces si elles sont distri-

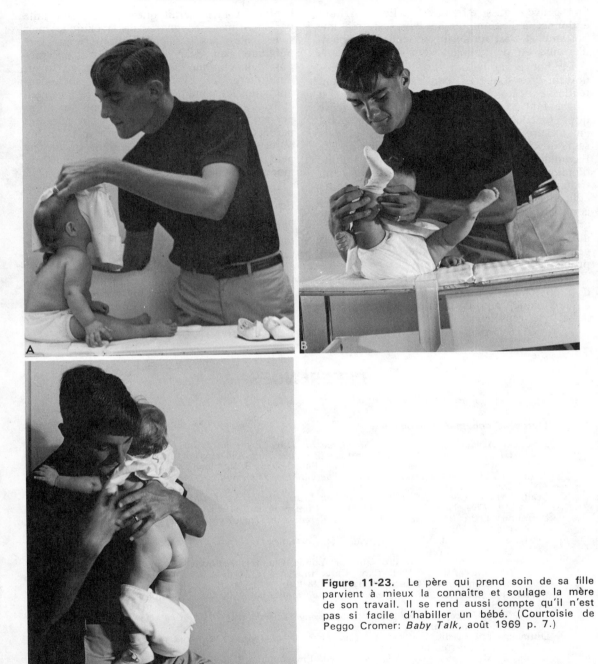

Figure 11-23. Le père qui prend soin de sa fille parvient à mieux la connaître et soulage la mère de son travail. Il se rend aussi compte qu'il n'est pas si facile d'habiller un bébé. (Courtoisie de Peggo Cromer: *Baby Talk*, août 1969 p. 7.)

buées pour répondre à des questions spécifiques et si elles sont lues avec les parents.

La principale motivation des parents demeure leur désir de garder leur enfant en bonne santé. S'ils sont indifférents à sa santé, ils ne profiteront probablement pas des renseignements qui leur sont donnés.

L'emploi du temps journalier de l'enfant doit être planifié avec la mère. Des suggestions pour aider à la croissance du jeune enfant peuvent aussi être offertes. La nourriture à donner à l'enfant ou au bébé est très importante et c'est un sujet sur lequel beaucoup d'erreurs ou de préjugés sont répandus.

Le but et le besoin des visites régulières doivent être soulignés, car les parents auront tendance à les considérer comme inutiles si leur enfant paraît bien portant. C'est la mère qui, étant continuellement avec l'enfant, est en mesure de remarquer les signes précurseurs de la maladie. Il est important qu'elle reconnaisse ces signes et comprenne l'utilité d'indiquer ses observations afin d'assurer un traitement efficace pour le bébé. Des cours collectifs peuvent être donnés aux mères sur certains sujets d'intérêt commun: comme, par exemple, le genre de vêtements appropriés aux conditions atmosphériques, les principes généraux de nutrition et le contrôle de certains problèmes du comportement.

Visites à domicile. La visite à domicile doit être faite après que l'enfant soit venu à la clinique, afin d'observer l'entourage familial, de renseigner la mère et d'examiner l'enfant. L'idéal serait que la visite soit faite par l'infirmière en charge de la clinique mais si ceci n'est pas possible, l'infirmière en santé publique s'en chargera et enverra un rapport à la clinique. Durant sa visite au foyer, l'infirmière doit évaluer le niveau socio-économique, les conditions sanitaires, le logement et les facilités récréatives qui sont aussi importantes à la santé de l'enfant qu'à celle des parents. À la maison, l'infirmière peut mieux observer les relations mère-enfant qu'elle ne peut le faire dans l'atmosphère plus ou moins officielle de la clinique.

Équipe multidisciplinaire

Dans ces cliniques, l'infirmière doit s'habituer à travailler en équipe. Elle doit collaborer avec les autres membres de l'équipe tout en ajoutant toujours son apport spécifique. Les infirmières, en améliorant leur compétence et en accroissant leur autonomie, peuvent participer à élever la qualité des soins dispensés aux parents et aux enfants.

RÉFÉRENCES

Livres et documents officiels

American Academy of Pediatrics: *Standards for Day Care Centers for Infants and Children Under 3 Years of Age.* Evanston, Ill., American Academy of Pediatrics, 1971.
Ames, L. B.: *Child Care and Development.* Philadelphie, J. B. Lippincott Company, 1970.
Anthony, E. J. et Koupernik, C. (édit): *The Child in His Family.* New York, John Wiley & Sons, Inc., 1970.
Beadle, M.: *A Child's Mind; How Children Learn During the Critical Years from Birth to Age Five.* New York, Doubleday & Company, Inc., 1970.
Brazelton, T. B.: *Infants and Mothers; Differences in Development.* New York, Delacorte Press, 1969.
Brody, S. et Axelrad, S.: *Anxiety and Ego Formation in Infancy.* New York, International Universities Press, 1970.
Brooks, M. R.: Stimulation Program for Young Children Performed by a Public Health Nurse as Part of Well Baby Care; in *ANA Clinical Sessions, 1970.* New York, Appleton-Century-Crofts, 1971, pp. 128-139.
Caplan, F. (édit.): *Les douze premiers mois de mon enfant.* Montréal, Éditions de l'Homme, 1973.
Cratty, B. J.: *Perceptual and Motor Development in Infants and Children.* New York, The Macmillan Company, 1970.
Dittmann, L. L. (édit.): *What We Can Learn from Infants.* Washington, D. C., National Association for the Education of Young Children, 1970.
Duvall, E. M.: *Family Development.* 4e éd. Philadelphie, J. B. Lippincott Company, 1971.
Erikson, E.: *Enfance et société.* 2e éd., Paris, Neuchâtel, Delachaux et Niestlé, 1966.
Escalona, S.: *Roots of Individuality.* Chicago, Aldine Pub. Co., 1968.
Freeman, R.: *Le nursing social.* Montréal, Holt, Rinehart et Winston, 1973.
Gesell, A., Ilg, F. et Bates, L.: *Infant and Child.* New York, Harper & Row, 3e éd., 1974.
Gouin-Décarie, T.: *Le développement psychologique de l'enfant.* 2e éd. Genève, Delachaux et Niestlé, 1973.
Illingworth, R. S. (édit.): *Development of the Infant and Young Child.* 4e éd., Baltimore, Williams & Wilkins Company, 1970.
Koupernik, C.: *Développement neuro-psychique du nourrisson.* Paris, P.U.F., 1968.
Laboratoires Ross: *Iron Nutrition in Infancy.* Columbus, Ohio, 1970.
Lambert-Lagacé, L.: *Comment nourrir son enfant.* Montréal, Éditions de l'Homme, 1974.
Lévy, J.: *L'éveil du tout-petit.* Paris, Éditions du Seuil, 1972.

Lewis, M.: *Clinical Aspects of Child Development*. Philadelphie, Lea & Febiger, 1971.
Mackeith, R. et autres: *Infant Feeding and Feeding Difficulties*. 4e éd. Baltimore, Williams & Wilkins Company, 1971.
McCammon, R. W.: *Human Growth and Development*. Springfield, Ill., Charles C Thomas, 1970.
Ministère de la Santé et du Bien-être social: *La mère canadienne et son enfant*. Division de l'hygiène maternelle et infantile. Ottawa, Gouvernement du Canada, 1967.
Piaget, J.: *Six études de psychologie*. Genève, Gonthier, 1964.
Prudden, S. et Sussman, J.: *La gymnastique des bébés*. Verviers, Marabout, 1975.
Richmond, P. G.: *An Introduction to Piaget*. New York, Basic Books, Inc., 1971.
Saul, L. J.: *Emotional Maturity: The Development and Dynamics of Personality*. 3e éd. Philadelphie, J. B. Lippincott Company, 1971.
Talbot, N. B., Kagan, J. et Eisenberg, L.: *Behavioral Science in Pediatric Medicine*. Philadelphie, W. B. Saunders Company, 1971.
White, B. L.: *Human Infants Experience and Psychological Development*. Englewood Cliffs, New Jersey, Prentice-Hall, 1971.

Articles

Aichlmayr, R. H.: Cultural Understanding: A Key to Acceptance. *Nursing Outlook*, 17:20, juillet 1969.
Alexander, M. M.: Homemade Fun for Infants. *Am. J. Nursing*, 70:2557, décembre 1970.
Alpert, J. J. et autres: Attitudes and Satisfactions of Low-Income Families Receiving Comprehensive Pediatric Care. *Am. J. Pub. Health*, 60:499, mars 1970.
Degrez, F.: Sevrage... sevrer. *L'enfant*, 41:469, 6, 1966.
Dodge, W. F. et autres: Patterns of Maternal Desires for Child Health Care. *Am. J. Pub. Health*, 60:1421, août 1970.
Freemon, B. L. et autres: How Do Nurses Expand Their Roles in Well Child Care? *Am. J. Nursing*, 72:1866, octobre 1972.
Gordis, L. et Markowitz, M.: Evaluation of the Effectiveness of Comprehensive and Continuous Pediatric Care. *Pediatrics*, 48:766, novembre 1971.
Ishida, M. et autres: Introducing Solid Foods to Infants. *Journ. Obst. & Gynec. Nursing*, 2:27, 5, 1973.
Kagan, J.: Do Infants Think? *Scientific American*, 226:74, mars 1972.
Kendall, N., Vaughan, V. C. et Kusakcioglu, A.: A Study of Preparation of Infant Formulas. A Medical and Sociocultural Appraisal. *Am. J. Dis. Child.*, 122:215, septembre 1971.
Kerber, J.: Alimentation du nourrisson normal. *Revue de l'infirmière et de l'assistante sociale*, 20:133, 2, 1970.
Klaus, M. H. et autres: Human Maternal Behavior at the First Contact with Her Young. *Pediatrics*, 46:187, août 1970.
Kravitz, H.: The Cotton-Tipped Swab: A Major Cause of Ear Injury and Hearing Loss. *Clin. Ped.*, 13:965, 11, 1974.
Krueger, J. M.: Spectographic Analysis of the Differing Cries of a Normal Two Month Old Infant. *Nursing Research*, 19:459, septembre-octobre 1970.
Parham, E.: The Effect of Early Feeding on the Development of Obesity. *Journ. Obst. & Gynec. Nursing*, 3:58, 3, 1974.
Porter, L. S.: The Impact of Physical-Physiological Activity on Infants' Growth and Development. *Nursing Research*, 21:210, mai-juin 1972.
Rivera, J.: The Frequency of Use of Various Kinds of Milk During Infancy in Middle and Lower Income Families. *Am. J. Pub. Health*, 61:277, février, 1971.
Saint-Macary, M.: Nouveau-né et nourrisson normaux. *Soins*, 1re partie: 18:41, 9, 1973. 2e partie: 18:19, 10, 1973.
Scahill, M.: Helping the Mother Solve Problems with Feeding Her Infant. *Journ. Obst. & Gynec. Nursing*, 4:51, 2, 1975.
Smitherman, C.: The Vocal Behavior of Infants as Related to the Nursing Procedure of Rocking. *Nursing Research*, 18:256, mai-juin 1969.
Spencer, V. L.: A Pilot Study to Determine Why Mothers Attend Child Health Conferences. *Canad. J. Pub. Health*, 60:116, mars 1969.
Tapia, J. A.: The Nursing Process in Family Health. *Nursing Outlook*, 20:267, avril 1972.
Warren, F.: Getting a Quick Reading on an Infant's Blood Pressure. *Nursing'75*, 5:13, 4, 1975.

12

pathologies des nourrissons nécessitant des soins immédiats ou de courte durée

L'hospitalisation du nourrisson constitue souvent une expérience nouvelle pour la mère et pour le bébé. Lorsque la mère est inquiète on devrait l'encourager à faire part de ses craintes au sujet de la santé de son enfant, l'amenant ainsi à surmonter l'anxiété qui peut perturber son bébé.

Il est évident que toute maladie, même très courte, peut perturber l'état émotif de l'enfant. Surtout si, lors de l'hospitalisation, il est privé de la présence maternelle, s'il subit de longues périodes d'immobilisation pour recevoir des traitements ou si l'alimentation est supprimée temporairement.

PATHOLOGIES RESPIRATOIRES

VOIES RESPIRATOIRES DU NOURRISSON. Les voies respiratoires du bébé sont de petites dimensions. C'est la raison pour laquelle toute obstruction causée par de l'œdème, des muco-sités ou par un corps étranger peut avoir de sérieuses conséquences. Si l'obstruction est étendue et haut placée dans les voies respiratoires, elle affecte le poumon entier; si elle est basse, seuls les tissus au-dessous du point obstrué seront atteints.

MALADIES DES VOIES RESPIRATOIRES. *Incidence.* Les maladies respiratoires, un des plus grands problèmes de santé chez les enfants, figurent encore parmi les 5 grandes causes de mortalité infantile. L'âge de l'enfant détermine en grande partie le type de maladie respiratoire dont il sera affligé et les symptômes qui apparaîtront.

Malgré leur fréquence chez les nourrissons, il est difficile de considérer les infections respiratoires comme des entités cliniques distinctes, car la muqueuse des voies respiratoires est continue et s'étend du nez aux ramifications bronchiques. Elle tapisse les parois des sinus et pénètre jusqu'à l'oreille moyenne par la trompe d'Eustache et une infection des voies respiratoires supérieures s'étendra souvent aux organes adjacents ou aux voies respiratoires inférieures.

Épidémiologie. L'air véhicule les germes infectieux d'une personne à l'autre. L'enfant inspire les microbes transportés par de minuscules gouttelettes d'eau ou par des particules de poussière. Ces microbes peuvent aggraver l'infection de l'enfant déjà atteint et qui, à son tour, en contaminera d'autres.

Ces germes pathogènes meurent rapidement au grand air, grâce à l'action des rayons ultra-violets du soleil et parce que cette température est défavorable à leur croissance. En été, parce que les bébés et les enfants sont plus souvent à l'extérieur, et que les maisons sont mieux aérées, les grippes sont moins fréquentes. Mais en hiver, quand on garde les enfants à l'intérieur, on facilite la contamination croisée et les grippes se propagent dans la famille, et aussi aux compagnons de jeux ou de classe. Durant les premières années scolaires, les enfants sont plus sujets aux infections des voies respiratoires supérieures parce qu'ils y sont plus fréquemment exposés et qu'ils n'ont pas encore développé suffisamment de résistance. Les enfants infectés, d'âge préscolaire et scolaire, sont donc une source d'infection pour les bébés dont la résistance aux maladies est encore très faible.

Étiologie. L'infection demeure le facteur étiologique le plus commun des maladies respiratoires de la période postnatale. Le nourrisson peut également aspirer des corps étrangers ou des substances irritantes contenant de l'huile ou des produits chimiques comme le stéarate de zinc contenu dans certaines poudres.

Une infection aiguë peut être causée par des virus ou des bactéries. Depuis plusieurs années, on reconnaît le virus de l'influenza et l'hemophilus influenzae comme les principaux organismes causant les infections respiratoires. Récemment, plusieurs autres virus ont cependant été isolés, tels les adénovirus, les virus Coxsackie, le virus ECHO (Enteric Cytopathegenic Human Orphan) et le virus SR (virus syncytial respiratoire).

Soins infirmiers généraux

Repos. On ne saurait exagérer l'importance du repos au cours de la période aiguë de ces maladies. L'enfant ressent le besoin de dormir: on le tient à l'écart des bruits et des mouvements habituels de la maison, des fatigues causées par les visites ou les activités des frères et sœurs. À l'hôpital, on doit éviter les occasions de faire pleurer le nourrisson, car les pleurs le fatiguent beaucoup.

Ingestion de liquide. Le bébé n'absorbe que de petites quantités de liquide à la fois et on doit lui en offrir très souvent. Parce qu'il est incapable de téter et de respirer en même temps, on lui ménage plusieurs pauses lorsqu'il tète ou qu'il prend son biberon. Il faut davantage de liquide à l'enfant assez âgé pour boire à la tasse. De petits verres, de jolies tasses, des chalumeaux gaiement colorés, facilitent l'absorption du liquide. Il est important que l'enfant boive des jus, du jello liquide, de l'eau glucosée ou d'autres liquides clairs à intervalles rapprochés afin de bien l'hydrater et de liquéfier ses sécrétions. Le lait rend souvent les sécrétions plus visqueuses et son apport devrait être diminué.

Humidité. On devrait maintenir la concentration de l'humidité dans la chambre entre 80 et 90%, de manière à liquéfier les sécrétions des voies respiratoires et à réduire ainsi la toux. D'excellents humidificateurs se vendent dans le commerce. Un récipient peu profond, rempli d'eau ou des serviettes mouillées placées sur un radiateur, jouent le même rôle, mais, à moins que le radiateur ne soit très chaud, l'évaporation sera lente ce qui n'augmentera pas suffisamment le taux d'humidité. On maintiendra la température de la pièce aux environs de 21°C.

Drainage nasal. On facilite le drainage des sécrétions nasales en plaçant l'enfant sur l'abdomen et en surélevant le pied du lit. À l'hôpital, on peut utiliser un appareil aspirateur, en tenant compte du fait qu'il peut blesser les muqueuses.

Une méthode plus efficace pour extraire les sécrétions, sans utiliser d'appareil, est la suivante: on instille une goutte de soluté salin physiologique dans chaque narine; puis, à l'aide d'un chiffon humide, on effectue des pressions douces, régulières et rythmiques, à partir de la racine du nez jusqu'aux bords des narines. On obtient ainsi une meilleure évacuation des sécrétions.

Gouttes nasales. On n'utilise les gouttes nasales médicamenteuses que lorsque le nez de l'enfant est obstrué, au maximum toutes les 3 heures et ceci durant les deux ou trois premiers jours seulement. Il s'agit de provoquer une vaso-constriction au niveau de la muqueuse, de diminuer l'œdème qui cause l'impression d'étouffement si caractéristique, et de réduire un écoulement nasal excessif. On instille les gouttes dans le nez du bébé 15 à 20 minutes avant l'heure des repas et au moment du coucher. Un premier jet dilue les sécrétions que l'on enlève avant d'appliquer une deuxième fois les gouttes. La deuxième instillation soulagera alors efficacement la congestion nasale. L'infirmière doit s'assurer que le nez du bébé est dégagé de toute sécrétion avant de le nourrir et de le mettre au lit.

À cause du danger de contamination, on utilise une bouteille et un compte-gouttes individuels. Un compte-gouttes en matière plastique ou en caoutchouc évite de blesser le nez de l'enfant. Si on utilise une seule bouteille pour plusieurs enfants, on doit disposer d'un compte-gouttes pour chaque enfant et ne jamais le remettre dans la bouteille après usage. On doit toujours tenir la bouteille de gouttes nasales hors de la portée de l'enfant.

Pour instiller les gouttes, on couche l'enfant sur le dos, la tête dépassant le bord du lit ou le cou posé sur une couverture roulée. Une légère rotation de la tête empêche les gouttes de couler directement dans le pharynx. L'infirmière maintient le visage avec sa main gauche qui encercle le menton et les joues, pendant qu'elle instille les gouttes avec sa main droite. Si une telle contrainte ne suffit pas et qu'une deuxième infirmière n'est pas disponible, on peut aussi envelopper l'enfant complètement comme une momie. Après l'instillation des gouttes, on maintient la tête du bébé plus basse que les épaules pendant une ou deux minutes. L'infirmière ou la mère peut garder le bébé sur ses genoux, dans la position qui lui sera la plus confortable, pourvu que sa tête soit projetée en arrière.

Seul l'enfant plus âgé peut utiliser le vaporisateur et encore faut-il exercer une surveillance étroite pour éviter qu'il n'en fasse un usage abusif.

Prévention de l'excoriation de la lèvre. L'excoriation de la lèvre supérieure, avec la possibilité d'infection qu'elle comporte, provient de l'irritation causée par l'écoulement nasal. L'application d'une crème adoucissante ou de vaseline prévient cette complication.

Médication. Administrer des médicaments aux petits enfants n'est pas toujours tâche facile. On écrase les pilules ou les tablettes et on les mélange à de l'eau ou du sirop, avant de les administrer à la cuillère. Si le nourrisson est quelque peu récalcitrant, il sera plus sûr d'administrer la médication avec un petit verre à médicament ou avec un compte-gouttes. On évitera ainsi les pertes, si le bébé remue ou ferme prématurément sa bouche. Il est toujours préférable d'offrir un biberon au nourrisson après l'ingestion d'un médicament.

Position. On change souvent la position de l'enfant. Le bébé respire mieux couché sur le côté car les sécrétions peuvent s'écouler à l'extérieur.

Il est bon d'alterner les positions déclive, semi-assise et latérale. La position dorsale est à éviter.

Nettoyage du nez. Dès que l'enfant peut comprendre, on lui enseigne la bonne méthode pour dégager les voies nasales. Il doit garder la bouche ouverte et souffler les sécrétions des deux narines à la fois. On ne devrait jamais lui dire: « Ferme la bouche et souffle fort » car les sécrétions peuvent alors s'engager dans la trompe d'Eustache et provoquer une otite moyenne.

Prévention. On doit isoler les enfants souffrant d'une infection des voies respiratoires de manière à éviter tout contact avec les enfants non atteints. Un enfant qui a une alimentation bien équilibrée ne contracte pas facilement la grippe ou le rhume. Les enfants acquièrent une résistance à l'infection en y étant exposés et en fabriquant les anticorps protecteurs. Les vaccins actuels contre la grippe ne sont pas utilisés pour les nourrissons.

Rhinopharyngite aiguë (Rhume ordinaire).

La rhinopharyngite aiguë, infection respiratoire la plus courante chez les bébés et les jeunes enfants, touche les sinus et le nasopharynx. La difficulté du traitement provient du fait que l'infection se propage rapidement, d'où la possibilité de complications sérieuses. Le tableau clinique du bébé ou de l'enfant diffère de celui de l'adulte.

Étiologie. Le rhume ordinaire est causé par un virus filtrant ou un groupe de virus qui provoquent une inflammation aiguë des voies respiratoires supérieures. Les bactéries, telles le pneumocoque, le streptocoque hémolytique ou le staphylocoque causent l'infection purulente qui vient presque toujours compliquer un rhume banal.

Facteurs favorisants. La résistance à l'infection varie suivant les individus. L'âge, l'alimentation, la fatigue, le degré de température du corps et l'état psychique peuvent influer sur la gravité ou l'évolution du rhume.

Immunité. On ne possède pas d'immunité prolongée contre le rhume. On doit donc protéger les enfants qui offrent en plus très peu de résistance à l'infection. De sérieuses complications sont à craindre pour les enfants qui vivent en groupe dans des écoles, dans des hôpitaux ou dans d'autres institutions.

Physio-pathologie. La lésion initiale est un œdème de la sous-muqueuse, suivi d'une infiltration leucocytaire. Il y a alors séparation des cellules épithéliales et destruction de l'épithélium nasal.

Manifestations cliniques. L'enfant devient irritable et agité. Il éternue et souffre d'un écoulement nasal fluide, qui par la suite deviendra purulent. Ces sécrétions irritent le bord des narines et la lèvre supérieure.

Il respire difficilement, la bouche ouverte, en raison de la congestion des muqueuses nasales. La gorge hyperhémiée devient douloureuse; certains ganglions lymphatiques cervicaux augmentent de volume. Souvent des troubles gastro-intestinaux comme des vomissements ou de la diarrhée s'ajoutent aux troubles respiratoires. Une température de 39°C à 40°C est courante chez les malades âgés de moins de 2 – 3 ans. Pour les enfants d'âge préscolaire, la température ne dépassera guère 39°C tandis que l'écolier ou l'adulte aura peu ou pas de fièvre.

L'anorexie, la toux, la fatigue, les courbatures sont courantes. L'obstruction des narines peut empêcher le bébé de téter, car il ne peut respirer par la bouche et sucer en même temps.

Diagnostic différentiel. Il est parfois difficile de diagnostiquer un rhume chez le petit enfant, car le tableau clinique ressemble souvent à celui de nombreuses maladies infectieuses: rougeole, coqueluche, poliomyélite ou syphilis congénitale. L'écoulement nasal d'une rhinite allergique peut laisser croire aux premiers symptômes d'une rhinopharyngite; il n'est cependant pas suivi d'écoulement purulent comme dans la grippe. Dans un cas d'allergie, les muqueuses nasales deviennent pâles et œdémateuses. Dans la rhinopharyngite, l'inflammation est évidente.

Complications. De sérieuses complications comme la sinusite, l'otite moyenne, la mastoïdite, l'abcès cérébral (dû à une extension de l'infection à partir de l'os mastoïde), la trachéite, la bronchite, la pneumonie, la pleurésie ou l'empyème se présentent plus souvent chez les bébés que chez les enfants plus âgés et sont causés par l'extension de l'infection aux structures adjacentes ou inférieures.

Traitement. Le traitement est largement symptomatique. À l'hôpital, on isole l'enfant. Il est important de maintenir un bon état nutritif par une diète convenable et des vitamines appropriées; on essaie d'augmenter l'ingestion de liquide. On garde l'enfant au lit pendant la période fébrile.

Il faut soulager la congestion nasale pour que le bébé puisse téter ou boire facilement. On instille du soluté salin physiologique en gouttes nasales et si cette mesure est inefficace, des gouttes médicamenteuses en solution aqueuse, telles que néosynéphrine (0,25%) ou éphédrine (0,5 à 1%) sont utili-

sées pour diminuer l'œdème et favoriser le drainage. Quelle que soit la médication, on emploie en général, pour les bébés et les jeunes enfants, la moitié ou le quart de la dose pour adulte. On ne doit jamais utiliser des gouttes nasales huileuses à cause du danger de pneumonie lipoïdique.

Les médicaments antipyrétiques font baisser la température. On donne habituellement 65mg (1 grain) d'aspirine en 2 ou 3 doses par jour. Le dosage basé sur le poids de l'enfant (65 mg par kg par 24 heures) est plus précis et plus sûr que celui qui est basé sur l'âge (1 grain par année d'âge par 24 heures). À l'enfant plus âgé on donne 0,3 g (5 grains) d'aspirine aux mêmes intervalles. On devrait cesser cette médication après quelques jours, car l'emploi abusif de salicylate peut intoxiquer l'organisme ou causer des effets secondaires sérieux. Une médication antipyrétique à base d'acétaminophène (Tempra-Tylénol) est préférée à l'aspirine.

Les sulfamides et les antibiotiques ne devraient pas être utilisés de façon routinière dans le traitement de la rhinopharyngite. Ils sont cependant indiqués en cas de complications ou d'infection prolongée. Il semble que les décongestionnants, les antihistaminiques et les expectorants n'aient que peu d'action sur les jeunes enfants. Il faut surtout éviter les antitussifs puissants qui diminuent le réflexe de la toux et favorisent par ce fait la broncho-aspiration des sécrétions du rhino-pharynx. On procède régulièrement au drainage nasal, l'enfant ne sachant pas encore se moucher.

Otite moyenne aiguë (purulente)

Étiologie et incidence. L'otite moyenne est une affection de l'oreille moyenne, d'origine infectieuse ou allergique. Suivant généralement une infection respiratoire supérieure, elle apparaît surtout pendant les mois les plus froids de l'année. Elle peut également suivre la rougeole ou la scarlatine.

Durant la première année de la vie, le principal agent causal est l'hémophilus influenzae. Le pneumocoque, le streptocoque bêtahémolytique ou le staphylocoque sont responsables des infections bactériennes aiguës. Chez les enfants plus âgés, l'hypertrophie des tissus adénoïdes autour de l'ouverture de la trompe d'Eustache, peut être la cause d'une otite moyenne séreuse récidivante, qui peut se transformer en otite purulente. L'otite moyenne est très commune chez les bébés, car la trompe d'Eustache qui relie le pharynx et l'oreille moyenne est plus courte, plus large et plus droite que chez l'enfant plus âgé. Le nourrisson repose la plupart du temps dans son lit, la tête tournée sur le côté et les sécrétions infectées trouvent un accès rapide et facile à travers la trompe d'Eustache vers la caisse du tympan.

Manifestations cliniques, diagnostic, évolution et complications. Au début de l'otite moyenne, l'œdème ferme très vite la trompe d'Eustache et empêche l'entrée de l'air dans la caisse du tympan, ce qui se traduit par la transsudation d'un liquide séreux dans l'oreille moyenne. À ce stade, l'otite est séreuse. La présence des organismes pathogènes entraîne l'infection du liquide en vase clos et provoque alors une otite infectieuse.

Les *symptômes* consécutifs ou concommitants de la nasopharyngite sont accompagnés d'une douleur de plus en plus forte, au fur et à mesure que la pression du liquide augmente dans l'oreille moyenne.

L'examen du tympan avec un otoscope permet de faire le *diagnostic*. Le tympan est bombé et moins luisant que normalement. S'il y a rupture tympanique, on peut faire un prélèvement des sécrétions de l'oreille moyenne, en vue d'une culture.

L'enfant plus âgé se plaindra de douleurs aiguës à l'oreille, mais certains bébés peuvent n'être qu'irritables, sans donner d'indices de souffrance au niveau de l'oreille. D'autres nourrissons vont tirer ou frotter leur oreille ou bouger la tête d'un côté à l'autre. L'infection évolue rapidement. La température atteint facilement 40°C. Elle est parfois accompagnée de convulsions chez les bébés ou de frissons chez l'enfant plus âgé. Le petit enfant agité, de mauvaise humeur, souffre de troubles gastro-intestinaux et d'anorexie. La fièvre et la douleur persistent jusqu'à ce que l'inflammation soit contrôlée par des traitements appropriés ou que la rupture spontanée du tympan, qui devrait toujours être évitée, permette l'écoulement de l'exsudat purulent.

Les *complications infectieuses* sont rares et résultent d'une médication inadéquate et insuffisante. Elles peuvent inclure l'otite moyenne chronique, la méningite, la mastoïdite, l'abcès cérébral, une thrombophlébite ou thrombose du sinus latéral et la septicémie. Si une mastoïdite se déclare, une mastoïdectomie peut s'avérer nécessaire. La complication la plus fréquente est la récidive suivie d'une surdité progressive. Lorsque la membrane tympanique éclate spontanément, l'excès de liquide s'écoule, mais très souvent, il en demeure une certaine quantité dans l'oreille moyenne. Cet exsudat devient fibrineux et entraîne graduellement la surdité. Chaque nouvelle otite aggrave le handicap.

Traitement et soins. Les gouttes nasales diminuent l'œdème de la muqueuse et la trompe d'Eustache redevient perméable. L'application de chaleur sèche sur l'oreille ainsi que l'aspirine aident à soulager la douleur. Les gouttes auriculaires ne sont pas employées de façon routinière puisque leur effet est très variable et qu'elles rendent plus difficile l'examen du conduit auditif. Lorsqu'elles sont prescrites, on les instille après les avoir fait réchauffer.

Une myringotomie ou paracentèse du tympan consiste à pratiquer une nette incision à un point précis de la membrane tympanique et à drainer complètement le contenu de l'oreille moyenne. Ceci permet de soulager la douleur causée par la pression, empêche la fissure irrégulière du tympan causée par une rupture spontanée et prévient la transformation fibrineuse du liquide non écoulé. Après une myringotomie, une ponction ou une rupture spontanée du tympan, le médecin prescrira probablement l'irrigation de l'oreille avec de l'eau oxygénée. Des gouttes auriculaires antibiotiques pourront être ordonnées après la culture des sécrétions de l'oreille.

Instillation de gouttes auriculaires. L'infirmière place l'enfant dans une position permettant aux gouttes de couler du conduit auditif externe jusqu'au tympan. Une deuxième infirmière tient la tête et les mains de l'enfant qui peut être aussi enveloppé comme une momie. Les gouttes seront réchauffées au préalable. L'enfant sera maintenu quelques minutes sur un côté avant l'instillation des gouttes dans l'oreille du côté opposé.

Lavage de l'oreille. Pour ce traitement, il faut « momifier » l'enfant, à moins que sa mère ou une autre infirmière ne soit disponible pour le maintenir. Avant l'âge de 3 ans, on tire le pavillon de l'oreille vers le bas et en arrière; si l'enfant a trois ans ou plus, on exerce la traction vers le haut et en arrière, de manière à faciliter le passage du liquide jusqu'au tympan. Les caractéristiques anatomiques de l'enfant justifient ces précautions. Il faut utiliser du soluté physiologique salin ou du peroxyde d'hydrogène.

Chaleur locale. Une bouillotte (la température de l'eau ne dépassant pas 46°C) enveloppée dans un sac de flanelle peut être placée sous l'oreille affectée.

Tampon auriculaire. L'usage d'un tampon de coton ouaté dans l'oreille est peu recommandé; il peut bloquer le conduit auditif externe et empêcher l'écoulement des sécrétions purulentes vers l'extérieur. Celles-ci sont alors refoulées vers la région mastoïdienne et propagent l'infection. De plus, l'insertion répétée de coton ouaté dans les oreilles enseigne à l'enfant à introduire des corps étrangers dans son conduit auditif.

Si le tampon de coton ouaté est utilisé, il devra être petit, inséré peu profondément et changé fréquemment. Il faut éviter de le mouiller lors des soins du bébé. Si cela arrive il faut assécher l'oreille et insérer un autre tampon.

Soins de la peau. En présence d'un écoulement abondant, on enduit la peau autour de l'oreille d'une crème protectrice, pour éviter l'irritation ou l'impétigo. S'il y a démangeaison, on devrait restreindre les mouvements du bébé ou lui mettre des « mitaines » pour empêcher qu'il ne se gratte et ne propage l'infection.

Prévention. La prévention et le traitement de la rhinopharyngite constituent le meilleur moyen d'éviter l'otite aiguë du norrisson. Pour les enfants plus âgés, il peut être nécessaire de procéder à l'adénoïdectomie.

Otite moyenne séreuse

L'otite moyenne séreuse se manifeste par une accumulation d'exsudat séreux non infecté ou de sécrétions mucoïdes dans l'oreille moyenne. Ce type d'otite moyenne fait souvent suite à une rhinite allergique qui bloque la trompe d'Eustache. La circulation d'air cesse donc entre la caisse du tympan et l'extérieur, et il se produit une transsudation séreuse qui remplit l'oreille moyenne. L'enfant n'a ni douleur, ni fièvre, mais peut se plaindre d'une sensation de plénitude dans l'oreille. Quand il éternue, quand il se mouche ou qu'il baille, la trompe d'Eustache peut redevenir temporairement perméable, la sensation de plénitude disparaît alors et l'audition s'améliore. Après quelques minutes, les symptômes réapparaissent car la trompe d'Eustache s'est refermée. En l'absence de micro-organismes pathogènes, le liquide ne s'infecte pas mais il épaissit peu à peu jusqu'à former une substance gluante (fibrine) qui tapisse la paroi et les osselets et cause l'otite adhésive. La surdité définitive peut en découler.

Traitement. Il faut utiliser des vasoconstricteurs nasaux et des antihistaminiques. Des audiogrammes permettent de déterminer le degré de surdité.

Si la surdité devient un problème, des aspirations répétées de l'oreille moyenne peuvent être nécessaires ou en dernier ressort, de pe-

tits tubes en matière plastique (tubes de Shea) peuvent être insérés à travers la membrane du tympan pour permettre un drainage palliatif permanent et maintenir dans la caisse du tympan une pression égale à la pression atmosphérique. Ce type d'otite ne peut être soigné que par un pédiatre et un oto-rhino-laryngologiste.

Bronchiolite aiguë et pneumonie interstitielle

Ces deux termes sont interchangeables particulièrement en parlant de la maladie chez le nourrisson ou chez le jeune enfant. Il est difficile de supposer une bronchiolite pure, sans atteinte du tissu interstitiel. Dans la bronchiolite, l'expulsion de l'air des alvéoles s'avère plus difficile et provoque la surdistension du poumon, la dyspnée et parfois, la cyanose.

Incidence, épidémiologie et étiologie. La majorité de ces infections apparaissent durant les 6 premiers mois de la vie, rarement chez les enfants de plus de deux ans.

Elles se manifestent le plus souvent en hiver ou au début du printemps. Plusieurs cas surviennent sporadiquement; on constate cependant une incidence accrue de bronchiolite, au cours d'épidémie d'infections des voies respiratoires supérieures parmi les enfants d'âge scolaire et chez les adultes. Le sexe et la race n'influent pas sur la susceptibilité à la bronchiolite.

La maladie semble d'étiologie virale. On a incriminé le virus respiratoire syncytial (RS) dans la majorité des bronchiolites du nourrisson, particulièrement en hiver. Quelques autres virus ont aussi été découverts comme agents causals.

Manifestations cliniques, diagnostic et diagnostic différentiel. Les symptômes de la bronchiolite apparaissent plusieurs jours après une infection des voies respiratoires supérieures et varient en gravité. Les symptômes respiratoires sont beaucoup plus importants que les signes de toxicité.

L'enfant a une toux sèche, persistante, avec dyspnée progressive. Il y a une inflammation diffuse de la muqueuse bronchique, il se forme un exsudat épais qui diminue le calibre des bronchioles. Physiologiquement, les bronchioles se dilatent à l'inspiration et se contractent à l'expiration; au cours de la maladie, l'air qui pénètre dans les alvéoles ne peut en ressortir lors de l'expiration. Les poumons se dilatent (emphysème); l'inspiration est difficile et la cage thoracique s'affaisse peu à l'expiration.

La température varie, se maintenant ordinairement entre 38°C et 38,5°C. Il n'y a pas de relations entre la fièvre et la gravité clinique de la maladie.

Les vomissements et la diarrhée présentent généralement peu de gravité, mais l'alimentation du bébé peut devenir un problème à cause de la dyspnée qui l'empêche de téter normalement. Le nourrisson est alerte, mais devient irritable et anxieux. La respiration est rapide et superficielle et on entend un grognement expiratoire caractéristique. L'enfant utilise ses muscles respiratoires accessoires et on constate un tirage susternal et sous-costal à l'inspiration. Les poumons se dilatent, l'hématose est perturbée. Le nourrisson cyanose ou devient très pâle. Le refus de boire et la perte d'eau par l'hyperventilation expliquent la déshydratation aiguë qui apparaît quelquefois. L'air ingéré par le nourrisson qui pleure entraîne des coliques qui accentuent le malaise et l'irritabilité du bébé.

Des examens fluoroscopiques et radiographiques montrent un emphysème obstructif de degré variable, avec ou sans infiltration parenchymateuse diffuse. Le nombre de globules blancs est normal; les cultures de nasopharynx demeurent négatives.

La maladie se manifeste par des symptômes qui la rendent difficile à différencier d'autres maladies comme l'asthme, la mucoviscidose avec lésions pulmonaires, la tuberculose miliaire, la coqueluche, l'aspiration de substances irritantes, l'empoisonnement aux salicylates et la broncho-pneumonie bactérienne.

Pronostic et complications. Le *pronostic* est généralement bon si l'enfant reçoit une thérapie de support, prompte et appropriée. Le taux de mortalité est bas mais la mort peut survenir par épuisement et anoxie.

Parmi les *complications* qui peuvent faire suite à un état aigu, on rencontre la bronchopneumonie bactérienne, l'otite moyenne, l'atélectasie pulmonaire avec abcès et l'insuffisance cardiaque.

Traitement. Le traitement vise tout particulièrement à maintenir l'oxygénation adéquate du sang. On place l'enfant dans une atmosphère à humidité élevée. La vapeur froide est préférable à la vapeur chaude. Ceci liquéfie les sécrétions et facilite l'expulsion des mucosités. On donne de l'oxygène aux nourrissons, même atteints de dyspnée légère, avant que n'apparaisse la cyanose. L'aspiration des sécrétions trachéo-bronchiques peut s'avérer nécessaire. On maintient la tête et le thorax de l'enfant légèrement surélevés. Cette position facilite la respiration, les organes abdominaux ne faisant pas pression sur le diaphragme. La thérapie antimicrobienne est utilisée seulement pour les enfants qui présentent une complication bactérienne et le traitement n'est commencé qu'après le prélèvement des sécrétions en vue de la culture. De grandes quantités de sédatifs ou d'opiacés ont tendance à déprimer les centres respiratoires et les réflexes de la toux. On donne cependant de petites doses de sédatif (phénobarbital) pour calmer un enfant placé dans une tente à humidité (Croupette). On augmente la quantité de liquide ingéré parce que la tachypnée favorise la déshydratation et le médecin peut ordonner des vitamines hydrosolubles.

Soins infirmiers. En planifiant les soins infirmiers d'un nourrisson gravement malade, on doit tenir compte de son état physique et émotif et on ne peut ignorer les réactions de ses parents.

Les parents anxieux et angoissés prennent probablement sur eux la responsabilité de l'état de l'enfant. Ils manquent souvent d'informations sur la maladie, sur son traitement et sur les soins à donner. La séparation d'avec l'enfant et les problèmes soulevés par son hospitalisation peuvent augmenter leur angoisse. Il faut leur expliquer le traitement et tous deux doivent recevoir un support moral, du réconfort et la permission de demeurer auprès de leur bébé aussi longtemps qu'ils le désirent.

L'infirmière doit observer l'état respiratoire de l'enfant et signaler immédiatement tout signe de détresse. Les modifications du pouls et de la température sont également significatives.

Soins particuliers. Une « croupette » aide à soulager ces enfants. Elle permet de procurer une quantité suffisante d'humidité et d'oxygène, à une température convenant au petit malade. L'enfant respire mieux avec une concentration plus élevée d'oxygène et l'humidité liquéfie les sécrétions dans les bronchioles, rendant la toux moins pénible. On peut utiliser de l'air sous pression pour propulser l'humidité si l'apport d'oxygène n'est pas nécessaire.

La tente de la « croupette », faite en plastique transparent, permet une surveillance plus facile de l'état du malade. Le tissu de plastique doit être bien tiré et replié adéquatement sous le matelas de façon à éviter les fuites d'oxygène et d'humidité.

L'oxygène ou l'air sous pression qui passe dans un récipient d'eau distillée procure l'humidité nécessaire. On nettoie soigneusement le filtre chaque fois que l'on remplit le bocal d'eau distillée. Le récipient placé à l'arrière

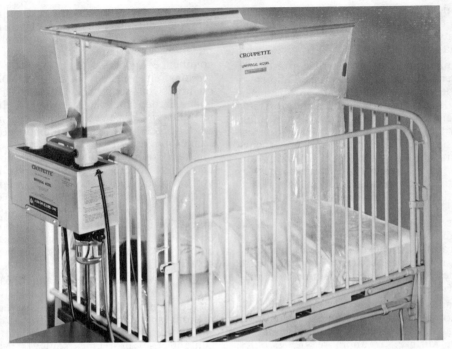

Figure 12-1. Dans la croupette, on peut donner à l'enfant de l'oxygène et de l'humidité tout en le sur-veillant étroitement. (Courtoisie Air Shields Inc., Hatboro, Penna.)

de la « croupette » contient de la glace en vue de rafraîchir la tente. On place une couverture de flanelle sur le drap pour permettre l'absorption de l'excès d'humidité. On couvre l'enfant d'un bonnet et d'une chemisette qui l'empêchent de prendre froid.

On change les couvertures et le linge de l'enfant dès qu'ils deviennent humides. Pour éviter de trop le déranger, on procède avec beaucoup de ménagement, profitant de l'heure de sa médication et de ses repas. Lorsque l'on maintient le nourrisson couvert, on peut éviter de changer ses vêtements trop souvent et de nuire à son repos.

On note le traitement de façon précise: la date et l'heure où l'on a installé l'enfant dans la « croupette » et où on l'a enlevé de celle-ci. Le débit d'oxygène est prescrit par le médecin.

On surveille attentivement la réaction de l'enfant au traitement, en notant sa coloration, son rythme respiratoire et son degré d'agitation. On donne au bébé un de ses jouets favoris pour lui tenir compagnie en évitant les animaux en peluche ou ceux pouvant produire des étincelles. Les jouets musicaux sont les plus appropriés étant donné leur effet régulateur sur la respiration.

On augmente l'ingestion de liquide en offrant souvent des jus entre les repas. Si l'in-

firmière ne peut retirer l'enfant de la « croupette », elle doit l'aider en soutenant sa tête et son dos d'une main, tandis qu'elle tient le biberon de l'autre. L'orifice de la tétine doit être assez large pour qu'il n'ait pas à se fatiguer en tétant trop vigoureusement, mais il ne doit pas être trop large afin d'éviter qu'il ne boive trop rapidement. Avant de faire boire l'enfant, on enlève les sécrétions nasales qui le forcent à respirer par la bouche. À ce moment et fréquemment, entre les repas, on doit aider le nourrisson à expulser des gaz, car il peut souffrir de coliques douloureuses, par suite d'aérophagie.

Seul le médecin peut ordonner les vitamines, les antibiotiques et les sédatifs, mais l'infirmière doit se rappeler que, pour l'enfant, respirer est laborieux, et que tout médicament doit être donné très lentement, en lui soulevant la tête.

Aspiration de corps étrangers

Étiologie, physio-pathologie, manifestations cliniques et diagnostics radiologiques. L'enfant peut avaler de petits objets, tels épingles de sûreté, pièces de monnaie, arachides, perles de colliers ou certains morceaux de jouets qu'il porte à sa bouche. La négligence des mères ou des infirmières qui laissent de tels objets à la portée de l'enfant, ou qui lui donnent des jouets non adaptés à son âge, est le plus souvent responsable de tels accidents.

Les lésions dépendent de la nature, du volume de l'objet et du degré d'obstruction des voies respiratoires. Une obstruction sérieuse peut causer de l'emphysème, de l'atélectasie ou un abcès pulmonaire.

Une particule de nourriture peut se loger dans les bronches et causer une obstruction inflammatoire distale. Dans ce cas, l'enfant souffrira de toux, de fièvre et d'une dyspnée continuelle révélant souvent un véritable abcès pulmonaire.

Les parents qui se sont rendus compte de la disparition d'un petit objet avec lequel l'enfant jouait, peuvent orienter le diagnostic même si la radiographie ne révèle pas de corps étranger. Certains objets sont visibles aux rayons X, ce qui en favorise l'extraction.

Les premiers *symptômes,* d'origine laryngée ou trachéale, sont la suffocation, la dyspnée, les nausées, la toux et une inspiration striduleuse. Si le corps étranger cause suffisamment d'obstruction, la cyanose peut se développer. On peut déterminer la localisation d'un corps étranger non opaque aux rayons X grâce aux effets produits dans la trachée ou les bronches.

Évolution. L'obstruction bronchique a de sérieuses conséquences, et le corps étranger doit être enlevé rapidement. Après quelques jours, il peut déclencher une infection purulente et un abcès pulmonaire. Éventuellement, l'emphysème et l'atélectasie apparaîtront.

Traitement. Une laryngoscopie ou bronchoscopie effectuée promptement, permettra l'extraction du corps étranger. Si l'objet s'est logé dans le larynx ou la trachée, une trachéostomie peut être nécessaire pour permettre la ventilation, jusqu'à ce qu'un traitement approprié puisse être appliqué.

On devrait traiter toute infection secondaire à l'aide d'agents antimicrobiens déterminés par la culture des spécimens prélevés.

Pronostic. Le pronostic dépend de la précocité du traitement. Néanmoins, de sérieuses complications ou même la mort peuvent survenir.

Prévention. La prophylaxie est évidente. On devrait garder hors de la portée des enfants les objets tels les jouets à petites parties démontables, les épingles de sûreté ou les noix. L'enfant plus âgé ne doit pas être autorisé à nourrir un bébé; le danger consiste à ce qu'il mette trop de liquide à la fois dans la bouche du bébé et que celui-ci ne suffoque;

on ne doit pas non plus l'autoriser à présenter au bébé des petits objets que celui-ci pourrait avaler. Il n'est pas prudent de laisser des enfants jouer avec des nourrissons, sans être surveillés par un adulte.

Les adultes ne devraient pas porter à leur bouche des épingles ou autres objets, car l'enfant pourrait être tenté de les imiter.

Pneumonie lipoïdique

Incidence, étiologie et manifestations cliniques. La pneumonie lipoïdique, que l'on observe plus fréquemment chez les enfants faibles et débiles, est causée par l'aspiration d'huile ou de substances huileuses. Il y a danger d'aspiration quand on emploie des gouttes nasales huileuses ou lorsqu'on administre, à l'enfant qui pleure, des substances comme de l'huile de foie de morue. Les huiles végétales semblent d'ailleurs moins irritantes que les huiles animales.

Un enfant qui déglutit difficilement ou qui est couché à plat sur son dos, risque d'aspirer le contenu de sa bouteille ou sa nourriture.

Le début de la maladie est insidieux. Une inflammation interstitielle proliférative apparaît suivie d'une dégénérescence fibreuse chronique. Au dernier stade de la maladie, on trouve une quantité de nodules localisés dans les poumons.

Aucune *manifestation clinique* n'est vraiment spécifique à cet état, ce qui en rend le diagnostic difficile. L'enfant a une toux sèche et non productive; sa respiration est rapide et difficile. À moins de surinfection, il ne souffre pas d'hyperthermie ou de leucocytose. Cependant la broncho-pneumonie demeure une complication fréquente.

L'image radiologique du poumon montre toutefois un tableau caractéristique de cet état.

Traitement, soins infirmiers, pronostic et prévention. Il n'y a pas de traitement spécifique pour la pneumonie lipoïdique, et une forme bénigne de la maladie peut persister pendant plusieurs mois avant que l'enfant ne guérisse. Les soins infirmiers en sont d'autant plus importants. On change l'enfant de position fréquemment afin de prévenir l'apparition d'une pneumonie hypostatique, et on l'isole afin d'éviter une infection secondaire. Le *pronostic* dépend de l'importance des lésions pulmonaires et de la gravité des infections secondaires éventuelles.

La *prévention* demeure plus négative que positive. On évite les gouttes nasales et les vitamines à base d'huile. On ne donne pas d'huile minérale ni d'huile de ricin par la bouche.

Si le bébé est sujet aux vomissements ou aux régurgitations, il faut toujours le placer sur le côté ou sur l'abdomen, après ses repas, ou encore le placer en position assise ou semi-assise.

Figure 12-2. Ces corps étrangers, n'ayant pas traversé spontanément le tube digestif, ont dû être extraits chirurgicalement par une laparotomie. (Gross: *The Surgery of Infancy and Childhood.*)

PATHOLOGIES GASTRO-INTESTINALES

Corps étrangers dans les voies gastro-intestinales

Étiologie. Un bébé, à la phase orale de son développement, éprouve du plaisir à tout porter à sa bouche. En suçant de petits objets, il peut lui arriver de les avaler. Les objets qui arrivent à l'estomac, sans obstruer l'œsophage, passeront généralement à travers les voies intestinales. Certains objets, cependant, ne traverseront pas le pylore ou les anses intestinales. Les objets pointus — aiguilles, épingles à cheveux, pinces à cheveux, épingles de sûreté ouvertes, cure-dents, etc. — peuvent perforer les intestins. Les objets localisés dans l'estomac peuvent généralement être enlevés par gastroscopie.

Traitement. Il n'y a pas de traitement spécifique si l'objet n'est pas retiré au moment d'une gastroscopie. On continue le régime alimentaire normal, sans laxatif ni diète spéciale. Une radiographie quotidienne permet de voir si l'objet progresse dans les voies intestinales, auquel cas une perforation n'est pas à craindre; par contre, si l'objet s'immobilise, l'intervention chirurgicale est recommandée, à cause du danger d'ulcération et de perforation de l'intestin. L'infirmière doit surveiller attentivement les signes de perforation: nausées, vomissements, sang dans les selles, rigidité ou sensibilité de l'abdomen et tout signe de douleur. Dès que la perforation semble imminente ou probable, il faut opérer l'enfant.

Soins infirmiers. Il n'y a pas de soins infirmiers particuliers autres que la surveillance de l'enfant pour déceler les signes éventuels de perforation. À chaque défécation, on place les selles dans un carré de tissu fin, placé sous un robinet largement ouvert, jusqu'à ce que les matières fécales se désagrègent et que l'objet, s'il est présent, devienne facilement repérable.

Intoxication à l'acide borique

L'empoisonnement à l'acide borique résulte de l'ingestion de cet acide ou de son utilisation sous forme de poudre ou de crème sur la peau de l'enfant, généralement à la région fessière. Des nausées, des vomissements, des douleurs abdominales, de la diarrhée et une démangeaison accompagnée de desquamation de la peau sont les symptômes ordinaires. Des signes d'irritation méningée, des convulsions et un coma peuvent suivre. Le taux de mortalité pour les bébés atteints de cette maladie est de 70%.

Le *traitement* de l'empoisonnement à l'acide borique demeure symptomatique. Une exsanguinotransfusion ou une hémodialyse peut être nécessaire. La prévention d'un tel accident peut être assurée par l'éducation des parents.

Diarrhée et vomissements

Les vomissements et la diarrhée du bébé ou de l'enfant sont les manifestations cliniques de diverses maladies. Ces deux conditions associées, constituent l'une des plus grandes causes de morbidité parmi les bébés et les jeunes enfants, surtout dans les pays où les conditions sanitaires et hygiéniques laissent à désirer, et où les traitements non scientifiques sont fréquents.

Des conditions sanitaires insuffisantes ou antihygiéniques ont des conséquences plus sérieuses pour les bébés que pour les jeunes enfants à cause de leur faible résistance à l'infection. Les vomissements et la diarrhée du nourrisson causent une perte importante de liquide marquée par des troubles électrolytiques. La mort est le plus souvent due aux effets de la déshydratation et des perturbations de l'équilibre acido-basique.

Pour comprendre l'importance de ces effets, il est nécessaire de réviser certaines notions fondamentales sur l'équilibre de l'eau et des électrolytes dans l'organisme.

L'eau et les électrolytes

Chaque cellule du corps baigne dans un liquide dont la composition est d'une importance vitale sur les activités cellulaires.

Eau. Un approvisionnement d'eau, suffisant et continuel, est nécessaire à la vie de tous les humains. Mais la déshydratation s'avère plus sérieuse chez l'enfant que chez l'adulte. L'eau représente à peu près 53% du poids du corps de l'adulte. Ce pourcentage atteint 70 à 83% pour le nourrisson. Cette proportion diminue rapidement dans les 6 premiers mois de la vie. La graisse étant anhydre, on trouve une plus grande proportion d'eau chez une personne mince, que ce soit un adulte ou un enfant.

Dans le corps humain, l'eau est répartie en trois compartiments séparés par des membranes semi-perméables: 1) liquide *intracellulaire* situé à l'intérieur des cellules; 2) liquide *intravasculaire* contenu dans les vaisseaux sanguins; et 3) liquide *interstitiel* situé dans les tissus, entre les espaces vasculaires et les cellules, similaire dans sa composition au plasma, exception faite de sa plus faible teneur en protéines.

Le liquide intravasculaire représente environ 5% du poids de l'organisme. Le plasma, la partie liquide du sang contient des protéines qui demeurent habituellement dans le courant circulatoire; l'eau et les électrolytes peuvent sortir des vaisseaux et se répandre dans les tissus avoisinants. Chez l'individu en santé, le volume du plasma demeure relativement stable. En cas d'hémorragie ou de déshydratation, le volume diminue et l'état de choc apparaît. Si le malade souffre d'hyperhydratation, l'activité du cœur sera perturbée et le liquide quittera les vaisseaux produisant de l'œdème aux poumons ou aux tissus sous-cutanés. La concentration du plasma en sels minéraux diffère de celle du liquide intracellulaire; les principaux constituants en sont le sodium et le chlorure.

Le liquide interstitiel occupe l'espace entre les vaisseaux et les cellules; ce liquide ressemble au plasma mais contient peu de protéines. Certains états pathologiques produisent une augmentation de liquide interstitiel révélée par l'œdème sous-cutané; un manque de liquide interstitiel conduit à la déshydratation. L'enfant possède proportionnellement plus de liquide interstitiel que l'adulte. Ce liquide représente environ 25% du poids du nouveauné; vers l'âge de deux ans il s'approche de la proportion de 15% qui est celle de l'adulte.

L'organisme possède les mécanismes nécessaires pour éviter les variations trop grandes des différents constituants. La déshydratation peut toutefois survenir à la suite de la déplétion d'eau dans l'un ou l'autre des trois grands compartiments.

Le liquide intracellulaire représente environ 35 à 40% du poids corporel. Chaque cellule doit recevoir l'oxygène et les éléments nutritifs dont elle a besoin. La quantité d'eau et de chlorure de sodium doit demeurer dans des limites extrêmement restreintes; le potassium est un de ses constituants importants.

Sources. L'eau provient d'abord des liquides ingérés et de certains aliments solides, tels les légumes ou les viandes, qui en contiennent un fort pourcentage. Elle est également fournie par le métabolisme, l'eau étant un produit d'oxydation formé durant les processus de dégradation des aliments.

Pertes d'eau. L'individu en bonne santé, subit une perte d'eau continuelle par la salive et par les selles. L'évaporation au niveau de la peau et des poumons contribue à diminuer la chaleur du corps; cette perte d'eau varie grandement, selon l'activité de la personne, la température ambiante et la constitution de l'individu. L'urine est surtout composée d'eau qui sert de véhicule à l'urée et à d'autres produits de déchets du métabolisme.

Lors de maladie, les pertes peuvent s'accroître à cause de la fièvre, de l'augmentation de la diurèse, de la diarrhée ou des vomissements. Si parallèlement, l'enfant n'absorbe pas assez de liquide, il présentera très vite des **signes de déshydratation,** tels que sécrétions épaisses, sécheresse de la bouche, perte de la turgescence de la peau, enfoncement des yeux et urine concentrée. La fontanelle antérieure du nourrisson peut également être déprimée.

En plus de la différence de proportion entre le poids total de l'eau, dans les cellules et les compartiments extracellulaires, il existe

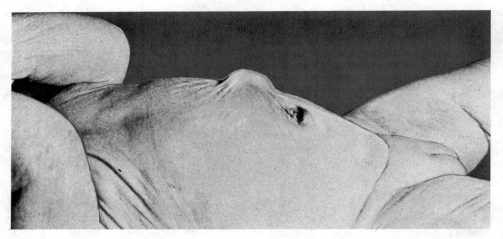

Figure 12-3. Perte de la turgescence de la peau chez un bébé gravement déshydraté. (Courtoisie du Dr Ralph V. Platou et de l'American Academy of Pediatrics.)

d'autres différences entre l'adulte et l'enfant. Le bébé absorbe et rejette plus d'eau que l'adulte, quand cette quantité est exprimée en millilitres par kilogramme de poids. Deux raisons expliquent cette différence: 1) la production de la chaleur de base par kilogramme de poids est deux fois plus élevée chez l'enfant que chez l'adulte. À cause de cela et parce qu'il a une plus grande surface corporelle proportionnellement à ses dimensions, l'enfant perd deux fois plus d'eau par kilogramme que l'adulte. 2) À cause du métabolisme plus rapide de l'enfant, il y a augmentation des produits du métabolisme et de leur élimination. Ce qui, à travers une plus grande quantité d'urine, suppose une dépense accrue de liquide.

Comme la quantité d'eau quotidienne que l'enfant élimine constitue à peu près la moitié du volume de son liquide extracellulaire, toute perte ou manque d'absorption d'eau affecte rapidement ses réserves extracellulaires.

Électrolytes. Les mouvements de liquide dans l'organisme dépendent en grande partie des variations électrolytiques; la concentration du sodium demeure particulièrement importante, mais d'autres éléments moins bien connus entrent aussi en ligne de compte.

Des produits chimiques en solution peuvent demeurer intacts ou se dissocier. Le dextrose, la créatine et l'urée sont des substances dont les molécules ne s'ionisent pas. Par contre, les *électrolytes* sont des substances qui, en solution, se dissocient en particules distinctes appelées *ions* et qui ont une fonction importante: celle de maintenir l'équilibre acido-basique de l'organisme. Tout ion transporte une charge électrique, positive ou négative.

Le sodium (Na^+), le potassium (K^+), le calcium (Ca^{++}) et le magnésium (Mg^{++}) sont des *cations* ou *ions* chargés positivement. Le chlore (Cl^-), le bicarbonate (HCO_3^-) et le phosphate (HPO_4^{--}) sont des *anions* ou *ions* négatifs.

Chaque compartiment d'eau a sa propre composition électrolytique. Le *milli-équivalent* (mEq.) indique le nombre de charges ioniques ou de liens électrovalents dans la solution ionisée de chaque compartiment. Bien que l'on connaisse la composition électrolytique normale de chacun des secteurs, seul le dosage des électrolytes du milieu intravasculaire peut être évalué avec précision étant donné la facilité d'obtenir un prélèvement sanguin pour fin d'analyse. Mais ceci ne donne pas une véritable évaluation des électrolytes dans les espaces cellulaire et interstitiel.

Sodium. La plus grande partie du sodium de l'organisme se trouve dans le milieu extracellulaire. Le taux du Na sérique est de 136-143 mEq./litre. La consommation moyenne quotidienne de Na compense les pertes normales. Un régime alimentaire équilibré suffit aux besoins en sodium; mais si une quantité additionnelle est requise dans la thérapie, on peut donner du chlorure de sodium en solution de 0,85 à 0,9%, ou du sang complet par voie parentérale.

L'élimination du sodium se fait en grande partie par l'intermédiaire des reins, et de la peau par le phénomène de la transpiration. L'excrétion augmente avec la hausse de la température ambiante, les exercices physiques, l'élévation de la température du corps ou la tension émotive. Une perte à travers la peau ne régularise pas la sécrétion du sodium; c'est simplement un sous-produit de la régulation de la température du corps. Normalement, l'excrétion du sodium s'effectue par le rein qui demeure le principal régulateur du taux de Na dans l'organisme.

Les hormones influent sur l'excrétion du sodium. L'hormone pituitaire antidiurétique (ADH), favorise la réabsorption de l'eau au niveau du tubule distal du néphron. Les hormones corticosurrénales, surtout l'aldostérone, influent sur la réabsorption du potassium (en la diminuant) et du sodium (en l'augmentant), réglementant ainsi la concentration de ces ions dans le sang qui circule. Chez l'enfant, l'échange d'eau entre les cellules et le liquide extracellulaire, est 3 à 4 fois plus rapide que chez l'adulte. Comme l'échange du sodium est également rapide, il y a des problèmes spécifiques dans le maintien de l'équilibre sodique chez le bébé.

Potassium. La plus grande partie du potassium échangeable se situe à l'intérieur de la cellule. Le potassium sérique varie entre 4,1 et 5,6 mEq. par litre. La moyenne quotidienne ingérée et excrétée s'équilibre en général, et un régime moyen normal satisfait les exigences du corps.

L'équilibre du potassium peut être maintenu même si l'absorption en est faible. L'ACTH, les gluco-corticoïdes et les minéralo-corticoïdes en augmentent l'excrétion rénale, tout en favorisant une rétention sodique.

La concentration de potassium dans le liquide interstitiel influe sur l'activité de toutes les cellules. L'hyperkaliémie produit un effet clinique sur le muscle cardiaque. Un faible taux de potassium extracellulaire peut provoquer des sensations de fatigue, de faiblesse, une perte de tonicité des muscles lisses et striés et une défaillance circulatoire peut survenir après un certain temps.

On ne donne pas de potassium à l'enfant tant que ses fonctions rénales laissent à désirer; autrement le taux de potassium sérique peut s'élever à un niveau dangereux. Les principales contre-indications à une thérapie au potassium sont une insuffisance surrénale et un fonctionnement rénal déficient, non corrigés par un traitement approprié.

Équilibre acido-basique. Une des plus importantes considérations dans la thérapie hydrique et électrolytique demeure l'équilibre acido-basique. Une solution est acide ou alcaline selon sa concentration en ions hydrogènes (H^+). Si la concentration des ions hydrogènes augmente, la solution devient plus acide; si cette concentration diminue, la solution devient plus alcaline. La quantité

d'ions hydrogènes dans une solution se définit par le concept du pH. Une solution neutre a un pH de 7; sa concentration en ions hydrogènes est égale au nombre d'ions OH^- présents. Au fur et à mesure que la quantité d'ions hydrogènes diminue, le pH augmente. En d'autres mots, une solution acide a un pH en-dessous de 7 et une solution alcaline a un pH au-dessus de 7.

En général, le liquide extracellulaire demeure à un niveau légèrement alcalin, son pH se situant entre 7,35 et 7,45. Si le pH s'élève au-delà de ce point, un état d'alcalose existe; si le pH baisse à un niveau inférieur, un état d'acidose prévaut. Dans le cas d'acidose, le milieu intérieur demeure cependant alcalin (c'est-à-dire au-dessus de 7), tout en étant moins alcalin que la normale. Un pH qui s'élève au-dessus de 7,7, ou tombe au-dessous de 7, met la vie du bébé en danger.

Il est important que les reins et les poumons fonctionnent normalement afin de maintenir l'équilibre acido-basique. Les reins tendent à excréter le surplus d'ions H^+ ou d'autres substances de manière à ce que le corps rejette les acides produits par le métabolisme. Le degré d'élimination du gaz carbonique par les poumons peut varier. L'alcalose provoque un ralentissement du rythme respiratoire; si le plasma devient trop acide, les poumons élimineront le gaz carbonique, légèrement acide, en augmentant le rythme et la profondeur de la respiration.

Les *substances-tampons* constituent un autre concept important. Une solution tampon tend à neutraliser les surplus d'ions hydrogènes ou à les libérer selon la nécessité. Les substances-tampons règlent l'équilibre acido-basique du corps humain.

Il y a plusieurs systèmes tampons dans l'organisme. Le système « acide carbonique ⇌ bicarbonate de sodium » est le plus important dans le liquide extracellulaire. Une perturbation de l'équilibre acido-basique provient souvent du déséquilibre dans ce système. Dans le liquide extracellulaire, on trouve une partie d'acide carbonique pour 20 parties de bicarbonate. Quand ce rapport est bouleversé, on assiste à une perturbation de l'équilibre acido-basique et le pH varie en conséquence.

Dans une situation clinique, le dosage de la concentration sanguine en bicarbonate indiquera l'importance du déséquilibre acido-basique. La quantité totale de gaz carbonique et la pression partielle de ce gaz seront aussi déterminées. Le gaz carbonique total dans le système veineux du bébé ou de l'enfant varie entre 18 et 27 millimoles par litre. Chez un enfant, la pression partielle du gaz carbonique (PCO_2) du sang veineux varie selon l'âge entre 33,5 et 45 mm de mercure (mmHg). L'acidose se présente quand les valeurs reliées à H_2CO_3 augmentent et celles liées au $NaHCO_3$ diminuent.

Buts de la thérapie hydrique et électrolytique. Le médecin peut prescrire une thérapie hydrique et électrolytique pour une ou plusieurs des raisons suivantes: pour suppléer à une ingestion insuffisante de nourriture, pour fournir un véhicule à la médication ou pour corriger un déséquilibre électrolytique.

Le remplacement de liquide et d'électrolytes s'avère extrêmement important dans le traitement des vomissements et de la diarrhée. Quand un enfant souffre de l'un ou de l'autre, on lui administre une solution de remplacement contenant les mêmes propriétés électrolytiques que celles du liquide perdu. On trouve dans le commerce plusieurs de ces solutions convenant à des besoins précis.

Précautions. Il faut tenir compte de la taille et du poids de l'enfant avant d'administrer des solutés de remplacement. Une trop grande quantité de liquide peut surcharger le système circulatoire, produire une défaillance cardiaque et provoquer un œdème aigu du poumon. Il faut également surveiller attentivement le rythme d'écoulement du liquide car, pour le très jeune enfant, même une petite quantité, administrée trop rapidement peut avoir de sérieuses conséquences.

Voies d'administration.

Voie orale. En présence de déshydratation l'apport quotidien de liquide par voie orale pour le nourrisson doit excéder les besoins normaux de 125 ml par kilogramme de poids corporel. Pour remplacer les pertes, l'enfant plus âgé devra recevoir entre 1500 et 3000 ml par jour. L'apport liquide doit comprendre des aliments riches en électrolytes, tels les soupes, les jus de fruits et le lait. Si la quantité de liquide est suffisante pour obtenir une diurèse satisfaisante, le déséquilibre électrolytique se corrigera de lui-même; une diurèse insuffisante signe l'incapacité du rein à rétablir l'équilibre hydrique et électrolytique.

Voie parentérale. Quand l'enfant ne boit pas suffisamment ou que la voie orale ne peut être utilisée, il faut administrer les liquides par voie parentérale: 1) sous la peau dans l'espace interstitiel ou 2) directement dans le courant circulatoire en injectant dans une veine périphérique. Si on injecte les liquides dans la cavité péritonéale, ils s'absorbent comme s'ils avaient été donnés par voie sous-cutanée.

Le liquide injecté par voie parentérale doit être stérile afin d'éviter l'infection locale ou générale toujours susceptible de se manifester. Les liquides donnés par voie sous-cutanée doivent être chimiquement neutres et leur composition doit être isotonique ou physiologique. Pour la thérapie intraveineuse, des liquides hypo ou hypertoniques peuvent être employés, mais produisent parfois de l'irritation aux parois vasculaires.

Nous avons parlé du soluté salin physiologique au début de ce chapitre. Une solution contenant entre 5 et 10% de glucose est également isotonique ou physiologique. L'eau distillée ou bi-distillée n'est pas isotonique et ne doit jamais être employée seule par voie intraveineuse ou sous-cutanée; elle pourrait endommager le tissus autour du point d'injection ou bien causer une hémolyse intravasculaire dont les conséquences peuvent être fatales.

La sorte et la quantité de liquide que le médecin prescrit dépendent des caractéristiques de la solution et des besoins de l'enfant. Il faut tenir compte des besoins normaux (thérapie de maintien), de la quantité de liquide déjà perdue (thérapie de remplacement) et des pertes actuelles ou probables dues à la maladie en cours (thérapie concomitante). Par voie intraveineuse, on peut donner des liquides contenant des électrolytes, des calories sous forme de glucose, du plasma, des acides aminés ou des vitamines.

Si la thérapie intraveineuse est insuffisante, la déshydratation s'accentue; si l'enfant reçoit trop de liquides par voie orale ou intraveineuse, il s'ensuit une surcharge vasculaire qui empêche le cœur de fonctionner normalement; l'excès de liquide s'échappera des vaisseaux pour causer de l'œdème au niveau des poumons ou de l'espace sous-cutané.

Les liquides qui ne contiennent que de l'eau ou ceux qui sont exempts de protéines traversent rapidement la paroi vasculaire et la surcharge sanguine diminue. Un nourrisson peut recevoir environ 30 ml par kilogramme en une seule injection et il peut tolérer jusqu'à 150 ml par kilogramme par jour si le liquide est perfusé de façon continue. Les quantités sont plus limitées s'il s'agit de sang ou de plasma qui renferment des protéines, puisque les protéines traversent très lentement la paroi vasculaire; la surcharge veineuse apparaît si l'enfant reçoit la perfusion trop rapidement. L'excès de liquide dans l'organisme peut provoquer des convulsions et une défaillance cardio-vasculaire.

Substances	Rôles principaux	Effets de la déplétion	Effets de l'excès	Principales sources
Eau	• Véhicule des électrolytes, permet échanges chimiques, température corporelle — lubrifiant	• Symptômes objectifs: urine très concentrée oligurie, soif, hyperthermie Autres sypmtômes: hyperconcentration du sérum (sodium) défaillance circulatoire	• Symptômes objectifs: urine diluée — polyurie, céphalée, confusion, nausées, vomissements, crampes et fourmillements musculaires, convulsions, coma Autres symptômes: hypoconcentration sérique, hypertension intracrânienne	• Tous les liquides, fruits, légumes, oeufs, viande
Sodium	• Maintien de pression osmotique, irritabilité musculaire et nerveuse	• Symptômes objectifs: nausées, vomissements, hypotension, diarrhée, céphalée, faiblesse musculaire, crampes abdominales Autres symptômes: diminution de volume du liquide extra-cellulaire, hémoconcentration, perte de l'élasticité tissulaire, microcardie	• Symptômes objectifs: excitation hypomaniaque, tachycardie, oedème Autres symptômes: augmentation du liquide extra-cellulaire, défaillance cardio-vasculaire, tendance à la déficience potassique	• Sel, viande, poisson, volaille, lait, fromage, jus de tomate, pain, beurre, céréales, marinades, cola
Potassium	• Maintien de la balance intracellulaire, régularité du rythme cardiaque, irritabilité musculaire et nerveuse	• Symptômes objectifs: apathie ou appréhension, léthargie, faiblesse musculaire, nausées, tachycardie Autres symptômes: iléus ou diarrhée, hypokaliémie, alcalose métabolique	• Symptômes objectifs: faiblesse musculaire, nausées, coliques, diarrhée modification de l'ECG Autres symptômes: hyperkaliémie, arrêt cardiaque	• Viande, poisson, volaille, céréales, fruits, jus (canneberge, raisin, pomme, orange, poire) bananes, thé, cola
Calcium	• Contraction musculaire, rythme cardiaque normal, irritabilité nerveuse, coagulation sanguine	• Engourdissements, fourmillements (nez, oreilles, ongles des doigts et des orteils) tétanie	• Peu de problèmes cliniques	• Lait, fromage à la pie, crème glacée, brocoli, crevettes
Magnésium	• Irritabilité musculaire et nerveuse	• Symptôme objectif: tétanie hypotonique Autre symptôme: fibrillation musculaire	• Peu de problèmes cliniques	• Lait, céréales
Chlorures	• Pression osmotique	• Peu de problèmes cliniques; se produit seulement après vomissements prolongés	• Peu de problèmes cliniques	• Sel, lait
Phosphates	• Constituant des os et des dents; système tampon, transport des acides gras, métabolisme des glucides et des lipides	• Hypophosphatémie, ostéomalacie, rachitisme	• Symptôme objectif: tétanie Autres symptômes: hyperphosphatémie, hypocalcémie	• Jaune d'oeufs, lait, céréales à grains entiers
Bicarbonates	• Équilibre acido-basique	• Acidose métabolique, augmentation du catabolisme protoplasmique, tendance aux pertes hydriques et électrolytiques	• Hyperglycémie, glycosurie, défaillance hépatique	• Oeufs, viande, volaille, bouillons, poisson

Figure 12-4. Déséquilibre hydrique et électrolytique. Extrait de M.A. Berry et C.B. Kerlin: « The Drops of Life: Fluid and Electrolytes. » *RN*, 33:37, septembre 1970.

Diarrhée

L'acidose métabolique apparaît à la suite d'une hausse des acides non volatiles ou d'une perte de bicarbonates de l'espace extracellulaire. On trouve par exemple de l'acidose métabolique dans les cas de diarrhée grave avec jeûne, à cause de la perte des ions de bicarbonate par la voie intestinale.

Incidence. La diarrhée est un symptôme d'une variété de conditions qui, groupées, constituent l'une des principales causes de morbidité et de mortalité parmi les bébés et les jeunes enfants à travers le monde.

Les aliments avariés constituent un milieu idéal pour la prolifération des bactéries. Dans les pays, à très bas niveau de vie, la mortalité infantile due aux désordres diarrhéiques atteint un taux très élevé. L'enfant nourri au sein échappe à l'une des plus grandes sources d'infection: le lait contaminé. On connaît bien les causes générales de la diarrhée, mais dans chaque cas particulier, on ne trouve les causes spécifiques qu'à l'aide d'examens de laboratoire.

Étiologie. Dans plusieurs cas, la cause de la diarrhée demeure difficile à déterminer. Les causes suivantes en sont généralement responsables: un excès de nourriture, un horaire ir-régulier, un régime alimentaire mal équilibré (mauvaise combinaison de protéines, lipides et glucides, trop grande quantité de sucre), de la nourriture avariée, souvent due à l'absence d'un réfrigérateur ou à un manque d'hygiène dans la préparation des repas.

Il est difficile de cerner les causes socio-économiques des troubles gastro-intestinaux. On retrouve souvent la contamination du lait ou d'autres produits alimentaires comme cau-se de diarrhée dans les groupes socio-écono-miquement faibles. Chez les autres, on re-marque surtout une infection par contact, di-rect ou indirect, avec un membre de l'entou-rage porteur de germes. Les microbes res-ponsables sont des bacilles coliformes patho-gènes, qui peuvent être extrêmement virulents ou des virus dont certains causent des mala-dies respiratoires chez les enfants et les adul-tes. Le staphylocoque doré cause également des troubles diarrhéiques; il arrive parfois que la diarrhée apparaisse parallèlement à une au-tre infection.

D'autres micro-organismes, tels que le Shi-gella (Shiga, Flexner, Sonne-Duval ou d'au-tres), et les bactéries du groupe des Salmo-nella peuvent agir comme agents étiologiques. Parfois la diarrhée provient de l'administration d'antibiotiques; certains germes peuvent de-venir pathogènes dans l'intestin, par suite d'un changement dans la flore normale à la suite d'une thérapie antibiotique. Parmi ces agents infectieux, on retrouve le *proteus mirabilis* et le *pseudomonas aeruginosa* (ou bacille pyo-cyanique).

L'allergie à certains aliments, l'émotion, la fatigue, le mauvais usage ou l'abus de laxatifs sont d'autres causes de diarrhée.

Diagnostic, manifestations cliniques et traitement.
Le médecin pose son *diagnostic* à partir de l'anamnèse et de l'examen clinique.

Les cultures de selles, répétées au moins trois fois et effectuées sur des prélèvements frais, obtenus à 8-10 heures d'intervalle, dé-termineront les agents en cause.

Les tests de laboratoire comprennent un bilan ionique et acido-basique (Astrup) ainsi que la détermination du taux et de la pression partielle du gaz carbonique, et du taux d'hé-moglobine et d'hématocrite.

Les *manifestations cliniques* d'une diarrhée légère diffèrent de celles d'une diarrhée grave. La diarrhée grave se manifeste de deux fa-çons: elle se développe graduellement ou frappe brutalement.

DIARRHÉE LÉGÈRE. Elle se manifeste par une hyperthermie légère, des vomissements éventuels, de l'irritation et un sommeil agité. L'enfant a des selles molles ou complètement liquides, à un rythme de 2 à 5 fois par jour. À ce point, l'acidose et la déshydratation de-meurent relatives, malgré une perte de 10% du poids corporel. Une perte de poids excé-dant ce taux indique une déshydratation sé-vère.

Traitement. Le traitement consiste à élimi-ner le lait et à réduire dans l'alimentation les graisses et les hydrates de carbone en vue d'alléger le travail des voies intestinales. On augmente l'ingestion de liquide sous forme de boissons gazeuses décarbonatées, de thé fai-ble, d'eau légèrement sucrée ou de jus de pomme. On évite l'eau pure pour prévenir une intoxication aqueuse suivie d'une aggra-vation du désordre électrolytique. On peut donner oralement un mélange de solution glu-cosée (5%) et de solution saline toutes les 3 ou 4 heures. Dans certains cas, le médecin peut ordonner une diète absolue (de 12 à 24 heures) suivie d'administration de glucose en solution saline et, plus tard, de lait écrémé coupé d'eau.

DIARRHÉE GRAVE. Les manifestations clini-ques de diarrhée grave *à début progressif* sont: une élévation de la température accompagnée de vomissements, d'anorexie et de douleurs abdominales. La diarrhée évolue: les selles deviennent verdâtres, chargées de bile, con-tenant des glaires et des traces de sang. Les selles plus fréquentes, 2 à 20 fois par jour, sont expulsées en jets. L'enfant accablé, ner-veux ou irritable peut également souffrir de convulsions. À cause de la **déshydratation,** la peau et les muqueuses deviennent sèches et perdent leur élasticité. Le pouls est rapide et faible, la fontanelle et les yeux enfoncés, la diurèse diminue et la perte de poids peut at-teindre 25% du poids initial du bébé. Ces signes de déshydratation proviennent surtout de la perte de liquide interstitiel.

Le pH diminue et l'acidose apparaît. Quand l'émission d'urine diminue et que les reins fonctionnent difficilement, l'acidose augmente à cause de l'accumulation des métabolites aci-difiants. La respiration devient plus profonde, alors que son rythme peut augmenter ou di-minuer.

Dans la diarrhée grave *à début rapide,* la température se situe entre 40°C et 41°C. L'en-fant est dans un état d'extrême prostration; il vomit et des signes toxiques apparaissent. Il est irritable, agité et peut avoir des convul-sions. La respiration est rapide et profonde.

La diarrhée, moins grave que dans les cas d'évolution graduelle, conduit quand même à l'acidose. L'affaissement de l'état général est dû à la perte de l'eau intracellulaire et à la diminution du volume plasmatique. Les signes de faiblesse de l'enfant sont la pâleur et l'hypotonie. Le taux de mortalité dans ces cas de diarrhée reste très élevé.

Dans les cas de diarrhée grave, il s'agit avant tout de remplacer la perte d'eau et de rétablir l'équilibre électrolytique. En comparant le poids actuel de l'enfant et son poids avant la maladie, on peut évaluer approximativement la quantité d'eau perdue. Des examens de laboratoire mesureront le déséquilibre électrolytique et le fonctionnement rénal. Spécifiquement, l'objectif de cette thérapie initiale est la restauration des fonctions rénales à l'aide de solutions hydratantes sans potassium, le maintien de l'apport hydrique et le remplacement du liquide perdu.

Une thérapie intraveineuse continue s'avère nécessaire pour les enfants très malades qui doivent rester à jeun, parfois pendant 48 heures.

Pour hydrater l'enfant, on peut administrer du liquide par voie sous-cutanée. On évite les solutions hypertoniques qui attirent le liquide avoisinant vers les lieux d'injection et peuvent précipiter le collapsus circulatoire. Des solutions hypotoniques ou isotoniques, auxquelles on ajoute une quantité d'hyaluronidase pour faciliter l'absorption locale, peuvent être administrées.

Quand le nombre de selles diminue et que les vomissements cessent, on peut commencer à faire absorber par voie buccale un mélange de glucose et d'électrolytes ou, selon les médecins, du Seven-up ou autre boisson gazeuse que l'on a laissé reposer pour enlever l'excès de gaz carbonique. L'eau de riz ou le thé faible salé (thé ringer) s'avèrent également très efficaces. On trouve, sur le marché, des préparations liquides qui contiennent les électrolytes nécessaires pour faire suite à la thérapie intraveineuse. Les jus de fruits, sauf le jus de pomme, demeurent trop irritants pour cette phase du traitement. Graduellement, si aucun signe de diarrhée ne réapparaît, on augmente la quantité des liquides pris par voie buccale. Des aliments pectiques, tels que pommes en purée, bananes mûres écrasées ou purée de carottes constituent habituellement les premiers aliments solides que tolère le bébé. Les céréales de riz diluées avec du jus de pomme, du lait écrémé ou d'autres laits commerciaux spécialement préparés (tel pregestimil), sont ensuite ajoutés. Progressivement, l'alimentation redevient normale, dans les 6 à 8 jours qui suivent. Le lait entier est toujours le dernier aliment réintroduit.

L'antibiothérapie spécifique débute aussitôt que l'on connaît les germes responsables.

Si le nourrisson fait de l'hyperthermie, des mesures rapides doivent être prises pour éviter les convulsions et une aggravation de la déshydratation. Les mesures les plus efficaces, chez le jeune enfant, sont: l'utilisation du matelas réfrigérant, les bains à l'eau tiède alcoolisée et l'administration d'un antipyrétique.

Prévention. L'allaitement maternel est encore le moyen préventif le plus efficace contre la diarrhée, surtout dans les foyers socio-économiquement faibles. On devrait enseigner à toutes les mères qui nourrissent leur enfant au biberon, la façon de préparer, de conserver le lait et de donner à boire à l'enfant. L'infirmière hygiéniste doit aider la mère à s'organiser adéquatement avec les moyens dont elle dispose. Pendant la saison chaude, on doit offrir fréquemment à boire au nourrisson, tout en réduisant temporairement la quantité de nourriture absorbée. On doit l'habiller suivant la température et non suivant la saison. En été, on doit le vêtir aussi légèrement que possible, mais le couvrir chaudement si la température se rafraîchit.

On tient le nourrisson à l'écart de tout contact avec les adultes ou les enfants ayant une infection, surtout intestinale; s'il souffre lui-même de diarrhée, on doit l'isoler pour éviter de propager l'infection. Les mesures d'hygiène publique ont une influence déterminante sur l'incidence de la diarrhée parmi les bébés. Pour conserver la santé il faut appliquer certaines mesures d'hygiène essentielles, telles que poubelles hygiéniques, eau saine, contrôle des insectes et des parasites. On doit apprendre à la mère à protéger le nourrisson contre les dangers de l'environnement qui demeurent hors de son contrôle. Par exemple, elle doit faire bouillir toute eau donnée au nourrisson, couvrir sa nourriture pour prévenir la contamination par les mouches, recouvrir son lit d'une moustiquaire pendant les saisons où les insectes sont nombreux.

Soins infirmiers. *Principes essentiels.* Quand un bébé gravement malade arrive à l'hôpital, l'infirmière doit être particulièrement attentive aux besoins de l'enfant et de ses parents. Dans le cas d'un nourrisson diarrhéique, elle doit l'isoler aussitôt et ce, jusqu'à ce que la cause de la diarrhée soit déterminée.

Elle doit connaître les *besoins et habitudes de l'enfant.* Si on doit le garder à jeun, il faut lui offrir un moyen de satisfaire son besoin de succion. On peut en discuter avec la mère et lui donner une tétine d'amusement. S'il l'accepte, on doit veiller à lui faire rendre fréquemment l'air qu'il a avalé en tétant. Il a besoin d'être entouré et réconforté quand sa mère ne peut lui rendre visite.

Il a également besoin d'être consolé quand on applique les contraintes nécessaires à la thérapie intraveineuse. Un bébé qui commençait à s'asseoir ou à se traîner peut trouver ces restrictions frustrantes. On peut l'aider à accepter un certain degré d'immobilisation en le berçant ou en bougeant rythmiquement son lit. Certains traitements peuvent être douloureux et il a besoin du réconfort de la présence maternelle. Si celle-ci ne peut rester à ses côtés, un des membres du personnel infirmier doit accorder à l'enfant toute l'attention et l'affection nécessaires.

Si l'enfant n'absorbe rien par voie buccale, ses lèvres deviennent très sèches, sa peau requiert des soins particuliers afin d'éviter des lésions. Il faut lui lubrifier les lèvres, changer sa position fréquemment et pratiquer des exercices passifs, si possible, pendant les périodes de contrainte.

Il faut réconforter la mère, surtout si elle se sent coupable de la maladie du bébé. Elle peut penser qu'elle n'a pas pris les précautions nécessaires en préparant les repas de l'enfant ou en ne le tenant pas à l'écart d'un autre enfant atteint d'infection. Quand elle vient voir l'enfant ou quand elle téléphone pour avoir des nouvelles, on lui fait part de ses progrès. Si l'état de l'enfant s'aggrave, le médecin la prévient et répond à ses questions. La mère peut s'inquiéter au sujet de choses essentielles aux yeux de l'infirmière, telles le rasage de la tête de l'enfant en vue de la thérapie intraveineuse; aussi doit-on la prévenir et lui expliquer la nécessité de tels procédés.

PARTICIPATION À UNE PONCTION VEINEUSE. L'infirmière participe aux ponctions veineuses destinées à obtenir des spécimens sanguins. Actuellement, la plupart des analyses sanguines, pour le nourrisson, peuvent être effectuées par micro-méthode, ce qui diminue beaucoup la quantité de sang à prélever. Une incision au bout du doigt fournit ordinairement assez de sang pour éviter la véritable ponction veineuse. Si l'examen ne peut absolument pas être pratiqué à partir d'un prélèvement effectué par micro-méthode, le sang doit être quelquefois prélevé dans la veine jugulaire externe, dans la veine fémorale ou, plus rarement, dans le sinus supérieur longitudinal, le nourrisson n'ayant pas de grosses veines dans la fosse antécubitale. Le médecin effectue alors la ponction. L'infirmière place l'enfant en position telle que le sang puisse être prélevé avec le moins de difficultés possibles pour le

médecin et le moins d'inconfort pour l'enfant. *On applique une pression ferme sur la veine jugulaire ou fémorale pendant plusieurs minutes après le retrait de l'aiguille et on surveille le point d'injection pendant une demi-heure pour déceler tout saignement.*

On utilise toujours une seringue stérile à cause des risques de réinjection de sang dans la veine. On peut se servir d'une aiguille n° 21 ou 22, même si une petite quantité de sang doit être prélevée, car plus le calibre de l'aiguille est petit, plus le risque de formation d'un caillot est grand.

Pour les nourrissons le moyen de contrainte appelé « momie » est utilisé pour les examens et les traitements qui s'appliquent à la tête ou au cou. On se sert d'un drap carré ou d'une couverture, dépendant de la taille de l'enfant, et de deux épingles de sûreté. Pour les méthodes d'application, voir les figures 12-6 et 12-7. On rassure le jeune enfant en lui parlant doucement ou en le caressant, car le procédé peut l'effrayer surtout s'il sait qu'il risque d'être suivi d'une autre expérience plus ou moins douloureuse.

Si la ponction est effectuée dans d'autres veines que les jugulaires ou les fémorales, l'infirmière peut procéder elle-même selon les lois de son état ou de son pays.

PARTICIPATION À LA THÉRAPIE INTRAVEINEUSE. Si l'enfant a eu des vomissements, s'il est inconscient, s'il souffre d'anorexie ou de déséquilibre électrolytique, si le médecin désire laisser reposer les voies gastro-intestinales, une thérapie intraveineuse peut s'avérer nécessaire. Les liquides utilisés lors d'une telle thérapie doivent être stériles, avoir un pH neutre ou presque neutre et la même isotonicité que le liquide interstitiel.

Quand des liquides sont administrés par voie intraveineuse, le médecin prescrit la quantité et le débit horaire. Si on surcharge la circulation par une administration trop rapide ou par une trop grande quantité de liquide, une défaillance cardiaque fatale peut se produire. Lors de perfusion intraveineuse continue, on peut administrer jusqu'à 150 ml de liquide par kilogramme de poids, par jour. L'infirmière arrive difficilement à régulariser le débit à 4 à 6 gouttes par minutes. Des dispositifs spéciaux permettent d'obtenir plusieurs micro-gouttes au lieu d'une seule goutte ordinaire. L'enfant reçoit environ 60 micro-gouttes par centimètre cube au lieu des 15 gouttes que laisse tomber le dispositif ordinaire. Certains appareils pour perfusion intraveineuse ont également un contrôle empêchant l'enfant de recevoir une trop grande quantité de liquide dans une courte période. On utilise un petit réservoir placé sur le trajet de la tubulure, qui va de la bouteille de soluté à l'aiguille. On le remplit toutes les

SURVEILLANCE DE PERFUSION INTRAVEINEUSE

Nom: *Gilles Dubé*   Date: *26 mars 76*

Solution: *Glucose 5%*   Format: *500 ml*

Médicaments(s) ajouté(s) : —

            —

            —

Type d'appareil: *Usuel avec micro-gouttes (60 gouttes au ml)*

Ordonnance: *400 ml/8 h*   Débit calculé: *50 gttes/min*

HEURE	QTÉ BOUT.	QTÉ ABSORBÉE	QTÉ DÉSIRÉE	DÉBIT	REMARQUES
8 h	500 ml	— —	— —	50 gttes/min	Début de la perfusion
9 h	450 ml	50 ml	50 ml	50 gttes/min	Bébé dort
10 h	375 ml	125 ml	100 ml	25 gttes/min	Ralentissement compensatoire
11 h	350 ml	150 ml	150 ml	50 gttes/min	Reprise du débit calculé
12 h					
13 h					
14 h					
15 h					
16 h	100 ml	400 ml	400 ml	50 gttes/min	Changement de service

N.B. À chaque service, inscrire le total de la quantité absorbée sur la feuillle de dosage des 24 heures.

Figure 12-5. Fiche de contrôle pour la thérapie intraveineuse.

heures et l'infirmière tient une comptabilité exacte de la qualité et de la quantité du liquide donné, de la quantité absorbée, de la rapidité du débit ou nombre de gouttes par minutes et de la quantité qui reste dans la bouteille (Fig. 12-5). Elle procède au réglage du nombre de gouttes quand l'enfant est au repos. Quand il pleure, la tension de ses muscles contracte les vaisseaux sanguins, le liquide coule plus lentement; une fois au repos, la rapidité du débit augmentera et les calculs s'avèreront inexacts.

L'infirmière qui installe une perfusion intraveineuse maintient l'enfant de manière à ce que l'endroit choisi soit immobilisé. On peut appliquer une contrainte momie si on pique dans une veine du cuir chevelu. On peut employer une contrainte momie modifiée si on choisit une autre partie du corps telle la main ou le pied. Les veines du nourrisson étant très petites, il est courant d'en choisir une au-dessus de la région temporale du crâne. Dans ce cas, on rase soigneusement cette région. La tête de l'enfant doit être immobilisée par une seconde personne en prenant soin de ne pas blesser l'enfant ni de gêner sa respiration.

Il est important que l'infirmière procède de façon aseptique et maintienne le matériel le plus propre possible. Il est recommandé d'utiliser un plateau à ponction veineuse dans lequel on trouve tout le matériel nécessaire:
—soluté physiologique salin
—seringue de 3 ou 5 ml
—aiguilles à cuir chevelu, numéro 22, 23, 24
—tampons imbibés d'alcool
—iode ou bétadine
—diachylons de différentes largeurs
—tampons ouatés secs
—demi-verre à médicament, bordé de diachylon.

L'infirmière doit toujours être accompagnée d'une deuxième personne pour procéder à la ponction. Elle doit se munir du soluté prescrit, d'un appareil à perfusion et d'une tige à soluté. Elle suspend le soluté à la tige, le branche à l'appareil à perfusion et fait le vide d'air à l'intérieur de la tubulure de matière plastique.

L'infirmière doit bien localiser la veine qu'elle veut ponctionner et désinfecter adéquatement avec de l'alcool à 70% ou de l'iode si elle choisit la région du cuir chevelu. L'aiguille à cuir chevelu est reliée à une seringue de 3 à 5 ml remplie de soluté physiologique salin et le vide d'air est effectué. L'infirmière appuie fermement un doigt environ 2.5 cm sous le point choisi pour la ponction afin d'immobiliser la veine. Après avoir placé le biseau de l'aiguille vers le haut, elle perce la peau

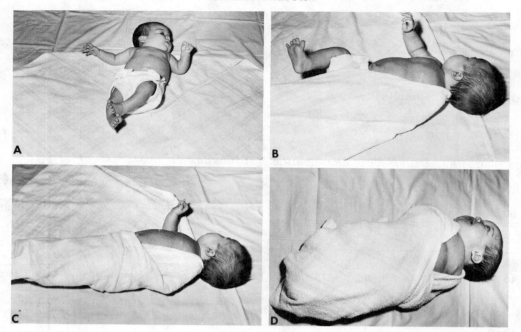

Figure 12-6. Technique pour « momifier » l'enfant. *A)* Plier la pointe d'une petite couverture. Placer le cou de l'enfant au niveau du pli. *B)* Ramener solidement un côté de la couverture sur l'épaule du bébé. *C)* Le reste de ce côté est plié et ramené sous le bébé, du côté opposé, de façon à entourer le corps. *D)* Procéder de la même façon pour le côté opposé.

à un angle de 45° à environ un centimètre de la veine choisie. Elle abaisse l'aiguille et ponctionne la veine en progressant parallèlement à la peau. Lorsque le sang revient dans le tube de matière plastique, il faut injecter du soluté salin pour vérifier la position de l'aiguille et celle-ci est ensuite branchée à l'appareil à perfusion.

Il faut immobiliser l'aiguille solidement avec des morceaux de diachylon et il faut parfois maintenir son angulation avec un tampon ouaté sec. Un demi-verre à médication fixé au-dessus de l'aiguille à cuir chevelu en garantit la solidité. On immobilise l'enfant de façon appropriée et le débit du soluté est ajusté.

Pour administrer du liquide intraveineux aux nourrissons on peut piquer d'autres veines que celles du cuir chevelu. Le soluté peut être injecté dans les veines du dos de la main, des parties flexibles du poignet, des pieds, des chevilles ou de la fosse anté-cubitale. Une dénudation des veines peut s'avérer nécessaire. Le médecin insère alors une certaine longueur de tube en plastique stérile dans la veine et le suture en place. L'enfant doit être immobilisé.

Un dispositif permettant à un tube de plastique de passer à travers l'aiguille qui est alors retirée, évite la dénudation veineuse. L'usage d'un tel cathéter diminue l'incidence d'infiltration des tissus sous-cutanés et la multiplication des ponctions pour l'enfant.

L'arrêt de l'écoulement du liquide pendant la thérapie intraveineuse implique une répétition de tout le traitement; l'infirmière responsable de l'enfant doit vérifier fréquem-

ment le débit, le lieu d'injection et s'assurer que l'aiguille est toujours dans la veine. Si la perfusion s'arrête et que le sang ne remonte pas dans l'aiguille, elle doit avertir le médecin ou l'infirmière responsable des perfusions intraveineuses. Il est à noter qu'il existe maintenant des pompes qui contrôlent le débit du soluté de façon électronique et qui évitent les perfusions trop rapides ou l'arrêt de l'écoulement parce que le bébé s'agite ou pleure.

L'infirmière est généralement responsable de la préparation des solutions intraveineuses et de l'addition des médicaments. Elle doit observer une technique aseptique rigoureuse et un calcul précis des dosages de médicaments. L'étudiante infirmière doit être surveillée jusqu'à ce qu'elle ait acquis l'expérience nécessaire. Elle doit connaître les règlements de l'institution où elle acquiert son expérience. L'aiguille doit être bien fixée dans la veine et seule l'immobilisation nécessaire doit être imposée à l'enfant.

PERFUSION SOUS-CUTANÉE. En prescrivant des liquides par voie sous-cutanée, le médecin spécifie une quantité totale de solution isotonique calculée d'après la taille et les besoins de l'enfant. La rapidité de l'écoulement n'est pas prescrite de façon spécifique comme dans la thérapie intraveineuse car la diffusion varie

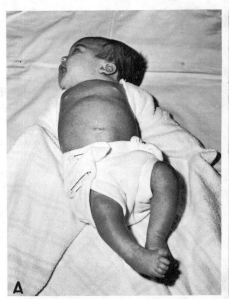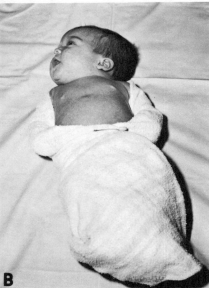

Figure 12-7.   Variation de momification pour exposer la poitrine du bébé. *A)* Tirer le côté de la couverture au-dessus de l'épaule et le ramener sous le bébé en couvrant bien le bras. Même technique pour l'autre côté. *B)* Envelopper les jambes avec ce qui reste de couverture et fixer solidement à l'aide d'une épingle de sûreté.

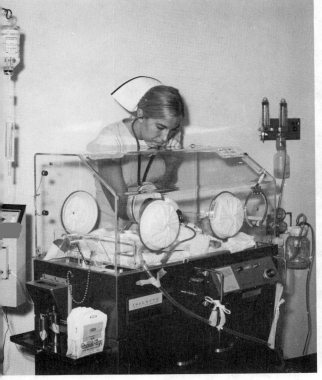

Figure 12-8.   La pompe à perfusion permet d'administrer en toute sécurité de toutes petites quantités de solution intraveineuse. Un oeil électronique contrôle le débit qui demeure constant. (Courtoisie de D.W. Wilmore, m.d., *Am. J, Nurs.*, 71(12): 2335, décembre 1971.)

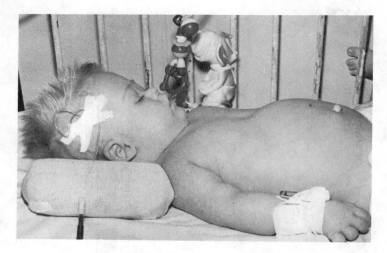

Figure 12-9. Soluté installé dans une veine du cuir chevelu. Les mains du bébé sont maintenues et la tête demeure droite à cause des sacs de sable appliqués des deux côtés. On suspend des jouets que le bébé peut regarder. (R. Kaye, J. D. Bridgers et D. M. Picou: Solutions and Techniques of Parenteral, Oral and Rectal Administrations. *Pediatric Clinics of North America.*)

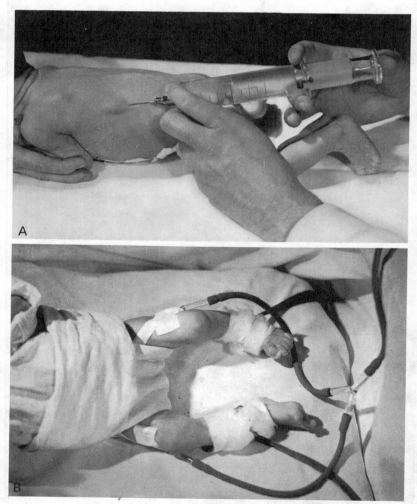

Figure 12-10. Hypodermoclyse. *A)* Injection à l'aide d'une seringue. Région dorsale. *B)* Aiguilles insérées à la face latérale de chaque cuisse, reliées à des tubes d'où le liquide s'écoule goutte-à-goutte. Les chevilles sont immobilisées. (Gross: *The Surgery of Infancy and Childhood.*)

selon les possibilités des tissus sous-cutanés. En vue de faciliter l'absorption des liquides, de l'hyaluronidase peut être injectée dans la zone de perfusion.

Pour le nourrisson, on peut déterminer plusieurs endroits pour une injection sous-cutanée, tels la région pectorale, le dos, la partie basse de l'abdomen ou les cuisses. Si on opte pour la région pectorale, la contrainte momie exposant la poitrine entière peut être appliquée pour immobiliser l'enfant. On insère les aiguilles latéralement et en-dessous des mamelons. Si on choisit le tissu sous-cutané du dos, on insère les aiguilles dans la partie supérieure du dos et le liquide est injecté à l'aide d'une grosse seringue. On peut administrer le liquide dans la partie basse de l'abdomen si le bébé ne doit pas subir une intervention chirurgicale à ce niveau. (Une telle intervention est fort improbable chez un enfant souffrant de diarrhée.) Les zones les plus fréquemment employées pour une injection sous-cutanée demeurent les faces latérales des cuisses. On maintient les bras et les jambes de l'enfant avec les moyens de contrainte habituels.

On observe une technique stérile rigoureuse, car des abcès sous-cutanés se développent parfois, à la suite de tels traitements. On ne doit pas insérer la pointe de l'aiguille près des vaisseaux fémoraux ou des saphènes et elle doit reposer entre la peau et les muscles.

Quelle que soit la région utilisée, un massage doux aidera à diffuser le liquide dans les tissus. Si l'endroit de l'injection devient pâle et dur, on changera la position de l'aiguille. On doit surveiller attentivement le débit de la perfusion pour éviter l'œdème par compression.

Quand un enfant reçoit du liquide par voie intraveineuse ou sous-cutanée, il est impératif que l'infirmière reconnaisse ses besoins de succion, d'affection et d'attention. Une tétine d'amusement, à moins qu'elle ne soit contre-indiquée, satisfera son besoin de succion. Il faut, si possible, lui permettre d'évacuer l'air qu'il aura avalé. Lui parler, jouer avec lui, installer un mobile devant lui ou lui faire écouter de la musique le réconforteront, autant que faire se peut, pendant le traitement.

RÉHYDRATATION PAR VOIE ORALE. Si l'enfant souffre d'une diarrhée légère ou a dépassé la phase aiguë d'une diarrhée grave, on lui administre des liquides par voie buccale. La quantité de liquide varie suivant sa taille et ses besoins. Les nourrissons doivent recevoir environ 125 ml par kilogramme de poids si on veut satisfaire leurs besoins normaux et finir de combler leur déficit hydrique.

Une infirmière adroite et patiente saura généralement encourager le nourrisson qui en est capable à prendre la quantité désirée de liquide. Elle devra fréquemment offrir le liquide prescrit. Le nourrisson qui ingère de petites quantités à la fois en retiendra probablement davantage que le nourrisson à qui l'on en donne trop en une seule fois. Forcer l'absorption de liquide provoque souvent des vomissements.

Avant de faire boire l'enfant, l'infirmière doit vérifier l'ordonnance du médecin pour s'assurer que rien n'a été changé, elle consigne ensuite les renseignements suivants: le type de nourriture, la quantité prise, le degré de l'appétit et les vomissements éventuels. Les aliments solides, tels les céréales de riz ou les bananes seront d'abord donnés en très petites quantités et augmentés graduellement jusqu'à ce que l'enfant reçoive une alimentation normale pour son âge.

CHANGEMENT DE POSITION. Si on doit immobiliser le nourrisson pendant de longues périodes ou s'il est trop malade pour bouger seul, il faut souvent le changer de position et lui faire faire des exercices passifs.

SOINS DE LA PEAU. Si le bébé vomit, on lave et on essuie soigneusement la peau de son visage et de son cou afin de prévenir l'excoriation. On nettoie le siège à chaque changement de couche afin de réduire le danger d'irritation et de fissures de la peau. Un lavage fréquent à l'eau tiède, suivi d'un asséchage adéquat est la meilleure méthode pour maintenir l'intégrité de la peau. Toutefois, si l'irritation apparaît, des pâtes à base de zinc ou d'aluminium sont les plus indiquées sauf s'il y a allergie. Si des excoriations apparaissent quand même sur la peau, on couche l'enfant sur l'abdomen, le siège à découvert. L'infirmière devra surveiller attentivement un nourrisson débile, afin de prévenir la suffocation quand il est placé dans cette position.

En plus d'exposer le siège à l'air, on peut faire sécher les lésions par la chaleur. Toute huile doit être enlevée de la peau avant le traitement. On utilise une lampe flexible porteuse d'une ampoule de 25 W. On place l'ampoule à 30 cm au-dessus de l'enfant et on expose le siège à la chaleur pendant trente minutes, plusieurs fois par jour, suivant l'état de l'enfant. Il faut veiller à ce que l'ampoule ne touche pas au drap et qu'elle soit bien fixée.

CONTRÔLE DE LA TEMPÉRATURE CORPORELLE. On prend la température du nourrisson diarrhéique sous l'aisselle pour éviter une stimulation des intestins en introduisant un thermomètre dans l'anus.

Il faut noter que le nourrisson présente souvent une hyperthermie très marquée, surtout lors de maladies infectieuses atteignant les oreilles et les voies urinaires. Les mesures décrites ici s'appliquent donc dans d'autres circonstances que la diarrhée infectieuse. Il est essentiel que l'infirmière maîtrise les mesures hypothermiques afin de prévenir les convulsions fébriles chez le nourrisson.

Mesures hypothermiques. Tout d'abord, il est important de vêtir l'enfant légèrement et d'enlever tout surplus de couverture. On doit vérifier la température de la chambre et de la tente d'oxygène ou d'humidité si le bébé y est placé. Dès que la température corporelle s'élève au-dessus de 37,7°C, il importe de stimuler l'hydratation du nourrisson tout en lui donnant une diète plus légère. Si le bébé peut s'asseoir dans le bain, on remplit ce dernier d'eau tiède additionnée d'alcool et on ajoute de l'eau froide tant que le bébé le tolère. Ces bains peuvent être répétés fréquemment. Si le bébé est alité, on pratique un bain d'éponge en utilisant les mêmes principes. Un antipyrétique augmente la valeur du traitement. Si la fièvre du bébé ne diminue pas, un matelas réfrigérant peut être employé avec avantage. Il est à souligner que les frictions alcoolisées peuvent endommager la peau et que le massage amène parfois une production de chaleur; une partie de l'alcool peut être absorbée par la peau. Les sacs de glace peuvent brûler l'enfant ou entraîner une chute trop rapide de la température. Les variations brusques de température peuvent également provoquer des convulsions.

Si la température du bébé se situe au-dessous de la normale, il faut le couvrir davantage et/ou le réchauffer avec une bouillotte (46°C) enveloppée de flanelle. On doit s'assurer que la bouillotte ne coule pas. Le nourrisson très jeune est placé dans un incubateur.

Prélèvement et culture des selles. Le médecin peut demander que les selles soient gardées pour qu'il puisse les examiner. L'infirmière enveloppera la couche contenant les selles les plus récentes, la déposera dans un contenant réservé à cet usage, jetant les spécimens recueillis antérieurement. Elle devra toujours noter les caractéristiques de chaque selle: couleur, quantité, consistance, présence de sang ou de pus et odeur. Si une culture des selles est requise, on fait le prélèvement de la couche immédiatement après l'évacuation en utilisant un applicateur stérile. On met le spécimen dans un tube ou une boîte stérile et on l'envoie tout de suite au laboratoire. Si le spécimen ne peut être acheminé immédiatement au laboratoire, on doit le conserver au réfrigérateur.

Il faudra noter la *fréquence d'évacuation* et essayer d'évaluer la quantité émise lors de chaque miction.

Soins des lèvres. Si les lèvres deviennent sèches, par suite de déshydratation, on appliquera de la glycérine ou la crème employée habituellement par l'hôpital. On peut mouiller les lèvres de l'enfant avec une serviette humide. Il existe aussi des bâtonnets imbibés de glycérine et de citron qui peuvent être utiles dans ce cas.

Techniques d'isolement. Si la diarrhée est infectieuse et se propage par les matières fécales, on applique la technique d'isolement incluant le port de la blouse. Un isolement strict protège les autres enfants et le personnel.

L'emploi des couches et des biberons uni-services allège beaucoup le fardeau de la technique d'isolement. Il faudra les jeter ensuite de façon à ne pas propager l'infection.

Vomissements

L'alcalose métabolique découle de la perte d'un acide fort. Elle apparaît dans les cas de vomissements graves qui produisent une perte importante de l'acide chlorhydrique de l'estomac.

Les vomissements constituent un des symptômes les plus courants chez le bébé ou le jeune enfant. Il n'est pas nécessaire de s'inquiéter indûment de vomissements occasionnels chez un enfant en bonne santé, alors que des vomissements fréquents requièrent des soins médicaux. Des vomissements persistants peuvent s'avérer sérieux non seulement par leur signification étiologique, mais aussi parce qu'ils précipitent la déshydratation et un déséquilibre électrolytique menant à l'alcalose. L'alcalose qui accompagne les vomissements importants provient des pertes de chlorures et de potassium. Le sodium passe alors dans le liquide intracellulaire qui perd ses ions K^+. Le liquide intracellulaire a gagné des ions sodium et perdu des ions potassium. Les ions potassium doivent être remplacés si l'on veut que l'équilibre ionique normal à l'intérieur de la cellule soit rétabli. Dès que la fonction rénale et la réhydratation sont assurées, on doit administrer du potassium. Si l'alcalose s'aggrave on doit craindre les convulsions et la tétanie.

Finalement, si un enfant n'est pas traité ou s'il n'arrive pas à garder de liquide, il peut montrer des signes de *cétose d'inanition*. Les conséquences des vomissements étant des plus sérieuses, tous les efforts doivent être faits pour en déterminer la cause et instituer un traitement médical immédiat.

VOMISSEMENTS DUS À DES CAUSES PHYSIQUES. Une *mauvaise technique alimentaire* peut causer des vomissements chez les enfants en bonne santé. Une trop grande quantité de nourriture mène à une distension gastrique, qui à son tour, provoque la régurgitation. La *régurgitation* est le type de vomissements par lequel les aliments non digérés sont expulsés par petites quantités, sans effort et coulent de la bouche du bébé.

Pour les bébés qui ne peuvent prendre et garder une grande quantité de lait à la fois, le *traitement* consiste à concentrer davantage le lait; ainsi le bébé recevra quand même la quantité nécessaire de calories. Si on nourrit l'enfant sur demande, et s'il boit trop et trop souvent on essaie de réduire les vomissements en diminuant la fréquence des repas. S'il boit trop rapidement, il en résultera une dilatation gastrique. On doit faire boire ce type de bébé avec une tétine à petits trous, de telle sorte que le repas puisse passer lentement de l'estomac aux intestins. Si le bébé avale beaucoup d'air, une distension gastrique et des vomissements subséquents en résulteront. L'air poussé par le lait dans les intestins causera une distension abdominale et des coliques. Pendant l'alimentation, on doit placer le bébé fréquemment en position verticale, pour lui permettre de rendre ses gaz. Lorsqu'il aura terminé son biberon, on le couchera sur l'abdomen ou sur le côté droit afin de permettre au liquide absorbé de passer facilement de l'estomac aux intestins et à l'air d'être aisément évacué; dans ces positions, il y a peu de chances que l'air rejeté entraîne le lait jusqu'à la bouche.

Parfois les bébés vomissent à cause des mucosités logées dans l'arrière gorge. Il est alors souhaitable d'aspirer ses sécrétions naso-pharyngées avant le repas.

Une nourriture inadéquate cause souvent les vomissements. L'irritation de l'estomac peut provenir d'un lait contenant trop de glucides ou de lipides. L'excès de lipides ralentit l'évacuation de l'estomac, d'où fermentation menant à l'irritation. En donnant à l'enfant une alimentation appropriée à ses besoins nutritifs, on préviendra ou traitera cet état.

Des aliments auxquels le bébé est allergique, des aliments trop assaisonnés, des mets nouveaux ou même des morceaux de nourriture solide s'il n'y est pas habitué, peuvent causer les vomissements.

Des infections ou d'autres maladies non intestinales s'accompagnent souvent de vomisse-ments. Parmi ces causes, on remarque l'infections des voies respiratoires supérieures et des oreilles ainsi que les maladies contagieuses aiguës. Par exemple des vomissements accompagnent souvent une quinte de toux dans la coqueluche. Quand les conditions infectieuses sont éliminées, les vomissements cessent.

L'hydrocéphalie, l'hémorragie intracrânienne, l'encéphalite et la méningite peuvent provoquer des vomissements qui ne sont pas synchronisés avec l'heure des repas, mais étroitement liés aux périodes d'augmentation de la pression intracrânienne. Le seul traitement pour ce type de vomissement est de réduire la pression intracrânienne.

L'obstruction du tractus gastro-intestinal peut provoquer des vomissements. Dans la période néonatale, les vomissements peuvent provenir de l'obstruction congénitale des intestins ou du canal biliaire. Plus tard, une sténose du pylore, une intussusception, un volvulus, une hernie étranglée, ombilicale ou inguinale, peuvent également causer une obstruction digestive et provoquer des vomissements. L'obstruction intestinale traitée, ceux-ci cesseront. Une faiblesse du cardia peut aussi être responsable des vomissements.

VOMISSEMENTS DUS À DES CAUSES ÉMOTIVES. Un certain type de vomissements est volontaire, comme dans le mérycisme. Ceci consiste à ramener volontairement de l'estomac à la bouche, de petites quantités de nourriture, peu de temps après l'absorption des repas. Le bébé ramène la nourriture dans la bouche en manipulant la langue ou en introduisant les doigts aussi loin que possible au fond de la gorge. Il peut ravaler la nourriture, mais elle coulera plus probablement hors de la bouche.

On ne connaît pas toujours les causes de ce comportement. Il se peut que l'enfant n'aime pas la nourriture qu'on lui donne ou encore qu'il rejette la personne chargée de le nourrir. Le mérycisme peut encore être dû à la tension émotive de l'entourage. Les relations déficientes parents-enfant, à travers lesquelles l'enfant manque d'affection ou d'attention, peuvent également causer cette habitude. Quelle qu'en soit la raison, le mérycisme peut provoquer la mort par inanition.

Traitement. Le traitement suggéré consiste en une psychothérapie pour la mère et en une réorientation des relations parents-enfant. Procurer à l'enfant plus de marques d'affection et jouer tranquillement un moment avec lui, après les repas, s'est souvent avéré efficace. Fort heureusement, c'est une habitude qu'il perdra si les conditions se modifient et si on peut l'empêcher de la pratiquer pendant quelque temps. Si on applique une bonne méthode de conditionnement, cela suffit souvent à faire disparaître ce genre de vomissements.

Soins infirmiers. En plus de corriger les causes immédiates des vomissements, s'il y a déshydratation et alcalose on a recours parfois à l'injection de liquides par voie parentérale et à une thérapie électrolytique.

Il faut alors faire l'évaluation de la fonction rénale et de la déshydratation. L'infirmière doit noter et évaluer la quantité d'urine évacuée. On retarde le traitement à base de potassium jusqu'à ce que cette évaluation ait été établie.

Dans le cas où les vomissements persistent, on peut donner des médicaments sous forme de suppositoire. Pour insérer un suppositoire, l'infirmière doit le lubrifier, le pousser doucement dans le rectum et tenir les fesses pressées l'une contre l'autre jusqu'à ce que la tendance à l'expulsion soit passée.

L'infirmière doit se lier d'amitié avec l'enfant, lui permettant ainsi de se sentir en sécurité quand elle lui prodigue ses soins. On doit éviter d'administrer les médicaments ou les traitements aux heures des repas.

On observe avec soin la technique d'alimentation de l'enfant en vue de découvrir certaines causes prédisposant aux vomissements. La position correcte est la même que celle adoptée quand le bébé est nourri au sein. On élève sa tête et ses épaules, alors que son corps est entouré du bras de l'infirmière. Une douce pression de son corps contre celui de l'infirmière est signe d'affection. Si l'enfant doit rester alité, on élève quand même sa tête et ses épaules si son état le permet. Il doit boire lentement et si l'infirmière le tient sur ses genoux, elle doit lui faire rendre ses gaz fréquemment. S'il est au lit, il faut si possible lui faire rendre ses gaz ou alors lui permettre de longues périodes de repos. Il éructera probablement avant que la tétine soit à nouveau introduite dans sa bouche. En élevant la tête du lit après le repas ou en asseyant le bébé pendant une demi-heure, on minimise les risques de vomissements. On remue alors l'enfant le moins possible, car le calme diminue les possibilités de vomissements.

Il est important de prévenir l'aspiration des vomissements. On tourne la tête de l'enfant sur le côté de manière à permettre au liquide rejeté de couler hors de sa bouche. Les soins de la peau sont importants ensuite. On nettoie et on essuie le visage. On porte une attention particulière au plis du cou et à la région rétroauriculaire.

L'infirmière prend note du temps écoulé entre les repas et les vomissements, évalue la quantité, l'odeur, le type, la couleur et la consistance du rejet, observe si le bébé semble nauséeux avant les vomissements ainsi que le type de ces derniers: mérycisme, régurgitations, vomissements violents ou en jets.

Salmonelloses

Incidence, étiologie, pathologie, manifestations cliniques et diagnostic. La salmonellose demeure un des plus sérieux problèmes d'hygiène publique. C'est parmi les bébés et les jeunes enfants que le pourcentage de ces infections reste le plus élevé. Elles sont causées par un certain nombre de germes flagellés apparentés par leur structure antigénique. Certains organismes caractéristiques de ce groupe provoquent chez les humains une infection semblable à la typhoïde. L'infection fait généralement son apparition après une ingestion d'aliments contaminés et peut durer très longtemps, particulièrement chez les bébés. Récemment il a été prouvé qu'une tortue, animal cher aux enfants et les poussins qu'on leur donne à l'occasion de Pâques, peuvent être porteurs de la maladie. On devrait donc enseigner à l'enfant à se laver les mains avec soin après avoir touché ses petits animaux. On ne devrait jamais vider l'eau du bol de la tortue dans l'évier de la cuisine.

Les changements pathologiques majeurs comprennent une entérite aiguë et une nécrose superficielle des tissus lymphoïdes du tube digestif.

Les *manifestations cliniques* sont des maux de tête, des nausées accompagnées de vomissements, des douleurs abdominales et de la diarrhée. Une élévation de la température, une pulsation dicrote, de la somnolence, du méningisme et une éruption lenticulaire peuvent apparaître. La toxémie, une extrême déshydratation et un collapsus circulatoire entraîneront la mort.

Pour faire le *diagnostic*, on isole le microbe et on démontre la présence d'un taux significatif d'agglutinines dans le sérum de l'enfant (test de Widal).

Complications et pronostic. Parmi les *complications* éventuelles figurent: l'ostéomyélite, la méningite, des abcès des tissus mous et la bronchite. Le taux de mortalité dépend d'un diagnostic précoce et du traitement.

Traitement et soins infirmiers. Le traitement et les soins infirmiers consistent à isoler parfaitement le nourrisson infecté, à supprimer l'alimentation par la bouche et à administrer des liquides parentéraux. Le chloramphenicol semble être le médicament de choix. On le donne parfois en association avec la tétracycline et il arrive qu'on le remplace par l'ampicilline. Les soins infirmiers sont les mêmes que ceux accordés à un enfant souffrant de diarrhée et de vomissements.

Une fois le diagnostic établi, l'infirmière en santé communautaire visitera la maison du bébé afin d'aider la mère à prévenir une récidive de l'infection et à déceler si un autre membre de la famille présente des symptômes similaires à ceux du malade. Le service de santé municipal effectuera une enquête épidémiologique pour retrouver l'origine de la contamination et les porteurs de germe.

Sténose hypertrophique congénitale du pylore

Incidence et physio-pathologie. Cette pathologie constitue l'anomalie du tractus digestif la plus commune chez le nourrisson. On la trouve fréquemment dans certaines lignées familiales, chez les premiers nés et chez les garçons. Cette anomalie est très rare parmi la race noire.

Au point de vue physiopathologique, il y a augmentation de la taille de la musculature circulaire du pylore. L'hypertrophie est généralement de la grosseur et de la forme d'une olive. La musculature fortement épaissie et la masse tumorale qui en résulte, réduisent l'ouverture du canal pylorique. Ceci empêche l'estomac de se vider. La musculature de l'estomac s'hypertrophie alors, en raison de l'effort requis pour forcer la nourriture à traverser le pylore contracté.

Manifestations cliniques, signes radiologiques et tests de laboratoire. Des symptômes apparaissent chez les nourrissons de 2 à 4 semaines et on peut diagnostiquer seulement à ce moment cette maladie congénitale. Les vomissements qui apparaissent pendant et après les repas constituent le symp-

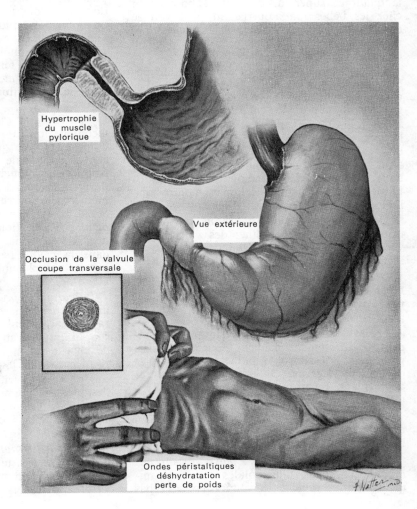

Figure 12-11. Sténose du pylore. (Copyright, The Ciba Collection of Medical Illustrations, par Frank H. Netter, m.d.)

Hypertrophie du muscle pylorique

Vue extérieure

Occlusion de la valvule coupe transversale

Ondes péristaltiques déshydratation perte de poids

tôme initial. Au début peu importants, ils deviennent progressivement plus violents jusqu'à devenir des vomissements en jets. Les matières vomies ne contiennent pas de bile, mais peuvent inclure des mucosités et des filets de sang qui traduisent la souffrance gastrique. L'enfant garde peu de nourriture et il a toujours faim. Il acceptera un nouveau biberon immédiatement après avoir vomi et il le vomit de nouveau. Le poids demeure stationnaire ou diminue. Le nourrisson acquiert l'apparence typique de l'enfant sous-alimenté: il ressemble à un petit vieillard. Parce que très peu de nourriture traverse le pylore, les selles diminuent en fréquence et en quantité. Dans quelques cas, cependant, une diarrhée d'inanition apparaît.

On reconnaît la sténose pylorique à la déshydratation accompagnée d'une faible turgescence de la peau, à la dilatation de l'épigastre, à la présence d'une masse, de la forme d'une olive, localisée par palpation dans le quadrant supérieur droit de l'abdomen et chez les bébés mal nourris, on peut voir le contour de l'estomac dilaté et les ondes péristaltiques passant de gauche à droite pendant et après les repas.

L'alcalose métabolique et une déplétion potassique apparaissent à la suite des pertes d'acide chlorhydrique. Il y a hausse du pH sanguin et diminution des chlorures plasmatiques.

Le repas baryté montre l'élargissement de l'estomac, le rétrécissement et l'allongement du pylore, l'augmentation des ondes péristaltiques et une rétention anormale du baryum dans l'estomac. Une radiographie pratiquée plusieurs heures après le repas montre que l'estomac ne s'est que partiellement vidé.

Les *résultats de laboratoire* indiquent une urine concentrée et alcaline; des valeurs élevées d'hémoglobine et d'hématocrite prouvent l'hémoconcentration.

Diagnostic. Le *diagnostic* est généralement établi sans difficulté; cependant la sténose pylorique peut être confondue avec le pylorospasme.

Traitement. Peu de médecins recommandent un traitement médical pour la sténose pylorique. S'il se solde par un échec, l'état de l'enfant s'aggrave et les risques opératoires augmentent. Le pronostic est excellent si l'intervention est précoce.

On prolonge rarement le traitement médical, à moins qu'il n'y ait des signes évidents d'amélioration de l'état de l'enfant.

TRAITEMENT MÉDICAL. *Épaississement des repas.* Les repas plus solides sont mécaniquement plus difficiles à vomir que les repas

liquides. On peut épaissir le lait avec de la farine d'orge ou des céréales précuites, dont les polysaccharides ont été réduits en sucres plus simples. Quand l'enfant vomit immédiatement après le repas, on le fait manger à nouveau.

Lavage d'estomac. Quand il y a dilatation gastrique, un lavage d'estomac prévient l'aggravation de la distension et l'apparition des vomissements éventuels.

Médication. Des médicaments antispasmodiques comme l'atropine, permettent aux muscles lisses du pylore de se relâcher. On donne ces médicaments 15 à 20 minutes avant les repas. Si l'atropine est ordonnée, on doit toujours utiliser une solution fraîchement préparée. La plupart des enfants ont une tolérance relativement élevée à ce médicament quoique certains d'entre eux montrent des signes d'idiosyncrasie. La dose est graduellement augmentée jusqu'à ce que les vomissements s'arrêtent, puis elle est progressivement diminuée. Si on doit suspendre temporairement la médication, on donne une plus petite dose quand il faut l'administrer de nouveau. Si le visage devient rouge, si les pupilles se dilatent ou s'il y a élévation de la température, il faut aviser immédiatement le médecin qui arrêtera probablement la médication ou en diminuera la posologie.

TRAITEMENT CHIRURGICAL. On applique la technique opératoire de Fredet-Ramstedt: la pyloromyotomie qui consiste à faire une incision longitudinale du muscle circulaire hypertrophié sans toucher la membrane muqueuse du pylore. Quand l'orifice a été dilaté de cette manière, la nourriture y passe plus facilement. Si la muqueuse pylorique a été sectionnée pendant l'opération, il y a danger de péritonite due à l'écoulement des sécrétions gastriques dans la cavité péritonéale. Si le muscle n'a pas été complètement incisé, l'obstruction peut persister.

Préparation préopératoire. L'équilibre hydro-électrolytique doit être rétabli avant l'opération, car un enfant déshydraté risque de mal supporter l'opération et il peut entrer en état de choc pendant l'anesthésie.

Juste avant l'opération, on introduit une sonde naso-gastrique qui permet de laver l'estomac et d'en retirer l'air accumulé. La vacuité de l'estomac facilite l'acte chirurgical et réduit l'incidence des vomissements postopératoires.

Soins infirmiers. *Examen préopératoire.* L'infirmière assiste le médecin, pour déterminer la présence d'ondes péristaltiques gastriques visibles à travers la paroi abdominale. Une bouteille d'eau stérile, un bavoir et une lampe de poche constituent l'équipement nécessaire.

On couche le bébé sur le dos, le visage tourné du côté gauche, l'abdomen exposé. Pendant que l'infirmière fait boire de l'eau au bébé, le médecin tient la lampe de poche au-dessus de l'abdomen, du côté gauche. Il se met du côté droit du bébé et observe l'abdomen. Si les ondes péristaltiques sont présentes, elles seront clairement visibles.

MÉTHODE DE NUTRITION. On nourrit l'enfant lentement, et on le fait éructer avant et pendant les repas afin d'éliminer l'air qui pourrait dilater l'estomac et provoquer les vomissements. Après les repas, on le bouge le moins possible et avec précaution. On couche l'enfant sur le côté droit ou sur l'abdomen, et on élève légèrement la tête du lit. On peut aussi asseoir le nourrisson sur un petit siège pour bébé. S'il vomit après le repas, on le fait manger à nouveau à moins d'une prescription contraire.

La tenue d'un dossier exact et précis s'avère ici d'une grande importance. On doit tout noter: la faim apparente du bébé, le type et le volume des vomissements, la présence d'ondes péristaltiques et ses pleurs avant ou après les vomissements.

AUTRES SOINS. Le bébé doit être pesé quotidiennement, toujours à la même heure et sur la même balance. Il faut être très précis, car le poids indique approximativement le degré de déshydratation et de malnutrition.

Il faut protéger le bébé contre tout danger d'infection. À moins que tous les autres enfants infectés de l'unité de pédiatrie ne soient isolés, le bébé doit l'être, pour sa propre protection. On évite tout contact avec les infirmières et les visiteurs atteints de quelque infection que ce soit.

On change fréquemment la position du bébé pour prévenir une pneumonie hypostatique. On le tient bien au chaud, utilisant des couvertures et des bouillottes si cela est nécessaire ou, mieux encore, un incubateur dont la température peut facilement être réglée.

Le dosage des ingesta et excreta et la prise régulière de la température apportent des renseignements précieux pour connaître l'état général du nourrisson.

Les SOINS PRÉOPÉRATOIRES immédiats comportent un ou deux bains au savon antiseptique, un nettoyage adéquat des fosses nasales et l'administration de la prémédication prescrite.

SOINS POSTOPÉRATOIRES. On donne du liquide par voie intraveineuse pendant les premiers jours après l'opération afin que l'enfant reçoive sa quantité de liquide requise quotidiennement.

La position du bébé est importante. On le couche sur le côté droit ou sur l'abdomen, si c'est possible; ces positions aident à la digestion des liquides ou du lait et empêchent également l'enfant d'aspirer ses vomissements. Durant les premières 24 ou 48 heures postopératoires l'infirmière peut aspirer, à basse pression, les sécrétions gastriques du nourrisson pour prévenir la distension de l'estomac et les vomissements. On place ensuite l'enfant en position semi-assise, ce qui prévient également les vomissements, les rendant mécaniquement difficiles. On doit le changer fréquemment de position en évitant toutefois de le fatiguer.

L'infirmière doit surveiller tous les *signes de choc*: pulsation rapide et faible, pâleur et agitation. Si les symptômes de choc apparaissent, on place le nourrisson en position déclive et on le réchauffe adéquatement. Le nourrisson est souvent placé dans un incubateur pendant les premières 48 heures postopératoires. Il est important d'observer la dilatation abdominale qui peut être causée par l'air qu'aurait avalé le nourrisson, mais également par une infection du péritoine.

Chaque médecin a sa méthode concernant l'alimentation postopératoire. La plupart des médecins utilisent le régime de Down dans lequel on commence à nourrir le bébé 4 à 6 heures après l'opération. On lui fait boire fréquemment de 15 à 30 ml d'eau glucosée à 5%. On en augmente graduellement la quantité et on y substitue bientôt une solution diluée de lait écrémé et d'eau que l'on modifie progressivement jusqu'à ce que l'enfant prenne la quantité normale de lait pour son âge. S'il vomit, on ralentit la réalimentation ou on procède à une réduction temporaire de la quantité de nourriture administrée par voie buccale.

Si le bébé est nourri au sein, la mère extrait son lait que l'on donnera au bébé aussitôt qu'il pourra le tolérer. Dans les 3 ou 4 jours qui suivent l'opération, on devrait normalement pouvoir le remettre au sein.

La méthode d'alimentation est la même que celle appliquée pendant la période préopératoire. On peut utiliser un compte-gouttes pour les premiers repas, mais on donne le biberon ou le sein aussi vite que possible, afin de satisfaire le besoin de succion de l'enfant.

Pour prévenir l'infection de la plaie, on place la couche de manière à éviter qu'elle ne vienne en contact avec le pansement.

Avant que le bébé quitte l'hôpital, sa mère doit recevoir un enseignement approprié. Elle

Tableau 12-1. *Régime de Down modifié*

(retour à l'alimentation normale en 24 heures après une pyloromyotomie)

Heure			Eau glucosée	Lait	Remarques
1.			10 ml	—	
2.	30 min	plus tard	10 ml	—	
3.	30 min	plus tard	10 ml	—	
4.	30 min	plus tard	15 ml	—	
5.	1 h	plus tard	15 ml	5 ml	
6.	1 h	plus tard	20 ml	—	
7.	2 h	plus tard	15 ml	10 ml	
8.	2 h	plus tard	25 ml	—	
9.	2 h	plus tard	15 ml	20 ml	
10.	2 h	plus tard	35 ml	—	
11.	2 h	plus tard	15 ml	30 ml	
12.	2 h	plus tard	45 ml	—	
13.	2 h	plus tard	10 ml	40 ml	
14.	2 h	plus tard	50 ml	—	
15.	2 h	plus tard	10 ml	50 ml	
16.	2 h	plus tard	60 ml	—	
17.	2 h	plus tard	—	60 ml	

Ensuite, donner 60 à 90 ml toutes les 3 heures pendant 24 heures puis 120 ml toutes les 4 heures selon l'appétit du bébé.

doit apprendre à bien appliquer la couche et à observer la plaie opératoire. Elle doit signaler au chirurgien toute rougeur qui apparaît ou tout autre changement important. On doit lui dire de ne pas baigner l'enfant dans une baignoire jusqu'à ce que l'incision soit complètement guérie. Elle doit être renseignée sur l'importance de se présenter au rendez-vous médical pour vérifier l'état postopératoire du bébé.

Pronostic. Le pronostic est excellent. Un soulagement complet suit l'intervention chirurgicale. Le taux de mortalité est bas, si l'enfant est opéré avant qu'il ne soit trop déshydraté ou sous-alimenté.

Spasme du pylore

Dans le *spasme du pylore*, il n'y a pas de lésions anatomiques du pylore. Le spasme se produit chez les bébés hyperactifs, provoquant des vomissements fréquents, souvent en jets, comme dans la sténose pylorique.

Le *traitement* du spasme pylorique consiste à alimenter l'enfant adéquatement et à administrer des médicaments antispasmodiques tels que l'atropine. La sédation améliore la situation et du phénobarbital peut être employé. Certains médecins peuvent prescrire une nourriture épaisse ou des repas par petites cuillerées.

(Voir traitement médical de la sténose du pylore, page 318).

Intussusception

Incidence et étiologie. *L'intussusception* consiste en l'invagination d'une partie de l'intestin dans l'autre. L'intussusception et la hernie inguinale étranglée sont les deux types les plus fréquents d'obstruction intestinale mécanique acquise chez le bébé. Plus de la moitié des nourrissons souffrant d'intussusception n'ont pas encore atteint l'âge d'un an. La plupart des autres cas apparaissent au cours de la deuxième année, surtout chez le garçon précédemment en bonne santé.

L'étiologie est indéterminée. Souvent, on ne trouve pas de cause précise. On a incriminé l'hyperpéristaltisme et la grande mobilité intestinale du bébé surtout au niveau du cæcum et de l'iléon. La diarrhée, la constipation, des polypes intestinaux agissant comme un corps étranger ou encore l'inflammation des tissus lymphatiques de l'intestin peuvent être des causes immédiates. L'intussusception se produit parfois autour d'un diverticule de Meckel. On a aussi associé l'intussusception aux infections intestinales virales, surtout celles qui atteignent les plaques de Peyer.

Physio-pathologie et manifestations cliniques. Généralement, la partie supérieure de l'intestin s'introduit dans la partie basse, dans la majorité des cas au niveau de la valvule iléo-cæcale.

La circulation est arrêtée dans la partie invaginée. Il en résulte de l'œdème. Dans certains cas, la réduction s'effectue spontanément, mais généralement la nécrose apparaît au niveau de l'intussusception. La partie étranglée peut se perforer, causant ainsi la péritonite et la mort.

Les *manifestations cliniques* résultent de la gravité de l'obstruction intestinale. Le début est brutal chez un nourrisson en bonne santé. L'étendue et la gravité des signes physiques anormaux dépendent de la durée des symptômes. De fortes douleurs abdominales apparaissent, que le bébé traduit en agitant ses jambes et en les relevant sur son abdomen. Il pleure. Au début, entre les spasmes, il peut reposer tranquillement. Mais la douleur devient progressivement plus aiguë. Des vomissements font leur apparition, d'abord alimentaires, ils deviennent ensuite bilieux. Ils peuvent être suivis de vomissements fécaloïdes, suivant le niveau de l'intussusception. Une ou deux selles molles sont suivies de décharges contenant du sang et des mucosités (selles glaireuses) à peu près 12 heures après l'attaque. Par la suite, l'enfant n'évacue plus de matières fécales.

Il est d'abord agité puis prostré. Sa température peut monter jusqu'à 41°C ou 42°C. Le choc et la déshydratation apparaissent. Une masse tumorale, généralement de la forme d'une saucisse, peut être palpée au siège de l'intussusception. Le toucher rectal permet de reconnaître la localisation iléo-cæcale.

Diagnostic et traitement. Le *diagnostic* est généralement facile, s'il y a un ténesme soudain, des douleurs abdominales, des vomissements, expulsion de sang et de mucosités par le rectum, une masse au niveau de l'abdomen et de la prostration. Après un lavement baryté, une radiographie laissera voir l'intussusception qui prend l'aspect d'un bouchon renversé après lequel il n'y a plus aucun passage de baryum.

TRAITEMENT MÉDICAL. La réduction médicale est pratiquée par un chirurgien sous contrôle fluoroscopique, après un grand lavement baryté. L'intussusception est réduite par pression hydrostatique. On ne touche pas à l'abdomen pendant le traitement. Si la manœuvre réussit, le petit intestin se remplira de baryum et la masse disparaîtra; si elle échoue, l'opération sera pratiquée. Ce procédé n'est pas sans risque. On doit aviser le personnel de la salle d'opération de la possibilité d'une intervention chirurgicale si le traitement médical échoue. Ce dernier ne sera appliqué que si l'intussusception n'est pas ilio-iléale et si le nourrisson n'est ni prostré, ni déshydraté. Il est rarement indiqué.

TRAITEMENT CHIRURGICAL. Le nourrisson est préparé pour l'intervention. On applique certaines mesures qui ont pour effet de prévenir le choc opératoire et de corriger le déséquilibre hydro-électrolytique. L'opération doit être effectuée aussitôt que possible. Si le chirurgien découvre de la gangrène ou une masse irréductible, il résèque le segment atteint. Généralement, il se contente de la réduction de l'intussusception. La plupart des médecins encouragent l'intervention chirurgicale qui permet de réduire l'intussusception et d'explorer toutes les causes possibles, y compris le polype intestinal.

Soins infirmiers. SOINS PRÉOPÉRATOIRES. Il faut procéder à une bonne hydratation avant l'opération; la thérapie hydro-électrolytique permet de minimiser les dangers de choc opératoire. Le drainage gastrique continu est de règle; l'infirmière doit observer si le drainage est régulier et doit en évaluer la quantité avec précision. Des antibiotiques doivent être donnés en dose suffisante pour obtenir une concentration sanguine adéquate lors de l'intervention.

SOINS POSTOPÉRATOIRES. Les soins infirmiers après une simple réduction sont largement symptomatiques. Les solutés intraveineux cessent avec le retour à une alimentation normale. Généralement, on donne des repas liquides, clairs, dès la reprise de l'activité péristaltique et l'arrêt des vomissements. Il est absolument nécessaire de garder la zone opératoire propre et sèche.

S'il y a eu résection intestinale, on donne des liquides par voie parentérale pendant plusieurs jours et une succion gastro-intestinale permet d'éviter le ballonnement. On fait un dosage précis du drainage, toute perte de liquide ou d'électrolytes devant être remplacée. L'infirmière doit noter les symptômes d'un choc postopératoire ou d'une péritonite. Elle doit signaler immédiatement tout changement dans les signes vitaux, la coloration, la dilatation abdominale ou l'odeur de la plaie abdominale.

L'intussusception peut se produire pendant la seconde partie de la première année alors que le petit enfant, non seulement ne peut se passer de sa mère, mais risque d'être effrayé par des étrangers; l'importance de recevoir de fréquentes visites de sa mère est à souligner. Ces enfants réagissent mal aux figures étrangères de l'environnement hospitalier. L'intussusception constitue une situation grave et la mère cherchera à exprimer son émotion et son

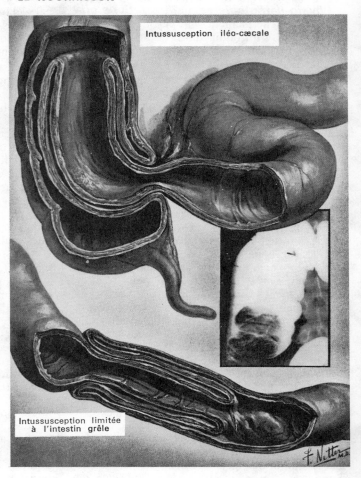

Intussusception iléo-cæcale

Intussusception limitée
à l'intestin grêle

Figure 12-12. Intussusception.
(Copyright, The Ciba Collection of Medical Illustrations
par Frank H. Netter, m.d.)

inquiétude en apprenant l'état de l'enfant ainsi
que les reproches qu'elle s'adresse pour ne pas
l'avoir conduit chez le médecin aux premiers
signes de douleur ou de changement dans ses
selles.

Pronostic. Le pronostic est bon si l'opération est effectuée sans délai. Les chances
de succès sont directement liées à la durée
de l'évolution avant l'intervention. Après 24
heures, le taux de mortalité devient élevé. La
mort, dans les cas non traités, résulte de
l'épuisement et survient dans les 2 à 3 jours
qui suivent le début de la maladie. Une réduction spontanée peut se produire dans certains
cas. Les rechutes sont rares après l'opération.

Hernie inguinale

*Incidence, étiologie et physio-patholo-
gie.* La hernie inguinale, plus fréquente chez
les garçons que chez les filles peut-être uni-

latérale ou bilatérale, congénitale ou apparaître après la naissance.

Pendant la vie embryonnaire, les testicules
migrent de l'abdomen vers le scrotum à travers
le canal inguinal; un sac de péritoine les précède, formant ainsi un tube relié à la cavité
péritonéale. Après la descente des testicules,
le tube s'atrophie et il n'existe normalement
pas de lien entre l'abdomen et le scrotum.
Le liquide péritonéal et une partie de l'intestin
peuvent toutefois s'y introduire et constituer
une hernie si le canal est mal fermé. La taille
de la hernie peut varier selon qu'elle s'étend
jusqu'à l'anneau inguinal externe ou jusque
dans le scrotum.

Bien que le sac herniaire soit présent à la
naissance, la hernie peut n'apparaître que vers
le 2e ou 3e mois, après la naissance. À ce
moment, le bébé pousse des cris vigoureux qui
font augmenter suffisamment la pression intra-
abdominale pour ouvrir le sac et forcer le li-

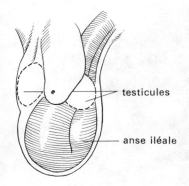

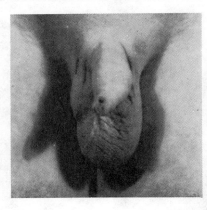

Figure 12-13. Hernie inguinale gauche. (Photographie de Gross, R.: *The Surgery of Infancy and childhood.* Philadelphie, W. B. Saunders Co.)

testicules

anse iléale

quide péritonéal où l'intestin à y pénétrer; ce qui provoque l'apparition d'une saillie dans la région inguinale ou au scrotum.

Chez les nourrissons de sexe féminin, un ovaire peut être poussé dans le sac herniaire par suite de l'augmentation de la pression intra-abdominale.

Manifestations cliniques. Le sac herniaire vide ne cause pas de symptômes. S'il contient une anse intestinale non fixée, une obstruction incomplète des intestins survient: cette hernie est *réductible*. Le bébé exprime son malaise et sa douleur par de la mauvaise humeur. La constipation et l'anorexie peuvent apparaître.

Si une boucle intestinale est incarcérée ou adhérente au sac, tous les symptômes de l'obstruction intestinale se manifestent. La hernie est appelée *irréductible* et *incarcérée*. Il y a danger de strangulation des intestins (*hernie étranglée*) avec arrêt de la circulation sanguine et en dernier lieu, gangrène. L'incarcération survient le plus fréquemment dans les 6 premières semaines de la vie. Le symptôme caractéristique d'une hernie étranglée est l'apparition d'une inflammation ferme et irréductible au-dessous du canal inguinal. Le bébé peut vomir et devenir très irritable. Plus tard, il y a arrêt du transit intestinal, distension abdominale, augmentation des vomissements, leucocytose et fièvre.

Le médecin peut quelquefois parvenir à réduire une hernie incarcérée dans les 12 heures qui suivent son apparition. En cas d'échec, l'intervention chirurgicale s'impose, accompagnée, dans les cas graves, d'une résection intestinale. En cas de réussite, la herniorraphie est quand même effectuée lorsque le bébé est complètement rétabli.

Si la strangulation survient avant l'opération, le bébé souffre beaucoup et les symptômes d'obstruction complète apparaissent. Là en-

core, seule l'opération immédiate peut soulager le malade.

Diagnostic et traitement. On établit le *diagnostic* sur l'histoire de l'apparition intermittente d'une masse dans la région inguinale, sur l'examen physique permettant de palper un sac qui se remplit quand l'enfant pleure, mais qui peut être réduit facilement.

Chez les enfants en bonne santé, les chirurgiens préfèrent pratiquer l'intervention chirurgicale dès que l'anomalie est diagnostiquée. L'opération consiste à enlever le sac herniaire et à bien fermer l'anneau interne du canal inguinal. Les bébés supportent très bien cette opération. Pour la majorité des enfants, elle écarte définitivement le danger de strangulation, d'œdème et de gangrène.

Si l'incarcération survient avant l'opération, un sac de glace placé sur la région peut aider à réduire l'œdème. Le pied du lit surélevé empêche le contenu abdominal de passer dans l'anneau. Si la réduction manuelle, faite sous sédation, ne réussit pas, l'intervention chirurgicale doit être pratiquée immédiatement.

Soins infirmiers. Avant l'intervention, on essaie d'éviter les pleurs et la tension qui tendent à accroître la pression intra-abdominale et augmentent le volume de la hernie. La constipation cause aussi une hausse de la pression intra-abdominale et doit être évitée.

Il est d'usage d'observer « rien par la bouche après minuit » pour tout malade devant être opéré le lendemain. Chez les petits enfants (particulièrement chez le jeune bébé), une telle prescription peut conduire à la déshydratation, s'ils ont pleuré, s'ils ont manqué des repas précédents ou s'ils ne doivent être opérés que tard dans la journée. Ceci explique que la majorité des anesthésistes permettent l'hydratation du nourrisson, sauf durant les quatre heures précédant l'intervention.

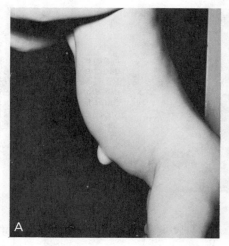
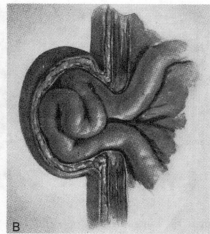

Figure 12-14. Hernie ombilicale. *A)* Vue de côté. *B)* Coupe sagittale. (Copyright, The Ciba Collection of Medical Illustrations par Frank H. Netter, m.d.)

SOINS POSTOPÉRATOIRES. Après une herniorraphie inguinale, le principal problème consiste à prévenir l'infection de l'incision en gardant la plaie opératoire propre et sèche.

On reprend généralement l'alimentation quelques heures après l'opération, excepté si une résection intestinale a été pratiquée. Le bébé doit être pris dans les bras pendant les repas. Après une herniorraphie inguinale simple, l'enfant peut être aussi actif qu'il le désire.

Hernie ombilicale

Étiologie, incidence et manifestations cliniques. Une hernie ombilicale est due à la fermeture imparfaite ou à la faiblesse de l'anneau ombilical. Ces hernies se présentent parmi toutes les races, mais sont plus communes chez les enfants de race noire.

Elle se manifeste par une protubérance quand l'enfant pleure ou est tendu. La hernie se réduit facilement par une pression douce sur l'anneau fibreux ombilical. Le contenu de cette hernie est l'intestin grêle et l'épiploon.

Sa taille varie de moins d'un centimètre à cinq centimètres de diamètre.

Pronostic, traitement et soins infirmiers. La plupart des petites hernies ombilicales disparaissent sans traitement, mais l'opération peut être nécessaire s'il n'y a pas de réduction spontanée. Ces hernies causent rarement l'incarcération ou un étranglement des intestins, durant l'enfance.

Les médecins diffèrent d'opinion quant à l'efficacité de la réduction et du port d'une bande abdominale. Si le médecin prescrit un bandage, on peut utiliser le procédé suivant.

On badigeonne la zone à couvrir de teinture de benjoin pour protéger la peau et pour aider l'adhésif à mieux coller à la peau. On laisse sécher le benjoin.

On réduit d'abord la hernie en repoussant doucement le contenu abdominal à travers l'anneau ombilical. On ramène vers le milieu les côtés des parois abdominales adjacentes de façon à former un pli dans la peau. On applique une bande adhésive de 5 cm sur l'abdomen en passant au-dessus du repli de la peau et en serrant fortement.

Auparavant, l'intervention chirurgicale était pratiquée si la hernie présentait un volume important ou s'incarcérait. La tendance actuelle est de corriger la plupart des hernies ombilicales, par mesure prophylactique, de façon à prévenir l'incarcération tardive à l'âge adulte et les complications sérieuses qui peuvent en découler.

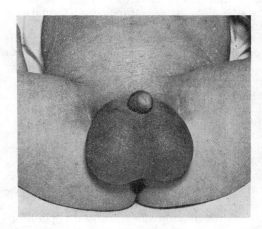

Figure 12-15. Hydrocèle bilatérale. (Davis et Rubin: *DeLee's Obstetrics for Nurses.* 17e éd.)

Les *soins infirmiers* postopératoires ne requièrent aucune technique spéciale. L'enfant peut être aussi actif qu'il le désire. On reprend aussitôt une alimentation normale. Les bandages appliqués au moment de l'opération doivent être tenus propres et secs afin de prévenir l'infection de l'incision.

PATHOLOGIES GÉNITO-URINAIRES

Hydrocèle

Une hydrocèle est une accumulation de liquide autour des testicules ou le long du cordon spermatique. Elle peut être congénitale ou apparaître durant l'enfance. L'hydrocèle doit être différenciée d'une hernie inguinale. Une hydrocèle présente l'image d'un sac fluctuant, ovale, translucide et tendu. Le liquide généralement se résorbe durant la petite enfance, mais dans le cas contraire, une correction chirurgicale sera nécessaire.

Pyélonéphrite (Pyélite)

Incidence et étiologie. La pyélonéphrite est une infection rénale qui atteint le bassinet et le tissu rénal interstitiel, et qui s'étend ordinairement aux structures adjacentes: uretères et vessie.

Très fréquente au cours de l'enfance, son incidence est surtout élevée entre deux mois et deux ans, période pendant laquelle l'enfant porte encore des couches. Les filles en sont généralement plus souvent atteintes que les garçons, l'urètre féminin étant plus court que l'urètre masculin. De plus, la contamination du méat urinaire par les selles est plus facile chez la fille que chez le garçon.

L'infection provenant des germes contenus dans une couche souillée, pénètre dans l'urètre, contamine la vessie et peut s'étendre jusqu'aux reins par voie ascendante. L'infection pénètre ordinairement dans les voies urinaires par l'urètre, mais peut également être apportée par les vaisseaux sanguins ou lymphatiques. Les malformations congénitales qui causent une obstruction de l'arbre urinaire, sont des facteurs prédisposants parce que la stase de l'urine est associée aux infections chroniques des voies urinaires. Ces infections répétées permettent souvent de diagnostiquer une malformation obstructive.

Le colibacille provoque la majorité des pyélonéphrites. Le staphylocoque, le streptocoque hémolytique et le streptococcus fæcalis peuvent aussi causer de telles infections. Les infections chroniques peuvent provenir de nombreuses variétés de microbes dont les proteus et le pseudomonas.

Physio-pathologie, manifestations cliniques et résultats de laboratoire. Il y a des changements inflammatoires au niveau du bassinet et de tout le rein et, chez la majorité des enfants, ceux-ci s'étendent aux uretères et à la vessie. Dans la pyélonéphrite chronique, il y a diminution de la fonction rénale provoquée par les cicatrices du parenchyme rénal. Éventuellement, le rein s'atrophie et le tissu rénal est détruit.

Les *aspects cliniques* varient. Les symptômes urinaires ne sont pas toujours présents. Le début est brusque ou progressif; la fièvre peut atteindre 40,3°C. La prostration, la pâleur et l'anorexie apparaissent. Les vomissements et la diarrhée surviennent, provoquant la déshydratation. L'enfant souffre de mictions impérieuses, de pollakiurie et de dysurie. Il est irritable et sujet aux convulsions.

La douleur et la sensibilité des reins sont des signes de cette maladie. L'infection chronique peut durer des mois ou des années, causant de l'anémie et ralentissant le développement physique de l'enfant. Éventuellement un fonctionnement rénal déficient et de l'hypertension peuvent en résulter.

Les examens de *laboratoire* comportent l'analyse et la culture des urines ainsi que le décompte des globules blancs. Une hématurie légère ou modérée et la cylindrurie peuvent être mises en évidence.

Diagnostic et traitement. Le *diagnostic* est fait à partir du pus et des microbes trouvés dans les urines. S'il y a pyurie récurrente ou persistante, on doit avoir recours à une urographie rétrograde ou intraveineuse. Il peut y avoir des anomalies neurologiques ou structurales qui causent la stase urinaire ou l'infection prolongée.

La cystographie mictionnelle est nécessaire pour confirmer la dilatation urétérale ou le reflux vésico-urétéral.

Pendant la période fébrile, le *traitement* générral comprend repos et médicaments analgésiques, si cela est nécessaire. Les antibiotiques ou les sulfamides permettent de raccourcir la durée de la maladie et d'éviter les troubles rénaux progressifs. On utilise surtout les sulfamides contre les infections des voies urinaires. L'acide mandélique agit comme agent antiseptique urinaire, seulement si l'urine peut être maintenue acide par une médication, la méthionine, par exemple, ou un régime approprié. Le nitrofurantoïne (Furadantin) est un agent bactériostatique et bactéricide efficace contre la plupart des microbes pathogènes des voies urinaires.

Pendant la période aiguë, on encourage l'enfant à ingérer de grandes quantités de liquide pour diluer l'urine. Des transfusions peuvent être recommandées pour combattre l'anémie. En présence de malformations rénales obstructives, une correction chirurgicale peut être tentée afin de prévenir les récidives de l'infection.

Soins. Pour obtenir un spécimen d'urine destiné à une culture, on effectue de plus en plus rarement un cathétérisme vésical et, dans la plupart des hôpitaux, le prélèvement par mi-jet, après désinfection, est devenu une technique établie. Il s'agit, avant tout, d'éviter la contamination du spécimen. Chez le nourrisson, il importe de désinfecter les organes génitaux au Zéphiran 1:1000 après avoir procédé à un lavage minutieux au savon antiseptique et à l'eau stérile. On applique un collecteur d'urine stérile et le spécimen est recueilli de façon aseptique dans un récipient stérile.

Si le cathétérisme s'avère absolument nécessaire, on procède comme pour l'adulte. Deux infirmières doivent être présentes, l'une encourage l'enfant, le maintient délicatement, l'autre effectue doucement la technique en essayant de bien voir le méat urinaire avant d'insérer le cathéter. Il est important de se rappeler que la vessie du jeune enfant est située plus à l'avant et plus au-dessus de la symphyse pubienne que celle de l'adulte. L'urètre se situe juste sous la symphyse. Frapper la paroi, pour essayer de localiser l'orifice, risque de blesser les muqueuses délicates de l'enfant. Aussi est-il impérieux d'utiliser un cathéter dont le calibre est adapté à l'âge de l'enfant.

Si aucune obstruction n'a été décelée et que l'infection provient probablement d'une contamination par les selles, l'infirmière doit enseigner à la mère les mesures d'hygiène essentielles. Le papier hygiénique doit être utilisé du méat urinaire vers l'anus, soit d'avant en arrière. Elle doit s'assurer que la mère connaît la meilleure façon de laver soigneusement le périnée et d'éviter le contact prolongé du méat urinaire avec les selles. La mère doit comprendre le lien qui existe entre ces soins et l'infection urinaire.

Cryptorchidie
(Testicules non descendus)

Pathogénèse, traitement et pronostic. La cryptorchidie est l'absence d'un ou des deux testicules dans le scrotum. Chez l'embryon, les testicules se développent dans l'abdomen, sous les reins. Pendant les deux derniers mois de la vie intra-utérine, ils descendent dans le scrotum. Si les testicules, en passant par le canal inguinal – qui se referme après leur passage – ne sont pas descendus à la naissance, ils migrent ordinairement quelques jours ou moins plus tard. Après ce laps de temps, s'ils ne sont pas descendus, ils migrent rarement spontanément dans le scrotum avant la puberté. Les testicules cryptorchides peuvent rester dans la cavité abdominale ou dans le canal inguinal.

À la puberté, normalement, ils augmentent de volume et développent une activité androgénique et spermatogénique. Les testicules cryptorchides se trouvent à une température plus élevée dans l'abdomen qu'à leur place normale – le scrotum – ce qui inhibe la spermatogénèse et cause, à la longue, des lésions irréversibles et la stérilité.

L'insuffisance testiculaire postpubertaire se traduit par un manque de spermatozoïdes. Les caractères sexuels secondaires apparaissent quand même grâce aux hormones surrénales. Il y a une plus grande incidence de dégénérescence testiculaire néoplasique au cours de la vie adulte.

Le testicule qui demeure dans le canal inguinal est plus vulnérable aux traumatismes que s'il se trouvait dans le scrotum. Des troubles émotifs peuvent survenir, particulièrement à l'âge scolaire, quand le jeune garçon découvre qu'il est différent de ses compagnons.

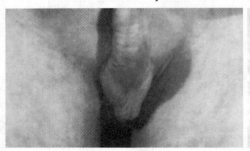 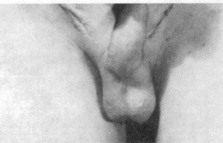

Figure 12-16. Cryptorchidie bilatérale chez un enfant de dix ans. *Gauche:* le scrotum n'est pas développé. *Droite:* après l'opération les testicules sont en place. (Extrait de Gross, R.: *The Surgery of Infancy and Childhood.* Philadelphia, W.B. Saunders.)

La préservation de la fertilité est le facteur le plus important dont il faut tenir compte dans le traitement. Certains médecins pensent qu'il faut essayer une thérapie endocrinienne pendant la période préscolaire. Un tel traitement a des chances de succès quand il n'y a pas de hernie; toutefois, la hernie est malheureusement présente dans plus de la moitié des cas. L'hormone gonadotrophique utilisée en doses excessives peut conduire à la puberté précoce. La dégénérescence cancéreuse du testicule affecté peut se produire même chez les garçons qui ont subi une orchidopexie au moment de la puberté ou après cette période.

Plusieurs médecins estiment que l'orchidopexie devrait être pratiquée dans tous les cas d'obstruction mécanique. Ils préfèrent opérer pendant le jeune âge, à cause du problème de la préservation de la fertilité et aussi en raison de l'augmentation de l'angoisse de castration pendant la période préscolaire. D'autres chirurgiens préfèrent retarder l'opération jusqu'à l'âge scolaire.

Quand l'enfant revient de la salle d'opération, il a une suture de traction dans la partie basse du scrotum, reliée à une bande de caoutchouc attachée à la face antéro-supérieure de la cuisse par des points ou un ruban adhésif. Ceci fixe le testicule au scrotum. On enlève ce lien après une semaine environ. L'infirmière ne doit pas déranger cette traction mécanique en transportant l'enfant et doit prévenir la contamination de la ligne de suture.

Si un testicule est absent ou s'il a dû être enlevé, une chirurgie plastique peut être effectuée afin de permettre à l'enfant d'être semblable à tous les autres garçons, ce qui évitera un problème psychologique éventuel.

Le *pronostic* est bon si le testicule est placé dans le scrotum avec succès et si aucun changement n'est survenu avant le traitement.

PATHOLOGIES NEUROLOGIQUES

Méningite

Définition. La méningite est une infection des méninges habituellement aiguë et secondaire. Elle peut être: 1) purulente ou bactérienne, 2) à liquide clair ou virale, 3) tuberculeuse. La méningite purulente est la plus fréquente chez le nourrisson.

Étiologie, incidence, symptomatologie. Chez le nouveau-né ou le très jeune nourrisson, le bacille coliforme est l'agent causal le plus fréquent. Chez le bébé de plus de 3 ou 4 mois, et chez le jeune enfant jusqu'à 5 ans, l'hémophilus influenzæ est l'agent causal habi-

tuel. Le méningocoque et le pneumocoque sont fréquemment responsables de la méningite, et ces cocci peuvent atteindre des enfants de tout âge. En temps d'épidémie, c'est le méningocoque qui est incriminé.

La majorité des cas de méningite surviennent avant l'âge de 5 ans, et la plus grande incidence se situe entre 6 mois et 2 ans. Les garçons, pour une raison inexpliquée, sont deux fois plus atteints. Les méningites à hémophilus prédominent en automne et en hiver et celles à pneumocoque et à méningocoque surviennent à la fin de l'hiver et au printemps.

Plus l'enfant est jeune, plus la symptomatologie est générale. Toutefois, le tableau clinique classique inclut: 1) fièvre élevée pouvant entraîner des convulsions 2) vomissements en jets, sans nausée 3) raideur et douleur à la nuque 4) bombement ou tension des fontanelles 5) irritabilité et hyperesthésie. Les signes de Kernig et de Brudzinski peuvent être mis en évidence. La méningite à méningocoque s'accompagne souvent d'une éruption pétéchiale.

Diagnostic, pronostic, traitement. Des hémocultures répétées, si possible, et dont l'une est effectuée avant l'institution du traitement antibiotique, peuvent permettre l'identification de l'agent causal. La ponction lombaire et l'analyse du liquide céphalo-rachidien permettent de confirmer le processus infectieux.

Le taux de mortalité demeure toujours assez élevé (6-10%), surtout pour les nourrissons très jeunes. Des complications cérébrales sont à redouter essentiellement pour les enfants de moins de 5 ans, étant donné que 90% du développement cérébral s'effectue durant ces premières années. Les complications les plus fréquentes sont l'hématome sous-dural, l'hydrocéphalie, le retard mental, la surdité, le strabisme et un certain degré de paralysie. Plus le traitement est précoce, réduisant rapidement l'inflammation et les possibilités d'adhérences, moins on rencontre de complications.

Le *traitement spécifique* est essentiellement médicamenteux et est institué immédiatement après le prélèvement pour hémoculture. Il consiste, ordinairement, en une association d'antibiotiques donnés par voie intraveineuse pendant huit à dix jours. Des mesures palliatives peuvent être nécessaires pour traiter l'état de choc, les difficultés respiratoires, la déshydratation et les convulsions.

Soins infirmiers. L'infirmière doit agir avec diligence et préparer rapidement ce qui est nécessaire pour l'hémoculture, la ponction lombaire et l'installation d'une perfusion intraveineuse, pour permettre une institution plus rapide du traitement. Elle doit prendre des mesures hypothermiques dès l'arrivée de l'enfant, de façon à prévenir les convulsions fébriles. Si les convulsions surviennent, elle doit protéger l'enfant d'accidents secondaires, observer soigneusement les gestes de celui-ci et administrer dès que possible les médicaments appropriés.

La surveillance de la perfusion intraveineuse et les soins à apporter à un enfant déshydraté ont été précédemment étudiés. L'infirmière doit se rappeler que l'enfant souffre d'hyperesthésie et être très douce en le touchant ou en le bougeant. Elle doit grouper tous les soins, le plus possible, pour favoriser le repos et le calme du nourrisson. Elle doit éviter le bruit ou la lumière vive qui irritent l'enfant. Toutefois, une présence rassure l'enfant et ses parents durant cette période terrifiante de la maladie. Une surveillance très minutieuse de l'état neurologique de l'enfant permet de déceler précocement une évolution vers l'encéphalite.

Encéphalite

L'encéphalite est une inflammation aiguë ou chronique de l'encéphale. Elle peut avoir les mêmes causes que la méningite ou être secondaire à une maladie contagieuse comme la rougeole, la varicelle, les oreillons.

La *symptomatologie* est la même que celle de la méningite, mis à part le caractère plus prononcé du syndrome neurologique. Les convulsions sont fréquentes. L'état de conscience évolue de la somnolence au coma progressif et à l'inconscience complète.

Les *séquelles* sont plus fréquentes et plus graves que dans la méningite. Le traitement et les soins infirmiers sont les mêmes que pour la méningite, sauf si l'encéphalite est sclérosante et subaiguë à la suite d'une rougeole. Il n'y a alors aucun traitement efficace connu pour arrêter l'évolution vers la mort.

Il n'existe pas de vaccin protégeant contre la méningite ou l'encéphalite. L'encéphalite peut également survenir à la suite de la vaccination contre la coqueluche ou la variole.

INFECTION VIRALE

Roséole infantile

Étiologie et incidence. La roséole infantile semble être causée par un virus filtrant, bien qu'aucun germe n'ait été identifié comme agent causal. On ne connaît pas le mode de contamination de cette infection. La maladie frappe également les deux sexes, généralement entre 6 et 8 mois, mais peut aussi atteindre les enfants de trois ans ou plus. L'incidence de cette maladie est sporadique; aucune épidémie n'a jamais été enregistrée.

Manifestations cliniques, diagnostic, traitement et complications. L'attaque est brutale, avec une température aussi élevée que 39,5°C à 40,5°C. Des convulsions peuvent survenir. Le bébé, irritable, somnolent et anorexique, n'apparaît pas, avec une telle fièvre, aussi malade qu'il le devrait. La température tombe brusquement, après deux ou trois jours, et une éruption maculaire ou maculopapulaire apparaît. L'éruption est localisée principalement sur le tronc, le cou et derrière les oreilles, et moins souvent sur la face et aux extrémités.

Il peut y avoir confusion avec la rougeole ou la rubéole. Dans la roséole, il n'y a ni symptômes catarrhéiques, ni points de Koplik, comme dans la rougeole, et la température est trop élevée pour que ce soit la rubéole.

En quelques heures, l'éruption commence à s'atténuer et disparaît généralement au bout de deux à trois jours. On peut rencontrer une adénopathie occipitale et postauriculaire. Le traitement est symptomatique et les complications, comme l'encéphalopathie résiduelle, sont rares.

Soins infirmiers. L'isolement de l'enfant n'est pas nécessaire. Au moment où l'éruption apparaît et que le diagnostic est fait, l'enfant n'est probablement plus contagieux, s'il l'a jamais été.

SYNDROME DE LA MORT INOPINÉE DU NOURRISSON

Incidence, théories sur l'étiologie, pathologie et prévention. Chaque année, on découvre un nombre de plus en plus élevé d'enfants morts dans leur lit, pour des raisons inexpliquées. Le taux de mortalité due à ce syndrome serait de 2 à 3 décès pour 1000 naissances vivantes dans les régions urbaines. Le faible poids à la naissance augmente le risque et plus d'un enfant par famille peut succomber de cette façon. Ces enfants apparaissent généralement bien développés et bien nourris; ils ont le plus souvent entre deux et quatre mois. Ces décès surviennent le plus fréquemment chez les garçons, pendant les mois froids de l'année, surtout entre minuit et neuf heures du matin. Ils atteignent le plus souvent les bébés de familles économiquement faibles, vivant dans des zones urbaines. À l'autopsie, on ne découvre que des changements pathologiques négligeables. Le thymus apparaît légèrement hypertrophié, mais demeure dans les limites de la normale; on trouve quelquefois des pétéchies au thymus, aux poumons et au cerveau; une légère inflammation du larynx est quelquefois présente et les surrénales peuvent être légèrement diminuées de volume comme c'est quasi normal chez le bébé en santé. La quantité de graisse brune autour des surrénales serait augmentée.

La suffocation, l'aspiration accidentelle du contenu gastrique causant un laryngospasme, la bactériémie, l'hypogammaglobulinémie, un traumatisme de la colonne vertébrale, et l'allergie au lait ou à d'autres substances, ont été invoqués comme causes possibles. Certains médecins tentent de démontrer que ces morts tragiques sont presque toujours dues à une infection virale soudaine et très brutale des voies respiratoires. Toutefois, ceci n'est pas encore prouvé. Lors d'études épidémiologiques, on a constaté que les mères de ces nourrissons fumaient plus que la moyenne des parturientes durant leur grossesse et que le pourcentage de bébés allaités au sein était plus bas que dans la population en général.

L'hypothèse explicative qui prévaut actuellement est que la mort inopinée serait due à une immaturité ou dysfonction du système autonome de ces bébés. Il semble que l'on ait pu démontrer que les bébés ayant survécu, après avoir été ranimés, étaient sujets à des périodes d'apnée dépassant 20 secondes. De courtes périodes d'apnée durant le sommeil sont fréquentes chez les jeunes nourrissons, particulièrement les prématurés, mais si le bébé ne possède pas les mécanismes pour recommencer à respirer, il peut décéder doucement lors d'un épisode apnéique. Les soins intensifs néonatals sont équipés de moniteurs électroniques dont l'alarme se déclenche si le bébé cesse de respirer plus de 10 secondes. Des recherches sont actuellement en cours pour découvrir si de tels appareils peuvent être utilisés pour des bébés qui semblent les plus vulnérables au syndrome de mort inopinée du nourrisson.

La prévention peut seulement viser à une surveillance étroite des nourrissons, surtout de ceux âgés de 0 à 6 mois.

La mort bouleverse n'importe quelle famille, mais quand un enfant, en bonne santé apparente, est trouvé mort dans son lit, ses parents peuvent être complètement désemparés et se sentir coupables. On doit les convaincre qu'il n'y a eu ni suffocation, ni infection évidente et qu'ils n'auraient pu en aucun cas éviter ce drame en consultant un médecin. Ils ne sont en rien responsables de la mort de leur enfant. Les jeunes enfants, qui ont parfois souffert de l'arrivée du nouveau bébé, peuvent rapidement avoir à évoluer au milieu d'une famille bouleversée par des accusations extérieures au milieu familial, tout en supportant leurs propres sentiments de culpabilité et la surprotection de leurs parents.

Des parents, ayant perdu leur bébé dans ces conditions, se sont organisés en groupe à travers les États-Unis, dans le but de s'accorder un support mutuel pendant leur deuil, et pour éduquer le public face au problème soulevé par le décès subit et inexpliqué de nourrissons. Chacun des parents qui a perdu un bébé de cette manière a également besoin du support moral et de l'affection des membres de l'équipe de santé.

RÉFÉRENCES

Livres et documents officiels

Bergman, A. B., Beckwith, J. B. et Ray, C. G.: *Sudden Infant Death Syndrome*. Seattle. Washington, University of Washington Press, 1970.

Burgess, A.: *The Nurse's Guide to Fluid and Electrolyte Balance*. New York, McGraw-Hill Book Company, Inc. 1970.

Dickens, M. L.: *Fluid and Electrolyte Balance*. 2e éd. Philadelphie, F. A. Davis Company, 1970.

Geertinger, P.: *Sudden Death in Infancy*. Springfield, Ill. Charles C Thomas, 1968.

Laboratoires Abbott: *L'eau et les électrolytes*, 2e éd., 1969.

MacKeith, R. et autres: *Infant Feeding and Feeding Difficulties*. 4e éd. Baltimore, Williams & Wilkins Company, 1971.

Paque, C., Huet, M. et Rey, J.: *Un état diarrhéique chez l'enfant*. Paris, Maloine, 1968.

Plumer, A. L.: *Principles and Practice of Intravenous Therapy*. Boston, Little, Brown and Company, 1970.

Raffensperger, J. G. et autres: *Acute Abdomen in Infancy and Childhood*. Philadelphie, J. B. Lippincott Company, 1970.

Reed, G. M. et Sheppard, V. F.: *Regulation of Fluid and Electrolyte Balance*. Philadelphie, W. B. Saunders Company, 1971.

Taylor, W. H.: *Fluid Therapy and Disorders of Electrolyte Balance*. 2e éd. Philadelphie, F. A. Davis Company, 1970.

Young, D. G. et Weller, B. F.: *Baby Surgery*. Milton Road, Aylesbury, Bucks, England, Harvey Miller & Medcalf Ltd., Publishers, 1971.

Articles

Anderson, F. P. et autres: An Approach to the Problem of Noncompliance in a Pediatric Outpatient Clinic. *Am. J. Dis. Child.*, 122:142, août 1971.

Arnal, J.: Diarrhées. *Soins*, XI:49, 2, 1966.

Aubin, G. et autres: Les bronchiolites. *Union méd. du Can.*, 97:773, juin 1968.

Berchel, C.: Rhinopharyngites à répétition de l'enfant. *Soins*, 19:37, 14, 1974.

Bergman, A. B.: Sudden Infant Death. *Nursing Outlook*, 20:775, décembre 1972.

Blair, J. et Fitzgerald, J.: Treatment of Nonspecific Diarrhea. *Clin. Ped.*, 13:333, 4, 1974.

Bouquier, J.: Convulsions hyperpyrétiques du nourrisson et du jeune enfant. *Soins*, 17:33, 6, 1972.

Clavé, M.: Les Angines. *La revue de l'inf.*, 23:29, 1, 1973.

Clotteau, J. E.: Sténose du pylore chez le nouveau-né. *Soins*, 19:15, 6, 1974.

Cragg, C. et Taine, A.: La méningite purulente chez l'enfant. *Inf. Can.*, 15:13, 3, 1973.

Dayton, D. H.: Early Malnutrition and Human Development *Children*, 16:210, novembre-décembre 1969

Donn, R: Intravenous Admixture Incompatibility. *Am. J. Nursing*, 71:325, février 1971.

Downs, A. W. et Cleland, V. S.: Bacteriuria and Urinary Tract Infection in Infancy and Childhood: A Review. *Nursing Research*, 20:131, mars-avril 1971.

Drachman, R.: Acute Infectious Gastroenteritis. *Ped. Clin. N. Amer.*, 21:711, 3, 1974.

Fontaine, G. et autres: Les états d'acidose. *La médecine infantile*, 77:521, 7, 1970.

Friedman, S.: Psychological Aspects of Sudden Unexpected Death in Infants and Children. *Pediat. Clin. N. Amer.*, 21:103, 1, 1974.

Guibert, J. M.: Moyens de diagnostic et de surveillance de l'infection urinaire. *La revue de l'inf.*, 24:41, 1, 1974.

Hardy, J. M.: Hernies inguinales, hernies crurales. *Soins*, 18:9, 10, 1973.

Howie, V. et Ploussard, J.: Treatment of Serious Otitis Media with Ventilatory Tubes. *Clin. Ped.*, 13:919, 11, 1974.

Kee, J. et Gregory, A.: The ABC's and mEq's of Fluid Imbalance in Children. *Nursing '74*, 4:28, 6, 1974.

Keto, D. et Heller, R.: Acute Respiratory Infections. *Ped. Clin. N. Amer.*, 21:683, 3, 1974.

Khan, A. et Pryles, C.: Urinary Tract Infection in Children. *Am. J. Nursing*, 73:1340, 8, 1973.

Kraus, S. A. et autres: Further Epidemiologic Observations on Sudden Unexpected Death in Infancy in Ontario. *Canad. J. Pub. Health*, 62:210, mai-juin 1971.

Labrune, B.: Pneumopathies aiguës chez l'enfant. *Soins*, 18:19, 3, 1973.

Langworth, J. et Steele, R.: Commentaires sur la mort inattendue du nourrisson. *Inf. Can.*, 8:37, septembre 1966.

Lecomte, E.: Angines et otites. *Soins*, 18:5, 8, 1973.

Lintzen, J. P.: Aspects cliniques et thérapeutiques des otites moyennes aiguës de l'enfant. *Soins*, 19:5, 14, 1974.

Menking, M. et autres: Rumination – A Near Fatal Psychiatric Disease of Infancy. *New Eng. J. Med.*, 280:802, 10 avril, 1969.

Michener, W. M. et Law, D.: Parenteral Nutrition: The Age of the Catheter. *Pediat. Clin. N. Amer.*, 17:373, mai 1970.

Mindlin, R. L.: Medical Care of Urban Infants: The Common Complaints. *Pediatrics*, 45:614, avril 1970.

Murray, J. D.: The Continuing Problem of Purulent Meningitis in Infants and Children. *Ped. Clin. N. Amer.*, 21:967, 4, 1974.

Nivelon, J. C.: L'infection urinaire chez l'enfant. *La revue de l'inf.*, 24:323, 4, 1974.

Olier, C.: Pathologie courante du canal inguinal chez l'enfant. *Revue de l'inf.*, 21:139, 2, 1971.

Ouellette, E.: The Child who Convulses with Fever. *Ped. Clin. N. Amer.*, 21:467, 2, 1974.

Patterson, K. et Pomeroy, M.: Sudden Infant Death Syndrome. *Nursing '74*, 4:85, 5, 1974.

Roget, J. et autres: Les vomissements du nourrisson et de l'enfant. *La médecine infantile*, 76:5, 1, 1969.

Salk, L.: Sudden Infant Death: Impact on Family and Physician. *Clinical Pediatrics*, 10:248, mai 1971.

Spicher, C.: Nursing Care of Children Hospitalized with Infections. *Nursing Clin. N. Amer.*, 5:123, mars 1970.

Stine, O. C. et Chuaqui, C.: Mothers' Intented Actions for Childhood Symptoms. *Am. J. Pub. Health*, 59:2035, novembre 1969.

Terdiman, F. et Terdiman, M.: Traitement des infections urinaires. *Soins*, 19:23, 16, 1974.

Thieffry, J. C.: Le lait dans les régimes d'exclusion chez l'enfant. *Soins*, 17:37, 8, 1972.

Thibert, R. et Beigue, C.: Otite séreuse et allergie. *Union méd. du Can.*, 97:67, janvier 1968.

Trotoux, J. et Gehanno, P.: Problèmes thérapeutiques actuels devant une otite chronique. *La revue de l'inf.*, 24:529, 6, 1974.

Valman, H. B. et Wilmers, M. J.: Use of Antibiotics in Acute Gastro-enteritis Among Infants in Hospital. *Lancet*, 1:1122, 7 juin 1969.

Vandekerkove, M.: La méningite cérébro-spinale. *Soins*, 20:15, 7, 1975.

Williams, T.: Responses of a Twelve-Month-Old Girl to Physical Restraint During Hospitalization. *Maternal-Child Nursing Journ.*, 4:109, 2, 1975.

Wilmore, D. W.: The Future of Intravenous Therapy. *Am. J. Nursing*, 71:2334, décembre 1971.

13 pathologies des nourrissons nécessitant des soins de longue durée

Au cours de sa première année de vie, une maladie, même de quelques mois, peut retarder grandement le développement de l'enfant. Apprendre à avoir confiance en son entourage est une des tâches les plus importantes de cet âge et il est essentiel que le nourrisson hospitalisé garde sa foi en la protection affective de ses parents et apprenne que d'autres personnes peuvent lui prodiguer soins physiques et affection. Il faudrait encourager la mère à consacrer le plus de temps possible à son enfant hospitalisé.

La réaction de la mère à l'égard de l'enfant qui a une maladie de longue durée, dépend naturellement de la gravité de cette maladie. Si elle est grave et le pronostic incertain, la mère éprouve une tension émotive prolongée. Elle peut réagir en surprotégeant son bébé. Par la suite, l'enfant manquera peut-être d'initiative et ne tentera pas de découvrir de nouvelles activités musculaires. Même tout petit, le nourrisson essaie de compenser le manque de maîtrise sur son environnement par un contrôle sur les adultes qui lui donneront ce qu'il désire et feront pour lui ce qu'il est incapable de faire par lui-même.

L'infirmière doit connaître les activités permises par le médecin et, à l'intérieur de ce champ d'actions, donner à l'enfant toutes les possibilités d'apprentissage. Ceci ne s'applique pas seulement à son activité physique, mais aussi à son évolution psychologique et émotive.

Il faut aussi permettre à la mère d'exprimer ses sentiments et de cette façon soulager dans une certaine mesure sa tension émotive. Des heures ouvertes de visite lui donneront la possibilité d'observer les infirmières qui soignent son enfant. Elle pourra discuter avec elles des techniques de réadaptation qui permettent au nourrisson de découvrir de nouvelles activités physiques ou de jouer seul sans avoir besoin d'une attention constante.

La mère peut devenir très dépendante de l'infirmière, mais lorsqu'elle est intégrée à l'équipe, son sentiment de frustration diminue. Elle comprend que les infirmières excellent dans leur travail professionnel, mais qu'elle-même est indispensable pour satisfaire les besoins d'affection et de sécurité de son enfant.

TROUBLES DE LA NUTRITION (MALADIES CARENTIELLES)

Le régime du nourrisson et du jeune enfant est quelquefois insuffisant en éléments nutritifs essentiels, c'est-à-dire protides, lipides, glucides, vitamines ou minéraux. Bien que plusieurs facteurs puissent engendrer des maladies carentielles, le problème fondamental provient habituellement d'un apport insuffisant de nourriture. Parfois, il peut y avoir une absorption déficiente d'une ou plusieurs composantes alimentaires. Les maladies par carence s'avèrent particulièrement dangereuses durant la petite enfance, parce que c'est la période où la croissance est la plus rapide et où l'organisme humain a besoin d'un régime adéquat, contenant tous les éléments nutritifs essentiels. On peut constater la carence d'un seul ou de plusieurs éléments nutritifs.

Malnutrition (Athrepsie — Marasme)

Incidence, étiologie et diagnostic. La malnutrition s'observe beaucoup moins en Amérique du Nord et en Europe qu'auparavant. Mais dans les pays du tiers-monde, elle constitue un des problèmes auxquels l'Organisation Mondiale de la Santé s'intéresse intensément.

La malnutrition est un terme général désignant un état d'hyponutrition accompagné le plus souvent de carences vitaminiques spécifiques.

La cause fondamentale réside dans le fait que l'enfant ne reçoit pas une alimentation satisfaisante ou est incapable d'assimiler des éléments nutritifs en quantité suffisante pour les besoins métaboliques de son organisme, ce qui entraîne l'épuisement des réserves tissulaires. La cause spécifique peut être une ingestion inadéquate ou un régime mal équilibré; de mauvaises habitudes alimentaires; une malformation physique comme une fissure labiale ou palatine; des anomalies digestives ou cardiaques; des maladies s'accompagnant de malabsorption (en général, ce sont des maladies chroniques, comme la mucoviscidose); des infections génératrices d'anorexie qui diminuent la capacité de digestion de l'enfant et qui en même temps augmentent son besoin en apport calorique; des pertes par vomissements ou diarrhée. Des problèmes affectifs engendrés, par exemple, par une perturbation des rapports mère-enfant peuvent entraîner la dénutrition.

On reconnaît la malnutrition en s'appuyant sur les symptômes évidents établis lors d'un examen physique, sur un retard de croissance ou sur le dosage des divers constituants du sang. L'analyse de l'alimentation d'un groupe permet d'identifier les enfants risquant de présenter un état de malnutrition.

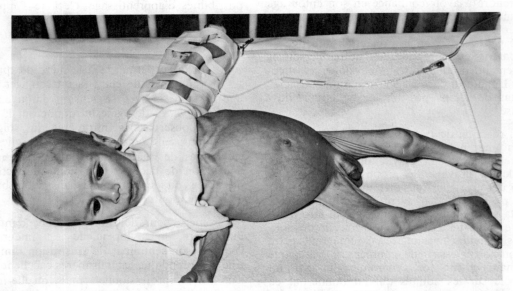

Figure 13-1. L'incapacité d'assimiler la nourriture conduit à la malnutrition. On constate une disparition du tissu adipeux sous-cutané. La peau est plissée aux extrémités et l'abdomen est proéminent.

Manifestations cliniques et examens de laboratoire. On reconnaît les maladies carentielles par l'absence de prise pondérale, suivie éventuellement d'une perte de poids. La croissance du squelette et du cerveau se poursuit, le corps est long et la tête large en comparaison du poids total. Pour maintenir le métabolisme de base, le corps consomme ses propres lipides et protéines. Le tissu adipeux sous-cutané disparaît, mais il demeure plus longtemps dans les pannicules de succion des joues, ce qui donne au visage une rondeur factice. Les yeux sont creux, les traits tirés et quand les pannicules de succion disparaissent, l'enfant ressemble à un vieillard. La peau perd son élasticité et se ride sur toute sa surface. L'enfant cesse toute activité, ses muscles sont habituellement flasques et relâchés, son cri devient faible et strident.

Comme le volume sanguin diminue et qu'il souffre d'anémie, son teint devient grisâtre. On constate un abaissement de la température corporelle, une bradycardie et une diminution du métabolisme basal. Il digère mal, mange sans appétit, présente de la constipation ou une diarrhée spécifique contenant du sang et du mucus. Le nourrisson résiste mal aux infections; il peut souffrir de rachitisme, de scorbut, de tétanie à la suite de carences nutritionnelles. On peut également noter un œdème par hypoprotidémie.

Les *examens de laboratoire* montrent une anémie hypochrome sévère, en général les protéines plasmatiques diminuent, mais en cas d'hémoconcentration, leur taux peut paraître faussement normal.

Complications. Il peut souffrir d'infections intercurrentes comme le muguet, la bronchite ou la pyélonéphrite. On observe des infections de la peau comme la furonculose et même des escarres aux points de pression osseuse (l'occiput, les talons, les genoux et le bassin). Une anémie nutritionnelle due à un manque de fer peut se développer. L'œdème apparaît quand le corps, en état de carence protéique secondaire à une alimentation insuffisante, utilise ses réserves tissulaires et ses propres protéines plasmatiques. L'œdème nutritionnel s'observe chez des enfants qui souffrent de malnutrition depuis plusieurs mois. Si on lui donne des protéines en quantité suffisante et si l'état de l'enfant s'est amélioré au point que son organisme est capable d'absorber les protéines ingérées, l'œdème disparaît.

Traitement, soins et pronostic. Le but du traitement consiste à fournir suffisamment d'éléments nutritifs pour garder le bébé en vie et ensuite lui assurer une croissance et un développement normaux. La thérapie intraveineuse essayée autrefois, avait remporté peu de succès; on s'était heurté aux difficultés causées par son administration prolongée, l'intoxication et l'apport calorique insuffisant. L'hyperalimentation, une nouvelle méthode d'alimentation parentérale, a permis de surmonter ces problèmes.

L'HYPERALIMENTATION consiste à administrer par voie intraveineuse une solution de glucose et d'acides aminés (hydrolysat de fibrine) à laquelle on ajoute des électrolytes et des vitamines selon les besoins du nourrisson. La perfusion régulière et ininterrompue nécessite une pompe reliée à un cathéter qui pousse le liquide dans la veine cave supérieure. Le traitement peut durer jusqu'à deux mois selon les besoins de l'enfant. L'administration de plasma fournit les oligoéléments et les acides gras essentiels; les transfusions sanguines ou les injections intramusculaires corrigent la déficience en fer.

La solution hypertonique doit couler à un rythme lent et uniforme dans un vaisseau de calibre suffisant pour assurer une dilution rapide tout en évitant l'irritation vasculaire et la thrombose veineuse. On utilise un cathéter de silicone qui pénètre dans la veine jugulaire ou la veine sous-clavière et se rend à la veine cave supérieure; la partie extérieure du cathéter est glissée sous la peau du cou et de la tête pour sortir au niveau du cuir chevelu. Cette dernière précaution facilite le nettoyage de la plaie, prévient en grande partie le retrait accidentel du cathéter tout en rendant plus faciles les soins normaux du nourrisson. On applique un onguent antibiotique et un pansement stérile sur le cathéter replié au-dessus du point d'insertion; cette précaution permet d'éviter l'infection et le retrait par inadvertance du tube de perfusion. Le tube n'est pas changé pendant le traitement sauf s'il est obstrué par des caillots ou des médicaments ou encore s'il est déplacé accidentellement. Un filtre spécial est ajouté au système de perfusion pour empêcher la pénétration de particules ou de micro-organismes qui pourraient contaminer la solution.

Certaines complications peuvent se produire en cours de traitement. Si la qualité de glucose administrée dépasse la production d'insuline, la glycosurie apparaît, suivie d'une diurèse osmotique. La surcharge vasculaire et l'hyperhydratation découlent de l'administration exagérée de liquide. La solution d'acides aminés entraîne quelquefois la toxicité ou l'aminoacidurie.

Les points suivants permettent de suivre l'évolution du traitement: le dosage strict des urines, la pesée quotidienne, la recherche du glucose urinaire, l'étude de la concentration des électrolytes sanguins et de la glycémie, l'hématrocite et l'osmolarité sérique. D'autres tests sont effectués régulièrement pour vérifier le fonctionnement hépatique.

Ces enfants ont besoin de soins continus. Le danger de septicémie explique la nécessité de l'asepsie la plus stricte au point d'entrée du cathéter. On n'utilise pas le tube de perfusion pour injecter les médicaments ou préléver les échantillons de sang à cause du danger de contamination ou d'occlusion. Toute élévation de la température corporelle peut signifier l'apparition d'une infection ou d'une réaction antigénique à la solution perfusée.

L'administration importante de glucose amène quelquefois une diurèse exagérée produisant une déshydratation grave et rapide d'où la nécessité d'effectuer le dosage qualitatif quotidien du sucre urinaire. En présence d'une quantité moyenne ou importante de glucose, il faut ralentir le rythme de la perfusion ou diminuer sa concentration en glucose. Si le médecin prescrit d'administrer de l'insuline, il faut surveiller l'apparition des signes d'hyper ou d'hypoglycémie.

L'alimentation par voie orale remplace ou fait suite à l'hyperalimentation intraveineuse. On donne d'abord une diète légère et hypocalorique; l'enfant peut souffrir de vomissements et de diarrhée si on augmente trop rapidement l'apport en calories. Le premier repas doit être du lait maternel dilué ou à défaut, du lait acidifié écrémé. Il faut augmenter progressivement la teneur en protéines et en glucides. L'augmentation de la teneur en lipides doit être plus lente que celle des glucides, puisque les graisses demeurent plus difficiles à digérer. Les besoins nutritifs atteignent environ 200 calories par kilogramme par jour, avant que ces enfants commencent à prendre du poids. Il faut augmenter la quantité de protéines pour permettre la reconstitution des tissus.

Si c'est nécessaire, on corrige la déshydratation par l'administration de liquide par voie parentérale. Des transfusions de sang en petite quantité, mais fréquentes, peuvent être nécessaires pour combattre l'anémie et augmenter la résistance à l'infection. La médication permet de pallier à certaines carences alimentaires. Les injections intramusculaires d'extraits de foie frais, tous les deux ou trois jours pendant plusieurs semaines, peuvent être utiles. Il faut fournir des vitamines A, B, C et D à doses normales ou plus élevées.

Il faut traiter les complications telles que les infections intercurrentes ou les affections de la peau.

Le *pronostic* dépend de la gravité de l'état de l'enfant, de sa taille et de la présence d'une infection. Des enfants en état de malnutrition grave peuvent entrer en collapsus et mourir subitement. C'est ce qui arrive le plus souvent aux enfants qui continuent à perdre du poids après l'institution du traitement, et qui présentent une chute de température accompagnée d'un pouls lent et d'un état de choc. Ces enfants peuvent avoir contracté une infection grave contre laquelle ils n'ont aucune résistance.

Soins infirmiers. Il faut maintenir normale la température du corps. Si l'enfant présente de l'hypothermie, il faut le placer dans un incubateur ou le couvrir à l'aide de vêtements et de couvertures supplémentaires. On utilise des bouillottes en tenant compte des précautions déjà mentionnées. Pour éviter les infections, surtout la moniliase buccale, il faut stériliser les biberons, les cuillers, les assiettes, etc. Il faut varier fréquemment la position du nouveau-né, pour prévenir une pneumonie hypostatique, éviter les zones de pression sur les proéminences osseuses et les infections de la peau. On l'isole pour sa propre protection, et le personnel infirmier qui s'en occupe doit être exempt de toute infection.

Il faut veiller à respecter scrupuleusement le régime prescrit par le médecin et vérifier l'ordonnance avant chaque repas. Il faut nourrir l'enfant lentement et permettre des éructations fréquentes. Le bébé doit se sentir en sécurité dans les bras de l'infirmière, entouré de chaleur physique et d'affection.

Si on craint un collapsus, on place l'enfant gravement malade sous surveillance constante afin de déceler le moindre signe précurseur: chute de température, pouls lent, cyanose, coloration « terreuse » de la peau et froideur des extrémités.

L'infirmière participera à l'administration parentérale de liquide ou de sang. Elle notera soigneusement la quantité de nourriture absorbée, refusée ou vomie, par l'enfant et s'il a bu ou mangé avec avidité ou indifférence. Il est important pour le médecin de connaître le nombre et la nature des selles et de savoir si l'abdomen est distendu. Il faudrait aussi peser l'enfant tous les jours pour déterminer exactement toute perte ou tout gain de poids.

Prévention. La prévention de la malnutrition est une des fonctions essentielles de l'équipe de santé. La quantité de nourriture doit être appropriée et la technique de l'ali-

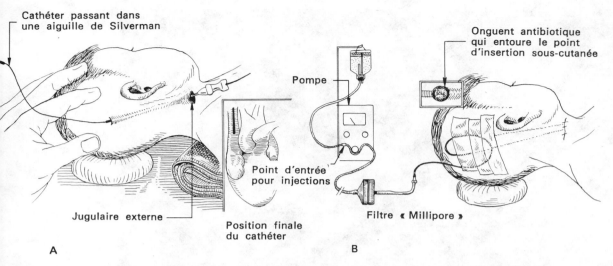

Figure 13-2. Techique d'*hyperalimentation*: *A)* L'installation du cathéter de silicone dans la veine cave supérieure. *B)* L'administration du liquide d'hyperalimentation (liquide, pompe et filtre). (R.M. Filler: Long-term total parenteral nutrition in infants. New Eng. J. Med., 281,(11):592, septembre 1969.) (Dessin adapté par S. Rosenthal.)

mentation adéquate pour que l'enfant profite au maximum de son régime.

Parmi les facteurs importants de la prévention de la malnutrition, signalons le traitement précoce des maladies et infections pouvant être en cause, et la prévention des troubles émotifs.

Kwashiorkor

Le kwashiorkor, syndrome prédominant chez les peuples du tiers-monde, dans les régions tropicales et subtropicales, est une forme de malnutrition due à une carence en protéines et, secondairement, en d'autres éléments nutritifs.

Ce terme de kwashiorkor, peut signifier « homme rouge » à cause de la couleur des cheveux des gens atteints ou encore « enfant détrôné », c'est-à-dire celui qui a dû laisser le sein à l'arrivée d'un nouveau bébé. La maladie peut apparaître entre 4 mois et 5 ans et ces enfants sont particulièrement sensibles aux infections.

Une coutume de certaines régions africaines veut que le bébé soit sevré dès qu'apparaissent les signes d'une prochaine grossesse. On nourrit ensuite l'enfant avec une racine dont on fait une bouillie sucrée qui calme momentanément l'appétit, mais dont l'apport calorique est faible et la teneur en protéines pratiquement nulle. Les protéines sont nécessaires à la croissance normale et les symptômes de carence apparais-

sent si l'apport en acides aminés essentiels est insuffisant, s'ils sont mal absorbés par l'organisme ou s'ils sont éliminés en quantité excessive dans les selles.

On constate alors les symptômes suivants: retard ou arrêt du développement et de la croissance, perte du tonus musculaire, manque d'énergie, faible résistance aux infections et présence d'œdème. On rencontre de la diarrhée et des dermatites; les troubles de pigmentation et le vitiligo peuvent apparaître. Les cheveux sont secs et cassants, leur couleur tourne au jaune, au rouge ou au gris à la suite des troubles de pigmentation. Les malades sont particulièrement sensibles aux infestations parasitaires et aux infections, surtout à la rougeole. En plus de souffrir d'anorexie, de vomissements et de faiblesse musculaire, l'enfant devient irritable et apathique. La cardiomégalie et la splénomégalie peuvent survenir.

L'œdème nutritionnel se développe à mesure que le taux d'albumine sérique diminue; d'autres perturbations sanguines accompagnent l'anémie et les carences vitaminiques.

Le traitement comprend l'administration d'eau et d'électrolytes. Les médicaments appropriés permettent de combattre les infections et les infestations. À long terme, il faut fournir une alimentation qui contient suffisamment de calories et surtout des protéines d'une valeur biologique élevée. Trop souvent, l'enfant qui survit souffre d'un retard de croissance et de dommages cérébraux irréversibles.

Figure 13-3. La croissance du bébé nourri au sein est normale. L'aîné est déjà atteint de kwashiorkor. (Jane F. McConnell: The Deposed One. *Am. J. Nursing*, vol. 61.)

Malnutrition engendrée par une perturbation des relations mère-enfant (Retard de croissance)

Étiologie, diagnostic et manifestations cliniques. Le diagnostic « retard de croissance » ou retard saturo-pondéral s'applique aux enfants qui présentent une malnutrition grave et un développement physique et psychique défectueux. On en attribue la cause à une perturbation des relations mère-enfant. Habituellement, ces enfants sont irritables, apathiques et anorexiques; ils peuvent souffrir de vomissements et de diarrhée. Leur développement social est perturbé, par exemple, ils refusent tout contact visuel en se couvrant les yeux avec les bras et ils sont physiquement sous-développés. Bien que ces nourrissons ne soient pas séparés de leur mère, leurs symptômes s'apparentent au syndrome de la dépression anaclitique.

Ces enfants présentent un problème de diagnostic et de thérapie parce qu'il faut éliminer un état physiopathologique tel qu'une anomalie congénitale ou une infection, avant d'incriminer une perturbation des relations parents-enfant.

On croit que le problème fondamental d'un enfant organiquement normal, mais qui est déprimé et refuse de s'épanouir, se trouve du côté des parents: soit une mère névrotique ou immature qui ne considère pas l'enfant comme le sien ou qui, en refusant de lui reconnaître une personnalité autonome ou en le rejetant, ne comprend pas les besoins de dépendance de son bébé ou doute de ses propres capacités d'éducatrice; soit un père détaché à la fois de la mère et de l'enfant.

Une mère perturbée à ce point, non seulement n'alimente pas adéquatement son bébé, mais elle ne réussit pas davantage à lui fournir les stimulations sensorielles, tactiles et verbales nécessaires à son développement.

Traitement et soins infirmiers. Le traitement de ces enfants est complexe; il nécessite la collaboration d'un pédiatre, d'un psychiatre, d'une infirmière et d'une travailleuse sociale. L'histoire médicale de la famille et de l'enfant est essentielle et précède l'évaluation pédiatrique et psychiatrique. Une entrevue non directive permet ensuite de compléter l'étude sur le plan social. Le médecin est responsable du diagnostic qui sera basé sur des examens physiologiques de l'enfant et sur la recherche des antécédents familiaux; il s'occupera de guider la famille dans son ensemble. La travailleuse sociale, en collaboration avec les autres membres de l'équipe, fournira aux parents, temporairement, un support moral, sans esprit de critique et de rivalité. Elle doit les aider à neutraliser les facteurs de tension qui les empêchent d'assumer pleinement leur rôle de parents. La mère surtout a besoin d'aide pour trouver des satisfactions dans son rôle. L'infirmière doit coordonner les soins de l'enfant, apprendre à la mère à prodiguer des soins appropriés, et transmettre aux parents ses propres observations au sujet de leur enfant. Elle doit partager ses connaissances avec l'infirmière en santé communautaire si celle-ci se rend à domicile pour aider la famille. Il faut accorder aux parents le temps d'exprimer leurs sentiments. Si l'on veut que le traitement soit fructueux, il faut que s'établisse une certaine communication entre l'équipe de santé et les parents. L'aide psychologique et même psychiatrique peut s'avérer la clé du succès de la thérapie et un programme d'aide à long terme doit être planifié avant le retour du bébé à la maison.

Pronostic et prévention. Le pronostic pour les enfants qui ont des difficultés de croissance est le même que pour ceux qui souffrent d'une très grave malnutrition. Tout dépend de la gravité et de la durée de cet état, et aussi de la présence d'infection. Il est important que dès la conception d'un enfant, toute l'équipe de santé travaille toujours en vue de favoriser de saines relations parents-enfant.

Carences vitaminiques

Malgré la hausse continuelle du niveau de la vie dans les pays industrialisés, on ne réussit pas à supprimer les syndromes de carences vitaminiques qui atteignent des enfants de toutes les strates de la société. La fréquence du rachitisme demeure étonnamment élevée dans les milieux défavorisés en Amérique du nord.

Rachitisme

Étiologie et incidence. Le rachitisme est une maladie carentielle des enfants en période de croissance, provenant d'un manque de vitamine D, une vitamine liposoluble.

Comme la vitamine D augmente l'absorption intestinale du calcium et du phosphore et diminue l'excrétion rénale en phosphates, une carence de cette vitamine entraîne une perturbation de la concentration de calcium et de phosphore dans le sang, les liquides tissulaires et les os.

Les facteurs prédisposant au rachitisme sont: 1) L'hérédité des gens à peau foncée, vivant dans des régions tempérées et ne profitant pas des rayons solaires pour transformer leur provitamine en vitamine D. 2) L'âge: le rachitisme peut se manifester en tout temps, de trois mois à trois ans. 3) La prématurité: la prématurité prédispose au rachitisme parce qu'à la naissance les réserves de calcium et de phosphore sont insuffisantes pour la croissance exceptionnellement rapide de l'enfant. 4) Rayonnement solaire réduit: les nuages, le brouillard, la poussière, la fumée en suspension dans l'air ou une vitre ordinaire diminuent l'activité des rayons ultra-violets. 5) La saison: la plupart des cas de rachitisme apparaissent à la fin de l'hiver et au début du printemps.

Physio-pathologie et manifestations cliniques. Les manifestations du rachitisme sont surtout évidentes sur le squelette; elles varient avec l'âge de l'enfant et le stress que subit l'os affecté. La lésion la plus marquée de la structure osseuse consiste en l'arrêt de calcification de l'épiphyse. Une tuméfaction visible naît dans cette zone de l'os. Les muscles sont peu développés et hypotoniques.

Dans le rachitisme avancé, la tête paraît plus volumineuse et a une forme carrée, vue d'en haut. On constate un retard dans la fermeture de la fontanelle antérieure. La palpation du crâne révèle des zones molles qui crépitent sous la pression: c'est le *craniotabès* qui s'observe surtout au niveau de l'os occipital.

Au niveau du thorax, on observe le « chapelet costal », augmentation de volume ou nouures des articulations chondrocostales et le « sillon de Harrisson », une dépression horizontale qui se développe le long du bord intérieur du thorax et qui correspond aux insertions costales du diaphragme. La position assise peut révéler une cyphose; une scoliose avec une déformation concomitante du bassin est très courante. Ces dernières lésions, (chez les femmes) si elles deviennent définitives, accroîtront les dangers de l'accouchement.

Des jambes arquées ou des genoux cagneux (genu valgum), accompagnés de pieds plats, sont les déformations les plus évidentes au niveau des extrémités. On observe aussi un élargissement épiphysaire des poignets et des chevilles (bourrelets épiphysaires).

Plus tard, l'enfant en position assise, se tient à la façon d'une grenouille. En raison de la faible croissance osseuse et de l'hypotonie musculaire, il subit un retard du développement moteur et de la dentition.

Le ventre proéminent est fonction de la faiblesse de la musculature abdominale et peut entraîner la constipation. L'enfant peut souffrir d'une anémie nutritionnelle et offrir une faible résistance aux infections respiratoires.

Diagnostic. Des cas bénins et précoces peuvent être diagnostiqués en déterminant les taux sériques du calcium, du phosphore inorganique et des phosphatases alcalines. Le diagnostic de rachitisme avancé s'appuie habituellement sur des manifestations cliniques évidentes, une histoire de carence en vitamine D et l'aspect des radiographies des os.

Traitement. L'administration orale de fortes doses de vitamine D, généralement de 1500 à 5000 U.I. par jour, pendant un mois environ, amènera habituellement la guérison.

Prévention. On doit donner la dose règlementaire de vitamine D aux nourrissons soumis à l'allaitement maternel comme à ceux qui ne le sont pas, pour satisfaire les besoins quotidiens estimés à 400 U.I. par jour. Ceci s'avère spécialement important au cours des mois d'hiver.

Soins infirmiers. Avant le départ pour la maison, on doit indiquer à la mère l'importance de la vitamine D pour son enfant. On doit aussi expliquer le traitement s'il souffre déjà de rachitisme. On ne doit hospitaliser que les nourrissons atteints d'un rachitisme grave ou d'une infection concomitante.

Il faut manier les enfants rachitiques avec douceur et les changer souvent de position. Pour éviter les déformations, il faut les empêcher de porter tout leur poids sur la colonne vertébrale ou les jambes, durant leur maladie. Il faut éviter toute pression sur la poitrine en les prenant, et toute pression sur les fémurs en mettant la couche trop serrée. Une position appropriée diminue les risques de déformation. Si on couche constamment l'enfant sur le dos ou sur un côté, sa tête et sa poitrine seront aplatis. Il doit être couché sur un matelas dur.

L'administration de la vitamine D ne présente aucun problème, à moins qu'on emploie une solution huileuse. Il faut veiller alors à ce que l'enfant n'aspire absolument aucune goutte de la substance.

La prévention de l'infection revêt ici une importance capitale. Des changements fréquents de position, pour prévenir les déformations, diminueront aussi le danger d'une infection de longue durée. Le médecin peut prescrire des bains de soleil à l'enfant.

Pronostic. Le rachitisme ne cause jamais directement la mort. Les déformations mineures disparaissent en général durant la période préscolaire. Les déformations graves seront traitées par ostéotomie.

Tétanie infantile nutritionnelle (Tétanie par avitaminose D)

Incidence et manifestations cliniques. La tétanie nutritionnelle infantile est causée par une ingestion et une absorption déficientes de la vitamine D. Cette affection est invariablement associée au rachitisme, mais tous les enfants rachitiques ne souffrent pas de tétanie.

On rencontre également la tétanie au début du traitement anti-rachitique par la vitamine D. La chute de la calcémie par suite de l'accroissement des dépôts de calcium dans l'os rachitique, ainsi qu'une insuffisance transitoire des parathyroïdes expliqueraient le phénomène.

Ce type de tétanie a la même incidence saisonnière que le rachitisme et survient au même âge.

On rencontre la tétanie sous forme latente ou manifeste. La spasmophilie ou *tétanie latente* se caractérise par une augmentation de l'excitabilité neuromusculaire et la calcémie se maintient légèrement au dessous de 7 à 7,5 mg pour 100 ml.

L'affection peut être mise en évidence par les quatre moyens mécaniques ou électriques suivants:

1) **Signe de Chvostek:** (signe du nerf facial). Il s'agit de percuter la zone située sous l'os malaire, territoire où le nerf facial passe très superficiellement. La réaction consiste en une contraction unilatérale des muscles faciaux autour de la bouche, du nez et de l'œil.

2) **Signe de Trousseau:** Il s'agit de faire apparaître le spasme carpien décrit un peu plus loin, en continuant de comprimer fermement le bras pendant deux ou trois minutes après que la main soit devenue exsangue.

3) **Signe d'Erb:** On place une électrode stimulante juste au-dessous de la tête du péroné, sur le trajet du nerf péronier. L'hyperexcitabilité neuro-musculaire provoque une flexion dorsale et une abduction du pied.

4) **Signe péronier:** Le patient fléchit légèrement le genou; la percussion du nerf péronier provoque une flexion dorsale et une abduction du pied.

La *tétanie manifeste* est caractérisée par une calcémie nettement inférieure à 7 mg pour 100 ml, des convulsions qui ressemblent beaucoup à des crises épileptiques et la mise en évidence du *spasme carpo-pédal*. Les contractures qui se manifestent à l'extrémité du membre supérieur lui donnent l'attitude caractéristique de la main d'accoucheur; le pouce est attiré vers la paume; la main se creuse en cuvette et se porte en abduction; l'avant-bras se fléchit sur le bras. L'extrémité inférieure se déforme: le pied, en extension, se présente en varus équin, les orteils sont fléchis et le pied se creuse. Ces contractures musculaires, toniques, rendent toute tentative de redressement douloureuse.

On peut également constater un *laryngospasme* caractérisé par une dypsnée inspiratoire qui rappelle le chant du coq. Il peut provoquer des périodes d'apnée au cours desquelles le nourrisson cyanose.

Diagnostic et traitement. Le *diagnostic* repose sur les manifestations cliniques et les données du laboratoire qui montrent une diminution du calcium sérique; le phosphore sérique peut être bas, normal ou élevé, mais les phosphatases alcalines sont augmentées.

Pour replacer la calcémie à son niveau normal, on administre du calcium sous forme de chlorure ou de gluconate. Le chlorure de calcium s'administre par voie orale. Le gluconate de calcium doit être donné par voie intraveineuse, car les risques de nécrose interdisent les voies sous-cutanée ou intramusculaire.

On contrôle la plupart des crises convulsives par l'oxygénothéraphie et l'administration de gluconate de calcium intraveineux. On peut également avoir recours au phénobarbital intramusculaire. Certains cas extrêmes de laryngospasme nécessitent une intubation d'urgence.

On commencera à administrer aussitôt que possible de la vitamine D et du calcium par voie orale.

Soins infirmiers. Les soins infirmiers sont de la plus grande importance. C'est l'infirmière qui administre les médicaments prescrits.

Elle doit avoir préparé un abaisse-langue recouvert de gaze pour empêcher l'enfant de se mordre la langue en cas de crise convulsive. Elle garde de l'oxygène et le matériel d'intubation à proximité pour parer aux convulsions et au laryngospasme, et elle doit savoir pratiquer la respiration artificielle.

Pronostic et prévention. Le *pronostic* est bon, sauf si le traitement est tardif. La mort peut résulter d'un laryngospasme ou d'une insuffisance cardiaque.

Avant de renvoyer l'enfant chez lui, il faut que le médecin et l'infirmière signalent à la mère l'importance de la vitamine D pour tous les enfants en période de croissance.

Le *traitement préventif* est le même que celui du rachitisme.

Scorbut

Incidence et étiologie. Le scorbut est une manifestation d'avitaminose C (acide ascorbique). Cette vitamine est instable et détruite par la chaleur; en solution aqueuse, elle est menacée par l'oxydation et un pH alcalin. En général, on donne la vitamine C aux enfants sous forme de jus d'orange frais, non bouilli. Il faut éviter l'exposition du jus d'orange à l'air ambiant et le conserver dans des récipients fermés. Le jus d'une orange fraîchement pressée demeure encore l'idéal.

Comme la vitamine C n'est pas synthétisée par l'organisme, l'apport total doit provenir de l'alimentation. Un apport adéquat au cours de la grossesse assure toutefois au nouveau-né des réserves suffisantes pour une certaine période.

Le scorbut peut survenir à tout âge, mais surtout entre six mois et deux ans. Il est moins fréquent qu'autrefois.

Physio-pathologie, diagnostic et manifestations cliniques. L'avitaminose C entrave la formation du tissu collagène et se répercute sur la dentine, les tissus osseux et cartilagineux et sur l'endothélium vasculaire. C'est pourquoi les manifestations cliniques comportant une tendance hémorragique apparaissent d'abord au niveau des dents et des os. La disparition de la substance intercellulaire dans le tissu vasculaire semble responsable de la diathèse hémorragique.

Le *diagnostic* est habituellement basé sur l'histoire clinique, l'examen radiologique et les symptômes.

L'examen radiologique montre des modifications au niveau des os longs, aux régions métaphysaires et épiphysaires. Au stade de guérison, les hématomes sous-périostés donneront des images radiologiques très caractéristiques.

Il s'avère parfois difficile de différencier le scorbut de l'arthrite, de l'ostéomyélite ou de la poliomyélite par suite de l'hyperesthésie des membres et de la douleur provoquée par le mouvement. On peut confondre le scorbut avec la dysenterie, la néphrite hématurique ou une dyscrasie sanguine.

Les *manifestations cliniques* apparaissent à la suite d'une période variable de carence vitaminique. L'enfant devient irritable et tendu. La douleur provoque une pseudo-paralysie, tout mouvement le fait souffrir et il garde ses membres inférieurs en position de grenouille, ce qui semble pour lui la position la plus confortable.

Des hémorragies peuvent se produire dans la peau, les muqueuses et les parties molles autour des yeux, et les pétéchies sont nombreuses. Les gencives bleues-violacées présentent de l'œdème et saignent facilement. On trouve de l'hématémèse et du méléna.

La subluxation du sternum à la jonction costo-chondrale détermine l'apparition d'un «-chapelet costal scorbutique » dont les grains sont plus pointus que dans le « chapelet rachitique » qui, lui, provient d'un élargissement des épiphyses ramollies.

La température de l'enfant peut s'élever jusqu'à 39,5°C. Consécutive à l'anorexie et aux hémorragies, l'anémie apparaît et le rythme de croissance ralentit.

Traitement. Le traitement spécifique consiste à administrer quotidiennement de fortes doses de vitamine C, soit 90 à 120 ml de jus d'orange ou 100 à 200 mg d'acide ascorbique, par voie orale ou parentérale. Après plusieurs jours de ce traitement, on reviendra aux doses normales. Un régime approprié est recommandé comme mesure de soutien. Des transfusions peuvent s'avérer nécessaires en cas d'anémie grave.

Soins infirmiers. Les soins infirmiers portent sur le régime, les médicaments et la prévention de la douleur et de l'infection. Durant la crise aiguë, il faudrait nourrir l'enfant dans la position où il semble se sentir le mieux.

La pseudo-paralysie du scorbut constitue le principal problème de soin. On doit agir avec une grande douceur dans le maniement de l'enfant. Pour changer sa couche, on évite de soulever les fesses en levant les jambes comme on fait habituellement pour un enfant bien portant. On peut mettre un arceau pour éviter toute pression douloureuse de la literie sur le corps de l'enfant.

Il faut grouper les soins infirmiers et les traitements pour accorder à l'enfant de grandes périodes de repos, et lui éviter les manipulations inutiles. Il faut cependant assurer à ce nourrisson la sécurité d'une présence et des stimulations sensorielles mesurées telles que musique, mobiles colorés.

La prévention de l'infection s'avère de la plus haute importance. Il faut changer fréquemment la position de l'enfant et rincer sa bouche après chaque repas.

Pronostic et prévention. Le pronostic est excellent si le traitement est adéquat. La douleur cède en quelques jours et la croissance reprend rapidement.

La *prévention* consiste à fournir à l'enfant un régime suffisamment riche en vitamine C durant toute l'enfance. On recommande pour l'enfant un apport quotidien de 30 à 50 mg d'acide ascorbique et de 45 à 60 mg pour l'adolescent.

Éducation. On doit enseigner aux mères de famille que la vitamine C disparaît rapidement du jus d'orange si on y ajoute de l'eau chaude ou si on le laisse à l'air libre. On doit aussi lui procurer une liste d'aliments riches en vitamine C.

TROUBLES GASTRO-INTESTINAUX

Syndrome cœliaque

Le syndrome cœliaque est un état d'insuffisance nutritionnelle chronique du nourrisson et de l'enfant, caractérisé par un arrêt de croissance, la fonte musculaire, l'amaigrissement des extrémités et des fesses, la distension abdominale, des selles pâles, abondantes et nauséabondes, une anorexie importante et enfin la mise en évidence d'une carence en vitamines liposolubles et en sels minéraux.

Le syndrome cœliaque comprend deux maladies relativement communes: la maladie cœliaque vraie ou idiopathique et la mucoviscidose que nous étudierons de façon plus approfondie. D'autres maladies entrent également dans ce cadre: l'obstruction mécanique du cycle de la digestion et/ou de l'absorption, les carences

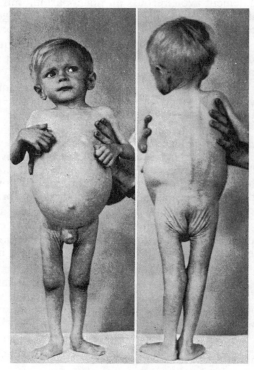

Figure 13-4. Enfant de 2 ans et 10 mois atteint d'une maladie cœliaque. (Murray Davidson. *Pediatrics* de Holt, McIntosh et Barnett. 13 éd. N.Y. Appleton-Century-Crofts, 1962.)

alimentaires graves comme la famine et le kwashiorkor, les allergies gastro-intestinales et les infections digestives chroniques.

Maladie cœliaque
(Entéropathie induite par le gluten)

Incidence et étiologie. La maladie cœliaque est caractérisée par une malabsorption intestinale chronique, traduite par le passage des graisses et autres éléments nutritifs dans les selles. La maladie affecte les deux sexes, le nourrisson comme l'enfant plus âgé et surtout ceux de race blanche. La maladie cœliaque des enfants semble rattachée à la sprue non-tropicale des adultes et on peut observer des cas chez différents membres de la même famille. On en attribue la cause à une anomalie congénitale du métabolisme avec ou sans réaction allergique. L'enfant ne tolère pas le **gluten** qui est la fraction protéique du blé et du seigle. Des infections systémiques et des troubles affectifs et psychiques peuvent déclencher une *crise cœliaque.*

Physio-pathologie et manifestations cliniques. Les *manifestations cliniques* typiques s'observent dès l'âge de six mois et peuvent se prolonger jusqu'à l'âge de cinq ans. On remarque de fréquents épisodes de diarrhée, surtout en présence d'infections respiratoires. L'enfant souffre souvent d'une anorexie déterminant un retard de croissance. La perte de poids, ordinairement importante, peut cependant varier à cause de l'œdème. La fonte musculaire atteint surtout les fesses, les plis de l'aine, les aisselles et les membres. Par contre, le visage demeure arrondi mais jaunâtre, anémique; les joues sont rouges avec de grands cernes bruns ou de l'œdème sous les yeux, ce qui donne à l'enfant une expression triste et craintive. On constate une absence de force musculaire, un retard dans l'apparition des dents et l'âge épiphysaire est au-dessous de la normale.

La *distension abdominale* dépend d'une collection hydro-aérique dans un intestin hypotonique et d'une grande faiblesse musculaire au niveau de la paroi abdominale.

Les symptômes nerveux, heureusement réversibles, se manifestent par une irritabilité où les accès de colère alternent avec une tendance exagérée à la timidité. L'enfant dort mal, il crie, grince des dents; la diaphorèse est fréquente et les extrémités sont ordinairement froides.

Au cours de la *crise cœliaque,* il se produit une diarrhée aqueuse accompagnée de vomissements entraînant une déshydratation et un état d'acidose. Cette crise risque parfois d'entraîner la mort si elle n'est pas rapidement et correctement traitée.

Le caractère des selles varie suivant la gravité de la maladie et la nature du régime. La selle cœliaque typique est abondante, plus pesante qu'une selle normale. Le nombre de selles augmente beaucoup au cours des crises. La selle est molle, mousseuse et en outre, nauséabonde. Le pourcentage de graisse (esters et acide gras libres) n'augmente que faiblement dans l'entéropathie induite par le gluten. Lors de l'amélioration clinique, les selles deviennent moulées et normalement colorées.

La carence protéique est modérée. Un taux de protéines sériques plus bas que 5 g pour 100 ml indique que l'enfant est gravement malade. La perte de substances minérales (calcium et fer) varie avec la gravité de l'affection.

Traitement. *Le traitement repose sur l'instauration du régime éliminant totalement le gluten.* On diminue les lipides, et il faut assurer un apport protéique variant entre 6 et 8 g par kg de poids et par jour. Si l'enfant est très malade, on lui donnera du lait écrémé ou protéiné et sucré avec du glucose, du sucrose ou de la poudre de banane. On ajoute progressivement d'autres aliments tous les deux ou trois jours, un à la fois, comme des œufs, du fromage, des fruits, des légumes et de la viande. Tous les aliments contenant du blé et du seigle sont prohibés.

Un apport hydrique et calorique est essentiel pour satisfaire les besoins normaux de l'enfant. Monosaccharides et disaccharides sont bien tolérés, mais les polysaccharides doivent être évités. Il faut donner aux parents la liste des produits alimentaires contenant du gluten et éliminer du régime certaines sauces, pains de viande ou poudings vendus sur le marché, parce que ces produits sont préparés avec de la farine de blé. Les parents doivent apprendre à lire les étiquettes et à rechercher si le produit contient du blé ou du seigle.

Soins infirmiers. Les soins infirmiers consistent non seulement à aider les parents à accepter l'état physique, mais aussi les problèmes de comportement de leur enfant qui est souvent irritable et difficile. L'infirmière doit avoir une attitude de compréhension bienveillante à leur égard. Ils peuvent se sentir coupables de la maladie de l'enfant, et le surprotéger.

Durant son hospitalisation, l'enfant peut avoir besoin de l'aide affective et du support émotif de l'infirmière. Il est anxieux et malheureux du fait qu'on le prive de nourriture. Ses parents devraient lui rendre visite très souvent ou, si possible, rester avec lui. Quand il a faim, il se sent frustré et en colère; il peut manifester des accès de mauvaise humeur ou être prostré. L'enfant, privé de ses aliments préférés devrait pouvoir exprimer librement son ressentiment par des pleurs ou des paroles. L'infirmière compréhensive l'aidera à s'exprimer et lui montrera sa sympathie s'il pleure. Nourrir l'enfant pose un problème. Bien que la faim puisse être la cause fondamentale de son irritabilité, l'appétit de l'enfant est capricieux. Il faudrait le nourrir lentement, par petites quantités. Il ne faut pas le forcer à manger; quand il se sentira mieux, il mangera davantage. De nouveaux aliments peuvent être introduits, un à la fois, et offerts parmi ceux qu'il aime. S'il refuse un aliment particulier, il faut le signaler à la diététicienne. Cet aliment doit être éliminé du régime et être repris un peu plus tard. Des problèmes peuvent surgir à la maison lorsque l'enfant constate qu'il a un régime différent des autres enfants de la famille. Il peut désirer ce qu'ils mangent plutôt que sa propre diète.

Il est important de consigner par écrit toute absorption alimentaire. L'infirmière doit noter la nature et la quantité des aliments ingérés, l'appétit de l'enfant et sa réaction aux différents aliments. Pour tout apport nouveau au régime elle doit noter la nature des selles, le comportement de l'enfant et le degré de distension abdominale.

On doit absolument prévenir l'infection. Comme l'enfant est anémique et sous-alimenté il faut observer une hygiène correcte. Il transpire abondamment et doit être gardé au sec. Il faut le bouger fréquemment, s'il est alité et a tendance à garder la même position. Il est utile de placer ces nourrissons dans de petites chaises ou « sauteuses » afin que leur abdomen volumineux ne nuisent pas aux mouvements respiratoires.

Les enfants qui souffrent de maladie cœliaque restent souvent isolés. Comme les jeux actifs demandent trop d'efforts, ils préfèrent les jeux calmes. Souvent leur abdomen volumineux les empêche de ramper ce qui retarde l'apprentissage de la marche. Le jeune enfant peut présenter une certaine régression dans son comportement. L'infirmière doit être patiente et pourvoir à son besoin de sécurité. Lorsque l'état physique s'améliore, le comportement psychologique change aussi; il abandonne alors les habitudes non appropriées à son âge et recherche la compagnie d'autrui.

Enseignement à donner à la mère. Les parents devraient connaître les causes sous-jacentes et le traitement de la maladie de leur enfant, afin de pouvoir lui donner des soins appropriés à son retour à la maison. Au cours de ses entretiens avec la mère, l'infirmière doit souligner: 1) la nécessité de prévenir l'infection et de maintenir un climat calme et sécurisant; 2) l'importance du respect scrupuleux de la diète; 3) la nécessité d'une surveillance médicale continue. Il faut éviter d'effrayer la mère et il faut lui donner un enseignement progressif. Il serait bon de la rassurer en lui donnant les quelques petits livres de recettes sans gluten qui existent dans le commerce. On peut aussi lui procurer des listes de produits alimentaires bien connus qui ne contiennent aucun gluten. Ces listes ont notamment été publiées par plusieurs compagnies de céréales. La mère s'apercevra ainsi qu'elle peut garder une apparence normale à la diète de son enfant. Par exemple, elle se rendra compte qu'elle peut satisfaire le besoin de l'enfant en pain et en gâteau grâce à des substituts farineux sans gluten.

Si elle est trop inquiète, elle risque de surprotéger son enfant et de restreindre le champ de ses activités au-delà des limites établies par le médecin. Cette attitude s'avère surtout nuisible pour la santé mentale du nourrisson et du jeune enfant qui n'ont pas de contact avec un professeur ou d'autres travailleurs professionnels qui pourraient neutraliser les attentions excessives de la mère.

Pronostic. En raison d'une meilleure compréhension de la maladie cœliaque, d'un emploi plus courant de la réhydratation parentérale, du traitement diététique et du contrôle de l'infection à l'aide des antibiotiques, le taux de mortalité dans cette affection est bas. La guérison est longue et entrecoupée de rechutes. L'évolution est caractérisée par des phases d'amélioration et de crise. Comme la maladie cœliaque est une anomalie constitutionnelle, la guérison est rarement totale, mais les manifestations cliniques diminuent à mesure que l'enfant vieillit. Toutefois, il peut présenter de la sprue à l'âge adulte.

Mucoviscidose (Fibrose kystique du pancréas)

Incidence et étiologie. La mucoviscidose se transmet selon le mode mendélien récessif. Pour qu'un enfant soit atteint de cette maladie, les parents doivent être tous les deux porteurs du gène autosome pathologique. Dans ce cas, la mère court un risque de 25% à chaque grossesse de mettre au monde un enfant atteint de la maladie et de 50% qu'il soit porteur du gène. On peut souvent identifier le sujet hétérozygote par le test de sudation.

La fibrose kystique est une maladie chronique qui demeure actuellement le problème respiratoire majeur dans la population infantile. D'une façon générale, sa fréquence varie entre 1 pour 1000 et 1 pour 2000. Les deux sexes sont atteints d'une façon égale. *L'incidence* est plus fréquente chez les Caucasiens et rare chez les nourrissons de race noire. Elle semble inexistante chez les orientaux.

Physio-pathologie et manifestations cliniques. Il y a une altération globale et générale des glandes exocrines de l'organisme. Les plus touchées sont le pancréas exocrine, les glandes muqueuses bronchiques, les glandes salivaires et sudoripares et les canalicules biliaires. Le processus pathologique est semblable pour toutes les glandes: la sécrétion s'épaissit, distend les canalicules et éventuellement obstrue leur passage. L'organe s'atrophie et son tissu spécifique est remplacé par du tissu fibreux.

Deux syndromes cliniques apparaissent: le *syndrome respiratoire* et le *syndrome digestif*.

Le *syndrome respiratoire,* souvent le plus précoce et le plus grave, se manifeste par une toux non productive, mais souvent suivie de vomissements. L'enfant souffre d'une dyspnée expiratoire et éventuellement de cyanose. À mesure que les sécrétions épaissies s'accumulent dans l'arbre bronchique, les cils vibratiles sont détruits, il se forme des bouchons muqueux qui provoquent l'apparition de l'emphysème et de l'atélectasie de résorption. Peu à peu, la transformation fibreuse du poumon amène les symptômes du « cœur pulmonaire » ou de l'insuffisance cardiaque droite. L'enfant présente de l'hippocratisme digital et de la tachycardie. Des infections respiratoires répétées, le plus souvent causées par le staphylocoque doré, viennent compliquer l'état précaire de l'enfant, mais demeurent souvent le point de départ de l'investigation. Des foyers de broncho-pneumonie et parfois des abcès bronchiectasiques, se développent et mettent sa vie en danger.

Le *syndrome digestif*: se confond avec le syndrome cœliaque. Le suc pancréatique épaissi ne conduit plus les enzymes pancréatiques au duodénum. La déficience en enzymes pancréatiques donne lieu aux manifestations de la malabsorption. Ce syndrome peut débuter à la naissance (environ 10% des cas) par l'apparition d'un iléus méconial. La mucovicidose est alors diagnostiquée très tôt. Dans la majorité des cas, l'enfant semble normal à la naissance. Les selles sont d'abord molles, mais ni plus graisseuses, ni plus fréquentes que chez les autres nourrissons. Lorsque l'alimentation solide est augmentée et que le bébé reçoit de la vitamine D en solution huileuse, ses selles deviennent mousseuses et nauséabondes, puis graisseuses, abondantes, fréquentes et pâles. Le nourrisson ne gagne plus de poids, ses réserves tissulaires fondent et toutes les manifestations du syndrome cœliaque apparaissent: croissance retardée, peau flasque, absence de

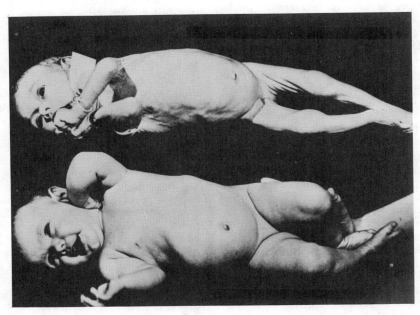

Figure 13-5. Mucoviscidose du pancréas. Avant le traitement, les manifestations du syndrome « cœliaque » sont présentes. Après le traitement, l'enfant paraît normal. (Courtoisie des Laboratoires Pfizer.)

tissu sous-cutané (sauf au niveau des joues), abdomen distendu et protubérant. L'enfant conserve un bon appétit en l'absence d'infections respiratoires.

Il est à noter que, très souvent, l'un ou l'autre des syndromes prédomine. Une autre manifestation secondaire est une sueur salée due à une forte concentration en chlorure de sodium et de potassium. Très souvent, la mère note ce goût en embrassant son bébé. La salive aussi s'épaissit et renferme une quantité accrue de chlore et de sodium. Plus tardivement, des symptômes de cirrhose hépatique peuvent apparaître.

À mesure que le processus pathologique évolue, l'enfant devient plus fatigué et facilement irritable. Ce comportement peut rendre plus difficile l'acceptation des multiples mesures de soins qu'il doit subir chaque jour.

Diagnostic.   Le diagnostic est basé sur l'anamnèse, l'examen physique, les tests de laboratoire et les examens radiologiques.

Le laboratoire met en évidence un manque d'enzymes pancréatiques (trypsine, lipase, amylase et carboxypeptidase). Il n'y a pas ou il y a peu de ces enzymes dans le suc duodénal, que l'on a recueilli par intubation et aspiration. En pratique, seule la recherche de trypsine s'avère nécessaire, parce qu'une absence de trypsine étaye solidement le diagnostic de mucoviscidose. On peut pratiquer le test de l'activité trypsique sur un échantillon de selles déposé sur une pellicule. Si l'enzyme est présente, elle digère la couche gélatineuse de la plaque radiologique. Toutefois, ce test a peu de valeur parce que des enzymes protéolytiques d'origine bactérienne peuvent effectuer le même travail et fausser le résultat. Une technique de dépistage rapide consiste à placer la main du malade sur une plaque de gélose imprégnée de nitrate d'argent. Si le taux de chlorure dans la sueur est élevé, l'empreinte de la main se dessine nettement sur la plaque, par formation de chlorure d'argent.

Le *diagnostic* de la mucoviscidose a été simplifié grâce à l'amélioration du test de la sudation. Auparavant la méthode thermique, longue, ardue et dangereuse était la seule possible. Aujourd'hui, le test peut se pratiquer en quelques minutes. Il s'agit de nettoyer l'avant-bras de l'enfant avec de l'eau distillée stérile, puis une petite gaze imbibée de pilocarpine est déposée sur la région préparée et fixée solidement. Par l'intermédiaire d'une électrode, un faible courant provoque l'iontophorèse. Après quelques minutes la gaze est enlevée et la lecture est faite grâce à une électrode reliée à un analyseur calibré. Tout résultat indiquant un

taux de chlorure supérieur à 60 milli-équivalents est anormal. Un résultat entre 50 et 60 mEq. requiert une investigation plus poussée. Le test de sudation peut s'effectuer de différentes façons, selon le type d'appareil utilisé, mais les principes demeurent toujours les mêmes.

Les enfants atteints de mucoviscidose ont des concentrations de sodium à peu près quatre fois plus élevées, dans les cheveux et les ongles, que les enfants normaux. Une analyse biochimique des ongles et des cheveux confirme avec exactitude ce diagnostic.

Il est possible aussi de déceler une absorption défectueuse des graisses. L'examen microscopique de selles diluées démontrera une excrétion fécale accrue de graisses. L'hypocholestérolémie s'avère constante et, est en partie, secondaire à un trouble d'absorption des lipides. Comme les graisses sont mal absorbées, la vitamine A, une vitamine liposoluble, doit être administrée sous forme aqueuse.

Les radiographies révèlent des lésions intestinales et pulmonaires, entre autres l'emphysème obstructif généralisé, l'atélectasie, la broncho-pneumonie, les bronchiectasies et les abcès bronchiolectasiques. Dans les cas avancés, on constate une hypertrophie ventriculaire droite.

Traitement.   Les efforts de tous les membres de l'équipe de santé sont requis, qu'il s'agisse du médecin, de l'infirmière, du travailleur social, de la physiothérapeute ou du conseiller génétique. Le traitement à long terme doit être planifié avec soin et une surveillance étroite demeure essentielle même quand l'enfant n'est pas sous traitement médical. Le traitement étant palliatif, le malade doit le suivre durant toute sa vie. Pour maintenir un bon état nutritionnel il faut assurer au nourrisson un *régime alimentaire* équilibré apportant une grande quantité de protéines (4 g par kg de poids) et une quantité normale de graisses. Si l'enfant ne supporte pas cette diète, il faut la modifier pour contrôler le volume des selles et leur teneur en graisse. Pour les nourrissons, on recommande un biberon de lait protidique enrichi de poudre de lait écrémé. On peut y ajouter de la poudre de banane et du glucose. D'autres aliments digestibles et à teneur élevée en protéines et basse en graisse et amidon peuvent être donnés, comme du fromage blanc, des viandes maigres, des fruits (surtout des bananes) et des légumes: 125 à 200 calories par kilogramme de poids doivent constituer l'apport calorique quotidien (puisque l'enfant perd 50% de la valeur calorique des aliments dans les selles). On doit saler abondamment les aliments; en été et par temps chaud, il faut fournir un supplément de sel.

La médication spécifique de la mucoviscidose demeure l'enzyme pancréatique. La dose varie suivant l'âge de l'enfant, ses besoins et la sorte de produit enzymatique utilisé. On donne ces enzymes avant chaque repas et avant chaque collation, pour remplacer les enzymes pancréatiques nécessaires à la digestion des aliments et que l'organisme de l'enfant ne peut pas produire. De cette façon, l'état des selles s'améliore. Il faut fournir également de fortes doses de vitamines A, D, E, K en solution aqueuse.

La prévention de l'infection, surtout de l'infection respiratoire, s'avère de la plus grande importance. Il faut éloigner l'enfant des autres malades et du personnel hospitalier qui souffrent d'infections respiratoires et l'hospitalisation doit être aussi brève que possible. Ceci suppose que la mère apprenne comment soigner son enfant à la maison. L'administration d'antibiotiques, oralement et en aérosol, à titre prophylactique, semble indiquée pour réduire le danger d'infection respiratoire. Si, cependant, l'enfant contracte une infection, il faudra lui administrer les antibiotiques appropriés à doses massives.

On administre de la *digitaline* et des *diurétiques* en cas d'insuffisance cardiaque. L'oxygène diminue la cyanose provoquée par l'accumulation des sécrétions bronchiques ou par l'insuffisance cardiaque.

La codéine et les autres médicaments qui suppriment le réflexe de la toux sont aussi dangereux que les substances produisant un assèchement des sécrétions. Si l'enfant souffre de constipation, il faut tout d'abord corriger son alimentation et adapter la quantité d'enzymes pancréatiques qu'il reçoit avant de lui administrer des médicaments qui ramollissent les selles.

Afin d'aider à la liquéfaction des sécrétions, l'enfant dort sous une *tente à humidité* à chaque sieste et pour toute la nuit. Ces tentes fonctionnent par air comprimé et l'oxygène n'est utilisé que si cela est précisé. De l'eau distillée ou plus souvent une substance tensoréductrice, telle que le propylène glycol, sert à former la buée d'humidité. Lorsque l'état de l'enfant s'aggrave ou lorsqu'il souffre d'une infection, il peut rester continuellement sous la tente.

Pour obtenir une liquéfaction plus immédiate des sécrétions et aussi pour pratiquer une antibiothérapie directe, l'*aérosolthérapie* est utilisée avant chaque séance de *massothérapie*.

Elle est effectuée à l'aide d'un masque et le plus souvent à l'aide d'un appareil à pression positive intermittente. Lorsque les poumons sont gonflés par une pression positive durant l'inspiration, on peut administrer l'aérosol à toutes les zones aérées, ce qui cause une amélioration du drainage bronchique et de la fonction pulmonaire. Plusieurs types de machines peuvent être employés. Suivant l'état de l'enfant, on applique le traitement quatre fois par jour, ou toutes les deux ou trois heures, et on le poursuit jusqu'à l'épuisement des médicaments dans le nébuliseur. Dans les cas graves, la thérapie par aérosol se poursuit sans interruption, avec une pression maintenue à la fois lors de l'inspiration et lors de l'expiration. À la solution d'aérosol, en plus des antibiotiques, on peut ajouter des mucolytiques, des bronchodilatateurs et des décongestionnants bronchiques.

Le drainage postural, le tapotement et la vibration aident l'enfant à éliminer les sécrétions mucoïdes épaisses des bronches.

Le but spécifique du *drainage postural* est d'amener les différentes branches de l'arbre bronchique dans une position telle que le drainage de la bronche et du segment de poumon qu'elle alimente en soit facilité. On place donc l'enfant successivement en 8 ou 9 positions différentes de façon à ce que chaque lobe pulmonaire puisse être adéquatement drainé. Pour le nourrisson, le drainage postural peut être effectué en plaçant celui-ci sur les genoux et le long des jambes de sa mère ou de son infirmière, alors que pour l'enfant plus âgé on se sert d'un lit articulé ou d'un autre appareil approprié. On obtient un drainage plus efficace, si on varie progressivement la position de l'enfant au cours du traitement.

La technique du *tapotement* peut s'effectuer de plusieurs façons. La plus usuelle consiste à ouvrir la main, à former un angle d'environ 120° et à pratiquer la percussion sans utiliser directement ni la paume ni les doigts. C'est l'air comprimé à l'intérieur de la main, qui exerce une pression sur les zones tapotées. Le poignet doit être alternativement en flexion et en extension tout au long du traitement. La percussion déloge les bouchons de mucus des bronches. L'air peut alors s'infiltrer derrière le mucus et l'aider à remonter vers la trachée.

La *vibration* est une autre technique qu'on applique seulement pendant l'expiration. L'infirmière place une main sur l'autre ou une main de chaque côté de la cage thoracique de l'enfant et applique de légers et doux mouvements vibratoires. Il existe maintenant une machine à percussions vibratoires qu'on peut

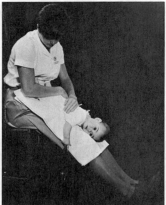

Lobe inférieur, segment postérieur; angulation: 45°. Couché sur le ventre, tapoter les dernières côtes, des deux côtés.

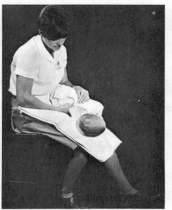

Lobe inférieur, segment latéral droit, angulation: 20° à 25°. Couché sur le côté, genoux pliés, si possible, ou plus confortable, tapoter sur les dernières côtes. N.B.: répéter de l'autre côté.

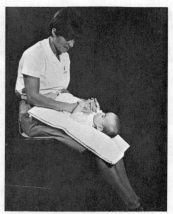

Lobe inférieur, segment antérieur, angulation: 20° à 25°. Couché sur le dos, genoux et hanches pliés si plus confortable, tapoter sur les dernières côtes.

Lobe moyen droit et lingula, angulation: 15°. Couché sur le côté droit, soulever et supporter le dos de l'enfant, de l'épaule à la hanche droite, donnant une rotation de 45°, tapoter au niveau du mamelon gauche. N.B.: répéter de l'autre côté.

Lobe inférieur, segment apical, position horizontale. Couché à plat ventre, un coussin sous l'abdomen si nécessaire, tapoter les dernières côtes en bas des omoplates des deux côtés.

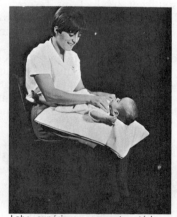

Lobe supérieur, segment antérieur, position horizontale. Couché sur le dos, genoux et hanches fléchis si plus confortable, tapoter en dessous de la clavicule des deux côtés.

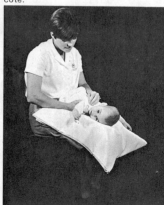

Lobe supérieur, segment postérieur droit, position horizontale. Couché à plat sur le côté gauche, le bras gauche ramené en arrière, supporter le côté droit de l'enfant, tapoter au niveau de l'omoplate droite.

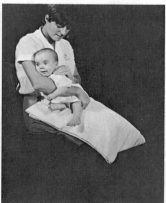

Lobe supérieur, segment postérieur gauche. L'enfant assis sur vous, ses jambes tombant vers la droite, tourner sa poitrine vers vous avec son bras droit en arrière; supportez-le avec votre bras droit en l'appuyant sur vous, tapoter au niveau de l'omoplate gauche.

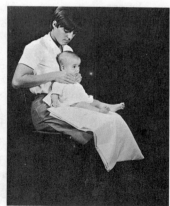

Lobe supérieur, segment apical, enfant assis et appuyé sur vous ou sur un oreiller, tapoter en avant entre l'épaule et le cou.

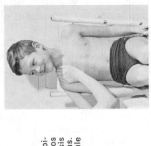

1. Lobe inf.: segm. post.: angulation: 45°. Couché sur le ventre. Tapoter les dernières côtes.

2. Lobe inf.: segm. lat. droit: angulation: 20 à 25°. Couché sur le côté gauche, genoux pliés. Tapoter sur les dernières côtes. N.B.–Faire l'inverse pour l'autre côté.

3. Lobe inf.: segm. antérieur. Couché sur le dos un oreiller sous les genoux. Tapoter sur les dernières côtes.

4. Lobe moyen: Lingula: angulation de 15°. Couché sur le côté droit, glisser sur un oreiller roulé dans le dos, y appuyer le patient. Tapoter au niveau du mamelon gauche. N.B.–Faire l'inverse pour l'autre côté.

5. Lobe inf.: segm. apical: position horizontale. Couché à plat ventre. Tapoter sur les dernières côtes, en bas des omoplates.

6. Lobe sup.: segm. antérieur–Position horizontale. Couché sur le dos, un oreiller sous les genoux. Tapoter en dessous de la clavicule.

7. Lobe sup.: segm. postérieur droit.–Position horizontale. Couché à plat ventre, le bras gauche le long du corps, glisser un oreiller sous le côté (de l'épaule à la hanche). Faire appuyer le bras droit et plier les genoux. Tapoter au niveau de l'omoplate droite.

8. Lobe sup.: segm. postérieur gauche: en position demi-assise, bras droit en arrière, bras gauche relevé et la poitrine appuyés sur des oreillers, genoux pliés.
–Avec un bébé, l'asseoir sur vous, les jambes vers la droite, tourner sa poitrine vers vous et appuyer sur votre poitrine Tapoter au niveau de l'omoplate gauche.

9. Lobe sup.: segm. apical. Patient assis, dos appuyé. Si petit, assis et appuyé sur vous. Tapoter entre l'épaule et le cou

Figure 13-6. Traitements de physiothérapie respiratoire pour améliorer la condition pulmonaire de l'enfant. Sur ces photos les traitements sont exécutés par une physiothérapeute. Il est indispensable que l'infirmière qui fait partie de l'équipe de santé connaisse parfaitement les positions de drainage. (Courtoisie du département de physiothérapie de l'Hôpital Ste-Justine).

employer à la place de la vibration manuelle. Elle peut être actionnée à la maison par les parents ou par l'enfant lui-même. Tout au long de l'application de ces deux techniques, et à la fin du traitement, on demande à l'enfant de tousser et d'expectorer le plus possible, s'il est assez âgé pour le faire.

Une physiothérapeute peut enseigner aux infirmières et aux parents la technique du drainage postural, du tapotement et de la vibration. La physiothérapeute peut aussi faire des suggestions qui facilitent le traitement à la maison. Elle doit souligner le fait que la *douceur* est capitale dans l'application de ces techniques. Des secousses ou des coups trop brusques auront comme seul résultat le refus de l'enfant de poursuivre la thérapie.

Complications. Le prolapsus rectal, dû à un amaigrissement des fesses, à l'abondance des selles et à la faiblesse de la musculature dans la zone rectale demeure une complication possible surtout entre six mois et deux ans.

« Un coup de chaleur » peut survenir lorsque la température ambiante est élevée et que l'enfant perd beaucoup d'électrolytes dans la sueur. L'enfant peut souffrir d'ostéoporose parce qu'il ne peut utiliser la vitamine D en solution huileuse, et ne profite donc pas du calcium ingéré pour la croissance de ses os. Toutefois, ces enfants souffrent rarement de rachitisme. On constate une carence en vitamine A, à moins de l'administrer sous forme hydrosoluble. Pour les enfants dépassant l'âge scolaire, l'apparition d'un diabète est à redouter à cause de la désorganisation progressive des îlots de Langerhans. Habituellement, une modification de la diète peut suffire, mais il faut parfois administrer de l'insuline. Le cœur se fatigue à cause de l'effort exigé pour pomper le sang dans le poumon fibrosé. Le « cœur pulmonaire » caractérisé par une hypertrophie ventriculaire droite, entraîne souvent la mort.

L'apparition de polypes de la muqueuse nasale, de sinusite, d'intussusception ou de constipation est toujours possible. L'enfant souffre souvent d'un retard de maturation sexuelle et les garçons, devenus adultes, sont souvent stériles. Les femmes peuvent devenir enceintes mais les risques de la grossesse augmentent avec la gravité de l'atteinte pulmonaire.

Plus tard, la dégénérescence cirrhotique du foie est une complication redoutable. L'enfant peut alors développer une hypertension portale et des varices œsophagiennes. Si ces dernières se rompent, la vie de l'enfant est en danger sauf si un traitement prompt et efficace est appliqué. Une chirurgie palliative, l'anastomose porto-cave peut devenir nécessaire.

Soins infirmiers. Une fois le diagnostic établi et les premiers jalons du traitement bien posés, l'enfant demeure à la maison et n'entre à l'hôpital que si une complication grave se déclare, telle une infection pulmonaire. Lors de la première hospitalisation de l'enfant, l'infirmière qui en prend soin enseigne à la mère les soins qu'elle devra bientôt lui prodiguer elle-même. L'enfant plus vieux apprendra à assumer une partie de son traitement. L'infirmière doit aider la famille à se rendre compte du changement que la maladie de l'enfant apporte à son mode de vie. La planification à long terme doit se faire avant le départ pour la maison.

L'état nutritif de l'enfant s'avère important. L'infirmière et les parents doivent faire preuve de patience à son égard, aux heures des repas ou lorsqu'il prend son biberon. Le malade a tendance à être irritable, il tousse, vomit facilement et respire souvent avec difficulté. Pour faciliter l'alimentation de l'enfant, l'infirmière doit s'assurer que l'aérosolthérapie et la massothérapie ont d'abord eu lieu. Ces traitements améliorent la fonction pulmonaire et favorisent ensuite l'ingestion de nourriture. Si l'enfant a expectoré, il est important de lui rincer la bouche ou de lui faire brosser les dents avant le repas, étant donné le mauvais goût des sécrétions. Il est important aussi que l'enfant puisse prendre ses médicaments (enzymes pancréatiques), avec des aliments ou jus qu'il aime, car cette médication précède tous les repas. Lorsque l'enfant est trop jeune pour avaler ces enzymes sous forme de capsules, la médication peut être mêlée à des aliments froids. Il faut le nourrir par petites quantités, mais fréquemment, pour ne pas le fatiguer par des efforts prolongés. Des éructations fréquentes évitent la distension abdominale. Le régime doit être aussi varié que possible, en tenant compte de l'âge de l'enfant et de sa capacité de digestion. L'infirmière doit noter soigneusement la réaction de l'enfant à tout aliment nouveau, la nature des selles après cet apport et au cours des jours qui suivent.

Il est important que l'infirmière et les parents acceptent les changements que l'on constate dans la personnalité de l'enfant, lorsque sa maladie se prolonge de plusieurs mois. Au cours des phases aiguës de sa maladie, affection et gentillesse l'aident à développer son sentiment de sécurité et le préparent à retrouver une vie normale.

Les soins de la peau revêtent une grande importance. Il faut nettoyer soigneusement le siège après chaque selle et appliquer un onguent neutre pour le protéger des selles ultérieures. Si la peau s'irrite il faut l'exposer à l'air ou à la chaleur sèche d'une lampe électrique.

Une propreté méticuleuse de toute la région fessière aidera à réduire l'odeur pénétrante des selles. Un purificateur, bien qu'utile, ne doit pas devenir un substitut de la propreté.

Des éruptions cutanées peuvent se produire aux proéminences osseuses. Lors des phases aiguës, il faut donc changer fréquemment la position du malade et garder le corps entier dans un état de propreté méticuleuse, pour prévenir les plaies de décubitus. De plus, le changement de position diminue le risque de pneumonie hypostatique. Même si l'enfant est assez âgé pour se mouvoir tout seul, il peut être trop faible pour le faire lui-même et cette responsabilité incombe à l'infirmière.

Il ne faut pas habiller l'enfant trop chaudement, mais il est essentiel qu'il ne prenne pas froid; s'il transpire, il faut changer ses vêtements immédiatement.

L'infirmière se chargera parfois de l'application des techniques de drainage postural, de tapotement et de vibration. Elle contribuera

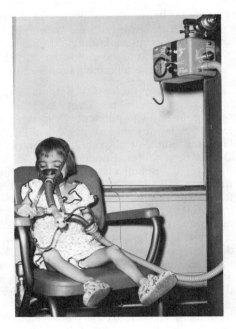

Figure 13-7. L'appareil fournit une pression positive qui vaporise le médicament à l'intérieur des bronches.

aussi à l'exécution des traitements par inhalation et aérosol. C'est elle qui expliquera à l'enfant, dès qu'il sera assez âgé pour le comprendre, qu'il doit prendre une inspiration profonde sous la pression douce et régulière et qu'un fin nuage de médicament pénétrera toutes les zones de ses poumons. Il faut mettre l'enfant en position correcte et l'aider à se soulever. Cette position donne plus d'espace aux mouvements du diaphragme et permet donc une inspiration plus profonde. Il faut l'encourager à inspirer lentement et profondément la première fois et à être détendu au cours du traitement. L'infirmière peut faire une démonstration personnelle qui aidera l'enfant à comprendre ce que l'on désire de lui. Un tissu doux sur le thorax diminue les contrecoups du tapotement.

S'il est effrayé par ces techniques, il faut l'aider à exprimer sa crainte. Ces enfants profitent beaucoup de la thérapie par le jeu, étant donné que leurs angoisses sont trop fortes pour être exprimées verbalement. Il est important qu'ils puissent dessiner ou peindre librement, qu'ils soient même encouragés à le faire et qu'ils puissent répéter leurs traitements sur des poupées à l'aide d'équipement médical ou de marionnettes. L'infirmière tente d'observer attentivement tous ces jeux et de déceler les appréhensions et les incompréhensions de l'enfant. Très souvent, il sera utile de lui fournir, simultanément, des activités lui permettant de libérer son agressivité, comme des clous à enfoncer dans des planchettes. Finalement, la plupart des enfants coopèrent à leur traitement parce qu'ils se rendent compte qu'ils se sentent mieux après ou parce qu'ils se résignent à l'inévitable; un certain degré de passivité n'est pas rare. Chacun doit posséder son propre masque. L'appareil utilisé doit être nettoyé entre chaque usage.

Lorsque l'antibiothérapie par voie orale et par aérosol ne suffit plus, il faut recourir à la médication donnée par voie intraveineuse. La voie intramusculaire est très peu utilisée en raison de l'atrophie des muscles. L'infirmière doit surveiller attentivement la perfusion intraveineuse et ne pas faire croire à l'enfant que ce traitement est relié à son alimentation déficiente. Celui-ci se croirait alors responsable de l'aggravation de son état et deviendrait très anxieux. L'administration d'antibiotiques par voie intraveineuse est surtout utilisée lorsque le malade a une broncho-penumonie.

Le rapport des observations doit être complet pour que le médecin puisse avoir une vue claire de l'état de l'enfant. Il faut faire une description détaillée des selles, comportant la couleur, la consistance et le volume. Il faut

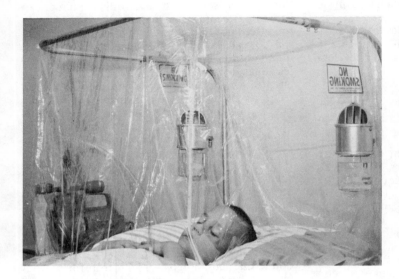

Figure 13-8. Tente à forte humidité pourvue d'un moteur à air comprimé et de deux nébulisateurs. Cet appareil fournit une humidité très dense et s'avère très utile pour le traitement de la mucoviscidose. (M. Green et R. J. Haggerty [Eds]: dans *Ambulatory Pediatrics*.)

noter le genre et la quantité des aliments consommés ou refusés. Tout gain ou perte de poids est noté ou consigné sur un graphique. Le teint de la peau a une valeur de diagnostic. L'infirmière doit déceler les signes de prolapsus rectal, et noter tous les symptômes relatifs à cet état. Si l'enfant tousse, le médecin désire connaître la nature et la fréquence de la toux. Les nourrissons pleurent pour plusieurs raisons, mais les larmes sont aussi un signe de malaise ou de douleur. Le moment, le genre et la fréquence des pleurs s'avèrent importants à la fois pour le diagnostic et pour l'appréciation de l'effet des traitements. Une description des pleurs est utile, non seulement pour juger de l'état physique de l'enfant, mais aussi pour évaluer les perturbations psychologiques qui accompagnent souvent des transformations physiques.

La *prévention* de l'infection doit demeurer une préoccupation constante.

L'éducation des parents est tout aussi importante. Des entretiens avec les parents doivent permettre la continuation à la maison du traitement reçu à l'hôpital. La mère doit être mise au courant du régime alimentaire et il faut s'assurer qu'elle a bien compris le but du régime et la meilleure façon de le rendre acceptable à son enfant. Elle devra aussi connaître et accepter psychologiquement le plan de traitement prévu par le médecin. Ce plan comporte une surveillance médicale, des mesures d'hygiène, la prévention de l'infection, du repos en fonction des besoins de l'enfant, l'administration des médicaments, l'aérosolthé-

rapie, la massothérapie et l'utilisation d'une tente à humidité à la maison. L'infirmière ne se contentera pas d'enseigner à la mère les procédures à suivre, mais elle lui expliquera leur but et les résultats espérés. Elle devra aussi souligner l'importance des médicaments prescrits par le médecin, et expliquer la meilleure façon de les administrer.

Il est difficile pour la mère d'accepter la régression probable de l'état de l'enfant au cours d'infections respiratoires, même légères, surtout si elle s'accuse elle-même de négligence ou si chaque phase aiguë ravive sa culpabilité d'avoir transmis une telle maladie à son enfant.

L'infirmière doit aider les parents à assumer leurs responsabilités dans les soins de l'enfant pour qu'ils puissent l'encourager à respecter les limites imposées. Avant la sortie de l'hôpital, elle doit s'assurer que les parents maîtrisent bien le fonctionnement de la tente à humidité, du nébulisateur et des techniques de drainage. Ils doivent savoir que la literie deviendra humide en moins de quatre heures, sous la tente; l'infirmière peut leur donner des moyens pour préserver malgré tout le confort et le sommeil de l'enfant (par exemple, ne pas border les couvertures sous le matelas, de façon à changer facilement celle du dessus avant d'aller eux-mêmes dormir). Elle peut aussi suggérer diverses façons de procéder au drainage postural afin que l'enfant coopère plus facilement. Si les parents ne possèdent pas de lit articulé, ce qui est fréquent, l'infirmière peut suggérer au père de fabriquer des blocs de bois pour remonter le pied du lit lorsque c'est nécessaire. Une planche à repasser bien immobilisée peut aussi servir de table de drainage; le père peut construire lui-même une table appropriée. Très souvent ce genre d'efforts aide les parents à se déculpabiliser.

Il est à craindre que les parents surprotègent l'enfant et, par là même, nuisent à son développement normal. Il faut l'aider à s'adapter le mieux possible à son handicap.

L'infirmière doit quand même être réaliste dans son dialogue avec les parents, et se rappeler qu'ils connaissent la gravité et le pronostic de la maladie. Les encourager à intégrer l'enfant dans les activités de la famille et de l'entourage est souhaitable. Il faut aussi se rappeler qu'il y a souvent plus d'un enfant dans la même famille et, autant que possible, les autres ne devraient pas être lésés. Mais pratiquement les parents ont à consacrer une telle somme de temps à l'enfant malade qu'ils peuvent ne pas percevoir tous les besoins de celui qui apparemment requiert moins de soins.

Le diagnostic d'une mucoviscidose entraîne des problèmes psychologiques et financiers pour la famille. On doit l'informer des possibilités qu'offre la collectivité pour assister l'enfant atteint de cette maladie. Il faut signaler aux parents l'existence de la fondation canadienne pour la fibrose kystique qui procure aux familles l'équipement nécessaire. Il existe plusieurs centres locaux dont les services sont variés. Les parents doivent aussi savoir où se trouvent les cliniques spécialisées en mucoviscidose.

Il faut permettre aux parents d'exprimer leur sentiment de culpabilité et les réconforter le mieux possible. Souvent, les parents se séparent ou divorcent peu de temps après l'annonce de la maladie de leur bébé, surtout si un ou quelques autres enfants de la famille souffraient déjà de mucoviscidose. La charge physique et émotive peut devenir trop lourde à supporter surtout si l'un des enfants décède. Il est bon de mettre les parents en contact avec d'autres familles qui éprouvent les mêmes problèmes et parfois des sessions de thérapie ou de dynamique familiale peuvent les aider.

Pronostic. Le pronostic est incertain, mais assez mauvais en cas d'atteinte grave. Il appert que la moitié de ces enfants meurent avant l'âge de 10 ans et 80% avant l'âge de 20 ans. Il semble que le garçon affecté d'une mucoviscidose soit stérile à l'âge adulte. Toutefois, cette donnée est établie sur le petit nombre de garçons qui ont survécu jusqu'à l'âge adulte. La mort peut provenir d'une malabsorption importante, d'une grave infection respiratoire ou d'une défaillance cardiaque. L'infirmière peut être d'un grand secours à ce moment-là pour les parents, surtout s'ils connaissent la cause génétique de la maladie et même s'ils en connaissaient le pronostic. Une assistance spirituelle peut grandement aider certains parents.

Plus d'enfants affectés de mucoviscidose atteignent maintenant l'âge adulte, mais ils parviennent souvent avec difficulté à acquérir une maturité émotive. Leur attention est depuis trop longtemps centrée sur leur maladie et l'avenir leur semble bien incertain. Les problèmes surviennent surtout au moment de l'adolescence et il faut alors impliquer les enfants de façon active dans la planification du traitement. Ils se rebellent souvent contre la nécessité d'une thérapie continue; ils se sentent atteints dans leur estime de soi à cause de leur incapacité à participer à des sports violents ou par leur difficulté à établir des relations d'amitié avec le sexe opposé. Leur image corporelle est déformée; ils se savent moins vigoureux, plus petits et se pensent moins attirants que leurs camarades. La possibilité qu'ils puissent un jour avoir une famille demeure encore aléatoire. Le fait de côtoyer la mort depuis des années influe sur leur façon de voir les événements et la vie.

Prolapsus et procidence du rectum et du sigmoïde

Incidence et étiologie. Le *prolapsus* du rectum consiste en un glissement de la muqueuse du rectum qui peut sortir de l'anus. La *procidence* est la descente anormale de toutes les tuniques du rectum et/ou du sigmoïde, avec ou sans protrusion par l'anus.

Ces *affections* s'observent surtout durant la première année, mais elles peuvent survenir jusqu'à l'âge de trois ans.

Tout facteur provoquant une élévation subite de la pression intra-abdominale et toute faiblesse importante de la musculature peuvent déclencher un prolapsus qui peut atteindre 12 à 15 cm de longueur et prendre une forme sphérique ou boudinée. La malnutrition, la diarrhée ou la constipation sont des facteurs adjuvants. Le prolapsus ou la procidence peut récidiver quand l'enfant pousse pour déféquer, si le sphincter est relâché et les muscles pelviens affaiblis.

Manifestations cliniques. La muqueuse ou la paroi qui fait saillie remonte d'abord d'elle-même après la défécation. À la longue, la réinsertion digitale devient nécessaire.

Traitement, soins infirmiers et pronostic. Le traitement causal s'avère essentiel. En cas de malnutrition, il faut veiller à corriger le poids de l'enfant par un régime approprié, à combattre la constipation par l'administration d'huile minérale et à instaurer des habitudes correctes de défécation. On traitera la diarrhée si elle semble à l'origine de la pathologie.

On peut rapprocher les fesses à la main ou avec un diachylon lors des défécations. La pression manuelle demeure toutefois préférable, si l'enfant est capable d'indiquer le moment des selles, parce qu'il est plus facile de diriger le passage du bol fécal.

Il est bon de maintenir l'enfant en position déclive pendant la réduction digitale. On peut enrouler du papier hygiénique autour du doigt, l'insérer dans l'ouverture du prolapsus, pousser le tout vers le rectum. Le papier colle alors à la muqueuse et y reste fixé lors du retrait du doigt. Ramolli par l'humidité du rectum, il passera dans la prochaine selle.

Dans les cas rebelles, une intervention chirurgicale peut s'avérer nécessaire. Avec un traitement adéquat, le pronostic est généralement bon.

Atrésie biliaire

Étiologie, physio-pathologie, manifestations cliniques et pronostic. On attribue la cause de l'atrésie biliaire à un défaut, partiel ou complet, du développement des voies biliaires. La bile s'accumule dans le foie au lieu d'entrer dans le tractus intestinal. Les pigments biliaires pénètrent dans le sang et l'ictère apparaît.

Le tableau clinique comprend l'ictère, un foie volumineux, une vésicule biliaire absente ou déformée, une rate augmentée de volume ainsi que de l'ascite, par suite de l'obstruction portale que détermine la cirrhose biliaire.

L'enfant semble ordinairement normal à la naissance. Un ictère apparaît progressivement vers la deuxième ou troisième semaine de vie et devient rapidement très marqué. La réaction de Van den Berg est positive. Les pigments biliaires colorent l'urine. Par suite de leur forte teneur en graisse et de l'absence des pigments et des sels biliaires, les selles, blanches et argileuses, ont la consistance du mastic. L'infection cause une toxémie inhabituelle. Les temps de saignement et de coagulation sont allongés. Le taux de prothrombine s'abaisse. L'absorption des graisses, des vitamines liposolubles (A, D, E, et K) et du calcium est faible.

En l'absence complète de voies biliaires, aucun espoir n'est permis, bien qu'on ait observé des survies de quelques années. La greffe hépatique peut prolonger la vie de l'enfant.

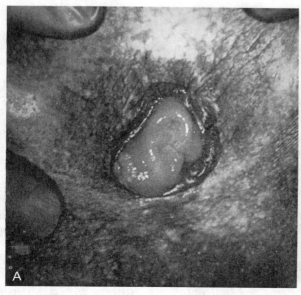 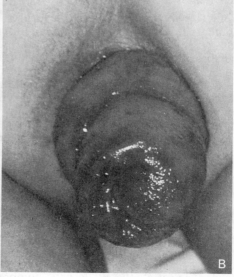

Figure 13-9. *(A)* Prolapsus partiel du rectum — seule la muqueuse rectale sort par l'orifice anal. *(B)* Procidence du rectum — toutes les couches de la paroi intestinale sont atteintes par cette pathologie. Elle se manifeste ici par une masse boudinée dont l'extrémité montre la lumière de l'intestin. (P. Hanley et M. O. Hiner dans *Christopher's Minor Surgery*, de Oschsner et DeBakey, 8e éd.)

Traitement et soins infirmiers. Le régime est élevé en protéines et pauvre en graisses. On donne les vitamines liposolubles A, D, E et K en solution aqueuse. Il faut protéger l'enfant contre l'infection. On administre des antibiotiques si une infection se produit.

Le *traitement chirurgical* est indiqué à l'âge de un ou deux mois s'il semble possible de reconstruire les voies biliaires. Pendant la période postopératoire, il faut surveiller l'apparition des symptômes de choc. On devrait changer fréquemment la position de l'enfant tout en prévenant un traumatisme de la plaie. Comme la cicatrisation s'effectue de façon irrégulière, il faut examiner les saignements de la plaie. Il faut observer la distension de l'abdomen, provoquée par une accumulation de liquide péritonéal ou une occlusion intestinale. On peut pratiquer une aspiration gastrique jusqu'à ce qu'on perçoive des mouvements péristaltiques. Le chirurgien peut ordonner des irrigations du cathéter gastrique avec une solution saline chaude, pour maintenir sa perméabilité. On emploie parfois un tube rectal pour soulager une distension abdominale ultérieure.

On nourrit l'enfant par voie parentérale, jusqu'à ce qu'il puisse le faire par voie orale. Si l'intervention réussit, les selles prendront un aspect plus normal lorsqu'on commencera à le nourrir par voie orale. Il faut faire une description soigneuse et complète de l'apparence des selles.

On effectue actuellement des recherches sur la technique de la transplantation du foie, chez des enfants souffrant d'atrésie biliaire. Le développement de cette technique chirurgicale est trop récent pour que l'on puisse en évaluer les résultats à long terme. Jusqu'à maintenant les enfants n'ont pas survécu cinq ans après la transplantation.

Maladie de Hirschsprung
(Mégacôlon aganglionnaire congénital)

Étiologie, incidence et pronostic. Cette pathologie consiste en une augmentation anormale du volume du côlon.

Le mégacôlon provient d'une absence congénitale des ganglions parasympathiques dans le côlon distal, causant une atrophie du segment atteint (avec absence complète de péristaltisme) et une accumulation de matières fécales en amont. La portion indemne de l'intestin (précédant la région privée de ganglions) se dilate, s'hypertrophie considérablement, puis s'amincit. L'absence de péristaltisme dans le segment atteint et la détérioration de la portion saine conduisent à la constipation opiniâtre et éventuellement à la distension abdominale.

Cette maladie prédomine chez les garçons. Les symptômes peuvent se présenter dès la naissance, ou apparaître au cours de la première année.

Sans traitement, le mégacôlon congénital conduit à la mort dans 75% des cas.

Manifestations cliniques. L'enfant souffre d'une constipation opiniâtre. Souvent, dès la naissance, on constate une absence de méconium. Il vomit, l'abdomen est distendu et des selles liquides alternent avec des périodes de constipation au cours des premières semaines de la vie.

L'évolution ultérieure comprend une constipation marquée, avec une distension de l'abdomen que déterminent les matières et les gaz. La flatulence peut devenir si importante qu'elle gêne la respiration. Les selles, que l'on doit provoquer le plus souvent par des lavements et des laxatifs, sont très fragmentées, enrubannées ou liquides. La malnutrition entraîne un retard staturo-pondéral. On note l'apparition de veines superficielles sur l'abdomen; on peut palper les matières fécales à travers la paroi abdominale amincie. Les douleurs abdominales, les vomissements et l'hyperthermie accompagnent les épisodes fréquents de sub-occlusion intestinale.

Diagnostic. Le diagnostic est basé sur les manifestations cliniques. Si l'enfant souffre de diarrhée, comme c'est souvent le cas dans la première enfance, il devient difficile de différencier le mégacôlon de la mucoviscidose. On peut y parvenir en recherchant la trypsine dans le liquide duodénal et en pratiquant le test de sudation. Le lavement baryté montre une image caractéristique de rétrécissement. Après l'examen, le baryum doit être éliminé immédiatement par une irrigation du côlon. On ne retrouve pas de matières fécales lors du toucher rectal, malgré la distension abdominale marquée. La biopsie intestinale permet de confirmer un diagnostic difficile.

Traitement. On donne des lavements fréquents ou quotidiens pour évacuer les selles lorsqu'elles s'accumulent. Le médecin peut prescrire des lavements de rétention, à base d'huile minérale ou d'huile d'olive que l'on fait suivre d'une irrigation colique.

Si l'état de l'enfant le permet, on procède à l'ablation du segment colique rétréci. Selon la technique de Swenson, la partie rétrécie du côlon est descendue à travers le sigmoïde et le rectum, et l'anastomose entre les parties saines est effectuée. Le segment atteint est ensuite réséqué.

La technique opératoire de Duhamel est plus récente. Elle consiste à préserver le rectum et ses fonctions, par une longue anastomose latéro-latérale effectuée entre le rectum et la partie proximale du côlon renfermant des ganglions normaux. Cette technique rétablit un rythme normal de défécation.

Si l'état du bébé ne permet pas l'intervention, ce qui est le cas le plus fréquent, on pratique une colostomie temporaire en vue d'assurer la survie et de permettre d'attendre un moment plus favorable pour l'intervention. La colostomie se pratique sur le segment colique en amont du segment pathologique. Les soins du bébé colostomisé ont été décrits précédemment.

Soins infirmiers. Comme ces enfants sont sous-alimentés, apathiques et gênés par la distension abdominale et les nausées, une bonne hygiène générale s'impose. Des apports alimentaires fréquents, mais par petites quantités, valent mieux que trois grands repas par jour. On donne un régime faible en résidus pour maintenir des selles molles et faciliter ainsi leur évacuation. L'infirmière doit noter l'appétit de l'enfant, la fréquence et la nature des selles. Une dose quotidienne d'huile minérale est ordinairement ajoutée à la diète. Comme la distension abdominale gêne la respiration, l'enfant semble plus à l'aise dans une position semi-Fowler. On peut le placer en position assise et le soutenir avec des sacs de sable et des oreillers. Les petites chaises de bébé sont conseillées dans ces cas.

Les *soins préopératoires* consistent à nettoyer l'intestin par des lavements répétés et des irrigations du côlon au moyen de solutions

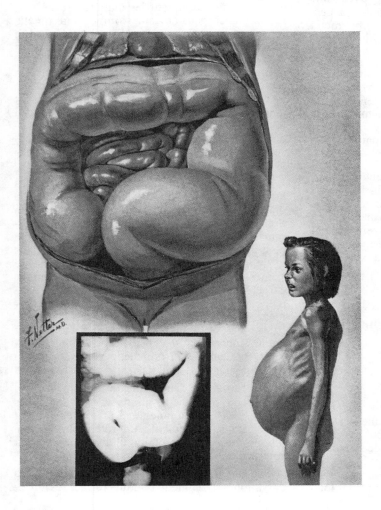

Figure 13-10. Mégacôlon. (Collection CIBA d'illustrations médicales, par Frank H. Netter, m.d.)

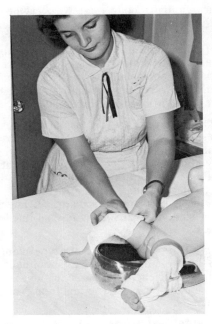

Figure 13-11. Position de l'enfant pour un lavement. On place la tête et le dos de l'enfant sur un oreiller; les fesses reposent sur le bord du bassin de lit que l'on a recouvert d'une couche pliée pour éviter le contact de la peau avec le métal. Une autre couche passe sous le bassin et ses extrémités servent à maintenir les jambes en position.

salines physiologiques. Il faut se rappeler que l'usage de l'eau du robinet peut provoquer une intoxication pouvant mettre la vie de l'enfant en danger. Le médecin peut prescrire des agents chimiothérapiques pour diminuer la flore bactérienne.

La technique du lavement est semblable à celle employée chez l'adulte, avec quelques modifications rendues nécessaires par l'anatomie et la physiologie de l'enfant. L'infirmière doit se rappeler que, dans le cas actuel, soit au niveau du segment rétréci, soit au niveau de la portion dilatée et amincie, la perforation constitue une des complications majeures du traitement médical dans le mégacôlon congénital. Il peut arriver que l'enfant ne puisse évacuer un lavement et que l'irrigation colique doive se faire avec une poire asepto adaptée au tube rectal. On injecte environ 30 à 50 ml de solution saline et une quantité semblable est retirée. Le traitement est poursuivi jusqu'au retour du liquide clair. Il peut durer une heure complète chaque jour et on comprend l'importance qu'il y a à l'effectuer dans une am-

biance détendue et de façon à ce que l'enfant puisse quand même jouer pendant cette période. Dans certains hôpitaux, l'infirmière n'administre pas de lavements à ce type de nourrissons.

1) On emploie un cathéter rectal n° 10 à 12 que l'on introduit de 5 à 10 cm dans le rectum. La progression du tube doit s'effectuer lentement et doucement.

2) La température de la solution doit être de 40,5°C.

3) On utilise une solution saline physiologique (jamais l'eau du robinet) obtenue en dissolvant une mesure de sel dans un litre d'eau.

4) Il ne faut pas administrer plus de 300 ml de solution à un nourrisson, sauf si le médecin prescrit une quantité plus grande.

5) L'enfant est mis en position dorsale, la tête et le dos reposant sur un oreiller. On place les fesses sur le bassin de lit couvert préalablement d'une couche pliée qui fera un coussin doux sous la région lombaire inférieure. Une autre couche maintient les jambes écartées de part et d'autre du bassin de lit.

6) On garde le récipient contenant la solution du lavement à 30 ou 45 cm au-dessus du niveau des hanches de l'enfant, pour que la solution puisse s'écouler lentement, par gravité.

7) On note soigneusement les résultats du lavement dans le dossier de l'enfant.

La mère doit apprendre la technique du lavement ou de l'irrigation colique pour assurer des soins appropriés à son enfant lors du retour à la maison. Si le médecin prescrit des lavements existant dans le commerce, il faut initier la mère à leur emploi.

Pour un lavement huileux, on peut utiliser la même technique ou adapter une seringue au tube rectal. On donne habituellement de 75 à 150 ml d'huile à 38°C. On doit ensuite exercer une pression sur l'anus afin d'éviter le rejet de la solution. Il faudrait donner un lavement irriguant après trente à quarante minutes de rétention.

En phase *postopératoire*, le médecin peut prescrire des antibiotiques, en vue de réduire le danger d'infection.

On prend la température par voie axillaire plutôt que rectale jusqu'à la fin de la cicatrisation.

Il faut noter soigneusement la quantité de liquides absorbés et excrétés et faire une description des selles. La région péri-anale doit être gardée propre en tout temps, mais surtout après une intervention chirurgicale de correction. Si on a pratiqué une colostomie, il faut appliquer les soins décrits lors de la correction de l'anus imperforé.

Complications. Il faut craindre la malnutrition et les ulcères de la muqueuse intestinale, qui provoquent une diarrhée, une perforation et une péritonite (rare mais possible).

Évolution et pronostic. Les formes bénignes du mégacôlon peuvent disparaître ou s'améliorer lorsque l'enfant grandit. La flatulence ne crée pas de sérieuses difficultés au cours des premières années, mais peut causer de grands embarras à l'enfant d'âge scolaire.

La correction chirurgicale donne d'excellents résultats.

Mégacôlon psychogénique

Il peut être difficile de distinguer le mégacôlon psychogénique du vrai mégacôlon aganglionnaire. La cause de ce syndrome réside en un antagonisme profond entre la mère et l'enfant. Le traitement consiste en laxatifs, suppositoires, apport plus grand de liquides et surtout apprentissage de bonnes habitudes intestinales. Cet état survient habituellement en période préscolaire, et est présenté ici parce que les symptômes peuvent être semblables à ceux du mégacôlon congénital. Si l'on veut que le traitement soit efficace, il faut comprendre l'attitude des parents et de l'enfant face aux habitudes intestinales. Une thérapie familiale peut s'imposer.

PATHOLOGIES DU SANG

Les anémies du nourrisson et de l'enfant

Étiologie, manifestations cliniques et pronostic. L'anémie, anomalie sanguine que l'on trouve le plus souvent chez l'enfant, se présente sous plusieurs formes; les plus courantes sont dues 1) à un défaut de production d'hématies ou d'hémoglobine et 2) à une perte excessive d'hématies. Une *baisse de production d'hématies ou d'hémoglobine* provient 1) d'une carence dans la moelle osseuse d'une ou plusieurs substances nécessaires à la formation des globules, 2) d'une diminution de la fonction de la moelle osseuse et 3) de déficits nutritifs spécifiques (fer).

Une perte excessive de globules rouges peut être secondaire à une hémorragie, telle l'hémorragie aiguë du nouveau-né, une colite ulcéreuse chronique ou une hémolyse sanguine. Les causes les plus communes de l'hémolyse sont 1) une anomalie congénitale des érythrocytes ou de l'hémoglobine: thalassémie et sphérocytose héréditaire, et 2) des anomalies acquises de l'érythrocyte ou de son milieu ambiant: anémies hémolytiques toxiques dues aux poisons ou aux médicaments, anémies hémolytiques des brûlés et des immunisations passives comme l'érythroblastose fœtale.

Si l'anémie peut avoir plusieurs causes, ses manifestations cliniques varient peu. Au début, l'enfant est vite fatigué, faible et apathique. Les symptômes ultérieurs sont la pâleur, les palpitations cardiaques et la tachycardie. Finalement, on note une lenteur mentale et physique, une hypertrophie cardiaque et une incapacité à s'adonner aux activités habituelles de l'enfance.

Le *pronostic* varie d'après le type d'anémie. Quand l'anémie est fatale, c'est habituellement dû à une déficience cardiaque et à une incapacité à maintenir une circulation sanguine normale.

Traitement et soins infirmiers. Le traitement et les soins infirmiers dépendent de la gravité de l'affection, de sa cause et de l'âge de l'enfant.

Des *transfusions* améliorent l'état de l'enfant, son appétit et son caractère. Il devient plus actif. Une transfusion peut être vitale quand l'anémie perturbe la fonction cardiaque. L'infirmière doit noter tout signe de malaise, comme l'agitation, les pleurs ou les cris, une hausse de température, un frisson ou une éruption cutanée, qui peuvent traduire une réaction de rejet à la transfusion. On peut constater des modifications cardio-vasculaires et une altération de la coloration de la peau. Il faut suivre de près les changements dans l'aspect des urines, leur quantité et tout phénomène hémorragique. Dès que l'infirmière note de tels symptômes, elle doit arrêter la transfusion et avertir immédiatement le médecin.

Un des problèmes de la transfusion chez les nourrissons est l'obstruction de l'aiguille par la paroi de la veine. Pour prévenir ceci, on peut injecter lentement le sang avec une seringue. L'infirmière assiste le médecin qui applique cette technique. Il faut prendre beaucoup de précautions pour empêcher la formation de bulles d'air et pour prévenir la contamination du piston de la seringue.

Les médicaments les plus habituellement administrés sont le fer, les vitamines C et B_{12}, l'acide folique et l'extrait de foie. On donne du fer si l'anémie provient d'une carence alimentaire ou d'une perte de fer secondaire à une hémorragie. Il est ingéré par voie orale sous forme de sulfate ferreux, mieux absorbé que le sel ferrique. Il faut signaler à la mère que l'absorption de fer amène des selles vert-foncé ou noires. Il faut l'administrer entre les repas, quand l'estomac ne contient plus de produits lactés ni de céréales qui inhibent l'absorption du fer. En cas de nécessité, on peut aussi administrer le fer par voie intra-veineuse ou intramusculaire.

On prescrit de la vitamine C pour corriger l'anémie causée par le scorbut, de l'extrait de foie, de la vitamine B_{12} ou de l'acide folique pour le traitement des anémies mégaloblas-tiques.

Une splénectomie peut être pratiquée à cause de sa valeur palliative ou pour supprimer la pression d'une rate hypertrophiée sur les organes abdominaux.

Il est très important de préparer les parents aux soins continus qu'exige le jeune enfant atteint d'une anémie. Au cours des entretiens avec la mère, le médecin ou l'infirmière vont reprendre dans son ensemble le problème de la santé générale de l'enfant. Une bonne hy-giène comprend le régime, le repos, le soleil et l'air frais qui aideront l'enfant à résister aux infections. Il faut l'habiller en fonction de la température et l'éloigner des enfants et des adultes qui ont des rhumes, des maux de gorge ou autres infections.

Lorsque le bébé grandit, sa mère devrait favoriser son désir d'indépendance, dans la mesure où son âge et son état physique le lui permettent. Des périodes de jeu libre devraient alterner avec des périodes de jeu contrôlé et tranquille. Il ne faut jamais le laisser dépasser ses forces, mais lui apprendre, lorsqu'il grandit, à se protéger contre l'abus de ses forces et les tensions émotives.

Il faudrait éviter une hospitalisation prolon-gée, sauf si les conditions familiales sont défa-vorables ou que son état l'exige. Il n'y a pas si longtemps, les enfants qui souffraient d'anémies chroniques comme la thalassémie ou la sphé-rocytose restaient longtemps à l'hôpital afin de recevoir des transfusions sanguines. Ces pério-des d'éloignement de la maison, des parents, et plus tard de l'école, étaient défavorables à son développement psychologique normal. Souvent, les enfants avaient peur de l'hôpital et chaque hospitalisation devenait plus difficile que la précédente. Ils manquaient de sécurité tant aux points de vue physique que psychique et on constatait aussi une anxiété chronique comportant des craintes illogiques et non fon-dées. Toute leur vie et celle de leur famille étaient centrées sur leur maladie.

Aujourd'hui, on hospitalise les enfants pour l'établissement du diagnostic et les premières transfusions. Dans l'unité de pédiatrie, ils sont libres de parler et de jouer avec les autres enfants. Ils comprennent la relation entre la transfusion et la sensation de bien-être qu'ils éprouvent après celle-ci. Les enfants coopèrent mieux quand ils sont familiarisés avec l'équi-pement, la technique et les gens qui s'en occu-pent. Il faut leur permettre de manier les appareils et de participer à leur traitement par exemple, en nettoyant la zone de l'injection avant le début de la transfusion.

Si l'enfant doit être admis à l'hôpital pour une période plus longue, en vue d'un examen, de tests de laboratoire ou d'un traitement, le personnel infirmier doit être attentif à ses problèmes et tenter de rendre son séjour le plus agréable possible. Le personnel doit noter ses goûts ou ses répugnances alimentaires, ses jouets préférés, et conserver ces renseignements d'une hospitalisation à l'autre. Souvent ces enfants, lors de leur retour à l'hôpital, consi-dèrent les infirmières comme des amies et ne se sentent pas menacés.

Il faudrait éduquer l'enfant anémique en fonction de son entourage et de son état. S'il n'est pas capable d'aller à l'école, il faudrait lui donner des leçons à domicile. Dans beaucoup de villes, la commission scolaire en-voie des professeurs à la maison ou à l'hôpital, pour instruire les enfants incapables de se rendre à l'école.

L'anémie hypochrome due à une carence en fer

Étiologie, incidence et physio-patholo-gie. L'anémie ferriprive de l'enfant demeure l'un des troubles nutritifs les plus fréquents dans les pays industrialisés. Il est facile de la prévenir et son traitement apporte d'excellents résultats.

Si l'hémoglobine n'est pas synthétisée, il en résulte une pâleur des érythrocytes. Cette hypo-chromie s'accompagne d'une diminution du volume des globules ou microcytose. Si l'ané-mie est évidente, comme le nombre des glo-bules rouges peut l'indiquer, les taux d'hémo-globine et d'hématocrite diminuent et on peut diagnostiquer une anémie hypochrome.

La cause réside presque toujours dans une carence en fer dans l'alimentation ou un trouble de l'absorption du fer. Le jeune enfant ne produit de l'hémoglobine que si son régime lui fournit un apport suffisant de fer; l'apport minimum quotidien est de 15 mg chez l'adulte. La ration quotidienne d'un enfant souffrant d'une anémie ferriprive est de 6 mg/kg de fer élémentaire, trois fois par jour.

La fréquence des carences en fer est maximale aux périodes de croissance rapide. Le prématuré grandit vite à l'âge de trois ou quatre mois et est prédisposé à l'anémie hypochrome. Les enfants nés à terme ont des réserves de fer plus grandes que les enfants prématurés, et un régime pauvre en fer, ne comportant que du lait, des pommes de terre et des céréales, ne porte habituellement pas à conséquence avant l'âge de six mois. Le risque augmente jusqu'à deux ans pour l'enfant né à terme. À deux ans, le rythme de croissance diminue, les enfants partagent le régime plus varié de la famille et l'incidence de l'anémie diminue.

Une diète pauvre en fer peut indiquer des conditions sociales et économiques déficientes: faible revenu des parents, ignorance des besoins diététiques de l'enfant ou indifférence à l'égard de ceux-ci. Souvent, il ne connaissent pas la technique d'alimentation, manquent de temps, ou tout simplement ne veulent pas prendre la peine d'habituer l'enfant à se nourrir d'aliments solides contenant du fer.

L'anémie est rarement causée par des difficultés d'absorption ou par des vomissements prolongés. Même lorsque l'enfant a un régime approprié à son âge, des troubles de l'absorption tels qu'on en observe lors de diarrhées chroniques ou de la maladie cœliaque, peuvent engendrer une carence en fer.

Manifestations cliniques. Les signes habituels de l'anémie grave comprennent l'hypotonie généralisée, un retard du développement moteur, la faiblesse et une pâleur extrême. On retrouve quelquefois une hypertrophie cardiaque, un souffle systolique et une splénomégalie. Les hématies peuvent se chiffrer à moins de 2 500 000/ml; elles sont hypochromes et de petite taille; l'hémoglobine peut descendre en dessous de 5 g.

Traitement. Le traitement consiste à corriger les anomalies causales. Un régime adéquat comporte des légumes et de la viande en plus des apports supplémentaires de vitamines. La vitamine C (acide ascorbique) semble favoriser l'absorption du fer. On donne du fer surtout sous forme inorganique. Le sulfate ferreux est peu onéreux, facilement disponible et possède une teneur élevée en fer. Comme

son absorption demeure limitée et peut provoquer des vomissements, il vaut mieux donner la dose journalière en deux ou trois fois. D'autres préparations existent, mais leur teneur en fer est moins élevée et l'on doit donner de plus grandes doses. On peut administrer le fer par voie parentérale, mais on utilise rarement ce moyen si l'enfant tolère la thérapie par voie orale. Certains de ces produits provoquent une irritation à l'endroit de l'injection intramusculaire et peuvent entraîner des troubles systémiques.

Une transfusion sanguine est ordonnée si l'état de l'enfant est sérieux, spécialement en cas de défaillance cardiaque. Des petites transfusions de culots de globules rouges ont également une valeur thérapeutique certaine.

Soins infirmiers. Les nourrissons souffrant d'une carence en fer paraissent habituellement irritables. Il faut donc les nourrir lentement. Lorsque l'anémie s'améliore, l'enfant manifestera plus d'appétit pour les aliments autres que le lait. La ration lactée journalière ne doit pas dépasser un litre. On ajoute des aliments semi-solides et solides au régime, en procédant de la même façon que pour les bébés plus jeunes.

Il faut protéger l'enfant contre la contamination provenant surtout du personnel infirmier qui souffre d'infections respiratoires.

Les entretiens avec la mère sont importants, étant donné que la prévention des difficultés ultérieures réside dans les soins à long terme qu'elle donnera à l'enfant. Il faut lui signaler que les selles deviendront foncées ou noires à cause de l'absorption de fer. Les parents peuvent s'inquiéter de la coloration des selles s'ils n'en connaissent pas la cause.

Comme le fer peut tacher temporairement les dents, on administre la solution avec un compte-gouttes de façon à ne pas les toucher. Aux enfants plus âgés on fait boire des préparations liquides avec une paille. On peut aussi mélanger le fer à un jus de fruit ou le diluer avant de l'administrer aux bébés. Il faut toutefois se rappeler que le lait forme avec le fer, des sels insolubles et qu'il vaut mieux donner le médicament entre les repas. Du fer en comprimé ou les préparations liquides plus récentes qui peuvent être administrées sans paille sont sans effets sur les dents.

Pronostic. Généralement, le *pronostic* est bon quand on donne du fer, des vitamines et un régime approprié. La guérison survient habituellement au bout de quatre à six semaines, mais le traitement continue pendant douze semaines. Le pronostic est variable si l'enfant souffre d'une infection concomitante.

Thalassémie (Anémie méditerranéenne, Anémie de Cooley)

Définition, étiologie et incidence. La thalassémie est une anémie héréditaire où l'on trouve des globules rouges de forme anormale (anisocytose, poïkilocytose) contenant un taux d'hémoglobine inférieur à la normale (hypochromie). On constate deux formes de thalassémie: la *thalassémie mineure* chez le porteur *hétérozygote* de la maladie et la *thalassémie majeure* chez l'enfant *homozygote,* pour le gène anormal. On en trouve une incidence particulière chez les enfants originaires du bassin de la Méditerranée, surtout de l'Italie, de la Grèce et de la Sicile. L'incidence est aussi élevée chez les gens de race noire, les orientaux et les Juifs.

Physiopathologie. La pathologie consiste en une anémie microcytaire hypochrome. L'anomalie spécifique réside dans la production de globules anormaux, plus rapidement détruits que les globules rouges normaux. Le tissu hématopoïétique essaie de compenser cette anomalie en produisant une quantité plus élevée d'hémoglobine fœtale, mais le transport de l'oxygène demeure toutefois perturbé. Un grand nombre d'érythrocytes nucléées et de réticulocytes sont rapidement détruits par le système réticulo-endothélial; l'enfant souffre alors d'anémie.

Manifestations cliniques. THALASSÉMIE MINEURE: l'anémie est discrète, les modifications globulaires modérées, et l'enfant porteur d'un gène unique ne présente que peu de symptômes. La maladie n'est souvent découverte qu'au cours d'examens de laboratoire de routine ou alors d'une recherche spécifique de la maladie chez les membres d'une même famille. La THALASSÉMIE MAJEURE se manifeste par une anémie grave, inexorable, progressive et incompatible avec une survie prolongée. L'enfant semble normal à la naissance et les symptômes se développent ordinairement au cours de la première année. La pâleur est manifeste, surtout au niveau des muqueuses. Le travail accru de la rate provoque une splénomégalie progressivement évolutive; le foie augmente de volume et l'enfant souffre quelquefois d'une distension abdominale qui peut amener les symptômes de l'insuffisance cardiaque. Une lymphadénopathie apparaît et les lésions squelettiques sont marquées. On observe un retard du développement physique et une modification de la physionomie par l'épaississement des os plats de la face et du crâne, souvent accompagnée d'une protrusion des dents causée par une croissance exagérée du maxillaire. Les mains sont larges et massives.

Traitement. Ces enfants supportent assez bien un taux d'hémoglobine relativement bas, mais il est indispensable de faire de fréquentes transfusions sanguines pour corriger l'anémie. L'emploi des culots globulaires fournit un apport suffisant d'hémoglobine et évite la surcharge vasculaire au cours du traitement.

L'hémosidérose, dépôt excessif de fer au niveau de tous les tissus, vient souvent compliquer le traitement à base de transfusions sanguines. L'insuffisance cardiaque traduit la sidérose myocardique et répond mal aux traitements habituels. On essaie, de façon expérimentale, de produire une élimination accrue du fer par les urines en administrant certains médicaments spécifiques. L'administration de fer par voie orale risque d'aggraver dangereusement l'hémosidérose. En cas de splénomégalie massive, la splénectomie élimine la gêne mécanique. Elle permet également d'espacer les transfusions et de normaliser la croissance.

Anémie à cellules falciformes (Drépanocytose)

La drépanocytose est une anémie hémolytique persistante, due à une anomalie dans la synthèse de l'hémoglobine. On trouve dans le sang des enfants atteints, une hémoglobine anormale (hémoglobine S) qui, sous une pression réduite d'oxygène, est responsable de l'aspect falciforme des globules rouges.

On observe deux formes de drépanocytose: la *drépanocytose mineure* chez le porteur *hétérozygote* (un seul gène est présent) qui prend le nom de « trait drépanocytaire » et la *drépanocytose grave* chez l'enfant *homozygote.*

Elle s'observe surtout chez les enfants de race noire, rarement chez les Caucasiens.

Physio-pathologie. La pathologie consiste en une anémie hémolytique persistante, avec des périodes de crises douloureuses passagères. Les globules rouges anormaux (falciformes) ont tendance à s'agglomérer dans les capillaires; l'anoxie localisée provoque la formation de nouvelles cellules falciformes qui augmentent à leur tour les lésions anoxiques. La douleur localisée révèle les lésions sous-jacentes. Les infarctus sont fréquents au niveau des organes anoxiques, et peuvent apparaître dans les os, les reins, les poumons, l'abdomen, le cerveau et le cœur. La rate demeure cependant l'organe le plus sérieusement touché, par suite de sa fonction hématopoïétique. Les infarctus spléniques répétés peuvent entraîner une fibrose importante, éventuellement suivie d'une atrophie de l'organe.

Manifestations cliniques. Le trait drépanocytaire demeure quasi asymptomatique et seule la recherche spécifique de la pathologie permet de le révéler.

La drépanocytose n'est pas apparente à la naissance. Quand l'hémoglobine fœtale disparaît vers l'âge de trois mois, les cellules falciformes commencent à se former et les manifestations cliniques apparaissent souvent avant l'âge d'un an. La crise drépanocytaire en constitue ordinairement l'élément initial. L'enfant ressent de fortes douleurs aux membres et à l'abdomen; il est excessivement pâle, souffre de vomissements, d'hyperthermie, de lombalgies accompagnées d'hématurie, de convulsions, de raideur de la nuque et de troubles cérébraux. Un ictère se manifeste, quelques jours après la crise, et traduit la libération de la bilirubine lors de l'hémolyse des globules anormaux. Entre les crises, l'enfant demeure pâle, anémié et conserve souvent son teint ictérique. Il se développe quand même de façon relativement normale mais présente une morphologie particulière: ses membres longs et graciles contrastent avec un thorax court, en tonneau, et un abdomen protubérant. Il peut souffrir d'insuffisance cardiaque à la suite d'anémie prolongée et l'atrophie de la rate succède à une splénomégalie importante et persistante.

Traitement. L'enfant qui souffre de drépanocytose a ordinairement un taux d'hémoglobine inférieur à la normale (6-9 g pour 100 ml) qui peut encore s'abaisser lors des crises. Chaque enfant tend à se stabiliser à son propre taux et toute élévation consécutive à une transfusion sanguine reste temporaire. La réticulocytose s'élève entre 5 et 25/100 ml et les valeurs maximales s'observent une semaine après les crises. Le traitement consiste à soutenir l'état général par des transfusions et à protéger l'enfant contre les infections. Le traitement des crises comporte l'apaisement de la douleur et la conservation de l'hydratation. Lorsque le taux d'hémoglobine s'abaisse rapidement, on donne de l'oxygène. La splénectomie ne modifie habituellement pas l'évolution de la maladie. Les crises tendent à s'espacer avec la croissance et plusieurs de ces enfants parviennent sans trop d'encombre à l'âge adulte. Étant donné le grand nombre d'enfants atteints aux États-Unis, ce pays consacre beaucoup d'énergie à la recherche sur cette maladie.

Plusieurs traitements expérimentaux, par exemple l'administration d'urée par voie orale pendant la crise, sont actuellement en cours.

PATHOLOGIE ENDOCRINIENNE

Crétinisme (Hypothyroïdie congénitale) (Myxœdème congénital)

Le myxœdème juvénile apparaît plus tardivement que le crétinisme et ses manifestations en sont moins importantes.

Définition, étiologie. Le crétinisme consiste en une insuffisance congénitale de la sécrétion de la glande thyroïde, provoquée par une anomalie embryologique dans laquelle la glande est absente ou rudimentaire et incapable de synthétiser l'hormone thyroïdienne, la thyroxine.

Manifestations cliniques. L'enfant paraît normal à la naissance et les symptômes se développent au cours des premières semaines ou des premiers mois de la vie. L'évolution en est insidieuse et la mère peut tarder à noter les symptômes.

L'apparence physique de l'enfant est assez particulière, c'est un nourrisson petit, indolent, sans vie. Il pleure très peu et la mère peut être fière de son « bon caractère ». Il tête toutefois difficilement, et le passage à l'alimentation solide demeure très aléatoire. La tête devient bombée, volumineuse, les cheveux sont implantés bas, la face est blême, œdémateuse, les paupières bouffies. L'écart entre les yeux semble très large, la bouche est entrouverte, la langue épaisse et sortie; la salive coule continuellement à l'extérieur de la bouche. La base du nez est large et plate; la peau, infiltrée de liquide, demeure trop sèche en surface. Les ongles et les cheveux sont secs et cassants. On trouve fréquemment des hernies abdominale, ombilicale ou inguinale.

Le *retard osseux* est manifeste et peut aller jusqu'au nanisme. L'occiput est bombé, la fontanelle antérieure largement ouverte. Le retard de la dentition s'accompagne de caries faciles. Le cou paraît court et épais; les membres sont courts, les mains et les pieds larges et épais.

L'enfant présente des *troubles fonctionnels.* Il souffre d'anorexie, de constipation opiniâtre, sa température plus basse que la normale explique sa frilosité, le pouls demeure lent.

On trouve également un *retard moteur* important. L'enfant tarde à s'asseoir, à se tenir debout, à marcher. Il manque globalement d'intérêt envers toute activité, parle tard et très peu. Le *retard sexuel* se manifeste fréquemment par une cryptorchidie. Si l'enfant parvient à l'adolescence, on constate une absence de développement génital et un retard considérable dans l'apparition, d'ailleurs peu marquée, des caractères sexuels secondaires.

Laboratoire. Comme les symptômes apparaissent progressivement, le diagnostic précoce peut s'avérer difficile. On peut mettre en évidence un abaissement du métabolisme basal, une hypercholestérolémie dont les chiffres varient entre 250 à 600 mg/100 ml, alors que le taux normal est compris entre 100 et 250 mg/100ml dont 60 à 75% est du cholestérol estérifié. La baisse de l'iode protéique sanguin (PBI) et la diminution de la fixation thyroïdienne de l'iode 131 aide à préciser le diagnostic.

Traitement. On devra donner le plus tôt possible après la naissance, pour éviter le déficit important qui se produit sans traitement, des extraits thyroïdiens qui constituent une médication substitutive qui devra être poursuivie durant toute la vie. On commence par une quantité peu importante pour en arriver au dosage maximum que l'enfant pourra prendre sans manifester de symptômes d'intoxication. La médication devra être ajustée ultérieurement, au moment de la puberté et en période génitale active.

Pronostic. Il demeure bon si l'enfant est traité adéquatement. Le déficit mental trouvé au moment de l'institution du traitement est rarement comblé, mais le développement physique et moteur peut atteindre les normes habituelles. Sans traitement, l'enfant se rend rarement à l'âge adulte et la mort survient ordinairement au cours d'une infection intercurrente.

Soins infirmiers. L'infirmière qui évolue dans un centre de santé joue un grand rôle dans le dépistage de la maladie. Une fois le traitement établi, elle devra être capable de reconnaître les symptômes de surdosage de l'hormone thyroïdienne soit, la tachycardie, la perte de poids, les vomissements et la diarrhée, les coliques et l'excitabilité. Elle doit faire comprendre aux parents l'importance de l'hygiène dentaire, de la régularité du traitement thyroïdien de substitution et de la surveillance

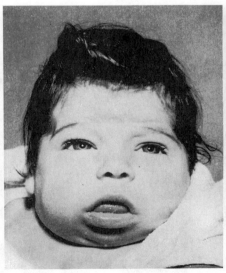
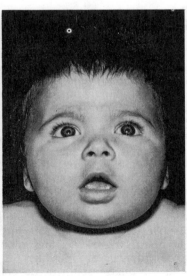

A   B

Figure 13-12. *(A)* Hypothyroïdie congénitale chez une fillette de six mois. Depuis la naissance, elle souffrait de troubles alimentaires, de constipation, et d'une rhinorrhée persistante. Très apathique, elle ne souriait pas et ne pouvait maintenir sa tête droite. Figure bouffie, cheveux implantés bas. *(B)* Après quatre mois de traitement aux extraits thyroïdiens, l'œdème de la face a disparu, les cheveux sont normaux et la fillette semble beaucoup plus éveillée. (A. M. DiGeorge dans *Textbook of Pediatrics* de W. Nelson.)

médicale continue. Il ne faut toutefois pas leur donner de faux espoirs. Le développement mental de l'enfant peut ne jamais être adéquat si le traitement n'a pas été institué dès la naissance.

ERREURS CONGÉNITALES DU MÉTABOLISME

Phénylcétonurie

Incidence, étiologie, manifestations cliniques.
La phénylcétonurie est une, maladie rare. On estime sa fréquence à un bébé sur 10 000 naissances vivantes. Elle affecte également les deux sexes et la plupart des enfants atteints ont les yeux bleus et les cheveux blonds.

Le trouble provient d'une anomalie congénitale dans le métabolisme de la phénylalanine. La phénylalanine est un acide aminé essentiel, présent dans tous les aliments qui contiennent des protéines. Son métabolisme est bloqué, au moment de sa transformation en tyrosine, par suite d'une déficience enzymatique. La phénylalanine s'accumule dans le sang et les corps phényloétoniques s'éliminent par les urines. Le mécanisme physio-pathologique amenant la détérioration mentale est actuellement peu connu. Le métabolisme de la mélanine étant également perturbé, ces enfants sont en général hypopigmentés.

La phénylcétonurie est transmise par un gène récessif autosome. La majorité des enfants atteints sont issus de deux hétérozygotes porteurs du gène. Lors de chaque grossesse, il y a une chance sur quatre que l'enfant soit normal, deux sur quatre qu'il soit porteur de l'anomalie, et une sur quatre qu'il soit atteint de phénylcétonurie.

Les *manifestations cliniques* se révèlent aux environs de quatre mois, quand la mère peut remarquer, chez l'enfant, une odeur particulière et un développement anormal. Le développement cérébral étant perturbé, il en résulte un retard mental à des degrés divers. Auparavant, on appelait cette affection *oligophrénie phénylpyruvique*. Des symptômes neurologiques apparaissent; le nourrisson et le jeune enfant sont irritables, désordonnés et colériques. Environ un malade sur quatre souffrira de convulsions et d'eczéma.

Diagnostic.
Le diagnostic est basé sur un simple test des urines pour découvrir les corps phénylcétoniques et sur un test sanguin pour démontrer la hausse de phénylalanine. Les corps phénylcétoniques apparaissent habituellement dans l'urine quand le taux plasmatique de phénylalanine dépasse approximativement 15 mg pour 100 ml. On emploie les mêmes gué des lois mandataires concernant l'usage de régime. Plusieurs gouvernements ont promultests pour le diagnostic et pour l'institution du ces tests afin de procéder à un dépistage systématique de la maladie.

Le *test de l'urine* s'effectue avec du chlorure de fer. Il n'est utile que lorsque le bébé est âgé d'au moins quatre semaines. On pratique ce test dans beaucoup d'hôpitaux et dans plusieurs cabinets pédiatriques pour détecter de façon précoce cette maladie. Une goutte de solution de 5 à 10% de chlorure de fer sur une couche récemment mouillée, la teindra d'une coloration verte en présence des corps phénylcétoniques. Si l'urine est normale, la couche restera jaune. Il faut répéter ce test à intervalles réguliers, étant donné que les résultats ne sont pas toujours positifs chez certains enfants atteints de phénylcétonurie. On peut effectuer le test à l'aide de bâtonnets « Phénistix » qui changent de couleur immédiatement quand on les plonge dans l'urine anormale.

Pendant plusieurs années, le test de l'urine fut la méthode universelle pour déceler cette maladie. Cependant, à l'heure actuelle, le test de Guthrie constitue la technique la plus remarquable. Il s'agit d'un simple test sur papier poreux effectué avec du sang prélevé au talon des nouveau-nés, le jour où ils quittent la pouponnière. Comme la concentration plasmatique de phénylalanine ne s'élève qu'au moment des premières absorptions de lait, et qu'elle augmente progressivement par la suite, on doit

Figure 13-13. Phénylcétonurie chez deux sœurs. La plus âgée semble très retardée; l'autre dont traitement a été institué précocement présente un aspect normal. (Courtoisie de la « National Association for Retarded Children ».)

pratiquer un second test environ quatre à six semaines plus tard. Plus le diagnostic est précoce, plus vite le traitement sera mis en route et meilleur sera le pronostic. Si on ne pratique pas ces tests avant que le médecin ou la mère soupçonne la maladie, l'enfant aura déjà subi des dommages cérébraux. Récemment des médecins ont préconisé des programmes de prévention pour trouver les femmes enceintes qui peuvent avoir des taux élevés de phénylalanine susceptibles d'amener un retard mental chez le nouveau-né.

Traitement et soins infirmiers. Comme les manifestations cliniques de la phénylcétonurie sont reliées à l'accumulation de la phénylalanine non métabolisée, on peut contrôler ce trouble en empêchant la prise de phénylalanine dès la toute première enfance. Comme tous les aliments naturels contiennent de la phénylalanine, sauf les huiles pures, la fécule pure et le sucre blanc, on instituera un régime à base de Lofenalac, un lait synthétique fournissant les protéines nécessaires à la croissance et aux reconstitutions tissulaires et contenant très peu de phénylalanine. Les autres aliments permis dans le régime contiennent un pour cent de protéines, comme les fruits, (surtout les pommes) et les légumes. Les céréales comme le tapioca et la fécule de maïs, le sucre et le beurre sont habituellement permis à volonté. Sont à supprimer, le pain, la viande, le poisson, la volaille, tous les types de farine, le fromage, le lait, les noix et produits à base de noix, les œufs et les légumineuses. La compagnie Mead Johnson met à la disposition du public une table des équivalents de la phénylalanine. Le traitement doit être adapté individuellement, d'après la réaction du sujet à la thérapie. On peut en juger par le taux de phénylalanine dans le sang et les urines, l'amélioration du développement physique et mental et la régression des symptômes.

L'infirmière doit être consciente du coût de ce régime alimentaire et de sa signification pour certains groupes culturels, si elle veut comprendre la réaction de certains parents devant cette restriction drastique dans la diète de leur enfant.

Comme il a un régime restreint, il faut évaluer fréquemment l'état nutritif et le taux d'hémoglobine de l'enfant. Des tests d'intelligence et d'autres évaluations de la capacité intellectuelle permettent de suivre l'évolution mentale de ceux dont le traitement a été entrepris précocement.

Il faut observer ces enfants pour mettre en évidence tout symptôme de trouble dermatologique ou neurologique. Les infirmières doivent souligner, dans leurs entretiens avec les parents, l'importance des examens complets du nouveau-né, pour que cette maladie, si elle existe, soit diagnostiquée et traitée le plus vite possible. Une thérapie suivie est fort onéreuse pour la famille de l'enfant, mais une aide financière peut être obtenue grâce à certains fonds privés ou publics. Plusieurs gouvernements offrent gratuitement le lait spécial « Lofenalac ».

Pronostic. Le pronostic est tributaire de la précocité de l'institution du traitement diététique. Si la thérapie a commencé dès la période néonatale, le pronostic est excellent. S'il y a eu délai, ne fut-ce que de quelques mois, un certain degré de retard mental persistera. Si la mise en route du traitement se fait après l'âge de trois ans, on constatera souvent une amélioration des lésions cutanées ainsi que de la personnalité et du comportement de l'enfant, mais pas de son arriération mentale. Beaucoup de médecins croient que si on maintient ce régime jusqu'à l'âge de six ans, on peut prévenir la plupart des lésions cérébrales. L'arrêt des restrictions diététiques améliore très souvent le climat psychologique de la famille, quand l'enfant est parvenu à cet âge. D'après certaines études récentes, il semble que cette suspension du traitement s'accompagne d'une faible régression du Q.I. compensée par l'amélioration de l'attitude de l'enfant qui peut commencer à fréquenter l'école avec un régime semblable à celui de ses compagnons. La plupart des pédiatres maintiennent toutefois un régime diététique modifié, jusqu'à l'âge de douze ans, âge auquel la croissance cérébrale est en général terminée. Le médecin peut suspendre la diète pendant une semaine et observer les réactions de l'enfant. De cette manière, il peut cesser le traitement à un moment plus sûr pour la santé de l'enfant. Les filles qui ont souffert de phénylcétonurie dans leur enfance doivent reprendre leur régime restreint en phénylalanine lorsqu'elles sont susceptibles d'être enceintes.

Galactosémie

Incidence, étiologie, manifestations cliniques et diagnostic. La galactosémie est une anomalie congénitale du métabolisme du galactose. C'est une anomalie assez rare qui se transmet selon le mode récessif autosomal et réside en l'absence de l'enzyme galactose - 1 - phostate uridyl transférase qui transforme le galactose en glucose au niveau du foie. On ne trouve pas de galactose à l'état libre dans les aliments, cependant la digestion du lactose du lait libère dans l'intestin du glucose et du galactose, absorbés sous cette forme par les villosités intestinales. La galactosémie est in-apparente à la naissance. Cependant, lorsque le régime lacté est bien institué, environ une ou deux semaines après la naissance, la galactosémie s'élève, dépasse le seuil rénal et la galactosurie apparaît.

La maladie se manifeste par de l'anorexie, des vomissements et un retard staturo-pondéral. Éventuellement, on observe une splénomégalie et une hépatomégalie liées à une cirrhose du foie. L'enfant présente un retard mental profond; des cataractes apparaissent. L'enfant souffrant de dénutrition extrême, de léthargie et d'émaciation meurt au cours d'un épisode infectieux, ou par suite de son insuffisance hépatique.

Traitement et soins infirmiers. Cette anomalie doit être décelée très tôt et il faut supprimer le lait du régime avant l'apparition des lésions irréversibles au cerveau et au foie. On donne une alimentation sans lactose, à base de substituts du lait faits d'hydrolysats de caséine. Il faut éliminer radicalement le lait, les laitages et les comprimés contenant du lactose pendant au moins les trois premières années de la vie. La persistance des cataractes requiert un traitement chirurgical.

Hypoglycémie

Incidence, étiologie, manifestations cliniques, traitement et pronostic. Au cours des dernières années, on a diagnostiqué une hypoglycémie, non seulement chez des nourrissons de mères diabétiques, mais aussi chez des bébés de mères non-diabétiques. On observe le plus souvent ce trouble, chez des nourrissons de sexe masculin de faible poids à la naissance et dont la mère a souffert de toxémie lors de la grossesse.

On croit que la cause de ce type d'hypoglycémie provient de l'insuffisance des réserves de glycogène dans le foie avant la naissance et d'un hyperinsulinisme fonctionnel après la naissance. L'explication la plus probable est une anomalie enzymatique congénitale, mais la cause réelle demeure inconnue.

Les *manifestations cliniques* apparaissent très tôt après la naissance, et durant toute la première enfance. On observe des tremblements, des convulsions, de la somnolence, des périodes de détresse respiratoire et de cyanose, des cris anormaux et des difficultés d'alimentation.

Le *traitement* consiste à administrer une solution de glucose par voie intraveineuse jusqu'à stabilisation du taux plasmatique du glu-cose. On peut aussi administrer de l'A.C.T.H. pour maintenir la glycémie normale. Cette affection peut réapparaître durant l'enfance.

Le *pronostic* vital est bon; cependant ces enfants peuvent être handicapés intellectuellement parce que le cerveau a un besoin essentiel et constant de glucose.

Agammaglobulinémie (Maladie de Bruton)

Incidence, étiologie, manifestations cliniques et diagnostic. L'agammaglobulinémie est une anomalie rare, dans laquelle l'enfant est incapable de former la gamma-globuline. Un gène récessif, lié au sexe, transmet l'anomalie; ordinairement, seuls les garçons sont affectés, et la mère elle-même ne présente aucune manifestation pathologique, bien qu'elle ait transmis la maladie.

La protection maternelle, trans-placentaire, agit chez le nouveau-né jusqu'à l'âge de six mois environ. Par la suite, l'enfant, incapable de former ses propres anticorps aux antigènes bactériens, devient spécialement sujet aux infections à bactéries pyogènes, (staphylocoques, streptocoques, pneumocoques et méningocoques). L'enfant ne peut développer d'anticorps même après des vaccins répétés (anatoxine diphtérique ou vaccin antityphique) et il souffre d'infections à répétition. Il semble toutefois que la réaction aux infections virales demeure normale. Le peu d'abondance du tissu lymphoïde constitue un signe habituel, et le dosage des gamma-globulines par l'immunophorèse permet de faire le diagnostic. Une agamma-globulinémie acquise peut apparaître plus tard dans la vie, et celle-ci affecte également les deux sexes.

Traitement et soins infirmiers. Il s'agit d'abord de prévenir les infections et on les traite immédiatement lorsqu'elles surviennent. Des injections intramusculaires mensuelles de gamma-globulines maintiendront le patient en vie. Les infections aiguës sont jugulées par la chimiothérapie antibactérienne.

En essayant d'éviter des infections à son enfant, une mère risque de trop le protéger. L'infirmière doit l'aider à adopter une saine attitude en dépit de la maladie de l'enfant.

Maladie de Tay-Sachs (Idiotie familiale amaurotique)

Définition, étiologie et incidence. L'idiotie familiale amaurotique, dégénérescence cérébro-maculaire, est une anomalie congénitale du métabolisme des lipides, causée par une déficience enzymatique. Elle se transmet sur le mode récessif autosomal. On la rencontre surtout chez les enfants issus de parents juifs d'Europe orientale.

Manifestations cliniques. L'enfant semble normal à la naissance. Vers l'âge de six mois, les parents notent une apathie inquiétante, une régression motrice accompagnée de faiblesse musculaire et d'une incapacité de l'enfant à fixer normalement son regard. La maladie évolue lentement, et vers l'âge d'un an, on trouve un enfant flasque et gras, mais qui souffre cependant d'hyperréflexie, d'une dégénérescence musculaire évidente et de *cécité*. Il présente bientôt des convulsions, de la spasticité accompagnée de décérébration et une démence croissante. L'enfant meurt vers l'âge de trois ans, dans un état de dénutrition extrême ou d'une infection intercurrente.

Diagnostic. Le diagnostic prénatal a été rendu possible grâce à l'amniocentèse et à l'analyse du tissu et du liquide embryonnaire. Les parents, s'ils le désirent, peuvent alors envisager la possibilité d'un avortement. Une simple analyse sanguine permet de déceler les porteurs de la maladie. Chez le bébé, les taches rouge-cerise sur la macula sont pathognomoniques. À l'autopsie, on trouve un cerveau dur, atrophié, infiltré de lipides et une atrophie optique. Tout au long de l'évolution, le sang et le liquide céphalo-rachidien sont toutefois demeurés dans les limites de la normale.

Traitement et soins infirmiers. On ne connaît pas de traitement. La famille doit être avisée de l'évolution clinique probable. Il faudrait l'informer des ressources communautaires qui peuvent l'aider

Le but des soins infirmiers se résume à assurer à l'enfant le plus de confort possible. Comme il sursaute facilement, il faut réduire au maximum les stimuli. Il faut maintenir la nutrition et éventuellement, on peut avoir recours au gavage.

Comme l'enfant est émacié, il faut bien prendre soin de sa peau. On doit le tourner fréquemment, pour éviter les escarres de la peau et pour diminuer les risques de pneumonie.

Les parents supportent difficilement la détérioration graduelle de l'état de l'enfant. Ils ont besoin de beaucoup de sympathie, surtout qu'ils savent la maladie héréditaire. Comme elle est due à une anomalie récessive, les parents se sentent responsables des souffrances de l'enfant. Le rabbin peut les réconforter, mais les parents se tourneront vers le médecin et l'infirmière pour exprimer leur peine de voir la dégénération continue de l'état de l'enfant. Il faut toutefois insister sur le fait qu'on peut maintenant prévenir la naissance d'enfants atteints de cette maladie.

Tyrosinémie

Incidence, étiologie, manifestations cliniques et diagnostic. La tyrosinémie est une affection génétique rare sauf dans la province de Québec, spécialement dans la région du Saguenay-Lac-St-Jean où l'incidence de la maladie atteint le taux incroyable d'un enfant malade pour 450 à 500 naissances. Une personne sur 20 serait porteuse du gène anormal.

La tyrosinémie se transmet selon le mode récessif autosomal et se caractérise par la déficience de l'enzyme oxydase d'acide parahydro-oxy-phénylpyruvique, enzyme essentielle au catabolisme de la tyrosine. Les taux sanguins de tyrosine, phénylalanine et méthionine s'élèvent.

L'enfant, ordinairement blond, présente une déficience hépato-cellulaire progressivement fatale. Il souffre de troubles gastro-intestinaux, d'hépatosplénomégalie avec hypertension portale, de phénomènes hémorragiques, de fièvre, de convulsions et d'un rachitisme vitamino-résistant.

Le *diagnostic,* établi d'après un examen sanguin, peut se faire très tôt dans la vie, surtout pour les nourrissons les plus susceptibles d'être atteints.

Traitement et soins infirmiers. Une diète restrictive en phénylalanine et en tyrosine permet de prolonger d'une ou deux années la vie du malade. Des essais thérapeutiques avec le pyridoxine, la cystine, l'ATP, laissent croire qu'un traitement plus efficace est en voie d'être développé.

Le rôle de l'infirmière consiste surtout à aider les parents à comprendre la nature et l'origine de la maladie. Ils doivent bien comprendre la diète qui est difficile à appliquer, et être préparés graduellement à la détérioration probable de l'état de leur enfant. On peut les mettre au courant des recherches en cours et les référer à un conseiller génétique.

PATHOLOGIES DE LA PEAU

Eczéma infantile
(Dermite atopique)

Définition. Lésion cutanée consistant en une dermatite due à l'hypersensibilité de l'enfant à une substance étrangère. La maladie peut apparaître peu après la naissance, mais demeure rare chez les enfants nourris au sein; elle peut guérir spontanément vers l'âge de deux ou trois ans, mais est fréquemment suivie de manifestations asthmatiques.

L'eczéma affecte également les deux sexes, toutes les races et se manifeste en tout temps. Il s'observe surtout au cours de l'hiver et tend à diminuer en été. Il atteint surtout le nourrisson gras et bien nourri dont l'état de santé est par ailleurs excellent.

Étiologie. Les principaux agents susceptibles d'agir sur le nourrisson sujet à l'eczéma sont certains *aliments*: le lait de vache, le blanc d'œuf, le blé, les oranges, le porc et le chocolat; des *inhalants*: les pollens, les poussières et les moisissures; des *substances de contact*: la laine, les poils, la poussière, etc.

Plusieurs facteurs peuvent favoriser l'apparition de la maladie. On trouve d'abord une *tendance familiale* certaine et, très souvent, les parents ont ou ont déjà souffert de manifestations allergiques, (asthme, urticaire).

L'état de la peau de l'enfant joue aussi un rôle important. La séborrhée ou l'érythème fessier accompagnent souvent l'eczéma, même si le bébé est bien soigné par sa mère. On trouve chez lui une teneur en sels et en eau plus élevée que chez le nourrisson normal. Parmi les *sources* possibles *d'irritation*, citons: les savons, le froid, la lumière solaire intense, l'irritation déterminée par les habits, des vêtements en laine ou de petites infections cutanées. Certains médecins estiment que la *suralimentation*, surtout en hydrates de carbone et en graisse, peut exercer un effet nocif sur les nourrissons portés à l'eczéma. Ceci est difficile à prouver, bien qu'on ait constaté une amélioration chez des enfants obèses après une perte de poids résultant d'une restriction glucidique et lipidique.

On croit qu'il peut aussi exister une perturbation dans les relations *mère-enfant* chez les nourrissons et les enfants qui souffrent d'eczéma ou de toute autre allergie. Les parents d'enfants allergiques ont été décrits comme surprotecteurs et anxieux ou comme hostiles et exigeants. Personne n'a réussi à évaluer si c'est la maladie de l'enfant qui amène un certain rejet de la part des parents, ou si l'attitude des parents provoque la pathologie.

Manifestations cliniques. Les lésions débutent par une éruption érythémateuse suivie de formation de vésicules très fines (liquide séreux). Les vésicules suintent et il se forme des croûtes jaunâtres. La peau sèche, desquame et s'épaissit. Ces lésions prurigineuses ont l'aspect de plaques irrégulières et sont surtout localisées aux plis cutanés, au cou, au front, au cuir chevelu et aux joues. Le grattage des lésions provoque des fissures pouvant s'infecter et produire de l'impétigo.

On ne vaccine ordinairement pas ces enfants contre la variole, à cause du danger de dissémination du vaccin (vaccine généralisée).

Le prurit intense peut rendre l'enfant irritable; l'insomnie et les pleurs sont fréquents. L'impétigo (surinfection au streptocoque) accompagne souvent une hyperthermie légère.

Traitement et soins infirmiers. Même un traitement intensif n'amène pas toujours la guérison, mais il peut soulager la plupart des malades.

Il faut informer la mère de l'évolution probable de la maladie, du traitement et des soins à donner. Il faut qu'elle sache que ces enfants sont sujets aux infections de la peau et des voies respiratoires. Chaque fois que cela semble possible, on essaie de soigner le nourrisson à la maison, à cause du danger d'infection à l'hôpital. L'hospitalisation peut s'avérer nécessaire, seulement, en présence d'une infection secondaire ou lorsque son état exige des soins plus intensifs et un traitement local que la mère ne peut plus donner. Parfois, il y a moins d'irritation externe dans le milieu hospitalier, et on peut maintenir d'une façon plus stricte le régime diététique. Lorsque la mère est épuisée à la suite des soins prodigués, on doit hospitaliser l'enfant dans son propre intérêt et dans celui de sa mère.

À l'hôpital, il faut tenir ce nourrisson à l'écart non seulement des enfants récemment vaccinés, mais aussi de toutes les personnes porteuses d'infections à virus et à cocci. Ces enfants se sentent mal à l'aise et ont besoin de soins maternels. Dans la mesure du possible, les mères doivent les visiter souvent et les infirmières doivent leur accorder une attention toute spéciale.

Dans le traitement local, les contraintes sont importantes, et il faut les utiliser uniquement

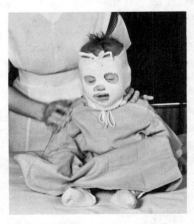

Figure 13-14. Masque facial facilitant le traitement de l'eczéma.

quand elles deviennent nécessaires pour prévenir le grattage. Ces enfants se grattent au lieu de crier lorsqu'ils sont en colère ou lorsqu'ils se sentent frustrés. L'infirmière doit inciter l'enfant à s'extérioriser en encourageant le jeu actif ou le mouvement physique. Des entraves deviennent nécessaires en l'absence de la mère ou de l'infirmière.

Pour ces nourrissons on utilise différents types d'entraves: un manchon rigide pour les coudes, une chemisette à manche fermée, un masque facial, des contraintes localisées aux chevilles et aux poignets. On peut employer toutes les protections nécessaires, mais on doit les vérifier fréquemment pour éviter qu'elles ne perturbent la circulation. On peut emprisonner les mains et les pieds dans des chaussettes de coton, après avoir coupé les ongles ras pour prévenir les lésions de grattage.

Il faut veiller à mettre ces entraves avec douceur, d'une façon solide et seulement lorsque c'est nécessaire. Il faut les enlever de temps en temps pour accorder un peu de liberté de mouvement. Si l'enfant souffre d'un prurit intense, il faut enlever une seule contrainte à la fois, pour que l'infirmière ou la mère puisse facilement l'empêcher de se gratter. Toutefois, si on intéresse immédiatement le bébé à un jeu amusant, il occupera ses mains et ne se grattera pas. S'il a un accès de grattage, l'amélioration constatée depuis plusieurs semaines peut disparaître, et la peau redevenir ouverte à l'infection.

Il faut prendre souvent l'enfant dans les bras, et le changer de position le plus souvent possible pour prévenir les infections respiratoires, surtout la pneumonie. Il faut lui accorder des périodes de jeu surveillé en dehors de son berceau pour réduire au minimum la colère provoquée par l'immobilisation et lui donner la possibilité de connaître son environnement s'il est assez âgé pour marcher. De longues périodes de jeu dans l'eau diminuent le prurit et permettent à l'enfant de bouger librement.

D'épaisses feuilles de cellophane ou de plastique transparent, placées sous le nourrisson, préviendront les frottements sur la literie et empêcheront l'absorption de la pommade par les draps. Si les parents n'ont pas les moyens d'acheter des feuilles neuves, on pourra utiliser une vieille nappe en plastique.

Baigner le nourrisson fait partie du traitement; en général il est préférable d'employer un savon neutre, non irritant. Souvent, le médecin prescrira une huile minérale à ajouter à l'eau du bain. Lorsque la surface corporelle est couverte de croûtes, on l'enduit d'une solution antiseptique douce avec des compresses imbibées de cette solution. Une application de compresses saturées de soluté physiologique, poursuivie pendant un jour ou deux de façon à ce que la peau reste constamment humide, permet de faire tomber les croûtes. Si des surfaces cutanées étendues sont couvertes de papulo-vésicules, le médecin peut prescrire un bain d'amidon et de bicarbonate de soude. On garde l'eau du bain à une température de 35°C. et on y baigne l'enfant le plus longtemps possible. On peut employer des jouets flottants pour l'amuser. L'infirmière doit garder l'enfant constamment occupé, de façon à prévenir efficacement le grattage. Elle doit donc prévoir une variété de jouets avant de préparer l'enfant pour son bain.

On évite de sortir l'enfant par temps froid ou venteux. À l'intérieur, on l'habille aussi légèrement que possible pour éviter l'échauffement et l'irritation de la peau. Il ne faut pas utiliser de couvertures de laine puisque l'enfant peut y être sensible. Il faut changer les couches dès qu'elles sont souillées pour empêcher l'irritation des fesses.

Pour nourrir l'enfant, on le tient de la même manière que les enfants en bonne santé. Il a besoin d'amour pour son évolution psychologique. Le fait de le prendre favorisera un changement de position et préviendra les difficultés respiratoires. Une tétine d'amusement le calme et réduit la tension durant sa première année d'existence.

Le *traitement* des lésions requiert l'application de différents topiques, variant selon la sorte de lésions. Les pommades, qu'il faut éviter de mettre sur les lésions suintantes, doivent être appliquées par un mouvement qui les fait pénétrer dans la peau. Il est inutile d'appliquer une pommade sur des croûtes déjà formées. On les enlève d'abord en appliquant des compresses salées ou en les frottant avec de la vaseline liquide.

Il est facile, pendant un jour ou deux, de préparer un masque facial en gaze ou en jersey de coton pour maintenir la lotion en contact étroit avec la peau. Il suffit de faire des ouvertures aux endroits correspondant aux yeux, au nez et à la bouche. On fait des points aux ouvertures pour empêcher les mailles de filer; on fixe le masque sur la tête de l'enfant avec des cordons. L'utilisation de « retelast » élimine la nécessité de l'ourlet et de l'emploi des cordons. Il faut veiller à ce que le masque ne soit pas trop serré pour éviter d'irriter les lésions.

Lorsque la surface est sèche, rouge et papuleuse, le médecin peut prescrire une pommade au goudron. Il faut appliquer cette pommade aussi souvent que nécessaire pour que la peau en reste enduite. On couvre ensuite la région avec un pansement sec. Parfois, on insère une pièce de cellophane entre l'onguent et le pansement. Chaque jour, avant d'appliquer de la pommade fraîche au goudron, il faut retirer soigneusement l'ancienne avec de la vaseline liquide. Si de grandes surfaces cutanées sont couvertes de papulo-vésicules, on peut, en mettant l'enfant dans un bain d'amidon, retirer la pommade.

L'infirmière doit signaler à la mère qu'il faut conserver la pommade au goudron dans des pots soigneusement fermés pour empêcher l'évaporation de ses constituants volatiles. Il faut éviter d'exposer l'enfant aux rayons du soleil, car la photo-sensibilisation peut causer une plus grande irritation cutanée. Quand l'état de la peau s'est amélioré, on remplace le goudron par une substance plus douce. Les taches de goudron s'enlèvent en les frottant avec un corps gras avant le lavage.

L'état de la plupart des enfants s'améliore sous l'effet du traitement local; mais si on ne constate pas de progrès, il faut prendre d'autres mesures, notamment éviter les allergènes spécifiques et modifier l'environnement.

Il faut éviter les contacts avec les allergènes. La chambre de l'enfant doit être scrupuleusement propre, facile à nettoyer, sans tapis, rideaux lourds ou décorations propres à attirer la poussière. Le ménage doit être fait tous les jours, hors de la présence de l'enfant, avec un linge humide qui absorbe la poussière.

Tous les éléments du lit doivent être lavés périodiquement. Les draps et les couvertures doivent être de coton (pas de laine ou de tissu synthétique). L'oreiller de caoutchouc mousse est idéal. L'enfant doit porter des vêtements légers, moyennement chauds, facilement lavables (coton). Sa chambre doit être exposée périodiquement au soleil. On lui donne des jouets lavables, évitant les animaux de peluche et les jouets qui retiennent la poussière. On ne doit tolérer aucun animal domestique dans la maison.

Pour le nourrisson, les régimes d'élimination constituent la méthode d'investigation la plus utile. On doit donner à la mère une liste des aliments permis plutôt que de ceux qui sont interdits. On peut inclure des vitamines synthétiques au régime. Progressivement, on ajoute de nouveaux aliments, mais toujours un seul à la fois, et on doit surveiller les réactions allergiques et les noter. De cette façon, on établit un régime éliminant les allergènes.

Les tests cutanés comme moyen de dépistage ne sont pas très valables avant l'âge de deux ans ou pour l'enfant entièrement couvert de lésions.

Beaucoup de nourrissons souffrant d'eczéma sont allergiques au lait de vache et on doit les nourrir avec des substituts lactés, tel le Pro Sobee. Certains enfants supportent le lait de vache bouilli; la valeur protéique s'en trouve altérée et il devient moins allergène. Pour cette raison, on emploie souvent le lait évaporé dans le traitement de ces nourrissons.

Aux enfants sensibles au lait de vache sous toutes ses formes, on peut donner du lait de chèvre, des substituts protéiques de légumes, des formules à base de viande ou de caséine hydrolysée. On trouve dans le commerce des substituts protéiques de légumes, surtout à base de soja, sous forme liquide ou en poudre. Avec toute formule de substitution, il faut donner des vitamines C et D aussi bien que les autres vitamines essentielles.

On peut prescrire différents traitements non spécifiques. Les techniques visant à provoquer une déshydratation légère s'avèrent utiles dans le traitement de l'eczéma. Une restriction de sodium peut diminuer la tendance à la rétention aqueuse.

Dans l'eczéma diffus et rebelle, on peut utiliser les corticostéroïdes par voies générale et locale. Le traitement des infections cutanées, ou de toute autre infection, par l'administration orale ou parentérale d'un antibiotique approprié, constitue un point essentiel de la thérapeutique. On peut donner de légers calmants en cas d'insomnie.

Il est important d'établir un graphique signalant l'état de la peau (changements dans l'apparence, la localisation des éruptions et l'aspect général des régions infectées), la réaction aux aliments (à la fois le lait et ce qu'on ajoute au régime), les traitements donnés, les manifestations allergiques additionnelles comme l'asthme et la rhinite, le degré de gêne causé par le prurit et les modifications du comportement.

Les soins *psychologiques* sont aussi importants que les soins physiques. Ces enfants doivent recevoir au moins autant d'attention et d'affection que les enfants normaux. Même si leur aspect ne porte pas l'infirmière à les prendre, à les dorloter et à jouer avec eux, il faut les entourer d'affection pour éviter tout sentiment de frustration. L'infirmière ou la mère peut revêtir une blouse ou un tablier pour protéger ses vêtements du contact de la pommade.

Il faut donner à l'enfant des jouets adaptés à son âge, lavables, sans danger, mous si possible et à surface lisse. Il faut éviter les jouets rembourrés de laine ou de plume qui risquent d'être allergènes.

L'infirmière doit comprendre les besoins des parents. Certaines mères ont l'impression qu'elles ont mal accompli leur rôle, d'autres protègent à l'excès leur enfant et d'autres encore craignent qu'il souffre d'une infection chronique qui entraînera des cicatrices au visage et un retard de développement. L'infirmière encouragera la mère à exprimer ce qu'elle ressent sur l'état de l'enfant et lui enseignera les soins que son état nécessite. Le fait d'aider la mère à surmonter ses craintes, pendant le séjour de l'enfant à l'hôpital, assurera à celui-ci de meilleurs soins à la maison.

L'infirmière doit enseigner aux parents les méthodes de la thérapeutique locale et le régime à donner. Elle doit montrer à la mère comment appliquer les entraves et comment procurer de l'exercice et de la distraction à l'enfant. Elle doit l'aider à trouver de nombreux moyens pour compenser l'absence de cajoleries et de baisers dont les enfants raffolent et pour lui procurer un environnement heureux afin qu'il puisse mener une vie aussi normale que possible, malgré l'entrave de ses mains et les applications locales de pommade. Il faut laisser l'enfant circuler autour de son berceau, de son parc ou de sa chambre; il doit sentir qu'il fait partie de la famille, qu'il a une activité normale. Il faut souvent satisfaire ses désirs afin qu'il ne se sente pas frustré par la gêne provoquée par le prurit. Il faudrait donner à la mère l'occasion d'en prendre soin à l'hôpital avec l'aide des infirmières. Ceci diminuera son appréhension lorsqu'elle le soignera à la maison.

Pronostic. Le pronostic est bon même si l'évolution semble parfois décourageante. Les parents ont tendance à perdre courage, surtout s'ils ont fait tout leur possible pour soigner l'enfant. L'infirmière doit les aider à comprendre la situation d'une manière réaliste et sans inquiétude injustifiée vis-à-vis de la gêne évidente de l'enfant. L'eczéma du nourrisson finit par disparaître spontanément, dans la plupart des cas, vers la fin de la deuxième année de la vie. On parvient quelquefois à enrayer la maladie plus tôt, si on réussit à éliminer les allergènes qui la provoquent. Après l'âge de deux ans, d'autres manifestations allergiques peuvent se manifester, comme l'asthme et la rhinite allergique (rhume des foins).

Si une infection se présente au cours de l'hospitalisation de l'enfant, le pronostic peut être moins bon, mais tout dépend de la gravité de son état. Pour prévenir ce danger, le séjour à l'hôpital devrait être aussi bref que possible.

TROUBLES DU SYSTÈME NERVEUX

Tétanie

La tétanie est un état d'hyperexcitabilité neuro-musculaire. Cet état peut survenir au cours d'un certain nombre d'affections différentes. Les formes cliniques de la tétanie peuvent être divisées en deux groupes: celles causées par un abaissement de la calcémie (tétanie hypocalcémique) et celles liées à un état d'alcalose (tétanie par alcalose).

Dans la tétanie hypocalcémique du nouveau-né, c'est-à-dire au cours de la première semaine de la vie, l'hypocalcémie est due à un hypofonctionnement des glandes parathyroïdes. L'insuffisance en vitamine D et la maladie cœliaque sont les causes les plus fréquentes de tétanie hypocalcémique.

La *tétanie par alcalose* survient quand l'équilibre acido-basique se déplace vers l'alcalose. Elle n'est pas liée à des modifications de la calcémie et de la phosphorémie. Elle survient dans des états qui engendrent une hyperventilation, ou une perte de chlorures, par des vomissements répétés. On l'observe parfois dans les sténoses du pylore et les occlusions intestinales hautes.

Convulsions

Au cours de la crise convulsive, il se produit au niveau du cerveau des décharges électriques paroxystiques que l'on peut déceler à l'électro-encéphalogramme. Les convulsions peuvent être le signe d'une atteinte cérébrale.

Incidence, étiologie. Les convulsions constituent plus souvent un symptôme qu'une maladie en soi. Elles se manifestent fréquemment pendant l'enfance, surtout au cours des deux premières années de la vie.

Chez le nouveau-né, l'anoxie et les hémorragies intracrâniennes, ainsi que les malformations congénitales du cerveau, en demeurent les causes les plus fréquentes.

Durant la première enfance, les infections aiguës du système nerveux central ou d'autres parties de l'organisme, accompagnées d'hyperthermie, en sont surtout responsables. Il existe d'autres causes moins fréquentes, telles la tétanie, l'épilepsie idiopathique, l'hypoglycémie, les intoxications au plomb ou à certains médicaments, l'asphyxie, certaines maladies dégénératives du système nerveux central et les traumatismes postnatals. Les convulsions peuvent être une complication rare de l'immunisation contre la coqueluche.

Plus tard, au cours de l'enfance, les convulsions fébriles se font plus rares; les crises convulsives indiquent le plus souvent que l'enfant souffre d'épilepsie idiopathique, d'une tumeur cérébrale ou de glomérulonéphrite.

Soins infirmiers.   Bien que les enfants meurent rarement au cours de crises convulsives, il existe peu de symptômes qui effraient à ce point les parents. L'infirmière doit se montrer compréhensive envers leur crainte et les aider à adopter une attitude réaliste face à l'état de l'enfant. Il faut leur dire que même si 7% des nourrissons ont des convulsions, peu cependant subissent des dommages permanents. Dans les autres cas, la convulsion révèle un état pathologique profondément enraciné.

L'infirmière doit placer l'enfant qui a eu une convulsion, ou qui est susceptible d'en avoir, à un endroit où on peut le surveiller constamment. Elle doit fréquemment observer l'enfant, le soigner en cas de convulsion, et rendre compte du processus convulsif avec précision au médecin.

À l'approche d'une convulsion, le jeune enfant peut montrer des changements de comportement, tels l'irritabilité, l'agitation ou l'apathie. On doit signaler de tels changements dans le rapport. L'infirmière doit noter les différents types de mouvements, cloniques (mouvements saccadés et trépidants) ou toniques (l'enfant devient raide et les muscles sont en état de contraction constante), le moment où les convulsions commencent et cessent, les régions du corps impliquées, le degré de sudation, les mouvements des yeux et les modifications de la pupille, l'incontinence (qui sera influencée, non seulement par la gravité de la crise, mais aussi par une distension de la vessie au moment de la convulsion), le rythme respiratoire, la coloration, la position du corps, l'écume à la bouche ou les vomissements, le degré apparent de conscience durant la crise et le comportement de l'enfant après qu'il ait repris conscience.

PRÉCAUTIONS À PRENDRE EN CAS DE CRISE. Il faut protéger l'enfant contre les traumatismes. Il faut retirer du lit tous les jouets durs sur lesquels il peut se blesser. On garde un abaisse-langue recouvert de gaze à proximité du lit afin de pouvoir l'insérer entre les dents et ainsi empêcher l'enfant de se mordre la langue au début de la crise. Il faut éviter de blesser la bouche en plaçant le bâtonnet. Il faudrait capitonner les barreaux du berceau sans nuire à la vision de l'enfant, ni à celle de l'infirmière qui doit facilement voir l'enfant. Si l'enfant a des convulsions répétées, on garde près du lit un appareil aspirateur pour éliminer les sécrétions accumulées dans le nasopharynx, et un appareil à oxygène au cas où il aurait des difficultés respiratoires. On garde habituellement sous la main une seringue contenant un médicament anticonvulsif qui peut être administré dès le début de la crise.

Si l'enfant a de la fièvre, il importe d'utiliser des moyens appropriés pour abaisser sa température, tels l'usage d'un matelas réfrigérant ou un bain tiède dont on laisse l'eau se refroidir progressivement. Si le petit enfant est conscient et refuse de s'aliter, l'infirmière, après avoir revêtu un tablier en plastique, peut le prendre sur ses genoux pour lui donner le bain. S'il est assez âgé, il peut participer au traitement.

Convulsions fébriles

Incidence et diagnostic.   Environ 7 pour cent de l'ensemble des enfants ont des convulsions fébriles entre l'âge de six mois et deux ou trois ans. Après la septième année, de telles crises deviennent extrêmement rares. Les garçons en souffrent plus souvent que les filles, et il semble exister une certaine prédisposition familiale.

La plupart des convulsions qui surviennent avant l'âge scolaire constituent le symptôme initial d'une maladie fébrile. Dans ces cas, une convulsion devient équivalente au « frisson » de l'adulte dans les mêmes conditions. Il faut examiner tout enfant qui a une convulsion fébrile, pour éliminer la possibilité d'autres causes éventuelles.

Traitement, pronostic et soins infirmiers.   Le *traitement* consiste à contrôler la crise à l'aide de sédatifs, comme le phénobarbital sodique. La dose dépend de l'âge et de la taille du bébé et du contrôle de la maladie sous-jacente. Il convient d'instituer un traitement à l'aide de médicaments antipyrétiques ou de bains tièdes et de donner des antibiotiques si c'est nécessaire. Il faut parfois procéder à une aspiration nasopharyngienne, en présence de sécrétions abondantes, et à une inhalation d'oxygène si le malade devient cyanosé au moment de la crise. Il est important d'éviter les écarts brusques de température qui prédisposent aux convulsions. Les sacs de glace sont contre-indiqués. De plus, l'enfant doit boire beaucoup et recevoir ses médicaments à heures précises et régulières. On doit le vêtir légèrement tout en maintenant un environnement confortable.

Le *pronostic* dépend de l'étiologie de la manifestation. Une convulsion fébrile unique entraîne rarement une épilepsie chronique.

L'apparition de plusieurs convulsions fébriles est souvent suivie de convulsions « non fébriles » spontanées. Après une crise convulsive, l'enfant subit plusieurs encéphalogrammes de contrôle pour vérifier s'il y a dommage cérébral.

Les *soins infirmiers* immédiats restent les mêmes quelle que soit l'étiologie de la crise convulsive.

Il est très important que les parents sachent que l'enfant qui a eu une convulsion fébrile est plus prédisposé qu'un autre nourrisson à subir d'autres crises convulsives. On doit donc leur enseigner à prendre la température de l'enfant et à utiliser les moyens antipyrétiques appropriés. Ils doivent aviser le médecin ou l'infirmière qui donnent les immunisations de façon à ce que l'inoculation contre la coqueluche soit reportée à plus tard.

Hématome sous-dural

Étiologie et incidence. Un hématome sous-dural consiste en l'accumulation de sang et de sérosités entre la dure-mère et l'arachnoïde. L'hématome sous-dural, ordinairement bilatéral, est fréquent chez les garçons; son incidence croît entre deux et quatre mois et diminue ensuite jusqu'au seizième mois où il devient assez rare.

L'anoxie et les hémorragies au moment de la naissance peuvent en constituer la cause, mais les traumatismes répétés chez l'enfant en sont plus souvent responsables. Le scorbut et les anomalies de la crase sanguine en augmentent le risque. La méningite peut aussi constituer un facteur étiologique.

Physio-pathologie. Un traumatisme provoque la déchirure ou la rupture de petites veines sous-durales, et l'hémorragie qui s'ensuit

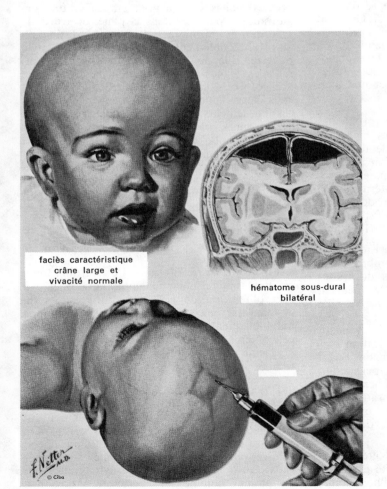

faciès caractéristique
crâne large et
vivacité normale

hématome sous-dural
bilatéral

Figure 13-15. Hématome sous-dural. (Copyright, Collection CIBA d'illustrations médicales, par Frank H. Netter, m.d.)

demeure emprisonnée dans l'espace crânien. Il se forme un sac membraneux qui entoure le liquide; la masse comprime le cerveau sous-jacent; celui-ci peut éventuellement s'atrophier.

Les *manifestations cliniques* varient. Dans l'hématome sous-dural aigu, en général à la suite d'un traumatisme, on note rapidement les signes d'accroissement de la pression intra-crânienne. Dans l'hématome sous-dural chronique, les manifestations cliniques sont moins caractéristiques. La mère note que l'enfant souffre d'anorexie, d'irritabilité, d'agitation, de vomissements ou de convulsions. L'enfant qui ne gagne pas de poids et qui ne se développe pas normalement, peut avoir un hématome sous-dural chronique.

Lors de l'interrogatoire de la mère, on apprend que d'autres signes existent comme des poussées de fièvre récidivantes, des réflexes exagérés, une fontanelle bombée et tendue, un crâne volumineux et une inégalité pupillaire. Il est important de connaître le degré d'intensité ou de fréquence de ces signes. On peut constater un élargissement des sutures crâniennes. L'enfant peut souffrir d'une anémie due à une déperdition sanguine. Le liquide céphalo-rachidien, souvent hypertendu, renferme des hématies, un excès de leucocytes, et une augmentation du taux des protéines.

Le *diagnostic* pose souvent des problèmes à cause du caractère insidieux des signes et des symptômes. On l'établit à l'aide de ponctions sous-durales bilatérales qu'on effectue assez facilement chez le nourrisson, en introduisant l'aiguille dans le coin latéral de la fontanelle ou plus loin sur la ligne de suture. Chez les enfants plus âgés, il faut pratiquer des trous de trépan pour introduire l'aiguille.

Traitement. Le traitement consiste à évacuer l'hématome et à retirer la membrane qui l'entoure. Il existe trois méthodes de traitement de l'hématome sous-dural: le médecin peut à plusieurs reprises aspirer à l'aiguille le contenu de la lésion jusqu'à ce qu'elle s'assèche ou que tous les symptômes aient disparu; il peut procéder à une dérivation chirurgicale comme dans l'hydrocéphalie ou il peut pratiquer une craniotomie permettant d'exciser la membrane. En cas d'hématomes bilatéraux, les craniotomies sont pratiquées à quelques jours d'intervalles. Cette opération doit quelquefois être suivie d'une des deux techniques précédentes.

Pronostic. Il varie suivant le degré d'atrophie cérébrale. Le taux de mortalité est fonction de la cause sous-jacente de l'hématome.

Soins infirmiers. Une des responsabilités principales de l'infirmière est le dépistage précoce permettant un traitement rapide du jeune enfant souffrant d'un hématome sous-dural, pour que le cerveau puisse se développer normalement. Si l'application du traitement est retardée, le cerveau subira des dommages et il en résultera un retard mental.

Il faut placer l'enfant sur un matelas de caoutchouc mousse ou une peau de mouton et le tourner fréquemment pour prévenir les zones de pression sur la peau. Le médecin, ou l'infirmière qui l'assiste lors de l'évacuation du liquide sous-dural, doit raser la partie antérieure du cuir chevelu de l'enfant et la nettoyer soigneusement. Il faut le tenir solidement pour éviter tout mouvement inattendu qui pourrait le blesser.

Après le drainage par ponction ou craniotomie, l'infirmière doit surveiller le pansement. Si du liquide suinte, il faut ajouter des compresses sèches stériles pour empêcher tout organisme de pénétrer dans la plaie, et avertir le médecin. L'infirmière doit faire la distinction entre un écoulement séreux et une hémorragie ouverte. Elle doit aussi reconnaître chez l'enfant les signes d'une pression intracrânienne accrue. On doit tenir continuellement l'enfant sous surveillance pour l'empêcher de retirer ses pansements; si ce n'est pas possible, on emprisonne ses mains dans des manchons. Avant d'appliquer ces dispositifs, tout effort doit être tenté pour l'apaiser, étant donné qu'ils pourraient l'agiter davantage et augmenter la pression intracrânienne. Nous discuterons des soins neuro-chirurgicaux en étudiant les tumeurs cérébrales.

Neuroblastome

Étiologie et incidence. Le neuroblastome est une tumeur maligne embryonnaire, due à la prolifération de cellules indifférenciées du système nerveux sympathique. Il se développe habituellement dans la glande surrénale. C'est probablement, après la tumeur cérébrale, l'une des tumeurs malignes les plus communes chez le nourrisson et l'enfant.

Physio-pathologie, symptômes, traitement et diagnostic. Les neuroblastomes sont des tumeurs dures, nodulaires et non encapsulées qui envahissent les tissus voisins. On diagnostique souvent cette tumeur d'une façon tardive, parce que les symptômes en sont généraux. On peut attribuer à plusieurs causes des symptômes comme une perte de poids, une douleur abdominale et des problèmes d'alimentation. Parmi les autres symptômes figure une exophtalmie ou un gonflement de l'abdomen. On établit le diagnostic d'après les antécédents, l'examen physique et les radiographies du squelette.

Comme la tumeur s'infiltre dans d'autres tissus, les métastases se fixent fréquemment dans le foie, la peau et les os, ce qui rend impossible l'ablation complète de la lésion. Après la chirurgie, l'irradiation ou la chimiothérapie, ces tumeurs régressent parfois spontanément. En chimiothérapie, signalons entre autres le cyclophosphamide (Cytoxan) et la vincristine.

En général, le pronostic est plus défavorable pour les enfants ayant un neuroblastome que pour ceux souffrant d'une tumeur de Wilms; mais on a vu des guérisons ou des maturations spontanées dues à des causes inconnues.

Soins infirmiers. L'infirmière en santé communautaire contribue dans une grande mesure à dépister et signaler ces cas. Le rôle de l'infirmière, à l'hôpital, consiste à aider l'enfant physiquement et psychologiquement. Elle collabore aux tests de diagnostic et donne les soins pré et postopératoires. Comme le pronostic reste défavorable pour la plupart de ces enfants, l'infirmière peut avoir l'occasion de revoir le rôle qu'elle peut jouer et l'aide qu'elle peut apporter aux parents dont les jeunes enfants sont acculés à la mort.

MALFORMATIONS DU SQUELETTE

Craniosynostose

Étiologie et physio-pathologie. La craniosynostose consiste en la fermeture prématurée d'une ou de plusieurs sutures crâniennes. La croissance des os entourant la suture déficiente s'en trouve réduite; il se produit une croissance compensatrice dans les autres régions. Il en résulte diverses déformations crâniennes selon la localisation de l'anomalie. Comme on trouve en général d'autres anomalies osseuses que la craniosynostose, on croit que le squelette a été atteint très tôt au cours de la vie embryonnaire.

Manifestations cliniques. Quand la suture sagittale est atteinte, le crâne est élevé et aplati latéralement, c'est la *scaphocéphalie.* Elle peut être accompagnée de symptômes d'hypertension intracrânienne. *L'oxycéphalie* suit la fermeture précoce de la suture coro-

nale. Certaines complications peuvent se produire quand le cerveau se trouve comprimé. L'enfant peut souffrir de céphalées, de perte de vision et de convulsions. On peut rencontrer de l'exophtalmie, du strabisme, du nystagmus et un œdème papillaire. Un retard mental peut exister, mais beaucoup d'individus porteurs de craniosynostose vivent tout à fait normalement et ne présentent jamais de symptômes. La syndactylie demeure l'anomalie la plus fréquemment associée à la craniosynostose.

Traitement. Le traitement chirurgical de la pathologie permet d'éviter les troubles cérébraux s'il est pratiqué précocement et les résultats esthétiques en seront meilleurs. L'intervention consiste à pratiquer une incision le long de la suture et à insérer un tube de polyéthylène qui va empêcher la réunion des parties osseuses.

Soins infirmiers. L'infirmière joue un rôle important dans le dépistage précoce de ces cas. Souvent l'infirmière en santé communautaire est la première à observer cet état chez un enfant apparemment normal. Elle ne peut pas établir le diagnostic, mais doit rapporter le cas à un médecin.

Les soins infirmiers, après l'opération, sont les mêmes qu'après une craniotomie lors d'une tumeur au cerveau.

Pronostic. Le pronostic est excellent, si on institue le traitement avant que ne surviennent des lésions permanentes au cerveau. Une révision de la craniotomie peut s'avérer nécessaire, à cause de la croissance rapide des os déterminant une fermeture des sutures.

TROUBLES PSYCHIQUES

Causes de l'anxiété chez le nourrisson. Tout nourrisson est amené à éprouver des sentiments inévitables de frustration, parce que, fondamentalement, « il veut ce qu'il veut, quand il le veut ». Il peut vouloir le biberon quand on lui donne des aliments solides, être porté quand on lui apprend à marcher, etc.

Ces frustrations lui apportent douleur et anxiété. Progressivement, il s'aperçoit qu'il peut surmonter lui-même ces situations gênantes en adoptant de nouvelles méthodes de comportement, par exemple en apprenant à marcher et à manger des aliments solides. C'est pourquoi il accepte de maîtriser de nouvelles techniques. Initialement, il se sent frustré et gêné par suite de la limitation de ses capacités. De nouveaux apprentissages apportent éventuellement de nouveaux plaisirs et moins de frustration.

L'enfant veut apprendre de nouvelles habiletés uniquement s'il a vécu une période de satisfaction optimale avec son ancien mode de comportement. Il faudrait laisser l'enfant expérimenter les inévitables frustrations de la vie, mais lentement et à petites doses. Les frustrations brusques et trop importantes, comme par exemple le sevrage rapide, ont un effet défavorable sur la personnalité qui se forme.

Comportement du nourrisson anxieux. Le nourrisson peut réagir de trois façons: il peut être irrité contre la cause qui provoque sa gêne et la combattre; il peut s'en éloigner sans lutter; ou bien il peut rester passif et ne rien faire.

ANXIÉTÉ PROVOQUÉE PAR UNE FRUSTRATION ALIMENTAIRE. Les jeunes enfants qui se sentent frustrés dans le processus alimentaire réagiront de la seule façon qu'ils connaissent, en gigotant, en criant et en remuant constamment leur corps. Lorsque l'enfant nourri au sein ne peut prendre une quantité suffisante de lait à cause de mamelons invertis, il peut régurgiter tout ce qu'il a déjà pris, s'éloigner et refuser de téter ou s'endormir. De même, l'enfant sevré trop brusquement aura les mêmes problèmes de comportement.

Le bébé peut réagir de la même façon à des aliments qui sont nouveaux, trop chauds, contiennent des gros morceaux ou demandent trop d'efforts de mastication. Dans une telle situation, il peut vomir à plusieurs reprises, éloigner sa tête ou rester immobile et refuser de participer au processus de l'alimentation.

Chacune de ces réactions affecte directement l'alimentation. Si l'enfant rejette la responsabilité de sa gêne sur sa mère, il peut se détourner d'elle lorsqu'elle s'approche de lui, refuser de manger, crier lorsqu'elle le touche ou, lorsqu'il est un peu plus âgé, faire exactement le contraire de ce qu'elle lui demande.

ANXIÉTÉ PROVOQUÉE PAR UNE FRUSTRATION DE SUCCION. Si son désir de succion est frustré, le nourrisson sucera des objets non nutritifs, comme son pouce, sa tétine, sa couverture ou ses jouets. Il continuera la succion au-delà de deux ou trois ans, moment où en principe il devrait avoir abandonné cette habitude.

Si les parents permettent la succion d'objets non-nutritifs, l'enfant obtiendra la satisfaction dont il a besoin. Si, au contraire, les parents empêchent la succion, l'enfant peut refuser toute nourriture ou bien arrêter complètement son habitude de succion et trouver un plaisir morbide dans la frustration.

ANXIÉTÉ PROVOQUÉE PAR UN MANQUE D'AMOUR DE LA PART DES PARENTS ET PAR UNE FRUSTRATION ACCABLANTE QUE LE NOURRISSON NE PEUT SURMONTER. On peut observer chez la plupart des enfants, à un moment donné au cours de la première année, des formes d'anxiété causée par une frustration alimentaire ou de succion. Certains enfants doivent faire face à une anxiété écrasante, à la suite du manque d'intérêt et d'amour de la part de leurs parents. Ces enfants se laissent quelquefois mourir d'inanition. L'histoire suivante peut illustrer une telle situation:

Alain, un enfant de deux ans, admis à l'unité pédiatrique, pèse 4 kg à son arrivée; il souffre de lésions cutanées infectées, de malnutrition et de déshydratation.

On ne peut retrouver son dossier de naissance et on connaît seulement les détails suivants: né d'une mère célibataire de 15 ans, celle-ci disparaît tôt après son accouchement, laissant le bébé à sa sœur qui se marie et donne le bébé à une voisine. Pendant les deux années qui suivent, il passe d'une voisine à l'autre jusqu'à ce qu'une femme le recueille et s'y attache. Les efforts de celle-ci restent vains car Alain a déjà trop souffert et le retard physique et émotif ne peut plus être comblé. Il refuse le biberon et l'on n'observe aucune réaction émotive. À son arrivée à l'hôpital il reçoit des gavages, une thérapie intraveineuse intensive, des antibiotiques et beaucoup de soins, mais meurt malgré tout quelques jours plus tard.

Symptômes. Parmi les symptômes de l'anxiété, signalons les cris excessifs, les insomnies, l'agitation ou des mouvements rythmés de balancement, et parfois de vomissements. L'enfant qui souffre d'une anxiété trop grande peut faire de la dépression accompagnée de cris et de pleurs à l'approche d'étrangers et d'un arrêt de développement physique et psychique.

Les troubles de la nutrition, allant du refus de manger aux vomissements répétés, sont courants. Finalement, un marasme peut se développer et l'enfant peut mourir d'inanition.

Un comportement antagoniste consiste à ne pas aimer la compagnie des parents, à refuser la joie des relations avec eux ou à faire exactement le contraire de ce qu'on lui demande.

Traitement et soins infirmiers. La prévention des troubles psychiques demeure de loin préférable au traitement de l'enfant perturbé. Beaucoup de mères désirent procurer affection et chaleur à leurs enfants et pourtant les rejettent à des degrés divers, du moins en apparence, parce que leur mari, parent ou voisin désapprouvent une attitude vraiment maternelle à l'égard de l'enfant; d'autres mères veulent donner des soins affectueux à leur bébé, mais en sont séparées par suite de leur propre maladie ou de celle d'autres membres de la famille.

On pourrait beaucoup aider ces mères en les éduquant sur les besoins affectifs des nourrissons. Une pareille éducation, donnée durant la période prénatale, les rendrait plus sûres de leur propre jugement et moins sensibles à la désapprobation d'autrui. La compréhension intellectuelle n'est pas un remède universel pour de tels problèmes, mais l'appui d'une autorité extérieure est rassurant. Le médecin ou l'infirmière peut aider de telles femmes à se fier à leurs propres sentiments maternels pour guider leur comportement. Les mères qui souffrent elles-mêmes d'une carence émotive grave ne se rendent pas toujours compte des besoins d'amour de l'enfant et sont donc incapables de lui donner cet amour.

Lorsqu'on traite un enfant pour un trouble psychologique, il faut d'abord en trouver la cause. Il faut comprendre clairement quel besoin a été frustré. Il est important, à la fois pour la mère et le médecin, d'agir avec l'enfant comme s'il était un peu plus jeune qu'au moment de l'expérience traumatisante. Par exemple, si l'enfant réagit violemment aux aliments solides nouveaux, sa mère doit cesser de lui en présenter. Il faut, ensuite, réintroduire progressivement les aliments sans obligation ni pression indue.

Parfois les difficultés d'alimentation, vomissements ou refus de manger, peuvent devenir tellement graves qu'il s'avère nécessaire de séparer l'enfant de sa mère pour un certain temps. Il peut être soigné à la maison par une personne affectueuse ou être hospitalisé. Souvent, ces enfants commencent à bien manger après une courte période d'adaptation à leur nouvelle situation. Au cours de la séparation, il faudrait conseiller les parents pour qu'ils puissent créer un environnement plus chaleureux pour l'enfant lors de son retour à la maison.

Si l'enfant est hospitalisé, c'est à l'infirmière qu'il incombe de donner les soins affectueux et tendres dont l'enfant a besoin. Elle doit le tenir bien près d'elle et manifester de façon tactile toute la chaleur de son affection. Elle doit le serrer doucement dans ses bras et être gentille et patiente lorsqu'elle lui donne à manger. Souvent, l'infirmière peut montrer à la mère comment serrer doucement l'enfant dans ses bras pour le nourrir et lui donner les soins affectueux dont il a besoin.

SYNDROME DE L'ENFANT BATTU OU MALTRAITÉ

Incidence, étiologie, découvertes cliniques, diagnostic et pronostic. Les mauvais traitements infligés aux enfants constituent un des plus graves problèmes auxquels sont confrontés les membres de l'équipe pédiatrique. On ne connaît pas réellement le nombre d'enfants maltraités, mais il semble qu'il augmente surtout dans les grandes zones métropolitaines. Il semble n'y avoir aucune corrélation entre l'incidence des mauvais traitements et le niveau d'instruction, le statut social ou le revenu des parents. Le problème paraît surtout relié aux tensions familiales ou économiques et à l'attitude des parents qui rejettent sur l'enfant leurs propres frustrations et s'en servent comme bouc émissaire.

L'enfant maltraité (habituellement un nourrisson ou un jeune enfant au-dessous de trois ans) est celui qui a subi des dommages corporels et, par conséquent, des perturbations psychiques de la part d'un adulte, à un degré tel que le cas attire l'attention d'un médecin ou d'un autre membre de l'équipe de santé. Souvent, cet enfant a déjà été soigné pour prématurité ou retard staturo-pondéral.

L'adulte peut blesser l'enfant en lui infligeant des brûlures, en le lançant n'importe où, en le frappant brutalement ou en lui tordant les membres, causant ainsi de grandes contusions, des égratignures, des brûlures, des hématomes et des fractures des os longs, des côtes ou du crâne. Le manque de soins, qu'on constate fréquemment chez ces enfants, provient d'un défaut chronique de certains adultes incapables de protéger l'enfant contre un danger physique évident ou de le soigner adéquatement. On constate souvent chez les enfants battus une mauvaise hygiène de la peau et un certain degré de malnutrition.

On établit le *diagnostic* sur l'aspect des radiographies où l'on constate des lésions osseuses parvenues à différents stades de cicatrisation, ce qui indique une suite de traumatismes. De pareilles lésions sont survenues à différentes époques antérieures à l'examen et à l'hospitalisation.

La base principale d'identification d'un tel problème repose sur le jugement d'une personne compétente, étant donné qu'habituellement, l'enfant est trop jeune pour se plaindre et que les parents ne voudront pas admettre leurs pratiques abusives. Le facteur étiologique s'appuie sur des parents ou des substituts qui ont un défaut caractériel et dont les impulsions agressives ont tendance à s'exprimer librement quand ils sont sous tension. Les parents eux-mêmes peuvent avoir été soumis à des abus quand ils étaient enfants et souffrir de carences affectives sérieuses. Dans certains cas, le père ou la mère peut se libérer de sa colère sur un enfant en particulier, parce qu'il est le symbole de quelqu'un ou de quelque chose qui un jour a causé son malheur. Un enfant illégitime est souvent visé. De tels parents ne donnent pas spontanément des renseignements sur l'enfant, ils se contredisent eux-mêmes quand ils font la description de la blessure, s'irritent lorsqu'on les questionne sur l'enfant, se fâchent à cause de sa blessure et ne manifestent pas de sentiment de culpabilité à l'égard de leur manque de soins à son endroit. Souvent, ils disparaissent peu de temps après l'admission de l'enfant à l'hôpital, ne lui rendent pas visite et ne sont nullement intéressés aux soins qu'on lui donne. Ces parents s'intéressent surtout à eux-mêmes, ils sont souvent à la charge de l'état, ils critiquent l'enfant et il n'y a chez eux aucune attention à l'égard des sentiments que celui-ci pourrait éprouver. Ils renversent les rôles et agissent envers les besoins alimentaires et affectifs de leur enfant comme ils le feraient envers leurs propres parents.

Les *manifestations typiques* du comportement d'un enfant négligé et maltraité sont des cris teintés d'une note désespérée, ou au contraire des pleurs peu nombreux même quand il est mal à l'aise, aucune attente de réconfort de la part des parents et de l'appréhension quand on le touche. Il semble rechercher la sécurité, en essayant d'évaluer la situation pour découvrir ce qui arrivera par la suite, plutôt qu'en cherchant un contact avec ses parents. Les enfants aimés et soignés cherchent leur sécurité auprès de leurs parents; les enfants maltraités supportent la vie seuls, sans espoir réel de sécurité dans un monde qui les blesse.

Le *pronostic* est variable. L'incidence de la mort est grande chez ces nourrissons, mais plus grands encore sont les dommages causés à la santé physique et mentale de ceux qui survivent.

Traitement, soins infirmiers et prévention. Dans ce syndrome, la prévention primaire est la plus importante. Il est essentiel d'assurer un soutien émotif et financier aux mères qui sont adolescentes, célibataires ou abandonnées. Durant la période prénatale, l'infirmière doit chercher à identifier les parents vulnérables et tenter de les aider à résoudre les problèmes avec lesquels ils sont confrontés. Il faut expliquer la dynamique des relations parents-enfant et faire comprendre les besoins et les réactions des nourrissons. Quand l'infirmière se rend à la maison, elle doit permettre aux parents d'enfants prématurés ou handicapés d'exprimer leur fatigue et quelquefois leur sentiment d'hostilité pour éviter que les tensions émotives ne précipitent les sévices corporels.

Chez tout enfant présentant de multiples lésions osseuses, il faut envisager une radiographie du crâne et un drainage sous-dural. Il faut réduire et immobiliser les fractures des os longs. Les soins infirmiers dépendent donc du traumatisme spécifique que présente l'enfant. Celui-ci exige de bons soins physiques et beaucoup d'amour.

La prévention des récidives implique la coopération des médecins, du département de police, des agences de service social, des infirmières et de la société en général. L'infirmière doit absolument connaître l'existence de ce syndrome, parce que c'est elle, soit à l'hôpital, soit dans une agence de santé, qui peut être la première à voir un enfant qui présente un traumatisme évident. L'infirmière peut aussi reconnaître certains indices que nous avons mentionnés plus haut. D'une façon plus spécifique, quand l'infirmière voit un enfant qui porte les marques de graves contusions ou d'autres blessures corporelles et qu'elle croit qu'il a été maltraité, voici ce qu'elle devrait faire: elle doit noter ses observations sur l'état physique de l'enfant comme elle le ferait pour tout autre patient, mais elle ne doit pas inscrire au dossier qu'elle pense que l'enfant a pu être maltraité; toutefois, si l'adulte qui accompagne l'enfant signale que l'enfant a été battu, l'infirmière peut noter ce qu'elle a appris et mettre entre guillemets les paroles citées ainsi que le nom de leur auteur. Elle doit rapporter verbalement ses observations au médecin et lui montrer le dossier de l'enfant. En général, c'est le médecin ou l'équipe médicale qui a la responsabilité de faire le rapport de la violence exercée contre certains enfants. L'infirmière en chef cependant doit être au courant de la politique de l'agence et des lois du pays où elle se trouve.

Le rôle de l'infirmière consiste à dépister les cas et à rapporter au médecin toute indication de sévices qu'elle pourrait avoir vue, à entrer en contact avec ces familles pour se rendre compte de leurs problèmes et à soigner l'enfant après son admission à l'hôpital. En travaillant avec les parents d'enfants négligés et maltraités, une approche non-critique et non-répressive s'avère nécessaire pour les empêcher à l'avenir d'extérioriser leurs frustrations sur leurs enfants. L'infirmière aura peut-être quelque difficulté à réaliser ce genre d'approche à cause d'un sentiment de colère ou de dégoût qu'elle pourrait ressentir à l'égard des parents.

Elle doit travailler avec les autres membres de l'équipe de santé. Après avoir signalé immédiatement le cas, les services sociaux entreprennent une investigation rapide et approfondie de chaque famille, étant donné que les parents d'enfants maltraités changent souvent de médecin et d'hôpital pour éviter qu'on relie le traumatisme actuel avec les blessures antérieures. Dans la majorité des hôpitaux on a maintenant mis sur pied des comités spéciaux auxquels on soumet pour enquête et analyse tous les cas d'enfants que l'on soupçonne d'avoir été maltraités. Ces comités sont habituellement composés d'un pédiatre, d'un psychiatre, d'une infirmière et d'une travailleuse sociale. En cas de doute, chaque membre du comité recueille des données pertinentes. Le pédiatre prescrit les examens nécessaires et évalue l'état physique de l'enfant, l'infirmière observe les réactions de l'enfant et celles de ses parents lorsqu'ils le visitent, le psychiatre procède à l'évaluation psychiatrique des parents alors que la travailleuse sociale évalue le milieu et les caractéristiques socio-économiques de la famille. Le comité prend alors les décisions qui s'imposent quant à l'avenir de l'enfant.

Il existe de plus en plus de lois qui protègent les enfants et obligent tout adulte qui a des soupçons à dénoncer les parents ou autres personnes qui maltraitent les enfants. La société tente d'établir un équilibre entre les droits des parents et ceux de leurs enfants.

Dans certains grands centres urbains, on a constitué des groupes formés de parents qui ont déjà maltraité leurs enfants. Ces groupes fonctionnent sur le modèle des « alcooliques anonymes ». Chacun n'est connu que par un prénom et les membres s'entr'aident de façon à résister à l'impulsion de maltraiter l'enfant. Des psychologues et des travailleurs sociaux animent ces groupes; ils tentent de réadapter les parents et de les amener à adopter un comportement parental approprié.

À long terme, la prévention consiste à éviter que ne se transmette le type de privation sociale qui a déterminé la négligence et les mauvais traitements des enfants. Il faut veiller à ce que les enfants qui survivent à de pareils traitements ne créent pas une future génération de parents qui eux non plus ne seront pas capables d'élever leurs enfants avec amour et compréhension.

RÉFÉRENCES

Livres et documents officiels

Basset, A. et Maleville, J.: *Les eczémas et leur traitement dans l'exercice journalier de la médecine praticienne.* Paris, Maloine, 1970.

Belmonte, M.: *Fibrose kystique : un manuel pour parents.* Québec, Association de fibrose kystique du Québec, 1965.

Dekaban, A.: *Neurology of Early Childhood.* Baltimore, Williams & Wilkins Company, 1970.

Denyes, M. J.: Child with Hirschsprung's Disease Uses a Nurse to Gain Ego Strength; in *ANA Clin. Sess.,* 1968, New York, Appleton-Century-Crofts, 1968, pp. 155-161.

Fondation canadienne de la fibrose kystique: *La fibrose kystique. Votre enfant et la fibrose kystique. A Cystic Fibrosis Child Is in Your Class. Il faut vaincre la fibrose kystique. Guide de diagnostic et de traitement pour la maladie fibrokystique du pancréas ou mucoviscidose.*

Fontana, V. J.: *The Maltreated Child: The Maltreatment Syndrome in Children.* 2e éd. Springfield, Ill., Charles C Thomas, 1971.

Gil, D. G.: *Violence Against Children; Physical Abuse in the United States.* Cambridge, Mass., Harvard University Press, 1970.

Kempe, C. H. et Helfer, R. E. (édit.): *Helping the Battered Child and His Family.* Philadelphie, J. B. Lippincott Company, 1972.

Kempe, H.: *Enfant victime de sévices.* Folia Traumatologia, Suisse, Ciba-Geigy 1975.

MacKeith, R. et autres: *Infant Feeding and Feeding Difficulties.* 4e éd. Baltimore, Williams & Wilkins Company, 1971.

Matson, D. D.: *Neurosurgery of Infancy and Childhood.* 2e éd Springfield, Ill., Charles C Thomas, 1969.

Mauer, A. M.: *Pediatric Hematology.* New York, McGraw-Hill Book Company, Inc., 1969.

Pillsbury, D. M.: *A Manual of Dermatology.* Philadelphie, W. B. Saunders Company, 1971.

Song, J.: *Pathology of Sickle Cell Disease.* Springfield, Ill., Charles C. Thomas, 1971.

Articles

Allaneau, C.: La maladie cœliaque. *Soins,* 18:37, 1, 1973.

Allaneau, C.: La drépanocytose. *Soins,* 17:7, 1, 1972.

Asfar, M. et Duches, D.: À propos d'un cas de mérycisme. *La médecine infantile,* 73:5, janvier 1966.

Barbero, G. et Shaheen, E.: Environmental Failure to Thrive. A Clinical View. *J. Pediat.,* 71:639, 1967.

Belmonte, M. M.: Aspects psychiques et émotifs dans la fibrose kystique du pancréas. *Union méd. du Can.,* 98:1943, novembre 1969.

Belmonte, M. M.: La maladie fibro-kystique du pancréas: Pronostic et traitement. *Union méd. du Can.,* 96:1541, décembre 1967.

Bensabel, H.: Les occlusions néo-natales de la maladie de Hirschsprung. *La médecine infantile,* 76:751, 9, 1969.

Chamberlain, N.: The Nurse and the Abusive Parent. *Nursing '74,* 4:72, 10, 1974.

Coffey, J.: The Whiplash Shaken Infant Syndrome. *Pediatrics,* 54:396, 4, 1974.

Colley, R. et Phillips, K.: Helping with Hyperalimentation. *Nursing '73,* 3:6, 7, 1973.

Crozier, D.: Cystic Fibrosis: A Not-so-Fatal Disease. *Ped. Clin. N. Amer.,* 21:935, 4, 1974.

Deitel, M.: La suralimentation par voie intraveineuse. *Inf. Can.,* 15:9, 8, 1973.

Deschamps, J. P.: Le syndrome digestif de la fibrose kystique du pancréas. *La médecine infantile,* 76:805, 10, 1969.

Donnère. R.: Hypothyroïdie de l'enfant. *Soins,* 18:5, 5, 1973.

Filler, R. M. et autres: Long-Term Total Parenteral Nutrition in Infants. *New Eng. J. Med.,* 281:589, 11 septembre 1969.

Guibert, J. P.: Hématome sous-dural du nourrisson. *Soins,* 18:37, 5, 1973.

Hennequet, A.: La mucoviscidose ou maladie fibro-kystique du pancréas. *La revue de l'inf.,* 21:115, 2, 1971.

Hopkins, J.: The Nurse and the Abused Child. *Nursing Clin. N. Amer.,* 5:589, décembre 1970.

Hurwitz, I. et autres: Intellectual Development after Severe Malnutrition in Infancy. *Pediatrics,* 54:306, 3, 1974.

Jean, R. et autres: Aspects actuels de la maladie cœliaque de l'enfant. *La revue de pédiatrie,* 7:563, 8, 1971.

Jeliu, G.: L'enfant maltraité. *Le méd. du Québec,* 10:12, 11, 1975.

Johnson, F. P. et Hatcher, W.: The Patient With Sickle Cell Disease. *Nurs. Forum,* 13:259, 3, 1974.

Johnson, M. E. et Fassett, B. A.: Bronchopulmonary Hygiene in Cystic Fibrosis. *Am. J. Nursing,* 69:320, février 1969.

Justice, P. et Smith, G.: Phenylketonuria, *Am. J. Nursing,* 75:1303, 8, 1975.

Klein, A. H., Meltzer, S. et Kenny, F. M.: Improved Prognosis in Congenital Hypothyroidism Treated Before Age Three Months. *J. Pediat.,* 81:912, novembre 1972.

Koel, B. S.: Failure to Thrive and Fatal Injury as a Continuum. *Am. J. Dis. Child.,* 118:565, octobre 1969.

Krueger, R. H.: Some Long-Term Effects of Severe Malnutrition in Early Life. *Lancet,* 2:514, 6 septembre 1969.

Labrune, B.: Examen des fontanelles et des sutures crâniennes chez l'enfant. *Revue du praticien,* XX:4835, 30, novembre, 1970.

Lauer, B. et autres: Battered Child Syndrome. *Pediatrics,* 54:67, 1, 1974.

Leonard, M. F., Rhymes, J. P. et Solnit, A. J.: Failure to Thrive in Infants. A Family Problem. *Am. J. Dis. Child.,* 111:600, 1966.

Lhuillier, N.: Traitement de l'eczéma. *Soins,* 19:19, 9, 1974.

Marcotte, A. A.: La fibrose kystique. *Inf. Can.,* 17:18, 4, 1975.

Meloche, B.: Craniosténose. *Union méd. du Can.,* 96:1064, septembre 1967.

Miller, C. et autres: Factors Contributing to Child Abuse. *Nursing Research,* 24:293, 4, 1975.

Murdock, C. G.: The Abused Child and the School System. *Am. J. Pub. Health,* 60:105, janvier 1970.

Olson, R.: Index of Suspicion: Screening for Child Abusers. *Am. J. Nursing*, 76:108, 1, 1976.

Orsini, A. et autres: Les troubles du métabolisme du fer chez l'enfant. *La médecine infantile*, 75:635, 9, 1968.

Pasticier, A.: Le kwashiorkor. *La revue de l'inf.*, 24:19, 1, 1974.

Paupe, J. et autres: Rachitisme. *La médecine infantile*, 77:243, 4, 1970.

Pearson, H. A.: Progress in Early Diagnosis of Sickle Cell Disease. *Children*, 18:222, novembre-décembre 1971.

Perelman, R.: Mucoviscidose. *Médecine infantile*, 79:549, 7, 1972.

Perelman, R.: La maladie cœliaque. *Médecine infantile*, 79:573, 7, 1972.

Pierson, M.: L'avenir éloigné des enfants hypothyroïdiens. *Arch. franç. péd.*, 27:337, 4, 1970.

Pinney, M. S.: Postural Drainage for Infants: A Better Approach. *Nursing '72*, 2:45, octobre 1972.

Rain, J. D.: Anémies hypochromes. *Soins*, XV:149, 4, 1970.

Rayanud de Lage, C.: Rachitisme carentiel. *Soins*, 17:7, 4, 1972.

Rhymes, J. P.: Working with Mothers and Babies Who Fail to Thrive. *Am. J. Nursing*, 66:1972, 1966.

Sibinga, M. S. et Friedman, C. J.: Complexities of Parental Understanding of Phenylketonuria. *Pediatrics*, 48:216, août 1971.

Silver, H. K. et Finkelstein, M.: Deprivation Dwarfism. *J. Pediat.*, 70:317, 1967.

Stadnyk, S. et Bindschadler, N.: A Camp for Children with Cystic Fibrosis. *Am. J. Nursing*, 70:1691, août 1970.

Stainton, C.: Le trauma non accidentel chez les enfants. *Inf. Can.*, 17:20, 12, 1975.

Steinschneider, R.: Mucoviscidose. *Soins*, 18:19, 7, 1973.

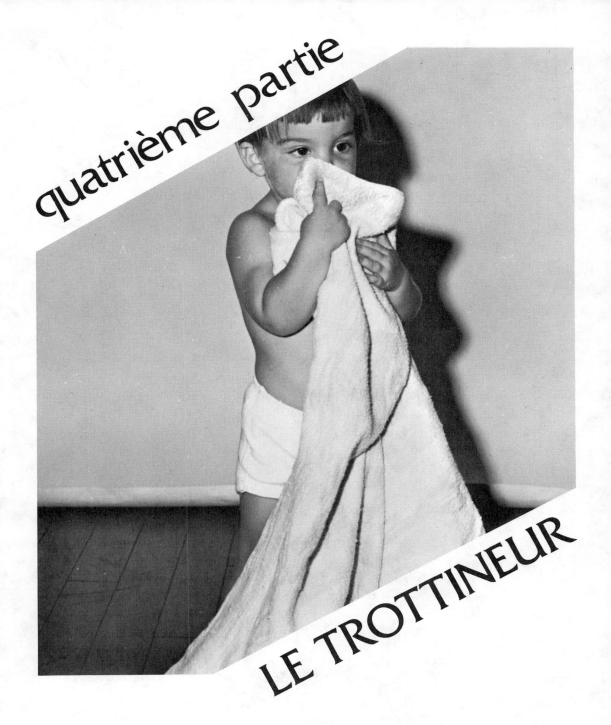

quatrième partie

LE TROTTINEUR

14
le trottineur normal: croissance, développement, soins

Au moment de son premier anniversaire, l'enfant a déjà appris, en grande partie, à faire confiance aux adultes qui prennent soin de lui ou à s'en méfier, selon les expériences qu'il a vécues. Son attitude pourra se modifier au cours de l'enfance et de l'adolescence, mais il demeure qu'elle influe sur ses perceptions et ses comportements durant ses deuxième et troisième années.

Au fur et à mesure que l'enfant progresse d'une dépendance passive vers un échange actif avec les personnes de son entourage, la société, et plus spécifiquement la famille, l'incitent à agir en conformité avec les normes sociales reconnues. L'exigence culturelle primordiale requise du trottineur est l'apprentissage du contrôle de ses sphincters.

Les parents du trottineur doivent apprendre à accepter les changements qui accompagnent la croissance et le développement de leur enfant. Celui-ci devient plus mobile et commence à affirmer son indépendance. Il peut arriver que les parents, la mère en particulier, aient retiré énormément de satisfaction à s'occuper d'un nourrisson totalement dépendant. Il leur est ensuite pénible d'accepter le nouveau désir de liberté de l'enfant qui souhaite explorer son environnement et affirmer son indépendance.

APERÇU DU DÉVELOPPEMENT ÉMOTIF DU TROTTINEUR

Sentiment d'autonomie

Alors que l'enfant cesse d'être un nourrisson pour devenir un trottineur, il se sert de ses capacités croissantes, afin d'apprendre à se suffire à lui-même et de développer son *sentiment d'autonomie*. Il fait connaître ses désirs à ceux qui l'entourent afin d'obtenir ce qu'il veut. Il montre clairement qu'il peut penser et qu'il entend se servir de sa volonté. S'il a appris à faire confiance aux autres, il accepte d'être guidé gentiment, de façon compréhensive dans ses nouveaux apprentissages. Toutefois, s'il est contrarié, il se fâche et déteste ceux-là mêmes qu'il a appris à aimer, soit sa mère, son père, ses frères et sœurs, son infirmière.

La réaction des êtres aimés à la colère de l'enfant joue un rôle important dans sa formation. Si ces personnes manifestent leur amour à l'enfant tout en lui refusant une demande déraisonnable, le trottineur oublie sa colère et préfère conserver une relation harmonieuse et gratifiante avec ceux qui lui prouvent amour

Figure 14-1. Le tout-petit a besoin de sécurité, mais aussi d'une certaine indépendance pour explorer son entourage. (H. Armstrong Roberts.)

et sécurité. Une acceptation positive des faits est un facteur d'apprentissage important pour le trottineur.

L'amour compréhensif se manifeste envers l'enfant de cet âge par l'octroi de la liberté dont il peut se servir en toute sécurité, et par l'aide exigée pour le maintenir en sécurité dans un milieu qu'il ne peut maîtriser et qui l'oblige à dépendre des autres pour satisfaire ses besoins somatiques. Cet amour se manifeste également en guidant l'enfant pour lui éviter des dangers inhérents aux situations sociales changeantes dont il se sent le point de mire.

Dans la mesure où il a appris à accepter, durant la première enfance, d'être guidé et de demander de l'aide, si c'est nécessaire, le trottineur a atteint un nouveau stade dans la maîtrise de soi, sans pour autant perdre l'estime de lui-même. S'il n'a pas appris à se débrouiller dans la mesure de ses capacités et à l'intérieur des limites imposées par ceux qui prennent soin de lui, et — ce qui est encore plus important — à accepter l'aide de l'adulte dans des situations qui le dépassent, l'enfant ressent de l'insécurité devant les problèmes physiques et sociaux de la vie courante. Il se replie sur lui-même, développe un sentiment de doute de lui-même et des autres, un sentiment somme toute compa-

rable à la honte chez l'adulte. Il évite alors les expériences nouvelles et a, par conséquent, moins d'occasions d'acquérir des habiletés nouvelles que le trottineur autonome.

LES BESOINS DU TROTTINEUR

Les besoins fondamentaux du trottineur sont identiques à ceux du nourrisson. Il lui faut de la sécurité et de l'amour, mais en plus une indépendance progressive.

Amour et sécurité

L'enfant aimé grandit dans un climat de sécurité ce qui l'encourage à se fixer des objectifs de plus en plus importants parce qu'il se sent prêt à expérimenter. Cette sécurité lui permet aussi de supporter les frustrations que subit tout enfant au cours de son développement.

Filles et garçons accordent leur première affection à leur mère parce que c'est elle qui leur prodigue avec tendresse les soins essentiels et immédiats. Outre les exigences corporelles, l'enfant ressent le besoin des plaisirs de la sociabilité qu'il va de plus en plus reporter sur son père en lui manifestant un attachement croissant. Dans une famille où le père donne à l'enfant, depuis sa naissance, les mêmes soins que la mère, celui-ci se sent généralement en sécurité avec l'un ou l'autre de ses parents. Mais beaucoup d'enfants n'arrivent guère à connaître leur père avant la deuxième année, quand il joue, se promène avec l'enfant, l'amène avec lui. Cependant ces trottineurs continueront à rechercher leur mère s'ils se sentent malades ou s'ils requièrent des soins physiques.

Durant ses deuxième ou troisième années, parfois un peu plus tard, l'enfant peut s'attacher à un objet qui devient très important pour lui et semble être une source de sécurité. *Cet objet transitionnel ou de sécurité* serait une étape dans le processus de séparation de l'enfant d'avec sa mère. L'objet peut être une couverture, une couche ou un jouet. L'enfant l'aime, le cajole, le couche dans son lit. Très souvent, l'objet transitionnel se salit, se brise, mais l'enfant lui conserve son attachement et s'inquiète si l'objet est lavé et risque d'être modifié un tant soit peu.

Indépendance progressive

L'indépendance s'acquiert petit à petit et ne doit être accordée à l'enfant que dans certaines situations où il peut éviter des traumatismes physiques ou affectifs. L'indépendance totale doit lui être refusée tant qu'il est trop jeune pour s'en servir sans danger, car une expérience malheureuse peut le rendre craintif et incapable d'expérimenter de nouvelles habiletés.

Satisfaction de ses besoins

Le trottineur, auquel les parents accordent une indépendance progressive lui permettant de réussir des expériences nouvelles, développe un sentiment d'autonomie et de débrouillardise. Il découvre qu'il peut effectuer des choix avec l'aide de ses parents. Il peut décider s'il jouera par terre ou sur la chaise, s'il mangera ou rejettera la nourriture qu'on lui offre, s'il accueillera un visiteur ou se cramponnera à la jupe de sa mère. Tôt ou tard, il apprendra que, parmi des quantités de choses qu'il veut faire, certaines lui sont impossibles et d'autres interdites. Il apprend facilement qu'il ne peut toucher à tout ce qu'il désire, puisqu'on place certains objets hors de sa portée. Il lui faut plus de temps pour comprendre que, bien qu'il n'y ait pas de danger physique à accomplir certaines activités, ses parents les lui défendent pour une raison qu'il ne peut saisir.

L'enfant désire souvent exécuter des tâches pour lesquelles il n'est pas physiquement prêt. La montée d'un escalier constitue un exemple de sa persistance. Le trottineur qui a un frère ou une sœur légèrement plus âgé que lui, essaie d'accomplir un grand nombre d'activités qu'il ne réussit pas toujours.

Le développement de son système musculaire s'accompagne d'habiletés motrices rudimentaires, mais l'enfant découvre qu'il ne peut les coordonner pour accomplir une activité contrôlée aussi aisément que des enfants plus grands. Bien qu'il ait appris à marcher, à tenir et à relâcher, à saisir et à manipuler des objets, il est souvent frustré dans ses efforts pour diriger ses mains et ses pieds. La première enfance demeure un âge de frustrations.

Une partie importante de l'apprentissage du tout-petit consiste à régulariser ses activités, ce qui représente un véritable défi pour l'adulte qui veut guider l'enfant. Le trottineur ne peut se rendre compte des conséquences de ses actes. Même en l'absence de tout danger d'être blessé, il peut se rendre ridicule et amener les autres à rire à ses dépens. Ceci blesse son amour-propre, s'il ne peut se joindre à leur hilarité.

Graduellement, l'enfant doit avoir accès à de nouvelles expériences tout en continuant à être protégé. L'une des raisons justifiant le contrôle des activités du trottineur par l'adulte est de lui éviter des échecs qui pourraient diminuer son estime de lui-même. Il est donc évident qu'un adulte ne doit jamais se servir de la honte ou du ridicule comme punition ou comme réprimande. La honte donne à l'enfant l'impression d'être encore plus petit qu'il ne l'est; si on humilie l'enfant trop souvent, il obéira si on l'observe et il agira comme bon lui semble en d'autres circonstances. Un tel comportement peut engendrer des accidents graves.

Une attitude négative, normale jusqu'à un certain point, peut paraître plus profonde qu'elle ne l'est en réalité. La réponse « non, non » ne veut pas toujours dire que l'enfant ne fera pas ce qu'on lui demande. Elle peut signifier: « Ne prends pas cet air fâché, maman », ou bien, « Je ne sais pas ce que tu veux dire ». « Non » est un son facile à reproduire. L'enfant l'utilise peut-être davantage pour son plaisir que pour exprimer un sentiment négatif. Même dans le cas d'un bambin de deux ou trois ans, il est possible que ce « non » ne constitue pas un refus, mais plutôt une réponse vague à des demandes non comprises. Trop souvent, cependant, il signifie que l'enfant ne fera pas ce que l'adulte lui demande. Et son insolence tend à augmenter devant la colère de l'adulte, car, indécis, ne sachant ce qu'il doit faire, il suit son exemple et adopte des expressions de colère. Il manque de vocabulaire pour communiquer ses sentiments et il frappe alors l'adulte, fait une crise de colère ou devient apathique et maussade. Quoiqu'une certaine résistance aux demandes fasse partie de l'acquisition progressive d'une saine indépendance, cette attitude peut se généraliser et s'installer chez l'enfant qui n'est pas dirigé par un adulte conséquent et aimant. S'il n'est pas corrigé, ce comportement risque de constituer un facteur d'inadaptation. Les parents ou leurs substituts doivent comprendre qu'il est aussi important de préserver leur dignité aux yeux de l'enfant que de respecter sa personnalité en pleine croissance. Le nourrisson qui a appris à faire confiance aux autres, acquerra normalement un sentiment d'autonomie durant les deux années qui suivront. Pour ce faire, on doit le respecter en tant qu'individu et l'aider à intérioriser les normes sociales de son groupe, afin qu'il *désire* faire ce qui est demandé et qu'il se sente mal à l'aise s'il déroge aux normes. Cette étape du développement requiert au moins deux ans pour être partiellement accomplie et l'enfant, s'il est bien guidé, la perfectionnera tout au long de sa croissance.

L'éducation sphinctérienne

Contrôler ses mictions et ses défécations constitue l'apprentissage le plus personnel que le trottineur a eu à accomplir depuis sa naissance. Il préfèrerait continuer à uriner et à déféquer au moment où il ressent une tension et à l'endroit où il se trouve. Toutefois, pour s'intégrer dans la société, il doit apprendre à renoncer à son confort et à supporter la frustration d'attendre. L'éducation sphinctérienne demeure une étape difficile pour le jeune enfant, surtout si sa famille attache une très grande importance à l'acquisition de la propreté. Si la mère y ajoute une connotation morale, (l'enfant devient méchant s'il se salit et sage s'il reste propre), le petit qui ne peut demeurer propre et au sec commence à ressentir des sentiments de culpabilité et d'anxiété, parce qu'il est incapable de satisfaire les adultes qui s'occupent de lui.

Le nourrisson vivait selon le *principe du plaisir* (il veut ce qu'il veut quand il le veut). Le trottineur doit commencer à accepter le *principe de la réalité* (il renonce à un plaisir dans l'immédiat afin d'avoir un autre plaisir plus tard). Dans le cas présent, le tout-petit doit renoncer au plaisir d'excréter où et quand il le veut, afin d'obtenir l'approbation de sa mère. S'il n'a pas établi avec elle une relation de confiance, il désirera moins contrôler ses sphincters.

D'autres facteurs influent sur cet apprentissage. Si l'enfant voit des sœurs ou frères aînés utiliser la toilette, il pourra vouloir en faire autant. Devenu plus actif, il trouve ses habits mouillés plus gênants. Si d'autres enfants montrent du doigt le gâchis qu'il a fait et se moquent de lui, il rira peut-être, mais commencera à faire le lien entre la rétention et le style de vie de l'enfant plus âgé qu'il tente d'imiter.

L'apprentissage d'une nouvelle habileté est difficile avant que le trottineur ait atteint le stade du développement où il désirera apprendre et où physiquement, il sera capable de le faire sans un trop grand effort. Si on l'incite à apprendre avant d'être prêt, des attitudes défavorables peuvent apparaître. Laisser passer ce stade optimum serait aussi erroné, car le trottineur serait ainsi privé du bonheur d'exercer son habileté nouvelle. Il manquerait aussi la satisfaction d'être félicité par les adultes en accomplissant une performance normale pour son âge.

L'âge pour commencer l'éducation sphinctérienne. Il faut commencer l'éducation sphinctérienne quand l'enfant est prêt tant aux points de vue psychologique que

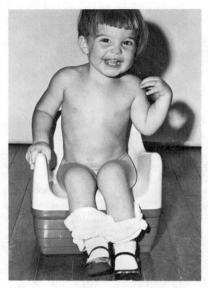

Figure 14-2. Le trottineur doit se sentir en sécurité lorsqu'on le place sur une chaise percée. Il doit être capable d'atteindre le plancher avec ses pieds et pouvoir s'appuyer confortablement contre le dos et sur les bras de la chaise.

physiologique. Lorsqu'il peut se mettre debout tout seul, ceci indique que la myélinisation a atteint le niveau de l'innervation anale. Il est inutile et frustrant pour l'enfant de commencer l'éducation des sphincters avant la formation des voies nerveuses qui lui permettent de contrôler et d'évacuer ses excrétions, lorsque sa mère le lui demande.

L'enfant indique qu'il est psychologiquement prêt pour cet apprentissage lorsqu'il prend plaisir à répéter des actes pour obtenir le sourire et les compliments de sa mère et qu'il a saisi la différence entre « donner » et « recevoir »; lorsque l'enfant est capable d'indiquer qu'il est souillé, il peut saisir les buts de l'entraînement à la propreté. L'enfant commence à indiquer qu'il a uriné *avant* de signaler qu'il a besoin d'uriner.

Pour la moyenne des enfants, l'éducation sphinctérienne peut débuter durant la deuxième année, mais si l'enfant ne comprend pas ce que l'on attend de lui, l'expérience doit être remise à plus tard. Si cette éducation est commencée trop tôt, par l'enfant, il ne retiendra ni expulsera volontairement ses excréments, même si sa mère a l'impression de réussir en le mettant sur sa chaise-toilette au moment où la tension cause l'ouverture de l'un ou l'autre ou des deux sphincters. La réussite durera tant que l'absorption quotidienne de la nourriture solide et des liquides restera la même, mais toute modification d'horaire risquera de changer l'heure de l'excrétion et le petit salira alors sa couche ou sa culotte. Sa mère peut interpréter ce changement comme une régression et, soit se décourager, soit gronder le jeune enfant.

L'éducation du sphincter anal est plus facile que celle du sphincter vésical, car le nombre de selles par jour est inférieur au nombre des mictions. Le contrôle de la vessie peut commencer un ou deux mois après l'établissement plus ou moins complet du contrôle anal, ou lorsque l'enfant est capable de passer deux ou trois heures sans miction. Des facteurs externes, tels un déménagement ou la naissance d'un autre enfant, peuvent rendre un peu plus difficile le processus de l'éducation sphinctérienne.

Méthode d'éducation sphinctérienne.

La première étape consiste à observer chez l'enfant l'heure habituelle de la défécation et à l'habituer à la mentionner. Un peu avant ce moment, on doit l'asseoir sur un siège percé ou sur une chaise-toilette où il se sent en sécurité. Il doit pouvoir appuyer ses bras et ses pieds. Il ne doit pas avoir de nourriture ou de jouets à ce moment, car son attention serait distraite au lieu d'être concentrée sur la raison pour laquelle il est sur la chaise. La mère ou l'infirmière doivent lui indiquer par leurs gestes et leur ton de voix qu'elles s'attendent à ce qu'il évacue à cet endroit et à ce moment. Il faudrait choisir pour désigner cet acte un terme précis et facile à comprendre pour tout le monde. Ceci est important, car un grand nombre d'enfants à la maternelle ou en visite chez des amis adultes ne savent pas faire comprendre qu'ils veulent évacuer; les autres ne comprennent pas les mots dont ils se servent. Le terme utilisé et enseigné par la mère de l'enfant reflète souvent le milieu social des parents. L'infirmière ne doit jamais paraître dégoûtée en entendant un mot prononcé par un enfant, mais peut toutefois lui apprendre un terme plus approprié.

Il faut à la mère une grande patience, car l'enfant n'apprend que par de multiples tentatives. L'entraînement ne doit pas créer de tension ni chez la mère, ni chez l'enfant. Une attitude détendue facilitera les choses. Puisque l'éducation sphinctérienne s'échelonne généralement sur une ou deux années, rien ne presse. L'enfant doit être félicité et embrassé quand il va à la selle ou quand il urine dans la cuvette des cabinets ou dans la chaise percée. Mais s'il ne réussit pas, sa mère doit conserver une attitude neutre, car l'enfant de cet âge a encore de la difficulté à évacuer volontairement.

Quand il est assez vieux pour aller tout seul à la toilette, l'enfant doit avoir des vêtements qu'il peut ôter et remettre sans aide, afin de devenir plus indépendant. Le pantalon d'un garçon doit être facile à descendre ou à ouvrir au moyen d'une fermeture-éclair. La culotte d'une fillette doit avoir un élastique à la taille pour pouvoir être descendue facilement sous le genou. Il est utile de placer des marches près de la toilette familiale (pourvue ou non d'un siège spécial), pour permettre à l'enfant de s'y asseoir sans aide. Un garçon apprend à uriner debout lorsqu'il observe les autres enfants ou son père. En montant sur un tabouret, il pourra uriner dans la cuvette des cabinets sans mouiller le plancher. Après le début de l'entraînement, il est important de changer l'enfant dès qu'il est mouillé pour l'habituer au confort d'être au sec. Il est bon d'utiliser des culottes de transition qui lui font comprendre que le temps des couches est passé et que l'on attend de lui un nouveau comportement.

Il ne faudrait se servir de lavements, de laxatifs ou de suppositoires que sur ordonnance médicale. La mère doit savoir qu'il n'est pas nécessaire que l'enfant ait chaque jour une évacuation intestinale.

L'âge où se termine l'éducation sphinctérienne.

L'enfant moyen, sain, intelligent et raisonnablement entraîné, acquiert le contrôle de son intestin entre 18 et 24 mois. Le contrôle de la vessie pendant les heures d'éveil peut être bien acquis dès l'âge de deux ans, et pendant le sommeil, vers sa troisième année. La continence, la nuit, ne doit pas être précipitée. Il n'est pas souhaitable de réveiller l'enfant pour l'amener à la toilette, car il peut rester éveillé pendant des heures après avoir été remis au lit. On peut essayer de ne pas lui donner à boire après le souper, mais si l'enfant n'est pas prêt physiologiquement, ce moyen ne l'aidera pas suffisamment. D'ailleurs, il risque d'avoir soif et de pleurer pour avoir de l'eau pendant la nuit.

L'entraînement pendant l'hospitalisation.

Si l'enfant n'a pas atteint son contrôle sphinctérien avant d'entrer à l'unité pédiatrique, il ne faudrait pas lui demander d'utiliser le bassin de lit, l'urinal ou la chaise percée durant son hospitalisation. Il manquerait de motivation pour apprendre, car il n'aime personne suffisamment pour vouloir modifier son comportement par désir de plaire. De plus, on doit lui éviter la tension associée au changement d'habitudes et à l'acquisition d'habiletés nouvelles.

Si, à l'admission de l'enfant, la mère dit qu'il a atteint son contrôle sphinctérien, on doit noter ce fait sur le plan de soins. On enregistre aussi la technique utilisée par la mère et les mots que l'enfant associe à l'évacuation. Si l'enfant est assez âgé pour comprendre, on lui montre l'équipement de l'hôpital, tel le bassin de lit et l'urinal. L'infirmière doit essayer de conserver le même horaire qu'à la maison, mais ne doit pas s'inquiéter s'il se mouille ou se salit, et ne doit en aucun cas manifester sa désapprobation. L'infirmière doit expliquer à la mère, pour qu'elle ne soit pas déconcertée par ce comportement, que l'enfant malade dans un milieu étranger régresse souvent et perd les habiletés nouvellement acquises. Quand il est rétabli, il regagne son ancien contrôle.

La signification de l'éducation sphinctérienne pour l'enfant.

On demande maintenant au trottineur de faire ce que veut sa mère, tandis qu'auparavant, elle le soignait avec amour sans demander d'autre réponse que sa dépendance affectueuse. Jusqu'alors sans responsabilité, il doit désormais apprendre à être, en partie, responsable de lui-même.

Le barbouillage avec des selles.

Le jeune trottineur n'a pas encore acquis le dégoût de l'adulte pour les excréments. Il aime manipuler ses selles et les utiliser pour barbouiller le plancher, les murs ou les meubles. Un tel comportement se manifeste entre les âges de quinze et vingt-quatre mois. L'enfant considère ses selles comme une partie de lui-même et, dans ce sens, elles représentent un cadeau. De plus, ce terme « cadeau » est souvent utilisé par l'adulte qui préside à l'entraînement à la propreté. Il ne comprend pas pourquoi on les jette quand on l'a incité à les évacuer dans la chaise percée. Voici un avantage de la cuvette des toilettes: il peut chasser l'eau lui-même et regarder les selles disparaître avec un sentiment d'accomplissement. Toutefois, il faut se rappeler que plusieurs trottineurs sont effrayés par la chasse d'eau et craignent d'être emportés dans le tourbillon. Il est important de remettre l'enfant debout avant d'actionner la chasse d'eau et de lui expliquer calmement ce qui se passe.

Les parents ou l'infirmière doivent accepter le sentiment de l'enfant au sujet de ses selles et ne jamais exprimer une forte désapprobation quand il en met sur lui-même ou sur un objet. Son désir de barbouiller doit être satisfait avec de la pâte à modeler, du sable humide ou de la boue qu'il peut manipuler. Plus tard, il aura du plaisir à faire de la peinture digitale, avec des couleurs vives, claires et gaies sur de grandes feuilles de papier.

L'enfant n'aura pas l'occasion de répandre ses selles si on le nettoie immédiatement après son évacuation. Il faut bien fermer sa couche pour que ses mains ne puissent y pénétrer. Une fois qu'il aura appris à utiliser la chaise percée ou la toilette, le problème du barbouillage disparaîtra de lui-même.

L'influence de l'éducation sphinctérienne sur la personnalité de l'enfant.

L'enfant devient souvent ambivalent à l'égard de sa mère durant cette période. Il l'aime, mais elle lui demande de sacrifier le confort apporté par l'évacuation libre et il en ressent de la frustration. Son attitude ambivalente se compose d'amour et de haine, tout à la fois. Il est capable de la frapper et de la quitter, puis, une minute plus tard, de se tourner vers elle pour être réconforté. Si elle conserve une attitude amicale et compréhensive, l'amour chez l'enfant prévaudra sur l'hostilité. Il est important d'atténuer ses frustrations afin qu'il ne conserve pas de cette période des sentiments d'hostilité, de rébellion, de rancune et de ressentiment.

Résumé.

Si la mère sait manifester son amour à son enfant, il sera incité à lui plaire et collaborera à son éducation sphinctérienne sans trop de difficultés. Si elle a confiance en son intelligence et en son désir de faire ce qu'elle lui demande, elle pourra s'attendre à un apprentissage sans difficultés majeures et assez rapide.

Si, par contre, la mère manifeste un dégoût pour tout le processus de l'évacuation, l'enfant aura honte de son corps, pourra se croire indigne d'affection et même penser qu'il est « méchant », parce qu'il ne réussit pas immédiatement à atteindre la propreté. Éventuellement, il peut croire que toute fonction physique doit être soumise à un contrôle sévère. Cette attitude pourra s'étendre à toutes ses activités au point que l'enfant aura sans cesse peur de déplaire à sa mère ou à d'autres adultes. Dans son esprit, une propreté exagérée devient synonyme de perfection. Malheureusement, son désir de rester propre inhibe son jeu actif normal. Un tel enfant manque de spontanéité, de créativité. Il craint de se salir en jouant et reste à l'écart quand d'autres enfants font des gâteaux de boue. Il peut développer une attitude tenace qui consiste à vouloir plaire à tous ceux qui ont autorité sur lui, à cause de la peur qu'il ressent de perdre leur approbation.

Non seulement il voudra être parfait lui-même, mais il s'attendra à ce que ses amis le soient aussi. Il deviendra rigide, inflexible et lié par des rites nécessaires qui, à son sens, réduiront le risque de déplaire à quelqu'un et, par conséquent, diminueront son anxiété.

L'apprentissage du langage

Apprendre à parler est un long processus qui prend racine dans le cri du nouveau-né. Le bébé passe lentement des sons réflexes au gazouillis, au babillage et finalement aux mots qui ont une signification pour lui et l'entourage. Toutefois, le nourrisson se sert plus souvent des mains et des bras pour exprimer ses désirs.

Entre un an et trois ans, l'enfant progresse dans sa compréhension d'autrui et dans l'expression verbale de ses sentiments et de ses idées. Le nourrisson et le trottineur peuvent cependant continuer à communiquer par des gestes, à tendre les bras ou à sourire lorsqu'ils veulent que l'adulte les prenne, même s'ils sont capables de dire ce qu'ils veulent.

Bien avant de pouvoir former des phrases, l'enfant comprend la signification d'un grand nombre de mots. Le regard de sa mère, ses gestes et le ton de sa voix, l'aident à saisir le sens de ce qu'elle dit. Elle peut lui apprendre un nouveau mot si elle montre du doigt un objet tout en prononçant le terme qui le désigne. Ou bien, lorsqu'il s'intéresse à un objet, une poupée par exemple, elle peut lui faire répéter le mot quand elle le lui donne.

Motivation du langage.

Pour parler, l'enfant doit avoir des relations satisfaisantes avec sa mère. Il n'a de motivation pour parler que s'il pense qu'elle va répondre; si l'effort n'est pas rentable, il n'aura pas d'intérêt à le faire. Il parle pour exprimer ses besoins. Quand il dit « ma-man », il exprime le besoin d'avoir toutes les choses agréables qu'elle fait pour lui. S'il dit « ma-man » et montre du doigt un objet, c'est pour dire « Donne-moi ça, s'il te plaît ». Quand il a appris le nom de chaque objet, il l'utilise, par exemple: tasse, chien. S'il reçoit tout ce qu'il désire sans demander, il a peu de motivation pour parler jusqu'au moment où il ressent le besoin de mots qui expriment des attitudes, des idées, des émotions.

En général, le premier langage de l'enfant exprime ses désirs. Ceci est suivi de mots ou de phrases indiquant des idées ou bien la fonction des objets, telle que l'enfant la perçoit. L'enfant apprend assez tôt la valeur de la parole dans les relations sociales agréables. Il éprouve beaucoup de plaisir à parler et parle à tous ceux qu'il rencontre, à ses jouets, à ses animaux ou à lui-même. Même s'il ne possède que quelques mots, il les utilise pour se renseigner sur lui-même, les autres et les objets. S'il dit « sortir », ce n'est pas qu'une demande; l'enfant veut aussi savoir s'il ira dehors. Quand il dit « chien », il demande peut-être où se trouve son animal favori.

Modes d'apprentissage.

Un jeune enfant doit avoir un bon modèle, sinon il n'apprendra pas à parler correctement. Il imitera un langage incorrect aussi facilement qu'un langage sans fautes, peut-être plus facilement même, car le premier s'avère souvent plus simple, direct et probablement accompagné de gestes. Si un adulte utilise le babil enfantin pour lui parler, l'enfant n'a pas de modèle pour apprendre les termes exacts qui correspondent aux expériences et aux attitudes. Il a besoin, non seulement d'un *modèle* qui lui parle, mais aussi d'une occasion pour répondre et utiliser le mot immédiatement. S'adressant aux jouets, aux animaux et à lui-même, il apprend à utiliser des mots; mais puisqu'il n'entend alors que lui-même, il peut prendre l'habitude de prononcer et d'utiliser les mots de façon incorrecte.

Il existe parmi les étapes de l'apprentissage de la parole, une période pendant laquelle l'enfant fait peu de progrès. Ceci survient quand l'enfant apprend à marcher et s'y intéresse tellement qu'il ne prête pas beaucoup d'attention à l'acquisition de nouveaux mots. Néanmoins, le nombre de mots qu'il comprend semble augmenter.

L'enfant peut pleurer à cause de la frustration née d'un vocabulaire limité, car, malgré ses efforts pour exprimer ses désirs ou ses sentiments, il n'obtient pas ce qu'il veut. Il continue à frapper quand il se fâche, et pleure

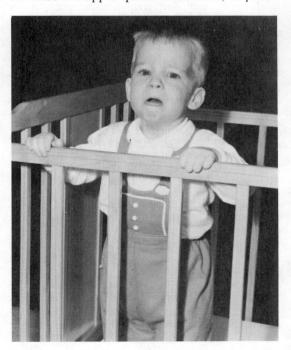

Figure 14-3. Le tout-petit pleure, car il n'arrive pas à exprimer ses besoins avec des mots.

quand il est blessé. Il n'est pas encore capable, aux points de vue physiologique et psychologique, de maîtriser ses gestes et d'utiliser des mots pour exprimer son désaccord ou sa peine. Plus tard, au lieu de frapper sa mère ou un camarade, il pourra s'exprimer en disant: « Je te déteste! » ou « Je veux que tu partes »; et au lieu de pleurer quand il ne peut sortir pour jouer, il pourra dire: « Pourquoi la pluie? Je veux jouer », ou simplement geindre: « Je veux sortir pour jouer ». Dans chaque cas, il demande le réconfort sollicité par ses pleurs lorsqu'il était un bébé. Même quand il peut parler, si ses émotions sont trop fortes pour qu'il puisse les maîtriser, les mots sont inadéquats et il retrouve les expressions infantiles de colère et de déception. Chaque fois qu'il parle ou pleure, l'enfant a besoin qu'on l'accepte, lui et ses sentiments, même s'ils peuvent paraître déraisonnables. Les pleurs sont des signes de détresse chez le trottineur, comme ils le sont chez le nourrisson.

Des exemples d'une telle situation surviennent souvent à l'hôpital. Quand un enfant croit qu'il sera blessé par une injection et se trouve rassuré par ce qu'on lui dit, on peut vérifier sa compréhension de la communication verbale et sa capacité d'exprimer sa peur par des mots. Il a besoin d'une explication simple, de témoignages d'affection verbaux et physiques pour ne pas penser que ces adultes inconnus veulent lui faire du mal (en termes techniques, qu'ils l'attaquent). L'infirmière, dans une telle situation, doit se garder de dire « Ne pleure pas », car ceci indiquerait un manque de compréhension de la manière dont l'enfant voit la situation. Il est encore trop jeune pour ne pas avoir peur de la douleur. L'infirmière ou la mère doit lui expliquer la nature et la raison du traitement, en des termes qu'il peut comprendre. Si c'est possible, sa mère devrait être présente pour le tenir; sinon, une des infirmières qu'il connaît ou considère comme amie, doit la remplacer. L'infirmière doit lui dire qu'elle sait qu'il a peur, mais que tout sera bientôt fini.

La formation du vocabulaire. Les premiers mots que l'enfant apprend sont des noms qui ressemblent aux sons qu'il a babillés (maman, pa-pa) à la phase syllabique. Il a retenu « ma-man » plutôt que « da-dan » à cause des gratifications reçues chaque fois qu'il agençait ces deux syllabes. Il essaie ensuite, des mots plus difficiles, jusqu'à pouvoir dire les noms des objets et des personnes de son milieu quotidien. Puis il apprend des *verbes* qui traduisent les actions qu'il observe autour de lui: courir, donner, prendre. Il commence à utiliser des *adjectifs* à partir de dix-huit mois environ.

Les premiers sont généralement « bon » et « mauvais », car il les entend souvent. Les premiers *adverbes* qu'il utilise sont ordinairement « ici » et « où ». Ce sont des mots employés par sa mère quand elle lui parle. En dernier lieu, il apprend la signification des *pronoms*. Il les confond, car ils varient selon la personne qui les utilise. Jean est « moi » et « je » pour lui-même, mais « toi » pour sa mère quand elle s'adresse à lui et « il » quand elle parle de lui à son père. La même confusion existe quant aux autres *pronoms*.

Le nombre de mots que l'enfant utilise dépend de sa motivation, de son intelligence et de la stimulation à parler qu'il a reçue. Habituellement, vers neuf mois, le nourrisson peut dire de façon significative « maman » et « pa-pa ». À un an, l'enfant ajoute deux ou trois mots. Entre 18 mois et trois ans, son vocabulaire s'accroît considérablement. Il peut posséder 300 mots à 2 ans et 900 mots à trois ans. L'acquisition plus ou moins rapide d'un vocabulaire étendu dépend du sexe de l'enfant, de sa position à l'intérieur de la famille, de la valeur du langage dans sa famille et du statut socio-économique de celle-ci.

Formation des phrases. Le premier effort de l'enfant pour former des phrases consiste à joindre deux mots et à les compléter par des gestes. Ensuite les phrases contiennent un nom, un verbe et, parfois, un adjectif et un adverbe, par exemple, « Bébé va dehors ».

Retard du langage. L'enfant normal commence à parler dès son quinzième mois environ. S'il ne prononce pas quelques mots à l'âge de deux ans, il faudrait chercher la cause de ce retard. Voici quelques-unes des causes courantes.

L'INTELLIGENCE. La parole est retardée chez les enfants d'intelligence faible. La richesse du vocabulaire dépend beaucoup de l'intelligence.

LE MILIEU SOCIAL ET CULTUREL. Les enfants des milieux sociaux défavorisés accusent souvent un retard dans le développement du langage, à cause des modèles inadéquats qu'ils imitent. Ceux qui vivent en institution également peuvent être très retardés dans ce domaine, car les adultes leur parlent rarement en tant qu'individus, et lorsqu'ils le font, la conversation tend à se limiter à ce que l'enfant doit ou ne doit pas faire.

LA MALADIE. Le développement du langage s'effectue plus lentement chez les enfants malades et longtemps hospitalisés parce qu'ils ont moins de contacts avec d'autres enfants et que leurs besoins sont satisfaits sans qu'ils les expriment verbalement. Le jeune malade qui reçoit beaucoup de soins des adultes à la maison, peut élargir rapidement son vocabulaire. C'est l'enfant hospitalisé qui risque d'être retardé. Toutefois, un jeune trottineur hospitalisé et immobilisé dont on s'occupe efficacement peut développer son langage plus rapidement, car la marche n'interfère pas sur son apprentissage du langage.

LE NÉGATIVISME. L'enfant peut décider de ne rien dire parce qu'on l'a obligé à parler avant qu'il ne soit prêt. Il est possible qu'on se soit moqué de sa prononciation infantile et que son image de soi en ait été blessée ou amoindrie.

LA SURDITÉ. Si l'enfant ne peut entendre ce que les autres disent, il ne peut les imiter et, par conséquent, ne parlera pas sans une aide appropriée. Même dans ce cas, il aura un vocabulaire plus restreint, une prononciation parfois déficiente et une étrange voix neutre.

LE SEXE. Les garçons parlent, en général, plus tard, ont un vocabulaire moins riche et font plus d'erreurs grammaticales.

LE BILINGUISME. L'apprentissage de deux langues à la fois peut retarder le langage de l'enfant de moins de cinq ans et créer une certaine confusion dans le vocabulaire et la grammaire. Ces affirmations sont actuellement le sujet de controverses de la part des spécialistes.

Le développement culturel

En plus du contrôle sphinctérien et du langage, le tout-petit doit apprendre de nombreux comportements. Il apprend à se laver et à se brosser les dents. Il comprend ce que veut sa mère lorsqu'elle désire qu'il soit propre ou qu'il range ses jouets.

L'enfant tend à maîtriser globalement son petit monde. Apprendre à faire quelque chose tout seul lui procure un vrai sentiment de contrôle, d'indépendance et d'autonomie. Ses parents devraient l'aider à apprendre et devraient souligner son succès. S'ils ne lui manifestent pas leur approbation de façon compréhensible il sera déchiré entre, d'une part, l'expérience agréable d'agir indépendamment et, d'autre part, la désapprobation de ses parents. Sachant ce qu'ils désapprouvent, il doit choisir entre le plaisir de faire ce qu'il veut et sa volonté de plaire à ses parents. C'est au moyen de telles décisions qu'à la longue, l'enfant apprend à porter des jugements appropriés, optant pour ce qui est considéré comme juste dans son groupe culturel. Sa motivation essentielle réside dans son amour pour ses parents, un

amour acquis dans sa première année et renforcé durant l'enfance.

Les traits de caractère du trottineur

Le négativisme

Dans son désir d'indépendance ou d'autonomie, l'enfant veut faire de nombreuses choses qu'il ne devrait pas faire. Depuis sa première enfance, il entend souvent sa mère dire « non » à ses tentatives pour s'affirmer. Peu à peu, il apprend à se servir de ce mot et à dire « non », « je ne veux pas » d'une façon assez têtue. Il affirme ainsi son pouvoir en contrôlant les demandes de ceux qui l'aiment. La tâche requise par son développement, à cette période, consiste à freiner ses réactions négatives et à adapter son comportement aux normes sociales de ceux qui détiennent l'autorité.

Chaque enfant traverse cette période de négativisme au cours de son évolution. L'âge de deux ans a été appelé l'âge du « non-non » ou « les terribles deux ans ». L'enfant veut agir en tant qu'individu et donne l'impression de préférer la puissance – le pouvoir de décision – au plaisir procuré par l'activité défendue. Cependant, s'il est frustré dans l'accomplissement de ce qu'il veut faire sans aide, ou bien quand la réaction des parents lui montre qu'ils ne sont pas d'accord, il peut très bien se tourner vers les adultes qui étaient les objets de son agressivité, pour avoir du réconfort dans la situation désagréable qu'il a créée.

Parfois, il veut être à la fois dépendant et indépendant. Par exemple, quand on lui offre de la crème glacée, il peut dire « non », puis la manger rapidement malgré sa réponse.

Un enfant peut agir de manière négative parce qu'il ne peut tolérer la frustration d'un désir. Il ne peut accepter les restrictions posées par ses parents et, en même temps, n'arrive pas à trouver un moyen acceptable pour obtenir ce qu'il désire. Quand il dit « non », il se sent tout aussi puissant que ses parents.

Quelquefois, un enfant paraît négatif, sans l'être véritablement. Il n'a aucune objection à faire ce que ses parents désirent, mais ne veut pas cesser une activité qui l'amuse, par exemple, s'il joue avec plaisir et qu'on lui demande de ranger ses jouets pour aller au lit.

La période de négativisme, en général, demeure assez courte si on comprend les besoins de l'enfant. Il lui faut l'amour de ses parents pour apprendre à satisfaire son besoin d'indépendance, d'une façon socialement acceptable.

*Comment réagir au comportement né-
gativiste.* Un adulte ne doit pas adopter
un comportement autoritaire pour vaincre
l'opposition de l'enfant. Une opposition directe
augmente son désir de manifester son indépendance. L'adulte ne doit pas donner trop d'ordres stricts au tout-petit ou interrompre trop
souvent ses activités.

La mère doit permettre à l'enfant d'assumer
de petites responsabilités, par exemple le rangement de ses jouets à l'heure du coucher.
Ceci permet au trottineur de sentir que lui et
l'adulte travaillent pour atteindre un but commun, plutôt que d'avoir l'impression qu'il est
obligé de faire ce que veut l'adulte. Quand la
mère place de la nourriture devant un petit de
deux ans, elle peut lui en offrir quelques cuillerées, en lui parlant doucement. L'enfant sai-
sira alors la cuillère et se nourrira lui-même.

La mère doit reconnaître les signes d'indépendance chez l'enfant. Ceci augmente l'estime
de soi du petit et le porte à coopérer davantage.
On l'aide ainsi à se sentir important. Tout enfant apprend à se connaître par l'intermédiaire
des personnes importantes de son milieu (surtout des membres de sa famille). Si la mère a
une conception valorisante de l'enfant, il aura,
pour sa part, une image agréable de lui-même.
S'il s'accepte à cet âge, il pourra accepter les
autres.

Le comportement ritualiste

Le trottineur a souvent un comportement
ritualiste. Il accompagne de rites des tâches
simples, car il sait pouvoir se contrôler de
cette façon. Ce comportement est fréquent entre deux ans et quatre ans; il atteint son maximum vers l'âge de deux ans et demi. En vieillissant, l'enfant a moins besoin d'une routine
stricte, car il est plus sûr de lui-même et peut
mieux s'adapter aux changements. Les adultes
doivent accepter ces rites lors d'activités telles
que le bain (il suspend sa serviette d'une certaine façon), le repas (sa bavette se porte toujours de la même manière) et le coucher (sa
couverture préférée le recouvre toujours dans
son lit). La mère économise ainsi du temps
et de l'énergie et donne à l'enfant un sentiment
de sécurité et de maîtrise de soi.

La lenteur à obéir

Le tout-petit apprend progressivement la
différence entre ce qu'il peut faire et ce qu'il
doit éviter; quand il ne peut se décider entre
deux actes, il accomplira habituellement les
deux. Par exemple, lorsque sa mère l'oblige à
quitter son jeu pour se servir de la chaise

percée, il aura tendance à finir son jeu d'abord,
puis à uriner en se rendant à la toilette. Ceci
résulte en partie de sa nervosité et de sa hâte
à faire ce que sa mère a demandé. Quand
l'expérience aura appris à l'enfant à choisir
entre deux actes, il saura prendre plus rapidement des décisions plus sensées.

Les accès de colère

Les accès de colère ont lieu quand l'enfant
ne peut contrôler ses impulsions devant les
exigences de la réalité. Il se sent frustré et
réagit de la seule façon qu'il connaisse — par
une violente activité physique et par des larmes. Si on ne lui offre pas une solution de
rechange, il se livre à une crise de colère. Ce
comportement se manifeste le plus fréquemment vers deux et trois ans. S'il persiste à
l'âge scolaire, il faudrait faire voir l'enfant à
des professionnels de la santé.

Les enfants hospitalisés peuvent avoir des
accès de colère causés par la peur de l'inconnu et l'éloignement de ceux qu'ils aiment. Ils
ont besoin d'aide pour comprendre ce milieu
et les soins qu'ils y reçoivent. Ils ont aussi
besoin de la sécurité fournie par de fréquentes
visites de leurs parents.

Lors d'un accès de colère, l'enfant ignore
totalement la réalité de la situation. Il ne peut
entendre ce qu'on lui dit ni y réagir, à moins
que ceci le saisisse suffisamment et pénètre
jusqu'à sa conscience.

La décharge de son émotion par une activité
musculaire sera, soit sans objet, soit dirigée
contre lui-même. Il pourra cogner sa tête ou
s'infliger d'autres douleurs. Il s'attaquera rarement à l'adulte qui cause sa crise.

*Comment réagir devant un accès de
colère.* L'enfant ne doit pas être l'objet
d'une attention anxieuse, mais doit être observé et protégé contre les accidents. Une contrainte augmente sa fureur, car elle limite le
seul moyen connu de l'enfant pour décharger
sa colère. S'il nuit à un autre enfant ou à un
adulte, ou s'il casse un objet précieux, il se
sentira coupable une fois la crise terminée.

Sa tension sera mitigée, si on peut l'écarter
de la cause immédiate de sa crise, pour être
avec un adulte dont il est sûr d'être aimé. Cet
adulte, généralement sa mère, doit être calme
et patient envers lui, mais ne doit pas lui
prêter trop d'attention, avant que l'enfant ne
montre qu'il est prêt à recevoir le réconfort
affectueux dont il a besoin après sa crise.

Les soins à la suite d'un accès de colère.
On recommande de faire le moins de commentaires possibles sur le comportement de

l'enfant pendant un accès de colère. On ne doit pas le punir. S'il veut coopérer, il sera soulagé par le fait qu'on lui lave la figure et les mains. On peut lui donner un jouet pour le distraire de l'expérience qu'il vient de subir. Son bouleversement est tel qu'il doit se calmer avant de recevoir de la nourriture.

Mesures préventives. La mère, puisqu'elle connaît l'enfant, peut prévoir l'accès de colère. Elle doit essayer de lui montrer de meilleurs moyens de résoudre son problème et lui proposer une solution socialement plus acceptable pour exprimer sa colère et sa frustration. De plus, un enfant a souvent peur de sa propre agressivité et de l'état désagréable qui en résulte. On devrait l'aider à décharger sa tension d'une façon permise, telle que par l'exercice physique ou le jeu symbolique.

L'enfant malade peut, avec un marteau, enfoncer des bâtons en caoutchouc dans une planche trouée ou lancer des ballons sur des quilles. À la maison un grand nombre d'activités lui permettent de libérer son agressivité. Dehors, il peut creuser des trous au jardin, ramasser des feuilles ou de la neige. À l'intérieur, il peut marteler des chevilles en bois ou bâtir une tour de cubes, puis la démolir.

Si l'accès de colère résulte d'un refus de la part d'un adulte, ce dernier doit rester ferme et ne pas céder à la demande de l'enfant. Par un comportement logique seulement, l'adulte permettra à l'enfant d'adopter une attitude raisonnable.

Il arrive parfois qu'un enfant s'isole quand il sent monter sa colère ou une tension nerveuse. Ceci est acceptable comme mesure temporaire, mais s'il se renferme toujours, il faudra l'aider à affronter ses problèmes d'une façon plus directe et plus saine.

La discipline

La discipline a pour objectif la *maîtrise de soi*. Elle ne consiste donc pas uniquement à obliger l'enfant à obéir à l'autorité de l'adulte. Pour être efficace, la discipline doit accompagner la formation personnelle, qui consiste à apprendre comment vivre aisément avec autrui. La discipline qui se veut constructive doit aider l'enfant à canaliser ses désirs moins acceptables, irréalistes ou vains, dans des voies socialement approuvées et efficaces. Cette socialisation commencée par les parents doit se poursuivre sans nuire à l'individualité ou à la créativité de l'enfant.

À mesure que s'effectue son apprentissage de la maîtrise de soi, l'enfant commence à se sentir plus en sécurité et moins inquiet. Il a besoin de l'aide des adultes pour accepter ses sentiments et les contrôler d'une manière constructive. Une relation positive parents-enfant s'avère nécessaire pour atteindre ces buts.

La discipline est un terme large comprenant une grande partie des relations entre la mère, ou un autre adulte, et l'enfant. Les parents utilisent la discipline pour établir des limites, donner des permissions, aider l'enfant à comprendre les normes culturelles et le guider vers un comportement socialement acceptable. Les parents et l'enfant reconnaissent difficilement comme de la discipline ces nombreux aspects qui font partie de la vie familiale et de l'expression d'un heureux rapport parents-enfant. La façon dont les parents envisagent la question de la discipline constitue peut-être le meilleur indice de leur attitude envers l'enfant.

L'établissement des limites. Il faut établir des limites au comportement de l'enfant pour l'aider à se sentir en sécurité; sans cadre, il subira sans cesse les conséquences d'erreurs qu'il ne pouvait guère éviter par lui-même. Les petits ne savent pas toujours distinguer le permis du défendu; ils doivent l'apprendre de leurs parents. Quand on lui impose des limites, l'enfant peut se fâcher au début, mais il comprendra, par la suite, que ses parents, mieux que lui, peuvent créer des situations agréables. C'est ainsi que sa confiance en l'adulte, acquise durant sa première année, s'accroît.

Les parents qui établissent chez le tout-petit des habitudes de comportement qui lui gagnent des amis et lui donnent une image de soi acceptable, remplissent une partie importante de leur fonction éducative.

La discipline constructive. Les parents doivent demeurer raisonnables quant à leurs exigences et tolérer un peu de retard dans la réaction de l'enfant. Ils ne devraient, ni trop s'inquiéter pour des petits détails dans le comportement de l'enfant, ni dire « non » trop souvent, et encore moins exiger de l'enfant qu'il se comporte d'une façon qui outrepasse ses capacités.

L'enfant, ayant compris le plaisir de coopérer avec ses parents, conservera la même attitude vis-à-vis des autres adultes. En récompense, il sera aimé et intégré dans nombre de situations agréables où il pose les fondements d'une auto-discipline. Un tel enfant est libre de s'épanouir, mais reçoit l'aide dont il a besoin pour résoudre ses problèmes. On lui accorde son indépendance graduellement, mais il n'est pas forcé de l'assumer prématurément. L'adulte doit, autant que possible, faire des

Figure 14-4. Les mères mettant quelquefois, avec insouciance, des objets tentants à la portée des enfants sont directement responsables des accidents. (Photographie de M. Lew Merrim et du magazine *Baby Talk.*)

actions *avec* l'enfant, au lieu de les faire *pour lui,* de sorte que celui-ci désire adopter le comportement souhaitable qu'on lui montre.

On doit éviter à l'enfant des craintes inutiles, mais lui apprendre plutôt à affronter progressivement les situations qui l'effraient.

Si la mère n'est pas *logique* dans sa discipline, ou si les adultes près de l'enfant ne montrent pas de cohérence dans ce qu'ils lui demandent, il devient confus et ne peut utiliser sa raison croissante pour déterminer ce qui arrivera s'il agit d'une manière ou d'une autre. Même s'il est motivé par son amour pour l'adulte à faire ce qui lui est demandé, souvent il désobéira, parce que l'autre parent qu'il aime également lui a demandé de faire tout le contraire.

La punition.   Il faut prévoir une forme de punition pour l'enfant qui enfreint les règles qu'il comprend et qui sont renforcées par chaque adulte responsable de sa discipline. On doit permettre à l'enfant qui a mal agi de conserver son estime de soi et ne jamais utiliser la honte comme punition. De même, l'affection ne doit pas servir à « acheter » le bon comportement et on ne doit pas laisser l'enfant croire que ses parents ne l'aiment plus à cause de sa conduite inacceptable.

Certains parents se blâment pour l'hostilité ou la colère qu'ils ressentent parfois à l'égard de leur enfant. Certaines infirmières, aussi, peuvent avoir de tels sentiments. Ces personnes ne punissent jamais un enfant, car elles considèrent toute punition comme une expression de colère. Ceci est une erreur. La punition constitue un instrument utile, si on l'utilise avec discernement. Elle décharge l'atmosphère pour permettre une relation nouvelle et souvent plus saine. L'enfant n'aura pas de ressentiment s'il pense qu'il « l'a méritée ». Il doit subir sa punition, pleinement conscient que l'adulte continuera à l'aimer. La punition ne doit jamais avoir l'air d'une revanche de l'adulte en colère. La peur d'être puni doit être réduite au minimum. L'enfant apprend la nécessité de l'obéissance, au fur et à mesure qu'il grandit, et décide progressivement par lui-même ce qu'il fera ou évitera.

Si c'est possible, on devrait montrer à l'enfant que la punition découle logiquement de sa décision erronée. Quand l'enfant se brûle la main parce qu'il touche au four chaud, il voit le résultat de sa désobéissance, mais il sait aussi que ce n'est pas sa mère qui lui a infligé la douleur. De même, une punition qui suit immédiatement l'acte répréhensible et qui se situe dans le même ordre d'idée rend l'enfant conscient de son erreur.

Si un enfant se sent coupable pour une chose faite à l'insu de sa mère et pour laquelle il n'a pas été puni, il pourra accomplir exprès un acte défendu afin d'être puni, diminuant ainsi son sentiment de culpabilité vis-à-vis de sa première faute. Certains enfants, méconnus ou rejetés par leurs parents, peuvent rechercher une punition pour obtenir une réaction quelconque. Quoiqu'elle ne soit pas une réponse affectueuse, l'enfant la préfère à un manque total d'attention.

L'enfant ne doit pas être puni pour des sentiments qu'il éprouve naturellement comme la jalousie à l'égard d'un nouveau petit frère. Il importe de l'amener à croire qu'il est dans l'erreur s'il se sent moins aimé et ne pas le gronder s'il n'apprend que lentement à aimer le nouveau venu. De plus, les punitions ne doivent jamais être cruelles ni comporter de sévices corporels.

L'infirmière qui prodigue des soins aux enfants hospitalisés doit respecter les mêmes règles de discipline que celles de la mère. Les étudiantes-infirmières n'y parviennent pas toujours étant donné leur conception de la discipline et de l'autorité.

Résumé du développement émotif

Les problèmes de cette période sont axés, pour la plupart, sur le *besoin d'autonomie* du trottineur. Il lui faut apprendre à se retenir et à se relâcher comme, par exemple, dans son éducation sphinctérienne. Il a besoin d'être soutenu pour régler le conflit entre la mise en œuvre de ses capacités nouvellement découvertes et son besoin toujours présent de sécurité et d'amour. Il faut le féliciter pour ce qu'il accomplit et surtout pour sa maîtrise de soi.

Les parents doivent se rappeler que l'enfant a devant lui beaucoup de temps pour achever l'évolution entamée au cours de sa deuxième année. Ils ne doivent pas essayer de le forcer trop rapidement à adopter un comportement plus mûr, sinon, au lieu de se plier, l'enfant peut se révolter et faire échouer les efforts des parents. Il risque ainsi de souffrir de négativisme.

Deux catégories de parents risquent de subir des échecs durant cette période, ceux qui demandent trop à l'enfant et ceux qui le laissent tout faire. De tels parents n'aident nullement l'enfant dans son effort pour atteindre la maturité.

APERÇU
DE LA CROISSANCE PHYSIQUE
ET DU DÉVELOPPEMENT

La croissance physique et le développement moteur ralentissent entre un an et trois ans. Cette période est surtout marquée par un accroissement de la force musculaire et un perfectionnement des habiletés. À la fin de la deuxième année, l'enfant utilise les principaux types d'activité musculaire. Les habiletés acquises se perfectionnent, permettant moins d'erreurs, plus de vitesse, des mouvements plus réguliers, plus harmonieux. Après l'acquisition des habiletés motrices fondamentales, le champ de ses capacités s'élargit et dépend de l'intérêt de l'enfant, de son milieu et de son intelligence.

Effets d'un retard moteur. Certains enfants n'atteignent pas, comme la plupart des autres, les étapes du développement enfantin aux âges approximatifs indiqués au chapitre 11. Ceux-ci ne souffrent pas seulement d'un retard moteur, mais ils sont habituellement privés de contacts avec d'autres enfants et d'une évolution sociale normale. Le jeune enfant, dont le développement moteur est lent, ne peut se joindre aux jeux des enfants qui savent courir et grimper. Il reste à l'écart, ou se voit exclu de leurs jeux, et peut acquérir des sentiments d'infériorité et d'agressivité qui seront plus tard les racines d'un comportement antisocial.

Séquence de la croissance et du développement. Les tableaux qui apparaissent aux pages 397 et suivantes, illustrant la croissance et le développement du trottineur, ne donnent que des moyennes d'âge auxquelles la majorité des enfants réussissent les activités décrites. Ils ne représentent pas le trottineur typique, mais simplement un cadre de référence pour interpréter le comportement du trottineur. En lisant ces tableaux on doit tenir compte de l'individualité et des facilités d'apprentissage du trottineur.

LE JEU

Les objectifs: L'importance du jeu croît avec l'enfant. 1) Le *développement physique* s'améliore grâce au jeu. Les muscles se développent, et presque toutes les parties du corps sont exercées. Un surcroît d'énergie se dépense dans un jeu actif. 2) Le *développement social* est stimulé quand le tout-petit prend part à des activités avec d'autres enfants. Même si l'interaction sociale est limitée à cet âge, l'enfant apprécie le *jeu parallèle* (aux côtés d'un autre enfant, non pas *avec* lui). 3) La *valeur thérapeutique* du jeu est autant psychologique que physiologique, car il canalise les impulsions et permet leur expression d'une façon acceptable, tant pour l'enfant que pour l'adulte. Par exemple, un enfant en colère peut soulager sa tension en frappant des planches avec un marteau ou en martelant un ballon. 4) Le jeu est *éducatif*. Le tout-petit, qui joue avec toutes sortes de jouets, apprend à connaître les couleurs, les formes, les grandeurs et les textures du matériel de jeu. 5) Le jeu permet une première approche des *valeurs morales*. L'enfant commence à distinguer le permis du défendu. Il commence à apprendre à ne pas faire mal aux autres enfants, en jouant de façon brutale.

Le trottineur est fort possessif à l'égard de ses jouets. Il les serre contre lui, disant « À moi, à moi ». Mais il apprend, peu à peu, l'importance du partage malgré sa répugnance à prêter ses jouets. On ne doit pas l'obliger à prêter ses jouets avant qu'il arrive à l'âge de comprendre que jouer avec d'autres implique qu'il renonce à certains plaisirs, afin d'avoir la satisfaction de participer à des projets communs.

Ce qui caractérise le jeu. Chaque âge jouit de sa propre façon de jouer. Certaines activités sont communes à tout âge, peu importe le milieu où l'enfant est élevé. Généralement, les enfants aiment s'amuser avec des jouets jusqu'à leur huitième année. Puis, ils préfèrent les jeux qui favorisent l'activité musculaire; ils aiment courir, par exemple. À partir de cet âge, les jeux ou les sports régis par des règlements stricts, prennent une importance primordiale.

Chez le trottineur, le jeu est actif et dépend de son développement psycho-moteur. Vers 13-14 mois la marche en soi est un jeu captivant. L'enfant acquiert aussi une plus grande habileté à se servir de ses bras. À quinze mois, il aime lancer des objets et les ramasser ensuite, les mettre dans des récipients et les en ressortir.

À dix-huit mois, il est extrêmement actif. Puisque son attention est de courte durée, il se déplace librement et fouille partout. L'adulte a de la difficulté à l'empêcher d'explorer les tiroirs. Son équilibre s'est amélioré, et il tire des jouets derrière lui ou porte une poupée ou un animal en peluche dans ses bras. Il aime jouer seul ou regarder jouer les autres, mais n'a pas appris à se livrer avec d'autres à des jeux de groupe. Il remarque les activités de ses parents et essaie de les imiter.

L'enfant de deux ans s'attarde à ses activités plus longtemps qu'un plus petit. Il flâne au cours de ses jeux. Il s'amuse à manipuler le matériel de jeu; il aime pétrir, tapoter, toucher la boue, le sable ou la pâte à modeler. Il joue avec des poupées, enfile de grosses perles et place ses cubes dans un wagon.

Dans le *jeu parallèle,* il se livre aux côtés d'un autre enfant à des activités, telles que la fabrication de gâteaux de glaise. Même si les enfants ne jouent pas effectivement ensemble, ils se stimulent l'un l'autre et le jeu de chacun dure plus longtemps. Il veut être l'ami des autres enfants, mais ne sait comment s'y prendre. Dans ses tentatives, il peut s'attaquer à un autre compagnon, c'est pourquoi un adulte doit toujours surveiller des enfants jouant ensemble. (Suite page 403.)

Tableau 14-1. *Schéma du développement, 15 mois à 2½ ans*

---

15 MOIS

Contrôle moteur (voir aussi fig. 14-5)

À cet âge le trottineur a atteint un palier dans son développement moteur.
Marche seul à 14 mois, mais les pieds écartés pour maintenir son équilibre.
Lorsque cet apprentissage est terminé, marcher devient un jeu pour lui.
Monte l'escalier à quatre pattes.
Construit une tour de 2 cubes.
Lance des objets, les ramasse, les relance. Ceci montre sa nouvelle aptitude à relâcher un objet qu'il tient.
Ouvre des boîtes.
Met son doigt dans des trous.
Tient une tasse en l'entourant de ses doigts. Il a tendance à l'incliner trop vite et à laisser tomber le contenu.
Tient une cuillère et la plonge dans une assiette. Il ne peut pas très bien remplir la cuillère. S'il la porte à sa bouche, il peut la retourner et en verser le contenu sur lui.

Langage et socialisation

Utilise un jargon.
Nomme des images ou des objets familiers.
Répond à des commentaires familiers.
Vocalise ses désirs et montre du doigt l'objet voulu.
Caresse les images dans un livre et tourne les pages.
Fait savoir si sa couche est mouillée.

---

18 MOIS

Développement physique

La fontanelle antérieure est généralement fermée (peut être fermée dès le 12e mois).
L'abdomen est protubérant.

Contrôle moteur (voir fig. 14-6)

Marche et court, les pieds un peu écartés, mais avec plus de stabilité. Il tombe rarement.
Traîne un jouet derrière lui.
Pousse des meubles légers autour de la pièce.
Peut marcher vers le côté et faire marche arrière.
Monte l'escalier et grimpe sur les meubles.
S'assied sur une petite chaise.
Lance un ballon dans une boîte, pousse un cube dans un orifice.
Gribouille vigoureusement. Essaie de tracer des lignes droites.
Distingue entre des coups de crayon droits et courbes.
Peut construire une tour de 3 cubes.
Porte une tasse à ses lèvres, boit bien et renverse rarement le contenu. Tend la tasse à sa mère, ou la laisse tomber à terre.
Peut remplir sa cuillère, mais a de la difficulté à la mettre dans sa bouche. Tend à retourner la cuillère dans sa bouche. En renverse souvent le contenu.

Langage et socialisation

Sait 10 mots.
Utilise des phrases composées d'adjectifs et de noms.
Transfère rapidement son attention d'une chose à une autre. Se déplace rapidement. Explore des tiroirs et des armoires. Met son nez partout.
A une nouvelle conscience des étrangers.
Commence à avoir des accès de colère s'il est contrarié.
Peut résister au sommeil pendant quelque temps après avoir été mis au lit. Appelle sa mère.
Peut contrôler ses évacuations intestinales.
Peut barbouiller avec ses selles.
S'il suce son pouce, l'habitude atteint son point culminant, commençant juste avant le sommeil pour durer toute la nuit.
Se plaît à jouer seul ou à regarder les activités des autres.
Serre son ours en peluche ou sa poupée.
Commence à préférer un jouet ou un objet favori; par exemple une couverture.

Figure 14-5.   L'enfant de 15 mois *A)* marche seul, *B)* monte l'escalier à quatre pattes, *C)* construit une tour de 2 cubes, *D)* tient une tasse en l'entourant de ses doigts, *E)* saisit une cuillère mais renverse son contenu, *F)* caresse une image dans un livre.

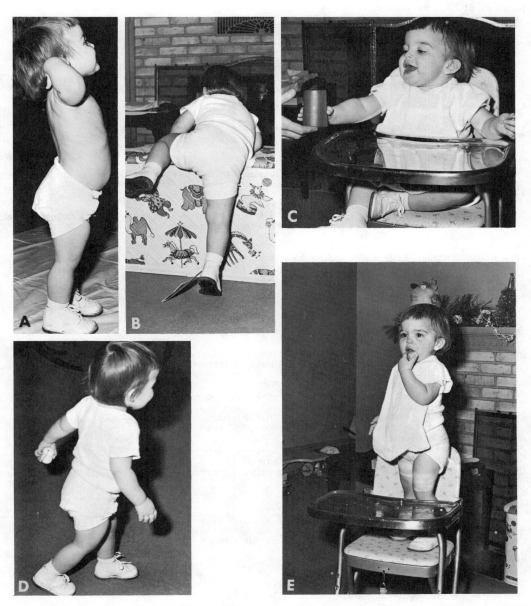

Figure 14-6. L'enfant de 18 mois *A)* a un abdomen protubérant, *B)* grimpe sur un haut coffre à jouets, *C)* tend sa tasse à sa mère, *D)* se déplace rapidement et s'amuse à tirer ses jouets derrière lui, *E)* commence à avoir des accès de colère. Cette enfant manifeste une frustration croissante, car elle veut descendre de sa chaise. Elle eut un accès de colère peu après la prise de cette photo.

Tableau 14-1.   *Schéma du développement, 15 mois à 2½ ans (suite)*

---

2 ANS

Développement physique
    Poids: 12 à 13 kg environ.
    Taille: 80 à 82,5 cm (un gain de 7,5 à 10 cm au cours de la 2e année).
    Pouls: 90-120 par minute.
    Respiration: 20-35 par minute.
    Dentition: 16 dents temporaires environ.
    L'abdomen est moins protubérant qu'à 18 mois.

Contrôle moteur (voir fig. 14-7)
    A une démarche plus assurée, plus régulière.
    Peut courir de façon plus contrôlée, tombe moins souvent, et peut faire une fugue.
    Peut sauter de façon rudimentaire. Tombe lors des premiers essais, car son corps est propulsé en avant.
    Monte et descend l'escalier en mettant les deux pieds à la fois sur une même marche et en se tenant à la rampe ou au mur.
    Construit une tour de 5 cubes ou plus. Peut former un train avec des cubes.
    Peut ouvrir les portes en tournant la poignée.
    Gribouille d'une façon plus contrôlée qu'à 18 mois. Imite le coup de crayon vertical.
    Boit bien dans un verre d'une seule main.
    Peut mettre une cuillère dans sa bouche sans la retourner.

Langage et socialisation
    A un vocabulaire de 300 mots environ. Peut utiliser des pronoms et nomme des objets familiers. Peut raconter ses expériences. Ne se sert plus de jargon.
    Fait des phrases de 3 ou 4 mots.
    Transfère son attention moins rapidement qu'à 18 mois.
    Se comporte comme si les autres enfants étaient des objets, pour les serrer dans ses bras ou bien les écarter. Voudrait se faire des amis, mais ne sait pas comment s'y prendre.
    Ne demande pas souvent de l'aide.
    Obéit à des commandements élémentaires.
    Aide à se déshabiller. Peut enfiler des habits simples.
    Maîtrise son intestin et sa vessie pendant la journée. Exprime son besoin d'aller à la toilette.
    Peut encore barbouiller avec ses selles.
    Suce moins son pouce.
    Ne distingue pas entre le permis et le défendu.
    A moins d'accès de colère relativement violents.
    Est fier de ses habiletés motrices.
    Peut craindre le départ des parents.
    Manifeste plus d'individualité.
    Se plaît au jeu parallèle – pas d'interaction avec d'autres enfants, même s'ils ont une activité identique. L'interaction, si elle a lieu, consiste à saisir les jouets, à donner des coups de pied ou à tirer les cheveux des autres.
    Manipule le matériel de jeu. Flâne souvent.
    Se plaît à jouer avec des poupées, à placer des perles dans une boîte pour les renverser ensuite, à tirer un wagon de cubes empilés.
    Ne peut partager ses possessions. A un sens très net de ce qui est « à moi », mais pas de conscience de ce qui est « à toi ».
    Apprend à ranger ses jouets.
    Aime entendre raconter des histoires illustrées avec des images.
    Commence des jeux qui imitent les activités des parents.
    Prend au lit son jouet préféré, ce qui l'aide à se calmer. Exprime beaucoup de demandes avant de se coucher.

---

30 MOIS (2½ ANS)

Développement physique
    Possède toute sa première dentition temporaire: 20 dents.

Contrôle moteur
    Marche sur la pointe des pieds.
    Se promène sur un petit véhicule.
    Se tient debout sur un seul pied.
    Peut lancer un gros ballon à une distance de 1,20 à 1,50 m.
    Empile 7 ou 8 cubes les uns sur les autres.
    Copie une ligne horizontale ou verticale.

Langage et socialisation
    Les accès de colère peuvent persister.
    Durant les 2e et 3e années, le trottineur commence à développer un concept du moi à partir des comportements des personnes qui ont une signification pour lui – ses parents et d'autres adultes qui l'aiment. Il commence à prendre conscience de lui-même en tant qu'individu, à comprendre quand il peut contrôler certains aspects de son comportement afin de se conformer aux exigences sociales.

Figure 14-7.   L'enfant de 2 ans *A)* monte et descend l'escalier en mettant les deux pieds à la fois sur une même marche et en tenant la rampe, *B)* peut construire une tour de 5 cubes ou plus, *C)* peut ouvrir une porte en tournant la poignée, *D)* aide à se déshabiller.

Figure 14-8. L'enfant de 2½ ans *A)* marche sur la pointe des pieds, *B)* se promène sur un véhicule pour enfants, *C)* peut se tenir debout sur un seul pied, *D)* lance un gros ballon à une distance de 1,20 à 1,50 m, *E)* empile 7 ou 8 cubes les uns sur les autres, *F)* dessine en copiant une ligne horizontale ou verticale.

Par rapport à l'enfant de deux ans, celui de deux ans et demi utilise ses muscles de façon plus raffinée. Il aime manipuler des cubes et des ballons plus petits, mais il a encore besoin de cubes et de ballons plus gros pour jouer. Il a également une coordination motrice assez développée pour se servir d'un petit véhicule enfantin.

Le jeu, à cette période, est ordinairement libre, *spontané,* sans règles. L'enfant explore et s'arrête à volonté. Puisque sa coordination motrice demeure imparfaite, il risque d'être destructif. Il faut examiner ses jouets avec soin pour voir s'il peut se blesser sur des parties cassées. Il ne les casse pas volontairement, mais en les explorant — il les secoue, les pousse et les agite — il leur fait parfois subir des traitements qu'ils ne peuvent supporter. Les jouets peuvent également servir de projectiles lors des crises de colère.

Dès la fin de la deuxième année, la plupart des enfants commencent à imiter les activités quotidiennes des adultes de leur entourage, comme, par exemple, mettre la table. Si les trottineurs jouent avec des plus grands, ils peuvent reconstituer des situations complètes avec parents, maison de poupée, meubles. Quand ils jouent avec des enfants d'âge pré-

Figure 14-10. Un trottineur peut s'attaquer à un autre enfant parce qu'il ne sait pas jouer avec des compagnons. (H. Armstrong Roberts.)

scolaire, les trottineurs assument le rôle des enfants de la famille dont les parents sont les grands de quatre ou cinq ans.

Même le jeune trottineur utilise le jeu *constructif* et fait des gâteaux de glaise, creuse des trous dans le sable et manipule la pâte à modeler. Il aime aussi les crayons et s'en sert pour dessiner ou pour gribouiller sur du papier. Le produit n'est généralement pas utilisable, mais il a une grande valeur éducative. Le tout-petit aime remuer ses bras, marquant le rythme de la musique. Il aime chanter les chansons simples, mais ne peut coordonner avec la musique les mouvements complexes de son corps.

Le tout-petit, à cause de la courte durée de son attention, a besoin d'une grande variété d'activités et de jouets pour rester occupé. L'enfant de deux ans peut quitter rapidement une activité pour une autre, mais y retourner par la suite. Il passe la plupart de ses heures de veille à jouer ou à explorer.

Le jeu du trottineur n'est pas organisé. Il joue quand et où il le veut. Tout peut être prétexte à jouer et il n'a pas besoin d'endroits particuliers, ni de vêtements spéciaux.

Le choix du matériel de jeu. Il faut se souvenir des goûts et caractéristiques du trottineur lors du choix de ses jouets. Il est actif et curieux. Il explore son milieu, utilisant plutôt sa force musculaire. Il aime tirer et pousser des jouets, pédaler, se promener sur un véhicule (stable) et s'asseoir sur un cheval berçant. Les jouets qui s'ouvrent et se ferment

Figure 14-9. Ce tout-petit vient de découvrir un nouveau jeu, dérouler le papier hygiénique. (Courtoisie de Mme Erika Stone et du magazine *Baby Talk.*)

Figure 14-11. L'enfant de 2½ ans développe la maîtrise des petits muscles et en est fier.

le captivent. Il aime jouer avec des poupées et des animaux en peluche. Ses activités de manipulation et de construction comprennent des jeux avec du sable, dans de l'eau, avec de la pâte à modeler, de la peinture digitale, des cubes, des planches (larges) à chevilles, des marteaux de caoutchouc et des crayons de cire, épais et gros. Il aime se faire raconter des histoires, pendant qu'il regarde les images de son livre.

Facteurs de sécurité dans le choix des jouets. Le tout-petit a besoin de jouets avec lesquels il peut jouer en toute sécurité. Il ne faut pas lui donner de jouets acérés, qui ont des arêtes rugueuses, des parties amovibles, qui sont inflammables, ou trop petits comme des billes ou des pièces de monnaie, de peur qu'il ne les aspire ou ne les avale. Les jouets colorés avec de la peinture contenant du plomb sont dangereux, car l'enfant qui les suce ingère un peu de peinture et peut s'intoxiquer. Lors de l'achat d'un jouet, il faut toujours rechercher la mention « non toxique ».

SOIN DES TROTTINEURS

La mère ou l'infirmière doit adapter son comportement à la différence de taille entre elle et l'enfant. Par exemple, lorsqu'elle parle avec l'enfant, l'infirmière doit s'accroupir afin d'être au niveau de ses yeux. Si elle se penche seulement, son image sera écrasante pour le jeune enfant. Le tout-petit n'a pas la résistance physique de l'adulte; il apprécie un toucher léger et une voix douce.

Les attitudes adultes doivent aussi s'adapter à son niveau de compréhension et à sa tolérance à la frustration. Un surcroît de choix le confond, car il ne saisit pas ce que chaque option implique. Il est alors possible que l'enfant ne demande pas ce qui lui ferait le plus plaisir. Il est toutefois souhaitable que l'enfant commence à prendre des décisions simples. Lorsqu'il n'y a pas de choix pour l'enfant, comme se laver les mains avant le repas, des directives douces et positives doivent être utilisées. Le tout-petit, qui a appris à avoir confiance en autrui, comprendra qu'on lui impose des limites, parce qu'on s'intéresse à lui et qu'on veille sur sa sécurité et son bonheur. Demander au trottineur s'il veut accomplir une activité, alors qu'il ne peut répondre non, est susceptible de provoquer frustration et accès de colère.

Les adultes oublient souvent qu'au cours de ses soins quotidiens, le trottineur développe son concept du moi et que son image de lui-même se forme d'après l'attitude des autres envers lui et son comportement. Il est sensible aux expressions faciales de ceux qui l'entourent, y lisant leurs réactions à ce qu'il fait et à ses efforts pour communiquer verbalement.

Le bain

Il est plus simple de donner le bain au trottineur qu'au nourrisson. Il faut que le bain fasse partie d'un horaire régulier qui cadre avec celui de sa mère et du reste de la famille. Beaucoup de mères pensent qu'un bain avant le repas du soir détend l'enfant et établit une atmosphère tranquille avant l'heure du coucher. On peut le baigner dans la baignoire des adultes, mais il faut l'avoir lavée et séchée avant d'y faire couler l'eau pour le bain de l'enfant. Un tapis de caoutchouc l'empêchera de glisser ou de tomber; il doit apprendre très tôt à ne pas jouer avec les robinets. Un adulte doit toujours demeurer avec l'enfant qui est dans l'eau. On évitera les brûlures en ne laissant pas entrer l'enfant dans la baignoire pendant qu'elle se remplit.

Les soins dentaires

La prévention des caries des dents de lait s'avère importante. L'hygiène de la bouche et un régime adéquat sont essentiels à la protection contre la carie.

Dès l'éruption de la dentition temporaire, les dents doivent être brossées. On doit apprendre à l'enfant de deux ans comment utiliser une petite brosse à dents, allant de la gencive vers la couronne. On brosse les dents, non seulement pour les nettoyer, mais aussi pour stimuler les gencives. L'enfant doit apprendre à laver sa brosse à dents et à la ranger adéquatement. Il faut apprendre à l'enfant de trois ou quatre ans à se brosser les dents après chaque repas, et spécialement avant de se coucher. Le faire lui-même affermit son intérêt envers la propreté de ses dents et l'aide à établir une habitude qui lui sera utile pendant tout son développement. Au début, il ne saura pas se servir de la brosse parfaitement, mais il deviendra plus habile avec la pratique. Sa mère surveillera ses efforts aussi longtemps qu'il le faudra.

Les vêtements

Les vêtements devraient être de couleurs claires ou vives, celles que les enfants aiment. Les couleurs vives ont aussi une certaine valeur dans la prévention des accidents, permettant aux enfants d'être facilement visibles, réduisant donc le risque qu'un véhicule les blesse.

Il faudrait aux habits de gros boutons et des boutons-pression, faciles à manipuler, placés là où l'enfant peut les atteindre. Une petite fille doit porter une culotte facile à descendre et un garçon, un pantalon à fermeture-éclair dont il peut s'occuper lui-même. Chaque vêtement doit être facile à mettre et à enlever, pour que l'enfant puisse apprendre à s'habiller et à se déshabiller.

Le tout-petit, faisant son apprentissage sphinctérien, pourra, dès l'âge de deux ou trois ans, aller seul aux toilettes. Lorsque la mère décide que l'enfant est prêt, une culotte d'entraînement peut remplacer les couches. Si l'on met un sous-vêtement propre chaque fois que l'enfant se mouille, même légèrement, il s'habituera au confort d'être sec. Il se sent « aussi grand » que ses frères et sœurs, quand il ne porte plus de couches et peut être changé debout. Une fois habitué à des sous-vêtements, l'enfant ne devrait pas, si possible, porter de couches, sauf pour dormir. Un sous-vêtement propre encourage l'enfant à rester sec.

Les vêtements pour jouer à l'extérieur doivent être chauds, sans être encombrants, puisque l'enfant aime le jeu actif et est contrarié de ne pouvoir remuer aisément. Il doit avoir des bottes pour la pluie et la neige, et un manteau imperméable avec un capuchon ou une casquette. Il est à noter qu'en habituant l'enfant à être trop vêtu, on diminue sa résistance au froid.

Les chaussures

L'enfant qui apprend à marcher n'a pas besoin de souliers; marcher pieds nus favorise le développement harmonieux des structures du pied.

La chaussure sert à protéger du froid ou de ce qui peut blesser le pied; on doit la choisir en fonction du développement de ses pieds et de sa posture. La chaussure doit avoir une semelle ferme et une forme qui suit la configuration du pied, c'est-à-dire, droite à l'intérieur, large au bout et relativement étroite au talon. La semelle ne doit comporter aucun talon, même bas, et doit être rugueuse ou côtelée, afin que l'enfant ne glisse pas; elle doit être deux centimètres plus longue et un centimètre plus large que le pied.

Le pied du petit enfant grandit vite. Il est donc préférable d'acheter des chaussures à prix modéré qui dureront jusqu'à ce qu'elles deviennent trop petites, puis de les remplacer par d'autres d'une pointure supérieure. Si la mère achète des chaussures dispendieuses, elle aura tendance à vouloir s'en servir trop longtemps. Ce faisant, elle risquera de forcer pour faire entrer les pieds de l'enfant dans des chaussures trop petites. Il sera alors non seulement gêné, mais son pied pourra être déformé par la pression d'une chaussure qui le serre; de mauvaises habitudes de marche peuvent en résulter. Les chaussures orthopédiques sont inutiles si l'enfant a des pieds normaux.

L'air, le soleil, et l'exercice

Le tout-petit est actif, curieux, et aime jouer dehors. Quoique l'enfant de dix-huit mois puisse se méfier des étrangers, il aime regarder jouer les autres enfants, s'il est avec sa mère. Il trouve du plaisir au jeu parallèle, mais n'est pas encore prêt pour le jeu collectif. Vers son troisième anniversaire, il arrive au stade où il fait des gestes amicaux aux enfants de son âge et essaie de se joindre aux jeux de groupe. Il aime faire des gâteaux de boue, des trous dans le sable ou, s'il fait chaud, patauger dans l'eau. En hiver, il aime jouer pendant quelque temps dans la neige, mais il ne peut la manipuler comme la boue ou le sable et tolère mal le froid en général.

Le tout-petit a besoin de jouer librement dans des endroits où il peut se promener sans risque. Néanmoins, un adulte doit être à proximité, car on ne peut prévoir les gestes de l'enfant. Malgré son désir de courir librement et de ne pas entendre constamment dire « non, non », il se sent plus en sécurité s'il sait qu'un adulte est avec lui.

Le sommeil

La durée de sommeil de l'enfant, dépend de son âge, de sa santé, de son état de tension, de son activité pendant la journée et de la profondeur de son sommeil. D'un an à trois ans, le temps de sommeil nécessaire diminue progressivement. L'enfant peut résister au sommeil pendant quelques temps après avoir été mis dans son lit; il peut réclamer sa mère en pleurant, demander un verre d'eau ou toute autre chose qui lui assurera de la compagnie.

À deux ans, l'enfant suit ordinairement un rite, sur lequel il insiste lorsqu'il se couche. Entre un et demi et trois ou quatre ans, il aime se coucher avec un jouet préféré. On devrait le lui permettre, puisque cela le détend. Il renoncera à cette habitude, de lui-même, en grandissant. Certains enfants adoptent d'autres moyens pour se détendre avant de s'endormir, tels que remuer la tête, chanter ou parler tout seul. Il ne faut pas imposer de contraintes à ces comportements, car cela ne ferait qu'augmenter sa tension et retarder le sommeil. L'enfant normal abandonne ces habitudes vers trois ans ou peu après, mais il peut les retrouver en période de tension comme, par exemple, lorsqu'il se trouve à l'hôpital.

Le tout-petit dort, en moyenne, douze à quatorze heures sur vingt-quatre, incluant la sieste d'une à deux heures. Il est rare que l'enfant ne s'oppose pas à faire la sieste, mais la mère ne doit pas accorder trop d'importance à son refus de dormir. Elle doit dévêtir l'enfant légèrement, lui donner de l'eau à boire, l'amener à la toilette, puis le mettre confortablement dans son lit. Elle doit fermer les volets ou les rideaux et fermer la porte de la chambre. L'enfant peut avoir un jouet dans son lit, mais s'il en a plusieurs, il aura tendance à les manipuler les uns après les autres, ce qui l'empêchera de dormir. La mère doit s'en tenir strictement à l'heure prévue pour la sieste, même si l'enfant ne dort pas. Ordinairement, le trottineur refuse la sieste par désir d'affirmer son autonomie et s'endort lorsqu'il est mis au lit.

Les cauchemars ou la peur du noir sont à prévoir vers trois ans, mais sont ordinairement plus fréquents à l'âge préscolaire.

Mesures de sécurité

Importance de la prévention des accidents.

Les accidents demeurent la principale cause de mortalité parmi les tout-petits, et entraînent ainsi de nombreuses invalidités et cicatrices permanentes. La majorité des accidents se produit dans, ou près de la maison. Dans un ordre approximatif de fréquence, la mort est causée par: les véhicules à moteur, les brûlures, les empoisonnements, les noyades et les chutes.

Une surveillance attentive est essentielle pour prévenir les accidents.

Même si on constate des progrès dans la prévention des accidents, leur nombre n'a pas diminué aussi rapidement que celui des maladies graves qui étaient jadis les causes majeures de la mort ou de l'invalidité permanente des trottineurs.

Les adultes doivent savoir apprécier le degré de liberté qu'il faut accorder à chaque enfant pour favoriser son développement, mais aussi pour le protéger. Si le trottineur se fait mal, l'adulte doit le consoler, mais expliquer en termes intelligibles la raison de sa blessure et lui donner une leçon de cause à effet, quant aux activités dangereuses et susceptibles de produire de la douleur.

L'infirmière doit assumer la responsabilité d'apprendre aux parents et aux enfants l'importance de la protection contre les accidents, et ceci à chaque entretien, soit à l'hôpital, soit à la clinique, soit à la maison. Le moyen le plus efficace de prévenir les accidents est de fournir à l'enfant des expériences contrôlées et graduées, tout en surveillant son environnement et ses jouets. Il est à souligner que les recherches récentes font ressortir que les accidents surviennent surtout dans des familles ayant des problèmes sérieux et chez des enfants affligés de certains troubles de comportement. Certains enfants semblent plus sujets aux accidents soit à cause de leur audace, de leur distraction ou d'autres causes non élucidées.

Quelques périls précis.

Il est normal que le tout-petit tombe souvent. D'habitude il tombe assis ou à plat ventre sans se faire mal, mais s'il tombe dans un escalier ou d'une certaine hauteur, il peut se blesser sérieusement. Il peut aussi tirer sur une nappe et faire tomber sur lui des objets qui peuvent le blesser, car il ne voit pas le dessus de la table. Des napperons offrent des avantages pratiques et plus de sécurité que les nappes.

On peut satisfaire la curiosité de l'enfant pour ce qu'il y a sur la table ou ce que la mère y fait, en le soulevant ou en le plaçant dans sa chaise. L'enfant moyen est assez grand, à deux ans, pour regarder sur la table s'il est sur la pointe des pieds, mais cette position est inconfortable et n'offre pas une vue complète. De plus, l'enfant est instable et s'il tend la main pour prendre quelque chose, il peut soudainement perdre son équilibre. Ceci le frustre et risque de provoquer un accès de colère ou de larmes.

Mesures de sécurité précises.   Des mesures de sécurité doivent être élaborées pour prévenir les accidents qui risquent d'arriver dans la vie quotidienne de l'enfant.

LES ACCIDENTS DE VÉHICULES À MOTEUR. On apprend au petit enfant à tenir la main de l'adulte pour traverser la rue. On lui rappelle qu'il faut traverser au coin de la rue, plutôt qu'au milieu d'un pâté de maisons. S'il y a des feux, on apprend à l'enfant que le vert signifie « Va » et le rouge « Arrête ». Il est trop jeune pour évaluer la vitesse d'une auto qui avance, par rapport au temps qu'il lui faut pour traverser; mais il l'apprendra, peu à peu, en traversant avec des adultes qui ne le bousculent pas, au changement de feux.

Il faut toujours surveiller un tout-petit, dans une certaine mesure, mais surtout lorsqu'il joue dehors sur son petit véhicule, tricycle ou luge, afin d'éviter qu'il ne sorte rapidement dans la rue entre des voitures en stationnement, ou qu'il ne fasse une glissade vers une artère de circulation. Les parents doivent faire attention lorsqu'ils entrent ou sortent l'auto du garage en marche arrière, car il est difficile de voir un petit enfant qui se trouve directement derrière la voiture.

Le taux de blessures subies par des enfants en promenade dans l'automobile des parents augmente avec le nombre de voitures sur la route. Le danger est le même pour l'enfant que pour l'adulte lors d'une collision ou d'un renversement. On doit l'attacher avec une ceinture de sécurité, pour qu'il ne soit pas propulsé hors de la banquette si la voiture s'arrête brusquement ou subit un accident. Quand un enfant se tient debout sur le siège à côté du conducteur, un arrêt brusque peut le projeter en avant.

LES BRÛLURES. Les allumettes doivent être tenues hors de la portée des jeunes enfants, même si peu d'entre eux savent s'en servir. Dans la cuisine, il faut surveiller de près les enfants, pour qu'ils ne tombent pas contre une cuisinière chaude, ni ne fassent un examen de ses plaques séduisantes avec leurs poêlons et leurs casseroles. Les casseroles avec anses, ou dont le manche est tourné vers l'arrière de la cuisinière, auront moins tendance à attirer son attention et seront moins faciles à toucher que celles dont le manche dépasse à portée de l'enfant. Un radiateur chaud peut causer une brûlure de moindre importance, si un enfant tombe dessus. Les radiateurs modernes en retrait, protégés par un écran fixe, éliminent ce danger. Le tout-petit s'intéresse aux prises électriques et peut y enfoncer une épingle ou un autre morceau de métal. Des fiches de sûreté l'en empêcheront.

LA NOYADE. Les enfants aiment jouer dans l'eau, mais s'ils tombent, ils ne pourront peut-être pas émerger, même d'un endroit peu profond; s'ils tombent dans une grande piscine, ils seront complètement sans défense. Il y a aussi le risque qu'ils se noient à la maison. On ne devrait pas les laisser seuls dans la salle de bain, quand la baignoire est remplie d'eau. La baignoire est glissante et l'enfant peut tomber dans l'eau quand il grimpe sur le bord pour y entrer. S'il se cogne la tête ou tombe dans l'eau très chaude, il pourra s'évanouir et se noyer avant que sa mère n'arrive pour le secourir. Le baquet d'autrefois ne s'utilise que rarement, sauf dans certaines régions rurales. Des accidents graves arrivaient, quand la mère y avait versé de l'eau chaude, puis était partie chercher un seau d'eau froide. Si l'enfant, en son absence, examinait le baquet et y tombait, il était brûlé, même si on le secourait pour éviter une noyade. Des seaux remplis d'eau chaude pour laver le plancher représentent aussi un danger pour des jeunes enfants.

LES CHUTES. L'enfant aime grimper. Avant que sa coordination musculaire et son jugement soient suffisamment développés pour lui permettre de grimper en sécurité, il faudrait prévoir un équipement adapté (par exemple, des petites caisses en bois), et surveiller toutes ses escalades.

Les enfants aiment regarder par la fenêtre, mais sont si petits qu'ils montent souvent sur une chaise pour voir ce qui se passe dehors. Debout sur une chaise ou sur le rebord d'une fenêtre, ils risquent de perdre l'équilibre et de tomber en avant. Chaque fenêtre devrait avoir un grillage que l'enfant ne peut ouvrir.

Une chute dans l'escalier est dangereuse. Un portail devrait être posé en haut et en bas de l'escalier. Les maisons d'un seul étage éliminent le risque de chutes de ce genre. Si la maison a un sous-sol, la porte de l'escalier devrait être fermée à clef.

Les chutes du balcon étaient, autrefois, une source fréquente de blessures pour les petits enfants. Il n'y a plus de danger dans les im-

Figure 14-12. La curiosité du tout-petit peut le mettre en danger. *A)* Des prises électriques et des rallonges usées peuvent être aussi funestes que la chaise électrique. Obstruez les prises et maintenez les rallonges en bon état. (Prudential Insurance Company of America et O. E. Byrd: *Health,* 4e édition). *B)* Une barrière autour du jardin l'empêchera d'errer près d'une piscine ou d'un étang. Apprenez-lui très tôt à nager. *(ibid.) C)* Le tout-petit risque de grimper haut et de tomber. (H. Armstrong Roberts.) *D)* Il peut goûter ou avaler ce qu'il trouve dans cette armoire qui contient des produits de nettoyage et des insecticides. (Photo: Peter Knowlden, Stanford Medical Center; d'O. E. Byrd: *Health,* 4e édition.) *E)* Les médicaments doivent être gardés hors de la portée de l'enfant. (Metropolitan Life Insurance Company.) *F)* Les portes doivent être enlevées des réfrigérateurs non-utilisés pour que les petits enfants ne puissent s'y enfermer. *G)* L'adulte qui recule son auto sans avoir regardé à l'arrière risque d'écraser le trottineur qu'il ne voit pas dans son rétroviseur. *H)* Le trottineur peut s'ébouillanter s'il tire sur le manche de la casserole. *(H. Armstrong Roberts.)*

meubles modernes, surtout dans des complexes urbains, où chaque balcon a son grillage.

Le côté amovible du berceau devrait rester solidement attaché en haut, pour empêcher l'enfant de tomber s'il s'y s'appuie.

L'EMPOISONNEMENT. L'empoisonnement se produit le plus souvent entre un et quatre ans. Les enfants sont curieux quant au goût des substances et peuvent souvent ingérer des liquides, des poudres ou même des solides, qu'ils trouvent dans la maison. Les substances les plus dangereuses pour le jeune enfant sont les médicaments et les produits détersifs.

Les médicaments sont souvent toxiques si l'on en ingère une grande quantité. L'enfant risque d'avaler le contenu d'un flacon, s'il s'agit d'un médicament sans saveur, ou d'un remède dont le goût désagréable est camouflé par un sirop doux ou une couche de sucre. Si on lui présente une pilule en disant « Prends le bonbon! » il est à craindre qu'il vide ensuite toute la bouteille. Toute substance nuisible doit rester hors de la portée du jeune enfant, et les poisons ménagers ou médicinaux doivent être enfermés dans des armoires verrouillées ou placés sur des étagères assez hautes pour que les enfants ne puissent les attraper. On ne doit jamais garder de substances nuisibles dans des récipients destinés à la nourriture. Un produit dangereux doit toujours être rangé au même endroit.

Il faut apprendre aux mères comment agir si un enfant ingère une substance nuisible. Elle doit téléphoner immédiatement au médecin ou à la clinique, ou bien, si elle habite près d'un hôpital, conduire l'enfant à la salle d'urgence. Si elle habite dans une ville dotée d'un centre pour le contrôle des poisons, elle doit y téléphoner sans délai et si elle sait quelle substance l'enfant a ingéré, ainsi que la quantité approximative, elle doit fournir ces renseignements de manière claire et précise. Si l'enfant a avalé le contenu d'une bouteille ou d'une boîte dont les ingrédients sont indiqués, elle doit également donner ces renseignements. Le centre lui expliquera comment procéder au traitement d'urgence et fournira, éventuellement, un transport rapide à l'hôpital. Une voiture de police est toujours disponible dans la plupart des villes. Le récipient d'où le poison a été pris doit être donné au médecin traitant. Si l'enfant vomit spontanément, ou après avoir avalé un émétique, le vomissement doit être soumis à un examen chimique. Ceci est particulièrement important si la mère ne sait pas ce que l'enfant a pris, ou si elle ne connaît pas les ingrédients d'un produit commercial quelconque.

Dans certaines villes, l'infirmière visiteuse a la responsabilité de voir l'enfant après son retour de l'hôpital. Elle aide les parents à corriger la situation qui a entraîné l'accident, et leur donne une explication plus complète sur la croissance et sur le développement de leur enfant, dans le but d'éviter d'autres accidents.

LES PIÈGES QUE SONT LES VIEUX RÉFRIGÉRATEURS. Un réfrigérateur désaffecté, dont la porte ferme hermétiquement, constitue un danger pour tout enfant. Si un jeune enfant se glisse à l'intérieur et que la porte se referme, il pourra suffoquer avant d'être libéré. Pour éviter ce genre d'accident, il faut enlever la porte ou la fermer avec un cadenas ou mieux encore détruire l'appareil.

Le contrôle de la santé

Il est important, au cours des deuxième et troisième années, de prévoir des visites chez le médecin ou au centre de santé. Ces visites peuvent avoir lieu tous les deux à quatre mois durant la deuxième année, et par la suite deux fois par an, pour assurer un contrôle suivi. Les anomalies se dépistent ainsi précocement, et de sérieuses infirmités peuvent être évitées. Le médecin ou l'infirmière enregistre le progrès de la croissance, donne des conseils concernant les mesures de sécurité, la nutrition, l'établissement de bonnes habitudes, et la prévention ou la correction d'habitudes idésirables. On procédera à des immunisations afin de continuer le programme préventif déjà exposé.

Ces visites permettent d'établir une relation amicale qui sera utile plus tard, si l'enfant est malade, et surtout s'il est hospitalisé.

Les soins dentaires et le contrôle de l'hygiène orale quotidienne prennent de l'importance dès que l'enfant possède toute sa dentition temporaire, soit entre deux ans et deux ans et demi. On doit amener l'enfant chez le dentiste tous les quatre ou six mois. Le dentiste moderne, comme le médecin, établit avec l'enfant un rapport qui sera précieux par la suite lorsque des traitements s'imposeront. Le nettoyage des dents, l'application d'un produit à base de fluor, et le traitement de caries superficielles, ne provoquent en général aucune douleur. Le dentiste devrait avoir, envers les enfants, une attitude sympathique, leur expliquer ce qu'il fait et leur permettre de toucher à ses instruments.

LA NUTRITION

La nutrition joue un rôle important dans la santé et la croissance normale de l'enfant. Son régime doit comporter les valeurs nutritives essentielles à son organisme pour lui fournir l'énergie nécessaire et pour maintenir, remplacer et promouvoir la croissance des tissus.

La nourriture doit être répartie en trois repas convenablement espacés. L'enfant a besoin de goûters nutritifs entre ses repas, surtout s'il est très actif. Il sera capable de manger les repas équilibrés, variés et simples qu'on lui donne, s'il n'est pas rendu trop irritable par une faim excessive.

L'influence de la croissance et du développement sur les habitudes alimentaires.

Pendant sa deuxième année, l'enfant a besoin de moins de nourriture qu'auparavant, car sa croissance est moins rapide et il s'intéresse à cet âge davantage à son milieu physique et social. Beaucoup d'enfants manifestent de l'anorexie (*anorexie physiologique*). La mère ne doit pas s'alarmer et se rappeler qu'il faut à l'enfant moins de calories par unité de poids. Il a peut-être acquis des préférences alimentaires, en imitant ses parents ou ses frères et sœurs. Il peut même refuser la nourriture pendant une courte période. Il ne faudrait pas l'obliger à manger. À moins qu'il soit atteint d'une maladie organique, un enfant n'aura de sérieuses difficultés alimentaires que si les adultes ont essayé de lui imposer la qualité et la quantité de ce qu'il doit manger. Si on le force à prendre de la nourriture quand il refuse ses repas, il sera tenté de se révolter, et un véritable problème alimentaire s'ensuivra.

Il faudrait donner à l'enfant une liberté de choix raisonnable quant à la quantité et au genre de nourriture qu'il mange. On doit respecter ses préférences et ses aversions majeures. L'enfant qui n'aime pas certains aliments essentiels devrait être amené graduellement à les accepter; ou bien ils devraient être inclus dans son régime sous une forme déguisée, par exemple en introduisant des carottes en purée dans la purée de pommes de terre. Une crème, un flan (au lait) ou un yaourt fournirait un apport additionnel de lait.

Parfois, un enfant sera exigeant, non seulement pour ce qu'il veut manger, mais aussi pour la vaisselle qu'il utilise et la manière dont la nourriture est présentée. Il aime se servir des ustensiles, même s'il est lent et maladroit. La mère doit se montrer souple et être d'accord avec lui si la question est sans gravité, car s'il est traité ainsi, l'enfant se sentira important et les rapports mère-enfant seront renforcés positivement.

Beaucoup d'enfants sont négativistes à cet âge, surtout quand il s'agit de s'alimenter. Ils peuvent essayer de savoir jusqu'à quelles limites

Figure 14-13. Une enfant de 2 ans peut mettre une cuillère dans sa bouche sans renverser son contenu. Elle peut s'en servir, manger assez bien la plupart des aliments, si elle a déjà eu l'expérience antérieure de s'alimenter elle-même.

leurs parents leur permettront d'agir à leur guise. Or, certaines limites s'imposent. Un enfant est mal à l'aise et souvent craintif si on le laisse tout faire selon sa fantaisie. Il peut refuser de manger, puis avoir faim peu après le repas. Il peut se sentir malade s'il mange trop ou trop rapidement.

L'activité influe sur l'appétit d'un enfant. S'il est raisonnablement actif, son appétit sera stimulé; mais s'il continue longtemps l'exploration curieuse de son entourage, il sera trop fatigué. Un repos avant chaque repas sert à diminuer sa fatigue et sa résistance aux suggestions des adultes. Par ailleurs, un repas peut interrompre son jeu et, par conséquent, il risque de résister s'il est appelé à table.

L'attention du tout-petit étant de courte durée, il lui arrive de quitter la table avant d'avoir fini de manger. Si on l'oblige à demeurer en place, il peut avoir un accès de colère. Ses nouveaux intérêts peuvent souvent servir à le ramener à la table. S'il est allé chercher son ours en peluche, sa mère peut lui dire : « Tiens, faisons une place à table pour ton ourson ».

L'enfant de cet âge observe un rite en mangeant; il peut avoir une grande préférence pour certains ustensiles, certaines assiettes. Il peut insister sur un ordre particulier dans ce qu'il mange. L'adulte ne devrait jamais lui imposer ses propres habitudes, car à cet âge les rites trouvent une place normale dans son développement. Ceux-ci tendront à coïncider avec les coutumes de la famille, si l'enfant est intégré au groupe familial, au lieu d'en être écarté en tant que « bébé ». Il y a maintes raisons pour faire manger un enfant de trois ans en compagnie de ses parents et de ses frères et sœurs; de cette façon, il aura beaucoup moins tendance à acquérir des fantaisies alimentaires que s'il mange tout seul. Les très jeunes enfants sont trop petits pour apprendre « de bonnes manières » à table, mais si toute la famille a de bonnes habitudes, le trottineur les imitera. Le repas est une occasion de rencontre familiale et le trottineur ne devrait pas en être exclu, même s'il y participe du haut de sa chaise d'enfant.

La latéralisation se développe durant cette période. Il faudrait permettre à l'enfant d'utiliser l'une ou l'autre main pour manger. Sa cuillère doit être placée devant lui de sorte qu'il puisse la prendre avec la main qu'il préfère.

Il est souhaitable d'offrir une variété d'aliments, pour que l'enfant apprenne à apprécier les goûts divers. Il est souvent difficile d'ajouter de nouveaux aliments, parce que la discrimination gustative, développée chez l'enfant, lui permet de découvrir et d'évaluer les nouvelles textures, les nouvelles saveurs.

Développement de l'habileté à se nourrir. La capacité et le désir de se nourrir seul diffère d'un enfant à l'autre. Cependant, voici la progression typique dans ce domaine.

12-15 mois – Il boit dans une tasse qu'il tient lui-même.

15-18 mois – Il tient sa propre cuillère. La mère devrait étaler un journal par terre, et l'enfant devrait porter un bavoir qui le protège bien. On ne devrait pas insister pour l'aider, mais offrir de l'aide s'il en a besoin. La vaisselle doit être incassable.

24 mois – Il se nourrit assez bien seul, s'il a été initié assez tôt. Sa mère, pour sa part, ne devrait pas le faire manger sous le prétexte d'éviter des saletés.

Le régime alimentaire. Le tableau 14-2 indique les rations nutritives recommandées pour les enfants entre un et trois ans.

Suggestions précises. Dès l'âge de dix-huit mois ou deux ans, l'enfant devrait manger la même nourriture que les adultes et aux mêmes heures que toute la famille. On pourrait retenir les conseils suivants.

1) Servir de petites quantités d'aliments. L'enfant aime les aliments simples, et les mange un à la fois.

2) Hacher ou émincer les aliments.

3) Donner des aliments crus ou en bâtonnets que l'enfant peut facilement saisir et porter à sa bouche: céleri, carottes coupées, cubes de fromage, etc.

4) Le régime quotidien doit inclure (un régime déterminé tiendra compte de la culture de la famille et des préférences qu'elle engendre):

   a) une portion de viande ou de poisson; un œuf ou du fromage chaque jour

   b) une portion de foie (ou plus) par semaine

   c) deux portions ou plus par jour de légumes verts et jaunes

   d) deux portions ou plus de fruits par jour dont un jus d'agrumes ou d'autres fruits crus ou en compote

   e) des céréales et du pain (assez pour fournir les calories nécessaires)

   f) du beurre ou de la margarine

   g) du lait, au maximum un demi-litre, une partie de celui-ci peut être utilisée pour la préparation des mets, ou mélangée à des céréales.

5) Faire en sorte que l'enfant mange à sa faim, des aliments nutritifs, évitant de lui donner trop de bonbons, de gâteaux ou de crème glacée, etc. Des goûters nutritifs peuvent se donner entre les repas.

6) Donner les vitamines suggérées par le médecin.

7) Puisque l'enfant croît moins rapidement, il mangera moins qu'à la fin de sa première année.

Aliments à éviter. Le jeune enfant ne regrette pas ce qu'il n'a jamais eu et ce dont il n'a pas besoin. Les aliments à éviter sont le chocolat, le sucre, de grandes quantités de graisse (difficile à digérer), des noix et des pépins (qui risquent d'être insuffisamment mâchés ou aspirés), des aliments assaisonnés et des stimulants, comme le thé et le café.

L'importance de saines habitudes alimentaires. Durant la deuxième année jusqu'à l'âge scolaire, se développent les habitudes et les attitudes alimentaires qui tendent à demeurer toute la vie. Trois ou quatre repas simples, par jour, devraient être servis à des intervalles réguliers, dans une atmosphère où l'enfant se sent en sécurité. Certains enfants, qui mangent peu à la fois, ont besoin d'une collation le matin, l'après-midi ou le soir. Le goûter ne devrait pas être servi à un moment ou en une quantité qui affecte l'appétit normal à l'heure du repas.

LA SÉPARATION

Signification pour le tout-petit. Même si sa sécurité dépend des deux parents, le

Tableau 14-2. *Rations quotidiennes nutritives recommandées pour les enfants âgés de 1 à 3 ans*

	1 – 2 ANS POIDS – 12 kg TAILLE – 81 cm		2 – 3 ANS POIDS – 14 kg TAILLE – 91 cm	
Calories	1 100		1 250	
Protéines	25	g	25	g
Vitamines liposolubles				
Vitamine A	2 000	U.I.	2 000	U.I.
Vitamine D	400	U.I.	400	U.I.
Vitamine E	10	U.I.	10	U.I.
Vitamines hydrosolubles				
Acide ascorbique (vit. C)	40	mg	40	mg
Acide folique	0,1	mg	0,2	mg
Acide nicotinique (équivalents)	8	mg	8	mg
Riboflavine	0,6	mg	0,7	mg
Thiamine	0,6	mg	0,6	mg
Vitamine B_6	0,5	mg	0,6	mg
Vitamine B_{12}	2,0	μg	2,5	μg
Minéraux				
Calcium	0,7	g	0,8	g
Phosphore	0,7	g	0,8	g
Iode	55	μg	60	μg
Fer	15	mg	15	mg
Magnésium	100	mg	150	mg

trottineur est plus lié à sa mère qu'à tout autre adulte ou qu'à ses frères et sœurs. Il sait que sa mère est une personne très spéciale. Le besoin qu'il a de son amour est aussi grand que son besoin de nourriture. Son attachement à elle est possessif et égoïste. Il croit qu'elle peut le protéger contre tout danger.

Dès la fin de sa première année, l'enfant se rend compte que sa mère est celle qui l'aime, le protège et lui fournit des expériences agréables. Il croit ne pouvoir survivre sans elle. Pour cette raison, il a peur quand il la perd de vue. Le jeu enfantin de « coucou » constitue pour l'enfant un moyen de maîtriser sa peur d'être séparé de sa mère. Puisqu'il peut la faire revenir facilement, il découvre qu'il peut ainsi maîtriser son anxiété avec plus de facilité. Il se rend compte plus tard, dans le jeu de « cache-cache », que sa mère le cherchera, si elle ne le voit pas. Ainsi, il apprend peu à peu que sa propre action suffit pour faire revenir sa mère.

Nous savons, d'après son comportement, qu'un enfant a besoin de sa mère ou d'un substitut stable et aimant, comme compagnie quasi constante jusqu'à son troisième anniversaire. À l'âge préscolaire, il acquiert une plus grande maîtrise de sa peur d'être séparé d'elle et il apprend à la partager avec d'autres.

Nécessité d'une séparation progressive. Le jeune enfant ne peut comprendre pourquoi il doit être séparé de sa mère. Or, en évoluant, il prend conscience du fait qu'il existe d'autres personnes (son père, des frères et sœurs), que sa mère aime aussi. Il peut avoir du ressentiment à leur égard; cependant sa mère veut que les autres l'aiment et que, lui les aime aussi. À ce stade, il faut aider l'enfant à accepter ses frères et sœurs, mais il faut également lui montrer que, s'il est hostile envers eux quelquefois, il sera aimé tout de même. Il faut subvenir à tous ses besoins, car, pour lui, cela signifie être aimé. Puisque la mère s'attend à ce que le jeune enfant, sécurisé par son amour, ressemble à ses frères et sœurs, il reçoit ainsi ses premières leçons de socialisation.

Pendant cette évolution, sa mère peut travailler en dehors du foyer, ou continuer ses études, et ne plus être constamment avec lui. Elle peut tomber malade ou aller à l'hôpital pour accoucher de nouveau. L'enfant lui-même, s'il est malade ou blessé, peut être hospitalisé. Il est bon de préparer graduellement le trottineur à se séparer de sa mère en introduisant quelques adultes dans sa vie, tels grands-parents, oncles, tantes ou amis. De plus, il est utile que le trottineur soit quelquefois gardé à la maison par une autre personne que sa mère afin que, progressivement, il assume son individualité et puisse supporter une séparation inévitablement plus longue.

Durant les deuxième et troisième années, le trottineur commence à développer un concept du moi, à partir des comportements des personnes auxquelles il est attaché – ses parents et d'autres adultes qui l'aiment. Il commence à prendre conscience de lui-même en tant qu'individu, à savoir qu'il peut contrôler certains aspects de son comportement afin de se conformer aux exigences de sa société.

RÉFÉRENCES

Livres et documents officiels

Gesell, A. et Ilg, F.: *Le jeune enfant dans la civilisation moderne.* Paris, P.U.F., 6ᵉ éd. 1967.
Illingworth, R. S. (édit.): *The Normal Child: Some Problems of the First Five Years and Their Treatment.* 4ᵉ éd. Baltimore, Williams & Wilkins Company, 1970.
Langevin, C.: *Le langage de votre enfant.* Québec, P.U.L., 1970.
Leriche, A. M.: *La peur.* Paris, Armand Colin, 1975.
Lidz, T.: *The Person: His Development Throughout the Life Cycle.* New York, Basic Books, Inc., 1968.
Ministère de la Santé nationale et du Bien-être social: *Le sommeil. La jalousie. La destructivité. Il suce son pouce. Habitudes alimentaires. La colère. La discipline. La peur.* Division de l'hygiène mentale, Ottawa, Gouvernement du Canada.
Ministère de la Santé nationale et du Bien-être social: *Croissance de un an à six ans.* Division de l'hygiène maternelle et infantile. Ottawa, Gouvernement du Canada.
Seeman, M.: *Les troubles du langage chez l'enfant.* Québec, P.U.L., 1967.
Senn, M. J. E. et Solnit, A. J.: *Problems in Child Behavior & Development.* Philadelphie, Lea & Febiger, 1968.
Yamamoto, K.: *The Child and His Image: Self Concept in the Early Years.* Boston, Houghton-Mifflin Company, 1972.

Articles

Austin, G., Foster, W. et Richards, J. C.: Pediatric Screening Examinations in Private Practice. *Pediatrics,* 41:115, janvier 1968.
Azarnoff, P.: A play Program in a Pediatric Clinic. *Children,* 17:218, novembre-décembre 1970.
Degrez, F.: Le savez-vous? Il marche. *L'enfant,* 43:207, 3, 1968.
Done, A. K. et autres: Evaluations of Safety Packaging for the Protection of Children. *Pediatrics,* 48:613, octobre 1971.
Engleman, J. L., Engleman, E. G. et Fink, D. L.: Playroom in the Out-patient Clinic. *Hospitals,* 44:46, 1 novembre 1970.
Kohler, W. et autres: Sleep Patterns in 2-Year-Old Children. *J. Pediat.,* 72:228, 2, 1968.
Lane, M. F. et autres: Child-Resistant Medicine Containers: Experience in the Home. *Am. J. Pub. Health,* 61:1861, septembre 1971.
Milis, M.: Comment faciliter l'acquisition du langage. *L'enfant,* 43:119, 2, 1968.
Robischon, P.: Pica Practice and Other Hand-Mouth Behavior and Children's Developmental Level. *Nursing Research,* 20:4, janvier-février 1971.
Scherz, R. G., Latham, G. H. et Stracener, C. E.: Child-Resistant Containers Can Prevent Poisoning. *Pediatrics,* 43:84, janvier 1969.
Sims, N. H., Seidel, H. M. et Cooke, R. E.: A Structured Approach to the Use of Physician Extenders in Well-Child Evaluations. *J. Pediat.,* 79:151, juillet 1971.
Smith, D. E. et autres: The Hippie Communal Movement: Effects on Child Birth and Development. *Am. J. Orthopsychiat.,* 40:527, avril 1970.
Spencer, V. L.: A Pilot Study to Determine Why Mothers Attend Child Health Conferences. *Canad. J. Pub. Health,* 60:116, mars 1969.
Stehbens, J. A. et Silber, D. L.: Parental Expectations in Toilet Training. *Pediatrics,* 48:451, septembre 1971.

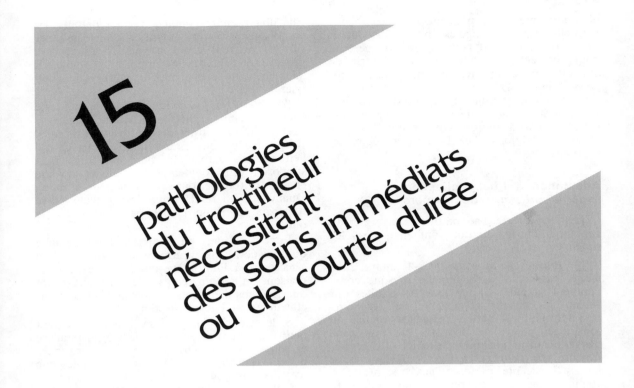

15
pathologies du trottineur nécessitant des soins immédiats ou de courte durée

HOSPITALISATION DU TROTTINEUR

Dans l'esprit du jeune enfant ses parents sont indispensables à sa survie. C'est pourquoi, quand ceux-ci le conduisent à l'hôpital et le confient au personnel hospitalier, il peut donner une fausse interprétation à la raison de la séparation. Il peut voir dans l'hospitalisation une punition pour quelque chose qu'il a fait ou la considérer comme une perte totale de leur amour. L'enfant ne sait plus ce qu'on attend de lui dans cette situation étrange; il craint d'être lésé physiquement et il peut devenir très anxieux s'il croit qu'il ne reverra plus ses parents. Ceci peut amener un retour à un comportement infantile: il devient plus exigeant et égocentrique.

L'infirmière doit reconnaître ce besoin qu'éprouve l'enfant de régresser. Elle doit gagner sa confiance pour qu'il accepte de dépendre d'elle durant sa maladie. Le jeune enfant malade peut devenir méfiant à l'égard des adultes et l'infirmière doit l'aider à reprendre confiance envers autrui.

Le traumatisme de la séparation menace surtout les jeunes enfants âgés de 7 ou 8 mois jusqu'à 3 ans. L'enfant établit à ce moment la différence entre les étrangers et les personnes qui prennent habituellement soin de lui et il est très dépendant de l'adulte.

Plusieurs facteurs entrent en jeu dans les réactions plus ou moins vives du trottineur à l'hospitalisation et à la séparation de sa famille: la qualité de sa relation affective avec sa mère, son niveau de développement, la fréquence et la durée des séparations antérieures, la préparation de l'enfant à l'hospitalisation actuelle, les conditions entourant son admission, la durée des visites de ses parents ainsi que leurs réactions.

L'adaptation du trottineur au milieu hospitalier et à sa maladie dépend de la qualité des soins qui lui sont prodigués, de la stimulation sensori-motrice qu'il reçoit et de sa propre personnalité.

Réactions spécifiques du trottineur hospitalisé

Lors de son hospitalisation, le jeune enfant éprouve des craintes fondamentales: peur de perdre l'amour de ses parents, peur de l'inconnu et peur d'être puni. Trop jeune pour qu'on puisse le raisonner, il sait seulement que son

415

père ou sa mère ne répondent pas à ses appels. Virtuellement, son angoisse nuit à l'évolution de sa personnalité et peut s'avérer dangereuse pour son état physique. Il peut souffrir de difficultés de comportement, mal dormir, régresser dans ses habitudes de propreté et exprimer colère et chagrin de façon excessive. Son anxiété peut l'empêcher de jouer comme il le faisait à la maison. On rencontre surtout de telles réactions chez l'enfant de deux ou trois ans.

Adaptation à l'hospitalisation sans la présence de la mère

Les étapes de l'adaptation apparente de l'enfant à l'hospitalisation sont en général les suivantes:

1) *Phase de protestation.* L'enfant submergé par son chagrin appelle presque constamment sa mère. Il repousse les adultes qui veulent le consoler et peut refuser les soins de l'infirmière. Il hurle, secoue les ridelles de son lit et pleure de détresse. Ne possédant pas de concepts adéquats de temps et d'avenir, il pense que sa mère l'a abandonné pour toujours. Il accepte parfois d'être réconforté à condition de ne pas regarder le visage de l'adulte qui le berce. L'infirmière doit respecter la peine profonde de l'enfant et ne pas exiger qu'il camoufle ses sentiments. Elle doit l'assurer que sa maman reviendra et demeurer près de lui, même s'il ne semble pas apprécier sa présence. Peu à peu, il acceptera d'être consolé.

2) *Phase de retrait.* L'enfant sombre dans un état dépressif. Il se retire en lui-même, accepte les soins sans réagir et n'appelle plus sa mère. Il peut sucer son pouce, s'attacher désespérément à un objet qui lui vient de sa mère et régresser vers des comportements antérieurs. L'enfant continent peut souiller son lit, celui qui avait commencé à parler peut cesser de s'exprimer verbalement. Il peut même refuser de quitter l'endroit où il a vu sa mère pour la dernière fois. Il présente une poignante expression de désespoir. De courtes visites de ses parents le perturbent encore davantage, parce qu'il n'a pas le temps d'exprimer la gamme des sentiments qu'il éprouve: colère, ressentiment, haine, amour, chagrin, que déjà ils le quittent de nouveau pour retourner à la maison.

L'infirmière peut aider le trottineur en lui offrant une présence amicale stable et en l'assurant que sa mère l'aime toujours et qu'elle reviendra le voir. Elle doit stimuler l'enfant à exprimer ses sentiments, surtout par le jeu.

Elle doit prendre contact avec les parents, les encourager à visiter l'enfant et à lui téléphoner s'ils ne peuvent venir le voir. Si l'infirmière procure à l'enfant un complément maternel adéquat, cette phase peut ne durer que quelques heures.

3) *Phase de négation.* Si l'enfant reste assez longtemps à l'hôpital, il atteint finalement le stade où toute trace de dépression a disparu. Il éprouve un plus grand intérêt pour ce qui l'entoure et semble être heureux. Il ne peut supporter plus longtemps la violence de son chagrin et refoule tout sentiment pour sa mère. Quand elle lui rend visite, c'est à peine s'il la remarque et il ne pleure pas quand elle le quitte.

Lors du départ de l'hôpital, il est possible qu'il ne désire pas rentrer à la maison et qu'il s'accroche à l'infirmière qui le soignait. À la maison, un certain temps peut s'écouler avant que les liens mère-enfant redeviennent ce qu'ils étaient avant l'hospitalisation.

Si le séjour à l'hôpital se prolonge, l'enfant peut finalement s'habituer à la vie hospitalière et, apparemment, n'avoir besoin ni de sa mère ni des infirmières. L'atteinte psychologique n'est pas toujours durable, toutefois certains enfants peuvent être gravement troublés et perdre la faculté d'établir des liens significatifs avec autrui.

Il arrive souvent que le jeune malade devienne l'enfant gâté de toute l'équipe. Néanmoins, personne n'a vraiment le temps ni un intérêt suffisant pour former la relation affectueuse nécessaire à sa stabilité, à la promotion de sa croissance et de son développement. Cette situation est dangereuse parce que l'équipe a l'impression de cajoler, de gâter l'enfant, alors qu'elle ne fait qu'entretenir le vide émotif de sa vie.

Ces réactions du trottineur ont été décrites surtout par J. Robertson et J. Bowlby dans les années 1950. Il est possible maintenant d'éviter la douloureuse et poignante deuxième phase et d'empêcher la réorganisation pathologique de la personnalité traduite par la troisième phase. Lorsque la mère peut cohabiter avec l'enfant ou lui rendre visite quotidiennement ou encore lorsqu'un substitut maternel adéquat et stable est fourni à l'enfant, on peut prévenir des dégâts émotifs qui semblaient trop facilement inévitables à l'équipe de santé.

Hospitalisation du trottineur sans la présence de la mère

Voici quelques raisons qui font que toutes les mères ne peuvent séjourner à l'hôpital avec leur enfant. 1) On ne peut prendre des dispositions pour le soin des autres enfants à la maison; 2) certains enfants, psychiquement perturbés, semblent plus troublés par la présence de la mère que lorsqu'ils sont seuls, toutefois les recherches sont loin d'être concluantes à ce sujet; 3) quelques mères trop anxieuses et désorientées s'avèrent incapables de soigner leur enfant malade; elles pourraient être encouragées à demeurer avec l'enfant et à ne participer que progressivement à ses soins; 4) l'aménagement de nombreuses unités pédiatriques ne permet pas toujours la possibilité de cohabitation mère-enfant et le personnel n'encourage pas les parents à demeurer auprès de l'enfant pendant de longues périodes. En fait, les première et dernière raisons sont les plus fréquentes.

Visite de la mère. Le jeune enfant séparé de sa mère a beaucoup de difficulté à vaincre la peur de perdre ses parents pour toujours. Il ne peut comprendre la nécessité d'une telle séparation ni les règlements de l'hôpital qui interdisent la présence de sa mère à certains moments. Il croit donc que celle-ci ne veut pas rester avec lui. Il est irrité, se sent seul et effrayé. Ces sentiments de colère, de frayeur et de solitude désespérée s'avèrent préjudiciables au point de vue psychologique et, par interaction psychosomatique, le deviennent également au point de vue physiologique.

Figure 15-1. La panique s'empare de cette fillette au moment où sa mère doit la quitter.

Quand sa mère lui rend visite, il exprimera une émotion très vive. Cette réaction est saine, parce qu'elle lui évite de refouler des sentiments qu'il pourrait exprimer plus tard de façon détournée ou inappropriée. Cette réaction peut survenir dès que l'enfant voit sa mère, au cours de la visite, ou lorsqu'elle est sur le point de le quitter. Si, en dépit de sa colère, il s'accroche à elle et pleure, la mère peut s'en trouver tellement affligée qu'elle redoutera une nouvelle visite. En même temps, cependant, elle peut éprouver une certaine satisfaction face à cette évidente manifestation de dépendance. L'infirmière doit comprendre et expliquer à la mère la signification du comportement de l'enfant et, si possible, l'encourager à rester plus longtemps avec lui.

Visites de durée illimitée. Un nombre sans cesse grandissant d'hôpitaux permettent des visites à toute heure du jour. Même si cet arrangement ne satisfait pas aussi pleinement l'enfant que la présence continuelle de sa mère, il reste de loin préférable aux visites limitées à certaines heures de la journée.

Quand ses parents sont avec lui, l'enfant peut exprimer ses sentiments d'angoisse et de colère, plutôt que de les refouler jusqu'à ce qu'il soit de retour à la maison.

Le personnel hospitalier a souvent l'impression que ces visites, à toute heure de la journée, créent une certaine confusion dans l'organisation de l'unité de soins. On peut éviter cet embarras, si on montre aux parents la manière de s'occuper de l'enfant et si on intègre leurs services à la routine quotidienne. En général, les heures de visite sans restriction améliorent les relations entre les parents et le personnel hospitalier.

Si la mère se trouve dans l'impossibilité de visiter souvent son enfant, l'infirmière doit comprendre la solitude et l'anxiété du petit malade. Elle doit lui dire qu'elle sait qu'il désire sa mère et veut rentrer à la maison avec elle. Elle ne doit pas essayer de la lui faire oublier. Elle doit plutôt l'aider à comprendre que les liens étroits qui l'unissent à sa mère ne sont pas rompus, même si celle-ci n'est pas présente. L'infirmière doit lui rendre la vie aussi agréable que possible.

Parmi les mesures qui peuvent aider l'enfant à se sentir en sécurité signalons, entre autres, le fait de lui permettre d'avoir avec lui son jouet préféré ou sa couverture favorite, de lui donner un mouchoir, un gant ou tout autre objet appartenant à sa mère lui rappelant qu'elle doit revenir, de lui procurer des cartes à envoyer à sa mère ou de collectionner celles que celle-ci lui envoie. Si c'est possible, il peut téléphoner fréquemment à ses parents.

Quand elle quitte l'enfant, la mère doit essayer d'être ferme et sincère, en lui expliquant les motifs de son départ et en lui indiquant le moment de son retour. Elle ne doit pas quitter l'unité à l'insu de l'enfant parce qu'elle craint ses pleurs. L'infirmière doit rester avec lui après les heures de visite jusqu'à l'apaisement de la douleur causée par le départ de sa mère.

Si la mère ne peut rester avec l'enfant ou lui rendre visite souvent, il faudrait l'intégrer à un petit groupe de malades dont une seule infirmière s'occupe régulièrement. Il faudrait qu'elle soit remplacée durant ses jours de repos par une infirmière que les enfants connaissent bien. On peut suggérer aux parents d'apporter à l'enfant des photographies de sa famille et de son animal favori, s'il y a lieu.

Problèmes que posent les soins du trottineur quand sa mère est absente

Rotation du personnel. Plusieurs infirmières et auxiliaires s'occupent des soins quotidiens de l'enfant, de sorte qu'aucune ne s'attache réellement à lui. L'enfant recherche alors des satisfactions matérielles, et établit des relations superficielles avec tout adulte qui l'approche. Lorsque différentes infirmières ont à s'occuper du trottineur, il s'avère spécialement important pour elles de suivre le plan de soins spécifiques établi pour l'enfant. En agissant ainsi, chaque infirmière connaîtra les jouets et les aliments favoris, sa façon préférée de prendre un médicament et le moment le plus favorable pour lui donner ses traitements. On tentera ainsi d'obtenir une certaine uniformité dans les soins. L'infirmière ne doit jamais brusquer l'enfant, ni exiger qu'il la traite en amie s'il la voit pour la première fois. Elle doit se souvenir que l'enfant doit une fois de plus, s'adapter à un adulte qu'il ne connaît pas et apprendre à lui faire confiance.

Pour favoriser une alimentation appropriée. Très souvent, un jeune enfant malade refuse de prendre la quantité de liquides ou d'aliments nécessaire pour accélérer sa guérison. Certaines infirmières s'inquiètent quand un jeune enfant refuse de manger, parce que ceci va à l'encontre de l'idée qu'elles ont d'elles-mêmes en tant que substitut maternel. Elles doivent se rappeler qu'il y a une cause à tout comportement, et que si elles peuvent la trouver et agir en conséquence, très souvent, le comportement se modifiera. En d'autres termes, le fait de forcer l'enfant à manger n'apportera pas de solution au problème.

Voici quelques raisons qui peuvent expliquer les problèmes d'alimentation: l'enfant ne grandit plus aussi rapidement que durant sa première année et ses besoins en nourriture ont diminué; il est en période de négativisme, en conflit entre l'acceptation de sa dépendance vis-à-vis des autres et l'affirmation de sa propre personnalité; il réagit au traumatisme causé par son hospitalisation et la séparation d'avec les parents; il peut ne pas aimer les aliments servis à l'hôpital, ou il souffre d'une anorexie provoquée par sa maladie. L'infirmière qui prend conscience des différentes raisons de ce comportement, peut encourager la mère à rendre des visites plus fréquentes, surtout aux heures des repas, et être elle-même détendue quand elle encourage l'enfant à manger. Elle devrait lui consacrer plus de temps, pour gagner sa confiance et lui accorder plus d'indépendance dans la mesure de ses possibilités, ou lui permettre d'être dépendant s'il le désire. Elle peut demander à la mère une liste des aliments préférés de l'enfant, transformer la période de repas en jeux. Une fois que l'enfant acquiert le contrôle de lui-même, son appétit s'améliore assez souvent. L'infirmière doit comprendre qu'un enfant heureux et en bonne santé mangera sans beaucoup d'aide, mais qu'un enfant malheureux et malade ne mangera que s'il est aidé par des adultes compréhensifs.

Contrôle des sphincters ou habitudes de toilette. L'enfant séparé de sa mère peut régresser dans ses fonctions corporelles et sociales et son contrôle sphinctérien s'en trouve perturbé. L'infirmière doit connaître le stade de développement de l'enfant avant son admission à l'hôpital. Elle doit questionner la mère sur les méthodes (équipement, mots et fréquence des « séances » sur le siège de toilette ou sur le pot) employées à la maison afin que l'on puisse, dans la mesure du possible, les continuer à l'hôpital. L'infirmière doit éviter d'être trop stricte ou trop exigeante, étant donné que l'enfant subit une tension émotive très forte due à l'impression d'abandon qu'il ressent. Il faut lui apprendre l'usage du bassin de lit et de l'urinal en présence de sa mère; son approbation le motivera à employer le nouvel équipement.

Si un jeune enfant n'a pas encore acquis d'habitudes de propreté, il ne faut pas essayer de les lui inculquer lors de son séjour à l'hôpital. Si sa convalescence se prolonge, on pourra commencer l'apprentissage lorsqu'il se sentira plus fort. Si l'on veut que l'expérience réussisse, sa mère et une infirmière pour laquelle l'enfant éprouve de l'affection doivent s'en occuper.

L'infirmière peut éprouver une certaine répulsion en voyant couches, vêtements et lit souillés par l'urine et les selles de l'enfant qui s'est amusé à les étendre autour de lui. Elle doit apprendre à contrôler ses sentiments et à comprendre le plaisir instinctif qu'éprouve le jeune enfant face aux substances qu'il excrète.

Il faut que l'infirmière se prépare à accepter certains « accidents » qui se produiront inévitablement. Les jeunes enfants, qui ont acquis les contrôles vésical et anal, ont tendance à être troublés lorsqu'un « accident » arrive. Il est essentiel qu'ils ne lient pas de tels événements à une attitude de rejet de la part des infirmières.

Certains enfants se souillent dans le but d'attirer l'attention, de punir les parents qui les ont laissés à l'hôpital, ou en guise de représailles contre les infirmières qui manquent de compréhension face à leurs besoins. Ils peuvent refuser de demander le bassin de lit ou l'urinal. Si l'infirmière réprimande un enfant à la suite d'un « accident », celui-ci peut recommencer son « exploit » pour attirer son attention ou l'ennuyer.

L'infirmière doit s'efforcer de découvrir la cause de ce comportement et par toutes sortes de moyens démontrer à l'enfant que l'on s'occupe de lui et ainsi, l'aider à coopérer. Celui qui a recours à de tels procédés se trouve dans un état de trouble émotif et l'infirmière doit l'aider à résoudre son problème d'une manière plus satisfaisante. Elle ne doit pas oublier que quantité de jeux, tels que terre glaise, seau et pelle etc. permettent à l'enfant de satisfaire, de façon symbolique les besoins, normaux à cet âge, de salir, remplir et vider.

Hospitalisation du jeune enfant avec la présence de la mère

Le meilleur moyen d'éviter le traumatisme d'une hospitalisation à un enfant est de le soigner à domicile lorsqu'il est malade. S'il est indispensable qu'il reçoive des soins à l'hôpital, on ne doit ménager aucun effort pour permettre à sa mère de demeurer avec lui.

À leur arrivée à l'unité pédiatrique on conduit d'abord l'enfant et sa mère jusqu'au lit. L'infirmière doit avoir une attitude amicale, permettre à la mère de s'asseoir et de se détendre. Même si l'infirmière manifeste un intérêt affectueux à l'enfant, elle ne doit pas jouer le rôle de substitut de la mère.

Les formalités d'admission doivent être soigneusement expliquées. L'infirmière doit accepter que la mère extériorise son anxiété et lui expliquer comment elle peut aider son enfant en milieu hospitalier.

Comme l'enfant adopte souvent les attitudes de sa mère, celle-ci doit être aussi calme que possible et lui procurer un support psychologique. Par son attitude coopérative avec l'infirmière, elle augmentera la confiance de l'enfant envers celle qui le soigne. Elle peut expliquer à l'enfant les habitudes de l'hôpital et la façon de se servir de l'équipement nouveau. S'il ne peut employer le pot, la mère lui expliquera l'emploi du bassin de lit et de l'urinal en des mots qu'il comprendra. Elle peut le déshabiller elle-même et lui mettre ses vêtements d'hôpital si c'est nécessaire. Dans certains hôpitaux, les enfants portent leurs vêtements habituels au cours de la journée.

L'infirmière doit s'informer auprès de la mère des méthodes qu'elle emploie à la maison pour que le personnel hospitalier puisse les suivre le plus fidèlement possible. Si l'état de l'enfant le permet, l'infirmière doit présenter la mère et l'enfant aux autres parents et enfants. Elle doit renseigner la mère sur toutes les facilités qui existent dans l'unité pour que celle-ci puisse participer convenablement aux soins de l'enfant. La mère doit expliquer à l'enfant qu'elle restera avec lui, afin de lui éviter tout sentiment de crainte à la vue de ceux qui sont restés seuls.

On place dans l'unité ou dans la chambre de l'enfant un lit pliant ou une chaise-lit pour la mère. Elle peut ainsi y rester jour et nuit.

Le personnel hospitalier ne comprend pas toujours les avantages qu'il y a à ce que la mère demeure avec son enfant et redoute les difficultés qui peuvent se présenter. Toutefois, plus on permet à la mère de satisfaire ses sentiments maternels en soignant son enfant (le nourrir et le baigner), moins elle sera anxieuse. Elle l'aidera à suivre son régime si elle en comprend la nécessité. Si l'état physique de l'enfant le permet, elle pourra poursuivre son éducation et lui faire prendre des habitudes de propreté, durant son séjour à l'hôpital.

Dans une unité où les mères donnent des soins à leurs enfants, c'est l'infirmière qui doit déterminer dans quelle mesure elles peuvent y participer. En général, elles sont capables de donner les traitements de routine, mais l'infirmière doit leur enseigner toute nouvelle technique, ou méthode de soin qu'exige l'état de l'enfant. Il ne faut jamais obliger une mère à utiliser des procédés qu'elle se sent incapable d'employer parce que, comme l'enfant, elle éprouve une grande tension qui peut la rendre moins habile qu'à la maison. La plupart des mères aideront l'enfant à traverser ces expériences difficiles, à condition qu'elles se sentent soutenues par le médecin et l'infirmière. À certains moments, cependant, il n'est pas prudent de laisser la mère près de son enfant; lorsqu'elle est incapable de se contrôler par exemple, l'effet sur l'enfant pourrait être désastreux. L'infirmière doit alors l'inviter à la suivre, lui permettre d'exprimer son anxiété et sa colère et lui fournir le réconfort nécessaire avant qu'elle ne retourne auprès de l'enfant. Si elle décide de partir, elle doit être encouragée à aller d'abord avertir l'enfant.

Si l'hospitalisation de l'enfant se prolonge, il faudrait inciter la mère à quitter de temps en temps la chambre du petit malade, à prendre des repas chez elle et à consacrer de plus en plus de temps aux autres membres de la famille. Elle a également besoin de penser à elle et de satisfaire ses besoins personnels, afin de récupérer les forces nécessaires pour affronter la maladie de son enfant.

Le trottineur et les injections intraveineuses

L'enfant n'aime pas les injections. La peur qu'il ressent variera selon l'âge, les expériences antérieures, la force de caractère et l'intelligence, la crainte de la douleur et les phantasmes de l'enfant quant à son intégrité corporelle. L'attitude des parents et de l'infirmière joue un rôle important dans l'acceptation ou le refus du traitement.

Même si parfois le trottineur réagit peu au moment de l'injection et qu'il semble moins traumatisé que l'enfant plus âgé, il protestera par la suite et tentera d'enlever les contraintes qui l'empêchent de se mouvoir librement. Quand c'est possible, il est excellent de prendre l'enfant et de le bercer de temps à autre en prenant les précautions nécessaires pour ne pas déloger l'aiguille de perfusion. Il faut lui procurer des distractions appropriées à son âge.

Le trottineur considère souvent son hospitalisation comme une punition et une forme d'abandon de ses parents et il peut interpréter l'injection ou la perfusion comme un geste de représailles de l'équipe médicale. Afin de minimiser les réactions agressives de l'enfant, toute la technique doit d'abord être bien expliquée, en indiquant le but de chaque pièce d'équipement. Si c'est possible, il devrait avoir la permission de jouer avec le matériel et de pratiquer le traitement sur une poupée. Il peut quand même pleurer pendant le traitement,

mais il ne gardera pas le souvenir d'un complot ou d'un geste malveillant délibéré à son égard. L'attitude plus que les paroles de l'infirmière mettent l'enfant en confiance et il comprendra qu'on ne veut pas le blesser même s'il ne saisit pas vraiment toutes les explications qu'on essaie de lui donner.

Les explications rassurent aussi les parents et leur présence facilite le contact au moment du traitement. S'ils sont trop anxieux, il est préférable qu'ils s'absentent un moment, mais l'infirmière doit alors compter avec l'anxiété que cause le départ des parents en plus de la peur du traitement. Ceci est toutefois préférable au fait de garder près du lit des parents trop anxieux qui rendent la situation encore plus tendue. Un bon contact tout au long de l'hospitalisation aide grandement les parents à fournir à leur enfant un soutien adéquat.

Récapitulation du rôle de l'infirmière dans le soin du trottineur

Bien qu'on ait discuté du rôle de l'infirmière dans les soins de l'enfant malade, on reverra ici quelques points importants sur l'aide à apporter au trottineur et à ses parents.

L'expérience de l'hospitalisation ne devrait pas entraver l'évolution psychologique du jeune enfant si l'infirmière l'aide à assimiler cette expérience, augmente sa capacité d'adaptation à de nouvelles situations et renforce les liens entre la mère et l'enfant. L'infirmière doit être considérée comme une amie qui aide l'enfant et ses parents. Un support affectif ne sera pas accepté si l'infirmière n'est pas aimée, respectée et importante aux yeux des membres de la famille. Si elle veut être efficace elle doit être consciente de leurs sentiments et de leurs besoins et être prête à y répondre. Elle doit aider à diminuer tension et anxiété en partageant leurs inquiétudes, en s'intéressant à leurs problèmes et en les aidant à s'adapter à la situation. L'infirmière doit considérer cette anxiété comme naturelle, même si elle peut entraîner un comportement qui semble injustifié. On parvient à comprendre ce comportement si on le considère comme une contribution au maintien de l'équilibre de l'individu.

Il est important que l'infirmière se fasse l'interprète du comportement de l'enfant auprès des parents et leur en explique les causes. Elle doit les aider à réagir à ces comportements de façon appropriée et constructive. Elle doit aussi les avertir des réactions probables de l'enfant lorsqu'il quittera l'hôpital, car il risque de devenir temporairement exigeant, agressif et dépendant.

La meilleure façon de soutenir un enfant consiste à tenter de soulager d'une manière affectueuse la douleur physique ou le chagrin. L'infirmière ne doit pas seulement dire qu'elle prendra soin de l'enfant. Elle doit le soigner physiquement comme elle le faisait pour le nourrisson, mais elle doit aussi l'aider à se familiariser avec son nouvel environnement, l'aider à s'adapter aux habitudes de l'unité et les rendre plus souples si c'est nécessaire; enfin l'aider à supporter la douleur ou la tension qu'il aura à subir au cours de son séjour à l'hôpital. Pour accomplir son rôle de façon efficace, l'infirmière ne doit pas oublier que le trottineur a besoin d'être préparé à tout traitement ou événement nouveau et que des moyens appropriés doivent lui être fournis pour qu'il assimile ces expériences. Les paroles ou les actions de l'infirmière feront aussi comprendre au jeune enfant qu'il ne sera pas puni s'il régresse ou s'il s'irrite, mais au contraire, qu'il sera accepté comme un individu qu'on aime et qu'on respecte.

Préparation à l'hospitalisation

Des enfants de cet âge ne peuvent pas vraiment comprendre l'idée que leur mère les quittera. Il faut surtout mettre l'accent sur la façon dont la mère et l'enfant communiqueront durant l'hospitalisation. Les parents peuvent réduire une certaine part d'inconnu en expliquant à l'enfant les techniques simples, telles que pesée, prise de température etc. Une journée ou deux avant l'hospitalisation, la mère peut lire un conte au sujet d'un enfant hospitalisé et dire à l'enfant qu'il a lui aussi une maladie qu'il faut traiter.

PATHOLOGIES AIGUËS DU TROTTINEUR

Abcès rétropharyngé

Étiologie et incidence.   Un abcès rétropharyngé atteint un ou plusieurs ganglions lymphatiques, normalement présents chez l'enfant. Il fait suite, ordinairement, à une infection rhinopharyngée bactérienne ou, plus rarement, à l'ingestion d'un corps étranger. Il apparaît surtout au cours des trois premières années de la vie; il devient rare après cette période, en raison de l'atrophie normale de ces ganglions. Sa fréquence a décru au cours de ces dernières années, même chez le jeune enfant, grâce à une meilleure surveillance médicale et à une thérapeutique plus efficace des infections des voies respiratoires supérieures.

Manifestations cliniques, diagnostic et diagnostic différentiel.   L'abcès rétropharyngé apparaît plus ou moins brutalement au cours d'une infection des voies respiratoires supérieures. La déglutition devient difficile et douloureuse, l'hypersalivation constitue un symptôme caractéristique. Pour soulager la douleur et pour déglutir plus facilement, l'enfant a tendance à garder la bouche ouverte. Il rejette la tête vers l'arrière, il crie quand on le bouge. A l'examen, on voit bien l'œdème de la paroi postérieure du pharynx, si l'abcès est haut situé. L'enfant respire bruyamment; en présence d'un œdème important, il peut avoir une respiration stertoreuse et même de la dyspnée. La fièvre s'élève habituellement et la prostration devient marquée.

Le *diagnostic* repose sur l'examen du pharynx. La masse apparaît ordinairement plus volumineuse d'un côté. Le médecin peut employer un laryngoscope pour examiner la gorge de l'enfant; il peut palper le cou ou demander une radiographie.

Traitement.   L'antibiothérapie précoce amène souvent une régression de l'infection sans formation d'abcès. On peut mettre des compresses humides, chaudes, sur le cou de l'enfant pour soulager la douleur et accélérer la maturation de l'abcès. Pour que ce traitement soit efficace, il faut changer les compresses, au moins toutes les dix minutes. Des compresses froides nuisent à la guérison. Quand l'abcès devient fluctuant, il faut l'ouvrir; le médecin pratique une incision et retire le pus par aspiration, en gardant la tête de l'enfant plus basse que le thorax pour favoriser le drainage et éviter la broncho-aspiration du liquide purulent. Après l'intervention, il faut pratiquer de fréquentes aspirations pharyngées. L'arrêt cardiaque et l'hémorragie pharyngée par rupture d'une branche de la carotide sont toujours possibles mais très rares. Il faut continuer l'antibiothérapie puisque le streptocoque B hémolytique demeure l'agent causal le plus fréquent.

On ne pratique pas d'anesthésie générale pour les raisons suivantes: 1) elle abolirait le réflexe de la toux et l'enfant pourrait aspirer du pus; 2) elle empêcherait l'usage des muscles accessoires de la respiration; et 3) l'enfant peut être incapable de respirer sous l'effet de l'anesthésique, avant le drainage de l'abcès.

Soins infirmiers.   Les soins infirmiers comprennent l'assistance au médecin lorsqu'il examine la gorge et incise l'abcès, ainsi que les soins postopératoires. Au cours de l'examen de la gorge, on peut retenir l'enfant à l'aide de moyens de contrainte. L'infirmière lui immobilise la tête en appliquant les mains de chaque côté du visage. Il faut bien le maintenir pour que l'examen puisse s'effectuer rapidement et avec douceur, sans abimer la paroi du pharynx et avec un minimum de douleur et d'effroi.

Durant l'incision, on maintient l'enfant comme pour l'examen de la gorge. L'infirmière tient la tête de l'enfant plus bas que le corps, pour prévenir l'aspiration du pus.

Après l'incision, on lui fait prendre la position déclive favorable au drainage de la bouche. On élève le pied du lit et on place l'enfant sur l'abdomen, un oreiller sous la poitrine, de façon à ce que le pus de l'abcès s'écoule par la bouche plutôt que dans le pharynx. Des contentions peuvent s'avérer nécessaires si l'enfant s'agite ou essaie de changer de position. Il est préférable qu'une infirmière ou sa mère demeure à ses côtés.

Il faut encourager l'enfant à boire dès qu'il peut avaler. On doit l'observer soigneusement afin de déceler les symptômes de détresse respiratoire et d'hémorragie. De fréquentes déglutitions peuvent être un indice de saignement et doivent être signalées rapidement.

Pronostic. Le pronostic est favorable si l'on incise l'abcès dès qu'il devient fluctuant et que l'on administre une médication anti-infectieuse appropriée. Un abcès non traité peut se rompre spontanément et l'enfant peut en aspirer le pus.

La mort peut survenir dans les cas non traités et lorsqu'on conduit l'enfant chez le médecin quand la mort par anoxie est imminente. La mort subite peut suivre un œdème de la glotte, une compression du larynx, une rupture de l'abcès dans le larynx ou une érosion de vaisseaux sanguins qui entraîne une hémorragie grave. Parmi les autres causes de décès figurent la pneumonie et les abcès pulmonaires, mais ces risques sont moins immédiats et moins fréquents.

INFECTIONS AIGUËS
DU LARYNX

L'infection aiguë du larynx se présente surtout chez le très jeune enfant dont les voies respiratoires très étroites s'obstruent plus facilement que celles de l'enfant plus âgé.

En plus du larynx, d'autres parties du tractus respiratoire sont habituellement atteintes. Les signes fonctionnels sont l'aphonie, la raucité de la voix, la dyspnée, le stridor et un tirage inspiratoire (inter-costal, sus-sternal, sous-costal et sous-sternal).

Le diagnostic est basé sur les résultats de la laryngoscopie et des examens bactériologiques.

Faux croup (ou laryngite striduleuse aiguë)

Etiologie et incidence. Le faux croup est une inflammation légère du larynx. La manifestation clinique dominante est un spasme laryngé qui provoque une obstruction respiratoire partielle. L'étiologie demeure inconnue, mais une infection virale ou même bactérienne précède ordinairement la crise.

Le faux croup atteint surtout les enfants entre deux et quatre ans, mais peut survenir chez tout enfant, jusqu'à l'âge de cinq ans. Dans certains cas, il semble exister une prédisposition familiale ou individuelle. L'enfant « nerveux » semble plus souvent atteint que l'enfant calme. Certains enfants prédisposés subissent plus d'une attaque et elles apparaissent presque toujours au cours de la nuit.

L'infection laryngée, souvent précédée d'une infection légère des voies respiratoires supérieures, se manifeste surtout quand l'enfant dort dans une chambre froide dont le taux d'humidité est trop bas. Le seul fait de transporter l'enfant d'une chambre chaude où il a passé la journée à une chambre à coucher plus fraîche, peut déclencher la crise dyspnéique.

Le faux croup n'est pas contagieux et il faudrait le signaler aux parents qui craignent que l'infection ne se transmette à d'autres enfants en bas âge. Le faux croup les effraie souvent parce qu'ils ont l'impression que l'enfant étouffe. Pourtant, les enfants ne meurent pratiquement jamais du faux croup sauf si le spasme entraîne une obstruction respiratoire complète et qu'aucun traitement rapide n'est institué.

Manifestations cliniques et diagnostic. Les manifestations cliniques apparaissent, la plupart du temps, chez un enfant qui semblait en bonne santé ou ne présentait que de légers symptômes d'une infection des voies respiratoires supérieures tels une rhinorrhée ou une certaine raucité de la voix. Le début de la crise est d'autant plus dramatique qu'elle survient souvent durant le sommeil.

Lors d'une attaque typique, l'enfant est réveillé au début de la nuit par une dyspnée inspiratoire bruyante et une toux forte, métallique et aboyante. La toux réveille les parents qui trouvent l'enfant assis sur son lit; son visage

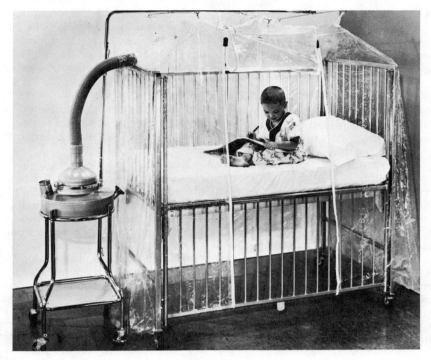

Figure 15-2.   On peut obtenir une atmosphère saturée d'humidité à l'aide de la tente Walton où l'enfant jouit d'une complète liberté de mouvement.

est rouge vif, il respire difficilement et il est très effrayé, car il a l'impression d'étouffer. Il tient sa gorge avec ses doigts crispés, il a une cyanose des lèvres et des extrémités, un battement des ailes du nez, un tirage et une diaphorèse intense. La voix est rauque et le pouls accéléré. La température dépasse rarement 38,5°C. Ces symptômes s'atténuent au bout d'une à trois heures et la gravité du spasme diminue, bien que plusieurs accès puissent se répéter au cours de la même nuit. Le lendemain, l'enfant peut avoir une toux grasse et la voix rauque.

Les crises moins graves se manifestent par une toux croupeuse et une dyspnée légère.

Le *diagnostic* est basé sur l'histoire médicale des difficultés respiratoires et l'absence d'autres manifestations cliniques. Le médecin doit distinguer le faux croup de la laryngite diphtérique, du laryngospasme, de la tétanie, de la laryngite aiguë à streptocoques ou de l'épiglottite.

Traitement.   Le traitement consiste à faire céder le spasme. Il faut placer l'enfant dans une atmosphère saturée de vapeur froide, ce qui tend à liquéfier les sécrétions de la gorge et à diminuer le spasme. Le médecin peut prescrire un émétique comme le sirop d'ipéca pour déclencher un vomissement qui diminuera le spasme laryngé. On peut répéter la dose une ou deux fois, si c'est nécessaire. Après que l'enfant a vomi, on peut donner un sédatif comme le phénobarbital. La chimiothérapie n'est pas nécessaire sauf si l'infection est grave. L'intubation ou la trachéotomie s'avère rarement nécessaire.

Soins infirmiers.   En tout premier lieu, il faut de l'humidité. Si l'enfant est hospitalisé, on doit lui montrer l'équipement et lui expliquer la technique s'il est assez âgé pour la comprendre. La vapeur d'eau sert à liquéfier les sécrétions, et la chaleur locale, si elle est prescrite, tend à réduire le spasme musculaire et à soulager l'inflammation de la muqueuse laryngée. On peut ajouter des agents médicamenteux à l'eau, mais c'est la vapeur d'eau qui est vraiment efficace.

À domicile, l'humidité froide peut être obtenue à l'aide d'un vaporisateur à vapeur froide. À l'hôpital on obtient de la vapeur froide à l'aide d'une tente à haute humidité, en utilisant de l'oxygène, ou de l'air comprimé si l'état de l'enfant ne nécessite pas d'oxygène. On préfère, souvent, l'humidité froide à la vapeur chaude, parce que l'air froid peut diminuer la température du corps de l'enfant, tandis que la vapeur chaude tend à l'augmenter.

Il existe actuellement des tentes fonctionnant à ultra-sons et qui procurent une vapeur froide beaucoup plus dense que celle des « croupettes » ordinaires. Elles sont spécialement utiles dans les cas de faux croup et de mucoviscidose.

Dans certains hôpitaux pédiatriques, on place le petit malade atteint de faux croup dans une chambre à haute humidité, ce qui lui évite le traumatisme de se sentir isolé sous une tente de dimension restreinte.

MODIFICATIONS DE LA TECHNIQUE DE L'HÔPITAL LORSQU'ON L'APPLIQUE À LA MAISON. La façon la plus simple de procurer de l'humidité à un enfant souffrant de faux croup, consiste à laisser couler de l'eau chaude dans le bain ou la douche, d'amener l'enfant à la salle de bain et de fermer la porte. On ne peut prolonger cette méthode longtemps, car la vapeur peut abîmer les murs et la quantité d'eau chaude s'épuise rapidement. Elle procure, cependant, un soulagement d'urgence qui suffit souvent à faire céder la crise ou qui permet d'attendre l'installation d'un humidificateur à vapeur froide.

AUTRES POINTS À SOULIGNER POUR LES SOINS INFIRMIERS. Comme le sirop d'ipéca déclenche un vomissement, l'infirmière ou la mère doit rester près de l'enfant jusqu'à ce qu'il ait vomi. Il est déjà anxieux en raison de sa détresse respiratoire et les vomissements augmentent sa tension. Le fait de souiller son lit et ses vêtements en vomissant peut l'effrayer, même s'il sait qu'on ne lui reprochera pas l'incident. Après que l'enfant a vomi, le médecin peut prescrire un sédatif, habituellement du phénobarbital.

Quand la crise est passée, l'infirmière peut expliquer à la mère l'état de l'enfant, la raison du traitement, de la médication et l'évolution de la maladie. La mère sera alors moins effrayée si une seconde crise se produit la nuit suivante.

Pour que le médecin puisse disposer de toute information essentielle pour le diagnostic et le traitement, l'infirmière doit observer tous les signes et symptômes, à la fois objectifs et subjectifs, dans la mesure où l'enfant est capable de les communiquer. Elle doit essayer d'instruire la mère de l'importance et de la signification de ces observations.

Les symptômes les plus importants à observer au cours d'une crise sont la coloration de l'enfant, le rythme et la nature des inspirations, le degré d'agitation, d'anxiété ou de prostration et la présence de cyanose.

Si les difficultés respiratoires de l'enfant augmentent, le diagnostic peut alors s'en trouver modifié et le médecin doit en être averti aussitôt. Au début d'une épiglottite, les symptômes peuvent ressembler à ceux de la larygite striduleuse et une trachéotomie ou une intubation d'urgence peut s'avérer nécessaire.

Pronostic et prévention. Le *pronostic* de la laryngite striduleuse est toujours bon, même si les parents et l'enfant peuvent en être vraiment effrayés.

Il n'existe pas de *mesures préventives* spécifiques, mais il faudrait éviter les situations qui augmentent la probabilité d'une attaque de faux croup spasmodique chez les enfants plus suceptibles de faire une crise. S'il y a des signes d'une crise imminente, comme une toux suspecte ou une raucité de la voix, particulièrement au cours de la nuit suivant une crise, il faut prendre des mesures générales de prévention. Il faut administrer une dose subvomitive d'ipéca ainsi qu'une dose sédative de phénobarbital, et faire régner dans la chambre à coucher une atmosphère modérément chaude (21°C) et humide. Il faut également éviter l'excès de poussière et de fumée qui peuvent contribuer à déclencher la crise. Il est toujours recommandé de faire examiner, au point de vue allergique, un jeune enfant qui a fréquemment des attaques de faux croup.

Épiglottite aiguë

Étiologie, incidence et manifestations cliniques. Il s'agit d'une infection grave, rapidement évolutive de l'épiglotte et des tissus avoisinants. Elle est causée par l'hémophilus influenzae B, le pneumocoque, un streptocoque de type A et par certains virus. Elle apparaît surtout sous les climats tempérés; le plus souvent l'hiver et dans les zones urbaines polluées. Elle atteint, en particulier les trottineurs et constitue une véritable urgence pédiatrique.

L'enfant souffre d'abord d'une légère infection des voies respiratoires supérieures. Brusquement, apparaît un tableau de détresse respiratoire comportant un sifflement inspiratoire, du tirage et de la toux. Le timbre de la voix est voilé, la température oscille entre 38°C et 40°C. L'enfant souffre de dysphagie, il bave et s'agite; il tient parfois son cou en hyperextension. Certains enfants peuvent glisser vers l'état de choc avec pâleur extrême ou cyanose. À l'examen, l'épiglotte apparaît œdémateuse et de couleur framboisée. La trachéotomie d'urgence est parfois nécessaire pour sauver la vie de l'enfant; une aiguille de gros calibre ou un trocart (12 – 15) piqué dans le cou jusqu'à la trachée permet de gagner du temps et de rassembler le matériel nécessaire à la trachéotomie.

Traitements et soins.   Les soins sont similaires à ceux que reçoit l'enfant atteint de faux croup ou de laryngo-trachéo-bronchite.

L'enfant doit respirer un air saturé d'humidité. L'infirmière doit veiller à l'administration de l'oxygène s'il y a lieu et à l'hydratation par voies orale ou parentérale. Si l'état du trottineur s'aggrave, elle doit préparer les parents et l'enfant à la perspective d'une trachéotomie.

Laryngo-trachéo-bronchite

Incidence et étiologie.   La laryngo-trachéo-bronchite est une inflammation aiguë du larynx, de la trachée et des bronches. Cette *infection* survient principalement au cours des trois premières années de la vie.

Un certain nombre de bactéries et de virus peuvent en être la cause. Parmi les principaux micro-organismes, citons: l'*Hemophilus influenzæ*, le streptocoque hémolytique, le pneumocoque et le staphylocoque.

Physio-pathologie, manifestations cliniques et diagnostic.   On trouve une inflammation des tissus du larynx, de la trachée et des bronches. Dans certains cas, il y a un exsudat purulent qui forme des croûtes. Si celles-ci s'accumulent, elles peuvent obstruer les voies respiratoires.

Une infection aiguë des voies respiratoires supérieures précède habituellement l'apparition des premiers symptômes. Le début peut toutefois apparaître brutalement et l'enfant présente de l'hyperthermie, de la prostration et une dyspnée extrême. La dyspnée inspiratoire initiale, d'origine laryngée, est bientôt suivie d'une dyspnée expiratoire qui indique une atteinte des bronches.

L'enfant peut s'agiter par suite du manque d'oxygène. Il présente un enrouement ou une aphonie, et un tirage sous et sus-sternal. Finalement, sa coloration peut devenir gris cendré ou cyanosée. La température s'élève généralement aux environs de 40°C et 40,5°C, et des convulsions fébriles peuvent se produire. On observe habituellement une toux persistante qui, dans les lésions plus exsudatives, devient grasse, bruyante et rauque. En présence d'un exsudat plus épais, la toux s'affaiblit, et quand l'obstruction est pratiquement complète, on perçoit à peine les mouvements respiratoires et la dyspnée peut être extrême.

Pour confirmer le *diagnostic,* il faut effectuer un prélèvement direct pour culture microbienne et antibiogramme (l'Hemophilus influenzæ est l'agent causal le plus fréquent). Il sera également nécessaire de pratiquer des hémocultures. Pour éliminer la possibilité d'une diphtérie, il faut rechercher les membranes caractéristiques et faire un prélèvement direct pour isoler le bacille de Klebbs-Loëffler. Des examens fluoroscopiques et bronchoscopiques écartent la possibilité de la présence d'un corps étranger dans le larynx ou dans les bronches.

Pronostic.   Le *pronostic* dépend de la gravité de l'infection, de l'âge du patient, de la durée de l'évolution avant l'institution du traitement et du type de thérapeutique. La mort est due à l'infection elle-même, à une pneumonie secondaire à l'infection ou à l'obstruction respiratoire. Dans de rares cas, une septicémie peut entraîner la mort.

Traitement.   La base du traitement de la laryngo-trachéo-bronchite consiste: a) à fournir de l'oxygène en quantité suffisante, dès que les muscles respiratoires accessoires sont utilisés pour la respiration (battements des ailes du nez); il ne faut pas attendre l'apparition de la cyanose; b) à humidifier l'air suffisamment pour liquéfier les sécrétions et prévenir la formation des croûtes. On emploie de l'humidité froide; c) on peut administrer des antibiotiques si l'infection est d'origine bactérienne. Les antibiotiques sont généralement inefficaces en présence d'une infection virale. Ils peuvent toutefois servir à éviter la surinfection bactérienne qui pourrait survenir.

La *trachéotomie* peut sauver la vie du patient quand l'obstruction des voies respiratoires devient suffisamment grave. Elle consiste à faire une incision dans la trachée ce qui rétablit la perméabilité des voies aériennes et permet le drainage des sécrétions. En général, les indications de la trachéotomie sont: la prostration accompagnée de pâleur extrême ou de cyanose qui précède le collapsus cardio-vasculaire et la pénétration de quantités minimes d'air dans les poumons malgré les mouvements respiratoires. Le médecin pratique l'incision horizontale juste au-dessous du premier anneau de la trachée et insère une canule spéciale qui permet l'entrée de l'air dans les voies respiratoires. Il faut éviter les opiacés et l'atropine qui ont tendance à atténuer les réflexes tussigènes protecteurs et à assécher les sécrétions. Si des signes de défaillance cardiaque apparaissent, on peut digitaliser l'enfant. Il faut combattre la déshydratation en administrant de fortes quantités de liquides, habituellement par voie parentérale.

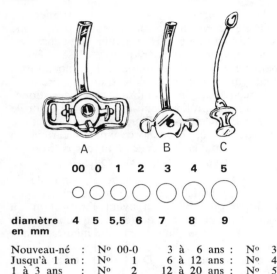

Figure 15-3. Pièces de la canule de trachéotomie. *A)* Canule externe. *B)* Canule interne. *C)* Mandrin. Le diagramme indique le calibre des canules employées aux différents âges. (Diamètre en millimètres.)

00	**0**	**1**	**2**	**3**	**4**	**5**

diamètre | 4 | 5 | 5,5 | 6 | 7 | 8 | 9
en mm

Nouveau-né   : N° 00-0   3 à 6 ans   : N° 3
Jusqu'à 1 an : N° 1   6 à 12 ans : N° 4
1 à 3 ans   : N° 2   12 à 20 ans : N° 5

Soins infirmiers. L'infirmière doit observer l'enfant souffrant d'une laryngo-trachéo-bronchite ou d'une épiglottite et noter toute indication de fatigue ou de détresse respiratoire qui se manifesteront par l'agitation, la tachycardie, l'hyperthermie, la dyspnée ou le tirage.

L'infirmière doit aussi établir une relation de confiance avec l'enfant pour qu'il accepte plus facilement les soins surtout si une trachéotomie s'avérait nécessaire. Elle doit tenter de soulager l'anxiété des parents et de l'enfant face aux symptômes de détresse respiratoire.

SOINS D'UN ENFANT TRACHÉOTOMISÉ. Il est essentiel de maintenir la canule trachéale perméable parce qu'elle assure le passage de l'air et le drainage pulmonaire. La canule peut s'obstruer ou se déplacer et la vie de l'enfant peut être mise en danger. On peut éviter ces accidents grâce à des soins intelligents et à une observation attentive de l'état de l'enfant. L'infirmière doit être préparée à donner des soins d'urgence, s'il y a lieu.

L'infirmière doit employer tous les moyens possibles pour réduire l'anxiété de l'enfant. Il est essentiel qu'elle ait confiance en elle-même pour donner les meilleurs soins possibles et pour inspirer confiance à la fois à l'enfant et à ses parents.

Après une trachéotomie, la présence continue d'une infirmière auprès de l'enfant est nécessaire. Souvent, le trottineur trachéotomisé sera transféré dans une unité de soins intensifs pédiatriques. L'infirmière doit observer et noter les signes de danger comme l'agitation, la fatigue extrême, la dyspnée, la cyanose ou la pâleur, la fièvre, la tachycardie, le tirage et les respirations bruyantes. Elle doit aussi surveiller les saignements et les signes d'infection autour de l'incision.

Il est important de contrôler certaines caractéristiques de l'environnement. En principe, l'air inspiré est filtré, réchauffé et humidifié dans les voies respiratoires supérieures; dans la situation présente il faut veiller à ce que l'air que l'enfant inspire soit humidifié et réchauffé avant de pénétrer dans la canule trachéale. La température de la pièce doit s'élever aux environs de 26,5°C. Pour humidifier l'air, on emploie un humidificateur ou on place l'enfant dans une tente ou une chambre à haute humidité. Un apport d'oxygène est parfois nécessaire; on conserve toujours à portée de la main, un appareillage d'urgence.

On garde près du lit un appareil aspirateur pourvu d'une pression négative suffisante.

On doit également disposer d'un plateau contenant un équipement stérile pour les soins de routine de la trachéotomie et pour les soins d'urgence.

Un tel équipement comporte des canules trachéales de remplacement (interne et externe), des cordons, deux pinces hémostatiques, des ciseaux, un mandrin, des nettoyeurs de canule (cure-pipes), des bandages et pansements de gaze, un compte-gouttes ou une seringue et une aiguille, des abaisse-langue, un cathéter (n° 8 à 10) pourvu d'orifices supplémentaires aux extrémités pour faciliter l'aspiration et un cathéter à extrémité ouverte en sifflet que l'on emploie pour éliminer les sécrétions de la canule trachéale. En plus, il doit y avoir un flacon bien fermé contenant de l'eau oxygénée, du Zéphiran ou du bicarbonate de soude pour nettoyer la canule trachéale, un flacon fermé de soluté physiologique salin et un flacon fermé de vaseline stérile ou de la gaze imbibée de vaseline. Il faut identifier les flacons sur les côtés et sur le couvercle pour éviter les erreurs. On peut employer de la vaseline stérile pour enduire la région cutanée autour de la canule. On applique la vaseline avec un abaisse-langue.

Soin de la canule trachéale et de l'incision. L'infirmière doit se laver les mains avant de toucher la canule trachéale et l'équipement. Elle retire la canule interne et la nettoie en la trempant dans de l'eau oxygénée, du bicarbonate de soude, ou une autre solution; ensuite, elle fait passer les nettoyeurs de tube et de la gaze à travers la canule pour enlever

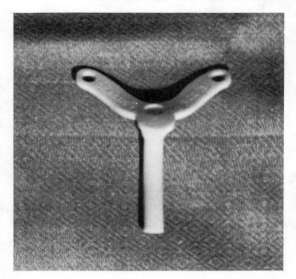

Figure 15-4. Le tube de trachéotomie pédiatrique fait de Silastic élimine les problèmes inhérents au tube métallique classique. Plus flexible il risque moins de créer un traumatisme tissulaire et une irritation; il se forme peu de croûtes dans l'orifice et la canule externe n'est pas nécessaire. (G. H. Conner, D. Hugues, M. J. Mills, B. Rittmanic, L. V. Sigg., *Am. J. Nurs.*, 72:68-77, janvier 1972.)

toutes les sécrétions qui pourraient s'y trouver. Elle aspire les sécrétions situées dans la canule externe et l'arbre trachéo-bronchique (la profondeur de l'aspiration dépend de la ligne de conduite adoptée par le personnel médical). Si l'obstruction persiste ou si le médecin l'a prescrit avec chaque aspiration, on instillera quelques gouttes de soluté physiologique dans la canule avant l'aspiration, à l'aide d'un compte-gouttes ou d'une seringue. Cette mesure stimule le réflexe de la toux, liquéfie les sécrétions et aide à déloger les croûtes.

On pince le cathéter d'aspiration pendant qu'on l'insère dans la canule externe jusque dans la bronche (on peut employer un tube de verre en Y pour que le vide puisse se faire sur une simple pression du doigt). Il faut insérer le cathéter lentement et doucement, sans aspirer, et le retirer en aspirant tout en faisant des mouvements giratoires qui permettent de bien nettoyer l'intérieur de la bronche et préviennent les traumatismes tissulaires. On rince ensuite le cathéter au soluté physiologique.

Pour que le tube puisse pénétrer dans une bronche, on fait tourner la tête de l'enfant du côté opposé. La précipitation nuit à une aspiration correcte; l'infirmière doit calmer l'enfant, ne pas effectuer des mouvements de va-et-vient qui irritent la muqueuse et laisser au patient le temps de se reposer entre chaque aspiration. Chaque aspiration ne doit pas dépasser 10 secondes, de façon à ne pas priver le malade d'oxygène d'une façon prolongée. La pression utilisée, chez le jeune enfant, ne doit pas excéder 100 mm de Hg.

On répètera l'opération aussi souvent qu'il le faudra pour conserver la perméabilité des voies respiratoires. On remet la canule interne en place, après l'avoir nettoyée bien à fond et s'être assuré qu'il ne reste pas, à l'extrémité de la canule externe, des sécrétions qui pourraient s'accumuler et créer éventuellement une obstruction.

Si une dyspnée ou un état d'agitation persiste après l'aspiration de l'arbre trachéo-bronchique, les voies respiratoires inférieures doivent être explorées. Le médecin peut lever l'obstruction à l'aide d'un examen bronchoscopique, si c'est nécessaire.

La fréquence des aspirations dépend des besoins de l'enfant. Immédiatement après la trachéotomie, on fait habituellement une aspiration tous les quarts d'heure, et ultérieurement toutes les demi-heures ou toutes les heures. La fréquence diminue progressivement avec l'amélioration de l'état de l'enfant.

Si l'infirmière doit changer le pansement qui entoure la canule trachéale, elle nettoie la région périphérique avec de l'eau oxygénée, l'assèche et l'enduit de vaseline stérile à l'aide d'un abaisse-langue. Elle découpe un carré de gaze selon les contours de la canule et le glisse sous la canule et les rubans, ce qui le maintient en place.

La prévention des accidents est importante dans le soin de ces enfants. Le jeune enfant ne comprend pas la nécessité de laisser la canule en place et on peut employer les contentions du coude ou d'autres contraintes pour l'empêcher d'y toucher. L'enfant agité et qui n'a rien pour se distraire peut essayer d'introduire des morceaux de nourriture ou des détritus dans la canule. Si l'enfant est assez vieux, on peut lui expliquer l'importance de la trachéotomie et essayer de gagner sa collaboration.

L'infirmière doit s'assurer que la canule interne est bien fixée en place et ne risque pas de sortir, que les cordons sont correctement fixés au tube et bien attachés pour que le tube soit maintenu fermement dans une position correcte et que l'enfant ne puisse pas le déloger.

Si l'enfant cesse de respirer à la suite d'une obstruction quelconque, il faut retirer la canule interne, aspirer à fond la canule externe et la trachée et administrer de l'oxygène par la canule trachéale.

Si par accident la canule externe est retirée de la trachée, le médecin doit insérer la canule trachéale de rechange. L'infirmière maintient ouverte l'incision de la trachée à l'aide d'une pince hémostatique, tandis qu'une autre infirmière appelle d'urgence le médecin. Il faudrait administrer de l'oxygène à travers l'incision. On peut pratiquer la respiration artificielle; la méthode est celle qu'on pratique habituellement sur les enfants, avec cette différence fondamentale que l'infirmière met sa bouche sur l'ouverture du cou plutôt que sur la bouche de l'enfant.

Avant *d'enlever définitivement* la canule trachéale, on en bouche l'ouverture partiellement avec un bouchon stérile. Ceci oblige l'enfant à respirer par le nez, tout en permettant une entrée d'air supplémentaire à travers la trachéotomie. Quand il est capable de supporter une occlusion complète de l'orifice trachéal, on place le mandrin pour l'obstruer tout à fait. Si l'enfant n'est pas gêné, on peut finalement retirer la canule et mettre un pansement stérile sur l'incision. L'enfant doit être sous une surveillance étroite durant plusieurs

jours, car il peut être incapable d'expectorer complètement ses sécrétions et il est à craindre qu'elles s'accumulent dans les bronches entraînant une élévation de la température et de l'agitation, signes de surinfection.

Il y a peu d'affections au cours desquelles le rapport des observations de l'infirmière et les soins à donner à l'enfant sont plus importants que lorsqu'on soigne un enfant qui a une trachéotomie. Chaque fois qu'on aspire la canule, il faut noter la durée de la séance, la quantité retirée, la consistance et la nature des sécrétions aspirées (voir si elles contiennent du sang, du mucus et des croûtes), et aussi noter si l'enfant respire plus facilement après l'aspiration. Il faut noter le moment où l'on retire la canule trachéale interne pour la nettoyer ainsi que la réaction de l'enfant.

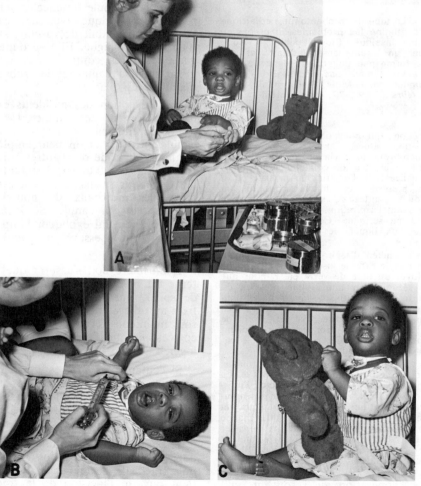

Figure 15-5.   Soins de trachéotomie. *A)* L'infirmière nettoie la canule interne avec un cure-pipe. On marque les récipients sur le côté et sur le couvercle afin d'éviter de les interchanger en les fermant. *B)* Elle aspire les sécrétions après avoir instillé quelques gouttes de soluté physiologique dans la canule. *C)* Après le traitement, l'enfant s'amuse à aspirer son animal favori.

Les soins psychologiques sont d'une importance extrême. Après une trachéotomie, la présence continuelle d'une infirmière au chevet de l'enfant s'avère essentielle. Il serait préférable de garder l'enfant dans une unité de soins intensifs.

Livré à lui-même, l'enfant court un danger physique certain et il a besoin de support affectif. Son état physique lui inspire la crainte de rester seul; l'agitation et l'anxiété favorisent l'apparition de la dyspnée. L'enfant trachéotomisé ne peut crier ou appeler l'infirmière; comme il ne sait pas toujours, au début, respirer à l'aide d'un tube, il faut craindre l'obstruction. Périodiquement, et pendant quelques secondes, l'infirmière peut obturer partiellement la canule trachéale de façon à ce que l'enfant réentende sa voix ou ses pleurs. Cette manière d'agir a souvent un effet rassurant et calmant sur l'enfant. Il est effrayé et l'infirmière augmente sa crainte quand elle aspire la canule; quand il sera habitué à ce traitement et qu'il se rendra compte que cela le soulage, il apprendra à se fier à l'infirmière. On peut expliquer à un enfant plus âgé l'importance du tube, mais un jeune enfant ne comprendra son utilité que lorsque l'expérience lui aura appris qu'il se sent mieux après qu'il a été libéré de ses sécrétions. Il peut, en guise de jeu, faire une aspiration à son jouet favori et revivre la scène à sa façon.

Avant que le jeune enfant ne soit habitué à la canule trachéale, il a peur d'absorber du liquide. En mettant de petites quantités de liquide ou d'aliments dans sa bouche, il apprendra que le fait d'avaler ne lui cause que peu ou pas de douleur.

Toute agitation doit lui être évitée, mais il faut laisser l'enfant s'amuser selon son âge et ses capacités tout en le surveillant étroitement pour qu'il ne déloge pas la canule.

AUTRES POINTS À SOULIGNER DANS LE SOIN DE L'ENFANT. Il faut prendre les signes vitaux selon la prescription du médecin ou, plus fréquemment, d'après les observations de l'infirmière. Si l'enfant n'est pas capable de changer de position, l'infirmière doit le bouger fréquemment pour prévenir une accumulation de sécrétions. La position semi-Fowler semble la plus confortable. Il faut nettoyer la bouche, surtout si l'enfant ne prend pas suffisamment de liquide et qu'il semble avoir la bouche sèche. Il faut combattre la déshydratation en administrant de grandes quantités de liquides — de préférence chauds — par voie orale. S'il ne prend pas la quantité désirée, on administre des liquides par voie parentérale. On peut augmenter l'hydratation par voie orale en présentant, à intervalles réguliers, de petites quantités de n'importe quel liquide que l'enfant aime.

Le médecin peut laisser rentrer l'enfant chez lui avant d'avoir enlevé la canule trachéale. Dans ce cas, il faut instruire progressivement la mère des soins à donner à l'enfant avant qu'il quitte l'hôpital. Des diapositives et des films en boucle peuvent favoriser l'apprentissage. Une infirmière en santé communautaire le visite chaque jour à la maison et on donne à la mère des rendez-vous périodiques à la clinique externe de l'hôpital.

Toutes les mères ne peuvent assumer la responsabilité de ce traitement, mais lorsque l'une d'elles connaît les soins à donner à son enfant et que celui-ci s'est habitué à vivre avec la canule et à coopérer aux soins que son état nécessite, il est préférable qu'il soit à la maison plutôt qu'à l'hôpital. On doit enseigner à la mère non seulement les techniques à appliquer, mais aussi les observations à faire au sujet de l'état de l'enfant et ce qu'il convient de rapporter au médecin. Il faut lui indiquer aussi où elle peut se procurer l'équipement nécessaire et l'oxygène en cas d'urgence.

La mère doit prendre beaucoup de précautions lorsqu'elle baigne l'enfant ou lorsqu'il se trouve près d'une piscine en compagnie d'autres enfants; s'il lui arrivait d'être momentanément submergé, l'eau pénètrerait dans la canule trachéale et atteindrait directement les poumons, ce qui entraînerait la noyade. L'accès au bac de sable doit être limité et l'enfant étroitement surveillé à cause du danger de broncho-aspiration qui le guette.

Il peut être de bonne politique de ménager des rencontres entre parents d'enfants trachéotomisés; ils peuvent échanger des informations sur les soins quotidiens à donner à la maison, sur la façon d'expliquer la maladie et le traitement aux grands-parents, aux frères et sœurs, aux voisins, aux visiteurs; ils peuvent également se communiquer des renseignements sur l'aide familiale temporaire ou sur un service de gardienne qui leur permette de faire relâche et sur les ressources financières disponibles pour les familles aux prises avec ces problèmes.

Pneumonies

La classification des pneumonies peut varier selon que l'on utilise pour les identifier la localisation, l'étiologie, les lésions anatomiques ou la réaction au traitement anti-infectueux. Aucune classification clinique des pneumonies ne donne entière satisfaction.

Quel que soit le type de pneumonie, les régions pulmonaires atteintes manquent d'oxygène parce que les alvéoles sont remplies d'un exsudat inflammatoire. Par suite de ce fait, et aussi parce que l'enfant respire peu profondément en raison de la douleur que lui cause l'inspiration, la saturation du sang en oxygène se trouve invariablement réduite.

Étant donné qu'il y a diverses formes de pneumonie et que certaines formes affectent plus particulièrement un ou plusieurs groupes d'âge, nous n'en étudierons ici que certains types. La pneumonie du nouveau-né et la pneumonie par aspiration ont été étudiées au chapitre 9, la pneumonie interstitielle ou bronchiolite et la pneumonie lipoïdique au chapitre 12.

Nous verrons ici les pneumonies à pneumocoques et à staphylocoques. Les soins infirmiers qui pourraient s'appliquer à tous les autres types demeurent essentiellement les mêmes pour le jeune enfant.

Pneumonie à pneumocoques

Étiologie, incidences et facteurs prédisposants. La pneumonie à pneumocoques est caractérisée par la formation d'un bloc de condensation plus ou moins important, au niveau d'un ou de plusieurs lobes pulmonaires. Elle est provoquée par le pneumocoque, dont on a identifié environ quatre-vingts types. Certains types s'observent plus fréquemment, à certains âges particuliers.

Jadis, le pneumocoque était la cause principale de pneumonie chez les nourrissons et les jeunes enfants. Au cours des dernières années, on a observé une nette chute de fréquence en raison de la réaction rapide aux sulfamides ou aux antibiotiques, administrés à un stade précoce de l'infection.

La pneumonie lobaire, dans laquelle on rencontre une atteinte d'un ou de plusieurs lobes du poumon, s'observe souvent au-delà de la première année. La forme disséminée, comme la bronchiolite, est relativement plus fréquente chez le nourrisson.

On rencontre surtout la pneumonie à la fin de l'hiver et au début du printemps; elle apparaît sous forme endémique dans les régions tempérées. Plusieurs membres d'une famille peuvent être porteurs de germes, bien qu'il soit rare d'observer plusieurs cas au sein d'une même famille. Une bonne partie de la population a développé des anticorps à de nombreux types de pneumocoques.

Les *facteurs prédisposants* sont l'âge (la fréquence la plus élevée se situe au cours de la deuxième année de vie), et la diminution de la résistance à l'infection due à la malnutrition, la débilité, la présence d'une autre infection ou à un grave refroidissement du corps.

Physio-pathologie et manifestations cliniques. Les pneumocoques atteignent les poumons par les voies respiratoires. Ils provoquent, au niveau des alvéoles, une réaction inflammatoire caractérisée par une congestion très marquée des capillaires alvéolaires. Les capillaires laissent filtrer du plasma et des globules qui, libérés à l'intérieur de l'alvéole, se coagulent pour former un bloc solide. Le bloc de condensation peut atteindre un lobe entier et le poumon prend l'aspect brun-rouge du foie. C'est l'« hépatisation » lobaire. Il se produit bientôt un envahissement du lobe par les leucocytes qui luttent contre le pneumocoque, provoquent la formation de pus et permettent la liquéfaction du bloc de condensation. Au début, après un épisode de toux sèche et non productive, des expectorations rouillées (sanguinolentes) et excessivement visqueuses apparaissent; elles deviennent ensuite franchement purulentes et cessent avec la guérison de la maladie.

L'enfant n'a pas toujours une symptomatologie caractéristique. Le début de la maladie est fréquemment précédé de signes d'infection des voies respiratoires supérieures. L'enfant plus âgé présente souvent un frisson important (frisson solennel); chez l'enfant plus jeune, où les manifestations nerveuses sont fréquentes, on observe souvent un épisode convulsif comme premier symptôme. La toux et les expectorations évoluent selon les caractéristiques expliquées plus haut. Il faut toutefois se souvenir que les expectorations rouillées, signe pathognomonique de la pneumonie franche lobaire aiguë de l'adulte, se manifestent rarement chez l'enfant qui, d'ailleurs, n'expectore que très peu. La température atteint rapidement 39,5°C ou 40°C, avec ou sans oscillation quotidienne marquée. L'évolution de l'affection non traitée se termine, habituellement, chez le grand enfant par une chute thermique abrupte, entre le 5e et le 9e jour. C'est ce qui marque le point tournant de la maladie.

Le rythme de 30 à 50 respirations par minute est normal chez le grand enfant; il oscille entre 40 et 80 respirations chez le nourrisson. Le pouls est accéléré, mais pas autant que le rythme respiratoire. La force et le rythme du pouls représentent des indices pour le pronostic de la maladie. Il faut autant se méfier du pouls faible et rapide que du pouls très lent. La douleur thoracique, due à l'atteinte pleurale, est accentuée par la toux et les mouvements respiratoires. Elle peut irradier dans l'abdomen. L'expansion thoracique diminue afin de réduire la douleur pleurale. Les muscles respiratoires accessoires peuvent entrer en jeu, déterminant le tirage; le battement des ailes du nez demeure l'un des signes les plus constants chez les enfants.

Le jeune enfant a souvent des symptômes gastro-intestinaux. Au début de la maladie, on peut observer des vomissements ou de la diarrhée et habituellement de l'anorexie au cours de l'évolution. Le grand enfant peut se plaindre de maux de tête, accompagnés parfois d'une raideur de la nuque.

Diagnostic, diagnostic différentiel et complications.

L'examen du thorax est capital pour diagnostiquer une pneumonie. Le médecin détermine le nombre et l'étendue des foyers pneumoniques en fonction des râles, des bruits à l'auscultation et de l'évidence d'une condensation. L'examen radiographique peut confirmer l'existence de la condensation et dépister certaines complications, telles qu'une pleurésie purulente ou une atélectasie.

Les examens de laboratoire peuvent montrer une chute discrète du nombre des globules rouges et de l'hémoglobine. La leucocytose s'élève généralement de 16 000 à 40 000 par millimètre cube. Les urines sont, en général, fortement teintées, très denses et peu abondantes. On note habituellement une acétonurie et une albuminurie modérée. Dans la plupart des cas, on trouve des pneumocoques dans les sécrétions rhino-pharyngées. Les hémocultures peuvent être positives, selon les cas.

Il faut différencier la pneumonie lobaire d'une atélectasie et d'un épanchement pleural; s'il y a une forte douleur abdominale, on pense aussi à une gastro-entérite ou à une appendicite. Si les symptômes nerveux prédominent, on peut craindre une méningite.

La pleurésie demeure une des complications habituelles; elle existe à un certain degré dans presque toutes les formes de pneumonie. L'administration d'antibiotiques et de sulfamides a considérablement réduit la fréquence des autres complications. La distension de l'abdomen (tympanisme abdominal) demeure une complication sérieuse qui traduit généralement un iléus paralytique, si elle persiste. Un empyème et la méningite sont des complications excessivement rares.

Traitement et soins infirmiers.

On peut soigner l'enfant à domicile, si le milieu familial s'avère satisfaisant et si la mère ou un autre adulte de la famille peut prendre soin du petit malade. C'est au médecin ou à l'infirmière qu'incombe la responsabilité d'enseigner à la mère comment soigner son enfant. L'administration d'antibiotiques donne de bons résultats et la mère peut facilement s'en charger à la maison. Si on institue le traitement dès le premier signe de pneumonie, l'administration d'oxygène (difficile et dangereuse à domicile) s'avère rarement nécessaire. Le développement de complications graves nécessitera le transport de l'enfant à l'hôpital.

La plupart des *soins infirmiers* sont symptomatiques et fonction des besoins personnels de l'enfant. Il doit avoir beaucoup de repos, à la fois physique et psychologique, et il faut le déranger le moins possible.

Dès l'apparition du premier signe de pneumonie, le médecin prescrit l'administration d'un sulfamide ou d'un antibiotique. La pénicilline prescrite à fortes doses, semblerait être le remède d'élection. Cette thérapeutique demeure importante au cours de toute l'évolution de la maladie. On doit poursuivre l'antibiothérapie au moins quatre ou cinq jours après le retour de la température à la normale.

Il faut une ration suffisante de liquides pour combattre la déshydratation et maintenir une diurèse de densité moyenne qui facilite l'excrétion des produits toxiques et demeure essentielle pour éviter les complications rénales, au cours du traitement par les sulfamides. À l'hôpital, en cas de vomissements, on administre les liquides par voie parentérale. Lorsque l'enfant se sent mieux, l'anorexie disparaît complètement.

L'enfant a tendance à se coucher sur le côté atteint, pour diminuer la douleur. Il faut le changer fréquemment de position dans son lit, de façon à éviter la gêne respiratoire et à faciliter le drainage trachéo-bronchique.

En cas de fièvre, on utilise les mesures antipyrétiques décrites à la page 294.

L'administration d'oxygène à l'aide d'un cathéter ou d'une tente apaisera l'agitation et préviendra une dyspnée grave, avec ou sans cyanose. L'oxygénothérapie précoce réduira considérablement le besoin de sédatifs et d'analgésiques. Dans les cas graves, on associe l'aspirine et le phénobarbital.

La convalescence doit être suffisamment longue, même si l'enfant paraît guéri à la suite du traitement anti-infectieux. On peut évaluer le retour à la normale par la reprise du poids antérieur et par l'absence de fatigue à la suite d'une activité journalière moyenne. La guérison complète prend habituellement deux semaines.

Pronostic et prévention.

L'évolution et le pronostic des pneumonies à pneumocoques

ont été complètement bouleversés par les sulfamides et les antibiotiques qui ont sensiblement réduit le taux de mortalité. Maintenant, la température revient à la normale vingt-quatre heures après le début d'un traitement satisfaisant. Simultanément, l'état clinique de l'enfant s'améliore et les complications sont devenues extrêmement rares. Lorsque le traitement est précoce, le taux de mortalité est habituellement inférieur à 1% chez les nourrissons et les enfants.

La *prévention* consiste à éviter que l'enfant vienne en contact avec les patients atteints de pneumonie et à maintenir son état général à un niveau optimal.

Pneumonie à staphylocoques

Étiologie, incidence, manifestations cliniques, physio-pathologie et diagnostic. Au cours de ces dernières années, la pneumonie à *staphylocoque doré* est devenue le type le plus important de pneumonie pédiatrique. Ce nouvel état de fait provient surtout de l'apparition de souches virulentes de staphylocoques, résistantes aux antibiotiques courants.

L'enfant peut contracter l'infection à staphylocoques à l'hôpital, à la maison ou au sein d'autres collectivités. Elle débute souvent par une infection cutanée, et l'enfant peut alors héberger des staphylocoques virulents au niveau du rhino-pharynx, ce qui peut éventuellement provoquer une pneumonie.

L'affection débute brusquement. On trouve de multiples lésions pneumoniques, avec destruction du tissu pulmonaire et formation d'abcès. Les lésions situées près de la périphérie, érodent souvent la plèvre, déterminant un pneumothorax ou une pleurésie purulente. Les autres manifestations cliniques ressemblent à celles de la pneumonie à pneumocoques.

Une radiographie du thorax conduit au diagnostic en mettant en évidence des lésions multiples. Les cultures des sécrétions rhinopharyngées révèlent habituellement l'agent causal et l'hémoculture est souvent positive.

Traitement et soins infirmiers. L'isolement strict et une surveillance constante constituent les deux points essentiels du *traitement* d'une pneumonie à staphylocoques. Il faut administrer un antibiotique qui agit sur les souches de staphylocoques habituellement trouvés dans les hôpitaux; parmi ces antibiotiques semi-synthétiques, citons la méthicilline, l'oxacilline et la nafcilline. On ne connaît, actuellement, aucun antibiotique capable d'agir sur toutes les souches à la fois. Il faut modifier l'ordonnance initiale d'après les résultats de l'antibiogramme et la réaction clinique de l'enfant.

Un traitement général de soutien comprend l'administration d'oxygène et le maintien de l'équilibre hydro-électrolytique. L'infirmière doit surveiller chez l'enfant, tout symptôme de développement éventuel d'un pneumothorax suffocant, par exemple, une douleur thoracique brusque, une dyspnée ou une cyanose qui apparaissent subitement.

Pronostic. Le pronostic dépend d'un diagnostic précoce, de l'emploi d'un antibiotique approprié, de l'absence de complications et de l'état physique de l'enfant avant la maladie. Plusieurs enfants, porteurs d'une malformation congénitale ou d'une maladie débilitante, meurent, en bas âge, des conséquences d'une infection pulmonaire à staphylocoques.

Parasites intestinaux

Les enfants qui souffrent de parasites intestinaux présentent peu ou pas de symptômes. Le grattage du nez, les grincements de dents et un sommeil agité, que l'on attribuait jadis à des infestations intestinales, sont plus probablement attribuables à des troubles psychologiques divers et révèlent la grande nervosité de l'enfant.

L'oxyurose et l'ascaridiose constituent les deux infestations parasitaires les plus courantes chez les jeunes enfants.

Oxyurose

Étiologie. L'oxyurose est une parasitose due au vers plat *Enterobius vermicularis* (Oxyurus vermicularis), qui envahit le cæcum et l'appendice où s'effectue la reproduction.

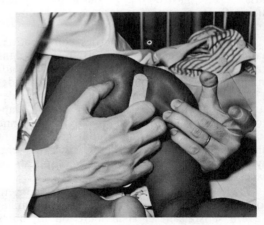

Figure 15-6. On pratique le test au « scotch tape » tôt le matin, afin de prélever les vers ou les œufs (oxyures) au niveau de l'anus.

L'oxyure adulte est blanc et d'apparence fusiforme. Le mâle adulte mesure de 2 à 5 mm de longueur, et la femelle de 8 à 13 mm.

Épidémiologie et physio-pathologie.

L'oxyurose constitue la variété la plus fréquente des parasitoses. La contamination se fait de personne à personne ou par la terre souillée. Les enfants y sont particulièrement exposés. L'oxyure dépose des œufs au pourtour de l'anus, ce qui provoque une réaction inflammatoire prurigineuse. L'enfant peut se contaminer à partir de son linge ou de la literie souillée, mais le plus souvent, il gratte les lésions, ramassant les œufs sous les ongles, et les porte à la bouche. Les œufs reprennent ainsi un nouveau cycle de vie et arrivent à maturité dans le tube digestif. La contamination peut également se produire par des œufs aéroportés. Les œufs fécondés demeurent infestants pendant environ neuf jours.

En résumé, la route d'infestation s'accomplit de l'anus aux doigts et des doigts à la bouche, ou bien de l'anus aux vêtements, des vêtements aux doigts et des doigts à la bouche, ou de la terre souillée aux doigts et à la bouche.

Les œufs que l'enfant avale éclosent au niveau du duodénum et les larves qui en sortent gagnent directement le cæcum et l'appendice. Elles deviennent adultes en quarante-cinq jours ou moins. Les vers s'accrochent à la muqueuse du cæcum et de l'appendice. Les femelles gravides vivent dans le rectum et sortent par l'orifice anal, ordinairement le soir, causant un prurit important, et elles y déposent plusieurs milliers d'œufs qui deviennent infestants en quelques heures. Les femelles oxyures gravides peuvent pénétrer dans l'appareil génital de la petite fille et provoquer une vaginite, une salpingite, s'enkyster dans les trompes ou dans la cavité péritonéale. Les vers causent souvent un prurit intense, et le grattage inévitable provoque des excoriations cutanées ainsi qu'une surinfection.

L'infestation ne se fait d'habitude qu'en introduisant des œufs dans la bouche.

Manifestations cliniques.

Les manifestations cliniques sont variables. Parfois, il n'y a pas d'autre symptôme que le purit anal au cours de la nuit, ce qui amène chez l'enfant irritabilité et agitation. Le prurit anal se complique souvent d'une infection bactérienne de la peau et d'une atteinte eczémateuse. On rencontre chez la petite fille une vaginite qui se manifeste par une irritabilité, une anoxerie, un amaigrissement et des insomnies, qui peuvent produire des troubles affectifs chroniques. Une éosinophilie peut s'observer chez certains enfants ainsi que des symptômes d'appendicite chronique.

Diagnostic.

Un diagnostic final peut être établi, si l'on voit, lors de l'examen, des vers qui sortent de l'intestin. La technique la plus simple et la plus efficace pour établir le diagnostic consiste à placer un ruban cellophane adhésif sur la peau périanale, où les œufs seront recueillis (test au scotch tape). On effectue le test, tôt le matin, avant le réveil spontané de l'enfant. Après le prélèvement, on retourne la face adhésive et on l'étale à plat sur une lame de verre, où on peut l'examiner au microscope. Au lieu de ruban adhésif, on peut employer un ruban conçu spécialement dans ce but. On trouve rarement des œufs dans les selles.

Traitement.

Par le traitement on vise à détruire les œufs et les vers intestinaux, et à prévenir une réinfestation exogène.

Le violet de gentiane constituait autrefois le traitement spécifique de l'oxyurose. Deux médicaments sont apparus, depuis lors, sur le marché. Le citrate de pipérazine (Antepar), présenté sous forme de sirop parfumé aux fruits, sous forme de tablettes ou de biscuits. Le dosage est calculé en fonction du poids de l'enfant; il varie de 250 mg à 2 g à donner une fois par jour, après le lever, pendant sept jours. Il constitue une thérapie efficace et très active qui, aux doses prescrites, n'entraîne aucun incident. Le pamoate de pyrvinium (Vanquin ou Povan) est un oxyuricide à dose unique, efficace et non toxique. Le médicament est présenté sous forme de tablettes et le dosage est de 5 mg par kg de poids corporel. Il donnera aux selles ou aux vomissements une coloration rouge; il tache les vêtements. Il faut signaler aux parents que l'enfant peut occasionnellement vomir la médication.

On doit traiter simultanément tous les sujets infestés d'une même famille ou d'un même groupe. Même si les oxyures ont complètement disparu d'une maison, les contacts extérieurs risquent de provoquer des réinfestations.

Soins infirmiers.

Pour prévenir une réinfestation, il faut recouvrir les mains de l'enfant de mitaines ou de chaussettes pour qu'il ne puisse pas recueillir des œufs sous les ongles quand il se gratte la région périanale. Il faut couper les ongles ras et veiller à garder les mains bien propres, surtout le matin et avant les repas. L'enfant devrait porter une couche bien serrée ou un pyjama-combinaison, pour qu'il ne puisse toucher la région infestée. Il faut nettoyer bien soigneusement l'anus au savon et à l'eau après chaque selle, et appliquer une crème adoucissante pour soulager le prurit. Il faut nettoyer tous les jours le siège de la toilette. Les draps, les sous-vêtements, les pyjamas et les serviettes de toilette de l'enfant doivent être bouillis pour tuer les œufs qui se trouvent souvent sur le linge. À l'hôpital, il faut empêcher que l'enfant n'infeste les autres malades. Il faut nettoyer et stériliser son bassin de lit, après chaque emploi.

Les vers peuvent être évacués de l'intestin par un lavement, des cathartiques ou autres médicaments prescrits par le médecin. Cette phase de la thérapeutique est rarement nécessaire.

L'infirmière doit expliquer à la mère que ces parasites ne constituent pas un signe de malpropreté, afin qu'elle ne se sente pas coupable de l'infestation de son enfant.

Pronostic et prévention. Le *pronostic* est habituellement bon.

La *prévention* consiste à respecter une hygiène scrupuleuse, à la fois personnelle et collective.

Ascaridiose

Étiologie et épidémiologie. L'ascaridiose est due à un nématode, l'*Ascaris Lumbricoides*. Le ver adulte, comparable à un ver de terre blanc ou rose, mesure de 15 à 40 cm de longueur. On trouve ces vers dans les pays chauds et dans les zones tempérées du Nord et du Sud. L'œuf fécondé peut survivre à presque toutes les intempéries, sauf si l'atmosphère ambiante est vraiment très chaude ou très froide. On trouve l'œuf dans les selles d'une personne infestée et dans le sol contaminé. Là où l'on n'utilise pas les cabinets d'aisance, les œufs fécondés viennent en contact avec le sol. L'œuf commence à se développer s'il se trouve en milieu chaud et humide et, au bout de neuf jours, la larve a atteint un premier stade. La larve mue une fois et, pendant une semaine, l'œuf devient infestant. Il n'éclôt pas sur le sol, mais uniquement après avoir été avalé.

Tous les jeunes enfants peuvent déposer leurs excréments là où ils jouent et, ainsi, ensemencer le sol. Les engrais organiques peuvent également en être responsables. Les œufs se développent à la surface du sol, et les enfants peuvent se contaminer en portant leurs doigts ou leurs jouets à la bouche, en avalant de la boue ou en mangeant des légumes non lavés. Beaucoup d'enfants âgés de un à dix ans sont infestés par les ascaris et peuvent contaminer d'autres enfants et les adultes.

Physio-pathologie, manifestations cliniques et diagnostic. Lorsque les œufs d'Ascaris atteignent le duodénum, ils éclosent; les larves pénètrent dans la muqueuse intestinale et elles envahissent le système veineux ou lymphatique. Elles passent habituellement par le foie et se rendent aux poumons en suivant la circulation veineuse.

Les larves traversent la paroi des capillaires pulmonaires et pénètrent dans l'alvéole où une réaction inflammatoire empêche la remontée vers les bronches. Après avoir mué une deuxième fois, au niveau des alvéoles, les larves remontent l'arbre bronchique, passent par l'épiglotte, descendent vers l'estomac et l'intestin grêle où elles se fixent et parviennent à maturité.

Les vers peuvent être évacués avec les selles, être rejetés dans les vomissements ou s'échapper par les narines. L'obstruction du canal appendiculaire, la perforation intestinale, l'obstruction du cholédoque, l'envahissement du parenchyme hépatique ou de la cavité pleurale peuvent également se produire.

Les *manifestations cliniques* dépendent de l'endroit où se trouvent les parasites. Les larves qui ont envahi les alvéoles pulmonaires peuvent provoquer une pneumonie atypique. Ces larves migratrices causent parfois une allergie qui se manifeste par de l'asthme, de l'urticaire et une éosinophilie. L'infestation intestinale peut passer inaperçue ou se manifester par des nausées, des vomissements, une anorexie, une perte de poids, de l'insomnie, une fièvre légère, de la nervosité, de l'irritabilité ou une asthénie physique et psychique. L'enfant se plaint surtout de coliques intestinales. Un amas serré de vers dans la lumière de l'intestin, peut provoquer une occlusion qui peut aller jusqu'à la perforation, l'invagination ou l'iléus paralytique.

La découverte d'œufs à l'examen microscopique des selles, permet de faire le *diagnostic* qui est parfois évident quand des vers sont émis dans les selles, vomis, ou rejetés par le nez.

Traitement, pronostic et prévention. Le citrate de pipérazine (Antépar) est le remède de choix et il a été décrit à la page précédente. Le médecin prescrit de 1 à 3,5 g selon le poids de l'enfant, une fois par jour, deux jours de suite. Cette médication ne nécessite aucune adjonction médicamenteuse et est exempte d'effets secondaires, si l'on s'en tient au dosage normal.

Le *pronostic* est excellent, à condition d'administrer un anthelminthique spécifique. Il varie lorsque des complications secondaires surgissent, telles une pneumopathie, une occlusion ou une perforation de l'intestin.

Les *mesures de prévention* s'avèrent essentielles dans les régions très infestées où le cycle recommence environ tous les trois mois. Ces mesures comprennent un traitement sanitaire des excréments, l'éducation du public, une surveillance des endroits de villégiature et le réaménagement du sol contaminé en retournant la terre pour en enterrer la surface infestée. Enfin, tous les sujets atteints doivent être correctement traités, si l'on veut que les mesures de prévention donnent des résultats.

Accidents

Nous ne pouvons étudier ici toutes les catégories d'accidents; nous considérerons les soins donnés aux enfants après les accidents les plus habituels. Parmi ceux-ci, il y a l'introduction de corps étrangers dans le nez ou les oreilles, les empoisonnements, les brûlures et les fractures du fémur.

Corps étrangers dans le nez

Incidence et types. Ce type d'accident se produit fréquemment à l'âge du trottineur. Le nourrisson n'est apparemment pas intéressé par un orifice aussi petit que la narine, et le grand enfant sait qu'il ne doit rien y introduire. Un jeune enfant introduit de petits corps étrangers dans son nez, par exemple, des grains de chapelet, des cailloux, des noyaux de cerise, des pois, des pépins de melon ou n'importe quel petit objet en sa possession.

Manifestations cliniques et diagnostic. Il est rare que l'enfant fasse pénétrer un objet très loin dans son nez. Des efforts maladroits pour l'enlever peuvent, cependant, le repousser en arrière. Le premier symptôme qui éveillera l'attention de la mère est la douleur provoquée par la palpation, une gêne respiratoire et parfois des éternuements. Les légumes, tels que les fèves et les pois augmentent de volume en absorbant du liquide et leur présence se manifeste assez vite après l'accident. L'objet dur, inorganique, peut demeurer en place pendant des mois, sans révéler sa présence. En général, cependant, sa présence se décèle par une irritation de la muqueuse, de l'œdème, de l'obstruction et par un écoulement sanguinolent et purulent.

Le *diagnostic* est établi après un examen au spéculum ou au rhinoscope.

Traitement. En demandant à l'enfant de se moucher fortement, pendant que l'on comprime la narine indemne, on parvient parfois à expulser le corps étranger. Lorsqu'il est plus profondément enfoncé, le médecin pulvérise dans la cavité nasale un anesthésique local et tente l'extraction sous vision directe.

Corps étrangers dans l'oreille

Incidence, types et traitement. Ce genre d'accident se produit habituellement vers la 2ème ou 3ème année de vie. L'enfant peut introduire dans son oreille tout objet petit, qu'il soit dur ou mou.

Si l'enfant coopère, on enlève doucement l'objet visible et facile à atteindre; sinon il vaut mieux recourir à l'anesthésie générale. Il faut éviter l'irrigation des particules organiques, comme des fèves ou des pois, qui, en absorbant de l'eau, peuvent augmenter de volume. En certaines circonstances, le médecin peut être amené à pratiquer une incision rétro-auriculaire.

Si un insecte pénètre dans l'oreille, l'enfant entend un vrombissement qui l'effraie. Il faut noyer l'animal en injectant quelques ml d'eau dans le canal auditif externe, avant de l'extraire délicatement avec des pincettes.

Pour enlever un petit bouchon de cérumen qui, techniquement, n'est pas un corps étranger, on procède avec douceur et précaution à l'aide d'un écouvillon ou d'une curette. Il faut d'abord ramollir les bouchons volumineux avec de l'huile ou une solution savonneuse détergente, avant de les enlever par des lavages à l'eau tiède.

Empoisonnement

L'empoisonnement est un état morbide causé par l'ingestion d'une substance toxique. Une quantité de produits toxiques est à la portée de la curiosité naturelle d'un enfant sans surveillance ou inexpérimenté.

Notre étude se limitera aux poisons que les enfants prennent par la bouche. Un enfant peut recracher un poison désagréable au goût, mais il peut aussi en avaler une certaine quantité. Il peut même en prendre plusieurs bouchées. Nous considérons comme toxique toute substance qui, lorsqu'elle est ingérée, même en quantités infimes, est susceptible de nuire aux tissus et de perturber les fonctions organiques.

Les poisons peuvent comprendre 1) ceux que l'enfant trouvera probablement dans l'armoire à pharmacie, comme l'aspirine, les contraceptifs oraux, les somnifères ou les tranquillisants, ou encore ceux qu'il trouvera dans une armoire de cuisine, comme des détergents de toutes sortes, des insecticides mal rangés ou de violents poisons exterminateurs d'insectes, de rats ou de souris; 2) ceux qui ont un effet corrosif immédiat, comme la soude caustique ou le phénol; et enfin, 3) d'autres dans lesquels une culture de bactéries a produit des toxines, comme dans différents produits alimentaires.

Les intoxications alimentaires dues à des toxines bactériennes, requièrent le même type de soins que les autres gastro-entérites et on ne les mentionne ici que pour souligner l'importance de se débarrasser rapidement de tout aliment avarié. Ces intoxications bactériennes sont plus fréquentes en été, dans les zones défavorisées des milieux urbains. Les produits laitiers, les salades et les viandes se conservent mal sans une bonne réfrigération et sont une source fréquente d'intoxication alimentaire.

Il faut aussi distinguer les poisons qui agissent dans un délai assez court, comme une dose trop forte de somnifères ou de cyanure (mort-aux-rats), et ceux qui ont un effet lent, mais cumulatif, comme une ingestion chronique de petites quantités de peinture qui contient du plomb.

Incidence, diagnostic, manifestations cliniques et traitement. *Principes généraux:* actuellement, les décès d'enfants âgés de plus d'un an sont essentiellement dus aux accidents et aux intoxications. L'intoxication, chez les enfants, est toujours liée à un manque de surveillance ou à une négligence d'un adulte qui laisse des substances toxiques à leur portée. Environ 500 enfants au-dessous de cinq ans meurent chaque année aux États-Unis, des suites d'une ingestion de substances toxiques que l'on trouve habituellement dans l'armoire à pharmacie ou dans un réduit de cuisine. Beaucoup plus encore souffrent d'infirmités permanentes, comme des atteintes hépatiques, une constriction de l'œsophage ou des lésions glomérulaires.

On emploie plus de 500 produits toxiques à la maison. Parmi ceux-ci, il y a les produits d'entretien, les détergents, les agents de blanchiment, les insecticides, les métaux lourds, les solvants de peinture, les cirages, le kérosène, les cosmétiques et les médicaments, comme l'aspirine, les contraceptifs oraux, les hypnotiques, les sédatifs et les tranquillisants. La législation oblige les fabricants à inscrire la mention « DANGER » sur les récipients contenant des substances toxiques. Les associations de consommateurs essaient de forcer les fabricants à inscrire sur les étiquettes la composition chimique du contenu et l'antidote approprié en cas d'accident. Plusieurs produits corrosifs contiennent maintenant ces détails sur leur étiquette.

Les enfants de 1 à 4 ans sont les plus vulnérables aux intoxications. Au-dessous de cinq ans, les intoxications sont plus fréquentes chez les garçons que chez les filles. Sans doute, les garçons prennent-ils plus de risques que les filles et sont-ils plus actifs. La fréquence et les causes des intoxications varient suivant les régions et selon qu'il s'agisse d'une population rurale ou urbaine. Il y a aussi une différence d'après les classes sociales.

Dans tous les cas d'ingestion de poison à action rapide, il faut faire immédiatement le *diagnostic* pour que l'on puisse administrer l'antidote avant l'absorption du poison par l'organisme. Pour cette raison, la mère ou l'infirmière doit essayer de décrire au médecin le déroulement complet de l'accident. Souvent, cependant, elles ne savent pas ce que l'enfant a pris, et même s'il a vraiment absorbé du poison. On peut simplement croire que l'enfant souffre d'un malaise soudain et le conduire chez le médecin quelque temps après l'ingestion du produit toxique. Il peut s'avérer fatal de croire que les symptômes de l'enfant sont dus à une maladie quelconque retardant ainsi le traitement de l'intoxication.

En premier lieu, il faut s'efforcer d'identifier le poison. On retrouve quelquefois le récipient qui contenait le produit toxique; l'enfant plus âgé peut raconter ce qui s'est passé et donner des indications précieuses. Il faut conserver les vomitus et les urines recueillis après l'accident, car leur analyse peut permettre de connaître la nature du produit et sa quantité approximative. On peut quelquefois identifier le poison par l'odeur caractéristique de l'haleine de l'enfant.

L'examen spectroscopique du sang montrera la présence ou l'absence de méthémoglobine, de sulfhémoglibine et de carboxyhémoglobine. On emploie le colorimètre photo-électrique pour mettre en évidence des traces de plomb, de thymol et de beaucoup d'autres substances toxiques. On peut faire des radiographies des os pour déceler une intoxication au plomb et au bismuth.

On trouve des renseignements précis sur les manifestations cliniques et le traitement des différentes intoxications dans des manuels appropriés ou au centre d'intoxication local, s'il existe.

Parmi les *symptômes* cliniques habituels d'une intoxication, on trouve 1) les troubles gastro-intestinaux: (a) douleur abdominale, (b) vomissements, (c) anorexie, (d) diarrhée; 2) les symptômes cardio-respiratoires: (a) choc, (b) collapsus, (c) cyanose inexpliquée; 3) les troubles neurologiques centraux: (a) perte soudaine de la conscience, (b) convulsions.

Ces manifestations cliniques ne sont pas spécifiques au petit enfant et peuvent indiquer une maladie aiguë aussi bien qu'une intoxication.

On peut résumer comme suit les principes généraux du *traitement, en cas d'ingestion de poison:*

1) En cas d'intoxication aiguë, il faut conserver son sang-froid, afin de pouvoir établir le traitement et exécuter les prescriptions du médecin.

2) Il faut éviter une manipulation excessive de l'enfant et un traitement exagéré, comme de trop grandes doses de sédatifs, de stimulants ou d'antidotes qui peuvent causer plus de tort que le poison lui-même.

3) Un traitement rapide est nécessaire. Dans la plupart des cas d'intoxication, l'efficacité de l'antidote dépend du laps de temps entre l'ingestion du poison et l'administration de l'antidote.

La première chose à faire consiste à provoquer un vomissement. La meilleure façon d'obtenir un vomissement rapide, abondant et sans trop de manipulation de l'enfant, est de lui administrer une petite dose (15 ml) de sirop d'ipéca. Ce produit devrait se trouver dans toutes les pharmacies familiales. Si les parents n'ont pas de médicaments sous la main, ils peuvent donner un verre d'eau salée ou tiède à l'enfant et alors, tout en maintenant sa tête basse, exciter la partie postérieure du pharynx avec le doigt, une cuiller ou un abaisse-langue, jusqu'à ce qu'un vomissement s'ensuive. Si l'enfant ne réussit pas à vomir, on peut lui faire boire du lait ou de la crème en abondance pour retarder l'absorption du poison ingéré. *Il ne faut jamais faire vomir un patient comateux, ou un sujet qui vient d'avaler une base coustique ou du kérosène.*

Après cela, il faut immédiatement amener l'enfant chez un médecin, à l'hôpital ou à une clinique d'intoxication, en apportant le flacon ou le récipient d'où l'enfant a pris le poison, pour que le médecin puisse l'examiner. Il faut aussi apporter le contenu gastrique vomi par l'enfant et les urines qu'il aurait pu émettre.

S'il n'a pas été possible de provoquer un vomissement, ou si l'on a des raisons de croire que tout le poison n'a pas été vomi quand l'enfant arrive à l'hôpital, on doit lui donner une dose de sirop d'ipéca, s'il n'en a pas reçu plus d'une dose. Cette médication est encore plus efficace que le lavage gastrique. Toutefois, l'enfant peut aussi subir ce dernier traitement à son admission à l'hôpital.

L'apomorphine, administrée par voie sous-cutanée, provoque habituellement un vomissement immédiat, et le médecin peut choisir de l'administrer. L'apomorphine provoque des dépressions respiratoires, et il ne faut pas l'utiliser si l'enfant est dans le coma, si le toxique a perturbé l'appareil respiratoire, ou encore, si la respiration est lente et pénible.

On administre, si possible, un antidote spécifique, s'il en existe un. L'étiquette figurant sur le flacon peut aider à le déterminer. Sinon, il faut appeler un centre d'intoxication pour obtenir le renseignement. On administre l'antidote, même si l'estomac a été complètement évacué par le lavage, pour combattre les effets du poison qui aurait pu être absorbé par l'organisme.

On applique un traitement de soutien général et symptomatique, en cas de choc ou de troubles métaboliques. Le médecin peut prescrire l'oxygénothérapie et l'administration de liquides et d'électrolytes par voie parentérale. On doit envisager des exsanguino-transfusions ou des séances d'épuration extra-rénale, à la suite de certaines intoxications.

L'ANTIDOTE UNIVERSEL. Si le toxique demeure inconnu, le charbon pur activé est l'adsorbant de choix à administrer, étant donné qu'il est efficace contre presque tous les produits chimiques et même sous des pH défavorables. On lui adjoint un purgatif pour en favoriser l'excrétion qui entraîne le poison. Le charbon pur activé est plus efficace et plus rapide que le classique antidote universel, dont la composition est la suivante:

Charbon pulvérisé (obtenu à partir de toasts brûlés)	2 parties
Oxyde de magnésium (lait de magnésie)	1 partie
Acide tannique (thé fort)	1 partie

Le charbon inerte provenant des « rôties brûlées » est tout à fait inefficace. On croyait que le charbon pulvérisé absorbait le phénol et la strychnine; l'oxyde de magnésium neutralise les acides et l'acide tannique précipite les alcaloïdes, certains glucosides et beaucoup de métaux.

INTOXICATION AUX SALICYLATES. L'aspirine est employée si couramment à la maison que les parents ne se rendent pas compte du danger qu'elle représente pour les enfants. Quand on laisse à leur portée des cachets d'aspirine agréablement parfumés, il peut arriver qu'ils en absorbent une grosse quantité. On a donc fait plusieurs recommandations dans le but de réduire le nombre des intoxications accidentelles. On préconise la vente des comprimés d'aspirine en petites quantités, pour que l'enfant ne puisse en prendre beaucoup à la fois, même en vidant toute une bouteille. On peut aussi les vendre en flacons difficiles à ouvrir, ou éviter de leur donner l'apparence ou la saveur de bonbons qui les rendent si tentants pour le jeune enfant. L'intoxication peut aussi se produire par suite d'un surdosage thérapeutique, à la suite d'un emploi excessif de poudre ou de pommade d'acide salicylique sur des lésions cutanées étendues, ouvertes et suintantes.

Les manifestations cliniques comprennent une hyperventilation, déterminant une alcalose respiratoire qui engendre un état confusionnel et un coma. L'acidose métabolique peut se superposer à l'alcalose respiratoire. Elle est due à une compensation rénale qui engendre une perte des bases fixes du corps. Les signes toxiques précoces sont suivis d'une acido-cétose. Les dérivés salicylés inhibent la formation de prothrombine dans le foie, causant des manifestations purpuriques. On peut observer chez l'enfant une anorexie, des vomissements, de la diaphorèse et une hyperpyrexie qui engendrent la déshydratation.

Le traitement immédiat d'une intoxication aiguë à l'aspirine consiste en l'administration de sirop d'ipéca suivie au besoin d'un lavage gastrique. On administre par voie intraveineuse des liquides contenant des électrolytes et des hydrates de carbone pour accélérer l'excrétion des salicylates dans l'urine. On injecte de la vitamine K par voie intramusculaire. On peut également avoir recours à l'exsanguino-transfusion, à la dialyse péritonéale ou à l'hémodialyse dans les cas extrêmes.

INTOXICATION AU KÉROSÈNE (pétrole distillé). L'intoxication au pétrole se produit parce que les jeunes enfants avalent du kérosène, du benzène, de l'essence, de l'huile de naphte ou quelqu'autre substance abandonnée négligemment autour de la maison. Ces substances sont rapidement absorbées par le tube digestif. Le traitement immédiat consiste à faire avaler à l'enfant 1,5 ml d'huile minérale par kilogramme de poids, ce qui ralentit l'absorption; puis on commence le lavage gastrique. Il est préférable de pratiquer un lavage plutôt que de provoquer un vomissement par émétique, à cause du danger d'aspiration de la substance huileuse qui pourrait provoquer une broncho-pneumonie lipoïdique. Lorsqu'on évacue le contenu gastrique, il faut maintenir la tête de l'enfant plus basse que ses hanches. Il faut prendre beaucoup de précautions pour éviter toute aspiration de la substance ingérée, et certains médecins estiment qu'il faut éviter de pratiquer ce traitement. L'intoxication qui peut également se produire par inhalation massive, s'accompagne d'euphorie, d'une démarche ébrieuse, de céphalées suivies de perte de conscience et de cyanose. En cas d'inges-

tion, les signes nerveux sont précédés d'une gastro-entérite.

Le traitement ultérieur comporte des analeptiques, l'administration prophylactique d'un antibiotique par voie intramusculaire, de l'oxygène et une transfusion en cas de méthémoglobinémie. Une pneumonie et des complications rénales peuvent se produire ultérieurement.

INTOXICATION PAR LES PRODUITS CHIMIQUES CORROSIFS. Les produits chimiques corrosifs, comme la soude, détruisent les tissus qui entrent en contact avec eux. La soude demeure une des sources les plus fréquentes d'intoxication chez les enfants. Les produits à base de soude et de potasse comprennent les poudres à lessiver ou à nettoyer les tuyauteries, les solvants de peinture et les désinfectants.

Ces substances engendrent une irritation locale intense de la bouche, du pharynx, de l'œsophage et de l'estomac. Les symptômes sont la douleur, l'incapacité d'avaler et la prostration. Les muqueuses atteintes blanchissent immédiatement après l'accident, mais plus tard elles deviennent brunes, ulcérées et œdémateuses. L'œdème entraîne parfois une obstruction respiratoire et une trachéotomie peut s'avérer nécessaire. On doit instituer une corticothérapie précoce, afin de lutter contre l'œdème et les sténoses cicatricielles consécutives. Le pouls est faible et rapide, et l'enfant peut présenter un collapsus.

Si l'enfant survit, les symptômes aigus se calment, mais une sténose de l'œsophage apparaît souvent après quatre à huit semaines, par suite d'un rétrécissement cicatriciel. Si l'obstruction est importante, l'enfant peut être incapable d'avaler des aliments ou même du liquide.

Le traitement immédiat consiste à neutraliser le produit chimique avec du vinaigre dilué ou du jus de citron. On peut soulager la douleur à l'aide de sédatifs, d'huile d'olive ou de lait. Il faut éviter le lavage gastrique et les émétiques, par crainte d'une perforation de la muqueuse nécrotique. Une corticothérapie précoce, suivie d'une œsophagoscopie dès que c'est possible sans danger, diminuent les risques de sténose permanente.

Si l'enfant ne peut avaler, on l'alimente par voie parentérale. Pour éviter une sténose permanente de l'œsophage, le médecin peut passer dans l'œsophage un cathéter en caoutchouc de dimension appropriée et dont l'extrémité est alourdie par un poids (bougie). On applique le premier traitement quatre jours environ après l'accident. Si la sténose persiste, les dilatations par bougie sont poursuivies 2 à

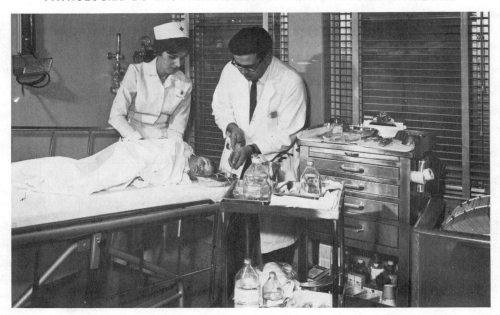

Figure 15-7. Salle de traitement d'urgence contre les intoxications. Le médecin procède au lavage gastrique et l'infirmière maintient délicatement l'enfant dans la position appropriée. Tout le matériel d'urgence est disponible en permanence dans cette pièce. (Courtoisie de l'Hôpital Sainte-Justine, Montréal.)

3 fois par semaine, au moins pendant un an. Progressivement, on augmente la dimension des bougies. En présence d'une obstruction complète, on peut nourrir l'enfant par gastrostomie, et cela jusqu'à ce que l'œsophage soit suffisamment dilaté. Les dilatations peuvent alors s'effectuer soit par voie rétrograde, soit par voie descendante. Lorsque l'œsophage reprend son diamètre optimal, les dilatations peuvent être graduellement espacées tous les mois, puis tous les six mois, et finalement, une fois par année. À la fin de la croissance, les dilatations sont accomplies selon les besoins.

Soins infirmiers. L'infirmière doit empêcher les parents anxieux de trop énerver l'enfant ou de le manipuler. On doit recueillir tous les échantillons de vomissements et d'urine pour les examens de laboratoire. L'infirmière assiste le médecin lorsqu'il procède au lavage gastrique ou le fait elle-même, d'après l'ordonnance.

Il faut maintenir l'enfant correctement, le visage tourné d'un côté. On introduit une sonde bien lubrifiée et de gros calibre, selon l'âge et le contenu gastrique. On fixe un appareil d'aspiration. Il faut injecter et aspirer une petite quantité de solution de lavage (150 à 200 ml) autant de fois qu'il le faut pour retirer toutes traces de poison. On emploie ordinairement deux à quatre litres de solution.

Pour une évacuation immédiate de l'estomac, on administre du sirop d'ipéca. On peut utiliser de l'eau, des solutions diluées de sel et de bicarbonate de soude, en attendant de disposer d'une solution plus satisfaisante. Ultérieurement, on emploiera du charbon activé, de l'acide tannique, de l'oxyde de magnésium ou une autre solution, selon le poison que l'enfant a ingéré.

Le lavage gastrique ne peut être pratiqué dans les cas suivants: dans les intoxications par les produits corrosifs — parce qu'il peut se produire une perforation de l'œsophage —; après l'ingestion de strychnine, parce que l'excitation provoquée par le tube de lavage peut déterminer une convulsion mortelle.

L'infirmière doit surveiller tout signe d'excitation ou de dépression du système nerveux central. L'excitation se manifeste par des convulsions, une agitation, un état de confusion et du délire. La dépression se manifeste par la stupeur et le coma.

Il peut y avoir des symptômes de dépression respiratoire, d'œdème pulmonaire et de broncho-pneumonie. La respiration artificielle, l'oxygénothérapie et le maintien de la perméabilité des voies respiratoires peuvent s'avérer nécessaires pour soulager l'oppression.

L'infirmière doit observer tout signe de collapsus circulatoire périphérique ou de défaillance cardiaque. L'administration de liquides ou de digitaline, par voie intraveineuse, peut être requise.

L'infirmière doit observer la fréquence des émissions d'urine et en recueillir des échantillons, d'après les directives du médecin. L'importance de l'atteinte rénale est variable. L'aspect le plus important du traitement, en relation avec l'influence du poison sur les reins, est l'administration judicieuse d'électrolytes et de liquides.

La régulation thermique est souvent perturbée; il importe donc de prendre la température de l'enfant à des intervalles réguliers et fréquents, et de signaler au médecin toute hypothermie ou hyperthermie.

L'enfant intoxiqué est sensible aux infections. On l'isole des autres enfants, et une infirmière qui est atteinte, ne fût-ce que d'une infection légère, ne doit pas le soigner. On administre les antibiotiques, d'après l'ordonnance du médecin.

L'enfant et ses parents ont besoin du soutien affectif de l'infirmière, particulièrement si l'enfant souffre. La mère peut se sentir coupable et se reprocher l'accident. Il faut l'aider à surmonter son expérience traumatisante. Des soins judicieux et compréhensifs sont essentiels. L'enfant qui doit subir des dilatations répétées a presque toujours besoin d'une thérapie par le jeu et ses parents doivent être conseillés et soutenus judicieusement. Certains peuvent apprendre à pratiquer les dilatations œsophagiennes et éviter à l'enfant des séjours répétés à l'hôpital. Ces parents comptent beaucoup sur le soutien de l'infirmière.

Prévention. Dans la majorité des cas, les intoxications accidentelles des jeunes enfants sont dues à une certaine négligence des adultes qui s'en occupent. Une étude scientifique récente a démontré que les enfants qui s'empoisonnent appartiennent souvent à des familles instables. Parfois le père est absent, la mère a souvent des ennuis matrimoniaux ou sexuels. En général, les enfants perturbés émotivement ont plus d'accidents que les autres. La responsabilité immédiate repose sur les parents de l'enfant. Mais, sont également responsables, tous les membres de l'équipe de santé qui enseignent aux parents l'hygiène et les soins des enfants.

Il faut garder tous les produits dangereux hors de la portée du jeune enfant, sur une étagère élevée ou, encore mieux, dans une armoire fermée à clef. Tous les médicaments, les produits d'entretien et les produits toxiques doivent être gardés dans leur récipient d'origine, car celui-ci est clairement étiqueté, et aucun adulte prudent ne les laissera à la portée de l'enfant. Si l'on range des substances toxiques dans des récipients alimentaires, on risque que quelqu'un les dépose en un endroit d'où l'enfant pourra les prendre et en goûter le contenu. La même précaution s'impose pour les matières inflammables. Il faut également protéger les enfants contre les intoxications par des aliments avariés; on préviendra ainsi les intoxications bactériennes.

Brûlures

Incidence et classification. On appelle brûlure toute destruction tissulaire causée par la chaleur. La chaleur peut être sèche, si elle provient d'un radiateur ou d'un poêle, d'allumettes enflammées ou d'un fil électrique sous tension; ou humide, si elle provient d'une tasse de café brûlant, de soupe chaude renversée sur l'enfant, ou d'un robinet d'eau chaude ouvert pendant que ce dernier se trouve dans la baignoire. Sont également à l'origine de brûlures: les agents chimiques, l'électricité, la surexposition aux rayons ultra-violets et aux rayons X et l'exposition aux substances radio-actives. Les brûlures constituent une des lésions accidentelles les plus fréquentes chez le nourrisson et l'enfant et la plupart auraient pu être prévenues. Les brûlures des nourrissons se produisent principalement à la maison, tandis que pour le grand enfant, cet accident survient à la maison, à l'école ou au jeu.

La classification des brûlures se fait d'après le degré (profondeur de la destruction tissulaire) et le pourcentage de la surface cutanée affectée. Chez l'enfant, le pourcentage de la surface atteinte importe encore plus que la profondeur des brûlures. Une brûlure *superficielle* ou du *premier degré* affecte *uniquement l'épiderme*. Il y a une rougeur de la peau, accompagnée de douleur et d'œdème. Les tissus se régénèrent sans difficulté dans les brûlures superficielles. Une brûlure du *second degré* détruit les *couches superficielles* de la peau et provoque des lésions tissulaires profondes. La région affectée est rouge, couverte de vésicules, et très douloureuse. Des cicatrices peuvent se produire, mais la peau se régénère à partir des cellules épithéliales actives qui restent. Une brûlure du *troisième degré amène la destruction* de l'épiderme et d'une partie du derme. La région brûlée peut paraître carbonisée. Il y a destruction des terminaisons nerveuses, des glandes sudoripares et des follicules pileux. Les brûlures du troisième degré nécessitent des greffes.

Tout enfant ayant une brûlure de 5 à 12% ou plus de sa surface cutanée doit être admis à l'hôpital pour un traitement. On peut évaluer approximativement cette surface à l'aide de la

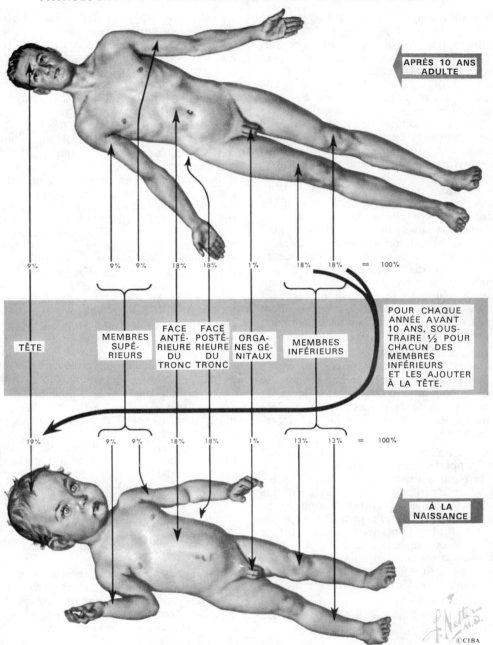

APRÈS 10 ANS
ADULTE

9%   9%   9%   18%   18%   1%   18%   18%   =   100%

| TÊTE | MEMBRES SUPÉRIEURS | FACE ANTÉRIEURE DU TRONC | FACE POSTÉRIEURE DU TRONC | ORGANES GÉNITAUX | MEMBRES INFÉRIEURS |

POUR CHAQUE ANNÉE AVANT 10 ANS, SOUSTRAIRE ½ POUR CHACUN DES MEMBRES INFÉRIEURS ET LES AJOUTER À LA TÊTE.

19%   9%   9%   18%   18%   1%   13%   13%   =   100%

À LA NAISSANCE

©CIBA

Figure 15-8. La « règle de neuf » permet de calculer l'étendue des brûlures. (Illustrations de Frank H. Netter, m.d., dans le Clinical Symposia de Ciba; John W. Chamberlain, m.d.; Kenneth Welch, m.d.; Thomas S. Morse, m.d.)

« règle de neuf » pour le nourrisson, l'enfant et l'adulte. Cette règle est utilisée pour obtenir une évaluation rapide, mais ensuite le calcul de la surface brûlée, chez le nourrisson et l'enfant, est effectué grâce à un graphique modifié beaucoup plus précis.

Problèmes associés aux brûlures; traitement et soins infirmiers. Le traitement d'un enfant brûlé vise d'abord à lui sauver la vie, et ensuite, à le protéger contre l'infection et à préserver ou rétablir autant que possible son apparence et ses capacités.

Le déséquilibre hydro-électrolytique présente un sérieux problème. Peu après la brûlure, il y a une diminution du volume plasmatique. Les électrolytes, l'eau et les protéines s'échappent des vaisseaux et sont emprisonnés autour de la brûlure. L'organisme est déshydraté, une hémoconcentration s'ensuit. Au cours des quarante-huit premières heures, si la brûlure couvre un quart à un cinquième de la surface du corps de l'enfant, la perte de liquide encouru peut causer l'apparition du choc hypovolémique. Les érythrocytes diminuent par l'hémolyse et le saignement dans la région atteinte. De grandes quantités de sodium envahissent le liquide œdémateux de la région brûlée, et il y a une substitution consécutive de potassium intracellulaire par du sodium. Le malade peut présenter une hyponatrémie. Souvent, l'acidose se développe. L'hypovolémie, l'hémoconcentration et la déshydratation causent une insuffisance circulatoire rénale. Le rein peut difficilement éliminer le potassium excédentaire et les déchets azotés. L'infection peut retarder la réabsorption du liquide œdémateux dans la région brûlée.

Le *traitement immédiat* d'une brûlure du premier degré consiste à nettoyer la région atteinte, à l'enduire d'une petite couche de pommade contenant un anesthésique local, et à administrer des analgésiques. On peut alors mettre un bandage stérile, pour ne pas aggraver la douleur.

Une autre méthode de traitement immédiat consiste à appliquer des sacs d'eau glacée ou à plonger la région atteinte dans de l'eau glacée, à laquelle on peut ajouter un antiseptique Ce traitement qui peut entraîner une hypothermie à des degrés divers, peut être appliqué lorsque les brûlures atteignent une surface cutanée égale ou supérieure à 20%. On peut prolonger ce traitement jusqu'à ce que toute douleur ait disparu. On calme ainsi la douleur, et l'on diminue l'œdème, la perte de liquide et le risque d'infection.

Quand un enfant a des brûlures plus sérieuses qui nécessitent une hospitalisation, il faut le placer dans une chambre privée avec eau courante et bain. Il faut veiller à disposer d'un équipement et d'une literie stériles. Le personnel qui soigne l'enfant doit revêtir blouse et gants stériles. On peut aussi exiger des masques, des bonnets et des protège-chaussures stériles. L'équipement qui doit être prêt dans la chambre de l'enfant, comporte le matériel pour les intraveineuses et le plateau pour les dénudations veineuses, les solutions intraveineuses, du plasma sanguin, un plateau de cathétérisme vésical avec des sondes Foley

de calibre approprié, un récipient stérile pour recueillir les urines, un plateau en cas de trachéotomie d'urgence et des canules trachéales de calibre adéquat, un arceau si on utilise la technique « ouverte », un appareil aspirateur avec des cathéters, et un masque à oxygène adapté à l'enfant et fixé à une source d'oxygène.

Pour les brûlures du deuxième et du troisième degré, le premier problème consiste à combattre l'état de choc. Il faut placer l'enfant sur un drap stérile. On donne de la morphine, de la codéine ou un autre calmant. On administre par voie intraveineuse du plasma et d'autres liquides pour rétablir l'équilibre électrolytique. Il faut garder l'enfant au chaud; on élève la température de la chambre à 25,5°C–26,5°C ou on emploie un arceau chauffant ou des lampes infra-rouges si on utilise la technique « ouverte ». Une chaleur excessive peut, cependant amener une dilatation des vaisseaux sanguins périphériques et augmenter les troubles circulatoires. En vue des transfusions, il faut déterminer les taux d'hématocrite et d'hémoglobine, le groupe sanguin et l'épreuve de compatibilité sanguine (cross match). On effectue très souvent d'autres prélèvements sanguins pour établir le bilan protéique et ionique.

On installe une sonde à demeure et on fait des analyses d'urine. La mesure du débit urinaire devient ici d'une importance primordiale. On mesure toutes les heures la quantité d'urine émise et l'on contrôle le débit des solutés intraveineux pour maintenir la diurèse entre 50 et 100 ml/h. Si le débit urinaire descend sous 30 ml à l'heure, il faut avertir immédiatement le médecin qui prendra les mesures correctives qui s'imposent. La densité urinaire est aussi mesurée toutes les heures de façon à suivre de près le fonctionnement rénal.

S'il faut débrider, une anesthésie appropriée est essentielle. On doit administrer de l'oxygène pour combattre l'anoxie. On peut pratiquer une trachéotomie d'urgence, si des difficultés respiratoires surviennent. En cas de choc, il faut surélever le pied du lit. On injecte de l'anatoxine ou/et de l'antitoxine tétanique, ainsi que du sérum anti-gangréneux. Il convient également d'instituer un traitement anti-infectueux à l'aide d'antibiotiques.

Les problèmes de perturbation électrolytique marquent l'évolution des 48 premières heures. La fuite des électrolytes et du plasma exige une réhydratation adéquate. Par ailleurs, deux jours environ après l'accident, la fuite plasmatique cesse brutalement, la diurèse revient à la normale, le volume sanguin se rétablit et le patient peut souffrir de surcharge vasculaire. L'œdème aigu du poumon constitue une menace grave si l'on néglige de contrôler le débit des solutés intraveineux, au cours de cette période. La diurèse constitue un indice précieux des changements qui surviennent à ce moment.

Durant les premiers jours suivant son admission à l'hôpital, l'enfant peut souffrir de la soif causée par la déshydratation. Initialement, on restreindra probablement l'administration orale des liquides. On essaie de faire boire à l'enfant des préparations à base d'électrolytes qui, malgré leur saveur détestable, demeurent très efficaces comme adjuvant à la thérapie intraveineuse. Plusieurs enfants refusent catégoriquement ce genre de besoin et l'on peut pallier avec du « Seven-Up » ou autre soda que l'on aura pris soin de décarbonater. Les jus de fruits sont, en général, bien acceptés des enfants, mais peuvent provoquer des nausées et des vomissements.

L'opinion est très partagée parmi les médecins en ce qui concerne le traitement local, et l'infirmière suit évidemment les prescriptions du médecin traitant. Dans la *technique « ouverte »*, il n'y a pas de pansements. La région brûlée est exposée à l'air libre, pour qu'une escarre se forme et que la peau guérisse sous les croûtes. Avec cette méthode, on rencontre moins de perturbations thermiques. On peut déplacer le brûlé si l'étendue des brûlures n'est pas trop grande, et il y a moins d'odeurs désagréables. D'habitude, on préfère cette méthode pour les brûlures de la figure, des articulations et des parties génitales. Le risque d'infection est cependant plus grand. Une des méthodes employées pour prévenir l'infection consiste à isoler l'enfant sous une tente en plastique pourvue de hublots à travers lesquels on peut donner les soins. Le problème réel lorsqu'on emploie un tel dispositif est l'isolement de l'enfant auquel on peut difficilement apporter

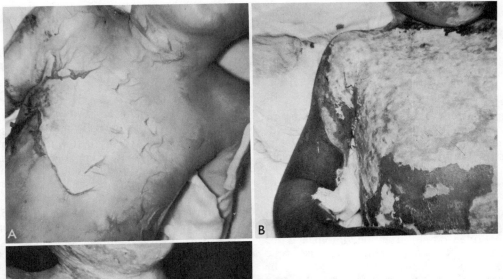

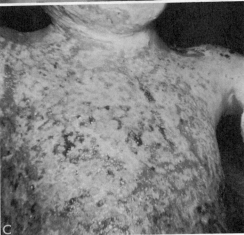

Figure 15-9. Brûlures traitées au nitrate d'argent. *A)* Brûlures par les flammes, atteignant 30% de la surface corporelle. Le durcissement et la décoloration des tissus permettent de soupçonner une brûlure du 3ème degré. *B)* Après 10 jours d'application d'une solution à 0,5% de nitrate d'argent, le coagulat de protéines rend difficile l'évaluation de la profondeur de la lésion. *C)* Après 3 semaines de traitement, de nombreuses zones de tissu de granulation sont apparues et se recouvrent de tissu épithélial. À l'examen bactériologique, on ne retrouve pas d'organismes pathogènes. (Krizek dans *Management of Trauma*, de W. F. Ballinger, R. B. Rutherford et G. D. Zuidema.)

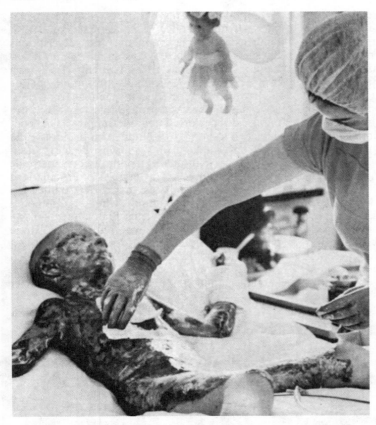

Figure 15-10. Application d'acétate de sulfamylon. L'infirmière applique la crème avec un gant stérile sur un enfant brûlé à 50% de sa surface corporelle. (Sister Mary Claudia: *Am. J. Nurs.* 69(4) : 755-757, avril 1969.)

un appui affectif. La chambre stérile constitue également une solution satisfaisante. Tout ce qui vient en contact avec l'enfant doit être stérilisé et l'infirmière doit employer une technique aseptique stricte (chap. 4).

La *technique du pansement compressif* est une autre forme de traitement. La brûlure est d'abord soigneusement débridée et nettoyée chirurgicalement. Puis, on recouvre toute la surface brûlée d'une gaze fine, imbibée d'une solution ou pommade médicamenteuse, que l'on couvre de plusieurs couches de gaze sèche et épaisse, puis d'un bandage serré. Le tout doit se faire dans des conditions de stricte asepsie. La pose d'un bandage serré assure la compression qui aide à contrôler la perte de plasma provoquée par les brûlures. On laisse ce pansement en place pendant deux ou trois semaines. En cas d'élévation thermique, ou si une odeur nauséabonde se dégage du pansement, on le retire pour traiter l'infection. Certains chirurgiens préfèrent un léger plâtre de Paris aux pansements compressifs. L'infection constitue le plus grand risque de cette méthode.

On utilise couramment diverses solutions et pommades pour le traitement des brûlures.

Parmi celles-ci, il y a la solution à 0,5 pour cent de nitrate d'argent, la pommade au sulfate de gentamycine, le Sulfamylon et une solution à base de silicone. On emploie fréquemment une solution de nitrate d'argent, l'onguent Sulfamylon et le nouveau mélange argent-sulfadiazine.

Si on emploie du nitrate d'argent à 0,5 pour cent, après le débridement, les pansements sont gardés constamment humides, le plus souvent à l'aide de cathéters irrigateurs. On les change deux ou trois fois par jour. Cette méthode diminue l'infection, ce qui permet des greffes plus précoces ou moins étendues et un meilleur résultat esthétique. Malheureusement le médicament cause une assez importante perturbation électrolytique. On peut prévenir cet inconvénient, en procurant des électrolytes par voie orale ou intraveineuse. Les fréquents changements de pansements sont très traumatisants et douloureux pour l'enfant. Si, cependant, l'infirmière se souvient des avantages de cette méthode thérapeutique, elle sera capable de soutenir l'enfant et se sentira moins tendue elle-même au cours du traitement.

En cas de catastrophe, la meilleure méthode de traitement des brûlures est la technique

Figure 15-11. *A)* Le bain-tourbillon assouplit les tissus, ramollit les zones nécrotiques et permet les exercices. *B)* Après le bain, l'infirmière, en blouse, gantée et masquée, pratique le débridement superficiel des zones nécrotiques, elle refait le pansement de manière aseptique. *C)* Un arceau empêche le frottement de la literie sur les tissus. Une tente en matière plastique permet à la chaleur dégagée par l'appareil de conserver l'enfant à une température confortable. (Le traitement de l'enfant brûlé.) (Courtoisie de l'Hôpital Sainte-Justine, Montréal.)

A

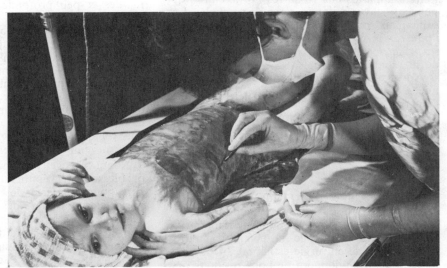

B

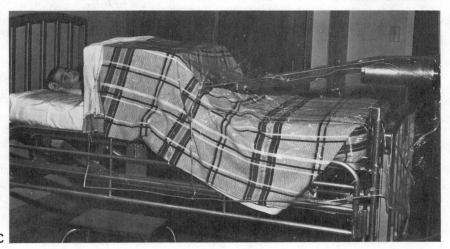

C

« ouverte », l'immobilisation et l'élévation du membre brûlé, et l'administration d'agents anti-infectieux pour prévenir l'infection.

Lorsque l'onguent Sulfamylon est utilisé, l'infirmière doit savoir que ce produit cause une sensation de brûlure, non seulement douloureuse, mais potentiellement terrifiante pour un enfant récemment brûlé. De plus, il importe de bien enlever la couche précédente avant d'en remettre de nouveau. Or, ce traitement, effectué très souvent dans le bain, entraîne des saignements qui peuvent paraître énormes à l'enfant qui voit l'eau se colorer en rouge. L'infirmière doit adapter ses explications à l'âge de l'enfant, de façon à le rassurer efficacement.

En cas de brûlures graves, une anémie peut apparaître vers le cinquième jour, ou plus tôt. On administre du fer et on fait des transfusions sanguines. Après la phase aiguë des premiers jours, apparaissent d'autres problèmes qui peuvent s'avérer fatals pour le malade. Les principaux problèmes sont la *dénutrition et l'infection.* À long terme, les *contractures et les cicatrices* grèvent lourdement l'évolution de la réhabilitation.

Après plusieurs jours, l'enfant souffre d'anémie, il est pâle et anorexique. La douleur, l'inactivité, les perturbations psychologiques qui commencent à se manifester, expliquent son manque flagrant d'appétit. Dans les cas graves, on peut procéder aux gavages. D'emblée, on essaie de donner au malade un régime riche en calories et en protéines qui lui fournit un apport très important en vitamines. La cicatrisation et la lutte contre l'infection dépendent en grande partie du facteur alimentaire.

Le *traitement ultérieur* d'un enfant brûlé comporte des greffes de la peau et d'autres interventions de chirurgie esthétique. Une greffe de la peau ne donnera de bons résultats que si l'on peut obtenir une base propre, sans infection et granuleuse. Il faut ramollir les escarres produites par le traitement « ouvert », avec des compresses salines humides ou des bains tourbillonnants, en vue de préparer la plaie pour la greffe. Toute infection doit être nettoyée et supprimée avant l'intervention.

Presque tous les enfants qui souffrent de brûlures nécessitant des greffes doivent subir des bains quotidiens et des débridements périodiques. L'un et l'autre traitements peuvent être douloureux et ils effraient surtout l'enfant. Il est très important d'adapter à chaque enfant une méthode de manipulation afin de le transporter sans douleur dans le bain et hors du bain. L'infirmière doit aider son petit patient à faire face à ses traitements de façon à éviter des problèmes psychologiques graves. À ce stade de la thérapeutique, presque tous les enfants ont des pansements et il est important de ne pas utiliser la méthode circulaire pour les appliquer, car ils entravent la circulation et sont difficiles à enlever dans le bain.

Il existe deux types de greffes: *l'homogreffe,* dans laquelle le greffon est emprunté à un autre sujet, et *l'autogreffe,* dans laquelle le greffon provient du sujet lui-même. On n'emploie la peau d'un donneur que pour couvrir des brûlures étendues, en attendant que la condition physique du patient soit suffisamment bonne pour subir une greffe de sa propre peau.

La planification des *soins infirmiers* dépend de la localisation et de l'étendue des brûlures, des besoins de l'enfant et du type de traitement prescrit. L'infirmière doit observer et noter les signes de choc (température subnormale, basse pression sanguine, pouls rapide, respirations rapides et peu profondes, et pâleur extrême) et l'évidence de toxicité. Une toxicité se manifeste d'habitude en un ou deux jours, et s'accompagne de température élevée, de prostration, de cyanose, d'un pouls rapide, d'une diminution des émissions d'urine et d'œdème marqué. Si l'on ne combat pas l'état toxique, le coma et la mort peuvent en résulter. Il faut observer aussi chez l'enfant la gêne abdominale ou le saignement gastro-intestinal, indiquant l'apparition de *l'ulcère de Curling* qui peut survenir chez les brûlés.

Il faut protéger l'enfant contre toute infection ou blessure de l'épithélium délicat qui se régénère pour remplacer les tissus détruits. Il faut porter des masques, des blouses et des gants stériles. Toute la lingerie utilisée pour l'enfant doit être stérilisée. Il faut se souvenir que bien des brûlés qui avaient survécu au choc initial, sont morts dans les semaines subséquentes d'une infection contractée en milieu hospitalier. Le Pseudomonas Aeroginosa (bacille pyocyanique) que l'on reconnaît à son pus bleu vert, contamine souvent les brûlures et il résiste à nombre d'antibiotiques ordinaires.

Si l'on utilise la technique « ouverte », on peut placer au-dessus du corps de l'enfant un arceau chauffant recouvert d'un drap stérile. Si les lésions touchent ou collent au drap stérile, on peut, avec l'autorisation du médecin, enduire le drap d'une mince couche de gelée lubrifiante, ce qui réduira les picotements et la douleur lorsque l'enfant est déplacé et touche au drap. On peut aussi coucher l'enfant sur des feuilles de « saran » (plastique mince et très flexible) stériles. La peau de l'enfant y adhère moins qu'aux draps et les changements de position sont moins douloureux.

Pour les enfants ayant des brûlures étendues, on peut employer un lit spécial (Stryker, circo-électrique, Bradford) ; on prévient ainsi la contamination des régions brûlées et on facilite la prise des échantillons d'urine si l'on n'a pas inséré de sonde dans la vessie. On doit maintenir le corps dans un bon alignement et changer fréquemment la position du brûlé avec un minimum de douleur.

Il faut mettre l'enfant dans une bonne position pour éviter les déformations qui peuvent résulter des contractures. Si la surface antérieure du cou est brûlée, on placera un rouleau sous les épaules pour favoriser l'hyperextension et prévenir une contracture et la formation de cicatrices vicieuses. L'emploi d'une planchette verticale prévient un affaissement des pieds lorsque l'enfant est en décubitus dorsal. Lorsqu'on le couche sur l'abdomen, on place un oreiller sous chaque jambe pour empêcher la pression sur les orteils. Il faut tourner l'enfant toutes les deux heures et donner des soins à la peau pour prévenir les lésions de pression. On masse doucement la peau saine qui entoure les régions brûlées avec une lotion adoucissante, approuvée par le médecin. Il faut garder l'enfant au sec pour prévenir la gêne et la contamination des zones brûlées. Si la main est brûlée, il est important de bien séparer les doigts par un pansement approprié. Les exercices passifs et actifs préviennent les contractures et les raideurs articulaires.

Certains hôpitaux disposent de bains tourbillonnants (Whirlpool) qui permettent au physiothérapeute de faire effectuer à l'enfant de nombreux mouvements sous l'eau, tout en aidant à détacher les plaques de tissus nécrotiques que l'on enlève ensuite par débridement. Les exercices rassurent l'enfant sur ses capacités et il est ensuite plus facile pour l'infirmière de les lui faire répéter.

Sauf si ses bras et ses mains sont brûlés, il faut donner à l'enfant des jouets et du matériel qui lui permettent de jouer tout seul. Il faut également lui faire la lecture, et lui montrer les images du livre. Il faut placer son lit de façon à ce qu'il puisse voir les autres enfants jouer. Il apprécie un tourne-disques, une radio ou un téléviseur.

Il n'est pas toujours facile de donner des soins à un enfant gravement brûlé, à cause de son apparence, d'une odeur possible et parfois d'une réaction agressive lorsque l'on change ses pansements. Les infirmières doivent reconnaître leurs sentiments et les dominer, de façon à s'occuper de l'enfant d'une manière efficace. Toutefois, l'infirmière se doit aussi d'être techniquement très compétente pour parvenir à bouger l'enfant et à changer ses pansements avec un minimum de douleur. Elle doit bien connaître les façons de saturer le pansement de liquide avant de l'enlever, ce qui évite les suintements sanguins trop abondants. Elle doit être assez sûre d'elle pour prévoir toutes les étapes du traitement et faire participer l'enfant aux moments appropriés.

Réhabilitation, réactions des parents et de l'enfant, pronostic et traitement. Le but de la *rééducation* est d'aider l'enfant brûlé à se développer en tirant le meilleur parti de ses capacités dans les limites de ses infirmités. Il faut également aider l'enfant et ses parents à accepter les cicatrices et toute autre handicap qu'il peut avoir. Une thérapie rééducative et physique est parfois indispensable après une brûlure grave. On peut aussi signaler le cas de l'enfant à la travailleuse sociale pour évaluer la situation financière de sa famille et la secourir le cas échéant.

La réaction des parents et de l'enfant au traumatisme varie selon les cas. L'enfant peut devenir craintif et anxieux, par suite de la peur éprouvée lors de l'accident, de sa douleur extrême et de la séparation de ses parents pour une longue période. Il peut aussi se sentir coupable s'il a été brûlé lorsqu'il se livrait à une activité défendue par ses parents ou contre laquelle ils l'avaient mis en garde. La plupart des enfants brûlés présentent un comportement agressif suivi de périodes de régression et de dépression. Il est très important qu'ils soient soignés par un personnel stable. Les parents peuvent également éprouver un sentiment de culpabilité s'ils pensent avoir manqué de surveillance. Ils peuvent faire preuve d'une compassion excessive à son égard ou manifester une attitude surprotectrice.

L'enfant, tout comme les parents, a besoin d'être rassuré et compris. L'infirmière doit découvrir ses craintes et y apporter un réconfort approprié. Si l'enfant doit retourner à l'hôpital pour une intervention réparatrice, il faut l'encourager à faire face à une autre période douloureuse. On doit l'amener à exprimer son agressivité par le jeu, s'il ne peut l'exprimer en paroles. Il faut aussi l'engager à crier s'il le désire, quand il subit un traitement douloureux. Assisté par une infirmière qu'il connaît et en qui il a confiance, il sera plus apte à supporter la souffrance. Cette expression de ses émotions facilitera son adaptation à la maladie et améliorera ses relations avec ses parents après sa guérison.

En général, le *pronostic* dépend de l'étendue et de la profondeur de la brûlure. Au cours de la phase aiguë, la mort est essentiellement due au choc, à des perturbations de la masse sanguine, et à des désordres humoraux. Après cette période, la mort suit une toxémie, une infection locale ou intercurrente et une atteinte générale.

La *prévention* de ces accidents douloureux et souvent mortels, consiste en un vaste programme d'éducation des adultes et des enfants pour leur enseigner les dangers du feu. Il faut leur apprendre, non seulement les différents moyens par lesquels les enfants peuvent se brûler, mais aussi les aider à comprendre l'importance qu'il y a à apprendre à leurs enfants comment se débarrasser de leurs vêtements au cas où ils s'enflammeraient et comment s'échapper immédiatement, si un incendie survient à la maison. Les parents et leurs enfants devraient avoir de fréquents exercices de simulation d'incendie pour se familiariser avec les différentes sorties de secours, surtout s'ils vivent dans des habitations surpeuplées et mal protégées contre les incendies.

Fractures

Les os de l'enfant sont incomplètement minéralisés et possèdent encore une proportion cartilagineuse importante. Les fractures « *en bois vert* » sont donc relativement fréquentes. Il s'agit d'une fracture dans laquelle un côté de l'os est fracturé, l'autre côté étant courbé, le périoste demeurant intact. Cependant un traumatisme grave déterminera une fracture *complète*. Chez les jeunes enfants, la consolidation peut être accompagnée d'une difformité, mais celle-ci disparaît d'habitude durant le processus de croissance.

La fracture simple, chez l'enfant, n'est pas toujours douloureuse et n'entraîne pas toujours d'impotence fonctionnelle et d'œdème localisé. Si l'enfant refuse de se servir d'un membre après un traumatisme, il faut envisager l'éventualité d'une fracture insoupçonnée. La plupart de ces lésions sont traitées par manipulation fermée, traction ou appareil plâtré.

Un traumatisme grave est souvent accompagné d'une fracture ouverte qui requiert une intervention chirurgicale. La guérison est rapide et les séquelles peu nombreuses; la physiothérapie est habituellement inutile pour l'enfant normal. La déformation apparente au début s'amenuise avec le temps et disparaît éventuellement.

L'immobilisation prolongée dans un corset ou une culotte plâtré entraîne parfois une hypercalcémie, une complication rare qui hypothèque le système rénal.

Fracture du fémur

Incidence, étiologie, types et diagnostic. La plupart des blessures qui surviennent chez les jeunes enfants sont dues à des chutes. Le jeune enfant apprend à marcher. Il monte et descend les escaliers, il grimpe sur les chaises et en descend, et ces exercices sont une véritable joie pour lui. Même si une fracture du fémur n'est pas la seule blessure qu'il puisse subir, c'est probablement une des fractures sérieuses habituellement causées par l'une de ses nombreuses chutes.

Les escaliers devraient avoir des rampes pour que l'enfant puisse s'y tenir lorsqu'il monte ou descend une marche à la fois. L'idéal serait que l'accès aux escaliers soit fermé par une porte, tant en haut qu'en bas. A ce point de vue, la maison sans étage offre plus de sécurité pour le jeune enfant. En général, une porte que l'on peut fermer à clef barre l'entrée de la cave.

Une fracture du fémur, parfois accompagnée d'autres blessures sérieuses, survient aussi lorsque l'enfant est happé au passage d'une auto, tandis qu'il court dans la rue après une balle, ou lorsqu'il est renversé par une auto qui sort d'un garage ou d'un chemin. Si l'enfant est renversé par un de ses parents, ce facteur s'ajoutera à l'impact émotif de l'accident sur la famille. Le fait de grimper sur les montants du lit ou de sauter sur un matelas, peut déterminer des chutes graves et des traumatismes musculo-squelettiques.

Le *diagnostic* est établi d'après l'incapacité de l'enfant de porter des objets pesants, une douleur ressentie lors d'un mouvement, la position du membre et d'après la douleur locale. Les examens radiologiques confirment le diagnostic et la position des fragments cassés.

Traitement et soins infirmiers. On enlève délicatement les vêtements de l'enfant, d'abord du côté non blessé du corps, et ensuite du côté blessé. Il faut bouger aussi peu que possible le membre atteint. Il est parfois nécessaire de couper les vêtements.

Le médecin peut prescrire des applications froides ou des sacs de glace durant les vingt-quatre ou trente-six premières heures pour prévenir un œdème. L'aspirine ou un salicylate s'avère efficace pour soulager la douleur. De petites doses de narcotiques peuvent quelquefois être nécessaires.

La traction cutanée est exercée sur les deux jambes, grâce à des diachylons appliqués sur la peau et à un système de poids et de poulies. On applique la traction pour réduire la fracture, pour maintenir les os dans une position

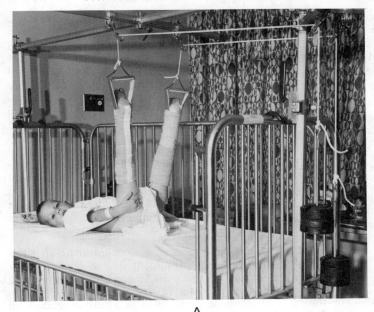

A

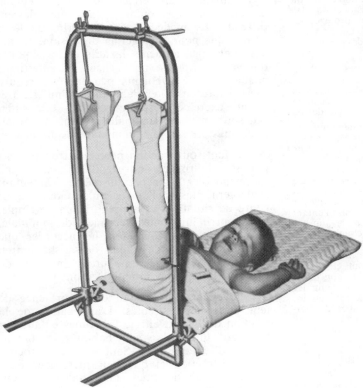

B

Figure 15-12. *A)* Traction de Bryant employée pour traiter une fracture du fémur chez le jeune enfant. Le contrepoids (pesées) doit être suffisant pour empêcher le siège de l'enfant d'appuyer sur le lit. (H. Armstrong Roberts.) *B)* Le cadre portatif pour traction pédiatrique (Stryker), grâce à sa maniabilité, facilite les soins. L'enfant peut même parfois retourner à la maison avec la traction. (Courtoisie de Stryker Corporation, Kalamazoo, Michigan.)

correcte et pour immobiliser les deux jambes et diminuer le spasme musculaire et la douleur. On appelle « *traction de Bryant* » le type d'appareil habituellement employé pour les enfants jusqu'à deux ans. C'est une méthode à suspension verticale.

Le principe fondamental du système à traction de Bryant est une extension bilatérale *de Buck* appliquée aux jambes. La technique est la suivante.

1) Raser les jambes si des poils s'y trouvent, et badigeonner la peau avec de la teinture de benjoin pour que l'adhésif tienne plus fermement à la peau. Le benjoin sert aussi de désinfectant pour la peau et soulage le prurit et l'excoriation sous l'adhésif.

2) On doit couper une bande de moleskine ou de bandage élastocrèpe pour chaque jambe; elle doit être assez longue pour recouvrir la jambe au-dessus du genou jusqu'au dessous du pied. Au centre de chaque bande, au niveau de la plante du pied, placer une planchette mince et plate de 7,5 cm de longueur et 2,5 cm plus large que la plus grande distance entre les malléoles. Il doit y avoir un trou au centre de la planchette où la corde de traction devra passer. Pour maintenir la planchette de bois en place, on doit placer un deuxième morceau de moleskine sur le côté, en face du pied de l'enfant. Cette bande de moleskine doit être aussi large que l'autre et assez longue pour passer au-dessus de la malléole sur un côté, en-dessous du pied et jusqu'au-dessus de la malléole sur l'autre côté. On fait ceci pour protéger les malléoles contre la pression de l'adhésif. On peut employer des attaches en métal au lieu de planchettes en bois.

3) On place en haut du lit deux barres longitudinales, ou une barre longitudinale et l'autre croisée, et on les attache solidement (cadre Balkan). On fixe une ou deux poulies à la barre, dans une position qui permettra d'appliquer la traction à l'angle désiré.

4) La moleskine est appliquée et maintenue en place à l'aide de gaze, de jersey de coton coupé de biais ou de bandages élastocrèpes. On passe une corde sur les poulies. On applique des poids suffisants *pour soulever légèrement du lit* les hanches de l'enfant. Les jambes doivent être disposées en angle droit par rapport au corps, et les fesses sont élevées de façon à ne pas toucher le lit. On doit employer une chemise de contention pour maintenir l'enfant à plat dans son lit et pour l'empêcher de tourner d'un côté à l'autre. L'enfant peut être couché sur le matelas de son lit ou bien être placé sur un cadre Bradford placé sur le lit. L'infirmière ne doit jamais bouger les poids une fois qu'ils ont été appliqués, en vue de maintenir une traction constante. Lorsqu'on bouge le lit, il ne faut pas soutenir les poids, ni non plus les laisser balancer à côté du lit. Après avoir appliqué la traction aux jambes de l'enfant, il faut la vérifier bien soigneusement, pour prévenir une compression des artères ou des traumatismes cutanés.

SOINS DE L'ENFANT SOUS TRACTION. L'infirmière doit surveiller les cordes de traction pour voir si l'alignement du corps de l'enfant est correct. Elle doit toucher fréquemment les orteils pour noter tout signe de trouble circulatoire. Les orteils doivent être roses et chauds.

La cyanose, le fourmillement ou la perte de sensibilité indique que le bandage est trop serré. L'infirmière doit s'assurer que les poids pendent librement et que les cordes se trouvent dans les rouages de la poulie. Dans l'appareil de Bryant, les petits enfants sont tentés de se tourner d'un côté à l'autre lorsqu'ils sont intéressés par ce qui se passe autour d'eux. Ceci modifie la traction égale exercée par les poids. Tout mouvement du corps est une indication que la chemise de contention n'est pas attachée correctement. L'infirmière doit toujours s'assurer que le siège de l'enfant est légèrement surélevé, sinon il exerce sur la traction un contrepoids qu'il faut éviter. Les couches de l'enfant doivent être changées dès qu'elles sont souillées.

Le fait d'être couché constamment en supination avec le frottement que le léger mouvement de la chemise de contention permet, a tendance à irriter le dos de l'enfant. Il nécessite donc de bons soins et l'infirmière doit lui frictionner fréquemment le dos et les fesses. Le lit doit être gardé sec et débarrassé de tout faux pli, miettes ou particules alimentaires.

Le manque d'exercice amène souvent la constipation chez l'enfant. L'abdomen devient distendu. Le médecin peut prescrire un léger cathartique pour soulager la distension. Il faut augmenter les aliments laxatifs et les liquides qui vont permettre une évacuation intestinale adéquate. Des lavements peuvent être requis, mais il faut en éviter l'emploi continu. De fréquents exercices respiratoires, tels que siffler ou souffler dans un ballon, sont essentiels pour prévenir la pneumonie hypostatique.

L'enfant sous traction peut être trop protégé par son infirmière, qui croit peut-être qu'il est incapable d'agir par lui-même. Un enfant s'adaptera plus facilement qu'un adulte à ce genre de situation, et apprendra, par exemple, à se nourrir lui-même avec une aide minimale. L'infirmière, toutefois, doit lui accorder une attention plus grande et plus de satisfaction en vue de préserver les ressources émotives de l'enfant durant son immobilisation.

Ces enfants ont besoin de la présence de leur mère à leurs côtés. L'application de la traction de Bryant effraie les jeunes enfants, et plus tard, quand ils y sont habitués, la contention rend le temps long. Sauf si on leur procure de la distraction et que leur mère leur rend des visites quotidiennes, l'hospitalisation peut s'avérer une expérience bien traumatisante.

Pronostic. Les fractures fémorales « en bois vert » guérissent vite chez les petits enfants. La consolidation se fait habituellement trois ou quatre semaines après le traumatisme. En général, quand la consolidation est en bonne voie, on applique un plâtre et l'enfant peut rentrer à la maison.

RÉFÉRENCES

Livres et documents officiels

Arena, J. M.: *Poisoning: Toxicology – Symptoms – Treatments.* 2e éd. Springfield, Ill., Charles C Thomas, 1970.

Arneson, S. A.: Changes in a Toddler's Mode of Adapting to Separation From His Mother During Daily Relationship Experiences with One Nurse; in *ANA Clin. Sess.,* 1968, New York, Appleton-Century-Crofts, 1968, p. 134-141.

Artz, C. P. et Moncrief, J. A.: *The Treatment of Burns.* 2e éd. Philadelphie, W. B. Saunders Company, 1969.

Dreisbach, R. H.: *Handbook of Poisoning: Diagnosis and Treatment.* 7e éd. Los Altos, Californie, Lange Medical Publications, 1971.

Jacoby, F. G.: *Nursing Care of the Patient with Burns.* Saint-Louis, C. V. Mosby Company, 1972.

Karelitz, S.: *When Your Child Is Ill.* New York, Random House, 1969.

Kintzel, K. C. (édit.): *Advanced Concepts in Clinical Nursing.* Philadelphie, J. B. Lippincott Company, 1971.

Matthew, H. et Lawson, A. A. H. (édit.): *Treatment of Common Acute Poisonings,* 2e éd. Baltimore, Williams & Wilkins Company, 1970.

Monafo, W. W.: *The Treatment of Burns: Principles and Practice,* Saint-Louis, Warren H. Green, 1971.

Petrillo, M. et Sanger, S.: *Emotional Care of Hospitalized Children: An Environmental Approach.* Philadelphie, J. B. Lippincott Company, 1972.

Shirkey, H. C. (édit.).: *Pediatric Therapy.* 4e éd. Saint-Louis, C. V. Mosby Company, 1971.

Talbot, N. B., Kagan, J. et Eisenberg, L.: *Behavioral Science in Pediatric Medicine.* Philadelphie, W. B. Saunders Company, 1971.

Varga, C.: *Handbook of Pediatric Medical Emergencies.* 5e éd. Saint-Louis, C. V. Mosby Company, 1972.

Articles

Ambler, M. C.: Disciplining Hospitalized Toddlers. *Am. J. Nursing,* 67:572, 1967.

Ammon, M.: The Effects of Music on Children in Respiratory Distress. *A.N.A., Clinical Sessions,* 1968, 127-133.

Aupézy, P.: Particularités du traumatisme crânien du nourrisson et de l'enfant. *La revue du Praticien,* XXI:1265, 8, 1971.

Barnes, C.: Support of a Mother in the Care of a Child with Esophageal Lye Burns. *Nurs. Clin. N. Amer.,* 4:53, 1, 1969.

Branstetter, E.: The Young Child's Response to Hospitalization: Separation Anxiety or Lack of Mothering Care. *Amer. Health Pub.,* 59:92, janvier 1969.

Boyd, E. M.: The Safety and Toxicity of Aspirin. *Am. J. Nursing,* 71:964, mai 1971.

Brooks, M. M.: Why Play in the Hospital? *Nursing Clin. N. Amer.,* 5:431, septembre 1970.

Calleia, P. et Boswick, J. A. Jr: A Home Care Nursing Program for Patients with Burns. *Am. J. Nursing,* 72:1442, août 1972.

Chabaux, C.: Intoxication par les produits ménagers. *Soins,* 20:3, 8, 1975.

Claudia, Sister M.: TLC and Sulfamylon for Burned Children. *Am. J. Nursing,* 69:755, avril 1969.

Deeths, T. M. et Breeden, J. T.: Poisoning in Children – A Statistical Study of 1 057 Cases. *J. Pediat.,* 78:299, février 1971.

Done, A. K. et autres: Evaluations of Safety Packaging for the Protection of Children. *Pediatrics,* 48:613, octobre 1971.

Editorial: The Do's and Don'ts of Traction Care. *Nursing '74,* 4:35, 11, 1974.

Estenne, B.: La chirurgie œsophagienne dans les brûlures par produits caustiques. *Soins,* 20:11, 8, 1975.

Fink, D. L. et autres: Improving Pediatric Ambulatory Care. *Am. J. Nursing,* 69:316, février 1969.

Genot, A. ,Messier, C. A. et Chicoine, L.: L'intoxication aux corrosifs. *Union méd. du Can.,* 97:279, mars 1968.

Gurevich, I.: Some New Concepts in Tracheostomy Suctioning. *RN,* 35-52, septembre 1972.

Haggerty, R. et autres: Childhood Poisoning. *Pediat. Clin. N. Amer..* 17, 3, 1970.

Harper, J. R. et Varakis, G.: Children in Adult Intensive Therapy Units. *Brit. Med. J.*, 1:810, 28 mars 1970.

Harpey, J. P.: Intoxications médicamenteuses accidentelles chez l'enfant. *Soins*, 20:33, 1, 1975.

Hartford, C.: The Early Treatment of Burns. *Nurs. Clin. N. Amer.*, 8:447, 3, 1973.

Henley, N. L.: Sulfamylon for Burns. *Am. J. Nursing*, 69:2122, octobre 1969.

Labrune, B.: Les accidents chez les enfants. *Soins*, 16:362, 8, 1971.

Lagardère, B.: Trois parasitoses digestives fréquentes. *Soins*, 16:449, 10, 1971.

Lecomte, E.: Les dyspnées laryngées de l'enfant. *Soins*, 17:7, 6, 1972.

MacLean, S.: Ipeca Syrup versus Apomorphine in Poisoning. *Journ. of ped.*, 82:121, 1973.

Margolis, J. A.: Psychosocial Study of Childhood Poisoning: A 5-Year Follow-up. *Pediatrics*, 47:439, février 1971.

McDonnell, C., Kramer, M. et Leak, A.: What Would You Do? *Am. J. Nursing*, 72:296, février 1972.

Miles, M. S.: Body Integrity Fears in a Toddler. *Nursing Clin. N. Amer.*, 4:39, mars 1969.

Minckley, B. B.: Expert Nursing Care for Burned Patients. *Am. J. Nursing*, 70:1888, septembre 1970.

O'Neil, J.: Evaluation and Treatment of the Burned Child. *Ped Clin. N. Amer.*, 22:407, 2, 1975.

Quinby, S. et Bernstein, N. R.: Identity Problems and the Adaptation of Nurses to Severely Burned Children. *Am. J. Psychiatry*, 128:58, juillet 1971.

Reeves, K. R.: Acute Epiglottitis – Pediatric Emergency. *Am. J. Nursing*, 71:1539, août 1971.

Scherz, R. G., Latham, G. H. et Stracener, C. E.: Child-Resistant Containers Can Prevent Poisoning. *Pediatrics*, 43:84, janvier 1969.

Stine, O. C. et Chuaqui, C.: Mothers' Intended Actions for Childhood Symptoms. *Am. J. Pub. Health*, 59:2035, novembre 1969.

Stoll, C. P.: Responses of Three Girls to Burn Injuries and Hospitalization. *Nursing Clin. N. Amer.*, 4:77, mars 1969.

Wiley, L.: Burn Care. *Nursing '72*, 2:32, juillet 1972.

Wright, L. et Fulwiler, R.: Long Range Emotional Sequelae of Burns: Effects on Children and Their Mother. *Pediat. Res.*, 8:931, 12, 1974.

16 pathologies du trottineur nécessitant des soins de longue durée

HOSPITALISATION DE LONGUE DURÉE

Une hospitalisation de longue durée provoque chez le trottineur un problème de carence maternelle plus sérieux que dans tout autre groupe d'âge.

Mesures préventives. Il faut éduquer le personnel hospitalier pour qu'il comprenne les besoins affectifs du jeune enfant et l'importance des visites fréquentes de ses parents pendant son séjour à l'hôpital. Si le coût excessif du transport ou le manque de temps dû à leur travail empêchent les parents d'aller voir leur enfant malade, la travailleuse sociale peut suggérer une solution pour leur venir en aide. Il faut tout mettre en œuvre pour que les jeunes enfants soit gardés et soignés à domicile. Si cela s'avère trop difficile, il faut les hospitaliser à proximité de leur logis et, si possible, les envoyer chez eux durant les fins de semaine et la vacances. On peut prendre des dispositions pour que les autres jeunes enfants de la famille fréquentent une maternelle ou une garderie de manière à libérer la mère afin qu'elle visite son enfant malade. On doit également autoriser les frères et sœurs plus âgés à lui rendre visite.

Les personnes qui s'occupent des jeunes enfants dont le séjour à l'hôpital est prolongé doivent être des membres permanents et stables de l'équipe de nursing, car le traumatisme de l'hospitalisation provient surtout de l'absence des parents. Une telle initiative aide le jeune enfant à développer sa personnalité, à établir des contacts qui l'aident à garder espoir, à prendre confiance en lui-même ou en ceux qui l'entourent, à apprendre à maîtriser sa colère et son sentiment de frustration. Les soins individuels des jeunes enfants préviennent certains traumatismes affectifs constatés chez les enfants soignés par un personnel qui change constamment.

1) Ce système de soins personnalisés doit être surtout employé pour les enfants qui exigent des soins de longue durée.

2) Il faut toujours attribuer le même personnel à un petit groupe d'enfants durant leur période d'hospitalisation. Ceci est possible si les soins sont donnés par une équipe permanente; des étudiantes en stage peuvent être admises en surnombre et tirer profit de cette expérience.

3) Les enfants dont la santé nécessite une hospitalisation de longue durée peuvent être placés dans des unités qui ressemblent à une

maison familiale et où ils jouissent d'une surveillance médicale. La majeure partie des
soins est dispensée par un personnel spécialisé connaissant les besoins des jeunes
enfants. Chaque membre du personnel agit
comme un substitut maternel pour un petit
groupe d'enfants. Les médecins viennent seulement en cas de nécessité. Dans ces petits
groupes familiaux, l'enfant peut se créer des
relations stables et mener une vie affective
satisfaisante.

4) Dans la mesure du possible, les enfants
gardés à l'hôpital doivent avoir autant d'activités récréatives que les enfants normaux. Ils
peuvent jouer, par exemple, avec de l'eau et
du sable, faire de la peinture digitale ou autre,
actionner des marionnettes, travailler avec des
blocs. Dans l'unité pédiatrique classique d'un
hôpital général, la pratique de telles activités
est peu courante. Cette carence provient plutôt du traditionalisme et d'une inertie face
au changement que de problèmes physiques
ou financiers. Les personnes en charge de ces
unités auraient avantage à s'inspirer des méthodes utilisées dans les hôpitaux pour enfants.

PATHOLOGIES
DE LONGUE DURÉE

Syndrome néphrotique idiopathique
(Néphrose lipoïdique)

Il n'existe aucune définition satisfaisante du
syndrome néphrotique, mais il se caractérise
par l'association des cinq signes suivants: des
œdèmes, une protéinurie abondante supérieure
à 3 g par 24 heures, une hypoprotéinémie inférieure à 60 g / 1, une hyperlipémie avec
hypercholestérolémie; une oligurie. Même si
certains types de néphrose peuvent apparaître
dès la naissance ou au cours de l'âge adulte,
nous nous bornerons dans ce chapitre à
étudier la néphrose lipoïdique idiopathique.

Étiologie, types et incidence. L'étiologie de la néphrose idiopathique demeure inconnue. On peut rarement associer le début
d'un syndrome néphrotique à une autre pathologie. Au cours de la maladie, les poussées
succèdent souvent à des infections aiguës.
Certains chercheurs considèrent la néphrose
lipoïdique comme une maladie immunitaire
puisqu'on a retrouvé dans le sang de certains
malades des anticorps antirénaux. De plus,
les symptômes s'amendent lors de l'administration de corticostéroïdes et de médicaments
immuno-suppresseurs.

La néphrose est une maladie du jeune enfant; elle se déclare vers l'âge de 2½ ans et
atteint plus souvent le garçon.

*Physio-pathologie, manifestations clini-
ques et examens de laboratoire.* Anatomiquement, les reins sont jaunâtres, infiltrés
de dépôts lipidiques et volumineux. Les
parois des capillaires glomérulaires sont épaissies et les tubules dilatés. Les lésions fondamentales sont au niveau des glomérules et ne
peuvent être constatées qu'au microscope
électronique.

Les lésions glomérulaires (épaississement de
la membrane basale des capillaires glomérulaires qui les rend perméables aux protéines)
produisent une perte excessive des protéines
plasmatiques dans les urines (protéinurie massive).

Cette réduction de protéines sanguines provoque une diminution de la pression oncoti-
que qui tend normalement à retenir l'eau dans
les vaisseaux. Le sérum transsude dans l'espace
extra-cellulaire, produisant ainsi de l'œdème.
L'hypovolémie est suivie d'oligurie et entraîne
une sécrétion accrue d'aldostérone qui vient
compliquer la gravité de l'œdème.

La maladie débute insidieusement. L'œdème est habituellement le premier symptôme
noté entre un an et trois ans. L'œdème débute
autour des yeux et des chevilles et se généra-

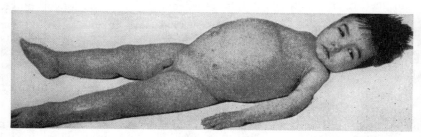

Figure 16-1.   Garçon de 4 ans, souffrant de néphrose. (M. I. Rubin dans Nelson *Textbook of Pediatrics.*
8e éd., 1964.)

lise par la suite. On constate une augmentation progressive, mais constante du poids de l'enfant en relation avec l'accumulation de liquide dans les tissus. Le phénomène peut évoluer pendant plusieurs semaines ou plusieurs mois. Le liquide s'accumule surtout dans la cavité péritonéale (*ascite*), le thorax (*hydrothorax*) et le scrotum (*hydrocèle*). Chez certains enfants, l'œdème peut devenir si important que la peau semble prête à se rompre; des vergetures peuvent apparaître par suite de l'étirement des fibres élastiques de la peau. L'œdème des tissus périphériques est déclive et se modifie selon les changements de position; il est blanc, mou, indolore, prenant le godet. Le débit urinaire varie à l'inverse de l'œdème.

Durant les phases œdémateuses, on peut observer d'autres signes cliniques, tels les hernies ombilicale et inguinales, la gêne respiratoire, le prolapsus rectal et la diminution de l'activité motrice. La pâleur paraît hors de proportion avec le degré de l'anémie; l'anorexie constitue un problème de soins. La malnutrition peut être sévère mais l'œdème masque la perte tissulaire. Des vomissements, une diarrhée et une distension abdominale peuvent survenir. La pression sanguine reste ordinairement normale, mais si l'enfant souffre d'insuffisance rénale avancée, on peut observer de l'hypertension. L'enfant demeure généralement afébrile. Les troubles de comportement concomitants comprennent l'irritabilité et la fatigabilité.

Les enfants atteints de néphrose sont sensibles à l'infection. Il est intéressant de noter qu'on observe habituellement une rémission à la suite d'une rougeole.

Une *crise néphrotique*, au cours de l'évolution de la maladie, peut produire des signes et des symptômes, tels que fièvre, douleur abdominale et parfois, lésions érysipéloïdes. Ils disparaissent en quelques jours et la diurèse peut redevenir normale.

Au stade terminal, l'enfant évolue vers l'insuffisance rénale et parfois cardiaque. Il peut présenter de l'hypertension, de l'urémie et de l'hématurie.

Les *examens* de l'urine et du sang permettent d'adapter le traitement aux besoins de l'enfant. La protéinurie constitue le signe biologique le plus important; la perte d'albumine peut atteindre jusqu'à 10 g ou plus par jour. Une hématurie persistante risque de compromettre sérieusement le pronostic. L'analyse urinaire permet aussi de mettre en évidence les corps bi-réfringents typiques. Les modifications sanguines concernent les protéines et les lipides. Il y a un abaissement de l'albumine sérique suffisant pour déterminer, à l'électrophorèse, une inversion du rapport albumine-globuline. On constate une élévation des lipides sanguins, particulièrement du cholestérol, pouvant atteindre 300 à 1 800 mg pour 100 ml de sang. On peut observer une anémie secondaire. La vitesse de sédimentation globulaire est accélérée.

Le *diagnostic* est basé sur les résultats des analyses urinaires et hématologiques. La biopsie rénale sous prémédication et anesthésie locale, permet de rechercher une étiologie précise, d'évaluer le pronostic et de guider la thérapeutique. À la suite de la ponction biopsique du rein, l'infirmière surveillera les signes vitaux, la quantité des urines et leur coloration (présence de sang, de caillots) ainsi que l'aspect du pansement. La complication immédiate de cet examen est l'hémorragie.

Complications et traitement.   Les complications sont rares depuis que les antibiotiques parviennent à juguler les infections autrefois redoutables. Le traitement consiste à prévenir et à contrôler les infections, à rétablir la fonction rénale, à contrôler l'œdème, à promouvoir une alimentation adéquate et une bonne hygiène mentale.

Il faut traiter rapidement les infections aiguës par un traitement antibactérien approprié et énergique.

On doit veiller à ce que l'enfant ait un régime bien équilibré, fournissant une quantité suffisante de protéines. Il faut parfois restreindre l'apport de sel durant les périodes d'œdème sévère et lors de la phase d'attaque de la corticothérapie. Les enfants acceptent difficilement les régimes pauvres en sel et ils souffriront probablement d'inappétence si on les limite à un tel régime. En phase aiguë ou oligurique, le médecin prescrit souvent une restriction de liquide. La ration quotidienne de liquide est basée sur le débit urinaire. L'enfant peut ingérer la même quantité que celle qu'il a excrétée la veille, plus 500 ml supplémentaires. De cette façon, la déshydratation ou la surcharge vasculaire sera évitée lors de la diminution de l'œdème.

Une diurèse importante entraîne la diminution de l'œdème. On utilise largement la thérapeutique hormonale dans le traitement de la néphrose. La corticothérapie est mise en œuvre dès que le diagnostic est posé. On administre les stéroïdes quotidiennement pendant quatre semaines environ. Il se produit alors une rémission clinique et une disparition progressive de la protéinurie. La dose de stéroïdes est graduellement diminuée afin de prévenir l'insuffisance surrénale aiguë consécutive au retrait brusque de la médication. Ordinairement, l'enfant reçoit une petite dose chaque jour ou tous les deux jours. Ce traitement d'entretien peut durer des mois ou des années. La détection précoce d'une infection fait partie intégrante du rôle de l'infirmière qui s'occupe d'un trottineur sous corticothérapie. Elle doit se rappeler que si le malade reçoit des stéroïdes, les symptômes habituels de l'infection seront supprimés par l'effet anti-inflammatoire du médicament. La corticothérapie suppose aussi de la part de l'infirmière une surveillance étroite du poids, de la tension artérielle et un dosage minutieux des liquides ingérés et excrétés. L'association de la cyclophosphamide et de stéroïdes donne d'excellents résultats et permet de diminuer la dose de chacun des deux médicaments évitant ainsi quelques effets secondaires pénibles. Les effets indésirables des immuno-suppresseurs seront indiqués en traitant de la leucémie au Chapitre 19.

Les diurétiques et l'aldactone, antagoniste de l'aldostérone, sont parfois utilisés, mais avec beaucoup de prudence, pour provoquer la diurèse et diminuer l'œdème. Il ne sont pas toujours efficaces et il faut habituellement compenser la perte de potassium qui apparaît lorsqu'ils déclenchent un débit urinaire suffisant.

Chez les malades cortico-résistants ou cortico-dépendants, les immuno-suppresseurs, surtout la cyclophosphamide, offrent une alternative de choix. Ces médicaments améliorent aussi considérablement le pronostic de la néphrose lorsque les stéroïdes sont contre-indiqués. Toutefois, les alkylants et les anti-métabolites exigent une évaluation fréquente de la formule sanguine, car ils peuvent provoquer une diminution sensible du nombre des éléments sanguins et une dépression de la moelle osseuse.

Les tentatives visant à élever la protéinémie par l'administration de plasma sanguin n'ont pas rencontré beaucoup de succès; cependant, le plasma, les albumines concentrées pauvres en sel ou d'autres substituts du plasma peuvent déclencher une diurèse temporaire.

Chez les malades porteurs d'une ascite abondante, une ponction du péritoine peut être nécessaire pour soulager la gêne cardio-respiratoire.

Le repos complet au lit ne devient nécessaire qu'en cas d'œdème important associé à d'autres symptômes. L'enfant peut se lever pour pratiquer des activités surveillées dès que son état le permet, mais on doit éviter tout contact avec des personnes atteintes d'infection.

Il est important de rassurer les parents et l'enfant. Le médecin dispensera aux parents appui et encouragement au cours de l'évolution de la maladie; il leur en expliquera la nature et le traitement. Dès que possible, les enfants doivent être traités à la maison et être conduits à l'hôpital uniquement pour un traitement particulier ou des soins spécialisés.

Soins infirmiers. Les soins infirmiers constituent la partie la plus importante du traitement. Il faut permettre aux parents des visites fréquentes ou prolongées et les encourager à participer aux soins de l'enfant. On évitera ainsi les effets nuisibles de l'absence maternelle et les parents peuvent lui exprimer leur affection et apaiser leur impression frustrante d'impuissance.

On doit protéger la peau œdémateuse contre tout traumatisme et infection. Il faut baigner souvent l'enfant, sans jamais le frotter vigoureusement, en accordant une attention spéciale aux parties moites du corps. On lave les organes génitaux du garçon plusieurs fois par jour, on les recouvre de poudre lénitive et on utilise un coussinet ou un support spécial pour les soutenir. Il ne faut jamais appliquer de pansement adhésif sur une peau œdémateuse. On place un oreiller entre les genoux quand l'enfant est couché sur le côté. Toutes les surfaces cutanées formant des plis ou susceptibles de se toucher doivent être séparées par un tissu doux pour prévenir l'intertrigo et l'excoriation par friction.

L'enfant peut avoir les yeux gonflés. L'irrigation avec une solution saline tiède prévient tout amas d'exsudat. On place l'enfant en position semi-assise pour diminuer la gêne causée par l'œdème.

Dans le but de prévenir une infection respiratoire, on garde l'enfant sec et au chaud, et on varie fréquemment sa position. À chaque changement de position, les parties œdémateuses doivent être adéquatement soutenues. Il faut éviter le contact avec d'autres enfants porteurs d'infection ou avec des membres du personnel atteints de maux de gorge ou de toute autre infection.

Un bon état nutritif est difficile à maintenir, étant donné que l'enfant n'a pas d'appétit durant les périodes d'œdème sévère. Il faut essayer de présenter les repas de façon agréable, sur des assiettes de couleur, et utiliser des pailles colorées pour la boisson. On présente de petites quantités d'aliments facilement digestibles, et on demande à l'enfant d'établir lui-même son menu. S'il doit subir une restriction de liquide, l'infirmière doit prendre garde de ne pas lui offrir d'aliments contenant beaucoup d'eau, mais qui n'apaisent pas la soif. On évite les soupes, les fruits en conserve, servis dans leur jus, etc... L'infirmière doit aussi planifier les ingesta pour 24 heures et s'assurer que l'enfant pourra boire un petit verre de liquide à sa collation du soir, par exemple. Le jeune enfant accepte mieux de petits verres pleins et plus fréquents que de rares et grandes quantités. L'infirmière doit se rappeler le développement psychologique de l'enfant et adapter son approche en conséquence.

Il faut peser l'enfant tous les jours ou deux ou trois fois par semaine. Le gain ou la perte de poids indique l'augmentation ou la régression de l'œdème.

Le dosage exact des liquides ingérés et excrétés est toujours de rigueur. Il est souvent difficile à faire, sinon impossible, avec des enfafnts qui ne sont pas encore tout à fait propres et qui peuvent régresser au cours de leur maladie. Pour obtenir un dosage adéquat, on peut employer le lit métabolique spécialement conçu pour laisser au malade le plus de liberté possible. Il repose sur un tissu perméable laissant filtrer l'urine qui s'écoule par un entonnoir et un tube, vers la bouteille déposée sous le lit. L'enfant demeure au sec et les selles ne contaminent pas la collection urinaire. Si l'enfant est propre le jour et ne présente qu'une incontinence nocturne, il est important de ne pas l'immobiliser inutilement, mais d'obtenir sa coopération. La nuit, il pourra reposer sur le lit métabolique, sur un filet résistant ou porter un collecteur d'urine.

Si l'ascite entrave la respiration, on place l'enfant en position demi-assise en attendant la paracentèse abdominale. L'infirmière doit expliquer la technique à l'enfant pour s'assurer de sa coopération. Il doit uriner juste avant le traitement pour qu'il y ait moins de risque de ponctionner la vessie. L'équipement et la technique varient suivant les hôpitaux. En général, les infirmières se partagent les responsabilités suivantes:

Infirmière nº 1: Installe l'équipement et prépare la région à ponctionner, recueille des échantillons de liquide ascitique pour culture et vérifie la coloration de l'enfant au cours de l'opération.

Infirmière nº 2: Explique au fur et à mesure la technique à l'enfant. Elle le place en position assise sur le bord du lit ou de la table d'examen et lui soutient le dos avec son corps. Elle emprisonne les mains de l'enfant dans les siennes. Aucune autre contrainte n'est nécessaire si l'enfant collabore. L'infirmière doit lui parler, lui permettre de regarder ce qui se passe ou distraire son attention selon ses réactions.

Il ne faut pas que le liquide d'ascite s'écoule trop rapidement ou trop abondamment de l'abdomen parce qu'une réduction rapide de la pression intra-abdominale peut entraîner une distension des veines abdominales profondes, réduire l'approvisionnement normal du cœur et provoquer un état de choc.

Après le traitement, on applique une bande abdominale et on met l'enfant au lit. L'infirmière doit soigneusement observer et noter la quantité de liquide drainé et l'état de l'enfant.

Durant les années préscolaires, le petit garçon qui a beaucoup d'imagination et est très vulnérable aux phantasmes de mutilation et de castration, peut croire qu'on lui a coupé le pénis, rendu peu apparent par l'étendue de l'œdème. L'infirmière doit demeurer avec l'enfant, le rassurer sur l'intégrité de son corps et lui donner des moyens d'exprimer symboliquement, surtout par le jeu, ses craintes qu'il n'ose pas formuler.

L'infirmière a un rôle important à jouer dans l'administration de la médication. Si l'enfant reçoit des immuno-suppresseurs, elle doit surveiller nausées et vomissements et en rendre compte au médecin qui ajoutera souvent des anti-émétiques au traitement. Si l'enfant développe une alopécie, elle doit avertir les parents que cette condition réversible est liée à la médication. Elle doit protéger efficacement le petit malade contre les infections étant donné la leucopénie secondaire possible.

Si l'enfant reçoit des stéroïdes, l'infirmière doit surveiller étroitement le poids, la tension artérielle, le dosage des ingesta et excréta, étant donné la rétention hydrosodique provoquée par ces médicaments. Elle doit prévenir l'ulcération gastrique, toujours menaçante, en administrant la médication avec des aliments ou un alcalin. Elle peut aussi réduire l'hypokaliémie secondaire en offrant de fréquents jus d'orange à l'enfant ou autres aliments riches, en potassium, car les corticostéroïdes entraînent une perte de cet électrolyte. Il est important aussi que parents et enfant sachent que les effets secondaires tels faciès lunaire, acné, sont transitoires et réversibles. Enfin l'infirmière doit s'attendre à une certaine instabilité de l'humeur au début et parfois durant une longue période de la corticothérapie.

Dès que l'état de l'enfant le permet, il faut autoriser des activités récréatives appropriées à son âge, ses goûts et son état de santé. La personne qui s'occupe des loisirs peut lui rendre visite, ou il peut aller dans la salle de jeu s'il n'y a pas de risque d'infection au contact des autres enfants.

Enseignement à donner à la mère lorsque son enfant quitte l'hôpital. Le médecin explique aux parents la nature de la maladie et son traitement. L'infirmière peut ultérieurement leur expliquer le régime de l'enfant, la nécessité d'une surveillance médicale continue, la manière de prévenir l'infection et de donner les soins à la peau. Elle doit insister sur le dosage des médicaments, leur fréquence et leurs effets secondaires. La mère doit bien connaître la médication qu'elle manipule et très bien comprendre le calendrier d'administration. Les parents doivent souvent apprendre à effectuer le dosage des protéines urinaires à l'aide d'un bâtonnet.

La discipline pose un problème sérieux au cours de toute maladie de longue durée chez le jeune enfant. Les parents doivent agir avec logique et savoir imposer les limites nécessaires. Une atmosphère familiale heureuse demeure sans doute le facteur le plus important. L'enfant collabore volontiers lorsqu'il vit dans un milieu heureux.

Pronostic. Il est difficile de prédire l'évolution d'une néphrose, mais elle se caractérise en général par des épisodes répétés d'œdème de durée variable. Le traitement anti-infectieux a nettement réduit la mortalité due aux infections. En fait, le syndrome néphrotique peut tout aussi bien évoluer vers la rémission que progresser, de rechute en rechute, vers une insuffisance rénale progressive. Grâce à la médication et à la greffe rénale, le pronostic semble actuellement favorable pour beaucoup d'enfants néphrotiques.

Acrodynie (pink disease, érythrœdème)

Étiologie, incidence et diagnostic. On n'en connaît pas la cause avec certitude. On croit que cette maladie est due à une intoxication, à une sensibilité inhabituelle ou à une idiosyncrasie envers le mercure. Parmi les sources d'empoisonnement par le mercure, citons le calomel, les pommades mercurielles, les produits de rinçage pour les couches, l'ingestion prolongée d'eau polluée ou de poissons intoxiqués par l'eau polluée où ils vivent. L'incidence de la maladie est très faible en général, mais elle peut être relativement fréquente dans des collectivités qui vivent de pêcheries, près d'étendues d'eau contaminées par le mercure; le diagnostic repose sur l'aspect clinique, l'évolution de la maladie et les tests biologiques.

Manifestations cliniques, examens de laboratoire et physio-pathologie. Les manifestations cliniques sont inhabituelles et caractéristiques. Le début est insidieux. L'enfant devient de plus en plus irritable et agité, plus rarement apathique. Les extrémités des doigts et des orteils prennent une teinte rose et

gonflent légèrement. Les malades souffrent de prurit aux mains et aux pieds. Plus tard, les paumes des mains et les plantes des pieds desquament. L'enfant se plaint de brûlures intenses; un érythème diffus et d'abondantes sueurs apparaissent. Les joues et le nez sont roses, les gencives rouges et gonflées. Les dents de lait, les ongles et les cheveux peuvent tomber. La pression sanguine s'élève, le pouls s'accélère. Habituellement, le malade n'a pas de fièvre sauf en cas de complications, telles la pyurie ou la broncho-pneumonie.

La personnalité de l'enfant change. L'hyperesthésie cutanée et musculaire explique qu'il refuse d'être pris dans les bras ou bercé. D'autres méthodes doivent être employées pour le distraire ou l'apaiser: mobiles suspendus, télévision, radio, etc.

On constate une diminution de l'activité musculaire, l'enfant est hypotonique. Il peut prendre des positions anormales: l'attitude dite de la prière mahométane est fréquente. Atteints de photophobie les enfants protègent leurs yeux de la lumière.

L'anorexie détermine une malnutrition. Comme l'enfant transpire abondamment, il boit beaucoup d'eau; des douleurs intenses l'empêchent de dormir. Il n'existe aucune anomalie urinaire en dehors de la présence de mercure. On n'observe aucune modification typique du point de vue pathologique.

Traitement. Le Dimercaprol (BAL, British anti-lewisite) administré par voie intramusculaire est efficace contre certains métaux lourds toxiques comme le mercure. Il provoque souvent des effets secondaires indésirables, tels que larmes, nausées, vomissements, salivation, maux de tête, sensation de brûlure, douleurs dentaires, transpiration, sensation d'oppression dans la poitrine, fièvre et agitation.

En général, les barbituriques agissent moins bien que le paraldéhyde administré par voie rectale dans une solution huileuse. On évite les opiacés, sauf en cas d'urgence. Une amélioration symptomatique a également été signalée avec la priscoline et la pénicillamine. Si une infection respiratoire survient, il faut la traiter avec des antibiotiques.

Le régime doit être riche en protides, en sels minéraux et en vitamines. Bien souvent, l'anorexie est si intense que l'on doit nourrir l'enfant par gavage. S'il refuse de boire suffisamment, il faut envisager un apport de liquide par voie parentérale.

Soins infirmiers. On adapte les soins aux changements de personnalité de l'enfant. L'infirmière doit demeurer ferme mais gentille, et réagir au comportement de l'enfant en espérant toujours l'amélioration éventuelle et même la guérison. Elle doit accepter les réactions de l'enfant et essayer d'alléger sa douleur et son anxiété.

Pour prévenir les blessures, il faut recouvrir l'intérieur du lit d'ouate ou de couvertures. Quand l'enfant se trouve dans sa chaise haute, il doit porter une chemise de contention, car il a tendance à tomber. Des manchons autour des coudes l'empêchent de se sucer les doigts ou de se tirer les cheveux.

On tient l'enfant aussi propre que possible, afin de réduire les risques d'infection cutanée à pyogènes. Les vêtements doivent être légers, de préférence en coton, et il faut les changer fréquemment lorsque les sueurs sont profuses.

L'inflammation des gencives complique les soins que l'on doit apporter à la bouche pour éviter l'infection. En raison de sa photophobie, on protège l'enfant de toute lumière violente.

Il faut prendre toutes les précautions nécessaires pour prévenir les infections respiratoires contractées auprès d'autres enfants ou des infirmières. Les sédatifs peuvent s'avérer nécessaires en cas d'insomnie ou pour prévenir une fatigue excessive. Si on administre du BAL, l'infirmière doit surveiller l'apparition des effets indésirables. On pèse régulièrement l'enfant pour déterminer la perte de poids. Durant la phase aiguë, ces enfants ont rarement envie de jouer; l'enfant aime que son infirmière lui fasse la lecture à haute voix ou lui permette d'entendre ses disques préférés. Les activités récréatives aident l'enfant, ainsi que ses parents, à s'adapter à sa condition de malade.

Complications, évolution, pronostic et prévention. Les *complications* qui peuvent survenir sont la pneumonie, la pyurie, la diarrhée et le prolapsus rectal. La maladie peut évoluer pendant plusieurs mois ou un an. Le taux de mortalité demeure peu élevé.

La maison constitue le meilleur endroit pour un enfant atteint d'acrodynie. On avertit les parents de la nature de la maladie et de son évolution prolongée. Il faut aussi leur apprendre à donner des soins appropriés.

La *prévention* consiste à éviter les médicaments mercuriels, à protéger l'enfant contre l'ingestion accidentelle de préparations à base de mercure et à favoriser des campagnes d'assainissement de l'environnement.

Le saturnisme

Étiologie, incidence et manifestations cliniques. On observe des cas d'intoxication au plomb, surtout chez les trottineurs âgés de dix-huit mois à trois ans. Le plomb pénètre dans l'organisme par le tube digestif, la peau ou les poumons. Les petits enfants, au moment de la poussée dentaire, ont tendance à sucer ou mâcher la peinture fraîche qui couvre le berceau, le mobilier et la charpente des fenêtres; ils s'intoxiquent également avec des jouets en plomb. Les charpentes et les murs non repeints permettent aux anciennes peintures au plomb de former des écailles qui tombent facilement à portée des jeunes enfants. Certains récipients en poterie peuvent aussi causer une intoxication.

Certaines vapeurs contenant du plomb peuvent provenir de la combustion d'essence ou de récipient contenant de la peinture au plomb. Cette forme d'intoxication demeure cependant très rare chez le jeune enfant.

Les murs des vieux immeubles sont souvent recouverts de couches de peinture successives dont le pourcentage de plomb était autrefois assez élevé. La peinture à usage extérieur renferme plus de plomb que celle utilisée à l'intérieur qui en contient moins de 1 pour cent.

Le plomb produit sur le système nerveux central des effets toxiques parfois définitifs et qui peuvent même s'aggraver au cours des années.

Les *manifestations cliniques* et la gravité de l'intoxication dépendent du degré de l'atteinte cérébrale.

Sauf dans les rares cas d'intoxication aiguë, la maladie apparaît insidieusement au fur et à mesure de l'absorption et de l'accumulation du plomb dans le sang et les tissus mous. Le plomb passe lentement des tissus mous à l'os; une partie est éliminée par les urines.

On rencontre le plus souvent l'intoxication saturnine au cours de l'été et elle suit une absorption accidentelle de sels de plomb ou d'inhalation de vapeurs toxiques. L'enfant présente des nausées, des vomissements, des douleurs abdominales. Les lésions rénales sont habituelles. Il peut avoir des convulsions, tomber dans le coma et mourir en état de choc après deux ou trois jours.

Les signes d'intoxication saturnine chronique dépendent du rythme et de l'importance des mouvements du plomb dans l'organisme. Les symptômes discrets sont variables: asthénie, perte de poids, irritabilité et vomissements, pâleur, céphalées, douleurs abdominales, anorexie et insomnie.

À cause de l'extrême fragilité du système nerveux central du jeune enfant, un contact relativement bref peut provoquer une encéphalite. On note l'apparition d'une anémie, de coliques, de névrites périphériques, d'une incoordination musculaire, de douleurs articulaires et d'une labilité du pouls. Des convulsions peuvent se produire, suivies de stupeur et de mort.

Diagnostic et traitement. On soupçonne le *diagnostic* d'après l'histoire du contact avec le plomb et des manifestations cliniques de l'intoxication: liseré bleu-gris aux gencives; zones plus denses aux extrémités des os longs, visibles à la radiographie; évidence de substance radio-opaque dans l'abdomen témoignant de l'absorption de substances étrangères et tests biologiques mettant en évidence la présence de plomb.

Le métabolisme de la porphyrine est perturbé dans l'intoxication au plomb. Il se produit une inhibition de la synthèse de l'acide delta-aminolévulinique et de la synthèse de la protoporphyrine à partir de cet acide. On trouve dans le sang et dans l'urine des quantités anormales d'acide delta-aminolévulinique et de porphobilinogène. Des recherches récentes ont permis de mettre au point un petit appareil portatif ultra-sensible qui rend possible la détection du plomb dans un échantillon de sang. S'il y a encéphalopathie, la pression du L.C.R. augmente et le liquide contient beaucoup de protéines et quelques cellules.

Le *traitement* d'urgence d'une intoxication aiguë consiste en un lavage d'estomac suivi d'une purgation au sulfate de magnésie. On institue une thérapie de support pour éviter l'apparition du collapsus cardio-vasculaire. Il faut donner du lait afin de former des sels de plomb insolubles dans l'intestin. Les sels de l'acide éthylène-diamine tétra-acétique (EDTA) augmentent l'excrétion du plomb par les urines. On administre habituellement l'EDTA en perfusions intraveineuses, car l'administration par voie orale retarde les effets du médicament. Le BAL accroît également l'élimination urinaire du plomb et récemment on a employé les deux produits en association. La pénicillamine peut être administrée pendant plusieurs jours pour provoquer l'élimination du plomb.

Une intoxication saturnine provient généralement de l'ingestion de petites parcelles de plomb durant un certain temps. Quand on amène un enfant à l'hôpital pour une intoxication saturnine chronique, il n'est pas certain qu'il ait ingéré du plomb récemment. Le plomb peut se trouver dans l'intestin, rarement dans l'estomac. C'est la raison pour laquelle on ne pratique habituellement pas de lavage gastrique. On peut appliquer les autres mesures spécifiques contre l'intoxication saturnine ai-

guë. Une ou plusieurs cures d'EDTA peuvent accroître l'excrétion du plomb.

L'objectif de la thérapeutique ultérieure est de réduire la teneur en plomb dans le sang et les tissus en favorisant l'excrétion rénale et les dépôts de plomb dans les os. On administre de grandes quantités de calcium, de phosphore et de vitamine D et on corrige le déséquilibre électrolytique (acidose) et les infections qui peuvent entraver le processus de dépôts.

On peut soulager les *coliques saturnines* par des antispasmodiques, tels que l'atropine ou les opiacés. On traite médicalement l'hypertension intracrânienne. Lors d'une *encéphalopathie* sévère, l'enfant peut souffrir d'une tension sanguine élevée, d'œdème papillaire, de bradycardie et de perte de conscience. Parmi les médicaments employés pour réduire l'hypertension intracrânienne, citons l'urée ou le mannitol qui s'administrent par voie intraveineuse. On peut aussi utiliser des stéroïdes. L'administration du phénobarbital par voie intramusculaire et de paraldéhyde par voie rectale peuvent juguler les convulsions dues à l'encéphalopathie. L'hypertension intracrânienne peut également être réduite par des ponctions lombaires répétées, en ne retirant qu'une faible quantité de liquide à la fois, en raison du danger extrême de hernie des amygdales cérébelleuses. Dans certains cas, on peut être amené à pratiquer une décompression chirurgicale par craniectomie. Il faut administrer de l'oxygène en cas de dépression respiratoire. On corrige les troubles hydro-électrolytiques en administrant des liquides par voie parentérale. Une rétention d'urine peut nécessiter l'installation d'une sonde à demeure.

Le traitement visant à débarrasser complètement les tissus du plomb peut prendre des mois, mais il demeure essentiel pour prévenir la récurrence des symptômes.

Soins infirmiers. Les soins infirmiers demeurent symptomatiques. Si l'enfant souffre de convulsions, il faut éviter toutes manipulations inutiles, car elles stimulent le système nerveux central. Les soins infirmiers doivent coïncider avec les périodes où l'on doit administrer les médicaments. Pour l'enfant qui présente une hypertension intracrânienne, il faut soigneusement observer les signes de détresse respiratoire et surélever sa tête pour en diminuer la tension.

On nourrit par gavage l'enfant comateux. Il faut le changer fréquemment de position et donner toujours des soins adéquats à la peau.

Pronostic et prévention. Le *pronostic* s'avère généralement défavorable. Environ la moitié des enfants atteints présentent des signes d'encéphalite et, chez ces sujets, le taux de mortalité se situe aux environs de 25%. Parmi ceux qui guérissent, un grand nombre présentent des séquelles définitives, neurologiques ou psychiques, comme l'arriération mentale. Après le traitement, une observation étroite s'impose durant une longue période pour prévenir des lésions ultérieures du système nerveux central. La fréquence des lésions nerveuses définitives s'accroît avec la durée du contact avec le plomb.

Il est normal pour tout enfant qui traverse sa période de « dentition » de porter à sa bouche et d'avaler un certain nombre de substances non comestibles. Le phénomène se manifeste au cours des deux premières années.

Les enfants atteints de *pica* (trouble de l'appétit consistant en une tendance à manger des substances non comestibles) peuvent continuer à ingérer du plomb durant de longues périodes. On doit supprimer toutes les sources de plomb de leur environnement et on doit les surveiller étroitement ainsi que leurs frères et sœurs afin qu'ils n'ingèrent pas de plomb provenant de sources qu'il est impossible d'éliminer.

Le traitement étant plutôt décevant, la *prévention* devient doublement importante. On a proscrit l'usage des peintures à base de plomb sur les jouets et le mobilier des enfants. Les peintres amateurs, à la maison, peuvent malheureusement peindre le mobilier avec de la peinture contenant du plomb. On rappelle constamment au public le danger qu'il y a à ingérer de la peinture. L'infirmière en santé communautaire participe à cette éducation lorsqu'elle visite des domiciles où il peut exister des sources d'intoxication saturnine. Un test très simple et peu coûteux a été mis au point récemment pour déterminer la quantité de plomb contenue dans une couche de peinture, même ancienne. On peut au besoin, enlever la peinture ou la recouvrir d'une autre couche non toxique.

Les enfants atteints, même s'ils ne présentent pas de symptômes spécifiques doivent être hospitalisés et traités de façon prophylactique. Une méthode rapide développée récemment permet de dépister l'intoxication au plomb à partir d'une simple goutte de sang prélevée au bout du doigt. Grâce à cette méthode, on peut effectuer le dépistage à peu de frais et sur une très grande échelle.

Dysfonction cérébrale manifeste

L'expression « dysfonction cérébrale manifeste », relativement nouvelle, groupe la paralysie cérébrale, le retard mental, l'épilepsie, l'autisme, des anomalies du comportement, divers troubles visuels et auditifs. L'origine de ces affections constitue le lien commun entre elles. Les lésions organiques amènent des manifestations neuro-motrices, divers troubles sensitifs et des anomalies du comportement ou de l'affectivité. On peut observer une ou plusieurs de ces manifestations chez un même malade. Le diagnostic repose habituellement sur le signe anatomique et clinique prédominant.

Paralysie cérébrale (Infirmité motrice cérébrale)

L'infirmité motrice cérébrale ou paralysie cérébrale est une expression courante pour désigner un contrôle inadéquat des muscles volontaires par suite d'une lésion de certaines parties du cerveau. Les causes, les manifestations cliniques, le traitement ou le pronostic sont variables. Le problème peut être bénin ou très sérieux. Toutefois, lorsque la lésion est

Figure 16-2. Jusqu'aux années '50, le plomb était utilisé dans la fabrication de la peinture d'intérieur. Dans les vieux immeubles, il faut se méfier des galettes de peinture qui se détachent des murs et des cadres de portes ou de fenêtres. (National Paint and Coatings Association, Inc.—USA.)

installée, on ne constate pas d'aggravation progressive et il devient possible d'établir un programme à long terme afin de développer les capacités de l'enfant.

Le *diagnostic* et le *traitement* s'avèrent particulièrement importants chez les jeunes enfants si on veut créer chez les parents une attitude réaliste et positive, de façon à ce que l'enfant acquière l'expérience nécessaire à un développement affectif normal. Bien que les manifestations physiques de cette affection aient été traitées depuis des années, ce n'est que récemment qu'on en a étudié les aspects intellectuels et affectifs.

Incidence et étiologie.
On estime que la paralysie cérébrale touche de 100 à 600 sujets sur 100 000.

L'étiologie spécifique demeure obscure. Plusieurs causes de lésion cérébrale provoquent cette maladie. Certaines sont claires, d'autres le sont moins. Nous avons déjà étudié les lésions cérébrales pouvant survenir avant la naissance ou au moment de l'accouchement ainsi qu'au cours de la première année. Parmi les causes de paralysie cérébrale citons l'hérédité, l'infection ou l'anoxie prénatales, l'agénésie cérébrale, l'anoxie postnatale (causerait 75% des cas), la narcose à la naissance, l'érythroblastose fœtale qui détermine le kernictère et l'hémorragie intracrânienne. Parmi les lésions qui peuvent se produire chez les nourrissons et les jeunes enfants, figurent l'in-toxication saturnine, les traumatismes crâniens avec hématome sous-dural, les lésions cérébrales dues à la fièvre, l'encéphalite, la méningite et l'hydrocéphalie. Chez nombre d'enfants, il existe une grande diversité de causes.

Diagnostic, types et manifestations cliniques.
Chez certains enfants on peut établir le *diagnostic* très tôt après la naissance. Il repose sur les symptômes suivants: croissance et développement retardés, atteinte musculaire, difficulté à sucer et à avaler, agitation ou irritabilité, crises convulsives, vomissements, pleurs faibles ou excessifs, cyanose ou pâleur. Chez d'autres enfants, on ne peut établir le diagnostic qu'au cours de la seconde année lorsque les symptômes neurologiques et moteurs typiques se manifestent.

Environ 75 pour cent des cas de paralysie cérébrale se classent en deux *types* principaux: la *spasticité* et l'*athétose*. La *spasticité* est caractérisée par l'hypertonie musculaire, l'hyperréflexie des extenseurs et les contractures rigides. C'est le type le plus habituel de paralysie cérébrale. L'*athétose* se manifeste par des mouvements involontaires, incoordonnés, de grande amplitude, affectant surtout les extrémités et le visage, et empêchant la coordination nécessaire pour faire les gestes les plus simples. L'athétose persiste au repos mais s'accentue lors d'un effort volontaire.

L'*ataxie* constitue un troisième type de paralysie cérébrale et se manifeste par la perte de la coordination et la perturbation de l'équilibre. Ces enfants marchent comme s'ils étaient en état d'ébriété. Un quatrième type marqué par la *rigidité,* se manifeste par une résistance exagérée de certains muscles fléchisseurs et extenseurs. Un cinquième type appelé *choréoathétoïde* est caractérisé par des tremblements qui produisent des mouvements rythmés involontaires. La paralysie flasque ou *atonique* constitue un sixième type.

Les *manifestations cliniques* varient avec le type ou les types de paralysie cérébrale de chaque enfant. On constate un retard du développement moteur, soit, par exemple, lorsque l'enfant apprend à s'asseoir, à marcher, à parler ou à se nourrir. Durant la première enfance, les infections, même légères, s'accompagnent de température élevée.

La spasticité constitue le signe le plus courant de l'atteinte motrice. L'enfant ne peut contrôler ses muscles volontaires; la personne qui l'examine n'y parvient pas elle non plus. Certains groupes musculaires, surtout au niveau des extrémités, présentent un tonus anormalement élevé qui maintient les membres dans des positions caractéristiques, et des déforma-

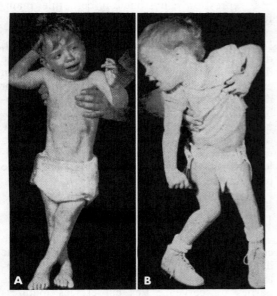

Figure 16-3. Paralysie cérébrale. *A)* Spasticité. *B)* Athétose. (Courville: dans *Cerebral Palsy — Advances in Understanding and Care.* New York, Association for the Aid of Crippled Children.)

tions posturales se produisent couramment. Les efforts volontaires de l'enfant pour mouvoir ces muscles amènent des mouvements asymétriques qui rendent la marche, l'alimentation et les mouvements coordonnés difficiles, voire impossibles. Les parties du corps habituellement atteintes sont les jambes, en position de *ciseaux* (l'enfant croise les jambes, et les pieds sont en équino-varus), les bras (le poing est serré, l'avant-bras fléchi et la partie supérieure du bras est pressée contre la paroi thoracique) et le tronc (extension du cou et rétraction des épaules).

La spasticité peut être de très légère à sévère. Chez les enfants très gravement atteints, la déglutition peut s'avérer difficile à cause de l'atteinte des muscles de la face, de la langue, des mâchoires et du pharynx.

Dans certains cas de spasticité, on constate un affaiblissement de quelques groupes musculaires. La faiblesse peut toutefois être présente même sans spasticité.

Les désignations topographiques s'identifient comme suit: on parle de *paraplégie* quand seuls les membres inférieurs sont atteints; l'atteinte de la moitié latérale du corps constitue une *hémiplégie* et la *quadriplégie* désigne l'atteinte des quatre membres. Des répartitions inhabituelles comprennent une *monoplégie* (un seul membre) ou une *triplégie* (trois membres). En plus des symptômes moteurs, toujours présents à des degrés divers l'enfant peut souffrir de plusieurs autres handicaps. D'après une compilation de plusieurs études, environ ⅓ des enfants atteints de paralysie cérébrale présenterait du strabisme. Deux tiers de ces malades seraient affligés de troubles d'élocution. Plus de 25 à 60% auraient des troubles épileptiformes. Environ ⅕ souffrirait de symptômes auditifs et près de 40% d'une arriération mentale plus ou moins importante.

Des troubles autres que ces problèmes physiques peuvent être dus à une lésion du cerveau, mais ils peuvent être causés ou accentués par la réaction des parents devant l'étendue du déficit. Des problèmes psychologiques et affectifs perturbent le développement de l'enfant plus que ses difficultés motrices. Les troubles de la vue, du langage ou de l'ouïe, les crises convulsives peuvent compliquer la situation et influer sur les rapports de l'enfant avec les autres membres de sa famille et ultérieurement, avoir des répercussions sur sa vie sociale.

L'enfant atteint de paralysie cérébrale est souvent instable sur le plan affectif en raison de son état physique, mais aussi du climat psychologique dans lequel il a vécu. Il a essentiellement besoin d'être accepté, aimé par ses parents, les enfants et les autres adultes. Son besoin naturel d'explorer l'environnement, de jouer, d'apprendre comme les autres enfants et de devenir indépendant est rarement satisfait. Il présente souvent une carence affective chronique.

Si l'enfant a des problèmes de langage, il peut être incapable de communiquer de façon normale avec les autres. S'il ne voit pas bien, il est privé de cette expérience unique que procure la lecture ou la vue des images, expérience nécessaire au développement normal. S'il ne peut pas écrire, il aura des difficultés supplémentaires à établir des relations satisfaisantes avec autrui.

Bien que le psychisme de ces enfants paraisse souvent affecté, beaucoup cependant jouissent d'une intelligence normale. Grâce à une éducation et un entraînement spécialisés, ils peuvent devenir des citoyens utiles à la société. Même ceux dont l'intelligence se situe au-dessous de la normale peuvent en arriver à gagner leur vie ou du moins, à se suffire à eux-mêmes.

Traitement et soins infirmiers. Le *traitement* des enfants atteints de paralysie cérébrale paraît être à un stade de transition. On propose des méthodes de traitement plus nouvelles. Comme beaucoup de discussions et de controverses s'élèvent au sujet de ces méthodes thérapeutiques, nous n'envisagerons ici que le traitement traditionnel.

On vise à assurer à l'enfant handicapé dès sa naissance une vie heureuse et équilibrée au cours de laquelle il pourra se réaliser pleinement dans les limites de ses capacités. Pour l'enfant qui a déjà été normal, mais qui devient handicapé à la suite d'une maladie, on doit viser à rétablir les capacités de l'enfant et à le faire progresser dans une voie aussi normale que possible.

Pour que les enfants atteints de paralysie cérébrale développent au maximum leurs possibilités, il faut les placer sous la surveillance d'une équipe spécialisée. Cette équipe est composée d'un ophtalmologiste, d'un orthopédiste, d'un psychologue ou d'un psychiatre, d'un physiothérapeute, d'un orthophoniste, d'un neurologue, d'un pédiatre, d'une travailleuse sociale, d'enseignants, d'infirmières et des parents de l'enfant.

Il est difficile d'identifier, au cours de la première et de la deuxième années, tous les enfants atteints de paralysie cérébrale. On peut dépister ces enfants à l'âge scolaire puisque la présence à l'école est obligatoire. Les enfants dont le cas n'est pas connu viennent d'ordinaire de familles à faible revenu, particulièrement dans les zones rurales isolées. Les parents de classe moyenne consultent facilement un médecin s'ils constatent que leur enfant n'est pas normal; en général ces derniers sont soignés par le même médecin depuis leur naissance. Les soins continus assurés par les infirmières en santé communautaire à partir de la naissance et poursuivis dans les cliniques et les centres de santé ont diminué le nombre des cas dépistés tardivement.

Avant d'entreprendre le traitement, il est nécessaire d'évaluer non seulement l'état physique de l'enfant, mais aussi ses capacités intellectuelles, puisque le traitement sera établi en fonction de ses possibilités. Il est difficile d'évaluer la capacité mentale d'un enfant avant qu'il soit assez âgé pour coopérer aux tests d'aptitude en utilisant ses capacités motrices. Grâce aux meilleures techniques disponibles, on établit un plan réaliste à court et à long terme; il faut le revoir périodiquement et évaluer les progrès accomplis.

Aucun traitement ne peut ramener à un niveau de fonctionnement normal un cerveau traumatisé à la naissance. Par le traitement on *vise à évaluer* correctement les possibilités physiques et mentales de l'enfant et à tirer le meilleur parti possible de celles-ci; à prévenir et à corriger les difformités par la physiothérapie et la chirurgie; à développer les capacités intellectuelles afin de rendre l'enfant apte, si possible, à se suffire à lui-même et à être utile à la société.

Il faut aider les parents à accepter l'enfant avec ses capacités et ses déficiences. Ils ont besoin de support pour apprendre à le soigner et à collaborer efficacement.

Les soins doivent aider à résoudre les problèmes reliés à la respiration, à l'alimentation, à l'élocution, au repos, au jeu et à l'éducation de l'enfant.

Les problèmes de respiration au cours des premiers mois de la vie sont dus à des lésions cérébrales ou à la présence de sécrétions dans la gorge. On peut retirer le mucus par aspiration. On change fréquemment le nourrisson de position pour diminuer sa gêne et éviter les complications respiratoires toujours menaçantes.

Des problèmes de nutrition peuvent provenir des difficultés de succion et de déglutition. L'enfant vomit facilement. Ces enfants requièrent pourtant une alimentation hypercalorique à cause de l'hypermotilité qui les caractérise. Pour l'aider à s'alimenter, il est bon de le nourrir lentement. L'infirmière doit faire preuve de patience quand elle lui donne une alimentation solide puisque souvent, il ne peut contrôler les muscles de sa gorge. Il faut de la dextérité pour nourrir ces enfants et elle ne s'acquiert que par l'expérience; l'infirmière ne doit pas se décourager si elle n'y réussit pas dès la première fois. Il s'avère encore plus difficile d'apprendre à l'enfant à se nourrir lui-même. Il a besoin d'une cuillère et d'une fourchette épointée (s'il est capable de contrôler convenablement sa main) munies d'un manche spécial pour qu'il puisse facilement les saisir. On doit fixer le plateau à la table pour que l'enfant ne le pousse pas quand il essaie de prendre des aliments.

Les problèmes d'élocution affectent beaucoup d'enfants affligés de paralysie cérébrale. Ces enfants ne parviennent pas à se faire comprendre verbalement, ce qui constitue une grande source d'agressivité et de frustration. Parfois, les parents élaborent un système qui pallie aux difficultés de communication, mais ils sont les seuls à le comprendre et l'enfant devient très dépendant d'eux et ne peut communiquer avec d'autres personnes. L'orthophonie n'aide qu'un petit nombre de cas. Une expérience pilote est en cours en Ontario, au Canada, pour valider la méthode de communication symbolique Bliss. Les enfants utilisent des cartes symboliques actionnées par des leviers pour exprimer une gamme d'émotions, de sentiments, de désirs ou d'observation. Cette méthode laisse entrevoir de grandes possibilités pour les enfants dont l'élocution est sérieusement perturbée.

Les problèmes de repos prennent une signification spéciale pour ces enfants qui sont sous tension constante, même lorsqu'ils essaient d'accomplir des actes simples que d'autres font inconsciemment. Bien que ces enfants se fatiguent vite, ils se détendent difficilement. Leur état nécessite de fréquentes périodes de repos, dans une chambre tranquille, avec le moins de stimuli possible. Ils ont besoin de calme avant d'aller au lit. L'administration de tranquillisants diminue la tension et favorise la détente.

Ces enfants doivent être éduqués avec compréhension. En sécurité et détendus, ils auront un meilleur contrôle de leurs mouvements que lorsqu'ils deviennent nerveux, en colère ou effrayés. L'adulte qui paraît ferme, mais non hostile, dans sa façon d'agir et dans ses paroles, non seulement obtient leur coopération, mais procure ainsi le climat social dans lequel ils sont capables de collaborer physiquement. Les succès obtenus par l'en-

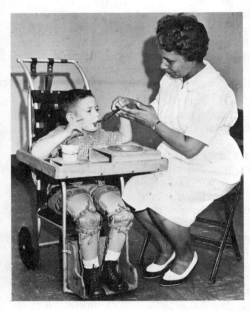

Figure 16-4. À gauche, un enfant ataxique qui apprend à se nourrir lui-même. Les supports pour tenir son bol et son verre, une paille pour boire et une cuillère pourvue d'une poignée lui facilitent la tâche. (United Cerebral Palsy.) En bas, chaise spéciale qui permet à l'enfant de garder une position confortable. (Courtoisie de l'Hôpital Sainte-Justine, Montréal.)

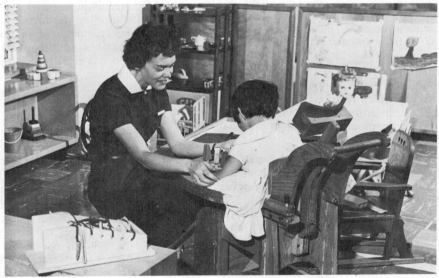

fant dans le contôle de ses muscles réduisent son sentiment de frustration. L'enfant paralysé est plus heureux avec des adultes qui établissent des limites à l'intérieur desquelles il peut agir avec succès; de ce fait, on constatera moins d'agressivité envers l'entourage. La détente est un art que l'enfant doit apprendre, car lorsqu'il sait se détendre, il réussit davantage à obtenir par lui-même ce qu'il désire.

Les problèmes de jeu sont multiples, mais ils peuvent être résolus avec succès. Aucun enfant ne mène une vie normale s'il ne joue pas. Cependant, le jeu doit être calme, sans excitation. Il faut de la créativité et de l'imagination pour trouver des jouets sûrs et éducatifs qui favorisent l'apprentissage, l'expression personnelle ou les relations avec les autres enfants. Quand l'enfant atteint l'âge scolaire, il doit chercher à jouer en groupe pour se faire des amis et apprendre à avoir d'heureux contacts avec ses semblables. Il doit se sentir leur égal, même s'il commet des maladresses qui gênent le jeu, ou s'il ne peut accomplir tout ce qu'ils font. Certaines mères craignent que leur enfant handicapé se sente perdu lorsqu'il joue sans elle. Mais elles doivent lui permettre certaines expériences, en autant qu'elles se situent à l'intérieur de ses limites, plutôt que de le soumettre à une surprotection constante. Il faut identifier correctement l'enfant, lorsqu'il est loin de ses parents, en lui mettant une épingle, une chaîne ou un bracelet munis d'un médaillon ou d'une plaque d'identification en métal.

L'éducation comporte la formation personnelle et sociale, aussi bien que l'apprentissage traditionnel. Elle doit être adaptée aux capacités de l'enfant pour qu'il éprouve de la joie à accomplir ce qu'on attend de lui. À l'école primaire, il faut adapter son travail à sa capacité mentale ainsi qu'à ses limites physiques. Dans la plupart des villes, il existe des écoles spécialisées ou des classes spéciales dans les écoles régulières. Dans ces classes ou écoles, les enseignants établissent des programmes d'éducation en fonction des besoins de petits groupes d'enfants dont les capacités sont à peu près identiques. Ces écoles s'occupent de la rééducation musculaire, de la physiothérapie et souvent, elles procurent l'aide psychologique nécessaire à l'enfant souffrant de problèmes affectifs.

Un avantage des écoles ou des classes spéciales: le mobilier est fonctionnel et les enfants peuvent ainsi travailler bien à l'aise. Leur inconvénient est de retarder parfois l'intégration de l'enfant dans le monde où il devra éventuellement évoluer.

Les enfants dont le handicap n'est pas trop important, peuvent fréquenter des classes régulières ou bien suivre certaines matières dans des classes spéciales et d'autres dans des classes régulières en compagnie d'enfants normaux. Le fait de travailler avec d'autres enfants contribuera à atténuer les sentiments d'infériorité et d'apitoiement sur eux-mêmes.

HOSPITALISATION. Lorsqu'un enfant atteint de paralysie cérébrale est admis à l'hôpital, les infirmières qui le soignent doivent se renseigner sur les méthodes de soins employées à la maison. Utilisés à bon escient, de tels renseignements favoriseront une transition moins traumatisante entre le domicile et l'hôpital, et fourniront à l'infirmière des connaissances qu'elle pourra utiliser auprès des autres patients. De plus, le niveau d'habileté de l'enfant pourra être maintenu ou amélioré.

Parfois, les parents ne connaissent pas les raisons de l'hospitalisation de l'enfant, le genre de traitement qu'il subira, ou la durée de son absence de la maison. Ils peuvent laisser l'enfant à contre-cœur à l'hôpital, parce qu'ils pensent qu'il souffrira plus qu'un enfant normal de l'absence maternelle. L'infirmière peut contribuer grandement à soulager l'anxiété des parents en les encourageant à demeurer avec l'enfant et à participer à ses soins, si c'est possible.

On doit organiser la vie quotidienne de l'unité pédiatrique d'un hôpital général, ou de l'hôpital pour enfants, en fonction de la croissance affective et physique des enfants. L'absence de la maison peut devenir une expérience enrichissante, particulièrement pour l'enfant surprotégé par sa famille.

Les soins physiques des enfants atteints de paralysie cérébrale consistent à prévenir les contractures et ceci peut sembler aberrant pour les parents. Ils ont essayé d'assurer à l'enfant le plus de confort possible en le laissant prendre et maintenir les positions qu'il aimait, aussi longtemps qu'il le désirait. Un physiothérapeute qualifié doit leur enseigner comment exécuter des exercices passifs d'extension, d'après les besoins spécifiques de l'enfant. On peut prescrire des attelles de correction. Habituellement, on ne les met que la nuit, mais des attelles aux jambes sont souvent nécessaires pour permettre à l'enfant de se tenir debout pendant la journée.

On peut utiliser des appareils pour aider l'enfant à mener une vie aussi normale que possible. S'il a des difficultés à se tenir droit ou à garder son équilibre, il peut se servir d'une chaise au dossier élevé, avec des bras et une plate-forme pour les pieds. S'il perd encore l'équilibre, des courroies le maintiendront en sécurité dans sa chaise.

Un équipement spécial permet à l'enfant de se nourrir lui-même. Cet équipement comporte des cuillères assez larges ou à manche incliné, des assiettes à rebord, des tasses à ventouse pour les empêcher de glisser et, enfin, des verres à couvercle percé d'un trou pour permettre l'introduction d'une paille.

En cas de difformité orthopédique, une intervention chirurgicale peut s'avérer nécessaire et peut nécessiter la section des nerfs conduisant aux extrémités spastiques, l'élongation du tendon d'Achille ou toute autre technique apte à améliorer le contrôle musculaire de l'enfant. Les soins du plâtre sont identiques à ceux que nous avons étudiés au chapitre précédent.

Si l'enfant ne contrôle pas encore tout à fait ses fonctions d'excrétion, on peut le placer sur un cadre de Bradford. Le traitement médical peut comporter des tranquillisants et des anti-

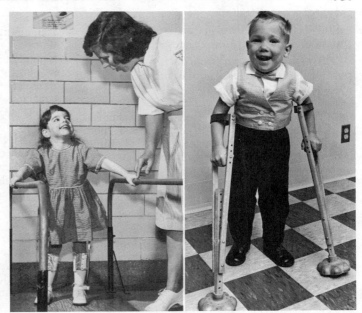

Figure 16-5. Apprentissage de la marche. L'enfant, après avoir pratiqué à l'aide de barres parallèles, marche avec des béquilles pourvues de pattes d'éléphants. (Courtoisie du Rehabilitation Institute of the Boston Dispensary et de F. H. Krusen dans *Handbook of Physical Medecine and Rehabilitation.*)

convulsivants. La physiothérapie s'avère importante pour prévenir les contractures et améliorer le contrôle du mouvement.

Les infirmières en santé communautaire et les infirmières de l'hôpital font partie de l'équipe qui s'occupe des enfants atteints de paralysie cérébrale. L'équipe s'occupe des enfants à la maison, à l'hôpital, dans les écoles et dans les camps d'été. Les infirmières enseignent aux parents la façon de donner les soins quotidiens à l'enfant et expliquent ses besoins aux autres membres de la famille et à ses enseignants. Au fur et à mesure qu'il grandit, ses contacts avec le monde extérieur augmentent. On admet même le jeune enfant à certaines écoles maternelles pour enfants handicapés et les enfants plus âgés fréquentent les camps d'été spéciaux où les groupes de jeu sont organisés en fonction de leurs besoins. Les infirmières entrent en contact avec les travailleuses sociales et les aident à coordonner leurs services avec le plan général de traitement établi par l'équipe pour chaque enfant.

Des associations pour paralysés cérébraux donnent des conseils aux parents dont l'enfant souffre de cette maladie. L'infirmière travaille en collaboration étroite avec les membres d'une telle organisation. Beaucoup ont des centres récréatifs et procurent une formation professionnelle aux adolescents. Chaque année, plus de centres contribuent à rechercher les causes et le traitement de la paralysie cérébrale

Figure 16-6. Tricycle avec dossier, ceinture de sécurité, appui-pied et système de poulie qui prévient la flexion plantaire. (Courtoisie du Minneapolis Curative Workshop et F. H. Krusen dans *Handbook of Physical Medecine and Rehabilitation.*)

et procurent des fonds pour la mise en application des résultats de la recherche sur l'éducation et la rééducation de ces enfants.

Enseignement aux parents. Il est important de conseiller les parents pour qu'ils modifient l'environnement familial de façon à faciliter le soin de l'enfant. Le père peut fabriquer des rampes, des pentes, des poignées, etc... Il peut concevoir un siège spécial pour le cabinet de toilette. La mère doit s'habituer à utiliser pour l'enfant des vêtements avec fermeture-éclair se terminant par une chaîne ou une boule, ou encore des vêtements avec attaches en Velcro.

Ils doivent comprendre qu'il faut se concentrer sur un seul apprentissage à la fois. Pour chaque nouvelle étape du développement, ils doivent penser à de nouveaux outils, s'adapter encore un peu plus. Ils doivent accepter de faire face aux frustrations et aux difficultés qu'il rencontre. Chaque nouvel apprentissage est un dur labeur pour l'enfant et il est facile d'être tenté de l'y soustraire au risque d'en faire un enfant sous-développé. Il faut aider ces parents et les soutenir pour qu'ils soient eux-mêmes capables de réconforter leur enfant.

Pronostic. Le pronostic dépend de la gravité de l'atteinte physique, de la capacité mentale et intellectuelle de l'enfant et du traitement disponible. En général, l'enfant doté d'une intelligence normale et qui reçoit un traitement adéquat s'améliore au point qu'il peut se suffire à lui-même et probablement réussir dans une profession adaptée à ses limites. Certaines formes de paralysie cérébrale constituent cependant un tel handicap physique qu'aucun traitement ne parvient à les améliorer. Les enfants souffrant de paralysie flasque ou choréo-athétosique grave ne peuvent guère bénéficier de la rééducation physique, même s'ils ont une intelligence normale. Parfois même il est impossible de les garder à domicile et ils doivent souvent être placés dans des institutions spécialisées.

Résumé. Le rôle de l'infirmière consiste à favoriser la prévention de la paralysie cérébrale, à contribuer au dépistage une fois qu'elle s'est produite et à aider à soigner au maximum les enfants atteints, en collaboration avec les autres membres de l'équipe de santé. L'objectif du traitement est que chaque enfant s'actualise pleinement dans les limites de ses capacités. Dans une atmosphère physique et sociale favorable, beaucoup d'enfants acquièrent une forte personnalité. Ils doivent cependant être aidés pour affronter la réalité, pour s'accepter eux-mêmes objectivement, et réussir à s'adapter aux problèmes causés par leurs han-

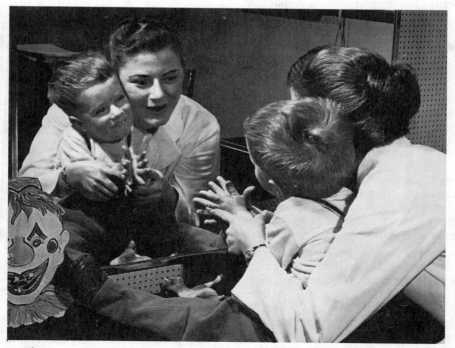

Figure 16-7. Évaluation de la parole et de l'ouïe. On fait subir les tests audiométriques, si on soupçonne une surdité. (M. Stewart: Role of the Nurse in Pediatric Rehabilitation. *Health News*, Vol. 33.)

dicaps. L'attitude de l'enfant vis-à-vis de lui-même et des autres se forme progressivement, dès le jeune âge, et une adaptation heureuse au cours de l'adolescence ou de la vie adulte est déterminée par les expériences vécues lorsqu'il était petit enfant. Les adultes sont tentés de lui faciliter la vie plutôt que de l'aider à affronter ses problèmes, à les résoudre lui-même et à accepter les expériences plus complexes qui se présentent lorsque l'enfant grandit. Le fait d'assumer ses propres responsabilités lui donne un sentiment de sécurité et de respect de lui-même. Si son handicap est trop important, il devra apprendre à accepter l'aide d'autrui.

Surdité

Importance du problème. Il existe plusieurs degrés de surdité. Une surdité bilatérale totale constitue un handicap sérieux. Le sourd est privé de tous les plaisirs que procure le son et il communique plus difficilement avec autrui.

On peut s'interroger sur l'acuité auditive d'un enfant de moins d'un an qui ne s'éveille pas quand on lui parle ou qu'il se produit un bruit; que l'on doit toucher pour qu'il sorte du sommeil; qu'on ne réussit jamais à consoler par des paroles ou des refrains et que la mère doit toujours prendre dans ses bras; qui ne joue pas ou très peu avec les sons ou les syllabes; qui n'est pas attiré par le son de la voix et qui ne comprend pas quand on l'appelle par son nom.

On peut également dépister des problèmes auditifs chez l'enfant plus âgé qui répond de façon inappropriée aux questions qu'on lui pose, qui penche sa tête ou prend des positions bizarres quand on lui parle; qui semble inattentif, qui ne répond pas aux questions, qui souffre de troubles de la parole ou qui communique avec autrui par des gestes plutôt qu'oralement. L'enfant partiellement ou complètement sourd peut sembler timide et peut se retirer volontairement à l'écart; il éprouve souvent des difficultés scolaires et peut déjà être perçu par ses parents et ses éducateurs comme un « enfant-problème ».

La surdité unilatérale est dépistée lorsqu'une circonstance accidentelle attire l'attention de la mère sur l'incapacité de l'enfant à entendre de l'oreille affectée. On doit traiter une surdité unilatérale, partielle ou totale de la même façon qu'une surdité bilatérale, bien que l'enfant ne soit pas aussi sérieusement handicapé dans ses relations sociales que l'enfant complètement sourd.

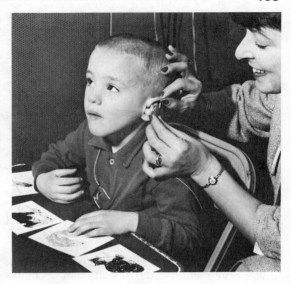

Figure 16-8. Adaptation d'un appareil acoustique à l'oreille d'un enfant atteint de surdité de conduction. (Irene B. Bayer and the New York League for the Hard of Hearing).

La surdité peut occasionner des problèmes de comportement et une mauvaise adaptation sociale. Les enfants sourds peuvent devenir agressifs et intraitables. On rencontre également parmi eux des enfants vifs, pourvus d'une intelligence normale ou au-dessus de la moyenne et remarquablement adroits.

Étiologie et diagnostic. La surdité peut être congénitale, ou acquise par une lésion du nerf auditif, du centre auditif cérébral ou d'un segment de l'oreille moyenne ou interne. Parmi les maladies qui entraînent la surdité, citons la rubéole congénitale, la syphilis congénitale, la méningite à méningocoques, l'encéphalite et l'otite moyenne chronique.

Un *diagnostic* précoce s'avère essentiel. On découvre souvent une surdité bilatérale partielle ou une surdité unilatérale au cours d'un examen physique de routine. Des épreuves auditives relativement simples peuvent déterminer la capacité auditive des nourrissons et des jeunes enfants. On donne d'abord un jouet à l'enfant. L'examinateur se place alors derrière ou à côté de l'enfant et il émet un son avec un sifflet, un hochet ou tout autre moyen de faire du bruit. Un enfant de plus de 3½ mois qui entend bien se tournera en direction du bruit et oubliera son jouet; l'enfant sourd ne réagira pas. Il existe aussi un audiomètre permettant d'identifier à la pouponnière, les nouveau-nés qui entendent bien. Toutefois, les autres bébés doivent être de nouveau investigués à l'âge de 6 mois parce qu'on ne peut affirmer avec certitude qu'ils souffrent de surdité. Étant donné l'état d'anxiété dans lequel vivent les parents en attendant le verdict et les perturbations possibles de la relation mère-enfant, on ne recommande pas de généraliser cette méthode de dépistage.

Chez les enfants qui ne sont pas sous surveillance médicale, la surdité peut être dépistée tardivement. Les examens auditifs plus raffinés comportent des tests audiométriques de sons purs de fréquences diverses, associés à des tests de langage et pratiqués dans une pièce insonorisée. À l'école, on pratique le dépistage des troubles auditifs grâce à des tests audiométriques de routine, lors de l'examen médical et on répète ces tests tous les trois ans. L'infirmière scolaire ou l'infirmière en santé communautaire peut s'en charger. Quand l'enfant a une acuité auditive de 70 pour cent ou moins par rapport à la normale, il ne peut entendre tout ce que le professeur ou ses compagnons de classe lui disent et il a besoin d'une aide spéciale pour assimiler le même contenu éducatif que les autres enfants.

Traitement. Un service spécialisé dans le traitement de l'enfant tout à fait ou partiellement sourd nécessite la collaboration d'un médecin, d'un otologiste, d'un audiologiste, d'un orthophoniste et peut-être d'un psychologue ou d'un psychiatre, d'une travailleuse sociale, d'une infirmière, de la famille et surtout de l'enfant lui-même.

Le dépistage précoce de la surdité s'impose si l'on veut assurer un développement adéquat du langage et de l'affectivité. Un entraînement demeure nécessaire pour la compréhension de l'expression du visage qui accompagne des mots d'approbation ou de désapprobation, de permission ou de refus et pour l'apprentissage de la lecture sur les lèvres. Cette dernière technique peut s'apprendre dès l'âge de 2½ ans ou trois ans, période à laquelle un enfant apprend normalement à s'exprimer par des phrases. La mère doit veiller à bien articuler quand elle parle, dans le but de favoriser la compréhension de l'enfant et d'aider le travail du spécialiste. Si les parents de l'enfant sont sourds, il doit apprendre deux systèmes de communication, l'un à la maison et l'autre avec le monde extérieur. On peut procurer très tôt une prothèse auditive à l'enfant.

S'il y a une perte sérieuse de l'acuité auditive, une éducation spéciale peut s'avérer nécessaire. Dans beaucoup de centres, on a organisé des écoles maternelles spéciales pour les enfants sourds et on leur apprend à parler en

dépit de leur surdité. À d'autres endroits, on doit retarder l'entraînement à la lecture sur les lèvres jusqu'à l'âge scolaire, parce qu'il n'y a pas de possibilités pour des enfants plus jeunes.

On peut enseigner aussi le langage par signes pour augmenter les possibilités de communication. L'apprentissage de la communication constitue la base de toute éducation.

On doit considérer les enfants sourds comme des enfants normaux, tout en tenant compte de leur grand handicap. Les adultes qui travaillent avec eux doivent faire preuve de patience. En attendant que l'enfant ait appris à communiquer par le langage on doit employer des signes. S'il a appris à écrire, on pourra communiquer avec lui plus facilement.

Rôle de l'infirmière. L'infirmière participe au dépistage de la surdité ou de la diminution de l'acuité auditive chez les nourrissons et les enfants que l'on amène à la clinique ou au centre de santé. L'infirmière scolaire pratique souvent les tests de routine pour dépister les troubles auditifs. Si un enfant qui a été malade paraît avoir des difficultés à comprendre ce que l'on dit en classe, le professeur peut l'envoyer chez l'infirmière pour un test auditif. L'infirmière scolaire rencontre régulièrement les enfants dont on connait les troubles d'audition pour surveiller l'application du programme de traitement déterminé par le médecin. Les infirmières travaillent en collaboration étroite avec le personnel enseignant des écoles régulières ou spécialisées. Dans les cliniques pour enfants sourds, les infirmières ont un contact direct avec l'enfant et sa mère.

Comme tout enfant normal, l'enfant sourd déteste qu'on le singularise et il n'aime pas qu'on attire l'attention sur son handicap ou qu'on le traite de façon différente des autres. Le degré de surdité constitue d'ailleurs une variable importante et qui détermine en partie le traitement que recevra l'enfant. L'apprentissage de l'enfant sourd suppose que sa mère ou la personne qui en est responsable lui consacrera beaucoup de temps. Elle doit se placer face à lui sous un bon éclairage quand elle lui parle et elle doit bien se garder de crier ou de prononcer de façon exagérée. Elle doit s'en tenir à un langage normal, bien articulé et bien modulé. Quand il connaît la lecture labiale, elle doit s'assurer qu'il voit bien sa bouche quand elle parle et elle peut attirer d'abord son attention en le touchant légèrement. Si l'enfant entend bien d'une oreille, il faut bien sûr, se placer de ce côté pour lui parler. Si l'enfant ne comprend pas ce qu'on lui dit, on écrit les mots-clés ou on utilise un synonyme ou une autre tournure de phrase pour obvier à la difficulté. L'enfant d'âge préscolaire se guide souvent sur l'expression faciale quand il comprend mal ce qu'on lui dit.

L'enfant sourd présente souvent des difficultés d'élocution. La compréhension du langage est facilitée par l'observation de l'expression faciale; il faut l'encourager à s'intéresser à des activités, telles que la lecture à haute voix, l'épellation et la diction.

L'adolescent cherche souvent à nier son handicap; il faut faire preuve de tact et répéter de façon différente la phrase qu'il n'a pas comprise et ne pas souligner le manque de compréhension.

Il faut surveiller attentivement l'apparition des premiers signes d'infection des voies respiratoires supérieures; ces enfants devraient jouir d'une surveillance médicale plus étroite autant pour traiter immédiatement toute infection que pour déceler les modifications du degré de surdité.

Pronostic.   Le pronostic dépend du degré et de la nature de l'état pathologique ou de la malformation et aussi du traitement que l'enfant a reçu. Le traitement adéquat dépend souvent de la présence de centres spécialisés possédant l'équipement nécessaire et un personnel compétent.

Le pronostic demeure excellent, pour la plupart des enfants sourds, si on le définit en termes de capacité à mener une vie normale. Si l'enfant est à la fois sourd et aveugle, ou s'il souffre de déficience mentale, le pronostic devient moins favorable quant à son intégration harmonieuse dans la société.

Prévention.   La prévention de la surdité acquise consiste surtout dans la prévention des maladies infectieuses qui s'attaquent volontiers à l'oreille, surtout les infections des voies respiratoires supérieures. Il est difficile, sinon impossible, de prévenir toutes les infections, mais on doit instituer un traitement rapide qui diminue l'incidence de ces complications désastreuses.

L'accumulation de cérumen trouble l'audition et peut entraîner une lésion de l'oreille. Les bouchons de cérumen doivent être retirés par un médecin. On doit traiter rapidement les infections des sinus et des adénoïdes. Il faut proscrire les médications oto-toxiques ou, du moins, les employer avec une extrême circonspection.

La surdité des enfants est rarement causée par un traumatisme. Néanmoins, lorsque l'enfant met un objet pointu dans son oreille, il peut blesser son tympan. Des lésions de l'oreille externe affectent peu l'audition. Des traumatismes crâniens peuvent perturber les centres de l'audition et de la parole.

Cécité

L'enfant est habituellement hypermétrope à la naissance. Il possède une vision périphérique jusqu'à ce que la vision centrale commence à se développer vers l'âge de six semaines. La cornée est presque normale à la naissance, mais le cristallin a encore besoin de maturation. L'enfant de trois mois peut suivre un objet avec ses deux yeux, dans toutes les directions; si le mouvement des yeux n'est pas synchronisé, il souffre peut être de strabisme ou d'amblyopie.

Étiologie et importance du problème. L'enfant peut naître aveugle ou le devenir par suite d'une fibroplasie rétro-lenticulaire, d'un traumatisme, d'une infection acquise au cours de l'accouchement, (ophtalmie néonatale), ou d'une syphilis congénitale. Les maladies qui entraînent la cécité au cours de l'enfance demeurent relativement peu nombreuses.

L'explosion de bouteilles de boisson gazeuse et de pétards ainsi que certains jouets peuvent occasionner des blessures oculaires.

Les enfants qui ont des troubles visuels peuvent se frotter souvent les yeux, loucher, froncer les sourcils lorsqu'ils essaient de voir à distance ou tenir leurs livres d'images trop près des yeux.

La définition légale de la cécité se base sur une acuité visuelle d'au plus 20/200 dans le meilleur œil après correction. Les enfants partiellement aveugles possèdent une acuité visuelle qui se situe entre 20/70 et 20/200 dans le meilleur œil, après une correction appropriée. Les enfants, comme les adultes, peuvent souffrir de myopie (vision de près seulement), d'astigmatisme (défaut de courbure des milieux réfringents de l'œil, rendant impossible la convergence en un seul point des rayons homocentriques) ou d'hypermétropie (vision de loin seulement).

Les enfants aveugles ou qui ont une vision très déficiente demandent une éducation spéciale. On peut améliorer leur état par un traitement médical ou une intervention chirurgicale et par le port de verres correctifs. Ils peuvent avoir besoin d'aide pour acquérir l'habileté nécessaire pour effectuer les soins personnels et les activités de la vie quotidienne. On les éduque par l'intermédiaire de l'ouïe ou du toucher. L'enfant doté d'une intelligence

A

Figure 16-9. L'enfant totalement aveugle doit développer au maximum ses sens de l'ouïe et du toucher pour compenser partiellement son handicap. *A)* Étude du Braille. *B)* L'enfant apprend à écouter avec un tourne-disque. (Courtoisie du « New York State Commission for the Visually Handicapped ».)

B

normale est capable de suivre à l'école les mêmes cours que les enfants normaux, même si ses progrès peuvent être moins rapides. Si l'enfant aveugle ne reçoit pas la même éducation que les autres enfants, il n'acquiert pas les intérêts, les attitudes et les possibilités que possèdent ses compagnons.

Traitement. Le but du traitement consiste à rendre ou à améliorer la vision ou à prévenir des troubles visuels ultérieurs. Si le trottineur doit porter des lunettes, celles-ci doivent pouvoir résister à tous les chocs; les lentilles incassables et les montures de plastique épais diminuent le danger d'accident.

On inscrit l'enfant d'âge scolaire totalement aveugle dans une école spécialisée ou dans une école normale où il existe une classe pour des enfants qui présentent des problèmes visuels.

On a créé des classes spéciales dans les écoles publiques et privées pour les enfants dont la vision est réduite à un point tel qu'ils sont incapables de suivre l'enseignement scolaire habituel. La technique utilisée se base sur un enseignement auditif et l'apprentissage de la lecture par le système Braille, fondé sur des techniques palpatoires. Pour les enfants dont la vision n'est pas complètement perdue, on imprime des livres en gros caractères de façon à réduire la fatigue oculaire. On accorde une attention particulière à l'éclairage et à l'attitude correcte de l'enfant pendant la lecture.

Les enfants atteints de cécité partielle peuvent fréquenter les classes régulières, à condition qu'un professeur spécialisé dans l'éducation des enfants aveugles les aide quand c'est nécessaire. De tels contacts favorisent les occasions de se faire des amis et de participer aux activités des enfants normaux. Le fait d'appartenir à un groupe normal encourage un développement social et affectif adéquat.

On aide les parents à comprendre les besoins de leur enfant aveugle. Une cécité congénitale ou qui se développe tôt dans l'enfance empêche l'enfant de connaître ce que les autres perçoivent. La mère doit employer les mots dans un contexte qui donne à l'enfant une idée de leur signification. Les petits aveugles doivent manipuler le plus possible ce qui les entoure. Ils peuvent pétrir de la terre ou de la pâte à modeler, ils peuvent tisser ou peindre pour apprendre à « percevoir ». On peut leur faire entendre des sonnettes, des boîtes à musique et des disques pour qu'ils connaissent le « son » et développent une perception auditive très grande.

Il faut aider les parents à comprendre les soins spéciaux qu'exige l'enfant atteint de cécité partielle ou totale. On a toujours tendance à le surprotéger et il semble souvent difficile de lui accorder la liberté qu'il doit avoir pour acquérir l'habileté et l'expérience nécessaires pour devenir un adulte. On donne ordinairement une formation professionnelle à l'aveugle; celui qui le désire peut recevoir une éducation supérieure et une préparation aux carrières qui lui sont accessibles.

Rôle de l'infirmière. Un dépistage précoce de la cécité ou des troubles visuels demeure essentiel pour le traitement et l'éducation de l'enfant. On doit faire évaluer la vision du nourrisson qui n'essaie pas de saisir son biberon ou ses jouets et qui ne sourit pas quand sa mère lui sourit, qui se heurte au mobilier, qui n'est pas intéressé, même par de grandes images et qui ne réagit pas aux mouvements des autres gens. Les cas de cécité non rapportés sont rares depuis que l'on a amélioré la surveillance médicale des enfants de toutes les classes sociales.

L'enfant aveugle a besoin d'être heureux comme les autres enfants. Il est plus sensible que les enfants normaux à l'attitude des adultes à son égard. L'infirmière qui s'occupe de l'enfant aveugle sait qu'il peut interpréter son humeur par une inflexion de sa voix, comme d'autres enfants le font en voyant un sourire ou un froncement de sourcils.

À l'hôpital, l'infirmière guide d'abord l'enfant dans son nouvel environnement et le dirige jusqu'à ce qu'il se soit familiarisé avec les bruits de l'unité de soins. En lui présentant les enfants, elle peut faciliter les premiers contacts en disant: « Jean ne peut te voir, essaie de lui sourire dans ta voix. » Elle doit parler à l'enfant avant de le toucher et bien s'identifier. La préparation aux différentes techniques de soins devient d'une importance capitale pour le jeune aveugle; toucher les pièces d'équipement le sécurise et on doit le laisser faire tout ce qu'il peut par lui-même. Le personnel infirmier doit lui fournir la stimulation sensorielle et psycho-motrice dont il a besoin.

L'infirmière peut aider les parents de plusieurs manières. Il est bon d'appuyer sur la nécessité de procurer à l'enfant de l'amour, de la sécurité et de développer son sens d'appartenance à la famille; l'importance des contacts physiques et de la stimulation sensorielle ne doit pas être sous-estimée. Les parents doivent reconnaître le moment où l'enfant est prêt pour de nouvelles expériences et lui accorder la liberté de mouvement et la mobilité nécessaires pour l'exploration de son environnement. Il faut parler beaucoup à l'enfant aveugle et essayer de développer ses autres sens par une stimulation appropriée. Il faut le traiter de la façon la plus normale possible, mais faire preuve de patience s'il accuse un certain retard, par exemple dans l'apprentissage de la propreté, dans la capacité de se nourrir seul ou dans l'établissement de son rythme de sommeil. Il doit se développer comme tout autre enfant sans ressentir de peurs inutiles ou un sentiment intense de culpabilité. Il a besoin en vieillissant de connaître la plupart des expériences normales de l'enfance et de l'adolescence.

Action de la société. Comme les parents, la société peut avoir tendance à trop protéger l'enfant aveugle. Une partie de la responsabilité de l'infirmière consiste à orienter la compassion des gens vers des actions utiles. Dans certaines villes, on a créé des centres récréatifs pour des enfants d'âge préscolaire où les jeunes aveugles peuvent jouer avec d'autres enfants. Le terrain de jeu et l'équipement sont adaptés à leurs besoins et ils y bénéficient d'une surveillance adéquate. De tels jeux aident ces enfants à s'adapter à la société; ils servent de base aux contacts avec ceux qui voient et développent une capacité normale de participation aux activités de groupe.

Pronostic. Le résultat du traitement varie d'après chaque enfant et on ne peut faire d'affirmations générales. De grands progrès ont été faits dans la prévention de la cécité causée par la gonorrhée et la syphilis et grâce aux meilleurs soins des enfants prématurés, on rencontre moins de cas de cécité causée par une fibroplasie rétro-lenticulaire.

Le pronostic de la santé mentale est bon. L'enfant aveugle de naissance s'adapte habituellement mieux à son handicap que celui qui devient aveugle à la suite d'une infection ou d'un traumatisme. Les relations parents-enfant demeurent plus importantes que toutes les mesures que la société peut prendre pour aider l'enfant aveugle. C'est la société, toutefois, qui procure l'éducation et qui donne à l'aveugle une situation dans l'industrie ou emploie ses services professionnels. Les enfants qui présentent des troubles visuels devraient devenir des adultes se suffisant à eux-mêmes et remplissant tous les rôles d'un adulte normal. Celui qui est atteint de cécité totale peut trouver plus difficile de s'acquitter de ses fonctions dans la société. Le succès repose en grande partie sur un entraînement précoce et un développement poussé de ses possibilités.

L'enfant handicapé d'une façon chronique

Pour se développer dans les limites de leurs capacités, les enfants handicapés ont besoin du sentiment de sécurité que seuls des parents affectueux peuvent leur donner.

Il n'est pas facile d'être des « parents parfaits » pour des enfants handicapés. Il faut aider l'enfant à grandir normalement Une personnalité handicapée entrave plus souvent l'adaptation sociale que l'état physique. Un enfant ne souffre de problèmes émotifs que lorsqu'il manque de satisfactions affectives et d'occasion de développer ses capacités.

Il faut du temps aux parents pour se remettre du choc et de la frustration qu'ils ont éprouvés en voyant leur enfant anormal. Ils redoutent les responsabilités supplémentaires qu'ils auront à prendre et ils craignent surtout l'attitude de la société envers eux et envers l'enfant. L'anxiété et l'hostilité entrent en conflit avec l'amour naturel qu'ils ressentent pour l'enfant. Ils peuvent à la fois avoir besoin d'une aide financière et de conseils spécialisés pour remplir leur rôle astreignant.

Un enfant handicapé perturbe non seulement les relations parents-enfant, mais aussi les relations entre les autres membres de la famille. Les parents peuvent réagir de différentes façons avec leur enfant malade. Ils peuvent méconnaître l'existence du handicap ou trop protéger l'enfant pour masquer leurs sentiments négatifs à son égard. Ils peuvent le rejeter ouvertement et ne pas lui donner l'amour et la sécurité dont il a besoin et lui refuser le statut d'un enfant bien accepté. Ils peuvent même le priver de contacts extérieurs qui l'aideraient à s'adapter aux autres gens.

Les parents peuvent ignorer son aptitude à apprendre parce qu'ils l'en jugent incapable ou parce qu'ils le surprotègent.

On assure de l'aide aux parents, grâce à l'équipe de santé formée par un médecin, une travailleuse sociale, un psychologue ou un psychiatre, une infirmière et d'autres professionnels, selon les problèmes de l'enfant. L'infirmière doit comprendre les relations normales parents-enfant, le processus de dé-

Figure 16-10. L'infirmière aide l'enfant aveugle à s'orienter dans son nouveau milieu. (Courtoisie de l'Hôpital Sainte-Justine, Montréal.)

veloppement et les besoins de l'enfant. Elle doit savoir comment aider les parents à accepter les problèmes que cause le handicap de l'enfant et enfin il faut qu'elle connaisse suffisamment les parents pour les soutenir au moment où ils sont prêts à collaborer. L'enseignement de techniques de soins, avant que la mère ne soit disposée à les apprendre, n'engendrera que frustration et échec.

L'infirmière peut être d'un grand secours pour les parents au cours des périodes difficiles. Elle doit croire en leur capacité de soigner l'enfant et de lui procurer amour et sécurité. Elle doit leur faire comprendre, par sa façon d'agir, qu'elle connait leurs sentiments et désire leur procurer soutien et assistance.

La réaction de l'enfant à l'aide qu'on lui procure constitue l'épreuve finale du succès. Si l'enfant handicapé sent que ses parents sont anxieux et frustrés, il se sentira peu aimé et il pourra se réfugier dans un monde imaginaire. Certains enfants éprouvent uniquement de la compassion pour eux-mêmes, certains essaient de blesser les autres comme eux-mêmes ont été blessés et d'autres recherchent des punitions pour leurs propres sentiments négatifs.

Les enfants, qui se sentent aimés et acceptés, feront plus d'efforts pour surmonter les limites imposées par leurs handicaps et éprouveront un sentiment de satisfaction dans l'accomplissement de gestes, même restreints. Ces enfants réussissent souvent au-delà de ce qu'on attendait d'eux. L'enfant handicapé n'a pas surtout besoin de pitié ou de compassion; il a besoin d'être compris et de savoir que les autres acceptent qu'il soit différent d'eux et lui accordent un statut égal.

L'infirmière doit être consciente de ses propres sentiments. Si elle éprouve de la répugnance ou de la crainte, elle ne doit pas en être gênée. Le fait de reconnaître ces sentiments est le premier pas d'un changement vers une attitude positive.

Quand l'enfant handicapé est capable de quitter sa famille pour de plus longues périodes, il faut lui fournir une pièce d'identité (carte, bracelet, médaillon).

Les parents ont besoin de loisirs s'ils veulent continuer à aider leur enfant handicapé. L'aide d'autres membres de la famille, de voisins ou d'amis devient nécessaire pour qu'ils puissent s'éloigner pendant quelques heures, à intervalles réguliers. L'adhésion aux organismes regroupant les parents d'handicapés favorise la discussion de problèmes communs et la découverte de solutions originales.

Le rôle des parents et surtout de la mère s'avère fondamental pour que l'enfant développe sa capacité de communiquer, élabore son image corporelle et acquière une perception positive de lui-même; l'influence des parents peut toutefois être modifiée dans un sens positif ou négatif quand se produisent des expériences agréables ou désagréables avec l'entourage. Malgré un climat familial propice, l'enfant peut être perturbé psychologiquement par une attitude de mépris, de crainte ou de dédain de la part de personnes qu'il rencontre hors de sa famille.

Anxiété du trottineur

Quand un jeune enfant paraît anxieux, c'est que le conflit entre ses désirs instinctifs et les exigences de son entourage s'avère trop difficile à supporter. Les manifestations de l'anxiété à cet âge peuvent se traduire par le refus d'aller au lit, par un comportement « craintif » au cours de la journée, par un sommeil agité et par des perturbations dans le contrôle des sphincters anal et vésical.

L'acquisition de la propreté devient souvent une source aiguë d'anxiété. Même pour les enfants qui ont acquis un contrôle satisfaisant, on peut observer des défaillances occasionnelles; l'enfant peut jouer avec ses selles même s'il en avait perdu l'habitude. Si un enfant a été éduqué d'une manière trop sévère dans ce domaine, il peut redouter de faire fonctionner ses intestins. La constipation résulte d'un sentiment d'opposition de l'enfant envers sa mère lorsque celle-ci a fait quelque chose qui ne lui plaît pas. L'anxiété de l'enfant au sujet de son alimentation peut créer des problèmes de nutrition.

L'enfant peut régresser vers des plaisirs infantiles, comme par exemple, la succion. Il peut commencer à *bégayer*. Ce comportement traduit souvent une tension excessive due le plus souvent à des exigences exagérées de la part des parents.

Certains jeunes enfants, par suite d'une éducation de la propreté trop sévère, deviennent excessivement propres, ne se souillant plus d'aucune manière pour éviter de déplaire à leur mère.

Un enfant qui souffre d'anxiété sera incapable d'avoir des relations affectueuses satisfaisantes avec un adulte et ne développera pas son sens de l'autonomie. Il sera plutôt envahi par la honte et doutera de ses propres capacités. Il faut l'aider à acquérir un amour réel pour sa mère. Celle-ci doit l'encourager à participer à des activités qu'il considère comme malpropres — jouer avec du sable, de la pâte à modeler ou de la peinture. Tout en riant, elle doit le féliciter lorsqu'il est sale après avoir joué. Si, au contraire, l'enfant se salit pour prouver son hostilité envers sa mère, elle doit accepter cette hostilité comme étant normale pour un enfant de cet âge, de la même façon qu'elle accepte ses manifestations d'affection.

Un traitement adéquat de l'anxiété doit être institué très tôt dans la vie, pour que l'enfant ait une enfance heureuse et un développement affectif normal. Non traitée, l'anxiété de l'enfant s'enracine et devient une réaction habituelle qui peut persister jusqu'à l'âge adulte.

RÉFÉRENCES

Livres et documents officiels

Association de paralysie cérébrale du Québec: *L'enfant atteint de paralysie cérébrale.* L'association de paralysie cérébrale du Québec, Montréal.

Courbeyre, J.: *Les handicapés moteurs et leurs problèmes.* Paris, Laffont, 1969.

Cratty, B. J.: *Movement and Spatial Awareness in Blind Children and Youth.* Springfield, Ill., Charles C Thomas, 1971.

Debuskey, M. (édit.): *The Chronically Ill Child and His Family.* Springfield, Ill., Charles C Thomas, 1970.

Finnie, N. R. et Haynes, U. (édit.): *Handling the Young Cerebral Palsied Child at Home.* New York, E. P. Dutton and Company, 1970.

French, E. L. et Cliford, S. J.: *Comment aider un enfant handicapé.* Paris, Laffont, 1968.

Hofmann, R. B.: *How to Build Special Furniture and Equipment for Handicapped Children.* Springfield, Ill., Charles C Thomas, 1970.

Keats, S.: *Cerebral Palsy.* Springfield, Ill. Charles C Thomas, 1970.

Lowenfeld, B.: *Our Blind Children: Growing and Learning with Them.* 3e éd. Springfield, Ill., Charles C Thomas, 1971.

Myklebust, H. R.: *Your Deaf Child: A Guide for Parents.* Springfield, Ill., Charles C Thomas, 1970.

Noland, R. L. (édit.): *Counseling Parents of the Ill and the Handicapped.* Springfield, Ill., Charles C Thomas, 1971.

Robaye-Geelen, F.: *L'enfant au cerveau blessé.* Bruxelles, Charles Dessart, 1969.

Sheehan, J. G. (édit.): *Stuttering: Research and Therapy.* New York, Harper & Row, 1970.

Sultz, H. A. et autres: *Long-Term Childhood Illness.* Pittsburgh, University of Pittsburgh Press, 1972.

Ulrich, S.: *Elizabeth.* Ann Arbor, The University of Michigan Press, 1972.

West, P.: *Words for a Deaf Daughter* New York, Harper & Row, 1970.

Wolf, J. M.: et Anderson, R. M.: *The Multiply Handicapped Child.* Springfield, Ill., Charles C Thomas, 1969.

Articles

Borel-Maisonny, S.: Surdité de l'enfance. *Soins*, 19:47, 14, 1974.

Carty, R.: Patients Who Cannot Hear. *Nursing Forum*, 11:290, 3, 1972.

Diamond, F.: A Play Center for Developmentally Handicapped Infants. *Children*, 18:174, septembre-octobre 1971.

Dumas, R: Le syndrome néphrotique de l'enfant. *Médecine infantile*, 80, 4, 1973 (numéro spécial).

Feingold, M., Fain, T. et Gellis, S. S.: State-Wide Information Center for Handicapped Children. *J. Pediat.*, 77:830, novembre 1970.

Gozali, J. et Moogk, H.: Le besoin d'approbation. *Inf. Can.*, 9:31, septembre 1967.

Graham, A. B.: Counseling Parent and Teacher Regarding the Effects of Mild Hearing Loss. *Trans. Amer. Acad. Opht. Otol.*, 80:73, 1, 1975.

Hawke, W.: La paralysie cérébrale: Le malade et sa famille. *Inf. Can.*, 9:39, février 1967.

Haynes, U. H.: Nursing Approaches in Cerebral Dysfunction. *Am. J. Nursing*, 68:2170, octobre 1968.

Knox, L. L. et McConnell, F.: Helping Parents to Help Deaf Infants. *Children*, 15:183, septembre-octobre 1968.

Kopito, L., Briley, A. M. et Schwachman, H.: Chronic Plumbism in Children. *J. A. M. A.*, 209:243, 14 juillet, 1969.

Laumond, D.: Le Comportement de l'enfant sourd. *La revue de pédiatrie*, 7:87, 2, 1971.

Lecomte, E.: Les surdités. *Soins*, 18:5, 4, 1973.

Linshaw, M. et autres: Management of the Nephrotic Syndrome. *Clin. Ped.*, 13:45, 1, 1974.

Marcellus, D. et Hawke, W. A.: Survey of Attitudes of Parents of Children with Cerebral Palsy in Windsor and Essex County. Ontario. *Canad. Med. Ass. J.*, 95:1242, 10 décembre, 1966.

Monroe, J. M. et Komorita, N. I.: Problems with Nephrosis in Adolescence. *Am. J. Nursing*, 67:336, 1967.

Natali, R.: La surdté et son traitement. *La revue de l'infirmière*, 21:441, 5, 1971.

Natali, R.: Les possibilités actuelles du traitement de la surdité. *La revue de l'infirmière*, 24:621, 7, 1974.

Neumann, H. H.: Pica – Symptom or Vestigial Instinct? *Pediatrics*, 46:441, septembre 1970.

O'Brien, M., Owens, M. et Ralph, J.: La réadaptation sociale des petites victimes de la thalidomide. *Inf. Can.*, 9:34, janvier 1967.

Payne, P. D. et Payne, R. L.: Behavior Manifestations of Children with Hearing Loss. *Am. J. Nursing*, 70:1718, août 1970.

Portmann, M.: L'étiologie des surdités. *La revue de pédiatrie*, 7:7, 1, 1971.

Portmann, M.: Le dépistage de la surdité infantile et la conduite de l'examen audiométrique. *La revue de pédiatrie*, 7:21, 1, 1971.

Pothier, P. C.: Therapeutic Handling of the Severely Handicapped Child. *Am. J. Nursing*, 71:321, février 1971.

Praud, E.: Les accidents de la corticothérapie. *Soins*, 16:371, 8, 1971.

Raimbault, G. et Royer, P.: Problèmes psychologiques dans les néphropathies chroniques de l'enfant. *La revue de neuropsychiatrie infantile*, 17:835, 12, 1968.

Raynaud de Lage, C.: Syndrome néphrotique. *Soins*, 17:29, 7, 1972.

Reed, A. J.: Lead Poisoning: Silent Epidemic and Social Crime. *Am. J. Nursing*, 72:2180, décembre 1972.

Robischon, P.: Pica Practice and Other Hand-Mouth Behavior and Children's Developmental Level. *Nursing Research*, 20:4. janvier-février 1971.

Siegel, N. J. et autres: Long-Term Follow-up of Children with Steroid-responsive Nephrotic Syndrome. *J. Pediat.*, 81:251. août 1972.

Tcherdakoff, P.: Syndromes néphrotiques. *La revue de l'infirmière*, 23:595, 7, 1973.

Waechter, E. H.: Developmental Correlates of Physical Disability. *Nursing Forum*, 9:90, 1, 1970.

cinquième partie

L'ENFANT
D'ÂGE PRÉSCOLAIRE

17
l'enfant d'âge préscolaire: croissance, développement, soins

APERÇU DU DÉVELOPPEMENT ÉMOTIF

Durant la période préscolaire, les parents doivent accepter le fait que leur enfant s'intéresse de plus en plus aux activités du monde extérieur. Ils doivent, eux aussi, évoluer et apprendre à se détacher de leur enfant qui grandit. Ils doivent permettre à l'enfant de s'exprimer librement et de faire preuve d'initiative tout en lui imposant certaines limites.

L'enfant à l'âge préscolaire, ayant appris à accorder sa confiance aux autres et ayant pris conscience de son individualité, est prêt à découvrir ses possibilités. Il doit maintenant acquérir méthodiquement certaines connaissances pour développer sa personnalité. Il observe les adultes, essaie d'imiter leur comportement et attend, avec impatience, le moment où il pourra partager leurs activités.

L'enfant, à l'âge préscolaire, est imaginatif et créatif. Empêché de participer concrètement au monde des adultes, il prétend néanmoins en faire partie à travers ses jeux. L'objet le plus simple peut alors représenter pour lui des réalités concrètes. Par exemple, plusieurs boîtes en carton ou des blocs de bois peuvent former un train, ou quelques petites boîtes en carton peuvent meubler une maison de poupée: elles deviennent un lit, un bureau, une chaise ou une table.

L'enfant apprend rapidement que les différents matériaux sont liés à des fins spécifiques. Il comprend aussi suffisamment le langage pour communiquer verbalement. Ce fait augmente son habileté à profiter de l'expérience d'autrui et à comprendre ce qu'il n'a pas encore expérimenté lui-même. Il interroge presque continuellement les autres sur l'univers, les hommes et leurs activités. Il peut poser ses questions de façon persistante ou bruyante ou à des moments inopportuns. Il cherche des explications aux phénomènes de son environnement en terme de causalité et de fonction. Des réponses à ses interrogations l'aident à organiser son univers et à devenir plus indépendant des adultes.

L'enfant d'âge préscolaire est aussi vigoureux dans ses activités physiques que dans

481

ses activités intellectuelles. Il bouge librement et violemment. Durant le jeu, il lui arrive de bousculer les autres enfants, volontairement ou accidentellement. Il s'amuse en exerçant sa motricité globale, mais il peut aussi fixer son attention sur un ouvrage exigeant un début de raffinement de l'activité musculaire.

L'influence des parents détermine presqu'exclusivement le comportement du trottineur; cette même influence diminue progressivement pour l'enfant d'âge préscolaire.

Le problème essentiel qui se pose à l'enfant de cet âge demeure l'apprentissage de la vie et des relations humaines. Il doit tenter de s'affirmer sans risquer de se sentir coupable. S'il est apte à résoudre ce problème, il fera preuve *d'initiative,* à l'intérieur des limites de ce qui lui est permis. S'il échoue, il ressentira une sorte d'accablement et développera alors un *sentiment de culpabilité.*

Les enfants d'âge préscolaire peuvent nourrir un sentiment de culpabilité à propos d'initiatives dont les parents désapprouvent la réalisation, ou à propos de simples pensées ou phantasmes que réprouve déjà leur conscience personnelle.

Si l'enfant fait preuve d'initiative et affirme une personnalité saine, les parents comme les adultes de son entourage doivent encourager ses projets et favoriser l'exercice de son imagination. Ils doivent alors restreindre les punitions, pour actes jugés pernicieux sur le plan moral, ou tellement inacceptables sur le plan social, que le résultat pourrait s'avérer fâcheux ou nuisible à l'enfant et à sa famille.

Les enfants à l'âge préscolaire ont hâte de ressembler à leur père ou à leur mère. À travers le comportement de leurs parents, ils apprennent les rôles de l'adulte et leurs jeux deviennent une occasion propice à imiter ces derniers. Peu à peu, ils s'habituent à communiquer avec les autres, d'abord avec les enfants, leurs semblables, puis avec les adultes, et ils tirent de ces échanges un immense plaisir. Les parents se doivent d'encourager ces efforts de coopération, et de fournir ainsi à leur enfant l'occasion de s'intégrer davantage à la famille, en participant à ses responsabilités, voire à ses décisions. Si cette occasion est refusée à l'enfant, si son initiative est réprimée, s'il est, de ce fait, trop souvent frustré dans son aspiration à la maturité, il devient vétilleux, perd son temps et gaspille son énergie à des activités futiles. Cet enfant risque de développer une conscience rigide qui exercera un contrôle trop sévère sur son comportement. Il peut, en outre,

nourrir de la rancœur à l'égard des adultes qui restreignent son comportement normal.

Tout au cours de l'enfance et de l'adolescence, l'initiative de l'enfant doit être encouragée. Si tel n'est pas le cas, un excellent début peut vite tourner à l'échec.

L'enfant à l'âge préscolaire et sa famille

La phase œdipienne. Dès leur jeune âge, les enfants de l'un et l'autre sexes manifestent leur affection et s'attachent davantage à leur mère, plus près d'eux que leur père, généralement absent du foyer durant la journée. De l'âge de trois ans à l'âge de six ans, un changement s'opère. La petite fille s'intéresse davantage à son père, tandis que le petit garçon demeure attaché à sa mère. Ce changement de l'objet-amour influence le comportement des enfants à l'égard des parents et modifie le rôle qu'ils s'attribuent au cours de leurs jeux. La fille est « la petite fille à papa » et s'attribue le rôle d'épouse et de mère. Le garçon est « le petit garçon à maman ». Mais, peu à peu, celui-ci se masculinise et, dans ses jeux, modèle son comportement sur celui du père.

Durant cette période, la petite fille peut développer un sentiment de possession à l'égard du père et être jalouse de l'amour que celui-ci porte à sa mère. Le petit garçon, de son côté, peut développer un sentiment de possession à l'égard de sa mère et se dresser en rival amoureux contre le père. Les enfants nourrissent ainsi de l'agressivité à l'égard du parent du même sexe. Habituellement, ils dissimulent leurs sentiments véritables mais, à l'occasion, ils manifestent ouvertement leur hostilité. Ils lanceront par exemple au parent de leur sexe: « Je te hais, va-t'en! » Une telle attitude est susceptible d'inspirer à l'enfant un sentiment d'anxiété, voire de culpabilité, et de l'amener à craindre le ressentiment du parent du même sexe. L'enfant est cependant en conflit avec lui-même car, tout en détestant le parent de son sexe, il l'aime réellement quoique d'un amour moins intense que celui éprouvé pour le parent du sexe opposé. Les jeux des enfants, entre trois ans et six ans, trahissent d'ailleurs ce conflit d'amour et d'aversion. Mais, indépendamment du sexe, les enfants aiment leur père et leur mère pour l'attention et l'affection que ceux-ci leur témoignent. Durant cette période conflictuelle, les parents doivent témoigner à leurs enfants davantage de compréhension et d'affection.

À mesure qu'il grandit et évolue vers la maturité, le petit garçon modèle son comportement sur celui de son père. La petite fille imite sa mère. Dans la poursuite d'un développement émotif normal, l'enfant doit réprimer ses sentiments sexuels à l'égard du parent du sexe opposé et s'identifier au parent du même sexe. Au terme de cette évolution, le garçon ne cherche plus à prendre la place de son père; il veut simplement lui ressembler. La fille ne cherche plus à se substituer à la mère; elle est impatiente de grandir pour, un jour, avoir, à son tour, des enfants qui seront siens. L'enfant devient l'ami de ses parents, sans considérer l'un ou l'autre comme objet d'amour spécifique. La famille prend alors toute sa signification comme objet d'amour. Le conflit est résolu.

Malheureusement, certains enfants ne font pas ce transfert de sentiments. Il arrive que le petit garçon conserve un amour possessif pour sa mère et la petite fille un amour exclusif pour son père. Par suite d'une telle fixation à l'âge préscolaire, ces enfants deviennent inaptes à franchir les étapes subséquentes de leur développement. Ils auront besoin, dans les années futures, d'un guide sûr afin de normaliser ces rapports avec leurs parents.

Il est de toute première importance, à ce stade du développement de l'enfant, que les parents, en tant qu'individus, soient pleinement acceptés de leur milieu. Si tel n'est pas le cas, si les parents ne répondent pas à un certain conformisme social, l'enfant adopte des comportements et développe des attitudes qui, un jour, nuiront à son évolution normale.

L'enfant unique et l'enfant adopté.
L'enfant unique est le centre d'intérêt exclusif au foyer. S'il est issu de parents jeunes, il est quelque peu favorisé par rapport à celui dont les parents sont plus âgés, car il sera probablement entouré de cousins de son âge et l'attention que lui porte ses parents est moins imprégnée d'anxiété.

Le premier enfant est un enfant unique jusqu'à l'arrivée du second. Les parents jeunes sont cependant mieux préparés à recevoir ce deuxième enfant et son attente équivaut presque à sa présence réelle. Le premier enfant n'est alors plus considéré comme unique. Ceci n'est pas le cas du premier enfant issu de parents plus âgés, car malgré le désir de ces derniers, il demeure bien souvent unique.

Les problèmes soulevés à propos de l'enfant unique se posent, avec plus d'acuité, lorsque l'enfant acquiert ce statut à la mort d'un petit frère ou d'une petite sœur.

L'enfant adopté pose souvent les mêmes problèmes que l'enfant unique. Il arrive en effet que l'enfant soit adopté au moment où les conjoints ont la preuve de leur stérilité ou encore pour combler la perte d'un enfant unique.

Il devient de plus en plus difficile d'adopter un enfant en bas âge; les listes d'attente sont très longues et les parents doivent souvent patienter pendant un ou deux ans avant de pouvoir réaliser leur rêve. Toutefois, il faut se rappeler que les services sociaux peuvent encore présenter pour adoption des enfants dont l'âge dépasse celui que les parents adoptifs éventuels trouvent habituellement attirant. Ces enfants n'ont pas été adoptés bébés pour diverses raisons: abandon tardif par une mère célibataire qui a essayé en vain d'élever seule son enfant; rupture des liens conjugaux sans qu'aucun des parents désire garder les enfants; mort des deux parents ou d'un seul d'entre eux; enfants souffrant d'une difformité physique ou d'un problème psychologique ou émotif; enfants d'origine raciale mixte. Certains enfants sont placés en foyer nourricier ou en institution sans que les parents s'en occupent tout en refusant leur mise en adoption.

De nos jours, plusieurs enfants sont disponibles pour l'adoption; toutefois leur nombre a sensiblement diminué à cause de la plus grande facilité d'accès aux moyens anticonceptionnels, à la libéralisation des lois sur l'avortement (du moins dans certains pays) et surtout parce que plusieurs mères célibataires décident d'élever elles-mêmes leur enfant. Les parents adoptifs éventuels recherchent surtout des nourrissons sains et normaux. Les enfants handicapés, tant physiquement qu'émotivement, ou ceux qui naissent de parents de races différentes peuvent ne jamais être adoptés.

L'infirmière qui prend soin de ces bébés n'a pas la liberté de divulguer d'informations concernant les parents de l'enfant et ne doit jamais parler d'eux, si elle les connaît. L'enfant adopté développe ordinairement les mêmes relations chaleureuses avec ses parents que les autres enfants de la famille.

On devrait se fier à une agence officielle d'adoption plutôt qu'à un médecin ou un « ami » pour le choix de l'enfant, car les agences ont certains critères de placement qui tiennent compte du statut physique, émotif, financier et social des parents adoptifs ainsi que de la condition physique et émotive de l'enfant. Ceci ne garantit pas le succès de l'adoption, mais aide à en assurer la réussite.

Il est préférable de révéler à l'enfant son adoption avant que ce statut ne prenne pour lui une signification trop grande. Tout jeune il accepte l'explication que ses parents adoptifs avaient besoin de lui et qu'ils sont allés le chercher. À mesure qu'il grandit, il peut cependant s'estimer différent des autres ou attribuer défenses et punitions au fait qu'il ait été adopté. Il peut imaginer que ses parents ne lui portent pas toute l'affection qu'ils auraient témoignée à leur propre enfant. Mais il faut noter que le nombre croissant d'adoptions, au cours des dernières années, normalise quelque peu la situation de l'enfant adopté, en la rendant plus courante, et réduit de beaucoup la charge d'émotion qui s'y rattache.

Le nombre des familles nombreuses, telles qu'elles existaient il y a quelques années, a diminué de façon rapide avec l'apparition des mesures de planification familiale. L'enfant unique bénéficie de la fréquentation précoce d'une prématernelle qui facilite son intégration au monde des enfants de son âge. Ces problèmes (enfant unique, adopté ou non et enfants de familles réduites) vont probablement ouvrir la voie à une meilleure organisation des services de prématernelles pour faciliter à ces enfants la socialisation et le premier contact avec le monde de l'éducation.

La naissance d'un frère ou d'une sœur et ses conséquences. *Puisque tout changement est susceptible de provoquer un traumatisme à l'enfant,* les parents doivent même le préparer à l'emménagement dans un nouveau domicile. Ils doivent, de la même façon, le préparer à la naissance d'un petit frère ou d'une petite sœur. Ils doivent l'habituer à l'idée que désormais il ne sera plus enfant unique. Inévitablement, l'apparition d'un nouveau-né prive en quelque sorte l'enfant de l'attention exclusive des parents et cette situation nouvelle peut être perçue, par celui-ci, comme une désaffection à son égard. Cette situation est en effet difficilement acceptable pour le trottineur et l'enfant d'âge préscolaire, dont l'amour se porte persqu'exclusivement vers ses parents.

L'enfant se sent rejeté et nourrit souvent un sentiment de jalousie qui peut se manifester de deux façons: soit *directement,* par un aversion ouverte pour le bébé, soit indirectement par une affection trop excessive à son égard. Dans l'un et l'autre cas, l'enfant joue le rôle d'un martyr et cette attitude peut persister toute sa vie durant. Habituellement, il manifeste une aversion ouverte et directe pour le nouveau-né et il lui arrive de faire des remarques désobligeantes à son sujet. Si les parents le réprimandent, il peut se sentir cou-

pable et « rationaliser » d'une façon enfantine. Il peut, par exemple, prendre comme prétexte pour frapper le bébé le fait que ce dernier a pris « sa » couverture, en feignant d'ignorer que c'est la mère qui a donné la couverture au bébé. Puis, quelques mois plus tard, lorsque le bébé emprunte ses jouets, il peut les saisir brusquement en disant: « C'est à moi! » Lorsque la mère intervient, il boude ou frappe le bébé ou même sa mère. Un tel déplacement de l'hostilité vers ses parents est fréquent.

La jalousie de l'enfant peut aussi se manifester d'une façon indirecte par une certaine maladresse dans ses relations avec le bébé. S'il se sent profondément coupable et s'il est incapable de manifester ouvertement sa jalousie, il peut aller jusqu'à laisser tomber volontairement le bébé lorsqu'on lui demande de le tenir.

L'hostilité envers la mère se manifeste également de diverses façons. L'enfant peut s'attaquer à elle, physiquement ou verbalement, ou bien l'ignorer complètement. Il peut aussi diriger cette hostilité vers d'autres adultes comme, par exemple, son institutrice ou son éducatrice. L'enfant peut régresser et exiger une attention égale à celle portée au bébé, refuser de boire dans une tasse pour revenir au biberon, ou se souiller de telle façon que

Figure 17-1. Les compagnons imaginaires viennent et repartent au gré de l'enfant. Les enfants uniques ou solitaires se créent souvent des compagnons; les enfants de famille nombreuse peuvent aussi en éprouver le besoin. (*Baby Talk*, octobre 1970, p. 10.)

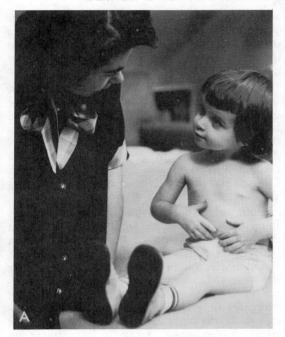

Figure 17-2. L'attente du nouveau bébé. « Quand je serai grande, est-ce que j'aurai, moi aussi, un bébé dans mon ventre? » (Courtoisie de George H. Padginton, Hamburg, New York et du *Baby Talk Magazine*, mai 1967.)

la mère doive lui porter les mêmes soins de propreté qu'au bébé. Cette régression n'est que temporaire et la mère doit l'accepter. Si, toutefois, elle se prolonge indûment, une consultation auprès du pédiatre ou d'un psychologue sera nécessaire. Il arrive que l'enfant n'extériorise pas cette jalousie, ce qui l'empêche de résoudre son problème et peut avoir pour effet de compromettre le contrôle de sa jalousie durant toute son enfance ou même durant toute sa vie.

L'enfant peut manifester sa jalousie dès qu'il apprend que sa mère est enceinte, au 5e ou au 6e mois de la grossesse. Aussi n'est-il pas prudent d'annoncer trop tôt la naissance du bébé, surtout dans le cas d'un enfant d'âge préscolaire.

Avant la naissance du bébé, la mère peut remédier efficacement à la jalousie de l'enfant en étant plus attentive à son égard et en essayant de lui communiquer le plaisir qu'elle éprouve à partager son affection avec celui qui viendra. Elle doit préparer l'enfant à la venue du nouveau-né, même si elle est consciente qu'il est encore trop jeune pour comprendre tous les changements qui s'opéreront au sein de la famille. Les parents doivent également favoriser les échanges de vues avec l'enfant et même encourager l'expression de l'hostilité que ce dernier peut déjà nourrir à l'égard du nouveau-né.

Un ouvrage illustré traitant de la maternité peut aider l'enfant à saisir le sens de tous les préparatifs auxquels s'adonne sa mère. Avant même que l'enfant soit au courant de la naissance prochaine, il est souhaitable de l'inscrire à la maternelle pour favoriser les contacts extérieurs et créer de nouveaux intérêts qui le distrairont au moment opportun.

La mère peut remédier efficacement à la jalousie de l'enfant de plusieurs façons. Elle ne laissera jamais seul avec le bébé l'enfant qui manifeste l'intention de blesser ce dernier. Un autre moyen efficace consiste à donner à l'aîné un animal, une poupée ou quelqu'autre objet dont il aura à prendre soin, comme la mère prend soin du bébé. L'enfant se familiarisera alors avec le rôle qu'il doit jouer, au sein de la famille, face au nouveau venu.

Les questions d'ordre sexuel demandent des explications claires, adaptées au vocabulaire de l'enfant et à sa capacité de comprendre le processus sexuel. La mère peut également amener l'enfant à faire la distinction, inhérente à la différence d'âge, entre ses besoins et ceux du bébé. L'enfant, par exemple, nettoie ses dents tandis que le bébé n'a pas encore de dentition. Il marche, court et joue, tandis que le bébé est porté dans les bras ou placé dans un landau; dans l'automobile, il s'assoit sur le siège, entre son père et sa mère, tandis que le bébé est couché dans son lit, sur le siège arrière, ou demeure dans les bras de sa mère. La mère doit en profiter pour jouer avec l'aîné pendant que le bébé dort dans une autre chambre. Dans la mesure du possible, l'enfant devrait tenir compagnie à son père durant la soirée pendant que la mère prend soin du bébé. Il faudrait enfin éviter, en présence de l'enfant plus âgé, toute effusion excessive de tendresse à l'égard du bébé. Ceux qui assistent à la cérémonie du baptême devraient penser à apporter un petit présent à l'aîné, en même temps qu'un cadeau pour le nouveau-né. Les attentions prodiguées au bébé ne devraient d'ailleurs pas faire oublier la présence de l'enfant qui peut facilement en éprouver de la rancœur et du ressentiment.

Les besoins de l'enfant d'âge préscolaire

L'enfant d'âge préscolaire a autant besoin d'indépendance que de sécurité. Il a aussi

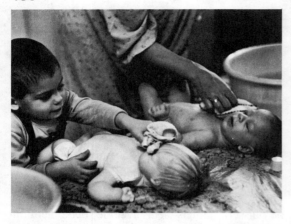

Figure 17-3. Prévention de la jalousie chez l'aîné. Ce petit garçon donne le bain à une poupée
pendant que sa mère lave le nouveau-né. (Erika et
Bill Stone: *Today's Health*, janvier 1964.)

besoin de l'affection et de la compréhension
de ses parents. Cependant, à l'intérieur de ce
monde de sécurité et d'affection que constitue
la famille, il recherche les occasions de manifester son désaccord, voire son hostilité, qu'il
exprime, à mesure qu'il grandit, tant par la
parole que par les actes. Il recherche également les occasions de s'attribuer davantage
de responsabilités et de souligner aussi son
indépendance. Il découvre la signification de
ces réalités et en saisit mieux les implications.

L'enfant se sent aimé et en sécurité lorsqu'il
est entouré de son père et de sa mère avec
qui il a des contacts quotidiens. Mais, en plus
de lui témoigner leur affection, les parents doivent veiller à son éducation et le guider vers
la maturité: 1) par l'échange verbal avec ses
parents, l'enfant apprend à s'exprimer et à
communiquer avec les autres. 2) Au foyer, il
apprend à assumer plus de responsabilités, tout
en faisant l'apprentissage de son indépendance.
3) De ses parents, il acquiert aussi les connaissances dont il a besoin pour atteindre la
maturité. Parmi les connaissances acquises à
cet âge, les plus importantes concernent sans
doute la sexualité et la religion et *les attitudes
à adopter vis-à-vis de celles-ci importent plus
que les connaissances elles-mêmes.*

L'enfant à l'âge préscolaire s'intéresse ensuite au monde extérieur, cherchant à résoudre
les « pourquoi » et les « comment » de la vie.

Besoins de l'enfant
d'âge préscolaire

Discipline. Les restrictions apportées au
comportement de l'enfant doivent être constamment maintenues, car ces restrictions servent de critères à l'enfant pour évaluer ou
prévoir les réactions des autres devant ses
attitudes ou ses actes. Il lui est ainsi possible
de façonner un comportement raisonnable et
acceptable.

Ces restrictions, bien établies par les parents,
inspirent à l'enfant un sentiment de sécurité
qui lui fait défaut lorsqu'il lui est permis de
tout décider par lui-même, même dans les
domaines qui dépassent son entendement. Les
deux parents doivent s'entendre pour offrir à
l'enfant une discipline logique et cohérente.
Ce qui est permis avec maman ne doit pas
être défendu par papa et vice versa.

Pour aider l'enfant à réaliser ses aspirations
immédiates ou pour lui faciliter l'établissement
de bonnes relations avec le monde adulte, on
peut lui faire des suggestions positives. Mais
il faut éviter, autant qu'il se peut, de lui donner
des ordres. Les ordres sont rarement nécessaires et ils sont plus efficaces lorsqu'ils sont
présentés de manière à ce que l'enfant participe à la décision. On ne doit pas non plus
parler à l'enfant de façon à lui inspirer un
sentiment de crainte ou de culpabilité, mais
plutôt tenter de le convaincre du rôle utile
des parents, capables, non seulement de surveiller ses activités et ses relations avec l'entourage, mais aussi de l'aider à résoudre ses
problèmes. Le libre choix des actes ne doit
être laissé à l'enfant que dans le cas où il fait
réellement preuve d'une aptitude à déterminer
lui-même la conduite à suivre, et cela même
s'il ne comprend pas toujours qu'il est dans
son intérêt de limiter sa liberté. Cette aptitude
à déterminer la conduite à suivre s'acquiert par
l'expérience et sous la surveillance étroite des
parents. Il faut cependant encourager l'enfant
à agir autant que possible par lui-même, lui
facilitant ainsi l'apprentissage de son indépendance.

Dans les jeux, les adultes ne doivent pas
commettre l'erreur de se substituer à l'enfant,
mais plutôt l'aider à profiter au maximum de
ses activités. Il faut par exemple, éviter de
dessiner des modèles que l'enfant copie ensuite, ce qui ne lui laisse pas l'occasion d'exercer
sa créativité. Les parents doivent toutefois
prêter leur assistance chaque fois que cela
est nécessaire. Ce comportement vise à donner
de la confiance à l'enfant.

Apprentissage du langage. L'enfant à
l'âge préscolaire apprend à communiquer ses
idées et ses sentiments dans une langue plus
précise et plus variée que celle utilisée par
le trottineur. Il pose continuellement des questions, se renseigne sur le monde extérieur en

cherchant la signification des connaissances acquises par les sens. Il interroge sur tout ce qui retient son attention: Pourquoi? Comment? Qui? Quand? Où?...

Durant la période préscolaire, l'enfant emploie des phrases de plus en plus longues et complexes. C'est la période où le vocabulaire se développe rapidement. Entre deux et six ans, l'enfant découvre environ 600 mots par année, principalement par les réponses que les adultes fournissent à ses questions. Il en acquiert d'autres en écoutant les adultes et les enfants qu'il fréquente. Il peut apprendre des mots dont les parents lui défendent l'usage, tels les termes incorrects, ceux empruntés à l'argot ou tout autre jugé inacceptable. Habituellement, si les adultes ne prêtent aucune attention lorsque l'enfant prononce ces mots, en feignant de ne pas les entendre, ils disparaîtront bientôt de la conversation de l'enfant. Une analyse des questions que pose l'enfant démontre sa soif de connaissance, en même temps qu'un accroissement de sa confiance. Les réponses données à ses questions devraient l'aider à mieux comprendre son milieu et à mieux saisir le rôle qu'il est appelé à y jouer, en même temps qu'elles devraient lui procurer une plus grande sécurité.

Les questions que pose un enfant de 3 ans sont relativement simples si on les compare à celles que pose un enfant de 4 ans ou de 5 ans qui veut comprendre le fonctionnement des choses. Ces questions demandent des explications détaillées que les adultes ne sont pas toujours en mesure de fournir.

Tout adulte doit se rappeler la règle à suivre à propos des réponses à fournir aux enfants et aux adolescents: dire la vérité telle qu'il la connaît. Si un mensonge est commis, l'enfant perdra confiance en celui qui s'en rend coupable et sa confiance en général en sera amoindrie. *La réponse doit être donnée dans des termes facilement intelligibles pour l'enfant.* Si un adulte ignore la réponse, il doit l'avouer à l'enfant, et ils pourront ensuite chercher la réponse ensemble.

L'éducation sexuelle.   Au cours des années préscolaires, l'éducation sexuelle suppose l'acquisition de connaissances spécifiques qui aident l'enfant à développer une attitude réaliste face à la sexualité. L'amour, le respect et la confiance que les époux ont l'un pour l'autre, donnent aux enfants un bon exemple à suivre. Dans une telle famille, l'enfant se définit rapidement comme un garçon ou une fille et apprend que chaque sexe a un rôle spécifique à jouer dans la vie. Les attitudes et les senti-ments que l'enfant acquiert influent grande-ment sur ses relations avec ses parents et plus tard, avec son conjoint et ses enfants.

On adapte le contenu à enseigner et la méthode d'éducation sexuelle aux besoins de l'enfant, mais certains principes généraux demeurent à la base de cet enseignement. L'enfant peut poser des questions simples sur le plan sexuel à partir de l'âge de 3 à 4 ans, mais certains ne s'informent pas avant 6 ans. Les différences individuelles dépendent de l'environnement de l'enfant et de son degré de maturité. *Les renseignements doivent répondre à l'intérêt de l'enfant et s'insérer naturellement dans la vie familiale.* Il faut éviter la simple description de faits physiques qui ne collent pas à la vie de tous les jours. En général, lorsqu'il pense à poser des questions, le petit peut comprendre des réponses simples et précises.

On donne l'éducation sexuelle à la maison ou à l'école. Des parents sincères et attentifs, capables d'aborder le sujet avec simplicité, sont les premiers à donner de bonnes explications à l'enfant. L'école joue tout au plus un rôle de suppléance, si l'éducation reçue à la maison s'avère insuffisante. L'information reçue à l'extérieur de ces deux foyers de renseignements risque non seulement d'être erronée, mais donne en plus une impression de mystère et de culpabilité.

Les parents doivent répondre honnêtement et directement aux questions en adaptant l'information au développement physiologique et psychologique de leur enfant. Tout en évitant de trop élaborer sur le sujet, il est bon de répondre immédiatement aux questions spontanées. L'attitude des parents compte souvent plus pour l'enfant que la réponse elle-même et une impression favorable lui permet d'oublier le problème pour quelque temps.

L'enfant d'âge préscolaire pose surtout des questions concernant la grossesse et la naissance, et son intérêt coïncide souvent avec une grossesse de sa mère ou la rencontre d'une femme enceinte. Après avoir appris que le fœtus se développe dans l'abdomen maternel, l'enfant s'interroge sur la grosseur du bébé, son confort dans l'utérus et les circonstances qui accompagnent la naissance. L'enfant rencontre des femmes enceintes, on parle ouvertement du sujet à la radio et à la télévision, les enfants des milieux ruraux ont connaissance de la reproduction des animaux domestiques. Quand le bambin demande: « D'où les bébés viennent-ils? », il faut chercher à savoir ce qu'il sait et surtout ce qu'il a pu imaginer et déformer à ce sujet. Une réponse franche, une attitude positive permettent à l'enfant de recevoir l'information sans honte ou anxiété.

Durant la période préscolaire, il ne peut comprendre les implications morales de la sexualité; on met surtout l'accent sur l'aspect physiologique de la question en appuyant sur son intégration à la vie familiale.

L'enfant hospitalisé peut poser aux infirmières les mêmes questions que celles qu'il pose à la maison. On doit lui répondre avec honnêteté et simplicité. Si la mère est présente, on lui laisse l'initiative de la réponse et on peut ensuite en discuter avec elle. Si l'infirmière se trouve obligée de répondre en présence de la mère, elle doit s'assurer que celle-ci comprend bien ce que l'on dit à son enfant.

On éviterait bien des problèmes au moment de l'adolescence, si l'on savait répondre franchement et calmement aux questions de l'enfant d'âge préscolaire. Les idées fausses qu'il peut entretenir empêchent le développement harmonieux de sa personnalité et peuvent déclencher de véritables problèmes psychologiques.

L'éducation religieuse. L'éducation religieuse dépend essentiellement de l'attitude des parents envers cet aspect de la vie. On ne peut garder l'enfant spirituellement neutre jusqu'à sa majorité car, malgré le désir de certains parents, il entend les autres enfants parler de religion, il reçoit des cours de catéchèse à l'école, il voit des églises et des images religieuses. Les explications des parents revêtent une extrême importance pour leur petit, mais si leurs actes ne correspondent pas à leur enseignement, il s'en rendra vite compte et ne saura plus que penser. Si on donne une éducation religieuse à l'enfant on doit rendre la religion attrayante et ne jamais forcer l'enfant à adopter des attitudes qu'il ne comprend pas ou qu'il rejette.

On peut difficilement influencer l'éducation religieuse de l'enfant hospitalisé. On essaie de le faire répondre à ses propres questions, en l'aidant à expliciter sa pensée et à rafraîchir ses connaissances. Un prêtre ou un ministre peuvent également aider l'enfant et ses parents dans les circonstances difficiles. L'essentiel réside toujours dans la simplicité des réponses et le respect des croyances et des sentiments d'autrui.

Anxiété de l'enfant d'âge préscolaire

Les sources d'anxiété et de tension chez l'enfant d'âge préscolaire proviennent de lui-même ou de l'environnement. Un besoin non satisfait ou une augmentation du nombre et de l'intensité de ses craintes intérieures peut en provoquer l'apparition. Il mobilise alors ses mécanismes de défense pour combattre les dangers qui le guettent.

Voici les *principales causes* d'anxiété au cours de la période préscolaire: l'enfant peut craindre que ses parents l'abandonnent, ne l'aiment plus, ou avoir peur d'être puni pour des méfaits ou des pensées dont il se sent coupable. Il craint énormément les blessures physiques, la mutilation.

L'HOSPITALISATION. Si l'enfant n'y a pas été suffisamment préparé ou si elle se produit à la suite d'un accident causé par une désobéissance, l'hospitalisation peut causer un véritable traumatisme psychologique dont les facteurs aggravants sont l'absence des parents et la peur d'être mutilé.

PERTE DE L'AMOUR PARENTAL. Pour un enfant d'âge préscolaire, l'amour parental se manifeste par la présence continue du père et de la mère; la séparation signifie la perte de l'amour. Nous étudierons les conséquences de la perte d'un ou des parents pour le développement normal d'un enfant de cet âge.

PERTE D'UN PARENT. L'absence temporaire d'un parent peut causer des conflits d'adaptation au moment du retour à la vie normale. On trouve des exemples typiques lorsque la mère a été longtemps hospitalisée ou que le père a dû aller chercher du travail à une grande distance du foyer ou à l'étranger.

L'enfant qui a perdu un parent à la suite d'un décès ou d'un divorce, vit dans un foyer physiquement et psychologiquement incomplet. La mort ne provoque ordinairement pas le même degré d'anxiété que le divorce, généralement précédé d'une période perturbée, où les parents se dressent l'un contre l'autre tout en cherchant à s'attacher l'enfant par tous les moyens. On a beaucoup traité au cours des dernières années des effets du divorce des parents sur l'équilibre émotif des enfants qui vivent ces situations de stress. Il semble toutefois que si les parents ne demeurent ensemble qu'en fonction du bien de l'enfant, l'atmosphère familiale et les relations conjugales perturbées créent un climat désastreux pour le développement émotif des enfants. Les parents ont quelquefois intérêt à divorcer s'ils ne peuvent pas régler leurs différends. Le tribunal accorde ordinairement la garde de l'enfant à la mère et le droit de visite au père. Il se peut que l'enfant ne comprenne pas l'antagonisme entre ses parents, alors qu'ils ont en commun

Figure 17-4. L'enfant se sent seul en l'absence de ses parents. (H. Armstrong Roberts.)

l'amour qu'ils éprouvent à son endroit. Il va sans dire que l'enfant aimé seulement par un parent ou totalement privé d'affection parentale est lésé d'un droit naturel.

Le garçon d'âge préscolaire qui vit sans son père est privé d'une image masculine, à laquelle il peut s'identifier, contre laquelle il peut devenir agressif et de qui il peut apprendre le rôle que joue un homme dans la maison, la collectivité ou le pays. La mère peut étouffer son fils par un amour initialement destiné à son mari. Il peut s'habituer à regarder la vie selon une optique féminine.

L'absence de la mère perturbe le garçon de façon différente et il peut retrouver un substitut maternel en la personne d'une grand-mère, d'une tante ou d'une simple employée. Le garçon, à l'âge préscolaire, peut régresser après le départ de la mère, jusqu'à ce qu'il accepte son substitut. L'enfant très profondément touché peut craindre d'aimer une autre femme, car il a peur de souffrir encore à la suite d'une nouvelle séparation.

L'effet de l'absence de la mère sur la petite fille soulève les mêmes problèmes. Elle n'aura personne à combattre pour gagner l'amour de son père; l'identification à la mère et l'apprentissage de son rôle féminin seront perturbés. Elle peut contracter une vision masculine de la vie familiale et communautaire, si aucun substitut maternel ne lui est offert.

La fille privée de son père peut devenir trop étroitement attachée à sa mère puis avoir peur d'aimer un homme et d'être blessée par sa perte. On entrevoit les problèmes qui pourront se présenter au moment de l'adaptation psychologique à l'autre sexe et de l'établissement de relations amoureuses saines et équilibrées.

Lorsqu'un parent se retrouve seul avec des enfants, il requiert habituellement de l'aide pendant qu'il travaille. Les petits peuvent être pris en charge par une auxiliaire familiale, un centre de jour ou une maternelle. Parfois, le parent choisit d'adhérer à une commune. Le nombre de plus en plus important de familles communautaires amène une nouvelle structure où les enfants s'intègrent et doivent apprendre à fonctionner. Il ne s'agit plus ici de la famille verticale où les différentes générations étaient représentées, mais de la réunion de plusieurs jeunes adultes qui élèvent ensemble les enfants du groupe en gardant parfois une certaine autonomie dans l'éducation de leurs propres enfants. Les effets à long terme de cette nouvelle cellule familiale sur le psychisme de l'enfant restent encore à évaluer.

PERTE DES DEUX PARENTS. La séparation complète d'avec les parents constitue un traumatisme extrême que l'enfant exprime ordinairement de façon non verbale. Il peut présenter des réactions somatiques ou régresser et recommencer à se mouiller, refuser de coopérer avec ceux qui veulent l'aider et développer beaucoup d'agressivité. Il faut éviter de gronder ou de punir l'enfant pour une telle réaction à la perte parentale, mais plutôt le traiter avec bonté et l'encourager à exprimer ses sentiments. Cet enfant, par suite de son complexe d'Oedipe, peut se sentir coupable de la mort ou du départ du parent du même sexe et il doit retrouver le plus tôt possible un objet d'amour et de sécurité. Les tuteurs doivent donc remplacer aussitôt que possible les parents absents et faire des efforts pour conquérir l'amour et la confiance de l'enfant; une aide psychologique s'avère quelquefois nécessaire pour surmonter le traumatisme.

Si la mort, ou le divorce des parents, laisse un enfant sans foyer et qu'on ne lui trouve pas de tuteur, il sera probablement placé en institution, dans un foyer nourricier ou dans une famille adoptive.

SOINS INSTITUTIONNELS. Aujourd'hui, les orphelinats ou centres d'accueil pour enfants servent de refuge jusqu'à ce qu'un foyer nourricier ou une famille adoptive puisse accepter l'enfant sans parents ou que le parent unique puisse recevoir de l'aide domestique, ou organiser le séjour de l'enfant dans un centre de jour ou une garderie. Malheureusement, beaucoup d'orphelinats manquent d'espace, à cause du nombre imposant d'enfants abandonnés et du délai nécessaire pour obtenir le placement. De plus, certains enfants demeurent en institution parce que la société hésite à retirer aux parents des responsabilités qu'ils sont parfois incapables d'assumer. Beaucoup de parents irresponsables abandonnent leurs enfants sans céder leurs droits légaux de sorte que ceux-ci ne peuvent pas être adoptés et jouir d'une vie normale.

Les institutions pour soins temporaires fonctionnent habituellement comme une réunion de petites familles, chacune dirigée par des « parents ». Les enfants vivent comme ceux du voisinage et on essaie de créer une atmosphère familiale dans chacune de ces unités. Les enfants sains ne vivent habituellement pas en institution, sauf pour de courtes périodes.

SOINS EN FOYER NOURRICIER. Une institution, même bien organisée, ne peut satisfaire les besoins d'un enfant comme un foyer nourricier peut le faire. Les parents nourriciers, qui aiment vraiment les enfants, connaissent leurs besoins et possèdent suffisamment de maturité pour accepter leur départ vers une famille adoptive. Malheureusement, tous les parents nourriciers ne possèdent pas ces qualités et nombreux sont les enfants qui changent continuellement de foyer et ne parviennent jamais à acquérir ce sentiment de sécurité qui leur fait si cruellement défaut. La travailleuse sociale devient quelquefois le seul adulte avec qui l'enfant établit une relation de confiance au long des années passées en institutions ou en foyers nourriciers.

SOURCES D'ANXIÉTÉ AUTRES QUE LA PERTE PARENTALE. Les parents très sévères ont des enfants qui se sentent constamment coupables et qui craignent beaucoup les punitions. L'ogre de l'enfant moderne est la personne qui le punira de sa méchanceté réelle ou imaginaire. L'anxiété la plus commune et qui semble particulièrement inévitable provient de l'incompatibilité entre l'enseignement prodigué par certains parents et leur propre façon d'agir.

Anxiété contagieuse. Cette forme d'anxiété s'acquiert d'un adulte, généralement la mère. Celle qui se contrôle bien dans les circonstances difficiles et qui vit sans anxiété véritable en période calme, a des enfants peu portés à l'anxiété. On observe souvent l'anxiété contagieuse chez l'enfant hospitalisé. La mère qui ne peut cacher sa peur lorsqu'elle voit son en-

fant malade, le rend nécessairement anxieux et l'infirmière peut les aider tous deux à regarder l'hospitalisation de façon plus objective.

Anxiété vraie ou objective. Celle-ci dépend de la capacité de l'enfant à comprendre la nature du danger qui le menace et de sa propension à élaborer des phantasmes à partir d'événements concrets. Il est inutile d'essayer de convaincre un enfant que l'éclair et le tonnerre ne présentent pas de danger, s'il n'en comprend pas la cause. L'enfant hospitalisé ou qui rend visite au médecin a peur des injections, car il sait par expérience qu'elles causent de la douleur. On contrôle les peurs objectives de l'enfant de cet âge en tenant compte de son degré de maturité et de son type d'imagination. Il a vraiment peur, même de choses non dangereuses, car il connaît mal le monde dans lequel il vit. L'adulte doit l'aider à vaincre ses craintes pour éviter qu'elles ne persistent à l'âge adulte. Certaines situations comportent un véritable risque et il doit apprendre à y faire face intelligemment ou à les éviter. C'est ainsi qu'on lui enseigne à traverser les rues quand les feux de circulation le lui permettent. L'enfant de cet âge a peur de se blesser, de se perdre ou d'être abandonné; il craint les animaux énormes et bruyants. La crainte augmente quand l'enfant se trouve seul ou parmi des étrangers. L'adulte doit savoir que l'imagination débordante de l'enfant d'âge préscolaire, le rend souvent plus craintif que le trotteur.

L'anxiété profonde. Différente de la peur, elle atteint l'enfant qui se sent mal aimé ou qui a peur de perdre l'affection des siens. La masturbation et l'arrivée d'un petit frère ou d'une petite sœur constituent souvent les éléments provocateurs. Tout paraît dangereux à l'enfant; la menace demeure vague, mobile, mais omniprésente.

Les cauchemars de l'enfant d'âge préscolaire proviennent souvent de conflits émotifs non résolus ou de phantasmes dus à son imagination trop fertile. Peu à peu, ils s'espacent et il est rare qu'une aide extérieure soit requise pour régler ce problème.

L'enfant anxieux a surtout besoin de sécurité et d'amour. Quand la tension est trop forte, sa mère devrait le prendre dans ses bras et le bercer doucement pour le calmer. Une fois détendu, l'enfant peut parvenir à exprimer son anxiété, le plus souvent à travers ses jeux ou des histoires qu'il invente. Le rôle de l'adulte consiste à supporter l'enfant psychologiquement et à chercher à le comprendre. On peut éviter bien des angoisses aux enfants en essayant d'imaginer leur réaction face à une situation nouvelle. Voir avec les yeux de l'enfant pousse l'adulte à mieux le préparer psychologiquement aux événements qui l'attendent.

Problèmes de comportement de l'enfant d'âge préscolaire

Succion du pouce

Sucer son pouce ne constitue pas un problème pour l'enfant. Ses parents peuvent toutefois s'imaginer avoir raté son éducation et devenir intransigeants à son endroit. Ils peuvent le punir, le cajoler et le ridiculiser alternativement, afin de lui faire perdre cette habitude. Les parents n'ont pas à craindre de blessures au pouce ou de malformations à la mâchoire, à moins que l'enfant ne souffre de problèmes d'auto-mutilation, ou encore que l'habitude se prolonge au cours de la période scolaire. La mâchoire se redresse ordinairement après la disparition de l'habitude.

L'enfant qui suce son pouce a peut-être été privé du plaisir de sucer au cours de la petite enfance; il a peut-être manqué d'affection, de sécurité ou a été insatisfait de la vie. Son sentiment de frustration augmente avec les pressions que l'on exerce sur lui pour corriger son comportement.

Les adultes qui l'entourent doivent l'observer attentivement pour savoir à quels moments la tentation devient irrésistible, et le combler alors de plus d'affection et de sécurité. Il est important de trouver la cause du problème. L'enfant se sent-il délaissé, surexcité ou ennuyé? A-t-il assez de jouets ou se sent-il de trop? Même si l'enfant se débarrasse de cette habitude vers l'âge de 5 ou 6 ans, il faut s'assurer que la cause réelle est corrigée, car il pourrait compenser par une autre habitude, afin de combler son besoin de plaisir et de confort.

Problèmes alimentaires

L'enfant d'âge préscolaire peut se découvrir un amour immodéré pour certains aliments (rarement la viande ou les légumes) et un dégoût subit, souligné par des cris, pour d'autres aliments. Cette situation peut créer une tension qui risque de s'aggraver avec le temps surtout si l'enfant résiste aux pressions parentales ou si les parents ne s'entendent pas sur une politique cohérente à ce sujet.

Énurésie

On dit que l'enfant souffre d'énurésie quand il mouille systématiquement et involontairement son lit après l'âge de 4 ou 5 ans. L'enfant normalement propre, qui mouille son lit de temps à autre, n'entre pas dans cette catégorie.

Les causes d'énurésie comprennent l'absence d'éducation sphinctérienne, une maladie organique, un facteur héréditaire ou congénital, un entraînement à la propreté trop précoce, trop sévère ou prolongé. Les parents devraient considérer la période d'apprentissage comme une simple étape de l'éducation et attendre que l'enfant y soit prêt physiquement et psychologiquement. Il faut éviter de dramatiser, d'utiliser les menaces, les punitions ou les promesses de récompense qui fixent l'attention de l'enfant et l'empêchent d'évoluer normalement dans d'autres domaines.

L'enfant qui a maîtrisé le contrôle de ses sphincters, peut recommencer à mouiller son lit quand il affronte des situations trop lourdes pour lui, comme la mort d'un membre de la famille ou l'arrivée d'un petit frère sans qu'il y ait été préparé. On peut essayer de donner moins de liquides pendant la soirée, mais les résultats de cette méthode demeurent très aléatoires. De nombreuses mères de famille lèvent les enfants de 3 à 5 ans avant d'aller elles-mêmes au lit et cessent graduellement cette habitude à mesure que l'enfant vieillit et ne se mouille plus la nuit.

Il faut faire comprendre à l'enfant qu'il perdra éventuellement cette habitude et l'aider à adopter une attitude positive face à son problème. Il doit vouloir rester sec et avoir confiance dans sa capacité de contrôler l'élimination. Les enfants hyperactifs ou agités pendant la journée, peuvent être tellement épuisés à l'heure du coucher qu'ils sont incapables de sortir de leur sommeil pour aller uriner. Certains facteurs d'environnement peuvent également expliquer l'énurésie, tels un grand couloir noir que l'enfant doit suivre pour se rendre à la salle de bain, une répugnance à quitter un lit chaud pour une salle de bain froide ou la peur du silence nocturne. Les adultes devraient analyser la situation, reconnaître un tel problème, s'il existe, et y apporter une solution satisfaisante.

L'énurésie provient parfois d'une cause physique et un examen médical devient nécessaire, si les moyens d'éducation habituels n'ont pas porté fruits. L'enfant peut souffrir de diabète, d'une vessie irritable, de petit calibre ou d'une infection chronique des voies urinaires. Une étude des différents facteurs qui peuvent contribuer à l'énurésie doit d'abord éliminer les causes physiques. Si on ne découvre pas de problème organique ou émotif grave, l'enfant peut être traité pendant deux mois avec une médication spécifique (Tofranil). Beaucoup d'enfants cessent d'être énurétiques avec cette médication, mais environ la moitié rechute lorsqu'elle est cessée. Certains moyens mécaniques (lit avec alarme) peuvent être utilisés si parents et enfant acceptent cette solution qui donne d'excellents résultats immédiats et à long terme.

Encoprésie

On considère qu'un enfant souffre d'encoprésie s'il refuse de se rendre à la salle de toilettes pour aller à la selle et qu'il a dépassé l'âge physiologique de l'entraînement à la propreté. Si le problème persiste après l'âge de 3 à 4 ans, on peut envisager la présence d'un problème émotif. Un entraînement trop rigoureux à la propreté ou une perturbation plus ou moins profonde des relations entre la mère et son enfant peuvent causer ce phénomène.

L'enfant qui a acquis le contrôle de son sphincter peut bloquer quasi volontairement son mécanisme de défécation. Les symptômes qui se produisent alors peuvent simuler le mégacôlon. L'abdomen est distendu par les gaz et les matières fécales, une diarrhée apparaît à cause de l'irritation de la paroi intestinale. En l'absence d'un mégacôlon, l'enfant bénéficiera d'un traitement psychiatrique qui englobera éventuellement toute sa famille.

Égoïsme

L'enfant acquiert difficilement la notion du partage. Il doit développer suffisamment son instinct de propriété avant de pouvoir céder ses jouets. Quelques possessions personnelles l'aideront à se reconnaître comme un être autonome et il décidera lui-même s'il les prêtera ou non. Les parents doivent éviter de régler les différends en donnant systématiquement le jouet à l'enfant plus jeune, au visiteur ou à la petite fille qui veut se l'approprier. On peut toujours donner un jouet-substitut à celui qui réclame. Le jeu de groupe, qui commence à cet âge, permet à l'enfant de comprendre les autres et facilite l'apprentissage de la coopération et du partage.

Mauvais langage

Le mauvais langage a plus d'importance pour l'adulte que pour l'enfant. Celui-ci joue avec les mots pour le plaisir de les manipuler, il répète sans comprendre des sons que les adultes et les autres enfants émettent, et peut prendre un malin plaisir à choquer l'adulte quand il se rend compte de sa réaction horrifiée face à certains termes. Il commence à exprimer verbalement ses sentiments et ses paroles dépassent souvent sa pensée réelle, tout en exprimant exactement ce qu'il ressent à ce moment précis.

Plusieurs attitudes permettent de résoudre ce problème, mais il faut surtout éviter de le dramatiser. On peut répéter le mot en enlevant toute consonnance émotive, faire dire des mots plus difficiles comme « Mississipi », ce qui détournera son attention, le distraire avec un nouveau jeu ou simplement expliquer à l'enfant que ce mot n'est pas joli ou mal accepté dans notre société.

Blessures faites à un tiers

Les petits enfants peuvent se blesser entre eux quand ils jouent ensemble. Si la blessure est accidentelle, l'incident sera oublié sans être imputé à personne. On ne doit jamais tolérer qu'un enfant inflige volontairement des blessures aux autres. Il faut protéger le groupe contre celui qui cherche à mordre, griffer, frapper ou tirer les cheveux de ses compagnons. Il sera alors nécessaire qu'un adulte l'aide à contrôler ses actes et l'empêche de blesser les autres enfants.

Celui qui agit de la sorte est souvent un enfant inquiet, jaloux ou frustré. Son comportement résulte de son état mental et ne doit pas être toléré. Il serait utile qu'une personne qui l'aime profondément puisse le contrôler et prévenir les déplaisantes conséquences de sa façon d'agir. Il faut qu'un tel enfant sache qu'il y a des limites au-delà desquelles il n'est pas permis d'aller. L'enfant ne doit en aucun cas, subir le même sort qu'il vient d'infliger à son camarade. On ne doit pas le traiter en enfant méchant, ni l'obliger à s'excuser auprès de celui à qui il a causé le tort. En aucune circonstance, il ne devra se sentir rejeté par les adultes qui sont responsables de lui.

L'adulte doit être positif devant cette tendance qu'ont les enfants de se blesser entre eux. Il est bien évident que lorsqu'un enfant veut lancer une pierre, mordre ou frapper, l'adulte doit l'en empêcher. Si le mal est déjà fait, il faut apaiser le blessé, conduire l'autre dans un endroit plus calme et l'aider à se contrôler. Durant ce temps, l'attention des autres enfants devrait être dirigée vers des activités qu'ils aiment et dès que possible, celui qui a causé le désordre devrait rejoindre le groupe.

Lorsqu'on sait qu'un enfant est susceptible de se quereller alors qu'il participe à des jeux de groupe, on doit enlever tous les objets ou jouets pouvant occasionner des blessures.

L'enfant qui veut toujours blesser les autres devrait être aidé à s'identifier au groupe. Des exercices physiques lui permettront de dépenser son surplus d'énergie et de se défouler. Il faut le féliciter lorsqu'il se conduit convenablement en groupe et même lorsqu'il est seul. La cause de ses problèmes doit toutefois être recherchée et traitée si possible.

La destruction

Tous les enfants, à l'occasion, brisent des objets et c'est tout à fait normal. Les parents doivent différencier entre destruction accidentelle et intentionnelle. La cause accidentelle de la destruction est due à l'excès d'énergie de l'enfant et à sa curiosité sans limite. En dépit des dommages possibles, les parents ne devraient pas limiter trop sévèrement les activités physiques et la curiosité de leur enfant, sous prétexte que des objets de grande valeur risquent d'être détruits.

Pour éviter de tels accidents, ils doivent mettre à l'abri les objets précieux et laisser à l'enfant un grand espace où il pourra jouer sans endommager les meubles de la maison. Ils doivent comprendre que les enfants n'accordent pas la même importance aux objets matériels que les adultes. Pour lui permettre de libérer son énergie, on lui donnera des jouets résistants.

Il sera cependant utile d'imposer à l'enfant certaines limites quant à l'utilisation de ses jouets et des objets appartenant aux adultes, afin qu'il sache faire la différence entre ce qui est sa propriété et celle des autres. Le progrès sera lent, mais il apprendra peu à peu à utiliser avec soin les objets qui ont de la valeur. L'enfant qui aime ses parents est profondément peiné lorsqu'il brise des objets auxquels ils sont attachés, même s'il sait qu'il ne sera pas puni pour sa maladresse.

L'enfant qui détruit intentionnellement est habituellement un enfant malheureux, incapable de contrôler ses sentiments de jalousie, d'abandon, d'agressivité ou de colère. Il peut se sentir mal aimé, détesté par ses semblables, ou ennuyé par des jeux inappropriés à son âge ou à son stade de développement. Parfois ces enfants semblent désirer se faire punir, ce qui constitue pour eux un moyen d'attirer l'attention. La cause de cette attitude doit être trouvée et traitée en conséquence. Les parents ne doivent dans ce cas, ni gronder ni punir, mais plutôt diriger l'énergie de l'enfant vers des activités appropriées.

La masturbation

Les parents acceptent plus ou moins le fait que la masturbation soit une expérience universelle chez les jeunes enfants. Le bébé découvre une sensation plaisante accompagnant la manipulation des organes génitaux et n'ayant d'ailleurs pour lui aucune autre signification.

Chez l'enfant d'âge préscolaire, la masturbation est plus fréquente et est accompagnée d'imagination. Chez l'adolescent, la masturbation est utilisée pour satisfaire un désir d'excitation sexuelle, car notre culture n'accepte pas facilement les relations hétérosexuelles à cet âge.

L'enfant qui se masturbe plus que normalement ne devrait pas être puni; il devrait au contraire être aidé à résoudre son problème. L'enfant qui a découvert le plaisir venant de la masturbation devrait être amené à connaître d'autres plaisirs compensateurs.

L'éducation sexuelle ne résout pas le problème de la masturbation, elle peut toutefois faire comprendre l'origine du plaisir, le démystifier en quelque sorte et faire connaître à l'enfant les rôles divers des organes génitaux.

Il ne faut pas réprimander l'enfant qui se masturbe, mais cette habitude peut l'empêcher de goûter à d'autres plaisirs absolument nécessaires à sa croissance et à son développement. Comme n'importe quel plaisir pratiqué dans l'isolement, il prévient toute interaction sociale.

Si le phénomène de la masturbation est mal contrôlé ou excessif à l'âge préscolaire, il peut amener une fixation auto-érotique. L'enfant éprouvera plus de plaisir en lui-même que lors de ses relations avec les autres.

Les parents doivent savoir que la masturbation ne produit pas de troubles nerveux, d'affaiblissement cérébral ou de dommages aux organes génitaux, et une condamnation parentale peut induire chez l'enfant un dommage psychologique ou émotif durable ou permanent.

L'adolescent qui se masturbe excessivement se limite socialement. Il est seul et malheureux. Il a besoin d'aide et non d'une condamnation morale.

La honte et la menace reliées à cette activité peuvent forcer l'enfant à répudier toute sensation sexuelle. Ceci conduit éventuellement à l'impuissance pour l'homme et à la frigidité pour la femme. Ces deux conditions nuisent à un mariage heureux et augmentent sensiblement la disposition aux maladies mentales.

Il faut se rappeler que chez l'enfant d'âge préscolaire, la masturbation excessive n'est pas un processus pathologique en soi, mais le symptôme d'une pauvre hygiène mentale. Les enfants élevés trop sévèrement, ceux qui s'ennuient parce qu'ils n'ont pas de compagnons de jeu, sont plus susceptibles de pratiquer la masturbation avec excès.

APERÇU DU DÉVELOPPEMENT PHYSIQUE, SOCIAL ET MENTAL

Croissance et développement physiques

L'enfant croît relativement lentement durant la période préscolaire, mais il se transforme de trottineur joufflu en enfant vigoureux. Il gagne environ 2,5 kg par année. L'enfant moyen de 6 ans a doublé le poids qu'il avait à 1 an. Durant la période préscolaire, l'enfant croît d'environ 5-6 cm par année. La hauteur moyenne d'un enfant de 6 ans est de 1 m, environ le double de sa taille à la naissance. À la fin de la période préscolaire, l'enfant paraît grand et menu, car il grandit plus qu'il ne gagne de poids.

On peut s'attendre à une augmentation de la taille et du poids des enfants qui reçoivent actuellement des meilleurs soins d'hygiène et une alimentation appropriée.

Une meilleure coordination musculaire permet à l'enfant de mieux explorer son environnement physique tout comme son développement cognitif élargit ses harizons.

À l'âge de 6 ans, il marche comme un adulte, ayant perdu la lordose de l'enfance. Durant les années préscolaires, un enfant hyperactif peut acquérir une mauvaise posture, à moins que des mesures préventives ne soient prises.

En général, après la 2e année, le développement moteur de l'enfant consiste essentiellement en une amélioration de la force et de l'habileté. Peu d'habiletés nouvelles sont acquises. Lorsqu'un enfant atteint l'âge de 5 ans, sa vitesse et son habileté musculaires le rendent davantage indépendant des autres.

Lorsque l'enfant est au repos, le rythme du pouls varie entre 90 et 110 à la minute et le nombre de respirations par minute est de 20. La tension artérielle est de 85/60.

Développement mental et social

L'enfant de cet âge a développé une certaine conscience et il a intégré les valeurs et les normes de son groupe. Il a commencé à développer la compréhension de concepts, tels que l'amitié, l'acceptation des responsabilités, l'indépendance (certains enfants démontrent leur indépendance en se sauvant de la maison), la durée, les relations spatiales, les mots abstraits et les chiffres. La capacité d'attention augmente.

Caractéristiques du développement physique, social et mental

Pour l'éducation d'un enfant, il faut considérer son développement complet et non seulement son âge chronologique; ceci exige une connaissance individuelle de l'enfant. Pour savoir à quel point le développement peut dévier des normes, il faut regarder la moyenne du comportement des enfants de tel groupe d'âge. Aucun enfant ne correspond parfaitement à la moyenne dans tous les domaines du développement; il peut être avancé dans un domaine et retardé dans l'autre.

Même si le développement ne procède pas au même rythme pour tous, l'ordre de ses séquences est toujours le même.

Le moment où tel comportement s'acquiert est une question d'individu. Ceci est le point le plus important à retenir dans l'application du concept de croissance et de développement d'un enfant en particulier.

L'enfant de trois ans. L'enfant de 3 ans est moins négatif que l'année précédente; ses crises de colère s'espacent, il comprend mieux la signification des mots et on peut lui donner des explications simples des phénomènes qui l'entourent. Il acquiert rapidement de l'expérience et s'intéresse à toute activité nouvelle. Au cours de cette période, l'activité mentale et l'expression verbale se substituent progressivement à l'activité physique dans l'expression des émotions. Par exemple, l'enfant de trois ans dira « Je te déteste » au lieu de frapper ou de lancer des objets. L'action violente encore possible est, de toute façon, accompagnée de paroles qui expriment ce qu'il ressent et diminuent son agressivité physique.

Les acquisitions suivantes caractérisent le développement moteur de l'enfant de 3 ans:

conduit un tricycle en utilisant les pédales
marche en reculant
monte un escalier en alternant les pieds
descend seul un escalier et saute la dernière marche
essaie de danser malgré un certain manque d'équilibre
verse facilement un liquide d'un contenant dans un autre
commence à utiliser des ciseaux
enfonce de grosses chevilles de bois dans une planche, avec un marteau
enfile de gros grains sur une corde
construit une tour de 9 ou 10 blocs
essaie de dessiner une image
copie un cercle ou une croix
se déshabille seul; peut déboutonner ses vêtements si les boutons sont devant ou sur les côtés
aide sa mère à l'habiller
pense à aller aux toilettes s'il n'est pas trop occupé
lave ses mains, se brosse les dents
mange seul
aide à essuyer la vaisselle ou à épousseter.

Acquisition du langage, socialisation et habileté mentale. L'enfant de 3 ans se sent à l'aise dans son univers s'il a acquis un sentiment de sécurité au cours de la première enfance. Il a normalement atteint le développement suivant:

a un vocabulaire de 900 mots ou plus
parle couramment et avec confiance. S'inquiète peu de savoir si quelqu'un l'écoute
répète une phrase de 6 syllabes
emploie le pluriel
peut chanter de courtes chansons enfantines
sait à quel sexe il appartient
se socialise progressivement
accepte plus volontiers d'attendre son tour ou de céder en jouant
ne se mouille plus la nuit
peut répéter trois chiffres dans l'ordre
commence à s'intéresser aux couleurs
sait son nom de famille
a une petite compréhension du passé, présent et futur
peut nommer les figures sur une image.

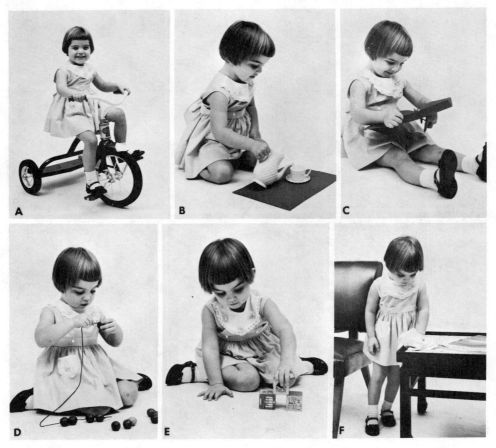

Figure 17-5. L'enfant de 3 ans. *A)* se sert des pédales de son tricycle, *B)* verse adroitement du liquide dans une tasse, *C)* commence à se servir de ciseaux, *D)* peut enfiler de grosses perles sur une corde, *E)* fabrique un pont à l'aide de 3 blocs, *F)* aide à épousseter.

L'enfant de 3 ans garde un certain rituel dans plusieurs de ses activités, comme ranger ses jouets et aller au lit. Amical et souriant, il veut plaire aux autres quoiqu'il puisse être jaloux de ses semblables. Il peut avoir peur de la noirceur et des animaux.

L'enfant de quatre ans. L'enfant de 4 ans est plus bouillant et impétueux que l'année précédente. Les parents exigent souvent trop de ses capacités et veulent corriger à tout prix ses manières et son langage. Les défenses et les permissions prennent une importance grandissante. Son agressivité est souvent dirigée contre ses parents et ses sautes d'humeur sont aussi fréquentes qu'inattendues.

Les acquisitions suivantes caractérisent le développement moteur de l'enfant de 4 ans:

grimpe et saute facilement
monte et descend un escalier sans tenir la rampe, utilisant alternativement les deux pieds
lance une balle avec extension du bras
découpe bien avec des ciseaux
copie un carré
construit un mur de 5 blocs à l'aide d'un modèle
lace ses souliers.

Acquisition du langage, socialisation et habileté mentale. Un enfant de 4 ans:

possède un vocabulaire de 1500 mots et plus
exagère, se vante et potine sur ses camarades
raconte facilement à l'extérieur ce qui se passe à la maison
parle avec un compagnon imaginaire, la plupart du temps du même âge et du même sexe. Il cesse habituellement ses relations avec un être imaginaire vers l'âge de 6 ans
participe activement aux jeux collectifs; les activités de groupe durent plus longtemps
fait des commissions à l'extérieur de la maison

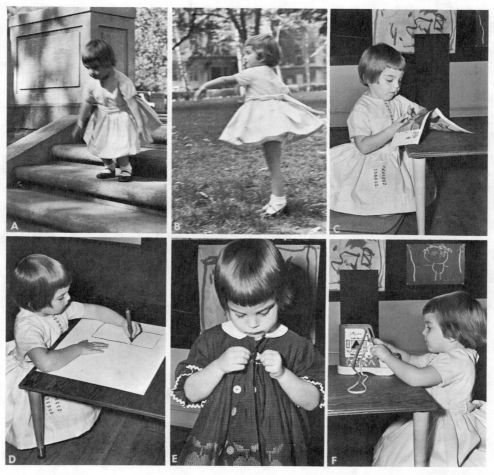

Figure 17-6. L'enfant de 4 ans *A)* saute adroitement, *B)* lance une balle, *C)* découpe des images avec des ciseaux, *D)* copie un carré, E) peut boutonner ses vêtements si les boutons sont devant ou sur le côté, *F)* lace ses souliers.

tend à être égocentrique et impatient
est fier de ses exploits
est agressif physiquement et verbalement; peut
    se sauver du foyer
nomme successivement 3 objets qu'il connaît
compte jusqu'à 3; répète 4 chiffres; apprend le
    concept numérique
connaît son âge
reconnaît la plus longue de deux lignes
compte 4 sous
nomme une ou plusieurs couleurs
possède un début de perception spatiale.

L'enfant de cinq ans. C'est un âge
agréable pour l'enfant, pour ses parents et
pour son éducateur. Moins révolutionnaire
qu'à quatre ans, il connaît mieux les rouages
de la société et accepte de s'y intégrer. Plus
fort, jouissant d'une meilleure coordination
musculaire, raisonnant plus facilement, il se

sent moins frustré par les obstacles de son
entourage. Il devient plus responsable de ses
actions, mais on doit encore l'aider à s'adapter au groupe.

Le grand changement physique qui se manifeste est la perte de la première dent de lait.

Les acquisitions suivantes caractérisent le
développement moteur de l'enfant de cinq ans:

peut courir et jouer en même temps
saute à la corde
saute 3 à 4 marches
peut se balancer sur un seul pied pendant 8 se-
    condes
range soigneusement ses jouets dans une boîte
sait se servir d'un marteau et frapper sur un clou
trace des lettres bien formées
plie du papier en diagonale
écrit son prénom

Figure 17-7. L'enfant de 5 ans *A)* saute à la corde, *B)* glisse en patins à roulettes, *C)* noue ses lacets,
D) dessine un bonhomme, *E)* copie un triangle, *F)* explique la signification de son dessin à ses camarades
de la maternelle.

dessine un bonhomme facilement reconnaissable
copie un triangle
se lave les mains sans mouiller ses vêtements
s'habille seul
réussit à faire les boucles pour lacer ses souliers.

À l'âge de cinq ans, l'enfant a beaucoup acquis au point de vue moteur, si on lui a fourni suffisamment de moyens d'apprentissage. Il a un bon équilibre et un excellent contrôle moteur.

Acquisition du langage, socialisation et habileté mentale.   L'enfant de cinq ans:

a approximativement un vocabulaire de 2100 mots
répète une phrase de 10 syllabes et plus
parle constamment
peut nommer au moins quatre couleurs, habituellement les rouge, vert, jaune et bleu. Certains enfants savent très bien différencier des couleurs plus subtiles
étudie les liens familiaux: oncles, tantes, cousins
demande la signification des mots
pose des questions pertinentes
détermine entre deux poids, celui qui est le plus lourd (après expérimentation)
identifie les pièces de monnaie courante
compte 10 pièces de monnaie
nomme les jours de la semaine et perçoit la semaine comme une unité de temps
refait un rectangle formé de deux pièces coupées en diagonale
ne s'enfuit plus de la maison.

À l'âge de cinq ans, l'enfant se prend au sérieux, est fier de ce qu'il réussit et veut assumer de plus en plus de responsabilités.

Résumé succinct

L'enfant d'âge préscolaire a intégré l'enseignement et les valeurs de ses parents. Plus indépendant physiquement et émotivement, il peut s'absenter ou supporter plus facilement l'absence de ses parents pour une courte période. Comme il veut faire de son mieux et plaire à ses parents, il agit en leur absence comme ils lui ont appris à le faire, en suivant les principes de base qu'ils lui ont inculqués.

LE JEU

Le jeu permet à l'enfant de développer sa personnalité, d'apprendre à faire face à la réalité et à contrôler ses émotions. Il devient capable, grâce au jeu, d'exprimer ses sentiments de colère ou d'amour. Les enfants de cet âge s'infligent entre eux moins de blessures que les plus jeunes et ils ont pitié de celui qui tombe ou se blesse.

Jeu de groupe.   L'enfant passe progressivement du jeu solitaire et parallèle au jeu de groupe. Il peut y avoir continuité dans l'activité du groupe même si les participants changent continuellement; certains enfants rejoignent ou quittent le groupe à leur gré. Ils aiment le jeu de groupe, mais sentent le besoin de s'isoler de temps en temps; tout seul, l'enfant joue à ce qui lui plaît, comme bon lui semble. Le jeu de groupe, vaguement organisé, se déroule en dépit du dirigisme ou de l'agressivité de certains participants.

À mesure qu'avance la période préscolaire, un type de jeu plus structuré apparaît. Les membres du groupe changent moins souvent, mais la structure manque de cohésion et de stabilité. Dans un tel groupe, l'enfant-type joue successivement le rôle de dirigeant et de dirigé.

Les caractéristiques du jeu.   Jouer est le propre de l'enfant et il le fait d'une façon très active. Il grimpe, court, frappe, ferme les portes avec bruit et la répétition de ces gestes permet un développement moteur harmonieux.

Les enfants imitent la vie sociale de l'adulte et se préparent à la vie réelle. Ils deviennent tour à tour le père, la mère, le pompier, l'épicier, le chauffeur de camion ou le professeur. Le changement de rôle se fait au rythme du déplacement des intérêts et des expériences nouvelles. Malgré le caractère hautement imaginatif de leurs jeux, les enfants restent conscients de la différence entre la réalité et leur monde imaginaire. L'enfant qui s'identifie à un indien sait fort bien que ce n'est qu'un jeu.

Beaucoup de thèmes de jeu proviennent de la confusion qui règne dans l'esprit de l'enfant à la suite d'expériences de la vie réelle comme la mort d'une grand-mère ou la naissance d'un petit frère. Ces thèmes favorisent l'expression d'un besoin de destruction, d'agressivité, de force; ils permettent à l'enfant d'exprimer ses vrais sentiments.

Il existe un problème potentiel dans l'engouement actuel de la société pour les poupées représentant des personnages très ressemblants ou anatomiquement très bien faits, ou pour des jouets qui imitent des objets de consommation courante pour l'adulte. La société place l'enfant dans une situation où son intelligence et sa créativité ne sont en aucune façon stimulées; la multiplication de ces jouets et de ces jeux conduit très rapidement les enfants vers la course à la consommation.

L'ENFANT DE TROIS ANS. Si l'enfant de trois ans aime les jeux actifs, il écoute volontiers les chansons enfantines qu'il dramatise ensuite. Il se socialise progressivement et se joint à des groupes de 2 ou 3 enfants, où les arrivées compensent les défections, où les changements d'activités très fréquents ne correspondent pas nécessairement à l'arrivée d'un nouveau membre ou au départ de l'initiateur du jeu. À trois ans, l'enfant commence à céder

Figure 17-8. La petite fille imite les activités de sa mère.

devant la volonté d'autrui et le jeu d'équipe devient possible. Il aime le contact physique d'autres enfants; il joue dans le sable et dans l'eau, s'amuse avec des jouets qu'il peut tirer ou vider. Construire avec des blocs, coller et découper constituent les activités tranquilles qu'il préfère.

La vie réelle le fascine: jouer à la poupée consiste à la mettre au lit et à faire la dînette. Son imagination transforme une boîte de carton en lit miniature et quelques morceaux de papier en service à thé.

L'ENFANT DE QUATRE ANS. Le jeu permet à l'enfant de 4 ans d'acquérir une plus grande maturité physique et sociale. Deux ou trois enfants du même sexe se groupent et acceptent de jouer ensemble. Ils veulent bien céder aux autres, mais ont encore tendance à vouloir dominer le groupe. Leurs jeux, très fantaisistes, foisonnent d'erreurs volontaires qui font leurs délices. Ces enfants ont des idées assez compliquées qu'ils ne peuvent réaliser faute de dextérité et de patience; ils ne savent pas planifier, comme le font des enfants plus âgés. Ils manipulent beaucoup mieux les matériaux que l'année précédente; ils adorent se déguiser et jouer à la vie réelle. Par le jeu, la fillette et son frère apprennent les rôles qu'ils tiendront plus tard. Ils jouent à tenir la maison, ils aident leur mère à nettoyer, à laver la vaisselle, à épousseter, à repasser et à repriser les vête-

ments. Les jeux d'expression, tels que la peinture digitale ou le modelage, sont populaires à cet âge.

L'enfant perçoit mal les formes, mais il aime les casse-tête où il procède par tâtonnement. Il range volontiers ses jouets, mais on doit le lui rappeler souvent. À l'école, la compagnie d'autres enfants qui accomplissent ce travail constitue un stimulant suffisant.

L'ENFANT DE CINQ ANS. Il s'intéresse à diverses activités, il aime courir et sauter. La compétition se manifeste par la phrase « je suis capable, pas toi... » qu'il lance à tout propos. Le groupe atteint maintenant 5 ou 6 membres, l'amitié qui les lie s'avère plus forte et plus durable. Même s'il doit y travailler longtemps, l'enfant de cinq ans veut finir ce qu'il a commencé. Les vêtements d'adulte qu'il revêt rendent ses jeux plus réels et plus intéressants.

Figure 17-9. Grand-père aime aider sa petite-fille dans les passages difficiles. (Wallace Pharmaceuticals)

Figure 17-10. L'enfant d'âge préscolaire adore la peinture A) peinture digitale, B) peinture à l'eau. (H. Armstrong Roberts.)

Il adore découper des images, travailler avec du papier peint ou réaliser un projet, tel qu'une maison ou un bateau à l'aide de larges blocs. Au cours de la dernière année préscolaire, l'enfant devient plus coopératif, sympathique et plus généreux avec ses jouets. Intéressé au monde extérieur, il adore les excursions et ne se lasse pas d'entendre parler de choses qu'il ne connaît pas.

Le choix des matériaux de jeu. On base le choix des matériaux de jeu sur des principes généraux d'utilité, de sécurité et de rendement comme pour les enfants plus jeunes. Ce groupe préfère les jouets d'entretien ménager, les appareils de terrain de jeu comme une boîte de sable, une glissoire et une balançoire, les jouets pour jeux actifs, tels que ballons, voitures, tricycles et autres véhicules. De larges blocs pour la construction d'escaliers et de ponts aident au développement musculaire et à l'acquisition des principes de base de la physique. Les matériaux à manipuler comme la plasticine, la peinture à l'eau, la peinture digitale et les jouets musicaux permettent une

Figure 17-11. À la prématernelle et à l'école maternelle, on facilite l'apprentissage de nouvelles habiletés et l'intégration dans un univers d'enfants du même âge. (H. Armstrong Roberts)

activité plus calme. Les enfants ont besoin d'un ensemble à découper et à peindre, de craies à colorier et de livres d'histoires que les adultes leur liront.

Rôle de l'adulte dans le jeu. L'enfant a besoin d'aide pour s'acclimater aux autres et apprendre à les respecter. Il veut plaire à ses parents et à son éducateur. S'il craint l'adulte, il peut coopérer en sa présence, mais perdre tout contrôle quand il se retrouve seul sans point d'appui. Pour réussir à s'amuser en groupe, les enfants ont souvent besoin de la présence sécurisante d'un adulte.

Certains parents croient fermement aux vertus éducatrices de la télévision, d'autres y voient un moyen commode d'assurer un peu de paix dans l'univers familial. On s'interroge sur l'innocuité de telles méthodes sur le développement intellectuel de l'enfant et sur la mise en valeur de sa personnalité. On ne connaît pas encore très bien la corrélation qui existe entre la violence montrée à la télévision et le degré d'agressivité que l'on retrouve chez les jeunes enfants.

L'ÉCOLE MATERNELLE

Dans les maternelles, on accueille les enfants de 4 et 5 ans. Plusieurs raisons poussent les parents à y inscrire leur enfant: le besoin d'une expérience éducative pour compléter celle reçue à la maison, le besoin de l'expérience socialisante du contact avec d'autres enfants et le travail de la mère hors du foyer. L'apprentissage, l'expérimentation, l'exercice d'imagination, les activités créatrices, la solution de problèmes et la socialisation figurent parmi les objectifs de l'école maternelle.

Valeur de l'école maternelle. La maternelle favorise la croissance et le développement et améliore l'état général de l'enfant. Elle augmente sa capacité d'action, sa confiance en lui-même et son sentiment de sécurité dans des situations variées. Placé dans un milieu planifié pour combler ses besoins et sous surveillance spécialisée, sa connaissance de lui-même et des autres se développe plus facilement et il devient mieux armé pour contrôler ses émotions. En plus, la maternelle favorise l'expression par l'art, la musique et le rythme.

Préparation à l'école maternelle. Même si l'enfant semble en sécurité pendant de courtes absences de sa mère, celle-ci doit se rendre compte que l'école maternelle peut devenir pour lui une expérience très frustrante. Sans préparation adéquate, il peut chercher à s'en protéger par un manque complet de coopéra-

tion ou une attitude de rejet. Chaque enfant possède déjà sa propre expérience de vie et interprète son entrée à la maternelle à partir de celle-ci. La mère doit elle-même avoir confiance dans l'école choisie avant d'entreprendre le processus d'intégration de l'enfant à ce nouveau milieu. La première étape consiste à visiter les lieux entre les heures d'activités pour le familiariser avec l'environnement et lui permettre de rencontrer son futur éducateur.

Le succès de ces premiers contacts aide les parents à prendre la décision finale de l'inscription à l'école. La capacité de l'enfant à tirer profit de l'expérience, son affection pour son professeur et pour les autres enfants, la certitude du retour de sa mère après la journée et la connaissance de la routine quotidienne favorisent une heureuse adaptation à cette situation nouvelle.

L'infirmière qui visite les maternelles doit s'assurer qu'à l'inscription on interroge la mère sur l'histoire de santé de son enfant. Elle doit veiller à ce que les habitudes hygiéniques soient enseignées et valorisées et qu'une chambre d'isolement soit toujours disponible pour l'enfant qui serait malade, fiévreux ou fatigué.

SOIN DE L'ENFANT D'ÂGE PRÉSCOLAIRE

L'enfant d'âge préscolaire commence à prendre soin de lui-même. En sécurité dans son milieu, il apprend à manger sans trop d'éclaboussures, à se vêtir et à se dévêtir, à se laver la figure et les mains et à se brosser les dents. Il n'arrête cependant pas ses jeux pour aller aux toilettes avant qu'une urgence ne survienne. Même si la mère trouve plus facile et plus simple de prendre soin de l'enfant elle-même, elle doit l'encourager à devenir progressivement plus indépendant. Il est naturellement lent et souvent désordonné dans ses mouvements. On doit l'aider à se baigner, à attacher ses lacets, à boutonner ses vêtements; à la fin de cette période il est capable de brosser et de peigner ses cheveux et on doit l'y encourager.

La mère doit planifier la journée de l'enfant pour éviter la précipitation avant le repas ou le départ pour l'école. Son horaire quotidien comprend des activités bruyantes, des jeux reposants et des périodes de sieste pour les plus jeunes. La mère doit prendre le temps de cajoler son enfant, de lui parler beaucoup et de lui prouver qu'elle aime l'avoir avec elle dans la maison. Elle doit le prendre sur ses genoux, lui faire la lecture, lui chanter des chansons enfantines. Au cours de la journée, elle le protège des accidents ou des expériences qui pourraient nuire à son développement physique ou émotif.

Sommeil

L'enfant joue si intensément qu'il oublie de dormir et refuse souvent d'aller au lit. L'enfant de 3 ans a souvent un sommeil agité; ses cauchemars correspondent à ses craintes réelles ou imaginaires. Cet enfant se lève souvent la nuit, erre dans la maison ou veut aller dormir avec ses parents. L'enfant a de la difficulté à saisir que son rêve est une expérience personnelle. Il peut demander à un adulte qui y a fait une apparition pourquoi il s'y est comporté d'une façon particulière. Partager la chambre d'un frère ou d'une sœur plus âgé, qui a dominé ces craintes, contribue à le rassurer. Les siestes diurnes doivent compenser ce manque de sommeil.

L'enfant de 4 ans ne veut plus faire la sieste et on ne peut l'y obliger sans forcer sa résistance. La mère doit toutefois insister pour une période de calme et de repos dans une chambre sombre: une musique reposante, son jouet favori aident à la détente et l'enfant s'endort souvent malgré lui.

Vers l'âge de 5 ans, l'enfant moyen dort paisiblement toute la nuit et n'a plus besoin de sieste. L'hyperactif et l'agité ont encore besoin d'une période de repos au cours de l'après-midi. Dans la plupart des maternelles, on fait la sieste sur un petit tapis ou sur une serviette que l'enfant plie et entrepose ensuite dans son casier personnel.

Mesures de sécurité

Ayant plus de liberté que le tout-petit, l'enfant d'âge préscolaire se blesse souvent loin de la maison. Son sens aigu de l'initiative et son désir d'imiter l'adulte le placent parfois dans des situations difficiles et dangereuses. Il peut tomber, jouer avec des allumettes, ouvrir le gaz ou le robinet d'eau chaude, s'électrocuter avec une prise de courant mal isolée, s'enfermer dans une glacière ou un réfrigérateur abandonné dont la porte n'a pas été enlevée. S'il est très libre et non surveillé, il risque de s'approcher de véhicules motorisés ou de piscines.

On ne peut tenir l'enfant éloigné de tous les dangers qui le menacent, mais des mesures de protection s'imposent. Lui en expliquer la rai-

son l'aide à les accepter et surtout à les suivre. On lui enseigne les principes de sécurité; certains jeux enseignent les « précautions » à prendre dans certaines situations familières, comme traverser les rues, monter en tricycle ou en canot-automobile. À mesure qu'il apprend à connaître le danger, on peut progressivement lui laisser prendre en main sa propre sécurité, sans toutefois lui faire entièrement confiance, vu son très jeune âge.

La fréquence des empoisonnements s'explique par la curiosité de l'enfant qui explore les armoires de la cuisine, de la salle de bain et du sous-sol, par le désir d'imiter les parents ou par l'attrait du médicament lui-même qui ressemble souvent à du chocolat enrobé de sucre coloré dont les enfants sont si friands.

Les premiers soins, étudiés au chapitre 15 sont facilités par le fait que le bambin d'âge préscolaire peut identifier le médicament, indiquer approximativement le niveau du médicament dans la bouteille et collaborer à l'initiation du traitement d'urgence.

L'éducation sexuelle générale et la mise en garde contre les maniaques sexuels ne devraient pas coïncider. On enseigne à l'enfant à refuser les cadeaux des étrangers ou une promenade en auto sans le consentement de ses parents, à éviter de marcher seul dans les rues isolées. Il est quasi criminel de laisser des enfants de cet âge libres de vagabonder dans les rues après la tombée de la nuit. L'enfant doit connaître le poste de police local où il peut obtenir refuge, protection et aide en l'absence des parents ou s'il s'est perdu. Tous les enfants de cet âge devraient connaître leur adresse, leur numéro de téléphone et le prénom de leur père pour faciliter d'éventuelles recherches. S'il en est incapable, une médaille contenant ces renseignements doit être attaché à ses vêtements ou à son cou.

Surveillance de la santé

Les visites annuelles ou bi-annuelles chez le médecin ou à une clinique de santé permettent de procéder à un examen approfondi de l'état général et aux examens nécessaires de la vue et de l'ouïe. Le médecin ou l'infirmière inscrit la croissance staturale et pondérale, donne ses recommandations sur le régime et les problèmes qui peuvent survenir dans les soins de l'enfant et complète le programme de vaccination.

On ne peut exagérer l'importance des soins dentaires. Les caries des dents de lait commencent ordinairement entre 3 et 6 ans et ont

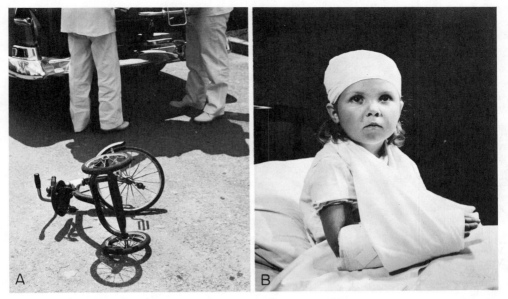

Figure 17-12. À l'âge préscolaire: une plus grande liberté d'action et un manque de maturité peuvent être la cause d'accidents. Une incursion en tricycle dans la rue peut conduire l'enfant à l'hôpital. (H. Armstrong Roberts.)

tendance à s'étendre rapidement. Les dents de lait servent de guides pour les dents permanentes et on doit les maintenir en bon état jusqu'à l'apparition de celles-ci. Si elles tombent, les dents permanentes poussent de façon irrégulière ou en mauvaise position.

On retrouve, parmi les facteurs de caries, une tendance idiopathique à la carie, la position des dents, la formation de fissures pendant le développement dentaire, la présence de sucres fermentés ou de bactéries produisant des acides qui décalcifient les dents ainsi que la basse teneur en fluor dans les dents.

Une excellente condition générale réduit la probabilité de carie. Les soins dentaires font partie intégrante des soins hygiéniques quotidiens normaux. On fait brosser les dents après chaque repas et l'ingestion de sucre raffiné doit être limitée. Lorsque l'enfant doit aller se coucher, après le brossage des dents, on déconseille le lait, les sucreries ou les biscuits. L'ingestion d'eau fluorée constitue une mesure préventive.

Alimentation

À cause d'un besoin d'exploration poussé et d'une croissance relativement lente, l'enfant d'âge préscolaire est moins intéressé à manger que le nourrisson. Les tentatives pour le forcer aboutissent souvent à un refus plus sérieux et à un durcissement des positions respectives qui nuisent à la solution agréable du problème. Son appétit augmente à mesure qu'il approche de l'âge scolaire. Un milieu calme sans trop

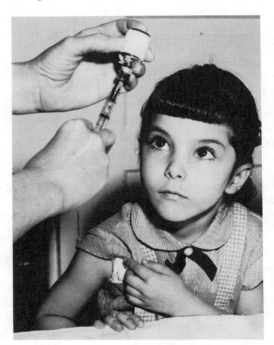

Figure 17-13. La poursuite de l'immunisation contre les maladies infectieuses de l'enfance constitue une partie importante du programme de santé. (H. Armstrong Roberts.)

Tableau 17-1. *Rations quotidiennes nutritives recommandées pour les enfants âgés de 3 à 6 ans*

	3 – 4 ans Poids – 16 kg Taille – 100 cm		4 – 6 ans Poids – 19 kg Taille – 110 cm	
K calories	1 400		1 600	
Protéines	30	g	30	g
Vitamines liposolubles				
Vitamine A	2 500	U.I.	2 500	U.I.
Vitamine D	400	U.I.	400	U.I.
Vitamine E	10	U.I.	10	U.I.
Vitamines hydrosolubles				
Acide ascorbique	40	mg	40	mg
Acide folique	0,2	mg	0,2	mg
Acide nicotinique (équivalents)	9	mg	11	mg
Riboflavine	0,8	mg	0,9	mg
Thiamine	0,7	mg	0,8	mg
Vitamine B_6	0,7	mg	0,9	mg
Vitamine B_{12}	3	μg	4	μg
Minéraux				
Calcium	0,8	g	0,8	g
Phosphore	0.8	g	0,8	g
Iode	70	μg	80	μg
Fer	10	mg	10	mg
Magnésium	200	mg	200	mg

de distractions, une période de repos avant le repas, de la jolie vaisselle, une chaise et une table confortables, une quantité limitée de nourriture à chaque service favorisent l'alimentation. Ces enfants aiment la nourriture simple, bien présentée, dans des plats séparés. Chaque enfant a ses préférences et on ajoute progressivement d'autres aliments pour améliorer la variété du menu. On en offre d'abord une cuillérée à thé et, s'il accepte, on en ajoute une deuxième. S'il refuse la nouvelle nourriture, on doit attendre qu'il en ait oublié le goût pour lui en offrir de nouveau.

L'enfant de trois ans utilise une cuillère, celui de cinq ans, une fourchette. On doit servir, à chaque repas, de la nourriture qu'il peut prendre avec les doigts, car c'est la méthode qu'il préfère entre toutes. Vers l'âge de 4 ou 5 ans, l'enfant peut manger une nourriture d'adulte. À cet âge, la plupart des enfants n'aiment pas les mets fortement épicés ou préparés avec une sauce.

L'attitude des parents influe sur les enfants d'âge préscolaire. Ceux-ci mangent mieux si tous les convives aiment la nourriture. L'effet est désastreux si le père critique le repas et si la mère mange parcimonieusement de crainte de prendre du poids. On ne doit pas obliger l'enfant à manger. On évite les distractions à table et on lui sert de petites portions, en lui laissant suffisamment de temps pour les absorber. Il devrait être défendu de grignoter entre les repas, tout en permettant une collation au cours de l'avant-midi et de l'après-midi. L'enfant s'identifie aux membres de sa famille; il aime prendre ses repas avec eux et se joindre à la conversation. C'est le moment idéal dont devraient profiter les parents pour répondre aux questions de leurs enfants.

Les enfants de 4 à 5 ans ont généralement des manières acceptables à table, mais on ne doit pas mettre trop d'emphase sur les détails. Les accidents ne devraient jamais devenir une cause d'émoi. Les enfants plus âgés veulent dresser le couvert, laver la vaisselle et le fait d'aider leur mère provoque plus d'intérêt pour le repas.

Il faut évaluer les facteurs suivants chez l'enfant qui refuse systématiquement de manger: l'excès de nourriture entre les repas, les troubles émotifs, l'épuisement ou l'imitation d'adultes qui ont un pauvre appétit. L'enfant malade ou porteur de caries dentaires peut refuser de manger à cause de nausées ou d'un mal de dents. Quelquefois il prend de mauvaises habitudes alimentaires pour attirer l'attention ou pour exprimer une rivalité entre ses frères et sœurs. On doit éliminer les causes du problème pour le plus grand bien physique et mental de l'enfant.

Figure 17-14. Les fruits constituent la collation idéale pour les enfants.

LES EFFETS DE LA SÉPARATION

L'enfant de 4 à 5 ans demeure anxieux quand on le laisse avec des étrangers, mais il peut comprendre la nécessité de la séparation. Sa notion du temps est très incomplète et des explications adaptées et concrètes lui sont nécessaires pour comprendre que son attente se terminera par le retour de sa mère. Un enfant de cet âge peut pleurer quand il revoit sa mère après une séparation. Il sent qu'il peut manifester ses émotions, maintenant qu'elle est présente pour le consoler. L'enfant laissé dans une garderie, une maternelle ou un hôpital se sent rassuré par la visite de sa mère qui lui montre ainsi qu'elle l'aime encore et le ramènera à la maison.

Livres et documents officiels

Ansfield, J. G.: *The Adopted Child.* Springfield, Ill., Charles C Thomas, 1971.
Bergé, A.: *L'éducation sexuelle chez l'enfant.* Paris, P. U. F., 1968.
Bergeron, G. et Bergeron, T.: *De l'amour aux enfants.* Paris, Le Centurion, 1975.
Child Welfare League of America, Inc.: *The Changing Dimensions of Day Care.* New York, Child Welfare League of America, Inc., 1970.
DiLeo, J. H.: *Young Children and Their Drawings.* New York, Bruner, Mazel, Publishers, 1970.
Grollman, E. A. (édit.): *Explaining Divorce to Children.* Boston, Beacon Press, 1969.
Hardy, W. G. (édit.): *Communication and the Disadvantaged Child.* Baltimore, Williams & Wilkins Company, 1970.
Ministère de l'Education: *La maternelle.* Gouvernement du Québec.
Ministère de la Santé nationale et du Bien-être social: *Protection par l'immunisation.* Division de l'hygiène maternelle et infantile, Goouvernement du Canada.
Ministère de la Santé nationale et du Bien-être social: *L'éducation sexuelle. Le bégaiement. La mauvaise prononciation. Habitudes nerveuses. L'obéissance. Mensonge et vol. La timidité. Jeu et compagnons de jeu. Les yeux.* Division de l'hygiène mentale, Gouvernement du Canada
Ministère des Affaires sociales: *Normes de garderie de jour.* Gouvernement du Québec, 1972.
Piaget, J.: *Six études de psychologie.* Genève, Gonthier, 1964.
Rice, E. P., Ekdahl, M. C. et Miller, L.: *Children of Mentally Ill Parents.* New York, Behavioral Publications, 1971.

Articles

Ambrosino, L.: Do Children Believe TV? *Children Today*, 1:18, novembre-décembre 1972.
Anonsen, D.: L'enfant hyperactif. *Inf. Can.*, 17:18, 5, 1975.
Bacharach, J. A. et autres: Vision Testing by Parents of 3½-Year Old Children. *Pub. Health Rep.*, 85:426, mai 1970.
Chamberlain, R.: Management of Preschool Behavior Problems. *Ped. 'Clin. N. Amer.*, 21:33, 1, 1974.
Curzon, M.: Dental Implications of Thumb-Sucking. *Pediatrics*, 54:196, 2, 1974.
Delthil, S. et autres: Dépistage des troubles de l'acuité visuelle à l'école maternelle. *La revue du praticien*, XIX:95, 11, 1969.
Gabriel, H. P.: Identification of Potential Emotional and Cognitive Disturbances in the 3 to 5 Year Old Child. *Pediat. Clin. N. Amer.*, 18:179, février 1971.
Grotberg, E. H.: What Does Research Teach Us About Day Care: For Children Over Three. *Children Today*, 1:13, janvier-février 1972.
Heagarty, M. et autres: Sex and the Preschool Child. *Am. J. Nursing*, 74:1479, 8, 1974.
Hines, J. D.: Father – The Forgotten Man. *Nursing Forum*, 10:176, 2, 1971.
Hunter, G. T.: Screening Tests for Head Start Children. *Pediat. Clin. N. Amer.*, 18:159, février 1971
Irwin, T.: First Child? Middle Child? Last Child? Only Child? What's the Difference? *Today's Health*, 47:26, octobre 1969.
Johnson, W. R.: Sex Education and the Nurse. *Nursing Outlook*, 18:26, novembre 1970.
Launay, C.: Les troubles du comportement chez l'enfant adopté. *La revue de l'infirmière*, 22:155, 2, 1972.
Silber, D.: Encopresis: Discussion of Etiology and Management. *Clin. Pediat.*, 8:225, 4, 1969.
Smith, D. E. et autres: The Hippie Communal Movement: Effects on Child Birth and Development. *Am. J. Orthopsychiat.*, 40:527, avril 1970.
Waechter, E. H.: Recent Research in Child Development. *Nursing Forum*, 8:374, 4, 1969.
Wilbur, C. et Aug, R.: Sex Education. *Am. J. Nursing*, 73:88, janvier 1973.
Woodward, P. et Brodie, B.: The Hyperactive Child: Who Is He? *Nurs. Clin. N. Amer.*, 9:727, 4, 1974.
Wootton, M., Wood, S. et Barnes, K.: Shaping Preschoolers' Play Behaviour in the Child Health Conference Waiting Area. *Canad. J. Pub. Health*, 61:10, janvier-février 1970.

18

pathologies de l'enfant d'âge préscolaire nécessitant des soins immédiats ou de courte durée

HOSPITALISATION DE L'ENFANT D'ÂGE PRÉSCOLAIRE

L'hospitalisation crée généralement une anxiété moins profonde à l'enfant d'âge préscolaire qu'à l'enfant plus jeune. Ceux qui ont connu une adaptation satisfaisante à l'école maternelle et qui sont habitués à accepter l'absence temporaire de leur mère s'adaptent mieux à l'hospitalisation que ceux qui ont constamment vécu avec elle et n'en ont jamais été séparés. Néanmoins, les enfants d'âge préscolaire ont besoin de la sécurité que leur procure la présence de leur mère. Plus celle-ci peut demeurer avec l'enfant, moins il souffrira de troubles émotifs pendant et après l'hospitalisation. Si elle ne peut être présente, l'enfant peut manifester, par la suite, un désir excessif d'affection et même une attitude de revanche.

Préparation en vue de l'hospitalisation.
L'enfant d'âge préscolaire, en raison de sa compréhension accrue du langage, peut être mieux préparé pour l'hospitalisation que le trottineur.

Cette préparation sera probablement mieux réussie si les parents s'en chargent. Ils devraient assurer l'enfant de leurs visites fréquentes et de son retour à la maison dès qu'il sera assez bien pour quitter l'hôpital.

Une explication détaillée peut ne pas être à sa portée, mais on doit lui expliquer la vérité le plus simplement possible. Les jeunes enfants peuvent se sentir coupables d'être malades. L'enfant qui s'est brûlé en jouant avec des allumettes, malgré la défense expresse de ses parents, a besoin d'être assuré que ses douleurs ne constituent pas une punition, mais la conséquence d'un jeu dangereux. Certains parents provoquent cette réaction de culpabilité par des menaces telles que: « Si tu ne bois pas ton lait, tu ne deviendras pas grand et fort, tu seras malade ». Quand l'enfant tombe malade, il peut croire qu'il mérite le blâme et qu'il est ainsi envoyé à l'hôpital en punition, probablement pour toujours. On ne doit jamais menacer un enfant de cette manière, et quand l'hospitalisation devient nécessaire, la véritable raison doit lui en être donnée. Comme l'enfant d'âge préscolaire semble particulièrement conscient des handicaps, mutilations et blessures des autres enfants et qu'il craint les accidents physiques, on doit l'encourager à parler de ses craintes et à poser des questions au sujet des problèmes qui le préoccupent. Une explication véridique minimise les distorsions de la réalité et réduit son anxiété.

L'enfant se représente l'hôpital comme un lieu étrange. Il peut avoir entendu des adultes parler d'hospitalisation et de maladies, en termes mystérieux. Ce qu'il voit en arrivant à l'hôpital peut n'être pas alarmant en soi, mais tout paraît si différent de ce à quoi il est habitué à la maison, qu'il est pris de peur à l'idée de ce qui pourrait lui arriver dans cette ambiance nouvelle.

Quelques jours avant une hospitalisation, la mère doit expliquer à l'enfant ce qu'est une unité pédiatrique et souligner les similitudes avec sa vie quotidienne plutôt qu'appuyer sur les différences. Avant son admission, l'enfant peut faire une tournée des endroits de l'hôpital qu'il verra durant son hospitalisation. Il posera alors les questions qui lui viendront à l'esprit; par exemple, voyant un lit, il peut questionner sur la vie de nuit à l'hôpital et être rassuré par les explications de sa mère. Lors de ces tournées, il faut éviter de semer la confusion dans l'esprit de l'enfant en lui montrant trop d'endroits ou en lui présentant trop de gens. Il est habituellement souhaitable de se limiter à la chambre, à la salle de jeux et à la cuisine, ainsi qu'aux infirmières et aux éducatrices. Il n'est cependant pas sage de parler de l'hôpital longtemps avant l'admission, pour éviter que l'enfant se fasse de fausses idées qui augmenteront son anxiété. Il faut surtout craindre l'apparition de l'anxiété chez l'enfant qui a connu une personne décédée au cours d'une hospitalisation.

La mère peut dire à l'enfant qu'il aura à l'hôpital un lit semblable à son petit lit à la maison, mais d'une couleur différente; qu'il prendra ses repas au lit ou à table avec d'autres enfants. L'usage du bassin de lit ou de l'urinoir surprend souvent l'enfant. Cette source d'anxiété peut être éliminée si la mère explique à l'enfant qu'ils sont utilisés quand il doit rester au lit et ne peut se rendre à la salle de toilette.

Les uniformes des infirmières et des médecins effraient souvent l'enfant, parce qu'ils leur donnent un aspect différent de celui des adultes qu'il connaît. L'anxiété que provoquent ces détails de la vie à l'hôpital pourrait être allégée si l'on offrait à l'enfant un livre d'images expliquant l'environnement physique et social. Plusieurs hôpitaux distribuent de tels livres au moment de l'admission et l'enfant peut les colorier pendant son séjour à l'hôpital. D'autres hôpitaux et certaines compagnies ont préparé des films et des bandes magnétoscopiques pour préparer l'enfant à l'hospitalisation et l'aider à faire face aux divers événements qui surgissent durant un séjour à l'hôpital.

Certaines maternelles ont inclus dans leur programme une visite d'une unité pédiatrique, de façon à familiariser l'enfant bien portant avec cet univers spécial. D'autres maternelles invitent des infirmières qui viennent présenter d'une façon accessible et adaptée, ce qu'est un hôpital et une hospitalisation.

Si des frères ou sœurs aînés ont déjà été hospitalisés, ils peuvent rassurer l'enfant en lui faisant remarquer qu'ils sont bien revenus à la maison. Ils peuvent lui raconter qu'ils ont eu des crèmes glacées ou qu'une animatrice de jeux leur apportait des jouets, ou qu'une infirmière avait fabriqué un bonnet de papier qui ressemblait à sa coiffe. Ces aînés connaissent les détails de la vie d'hôpital qui peuvent vraiment intéresser un enfant.

Les parents doivent également préparer l'enfant pour les expériences désagréables. Par exemple, s'il doit être opéré, ils peuvent utiliser des marionnettes pour lui expliquer ce qui lui arrivera et lui permettre de jouer son rôle de malade. Ils doivent lui parler de son passage à la salle d'opération, et l'assurer qu'ils seront dans sa chambre à son retour.

Les parents devraient connaître la forme d'anesthésie qui sera choisie. Si elle doit être administrée avec un masque, on joue à simuler cette technique. Une serviette peut servir de masque et on devrait suggérer à l'enfant de respirer profondément et de faire semblant de s'endormir. Selon son âge, la conception de respiration profonde peut être expliquée en lui disant de respirer comme s'il allait gonfler un ballon ou comme lorsqu'il court rapidement. Les parents peuvent respirer avec lui pour lui montrer comment on doit procéder. Il devrait comprendre que cela entraîne quelque inconfort.

Il n'est pas recommandé d'expliquer toutes les techniques qui peuvent être employées. Ce qui est important c'est que l'enfant sache que ses parents sont au courant de ce qui va lui arriver.

On doit lui laisser le plaisir d'emballer sa brosse à dents et les autres articles qu'il apportera à l'hôpital et de choisir les vêtements qu'il portera pour retourner à la maison, ce qui l'assure encore plus qu'il y reviendra.

Si l'enfant a un jouet ou une couverture qu'il préfère et qui lui donne un sentiment de sécurité quand il est effrayé ou fatigué, il doit pouvoir l'apporter à l'hôpital. Cet objet sert de lien avec la maison et le réconforte dans les moments de tension. Le personnel infirmier doit reconnaître l'importance d'un tel objet et le protéger pour qu'il ne soit ni perdu, ni abîmé par les autres enfants.

Trop souvent, les parents sont incapables de préparer efficacement l'enfant à cause de l'anxiété que soulève chez eux son hospitalisation. Il se peut qu'ils ne lui disent rien du tout, ou que, par ignorance, ils lui donnent une fausse impression de ce qui va se passer. Le pédiatre ou l'infirmière de la clinique peuvent alors expliquer aux parents le genre de vie que mènera l'enfant à l'hôpital et les traitements qu'il devra subir. De toute façon, l'infirmière doit toujours s'enquérir du type de préparation que l'enfant a reçu et en tenir compte par la suite.

Les infirmières de certaines unités pédiatriques visitent les enfants à domicile pour leur expliquer ce qu'est une infirmière et une hospitalisation. En général, elles apportent de l'équipement médical et de soin, réel et miniature, des poupées, des images, des crayons. L'enfant qui joue avec le matériel se familiarise de façon détendue avec des faits susceptibles de devenir anxiogènes. Cette initiative peut épargner beaucoup d'anxiété aux parents et à l'enfant et faciliter le séjour à l'hôpital.

Réactions de l'enfant à l'hospitalisation.
La réaction de l'enfant d'âge préscolaire, face à une maladie sérieuse, dépend en grande partie de l'anxiété de ses parents et de la façon dont il a été préparé à la séparation par des expériences antérieures.

Pendant l'hospitalisation, l'enfant perçoit ses parents différemment, car leur rôle de protection se trouve affaibli par les circonstances. Ils ne peuvent éviter à l'enfant le malaise et la douleur causés par sa maladie, et il ne comprend pas pourquoi ils permettent aux médecins et aux infirmières de le faire souffrir. Il s'effraie de l'impuissance de ses parents et leur reproche leur défaillance. Les parents doivent comprendre ces sentiments et procurer aide et réconfort, même si les souffrances de l'enfant n'en sont pas soulagées. L'enfant n'a pas seulement besoin d'entendre

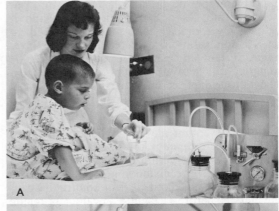
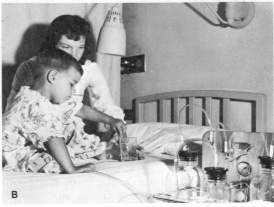

Figure 18-1. *A)* L'infirmière explique à l'enfant la technique de l'aspiration. *B)* Celui-ci se familiarise avec l'équipement, ce qui diminue son anxiété au moment du traitement. (Margo Smith, Université de Californie.)

exprimer verbalement l'affection de ses parents, mais il doit surtout en sentir la chaleur.

Même si l'enfant d'âge préscolaire est habituellement curieux et cherche à explorer le monde qui l'entoure, il devient très anxieux au sujet de son intégrité corporelle pendant l'hospitalisation. L'enfant connaît mal les fonctions physiologiques et il élabore des théories fantaisistes pour s'expliquer ce qui se passe à l'intérieur de son corps. Quand le technicien de laboratoire prélève un échantillon sanguin, il peut craindre de mourir exsangue et la pipette du micro-prélèvement peut être associée à un processus satanique pour le vider lentement de tout son sang. L'infirmière qui connaît les craintes de l'enfant peut minimiser son appréhension par des explications appropriées et un support psychologique adéquat pendant le prélèvement.

Les techniques qui touchent le périné risquent de traumatiser encore davantage. Il est donc préférable de prendre la température par voie buccale dès que l'enfant peut collaborer et qu'il n'y a pas de contre-indication médicale. S'il doit subir un cathétérisme ou un lavement, il faut lui permettre de manipuler le matériel qui sera utilisé, lui donner des explications adaptées et le laisser procéder au traitement sur une poupée spécialement prévue à cet effet.

Le jeune enfant n'a pas la notion du temps et il peut croire qu'il sera malade pour toujours. Il ne peut comprendre la douleur et a le sentiment d'être abandonné. À cause de son état physique et émotif, il peut souffrir de cauchemars et perdre la faculté d'évaluer la réalité comme il le pouvait avant d'être malade. L'étrangeté de l'environnement fait surgir la crainte que de nouveaux dangers soient imminents. Il peut devenir de plus en plus dépendant, perdre le goût de ses activités passées et concentrer son attention sur la partie de son corps la plus atteinte par sa maladie.

Après avoir aidé les parents à contrôler leur propre anxiété on peut, avec eux, aider l'enfant à faire face à la réalité, à comprendre et à accepter sa maladie, et à entretenir des intérêts normaux en dépit de son état. L'infirmière doit comprendre qu'elle a la responsabilité de fournir un support émotif aux parents et à l'enfant. Elle doit savoir que la guérison d'un enfant malheureux et anxieux est retardée par son état émotif, que ses progrès ne sont pas les mêmes que ceux d'un enfant heureux qui n'est ni profondément frustré, ni déprimé.

Dans certains hôpitaux, une personne spécialement désignée, infirmière, travailleuse sociale ou éducatrice, organise des rencontres avec les parents et les enfants, ou seulement entre les parents, afin de les aider à résoudre les problèmes qui peuvent se présenter au cours de l'hospitalisation. Ces réunions s'avèrent spécialement importantes si l'enfant est hospitalisé pendant de très longues périodes ou à intervalles rapprochés, ou encore s'il fait un séjour à l'unité des soins intensifs. Les parents perçoivent la vie de l'unité sous un autre jour que les infirmières et leurs suggestions amènent souvent des changements dans les politiques établies.

Rôle des parents au cours de l'hospitalisation.
Si on enlève à la mère toute possibilité de s'occuper elle-même de son enfant hospitalisé, elle peut ressentir ce refus comme un blâme des soins qu'elle lui donnait à la maison et développer un sentiment de culpabilité. Elle peut désirer ardemment le retour de l'enfant au foyer et idéaliser la période où il était encore à la maison. L'enfant normal n'a pas que des qualités, mais ses défauts disparaissent de la mémoire de la mère

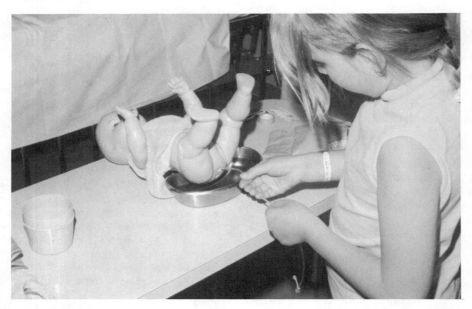

Figure 18-2. Fillette d'âge préscolaire qui pratique sur sa poupée un traitement qu'elle doit bientôt subir. (Courtoisie de l'École des sciences infirmières de l'Université Laval, Québec.)

qui s'ennuie au foyer et à qui l'on n'accorde que de brèves heures de visite.

Malheureusement, l'enfant qui s'est cru abandonné parce qu'on l'a privé de la présence de ses parents, réagit de façon négative à son retour à la maison. Il devient souvent très irritable, exigeant et les parents devant ces réactions ressentent une fois de plus leur incompétence, ce qui augmente leur sentiment de culpabilité, surtout si l'enfant s'est conduit de façon exemplaire à l'hôpital. Il faut faire comprendre à la mère que sa compétence et l'amour de son enfant ne sont pas en cause; la réaction de l'enfant provient du traumatisme de l'hospitalisation. Elle doit surtout éviter de réagir en devenant elle-même exigeante, irritable ou larmoyante; l'amour et la sécurité finiront par avoir raison de la réaction défensive de l'enfant et leurs relations redeviendront bientôt ce qu'elles étaient auparavant.

Ces réactions malheureuses que nous venons de décrire se produisent rarement quand on permet à la mère ou aux parents de participer de façon active aux soins de l'enfant pendant son séjour à l'hôpital. En contact étroit avec le personnel, les parents demeurent objectifs à l'égard de l'enfant, de sa maladie et des soins qu'il reçoit. De retour à la maison, il ne sentira pas le besoin de défouler ses sentiments négatifs sur ses parents et le retour à la vie normale se fera sans heurts.

Soins physiques

Bain et vêtements. Chaque enfant devrait recevoir les mêmes soins physiques que chez lui. On doit tenir compte des renseignements obtenus par le questionnaire au moment de l'admission.

L'infirmière peut ainsi savoir jusqu'à quel point l'enfant peut se baigner lui-même ou se brosser les dents. S'il en est physiquement capable, elle doit le laisser s'occuper de lui-même, comme il le faisait à la maison. S'il le désire, elle l'aide jusqu'à ce qu'il soit prêt à se débrouiller seul. L'infirmière a une excellente occasion de lui enseigner de bonnes règles d'hygiène, tout en lui prodiguant ses soins quotidiens. Au moins une fois par semaine, il faut laver la tête des enfants qui ne sont pas trop malades et qui peuvent le supporter.

Si l'enfant est assez âgé, on doit le laisser choisir ses vêtements pour la journée. Des pyjamas ou autres tenues de jour, aux couleurs vives et ressemblant à ceux qu'il porte habituellement à la maison, sont préférables à la chemise d'hôpital blanche et ouverte dans le dos. Il est désagréable pour un enfant d'âge préscolaire d'être vêtu de façon uniforme. L'infirmière doit s'assurer que le petit garçon ne trébuche pas à cause de pantalons trop longs ou que la petite fille ne se sente mal à l'aise à cause d'une robe trop serrée.

Alimentation. L'alimentation peut constituer un défi. Pendant que l'enfant est confiné au lit, il est particulièrement important de placer les aliments à sa portée et de l'installer confortablement pour le repas. Si on lui permet de s'asseoir, on supporte son dos avec un appui ou avec un oreiller placé contre la tête du lit. On dépose son plateau sur une table de lit de couleur attrayante. L'infirmière l'aide à manger s'il éprouve des difficultés à le faire lui-même. Tout problème d'alimentation que l'infirmière ne peut régler doit être communiqué à l'infirmière-chef ou à la diététicienne.

Le service des repas pour l'enfant qui peut se déplacer devrait suivre le procédé utilisé dans les maternelles. On peut faire sonner une cloche un peu avant de servir le repas. À ce signal, l'enfant arrête de jouer et on commence les préparatifs. En suivant la même routine, chaque jour, on en fait une habitude et le moment du repas en est facilité. Les repas doivent être précédés d'une période calme, durant laquelle les enfants se détendent. Une attitude positive envers les repas stimule de bonnes habitudes alimentaires. On donne le bassin de lit ou l'urinoir aux enfants couchés et on leur fait se laver les mains.

On devrait servir à une table commune les enfants dont l'état le permet. Ceux qui suivent un régime particulier ou qui sont limités dans leurs activités ont parfois besoin d'une attention spéciale.

La hauteur des chaises doit être proportionnée à celle de la table pour que les pieds de l'enfant puissent toucher le sol. Les assiettes doivent être attrayantes et les fourchettes et cuillères de dimension appropriée. Tout l'équipement qui n'est pas jeté après usage doit être stérilisé. Des chalumeaux aux couleurs vives encouragent l'absorption de liquide.

Il faut offrir une variété d'aliments complets. On permet souvent aux enfants de choisir leur menu, comme le font les adultes. Des repas légers sont préférables et il faut présenter les aliments de manière à stimuler leur appétit. On peut servir le pain et le beurre sous forme de sandwich, pour qu'ils puissent les manipuler plus aisément. On coupe la viande et les légumes de façon appropriée. Si on sert le repas sur un chariot roulant, on peut amener celui-

Figure 18-3.   Petite fille qui s'amuse malgré ses sondes urétérales et vésicale. (Courtoisie de l'École des sciences infirmières de l'Université Laval, Québec.)

ci à la table ou au lit et l'enfant a la possibilité de choisir ce qu'il veut. Un repas servi de cette manière constitue une expérience plus agréable qui permet à l'enfant une participation active à son alimentation.

L'atmosphère devrait être enjouée, les enfants conversant joyeusement. Un adulte aide ceux qui en ont besoin et sa présence recrée une atmosphère familiale.

Certains parents apportent fréquemment des bonbons et des friandises aux enfants hospitalisés. Ces aliments diminuent l'appétit du malade, l'amènent à refuser des mets plus nutritifs et causent souvent une dérogation à la diète prescrite. La politique de l'unité pédiatrique doit être très claire à ce sujet et il faut expliquer aux parents les raisons des restrictions imposées.

Repos

On peut rencontrer certaines difficultés aux heures de sieste et au coucher. La chambre doit être dans l'obscurité et chaque enfant prêt, ou bien à dormir, ou bien à jouer calmement dans son lit s'il ne fait pas habituellement de sieste à la maison. Si l'infirmière exige que tous les enfants dorment au moment de la sieste, un ou deux d'entre eux peuvent tenir tous les autres éveillés par leur opposi-

tion à une exigence si déraisonnable. Il ne faut jamais envoyer un enfant au lit en guise de punition, car cette pratique risque de rendre l'heure du coucher très pénible pour l'enfant et pour son entourage.

Activités

Le jeu est le propre de l'enfant, et l'enfant malade a autant, sinon plus, besoin de jouer à l'hôpital. Les suggestions et explications données au chapitre 5 sur le jeu de l'enfant hospitalisé s'appliquent aussi ici. L'infirmière doit se rappeler que c'est surtout à l'âge préscolaire que l'enfant utilisera les marionnettes, les jeux avec poupées et équipement médical et les jouets qui permettent d'imiter la vie adulte.

L'enfant trop faible pour quitter son lit peut regarder la télévision avec ses copains. S'il est très malade, on doit veiller à lui éviter les émissions violentes ou trop excitantes.

L'infirmière doit tenter de compléter les soins d'hygiène et les traitements assez tôt le matin pour permettre aux enfants de se rendre à la salle de jeu. Elle doit encourager certains petits à la quitter et à gagner la salle de jeu, mais elle doit éviter de laisser un jeune malade seul dans sa chambre, si c'est possible.

GLOMÉRULONÉPHRITE AIGUË

Définition.   Affection caractérisée anatomiquement par une inflammation non bactérienne et non suppurative des capillaires glomérulaires.

Incidence, étiologie et physio-pathologie.   La glomérulonéphrite aiguë constitue la forme la plus commune de néphrite chez les enfants. Approximativement 66% des cas se manifestent avant l'âge de sept ans. On la remarque rarement chez les moins de trois ans et elle atteint plus souvent les garçons.

La glomérulonéphrite est une réaction de type immunologique qui apparaît à la suite d'une infection à streptocoque bêta hémolytique, au niveau des voies respiratoires supérieures ou de la peau.

La néphrite peut faire suite à la fièvre scarlatine ou à une autre infection streptococcique, telle que l'impétigo ou l'eczéma impétiginé et se présente habituellement une à trois semaines après le début de l'infection.

Les reins sont pâles et hypertrophiés. Sur les surfaces corticales et dans le parenchyme, on constate de petites hémorragies punctiformes. Les glomérules paraissent larges et relativement avasculaires. Les capillaires des glomérules laissent passer des protéines et des cellules dans le filtrat glomérulaire. Les cellules des tubules sont granuleuses et œdémateuses. Des lésions capillaires se manifestent. On peut obtenir un fragment de tissu rénal, par une biopsie à l'aiguille, afin de recueillir certaines informations au sujet du processus pathologique. Les lésions laissent supposer un processus antigénique au niveau des capillaires glomérulaires.

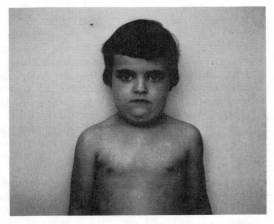

Figure 18-4.   Oreillons: noter l'oedème bilatéral des parotides qui provoque une dysphagie importante. (Voir page 526.)

Manifestations cliniques et diagnostic. La glomérulonéphrite peut se présenter comme une maladie anodine qui passe inaperçue ou se déclarer brusquement, accompagnée de *manifestations cliniques* graves, comme céphalée, malaise, hyperthermie, hypertension, oligurie ou anurie, et éventuellement une décompensation cardiaque provoquant la mort.

Dans les cas habituels, l'enfant ne semble pas très atteint, mais présente toujours de l'hématurie microscopique et quelquefois macroscopique. L'urine est trouble et foncée. On trouve parfois un œdème léger autour des yeux; l'œdème généralisé demeure rare à moins que l'enfant ne souffre de défaillance cardiaque. La température, au début, peut s'élever à 40° C, mais, au cours des jours suivants, tombe à 37,7° C et reste à ce niveau jusqu'à ce que les reins guérissent. L'enfant se plaint de maux de tête, d'anorexie, de vomissements, de constipation ou de diarrhée. L'hypertension se manifeste quelquefois et on peut enregistrer des lectures de l'ordre de 200/120 mm de mercure.

L'oligurie est manifeste. L'urine contient de l'albumine, des globules rouges, quelques globules blancs et des cylindres, et a une densité élevée. L'azotémie s'élève. L'anémie peut se déclarer. Le taux de sédimentation globulaire corrigée est élevé.

L'encéphalopathie hypertensive peut apparaître. L'enfant est somnolent, il se plaint de céphalée, de diplopie. Il peut avoir des convulsions et vomir. Il présente de la bradycardie. Les symptômes cérébraux disparaissent avec la chute de la pression artérielle.

L'amélioration clinique survient après une ou deux semaines. L'urine redevient normale après six semaines ou plusieurs mois plus tard.

Approximativement, les trois quarts des enfants souffrant de glomérulonéphrite ont des troubles cardiaques transitoires. La défaillance du cœur peut provoquer la mort, mais si l'enfant guérit, on constate un rétablissement complet de la fonction cardiaque.

L'histoire clinique d'une infection antérieure, la présence de l'hématurie, l'œdème léger et l'albuminurie permettent de poser le diagnostic.

D'autres diagnostics peuvent être possibles comme la pyélo-néphrite aiguë, le scorbut et une dyscrasie sanguine.

Traitement.   Le traitement demeure symptomatique. Il faut garder le lit durant les phases aiguës ou jusqu'à la cessation de l'hématurie. L'opinion médicale est très partagée à ce sujet: certains médecins n'ordonnent jamais le repos au lit, alors que d'autres recommandent deux semaines de repos. Par la suite, un peu d'activité n'affecte pas le cours de la maladie. On doit examiner l'urine à intervalles fréquents. Il faut protéger l'enfant contre le refroidissement, la fatigue et éviter tout contact avec des personnes souffrant d'infection respiratoire. Au début, on donne une diète hypercalorique, pauvre en protéines, à base de lait et de jus de fruits sucrés. Après la phase aiguë, l'enfant peut avoir une alimentation contrôlée et ensuite un régime régulier. En présence d'œdème grave, on peut limiter l'apport de sel. Si l'azotémie s'élève, on peut diminuer l'apport protéique.

À cause de la présence de streptocoques dans les cultures pharyngées, la pénicilline, administrée par voie parentérale, demeure l'antibiotique de choix pendant la phase aiguë. On peut continuer à l'administrer oralement, pendant les deux ou trois mois qui suivent la crise, de manière à diminuer les risques de récidive de l'infection à streptocoques.

Si la tension artérielle s'élève, ce qui est révélateur de vaso-constriction, une défaillance cardiaque ou une encéphalopathie peuvent se développer. Si la tension artérielle dépasse 140/95, on peut donner en injection intramusculaire une combinaison de réserpine et d'hydrochlorure hydrolazine (Aprésoline). Ces médicaments hypotenseurs réduisent la tension rapidement et exigent une surveillance étroite. Ils peuvent être donnés oralement en doses fractionnées, après la dose initiale.

Il faut restreindre les liquides si l'enfant présente une hypertension grave, à moins que la diurèse ne soit abondante.

Un enfant souffrant d'une encéphalopathie hypertensive avec convulsions peut avoir besoin de sédatifs et d'oxygène. S'il présente une défaillance cardiaque, des opiacés, de la digitaline et de l'oxygène peuvent être indiqués. Il est nécessaire de suivre l'état cardiaque après la disparition des symptômes.

Si le débit urinaire décroît, l'acidose, l'œdème et l'urémie peuvent se développer. Il faut augmenter la diurèse et l'excrétion des déchets du métabolisme, en offrant suffisamment de liquide à l'enfant. S'il vomit, on peut donner le liquide par voie intraveineuse pour empêcher la déshydratation et l'acidose. Les solutions contenant du potassium s'avèrent dangereuses en présence d'oligurie ou d'anurie. Il faut prendre des mesures pour réduire l'hyperkaliémie quand le taux de potassium sérique atteint 6 mEq/l. Si l'hyperkaliémie persiste, il faudra éventuellement soumettre l'enfant à la *dialyse péritonéale*.

Cette technique sert à corriger l'urémie, l'acidose et certains déséquilibres électrolytiques, tels que l'hyperkaliémie. C'est une forme d'hémodialyse où le péritoine fait office de membrane semi-perméable. On perfuse une solution hypotonique dans la cavité péritonéale, les substances de déchets traversent la membrane et pénètrent dans le liquide de dialyse. À chaque quantité de liquide perfusé doit correspondre une quantité semblable de liquide excrété par un trocart inséré dans l'abdomen et relié à une bouteille fixée au sol. Il faut suivre une technique aseptique stricte. La vérification des signes vitaux, le dosage des liquides et la pesée sont essentiels et il faut continuer d'observer l'enfant pendant 12 à 36 heures après le traitement. Les complications demeurent extrêmement rares et aucun pontage artério-veineux n'est nécessaire comme c'est le cas pour l'hémodialyse. Une transplantation rénale peut éventuellement devenir nécessaire si l'enfant évolue vers l'insuffisance rénale.

On ne devrait procéder à l'amygdalectomie et à l'adénoïdectomie que plusieurs mois après la phase aiguë de la maladie, et l'administration de pénicilline devrait précéder et suivre l'opération pour prévenir l'infection streptococcique.

Soins infirmiers. Le repos au lit est souvent nécessaire durant la phase aiguë de la gloméro-néphrite et jusqu'à ce que l'urine ne contienne plus de globules sanguins. L'infirmière doit empêcher l'enfant d'avoir froid en l'habillant chaudement et, quand il est au lit, en le couvrant avec une couverture légère, mais qui le tienne au chaud. Il faut le placer dans une chambre bien ventilée et tiède, à l'écart des enfants souffrant d'infection.

On note les signes vitaux régulièrement; on doit prendre la tension artérielle fréquemment, parce que des changements soudains peuvent survenir qu'il faut signaler immédiatement. L'infirmière doit observer les signes d'encéphalopathie hypertensive. Quand ils se présentent, l'enfant doit être placé dans son lit avec les montants levés. L'infirmière devrait toujours s'assurer que les médicaments nécessaires lors de complications sont disponibles et à la portée de la main.

Les soins de la peau sont très importants. On doit aussi suivre à la lettre les ordonnances médicales concernant les aliments solides et liquides. La quantité de liquide permise par vingt-quatre heures doit être répartie au cours de la journée et offerte par petites doses à intervalles réguliers. Il faut en administrer la plus grande partie pendant le jour pour que l'enfant puisse dormir suffisamment pendant la nuit. Le dosage des liquides ingérés et excrétés demeure primordial. On pèse l'enfant à la même heure, chaque jour pour suivre l'évolution de l'œdème. L'infirmière doit noter la présence et l'importance de l'œdème périorbital. Plusieurs des soins s'appliquant à l'enfant souffrant d'un syndrome néphrotique s'appliquent dans le cas présent.

Quand l'enfant peut se lever, il faut lui proposer des activités tranquilles et des jeux calmes.

Pronostic.   Le pronostic est généralement bon dans l'enfance, mais il varie d'un enfant à l'autre. Une seconde attaque demeure peu fréquente, mais l'enfant qui n'est pas complètement guéri peut présenter une récidive lorsqu'il contracte une autre infection des voies respiratoires ou qu'il subit une amygdalectomie. Le cours de la glomérulonéphrite peut varier de 10 jours à un an. La néphrite chronique se développe dans un très petit nombre de cas. L'enfant peut être emporté rapidement si la glomérulo-néphrite se complique d'une encéphalopathie hypertensive aiguë.

VULVO-VAGINITE

La vulvo-vaginite se manifeste avec une certaine fréquence après la deuxième année. Il en existe deux types: la vaginite non gonococcique commune et la vaginite gonococcique dont la fréquence diminue.

Les infections vaginales se présentent plus souvent avant la puberté, parce que la muqueuse du vagin impubère est tapissée d'une couche épithéliale très mince et que les sécrétions vaginales sont neutres au lieu d'être acides comme c'est le cas pour les adultes. Comme un épithélium vaginal épais et une propriété acide protègent contre les infections, l'enfant demeure généralement plus exposée à l'infection vaginale.

Vulvo-vaginite non gonococcique

Étiologie, manifestations cliniques, traitement et pronostic.   Tout agent pathogène, tel que bactérie, virus, parasite ou champignon, peut causer une vaginite non gonococcique.

Si une fillette n'est pas propre, s'introduit des corps étrangers dans le vagin ou souffre d'oxyurose, la vulvo-vaginite peut en résulter.

Si la vaginite ne cède pas au traitement, le médecin doit s'inquiéter de la présence d'un corps étranger, cause d'irritation et d'infection subséquente.

Des organes génitaux rouges et œdématiés, une sécrétion vaginale et, dans certains cas, une mauvaise odeur, peuvent indiquer une vulvo-vaginite.

Le *traitement* est à la fois systémique et local. Il faut améliorer l'état de santé de l'enfant et trouver la cause primaire de l'infection. Les organes génitaux doivent être rigoureusement propres. Si l'agent causal est le Candida Albicans qui cause aussi le muguet, on applique localement du Mycostatin ou une solution à 1% de violet de gentiane. On peut aussi administrer le Mycostatin par voie systémique. On traite les infections bactériennes à l'aide d'antibiotiques spécifiques. Tout corps étranger doit être enlevé et on traite l'oxyurose si c'est indiqué. La disparition de la cause et un traitement approprié assurent la guérison dans la plupart des cas.

Vaginite gonococcique

Étiologie, manifestations cliniques et diagnostic.   Le *gonocoque*, agent causal de la gonorrhée, peut pénétrer dans le vagin de l'enfant au moment de la naissance, par les mains contaminées des personnes qui assistent à l'accouchement. Plus tard la mère peut contaminer son bébé. L'infection peut aussi être communiquée par des objets fraîchement contaminés. La sécrétion varie d'une sérosité claire et aqueuse à un mucus épais, jaunâtre et purulent. On note une rougeur de la vulve et du vagin généralement accompagnée de dysurie, de fièvre et d'une excoriation de la peau des cuisses.

On établit le *diagnostic* d'après les résultats de l'analyse des sécrétions du vagin ou du col de l'utérus.

Complications et traitement.   Les *complications* sont beaucoup moins fréquentes chez les enfants que chez les adultes.

Le *traitement* général consiste à observer une propreté méticuleuse. La pénicilline demeure le médicament le plus fréquemment utilisé. L'enfant doit subir un autre examen bactériologique deux semaines après la fin du traitement.

Soins infirmiers.   Pendant qu'elle baigne un enfant, l'infirmière doit examiner les organes génitaux pour dépister les sécrétions et en avertir le médecin. Dans les institutions et à domicile, la douche demeure préférable à la baignoire, étant donné que les mesures de désinfection ne sont pas toujours suivies.

On isole l'enfant jusqu'à sa guérison complète. L'infirmière doit appliquer rigoureusement la technique d'isolement pour ne pas transmettre l'infection à d'autres enfants et ne pas se contaminer elle-même. La fillette ne doit pas retourner à la garderie ou à l'école maternelle avant que l'infection soit complètement guérie.

Pronostic. Le pronostic demeure bon avec un traitement adéquat; sans traitement, l'infection peut persister longtemps, quelquefois jusqu'à la puberté.

STRABISME

On rencontre deux sortes de strabisme: le strabisme paralytique et le strabisme non paralytique. Le strabisme *paralytique* est caractérisé par une atteinte d'un ou de plusieurs groupes musculaires à la suite d'un traumatisme, d'une paralysie congénitale ou d'une compression nerveuse. L'enfant est incapable de bouger l'œil malade ou il manque totalement de contrôle sur les mouvements oculaires. L'angle de dérivation entre les deux yeux varie avec les mouvements oculaires et aucune fusion de l'image n'est possible. Un œil bouge et l'autre reste immobile. Le traitement de cette sorte de strabisme reste peu encourageant.

Le strabisme *non paralytique* se caractérise par un mauvais alignement des yeux. Les deux yeux bougent en même temps et l'angle de dérivation ne varie pas.

Le strabisme non paralytique peut être convergent (regarde en dedans), divergent (regarde à l'extérieur) ou vertical (les yeux ne sont pas à la même hauteur).

Le *strabisme convergent* s'avère le plus fréquent, mais on ne peut le reconnaître avant l'âge de six mois.

Le strabisme peut aussi être *monoculaire* (un seul œil dévie) ou *alternatif* (l'un et l'autre œil dévient); le strabisme d'*accomodation* est dû à l'hypermétropie.

L'enfant normal semble très souvent présenter un strabisme à la naissance, et ceci peut persister jusqu'à l'âge de six mois, moment où la coordination oculaire se perfectionne. D'autres enfants semblent souffrir de strabisme parce qu'ils présentent un épicanthus (pli cutané du côté interne de l'œil). Cette dernière affection est appelée « faux strabisme » et aucun traitement n'est nécessaire.

L'enfant âgé de plus de six mois qui présente un strabisme doit être examiné par un médecin. Il faut agir avant la fin de la première année (entre 6-9 mois serait l'idéal), car les réflexes qui règlent la fusion de l'image se développent durant cette période et la macula (tache jaune) devient le centre principal de la rétine.

L'enfant qui louche voit deux images différentes (diplopie). Le cerveau réagit en supprimant une de ces images et fait usage de l'œil qui voit le mieux. La région du cerveau qui régit la vision de l'œil inutilisé arrêtera alors de se développer. Si on ne prend pas, au plus tôt, les mesures correctives appropriées, il s'ensuivra une perte de la vision de l'œil le plus faible, ce qui constitue l'*amblyopie de suppression*. Le traitement chirurgical, appliqué alors, ne sera fait que pour rétablir l'esthétique du visage afin d'éviter à l'enfant l'effet traumatisant des moqueries des camarades d'école.

Certains facteurs peuvent accélérer l'évolution du strabisme: perturbation émotive, débilité, peur, milieu.

La cause la plus fréquente du strabisme demeure l'*hypermétropie*.

— Normalement, *quand on regarde au loin,* les yeux sont parallèles (6 mètres).
L'hypermétrope, dont l'œil est congénitalement trop petit, doit faire un effort d'accommodation pour voir clairement à cette distance.

— Normalement, *quand on fixe de près,* les yeux convergent légèrement.
L'œil hypermétrope, qui doit déjà faire un effort d'accomodation dans la vision normale, devra effectuer un double effort dans la vision rapprochée. Quand l'effort devient trop important, l'équilibre entre la fusion et l'accommodation est perturbé et le strabisme apparaît.

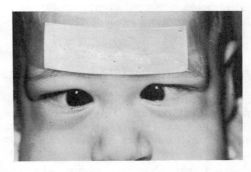

Figure 18-5. Strabisme convergent bilatéral. (Dr Arnold Patz de Baltimore dans Schaffer: *Diseases of the Newborn.*)

Manifestations cliniques et traitements.
L'enfant atteint de strabisme peut être incapable de synchroniser quand il regarde dans certaines directions. Il décrit difficilement ce qu'il voit. Il peut pencher la tête pour réussir à voir une seule image ou fermer un œil pour éliminer l'une des deux images. Il peut paraître malhabile, trébucher ou être incapable de saisir des objets avec précision.

Le premier pas dans la correction du strabisme est d'empêcher la double vision, en obstruant l'œil qui fixe, ce qui oblige l'œil faible à travailler. Il faut laisser le bandeau sur l'œil toute la journée et s'assurer qu'il le recouvre complètement. On peut aussi utiliser des lunettes dont on recouvre l'une des lentilles. Ce traitement peut être nécessaire pendant des semaines et des mois, pendant que l'enfant s'efforce de développer l'œil qui dévie. Le bandeau couvrant l'œil sain ou les lunettes opaques peuvent se révéler traumatisants pour l'enfant qui a de la difficulté à voir adéquatement. Il refuse parfois de les porter et les parents ont besoin d'aide pour imaginer les moyens d'encourager l'enfant à le faire (exemple: jouer au pirate). Dès l'âge de 14 mois les enfants peuvent porter des lunettes pour corriger l'hypermétropie et l'exercice de leurs muscles oculaires est efficace pour développer la fusion des images.

On entreprend le traitement chirurgical chez les enfants dont l'état ne s'est pas amélioré à la suite des exercices ou du port des lunettes. On pratique l'opération à l'âge de trois ou quatre ans, si l'on veut obtenir le parallélisme des yeux et la vision binoculaire. La chirurgie consiste à allonger ou à raccourcir les structures extra-oculaires. Certains ophtalmologistes la pratiquent d'emblée, et très tôt dans la vie, sans essayer les traitements correcteurs dont nous venons de parler.

L'enfant est ordinairement hospitalisé pour subir une cure de strabisme. Sa mère devrait le préparer avant son entrée à l'hôpital. L'enfant s'inquiète souvent de l'intégrité de ses yeux à la suite de l'intervention et il est bon de lui mentionner que le chirurgien opère à l'extérieur de l'œil et qu'il ne court aucun risque de perdre la vue. On explique également à la mère que la solution employée pour désinfecter la région opératoire peut teinter la peau en rouge et que ceci peut la surprendre au retour de la salle d'opération.

Autrefois, les patients gardaient le lit pendant plusieurs jours après l'opération, dans l'obscurité la plus complète. Aujourd'hui, le médecin n'obstrue qu'un œil (et pas toujours) et le patient peut ordinairement quitter l'hôpital dès le lendemain de l'intervention.

Si, par hasard, les deux yeux doivent être obstrués, l'enfant doit en être averti par le chirurgien avant l'opération (si c'est possible) et il est bon que sa mère demeure près du lit lors de son réveil.

Soins infirmiers.　L'infirmière doit aider autant la mère que l'enfant à comprendre l'importance des exercices oculaires et du port des lunettes recommandés par l'ophtalmologiste. L'enfant doit apprendre comment protéger ses lunettes quand il joue et comment les entretenir. Un verre incassable est essentiel pour les lentilles et on doit remplacer immédiatement une lentille abimée. L'enfant résiste souvent au port de lunettes, étant donné qu'il voit moins bien en les portant, puisqu'elles visent à faire travailler l'œil faible. Il faut lui fournir des explications détaillées et adaptées à sa compréhension.

Après l'intervention chirurgicale, sa mère ou l'infirmière l'empêche gentiment d'enlever ses pansements. Pour le distraire, on peut lui lire ou lui raconter des histoires, lui faire écouter la radio et des enregistrements sur disque.

On lui donne une alimentation régulière aussitôt qu'il n'a plus de nausées. Les enfants, dans ce cas, aiment qu'on leur dise ce qu'ils mangent pendant que la mère ou l'infirmière les nourrit. Après l'opération, l'infirmière peut expliquer à la mère les exercices recommandés par l'ophtalmologiste. Elle peut aussi aviser l'institutrice de la maternelle ou l'infirmière de l'école que les exercices doivent être continués régulièrement.

Pronostic.　Plus tôt on entreprend le traitement, meilleurs sont les résultats et les chances d'éviter les troubles de la personnalité. Si l'acuité visuelle a été affectée, une réduction définitive de la vue est à prévoir. Un résultat esthétique garde cependant toute son importance.

AMYGDALECTOMIE ET ADÉNOÏDECTOMIE

Les amygdales et les adénoïdes sont des organes lymphoïdes qui servent de défense contre les infections des voies respiratoires. L'exérèse de ces formations est nécessaire dans certains cas bien précis, mais il n'est pas indiqué de la pratiquer systématiquement comme on le préconisait il y a quelques années. L'usage d'antibiotiques contre les infections des voies respiratoires a rendu possible d'obvier à l'amygdalectomie et à l'adénoïdectomie chez beaucoup d'enfants.

Les *indications* habituelles sont l'amygdalite aiguë franchement récidivante, l'amygdalite chronique grave ou l'otite moyenne à répétition accompagnée d'une adénopathie satellite, les abcès péri- ou rétro-amygdaliens, une maladie auto-immune comme le rhumatisme articulaire aigu ou la gloméarulo-néphrite, pour essayer d'en prévenir les récidives.

On doit se souvenir que le amygdales sont normalement plus grosses durant la seconde enfance qu'au cours des années qui suivent. Chez de nombreux enfants, cependant, les amygdales restent petites et logées derrière les piliers du voile du palais.

L'obstruction à la respiration et à la déglutition semble plus souvent due aux végétations adénoïdes qu'aux amygdales. Les adénoïdes, spécialement sur la paroi postérieure ou la voûte du naso-pharynx, peuvent s'hypertro-

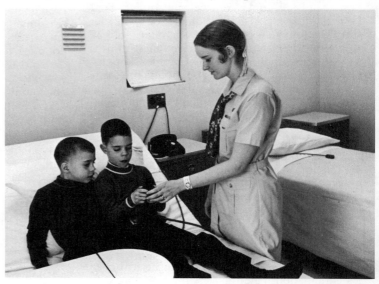

A

Figure 18-6. *A)* Les enfants manipulent les contrôles électriques du lit articulé et se familiarisent avec l'environnement hospitalier. (A. Rosenthal: *Today's Health,* août 1970, p. 54. Photo par Tom Bergman. *B)* Après avoir inspecté le matériel, on joue à « faire semblant ». (B. N. Abbott, P. Hansen, et K. Lewis: *Am. J. Nursing.:* 70(11):2360, nov. 1970.)

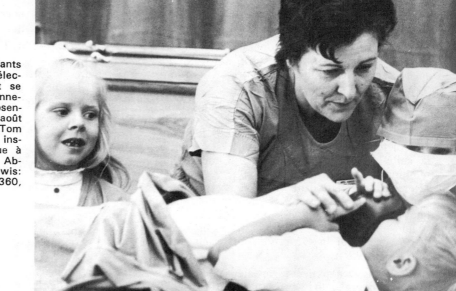

B

phier, diminuer le calibre du nasopharynx et obstruer la trompe d'Eustache, provoquant souvent une otite séreuse. Les manifestations cliniques incluent la respiration par la bouche, la rhinite chronique et quelquefois une expression faciale terne (facies adénoïdien). La voix peut être assourdie et nasale. Une toux persistante peut se manifester. L'otite moyenne chronique adhésive ou suppurée se produit très souvent et l'enfant devient sourd, à moins que la trompe d'Eustache ne soit dégagée.

La décision de pratiquer l'amygdalectomie ou l'adénoïdectomie dépend de l'état de ces tissus. On enlève habituellement les amygdales et les végétations adénoïdes en même temps, quoique l'état de l'enfant puisse indiquer qu'une ablation séparée est recommandable.

Âge pour l'opération. L'amygdalectomie et l'adénoïdectomie sont rarement nécessaires avant l'âge préscolaire. On retarde cependant l'opération aussi longtemps que possible pour deux raisons: 1) l'affection peut se corriger d'elle-même, puisqu'il se produit normalement une atrophie de ces structures durant l'âge scolaire et 2) l'opération est psychologiquement plus traumatisante pour l'enfant d'âge préscolaire que pour l'écolier.

Moment idéal pour la chirurgie. On peut pratiquer l'amygdalectomie et l'adénoïdectomie à n'importe quel moment de l'année, depuis que l'immunisation contre la poliomyélite est devenue une pratique répandue. Les grippes et les maux de gorge sont plus courants en hiver, mais des agents antibactériens sont administrés pour réduire le danger de telles affections secondaires.

On doit attendre quatorze à vingt et un jours après une infection aiguë, pour pratiquer l'amygdalectomie et l'adénoïdectomie. Si l'enfant souffre d'une infection chronique des amygdales et des végétations adénoïdes ou s'il présente une maladie auto-immune, le médecin prescrit un antibiotique, pendant quelques jours, avant et après l'opération.

Préparation opératoire. Il faut expliquer aux parents la nature de l'opération et les aider à préparer l'enfant pour son admission à l'hôpital. On doit expliquer au petit ce que sont les amygdales, lui dire où elles logent et bien spécifier que rien d'autres ne sera touché. On doit le renseigner sur le genre d'opération qu'il doit subir, lui dire qu'il aura mal à la gorge, mais que ses parents seront là au retour de la salle d'opération. L'infirmière de la clinique ou du bureau du médecin peut aider la mère, si celle-ci ne sait comment préparer l'enfant en des termes adaptés à son dévelop-

pement. Si la mère semble incapable de le faire, l'infirmière joue ici un rôle de suppléance, tout en tenant compte des réactions des parents dont les craintes égalent peut-être celles de l'enfant. Il est important de demander à l'enfant ce qu'il a compris et de lui permettre de jouer à pratiquer l'intervention sur une poupée. On peut alors voir ce qu'il a mal interprété et déceler des peurs spécifiques telles: ne plus s'éveiller, saigner à mort, etc . . . Tout ce qui a été dit précédemment s'applique à n'importe quelle intervention chirurgicale.

On recherche habituellement le temps de saignement et de coagulation avant l'opération. On utilise un barbiturique associé à de l'atropine, comme prémédication. On exclut les aliments et les liquides plusieurs heures avant l'opération.

Soins postopératoires. À son retour de la salle d'opération, on place l'enfant en position déclive pour faciliter le drainage des sécrétions et empêcher qu'il n'aspire ses vomissements. On doit l'observer constamment jusqu'à ce qu'il soit réveillé, fréquemment par la suite et ce, pendant plusieurs heures. Son pouls – vitesse et qualité – ses vomissements et une tendance à déglutir fréquemment peuvent révéler une hémorragie. Le matériel nécessaire pour arrêter l'hémorragie et l'appareil aspirateur doivent être prêts pour les cas d'urgence. Le repos au lit est indiqué pour le reste de la journée et des périodes de repos sont nécessaires au cours des jours suivants.

De la glace broyée peut être donnée quand l'enfant s'éveille. Des sucettes de glace colorées sont plus attrayantes pour l'enfant et l'encouragent à prendre plus de liquide. Certains médecins interdisent l'absorption de glace, car les mouvements de succion peuvent endommager les tissus opérés. On commence à hydrater l'enfant aussitôt que la nausée subséquente à l'anesthésie a disparu, d'abord avec des jus de fruits synthétiques non acides et plus tard avec des jus de fruits naturels qui sont plus irritants pour la gorge que les précédents. Dans plusieurs hôpitaux, on donne à l'enfant du lait et de la crème glacée durant la période postopératoire immédiate. Toutefois, ces aliments sont considérés aussi comme des milieux de culture excellents, favorisant l'infection; aussi sont-ils bannis par plusieurs médecins. On tente d'éviter tout contact avec les sources d'infection. L'aspirine peut être administrée quoique l'acétaminophène (Tylénol-Tempra) lui est préféré si l'enfant a tendance à saigner. Un collier de glace appliqué contre la gorge diminue la douleur et le risque d'hémorragie, mais certains enfants tolèrent mal le poids du sac sur leur gorge douloureuse.

Complications. Les complications possibles sont l'hémorragie postopératoire, l'abcès pulmonaire, la septicémie et la pneumonie. L'hémorragie, la complication la plus commune, peut être contrôlée par tamponnement ou ligature. L'enfant qui déglutit constamment en dormant ou qui vomit du sang rouge, saigne probablement et le médecin doit en être avisé. Le contrôle régulier des signes vitaux peut permettre de déceler un état de choc progressif. Une transfusion peut être indiquée.

Réaction de l'enfant à l'opération. Les enfants qui sont capables d'intégrer cette expérience et qui ont peu de séquelles émotives malheureuses sont habituellement ceux qui ont été capables d'avoir confiance dans le personnel médical et paramédical, de s'extérioriser librement tant avant qu'après l'intervention et qui ont été préparés efficacement à l'hospitalisation, à la chirurgie et aux suites postopératoires. On a pu relier la préparation psychologique préopératoire ainsi que la présence continue de la mère à une diminution marquée du temps d'anesthésie et de la fréquence des hémorragies postopératoires.

Sortie de l'enfant de l'hôpital. On remet aux parents des instructions précises à propos des soins à prodiguer à l'enfant à la maison et au sujet des symptômes qui indiqueraient qu'il doit être vu immédiatement par le médecin. De tels symptômes sont de constants maux d'oreilles, de fréquentes déglutitions et des vomissements de sang; vers le 10e jour postopératoire le danger d'hémorragie augmente légèrement. L'enseignement devrait inclure: 1) des conseils sur le repos à observer, les liquides et les aliments à donner, et la nécessité d'éviter les infections, 2) l'information au sujet des médicaments ordonnés par le médecin, et 3) si l'enfant n'est pas sous la surveillance d'un médecin, le nom et le numéro de téléphone du chirurgien qui doit être appelé, au cas où la mère aurait besoin de conseils ou de soins urgents pour l'enfant, et l'adresse de l'endroit où l'enfant devra être amené pour des examens de contrôle.

MALADIES CONTAGIEUSES

L'univers de l'enfant d'âge préscolaire s'élargit. Il participe à des activités où il rencontre d'autres enfants, et par conséquent, il entre en contact avec les causes de maladies contagieuses. Quelques-unes de ces maladies peuvent être évitées par une immunisation; d'au-

tres qui ne peuvent être prévenues surviennent plus fréquemment dans ce groupe d'âge que dans aucun autre. Cependant, des complications sérieuses, communes dans le passé, deviennent moins fréquentes actuellement, par suite du diagnostic et du traitement précoces.

Les taux de morbidité et de mortalité dues aux maladies contagieuses ont décliné d'une façon spectaculaire durant les dernières décades; cependant, des recherches continues et leur application en médecine préventive et curative demeurent toujours nécessaires.

Définitions. Les définitions suivantes sont présentées comme une révision des éléments que l'étudiant a probablement déjà appris précédemment.

Une maladie contagieuse est causée par un agent infectieux ou son produit toxique et se transmet d'une personne infectée, d'un animal malade, ou de matériel contaminé, à une personne en santé. Les *sources d'infection* peuvent être l'homme, les insectes, les animaux ou les facteurs environnants, tels que la poussière, l'eau ou les aliments contaminés. *L'agent causal* peut être une bactérie, une levure, une moisissure, un protozoaire, un virus et un rickettsie.

Les maladies contagieuses peuvent être endémiques, épidémiques ou pandémiques. Une maladie *endémique* est celle qui se manifeste chez un nombre limité de personnes, dans une région donnée et à un taux relativement constant. Une maladie *épidémique* se manifeste par une incidence soudaine et importante d'une maladie particulière dans une région donnée. Une maladie est *pandémique* lorsque de nombreux cas se manifestent simultanément sur une grande aire géographique.

La *virulence* se définit comme la capacité du micro-organisme à transmettre la maladie ou comme l'aptitude du microbe à rendre inefficaces les défenses que lui oppose la personne infectée. Une contamination récente influence dans une large mesure la virulence. La période *d'incubation* d'une maladie contagieuse est celle qui s'écoule entre la contamination et l'apparition des symptômes initiaux. La période de *communicabilité* est le temps pendant lequel une personne infectée peut transmettre la maladie, directement ou indirectement, à une autre personne.

Un *porteur de germes* est un individu ou un animal qui porte en lui le germe spécifique d'une maladie sans en manifester les symptômes, quoiqu'il puisse contaminer son entourage. Un « contact » est une personne ou un

(Suite page 534.)

PLANCHE 3

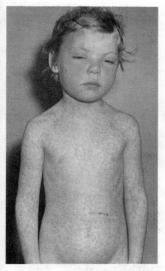

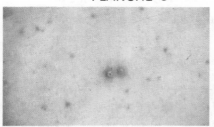

2. Varicelle. Noter les différents stades des lésions: (macules, papules et vésicules présentes au même moment). (Courtoisie du Dr. P.F. Lucchesi.)

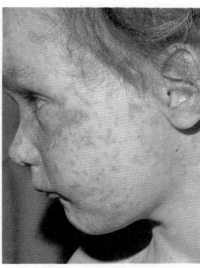

1. Rougeole. Des macules petites, rondes ou ovales, rouge-brun, partiellement rattachées, disséminées sur toute la surface du corps. Photophobie. Catarrhe oculo-nasal.*

3. Rubéole. (Courtoisie de Korting, G.W., *Hautkrankheiten bei Kindern und Jugendlichen*. F.K. Schattauer Verlag, 1969.)

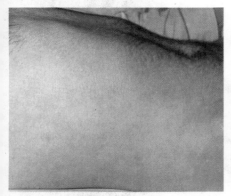

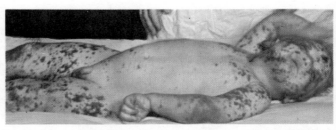

4. Fièvre scarlatine. Inflammation diffuse rose-rouge de la peau avec des lésions papulaires punctiformes. L'éruption est plus apparente au niveau des plis cutanés.*

5. Meningococcémie fulgurante. Apparition des premiers symptômes 36 heures avant l'admission avec vomissements et hyperthermie. Mort 8 heures après l'admission. (Nelson, Vaughn, Mckay: *Textbook of Pediatrics.* 9e éd. Philadelphie, W.B. Saunders Co., 1969, p. 628.)

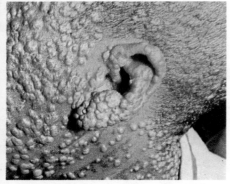

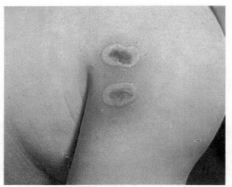

6. Variole. Éruption généralisée, avec des pustules siégeant sur une base érythémateuse, associée à des symptômes systémiques graves. Contrairement à la varicelle, toutes les lésions se développent en même temps.*

7. Vaccin antivariolique. Entre le septième et le neuvième jour après l'inoculation, la vésicule initiale se transforme en une grosse pustule nécrotique. La région environnante prend l'apparence de l'érysipèle et on constate une adénopathie satellite.*

* Extrait de *Frieboes & Schonfeld's Color Atlas of Dermatology*, par J. Kimmig & M. Janner. Édition américaine traduite et revisée par H. Goldschmidt. Georg. Thieme Verlag, Stuttgart, 1966.)

Tableau 18.1　Maladies contagieuses

MALADIE	INCUBATION	PÉRIODE CONTAGIEUSE	AGENT CAUSAL	MODE DE CONTAMINATION	MANIFESTATIONS CLINIQUES
Coqueluche	5 à 21 jours	Quatre à six semaines après le début de la maladie	Bordetella pertussis. Cocco-bacille de Bordet et Jengou	Contact direct ou indirect avec sécrétions du larynx et des bronches de personnes infectées	Maladie qui atteint surtout l'enfant de moins de 3 ans. Coryza, toux sèche qui augmente pendant environ 2 semaines. Généralement, elle se manifeste surtout la nuit par de fortes quintes de toux au cours d'une seule expiration, ensuite par une inspiration rapide et profonde (chant du coq) suivie d'une autre quinte. L'accès se termine fréquemment par l'expectoration d'un mucus limpide et adhérent, très contagieux pendant les premiers jours. Souvent les quintes typiques n'apparaissent pas chez le jeune bébé et chez l'adulte. La période de toux paroxystique peut durer 1 ou 2 mois. La dyspnée et la fièvre peuvent se manifester. Des vomissements sont possibles après la toux. La lymphocytose est présente
Diphtérie Croup	2 à 5 jours ou plus longue	Plusieurs heures avant le début de la maladie jusqu'à ce que les bactéries disparaissent des voies respiratoires (2 à 4 semaines)	Corynebacterirum Diphteriæ ou Bacille de Klebs-Lœffler	Mucosités émanant des voies respiratoires d'un malade ou d'un porteur de germes	Manifestations systémiques et locales. Membranes recouvrant les voies respiratoires supérieures, nez ou pharynx et larynx, entourées d'une zone rouge terne à l'endroit envahi par les bacilles. Toux rauque et grasse avec respiration striduleuse. Toxine cause du malaise et de la fièvre. (Les toxines ont une affinité pour les tissus nerveux et cardiaques.) Paralysie respiratoire et paralysies musculaires multiples possibles

TRAITEMENT ET SOINS INFIRMIERS	COMPLICATIONS	IMMUNITÉ
Symptomatique. On peut donner du sérum anti-coquelucheux. On doit protéger l'enfant des infections secondaires. Les antibiotiques peuvent diminuer la période de contagiosité, mais ne chargent pas le cours de la maladie. Ils aident à prévenir les infections secondaires. Repos mental et physique pour prévenir les crises de toux. Air humide tiède. L'oxygène peut être nécessaire. Refroidissements à éviter. Repas légers et fréquents pour maintenir le statut nutritif. Réalimentation si l'enfant vomit. Des anti-émétiques s'avèrent utiles. Des doses modérées de sédatif peuvent être administrées pour calmer l'enfant	Très sérieuse maladie durant l'enfance à cause des complications de broncho-pneumonie. L'otite moyenne, la malnutrition, la bronchiectasie et l'atélectasie peuvent se présenter. Une hémorragie peut se manifester pendant les crises aiguës de toux. L'encéphalite est possible	*Immunisation active:* vaccin vivant atténué. Peut être administré combiné: diphtérie, coqueluche et tétanos. *Immunisation passive:* la gamma-globuline préparée à partir d'un sérum humain hyperimmunisé. Aucune preuve d'immunisation trans-placentaire. *Immunisation spontanée:* la maladie confère une immunité assez longue, mais une seconde attaque peut se produire à l'âge adulte. *Test:* titrage d'agglutinine et fixation du complément et test de protection des souris
Les buts du traitement sont de neutraliser les toxines à l'aide d'antitoxine diphtérique et d'antibiotiques afin d'éliminer les bacilles et d'empêcher l'obstruction de la respiration. Des anatoxines sont administrées pour immuniser les contacts. Repos strict au lit. Gargarismes et désinfectants de la gorge peuvent être ordonnés. Le gavage ou l'administration parentérale d'aliments peut devenir nécessaire en cas de paralysie. Surveillance de la détresse respiratoire et des paralysies musculaires. L'équipement pour l'aspiration devrait être sous la main. Oxygène et trachéotomie d'urgence peuvent s'avérer nécessaires en cas de paralysie respiratoire	La complication immédiate: obstruction respiratoire par les membranes ou œdème laryngé. L'absorption de la toxine peut provoquer une atteinte à tous les niveaux du système nerveux: paralysie respiratoire ou motrice. Myocardite	*Immunisation active:* l'anatoxine de Ramon, associée à d'autres antigènes dans D.C.T. *Immunisation passive:* (1) le nouveau-né l'acquiert par voie placentaire d'une mère immunisée; elle dure environ 6 mois. (2) Injection d'antitoxine diphtérique; l'effet dure 2-3 semaines. *Immunisation spontanée:* la maladie confère une immunité habituellement persistante. *Le test de Schick.* Injection intradermique de la toxine de la diphtérie. Si la personne est immunisée, il n'y a aucune réaction. Si elle n'est pas immunisée, une vésicule se produit. Test positif: anatoxine nécessaire. Culture des sécrétions nasopharyngées

Tableau 18.1 *Maladies contagieuses (suite)*

MALADIE	INCUBATION	PÉRIODE CONTAGIEUSE	AGENT CAUSAL	MODE DE CONTA-MINATION	MANIFESTATIONS CLINIQUES
Grippe (Influenza)	24 à 72 heures	Inconnue, probablement au début et durant la période fébrile; ordinairement 3 jours	Virus du type A et B et sous-type C	Infection aérogène – contact direct – gouttelettes de sécrétions respiratoires. Réservoir humain	Manifestations respiratoires. Début soudain avec frisson, fièvre, douleurs musculaires. Coryza et toux pénible. Si l'infection est sévère et s'étend aux voies respiratoires, la dyspnée peut se développer
Hépatite infectieuse	Type A: 14 à 20 jours. Type B: environ 3 mois.	Peu de jours avant, à un mois après le début. Type B: on l'ignore; peut-être pendant des années	Virus du type A – pénètre par voie digestive: liquides ou solides contaminés. Virus du type B – hépatite sérique: par voie parentérale. Seringue contaminée. Sang-sérum-plasma contaminés	Souche A: contamination orale par les excréments, aliments, lait ou eau contaminés. Souche B: sang et sérum contaminés. Réservoir humain	Les manifestations peuvent être légères ou sévères; varient d'une fièvre légère avec anorexie, malaise général, nausées, vomissements, goût amer dans la bouche à des douleurs abdominales avec un ictère léger ou grave, un coma et la mort. La leucopénie se manifeste précocement. On trouve de la bile dans les urines; les selles sont de la couleur de l'argile (elles sont contagieuses). Les tests de la fonction hépatique s'avèrent utiles pour le diagnostic

TRAITEMENT ET SOINS INFIRMIERS	COMPLICATIONS	IMMUNITÉ
Symptomatique. Repos au lit et liquides en abondance. Les antibiotiques et les sulfamides peuvent empêcher les infections secondaires. Des antipyrétiques, des potions pour contrôler la toux et des analgésiques peuvent être administrés	Dans les cas sévères, l'œdème pulmonaire et la défaillance cardiaque. Les contaminations secondaires peuvent produire l'infection bactérienne des voies respiratoires surtout chez les jeunes enfants, les vieillards et les débiles	*Immunisation active:* vaccins *Immunisation passive:* aucune *Immunisation spontanée:* on ne connaît pas la durée de l'immunité à la suite de la maladie *Test:* aucun
Symptomatique. Le repos au lit constitue le traitement de base. Diète hypercalorique, riche en glucides et en protéines et pauvre en lipides. On sert les aliments en petites portions attrayantes et fréquemment. Les raisons principales d'une hospitalisation sont des vomissements continus et un état toxique qui se développe. Les liquides peuvent être administrés parentéralement. On doit prendre des précautions entériques: l'enfant est sous surveillance stricte, le bassin de lit est stérilisé après chaque usage. On utilise des gants à jeter après usage pour manipuler les récipients contenant des selles, pour administrer les lavements et pour faire les prélèvements de sang. On recommande les seringues et les aiguilles à jeter après usage pour les prélèvements de sang et la thérapeutique parentérale. On protège les voies respiratoires d'une infection éventuelle. On évite d'administrer de la morphine, des barbituriques et des sulfamides qui surchargent lourdement la fonction hépatique perturbée. La somnolence inhabituelle, la confusion mentale et l'anorexie extrême indiquent la détérioration de la fonction hépatique. De fortes doses de stéroïdes peuvent arrêter le progrès de la maladie si une obstruction irréversible du foie ne s'est pas manifestée. *Prévention:* lavage méticuleux des mains après évacuation intestinale, propreté des toilettes (bol et siège), stérilisation de la nourriture et de l'eau avant leur usage. Ne pas accepter comme donneurs de sang des gens ayant déjà souffert d'ictère. Stérilisation du matériel d'injection	Rechutes possibles. La fonction hépatique peut rester perturbée pendant quelque temps. L'atrophie du foie (fatale) demeure exceptionnelle	*Immunisation passive:* la gamma-globuline combinée après une période de contact connue. *Immunisation spontanée:* le degré d'immunité acquise par la maladie est inconnu. *Test:* aucun

Tableau 18.1 *Maladies contagieuses (suite)*

MALADIE	INCUBATION	PÉRIODE CONTAGIEUSE	AGENT CAUSAL	MODE DE CONTA-MINATION	MANIFESTATIONS CLINIQUES
Infection à streptocoque hémolytique (angine streptococcique et fièvre scarlatine)	1 à 5 jours	Du début à la guérison: 2 à 3 semaines au total. Plus longtemps parfois	Streptocoque hémolytique Bêta, groupe A	Transmission directe ou indirecte par les sécrétions contaminées du nez et de la gorge. Par lésions cutanées	Les symptômes initiaux de la fièvre scarlatine se manifestent par une angine streptococcique. Le microbe peut avoir son siège dans une blessure ou dans une brûlure. Les toxines produites sont absorbées par le flux sanguin. La fièvre scarlatine se manifeste par la céphalée, la fièvre élevée à 39,5° C −40°C pendant plusieurs jours, un pouls rapide, la soif, les vomissements, la lymphadénite ou le délire. L'angine est manifeste, accompagnée d'une cellulite de la gorge. La langue est recouverte d'un enduit blanchâtre, les bords en sont rouges. Elle devient rouge-vif (framboisée) après 3-4 jours; rouge et lisse par desquamation au 8e jour (vernissée). L'éruption comprend un énanthème (pharynx surtout) et exanthème d'abord, au niveau des plis, puis se généralisant, épargnant généralement la face. Couleur rouge franc sans intervalles de peau saine. S'efface légèrement à la pression. Desquamation en lambeaux pendant 2 à 5 semaines
Oreillons (parotidite infectieuse) ou maladie ourlienne	14 à 21 jours	Un à six jours avant les premiers symptômes et jusqu'à ce que l'inflammation disparaisse	Virus ourlien: il peut être isolé dans la salive, le sang et le L C R	Contact direct ou indirect avec la sécrétion salivaire de la personne infectée. Réservoir humain seulement	Les glandes salivaires sont principalement affectées, surtout les glandes parotides. L'orifice du canal de Sténon est rouge et œdématié. Douleur et gonflement apparaissent d'abord unilatéralement, ensuite bilatéralement. L'enfant peut avoir des difficultés à avaler, des maux de tête, de la fièvre ou autres malaises. La localisation nerveuse est possible

TRAITEMENT ET SOINS INFIRMIERS	COMPLICATIONS	IMMUNITÉ
La pénicilline, les tétracyclines, une quantité adéquate de liquide, repos au lit, analgésiques. Les soins de la bouche s'avèrent importants. On établit la diète au goût de l'enfant: liquide, molle ou régulière. Chez les enfants plus âgés on pratique des irrigations de la gorge avec de l'eau salée tiède. On augmente l'humidité pour les enfants atteints d'infection sévère des voies respiratoires supérieures. On fait des applications chaudes ou froides sur les ganglions lymphatico-cervicaux	1. Complications dues à la toxine: R.A.A. glomérulonéphrite polyarthrite 2. L'érysipèle, la fièvre puerpérale streptococcique sont dues au streptocoque 3. Infections également causées par le streptocoque ou une surinfection bactérienne: adénite, otite, mastoïdite, ostéomyélite, péritonite, septicémie, impétigo contagieux, infections de plaies cutanées	*Immunisation active:* aucune *Immunisation passive:* aucune *Immunisation spontanée:* l'immunité contre la toxine érythrogénique semble permanente, mais une deuxième scarlatine est possible par une forme immunologique différente de la toxine. L'immunisation contre le streptocoque lui-même est actuellement inexistante *Test:* la réaction de Dick consiste en injection intradermique de toxine streptococcique. Chez les personnes atteintes, l'érythème apparaît lors de l'injection. Les personnes immunisées ne présentent pas de réaction
Application locale chaude ou froide sur les glandes salivaires pour soulager la douleur. On donne du liquide ou des aliments mous. Les aliments acides (ex.: jus d'orange) peuvent augmenter la douleur. Repos au lit jusqu'à ce que l'inflammation disparaisse.	Les complications sont moins fréquentes chez les enfants que chez les adultes. La méningo-encéphalite, l'inflammation des ovaires ou des testicules, la surdité peuvent en résulter	*Immunisation active:* vaccin antiourlien (vivant atténué) *Immunisation passive:* 1) l'immunité trans-placentaire est possible pour les nouveau-nés. 2) la gamma-globuline plutôt qu'un sérum contenant des anticorps concentrés *Immunisation spontanée:* la maladie confère l'immunité permanente *Test* de fixation du complément – hémoagglutination

Tableau 18.1   *Maladies contagieuses (suite)*

MALADIE	INCUBATION	PÉRIODE CONTAGIEUSE	AGENT CAUSAL	MODE DE CONTAMINATION	MANIFESTATIONS CLINIQUES
Poliomyélite antérieure aiguë (paralysie infantile)	5 à 14 jours	Durant la période d'infection, aux derniers moments de la période d'incubation et la première semaine de la période aiguë	Virus. Types 1) (Brun-hilde) 2) Lansing 3) Leon	Contamination orale par les excrétions intestinales et pharyngiennes. Réservoir humain. Le lait peut servir de véhicule	Maladie grave. Le virus se fixe sur les cornes antérieures motrices de la moelle épinière ou sur les noyaux moteurs de bulbe rachidien. Pas de troubles sensitifs. Les types de poliomyélite incluent les formes: avortée, non paralytique, paralytique spinale et paralytique bulbaire. Les manifestations cliniques peuvent varier des formes anodines à celles très sévères, après la période asymptomatique suivant l'attaque initiale. Les symptômes ultérieurs incluent la céphalée, la nausée, les vomissements, les algies musculaires, la raideur de la nuque et de la colonne vertébrale, des changements dans les réflexes et la paralysie ordinairement asymétrique. Le signe du trépied montre l'atteinte méningée. L'examen du liquide céphalo-rachidien révèle une augmentation du nombre de protéines et de cellules, mais le liquide est rarement trouble
Rougeole	10 à 12 jours	3 à 4 jours avant l'éruption jusqu'à cinq jours après	Virus de la rougeole. Isolement du virus des sécrétions du nez et de la gorge	Contact direct ou indirect avec sécrétions respiratoires. La transmission aéroportée est probable en certains cas. Source humaine seulement. Centres urbains: épidémies relativement bénignes tous les 2 à 4 ans Régions rurales: épidémies moins fréquentes – plus graves Régions très isolées: (îles – Arctique) épidémies très rares – létalité élevée	Le fœtus peut contracter la rougeole dans l'utérus, si la mère a la maladie. Phase prodomique caractérisée par un catarrhe oculo-nasal fébrile et la présence du signe de Koplik à la face interne des joues. Les yeux sont rouges, larmoyants. L'enfant souffre de photophobie. Écoulement nasal, toux rauque, râles bronchiques. Koplik: 80% des malades. Température: 39,5°C pour 4-5 jours. Adénopathie. Éruption; 3e ou 4e jour. Des papules rouge foncé caractéristiques apparaissent d'abord à la face, s'étendent au corps et aux membres. Les papules disparaissent à la pression L'éruption pâlit après 2 jours. Desquamation après 5 jours

TRAITEMENT ET SOINS INFIRMIERS	COMPLICATIONS	IMMUNITÉ

Les parents autant que l'enfant ont besoin de réconfort et d'assurance, parce que le mot « polio » lui-même les épouvante. Le traitement et les soins infirmiers sont symptomatiques. Éviter la fatigue. Placer l'enfant sur un matelas rigide avec un support pour les pieds. Éviter la pression sur les orteils quand l'enfant est couché sur l'abdomen, en tirant le matelas par-dessus le pied du lit et en laissant les pieds pendre au-delà du bout du matelas; quand l'enfant est couché sur le dos, utiliser un support pour soutenir les pieds. Changer fréquemment le malade de position. Maintenir un bon alignement du corps. Donner une quantité d'aliments et de liquide appropriée à la gravité de la maladie. La physiothérapie peut être nécessaire ainsi que des applications de chaleur humide pour soulager les douleurs musculaires. Une thérapeutique est requise pour prévenir la contracture des muscles qui raccourcissent et atténuer l'incapacité résiduelle. La manipulation des extrémités affectées, pour les exercer à certains angles d'articulation, peut être tentée par l'infirmière avec la permission du médecin. Une prophylaxie antibactérienne doit être prescrite. La cathétérisation de la vessie distendue peut s'avérer nécessaire. Comme les selles contiennent le virus, elles doivent être considérées comme contagieuses. Dans la poliomyélite bulbaire, la thérapeutique consiste à maintenir le pharynx propre et à assurer un drainage postural pour empêcher l'aspiration des sécrétions. Parfois, l'alimentation par gavage, l'injection de liquide par voie parentérale, la trachéotomie, l'usage de l'appareil respirateur et l'apport d'oxygène sont nécessaires; il faut également prévenir l'infection intercurente. Une réhabilitation prolongée peut être utile, incluant l'usage de supports métalliques et/ou des interventions chirurgicales

Troubles émotifs, dilatation gastrique, méléna, paralysie transitoire de la vessie peuvent se présenter comme des complications. On peut considérer comme complications les séquelles paralytiques ordinairement unilatérales non disparues après 18 mois

Immunisation active: vaccin antipoliomyélitique: Sabin oral: virus vivants atténués
Immunisation passive: les nouveau-nés l'obtiennent par voie placentaire d'une mère immunisée. La gamma-globuline protège le sujet-contact
Immunisation spontanée: peut s'acquérir d'une infection apparente ou insoupçonnée
Test: recherche du virus dans la gorge et les selles. Le virus reste présent 3 à 6 semaines dans les selles. À l'époque des épidémies, les enfants ne devraient avoir que des contacts limités ou pas de contact du tout avec des personnes hors de la famille

Symptomatique. Garder l'enfant au lit jusqu'à ce que la fièvre et la toux disparaissent. Tamiser la lumière dans la chambre pour le confort de l'enfant. L'empêcher de toucher à ses yeux et utiliser une solution physiologique pour soulager l'irritation. Augmenter l'humidité dans la chambre pour soulager la toux. Encourager l'absorption de liquides pendant les accès de fièvre. Administrer la gamma-globuline pour modifier le cours de la maladie et réduire les complications. Combattre les complications par une thérapeutique antibactérienne

Varient avec le degré de sévérité de la crise. L'otite moyenne, la pneumonie, la trachéo-bronchite, la néphrite suivent une surinfection.
L'encéphalite due au virus morbilleux est possible et laisse des séquelles. L'encéphalite subaiguë sclérosante, mortelle, peut survenir à la suite de la rougeole et n'est pas reliée à la gravité de l'infection virale

Immunisation active: 1) vaccin antimorbilleux vivant; 2) vaccin actif atténué plus gamma-globuline; 3) vaccin de microbes morts (la durée de l'immunité est inconnue)
Immunisation passive: gamma-globuline. Le nouveau-né reçoit l'immunisation de sa mère par voie placentaire. Durée: 6 mois
Immunisation spontanée: la maladie confère l'immunité permanente
Test: titrage des anticorps

Tableau 18.1   *Maladies contagieuses (suite)*

MALADIE	INCUBATION	PÉRIODE CONTAGIEUSE	AGENT CAUSAL	MODE DE CONTA-MINATION	MANIFESTATIONS CLINIQUES
Rubéole	14 à 21 jours	Durant la période prodromique et pendant quatre jours au moins	Virus. L'isolement est possible dans des laboratoires spécialisés	Par le contact direct ou indirect avec les sécrétions du nez et de la gorge de personnes infectées. Réservoir humain seulement. Transmission aéroportée possible	Signes généraux minimes. Fièvre légère, coryza bénin. L'éruption polymorphe consiste en petites macules roses ou rouge pâle se changeant en papules, qui disparaissent à la pression. L'éruption s'évanouit en trois jours. Hypertrophie des ganglions lymphatiques rétro-auriculaires cervicaux et occipitaux. Pas de tache de Koplik ni de photophobie comme dans la rougeole
Tétanos	3 à 21 jours	Non transmissible de personne à personne	Bacille Clostridium Tetani ou bacille de Nicolaïer	Les bacilles se trouvent dans le sol et entrent dans l'organisme par le biais d'une blessure. Les blessures profondes dues à des objets pénétrants et les brûlures sont des lésions qui permettent à ce bacille anaérobique de pénétrer facilement	Début sévère et graduel. Les bacilles produisent une puissante toxine ayant une affinité pour le système nerveux. Les manifestations cliniques incluent la rigidité des muscles, des spasmes, de l'hyperirritabilité, des convulsions, la céphalée, la fièvre. Le trismus, ou inaptitude à ouvrir la bouche, apparaît. Le spasme des muscles du visage provoque le rictus sardonique. L'opisthotonos, une courbure du dos vers l'arrière, se traduit par la contracture des muscles extenseurs de la colonne vertébrale. Les tétanospasmes cliniques peuvent être déclenchés par de légères incitations motrices externes. Il n'y a pas de perte de conscience. Les urines peuvent être retenues à cause du spasme des muscles urétraux. Le spasme musculaire du larynx et de la poitrine peut causer la cyanose et l'asphyxie. Le métabolisme basal s'élève à cause de l'hyperirritabilité musculaire intense. La mort peut résulter de la pneumonie d'aspiration et de l'épuisement

TRAITEMENT ET SOINS INFIRMIERS	COMPLICATIONS	IMMUNITÉ
Symptomatique. Repos au lit jusqu'à ce que la fièvre tombe	Risque de malformations congénitales importantes chez le fœtus quand la mère contracte la maladie au cours du premier trimestre de la grossesse. Les malformations les plus fréquentes sont les cataractes congénitales, les affections cardiaques et la surdi-mutité. La mort in utero est fréquente	*Immunité active:* vaccin antirubéoleux vivant atténué *Immunisation passive:* gamma-globuline dont la valeur est d'ailleurs contestée *Immunisation spontanée:* la maladie confère l'immunité *Test:* la réaction d'inhibition – hémagglutination pour la détection des anticorps de la rubéole
Après la blessure et durant la maladie, les toxines devraient être neutralisées par des antitoxines. Le test de sensibilité au sérum doit être pratiqué avant l'administration de l'antitoxine. La pénicilline est efficace contre les bacilles du tétanos. La blessure doit être nettoyée méticuleusement. Tous les instruments de l'hôpital contaminés par le bacille doivent être stérilisés parfaitement. De bons soins de soutien requièrent la présence constante de l'infirmière et du médecin si possible. On place l'enfant dans un chambre sans lumière et on évite toute stimulation qui peut provoquer des spasmes. Une médication composée de médicaments pour détendre les muscles, de sédatifs et de tranquillisants aidera à contrôler les tétanospasmes. L'enfant doit être détendu, mais pas trop assoupi. La trachéotomie peut être nécessaire si les laryngo-spasmes se manifestent. L'administration parentérale de liquides, l'oxygénothérapie, la réanimation, l'aspiration des sécrétions, l'utilisation du gavage et la cathétérisation vésicale peuvent être nécessaires	Obstruction du larynx, anoxie, atélectasie et pneumonie	*Immunisation active:* l'anatoxine est un antigène puissant. Elle peut être donnée en conjonction avec les immunisations contre la diphtérie et la coqueluche *Immunisation passive:* les nouveau-nés acquièrent par voie placentaire une antitoxine, mais elle est inefficace pour les protéger. L'immunisation passive résulte d'une injection de globuline immunisée, ou d'antitoxine administrée peu d'heures après la blessure *Test:* aucun

Tableau 18.1   Maladies contagieuses (suite)

MALADIE	INCUBATION	PÉRIODE CONTAGIEUSE	AGENT CAUSAL	MODE DE CONTA-MINATION	MANIFESTATIONS CLINIQUES
Varicelle	10 à 21 jours. Invasion 12 à 24 heures	Une journée avant l'apparition à six jours après l'apparition des premières vésicules	Virus de la varicelle et du zona. Isolement du virus difficile	Source humaine seulement. Contact direct ou indirect avec les vésicules. Les croûtes sèches ne sont pas contagieuses	Malaise général, fièvre légère, anorexie, céphalée. Macules, papules, vésicules, croûtes, apparaissent par poussées successives. Lésions d'âges différents. Prurit. Lymphadénopathie généralisée
Variole	12 jours	Un à deux jours avant les premiers symptômes et jusqu'à ce que les croûtes tombent. 2 à 4 semaines	Virus	Contact direct ou indirect, salive et lésions. Les croûtes sèches sont contagieuses. Réservoir humain	Début soudain avec vomissement et céphalée, forte fièvre, courbatures générales. Les éruptions ont lieu peu de jours après le début de la maladie (4-5 jours). Évolution progressive: macules, papules, vésicules, pustules. Les vésicules présentent une ombilication. La prostration et les convulsions peuvent se manifester. Les lésions individuelles apparaissent par groupe et progressent ensemble. Les muqueuses de la bouche et des yeux peuvent être attaquées. Les cicatrices dépendent de l'étendue et de la profondeur des éruptions

TRAITEMENT ET SOINS INFIRMIERS	COMPLICATIONS	IMMUNITÉ
Symptomatique. Empêcher l'enfant de se gratter. Tenir les ongles courts et propres. Administrer un sédatif si c'est nécessaire. Utiliser les lotions calmantes pour soulager les démangeaisons. Si une infection secondaire se déclare, recourir aux antibiotiques ou à la chimio-thérapie	Peut être fatale si le patient est sous corticothérapie. Invasion secondaire respiratoire et rénale. Encéphalite rare. Zona à l'âge adulte. Infection des lésions de grattage: furonculose, impétigo	*Immunisation active:* aucune *Immunisation passive:* aucune pour l'enfant sain. L'enfant malade peut recevoir de la gamma-globuline pour le protéger *Immunisation spontanée:* la maladie confère une immunité quasi permanente *Test:* aucun
Aucun traitement spécifique, excepté les antibiotiques et les sulfamides pour les infections secondaires. Soin des yeux, hygiène orale et diète selon la tolérance. Les cas sévères peuvent requérir des sédatifs, du liquide administré parentéralement, et des gavages. L'oxygène, les transfusions de sang et la digitaline peuvent être indiqués	La laryngite, la broncho-pneumonie et l'encéphalite. Les enfants affectés d'eczéma peuvent contracter une vaccine généralisée si on leur administre le vaccin ou s'ils viennent en contact avec un enfant vacciné	*Immunisation active:* vaccination par la méthode de pression multiple *Immunisation passive:* la gamma-globuline de personne immunisée peut modifier le cours de la maladie *Test:* aucun

animal exposé à une infection par la rencontre d'une personne ou d'un animal infecté.

L'immunité est l'aptitude du corps contaminé à résister à l'agent infectieux. La protection contre les maladies spécifiques est due à la présence d'anticorps qui peuvent affaiblir ou détruire l'agent causal ou neutraliser ses toxines. *L'immunité naturelle* est présente quand elle existe alors que la personne n'a pas eu la maladie et qu'elle n'a jamais reçu d'immunisation spécifique. *L'immunité acquise* peut être spontanée ou provoquée. On acquiert *l'immunité spontanée* à la suite d'une maladie qui provoque la formation d'anticorps. *L'immunité artificielle ou provoquée* peut être active ou passive. On acquiert *l'immunité active* par la vaccination qui consiste en l'inoculation d'une suspension de micro-organismes morts ou affaiblis, ou de toxines spécifiques modifiées. Ces substances agissent comme des antigènes et produisent l'immunité en stimulant la formation d'anticorps qui protègent l'organisme contre les menaces de l'agent infectieux. L'immunisation active contre les maladies contagieuses courantes a été discutée en relation avec la surveillance sanitaire dans les différents groupes d'âge. *L'immunité passive* agit rapidement, mais son effet est de courte durée. Elle s'acquiert par le transfert d'anticorps de la mère au fœtus ou par l'administration d'un sérum qui contient des anticorps de personnes ou d'animaux immunisés. On utilise l'immunisation passive pour modifier la maladie, si une personne est soupçonnée d'infection ou est déjà infectée. Quoiqu'on puisse employer des types variés de sérum pour une immunisation passive, la gamma-globuline demeure la source la plus fréquente d'anticorps humains. Le sérum qui provient de l'animal s'avère souvent très efficace, mais il demeure très antigénique.

Cuti-réaction. Elle peut être pratiquée pour déterminer l'immunité contre certaines maladies. Les *tests* les plus sûrs et les plus communément utilisés sont la réaction de *Dick* qui détermine la sensibilité à la scarlatine et la réaction de *Schick* qui détermine la sensibilité à la diphtérie.

Le *traitement* des maladies contagieuses consiste à aider l'organisme à résister à l'invasion de l'agent causal. Les recherches récentes sur l'interféron, une protéine produite par l'organisme, démontrent que les cellules traitées à l'interféron ne permettent pas la croissance virale normale. Il s'ensuivrait que l'interféron est impliqué dans la guérison naturelle des maladies à virus. Des études plus poussées permettront de déterminer si l'on peut utiliser l'interféron en thérapeutique contre quelques-uns des virus causant des maladies contagieuses. La *prévention* repose sur l'immunité acquise et l'absence de contacts avec l'organisme causal. Des programmes d'immunisations très vastes ont permis de contrôler la propagation de plusieurs maladies d'enfants. La *quarantaine* signifie une limitation de la liberté de mouvements de personnes ou d'animaux exposés à une maladie contagieuse, une période égale à la plus longue durée d'incubation habituelle de la maladie.

On n'hospitalise les enfants atteints d'une maladie contagieuse que s'ils requièrent des soins spéciaux. Ils peuvent être admis dans un *hôpital général* qui possède des locaux d'isolement appropriés. Tout le personnel chargé des soins de tels enfants doit connaître les techniques d'isolement et les appliquer correctement.

Complications. Les enfants souffrant d'encéphalite à la suite d'une maladie contagieuse comme la varicelle, les oreillons, la coqueluche ou la méningite, peuvent éventuellement souffrir de retard mental. On peut éviter la plupart des complications des maladies contagieuses communes, si on donne des soins adéquats à l'enfant au début de sa maladie. Toutefois, certaines d'entre elles demeurent impossibles à prévoir ou à éviter, telle la leuco-encéphalite subsclérosante à la suite d'une rougeole.

La signification de l'isolement pour l'enfant, ses parents et son infirmière. Quand un enfant est isolé, pour sa protection comme dans le cas de brûlures, ou pour la protection des autres, s'il souffre d'une maladie contagieuse, il est physiquement séparé de tous, aussi bien des enfants que des adultes. De plus, les mesures d'isolement peuvent affecter psychologiquement le comportement des autres à son endroit. L'enfant peut se sentir oublié si l'infirmière ne le visite pas fréquemment pour le distraire ou jouer avec lui. Il peut aussi se sentir abandonné si ses parents ne s'approchent pas de lui quand ils viennent le voir, soit parce qu'ils craignent de rapporter l'infection aux autres enfants de la maison ou que les règlements de l'hôpital interdisent les visites dans les chambres contaminées.

En plus de ces sentiments d'abandon et de solitude, l'enfant peut aussi se méfier de l'uniforme et probablement du masque et des gants que les médecins et les infirmières portent quand ils s'occupent de lui. Il peut aussi être troublé par la façon étrange dont ses parents sont vêtus quand ils le visitent. L'enfant peut se croire malpropre si on ne le touche qu'avec des gants et se sentir rejeté parce qu'on maintient la porte de sa chambre fermée.

L'infirmière doit expliquer, tant aux parents qu'à l'enfant, les raisons de cet isolement. Si les parents peuvent saisir cet enseignement, ils sont plus à même de coopérer et de comprendre les besoins de l'enfant. Il faut lui procurer des jouets qui pourront être nettoyés à fond ou jetés quand l'isolement aura pris fin.

En résumé, l'infirmière doit être consciente de ses propres sentiments envers l'enfant isolé et être attentive aux appréhensions possibles des parents. Elle doit aussi se rendre compte de la solitude et de la crainte de l'enfant qui n'est pas capable de comprendre les précautions qui accompagnent les soins qu'on lui prodigue.

RÉFÉRENCES

Livres et documents officiels

American Academy of Pediatrics: *Report of the Committee on Infectious Diseases* 1970. 16e éd. Evanston, Ill. American Academy of Pediatrics, 1971.
American Hospital Association: *Infection Control in the Hospital.* Revised ed. Chicago, Ill., American Hospital Association, 1970. ,
American Public Health Association: *Control of Communicable Diseases in Man.* 11e éd. Washington, D. C., American Public Health Association, 1970.
Fox, J. P., Hall, C. E. et Elveback, L. R.: *Epidemiology: Man and Disease.* New York, MacMillan Company, 1970.
Institut de microbiologie et d'hygiène de l'Université de Montréal: *Immuno-séro-globuline. Vaccin antitypho-paratyphoïde A et B. Vaccin D. C. T. associé. Vaccination antivariolique. Vaccin anti-poliomyélitique vivant, oral. Vaccin T. A. B. T. associé. Virusvaccin anti-influenza polyvalent. Anatoxine tétanique. Antitoxine tétanique. Sérum antirabique. Anatoxine diphtérique. Toxine diphtérique (test de Schick). Antitoxine diphtérique. Réactions sériques; prévention et traitement,* Montréal.
Krugman, S. et Ward, R.: *Infectious Diseases of Children.* 4e éd. Saint-Louis, C. V. Mosby Company, 1968.
Laboratoires Ross: *Les maladies exanthémateuses de l'enfant et du nourrisson. Vaccination antivariolique.* Columbus, Ohio.
Lockwood, N. L.: Effect of Situational Doll Play upon the Preoperative Stress Reactions of Hospitalized Children; in *ANA Clinical Sessions,* 1970. New York, Appleton-Century-Crofts, 1971, pp. 113-120.
Ministère de la Santé: *Le vaccin prévient la polio. La poliomyélite. La rougeole. La coqueluche, La scarlatine. La rubéole. Le tétanos. La diphtérie.* Gouvernement du Québec.
Nossal, G. J. V.: *Antibodies and Immunity.* New York, Basic Books, Inc., 1969.

Articles

Abbott, N. C., Hansen, P. et Lewis, K.: Dress Rehearsal for the Hospital. *Am. J. Nursing,* 70:2360, novembre 1970.
Apt, L et autres: Emotional Aspects of Hospitalization of Children for Strabismus Surgery. *Ann. Ophtalmol.,* 6:11, 9, 1974.
Ayliffe, G. A. J. et autres: Varieties of Aseptic Practice in Hospital Wards. *Lancet,* 2:1117, 22 novembre 1969.
Balon, M. et Ollivier-Farcat, M.: Le strabisme et son traitement. *Soins,* 20:45, 3, 1975.
Bernard, D.: Glomérulonéphrites aiguës. *Soins,* 19:5, 16, 1974.
Brown, M.: What You Should Know About Communicable Diseases. *Nursing '75,* 5:70, 9, 1975 (I), 5:56, 10, 1975 (II), 5:55, 11, 1975 (III). ,
Calamy, G. et Razavet, B.: Infections à streptocoques. *Soins,* 20:3, 7, 1975.
Clavé, M.: Les fièvres éruptives de l'enfant. *La revue de l'infirmière,* 25:577, 7, 1975.
Cranston, L.: Les maladies contagieuses. *Inf. Can.,* 18:12, 2, 1976.
Crawford, C. F. et Palm, M. L.: «Can I Take My Teddy Bear?» *Am. J. Nursing,* 73:286, février 1973.
Dison, N.: Tonsillectomy: Mother's View. *Am. J. Nursing,* 69:1024, mai 1969.
Gagnon, R. et Gohier, L.: Le traitement orthoptique des strabismes divergents intermittents. *Union méd. du Can.,* 99:1490, août 1970.
Geoffroy, G. et autres: Cette effroyable complexité qu'est le cerveau *Inf. Can.,* 13:24, 3, 1971.
Gervais, M. et Drummond, K.: L'hématurie récidivante chez l'enfant. *Union méd. du Can.,* 99:1234, juillet 1970.

Gochman, D. S.: Children's Perceptions of Vulnerability to Illness and Accidents. *Pub. Health Rep.*, 85:69, janvier 1970.

Grosbuis, S. et Goulon, M.: La prévention du tétanos. *La revue de l'infirmière*, 24:807, 9, 1974.

Hiles, D.: Strabismus. *Am. J. Nursing*, 74:1082, 6, 1974.

Korsch, B. M. et autres: Experiences with Children and Their Families During Extended Hemodialysis and Kidney Transplantation. *Pediat. Clin. N. Amer.*, 18:625, mai 1971.

Labrune, B.: Traitement de la rougeole chez l'enfant. *Soins*, 17:27, 3, 1972.

Labrune, B.: Varicelle et zona. Soins, 19:4, 1, 1974.

Lecomte, E.: Amygdalectomie. *Soins*, 16:341, 8, 1971.

MacCarthy, J. et Morison, J.: An Explanatory Test of a Method of Studying Illness Among Preschool Children. *Nursing Research*, 21:319, juillet-août 1972.

Manuel, C.: Le tétanos. *Soins*, 20:9, 7, 1975.

Marsault, M.: Le strabisme de l'enfant. *Soins*, 16:5, 1, 1971.

Mostow, S. R.: Why Influenza Vaccine Does Not Do the Job. *Am. J. Nursing*, 70:2126, octobre 1970.

Mumby, D.: Une ville canadienne fait face au problème de la rougeole. *Inf. Can.*, 10:32, janvier 1968.

Richard, M.: Le strabisme. *La revue de pédiatrie*, 9:621, 10, 1973.

Schultz, N. V.: How Children Perceive Pain. *Nursing Outlook*, 19:670, octobre 1971.

Smith, D. H. et Peter, G.: Current and Future Vaccines for the Prevention of Bacterial Diseases. *Pediat. Clin. N. Amer.*, 19:387, mai 1972.

Spicher, C.: Nursing Care of Children Hospitalized with Infections. *Nurs. Clin. N. Amer.*, 5:123, 1, 1970.

Whitson, B. J.: The Puppet Treatment in Pediatrics. *Am. J. Nursing*, 72:1612, septembre 1972.

Vergnon, L. et Meaux, L.: Soins aux amygdalectomisés. *Soins*, 19:25, 14, 1974.

Ziring, P. R., Florman, A. L. et Cooper, L. Z.: The Diagnosis of Rubella. *Pediat. Clin. N. Amer.*, 18:87, février 1971.

19

pathologies de l'enfant d'âge préscolaire nécessitant des soins de longue durée

IMPACT D'UNE PATHOLOGIE DE LONGUE DURÉE SUR L'ENFANT D'ÂGE PRÉSCOLAIRE ET SA FAMILLE

L'enfant atteint d'une maladie chronique connaît une période d'alitement prolongée, ou des périodes brèves, mais fréquentes, de repos complet. Ceci constitue une rude épreuve pour l'enfant d'âge préscolaire, car alors, ses activités physiques et ses rapports avec d'autres enfants sont réduits au minimum. À l'hôpital, les soins à donner à l'enfant atteint de maladie chronique sont complexes; à la maison, ils posent des problèmes graves à la mère qui doit, la plupart du temps, donner les soins nécessaires à l'enfant tout en continuant ses activités habituelles. Elle peut devenir surmenée et irritable avec toutes les conséquences que cela comporte sur l'atmosphère familiale.

L'infirmière peut souvent offrir des suggestions pour alléger le poids de ce fardeau. La mère devrait d'abord accepter le fait qu'elle a besoin de repos et qu'il est inutile de s'épuiser à la tâche. Elle peut partager certaines de ses responsabilités avec son mari; ou compter sur les autres enfants, sur d'autres membres de la famille ou sur les voisins pour l'aider dans l'entretien de sa maison.

Placer l'enfant dans le vivoir plutôt que dans une chambre située à l'étage supérieur ou éloignée du centre de la maison, évite à la mère un va-et-vient épuisant et l'enfant sent davantage qu'il participe à la vie familiale.

Même si la mère ne peut demeurer continuellement au chevet de l'enfant, il est important que celui-ci puisse s'adonner à certains jeux. S'il est capable de s'asseoir, on place une table sur son lit, pour qu'il puisse se distraire en dessinant.

Durant ses travaux ménagers, la mère risque d'oublier l'heure exacte à laquelle un médicament doit être donné. Une horloge munie d'une sonnerie lui rappellera l'heure de la prochaine dose; une table de chevet, sur laquelle on a placé des cuillères propres et un carafon d'eau, lui évite des déplacements inutiles.

Une maladie chronique crée aussi des difficultés aux frères et sœurs du malade qui trouvent qu'on le favorise et qu'il retient beaucoup trop l'attention des adultes. Ceci accentue la rivalité qui existe normalement entre frères et sœurs. On doit leur faire comprendre que le malade nécessite une attention particulière, mais qu'on ne le préfère pas aux autres.

Les enfants, sains ou malades, craignent que les parents ne comprennent pas leur frayeur devant la maladie et la souffrance. Les frères et sœurs, s'ils sont assez grands pour associer la maladie à la mort, peuvent développer une peur réelle de la mort, non seulement pour le malade, mais aussi pour eux-mêmes. Les parents doivent leur expliquer franchement, dans des mots qu'ils peuvent comprendre, l'état de celui qui est malade. S'il existe des restrictions quant à ses activités physiques, on devrait les expliquer à ses frères et sœurs.

La jalousie des autres enfants devient assez intense pour qu'ils souhaitent parfois malheur à l'enfant malade et de telles pensées engendrent un sentiment de culpabilité. S'il survient une aggravation dans son état, ils s'en sentiront responsables, et leur sentiment de culpabilité prendra des proportions troublantes. De tels sentiments sont la conséquence normale d'un conflit émotif lié à la présence de l'enfant malade dont les besoins deviennent prioritaires sur ceux des autres. Au fur et à mesure de l'amélioration de son état, le malade doit s'adapter à sa nouvelle situation. Il lui arrivera de désirer ardemment le temps où son état réclamait une attention constante. Il peut devenir exigeant et facilement mécontent s'il n'obtient pas ce qu'il désire et sa réadaptation à une vie normale peut durer plusieurs semaines. Les parents doivent se montrer patients et compréhensifs, lui donner l'affection dont il a besoin, mais sans exagération.

Si à la suite d'une maladie, l'enfant souffre d'une incapacité ou d'une réduction plus ou moins importante de son activité, les membres de la famille doivent en comprendre les raisons et en avertir les professeurs et les autres adultes appelés à entrer en contact avec lui afin d'obtenir une certaine constance dans la réhabilitation. On doit l'encourager à faire les choses dont il est capable. Il faut éviter de manifester une trop grande attention à son incapacité et l'aider à se centrer sur ses possibilités, même si l'on reconnaît qu'il souffre d'un handicap.

MALADIES CHRONIQUES

Leucémie

Incidence et étiologie. Le cancer est, après les accidents, la principale cause de mortalité chez l'enfant; la leucémie en est le type le plus fréquent. Plus de 50% des cas de leucémie surviennent avant l'âge de cinq ans.

Il s'agit d'un processus néoplasique atteignant les organes hématopoïétiques (mœlle osseuse, tissus lymphoïde et réticulo-endothélial) et caractérisé par une surproduction de globules blancs et de leurs cellules-souches qui envahissent le sang périphérique. Le taux normal des globules blancs varie de 5 000 à 10 000/mm³; dans la leucémie, ce taux peut dépasser 50 000/mm³.

Durant l'enfance, on rencontre surtout la leucémie aiguë. On ne connaît à la maladie aucun facteur social, géographique ou socio-économique caractéristique. On fait actuellement des recherches sur les possibilités d'une origine virale. On étudie également la relation qui existe entre le mongolisme et la leucémie. Certains psychologues tentent de relier l'apparition d'une leucémie à des traumatismes psychologiques divers. On songe aussi à une prédisposition génétique.

Types, physio-pathologie et manifestations cliniques. Il est possible de classifier les leucémies en fonction de la variété de globules blancs augmentés (polynucléaires ou mononucléaires), mais il s'avère parfois difficile de reconnaître le type de leucémie dont souffre l'enfant. La leucémie aiguë lymphoblastique semble plus fréquente que la leucémie aiguë myéloblastique, mais elles demeurent souvent très difficiles à distinguer à cause du manque de maturité des cellules. On rencontre également la leucémie aleucémique où le taux de leucocytes s'abaisse et où les leucoblastes passent très peu dans la circulation. Une ponction médullaire révèle alors la maladie. Des formes subaiguës ou chroniques apparaissent rarement chez l'enfant. Cependant, avec la chimiothérapie moderne, la forme aiguë peut avoir une évolution beaucoup plus longue qu'antérieurement.

Les conséquences pathologiques de la leucémie découlent surtout de l'augmentation des globules blancs immatures, de la chute des thrombocytes et de l'atteinte secondaire de certains organes. Les leucoblastes se multiplient rapidement, mais ne peuvent accomplir les fonctions des cellules arrivées à maturité (leucocytes). La production des autres éléments figurés du sang s'en trouve rapidement réduite. Ainsi, l'abaissement du nombre des plaquettes explique les manifestations hémorragiques. L'anémie est manifeste. Le foie, la rate et les ganglions lymphatiques sont augmentés de volume. On observe des modifications des reins et des os. Des zones d'ulcérations et secondairement d'infections apparaissent à des points divers de l'organisme. En plus des manifestations spécifiques à un type précis de leucémie, il existe des manifestations communes à tous les types.

Le début peut être rapide ou progressif. Les pétéchies apparaissent sur tout le corps. L'enfant est pâle et souffre d'anorexie, d'épistaxis, de vomissements, de perte de poids, de faiblesse, de fatigabilité, de palpitations et de dyspnée. La température est élevée. L'hyper-

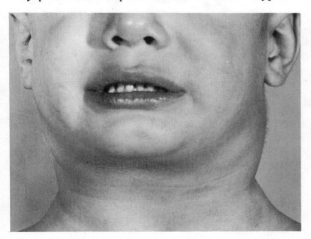

Figure 19-1. Lymphadénopathie bilatérale chez un enfant souffrant d'une leucémie lymphoblastique aiguë. (J.E. Lunceford, *Nurs. Clin. N. Amer.*, vol 2, n° 4, déc. 1967.)

trophie des ganglions lymphatiques cause des douleurs abdominales épisodiques. L'anémie s'aggrave au fur et à mesure de l'évolution de la maladie. Quand le taux des plaquettes diminue, l'enfant saigne facilement et un traumatisme léger produit une ecchymose importante; des lésions nécrotiques se développent, lesquelles peuvent secondairement s'infecter. Des zones hémorragiques peuvent marquer les muqueuses, les os et les organes nobles.

Les *manifestations cliniques* dépendent de l'organe ou du tissu atteint par les cellules leucémiques. L'hématurie traduit une hémorragie de l'arbre urinaire. Des lésions ulcératives et nécrotiques peuvent se produire au niveau du rectum et des zones périrectales; il y a une ulcération des gencives. Le foie et la rate augmentent de volume et une lymphadé-

nopathie apparaît spécialement au niveau des ganglions profonds. L'enfant se plaint de douleurs aux jambes ou aux articulations causées le plus souvent par des hémorragies sous-périostées ou articulaires. La douleur peut aussi être causée par la nécrose avasculaire ou par la destruction du tissu osseux par les cellules leucémiques. Une augmentation des foyers leucémiques au niveau du système nerveux central résulte d'une famille des agents antileucémiques à traverser la barrière méningée.

Diagnostic et traitement. Les éléments du *diagnostic* sont les manifestations cliniques et le frottis sanguin qui permet de déceler les cellules immatures dans le sang périphérique. On observe une anémie. Les manifestations cliniques laissent supposer l'existence d'une leucémie. La formule sanguine complète révèle une baisse des hématies et des plaquettes. On trouve des leucoblastes dans la circulation et on note une augmentation considérable des leucocytes sauf en cas de leucémie aleucémique où le nombre des globules blancs diminue considérablement. L'examen de la moelle osseuse obtenue par aspiration ou par prélèvement chirurgical demeure nécessaire pour le diagnostic de la leucémie. La moelle osseuse montre un tissu leucopoïétique anormal et quelques éléments hématopoïétiques normaux. Des radiographies des os longs révèlent des modifications des os.

Le *traitement* débute aussitôt que le diagnostic est posé. Les caractéristiques de la maladie ainsi que son traitement devraient être discutés avec les parents. Il n'existe pas de guérison et le traitement demeure palliatif. Un traitement adéquat prolonge ordinairement l'évolution de la maladie et assure à l'enfant un confort relatif pendant cette période.

Les principaux agents antileucémiques se recrutent parmi les médicaments suivants: les corticoïdes, les antimétabolites et les antimitotiques.

Les *corticoïdes* produisent une lympholyse; ils stimulent le fonctionnement de la moelle osseuse d'où élévation des éléments figurés normaux du sang; ils augmentent la résistance capillaire contrôlant ainsi la tendance aux hémorragies; ils améliorent l'état général en augmentant l'appétit et en produisant un état de bien-être. L'administration de corticoïdes produit un soulagement rapide des symptômes chez l'enfant atteint de leucémie aiguë. La rémission de la maladie peut aller de quelques semaines à quelques mois. Des effets secondaires, tels que faciès lunaire et rétention hydrosodique se produisent lors de l'administration de fortes doses ou d'un traitement prolongé.

L'effet anti-inflammatoire des corticoïdes exige une surveillance accrue pour déceler l'apparition des symptômes d'infection. L'ulcère gastro-duodénal peut également apparaître au cours du traitement. Quand les symptômes de leucémie réapparaissent après une période de rémission le traitement peut être repris.

Les *antimétabolites* privent les cellules de certains facteurs nécessaires à leur synthèse, à leur division ou à leur formation, en agissant par un phénomène d'antagonisme avec ces facteurs. On trouve des antifoliques, des antipuriniques et des antipyrimidiques et le plus communément employé est l'aminoptérine (Méthotréxate) qui interfère avec le métabolisme de l'acide folique. L'acide folique est essentiel à la synthèse des nucléo-protéines requises pour la multiplication rapide des globules blancs. Ces médicaments sont toxiques et peuvent causer une dépression de la moelle osseuse et des saignements gastro-intestinaux. Les symptômes d'intoxication comprennent les ulcères de la bouche, la diarrhée et l'alopécie. La 6-mercaptopurine (Purinéthol) agit différemment des antagonistes de l'acide folique; c'est un antipurinique. La principale manifestation de toxicité liée à la 6-mercaptopurine est la perturbation de l'hématopoïèse. L'enfant dont l'état s'améliore avec le méthotréxate ou la 6-mercaptopurine, sera vu par le médecin à intervalles rapprochés. Les rémissions durent habituellement de quatre à sept mois.

Les *antimitotiques* inhibent la division cellulaire et bloquent l'évolution de la mitose. On en trouve deux principales catégories: les alkylants et certains extraits végétaux comme la vincristine (Oncovin). Un agent alkylant, le cyclophosphamide (Cytoxan ou Procytox) peut être donné oralement ou parentéralement pour le traitement palliatif de la leucémie. Les effets toxiques de ce médicament comprennent la dépression de la moelle osseuse, l'alopécie et la cystite hémorragique. Lors de l'emploi de la vincristine, une toxicité sensorielle et neuro-musculaire, aussi bien que la constipation, peuvent se manifester. Ces différents médicaments doivent être administrés de façon cyclique et selon différentes combinaisons afin d'éloigner les rechutes.

La *daunorubicin* est un antibiotique qui perturbe la synthèse des acides nucléiques. Il diminue la multiplication des cellules leucémiques, mais cause des dommages à la moelle osseuse et au niveau du système cardio-vasculaire. Il peut susciter une éruption et entraîner la diarrhée.

La *L-Asparaginase* est une enzyme employée de façon expérimentale dans le traitement de la leucémie. La L-Asparaginase empêche la cellule leucémique d'assimiler l'asparagine indispensable à la synthèse protéique. La cellule saine peut produire elle-même cet acide aminé. Ce nouveau médicament peut toutefois produire des anomalies de la coagulation et des troubles hépatiques. Une réaction anaphylactique que l'on traite avec des antagonistes de l'histamine peut survenir.

Certains autres médicaments en essai donnent des espoirs, tels l'hydrea et le cytosar.

Ordinairement le médecin suit un protocole d'emploi et utilise ces divers médicaments en alternance et en association. Dans la leucémie chronique, le busulfan (Myleran), un dérivé de la moutarde azotée, est utilisé avec succès.

À mesure que la maladie progresse, l'organisme devient graduellement résistant aux médicaments, le soulagement devient de plus en plus difficile à obtenir et les rémissions sont plus courtes.

On donne des antibiotiques pour le contrôle des infections intercurrentes. L'administration de sang complet ou de culots globulaires permet de corriger une anémie sévère (hématies), d'arrêter les saignements (plaquettes) et de combattre l'infection (leucocytes). Des sédatifs sont administrés si c'est nécessaire et les analgésiques contrôlent la douleur, surtout en phase terminale.

Environ le quart des enfants leucémiques souffrent d'une infiltration leucémique des méninges et d'une hypertension intracrânienne consécutive. On peut alors injecter du méthotrexate directement dans le liquide céphalo-rachidien ou utiliser la radiothérapie.

Une ponction de la moelle osseuse s'avère nécessaire pour le diagnostic et l'évaluation du traitement. On l'effectue au niveau du sternum ou de la crête iliaque et on doit renseigner l'enfant sur le but et la technique de l'examen. Il doit savoir qu'on le maintiendra doucement, mais fermement pour éviter les mouvements qui pourraient provoquer un traumatisme, qu'il sentira la désinfection de la peau, l'injection de l'anesthésique local et la forte pression du trocart au niveau de la surface osseuse. On doit l'avertir du bruit qu'il entendra et l'assurer que son os ne sera pas fracturé. Après la ponction, on doit le surveiller, car il peut se produire un saignement qu'il faudra contrôler à l'aide d'un pansement compressif.

Lorsque l'enfant présente une rémission, tous les signes biochimiques et physiopathologiques de la maladie disparaissent. L'enfant redevient sain pour des périodes variant de quelques jours à plusieurs mois. Des rémissions qui ont duré plusieurs années se sont produites dans quelques rares cas.

Soins infirmiers. L'enfant atteint de leucémie n'est généralement hospitalisé qu'au moment du diagnostic, pour la mise au point du traitement, lors de périodes transitoires d'exacerbation et à la phase terminale. Pendant les rémissions, il vit au sein de sa famille et mène une vie relativement normale pour son âge. Bien que cela puisse être difficile pour les parents, ils doivent créer une atmosphère heureuse et aussi peu anxiogène que possible. Il faut éviter de traiter l'enfant avec trop de tolérance ou d'indulgence et le priver ainsi de la sécurité d'une saine discipline.

Le soin de l'enfant leucémique est basé en partie sur les signes, les symptômes et les complications de la maladie, mais aussi et surtout, sur les complications et les effets secondaires engendrés par les médicaments utilisés pour la combattre.

L'enfant est presque constamment menacé d'*infection*. La perturbation des leucocytes constitue une des facettes de la maladie et le traitement lui-même produit une baisse considérable des globules blancs dont le taux ne revient que progressivement à la normale. De plus, les stéroïdes masquent les symptômes qui permettent de déceler une infection. Il faut donc signaler immédiatement tout signe possible d'infection; la gamma-globuline peut quelquefois être administrée quand le contact avec une maladie infectieuse est très évident (ex: la varicelle...).

Dans certains centres pédiatriques, on place les enfants atteints de leucémie dans un environnement strictement stérile, pour pallier le manque de défenses organiques causé par la médication. Ceci nécessite un isolement protecteur faisant appel à un type de lit en matière plastique, isolant tout le corps, et comprenant des hublots à travers lesquels l'infirmière donne les soins. On peut également utiliser une chambre que l'on désinfecte au préalable et où les infirmières et les visiteurs ne circulent que vêtus d'une blouse, d'un bonnet, d'un masque et de gants stérilisés. Nous avons déjà insisté sur l'impact psychologique d'un tel isolement sur l'enfant malade.

Certains soins sont semblables à ceux prodigués lors d'une *anémie*. L'infirmière doit manier le corps de l'enfant très *doucement*, surtout quand les extrémités sont douloureuses au toucher. L'hygiène de la bouche est nécessaire et doit être pratiquée avec le plus grand soin pour prévenir un traumatisme des gencives saignantes, spécialement s'il y a des ulcères.

Si ces enfants ont la gorge enflammée, il est préférable qu'ils s'abstiennent de parler ou de manger. Ils sont sujets aux infections et il faut les préserver de tout refroidissement. Une hydratation adéquate s'avère importante. Pour éviter les nausées, on donne fréquemment à l'enfant de petites quantités de sa boisson favorite. On fait le dosage des liquides ingérés et excrétés.

On sert à l'enfant des repas bien équilibrés, composés d'aliments qu'il aime. Il ne faut pas le réveiller pour le faire manger, car le repos lui est tout aussi nécessaire que la nourriture.

Le danger d'hémorragie est proportionnel à l'insuffisance plaquettaire. L'infirmière doit signaler non seulement l'importance, mais aussi l'origine des saignements. Il est difficile d'obtenir de l'enfant des renseignements précis sur son état, il faut donc noter en détail toutes ses plaintes et les gestes qui révèlent la douleur. Étant donné que les plus légers traumatismes peuvent causer des hémorragies, on capitonne très souvent le lit et le fauteuil roulant. Cette précaution doit être expliquée à l'enfant et aux parents pour prévenir des interprétations erronées de leur part. Il faut éviter les injections dans la mesure du possible; si elles s'avèrent indispensables, elles doivent toujours être suivies de compression locale. L'utilisation d'une peau de mouton synthétique permet d'éviter l'apparition de plaies de décubitus. La tenue du dossier est d'une extrême importance. L'infirmière doit signaler immédiatement l'apparition des signes d'infection et

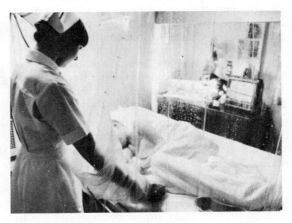

Figure 19-2. Tente d'isolement. Un environnement complètement stérile protège l'enfant dont la vie serait menacée par l'apparition d'une infection. Il s'agit d'enfants dont le système immunitaire est déficient, qui souffrent de brûlures graves ou dont la leucopénie provient d'une maladie ou d'un traitement. (Courtoisie du Children's Hospital de Philadelphie.)

d'hémorragie et savoir reconnaître les manifestations de l'envahissement des méninges. Tous les changements qui se produisent dans l'humeur ou le comportement de l'enfant doivent donc être notés avec précision.

L'enfant qui souffre devient souvent irritable; s'il reçoit en plus un traitement prolongé par voie intraveineuse, la douleur et l'immobilité liées à ce traitement peuvent le rendre très nerveux. Ceux qui l'entourent doivent être patients et essayer de créer une atmosphère calme dans laquelle il subira le moins de frustrations possibles. On encourage la mère à demeurer avec son enfant. Elle peut ainsi lui procurer les soins, l'amour constant et la distraction dont il a besoin, et apprendre à le soigner en vue du retour au sein de sa famille. Les parents donnent une affection naturelle et positive s'ils ont la permission de participer aux soins de leur enfant pendant son séjour à l'hôpital. L'enfant à qui l'on permet de collaborer à son traitement sent moins sa dépendance envers le personnel et même envers ses parents. Il peut surveiller la perfusion intraveineuse, faire lui-même le dosage de ses ingesta et excreta et nettoyer sa bouche avec les tampons glycérinés.

Il est nécessaire que l'enfant soit conscient des complications reliées au traitement qu'il subit. Il doit connaître par exemple la nécessité de l'isolement à la suite de la baisse des globules blancs, il doit s'habituer à signaler à sa mère ou à l'infirmière qu'il a été à la selle puisque la vincristine comporte un grand risque de constipation. Quand le traitement employé comporte un risque d'alopécie, l'enfant devra être psychologiquement préparé à la chute de ses cheveux. Souvent, les parents lui font porter une perruque, car la repousse des cheveux est lente et l'enfant souffre énormément de son aspect qui provoque fréquemment la risée de ses camarades de classe pendant les périodes de rémissions.

Durant sa maladie, l'enfant peut avoir des nausées, être fatigué et se sentir délaissé. Les parents qui ont accepté de faire face à la maladie peuvent grandement aider leur enfant. Étant donné que celui-ci peut être malade pendant plusieurs mois, avec des périodes de rémissions et d'exacerbations, les parents ont besoin du réconfort du médecin et de l'infirmière.

L'enfant traité à domicile peut être appelé à retourner périodiquement à la clinique externe pour recevoir des transfusions, des médicaments anti-leucémiques ou subir des examens de contrôle. Les parents peuvent contribuer aux soins en surveillant la vitesse du débit de la transfusion ou en préparant l'enfant pour les examens. L'infirmière doit se rappeler, cependant, qu'elle est responsable des traitements de l'enfant.

Les soins en phase terminale s'avèrent difficiles. Les parents sont conscients que l'enfant arrive au terme de sa vie, cependant ils continuent d'espérer sa guérison. Les infirmières doivent accepter les exigences des parents pendant la maladie de leur enfant à cause de l'intense anxiété qu'ils éprouvent. L'enfant a besoin de soutien moral et physique, car il devient terriblement anxieux et souvent même très souffrant tant qu'il garde sa lucidité. Son nez et sa gorge doivent être propres, ses lèvres et sa bouche humides. Il faut le rafraîchir fréquemment et changer sa position aussi souvent que possible sans le fatiguer, afin de prévenir des escarres de décubitus. On lui donne des sédatifs et des analgésiques selon ses besoins.

Pour assister l'enfant mourant et ses parents, l'infirmière devra accepter la façon dont ils expriment leur peur et leur peine. Pour ce faire, elle doit essayer d'analyser ses propres sentiments envers la mort. Quand l'enfant gravement malade devient inconscient, l'infirmière doit rester à son chevet avec les parents afin qu'ils sachent que tout ce qui demeure possible sera fait pour l'enfant. Si l'infirmière les laisse seuls avec le mourant, ils peuvent penser qu'elle se dissocie de leur tourment ou qu'elle rejette leur chagrin. Si les parents ne peuvent pas être présents, l'infirmière devra rester constamment avec l'enfant, afin d'éviter qu'il se sente seul et qu'il ait peur que personne ne lui vienne en aide lorsqu'il souffre. Les autres enfants de l'unité peuvent sentir la tension de l'infirmière et des adultes présents. Ils ont besoin de réconfort surtout si l'un d'eux se sait également atteint de leucémie et qu'il est conscient de son évolution et de son pronostic. Il est difficile de savoir si l'on doit dire à l'enfant leucémique qu'il souffre d'une maladie fatale. Les parents, aidés le plus souvent par les membres de l'équipe de santé, prennent la décision qui leur semble la plus acceptable, même si elle n'est pas toujours au bénéfice de l'enfant.

L'enfant qui comprend sa maladie, même s'il n'en saisit pas toutes les implications, collabore beaucoup mieux au traitement et garde sa confiance aux adultes qui le soignent. Les parents peuvent difficilement conserver une attitude positive, non défaitiste devant l'évolution de l'état de leur enfant; le personnel peut jouer un grand rôle de support pour les rendre capables d'aider efficacement leur enfant.

Complications et pronostic. Les complications sont dues à une insuffisance d'éléments figurés sanguins normaux. Il peut se produire des hémorragies intracrâniennes et viscérales; l'hémorragie intracrânienne cause le plus souvent le décès. La mort peut être due soit à la maladie elle-même, soit à une infection intercurrente ou à l'association des deux.

En l'absence de traitement, la maladie évolue généralement dans le sens d'une détérioration rapide avec décès dans les deux à six mois. Lorsqu'elle est traitée, la leucémie aiguë peut se transformer en leucémie chronique et l'enfant peut survivre de un à trois ans ou plus. Quand l'enfant aura atteint le stade terminal de sa maladie, se posera la question délicate de savoir s'il est nécessaire de le maintenir en vie par des moyens mécaniques.

L'IMPACT D'UNE MALADIE FATALE SUR L'ENFANT ET SES PARENTS

L'annonce que l'enfant souffre d'une maladie fatale, à plus ou moins brève échéance, a un impact émotif intense sur les parents et souvent sur l'enfant lui-même. Les membres du personnel qui participent aux soins subissent aussi les contrecoups et les effets du drame qui se joue en leur présence. Le deuil commence vraiment au moment du diagnostic et la force de la douleur peut atteindre à ce moment un sommet culminant.

On s'interroge souvent sur l'opportunité d'informer l'enfant de la gravité de sa maladie. Que l'on essaie de lui cacher la vérité, qu'on lui mente ou qu'on lui parle franchement, l'enfant est habituellement conscient de son état, il « sent » ou « pressent » la vérité. Les enfants d'âge scolaire entrevoient la possibilité de leur fin prématurée. L'enfant plus jeune ne craint souvent que la douleur physique, la mutilation et surtout, la séparation d'avec ses parents et sa famille.

Les parents peuvent établir une relation de confiance avec leur enfant, s'ils parviennent à communiquer de façon positive. Ils doivent lui faire saisir qu'ils comprennent ses préoccupations et qu'ils ont à cœur son confort physique et émotif. Cette attitude ouverte permet à l'enfant d'avoir confiance, de croire qu'on n'essaie pas de lui mentir et il peut alors exprimer ses craintes et son anxiété sans avoir peur que les adultes se retirent derrière un paravent et des clichés optimistes vides de sens. L'enfant qui comprend sa maladie collabore beaucoup mieux au traitement. Si les parents tentent de camoufler la vérité à l'enfant, celui-ci réagit en taisant ses véritables sentiments; il essaie à son tour de les protéger. Les communications positives deviennent quasi impossibles et l'enfant se sent de plus en plus seul et désemparé.

Les parents sont susceptibles de présenter toutes sortes de réactions à l'annonce de la mort éventuelle de leur enfant. Ils peuvent rationaliser à l'extrême, refuser d'accepter la maladie, devenir hyperactifs ou encore irritables ou déprimés. Ils s'interrogent beaucoup sur la façon dont l'enfant mourra. Il est bon que l'équipe de santé se penche sur ce problème avec les parents; leur imagination les emporte et leurs craintes sont très souvent irrationnelles ou inattendues.

Les membres de la famille peuvent s'imaginer que le père s'éloigne d'eux au moment où ils en ont le plus besoin; leurs amis et les gens de l'entourage partagent parfois cette opinion et oublient que l'aide qu'ils pourraient fournir au père lui permettrait à son tour de donner du support à sa famille. Il est bon de lui faire exprimer ses sentiments, sa peine et les raisons qui lui font éviter le contact avec l'enfant malade, ce qui rend la situation encore plus pénible pour toute la famille.

Les frères et les sœurs de l'enfant malade montrent aussi parfois des changements de comportement qui indiquent les difficultés qu'ils traversent. Ils peuvent souffrir d'une gamme de maladies: anxiété de séparation, céphalée, douleurs abdominales, énurésie, dépression, difficultés d'apprentissage et phobie scolaire. Ils se sentent parfois coupables pour des gestes ou des sentiments négatifs qu'ils ont ressentis envers le petit malade et craignent que ce qui lui arrive n'en soit la conséquence; ils peuvent également craindre de tomber eux-mêmes malades. Ils se sentent peut-être rejetés par les parents qui portent toute leur attention sur celui qui est menacé. Les membres de l'équipe de santé doivent prévoir ces réactions et donner du support à tous les membres de la famille. Il ne faut pas oublier les grands-parents qui peuvent s'avérer d'un grand secours pour aider les parents, comme ils peuvent rendre la situation encore plus difficile si leurs réactions sont mal contrôlées.

Les membres de la famille peuvent s'aider mutuellement ou chercher un soutien de l'extérieur. Le prêtre ou le pasteur encourage la famille dont les sentiments religieux la portent à se tourner vers ce réconfort. Le médecin de famille a également un rôle à jouer. Il arrive toutefois que certaines familles lui en veuillent puisque c'est souvent lui qui a apporté la mauvaise nouvelle de la maladie de l'enfant et qu'il ne peut offrir à lui seul tous les services que les membres du service hospitalier sont à même de leur procurer.

L'hématologue ou le pédiatre planifie le traitement et l'explique aux parents et à l'enfant s'il y a lieu; la travailleuse sociale résout les problèmes de logement et de transport qui se présentent et offre son aide pour apporter une solution aux problèmes financiers. L'infirmière joue un rôle primordial, car elle sera en contact avec l'enfant et sa famille à chaque séjour à l'hôpital et quelquefois aussi à la maison.

Dans certains hôpitaux, on organise une rencontre entre les parents, le psychiatre et les autres membres de l'équipe pour faciliter la planification des soins à long terme. Chaque individu réagit à une situation de stress selon sa personnalité, ses croyances religieuses, son expérience, sa capacité d'accepter l'aide extérieure et sa perception de la situation telle qu'il la vit. Au cours de la rencontre qui peut être répétée à l'occasion, les parents peuvent exprimer leurs sentiments, recevoir des réponses satisfaisantes aux multiples questions qu'ils se posent et mesurer l'intérêt de l'équipe de santé à leur égard.

Les membres de l'équipe, dont le rôle consiste habituellement à promouvoir le retour à la santé, acceptent souvent très mal l'idée que la maladie d'un enfant puisse être fatale. La frustration et les sentiments dépressifs les assaillent surtout au moment où l'enfant fait une rechute; l'agressivité vient se greffer sur ces sentiments. À l'approche de la mort, les parents sont trop souvent laissés à eux-mêmes, les membres de l'équipe ne pouvant réagir contre l'anxiété qui les envahit à leur contact; l'aspect négatif de cette réaction conduit d'ailleurs à un sentiment envahissant de culpabilité. Pour rompre ce cercle de réactions, les membres de l'équipe doivent discuter entre eux de leurs sentiments envers la mort, envers les enfants malades et leurs parents. Dans certaines unités pédiatriques, des contacts fréquents avec le psychiatre permettent aux infirmières de recevoir l'aide dont elles ont besoin.

À la mort de l'enfant, le soulagement et la douleur alternent dans le cœur des parents. Les souffrances du petit leucémique sont terminées et ils n'auront plus à s'inquiéter à son sujet ou à craindre le moment et les circonstances de sa mort. Les parents sont douloureusement conscients de leur ambivalence et il peut être cruel de le leur rappeler en disant: « Votre enfant est beaucoup mieux ainsi, il a cessé de souffrir! » Certains parents deviennent agressifs au moment de la mort et il ne faut pas considérer leurs paroles comme un blâme de leur part, mais comme l'expression de leur douleur.

Les frères et les sœurs réagissent de différentes manières: certains expriment leurs sentiments en pleurant ou en parlant du mort, d'autres s'expriment par le jeu, par des changements de comportement et certains craignent de mourir aussi de leucémie. Ils peuvent mettre la mort de l'autre enfant sur le compte de sentiments hostiles qu'ils ont ressentis à son égard pendant ou avant sa maladie. Les réactions n'apparaissent pas toujours au moment du décès, mais se présentent parfois quelques temps après. Il est possible que les parents, accablés par leur peine, ne puissent pas répondre aux besoins de l'enfant qui se retrouve seul devant sa propre douleur.

Si les parents ou d'autres membres de la famille ne réussissent pas à accepter la mort de l'enfant, certaines réactions négatives peuvent apparaître après quelques temps: changements de comportement, dépression, réactions de conversion ou problèmes psychosomatiques. Une aide psychiatrique devient alors nécessaire. Une visite des parents à l'hôpital quelques temps après la mort leur permet d'exprimer les sentiments qui les habitent; ils peuvent à cette occasion recevoir le rapport de l'autopsie s'ils avaient accordé leur consentement au moment de la mort et ils peuvent discuter des réactions qu'ils ont eues depuis cet instant. Une aide à long terme peut être décidée si cela semble nécessaire.

Des associations de parents d'enfants leucémiques ont été formées pour aider à résoudre les problèmes qui se présentent pendant la maladie de l'enfant, pour permettre l'échange d'informations et de connaissances, pour procurer de l'aide psychologique et émotive et pour promouvoir la recherche pour vaincre la leucémie.

L'hémophilie

Incidence. L'hémophilie n'est pas une entité simple, mais un syndrome résultant de différentes perturbations innées des mécanismes de la coagulation sanguine.

Le phénomène de la coagulation s'effectue en trois phases et est déclenché par un traumatisme vasculaire. Le tissu et les plaquettes

Maladies hémorragiques

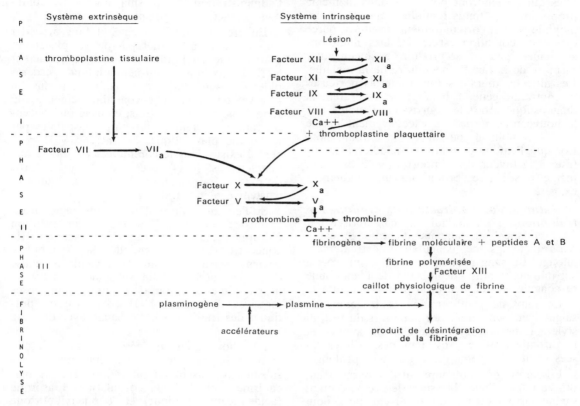

Figure 19-3. Phénomène physiologique de la coagulation. (Extrait de *Textbook of Pediatrics*, 9e éd. Nelson, W.E., Vaughn, V.C. et McKay, R.J., édit. Philadelphia, W.B. Saunders Company, 1969.)

lésés libèrent la thromboplastine tissulaire et plaquettaire qui s'associent à huit facteurs coagulants et forment la thromboplastine plasmatique. Cette dernière déclenche la deuxième phase, durant laquelle la prothrombine, enzyme inactive formée au foie en présence de vitamine K, est transformée en thrombine en présence d'ions calcium et de 6 autres facteurs coagulants. La thrombine est une enzyme active qui, au cours de la troisième phase, amène la transformation du fibrinogène en fibrine moléculaire. La fibrine moléculaire polymérise et forme le caillot de fibrine auquel adhèrent les hématies et les plaquettes. Par la suite survient la rétraction du caillot puis sa lyse sous l'action de la plasmine.

L'hémophilie A provient d'une déficience du facteur VIII, la globuline antihémophilique (GAH); *l'hémophilie* B (maladie de Christ-

mas) provient d'une déficience du facteur IX, élément de la thromboplastine plasmatique (PTC); et *l'hémophilie* C est causée par le manque de facteur XI, antécédent de la thromboplastine plasmatique.

D'autres facteurs peuvent être absents, mais l'hémophilie A et B constituent les types les plus courants. L'hémophilie A demeure la forme classique de la maladie. Les soins sont approximativement les mêmes pour tous les autres types d'hémophilie qui ne seront pas traités dans ce chapitre.

L'hémophilie A est une maladie héréditaire, à caractère récessif, transmise par le chromosome sexuel X et dont le caractère essentiel est l'allongement du temps de coagulation. Elle atteint le garçon, après avoir été transmise par une mère asymptomatique porteuse d'un seul chromosome X hémophile.

Le père hémophile transmet le gène pathologique à toutes ses filles qui pourront, dans une proportion 1 : 2, le transmettre à leurs garçons qui deviendront hémophiles et à leurs filles qui deviendront porteuses dans la même proportion. Un fœtus féminin homozygote hémophile meurt ordinairement in-utero parce que cette condition est létale. Des mutations spontanées peuvent se produire et aucun autre membre de la famille ne souffre de la maladie. Les filles du mutant seront toutefois porteuses du nouveau gène. L'hémophilie est rarement diagnostiquée chez le nourrisson, à moins que le nouveau-né ne saigne excessivement par le cordon ombilical ou après la circoncision. Lorsque l'enfant grandit, la maladie se manifeste à la faveur de n'importe quelle blessure, même très légère, produisant un saignement exagéré.

Pathogénie, manifestations cliniques et traitement.

La maladie est caractérisée par une tendance au saignement prolongé causé par un temps de coagulation extrêmement allongé. Le sang normal se coagule en trois à six minutes tandis que le sang de l'hémophile se coagule en une heure ou parfois davantage.

Le taux de prothrombine et le temps de saignement demeurent normaux lors du test au stylet. L'incision est généralement petite, et la thromboplastine provenant des cellules lésées suffit à prévenir un saignement prolongé.

L'hémorragie peut apparaître spontanément ou résulter d'une blessure légère. L'enfant saigne surtout du nez ou au niveau du genou. Les hémorragies intra-articulaires (hémarthrose) sont extrêmement douloureuses puisque le saignement s'effectue dans un espace restreint. Les traumatismes répétés produisent l'arthrite hémophilique qui s'accompagne de raideur articulaire, de boiterie et même d'impotence fonctionnelle. Le *traitement* comprend l'administration de sédatifs ou de narcotiques, l'immobilisation avec des attelles ou une coquille plâtrée et le refroidissement local. Après l'immobilisation, la physiothérapie prévient l'apparition des contractures. Un arceau protège la partie atteinte et évite le poids des couvertures sur le membre malade. Il faut bouger l'enfant avec précaution pour éviter d'autres hémorragies. Une hémorragie importante se manifeste par de l'anémie, une augmentation des plaquettes et une leucocytose. Si des hémorragies répétées constituent une menace pour les articulations, un traitement orthopédique peut devenir nécessaire.

Le *traitement* immédiat d'une blessure ouverte consiste à bien nettoyer la plaie et à placer au niveau de la lacération une mousse de fibrine ou de thrombine. On peut arrêter l'hémorragie locale par pression, par refroidissement local, par transfusion sanguine et par l'administration de plasma concentré contenant le facteur coagulant nécessaire.

En présence d'hémorragie, il faut procéder tout de suite à la thérapie de remplacement pour augmenter le taux plasmatique de facteur VIII. La globuline anti-hémophilique perd rapidement son efficacité dans le sang mis en réserve; on donne par voie intraveineuse, du sang frais, du plasma frais, congelé ou concentré tout en évitant la surcharge vasculaire par le liquide plasmatique. Le facteur VIII concentré existe dans le commerce. Le moins dispendieux est le cryoprécipité obtenu à partir du plasma frais; d'autres formes plus coûteuses existent également.

Si l'enfant souffre d'une hémorragie intra-crânienne ou s'il doit subir une intervention chirurgicale, l'administration de facteur VIII concentré devient essentielle. Si l'hémophile devient réfractaire au traitement à cause de la production d'une substance inhibitrice, la globuline IgC, on doit donner des doses massives de facteur VIII concentré ou pratiquer des transfusions d'échange avec du sang frais.

Le choix d'un analgésique s'avère d'une extrême importance puisque plusieurs de ces substances nuisent ou interfèrent avec le mécanisme normal de la coagulation. L'aspirine (acide acétylsalicylique) et le phénylbutazone inhibent le rôle normal des plaquettes et prolongent le temps de saignement. On peut utiliser sans danger l'acétaminophène et la mépiridine.

À la maison, des transfusions périodiques de cryoprécipité préviennent les hémorragies et en diminuent l'importance si l'enfant se blesse. Si la mère ne peut apprendre à les administrer elle-même, on peut conduire l'enfant à l'hôpital pour qu'il puisse recevoir sa transfusion et le ramener aussitôt chez lui.

Soins infirmiers.

À cause des hospitalisations répétées pour transfusions et traitements, il est nécessaire que l'infirmière comprenne l'attitude de l'enfant et de sa famille envers la maladie et l'hospitalisation.

Autant que possible on doit manipuler l'enfant avec précaution et l'infirmière doit surveiller les signes de douleur ou de pression, car le saignement peut se produire à n'importe quel endroit dans l'organisme. Si on demande à l'hémophile comment il préfère être bougé, ses douleurs et son sentiment d'impuissance s'en trouvent diminués. Autant que possible, on donne les médicaments par voie buccale. Si les injections deviennent nécessaires, on doit en choisir l'endroit avec précaution en variant fréquemment pour plus de sécurité. On injecte le médicament lentement puis on exerce une pression à l'aide du doigt ou d'un pansement compressif pendant au moins cinq minutes. Pour prélever des échantillons de sang, il faut choisir des veines superficielles car le danger d'hémorragie devient extrêmement grave si on utilise la fémorale ou la jugulaire.

Pour protéger le nourrisson hémophile, on lui donne des jouets mous; les côtés du lit et du parc sont rembourrés pour lui éviter des blessures lorsqu'il commence à se tenir debout et à marcher; on doit le protéger contre les accidents. Au cours de sa croissance, l'enfant devient plus actif et ses parents ont à songer à la fois au danger d'une blessure et à la nécessité d'une vie normale. Les professeurs et l'infirmière de l'école doivent être mis au courant de sa maladie et des problèmes qui y sont liés. Les adultes qui surveillent ses activités doivent essayer d'éviter la surprotection et lui permettre d'agir dans les limites de sa sécurité. L'enfant sain aime jouer avec ses camarades. Puisque l'hémophile semble normal, il peut chercher à cacher sa maladie pour suivre ses amis et gagner ainsi leur confiance et leur respect. Au contraire, s'il s'isole, il se sent abandonné, rejeté par le groupe et devient trop dépendant des adultes qui l'entourent.

L'infirmière essaie de lui procurer un support discret et continu. Pendant les périodes où l'enfant ne saigne pas, les parents peuvent devenir moins conscients de la nécessité de la surveillance médicale et l'infirmière doit insister sur ce point. L'enfant doit également recevoir des soins dentaires optimum et ce, très tôt, afin d'éviter d'éventuelles extractions dentaires. Si une telle intervention devient nécessaire, l'hémophile doit être hospitalisé.

L'enfant atteint d'une maladie chronique, telle que l'hémophilie, s'absente souvent de son milieu scolaire. Quand il ne va pas à l'école, il est quelquefois possible de maintenir le contact avec le milieu scolaire par liaison téléphonique. À cause de la nature chronique de la maladie, l'enfant et sa famille peuvent avoir besoin d'aide psychologique et financière. Les transfusions de sang ou de plasma peuvent devenir un problème sérieux pour les parents qui doivent pouvoir se rendre rapidement à l'hôpital à n'importe quel moment de la journée.

Pour aider l'enfant atteint d'arthrite hémophilique à se réadapter, on peut avoir recours à la chirurgie ou à l'emploi d'atelles, de plâtres, de béquilles ou d'une chaise roulante. Dans plusieurs pays, des associations existent pour fournir aux parents d'hémophiles l'aide dont ils besoin pour assurer une vie normale à leur fils.

La mère peut se sentir coupable d'avoir donné naissance à un enfant hémophile. Elle peut développer de la rancœur et de l'agressivité à la suite des soins intenses que son état exige. Le père peut rejeter l'enfant ouvertement ou de façon inconsciente parce que son fils ne peut se mesurer aux autres garçons sur le plan physique ou sportif. L'enfant surprotégé par une mère anxieuse risque de devenir égocentrique et craintif. Il s'éloigne alors des autres enfants et devient dépendant des adultes. Il peut se servir de sa maladie pour manipuler ses parents et se placer intentionnellement dans des situations dangereuses. Le père de l'enfant hémophile a souvent de la difficulté à accepter les réactions de son épouse et de son garçon. Les études démontrent que les saignements sont très souvent associés à des situations anxiogènes ou à des traumatismes psychologiques. Si les parents reçoivent une aide appropriée, ils peuvent aider leur enfant à développer son autonomie et son sens de l'initiative et à acquérir une personnalité saine.

Pronostic. Le pronostic demeure incertain. Souvent, des saignements légers alternent avec des hémorragies sévères suivant un rythme quelquefois associé au stress que subit l'enfant. La tension émotive reflète parfois les relations difficiles avec les parents, mais provient aussi de différends avec les frères et sœurs ou d'autres personnes de l'entourage. La mort peut suivre une hémorragie intracrânienne ou une autre hémorragie grave. Les méthodes modernes de traitement, sang frais, cryo-précipités, permettent de contrôler plus efficacement l'évolution de la maladie, de diminuer ou de raccourcir les séjours à l'hôpital.

Purpura

Des hémorragies spontanées caractérisent la maladie connue sous le nom de purpura. Ces hémorragies se produisent au niveau de la peau, des muqueuses ou des organes internes. De telles hémorragies sont possibles dans toute condition où il existe une diminution du nombre des plaquettes sanguines ou une fragilité de la paroi des capillaires. Des pétéchies ou de minuscules hémorragies cutanées peuvent également apparaître lors de réactions allergiques.

Deux types de purpura sont décrits dans ce chapitre: le purpura idiopathique thrombocytopénique et le purpura anaphylactoïde.

Purpura thrombocytopénique idiopathique

Étiologie, incidence, manifestations cliniques et signes de laboratoire. Le purpura est associé à une diminution du nombre des plaquettes sanguines, causées par des facteurs extérieurs aux plaquettes elles-mêmes. La maladie est particulièrement fréquente entre trois et sept ans. Elle est rare chez l'enfant de race noire. Durant l'enfance, on rencontre surtout la forme aiguë. La maladie peut apparaître brusquement à la suite d'une infection respiratoire légère ou d'une rougeole. On note de la fièvre et un état de prostration; elle est caractérisée par de petites hémorragies au niveau de la peau, des membranes et des autres tissus. De larges ecchymoses peuvent être dues à des traumatismes. Dans sa forme grave, la maladie peut être accompagnée d'hémorragies vaginales, nasales, urinaires, et gastro-intestinales. On doit craindre l'hémorragie cérébrale.

La forme chronique, rare chez l'enfant, apparaît progressivement. Elle se manifeste par des saignements prolongés à la suite de blessures et par des ecchymoses importantes au moindre traumatisme. L'évolution est cyclique, les périodes de rémission alternent avec des périodes de saignement excessif.

Les *examens de laboratoire* confirment le diagnostic. La numération des plaquettes est toujours au-dessous de 100 000/mm³ de sang (la normale est de 200 000 à 500 000). Dans la forme chronique, on note une déficience en fer qui résulte des pertes sanguines. Les temps de saignement et de coagulation sont normaux, mais la rétraction du caillot s'effectue d'une façon anormale. L'analyse de la moelle osseuse élimine la possibilité d'une leucémie.

Traitement, évolution et pronostic. Le traitement conservateur fait appel à des transfusions sanguines, aux antibiotiques, au repos au lit lors des hémorragies modérées et graves et à une diète bien équilibrée, riche en vitamines. En cas de saignement grave, on donne du plasma riche en plaquettes ou du sang frais complet. L'ACTH ou la cortisone réduisent la durée des récidives mais ne sont qu'un traitement palliatif. Une splénectomie peut être pratiquée si la maladie persiste pendant six à douze mois ou si le malade présente des hémorragies graves. La splénectomie peut amener des périodes de rémission durable chez l'enfant porteur de la forme chronique. L'opération modifie les symptômes des enfants qui n'ont pas été guéris.

La majorité des enfants porteurs de la forme aiguë guérissent en quelques mois avec un traitement conservateur. L'hémorragie intra-crânienne est rare mais demeure la principale cause de décès. Les filles affligées de purpura chronique doivent ordinairement subir une splénectomie avant le début de leurs menstruations.

Purpura anaphylactoïde (syndrome de Schoënlein-Hénoch)

Le syndrome de Schoënlein-Hénoch ou purpura anaphylactoïde est une maladie systémique polymorphe. On trouve des lésions cutanées et viscérales.

Incidence et étiologie. La maladie n'est pas rare; elle affecte toutes les races et apparaît surtout entre trois et sept ans.

La cause en est inconnue. Le début peut suivre un contact avec une substance spécifique. Dans de tels cas, le rôle de l'allergie semble important. Le début peut survenir après une infection du tractus respiratoire supérieur causée par le streptocoque hémolytique.

Manifestations cliniques et signes de laboratoire. Très souvent à la suite d'une infection, *une série de symptômes* différents font leur apparition. Des douleurs abdominales et articulaires peuvent se manifester au début. Une éruption cutanée apparaît alors au niveau des jambes et de la région fessière, pour s'étendre au visage, aux bras et au tronc. L'éruption se présente d'abord sous forme d'urticaire, suivie de lésions érythémateuses maculo-papulaires. Finalement, les lésions deviennent pétéchiales ou purpuriques, changeant du rouge au pourpre ou ocre avant de disparaître. On trouve des lésions d'âges différents. Des hémorragies et de l'œdème peuvent se produire au niveau des tractus gastro-intestinal et urinaire. On observe généralement un malaise et un état subfébrile.

On rencontre des douleurs abdominales de type colique, des vomissements et du méléna. L'atteinte rénale se manifeste par de l'albuminurie et de l'hématurie et environ la moitié des enfants qui ont les reins atteints souffrent aussi d'hypertension ou d'azotémie élevée. Les articulations, généralement les genoux et les chevilles, peuvent être affectées. On note alors de la douleur, de l'œdème et une limitation de mouvement qui peuvent faire penser à la fièvre rhumatismale. L'œdème cérébral et l'hémorragie peuvent causer des convulsions et le coma.

Les *analyses de laboratoire* ne révèlent rien d'anormal, si ce n'est que la vitesse de sédimentation est élevée. Les pertes importantes de sang précèdent l'anémie. Les temps de saignement et de coagulation, la rétraction du caillot et le taux des plaquettes demeurent inchangés.

Traitement, complications, évolution et pronostic. Il n'y a pas de *traitement* spécifique. En présence d'une allergie (substances alimentaires, bactéries, médicaments ou pollen) on mettra l'enfant à l'abri de l'allergène. Si le purpura suit une infection bactérienne, on élimine l'agent pathogène par un traitement approprié. Au cours de la phase aiguë, l'alitement est nécessaire et on doit surveiller étroitement l'état rénal et cérébral. Les corticostéroïdes peuvent modifier les symptômes, mais ils ne raccourcissent pas l'évolution de la maladie. On donne des transfusions sanguines si c'est nécessaire.

Des *complications* rénales suivies d'une insuffisance rénale peuvent apparaître plusieurs années après la phase aiguë de la maladie. L'*évolution* et le *pronostic* demeurent extrêmement variables. La maladie peut durer de six semaines à un ou deux ans. Généralement, elle disparaît après quelques jours. L'enfant peut mourir d'une atteinte gastro-intestinale ou rénale, d'hypertension ou d'une hémorragie intracrânienne.

Allergie

Étiologie et facteurs prédisposants. Le terme allergie définit une altération de la réaction tissulaire à une ou plusieurs substances. Quand un antigène ou un corps étranger pénètre dans l'organisme, celui-ci se défend en élaborant des anticorps qui agissent sur le corps étranger pour le détruire ou le transformer en une substance inoffensive. Chez les individus allergiques, il se produit, au cours de cette réaction, une libération excessive d'histamine, responsable des effets allergiques défavorables. Dans presque tous les cas, les anticorps sont déjà présents, élaborés à la suite d'agressions antigéniques antérieures. L'agression peut se produire par inhalation, par absorption cutanée, par ingestion ou par injection parentérale.

L'antigène est toujours de nature protéique et provient ordinairement d'une espèce animale différente. Les glucides, les lipides ou certains produits chimiques peuvent être associés à des protéines et agir comme antigène.

L'allergie est en partie héréditaire (dans ce cas, on parle d'atopie), en partie liée à l'allergène lui-même; elle dépend aussi du degré et de la durée de l'exposition à l'allergène. Quoique tout individu soit potentiellement allergique, la susceptibilité à l'allergie varie beaucoup. On retrouve un facteur héréditaire chez environ 75% des enfants allergiques, mais ceux-ci n'ont pas toujours les mêmes manifestations allergiques que leurs parents et ne réagissent pas nécessairement aux mêmes allergènes. *Ce qui est transmis, c'est la vulnérabilité générale de l'organisme à l'allergie.*

Le fœtus peut subir une sensibilisation passive qui ne se manifestera qu'après son premier contact avec l'allergène. Les nourrissons et les enfants plus âgés qui ont souffert de graves problèmes gastro-intestinaux pourront développer une sensibilité à certaines protéines non transformées qui ont gagné la circulation sanguine à la faveur d'une augmentation de la perméabilité de la paroi intestinale. On ne peut nier l'importance des facteurs psychologiques et du stress dans le développement de l'allergie. Plusieurs recherches s'effectuent afin de dégager les traits de la personnalité de l'enfant allergique et les caractéristiques de la relation parents-enfant. En général, on trouve une anxiété et une dépendance excessive de la part de l'enfant, et la mère semble surprotectrice. Ces recherches ne sont pas concluantes, mais l'infirmière doit s'attendre à trouver une atmosphère tendue lorsqu'elle soigne un enfant allergique.

Manifestations cliniques, diagnostic et signes de laboratoire. Les *manifestations cliniques* varient beaucoup et dépendent de l'âge de l'enfant. Un nourrisson porteur d'eczéma souffrira éventuellement d'asthme ou de rhinite allergique. De nouvelles sensibilités peuvent apparaître chez l'enfant, tandis que les anciennes se maintiennent ou diminuent.

Un enfant présentant des manifestations allergiques devra subir des tests cutanés afin d'identifier la ou les substances en cause. Quoique les enfants réagissent aux tests d'allergie de la même manière que les adultes, leurs réactions sont interprétées à la lumière des signes cliniques et l'exactitude des résultats est douteuse si on administre les tests avant l'âge de deux ans. Certains chercheurs sont en train de mettre au point une méthode de titrage d'anticorps qui nécessiterait deux prélèvements sanguins et éviterait les tests cutanés. On peut également isoler les allergènes alimentaires en donnant à l'enfant une diète par élimination. Ceci permet de déterminer l'agent causal pour un enfant dont la diète inclut uniquement quelques aliments. Il faut éliminer certains aliments de la diète et surveiller étroitement ses réactions à d'autres aliments.

Sauf dans le cas d'asthme aigu, on rencontre généralement une éosinophilie sanguine. L'éosinophilie dans les sécrétions nasales peut apparaître dans n'importe quelle manifestation allergique.

Traitement, pronostic et prophylaxie.

Le médecin cherche à obtenir l'histoire détaillée de l'enfant et de sa famille et les parents doivent accepter la possibilité d'un traitement à long terme. On peut tenter trois méthodes de traitement: éliminer l'allergène en cause, hyposensibiliser l'organisme à l'allergène spécifique connu ou modifier la réaction de l'organisme.

Le moyen probablement le plus efficace pour traiter une allergie alimentaire consiste à éliminer du régime l'aliment responsable. Il faut tout de même veiller à ce que la diète réponde aux besoins énergétiques de l'enfant. On peut le soustraire partiellement au contact de la poussière et d'autres allergènes agissant par contact ou inhalation.

Il n'existe pas de méthode exacte pour déterminer le dosage nécessaire à la désensibilisation à partir d'un allergène connu. Pour les substances inhalées, on pratique généralement la désensibilisation par injection d'extraits de la substance, à doses croissantes. La quantité initiale est la plus petite dose qui, donnée par voie sous-cutanée, produit une réaction intradermique. Les doses subséquentes sont progressivement augmentées et données à intervalle de trois à cinq jours. À aucun moment on ne donnera la quantité à laquelle se produisent des symptômes. On obtient la désensibilisation aux aliments en donnant des quantités croissantes de la substance alimentaire responsable des manifestations allergiques. Il faut souligner que la désensibilisation donne des résultats mitigés. Elle diminue la gravité des symptômes et modifie le cours de l'histoire allergique, mais elle ne guérit pas la maladie et ne soulage pas entièrement tous les symptômes.

La troisième méthode de traitement consiste à modifier la réaction de l'organisme à l'allergène en cause. On vise à réduire la tension émotive des parents et de l'enfant, car l'état psychologique influe sur les réactions de l'organisme. Il faut traiter toute perturbation endocrinienne. Certains médicaments contribuent à diminuer les symptômes: ce sont les antihistaminiques, les adrénergiques, tels l'épinéphrine et l'éphédrine, les xanthines, la corticotrophine (ACTH) et les corticostéroïdes. Il faut éliminer les infections respiratoires parce qu'elles prédisposent à l'allergie. La déshydratation diminue la réaction allergique. Le repos et l'amélioration de l'état général contribuent à atténuer les manifestations allergiques.

L'allergie à une substance ne peut pas être guérie, mais elle peut être suffisamment bien contrôlée pour ne plus produire de symptômes. On doit tenter de supprimer partiellement ou complètement l'allergène du milieu ambiant des personnes sensibilisées. Il est important que les enfants nés de parents allergiques n'entrent pas trop tôt en contact avec les substances susceptibles de produire une réaction indésirable.

Si un ou les deux parents sont allergiques, il y a un risque marqué de sensibilisation au lait de vache et l'idéal serait l'allaitement maternel ou la substitution de lait à base de graminés comme le soya (Pro-Sobee). Plus tard, il faut éviter d'ajouter à la diète deux aliments à la fois. En effet, si le mélange de nouveaux aliments produit une manifestation allergique, il est alors difficile de reconnaître l'allergène en cause. On évite de donner aux enfants nés de parents allergiques certains aliments causant généralement l'allergie, tels le lait de vache, les œufs, le chocolat, le germe de blé et les oranges.

Types d'allergie chez l'enfant.

Les plus importantes manifestations allergiques de l'enfant sont l'eczéma, l'asthme, la rhinite allergique et les maladies sériques. Les atteintes chroniques du nez, de la gorge et du tractus gastro-intestinal peuvent également être d'origine allergique.

Asthme

Incidence, étiologie et physio-pathologie.

L'asthme est une maladie pulmonaire souvent due à une allergie. On considère l'eczéma infantile comme un signe avant-coureur de l'asthme. La maladie atteint rarement le nourrisson; son *incidence* croît à partir de l'âge de trois ans.

L'asthme peut être déclenché par certains aliments, certaines substances inhalées ou des infections, particulièrement celles du système respiratoire. La crise peut suivre une activité vigoureuse, l'exposition au froid ou une émotion. Les attaques se produisent souvent après le coucher car, dans son lit, l'enfant est en contact avec les plumes de l'oreiller, la laine des couvertures, les jouets rembourrés et même la poussière du milieu ambiant. De plus, les peurs sont plus intenses à ce moment de la journée.

L'asthme apparaît parfois à la suite d'une expérience psychologique traumatisante. La tension émotive chronique qui sévit dans certaines familles peut précipiter des crises asthmatiques répétées. Les crises successives peuvent à leur tour polariser l'anxiété des parents et ainsi s'établit un climat chargé d'émotivité. La psychothérapie peut devenir nécessaire pour diminuer l'anxiété et la tension émotive de l'entourage et permettre à l'enfant de mener une vie plus normale. Les membres de l'équipe de santé doivent saisir la nécessité d'un tel traitement. Il devient quelquefois indispensable de soigner l'enfant dans une institution où des soins complets pourront lui être prodigués.

Les bronches et les bronchioles subissent des modifications importantes. Au début, apparaissent un spasme de la musculature bronchique, un œdème de la muqueuse et la sécrétion d'un mucus épais et adhérent qui s'accumule dans la lumière de la bronche. Il s'ensuit une obstruction des voies respiratoires; au cours de la crise, tout l'air ne peut pas être expiré et demeure dans les alvéoles réalisant le tableau de l'emphysème obstructif. On entend des râles sibilants dus à la présence des sécrétions bronchiques. L'atélectasie suit une obstruction bronchique complète.

La durée de la crise d'asthme peut varier de quelques heures à quelques jours et l'enfant arrive éventuellement à expectorer le mucus. Le spasme disparaît. En présence d'infection, on peut observer d'autres problèmes respiratoires. D'ailleurs, la bronchite asthmatique et l'asthme ne sont pas faciles à différencier.

Manifestations cliniques et traitement.

L'asthme est caractérisé par des crises de dyspnée paroxystique à prédominance expiratoire. Le début peut être progressif avec des éternuements, une congestion nasale, de la rhinorrhée et une toux légère. Certaines crises apparaissent soudainement et se manifestent surtout la nuit. L'enfant adopte alors dans son lit la position assise qui facilite sa respiration. Il transpire abondamment et devient anxieux et agité. Les râles sibilants accompagnent surtout l'expiration; la toux peut être continue. Si les bronches deviennent obstruées par des bouchons muqueux, il se produit de l'atélectasie dans les zones que desservent ces bronches et le médiastin peut être déplacé du côté atteint. Les veines du cou deviennent distendues, mais la cyanose apparaît rarement. Au cours de la crise d'asthme, l'enfant ne devrait jamais être laissé seul. Toutefois, les parents deviennent extrêmement anxieux et leur anxiété peut contribuer à perturber davantage l'état émotif de l'enfant.

Avec un traitement approprié, une telle crise s'amende rapidement. L'attitude empreinte de calme de l'infirmière aide à réduire l'anxiété des parents et de l'enfant. Son rôle consiste également à observer l'effet des médicaments administrés ainsi que les effets secondaires qui peuvent apparaître en cours de traitement.

La crise non traitée peut durer plusieurs jours. Si l'enfant est en « status asthmaticus » ou état de mal asthmatique, la crise continue et il faut veiller à maintenir l'équilibre hydrique et à corriger l'acidose due à la rétention de l'acide carbonique. On peut être obligé de recourir à la ventilation mécanique avec pression positive intermittente ou continue. L'installation d'un tube endotrachéal favorise l'aspiration des sécrétions ou le lavage des bronches. Une trachéotomie peut devenir nécessaire. La percussion et le drainage postural facilitent l'écoulement du mucus. L'enfant souffrant de status asthmaticus doit demeurer sous surveillance constante dans une tente à oxygène et à haute humidité. L'enfant peut mourir au cours d'une de ces crises.

La façon la plus efficace de traiter l'asthme consiste à éliminer l'allergène en cause, qu'il soit alimentaire ou dans le milieu ambiant, sinon on doit entreprendre une cure d'hyposensibilisation aux allergènes spécifiques. L'enfant doit éviter la fatigue et le refroidissement et vivre dans un environnement physique et émotif adéquat.

Le médicament le plus efficace dans le traitement d'une crise aiguë d'asthme infantile est l'épinéphrine (adrénaline) donnée par voie sous-cutanée. L'enfant est soulagé en 3 à 5 minutes et la dose peut être répétée 2 fois à des intervalles de 20 minutes. L'infirmière doit surveiller la pulsation de l'enfant étant donné le risque de tachycardie que comporte ce médicament. On peut aussi administrer l'adrénaline en la vaporisant profondément dans la gorge au moment de l'inspiration. Par la suite, un adrénergique à plus longue action, tel l'éphédrine, peut être administré. Toutefois on préfère souvent les xanthines.

Les xanthines, surtout sous forme d'aminophylline, sont employées à doses filées pour obtenir une bronchodilatation stable et une respiration plus profonde. Il importe de bien vérifier la dose du médicament étant donné que la quantité toxique est très près de la dose thérapeutique. L'aminophylline produit des effets secondaires sérieux, tels vomissements, surexcitation, hématémèse, convulsions et coma. L'action de l'aminophylline est augmentée par l'administration d'adrénaline ou d'éphédrine.

On peut obtenir un soulagement rapide avec les corticostéroïdes. Ils peuvent être administrés d'abord par voie intraveineuse (solucortef) puis par voie buccale (prednisone). Le traitement à long terme avec ces dérivés hormonaux peut amener, entre autres effets secondaires, la suppression de l'activité surrénalienne, le retard de croissance et la dépendance de l'organisme envers le médicament. À court terme, les stéroïdes produisent souvent un état d'euphorie et d'excitation.

Une médication expectorante peut s'avérer nécessaire quoique l'hydratation constitue le meilleur moyen de fluidifier les sécrétions et de favoriser leur expectoration. L'iodure de potassium, trois fois par jour, semble être le médicament de choix.

Étant donné que la majorité des médicaments ci-haut décrits ont comme effet secondaire commun l'excitation, le médecin prescrit souvent un sédatif. Le phénobarbital est le plus couramment employé.

On place l'enfant, au plus tôt, dans une atmosphère suffisamment humide pour liquéfier ses sécrétions et faire cesser le spasme. Il faut bien hydrater l'enfant asthmatique afin de permettre une liquéfaction des sécrétions bronchiques. Des perfusions parentérales sont très souvent indiquées.

On peut donner de l'oxygène si c'est nécessaire dans le but de réduire l'anoxie et la cyanose. Si une atélectasie se produit par obstruction bronchique, une bronchoscopie est alors indiquée pour nettoyer les voies respiratoires.

On institue une thérapie antibactérienne quand l'enfant souffre d'une infection au moment d'une crise d'asthme. Après la phase aiguë, lorsque le spasme cède, l'aérosolthérapie et les drainages posturaux sont indiqués.

L'aérosolthérapie fait appel à une variété de médicaments. L'isoprotérénol apporte un soulagement rapide et améliore les échanges gazeux. Toutefois un dosage rigoureux s'impose étant donné la toxicité possible du médicament. De plus, il ne doit pas s'administrer conjointement avec l'épinéphrine si la condition cardiaque de l'enfant n'est pas excellente. Des mucolytiques, de l'éphédrine, du soluté salin et des antibiotiques peuvent faire partie de l'arsenal médicamenteux des aérosols. Toutefois, il est à souligner que des crises d'asthme ont été induites par des aérosols, qu'ils ont contribué à endommager irrémédiablement des muqueuses et qu'ils peuvent créer un effet de dépendance chez plusieurs patients. Des cas d'abus ont été rapportés et des morts sont survenues à la suite d'aérosols avec norépinéphrine. On tend de plus en plus à diminuer l'aérosolthérapie, surtout entre les crises aiguës.

On continue le traitement d'entretien par voie buccale. Les médicaments habituellement donnés incluent les sédatifs, les broncho-dilatateurs et les expectorants. On évite d'administrer régulièrement des stéroïdes étant donné leurs effets secondaires sérieux. L'enfant est toujours gardé dans une atmosphère suffisamment humide. Pour prévenir les infections respiratoires, l'enfant pourrait bénéficier d'un climat tempéré pendant les mois d'hiver. Certains médecins recommandent de petites doses d'antibiotiques comme moyen prophylactique contre les infections au cours de l'hiver. D'autres médecins recommandent l'emploi de vaccins qui réduisent l'incidence d'infections respiratoires. Certains médecins recommandent l'amygdalectomie et l'adénoïdectomie quand ces tissus constituent des foyers d'infection ou qu'ils obstruent les voies respiratoires.

Entre les périodes aiguës, un nouveau médicament qui prévient la crise d'asthme est maintenant utilisé. Le cromoglycate de sodium (Cromolyn-Intal) est une poudre que l'on doit vaporiser puis inhaler. Ce médicament aide à espacer les attaques, diminue la toux et les symptômes de malaises respiratoires. Il est utilisé entre les phases aiguës de la maladie. Dans le traitement d'un enfant asthmatique, le concours d'un allergologiste et d'un psychologue ou d'un psychiatre pour enfants peut devenir nécessaire.

Soins infirmiers. L'infirmière qui prend soin de l'enfant observe son comportement quand il se trouve avec d'autres enfants ou avec le personnel de l'hôpital, ainsi que ses réactions quand sa mère le visite. Un tel relevé s'avère d'une grande importance pour le médecin ou le psychiatre dans l'évaluation de la médication et des facteurs émotifs éventuels.

Il est important de garder l'enfant asthmatique en bonne santé. Il doit recevoir une diète équilibrée, riche en vitamines. Étant donné qu'il lui arrive de manger lentement à cause d'une difficulté respiratoire, il faut lui laisser suffisamment de temps pour se nourrir. Des petits repas fréquents semblent préférables à de copieux repas donnés à intervalles espacés.

L'enfant doit prendre suffisamment de repos dans un milieu aussi calme que possible. Il sera vraisemblablement plus confortable en position assise. On encourage les divertissements et les jeux appropriés à son âge et à sa condition physique.

Quoique l'infirmière doive être patiente avec l'enfant, elle établira des limites qu'il devra respecter. L'instabilité produit des conflits émotifs qui augmentent la difficulté respiratoire. La fréquentation scolaire est possible, mais il est bon de mettre le personnel de l'établissement au courant de l'état de santé de l'enfant. Il pourra ainsi mener une vie aussi normale que possible.

Enseignement aux parents. L'enseignement aux parents est essentiel parce qu'ils reçoivent des informations de plusieurs sources et deviennent très souvent anxieux et perplexes. Il est important qu'ils sachent quelles activités sont permises à l'enfant de façon à ne pas le limiter inutilement. Ordinairement, on lui permet de vivre normalement selon son âge, mais il lui faut éviter les activités qui provoquent un essoufflement rapide et excessif. L'enfant doit apprendre à mesurer sa tolérance et il doit surtout apprendre à connaître ses réactions et à se soigner graduellement lui-même.

Les parents doivent aussi organiser un environnement physique adéquat en éliminant le plus possible les tapis, les tentures et couvre-lits de laine, les oreillers de plumes et les jouets rembourrés ou en peluche. Dans la mesure du possible, ils doivent s'abstenir de garder des animaux à la maison. L'infirmière doit aussi les renseigner sur la médication que reçoit l'enfant, en insistant sur le dosage et les effets à surveiller. Ils doivent savoir que la médication a des effets secondaires de surexcitation. Ils seront moins portés à blâmer l'enfant pour son comportement hyperactif et trouveront plutôt des exutoires à son activité.

L'infirmière doit présenter son enseignement de façon à déculpabiliser les parents, à ne pas augmenter leur anxiété et à les aider à comprendre que l'enfant doit conserver son indépendance et son initiative.

Pronostic. Les crises d'asthme cessent très souvent au moment de la puberté, mais l'enfant peut alors présenter d'autres manifestations allergiques. Chez certains, l'asthme se poursuit au cours de la vie adulte sans créer de limitations sérieuses. Chez d'autres, un état de mal asthmatique se développe et handicape l'enfant dans ses activités.

Rhinite allergique

Étiologie et incidence. La rhinite allergique est une manifestation allergique touchant le tractus respiratoire supérieur. Les crises peuvent être permanentes. La rhinite allergique peut être induite par un pollen ou par l'inhalation d'autres substances. Les herbes (ragweed) et les roses peuvent causer la rhinite allergique chez les personnes sensibles. On parle de «fièvre des foins» quand la rhinite est saisonnière. On rencontre rarement la maladie avant l'âge de trois à quatre ans.

Manifestations cliniques et traitement. Les *manifestations cliniques* comprennent des éternuements par salves, un prurit intense et un encombrement nasal. On peut également observer un prurit, de l'érythème et un écoulement au niveau des conjonctives. La muqueuse du nez est pâle et œdémateuse. L'écoulement nasal, d'abord muqueux et abondant, peut devenir purulent à la suite d'une infection. La rhinite allergique demeure moins grave que les autres maladies allergiques. Le *moyen* le plus efficace de la traiter est d'essayer d'éliminer l'allergène de l'air ambiant. On emploiera au besoin un climatiseur et un système de filtration de l'air qui n'assureront toutefois qu'une protection à l'intérieur de la maison. Un changement de climat met souvent fin à la rhinite allergique.

Une désensibilisation doit être tentée dans la majorité des cas: elle est longue, mais souvent efficace pour un certain temps et en continuant de prendre des précautions particulières.

On emploie fréquemment des antihistaminiques, tels le bénadryl ou le pyribenzamine dans les cas de rhinite saisonnière. Les vaso-constricteurs, comme l'éphédrine, agissent généralement bien au niveau des muqueuses nasales, mais doivent être utilisés très prudemment étant donné leur toxicité rapide. L'épinéphrine ne sera employée que s'il existe un asthme associé.

Maladies sériques et réactions anaphylactiques

Incidence et étiologie. Toute personne est susceptible de souffrir d'une maladie sérique si on lui injecte suffisamment de sérum contenant des protéines étrangères. La maladie peut survenir à n'importe quel âge et chez les deux sexes. La cause la plus fréquente demeure l'injection prophylactique de sérum de cheval, quoique n'importe quel autre sérum puisse produire des manifestations cliniques.

L'injection de sérum suscite la production d'anticorps qui vont s'unir au sérum restant pour produire une réaction allergique.

L'injection de petites quantités de sérum peut sensibiliser un individu pour plusieurs années. Dans l'ensemble, les réactions graves ressemblent au choc anaphylactique et peuvent se produire chez des individus sensibilisés au sérum de cheval. Les réactions anaphylactiques sont moins fréquentes chez l'enfant que chez l'adulte. L'injection de produits ou de dérivés de la pénicilline ainsi que les piqûres d'insectes en demeurent les principales causes.

Manifestations cliniques, pronostic et prévention. Les *manifestations cliniques* peuvent être modérées ou graves. Le début de ces manifestations se situe en moyenne deux jours après l'injection du sérum avec des extrêmes allant de quelques heures à un mois. L'éruption cutanée, qui est la papule urticarienne, apparaît d'abord à l'endroit de l'injection, puis s'étend sur tout le corps. Dans les cas graves, du purpura et des éruptions exsudatives se produisent. Un œdème angioneurotique se développe au niveau des paupières, des lèvres, de la langue, des mains ou des pieds et un œdème généralisé (Quincke) peut être présent. Le prurit est intense. On peut rencontrer une adénopathie généralisée, une splénomégalie, de l'œdème et de la rougeur des articulations. Les douleurs musculaires, les céphalées, la fièvre et un malaise général sont fréquents. Dans les cas graves, on peut craindre les complications cérébrales et neurologiques.

Si la personne a été préalablement sensibilisée, les manifestations cliniques surviennent immédiatement après l'injection du sérum.

Quand on pratique le test cutané pour évaluer la sensibilité au sérum ou quand on administre le sérum lui-même, l'épinéphrine permet de contrôler les symptômes anaphylactiques éventuels. On utilise l'éphédrine au même titre que les antihistaminiques et les corticostéroïdes. Des compresses froides, des bains d'amidon et des lotions antiprurigineuses soulagent le prurit; des sédatifs et des salicylates seront prescrits pour apaiser l'enfant.

La réaction au sérum disparaît spontanément. Elle évolue généralement pendant un ou deux jours, mais peut aussi durer une semaine.

On doit pratiquer des tests de sensibilité avant l'injection de n'importe quel sérum étranger, spécialement si l'enfant a des antécédents d'eczéma, d'asthme ou de rhinite allergique. Si la zone d'injection devient rouge après vingt minutes, la réaction est considérée comme positive; on peut également pratiquer des tests ophtalmiques pour déterminer la sensibilité au sérum. La réaction est positive si l'œil devient rouge après quelques minutes. On peut administrer un antihistaminique de façon prophylactique pour éviter une maladie sérique.

Épilepsie

Les convulsions du nourrisson ont déjà été décrites. Les convulsions de l'enfant d'âge préscolaire indiquent généralement une épilepsie.

L'épilepsie est caractérisée par des crises répétées de perte de conscience ou d'obnubilation. Des spasmes musculaires toniques ou cloniques ou d'autres anomalies du comportement peuvent se produire. L'épilepsie n'est pas en elle-même une entité morbide spécifique, mais un terme général définissant une variété de crises convulsives à caractère répétitif.

On craint parfois ceux qui en sont atteints considérant l'épilepsie comme une maladie honteuse. Les membres de l'équipe de santé doivent faire comprendre au public et surtout aux membres de la famille du malade, le sens réel de cette maladie chronique. Il faut éviter de donner une information détaillée en une seule fois, mais renseigner progressivement de façon à dissiper le mystère et la crainte.

Il existe deux types étiologiques d'épilepsie: idiopathique et organique.

Épilepsie idiopathique. Plus de la moitié des enfants présentant des crises répétées avant la puberté, souffrent d'une épilepsie idiopathique. La cause de ces crises est inconnue. Un facteur génétique est postulé, mais l'hérédité est rarement démontrée cliniquement. L'électroencéphalogramme est habituellement anormal mais on ne trouve aucune lésion anatomique. Le début survient généralement entre quatre et huit ans. Dans 85% des cas, le traitement parvient à contrôler les crises.

Épilepsie organique. L'épilepsie organique provient de lésions anatomiques ou biochimiques focales ou diffuses du cerveau. Ces atteintes résiduelles peuvent être causées par une lacération directe du tissu cérébral au moment d'un accident ou par une hémorragie également due à un traumatisme ou à une maladie hémorragique; par des infections, telles la méningite et l'encéphalite; par l'anoxie, surtout secondaire à l'asphyxie néonatale; ou par des manifestations toxiques imputables au kernictère ou à un empoisonnement au plomb. Le cerveau peut également être le siège de modifications dégénératrices. Des pathologies congénitales, telles la phénylcétonurie ou l'hydrocéphalie, ou encore, des maladies, telles la syphilis ou la toxoplasmose peuvent engendrer des anomalies organiques au niveau du cerveau. Dans l'épilepsie organique, l'électroencéphalogramme est anormal dans la majorité des cas.

Manifestations cliniques et diagnostic. Les *manifestations cliniques* servent de base à une classification des crises: grand mal, petit mal, psychomotrice, focale et crise infantile myoclonique.

Chez l'enfant, *le grand mal* n'est pas toujours précédé d'aura comme chez l'adulte. Les enfants plus âgés peuvent avoir des céphalées, paraître irritables et léthargiques ou souffrir d'un malaise digestif juste avant la crise. Celle-ci consiste en une convulsion généralisée. On lui reconnaît une phase tonique et une phase clonique.

Le *spasme tonique* est une contraction involontaire, violente et persistante. Au début de la phase tonique, l'enfant pâlit soudainement, pousse un cri rauque, perd conscience et tombe. Les pupilles sont dilatées, les yeux révulsés, le faciès déformé. Les muscles du cou, de la face, du thorax, de l'abdomen et des membres deviennent rigides et le thorax est fixé en expiration forcée. L'enfant peut se mordre la langue. Étant donné l'arrêt des mouvements respiratoires, la cyanose apparaît. Cette phase dure environ de 10 à 20 secondes.

La phase *clonique* consiste en une alternance rythmique de contractions et de détentes musculaires. Les secousses deviennent de plus en plus fortes et moins fréquentes. La tête est agitée de mouvements violents de rotation et de flexion. Les mâchoires s'ouvrent et se ferment, la langue est projetée vers l'avant. Une écume abondante sort de la bouche.

Les sphincters se relâchent et il y a très souvent émission d'urines et de selles.

La crise se termine par une brusque détente, accompagnée d'un profond soupir. L'enfant tombe ensuite dans un sommeil profond, quasi comateux, et respire bruyamment. À son réveil, il se plaint parfois de céphalée et semble confus et stuporeux. Il ne garde aucun souvenir de ce qui s'est passé. L'enfant peut avoir des crises la nuit et s'apercevoir le matin que son lit est humide ou qu'il s'est mordu la langue.

Le *petit mal* est caractérisé par des pertes passagères de conscience accompagnées généralement de révulsion des yeux et de clignotement des paupières. On voit souvent des mouvements légers et rythmiques de la tête, des membres ou du tronc. L'enfant ne tombe généralement pas; il ne bave pas. À partir de trois ans, le petit mal se voit plus souvent chez les filles que chez les garçons. Ces attaques durent environ trente secondes, surviennent sans avertissement et ne laissent aucune séquelle. L'enfant peut faire plusieurs crises par jour, allant jusqu'à cent et plus, ou n'en avoir qu'une seule par mois. Il est généralement confus après la crise et ne garde aucun souvenir de l'épisode, ordinairement qualifié « d'absence » par son entourage.

Il existe un troisième type de crise, la crise *psychomotrice*. On la reconnaît difficilement parce qu'elle semble être une suite de mouvements volontaires, mais répétitifs et sans but. Généralement, on ne note pas de mouvements toniques ou cloniques. L'enfant peut avoir un léger aura et s'endormir après la crise. Il n'est généralement pas confus.

Les crises focales (épilepsie Bravais-Jacksonienne) peuvent être motrices, sensitives ou sensorielles. Les manifestations dépendent de la localisation de la lésion cérébrale responsable des décharges neurologiques anormales. Les crises jacksonniennes sont unilatérales et généralement cloniques. Les muscles atteints sont généralement ceux de la main, de la langue, de la face et du pied. La crise motrice focale typique débute par exemple au niveau de la main et s'étend à d'autres zones du corps du même côté suivant un tableau toujours identique. Le patient ne perd ordinairement pas conscience et il assiste à sa crise. On rencontre également des crises sensitives focales (fourmillement, engourdissement, brûlure) des crises sensorielles stéréotypées (hallucinations visuelles, auditives ou olfacto-gustatives).

On observe *les crises infantiles de type myoclonique* avant l'âge de deux ans et elles affectent un groupe de muscles. L'enfant baisse la tête et fléchit ses bras plusieurs fois par jour. Il peut aussi fléchir ses jambes sur son abdomen. Ce type de convulsions disparaît généralement à l'âge de trois ans et fait place au grand mal. Le type infantile est généralement accompagné de retard mental.

Le *diagnostic* se base sur l'histoire familiale, l'histoire médicale de l'enfant, l'aspect clinique des attaques et les anomalies variées à l'électroencéphalogramme. La radiographie du crâne est généralement indiquée. D'autres tests tels la pneumoencéphalographie et l'analyse du liquide céphalo-rachidien peuvent s'avérer nécessaires pour éliminer d'autres problèmes cérébraux.

Traitement. Durant la crise, il faut protéger l'enfant contre les blessures. On détache ses vêtements surtout au niveau du cou et on le tourne sur le côté de façon à lui éviter d'aspirer ses sécrétions. On donne de l'oxygène en cas de cyanose et de convulsions persistantes.

Une série prolongée de crises de grand mal s'appelle *status épilepticus*. On donne de l'oxygène et on administre du phénobarbital sodique par voie intramusculaire. L'environnement doit être calme au moment où l'enfant sort d'une crise prolongée. Il a besoin d'être rassuré, ainsi que ses parents.

Par le traitement prolongé on vise les buts suivants: le contrôle des convulsions ainsi que l'éducation de la famille et de l'entourage, de façon à ce qu'ils acceptent l'enfant et qu'ils l'aident à mener une vie normale. Le traitement comprend les anticonvulsivants, les soins généraux et la psychothérapie, si c'est nécessaire. La famille et l'enfant doivent développer une attitute positive envers la maladie. L'anxiété tend à augmenter la fréquence des crises. Si l'enfant est anxieux, le travailleur social, l'infirmière ou le psychiatre devront aider la famille à découvrir la source de l'anxiété.

Le choix des anticonvulsivants et leur dosage varient selon l'enfant et la forme de la crise.

Le Dilantin (diphenylhydantoïne sodique) est un anticonvulsivant efficace. L'administration de Dilantin peut donner lieu à une hypertrophie douloureuse, mais non hémorragique des gencives qui ne requiert aucun traitement spécial. La somnolence et l'ataxie se manifestent avec l'administration de fortes doses.

On emploie souvent le phénobarbital pour traiter les cas de grand mal. Une éruption cutanée maculo-papulaire, de la somnolence et de la fièvre se produiront si l'enfant souffre d'une idiosyncrasie au phénobarbital.

L'éthosuccimide (Zarontin) est actuellement le médicament de choix dans le petit mal. Il est en effet moins toxique que les autres composés. Le Milontin et le Célontin sont similaires. Le Trimédone (triméthadione) s'avère parfois efficace dans le traitement du petit mal. Ce médicament peut toutefois augmenter la fréquence des crises de grand mal de l'enfant qui en est également atteint, et le phénobarbital ou le Dilantin devront alors être prescrits. L'emploi prolongé ou excessif peut produire de la somnolence, des nausées, de la photophobie ou des éruptions cutanées. Une anémie aplastique apparaît parfois. La Mysoline (primidone) peut être donnée contre le grand mal et les crises psychomotrices. Ses effets secondaires sont la somnolence et l'ataxie.

Chez certains enfants dont l'état est difficile à contrôler par la médication, un régime cétogénique lié à une restriction liquidienne a été recommandé. Ce traitement amenait une réduction des crises convulsives. Toutefois, les effets secondaires biologiques et émotifs étaient importants et ce régime n'est plus guère employé que dans des cas bien particuliers.

Soins infirmiers. L'infirmière doit noter immédiatement toutes ses observations, car le médecin est rarement présent quand l'enfant fait sa crise. Quoiqu'il soit nécessaire de surveiller étroitement le malade, on évite de lui faire sentir qu'il est incapable de rester seul. Les soins physiques lors de crises sont semblables à ceux de l'enfant durant une convulsion. Il s'agit surtout d'éviter les blessures.

L'infirmière doit essayer de diminuer l'anxiété de l'enfant. Elle lui évite les stimulations inutiles et lui offre des distractions appropriées à son âge. Il faut choisir ses jouets de façon à ce qu'il ne puisse se blesser au cours d'une crise. L'infirmière doit être présente au moment des tests de diagnostic que l'on aura d'abord expliqués à l'enfant. Elle veille à ce qu'il prenne ses anticonvulsivants et surveille leurs effets secondaires.

On observe les relations entre l'enfant et ses parents afin de noter éventuellement le rejet ou la surprotection de l'enfant. Il doit être suivi afin de discerner des traits d'égocentrisme et d'instabilité émotive. Les comportements se développent selon l'attitude des adultes face à l'enfant et à sa maladie. Les parents et l'enfant doivent comprendre l'importance de poursuivre le traitement médical pour contrôler les convulsions.

Évolution et pronostic. Étant donné que l'enfant se sent mieux à la maison qu'à l'hôpital, si la mère est capable de le soigner, l'enfant retourne chez lui où il doit avoir une vie aussi normale que possible. Il faut planifier des activités de plein air. Si les convulsions sont bien contrôlées et si intellectuellement l'enfant est normal il peut fréquenter l'école. L'attitude des adultes et le traitement qu'ils appliquent lors d'une crise influent sur l'attitude des autres enfants envers le malade. Assumer le rôle de parents d'un enfant épileptique est difficile; être épileptique l'est encore plus. Les parents et l'enfant ont besoin de support, d'être rassurés et encouragés. La fréquence des crises doit être réduite le plus possible de façon à ne pas entraver les activités de l'enfant. Les troubles de la personnalité sont minimisés si les parents traitent l'épileptique comme un enfant normal.

Le *pronostic* dépend des handicaps éventuels, psychiques ou physiques, dont pourrait souffrir l'enfant, de l'efficacité du traitement médical et de l'attitude de l'entourage. L'enfant bien traité, qui ne développe pas de troubles psychologiques, peut s'attendre à mener une vie normale.

Il faut enseigner aux parents à protéger l'enfant pendant la crise. Ils doivent surtout rester calmes: ne pas essayer de bouger l'enfant, ni de le retenir; placer un oreiller sous sa tête et essayer d'insérer un objet mou entre ses dents (ils peuvent préparer à l'avance des abaisse-langue entourés de bandage); ils doivent éloigner les objets qui pourraient le blesser; desserrer les vêtements autour du cou; éponger la salive pour faciliter la respiration.

Les parents apprendront graduellement à l'enfant les limites légales que peut lui imposer sa maladie. L'infirmière scolaire a un grand rôle d'éducation à effectuer auprès des professeurs.

Le retard mental

Incidence et étiologie. Le retard mental désigne un fonctionnement intellectuel général en-dessous de la moyenne, qui amène des difficultés d'adaptation et dont l'origine se situe durant la période de développement de l'individu. (Définition de l'Association américaine de la déficience mentale.) L'arriération mentale ne constitue pas une entité pathologique, mais un ensemble de symptômes dus à des causes multiples et variées. Elle se manifeste chez 3 à 4% de la population.

L'hérédité peut en être la cause; dans certains cas, on peut retrouver le retard mental tout au long d'une lignée généalogique. Cependant, il existe tellement d'autres facteurs qu'il est difficile de cerner le rôle de l'hérédité. On peut classer certains de ces facteurs de la façon suivante: 1) les causes *prénatales* (héréditaires ou congénitales), telles la phénylcétonurie, le crétinisme (hypothyroïdie), le mongolisme (syndrome de down), certaines malformations crâniennes, des infections maternelles, comme la rubéole ou la syphilis, l'irradiation de la mère, l'anoxie; 2) les causes *néonatales* comprenant l'hémorragie intracrânienne, la prématurité, l'anoxie, les traumatismes lors de l'accouchement, l'iso-immunisation (kernictère); 3) des causes *postnatales*, telles les traumatismes crâniens ou les hémorragies, les infections, par exemple la méningite, les

thromboses cérébro-vasculaires, l'anoxie, les néoplasies, les convulsions répétées et la privation sensorielle et/ou maternelle. Il faut souligner que pour environ le tiers des retards mentaux, la cause demeure totalement inconnue.

Le diagnostic. Des facteurs comme l'épilepsie, la paralysie cérébrale, la malnutrition, les troubles émotifs, la cécité, la surdité et les troubles du langage conduisent parfois au diagnostic incorrect de retard mental et empêchent l'enfant d'accéder à un développement mental optimum.

Le diagnostic définitif de la déficience mentale ne sera posé qu'après une étude approfondie de la famille et de l'enfant, par une équipe composée des membres suivants: pédiatre, psychologue, psychiatre, travailleur social, infirmières en santé communautaire et en pédiatrie. Afin de pouvoir collaborer avec les autres membres de l'équipe, l'infirmière doit posséder une bonne connaissance des ressources communautaires et servir également de lien entre l'équipe et les parents. Certains centres, rattachés à des écoles de médecine, ont été créés pour la recherche, le diagnostic et la planification de soins individuels pour le déficient mental.

On peut quelquefois reconnaître l'atteinte mentale profonde, dès la naissance, quand l'enfant ne peut apprendre à boire au sein ou au biberon à cause d'une déficience de son réflexe de succion. On doit considérer la possibilité de retard mental, si un enfant de trois mois, vivant dans un milieu adéquat, ne se développe pas normalement. Au cours de la première enfance, avant que l'enfant n'apprenne à parler, on peut évaluer grossièrement ses capacités mentales selon ses capacités motrices. S'assoit-il, se tient-il debout et marche-t-il dans les limites normales pour son âge? Un handicapé mental montre de la lenteur à parler, à manger seul et à faire sa toilette. Jusqu'à l'âge préscolaire, la lenteur du développement peut être méconnue, mais le problème apparaît aussitôt que l'enfant se trouve avec d'autres enfants normaux d'âge préscolaire. Un enfant très légèrement atteint peut évoluer à travers la première enfance et les années préscolaires sans signe de retard mental. Son handicap ne deviendra manifeste qu'une fois à l'école, au moment de comprendre des notions abstraites.

On doit rechercher les causes d'un retard du développement chez tout enfant qui présente un retard de développement physique ou moteur. Il faut procéder à un examen minutieux afin d'éliminer une cause physique qui pourrait bénéficier d'un traitement précis.

On évalue la capacité mentale par les tests d'intelligence et les autres moyens disponibles et il faut étudier les réactions émotives et l'adaptation sociale de l'enfant. Les caractéristiques de la personnalité du déficient mental sont variables. Certains enfants sont calmes et gais et se comportent bien avec les autres enfants et avec les adultes; d'autres par contre, deviennent agités, irritables et désobéissants. Ces comportements influent énormément sur l'adaptation sociale. Les enfants peu intelligents semblent généralement gauches dans leurs mouvements et réagissent lentement aux stimulations.

Classification et manifestations cliniques. On peut classifier l'arriération mentale en trois catégories: 1) les enfants *légèrement retardés mais éducables,* ont un quotient intellectuel entre 51 et 80 et peuvent atteindre un âge mental de huit à douze ans; 2) les enfants *modérément arriérés ou semi-éducables* présentent un quotient intellectuel entre 31 et 50. Ils peuvent atteindre un âge mental de trois à sept ans; 3) les enfants qui sont *gravement retardés et complètement dépendants* présentent un quotient intellectuel entre zéro et trente et peuvent atteindre un âge mental de zéro à deux ans.

Les enfants légèrement retardés mais éducables peuvent prendre soin d'eux-mêmes, apprendre à être utiles à la maison et à la collectivité en exécutant des travaux simples. Les enfants modérément retardés peuvent prendre soin d'eux-mêmes, apprendre à parler, acquérir un comportement social acceptable. Leur habileté à se concentrer varie, mais sans jamais être soutenue. Il faut les maintenir toujours dans un cadre précis. Certains enfants très arriérés sont incapables de parler ou de marcher avant l'âge de cinq ans. Ils exigent une surveillance et des soins constants. Bien qu'ils puissent progresser lentement, on les confie généralement à une institution.

Conduite à adopter envers le déficient mental. Les parents, l'école, la collectivité et le gouvernement ont tous une part de responsabilité. L'étape initiale consiste à informer les parents du problème. Il faut évidemment attendre que le diagnostic soit définitivement établi. Bien que les parents soupçonnent ce diagnostic, ils l'entrevoient avec une grande anxiété et sa confirmation peut déclencher chez eux un sentiment de culpabilité. Ils doivent comprendre et accepter le problème pour se départir de ce sentiment de culpabilité et faire face à leurs responsabilités. Aussitôt que possible, ils doivent, avec d'autres membres de l'équipe de santé, établir des plans réalistes pour le soin de l'enfant. Le programme dépendra de leurs propres réactions envers l'handicapé, du degré d'arriération mentale de celui-ci et des ressources communautaires de la région où ils vivent.

Si la cause du retard mental peut être trouvée et traitée, tout effort devra être fait pour aider l'enfant. Dans le cas de crétinisme, on donne des extraits thyroïdiens; dans les cas d'hématome sous-dural, d'hydrocéphalie ou de craniosynostose, on procède à une opération; dans les cas de phénylcétonurie, on établit une diète appropriée.

Il faut évaluer avec les parents les possibilités de l'enfant et avoir une idée réelle de ses aptitudes. Les parents et les professeurs n'exerceront aucune pression en vu de forcer un enfant retardé à étudier, car de tels efforts conduisent à la frustration, cause de troubles émotifs additionnels. Tout comme l'enfant normal, il a besoin d'aide, de sécurité et d'affection de la part des parents et des professeurs, mais ce besoin dure plus longtemps chez lui du fait de sa grande dépendance. Dans le programme établi, on devra tenir compte des ressources du milieu pour que l'enfant puisse utiliser ses capacités à leur maximum. Certains enfants évoluent mieux en institution, pour d'autres les soins à domicile conviennent davantage.

Certains enfants profitent d'un séjour dans une garderie ou dans une école spécialisée où ils apprennent à prendre soin d'eux-mêmes et à étudier si possible. L'enfant peut cependant fréquenter l'école régulière si on trouve un programme approprié à son handicap intellectuel. Ces programmes favorisent l'intégration de l'enfant dans son milieu social. Ces décisions importantes devront finalement être prises par les parents; toutefois, l'équipe de santé peut les orienter en se basant sur le diagnostic.

Avant de pouvoir établir un programme réaliste, il faut d'abord que les parents de l'enfant retardé acceptent le diagnostic, sans quoi ils continueront à chercher une raison médicale à son état et un moyen de le guérir. Quand ils auront accepté le diagnostic et le plan de traitement, ils pourront obtenir un support moral en rencontrant un groupe de parents ayant les mêmes problèmes qu'eux et en se joignant à leur association locale de parents d'enfants déficients mentaux.

Les sœurs et frères d'un enfant handicapé et particulièrement ceux d'un arriéré mental

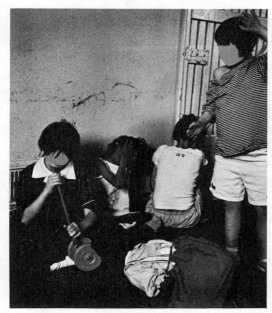

Figure 19-4. Enfants mentalement retardés qui vivent dans une institution où aucune activité n'est planifiée pour eux. Ils passent la journée entière dans une pièce vide, à ne rien faire. (B. Blatt et F. Kaplan: « Christmas in Purgatory » *A photographic Essay on Mental Retardation.* Boston, Allyn and Bacon, 1966.)

se sentent souvent négligés parce que la mère consacre beaucoup de temps à l'enfant handicapé. Aussi certains enfants régressent-ils pour se mettre au niveau du retardé mental, afin d'obtenir les mêmes attentions que lui. Si les parents comprennent la signification de ce comportement et donnent beaucoup d'attention à l'enfant, cette phase se terminera rapidement. Plus tard, ils hésitent parfois à amener des amis chez eux par crainte d'être rejetés subséquemment à cause de l'enfant retardé; ils peuvent hésiter à se marier parce qu'ils craignent l'hérédité. Il faut donner une explication franche et appropriée aux frères et sœurs de l'enfant arriéré, pour leur donner une vision réaliste de la situation. L'enfant déficient peut apporter beaucoup à ses frères et sœurs en leur faisant découvrir l'univers des handicapés. Ils ont l'occasion d'apprendre la compassion et la tolérance. Ils peuvent apprécier différemment ce que d'autres prennent pour acquis: une intelligence normale.

Soins infirmiers. L'infirmière peut être la première à déceler les signes d'arriération mentale. Elle peut voir l'enfant à la clinique externe de l'hôpital ou à la maison. Étant donné ses connaissances sur le développement et la croissance, elle peut se rendre compte

d'un retard que les parents n'auront pas été à même d'apprécier; elle devra faire part de ses observations au médecin qui, avec les autres membres de l'équipe, arrivera à déterminer le degré de l'arriération et éventuellement sa cause.

L'infirmière doit faire partie de l'équipe qui planifie et exécute les recommandations pour les soins de l'enfant à domicile. La *méthode du conditionnement*, jugée actuellement comme la plus efficace pour enseigner à ce type d'enfant, est basée sur les caractéristiques de la personnalité de l'enfant déficient: inhabileté à se concentrer, à établir facilement des relations humaines, comportement monotone et répétitif, difficulté à attendre ou à changer d'environnement.

Le conditionnement instrumental se fonde surtout sur le *renforcement du comportement* désirable. La gratification doit être *immédiate, adaptée et systématique*. Cette méthode est utilisée pour promouvoir l'acquisition de comportements nouveaux et pour faire disparaître des comportements inappropriés. Les récompenses (nourriture, friandises ou louanges) doivent être données immédiatement et systématiquement lorsque la conduite de l'enfant a été bonne; si le contraire se produit, on ne doit pas le récompenser et conserver une attitude neutre. Ces techniques rendent possible l'apprentissage de comportements plus évolués quand ceux-ci restent dans les limites des capacités de l'enfant. On peut ainsi obtenir des modifications du comportement dans l'entraînement à la toilette, l'apprentissage de l'alimentation, de l'habillement et diminuer des tendances destructives. Cette technique exige *patience et répétition* de la part de ceux qui l'utilisent. L'infirmière doit expliquer clairement à la mère que, malgré l'âge chronologique de l'enfant, ses besoins sont fonction de son âge mental.

Pour l'apprentissage de la propreté, on place d'abord l'enfant sur le siège des toilettes toutes les deux heures, et graduellement ce programme est modifié pour s'adapter à la routine familiale. Pour obtenir une élimination régulière, on servira les repas toujours à la même heure. Si on emploie une chaise percée, celle-ci ne doit pas être déplacée afin de faciliter l'apprentissage. La mère explique à l'enfant en termes simples et par gestes ce qu'il a à faire et le récompense quand il y parvient. Comme pour un enfant normal, il faut éviter les reproches si un « accident » se produit. Pour apprendre à l'enfant à s'habiller seul, on lui procure des vêtements faciles à mettre, à enlever et à ranger, de façon à ce qu'il puisse

Figure 19-5.   Ces enfants mentalement retardés apprennent par le jeu à mieux coordonner leur activité musculaire. (Charles P. Jubenville, Ed. D., Director, Daytime Care Centers.) (*Nursing Outlook*, Juill. 1960.)

les retrouver facilement. Des vêtements avec fermeture-éclair, boutons et cordelettes l'aident à développer son habileté. Pour enseigner à l'enfant retardé à manger seul, la mère suivra les mêmes principes généraux qui ont été décrits pour l'enfant normal, mais en ralentissant considérablement le rythme d'apprentissage.

Pour discipliner le déficient mental, on emploie les mêmes principes généraux que pour la moyenne des enfants. Ces principes supposent une constance dans les exigences, l'emploi d'un vocabulaire simple et l'établissement d'une routine dans sa vie quotidienne. Si une punition est nécessaire, elle doit suivre immédiatement les méfaits, pour que l'enfant puisse faire la relation entre les deux. L'enfant arriéré a besoin de stimulation venant de son entourage afin de mener à bien son développement. Il a besoin comme tout autre, et sinon davantage, d'un objet à regarder, de sons à entendre, d'un article à manipuler. Quand un tel enfant est hospitalisé, l'infirmière doit demander à la mère de lui expliquer de façon détaillée la routine à laquelle l'enfant est habitué à la maison. Le rôle spécifique de l'infirmière est de maintenir ses habiletés acquises, de lui faire pratiquer l'apprentissage en cours et de le surveiller afin qu'il ne puisse pas se blesser. Une discipline trop sévère ne lui convient pas. On lui donne des jeux simples offrant un

plaisir immédiat pour orienter son attention vers une activité acceptable.

L'infirmière aide l'enfant dans le choix des jeux en se basant sur l'âge mental et non sur l'âge chronologique. Elle doit comprendre que son attention est de courte durée, l'encourager pour ses succès et lui trouver des activités appropriées.

La période de la puberté et de l'adolescence, difficile à traverser pour tous les parents, devient encore plus angoissante pour les parents de l'enfant débile. Ils doivent tenter de satisfaire les besoins sociaux et émotifs de leur enfant tout en le maintenant à l'intérieur d'un cadre sûr. Il existe de petits livrets qui expliquent les menstruations à la fillette retardée et la sexualité en général, aux enfants déficients des deux sexes.

Pronostic, prévention et planification pour le futur.   À moins que l'enfant ne soit sérieusement retardé, l'espérance de vie est à peu près celle d'un enfant normal. Son adaptation à la société dépendra de son degré d'arriération et du profit qu'il saura tirer de ses ressources mentales. De grands pas ont été faits dans la prévention des causes et des problèmes reliés à l'arriération. Des recherches sont actuellement en cours pour trouver des moyens de réduire son incidence. Le dépistage plus systématique des maladies métaboliques chez le nouveau-né réduira éventuellement le nombre de retardés mentaux. Les associations pour l'arriération mentale offrent à la fois des services aux parents et aux enfants et stimulent les recherches pertinentes. Toutefois, de grands efforts doivent être faits pour augmenter les fonds nécessaires à la recherche, à la préparation de personnel qualifié pour les soins aux retardés, à la création de groupes de parents et à l'établissement de programmes pour venir en aide à ces enfants. L'ouverture d'écoles vraiment adaptées et d'ateliers protégés, endroits où les handicapés mentaux peuvent travailler et gagner leur subsistance, offre de nouveaux espoirs. Il reste encore beaucoup à faire dans ce domaine.

PROBLÈMES ÉMOTIFS

À l'âge préscolaire, les deux problèmes émotifs les plus souvent rencontrés sont: les phobies ou craintes irrationnelles et les crises de colère.

Les phobies

Généralement, les enfants ressentent un certain nombre de craintes face à la vie quotidienne. De leurs parents qui doivent les protéger, ils apprennent à connaître les dangers, tels le feu, les couteaux tranchants ou encore une rue passante; ils ont toutefois peur de certaines choses ne pouvant leur causer aucun tort. Ils peuvent avoir peur de l'obscurité, des bruits et des fantômes. Les garçons craignent généralement d'être blessés, tandis que les filles n'aiment pas l'obscurité et les bruits étranges. L'incidence de ces craintes demeure très élevée pendant la période préscolaire.

Quand une peur irraisonnée produit chez l'enfant un état de panique, on parle de phobie. L'affection de l'adulte n'arrive pas à le rassurer et à faire disparaître sa terreur. Si la cause de la phobie est liée à une réalité, par exemple la crainte d'un chien réellement capable de lui causer du tort, le problème ne semble pas grave. Si la cause n'est pas liée à une réalité, l'enfant est malade émotivement. Le vrai problème n'est pas dans l'objet de la phobie, mais dans un conflit émotif actuellement insoluble. La plupart des enfants guérissent de leur phobie, mais ils ont besoin d'aide. La façon la plus efficace consiste à leur faire prendre progressivement contact avec la situation ou l'objet, pour qu'ils aient l'occasion de l'examiner ou de l'ignorer. L'adulte doit

aussi les aider activement à participer à des situations terrifiantes ou liées à l'objet de leur crainte.

Parfois, le fait de démontrer que la situation ou l'objet ne présente vraiment aucun danger ou le fait que d'autres enfants n'aient pas peur, les aide à se maîtriser. Il ne faut en aucun cas les obliger à entrer brusquement en contact avec l'objet de la crainte ou agir comme si celle-ci n'existait pas.

On encourage l'enfant à être plus indépendant et à fréquenter d'autres enfants. On doit lui permettre d'exprimer verbalement son hostilité ou de s'engager dans des jeux actifs afin de libérer ses émotions. L'enfant dont la phobie limite sérieusement l'activité doit rencontrer un psychiatre ou un psychologue pour enfants.

Accès de colère

Les crises de colère sont normales pendant la période où l'enfant apprend à marcher, mais l'augmentation de leur fréquence et de leur gravité pendant la période préscolaire indique que l'enfant n'a pas appris à résoudre les frustrations normales de la croissance. Au cours d'un accès de colère, l'enfant semble perdre conscience de son entourage et de la réalité. Il dépense une grande quantité d'énergie musculaire, frappant sur tout ce qui l'entoure et sur lui-même, mais rarement sur l'adulte responsable de ses frustrations. La réaction de l'enfant semble habituellement disproportionnée à la cause apparente du conflit. L'extériorisation de la frustration prouve que l'enfant est en réalité fâché contre lui-même. Épuisé par sa grande activité physique, il est rempli de remords parce qu'il reconnaît avoir agi comme un petit enfant.

Les accès de colère se voient chez tous les enfants. Si ces accès sont graves ou prolongés ou encore s'ils se manifestent fréquemment, il semble que l'enfant ne se soit pas développé comme il aurait dû. Il est probable que l'enfant faisant des accès pathologiques de colère a connu une grande tolérance pendant son développement et n'a pas appris à maîtriser ses impulsions ou à réagir dans les limites normales de ses frustrations. Le traitement de ces enfants consiste à leur apprendre à contrôler leurs désirs infantiles et à les aider à rechercher des moyens raisonnables de satisfaction. L'infirmière peut aider l'enfant en le félicitant d'avoir maîtrisé certaines impulsions et en lui donnant l'occasion d'exprimer son agressivité par des moyens acceptables. Il est essentiel que cet enfant reçoive beaucoup d'attention lorsqu'il n'est pas en colère et que ses crises soulèvent le moins d'émoi possible.

Les *accès de colère pathologiques* peuvent se produire si l'on a trop rapidement obligé l'enfant à être indépendant et à exercer un contrôle rigide de son comportement. Il tente désespérément d'avoir une conduite qui reçoive l'approbation de ses parents. Le traitement consiste à diminuer cette rigueur dans les demandes; ainsi pourra-t-il agir en accord avec son âge. Avec un traitement psychiatrique, de tels enfants apprennent à se contrôler et à évoluer normalement.

PROBLÈME PSYCHIATRIQUE

Schizophrénie de l'enfant — autisme

Incidence. On constate une augmentation du nombre des enfants d'âge préscolaire atteints de maladie mentale et admis dans les départements de pédiatrie ou de psychiatrie infantile. Un meilleur diagnostic permet de séparer les enfants atteints de retard mental et ceux atteints de maladie mentale et de leur appliquer un traitement plus adéquat.

La distinction entre les différentes maladies émotives de l'enfance est devenue beaucoup plus claire au cours des années. On croit que l'enfant qui souffre d'« autisme » en présente les symptômes dès les premiers mois de sa vie (Kanner). Ces enfants n'aiment pas qu'on les prenne, se replient sur eux-mêmes et semblent vivre dans un monde de rêve qui n'appartient qu'à eux seuls. L'enfant qui souffre de « schizophrénie » s'est tout d'abord développé normalement avant de présenter des changements de comportement. Il réagit au contact d'autrui même s'il semble confus ou anxieux. L'enfant retardé présente avec les deux premiers une analogie des symptômes qui rend la distinction difficile au premier abord.

Manifestations cliniques. En général, les enfants d'âge préscolaire qui souffrent de problèmes émotifs ne présentent pas un développement de la personnalité qui correspond à leur âge chronologique. Leur mode de pensée, leur comportement et leurs moyens de communication ressemblent à ceux du trottineur. Leur développement a été irrégulier aux points de vue émotif, social et intellectuel.

Les membres de l'équipe de santé doivent veiller à ce que les parents ne se laissent pas envahir par des sentiments de culpabilité et de honte. Plusieurs d'entre eux avaient saisi depuis longtemps que l'enfant ne se développait

pas normalement, mais souvent les indices étaient insuffisants pour qu'un diagnostic puisse être fait avant que l'enfant ait atteint l'âge préscolaire.

La rupture de communication avec l'entourage est généralement observée entre trois et cinq ans, mais peut se voir aussi à partir de la deuxième année. Bien qu'ils aient appris à parler, ils ne semblent pas éprouver le besoin de le faire, ni être capables de communiquer dans un langage cohérent.

Ces enfants n'arrivent pas à distinguer le réel de l'irréel, et ceux qui sont atteints gravement, ou très tôt, sont incapables de faire la différence entre eux-mêmes et les personnes qui les entourent. La faculté de percevoir le réel se développe dans les premières années de la vie d'un enfant qui reçoit les soins et l'amour d'une mère adulte. Chez l'enfant schizophrénique, cette faculté n'est pas totalement développée ou est diminuée.

L'enfant qui manifeste un comportement autistique erre dans les endroits retirés où les contacts humains sont peu fréquents. Il obtient une satisfaction orale en portant à la bouche des objets variés et il doit être protégé

Figure 19-6. L'observatrice peut analyser et évaluer le comportement de l'enfant au jeu. L'enfant ne voit pas l'observatrice; ses réactions plus naturelles permettent d'évaluer son statut intellectuel et émotif. (Byrd: *Health*, 4e éd.)

contre l'ingestion de substances nocives. Il refuse ordinairement tout contact tactile.

Certains enfants présentent un *autisme grave* ne peuvent pas s'adapter à des routines organisées et tout effort en ce sens conduit à une augmentation des accès de colère, de la masturbation et de l'anxiété. Quand il leur est permis de rester seul, ils s'adonnent à des préoccupations corporelles, telles sucer leur pouce ou autres objets et se frapper la tête. D'autres enfants supportent mal les changements dans la routine établie et demeurent inflexibles dans leur comportement. Ces enfants font souvent des gestes bizarres avec leurs mains et peuvent devenir très violents. Certains ne parlent jamais et d'autres présentent de l'écholalie. Leur capacité de jouer est profondément perturbée.

Conduite à tenir. L'enfant atteint de psychose grave peut bénéficier de soins à domicile et de l'emploi des techniques de conditionnement. Quand il est hospitalisé, l'infirmière doit lui apporter la sécurité, l'acceptation et l'amour qui lui manquent. Les infirmières deviennent des agents thérapeutiques qui agissent en collaboration étroite avec le psychiatre.

Les traitements ultérieurs viseront à rendre l'enfant capable d'identifier son propre corps, d'intégrer le concept du moi, de développer des relations positives avec d'autres personnes et à le protéger de ses impulsions destructrices. L'infirmière doit essayer de voir le monde de la même façon que l'enfant, de développer une empathie lui permettant de comprendre son comportement. Quand l'état de l'enfant s'améliore, on introduit une routine progressive; ceux qui ont un comportement rigide ou stéréotypé sont amenés à tolérer quelque souplesse dans la routine et dans le jeu. Le but du programme est d'établir un cycle de repos et d'activités et d'apprendre à l'enfant à s'aider lui-même en faisant sa toilette, en s'habillant et en mangeant seul. À un stade moins avancé de la maladie mentale, l'enfant peut fréquenter des centres où il côtoie des enfants normaux et des enfants ayant également des problèmes. De nombreux parents émotivement perturbés reçoivent aussi une psychothérapie pendant que leurs enfants sont sous traitement.

Pronostic. Le pronostic est d'autant plus réservé que l'autisme a débuté tôt, car de tels enfants présentent des problèmes thérapeutiques difficiles. Les thérapies par le jeu et par un milieu favorable sont les plus usuelles et donnent des résultats variables. Il existe certains centres aux États-Unis consacrés uniquement à ces enfants. La cause demeurant difficile à cerner, le traitement ne peut être qu'empirique. Certaines recherches sont en cours pour retrouver une étiologie biologique à cette pathologie.

RÉFÉRENCES

Livres et documents officiels

Adams, M.: *Mental Retardation and Its Social Dimensions.* New York, Columbia University Press, 1971.

Alagille, D.: *L'hémophilie.* Paris, J. B. Ballière et fils, 1970.

Axline, V. M.: *Play Therapy.* New York, Ballantine Books, Inc., 1969.

Barnard, K. E. et Powell, M. L.: *Teaching the Mentally Retarded Child: A Family Care Approach.* Saint-Louis, C. V. Mosby Company, 1972.

Blodgett, H. E.: *Mentally Retarded Children: What Parents and Others Should Know.* Toronto, Ontario, Copp Clark Company, 1971.

Boshes, L. D. et Gibbs, F. A.: *Epilepsy Handbook.* 2ᵉ éd. Springfield, Ill., Charles C Thomas, 1971.

Carter, C. H.: *Handbook of Mental Retardation Syndromes.* 2ᵉ éd. Springfield, Ill., Charles C Thomas, 1970.

Compagnie Kotex: *Comment expliquer la menstruation à une fillette attardée.* Documentation du Centre des cycles de la vie, Ontario.

Debuskey, M. (édit.): *The Chronically Ill Child and His Family.* Springfield, Ill., Charles C Thomas, 1970.

Easson, W. M.: *The Dying Child: The Management of the Child or Adolescent Who is Dying.* Springfield, Ill. Charles C Thomas, 1970.

Fagin, C. W. (édit.): *Nursing in Child Psychiatry. Saint-Louis,* C. V. Mosby Company, 1972.

Fontana, V. J.: *Practical Management of the Allergic Child.* New York, Appleton-Century-Crofts, 1969.

Foster, G. W. et autres: *Child Care Work with Emotionally Disturbed Children.* Pittsburgh University of Pittsburgh Press, 1972.

Fredlund, D. J.: Nurse Looks at Children's Questions About Death: in *ANA Clin. Sess.*, 1970, New York, Appleton-Century-Crofts, 1971, pp. 105-112.

French, E. L. et Scott, J. C.: *Comment aider un enfant handicapé.* Paris, Laffont, 1968.

Grollman, E. A.: *Talking About Death: A Dialogue Between Parent and Child.* Boston, Beacon Press, 1970.

Hallas, C. H. (édit.): *The Care and Training of the Mentally Subnormal.* 4e éd. Baltimore, Williams & Wilkins Company, 1971.

Kanner, L.: *Child Psychiatry.* 4e éd Springfield, Ill. Charles C Thomas, 1971.

Kugelmass, I. N.: *The Autistic Child.* Springfield, Ill. Charles C Thomas, 1970.

Levinson, A.: *L'enfant mentalement retardé.* Paris, Éd. du Centurion, 1968.

Livingston, S. et Bruce, I. M.: *Comprehensive Management of Epilepsy in Infancy, Childhood and Adolescence.* Springfield, Ill., Charles C Thomas, 1972.

Ministère de la Santé nationale et du Bien-être social: *L'arriération mentale au Canada. L'enfant arriéré. L'épilepsie.* Division de l'hygiène mentale, Gouvernement du Canada.

Molloy, J. S.: *Teaching the Retarded Child to Talk.* London, University of London Press, 1970.

Noland, R. L. (édit.): *Counseling Parents of the Ill and the Handicaped.* Springfield, Ill., Charles C Thomas, 1971.

Paisse, J. M.: *L'univers symbolique de l'enfant arriéré mental.* Paris, Dessart, 1975.

Shaw, C. R. et Lucas, A. R.: *The Psychiatric Disorders of Childhood.* 2e éd. New York, Appleton-Century-Crofts, 1970.

Tredgold, R. F. et Soddy, K. (édit.): *Mental Retardation.* 11e éd. Baltimore, Williams & Wilkins Company, 1971.

Articles

Antoine, H. M.: La ponction sternale. *Soins*, 19:48, 17, 1974.

Arfi, S.: L'épilepsie. *Soins*, 19:4, 12, 1974.

Balthazar, E. E., English, G. E. et Sindberg, R. M.: Behavior Changes in Mentally Retarded Children Following the Initiation of an Experimental Nursing Program. *Nursing Research*, 20:69, janvier-février 1971.

Benoît, P. et autres: Les soins à domicile pour l'enfant leucémique. *Inf. Can.*, 16:14, 4, 1974.

Benoliel, J. Q.: The Concept of Care for a Child with Leukemia. *Nursing Forum*, 11:194, 2, 1972.

Berni, R., Dressler, J. et Baxter, J. C.: Reinforcing Behavior. *Am. J. Nursing*, 71:2180, novembre 1971.

Binger, C. M. et autres: Childhood Leukemia: Emotional Impact on Patient and Family. *New England J. Med.*, 280:414, 20 février 1969.

Bizet, M.: Leucémie aiguë lymphoblastique. *Soins*, 19:9, 17, 1974.

Cotte, J. et autres: Le dépistage des anomalies métaboliques entraînant une arriération mentale évitable. *Pédiatrie*, XXIII:443, 4, 1968.

Cragg, C.: L'infirmière et l'enfant leucémique. *Inf. Can.*, 12:41, mai 1970.

Crosby, M. H.: Control Systems and Children with Lymphoblastic Leukemia. *Nursing Clin. N. Amer.*, 6:407, septembre 1971.

Field, W. E.: Watch Your Message. *Am. J. Nursing*, 72:1278, juillet 1972.

Florent, J.: Hémophilie et chirurgie. *Revue de l'inf., et ass. soc.*, 19:357, 4, 1969.

Geis, D. P. et Rochon, D.: Home Visits Help Prepare Preschoolers for Hospital Experience. *Hospitals*, 40:83, février 1966.

Gentile, J. M. et Pépin, J. M.: Leucémie et virus. *Union méd. du Can.*, 98:1335, août 1969.

Godard, N.: Asthme de l'enfant. *La revue de l'infirmière*, 23:33, 1, 1973.

Goldfogel, L.: Working with the Parent of a Dying Child. *Am. J. Nursing*, 70:1675, août 1970.

Gonzales, J.: Déficiences mentales. *Soins*, XV:293, 7, 1970.

Hyde, N. D.: Play Therapy: The Troubled Child's Self-Encounter. *Am. J. Nursing*, 71:1366, juillet 1971.

Jacquillat, C. et autres: Traitement des leucémies aiguës. *La revue de l'infirmière*, 23:105, 2, 1973.

Jean, R. et autres: L'asthme infantile. *Médecine infantile*, 78:5, 1, 1971.

Kiger, J. P. et Pariente, R.: Asthme. *La revue de l'infirmière*, 25:477, 6, 1975.

Koop, C. E.: The Serioously Ill or Dying Child: Supporting the Patient and the Family *Nursing Clin. N. Amer.*, 16:555, août 1969.

Kyle, J. et Savino, A.: Teaching Parents Behavior Modification. *Nurs. Outlook*, 21:717, 11, 1973.

Labrune, B.: Hémophilie. *Soins*, 17:7, 9, 1972.

Lazerson, J.: Hemophilia Home Transfusion Program: Effect on School Attendance. *J. Pediat.*, 81:330, août 1972.

Leath, J. R. et Flournoy, R. L.: Three Year Follow-up of Intensive Habit-Training Program. *Ment. Retard.*, 8:32, juin 1970.

Loisel, J. P. et autres: Traitement des leucémies lymphoïdes chroniques. *La revue de l'infirmière*, 22:641, 7, 1972.

Loogood, J.: Selection of Patients for Cromolyn Therapy. *Clin. Ped.*, 13:428, 5, 1974.

Mamula, R. A.: The Use of Developmental Plans for Mentally Retarded Children in Foster Family Care. *Children*, 18:65, mars-avril 1971.

Martin, C.: À Propos de la débilité mentale chez l'enfant. *La revue de l'infirmière*, 22:985, 10, 1972.

Maxwell, J. E.: Home Care for the Retarded Child. *Nursing Outlook*, 19:112, février 1971.

Middleton. A. B. et Pothier, P. C.: The Nurse in Child Psychiatry – An Overview. *Nursing Outlook*, 18:52, mai 1970.

Misset, J. L.: Les antimitotiques. *Soins*, 19:25, 15, 1974.

Miya, T. M.: The Child's Perception of Death. *Nursing Forum*, 11:214, 2, 1972.

Noble, M. A.: Nursing's Concern for the Mentally Retarded Is Overdue. *Nursing Forum*, 9:192, 2, 1970.

Pattullo, A. W. et Barnard, K. E.: Teaching Menstrual Hygiene to the Mentally Retarded. *Am. J. Nursing*, 68:2572, décembre 1968.

Paupe, G. et Dalayeun, H.: Indications et conduite pratique de l'enquête allergologique et de la désensibilisation spécifique dans les syndromes respiratoires de l'enfant. *La revue de pédiatrie*, VI:671, 10, 1970.

Piguet, H.: Le traitement de l'hémophilie. *La revue de l'infirmière*, 24:399, 5, 1974.

Revier, D.: Les épilepsies. *La revue de l'infirmière*, 22:33, 4, 1972 (I), 22:43, 5, 1972 (II).

Rodman, M. J.: Anticancer Chemotherapy. 1. The Kinds of Drugs and What They Do. *RN*, 35:45, février 1972.

Rodman, M. J.: Anticancer Chemotherapy. 3. Against the Leukemias and Lymphomas. *RN*, 35:49, avril 1972.

Sadler, J.: The Long-Term Hospitalization of Asthmatic Children. *Ped. Clin. N. Amer.*, 22:173, 1, 1975.

Samter, M.: Bronchial Asthma: New Definition for an Old Disease. *Clin. Ped.*, 13:406, 5, 1974.

Stern, H. et autres: Microbial Causes of Mental Retardation. *Lancet*, 2:443, 30 août 1969.

Turner, R.: A Method of Working with Disturbed Children. *Am. J. Nursing*, 70:2146, octobre 1970.

Waechter, E. H.: Children's Awareness of Fatal Illness. *Am. J. Nursing*, 71:1168, juin 1971.

Warren, B.: Maintaining the Hemophiliac at Home. *Nursing '74*, 4:75, 1, 1974.

Warren, S. A. et Burns, N. R.: Crib Confinement as a Factor in Repetitive and Stereotyped Behavior in Retardates. *Ment. Retard.*, 8:25, juin 1970.

Williams, A.: Classification and Diagnosis of Epilepsy. *Nurs. Clin. N. Amer.*, 9:747, 4, 1974.

sixième partie

L'ENFANT
D'ÂGE SCOLAIRE

20

l'enfant d'âge scolaire: croissance, développement, soins

DÉVELOPPEMENT ÉMOTIF

Quand leur enfant atteint l'âge scolaire, les parents doivent apprendre à s'adapter à ce qui semble être une période de rejet. Il manifeste une indépendance nouvelle envers eux et les valeurs qu'ils ont essayé de lui inculquer. Les parents peuvent en ressentir de la peine, de la déception et de la colère. Cependant, en dépit des apparences, l'enfant a encore besoin d'une aide discrète qui tienne compte de ses désirs d'indépendance.

Avant son sixième anniversaire, l'enfant doit avoir appris à faire confiance aux autres et avoir acquis une certaine autonomie. En principe, il doit être capable de se tirer d'affaire dans son milieu habituel, soit par ses expériences personnelles, soit en questionnant ses parents et d'autres adultes. Il doit avoir acquis un sens de l'initiative, et ses activités devraient être contrôlées jusqu'à un certain point par sa conscience.

Les différentes étapes que franchit l'enfant avant l'âge de six ans sont probablement les plus importantes pour le développement d'une personnalité saine. Les enfants dont le dévelop-pement se trouve faussé durant les premières années de la vie, risquent de demeurer handi-capés à moins qu'on ne leur vienne en aide. Il y a des exceptions, certes, parce que les expé-riences vécues plus tard dans l'enfance et pen-dant l'adolescence influent aussi sur l'orienta-tion du développement émotif.

Le sens du travail. Entre 6 et 12 ans, l'enfant acquiert le sens du travail et désire participer concrètement aux activités de son milieu. Il trouve en lui-même la motivation qui lui permettra de s'engager dans une activité qui lui apportera la certitude de sa propre va-leur. Même avant 6 ans, un enfant peut mon-trer qu'il aime se rendre utile, qu'il veut réa-liser des choses et qu'il veut apprendre à les bien faire.

Ces années sont habituellement une période de calme apparent, et il est peu probable de noter des revirements brusques d'attitude. L'en-fant progresse régulièrement vers l'âge adulte. Il absorbe des connaissances et acquiert une adresse qui lui permettront d'apporter une con-tribution utile à la société. Il apprend à co-opérer au sein d'un groupe, à suivre les règles du jeu et à se conformer à des normes de sociabilité; sa vie devient une expérience positive pour lui et pour ceux qui le côtoient. La période d'âge scolaire est caractérisée tour à tour par le conformisme et la rébellion devant l'autorité de l'adulte.

Au lieu d'acquérir le sens du travail, l'enfant peut commencer à ressentir ou bien à intensifier des sentiments *d'infériorité* et *d'insuffisance*. Il y a plus de risques que ceci se produise s'il n'a pas parcouru avec succès les premières étapes du développement de sa personnalité.

Le développement intellectuel.

Entre 7 et 12 ans, l'enfant abandonne les analogies, les intuitions pour commencer à raisonner de façon logique. Toutefois, il ne peut appliquer sa logique que lorsque les données du problème sont représentées concrètement. Il procède par essais et erreurs lorsqu'il a à résoudre une énigme abstraite.

L'enfant peut maintenant effectuer des associations, des relations et sa pensée est réversible. Il acquiert progressivement les notions de conservation de la matière, de poids et de volume. C'est aussi à cette période de la vie que l'enfant saisit le concept du temps objectif. Il peut faire la différence, sans problème, entre le matin et l'après-midi, entre les saisons et entre les années.

Le jugement moral.

C'est à l'âge scolaire que l'enfant dépasse la conscience extrinsèque enfantine pour développer un jugement moral approprié. Il commence à appliquer dans sa conduite, même sans surveillance, des valeurs que lui ont inculquées ses parents. Ce n'est que vers 9 ans que l'enfant cesse de tricher et de mentir régulièrement pour s'échapper d'une situation fâcheuse. Alors qu'à l'âge préscolaire, l'enfant juge les actes selon leurs résultats, l'enfant d'âge scolaire évalue maintenant les actions en tenant compte des intentions de celui qui les accomplit.

À la fin de l'âge scolaire, l'enfant développe un sens aigu de la justice et de l'honneur. Il est fréquent d'entendre les enfants s'exclamer: « Ce n'est pas juste ». Ils élaborent des règles de jeux et de conduite très complexes qui doivent être suivies par tous les membres du groupe.

Le sens de l'humour.

Le sens de l'humour est une nouveauté dans le développement de l'enfant d'âge scolaire. L'enfant commence à rire de ce qu'il craint ou de ce qui l'angoisse comme le font les adultes. Même si son sens de l'humour est encore boîteux, il découvre une façon moins enfantine d'exprimer ses préoccupations, ses peurs, son anxiété. Toutefois, les procédés qu'il utilise pour faire de l'humour sont parfois si faibles qu'il met à nu les appréhensions qu'il voulait camoufler. Il est très important à cet âge de savoir des « histoires », des devinettes. Il est remarquable de constater que les mêmes histoires et devinettes se racontent depuis des siècles et ce, en plusieurs langues.

L'enfant et l'école.

À l'école, l'enfant doit accomplir une tâche qui se continuera durant toute son enfance. S'il y est préparé adéquatement, si on a tenu compte de ses besoins de croissance et s'il réussit, l'expérience de l'école aura une influence positive sur le développement de sa personnalité. S'il ne réussit pas à l'école parce qu'il n'est pas particulièrement brillant, il aura une mauvaise opinion de lui-même et s'il a trop de difficulté à s'adapter au milieu environnant pour s'y faire des amis, il pensera que personne ne peut l'apprécier. Il restera peut-être à l'école en acceptant passivement son infériorité, ou encore, il la quittera aussitôt que la loi l'y autorisera. Il peut aussi développer des problèmes de comportement. Toutefois, des instituteurs qualifiés peuvent prévenir la détérioration de la personnalité de l'enfant.

Il est important d'adapter l'expérience scolaire aux besoins de l'enfant en pleine croissance.

L'école n'est pas le seul endroit où l'enfant peut acquérir un sentiment de compétence et un sens du travail. L'enfant peut se voir confier des travaux utiles à la maison. Les parents peuvent lui déléguer des responsabilités qui contribuent au bonheur et au bien-être de toute la famille. Ces travaux et responsabilités ne doivent pas être ceux dont les adultes ne veulent pas se charger eux-mêmes, mais ils doivent résulter d'une division adéquate du travail, donnant à l'enfant ce qui convient à ses capacités. Ce travail ne doit pas empêcher l'enfant d'étudier, d'accepter de menus travaux à l'extérieur de la maison, ou encore de jouer avec d'autres membres de la famille ou des amis.

Les organisations sociales pour les enfants, telles les Clubs 4-H, les Guides, les Scouts, les Jeunes Naturalistes, soulignent à la fois ces deux aspects « récréation et travail ».

L'enfant d'âge scolaire doit dépasser le stade où il dépendait entièrement de sa famille et il doit apprendre à trouver du plaisir en compagnie des jeunes de son âge et des adultes qui l'entourent. Il doit posséder suffisamment de connaissances pour communiquer avec des adultes hors de l'école et, de cette façon, apprendre les caractéristiques de la société dans laquelle il vit. Il doit progresser dans la compréhension des concepts, de la logique et des moyens de communication.

L'enfant devrait acquérir à l'école une saine perception de lui-même en tant que personne. Il doit apprendre à s'entendre avec des compagnons de son âge, tout en continuant d'agir selon sa conscience et son échelle de valeurs. Il s'acquitte lui-même de ses soins d'hygiène. Il doit savoir lire, écrire, compter et avoir acquis assez d'adresse pour pratiquer les jeux de son âge.

Vers son 12ᵉ anniversaire, il devrait avoir acquis des attitudes positives envers les groupes sociaux, raciaux, économiques et religieux. Il devrait avoir appris les concepts essentiels à sa participation à la vie quotidienne de son environnement.

L'enfant d'âge scolaire, sa famille, ses amis

Relations avec les parents. L'enfant entre six et douze ans élargit ses horizons sociaux au-delà des limites familiales. Même s'il compte encore sur l'amour de ses parents, il accorde de plus en plus d'importance à la compagnie des jeunes de son âge et des adultes qu'il rencontre.

À l'âge scolaire, la crise œdipienne se résout ordinairement. L'enfant aime et respecte le parent du sexe opposé et s'identifie au parent du même sexe qu'il essaie d'imiter. À travers l'imitation de ce parent, il apprend son propre rôle social et sexuel.

Durant cette période, il acquiert progressivement une indépendance tant idéologique que physique et émotive. Il recueille des idées nouvelles des adultes qui l'entourent: professeurs, parents d'amis, policiers, vedettes de télévision, journalistes et auteurs de manuels de classe ou de romans. Il y aura souvent des divergences entre ces points de vue nouveaux et ceux de ses parents, surtout si l'enfant vit dans une société cosmopolite et hétérogène. Les adultes qui le côtoient doivent l'aider à comprendre et à résoudre ces conflits afin qu'il ne heurte pas cruellement ses parents et qu'il ne perde pas le respect qu'il a pour eux et pour lui-même.

L'éducation sanitaire est l'un des aspects de l'éducation générale moderne dans les écoles publiques. Des habitudes de santé, telles que le bain quotidien, acceptées par les enfants, peuvent sembler inutiles à leurs parents. Le bain quotidien n'est peut-être pas possible dans un logement surpeuplé. Un conflit naît ici entre ce que l'enfant apprend à l'école et à la maison, et cette situation engendre une tension dans les relations entre parents et enfants.

L'enfant d'âge scolaire prend conscience de sa propre personnalité et n'admet plus les limites rigides que ses parents peuvent continuer à lui imposer. Les démonstrations d'affection en public lui déplaisent, s'il n'est pas malade ou en danger, il ne se laisse plus embrasser et détourne le visage et les parents peuvent en ressentir un certain désarroi. D'autres conflits émotifs naissent à cause des nouveaux concepts que l'enfant a découvert hors du milieu familial, de ses efforts d'indépendance et d'un désintéressement apparent devant les démonstrations d'affection. Les parents ne doivent cependant pas être surpris si l'enfant se tourne vers eux en quête de protection et d'affection quand il se sent menacé par la maladie ou la douleur.

Les parents ont besoin d'aide pour comprendre la croissance et le développement normaux de leurs enfants quand naissent de tels conflits. Il leur est possible de discuter de ces questions avec les professeurs de l'enfant, seuls ou pendant les réunions parents-maîtres, avec le médecin, le conseiller religieux ou l'infirmière lors d'une visite à la maison ou d'un séjour de l'enfant à l'hôpital.

Il y a certains principes de base qui peuvent guider les parents au cours de cette période. Tout d'abord, ils doivent demeurer des parents pour l'enfant et non pas chercher à jouer au copain ou à l'ami. Par ce comportement, ils priveraient l'enfant d'une richesse inestimable et difficilement remplaçable: ses parents. Ils doivent l'inviter à communiquer avec eux, mais ne jamais le forcer à parler, car il a droit à son intimité et à ses secrets. Les parents servent d'exemple pour leurs enfants. Ils ne peuvent s'attendre à voir ceux-ci respecter les lois de la société s'ils ne le font pas eux-mêmes. Il faut que les deux parents sachent demeurer constants dans les limites qu'ils imposent à la conduite de leur enfant; même si celui-ci ressent quelque frustration sur le moment, il comprendra finalement que cet intérêt est la preuve de leur amour pour lui. Les parents devraient voir leur enfant tel qu'il apparaît aux autres, et non pas comme une extension idéalisée d'eux-mêmes. Et enfin, il est très mauvais de comparer entre eux les enfants d'une même famille; chaque enfant a le droit d'être accepté pour ce qu'il est, différent de ses frères et sœurs et de ses cousins.

Relations avec les frères et sœurs. L'enfant d'âge scolaire est de plus en plus influencé par le fait qu'il est un enfant unique ou un membre d'une famille nombreuse. L'enfant unique est le centre de la famille; quand il sort de son cercle familial pour se faire des amis parmi les enfants de son âge, il s'attend encore à être le centre du groupe, et s'effraie quand il découvre qu'il ne l'est pas. Il s'acclimate difficilement à l'échange d'égal à égal, base de la vie sociale avec les autres enfants. L'enfant unique qui réussit à s'intégrer comme membre d'un groupe trouve parfois moins amusant de jouer seul; il peut en venir à détester sa solitude et souhaiter ardemment avoir des frères et des sœurs. Seul récipiendaire de toute l'affection et de toute l'autorité de ses parents, il est souvent restreint dans sa liberté.

Les enfants de familles nombreuses ont aussi leurs problèmes. Ainsi la jalousie peut apparaître même dans les familles où tous s'aiment. Le phénomène est moins aigu pour les enfants qui ont dépassé six ans, mais il existe encore. Un aîné peut envier l'attention que reçoivent les plus jeunes à la maison. Il peut s'offenser du fait qu'un jouet dont il ne se sert plus soit brisé par un enfant plus jeune et du fait qu'on attende de lui, malgré ses sentiments, qu'il aime et souvent surveille ses frères et sœurs.

Si l'enfant d'âge scolaire est lui-même un benjamin, il peut envier à l'aîné sa liberté et son habileté. La jalousie de l'enfant d'âge scolaire envers ses frères et sœurs, plus jeunes et plus vieux, peut en fait augmenter s'il persiste à vouloir conserver sa supériorité sur un plus jeune ou à égaler un plus vieux. La réussite scolaire est une des causes principales de jalousie à cet âge, tout particulièrement pour l'enfant qui est intellectuellement moins doué que ses frères et sœurs.

Les enfants d'âge scolaire préfèrent souvent la compagnie de leurs amis à celle de leurs frères et sœurs. Les relations avec un ami sont moins émotives et les parents risquent moins d'intervenir. L'enfant choisit ses amis; la relation avec ses frères et sœurs lui est imposée par la nature et il ne peut pas s'en libérer volontiers. Idéalement, l'expérience de vie avec les frères et sœurs devrait faciliter l'adaptation d'un enfant à la société, mais cette expérience ne remplace pas une amitié personnelle.

Relations avec les amis.   Comme l'enfant s'éloigne psychologiquement de la maison, ses amis prennent de plus en plus d'importance pour lui. Il apprend à faire partie d'un groupe et sa vie sociale débute. Au cours de cette étape, les enfants ont tendance à se tenir à l'écart de l'autre sexe et même à le déprécier. Chaque sexe découvre son langage, ses activités et la façon de se conduire. Garçons et filles apprennent lentement à rivaliser, puis à coopérer.

Les enfants d'âge scolaire peuvent être cruels les uns envers les autres. Ils décèlent avec une remarquable perspicacité ce qui est différent

Figure 20-1.   Pendant les années scolaires, les amis prennent de plus en plus d'importance. Les enfants de chaque sexe possèdent leur propre langage et des activités spécifiques. (H. Armstrong Roberts.)

ou inusité chez les autres et un abus de taquinerie est commun aux enfants de cet âge. Certains enfants, différents de quelque façon, sont tenus à l'écart des groupes, ridiculisés et parfois même persécutés. Les enfants peuvent également être cruels envers des adultes qu'ils n'aiment pas.

Les bandes ou les groupes. Les enfants d'âge scolaire ont découvert que leurs parents ne sont pas omnipotents, qu'ils font des erreurs et qu'ils ont peur parfois. Les jeunes cherchent alors à se confier à leurs amis; ils se lient d'amitié et se joignent à des groupes de leur propre sexe. Un tel groupe peut être simplement une réunion d'amis ou une société secrète ou encore une bande anti-sociale, suivant les besoins des enfants qui y appartiennent. Entre eux, les enfants discutent des problèmes auxquels ils ont à faire face, de leurs théories sur la vie, la mort et les questions sexuelles; ils partagent les attitudes, les valeurs et les croyances de leurs amis. Celles-ci varient par la suite, mais la première empreinte émotive dure souvent jusqu'à l'âge adulte. Les émissions de télévision influent aussi sur la vision de la réalité de l'enfant d'âge scolaire.

Les tendances agressives du garçon trouvent un exutoire dans la bataille: soit d'une façon organisée, comme dans le baseball ou le football, soit en jouant aux policiers et aux voleurs ou aux Indiens et aux cowboys. Malheureusement, certains de ces groupes juvéniles dirigent leur agressivité, non pas contre des enfants de leur âge et à l'intérieur d'un jeu, mais contre d'autres jeunes ou contre des adultes avec des intentions qui n'ont rien à voir avec le jeu. Quand cela se produit, la voie est ouverte à la délinquance.

Les filles aussi forment des groupes distincts et discutent de leurs problèmes personnels. Toutefois, elles ne s'orientent habituellement pas vers les démonstrations d'agressivité et d'hostilité que l'on peut voir dans les bandes de garçons.

Vers la fin de la période scolaire, les enfants savent ce que sont la compétition, le compromis et la coopération, de sorte qu'ils peuvent agir sans l'aide des adultes. Ils ont appris à se conformer aux règles de la société et ont acquis un sens des responsabilités au sujet de questions qu'ils savent importantes.

Les parents devraient comprendre et accepter les activités de leurs enfants d'âge scolaire et être prêts à leur accorder l'indépendance nécessaire. Trop souvent, la mère seule s'intéresse à ces questions et elle comprend plus difficilement les sujets qui intéressent son fils.

Le garçon a tout particulièrement besoin de l'intérêt affectueux de son père.

APERÇU DU DÉVELOPPEMENT PHYSIQUE, SOCIAL ET MENTAL

Développement physique. Pendant les années scolaires, l'enfant grandit de plus en plus lentement, mais prend du poids. Il perd le plus souvent sa maigreur des années précédentes. La croissance, en général, est lente, jusqu'à la poussée qui précède la puberté. La coordination musculaire s'améliore graduellement; la posture doit être bonne (la lordose antérieure est disparue). Le tissu lymphoïde atteint le point culminant de son développement au cours des premières années d'école. Les sinus frontaux sont assez bien développés vers six ans. À partir de ce moment, tous les sinus peuvent devenir des foyers d'infection.

C'est à cette période qu'apparaissent les dents permanentes. Les molaires sont les premières à poindre vers 6 ans et constituent le pivot de l'arche dentaire permanente. La mâchoire plutôt petite du jeune enfant s'est allongée vers l'avant pour donner l'espace nécessaire aux dents permanentes.

La température, le pouls et la respiration se rapprochent des normes de l'adulte. La température normale est de 37°C. Le rythme respiratoire varie de 18 à 26 par minute selon l'âge de l'enfant.

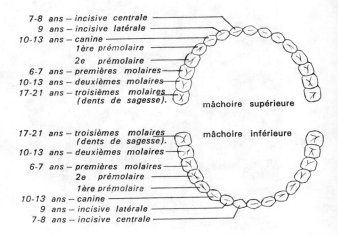

7-8 ans — incisive centrale
9 ans — incisive latérale
10-13 ans — canine
1ère prémolaire
2e prémolaire
6-7 ans — premières molaires
10-13 ans — deuxièmes molaires
17-21 ans — troisièmes molaires
(dents de sagesse).

mâchoire supérieure

17-21 ans — troisièmes molaires
(dents de sagesse).
10-13 ans — deuxièmes molaires
6-7 ans — premières molaires
2e prémolaire
1ère prémolaire
10-13 ans — canine
9 ans — incisive latérale
7-8 ans — incisive centrale

mâchoire inférieure

Figure 20-2. Dentition permanente. L'éruption de ces dents survient entre 6 et 21 ans.

Figure 20-3. Plus un enfant vieillit, plus il devient difficile d'établir des normes de développement physique, de conduite, d'habileté. Ces deux enfants ont six ans, mais il existe entre eux une différence évidente de taille.

Figure 20-4. Les enfants de six ans aiment l'activité physique, mais leurs mouvements ne sont pas aussi coordonnés que ceux des enfants plus âgés. (H. Armstrong Roberts.)

Les changements d'ordre physique indicateurs de la puberté peuvent commencer à apparaître vers la fin de cette période.

Développement social et mental. À l'école, l'enfant a la possibilité d'élargir ses contacts sociaux en même temps qu'il développe ses capacités mentales. Les horaires de nombreuses écoles sont plus courts pour les enfants de six à huit ans que pour les autres plus âgés. Ceci rend plus facile la transition de la vie au foyer à celle de l'école ainsi que l'adaptation à de nouvelles expériences.

POINTS IMPORTANTS DU DÉVELOPPEMENT SOCIAL ET MENTAL

Plus l'enfant vieillit, moins il devient possible d'établir des normes rigides de conduite et de capacités. De telles normes servent tout au plus de références à ce qui se produit souvent à un certain âge. L'étudiant devrait se rappeler, tel que vu au chapitre 2, que le développement ne suit pas toujours une courbe ascendante régulière. Il y a des périodes d'accélération, des plateaux, et même des retards dans certains domaines, pendant que le reste du développement se poursuit à un rythme normal. Toutefois, chez l'enfant, la croissance physique et le développement mental et émotif sont intimement liés. Les *différences individuelles,* dues à l'état de santé, l'environnement familial, social et communautaire, deviennent de plus en plus prononcées à mesure que l'enfant vieillit.

Six ans

La sixième année est l'année de transition, de changements physiques et psychologiques que la société a adoptée comme moment favorable à l'entrée à l'école. C'est une période difficile pour les parents, et aussi pour l'enfant parce qu'il veut se charger de responsabilités de plus en plus grandes alors qu'il n'a pas encore les moyens de prendre des décisions éclairées. Ordinairement, il est émotif et tendu, centré sur lui-même et très démonstratif. Il aime diriger les autres, mais est blessé facilement par les critiques qu'il soulève. Il a le goût de tout entreprendre, mais n'est pas pressé de terminer ce qu'il commence. Il peut montrer du défi et de l'impolitesse envers les adultes et ceci est le résultat de ses réactions émotives instables.

Les enfants de six ans ressentent une tension parce qu'ils vieillissent et quittent la sécurité de la maison pour aller à l'école. L'enfant

Figure 20-5. L'enfant de six ans *A)* a un sens de l'équilibre amélioré, de sorte qu'il peut sauter et courir le long d'une marque de craie, *B)* il peut facilement lancer et attraper une balle, *C)* il fait aisément des boucles, *D)* il peut dessiner une personne avec des détails qui n'y étaient pas auparavant.

éprouve une nouvelle vague d'anxiété devant la séparation, phénomène courant, même pendant l'adolescence. L'école maternelle est une expérience de transition qui atténue ces réactions. Il veut encore jouer au petit enfant; l'amour et les félicitations des parents gardent leur importance.

Les garçons et les filles jouent ensemble. Leurs jeux ont de fortes chances de se terminer par des querelles auxquelles participent également les deux sexes.

L'enfant de six ans peut être troublé par certaines questions qu'il s'est posées sur la sexualité pendant la période précédant l'âge scolaire. Il peut se livrer à des jeux sexuels. Même s'il parle du mariage, il prête peu d'attention à son aspect sexuel et peut demander à quelqu'un de sa famille d'être son conjoint. Il peut aussi vouloir que sa mère ait un bébé, même s'il y en a déjà un dans la famille.

Développement physique et contrôle moteur. Le développement physique et le contrôle moteur se voient dans les caractéristiques et les capacités changeantes de l'enfant de six ans. La perte des dents temporaires continue et les dents permanentes, les molaires de six ans, apparaissent. À l'école, il est plus souvent exposé aux infections que chez lui et les problèmes oto-rhino-laryngologiques sont fréquents. Il semble être en mouvement perpétuel. Il aime bien l'activité physique, mais ses mouvements deviennent gauches à la suite de la fatigue due à un surcroît d'exercice; il saute, fait des culbutes, lutte avec d'autres enfants. Son sens de l'équilibre s'est amélioré: il grimpe, saute à la corde, sautille et court bien. Garçons et filles peuvent marcher avec assurance sur une marque de craie et apprendre à patiner; ils peuvent conduire une bicyclette.

Ces enfants peuvent lancer et attraper une balle. Ils sont conscients que leurs mains sont des instruments dont ils peuvent se servir. Ils peuvent marteler, construire des structures simples, attacher leurs vêtements et lacer leurs chaussures.

Langage, socialisation et capacité intellectuelle. L'enfant de six ans contrôle pratiquement toutes les formes de structures de phrase. Il a acquis le langage et n'expérimente plus avec les mots. Il pose des questions qui expriment sa pensée. Il se sert du langage comme d'un outil et moins pour le plaisir de parler, comme il le faisait avant l'âge scolaire. Il peut utiliser le langage agressivement, en se servant d'expressions grossières ou même de jurons. Il parle pour partager l'expérience des autres et il cherche à en apprendre davantage au sujet de sa famille et de sa parenté. Il définit encore les objets en fonction de leur usage: une chaise est quelque chose sur laquelle on peut s'asseoir, une cuillère est quelque chose avec laquelle on mange. Cependant, il a une certaine conception des mots abstraits; il sait différencier le matin de l'après-midi. Il distingue la main droite de la main gauche, il peut compter jusqu'à 20 ou plus, mais quand il écrit, il peut inverser un ou deux chiffres ou les lettres majuscules. Puisqu'il est maintenant capable de discerner les formes, il peut lire et décrire les objets qu'il voit sur les images. Il dessine une personne avec des détails qui ne figuraient pas dans ses dessins précédents, comme les mains, le cou et les vêtements. Il distingue ce qu'il trouve joli de ce qui lui semble laid, quand on lui montre une série de visages. Il est capable d'obéir à trois ordres donnés successivement, par exemple: « essuie-toi les mains, mets les plats sur la table et ferme la porte ».

Sept ans

Sept ans est l'âge de l'assimilation, une période de quiétude. L'enfant présente moins de problèmes qu'à six ans, il est plus souvent calme qu'exubérant. De nombreux professeurs trouvent qu'à l'élémentaire les groupes de deuxième année sont les plus faciles. L'enfant a des relations moins intenses avec les autres. Il ne cherche pas les ennuis, mais il aime bien taquiner, et ceci entraîne des complications avec les plus jeunes et avec les adultes qui les défendent. Il aime jouer seul, quoiqu'il préfère le jeu en groupe. Quand il joue, il est plus passif que l'enfant de six ans.

Figure 20-6. L'enfant de sept ans *A)* peut jouer à la marelle, *B)* sait quel est le mois, surtout s'il s'y trouve un événement agréable comme l'Halloween, *C)* est un membre coopératif dans la famille.

L'enfant de sept ans idéalise sa famille et ressent à la fois une infériorité personnelle et une certaine colère lors d'échecs, même mineurs, de l'un de ses membres. Son sens de l'éthique se développe; il a conscience du bien et du mal dans la conduite des autres et dans la sienne. Il se peut, que motivé par son sentiment de justice, il dénonce un camarade. Il est maintenant un membre coopératif de la famille et recherche l'approbation de ses parents. Les parents doivent respecter sa vie intérieure, ses poussées de tristesse et ses périodes de soudaine timidité. C'est pendant cette période qu'il devient conscient de lui-même et des autres.

L'enfant de sept ans est plus timide au sujet des questions sexuelles et s'adonne moins à de tels jeux. Plusieurs enfants de sept ans aimeraient avoir un frère ou une sœur bébé. L'enfant de sept ans peut éprouver un sentiment d'amour pour quelqu'un de l'autre sexe dans les limites de son développement émotif.

Développement physique et contrôle moteur. Le niveau d'activités diminue à sept ans, mais il varie beaucoup d'un enfant à l'autre. L'enfant a une caractéristique qui ennuie ses aînés, mais qui le fascine, lui et ceux de son âge, des dents vacillantes.

Les livres qu'il lit ne sont plus écrits plus gros que la normale, car à sept ou huit ans, ses yeux sont complètement développés. Sa posture est plus tendue et plus prête au mouvement que celle de l'enfant plus jeune.

Garçons et filles aiment le patinage et les autres sports actifs. Il commence cependant à y avoir une division entre sports masculins et féminins. Les filles sautent à la corde et jouent à la marelle, jeux auxquels les garçons ont tendance à s'adonner pour taquiner seulement. Même si les enfants de sept ans sont actifs, ils aiment les jeux où ils peuvent s'asseoir et se reposer.

Langage, socialisation et capacité intellectuelle. L'enfant a une bonne notion du temps et de l'espace. Il sait quel est le mois et quelle est la saison, surtout les mois où surviennent des événements qui l'intéressent particulièrement (Noël ou son anniversaire). Il commence à lire l'heure sur l'horloge ainsi que les minutes.

Il devient plus habile de ses mains, et il préfère souvent se servir d'un crayon et d'une gomme à effacer que des craies à colorier. Il peut écrire plusieurs phrases en lettres moulées, bien que les lettres deviennent plus petites vers la fin de la ligne. Il inverse moins souvent les lettres et corrige ses erreurs. Il peut répéter cinq chiffres à la suite et trois chiffres à rebours, compter par deux et par cinq, saisir l'idée de base de l'addition et de la soustraction, recopier un losange sans le confondre avec un carré et dire quelles sont les parties qui manquent dans une image incomplète. Il est capable de maintenir son attention plus longtemps, et il aime répéter des activités qui lui apportent une satisfaction. Il se suffit mieux à lui-même, il a besoin de très peu d'aide pour s'habiller, se déshabiller et se mettre au lit. Dépendant du type d'éducation religieuse qu'il reçoit, son intérêt peut grandir à propos de questions, telles la place de Dieu dans le monde, la situation et la description du paradis.

Huit ans

L'enfant de huit ans est communicatif et veut tout faire. C'est l'âge où les expériences se diversifient. Il est plus créateur et plus actif quand il joue ou travaille seul, mais il a besoin de la compagnie et de l'approbation des autres enfants et il les recherche. Plein d'énergie, enthousiaste, il veut que les adultes le trouvent important. Il veut assumer des responsabilités et étendre son influence sur la culture de son groupe en montant des spectacles dramatiques et en inventant de nouvelles façons d'accomplir les tâches. Il essaie de comprendre les idées et les valeurs des adultes en écoutant ce qu'on lui dit. Il apprend par expérience, et par les autres, ce qui est nécessaire à la vie de groupe. Si ces capacités intellectuelles sont d'un niveau normal ou supérieur, il s'intéresse beaucoup à la lecture, aux activités de groupe et scolaires, particulièrement aux sciences qu'il relie aux avions, aux bateaux et aux voyages dans l'espace. Il aime la science-fiction. Le culte d'un héros commence à cet âge.

Il aime faire partie de clubs s'ils ne sont pas régis trop sévèrement, et prend au sérieux les particularités du groupe. Les enfants de huit ans semblent très conscients de l'identité sexuelle et choisissent des amis du même sexe qu'eux. Les garçons sont volontiers cachottiers au sujet de leur petite amie, surtout s'il s'agit d'une nouvelle voisine. Ils montrent un intérêt moins ouvert pour les sujets sexuels qui dépassent leur compréhension, mais peuvent poser des questions au moment opportun. Les mères doivent faire comprendre à leurs enfants qu'il est préférable de ne pas discuter des réponses à leurs questions sur la sexualité avec frères et sœurs ou amis. L'intérêt sexuel est souvent camouflé, à cet âge, dans les devinettes et les histoires que les enfants se racontent.

L'enfant de huit ans se conduit de son mieux quand il y a des visiteurs ou lorsqu'il est hors de la maison.

Développement physique et contrôle moteur.

Il se produit des changements subtils dans l'aspect physique d'un enfant de huit ans; les bras allongent en proportion du corps et les mains sont aussi proportionnellement plus grandes. Ses mouvements deviennent plus coordonnés, plus gracieux et plus assurés. Ses jeux changent puisqu'il vieillit. Il aime maintenant marcher en forêt, jouer à la balle et à des activités comme les jeux de piste.

Le garçon veut améliorer son habileté à la boxe et à la lutte; la fille saute à la corde et joue à la marelle. Les garçons et les filles aiment patiner sur patins à roulettes. Ils sont expressifs et accompagnent la parole de gestes descriptifs.

Langage, socialisation et capacité intellectuelle.

À l'école, l'enfant de huit ans écrit mieux les lettres régulières que moulées, et aime bien cette nouvelle capacité. Dans les tests destinés aux enfants de cet âge, on demande de nommer de mémoire les ressemblances et les différences entre deux objets — par exemple une balle et un bloc — et de compter à rebours à partir de vingt. À l'école et dans la vie quotidienne, il manifeste de nouvelles possibilités. Il commence à comprendre la perspective dans le dessin. Il peut nommer les jours de la semaine et a une idée du nombre de jours qui doivent s'écouler avant qu'un événement attendu avec joie arrive — un congé, son anniversaire ou, s'il est à l'hôpital, ce jour spécial où il reviendra à la maison.

Certains enfants de cet âge sont intéressés par l'éducation religieuse.

Figure 20-7. L'enfant de huit ans *A)* aime les jeux d'adresse qui font appel aux petits muscles de la main, *B)* affiche un intérêt marqué pour les sciences, *C)* a des mouvements plus sûrs en patinant, *D)* présente un meilleur équilibre.

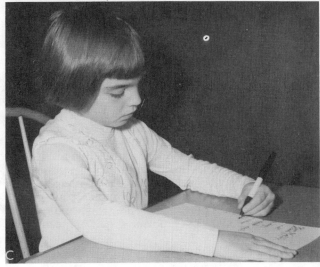

Figure 20-8. L'enfant de neuf ans, *A)* préfère encore les compagnons de jeu de son propre sexe, *B)* prend soin d'un enfant plus jeune ou d'un animal domestique, *C)* écrit avec une dextérité manuelle qui s'améliore constamment.

Neuf ans

L'enfant de neuf ans commence à prendre part aux discussions de famille. Il est moins agité que l'enfant de huit ans et s'intéresse plus aux activités familiales. Il se sent obligé de montrer aux autres qu'il est un individu, et ne tient pas compte de l'autorité des adultes quand elle entre en conflit avec des idées ou des valeurs de son groupe d'âge. Les professeurs trouvent qu'il est difficile d'enseigner aux groupes de quatrième année. En élargissant son champ d'expériences hors de la maison il accède à une indépendance plus grande. Il peut accepter qu'on le blâme pour ses actions, assumer la responsabilité de la surveillance de ses plus jeunes frères et sœurs et réussir à conserver un certain ordre dans sa chambre. Il a ses propres motivations et il a plus tendance à terminer ce qu'il commence.

Il évolue entre l'enfance et la jeunesse dans ses actions et ses pensées. Le culte du héros s'accentue. Les filles préfèrent encore jouer avec les filles et les garçons avec les garçons. L'aspect « reproduction » de la question sexuelle les préoccupe moins qu'à huit ans. Cela dépend toutefois de la façon dont on leur a répondu quand ils ont manifesté un désir d'information sur la conception et la naissance des enfants. L'enfant de neuf ans ressent toujours un sentiment d'urgence, comme s'il était dans une course perpétuelle contre la montre.

Développement physique et contrôle moteur. Ces enfants ont un éventail plus large de possibilités que durant leurs trois premières années d'école. Normalement, la coordination de la main avec la vue est développée et l'enfant devient habile dans les activités manuelles. En général, les enfants de cet âge peuvent se servir de chacune de leurs mains indépendamment.

L'enfant travaille et joue beaucoup et il aime pouvoir montrer sa capacité motrice et sa force; il manifeste aussi un grand intérêt pour les compétitions sportives comme le base-ball ou le hockey.

Langage, socialisation et capacité intellectuelle. Ses nouvelles capacités intellectuelles consistent à décrire des objets usuels et non plus à les définir par leur usage comme à six ans, répéter les mois de l'année en ordre, savoir la date, dire l'heure avec exactitude, écrire (habituellement en petites lettres de grosseur égale), comparer les choses qu'il lit avec la réalité, donner exactement la monnaie de vingt-cinq sous, classer par ordre de poids cinq objets, multiplier et diviser (division simple) et répéter quatre nombres à rebours (c'est là une partie habituelle d'un test intellectuel courant). Il a également acquis les concepts de la conservation du poids et de la matière.

L'enfant se suffit à lui-même dans ses besoins corporels; il s'agit là d'un grand pas hors de l'enfance, vers l'indépendance adulte. Il a appris les bonnes manières à table et les applique sans que ses parents soient obligés de les lui rappeler. Même s'il a moins peur que lorsqu'il était plus jeune, il est devenu plus préoccupé par les problèmes qu'il rencontre.

Dix ans

L'enfant normal de dix ans est au début de la période préadolescente. La fillette avance plus vite vers la puberté. L'enfant de dix ans est encore plus raisonnable que celui de neuf ans, parce qu'il a acquis une maîtrise plus grande de lui-même et de son environnement. Il manifeste plus de courtoisie envers les adultes, il a de meilleures manières et une plus grande capacité à se diriger lui-même. Ses intérêts sont variés et il commence à penser clairement aux problèmes sociaux et aux préjugés raciaux. Des talents particuliers se révèlent à cet âge.

L'enfant s'adapte plus facilement à la routine de la maison; il peut vivre selon des règles et tolère les frustrations. Il entre dans un âge où le besoin d'activités de groupe est à son maximum. Pour lui, atteindre un but pour le groupe est plus important que ses propres idées ou ses désirs. Il est capable de grande loyauté et d'un culte intense du héros; ce sont deux qualités qui facilitent l'intégration au groupe.

L'enfant de dix ans s'intéresse aux questions sexuelles, mais a plus tendance à discuter de ce sujet avec ses compagnons qu'avec ses parents. Garçons et filles s'intéressent à leurs organes sexuels, seuls ou lors de jeux sexuels.

Hors de l'école, les deux sexes se mêlent peu. Quoique des baisers puissent être échangés à l'occasion de jeux organisés par les adultes, ces jeux ne sont pas spontanément repris par les enfants. Ils se taquinent les uns les autres à propos d'amis de l'autre sexe.

L'enfant de dix ans veut être indépendant. L'adulte doit donc formuler ses demandes avec précision et tact. Les ordres négatifs sont un affront à sa propre estime. La force de la suggestion est importante à cet âge et peut être employée dans l'éducation de l'enfant.

Développement physique et contrôle moteur. Comme le corps de l'enfant se développe, les différences sexuelles deviennent plus prononcées. Les garçons et les filles deviennent de plus en plus habiles et ils désirent atteindre la perfection dans des activités souvent très complexes. Les filles ont plus d'aisance que les garçons, en partie à cause de leur maturité plus précoce.

Langage, socialisation et capacité intellectuelle. L'enfant conçoit maintenant les situations en termes de cause à effet. Il a une certaine compréhension des principes régissant les relations humaines et veut accomplir de grandes choses dans la vie.

Son éducation est plus avancée et il se sert de ce qu'il sait et des capacités qu'il a acquises dans la vie quotidienne. Il peut écrire pendant assez longtemps et ce, à une vitesse constante. Il aime les histoires mystérieuses, la science-fiction et les pratiques de magie. Il peut se servir de chiffre dépassant 100 et faire des fractions simples.

Dix à douze ans (Préadolescence)

Les années entre dix et douze ans sont identifiées par le nom de préadolescence. C'est une période de croissance et de développement rapides, au cours de laquelle de nombreux problèmes surgissent. À mesure qu'il approche de l'âge adulte, l'enfant critique de plus en plus les adultes, les comparant à l'image qu'il s'est faite de l'homme ou de la femme qu'il a

Figure 20-9. L'enfant de dix — onze ans, *A)* participe à part entière aux activités du groupe (construire une cabane où l'on pourra parler et partager des secrets), *B)* son intérêt dépasse maintenant les bornes de la vie familiale, *C — D)* développe de nouvelles capacités: apprend à tricoter et à jouer d'un instrument de musique.

l'intention de devenir. Il oscille entre la dépendance et l'indépendance et se replie sur lui-même plutôt que d'exprimer sa colère quand il est frustré. Il se rebelle parfois contre les habitudes familiales de propreté et d'habillement.

Les amis de son groupe sont extrêmement importants pour lui; il partage leurs attitudes et se confie à eux plutôt qu'à ses parents. Il prend une part enthousiaste à des projets communautaires comme recueillir des vêtements usagés pour les œuvres charitables ou des vieux journaux pour les Scouts.

Il est capable d'auto-critique. Il aimerait se libérer financièrement de ses parents; il est heureux de faire de petits travaux après l'école et pendant les vacances. Il recherche un ami adulte du même sexe à qui il peut s'identifier et exprimer ses critiques au sujet de ses parents. Le calme et le contrôle de l'enfant de dix ans disparaissent graduellement à onze et douze ans. Il devient taquin, négligent, exhibitionniste et négativiste. Il essaie de maîtriser la réalité et se prépare à l'adolescence. Il s'intéresse au fonctionnement des choses et il est curieux au sujet du monde en général, mais son intérêt pour les connaissaces académiques peut diminuer.

Il a besoin d'acquérir une personnalité encore plus forte pour pouvoir apporter de saines solutions aux problèmes de l'adolescence. L'adulte qui est responsable d'un préadolescent, à la maison, dans la collectivité ou à l'école doit accepter le fait que l'enfant a besoin de se rebeller et de déprécier les autres afin de résoudre son propre conflit entre la dépendance et l'indépendance. Il dépend des autres, mais n'aime pas qu'on lui fasse sentir qu'il est encore un enfant. Il rejette ses parents parce qu'il ne veut pas se sentir dépendant; il comble ses besoins de dépendance avec d'autres adultes. L'adulte qui se trouve élu par un préadolescent doit agir avec circonspection et sagesse. Il doit accepter l'enfant et cependant lui indiquer des limites dans sa conduite, comme le faisaient les parents quand l'enfant était plus jeune. Le préadolescent doit être guidé pour canaliser ses sentiments et son énergie, dans des sports ou un travail compatibles avec cette phase de croissance et de développement. Il a besoin d'aide afin de pouvoir s'accepter dans ce nouveau rôle de préadolescent. Les adultes, dans son milieu, doivent l'aider à s'estimer lui-même à sa juste valeur, et à renforcer sa personnalité de façon à le préparer adéquatement aux problèmes de l'adolescence.

Développement physique et contrôle moteur. Les enfants de ce groupe d'âge ont une grande énergie et sont constamment actifs. Leur contrôle musculaire est bon et leur habileté nouvelle égale presque celle des adultes. Ils semblent tendus et soulagent cette tension en tapant du pied ou en battant la mesure avec les doigts sur la table. Les molaires de douze ans apparaissent, ce sont les dernières dents à apparaître pendant l'enfance. La poussée de croissance de la préadolescence apparaît plus tôt chez les filles que chez les garçons, mais les filles sont dépassées par les garçons quant à l'endurance et la force physique.

Langage, socialisation et capacité intellectuelle. Avant douze ans, un enfant peut habituellement définir certaines notions abstraites comme l'honnêteté et la justice. Le développement de son vocabulaire et de sa diction dépend de son intelligence, de son expérience et de son milieu. Les enfants de ce groupe peuvent cerner la morale d'une histoire. Leurs intérêts et leurs recherches intellectuelles varient et s'expriment dans leur intérêt pour les questions mondiales, aussi bien passées que présentes et par leur attitude devant les problèmes sociaux, surtout ceux qui touchent à leur vie quotidienne.

Ils sont intéressés par les questions de santé. Ils veulent savoir pourquoi on doit se couvrir la bouche quand on tousse. Ils sont capables de se soigner dans les situations ordinaires, mais sous la surveillance d'adultes sympathiques. Ils sont capables d'assumer une certaine responsabilité quant aux soins à donner aux plus jeunes. Leurs rapports avec les enfants et les adultes s'étendent bien au-delà des limites du foyer.

Le groupe d'amis est très important pour le jeune de onze ans. C'est la période où l'on partage des secrets. On peut même inventer un langage codé et l'employer exclusivement dans le cercle restreint. Ces enfants préfèrent encore jouer avec des jeunes de leur propre sexe, mais ils acceptent des compagnons de l'autre sexe dans leurs activités.

L'ÉCOLE

La fréquentation de l'école est un aspect important de la vie de l'enfant durant sa croissance. L'école est l'institution de la société, destinée à servir d'instrument formel pour l'éducation des enfants. Le but de l'école est d'aider chaque enfant à actualiser ses possibilités. Cela sous-entend qu'elle doit aider chaque enfant à développer *son sens du travail.*

Les instruments de base pour atteindre cet objectif sont les moyens de communication et les mathématiques. L'enfant qui maîtrise ces deux outils peut alors étendre le champ de ses connaissances et inclure l'histoire, la géographie, les sciences et les arts.

À partir des premières années, le programme scolaire fournit une expérience qui contribue au développement social de l'enfant. Idéalement, il devrait apprendre à l'école à penser d'une façon critique, à porter des jugements basés sur un raisonnement, à accepter la critique, à coopérer avec les autres et à être tour à tour chef ou membre d'un groupe selon les occasions. Il devrait y faire l'apprentissage de l'estime de soi et du respect des autres.

La fréquentation de l'école est importante pour tous les enfants, peu importe leur groupe socio-économique et leur niveau d'intelligence. L'organisation du programme d'études devrait être telle que chaque enfant puisse éprouver un sentiment de succès dans un certain domaine.

Tous les enfants ne sont pas capables d'exceller intellectuellement. L'école devrait aider chacun à réaliser ses potentialités et à trouver une satisfaction réelle à réussir dans les activités sportives, manuelles ou artistiques, sinon dans des domaines académiques.

Préparation à l'école.

Les enfants ne sont pas tous prêts pour la scolarité au même âge chronologique. Si l'enfant s'est bien adapté à l'école maternelle, il aura probablement peu de difficultés à s'habituer à la vie de l'école. Il voit la fréquentation de l'école comme une responsabilité normale de l'enfance.

Aussitôt que l'école commence, l'enfant est séparé physiquement de son foyer. Celui qui n'y est pas préparé devient parfois anxieux ou craintif envers le professeur, ce nouvel adulte qui se charge d'une partie de sa vie. Il peut être effrayé de se trouver séparé de ses parents au milieu d'un groupe d'enfants différents de ceux qu'il a connus jusqu'alors. Cependant, s'il a fréquenté la maternelle, il a des amis en première année, et il peut connaître l'édifice de l'école. Si un plus jeune de la famille entre à l'école maternelle, il se fera son protecteur et l'initiera à sa nouvelle vie.

La préparation pour l'expérience scolaire devrait être la même que celle pour l'entrée à l'école maternelle (voir chapitre 17). L'enfant doit connaître son nom au complet et son adresse avant d'entrer à l'école, et apprendre certaines règles de sécurité, comme la façon de traverser les rues. Il doit être capable de s'occuper de lui-même à peu près entièrement, en ce qui concerne ses vêtements et sa toilette. Il devrait subir un examen médical et avoir reçu les vaccins nécessaires.

La mère doit conduire l'enfant à l'école avant le début des classes pour l'aider à s'orienter dans l'édifice et pour rencontrer son professeur, si c'est possible. Il faut parler positivement de l'école en tout temps et surtout à l'enfant sur le point d'y entrer. Les aînés présentent l'école comme une réalité de tous les jours pour tous les enfants de six ans et comme une supériorité sur les plus jeunes. Après le début des classes, si l'enfant demeure craintif et réticent, la mère devrait rencontrer le professeur et discuter avec lui des meilleurs moyens à utiliser. Avant que les parents laissent un enfant partir seul pour l'école, ils doivent être certains qu'il connaît le chemin pour s'y rendre. En général, la distance jusqu'à l'école n'excède pas celle d'une courte marche ou alors l'enfant s'y rend en autobus scolaire.

Un problème qui peut surgir après que l'enfant se soit familiarisé avec son nouvel environnement est qu'il soit plus intéressé à se faire de nouveaux amis qu'à acquérir de nouvelles connaissances, surtout si aucun de ses amis du voisinage, du jardin d'enfants ou de la maternelle ne se trouve dans sa classe à l'école.

Les parents ne devraient pas exiger trop des enfants à leur retour de l'école. Ils ont été astreints à une journée de travail scolaire et à une récréation surveillée, ces deux types d'activités étant planifiés pour promouvoir la croissance et le développement. Même si l'enfant doit se charger de certaines responsabilités à la maison, il faut qu'il ait aussi le temps de jouer avec ses frères et sœurs, ses amis et aussi d'être seul. Ce dernier besoin est souvent négligé même par les parents consciencieux.

Pendant la période d'orientation de l'enfant, aussi bien que durant toute sa vie scolaire, les parents doivent l'encourager à raconter ses expériences scolaires. Cela perfectionne sa capacité de communiquer et l'aide à prendre conscience de lui-même comme d'un individu à part entière. L'intérêt que manifeste ses parents envers l'école et envers les activités de l'enfant motive en premier lieu son désir de s'instruire.

Si l'enfant refuse d'accepter l'école, s'il y est chroniquement malheureux ou s'il n'apprend pas au rythme souhaité, ses parents doivent essayer d'en découvrir les causes, avec l'aide du professeur ou d'un autre membre du personnel de l'école.

LE JEU ET LE TRAVAIL

Le jeu est un outil d'apprentissage pour l'enfant, et ses jeux changent au fur et à mesure que son développement se poursuit. L'enfant d'âge scolaire ajoute des détails réalistes à son jeu, et cependant il devient en même temps plus imaginatif. Il ne mêle plus phantasme et réalité comme à l'âge préscolaire. Il a ses rêveries, mais les garde pour lui sans les partager avec ses parents.

En général, le temps passé au jeu et le nombre d'activités de jeu diminuent à mesure que l'enfant vieillit. Cependant, le temps consacré à une activité en particulier s'allonge, parce que sa capacité d'attention augmente et que l'enfant prend plus d'intérêt à ce qu'il fait. Le jeu, pendant l'âge scolaire, devient plus organisé, plus compliqué, plus compétitif et jusqu'à un certain degré, moins actif physiquement. L'enfant se plaît à des jeux comportant beaucoup de règles strictes. Il commence à s'intéresser à un passe-temps ou à des collections diverses et, ce faisant, il collectionne des données et des connaissances au sujet du monde dans lequel il vit.

Alors que l'enfant participe à des jeux de compétition, comme le football, le baseball ou la course à pied, il a besoin de l'aide des adultes pour apprendre les règlements. Cependant, l'adulte ne devrait pas diriger les jeux, car les enfants réagissent mieux quand ils les organisent eux-mêmes. C'est au cours de ces expériences qu'ils apprennent à se gouverner et à diriger leurs activités.

Une autre responsabilité des parents pendant ces années est d'aider l'enfant à apprendre à travailler. Il faut l'encourager à participer aux travaux de la maison. Il se peut qu'on prenne plus de temps à se faire aider d'un enfant qu'à faire le travail soi-même, mais, à long terme, l'adulte y gagnera et l'enfant développera son sens du travail. Si on ne lui permet pas d'aider les autres lorsqu'il est jeune, il peut, plus tard, ne pas manifester d'esprit d'entr'aide. Le travail qu'on lui demande devrait contribuer au bien-être du groupe.

Aussitôt que l'enfant est intéressé à gagner l'argent suffisant à ses menues dépenses (ceci vers 10-11 ans) il faut l'aider à décider quel genre de travail il aimerait faire: livrer les journaux, entretenir les pelouses, surveiller les enfants, etc. L'attitude qu'il adopte vis-à-vis de son travail pendant ces premières années est importante et contribue à faire de lui le travailleur qu'il sera à l'âge adulte.

SIX À HUIT ANS

De six à huit ans, l'enfant s'intéresse surtout à son environnement immédiat et au moment présent. Il a besoin, dans le jeu, de trouver une chance d'exprimer ses sentiments et de se sentir accepté des autres. Ses jeux doivent convenir à ses intérêts et à sa capacité de concentration. Comme il en sait plus au sujet de la vie familiale qu'au sujet de toute autre façon de vivre, il aime jouer au papa et à la maman. Il imite aussi les différents travailleurs avec lesquels il est en contact: marchand, laitier ou cheminot. L'adulte peut apprendre à mieux connaître l'enfant, en observant ses jeux.

Six ans

L'enfant de six ans joue avec de plus en plus de diversité et de mouvement. Garçons et filles prennent part aux mêmes activités. Par exemple, ils aiment peindre et colorier, découper et coller. Les garçons aiment dessiner des avions, des trains et des bateaux; habituellement, les filles préfèrent dessiner des personnages et des maisons. Les garçons aiment à creuser plus que les filles, quoique ce soit l'une des activités favorites de tous les enfants. Les garçons ont plus souvent une bicyclette que les filles, mais ils veulent tous apprendre à la conduire. S'ils n'en ont pas une à eux, ils empruntent celle d'un frère plus âgé ou d'une grande sœur, ou encore d'un ami. Les enfants des deux sexes aiment bien la course, jouer à cache-cache, se promener en patins à roulettes et se baigner. Les filles aiment sauter à la corde.

Garçons et filles aiment « faire semblant », mais il y a une différence entre les sexes. Les garçons se prétendent conducteurs, mécaniciens ou soldats, ou ils imitent un autre rôle masculin qui comporte beaucoup d'activités. Les filles se costument et jouent à la mère ou au professeur, en utilisant des enfants plus jeunes ou des poupées en guise de bébés. C'est l'âge où elles jouent le plus à la mère et tous les jouets qui se rattachent à ce jeu ajoutent au plaisir de l'enfant. Sans distinction de sexes, les enfants de cet âge collectionnent toutes sortes de choses: des pièces de monnaie, des images ou n'importe quel objet qui frappe leur imagination.

Les enfants de six à huit ans aiment exercer leur mémoire, regarder des livres de bandes dessinées, jouer à de simples jeux de société, écouter la radio et regarder la télévision.

Garçons et filles peuvent jouer ensemble au père et à la mère, mais les garçons ne jouent pas à ces jeux entre eux. Les garçons aiment particulièrement les jeux qui consistent à se cacher et à tirer sur l'ennemi. Ils sont intéressés par les jeux de construction et de transport.

Les jouets appréciés des filles sont les poupées et tous les accessoires pouvant les accompagner, les balançoires, les cuisinières, les valises et les ensembles de maquillage. Les garçons aiment les trains électriques, les avions, les bateaux, les camions et les automobiles.

Sept ans

Le jeu à sept ans est moins exubérant et l'enfant y introduit moin d'innovations. Il est plus persévérant dans ses intérêts de jeu. Il aime les livres drôles et simples et il aime à colorier dans les livres qui ont des images convenant à son âge. Il aime les jeux de société, les casse-tête chinois, la magie et les tours. Il accepte facilement de jouer seul, s'il ne trouve pas de compagnons et il réussit à

Figure 20-10. L'enfant de huit ans *A) B)* aime bien faire du théâtre, *C)* apprécie les collections.

planifier ses activités. Il choisit à la télévision les émissions où il y a beaucoup de tir et de folles galopades. Il aime à inventer, et ensuite à construire, des jouets et des cadeaux pour ses parents, se servant de boîtes de céréales, de caisses de fruits et même de boîtes d'empaquetage. Les filles aiment à dessiner des robes pour leurs poupées.

Ces enfants collectionnent de tout sans se préoccuper de la qualité: ils conservent les cailloux, les capsules de bouteilles et presque tout ce qu'ils trouvent qui sort de l'ordinaire.

Ils exigent plus de réalisme dans leurs jeux. Ils ont besoin de fusils et de munitions pour jouer aux cowboys et aux Indiens, ou aux policiers et aux gendarmes. Toutes les « mamans » de sept ans veulent des poupées de la taille d'un vrai bébé, qui peuvent boire au biberon et mouiller leur couche. Elles apprécient les poupées qui ont des cheveux que l'on peut brosser et peigner.

Les enfants des deux sexes aiment les jeux actifs. Les filles préfèrent la marelle et le saut à la corde. Les garçons courent, jouent à la balle et grimpent aux arbres. Tous jouent aux billes, conduisent bien une bicyclette, et apprennent la natation sous surveillance. S'ils en ont la possibilité, ils apprennent le ski.

Huit ans

Huit ans est un âge actif, où des intérêts variés se manifestent. Les jeux non surveillés entre enfants de huit ans deviennent bruyants et se terminent souvent en disputes. Ils n'aiment pas jouer seuls. Avec un adulte, ils exigent une participation entière. Leurs dessins illustrent des scènes d'action.

Les filles aiment à mélanger la pâte pour les biscuits, faire des gelées dans de jolis moules, glacer les gâteaux et essayer des recettes de cuisine faciles. Les garçons aiment les ensembles de chimie simples et l'équipement pour construire un système de télégraphe. Ils aiment le théâtre, la bataille et les jeux de pompier. Les filles aiment aussi le théâtre quoique d'un genre plus artistique et elles veulent toujours un auditoire.

Les garçons et les filles de cet âge aiment la magie et font des collections, mais ils sont maintenant conscients de la qualité; ils classent et organisent leurs collections. Ils conservent les cailloux, les roches, les billes, les cartes d'étoiles de baseball, d'automobiles, les poupées de papier, les cartes de souhaits et d'autres objets semblables.

Les enfants de huit ans commencent à former des clubs assez peu organisés, qui ne durent pas longtemps. Ils ont des mots de passe secrets qui doivent être donnés afin d'obtenir la permission d'entrer dans la maison du club, la hutte ou la cachette.

Ils aiment les sports variés suivant les saisons. Ils s'intéressent à des jeux comme les échecs et les dames. Ils peuvent inventer leurs propres règles pour d'anciens jeux, allant souvent jusqu'à en faire en quelque sorte un jeu nouveau. Les règles ne durent peut-être pas longtemps, mais tous doivent s'y conformer tant qu'elles existent. Les enfants de cet âge n'acceptent pas facilement de perdre et quittent souvent le groupe s'ils sont vaincus.

La plupart des enfants de huit ans lisent suffisamment bien pour apprécier les classiques de l'enfance comme les récits de voyage et la géographie. Les bandes dessinées demeurent toutefois les grandes favorites. Ce sont ces enfants qui désirent le plus ardemment les prix et les objets que l'on peut obtenir avec les coupons publicitaires. Ils ont autant de plaisir que les adultes à recevoir du courrier. La radio et la télévision prennent une grande importance dans leur vie. Ils aiment les histoires d'aventure, de science-fiction et les récits mystérieux.

NEUF ANS A DOUZE ANS

L'intérêt des enfants de ce groupe d'âge s'étend dans le temps et l'espace, ils reculent dans l'histoire et se projettent dans l'âge interplanétaire. Ils aiment les histoires qui ne comportent pas de morale, mais qui donnent des exemples de courage, de bonté, d'endurance et d'aventure. Ils se sentent responsables et veulent rendre service. Ils éprouvent une satisfaction à contribuer à une activité de groupe et ils commencent à développer la fidélité au groupe qui caractérise les adolescents. Ils sont maintenant capables d'assimiler les conseils relatifs aux avantages d'une conduite réfléchie. Ils s'intéressent à leur avenir d'une certaine façon puisqu'ils disent: « Quand je serai grand ... » Les parents doivent observer leurs penchants naturels, quoique les décisions au sujet de leur profession future ne puissent être prises avant l'adolescence.

Neuf ans

L'enfant de neuf ans joue et travaille très fort, souvent jusqu'à s'exténuer. Il est occupé par des activités de son choix; il aime lire, écouter la radio, regarder la télévision durant des heures. Les garçons jouent au football ou au baseball et les filles jouent à la mère pendant de longues heures.

Les garçons comme les filles aiment les sports actifs. Ils sont assez vieux pour vouloir améliorer leurs performances et il y a maintenant un but dans leur jeu. Les garçons dérangent souvent les adultes et les autres enfants quand ils se chamaillent.

Les enfants de neuf ans lisent beaucoup, et plusieurs fois, leurs livres préférés. Ils lisent souvent les classiques juniors, mais les bandes dessinées et les livres d'aventure, de guerre et d'humour basés sur des situations familiales retiennent encore leur attention.

Plusieurs enfants s'intéressent à la musique et suivent des leçons à l'école ou chez un professeur particulier. Souvent, ils s'appliquent à atteindre un plus grand perfectionnement et y parviennent par de longues heures de pratique. Les talents, surtout dans les arts, se manifestent à cet âge. Ils veulent tous aller au cinéma.

Dix ans

Les différences sexuelles dans les jeux sont prononcées chez les enfants de dix ans. Les garçons et les filles essaient de bien se conduire en société. À l'école, ils travaillent rapidement, aimant bien le défi du calcul mental.

L'enfant de dix ans a tellement conscience d'avoir besoin du support des enfants de son âge qu'il tiendra plus à leur opinion qu'à celle de ses parents. Il s'intéresse au bien-être et à la justice sociale. Il fait preuve de loyauté envers son groupe et n'en colporte pas les secrets. Il peut cultiver l'image d'un héros.

À la radio et à la télévision, les goûts de l'enfant de dix ans sont ceux de l'enfant de neuf ans. Les garçons rejettent les histoires d'amour, mais les filles réagissent différemment.

Les filles aiment dramatiser les situations de la vie réelle et les sujets de ces jeux tournent souvent autour de fiançailles et de mariages. Cependant, quelques-unes jouent encore à la poupée, adoptant le rôle de la maman qui « élève ses enfants ». Elles s'intéressent de plus en plus à leur apparence.

Onze ans

L'enfant de onze ans est plein d'énergie et de dynamisme. Il explore différents domaines et s'intéresse intensément aux activités de groupe. Son intérêt pour l'école peut diminuer, surtout s'il n'est pas bon élève. Le jeu n'est plus le centre de sa vie et la compagnie des autres devient plus importante.

Même si ces enfants semblent maladroits dans leurs activités à la maison, ils sont devenus très habiles au jeu. Tout les intéresse. C'est l'âge du clan, et le groupe possède sa propre hutte ou sa maison dans les arbres. L'intérêt de l'enfant pour la lecture et le cinéma augmente; les personnages rencontrés dans les récits lui semblent vivants, il aimerait les connaître ou peut-être les punir d'une façon ou d'une autre.

Douze ans

L'enfant de douze ans est enthousiaste, à tel point qu'il oublie les conséquences de ses actes. Même s'il demeure membre de son groupe, il aime la solitude. Il s'engage dans le sport organisé avec un esprit d'équipe plus développé et se laisse moins distraire par ce qui est extérieur au jeu. Il a moins besoin de louanges que l'année précédente. L'élargissement de ses intérêts se manifeste par un désir de correspondre avec un autre jeune d'un pays éloigné.

Les enfants de douze ans veulent gagner de l'argent, non pas en faisant les courses pour leurs parents ou d'autres petits travaux, mais dans le cadre d'un projet organisé, surtout à deux, qui motive leur désir de réussite. Ils peuvent également s'intéresser à la publication d'un journal et nombreux sont ceux qui vendent des journaux. À cet âge, garçons et filles ont encore tendance à se tenir éloignés les uns des autres.

SOINS

Soins physiques

Bain, habillement et toilette. Les enfants entre six et douze ans sont en général capable de se baigner, de s'habiller et de faire leur toilette, mais ils ont besoin d'aide pour des détails, tels que le soin de leurs ongles, la bonne tenue de leurs vêtements et même la propreté. Il y a, évidemment, des différences individuelles; certains enfants ne peuvent pas supporter de se faire nettoyer les oreilles, d'autres n'aiment pas se faire brosser les cheveux, ni se faire coiffer. Dans ce domaine, les différences entre les sexes sont accusées: les filles sont en général plus soigneuses de leur apparence que les garçons.

L'enfant de six ans a besoin d'aide, même s'il ne l'accepte pas facilement. Il est désordonné et doit être surveillé. S'il se déshabille, il laisse tomber ses vêtements ou les jette de tous côtés. L'enfant de sept ans y met le temps, mais il finit habituellement ce qu'il commence. L'enfant de huit ans est plus efficace. À partir de neuf ans, les enfants semblent plus responsables dans le choix de leurs vêtements qu'ils adaptent suivant l'occasion et la température, et qu'ils replacent à l'endroit réservé à cet effet. Ils peuvent s'occuper de leur toilette et de leur bain, mais il arrive qu'on doive leur rappeler de se brosser les dents ou de se laver soigneusement les mains, et certains ont besoin d'aide pour peigner leurs cheveux longs.

Sommeil

Le sommeil de l'enfant d'âge scolaire est plutôt agité. La crainte, sous forme de terreurs nocturnes ou de cauchemars, l'empêche de dormir calmement. La peur de la mort est une angoisse nouvelle à cet âge. L'heure du coucher devrait être particulièrement tranquille, soulignant l'interdépendance des parents et de l'enfant. C'est le moment propice aux confidences, aux questions et aux discussions.

Il est possible que l'enfant, en vieillissant, veuille décider de l'heure à laquelle il va se coucher. Les parents doivent alors juger combien d'heures de sommeil lui sont nécessaires et veiller à ce qu'il se couche à temps. La durée de sommeil indispensable diminue avec l'âge. L'enfant de six ans peut avoir besoin de onze à douze heures de sommeil, alors que l'enfant de douze ans n'a besoin en général que de dix heures.

Mesures de sécurité

Avec l'élargissement constant du champ d'activités de l'enfant d'âge scolaire, les parents ne peuvent pas espérer être toujours présents pour éviter les accidents. Si les parents et les professeurs de la maternelle et de l'élémentaire ont mis l'accent sur les mesures de sécurité, un enfant devrait être prêt à instaurer, à partir de ses expériences antérieures, son propre système de sécurité, de façon à éviter les dangers qu'il rencontre sur son chemin.

Entre six et douze ans, les accidents les plus fréquents, mortels ou non, sont les *accidents de la route*. Les enfants peuvent traverser la rue au feu rouge ou entre des autos stationnées, ou se faire blesser lorsqu'ils sont en automobile ou à bicyclette.

La deuxième cause d'accidents est la *noyade*. L'enfant doit apprendre à nager le plus tôt possible. On devrait également lui enseigner les mesures de sécurité dans l'eau et les techniques de réanimation.

Les accidents entraînant des blessures aux yeux sont fréquents pendant les années d'école.

Les enfants doivent porter l'équipement protecteur nécessaire quand ils ont une activité impliquant certains risques.

D'autres accidents se produisent aussi quand les enfants patinent, lorsqu'ils sont en autobus scolaire ou qu'ils jouent avec d'autres enfants ou avec des animaux.

SANTÉ

La responsabilité de la santé des enfants revient aux parents. La santé de l'enfant à l'école est influencée à la fois par la surveillance médicale du médecin de famille et du dentiste, par l'éducation sanitaire qu'il reçoit de ses parents et de ses professeurs, par son environnement au foyer et à l'école, par le programme de santé de la collectivité où il vit et enfin par les services directs assurés à l'école.

Examen de santé préscolaire

Chaque enfant devrait subir un examen de santé préscolaire. Sa taille, son poids, sa pos-

Figure 20-11. L'enfant de douze ans aime gagner son argent de poche en travaillant. (H. Armstrong Roberts.)

ture, son ouïe et sa vue devraient être vérifiés soigneusement. Les problèmes scolaires des premières années proviennent souvent d'une déficience de l'ouïe ou de la vue. Si l'enfant doit porter des lunettes pour corriger un défaut de vision, il lui faut des lentilles incassables afin d'éviter les accidents. Un examen de ses dents et la correction des imperfections dentaires sont nécessaires. Pour que l'enfant profite le plus possible de l'école, il faut qu'il soit en bonne santé.

Le médecin continuera le programme d'immunisation contre les maladies contagieuses dont il a été question au chapitre 11.

L'examen préscolaire devrait se pratiquer au printemps, avant que l'enfant n'entre à l'école, afin que le traitement de toute anomalie ou de tout symptôme puisse se faire avant la rentrée scolaire.

Les parents devraient veiller à ce que l'enfant subisse un examen médical complet chaque année. S'il semble malade, on le conduit chez le médecin. L'examen de ses dents devrait être fait deux fois par année ou aussi souvent que le dentiste le recommande.

Programme de santé scolaire

Le programme de santé à l'école est un aspect important du programme global de santé. Le but principal du programme scolaire est de maintenir, améliorer et promouvoir la santé de chaque enfant à l'école. Une surveillance adéquate des aspects physique, mental, émotif et social de la vie à l'école en fait normalement partie. Le programme comprend aussi la planification du cours d'éducation sanitaire et de nutrition, et la mise en application de ces instructions dans la vie habituelle des enfants pendant les heures d'école. Il faut y inclure la prévention des accidents, l'organisation des loisirs et l'éducation physique.

L'infirmière scolaire veille à ce que tous les enfants subissent des examens physiques réguliers et bénéficient d'une surveillance continue, de façon à ce qu'ils reçoivent les soins dont ils ont besoin. L'éducation des parents est aussi nécessaire. Un travail d'équipe des parents, des professeurs, des infirmières et des médecins, tant à la maison qu'à l'école, est essentiel. Les médecins de famille doivent connaître le programme de santé scolaire et voir comment il complète leurs propres soins. Le dentiste et tout le personnel spécialisé rattaché à l'école devraient également coopérer.

Les services préventifs devraient être établis pour éviter la carie dentaire, les accidents, les troubles émotifs, la malnutrition, les maladies dues à l'infection, le milieu insalubre et le manque de soins après une maladie.

Problèmes de santé pendant l'âge scolaire

Un des problèmes inhérents à la fréquentation scolaire est l'exposition aux maladies contagieuses. Il n'y a pas de danger quand il s'agit de maladies contre lesquelles l'enfant est immunisé ou qu'il a déjà contractées avant son entrée à l'école. Il faut que la mère connaisse les règlements de l'école et garde l'enfant à la maison quand il a de la fièvre, un rhume, une éruption, ou tout autre symptôme de maladies contagieuses, pour éviter de contaminer les autres enfants.

Un autre problème de soins qui se présente à l'école est celui de fournir les services nécessaires aux enfants handicapés. Il faut informer les membres du personnel scolaire du programme de réhabilitation de l'enfant et de la participation que l'on attend d'eux.

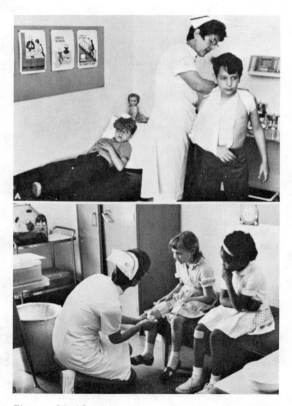

Figure 20-12. Une des nombreuses responsabilités de l'infirmière scolaire consiste à prodiguer des soins d'urgence aux enfants blessés ou malades. (Courtoisie de M. Rigenberg et *RN*, 32:57-58, sept. 1969.)

Un troisième problème concerne les enfants plus âgés, que l'on doit informer des changements qui se produiront chez eux à la puberté. Bien que les parents doivent discuter de ces questions avec leurs enfants, afin de maintenir de bonnes relations parents-enfants, il se peut qu'une infirmière ou un professeur en discute aussi avec l'enfant individuellement ou en classe. Il est bon de mettre l'accent sur l'universalité de l'expérience, ce qui rend la discussion moins personnelle et plus objective. Les parents ont le droit de savoir ce qu'on enseigne à ce sujet à leurs enfants. Une présentation illustrée devrait compléter la discussion. On choisit le matériel didactique selon l'intérêt, l'âge chronologique du groupe et le niveau de compréhension de chaque enfant. Il faut insister sur les faits et les présenter de façon adulte, amicale. L'enfant qui n'est pas préparé aux changements physiques qui accompagnent la puberté peut être terrifié quand ils se produisent.

La société nord-américaine stimule trop les enfants de onze ou douze ans à avoir un « ami régulier » et de nombreux parents ont de grandes hésitations quant aux limites à imposer à leurs enfants de cet âge. Ceux-ci ne sont pas prêts émotivement aux fréquentations sérieuses garçon-fille, et seront soulagés de se voir refuser fermement certaines permissions.

Un quatrième problème qui a surgi au cours des dernières années est celui de l'abus du tabac et des drogues. Comme le nombre des adeptes augmente, même chez les enfants qui n'ont pas encore atteint la puberté, de nombreux médecins et éducateurs croient que les programmes d'éducation sur ces sujets devraient commencer à l'école élémentaire.

NUTRITION

Chez l'enfant d'âge scolaire, les besoins caloriques par unité de poids continuent de diminuer, mais les besoins nutritifs demeurent relativement plus élevés que pour une personne adulte.

Le tableau 20-1 indique les besoins nutritifs des enfants d'âge scolaire.

L'enfant de cet âge mange habituellement bien et a moins de caprices alimentaires que

Tableau 20-1. *Diète quantitative quotidienne pour les enfants d'âge scolaire (6 à 12 ans)*

	6 – 8 ANS POIDS – 23 kg TAILLE – 121 cm	8 – 10 ANS POIDS – 28 kg TAILLE – 131 cm	10 – 12 ANS GARÇONS POIDS – 35 kg TAILLE – 140 cm	10 – 12 ANS FILLES POIDS – 35 kg TAILLE – 142 cm
Calories	2 000	2 200	2 500	2 250
Protéines	35 g	40 g	45 g	50 g
Vitamines liposolubles				
Vitamine A	3 500 U.I.	3 500 U.I.	4 500 U.I.	4 500 U.I.
Vitamine D	400 U.I.	400 U.I.	400 U.I.	400 U.I.
Vitamine E	15 U.I.	15 U.I.	20 U.I.	20 U.I.
Vitamines hydro-solubles				
Acide ascorbique	40 mg	40 mg	40 mg	40 mg
Acide folique	0,2 mg	0,3 mg	0,4 mg	0,4 mg
Acide nicotinique (équivalents)	13 mg	15 mg	17 mg	15 mg
Riboflavine	1,1 mg	1,2 mg	1,3 mg	1,3 mg
Thiamine	1 mg	1,1 mg	1,3 mg	1,1 mg
Vitamine B_6	1 mg	1,2 mg	1,4 mg	1,4 mg
Vitamine B_{12}	4 μg	5 μg	5 μg	5 μg
Minéraux				
Calcium	0,9 g	1 g	1,2 g	1,2 g
Phosphore	0,9 g	1 g	1,2 g	1,2 g
Iode	100 μg	110 μg	125 μg	110 μg
Fer	10 mg	10 mg	10 mg	18 mg
Magnésium	250 mg	250 mg	300 mg	300 mg

l'enfant plus jeune. Les problèmes dans ce domaine sont plutôt liés à l'heure des repas, (par exemple, si le repas est à la même heure qu'une émission préférée), qu'en relation avec le contenu et la quantité fournis aux repas. Comme il se peut qu'un enfant ait faim après l'école, un goûter lui sera nécessaire. Dans ce cas, le lait et les fruits sont préférables aux bonbons et aux biscuits.

Comme l'enfant veut agir de la même façon que ses compagnons, il voudra s'alimenter comme eux, soit d'un casse-croûte soit d'un repas à la cafétéria. Si le repas du midi n'est pas adéquat, les repas du matin et du soir doivent compenser.

Les enfants d'âge scolaire peuvent aider leur mère à l'heure des repas, participer à l'élaboration du menu, aller aux provisions et laver la vaisselle. Même si ces activités développent le sens du travail, les parents ne devraient pas les exiger trop souvent de leurs jeunes enfant qui passent beaucoup de temps à l'école et ont besoin de jouer au grand air.

Habitudes à table. L'heure des repas devrait être un moment agréable et reposant, mais de nombreux parents en font une période éducative et mettent trop d'emphase sur les bonnes manières. Les habitudes de l'enfant à table s'amélioreront à mesure qu'il grandira.

L'enfant de six ans mange goulûment, laisse tomber de la nourriture, la rattrape et parle beaucoup pendant qu'il mange. Il est plus intéressé à sa nourriture au début du repas qu'à la fin. Il a bon appétit. Il peut refuser d'employer une serviette de table.

L'enfant de sept ans parle moins au repas. Il se peut qu'il mange vite, mais il se calme progressivement. Sa serviette peut ne pas rester en place.

Les enfants de huit et neuf ans mangent plus proprement, se servent de serviettes comme les plus âgés. Ils ont tendance à avoir de meilleures manières hors de la maison que chez eux.

Les enfants de dix et onze ans mangent comme les adultes et leurs manières copient celles de leurs parents, que ce soit à la maison ou ailleurs.

Les manières des enfants s'amélioreraient plus vite si l'on insistait moins sur la question. Une atmosphère amicale et joyeuse à table est le meilleur stimulant de leur appétit.

EFFETS DE LA SÉPARATION

Si l'enfant a connu des relations agréables avec ses parents, il sera peu traumatisé par une courte séparation. L'enfant d'âge scolaire a appris à établir des relations avec d'autres adultes que ses parents et il n'est pas perturbé émotivement par le fait d'être laissé avec des étrangers. Il connaît la signification du temps et supporte mieux l'absence de ses parents. Il sait à quel moment ils reviendront. Cependant, une séparation prolongée, durant des semaines ou des mois, comme une longue hospitalisation, risque d'entraîner un traumatisme émotif. Si ses parents ne lui rendent pas visite régulièrement, surtout s'il sait que cela leur serait possible, il se sent rejeté et sa tension aggrave le stress de sa maladie ou de sa blessure. Les raisons d'une séparation prolongée doivent lui être expliquées d'une façon objective et réaliste par un adulte sympathique, de préférence un de ses parents. En plus des visites habituelles, d'autres preuves de l'amour de ses parent devraient lui être données durant ce temps de crise.

RÉFÉRENCES

Livres et documents officiels

American Academy of Pediatrics: *Report of the Committee on School Health of the American Academy of Pediatrics.* Evanston, Ill., American Academy of Pediatrics, 1966.
Anderson, C. L.: *School Health Practice.* 4e éd. Saint-Louis, C. V. Mosby Company, 1968.
Bower, E.M.: *Early Identification of Emotionally Handicapped Children in School.* 2e éd. Springfield, Ill., Charles C Thomas, 1970.
Frommer, E. A.: *Voyage Through Childhood into the Adult World; A Description of Child Development.* New York, Pergamon Press, 1969.
Gagnon, F. et Desjardins, J. Y.: *Ton sexe et l'autre... un message aux 10-12.* Montréal, Sextant: atelier de sociologie, 1968.
Gesell, A. et Ilg, F.: *L'enfant de 5 à 10 ans.* 3e éd., Paris, P.U.F., 1963.
Grout, R. E.: *Health Teaching in Schools.* 5e éd. Philadelphie, W. B. Saunders Company, 1968.

Hanlon, J. J. et McHose, E.: *Design for Health; School and Community*. 2e éd. Philadelphie, Lea & Febiger, 1971.

Lawrence, M. M.: *The Mental Health Team in the Schools*. New York, Behavioral Publications, 1971.

McKevitt, R., Stobo, E. C. et Shoobs, D.: *Mental Health and the Work of the School Nurse*. New York, Teachers College, Columbia University, Teachers College Press, 1969.

Maïco Hearing Service: *Pourquoi et comment effectuer les tests audio-métriques*. Montréal.

Ministère de l'Éducation: *Votre enfant a-t-il des difficultés à s'adapter à la vie scolaire?* Gouvernement du Québec.

Ministère de la Santé nationale et du Bien-être social: *La confiance en soi-même: comment la donner à mon enfant? L'enfant brillant: comment l'aider? L'argent de poche. La préparation à l'école*. Division de l'hygiène mentale, série: « Formation de l'enfant ». Gouvernement du Canada.

Nemir, A.: *The School Health Program*. 3e éd. Philadelphie, W. B. Saunders Company, 1970.

Opie, I. et Opie, P.: *Children's Games in Street and Playground*. New York, Oxford University, 1969.

Piaget, J.: *Le langage et la pensée chez l'enfant*. Suisse, Delachaux et Niestlé, 1966.

Piaget, J.: *Le jugement et le raisonnement chez l'enfant*. Suisse, Delachaux et Niestlé, 1963.

Stobo, E. C. et autres: *Report of the Nurse in the Elementary School; Promotion of Mental Health*. New York, Teachers College, Columbia University, Teachers College Press, 1968.

Articles

Barbour, A., Ager, C. et Sundell, W.: A Survey of Denver Public School Nurses to Explore Their Concepts Related to Expanded Role Functioning. *J. School Health*, 40:546, décembre 1970.

Barnes, K. E. et autres: The Effects of Various Persuasive Communications on Community Health: A Pilot Study. *Can. J. Pub. Health*, 62:105, mars-avril 1971.

Blaser, L. E. et Scharf, R. H.: School Teachers as Casefinders. *Nursing Outlook*, 19:460, juillet 1971.

Bourne, I. B.: A Pilot Project for Improvement of School Health Services. *J. School Health*, 41:288, juin 1971.

Bury, I. B.: A Study of the Effects of Air Pollution on Children. *J. School Health*, 40:510, novembre 1970.

Cauffman, J. G. et autres: Health Care of School Children: Variations Among Ethnic Groups. *J. School Health*, 39:296, mai 1969.

Cauffman, J. G. et autres: The Nurse and Health Care of School Children. *Nursing Research*, 18:412, septembre-octobre 1969.

Cornwell, G.: The Differential Sexual Socialization of School Children. *Nursing Forum*, 10:401, 4, 1971.

Crosby, M. H. et Connolly, M. G.: The Study of Mental Health and the School Nurse. *J. School Health*, 40:373, septembre 1970.

Dodge, W. F. et autres: Patterns of Maternal Desires for Child Health Care. *Am. J. Pub. Health*, 60:1421, août 1970.

Eisner, V., Cobb, O. et Tortosa, R.: The effectiveness of Health Screening in a School Program for Migrant Children. *Pediatrics*, 49:128, janvier 1972.

Gendel, E. S. et Green, P. B.: Sex Education Controversy – A Boost to New and Better Programs. *J. School Health*, 41:24, janvier 1971.

Gochman, D. S.: Some Correlates of Children's Health Beliefs and Potential Health Behavior. *J. Health Soc. Behav.*, 12:148, juin 1971.

Hawkins, N. G.: Is There a School Nurse Role? *Am. J. Nursing*, 71:744, avril 1971.

Lamer, L.: Dépistage des troubles visuels chez l'écolier et chez l'adulte. *Bull. de la soc. d'hyg. et de méd. prév. de la prov. de Québec*, 20:7, 3 à 6, 1967.

Marshall, C. L. et autres: Attitudes Toward Health Among Children of Different Races and Socioeconomic Statut. *Pediatrics*, 46:422, septembre 1970.

Murphy, D. C.: The Therapeutic Value of Children's Literature. *Nursing Forum*, 11:141, 2, 1972.

O'Brien, M. J.: Team Nursing in School Health. *Nursing Outlook*, 17:28, juillet 1969.

Osofsky, H. J. et Osofsky, J. D.: Let's Be Sensible About Sex Education. *Am. J. Nursing*, 71:532, mars 1971.

Paquin, A. et autres: La santé de l'enfant dans le Montréal métropolitain français et son acheminement vers la maturité. *Union méd. du Can.*, 95:445, avril 1966.

Shephard, R. J. et autres: Working Capacity of Toronto School Children. *Canad. M. A. J.*, 100:560, 22 mars 1969.

Stamler, C. et Palmer, J. O.: Dependency and Repetitive Visits to the Nurse's Office in Elementary School Children. *Nursing Research*, 20:254, mai-juin 1971.

Stephens, M. M. Rounthwaite, F. J. et Hutchison, D. A.: Identification of Hearing Loss in School Children: A Model Program and Results. *Canad. J. Pub. Health*, 61:297, juillet-août 1970.

Tuthill, R. W. et autres: Evaluating a School Health Program Focused on High Absence Pupils: A Research Design. *Am. J. Pub. Health*, 62:40, janvier 1972.

Zazzo, B.: L'image de soi chez l'enfant de 6 à 12 ans. *La revue de neuropsychiatrie infantile*, 17:479, août 1969.

21

pathologies de l'enfant d'âge scolaire nécessitant des soins immédiats ou de courte durée

HOSPITALISATION DE L'ÉCOLIER

Il y a actuellement beaucoup plus d'enfants de six à douze ans qui reçoivent des soins médicaux qu'il n'y en avait autrefois; cette augmentation est due en partie aux progrès de la médecine et aussi à une philosophie différente en ce qui a trait au soin des enfants. La durée du séjour à l'hôpital a cependant diminué considérablement pour chaque enfant et on tend de plus en plus à encourager l'élaboration d'un traitement que l'enfant pourra recevoir à la clinique externe ou au centre local de santé. Cette nouvelle orientation revêt une importance considérable quand on se rappelle les conséquences désastreuses qui se produisent quand on sépare longtemps l'enfant de son milieu familial et scolaire et qu'on l'éloigne de ses amis.

En règle générale, l'enfant d'âge scolaire accepte plus facilement la maladie et la séparation d'avec ses parents que l'enfant d'âge préscolaire. Sa réaction devant l'hospitalisation dépend de sa personnalité et de la nature de ses rapports avec ses parents.

Préparation à l'hospitalisation On doit donner à l'enfant d'âge scolaire à peu près la même préparation à l'hospitalisation qu'à l'enfant de moins de 6 ans. À cause de sa connaissance du langage, l'écolier comprend généralement mieux les explications qu'on lui donne et il peut lire des brochures concernant l'hospitalisation. On doit lui dire la vérité sur l'expérience qui l'attend. Si c'est possible on l'assure que ses parents iront le voir souvent, qu'ils lui enverront des cartes postales et lui téléphoneront afin qu'il sache qu'ils pensent à lui.

Comportement de l'enfant lors de l'hospitalisation. En dépit de la préparation qu'ils ont pu recevoir, la plupart des enfants d'âge scolaire s'imaginent avoir eux-mêmes provoqué leur maladie ou en être responsables d'une façon quelconque, par exemple, parce qu'ils ont désobéi.

Les enfants entre six et huit ans présentent une attitude ambivalente: tantôt ils se conforment à l'autorité des adultes, tantôt ils s'insurgent contre elle. Si l'enfant se révolte, il se sent coupable et s'attend à une punition. Lorsque l'hospitalisation résulte de tels actes de rébellion, l'enfant considèrera le traitement comme une punition. Le tout jeune écolier, éloigné de sa mère, ressent de nouveau l'anxiété de la séparation. Cette anxiété se manifeste parfois, pendant l'hospitalisation, par de l'énurésie, des frayeurs nocturnes, de l'insomnie, le rongement des ongles, etc.

Puisque l'enfant de huit à dix ans présente une personnalité plus structurée, il réagit de façon mieux adaptée aux restrictions et aux exigences des adultes qui prennent soin de lui. Jusque vers l'âge de neuf ans, l'enfant n'a qu'une vague idée des fonctions de son propre organisme et, encore à ce moment-là, il peut avoir des idées complètement fausses associées à des notions de vérité. Il peut croire qu'il souffre de diabète, parce qu'il a mangé trop de desserts; d'une affection respiratoire, parce qu'il n'a pas porté de manteau; d'un saignement de nez, parce qu'il a trop joué. Il ne possède qu'une idée imprécise des causes de la maladie et peut même croire qu'il a été désigné pour subir une punition méritée par son groupe d'amis tout entier.

L'enfant de 10 à 12 ans a déjà connu des situations de stress à l'école ou ailleurs et il est moins facilement bouleversé par l'épreuve de l'hospitalisation. Cependant, il risque de souffrir du manque d'intimité, surtout si les changements corporels qui accompagnent la puberté commencent à se manifester. Son absence de l'école et la crainte de perdre ses amis peuvent l'angoisser, comme, d'ailleurs, la peur de rester infirme ou diminué à la suite de la maladie ou de l'accident.

L'écolier hospitalisé peut devenir très coléreux ou très anxieux, craintif ou capricieux. En général, les enfants n'aiment pas rester au lit, parce que le mouvement a pour eux une importance vitale. De l'activité de l'enfant dépend dans une grande mesure sa maîtrise du monde extérieur et de ses impulsions. Il relie sa motilité au fait d'être vivant. *L'immobilité constitue sans doute l'aspect le plus difficile de la maladie de l'enfant.* Lorsqu'on réduit son activité, il devient anxieux et cette anxiété entraîne un besoin de plus grande activité. Alité, il ne peut pas extérioriser ses sentiments profonds et il peut devenir déprimé, exigeant, capricieux. Il régresse souvent dans son développement cognitif. Hors de la présence d'adultes, il peut se livrer à un excès d'exercices ou demeurer figé de peur. S'il doit rester complètement immobile, le malade peut devenir passif et se soumettre au traitement avec une résignation désespérée. Il faut l'aider à comprendre sa maladie, les raisons de son immobilisation et lui faire prendre une part de responsabilité dans son propre traitement.

L'enfant d'âge scolaire exprime difficilement ses sentiments et ses émotions même s'il décrit avec aisance la plupart de ses activités. L'écolier hésite entre les réactions du bébé qui pleure pour s'exprimer et celles de l'enfant plus âgé qui peut exprimer les craintes qui l'agitent quand il se sent menacé.

L'écolier hospitalisé craint la mutilation et la mort. Il développe ces peurs à travers les expériences qu'il vit, mais elles sont surtout renforcées par ses lectures, les discussions avec ses amis et les émissions qu'il regarde à la télévision. Il craint particulièrement le « sommeil » de l'anesthésie; toutes ces craintes peuvent paraître irrationnelle, mais prennent leurs véritables proportions si on les considère du même œil que l'enfant. S'il lance à un copain au moment de son départ pour la salle d'opération: « Rendez-vous à la morgue! », il pense sûrement plus qu'à moitié ce qu'il dit en plaisantant.

L'enfant de cet âge lutte contre la peur de différentes manières, mais il a surtout tendance à afficher un air d'assurance et de bravade, en particulier devant les autres enfants. Si l'infirmière en qui il a confiance demeure auprès de lui durant les moments les plus angoissants, il est moins effrayé par l'épreuve et son moi en sera renforcé.

L'enfant hospitalisé cherche souvent à être vêtu exactement comme ses voisins de chambre afin de diminuer l'impression qu'il ressent d'être différent des autres; le jeu sert aussi de soupape surtout s'il s'agit d'imaginer une situation qui le rend anxieux. La magie des mots ou des gestes diminue ou neutralise la crainte de la mort ou la peur de sentiments agressifs; l'écolier peut croiser les doigts et les garder « fixes » en subissant un traitement qui lui fait peur ou qu'il sait douloureux.

Bref, pendant son hospitalisation, l'enfant d'âge scolaire peut se sentir coupable, angoissé ou en colère. De telles émotions retardent éventuellement sa guérison, si elles ne trouvent pas de voies d'expression acceptables.

L'infirmière et l'écolier.   L'écolier a besoin d'infirmières qui comprennent son niveau de croissance et de développement, ses besoins et les expériences qui lui sont nécessaires pour assurer une croissance ininterrompue de sa personnalité durant son séjour à l'hôpital. L'infirmière doit lui apporter chaleur, amitié et justice, même s'il lui faut imposer des limites à son comportement et s'efforcer de voir en chaque enfant une personne qui souffre des frustrations inévitables dues à la maladie ou à l'infirmité. Elle doit tenter de lui procurer des satisfactions qui lui rendront sa maladie plus supportable.

L'infirmière doit aider l'enfant à résoudre ou à surmonter son sentiment de culpabilité, sa peur du mal physique et l'anxiété résultant de son immobilisation. L'enfant, que son état préoccupe beaucoup, en parle moins que celui que la chose affecte moins profondément. L'infirmière doit employer toute son ingéniosité à briser le mur dressé entre elle et le malade.

Les amis demeurent l'élément important de la vie d'un enfant d'âge scolaire et ce, qu'il soit à la maison ou à l'hôpital. Dès son arrivée à l'unité de soins, il faut le présenter aux autres et nommer les enfants qui l'entourent; il faut placer les lits de telle sorte que les malades puissent facilement bavarder entre eux. On doit leur permettre de choisir entre deux possibilités, aussi souvent que cela est possible, en évitant de les confronter avec un choix qui serait par la suite inacceptable pour le personnel. Par exemple, si l'infirmière demande « Veux-tu aller au lit? » et que l'enfant répond « Non », un conflit peut facilement s'ensuivre.

Pour pratiquer un traitement douloureux, l'infirmière doit prendre soin d'isoler l'enfant après lui avoir expliqué la technique, afin qu'il ne perde pas tout son prestige devant ses amis s'il lui arrivait de pleurer. La communication doit se faire sur un ton amical et positif.

L'infirmière peut faire comprendre à l'enfant qu'elle le respecte comme individu en ajoutant « s'il vous plaît » à ses demandes et « merci » quand il obtempère à une requête. Elle doit appuyer sur l'aspect positif du comportement de l'enfant et éviter l'énoncé de jugements de valeur du style : « Tu es méchant! » quand il a mal agi. Il est plus sage de lui dire : « Il ne faut pas blesser Jeannot » et établir clairement les limites qu'il ne faut pas dépasser même quand il est en colère. Il faut se rappeler qu'en traitant l'enfant honnêtement, on augmente sa confiance en autrui.

Il ne faut jamais faire de « chantage affectif ». Il est inadmissible de dire des phrases comme « Le médecin ne te laissera pas rentrer chez toi si tu refuses de manger » ou bien « Ta mère ne pourra venir te voir si tu n'obéis pas! » et ceci mène rapidement à la faillite des relations harmonieuses entre l'infirmière et l'enfant. Celle qui sait écouter et qui se met à la portée des petits malades gagne facilement leur confiance et leur coopération.

En règle générale, les enfants n'aiment pas parler de leurs sentiments avec des adultes; l'infirmière doit toutefois leur faire comprendre que la maladie peut vous frapper que vous soyez « bon » ou « méchant ». Elle doit encourager l'écolier à exprimer ses idées sur la raison de sa maladie et le renseigner quant aux véritables causes de son état. Elle doit employer des moyens concrets pour lui en expliquer l'aspect physiologique et la nécessité de l'inactivité qui en découle. Des images ou des modèles d'organes, des reproductions en matière plastique, des transparents représentant l'homme et la femme, des dessins sommaires du corps permettent d'expliquer la technique de certains traitements. L'infirmière l'aide à dominer ses craintes en lui expliquant ce qu'on lui fera et en lui disant que le traitement le soulagera à la longue, même si cela lui fait mal pendant quelque temps; en le laissant manipuler les instruments à utiliser et en lui permettant de l'aider pendant qu'elle le soigne, l'infirmière atténue les phantasmes de l'enfant. Il est aussi important de lui expliquer les traitements des autres enfants si c'est possible pour mettre un frein à son imagination débordante. L'enfant d'âge scolaire a terriblement peur de perdre son contrôle et craint que l'on se moque de lui. L'infirmière doit l'assurer, avant un traitement douloureux, qu'il pourra pleurer ou grimacer sans qu'on le qualifie de « bébé ». Ceci lui évitera de s'imposer des règles impossibles et de régresser ensuite profondément.

À mesure que l'enfant grandit et traverse l'âge scolaire, il est curieux et a hâte d'apprendre. L'infirmière devra adapter son enseignement aux possibilités de compréhension et aux besoins de celui-ci. Une ambiance de chaleureuse sympathie l'encourage à parler librement avec elle de ses difficulté, de ses craintes et de ses caprices, de sa maladie ou de sa blessure. Bien que l'enfant de six à douze ans soit mieux préparé qu'un enfant plus jeune à résister au stress, on doit lui fournir l'occasion de discuter de ce qui l'inquiète avec un adulte, ses parents ou une infirmière en qui il a confiance.

Si l'enfant ne peut exprimer ses sentiments, on peut lui fournir du matériel de dessin ou de bricolage pour qu'il y parvienne de façon non verbale. Les activités de groupe sont souvent plus stimulantes et l'enregistrement d'une conversation animée peut facilement servir de base à un dialogue plus profond. L'enfant capable de s'exprimer par écrit aime corrrespondre avec ses amis, à qui il confie ses sentiments envers l'hospitalisation et les traitements qu'il doit subir. L'infirmière doit être capable de déceler les éléments qui lui permettront d'aider l'enfant à s'exprimer et à comprendre ce qui lui arrive.

Le sentiment de colère, dont nous avons parlé précédemment, peut se manifester chez l'enfant soit verbalement, soit par des actes. L'enfant ira jusqu'à dire à l'infirmière qu'il la déteste, bien qu'il sache qu'elle lui donne de bons soins. Il peut aussi refuser de faire ce

Figure 21-1. L'écolier a besoin d'activités créatrices qui rendent plus agréable son séjour à l'hôpital, même s'il n'y reste pas suffisamment longtemps pour aller en classe avec les autres petits malades.

qu'elle lui demande. L'infirmière compréhensive accepte l'émotion de l'enfant, mais ne lui permet pas de la manifester de façon trop brutale. Elle pourrait dire: « Je me rends compte que tu es très en colère, mais je ne peux pas te permettre de jeter tes livres sur le plancher. Veux-tu me dire ce que tu ressens? » Si l'infirmière est calme, l'enfant pourra exprimer son émotion verbalement sans avoir recours à d'autres manifestations. Parfois, il suffit de donner corps à l'émotion en disant: « Alors, tu es en colère, Jean? », pour que l'enfant se sente compris, ce qui l'incite à d'autres confidences.

Lorsque les enfants d'âge scolaire subissent plusieurs frustrations durant la journée, et qu'ils doivent se maîtriser rigoureusement, souvent ils se détendent et donnent libre cours à leur agressivité au moment où l'infirmière du soir est seule. Elle peut avoir à faire face à des batailles d'oreillers, des disputes, des jouets jetés sur le plancher ou des boulettes de papier lancées d'un lit à l'autre. Le meilleur moyen de régler cette situation consiste à la prévenir. Il faut fournir aux enfants l'occasion de libérer leur agressivité, par certaines activités constructives surtout au cours de la journée. Les patients ambulants, comme les alités, peuvent avoir des activités physiques, symboliques ou artistiques leur permettant d'exprimer adéquatement leurs émotions.

L'infirmière peut également permettre à l'enfant alité d'organiser lui-même son horaire, stimulant ainsi sa confiance en son autonomie. Elle doit aller le voir souvent et si c'est possible approcher assez près de son lit celui d'un autre enfant, pour qu'ils puissent jouer en-

semble. Si cela l'amuse, l'enfant peut aussi établir lui-même un règlement lui permettant de rester calme. Si l'agressivité continue, il faut en avertir le médecin qui pourra recommander une aide psychologique ou prescrire un traitement approprié.

L'enfant de cet âge a des idées préconçues quant aux infirmières. S'il découvre chez elles une ressemblance avec des qualités des parents, il aura peut-être avec elles le même comportement qu'avec eux. À ce moment-là, son comportement envers l'infirmière pourra ne pas dépendre de son attitude à elle, mais de la manière dont il se conduit avec sa mère. On aura alors un indice de ce que fut son expérience passée et cela pourra servir de guide pour l'élaboration du plan de soins.

Normalement, l'enfant d'âge scolaire n'aime pas qu'un adulte se penche sur lui et le protège, mais lorsqu'il est blessé ou malade, il souhaite recevoir protection et appui. Un garçon, surtout, voit dans l'infirmière une menace à son indépendance; pourtant, au moment d'un traitement douloureux, il a lui-même recours au support rassurant de l'infirmière.

Les infirmières doivent trouver des moyens d'aider les enfants convalescents à être heureux de façon constructive. Les enfants hospitalisés pourront continuer leurs collections et en commencer de nouvelles avec des objets plus faciles à trouver dans un hôpital, tels les bouteilles d'antibiotiques vides, les tasses de papier ou les cartes de vœux. L'infirmière peut les aider à rassembler divers objets de soin qu'ils seront fiers de montrer à leurs camarades, quand ils seront sortis de l'hôpital. De plus, ce genre de collection permet à l'enfant d'acquérir de nouvelles connaissances et de maîtriser jusqu'à un certain point, un environnement déroutant.

Les convalescents peuvent lire, participer à des jeux calmes, écouter la radio ou des disques, regarder la télévision. L'infirmière doit surveiller ces activités, afin d'éviter que les enfants ne s'agitent ou ne se fatiguent. Les écoliers qui aiment prendre des responsabilités et s'occuper d'enfants plus jeunes peuvent rendre des services pendant leur convalescence. Ceci les aide à reprendre confiance en se sentant importants et en participant à des expériences nouvelles. Aider au nettoyage et au rangement de la salle de jeux et de la classe, s'amuser à ranger le matériel de l'unité et à passer les collations les occupe et les divertit. Souvent, ils rendent service en aidant les plus petits à manger, en leur lisant des histoires ou en jouant avec eux. Les enfants plus âgés s'identifient ainsi aux adultes du secteur, ce qui leur apporte une sécurité supplémentaire.

Soins physiques de l'enfant. Les enfants d'âge scolaire qui ont appris à devenir indépendants, sont gênés quand l'infirmière doit prendre soin d'eux; ceci est le cas particulièrement pour ceux qui ont 10 ans et plus. L'enfant d'âge scolaire peut prendre soin de lui-même, soit prendre un bain, manger, s'habiller seul, etc., à moins d'être trop malade ou handicapé pour le faire. S'il en est incapable, l'infirmière doit l'aider à accepter la situation et à collaborer plutôt que de l'obliger à céder parce que c'est de règle à l'hôpital. Pour l'enfant, de tels soins en font un « bébé » et menacent son intégrité. Il comprend mieux la situation si on lui parle des mêmes soins donnés aux adultes. L'enfant de cet âge a ordinairement développé un sens prononcé de la pudeur et lors des soins physiques, on doit veiller à respecter son intimité dans la mesure du possible. Il est bon de rappeler cette caractéristique du développement à tous les membres de l'équipe de santé. On encourage l'enfant à reprendre son indépendance dès qu'il devient physiquement apte à le faire. Il a normalement très hâte de se débrouiller seul. Ceci est une des raisons pour lesquelles les enfants d'âge scolaire aiment porter des vêtements ordinaires plutôt que des chemises d'hôpital; ils se rendent compte alors qu'ils sont moins malades. L'enfant plus âgé peut et doit avoir l'occasion de collaborer avec ses parents pour aider l'équipe de santé.

Les écoliers connaissent les mots employés dans leur milieu pour désigner la miction, la défécation et les organes de reproduction. L'infirmière doit comprendre que l'enfant a appris ces expressions et ces attitudes chez lui ou avec ses amis. À l'école, lorsqu'il veut uriner il demande la permission de sortir; cette formule ne convient pas, lorsqu'il est à l'hôpital. Lui faire honte s'il emploie les seules expressions qui lui sont familières, donne à l'enfant l'impression qu'il vit parmi des étrangers qui ne l'aiment pas. Il évitera de le dire à l'infirmière s'il lui faut de nouveau aller aux toilettes. L'enfant plus âgé aura peut-être l'impression que l'infirmière le rejette surtout s'il vient d'un milieu socio-économique défavorisé. Son sens des valeurs, l'image qu'il se fait de lui-même sont ternis et cela peut le pousser à se replier sur lui-même. On peut toutefois en profiter pour enseigner à l'enfant les vrais termes à employer, sans ridiculiser son vocabulaire antérieur.

Entre huit et onze ans, on rencontre parfois chez l'enfant la phobie du sommeil qu'il associe à la peur de la mort, surtout s'il vient d'en découvrir l'irréversibilité. Cette crainte peut se manifester à l'hôpital, surtout s'il croit que l'opération qu'il va subir peut porter atteinte à son intégrité corporelle. L'infirmière doit rassurer l'enfant et demeurer avec lui jusqu'à ce qu'il soit calmé.

L'école à l'hôpital. Les enfants qui subissent une courte hospitalisation n'ont pas le temps de s'intégrer à l'école de l'hôpital. Néanmoins, l'enfant peut avoir besoin de continuer ses travaux scolaires. Il peut recevoir ses devoirs de son institutrice habituelle, par l'intermédiaire de ses camarades, ou être aidé par une institutrice de l'hôpital. Voir au chapitre suivant pour une étude plus détaillée de l'instruction de l'enfant hospitalisé.

PATHOLOGIES AIGUËS

Épistaxis (hémorragie nasale ou saignement de nez)

Incidence, étiologie, manifestations cliniques, traitement et soins infirmiers. L'épistaxis apparaît souvent durant l'enfance, surtout à l'âge scolaire, mais son incidence diminue après la puberté. Elle est provoquée par un traumatisme externe, une rhinite, la présence d'un corps étranger, le fait que l'enfant se mouche trop vigoureusement ou qu'il se gratte le nez. La tension et l'excitation émotive ou physique suffisent parfois à provoquer le saignement de nez. Lorsque l'état circulatoire, rénal ou émotif produit une élévation de la tension sanguine, il peut en résulter une hémorragie nasale. Celle-ci peut provenir d'une dyscrasie sanguine ou d'une infection. L'épitaxis peut se produire chez les jeunes filles au moment de leur menstruation.

L'attaque est subite. Le sang peut couler des deux narines. Le saignement, généralement minime, s'arrête spontanément, mais il peut devenir fatal, si l'enfant souffre d'une maladie hémorragique.

On fait prendre à l'enfant une position presque verticale, en lui demandant de ne pas se moucher. On desserre ses vêtements autour du cou. Un sac de glace posé sur l'arête du nez peut être utile. On exerce une pression délicate, mais ferme, des ailes du nez contre la cloison. On peut appliquer sur la muqueuse nasale, au moyen d'un applicateur, une solution d'épinéphrine (ce produit est un vasoconstricteur). Le médecin peut cautériser le point de saignement au nitrate d'argent. Dans les cas plus graves, il peut être nécessaire d'effectuer un paquetage nasal ou de garnir les narines de thrombo-plastine ou de mousse fibrineuse (Gelfoam). En cas de maladie hémorragique (hémophilie), la transfusion peut s'imposer si la perte de sang a été importante.

Infections respiratoires et maladies contagieuses

Incidence et soins. Si l'enfant n'a pas eu les maladies contagieuses ordinaires à l'âge préscolaire, il est susceptible de les contracter après son entrée à l'école, où il sera en contact étroit avec plusieurs enfants. Pour la même raison, cet enfant est sujet aux infections respiratoires qui sont la première cause d'absentéisme à l'école. Ceci est surtout vrai, s'il vient d'une petite famille où il a été très protégé, ou s'il vient d'un milieu rural où les infections sont moins fréquentes. Le plus grand nombre d'infections se manifeste dès la première année d'école, pour décroître par la suite.

L'enseignement de méthodes d'hygiène commence dès les premières années d'école. On doit apprendre à l'enfant à couvrir sa bouche avec son mouchoir quand il tousse et à tourner sa figure vers le sol surtout à table où un accès de toux peut répandre des gouttelettes sur les aliments. Il ne doit pas se contaminer les mains pour ensuite contaminer les jouets, les livres, les poignées de porte et autres objets.

On doit apprendre aux enfants à se laver les mains lorsqu'elles sont contaminées et toujours avant de manger. Il est indispensable, mais difficile, de leur enseigner de ne pas s'offrir l'un à l'autre des bouchées de bonbons, des morceaux de pomme, de lécher la même crème glacée, de sucer les mêmes bonbons, de boire à la même bouteille ou avec le même chalumeau, parce qu'ils trouvent amical ou généreux de partager ce qu'ils ont.

On doit tenir les enfants éloignés d'autres enfants souffrant d'infections respiratoires.

L'enfant ainsi infecté ne devrait pas aller à l'école. S'il s'y rend et que l'instituteur ou l'institutrice constate qu'il est malade, il (ou elle) ou l'infirmière de l'école peut le renvoyer à la maison, pourvu qu'il y ait quelqu'un pour prendre soin de lui, ou téléphoner à sa mère de venir le chercher. S'il n'y a pas d'adulte chez lui pour le recevoir, on garde l'enfant à l'infirmerie. S'il n'y a pas d'infirmerie à l'école et que son état le permet, on le place à l'arrière de la classe, à distance des autres enfants. Si quelqu'un vient chercher l'enfant, on lui explique comment en prendre soin. De telles recommandations comprennent la technique d'isolement à domicile, la préparation des sacs de papier pour recevoir les mouchoirs de papier de l'enfant, etc. S'il y a lieu, on recommande aussi l'immunisation.

LA TEIGNE (tinea)

La teigne est une infection superficielle à champignons (tricophyton), classifiée selon la région du corps qui est atteinte ou selon la forme de lésion qui en résulte. Plusieurs sortes de champignons sont susceptibles de produire la teigne et il est indispensable de faire faire un examen de laboratoire pour trouver le traitement adéquat. Tous les types de teignes sont contagieux.

Mycose du cuir chevelu (Tinea capitis)

Incidence et étiologie. Cet état est presque limité aux enfants et surtout aux enfants négligés. C'est un problème grave dans les écoles situées dans des milieux urbains socio-économiquement faibles ou défavorisés. La cause la plus fréquente de la teigne est le « *Microsporum audouini* » qui se transmet entre êtres humains. Le *microsporum canis* se propage de l'animal à l'enfant. La teigne tend à disparaître spontanément à la puberté.

L'infection peut débuter à la racine d'un seul cheveu, mais elle s'étend en cercle et forme des lésions qui atteignent jusqu'à 5 cm de diamètre. Les spores envahissent la base du cheveu et le font casser au ras de la peau, laissant un espace chauve; le cuir chevelu devient rouge et des écailles grises se forment. Une infection secondaire peut se développer et l'enfant se plaint d'une faible démangeaison.

Diagnostic, traitement et pronostic. On établit le *diagnostic* en examinant le cuir chevelu sous les rayons ultraviolets d'une lampe spéciale. On doit également pratiquer l'examen microscopique de cheveux tombés.

La griséofulvine prise par voie orale peut guérir les lésions en 7 à 10 jours. On peut

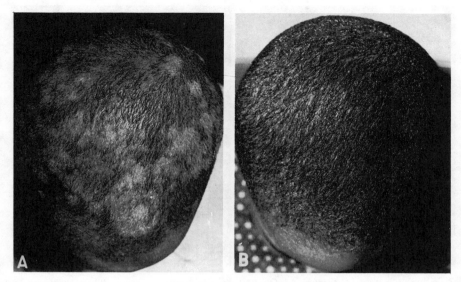

Figure 21-2. *A)* Teigne du cuir chevelu, non inflammatoire, causée par microsporum audouini. *B)* Dix jours plus tard, après emploi de griséofulvine (1 g/jr pendant un mois). (Pillsbury, Shelley et Kligman: A Manual of Cutaneous Medicine.)

également employer un onguent antifongique. Recouvrir la tête d'un linge ou d'un bonnet en jersey (tricot), qu'il faut laver et faire bouillir chaque jour, évite d'étendre l'infection. On considère que l'enfant est complètement guéri lorsque l'examen microscopique et la culture sont négatifs. Le pronostic est bon.

Mycoses de la peau
(Tinea corporis; tinea cruris)

Il y a deux types de mycoses de la peau: la tinea corporis et la tinea cruris.

Les lésions de la *tinea corporis* se situent au niveau du cou, de la figure, des avant-bras et des mains. Elles débutent par des plaques rondes ou un peu irrégulières, d'un rose rougeâtre, de la grosseur d'un petit pois, squameuses et légèrement soulevées. Le centre se dégage et la périphérie s'étend. Les lésions prennent alors la forme d'un anneau et provoquent un léger prurit.

Les lésions de la *tinea cruris* se situent au niveau de l'aine. La chaleur locale qui se dégage dans la région provoque de l'inflammation, du prurit et une surinfection, sous forme de petites pustules.

Traitement et pronostic. La griséofulvine, associée au classique topique antifongique (onguent renfermant du soouffre et de l'acide solicylique), constitue un traitement adéquat. Pour les lésions œdémateuses et exsudatives, on emploie des pansements humides antiseptiques (solution Burrow) ou du permanganate de potasse. Quand elles sont traitées, les mycoses jouissent d'un excellent pronostic.

Mycose des pieds (pied d'athlète)
(Tinea pedis)

Incidence. C'est pendant les mois d'été que cette mycose est fréquente parmi les enfants d'âge scolaire. L'infection provient des autres enfants et des adultes; les endroits où les gens vont pieds nus — comme les piscines — en favorisent la transmission. L'infection apparaît habituellement au 4ème espace interdigital; elle se manifeste par la macération de l'épithélium et la desquamation subséquente. La surface à vif présente souvent des fissures; l'intensité du prurit porte l'enfant à se gratter et la maladie s'étend.

Traitement et prévention. On applique de l'onguent ou on fait tremper les pieds dans une solution antiseptique. Il faut stériliser ou détruire les bas ou autres vêtements contaminés par le champignon. Des chaussures légères, bien aérées, empêchent l'aggravation provoquée par la transpiration.

Par mesure de protection, les enfants devraient porter des souliers pour marcher dans les endroits publics. Les personnes infectées doivent se tenir à distance des piscines, des vestiaires, des gymnases et autres endroits où l'infection est susceptible de se propager.

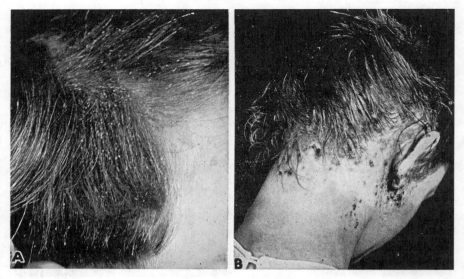

Figure 21-3.   Pédiculose ou phtiriase. *A)* On voit de nombreuses lentes. *B)* Des lésions d'impétigo se produisent souvent après que l'enfant s'est gratté. (Lewis: *Practical Dermatology*, 2e éd.)

Pédiculose

Types, étiologie et incidence.   Il y a trois types de pédiculose chez les enfants: 1) pediculosis capitis ou infestation par les poux de tête, très fréquente chez les enfants recevant peu de soins; 2) pediculosis corporis ou infestation par les poux de corps; 3) pediculosis pubis ou infestation par les morpions (poux du pubis). Comme le pou de tête est le plus fréquent chez les enfants, ce sera le seul dont nous traiterons ici.

Comme son nom l'indique, le pou de tête vit sur le cuir chevelu: ses œufs ou lentes, grisâtres, translucides, de forme ovale collent au cheveu. Ils éclosent au bout de trois ou quatre jours. Ils se transmettent facilement d'un enfant à l'autre, à l'école et dans les quartiers populeux. On les trouve le plus souvent chez les enfants qui portent les cheveux longs.

Manifestations cliniques.   Il y a une forte démangeaison du cuir chevelu. En se grattant, l'enfant produit des éraflures avec exsudation séreuse, purulente ou sanguine. Il se forme une croûte et les cheveux collent et s'emmêlent. Les lésions sont accompagnées d'une adénopathie cervicale. Il peut également y avoir des égratignures sur la figure et le cou.

Traitement et soins infirmiers.   Ils sont efficaces pour enrayer la pédiculose. Le but du traitement est de tuer les poux, de dévitaliser les lentes et de soulager l'enfant. Il faut enrayer l'inflammation. On doit nettoyer à sec, ou laver et repasser les vêtements et saupoudrer les chapeaux avec une poudre de talc antiseptique. Il existe sur le marché plusieurs médicaments, sous forme de shampoing, qui permettent de débarrasser l'enfant des poux et des lentes à la suite d'un ou de quelques lavages. Pour enlever les lentes on peigne les cheveux avec un peigne fin trempé dans du vinaigre chaud. Si les cheveux sont très infestés, on peut les couper au ras du cuir chevelu. S'il y a des pustules sur le cou et sur la figure, on utilise un antibiotique. On doit prévenir les enfants de ne pas s'échanger les chapeaux entre eux. Il faut également examiner les autres membres de la famille en cas d'infestation et en profiter pour faire l'éducation sanitaire.

La gale

Étiologie et manifestations cliniques. La gale est causée par un *sarcopte,* un parasite spécifique. La femelle creuse des sillons sous la peau pour y déposer ses œufs. Le parasite se transmet facilement d'une personne à l'autre. Les parties vulnérables du corps sont généralement humides et la peau en est mince: entre les doigts ou les orteils, sur les poignets, aux aisselles, à l'abdomen et aux régions génitales. On peut facilement voir sous la peau le sillon que creuse le parasite: il est superficiel et d'une longueur d'environ 1,5 cm. Des infections secondaires, sous forme de papules, vésicules ou pustules, peuvent en résulter. Le prurit est intense.

Traitement et soins infirmiers.   Le but du *traitement* est de détruire le parasite et de

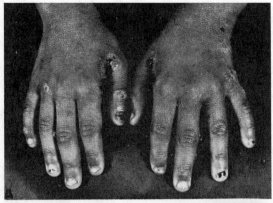

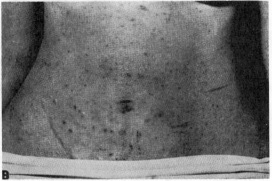

Figure 21-4. Gale. *A)* Sillons interdigitaux et excoriations avec pyodermite secondaire. *B)* Excoriations sur l'abdomen et lésions ombilicales. (Lewis: *Practical Dermatology*, 2e éd.)

soulager le prurit. Le traitement consite en un bain chaud, suivi de trois applications d'un antiseptique spécifique, une toutes les douze heures. La dernière application est suivie d'un autre bain chaud. On traite l'infection bactérienne secondaire par des antibiotiques. Toutes les personnes infectées dans une maison doivent recevoir simultanément le même traitement pour détruire tous les parasites. Il faut nettoyer à sec ou faire bouillir tout le linge et la literie contaminés.

Dermatite de contact (herbe à puce)

Incidence, étiologie et manifestations cliniques. La dermatite de contact est celle que l'on rencontre le plus souvent au cours de l'âge scolaire. Différents allergènes, aéroportés, liés aux vêtements ou aux souliers ou fixés aux parois d'un jouet peuvent provoquer la réaction allergique; il semble toutefois que la source la plus fréquente d'allergène soit les plantes et leur pollen, aux saisons qui leur sont propres. L'herbe à puce (Rhus toxicodendron) demeure l'agent le plus fréquemment rencontré.

Les enfants ayant atteint l'âge scolaire sont beaucoup plus libres d'explorer la nature et rencontrent fréquemment des plantes à potentiel allergénique important.

La réaction organique à l'allergie de contact varie d'une simple rougeur avec œdème jusqu'à la formation de vésicules accompagnées d'un prurit important. La réaction se manifeste habituellement sur la surface venue directement en contact avec la plante, mais le grattage ou le frottement favorise la migration des lésions, même aux endroits où le contact cutané direct ne s'est pas produit. Sans contact ultérieur avec l'allergène, la guérison spontanée, sans complications infectieuses, se produit après deux semaines environ.

Traitement, soins et prévention. Le traitement de l'herbe à puce consiste d'abord à éliminer complètement tout contact avec la substance allergène et à utiliser des corticostéroïdes de façon locale et systémique pour réduire les réactions inflammatoires. Les médicaments agissent surtout avant la formation des vésicules. La calamine en application locale parvient à réduire relativement le prurit.

Cette sorte de dermatite de contact peut être éliminée en évitant tout contact avec la substance allergène. On doit enseigner aux enfant la forme des feuilles de l'herbe à puce et les endroits où elle est le plus susceptible de se trouver dans les champs. Il est évident que plusieurs sortes de plantes présentent des caractéristiques similaires à l'herbe à puce, mais l'enfant reconnaît vite les plantes auxquelles il est allergique.

S'il y a un contact, un bon lavage au savon et à l'eau courante diminue nettement la gravité de la dermatite. Certains médecins tentent au printemps l'hyposensibilisation de l'organisme à l'allergène.

L'ostéomyélite

Incidence, étiologie et pathogénèse. L'incidence de l'ostéomyélite est surtout fréquente parmi les enfants de cinq à quatorze ans, et atteint deux fois plus les garçons que les filles. L'ostéomyélite aiguë est due au dépôt, dans les os, de bactéries provenant d'une infection primaire, habituellement cutanée, telle que furonculose, impétigo ou brûlures infectées. Elle peut aussi se produire par contamination directe à la suite d'une fracture ouverte.

L'organisme causal le plus fréquent, le staphylocoque doré hémolytique, pénètre par les vaisseaux sanguins et se fixe à la métaphyse de l'os. L'infection s'étend latéralement le long de la plaque épiphysaire, pénètre le cortex et s'introduit sous le périoste provoquant un abcès. La moelle de l'os peut s'infecter. L'os mort forme un séquestre qui peut être expulsé ou absorbé. Le périoste forme un nouvel os qui peut recouvrir entièrement l'os nécrosé.

Manifestations cliniques et diagnostic. La première *manifestation clinique* de l'ostéomyélite hématogène est un furoncle ou une autre infection de la peau. Une semaine ou deux plus tard, se produisent brusquement des malaises, de la fièvre, des frissons et des vomissements. L'enfant ressent une douleur aiguë localisée au niveau de l'os atteint, habituellement le genou, le coude, la hanche ou l'épaule; toutefois, des os plats, tels le crâne, la colonne ou le bassin peuvent aussi être infectés. On trouve des signes d'inflammation localisés au niveau de l'os atteint: douleur, chaleur, rougeur, œdème. L'enfant devient très malade et présente des symptômes toxiques.

Le *diagnostic* est confirmé par les examens de laboratoire. La leucocytose atteint des chiffres de 15 000 à 25 000. La culture sanguine est généralement positive et révèle l'organisme d'origine. Des radiographies peuvent être prises après modification de l'os, soit dix jours ou plus après l'apparition des symptômes.

Traitement, pronostic et complications. Habituellement, on administre des antibiotiques agissant contre plusieurs variétés de staphylocoques, tant que l'organisme pathogène n'est pas identifié de façon précise. On applique une attelle pour immobiliser le membre et soulager la douleur. On administre des analgésiques et on draine l'abcès, si c'est nécessaire. Si la destruction osseuse est très avancée, la lésion doit être complètement extirpée pour que la guérison puisse s'accomplir.

L'*évolution* et le *pronostic* dépendent d'un traitement précoce, continué pendant une période suffisamment longue. Une antibiothérapie précoce et appropriée donne d'excellents résultats. Il faut prévoir des soins à long terme si les jambes sont atteintes et la jambe malade présente souvent un raccourcissement résiduel. Le taux de mortalité a beaucoup diminué depuis l'utilisation d'agents antibactériens spécifiques.

Si le traitement n'est pas approprié ou s'il est arrêté trop rapidement, l'infection peut se propager à la capsule articulaire soit directement, soit en utilisant le courant sanguin et produire une *arthrite septique*. Il faut aspirer du liquide synovial pour analyse, culture et antibiogramme. Les symptômes et le traitement sont similaires à ceux de l'ostéomyélite, mais la douleur est intense. Si l'antibiothérapie n'agit pas suffisamment, il faut pratiquer une ponction articulaire pour vider l'épanchement; il faut surtout craindre la destruction de l'intérieur de la capsule articulaire et la formation de tissu cicatriciel qui altère grandement la fonction de l'articulation. Le drainage chirurgical devient particulièrement important si l'arthrite septique touche l'articulation de la hanche (coxo-fémorale), vu le danger de destruction de la tête fémorale et la luxation éventuelle qui s'ensuivrait. À la suite de telles complications, l'enfant peut demeurer handicapé ou nécessiter de nombreuses interventions chirurgicales.

Fracture supracondylienne de l'humérus

Incidence, étiologie, physio-pathologie et manifestations cliniques. Les fractures supracondyliennes se produisent fréquemment durant l'enfance; elles surviennent le plus souvent quand l'enfant grimpe, escalade ou participe à un sport qui requiert de l'adresse. La fracture supracondylienne de l'humérus se produit juste au-dessus du coude et est causée par un choc direct au bras.

Le fragment distal est déplacé postérieurement et il y a compression de l'artère brachiale, diminuant ainsi la circulation artérielle dans l'avant-bras. En plus l'œdème et l'hémorragie nuisent au retour du sang veineux en provenance de l'avant-bras. Ces deux facteurs combinés peuvent produire une paralysie ischémique grave.

Diagnostic, traitement et soins infirmiers. Il est indispensable de réduire la fracture, au plus tôt et de manière adéquate, et de rétablir la circulation aller et retour, dans l'avant-bras. Le chirurgien replace, en les manipulant, les os légèrement déplacés. On applique une attelle pour maintenir le coude en position de flexion. On peut placer le bras dans un appareil de suspension afin de réduire l'œdème. On prendra des radiographies pour vérifier la position des fragments. Il faut immobiliser le bras pendant trois à quatre semaines. La fracture guérie, l'enfant recouvre habituellement la mobilité par ses propres moyens sans exercices spéciaux.

En présence d'un œdème important au moment de la blessure, on a recours à la traction et à la suspension pour réduire la fracture. Il faut vérifier la coloration de la peau et la pulsation radiale, lors de ces traitements.

À son arrivée à l'hôpital, l'enfant est généralement anxieux, malheureux et peut se sentir coupable si la blessure est survenue à un moment où il faisait quelque chose de défendu. Comme on n'a pas eu le temps de le préparer à l'hospitalisation, l'infirmière qui s'occupe de lui doit être amicale et compréhensive.

L'infirmière vérifie fréquemment la pulsation radiale et la coloration du bras, environ toutes les trente minutes habituellement. Elle continue ses observations pendant les premières vingt-quatre à quarante-huit heures après la blessure. Si l'enfant se plaint d'engourdissement, si les doigts paraissent froids ou décolorés, ou si le pouls est faible, elle doit aussitôt avertir le médecin.

Dès son admission à l'hôpital, on place l'enfant sur un matelas ferme. L'emploi de sacs de glace peut réduire l'œdème et soulager la douleur. Les sacs devront être bien enveloppés et ne contenir que quelques petits morceaux de glace. On les placera en-dessous, et non au-dessus du bras, pour éviter que leur poids ne repose sur la partie blessée.

Pour éviter qu'il se sente trop dépendant, on encourage l'enfant à faire le plus de choses possibles par lui-même; on lui procure des activités convenant à ses limitations physiques.

Appendicite

Incidence, étiologie, physio-pathologie et manifestations cliniques. L'appendicite survient rarement pendant les deux premières années de la vie, mais son *incidence* augmente ensuite jusqu'à l'adolescence.

La cause en demeure souvent inconnue. L'obstruction, surtout par des matières fécales, semble le principal facteur dans la majorité des cas; l'obstruction peut aussi être causée par une infection ou une allergie. Les organismes que l'on trouve dans l'appendice comprennent le *streptocoque*, le *staphylocoque doré* et le *colibacille*. Les oxyures peuvent aussi être une cause d'inflammation.

La muqueuse est rouge et ulcérée. Le canal est distendu, ce qui nuit à l'irrigation sanguine. Les bactéries peuvent s'échapper par la paroi et provoquer une péritonite diffuse ou un abcès circonscrit par l'intestin et l'épiploon.

Les *manifestations cliniques* sont diverses. L'attaque peut être brutale ou suivre une gastro-entérite. Il peut y avoir des nausées, des vomissements, des douleurs abdominales, de la constipation ou de la diarrhée, une sensibilité localisée, et l'absence de mouvement péristaltique, sauf en présence de diarrhée. Chez les enfants, la douleur abdominale peut ne pas se situer au point de Mac Burney, dans le quadrant inférieur droit. De plus, l'enfant ne sait pas toujours désigner le siège exact de la douleur.

Parmi les autres manifestations on trouve de l'anorexie, une leucocytose bénigne

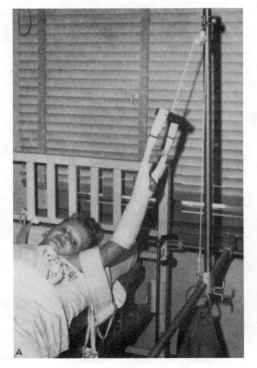

Figure 21-5. *A)* La traction de Dunlop utilisée pour le traitement de la fracture supracondylienne de l'humérus. (De J.C. Wilson, *Ped. Clin. N. Amer.* 14:3,659, 1967.) *B)* Le même traitement vu par un enfant. Le dessin aide l'enfant à vaincre son anxiété. (Courtoisie du Children's Hospital de Philadelphie.)

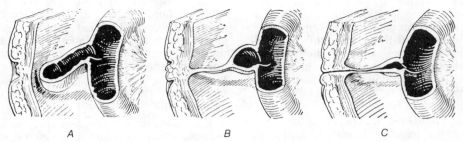

Figure 21-6. Diverticule de Meckel de l'iléon. *A)* Cul-de-sac ordinaire. *B)* Diverticule relié à l'ombilic par une bride. *C)* Diverticule avec fistule à l'ombilic. (Arey: *Developmental Anatomy.* 6e éd.)

(12 000 à 15 000 cellules), une fièvre entre 38° C et 39° C, un faciès congestionné, un pouls et rythme respiratoire rapides, de l'agitation, de l'irritabilité, et de l'insomnie.

Diagnostic, traitement, soins infirmiers, complications et pronostic. La difficulté de diagnostiquer l'appendicite est accrue pendant l'enfance, période au cours de laquelle des symptômes similaires peuvent être produits par des causes différentes. Ainsi, par exemple, pour l'enfant souffrant d'une infection des voies respiratoires, la douleur abdominale peut indiquer une pneumonie naissante ou une adénite mésentérique. Les symptômes provoqués par l'inflammation du diverticule de Meckel ou la gastro-entérite rappellent ceux de l'appendicite ou de l'irritation du péritoine apparaissant lors d'une fièvre rhumatismale; d'où la nécessité d'examens répétés avant l'établissement d'un diagnostic définitif.

Après l'établissement du diagnostic, dès que l'état de l'enfant le permet, l'appendicectomie — ablation chirurgicale de l'appendice — doit être effectuée le plus tôt possible. Suspendre l'alimentation, établir l'hydratation par voie intraveineuse et réduire la température rectale au-dessous de 39° C constituent les préparatifs pré-opératoires routiniers. Le médecin peut prescrire des antibiotiques pour prévenir ou minimiser le danger de péritonite. L'administration de purgatifs est contre-indiquée. L'opération est effectuée immédiatement après l'admission ou le plus tôt possible.

À la suite de l'appendicectomie, la convalescence s'effectue rapidement et l'enfant peut généralement retourner à l'école deux semaines après l'opération. Dans un cas de péritonite, d'abcès péritonéal ou appendiculaire, l'aspiration gastrique continue, la chimiothérapie et l'administration de liquides parentéraux deviennent nécessaires. Pour faciliter la circonscription de l'infection, on place l'enfant en position semi-assise. On lui permet de se lever

aussitôt que possible, même si le tube de succion gastrique est encore en place. La convalescence est évidemment plus longue que pour une appendicite simple.

Les *soins* de l'enfant qui a subi une appendicectomie sont habituellement simples et similaires à ceux que l'on donne aux adultes.

Parmi les *complications* possibles, il faut compter l'abcès localisé et la péritonite secondaire étendue. Des complications peuvent survenir à la suite d'une perforation de l'appendice provoquée par un purgatif que les parents ont pu administrer à l'enfant (traitement du profane pour une douleur abdominale infantile) ou par le silence de l'enfant qui, plus intéressé à jouer, n'a pas fait part de son malaise à sa mère.

Avant l'apparition d'une perforation, l'opération est bénigne. Et, même dans le cas d'une perforation, le risque demeure relativement minime, mais l'hospitalisation de l'enfant est un peu plus longue. Il faut cependant se rappeler que l'appendicite non traitée peut conduire à la mort par péritonite.

Le diverticule de Meckel

Étiologie, physio-pathologie et manifestations cliniques. La persistance du conduit omphalomésentérique, s'étendant de la fin de l'iléon au cordon ombilical, amène la formation d'un diverticule de Meckel. Il naît de l'iléon, mais n'est généralement pas relié à l'ombilic. Un diverticule de Meckel peut atteindre de 1,5 à 8 cm de longueur et être tapissé de muqueuse intestinale ou gastrique.

Ce n'est généralement pas le diverticule qui cause les symptômes. Les complications apparaissent lorsque la muqueuse sécrète des ferments, pouvant provoquer des ulcérations dans l'iléon ou dans le diverticule, ce qui peut conduire à une hémorragie massive, à une perforation et à une péritonite. Le diverticule peut être la cause d'adhérences intestinales, de strangulation ou d'invagination, ayant comme résultat l'obstruction intestinale.

Lorsqu'il y a hémorragie, les selles sont d'abord noires et ensuite rouge vif. L'hémorragie est accompagnée de pâleur et d'un accroissement du rythme des pulsations. Un retard dans les transfusions peut entraîner la syncope et la mort.

Le seul moyen pour confirmer le diagnostic est la découverte du diverticule.

Traitement et soins infirmiers. La présence d'hémorragie rend les transfusions nécessaires et l'ablation chirurgicale du diverticule s'impose.

Après l'intervention, les *soins infirmiers* sont les mêmes que ceux requis à la suite d'une autre opération abdominale.

RÉFÉRENCES

Livres et documents officiels

Clarke, L.: *Can't Read, Can't Write, Can't Talk Too Good Either.* New York, Walker and Co, 1973.
Cantwell, D. (édit.): *The Hyperactive Child.* New York, Spectrum Pub., 1975.
Lampe, K. F. et Fagerstrom, R.: *Plant Toxicity and Dermatitis.* Baltimore, Williams & Wilkins Company, 1968.
Pillsbury, D. M.: *A Manual of Dermatology.* Philadelphie, W. B. Saunders Company, 1971.

Articles

Aufranc, O. E., Jones, W. N. et Bierbaum, B. E.: Open Supracondylar Fracture of the Humerus. *J. A. M. A.,* 208:682, 28 avril 1969.
Berman, B. A.: Common Dermatologic Conditions Seen by the Pediatric Allergist. *Pediat. Clin. N. Amer.,* 16:193, février 1969.
Bertin, P. et autres: Complications des appendicectomies chez l'enfant. *La revue de pédiatrie,* 9:131, 3, 1973.
Blais, N.: Quand l'école vient à nous. *Inf. Can.,* 10:38, février 1968.
Davenport, H. T. et Werry, J. S.: The Effect of General Anesthesia, Surgery and Hospitalization upon the Behavior of Children. *Am. J. Orthopsychiat.,* 40:806, octobre 1970.
Duperrat, B. et autres: Maladies du cuir chevelu. *La médecine infantile,* 72:7, 1, 1965.
Epstein, E.: Contact Dermatitis in Children. *Pediat. Clin. N. Amer.,* 18:839, août 1971.
Erickson, F.: When 6- to 12-Year Olds Are Ill. *Nursing Outlook,* 13:48, juillet 1965.
Gould, W. M.: Superficial Fungal Infections. *Med. Times,* 97:227, octobre 1969.
Green, C.: Larry Thought Puppet-Play Childish. *Nursing '75,* 5:30, 3, 1975.
Hardin, D.: The School-Age Child and the School Nurse. *Am. J. Nursing,* 74:1476, 8, 1974.
Howe, J.: Children's Ideas About Injury. *ANA Regional Clinical Conferences,* American Nurses' Association, 1967. New York, Appleton-Century-Crofts, 1968, 189.
Lipton, G. L. et Roth, E. I.: Rape, a Complex Management Problem in the Pediatric Emergency Room. *J. Pediat.,* 75:859, novembre 1969.
Orentreich, N.: Disorders of the Hair and Scalp in Childhood. *Pediat. Clin. N. Amer.,* 18:953, août 1971.
Pellerin, D. et Bertin, P.: L'appendicite de l'enfant. *La revue de pédiatrie,* 9:109, 3, 1973.
Petrillo, M.: Preventing Hospital Trauma in Pediatric Patients. *Am. J. Nursing,* 68:1468, 1968.
Roueché, B.: Poison Ivy: « Its Purpose Has Yet to Be Established ». *Today's Health,* 49:38, mai 1971.
Smith, V.: A Study of Injuries. *J. School Health,* 41:108, février 1971.
Van Kote, G.: Les appendicites de l'enfant. *Soins,* 20:13, 1, 1975.
Villermay, D.: Les épistaxis. *La revue de l'inf.,* 25:401, 5, 1975.
Wehrlin, N. et Clavé, M.: L'appendicite aiguë. *La revue de l'Inf.,* 22:767, 8, 1972.
Wexler, L.: Gamma Benzene Hexachloride in Treatment of Pediculosis and Scabies. *Am. J. Nursing,* 69:565, mars 1969.

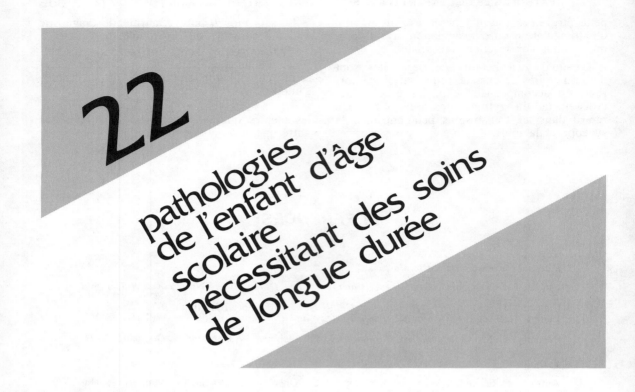

22

*pathologies
de l'enfant d'âge
scolaire
nécessitant des soins
de longue durée*

RÉADAPTATION DE L'ENFANT D'ÂGE SCOLAIRE

La réadaptation commence le plus vite possible après le dépistage de la maladie et continue pendant toute sa durée jusqu'à ce que l'enfant soit rétabli de façon satisfaisante. La réadaptation est fondée sur l'idée que toute personne doit être aidée à recouvrer une santé mentale et physique optimale. Si l'enfant souffre de plusieurs handicaps ou d'une maladie chronique, on se donne pour objectifs de prévenir d'éventuelles complications, d'aider à atteindre le développement désirable, tout en renforçant la résistance sur le plan psychologique. Ainsi, la réadaptation devient un but important de l'ensemble des soins donnés à l'enfant. Pour y parvenir, l'infirmière doit collaborer étroitement avec les autres membres de l'équipe de santé.

À partir de l'âge scolaire, l'enfant doit assumer une responsabilité croissante en vue de son propre rétablissement. La compréhension de cette nécessité assurera· sa participation. C'est donc à l'infirmière qu'incombe la tâche délicate d'en expliquer l'importance à l'enfant et de l'amener à coopérer.

Pour aider le jeune patient à atteindre cet objectif, ses aspirations doivent être prises en considération et l'infirmière devra les découvrir en conversant avec lui. Elle doit, en outre, fournir tous les renseignements appropriés aux autres membres du personnel soignant. Tous ont le devoir et la responsabilité de faire en sorte que chaque enfant, handicapé ou non, occupe le moment venu la place qui lui reviendra dans la société.

L'école au sein même de l'hôpital. La période scolaire est essentielle pendant la croissance et le développement de l'enfant. Il est donc de la plus haute importance que l'enfant hospitalisé bénéficie d'un contact permanent avec le milieu scolaire. Lorsque l'enfant ne peut aller à l'école, l'école doit venir à lui. Pour l'enfant plus âgé, la fréquentation scolaire représente un « métier », et il y accorde autant d'importance que l'adulte en attache à sa profession. Pour cette raison, de nombreux hôpitaux offrent des cours aux enfants hospitalisés. Ces cours pourront être suivis par des enfants sérieusement atteints, mais surtout par des malades chroniques ou des convalescents. Ils auront pour effet de maintenir le petit malade au niveau des enfants de son âge, à la fois sur le plan académique et sur le plan social,

Figure 22-1. La fréquentation de l'école en milieu hospitalier fait partie intégrante du programme de réadaptation. (Courtoisie de l'Hôpital Sainte-Justine, Montréal.)

tout en réduisant au minimum les inconvénients que risque d'entraîner son hospitalisation. Le fait de les suivre lui donne l'occasion de s'exprimer et d'utiliser son temps de manière constructive. En outre, ces cours lui apportent à l'hôpital une part de l'atmosphère familière du monde extérieur.

Les règlements concernant les heures de visite étant assouplis, les parents peuvent plus souvent rendre visite à leur enfant. Ceci offre une occasion unique aux professeurs et aux parents de communiquer, et ces derniers deviennent le lien entre l'école habituelle de l'enfant et celle de l'hôpital.

L'observation des réactions du petit malade à l'égard des cours et du travail scolaire aide le personnel à le comprendre. Parfois, ses attitudes ont une grande signification pour le médecin, l'infirmière ou les autres membres du personnel en contact avec lui. Elles sont révélatrices de ses motivations, de ses possibilités, de la satisfaction qu'il retire de son travail, et de la mesure dans laquelle il a appris à agir efficacement. Ses réactions reflètent sa personnalité, de même que l'influence qu'exerce sur lui son milieu familial et scolaire.

Dans beaucoup d'hôpitaux, l'enfant reçoit la visite d'un professeur, soit à son chevet, soit dans une classe aménagée spécialement pour recevoir des fauteuils roulants ou des lits. Les classes ont l'équipement habituel, comprenant un tableau, des tables et des chaises. Le temps consacré à l'étude est court et aucun enfant ne travaille sous tension. On adapte son programme scolaire à son état physique.

Les enfants hospitalisés ne manquent pas seulement l'école, mais perdent aussi, bien d'autres occasions de s'instruire. Ils devraient profiter de toutes celles qui sont conciliables avec la vie de l'hôpital. Ils peuvent apprendre certains faits concernant leur corps ou les moyens de prévenir la maladie. On peut les renseigner sur les méthodes de laboratoire et l'équipement médical. Les jeunes convalescents peuvent être amenés en pique-nique ou participer à des excursions. Pour ceux qui ne peuvent quitter l'hôpital, on organise parfois des présensations de films ou des expositions. Les enfants d'âge scolaire s'ennuient et deviennent renfermés s'ils n'ont pas l'occasion d'enrichir leurs connaissances.

Il arrive que le petit malade ait à poursuivre chez lui une longue convalescence pouvant varier d'une à plusieurs semaines ou plusieurs mois. S'il dispose, dans son quartier, d'un service téléphonique le reliant directement à l'école, il pourra à distance participer aux cours réguliers. Il poursuivra ainsi son éducation sans avoir le sentiment d'être laissé à l'écart. Si un tel service n'est pas accessible, un professeur peut venir chez lui poursuivre son instruction afin qu'il soit en mesure de rejoindre sa classe après sa guérison complète.

PATHOLOGIES DE LONGUE DURÉE

Fièvre rhumatismale (Rhumatisme articulaire aigu ou maladie de Bouillaud)

Maladies du collagène. Les maladies du collagène sont un groupe de maladies caractérisées par une altération de la substance fondamentale du tissu conjonctif, et suivies par des changements dans les fibrilles du collagène. Habituellement, on constate une atteinte du tissu conjonctif de tous les organes et des petits vaisseaux sanguins. Voici quelques maladies du collagène (elles constituent des entités cliniques différentes, mais présentent certains symptômes communs): la fièvre rhumatismale, l'arthrite rhumatoïde, la périartérite noueuse, le lupus érythémateux disséminé, la sclérodermie et la dermatomyosite. Toutes ces maladies réagissent de façon symptomatique à la corticotrophine (ACTH) ou aux corticostéroïdes, pendant un certain temps. Le problème fondamental de ces pathologies est le dépôt de matière fibrinoïde dans les tissus. Sur le plan histopathologique, la fibrinoïde forme des dépôts de plus en plus importants dans la lumière et les parois des vaisseaux sanguins ainsi que dans les tissus conjonctifs environnants.

Définition, étiologie, incidence et physio-pathologie. La fièvre rhumatismale (R.A.A.) est une maladie systémique caractérisée par de fréquentes rechutes et qui apparaît à la suite d'infections à streptocoques bêta hémolytiques du groupe A. L'importance étiologique de ce facteur repose sur l'épidémiologie clinique, comme le montre son association avec une pharyngite qui précède de une à trois semaines la fièvre rhumatismale, et sur la réaction immunologique que l'on constate lors de la réaction antigènes-anticorps. Une streptolysine provoque la formation d'anticorps dans le sang du patient. Celle-ci peut être évaluée en titrant les antistreptolysines O (titrage ASO). Le taux d'anticorps reflète l'intensité de la réaction tissulaire et aide à établir le diagnostic.

L'apparition de la fièvre rhumatismale se déroule comme suit: 1) infection initiale à streptocoques bêta hémolytiques du groupe A (pharyngite ou scarlatine), 2) une phase latente ou asymptomatique se prolongeant habituellement d'une à trois semaines et 3) apparition des symptômes de la fièvre rhumatismale.

La fièvre rhumatismale constitue pour l'enfant l'une des causes majeures de maladie chronique et de mort. *L'incidence* la plus élevée se situe entre cinq et quinze ans; la plupart des premières poussées surviennent entre six et huit ans. La maladie prédomine dans les régions tempérées. Le climat paraît jouer un rôle plus important que la susceptibilité raciale; il existe une incidence saisonnière qui varie suivant les régions, mais qui suit toujours la courbe et la fréquence des maladies streptococciques.

Les logis surpeuplés et un manque général d'hygiène constituent des facteurs prédisposants que l'on rencontre surtout dans les zones urbaines et chez les groupes socio-économiquement faibles. La maladie peut atteindre plusieurs membres d'une même famille, ce qui fait penser à une prédisposition héréditaire possible, mais non prouvée actuellement.

La fièvre rhumatismale se manifeste surtout au niveau du tissu conjonctif du cœur, des artères, des articulations et du tissu sous-cutané. Elle se traduit par un processus pathologique en trois phases: 1) la phase proliférative pendant laquelle s'observent œdème et formation de nodules soit intracardiaques (*nodules d'Aschoff*) soit sous-cutanés (*nodules de Meynet*), 2) la phase exsudative suit et 3) à la phase cicatricielle, la résorption de l'exsudat s'effectue; des adhérences peuvent se former (péricardite constrictive), la valvule mitrale peut s'épaissir et les cordages tendineux se raccourcir, produisant le tableau clinique d'une sténose mitrale.

Quoique les complications puissent résulter d'une première atteinte grave, elles sont ordinairement liées à des récidives fréquentes. Elles ne deviennent parfois manifestes que plusieurs années après l'atteinte rhumatismale.

Manifestations cliniques. Les manifestations cliniques de la fièvre rhumatismale sont souvent variées et peu spécifiques. Afin de clarifier la question et de faciliter le diagnostic, les symptômes ont été classés par Jones en 1) manifestations majeures et 2) manifestations mineures. Ce tableau a été accepté par l'American Heart Association en 1965 et par la majorité des praticiens.

Symptômes majeurs. Ils incluent la cardite, la polyarthrite, la chorée de Sydenham, les nodules sous-cutanés et l'érythème marginé.

Cardite. Elle survient dans près de 40% des cas et surtout chez les plus jeunes enfants. Elle est surtout caractérisée par une tachycardie persistant au repos et sans corrélation avec la fièvre. On décèle presque toujours des murmures cardiaques significatifs. L'enfant peut avoir une fièvre modérée et une légère cyanose. Cette manifestation de la fièvre rhumatismale rend le pronostic plus incertain. Même lors de la première atteinte, l'enfant peut présenter des signes de défaillance cardiaque.

Polyarthrite migratrice. Cette arthrite est accompagnée de signes locaux d'inflammation,

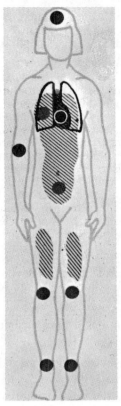

Figure 22-2. Localisation du processus rhumatismal aigu. (Disease Panorama on Rheumatic Fever. Courtoisie de Schering Corporation.)

Symptômes mineurs. 1) On peut constater une fièvre modérée, surtout à la fin de l'après-midi. La fièvre persiste plus longtemps, s'il y a atteinte cardiaque. 2) L'arthralgie sans signes locaux d'inflammation peut aussi être observée. 3) Les épistaxis et parfois même du purpura sont présents dès le début de la maladie et signalent l'atteinte collagénique au niveau des petits vaisseaux. 4) Les douleurs abdominales peuvent être assez importantes pour orienter faussement le diagnostic. Elles seraient dues à une adénopathie mésentérique ou à une irritation du péritoine.

Les manifestations, accompagnant toute maladie grave, telles qu'anorexie, pâleur, perte de poids peuvent aussi faire partie du tableau.

Diagnostic. Le diagnostic du R.A.A. peut s'avérer difficile, car beaucoup d'autres affections présentent des manifestations cliniques similaires, on doit interpréter chaque test de laboratoire à la lumière des autres résultats et du tableau clinique général.

Les tests de laboratoire sont importants pour le diagnostic et l'évaluation de la maladie. Les résultats positifs aux tests suivants font partie des *manifestations objectives mineures* du tableau de Jones: 1) La recherche de la protéine C (C.R.P.A.) qui est normalement absente dans le sang, mais se retrouve dans les processus rhumatismaux. 2) Le titrage positif des antistreptolysines ou des antihyaluronidases. 3) L'accélération de la vitesse de sédimentation. 4) La leucocytose.

elle réagit favorablement aux salicylates et se loge aux articulations majeures (genoux, chevilles, coudes). Elle est migratrice, car sa localisation varie d'un jour à l'autre, mais elle ne laisse pas de séquelles.

La chorée de Sydenham ou danse de Saint-Guy est une affection du système nerveux central qui s'observe plus fréquemment chez des enfants plus âgés. (voir p. 615).

Nodules sous-cutanés. Ce sont de petites nodosités dures, de diamètre variable, qui siègent sous la peau au niveau des articulations, des tendons extenseurs, du cuir chevelu et le long des apophyses épineuses vertébrales. Ils sont difficiles à mettre en évidence et on doit les rechercher. La peau qui les recouvre demeure mobile et ils ne sont pas douloureux. Ils indiquent ordinairement une activité rhumatismale sévère.

Érythème marginé. Cette éruption apparaît surtout sur le tronc et aux extrémités. La lésion typique consiste en une rougeur circulaire présentant un centre blanc. Elle disparaît sans aucun traitement et peut passer inaperçue.

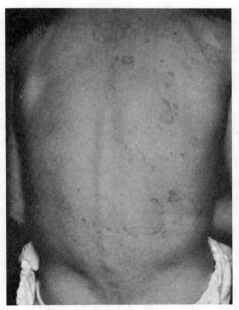

Figure 22-3. Érythème marginé. (Nadas: *Pediatric Cardiology.* 2e éd.)

Les électrocardiogrammes peuvent établir l'évidence d'une cardite. L'intervalle P-R est souvent allongé en présence d'une cardite. On pose un diagnostic de R.A.A. lorsque l'enfant présente au moins deux symptômes majeurs ou un majeur et deux manifestations mineures.

Traitement. Comme le traitement d'un enfant atteint de R.A.A. constitue un problème de longue durée, il concerne spécialement les membres suivants de l'équipe de santé: médecins, infirmières de l'unité pédiatrique, éducateurs, infirmières en santé communautaire et travailleur social.

Aucun traitement spécifique ne s'est avéré capable de mettre fin à l'activité du processus rhumatismal. Le repos au lit demeure essentiel jusqu'à ce que la protéine C disparaisse, que le pouls redevienne normal, que la vitesse de sédimentation ralentisse, que la douleur s'efface et que le taux d'hémoglobine soit redevenu normal. Il faut que l'enfant reprenne du poids avant de pouvoir se livrer à des activités. En réduisant le travail du cœur au minimum, on favorise la guérison avec un minimum de tissu cicatriciel.

Les dérivés salicylés demeurent une médication de choix. Ils abaissent la fièvre, soulagent les douleurs et mettent fin à la polyarthrite. Il faut noter les réactions toxiques comme les tintements d'oreilles, les nausées, les vomissements, les céphalées, l'hyperpnée ou le purpura. D'habitude, on administre les salicylates par voie orale. On peut utiliser de l'aspirine (acide acétylsalicylique) ou du salicylate de soude. On poursuit cette thérapie jusqu'à ce que la recherche de protéine C soit négative et que la vitesse de sédimentation ait diminuée. L'aminopyrine ou la phénylbutazone (Butazolidine) peut être employée pour les enfants qui ne peuvent tolérer les salicylates.

On a obtenu des résultats identiques avec l'ACTH ou des corticostéroïdes. On préfère la prednisone parce qu'elle a moins tendance à provoquer une rétention hydro-sodique que la cortisone. On utilise cette médication à cause de son effet anti-inflammatoire puissant qui raccourcit le processus rhumatismal et diminue les risques de séquelles cardiaques. Étant donné leurs effets secondaires importants, on tend à les employer seulement s'il y a cardite sans hypotension. Ce qui a été dit précédemment sur les effets secondaires et toxiques de cette médication peut s'appliquer ici.

Des narcotiques deviennent parfois nécessaires pour soulager les douleurs ainsi que des sédatifs, comme le phénobarbital, pour diminuer l'appréhension. L'administration d'oxygène peut s'avérer nécessaire. La digitaline peut être indiquée en cas d'insuffisance cardiaque.

Soins infirmiers. PHASE AIGUË. Pendant la phase aiguë de la fièvre rhumatismale, le repos est capital afin de réduire le travail du cœur. Il faut expliquer à l'enfant la nécessité d'un repos absolu, tout en l'assurant que cette période de restriction ne se prolongera pas indûment. Le lit doit avoir un matelas ferme, ce qui favorisera une bonne position et sera moins inconfortable qu'un matelas qui s'affaisse. On peut relever la tête du lit si l'enfant souffre de dyspnée ou s'il semble plus à l'aise dans cette position. Lorsqu'on élève la tête du lit, on doit appuyer les bras sur des coussins afin d'alléger leur poids, ce qui évite une trop forte tension sur les épaules. Si les coussins sont de taille adéquate, ils facilitent les mouvements respiratoires de l'enfant et évitent que ses bras n'exercent une pression sur son abdomen lorsqu'il les croise. Il faut maintenir un bon alignement des jambes et soutenir les pieds avec un support vertical pour éviter le pied tombant et la rotation externe de la hanche. Un arceau empêche la literie d'exercer une pression sur ses orteils.

On exécute les soins à intervalles réguliers, afin qu'entre temps l'enfant puisse jouir d'un repos absolu sans être dérangé. Il ne faut pas le déplacer inutilement puisque tout mouvement physique est douloureux. Les gestes de l'infirmière doivent être sûrs, et elle doit agir sans brusquerie afin d'inspirer confiance à l'enfant. Si elle lui fait mal, il deviendra nerveux, craintif et ne voudra pas qu'on le touche.

L'infirmière doit lui expliquer ce qu'elle veut faire: par exemple, prendre sa température ou le soulever. Le médecin détermine ce que le petit malade peut faire par lui-même. S'il devient irritable ou agité, le médecin lui permettra, dans certains cas, une activité limitée, bien que les résultats de laboratoire ne soient pas normaux. L'infirmière doit assurer à l'enfant un calme émotif aussi bien que le confort physique; elle doit prévoir ses besoins et les satisfaire afin d'apaiser son anxiété.

Le séjour prolongé au lit suppose le danger d'apparition de points de pression due à la compression constante du tissu œdémateux, à l'humidité causée par la transpiration et à la chaleur locale produite par l'hyperthermie. Il faut assurer les soins de la peau de façon régulière, surtout au niveau du dos et des fesses et l'on doit parfois se servir de moyens mécaniques: peau de mouton, coussin de caoutchouc mousse ou matelas à pression alter-

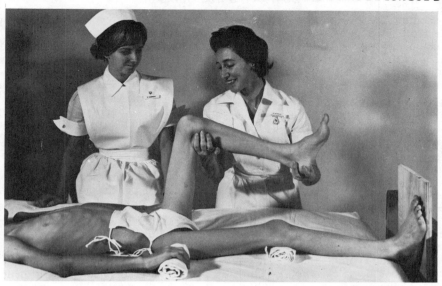

Figure 22-4. Position dorsale qui répond aux exigences de la bonne posture. Noter les serviettes roulées qui épousent les contours et le support pour le pied. Noter également la façon de tenir le membre pour exécuter les exercices passifs. (Courtoisie de l'Hôpital Sainte-Justine, Montréal.)

native. Toutefois, les changements réguliers de position restent la meilleure façon d'éviter les plaies de décubitus, de favoriser l'expansion pulmonaire et d'empêcher l'ankylose des extrémités. Il faut manipuler l'enfant avec précaution, en faisant attention aux articulations douloureuses. On masse ses coudes avec une lotion, car le contact des draps peut provoquer de l'irritation. Il faut aider l'enfant à se servir du bassin de lit quand c'est nécessaire. Si l'enfant respire par la bouche ou ne prend qu'une quantité limitée de liquide, il faut apporter une attention particulière aux soins de la bouche.

Une alimentation fréquente, par petites quantités, est préférable aux repas servis à intervalles réguliers. Les aliments doivent être légers et nourrissants. On ne doit pas le forcer à manger, ni lui permettre les excès de table qui risqueraient de le rendre obèse, vu son manque d'activité. Il faut placer l'enfant dans une position appropriée pour les repas, et s'il ne peut le faire seul, l'infirmière doit l'aider à se nourrir. Si l'enfant souffre d'anorexie, il peut devenir nécessaire de lui donner de petites transfusions de sang ou de plasma.

On administre généralement l'oxygène sous une tente, après avoir expliqué le procédé au petit patient. L'enfant d'âge scolaire, contrairement aux plus jeunes, ne s'en effraie généralement pas. Il faut lui donner une sonnette pour appeler son infirmière au besoin, et des vêtements appropriés pour éviter qu'il ne prenne froid.

Les notes des infirmières doivent être complètes et précises. Le rythme et la nature du pouls indiquent bien les progrès de l'enfant. Si le médecin le prescrit, il faudra prendre le pouls aussi bien la nuit que le jour, et pendant une minute entière. Avant chaque dose de digitaline, l'infirmière doit prendre le pouls du malade et si elle remarque quelque changement dans sa nature ou dans son rythme (ralentissement) elle doit avertir le médecin avant d'administrer le médicament. Les critères permettant d'évaluer les progrès de l'enfant comprennent la nature du pouls au repos et la rapidité avec laquelle il redevient normal après un exercice modéré. En présence de lésions cardiaques évidentes, l'activité du petit malade restera limitée.

En général, on pratique un dosage rigoureux des ingesta et excreta, et si possible, l'enfant devrait le consigner lui-même, par écrit. Lorsqu'on restreint l'absorption de liquide, on doit lui fournir un horaire à suivre. Il faut également enregistrer la nature et la quantité des aliments et on doit expliquer à l'enfant l'importance et l'utilité de ces divers contrôles. L'infirmière doit aussi observer et noter l'état émotif de l'enfant, la fatigue, le rythme respiratoire, l'orthopnée, la dilatation des veines du cou, la toux, la coloration de la peau, des lèvres, des ongles, des lésions cutanées et l'œdème.

Le personnel soignant doit comprendre et évaluer dès le début l'attitude des parents à l'égard de l'enfant et de sa maladie. Cette attitude varie de l'indifférence apparente jusqu'à l'inquiétude extrême. Il faut aider les parents à adopter une attitude positive à l'égard de la maladie, en prévision d'une réadaptation complète.

SOINS DE CONVALESCENCE. L'aspect probablement le plus important de la convalescence consiste à garder l'enfant heureux et satisfait. Ces enfants se sentent facilement déprimés parce qu'ils voient d'autres malades sérieusement atteints entrer à l'hôpital, guérir et rentrer chez eux, alors qu'eux-mêmes restent confinés au lit. Les activités du malade ne doivent pas dépasser les limites permises par le médecin. Au fur et à mesure que son état s'améliore, l'enfant peut prendre davantage soin de lui-même (se nourrir, se laver, etc.). Si le travail scolaire lui est permis, l'enfant a la satisfaction de se sentir au niveau de sa classe et, en outre, cela lui permet d'envisager le jour où il quittera l'hôpital. Les soins récréatifs l'aident en lui offrant de nouveaux centres d'intérêt, de nouvelles occasions d'apprendre.

Les activités recommandées comprennent la peinture digitale, la fabrication de bijoux avec des macaronis coupés puis enfilés, la confection de marionnettes, la sculpture de savon, le dessin au pochoir, la fabrication de maquettes d'avions ou de bateaux, les jeux de construction, le tricot, etc. Les collections d'objets qui intéressent les enfants sont appropriées. Ces enfants aiment aussi les jeux de devinettes qui ont pour la plupart une valeur éducative. L'enfant qui accepte ces activités trouvera plus facile de jouer calmement ou d'accepter un rôle physiquement inactif dans les jeux auxquels il participera avec ses amis une fois qu'il aura quitté l'hôpital.

À l'hôpital, la période de jeux doit être courte et suivie d'une période de lecture, de musique ou de récit d'histoires pendant laquelle l'enfant se détend. Le temps passé hors du lit augmente graduellement. On peut lui placer une chaise confortable (non pas un fauteuil roulant) près de la fenêtre et donner au jeune patient ses jouets préférés qui lui assurent une activité tranquille. L'infirmière utilise le fau-

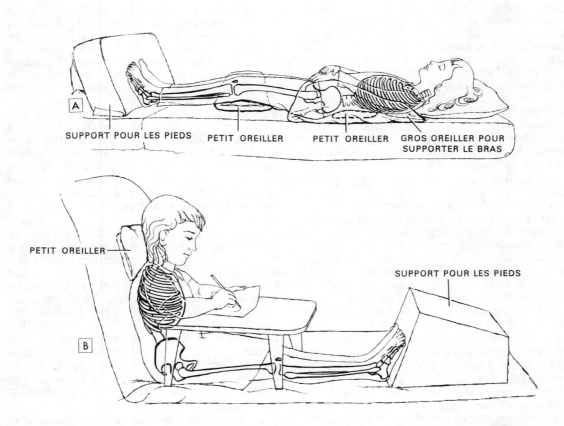

SUPPORT POUR LES PIEDS   PETIT OREILLER   PETIT OREILLER   GROS OREILLER POUR SUPPORTER LE BRAS

PETIT OREILLER

SUPPORT POUR LES PIEDS

Figure 22-5.   Pour obtenir un bon alignement du corps. *A)* En position dorsale. *B)* En position assise.

teuil roulant pour lui faire explorer le milieu. Après plusieurs semaines ou mois, on lui donne la permission de marcher, mais sous un contrôle sévère pour qu'il n'en abuse pas.

La maison est pour lui le meilleur endroit où poursuivre sa convalescence. Si cela s'avère impossible à cause de l'encombrement ou d'un manque général de commodités, on le dirige vers un hôpital de convalescence où tout est organisé pour donner à l'enfant la sécurité émotive dont il a besoin, où il trouve des occasions de s'amuser, de s'instruire, de travailler et de mener une vie de groupe tout en améliorant sa santé physique. Une infirmière en santé communautaire ou une infirmière visiteuse juge si la maison offre les critères requis avant que l'enfant n'obtienne son congé de l'hôpital. Dans certains cas, on peut envoyer l'enfant dans un foyer nourricier qui correspond à ses besoins, ce qui reste très difficile à trouver.

La reprise des activités normales s'échelonne sur une période de plusieurs semaines ou de plusieurs mois. Si on envoie l'enfant dans un hôpital de convalescence ou dans un foyer, il faut l'aider à faire des projets, lui présenter ceux à qui il sera confié et l'informer des plans établis. Ses parents doivent rester en contact avec lui puisque cette situation n'est que provisoire. Avant que l'enfant ne quitte l'hôpital, il est indispensable d'établir un plan de soins pour lui, avec ses parents ou avec ceux qui en auront la garde. Il faut aussi satisfaire ses besoins psychologiques. On lui accorde une indépendance croissante, tout en évitant certains troubles du comportement. Tous les aspects de son traitement doivent être étudiés. Si un certain équipement devient nécessaire, tel que des tables pour le lit ou des appuie-tête, on peut montrer aux parents comment les fabriquer avec des caisses, et s'ils ne peuvent être fabriqués à la maison, ou que les parents ne peuvent se permettre d'en acheter, on leur indique les agences où ils peuvent s'en procurer.

L'atmosphère de la maison doit être agréable. L'enfant doit avoir le même genre d'activités tranquilles qu'à l'hôpital. Dans certaines villes, la commission scolaire envoie un professeur itinérant, ou fait installer une ligne téléphonique reliant sa chambre à la classe de l'école qu'il devrait fréquenter. Cela lui permet de suivre l'enseignement donné à ses camarades et d'y participer dans une certaine mesure. Les centres de jour où l'enfant peut à la fois recevoir les soins qu'il requiert et l'instruction propre à son âge conviennent particulièrement bien dans ce cas.

On ne doit pas attacher une importance excessive à l'état cardiaque de l'enfant. Il faut l'aider à acquérir pleinement confiance en lui-même et lui apprendre à fixer ses propres limites d'activité. On doit garder présent à l'esprit le véritable but de la convalescence: permettre à l'enfant de retrouver sa place dans la société avec le moins de traumatisme émotif possible.

Lorsqu'il retourne à l'école, on doit informer le professeur et l'infirmière de l'école des soins spéciaux qu'il requiert. Ils doivent comprendre la nature de sa maladie et, par la suite, aider les autres enfants à accepter la différence entre la routine quotidienne du petit convalescent et la leur; par exemple il prendra l'ascenseur, ou ses heures de cours seront moins longues.

Les parents et l'enfant doivent comprendre l'importance des visites à la clinique ou chez le médecin de famille pour les soins prophylactiques et les soins dentaires. On peut s'adresser au service social qui facilitera le transport pour aller à ces visites. Les parents doivent comprendre et accepter la routine quotidienne de l'enfant et être en mesure de reconnaître les infections respiratoires et cutanées, peut-être causées par le streptocoque, et recourir aux soins nécessaires lorsqu'elles se manifestent. Il est difficile pour la mère de soigner l'enfant à la maison, surtout si elle en a plusieurs autres dont quelques-uns en bas âge, ou encore si elle doit travailler à l'extérieur. Se rendre avec une grande régularité aux rendez-vous de la clinique, si les transports publics ne sont pas adéquats ou si elle doit chercher une gardienne pour de plus jeunes enfants, constitue d'emblée un handicap d'importance.

Un problème plus délicat se pose lorsque l'enfant est suffisamment rétabli pour ne plus avoir besoin de soins professionnels. La mère n'a donc plus le secours des médecins, des infirmières et des travailleuses sociales à un moment où elle a encore besoin d'aide sur le plan psychologique pour mener à bien la convalescence de l'enfant. L'infirmière en santé

Figure 22-6. L'auteur de ce dessin est un écolier très malade, dont les besoins d'amour et d'acceptation n'ont pas été comblés au cours d'une longue hospitalisation. Incapable d'exprimer son sentiment d'impuissance, il en fit un dessin. (Courtoisie de Miss Mary Brooks.)

communautaire, si elle lui rend visite, peut l'aider à résoudre une partie importante de ses problèmes au moment où ils surgissent.

Les parents d'un adolescent ayant souffert de rhumatisme articulaire craignent l'entrée de l'enfant dans la vie adulte. Ils tentent souvent de lui faire prendre un métier sédentaire qui ne correspond pas nécessairement à ses aspirations. Ils peuvent essayer de le dissuader de se marier et si l'enfant est une fille, les parents ont très peur pour elle de la grossesse et de l'accouchement. Il faut étudier ces divers problèmes en équipe afin de ne pas laisser de faux problèmes brimer inutilement la vie de l'adolescent.

Pronostic et prévention.   Il semble que le taux de mortalité ait diminué, aussi bien après la première attaque qu'après une rechute de fièvre rhumatismale. Les rechutes surviennent surtout durant l'enfance et diminuent après la puberté.

Une atteinte cardiaque grave résulte souvent d'une série de poussées rhumatismales. Le pronostic s'assombrit pour les enfants qui subissent leur première crise avant l'âge de six ans, parce qu'ils souffrent d'habitude d'une cardite accompagnée de séquelles cardiaques. Si l'enfant présente une maladie valvulaire chronique par suite d'une pancardite rhumatoïde, son cœur va s'hypertrophier à cause du travail accru. Au début, on peut entendre uniquement un murmure cardiaque. Quand la décompensation cardiaque s'installe, la circulation s'altère et le sang s'accumule dans le système veineux. Il en résulte de l'œdème, de l'ascite, de la congestion pulmonaire et hépatique, de la dyspnée et de la cyanose. Le traitement de la défaillance cardiaque de l'enfant ressemble à celui de l'adulte et comprend une réduction du travail du cœur par le repos au lit et la sédation. Le traitement ultérieur comprend l'administration d'oxygène pour soulager la dyspnée, de la digitaline pour ralentir le travail du cœur et des diurétiques pour diminuer l'œdème. Le régime prescrit contient habituellement peu de sel. Les restrictions de liquide varient. Souvent, l'atteinte cardiaque est si grave qu'elle constitue un handicap pour l'adolescent ou l'adulte dans sa vie familiale ou sociale.

Le *pronostic* demeure bon pour les enfants qui n'ont pas de complications cardiaques. Même chez l'enfant gravement atteint, il est rare que l'on effectue un remplacement valvulaire, comme on le fait pour les adultes.

On n'observe généralement aucune séquelle définitive tant articulaire (consécutive à une polyarthrite rhumatismale) que nerveuse centrale (à la suite d'une chorée).

La *prophylaxie* de la fièvre rhumatismale consiste à prévenir toute infection à streptocoques bêta hémolytiques du groupe A. La prévention de la première crise consiste à éliminer les streptocoques des voies respiratoires

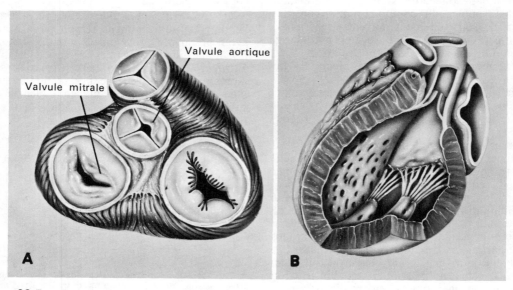

Figure 22-7.   Cœur présentant des séquelles rhumatismales. *A)* Vue supérieure du cœur montrant une insuffisance aortique et une sténose mitrale. *B)* Dissection du cœur montrant une fibrose de la valvule mitrale et un épaississement des cordages tendineux. (De Disease Panorama on Rheumatic Fever. Courtoisie de Schering Corporation.)

supérieures quand l'enfant souffre d'une pharyngite. On donne de la pénicilline, de préférence par voie orale, pendant dix à quatorze jours, sauf dans les cas où l'on craint que le patient ou ses parents n'oublient la médication.

Il faut prévenir les rechutes, car chaque crise augmente le risque de lésions cardiaques. Il faut éloigner l'enfant des personnes porteuses d'une infection des voies respiratoires supérieures. En cas de contamination, on demande à l'infirmière scolaire de faire un prélèvement des sécrétions pharyngées afin de pratiquer une culture. D'une façon idéale, il faudrait qu'il vive dans un climat chaud et qu'il dispose d'un espace vital suffisant. Comme mesure prophylactique le médecin prescrit une injection intramusculaire de pénicilline à action prolongée, une fois par mois pendant quelques années, ou l'on administre de la pénicilline par voie orale, tous les jours, après la crise initiale. Il est essentiel pour l'infirmière de souligner, à la fois aux parents et à l'enfant, l'importance de cette médication préventive. Les parents peuvent recourir à un service de bien-être social pour obtenir une aide financière.

On effectue actuellement des recherches intensives pour mettre au point un vaccin antistreptococcique qui éliminerait éventuellement les ravages de la fièvre rhumatismale et de la glomérulo-néphrite. De nombreuses recherches demeurent encore nécessaires pour connaître l'efficacité réelle de ce vaccin.

Si l'enfant doit subir une amygdalectomie ou une extraction dentaire, on lui administre une dose plus forte de pénicilline pour prévenir l'endocardite bactérienne.

Aspects en santé publique. On a absolument besoin de programmes conjoints communautaires pour assurer la prévention et le dépistage du R.A.A. ainsi que la planification à long terme du soin de ces enfants. De meilleures conditions de vie dans les milieux à faibles revenus et de meilleurs programmes de santé dans les écoles demeurent essentiels pour prévenir cette grave maladie. Dans certaines villes, une meilleure coordination des efforts de l'équipe de santé serait souhaitable pour aider ces petits patients ainsi que leurs parents.

Chorée de Sydenham (Danse de Saint-Guy)

Incidence, manifestations cliniques et diagnostic. La chorée de Sydenham, une affection du système nerveux central, constitue l'une des manifestations cliniques majeures du processus rhumatismal. Elle s'observe le plus souvent chez les filles entre sept et quatorze ans. Certains croient que la maladie est plus courante dans certaines familles (l'hérédité

jouerait donc un rôle), et qu'elle atteint surtout les personnes nerveuses. Elle se raréfie après la puberté.

La chorée de Sydenham est caractérisée par des mouvements involontaires, incontrôlés et irréguliers, impliquant une partie ou l'ensemble des muscles volontaires.

Les *manifestations cliniques* peuvent être bénignes ou graves. Le début est progressif. L'enfant devient de plus en plus nerveux et ses mouvements, qu'il ne contrôle plus, l'affectent beaucoup. Ces mouvements n'ont rien à voir avec des tics, et sont beaucoup plus prononcés. Au début, l'enfant laisse tomber les objets, il trébuche fréquemment et renverse ses aliments à table. Il grimace et écrit difficilement. L'effort et la fatigue accentuent les mouvements qui cessent cependant au cours du sommeil. L'asthénie musculaire est fréquente et empêche l'enfant de marcher ou même de s'asseoir. Il parle indistinctement et on le comprend difficilement. Il a des difficultés pour s'habiller, lacer ses chaussures ou boutonner un vêtement. Il devient parfois incapable de se nourrir et il peut avoir de la difficulté à avaler. Certains enfants souffrent d'incontinence. L'instabilité émotive se manifeste par des rires et des pleurs, et l'enfant passe rapidement de la dépression à l'exaltation. D'habitude, l'enfant n'a pas de fièvre. L'enseignant peut facilement reconnaître les premiers signes de la chorée: l'enfant n'est pas capable de rester assis en classe, il fait des grimaces et il y a des signes évidents de changement dans son écriture. Il faudrait renseigner les éducateurs sur les premiers signes d'une maladie comme la chorée qui affecte les enfants à l'âge scolaire.

Le médecin pose le diagnostic à partir des manifestations cliniques. Les plus importantes consistent en un accroissement des mouvements choréiformes quand l'enfant est tendu, une aggravation des troubles de la parole, et enfin, une physionomie excessivement changeante, passant instantanément du rire aux larmes. Les tests de laboratoire comme la vitesse de sédimentation, le nombre le leucocytes et le dosage de l'antistreptolysine O, peuvent être normaux, et la réaction de la protéine C peut être négative.

Traitement, soins infirmiers et pronostic. Le traitement et les soins infirmiers ont pour but de soulager les symptômes. Étant donné qu'il n'y a pas vraiment de traitement efficace, les soins infirmiers s'avèrent d'une importance primordiale.

On procure à l'enfant un repos mental et physique absolu. Il doit avoir une chambre particulière ou partager une chambre avec quelques enfants soigneusement choisis pour satisfaire ses besoins de compagnie. Des bains chauds et prolongés peuvent avoir un effet sédatif et on peut administrer des tranquillisants, tels le phénobarbital. L'infirmière fait manger l'enfant quand il ne peut s'alimenter seul. Il faut rembourrer les côtés du lit avec des draps, des couvertures ou des coussins pour éviter les blessures. Il faut veiller à ce qu'il ne puisse se blesser avec ses jouets. L'infirmière doit prévoir ses besoins: attendre le bassin de lit augmente sa nervosité. L'exercice, aussi bien mental que physique, lui sera permis graduellement, suivant les recommandations du médecin, au fur et à mesure que son état s'améliorera. Puisque cet enfant bouge constamment, il doit être alimenté fréquemment, en suivant un régime léger et nourrissant, riche en protéines et en fer, comprenant des suppléments de vitamines. Il est préférable de le nourrir avec une cuillère plutôt qu'avec une fourchette.

Les soins de la peau sont importants. Les bains qui le calment font aussi partie des soins cutanés. Les mouvements constants produisent une irritation de la peau des coudes et des genoux. On doit le masser avec une lotion ou un onguent et le vêtir d'un pyjama en tissu doux pour protéger sa peau des frictions sur les draps. S'il souffre d'incontinence, on change sa literie aussitôt qu'elle est souillée ou mouillée, et la peau du siège et des organes génitaux est soigneusement lavée et séchée. Les soins psychologiques sont aussi importants que les soins physiques. L'infirmière doit être patiente et compréhensive. Les mouvements de l'enfant entravent ses activités, et du point de vue émotif, il est très instable et irritable. Il faut le laisser prendre soin de lui-même autant que le médecin le permet, car cela lui donne un sentiment d'indépendance. Il a besoin à la fois d'affection et de gaieté dans ses contacts avec ses parents et son infirmière. Les relations parents-enfant ont pu être tendues avant que son état ne devienne assez évident pour qu'on le conduise chez le médecin. Certains parents se sentent coupables de l'avoir blâmé de sa maladresse incontrôlable; d'autres comprennent mal que sa conduite irritante était et reste due simplement à sa maladie, sans que l'enfant puisse la contrôler. Ils doutent que sa guérison rétablisse un comportement normal. L'attitude compréhensive de l'infirmière les aidera à voir la situation objectivement et à donner à l'enfant le soutien émotif dont il a grandement besoin.

L'enfant convalescent peut suivre des cours à la maison ou dans une école spéciale, où les heures d'étude sont brèves et tout le programme éducatif adapté à ses besoins. Pendant sa convalescence, il faut lui fournir des jouets qui lui permettront d'exercer ses muscles principaux, puis les petits muscles plus précis.

Le *pronostic* est bon. La guérison apparaît spontanément après huit ou dix semaines. Les rechutes demeurent possibles, mais la guérison est d'ordinaire complète. On évalue les progrès de l'enfant par son écriture; on lui demande donc chaque jour d'écrire son nom. Cette maladie est rarement fatale, mais la mort peut survenir par épuisement ou atteinte cardiaque.

Arthrite Rhumatoïde (Maladie de Still)

Une des affections que l'on peut facilement confondre avec le rhumatisme articulaire aigu est une maladie chronique systémique: l'arthrite rhumatoïde. Cette pathologie débute surtout entre 2 et 4 ans. Toutefois, les handicaps dont elle est la cause se manifestent surtout à l'âge scolaire.

Étiologie, physio-pathologie, manifestations cliniques et diagnostic. L'étiologie est inconnue, elle n'a aucun rapport avec une infection aux streptocoques du groupe A comme la fièvre rhumatismale. Il semble que la maladie constitue une réaction à un stress; elle se produit au cours du printemps, dans les régions tempérées et atteint surtout les filles.

La *physio-pathologie* comprend des lésions articulaires atteignant les synoviales, les capsules articulaires et les ligaments. Une ankylose fibreuse ou osseuse et des contractures en flexion peuvent entraîner des difformités permanentes. Une cardite peut se produire. La vitesse de sédimentation est accélérée et la recherche de la protéine C est positive. Le titrage de l'antistreptolysine O est rarement élevé.

Les *symptômes* peuvent se manifester brutalement, avec de la température s'élevant jusqu'à 41°C, avec ou sans signes articulaires, ou apparaître d'une façon très insidieuse. Les coudes, les épaules, les poignets, les genoux et les chevilles peuvent être atteints d'une façon symétrique. On peut rencontrer une perturbation de la croissance osseuse. L'enfant évite tout mouvement articulaire; les doigts sont tuméfiés « en fuseau »; il peut souffrir d'anorexie, paraître anxieux et préférer la solitude. On trouve parfois une éruption maculaire sur la peau. Les symptômes articulaires sont souvent tardifs. Il est fréquent de rencontrer une péricardite ou une uvéite associée. L'évolution se caractérise par des poussées récidivantes suivies de rémissions et ce, jusqu'à la puberté; on a signalé cependant des poussées au cours de l'âge adulte.

Il peut être difficile de distinguer l'arthrite rhumatoïde de la fièvre rhumatismale, de l'ostéomyélite ou de la leucémie.

Traitement, soins infirmiers et pronostic. Le *traitement* doit être compris par les parents et par l'enfant, car la maladie peut être chronique et son évolution imprévisible. La thérapie requiert les services de plusieurs membres de l'équipe médicale, sous l'autorité du pédiatre ou du médecin de famille. Elle consiste surtout à conserver la fonction de l'articulation, à éviter les difformités résiduelles et à promouvoir le développement et la croissance normale de l'enfant.

Les éléments de la réadaptation comprennent le diagnostic précoce, le soulagement de la douleur, la correction des difformités ainsi que l'acceptation de la maladie par l'enfant et sa famille.

On peut administrer des agents anti-inflammatoires, tels de fortes doses d'aspirine et, en ce cas, l'infirmière doit surveiller constamment l'apparition des symptômes toxiques. On peut aussi donner de la prednisone, mais les symptômes réapparaissent le plus souvent à l'arrêt du traitement. Au cours de la phase aiguë de l'arthrite rhumatoïde, il se peut que l'enfant ait besoin d'être nourri, lavé et habillé par l'infirmière parce que ses mains sont gravement affectées. Plus tard, il faut intensifier les activités de l'enfant afin de préserver l'intégrité du tissu osseux et le fonctionnement articulaire. L'activité normale de l'enfant joue souvent le rôle d'exercices non spécifiques. La physiothérapie peut s'avérer essentielle pour éviter le raccourcissement des tendons fléchis par la douleur. Une fois qu'on a jugulé l'inflammation des articulations, il faut les étendre au maximum, au moins une fois par jour. Il faut coucher l'enfant sur un matelas dur et l'encourager à se tenir à plat plutôt que sur le côté, ce qui demeure pour lui une position plus confortable, mais favorise l'apparition des difformités. Comme ces enfants seront probablement plus actifs à la maison qu'à l'hôpital, il faudrait qu'ils quittent l'hôpital le plus tôt possible.

Il faut aider les parents à se familiariser avec les soins que requièrent ces enfants. Ils doivent apprendre les exercices que l'enfant doit effectuer à la maison, comment préparer les bains chauds et les applications de paraffine et la façon d'utiliser les attelles provisoires, s'il y a lieu. En effet, en donnant aux enfants des bains chauds dans la matinée, on réduit la raideur des articulations, raideur qui s'est formée au cours de la nuit. De plus, l'emploi d'attelles au cours de la nuit aide à prévenir les contractures déformantes. Comme l'arthrite rhumatoïde est une maladie de longue durée les parents, tout comme l'enfant, ont besoin du soutien des membres de l'équipe de santé. Il faut apaiser l'inquiétude de l'écolier au sujet de sa maladie pour qu'il puisse supporter toute recrudescence possible des symptômes. Il faut l'encourager à fréquenter l'école et à participer à des activités modérées.

La maladie évolue par poussées successives de rémission et d'exacerbation qui tendent à devenir moins graves à mesure que la puberté approche. Le pronostic de vie est bon, mais une certaine proportion des sujets atteints souffriront de difformités définitives. La chirurgie orthopédique reste indiquée dans certains cas.

Diabète sucré

Incidence, physio-pathologie. Dans le diabète sucré, le corps s'avère incapable de métaboliser les glucides à cause d'une production insuffisante d'insuline, hormone produite par les cellules bêta des Îlots de Langerhans du pancréas. On constate aussi une perturbation du métabolisme des lipides et des protéines. On estime que le diabète de l'enfant représente environ 5% de l'ensemble des cas de diabète. Peu fréquent, il semble constituer toutefois une affection beaucoup plus sérieuse que le diabète de l'adulte. C'est une maladie héréditaire, transmise selon le mode récessif, mais tous les mécanismes liés à cette transmission ne sont pas connus.

On appelle *diabète juvénile*, le diabète qui débute avant l'âge de vingt ans. Il faut le distinguer du *diabète insipide* qui est une maladie du lobe postérieur de l'hypophyse ou de l'hypothalamus.

Comme il y a une déficience en insuline dans le diabète sucré juvénile, une acidose diabétique, le coma et la mort peuvent en résulter. L'hyperglycémie se produit, qui, lorsqu'elle dépasse le seuil rénal, cause une glycosurie. Toutefois, chez l'enfant, la glycosurie légère se rencontre sans hyperglycémie.

La quantité de sucre à éliminer entraîne une déperdition simultanée d'eau. La diurèse augmente, la déshydratation et une perturbation électrolytique apparaissent.

Le glucose n'étant pas utilisé par les cellules, un catabolisme tissulaire s'ensuit. Les réserves glycogéniques s'épuisent; les protéines et les lipides sont oxydés de façon à compenser la déficience glucidique. Les lipides donnent des produits de dégradation acides, les corps cétoniques, qui conduisent à l'acidose métabolique et à la cétonurie.

Les infirmières doivent être attentives afin de déceler le diabète chez les enfants, surtout si d'autres cas existent dans la famille. Il faut indiquer aux parents les symptômes précoces possibles, comme par exemple, une soif inhabituelle de l'enfant ou un besoin fréquent d'uriner.

Manifestations cliniques, études de laboratoire et diagnostic.

Le diabète peut se développer lentement ou être décelé pour la première fois lors d'un coma diabétique. Les symptômes de diabète se manifestent plus rapidement chez l'enfant que chez l'adulte. Leurs symptômes cardinaux sont: *Polyurie.* La quantité de sucre à éliminer entraîne une perte d'eau considérable. L'enfant demande fréquemment d'aller à la toilette et très souvent il commence à présenter de l'énurésie. La mère en changeant les draps, peut être alertée par l'urine collante de l'enfant. *Polydipsie.* La perte d'eau et la concentration sanguine élevée en glucose stimulent la soif. L'enfant est mal à l'aise et demande souvent à boire. *Polyphagie.* Le manque d'utilisation du glucose par l'organisme entraîne une baisse d'énergie et stimule le mécanisme de la faim. L'enfant a un appétit vorace qui surprend ses parents. *Perte de poids.* Elle provient de la déshydratation et de la non-utilisation des calories consommées. Ce dernier symptôme lié à un bon appétit amène ordinairement les parents à consulter le médecin.

Les *symptômes* du coma diabétique ou acidosique sont une agitation progressive accompagnée de vomissements et de douleurs abdominales. La peau est rouge et sèche et l'haleine acétonique. Lorsque le coma s'installe, on observe une respiration de Kussmaul. La pulsation est rapide et faible.

Le *diagnostic* repose sur les antécédents de la famille et de l'enfant, sur les manifestations cliniques et sur les données du laboratoire. En cas de glycosurie, il faut rechercher le taux de la glycémie. Si la concentration de sucre dans le sang est supérieure à 150 mg/100 ml chez l'enfant, on tente un test de tolérance au glucose. L'acidose diabétique est associée à une diminution du pH sanguin et une hypokaliémie. On trouve souvent de l'albumine et des cylindres dans l'urine.

Traitement.

Le *traitement* du diabète juvénile repose sur cinq principes essentiels: l'administration d'insuline, une diète adéquate, l'enseignement aux parents, une hygiène normale de vie et l'acceptation de la maladie par l'enfant et ses parents.

L'*insuline* est toujours requise au début du diabète juvénile. Après 3 ou 4 mois de traitement, une période de rémission survient pendant laquelle on peut quelquefois cesser ce traitement. Ceci peut durer quelques jours ou quelques mois, mais cette période demeure toujours transitoire. L'administration d'insuline vise à maintenir la glycémie dans les limites normales. Elle est toujours nécessaire dans le diabète juvénile, car les Îlots de Langhérans deviennent non fonctionnels et ne peuvent être stimulés par des hypoglycémiants oraux. On utilise *l'insuline ordinaire* et *l'insuline semilente* (N.P.H. et lente). Ces diverses insulines peuvent être mélangées dans une même seringue.

On dose l'*insuline* selon les résultats de la recherche du sucre urinaire. Ces tests sont effectués avant chaque repas et au coucher. Il est recommandé d'effectuer le test sur une deuxième miction afin d'être sûr que l'urine vient d'être sécrétée. Il peut être difficile d'obtenir deux mictions du très jeune enfant et il est préférable d'analyser chaque urine émise. De nombreux tests, faciles à effectuer, ont été mis au point par diverses compagnies.

La dose d'insuline peut aussi être modifiée selon le régime alimentaire, l'activité physique et les infections. Si l'enfant mange peu, est hyperactif ou prend un repas plus tard qu'à l'habitude, il peut souffrir d'un choc hypoglycémique. Les symptômes sont la somnolence, la moiteur de la peau, la diaphorèse profuse, la pâleur et une sensation de faim. Si l'enfant ingère immédiatement un concentré sucré, l'équilibre se rétablit promptement; sinon, il peut devenir comateux et avoir besoin d'une injection intramusculaire de glucagon ou d'une administration parentérale de glucose.

Un réajustement de la posologie peut être nécessaire en fonction de la croissance de l'enfant. Les troubles émotifs et les infections intensifient aussi le besoin d'insuline. En général, le diabète de l'enfant est plus difficile à équilibrer que celui de l'adulte.

La diète de l'enfant peut être libre ou calculée. Si on utilise le *régime libre*, il reçoit une diète normale pour son âge. Il n'évite que les concentrés sucrés, tels miel ou confitures. Il doit consommer une quantité à peu près égale d'aliments chaque jour et suivre un horaire régulier. Si le médecin prescrit une *diète calculée*, tous les aliments doivent être évalués quant à leur valeur réelle en glucides, lipides et protides. Ils doivent aussi être pesés. Une table d'échanges permet de varier les menus et d'éviter les erreurs. Le régime doit satisfaire la faim et les besoins de l'organisme et être adapté à la dose d'insuline. Selon les exercices physiques prévus, l'enfant doit apprendre à supprimer ou à augmenter ses collations. Les parents doivent bien comprendre le traitement diététique.

Les trois derniers points du traitement relèvent surtout des soins infirmiers et nous en traiterons sous ce titre.

Si l'enfant présente un coma acidosique, un traitement intensif devient nécessaire. On effectue rapidement la recherche du glucose et de l'acétone dans l'urine. On doit procéder à des prélèvements sanguins en vue de déterminer la glycémie et la balance acido-basique. En plus d'une thérapie intraveineuse l'enfant reçoit de l'insuline, des électrolytes, du glucose et de l'eau. Il peut avoir besoin de bicarbonate de soude en cas d'acidose prononcée. Un lavage d'estomac peut s'avérer nécessaire. Dès que l'état de l'enfant le permet, on le réalimente par voie orale. Une surveillance très étroite s'impose parce qu'il peut facilement évoluer vers un état hypoglycémique.

Soins infirmiers. Il s'agit surtout d'aider l'enfant diabétique ainsi que ses parents à développer des attitudes positives à l'égard de la maladie. Le problème central consiste probablement à leur faire admettre le fait que l'enfant peut être sain et actif s'il suit fidèlement son régime et si l'insuline est adaptée à ses besoins. L'infirmière doit écouter les parents lorsqu'ils expriment leurs sentiments au sujet de la maladie. Elle doit essayer de convaincre à la fois les parents et l'enfant de l'importance de la stabilité dans le régime recommandé, le dosage de l'insuline et les activités quotidiennes.

Il faut encourager l'enfant diabétique à exprimer ce qu'il ressent envers sa maladie, son traitement. Beaucoup d'enfants ont l'impression d'être punis à cause des restrictions alimentaires et des injections qu'ils doivent subir ou se donner. Il faut répondre à leurs questions et encourager le jeu pour réduire l'anxiété.

Si on lui permet un régime libre, l'enfant aura peu de problèmes pour s'alimenter. Si on le soumet à un régime strict, l'infirmière doit lui apprendre à contrôler lui-même sa diète. Elle enseignera à la mère la nécessité d'aider l'enfant à se conformer à sa vie réglée, et elle lui donnera les moyens de réaliser cette tâche. Il faut que l'enfant se livre à des activités après le repas. Il faut tenir aussi loin que possible tout aliment tentant, mais interdit. Néanmoins, les enfants d'âge scolaire doivent apprendre à se priver des aliments défendus tandis que les autres en mangent. Il est important d'insister sur les aliments permis et d'utiliser tous les substituts possibles pour les aliments défendus. On doit présenter les repas d'une façon attrayante. Il faut autoriser et préparer des collations à l'heure du coucher et entre les repas. Il faut faire comprendre à l'enfant qu'il ne sera pas puni, ni grondé s'il avoue les entorses faites au régime, mais qu'il peut tomber subitement malade s'il s'en abstient.

On ne doit pas tenter de cacher le fait que l'enfant souffre de diabète. Lui-même et ceux qui l'entourent doivent en être bien conscients pour comprendre les restrictions de son régime et la nécessité d'une vie régulière. L'enfant diabétique doit assumer sa part de responsabilités familiales et se mesurer avec ses camarades de classe sur une base d'égalité. Il ne doit pas considérer son diabète comme un handicap ou s'abriter derrière lui pour réclamer de l'indulgence.

Le tableau 22-1 sera d'une grande utilité lors du traitement de l'enfant à l'hôpital et à la maison. Cette information aidera les parents, mais elle ne peut remplacer les renseignements individuels que les médecins, les infirmières et les diététiciennes leur donnent. La compréhension des soins reçus à l'hôpital assure non seulement une meilleure coopération entre l'enfant, ses parents et les infirmières, mais elle demeure la base de l'acceptation et de l'observation du programme des soins à domicile. L'infirmière doit bien connaître les informations que donne le tableau. L'étudiante trouvera qu'il s'agit là d'une aide pour apprendre les soins de l'enfant diabétique et pour les enseigner aux parents et aux enfants.

L'infirmière doit prévoir plusieurs sessions d'enseignement afin de bien faire comprendre aux parents et à l'enfant les soins qui seront désormais nécessaires. Elle peut fournir aux parents un feuillet explicatif sur le diabète juvénile, leur demander de le lire en notant leurs questions et en discuter avec eux par la suite. Il est important que les parents puissent s'exprimer sur le diabète de leur enfant et accepter cette nouvelle réalité avant qu'un enseignement formel ne leur soit donné.

En général, on commence par enseigner aux parents et à l'enfant ce que sont les tests de recherche de sucre et d'acétone urinaires. Ils doivent en connaître les buts, savoir les effectuer et en noter les résultats. On leur montre comment préparer un cahier pratique de notation où figurent chaque jour les résultats de 4 dosages quotidiens de sucre urinaire, le dosage occasionnel d'acétone, la dose d'insuline et les réactions particulières de l'enfant. L'enfant peut inscrire ses résultats en utilisant des crayons de couleurs différentes.

On poursuit l'enseignement en présentant les sortes d'insuline, en expliquant comment préparer et administrer l'injection. Les parents apprennent comment préparer un plateau comprenant tout le matériel nécessaire pour l'injection. On fournit aux parents et à l'enfant

Tableau 22-1. *Soins de l'enfant diabétique.*

1. Soins de la peau:
   a. Donner des bains fréquents, au moins tous les deux jours.
   b. Fournir des souliers qui peuvent être facilement changés lorsque l'enfant grandit.
   c. Apprendre à l'enfant à rendre compte de toute blessure ou excoriation et la soigner rapidement.

2. Protection constante contre l'infection:
   a. Vêtir l'enfant de façon adéquate selon la température et non la saison.
   b. Éloigner l'enfant de toute personne souffrant d'une infection des voies respiratoires ou d'une autre infection.
   c. Avertir le médecin dès que possible en cas d'infection.
   d. Augmenter légèrement la dose d'insuline ou supprimer les collations en cas d'infection.
   e. Immuniser l'enfant contre les maladies contagieuses communes.

3. Élimination normale.

4. Exercices réguliers:
   a. À l'hôpital, maintenir l'enfant aussi occupé qu'il le serait à la maison.
   b. À la maison, l'encourager à pratiquer régulièrement des exercices modérés.
   c. Adapter la diète au programme d'exercices de l'enfant.

5. Précision dans la collecte des spécimens d'urine:
   a. Demander à l'enfant d'uriner à 20 ou 30 minutes d'intervalles avant chaque repas et au moment d'aller se coucher. Analyser la deuxième miction et inscrire les résultats. Les parents et l'enfant doivent apprendre la technique.
   b. Veiller à ce que l'enfant ne dilue pas l'urine ou n'inscrive pas un faux résultat pour dissimuler une infraction à son régime.

6. Régime alimentaire:
   a. À l'hôpital, laisser manger l'enfant avec les autres diabétiques, car il acceptera ainsi, plus facilement, son régime.
   b. Apprendre à l'enfant à s'en tenir au régime ordonné. Lui donner la liste des aliments équivalents, si cela lui est permis.
   c. Aider l'enfant à respecter son régime en lui assurant une variété d'aliments.
   d. Apprendre à l'enfant à planifier lui-même son propre régime dès que possible.
   e. Renseigner les parents sur les livres de recettes pour diabétiques.

7. Administration d'insuline:
   a. Les parents doivent comprendre la nécessité des injections d'insuline et la technique d'administration.
   b. La mise sur le marché d'insuline à concentration unique (100 U/cc) facilite beaucoup les soins.
   c. Les enfants de huit à dix ans peuvent apprendre généralement à se donner eux-mêmes les injections d'insuline. L'âge auquel l'enfant devient responsable de ses soins dépend de sa personnalité et du mode d'éducation qu'il a reçu. S'il a été plutôt surprotégé jusqu'à maintenant, il peut considérer comme une punition d'être subitement responsable de lui-même. Il semble que les enfants que l'on a astreint très tôt à assumer toutes les responsabilités de leurs soins traversent une période orageuse à l'adolescence.

---

s'il est assez âgé, 2 bouteilles, une seringue et une orange pour s'exercer à préparer et à donner l'injection. L'enfant peut aussi donner des injections à une poupée. Lorsqu'ils sont prêts, les parents administrent l'insuline à l'enfant ou l'enfant se pique lui-même. Le moment est alors venu pour eux d'apprendre comment reconnaître les réactions hypo et hyperglycémiques et leurs traitements immédiats.

L'enseignement de la diète est donné ha-bituellement par la diététicienne et l'infirmière renforce les données fournies. Celle-ci poursuit son enseignement sur le soin des dents, de la peau, des yeux et des pieds. Elle renseigne les parents sur l'Association du diabète, sa revue et les camps d'été.

Avant que l'enfant quitte l'hôpital, ses parents, et lui-même si cela est possible, doivent connaître la diète, savoir le rôle et les caractéristiques de l'insuline, pouvoir donner l'injection, reconnaître les signes hypo et hyper-

Tableau 22-1. *Soins de l'enfant diabétique. (Suite)*

1) Donner une explication simple. Après que l'infirmière ait donné une première explication, un autre enfant diabétique peut aider mieux qu'un adulte, ayant plus d'empathie pour expliquer le comment et le pourquoi de chaque geste.

2) Laisser l'enfant ou les parents s'exercer sous surveillance. Varier l'endroit de l'injection: le haut des bras gauche et droit, les cuisses gauche et droite, les fesses gauche et droite et l'abdomen. Il est utile de confectionner pour l'enfant des modèles en carton que l'on perfore d'orifices situés à 12 mm (½") de distance chacun, tant horizontalement que verticalement. Ceci permet d'utiliser tous les endroits possibles et d'alterner plus sûrement. Cette mesure aide à prévenir les complications lipo-dystrophiques. Vis-à-vis de chaque orifice on peut inscrire la date à laquelle a été donné l'injection.

3) Vérifier les doses mesurées par l'enfant ou les parents et s'assurer de leur précision.

4) S'assurer que l'enfant ou les parents utilisent l'insuline à la température de la pièce, parce que l'insuline froide favorise les complications cutanées de l'injection.

5) S'assurer que l'enfant ou les parents utilisent une aiguille de 6 à 12 mm (¼ ou ½ pouce) de longueur.

6) Pincer la peau ou apprendre à l'enfant à le faire; cela permet de détacher le tissu sous-cutané.

7) Donner l'injection dans le tissu sous-cutané profond, *à un angle de 90°.*

8. Rapports:

L'enfant doit apprendre à faire un rapport quotidien des doses d'insuline, du régime, des résultats d'analyse d'urine.

9. Réactions hyper ou hypoglycémiques:

a. Si l'enfant présente une réaction difficilement identifiable, il n'y a pas de danger à lui donner du sucre par voie orale.

b. Si l'enfant présente une réaction hypoglycémique, on lui donne ou il prend lui-même un concentré sucré. S'il ne peut avaler, ses parents peuvent lui administrer une injection intramusculaire de glucagon. Il est bon que l'on essaie de tester un échantillon d'urine. Le médecin doit être averti si l'enfant est devenu comateux.

c. Si l'enfant présente une réaction hyperglycémique, on omet sa collation, on lui fait boire une boisson chaude non sucrée, et on le stimule à exercer une activité physique. Un échantillon d'urine doit être analysé et le médecin averti si la réaction s'aggrave.

10. Rôle de l'enfant dans sa guérison:

a. Garder l'enfant sous surveillance aussi longtemps que nécessaire, mais lui donner de l'indépendance dès que possible.

b. S'assurer de sa collaboration pour:

1) Contrôler volontairement son régime, pour que les autres enfants ne puissent le tenter.
2) Pratiquer régulièrement ses exercices.
3) Rendre compte honnêtement de toute transgression aux ordres du médecin.
4) Ne pas tromper ses parents en simulant une réaction insulinique.
5) Porter constamment une carte d'identité ou une médaille avec l'inscription « je suis diabétique », ainsi que son nom, son adresse, son numéro de téléphone et ceux de son médecin traitant.

c. Diriger l'enfant vers une adolescence normale en comprenant son agressivité, son inhibition ou sa révolte contre les restrictions Le mener à une vie adulte normale où il jouera son rôle dans la société.

11. Diabète et ressources communautaires:

a. Renseigner les parents sur les associations pour diabétiques et leurs périodiques.

b. Renseigner les parents sur les camps d'été pour enfants diabétiques.

---

glycémiques, être capable d'effectuer les dosages urinaires de sucre et d'acétone, d'en noter les résultats et de pouvoir en fournir une interprétation sommaire. Si cela ne peut être atteint avant le congé de l'enfant, une infirmière en santé communautaire se rendra régulièrement au domicile de l'enfant.

Le professeur et l'infirmière scolaire doivent être au courant de la maladie de l'enfant, ainsi que des manifestations possibles de choc et de coma, afin de pouvoir l'aider en cas d'urgence. Les parents de l'enfant et l'infirmière scolaire doivent avoir les trousses d'urgence contenant du glucagon au cas où l'enfant ferait un choc hypoglycémique. Ils doivent se rendre compte qu'une réadmission à l'hôpital sera nécessaire pour une évaluation et un ajustement du régime et du dosage de l'insuline.

L'infirmière scolaire peut aussi aider l'enfant pour recueillir et pour analyser des échantillons d'urine, en lui trouvant un endroit où il lui sera possible de le faire privément.

Tableau 22-2. *Réactions hypo et hyperglycémiques*

	HYPOGLYCÉMIQUES	HYPERGLYCÉMIQUES
Causes:	– trop d'insuline – insuffisance de nourriture – exercice accru – repas retardé	– insuffisance d'insuline – excès de nourriture – infection – stress émotif
Symptômes:	– sudation profuse – céphalée – sensation de faim – vue affaiblie – tremblements – pâleur – ne peut être réveillé après le sommeil	– sécheresse de la peau – douleur abdominale – perte de l'appétit – soif, sécheresse de la bouche – nausées, vomissements – rougeur du visage
Conduite:	– donner du sucre – cesser d'administrer l'insuline – tester l'urine – faire reposer l'enfant – donner du glucagon i.m. si l'enfant ne peut ingérer de sucre per os	– faire boire des boissons chaudes non sucrées – donner de l'insuline – tester l'urine – coucher l'enfant – appeler le médecin
Prévention:	– si l'enfant présente plusieurs dosages urinaires négatifs, ajouter une collation et diminuer les exercices	– si l'enfant présente plusieurs dosages urinaires très positifs, stimuler l'activité et supprimer une collation.

S'ils s'y rendent de leur plein gré les enfants diabétiques apprendront beaucoup au sujet de leur maladie, en fréquentant un camp d'été pour diabétiques. Les programmes varient d'un camp à l'autre, mais tous visent à développer chez le jeune diabétique un sentiment de confiance, d'estime de soi et d'indépendance.

À l'approche de l'adolescence, l'enfant a des besoins alimentaires accrus du fait de sa croissance. Comme il veut être sur un pied d'égalité avec ses compagnons, il mange tout ce que les autres consomment, même s'il sait que cela peut lui être néfaste. Cet enfant a besoin d'aide et de compréhension pour contrôler sa maladie. Si on le punit pour ses écarts alimentaires, il pourra commettre d'autres imprudences. Il faut adapter le régime à ses besoins particuliers.

Au cours de l'adolescence, les difficultés du jeune diabétique tendent à s'accentuer. L'adolescent éprouve un désir d'indépendance et se révolte contre toutes les restrictions exigées par son état; les parents, par contre, cherchent à le protéger et le tiennent donc sous leur dépendance. Les adolescents s'interrogent quant à leur avenir sexuel, ils se demandent s'ils pourront se marier et avoir des enfants normaux. Ils s'inquiètent au sujet de leur futur travail. La travailleuse sociale ou l'infirmière en santé communautaire avec les autres membres de l'équipe, peuvent aider à la fois les parents et le jeune pour que l'adolescent puisse parvenir à l'âge adulte sans traumatisme psychologique sérieux. L'assistance d'un psychiatre peut s'avérer nécessaire en certains cas.

Complications, évolution et pronostic. Les *complications* sérieuses du diabète surviennent ordinairement 15 à 20 ans après son début, ce qui signifie à l'âge adulte dans les cas de diabète juvénile. Le retard de croissance et de développement, l'absence d'apparition des caractères sexuels secondaires et l'aménorrhée s'observent chez les enfants dont le diabète n'a pas été équilibré pendant longtemps. La gangrène, les rétinopathies, les cataractes et l'artériosclérose surviennent après plusieurs années d'évolution. Chez l'enfant diabétique insuffisamment traité, les infections sont fréquentes et elles ont tendance à guérir difficilement; parmi les plus fréquentes, citons les caries dentaires, les infections des voies respiratoires, des voies urinaires basses et les infections cutanées.

Les complications liées aux injections d'insuline sont la lipomatose ou la lipodystrophie. On comprend mal ce processus pathologique, mais des moyens préventifs sont donnés dans le tableau 22-1. On expérimente actuellement le traitement des lipodystrophies avec des injections d'insuline purifiée et les résultats sont très encourageants. L'allergie à l'insuline peut se rencontrer.

On n'a pas encore pu prouver que les complications tardives (après vingt ans) du diabète peuvent être prévenues par un contrôle adéquat. Des lésions dégénératives graves apparaissent chez des jeunes adultes qui ont souffert du diabète pendant plus de quinze ou vingt ans. Ces complications consistent essentiellement en une artériosclérose accompagnée d'hypertension, d'une atteinte rénale (glomérulo-sclérose) et d'altérations de la rétine.

La greffe d'Îlots de Langerhans donnerait des résultats spectaculaires chez l'animal. Si elle peut être réussie pour l'homme, le traitement du diabète en serait transformé.

Développement sexuel précoce (Puberté précoce)

Étiologie et traitement. On peut diagnostiquer un développement sexuel précoce quand les caractères sexuels secondaires apparaissent avant l'âge de huit ou dix ans.

On peut diviser ces enfants en deux groupes: ceux qui souffrent de puberté précoce vraie et ceux atteints de pseudo-puberté précoce, où il n'y a ni spermatogénèse, ni ovulation.

La plupart des cas de puberté précoce vraie sont dus à une maturation prématurée idiopathique de la fonction endocrine des glandes génitales. L'incidence en est sporadique ou familiale, mais il se produit une stimulation hypothalamique qui déclenche le mécanisme de maturation sexuelle et la puberté apparaît. Chez la fille, les seins augmentent de volume et le poil pubien commence à pousser. Un peu plus tard, les organes génitaux externes se développent, le poil axillaire apparaît ainsi que les premières menstruations (ménarche). Le garçon voit ses organes génitaux externes (verge et testicules) augmenter de volume et le poil pubien pousse. La production de sperme peut apparaître dans certains cas dès l'âge de cinq ans.

Ces modifications accompagnent une avance modérée de la croissance physique, de la taille, du poids et de l'ossification. La croissance accentuée du squelette peut aboutir à une soudure précoce des épiphyses, de sorte que la taille définitive reste quelquefois inférieure à celle qui aurait été atteinte autrement. Le médecin expliquera cet état aux parents et à l'enfant. Aucun traitement n'est nécessaire pour ces cas, mais la grossesse demeure possible chez la fillette.

Un second type de puberté précoce vraie est dû à une infection du système nerveux central, comme une encéphalite ou une lésion qui affecte l'hypothalamus ou le plancher du troisième ventricule. On peut observer chez ces enfants des convulsions ou un retard mental. Le traitement et le pronostic dépendent de la lésion causale.

Chez la fille, la puberté précoce peut provenir d'une tumeur de l'ovaire, d'une tumeur féminisante du cortex surrénalien, d'un syndrome de McCune-Albright ou de l'ingestion accidentelle d'œstrogènes. Elle peut apparaître chez le garçon qui souffre de lésions cérébrales, d'un syndrome adrénogénital, d'une tumeur des cellules de Leydig ou qui a absorbé accidentellement des substances androgènes.

Le *traitement* consiste surtout à soutenir l'enfant et ses parents au point de vue psychologique et à les aider à se rendre compte que les mêmes phénomènes se manifesteront chez les garçons de son âge quand ils auront eux-mêmes atteint la puberté. La cause doit être traitée si cela est possible. Le *pronostic* dépend de la lésion causale.

Traumatismes crâniens

Les enfants d'âge scolaire subissent des traumatismes crâniens par suite d'accidents d'auto, de chutes à bicyclette ou lorsqu'ils grimpent, ou s'ils se frappent la tête en jouant.

Commotion cérébrale

Définition, manifestations cliniques, traitement et soins infirmiers. La *commotion* cérébrale consiste en une perte temporaire de conscience sans qu'il y ait des lésions cérébrales. La *contusion* est également accompagnée de perte de conscience, mais des lésions microscopiques marquent la substance cérébrale. Lorsqu'il y a une *lacération* du cerveau, des changements macroscopiques s'observent sur la substance cérébrale. Les *manifestations cliniques* de la commotion cérébrale, causée par un coup brusque sur la tête, comprennent la perte brève de conscience, les céphalées, la pâleur, les vomissements, l'apathie et l'irritabilité. Si la perte de conscience se prolonge durant un certain temps avec des degrés divers d'amnésie, on doit établir le diagnostic de contusion cérébrale. Des convulsions peuvent se manifester.

Au cours des douze ou vingt-quatre heures qui suivent le traumatisme, il faut surveiller, au moins toutes les deux heures, le degré de conscience, noter les signes vitaux, le mouvement des yeux, l'état des pupilles, y compris leur forme et leur réaction. Toute altération de ces signes ou une aggravation de l'état stuporeux peut traduire une hypertension intracrânienne. Si l'enfant est très agité, on peut prescrire un sédatif qui risque cependant de masquer l'apparition des symptômes. Il faut capitonner les côtés du lit pour empêcher les blessures en cas de convulsion, et éviter d'attacher l'enfant ce qui augmente l'agitation. Il faut surveiller la diurèse et l'apparition d'un globe vésical, car la distension peut être une cause d'agitation continuelle.

Fracture du crâne

Manifestations cliniques, diagnostic, traitement et soins infirmiers. Les *manifestations cliniques* d'une fracture de la base crânienne comprennent une hémorragie auriculaire, nasale, pharyngée ou orbitaire bilatérale; une paralysie faciale périphérique ou un écoulement de liquide céphalo-rachidien par le nez ou l'oreille. On établit le *diagnostic* de la fracture en se basant sur les radiographies.

Traitement. Le traitement consiste à replacer l'os enfoncé du crâne. Les enfants ayant des fractures linéaires doivent recevoir le même *traitement* que ceux qui ont subi une commotion cérébrale. Il faut fermer chirurgicalement la fissure méningée, si elle existe. On administre des antibiotiques si c'est nécessaire.

Soins. Il faut surveiller les modifications des signes vitaux pour déceler à temps l'hypertension intracrânienne. Si du liquide céphalo-rachidien coule du nez ou de l'oreille, il ne faut surtout pas irriguer les narines ou le conduit auditif, et ne pas bourrer ces orifices de coton absorbant.

Hématome extra-dural

Manifestations cliniques, traitement et soins. On peut observer les *manifestations cliniques* de l'hématome extra-dural environ vingt-quatre heures après un traumatisme, même si l'enfant n'a pas de fracture du crâne. Le traumatisme crânien s'accompagne d'une brève perte de conscience, d'une reprise de conscience suivie d'un état de stupeur ou de coma. Quand le sang s'accumule entre l'os et la dure-mère, on observe une élévation de la pression artérielle, une dilatation pupillaire unilatérale et une hémiparésie.

En guise de *traitement*, le chirurgien doit pratiquer sans retard une intervention chirurgicale. L'épilepsie post-traumatique suit parfois un traumatisme crânien.

Les soins de l'enfant ayant souffert d'un traumatisme cérébral ressemblent grandement à ceux que l'on prodigue à l'enfant atteint d'une tumeur cérébrale. Souvent les parents ressentent un grand sentiment de culpabilité à cause de l'accident et les membres de l'équipe de santé doivent les aider à exprimer leurs émotions et à les assumer le plus objectivement possible.

Tumeur cérébrale

Étiologie, incidence, manifestations cliniques et types. Chez les enfants, les tumeurs cérébrales sont rarement dues à des métastases. Elles siègent, en général, au-dessous de la tente du cervelet alors qu'on observe l'inverse chez l'adulte.

Les tumeurs cérébrales sont six fois moins fréquentes chez les enfants que chez les adultes. L'*incidence* est la plus élevée entre 2 et 6 ans et ne varie pas durant toute la période scolaire.

Les *symptômes* révèlent une hypertension intracrânienne. L'enfant a des *vomissements* habituellement au cours de la matinée; à un stade plus tardif, les vomissements en jet apparaissent. On note de la *céphalée,* de la *diplopie* et une *augmentation du volume de la tête* si la tumeur survient avant la fermeture des fontanelles. L'enfant présente une altération de son état mental: léthargie, troubles de comportement, somnolence, ou état de stupeur qui évolue vers le coma et la mort. Très souvent, les premiers signes de changements dans la personnalité sont notés par le professeur de l'enfant ou par l'infirmière scolaire qui encourage les parents à faire examiner l'enfant. Les altérations des signes vitaux s'avèrent importants pour établir le diagnostic d'une hypertension intracrânienne. Les tumeurs infratentorielles amènent rarement les convulsions

Les autres manifestations cliniques dépendent du type et de la localisation de la tumeur.

On observe cinq types de tumeurs:

Le *médulloblastome* demeure la plus commune des tumeurs de l'enfance. Elle atteint surtout l'enfant entre 5 et 6 ans. C'est une tumeur très maligne, qui se développe rapidement et qui siège surtout au niveau du cervelet. L'enfant souffre d'ataxie, d'anorexie, de vomissements, de céphalée matinale et à l'examen du fond de l'œil, on trouve un œdème de la papille. L'enfant devient peu à peu somnolent et présente du nystagmus. Les survies sont habituellement inférieures à un an.

L'*astrocytome* qui se localise d'habitude dans le cervelet, peut survenir à tout âge, mais plus fréquemment vers la huitième année. Ses symptômes diffèrent sensiblement des signes habituels de tumeur cérébrale. Le début est insidieux et l'évolution très lente. On rencontre des signes de perturbations locales ou d'hypentension intracrânienne. L'enfant peut devenir ataxique, hypotonique, hyporéflexique, et souffrir de nystagmus. L'œdème de la papille est présent. Sans opération, le pronostic est très pauvre. Une exérèse chirurgicale totale est possible et l'on peut obtenir une guérison complète.

L'*épendymome* se trouve dans le quatrième ventricule ou dans l'un des ventricules latéraux du cerveau. L'hypertension intracrânienne est accompagnée d'autres symptômes selon la localisation de la tumeur: vomissements, céphalée, augmentation du volume de la tête, ataxie. L'hydrocéphalie apparaît chez le bébé. Le meilleur traitement demeure la décompression interne incomplète et la radiothérapie.

Le *craniopharyngiome* s'observe à la fin de la seconde enfance, la tumeur siège près de l'hypophyse. Les principaux symptômes proviennent de l'hypothalamus ou de l'hypophyse, par exemple le diabète insipide, l'arrêt de croissance, le myxœdème ou le retard de puberté. On trouve des perturbations du champ visuel, des troubles de la mémoire et/ou de la personnalité, de l'hypertension intracrânienne, suivie de vomissements et de céphalée. Une radiographie du crâne révèle un élargissement des sutures. L'ablation totale de la tumeur s'avère presque impossible. La radiothérapie permet souvent de freiner l'évolution pendant des années.

Les *gliomes du tronc cérébral* ont une fréquence maximale aux environs de la septième année. Les principales manifestations cliniques incluent les paralysies multiples des territoires des nerfs crâniens, l'ataxie du tronc et une perte sensitive minimale sans indication d'hypertension intracrânienne. Cette tumeur est inopérable, mais son évolution est lente et un traitement radiothérapeutique peut permettre à l'enfant de survivre pendant longtemps.

Diagnostic et traitement. Le *diagnostic* précoce d'une tumeur du cerveau peut s'avérer impossible à cause de son début insidieux. Le diagnostic se fonde sur l'histoire de l'apparition d'une hypertension intracrânienne ou de troubles cérébraux, et sur les données de l'examen physique. Un électro-encéphalogramme aide à localiser les tumeurs sustentorielles superficielles. Le pneumo-encéphalogramme peut donner des renseignements intéressants. Des radiographies peuvent montrer un élargissement des lignes de suture ou une calcification à l'intérieur de la tumeur. La ventriculographie, l'artériographie, la cartographie, l'étude du flot cérébral et le marquage aux isotopes aident à localiser la tumeur et à en déterminer le volume. Il ne faut pas pratiquer de ponction lombaire en présence d'une hypertension intracrânienne, car on risque de provoquer une hernie fatale du tronc cérébral.

Les symptômes des différents types de tumeurs peuvent aussi se rencontrer chez des enfants atteints d'encéphalite, d'abcès du cerveau ou de certaines maladies cérébrales dégénératives. Il faut d'abord éliminer ces maladies avant d'établir le diagnostic d'une tumeur du cerveau.

Le traitement est chirurgical ou radiothérapeutique. Une intervention enlèvera la plus grande partie possible de la tumeur. La radiothérapie donne des résultats dans certains cas. Les résultats de la neurochirurgie se sont améliorés depuis les récents progrès en anesthésiologie et en endocrinologie, surtout avec les corticostéroïdes. Même lorsqu'une guérison complète s'avère impossible, on parvient souvent à obtenir une amélioration fonctionnelle et à procurer à l'enfant quelques mois ou quelques années de vie relativement confortable.

Soins infirmiers. SOUTIEN ÉMOTIF. Les parents et l'enfant doivent rencontrer l'infirmière qui s'occupera de l'enfant après l'opération. Ils éprouvent bien sûr de l'anxiété et il faut les préparer, tout comme l'enfant à la neurochirurgie, à l'aspect du nouvel opéré, aux traitements et techniques qu'il faudra appliquer. Même si l'enfant semble inconscient, il faut éviter de tenir en sa présence des propos angoissants. Les parents ont besoin, de la part de l'infirmière, d'une compréhension et d'un soutien continus au cours des périodes pré et postopératoires.

SOINS PRÉOPÉRATOIRES ET OBSERVATION. On place l'enfant dans un lit pourvu de ridelles pour éviter les chutes, surtout s'il est inconscient, confus ou agité.

Le malade doit recevoir un régime nourrissant. S'il vomit, il faut lui donner de nouveau à manger, car ces vomissements sont souvent d'origine centrale et non précédés de nausées. On évite les lavements de crainte d'accentuer l'hypertension intracrânienne.

Les observations de l'infirmière sont de la plus haute importance pour aider le médecin à localiser la tumeur et évaluer l'hypertension intracrânienne. Elle doit inscrire de façon complète les plaintes et le comportement de l'enfant, en mentionnant les circonstances qui les ont provoqués. Elle doit noter spécifiquement le ralentissement et les modifications dans la nature du pouls, les changements progressifs ou brusques de la température corporelle, l'affaiblissement et les changements dans la nature du rythme respiratoire, surtout une respiration irrégulière, et enfin, toute altération de la tension artérielle, en particulier l'élévation de la pression systolique et toute autre modification des signes neurologiques.

Il faut noter les vomissements, les épisodes de céphalée, de léthargie ou de stupeur. L'infirmière doit décrire les convulsions en détail et prendre certaines précautions lors des crises. Si possible, elle doit s'informer s'il y a une limitation du champ visuel ou si l'enfant voit une image double ou un seul objet. Elle doit noter le degré et la localisation de la faiblesse musculaire, ainsi que l'incontinence ou la rétention urinaire et fécale et les manifestations de douleur et de malaise.

Les parents et l'enfant doivent savoir que l'on doit raser les cheveux avant une intervention intracrânienne. Le rasage peut être effectué à la chambre de l'enfant ou à la salle d'opération. L'infirmière doit expliquer à l'enfant que ses cheveux repousseront et elle peut demander aux parents d'apporter à l'avance des turbans qu'il pourra essayer. S'il doit être admis à l'unité des soins intensifs ou en chambre privée après l'intervention, il est essentiel de le prévenir ainsi que ses parents pour qu'ils n'interprètent pas ce changement comme un signe de complication postopératoire. Si le malade est en état de comprendre les explications, il faut le préparer psychologiquement à la chirurgie tel qu'expliqué précédemment au chapitre 10.

L'infirmière doit savoir où se trouve l'équipement d'urgence, tel l'oxygène, l'aspirateur, les gants stériles, le plateau à ponction ventriculaire, les médicaments d'urgence, et tous les autres accessoires et appareils dont elle pourrait avoir besoin.

SOINS POSTOPÉRATOIRES. Ces soins sont astreignants, et exigent de l'habileté et de l'expérience. Après l'intervention, l'état de conscience varie, en fonction de l'état d'éveil avant l'opération et selon la nature et la durée de celle-ci. L'assistance respiratoire peut être nécessaire pendant quelques heures après la fin de l'anesthésie.

On administre les liquides par voie parentérale et il faut noter soigneusement la quantité de liquide perfusé. Une administration trop rapide peut provoquer une dangereuse hypertension intracrânienne. Les soins de la bouche s'avèrent essentiels pour prévenir une parotidite ou une moniliase.

Immédiatement après l'opération, il faut coucher l'enfant à plat, du côté non atteint. Quand le risque de vomissements est passé, il faut le changer souvent de position pour empêcher des zones de pression et une pneumonie hypostatique. On ne couche habituellement pas l'enfant du côté opéré. Le chirurgien peut préférer que la tête soit légèrement élevée. Pour tourner l'enfant qui a été opéré dans la région du cervelet, il faut maintenir le corps en ligne droite, et procéder avec lenteur et délicatesse. En bougeant l'enfant, il faut bien soutenir sa tête, son cou et ses épaules de façon à ce qu'aucune partie du corps ne s'affaisse. Deux infirmières sont nécessaires pour bouger un enfant d'âge scolaire. Pour prévenir également la formation de plaies sur la tête ou le corps de l'enfant, on peut couvrir le matelas de caoutchouc mousse, mettre une peau de mouton sous les zones de pression

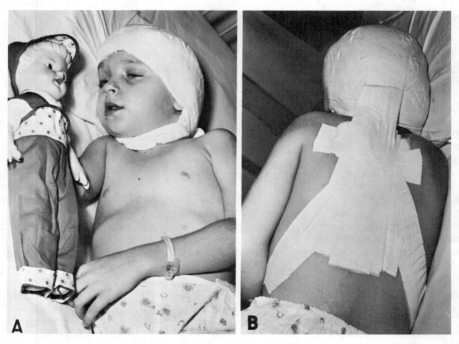

Figure 22-8.   Les pansements d'une craniectomie suboccipitale aident à maintenir la tête dans un alignement correct avec le corps de l'enfant, même lorsqu'il est sur l'abdomen. A) Vue frontale. B) Vue dorsale.

comme les oreilles ou le côté de la tête, ou employer un matelas pneumatique ou aquatique.

Il faut garder le patient propre et au sec en tout temps, et masser souvent le dos et la région autour des points de pression. Si une paralysie ou une spasticité des extrémités se produit, il faut employer des oreillers ou un autre support. On prévient un affaissement des pieds à l'aide d'un appui adéquat.

Pour déceler les signes d'hypertension intra-crânienne, on prend les signes vitaux selon l'ordonnance du médecin, tous les quarts d'heure au retour de la salle d'opération et ensuite moins souvent, selon l'évolution du malade.

On aspire les sécrétions nasopharyngées quand c'est nécessaire et on encourage l'enfant à inspirer profondément à intervalles réguliers.

Si un état de choc survient, on applique des couvertures chaudes. Il faut avoir à portée de la main, pour emploi immédiat, des stimulants d'urgence, des liquides pour la thérapie intra-veineuse et de l'oxygène. En général, on évite de soulever le pied du lit à cause du danger d'hypertension intracrânienne. L'infirmière doit indiquer immédiatement l'incontinence ou la rétention urinaire.

Il ne faut pas employer de moyens de contrainte, à moins qu'ils ne soient absolument nécessaires, parce que l'enfant peut les combattre et augmenter sa tension intracrânienne. Il faut les appliquer si l'enfant tire sur les bandages, essaie de retirer le tube intraveineux ou de gavage, ou s'il risque de se blesser lui-même. Dans ce cas, on peut utiliser des attelles pour les coudes et des mitaines pour les mains.

Si les pansements sur la tête deviennent humides par suite du drainage de la plaie opératoire, on entoure l'écoulement d'une ligne au violet de gentiane. Si la région souillée s'étend rapidement, ou si du sang apparaît sur le bandage, il faut en avertir le chirurgien. L'infirmière renforce le pansement avec des compresses stériles maintenues en place par un bandage supplémentaire. La contamination de la région opérée peut entraîner une méningite.

L'opération peut amener un œdème du visage, des paupières et du cerveau. Comme les sécrétions lacrymales ne peuvent s'écouler en cas d'œdème, les conjonctives risquent de s'assécher, de s'irriter et de s'infecter. Les irrigations salines chaudes, les gouttes oculaires ou l'application de compresses froides sur les paupières gonflées aident à prévenir cette complication. Certains médecins recommandent de garder les paupières fermées avec de petits morceaux de cellophane ou de les couvrir d'une coquille. En période pré ou postopératoire, on peut administrer des corti-

costéroïdes qui, en réduisant l'œdème, diminuent la pression intracrânienne.

L'hyperthermie peut être causée par un œdème intracrânien, une hémorragie à l'endroit de l'opération, ou un trouble du centre thermorégulateur; il faut alors prendre la température au moins toutes les demi-heures. Pour diminuer la fièvre, on peut déshabiller l'enfant et le couvrir d'un seul drap, réduire la température de la pièce, donner des bains d'éponge tièdes et alcoolisés, placer l'enfant sur un matelas réfrigérant, donner des lavements d'eau glacée ou des petits lavements de rétention contenant de l'aspirine. Quand la température a atteint un degré acceptable, il faut continuer une surveillance étroite, car elle demeure rarement stable. Si l'enfant ne peut avaler, on l'alimente par gavage; il faut signaler immédiatement la distension gastrique ou le ballonnement abdominal.

Dès que l'enfant a cessé de vomir et semble être capable d'avaler, on peut lui donner de petites quantités d'eau. On ajoute progressivement des liquides nourrissants et une diète molle. Il ne faut pas trop forcer l'hydratation et l'alimentation qui peuvent entraîner des vomissements qui augmenteraient la tension intracrânienne. On donne des aliments solides dès que l'enfant peut les tolérer.

À mesure que le malade se remet de son opération, il faut l'aider à acquérir une plus grande autonomie. Il faut lui donner l'occasion de jouer seul ou avec d'autres enfants. Les parents doivent comprendre qu'il faut lui permettre une certaine indépendance à la maison, mais qu'il a besoin d'une surveillance médicale constante après son départ de l'hôpital.

Évolution et pronostic. L'*évolution* dépend du type de tumeur. La maladie peut durer quelques semaines ou plusieurs années. Le taux de survie jusqu'à l'âge adulte demeure très bas.

Dysfonction cérébrale minimale

Incidence, étiologie, manifestations cliniques, diagnostic et traitement. L'expression « *dysfonction cérébrale minimale* » s'applique d'une façon assez vague à un groupe fort hétérogène d'enfants malades d'une façon chronique. Il s'agit là d'une étiquette qui ne désigne pas un diagnostic spécifique. Ce syndrome peut être dû à une lésion du cerveau, mais aussi à des anomalies de développement cytogéniques, génétiques et morphogéniques, ou à des anomalies du système nerveux central. Il semble que le nombre de ces enfants tende à augmenter, soit à cause de meilleures techniques de diagnostic, soit parce que leur survie est maintenant assurée grâce aux progrès de la science médicale.

Au cours de la période préscolaire, on remarque chez ces enfants des variations de comportement imprévisibles, des sautes d'humeur, une incapacité de fixer leur attention pendant une période normale pour un enfant de cet âge, un seuil de frustration très bas et un comportement bizarre à plusieurs points de vue.

On rencontre chez eux des difficultés de comportement et d'apprentissage qu'on n'observe parfois qu'après leur entrée à l'école. Ils se distinguent des autres enfants par des variations psychologiques, académiques et neurologiques. Ils peuvent avoir un ou plusieurs des problèmes suivants: incapacité à se concentrer, hyperactivité, impulsivité, irritabilité, réactions exagérées aux excitations ambiantes, et par la suite difficulté à concevoir et à comprendre un raisonnement abstrait. Leur intelligence est normale, à la limite inférieure ou supérieure, bien qu'ils puissent éprouver des difficultés à apprendre et c'est ainsi qu'on peut les distinguer du groupe des arriérés mentaux.

L'enfant qui se rend compte de la différence qui existe entre lui et ses compagnons peut développer des réactions émotives négatives. À mesure qu'il vieillit, des problèmes de comportement viennent s'ajouter au tableau clinique. Son immaturité devient plus flagrante et il éprouve souvent des sentiments d'anxiété à un degré anormal. Il agit de façon impulsive et regrette souvent ses actes par la suite. Il peut être incapable d'assumer son sentiment de culpabilité et devenir encore plus agressif. Il souffre fréquemment de troubles de l'audition ou de la vision. Les tests d'intelligence donnent des résultats variables et le résultat global est souvent décevant.

L'utilisation des amphétamines et de son proche voisin la Ritaline parvient à augmenter la capacité d'attention et à réduire les sautes d'humeur et le comportement agressif. Les tranquillisants diminuent l'irritabilité et l'impulsivité. Il est évident que l'enfant qui prend de tels médicaments doit demeurer sous surveillance médicale étroite. On craint actuellement la surconsommation, une certaine accoutumance et les effets à long terme de l'utilisation prolongée de ces médicaments.

Le *traitement* d'un tel enfant suppose la collaboration de toutes les personnes concernées, les parents, le pédiatre qui dirige l'équipe, des médecins spécialistes, des psychologues, le directeur de l'école, les enseignants, les travailleuses sociales, les infirmières scolaires et les infirmières pédiatriques quand l'enfant est admis pour diagnostic ou traitement.

Le comportement de l'enfant, ses résultats scolaires, les tests psychologiques, l'étude des antécédents médicaux et familiaux et enfin les examens médicaux et neurologiques, y compris un électroencéphalogramme, permettent d'évaluer l'état de l'enfant. Des résultats thérapeutiques positifs exigent une telle évaluation et un plan de soins établi d'après les ressources et les tendances de l'individu et de son entourage. Un milieu adapté et cohérent qui tient compte des problèmes multiples de l'enfant est plus efficace que l'administration massive de médicaments sédatifs ou tranquillisants.

En donnant la diète de Feingold qui élimine les colorants artificiels et les produits naturels à noyau salycilé, on a réussi à réduire la médication chez un bon nombre d'enfants et à la cesser complètement dans d'autres cas. Cette approche, liée à un milieu scolaire renouvelé, représente la tendance actuelle du traitement de ces enfants. Ils bénéficient d'un séjour dans des classes spécialement adaptées à leur état et à leurs besoins. Leur sentiment de frustration diminue quand des changements apportés dans l'environnement enlèvent une partie de leurs problèmes. Certaines techniques pédagogiques qui s'appuient sur l'application concrète des notions abstraites, l'attention individuelle et l'aide apportée aux parents peuvent également atténuer le problème. La psychothérapie peut quelquefois devenir nécessaire.

Le pronostic dépend de l'attitude des adultes qui s'occupent de l'enfant, de l'âge où le traitement a débuté et de l'adaptation de la famille à cette situation souvent frustrante. Certains enfants deviennent délinquants, socialement et intellectuellement retardés et même psychotiques. Si l'enfant réussit quand même à garder ou à développer la confiance qu'il a en lui-même et en autrui, son adaptation sera souvent normale quand il atteindra l'âge adulte.

Soins infirmiers. Le rôle de l'infirmière consiste à déceler les cas et à coopérer aux efforts de l'équipe qui doit établir le diagnostic, prodiguer les conseils aux parents, utiliser les techniques pédagogiques adéquates et offrir une psychothérapie occasionnelle.

Lors de l'hospitalisation, l'infirmière doit viser à contrôler les excitations ambiantes et procurer à l'enfant un environnement stable et structuré où il puisse s'épanouir. Comme l'enfant s'adapte difficilement à des changements de situations, l'infirmière doit veiller à la continuité des soins et éviter les situations qui engendrent de la tension; ceci est rendu possible grâce à la permanence des infirmières assignées à ses soins ou à la présence de la mère près de l'enfant. L'infirmière doit expliquer à l'enfant d'une manière simple et directe ce qu'on attend de lui. Elle doit le féliciter lorsqu'il se comporte comme on le désire. Il répondra favorablement à des directives compréhensibles et à l'approbation d'autrui. Une attitude confiante à l'égard de ses capacités améliore l'image qu'il se fait de lui-même.

Si la mère demeure à l'hôpital avec l'enfant, l'infirmière qui observe les relations mère-enfant peut déceler d'éventuels problèmes émotifs. L'enfant qui a des problèmes d'adaptation s'intégrera mal à la société si les parents refusent de reconnaître son état et le considèrent uniquement comme un « mauvais enfant ». L'infirmière doit aussi connaître les agences qui peuvent aider la famille. Il faut qu'on dise aux parents ce qu'ils peuvent attendre de l'enfant, actuellement et dans l'avenir, et il faut souligner qu'il s'améliorera probablement avec l'âge et la thérapie. Il faut quelquefois le confier un certain temps à des institutions spécialisées.

Maladie de Legg-Calvé-Perthes (Coxa Plana)

Cette maladie consiste en une nécrose avasculaire de la tête du fémur, d'étiologie inconnue, qui se manifeste par une boiterie et des douleurs intermittentes chez les garçons, plus rarement chez les filles, vers l'âge de cinq à dix ans.

Radiologiquement, on reconnaît 4 stades à la maladie. Le premier, celui de la nécrose, se manifeste par une densité augmentée, partielle ou totale, de l'épiphyse fémorale proximale. Le second stade, la fragmentation de la tête, correspond à la revascularisation. C'est le moment critique où la tête est affaiblie et où les forces de compression peuvent amener une déformation que l'on reconnaît au troisième stade par un aplatissement, un élargissement et des irrégularités variables de l'épiphyse. Le quatrième stade montre les séquelles de la maladie.

Les symptômes sont la claudication, la douleur à la hanche, les spasmes musculaires et la diminution de la motilité.

Le *traitement* consiste à empêcher ces déformations de se produire. Comme il n'existe pas de moyens de prévenir l'affaiblissement structural de la tête fémorale, on vise à ce que cette tête malléable soit bien contenue dans l'acétabulum.

En phase de synovite aiguë, on emploie la traction pour soulager la douleur et le spasme musculaire. Un traitement chirurgical, l'ostéo-tomie de Salter, tente une réorientation spatiale de la cavité acétabulaire.

Divers moyens permettent de maintenir le membre en abduction et rotation interne avec délestage total ou partiel, que ce soit par alitement, appareils ou plâtres.

Il est à noter que, quel que soit le traitement employé, celui-ci doit être entrepris au tout début de la maladie. Malgré tout, un certain pourcentage de ces enfants présente des séquelles qui nuisent à la bonne mécanique de la hanche et mènent à une ostéoarthrite précoce.

Soins. Il faut appuyer sur l'importance d'éviter le port du poids sur la hanche malade pendant plusieurs mois. L'enfant doit rester au lit, sur un matelas ferme posé au besoin sur une planche. Si le malade a été placé en traction, il peut se coucher à volonté sur le dos ou le ventre, mais on doit le tourner au moins toutes les quatres heures. Il faut l'encourager à bouger ses articulations et à faire des exercices musculaires. Si on a appliqué un plâtre, les soins sont les mêmes que ceux décrits au chapitre 10.

Le grand problème du traitement de la maladie de Legg-Perthes réside dans l'immobilisation prolongée. Il faut aider les parents à organiser la vie familiale en fonction de cette particularité et il faut surtout beaucoup d'ingéniosité pour distraire l'enfant qui ne se sent pas malade et que l'on doit garder occupé. Il peut devenir nécessaire de diriger l'enfant vers une institution spécialisée dans les soins pédiatriques à long terme.

Dystrophie musculaire

La dystrophie musculaire, qui existe sous plusieurs formes, peut se définir comme une affection dégénérative myopathique primaire, héréditaire, dont la véritable étiologie demeure inconnue.

Toutes les dystrophies musculaires présentent le même processus dégénératif. On constate d'abord une diminution de la perméabilité de la membrane cellulaire et une perte de certaines enzymes musculaires, surtout la créatine-kinase que l'on trouve alors dans la circulation sanguine. Les changements structuraux se caractérisent par une dégénérescence fibreuse et adipeuse qui correspond au degré de l'atrophie constatée chez le malade.

Classification des dystrophies musculaires. Étant donné que le processus pathologique demeure le même, on classifie habituellement les dystrophies musculaires selon la localisation de l'atteinte. On trouve 1) le type facio-scapulo-huméral 2) le type scapulopelvien (avec ou sans atteinte de la face) 3) le type pseudo-hypertrophique ou type Duchenne, le plus important et le plus fréquent. On rencontre également d'autres formes que nous ne ferons que citer, sans en faire l'étude: la dystrophie musculaire congénitale, la dystrophie musculaire oculaire et la dystrophie musculaire distale.

Manifestations cliniques. 1) Forme facio-scapulo-humérale. On constate une faiblesse des muscles de la face: les yeux restent ouverts, le patient ne peut plisser le front, froncer les sourcils, siffler ou montrer ses dents. Sa figure est sans expression et semble figée sous un masque. L'atteinte de la ceinture scapulaire varie beaucoup et se manifeste par une difficulté à lever les membres supérieurs. Cette forme peut apparaître à tout âge, mais elle débute ordinairement avant l'âge de 30 ans. Son évolution est lente et compatible avec une vie normale. 2) Forme scapulo-pelvienne: touche les ceintures osseuses et varie beaucoup quant à son intensité. Elle apparaît ordinairement entre 10 et 20 ans. 3) Forme pseudo-hypertrophique de Duchenne. Cette variété de dystrophie musculaire demeure la plus grave et la plus fréquente. Elle apparaît surtout chez les garçons et se manifeste fréquemment avant l'âge de six ans. L'enfant peut tarder à marcher, il tombe facilement, il refuse de courir, tombe souvent de son tricycle et monte difficilement les escaliers. Sa démarche devient chancelante à la suite de la faiblesse des muscles fessiers. Un des signes les plus précoces et quasi pathognomonique est la difficulté qu'éprouve l'enfant à se lever quand il est assis sur le sol. Il se lève en grimpant le long de ses propres jambes. Une fois debout, il doit conserver une base d'appui très large pour maintenir son équilibre, et le moindre choc le fait tomber.

L'enfant atteint de dystrophie musculaire présente une lordose importante, une hypertrophie symétrique du mollet, des muscles fessiers et des sous-épineux; occasionnellement, d'autres muscles peuvent être atteints, toujours de façon symétrique. Les muscles sont fermes, mais demeurent plus faibles que les muscles normaux. Par exemple, la faiblesse des muscles de la ceinture scapulaire peut être mise en évidence quand l'enfant glisse entre les mains de l'examinateur qui tente de le soulever en le prenant sous les bras.

L'atrophie s'installe progressivement et atteint d'abord les régions du bassin, des lombes et de l'épaule; la silhouette peut être conservée pendant assez longtemps à cause des dépôts de tissu adipeux et fibreux dans le muscle atrophique. Les articulations des han-

ches, des genoux, des chevilles, des épaules et des coudes deviennent afonctionnelles. Les contractures et la flaccidité des membres condamnent l'enfant à demeurer sur une chaise roulante ou au lit; l'évolution peut être précipitée par un épisode infectieux qui se solde pour l'enfant par une impotence accrue. À un stade plus avancé, le malade présente une obésité marquée qui masque les pertes musculaires ou au contraire, une cachexie extrême due à l'inanition. La cardiomégalie, l'insuffisance cardiaque et les troubles du rythme viennent souvent compliquer l'évolution.

Diagnostic. L'examen clinique, toujours important pour le diagnostic, est complété par le dosage des enzymes musculaires, surtout de la créatine-kinase, dont le taux est souvent augmenté dès la naissance, c'est-à-dire bien avant l'évidence clinique de la maladie. La biopsie du muscle révèle les modifications musculaires. La recherche de la créatine-kinase et la biopsie musculaire permettent très souvent de reconnaître les femmes porteuses (hétérozygotes) susceptibles de transmettre la maladie à leurs garçons, sans présenter elles-mêmes de symptômes d'atteinte musculaire. Les filles de ces porteuses peuvent également être hétérozygotes dans une proportion de 1:2. Il faut se rappeler que la dystrophie musculaire pseudo-hypertrophique se transmet par un gène lié au sexe, comme l'hémophilie.

Évolution et traitement. Il n'existe actuellement aucun traitement contre la dystrophie musculaire. Toute perte de la fonction musculaire est définitive et il faut essayer de conserver la fonction, même des muscles très faibles, le plus longtemps possible, car le processus demeure irréversible. Les exercices actifs, la physiothérapie et une vie aussi normale que possible retardent l'évolution. Il faut à tout prix éviter l'obésité qui se présente souvent et qui augmente l'impotence fonctionnelle.

Soins infirmiers. L'infirmière en santé communautaire peut jouer un rôle de dépistage qui s'avère important, s'il permet de ralentir l'évolution du processus et de permettre une survie plus longue à l'enfant. Une fois que le diagnostic est définitivement posé, une planification des soins permet d'établir un programme d'exercices et d'activités. L'enfant, ses parents, le médecin, l'infirmière et la physiothérapeute participent à l'élaboration de ce programme.

Il est bon que l'enfant fréquente l'école ordinaire le plus longtemps possible; on le dirige ensuite vers une école pour enfants handicapés. À mesure que l'impotence fonctionnelle s'ins-

Tableau 22-3. *Dystrophie musculaire:*
Critères cliniques du diagnostic différentiel entre les types I — II — III.
(Rossi, E.: Considérations cliniques sur les myopathies de l'enfant,
Union médicale du Cananda, 96:1351, novembre 1967.) (adapté)

TYPE	I	II	III
Désignation	facio-scapulo-humérale	scapulo-pelvienne	Duchenne
Hérédité	dominant autosomal	récessif autosomal	récessif, lié au sexe
Début	entre 10 et 30 ans	entre 10 et 20 ans	avant 10 ans (2-6 ans)
Localisation initiale	visage	extrémités supérieures	extrémités inférieures
Pseudo-hypertrophie	jamais	rarement	toujours
Évolution	bénigne	relativement grave	maligne
Survie	normale	légèrement raccourcie	très raccourcie, mort avant l'âge de 20 ans

talle, la lecture, la télévision et la radio peuvent aider à garder l'enfant occupé.

Il faut encourager ces enfants à demeurer indépendants et actifs le plus longtemps possible. Même s'ils semblent gauches et lents, il faut se rappeler que l'exercice est le seul moyen de préserver la force musculaire et que la fonction perdue n'est jamais retrouvée. La prévention des contractures s'avère de prime importance. Il faut enseigner à la mère les moyens mécaniques qui permettent de les éviter: planches sous le matelas et support contre le pied tombant. À un stade plus avancé, un trapèze fixé au dessus du lit, une rampe fixée au mur de la chambre de bain, facilitent les mouvements de l'enfant, sans que la mère ait à fournir un effort physique excessif. Vers la fin de sa vie, l'enfant est parfois confié à une institution qui se spécialise dans le soin de ces handicapés.

Problèmes dentaires

Les objectifs principaux de la pédodontie consistent à maintenir les dents en bon état, à prévenir la maladie, à traiter les anomalies et à restaurer la fonction. Les problèmes dentaires courants comprennent les caries dentaires, la malocclusion, les traumatismes et les anomalies de la coloration.

La *carie* constitue un des problèmes dentaires majeurs chez les enfants. Il semble y avoir une corrélation positive entre l'éducation de la santé des dents chez les parents et l'incidence de la carie dentaire chez les enfants. Il faut donc s'attendre à ce que le problème soit plus aigu dans les milieux défavorisés. Des facteurs génétiques, un régime adéquat, une bonne hygiène buccale et l'emploi du fluor jouent un rôle dans l'incidence de la carie.

Une *malocclusion* résulte d'une position anormale des dents, primitive ou secondaire à un trouble du développement des mâchoires. L'enfant peut présenter des difficultés à la mastication, une bouche déformée, des anomalies faciales, un langage défectueux, des troubles de la nutrition et des problèmes émotifs. Un dentiste doit évaluer l'anomalie lorsqu'elle se développe. Si la malocclusion est évidente, il faut consulter un orthodontiste spécialement formé pour diagnostiquer et traiter la malocclusion. Si les dents de lait tombent prématurément ou s'il y a une absence congénitale des dents, il faut commencer très tôt le traitement pour prévenir une malocclusion. Le traitement consiste soit à placer un appareil pour maintenir les espaces entre les dents, soit à déplacer la dent. L'orthodontie préventive aide beaucoup d'enfants.

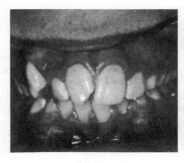 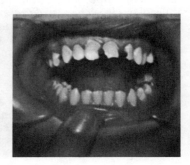

Figure 22-9. Il faut envoyer en clinique dentaire les enfants qui souffrent de malocclusion (gauche) ou de caries (droite). (Courtoisie de la Metropolitan Life Insurance Company.)

Les enfants ayant subi des *traumatismes* aux dents doivent être examinés immédiatement après l'accident. Le traitement dépend de la nature de la dent (de lait ou permanente), de son stade de développement, de la nature de la fracture et de l'état de la pulpe dentaire.

La *coloration* normale des dents permanentes est habituellement plus foncée que celles des dents de lait. Les parents craignent donc que les dents de leurs enfants soient définitivement ternies. Il faut leur dire que lorsque toutes les dents permanentes auront poussé, leur couleur sera probablement uniforme. Les dents peuvent se ternir sous l'effet d'agents extrinsèques comme certains médicaments. On peut faire enlever la plupart des taches en les faisant nettoyer par un dentiste.

PROBLÈMES ÉMOTIFS

Vers l'âge de six ans, l'enfant possède déjà une personnalité assez bien formée. Son comportement correspond à son développement physique et à l'atmosphère de son entourage. Il faut qu'il puisse perfectionner son corps et son esprit et entretenir des relations plus profondes avec des enfants et des adultes en dehors du milieu familial. Au cours de la même période, il doit également s'adapter à l'école.

Si au cours des années scolaires l'enfant a des problèmes de comportement qui indiquent des troubles psychiques, sa réaction ressemble à celle des adultes en face de difficultés. Il peut présenter des symptômes névrotiques comme le nervosisme, la succion du pouce, l'onychophagie et des peurs; la phobie de l'école; des troubles de conduite (l'enfant-problème); des troubles de langage comme le bégaiement; et des maladies psychosomatiques comme l'anorexie, la boulimie, la constipation, la colite, la douleur abdominale et l'énurésie.

Ces troubles, sérieux en eux-mêmes, peuvent aussi empêcher l'enfant de bien s'adapter à l'école. *Un échec scolaire peut donc avoir pour cause un trouble psychique tout autant qu'un retard mental.* L'enfant trop anxieux et tendu se concentre difficilement sur ses études, même s'il jouit d'une capacité intellectuelle suffisante.

L'enseignant et l'infirmière scolaire doivent se rendre compte de ces problèmes lorsqu'ils se manifestent. Ils devraient être capables de travailler avec les parents et autres membres de l'équipe dans le but d'aider l'enfant.

Phénomènes névrotiques

Chez l'enfant, il est difficile de distinguer une névrose d'un comportement normal. Certains comportements, lorsqu'ils persistent, doivent être considérés comme névrotiques.

Nervosisme

Étiologie et manifestations cliniques. Le terme nervosisme désigne un groupe de symptômes propres aux enfants physiquement ou psychiquement agités, surexcités ou timides, et qui se fatiguent vite.

La cause initiale de la nervosité peut être le poids permanent d'une anxiété, d'une tension ou encore d'une maladie grave. Certains enfants deviennent nerveux à cause d'une contrainte abusive des parents. D'autres enfants sont nerveux parce qu'ils se sentent inférieurs aux autres, s'excitent trop en jouant, ou partagent l'anxiété de leurs parents.

On peut facilement en reconnaître les *manifestations*. L'enfant est tendu et agité, le pouls et le rythme respiratoire s'accélèrent, les mouvements deviennent rapides et saccadés et les réactions de l'enfant sont trop rapides.

Traitement et pronostic. Le traitement peut dépendre d'un omnipraticien ou d'un psychiatre, selon la gravité du problème. Il faut procurer à l'enfant une nutrition adéquate, un sommeil calme et éviter de vouloir hâter de façon excessive son développement physique et psychique. L'enfant nerveux a besoin de support et on doit lui procurer un emploi du temps raisonnable. Parfois, il vaut mieux le soustraire à certaines influences anxiogènes du milieu familial.

Le *pronostic* varie selon la cause de la nervosité et le traitement offert à l'enfant.

Succion du pouce

La plupart des enfants cessent de sucer leur pouce vers l'âge de deux ans; d'autres aux environs de cinq ou six ans. Si cette habitude persiste à l'âge scolaire, il faut essayer de découvrir, dans la vie des parents et de l'enfant, la cause de ce comportement anormal. Il faut éviter les contentions ou les protège-pouce et ne pas mettre sur le pouce ou le doigt de lotions au goût désagréable.

Si l'enfant avait cessé cette habitude assez tôt pour la reprendre vers sept ou huit ans, c'est probablement qu'il a rencontré une difficulté qu'il ne peut résoudre et qu'il a régressé pour obtenir une satisfaction. Ces difficultés peuvent être causées par la naissance d'un frère ou d'une sœur, par le fait que la mère quitte la maison pour travailler, par la mort d'un parent qu'il aimait ou par le déménagement dans une nouvelle maison. Le traitement consiste à aider l'enfant à faire face à l'événement traumatisant.

Onychophagie

L'onychophagie indique une grande tension d'esprit. Si les parents s'y opposent d'une façon trop rigide, le traumatisme risque de créer un conflit parents-enfant. Une onychophagie grave peut avoir pour but de mortifier et d'ennuyer les parents. De plus, l'enfant en s'infligeant une blessure se punit lui-même de son hostilité à l'égard de ses parents. Il faut insister sur l'avantage d'avoir de beaux ongles plutôt que de rendre l'enfant honteux de son habitude. Il faut accroître sa confiance en lui-même et augmenter le sentiment de sécurité qu'il éprouve au sein du foyer.

Il se peut que l'enfant imite tout simplement un de ses parents qui a cette habitude. Celui-ci semble accepter ce comportement pour lui-même, sans le tolérer chez l'enfant.

Anxiété et peur

Tous les enfants doivent développer certains sentiments de peur devant les dangers qu'ils rencontrent, et cette peur s'avère salutaire, puisqu'elle éloigne l'enfant des dangers réels.

La peur de l'obscurité constitue l'une des frayeurs les plus courantes de l'enfance, et elle est due au fait que l'enfant se sent seul et abandonné dans le noir. Pour lui, la nuit peut être peuplée de personnages imaginaires dangereux. Les parents doivent le rassurer et lui affirmer qu'eux ne craignent pas l'obscurité.

Une anxiété paralysante remplace la peur quand par une déformation inconsciente de la réalité, la situation réelle se confond avec un conflit inconscient ou une expérience antérieure très angoissante. D'habitude, la signification exacte de l'expérience antérieure a été refoulée.

L'anxiété persiste si l'enfant donne une signification symbolique à ce qu'il craint, et il faut faire alors appel à un spécialiste.

Il ne faut pas exposer indûment les enfants à des situations anxiogènes. Quelles que soient les causes de la frayeur, ils sont mieux armés contre cette dernière lorsque des liens solides les unissent à leurs parents et que ceux-ci les encouragent à exprimer leur frayeur.

Phobie scolaire

Il s'agit là d'un symptôme et non d'une maladie. L'enfant refuse d'aller à l'école et préfère rester à la maison. Le problème se manifeste par des plaintes somatiques, la peur du professeur ou des autres enfants et l'anxiété devant toute situation qui se produit à l'école. En fait, ces enfants ont peur de quitter leurs parents, et ceux-ci craignent également la séparation. Le centre du problème est donc une interdépendance exagérée, surtout dans le duo mère-enfant.

La thérapie consiste à renvoyer l'enfant immédiatement à l'école, en lui signifiant qu'il n'a pas le choix. Si on n'y parvient pas, la responsabilité des parents est tout autant engagée que celle de l'enfant. Par la suite, la thérapie vise à corriger les problèmes sous-jacents dans les relations familiales, afin de prévenir les récurrences. S'il se produit d'autres manifestations, et si l'enfant semble psychiquement malade, il faut le référer à un psychiatre ou à un psychologue.

La phobie de l'école constitue souvent un « appel à l'aide » de la part de l'enfant. La coopération des différents professionnels qui peuvent l'aider, tels l'infirmière scolaire, le professeur, le directeur de l'école, le conseiller ou le travailleur social, le pédiatre et le psychologue ou le psychiatre constitue un élément essentiel du traitement. Il ne faut pas oublier d'inclure les parents dans la planification du traitement.

Figure 22-10. Des enfants qui font l'école buissonnière peuvent se livrer à des activités extrêmement dangereuses. (H. Armstrong Roberts.)

Troubles du comportement

Agressivité, toxicomanie

Étiologie, types, traitement et pronostic. L'enfant que les parents et les enseignants appellent un enfant-problème, essaie constamment de résoudre un problème et ne cherche pas à en constituer un. Les conduites anormales ne sont pas l'apanage d'une classe sociale particulière. D'habitude, elles se produisent parce que les besoins affectifs fondamentaux de l'enfant n'ont pas été satisfaits. Les moyens de solution de l'enfant demeurent grossiers et sa conception du problème peut être fausse. De tels enfants peuvent voler, faire l'école buissonnière, brutaliser les plus petits, raconter des histoires douteuses ou pratiquer des jeux sexuels.

Au cours des dernières années, ces enfants ont trouvé une certaine satisfaction à inspirer les vapeurs de colle. Sous l'influence de ces vapeurs, certains commettent des délits. Des recherches récentes tendent à démontrer que le fait de renifler de la colle constitue un danger d'altération des chromosomes et peut augmenter le danger de leucémie pour ces enfants. Ceux qui inhalent les gaz contenus dans les différents produits à vaporiser que l'on trouve dans le commerce risquent que le fluorocarbone concentré agisse sur le muscle cardiaque et cause de la fibrillation; la mort peut également survenir par le gel rapide des voies respiratoires sous l'action de ces substances délétères. Ces enfants qui ont appris les joies de l'intoxication peuvent avoir recours à l'alcool, aux narcotiques ou à d'autres drogues s'ils ne sont pas traités avant l'adolescence. L'enfant dirige quelquefois son agressivité contre ceux qu'il rend responsables de ses problèmes.

Pour aborder l'enfant, il importe que le psychiatre gagne sa confiance. Il faut éviter soigneusement toute attitude de reproche et l'encourager à raconter son histoire personnelle. Il faut que le traitement touche tous les aspects de la vie de l'enfant. Il nécessite la collaboration de toute l'équipe, les parents, le médecin, le professeur, le conseiller spirituel, le chef scout, la travailleuse sociale et l'infirmière. Il faut que l'enfant participe à l'élaboration du plan thérapeutique. On oriente d'habitude le traitement vers l'assainissement des relations parents-enfant et vers la neutralisation des sentiments d'infériorité de ce dernier.

Les perspectives sont généralement bonnes, si on donne à ces enfants l'aide compréhensive dont ils ont besoin.

Troubles du langage

Étiologie et incidence. Des causes nombreuses et complexes peuvent provoquer des troubles de langage. La fréquence des défectuosités de la parole est maximale entre quatre et onze ans. Les garçons sont plus souvent atteints que les filles. Tout problème de communication au cours de l'enfance risque de dégénérer en troubles permanents du langage ou du comportement.

Types, diagnostic et traitement. Il y a trois types de troubles de la parole: des troubles fonctionnels comme le bégaiement, des anomalies dues à des malformations anatomiques, comme la division palatine et la fissure labiale, et des anomalies dues à des lésions du système nerveux central, comme la paralysie cérébrale. Il faut considérer l'enfant dans son ensemble pour faire le diagnostic et prescrire le traitement. Celui-ci dépend du problème qui est à l'origine du trouble de la parole.

Bégaiement

Le bégaiement constitue le trouble fonctionnel du langage le plus courant. Il affecte plus souvent les garçons, les enfants de famille nombreuse et les gauchers. Ce problème de la parole est connu depuis l'antiquité et touche toutes les races. L'enfant est incapable de parler librement à cause de l'action incoordonnée et spasmodique des muscles de la phonation. On s'interroge sur la cause et plusieurs hypothèses sont à vérifier. Certains recherchent une cause génétique ou physique, d'autres tentent de retrouver une origine psychologique alors que plusieurs professionnels actuels pensent que le bégaiement s'installe à la suite d'un conditionnement involontaire. En effet, la plupart des enfant normaux traversent une période de bégaiement sporadique entre 2 et 4 ans et la façon dont les adultes se comportent à ce moment déterminerait la persistance ou la disparition du bégaiement. Certains experts estiment que la réaction de l'enfant peut être due à une contrainte qu'on veut imposer à sa nature, par exemple, en voulant transformer un enfant « gaucher » en « droitier ». Avant d'établir le traitement, il faut évaluer l'état physique, intellectuel et psychique de l'enfant et déterminer si le bégaiement est primaire ou secondaire.

Par le traitement, on cherche à réduire l'anxiété réactionnelle de l'enfant et à traiter tout autre problème découvert dans l'évaluation de santé. Si le bégaiement est primaire, le traitement porte sur les parents et le milieu dans lequel évolue l'enfant. Si le bégaiement est de type secondaire, accompagné de symptômes compensateurs, le traitement s'adresse alors au bègue lui-même. Il faut lui faire connaître et comprendre la nature de son affection. Les services d'une orthophoniste sont habituellement requis, plus rarement ceux d'un psychiatre.

Affections psychosomatiques

Étiologie. Une affection psychosomatique est un trouble physique qui a une origine psychologique. Les éléments organiques et psychiques s'imbriquent et le degré de la perturbation et la localisation du problème varient pour chaque enfant. Pour les enfants d'âge scolaire, plusieurs affections psychosomatiques sont liées au tractus gastro-intestinal, comme l'anorexie, la boulimie, la constipation, la colite ulcéreuse et la douleur abdominale. On peut également classer l'énurésie et l'asthme dans les affections psychosomatiques pédiatriques. Le diagnostic et le traitement reposent sur la responsabilité conjointe du pédiatre et du psychiatre.

Anorexie mentale

Cette affection est caractérisée par l'effort impitoyable que s'impose le sujet en refusant de s'alimenter et ne survient qu'en présence d'un trouble affectif profond. Il y a souvent un conflit intense entre la mère et la fille. Des idées fausses concernant la conception et la grossesse marquent souvent l'origine de toutes les idées fantastiques de l'enfant à propos de la sexualité. Au fur et à mesure que le jeûne se poursuit, l'appétit disparaît et des vomissements provoqués amènent une rapide perte de poids et des changements corporels dus à un manque d'aliments. Les symptômes attirent sur le malade l'attention de la famille qui lui manifestera une plus grande sympathie.

Le traitement consiste à rétablir l'équilibre électrolytique et à élargir le régime. L'hospitalisation s'avère souvent nécessaire. Il faut recourir à un psychiatre.

L'anorexie mentale est une affection chronique et le pronostic final demeure incertain, même lorsque le traitement médical et psychiatrique est adéquat.

Boulimie

On pense habituellement que la boulimie qui entraîne une obésité extrême est due, chez l'enfant, à un besoin d'amour qu'il confond avec la nourriture. Elle peut être due, cependant, à son désir de devenir grand et fort ou à d'autres facteurs affectifs. Le traitement s'avère généralement difficile. Bien souvent, les services conjoints d'un médecin et d'un psychiatre sont requis pour freiner les désirs alimentaires de l'enfant.

Constipation

Beaucoup de cas de constipation chez les enfants existent uniquement dans l'esprit des parents. Ils estiment que leur enfant est constipé parce qu'il ne va pas à la selle aussi souvent qu'ils le voudraient. Toutefois, il y a de vraies constipations qui peuvent provenir de facteurs affectifs.

Il y a deux causes principales à ce genre de constipation. La première se manifeste chez des enfants qui ont une aversion pour toute forme de saleté, particulièrement les excréments. Ces enfants, en période préscolaire ou au cours de la deuxième année, au moment où ils ne contrôlaient pas encore tout à fait les fonctions anale et vésicale, craignaient que leurs parents les punissent, même s'ils allaient à la selle à l'endroit et au moment voulus et de là, ont commencé à craindre toute défécation. Cette crainte précoce les a conditionnés à éprouver de l'anxiété au sujet de leurs selles, même lorsqu'ils les contrôlaient complètement. Ils ont par la suite entravé les mouvements normaux des intestins. Le traitement habituel pour ce genre de constipation consiste à ajouter une petite quantité d'aliments riches en résidus au régime et à favoriser les jeux dans lesquels l'enfant se salit. Une thérapie plus complète par le jeu donne d'excellents résultats. Aux enfants plus âgés, on peut expliquer l'importance des évacuations régulières.

L'autre type de constipation est dû au fait que l'on a exigé trop tôt que l'enfant devienne propre ce qui entraîne chez lui l'impression que l'excrétion constitue un acte d'hostilité envers ses parents. Cet enfant a besoin d'une aide psychiatrique pour découvrir et supprimer la crainte de ses propres réactions affectives.

Colite ulcéreuse chronique

Étiologie et incidence. La colite ulcéreuse consiste en une inflammation chronique de la muqueuse du gros intestin. Au cours des crises, la membrane devient hyperhémiée: elle saigne aisément, s'ulcère et se couvre parfois de pseudo-polypes; ceux-ci risquent éventuellement de se transformer en tumeurs malignes. Différentes théories tentent d'expliquer la maladie; on parle d'allergie, d'infection ou de somatisation. Plus d'une personne par famille peut être atteinte. L'enfant malade est habituellement dépendant, craintif, passif et semble attaché à sa mère d'une manière très ambivalente. Cette ambivalence se retrouve parfois aussi chez la mère qui peut rejeter l'enfant tout en lui consacrant tout son temps.

La pathologie peut débuter à l'âge préscolaire, mais la plus grande incidence se situe à la fin de l'âge scolaire.

Physio-pathologie et manifestations cliniques.
La colite ulcéreuse peut atteindre n'importe quelle portion du côlon, quoique les lésions débutent ordinairement au rectum et s'étendent graduellement. Tout le côlon peut être touché et dans quelques cas, le caecum et quelques centimètres d'iléon sont atteints. L'inflammation diffuse et superficielle rend la muqueuse rouge, friable et saignotante. Les abcès cryptiques très fréquents peuvent être découverts à la biopsie intestinale.

Le début peut être aigu ou insidieux. Le symptôme le plus important consiste en l'émission fréquente de petites selles contenant du mucus, du pus et du sang, parfois sous forme de diarrhée. En général, l'enfant ne présente pas de fièvre, de douleur abdominale ou de vomissement, mais ces symptômes peuvent se produire au cours de l'exacerbation de la maladie. La crise aiguë de colite se produit souvent la nuit et consiste en une diarrhée sanglante abondante, accompagnée de crampes abdominales, qui taxe lourdement la vitalité de l'enfant. Une hémorragie intestinale ou un prolapsus rectal constitue une complication occasionnelle. L'amaigrissement, l'anémie, des œdèmes de carence et des déficiences vitaminiques peuvent assombrir le pronostic. Il est à noter que certains enfants présentent des symptômes extra-intestinaux, tels arthrite, ictère, uvéite, thrombophlébite et retard staturo-pondéral.

Diagnostic et traitement.
Le diagnostic repose sur le tableau clinique, sur l'impossibilité de mettre en évidence un agent étiologique spécifique, sur la sigmoïdoscopie et la biopsie rectale. Dans les formes très avancées, le côlon prend l'aspect dit en « tuyau de plomb ».

Il est important de distinguer la colite ulcéreuse d'une autre pathologie qui lui ressemble: la *maladie de Crohn* ou entérite régionale granulomateuse. Les deux maladies donnent des symptômes similaires, sont d'étiologie indéterminée et ont une évolution chronique, mais leur physiopathologie et leur traitement diffèrent. Dans la maladie de Crohn, l'inflammation est profonde et régionalisée. L'iléon distal est le plus souvent atteint. La muqueuse est infiltrée de lymphocytes, de plasmocytes et de cellules géantes. Les fistules sont fréquentes. La fièvre et la douleur abdominale prédominent souvent sur la diarrhée.

On ne connaît pas de traitement spécifique pour la colite ulcéreuse. On donne normalement un régime léger, atoxique et sans résidus. Il faut fournir des vitamines et des sels minéraux supplémentaires. Des transfusions sanguines permettent de contrôler l'anémie. L'emploi de corticostéroïdes par voie rectale ou systémique amène souvent une amélioration passagère. L'usage à long terme de salazosulfapyridine réduit les crises aiguës de colite et permet à beaucoup de patients de vivre une existence normale. La plupart des effets secondaires peuvent être évités quand le comprimé est enrobé. Si le côlon se perfore ou si les crises se rapprochent, une colectomie est envisagée. Si la colectomie est totale, une iléostomie permet au patient de survivre, souvent sans ennuis médicaux sérieux par la suite. De toute façon, après une dizaine d'années d'évolution, le risque de cancérisation devient assez élevé pour que la colectomie soit effectuée de façon élective.

C'est en mettant en œuvre un ensemble cohérent de traitements à la fois pédiatriques et psychiatriques que l'on observe les résultats les plus encourageants. Il faut soulager les tensions qu'éprouve l'enfant du point de vue affectif et familial. À cette fin, les parents et l'enfant peuvent bénéficier d'une psychothérapie.

Évolution et pronostic.
L'évolution est chronique, coupée d'épisodes transitoires d'amélioration et d'aggravation. La maladie peut durer des années et la mort est habituellement due à l'épuisement lorsqu'aucune chirurgie n'a été effectuée.

Soins.
Il faut se rappeler qu'après que l'enfant a atteint le contrôle de ses sphincters, toute maladie qui suppose une remise en question de cette étape devient très traumatisante. Des soins infirmiers appropriés peuvent diminuer l'impact de la maladie sur le psychisme de l'enfant.

Si le malade est très maigre, il faut surveiller l'apparition des points de pression et chercher à protéger les proéminences osseuses. Il faut le garder au chaud et au sec. L'alimentation constitue souvent un problème, car le malade prend très souvent la nourriture en horreur. L'infirmière doit surveiller attentivement l'apparition des effets secondaires ou néfastes des médicaments.

La rédaction du dossier doit comprendre les observations sur le nombre, la quantité et la nature des selles. Un dosage strict des ingesta et des excréta s'impose. Il est important d'écouter l'enfant qui connaît son état et peut indiquer les aliments et les situations qui augmentent la fréquence et la fluidité des selles. L'infirmière doit surveiller l'apparition des complications, telles la distension abdominale, les nausées et vomissements ainsi que l'hémorragie.

Le repos physique et émotif s'avère essentiel; il faut faciliter le contact avec les autres malades et les membres de l'équipe doivent être chaleureux et sincères dans leurs relations avec l'enfant.

Certains acceptent leur maladie de façon stoïque et participent plus ou moins activement au traitement; l'infirmière doit évaluer la situation et prévoir avec les parents les problèmes qui risquent de se présenter à la maison. On doit appuyer sur l'importance des besoins intestinaux de l'enfant, de ses médicaments, de sa réaction à la maladie et des observations qui permettent de se rendre compte qu'il fait une rechute.

Si l'adolescent doit subir une iléostomie, il faut lui fournir une préparation psychologique extensive et un support émotif stable.

Douleur abdominale

La douleur abdominale récurrente, sans cause organique, est un symptôme fréquent pour les enfants d'âge scolaire. Elle survient à n'importe quel moment de la journée, sans relation avec les repas ou les défécations. Le degré de la douleur varie d'une gêne légère à une douleur grave. Une appendicectomie d'exploration ou une laparotomie ne règle pas les problèmes de l'enfant.

En général, ces enfants semblent avoir un comportement plus mûr, plus agréable et plus responsable que leurs compagnons. Leurs parents peuvent être exigeants pour eux-mêmes et pour les enfants et craindre que ceux-ci ne se développent pas au rythme normal. L'enfant, incapable d'apaiser l'anxiété de ses parents, cherche à être dirigé et rassuré et ne se développe pas aussi bien que les autres enfants de son âge. Ce comportement suffit à augmenter l'anxiété des parents à son sujet. Les services d'un médecin et d'un psychiatre peuvent devenir nécessaires.

Certains enfants qui se plaignent souvent de douleurs abdominales peuvent être porteurs d'un ulcère gastrique ou duodénal. Ils vivent habituellement dans des familles à problèmes. Leur âge se situe entre sept et neuf ans, mais ceci est très variable et l'ulcère peut apparaître à n'importe quel âge, même chez le nourrisson. Ces enfants sont perfectionnistes, désirent plaire à tout prix, sont très sensibles aux critiques, présentent une intelligence au-dessus de la normale et sont très énergiques. **La** douleur siège autour de l'ombilic ou de la

région épigastrique et est accompagnée de nausées et de vomissements.

Le diagnostic est fait selon les méthodes habituelles. Le traitement médical demeure le plus efficace; l'hémorragie et la perforation sont les uniques indications chirurgicales.

Énurésie

Cette expression signifie que les enfants mouillent leur lit au delà de l'âge de 4 ou 5 ans. Bien que ces enfants soient d'habitude normaux, il faut les soumettre à un examen physique pour éliminer des maladies comme le diabète, la pyélite ou l'épilepsie nocturne et à un examen psychologique pour éliminer un éventuel problème psychiatrique.

La majorité des enfants énurétiques ne présentent aucune pathologie anatomique, psychologique ou psychiatrique. Une énurésie passagère peut être due à un conflit psychologique, tel la jalousie envers un jeune bébé, le ressentiment envers les parents ou l'hospitalisation. L'énurésie peut aussi être un symptôme mineur d'un problème psychiatrique grave ou d'une maladie physique sérieuse. Toutefois, pour 75% des enfants, l'énurésie est idiopathique et l'histoire familiale poussée en révèle d'autres cas, souvent le père de l'enfant qui n'en avait jamais parlé auparavant.

Le traitement consiste à combattre la cause physique, psychologique ou psychiatrique lorsqu'elle existe. Dans les autres cas, le traitement peut présenter plusieurs facettes, mais inclut toujours un support émotif à l'enfant et à ses parents et la plus grande participation possible de l'enfant à son traitement. Pour certains enfants, un entraînement visant à augmenter la capacité vésicale peut réussir. Pour d'autres l'imipramine administrée pendant plusieurs mois donne de bons résultats. Le taux de succès varie de 30 à 60% et les effets secondaires du médicament peuvent être graves. Le conditionnement par appareil électrique semble être le traitement le plus efficace, son taux de succès atteint 80 à 90%, parfois dès la première session, quelquefois lors d'une deuxième série d'essais. On n'a pas trouvé de problème psychologique lié à ce traitement pour les enfants de plus de 7 ans et une amélioration de la personnalité et du rendement scolaire est flagrante quand l'énurésie est corrigée. Si on utilise ces appareils, il faut examiner soigneusement la peau de l'enfant chaque jour.

Il ne faut jamais ridiculiser un enfant énurétique ni le punir ou le blâmer pour son problème. Il importe de soutenir ces enfants dans leur estime de soi et leur apprendre à avoir une vision positive d'eux-mêmes.

Thérapie

Les parents peuvent commettre des erreurs sans que l'enfant en soit trop perturbé, alors que trop d'erreurs affectent son comportement. Les parents, trop impliqués dans la situation pour vraiment comprendre ce qui se passe peuvent être agacés par le comportement de l'enfant, mais sans prendre conscience du problème de base.

Parfois, le comportement d'un enfant est déroutant, même s'il s'agit seulement d'une manifestation de sa croissance. Ces parents ont uniquement besoin d'une explication sur le développement et la croissance normale d'un enfant. En général, aucune thérapie ne s'avère nécessaire.

Une aide professionnelle peut devenir utile cependant, si la cause du problème semble profonde et non comprise par les parents. Cette aide peut être requise si l'enfant a peur de quitter son niveau actuel de développement pour s'acheminer vers une plus grande maturité; s'il ne grandit et ne se développe pas suivant les normes habituelles; s'il est trop soumis ou trop agressif, ou s'il n'apprend pas en fonction de ses capacités; s'il ne peut vaincre ses frustrations, se comporter socialement comme devrait le faire un enfant de son âge ou enfin, s'il a des habitudes de comportement socialement inacceptables.

Sources et types. Une aide extérieure peut venir du médecin de famille, du pédiatre, d'un groupe de parents, d'enseignants ou de conseillers.

Les parents hésitent souvent à demander de l'aide pour des enfants qui ont des perturbations affectives. Ils ont l'impression de pouvoir résoudre eux-mêmes tous les problèmes qui se présentent. Le psychiatre doit demander un tableau détaillé du développement et des problèmes des parents aussi bien que de l'enfant. Il faudrait qu'il évalue les relations entre les parents et les autres membres de la famille.

Le psychiatre peut trouver que le comportement est typiquement celui d'un enfant de cet âge et il aidera les parents à résoudre les problèmes particuliers; il peut penser qu'il s'agit d'un trouble qui concerne surtout les parents et recommander un changement de milieu pour l'enfant et une aide sûre pour les parents; ou bien, il peut juger que c'est essentiellement le problème de l'enfant et demander à le voir fréquemment pour l'aider à comprendre son problème et découvrir d'autres moyens de le résoudre.

Une thérapie prolongée peut s'avérer nécessaire. Par moments, au cours d'une telle thérapie, le comportement de l'enfant peut empirer, parce qu'il extériorise les impulsions qu'il contrôlait auparavant. Les parents ont besoin de l'aide du psychiatre pour comprendre ce qui se passe dans les relations parents-enfant et pour savoir comment faire face au comportement de l'enfant. Le psychiatre ne divulgue aucun des renseignements de l'enfant sans sa permission. Ceci est difficile à comprendre pour les parents, mais il est essentiel qu'ils acceptent cet élément de la situation. En plus de la thérapie de l'enfant, il se peut que les parents soient aussi impliqués dans la psychothérapie. La thérapie familiale, réunissant l'enfant et ses parents, devient une expérience éducative et thérapeutique de plus en plus courante.

L'enfant perturbé affectivement peut être placé dans un foyer nourricier, un centre de jour ou un internat, dans un centre de traitement résidentiel structuré ou dans un hôpital psychiatrique. Ces différents types d'institutions procurent aux enfants souffrant de problèmes affectifs variés un moyen de recevoir la thérapie en dehors de leur milieu familial.

Rôle de l'infirmière. L'infirmière qui s'occupe d'enfants ayant des affections psychosomatiques ou des troubles affectifs doit être capable d'observer soigneusement leur comportement et de noter ce qu'elle entend, ressent et voit. Ces observations aident ceux qui traitent l'enfant, et sont même profitables aux infirmières spécialisées dans le soin de ces enfants.

Une coopération étroite avec le thérapeute s'avère essentielle. Celui-ci peut aider les infirmières à comprendre la signification du comportement qu'elles observent et les aider à procurer le genre de soins infirmiers que les enfants exigent. Les thérapeutes s'intéressent aux relations de l'enfant avec ses parents, ses semblables et les autres adultes. Ils aiment aussi connaître sa capacité d'adaptation à l'hôpital, à l'école et aux activités récréatives.

Des infirmières spécialisées en psychiatrie infantile sont nécessaires pour améliorer le soin des enfants affectés psychiquement.

Des réunions d'équipe s'imposent; elles incluent les médecins, les travailleuses sociales, les enseignants, les infirmières, les aides et le personnel auxiliaire qui a des contacts avec les enfants. Ces réunions aident à comprendre le soin de l'enfant, ainsi que la cause de son affection. De telles conférences peuvent aussi aider l'infirmière à comprendre sa propre personnalité et à améliorer par conséquent ses relations avec les malades dont elle a la responsabilité.

RÉFÉRENCES

Livres et documents officiels

Ames Company: *Comment soigner l'enfant atteint de diabète. M. Hypo est mon ami.* Rexdale, Ontario.

Bakwin, H. et Bakwin, R. M.: *Behavior Disorders in Children.* 4e éd. Philadelphie, W. B. Saunders Company, 1972.

Benoliel, J. Q.: Social Consequences of Diabetes Mellitus in Adolescence; in *Seventh Nursing Research Conference, Atlanta, Georgia, March 10-12, 1971.* New York, American Nurses' Association, 1971, pp. 53-72.

Debuskey, M. (édit.): *The Chronically Ill Child and His Family.* Springfield, Ill., Charles C Thomas, 1970.

Fischer, A. E. et Horstmann, D. L.: *A Handbook for the Young Diabetic.* 4e éd. New York, Intercontinental Medical Book Corp., 1972.

Foster, G. W. et autres: *Child Care Work with Emotionally Disturbed Children.* Pittsburgh, University of Pittsburgh Press, 1972.

Kanner, L.: *Child Psychiatry.* 4e éd. Springfield, Ill., Charles C Thomas, 1972.

Koos, W. T. et Miller, M. H.: *Intracranial Tumors of Infants and Children.* Saint-Louis, C. V. Mosby Company, 1971.

Marble, A. et autres: *Joslin's Diabetes Mellitus.* 11e éd. Philadelphie, Lea & Febiger, 1971.

Matson, D. D.: *Neurosurgery of Infancy and Childhood.* 2e éd. Springfield, Ill, Charles C Thomas, 1969.

Ministère de la Santé nationale et du Bien-être social: *Manuel d'hygiène dentaire.* Service d'hygiène dentaire, Gouvernement du Canada.

Ministère de la Santé nationale et du Bien-être social: *Il mouille son lit.* Division de l'hygiène mentale, série: « Formation de l'enfant », Gouvernement du Canada.

Noland, R. L. (édit.): *Counseling Parents of the Ill and the Handicapped.* Springfield, Ill., Charles C Thomas, 1971.

Robinson, C. H. et Lawler, M. R.: *Normal and Therapeutic Nutrition.* 14e éd. New York, Macmillan Company, 1972.

Sheehan, J. G. (édit.): *Stuttering: Research and Therapy.* New York, Harper & Row, 1970.

Sutow, W. W., Vietti, T. et Fernbach, D. J. (édit.): *Clinical Pediatric Oncology.* Saint-Louis, C. V. Mosby Company, 1972.

The Commission on Emotional and Learning Disorders in Children: *One Million Children: A National Study of Canadian Children with Emotional and Learning Disorders.* Toronto, Canada, The Commission of Emotional and Learning Disorders in Children, 1970.

Traisman, H. S.: *Management of Juvenile Diabetes Mellitus.* 2e éd. Saint-Louis, C. V. Mosby Company, 1971.

Varga, C.: *Handbook of Pediatric Medical Emergencies.* 5e éd. Saint-Louis, C. V. Mosby Company, 1972.

Waechter, E. H.: Death Anxiety in Children with Fatal Illness; dans *Fifth Nursing Research Conference, New Orleans, La., March 3-5, 1969.* New Work, American Nurses' Association, 1971, pp. 83-101.

Articles

La cardiopathie rhumatismale: aspects nouveaux. *Chronique O. M. S.*, 24:25, 1, 1970.

Alarcia, J. et Pinard, G.: Le bégaiement. *Union méd. du Canada*, 104:897, 6, 1975. ,

Anonsen, D. C.: L'enfant hyperactif. *Inf. Can.*, 17:18, 5, 1975.

Badoual, P.: Diabète sucré. *Soins*, XIV:437, 10, 1969.

Bierbauer, E.: Tips for Parents of a Neurologically Handicapped Child. *Am. J. Nursing*, 72:1872, octobre 1972.

Blanckaert, D. et autres: La polyarthrite rhumatoïde. *La revue de pédiatrie*, 10:123, 3, 1974.

Boone, J. et autres: Juvenile Rheumatoid Arthritis. *Ped. Clin. N. Amer.*, 21:885, 4, 1974.

Bontoux, D.: Surveillance par l'infirmière du traitement des rhumatismes inflammatoires. *Rev. Inf. et ass. Soc.*, 18:701, 7, 1968.

Brosseau, D.: L'enseignement au diabétique. *Inf. Can.*, 15:19, 9, 1973.

Bruce, C. B.: Le bégaiement. *Inf. Can.*, 15:33, 2, 1973.

Bundock, G.: Un rendez-vous avec « l'EMI scanner ». *Inf. Can.*, 17:19, 10, 1975.

Calvo, G.: Chorée de Sydenham. *Rev. inf. et ass. soc.*, 19:495, 5, 1969.

Carbonell, S.: Les troubles de la parole et du langage chez l'enfant. *La revue de pédiatrie*, 9:235, 5, 1973.

Choulot, J. J.: Le rhumatisme articulaire aigu. *Soins*, 20:5, 1, 1975.

Collier, B. N. et Etzwiler, D. D.: Comparative Study of Diabetes Knowledge Among Juvenile Diabetics and Their Parents. *Diabetes*, 20:51, janvier 1971.

Courrèges, J. P.: Rhumatisme articulaire aigu. *Soins*, 18:5, 9, 1973.

Courtecuisse, V. et Gutton, Ph.: Colites ulcéreuses idiopathiques de l'enfant. *La Revue du Praticien*, XX:4851, novembre 1970.

Dennison, D. et Fenimore, J. A.: A Heart-Sound Screening Program for Elementary Children. *J. School Health*, 41:349, septembre 1971.

Denson, R.: Le traitement contemporain de l'énurésie. *Union méd. du Canada*, 102:362, 2, 1973.

Dodge, W. F. et autres: Noctural Enuresis in 6 to 10-Year-Old Children. *Am. J. Dis. Child*, 120:32, juillet 1970.

Dugas, M. et autres: Le bégaiement. *La revue de pédiatrie*, 9:307, 6, 1973.

Ehrlich, R.: Diabetes Mellitus in Childhood. *Ped. Clin. N. Amer.*, 21:871, 4, 1974.

Feeney, R.: Preventing Rheumatic Fever in School Children. *Am. J. Nursing*, 73:265, février 1973.

Feingold, B.: Hyperkinesis and Learning Disabilities Linked to Artificial Food Flavors and Colors. *Am. J. Nursing*, 75:797, 5, 1975.

Forman, B. et autres: Management of Juvenile Diabetes Mellitus. *Pediatrics*, 53:257, 2, 1974.

Friez, P.: Conduite à tenir dans les troubles de la dentition et les altérations de la denture chez l'enfant. *La revue de l'inf.*, 23:5, 1, 1973 (I), 23:97, 2, 1973 (II).

Graid, R. et Homer, D.: Approaches to Inflammatory Bowel Disease in Childhood and Adolescence. *Ped. Clin. N. Amer.*, 22:835, 4, 1975.

Guthrie, D.: Diabetic Children: special needs, diet, drugs and difficulties. *Nursing '73*, 3:10, 3, 1973.

Guthrie, D. et Guthrie, R.: Juvenile Diabetes Mellitus. *Nurs. Clin. N. Amer.*, 8:587, 4, 1973.

Job, J. C.: Précocités et retards pubertaires. *La médecine infantile*, 74:629, 5, 1967.

Kennell, J. H. et autres: What Parents of Rheumatic Fever Patients Don't Understand About the Disease and Its Prophylactic Management. *Pediatrics*, 43:160, février 1969.

Kryk, H. et autres: Revue des tumeurs cérébrales. *Inf. Can.*, 17:23, 10, 1975.

Lafontaine, R.: Les dysfonctions cérébrales mineures chez l'enfant. *Le méd. du Québec*, 10:40, 11, 1975.

Lestradet, H.: Particularités du diabète chez l'enfant. *Rev. de l'inf. et ass. soc.*, 19:271, 3, 1969.

Mc Anarney, E. et autres: Psychological Problems of children with Chronic Juvenile Arthritis. *Pediatrics*, 53:523, 4, 1974.

Mc Farlane, J.: Children with Diabetes. *Am. J. Nursing*, 73:1360, 8, 1973.

McKendry, J. et Stewart, D.: Enuresis. *Ped. Clin. N. Amer.*, 21:1019, 4, 1974.

Mornet, P.: La maladie de Crohn. *La revue de l'inf.*, 23:917, 10, 1973.

Pendleton, T. et Grossman, B.: Rehabilitating Children with Inflammatory Joint Disease. *Am. J. Nursing*, 74:2223, 12, 1974.

Rossi, E.: Considérations cliniques sur les myopathies de l'enfant. *Union méd. du Can.*, 96:1351, novembre 1967.

Rossier, C.: Lecture et dyslexie. *La médecine infantile*, 75:47, 1, 1968.

Roy, J. Y., Colard, R. et Tétrault, L.: Aspects psychologiques de l'énurésie: enquête chez 36 jeunes sourds-muets. *Laval médical*, 42:193, février 1971.

Roy, J. Y., Colard, R. et Tétrault, L.: Aspects psycho-pharmacologiques de l'emploi de l'imipramine dans l'énurésie chez 26 sourds-muets. *Union méd. du Can.*, 99:1420, août 1970.

Taft, L.: The Care and Management of the Child with Muscular Dystrophy. *Dev. Med. Child. Neurol.*, 15:510, 8, 1973.

Turpin, J. C. et Dilpech, J.: Les tumeurs cérébrales de l'enfant. *La revue de pédiatrie*, 9:279, 5, 1973.

septième partie

L'ADOLESCENT

23

l'adolescent: croissance, développement, soins

Pour mieux différencier les termes employés dans ce chapitre, définissons les concepts suivants: la *prépuberté* est la période de croissance physique rapide qui accompagne l'apparition des caractères sexuels secondaires; la *puberté* commence avec les phénomènes de la menstruation, pour les filles, et de l'éjaculation du sperme, pour les garçons. Le terme *ménarche* désigne la première menstruation. L'*adolescence* commence avec l'apparition des caractères sexuels secondaires et se termine avec l'achèvement de la croissance somatique et l'atteinte d'une certaine maturité psychologique qui rendent l'individu capable de jouer son rôle dans la société. C'est une période de conflit, de tension, d'angoisse, mais aussi d'actualisation de soi. L'adolescence semble être un phénomène particulier à l'espèce humaine et certains considèrent que cette longue étape du développement, marquée de difficultés et de stress est propre à la culture occidentale.

Vers 10 ou 12 ans, l'enfant entre dans la dernière phase de son évolution avant d'atteindre l'âge adulte. Auparavant, il a appris à faire confiance aux autres sans, pour autant, perdre son autonomie. D'autre part, il a acquis graduellement le sens de l'initiative, et enfin le sens du travail, parce qu'il est capable d'accomplir des tâches bien définies.

Les adolescents ont deux étapes à franchir avant de réaliser pleinement leur personnalité. Celles-ci correspondent à l'acquisition d'un sentiment *d'identité* et ensuite, d'un sentiment *d'intimité*.

L'adolescence se termine graduellement pour faire place à la vie adulte. Dans la civilisation nord-américaine, ce phénomène se situe autour de la vingtième année, ou même plus tard, en raison de certains facteurs économiques et sociaux. Le jeune travailleur ou le jeune étudiant, l'adolescent parent, marié ou célibataire et le jeune qui demeure avec sa famille vivent différemment l'adolescence. Il est à souligner que l'adolescence n'existe pas chez les animaux, et les anthropologues ont démontré que le phénomène peut être très court ou absent dans certaines cultures.

Bien qu'on puisse situer les premières manifestations de la puberté autour de la dixième année, il est difficile de dire à quel moment précis se produit chacun des changements décisifs. De plus, au fur et à mesure que l'adolescent vieillit, les phases importantes de son évolution s'étendent sur une plus longue période. C'est pourquoi nous ne pouvons que décrire les transformations générales s'effectuant au cours de la prépuberté, de la puberté et de l'adolescence.

En somme, l'adolescence est essentiellement la période au cours de laquelle l'individu s'efforce de devenir adulte tout en gardant le désir inconscient de demeurer enfant.

De nombreux adolescents traversent une crise émotive dont on ne peut facilement prévoir l'issue. Une telle crise peut provoquer une régression dans le développement ou retarder la croissance et la maturation. Mais elle peut aussi révéler l'existence de problèmes émotifs jusque là insoupçonnés, et permettre de leur apporter des solutions satisfaisantes.

Durant cette période, les parents doivent se transformer pour s'adapter à leur adolescent et promouvoir son développement. Ils doivent être prêts à le laisser se détacher d'eux tout en l'assurant d'un soutien continu.

APERÇU GÉNÉRAL DU DÉVELOPPEMENT ÉMOTIF ET SOCIAL

La puberté

La puberté dure deux ans environ et forme une sorte de transition entre l'enfance et l'adolescence. Elle constitue le phénomène organique de cette dernière période. L'enfant est alors près d'atteindre sa taille adulte, et le développement de sa personnalité s'accompagne de changements physiques rapides. Cette poussée de croissance a lieu vers l'âge de 10 ans pour les filles, vers l'âge de 12 ans pour les garçons. Alors qu'au cours de leurs premières années d'école, les enfants offraient pour ainsi dire le même aspect physique, on voit maintenant s'accentuer les traits distinctifs qui vont les différencier les uns des autres selon leur sexe, leur taille et leur poids.

Pendant sa puberté, l'enfant subit des changements décisifs qui affectent sa personnalité. Ses facultés d'adaptation se développent progressivement, lui permettant de communiquer avec son entourage et d'aborder ses problèmes familiaux et scolaires avec une assurance accrue. Il s'intéresse aux jeux qui exigent, non seulement une habileté physique, mais aussi un esprit de groupe. L'amour renouvelé qu'il éprouve pour le parent du sexe opposé ne l'empêche nullement d'argumenter aussi bien avec son père qu'avec sa mère. Il est capable d'assumer des responsabilités toujours plus grandes et ses valeurs peuvent se différencier de celles de ses parents parce qu'il est de plus en plus influencé par les média de communication, les amis de son âge et la société en évolution dans laquelle il vit. Ceux-ci peuvent exiger que leur enfant prenne ses responsabilités à la maison, alors que pour lui, ce qui importe davantage, c'est de tenir ses promesses auprès de ses amis ou encore de terminer des projets commencés en groupe.

À première vue, le préadolescent semble pouvoir régler facilement ses problèmes émotifs. Ainsi, on serait porté à croire qu'il réagit sainement, quoique stoïquement, à la mort ou au divorce de ses parents, puisqu'il se plonge rapidement dans d'autres activités. Cependant, le problème peut surgir de nouveau, quelques années plus tard, parce qu'il n'avait pas été assimilé, mais refoulé.

Les parents se rendent vite compte que l'hostilité qui existait entre les garçons et les filles disparaît graduellement. Elle fait place alors à un intérêt évident pour les « rendez-vous », les soirées mixtes – spécialement, s'il s'agit de soirées dansantes – et pour les conversations sans fin sur le sexe opposé. Toutes ces manifestations ne prouvent pas que les enfants aient atteint leur maturité émotive, mais signifient plutôt que les jeunes essaient de sortir de l'enfance pour adopter le comportement des adolescents ou des adultes.

L'enfant se rend compte, toutefois, que ses premières tentatives pour agir comme un adulte sont vouées à l'échec. Il sait qu'il manque de maturité et que la plupart de ses activités sont encore centrées sur l'école, les amis, les jeux et la famille. Malheureusement, beaucoup de parents exigent de lui un intérêt pour le sexe opposé qu'il n'est pas encore prêt à éprouver. Parmi les raisons qui poussent les parents à agir de la sorte, la plus importante est certainement le désir de voir leur enfant avoir du succès auprès des deux sexes, et être bien accepté de son groupe d'amis. En général, de telles pressions sont nocives pour l'enfant.

Somme toute, la puberté demeure une période de calme relatif pour l'enfant et pour les adultes qui l'entourent. Le jeune semble autonome, et ses parents peuvent dialoguer avec lui et essayer de trouver des solutions à ses problèmes. Par ailleurs, dans son milieu social, on s'attend à ce qu'il souscrive aux exigences de son groupe. Les adultes demandent au préadolescent de respecter les règles de leur société.

L'adolescence et la jeunesse (sens de l'identité et sens de l'intimité)

Le passage de l'enfance à l'âge adulte ne se fait pas sans heurts. L'adolescence est une période de tension (stress) aussi bien pour les jeunes que pour leurs parents. L'adolescent doit prendre conscience de la réalité qui l'entoure et modifier son comportement pour être prêt à jouer son rôle d'adulte. Il remet en question tout ce qu'il tenait jusque là pour certain. Ce réveil intellectuel et émotif joint à la croissance rapide de son corps, lui cause une anxiété que les pressions du monde moderne rendent encore plus insupportables.

Les adolescents d'aujourd'hui subissent des influences que les générations précédentes n'ont pas connues. La vitesse à laquelle s'effectuent les changements sociaux, les guerres, la rapidité croissante des moyens de transport et des progrès technologiques engendrent des problèmes inconnus auparavant.

Un adolescent, au moment où il cherche à s'émanciper de sa famille, doit faire face à de nombreuses difficultés dont la plus importante consiste à se trouver un emploi. Les lois sur le travail, en limitant les possibilités d'emploi pour les très jeunes, ont sans doute corrigé des situations déplorables, mais n'en ont pas moins créé de nouveaux problèmes. Les lois sur l'instruction obligatoire deviennent extrêmement difficiles à appliquer en raison du nombre toujours croissant d'adolescents incapables de s'adapter à l'école, tels les retardés mentaux et ceux qui présentent de graves troubles de comportement.

Pour Erikson, le problème crucial de l'adolescence réside dans l'établissement de ce qu'il appelle le « sens de l'identité ». Pour un adolescent moderne, ce phénomène se traduit par ces mots: « Je ne peux parler de mes sentiments ou de mes problèmes parce qu'ils sont encore confus. Mes opinions sur la vie et sur les gens changent constamment parce que je n'ai pas fini de me découvrir moi-même ».

L'adolescent ne cesse de se demander quelle idée les autres se font et se feront de lui. Est-il à l'image de ce que la société attend de lui? C'est là une question qui relie tout le développement d'un individu, depuis la tendre enfance jusqu'à l'âge adulte.

Dans certaines civilisations, les adolescents ont un rôle mieux défini que dans la nôtre. Ils sont soumis à des rites d'initiation qui symbolisent leur entrée dans le monde des adultes. Il en est ainsi, par exemple, dans la

Figure 23-1. L'adolescente se demande qui elle est, et quel sera son rôle dans la société après ses études secondaires. (H. Armstrong Roberts.)

religion des Navajos où l'avènement de la puberté chez les filles est marqué par la cérémonie de la « Voie Sacrée ».

Dans la société nord-américaine, on pourrait donner une signification analogue aux cérémonies de diverses organisations de jeunes, comme la « promesse » scoute, à l'obtention d'un permis de conduire, à la remise des diplômes de fin d'études et à l'acquisition du droit de vote.

Pourtant, malgré toute l'importance qu'on leur accorde, ces cérémonies n'ont pas la même portée que les rites d'initiation: ceux-ci apportent la sécurité, mais aussi l'obligation de faire face aux responsabilités de la vie adulte.

Comme la société n'impose pas de lois rigides ou de tabous pour diriger le comportement des adolescents, ceux-ci les établissent eux-mêmes. Chaque groupe de jeunes adopte ainsi un certain nombre de préjugés, des règles générales de conduite, et même des façons particulières de s'habiller. Ces lois leur procurent un sentiment d'appartenance et d'estime de soi. Malheureusement, de telles limites tendent à exclurent de ces groupes un grand nombre de jeunes qui ont alors beaucoup plus de difficultés à acquérir des sentiments de sécurité et d'identité. De plus, ces règles poussent certains adolescents à adopter des comportements pour lesquels ils ne sont pas prêts, tels que les activités sexuelles ou la consommation de drogues dangereuses, par peur d'être rejetés du groupe.

Le jeune d'aujourd'hui est dominé par un sentiment d'inquiétude parce qu'il est aussi peu certain de ce qu'il est que de ce qu'il deviendra. L'éventail de possibilités qui s'offrent à lui, loin de le rassurer, ne réussit qu'à l'embrouiller davantage. De plus, son comportement est marqué par l'ambivalence, ce qui rend plus difficiles l'établissement de relations avec les adultes.

L'établissement du sens de l'identité dépend en grande partie du développement de la personnalité au cours de l'enfance. Si ce développement n'a pas été adéquat, il faut, pendant la puberté et l'adolescence, guider le jeune et le faire aider par des adultes responsables, en qui il a confiance.

L'adolescent qui ne se sent pas capable d'affronter la vie et qui a l'impression de se « disperser », peut devenir délinquant, névrotique ou psychotique. C'est le résultat de ce qu'on appelle la « diffusion des rôles ».

Bien qu'un sentiment d'identité soit difficile à acquérir, le jeune ne peut éviter les troubles émotifs, s'il ne réussit pas à l'atteindre. Il lui faut découvrir un sens à sa propre vie et apprendre à se découvrir et à s'accepter.

Jamais auparavant, l'adolescent n'avait eu à affronter les difficultés auxquelles il fait face aujourd'hui. Il doit essayer de se sauver lui-même, alors qu'il vit dans un monde marqué par l'instabilité des valeurs auxquelles on lui demande de croire, un monde sans cesse menacé de destruction.

À la fin de cette période, alors que l'adolescent devient un jeune adulte, il doit acquérir un « sens de l'intimité », vis-à-vis de lui-même d'abord, puis vis-à-vis des autres. Tant qu'il ne sera pas sûr de lui, il demeurera incapable d'établir les liens profonds d'amitié ou d'amour qui caractérisent le sentiment d'intimité.

Les relations entre les garçons et les filles commencent à s'établir au moment de la puberté, mais elles manquent alors d'intimité; elles consistent surtout à échanger des opinions sur des sujets d'intérêt commun. Pendant la dernière phase de l'adolescence, ces relations ont un autre but. Elles aident les jeunes à découvrir leur identité sexuelle et créent des liens plus étroits entre eux. Certains adolescents ont besoin d'expérimenter leur rôle sexuel, pas nécessairement physiquement, avant de pouvoir établir des liens hétérosexuels significatifs. Si un tel individu se lance dans un mariage prématuré, il va au-devant d'un échec certain car, se connaissant mal lui-même, il peut difficilement aimer l'autre.

L'adolescent se découvre lentement au point de vue sexuel, tout comme il se découvre progressivement à d'autres points de vue. Il accorde beaucoup d'importance à la sexualité, l'intégrant difficilement à l'amour. L'abus des relations sexuelles, malgré beaucoup de vantardise, est plutôt rare et traduit un déséquilibre.

Les problèmes de l'adolescent

Il y a cinq problèmes majeurs que l'adolescent doit résoudre s'il veut acquérir des sentiments d'identité et d'intimité et s'il veut atteindre une certaine maturité émotive. Ces problèmes sont les suivants: 1) l'intégration de la personnalité, 2) l'émancipation vis-à-vis des parents et de la famille, 3) l'adaptation au sexe opposé, 4) l'acceptation d'une nouvelle forme corporelle, après les changements rapides qui ont eu lieu au cours de cette période, 5) le choix d'une carrière.

Si le développement de l'enfant a été satisfaisant jusqu'à la puberté, ces problèmes seront plus faciles à résoudre, pourvu que les parents et les autres adultes lui offrent toute l'aide dont il a besoin. Cependant, il arrive souvent que des frictions, des malentendus surgissent entre les enfants et les parents et rendent la croissance plus difficile.

Intégration de la personnalité. L'avènement de l'adolescence coïncide normalement avec le début d'une intégration de la personnalité. Cela signifie que l'enfant devrait pouvoir affronter certaines situations difficiles et prendre l'initiative d'y faire face, sans quoi il devient un adolescent timide, inquiet, prêt à se replier sur lui-même au moindre problème, évitant tout contact avec les autres et rejetant les responsabilités chaque fois qu'il le peut. Livré à lui-même, il risque d'être très peu préparé à affronter la vie.

L'intégration de la personnalité n'est complète que lorsque l'adolescent est prêt à participer à la vie sociale en général, et non seulement aux aspects qui le touchent de près. Son *ambivalence* l'empêche d'évoluer rapidement vers la maturité. Il devient plus ouvert aux autres, mais pas nécessairement à ses proches. Il lui faut apprendre à moins critiquer les adultes et à accepter leurs points de vue même s'il ne partage pas leurs opinions. Il doit progressivement agrandir son champ d'activités et de rencontres. Son altruisme, sa volonté d'aider les autres, atteint un apogée. L'adolescent désire toujours « sauver le monde » et s'attacher à de grandes causes.

L'adolescent et sa famille. Les parents, les éducateurs et les autres adultes peuvent ne pas avoir la même influence qu'autrefois sur l'adolescent. Celui-ci éprouve souvent une certaine hostilité à leur égard; il est agressif et conteste leur autorité. Il est partagé entre son besoin de protection et son désir d'émancipation. Il doit lutter à la fois contre son amour inconscient pour le parent du sexe opposé et dominer les sentiments ambivalents qu'il éprouve pour le parent de son sexe.

Les parents s'accordent à dire que l'adolescence est un âge difficile et qu'ils ne comprennent pas le comportement de leurs enfants. Ils doivent savoir que les adolescents prennent peu à peu conscience de leur maturité et qu'ils peuvent, à l'occasion, avoir besoin d'aide.

Loin de vouloir s'identifier au parent du même sexe, l'adolescent essaie de s'en éloigner le plus possible. Il lui arrivera même de tourner ses parents en ridicule, à la maison, alors qu'avec ses amis il en parlera avec fierté. Son affection se porte bientôt sur d'autres adultes que ses parents. Ceci marque le début d'une série de petites crises qui caractérisent bien cette période. L'adolescent se met à aimer l'adulte, désire lui plaire, s'identifier à lui. Il lui emprunte certains traits de caractère, sa façon de parler, un de ses talents, et les intègre à sa propre personnalité. L'adulte-modèle, souvent un professeur, ne prend pas toujours conscience de l'influence qu'il peut avoir sur le jeune. Certains parents peuvent prendre ombrage de ce comportement chez leur enfant. Toutefois, il arrive que l'adulte qui attire le respect et la confiance d'un adolescent soit en mesure de l'aider mieux que ne le font les parents dont l'objectivité est moins évidente. Auprès de lui, l'adolescent apprend à se découvrir, à rendre sa pensée plus claire, à trouver des solutions à ses problèmes et à se conduire en adulte. Lorsque l'adolescent atteint ce dernier stade, il n'est plus soumis aux pressions extérieures. Il devient plus calme, plus sociable, et ses difficultés avec ses parents s'aplanissent. Si l'adolescent a besoin de compréhension et d'appui, il ne faut pas pour autant le traiter en enfant, mais en futur adulte. C'est de cette manière seulement qu'il pourra connaître ses limites et ses possibilités.

Il ne faut pas oublier que certains parents ont également besoin d'aide et de compréhension. Parfois, ayant eu eux-mêmes une adolescence orageuse, ils ressentent une vive appréhension devant les difficultés que rencontrent leurs enfants. Si personne ne les aide à voir clair en eux-mêmes, ils peuvent être soit trop sévères, soit trop indulgents; ces deux attitudes extrêmes sont également néfastes à l'adolescent, au moment où il traverse une étape cruciale de sa vie. Les parents qui n'ont jamais pratiqué l'introspection, qui ne se sont jamais remis en question ou qui vivent en deçà des normes qu'ils s'étaient fixés dans leur jeunesse,

peuvent être incapables de faire face aux vérités que leur dévoilent froidement leurs adolescents.

Les rapports de l'adolescent avec ses frères et sœurs peuvent être extrêmement tendus, particulièrement quand il a une jeune sœur qui a déjà atteint la puberté, et dont la croissance est par conséquent plus avancée. Cependant, au moment où ils abordent les problèmes de l'adolescence, une confiance réciproque s'établit entre le frère et la sœur. Leurs rapports respectifs avec les jeunes du sexe opposé s'en trouvent facilités, car ils ont appris, au contact l'un de l'autre, comment ils doivent se comporter.

Pour certains jeunes enfants, le frère ou la sœur adolescent tient lieu de père ou de mère. Cette sorte de substitution peut être dangereuse pour le jeune enfant qui comprend mal l'instabilité de l'adolescent.

Dans toutes les familles, il arrive un moment où les jeunes luttent pour obtenir leur indépendance. Alors que les parents s'efforcent de maintenir leur autorité et leur prestige, les enfants, eux, combattent pour gagner leur liberté. Le jeune qui engage une telle lutte devrait causer moins d'inquiétude que celui qui traverse cette période sans conflits apparents.

Cette période est pourtant la plus propice à l'épanouissement de la personnalité, parce que l'individu apprend alors à vivre par lui-même. Malheureusement, les parents s'adaptent difficilement à cette situation nouvelle et souvent briment les efforts d'indépendance de leur enfant. Le plus grand tort qu'ils puissent alors causer aux jeunes, c'est de leur déclarer qu'ils s'attendent au pire de leur part. Lorsqu'au contraire, ils s'attendent à ce qu'il y a de meilleur, les adolescents chercheront à ne pas les décevoir, sinon dans l'immédiat, du moins dans les choix qui engagent leur avenir.

Si l'émancipation du jeune n'est pas facile à réaliser, c'est parce que les deux parties en cause ont leurs problèmes. L'enfant a besoin que l'on prenne soin de lui, mais il n'est aucunement disposé à coopérer avec les adultes qui pourraient lui donner ce sentiment de sécurité qu'il recherche. Les parents ont aussi leurs problèmes, dont ils ne prennent pas toujours conscience. Tout d'abord, ils ont beaucoup de mal à partager avec les autres, l'amour de leur enfant. Ensuite, ils ont tendance à le croire incapable de se tirer d'affaire et cherchent alors à le dominer. Ils soutiennent que les jeunes courent des risques certains s'ils quittent la maison paternelle. De plus, il peuvent être incapables d'accepter que leur petit enfant est maintenant un être dont les désirs sexuels sont réels et normaux. La mère traverse souvent elle-même la difficile période de la ménopause. Dans cette situation tendue, le plus petit détail de la vie quotidienne peut provoquer un drame: l'heure à laquelle l'adolescent doit quitter la maison et être de retour, la permission ou le refus de se servir de l'auto, d'avoir une clé de la maison, de choisir ses vêtements, etc...

L'adolescent doit sans aucun doute s'émanciper, mais graduellement. Tout comme on demande aux parents de comprendre le rôle du jeune dans ce conflit, l'adolescent doit aussi faire l'effort de se pencher sur les problèmes de ses parents.

Si, au cours des six premières années de sa vie, l'enfant grandit dans un climat de confiance et d'entente, son adolescence sera une période positive de développement. Les parents doivent lui permettre de développer son jugement et ses aptitudes, lui dire la vérité et surtout éviter de lui chercher querelle ou de le ridiculiser.

Au cours des dernières années, les adolescents ont bénéficié d'une indulgence sans limite, sans doute en réaction contre la sévérité et la rigidité de l'éducation d'autrefois. Ce qui importe surtout, – et c'est là que réside le vrai problème – c'est de savoir donner aux adolescents la liberté dont ils ont besoin, sans cesser de les conseiller et de les guider. On voit alors l'anxiété disparaître graduellement, à mesure que leur indépendance devient un fait acquis; les relations avec leurs parents sont moins tendues parce qu'elles sont fondées sur une compréhension mutuelle et sur une plus grande maturité d'esprit.

L'adolescent et ses amis. L'adolescent a besoin de faire partie d'un groupe pour y puiser confiance et solidarité et être appuyé dans son rejet de l'influence des adultes. Être accepté par un groupe lui donne de la sécurité. Ses opinions lui sont dictées par les codes sociaux et éthiques de ce noyau auquel il appartient. Les manies même prennent de l'importance, qu'il s'agisse de la tenue vestimentaire ou du comportement général. L'adolescent peut ne pas chercher à exprimer son individualité au-delà des limites imposées par le groupe.

À partir de discussions très souvent passionnées, les membres d'un groupe finissent par établir certaines règles de vie. Ils formulent, puis adoptent des attitudes définies à l'égard de la morale, des coutumes religieuses et sociales. En somme, chaque cellule décide du comportement de ses membres, et devient un îlot de sécurité au milieu de la tempête générale. Ceci se maintient tant qu'un adulte autoritaire ou directif ne s'introduit pas dans le groupe.

L'adolescent qui a eu une puberté retardée risque d'avoir des problèmes émotifs aigus. Il peut se trouver exclu de son cercle d'amis, aussi bien que des groupes d'enfants plus jeunes ou plus âgés que lui. Il se sent inférieur, sur les plans physique et psychologique, et cela le diminue à ses propres yeux.

Des liens d'amitié unissent fréquemment deux ou trois camarades du même sexe. Les intérêts communs, l'âge et la personnalité de chacun sont autant de facteurs qui entrent en jeu, lorsque de telles relations s'établissent. Ces amitiés jouent un rôle important dans le développement de la personnalité. Ces amis dévoués et souvent inséparables ont une conscience aiguë de leurs besoins réciproques, et réagissent sans l'égoïsme que l'on note au cours des premières phases de la croissance. Ils se confient leurs idées, leurs secrets les plus intimes, leurs soucis et, ce faisant, acquièrent un sens des responsabilités et une loyauté qu'ils ne possédaient pas auparavant. Les jeunes ont une tendance évidente à déformer un peu la réalité quand ils parlent de leurs amitiés. Celles-ci aident l'adolescente à se détacher plus facilement de sa mère. Les garçons extériorisent leurs sentiments en s'adonnant à des jeux violents, en se querellant, ou même en se jouant des tours. Ils font preuve d'une grande loyauté envers leur groupe d'amis.

Puis, peu à peu, à côté de ces solides amitiés d'adolescents du même sexe, s'établissent des liens plus tendres avec des jeunes du sexe opposé.

L'adaptation au sexe opposé. Lorsqu'un adolescent est attiré par le sexe opposé, cet intérêt est d'abord voilé. Ainsi, un garçon qui aperçoit un groupe de filles, déploie toutes ses qualités physiques pour attirer leur attention. Il se persuade lui-même – et tente de persuader les autres – qu'il fait uniquement des exercices corporels. Les filles ricanent et chuchotent pour se faire remarquer.

Plus tard, c'est un véritable amour romantique qui naîtra entre une fille et un garçon et, généralement, ce dernier est de deux ans plus âgé que sa partenaire en raison du décalage qui existe entre leurs périodes respectives de croissance. Ces idylles sont de courte durée, mais elles ont l'avantage de livrer aux jeunes une connaissance de la personnalité du sexe opposé qui les aidera plus tard, lorsqu'ils seront prêts à aimer réellement.

Pour établir des relations hétérosexuelles, l'adolescent doit vaincre les tabous de sa conscience d'enfant, et s'en libérer totalement. Durant cette période de lutte et de perplexité, son anxiété devient intolérable; il tente désespérément de se contrôler. Il nie peut-être l'autorité de ses parents, mais peut la rechercher dans ces circonstances. Pour calmer son angoisse, il n'hésitera pas à se tourner vers la religion ou encore vers des préoccupations d'ordre intellectuel. Il en arrivera éventuellement à ne plus craindre ses impulsions et à goûter les joies nécessaires à son épanouissement.

Pour la plupart des adolescents, le mariage et la procréation se situent dans un avenir très proche. C'est pourquoi ils doivent apprendre à se connaître mutuellement, et ils le font au cours de soirées dansantes ou d'autres rencontres. Ils aiment se tenir par la main, s'embrasser, être dans les bras l'un de l'autre; et toutes ces manifestations physiques sont normales, pendant que l'adolescent développe ses sentiments d'identité et d'intimité, nécessaires afin de pouvoir éprouver et partager un sentiment d'amour.

Souvent, ce sont les parents qui s'opposent à cette connaissance du sexe opposé, de peur que leurs enfants ne se marient trop tôt et délaissent leurs études. Ils appréhendent aussi les maladies vénériennes et les grossesses prémaritales. Il faut pourtant que les parents comprennent que les jeunes doivent se développer et qu'ils admettent l'existence de leurs désirs. Si les relations entre les parents et les enfants sont excellentes, si les jeunes bénéficient d'une éducation sexuelle satisfaisante, et si, d'autre part, on leur enseigne à assumer leurs responsabilités et à respecter autrui, les adolescents adopteront à l'égard des questions sexuelles l'attitude que les adultes aimeraient leur voir prendre. Les jeunes doivent pouvoir se rencontrer sans inquiétude et sans honte.

Autrefois, les parents n'encourageaient pas leurs enfants à sortir « sérieusement » avec quelqu'un, de crainte de les voir s'exposer à une forte déception au moment de la rupture de ce qu'ils considéraient comme un demi-mariage. Aujourd'hui, les jeunes sortent « régulièrement », plutôt que « sérieusement ».

Donc, si l'enfant reçoit une éducation sexuelle appropriée, s'il est élevé par des parents aimants et responsables, les problèmes de l'adolescence seront surmontés. Quoiqu'il en soit, il a besoin d'être appuyé chaque fois qu'il doit régler des questions qui exigent une certaine maturité de jugement. Il faut l'aider à comprendre les principes sociaux et moraux qui règlent ses sorties et ses relations sexuelles, et à trouver les voies qui correspondent le mieux à ses intérêts. Les parents doivent être prêts à discuter des moyens contraceptifs avec leur fille et leur garçon. Ils ne doivent pas pousser indûment leurs enfants à s'en servir s'ils ne connaissent pas leurs activités sexuelles. Ceux-ci peuvent interpréter le comportement de leurs parents comme une pression à s'engager dans les relations hétérosexuelles. Toutefois, il faut présenter les moyens contraceptifs comme des éléments d'un comportement responsable.

Les menaces ont très peu d'influence sur les adolescents. Elles entraînent un comportement que les parents qualifient de répréhensible, parce que leur autorité et leurs principes sont alors rejetés.

Puisqu'en fin de compte, la conduite de l'adolescent dépend aussi bien de l'approbation des parents que des décisions du groupe auquel il appartient, il est indispensable que ce groupe soutienne des règles valables.

Maturité émotive

Personne n'atteint une maturité émotive complète. Il reste toujours des lacunes à combler, quoique la moindre étape de l'évolution ait une importance capitale dans l'épanouissement de la personnalité.

Théoriquement, l'individu qui a atteint cette maturité est capable d'affronter la réalité, de faire preuve de jugement, de se choisir un compagnon de vie, de construire un foyer et d'élever intelligemment ses enfants. Il devrait non seulement prendre ses responsabilités et jouir pleinement des activités qu'il entreprend individuellement ou en groupe, mais aussi maintenir un équilibre constant entre le devoir et le plaisir, pour éviter toute tension inutile. Enfin, ayant gagné une certaine assurance, il demeure modeste et accepte ses limites ainsi que celles imposées par la réalité.

Un être adulte doit se faire à l'idée que, dans une société, tous dépendent les uns des autres et que cette sorte de solidarité est à la base de la vie sociale. Il sait faire confiance aux autres, mais il sait aussi distinguer avec perspicacité ceux qui ne l'aiment pas et ceux que lui n'aime pas. C'est vers ce but que l'adolescent doit tendre. C'est à lui de décider du comportement à adopter et d'établir sa philosophie de la vie. Cependant, bien que relevant de lui seul, ses décisions n'en sont pas moins influencées par son milieu familial, son éducation scolaire et religieuse, et par toutes les expériences qu'il a vécues.

APERÇU GÉNÉRAL DU DÉVELOPPEMENT PHYSIQUE

Durant la puberté et l'adolescence, la maturation émotive est accompagnée d'une maturation physique. Plusieurs facteurs influent sur les développements physique et sexuel de l'adolescent: facteurs socio-économiques, alimentation, bagage génétique, type morphologique et état de santé. Au cours des derniers cents ans, on a constaté une accélération du développement sexuel des adolescents dans certaines régions du monde. Et par ailleurs, le développement physique entraîne des changements qui sont souvent la cause de troubles émotifs.

La puberté

La puberté est associée à la maturation sexuelle. Un ou deux ans avant cette période, la croissance est accélérée et on note des changements dans le poids et la taille, dans la forme du corps et enfin dans la physiologie générale, résultats de la maturation des gonades et de l'activité hormonale. Ces transformations se prolongent généralement jusqu'à la puberté, soit vers l'âge de 13 ans pour les filles et un ou deux ans plus tard pour les garçons. Les filles ont tendance à se développer plus rapidement que les garçons et gardent une certaine avance sur eux, jusqu'à l'âge adulte.

On s'interroge sur l'origine physiologique du déclenchement de la puberté, mais on connaît toutefois le mécanisme qui entre en jeu dans le phénomène lui-même. La stimulation neurohumorale provient de l'hypothalamus qui agit sur l'hypophyse. Par la suite, les hormones gonadotrophines pituitaires stimulent les cellules de Leydig des testicules qui produisent alors de la testostérone, et les cellules folliculaires de l'ovaire qui sécrètent des œstrogènes. On assiste simultanément à une augmentation des hormones androgènes du cortex surrénalien. L'action combinée de ces hormones produit l'apparition des caractères sexuels secondaires.

Les caractères sexuels qui se développent dépendent de la quantité et de la variété d'hormones produites. En effet, l'organisme humain produit simultanément des hormones mâles et femelles, mais à des degrés variables selon le sexe et la personne. L'homme produit surtout des hormones androgènes et la femme des œstrogènes. Les deux types d'hormones provoquent le développement et la fusion des épiphyses. Un ralentissement de la croissance s'observe après la puberté.

Pour les garçons, les changements physiques sont, par ordre d'apparition:
– le développement des organes génitaux,
– le développement du thorax,
– l'apparition de la pilosité au pubis, aux aisselles, sur le visage et sur le thorax,
– la mue de la voix,
– la production de spermatozoïdes,
– le développement rapide des épaules, à partir de l'âge de treize ans.

Les garçons peuvent se sentir troublés par les éjaculations nocturnes, c'est-à-dire la perte de liquide séminal pendant le sommeil. S'ils n'ont pas été prévenus du caractère normal de ce phénomène, ils peuvent s'imaginer qu'ils sont malades et que la masturbation et les obsessions sexuelles leur ont attiré cette forme de châtiment. Ils peuvent aussi croire qu'ils risquent une stérilité définitive. Les éjaculations nocturnes sont dues à l'activité des glandes sexuelles et ne doivent pas être un objet d'inquiétude. Si l'on n'a pas préparé les garçons à ce phénomène, ils s'informeront probablement auprès de leur père ou de leurs amis, parce qu'ils ont en général plus de facilité que les filles à parler entre eux de leurs problèmes.

Pour les filles, les changements débutent vers l'âge de douze ans et se produisent dans l'ordre suivant:
– élargissement du bassin,
– développement des seins,
– transformation des sécrétions vaginales,
– apparition du système pileux sur le pubis et aux esselles,
– déclenchement de la première menstruation, ordinairement après l'apparition de la pilosité pubienne, mais avant la croissance pileuse axillaire.

Menstruations. L'hypothalamus libère une hormone stimulante spécifique qui entraîne la production de l'hormone gonadotrophine par l'hypophyse. Cette hormone (FSH) agit sur le follicule ovarien et stimule la production d'œstrogènes par l'ovaire et la maturation de l'ovule. L'œstrogène favorise la prolifération et la vascularisation accrue de l'endomètre de l'utérus. Cette phase du cycle menstruel est appelée phase proliférative ou œstrogénique. Vers le 14e jour du cycle, l'ovule à maturité est libéré et sous la stimulation de l'hormone lutéinisante (LH) de l'hypophyse, le site d'expulsion de l'ovaire est fermé par des cellules qui forment le corps jaune, organe producteur de progestérone et d'œstrogène. La progestérone, en conjonction avec l'œstrogène, augmente la prolifération de l'endomètre et stimule sa fonction sécrétoire. L'utérus est ainsi préparé à l'implantation éventuelle de l'ovule fécondé. Cette phase du cycle menstruel s'appelle phase sécrétoire ou progestative. Si l'ovule n'est pas fécondé, le corps jaune s'atrophie, la production de progestérone s'arrête et celle des œstrogènes chute brutalement. L'endomètre hypertrophié se désintègre et les menstruations apparaissent. Le cycle d'une durée approximative de 28 à 30 jours, recommence par l'augmentation de la production des hormones hypophysaires stimulée par la baisse des hormones ovariennes.

Souvent mal renseignées sur le phénomène de la menstruation, les filles se sentent mal à l'aise; elles ont la pénible sensation que certaines fonctions de leur corps leur échappent, et considèrent leurs menstruations comme un fardeau. Si elles ont été préparées adéquatement, elles peuvent attendre l'événement avec impatience et en retirer énormément de fierté.

Certains parents évitent de parler des divers changements qu'entraîne la puberté. Les enfants doivent être renseignés avant la période pubère sur les différences anatomiques et fonctionnelles qui existent entre les deux sexes. On doit expliquer en quoi consiste l'ovulation, la fertilisation, la grossesse, l'accouchement et naturellement, on doit parler des menstruations avant qu'elles ne se produisent. En abordant ce sujet, certains parents ne font que transmettre à leurs enfants les croyances et les tabous dont ils ont été victimes eux-mêmes. Ils conseillent à leur fille de se reposer durant cette période et de ne participer à aucune activité lui donnant ainsi l'impression d'être malade.

La menstruation est un phénomène physiologique et il n'y a aucune raison de ralentir les activités pendant qu'elle se produit. Le sang perdu est rapidement remplacé. Si les mères affirment qu'il s'agit là d'un phénomène purement naturel, les adolescentes l'acceptent facilement.

C'est aux parents de convaincre les enfants que les questions sexuelles sont beaucoup plus complexes que la fausse image présentée sur les écrans ou dans les revues. C'est aussi aux parents qu'incombe la responsabilité de discuter avec leurs adolescents, de rectifier les erreurs et de mieux les informer.

On note d'autres changements physiques chez les enfants des deux sexes; les glandes sébacées de la figure, du dos et de la poitrine deviennent plus actives. La prédisposition à l'acné est grande à cet âge et est due à l'activité androgénique du cortex surrénalien. La transpiration augmente. Enfin, l'instabilité vaso-motrice est la cause de rougissements fréquents.

Le rythme de croissance en hauteur, après avoir suivi une courbe descendante entre la naissance et la puberté, s'accélère à la pré-adolescence. L'enfant approche de sa taille d'adulte. Au début de l'adolescence, on note surtout une augmentation de poids, ce qui donne aux jeunes une apparence trapue. Cette obésité joue un grand rôle sur les plans psychologique et physique.

Tous les systèmes organiques ne subissent pas le même rythme de croissance. Ainsi, les os se développent plus rapidement que les muscles qui les soutiennent, ce qui donne au corps une allure disgracieuse. D'autre part, les muscles ne se développent pas tous en même temps; les mains et les pieds grandissent plus rapidement que le reste du corps, si bien que les mouvements manquent en quelque sorte de coordination.

Comme le cœur et les poumons se développent en général plus lentement que les autres organes, la quantité d'oxygène absorbée est insuffisante, et l'adolescent peut en éprouver une lassitude constante.

Les jeunes, — et quelquefois même les parents — ne se rendent pas compte que l'adolescence n'est qu'une période de transition, et ils supportent mal toutes ces transformations. Pour combattre le sentiment d'infériorité qu'ils éprouvent, ils se mettent à se moquer des autres, s'imposent des exercices physiques, suivent un régime sévère; ils peuvent également chercher à attirer l'attention à tout prix, ou encore développer leurs facultés intellectuelles pour faire oublier leur corps. Il y en a qui s'effacent volontairement pour éviter toute comparaison avec les autres.

Les parents ne doivent pas ridiculiser les enfants qui traversent cette étape, d'autant plus qu'avec le temps ces difficultés physiques disparaîtront. Au contraire, ils doivent leur apprendre à s'accepter tels qu'ils sont, même si la forme actuelle de leur corps ne correspond pas à l'image dont ils rêvent.

À la puberté, l'enfant est envahi par des sensations et des sentiments nouveaux qu'il ne réussit pas à comprendre. C'est une des raisons pour lesquelles il se lasse très vite des choses qui lui avaient semblé intéressantes de prime abord. Ces abandons successifs lui donnent le temps d'assimiler les sensations nouvelles qu'il éprouve: ce phénomène se situe vers l'âge de treize ans. Il faut s'attendre aussi à ce que ses progrès scolaires s'en trouvent ralentis pendant un an environ. Au lieu de se moquer de lui, ses parents et ses professeurs doivent l'encourager et l'assurer que ce n'est là qu'un état passager.

L'activité motrice est, elle aussi, influencée par les changements corporels. Malgré la force physique qu'il acquiert progressivement, et malgré ses aptitudes générales, l'adolescent peut paraître lourd et gauche, sans doute parce qu'il s'adapte lentement à toutes les transformations qu'il subit, et parce qu'il redoute qu'on se moque de lui. Par ailleurs, sa croissance rapide requiert toutes ses ressources physiques et ne lui laisse que peu d'énergie pour poursuivre ses activités. Voilà pourquoi l'adolescent peut, une fois de plus, être sujet à la fatigue.

Les filles développent moins d'habileté motrice, sans doute parce que leur intérêt porte souvent sur d'autres activités que les sports et que la société valorise plus une attitude passive pour la jeune fille.

Au moment où surviennent ces changements, l'adolescent semble s'intéresser particulièrement à son apparence physique. Sachant à quoi il veut ressembler lorsqu'il sera adulte, il se sent angoissé s'il s'aperçoit que la réalité ne correspond pas à ce qu'il avait espéré. Il faut alors l'aider à apprécier son corps à sa juste valeur et à tirer profit de ses qualités.

L'adolescence

Après la puberté, la croissance ralentit, et la ligne générale du corps se transforme progressivement. Mais l'adolescent continue à vivre avec des systèmes organiques et des capacités fonctionnelles qui ne sont pas tous au même stade de développement.

À 15 ou 16 ans, les caractères sexuels secondaires sont développés et les organes sexuels ont atteint leur maturité. En général, il existe une stérilité relative entre 12 et 15 ans. En effet, pendant cette période, les ovaires se développent lentement, n'étant qu'à environ 30% de leur taille adulte lors de la première menstruation. Pour le garçon, le nombre de spermatozoïdes est habituellement insuffisant dans le sperme, pour qu'une fécondation soit possible.

À cet âge, les capacités motrices des jeunes sont égales à celles de l'adulte. Un adolescent peut accomplir des tâches qui exigent de la force musculaire et de l'adresse. Les parents doivent alors veiller à ce qu'il n'outrepasse pas ses capacités et se rendre compte que les autres aspects de sa personnalité ne sont pas aussi avancés que son développement physique.

Au sortir de l'adolescence, les jeunes possèdent l'apparence physique des adultes. Leur tête mesure environ ⅛ de la hauteur totale; et lorsque les dents de sagesse apparaissent, c'est-à-dire entre dix-sept et vingt-cinq ans, leur dentition est complète.

Les étapes de la maturation de l'adolescent s'échelonnent de l'âge de 12 ou 13 ans jusque vers l'âge de 20 ans. L'adolescent de 13 ans est donc très différent de celui qui est âgé de 19 ans. La tension et l'anxiété accompagnent souvent les changements physiques, émotifs, sociaux et intellectuels qui se produisent au cours de cette période.

PARTICULARITÉS DU DÉVELOPPEMENT PHYSIQUE, SOCIAL ET MENTAL

On comprend mieux la puberté et l'adolescence, si on les considère comme des périodes de maturation accélérée et non comme un laps de temps limité, au cours duquel l'évolution suit un cours régulier. Il serait artificiel de cloisonner les étapes de cette évolution, puisque la croissance ne se fait pas au même rythme dans tous les domaines, et que de nombreux facteurs déterminent ce rythme de croissance. Citons, par exemple, l'hérédité, la constitution physique, les caractéristiques raciales et nationales, le sexe, l'environnement – y compris l'environnement prénatal –, la situation socio-économique de la famille, la nutrition, le climat, la maladie, la position occupée dans la famille, l'intelligence, l'équilibre hormonal, et enfin les émotions.

L'école

Les adolescents se montrent de plus en plus capables de poursuivre des raisonnements abstraits. De plus, les sujets qu'ils abordent à l'école sont si complexes qu'ils nécessitent un vocabulaire plus riche et un langage plus évolué. Mais comme la maturité de l'esprit n'est pas en relation directe avec la croissance physique, les parents et les enseignants ne

Figure 23-2. Les étudiants du cours secondaire sont maintenant capables de raisonnements abstraits. Ils se sentent profondément engagés dans les sujets qui les intéressent. (H. Armstrong Roberts.)

doivent pas se laisser abuser par les apparences, et exiger d'un adolescent qu'il ait une mentalité d'adulte.

Les jeunes éprouvent une certaine difficulté à s'adapter à la vie scolaire. Il y en a beaucoup qui sacrifient leurs études aux activités parascolaires. Ils sont tellement tourmentés par leurs problèmes qu'ils ne réussissent pas à se concentrer longtemps sur leur travail. Puisque l'école reconnaît l'existence de ces problèmes, elle doit offrir des activités adéquates qui aident l'adolescent à satisfaire tous ses besoins.

Les aptitudes intellectuelles et l'intérêt porté aux études varient beaucoup d'un individu à l'autre. Certains excellent dans tous les domaines, alors que d'autres ne réussissent nulle part. La motivation de l'élève est étroitement reliée au but qu'il veut atteindre. Si sa future profession exige une grande préparation scolaire, il s'applique à ses études. S'il n'a pas un but vraiment précis à atteindre, il ne voit pas la nécessité de se donner du mal pour réussir brillamment ses études secondaires.

L'école n'offre pas uniquement une préparation conventionnelle et livresque. Elle permet aussi à l'adolescent d'exercer d'autres activités et de satisfaire son besoin de sécurité et de réussite. Elle ne doit pas négliger non plus l'intérêt qui pourrait le porter vers d'autres domaines, tels le travail manuel, la musique et les arts.

Les programmes scolaires devraient être établis en fonction du stade de développement des enfants, et non seulement en fonction de leur âge. Il se peut, en effet, que dans une même classe, soient groupés des prépubères, des pubères et de jeunes adolescents.

Il importe que les parents s'intéressent à la vie scolaire de l'adolescent et lui permettent d'assister à certaines activités sociales d'adultes, au sein de la collectivité. Il semble qu'à l'école secondaire, les manifestations sportives et les soirées dansantes soient très coûteuses, et que, pour cette raison, certains jeunes moins fortunés éprouvent un sentiment d'infériorité vis-à-vis de leurs camarades, et songent même à quitter l'école avant la remise des diplômes. La meilleure façon d'aider ces jeunes est de leur procurer le moyen de gagner l'argent qui leur est nécessaire.

Loisirs et travail

Pendant la puberté et l'adolescence, les loisirs et le choix d'un travail varient parfois avec le sexe des étudiants. Toutefois, ces différences tendent à s'amenuiser à mesure que garçons et filles sont traités sur un pied d'égalité.

Les filles s'intéressent plus aux soirées dansantes et aux aventures romanesques qu'à l'entretien de la maison. Elles aiment les films et les émissions de télévision. Elles passent des heures à se faire belles, en essayant de nouvelles coiffures, des produits de beauté et de nouveaux vêtements. Elles apprennent, parfois sans enthousiasme, à cuisiner, à faire le mé-

Figure 23-3. Les adolescents ne partagent pas tous les mêmes intérêts. *A)* Certains prennent plaisir à étudier. *B)* D'autres se complaisent dans les conversations interminables au téléphone. (H. Armstrong Roberts.)

nage et à coudre. Leur intérêt s'étend à d'autres domaines, tels que l'art, la poésie et la musique. Comme les garçons, elles aiment les conversations interminables au téléphone avec quelqu'un qu'elles viennent tout juste de quitter.

Les garçons, eux, s'intéressent à la compétition quelle qu'elle soit. Ils aiment généralement les sports. Ils s'intéressent aussi à la mécanique et à l'électricité, au point d'en faire leurs passe-temps favoris. Ils sont acceptés dans un groupe, non pas en fonction de leur belle apparence, mais en fonction de leur caractère viril, de leurs qualités physiques et de leur habileté manuelle.

Filles et garçons acceptent avec joie les travaux à temps partiel qui leur permettent de gagner leur argent de poche. Ils peuvent livrer les journaux, tondre le gazon, pelleter la neige ou garder les enfants. Bien que ces petites besognes n'aient aucun rapport avec leur profession future, elles leur donnent des responsabilités et révèlent leurs aptitudes au travail. L'adolescent apprend ainsi à travailler avec les autres et à collaborer également avec tout le monde, y compris ceux qui lui sont parfaitement indifférents. Il y puise la satisfaction d'avoir accompli consciencieusement son travail, et d'avoir en quelque sorte participé à la vie de la société. Les adolescents éprouvent toujours une vive satisfaction à se dépenser pour une noble cause. Et comme les sentiments altruistes sont très développés à cet âge, l'individu et le groupe mettent leurs efforts en commun en vue de réaliser de grandes choses.

Choix d'une carrière

L'adolescent doit se préparer à la vie adulte sur trois plans: devenir un citoyen, un travailleur, et enfin un parent. L'adolescent doit apprendre ce que chaque aspect signifie et requiert. Il est probable que son unique préoccupation immédiate soit de choisir une carrière. L'adolescent doit aussi se préparer à exercer un travail qui lui permettra de subvenir à ses besoins.

Choisir une profession, c'est savoir tenir compte de ses limites et de ses capacités. Le père qui a décidé d'être médecin ne doit en aucun cas pousser son fils à choisir la même profession que lui. Les jeunes contribuent mieux à la vie sociale en effectuant un travail qui les intéresse. Il est injuste qu'un adolescent sacrifie son choix à cause de son statut socio-économique. Les conseils qu'on lui donne lui éviteront bien des déceptions et lui permettront de faire des projets réalistes.

SOINS

L'adolescent, dont l'attention a été attirée par le sexe opposé, devient habituellement soucieux de l'effet qu'il produit sur les autres. Les parents s'étonnent de le voir soudain changer de comportement et s'inquiéter outre mesure de la propreté de sa tenue vestimentaire. Ils doivent alors le laisser complètement prendre en charge ses soins quotidiens, et tenter de s'assurer qu'il jouit bien de huit à neuf heures de sommeil par jour, et que son alimentation est suffisamment riche en calories.

Sécurité ou prévention

Malgré toutes les précautions prises à la maison, dans les écoles et par les organisations de jeunesse pour assurer la sécurité des jeunes, le taux d'accidents qui frappent les adolescents est désespérément élevé. La plupart de ces accidents sont causés par des véhicules motorisés. Dans l'espoir de réduire le taux de mortalité, de nombreuses écoles offrent des cours de conduite automobile.

Les adolescents doivent, avant tout, apprendre à maîtriser leurs réflexes s'ils veulent devenir des conducteurs émérites, et s'ils se soucient de leur vie et de celle des autres.

Les accidents les plus fréquents se produisent en motocyclettes, sport dont la popularité augmente chaque jour. Les filles qui se tiennent à l'arrière de ces véhicules peuvent se

Figure 23-4. Les adolescents peuvent manifester un grand intérêt pour la mécanique et l'électricité. Cet intérêt peut influencer le choix de leur carrière. (H. Armstrong Roberts.)

Figure 23-5. Les adolescentes deviennent parti-culièrement soucieuses de leur apparence physique. (H. Armstrong Roberts.)

brûler les jambes au contact du tuyau d'échappement, et garçons et filles risquent d'être projetés sur le sol. Comme, dans la plupart des cas, la mort est provoquée par des blessures à la tête, toute personne qui voyage en motocyclette – ou sur un véhicule du même genre – doit porter un casque de sécurité pour être protégée en cas d'accident. Les motoneiges et les mobylettes sont aussi la cause de nombreux accidents. Il serait important d'être plus sévère dans l'octroi des permis pour conduire ces véhicules et les infractions devraient être sévèrement punies.

Les noyades et les armes à feu constituent aussi une lourde menace pour les adolescents. Il faut apprendre aux jeunes à nager et à se servir sans danger d'une arme à feu, si toutefois, ils en ont vraiment besoin. Ils ne devraient évidemment pas jouer avec une arme chargée. Plusieurs adolescents sont blessés chaque année dans les sports de compétition. On s'interroge actuellement sur la valeur de certains sports, tels le football, durant cette période de la vie. On accorde de plus en plus d'attention à la protection que peuvent offrir des vêtements et un équipement adéquat au cours des activités sportives.

Enfin, dans certains cas, il faut prévenir les traumatismes physiques pour les adolescents qui entreprennent des tâches au-dessus de leurs forces.

La prévention des accidents est difficile à effectuer auprès des adolescents, parce qu'ils aiment frôler le danger et se stimulent souvent les uns les autres à faire preuve d'une bravoure irraisonnée et à ignorer les précautions nécessaires.

NUTRITION

Cette période de croissance nécessite une nutrition saine et appropriée. L'appétit des adolescents ne pose pas de problème et, en général, ils ont tendance à vider le réfrigérateur. Les filles peuvent avoir besoin de 2 400 calories par jour, et les garçons de 3 000 calories. Le tableau 23-1 donne les exigences alimentaires requises à différents âges, pour les garçons et pour les filles. Ces exigences ne sont pas identiques pour les adolescents des deux sexes, parce que les garçons atteignent une taille plus élevée et manifestent un intérêt marqué pour les activités physiques.

Quand les filles commencent à se soucier de leur apparence, elles s'inquiètent aussitôt de leur poids. Elles suivent alors une diète amaigrissante qui risque de mettre leur santé en danger. Les parents devraient surveiller ce régime, mais le plus discrètement possible. Les adolescents peuvent d'ailleurs apprendre à planifier eux-mêmes leurs repas, à faire les courses, à composer les menus de tous les jours et, partant, à connaître la base d'une alimentation saine. La nutrition se révèle d'une importance extrême pour la jeune femme, au cours de ses grossesses. Les parents et les éducateurs doivent renseigner les jeunes sur le régime alimentaire qui leur convient, car souvent, ils ont une fâcheuse tendance à boire beaucoup de boissons gazeuses et à manger de grandes quantités de pâtisseries et d'aliments à base de féculents. Lorsque l'esprit du groupe domine, c'est le groupe entier qu'il faut orienter vers de meilleures habitudes alimentaires. Adopter une alimentation riche en viandes et autres protéines, en légumes, en fruits, en céréales à grains entiers, et en produits laitiers, c'est se préparer une excellente santé pour l'avenir. Habituellement, les garçons mangent sans se faire prier, parce qu'ils aiment se sentir en forme pour participer aux jeux sportifs. Le menu des cafétérias étudiantes doit offrir des mets nourrissants plutôt que des repas économiques à base de pâtes alimentaires et de viandes bouillies; on doit vendre dans les machines distributrices des aliments nutritifs, tels noix et fruits au lieu de bonbons, boissons gazeuses, tartelettes et gâteaux.

Tableau 23-1. *Rations quotidiennes nutritives recommandées pour les préadolescents et les adolescents (12 à 18 ans)*

	GARÇONS			FILLES		
	12 – 14 ANS	14 – 18 ANS		12 – 14 ANS	14 – 16 ANS	16 – 18 ANS
POIDS	43 kg	59 kg		44 kg	52 kg	54 kg
TAILLE	15|1 cm	170 cm		154 cm	157 cm	160 cm
K calories	2 700	3 000		2 300	2 400	2 300
Protéines	50 **g**	60 g		50 g	55 g	55 g
Vitamines liposolubles						
Vitamine A	5 000 U.I.	5 000 U.I.		5 000 U.I.	5 000 UU.I.	5 000 U.I.
Vitamine D	400 U.I.	400 U.I.		400 U.I.	400 U.I.	400 U.I.
Vitamine E	20 U.I.	25 U.I.		20 U.I.	25 U.I.	25 U.I.
Vitamines hydrosolubles						
Acide ascorbique (c)	45 mg	55 mg		45 mg	50 mg	50 mg
Acide folique	0,4 mg	0,4 mg		0,4 mg	0,4 mg	0,4 mg
Acide nicotinique (équivalents)	18 mg	20 mg		15 mg	16 mg	15 mg
Riboflavine	1,4 mg	1,5 mg		1,4 mg	1,4 mg	1,5 mg
Thiamine	1,4 mg	1,5 mg		1,2 mg	1,2 mg	1,2 mg
Vitamine B_6	1,6 mg	1,8 mg		1,6 mg	1,8 mg	2,0 mg
Vitamine B_{12}	5 μg	5 μg		5 μg	5 μg	5 μg
Minéraux						
Calcium	1,4 g	1,4 g		1,3 g	1,3 g	1,3 g
Phosphore	1,4 g	1,4 g		1,3 g	1,3 g	1,3 g
Iode	135 μg	150 μg		115 μg	120 μg	115 μg
Fer	18 mg	18 mg		18 mg	18 mg	18 mg
Magnésium	350 mg	400 mg		350 mg	350 mg	350 mg

Durant cette période, environ 15% du nombre total de calories doit provenir des protéines, afin de maintenir une balance azotée positive. Celles-ci sont apportées par le lait, les œufs, la viande et le fromage. L'adolescent doit donc absorber jusqu'à 60 grammes de protéines par jour. De plus, il a besoin d'un demi litre à un litre de lait pour obtenir le calcium nécessaire et de 400 unités internationales de vitamine D par jour, pour accroître l'absorption digestive du calcium.

SURVEILLANCE MÉDICALE

L'*éphébiatrie* (du grec ephebos, qui signifie jeune, puberté) est une science nouvelle qui a pour but d'aider les adolescents à résoudre leurs problèmes. Les adolescents ont, en effet, des besoins spécifiques, et les médecins ne se sentent pas tous qualifiés pour les aborder. Les *éphébiatristes* sont donc les médecins qui soignent ces jeunes dont plusieurs sont sous traitement dans des cliniques spécialisées.

Au cours des dernières années, plusieurs cliniques pour adolescents ont été implantées dans différentes régions, et on y traite toutes sortes de problèmes relatifs aux jeunes. Ainsi, les cliniques de médecine générale sont consacrées à un âge particulier, et non à une maladie déterminée, et les spécialistes sont toujours à la disposition de l'adolescent.

Habituellement, les jeunes de douze à vingt et un an y reçoivent toute l'aide dont ils ont besoin, selon les problèmes qui les tourmentent, qu'ils soient d'ordre physique, émotif, social ou intellectuel. Le médecin s'intéresse à l'adolescent et à ses problèmes et établit une relation de confiance avec lui. Les parents peuvent avoir été préalablement consultés, mais les liens qui unissent le médecin à son patient demeurent les plus forts. L'adolescent est alors amené à se sentir entièrement responsable de sa santé.

Les soins prodigués à l'adolescent concernent quatre domaines: la croissance physique, les différentes activités, l'école et, enfin, le rôle des facteurs émotifs dans le développement général. Dans ces cliniques, les médecins traitent aussi les maladies qui atteignent généralement les jeunes (voir chapitre 25). Leur intérêt est centré sur l'adolescent lui-même et non sur un problème médical spécifique. Le médecin traitant ne devient pas automatiquement un spécialiste pour le traitement des adolescents.

Les adolescents ont besoin de parler de leurs problèmes, mais, sur un autre plan, ils ont aussi besoin de prendre des mesures préventives contre les maladies pour lesquelles ils ne sont plus immunisés.

Certains troubles physiques sont définitivement éliminés grâce à des soins appropriés. Ainsi, les étudiants doivent être soumis à des examens réguliers de la vue.

Ils ne doivent pas non plus négliger le soin des pieds; les garçons, parce qu'ils sont plus sportifs, risquent souvent d'être blessés aux pieds, et les filles, par souci d'élégance, portent souvent des chaussures inappropriées.

Les adolescents doivent, enfin, faire examiner leurs dents pour prévenir les caries. Celles-ci surviennent surtout entre l'âge de dix et vingt ans, et sont dues, très souvent, à l'excès de glucides et au manque d'hygiène dentaire.

Les jeunes devraient tirer profit de toutes les connaissances qu'on leur donne au sujet de leur santé. Ils doivent s'intéresser à la croissance, à la prévention des accidents, à la nutrition, à l'éducation sexuelle et à l'hygiène mentale. On doit signaler aux adolescents qui prennent l'habitude de fumer justement à cette période, les effets de la nicotine et du goudron. Et enfin, il faut donner aux jeunes filles l'habitude de s'auto-examiner les seins régulièrement, afin de dépister précocement toute tumeur.

Les principaux atouts de l'infirmière qui travaille avec les adolescents, soit individuellement, soit en groupe, consistent en son amour des jeunes, son honnêteté, son objectivité, son respect de la personne humaine et de sa vie privée. Elle doit être réceptive et aider l'adolescent à trouver lui-même les réponses à ses problèmes. Elle doit surtout comprendre le langage de l'adolescence pour établir une communication valable.

De nombreux adolescents sont gênés par l'apparition des caractères sexuels secondaires. Les filles voient leur poitrine prendre du volume et les garçons s'interrogent sur l'aspect de leurs organes génitaux, surtout s'ils se jugent différents de leurs compagnons. Quand l'adolescent a réussi à exprimer ses sentiments à ce sujet, des informations claires et simples parviennent à réduire l'anxiété qui l'habite.

Des questions surgissent aussi à propos des fréquentations, des relations prémaritales et des mesures anticonceptionnelles. Chaque sexe doit se rendre compte des sentiments de l'autre

sexe au sujet de ces mêmes problèmes et du genre de relation qu'il est possible d'établir entre eux. Ce choix dépend aussi de l'attitude des parents, des croyances religieuses, de la philosophie de la société dont ils font partie et de la conséquence de leurs actes sur leur santé physique et mentale.

Les discussions concernant la lutte pour l'indépendance envers la famille permettent de comprendre le sentiment de rébellion qui les anime.

Plusieurs adolescents pensent à quitter l'école qui ne semble plus répondre à leurs aspirations. L'infirmière peut les aider à découvrir les conséquences de leur geste et à étudier les possibilités qui s'offrent à eux si leur choix se fait dans ce sens. Si l'adolescent décide de continuer ses études, son succès dépendra de sa motivation, de son potentiel intellectuel, de son intérêt académique et de sa préparation antérieure. S'il décide de quitter l'école, il faut étudier avec lui les options qui lui sont offertes et appuyer sa décision tout en l'aidant à se fixer de nouveaux objectifs valables.

Au cours des entretiens, si l'infirmière et l'adolescent réussissent à établir une relation de confiance, les différences entre eux diminueront et ils pourront dialoguer efficacement. L'adolescent peut en arriver à comprendre qu'il est normal d'être anxieux et d'éprouver des sentiments contradictoires, mais qu'il peut s'aider s'il arrive à être capable d'en parler ouvertement. L'infirmière est une conseillère en santé et n'apparaît pas à l'adolescent comme un substitut de ses parents qui tente à son tour de le contrôler.

Sous le couvert de questions de routine apparemment anodines, les véritables problèmes ne tardent pas à apparaître si l'atmosphère est à la confiance et à la détente. Les problèmes de l'adolescent dépendent de ses antécédents familiaux, personnels et sociaux. Ils concernent habituellement les changements physiques et émotifs qui accompagnent la puberté, les façons d'y faire face, les relations entre les garçons et les filles, l'indépendance progressive de la famille et les plans d'avenir.

Au cours des entretiens, les sujets qui reviennent souvent sont la clarification de certains faits au sujet des menstruations, des maladies vénériennes, des moyens contraceptifs, de la grossesse, de l'avortement, des dangers de la cigarette, de l'alcool et de l'usage des drogues. Malgré l'abondante documentation, il existe encore beaucoup de confusion dans l'esprit des adolescents au sujet de ces problèmes.

CONSÉQUENCES DE LA SÉPARATION

Durant la puberté et l'adolescence, le jeune peut être séparé de ses parents pendant assez longtemps et il s'adapte assez facilement à cette situation, si son développement émotif a été satisfaisant. Il arrive souvent que les adolescents passent la nuit chez leurs amis, sous la surveillance des parents, ou vivent plusieurs semaines dans un camp d'été ou encore, soient inscrits dans des pensionnats, loin de la maison. Quoi qu'il en soit, la séparation est toujours pénible, au début, mais la nostalgie que ces adolescents éprouvent est vite chassée par l'intérêt qu'éveillent leurs nouvelles occupations.

RÉFÉRENCES

Livres et documents officiels

Caplan, G. et Lebovici, S. (édit.): *Adolescence: Psychosocial Perspectives*. New York, Basic Books, Inc., 1969.

Cole, L. et Hall, I. N.: *Psychology of Adolescence*. 7e éd. Toronto, Ontario, Holt, Rinehart and Winston, 1970.

Compagnie Kotex: *La joie d'être une fille. L'éveil de la féminité. Vous et votre fille.* Collection des Cycles de la vie, Toronto, Ontario.

Corporation canadienne Tampax: *Documentation éducative sur la menstruation*. Ontario, Canada.

Erikson, E. H.: *Identity – Youth and Crisis*. New York, W. W. Norton and Company, 1968.

Kogert, M.: Growth and Development in Adolescence. *Ped. Clin. N. Amer.*, 20:789, 4, 1973.

Gesell, A. et Ilg, F.: *L'adolescent de 10 à 16 ans*. 3e éd. Paris, P. U. F., 1965.

Ginott, H. G.: *Entre parents et adolescents*. Paris, Laffont, 1970.

Heald, F. P. (édit.): *Adolescent Nutrition and Growth*. New York, Appleton-Century-Crofts, 1969.

Hill, J. P. et Shelton, J. (édit.): *Readings in Adolescent Development and Behavior*. Englewood Cliffs, New Jersey, Prentice-Hall, Inc., 1971.

Johnson et Johnson Company: *Tu deviens femme. Maman, dis-moi... tout sur les menstruations*. Montréal, Québec.

Josselyn I. M.: *Adolescence*. New York, Harper and Row, 1971.

Kagan, J. et Coles, R.: *12 to 16, Early Adolescence*. New York, W. W. Norton, 1972,

Ministère de la Santé nationale et du Bien-être social. *Compréhension de la jeunesse*. Division de l'hygiène mentale, gouvernement du Canada.

Ministère de la Santé: *Les yeux clairs de l'adolescence*. Gouvernement du Québec.

Ray, O. S.: *Drugs, Society and Human Behavior*. Saint-Louis, C. V. Mosby Company, 1972.

Taylor, D. L. (édit.): *Human Sexual Development: Perspectives in Sex Education*. Philadelphie, F. A. Davis Company, 1970.

Articles

Bellaire, J.: Teenagers Learn to Care About Themselves. *Nursing Outlook*, 19:792, décembre 1971.

Daniels, A. M. et Krim, A.: Helping Adolescents Explore Emotional Issues. *Am. J. Nursing*, 69:1482, juillet 1969.

Duché, D. J.: Les problèmes psychologiques de la puberté. *Revue de l'inf.*, 22:23, 1, 1972.

Gendel, E. S. et Green, P. B.: Sex Education Controversy – A Boost to New and Better Programs. *J. School Health*, 41:24, janvier 1971.

Johnson, R. W.: Sex Education and the Nurse. *Nursing Outlook*, 18:26, novembre 1970.

Kogert, M.: Growth and Development in Adolescence. *Ped. Clin. N. Amer.*, 20:789, 4, 1973.

Macintyre, J. M.: Adolescence, Identity and Foster Family Care. *Children*, 17:213, novembre-décembre 1970.

Reiter, E. O. et Kulin, H. E.: Sexual Maturation in the Female *Pediat. Clin. N. Amer.*, 19:581, août 1972.

Semmens, J. P. et Semmens, J. H.: Sex Education of the Adolescent Female. *Pediat. Clin. N. Amer.*, 19:765, août 1972.

Sternlieb, J. J. et Munan, L.: A Survey of Health Problems, Practices and Needs of Youth. *Pediatrics*, 49:117, février 1972.

24 problèmes de la puberté et de l'adolescence reliés à la croissance et au développement

L'adolescent devient de plus en plus conscient de son corps et les parents ne voient pas toujours l'importance qu'il accorde à des problèmes, tels que l'acné, les défauts de posture, la fatigue, l'obésité ou les menstruations irrégulières. Il faut tenir compte de cet éveil, discuter avec lui du traitement et des règles hygiéniques qui peuvent améliorer son état et l'encourager à prendre son traitement en mains. Certains parents n'admettent pas l'évolution de leur enfant et ne peuvent le guider vers une meilleure compréhension des changements qui s'opèrent en lui, tout en le tenant au courant de son état physique.

De nombreux problèmes de l'adolescent proviennent des changements physiques et physiologiques qu'il subit et des conflits émotifs violents qui l'agitent. Devant l'importance de l'aspect psychosomatique de ces maladies, il devient essentiel d'établir des liens étroits entre le patient, les parents, le médecin, le professeur, le conseiller et l'infirmière scolaire.

En plus de conseils médicaux, l'adolescent a souvent besoin de parler avec une personne, étrangère à son milieu familial, qui accepte de discuter avec lui de sujets, tels que la sexualité, la religion, la mort, l'éducation et la drogue. L'adolescent peut s'exprimer sans avoir peur d'être jugé ou puni et devient ainsi plus objectif envers ses problèmes.

Acné

L'acné est une inflammation de la peau, atteignant les glandes sébacées et leur périphérie. Certains facteurs héréditaires et l'hyperactivité d'une sécrétion hormonale androgénique apparemment normale semblent en être les causes, mais l'acné est tellement fréquente qu'on la considère un peu comme une manifestation normale du développement sexuel.

On constate d'abord une hypersécrétion de sébum qui ne peut s'éliminer complètement à la surface de la peau; les pores se dilatent, la kératinisation durcit le sébum et irrite la glande sébacée. Les comédons ou points noirs apparaissent; ils sont suivis de papules superficielles et profondes qui, sans traitement,

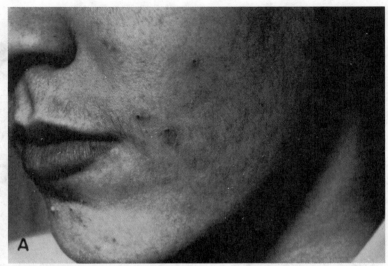

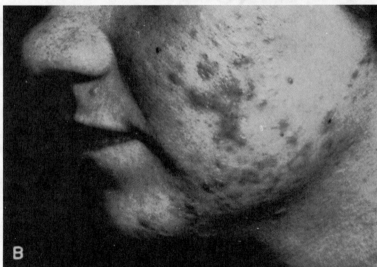

Figure 24-1. *A)* Grade 1— Une papule s'élève autour du comédon. *B)* Grade 2— Des lésions inflammatoires plus étendues entourent les comédons. (Pillsbury, D.M. Shelley, W.B. et Kligman, A.M.: *Dermatology.* Philadelphia, W.B. Saunders Company, 1956.)

deviennent des pustules et des kystes qui laisseront des cicatrices.

On remarque l'acné sur le front, le menton et les joues; le dos, les épaules et la poitrine peuvent aussi être atteints. Le prurit n'est pas toujours présent. L'adolescent souffrant d'acné peut se replier sur lui-même et en arriver à éviter tout contact social. Il peut éventuellement souffrir de problèmes émotifs.

Traitement et pronostic. Le traitement doit débuter aussitôt que possible afin d'éviter les cicatrices indélébiles. Un régime alimentaire équilibré, beaucoup de repos, l'exposition à la lumière solaire, la réduction des tensions émotives et de l'anxiété, une très grande propreté personnelle, contribuent à améliorer l'état général et l'état de la peau, mais n'a pas nécessairement d'effets sur l'acné.

Les sports et l'exercice peuvent améliorer l'état de la peau; la transpiration profuse amollit les comédons qui bloquent l'entrée de la glande sébacée et favorise l'expulsion de sébum. Il est recommandé de prendre un bon bain avec massage après un exercice violent.

Par le traitement local on s'attaque directement au problème. La peau doit être nettoyée au moins deux fois par jour avec un savon spécial à base d'antiseptique et contenant un kératolytique. L'eau chaude amollit les lésions, la kératolyse permet de les ouvrir et l'antiseptique assèche la peau et peut agir contre la saleté et les bactéries accumulées. Le but du traitement local est de décaper délicatement la peau et de la dégraisser pour prévenir la formation des comédons. La thérapie locale peut consister en l'application d'une préparation à base de soufre, ou d'un mélange de soufre et de résorcinol, un agent décapant ou kératolytique. La vitamine A, appliquée localement, réduit la formation des comédons. Il faut utiliser les nouvelles substances d'un seul côté du visage à la fois afin de pouvoir juger du résultat. Certaines préparations cosmétiquement acceptables ont été développées pour cacher les lésions, évitant ainsi le traumatisme psychologique qui accompagne souvent l'acné. Le médecin doit insister sur le danger de pincer et d'extirper soi-même les comédons, car cette pratique favorise la formation de cicatrices qui peuvent devenir permanentes. Toutefois, la chirurgie de l'acné inclut l'incision du comédon et le drainage de la glande sébacée. Ces soins, effectués avec des instruments stériles ne laissent pas de cicatrices.

Les crèmes antibiotiques peuvent aider, mais il est bon d'appliquer d'abord une mince couche sur un seul côté du visage afin d'en évaluer l'effet curatif et les réactions allergiques possibles.

Dans les cas très graves, on a recours à l'antibiothérapie systémique. Les tétracyclines sont l'antibiotique de choix et peuvent être administrées durant d'assez longues périodes sans effets secondaires graves. Parfois, l'association des tétracyclines avec la vitamine A augmente leur efficacité. Si l'adolescent réagit peu à la tétracycline, on peut essayer l'érythromycine. Dans les formes graves d'acné, on utilise les corticostéroïdes topiques en prenant soin d'en appliquer une couche très mince. La corticothérapie systémique est plus rarement tentée et seulement pour de courtes périodes.

Les traitements esthétiques comme le sablage et la dermabrasion n'améliorent pas toujours les cicatrices profondes qui suivent l'acné. L'acné disparaît d'habitude spontanément, et parfois très lentement, à la fin de l'adolescence ou au début de la vie adulte.

Perçage des oreilles

Beaucoup de jeunes filles désirent se faire percer les oreilles, car cette pratique est populaire dans la culture nord-américaine. Malheureusement, cette opération est souvent effectuée par la mère, une amie, un bijoutier ou l'adolescente elle-même. Certaines complications, comme la dermatite allergique au métal, la formation de croûtes, l'inflammation, le saignement, la formation de kystes ou de cicatrices chéloïdes peuvent survenir. Vu ces complications, les jeunes filles qui souffrent de diabète ou qui ont déjà présenté des cicatrices chéloïdes doivent demander à leur médecin de

pratiquer l'intervention; les parents doivent donner leur consentement si elles sont mineures. On ne doit pas utiliser de boucles d'oreilles contenant du nickel ou d'autres métaux comportant un danger de sensibilisation.

Défaut de posture

Il peut y avoir plusieurs causes à la mauvaise posture de l'adolescent. La croissance osseuse peut être plus rapide que l'accroissement musculaire et l'adolescent, très grand et très maigre, ne sait plus quelle attitude adopter; il se sent plus grand que ses condisciples et essaie de se replier sur lui-même. L'apparition des seins peut gêner l'adolescente qui courbe les épaules pour cacher ce symbole de sexualité. Des jeunes des deux sexes développent une mauvaise posture pour avoir regardé la télévision depuis très longtemps dans des fauteuils inappropriés. Le cou se porte vers l'avant et les épaules s'arrondissent. Les muscles antérieurs du cou et de la poitrine se raccourcissent et ceux de la région postérieure du cou et des épaules deviennent plus faibles.

Il est inutile de ridiculiser, d'embarrasser ou de menacer celui qui se tient mal. Un médecin

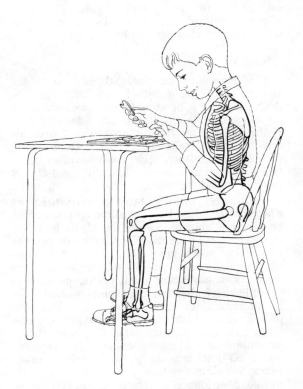

Figure 24-2. Le mobilier adapté à sa taille aide l'adolescent à acquérir des habitudes de bonne posture.

pourra déterminer si le problème est physique ou psychologique. Souvent, une bonne discussion à cœur ouvert peut régler les problèmes psychologiques reliés au développement sexuel. Si la cause semble être une croissance plus lente de la masse musculaire, il s'agit simplement d'attendre et d'encourager une posture adéquate. Une consultation en orthopédie élimine la possibilité d'une scoliose.

Fatigue

La fatigue de l'adolescent peut provenir de multiples facteurs comme une croissance physique extrêmement rapide, un surcroît d'activité, un manque de sommeil, une mauvaise alimentation, de l'anémie ou un problème émotif. Si la fatigue est excessive ou dure depuis trop longtemps, il faut faire une investigation plus approfondie pour en découvrir la cause.

Anémie

Avant la puberté, le taux d'hémoglobine est le même pour les deux sexes, alors qu'après le début des menstruations, les filles ont un taux inférieur de 2 grammes à la moyenne des garçons. Même si l'anémie hypochrome est moins fréquente qu'autrefois, elle peut encore produire des pertes de conscience et de la fatigue chez les adolescentes.

Obésité

L'accumulation de tissu adipeux est relativement fréquente pendant l'adolescence. Les deux sexes en sont atteints, spécialement dans les classes de faible niveau socio-économique. L'obésité de l'adolescent ne requiert ordinairement aucun traitement médical, mais il est pénible de constater que ses mauvaises habitudes alimentaires le condamnent peut-être à devenir un adulte obèse.

Étiologie, manifestations cliniques et diagnostic. Les besoins alimentaires varient en fonction du métabolisme basal, de la croissance et de l'activité. La suralimentation et l'inactivité proviennent de facteurs héréditaires, familiaux, raciaux, émotifs et parfois physiques. Un adolescent malheureux, porté à la solitude, peut chercher une compensation dans la nourriture, ce qui est loin de régler son problème, car l'obésité cause souvent une distorsion de l'image corporelle. Certaines mères présentent les aliments comme une récompense ou habituent le jeune à des quantités excessives de nourriture. S'il existe un problème de dépendance envers la mère, l'enfant se tourne vers la nourriture à la moindre difficulté.

Les problèmes endocriniens, comme l'hypothyroïdisme ou le syndrome de Cushing, les lésions crâniennes, sont des causes extrêmement rares d'obésité. Les mauvaises habitudes alimentaires en demeurent la cause la plus fréquente.

L'adolescent obèse est facile à reconnaître. Plutôt inactif, de taille plus élevée que la moyenne, il a une finesse de traits faciaux qui surprend au premier abord. L'excès de tissu adipeux est surtout localisé à la poitrine, à la partie supérieure des bras et des cuisses; la paroi abdominale est marquée de vergetures et chez le garçon, la verge apparaît toute petite, car elle est noyée dans le tissu adipeux.

Le jeune présente souvent des problèmes émotifs; gauche et maladroit, il participe le moins possible aux compétitions sportives où il réussit d'ailleurs assez mal. Le glissement épiphysaire est fréquent, ainsi que les pieds plats et le genou en valgus.

Il faut d'abord reconnaître les problèmes endocriniens et évaluer ensuite l'état émotif du patient. Une fiche complète de tout ce que l'enfant mange quotidiennement prouve ordinairement la suralimentation; après des repas normaux, les excès se produisent aux heures creuses de l'après-midi ou de la soirée.

Traitement et pronostic. La coopération de l'adolescent et de sa famille est essentielle pour assurer le succès de la cure, car on doit fréquemment changer les habitudes alimentaires de toute la famille. L'alimentation est établie d'après les besoins caloriques, mais on peut diminuer l'apport jusqu'à 1 000 ou 1 200 calories par jour, pour un enfant entre 10 et 14 ans. La diète doit être équilibrée, riche en résidus, sels minéraux et vitamines. La vitamine D permet une croissance normale. Les collations sont calculées dans l'apport calorique. Un programme d'exercices et d'activités accompagne le traitement diététique. L'idéal serait une perte de poids de 1 kg par semaine.

Il faut reconnaître les problèmes psychologiques avant d'établir le régime. L'adolescent doit être convaincu que le médecin et la diététicienne le respectent. Des rencontres avec des groupes d'adolescents obèses peuvent le stimuler. La psychothérapie peut être nécessaire, ainsi qu'une médication adéquate.

Les marottes alimentaires

Les marottes alimentaires dégénèrent souvent en mauvaise nutrition même dans les familles financièrement capables de s'offrir une diète équilibrée. La vogue est actuellement aux aliments dits « naturels » et aux aliments amaigrissants spéciaux. Certains adolescents s'adonnent aux marottes alimentaires dans l'espoir de maigrir ou de ne pas grossir, ou parce que ces aliments sont populaires et simples ou promettent force et beauté.

Manger constitue une expérience émotive: dès la naissance, elle requiert la coopération d'au moins une autre personne. De plus, les adolescents sont constamment à la recherche d'expériences nouvelles; celle de manger des aliments particuliers les aident à tolérer certains sentiments d'insatisfaction.

Il faut aider les adolescents à comprendre les principes d'une saine alimentation afin d'éviter les déficiences nutritives qui les guettent. Il est essentiel de manger tous les jours des aliments qui comprennent les éléments nutritifs indispensables.

Gynécomastie

L'hypertrophie de la glande mammaire chez l'homme s'appelle gynécomastie et peut être causée par l'hypersécrétion d'œstrogènes ou d'androgènes par les testicules au moment de la puberté. La gynécomastie peut survenir avant l'apparition des caractères sexuels secondaires masculins et disparaît habituellement après un ou deux ans. L'accroissement et l'hypersensibilité peuvent se produire à un ou aux deux seins. Le traitement hormonal n'est pas justifié, mais la chirurgie peut être indiquée si l'hypertrophie devient si apparente qu'elle risque de constituer un problème psychologique.

La gynécomastie est parfois transmise par un gène autosome dominant; elle peut aussi être associée à des tumeurs interstitielles du testicule ou à des tumeurs féminisantes des surrénales. Les autres causes possibles sont le syndrome de Klinefelter, certaines défaillances testiculaires et pour les garçons plus âgés, les maladies hépatiques et la paraplégie. L'enfant exposé accidentellement ou de façon thérapeutique aux œstrogènes peut également souffrir de gynécomastie.

La pseudogynécomastie apparaît chez l'enfant obèse dont les seins sont couverts d'un épais pannicule adipeux.

Le rôle de l'infirmière consiste à rassurer les parents et l'enfant, car une fois le diagnostic établi, il suffit d'attendre la résorption de la glande. Si les mamelons sont douloureux, il peut être bon de les couvrir d'un tissu doux pour éviter le frottement.

Menstruations irrégulières

Les premières menstruations se produisent ordinairement vers l'âge de 12-13 ans, variant de onze à quinze ans selon les jeunes filles. Il est normal que les premiers cycles soient anovulaires et il ne faut pas s'étonner de l'irrégularité et des variations quantitatives du flot menstruel. Au cours de la deuxième année, tout redevient normal, quoique certains cycles demeurent anovulaires, mais les problèmes sont peu nombreux. Ils se présentent surtout chez les filles obèses ou sous-alimentées, hyper ou hypoactives. Les troubles émotifs, les difficultés scolaires et la mauvaise adaptation sociale peuvent également se manifester par des menstruations irrégulières. Si le rétablissement de l'état général ou la correction des problèmes psychologiques ne suffisent pas à améliorer la situation, une évaluation du métabolisme basal et un examen gynécologique deviennent alors nécessaires. La grossesse peut être une explication plausible après une assez longue période d'aménorrhée secondaire.

Dysménorrhée

La dysménorrhée, ou douleurs menstruelles, est assez fréquente. On croit qu'elle provient de spasmes musculaires de l'utérus, encore mal expliqués. Habituellement, un bain chaud ou un coussin chauffant placé sur l'abdomen ou à la région lombaire, de l'exercice et un analgésique ou un sédatif doux parviennent à vaincre le malaise. Le médecin doit être consulté si la dysménorrhée devient un handicap. Il est à souligner que les cycles menstruels anovulaires ne produisent jamais de dysménorrhée.

Douleur à l'ovulation

Environ 14 jours avant le début de la période menstruelle, l'adolescente peut ressentir dans la région pelvienne, une douleur sourde qui irradie vers la cuisse. Ce malaise serait dû à la rupture et à l'hémorragie du corps jaune. Ce phénomène et la dysménorrhée disparaissent souvent après la naissance du premier enfant.

Ménorragie

On désigne sous ce nom les menstruations trop abondantes. La ménorragie est parfois le signe d'un problème organique et peut être si abondante que l'adolescente souffre de fatigue et d'anémie. Les causes possibles sont une maladie utérine, une anomalie de la sécrétion des ovaires ou de la glande thyroïde ou une dyscrasie sanguine, telle la leucémie ou le purpura. Si la ménorragie persiste, il faut consulter un gynécologue.

Syndrome prémenstruel

Certaines adolescentes se plaignent d'un malaise appelé syndrome prémenstruel caractérisé par une nervosité excessive, de la tension, un sentiment dépressif, une sensation de lourdeur aux jambes, de la céphalée et des nausées. Le syndrome qui persiste justifie un examen médical complet pour éliminer une cause organique. Le médecin prescrit parfois un diurétique ou un analgésique pour diminuer le malaise.

Soins. L'adolescente peut être très réticente quand elle doit subir un examen gynécologique. Pour diminuer son appréhension il serait bon de lui expliquer, au préalable, l'anatomie des organes génitaux, la façon de procéder à l'examen gynécologique et les buts précis de l'examen.

Il est à souligner que la médecine ne s'est jamais penchée sérieusement sur les problèmes reliés à la menstruation. On ignore les causes des douleurs menstruelles et on ne peut expliquer la vulnérabilité de certaines femmes à la dysménorrhée, au syndrome prémenstruel et à la migraine pendant les menstruations.

Masturbation

La masturbation est normale au cours de l'adolescence et joue un rôle dans le processus de maturation physique et émotive. L'adolescent qui a appris de ses parents que la masturbation est un acte coupable et qui se rend compte en même temps du plaisir que la masturbation procure, se trouve en situation conflictuelle. Il peut tenter de vaincre le dilemme en évitant toute stimulation sexuelle et en exerçant sur lui-même un contrôle sévère. La moindre rechute augmente sa culpabilité et le dégoût qu'il éprouve de lui-même. Il peut transposer le conflit au niveau somatique et se plaindre de faiblesse et de fatigue extrême, de symptômes et de malaises vagues et multiples. Certains adolescents tentent de sublimer leurs besoins sexuels ou s'adonnent à des activités sexuelles préliminaires avec des jeunes de l'autre sexe. L'excès dans la masturbation constitue habituellement le signe de la faillite de l'individu sur le plan des relations inter-personnelles. L'infirmière doit chercher à identifier les besoins de l'adolescent et à le diriger vers d'autres moyens de gratification. L'adolescent comblé au point de vue affectif cessera de se masturber de façon excessive et évoluera vers des relations satisfaisantes avec l'autre sexe.

Hyperthyroïdisme

Le goître exophtalmique est très rare à cette époque de la vie. Le métabolisme basal, diminué depuis le début de l'âge scolaire, s'élève immédiatement avant la puberté. Certains présentent un tableau d'hyperthyroïdisme, mais la quantité d'hormone produite n'atteint pas le seuil du goître exophtalmique. Le traitement comprend un régime riche en calories, un ralentissement des activités scolaires et sportives et quelquefois l'administration d'iode. Cette sorte d'hyperthyroïdie disparaît avec la maturité sexuelle.

Névroses mineures

L'adolescent présente souvent des signes névrotiques discrets; d'abord peu importants, ils apparaissent à la suite d'un stress ou d'une épreuve et ne persistent que si l'adolescent découvre que ces symptômes sont pour lui l'occasion de gratifications.

Les principales causes sont le manque de popularité, la pauvreté des performances athlétiques et les faibles résultats scolaires, la faillite dans la participation aux activités récréatives, l'échec dans l'émancipation vis-à-vis de l'autorité parentale, la culpabilité causée par la masturbation et la peur de la sexualité.

Les adolescents se plaignent le plus souvent d'insomnie, de cauchemars, de céphalées, de manque de concentration, de problèmes gastro-intestinaux et menstruels.

Il suffit, en général, d'aider l'adolescent et ses parents à trouver la raison du problème. Le médecin de famille ou l'infirmière scolaire sont les mieux placés pour évaluer les résultats et ils peuvent toujours demander une consultation en psychiatrie, si le besoin s'en fait sentir.

RÉFÉRENCES

Livres et documents officiels

Daniel, W. A.: *The Adolescent Patient*. Saint-Louis, C. V. Mosby Company, 1970.

Frank, S. B.: *Acne Vulgaris*. Springfield, Ill., Charles C Thomas, 1971.

Gallagher, J. R.: *Medical Care of the Adolescent*. 2e éd. New York, Appleton-Century-Crofts, 1966.

Hammar, S. et Eddy, J.: *Nursing Care of the Adolescent*. New York, Springer Pub. Co, 1966.

Kalafatich, A.: *Approaches to the Care of Adolescents*. New York, Appleton-Century-Crofts, 1975.

Meeks, J. E.: *The Fragile Alliance — An Orientation to the Out-Patient Psychotherapy of the Adolescent*. Baltimore, Williams & Wilkins Company, 1971.

Pillsbury, D. M.: *A Manual of Dermatology*. Philadelphie, W. B. Saunders Company, 1971.

Rowland, C. V. (édit.): *Anorexia and Obesity*. Boston, Little, Brown and Company, 1970.

Usdin, G. (édit.): *Adolescence: Medical Care and Counseling*. Philaldelphie, J. B. Lippincott Co, 1967.

Articles

Bellaire, J.: Teenagers Learn to Care About Themselves. *Nursing Outlook*, 19:792, décembre 1971.

Brown, F.: Sexual Problems of the Adolescent Girl. *Pediat. Clin. N. Amer.*, 19:759, août 1972.

Bryan, D. S.: Skin Problems of School Age Children and Youth — A Nursing Responsibility? *J. School Health*, 40:437, octobre 1970.

Cortese, T. A. et Dickey, R. A.: Complications of Ear Piercing. *Am. Fam. Physician GP*, 4:66, août 1971.

Fuszard, Sister M. B.: Acceptance of Authoritarianism in the Nurse by the Hospitalized Teen-Ager. *Nursing Research*, 18:426, septembre-octobre 1969.

Giroux, J. M. et Camirand, P.: Récentes théories sur la physiopathologie et le traitement de l'acné vulgaire. *Union méd. du Can.*, 99:1630, septembre 1970.

Guthrie, A. D. et Howell, M. C.: Mobile Medical Care for Alienated Youths. *J. Pediat.*, 81:1025, novembre 1972.

Hammar, S. L.: The Approach to the Adolescent Patient. *Ped. Clin. N. Amer.*, 20:779, 4, 1973.,

Kalisch, B. J.: The Stigma of Obesity. *Am. J. Nursing*, 72:1124, juin 1972.

Lore, A.: Adolescents: People, not Problems. *Am. J. Nursing*, 73:1232, 7, 1973.

Panaccio, V.: L'acné, problème toujours d'actualité. *Union méd. du Can.*, 97:63, janvier 1968.

Reisner, R.: Acne Vulgaris. *Ped. Clin. N. Amer.*, 20:851. 4, 1973.

Rigg, C. A. et autres: Is a Separate Adolescent Ward Worthwhile? *Am. J. Dis. Child.*, 122:489, décembre 1971.

Schowalter, J. E. et Lord, R. D.: The Hospitalized Adolescent. *Children*, 18:127, juillet-aooût 1971.

Seltzer, C. C. et Mayer, J.: An Effective Weight Control Program in a Public School System. *Am. J. Pub. Health*, 60:679, avril 1970.

Sloan, D.: Pelvic Pain and Dysmenorrhea. *Pediat. Clin. N. Amer.*, 19:669, août 1972.

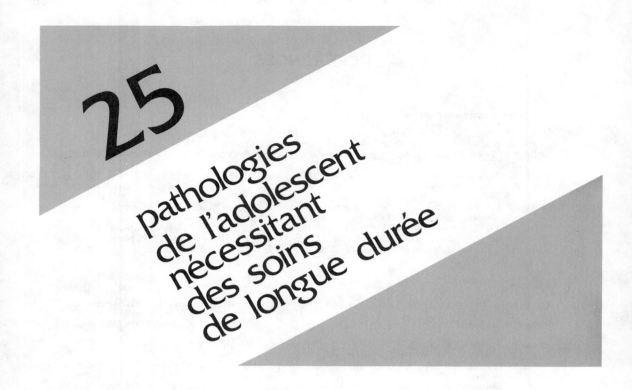

25

pathologies de l'adolescent nécessitant des soins de longue durée

EFFETS DE LA MALADIE SUR LES ADOLESCENTS

L'adolescence, période critique en soi, peut devenir une véritable pierre d'achoppement pour l'enfant handicapé. Il peut avoir quelque difficulté à acquérir son identité sexuelle, à se connaître lui-même, à s'émanciper de sa famille et choisir une carrière. Les aspects sociaux du handicap deviennent beaucoup plus apparents durant l'adolescence, et si l'enfant n'a pas déjà accepté la réalité dans laquelle il vit, il peut en devenir émotivement perturbé.

Les effets d'un handicap, tel que la surdité, la cécité, les troubles cardiaques, le diabète ou la paralysie cérébrale, tendent à rendre les enfants de tout âge hyper-dépendants des adultes et modifient de différentes façons le développement de leur personnalité. De tels handicaps peuvent limiter à la fois les relations sociales avec les autres enfants et la possibilité de libérer les émotions par l'activité physique. L'adolescent peut alors développer des sentiments de méfiance et d'infériorité; il manque de confiance en lui-même. Il peut s'avouer vaincu au départ ou chercher à punir autrui pour ses échecs.

La maladie prolongée durant l'adolescence peut avoir des effets désastreux sur le développement de la personnalité. L'adolescent souffrant d'une maladie chronique peut trouver difficile ou s'avérer incapable de développer des sentiments d'identité et d'intimité, tâches pourtant nécessaires à son développement.

L'adolescent handicapé qui réussit, avec ou sans aide extérieure, à traverser victorieusement cette période, deviendra probablement un adulte autonome et riche d'une expérience que beaucoup pourraient lui envier.

SOIN DE L'ADOLESCENT HOSPITALISÉ

L'adolescent se plaint souvent de vagues malaises physiques qui proviennent la plupart du temps de changements normaux auxquels il n'était pas préparé. Un examen physique sérieux et complet permet de déceler les problèmes réels et fournit également l'occasion de discuter avec lui des inquiétudes qui se cachent derrière ses malaises. L'anxiété diminue quand l'adolescent sait qu'il est en bonne santé ou qu'il peut recevoir de l'aide s'il est malade.

L'adolescent qui doit être hospitalisé doit recevoir au préalable une bonne préparation;

il faut lui fournir des explications sur les traitements, les examens et les interventions qu'il doit subir et il faut lui permettre de participer aux décisions qui le concernent.

L'adolescent, selon son degré de maturité, s'adapte habituellement assez bien à l'hôpital pourvu qu'il puisse garder un contact étroit avec sa famille et ses amis. Il tolère relativement bien une anxiété modérée et noue plus facilement qu'auparavant des relations nouvelles avec les adultes qu'il rencontre.

Il peut toutefois se sentir frustré parce que sa maladie perturbe ou interrompt sa vie scolaire, familiale ou sociale. Il peut trouver si pénible d'assumer les transformations qui accompagnent l'adolescence qu'il se sent submergé par les nouveaux problèmes qui se présentent à lui. Il défend jalousement l'image de force qu'il a lentement édifiée et il craint que la maladie ne le diminue ou lui cause un dommage irréparable. Tout comme l'enfant d'âge scolaire, il peut croire que la maladie constitue une punition pour des fautes plus ou moins réelles et que tous les plans qu'il avait élaborés en seront détruits. L'adolescent qui semblait fort et auto-suffisant peut se sentir soudainement faible et vulnérable; ne voulant pas en convenir et tentant de le cacher à ses amis, il cherche souvent à s'isoler.

Quand l'adolescent est hospitalisé dans une unité de soins pour adultes, il faut lui laisser le choix de se faire appeler par son prénom ou de se faire dire « monsieur » ou « mademoiselle ». Devant l'adulte qui partage sa chambre, il craint de paraître ridicule s'il a de la difficulté à choisir son menu du lendemain, s'il doit se servir du bassin de lit ou s'il ne sait pas trop comment occuper ses loisirs. Le bain complet au lit peut également devenir une source d'embarras et fournir un sujet de taquinerie dont l'adulte abuse parfois. S'il partage sa chambre avec un vieillard, l'ennui le guette, surtout s'il est immobilisé au lit et qu'il n'a pas de téléphone à sa portée. L'abus de conversations téléphoniques peut par contre gêner l'adulte qui a aussi droit à la tranquillité.

Les visiteurs que reçoit l'adolescent peuvent constituer un problème pour le personnel de l'unité de soins pour adultes; en effet, les jeunes se déplacent souvent en bandes et les limites sur le nombre de visiteurs permis ne sont guère respectées. Il suffit habituellement d'expliquer au jeune malade qu'un trop grand nombre de visiteurs perturbe les autres malades et gêne l'efficacité des soins; de plus, l'intensité du bruit peut dépasser les bornes acceptables. Si un groupe de jeunes fait brusquement irruption dans la chambre, on peut leur permettre une courte visite et leur expliquer en même temps les règles auxquelles ils devront se conformer à l'avenir. Les mesures cœrcitives sont la plupart du temps inutiles; elles risquent d'encourager l'adolescent à déroger aux règles et elles diminuent la crédibilité du personnel chez celui qui est malade. Il faut s'inquiéter davantage de l'adolescent qui ne reçoit pas de visiteurs et encore plus de celui qui ne désire pas en recevoir.

Dans les unités d'adultes, l'adolescent ennuie souvent les autres patients par ses activités bruyantes. Il peut également devenir très anxieux lorsqu'il reçoit des informations erronées de la part des patients adultes; il peut voir des scènes ou entendre des bruits qui sont susceptibles de le terrifier.

Dans les unités pédiatriques, l'adolescent peut être agacé par les pleurs des enfants plus jeunes, se sentir isolé parce qu'il n'a pas de camarades de son âge et être gêné par le manque d'intimité. Il peut souffrir des remarques de ses amis qui le traitent de « bébé » puisqu'il se trouve avec des enfants. Le matériel est parfois trop petit et il est très gênant de coucher dans un lit trop court, surtout devant les camarades.

Au cours des dernières années, on a créé dans certains hôpitaux des *unités spéciales* où les adolescents se retrouvent entre camarades du même âge. On croit que les médecins et les infirmières, qui se plaisent à travailler avec les jeunes, donneront des soins plus compréhensifs à leurs patients. De plus, les adolescents ont besoin d'une relation continue avec leur pédiatre, jusqu'à ce qu'ils atteignent l'âge adulte.

Dans les unités d'adolescents, l'environnement doit être aussi amical et simple que possible. Un tourne-disques dans la salle de séjour fournit une occasion de rencontre pour les patients ambulants. Un téléphone près du lit permet à l'adolescent de garder le contact avec ses amis et sa famille. On essaie d'être aussi peu rigide que possible au sujet des heures de visite. De plus, on permet à l'adolescent, dont l'appétit est ordinairement insatiable, de choisir au menu des aliments qui correspondent à ses goûts et que l'on trouve rarement en milieu hospitalier ordinaire. Les collations deviennent également plus fréquentes et plus substantielles. Des rencontres de groupe, organisées ou spontanées, facilitent les échanges entre les adolescents, favorisent la communication entre les malades et les membres de l'équipe et fournissent des occasions de donner un enseignement qui sera bien reçu.

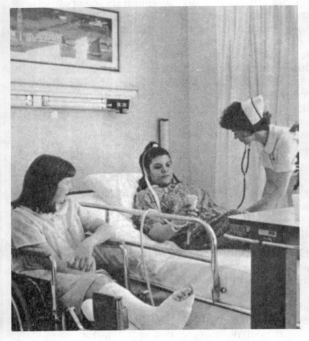

Figure 25-1. Les relations qui s'établissent avec le personnel infirmier et les camarades du même âge deviennent encore plus importantes quand l'adolescent est alité. (Extrait de Weinberg, S., Schonberg, C.E. et Grier, D.Y.: *Nursing Outlook*, 17:18, décembre 1968.)

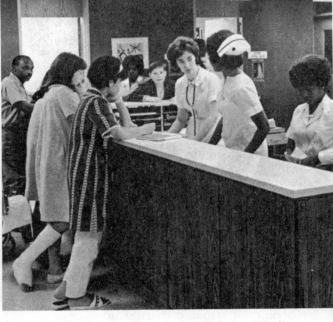

Figure 25-2. Le poste des infirmières est le lieu de prédilection où se réunissent les adolescents qui peuvent marcher. Ils écoutent avec intérêt tous les renseignements concernant les examens, la diète ou le programme scolaire. (Extrait de Weinberg, S., Schonberg, C.E. et Grier, D.Y.: *Nursing Outlook*, 17:18, décembre 1968.)

Les adolescents hospitalisés dans de telles unités possèdent, en général, suffisamment de maturité pour admettre qu'ils sont malades et pour essayer de s'adapter à la situation. Ils peuvent cependant protester au sujet de restrictions, telles qu'un régime spécial ou la nécessité du repos au lit. Ils veulent être renseignés sur leur maladie et les traitements qu'ils doivent subir. Les adolescents hospitalisés ont besoin de contact avec d'autres adolescents, de distraction et de respect en tant qu'individu.

L'adolescent qui provient d'un milieu socio-économique défavorisé réagit souvent à l'hospitalisation d'une manière tout à fait différente de ses compagnons plus favorisés. Après l'admission, il peut s'isoler de son nouveau milieu et devenir distant et apathique. Il peut éviter les activités créatrices qui l'aideraient à s'exprimer et refuser de se distraire par la lecture ou la conversation avec les autres malades ou le personnel. Souvent, il ne pose pas de question sur son état, subit les traitements de façon passive et ne demande pas d'aide ou de support au personnel. Il donne l'impression de préférer souffrir en silence et il s'isole de

l'entourage tout en suivant des yeux tout ce qui se passe autour de lui. Le personnel doit comprendre à quel point le milieu hospitalier s'appuie sur des valeurs de classe moyenne. L'adolescent en quête de son identité peut éprouver un véritable choc culturel lorsqu'il est hospitalisé et réagir en ressentant un profond sentiment d'infériorité et d'incompétence. Seule une attitude authentique de respect et d'acceptation peut amener l'adolescent défavorisé à accepter les soins et l'enseignement qui lui sont prodigués.

Rôle de l'infirmière dans le soin des adolescents

L'infirmière trouve parfois pénible de travailler avec les adolescents. En effet, le jeune homme peut se sentir gêné lorsqu'une jeune infirmière lui donne des soins personnels; la jeune fille peut hésiter à découvrir certaines parties de son corps devant quelqu'un qui a presque son âge. Souvent, les adolescents communiquent plus facilement avec une personne plus âgée et possédant plus de maturité. Toutefois, l'infirmière doit comprendre les sentiments des adolescents et apprendre à communiquer avec eux de façon efficace.

L'infirmière, peu importe son âge, doit aider l'adolescent à se sentir important. Elle doit le présenter aux autres patients, lui demander son avis sur les sujets qui le touchent et le faire participer à la planification de ses soins.

Les adolescents sont souvent imprévisibles; ils peuvent être émotivement instables et ambivalents, tiraillés entre leurs désirs de dépendance et d'indépendance. L'infirmière doit se rappeler que leur besoin de se sentir en sécurité, d'aimer et d'être aimés, d'être acceptés comme membre du groupe, peut quelquefois les empêcher de montrer leur angoisse à l'idée d'être malade et d'être hospitalisé.

L'infirmière compétente décèle rapidement l'hostilité et le rejet chez ces patients. Quand de tels sentiments deviennent évidents, elle doit souvent changer son approche afin d'obtenir leur coopération. Elle doit éviter d'argumenter inutilement et de leur donner des ordres tout en leur faisant confiance et en les traitant comme des adolescents, non comme des enfants.

Une certaine liberté d'action doit régner dans les unités d'adolescents, mais l'infirmière doit imposer des restrictions quand elles deviennent nécessaires. L'adolescent accepte parfois difficilement les règlements de l'hôpital qui lui semblent la prolongation de l'autorité parentale dont il essaie justement de se libérer. Les normes établies doivent rester suffisamment flexibles pour permettre à chaque individu de s'épanouir librement. Les restrictions doivent aller de pair avec les privilèges et ceux-ci font appel à la responsabilité de chacun. Par exemple, bien que le règlement exige que les visites se terminent à 21 heures, si pour l'anniversaire d'une adolescente, ses amis veulent continuer la fête jusqu'à 21 h 30 mn, on pourra le leur permettre. Ils doivent cependant comprendre que le bruit excessif peut déranger les autres patients; si bien qu'ils doivent assumer la responsabilité de demeurer relativement tranquilles. Ils doivent aussi accepter de tout remettre en ordre lorsque la fête sera terminée. Il faut surtout s'inquiéter de celui qui accepte trop facilement l'autorité du personnel et tenter de découvrir s'il s'agit d'une adaptation particulièrement bien réussie ou d'un écran permettant de dissimuler la régression ou la négation de la situation.

Certains adolescents acceptent difficilement les transformations physiologiques de la puberté. L'infirmière compétente peut leur venir en aide au moment de l'examen médical ou lorsqu'elle administre des traitements. Si elle reconnaît les craintes propres à cette phase de la croissance, elle va percevoir la signification cachée de certaines questions apparemment sans but. Elle peut expliquer que des craintes de cette sorte sont normales et qu'elle les comprend.

L'adolescente examinée par un médecin masculin ou l'adolescent soigné par une femme médecin ont souvent besoin du secours de l'infirmière pour vaincre l'embarras qu'ils ressentent. Celle-ci doit demeurer au chevet de l'adolescent s'il en exprime le désir. Après le départ du médecin, elle peut également en profiter pour éclaircir ou expliquer certains points restés obscurs.

Les adolescentes veulent paraître aussi attrayantes que possible, et l'usage des produits de beauté revêt pour elles une grande importance. L'infirmière doit comprendre que le fait d'aider une jeune fille à se coiffer d'une manière attrayante, même si elle est immobilisée dans un plâtre, constitue une partie essentielle de sa tâche.

Les adolescents hospitalisés tendent à former des groupes comme ils le font dans la vie normale. Ces groupes sont habituellement composés d'individus d'âges différents et fluctuent en fonction des arrivées et des départs incessants. Les jeunes souffrant de troubles similaires s'unissent souvent, comme par exemple, les scoliotiques de l'unité d'orthopédie. L'infirmière doit observer l'organigramme du groupe et son influence sur le chef de file facilitera souvent les rapports avec tous les autres membres. Elle doit identifier les adolescents rejetés ou traités en « souffre douleur » et intervenir le cas échéant.

Une des plus grandes craintes des adolescents consiste à perdre leur contrôle émotif devant leurs camarades. Si un adolescent doit affronter un traitement pénible, il peut être préférable de le retirer du groupe, afin qu'il puisse exprimer ses sentiments ouvertement plutôt que de pleurer en présence des autres et se sentir ensuite humilié.

L'adolescent qui doit subir une intervention chirurgicale sous anesthésie générale est soumis à une tension particulièrement grande et craint la période d'impuissance qui suivra. La rencontre d'autres opérés et le support de l'infirmière l'aident à surmonter ce sentiment pénible.

Celui qui doit demeurer immobile, soit en traction ou à la suite d'une intervention chirurgicale, est également soumis à un stress physique et émotif. Il se sent honteux, diminué et peut devenir anxieux, insécure, dépendant, agressif et hostile. Il se plaint de malaises physiques divers et son rythme de sommeil devient souvent perturbé. On peut diminuer les réactions négatives en discutant honnêtement avec lui de son état, en soulignant les progrès qu'il fait et en lui expliquant toutes les techniques de soin qu'il doit subir. L'adolescent qui dépend entièrement d'autrui pour ses soins physiques devient facilement très exigeant, éprouve des peurs irrationnelles et refuse les traitements; il peut au contraire devenir très dépendant et perdre son autonomie. On doit le rassurer et l'encourager à participer activement à ses soins.

Il est fréquent que l'adolescent hospitalisé recherche des contacts physiques avec l'infirmière: il veut se faire masser le dos ou il lui demande de lui tenir la main. Il faut se rappeler que le contact physique tout comme pour l'enfant demeure très important au point de vue physique et psychologique. L'infirmière très jeune peut se sentir troublée par ces exigences et celles-ci doivent être évaluées au cours des réunions d'équipe autant pour en cerner les implications que pour rassurer celle qui donne les soins. Dans ces situations, il est important que les infirmières établissent un contact chaleureux avec l'adolescent, mais qu'elles imposent toutes les mêmes limites à ses demandes.

L'adolescent qui est vivement intéressé à son propre cas, à son corps et à sa maladie, a fréquemment besoin d'explications détaillées. En lui fournissant de tels renseignements, l'infirmière doit être prête à répondre à ses questions et à le rassurer tout comme elle le fait avec des enfants plus jeunes. Elle doit consentir à demeurer un certain temps avec l'adolescent et à lui fournir l'appui dont il a besoin.

Les activités récréatives de l'adolescent consistent généralement à regarder la télévision, à écouter la radio et des disques ou à aider aux soins des plus jeunes enfants. Il faudrait aider l'adolescent à continuer son travail scolaire, afin qu'il puisse se retrouver au même niveau que ses camarades lorsqu'il quittera l'hôpital. Il est nécessaire de lui fournir des occasions d'exercer sa créativité, telles la rédaction d'une revue, la décoration de l'unité, etc... Au départ, il faut prendre contact avec le professeur ou l'infirmière de l'école, les informer de l'incapacité éventuelle de l'adolescent et les aider à comprendre les besoins physiques et psychologiques qui découlent de sa maladie. Il est bon de rappeler à son entourage que ses besoins fondamentaux demeurent ceux des adolescents normaux.

MALADIES PENDANT L'ADOLESCENCE

La poussée de croissance que subissent les adolescents les rend particulièrement vulnérables à certaines maladies qui peuvent avoir des effets déterminants sur leur processus de développement. Les accidents demeurent, cependant, la principale cause de décès à cette époque de la vie; le taux de décès par la maladie est relativement bas.

Tuberculose

La tuberculose est une maladie mondialement répandue. Bien que sa fréquence ait grandement diminué, elle demeure importante dans les pays sous-développés. Les méthodes utilisées pour contrôler la tuberculose ne peuvent être appliquées avec un succès égal dans tous les pays. Les programmes éducatifs, un standard de vie plus élevé, un diagnostic précoce et de meilleures méthodes de traitement s'avèrent essentiels pour en assurer le contrôle. L'Organisation Mondiale de la Santé (O.M.S.) joue un grand rôle dans la lutte contre cette infection.

Fréquence. Même si la tuberculose a autrefois été une cause majeure de mort pour l'adolescent, son incidence a grandement diminué au cours des dernières décades. Il faut toutefois se rappeler qu'elle demeure une menace particulière pour les jeunes de cet âge. Le fait que les adolescentes en soient atteintes plus tôt et plus souvent que les garçons peut être relié à leur maturation plus rapide. La fréquence augmente dans les milieux pauvres où la surpopulation et les conditions sanitaires sont précaires. La fréquence demeure élevée dans les régions périodiquement atteintes par les inondations et la famine. Le diagnostic précoce et les méthodes améliorées de traitement donnent à ces jeunes une bonne chance de guérison.

Étiologie et épidémiologie. La tuberculose est causée par le bacille de Koch (ou mycobacterium tuberculosis), dont les formes bovine et humaine produisent la maladie chez l'homme. Une personne peut contracter la tuberculose en buvant du lait contaminé, bien que cette forme de contamination ait presque complètement disparu dans les pays industrialisés, grâce à l'hygiène de l'industrie laitière: on tue le bétail malade, on interdit la vente du lait contaminé, on pasteurise tout le lait vendu sur le marché et on surveille les symptômes possibles de tuberculose chez les employés de l'industrie laitière.

Le bacille pénètre ordinairement dans l'organisme par les voies respiratoires et digestives. Il se répand surtout aujourd'hui par contact avec des sécrétions respiratoires aéroportées ou par contact direct avec des personnes atteintes. Les enfants contractent le plus fréquemment la maladie, à domicile, d'un adulte tuberculeux. C'est la raison pour laquelle il faut séparer le nouveau-né de sa mère tuberculeuse, de sorte que celle-ci ne puisse le contaminer en respirant ou en toussant pendant qu'elle le nourrit ou le soigne. Les jeunes enfants et les adolescents peuvent contracter la maladie au foyer, chez des amis ou par contact direct avec d'autres enfants tuberculeux. À tout âge, les enfants peuvent porter des objets contaminés à leur bouche. L'habitude peu sanitaire du partage des caramels, des bonbons, des verres à boire ou des ustensiles peut contribuer à répandre la maladie.

Facteurs prédisposants, genres d'infection et physio-pathologie. Les maladies chroniques, la fatigue et la malnutrition peuvent prédisposer à la tuberculose.

La *primo-infection* se produit au premier contact de l'organisme avec le bacille de Koch. Cette lésion initiale guérit d'habitude spontanément et le sujet devient porteur du bacille; il est tuberculisé et réagit au contact de l'extrait protéique du bacille (tuberculine). Le sujet atteint d'une primo-infection n'est pas tuberculeux et il ne le deviendra que si la primo-infection est suivie immédiatement d'une contamination massive, ou plus tardivement à la suite d'une réinfection qui produira chez lui la tuberculose-maladie. Le sujet tuberculisé jouit d'habitude d'une certaine immunité.

La primo-infection se produit habituellement dans l'enfance. Les progrès de l'hygiène ont beaucoup retardé ce premier contact avec le bacille et il s'avère essentiel aujourd'hui d'évaluer la sensibilité (allergie) de l'organisme à la tuberculine, avant de permettre aux jeunes adultes, tels les étudiants de la santé et les nouveaux employés d'hôpitaux, de venir en contact avec des doses massives de bacilles.

Les lésions de la primo-infection comprennent un chancre d'inoculation qui se calcifie ordinairement et une adénopathie satellite plus ou moins importante. La résistance individuelle et l'importance de l'invasion bactérienne déterminent l'étendue de cette première atteinte. Le sujet peut devenir tuberculeux s'il est immédiatement réinfecté, comme cela se produit quand un enfant vit avec un adulte atteint de tuberculose active. D'habitude, la primo-infection guérit d'elle-même et la réinfection surviendra au moment de l'adolescence ou au début de la vie adulte.

La primo-infection grave peut toutefois s'étendre à d'autres parties du poumon et produire des symptômes de pneumonie. Les bacilles peuvent se disséminer à partir des ganglions infectés. Les vaisseaux lymphatiques et sanguins transportent alors le micro-organisme et de nouveaux foyers d'infection apparaissent dans divers organes et dans les séreuses.

Quand l'infection généralisée se produit, on dit que l'enfant souffre de *tuberculose miliaire*. Cette sorte de tuberculose se produit généralement chez le bébé ou le très jeune enfant. La première attaque est ordinairement aiguë, accompagnée de poussées de fièvre et de symptômes pulmonaires. On peut rencontrer une splénomégalie, un ballonnement abdominal, de la prostration, de la dyspnée, de la toux et de la cyanose. Le taux de mortalité a été réduit par l'emploi de nouveaux médicaments.

Si la maladie affecte les méninges, il peut en résulter une *méningite tuberculeuse*. La tuberculose des ganglions lymphatiques mésentériques ou cervicaux, l'atteinte du péritoine, des os, des articulations, peuvent aussi se produire. Les os les plus souvent atteints sont la tête du fémur (*arthrite tuberculeuse de la hanche*), les doigts et les orteils (*dactylite tuberculeuse*) et les vertèbres (*spondylite tuberculeuse ou maladie de Pott*).

Si la résistance de l'enfant est bonne, la maladie reste localisée au poumon et aux ganglions avoisinants; la guérison de la lésion primaire et la calcification se produisent. Plus

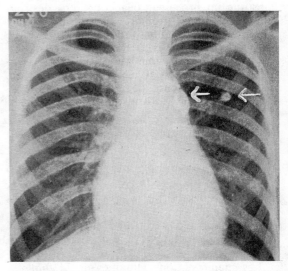

Figure 25-3. Nodule tuberculeux calcifié (droite) et ganglion lymphatique trachéo-bronchique (gauche). (R. H. High et W. E. Nelson, dans W. E. Nelson, *Textbook of Pediatrics*, 8e éd., 1964.)

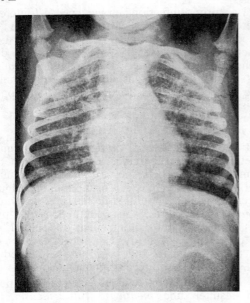

Figure 25-4. Tuberculose pulmonaire miliaire chez un garçon de 3 ans. (R. H. High et W. E. Nelson, dans W. E. Nelson, *Textbook of Pediatrics*, 8ᵉ éd., 1964.)

tard, à cause d'une résistance amoindrie, la lésion latente peut redevenir active.

La *tuberculose – maladie* se produit ordinairement durant l'adolescence ou au début de la vie adulte, soit à partir du foyer initial ou d'une nouvelle infection. Elle diffère de l'infection primaire à cause de la réaction allergique de l'organisme. La nouvelle infection constitue un processus beaucoup plus destructeur que la lésion primaire. Il peut se produire une réaction inflammatoire considérable avec destruction des tissus et formation de cavités. La guérison des lésions tuberculeuses s'effectue principalement par cicatrisation et fibrose. La lésion pulmonaire de la tuberculose apparaît normalement à l'apex du poumon.

Manifestations cliniques et diagnostic. Au cours de la *primo-infection,* les manifestations pulmonaires ne sont pas toujours évidentes. L'enfant peut se plaindre de malaise, de fatigue, d'anorexie, perdre du poids et devenir irritable. La plupart des primo-infections passent inaperçues. Si on soupçonne la tuberculose, mais qu'il n'y ait pas de symptômes apparents, le diagnostic peut s'effectuer par un test à la tuberculine et une radiographie pulmonaire.

Les manifestations cliniques de la *tuberculose secondaire* de l'adolescent peuvent ressembler à celles des adultes contaminés. La maladie peut se transformer en tuberculose pulmonaire, chronique et progressive, avec toux et expectorations, fièvre, hémoptysie, perte de poids et sueurs nocturnes.

On emploie deux sortes de *tuberculine* pour les *tests de diagnostic*: la tuberculine O.T. (Old Tuberculine) et le P.P.D. (Purified Protein Derivative), un dérivé purifié de protéines spécifiques. Les tests s'effectuent par scarification (Von Pirquet), application (Vollmer), intradermo-réaction (Mantoux) et piqûres multiples (Tine Test). Les plus usités, les tests de Mantoux et par piqûres multiples, seront expliqués.

LE TEST DE MANTOUX. Environ six semaines après l'infection, la présence d'allergie ou d'hypersensibilité aux protéines tuberculeuses peut être observée au moyen d'une réaction cutanée positive. On injecte une dose précise de tuberculine, par voie intradermique et on observe la réaction après 48 à 72 heures. Elle est positive si une surface d'au moins 5mm de diamètre présente un érythème et un durcissement évidents. On doit noter la mesure exacte de la réaction. Plus grande est la surface de réaction, plus important est le risque que l'enfant soit frappé d'infection tuberculeuse grave. Ce test est très efficace à condition d'être techniquement bien exécuté.

TINE TEST OU TEST À PONCTIONS MULTIPLES. Un disque en acier inoxydable, muni de 4 pointes enduites de O.T. concentrée, est pressé fermement contre la face interne de l'avant-bras, préalablement nettoyée avec de l'alcool ou de l'acétone. Les aiguilles pénètrent dans la peau, déposant la tuberculine dans le derme. On vérifie le résultat après 48 à 72 heures. On considère que la réaction est positive si le durcissement autour d'un ou plusieurs des points de ponction est de 2mm de diamètre ou plus. Les personnes qui présentent des réactions douteuses doivent subir le test de Mantoux.

SIGNIFICATION DES RÉACTIONS. Une réaction positive à la tuberculine signifie que la personne a été contaminée par le bacille de la tuberculose et qu'elle demeure allergique ou hypersensible aux protéines du bacille. La lésion tuberculeuse n'est pas nécessairement active au moment du test. Si la réaction allergique est très marquée, il faut penser à une tuberculose en évolution, surtout si l'enfant en présente les symptômes ou vit avec des adultes tuberculeux.

Une réaction négative peut signifier 1) que la personne n'a jamais été en contact avec le bacille de Koch et n'a pas fait la primo-infection; 2) qu'elle ne peut développer d'allergie à la tuberculine, ce qui ne change en rien son immunité contre le bacille; 3) qu'elle se trouve en état d'anergie: certaines personnes ont fait la primo-infection, mais ont perdu de façon durable ou temporaire la possibilité de réagir à la tuberculine; elles se trouvent en même temps dans un état de réceptivité spéciale à l'égard du bacille. Les principaux facteurs anergisants sont la présence de certaines maladies, telles la rougeole, la coqueluche, la grippe, la pneumonie, la typhoïde, les néoplasies ou certaines modifications de l'organisme qui accompagnent la puberté, la grossesse et la ménopause. Les adolescentes sont donc spécialement sujettes aux réinfections ou au réveil du foyer de primo-infection.

Tout enfant qui fait une réaction positive à la tuberculine doit subir un examen médical, passer une radiographie pulmonaire et subir des analyses de laboratoire qui permettent de connaître sa vitesse de sédimentation et le décompte de ses leucocytes. Il faut examiner les parents, les grands-parents, les frères et sœurs ou les personnes qu'il rencontre régulièrement, pour déceler un éventuel porteur de lésions pulmonaires actives.

Un diagnostic positif de tuberculose est établi si l'on trouve le bacille dans le contenu gastrique ou dans les sécrétions des voies respiratoires. Les jeunes enfants expectorent rarement, mais l'examen du contenu gastrique obtenu par aspiration est valable, car l'enfant déglutit habituellement ses sécrétions.

Avant le déjeuner, on procède au tubage gastrique en utilisant un tube de Levine. On retire un échantillon du contenu gastrique avec une seringue. On examine le sédiment ainsi obtenu afin de trouver le bacille tuberculeux par culture en laboratoire, injection sur cobaye ou par ces deux procédés à la fois. On devrait répéter le test trois fois avant de considérer que le résultat est négatif.

Traitement et soins infirmiers. Que l'on soigne le patient à la maison ou à l'hôpital, la planification du traitement dépend de la situation globale. Si l'on a trouvé un porteur quelconque dans son entourage, on doit éviter au patient un contact continu avec cette source d'infection.

Le malade devrait jouir d'un repos mental et physique. Le repos au lit peut s'avérer nécessaire. L'adolescent doit se conformer à un horaire quotidien régulier et éviter l'excès d'activités. On doit lui interdire l'école pour sa propre sécurité et celle de ses camarades. Une surveillance sanitaire demeure essentielle.

L'adolescent soigné à la maison devrait rester relativement isolé, afin d'empêcher que l'infection tuberculeuse ne se répande et afin de le protéger aussi contre d'éventuelles infections qui diminueraient davantage ses ressources physiques. La rougeole semble spéciale-ment dangereuse pour un individu atteint de tuberculose.

Il a besoin d'une diète adéquate, riche en protides, en calcium et en vitamines, particulièrement B, C et D. On ne devrait pas forcer l'enfant ou l'adolescent à manger, mais l'encourager à s'alimenter suffisamment. L'air frais et le soleil peuvent aider à sa guérison et ajouter à son bien-être.

Le malade reprend ses activités habituelles graduellement, à mesure que la lésion guérit. Afin de prévenir la dépendance excessive, il faut l'encourager à prendre soin de lui-même et à planifier son avenir. L'adolescent doit faire partie de l'équipe sanitaire, chargée de veiller à ses soins et à sa réadaptation. L'équipe comprend ses parents, le médecin, le travailleur social, le professeur et l'infirmière. Même pendant la convalescence, on doit l'aider à garder le contact avec ses amis. Un téléphone près de son lit et une correspondance active s'avèrent d'un grand secours pour l'aider à sentir qu'il fait encore partie d'un groupe et qu'il va y retourner.

Plusieurs médicaments ont été utilisés avec succès dans le traitement de la tuberculose, bien qu'aucun en particulier ne guérisse la maladie. Un traitement prolongé de 6 mois à un an est ordinairement nécessaire.

On administre la *streptomycine* par voie intramusculaire. Certaines complications peuvent apparaître au cours du traitement à long terme, surtout une détérioration du huitième nerf crânien entraînant la surdité. L'association avec un autre médicament autituberculeux empêche le développement précoce d'une résistance à la streptomycine.

L'*isoniazide* (INH, Rimifon), un antituberculeux peu toxique, peut contrôler les lésions progressives et s'avère efficace dans la prévention de la dissémination hématogène. Il peut être absorbé par voie orale ou par injection. Il constitue le médicament le plus efficace communément utilisé pour traiter la tuberculose. Il doit toutefois être associé à une autre substance antituberculeuse si la maladie est en phase active afin de prévenir la résistance précoce du bacille. Ce médicament produit une stimulation du système nerveux central qui peut amener de l'hyperactivité et des convulsions. Ces effets secondaires sont toutefois contrôlés par l'administration de pyridoxine. L'isoniazide peut provoquer aussi de fortes fièvres associées à de l'hyperesthésie qui font penser à une méningite.

On administre par voie orale, l'*acide para-amino-salicylique* (PAS). Moins efficace que la streptomycine ou l'isoniazide, le PAS peut également provoquer de l'irritation gastrique, mais il demeure valable parce qu'il empêche le développement de la résistance du bacille, à la fois à la streptomycine et à l'isoniazide. De plus, le PAS augmente l'efficacité de l'isoniazide. Il s'avère toutefois dangereux pour le jeune enfant à cause de la très grande quantité de médicament que l'on doit administrer pour obtenir un résultat positif.

Des combinaisons variées de ces médicaments ont réduit la durée de l'infection tuberculeuse et aussi de certaines formes secondaires de l'infection. Les *corticostéroïdes* sont souvent nécessaires dans le cas de méningite tuberculeuse pour prévenir l'hydrocéphalie. D'autres médicaments peuvent être employés dans les cas d'allergie, de résistance ou d'hyposensibilité. Le *rifampin*, un antibiotique, est une nouvelle médication antituberculeuse qui semble très efficace en association avec l'un ou l'autre des médicaments déjà discutés.

L'adolescent suffisamment motivé ne laissera pas tomber son traitement en cours de route. Il doit bénéficier de l'encouragement de ses parents et de l'équipe de santé, et l'infirmière en santé communautaire doit se rendre régulièrement à la maison pour renforcer l'enseignement déjà donné et évaluer l'attitude de la famille envers le traitement. Si l'adolescent tuberculeux ne prend pas ses médicaments, la maladie progresse et il faut trouver des moyens pour l'aider à penser à sa médication et à en assumer lui-même la responsabilité. Certains parents refusent d'accepter le traitement même s'il s'agit d'une thérapie préventive à laquelle on soumet l'enfant présentant une réaction positive à la tuberculine. L'infirmière doit donc jouer un rôle de support en ce qui concerne les médicaments et l'assiduité aux consultations médicales. Elle doit aussi aider l'adolescent et sa famille à comprendre la maladie, à poursuivre le traitement et à se départir des sentiments de honte ou de culpabilité qu'ils peuvent éprouver à ce sujet.

Pronostic, prévention et méthodes de contrôle. En général, le taux de mortalité est plus élevé chez le nourrisson et l'adolescent que chez l'enfant d'âge préscolaire ou scolaire.

La lésion primaire, ordinairement bénigne, peut devenir une infection foudroyante. Plus l'enfant est jeune, plus le danger est grand. Durant l'adolescence, cependant, le risque que se développe la tuberculose pulmonaire chronique et progressive augmente, soit à partir du foyer primaire, soit à partir d'une nouvelle infection. Avec des lésions secondaires, le pronostic dépend de la gravité de l'atteinte, du sexe, de l'âge et du milieu dans lequel vit l'enfant ou l'adolescent.

Au cours des dernières années, le traitement antimicrobien a empêché le développement de la tuberculose miliaire et de la méningite tuberculeuse chez les nouveau-nés et les trotineurs contaminés par la tuberculose. Ce traitement a aussi empêché que les enfants plus âgés contractent la maladie. Quand on administre de l'isoniazide pendant un an, au moment du virage de la cuti-réaction, le chancre d'inoculation ne progresse ordinairement pas et la dissémination hématogène se produit rarement. L'enfant ou l'adolescent qui a une réaction positive à la tuberculine doit recevoir une thérapie chimioprophylactique s'il contracte la rougeole ou la coqueluche.

Le seul moyen efficace de prévenir la tuberculose consiste à éviter les contacts avec des personnes contaminées. L'éducation du public est essentielle. Afin d'établir la résistance aux bacilles tuberculeux, on doit enseigner à la population à maintenir une nutrition adéquate et à éviter la fatigue et les infections débilitantes. On doit recommander de boire seulement du lait pasteurisé et faire comprendre la maladie et l'importance du diagnostic et du traitement précoces. Les centres urbains doivent organiser des programmes de détection et de santé publique pour le contrôle de la maladie incluant le traitement des patients contagieux, le dépistage, l'étude des contacts, la surveillance des patients dont la tuberculose a cessé d'évoluer, des unités mobiles pour les radiographies de dépistage et des mesures afin d'améliorer la santé de la collectivité.

On possède des moyens de développer l'immunité artificielle contre la tuberculose. On emploie la vaccination par le BCG (Bacille de Calmette et Guérin), surtout par voie intradermique. Pour effectuer des vaccinations de masse, on a essayé la méthode par vaporisation ultrasonique qui s'effectue sans douleur. Tout un groupe d'enfants peut être immunisé simultanément en respirant la vapeur saturée de vaccin antituberculeux. Cette méthode est au stade expérimental. On ne connaît pas encore la période de résistance à l'infection après l'emploi du BCG. Parce que le vaccin entraîne une réaction toujours positive au test à la tuberculine, les tests postérieurs à son administration demeurent sans valeur.

Mononucléose infectieuse

Définition, étiologie et épidémiologie. La mononucléose infectieuse est une maladie aiguë dont la cause semble être virale. On a récemment incriminé un virus de type herpétique appelé le virus EB, sans pouvoir tirer de conclusion définitive. La mononucléose apparaît surtout chez les enfants plus âgés et chez les adolescents, bien qu'on puisse la contracter à n'importe quel moment de la vie. Cette maladie n'est que modérément contagieuse, mais elle peut apparaître sous forme d'épidémie; cependant, on voit plus communément apparaître des cas sporadiques.

La période d'incubation dure environ une à deux semaines. La période de contagiosité demeure inconnue. Le mode de transmission s'effectue par contact direct avec une personne atteinte ou par les sécrétions salivaires aéroportées. Cette maladie peut être propagée par le baiser, d'où son appellation « maladie du baiser ».

Physio-pathologie, manifestations cliniques, diagnostic et diagnostic différentiel. La mononucléose infectieuse est une maladie généralisée qui cause une hypertrophie du tissu lymphoïde de tout l'organisme. Les *manifestations cliniques* varient d'une façon marquée, mais peuvent comprendre la fièvre, la pharyngite, l'amygdalite, une lymphadénopathie généralisée, habituellement non douloureuse, atteignant surtout les ganglions cervicaux, une splénomégalie, la production de lymphocytes anormaux et la présence d'anticorps hétérophiles. L'anorexie et un état de malaise général peuvent se produire. Une éruption cutanée se manifeste quelquefois au début de la maladie. L'hépatite accompagnée d'ictère apparaît communément. Les manifestations du système nerveux central peuvent inclure un syndrome de méningite aseptique, l'encéphalite ou la polyradiculite infectieuse (syndrome de Guillain-Barré). Des séquelles neurologiques, la pneumonite, la péricardite et le purpura thrombocytopénique viennent parfois compliquer la maladie.

Le *diagnostic* est basé sur les découvertes de laboratoire: un échantillon sanguin périphérique révèle la présence de lymphocytes anormaux. La leucocytose lymphocytaire se développe et peut atteindre des degrés leucémoïdes pendant les premières journées de la maladie. Le nombre total de leucocytes, généralement augmenté, peut cependant être normal ou diminué. Les polymorpho-nucléaires peuvent s'accroître au début, pour diminuer considérablement par la suite.

La recherche des anticorps hétérophiles peut faciliter le diagnostic. On a récemment développé un test sérologique extrêmement spécifique et sensible, le mono-test, qui s'effectue en deux minutes et dont les résultats semblent très sûrs.

Certaines pathologies peuvent être confondues avec la mononucléose infectieuse, ce sont la diphtérie, la pharyngite, la leucémie, la maladie de Hodgkin, l'hépatite, la scarlatine, les éruptions cutanées dues aux médicaments ou aux allergies, et parfois l'appendicite. Il faut aussi éliminer les maladies qui peuvent se compliquer de méningite aseptique, d'encéphalite ou de polyradiculite infectieuse.

Traitement, soins infirmiers, pronostic et prévention. Le *traitement* n'est pas spécifique; on vise surtout à soulager les symptômes. Il comprend le repos au lit et la diète hypercalorique. On doit tenir le patient sous observation pour déceler l'apparition des complications peu fréquentes de la maladie. Dans certaines formes graves, les stéroïdes peuvent être indiqués. On donne souvent des suppléments vitaminiques.

Le *pronostic* est ordinairement bon en l'absence de complications. La guérison est lente et la convalescence peut se prolonger pendant plusieurs semaines.

Il n'y a pas de moyens connus de *prévention* de la mononucléose infectieuse.

Scoliose

Définition. La scoliose consiste en une incurvation latérale en forme de S de la colonne vertébrale, ordinairement associée à une rotation.

Classification. Voir tableau 25.1.

On rencontre deux *sortes* de scoliose: la scoliose fonctionnelle et la scoliose structurale ou organique.

La scoliose *fonctionnelle* se corrige quand l'enfant se penche du côté de la courbure. La cause sous-jacente doit être traitée pour prévenir l'apparition des symptômes secondaires à un mauvais alignement des vertèbres et les changements structuraux qui peuvent éventuellement apparaître.

La scoliose *structurale* peut avoir de nombreuses causes. La plus fréquente demeure la scoliose idiopathique dont nous parlerons plus longuement. Sa classification est basée sur l'âge osseux au moment de l'apparition des symptômes.

A. La scoliose idiopathique de l'adolescent entraîne peu de déformation et de troubles fonctionnels. B. La scoliose juvénile apparaît entre 3 ans et la puberté. Elle survient huit fois sur dix chez la fille. Le pronostic dépend de l'âge de l'enfant à l'apparition de la lésion. Plus tôt elle apparaît, plus grave est le pronostic. Elle n'est pas inéluctable, mais peut s'aggraver dangereusement à la puberté.

Tableau 25-1.

Classification des scolioses

Fonctionnelles:
    Posturale
    Compensatoire (raccourcissement d'un membre)
    Antalgique
    Hystérique

Structurale ou *organique*:
    Idiopathique: 85% des cas:
            De l'adolescence
            Juvénile: entre 3 et 10 ans
            Infantile: – résolutive
                       – progressive

    Neuropathique : Paralysie post-polio-
                      myélitique
               Neurofibromatose
               Syringomyélie
               Myéloméningocèle
               Paralysie cérébrale

    Ostéopathique : Anomalies vertébrales
                      congénitales

    Myopathique   : Dystrophie musculaire
                      Arthrogrypose
                      Amyotonie congénitale

    Thoracogénique: Fusion costale
                      Post-thoracoplastie

    Métabolique   : Rachitisme
                      Ostéoporose

    Iatrogénique   : Post-radiothérapie

Figure 25-5. Corset de Milwaukee. Le corset a été modifié de façon à prendre appui sur le front au lieu du menton, ce qui pouvait amener des déformations mandibulaires. (Keiser. *Nursing Clinics of North America*, Sept. 1967.)

C. La scoliose idiopathique infantile se manifeste avant l'âge de trois ans; la forme résolutive se corrige spontanément, l'évolution de la forme progressive demeure toujours très grave. En période pubertaire, une aggravation notable est habituelle.

Manifestations cliniques. Elles apparaissent le plus souvent pendant les poussées de croissance. L'enfant ou l'adolescent ne présente pas de douleur avant la phase avancée de la maladie. Les symptômes varient selon la localisation précise de la scoliose. Les signes de la scoliose dorsale sont une saillie des côtes et de l'omoplate, et une élévation de l'épaule du côté convexe; du côté concave, on remarque un aplatissement des côtes, un sein plus petit que l'autre, un angle plus aigu à la taille. La tête s'incline ordinairement de ce côté. La scoliose lombaire se manifeste du côté concave par une hanche proéminente, un raccourcissement apparent du membre inférieur et une tendance à tenir le pied en équinisme. Quand l'enfant se tient debout, il fléchit son genou du côté convexe pour compenser le raccourcissement du membre opposé et rétablir son équilibre. Certains signes peuvent aider les parents à se rendre compte du problème, tels, une robe qui tombe mal sur les hanches, une épau-

le où la bretelle est toujours trop grande, un soutien-gorge qui s'ajuste mal.

Traitement. Le traitement varie selon la gravité de la lésion et l'âge de l'enfant. Dans tous les cas, une surveillance étroite et continue s'avère essentielle, spécialement dans les scolioses idiopathiques où l'évolution demeure imprévisible avant la fin de la croissance.

Différentes formes de traitement sont utilisées selon les milieux orthopédiques, mais toutes essaient d'empêcher l'aggravation de la scoliose et, si possible, de corriger la courbure déjà existante. Certains orthopédistes favorisent l'emploi de corsets correcteurs du type Milwaukee qui visent surtout à stabiliser la scoliose. Ils peuvent être utilisés comme traitement définitif ou comme traitement transitoire pour permettre une croissance plus prolongée de la colonne et éviter un trop grand raccourcissement du tronc lors de la fusion spinale qui s'effectue par une greffe osseuse.

La traction squelettique, le halo cranio-fémoral permet d'augmenter régulièrement la distance comprise entre le crâne et le bassin.

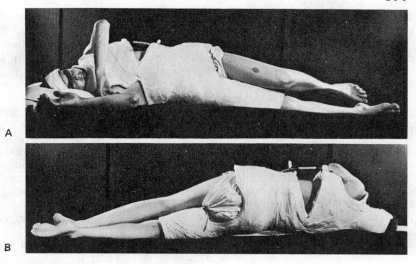

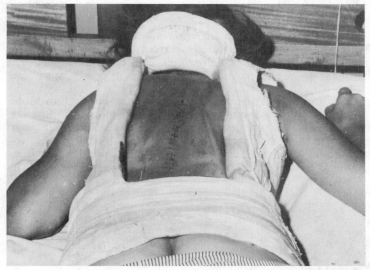

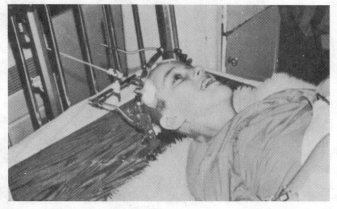

Figure 25-6. *A), B)* Plâtre à charnière (Risser). (Weibe: *Orthopedics in Nursing*.) *C)* Plâtre localisateur de Risser. Le découpage de la fenêtre dorsale a permis de pratiquer la fusion spinale. (Courtoisie du Dr. R.P. Keiser, *Nurs. Clin. N. Amer.*, 2(3):409, sept. 1967.) *D)* Traction halo-fémorale. On voit le cercle métallique fixé au crâne. (Courtoisie de D. Roberts, J. M., *Nursing Clin. N. Amer.*, 2(3):383, sept. 1967.)

La traction inférieure est appliquée à la base des fémurs et la contretraction est appliquée à la tête avec un cercle métallique en forme de halo. Cette sorte de traction est utilisée dans les cas graves, avant et après la fusion spinale.

D'autres techniques consistent en l'application d'un plâtre stabilisateur pour obtenir en période préopératoire une correction maximale de la courbure que l'on maintiendra par une arthrodèse vertébrale. Le plus connu est le plâtre à charnière de Risser. Il s'agit d'un corset plâtré qui couvre tout le tronc et une cuisse. Le plâtre est découpé en « coin » du côté convexe et une tige de distraction est appliquée de l'autre côté. On augmente la longueur de cette tige tous les jours et l'ouverture en coin du côté convexe se referme et entraîne une correction de la courbure. Une fusion spinale est alors pratiquée pour maintenir la correction.

Une autre forme de correction peut s'effectuer avec un plâtre stabilisateur qui s'arrête aux hanches et permet au patient de continuer à marcher. C'est le plâtre localisateur, également conçu par Risser.

La technique E.D.F. (élongation, dérotation et flexion latérale du rachis) vise en préopératoire à obtenir un assouplissement maximal des courbures par des exercices actifs et une amélioration fonctionnelle, surtout respiratoire. Après la fusion, on essaie d'obtenir une correction supplémentaire de la gibbosité à l'aide d'un système de compression par appareil pneumatique (ballon) placé sous le plâtre.

Dans la technique de Harrington, on obtient une correction chirurgicale interne au moyen de tiges métalliques. On applique une tige à compression du côté convexe et un distracteur du côté concave. Un système de crochets les tient en place. Une arthrodèse vertébrale apporte une stabilisation supplémentaire. Pour permettre la fusion de la greffe, un corset plâtré est appliqué en période postopératoire. Le patient demeure étendu sur un lit « Stryker » ou « Circ-O-Lectric » pendant plusieurs semaines.

Une technique plus récente (Dwyer) s'attaque directement aux corps vertébraux par voie antérieure trans-thoracique. L'avantage de cette méthode est le lever précoce et le fait que l'enfant n'a pas à garder un plâtre pendant plusieurs mois.

Soins infirmiers. L'infirmière en santé communautaire, surtout celle qui évolue en milieu scolaire, doit être capable de dépister chez les enfants les défauts de posture qui cachent une scoliose.

Lorsque les enfants sont hospitalisés pour un long traitement préopératoire, l'infirmière assiste le médecin et le physiothérapeute pour faire exécuter les exercices conçus pour le redressement de la scoliose, pour l'accroissement de la capacité respiratoire vitale et la

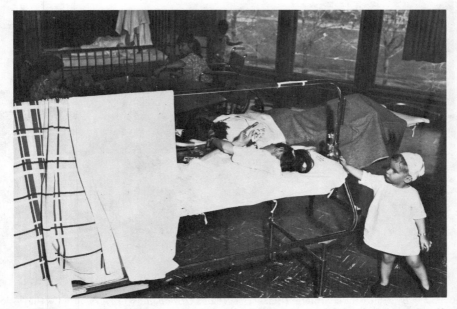

Figure 25-7. Deux fillettes opérées pour scoliose par la technique de Harrington. Leur séjour sur le lit Stryker est rendu plus agréable par leur présence réciproque. Noter la position ventrale et la position dorsale des fillettes. (Courtoisie de l'Hôpital Sainte-Justine, Montréal.)

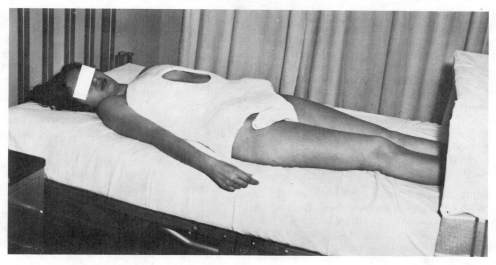

Figure 25-8. Corset plâtré que l'enfant devra porter pendant quelques mois après la correction de la scoliose par la méthode de Harrington. Ce corset sera ensuite remplacé par un autre plus léger, fait de matière plastique. (Courtoisie de l'Hôpital Sainte-Justine, Montréal.)

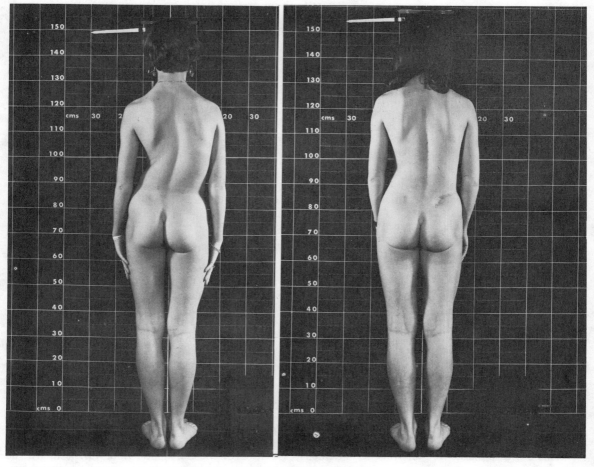

Figure 25-9. Scoliose. Correction interne par tiges de Harrington. N. B. La cicatrice de la hanche droite correspond à la prise du greffon pour l'arthrodèse. (Courtoisie de l'Hôpital Sainte-Justine, Montréal.)

stimulation du tonus musculaire. Comme ces patients se fatiguent facilement, les périodes d'exercice devraient alterner avec les périodes de repos. Les positions de repos peuvent être spécifiées par le médecin ou le physiothérapeute et peuvent être d'une aussi grande valeur que les exercices. On doit encourager l'adolescent à dormir sur un lit ferme, sans oreiller. On peut aussi recommander des exercices respiratoires qui préparent à l'opération. L'infirmière doit connaître les exercices à effectuer afin de pouvoir les faire pratiquer régulièrement.

Le jeune patient, dans un plâtre à charnière ou dans un plâtre plus léger, a besoin de soins infirmiers empreints de compréhension. Plusieurs jeunes malades craignent le séjour dans le plâtre ou la traction, soit parce qu'ils croient que leur croissance en sera arrêtée, ou parce qu'ils redoutent une longue période de dépendance. L'intérêt de l'adolescent devient centré sur son propre corps et il peut se désintéresser de ce qui l'entoure; son image corporelle déjà amoindrie par la scoliose peut en souffrir encore davantage. Il ne peut accomplir adéquatement les tâches de développement de cette étape de la croissance. L'immobilisation suscite chez l'adolescent des sentiments de rage, de chagrin, de crainte de la douleur corporelle, d'abandon et de culpabilité, le tout accompagné de désespoir et d'autodépréciation. Certains jeunes qui réagissent au stress par une activité accrue peuvent devenir désorganisés, désorientés et à la limite de la rupture d'avec la réalité.

L'infirmière et la famille doivent fournir de l'information, de l'encouragement et du support pour pallier ces craintes et ces réactions. La rencontre d'autres adolescents ayant déjà séjourné dans un plâtre ou une traction, et le fait de partager avec eux les mêmes sentiments éprouvés au cours de ces expériences aident à réduire l'anxiété de l'adolescent et lui permettent de faire face à la situation.

Le soin de la peau s'avère important. Les problèmes associés à ces techniques incluent l'excoriation de la peau autour des bords du plâtre et la création de points de pression sous le plâtre. L'infirmière doit s'assurer de l'intégrité de la peau, spécialement au niveau des côtes. Elle doit vérifier la cause de toutes les plaintes de douleur ou de malaise. L'infirmière ne doit pas permettre à l'adolescent de se gratter sous son plâtre, ce qui peut causer des lésions cutanées. On peut utiliser des médicaments ou faire passer de l'air frais, si la démangeaison persiste, mais on ne doit pas appliquer de poudre.

Il faut protéger la peau avec des pétales de tissu adhésif ou un tricot solidement fixé sur les bords du plâtre. On doit frictionner la peau fréquemment. On peut utiliser un léger coussinet pour alléger le malaise provenant de la pression du plâtre, mais un coussinet trop épais peut causer une pression encore plus grande. Du matériel à l'épreuve de l'eau doit protéger le plâtre autour des fesses et des parties génitales. On nettoie la peau à fond quand le patient se salit.

Après une intervention par la technique de Harrington, avant de poser le corset plâtré, on laisse le patient sur le lit Stryker ou le lit électrique pendant environ deux semaines afin de permettre la guérison de la plaie opératoire. Il faut expliquer à l'adolescent la raison de cette immobilisation et surtout le fonctionnement du lit mécanique.

Après la fusion vertébrale, on peut continuer l'immobilisation dans un plâtre ou un corset pendant 6 à 12 mois. Si on a prélevé un greffon tibial, on devrait manipuler le membre avec soin pendant au moins 8 semaines.

On planifie les soins de façon à satisfaire les besoins de l'adolescent au cours du traitement pré et postopératoire. Il peut séjourner à domicile ou dans un hôpital spécialisé dans les soins à long terme.

L'adolescent entouré d'appareils, dans un plâtre ou sur un lit spécial, se sent souvent dépersonnalisé. Il est important de l'aider à conserver son identité, à trouver des moyens de préserver sa féminité ou son apparence virile. Ces soins diminueront les réactions agressives et dépressives. Des distractions appropriées doivent être fournies en dépit des limitations physiques du patient. Il est important de donner à l'adolescent des moyens concrets de se situer dans le temps et l'espace durant cette immobilisation prolongée.

Une adolescente peut refuser de porter un corset parce qu'elle est « trop fatiguée » ou qu'elle pense que cela nuit à son apparence. Il se peut qu'elle ne veuille pas faire ses exercices, parce qu'elle est « trop affairée ». Les adolescents des deux sexes peuvent se révolter contre leur dépendance vis-à-vis des parents au moment de leur immobilisation plus ou moins complète. Les parents doivent être avertis de la possibilité de ces réactions et aidés à y faire face adéquatement.

Si l'adolescent porte un plâtre ou un corset, pendant une période prolongée, il peut se sentir isolé de ses camarades. Les parents pourront avoir besoin d'aide pour lui permettre de rester en contact avec ses amis. La planification d'un programme d'études à domicile favorise ce contact, tout en facilitant le retour éventuel à l'école.

Si l'adolescent fait ses exercices devant un miroir, il deviendra plus conscient de son maintien et se rendra compte de la correction créée par l'usage de ses muscles. La danse est également valable pour développer un meilleur équilibre.

Le *diagnostic* et le *traitement* précoces demeurent d'une importance capitale pour prévenir une difformité sérieuse. Il est dangereux de remettre à plus tard, en croyant que la croissance de l'adolescent réglera le problème.

Glissement de l'épiphyse fémorale

Étiologie et fréquence. La fermeture de la plaque épiphysaire qui marque le terme de la croissance du squelette est davantage reliée à l'âge physiologique qu'à l'âge chronologique et coïncide avec la maturité sexuelle. Cette caractéristique s'avère importante dans le cas du glissement épiphysaire qui demeure une des principales pathologies osseuses de l'adolescence. L'étiologie en est encore inconnue, mais les traumatismes et les changements hormonaux pourraient y jouer un certain rôle.

La phase de croissance maximum se situe, en moyenne, vers l'âge de 12 ans pour les filles, et entre l'âge de 14 et 15 ans pour les garçons. Habituellement, l'adolescent qui souffre d'un glissement de l'épiphyse fémorale est grand et lourd (type Fröelich) ou grand et mince (type longiligne).

Manifestations cliniques, diagnostic et traitement. Aux premiers stades, des signes de synovite apparaissent. L'adolescent boite légèrement du côté atteint. La tête fémorale peut glisser vers le bas et vers l'arrière, le col prend l'aspect d'un sabot de cheval, la portion distale étant plus élevée que la partie proximale. Le membre est en éversion; la rotation interne et l'abduction deviennent limitées. La douleur est quelquefois localisée dans le genou. L'évolution est insidieuse et l'atteinte est fréquemment bilatérale (15% des cas).

Le *diagnostic* est basé sur l'examen radiologique qui montre, à partir d'une radiographie latérale, que l'épiphyse fémorale capitale a glissé postérieurement et inférieurement. Le col du fémur prend l'apparence d'un sabot de cheval. Le diagnostic et le traitement précoces s'avèrent essentiels.

L'objectif principal du *traitement* est d'arrêter le glissement par une fixation interne, suivie de l'application d'un plâtre; le port du poids sur le fémur est évité par l'utilisation de béquilles jusqu'à la guérison. Dans les cas graves, l'ostéotomie, ou d'autres formes d'intervention, peuvent s'avérer nécessaires.

Comme cette maladie peut être bilatérale, il faut examiner soigneusement l'adolescent pour déceler les signes d'atteinte de la hanche opposée.

Tumeurs malignes de l'os

Les tumeurs malignes osseuses primaires les plus fréquentes sont l'ostéosarcome et le sarcome d'Ewing. Elles se produisent habituellement entre l'âge de 10 et 20 ans et apparaissent surtout chez les garçons.

La cause en demeure inconnue, mais l'hérédité pourrait être un facteur.

Les radiographies peuvent simuler une ostéomyélite aiguë. On doit établir un *diagnostic* prudent, à partir d'examens radiologiques et de biopsies chirurgicales.

Ostéosarcome (Sarcome ostéogénique)

Manifestations cliniques, diagnostic, traitement et pronostic. L'ostéosarcome apparaît plus fréquemment que le sarcome d'Ewing et implique ordinairement la métaphyse d'un os long – l'extrémité inférieure du fémur ou l'extrémité supérieure du tibia ou de l'humérus. On rencontre également d'autres localisations. Les *manifestations cliniques* sont la douleur et l'œdème de la partie atteinte. Le *diagnostic* est établi d'après des examens radiologiques qui révèlent la destruction de l'os et une néo-formation osseuse. Le seul traitement est l'amputation de l'extrémité atteinte. Le processus néoplasique peut atteindre la cavité médullaire, le périoste et les tissus mous environnants. Le sarcome produit souvent des métastases pulmonaires, bien que d'autres organes puissent également être atteints. Le taux de mortalité demeure élevé.

Soins infirmiers. Les soins infirmiers sont semblables à ceux prodigués aux patients atteints de sarcome d'Ewing.

Sarcome d'Ewing

Manifestations cliniques, diagnostic, traitement, soins infirmiers et pronostic. Le sarcome d'Ewing se produit habituellement dans la diaphyse d'un os long. Il peut aussi atteindre les os plats et les côtes. Les manifestations cliniques ressemblent à celles de l'ostéosarcome. Il peut y avoir de la fièvre et une leucocytose. Ordinairement, un seul os est atteint, au moment du diagnostic, mais d'autres os peuvent être affectés par la suite.

L'examen radiologique et l'étude histologique de la tumeur permettent de poser le *diagnostic*. Le *traitement* est insatisfaisant. La néoplasie réagit d'abord à la radiothérapie, mais les rémissions demeurent peu fréquentes. La radiothérapie associée à la chimiothérapie (ordinairement moutarde azotée ou cyclophosphamide) a connu certains succès thérapeutiques. L'amputation demeure le seul autre traitement utilisé.

À mesure que la maladie progresse, le patient souffre d'anémie, il devient pâle et se fatigue rapidement. L'optimisme du début de la maladie se transforme bientôt en dépression. Les parents, les visiteurs et les infirmières doivent essayer de fournir un support émotif, afin d'aider le patient à faire face au dénouement probable de sa maladie. Les soins décrits pour l'enfant malade à long terme et mourant s'appliquent ici.

Comme une fracture pathologique peut se produire à l'endroit ou près de l'endroit de la tumeur, l'infirmière doit manier l'extrémité avec douceur quand elle fait le lit ou quand elle baigne le patient. S'il peut marcher, il faut éviter les chutes. De telles fractures pathologiques peuvent être indolores; l'infirmière doit en rechercher les signes, si l'adolescent tombe ou subit un traumatisme.

On donne un régime riche en protides, en vitamines et en sels minéraux pour contrebalancer l'anémie progressive.

L'infirmière surveille les signes d'atteinte pulmonaire, tels les douleurs thoraciques, la toux et les expectorations sanglantes et les signale immédiatement. Comme dans le cas de l'ostéosarcome, les métastases pulmonaires se produisent fréquemment.

Réticulo-sarcome

Le sarcome d'Ewing doit être différencié du réticulo-sarcome (tumeur du canal médullaire), car son apparence radiologique n'est pas spécifique. Ce sarcome est diagnostiqué par biopsie osseuse. Cette tumeur est radiosensible. L'amputation peut toutefois s'avérer nécessaire. Pendant que le patient est sous radiothérapie, il faut protéger le membre avec une atelle ou avec un plâtre afin d'éviter les fractures. Après la radiothérapie, l'adolescent peut souffrir de lésions cutanées, de douleur ou de problèmes digestifs. La thérapie intraveineuse peut devenir nécessaire pour maintenir l'hydratation.

Retard de développement sexuel

Le retard pubertaire et la puberté précoce peuvent se produire chez les deux sexes. Les parents s'inquiètent d'un retard et l'enfant se sent seul et rejeté à mesure qu'il prend conscience de la marge de développement qui le sépare de ses amis. Son estime de soi et son image corporelle en sont affectés.

La puberté retardée chez la fille

Étiologie, manifestations cliniques et traitement. L'*hypogonadisme primaire* provient d'une agénésie ou d'une destruction ovarienne, causée par le retrait chirurgical ou la destruction radiologique. L'*hypogonadisme secondaire* peut être causé par une destruction ou une anomalie de l'hypophyse ou de l'hypothalamus ou encore par une grave maladie systémique amenant l'insuffisance secondaire de l'hypophyse, telle l'hypothyroïdie (crétinisme), le diabète incontrôlé, la mucoviscidose ou la tuberculose.

À la puberté chronologique, les *manifestations cliniques* deviennent évidentes. On constate l'absence de croissance pileuse et du développement caractéristique de la poitrine. Les organes génitaux demeurent infantiles et les menstruations n'ont pas lieu. Les épiphyses sont lentes à se fermer et la fillette présente des extrémités effilées. Si l'hypothalamus a été gravement atteint par une tumeur, on constatera occasionnellement de l'obésité en plus de l'infantilisme sexuel. Cette combinaison de manifestations cliniques est appelée *syndrome de Fröhlich*. Le *syndrome de Turner* dans lequel la fille possède 45 chromosomes et un seul chromosome sexuel retarde la puberté et amène une stérilité relative.

Le *traitement* de l'hypogonadisme primaire consiste en l'administration d'œstrogènes quand l'enfant a atteint l'âge de la puberté. On continue indéfiniment cette thérapie hormonale. Des menstruations ont lieu, mais sans ovulation; ces femmes demeurent donc stériles. La thérapie comporte des avantages d'ordre psychologique, en plus du fait qu'elle prévient la sénilité prématurée causée par le manque d'œstrogène. Dans l'hypogonadisme secondaire, le traitement causal peut amener un développement sexuel normal.

La puberté masculine retardée

Étiologie, manifestations cliniques, traitement et pronostic. La déficience du développement sexuel chez le mâle s'appelle *eunuchoïdisme*. L'absence ou la destruction des testicules ne produit aucun symptôme jusqu'à la puberté; ensuite les *manifestations* apparaissent: les organes génitaux n'augmentent pas de volume, les poils du pubis sont rares ou absents, la voix demeure infantile. La grande taille du garçon est due à la fermeture lente des épiphyses. L'excrétion des 17-cétostéroïdes est habituellement faible.

Le garçon qui souffre du *syndrome de Klinefelter* est habituellement porteur d'une anomalie chromosomique sexuelle. La forme XXY est la plus fréquente; la puberté est retardée, la fertilité perturbée et parfois le retard mental est présent. Le *traitement* consiste en une thérapie de substitution où l'on administre de la testostérone par voie orale ou intramusculaire. On peut obtenir des effets prolongés par l'implantation de capsules hormonales dans le tissu sous-cutané. La thérapie entraîne la masculinisation, mais la stérilité demeure.

PROBLÈMES SOCIAUX DURANT L'ADOLESCENCE

Parents adolescents célibataires

Dans la société nord-américaine, plusieurs milliers d'adolescentes célibataires sont enceintes chaque année. Pour ces jeunes, la transition s'effectue brutalement entre l'adolescence et le statut de parents. La plupart d'entre elles requiert une aide professionnelle pour faire face à cette crise avec un minimum de dommages physiques et psychologiques. Ce type de problème se rencontre dans toutes les couches de la société.

Les causes des grossesses non planifiées, chez les adolescentes, sont diverses. Sur le plan psychologique, on trouve un sentiment d'identité diffus, une recherche du défi, une oscillation entre la dépendance et l'indépendance, un besoin d'expérimenter et de s'affirmer, une quête illusoire d'amour et d'affection. Culturellement, l'usage accru d'alcool ou de stupéfiants qui diminuent les inhibitions, favorise l'apparition de grossesses non planifiées. L'ignorance, toujours actuelle, des sujets sexuels, doublée d'un non-emploi de moyens contraceptifs efficaces, favorisent la grossesse chez les adolescentes dont les valeurs et les normes encouragent de plus en plus les relations sexuelles précoces. Pour réduire le problème des naissances non désirées, les professionnels de la santé doivent s'attaquer aux causes réelles du problème et ne pas tenter de moraliser ou de suggérer des solutions toutes faites, imaginées dans un autre temps et pour un autre âge.

L'adolescente enceinte doit être aidée, tant à se comprendre elle-même et à s'accepter qu'à maintenir un état physique adéquat. L'infirmière scolaire qui la rencontre très souvent dès le début doit la diriger vers les ressources communautaires existantes. Le père adolescent ne doit pas être écarté, et s'il le désire, il doit être intégré dans la planification des soins pré et postnatals.

L'adolescente court un risque plus grand de présenter une toxémie gravidique que la femme plus âgée, et son bébé a plus de chance de naître prématurément. Ces risques sont d'autant plus importants que la diète de l'adolescente célibataire est le plus souvent mal équilibrée et qu'elle ne recourt aux services médicaux que le plus tard possible. L'infirmière a un grand rôle éducatif à jouer.

Selon le contexte familial et social, l'adolescente peut recourir à l'infirmière pour discuter de ses problèmes et de ses angoisses et pour effectuer son choix de continuer sa grossesse, de garder son enfant après la naissance ou de le placer pour adoption. L'infirmière doit posséder la maturité et les connaissances nécessaires pour offrir une aide appropriée.

Après l'avortement ou l'accouchement, selon le cas, il est important que l'infirmière offre un support continu à l'adolescente et un enseignement approprié sur les moyens contraceptifs. Dans beaucoup de régions, les moyens contraceptifs sont donnés gratuitement aux adolescentes susceptibles de redevenir rapidement enceintes.

Maladies vénériennes: syphilis et gonorrhée

L'incidence des maladies vénériennes, spécialement la gonorrhée, augmente à un rythme alarmant chez les adolescents, surtout chez ceux âgés de 15 à 19 ans. Ces adolescents proviennent de tous les milieux sociaux et économiques. Comme la plupart d'entre eux se soucie beaucoup de leurs corps, les symptômes de maladies vénériennes les inquiètent et les poussent souvent à se faire traiter. Quelques-uns ne se feront cependant pas aider, par crainte de faire connaître leur comportement ou d'être mal jugés.

C'est toute l'équipe de santé qui doit entreprendre le traitement pour que celui-ci soit un succès. Plusieurs aspects de la cure et du contrôle utilisés pour les adultes s'appliquent également aux adolescents, quoique des problèmes spéciaux surviennent pour ceux-ci.

Les deux maladies vénériennes les plus répandues sont la syphilis et la gonorrhée. Elles évoluent chez l'adolescent de la même façon que chez l'adulte.

Au début, la *syphilis* peut être asymptomatique ou donner des malaises si légers que la personne atteinte ne s'en rend même pas compte. Au premier stade de la maladie, on voit apparaître un chancre (lésion unique indolore) à l'endroit où le spirochète a pénétré dans l'organisme. Le chancre a l'aspect d'un durillon ou d'une vésicule et apparaît environ 21 jours après la contamination. Le stade secondaire commence entre deux et six mois après le premier contact; il peut aussi passer inaperçu malgré l'apparition d'une éruption (roséole syphilitique) ou de lésions à la bouche ou à la gorge, accompagnée parfois d'une hyperthermie légère. Les tests sérologiques ou l'examen au microscope permettent de poser le diagnostic. En l'absence de traitement, le spirochète peut occasionner des dommages organiques qui produiront après plusieurs années d'évolution une forme de paralysie générale ou de tabès. Le bébé d'une femme syphilitique peut souffrir de syphilis congénitale. Même si actuellement on est en train de mettre au point un vaccin antisyphilitique, il ne sera pas inoculé à un être humain avant plusieurs années.

Chez l'homme, la *gonorrhée* se manifeste deux à six jours après la contamination par une décharge purulente et une douleur cuisante au pénis lors de la miction. La femme qui souffre de gonorrhée peut présenter un écoulement vaginal purulent, de la dysurie et de la pollakiurie. Ces symptômes peuvent toutefois être totalement absents et la malade peut disséminer l'infection à son insu pendant longtemps, tandis que la gonorrhée progresse et se complique de salpingite, d'infection pelvienne, de péritonite et de stérilité. La femme qui accouche peut transmettre à son enfant l'ophtalmie purulente gonococcique, conséquence du passage du bébé dans le vagin contaminé. Chez l'homme, la gonorrhée atteint l'urètre postérieur et la prostate; sans traitement, la rétraction des canaux séminifères entraîne la stérilité. Pour les deux sexes, la gonorrhée peut se compliquer d'arthrite septique, de conjonctivite et d'endocardite. Il n'existe pas actuellement de test sérologique pour diagnostiquer la gonorrhée et les recherches se poursuivent en ce sens. Une culture positive de l'écoulement purulent permet de poser le diagnostic.

Ces deux maladies sont contractées par contact sexuel. Les problèmes majeurs pour les adolescents sont le traitement de la maladie, le dépistage et la prévention. Le dépistage précoce est spécialement important si la jeune fille est enceinte, afin que le traitement soit terminé avant la naissance de l'enfant.

Outre l'infirmière, plusieurs membres doivent s'intégrer à l'équipe de santé, afin d'assurer le contrôle des maladies vénériennes: a) les parents, qui contribuent à la formation d'une philosophie de la vie chez leur adolescent; b) le professeur qui distribue l'information nécessaire, conseille les adolescents et guide les jeunes, qui sont perturbés, vers des ressources appropriées; c) le travailleur social qui rencontre fréquemment les adolescents de divers milieux et qui peut aider l'infirmière à apprécier les causes du comportement de l'adolescent et à comprendre ce que la maladie signifie pour le patient; d) le médecin de famille qui peut instruire les jeunes patients au sujet des maladies vénériennes, les traiter au besoin, rapporter les cas à l'épidémiologiste et aider à localiser les sources d'infection; e) l'épidémiologiste, dont le rôle est de découvrir toutes les sources d'infection et tous les porteurs, afin de limiter la dissémination de l'infection.

Même si d'autres sources d'aide sont disponibles, beaucoup d'adolescents en détresse ont recours aux cliniques locales qui leur sont spécialement destinées et où le personnel est présent durant la soirée et la nuit, aux moments où il peut vraiment être utile. Les lignes téléphoniques ou d'entraide obtiennent également un succès qui s'explique par l'anonymat et les heures de présence des travailleurs. Le personnel, habituellement jeune, n'a pas pour mission de juger ou de modifier le comportement de l'adolescent, mais de l'aider à résoudre le mieux possible le problème auquel il est confronté.

Rôle de l'infirmière. L'infirmière doit connaître les signes et symptômes des maladies vénériennes et les reconnaître chez les étudiants. Elle doit être capable d'évaluer les plaintes, de référer ces adolescents au médecin et de conserver des dossiers médicaux adéquats sur tous les étudiants, de façon à être au courant de leurs problèmes individuels. Elle doit être accueillante et ne pas porter de jugement moral au sujet de ces maladies. Son rôle d'éducatrice sanitaire est particulièrement important.

L'infirmière à l'hôpital travaille de concert avec l'infirmière scolaire. Bien que la syphilis et la gonorrhée soient ordinairement traitées en clinique externe, les soins infirmiers pour les adolescents hospitalisés doivent tenir compte du fait que la période d'incubation de la syphilis et de la gonorrhée s'étendent sur plusieurs jours et quelques adolescents récemment admis peuvent manifester des symptômes au cours de l'hospitalisation.

Le chancre primaire de la syphilis et l'écoulement purulent de la gonorrhée sont hautement infectieux. Une technique d'isolement s'avère donc nécessaire.

Le traitement de choix demeure la pénicilline. Si le patient souffre de gonorrhée, on lui donne de la pénicilline durant quelques jours. Pour guérir la syphilis, la pénicillino-thérapie dure environ deux semaines. L'infirmière doit rechercher les effets secondaires indésirables de cet antibiotique au cours du traitement. D'autres antibiotiques doivent quelquefois être utilisés puisque certaines souches du spirochète ont développé une très haute résistance à la pénicilline.

L'infirmière doit encourager l'adolescent à revenir régulièrement se faire soigner. Elle doit connaître les mesures diagnostiques et thérapeutiques, de façon à les interpréter aux malades pour les éduquer et les rassurer. Les adolescents veulent des réponses honnêtes à leurs questions directes et l'infirmière doit être en mesure d'y répondre, si elle veut que son aide soit efficace.

Certains adolescents hésitaient autrefois à se faire soigner parce que le consentement de leurs parents était nécessaire pour le traitement. Depuis l'abolition de cette dernière exigence, il est plus facile d'atteindre les victimes de ces maladies. Il est fréquent qu'une seule personne soit le point de départ de la contamination dans une collectivité fermée et tous les contacts doivent être examinés et traités, ce qui est beaucoup plus facile si l'adolescent a la certitude que la vérité ne sera pas découverte par ses parents.

La seule façon de contrôler les maladies vénériennes chez les adolescents consiste dans l'approche multi-disciplinaire. L'infirmière doit comprendre sa responsabilité en tant que membre de l'équipe et participer à la réduction de ces maladies.

La délinquance juvénile

Fréquence et étiologie. Un délinquant est celui qui ne se conduit pas selon les normes établies par sa société ou sa collectivité. Fondamentalement, le comportement délinquant est antisocial et agressif, il est souvent précédé d'anxiété et de frustrations. Le comportement délinquant peut se manifester par le vol à l'étalage, l'école buissonnière, la fuite du foyer, le dommage et le vol à la propriété d'autrui (surtout les automobiles), la violence et les agressions sexuelles. La délinquance juvénile augmente chaque année dans la plupart des pays occidentaux.

Un ensemble de causes en est ordinairement responsable.

LA DÉLINQUANCE CAUSÉE PAR LA FORCE DES CIRCONSTANCES. Un exemple de cette sorte de délinquance est l'adolescent qui vole pour se procurer le nécessaire, par exemple sa nourriture. Dépenser autant d'argent que leurs amis apparaît à plusieurs adolescents comme une

nécessité. Ils peuvent voler afin de demeurer dans le groupe. Cette sorte d'adolescents est essentiellement normale et n'aime pas voler. Ils ont besoin d'un travail rémunéré et parfois de l'aide d'un adulte.

A

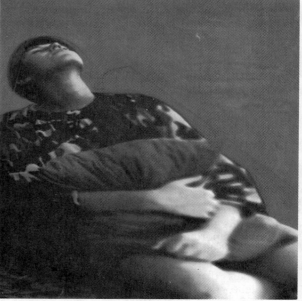

B

Figure 25-10. L'adolescent intoxiqué. *A)* Les parents ne devraient pas être les derniers avertis. (Metropolitan Life Insurance Company.) *B)* Sevrage. (Education Age, janv. fév., 1969.)

LA DÉLINQUANCE DUE À UN MILIEU SOCIO-ÉCONOMIQUE DÉFAVORISÉ. L'adolescent dont l'insécurité à la maison et dans la société est très grande, peut devenir délinquant. Enfant, il peut s'être senti rejeté ou incompris. En tant qu'adolescent, il peut s'engager dans un bande de jeunes dont il suit aveuglément les lois et dont il retire fierté et sécurité. Les lois du groupe peuvent l'inciter à des activités, telles le vol, la toxicomanie, les abus sexuels et même le meurtre. Ses démêlés avec la loi blessent davantage ses parents que lui-même. Il atteint à travers ses exploits un statut plus élevé dans son groupe.

Le traitement de cet adolescent peut être très difficile, puisque la base de l'insécurité est à la fois à la maison et dans la collectivité. Il consiste à éduquer l'adolescent et à l'aider à accepter les lois d'un nouveau groupe.

Un enfant qui a été élevé selon un système de valeurs et qui change ensuite de société, peut être considéré comme normal dans la première de ces sociétés, mais délinquant dans la seconde. Le traitement réside donc dans l'éducation et dans le fait d'aider le jeune à accepter les lois de ce nouveau groupe. En même temps, on doit aider son nouveau groupe social à comprendre le problème de l'adolescent.

LA DÉLINQUANCE CAUSÉE PAR UN RETARD MENTAL. Un adolescent mentalement retardé a besoin de soutien émotif continu et il demeure facilement influençable. Il ne peut distinguer clairement ce qui ne lui appartient pas ou ce qui lui arrivera à la suite de ses actes asociaux. Souvent, il ne différencie pas le bien du mal. S'il n'a pas reçu suffisamment d'amour, il peut développer un comportement agressif. Il peut être manipulé par des délinquants intelligents et souvent c'est lui qui sera appréhendé par les autorités. Il a besoin de protection, de formation et de surveillance.

DÉLINQUANCE DUE À LA NÉVROSE. Quelques adolescents deviennent délinquants parce qu'ils ont besoin d'être punis, afin d'éteindre un sentiment de culpabilité persistant et angoissant.

DÉLINQUANCE CAUSÉE PAR DES TROUBLES CARACTÉRIELS. Les délinquants peuvent être atteints de troubles caractériels qui produisent un comportement semblable à celui des adultes psychopathes. Ces adolescents semblent avoir des personnalités faibles. Ils sont incapables d'apprendre à partir de l'expérience vécue. Ils ne peuvent établir de relations significatives, même avec ceux qui essaient de les aider à résoudre leurs problèmes. Ils font exactement ce qu'ils veulent sans tenir compte des conséquences de leurs actes pour autrui et pour eux-mêmes. Ils peuvent nécessiter l'in-ternement et un traitement intensif, afin de protéger la société. On aurait pu identifier plusieurs de ces adolescents dans leur première enfance et leur donner un traitement adéquat. Trop souvent, on ne les aide pas avant qu'ils entrent en conflit avec la loi et les institutions appropriées à ces cas sont malheureusement trop rares.

DÉLINQUANCE CAUSÉE PAR DES TROUBLES ÉMOTIFS (PSYCHOSES). Les adolescents émotivement troublés ou psychotiques peuvent devenir délinquants. Leur comportement serait normal si le monde réel ressemblait à leur monde d'illusions. Cette sorte de délinquance est relativement rare au cours de l'adolescence, mais quand elle se produit, un traitement psychiatrique devient nécessaire.

Traitement, prévention et rôle de l'infirmière. Si l'on veut donner un traitement adéquat à l'adolescent, il faut insister, non sur l'acte délinquant pris isolément, mais sur l'individu dans sa totalité, à la maison et dans sa communauté, et sur les raisons pour lesquelles il a commis cet acte.

Dans les cours juvéniles, le personnel est mieux qualifié pour s'occuper de l'adolescent délinquant que dans les cours pour adultes. Les objectifs des cours juvéniles sont fondamentalement le diagnostic, la protection et l'éducation. Après une étude globale de l'individu, on planifie la réhabilitation en se basant sur son problème majeur et sur ce qui semble constituer la meilleure solution pour lui et la société.

On a fait plusieurs suggestions au sujet de la prévention: des écoles plus nombreuses et mieux adaptées, des terrains de jeu, des loisirs organisés et de meilleurs logements. Les autorités ont également recommandé qu'on donne plus d'attention aux enfants des groupes minoritaires. Les besoins fondamentaux de tous les enfants qui grandissent doivent être mieux compris si l'on veut prévenir la délinquance. Si l'on pouvait stabiliser les conditions de vie de tous les enfants, il y aurait probablement moins de délinquance.

Globalement, la prévention implique non seulement les délinquants en tant qu'individus, mais aussi les facteurs causals à l'œuvre dans la société. Pour réussir, tout effort préventif doit combiner les compétences de plusieurs disciplines. Si plus d'adultes acceptaient d'organiser ou de partager les activités des adolescents, beaucoup de jeunes dont l'image parentale est déficiente trouveraient des modèles positifs à imiter.

On peut faire appel à l'infirmière pour le soin des délinquants. Elle doit reconnaître que son patient est avant tout un individu et doit l'accepter comme tel, sans insister sur ses actes sociaux. Elle doit observer avec perspicacité son comportement, déceler ses appels à l'aide et travailler en étroite relation avec les autres membres de l'équipe de santé.

L'infirmière scolaire peut reconnaître aux signes suivants certains adolescents qui deviendront éventuellement délinquants: plaintes fréquentes de douleurs physiques vagues, accidents répétés, retrait des activités du groupe soit par une manifestation d'agressivité ou de passivité.

L'infirmière en santé communautaire doit aussi se servir de ses connaissances professionnelles, afin d'aider à prévenir, chez les jeunes enfants, la formation de traits de caractère qui mènent à la délinquance.

Toxicomanie

Des adolescents et même des enfants peuvent devenir physiquement ou psychologiquement dépendants des drogues. Ils peuvent commencer à prendre de la drogue pour le confort et le plaisir qu'elle procure. Plusieurs ont vu leurs parents se détourner de la réalité pour des paradis illusoires. L'usage des stupéfiants est aussi devenu un signe d'appartenance à la génération de la paix et de l'amour, à celle qui refuse la guerre et l'injustice. La prévention de la toxicomanie doit être axée sur une restructuration de la société, un changement des valeurs et un approfondissement de la communication entre les êtres humains, entre les parents et les enfants. On doit aider l'adolescent à établir ses propres valeurs et limites et à se fixer des buts dans la vie.

Les substances qui peuvent provoquer la dépendance physique et psychologique varient de la nicotine et de la marijuana à la colle, au fréon, à l'alcool et aux produits chimiques incluant les amphétamines, les barbituriques, l'acide lysergique diéthylamide (LSD) et les narcotiques.

Nicotine. On a consacré récemment beaucoup de publicité aux dangers de la cigarette, surtout aux effets possibles sur la santé des jeunes. Cependant, des enfants commencent encore à fumer alors qu'ils sont à l'école primaire ou pendant leur adolescence. Les écoles et les parents ont la responsabilité de renseigner les enfants sur les dangers de cette habitude.

Plusieurs écoles et de nombreux parents ont sévi durement contre les étudiants qui fument. Des directeurs d'école interdisent de fumer sur le terrain de l'institution et obligent les étudiants à prendre des cours sur les effets nocifs de la cigarette. Les parents n'influencent vraiment leurs enfants que par l'exemple, s'ils ne fument pas eux-mêmes. Si l'enfant riposte: « Si je ne fume pas, je ne serai pas accepté par mon groupe », les parents devraient faire remarquer qu'ils ont essayé de lui enseigner à suivre ses propres valeurs, à être indépendant, même si cela requiert beaucoup de volonté. Un adolescent accepte mieux de tels conseils d'adultes qu'il respecte que de ses parents.

Reniflement de la colle. On rencontre des enfants d'âge scolaire et des adolescents qui développent une accoutumance psychologique en inspirant les vapeurs toxiques du ciment à caoutchouc et de la colle à avion-jouet, parmi d'autres produits moins souvent utilisés. Des doses accrues sont nécessaires au drogué afin d'obtenir la réaction qu'il désire. L'utilisation de quantités considérables de ces substances peut mener à une folle gaieté, à l'intoxication, aux hallucinations, au crime et même à la mort. Plusieurs adolescents, en vieillissant, abandonnent la colle pour d'autres drogues.

Afin de prévenir les effets nocifs résultant du reniflement de la colle, on fabrique maintenant une sorte de colle qui ne s'évapore pas et s'avère non toxique pour l'organisme. Jusqu'à ce qu'on utilise ce produit, les propriétaires de magasin devraient rapporter au service de santé approprié tout accroissement soudain de la vente de colle aux jeunes gens. Les parents doivent faire examiner leur enfant par un médecin, s'ils soupçonnent qu'il a reniflé de la colle. Les professeurs devraient soupçonner fortement cette habitude si certains de leurs élèves sont irritables ou distraits ou deviennent excessivement somnolents en classe. De plus, une publicité adéquate devrait alerter le public au sujet de cette pratique et de ses dangers.

Reniflement du fréon. Le reniflement ou inhalation d'un gaz fluide frigorifiant, vendu en récipients aérosols, peut nuire à la santé. Quand le gaz arrive en contact avec la peau, il peut produire une engelure. Quand ils sont en contact avec une flamme à l'air libre ou une surface très chaude, les fréons se décomposent en gaz hautement irritants et toxiques. Respirés en fortes doses, les fréons ont un effet narcotique et peuvent causer des lésions pulmonaires, un spasme laryngé ou de l'anoxie. La mort peut résulter de l'inhalation de cette substance.

Alcool. L'alcool peut devenir un problème pour tout usager qui perd le contrôle de la quantité qu'il absorbe. Celui-ci développe une dépendance physiologique en même temps qu'une contrainte psychologique qui détruit son aptitude à se contrôler. L'alcoolisme est une maladie progressive et ultimement fatale, si l'alcoolique n'apprend pas à vivre sans sa drogue.

L'alcool est rapidement absorbé dans le sang. Ses effets physiologiques les plus prononcés touchent le cerveau, provoquant, selon la quantité ingurgitée, l'excitation, la disparition des inhibitions, la perte de contrôle corporel manifesté, par exemple, par une démarche ébrieuse, et finalement, l'hébétude et le sommeil.

On croit généralement que l'alcoolisme ne survient qu'à l'âge adulte. Cette croyance est fausse. Ce n'est pas l'âge chronologique ni le nombre d'années pendant lesquelles la personne a bu qui déterminent l'alcoolisme. Le critère important réside dans le contrôle de l'absorption ou la dépendance envers l'alcool. Un petit pourcentage d'alcooliques le sont depuis leur premier verre. La perte du contrôle de l'absorption ou alcoolisme peut se produire à un âge aussi jeune que 18 ans. On croit généralement que dans ces cas la seule solution réside dans l'abstinence complète.

Pour l'alcoolique, l'alcool est une drogue plutôt qu'un breuvage; il boit parce qu'il est déprimé, seul, courroucé ou nerveux. L'usage excessif et continuel de l'alcool affecte les capacités rationnelles de l'individu, diminue sérieusement ses possibilités de jugements critiques et détruit sa faculté d'auto-évaluation.

Durant l'adolescence, l'habitude de l'alcool apparaît plus fréquemment chez les garçons que chez les filles. On note l'abus d'alcool chez les adolescents des grandes villes, et encore plus fréquemment chez les adolescents des banlieues. L'excès de boissons, que la personne soit alcoolique ou non, est responsable de plusieurs accidents mortels sur les grandes routes.

On peut obtenir des conseils pour la thérapie des alcooliques de tout âge auprès du groupe appelé « Alcooliques Anonymes » (A.A.). D'autres organismes, tels l'Office de prévention et de traitement de l'alcoolisme et des autres toxicomanies (O.P.T.A.T.) sont d'un précieux secours, au Canada.

Le but de l'éducation moderne sur l'alcoolisme consiste à enseigner, par des moyens intelligents, la manière de boire de l'alcool. Dans une culture qui, généralement, approuve ce comportement, plusieurs jeunes gens acceptent ce modèle prédominant et consomment de l'alcool. Il s'agit donc d'influencer la sorte de buveurs qu'ils deviendront, plutôt que de prohiber l'usage de l'alcool. Quand on utilise l'alcool comme breuvage, comme apéritif, ou

comme symbole religieux ou culturel, ses effets sur la personnalité ne sont pas nocifs. Quand on l'utilise comme un agent d'intoxication et comme moyen d'éviter le stress, il devient un problème.

Amphétamines et barbituriques. Les amphétamines sont des drogues qui combattent la somnolence et la fatigue parce qu'elles sont des stimulants de la vigilance. On peut aussi les utiliser médicalement pour supprimer l'appétit. Les amphétamines les plus utilisées sont l'amphétamine (Benzédrine), la méthamphétamine (Méthédrine) et la dextro-amphétamine (Dexédrine). Ceux qui emploient des termes d'argot pour ces drogues, les nomment « pep pills », « speed », « bennies», « meth », etc . . .

Des doses normales d'amphétamines peuvent produire un sentiment de bien-être et de vivacité, mais des doses excessives causent de l'irritabilité et de la tension. Ces drogues provoquent la tachycardie, l'hypertension artérielle, l'accélération de la respiration, des céphalées et une sudation accrue. Ces effets sont dus au fait que ces drogues stimulent la libération de noradrénaline, une substance emmagasinée dans les terminaisons nerveuses.

Ces stimulants peuvent être mal employés par les jeunes, aussi bien que par des personnes de tout âge. Ceux qui en abusent peuvent les prendre par voie orale ou intraveineuse. L'absorption intraveineuse s'appelle « speeding » et peut produire une hépatite sérique, des abcès et une désorganisation progressive de la personnalité ou la mort. Dans les milieux « underground », on sait bien que « le speed tue ».

Les drogues stimulantes ne produisent pas de dépendance physique; cependant, l'organisme peut développer une tolérance, si bien que des doses de plus en plus fortes sont requises pour atteindre l'effet désiré. La dépendance psychologique peut se produire.

Les barbituriques sont des dépresseurs du système nerveux central. Ces drogues incluent le phénobarbital à action rapide (Nembutal), le secobarbital (Seconal), le phénobarbital à effet prolongé (Luminal), le butabarbital (Butisol) et l'amobarbital (Amytal). Les termes d'argot qui désignent les barbituriques à effet rapide sont, entre autres « goofball » et « barbs ».

Les barbituriques ralentissent l'action du muscle cardiaque, des muscles striés et des nerfs; ils réduisent les rythmes cardiaque et respiratoire et abaissent la tension artérielle. À doses élevées, ces drogues amènent la confusion, l'élocution pâteuse, la démarche titu-

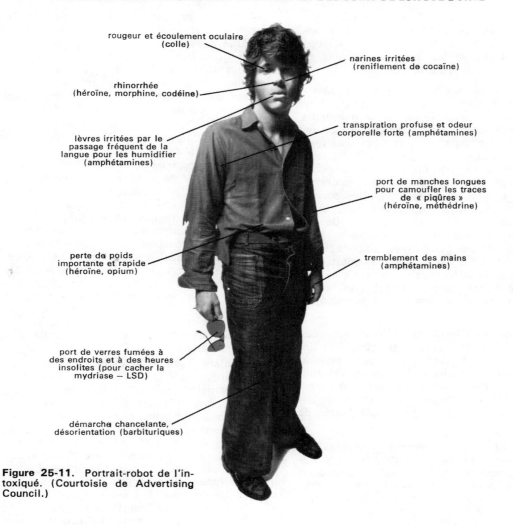

rougeur et écoulement oculaire
(colle)

narines irritées
(reniflement de cocaïne)

rhinorrhée
(héroïne, morphine, codéine)

transpiration profuse et odeur
corporelle forte (amphétamines)

lèvres irritées par le
passage fréquent de la
langue pour les humidifier
(amphétamines)

port de manches longues
pour camoufler les traces
de « piqûres »
(héroïne, méthédrine)

perte de poids
importante et rapide
(héroïne, opium)

tremblement des mains
(amphétamines)

port de verres fumées à
des endroits et à des heures
insolites (pour cacher la
mydriase — LSD)

démarche chancelante,
désorientation (barbituriques)

Figure 25-11. Portrait-robot de l'intoxiqué. (Courtoisie de Advertising Council.)

bante, la réduction de la capacité à se concentrer et à travailler, et peuvent ultimement provoquer la colère, l'agressivité ou le sommeil profond.

Les barbituriques, spécialement lorsqu'ils sont absorbés avec de l'alcool, peuvent être la cause d'accidents d'automobiles. Ils sont aussi, parce que l'on peut se les procurer facilement, une des principales façons que les gens emploient pour se suicider. Ces drogues entraînent la dépendance physique; ainsi, l'individu a besoin de doses de plus en plus fortes avant que l'organisme n'en ressente les effets. L'abstinence subite de ces drogues peut causer des nausées, des convulsions et la mort. L'abstinence graduelle sous contrôle médical peut prendre plusieurs semaines ou plusieurs mois, en réduisant régulièrement les doses.

Dans la plupart des pays, les amphétamines et les barbituriques tombent sous la juridiction de la « Loi des Aliments et Drogues ». On peut les obtenir légalement par ordonnance du médecin; cependant, beaucoup trop souvent, les adolescents en obtiennent illégalement ou en trouvent dans la petite pharmacie familiale où les adultes gardent leurs « médicaments pour les nerfs » . . .

Marijuana et haschich. Ces drogues se trouvent dans le chanvre indien, cannabis sativa, qui pousse dans les pays tempérés. Les fleurs et les feuilles de cette plante sont séchées et roulées, et on les fume en cigarettes ou avec une pipe. On peut aussi prendre ces substances sous forme de nourriture ou bien les renifler. Les cigarettes appelées « joints », « stricks », « reefers », ont une odeur sucrée quand on les fume. Le haschich est fabriqué à partir de la résine du cannabis et il peut être fumé ou inhalé directement. Sa concentration en THC, produit actif du cannabis, est plus élevée que celle de la marijuana.

L'usage de la marijuana (« pot », « grass ») a augmenté rapidement au cours des dernières années. Lorsque l'on fume de la marijuana, celle-ci entre dans le sang rapidement et agit sur le système nerveux et le cerveau. Les réactions physiques à cette drogue incluent la tachycardie, la rougeur aux yeux, la sécheresse de la bouche, l'abaissement de la température et une augmentation de l'appétit. Les personnes qui emploient la marijuana peuvent se mettre à parler fort et abondamment, devenir somnolentes et inhabiles à coordonner leurs mouvements. Elles peuvent se sentir excitées ou déprimées et subir de la distorsion dans leurs sens de la distance, du temps, de la couleur et de l'ouïe. Elles peuvent avoir de la difficulté à penser clairement et à prendre des décisions.

En doses plus fortes ou plus concentrées, la marijuana et le haschich peuvent être appelés des hallucinogènes, parce qu'ils peuvent causer des hallucinations visuelles ou des illusions. La paranoïa est une réaction commune. À long terme, ces drogues produiraient un désintéressement de la réalité et une baisse de l'énergie.

La marijuana et le haschich ne créent pas de dépendance physique. L'organisme ne développe probablement pas de tolérance et l'abstinence subite ne provoque pas de syndrome de sevrage. On croit cependant que l'utilisation régulière amène la dépendance psychologique.

Les personnes qui utilisent ces drogues peuvent éventuellement en venir à utiliser des narcotiques. Ceux qui abusent d'une drogue peuvent désirer changer ou être amenés à en utiliser d'autres, à cause de leurs contacts avec les usagers et les vendeurs de drogues et aussi par désir de nouvelles expériences.

Aux États-Unis et au Canada, la possession et la vente de marijuana et de haschich est encore un crime, puni par la loi fédérale. Si les adolescents enfreignent cette loi, leur éducation peut être interrompue et une ombre peut planer sur leur avenir à cause de leur casier judiciaire. En plus des aspects légaux, une jeune personne qui consomme régulièrement ces drogues peut trouver de plus en plus difficile de développer un sentiment d'identité, de s'adapter à la vie en tant qu'adulte et de développer un système de valeurs.

Acide lysergique diéthylamide (LSD).

L'acide lysergique diéthylamide est un produit chimique classé comme « hallucinogène », une drogue qui affecte l'esprit. Il produit des réactions mentales bizarres, provoquant une grave distorsion de la vue, de l'odorat, de l'ouïe et du toucher. D'autres drogues, qui sont aussi des hallucinogènes puissants, incluent la mescaline, la psilocybine, le DMT, le STP, etc . . .

Bien que l'usage du LSD (« Acide ») soit illégal dans la majorité des pays, sauf dans certains cas approuvés par le gouvernement, il est employé par de nombreuses personnes, soit pour expérimentation ou de façon régulière. On peut prendre du LSD sur un cube de sucre, un biscuit, ou d'autre nourriture; on peut le lécher sur un timbre-poste sur lequel on a placé la drogue. La réaction de l'organisme à cette drogue inclut la tachycardie, l'irrégularité respiratoire, l'élévation de la tension artérielle et de la température, le tremblement des extrémités, la dilatation des pupilles, la rougeur ou la pâleur du visage, les frissons, la nausée et l'anorexie. Cette drogue ne crée pas de dépendance physique et n'entraîne pas de syndrome de sevrage.

Les effets psychologiques de l'absorption de LSD comprennent la distorsion de la perception sensorielle, mais ne rendent pas les gens plus créateurs et ne les aident pas non plus à se trouver eux-mêmes. Les couleurs semblent plus brillantes, des dessins étranges peuvent surgir devant les yeux et les murs semblent bouger. Le goût, l'odorat, l'ouïe et le toucher semblent plus intenses que d'habitude. La notion du temps peut être perturbée, bien qu'il n'y ait pas de perte de conscience. Les usagers de cette drogue peuvent se sentir heureux et déprimés en même temps. Ils peuvent aussi perdre les notions d'espace et de gravité, si bien qu'il leur semble quelquefois qu'ils peuvent voler ou flotter dans l'air. Les usagers vous diront, selon leurs sensations éprouvées, qu'ils ont eu un « bon » ou un « mauvais voyage ».

L'usage prolongé de cette drogue peut diminuer la capacité de concentration et amener un retrait progressif de la réalité.

Il y a des dangers certains inhérents à l'usage du LSD. L'usager peut prendre peur, parce qu'il sent qu'il ne peut plus arrêter l'action de la drogue une fois qu'il l'a prise, ou alors, il peut être atteint de paranoïa. Pour les jeunes usagers surtout, l'effet de cette drogue peut s'avérer extrêmement terrifiant. Ils peuvent éprouver la récurrence des effets de la drogue longtemps après l'avoir prise. Ils peuvent devenir déprimés ou développer une affection psychiatrique chronique. L'usage de cette drogue peut aussi contribuer à des meurtres ou à des suicides. Certaines personnes peuvent souffrir de maladie mentale aiguë ou prolongée, après l'avoir prise.

Le danger le plus important associé à l'usage du LSD est la mort accidentelle, parce que la personne, sous l'effet de cette drogue, peut sauter d'une certaine hauteur, croyant qu'elle peut flotter ou voler, ou se précipiter devant un véhicule en mouvement, croyant qu'il ne peut en résulter aucun mal.

On étudie actuellement la possibilité que l'usage du LSD affecte les chromosomes, leur causant des dommages permanents et provoquant des anomalies chez les enfants de ceux qui ont employé cette drogue. On fait des recherches pour déterminer la façon dont ces changements pourraient se produire, puisqu'on ne constatera pas avant un certain temps le dommage génétique et psychologique total causé par le LSD à la population humaine.

Il y a des peines sévères pour quiconque produit illégalement, vend ou distribue le LSD. Les peines comprennent l'emprisonnement ou des amendes et peuvent être très sérieuses.

On effectue actuellement des recherches pour déterminer l'action exacte de la drogue, sa valeur pour les êtres humains, les façons de traiter ceux qui souffrent de ses effets et les caractéristiques culturelles des usagers.

Narcotiques. Le terme « narcotique » est employé pour désigner l'opium, un produit de la fleur de pavot, ses dérivés naturels, tels l'héroïne et la morphine, ainsi que les produits synthétiques imitant ses effets. La cocaïne, fabriquée à partir des feuilles de coca, aussi bien que d'autres drogues, peuvent aussi être considérées comme narcotiques. L'héroïne est le narcotique le plus couramment employé par les narcomanes.

La personne qui devient dépendante (« hooked ») d'un narcotique désire ardemment des doses répétées et plus considérables, parce que son corps développe une tolérance à cette substance. Lorsqu'elle est privée de drogue, elle tombe malade, et apparaissent alors la diaphorèse, les tremblements, les vomissements, la diarrhée et d'intenses douleurs abdominales. La dépendance psychologique se produit aussi, parce que la drogue est utilisée comme un moyen de fuir la réalité. S'il y a absorption suffisante de drogue, la mort peut en résulter.

Quand la personne prend de l'héroïne pour la première fois, elle peut sentir une réduction de ses craintes, un soulagement de ses soucis et un degré d'inactivité qui peut se transformer en stupeur. La drogue endommage certaines parties du cerveau ainsi que les nerfs.

Elle réduit la soif, la faim, les impulsions sexuelles et les sensations douloureuses. La malnutrition peut survenir quand cette drogue est employée pendant un certain temps. Les hépatites sériques sont fréquentes à cause du manque d'asepsie lors des injections intraveineuses et de l'utilisation de seringues et d'aiguilles contaminées. Les symptômes de sevrage apparaissent approximativement dans les 18 heures qui suivent le retrait de la drogue.

Les bébés nés de mères héroïnomanes peuvent être intoxiqués à leur naissance et présenter un syndrome de sevrage dangereux, peu après leur naissance.

Le principal objectif de l'héroïnomane est d'obtenir une provision continuelle de drogues. Il devra peut-être abandonner ses études ou son travail, parce qu'il sera souvent malade, à cause d'un manque ou d'une dose excessive. Il pourra éprouver des difficultés tant avec sa famille qu'avec la loi. S'il garde son habitude, il sera amené au crime, surtout au vol ou aux autres crimes contre la propriété, parce que sa dépendance coûte très cher. La possession illégale ou la vente de narcotiques est punissable par des amendes ou par l'emprisonnement.

La toxicomanie est une maladie et elle nécessite un traitement. Si la désintoxication réussit, la personne retourne dans son milieu où elle peut trouver difficile de ne pas revenir à l'usage des drogues. Une thérapie globale, incluant une réhabilitation physique, mentale, sociale et professionnelle doit être tentée, afin d'empêcher l'individu d'utiliser encore de l'héroïne et de gâcher sa vie.

On fait des recherches actuellement sur les effets des narcotiques, sur les usagers eux-mêmes et sur les antidotes qui peuvent être utilisés contre la dépendance à l'héroïne.

Le rôle de l'infirmière. Le rôle de l'infirmière face à l'adolescent qui utilise des drogues est complexe. Il importe d'abord qu'elle soit bien renseignée sur toutes les données de ce problème. Elle doit connaître les symptômes et les comportements produits par les diverses drogues, les traitements appropriés, ainsi que les ressources communautaires à la disposition de l'adolescent.

L'infirmière, soit à l'hôpital, soit en santé communautaire, doit être préparée à répondre aux questions sur l'usage des drogues, que celles-ci viennent de parents inquiets ou des adolescents eux-mêmes. Elle doit aussi connaître le matériel éducatif à sa disposition et l'utiliser pour éduquer le public.

On peut demander à l'infirmière scolaire ou à l'infirmière en santé publique de donner des cours à l'école ou dans la communauté, sur les méthodes d'identification des adolescents drogués, aussi bien que sur les différents aspects de l'utilisation de diverses drogues. L'infirmière peut aussi jouer un rôle extrêmement important dans la prévention de la toxicomanie et dans le dépistage des adolescents devenus drogués. Elle doit être sympathique et compréhensive, et s'abstenir de porter des jugements moraux ou absolus. Il faut écouter l'adolescent attentivement, essayer de le comprendre et l'encourager à utiliser les ressources possibles, telles que les médecins ou les cliniques spécialisées dans l'aide aux jeunes toxicomanes.

Puisque la thérapie actuelle et les soins infirmiers de l'adolescent drogué ne sont pas très différents de ceux de l'adulte intoxiqué, les détails de la réhabilitation ne seront pas discutés dans ce livre. Le dénominateur commun dans le traitement et le soin des personnes dépendantes des drogues est celui de la réduction de l'anxiété par la tranquillité, le calme et l'aide donnés dans un milieu thérapeutique par un être chaleureux et compréhensif. Une approche multi-disciplinaire a été trouvée utile dans plusieurs centres spécialisés dans ces soins.

PROBLÈMES PSYCHIATRIQUES DE L'ADOLESCENT

Psychonévroses graves

Les adolescents peuvent souffrir de psychonévroses graves. Ils peuvent accuser des symptômes de dépression sérieuse, d'hystérie, d'anxiété ou de retrait. Les adolescents plus âgés peuvent devenir anxieux et hypocondriaques. Ils peuvent aussi présenter des obsessions, de la compulsion et des phobies. Le médecin et l'infirmière peuvent avoir besoin de l'aide d'un psychiatre pour le soin de tels patients.

Réactions schizophréniques chez l'adolescent

Fréquence et étiologie. Bien que les réactions schizophréniques soient plutôt rares chez les enfants, elles constituent la plus importante maladie mentale pendant les années d'adolescence.

Il y a plusieurs théories au sujet des causes de la schizophrénie. Aucune n'a été prouvée. On ne sait jusqu'à quel point l'hérédité peut jouer. On soupçonne aussi un défaut biochimique ou neurologique à la base de cette maladie. La tension due à l'entourage et au déve-loppement, peut causer une faille dans l'apprentissage de la communication. Plusieurs auteurs soutiennent que l'enfant élevé dans un milieu où les actes contredisent les paroles, où les messages ne sont jamais clairs, développe progressivement une confusion dans sa communication et son comportement, et évolue vers la schizophrénie. D'autres études révèlent que le père du schizophrène est souvent faible ou absent, et sa mère surprotectrice ou froide. Toutefois, aucune recherche n'est concluante.

Manifestations cliniques et diagnostic. Le début peut sembler subit, mais les changements de personnalité se sont probablement échelonnés depuis des mois ou des années. On peut voir se développer la conduite suivante: a) rigidité dans l'adaptation aux personnes et situations de l'entourage. L'enfant ne peut tolérer aucune sorte de vie autre que la sienne. Il crée un rituel dans sa vie quotidienne et ne peut pas le changer rapidement; b) il commence à s'éloigner des autres. Il devient réservé et semble avoir seulement de brèves périodes de contact avec la réalité. Sa personnalité se désorganise progressivement; c) il y a une séparation émotive et intellectuelle entre la signification d'un acte et sa réaction à cet acte. Il peut rire quand une tragédie se produit. Il semble bizarre dans son comportement; d) il devient nonchalant, négligé, paresseux et semble satisfait quand il s'assied tout seul. Finalement, il se retire dans son propre monde, parce que la réalité lui est intolérable. Il a des illusions et des hallucinations. Sa conversation devient irrégulière et illogique.

Figure 25-12. L'adolescent schizophrène préfère s'asseoir seul, à l'écart des autres, pour se soustraire à la réalité et vivre dans son propre monde. (H. Armstrong Roberts.)

La maladie mentale est difficile à *diagnostiquer* durant l'adolescence, parce que les enfants et adolescents normaux peuvent, à un moment ou un autre de leur développement, présenter des manifestations semblables à celles décrites précédemment. C'est le degré auquel le comportement anormal se produit qui est important pour poser un diagnostic.

Traitement, soins infirmiers et pronostic. Il faut donner un *traitement* psychiatrique aussi promptement que possible. Les soins, pour qu'ils soient efficaces, doivent être dispensés par des adultes accueillants, chaleureux, qui prodiguent au jeune leur attention entière. Il faut fournir à l'adolescent, amour et acceptation, et lui offrir des expériences pouvant lui procurer des gratifications et un certain contrôle. On doit améliorer sa condition physique, et des soins spécialisés et compétents lui sont nécessaires.

Il est difficile d'être certain du *pronostic*. Même avec la thérapie et les soins en institution, le pronostic s'est avéré pauvre. Au cours des dernières années, on a obtenu un certain succès par thérapie intensive. La guérison est rare, mais le malade peut parvenir à une adaptation sociale satisfaisante. On effectue de plus en plus de recherches pour que le traitement de ces adolescents puisse être plus fructueux.

Suicide

Les tentatives suicidaires et le suicide ne sont pas rares chez les enfants et les adolescents. La fréquence de ces morts a presque doublé dans les dix dernières années. Ce problème est moins commun chez les enfants d'âge scolaire que chez les adolescents. La mort par suicide est plus fréquente chez l'homme, mais les tentatives de suicide sont plus nombreuses parmi les femmes. Le suicide se produit le plus souvent au printemps. Entre 5 et 19 ans, il est la troisième cause de décès au Canada, après les accidents et les néoplasies. Plusieurs suicides sont camouflés en accidents, tels les empoisonnements, les chutes, les électrocutions, les collisions d'automobiles et de motocyclettes.

Certains médecins croient que la fréquence relative des suicides chez les adolescents peut être portée au compte de l'insécurité actuelle de la société moderne qui, jointe à une chute des valeurs établies, produit la destruction plutôt que la consolidation de l'ego des jeunes gens. Plus spécifiquement, la plupart des enfants et des adolescents qui songent au suicide ou le commettent, sont des solitaires, provenant de foyers désorganisés et subissant un stress intolérable, habités par un sentiment d'échec, ne se sentant pas aimés ni désirés, et se considérant comme mauvais. Ils réagissent avec colère, ordinairement contre leurs parents. Ces sentiments engendrent la culpabilité qui mène à une tentative suicidaire, laquelle d'une certaine façon a pour but de punir leurs parents. Certains adolescents qui se suicident peuvent le faire dans un effort pour manipuler les autres, ou comme un signal de détresse ou parce qu'ils sont schizophrènes. Les adolescents

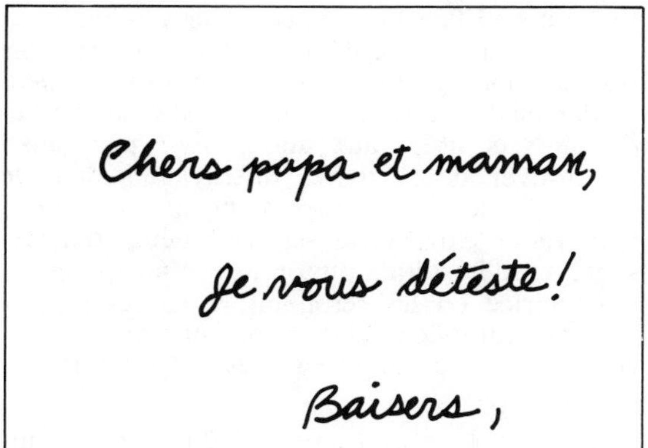

Chers papa et maman,

Je vous déteste!

Baisers,

Lucie

Figure 25-13. Lettre d'une adolescente qui va se suicider.

qui menacent de se suicider ou se suicident, sont en général des personnes impulsives et immatures, portées aux réactions exagérées, même devant des tensions mineures. Ils sont souvent blasés, hyperactifs et ont fréquemment fait l'école buissonnière ou des fugues; ils ont souvent des antécédents d'aventures sexuelles ou de dépression.

Chez les groupes d'âge scolaire et chez les adolescents, la dépression se manifeste souvent par la désobéissance, l'ennui, les accès continuels de mauvaise humeur, l'agitation, la fuite de la maison, l'école buissonnière et la propension aux accidents. Plusieurs adolescents déprimés extériorisent leur détresse par l'usage des drogues et les aventures sexuelles répétées. Ils accumulent les échecs à l'école, se montrent incapables de se concentrer, s'isolent, souffrent d'anorexie, perdent du poids, accusent de l'insomnie et autres plaintes, dont la plus commune est une fatigue excessive. Ils peuvent aussi être préoccupés par l'insignifiance de leur vie et le désir de la mort. La conception de la mort chez l'enfant dépend de l'âge. Cela explique en partie la fréquence plus faible de suicides chez les enfants plus jeunes que chez les adolescents.

Avant une tentative suicidaire, il y a ordinairement, mais pas toujours, un facteur déclenchant, tel une crise importante impliquant la discipline, une punition que le jeune juge injuste, un chagrin d'amour, la perte d'un parent par divorce ou par décès, ou une grossesse non planifiée. Les tentatives suicidaires se produisent presque toujours quand la personne se sent extrêmement seule.

Les adolescents déprimés ou qui ont menacé de se suicider requièrent un examen physique, neurologique et psychiatrique complet. Souvent, les personnes importantes dans la vie de l'adolescent, telles que les amis, les parents, les professeurs, peuvent fournir des observations pouvant être utiles à sa compréhension. Il faut aussi observer soigneusement le comportement de l'adolescent après son admission à l'hôpital, surtout ce qui peut révéler un désir d'autodestruction.

Après une période d'observation, tant les parents que le patient doivent prendre une part active à la thérapie menée, soit par un pédiatre expérimenté dans ce travail clinique, soit par un psychiatre pour enfants. Le médecin doit aider l'adolescent à munir son ego d'une force suffisante pour faire face à ses sérieux problèmes émotifs. Si l'adolescent n'a pas confiance en son médecin, il peut opposer de la résistance à sa thérapie, nier sa maladie et

fausser l'expression de ses sentiments comme moyen de fuir ce qu'il considère être une situation intolérable. Ces patients doivent recevoir des soins et être suivis durant au moins trois mois. La période consécutive à la crise aiguë est souvent la plus importante pour éviter les rechutes.

Soins infirmiers. Puisque les adolescents se suicident au cours d'une crise émotive à un moment où ils n'ont personne à qui parler, l'infirmière en contact avec des jeunes de cet âge doit être attentive aux signes précurseurs d'une tentative suicidaire. L'infirmière doit alors employer les moyens nécessaires afin d'obtenir de l'aide aussitôt que possible. Ceci est spécialement vrai pour ceux qui donnent des avertissements verbaux définis d'intention suicidaire. Les infirmières doivent aussi aider les parents à comprendre davantage le suicide et à découvrir les signes avertisseurs présuicidaires. Plusieurs centres de prévention du suicide ont été formés dans de grandes villes, afin de procurer de l'assistance quand elle est requise.

À cause de leurs sentiments extrêmes de solitude, plusieurs soi-disant cas de suicide sont faciles à ramener à la vie. Ils ne sont jamais entièrement certains qu'ils désirent mourir. Si quelqu'un dit: « Ne faites pas cela », très souvent, ils ne passeront pas à l'acte. Une relation de confiance chaleureuse doit être établie avec eux pour les aider à sortir de leur solitude et à s'adapter à la vie.

L'infirmière qui soigne un de ces jeunes doit le respecter et l'accepter, et lui fournir une protection contre l'autodestruction en réduisant les risques environnants jusqu'à ce qu'il soit en mesure d'assumer cette responsabilité lui-même. Elle doit soutenir sa confiance et son respect de lui-même. Quand il exprime ses sentiments d'infériorité, l'infirmière peut l'aider en lui faisant accomplir des tâches nécessaires et utiles aux autres. Elle peut aussi lui trouver des activités distrayantes dans le but de l'aider à exprimer d'une manière constructive et extravertie ses sentiments d'agressivité et d'hostilité, plutôt que d'une manière destructrice en les refoulant et en les retournant sur lui-même. Il faut encourager l'adolescent à planifier lui-même ses activités et ses soins.

L'aspect le plus important du rôle de l'infirmière est d'établir une relation thérapeutique avec l'adolescent. L'infirmière doit manifester un intérêt sincère, une compréhension rassurante et le protéger jusqu'à ce qu'il puisse dominer lui-même ses impulsions autodestructrices.

RÉFÉRENCES

Livres et documents officiels

Association canadienne antituberculeuse: *Comment détruire le germe de la tuberculose.* Montréal.

Association médicale canadienne et le ministère de la Santé nationale et du Bien-être social: *J'aime le danger!... et puis?* Ottawa, Canada.

Ayars, A. L. et Milgram, G. G.: *The Teenager and Alcohol.* New York, Richards Rosen Press, 1970.

Ayrault, E. W.: *Helping the Handicapped Teenager Mature.* New York, Association Press, 1971.

Bernstein, R.: *Helping Unmarried Mothers.* New York, Association Press, 1971.

Bloomquist, E. R.: *Marijuana; The Second Trip.* Rev. éd. Beverly Hills, Californie, Glencœ Press, 1971.

Collège des médecins et chirurgiens de la province de Québec: *Les Toxicomanies autres que l'alcoolisme.* Éducation permanente, Montréal.

Durocher, J.: *Drogues.* Montréal, Éditions de l'Homme, 1970.

Feinstein, S. C., Giovacchini, P. et Miller, A. A.: *Adolescent Psychiatry.* New York, Basic Books Inc., 1971, Vol. 1.

Friedman A. S. et autres: *Therapy with Families of Sexually Acting-Out Girls.* New York, Springer Publishing Company, Inc., 1971.

Grollman, E. A.: *Suicide Préventioon, Intervention, Postvention.* Boston, Beacon Press, 1971.

Institut de microbiologie et d'hygiène de l'Université de Montréal: *Notice sur le BCG. Cuti-BCG. Vaccination par la méthode des scarifications. Les recherches à l'Institut de microbiologie et d'hygiène de l'Université de Montréal et leur portée sur la santé publique,* Montréal.

Love, H. D.: *Youth and the Drug Problem: A Guide for Parents and Teachers.* Springfield, Ill., Charles C Thomas, 1971.

Ministère de la Santé: *La tuberculose. En garde contre la tuberculose. La pratique des épreuves à la tuberculine et de la Cuti-BCG en tuberculose. Le tabac et la santé. M. V. (Maladies vénériennes).* Gouvernement du Québec.

Ministère de la Santé nationale et du Bien-être social: *En toute confidence... aux adolescents. Maladies vénériennes, ce qu'il faut savoir. Syphilis et blennorragie.* Division de l'épidémiologie, Gouvernement du Canada.

Ordre des infirmières et infirmiers du Québec: *Le nursing en tuberculose.* Montréal, 1975.

Pannor, R.. Massarik. F. et Evans, B.: *The Unmarried Father: New Helping Approaches for Unmarried Young Parents.* New York, Springer Publishing Company, Inc., 1971.

Pierce, R. I.: *Single and Pregnant.* Boston, Beacon Press, 1970.

Shields, R. W.: *A Cure of Delinquents: The Treatment of Maladjustment.* New York, International Universities Press, 1971.

Société canadienne du cancer: *Fumer: plaisir ou risque.* Montréal.

Speck, R. V. et autres: *The New Families: Youth, Communes and the Politics of Drugs.* New York, Basic Books, Inc., 1972.

Wein, B.: *The Runaway Generation: A Study in Depth of Our Alienated Children.* Don Mills, Ontario, Musson Book Company, 1970.

Articles

Bame, K. B.: Halo Traction. *Am. J. Nursing,* 69:1933, septembre 1969.

Blais, N.: Une main tendue aux Victimes de la drogue. *Inf. Can.,* 12:22, octobre 1970.

Boegli, E. H. et Steele, M. S.: Scoliosis: Spinal Instrumentation and Fusion. *Am. J. Nursing,* 68:2399, 1968.

Braconnier, A.: Schizophrénie. *La revue de l'inf.,* 21:655, 7, 1971.

Broussole, P. et Quénard, O.: Toxicomanies et drogues. *La revue de l'inf.,* 23:89, 10, 1973.

Broutart, J. C.: Les scolioses. *Soins,* XV:461, 10, 1970.

Brown, M. A.: Adolescents and VD. *Nursing Outlook,* 21:99, 2, 1973.

Brown, W. J.: Acquired Syphilis, Drugs and Blood Tests. *Am. J. Nursing,* 71:713, avril 1971.

Calamy, G.: Syndromes mononucléosiques. *Soins,* 16:197, 5, 1971.

Claman, A. D., Williams, B. J. et Wogan. L.: Reaction of Unmarried Girls to Pregnancy. *Canad. Med. Assoc. J.,* 101:328, 20 septembre 1969.

Connell, E. B. et Jacobson, L.: Pregnancy, the Teenager and Sex Education. *Am. J. Pub. Health,* 61:1840, septembre 1971.

Curtis, F.: The Pregnant Adolescent. *Nursing '74,* 3:77, 3, 1974.

Feray, C., Lacoste, A. et Roy-Camille, R.: La scoliose essentielle du grand enfant et de l'adolescent. *La médecine infantile*, 76:583, 7, 1969.

Fleshman, R.: Eating Rituals and Realities. *Nurs. Clin. N. Amer.*, 8:91, 1, 1973.

Gabrielson, I. W. et autres: Suicide Attempts in a Population Pregnant as Teen-Agers. *Am. J. Pub. Health*, 60:2289, décembre 1970.

Gauthier, D.: Les hypogonadismes masculins. *Soins*, 20:11, 10, 1975.

Guimont, A.: La scoliose: étude des cas opérés par la technique de Harrington. *Union méd. du Can.*, 97:746, juin 1968.

Grunberg, J.: La primo-infection tuberculeuse. *Soins*, 18:5, 1, 1973.

Hanus, M.: À propos des toxicomanies: Le haschisch et le L. S. D. 25. *Soins*, 17:31, 3, 1972.

Hartman, E. E.: Involvement of a Maternity and Infant Care Project in a Pregnant School Girl Program in Minneapolis, Minnesota. *J. School Health*, 40:224, mai 1970.

Hustu, H. O. et autres: Treatment of Ewing's Sarcoma with Concurrent Radiotherapy and Chemotherapy. *J. Pediat.*, 73:249, 1968.

Juvenspan, H. et Courrèges, M.: La syphilis. *Soins*, 19:26, 1, 1974.

Kline, N. S. et Davis, J. M.: Psychotropic Drugs. *Am. J. Nursing*, 73:54, janvier 1973.

Labrune, B.: La mononucléose infectieuse. *Soins*, 20:21, 1, 1975.

Leverle, M. et Leverle, J.: Lymphosarcomes et réticulosarcomes de l'enfant. *Journées parisiennes de pédiatrie*, Paris, Flammarion, 1970, p. 203.

Lipp, M. R., Benson, S. G. et Allen, P. S.: Marijuana Use by Nurses and Nursing Students. *Am. J. Nursing*, 71:2339, décembre 1971.

Long, B. et Krepuck, D.: New Perspectives on Drug Abuse. *Nurs. Clin. N. Amer.*, 8:25, 1, 1973.

Lowenberg, J. S.: The Coping Behaviors of Fatally Ill Adolescents and Their Parents. *Nursing Forum*, 9:269, 3, 1970.

Marinoff, S. C. et Schonholz, D. H.: Adolescent Pregnancy. *Ped Clin. N. Amer.*, 19:795, août 1972.

Maxwell, M. B.: A Terminally Ill Adolescent and Her Family. *Am. J. Nursing*, 72:925, mai 1972.

Meyer, H. L.: Predictable Problems of Hospitalized Adolescents. *Am. J. Nursing*, 69:525, mars 1969.

Portal, A.: Les formes cliniques de la mononucléose infectieuse. *La revue de l'inf.*, 23:519, 6, 1973.

Reid, U. V.: Le dépistage de la scoliose idiopathique de l'adolescent. *Inf. Can.*, 18:18, 2, 1976.

Rigault, P. et autres: Les scolioses. *La revue de pédiatrie*, 10:527, 9, 1974 (numéro spécial).

Roberts, A. R. et Grau, J. J.: Procedures Used in Crisis Intervention by Suicide Prevention Agencies. *Pub. Health Rep.*, 85:691, août 1970.

Séguin-Langlois, M.: L'adolescente enceinte. *Inf. Can.*, 17:19, 6, 1975.

Stine, O. C. et Kelley, E. B.: Evaluation of a School for Young Mothers. *Pediatrics*, 46:581, octobre 1970.

Thenot, A.: Nouveaux médicaments antituberculeux. *Soins*, 16:331, 7, 1971.

Stone, M. L. et autres: Narcotic Addiction in Pregnancy. *Am. J. Obst. & Gynec.*, 109:716, 1er mars 1971.

Tiedt, E.: The Adolescent in the Hospital: An Identity-Resolution Approach. *Nursing Forum*, 11:120, 2, 1972.

DONNÉES STATISTIQUES
QUÉBÉCOISES ET CANADIENNES

Tableau 1. Taux de mortalité infantile et de mortinatalité, selon les provinces, au Canada, en 1972.

PROVINCES	MORTALITÉ INFANTILE [1]	MORTALITÉ NÉONATALE [2]	MORTALITÉ PÉRINATALE [3]
Québec	17,9	12,6	19,2
Ontario	15,3	11,1	19,1
Île du Prince-Édouard	19,4	12,9	21,7
Nouvelle-Écosse	16,8	9,5	16,4
Nouveau-Brunswick	17,3	12,5	22,5
Terre-Neuve	20,7	13,5	21,7
Manitoba	18,9	12,1	20
Saskatchewan	19,4	13,4	20,8
Alberta	17,5	12,4	18,6
Colombie-Britannique	16,8	11	16,3
Canada	17,1	11,9	19

[1] Mortalité d'enfants de moins de 1 an.
[2] Mortalité de bébés de moins de 28 jours.
[3] Mortalité de fœtus de plus de 27 semaines de gestations et de bébés de moins de 7 jours.

Tableau 2. *Répartition des décès, par jour, par semaine et par mois, au cours de la pre-mière année de vie, au Canada, en 1972.*

PÉRIODES DURANT LA PREMIÈRE ANNÉE	NOMBRE DE DÉCÈS	% DES DÉCÈS DANS LA PREMIÈRE ANNÉE DE VIE
1er jour	2459	41,4
2e jour	520	8,8
3e jour	265	4,5
4e jour	137	2,3
5e jour	101	1,7
6e jour	82	1,4
7e jour	62	1
1re semaine	3626	61,1
2e semaine	221	3,7
3e semaine	123	2,1
4e semaine	147	2,5
1er mois	4117	69,4
2e mois	430	7,2
3e mois	362	6,1
4e mois	279	4,7
5e mois	193	3,3
6e mois	143	2,4
7e mois	75	1,3
8e mois	93	1,6
9e mois	70	1,2
10e mois	67	1,1
11e mois	66	1,1
12e mois	43	0,7

Il est à noter que 41% des décès de la première année de vie surviennent le premier jour, 61,1% durant la première semaine et 70% durant le premier mois.

Tableau 3.   *Causes et taux de mortalité infantile, par sexe, au Canada, en 1972.*

CAUSES	SEXE MASCULIN	SEXE FÉMININ
Anomalies congénitales	405,5	359
Anoxémie, hypoxémie	373,1	275,9
Prématurité, débilité	215,9	182,8
Pneumonie	143,2	101,5
Anomalies du cordon et du placenta	106,3	70

Les causes de mortalité sont les mêmes pour les deux sexes, mais le nombre de décès féminins excède celui des décès de nourrissons masculins.

Tableau 4.   *Causes de décès, au-dessus de 1 an, par sexe et groupes d'âge, au Canada, en 1972.*

GROUPES D'ÂGE	SEXE MASCULIN	SEXE FÉMININ
1– 4 ans	1. Accidents	1. Accidents
	2. Anomalies congénitales	2. Anomalies congénitales
	3. Cancer	3. Cancer
	4. Pneumonie	4. Pneumonie
	5. Méningite	5. Entérite et maladies diarrhéiques
5– 19 ans	1. Accidents	1. Accidents
	2. Cancer	2. Cancer
	3. Suicide	3. Anomalies congénitales
	4. Anomalies congénitales	4. Suicide
	5. Maladies cardio-vasculaires	5. Pneumonie

Il existe une différence entre les sexes pour les causes de mortalité, et pour les taux de mortalité le nombre de décès de garçons excède celui des filles.

Tableau 5. Évolution du taux de mortalité infantile, de 1968 à 1973, au Québec

ANNÉES	TAUX
1968	21,7
1969	20,3
1970	20,6
1971	17,7
1972	17,9
1973	16,1

Tableau 6.   *Taux de mortalité infantile, selon les régions, au Québec, en 1973.*

RÉGIONS	NOMBRE DE DÉCÈS	TAUX DE MORTALITÉ INFANTILE
Bas Saint-Laurent	69	20,8
Saguenay et lac Saint-Jean	106	23,1
Québec	242	16,7
Trois-Rivières	92	18,8
Cantons de l'Est	49	14,4
Montréal métropolitain	386	14,5
Laurentides	79	13,6
Sud de Montréal	164	12,5
Outaouais	74	17,3
Nord-Ouest	60	23,5
Côte-Nord	44	19,3
Nouveau-Québec	16	40,2
Total	1381	16,1

Les disparités régionales sont évidentes et s'expliquent par le niveau de vie, l'accessibilité à des soins de qualité et la concentration, dans certaines régions, d'anomalies congénitales et de maladies héréditaires mortelles.

Tableau 7. *Évolution des taux de mortinatalité et de néonatalité, de 1968 à 1973, au Québec.*

ANNÉES	MORTINATALITÉ [1]	NÉONATLITÉ PRÉCOCE [2]	NÉONATALITÉ [3]
1968	12,8	14,2	15,6
1969	11,9	13,6	15
1970	12,9	13,2	14,7
1971	11,2	11,2	12,7
1972	10,5	11,2	12,7
1973	9,7	10,2	11,6

[1] Décès d'un fœtus de plus de 20 semaines de gestation.
[2] Décès d'un bébé entre 0 et 7 jours de vie.
[3] Décès d'un bébé entre 0 et 28 jours de vie.

Tableau 8.   *Taux de mortalité, selon le groupe d'âge et le sexe, au Québec, en 1973.*

GROUPES D'ÂGE	SEXE MASCULIN	SEXE FÉMININ	TAUX TOTAL
0 – 4 ans	4,4	3,4	3,9
5 – 9 ans	0,6	0,4	0,5
10 – 14 ans	0,5	0,3	0,4
15 – 19 ans	1,6	0,6	1,1
20 – 24 ans	0,7	1,4	2,1

Durant toute l'enfance et l'adolescence, c'est la première année de vie qui comporte le plus de risques de mortalité, surtout pour les garçons.

Tableau 9. *Causes de décès, selon les groupes d'âge, au Québec, en 1973.*

GROUPES D'ÂGE	CAUSES
0 – 1 an	1. Morbidité et mortalité néonatale 2. Anomalies congénitales 3. Maladies de l'appareil respiratoire 4. Accidents, empoisonnements, traumatismes 5. Maladies de l'appareil digestif
1 – 4 ans	1. Accidents, empoisonnements, traumatismes 2. Anomalies congénitales 3. Cancers 4. Maladies de l'appareil respiratoire 5. Maladies infectieuses
5 – 14 ans	1. Accidents, empoisonnements, traumatismes 2. Cancers 3. Maladies du système nerveux et des organes des sens 4. Anomalies congénitales 5. Maladies infectieuses
15 – 19 ans	1. Accidents, empoisonnements, traumatismes 2. Cancers 3. Maladies du système nerveux et des organes des sens 4. Maladies de l'appareil circulatoire 5. Maladies de l'appareil respiratoire
20 – 24 ans	1. Accidents, empoisonnements, traumatismes 2. Cancers 3. Maladies de l'appareil circulatoire 4. Maladies du système nerveux et des organes des sens 5. Anomalies congénitales

Il est à noter que les accidents sont la première cause de mortalité à partir de la 2e année de vie. Les anomalies congénitales et les cancers demeurent meurtriers tout au long de l'enfance.

index